RAND M^cNALLY

ZIP CODE FINDER

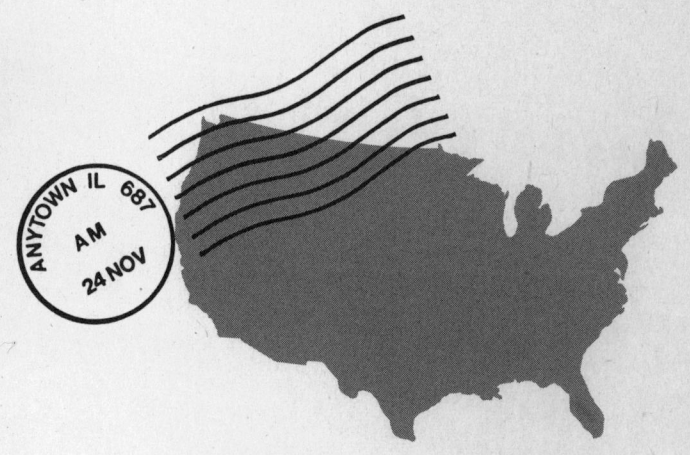

ANYTOWN IL 687
AM
24 NOV

Rand McNally Zip Code Finder
Table of Contents

INTRODUCTION

BASIC LISTINGS AND
3-DIGIT ZIP CODE MAPS

State	3-Digit Map	Listings	State	3-Digit Map	Listings
Newark		301	Pittsburgh		409
New Mexico	306-307	305	Rhode Island	82-83	419
New York	310-311	312	South Carolina	422-423	421
Bronx		313	South Dakota	428-429	430
Brooklyn		313	Tennessee	432-433	434
Far Rockaway		317	Memphis		441
Flushing		317	Nashville		442
Jamaica		320	Texas	448-449	450
Long Island City		321	Dallas		453
New York City		323	Fort Worth		456
Staten Island		330	Houston		458
North Carolina	334-335	333	San Antonio		465
Charlotte		336	Utah	470-471	472
North Dakota	348-349	347	Vermont	474-475	476
Ohio	352-353	354	Virginia	480-481	479
Cincinnati		356	Norfolk		489
Cleveland		357	Washington	496-497	495
Columbus		357	Seattle		501
Oklahoma	374-375	373	West Virginia	504-505	503
Oklahoma City		377	Wisconsin	514-515	513
Oregon	380-381	379	Milwaukee		521
Pennsylvania	386-387	385	Wyoming	526-527	528
Philadelphia		407			

MAJOR CITIES WITH 5-DIGIT ZIP CODE MAPS

City	5-Digit Map	City	5-Digit Map
Atlanta, GA	110	Minneapolis, MN	254
Boston, MA	226	New York, NY	324-325
Chicago, IL	133	Philadelphia, PA	408
Dallas, TX	454	San Francisco, CA	71
Detroit, MI	238	St. Paul, MN	256
Kansas City, KS	177	Washington, DC	91
Los Angeles, CA	65		

INTRODUCTION

The Rand McNally *Zip Code Finder* is a complete and convenient reference containing zip code listings for more than 120,000 places in the United States. Arranged alphabetically by state, these listings enable you to quickly and easily find zip codes. The *Zip Code Finder's* listings are visually enhanced by a detailed 3-digit zip code map for each state. These maps show the location of towns and cities within Zip Code Sectional Areas.

Listings for 50 major U.S. cities include zip codes for selected hospitals, military installations, hotels/motels, colleges, universities and financial institutions. Additionally the Washington, D.C. listing includes zip codes for government offices.

Included in the listings is a telephone number for each multiple zip code city. By using this number, you can readily determine which of the city's zip codes you need. Listings for cities with only two zip codes, one of which is for the delivery **area** and the other for **post office boxes**, do not include telephone numbers. Instead, footnotes designate which zip code is for the delivery area (*), and which zip code is for post office boxes (†). Five-digit zip code maps display zip code boundaries for each of thirteen multiple zip code cities.

The Rand McNally *Zip Code Finder* saves you time and money. Information provided on postal rates and regulations, plus the locations of post office business offices, helps you to mail economically and efficiently. Convenient listings of toll-free numbers for car rentals, airline reservations and hotel/motel accommodations place these services at your fingertips. In addition, telephone area code lists provide a helpful and economical reference when placing long-distance calls.

THE MEANING OF YOUR ZIP CODE

Zip codes, set up to improve mail distribution, define areas within the U.S.

The country is divided into ten geographic regions that consist of three or more states. Each of these regions is assigned a number 0-9. This number is the first digit of your zip code.

Within the ten geographic regions, states are further divided into smaller geographic units. The second and third digits of your zip code identify these units.

Together, the first three digits of your zip code identify either a particular Sectional Center or Multi-Coded City. Sectional Centers and Multi-Coded Cities have similar postal functions. A Sectional Center, usually the natural center of local transportation, is a large post office serving smaller surrounding post offices. The Multi-Coded City is a main city post office which serves its stations and branches within the city's neighborhoods.

The final two digits of your zip code identify the post offices served by the Sectional Center _or_ branches and stations served by the city post office.

The example below further illustrates the meaning of a 5-digit zip code:

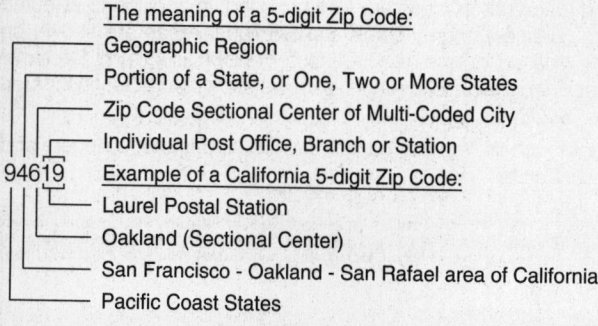

The meaning of a 5-digit Zip Code:
- Geographic Region
- Portion of a State, or One, Two or More States
- Zip Code Sectional Center of Multi-Coded City
- Individual Post Office, Branch or Station

94619   Example of a California 5-digit Zip Code:
- Laurel Postal Station
- Oakland (Sectional Center)
- San Francisco - Oakland - San Rafael area of California
- Pacific Coast States

USING THE ZIP CODE FINDER

Using the Rand McNally *Zip Code Finder* is easy. If you have the name of a city or town, but don't know its zip code, check the basic listings.

The basic listings are organized by state. Cities and towns are arranged alphabetically within each state.

Since it is not uncommon for the name of a city or town to occur more than once within a state, the *Zip Code Finder* differentiates between such cities or towns in several ways. First, if a city or town has the same name as another city or town, but is located in a different county, the *Zip Code Finder* will list the county in which the city or town is located. The county will be listed in parenthesis following the name of the city or town for all places that have a name which is identical to the name of another place within the same state. For example:

Altamont (Effingham County)	62411
Altamont (Madison County)	62035

In most cases, listing the county in which a city or town is located will differentiate between places with the same name. However, since the *Zip Code Finder* also lists townships and "towns"*, places that are "part of" other places, places that are defined by the Bureau of the Census, and several other types of localities, additional differentiation may be shown in parenthesis following the name of the place. For example:

Ashford	06278
Ashford (Town)	06250

In this case, the first listing refers to a single community that has the same name as the larger civil division which contains it and several other communities or places as well. The zip code for the larger civil division is shown in the second listing.

For places with more than one zip code, the *Zip Code Finder* provides the *range* of zip codes as shown below:

Belleville	62220-25
For specific Belleville Zip Codes call (618) 233-0391, or your local postmaster.	

In this example, the hyphenated numbers indicate the zip code range for Belleville. To obtain the zip code for a specific address within this multi-coded city, telephone your local postmaster or the number shown. (Listings for cities with only two zip codes, one for the delivery **area** and one for **post office boxes**, include footnotes that designate the nature of the zip code, * and † respectively.)

In addition to the telephone number for zip code information, a 5-digit zip code map is provided for each of the following cities:

- Atlanta, GA
- Boston, MA
- Chicago, IL
- Dallas, TX
- Detroit, MI
- Kansas City, KS
- Los Angeles, CA
- Minneapolis, MN
- New York, NY
- Philadelphia, PA
- San Francisco, CA
- St. Paul, MN
- Washington, D.C.

The 5-digit zip code map appears on the first full page following the beginning of the listing for each city shown above.

The *Zip Code Finder* also includes 3-digit zip code maps for the fifty states and the District of Columbia. More detailed maps of the 3-digit Sectional Areas around major urban areas are also provided. In addition to selected cities, towns and military bases, all state capitals, counties, county seats and Sectional Areas are shown on these maps. These maps provide a population key based on the 1980 Census of Population, and Sectional Centers are indicated by a circle around their respective population symbols. (Arrows show that a Sectional Area is served by a Sectional Center located in another Sectional Area.)

Zip Codes for selected hospitals, military installations, hotels, motels, banks, savings and loans, colleges, and universities are also listed for 50 of America's largest cities.

* In certain states, the civil divisions know as "townships" or "towns" have significant local importance. These civil divisions frequently include several distinct communities or places, and one of these places may bear the same name as the civil division. In the *Zip Code Finder*, "townships" are included in the listings for Illinois, Indiana, Michigan, Ohio, New Jersey and Pennsylvania, and "towns" are included for Connecticut, Maine, Massachusetts, New Hampshire, New York, Rhode Island, Vermont and Wisconsin.

STANDARD ABBREVIATIONS
FOR ADDRESSES

Listed below are two-letter state abbreviations which can be used in addressing mail.

Two-Letter State Abbreviations

Alabama AL	Kentucky KY	North Dakota ND
Alaska AK	Louisiana LA	Ohio OH
Arizona AZ	Maine ME	Oklahoma OK
Arkansas AR	Maryland MD	Oregon OR
California CA	Massachusetts MA	Pennsylvania PA
Colorado CO	Michigan MI	Rhode Island RI
Connecticut CT	Minnesota MN	South Carolina SC
Delaware DE	Mississippi MS	South Dakota SD
District of Columbia DC	Missouri MO	Tennessee TN
Florida FL	Montana MT	Texas TX
Georgia GA	Nebraska NE	Utah UT
Hawaii HI	Nevada NV	Vermont VT
Idaho ID	New Hampshire NH	Virginia VA
Illinois IL	New Jersey NJ	Washington WA
Indiana IN	New Mexico NM	West Virginia WV
Iowa IA	New York NY	Wisconsin WI
Kansas KS	North Carolina NC	Wyoming WY

SELECTED TOLL - FREE RESERVATION NUMBERS

To save you time and facilitate your reservations needs, the following toll-free reservation numbers are provided for selected lodging accommodations, car rental services and major airlines. (All numbers listed were effective at time of publication.)

AIRLINES

America West
800-235-9292

American
800-433-7300

Continental
800-525-0280

Delta
800-221-1212

Northwest
800-225-2525

Southwest
800-435-9792

TWA
800-221-2000

United
800-241-6522

U.S. Air
800-428-4322

HOTEL/MOTELS

Best Western
International, Inc.
800-528-1234

Days Inn
800-325-2525

Doubletree & Guest Quarters
800-424-2900

Embassy Suites
800-EMBASSY

Fairmont Hotels
800-527-4727

Harley Hotels
800-321-2323

Helmsley Hotels
800-221-4982

Holiday Inns
800-HOLIDAY

Howard Johnson's
Motor Lodges
800-654-2000

Hyatt Hotels Corp.
800-228-9000

Marriott
800-228-9290

Omni/Supranational
Hotels
800-843-6664

Preferred Hotels
800-323-7500

Quality Inns
800-228-5151

Radisson Hotels Int'l.
800-333-3333

Ramada Inns, Inc.
800-228-2828

Regent International
Hotels
800-545-4000

ITT Sheraton Hotels
& Motor Inns
800-325-3535

Stouffer Renaissance
Hotels & Resorts
800-HOTELS-1

Westin Hotels
800-228-3000

CAR RENTAL COMPANIES

Agency Rent-A-Car
800-321-1972
800-362-1794 (Ohio only)

Alamo Rent-A-Car
800-327-9633

Allstate Rent-A-Car
800-634-6186 (except NV)

Ace
Rent-A-Car
800-782-0511

Avis Reservations Center
800-331-1212 (Domestic)
800-331-1084 (International)

Budget Rent-A-Car
800-527-0700

Enterprise Rent-A-Car
800-325-8007

Hertz Corporation
800-654-3131

National Car Rental
800-328-4567

Payless Car Rental
800-PAYLESS

Sears Rent-A-Car
800-527-0770

Thrifty Rent-A-Car
800-367-2277

Value Rent-A-Car
800-327-2501

TELEPHONE AREA CODE AND TIME ZONE INFORMATION

The following tables list telephone area codes used in the United States. The first table is arranged in alphabetical order by state. The second table lists telephone area codes in numerical order.

The United States (including Alaska and Hawaii) is divided longitudinally into six time zones. If you were traveling from east to west, you would pass through the time zones in the following order: Eastern Standard Time (EST), Central Standard Time (CST), Mountain Standard Time (MST), Pacific Standard Time (PST), Alaska Time (AK), and Hawaii Time (HI).

Each time you enter a new time zone, it becomes one hour earlier. When it is 5 p.m. Eastern Standard Time (EST), it is 4 p.m. Central Standard Time (CST), 3 p.m. Mountain Standard Time (MST), etc. For your convenience, the appropriate time zone is listed in parentheses after each area code below. The map on pages 12 and 13 details the time zone boundaries.

Aphabetical List of Telephone Area Codes

Alabama
Birmingham (CST) 205
Montgomery (CST) 334
Alaska (AK-HI) 907
Juneau (AK) 907
Arizona
Phoenix (MST) 602
Tucson (MST) 520
Arkansas 501
Little Rock (CST) 501
California
Anaheim (PST) 714
Bakersfield (PST) 805
Eureka (PST) 707
Fresno (PST) 209
Long Beach (PST) 310
Los Angeles (PST) 213
Los Angeles-Suburban (PST) 818
Oakland (PST) 510
Riverside (PST) 909
Sacramento (PST) 916
San Diego (PST) 619
San Francisco (PST) 415
San Jose (PST) 408
Colorado
Colorado Springs (MST) 719
Denver (MST) 303
Connecticut 203
Hartford (EST) 203
Delaware 302
Dover (EST) 302
District of Columbia 202
Washington (EST) 202
Florida (CST,EST)
Jacksonville (EST) 904
Miami (EST) 305
Miami (EST) (cellular/beeper)* 954
Orlando (EST) 407
St. Petersburg (EST) 813
Tallahassee (EST) 904
Georgia
Atlanta (EST) 404
Columbus (EST) 706
Savannah (EST) 912
Hawaii (HI) 808
Honolulu (AK-HI) 808
Idaho (MST,PST) 208
Boise (MST) 208

Illinois
Chicago (CST) 312
Chicago-Suburban (CST) 708
Chicago-Suburban (CST)
(cellular/beeper)* 630
Peoria (CST) 309
Rockford (CST) 815
Springfield (CST) 217
West Frankfort (CST) 618
Indiana (CST,EST)
Evansville (EST) 812
Indianapolis (EST) 317
South Bend (EST) 219
Iowa
Council Bluffs (CST) 712
Des Moines (CST) 515
Dubuque (CST) 319
Kansas (CST,MST)
Topeka (CST) 913
Wichita (CST) 316
Kentucky (CST,EST)
Covington (EST) 606
Frankfort (EST) 502
Louisville (EST) 502
Louisiana
Baton Rouge (CST) 504
New Orleans (CST) 504
Shreveport (CST) 318
Maine 207
Augusta (EST) 207
Maryland
Annapolis (EST) 410
Rockville 301
Massachusetts
Boston (EST) 617
Lowell (EST) 508
Springfield (EST) 413
Michigan (CST,EST)
Detroit (EST) 313
Escanaba (EST) 906
Grand Rapids (EST) 616
Lansing (EST) 517
Warren (EST) 810
Minnesota
Duluth (CST) 218
Minneapolis (CST) 612
Rochester (CST) 507
St. Paul (CST) 612

TELEPHONE AREA CODE AND TIME ZONE INFORMATION, CONT'D.

Aphabetical List of Telephone Area Codes, continued

Mississippi	601	Pennsylvania		
Jackson (CST)	601	Allentown (EST)	610	
Missouri		Erie (EST)	814	
Jefferson City (CST)	314	Harrisburg (EST)	717	
Kansas City (CST)	816	Philadelphia (EST)	215	
St. Louis (CST)	314	Pittsburgh (EST)	412	
Springfield (CST)	417	Rhode Island	401	
Montana	406	Providence (EST)	401	
Helena (MST)	406	South Carolina	803	
Nebraska (CST,MST)		Columbia (EST)	803	
Lincoln (CST)	402	South Dakota (CST,MST)	605	
North Platte (CST)	308	Pierre (CST)	605	
Omaha (CST)	402	Tennessee (CST,EST)		
Nevada	702	Memphis (CST)	901	
Carson City (PST)	702	Nashville (CST)	615	
New Hampshire	603	Texas (CST,MST)		
Concord (EST)	603	Abilene (CST)	915	
New Jersey		Amarillo (CST)	806	
Elizabeth (EST)	908	Austin (CST)	512	
Newark (EST)	201	Beaumont (CST)	409	
Trenton (EST)	609	Dallas (CST)	214	
New Mexico	505	Fort Worth (CST)	817	
Santa Fe (MST)	505	Houston (CST)	713	
New York		Houston (CST) (cellular/beeper)	†	
Albany (EST)	518	San Antonio (CST)	210	
Binghamton (EST)	607	Tyler (CST)	903	
Buffalo (EST)	716	Utah	801	
Hempstead (EST)	516	Salt Lake City (MST)	801	
New York (EST)	212	Vermont	802	
New York (EST)	718	Montpelier (EST)	802	
New York (EST) (cellular/beeper)	917	Virginia		
North Carolina		Richmond (EST)	804	
Charlotte (EST)	704	Roanoke (EST)	703	
Greensboro (EST)	910	Washington		
Raleigh (EST)	919	Bellingham (PST)	360	
North Dakota (CST,MST)	701	Olympia (PST)	360	
Bismark (CST)	701	Seattle (PST)	206	
Ohio		Spokane (PST)	509	
Cincinnati (EST)	513	West Virginia		
Cleveland (EST)	216	Charleston (EST)	304	
Columbus (EST)	614	Wisconsin		
Toledo (EST)	419	Eau Claire (CST)	715	
Oklahoma		Madison (CST)	608	
Oklahoma City (CST)	405	Milwaukee (CST)	414	
Tulsa (CST)	918	Wyoming	307	
Oregon (MST,PST)	503	Cheyenne (MST)	307	
Salem (PST)	503			

Numerical List of Telephone Area Codes

Area Code	Location (Time Zone)	Area Code	Location (Time Zone)
201	New Jersey (EST)	213	California (PST)
202	District of Columbia (EST)	214	Texas (CST)
203	Connecticut (EST)	215	Pennsylvania (EST)
205	Alabama (CST)	216	Ohio (EST)
206	Washington (PST)	217	Illinois (CST)
207	Maine (EST)	218	Minnesota (CST)
208	Idaho (MST,PST)	219	Indiana (CST,EST)
210	Texas (CST)	301	Maryland (EST)
212	New York (EST)	302	Delaware (EST)

TELEPHONE AREA CODE AND TIME ZONE INFORMATION, CONT'D.

Numerical List of Telephone Area Codes, continued

Area Code...	Location (Time Zone)
303......	Colorado (MST)
304......	West Virginia (EST)
305......	Florida (EST)
307......	Wyoming (MST)
308......	Nebraska (CST,MST)
309......	Illinois (CST)
310......	California (PST)
312......	Illinois (CST)
313......	Michigan (EST)
314......	Missouri (CST)
315......	New York (EST)
316......	Kansas (CST,MST)
317......	Indiana (EST)
318......	Louisiana (CST)
319......	Iowa (CST)
334......	Alabama (CST)
360......	Washington (PST)
401......	Rhode Island (EST)
402......	Nebraska (CST,MST)
404......	Georgia (EST)
405......	Oklahoma (CST)
406......	Montana (MST)
407......	Florida (EST)
408......	California (PST)
409......	Texas (CST)
410......	Maryland (EST)
412......	Pennsylvania (EST)
413......	Massachusetts (EST)
414......	Wisconsin (CST)
415......	California (PST)
417......	Missouri (CST)
419......	Ohio (EST)
501......	Arkansas (CST)
502......	Kentucky (CST,EST)
503......	Oregon (MST,PST)
504......	Louisiana (CST)
505......	New Mexico (MST)
507......	Minnesota (CST)
508......	Massachusetts (EST)
509......	Washington (PST)
510......	California (PST)
512......	Texas (CST)
513......	Ohio (EST)
515......	Iowa (CST)
516......	New York (EST)
517......	Michigan (EST)
518......	New York (EST)
520......	Arizona (MST)
601......	Mississippi (CST)
602......	Arizona (MST)
603......	New Hampshire (EST)
605......	South Dakota (CST,MST)
606......	Kentucky (EST)
607......	New York (EST)
608......	Wisconsin (CST)

Area Code...	Location (Time Zone)
609......	New Jersey (EST)
610......	Pennsylvania (EST)
612......	Minnesota (CST)
614......	Ohio (EST)
615......	Tennessee (CST,EST)
616......	Michigan (EST)
617......	Massachusetts (EST)
618......	Illinois (CST)
619......	California (PST)
630......	Illinois (CST)*
701......	North Dakota (CST,MST)
702......	Nevada (PST)
703......	Virginia (EST)
706......	Georgia (EST)
707......	California (PST)
708......	Illinois (CST)
712......	Iowa (CST)
713......	Texas (CST)
714......	California (PST)
715......	Wisconsin (CST)
716......	New York (EST)
717......	Pennsylvania (EST)
718......	New York (EST)
719......	Colorado (MST)
800......	Inward Watts
801......	Utah (MST)
802......	Vermont (EST)
803......	South Carolina (EST)
804......	Virginia (EST)
805......	California (PST)
806......	Texas (CST)
808......	Hawaii (AK-HI)
810......	Michigan (EST)
812......	Indiana (CST,EST)
813......	Florida (EST)
814......	Pennsylvania (EST)
815......	Illinois (CST)
816......	Missouri (CST)
817......	Texas (CST)
818......	California (PST)
901......	Tennessee (CST)
903......	Texas (CST)
904......	Florida (CST,EST)
906......	Michigan (CST,EST)
907......	Alaska (AK-HI)
909......	California (PST)
910......	North Carolina (EST)
912......	Georgia (EST)
913......	Kansas (CST,MST)
914......	New York (EST)
915......	Texas (CST,MST)
917......	New York (EST)
918......	Oklahoma (CST)
919......	North Carolina (EST)
954......	Florida (EST)*

* probable new telephone area code, 1995
† to be selected

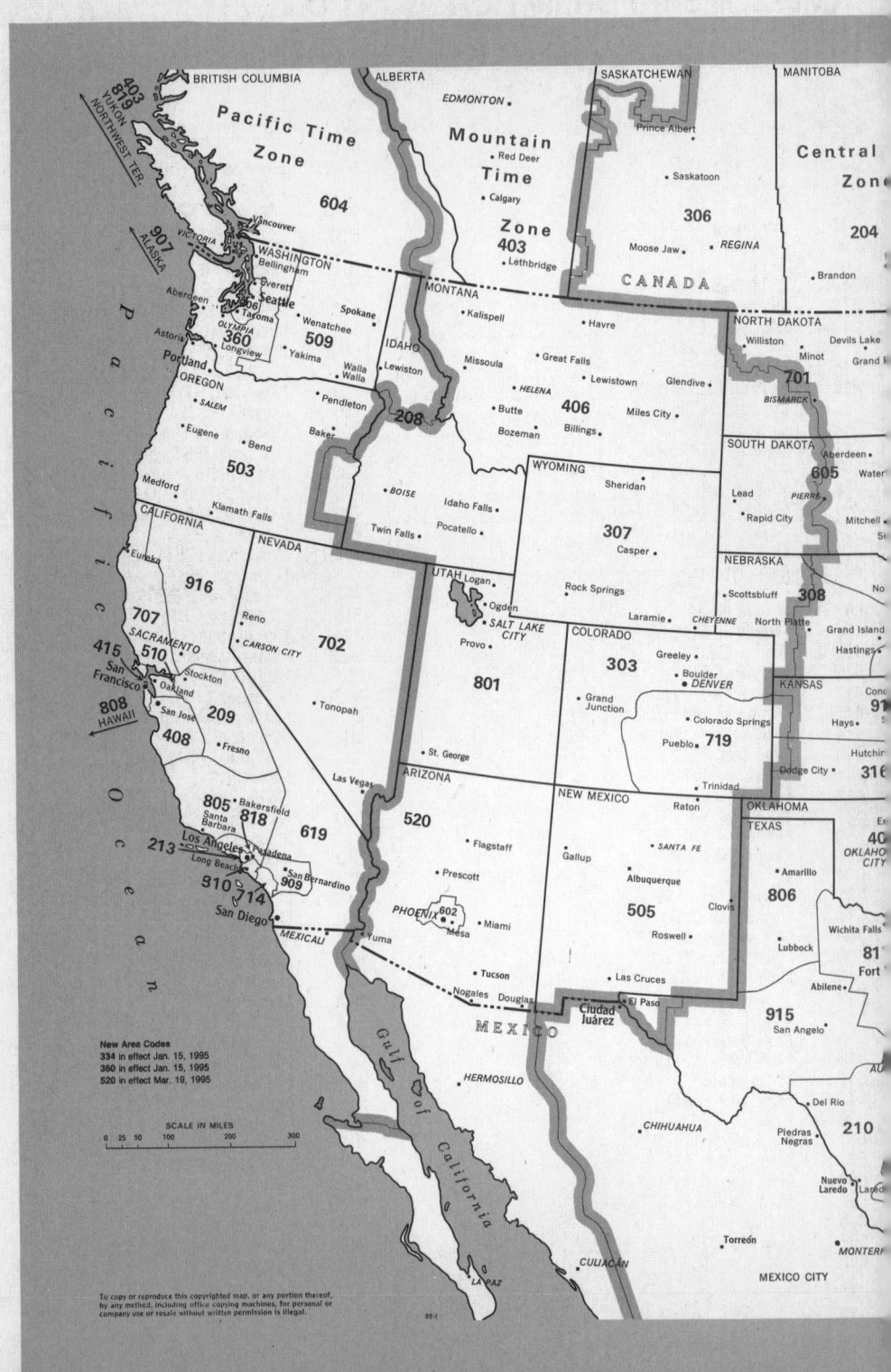

SMALL PARCEL RATES

Ground service rates for packages of 1 to 20 pounds are shown for the U.S. Postal Service, United Parcel Service (UPS), and Roadway Package System (RPS). Air freight rates for packages of 1 to 5 pounds and express letters, are also shown for selected air freight companies. (All rates shown were current at the time publication.)

In order to use the ground zone rate charts presented below for the U.S. Postal Service, United Parcel Service (UPS), and Roadway Package System (RPS), you will need to contact the carrier of your choice and request the zone chart that applies to your specific geographic location. This chart will enable you to determine the zone which corresponds to the destination of your parcel. Contact your local post office or UPS office; RPS may be contacted by calling the toll-free number which appears beneath the RPS Ground Zones Chart.

GROUND SERVICE RATES

United States Post Office Parcel Post Rates

First-Class Zone Rates (Priority Mail): All first-class mail weighing over 12 oz. Maximum weight is 70 lbs.; size is limited to 108 inches in combined length and girth.

Weight over 12 oz. and not exceeding	Zones					
	Local 1, 2 & 3	4	5	6	7	8
1 #	$ 2.90	$ 2.90	$ 2.90	$ 2.90	$ 2.90	$ 2.90
2 #	2.90	2.90	2.90	2.90	2.90	2.90
3 #	4.10	4.10	4.10	4.10	4.10	4.10
4 #	4.65	4.65	4.65	4.65	4.65	4.65
5 #	5.45	5.45	5.45	5.45	5.45	5.45
6 #	5.55	5.75	6.10	6.85	7.65	8.60
7 #	5.70	6.10	6.70	7.55	8.50	9.65
8 #	5.90	6.50	7.30	8.30	9.40	10.70
9 #	6.10	7.00	7.95	9.05	10.25	11.75
10 #	6.35	7.55	8.55	9.80	11.15	12.80
11 #	6.75	8.05	9.20	10.55	12.05	13.80
12 #	7.15	8.55	9.80	11.30	12.90	14.85
13 #	7.50	9.10	10.40	12.05	13.80	15.90
14 #	7.90	9.60	11.05	12.80	14.65	16.95
15 #	8.30	10.10	11.65	13.55	15.55	18.00
16 #	8.70	10.65	12.30	14.30	16.45	19.05
17 #	9.10	11.15	12.90	15.05	17.30	20.10
18 #	9.50	11.65	13.55	15.80	18.20	21.10
19 #	9.90	12.20	14.15	16.50	19.05	22.15
20 #	10.30	12.70	14.75	17.25	19.95	23.20

For additional rate information, call your local Post Office.

SMALL PARCEL RATES, CONT'D.

United Parcel Service (UPS)   (Commercial deliveries only.)

Ground Zones

Weight not to exceed	2	3	4	5	6	7	8
1 #	$ 2.35	$ 2.50	$ 2.74	$ 2.83	$ 2.92	$ 3.00	$ 3.07
2 #	2.37	2.54	3.02	3.13	3.35	3.45	3.70
3 #	2.47	2.71	3.22	3.38	3.65	3.76	4.09
4 #	2.58	2.87	3.35	3.55	3.79	3.99	4.38
5 #	2.70	3.00	3.43	3.64	3.97	4.18	4.61
6 #	2.81	3.08	3.49	3.71	4.14	4.37	4.76
7 #	2.92	3.15	3.55	3.76	4.26	4.57	4.99
8 #	3.03	3.22	3.62	3.84	4.40	4.80	5.37
9 #	3.14	3.30	3.68	3.94	4.56	5.09	5.80
10 #	3.25	3.40	3.75	4.07	4.73	5.44	6.23
11 #	3.34	3.50	3.84	4.26	4.99	5.78	6.68
12 #	3.43	3.62	3.95	4.47	5.27	6.15	7.13
13 #	3.50	3.74	4.07	4.69	5.57	6.56	7.60
14 #	3.58	3.88	4.23	4.92	5.88	6.94	8.09
15 #	3.66	4.04	4.40	5.17	6.19	7.35	8.57
16 #	3.74	4.21	4.57	5.41	6.52	7.75	9.03
17 #	3.82	4.36	4.74	5.62	6.82	8.13	9.50
18 #	3.89	4.51	4.91	5.85	7.13	8.53	9.97
19 #	3.99	4.62	5.09	6.06	7.47	8.91	10.44
20 #	4.13	4.78	5.28	6.32	7.77	9.29	10.91

For additional rate information, contact your local United Parcel Service office.

Roadway Package System (RPS)   (Commercial deliveries only.)

Ground Zones

Weight not to exceed	2	3	4	5	6	7	8
1 #	$ 2.35	$ 2.50	$ 2.74	$ 2.83	$ 2.92	$ 3.00	$ 3.07
2 #	2.37	2.54	3.02	3.13	3.35	3.45	3.70
3 #	2.47	2.71	3.22	3.38	3.65	3.76	4.09
4 #	2.58	2.87	3.35	3.55	3.79	3.99	4.38
5 #	2.70	3.00	3.43	3.64	3.97	4.18	4.61
6 #	2.81	3.08	3.49	3.71	4.14	4.37	4.76
7 #	2.92	3.15	3.55	3.76	4.26	4.57	4.99
8 #	3.03	3.22	3.62	3.84	4.40	4.80	5.37
9 #	3.14	3.30	3.68	3.94	4.56	5.09	5.80
10 #	3.25	3.40	3.75	4.07	4.73	5.44	6.23
11 #	3.34	3.50	3.84	4.26	4.99	5.78	6.68
12 #	3.43	3.62	3.95	4.47	5.27	6.15	7.13
13 #	3.50	3.74	4.07	4.69	5.57	6.56	7.60
14 #	3.58	3.88	4.23	4.92	5.88	6.94	8.09
15 #	3.66	4.04	4.40	5.17	6.19	7.35	8.57
16 #	3.74	4.21	4.57	5.41	6.52	7.75	9.03
17 #	3.82	4.36	4.74	5.62	6.82	8.13	9.50
18 #	3.89	4.51	4.91	5.85	7.13	8.53	9.97
19 #	3.99	4.62	5.09	6.06	7.47	8.91	10.44
20 #	4.13	4.78	5.28	6.32	7.77	9.29	10.91

For additional rate information, call 1-800-ROADPAK.

SMALL PARCEL RATES, CONT'D.

AIR FREIGHT RATES FOR SELECTED PRIVATE CARRIERS

With the exception of UPS, most private carriers offer a variety of services, including overnight and second-day delivery. Most provide free envelopes and shipping containers and offer discounts for drop-off by the sender.

All of the private carriers listed provide pick-up as well as delivery. Most have drop-off boxes available in convenient locations. Next-day air and second-day air delivery times vary by carrier.

For your convenience in obtaining additional information on rates for heavier shipments, multiple shipments and frequent shipper discounts, toll-free numbers have been included in the rate tables. (All rates shown were current at the time of publication. Rates are subject to change without notice.)

United Parcel Service (UPS)   (1-800-942-7127)

Next-Day Air Letter

$10.75 (Continental U.S.)

2nd-Day Air Letter

$5.75 (Continental U.S.)

Next-Day Air Package

Lbs.	Continental U.S.	AK & HI
1	$15.25	$20.50
2	16.00	22.00
3	17.50	23.50
4	19.00	25.00
5	20.75	26.75

2nd-Day Air Package

Lbs.	Continental U.S.	AK & HI
1	$ 6.00	$10.25
2	7.00	11.50
3	7.75	12.75
4	8.25	14.00
5	9.00	15.25

Federal Express (Fed Ex)   (1-800-238-5355)

Priority
Overnight Letter

$15.50 (up to 8 oz.)

Standard
Overnight Letter

$11.50 (up to 8 oz.)

Priority Overnight Service
(Pkg. delivery by 10:30 AM)

Lbs.	Price *
1	$22.50
2	24.25
3	27.00
4	29.75
5	32.50

Standard Overnight Service
(Pkg. delivery by 3:00 PM)

Lbs.	Price *
1	$15.50
2	16.50
3	17.50
4	18.50
5	19.50

Economy Service
(Pkg. delivery by
4:30 PM on 2nd day)

Lbs.	Price *
1	$13.00
2	14.00
3	15.00
4	16.00
5	17.00

SMALL PARCEL RATES, CONT'D.

Airborne (General office, 1-800-426-2323; Washington state, 1-800-562-2227)

Overnight Letter
(Delivery by 12:00 PM)

$14.00 * (up to 8 oz.)

Select Delivery Service
(Delivery by 3:00 PM)

$8.00 * (up to 8 oz.)

(The above rates are for Non-Discounted service.)

"Express One" Service
(Next day, door-to-door pkg. delivery)

Lbs.	Price *
2	$25.00
3	30.00
4	36.00
5	38.00

Emery (1-800-HI-EMERY)
For specific rate information call Emery's toll-free telephone number, listed above.

Burlington Air Express (1-800-CALL-BAX)
For specific rate information call Burlington's toll-free telephone number, listed above.

Contact the toll-free "800" telephone numbers for further information.

* Prices not applicable for shipments from Continental U.S. to or between Alaska and Hawaii.

U.S. POSTAL SERVICE BUSINESS CENTERS

The following is a list of the 95 Postal Business Centers that operate nationwide. In the event that you have questions about mailing procedures, rates or regulations, contact the appropriate Center. The listings below were current as of June, 1994.

ALABAMA

Birmingham   (205) 323-6510
351 24th St. N
Birmingham, AL   35203-9691

ALASKA

Anchorage   (907) 564-2823
3201 C St., Suite 505
Anchorage, AK   99503-3934

ARIZONA

Phoenix   (602) 225-5454
4949 E. Van Buren St., Room 8
Phoenix, AZ   85026-9605

Tucson   (602) 620-5108
1501 S. Cherrybell Stravenue
Tucson, AZ   85726-9605

ARKANSAS

Little Rock   (501) 227-6639
11324 Arcade Dr., Suite 3
Little Rock, AR   72212-4072

CALIFORNIA

Long Beach   (310) 494-2301
2300 Redondo Ave.
Long Beach, CA   90809-9694

Los Angeles   (213) 586-1843
7001 S. Central Ave., Room 264
Los Angeles, CA   90052-9602

Oakland   (510) 874-8600
1675 7th St., Room 120
Oakland, CA   94615-9641

Sacramento   (916) 923-4357
2035 Hurley Way, Suite 200
Sacramento, CA   95825-3209

San Diego   (619) 674-0400
11251 Rancho Carmel Dr., Room 266
San Diego, CA   92199-9606

San Francisco   (415) 550-6565
P.O. Box 193000
San Francisco, CA   94119-3000

San Jose   (408) 723-6262
P.O. Box 50014
San Jose, CA   95150-0014

Santa Ana   (714) 662-6213
3101 W. Sunflower Ave.
Santa Ana, CA   92799-9323

Van Nuys   (818) 374-4943
15701 Sherman Way
Van Nuys, CA   91409-9680

COLORADO

Denver   (303) 297-6118
1745 Stout St., Suite 101
Denver, CO   80266-9617

CONNECTICUT

Hartford   (203) 524-6491
141 Weston St.
Hartford, CT   06101-9631

DISTRICT OF COLUMBIA

Washington, DC   (301) 565-2177
8455 Colesville Rd., Suite 950
Silver Spring, MD   20910-3319

FLORIDA

Fort Lauderdale   (305) 527-6981
1900 W. Oakland Park Blvd.
Fort Lauderdale, FL   33310-9600

Jacksonville   (904) 260-8101
11250 Phillips Industrial Blvd. E
Jacksonville, FL   32256-3000

Miami   (305) 470-0803
2200 NW 72nd Ave., Room 525
Miami, FL   33152-9600

Orlando   (407) 826-5602
10401 Tradeport Dr., Room 103
Orlando, FL   32862-8901

Tampa   (813) 871-6245
4107 N. Himes Ave., Suite 203
Tampa, FL   33607-6600

West Palm Beach   (407) 697-2180
3200 Summit Blvd., Room 109
West Palm Beach, FL   33406-9602

GEORGIA

Macon   (912) 784-3917
P.O. Box 20777
Macon, GA   31205-0777

North Metro   (404) 717-3440
P.O. Box 599332
North Metro, GA   30159-9332

Savannah   (912) 235-4591
2 N. Fahm St.
Savannah, GA   31402-9600

HAWAII

Honolulu   (808) 423-3761
3600 Aolele St.
Honolulu, HI   96820-9623

ILLINOIS

Aurora   (708) 978-4455
3900 Gabrielle Lane
Aurora, IL   60599-9601

Carol Stream   (708) 260-5512
500 E. Fullerton Ave.
Carol Stream, IL   60199-9661

Chicago   (312) 765-4215
433 W. Van Buren St., Room 108
Chicago, IL   60607-9601

INDIANA

Indianapolis   (317) 464-6010
125 W. South St., Room 101
Indianapolis, IN   46206-9661

IOWA

Des Moines   (515) 251-2336
P.O. Box 189996
Des Moines, IA   50318-9605

KENTUCKY

Louisville   (502) 473-4200
P.O. Box 31660
Louisville, KY   40231-9660

LOUISIANA

New Orleans   (504) 589-1366
701 Loyola Ave., Room 1103
New Orleans, LA   70113-9680

MAINE

Portland   (207) 871-8567
125 Forest Ave.
Portland, ME   04101-9600

U.S. POSTAL SERVICE BUSINESS CENTERS, CONT'D.

MARYLAND

Baltimore   (410) 347-4358
900 E. Fayette St., Room 502
Baltimore, MD   21233-9661

MASSACHUSETTS

Boston   (617) 654-5725
25 Dorchester Ave., Room 1000
Boston, MA   02205-9602

Springfield   (413) 731-0306
1883 Main St.
Springfield, MA   01101-9600

Woburn   (617) 938-1450
P.O. Box 2336
Woburn, MA   01888-0336

Worcester   (508) 795-3608
4 East Central St.
Worcester, MA   01613-9602

MICHIGAN

Birmingham   (810) 901-4525
P.O. Box 9630
Birmingham, MI   48009-9630

Detroit   (313) 225-5445
1927 Rosa Parks Blvd.
Detroit, MI   48216-9620

Grand Rapids   (616) 776-6161
P.O. Box 999661
Grand Rapids, MI   49599-9661

MINNESOTA

Minneapolis   (612) 349-6360
100 S. First St., Room 119
Minneapolis, MN   55401-9617

MISSISSIPPI

Jackson   (601) 360-2700
401 E. South St., Suite 100
Jackson, MS   39201-9825

MISSOURI

Kansas City   (816) 374-9513
315 W. Pershing Rd., Room 104
Kansas City, MO   64108-9623

St. Louis   (314) 534-2678
2665 Scott Ave.
St. Louis, MO   63103-3048

MONTANA

Billings   (406) 255-6432
550 S. 24th St. W
Billings, MT   59102-6293

Missoula   (406) 329-2231
1100 W. Kent Ave.
Missoula, MT   59801-9625

NEBRASKA

Omaha   (402) 573-2100
5303 N. 91st Ave.
Omaha, NE   68134-9600

NEVADA

Las Vegas   (702) 361-9318
1001 E. Sunset Rd.
Las Vegas, NV   89199-9605

NEW HAMPSHIRE

Manchester   (603) 644-3838
955 Goffs Falls Rd.
Manchester, NH   03103-9671

NEW JERSEY

Bellmawr   (609) 933-6000
P.O. Box 9001
Bellmawr, NJ   08099-9996

Edison   (908) 777-0565
21 Kilmer Rd.
Edison, NJ   08899-9610

West Orange   (201) 731-4866
100 Executive Dr., Suite 390
West Orange, NJ   07052-9333

NEW MEXICO

Albuquerque   (505) 245-9480
1135 Broadway Blvd. NE, Room 147
Albuquerque, NM   87101-9601

NEW YORK

Albany   (518) 869-6526
1770 Central Ave.
Albany, NY   12205-4753

Buffalo   (716) 846-2581
1200 William St., Room 100
Buffalo, NY   14240-9661

Elmsford   (914) 345-1237
500 N. Saw Mill River Rd.
Elmsford, NY   10523-9650

Flushing   (718) 321-5700
14202 20th Ave., Room 123B
Flusing, NY   11351-9621

Hauppauge   (516) 582-7600
P.O. Box 7609
Hauppauge, NY   11760-9661

New York   (212) 330-2824
421 8th Ave., Room 4202H
New York, NY   10199-9619

Rochester   (716) 272-7220
P.O. Box 22908
Rochester, NY   14692-2908

NORTH CAROLINA

Charlotte   (704) 393-4481
2901 S. I-85 Service Rd.
Charlotte, NC   28228-9975

Greensboro   (910) 665-9740
P.O. Box 27499
Greensboro, NC   27498-9661

OHIO

Akron   (216) 996-9721
675 Wolf Ledges Pkwy
Akron, OH   44309-9600

Cincinnati   (513) 723-9900
990 Dalton Ave.
Cincinnati, OH   45203-9601

Cleveland   (216) 443-4401
2400 Orange Ave., Room 23
Cleveland, OH   44101-9998

Columbus   (614) 469-4336
850 Twin Rivers Dr.
Columbus, OH 43216-9601

OKLAHOMA

Oklahoma City   (405) 720-2675
7101 NW Expressway St., Suite 325
Oklahoma City, OK   73132-1598

OREGON

Portland   (503) 294-2306
P.O. Box 4029
Portland, OR   97208-4029

PENNSYLVANIA

Erie   (814) 878-0018
1314 Griswold Plaza
Erie, PA   16501-9631

Harrisburg   (717) 257-2108
1425 Crooked Hill Rd.
Harrisburg, PA   17107-9601

Lancaster   (717) 396-6994
1400 Harrisburg Pike
Lancaster, PA   17604-9601

Philadelphia   (215) 895-8046
P.O. Box 13416
Philadelphia, PA   19101-3416

U.S. POSTAL SERVICE BUSINESS CENTERS, CONT'D.

Pittsburgh   **(412) 359-8046**
1001 California Ave., Room 1007
Pittsburgh, PA   15290-9652

Southeastern   **(215) 964-6441**
1000 W. Valley Rd.
Southeastern, PA   19399-9604

PUERTO RICO

San Juan   **(809) 782-3929**
585 FDR Ave., Suite 211
San Juan, PR   00936-9623

RHODE ISLAND

Providence   **(401) 276-5038**
24 Corliss St., Room 355
Providence, RI   02904-9602

SOUTH CAROLINA

Columbia   **(803) 926-6310**
P.O. Box 929641
Columbia, SC   29292-9641

SOUTH DAKOTA

Sioux Falls   **(605) 339-8854**
320 S. 2nd Ave.
Sioux Falls, SD   57102-7574

TENNESSEE

Memphis   **(901) 576-2035**
P.O. Box 3463
Memphis, TN   38173-0463

Nashville   **(615) 885-9399**
525 Royal Pky., Room 327
Nashville, TN   37229-9601

TEXAS

Dallas   **(214) 393-6701**
951 W. Bethel Rd.
Coppell, TX   75099-9681

Fort Worth   **(817) 625-3600**
4600 Mark IV Pky., Suite 260K
Fort Worth, TX   76161-9681

Houston   **(713) 226-3349**
P.O. Box 250001
Houston, TX   77202-9610

North Houston   **(713) 985-4108**
4600 Aldine Bender Rd., Room 227
Houston, TX   77315-9610

San Antonio   **(210) 657-8578**
10410 Perrin Beitel Rd.
San Antonio, TX   78284-9623

UTAH

Salt Lake City   **(801) 974-2503**
1760 W. 2100 S
Salt Lake City, UT   84199-9625

VERMONT   **(800) 230-2370**

Vermont is served by the Postal Business Center in Springfield, Massachusetts.

VIRGINIA

Merrifield   **(703) 207-6800**
8409 Lee Hwy., Rooms 1-8
Merrifield, VA   22081-9621

Richmond   **(804) 775-6224**
1801 Brook Rd.
Richmond, VA   23232-9610

WASHINGTON

Seattle   **(206) 625-7016**
P.O. Box 24000
Seattle, WA   98124-4000

Spokane   **(509) 626-6733**
707 W. Main Ave., Suite 600
Spokane, WA   99299-9641

WEST VIRGINIA

Charleston   **(304) 340-4233**
P.O. Box 59661
Charleston, WV   25350-9661

WISCONSIN

Madison   **(608) 246-1245**
P.O. Box 14750
Madison, WI   53714-0750

Milwaukee   **(414) 287-2522**
P.O. Box 5008
Milwaukee, WI   53201-5008

	ZIP
Abanda	36274
Abbeville	36310
Abel	36258
Abercrombie	35042
Aberfoil	36089
Abernant	35440
Abernathy	36264
Acipcoville (Part of Birmingham)	35207
Ackerville	36768
Acmar	35094
Active	36793
Ada	36069
Adamsburg	35967
Adamsville	35005
Addison	35540
Adger	35006
Adler	36779
Ai	36264
Aimwell	36782
Airport Highlands (Part of Birmingham)	35206
Airport Station (Part of Mobile)	36608
Akron	35441
Alabama City (Part of Gadsden)	35904
Alabama Fork	35611
Alabama Port	36523
Alabama Shores	35660
Alabaster	35007
Alaga	36343
Alberta	36720
Alberta City (Part of Tuscaloosa)	35401
Alberton	36453
Albertville	35950
Alder Springs	35950
Aldrich	35115
Aldridge	35580
Aldridge Grove	35650
Alexander City	35010
Alexandria	36250
Alexis	35960
Aliceville	35442
Allen	36419
Allens Crossroads	35175
Allenton	36768
Allenton Station	36768
Allenville (Hale County)	36738
Allenville (Marengo County)	36738
Allgood	35013
Allsboro	35616
Allsop	36272
Alma	36501
Almeria	36089
Almond	36276
Alpine (DeKalb County)	35984
Alpine (Talladega County)	35014
Altadena Valley	35243
Alton	35015
Altoona	35952
America	35580
Andalusia	36420
Anderson (Etowah County)	35901
Anderson (Lauderdale County)	35610
Andrews Chapel	35619
Angel	36265
Annemanie	36721
Anniston	36201-07
For specific Anniston Zip Codes call (205) 236-6355, or your local postmaster.	
Anniston Army Depot	36201
Ansley	36081
Antioch (Calhoun County)	36253
Antioch (Covington County)	36420
Antioch (Pike County)	36081
Appleton	36426
Aqua Vista	35645
Aquilla	36558
Arab	35016
Ararat	36921
Arbacoochee	36264
Arbor Acres (Part of Huntsville)	35810
Ardell	35053
Ardilla (Part of Dothan)	36301
Ardmore	35739
Ardmore Highway (Part of Huntsville)	35816
Argo	35173
Argo Heights	35550
Arguta	36360
Ariton	36311

	ZIP
Arkadelphia	35033
Arkwright (Part of Vincent)	35178
Arley	35541
Arlington	36722
Armstead	35121
Armstrong	36089
Arona	35957
Arrowhead	36109
Arrowwood (Part of Tuscaloosa)	35405
Asberry	36272
Asbury (Dale County)	36360
Asbury (Marshall County)	35950
Ashbank	35578
Ashby	35035
Ashford	36312
Ashland (Clay County)	36251
Ashland (Madison County)	35811
Ashridge	35565
Ashville	35953
Aspel	35768
Athens	35611
Atkinson	36784
Atmore	36502-04
For specific Atmore Zip Codes call (205) 368-2871, or your local postmaster.	
Attalla	35954
Atwood	35571
Auburn	36830-49
For specific Auburn Zip Codes call (205) 821-3754, or your local postmaster.	
Augustin	36701
Aurora	35957
Aurora Springs	35616
Austinville (Part of Decatur)	35601
Autaugaville	36003
Avalon Park (Part of Hueytown)	35020
Avant	36033
Avery (Part of Stevenson)	35772
Avoca	35653
Avon	36312
Avondale (Part of Birmingham)	35222
Avondale Mill (Part of Alexander City)	35010
Avondale Village (Part of Pell City)	35125
Avon Park (Part of Birmingham)	35234
Awin	36768
Axis	36505
Ayres	35126
Babbie	36420
Bacon Level	36274
Bagley	35062
Bailey Cove (Part of Huntsville)	35802
Bailey Springs	35645
Baileyton	35019
Baileytown	35019
Baker Hill	36027
Bald Hill	36375
Baldwin Farms	36083
Balkum	36345
Ballplay	35903
Bangor	35079
Bankhead (DeKalb County)	35984
Bankhead (Walker County)	35580
Banks	36005
Bankston	35542
Barachias (Part of Montgomery)	36064
Barber	36312
Barfield	36266
Barlow	36558
Barlow Bend	36545
Barnes	36311
Barnesville	35570
Barnett Chapel	35572
Barnett Crossroads	36426
Barney	35550
Barnisdale Forest (Part of Birmingham)	35215
Barnwell	36532
Barrytown	36908
Barton	35616
Basham	35640
Bashi	36784
Basin	36323
Bass	35772
Bassetts Creek	36585
Batesville	36053
Battelle	35989

	ZIP
Battens Crossroads	36316
Battleground	35179
Battles Wharf	36532
Bay Minette	36507
Bayou La Batre	36509
Bay Shore Junction (Part of Prichard)	36610
Bayside (Mobile County)	36605
Bayside (Morgan County)	35603
Bay Springs	35960
Bayview	35005
Bazemore	35559
Beachwood Park (Part of Birmingham)	35212
Beamon	36360
Bean Rock	35175
Bear Creek	35543
Bear Point	36561
Beasons Mill	36264
Beatrice	36425
Beaty Crossroads (Part of Ider)	35981
Beauregard	36801
Beaverton	35544
Beaver Town	35442
Beck	36420
Beehive	36865
Bel Air (Jefferson County)	35210
Bel Air (Mobile County)	36616
Bel Air Mall (Part of Mobile)	36606
Belforest	36526
Belgreen	35653
Belk	35545
Bellamy	36901
Bellefontaine	36567
Bellefonte	35752
Bellefountaine	36582
Bellemeade	35630
Belle Mina	35615
Belleville	36401
Bellevue (Part of Gadsden)	35901
Bell Springs	35622
Bellview	36726
Bellwood (Geneva County)	36313
Bellwood (Jefferson County)	35064
Belmont	35470
Beloit	36759
Beltline (Part of Decatur)	35601
Belview Heights (Part of Tuscumbia)	35674
Bemiston (Part of Talladega)	35160
Bendale (Part of Birmingham)	35217
Benevola	35466
Benoit	35550
Bentley Hills (Part of Mountain Brook)	35216
Benton	36785
Ben Vines Gap (Part of Maytown)	35118
Berkley	35748
Berlin	35055
Bermuda (Conecuh County)	36401
Bermuda (Monroe County)	36460
Berney Points (Part of Birmingham)	35211
Berry	35546
Bertha	36353
Bessemer	35020-23
For specific Bessemer Zip Codes call (205) 428-9163, or your local postmaster.	
Bessemer Gardens (Part of Hueytown)	35020
Bessemer Homestead (Part of Bessemer)	35020
Bessie	35062
Bessie Junction	35062
Bethany	35452
Bethel (Barbour County)	36311
Bethel (Cullman County)	35057
Bethel (Limestone County)	35620
Bethlehem	36046
Beulah (Covington County)	36467
Beulah (Greene County)	35469
Beulah (Lee County)	36854
Beverly Station (Part of Birmingham)	35211
Bexar	35570
Bibbville	35188

	ZIP
Biddle Crossroads (Part of Henagar)	35978
Bigbee	36510
Big Creek	36301
Big Oak	35645
Big Springs	35188
Billingsley	36006
Billy Goat Hill	35960
Birdine	36740
Birdsong	35055
Birmingham	35201-61
For specific Birmingham Zip Codes call (205) 521-0451, or your local postmaster.	
Birmingham Green (Part of Birmingham)	35237
Birwat (Part of Tarrant)	35217
Bishop	35616
Biven	35214
Black	36314
Blackankle	35768
Black Creek	35207
Black Diamond	35023
Black Rock	36042
Blacksher	36507
Blackwood	36345
Bladon Springs	36919
Blanche	35973
Blanton	36854
Bleecker	36874
Blossburg	35073
Blount Springs	35079
Blountsville	35031
Blow Gourd	35049
Blue Creek	35023
Blue Creek Junction (Part of Bessemer)	35020
Blue Mountain	36201
Blue Pond	35959
Blue Ridge	36092
Blue Ridge Estates	35226
Blues Old Stand	36061
Blue Spring (Part of Huntsville)	35810
Blue Springs (Barbour County)	36017
Blue Springs (Blount County)	35031
Blue Springs (Covington County)	36467
Blue Springs Garden	35811
Bluff	35555
Bluff Park	35226
Bluff Spring	36251
Bluff Springs	36323
Bluffton	30138
Boar Tush	35565
Boaz	35957
Bobo (Fayette County)	35594
Bobo (Madison County)	35773
Boiling Springs	36271
Boldo	35501
Boley Springs	35546
Boligee	35443
Bolinger	36903
Bolivar	35740
Bolling	36033
Bomar	35960
Bon Air	35032
Bonita	36749
Bonneville	35611
Bonnie Doone	35611
Bon Secour	36511
Booth	36008
Boot Hill	36048
Boothtown	36521
Boozer Heights (Part of Oxford)	36203
Borden Springs	36262
Borden Wheeler Springs	36262
Borom	36860
Boston (Part of Brilliant)	35548
Boswell	36081
Bowles	36401
Bowmans Crossroads	35744
Boyd	35470
Boyd Crossing	35490
Boykin (Escambia County)	36426
Boykin (Wilcox County)	36723
Boyles (Part of Birmingham)	35217
Boylston (Part of Montgomery)	36110
Boys Ranch	36761
Bradford	35089
Bradley	36420
Bradleyton	36041
Braggs	36761
Branchville	35120

* Area Zip Code   † Post Office Boxes

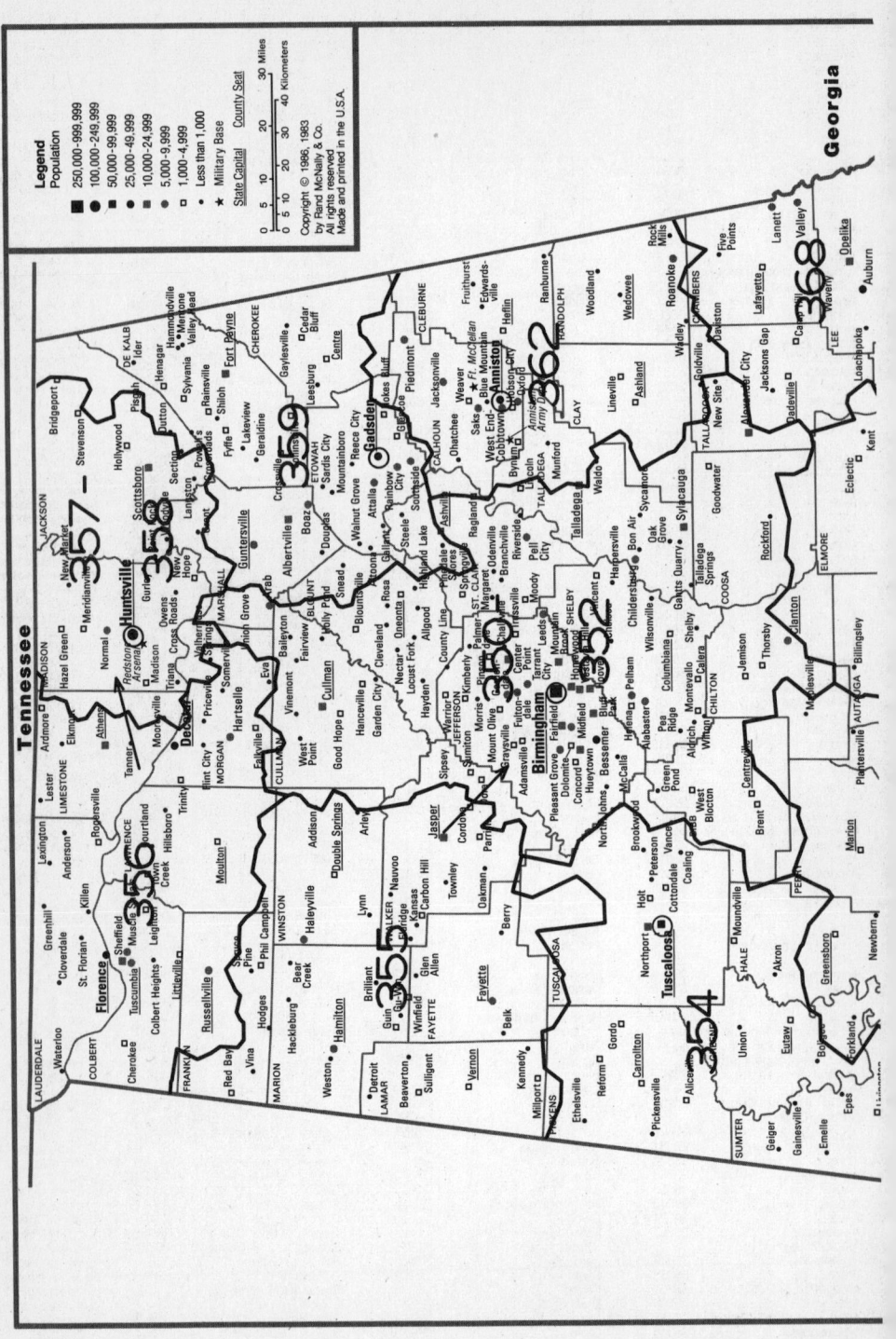

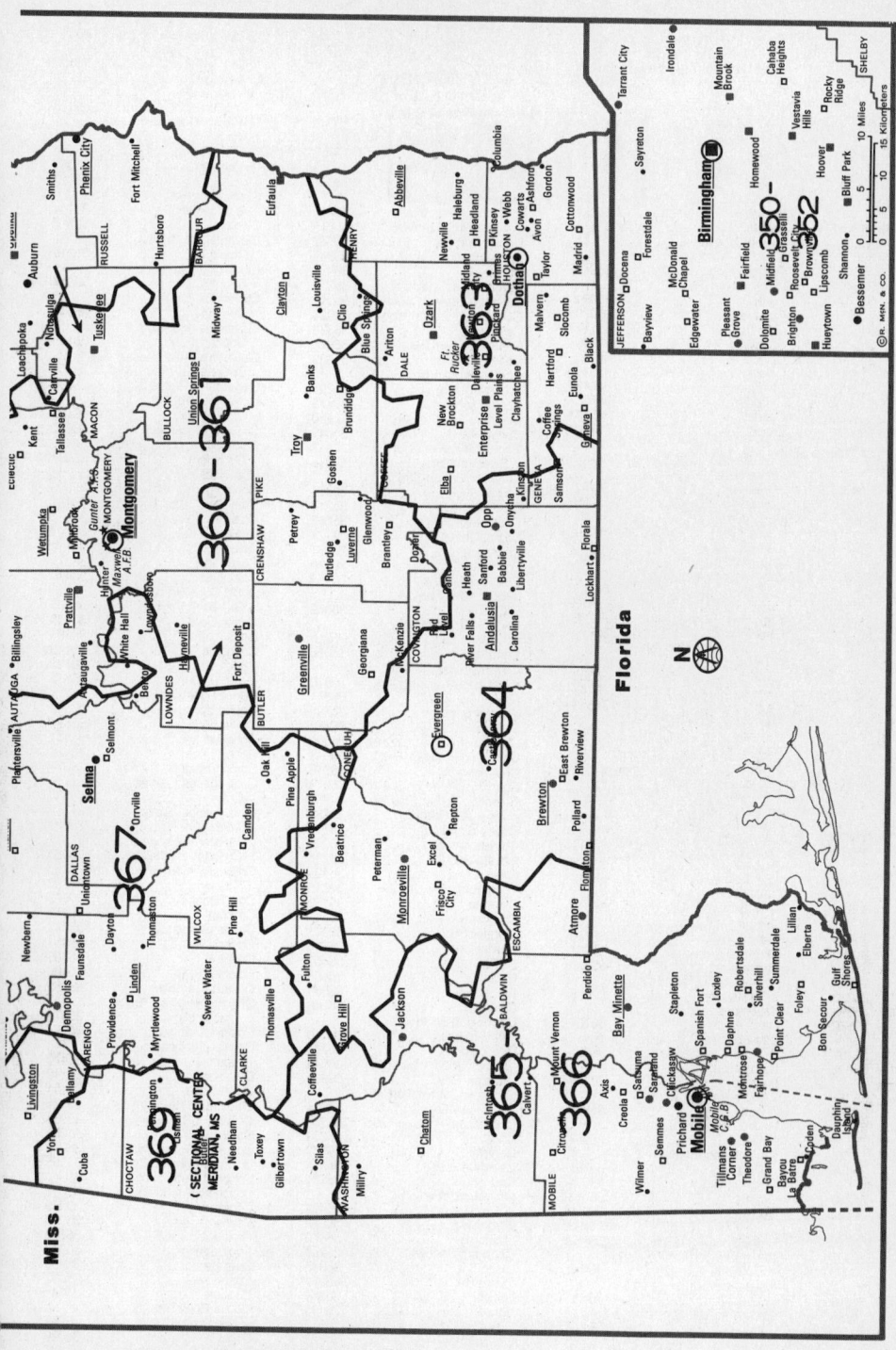

	ZIP
Brandontown (Part of Huntsville)	35805
Brannon Springs	36271
Brannon Stand	36301
Brantley (Crenshaw County)	36009
Brantley (Dallas County)	36703
Brantleyville	35114
Bremen	35033
Brent	35034
Brewersville	35470
Brewton	36426*
	36427†
Briar Hill	36035
Brick	35660
Bridgeport	35740
Bridgeville	35442
Bridlewood Forest Estates	35215
Brierfield	35035
Brighton	35020
Bright Star	35980
Brilliant	35548
Brisco Store	35772
Broadmoor (Part of Bessemer)	35020
Bromley	36507
Brompton	35094
Brookhurst (Jefferson County)	35215
Brookhurst (Madison County)	35810
Brookland	36453
Brookley (Part of Mobile)	36605
Brooklyn (Coffee County)	36467
Brooklyn (Conecuh County)	36429
Brooklyn (Cullman County)	35083
Brooks	36456
Brookside	35036
Brooksville (Blount County)	35031
Brooksville (Morgan County)	35670
Brookwood	35444
Brookwood Forest (Part of Athens)	35611
Brookwood Village (Part of Homewood)	35209
Broomtown	35973
Broughton	36274
Browns	36759
Brownsboro	35741
Browns Corner	35773
Browns Crossroad	36310
Browns Crossroads	36360
Browntown (Jackson County)	35978
Brown Town (Mobile County)	39451
Brownville (Clay County)	35072
Brownville (Conecuh County)	36401
Brownville (Jefferson County)	35211
Brownville (Tuscaloosa County)	35476
Bruceville	36089
Brundidge	36010
Brunnet Heights	35217
Brushy Pond	35033
Bryant	35958
Bryant's Lower Landing	36579
Bryce Hospital (Part of Tuscaloosa)	35401
Buchanan Peninsula	35616
Buckhorn (Madison County)	35761
Buckhorn (Pike County)	36081
Buck Island Shores	35976
Bucks	36512
Bucksnort	35747
Buena Vista	36425
Buena Vista Highlands (Part of Homewood)	35209
Buffalo	36862
Buggs Chapel	35763
Buhl	35446
Bull City	35468
Bullock	36009
Bullock Correctional Facility	36089
Burchfield	35444
Burgreen Corners	35758
Burks Gardens (Part of Tuscaloosa)	35401
Burkville	36752
Burl	36753
Burlington	36078

	ZIP
Burningtree Estates (Part of Decatur)	35603
Burningtree Mountain (Part of Decatur)	35603
Burns	36272
Burnsville	36703
Burnt Corn	36431
Burntout	35593
Burnwell	35038
Burstall (Part of Bessemer)	35020
Bushy Creek	36033
Butler	36904
Butler Springs	36030
Buttston	36853
Buyck	36080
Bynum	36253
Caddo	35673
Caffee Junction	35111
Cahaba	36767
Cahaba Heights	35243
Cahaba Hills (Part of Leeds)	35094
Cahaba River Estates	35020
Calcis	35178
Caldwell	35146
Caledonia	36753
Calera	35040
Calhoun	36047
Calumet	35580
Calvert	36513
Camden	36726
Camelot (Part of Huntsville)	35803
Cameronsville	35772
Campbell	36727
Campbells Crossroads	36266
Campbellville	35063
Camp Hill	36850
Camp Oliver	35130
Canoe	36502
Cantebury Heights (Part of Mobile)	36609
Cantelous Spur	36113
Canton Bend	36726
Capell	36726
Capitol Heights (Part of Montgomery)	36107
Capps	36353
Capshaw	35742
Carbon Hill	35549
Cardiff	35041
Carlisle	35957
Carlowville	36761
Carlton	36515
Carns	35746
Carolina	36420
Carolyn (Part of Montgomery)	36106
Carpenter	36507
Carriger	35611
Carr Mill	36251
Carrollton	35447
Carrville (Part of Tallassee)	36078
Carson	36548
Carter Grove	35750
Cartersville	35967
Cartwright	35620
Carver Court (Part of Tuskegee)	36088
Casemore	36742
Casey	36701
Castleberry	36432
Catalpa	36081
Catherine	36728
Catoma	36108
Cavalry Hill (Part of Huntsville)	35805
Cave Spring (Etowah County)	35954
Cave Spring (Madison County)	35763
Cave Springs	35674
Cecil	36013
Cedar Bluff	35959
Cedar Cove	35453
Cedar Fork	36482
Cedar Grove (Baldwin County)	36542
Cedar Grove (Covington County)	36420
Cedar Grove (Jackson County)	35772
Cedar Hill (Fayette County)	35555
Cedar Hill (Limestone County)	35739
Cedar Hill Estates	35674

	ZIP
Cedar Plains	35622
Cedar Point	35760
Cedar Springs	35265
Cedrum	35549
Center	35565
Centercrest	35215
Centergrove	35670
Center Hill (Cullman County)	35077
Center Hill (Lauderdale County)	35648
Center Hill (Limestone County)	35773
Center Point (Clarke County)	36524
Center Point (Jefferson County)	35215
Center Point Gardens	35215
Center Springs	35172
Center Star	35645
Centerville	36401
Centerwood Estates	35215
Central (Cullman County)	35055
Central (Elmore County)	36024
Central City	36330
Central Crossroads	35978
Central Heights	35633
Central Highlands (Part of Birmingham)	35206
Central Mills	36773
Centre	35960
Centreville	35042
Century Plaza (Part of Birmingham)	35210
Ceramic (Part of Phenix City)	36867
Chalkville	35215
Chalybeate Springs	35643
Champion	35121
Chance	36751
Chancellor	36316
Chandler Springs	35160
Chapel Hill (Chambers County)	36862
Chapel Hill (Jefferson County)	35216
Chapman	36015
Chapman Heights (Part of Huntsville)	35810
Chase	35811
Chastang	36560
Chatom	36518
Chelsea (Madison County)	35801
Chelsea (Shelby County)	35043
Cherokee	35616
Cherokee Bluffs	36078
Cherokee Forest (Part of Mountain Brook)	35223
Cherry Grove	35611
Chesson	36029
Chesterfield	30731
Chestnut	36425
Chestnut Grove	36010
Chetopa	35139
Chickasaw	36611
Chigger Hill	35971
Childersburg	35044
Chilton	36451
China	36401
China Grove	36081
Chinneby	36268
Chisholm (Part of Montgomery)	36110
Choccolocco	36254
Choctaw Bluff	36545
Choctaw City	36904
Choctaw Corner (Part of Thomasville)	36784
Chosea Springs	36207
Christiana	36258
Chrysler	36550
Chulafinnee	36264
Chunchula	36521
Circlewood (Part of Tuscaloosa)	35405
Citronelle	36522
Claiborne	36470
Clairmont Springs	35160
Clanton	35045
Clarksville	36524
Claud	36024
Clay	35048
Clay City	35532
Clayhatchee	36322
Clayhill	36784
Claysville	35976
Clayton	36016
Clear Springs	35121

	ZIP
Clearview (Covington County)	36028
Clearview (Crenshaw County)	36041
Cleveland (Blount County)	35049
Cleveland (Fayette County)	35542
Cleveland Crossroads	35072
Cliff Haven (Part of Sheffield)	35660
Clift Acres (Part of Madison)	35758
Clinton	35448
Clintonville	35351
Clio	36017
Clisby Park (Part of Montgomery)	36104
Clopton	36317
Cloverdale (Jefferson County)	35215
Cloverdale (Lauderdale County)	35617
Cloverdale (Mobile County)	36541
Cloverdale (Montgomery County)	36105
Cloverdale (Tuscaloosa County)	35401
Cloverdale Heights	35630
Cloverland (Part of Montgomery)	36105
Clowers Crossroads	36010
Clubview Heights (Part of Gadsden)	35901
Coal Bluff	36769
Coalburg	35068
Coal City	35131
Coal Fire	35481
Coaling	35449
Coalmont	35114
Coal Valley	35579
Coatopa	35470
Cobb City (Part of Glencoe)	35905
Cobbs Ford	36025
Cobb Town	36201
Cochrane	35442
Coden	36523
Cody	35555
Coffee Junction	35111
Coffee Springs	36318
Coffeeville	36524
Cohasset	36474
Coker	35452
Colbert Heights	35674
Cold Springs (Cullman County)	35033
Cold Springs (Elmore County)	36022
Coldwater (Calhoun County)	36260
Coldwater (Cleburne County)	36262
Cole Spring	35622
Collbran	35967
Collins Chapel	35045
Collinsville	35961
Collirene	36785
Coloma	35960
Colonial Gardens	35759
Colonial Heights (Part of Tuscumbia)	35674
Colony (Cullman County)	35077
Colony (Tuscaloosa County)	35476
Columbia	36319
Columbiana	35051
Columbus City	35976
Colwell	35905
Comer	36053
Concord (Blount County)	35049
Concord (Fayette County)	35555
Concord (Jefferson County)	35023
Congo	35959
Conifer	36078
Consul	36728
Cook Springs	35052
Cool Springs	35953
Coon Creek	35063
Coopers	35045
Coosa Court (Part of Childersburg)	35044
Coosada	36020
Coosa River	36022
Copeland	36558
Copeland Bridge	35961
Copper Springs	35120

	ZIP
Coppinville (Part of Enterprise)	36330
Corcoran (Part of Troy)	36081
Cordova	35550
Corinth (Bullock County)	36081
Corinth (Cullman County)	35179
Corinth (Randolph County)	36278
Corner	35180
Cornhouse	36274
Cornwall Furnace	35959
Corona	35579
Cortelyou	36585
Cotaco	35670
Cottage Grove	35089
Cottage Hill (Jefferson County)	35127
Cottage Hill (Mobile County)	36609
Cottondale	35453
Cottonton	36851
Cottontown	35646
Cotton Valley	36083
Cottonville	35747
Cottonwood	36320
Country Club Acres (Part of Athens)	35611
Country Club Estates (Madison County)	35201
Country Club Estates (Mobile County)	36608
Country Club Village (Part of Mobile)	36608
Country Estates (Jefferson County)	35215
Country Estates (Madison County)	36108
County Line (Blount County)	35172
County Line (Covington County)	36453
County Line (Pike County)	36034
Courtland	35618
Covin	35555
Cowarts	36321
Cox Beach (Part of Satsuma)	36572
Coxey	35611
Coy	36435
Cragford	36255
Crane Hill	35053
Crawford (Mobile County)	36608
Crawford (Russell County)	36867
Creek Stand	36089
Creeltown	35063
Creola	36525
Crescent Heights (Part of Lipscomb)	35020
Crestline (Part of Mountain Brook)	35213
Crestline Gardens (Part of Birmingham)	35210
Crestline Heights (Part of Mountain Brook)	35213
Crestline Park (Part of Birmingham)	35213
Crestview (Part of Mobile)	36609
Crestview Gardens (Part of Pell City)	35125
Crestwood (Part of Huntsville)	35807
Creswell	35078
Crews	35586
Crichton (Part of Mobile)	36607*
	36670†
Crockett Junction	35118
Cromwell	36906
Crooked Oak	35674
Cropwell (Part of Pell City)	35054
Crosby	36343
Cross Key	35620
Crossroads (Baldwin County)	36507
Cross Roads (Clarke County)	36570
Crossroads (Marshall County)	35976
Crosston	35126
Crossville (DeKalb County)	35962
Crossville (Lamar County)	35592
Crudup (Part of Reece City)	35954
Crumley Chapel	35214
Cuba	36907
Cullman	35055-57

For specific Cullman Zip Codes call (205) 734-6633, or your local postmaster.

	ZIP
Cullomburg	36919
Cunningham (Clarke County)	36727
Cunningham (Pickens County)	35442
Curry (Talladega County)	36268
Curry (Walker County)	35501
Currytown	36350
Curtis	36323
Curtiston (Part of Attalla)	35954
Cusseta	36852
Cypress	35474
Cyril	36912
Dadeville	36853
Daisy City	35214
Daleville	36322
Dallas (Blount County)	35172
Dallas (Madison County)	35801
Damascus (Coffee County)	36323
Damascus (Escambia County)	36426
Dancy	35442
Dancy Quarter (Part of Decatur)	35603
Danley	36323
Danville	35619
Danway	36801
Daphne	36526
Dargin	35040
Darlington	36726
Darwin Downs (Part of Huntsville)	35801
Dauphin Island	36528
Davis Hills (Part of Huntsville)	35805
Daviston	36256
Davisville	36083
Dawes	36601
Dawson	35963
Dawsons Mill	36749
Dayton	36731
De Armanville	36257
Deason Hill	35550
Deatsville	36022
Deavertown	35049
Decatur	35601-09

For specific Decatur Zip Codes call (205) 355-1211, or your local postmaster.

	ZIP
Deer Park	36529
DeFoor	35565
Delchamps	36523
Delmar	35551
Delta	36258
Demopolis	36732
Dempsey	35653
Deposit	35761
Detroit	35552
Devenport	36047
Dexter	36092
Diamond	35976
Dickert	36276
Dickinson	36436
Dillard	36360
Dilworth	35063
Dime	35581
Dixiana	35126
Dixie	36420
Dixieland	36867
Dixie Springs	35579
Dixon Corner	36544
Dixons Mills	36736
Dixonville	36426
Docena	35060
Dock	36037
Dogtown	35549
Dolcito (Part of Tarrant)	35217
Doliska (Part of Dora)	35130
Dolomite	35061
Dolonah	35023
Dora	35062
Doster	36311
Dothan	36301-04

For specific Dothan Zip Codes call (205) 794-8567, or your local postmaster.

	ZIP
Double Bridges (Henry County)	36310
Double Bridges (Marshall County)	35957
Doublehead	36862
Double Springs	35553
Douglas (DeKalb County)	35967
Douglas (Marshall County)	35964
Douglasville (Part of Birmingham)	35207
Downing	36052

	ZIP
Downs	36039
Downtown (Part of Huntsville)	35801
	35804

For specific Downtown Zip Codes call (205) 539-9686, or your local postmaster.

	ZIP
Downtown (Part of Montgomery)	36101-04

For specific Downtown Zip Codes call (205) 244-7500, or your local postmaster.

	ZIP
Downtown (Part of Tuscaloosa)	35401
Dozier	36028
Draper Correctional Center	36025
Drewry	36460
Drummond	35063
Dry Forks	36726
Dry Valley	35096
Dublin	36069
Duck Nest Springs	36268
Ducksprings	35954
Dudley	35490
Dudleyville	36850
Duke	36279
Dulin	35594
Duncan Crossroads	35771
Duncanville	35456
Dundee	36344
Dunn	36081
Dunns	36420
Dupree	36312
Dutton	35744
Duval (Part of Opp)	36467
Dyas	36507
Dyers Crossroads	35055
Eady City (Part of Valley)	36854
Eagle	35540
Earlytown	36453
Eastaboga	36260
East Birmingham (Part of Birmingham)	35204
East Boyles (Part of Birmingham)	35217
East Brewton	36426
Eastbrook (Part of Montgomery)	36109
East Brookwood	35444
Eastdale Mall (Part of Montgomery)	36123
Eastern Valley	35020
East Gadsden (Part of Gadsden)	35903
East Hampton (Part of Athens)	35611
East Haven	35215
East Irondale (Part of Irondale)	35210
East Killen (Part of Killen)	35645
East Lake Roebuck (Part of Birmingham)	35206
East Point	35055
East Side (Part of Tuscaloosa)	35404
East Tallassee (Part of Tallassee)	36023
East Thomas (Part of Birmingham)	35204
Eastwood (Blount County)	35121
Eastwood (Jefferson County)	35224
Eastwood Mall (Part of Birmingham)	35234
Ebenezer	35179
Echo	36350
Echola	35457
Echols Crossroads	35670
Echols Hills (Part of Huntsville)	35801
Eclectic	36024
Eddy (Part of Arab)	35016
Eden (Part of Pell City)	35125
Edgefield (Barbour County)	36016
Edgefield (Jackson County)	35772
Edgemont (Part of Homewood)	35209
Edgemont Park (Part of Homewood)	35209
Edgewater	35224
Edmonton Heights (Part of Huntsville)	35810
Edna	36922
Edwardsville	36261
Edwin	36317

	ZIP
Egypt	35952
Eight Mile (Part of Prichard)	36613*
	36663†
Elamville	36311
Elba	36323
Elberta	36530
Eldridge	35554
Elgin	35652
Eliska	36480
Elkmont	35620
Elkwood	38449
Ellards	35034
Elliotsville (Part of Alabaster)	35007
Ellisville (Baldwin County)	36551
Ellisville (Cherokee County)	35960
Elmore	36025
Elmore Correctional Facility	36025
Elrod	35458
Elsanor	36567
Elsmeade (Part of Montgomery)	36116
Elting (Part of Florence)	35630
Elyton (Part of Birmingham)	35204
Emelle	35459
Emerald Shores	35630
Empire	35063
Englewood	35405
English Village (Jefferson County)	35223
English Village (Madison County)	35802
Enon (Bullock County)	36053
Enon (Cullman County)	35179
Enon (Houston County)	36376
Enon (Pike County)	36005
Ensley (Part of Birmingham)	35218
Enterprise (Cottee and Dale Counties)	36330*
	36331†
Enterprise (Chilton County)	36091
Eoda	36420
Eoline	35042
Epes	35460
Equality	36026
Erin	36266
Escambia Correctional Center	36503
Escatawpa	36584
Estelle	36726
Estes Crossroads	36272
Estillfork	35745
Ethel	36081
Ethelsville	35461
Euclid Estates (Part of Mountain Brook)	35217
Eufaula	36027*
	36072†
Eulaton	36201
Eunola	36340
Eureka	35772
Eutaw	35462
Eva	35621
Evansboro	36913
Evansville	35441
Evergreen (Autauga County)	36006
Evergreen (Conecuh County)	36401
Ewell	36360
Excel	36439
Exmoor	36782
Fabius	35966
Fackler	35746
Fadette	36375
Fairdale	35042
Fairfax (Part of Valley)	36854
Fairfield (Covington County)	36420
Fairfield (Jefferson County)	35064
Fairfield (Lawrence County)	35650
Fairfield Highlands (Part of Midfield)	35064
Fairford	36553
Fairhope	36532*
	36533†
Fairmont	35611
Fairoaks	35477
Fairview (Chilton County)	35045
Fairview (Coffee County)	36323

	ZIP
Fairview (Conecuh County)	36401
Fairview (Cullman County)	35055
Fairview (DeKalb County)	35963
Fairview (Jefferson County)	35208
Fairview (Limestone County)	35611
Fairview (Marion County)	35564
Fairview (Mobile County)	36587
Fairview (Morgan County)	35601
Fairview (St. Clair County)	35131
Fairview (Winston County)	35540
Fairview West	35077
Falkville	35622
Fannie	36441
Farill	35959
Farley (Part of Huntsville)	35802
Farmersville	36761
Farmville	36801
Fatama	36726
Faunsdale	36738
Fayette	35555
Fayetteville	35150
Federal Prison Camp	36112
Fergusons Cross Roads	35972
Fernbank	35576
Fernland	36541
Fernwood Estates	35215
Fieldstown (Part of Gardendale)	35071
Fig Tree	36749
Finchburg	36444
Finley Crossing	36784
Fisher Crossroads (Part of Fort Payne)	35967
Fishhead	36258
Fish Pond	35643
Fish River	36555
Fisk	35750
Fitzpatrick	36029
Five Points (Blount County)	35049
Five Points (Chambers County)	36855
Five Points (Cleburne County)	36264
Five Points (Dale County)	36352
Five Points (Dallas County)	36767
Five Points (Elmore County)	36025
Five Points (Houston County)	36320
Five Points (Lawrence County)	35619
Five Points (Madison County)	35801
Five Points (Marshall County)	35755
Five Points (Walker County)	35501
Five Points East (Part of Irondale)	35210
Five Points West Shopping City (Part of Birmingham)	35208
Flat Creek	35130
Flat Rock (Clay County)	36266
Flat Rock (Jackson County)	35966
Flat Top	35062
Flatwood (Montgomery County)	36110
Flatwood (Walker County)	35549
Flatwood (Wilcox County)	36728
Fleetwood	35453
Fleming Meadows (Part of Huntsville)	35802
Flemington Heights (Part of Huntsville)	35802
Fleta	36043
Flint City (Part of Decatur)	35601
Flomaton	36441
Florala	36442
Floral Crest	35774
Florence	35630-33
For specific Florence Zip Codes call (205) 764-6961, or your local postmaster.	
Florette	35670
Flower Hill	35643
Floyd	36024
Foley	36535*
	36536†
Ford City	35660
Forest	35461
Forest Brook Estates	35226

	ZIP
Forestdale (Jefferson County)	35214
Forester	36067
Forester Chapel	36276
Forest Hill (Part of Mobile)	36608
Forest Hills (Calhoun County)	36203
Forest Hills (Jefferson County)	35064
Forest Hills (Lauderdale County)	35630
Forest Hills (Talladega County)	35044
Forest Home	36030
Forest Park (Jefferson County)	35222
Forest Park (Mobile County)	36608
Forkland	36740
Forkville	35565
Forney	35960
Fort Benning	31905
Fort Dale	36037
Fort Davis	36031
Fort Deposit	36032
Fort McClellan	36205
Fort Mitchell	36856
Fort Morgan	36542
Fort Payne	35967
Fort Rucker	36362
Fosheeton	35010
Fosters	35463
Fostoria	36761
Fountain	36460
Fountain Heights (Part of Birmingham)	35204
Four Mile	35186
Fowlers Crossroads	35542
Fowl River	36582
Fox	35401
Frances Heights (Part of Fultondale)	35068
Francisco	37345
Francis Mill	36271
Frankfort	35653
Franklin (Macon County)	36083
Franklin (Monroe County)	36444
Frankville	36538
Fredonia	36855
Freemanville	36502
Fremont	36749
French Mill	35611
Fridays Crossing	35121
Friendship (Covington County)	36467
Friendship (Elmore County)	36078
Friendship (Montgomery County)	36036
Frisco	36010
Frisco City	36445
Frisco Quarters (Part of Jasper)	35501
Frost (Part of Centreville)	35042
Fruitdale	36539
Fruithurst	36262
Fullers Crossroads	36049
Fullerton	35973
Fulton	36446
Fulton Bridge (Part of Hamilton)	35570
Fultondale	35068
Fulton Road (Part of Mobile)	36605
Fulton Springs (Part of Fultondale)	35068
Furman	36741
Fyffe	35971
Gadsden	35901-05
	35999
For specific Gadsden Zip Codes call (205) 547-6391, or your local postmaster.	
Gadsden Mall (Part of Gadsden)	35901
Gainer	36477
Gainestown	36540
Gainesville	35464
Gallant	35972
Galleria (Part of Hoover)	35244
Gallion	36742
Gamble	35501
Gandys Cove	35622
Gann Crossroad	35981
Gantt	36038
Gantts Junction (Part of Sylacauga)	35150
Gantts Quarry	35150
Garden	35442

	ZIP
Garden City	35070
Gardendale	35071
Garden Highlands	35211
Gardiners Gin	35550
Garland	36456
Garrards Crossroads	36375
Garth	35764
Gary Springs	35042
Garywood	35023
Gasque	36542
Gastonburg	36728
Gate City (Part of Birmingham)	35212
Gaylesville	35973
Gay Meadows (Part of Montgomery)	36111
Geiger	35459
General Mail Facility (Part of Montgomery)	36119
Genery	35020
Geneva	36340
Gentilly Forest (Part of Vestavia Hills)	35216
Georgetown	36521
Georgia (Part of Hartselle)	35640
Georgiana	36033
Gerald (Part of Level Plains)	36322
Geraldine	35974
Germania (Part of Birmingham)	35211
Gibsonville	36251
Gilbert Crossroads	35963
Gilbertown	36908
Gilbertsboro	35647
Giles	35188
Gilliam Springs (Part of Arab)	35016
Gilmore	35020
Gipsy	35620
Girard (Part of Phenix City)	36867
G.K.Fountain Correctional Center	36502
Gladstone	35806
Glass (Part of Valley)	36854
Gleandean (Part of Auburn)	36830
Glen Allen	35559
Glen City (Part of Pell City)	35125
Glencoe (Etowah County)	35905
Glencoe (Jefferson County)	35213
Glen Hills (Part of Bessemer)	35020
Glen Mary	35577
Glenn Acres	36608
Glen Oaks (Part of Fairfield)	35064
Glenville	36871
Glenwood	36034
Gnatville	36272
Godwin Estates	35215
Goldbranch	35183
Golden Springs (Part of Anniston)	36207
Gold Mine	35548
Gold Ridge (Cullman County)	35055
Gold Ridge (Lee County)	36879
Goldville	36255
Gonce	35772
Good Hope (Cullman County)	35055
Good Hope (Elmore County)	36024
Goodman	36330
Good Springs (Limestone County)	35610
Goodsprings (Walker County)	35560
Goodwater	35072
Goodway	36449
Goodyear (Part of Gadsden)	35903
Goose Pond Crossroads (Part of Scottsboro)	35768
Gordo	35466
Gordon	36343
Gordon Heights (Part of Lipscomb)	35020
Gordonsville	36785
Gorgas	35580
Goshen	36035
Gosport	36482
Graball (Part of Abbeville)	36310
Grady	36036
Graham	36263

	ZIP
Grand Bay	36541
Grangeburg	36343
Grant	35747
Grantley	36272
Granttown	36268
Grasselli (Part of Birmingham)	35211
Grassy	35016
Gravel Hill (Part of Russellville)	35653
Gravelly Springs	35630
Graymont (Part of Birmingham)	35204
Grays Chapel	35745
Grayson	35572
Graystone	35013
Graysville	35073
Grayton	36271
Greeley	35111
Green Acres (Part of Birmingham)	35228
Greenbrier (Lauderdale County)	35630
Greenbrier (Limestone County)	35758
Green Chapel	35971
Greenhill	35630
Green Lantern (Part of Montgomery)	36111
Green Meadows	36067
Green Pond	35074
Greensboro	36744
Greens Chapel	35049
Greensport	35953
Green Springs (Part of Homewood)	35219
Green Valley (Etowah County)	35903
Green Valley (Jefferson County)	35216
Greenville	36037
Greenwood (Clarke County)	36451
Greenwood (Jefferson County)	35020
Greenwood (Macon County)	36088
Greenwycke Village (Part of Huntsville)	35802
Griffith Bend	35160
Grimes	36301
Grove Hill	36451
Groveoak	35975
Grove Park (Jefferson County)	35209
Grove Park (Talladega County)	35044
Grovewood Estates	36108
Guerryton	36860
Guest	35967
Guin	35563
Gulf Crest	36521
Gulf Shores	36542*
	36547†
Gum Pond	35621
Gum Spring	35640
Gum Springs	35031
Gunter Air Force Base	36114-15
For specific Gunter Air Force Base Zip Codes call (205) 416-3938, or your local postmaster.	
Guntersville	35976
Gurley	35748
Guthery Crossroads	35053
Gu-Win	35563
Hackleburg	35564
Hackneyville	35010
Hacoda	36442
Hagler	35456
Haleburg	36319
Haleyville	35565
Half Acre	36763
Halls Crossroads	36445
Halltown	35582
Halsell	36912
Hamburg (Perry County)	36759
Hamburg (Wilcox County)	36768
Hamilton	35570
Hamilton Crossroads	36010
Hammondville	35989
Hamner	35460
Hampden	36722
Hanceville	35077
Hancock Crossroads	35771
Hannah (Part of Athens)	35611
Hannon	36860
Hanover	35136
Hardaway	36039
Harkins Crossroads	36251

	ZIP		ZIP		ZIP		ZIP
Harlem Heights (Part of Hueytown)	35023	Hissop	35089	Indian Hill (Part of Childersburg)	35044	Kaulton (Part of Tuscaloosa)	35401
Harmony (Covington County)	36420	Hobbs Island	35803	Indian Hills	35244	Keego	36426
Harmony (Lawrence County)	35650	Hobgood	35674	Indian Springs (Lauderdale County)	35630	Keener	35954
Harmony (Marshall County)	35950	Hoboken (Barbour County)	36027	Indian Springs (Mobile County)	36613	Kellerman	35468
Harpersville	35078	Hoboken (Marengo County)	36782	Indian Springs Village	35124	Kelly	36322
Harrell	36759	Hobson	36518	Indian Valley	35244	Kelly Springs (Part of Dothan)	36301
Harriman Park (Part of Birmingham)	35207	Hobson City	36201	Industrial City (Part of Hueytown)	35023	Kellyton	35089
Harrisburg (Bibb County)	35034	Hodge	35744	Industry	36033	Kendale Gardens	35630
Harrisburg (St. Clair County)	35125	Hodges	35571	Inglenook (Part of Birmingham)	35217	Kennedy	35574
Harrisville	35952	Hodges Store	35619	Ingram	35474	Kent (Elmore County)	36045
Hartford	36344	Hodgesville	36301	Inland	35121	Kent (Pike County)	36035
Hartselle	35640	Hodgewood	36921	Inmanfield	35540	Kenwood	35226
Harvest	35749	Hogglesville	35474	Ino	36453	Ketona (Part of Tarrant)	35217
Hatchechubbee	36858	Hog Jaw	35016	Institute	36778	Key	35960
Hatton	35672	Hokes Bluff	35903	Interburan Heights (Part of Fairfield)	35064	Keyno	35089
Havana	35474	Holiday Homes (Part of Huntsville)	35807	Inverness (Bullock County)	36089	Keys Mill	35761
Hawk	36280	Holiday Park Estates	35215	Inverness (Shelby County)	35242	Keystone (Part of Pelham)	35007
Hawthorn	36585	Holland Gin	35620	Ironaton	36268	Keyton	36330
Hayden	35079	Holley Crossroads	36272	Iron City	36207	Kilby (Part of Montgomery)	36114
Haynes	36067	Hollins	35082	Irondale	35210	Kilby Corrections Facility	36109
Haynes Crossing	35772	Hollis Crossroads	36264	Irvington	36544	Kilgore	35062
Hayneville	36040	Holly Grove	35587	Isabella	36750	Killen	35645
Haysland (Part of Huntsville)	35802-03	Holly Pond	35083	Isbell	35653	Killough Springs (Part of Birmingham)	35235
	35815	Holly Springs	35146	Ishkooda (Part of Birmingham)	35211	Kilpatrick	35950
For specific Haysland Zip Codes call (205) 883-0671, or your local postmaster.		Hollytree	35751	Isney	36919	Kimberly	35091
		Hollywood (Jackson County)	35752	Ivalee	35954	Kimbrel	35111
Haysland Estates (Part of Huntsville)	35802	Hollywood (Jefferson County)	35209	Ivanhoe (Part of Birmingham)	35222	Kimbrough	36769
Hays Mill	35620	Holman	36503	Jachin	36910	Kincheon	35045
Haywood	36280	Holman Prison	36502	Jack	36346	Kings Landing (Baldwin County)	36567
Hazel Green	35750	Holt	35404	Jackson (Choctaw County)	36921	Kings Landing (Dallas County)	36775
Hazen	36767	Holt Junction (Part of Tuscaloosa)	35401	Jackson (Clarke County)	36545	Kingston (Part of Birmingham)	35234
Headland	36345	Holtville	36022	Jackson Heights (Part of Mobile)	36609	Kingsway Terrace (Part of Birmingham)	35206
Healing Springs	36558	Holy Trinity	36859	Jackson Oak	36526	Kingtown	35652
Heath	36420	Homewood	35209	Jacksons Gap	36861	Kingville	35574
Hebron	35747	Honoraville	36042	Jacksonville	36265	Kinsey	36301
Hector	36029	Hoods Crossroads	35121	Jack Springs	36502	Kinston	36453
Heflin	36264	Hoover (Jefferson County)	35236	Jagger	35578	Kinterbish	36907
Heiberger	36756	Hoover (Madison County)	35749	Jamestown	35973	Kirbytown	35755
Helena	35080	Hope Hull	36043	Jamesville	36879	Kirk	35466
Helicon (Crenshaw County)	36036	Hopewell (Cherokee County)	35959	Jarrett (Part of Valley)	36854	Kirkland	36426
Helicon (Winston County)	35541	Hopewell (Cleburne County)	36264	Jasper	35501*	Kirklands Crossroads	36345
Henagar	35978	Hopewell (DeKalb County)	35950		35502†	Kirks Grove	35960
Henderson	36035	Hopewell (Jefferson County)	35020	Java	36010	Klein	35078
Hendrick Mill	35121	Hoppes	36535	Jay Villa	36401	Klondike	35580
Hendrix	35121	Hornady	36039	Jeddo	36480	Knightens Crossroads	36272
Henryville	35976	Horn Hill	36467	Jeff	35806	Knoxville	35469
Henson Springs	35544	Horton	35980	Jefferson	36745	Koenton	36558
Herbert	36401	Hortons Mill	35121	Jefferson Hills (Part of Birmingham)	35217	Kowaliga Beach	35010
Heron Bay	36523	Houston	35572	Jefferson Park	35210	Krafton (Part of Prichard)	36610
Hester Heights (Part of Russellville)	35653	Howard	35549	Jemison	35085	Kyles	35746
Hickory	35442	Howells Cross Roads	35960	Jena	35480	Kymulga	35014
Hickory Flat	36274	Howelton	35952	Jenifer	36268	Laceys Chapel	35020
Hickory Grove	35650	Howton	35453	Jericho	36756	Laceys Spring	35754
Hickory Hills (Lauderdale County)	35630	Hubbertville (Part of Glen Allen)	35555	Jernigan	36851	Lacon	35622
Hickory Hills (Morgan County)	35603	Hudson Gardens (Part of Lipscomb)	35020	Jerusalem Heights	35405	Ladiga	36272
Hideaway Hills	35645	Hudson Settlement	35501	Joe Wheeler Dam	35672	Ladonia	36867
Higdon	35979	Hueytown	35023	Johnsons Crossing	35077	Lafayette	36862
High Bluff	36344	Hueytown Crest (Part of Hueytown)	35020	Johnsonville	36401	Lagoon Park (Part of Montgomery)	36117
Highland (Part of Lineville)	36266	Huffman (Part of Birmingham)	35215	Jones	36749	Lake Coves	35630
Highland Home	36041	Huffman Gardens (Part of Birmingham)	35215	Jonesboro (Baldwin County)	36526	Lake Drive Estates (Part of Homewood)	35209
Highland Lake	35121	Hugo	36783	Jonesboro (Franklin County)	35653	Lake Forest	36526
Highland Park (Part of Montgomery)	36107	Huguley	36854	Jonesboro (Jefferson County)	35020	Lake Purdy	35242
Highmound	35980	Hulaco	35087	Jones Chapel	35057	Lakeside Acres	35645
High Point (DeKalb County)	35989	Hull (Part of Sumiton)	35063	Jones Crossroads	35611	Lakeside Highlands (Part of Florence)	35630
High Point (Marshall County)	35950	Humpton	35776	Jones Valley (Part of Birmingham)	35211	Lakeview (DeKalb County)	35971
High Ridge	36089	Hunter (Part of Montgomery)	36108	Jones Valley Estates (Part of Huntsville)	35802	Lakeview (Marshall County)	35976
Hightogy	35592	Huntsville	35801-24	Joppa	35087	Lakeview Highlands (Part of Muscle Shoals)	35660
Hightower	36263	For specific Huntsville Zip Codes call (205) 461-6602, or your local postmaster.		Joquin	36035	Lakewood (Jefferson County)	35234
Hillandale (Part of Huntsville)	35805	Huntsville Park (Part of Huntsville)	35807	Jordan (Elmore County)	36092	Lakewood (Limestone County)	35611
Hillard	35587	Hurricane	36507	Jordan (Washington County)	36518	Lakewood (Madison County)	35810
Hillman	35020	Hurtsboro	36860	Jordans Mill	35593	Lakewood Estates (Part of Bessemer)	35020
Hillman Gardens	35020	Hustleville	35950	Josephine	36530	Lamison	36728
Hillman Park	35020	Hustontown	35645	Joseph Springs	36207	Land	36904
Hillsboro (Lawrence County)	35643	Huxford	36543	Josie	36005	Landersville	35650
Hillsboro (Madison County)	35761	Hyatt	35980	Julia Tutwiler Prison for Women	36092	Lands Crossroads (Part of Rainsville)	35986
Hillsdale (Part of Jasper)	35501	Hybart	36444	Kahatchie	35044	Lane Springs	35616
Hilltop (Part of Bessemer)	35020	Hytop	35768	Kansas	35573	Lanett	36863
Hillview	35214	Idaho	36251	Kaolin (Part of Phenix City)	36867	Langdale (Part of Valley)	36854
Hinton	39355	Ider	35981			Langston	35755
Hirsch	36871	Independence	36067			Langtown	35650
		Indian Creek	36061				

Place	ZIP	Place	ZIP	Place	ZIP	Place	ZIP
Laniers	35014	Lock Six	35645	Magnolia Terminal	36722	Mexboro	36445
Lapine (Crenshaw County)	36041	Lock Three	35652	Majestic	35116	Mexia	36458
Lapine (Montgomery County)	36046	Locust Fork	35097	Malbis	36526	Mexia Crossing	36458
La Place	36075	Loflin	36851	Malcolm	36556	Micaville	36264
Larkinsville	35768	Logan	35098	Mall, The (Part of Huntsville)	35801	Middle Brooks Cross Roads	36879
Larkwood	35215	Logton	36081	Malone	36276	Middleton	36271
Lasca	36784	Lola City	35173	Malta	36502	Midfield	35228
Latham	36579	Lomax	35045	Malvern	36349	Midland City	36350
Lathamville	35962	London (Conecuh County)	36432	Mamie	36052	Midtown (Part of Mobile)	36604
Lattiwood	35950	London (Montgomery County)	36064	Manack	36752	Midway (Bullock County)	36053
Lauderdale Beach	35630	Long Island	35958	Manchester	35501	Midway (Butler County)	36042
Laurendine	36582	Longleaf Estates (Part of Decatur)	35603	Manila	36586	Midway (Chilton County)	36051
Lavaca	36911	Longview (Cullman County)	35179	Manley Crossroads	35758	Midway (Clay County)	35072
Lawley	36793	Longview (Shelby County)	35137	Manningham	36037	Midway (Lawrence County)	35650
Lawrence	35959	Longwood (Part of Huntsville)	35801	Mansion View	35630	Midway (Monroe County)	36768
Lawrence Cove	35621	Loop (Cherokee County)	35959	Mantua	35462	Miflin	36530
Lawrence Mill	35555	Loop (Mobile County)	36606	Maple Hill	38449	Mignon	35150
Lawrenceville	36310	Loree	36401	Maplesville	36750	Miles (Part of Fairfield)	35064
Leatherwood	36201	Lott	36613	Maplewood (Jefferson County)	35094	Millbrook	36054
Lebanon (Cleburne County)	36269	Lottie	36502	Maplewood (Madison County)	35758	Miller	36748
Lebanon (DeKalb County)	35961	Louisville	36048	Marble City Heights (Part of Sylacauga)	35150	Millers Ferry	36760
Lecta	36264	Love Hill	36312	Marble Valley	35150	Millertown	36613
Leeds	35094	Lovelace Crossroads	35630	Marbury	36051	Millerville	36267
Leeds Mineral Well (Part of Leeds)	35094	Loveless	35967	Marcoot	36862	Millport	35576
Leesburg	35983	Loveless Park	35020	Margaret	35112	Millry	36558
Leesdale (Part of Falkville)	35622	Lovick	35173	Margerum	35616	Mills Quarter's	36535
Leggtown	35620	Lower Peach Tree	36751	Marietta	35579	Milltown	36862
Le Grand	36105	Lowery	36453	Marion	36756	Mill Village (Part of Guntersville)	35976
Leighton	35646	Lowerytown	35184	Marion Junction	36759	Milstead	36075
Lenlock (Part of Anniston)	36201	Low Gap	35120	Markeeta	35094	Milton	36749
Lenox	36454	Lowndesboro	36752	Marl	36477	Mineral Springs	35085
Leon	36028	Lowry Mill	36346	Marley Mill	36360	Minooka	35040
Leroy	36548	Loxley	36551	Marlow	36580	Minor	35224
Leslie	36790	Loxley Heights	36551	Mars Hill (Part of Florence)	35630	Minor Terrace (Part of Childersburg)	35044
Lester	35647	Lucille	35184	Martins (Part of Birmingham)	35208	Minter	36761
Letcher	35776	Lugo	36027	Martintown	35752	Minvale (Part of Fort Payne)	35967
Letchers	36201	Lumbull	35543	Martinville	36502	Mitchell	36029
Letohatchee	36047	Luttrell	35971	Martling	35950	Mitchell Town	35645
Level Plains	36322	Luverne	36049	Marvel	35115	Mobile	36601-95
Levelroad	36276	Lydia	35967	Marvyn	36801	For specific Mobile Zip Codes call (205) 694-5917, or your local postmaster.	
Levert	36779	Lyeffion	36401	Marylee	35501		
Lewis	36350	Lynn	35575	Maryville	35954	Mobile Festival Centre (Part of Mobile)	36608
Lewisburg (Part of Birmingham)	35207	Lynn Crossing	35073	Massey	35619	Mobile Junction	35023
Lewiston	35462	Lynndale (Part of Montgomery)	36105	Masterson Mill	35650	Moffett	36587
Lexington	35648	Lynn Haven (Part of Tuscaloosa)	35404	Mastin Lake (Part of Huntsville)	35810-11	Mollie	36906
Liberty (Blount County)	35031	Lynns Park	35550	For specific Mastin Lake Zip Codes call (205) 852-2554, or your local postmaster.		Molloy	35586
Liberty (Butler County)	36037	Lytle	36477			Mon Louis	36523
Liberty (DeKalb County)	35957	Mabson	36360	Mathews	36052	Monroeville	36460*
Liberty City	36866	McCalla	35111	Mattawana	35121		36461†
Liberty Highlands	35210	McClure Town	36081	Maud	35616	Monrovia	35806
Liberty Hill (Franklin County)	35581	McCollum	35501	Maxine	35130	Montague	35740
Liberty Hill (Jackson County)	35966	McCord Crossroads	35960	Maxwell	35401	Monterey	36030
Libertyville	36420	McCulley Hill	35184	Maxwell Air Force Base (Part of Montgomery)	36112-13	Monterey Heights	36877
Lightwood	36022	McCullough	36502	For specific Maxwell Air Force Base Zip Codes call (205) 263-2450, or your local postmaster.		Monte-Sano (Part of Birmingham)	35228
Ligon Springs	35653	McDonald Chapel	35224			Montevallo	35115
Lillian	36549	McDowell	35470	Maxwellborn	36272	Monte Vista (Part of Gadsden)	35901
Lily Flag (Part of Huntsville)	35802	Macedonia (Cleburne County)	36273	Maxwell Heights (Part of Montgomery)	36113	Montgomery	36101-99
Lime	36274	Macedonia (Jackson County)	35771	Mayes Crossroads	35903	For specific Montgomery Zip Codes call (205) 244-7500, or your local postmaster.	
Lime Kiln	35616	Macedonia (Montgomery County)	36036	Mayfair (Jefferson County)	35209		
Limestone	36460	Macedonia (Walker County)	35501	Mayfair (Madison County)	35801	Montgomery Mall (Part of Montgomery)	36116
Lim Rock	35776	McElderry	36268	Maylene (Part of Alabaster)	35114	Monticello	36005
Lincoln (Madison County)	35810	McFarland Mall (Part of Tuscaloosa)	35405	Maynards Cove	35768	Montrose	36559
Lincoln (Talladega County)	35096	McGhees Bend	35960	Maysville	35748	Moody	35094
Lincoya Estates (Part of Vestavia Hills)	35216	McGinty (Part of Valley)	36854	Maytown	35118	Moorefield	36862
Lindbergh	35073	McIntosh	36553	Meadowbrook	35242	Moores Bridge	35476
Linden	36748	McKenzie	36456	Meadow Crossroads	36874	Moores Crossroad	35971
Lineville	36266	McKestes	35963	Meadow Hills (Part of Huntsville)	35810	Moores Crossroads	36274
Linwood	36081	McKinley	36728	Mechanicsville	36874	Moores Mill	35811
Lipscomb	35020	McLarty	35980	Media	35062	Mooresville	35649
Lisman	36912	McLendon	36851	Meeksville	36081	Moreland	35572
Little Oak	36081	McMullen	35442	Megargel	36457	Morgan (Part of Bessemer)	35020
Little River (Baldwin County)	36550	Macon	36271	Mehama	35653	Morgan City	35175
Little River (Cherokee County)	35959	McQueen	36066	Mellow Valley	36255	Moriah	35136
Little Rock	36502	McShan	35471	Melrose (Conecuh County)	36401	Morningside	35215
Little Shawmut	36863	McVay	36451	Melrose (Pickens County)	35471	Morris	35116
Little Texas	36083	McVille	35950	Melton	36776	Morvin	36762
Littleton (Etowah County)	35954	McWilliams	36753	Meltonsville	35755	Moshat	35960
Littleton (Jefferson County)	35073	Madison	35758	Melville	35541	Mosses	36040
Littleville (Colbert County)	35653	Madison Crossroads	35772	Melvin	36913	Mossy Grove	36081
Littleville (Winston County)	35565	Madison Square Mall (Part of Huntsville)	35806	Memphis	39341	Mostellers	35143
Live Oak Landing	36507	Madrid	36320	Mentone	35984	Motley	36276
Livingston	35470	Magazine (Part of Mobile)	36610	Mercury	35811	Moulton	35650
Loachapoka	36865	Magnolia	36754	Meridianville	35759	Moulton Heights (Part of Decatur)	35601
Loango	36474	Magnolia Beach (Part of Fairhope)	36532	Merry	36064	Moundville	35474
Locke Crossroads	35620	Magnolia Springs	36555	Mertz (Part of Mobile)	36606	Mountainboro	35957
Lockhart	36455						

* Area Zip Code   † Post Office Boxes

	ZIP
Mountain Brook (Jefferson County)	35223
Mountain Brook (Madison County)	35801
Mountain Brook Village (Part of Mountain Brook)	35223
Mountain Chest (Part of Guntersville)	35976
Mountain Creek	36051
Mountain Grove	35031
Mountain Home	35673
Mountain Park (Part of Birmingham)	35217
Mountain View (Part of Guntersville)	35976
Mountain Woods (Part of Vestavia Hills)	35216
Mountain Woods Park (Part of Vestavia Hills)	35216
Mount Andrew	36053
Mount Carmel (Jackson County)	35740
Mount Carmel (Marshall County)	35976
Mount Carmel (Montgomery County)	36046
Mount Hebron (Greene County)	35443
Mount Hebron (Marshall County)	35957
Mount Hester	35616
Mount Hope	35651
Mount Ida	36009
Mount Jefferson	36801
Mount Meigs	36057
Mount Nebo	36785
Mount Olive (Coosa County)	35072
Mount Olive (Jefferson County)	35117
Mount Pleasant (Coffee County)	36330
Mount Pleasant (Monroe County)	36480
Mount Rozell	35647
Mount Sinai	36113
Mount Star	35653
Mount Sterling	36904
Mount Union	36401
Mount Vernon (Cullman County)	35179
Mount Vernon (DeKalb County)	35967
Mount Vernon (Fayette County)	35555
Mount Vernon (Mobile County)	36560
Mount Willing	36032
Mount Zion	36069
Muck City	35650
Mud Creek (Jackson County)	35752
Mud Creek (Jefferson County)	35006
Mulga	35118
Mulga Mine	35118
Munford	36268
Murphy	35677
Murrays Chapel	35146
Muscadine	36269
Muscadine Junction	36269
Muscle Shoals	35661
Muscoda	35020
Mynot	35616
Myrick Chapel	36022
Myrtlewood	36763
Nadawah	36726
Naftel	36046
Nanafalia	36764
Nances Creek	36272
Napier Field	36301
Napoleon	36280
Nat	35776
Natchez	36425
Nathan (Part of Arley)	35541
Natural Bridge	35577
Nauvoo	35578
Navco (Part of Mobile)	36605
Nebo	35758
Nectar	35049
Needham	36915
Needmore (Marshall County)	35957
Needmore (Pike County)	36081
Needmore (Winston County)	35565
Neel	35640
Neenah	36726

	ZIP
Nellie	36726
Neshota (Part of Mobile)	36605
Nesmith (Cullman County)	35057
Ne Smith (Lawrence County)	35672
Nettleboro	36436
Newbern	36765
Newberry Crossroads	35960
New Brashier Chapel	35950
New Brockton	36351
Newburg	35653
New Castle	35119
New Center	35640
New Dora (Part of Dora)	35062
Newell	36270
New Georgia	35540
New Haven	35758
New Hill (Part of Lipscomb)	35020
New Home	35978
New Hope (Coffee County)	36010
New Hope (Cullman County)	35083
New Hope (Jackson County)	35768
New Hope (Madison County)	35760
New Hope (Shelby County)	35243
New Hopewell	36264
New Lexington	35546
New London	35054
New Market	35761
New Moon	35973
New Prospect (Autauga County)	36051
New Prospect (Hale County)	35441
New Sharon	35750
New Site	35010
Newsome (Part of Rainsville)	35986
Newton (Dale County)	36352
Newton (Houston County)	36301
Newtonville	35555
Newtown (Franklin County)	35653
New Town (Jackson County)	35772
Newville	36353
Nichburg	36475
Nicholsville	36784
Nitrate City	35660
Nixburg	36026
Nix Mill	35581
Nixons Chapel	35980
Noah	35960
Nokomis	36502
Nolandale (Part of Madison)	35758
Nolan Hills (Part of Madison)	35758
Normal (Part of Huntsville)	35762
Normandale Shopping Center (Part of Montgomery)	36111
North Arab (Part of Arab)	35016
North Athens (Part of Athens)	35611
North Birmingham (Part of Birmingham)	35207
North Courtland	35618
North Daye Hill	35749
North Elmore	36025
North Florence (Part of Florence)	35630
North Highlands (Part of Hueytown)	35020
North Johns	35006
North Mobile (Part of Chickasaw)	36611
Northport	35476
Northside (Part of Dothan)	36304
Northside Acres	35806
Northside Mall (Part of Dothan)	36303
North Smithfield Estates	35214
North Smithfield Manor (Part of Birmingham)	35207
North Vinemont	35179
North Walter	35055
Northwood Hills (Part of Florence)	35630
Norton	35803
Norwood (Part of Birmingham)	35234
Notasulga	36866
Nottingham	35014

	ZIP
Nuckols	36856
Nymph	36401
Oak	36535
Oak Bowery	36862
Oak Crossing (Part of Leeds)	35094
Oakdale	35611
Oakdale Acres	35611
Oak Grove (Autauga County)	36067
Oak Grove (Chilton County)	35085
Oak Grove (Franklin County)	35653
Oak Grove (Jefferson County)	35006
Oak Grove (Limestone County)	35739
Oak Grove (Mobile County)	36613
Oak Grove (Talladega County)	35150
Oak Hill (DeKalb County)	35962
Oak Hill (Wilcox County)	36766
Oakhurst (Part of Birmingham)	35207
Oakland	35630
Oakleigh Estates (Part of Gadsden)	35901
Oak Level	36262
Oakman	35579
Oakmulgee	36793
Oak Ridge (Morgan County)	35640
Oak Ridge (St. Clair County)	35125
Oak Ridge Park (Part of Birmingham)	35212
Oakville (Jefferson County)	35206
Oakville (Lawrence County)	35619
Oakwood (Part of Bessemer)	35020
Oakwood College	35896
Oakworth (Part of Decatur)	35601
Oaky Grove	36353
Oaky Streak	36037
Octagon	36748
Odena	35150
Oden Ridge	35621
Odenville	35120
Odom	36456
Ofelia	36266
Ohatchee	36271
Old Bethel	35646
Old Burleson	35593
Old Davistown	36201
Old Fabius	35966
Oldfield (Part of Sylacauga)	35150
Old Jonesboro	35215
Old Kingston	36067
Old Maylene (Part of Alabaster)	35114
Old Monrovia	35806
Old Nauvoo	35653
Old Samuel	36908
Old Spring Hill	36742
Old Texas	36768
Old Town (Conecuh County)	36401
Old Town (Dallas County)	36785
Oleander	35175
Oliver	35652
Ollie	36460
Olney	35442
Olustee	36081
Omaha	36274
O'Neal	35611
Oneonta	35121
Onycha	36467
Opelika	36801-03
For specific Opelika Zip Codes call (205) 745-3561, or your local postmaster.	
Opine (Clarke County)	36784
Opine (Covington County)	36467
Opp	36467
Orange Beach	36561
Orchard (Part of Mobile)	36618
Ord (Part of Gadsden)	35901
Orion	36081
Orrville (Dallas County)	36767
Orrville (Limestone County)	35671
Osanippa	36854
Osborn	36779

	ZIP
Oswichee	36856
Our Town	35010
Overbrook	35150
Overlook (Part of Mobile)	36608
Overton	35210
Owassa	36401
Owens Cross Roads	35763
Owenton (Part of Birmingham)	35204
Oxford	36203
Oxford Lake (Part of Oxford)	36203
Oxmoor	35211
Oyster Bay	36535
Ozark	36360*
	36361†
Painter	35962
Paint Rock	35764
Palestine	36262
Palmerdale	35123
Palmers Crossroads	36480
Palmetto	35481
Palmetto Beach	36542
Palos	35130
Panola (Crenshaw County)	36046
Panola (Sumter County)	35477
Pansey	36370
Paran	36274
Park City	36526
Parkdale	35072
Park Hill (Part of Pell City)	35125
Parkland (Part of Jasper)	35501
Parkway City (Part of Huntsville)	35801
Parkway Estates (Part of Huntsville)	35802
Parkwood	35020
Parrish	35580
Partridge Crossroads	35180
Patsburg	36049
Patton	35579
Patton Chapel (Part of Hoover)	35216
Paul	36469
Pauls Hill	35020
Pawnee	35217
Peacock	36451
Pea Ridge (Escambia County)	36426
Pea Ridge (Fayette County)	35546
Pea Ridge (Madison County)	35801
Pea Ridge (Marion County)	35563
Pea Ridge (Shelby County)	35115
Pearson	35456
Pebble	35565
Peeks Corner	35961
Peeks Hill	36271
Peets Corner	35611
Pelham	35124
Pelham Heights (Part of Anniston)	36201
Pell City	35125
Penfield Heights (Part of Birmingham)	35217
Penn	35619
Pennington	36916
Pennsylvania (Part of Satsuma)	36572
Penton	36862
Pentonville	35136
Pepperell (Part of Opelika)	36801
Perdido	36562
Perdido Beach	36530
Perdue Hill	36470
Perote	36061
Perry Chapel	36586
Perry Store	36453
Perryville	36701
Peterman	36471
Peterson	35478
Petersville	35633
Petrey	36062
Petronia	36785
Pettusville	35620
Peytonia Points	35660
Phalin	35456
Phelan	35055
Phenix City	36867-69
For specific Phenix City Zip Codes call (205) 298-7871, or your local postmaster.	
Phil Campbell	35581
Phillips Estates (Part of Bessemer)	35020

* Area Zip Code   ***† Post Office Boxes***

	ZIP
Phillipsville	36507
Phoenixville (Part of Birmingham)	35221
Pickensville	35447
Pickering	36758
Piedmont (Calhoun County)	36272
Piedmont (Madison County)	35801
Piedmont Springs	36272
Pierce	36587
Pigeon Creek	36037
Pike Road	36064
Pikeville	35768
Pilgrims Rest (Part of Southside)	35901
Pinckard	36371
Pinder Hill	35772
Pine Apple	36768
Pine Beach	36542
Pinebelt	36767
Pine Dale (Limestone County)	35739
Pinedale (Montgomery County)	36106
Pinedale Acres (Lauderdale County)	35645
Pinedale Acres (Limestone County)	35611
Pinedale Shores	35953
Pine Flat	36022
Pine Grove (Baldwin County)	36507
Pine Grove (Bullock County)	36053
Pine Grove (Cherokee County)	35960
Pine Grove (Lee County)	36801
Pine Grove (Tallapoosa County)	36850
Pine Hill (Randolph County)	36263
Pine Hill (Wilcox County)	36769
Pine Level (Autauga County)	36022
Pine Level (Coffee County)	36323
Pine Level (Montgomery County)	36065
Pine Mountain	35133
Pine Orchard	36471
Pine Ridge	35967
Pineview (Part of Irondale)	35210
Pinewood Terrace (Part of Childersburg)	35044
Piney	35960
Piney Bend	35593
Piney Chapel	35611
Piney Grove (Lawrence County)	35619
Piney Grove (Marion County)	35548
Piney Woods	36262
Pinkeyville	35072
Pinkney City	35214
Pinnell	36850
Pinson	35126
Pinson-Clay-Chalkville	35215
Pintlalla	36043
Pisgah (Jackson County)	35765
Pisgah (Limestone County)	35773
Pisgah (Montgomery County)	36036
Pittsview	36871
Plainview (Cleburne County)	36264
Plainview (DeKalb County)	35986
Plant City	36863
Plantersville (Dallas County)	36758
Plantersville (Talladega County)	35014
Plateau (Part of Prichard)	36610
Plaza De Malaga (Part of Mobile)	36685
Pleasant Acres	35811
Pleasant Gap	36272
Pleasant Grove (Chilton County)	35085
Pleasant Grove (Jackson County)	35772
Pleasant Grove (Jefferson County)	35127
Pleasant Grove (Marshall County)	35950
Pleasant Hill (Barbour County)	36027

	ZIP
Pleasant Hill (Choctaw County)	36908
Pleasant Hill (Dallas County)	36701
Pleasant Hill (Escambia County)	36502
Pleasant Hill (Franklin County)	35585
Pleasant Hill (Jefferson County)	35020
Pleasant Home	36420
Pleasant Plains	36312
Pleasant Ridge (Franklin County)	35653
Pleasant Ridge (Greene County)	35462
Pleasant Ridge (Pike County)	36034
Pleasant Site	35582
Pletcher	36750
Plevna	35761
Poarch	36502
Poarch Creek Indian Reservation	36502
Pocahontas	35549
Pogo	35582
Point Clear	36564
Polk	36785
Pollard	36441
Pollards Bend	35983
Ponderosa Estates	36575
Ponders	36853
Pondville	35034
Pool	35619
Pooles Crossroads	36274
Pools Crossroads	35045
Pope	36769
Poplarridge	35760
Poplar Springs (Marshall County)	35950
Poplar Springs (Winston County)	35578
Port Birmingham	35118
Porter	35005
Portersville	35961
Posey Mill	35565
Poseys Crossroads	36067
Postoak	36089
Potash	36274
Potter	36701
Powderly (Part of Birmingham)	35211
Powderly Hills (Part of Birmingham)	35211
Powell	35971
Powers	35474
Powhatan	35118
Powledge	36874
Praco	35130
Prairie	36728
Prairieville	36742
Pratt City (Part of Birmingham)	35214
Prattmont (Part of Prattville)	36067
Pratts	36016
Prattville	36066-67
For specific Prattville Zip Codes call (205) 365-6467, or your local postmaster.	
Prescott	35125
Preston	35768
Prestwick	36548
Priceville	35601
Prichard	36610
Pride	35674
Primitive Ridge	35184
Princeton	35766
Pronto	36081
Prospect	35578
Providence (Butler County)	36033
Providence (Cullman County)	35179
Providence (Marengo County)	36742
Providence (Walker County)	35579
Prudence	36871
Pruitton	35630
Pulaski Pike (Part of Huntsville)	35810
Pulltight	35548
Pumpkin Center (DeKalb County)	35967
Pumpkin Center (Morgan County)	35619
Pumpkin Center (Walker County)	35130

	ZIP
Pushmataha	36912
Putnam	36784
Pyriton	36266
Queenstown	35173
Quintard Mall (Part of Oxford)	36203
Quinton	35130
Quintown	35130
Rabb	36401
Rabbitown (Calhoun County)	36272
Rabbit Town (Marshall County)	35950
Rabbittown (Winston County)	35565
Rabun	36507
Ragland	35131
Raimund	35020
Rainbow	35758
Rainbow City	35906
Rainbow Mountain Heights	35758
Rainsville	35986
Ralph	35480
Ramer	36069
Ranburne	36273
Randolph	36792
Range	36473
Rash	35772
Rayburn (Part of Guntersville)	35976
Read's Mill	36279
Red Bank	35672
Red Bay	35582
Reddock Springs	36037
Red Eagle Honor Farm	36101
Red Hill (Blount County)	35063
Red Hill (Elmore County)	36078
Red Hill (Marshall County)	35976
Redland Heights (Part of Valley)	36854
Red Level	36474
Redmont Park (Part of Mountain Brook)	35213
Red Ore	35020
Red Rock	35674
Red Rock Junction	35616
Redstone Arsenal	35808-09
For specific Redstone Arsenal Zip Codes call (205) 881-8883, or your local postmaster.	
Redtown	36502
Reece City	35954
Reedtown (Part of Russellville)	35653
Reeltown	36078
Reform	35481
Regency (Part of Florence)	35630
Regent Forest	35226
Rehobeth	36301
Rehoboth	36720
Reid	35611
Remlap	35133
Renfroe	35160
Reno	35111
Repton	36475
Republic	35214
Rhoades	36453
Rhodesville	35630
Rice	35201
Richmond	36761
Richmond Hills (Part of Tuscumbia)	35674
Rideout Village (Part of Huntsville)	35806
Riderwood	36904
Ridgecrest	36105
Ridgeville (Butler County)	36030
Ridgeville (Etowah County)	35954
Ringgold	35973
Ripley	35611
Riverbend	35184
Riverdale (Part of Mentone)	35984
River Falls	36476
Rivermont (Colbert County)	35660
Rivermont (Lauderdale County)	35630
River Oaks Center (Part of Decatur)	35603
River Park	36532
Riverside (Blount County)	35031
Riverside (St. Clair County)	35135
Riverton	35616

	ZIP
River View (Chambers County)	36854
Riverview (Escambia County)	36426
Riverview (Tuscaloosa County)	35401
Riverwood (Part of Tuscaloosa)	35406
Roanoke	36274
Roanoke Junction (Part of Opelika)	36801
Roba	36089
Robbins Crossroads	35062
Roberta	35040
Roberts	36420
Robertsdale	36567
Robinsons	36752
Robinson Springs	36025
Robinsonville	36502
Robinwood	35217
Rock City (Jackson County)	35771
Rock City (Marion County)	35594
Rockdale	35020
Rocket	35808
Rockford	35136
Rock Hill	36426
Rock House	35771
Rockledge	35954
Rock Mills	36274
Rock Run	36272
Rock Spring (Part of Glencoe)	35905
Rock Spring Quarry (Part of Glencoe)	35905
Rock Springs (Blount County)	35031
Rock Springs (Choctaw County)	36904
Rock Stand	36274
Rockville	36545
Rockwest	36726
Rockwood	35653
Rocky Head	36311
Rocky Hill	35672
Rocky Hollow	35550
Rocky Ridge	35243
Rodentown	35957
Roebuck (Part of Birmingham)	35206
Roebuck Crest Estates (Part of Birmingham)	35215
Roebuck Forest (Part of Birmingham)	35235
Roebuck Gardens (Part of Birmingham)	35235
Roebuck Park (Part of Birmingham)	35215
Roebuck Plaza	35235
Roebuck Springs (Part of Birmingham)	35206
Roebuck Terrace (Part of Birmingham)	35206
Roeton	36010
Rogersville	35652
Rolling Hills (Part of Decatur)	35603
Rollins	36022
Romar Beach	36561
Rome	36420
Romulus	35446
Roper	35173
Rosa	35121
Rosalie	35765
Roseboro	37328
Rosebud	36766
Rosedale (Part of Homewood)	35209
Rose Hill (Covington County)	36028
Rose Hill (Jefferson County)	35210
Rosemont (Part of Birmingham)	35221
Rose Park (Part of Florence)	35630
Rosinton	36567
Rossland City	35555
Round Hill	36784
Round Mountain	35959
Rowells Crossroad	36879
Roxana	36879
Royal	35031
Ruffner (Part of Irondale)	35210
Russell Heights (Part of Leeds)	35094
Russell Mill (Part of Alexander City)	35010

* Area Zip Code † Post Office Boxes

Place	ZIP
Russell Village (Part of Decatur)	35603
Russellville	35653
Rutan	36518
Ruth	35016
Rutherford	36860
Rutledge	36071
Rutledge Heights (Jefferson County)	35064
Rutledge Heights (Madison County)	35816
Ryan	35115
Ryan Crossroads	35087
Ryland	35767
Saco	36081
Safford	36773
Saginaw	35137
Sahama Village (Part of Tuscaloosa)	35401
St. Bernard	35055
St. Clair	36752
St. Clair Correctional Facility	35120
St. Clair Springs	35146
St. Elmo	36568
St. Florian	35630
Saints Crossroads	35653
St. Stephens	36569
Saks	36201
Salem (Dallas County)	36767
Salem (Fayette County)	35546
Salem (Lee County)	36874
Salem (Limestone County)	35620
Salitpa	36570
Samantha	35482
Samford University (Part of Homewood)	35229
Samson	36477
Samuels Chapel	35952
Sandfield	36081
Sandfort	36875
Sandhurst Park (Part of Huntsville)	35802
Sand Rock	35961
Sandtown	35546
Sandusky (Part of Birmingham)	35214
Sandy Creek	36850
Sandy Ridge	36047
Sanford	36420
Sanie	35120
San Souci Beach (Part of Bayou La Batre)	36509
Santuck	36092
Sapps	35447
Saragossa	35578
Saraland	36571
Saratoga (Part of Albertville)	35950
Sardine	36441
Sardis (Bullock County)	36089
Sardis (Dallas County)	36775
Sardis (Walker County)	35550
Sardis City	35957
Sardis Springs	35611
Satsuma	36572
Saucer	36030
Saville	36041
Sawyerville	36776
Sayre	35139
Scant City	35016
Scarce Grease	35647
Scenic Heights (Part of Gadsden)	35901
Schenks	36279
Schmits Mill	35096
Schuster Springs	36768
Scotland	36471
Scotrock (Part of Alabaster)	35007
Scott City	35094
Scottland	36089
Scottsboro	35768
Scranage	36502
Scranton	36313
Scyrene	36436
Seaboard	36522
Seacliff (Part of Fairhope)	36532
Seale	36875
Sealy Springs (Part of Cottonwood)	36320
Searight	36028
Searles	35444
Section	35771
Segco	35580
Selbrook	36108
Selfville	35133
Sellers	36046
Sellersville	36318
Selma	36701-03
For specific Selma Zip Codes call (205) 874-4678, or your local postmaster.	
Selma Mall (Part of Selma)	36703
Selmont	36703
Selmont-West Selmont	36703
Seman	36024
Seminole	36567
Semmes	36575
Service	36919
Seven Hills	36601
Seymour Bluff	36542
Shacklesville	36033
Shades Crest Estates	35226
Shady Grove (Clay County)	35072
Shady Grove (Coffee County)	36323
Shady Grove (Franklin County)	35581
Shady Grove (Pike County)	36035
Shady Lane (Part of Huntsville)	35810
Shakespeare (Part of Montgomery)	36117
Shanghai	35611
Shannon	35142
Shawmut (Part of Valley)	36854
Shawnee	36726
Sheffield	35660-62
For specific Sheffield Zip Codes call (205) 383-0252, or your local postmaster.	
Shelby	35143
Shellhorn	36081
Sherman Heights (Part of Anniston)	36201
Sherwood Forest (Part of Florence)	35630
Sherwood Park (Part of Huntsville)	35206
Shiloh (DeKalb County)	35967
Shiloh (Marengo County)	36754
Shiloh (Pike County)	36005
Shinebone	36266
Shingle	35581
Shoals Acres	35645
Shopton	36029
Short Creek	35118
Shorter	36075
Shorterville	36373
Shortleaf (Part of Demopolis)	36732
Shottsville	35570
Shreve	36456
Sico	35150
Siddonsville	36738
Sigma	36319
Sikesville	36276
Silas	36919
Siloam	36907
Siluria (Part of Alabaster)	35144
Silver Cross	36919
Silverhill	36576
Silver Run	36268
Simcoe	35055
Simmons Crossroads	36879
Simmsville	35043
Sims Chapel	36553
Simsville	36089
Sipsey	35584
Six Mile	35035
Six Way	35603
Skaggs Corner (Part of Ider)	35978
Skeggs Crossroads	35072
Skinem	35750
Skinnerton	36401
Skipperville	36374
Skirum	35963
Skyland (Part of Tuscaloosa)	35407
Skyline	35768
Skyline Acres	35758
Skyline Estates	35226
Sky Ranch	35226
Skyview (Part of Bessemer)	35020
Slackland	35901
Slocomb	36375
Smithfield (Part of Birmingham)	35204
Smith Hill	35184
Smith Institute	35957
Smiths	36877
Smiths Crossroads (Part of Glencoe)	35903
Smithson	35020
Smithsonia	35630
Smoke Rise	35133
Smut Eye	36061
Smyer	36727
Smyrna	36301
Snead	35952
Snoddy	35462
Snowdoun	36105
Snow Hill	36778
Snowtown	35062
Socapatoy	35089
Society Hill	36801
Soleo	35072
Somerville	35670
South (Covington County)	36474
South (Montgomery County)	36116
South Calera (Part of Calera)	35040
South Gadsden (Part of Gadsden)	35901
South Gate Mall (Part of Muscle Shoals)	35660
South Guntersville (Part of Guntersville)	35976
South Haleyville (Part of Haleyville)	35565
South Highland (Part of Birmingham)	35205
South Lowell	35501
Southmont (Part of Montgomery)	36105
South Orchard	36582
South Park Estates (Part of Huntsville)	35802
South Sheffield (Part of Tuscumbia)	35674
Southside	35901
	35903
For specific Southside Zip Codes call (205) 547-6391, or your local postmaster.	
Southtown (Part of Guntersville)	35976
Southwood (Part of Homewood)	35209
Souwilpa	36919
Spanish Fort	36527
Speake	35619
Speed	36026
Speeds Water Mill	35466
Speigener	36022
Spivey's	36535
Sprague	36069
Springbrook (Part of Tuscaloosa)	35405
Springdale (Part of Tarrant)	35217
Springdale Mall (Part of Mobile)	36606
Springfield (Clarke County)	36784
Springfield (Lauderdale County)	35652
Springfield (Randolph County)	36274
Spring Garden	36275
Spring Hill (Barbour County)	36053
Spring Hill (Mobile County)	36608
Spring Hill (Pike County)	36081
Spring Hill (Walker County)	35549
Spring Valley (Colbert County)	35674
Spring Valley (Montgomery County)	36116
Springville	35146
Springville Lake Estates	35146
Sprott	36779
Spruce Pine	35585
Standard	35580
Standing Rock	36855
Stanley	36420
Stansel	35481
Stanton	36790
Stapleton	36578
Star	35576
State Line	36320
Statesville	36703
Steele	35987
Steele Crossing	37328
Steelwood	36551
Steenson Hollow (Part of Muscle Shoals)	35660
Steiner (Part of Montgomery)	36111
Sterrett	35147
Stevenson	35772
Stewart	35441
Stewartsville	35150
Stills Cross Road	36081
Stockdale	36268
Stockton	36579
Stokeley (Part of Andalusia)	36420
Stokes	35456
Stones	36054
Stoney Point	36022
Stotesville	35184
Stough	35555
Straight Mountain	35121
Strata	36046
Strawberry	35016
Stroud	36855
Studdards Crossroads	35549
Sturkie	36862
Suggsville	36482
Sulligent	35586
Sulphur Springs (Blount County)	35079
Sulphur Springs (DeKalb County)	30738
Sulphur Springs (Jackson County)	35966
Sulphur Springs (Madison County)	35761
Sumiton	35148
Summerdale	36580
Summerfield	36701
Summit	35031
Summit Farm	35023
Sumterville	35460
Sunflower	36581
Sunny Cove	36582
Sunny South	36769
Sunset Cove (Part of Huntsville)	35802
Sunset Mill Village (Part of Selma)	36701
Sunset Shores	36535
Sun Valley	35215
Surginer	36754
Susan Moore	35952
Suspension	36089
Suttle	36701
Swaim	35764
Swancott	35758
Swearengin	35768
Sweet Water	36782
Sycamore	35149
Sylacauga	35150
Sylvan Grove	36350
Sylvania	35988
Sylvan Springs	35118
Tabernacle (Coffee County)	36351
Tabernacle (Houston County)	36301
Tabor	35901
Taft	35973
Taits Gap	35121
Talladega	35160
Talladega Springs	35150
Tallahatta Springs	36784
Tallapoosa City (Part of Tallassee)	36078
Tallassee	36078
Tallaweka (Part of Tallassee)	36078
Talucah	35775
Tanner	35671
Tanner Crossroads	35671
Tanner Heights (Part of Hartselle)	35640
Tanner Williams	36587
Tanyard (Bullock County)	36061
Tanyard (St. Clair County)	35125
Tarentum	36010
Tarpley (Part of Birmingham)	35211
Tarrant	35217
Tarrant Heights	35217
Tasso	36767
Tattlersville	36524
Taylor	36301
Taylors Crossroads	36274
Taylorville	35405
Teals Crossroads	36311
Teasleys Mill	36052
Tecumseh	30138
Teddy	36426
Tenant	36274
Ten Broeck (Part of Lakeview)	35971
Tennala	35960

* Area Zip Code   † Post Office Boxes

	ZIP
Tennille	36010
Tensaw	36579
Terese (Part of Eufaula)	36027
Terry Heights (Part of Huntsville)	35805
Texasville	36016
Thach	35501
Tharptown	35653
Thatch	35620
The Cedars (Part of Florence)	35630
The Highlands (Etowah County)	35901
The Highlands (Madison County)	35810
Theodore	36582*
	36590†
The Ridge	36460
Thomas (Autauga County)	36067
Thomas (Jefferson County)	35214
Thomas Acres (Part of Bessemer)	35020
Thomas F. Station Correctional Center	36025
Thomas Hill (Part of Sylacauga)	35150
Thomaston	36783
Thomasville	36784
Thompson	36089
Thorn Hill	35565
Thornton	36853
Thorntontown	35652
Thorsby	35171
Three Notch	36053
Threet	35617
Thurston	36340
Tibbie	36583
Tilden	36761
Till	36033
Tiller Crossroads	36850
Tillery Crossroads	36854
Tillmans Corner	36619
Tinela	36481
Titus	36080
Toadvine	35020
Toddtown	36451
Tompkinsville	36916
Toney	35773
Toonersville	35652
Toulminville (Part of Mobile)	36610
Town Creek	35672
Towne West (Part of Mobile)	36618
Townley	35587
Toxey	36921
Trade	35053
Trafford	35172
Travis Bridge	36401
Tredegar	36265
Trenton	35774
Triana	35758
Trickem	36785
Trimble	35057
Trinity	35673
Trotwood Park (Part of Birmingham)	35206
Troy	36081
Trussville	35173
Tuckabatchie	36078
Tuckahoe Heights (Part of Gadsden)	35901
Tucker Crossroads	35959
Tumbleton	36345
Tunnel Springs	36471
Tupelo	35768
Turkestan	36753
Turkey Branch	36555
Turkeytown	35901
Turner Crossroads	36351
Tuscaloosa	35401-07
	35485-87
For specific Tuscaloosa Zip Codes call (205) 752-2521, or your local postmaster.	
Tuscumbia	35674
Tuskegee	36083
Tuskegee Institute	36087†
	36088*
Twilley Town	35130
Twin	35563
Twin Oaks (Part of Montgomery)	36123
Twinsprings	36027
Tyler	36785
Tyler Crossroads	36048
Tyson	36043
Tysonville	36075

	ZIP
Uchee	36858
Underwood (Lauderdale County)	35630
Underwood (Shelby County)	35115
Underwood Crossroads	35646
Underwood-Petersville	35630
Union (Etowah County)	35957
Union (Greene County)	35462
Union (Henry County)	36310
Union (Morgan County)	35670
Union (Tallapoosa County)	36853
Union Academy	36330
Union Grove (Chilton County)	35085
Union Grove (Cullman County)	35083
Union Grove (Jefferson County)	35005
Union Grove (Marshall County)	35175
Union Hill (Cleburne County)	36273
Union Hill (Limestone County)	35610
Union Hill (Morgan County)	35622
Union Springs	36089
Uniontown	36786
Unity (Autauga County)	36006
Unity (Coosa County)	35183
Unity (Tuscaloosa County)	35401
Universal Heights	35404
University (Part of Tuscaloosa)	35486
University Mall (Part of Tuscaloosa)	35401
University of Montevallo (Part of Montevallo)	35115
University of South Alabama (Part of Mobile)	36608
Upper Coalburg	35068
Upper Green Hill	35630
Upshaw	35540
Uriah	36480
Valdosta (Part of Tuscumbia)	35674
Valhermoso Springs	35775
Vallegrande	36703
Valley	36854*
	36872†
Valley Creek	35020
Valley Creek Junction	36758
Valley Head	35989
Valley View	35640
Vance	35490
Vanderbilt (Part of Birmingham)	35204
Vandiver	35176
Vangale	36782
Vaughn	36579
Vaughn Corners	35758
Verbena	36091
Verlie (Part of Alabaster)	35007
Vernledge	36049
Vernon	35592
Vernontown	35184
Vestavia Hills	35216
Vestavia Hills Centre (Part of Vestavia Hills)	35216
Vesthaven (Part of Vestavia Hills)	35216
Veterans Hospital (Part of Tuscaloosa)	35401
Veto	35620
Vick (Part of Centreville)	35042
Victoria	36323
Vida	36067
Vidette	36049
Vienna	35442
Viewpoint	35963
Vigo	36272
Village Creek (Part of Birmingham)	35207
Village Springs	35126
Villula	36871
Vina	35593
Vincent	35178
Vinegar Bend	36584
Vine Hill	36758
Vineland	36784
Vineland Park (Part of Hueytown)	35020
Vinemont	35179
Vinesville (Part of Birmingham)	35208
Virginia	35020
Virginia Shores	35660

	ZIP
Vocation	36480
Volanta (Part of Fairhope)	36532
Vredenburgh	36481
Vulcan City (Part of Birmingham)	35207
Waco	35653
Wacoochee Valley	36874
Wadley	36276
Wadsworth	36022
Wagar	36585
Wagarville	36585
Wahouma (Part of Birmingham)	35206
Walco (Part of Sylacauga)	35150
Waldo	35160
Walker Chapel (Part of Fultondale)	35068
Walkers Corner	35055
Walker Springs	36586
Walkerton (Part of Pell City)	35125
Wallace	36426
Walley	36584
Wallsboro	36092
Wall Street	35758
Walnut Grove	35990
Walnut Hill	36853
Walnut Park (Part of Gadsden)	35904
Walter	35077
Wannville	35752
Ward	36922
Ware	36078
Warrenton	35976
Warrior	35180
Warriorstand	36089
Warsaw	35477
Waterford (Part of Newton)	36352
Waterloo	35677
Water Valley	36908
Watson (Cherokee County)	35973
Watson (Jefferson County)	35181
Watsonville	36753
Watts Mill	36266
Wattsville	35182
Waugh	36109
Waverly	36879
Wawbeek	36502
Wayne	36782
Wayside	35594
Weatherly Heights (Part of Huntsville)	35802
Weaver	36277
Webb	36376
Webb Addition (Part of Scottsboro)	35768
Webster Chapel	35903
Wedgewood	36108
Wedgworth	36776
Wedowee	36278
Weed Crossroad	36009
Weeden Heights (Part of Florence)	35630
Weeks	36453
Wegra	35130
Wehadkee	36274
Wellington	36279
Welti	35055
Wende	36860
Wenonah (Part of Birmingham)	35211
Weogufka	35183
Weoka	36092
Wessington	35040
West (Part of Huntsville)	35805-08
For specific West Zip Codes call (205) 461-6617, or your local postmaster.	
West Alexandria	36250
West Bend	36524
West Blocton	35184
West End (Calhoun County)	36201
West End (Jefferson County)	35211
West End (Montgomery County)	36104
West End-Cobbtown	36201
West Ensley	35224
Western Hills (Part of Mobile)	36618
Western Hills Estates	35749
Western Hills Mall (Part of Fairfield)	35064
West Greene	35491

	ZIP
West Highlands (Part of Hueytown)	35023
West Huntsville (Part of Huntsville)	35807
West Jefferson	35130
West Lake Highlands (Part of Bessemer)	35020
Westlake Mall (Part of Bessemer)	35020
Westlawn (Part of Huntsville)	35807
West Monroeville (Part of Monroeville)	36460
Weston (Part of Hamilton)	35570
Westover	35185
West Point	35057
West Pratt (Part of Dora)	35062
West Sayre	35062
West Selmont	36703
West Side (Jefferson County)	35020
West Side (Montgomery County)	36108
West Wellington	36279
Westwood	35005
Wetumpka	36092
Whatley	36482
Wheat	35053
Wheeler	35618
Wheelerville (Part of Mobile)	36608
Whistler (Part of Mobile)	36612
White City (Autauga County)	36051
White City (Cullman County)	35077
White Hall	36040
Whitehead	35652
Whitehouse	35565
Whitehouse Forks	36507
Whiteoak (Colbert County)	35646
White Oak (Henry County)	36310
Whiteoak (Marshall County)	35950
White Plains (Calhoun County)	36207
White Plains (Chambers County)	36862
Whites Bluff	36767
Whitesboro	35957
Whitesburg (Part of Huntsville)	35802
Whites Chapel (Part of Moody)	35173
Whites Gap	36265
Whitesville	35957
Whitfield	36925
Whitney (Part of Ashville)	35953
Whiton	35962
Whorton	35960
Wicksburg	36352
Wiggins (Part of Babbie)	36420
Wigginsville	35611
Wiginton	35564
Wilburn	35033
Wiley (Montgomery County)	36105
Wiley (Tuscaloosa County)	35501
Wilkes (Part of Midfield)	35064
Wilkinstown	36081
Williamstown	35580
Willowbrook (Part of Huntsville)	35802
Willow Springs	36092
Wills Crossroads	36310
Wills Valley	35967
Wilmer	36587
Wilson Lake Shores	35660
Wilson Quarters	36303
Wilsonville	35186
Wilton	35187
Wimberly	36921
Winburn	35094
Windham Springs	35546
Windsor Highlands (Part of Homewood)	35209
Winfield	35594
Wing	36483
Wingard	36035
Winn	36545
Winninger	35776
Winslow	36003
Winterboro	35014
Winton	35670
Wolf Creek	35125
Wolf Springs	35672
Womack Hill	36908
Woodaire Estates	35215

* Area Zip Code **† Post Office Boxes**

	ZIP		ZIP		ZIP		ZIP
Woodbluff	36727	Woodley Park (Part of Montgomery)	36116	Wyatt	35130	Youngs Chapel	35903
Wooddale	35244	Woodmeadow (Part of Hoover)	35226	Wylam (Part of Birmingham)	35224	Yucca	35966
Woodford	35470			Wynnville	35952	Yupon	36555
Woodland (Macon County)	36866	Woodmont (Part of Hueytown)	35020	Yantley	36912	Zimco	36451
Woodland (Randolph County)	36280	Woodstock	35188	Yarbo	36558	Zion (Montgomery County)	36047
Woodland Forest	35405	Woodstock Junction	35188	Yelling Settlement	36526	Zion (Pickens County)	35466
Woodland Lake	35111	Woodville	35776	Yellow Bluff	36769	Zion City (Part of Birmingham)	35207
Woodlawn (Part of Birmingham)	35212	Woodward	35020	Yellow Creek Falls	35959		
		Woolfolk	36268	Yellowleaf	35186	Zion Heights (Part of Birmingham)	35207
Woodlawn Heights (Franklin County)	35653	Wren	35650	Yellow Pine	36539	Zip City	35630
Woodlawn Heights (Jefferson County)	35212	Wright	35677	Yerkwood	35062	Zoar	36323
		Wright Crossroads	36830	York	36925		
				Youngblood	36081		

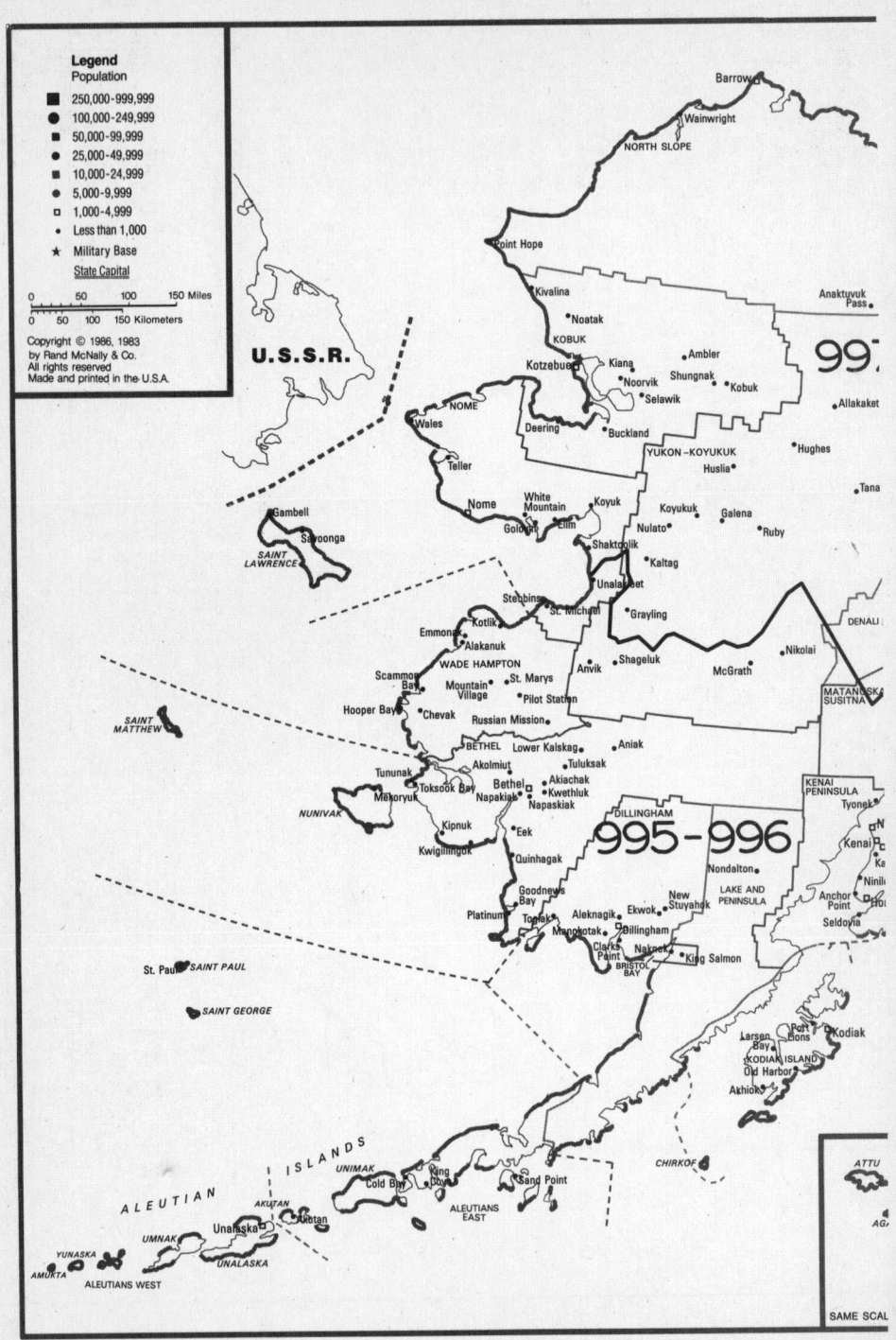

Legend
Population

- ■ 250,000-999,999
- ● 100,000-249,999
- ● 50,000-99,999
- ● 25,000-49,999
- ■ 10,000-24,999
- ■ 5,000-9,999
- □ 1,000-4,999
- • Less than 1,000
- ★ Military Base
- <u>State Capital</u>

0   50   100   150 Miles
0   50   100   150 Kilometers

U.S.S.R.

Barrow
Wainwright
NORTH SLOPE
Point Hope
Kivalina
Noatak
Anaktuvuk Pass
KOBUK
Kiana   Ambler
Kotzebue   Noorvik   Shungnak   Kobuk
Selawik   Allakaket
NOME   Deering   Buckland
Wales   YUKON–KOYUKUK   Hughes
Teller   Huslia
White   Koyuk   Tana
Nome   Mountain   Koyukuk   Galena
Golovin   Elim   Nulato   Ruby
Shaktoolik
Stebbins   Kaltag
Unalakleet
Kotlik   St. Michael   Grayling
Emmonak   DENALI
Alakanuk   Anvik   Shageluk   Nikolai
Scammon   WADE HAMPTON   McGrath
Bay   Mountain   St. Marys   MATANUSKA
Village   Pilot Station   SUSITNA
Hooper Bay   Chevak   Russian Mission
Aniak   KENAI
BETHEL   Lower Kalskag   PENINSULA
Tununak   Akolmiut   Tuluksak   Tyonek
Toksook Bay   Bethel   Akiachak
Mekoryuk   Napakiak   Kwethluk   Kenai
NUNIVAK   Napaskiak   DILLINGHAM
Kipnuk   Eek   995-996
Kwigillingok   Quinhagak   Nondalton
Anchor
LAKE AND   Point
Goodnews   PENINSULA   Seldovia
Bay   New
Platinum   Aleknagik   Ekwok   Stuyahok
Togiak   Manokotak   Dillingham
Clarks   Naknek
Point   King Salmon
St. Paul   SAINT PAUL   BRISTOL
BAY
SAINT GEORGE
Larsen   Port
Bay   Lions   Kodiak
KODIAK ISLAND
Old Harbor
Akhiok
Gambell
Savoonga
SAINT LAWRENCE
SAINT MATTHEW
CHIRKOF   ATTU
ISLANDS   AGA
ALEUTIAN   UNIMAK   King   Sand Point
Cold Bay   Cove   ALEUTIANS EAST
AKUTAN
Akutan
YUNASKA   UMNAK   Unalaska
AMURTA   UNALASKA
ALEUTIANS WEST   SAME SCAL

997

Kaktovik

uvuk
Pass.

97

llakaket

Fort Yukon •

• Tanana

College
Geist   **Fairbanks**
         • North Pole
Nenana •   FAIRBANKS
           NORTH STAR
Anderson •
DENALI
         Healy •
                Ft. • Delta
                Greely   Junction

Eagle •

Canada

SOUTHEAST
FAIRBANKS

• Big Delta

• Tok

ANUSKA
NA

VALDEZ – CORDOVA

• Talkeetna

Wasilla □ Palmer
□
onek •   • ANCHOR-
          AGE
          Anchorage

Nikishka □
enai □ Soldotna
□ Kasilof
Seward
Ninilchik
• Homer
a

Glennallen
• Copper Center

□ Valdez

Whittier   • Cordova

iak

N

SKAGWAY –
YAKUTAT –
ANGOON

• Yakutat

SKAGWAY –
YAKUTAT –
ANGOON
• Skagway

HAINES •
        Haines

JUNEAU

Hoonah
Pelican •   Tenakee
                Springs
        SITKA
                Angoon

Sitka   • Kake
              WRANGELL –
              PETERSBURG

• Petersburg

□ Wrangell

Port
Alexander

North Tongass
Highway

KETCHIKAN
GATEWAY

Ketchikan

Klawock
Craig

Hydaburg Metlakatla

PRINCE OF WALES –
OUTER KETCHIKAN

998 – 999

ATTU
• Shemya A.F.B.

4
AGATTU

KISKA

AMCHITKA

ALEUTIAN ISLANDS

ALEUTIANS WEST

SEMISO-
POCHNOI

TANAGA

Adak N.S.
KANAGA

ADAK

SEGUAM

ATKA

AMLIA

995 – 996

Can.

SCALE AS MAIN MAP

©R. M⁹N. & CO.

	ZIP
Adak Naval Station	99502
Adak Station	99502
Akhiok	99615
Akiachak	99551
Akiak	99552
Akutan	99553
Alakanuk	99554
Alatna (Part of Allakaket)	99720
Alcan	99764
Aleknagik	99555
Alexander	99695
Alitak	99697
Allakaket	99720
Ambler	99786
Amchitka	99501
Amook	99697
Anaktuvuk Pass	99721
Anchorage	99501-04
	99507-24
	99599

For specific Anchorage Zip
Codes call (907) 564-2842, or
your local postmaster.

	ZIP
Anchorage 5th Avenue Shopping Center (Part of Anchorage)	99501
Anchor Point	99556
Anderson	99744
Angoon	99820
Aniak	99557
Annette	99926
Anvik	99558
Arctic Village	99722
Atka	99547
Atmautluak	99559
Atqasuk	99791
Attu	99502
Auke Bay (Part of Juneau)	99821
Aurora (Part of Fairbanks)	99701
Aurora Lodge	99701
Baranof (Part of Sitka)	99835
Barrow	99723
Bartlett Cove	99826
Beaver	99724
Bell Island Hot Springs	99901
Beluga	99695
Bethel	99559
Bettles Field	99726
Big Delta	99737
Big Horn	99701
Big Lake	99652
Birch Creek	99740
Birch Estates	99701
Birchwood (Part of Anchorage)	99567
Bird (Part of Anchorage)	99540
Bjerremark (Part of Fairbanks)	99701
Black Sand	99689
Bluff	99762
Border	99780
Boswell Bay	99574
Boundary	99780
Boyd	99701
Brevig Mission	99785
Broadmoor Acres	99701
Brooks Lodge	99613
Browerville (Part of Barrow)	99723
Buckland	99727
Butte	99645
Campbell (Part of Anchorage)	99517
Candle	99752
Cantwell	99729
Cape Lisburne	99766
Cape Newenham	99576
Cape Newenham Air Force Station	99576
Cape Pole	99901
Cape Romanzof Air Force Station	99559
Cape Yakataga	99695
Carlanna (Part of Ketchikan)	99901
Central	99730
Chalkyitsik	99788
Chandalar	99701
Charcoal Point (Part of Ketchikan)	99901
Chase	99676
Chatanika	99712
Chatham (Part of Sitka)	99803
Chefornak	99561
Chena Hot Springs	99701
Chenega	99693
Chernofski	99685
Chevak	99563
Chickaloon	99674

	ZIP
Chicken	99732
Chignik	99564
Chignik Lagoon	99565
Chignik Lake	99548
Chiniak	99615
Chisana	99780
Chistochina	99586
Chitina	99566
Chuathbaluk	99557
Chugiak (Part of Anchorage)	99567
Circle	99733
Circle Hot Springs Station	99730
Clam Gulch	99568
Clark's Point	99569
Clear	99704
Clearwater Ranch	99737
Clover Pass	99901
Coffman Cove	99918
Cohoe	99610
Cold Bay	99571
Coldfoot	99701
College (Fairbanks North Star Borough)	99708
College Village (Part of Anchorage)	99504
Collegiate Park	99701
Colorado	99695
Cooper Landing	99572
Copper Center	99573
Copperville	99573
Cordova	99574
Cosna	99756
Cottonwood	99654
Council	99762
Covenant Life	99827
Craig	99921
Crooked Creek	99575
Crown Point	99631
Cube Cove	99850
Deadhorse	99734
Debarr Shopping Center (Part of Anchorage)	99504
Deering	99736
Delta Junction	99737
Denali National Park	99755
Derby Tract (Part of Fairbanks)	99701
Dillingham	99576
Dimond Center (Part of Anchorage)	99515
Dora Bay	99901
Dot Lake	99737
Douglas (Part of Juneau)	99824
Downtown (Part of Anchorage)	99501
	99510

For specific Downtown Zip
Codes call (907) 279-3062, or
your local postmaster.

	ZIP
Downtown (Part of Fairbanks)	99707
Driftwood Bay	99695
Dry Creek	99737
Duncan Canal	99833
Dutch Harbor	99692
Eagle	99738
Eagle River (Part of Anchorage)	99577
Eagle Village	99738
Eastchester (Part of Anchorage)	99520
Edna Bay	99901
Eek	99578
Egegik	99579
Eielson Air Force Base	99702
Eklutna (Part of Anchorage)	99567
Eklutna Housing Project (Part of Anchorage)	99645
Ekuk	99695
Ekwok	99580
Elfin Cove	99825
Elim	99739
Ellamar	99695
Emmonak	99581
English Bay	99603
Eska	99674
Ester	99725
Eureka (Matanuska-Susitna Borough)	99645
Eureka (Yukon-Koyukuk Census Division)	99756
Evansville	99726
Excursion Inlet	99850
Eyak	99574
Fairbanks	99701
	99706-12
	99775

	ZIP
	99790

For specific Fairbanks Zip
Codes call (907) 455-5405, or
your local postmaster.

	ZIP
False Pass	99583
Farewell	99627
Ferry	99743
Fire Lake (Part of Anchorage)	99577
Fishhook Junction	99645
Flat	99584
Fort Greely	99737
Fort Wainwright	99703
Fortymile Roadhouse	99737
Fort Yukon	99740
Four Corners	99645
Fox	99701
Fox River	99603
Freshwater Bay (Sitka Borough)	99803
Freshwater Bay (Skagway-Hoonah-Angoon Census Division)	99829
Fritz Cove (Part of Juneau)	99801
Fritz Creek	99603
Funter Bay	99850
Gakona	99586
Galena	99741
Gambell	99742
Game Creek	99829
Ganes Creek	99675
Geist	99701
Girdwood (Part of Anchorage)	99587
Glennallen	99588
Gold Creek	99695
Golovin	99762
Goodnews Bay	99589
Goodnews Mining Camp	99651
Graehl (Part of Fairbanks)	99701
Granite Mountain	99762
Grayling	99590
Gulkana	99695
Gustavus	99826
Haines	99827
Halibut Cove	99603
Hamilton Acres (Part of Fairbanks)	99701
Happy Valley	99556
Harding Lake	99701
Hawk Inlet	99850
Haycock	99753
Healy	99743
Healy Lake	99737
Herring Cove	99901
Hobart Bay	99850
Hogatza	99701
Hollis	99901
Holy Cross	99602
Homer	99603
Hoonah	99829
Hooper Bay	99604
Hope	99605
Houston	99694
Huffman (Part of Anchorage)	99511
Hughes	99745
Huslia	99746
Hydaburg	99922
Hyder	99923
Icy Bay	99695
Igiugig	99613
Iliamna	99606
Indian (Part of Anchorage)	99540
Indian River	99720
Island Homes (Part of Fairbanks)	99701
Ivanof Bay	99695
Jakolof Bay	99695
Jennie M.	99701
Johnston (Part of Fairbanks)	99701
Juneau	99801-11

For specific Juneau Zip Codes
call (907) 586-7138, or your
local postmaster.

	ZIP
Kachemak	99603
Kake	99830
Kako	99657
Kaktovik	99747
Kalifonsky	99610
Kalskag	99607
Kaltag	99748
Kanakanak	99576
Kantishna	99755
Karluk	99608
Kasaan	99901

	ZIP
Kashegelok	99668
Kasigluk	99609
Kasilof	99610
Kasitsna Bay	99695
Kenai	99611
Kenai Lake	99572
Kenai Packers Cannery (Part of Kenai)	99611
Kennicott	99588
Kenny Cove	99695
Kenny Lake	99573
Ketchikan	99901
Kiana	99749
King Cove	99612
King Salmon	99613
Kipnuk	99614
Kitoi Bay	99697
Kivalina	99750
Klawock	99925
Klukwan	99827
Knik	99654
Knudson Cove	99901
Kobuk	99751
Kodiak	99615-19

For specific Kodiak Zip Codes
call (907) 486-4721, or your
local postmaster.

	ZIP
Kodiak Station	99615
Kokhanok	99606
Kokrines	99768
Koliganek	99576
Kongiganak	99559
Kotlik	99620
Kotzebue	99752
Koyuk	99753
Koyukuk	99754
Kupreanof	99833
Kustatan	99682
Kwethluk	99621
Kwigillingok	99622
Labouchere Bay	99927
Lake Minchumina	99757
Lake Nancy	99688
Lake Otis (Part of Anchorage)	99511
Lakloey Hill	99701
Larsen Bay	99624
Lawing	99664
Lazy Mountain	99645
Lemeta (Part of Fairbanks)	99701
Lemon Creek (Part of Juneau)	99801
Lena Cove (Part of Juneau)	99801
Levelock	99625
Liberty	99738
Lignite	99743
Lime Village	99627
Little Diomede	99762
Little Port Walter	99835
Livengood	99701
Long	99768
Long Island (Matanuska-Susitna Borough)	99654
Long Island (Prince of Wales-Outer Ketchikan Census Division)	99922
Lost River (Nome Census Division)	99762
Lost River (Yakutat Borough)	99689
Lower Kalskag	99626
Lower Mendenhall Valley (Part of Juneau)	99801
Lutak	99827
McCarthy	99695
McGrath	99627
Mack	99701
McKinley Acres	99701
Main Office (Part of Anchorage)	99519
Manley Hot Springs	99756
Manokotak	99628
Mansfield Village	99760
Marshall	99585
Marvel Creek	99557
Mary's Igloo	99778
Matanuska	99645
May Creek	99695
Meade River	99791
Meadow Lakes	99654
Medfra	99627
Meekins Roadhouse	99645
Meier	99737
Mekoryuk	99630
Mendeltna	99588
Mendeltna Lodge	99645

* **Area Zip Code** † **Post Office Boxes**

	ZIP
Mendenhall (Part of Juneau)	99803
Mendenhall Flats (Part of Juneau)	99801
Mentasta Lake	99780
Metlakatla	99926
Meyers Chuck	99903
Midtown (Part of Anchorage)	99503
Minto	99758
Montana	99688
Moose Creek	99701
Moose Pass	99631
Moser Bay	99697
Mosquito Lake	99827
Mountain Point	99901
Mountain View (Part of Anchorage)	99508
Mountain Village	99632
Mount Edgecumbe (Part of Sitka)	99835
Mud Bay	99901
Muldoon (Part of Anchorage)	99504
Nabesna	99586
Naknek	99633
Napaimute	99557
Napakiak	99634
Napaskiak	99559
Naukati Bay	99925
Nelson Lagoon	99571
Nenana	99760
Nenana Native Village (Part of Nenana)	99760
Newhalen	99606
New Stuyahok	99636
Newtok	99559
Nightmute	99690
Nikiski	99635
Nikolaevsk	99556
Nikolai	99691
Nikolski	99638
Ninilchik	99639
Noatak	99761
Nome	99762
Nondalton	99640
Noorvik	99763
North Douglas (Part of Juneau)	99801
North Pole	99705
Northway	99764
Northway Junction	99764
Northway Village	99764
Nuiqsut	99789
Nulato	99765
Nunaka Valley (Part of Anchorage)	99504
Nunapitchuk	99641
Nyac	99557
Okagamute	99607
Old Andreafski	99658
Old Harbor	99643
Olnes	99701
Olsonville	99576
Oscarville	99559
Ouzinkie	99644
Palmer	99645
Paradise Hill	99602
Parks	99697
Paxson	99737
Pederson Point	99633
Pedro Bay	99647
Pelican	99832
Peninsula Point	99901
Pennock Island	99901
Perryville	99648

	ZIP
Petersburg	99833
Peters Creek (Part of Anchorage)	99567
Pilot Point	99649
Pilot Station	99650
Pitkas Point	99658
Pittman	99654
Platinum	99651
Pleasant Valley	99701
Point Baker	99927
Point Barrow DEW Station	99723
Point Higgins	99901
Point Hope	99766
Point Lay	99759
Point Whiteshed	99574
Polk Inlet	99922
Poorman	99768
Portage (Part of Anchorage)	99587
Portage Creek	99695
Port Alexander	99836
Port Alice	99901
Port Alsworth	99653
Port Armstrong	99836
Port Ashton	99695
Port Bailey	99697
Port Clarence	99790
Port Graham	99603
Port Heiden	99549
Port Lions	99550
Portlock	99663
Port Moller	99571
Port Protection	99901
Port Walter	99835
Port Williams	99697
Potter (Part of Anchorage)	99501
Primrose	99631
Prudhoe Bay	99734
Quartz Creek	99572
Queen	99576
Quinhagak	99655
Rainbow (Part of Anchorage)	99501
Rampart	99767
Red Devil	99656
Red Mountain	99603
Red Salmon	99633
Rego	99701
Ridgeway	99669
Rodman (Part of Sitka)	99835
Rogers Park (Part of Anchorage)	99508
Rowan Bay (Skagway-Hoonah-Angoon Census Division)	99835
Rowan Bay (Wrangell-Petersburg Census Division)	99836
Ruby	99768
Russian Jack (Part of Anchorage)	99514
Russian Mission	99657
St. George Island	99591
St. John Harbor	99929
St. Marys	99658
St. Marys Mission (Part of St. Marys)	99658
St. Michael	99659
St. Paul Island	99660
Salamatof	99611
Salcha	99714
Salmon Creek (Part of Juneau)	99801
Sand Lake (Part of Anchorage)	99522

	ZIP
Sand Point	99661
Savoonga	99769
Saxman	99901
Saxman East (Part of Saxman)	99901
Scammon Bay	99662
Scow Bay	99833
Seal Bay	99697
Selawik	99770
Seldovia	99663
Seward	99664
Shageluk	99665
Shaktoolik	99771
Shanley (Part of Fairbanks)	99701
Sheldon Point	99666
Shemya Air Force Base	99501
Shemya Station	99501
Shishmaref	99772
Shungnak	99773
Sitka	99835
Situk	99689
Skagway	99840
Skwentna	99667
Slana	99586
Slaterville (Part of Fairbanks)	99701
Sleetmute	99668
Snowball	99701
Snug Harbor	99572
Soldotna	99669
Solomon	99790
Sourdough	99586
South (Part of Anchorage)	99511
South Bjerremark	99701
South Naknek	99670
Spenard (Part of Anchorage)	99509
Sprucewood	99701
Squaw Harbor	99661
Starr Hill (Part of Juneau)	99801
Stebbins	99671
Steele Creek	99738
Steese	99710
Sterling	99672
Stevens Village	99774
Stony River	99557
Strelna	99566
Summit	99729
Summit Lodge	99586
Sunnyside	99832
Sunshine	99695
Suntrana	99743
Sutton	99674
Takotna	99675
Talkeetna	99676
Tanacross	99776
Tanana	99777
Tatalina	99627
Tatitlek	99677
Tee Harbor (Part of Juneau)	99801
Telida	99695
Teller	99778
Tenakee Springs	99841
Terror Bay	99697
Tetlin	99779
Thane (Part of Juneau)	99801
Thorne Bay	99919
Tiekel	99686
Tin City	99783
Togiak	99678
Tok	99780
Tokeen	99901

	ZIP
Toksook Bay	99637
Tonsina	99573
Totem Bight	99901
Totem Park	99701
Trapper Creek	99683
Tuluksak	99679
Tuntutuliak	99680
Tununak	99681
Turnagain (Part of Anchorage)	99517
Turnagain by-the-Sea (Part of Anchorage)	99517
Turnagain Heights (Part of Anchorage)	99517
Twin Hills	99576
Two Rivers	99716
Tyonek	99682
Uganik	99697
Ugashik	99613
Umiat	99701
Unalakleet	99684
Unalaska	99685
Ungalik	99684
University Center (Part of Anchorage)	99503
University Park	99701
Upper Mendenhall Valley (Part of Juneau)	99801
Upper Nickeyville (Part of Ketchikan)	99901
U.S. Coast Guard Station	99619
Usibelli	99743
Valdez	99686
Vank Island	99929
Venetie	99781
View Cove	99901
Wainwright	99782
Wales	99783
Ward Cove	99928
Wasilla	99687
	99654
For specific Wasilla Zip Codes call (907) 376-5327, or your local postmaster.	
Waterfall	99901
West Fairwest	99701
Westgate (Part of Fairbanks)	99701
West Juneau (Part of Juneau)	99801
West Point	99697
Westwood	99701
Whale Pass	99901
White Mountain	99784
Whites Crossing	99688
Whitestone Logging Camp	99829
Whitney (Part of Anchorage)	99501
Whittier	99693
Wilcox	99701
Wilcox Estates	99701
Wild Lake	99726
Willow	99688
Wiseman	99790
Womens Bay	99615
Woodland Park (Part of Anchorage)	99517
Wood River	99576
Wrangell	99929
Yakutat	99689
Yankee Creek	99675
Zachar Bay	99697

* Area Zip Code   **† Post Office Boxes**

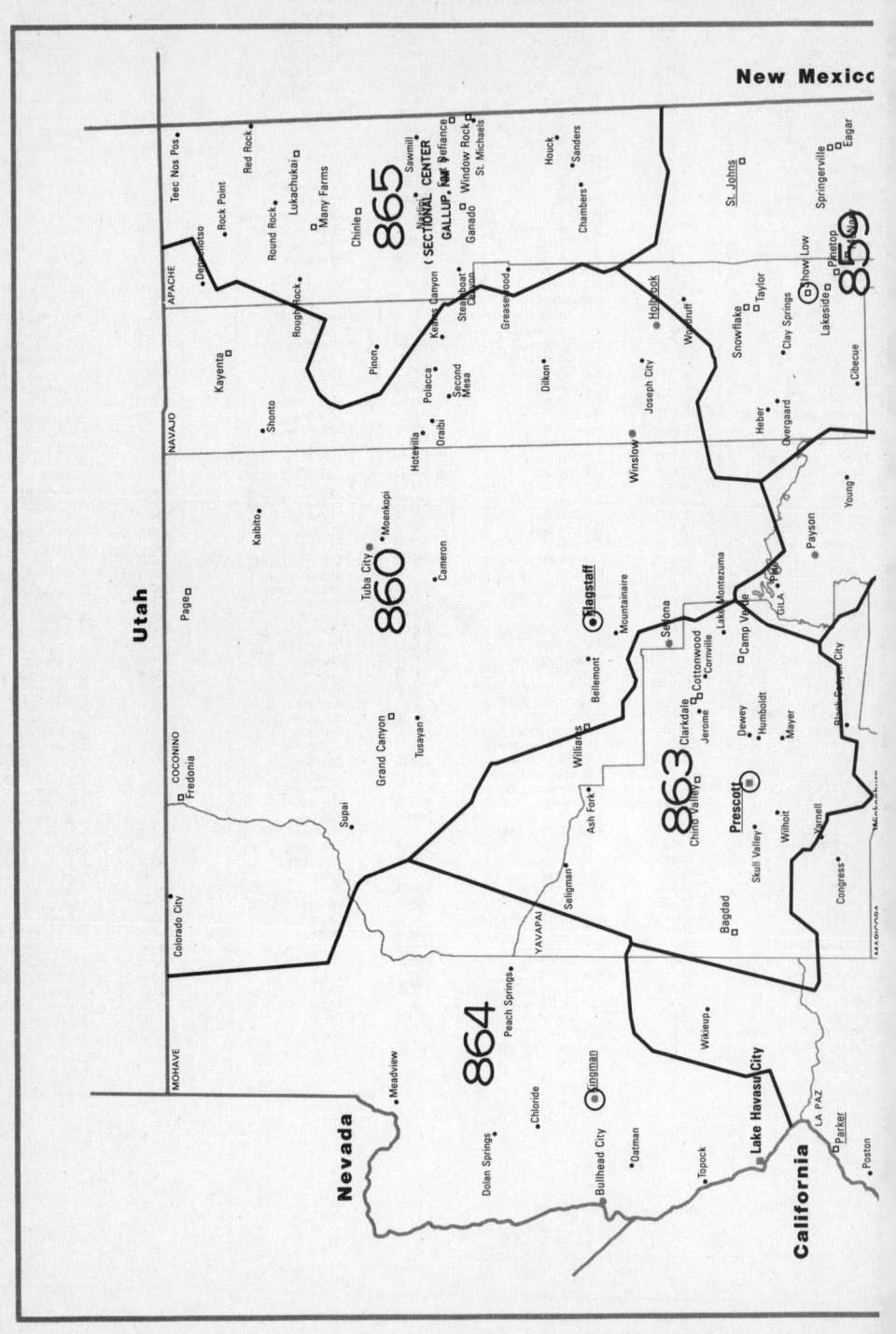

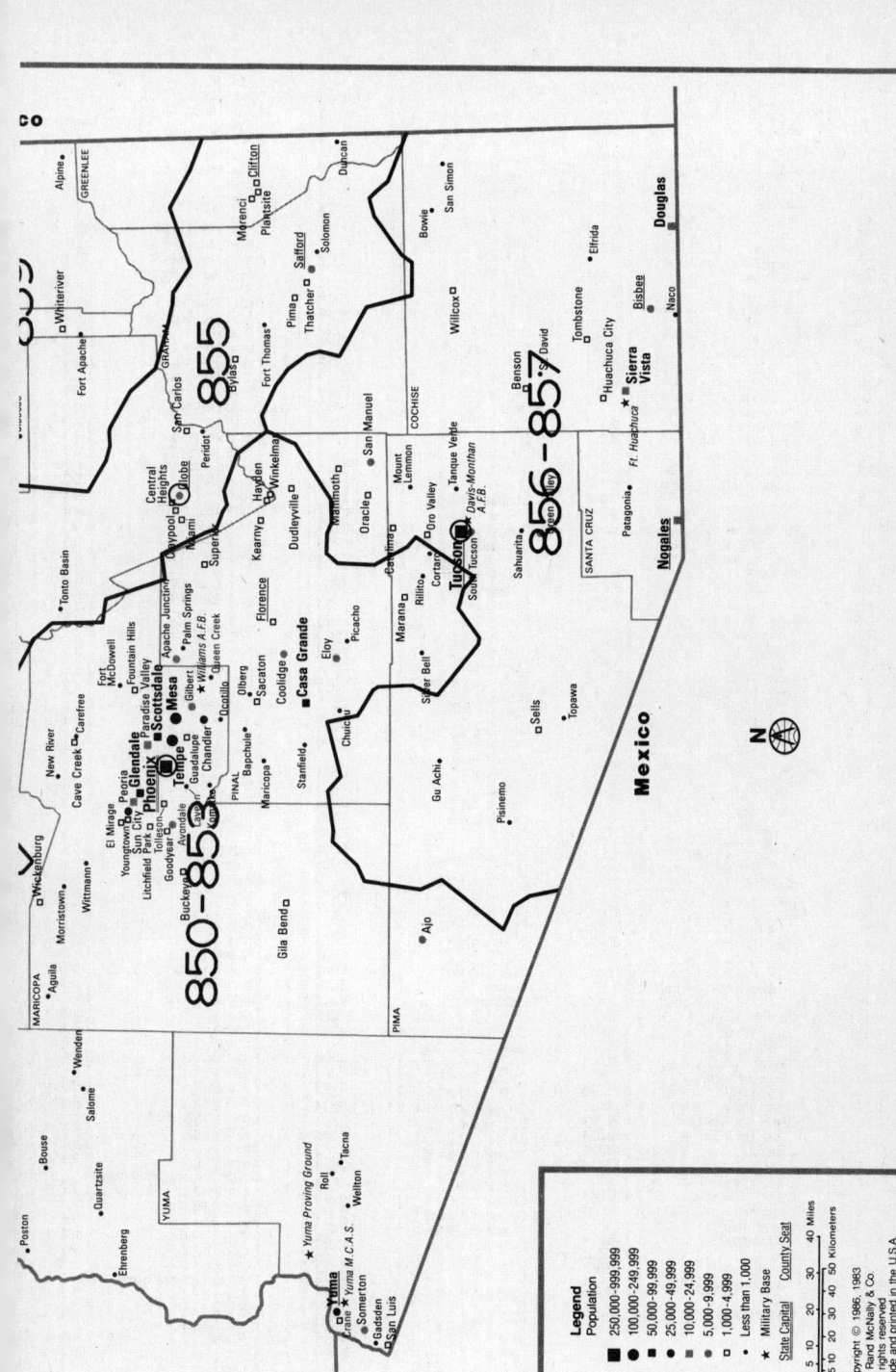

850-855

855

856-857

CO

GREENLEE

GRAHAM

COCHISE

SANTA CRUZ

Mexico

MARICOPA

PINAL

PIMA

YUMA

Alpine

Whiteriver

Fort Apache

Morenci • Clifton
Metcalf
Duncan
Plantsite

San Simon

Safford
Solomon
Bowie

Pima Thatcher
Bylas

Fort Thomas

Willcox

Bowie

Douglas

Efrida

Tombstone

Sierra Vista
Huachuca City
Fort Huachuca
Benson
David

Bisbee
Naco

Patagonia
Nogales

Tanque Verde

Davis-Monthan A.F.B.

Tucson
South Tucson

Sahuarita

Green Valley

Oro Valley
Mount Lemmon

Catalina

Cortaro
Rillito
Marana

Picacho

Topawa

Sells

Gu Achi

Pisinemo

Chiu

Silver Bell

Eloy

Casa Grande

Coolidge
Sacaton
Olberg
Florence
Queen Creek

Stanfield

Maricopa

Bapchule

Guadalupe
Chandler

Ocotillo
Gilbert

Mesa
Tempe
Scottsdale
Phoenix
Glendale
Peoria
Sun City
Youngtown
El Mirage

Litchfield Park
Goodyear
Avondale
Buckeye

Gila Bend

Ajo

Wickenburg

Aguila

Morristown

Wittmann

New River

Cave Creek Carefree

Tonto Basin

Fort McDowell

Paradise Valley
Fountain Hills
Apache Junction

Williams A.F.B.
Palm Springs

Cortaro

Tolleson

Central Heights

Claypool
Miami
Globe
San Carlos
Peridot

Hayden
Winkelman
Dudleyville
Mammoth

Kearny

Superior

San Manuel

Oracle

Superstition

Somerton
San Luis
Gadsden
Yuma
Yuma M.C.A.S.
Crane

Yuma Proving Ground
Roll
Wellton
Tacna

Salome

Wenden

Bouse

Quartzsite

Ehrenberg

Poston

Copyright © 1966, 1983
by Rand McNally & Co
All rights reserved
Made and printed in the U.S.A.

Legend
Population
250,000-999,999
100,000-249,999
50,000-99,999
25,000-49,999
10,000-24,999
5,000-9,999
1,000-4,999
Less than 1,000
★ Military Base
State Capital County Seat

0 5 10   20   30   40 Miles
0 5 10 20 30 40 50 Kilometers

	ZIP
Acres Foothills	85614
Adamana	86025
Adamsville	85232
Agua Caliente	85333
Agua Linda	85640
Aguila	85320
Ahwatukee	85044-45
	85048
	85076

For specific Ahwatukee Zip Codes call (602)407-2024, or your local postmaster.

	ZIP
Airpark (Part of Scottsdale)	85260
Ajo	85321
Akchin	85634
Ak-Chin Village	85239
Alamo Crossing	85357
Alchesay Flat	85941
Ali Chuk	85634
Ali Molina	85634
Allentown	86506
Alpine	85920
Amado	85645
Ames Acres	86047
Anegam	85634
Apache	88056
Apache Flats	85613
Apache Grove	85534
Apache Ho (Part of Apache Junction)	85220
Apache Junction	85217-20
	85278

For specific Apache Junction Zip Codes call (602) 982-2121, or your local postmaster.

	ZIP
Apache Wells (Part of Mesa)	85215
Araby	85364
Aravaipa	85292
Aravaipa Canyon	85292
Arcadia (Part of Phoenix)	85018
	85060

For specific Arcadia Zip Codes call (602) 407-2025, or your local postmaster.

	ZIP
Arcosanti	86333
Arivaca	85601
Arizola	85222
Arizona City	85223
Arizona Shores	85344
Arizona State Prison Complex-Douglas	85607
Arizona State Prison Complex-Florence	85232
Arizona State Prison Complex-Perryville	85338
Arizona State Prison Complex-Safford	85546
Arizona State Prison Complex-Tucson	85706
Arlington	85322
Artesa	85634
Artesia	85546
Ash Fork	86320
Avondale	85323
Avra Valley	85653
Aztec	85333
Baby Rock	86033
Bacobi	86030
Bagdad	86321
Bakerville (Part of Bisbee)	85603
Bald Mesa (Unit 1)	86024
Bald Mesa (Unit 2)	86024
Bapchule	85221
Bayless Shopping Center (Part of Apache Junction)	85220
Beardsley	85373
Beautys Estates (Part of Nogales)	85621
Beaver Dam	86432
Beaver Valley Estates	85541
Bella Vista Estates (Part of Sierra Vista)	85635
Bellemont	86015
Benson	85602
Beyerleville	85621
Big Park	86335
Biltmore Fashion Park (Part of Phoenix)	85016
Bisbee	85603
Bisbee Junction	85603
Bitahochee	86031
Bitter Springs	86036
Black Canyon City	85324
Black Hills (Part of Clarkdale)	86324
Blackwater	85228

	ZIP
Blue	85922
Blue Gap	86520
Blue Ridge	86024
Bluewater	85344
Bonita	85643
Bonita Creek	85541
Bouse	85325
Bowie	85605
Boys Ranch (Part of Queen Creek)	85242
Braemer (Part of Peoria)	85345
Branding Iron	85701
Brenda	85348
Bridge Canyon Country Estates	86337
Bridgeport	86326
Briggs Townsite (Part of Bisbee)	85603
Bryce	85543
Buckeye	85326
Buckhorn	85205
Buena Vista	85546
Bullhead City	86426
	86429-30

For specific Bullhead City Zip Codes call (602) 754-3717, or your local postmaster.

	ZIP
Bumble Bee	86333
Burnt Water	86512
Bushman Acres	86047
Bylas	85530
Cactus (Part of Phoenix)	85032
	85046
	85078

For specific Cactus Zip Codes call (602) 407-2026, or your local postmaster.

	ZIP
Cactus Flat	85546
Cactus Forest	85232
Calva	85530
Camelview Plaza (Part of Scottsdale)	85251
Cameron	86020
Camp Creek	85331
Camp Verde	86322
Camp Verde Indian Reservation	86322
Cane Beds	86022
Canelo	85611
Canoa Estates	85614
Canyon (Part of Mesa)	85201
Canyon Day	85941
Canyon Sights	86301
Capitol (Part of Phoenix)	85005
	85009

For specific Capitol Zip Codes call (602) 484-9014, or your local postmaster.

	ZIP
Carefree	85377
Carmen	85640
Carrizo	85901
Casa Blanca	85221
Casa Grande	85222
	85230

For specific Casa Grande Zip Codes call (602) 836-7221, or your local postmaster.

	ZIP
Casa Paloma I	85614
Casa Paloma II	85614
Casas Adobes	85704
Cascabel	85602
Cashion (Part of Avondale)	85329
Castle Canyon Mesa	86301
Castle Hot Springs	85342
Castle Rock Shores	85344
Catalina	85738
Catalina Foothills	85718
Cave Creek	85331
Cedar Creek	85941
Cedar Ridge	86020
Centerville (Part of Clarkdale)	86324
Central	85531
Central Heights	85501
Central Heights-Midland City	85532
Chambers	86502
Chandler	85224-26
	85244
	85248-49

For specific Chandler Zip Codes call (602) 963-6643, or your local postmaster.

	ZIP
Chandler Heights	85227
Chaparral (Part of Chandler)	85224
Cherry	86327
Chevelon	86001

	ZIP
Chiawuli Tak	85634
Chilchinbito	86033
Childs	85321
Chinle	86503
Chino de Manana (Part of Chino Valley)	86323
Chino Heights	86323
Chino Meadows (Part of Chino Valley)	86323
Chino Ranches	86323
Chino Valley	86323
Chloride	86431
Choulic	85634
Christopher Creek	85541
Chris-Town Center (Part of Phoenix)	85015
Chuichu	85222
Cibecue	85911
Cibola	85328
Cienega Springs	85344
Circle City	85342
Citrus Gardens	85201
Clarkdale	86324
Claypool	85532
Clay Springs	85923
Cleator	86333
Clifton	85533
Coal Mine Mesa	86045
Cobblestone Village (Part of Peoria)	85381
Cochise	85606
Cocopah Indian Reservation	85350
Colcord Estates	85541
College (Part of Tucson)	85722
Colorado City	86021
Colorado River Indian Reservation	85344
Comobabi	85634
Concho	85924
Concho Valley	85924
Congress	85332
Continental	85614
Continental Vistas	85614
Coolidge	85228
Coolidge Dam	85542
Co-op Village	85339
Copper Mine	86040
Copper Queen (Part of Bisbee)	85603
Cordes	86333
Cordes Juntion	86333
Cordes Lakes	86333
Cork	85536
Cornfields	86505
Cornville	86325
Coronada Foothills Estates	85718
Corona de Tucson	85747
Coronado (Part of Tucson)	85711*
	85732†
Coronado Unit	86047
Cortaro	85652
Cottonwood	86326
Cottonwood Station	86503
Cottonwood-Verde Village	86326
Country Club Estates (Cochise County)	85635
Country Club Estates (Pima County)	85614
Country Club Vistas I, II, III	85614
Country Life	85201
Cove	87420
Covered Wells	85634
Cowlic	85634
Cow Springs	86044
Crane	85364
Craycroft (Part of Tucson)	85712
Crestview (Part of Bisbee)	85603
Cross Canyon	86511
Crown King	86343
Cuckelbur	85222
Curley Horn Ranch	85629
Cutter	85501
Dam View	85344
Date	85332
Dateland	85333
Davis Dam (Part of Bullhead City)	86430
Davis-Monthan Air Force Base	85702
Del Rio	86323
Del Sol	85364
Dennehotso	86535
Desert (Part of Mesa)	85206

	ZIP
	85216

For specific Desert Zip Codes call (602) 985-6181, or your local postmaster.

	ZIP
Desert Air	85364
Desert Carmel	85222
Desert Harbor (Part of Peoria)	85381
Desert Hills (Mohave County)	86403
Desert Hills (Part of Green Valley)	85614
Desert Hills (Part of Tucson)	85718
Desert Meadows I	85614
Desert Meadows II	85614
Desert Meadows III	85614
Desert Sands (Part of Mesa)	85208
Desert Shadows	86438
Desert Steppes (Part of Tucson)	85710
Desert View	86023
Dewey	86327
Dewey-Humboldt	86329
Diamond Point	85541
Diamond Valley	86301
Dilkon	86047
Discovery at the Orchard (Part of Peoria)	85381
Dobson (Part of Mesa)	85202
	85272
	85274

For specific Dobson Zip Codes call (602) 829-9334, or your local postmaster.

	ZIP
Dolan Springs	86441
Dome	85365
Don Luis (Part of Bisbee)	85603
Dos Cabezas	85643
Double Adobe	85617
Douglas	85607-08
	85655

For specific Douglas Zip Codes call (602) 364-3631, or your local postmaster.

	ZIP
Downtown (Part of Flagstaff)	86001
Downtown (Part of Kingman)	86402
Downtown (Part of Phoenix)	85001-04
	85007

For specific Downtown Zip Codes call (602) 225-3434, or your local postmaster.

	ZIP
Downtown (Part of Tempe)	85281
Downtown (Part of Tucson)	85701*
	85702†
Dragoon	85609
Drake	86334
Dreamland Villa	85205
Drexel Heights	85746
Drippings Springs	85292
Dudleyville	85292
Dugas	86333
Duncan	85534
Eagar	85925
Eagle Creek	85533
East Flagstaff (Part of Flagstaff)	86001
East Fork	85941
East Plantsite (Part of Clifton)	85540
Eden	85535
Ehrenberg	85334
El Con Regional Shopping Center (Part of Tucson)	85716
Eleven Mile Corner	85222
Elfrida	85610
Elgin	85611
Ellison Creek	85541
El Mirage	85335
El Mirage (mobile home park)	85201
Eloy	85231
El Pueblecito (Part of Yuma)	85364
El Rio (Part of Tucson)	85745
Emery Park (Part of Tucson)	85706
Empire Landing	85344
Fairbank	85621
Fairways I	85614
Fairways II	85614
Fairways III	85614
Falcon (Part of Mesa)	85205

Place	ZIP
	85207
	85215
For specific Falcon Zip Codes call (602) 641-7699, or your local postmaster.	
Falcon Estates (Part of Mesa)	85203
Federal Correctional Institution (Graham County)	85546
Federal Correctional Institution (Maricopa County)	85027
Federal Correctional Institution (Pima County)	85706
Federal Prison Camp	85546
Fiesta Mall (Part of Mesa)	85202
Fiesta Park	85201
Fishers Landing	85365
Flagstaff	86001-04
For specific Flagstaff Zip Codes call (602) 527-2440, or your local postmaster.	
Flecha Caida Estates	85718
Florence	85232*
	85279†
Florence Junction	85219
Flowing Wells	85705
Floy	85924
Foothills North	85364
Forbing Park (Part of Prescott)	86301
Forest Lakes	85931
Fort Apache	85926
Fort Apache Indian Reservation	85941
Fort Apache Junction	85941
Fort Defiance	86504
Fort Grant	85644
Fort Lowell (Part of Tucson)	85712
	85715
	85749
For specific Fort Lowell Zip Codes call (602) 721-8503, or your local postmaster.	
Fort McDowell	85254
Fort McDowell Indian Reservation	85264
Fort Mohave Indian Reservation	86427
Fort Rock	86337
Fort Thomas	85536
Fortuna Foothills	85356
Fortuna Heights	85364
Fortuna Hills	85364
Fountain East	85201
Fountain Hills	85268*
	85269†
Fountain of the Sun (Part of Mesa)	85208
Foxfire (Part of Peoria)	85381
Foxwood (Part of Peoria)	85381
Franklin	85534
Fredonia	86022
Fresnal Canyon	85634
Friendly Corners	85231
Fry (Part of Sierra Vista)	85635
Gadsden	85336
Galena (Part of Bisbee)	85603
Ganado	86505
Geronimo	85536
Gibson	85321
Gila Acres	85364
Gila Bend	85337
Gila Bend Indian Reservation	85634
Gila Crossing	85339
Gila River Indian Reservation	85247
Gilbert	85233-34
	85296
	85299
For specific Gilbert Zip Codes call (602) 892-0010, or your local postmaster.	
Gisela	85541
Gladden	85320
Gleeson	85610
Glendale	85301-08
	85310-12
	85318
For specific Glendale Zip Codes call (602) 842-0099, or your local postmaster.	
Glen Ilah	85362
Globe	85501*
	85502†

Place	ZIP
Gold Canyon	85219
Golden Shores	86436
Golden Valley	86413
Goldfield	85219
Goodyear	85338
Goodyear Farms (Part of Litchfield Park)	85340
Gordon Canyon Estates	85541
Graham	85552
Grand Canyon	86023
Grand Canyon Caverns	86434
Grandview	86301
Grandview Estates	86301
Granite Dells	86301
Granite Oaks	86301
Grasshopper Junction	86401
Gray Mountain	86016
Greasewood	86505
Greaterville	85637
Greenback Valley	85553
Green Valley	85614*
	85622†
Greenway (Part of Glendale)	85306
Greer	85927
Gripe	85546
Groom Creek	86303
Guadalupe	85283
Gunsight	85634
Gu Oidak	85634
Guthrie	85533
Gu Vo	85634
Hacienda De Valencia	85201
Hackberry	86411
Haivana Nakya	85634
Hamilton Corner	85248
Hannagan Meadow	85922
Hano	86042
Happy Jack	86024
Harcuvar	85348
Harmony Villa	85201
Hassayampa	85343
Havasupai Indian Reservation	86435
Hawkins	85332
Hawley Lake	85930
Hayden	85235
Hayden Junction	85235
Heber	85928
Heber-Overgaard	85928
Hereford	85615
Hereford Hills	86323
Hermits Rest	86023
Hickiwan	85634
Hidden Springs	86020
Highland Park	85603
Highland Pines	86301
Higley	85236
Hillcrest	85546
Hillside	86301
Hilltop	85632
Ho Kay Gan	86301
Holbrook	86025
Holiday	85344
Holiday Hills	86301
Hollywood	85546
Hon Dah	85935
Hope	85348
Hopi (Part of Scottsdale)	85258
	85261
For specific Hopi Zip Codes call (602) 998-9444, or your local postmaster.	
Hopi Indian Reservation	86039
Horn	85333
Horse Mesa	85219
Horse Thief	86333
Hotason Vo	85634
Hotevilla	86030
Houck	86506
Huachuca City	85616
Huachuca Terrace (Part of Bisbee)	85603
Hualapai	86412
Hualapai Indian Reservation	86434
Hubbell	86505
Humboldt	86329
Hunt	85924
Hunters Point	86511
Hyder	85333
Immanuel Mission	86514
Indian Gardens	86336
Indian Ridge Estates	85715
Indian School (Part of Phoenix)	85014
Indian Wells	86031
Inscription House	86044
Inspiration	85532

Place	ZIP
Iron Springs	86330
Jackrabbit	85222
Jackson Acres	86301
Jacob Lake	86022
Jade Park North (Part of Phoenix)	85308
Jakes Corner	85541
Jeddito	86034
Jerome	86331
Johnson	85609
Joseph City	86032
Juniper Heights	86301
Kachina Gardens	86047
Kachina Village	86001
Kaibab	86022
Kaibab Indian Reservation	86022
Kaibab Lodge	86022
Kaibito	86053
Kaihon Kug	85634
Kaka	85321
Kansas Settlement	85643
Katherine	86430
Kayenta	86033
Keams Canyon	86034
Kearny	85237
Kelvin	85237
Kerwo	85634
Kingman	86401-02
For specific Kingman Zip Codes call (602) 753-2480, or your local postmaster.	
Kings Ranch	85217
Kingswood	86301
Kinlichee	86505
Kino (Part of Tucson)	85703*
	85705†
Kino Hills (Part of Nogales)	85621
Kino Springs	85621
Kinsley Ranch	85640
Kirkland	86332
Kirkland Junction	86332
Klagetoh	86505
Klondyke	85644
Kohatk	85634
Kohls Ranch	85541
Komatke	85339
Ko Vaya	85634
Kykotsmovi Village	86039
La Canada Norte	85629
Lake Havasu City	86403-06
For specific Lake Havasu City Zip Codes call (602) 855-2361, or your local postmaster.	
Lake Mead City	86444
Lake Mead Rancheros	86401
Lake Mohave	86430
Lake Montezuma	86342
Lakeside (La Paz County)	85344
Lakeside (Navajo County)	85929
Lampliter Village (Part of Clarkdale)	86324
La Palma	85222
La Quintas de Santo Tomas	85629
La Quintas Serenas	85629
Las Ligas (Part of Avondale)	85323
Laveen	85339
Leche-e Chapter	86040
Lees Ferry	86036
Leisure World	85206
Leupp	86035
Leupp Corner	86047
Liberty	85326
Ligurta	85356
Litchfield Greens (Part of Litchfield Park)	85340
Litchfield Park	85340
Little Acres	85501
Littlefield	86432
Little Tucson	85634
Lizard Acres	85373
Lochiel	85624
Loma Linda	85619
Loma Linda Estates	85533
Lone Star	85546
Long Valley	86001
Los Arcos Mall (Part of Scottsdale)	85257
Los Gatos	85255
Lowell (Part of Bisbee)	85603
Lower Miami	85539
Low Mountain	86503
Lukachukai	86507
Luke Air Force Base	85309
Lukeville	85341
Lupton	86508
Lynx Estates	86301

Place	ZIP
McDowell (Part of Phoenix)	85008
	85010
For specific McDowell Zip Codes call (602) 275-1997, or your local postmaster.	
McGees Settlement	85736
McGuireville	86335
McNary	85930
McNeal	85617
Madera Canyon	85706
Mammoth	85618
Many Farms	86538
Marana	85653
Marble Canyon	86036
Maricopa	85239
Maricopa (Ak-Chin) Indian Reservation	85239
Maricopa Village	85339
Marine Corps Air Station	85369
Mariposa Manor (Part of Nogales)	85621
Martinez Lake	85365
Maryvale (Part of Phoenix)	85019
	85031
	85033
	85063
For specific Maryvale Zip Codes call (602) 247-7664, or your local postmaster.	
Mayer	86333
Meadow Brook (Part of Yuma)	85364
Meadview	86444
Mennonite Mission	86505
Mesa	85201-16
	85240
	85274-77
For specific Mesa Zip Codes call (602) 969-9171, or your local postmaster.	
Mesa del Caballo	85541
Mesa Del Oro	85219
Mesa del Sol	85364
Mescal	85602
Metrocenter (Part of Phoenix)	85021
Mexican Town	85321
Mexican Water	86514
Miami	85539
Miami Gardens	85539
Middle Verde (Part of Camp Verde)	86322
Midland City	85501
Miller Valley (Part of Prescott)	86301
Miracle Valley	85615
Miramonte Acres (Part of Bisbee)	85603
Mishongnovi	86043
Mission (Part of Tucson)	85706
	85714
	85734
For specific Mission Zip Codes call (602) 746-3695, or your local postmaster.	
Mission Manor (Part of Tucson)	85706
Mobile	85239
Moccasin	86022
Moenave	86045
Moenkopi	86045
Mohave Valley	86440
Morenci	85540
Mormon Lake	86038
Morristown	85342
Mountainaire	86001
Mountain Club	86301
Mountain View (Cochise County)	85603
Mountain View (Maricopa County)	85203
	85213
	85275
For specific Mountain View Zip Codes call (602) 898-0995, or your local postmaster.	
Mountain View (Navajo County)	85935
Mountain View (Pima County)	85752
Mountain View Acres	85629
Mount Elden (Part of Flagstaff)	86001
Mount Lemmon	85619
Munds Park	86017
Na-Ah-Tee Canyon	86025
Naco	85620
Navajo	86509

*** Area Zip Code** **† Post Office Boxes**

	ZIP
Navajo Depot Activity	86015
Navajo Indian Reservation	86515
Navajo Mountain	86044
Navajo Spring	86036
Navajo Station	86505
Nazlini	86540
Nelson	86434
New Hope	85201
New Kingman-Butler	86401
New Oraibi	86039
New River	85027
New Tucson (Part of Tucson)	85747
Nicksville	85615
Nogales	85621
	85628
	85662
For specific Nogales Zip Codes call (602) 287-9246, or your local postmaster.	
Nogales West (Part of Nogales)	85621
Nolia	85634
Normal Junction (Part of Tempe)	85281
Northeast (Part of Phoenix)	85016
Northern Arizona University (Part of Flagstaff)	86011
Northern Hills	85704
North Komelik	85634
Northridge Park	86314
North Rim	86052
Northwest (Part of Phoenix)	85015
	85017
	85061
	85079
For specific Northwest Zip Codes call (602) 249-6344, or your local postmaster.	
Nortons Corner (Part of Chandler)	85225
Nutrioso	85932
Oak Knoll Village	86301
Oak Springs	86511
Oasis Park (Part of Apache Junction)	85220
Oatman	86433
Ocotillo	85248
Ocotillo Ranch	85629
Octave	85332
Olberg	85247
Old Columbine	85546
Old Oraibi	86039
Oracle	85623
Oracle Foot Hill Estates	85704
Oracle Junction	85737
Orange Grove Estates	85704
Oro Valley	85737
Osborn	85012-13
	85067
For specific Osborn Zip Codes call (602) 235-9118, or your local postmaster.	
Overgaard	85933
Page	86040
Page Springs	86325
Palm Springs (Part of Apache Junction)	85219
Palominas	85615
Palo Verde	85343
Pan Tak	85634
Papago (Part of Scottsdale)	85257
Papago Indian Reservation	85634
Paradise	85632
Paradise Valley	85253
Paradise Valley Mall (Part of Phoenix)	85032
Park Central Mall (Part of Phoenix)	85013
Parker	85344
Parker Strip	85344
Park Mall (Part of Tucson)	85711
Parks	86018
Pascua Yaqui Indian Reservation	85746
Patagonia	85624
Paulden	86334
Paul Spur	85607
Payson	85541*
	85547†
Peach Springs	86434
Pearce	85625
Peeples Valley	86332
Peoria	85345

	ZIP
	85380-82
For specific Peoria Zip Codes call (602) 979-1841, or your local postmaster.	
Peralta Estates	85219
Peridot	85542
Perkinsville	86323
Perryville	85326
Petrified Forest National Park	86028
Phoenix	85001-86
For specific Phoenix Zip Codes call (602) 225-3434, or your local postmaster.	
COLLEGES & UNIVERSITIES	
DeVry Institute of Technology-Phoenix	85021
University of Phoenix	85072
FINANCIAL INSTITUTIONS	
Bank of America, Arizona	85003
Bank One Arizona, N.A.	85004
Chase Bank of Arizona	85012
Citibank (Arizona)	85012
First Interstate Bank of Arizona, N.A.	85003
HOSPITALS	
Arizona State Hospital	85008
Carl T. Hayden Veterans Affairs Medical Center	85012
Good Samaritan Hospital Medical Center	85006
Healthwest Regional Medical Center	85016
John C. Lincoln Hospital and Health Center	85020
Maricopa Medical Center	85008
St. Joseph's Hospital and Medical Center	85013
HOTELS/MOTELS	
Arizona Biltmore	85016
Embassy Suites Hotel	85016
Embassy Suites Camelhead	85008
Doubletree Suites Hotel	85008
Holiday Inn-Corporate Center	85029
Hyatt Regency Phoenix	85004
Pointe Hilton Resort at Squaw Peak	85020
Ramada Inn Metrocenter	85029
Sheraton Greenway Inn	85023
MILITARY INSTALLATIONS	
Arizona Air National Guard, FB6021, Sky Harbor International Airport	85034
Pia Oik	85634
Picacho	85241
Picture Rocks	85653
Pima	85543
Pine	85544
Pinedale	85934
Pine Lake (Apache County)	85924
Pine Lake (Mohave County)	86401
Pine Lake (Yavapai County)	86301
Pine Springs	86506
Pinetop (Part of Pinetop-Lakeside)	85935
Pinetop Country Club	85935
Pinetop Lake Country Club	85935
Pinetop-Lakeside	85935
Pinion Pine Estates	86401
Pinnacle Peak Village	85255
Pinon	86510
Pioneer (Part of Mesa)	85210
Pirtleville	85626
Pisinemo	85634
Plantsite	85540
Plaza Del Rio (Part of Peoria)	85381
Polacca	86042
Poland Junction	86333
Pomerene	85627
Ponderosa Park	86301
Ponderosa Springs	85541
Portal	85632
Porter Creek Estates	85929
Porter Mountain Estates	85929

	ZIP
Poston	85371
Potato Patch	86301
Prescott	86301-04
	86313
For specific Prescott Zip Codes call (602) 778-1890, or your local postmaster.	
Prescott Canyon Estates	86301
Prescott Country Club	86301
Prescott Riviera	86301*
	86312†
Prescott Valley	86314
Presidential Estates	85616
Pueblo del Sol (Part of Sierra Vista)	85635
Pueblo del Sol Village I (Part of Sierra Vista)	85635
Pueblo Estates	85614
Pumpkin Center	85553
Quartzsite	85346*
	85359†
Queen Creek	85242
Queen Valley	85219
Querino	86506
Rainbow Valley	85326
Ranch del Sol	85296
Rancho Buena Vista	85629
Rancho del Rio	85344
Ranchos Carmela (Part of Sierra Vista)	85635
Rancho Verde	85364
Rancho Vista Hills	86301
Randolph	85222
Reata Pass (Part of Scottsdale)	85255
Redington	85602
Red Mesa	86514
Red Rock (Apache County)	87420
Red Rock (Pinal County)	85245
Red Valley	86544
Rillito	85654
Rimrock	86335
Rincon	85710*
	85731†
Rio Rico	85621
	85648
For specific Rio Rico Zip Codes call (602) 281-7223, or your local postmaster.	
Rio Rico East	85621
Rio Salado (Part of Phoenix)	85006
Rio Verde	85263
Riverside	85237
Riviera (Part of Bullhead City)	86439
	86442
For specific Riviera Zip Codes call (602) 758-5711, or your local postmaster.	
Rock Point	86545
Rock Springs	85026
Roll	85347
Rolling Hills Country Club Estates (Part of Tucson)	85710
Roosevelt	85545
Roosevelt Estates	85545
Roosevelt Resort	85545
Rough Rock	86503
Round Rock	86547
Royal Estates (Part of Nogales)	85621
Royal Oaks	86301
Rye	85541
Sacate	85221
Sacaton	85247
Sacaton Flats	85247
Sacred Mountain	86001
Safford	85546*
	85548†
Saginaw (Part of Bisbee)	85603
Sahuarita	85629
Sahuarita Heights	85629
St. David	85630
St. Johns	85936
St. Michaels	86511
Salado	85936
Salina	86503
Salome	85348
Salt River Indian Reservation	85256
Salt River Powder District Camp	85545
San Carlos	85550
San Carlos Indian Reservation	85550
Sanchez	85546

	ZIP
Sanders	86512
Sand Springs	86039
San Jose (Cochise County)	85603
San Jose (Graham County)	85546
San Lucy Village	85337
San Luis (Pima County)	85634
San Luis (Yuma County)	85349
San Manuel	85631
San Miguel	85634
San Pedro	85634
San Rafael Terrace (Part of Bisbee)	85603
San Simon	85632
Santa Cruz	85221
Santa Maria	85009
Santan	85247
Santa Rita	85640
Santa Rosa	85634
Santo Tomas	85629
Santo Tomas del Norte	85629
Santo Tomas Village	85629
San Xavier	85746
San Xavier Indian Reservation	85634
Sasabe	85633
Sawmill	86549
Schuchk	85634
Schuchuli	85634
Scottsdale	85250-52
	85254-62
	85264-65
	85267
	85271
For specific Scottsdale Zip Codes call (602) 949-7100, or your local postmaster.	
Scottsdale Fashion Square (Part of Scottsdale)	85251
Scottsdale Galleria (Part of Scottsdale)	85251
Seba Dalkai	86047
Second Mesa	86043
Sedona	86336
	86339-41
	86351
For specific Sedona Zip Codes call (602) 282-3511, or your local postmaster.	
Seligman	86337
Sells	85634
Sentinel	85333
Seven Springs	85331
Shadow Meadows	86323
Shaw Butte (Part of Phoenix)	85029
Sheldon	85534
Sherwood (Part of Mesa)	85204*
	85214†
Shipolovi	86043
Shongopovi	86043
Shonto	86054
Shopishk	85634
Show Low	85901
Shumway	85901
Sichomovi	86042
Sierra Adobe	85023-24
	85027
	85080
For specific Sierra Adobe Zip Codes call (602) 407-2036, or your local postmaster.	
Sierra Bonita	85643
Sierra Vista	85635-36
	85670-71
For specific Sierra Vista Zip Codes call (602) 458-2540, or your local postmaster.	
Sierra Vista Estates (Part of Sierra Vista)	85635
Sierra Vista Southeast	85615
Sil Nakya	85634
Silverbell (Part of Tucson)	85745
	85754
For specific Silverbell Zip Codes call (602) 622-5210, or your local postmaster.	
Site Six (Part of Lake Havasu City)	86403
Skull Valley	86338
Skyline Bel Aire Estates	85718
Skyway Village	85205
Smoke Signal	86503
Snowflake	85937
Solomon	85551
Somerton	85350
Sonoita	85637

*** Area Zip Code** **† Post Office Boxes**

	ZIP
Sonora Town	85233
South Bisbee	85603
South Central (Part of Phoenix)	85040
	85066
For specific South Central Zip Codes call (602) 268-1162, or your local postmaster.	
Southgate Mall (Part of Yuma)	85364
South Komelik	85634
South Santan	85247
South Tucson	85713*
	85725†
Springerville	85938
Spring Valley	86333
Sprucedale	85922
Stagecoach Acres	86301
Stanfield	85272
Stanton	85332
Stargo	85540
Starlight Pines	86024
Star Valley	85541
Steamboat Canyon	86505
Stoneman Lake	86024
Strawberry	85544
Sun (Part of Tucson)	85717
	85719
	85733
For specific Sun Zip Codes call (602) 881-1096, or your local postmaster.	
Sun City	85351
	85372-73
For specific Sun City Zip Codes call (602) 974-3623, or your local postmaster.	
Sun City Rancho Vistoso	85738
Sun City West	85375
Sunflower	85201
Sunizona	85625
Sun Lakes	85248
Sunnyslope (Part of Phoenix)	85020
	85022
	85068
For specific Sunnyslope Zip Codes call (602) 870-3947, or your local postmaster.	
Sunrise (Coconino County)	86047
Sunrise (Yavapai County)	86323
Sunrise Springs	86505
Sunset	85643
Sunset Acres	85603
Sunshine Acres (Part of Mesa)	85201
Sunsites	85625
Suntown (Part of Peoria)	85345
Sun Valley	86029
Supai	86435
Superior	85273
Superstition Estates (Part of Apache Junction)	85220
Superstition Springs Center (Part of Mesa)	85206
Supi Oidak	85634
Surprise	85374
Sweet Acres	86301

	ZIP
Sweetwater (Apache County)	87401
Sweetwater (Maricopa County)	85326
Sweetwater (Pinal County)	85221
Swift Trail Junction	85546
Tacna	85352
Tall Pines (Part of Show Low)	85935
Tapco	86324
Tat Momoli	85634
Tatria Toak	85634
Taylor	85939
Teec Nos Pos	86514
Tees To	86047
Tempe	85280-87
For specific Tempe Zip Codes call (602) 220-0258, or your local postmaster.	
Temple Bar Marina	86443
Tes Nez Iah	86033
Thatcher	85552
Theba	85337
The Foothills	85364
The Gap	86020
The Summit Estates (Part of Sierra Vista)	85635
Thomas Mall (Part of Phoenix)	85018
Three Points	85714
Three Way	85534
Tintown (Part of Bisbee)	85603
Tolani	86047
Tolleson	85353
Toltec (Part of Eloy)	85231
Tombstone	85638
Tonalea	86044
Tonkawa	86301
Tonopah	85354
Tonto Basin	85553
Tonto Hills	85331
Tonto Village	85541
Topawa	85639
Topock	86436
Toreva	86043
Tortilla Flat	85290
Totopitk	85634
Tovrea (Part of Phoenix)	85034
Tower Plaza Mall (Part of Phoenix)	85018
Town and Country (Part of Sierra Vista)	85635
Toyei	86505
Tremaine	85225
Tri-City Mall (Part of Mesa)	85201
Truxton	86434
Tsaile	86556
Tubac	85646
Tuba City	86045
Tucson	85701-37
	85740-54
For specific Tucson Zip Codes call (602) 620-5142, or your local postmaster.	
Tucson Country Club Estates	85715
Tucson Estates	85715
Tucson National Estates	85741

	ZIP
Tumacacori	85640
Turkey Flat	85546
Tusayan	86023
Tusconita	85706
Twin Arrows	86001
Twin Buttes	85629
Twin Knolls	85207
Two Story	86511
University of Arizona (Part of Tucson)	85717
Upper Wheatfields	86556
Utting	85348
Vahki	85221
Vail	85641
Vaiva Vo	85634
Valencia (Part of Buckeye)	85326
Valencia West	85746
Valentine	86437
Valle Verde del Norte	85629
Valley Farms	85291
Valley West Mall (Part of Glendale)	85301
Vamori	85634
Vandenberg Village	85708
Vaya Chin	85634
Velda Rose Estates	85205
Velda Rose Gardens	85201
Ventana	85634
Ventana Lakes (Part of Peoria)	85382
Venture Out	85201
Verde Lee Estates	85533
Verde Valley	85364
Verde Village (Part of Cottonwood)	86326
Vernon	85940
Vicksburg	85348
Vicksburg Junction	85348
Village Meadows (Part of Sierra Vista)	85635
Village of Oak Creek	86341
Villages of Green Valley	85614
Vista Grande (Part of Chino Valley)	86323
Vista Linda	85546
Waddell	85355
Wagoner	86332
Wahak Hotrontk	85634
Wahweap	86040
Walker	86301
Walnut Grove	86332
Walpi	86042
Warren (Part of Bisbee)	85603
Washington (Part of Phoenix)	85021
	85051
	85069
For specific Washington Zip Codes call (602) 407-2039, or your local postmaster.	
Washington Camp	85624
Washington Park	85541
Wellton	85356
Wenden	85357
Westbrook Village (Part of Peoria)	85382
West Chandler (Part of Chandler)	85224

	ZIP
Westfield (Part of Peoria)	85345
Westgate	85611
Westgreen Estates (Part of Peoria)	85345
West Plaza Shopping Center (Part of Phoenix)	85017
Westridge (Part of Phoenix)	85075
Westridge Mall (Part of Phoenix)	85033
West Sedona (Part of Sedona)	86340
Westward Quest	85201
Wheatfields	86515
Whetstone	85613
Whipple (Part of Prescott)	86313
Whippoorwill	86510
Whispering Hills (Part of Sierra Vista)	85635
Whispering Pines	85541
White Clay	86504
White Cone	86025
White Mountain Lake	85912
White Mountain Summer Homes	85935
Whiteriver (Navajo County)	85941
White Tanks	85326
Why	85321
Wickenburg	85358†
	85390*
Wide Ruin	86502
Wikieup	85360
Wildwood Estates	86301
Wilhoit	86332
Willcox	85643*
	85644†
Williams	86046
Williamson Valley	86301
Willow Beach	86445
Willow Canyon	85619
Willow Valley Estates	86440
Window Rock	86515
Winkelman	85292
Winona	86001
Winslow	86047
Winslow West	86047
Winwood	85603
Wittmann	85361
Woodruff	85942
Woodsprings	86505
Wrangler Ranch	85629
Yaqui (Part of Tucson)	85746
Yarnell	85362
Yava	86301
Yavapai Indian Reservation	86301
York	85534
Young	85554
Youngtown	85363
Yucca	86438
Yuma	85364-69
For specific Yuma Zip Codes call (602) 783-2124, or your local postmaster.	
Yuma East	85364
Yuma Proving Ground	85365

* Area Zip Code   † Post Office Boxes

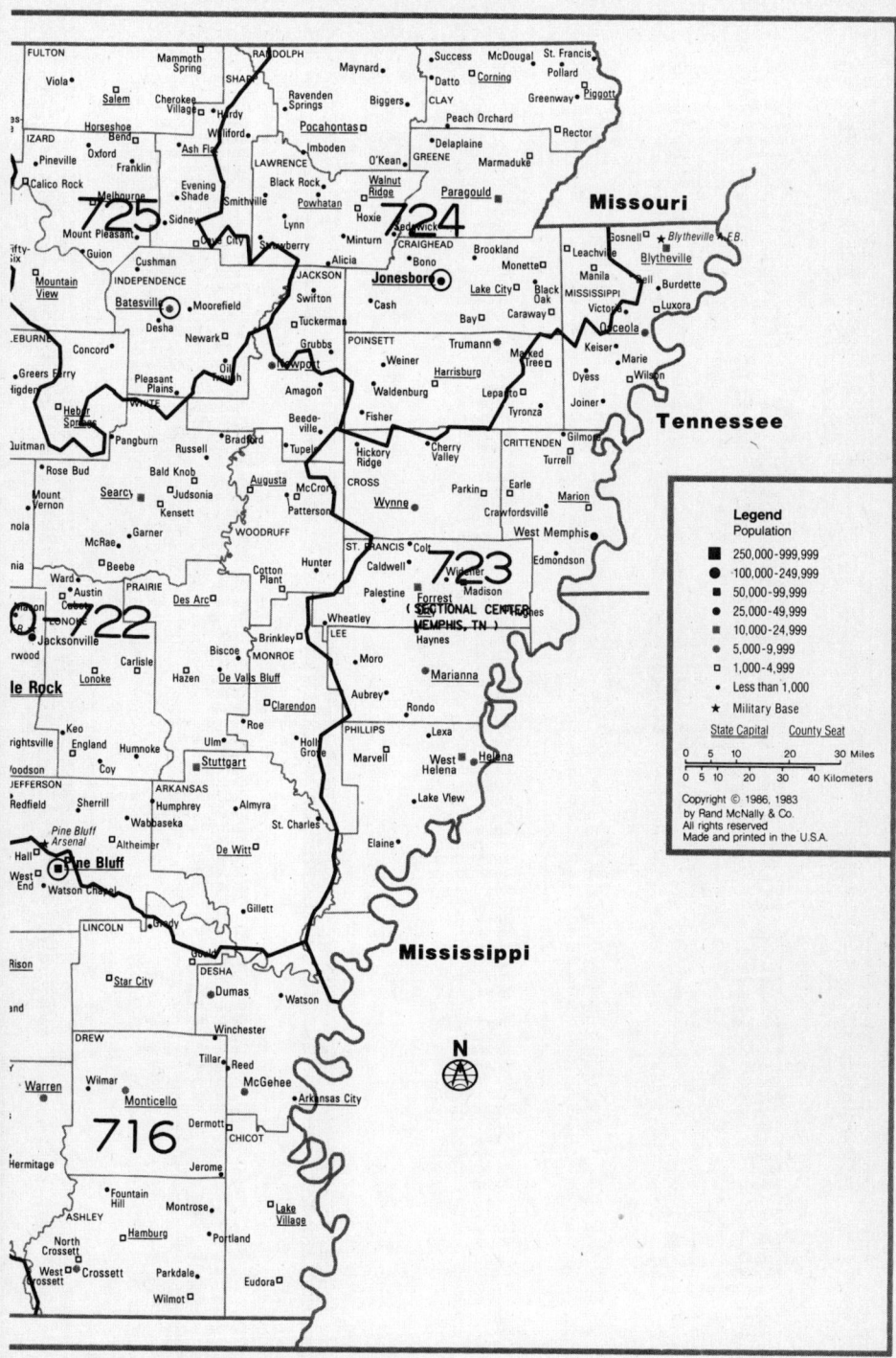

Legend
Population

■	250,000-999,999
●	100,000-249,999
■	50,000-99,999
●	25,000-49,999
■	10,000-24,999
●	5,000-9,999
□	1,000-4,999
•	Less than 1,000
★	Military Base

State Capital   County Seat

0 5 10   20   30 Miles
0 5 10   20   30   40 Kilometers

	ZIP
Abbott	72944
Aberdeen	72134
Acorn	71953
Ada	72001
Adkins Lake	71601
Adona	72001
Agnos	72513
Alabam	72740
Albert Pike (Part of Hot Springs)	71913
Albion	72143
Alco	72610
Alexander (Greene County)	72450
Alexander (Pulaski County)	72002
Algoa	72112
Alicia	72410
Alix	72820
Allbrook	71851
Alleene	71820
Allison	72560
Allport	72046
Alma	72921
Almond	72550
Almyra	72003
Alpena	72611
Alpine	71920
Alread	72031
Altheimer	72004
Alto	72354
Altus	72821
Aly	72857
Amagon	72005
Amanca	72376
Amboy (Part of North Little Rock)	72118
Amity	71921
Amy	71701
Andy	72376
Annieville	72434
Antioch (Perry County)	72070
Antioch (White County)	72012
Antoine	71922
Aplin	72126
Appleton	72822
Apt	72401
Arbor Grove	72433
Ard	72834
Arden	71822
Arkadelphia	71923
Arkana	71826
Arkansas City	71630
Arkinda	71836
Arkola	72940
Arlberg	72031
Armorel	72310
Armstrong	72482
Armstrong Springs	72143
Artesian	71744
Artist Point	72946
Ashdown	71822
Asher (Madison County)	72727
Asher (Pulaski County)	72204
Ash Flat	72513
Athelstan	72370
Athens	71971
Atkins	72823
Atlanta	71740
Attica	72455
Aubrey	72311
Augsburg	72847
Augusta	72006
Aurelle	71765
Aurora	72740
Austin (Conway County)	72031
Austin (Lonoke County)	72007
Auvergne	72112
Avilla	72002
Avoca	72711
Avon	71832
Back Gate	71639
Baker	72482
Balch	72009
Bald Knob	72010
Baldwin (Part of Fayetteville)	72701
Ballard	72513
Band Mill	72517
Banks	71631
Banner	72523
Barber	72927
Barcelona	72955
Bard	72450
Bardstown	72350
Barfield	72315
Barling	72923
Barney	72047
Barton	72312

	ZIP
Barton Eddins	72312
Bashe (Part of Fort Smith)	72901
Bass	72655
Bassett	72313
Batavia	72601
Batchelor	72366
Bates	72924
Batesville	72501*
	72503†
Battlefield	71801
Baucum	72117
Bauxite	72011
Baxter	71638
Bay	72411
Bayou Meto (Arkansas County)	72160
Bayou Meto (Lonoke County)	72086
Bay Village	72324
Bear Creek Springs	72601
Bearden	71720
Beaver	72613
Beaver Shores	72756
Beck	72348
Becton	72036
Beebe	72012
Bee Branch	72013
Beech Grove (Dallas County)	71742
Beech Grove (Greene County)	72412
Beedeville	72014
Beirne	71721
Bellaire	71638
Bella Vista	72714
Bellefonte	72601
Belle Meade	72348
Belleville	72824
Bells Chapel	72823
Bellville	71846
Belton	71852
Ben	72530
Ben Gay	72466
Ben Hur	72856
Ben Lomond	71823
Benton	72015
	72018
For specific Benton Zip Codes call (501) 778-2920, or your local postmaster.	
Bentonville	72712
Benton Work Release and Pre-Release Center	72015
Bergman	72615
Berryville	72616
Beryl	72032
Best	72756
Bethany	71833
Bethel	72450
Bethel Heights	72764
Bethesda	72501
Beulah	72017
Bevis Corners	72142
Bexar	72515
Bidville	72959
Bigelow	72016
Big Flat	72617
Big Fork	71953
Biggers	72413
Big Lake	72442
Big Springs	72657
Billingsley's Corner	71866
Billstown	71958
Bingen	71852
Birdell	72455
Birdeye	72314
Birdsong	72386
Birdtown	72157
Birta	72853
Biscoe	72017
Bismarck	71929
Blackburn	72959
Blackfish	72346
Black Fork	71953
Black Oak (Craighead County)	72414
Black Oak (Poinsett County)	72386
Black Rock	72415
Black Springs	71960
Blackton	72069
Blackville (Conway County)	72823
Blackville (Jackson County)	72112
Blakely	71931
Blakemore	72046
Blevins	71825
Bloomer	72933

	ZIP
Bloomfield	72734
Blossom	72392
Blue Ball	72833
Blue Eye	65611
Blue Hill	72118
Blue Mountain	72826
Blue Springs	71909
Blue Springs Village	72764
Bluff City	71722
Bluffton	72827
Blytheville	72315-19
For specific Blytheville Zip Codes call (501) 763-3690, or your local postmaster.	
Board Camp	71932
Bodcaw	71858
Bogg Springs	71944
Bolding	71747
Boles	72926
Bonanza	72916
Bondsville	72354
Bonnerdale	71933
Bono (Craighead County)	72416
Bono (Faulkner County)	72058
Booker	72117
Booneville	72927
Booster	72645
Boothe	72927
Boston	72752
Boswell	72516
Botkinburg	72031
Boughton	71857
Bowen	71940
Bowman	72437
Boxley	72740
Boyd	71837
Boydell	71658
Boyd Hill	71845
Boydsville	72461
Boynton	72438
Bradford	72020
Bradley	71826
Brady (Part of Little Rock)	72205
Bragg City	71726
Brakebill	72478
Branch	72928
Brasfield	72017
Bredlow Corner	72046
Brentwood	72959
Brewer	72044
Brickeys	72320
Briggsville	72828
Brighton	72450
Bright Star	71834
Brightwater	72756
Brinkley	72021
Brister	71740
Brockett	72455
Brockwell	72517
Brookland	72417
Brown's Crossing	71640
Brown Springs	72104
Brownstown	71846
Brownsville	72067
Bruins	72348
Brumley	72032
Brummitt	72160
Bruno	72618
Brush Creek	72084
Bryant	72022*
	72089†
Bryant Addition	72857
Buckeye	72438
Buckner	71827
Buck Range	71851
Buckville	71956
Buena Vista	71764
Buffalo City	72653
Buie	72129
Bullfrog Valley	72837
Bull Shoals	72619
Bunney	72414
Burdette	72321
Burg	71833
Burlington	72662
Burnville	72936
Buroak	72650
Burtsell	71962
Busch	72632
Bussey	71860
Butlerville	72176
Butterfield	72104
Byron	72576
Cabanol	72616
Cabot	72023
Caddo Gap	71935
Caddo Valley	71923
Cain	72946
Calamine	72466

	ZIP
Caldwell	72322
Cale	71828
Caledonia	71749
Calhoun	71753
Calico Rock	72519
Calion	71724
Calmer	71665
Calumet	72315
Camark	71701
Camden	71701
Cammack Village	72207
Camp	72520
Campbell Station	72473
Camp Joseph T. Robinson	72205
Canaan	72650
Canal Gardens	72348
Cane Creek	72150
Canehill	72717
Caney (Faulkner County)	72032
Caney (Hot Spring County)	71929
Caney Valley	71921
Canfield	71845
Cantwell	72422
Capps	72601
Capps City	71069
Caraway	72419
Carbon City	72855
Carden Bottoms	72834
Careyville	71765
Carlile Highland	72653
Carlisle	72024
Carmel	71671
Carmi	72438
Carolan	72927
Carpenter	71642
Carpenter Addition	71655
Carroll's Corner	72442
Carrollton	72611
Carryville	72454
Carson	72370
Carter Cove Use Area	72857
Carthage	71725
Casa	72025
Cash	72421
Cass	72949
Casscoe	72026
Catalpa	72854
Catcher	72956
Catholic Point	72027
Cathy Lake	72396
Cato	72114
Catron	72367
Caulksville	72951
Cauthron (Logan County)	72927
Cauthron (Scott County)	72958
Cavanaugh (Part of Fort Smith)	72901
Cave City	72521
Cave Creek	72501
Cave Springs	72718
Cecil	72930
Cedar Creek	72950
Cedar Grove	72534
Cedarville	72932
Center	72542
Center Hill (Greene County)	72450
Center Hill (White County)	72143
Center Point (Clark County)	71743
Center Point (Hempstead County)	71801
Center Point (Howard County)	71852
Center Point (Prairie County)	72064
Center Ridge (Clark County)	71921
Center Ridge (Cleburne County)	72543
Center Ridge (Conway County)	72027
Centerton	72719
Center Valley	72801
Centerville (Faulkner County)	72058
Centerville (Hempstead County)	71835
Centerville (Yell County)	72829
Central (Clark County)	71923
Central (Cross County)	72396
Central (Hot Spring County)	72104
Central (Sevier County)	71842
Central Baptist College (Part of Conway)	72032

	ZIP
Central City (Garland County)	71913
Central City (Sebastian County)	72941
Central Mall (Part of Fort Smith)	72903
Cerrogordo	71866
Chambersville	71766
Chapel Hill	71832
Charleston	72933
Charlotte	72522
Chasewood Landing	71969
Chatfield	72348
Chelford	72386
Cherokee City	72734
Cherokee Village	72525
	72529
For specific Cherokee Village Zip Codes call (501) 257-2662, or your local postmaster.	
Cherokee Village-Hidden Valley	72525
Cherry Hill (Perry County)	72126
Cherry Hill (Polk County)	71953
Cherry Valley	72324
Chester	72934
Chickalah	72834
Chicot Junction	71640
Chidester	71726
Childress	72447
Chimes	72645
Chismville	72943
Choctaw	72028
Choctaw Acres	72031
Christy Acres	72015
Chula	72857
Cincinnati	72769
Clarendon	72029
Clarkedale	72325
Clarkridge	72623
Clarks Corner	72394
Clarksville	72830
Clay	72143
Clear Lake (Grant County)	72150
Clear Lake (Mississippi County)	72315
Clear Point	72756
Clear Spring	71962
Cleveland	72030
Clifty	72756
Clinton	72031
Clover Bend	72433
Clow	71855
Clyde	72717
Coaldale	74937
Coal Hill	72832
Coffeeville	72020
Coffman (Greene County)	72450
Coffman (Lawrence County)	72433
Coldwater	72373
Coleman	71655
Colfax	72653
College City	72476
Collegehill	71752
College Station	72053
Collegeville	72002
Collins	71634
Colt	72326
Columbus	71831
Combs	72721
Cominto	71655
Compton	72624
Concord	72523
Congo	72015
Connells Point	72366
Conway	72032*
	72033†
Copper Mine	72756
Cord	72524
Corinth	72824
Corley	72855
Cornerstone	72004
Cornerville	71667
Corning	72422
Cotter	72626
Cotterneck	71742
Cottonbelt	71720
Cotton Plant	72036
Cottonshed	71851
Cottonwood Corner (Craighead County)	72447
Cottonwood Corner (Mississippi County)	72370
Council	72320
Cove	71937
Cowell	72856
Cowlingsville	71846
Coy	72037

	ZIP
Cozahome	72639
Crabapple Point	71724
Crabtree	72031
Cravens	72949
Crawfordsville	72327
Creigh	72366
Crigler	71667
Crockett	72454
Crocketts Bluff	72038
Crosses	72701
Crossett	71635
Crossroads (Cleburne County)	72131
Cross Roads (Hot Spring County)	71933
Crossroads (Izard County)	72566
Crossroads (Jackson County)	72112
Cross Roads (Little River County)	71866
Cross Roads (Logan County)	72863
Cross Roads (Madison County)	72738
Crossroads (Prairie County)	72040
Crows	72015
Crumpler	72644
Crumrod	72328
Crystal Hill	72118
Crystal Springs	71968
Crystal Springs Landing	71968
Cullendale (Part of Camden)	71701
Culpeper	72031
Cumi	72544
Cummins Unit	71644
Curtis	71728
Cushman	72526
Cypert	72366
Cypress Valley	72156
Dabney	72110
Daisy	71950
Dalark	71923
Dallas	71953
Dalton	72455
Damascus	72039
Danville	72833
Dardanelle	72834
Datto	72424
Davis Creek	72129
Dawn Hill Country Club	72761
Dayton	72940
DeAnn	71801
Deans Market	72921
Dean Springs	72921
Decatur	72722
Deckerville	72386
Deep Elm	71653
Deer	72628
Deerfield	72328
Delaney	72727
Delaplaine	72425
Delaware	72835
Delfore	72438
Delight	71940
Dell	72426
De Luce	72042
Denmark	72020
Dennard	72629
Denning	72821
Denton	72458
Denver	72638
Denwood	72386
De Queen	71832
Dermott	71638
De Roche	71929
Des Arc	72040
Desha	72527
Detonti	72011
De Valls Bluff	72041
Dewey (Chicot County)	71638
Dewey (White County)	72121
De Witt	72042
Dialion	71665
Diamond Bay	72531
Diamond City	72630
Diamondhead	71913
Dian (Part of Prescott)	71857
Diaz	72043
Dickey Heights	72768
Dicus	72476
Dierks	71833
Dillen	72854
Dixie (Craighead County)	72437
Dixie (Pulaski County)	72114
Dixie (Woodruff County)	72006
Dixieland Mall (Part of Rogers)	72756

	ZIP
Doddridge	71834
Dogpatch	72648
Dogtown	71832
Dogwood (Part of Blytheville)	72315
Dogwood Acres	71957
Dollarway (Part of Pine Bluff)	71602
Dolph	72528
Donaldson	71941
Dongola	72650
Doniphan	72143
Dora	72956
Double Bridges	72358
Douglas	71643
Douglas Corner	72205
Dover	72837
Dowdy	72524
Downtown (Part of Little Rock)	72201
Drakes Creek	72740
Drasco	72530
Driggs	72943
Dripping Springs	72955
Driver	72329
Dryden	72401
Dryfork	72740
Dublin	72863
Duff	72675
Dumas	71639
Durham	72727
Dutch Mills	72744
Dutton	72760
Dyer	72935
Dyess	72330
Eagle Mills	71720
Eagle Point	72531
Eagleton	71953
Earle	72331
East Black Oak	72386
East Camden	71701
East End	72065
Eastview	72351
Eaton	72458
Ebenezer	71764
Ebony	72364
Echo	72927
Economy	72823
Eden Isle	72543
Edgemont	72044
Edmondson	72332
Eglantine	72153
Egypt	72427
Elaine	72333
El Dorado	71730-31
For specific El Dorado Zip Codes call (501) 863-7571, or your local postmaster.	
Elevenpoint	72455
Elgin	72112
Elizabeth	72531
Elkins	72727
Elk Ranch	72632
Elliott	71701
Ellison	72152
Elm Springs	72728
Elm Store	65778
Elmwood	72601
Elnora	72455
El Paso	72045
Emerson	71740
Emmet	71835
Empire	71661
Enders	72131
Engelberg	72455
England	72046
English	72004
Enola	72047
Enterprise	72901
Eros	72633
Erwin	72112
Ethel	72048
Etna	72949
Etowah	72428
Euclid Heights (Part of Hot Springs)	71901
Eudora	71640
Eula	72675
Eureka Springs	72632
Evansville	72729
Evening Shade (Hempstead County)	71801
Evening Shade (Scott County)	72958
Evening Shade (Sharp County)	72532
Evening Star	72422
Everton	72633
Excelsior	72936

	ZIP
Fairbanks	72131
Fairfield (Part of Little Rock)	72209
Fairfield Bay	72088
Fairmont	72160
Fair Oaks	72397
Fairview (Chicot County)	71653
Fairview (Lonoke County)	72086
Fairview (Marion County)	72650
Fairview (Ouachita County)	71701
Fairview (Sevier County)	71841
Fairwood	71913
Falcon	71827
Falls Chapel	71846
Fallsville	72854
Fancy Hill	71935
Fannie	71970
Farelly Lake	72160
Fargo	72021
Farmington	72730
Farmville	71671
Farville	72417
Fayetteville	72701-04
For specific Fayetteville Zip Codes call (501) 442-8286, or your local postmaster.	
Felsenthal	71747
Felton	72360
Fender	72476
Fendley	71921
Fenter	72167
Ferguson	72328
Ferguson Crossroads	71837
Fern	72946
Ferndale	72208
Fifty-Six	72533
Figure Five	72956
Finch	72450
Fisher (Craighead County)	72421
Fisher (Poinsett County)	72429
Fitzgerald (Part of Diaz)	72112
Fitzgerald Crossing	72396
Fitzhugh	72006
Fivemile	72530
Flag	72645
Flat Rock	72847
Flint Springs	72583
Flippin	72634
Floodway	72442
Floral	72534
Florence	71655
Floyd	72143
Fomby	71822
Fontaine	72416
Fordyce	71742
Foreman	71836
Forest Grove (Columbia County)	71740
Forest Grove (Lafayette County)	71861
Forest Park (Part of Little Rock)	72207
Formosa	72031
Forrest City	72335
Fort Chaffee	72905
Fort Douglas	72854
Fort Lynn	71837
Fort Smith	72901-17
For specific Fort Smith Zip Codes call (501) 484-6370, or your local postmaster.	
Fortune	72373
Forty Four	72585
Forum	72740
Fouke	71837
Fountain Hill	71642
Fountain Lake	71901
Fourche	72016
Fourche Junction	72857
Fourche Valley	72827
Fourmile Hill	72143
Fox	72051
Francis	72601
Franklin	72536
Free Hope	71753
Frenchmans Bayou	72338
Frenchport	71701
Fresno	71643
Friendship (Cleveland County)	71665
Friendship (Columbia County)	71860
Friendship (Hot Spring County)	71942
Friley	72752
Fritz	72461
Fryatt	72554
Frys Mill	72386

***** Area Zip Code   † Post Office Boxes**

* **Area Zip Code**　　† **Post Office Boxes**

	ZIP		ZIP		ZIP		ZIP
Keo	72083	Liberty Valley	72010	Madding	72004	Mitchellville	71639
Kerlin	71753	Lick Mountain	72027	Madison	72359	Mixon	72927
Kerr	72142	Light	72439	Magazine	72943	Moark	72422
Kibler	72956	Limedale	72501	Magic Springs	72650	Mohawk	71740
Kimberley	71958	Limestone	72628	Magness	72553	Moko	72557
Kindall	72374	Lincoln	72744	Magnet Cove	72104	Monarch	72687
King	71841	Linder	72058	Magnolia	71753	Monette	72447
Kingsland	71652	Lisbon	71730	Main Street (Part of North		Monkey Run	72635
Kingston (Madison		Little Bay	71766	Little Rock)	72119	Monnie Springs	72135
County)	72742	Little Flock	72756	Mallet Town	72157	Monroe	72108
Kingston (Yell County)	72853	Little Garnett	71667	Mallory Spur	72348	Montana	72840
Kingswood Estates	72653	Little Italy	72016	Malvern	72104	Monte Ne Shores	72758
Kingtown	72366	Little Red	72121	Mammoth Spring	72554	Monterey	72373
Kirby	71950	Little River	72442	Mandalay	72442	Monticello	71655
Kirkland	71751	Little River Country Club	71866	Mandeville	75501	Montongo	71655
Knob	72436	Little Rock	72201-07	Manfred	71935	Montreal	72940
Knobel	72435		72209-95	Mangrum	72414	Montrose	71658
Knoxville	72845	For specific Little Rock Zip		Manila	72442	Moore	72856
Koch Ridge	72031	Codes call (501) 375-8148, or		Manning	71763	Moore Camp	71822
Lacey	71655	your local postmaster.		Mansfield	72944	Moorefield	72501
Laconia	72379	Little Rock Air Force Base	72099	Many Island	72554	Moreland	72801
LaCrosse	72584	Locke	72946	Maple	72616	Morgan	72118
Ladd	71601	Lockesburg	71846	Maple Corner	72374	Morganton	72013
Ladelle	71655	Locust Bayou	71701	Maple Grove	72472	Morning Star (Garland	
Lafe	72436	Locust Grove	72550	Maple Springs	72571	County)	71901
Lafferty	72561	Lodge Corner	72160	Marble	72740	Morning Star (Searcy	
La Grange	72352	Lodi	71943	Marcella	72555	County)	72650
Lake Bull Shoales Estates	72687	Logan	72761	Marche	72118	Morning Sun	72143
Lake Catherine	71901	Lollie	72106	Marc Lyn Estates	72687	Moro	72368
Lake City	72437	London	72847	Marianna	72360	Morobay	71651
Lake Dick	72004	Lonelm	72947	Marie	72395	Morrilton	72110
Lake Elmdale	72764	Lone Pine	72650	Marion	72364	Morris	71828
Lake Francis	72761	Lono	72084	Marked Tree	72365	Morrison Bluff	72863
Lake Hamilton	71913	Lonoke	72086	Marmaduke	72443	Morriston	72576
Lake Poinsett	72432	Lonsdale	72087	Marsden	71647	Morrow	72749
Lakeport	71653	Lookout (Benton County)	72756	Marsena	72650	Morton	72101
Lakeside (Garland		Lookout (Monroe County)	72134	Marshall	72650	Mosby	72328
County)	71901	Lorado	72401	Mars Hill	71860	Moscow	71659
Lakeside (Ouachita		Lorine	72455	Martindale	72204	Mosley	72834
County)	71701	Lost Bridge Village	72732	Martinville	72204	Mossville	72641
Lakeside Country Club	72065	Lost Cane	72442	Marvell	72366	Mounds (Crittenden	
Lakeside Terrace	72653	Lost Corner	72080	Marvinville	72842	County)	72376
Lakeview (Baxter County)	72642	Louann	71751	Marysville	71753	Mounds (Greene County)	72461
Lakeview (Conway		Louise	72376	Mason Valley	72712	Mountainburg	72946
County)	72110	Lowell	72745	Masonville	71654	Mountain Crest	72727
Lake View (Craighead		Lower Boydsville	72461	Massard (Part of Fort		Mountain Fork	71953
County)	72437	Lower Poplar Ridge	72414	Smith)	72901	Mountain Harbor	71957
Lake View (Phillips		Lower White Oak Lake	71726	Maumee	72675	Mountain Home	72653
County)	72342	Low Gap	72641	Maumelle	72113	Mountain Pine	71956
Lakeview Estates	71970	Luber	72560	Maxville	72521	Mountain Springs	72023
Lake Village	71653	Lucas	72927	Mayfield	72703	Mountain Top	72949
Lakeway	72687	Ludwig	72830	Mayflower	72106	Mountain Valley	71901
Lakewood (Jefferson		Lumber	71770	Maynard	72444	Mountain View	72560
County)	72004	Luna	71653	Maysville	72747	Mount Elba	71660
Lakewood (Pulaski		Lundell	72367	Mazarn	71933	Mount Elba Edition	71665
County)	72116	Lunenburg	72556	Meadow Cliff	72335	Mount Gayler	72959
Lakewood Estates	75501	Lunsford	72437	Meeks Settlement	71962	Mount George	72833
Lakewood Village (Part of		Lurton	72856	Melbourne	72556	Mount Hersey	72685
North Little Rock)	72116	Lutherville	72846	Mellwood	72367	Mount Holly	71758
Lamar	72846	Luxora	72358	Melrose	72550	Mount Ida	71957
Lamartine	71770	Lynch (Part of North Little		Mena	71953	Mount Judea	72655
Lambert	71929	Rock)	72117	Menifee	72107	Mount Moriah	71958
Lambrook	72353	Lynn	72440	Meridian	71635	Mount Olive (Bradley	
Landers	72472	Mabelvale (Part of Little		Meroney	71643	County)	71647
Landis	72650	Rock)	72103	Merrivale (Part of Little		Mount Olive (Conway	
Laneburg	71844	McAlmont	72117	Rock)	72209	County)	72127
Langford	72004	McArthur	71654	Mesa	72041	Mount Olive (Izard	
Langley	71952	McBrides	65733	Metalton	72601	County)	72556
Lanieve	72416	McCain Mall (Part of		Middlebrook	72444	Mount Olive (Washington	
Lansing	72327	North Little Rock)	72116	Middleton	72027	County)	72727
Lanty	72063	McCaskill	71847	Midland	72945	Mount Pisgah	72143
Lapile	71765	McClelland	72006	Midland (Part of Fort		Mount Pleasant (Izard	
La Plaza Acres	72143	McCormick	72472	Smith)	72904	County)	72561
Larkin	72584	McCreanor	72024	Midway (Baxter County)	72651	Mount Pleasant (Miller	
Larue	72756	McCrory	72101	Midway (Hot Spring		County)	75502
Latour	72355	McDonald	72373	County)	71941	Mount Sherman	72641
Lauratown	72433	McDougal	72441	Midway (Howard County)	71852	Mount Tabor	71956
Lavaca	72941	Macedonia (Columbia		Midway (Jackson County)	72479	Mount Vernon (Faulkner	
Lawson	71750	County)	71753	Midway (Lafayette		County)	72111
Lazy Acres	65733	Macedonia (Conway		County)	71845	Mount Vernon (Johnson	
Leachville	72438	County)	72063	Midway (Logan County)	72865	County)	72840
Lead Hill	72644	McElroy	72396	Midway (Nevada County)	71857	Mozart	72051
Lebanon	71846	McEntre	72476	Midway (White County)	72568	Muddyfork	71852
Lee Creek	72934	Macey	72447	Midway Corner	72376	Mulberry	72947
Lehi	72364	McFadden	72347	Milford	71846	Mull	72687
Leitner (Part of Pine Bluff)	71601	McGehee	71654	Mill Creek (Pope County)	72801	Murfreesboro	71958
Leola	72084	McGintytown	72058	Mill Creek (Sebastian		Murphys Corner	72112
Leonard	72461	McGregor	72036	County)	72901	Mustin Lake	71701
Lepanto	72354	McHue	72501	Mill Creek Estates	72687	Myron	72513
Leslie	72645	McJester	72121	Milligan Ridge	72442	Nady	72166
Lester	72437	McKamie	71860	Milltown	72936	Nail	72628
Letona	72085	Macks	72112	Milo	71646	Nance	72087
Levy (Part of North Little		McMilan Corner	71653	Mimosa Circle	72513	Nashville	71852
Rock)	72118	McNab	71838	Mineral	71841	Nathan	71852
Lewisville	71845	McNeil	71752	Mineral Springs	71851	Natural Dam	72948
Lexa	72355	McNutt	72476	Minorca	72444	Natural Steps	72135
Lexington	72031	Macon	72076	Minturn	72445	Naylor	72173
Liberty	72835	Macon Lake	71653	Mist	71646	Neal Springs	71842
Liberty Hall	72834	McRae	72102	Mitchell	72583	Nebo	71667

	ZIP
Needham	72437
Needmore	72958
Nelia	71953
Nelsonville	72466
Nettleton (Part of Jonesboro)	72401
Neuhardt	72376
Newark	72562
New Augusta (Part of Augusta)	72006
New Blaine	72851
Newburg	72556
New Dixie	72016
New Edinburg	71660
Newell	71730
New Gascony	72004
New Hope (Dallas County)	71763
New Hope (Drew County)	71655
New Hope (Hempstead County)	71801
New Hope (Independence County)	72501
Newhope (Pike County)	71959
New Hope (Pope County)	72801
New London	71765
Newnata	72657
Newport	72112
New Spadra	72830
New Summit (Part of Benton)	72011
New Town (Crawford County)	72921
Newtown (Jefferson County)	72004
Nimmo	72143
Nimmons	72461
Nimrod	72126
Nine Elms	72761
Noble Lake	71601
Nodena	72395
Noland	72455
Norfolk Lake Estates	72544
Norfork	72658
Norfork Village	72658
Norman	71960
Norphlet	71759
Norristown (Part of Russellville)	72801
North Bingen	71852
North Cedar (Part of Pine Bluff)	71601
North Crossett	71635
North Dardanelle	72801
Northern Ohio	72365
North Heights (Part of Texarkana)	75502
North Hughes	72348
North Little Rock	72113-20
	72124
	72190
For specific North Little Rock Zip Codes call (501) 758-1707, or your local postmaster.	
Northpoint	72135
Northwest Arkansas Mall (Part of Fayetteville)	72703
Norvell (Part of Earle)	72331
Nuckles	72020
Number Nine	72315
Nunley	71953
Oak Bower	71929
Oak Forest (Lee County)	72360
Oak Forest (Pulaski County)	72201
Oak Grove (Carroll County)	72660
Oak Grove (Clark County)	71728
Oak Grove (Hot Spring County)	72104
Oak Grove (Little River County)	71822
Oak Grove (Lonoke County)	72007
Oak Grove (Nevada County)	71858
Oak Grove (Perry County)	72070
Oak Grove (Pope County)	72801
Oak Grove (Pulaski County)	72118
Oak Grove (Sevier County)	71846
Oak Grove (Washington County)	72764
Oak Grove Heights	72450
Oakhaven	71801
Oak Hill	71822
Oakland	72661

	ZIP
Oaklawn (Part of Hot Springs)	71901
Oak Park (Part of Pine Bluff)	71603
Oark	72852
Oden	71961
O'Donnell Bend	72358
Ogden	71853
Ogemaw	71764
Oil Trough	72564
O'Kean	72449
Okolona	71962
Ola	72853
Old Alabam	72740
Old Austin	72007
Old Grand Glaise	72020
Old Hickory	72063
Old Jenny Lind	72901
Old Joe	72658
Old Town	72389
Old Union	71730
Old Weona	72472
Olio	72958
Oliver	72958
Olmstead	72116
Olvey	72601
Olyphant	72020
Oma	71964
Omaha	72662
Omega (Carroll County)	72616
Omega (Yell County)	72834
Onda	72774
One Horse Store	72160
Oneida	72369
Onia	72663
Onyx	72857
Opal (Polk County)	71953
Opal (White County)	72012
Oppelo	72110
Optimus	72519
Orion	72132
Orlando	72638
Osage	72638
Osage Mills	72712
Osage Village	72531
Osceola	72370
Ott	65626
Otto	72173
Otwell	72401
Ouachita	71763
Ouachita College (Part of Arkadelphia)	71923
Overcup (Conway County)	72110
Overcup (Woodruff County)	72101
Owensville	72087
Oxford	72565
Oxley	72645
Ozan	71855
Ozark	72949
Ozark Acres (Baxter County)	72635
Ozark Acres (Sharp County)	72482
Ozark Lithia	71901
Ozone	72854
Pace City	71751
Palestine	72372
Palmyra	71667
Pangburn	72121
Pankey (Part of Little Rock)	72212
Panther Forest	71653
Paradise Landing	72106
Paragould	72450*
	72451†
Paraloma	71846
Paris	72855
Parkdale	71661
Parkers	72206
Parkers Chapel	71730
Parkers-Iron Springs	72206
Park Grove	72029
Park Hill (Part of North Little Rock)	72116
Parkin	72373
Park Place	72320
Park Plaza (Part of Little Rock)	72205
Parks	72950
Parma	72044
Parmenter Addition	72315
Parnell	72023
Paron	72122
Parthenon	72666
Pastoria	72152
Patmos	71801
Patrick	72727

	ZIP
Patsville	71647
Patterson	72123
Pawheen	72438
Payneway	72472
Peach Orchard	72453
Pearcy	71964
Pea Ridge (Benton County)	72751
Pea Ridge (Desha County)	71674
Pearson	72131
Pecan Point	72350
Peel	72668
Pelsor	72856
Pencil Bluff	71965
Pendleton	71639
Penjur	72348
Pennington	72005
Pennys	71846
Penrose	72101
Peppers Landing	72041
Perla	72104
Perry	72125
Perrytown	71801
Perryville	72126
Peter Pender	72933
Peter Rock Acres	72031
Pettigrew	72752
Pettus	72086
Pettyville	72442
Pfeiffer	72501
Philadelphia	72401
Philander Smith College (Part of Little Rock)	72202
Phillips Bayou	72360
Phoenix Village (Part of Fort Smith)	72901
Pickens (Desha County)	71662
Pickens (White County)	72143
Pickering	71730
Piercetown	72641
Piggott	72454
Pike City	71958
Pilgrims Rest	72764
Pindall	72669
Pine Bluff	71601-13
For specific Pine Bluff Zip Codes call (501) 536-3535, or your local postmaster.	
Pine Bluff Arsenal	71602
Pine Bluff Southeast (Part of Pine Bluff)	71601
Pine City	72069
Pine Grove	71763
Pine Grove Valley	72944
Pine Ridge	71966
Pine Tree	72326
Pineville	72566
Piney (Garland County)	71913
Piney (Johnson County)	72847
Piney Grove	71845
Pinnacle	72135
Pisgah (Pike County)	71940
Pisgah (Yell County)	72834
Pitman	72444
Pitts	72421
Plainfield	71740
Plainview (White County)	72081
Plainview (Yell County)	72857
Plant	72031
Pleasant Grove (Craighead County)	72401
Pleasant Grove (Stone County)	72567
Pleasant Grove (Van Buren County)	72030
Pleasant Hill (Crawford County)	72947
Pleasant Hill (Cross County)	72396
Pleasant Hill (Garland County)	71901
Pleasant Hill (Nevada County)	71857
Pleasant Plains	72568
Pleasant Ridge	72632
Pleasant Valley (Carroll County)	72616
Pleasant Valley (Faulkner County)	72058
Pleasant Valley (Izard County)	72519
Pleasant Valley (Lafayette County)	71826
Pleasant Valley (Perry County)	72016
Pleasant Valley (Pope County)	72837

	ZIP
Pleasant View (Conway County)	72110
Pleasant View (Franklin County)	72949
Pleasure Heights	72745
Plumerville	72127
Plunketts	72017
Pocahontas	72455
Point Cedar	71921
Pollard	72456
Ponca	72670
Ponders	72476
Pontoon	72025
Poplar Grove	72374
Portia	72457
Portland	71663
Posey	72392
Possum Grape	72020
Postelle	72366
Post Oak	71658
Potter	71953
Potter Junction	71953
Pottsville	72858
Poughkeepsie	72569
Powhatan	72458
Poyen	72128
Prairie Creek	72756
Prairie Grove	72753
Prairie View	72863
Prattsville	72129
Prescott	71857
Preston	72032
Preston Ferry	72134
Price Place	65729
Prim	72130
Princedale	72373
Princeton	71725
Process City	71832
Proctor	72376
Promised Land (Mississippi County)	72315
Promised Land (Poinsett County)	72472
Providence	72081
Provo	71846
Pruitt	72648
Pumpkin Bend	72101
Pyatt	72672
Quarry Heights	72826
Quinn	71730
Quitman	72131
Raggio	72320
Ragtown	72069
Rainbow Island	72121
Ralph	72687
Rambo Riveria	72756
Ramsey	71742
Ramsey Hill	72501
Ranger	72824
Ratcliff	72951
Ratio	72333
Ravanna	55556
Ravenden	72459
Ravenden Springs	72460
Rawlison	72348
Ray Lee Addition	72801
Reader	71726
Readland	71640
Rea Valley	72634
Rector	72461
Redfield	72132
Redland	71857
Red Leaf	71653
Red Onion	72447
Red Springs	71743
Red Star	72752
Red Wing	71832
Reed	71670
Reedville	71639
Relfs Bluff	71667
Remmel	72112
Rena	72956
Republican	72058
Revel	72006
Rex	72031
Reydell	72133
Reyno	72462
Rich	72021
Richardson	72004
Richland View	72727
Richmond	71822
Richwood	72476
Richwoods	71923
Ridgeway	72601
Rio Vista	72010
Risher	72421
Rison	71665
Rivercliff Estates	72756
Riverdale	72941

	ZIP
River Mountain	72835
Riverside	72101
Rivervale	72377
Riverview	72110
Riverview Addition	72501
Rixey (Part of North Little Rock)	72117
Robertsville	72063
Robinson	72761
Rob Roy	72004
Rock Hill	71846
Rockport	72104
Rock Springs	71675
Rockwell (Garland County)	71901
Rockwell (Garland County)	71913
Rocky	71953
Rocky Hill	72629
Rocky Mound (Hempstead County)	71801
Rocky Mound (Miller County)	71837
Rodney	72519
Roe	72134
Rogers	72756-58
For specific Rogers Zip Codes call (501) 636-3301, or your local postmaster.	
Rogers Avenue (Part of Fort Smith)	72903
Rohwer	71666
Roland	72135
Rolla	72104
Romance (Lee County)	72136
Rondo (Lee County)	72355
Rondo (Miller County)	75502
Rosa	72358
Rosboro	71921
Rose Bud	72137
Rose City (Part of North Little Rock)	72117
Rose Hill	71655
Roseland	72442
Rose Meadow (Part of Little Rock)	72206
Roseville	72949
Rosie	72571
Ross	72846
Rosston	71858
Ross Van-Ness	71640
Rotan	72370
Round Pond	72394
Rover	72860
Rowell	71665
Roy	71852
Royal	71968
Royal Oak	72103
Rubicon	72015
Ruddell Hill	72501
Rudy	72952
Rule	72638
Rumley	72645
Rupert	72031
Rushing	72051
Russell	72139
Russellville	72801*
	72811†
Rutherford	72501
Rye	71665
Sacred Heart	72840
Saddle	72554
Saffell	72572
Sage	72573
Saginaw	71941
St. Charles	72140
St. Francis	72464
St. Joe	72675
St. Matthews	71752
St. Paul	72760
St. Vincent	72063
Salado	72575
Salem (Fulton County)	72576
Salem (Lee County)	72368
Salem (Pike County)	71943
Salem (Saline County)	72015
Salesville	72653
Saltillo	72032
Salus	72854
Sand Hill	72040
Sandtown	72501
Sandy Bend	71765
Sandyland	71762
Sandy Ridge	72315
Sans Souci	72370
Sarassa	71644
Saratoga	71859
Sardis	72011
Savoy	72704

	ZIP
Schaal	71851
Schaberg	72946
Schooley	71851
Schug	72450
Scotland	72141
Scott	72142
Scottsville	72837
Scott Valley	72360
Scranton	72863
Screeton	72064
Searcy	72143*
	72145†
Seaton	72046
Seaton Dump	72046
Sedgwick	72465
Sellers Store	72542
Selma	71670
Seyppel	72348
Shady	71953
Shady Grove (Faulkner County)	72058
Shady Grove (Fulton County)	72583
Shady Grove (Johnson County)	72830
Shady Grove (Mississippi County)	72442
Shady Grove (Nevada County)	71857
Shady Grove (Poinsett County)	72472
Shakertown	71923
Shannon	72455
Shannondale	72348
Shannon Hills	72103
Shannonville	72331
Sharman	71860
Sharum	72455
Shaw	72015
Shearerville	72346
Shelbyville	72521
Shell Lake	72346
Sheppard	71838
Sheridan	72150
Sherrill	72152
Sherwood	72120
Sherwood Hills	72105
Shiloh (Howard County)	71851
Shiloh (Pope County)	72801
Shippen	72351
Shirley	72153
Shoffner	72112
Shover Springs	71801
Sidney	72577
Sidon	72137
Signal Hill	72560
Siloam Springs	72761
Silver	71957
Silver Hill	72675
Silver Ridge (Cleburne County)	72530
Silver Ridge (Sevier County)	71846
Sims	71969
Simsboro	72348
Sitka	72482
Skunkhollow	72032
Slaytonville	72937
Slonikers Mill	72372
Slovak	72160
Smackover	71762
Smale	72021
Smearney	71647
Smithdale	72373
Smiths Corner	72368
Smithville (Lawrence County)	72466
Smithville (Miller County)	71834
Snow	72687
Snowball	72650
Snow Hill	71751
Snow Lake	72379
Snyder	71658
Social Hill	71104
Solgohachia	72156
Sonora	72764
South Bend	72076
South Crossett (Part of Crossett)	71635
Southern Hills	72601
Southern State College (Part of Magnolia)	71753
South Fort Smith (Part of Fort Smith)	72906
South Jacksonville (Part of Jacksonville)	72076
Southland (Craighead County)	72437

	ZIP
Southland (Phillips County)	72355
South Lead Hill	72644
South Lewisville	71845
South Ozark	72949
South Sheridan	72150
South Shore Park	72543
South Side (Independence County)	72501
South Side (Pulaski County)	72206
Southside (Van Buren County)	72013
Spadra	72830
Sparkman	71763
Spence Junction	72856
Spirit Lake	71845
Springdale	72762-66
For specific Springdale Zip Codes call (501) 751-4441, or your local postmaster.	
Springfield	72157
Springhill (Faulkner County)	72058
Spring Hill (Hempstead County)	71801
Spring Lake Estates	72653
Springtown	72767
Spring Valley (Independence County)	72501
Spring Valley (Pulaski County)	72210
Spring Valley (Washington County)	72764
Sprudel	71838
Stacy (Crittenden County)	72384
Stacy (Poinsett County)	72472
Stamps	71860
Standard-Umsted	71762
Stanford	72450
Star City	71667
State Capitol (Part of Little Rock)	72201
State Line (Columbia County)	71740
State Line (Lafayette County)	71861
State Services	72158
State University (Part of Jonesboro)	72467
Staves	71665
Stelltown	71940
Stephens	71764
Steprock	72159
Stevens Creek	72010
Stevens Landing	72472
Stokes	72455
Stonewall	72450
Stony Point	72070
Story	71970
Strangers Home	72410
Strawberry (Johnson County)	72846
Strawberry (Lawrence County)	72469
Stringtown	71842
Strong	71765
Stump City	72346
Sturkie	72578
Stuttgart	72160
Subiaco	72865
Success	72470
Sugar Grove	72927
Sugarloaf Lake	72937
Sulphur City	72701
Sulphur Rock	72579
Sulphur Springs (Benton County)	72768
Sulphur Springs (Jefferson County)	71603
Sulphur Springs (Johnson County)	72830
Sulphur Springs (Yell County)	72834
Summers	72769
Summerville	71744
Summit	72677
Sumpter	71647
Sunnydale	72081
Sunny Hill (Part of Searcy)	72143
Sunset (Crittenden County)	72364
Sunset (Washington County)	72959
Sunshine (Ashley County)	71661
Sunshine (Garland County)	71968
Supply	72444
Sutton	71835

	ZIP
Swain	72628
Swan Lake	72004
Sweden	72004
Sweethome (Montgomery County)	71957
Sweet Home (Pulaski County)	72164
Swifton	72471
Sycamore Bend	72348
Sylamore	72556
Sylvan Hills (Part of Sherwood)	72116
Sylvania	72176
Sylverino	75502
Tafton	72183
Talley	71740
Tall Trees	72322
Tamo	71644
Tanglewood	72756
Tannenbaum	72530
Tarry	71667
Tate	72927
Tates Bluff	71726
Taylor	71861
Tech (Part of Russellville)	72801
Tennessee	71655
Texarkana	75502
Thebes	71658
Thida	72165
Thompson Grove	72348
Thornburg	72126
Thorney	72727
Thornton	71766
Three Brothers	72653
Three Creeks	71749
Three Way	72370
Tichnor	72166
Tie Plant (Part of North Little Rock)	72117
Tillar	71670
Tilly	72679
Tilton	72347
Timber Lake Manor	72531
Timber Lane	71833
Timbo	72680
Tinsman	71767
Toad Suck	72016
Togo	72373
Tokio	71852
Toledo	71665
Tollette	71851
Tollville	72041
Toltec	72142
Tomahawk	72675
Tomato	72381
Tomberlin	72046
Toneyville (Part of Jacksonville)	72076
Tongin	72320
Tontitown	72770
Trammellville	72461
Traskwood	72167
Treasure Hills (Faulkner County)	72032
Treasure Hills (Pulaski County)	72207
Treat	72854
Trenton	72374
Troy	71764
Trumann	72472
Tucker	72168
Tuckerman	72473
Tuckertown	72321
Tucker Unit	72168
Tulip	71725
Tull	72015
Tully	72472
Tulot	72472
Tumbling Shoals	72581
Tupelo	72169
Turkey Scratch	72366
Turner	72383
Turrell	72384
Tuttle	72727
Twentythree	72010
Twin Groves	72039
Twin Lakes (Part of Little Rock)	72201
Twin Springs	72205
Twist	72331
Tyro	71639
Tyronza	72386
Ulm	72170
Umpire	71971
Union (Fulton County)	72576
Union (Sevier County)	71832
Union Hill	72020
Uniontown	72955
Unionville	71665

* Area Zip Code   **† Post Office Boxes**

	ZIP		ZIP		ZIP		ZIP
Unity	71852	Walnut Grove (Clay County)	72435	West Gum Springs (Part of Gum Springs)	71923	Winesburg	72401
University Mall (Part of Little Rock)	72205	Walnut Grove (Independence County)	72524	West Hartford	72938	Winfield	72958
University of Arkansas at Monticello (Part of Monticello)	71655	Walnut Grove (Van Buren County)	72031	West Helena	72390	Winfrey	72959
				West Line	74734	Wing	72860
				West Marche	72118	Winslow	72959
University of Central Arkansas (Part of Conway)	72032	Walnut Grove (Washington County)	72730	West Memphis	72301*	Winston Terrace (Part of Little Rock)	72201
					72303†	Winthrop	71866
Uno	72421	Walnut Grove (Yell County)	72842	West Pangburn	72121	Wirth	72554
Upper White Oak Lake	71726	Walnut Hill	71826	West Point (Benton County)	72734	Wiseman	72587
Urbana	71768	Walnut Ridge	72476			Witcherville	72940
Urbanette	72601	Walnut Springs	71842	West Point (White County)	72178	Witherspoon	71923
Ursula	72933	Walters	72438	West Ridge	72391	Witter	72776
Vaden	71923	Waltreak	72833	Westside (Part of Little Rock)	72211	Wittsburg	72396
Vail	72438	Wampler Spur (Part of Pine Bluff)	71601	Westville	72956	Witts Springs	72686
Valley Gin	71837			Westwood (Part of Little Rock)	72201	Wiville	72101
Valley Springs	72682	Ward	72176			Wolf Bayou	72530
Valley View	72401	Wardell	72350	Wharton	72740	Wonderview	72063
Van	72042	War Eagle	72756	Wheatley	72392	Woodberry	71744
Van Buren	72956	Warm Springs	72478	Wheeler	72775	Woodland	72830
Vandervoort	71972	Warner	71701	Wheeling	72576	Woodland Corner	72315
Vanndale	72387	Warren	71671	Whelen Springs	71772	Woodland Heights (Part of Little Rock)	72201
Varner Unit	71644	Washburn	72936	Whispering Springs	72067		
Vaughn	72712	Washington	71862	Whistleville	72442	Woodland Hills (Fulton County)	72542
Velvet Ridge	72010	Washita	71957	Whitaker	72432		
Vendor	72683	Watalula	72949	White	71635	Woodland Hills (Saline County)	72002
Verona	72618	Waterloo	71858	White Cliffs	71846		
Vesta	72933	Watkins Corner	72366	White Hall (Drew County)	71655	Woodlawn (Cleveland County)	71665
Vick	71647	Watson	71674	White Hall (Jefferson County)	71602		
Victoria	72370	Watson Chapel (Part of Pine Bluff)	71601			Woodlawn (Lonoke County)	72007
Village	71769			Whitehall (Lee County)	72320	Woodrow	72130
Vilonia	72173	Wattensaw	72086	Whitehall (Poinsett County)	72432	Woodson	72180
Vimy Ridge	72002	Waveland	72867			Wooster	72181
Vincent	72327	Waverly	72376	Whiteoak	72949	Worden	72010
Vine Prairie	72947	Wayton	72628	White Oak Bluff	71665	Wright	72182
Vineyard	72360	Webb City	72949	White Rock	72701	Wrights Corner	72010
Viney Grove	72753	Weber	72166	Whitetown	71961	Wrightsville	72183
Vinity Corner	72143	Wedington	72704	Whiteville	72635	Wrightsville Unit	72183
Viola	72583	Wedington Woods	72704	Whitmore	72394	Wycamp	72390
Violet Hill	72584	Weiner	72479	Whitton	72386	Wye	72016
Vista Shores	72732	Welcome	71861	Wickes	71973	Wyman	72701
Wabash	72389	Welcome Home	72650	Wideman	72585	Wynne	72396
Wabbaseka	72175	Weldon	72112	Widener	72394	Wyola	72959
Wakefield Village (Part of Little Rock)	72201	Wellford	71640	Wiederkehr Village	72821	Yale	72752
		Weona	72472	Wilburn	72179	Yancopin	71674
Walcott	72474	Wesley	72773	Wild Cherry	72576	Yancy	71855
Waldenburg	72475	Wesley Chapel	72110	Wildwood	72346	Yarbro	72315
Waldo	71770	Wesson	71749	Williamson	71842	Yardelle	72685
Waldron	72958	West (Part of Springdale)	72762	Williford	72482	Y City	72926
Walker (Columbia County)	71753		72766	Willisville	71864	Yellow Bayou	71653
Walker (White County)	72143	For specific West Zip Codes call (501) 750-3216, or your local postmaster.		Willow	72084	Yellville	72687
Walker's Corner	72142			Wilmar	71675	Yocana	71953
Walkers Creek	71861			Wilmot	71676	Yoestown	72921
Walkerville	71740	West Camden Heights (Part of Camden)	71701	Wilson (Mississippi County)	72395	Yorktown	71678
Wallace	71836	West Crossett	71635			Zachery	72366
Walnut	72854	West End (Part of Pine Bluff)	71601	Wilson (Pope County)	72823	Zent	72021
Walnut Corner (Greene County)	72416			Wilton	71865	Zinc	72601
		Western Grove	72685	Winchester	71677	Zion	72556
Walnut Corner (Phillips County)	72312	West Fork	72774	Windamere (Part of Little Rock)	72201	Zion Hill	72110

	ZIP
Aberdeen	93526
Acacia Acres	93291
Academy	93611
Acampo	95220
Actis Gardens	93501
Acton	93510
Adams Springs	95426
Adelaida	93446
Adelanto	92301
Adin	96006
Adobe Corners	92392
Aerial Acres	93523
Aetna Springs	94567
Afton	95920
Agate Bay	96140
Ager	96064
Agnew (Part of Santa Clara)	95054*
	95056†
Agoura (Part of Agoura Hills)	91301
Agoura Hills	91301*
	91376†
Agua Caliente	95476
Agua Caliente Indian Reservation	92262
Agua Dulce	91350
Aguanga	92536
Ahwahnee	93601
Airbase (Part of Santa Maria)	93454
Airport (Part of Oakland)	94614
Alabama Hills	93545
Alameda	94501-02
For specific Alameda Zip Codes call (510) 748-5366, or your local postmaster.	
Alamo	94507
Alamo Oaks (Part of Danville)	94526
Alamorio	92227
Albany	94706
Alberhill	92530
Albion	95410
Albrae (Part of Fremont)	94538
Alcatraz (Part of San Francisco)	94123
Alderbrook Tract (Part of Cupertino)	95014
Aldercroft Heights	95030
Alderpoint	95511
Alder Springs	93602
Alessandro (Part of Riverside)	92508
Alexander Valley	95441
Alhambra	91801-99
For specific Alhambra Zip Codes call (818) 289-9101, or your local postmaster.	
Alhambra Valley	94553
Alisal (Part of Salinas)	93905
Aliso Viejo	92656
Alleghany	95910
Allendale	95688
Allensworth	93219
Alliance (Part of Arcata)	95521
Allied Gardens (Part of San Diego)	92120
Almaden Plaza (Part of San Jose)	95118
Almaden Valley (Part of San Jose)	95120
Almanor (Part of Canyondam)	95923
Almanor	96020
Almonte	94941
Alondra	90249
Alpaugh	93201
Alpine	91901*
	91903†
Alpine Forest	93561
Alpine Heights	91901
Alpine Meadows	96146
Alpine Village (Riverside County)	92262
Alpine Village (Tulare County)	93265
Alta	95701
Altadena	91001-03
For specific Altadena Zip Codes call (818) 794-1147, or your local postmaster.	
Alta Heights (Part of Napa)	94559
Alta Hill	95945
Al Tahoe (Part of South Lake Tahoe)	96151
Alta Loma (Part of Rancho Cucamonga)	91701

	ZIP
	91737
For specific Alta Loma Zip Codes call (909) 987-3100, or your local postmaster.	
Alta Sierra (Kern County)	93285
Alta Sierra (Nevada County)	95949
Altaville (Part of Angels Camp)	95221
Alta Vista	93514
Alto (Part of Mill Valley)	94941
Alton	95540
Alturas	96101
Alvarado (Part of Union City)	94587
Alviso (Part of San Jose)	95002
Amador City	95601
Amarillo Beach (Part of Malibu)	90265
Ambassador (Part of Los Angeles)	90005
Ambler Park	93901
Amboy	92304
Ambrose	94565
American Canyon	94589
American House	95981
Anaheim	92801-25
For specific Anaheim Zip Codes call (714) 520-2600, or your local postmaster.	
FINANCIAL INSTITUTIONS	
United California Savings Bank	92805
HOTELS/MOTELS	
Anaheim Hilton & Towers	92802
Sheraton-Anaheim Hotel	92802
Anaheim Hills (Part of Anaheim)	92808
Anaheim Plaza (Part of Anaheim)	92801
Ana Verde (Part of Palmdale)	93551
Anchor Bay	95445
Anderson	96007
Anderson Springs	95461
Andrew Jackson (Part of San Diego)	92115
Angels Camp	95222
Angelus Oaks	92305
Angiola	93212
Angora Highlands	96150
Angwin	94508
Annapolis	95412
Annex III (Part of Los Angeles)	91405
Antelope	95843
Antelope Acres	93536
Antelope Valley Mall (Part of Palmdale)	93550
Antioch	94509*
	94531†
Antonio	93437
Anza	92539
Applegate	95703
Apple Valley	92307-08
For specific Apple Valley Zip Codes call (619) 247-7819, or your local postmaster.	
Aptos	95001†
	95003*
Aptos Hills-Larkin Valley	95003
Arbolada (Part of Ojai)	93023
Arbuckle	95912
Arcade (Los Angeles County)	90052
Arcade (Sacramento County)	95821
Arcadia	91006-07
	91066
	91077
For specific Arcadia Zip Codes call (818) 821-6300, or your local postmaster.	
Arcata	95521
Arch Beach Heights (Part of Laguna Beach)	92651
Arden	95825
Arden-Arcade	95821
Arden Fair Mall (Part of Sacramento)	95815
Arden Town	95825
Ardmore (Part of South Gate)	90280
Arena	95301
Argus	93562

	ZIP
Arlanza Village (Part of Riverside)	92505
Arleta (Part of Los Angeles)	91331
Arlington (Part of Riverside)	92503*
	92513†
Arlington Heights Estate	95934
Arlynda Corners	95536
Armistead	93527
Armona	93202
Army Point	94510
Army Terminal (Part of Oakland)	94626
Arnold	95223
Arnold Heights	92508
Aromas	95004
Arrowbear Lake	92382
Arrowhead Highlands	92325
Arroyo Grande	93420*
	93421†
Arroyo Vista (Part of Dublin)	94566
Artesia	90701-03
For specific Artesia Zip Codes call (310) 860-6694, or your local postmaster.	
Artois	95913
Arvin	93203
Arvin (labor camp)	93308
Ash Creek	96057
Ashland	94541
Asian Village (Part of Westminster)	92683
Asilomar (Part of Pacific Grove)	93950
Aspendell	93514
Asti	95425
Atascadero	93422*
	93423†
Athens	90047
Atherton	94027
Athlone	95333
Atlanta	95366
Atlantic Richfield Plaza (Part of Los Angeles)	90071
Atwater	95301
Atwood (Part of Placentia)	92601
Auberry	93602
Auburn	95602-04
For specific Auburn Zip Codes call (916) 885-7944, or your local postmaster.	
August	95201
Avalon	90704
Avalon Village (Part of Carson)	90745
Avenal	93204
Avery	95224
Avila Beach	93424
Avocado Heights	91746
Azusa	91702
Baden (Part of South San Francisco)	94080
Badger	93603
Bailey (Part of Whittier)	90601
Baker	92309
Baker Ranch	95631
Bakersfield	93301-89
For specific Bakersfield Zip Codes call (805) 861-4346, or your local postmaster.	
Bakersfield East (Part of Bakersfield)	93305
Bakersfield Plaza (Part of Bakersfield)	93308
Bakersfield South (Part of Bakersfield)	93304
Balance Rock	93260
Balboa (Part of Newport Beach)	92661
Balboa Bay Shores (Part of Newport Beach)	92663
Balboa Island (Part of Newport Beach)	92662
Balch Camp	93602
Balderson Station	95634
Baldwin Hills Regional Shopping Mall (Part of Los Angeles)	90067
Baldwin Lake	92314
Baldwin Park	91706
Baldy Mesa	92371
Ballarat	93562
Ballard	93463
Ballico	95303
Ballou (Part of Ontario)	91761
Balls Ferry	96007

	ZIP
Baltimore Park (Part of Larkspur)	94939
Bandini (Part of Commerce)	90040
Bangor	95914
Bankhead Springs	91934
Banner	92036
Banning	92220
Banta	95304
Barber City (Part of Westminster)	92683
Bard	92222
Bardsdale	93015
Barona	92040
Barona Indian Reservation	92040
Barrett	91917
Barrington (Part of Los Angeles)	90049
Barron Park (Part of Palo Alto)	94306
Barstow (San Bernardino County)	92311*
	92312†
Barstow (Fresno County)	93705
Barton (Part of Fresno)	93702
Base Line (Part of San Bernardino)	92410
Bassett	91746
Bassetts	96125
Bass Lake	93604
Bass Lake Height	93644
Batavia	95620
Baumberg (Part of Hayward)	94545
Baxter	95701
Bay (Part of Big Bear Lake)	92315
Bay Fair Mall (Part of San Leandro)	94578
Bayliss	95943
Bayo Vista	94572
Bay Park (Part of San Diego)	92110
Bay Point	94565
Bayshore (Part of Brisbane)	94005
Bayshore Mall (Part of Eureka)	95501
Bayside (Humboldt County)	95524
Bayside (Santa Clara County)	95131
	95134
	95164
For specific Bayside Zip Codes call (707) 822-1683, or your local postmaster.	
Bayview (Humboldt County)	95503
Bayview (San Francisco County)	94124
Bayview-Montalvin	94806
Bayview Park	94806
Baywood-Los Osos	93402
Baywood Park	93402
Beach Center (Part of Huntington Beach)	92648
Beale Air Force Base	95903
Bear Creek	95340
Bear Creek Estates	95006
Bear River Lake	95666
Bear River Pines	95945
Bear Valley (Alpine County)	95223
Bear Valley (Mariposa County)	95338
Bear Valley Springs	93561
Beaumont	92223
Beckwourth	96129
Bee Rock	93426
Bel Air (Part of Los Angeles)	90024
Bel Aire Estates (Part of Tiburon)	94920
Belden	95915
Bell	90201
Bella Vista (Contra Costa County)	94565
Bella Vista (Kern County)	93283
Bella Vista (Los Angeles County)	90022
Bella Vista (Shasta County)	96008
Belle Haven (Part of Menlo Park)	94025
Belleview	95370
Bellflower	90706*
	90707†
Bell Gardens	90201

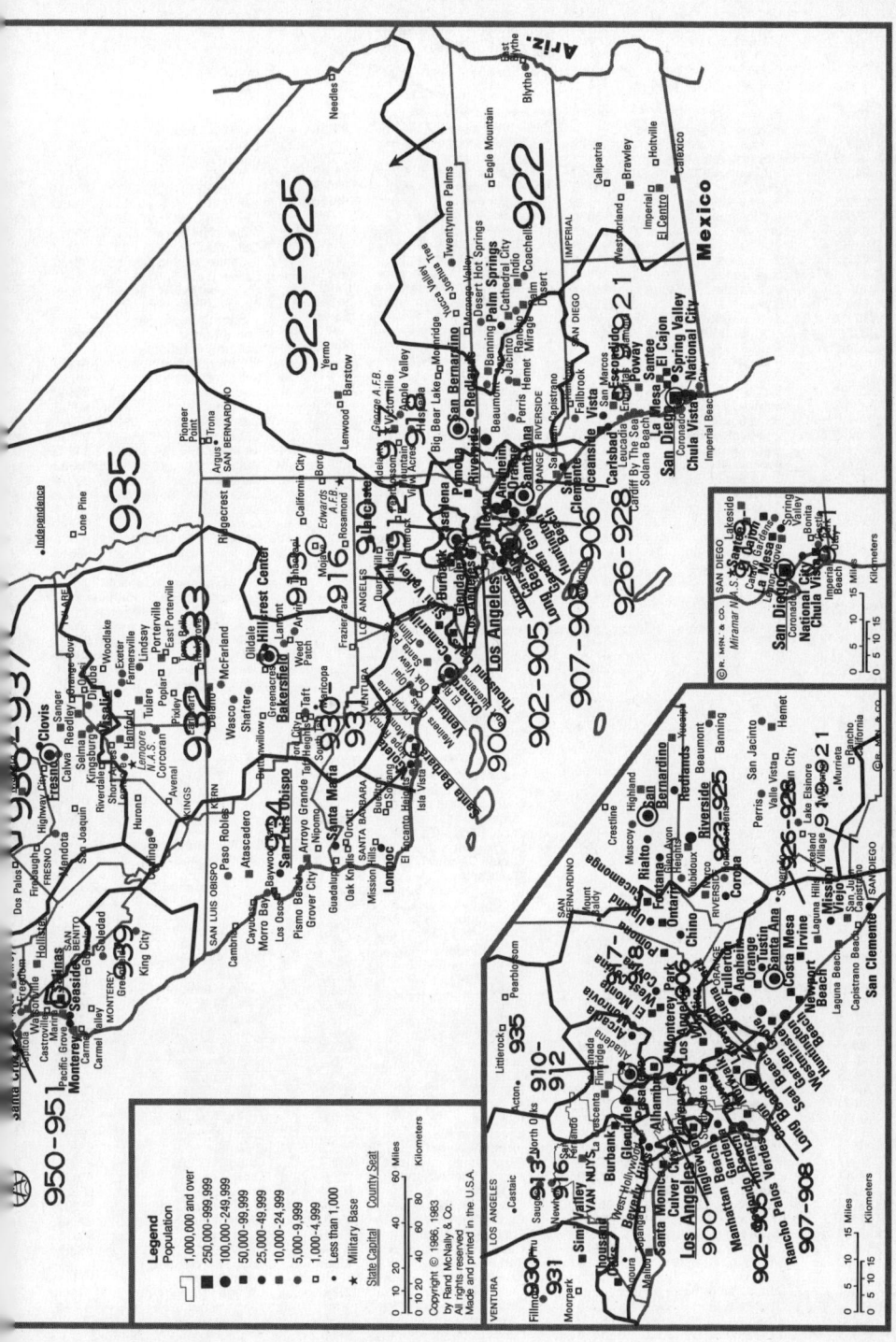

Name	ZIP
Bell Mountain	92392
Belltown	92509
Bel Marin Keys	94947
Belmont	94002*
	94003†
Belmont Shore (Part of Long Beach)	90803
Belridge Farms	93251
Belvedere (Los Angeles County)	90022
Belvedere (Marin County)	94920
Belvedere Gardens	90022
Belvedere-Tiburon (Part of Belvedere)	94920
Belvernon Gardens (Part of Tiburon)	94920
Benbow	95542
Bend	96080
Ben Hur	93653
Benicia	94510
Ben Lomond	95005
Benton	93512
Berenda	93637
Berkeley	94701-05
	94707-10

For specific Berkeley Zip Codes call (510) 649-3100, or your local postmaster.

Name	ZIP
Bermuda Dunes	92201
Bernal (Part of San Francisco)	94110
Berry Creek	95916
Berryessa (Part of San Jose)	95132
Berryessa Highlands	94558
Berryessa Park	94558
Berteleda	95531
Bertsch Terrace	95531
Bethany Park (Part of Scotts Valley)	95066
Bethel Island	94511
Betteravia	93454
Beverly (Part of Beverly Hills)	90212
Beverly Center (Part of Los Angeles)	90048
Beverly Hills	90209-13

For specific Beverly Hills Zip Codes call (310) 247-3400, or your local postmaster.

Name	ZIP
Bicentennial (Part of Los Angeles)	90048
Bieber	96009
Big Bar	96010
Big Basin	95006
Big Bear City	92314
Big Bear Lake	92315
Big Bend	96011
Big Chief	96161
Big Creek	93605
Big Eddy Estates	96028
Biggs	95917
Big Lagoon Park	95570
Big Meadows	95223
Big Oak Flat	95305
Big Pine	93513
Big Pine Indian Reservation	93513
Big River	92242
Big Springs	96064
Big Sur	93920
Big Trees	95018
Bijou (Part of South Lake Tahoe)	96156
Bijou Park (Part of South Lake Tahoe)	96156
Binghamton	95620
Biola	93606
Birch Hill	92060
Birch Meadow Acres	95945
Birdcage Walk	95610
Bird Rock (Part of San Diego)	92037
Birds Landing	94512
Bishop	93514*
	03515†
Bishop Acres	93263
Bishop Indian Reservation	93514
Bitterwater	93930
Bixby (Part of Long Beach)	90807
Bixby Knolls (Part of Long Beach)	90807
Black Bear	96031
Blackhawk	94506
Black Meadow Landing	92267
Black Point	94947
Blackrock	93526

Name	ZIP
Blackstone (Part of Fresno)	93710
Blackwells Corner	93249
Blairsden	96103
Blanco	93901
Blocksburg	95514
Bloomfield	94952
Bloomfield Acres (Part of Arcata)	95521
Bloomington	92316
Blossom Hill (Part of San Jose)	95123
Blossom Valley (Part of Mountain View)	94040
Blue Canon	95715
Blue Hills (Part of Saratoga)	95070
Blue Jay	92317
Blue Lake	95525
Blue Lakes	95493
Bluewater	92242
Bluff Creek	95546
Blythe	92225-26

For specific Blythe Zip Codes call (619) 922-6157, or your local postmaster.

Name	ZIP
Bodega	94922
Bodega Bay	94923
Bodfish	93205
Bolinas	94924
Bolsa (Part of Westminster)	92683
Bolsa Knolls	93906
Bombay Beach	92257
Bonadelle Ranchos	93637
Bonadelle Ranchos-Madera Ranchos	93637
Bonds Corner	92250
Bonita (Madera County)	93637
Bonita (San Diego County)	91902*
	91908†
Bonny Doon	95060
Bonnyview (Part of Redding)	96001
Bonsall	92003
Boonville	95415
Bootjack	95338
Boron	93516*
	93596†
Borosolvay	93562
Borrego Springs	92004
Borrego Wells	92004
Bostonia	92021
Boulder Creek	95006
Boulder Oaks	91962
Boulder Park	91934
Boulevard	91905
Bowman	95604
Box Springs	92507
Boyes Hot Springs	95416
Boyle (Part of Los Angeles)	90033
Boyle Heights (Part of Los Angeles)	90033
Boys Republic (Part of Chino Hills)	91710
Brackney	95005
Bradbury	91010
Bradford (Part of Hayward)	94541
Bradley	93426
Brandeis	93064
Branscomb	95417
Brawley	92227
Bray	96058
Brea	92621*
	92622†
Brea Mall (Part of Brea)	92621
Brentwood	94513
Briceburg	95345
Briceland	95542
Bridgehead	94509
Bridgeport (Mariposa County)	95338
Bridgeport (Mono County)	93517
Bridgeport (Nevada County)	95977
Bridgeville	95526
Brisbane	94005
Bristol (Part of Santa Ana)	92703
Broadmoor	94015
Broadway (Sacramento County)	95818
Broadway (San Mateo County)	94010
Broadway Manchester (Part of Los Angeles)	90003

Name	ZIP
Broadway Plaza (Part of Walnut Creek)	94596
Brockway	96143
Broderick (Part of West Sacramento)	95605
Brookdale	95007
Brookhurst Center (Part of Anaheim)	92804
Brooks	95606
Brookside Park (Part of Portola Valley)	94028
Browns Corner (Part of Woodland)	95695
Browns Valley	95918
Brownsville	95919
Bruceville	95758
Brundage (Part of Bakersfield)	93307
Brush Creek	95916
Bryant (Part of Long Beach)	90815
Bryn Mawr (Part of Loma Linda)	92318
Bryson	93426
Bryte (Part of West Sacramento)	95605
Buckeye (El Dorado County)	95634
Buckeye (Shasta County)	96003
Buckhorn Lodge	95666
Buckingham Park	95451
Buck Meadows	95321
Bucks Bar	95667
Bucks Lake	95971
Bucks Lake Lodge	95971
Bucktail	96052
Buellton	93427
Buena (Part of Vista)	92083
Buena Park	90620-22
	90624

For specific Buena Park Zip Codes call (714) 523-1960, or your local postmaster.

Name	ZIP
Buena Park Mall (Part of Buena Park)	90620
Buenaventura Plaza (Part of Ventura)	93003
Buena Vista (Amador County)	95640
Buena Vista (Sonoma County)	95476
Buffalo Hill	95634
Buhach	95340
Bummerville	95255
Burbank	91501-10

For specific Burbank Zip Codes call (818) 846-3155, or your local postmaster.

Name	ZIP
Burbank	95128
Burkett Acres (Part of Stockton)	95215
Burkett Gardens	95205
Burlingame	94010-12

For specific Burlingame Zip Codes call (415) 342-7694, or your local postmaster.

Name	ZIP
Burlingame Hills (Part of Burlingame)	94010
Burney	96013
Burnt Ranch	95527
Burrel	93607
Burrough	93667
Burson	95225
Butano Canyon	94060
Butte City	95920
Butte Creek	95928
Butte Meadows	95942
Buttonwillow	93206
Byron	94514
Cabazon	92230
Cabazon Indian Reservation	92201
Cabin Cove	93271
Cabrillo (Part of Long Beach)	90810
Cabrillo Estates	93402
Cache Creek	93501
Cachuma Village	93101
Cadiz	92319
Cahuilla	92539
Cahuilla Estates	92539
Cahuilla Hills	92260
Cahuilla Indian Reservation	92543
Cairns Corner	93247
Cajon Junction	92403
Calabasas	91302*
	91372†
Calabasas Highlands	91302

Name	ZIP
Calabasas Hills	91301
Calabasas Park	91302
Calaveras (Part of Stockton)	95207
Calaveras Yacht and Country Club Estates	95204
Calaveritas	95249
Calavo Gardens	91941
Calexico	92231*
	92232†
Calexico Lodge	91905
Calico	92398
Cal-Ida	95922
Caliente	93518
California City	93504*
	93505†
California Correctional Institution (Kern County)	93561
California Correctional Center (Lassen County)	96130
California Hot Springs	93207
California Medical Facility	95688
California Polytechnic State University-San Luis Obispo	93407
California Rehabilitation Center (Part of Norco)	91760
California State Prison-Amador	95640
California Valley	93453
Calimesa	92320
Calipatria	92233
Calistoga	94515
Calla	95336
Callahan	96014
Calpella	95418
Calpine	96124
Calville	95521
Calwa (Part of Fresno)	93725
Camanche Lake	95640
Camarillo	93010-12

For specific Camarillo Zip Codes call (805) 482-8894, or your local postmaster.

Name	ZIP
Camarillo Heights (Part of Camarillo)	93010
Cambria	93428
Cambrian Park	95124
Cambridge (Part of Palo Alto)	94306
Camden	93242
Camellia (Part of Sacramento)	95819
Cameo Acres (Part of Danville)	94526
Cameron Corners	91906
Cameron Creek Colony	93223
Cameron Park	95682
Camino	95709
Camino Heights	95709
Campbell	95008-09
	95011

For specific Campbell Zip Codes call (408) 452-4300, or your local postmaster.

Name	ZIP
Campbell Hot Springs	96126
Camp Connell	95223
Camp Evers (Part of Scotts Valley)	95066
Camp Meeker	95419
Camp Nelson	93208
Campo	91906
Campo Indian Reservation	91906
Campo Seco	95226
Camp Pendleton	92055
Camp Pendleton Marine Corps Base	92055
Camp Pendleton North	92055
Camp Pendleton South	92055
Camp Richardson	96150
Camp Sierra	93664
Camp St. Michael	95585
Camp Ten	95634
Camptonville	95922
Camp Wishon	93265
Camulos	93040
Canby	96015
Canebrake	93255
Canoga Annex (Part of Los Angeles)	91304
Canoga Park	91303-05
	91307-09

For specific Canoga Park Zip Codes call (818) 340-7525, or your local postmaster.

Name	ZIP
Cantil	93519
Cantua Creek	93608
Canyon	94516

* Area Zip Code   † Post Office Boxes

	ZIP
Canyon Acres (Part of Laguna Beach)	92651
Canyon Country (Part of Santa Clarita)	91351*
	91386†
Canyon Crest (Part of Riverside)	92507*
	92517†
Canyon Crest Heights (Part of Riverside)	92507
Canyondam	95923
Canyon Lake	92587
Capay (Glenn County)	95963
Capay (Yolo County)	95607
Capetown	95536
Capistrano Beach (Part of Dana Point)	92624
Capistrano Highlands (Part of Laguna Hills)	92653
Capital Hill (Part of Paso Robles)	93446
Capitola	95010
Capitol Square (Part of San Jose)	95133
Carbona	95376
Carbon Beach (Part of Malibu)	90265
Carbon Canyon (Part of Chino Hills)	91710
Cardiff By The Sea (Part of Encinitas)	92007
Cardwell (Part of Fresno)	93704
Caribou	95915
Carlotta	95528
Carlsbad	92008-09
	92018
For specific Carlsbad Zip Codes call (619) 729-2456, or your local postmaster.	
Carlton Hills (Part of Santee)	92071
Carmel	93921-23
For specific Carmel Zip Codes call (408) 625-4411, or your local postmaster.	
Carmel By The Sea (Part of Carmel)	93921
Carmel Highlands	93923
Carmel Hills	93923
Carmel Point	93923
Carmel Valley	93924
Carmel Woods	93923
Carmenita (Part of Santa Fe Springs)	90670
Carmet	94923
Carmichael	95608*
	95609†
Carnelian Bay	96140
Carpinteria	93013*
	93014†
Carquinez Heights (Part of Vallejo)	94590
Carriage Hills	91977
Carrick Addition	96094
Carson	90745-47
	90749
For specific Carson Zip Codes call (310) 549-2800, or your local postmaster.	
Carson Heights Mesa	93550
Carson Hill	95222
Carson Mall (Part of Carson)	90746
Cartago	93549
Caruthers	93609
Carvin Creek Homesites	96126
Casa Blanca (Part of Riverside)	92504
Casa Conejo	91359
Casa Correo (Part of Concord)	94521
Casa de Oro	91976*
	91977†
Casa de Oro-Mount Helix	91977
Cascadel Woods	93643
Casitas Springs	93001
Casmalia	93429
Caspar	95420
Cassel	96016
Castaic	91310
Castella	96017
Castellammare (Part of Los Angeles)	90272
Castle Air Force Base	95342
Castle Garden	95301
Castle Park (Part of Chula Vista)	91911
Castle Rock Springs	95461
Castlewood	94588

	ZIP
Castro City (Part of Mountain View)	94042
Castro Valley	94546
Castroville	95012
Catalina (Part of Pasadena)	91116
Cathedral City	92234*
	92235†
Catheys Valley	95306
Cawelo	93308
Cayucos	93430
Cazadero	95421
Cecilville	96031
Cedar (Part of Lancaster)	93534*
	93584†
Cedarbrook	93641
Cedar Crest	93605
Cedar Flat	96140
Cedar Glen	92321
Cedar Grove (El Dorado County)	95709
Cedar Grove (Fresno County)	93633
Cedarpines Park	92322
Cedar Ridge (Nevada County)	95924
Cedar Ridge (Tuolumne County)	95370
Cedar Slope	93265
Cedar Stock	96052
Cedar Valley	93644
Cedarville	96104
Center Avenue (Part of Huntington Beach)	92605
Centerpoint Mall (Part of Oxnard)	93033
Centerville (Alameda County)	94536
Centerville (Fresno County)	93657
Central City Mall (Part of San Bernardino)	92401
Central Valley	96019
Centre	95860
Century City (Part of Los Angeles)	90067
Century City Shopping Center (Part of Los Angeles)	90067
Ceres	95307
Cernan (Part of Vacaville)	95688
Cerritos	90701
Cerro Villa Heights (Part of Villa Park)	92667
Chalfant	93514
Challenge	95925
Challenge-Brownsville	95925
Challenger (Part of Los Angeles)	91303
Chambless	92319
Champagne Fountain (Part of Saratoga)	95070
Channel Islands	93030
Chapmantown (Part of Chico)	95926
Chapman Woods	91107
Chappo	92055
Charter Oak	91724
Chatsworth	91311-13
For specific Chatsworth Zip Codes call (818) 772-6675, or your local postmaster.	
Chatsworth Lake Manor	91311
Chawanakee	93602
Cheeseville	96037
Chemehuevi Indian Reservation	92363
Chemeketa Park	95030
Cherokee (Butte County)	95965
Cherokee (Nevada County)	95959
Cherokee Strip	93263
Cherry Creek Acres	95949
Cherryland	94541
Cherry Valley	92223
Chester	96020
Chestnut (Part of South San Francisco)	94080
Chicago Park	95712
Chico	95926-28
For specific Chico Zip Codes call (916) 343-5012, or your local postmaster.	
Chilcoot	96105
Childs Meadows	96061
Chili Bar	95667
China (Part of San Francisco)	94108
China Camp	94901

	ZIP
China Lake (Part of Ridgecrest)	93555
China Lake Naval Weapons Center	93555
Chinatown (Part of San Francisco)	94108
Chinese Camp	95309
Chino	91708†
	91710*
Chino Hills	91708
Chinowths Corner (Part of Visalia)	93277
Chinquapin	95389
Chiquita Lake	95634
Chiriaco Summit	92201
Cholame	93431
Chowchilla	93610
Christian Valley	95602
Christofferson	93610
Chrome	95963
Chualar	93925
Chuckwalla Valley State Prison	92225
Chula Vista	91909-15
For specific Chula Vista Zip Codes call (619) 422-9221, or your local postmaster.	
Chula Vista Shopping Center (Part of Chula Vista)	91910
Cima	92323
Circle Oaks	94558
Cisco	95728
Citrus	91702
Citrus Heights	95610-11
	95621
For specific Citrus Heights Zip Codes call (916) 725-2060, or your local postmaster.	
City Hall (Part of San Francisco)	94102
City Heights (Part of San Diego)	92105
City of Industry	91714-16
For specific City of Industry Zip Codes call (818) 855-6699, or your local postmaster.	
City Shopping Center, The (Part of Orange)	92668
City Terrace	90063
Civic Center (Alameda County)	94612
Civic Center (Fresno County)	93721
Civic Center (Los Angeles County)	91401
Civic Center (Marin County)	94903
Civic Center (Orange County)	92701
Civic Center (Orange County)	90633
Clairemont (Part of San Diego)	92117
Clam Beach	95521
Claremont	91711
Clarksburg	95612
Clarksville	95682
Clay	95638
Clayton	94517
Clear Creek (Lassen County)	96137
Clear Creek (Siskiyou County)	96039
Clearlake	95422
Clearlake Oaks	95423
Clearlake Park (Part of Clearlake)	95424
Clearlake Riviera	95541
Clements	95227
Cleone	95437
Cliff Haven (Part of Newport Beach)	92663
Clifton	90277
Clingans Junction	93675
Clinter (Part of Fresno)	93703
Clinton	95642
Clio	96106
Clipper Gap	95603
Clipper Mills	95930
Cloverdale (Shasta County)	96007
Cloverdale (Sonoma County)	95425
Clovis	93611-13
For specific Clovis Zip Codes call (209) 299-3118, or your local postmaster.	
Clyde	94520

	ZIP
Coachella	92236
Coalinga	93210
Coarsegold	93614
Coarsegold Creek Ranch	93614
Coarsegold Highlands	93614
Cobb	95426
Cockatoo Grove (Part of Chula Vista)	91910
Coddington Center (Part of Santa Rosa)	95401
Coddingtown (Part of Santa Rosa)	95401
Codora	95970
Coffee Creek	96091
Cohasset	95926
Coit	93640
Cold Fork	96080
Cole (Part of West Hollywood)	90046
Coleville	96107
Colfax	95713
College City	95931
College Grove Center (Part of San Diego)	92115
College Heights (Kern County)	93305
College Heights (San Bernardino County)	91786
College Heights (Santa Cruz County)	95003
College Park (Part of Thousand Oaks)	91360
College Plaza (Part of Oceanside)	92056
Collegeville	95206
Collier (Part of Los Angeles)	91307
Collierville	95220
Collinsville	94585
Colma	94014
Coloma	95613
Colonial (Part of Sacramento)	95820
Colonial Juarez (Part of Fountain Valley)	92708
Colonnade (Part of San Jose)	95172
Colony	92363
Colorado	90404-05
	90411
For specific Colorado Zip Codes call (310) 576-2610, or your local postmaster.	
Colorado River Indian Reservation	85344
Colton	92313
	92324
For specific Colton Zip Codes call (909) 825-0505, or your local postmaster.	
Columbia	95310
Columbus (Part of Bakersfield)	93306
Colusa	95932
Commerce	90040
Commonwealth (Part of Fullerton)	92632
Community Center (Part of Simi Valley)	93065
Comptche	95427
Compton	90220-24
For specific Compton Zip Codes call (310) 638-0394, or your local postmaster.	
Concepcion	93436
Concord	94518-22
	94524
	94527
For specific Concord Zip Codes call (510) 687-1500, or your local postmaster.	
Concord Naval Weapons Station	94520
Concow	95969
Conejo	93662
Conejo Valley (Part of Thousand Oaks)	91358
Confidence	95383
Convict Lake	93514
Cool	95614
Copco	96064
Copper Cove	95228
Copperopolis	95228
Copperwood (Part of Oceanside)	92054
Copsey Creek	95457
Corbin Village (Part of Los Angeles)	91364
Corcoran	93212

* Area Zip Code   † Post Office Boxes

	ZIP
Cordelia	94585
Cornell	91301
Corning	96021
Corona	91718-20
For specific Corona Zip Codes call (909) 737-0451, or your local postmaster.	
Corona Del Mar (Part of Newport Beach)	92625
Coronado	92118*
	92178†
Coronado Naval Amphibious Base	92155
Corona Mall (Part of Corona)	91720
Coronita	91720
Corral Beach (Part of Malibu)	90265
Corralitos	95076
Correctional Training Facility	93960
Corte Madera	94925
	94976
For specific Corte Madera Zip Codes call (415) 924-4463, or your local postmaster.	
Coso Junction	93549
Costa Mesa	92626-28
For specific Costa Mesa Zip Codes call (714) 546-5330, or your local postmaster.	
Cosumnes	95683
Cotati	94931
Coto De Caza	92679
Cottage Springs	95223
Cotton Center	93257
Cottonwood	96022
Coulterville	95311
Country Club (Contra Costa County)	94556
Country Club (San Joaquin County)	95204
Country Club Acres	93644
Country Club Centre	95825
Country Club Estates	93401
Country Club Plaza	95825
Country Modern	93501
County East Mall (Part of Antioch)	94509
Court (Part of Martinez)	94553
Courtland	95615
Covelo	95428
Covina	91722-24
For specific Covina Zip Codes call (818) 966-8391, or your local postmaster.	
Covington Mill	96052
Cowan Heights	92705
Cowell (Part of Concord)	94518
Coy Flat	93208
Coyote (Part of San Jose)	95013
Craf	92359
Crafton	92359
Crenshaw (Part of Los Angeles)	90008
Crenshaw-Imperial (Part of Inglewood)	90303
Crescent (Part of Beverly Hills)	90213
Crescent City	95531
Crescent City North	95531
Crescent Mills	95934
Cressey	95312
Crest	92021
Crestline	92325
Crestmore	92316
Crestmore Heights	92509
Creston	93432
Crest Park	92326
Crestview Village	95608
Crockett	94525
Cromberg	96103
Crossroads (Part of Santa Rosa)	95401
Crossroads Plaza (Part of Pico Rivera)	90661
Crowley Lake (Part of Mammoth Lakes)	93546
Crown Point (Part of San Diego)	92109
Crows Landing	95313
Crutcher (Part of Paramount)	90723
Crystal Court (Part of Costa Mesa)	92626
Crystal Cove	92651
Cucamongo	91729-30

	ZIP
	91739
For specific Cucamongo Zip Codes call (909) 987-4641, or your local postmaster.	
Cudahy	90201
Cuesta-by-the-Sea	93402
Culver City	90230-33
For specific Culver City Zip Codes call (213) 391-6374, or your local postmaster.	
Cummings	95454
Cunningham	95472
Cupertino	95014-16
For specific Cupertino Zip Codes call (408) 452-4300, or your local postmaster.	
Curry Village	95389
Curtiss Heights (Part of Arcata)	95521
Curtner (Part of Fremont)	94539
Cutler	93615
Cutten	95534
Cuyama	93214
Cypress	90630
Cypress South (Part of Cypress)	90630
Daggett	92327
Dairyland	93610
Dairyville	96080
Dales	96080
Daly City	94014-17
For specific Daly City Zip Codes call (415) 756-2303, or your local postmaster.	
Dana	96028
Dana Point	92629
Danby	92332
Danville	94526
Daphnedale Park	96101
Dardanelle	95314
Darrah	95338
Darwin	93522
Daulton	93637
Davenport	95017
Davis	95616*
	95617†
Davis Creek	96108
Day	96056
Dayton	95928
Day Valley	95076
Deane Brothers	91350
Dearborn Park	94060
Death Valley	92328
Death Valley Junction	92328
Decoto (Part of Union City)	94587
Deep Springs	89010
Deer Creek	96061
Deer Lick Springs	96076
Deer Park (Napa County)	94576
Deer Park (Santa Cruz County)	95003
Del Aire (Los Angeles County)	90250
Del Amo (Part of Torrance)	90503
Del Amo Fashion Center (Part of Torrance)	90503
Delano	93215*
	93216†
Del Dios	92029
Delevan	95988
Delft Colony	93618
Delhi	95315
Delkern	93307
Delleker	96122
Del Loma	96010
Del Mar (San Diego County)	92014
Del Mar (Santa Cruz County)	95060
Del Mesa	94904
Del Monte Forest	93953
Del Monte Heights (Part of Seaside)	93955
Del Monte Park (Part of Pacific Grove)	93950
Del Monte Shopping Center (Part of Monterey)	93940
Del Paso Heights (Part of Sacramento)	95838
Del Rey	93616
Del Rey Oaks	93940
Del Rio Woods	95448
Del Rosa (Part of San Bernardino)	92404
Del Sur (Part of Lancaster)	93536

	ZIP
Delta (Part of Stockton)	95201*
	95202†
De Luz	92028
Del Valle (Part of Los Angeles)	90015
Delways	95695
Democrat Hot Springs	93301
Denair	95316
Denny	95527
Denverton	94585
Derby Acres	93224
Descanso	91916
Desert	92364
Desert Beach	92254
Desert Center	92239
Desert Hot Springs	92240-41
For specific Desert Hot Springs Zip Codes call (619) 329-6933, or your local postmaster.	
Desert Lake	93516
Desert Shores	92274
Desert View Highlands	93550
Des Moines (Part of La Habra)	90631
Deuel Vocational Institution	95376
Devils Den	93204
Devore	92407
Devore Heights	92407
Diablo	94528
Diamond (Part of Santa Ana)	92704
Diamond Bar	91765
Diamond Heights (Part of San Francisco)	94131
Diamond Springs	95619
Diamond Springs Heights	95619
Di Giorgio	93217
Dillon Beach	94929
Dimond (Part of Oakland)	94602
Dinkey Creek	93664
Dinsmore	95526
Dinuba	93618
Discovery Bay	94513
Disneyland (Part of Anaheim)	92802
Dixieland	92273
Dixon	95620
Dixon Lane-Meadow Creek	93514
Dobbins	95935
Dockweiler (Part of Los Angeles)	90007
Dogtown (Calaveras County)	95249
Dogtown (Marin County)	94924
Doheny Park	92624
Dollar Point	96145
Dollar Ranch (Part of Walnut Creek)	94595
Dolomite	93545
Dominguez (Part of Carson)	90810
Donlon (Part of Oxnard)	93030
Donner (Part of Truckee)	96162
Donner Lake	96161
Don Pedro Camp	95329
Dorrington	95223
Dorris	96023
Dos Palos	93620
Dos Rios	95429
Douglas City	96024
Douglas Flat	95229
Downey	90239-42
For specific Downey Zip Codes call (310) 923-5465, or your local postmaster.	
Downieville	95936
Downtown (Part of Bakersfield)	93303
Downtown (Part of Burbank)	91502*
	91503†
Downtown (Part of Long Beach)	90801†
	90802*
Downtown (Part of Manhattan Beach)	90266
Downtown (Part of Ontario)	91761
Downtown (Part of Redding)	96001
Downtown (Part of Redwood City)	94064
Downtown (Part of Riverside)	92501*
	92502†
Downtown (Part of San Bernardino)	92401*

	ZIP
	92402†
Downtown (Part of San Diego)	92101*
	92112†
Downtown (Part of Sonora)	95370
Downtown Plaza (Part of Sacramento)	95814
Doyle (Lassen County)	96109
Doyle (Tulare County)	93258
Drakesbad	96020
Dryden Flight Research Center	93523
Drytown	95699
Duarte	91009†
	91010*
Dublin	94568
Ducor	93218
Dulzura	91917
Duncans Mills	95430
Dunlap	93621
Dunlap Acres (Part of Yucaipa)	92399
Dunmovin	93549
Dunneville Corners	95023
Dunnigan	95937
Dunsmuir	96025
Durham	95938
Dustin Acres	93268
Dutch Flat	95714
Eagle Lake Resort	96130
Eagle Mountain	92239
Eagle Rock (Part of Los Angeles)	90041
Eagle Rock Plaza (Part of Los Angeles)	90041
Eagle Tree	95690
Eagleville	96110
Earlimart	93219
Earp	92242
East (Part of Downey)	90239
East Anaheim Shopping Center (Part of Anaheim)	92806
East Applegate	95703
East Bakersfield (Part of Bakersfield)	93305
East Baldy Mesa	92371
East Bluff (Part of Newport Beach)	92660
East Blythe	92225
East Compton	90221
East Downey (Part of Downey)	90239
East Foothills	95127
East Fresno (Part of Fresno)	93727
Eastgate (Part of Beverly Hills)	90211
East Gridley	95948
East Guernewood	95446
East Hemet	92544
East Highlands	92346
East Irvine (Part of Irvine)	92650
East La Mirada	90638
Eastland Shopping Center (Part of West Covina)	91791
East Linda	95901
East Long Beach (Part of Long Beach)	90804
East Los Angeles	90022
East Lynwood (Part of Lynwood)	90262
Eastmont (Part of Oakland)	94605
Eastmont Mall (Part of Oakland)	94605
East Nicolaus	95659
Easton	93706
East Palo Alto (San Mateo County)	94303
East Palo Alto (Santa Clara County)	94303
East Pasadena	91107*
	91117†
East Porterville	93257
East Quincy	95971
East Richmond Heights	94805
Eastridge (Part of San Jose)	95122*
	95173†
East San Diego (Part of San Diego)	92105
East San Gabriel	91775
East San Pedro (Part of Los Angeles)	90731
East Santa Cruz (Part of Santa Cruz)	95060
Eastside Acres	93622

***** Area Zip Code   † Post Office Boxes**

	ZIP
Eastside Ranch	93622
East Sonora	95370
East Stockton (Part of Stockton)	95205
	95215
For specific East Stockton Zip Codes call (209) 983-6325, or your local postmaster.	
East Tustin	92705
East Vallejo (Part of Vallejo)	94590
East Ventura (Part of Ventura)	93003
Eastview (Part of Rancho Palos Verdes)	90734
Echo Lake	95721
Echo Park (Part of Los Angeles)	90026
Edendale (Part of Los Angeles)	90026
Edgemar (Part of Pacifica)	94044
Edgemont (Part of Moreno Valley)	92508
Edgemont Acres	92523
Edgewater Estates	91977
Edgewood	96094
Edison	93220
Edmundson Acres	93203
Edwards	93523*
	93524†
Edwards AFB (census designated place)	93523
Edwards Air Force Base	93524
Edwards Estates	93523
Edwards Palisades	93523
Eel Rock	95554
Eight Mile House	95709
El Bonita	95446
El Cajon	92019-22
For specific El Cajon Zip Codes call (619) 442-0727, or your local postmaster.	
El Camino	96035
El Camino North Shopping Center (Part of Oceanside)	92054
El Casco Lake	92373
El Centro	92243*
	92244†
El Cerrito (Contra Costa County)	94530
El Cerrito (Riverside County)	91720
El Cerrito Plaza (Part of El Cerrito)	94530
Elders Corner	95603
Elderwood	93286
El Dorado	95623
El Dorado Hills	95762
Eldridge	95431
El Encanto Heights	93117
El Granada	94018
Elizabeth Lake	93532
Elk	95432
Elk Creek	95939
Elk Grove	95758-59
For specific Elk Grove Zip Codes call (916) 685-5700, or your local postmaster.	
Elk Grove	95624
Elkhorn	95012
Elk River	95503
Elk River Corners	95503
Ellwood	93118
El Macero (Part of Davis)	95618
Elmhurst (Part of Oakland)	94603
Elmira	95625
El Mirador	93247
El Mirage	92301
El Modena (Part of Orange)	92667
El Monte	91731-34
For specific El Monte Zip Codes call (818) 443-8995, or your local postmaster.	
El Monte (Part of Concord)	94521
El Monte Park	92040
Elm View	93609
Elmwood (Part of Berkeley)	94705
El Nido	95317
El Portal	95318
El Porto Beach (Part of Manhattan Beach)	90266
El Pueblo	94565
El Rio	93030
El Rio Villa	95694
El Segundo	90245

	ZIP
El Sereno (Part of Los Angeles)	90032
El Sobrante	94803*
	94820†
El Sueno	93110
El Toro	92610
	92630
For specific El Toro Zip Codes call (714) 837-1220, or your local postmaster.	
El Toro Marine Corps Air Station	92709
El Toro Station	92709
El Verano	95433
Elverta	95626
El Viejo	95353*
	95354†
Emandal	95490
Embarcadero Postal Center (Part of San Francisco)	94105
Emerald Bay	92651
Emerald Lake Hills	94062
Emeryville	94608*
	94662†
Emigrant Gap	95715
Empire	95319
Encanto (Part of San Diego)	92114
Encinal (Part of Sunnyvale)	94087
	94090
For specific Encinal Zip Codes call (408) 245-0617, or your local postmaster.	
Encinitas	92023-24
For specific Encinitas Zip Codes call (619) 753-6446, or your local postmaster.	
Encino (Part of Los Angeles)	91316
	91416
	91426
	91436
For specific Encino Zip Codes call (181) 908-6919, or your local postmaster.	
Enterprise (Part of Redding)	96001
Erwin Lake	92386
Escalle (Part of Larkspur)	94939
Escalon	95320
Escondido	92025-27
	92029-33
	92046
For specific Escondido Zip Codes call (619) 745-1912, or your local postmaster.	
Escondido Junction (Part of Oceanside)	92054
Escondido Village Mall (Part of Escondido)	92027
Esparto	95627
Esplanade, The	93300
Essex	92332
Estrella	93451
Estudillo (Part of San Leandro)	94577
Etiwanda (Part of Rancho Cucamonga)	91739
Etna	96027
Ettersburg	95542
Eucalyptus Hills	92040
Eugene	95230
Eureka	95501-03
For specific Eureka Zip Codes call (707) 442-1768, or your local postmaster.	
Exeter	93221
Fairfax (Kern County)	93307
Fairfax (Marin County)	94930*
	94978†
Fairfield	94533
Fairhaven	95564
Fairmead	93610
Fairmont	93534
Fairmont Hospital	94578
Fairmont Terrace	94577
Fairmont (Part of El Cerrito)	94530
Fair Oaks (Sacramento County)	95628
Fair Oaks (San Joaquin County)	95205
Fairview (Alameda County)	94542
Fairview (Trinity County)	96052
Fairview (Tulare County)	93238

	ZIP
Fairway Park (Part of Hayward)	94544
Falk	95503
Fallbrook	92028*
	92088†
Fallbrook Junction	92055
Fallbrook Mall (Part of Los Angeles)	91307
Fallen Leaf	96151
Falling Springs	91702
Fallon	94971
Fall River Mills	96028
Fallsvale	92339
Famoso	93250
Fancher	93727
Farmers Market (Part of Los Angeles)	90036
Farmersville	93223
Farmington	95230
Fashion Valley Center (Part of San Diego)	92108
Fawnskin	92333
Fay Creek	93283
Feather Falls	95940
Feather River	96020
Feather River Inn	96103
Feather River Park	96103
Federal (Part of Anaheim)	92805
Federal (Part of Covina)	91723
Federal (Part of Los Angeles)	90012-13
For specific Federal Zip Codes call (213) 586-1723, or your local postmaster.	
Federal Building (San Francisco County)	94102
Federal Building (Ventura County)	93030
Federal Correctional Institution	94568
Federal Prison Camp	93516
Federal Terrace (Part of Vallejo)	94590
Fellows	93224
Felterwood	95531
Felton (census designated place)	95041
Felton	95018
Felton Grove	95018
Fernbridge	95540
Fernbrook	92065
Ferndale	95536
Fern Valley	92549
Fernwood	90290
Fetters Hot Springs	95476
Fetters Hot Springs-Agua Caliente	95476
Fickle Hill	95521
Fiddletown	95629
Fieldbrook	95521
Fields Landing	95537
Fig Garden (Part of Fresno)	93704
Fig Garden Village (Part of Fresno)	93704
Figueroa (Part of Los Angeles)	91001
Fillmore	93015*
	93016†
Fine Gold	93643
Finley	95435
Firebaugh	93622
Fire Mountain	96061
Firestone (Part of South Gate)	90280
Firestone Park	90001
First Street (Part of Oceanside)	92049†
	92054*
Fish Camp	93623
Fish Springs	93513
Fisk (Part of San Francisco)	94122
Fitchburg (Part of Oakland)	94621
Five Brooks	94950
Five Mile Terrace	95667
Five Points (Fresno County)	93624
Five Points (San Diego County)	92110
Flamingo Heights	92284
Flinn Springs	92021
Flint (Part of Los Angeles)	90057
Flintridge (Part of La Canada Flintridge)	91011
Florence	90001
Florence-Graham	90001

	ZIP
Florin	95828-29
For specific Florin Zip Codes call (916) 383-1606, or your local postmaster.	
Florin Mall (Part of Sacramento)	95823
Floriston	96111
Flosden Acres (Part of Vallejo)	94590
Flournoy	96029
Flower Village	93305
Fly in Acres	95223
Folsom	95630*
	95763†
Folsom Junction (Part of Folsom)	95630
Fontana	92334-37
For specific Fontana Zip Codes call (909) 822-8039, or your local postmaster.	
Foothill Farms	95841
Forbestown	95941
Ford City	93268
Forest	95910
Foresta	95389
Forest Falls	92339
Forest Glen	96041
Foresthill	95631
Forest Home (Amador County)	95669
Forest Home (San Bernardino County)	92339
Forest Knolls	94933
Forest Lake	95426
Forest Park	95006
Forest Ranch	95942
Forest Springs (Nevada County)	95949
Forest Springs (Santa Cruz County)	95006
Forestville	95436
Forks of Salmon	96031
Forrest Park	91350
Fort Baker	94965
Fort Barry	94965
Fort Bidwell	96112
Fort Bidwell Indian Reservation	96112
Fort Bragg	95437
Fort Cronkhite	94965
Fort Dick	95538
Fort Goff	96086
Fort Hunter Liggett	93928
Fort Independence Indian Reservation	93526
Fort Irwin	92310
Fort Jones	96032
Fort Mason (Part of San Francisco)	94123
Fort McArthur (Part of Los Angeles)	90731
Fort Miley (Part of San Francisco)	94121
Fort Mohave Indian Reservation	92363
Fort Ord	93941
Fort Ord Village (Part of Seaside)	93941
Fort Seward	95511
Fort Sutter (Part of Sacramento)	95816
Fortuna	95540
Fort Yuma	85364
Fort Yuma Indian Reservation	92283
Foster City	94404
Fountainhead Springs	93257
Fountain Valley	92708*
	92728†
Four Corners (Madera County)	93637
Four Corners (Kramer Junction)	93516
Four Corners (Part of Twentynine Palms)	92277
Fouts Springs	95979
Fowler	93625
Fox Creek	95528
Fox Hills (Part of Culver City)	90233
Fox Hills Mall (Part of Culver City)	90230
Fox Plaza (Part of San Francisco)	94102
Foy (Part of Los Angeles)	90017
Franciscan Park (Part of Daly City)	94014
Franklin (Napa County)	94559

* **Area Zip Code**   † **Post Office Boxes**

	ZIP
Franklin (Sacramento County)	95758
Frazier Park	93222†
	93225*
Fredericksburg	96120
Freedom	95019
Freeman Junction	93527
Freestone	95472
Fremont	94536-39
	94555
For specific Fremont Zip Codes call (510) 792-8654, or your local postmaster.	
Fremont Hub Shopping Center (Part of Fremont)	94538
French Camp	95231
French Corral	95960
French Gulch	96033
Fresh Pond	95726
Freshwater	95503
Freshwater Corners	95503
Fresno	93650
	93701-94
For specific Fresno Zip Codes call (209) 487-7700, or your local postmaster.	
Fresno Fashion Fair (Part of Fresno)	93710
Friant	93626
Friendly Hills	92252
Fruitland	95554
Fruitridge	95820
Fruitvale (Alameda County)	94601
Fruitvale (Kern County)	93308
Fruto	95988
Fullerton	92631-35
For specific Fullerton Zip Codes call (714) 525-3893, or your local postmaster.	
Fulton	95439
Gabilan (Part of Salinas)	93906
Gabilan Acres	93906
Galleria at South Bay, The (Part of Redondo Beach)	90277
Galleria at Tyler (Part of Riverside)	92503
Gallinas	94903
Galt	95632
Garberville	95542
Gardena	90247-49
For specific Gardena Zip Codes call (310) 327-9114, or your local postmaster.	
Garden Acres	95205
Garden Farms	93422
Garden Gate Village (Part of Cupertino)	95014
Garden Grove	92640-45
For specific Garden Grove Zip Codes call (714) 537-1301, or your local postmaster.	
Garden Valley	95633
Garden Village (Part of Daly City)	94015
Garey	93454
Garfield	93205
Garlock	93554
Gasoline Alley	95603
Gas Point	96022
Gasquet	95543
Gateway (Los Angeles County)	90232
Gateway (Nevada County)	96161
Gaviota	93117
Gazelle	96034
Geary (Part of San Francisco)	94121
Gene	92267
Genesee	95983
Genesee Plaza (Part of San Diego)	92111
George AFB (census designated place)	92392
George Air Force Base	92394
Georgetown	95634
George Washington (Part of San Diego)	92103
Gerber	96035
Gerber-Las Flores	96035
Geyserville	95441
Gilman Hot Springs	92583
Gilroy	95020*
	95021†
Glamis	92227
Glassell (Part of Los Angeles)	90065

	ZIP
Glen Arbor	95005
Glen Avon	92509
Glenbrook (Lake County)	95461
Glenbrook (Nevada County)	95945
Glenburn	96028
Glencoe	95232
Glencove (Part of Vallejo)	94590
Glendale (Los Angeles County)	91201-26
	91221-22
	91225-26
For specific Glendale Zip Codes call (818) 502-3202, or your local postmaster.	
Glendale (Humbolt County)	95521
Glendale Galleria (Part of Glendale)	91210
Glendora	91740-41
For specific Glendora Zip Codes call (818) 335-6957, or your local postmaster.	
Glen Ellen	95442
Glenhaven	95443
Glen Martin	92305
Glenn	95943
Glennville	93226
Glenoaks (Part of Burbank)	91504
Glenshire-Devonshire	96161
Glenview (Los Angeles County)	90290
Glenview (San Diego County)	92021
Glenwood	95066
Glorietta (Part of Orinda)	94563
Goffs	92332
Golden Hill (Part of San Diego)	92102
Golden Hills (Calaveras County)	95249
Golden Hills (Kern County)	93561
Golden Valley (Part of Santa Clarita)	91350
Gold Flat	95959
Gold Gulch	95018
Gold Hill	95667
Gold River	95670
Gold Run	95717
Goleta	93116-18
For specific Goleta Zip Codes call (805) 564-2266, or your local postmaster.	
Gonzales	93926
Goodyears Bar	95944
Gorda	93920
Gordon Valley	94585
Gorman	93243
Goshen	93227
Government Island (Part of Alameda)	94501
Graeagle	96103
Graham	90002
Granada Hills (Part of Los Angeles)	91344
Grand Avenue (Part of Santa Ana)	92705
Grand Central (Part of Glendale)	91201*
	91221†
Grand Lake (Part of Oakland)	94610
Grand Terrace	92313
Grandview	92311
Grangeville	93230
Granite Bay	95746
Granite Hill (Part of Grass Valley)	95945
Granite Hills	92019
Graniteville	95959
Grantville (Part of San Diego)	92120
Grapevine	93243
Grass Valley	95945
	95949
For specific Grass Valley Zip Codes call (916) 273-7233, or your local postmaster.	
Graton	95444
Grayson	95363
Greeley	93307
Greeley Hill	95311
Green (Part of Los Angeles)	90037
Greenacres	93308
Greenbrae	94904

	ZIP
Greenbrook (Part of Danville)	94526
Greenfield	93927
Greenmead (Part of Los Angeles)	90059
Green Meadows (Part of Davis)	95616
Greenspot	92359
Green Valley	91350
Green Valley Estates	94585
Green Valley Lake	92341
Greenview	96037
Greenview Acres (Part of Arcata)	95521
Greenville	95947
Greenwich Village (Part of Thousand Oaks)	91360
Greenwood	95635
Grenada	96038
Gridley	95948
Griffith (Part of Los Angeles)	90039
Grimes	95950
Grizzly Flats	95636
Grossmont (Part of La Mesa)	91942
Groveland	95321
Groveland-Big Oak Flat	95321
Grover Beach	93433*
	93483†
Guadalupe	93434
Gualala	95445
Guasti (Part of Ontario)	91743
Guatay	91931
Guerneville	95446
Guernewood Park	95446
Guernsey	93230
Guinda	95637
Gustine	95322
Hacienda (Alameda County)	94566
Hacienda (Sonoma County)	95436
Hacienda Heights	91745
Haiwee	93549
Halcyon	93420
Hales Grove	95585
Half Moon Bay	94019
Hall (Part of Union City)	94587
Halloran Springs	92364
Halls Corner	93245
Hallwood	95901
Hamburg	96050
Hamilton (Part of Palo Alto)	94301*
	94302†
Hamilton City	95951
Hammer Ranch (Part of Stockton)	95209
	95219
	95269
For specific Hammer Ranch Zip Codes call (209)957-7972, or your local postmaster.	
Hammil	93514
Hammonton	95901
Hancock (Part of Los Angeles)	90044
Hanford	93230-32
For specific Hanford Zip Codes call (209) 582-2507, or your local postmaster.	
Happy Camp	96039
Harbin Springs	95461
Harbin Springs Annex	95461
Harbison Canyon	92020
Harbor City (Part of Los Angeles)	90710
Harbor Island (Part of Newport Beach)	92660
Harbor Side (Part of Chula Vista)	91911
Hardman Center (Part of Riverside)	92504
Hardwick	93230
Harlem Springs (Part of Highland)	92346
Harmony	93435
Harmony Grove	92029
Harris	95542
Harrison Park	92036
Hartland	93603
Harvard	92398
Haskell Creek Homesites	96124
Haskins Resort	95971
Hat Creek	96040
Hathaway Pines	95233
Hatton Fields	93923
Havasu Lake	92363

	ZIP
Havilah	93518
Hawaiian Gardens	90716
Hawkins Bar	95563
Hawkinsville	96097
Hawthorne	90250*
	90251†
Hayfork	96041
Hayward	94540-45
	94557
For specific Hayward Zip Codes call (510) 783-2400, or your local postmaster.	
Hayward Highlands (Part of Hayward)	94542
Hazard	90063
Healdsburg	95448
Heather Glen	95703
Heber	92249
Helena	96048
Helendale	92342
Helm	93627
Hemet	92543-46
For specific Hemet Zip Codes call (909) 658-3263, or your local postmaster.	
Henderson (Part of Porterville)	93258
Henderson Center (Part of Eureka)	95501
Henderson Village	95240
Henley	96044
Henleyville	96021
Herald	95638
Hercules	94547
Heritage Ranch	93446
Herlong	96113
Hermosa Beach	90254
Hernandez	95023
Herndon (Part of Fresno)	93711
Hesperia	92340†
	92345*
Heyer	94546
Hickman	95323
Hidden Hills	91302
Hidden Lake Estate	93637
Hidden Lakes Estates	93626
Hidden Meadows	92025
Hidden Valley	95650
Hidden Valley Lake	95457
Highgrove	92507
Highland	92346
Highland Park (Kern County)	93308
Highland Park (Los Angeles County)	90042
Highlands	94402
Highway City (Part of Fresno)	93706
Highway Highlands (Part of Glendale)	91214
Hilarita (Part of Tiburon)	94920
Hildreth	93645
Hillcrest (Los Angeles County)	90301
Hillcrest (San Diego County)	92103
Hillcrest Center (Part of Bakersfield)	93306
Hillcrest Park	94590
Hillsborough	94010
Hillsdale (Part of San Mateo)	94403
Hillsdale Shopping Center (Part of San Mateo)	94403
Hills Flat (Part of Grass Valley)	95945
Hilltop (Contra Costa County)	94806
Hilltop (Kern County)	93307
Hillview (Part of San Jose)	95121
Hilmar	95324
Hilt	96044
Hilton	95436
Hinkley	92347
Hiouchi Valley	95531
Hirschdale	96161
Hi Vista	93535
Hoaglin	95595
Hobart (Part of Vernon)	90058
Hobart Mills	96161
Hobergs	95426
Hodge	92311
Holiday (Part of Anaheim)	92802
Holiday Lake (Part of Morgan Hill)	95037
Hollister	95023*
	95024†
Hollydale (Los Angeles County)	90280

	ZIP
Hollydale (Sonoma	
County)	95436
Hollywood (Part of Los	
Angeles)	90027-28
For specific Hollywood Zip	
Codes call (213) 586-1723, or	
your local postmaster.	
Hollywood Beach	93035
Hollywood by the Sea	93035
Hollywood Riviera (Part of	
Torrance)	90277
Holmes	95569
Holt	95234
Holtville	92250
Holy City	95044
Home Garden	93239
Home Gardens	91720
Homeland	92548
Homestead (Kern County)	93527
Homestead (Riverside	
County)	92539
Homestead (San Joaquin	
County)	95206
Homestead Valley	94941
Homewood	96141
Honby	91350
Honcut	95965
Honeydew	95545
Hood	95639
Hooker	96022
Hookston (Part of	
Pleasant Hill)	94523
Hoopa	95546
Hoopa Valley Indian	
Reservation	95546
Hope Ranch	93105
Hopeton	95369
Hope Valley	96120
Hopland	95449
Hornbrook	96044
Hornitos	95325
Horse Creek	96050
Horseshoe Bar	95650
Horton Plaza (Part of San	
Diego)	92101
Howard Landing	95690
Howest (Part of	
Burlingame)	94010
Hub City (Part of	
Compton)	90220
Hudson	95355-57
For specific Hudson Zip Codes	
call (209) 551-9444, or your	
local postmaster.	
Hughes (Part of Fresno)	93705
Hughson	95326
Humboldt Bay CGAS	95521
Humboldt Hill	95537
Hume	93628
Humphreys Station	93611
Hunters Valley	95325
Huntington (Part of	
Huntington Beach)	92646
Huntington Beach	92605
	92615
	92646-49
For specific Huntington Beach	
Zip Codes call (714) 847-5665,	
or your local postmaster.	
Huntington Center (Part of	
Huntington Beach)	92647
Huntington Harbor (Part of	
Huntington Beach)	92649
Huntington Lake	93629
Huntington Park	90255
Huron	93234
Hyampom	96046
Hyde Park (Part of Los	
Angeles)	90043
Hydesville	95547
Ida Jean Haxton (Part of	
Huntington Beach)	92647
Idlewild	93260
Idria	95023
Idyllwild	92549
Idyllwild-Pine Cove	92549
Ignacio	94947
Igo	96047
Imola	94558
Imperial	92251
Imperial Beach	91932-33
For specific Imperial Beach Zip	
Codes call (619) 423-4545, or	
your local postmaster.	
Imperial Crest (Part of	
Norwalk)	90650
Incline	95318
Independence	93526
Indian Beach	95443

	ZIP
Indian Falls	95934
Indian Hill Mall (Part of	
Pomona)	91767
Indian Lakes Estates	93614
Indian Mission	93602
Indianola	95503
Indian Springs	93644
Indian Wells (Kern	
County)	93527
Indian Wells (Riverside	
County)	92210
Indio	92201-03
For specific Indio Zip Codes call	
(619) 347-3442, or your local	
postmaster.	
Industrial (Part of Santa	
Ana)	92705
Inglenook	95437
Ingleside (Part of San	
Francisco)	94112
Inglewood	90301-12
For specific Inglewood Zip	
Codes call (310) 301-1230, or	
your local postmaster.	
Ingot	96008
Inland Center (Part of San	
Bernardino)	92408
Inskip	95978
Interlaken	95076
Inverness	94937
Inverness Park	94956
Inwood	96088
Inyokern	93527
Ione	95640
Iowa Hill	95713
Irish Beach	95459
Iron Mountain	92242
Irvine	92619
	92650
	92709-10
	92713-20
For specific Irvine Zip Codes	
call (714) 474-0407, or your	
local postmaster.	
Irvington (Part of Fremont)	94538
Irwin	95324
Irwindale	91706
Irwin Estates	92311
Island Mountain	95542
Isla Vista	93117
Isleton	95641
Ivanhoe	93235
Ivanpah	92364
Jacinto Grange	95943
Jackie Robinson	91103-04
For specific Jackie Robinson	
Zip Codes call (818) 304-7134,	
or your local postmaster.	
Jackson	95642
Jackson Gate (Part of	
Jackson)	95642
Jacumba	91934
Jalama	93436
Jamesburg	93924
Jamestown	95327
Jamul	91935
Janesville	96114
Japan Center (Part of San	
Francisco)	94115
Jarbo	95965
Jelly	96080
Jenner	95450
Jenny Lind	95252
Jesmond Dene	92026
Jimtown	95448
Johannesburg	93528
John Adams (Part of San	
Diego)	92116
Johnsondale	93238
Johnson Park	96013
John Steinbeck (Part of	
Salinas)	93901
Johnstonville	96130
Johnstown	92021
Johnsville	96103
Jolon	93928
Jonesville	95942
Joshua Hills (Part of	
Palmdale)	93550
Joshua Tree	92252
Julian	92036
Junction City	96048
June Lake	93529
June Lake Junction	93529
Juniper Hills	93543
Juniper Lake Resort	96020
Juniper Springs	92548
Jurupa	92509

	ZIP
Kaiser Center (Part of	
Oakland)	94612
Kaiser Eagle Mountain	92239
Kaweah	93237
Keddie	95971
Keeler	93530
Keene	93531
Kelly	96020
Kelsey	95643
Kelseyville	95451
Kelso	92351
Kennedy Meadow	95370
Kennedy Ranch	95449
Kensington	94707-08
For specific Kensington Zip	
Codes call (510) 649-3107, or	
your local postmaster.	
Kensington Park (Part of	
San Diego)	92116
Kentfield	94904
Kentwood-In-The-Pines	92036
Kent Woodlands	94904
Kenwood	95452
Keough Hot Springs	93514
Kerman	93630
Kern City (Part of	
Bakersfield)	93309
Kern Homes	93308
Kernvale	93240
Kernville	93238
Keswick	96001
Kettleman City	93239
Kevet (Part of Santa	
Paula)	93060
Keyes	95328
Kilkare Woods	94586
King (Part of Santa Ana)	92706
King City	93930
King Island	95219
King Salmon	95503
Kings Beach	96143
Kingsburg	93631
Kings Mall (Part of	
Hanford)	93230
Kingvale	95728
Kirkville	95645
Kirkwood (Alpine County)	95646
Kirkwood (Tehama	
County)	96021
Kit Carson	95644
Klamath	95548
Klamath Glen	95548
Klamath River	96050
Klinefelter	92363
Kneeland	95549
Knightsen	94548
Knights Ferry	95361
Knights Landing	95645
Knob	96076
Knotts Berry Farm (Part of	
Buena Park)	90620
Knowles	93653
Konocti	95451
Kono Tayee	95443
Korbel	95550
Krug (Part of St. Helena)	94574
Kyburz	95720
La Barr Meadows	95949
La Canada (Part of La	
Canada Flintridge)	91011
La Canada Flintridge	91011*
	91012†
La Costa (Los Angeles	
County)	90265
La Costa (San Diego	
County)	92008
La Costa Beach (Part of	
Malibu)	90265
La Crescenta	91214*
	91224†
La Crescenta-Montrose	91214
La Cresta (Kern County)	93305
La Cresta (San Diego	
County)	92020
La Cumbre Plaza (Part of	
Santa Barbara)	93105
Ladera	94028
Ladera Heights	90045
Lafayette	94549
La Grange	95329
Laguna	95758
Laguna Beach	92607
	92651-52
	92677
For specific Laguna Beach Zip	
Codes call (714) 494-4122, or	
your local postmaster.	
Laguna Creek	95758
Laguna Hills	92653*

	ZIP
	92654†
Laguna Hills Mall (Part of	
Laguna Hills)	92653
Laguna Lake (Part of San	
Luis Obispo)	93405
Laguna Niguel	92607
	92651
	92677
For specific Laguna Niguel Zip	
Codes call (714) 495-1510, or	
your local postmaster.	
Lagunitas	94938
Lagunitas-Forest Knolls	94933
La Habra	90631-33
For specific La Habra Zip	
Codes call (714) 992-5620, or	
your local postmaster.	
La Habra Fashion Square	
(Part of La Habra)	90631
La Habra Heights	90631
La Honda	94020
Lairport (Part of El	
Segundo)	90245
La Jolla (Part of San	
Diego)	92037-39
	92092-93
For specific La Jolla Zip Codes	
call (619) 454-7139, or your	
local postmaster.	
La Jolla (Part of Placentia)	92670
La Jolla Indian	
Reservation	92025
Lake Alpine	95223
Lake Arrowhead	92352
Lake Arrowhead (census	
designated place)	92317
Lake Christopher (Part of	
South Lake Tahoe)	96150
Lake City	96115
Lake Earl	95531
Lake Elsinore	92530-32
For specific Lake Elsinore Zip	
Codes call (909) 674-3720, or	
your local postmaster.	
Lake Forest	96145
Lakehead	96051
Lake Henshaw	92070
Lake Hills Estates	95762
Lake Hughes	93532
Lake Isabella	93240
Lake Kirkwood	95646
Lakeland Village	92530
Lake Los Angeles	93550
Lake Madera Country	
Estates	93637
Lake Marie Estates	93455
Lake Mary	93546
Lake Morena Village	91906
Lake Murray (Part of San	
Diego)	92119
Lake Nacimiento	93446
Lake Of The Pines	95603
Lake of the Woods	93225
Lake Pillsbury Homesites	95469
Lake Pillsbury Resort	95469
Lakeport	95453
Lake San Marcos	92069
Lakeshore	93634
Lakeshore Lodge	95971
Lakeside	92040
Lakeside Farms	92040
Lake Tamarisk	92239
Lakeview (Kern County)	93307
Lakeview (Riverside	
County)	92567
Lakeview (San Diego	
County)	92040
Lake View Terrace (Part	
of Los Angeles)	91342
Lakeville	94954
Lake Williams Estates	92386
Lakewood	90711-15
For specific Lakewood Zip	
Codes call (310) 866-1741, or	
your local postmaster.	
Lakewood Center Mall	
(Part of Lakewood)	90712
La Loma (Part of	
Modesto)	95354
Lamanda Park (Part of	
Pasadena)	91107
La Mesa	91941-44
For specific La Mesa Zip Codes	
call (619) 466-3283, or your	
local postmaster.	
La Mirada	90637†
	90638*
La Mirada Mall (Part of La	
Mirada)	90638

* **Area Zip Code**   † **Post Office Boxes**

	ZIP
Lamont	93241
Lanare	93656
Lancaster	93534-39
	93584-86

For specific Lancaster Zip Codes call (805) 948-1691, or your local postmaster.

Landers	92285
Land Park (Part of Sacramento)	95822
Landscape (Part of Berkeley)	94707
Lansdale (Part of San Anselmo)	94960
La Palma	90623
La Panza	93432
La Patera	93117
La Porte	95981
La Puente	91744-49

For specific La Puente Zip Codes call (818) 968-9311, or your local postmaster.

La Quinta	92253
Larabee	95569
La Riviera	95826
Larkfield	95403
Larkfield-Wikiup	95403
Larkspur	94939
Larson Tract	93240
Larwin Plaza (Part of Vallejo)	94590
Las Cruces	93117
La Selva Beach	95076
Las Flores (Los Angeles County)	90265
Las Flores (Tehama County)	96035
La Sierra (Part of Riverside)	92505*
	92515†
La Sierra Heights (Part of Riverside)	92505
Las Lomas	95076
Las Posas Estates	93010
Lathrop	95330
La Tijera (Part of Los Angeles)	90043
Laton	93242
Latrobe	95682
Laurel (Part of Oakland)	94619
Laurel Canyon	91605-06

For specific Laurel Canyon Zip Codes call (818) 503-0695, or your local postmaster.

Laurel Plaza (Part of Los Angeles)	91606
Laurelwood (Part of Los Angeles)	91604
La Verne	91750
La Vina	93637
Lawndale	90260-61

For specific Lawndale Zip Codes call (310) 679-0121, or your local postmaster.

Lawrence (Part of Danville)	94506
Laws	93514
Layman	96103
Laytonville	95454
Lazy Acre	93311
Lebec	93243
Lee	96020
Lee Vining	93541
Leggett	95585
Le Grand	95333
Leisure Acres	93643
Leisure Town (Part of Vacaville)	95687
Leisure World (Part of Seal Beach)	90740
Leliter	93527
Lemoncove	93244
Lemon Grove	91945*
	91946†
Lemon Heights	92705
Lemoore	93245
Lemoore Naval Air Station	93245
Lennox	90304
Lenwood	92311
Leona Valley	93551
Leucadia (Part of Encinitas)	92024
Lewiston	96052
Lexington Hills	95044
Liberty Acres	90250
Liberty Farms	95620
Libfarm	95620
Lido Isle (Part of Newport Beach)	92663

	ZIP
Likely	96116
Lily Valley	95255
Limco	93060
Lincoln	95648
Lincoln Acres	91947
Lincoln Heights (Part of Los Angeles)	90031
Lincoln Village (Los Angeles County)	90810
Lincoln Village (San Joaquin County)	95207
Linda	95901
Linda Vista (Los Angeles County)	91103
Linda Vista (San Diego County)	92111
Linda Vista (Santa Clara County)	95127
Lind Cove	93221
Linden	95236
Linden Avenue (Part of South San Francisco)	94080
Lindenwood (Part of Menlo Park)	94027
Lindsay	93247
Lingard	95333
Linnell	93292
Linns Valley	93226
Litchfield	96117
Little Lake	93542
Little Norway	95721
Little Reed Heights (Part of Tiburon)	94920
Littleriver	95456
Littlerock	93543
Little Saigon (Part of Westminster)	92683
Little Shasta	96064
Little Valley	96053
Live Oak (Santa Cruz County)	95062
Live Oak (Sutter County)	95953
Live Oak Acres (Tehama County)	96080
Live Oak Acres (Ventura County)	93022
Live Oak Canyon	91750
Live Oak Springs	91905
Livermore	94550*
	94551†
Livingston	95334
Llano	93544
Lobitos	94019
Lobo (Part of Stanton)	90680
Loch Lomond	95426
Locke	95690
Lockeford	95237
Lockhart	92347
Lockwood	93932
Lodgepole	93262
Lodi	95240-42

For specific Lodi Zip Codes call (209) 369-9545, or your local postmaster.

Lodoga	95979
Logan Heights (Part of San Diego)	92113
Loleta	95551
Loma (Part of Long Beach)	90814
Loma Linda	92354
Loma Mar	94021
Loma Portal (Part of San Diego)	92110
Loma Rica	95901
Lomas Santa Fe (Part of Solana Beach)	92075
Loma Verda (Part of Novato)	94949
Lomita	90717
Lomita Park (Part of San Bruno)	94066
Lompico	95018
Lompoc	93436-38

For specific Lompoc Zip Codes call (805) 736-4561, or your local postmaster.

London	93618
Lone Pine	93545
Lone Pine Indian Reservation	93545
Long Barn	95335
Long Beach	90801-53

For specific Long Beach Zip Codes call (213) 494-2371, or your local postmaster.

COLLEGES & UNIVERSITIES

	ZIP
California State University-Long Beach	90840

FINANCIAL INSTITUTIONS

Farmers & Merchants Bank of Long Beach	90802
Harbor Bank	90802
National Bank of Long Beach	90807

HOSPITALS

Long Beach Community Hospital	90804
Long Beach Memorial Medical Center	90806
St. Mary Medical Center	90801
Veterans Affairs Medical Center	90822

HOTELS/MOTELS

Hyatt Regency Long Beach	90802
Hotel Queen Mary	90802
Ramada Inn-Long Beach	90804

MILITARY INSTALLATIONS

Long Beach Naval Shipyard	90810
Naval Regional Contracting Center Detachment	90822
Supervisor of Shipbuilding, Conversion and Repair, Long Beach	90822
11th Coast Guard District, Long Beach	90802

Long Beach Plaza (Part of Long Beach)	90802
Longvale	95490
Lonoak	93930
Lonoke (Part of Gilroy)	95020
Lookout	96054
Lookout Ranchettes	96054
Loomis	95650
Loomis Corners	96003
Loraine	93518
Loree Estates	95014
Los Alamitos	90720*
	90721†
Los Alamitos Naval Air Station	90720
Los Alamos	93440
Los Altos	94022-24

For specific Los Altos Zip Codes call (415) 948-6000, or your local postmaster.

Los Altos Hills	94022
Los Altos Shopping Center (Part of Long Beach)	90815
Los Amigos (Part of Downey)	90240
Los Angeles	90001-68
	90070-99
	90101

For specific Los Angeles Zip Codes call (213) 586-1737, or your local postmaster.

COLLEGES & UNIVERSITIES

California State University-Los Angeles	90032
Loyola Marymount University	90045
Mount Saint Mary's College	90049
Northrop University	90301
Occidental College	90041
University of California-Los Angeles	90024
University of Southern California	90089

FINANCIAL INSTITUTIONS

American International Bank	90017
Bank of California, National Association	90071
Bankers Trust Company of California, N.A.	90071
California Commerce Bank	90017
California Federal Bank	90036
California Korea Bank	90010

	ZIP
Canadian Imperial Bank of Commerce	90071
Cathay Bank	90012
Century Bank	90010
Dai-Ichi Kangyo Bank of California	90013
East-West Federal Bank, F.S.B.	90012
Family Savings Bank, F.S.B.	90016
Far East National Bank	90012
First Business Bank	90071
First Interstate Bank of California	90017
First Los Angeles Bank	90067
First Public Savings Bank, F.S.B.	90012
Founders National Bank of Los Angeles	90008
General Bank	90012
Guardian Bank	90017
Hancock Savings Bank	90004
Hanmi Bank	90010
Highland Federal Bank	90041
Home Savings of America, F.S.B.	90010
Manufacturers Bank	90071
Marathon National Bank	90064
Mercantile National Bank	90067
Metrobank	90024
Standard Savings Bank	90012
Sterling Bank	90010
Tokai Bank of California	90014
Western Bank	90024

HOSPITALS

California Medical Center-Los Angeles	90015
Cedars-Sinai Medical Center	90048
Childrens Hospital of Los Angeles	90027
Hospital of the Good Samaritan	90017
Kaiser Foundation Hospital	90027
LAC-King-Drew Medical Center	90059
LAC-University of Southern California Medical Center	90033
St. Vincent Medical Center	90057
University of California Los Angeles Medical Center	90024
Veterans Affairs Medical Center-West Los Angeles	90073

HOTELS/MOTELS

Biltmore Hotel	90071
Holiday Inn-Downtown	90017
Hyatt Regency Los Angeles-at Broadway Place	90017
Los Angeles Hilton & Towers	90017
New Otani Hotel & Garden	90012
Sheraton Grande	90071
University Hilton-Los Angeles	90007
Westin Bonaventure	90071

MILITARY INSTALLATIONS

Los Angeles Air Force Station	90009
Military Airlift Command United States Army Engineer District, Los Angeles	90045
	90053
Los Banos	93635
Los Berros	93420
Los Cerritos Center (Part of Cerritos)	90703
Los Coyotes Indian Reservation	92086
Los Deltos	93622
Los Feliz (Part of Los Angeles)	90027
Los Gatos	95030-32

For specific Los Gatos Zip Codes call (408) 452-4300, or your local postmaster.

Los Molinos	96055
Los Nietos	90606
Los Olivos	93441

---

* Area Zip Code   † Post Office Boxes

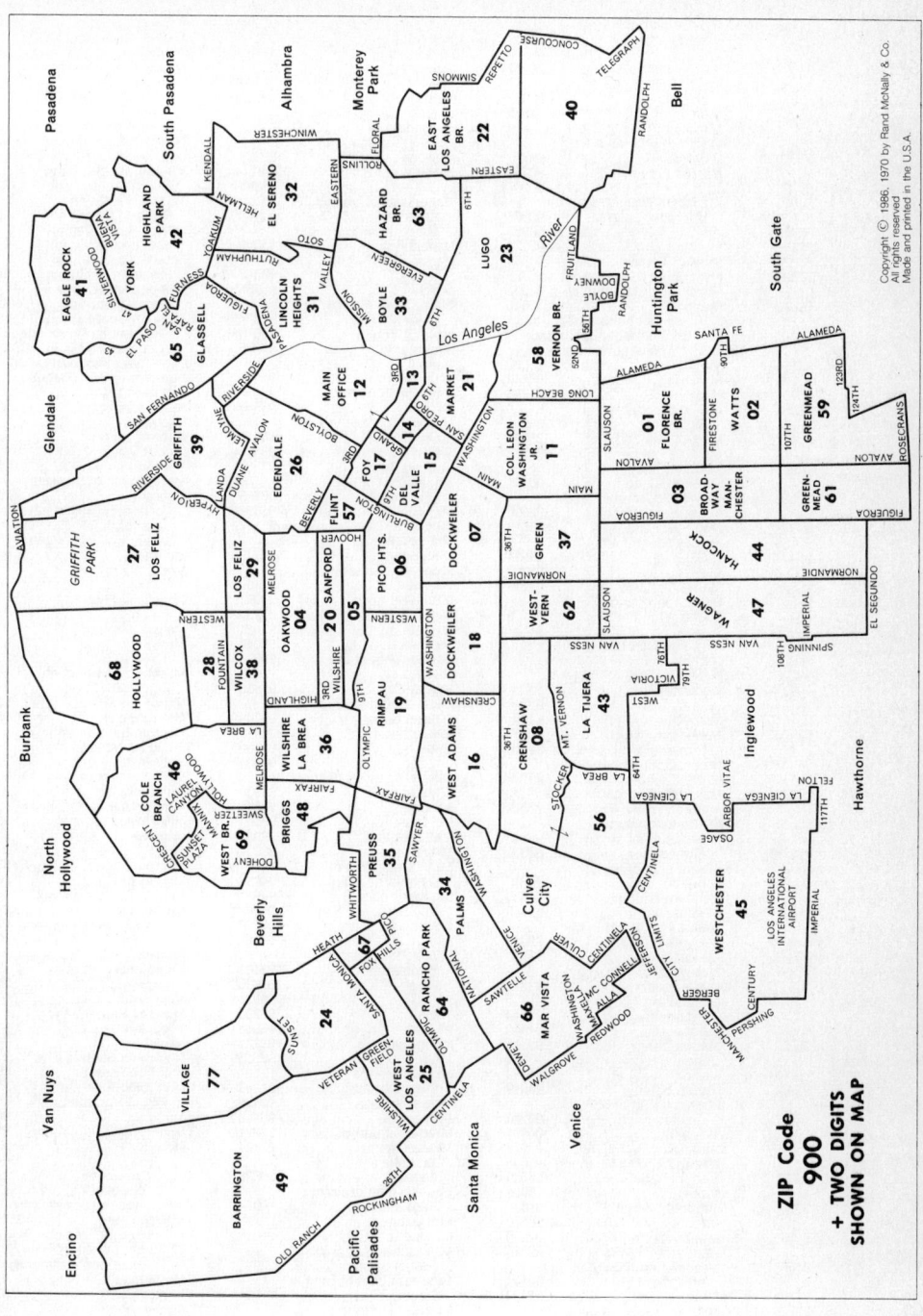

ZIP Code
900
+ TWO DIGITS
SHOWN ON MAP

* Area Zip Code   † Post Office Boxes

	ZIP
Moonridge (Part of Big Bear Lake)	92315
Moonstone	95570
Moorpark	93020*
	93021†
Moorpark Home Acres	93021
Morada	95212
Moraga	94556
	94570
	94575
For specific Moraga Zip Codes call (510) 376-4948, or your local postmaster.	
Morena	92040
Moreno	92554-55
For specific Moreno Zip Codes call (909) 656-2590, or your local postmaster.	
Moreno Valley	92552-57
For specific Moreno Valley Zip Codes call (909) 656-2590, or your local postmaster.	
Moreno Valley Mall at Towngate (Part of Moreno Valley)	92508
Morgan Hill	95037*
	95038†
Mormon Bar	95338
Morningside Park (Part of Inglewood)	90305
Morongo Indian Reservation	92220
Morongo Valley	92256
Morro Bay	93442*
	93443†
Morro Palisades	93402
Moss Beach	94038
Mossdale	95330
Moss Landing	95039
Mountain Center	92561
Mountain Gate	96003
Mountain House (Alameda County)	95376
Mountain House (Butte County)	95916
Mountain Meadow	96091
Mountain Mesa	93240
Mountain Pass	92366
Mountain Ranch (Calaveras County)	95246
Mountain Ranch (Madera County)	93638
Mountain Rest	93664
Mountain Spring	91934
Mountain View (Kern County)	93307
Mountain View (Santa Clara County)	94039-43
For specific Mountain View Zip Codes call (415) 967-5721, or your local postmaster.	
Mountain View Acres	92392
Mount Aukum	95656
Mount Baldy	91759
Mount Bullion	95338
Mount Eden (Part of Hayward)	94557
Mount Hamilton	95140
Mount Hannah Lodge	95451
Mount Hebron	96058
Mount Helix	91941
Mount Hermon	95041
Mount Laguna	91948
Mount Shasta	96067
Mount Signal	92231
Mount View	94553
Mount Whitney	93545
Mount Wilson	91023
Mt. Roberta	95066
Mugginsville	96032
Muir (Part of Willits)	95490
Muir Beach	94965
Muir Woods	94941
Murietta	93640
Murphys	95247
Murray Park (Part of Larkspur)	94939
Murrieta	92562-64
For specific Murrieta Zip Codes call (909) 677-5927, or your local postmaster.	
Murrieta Hot Springs	92563
Muscoy	92405
Myers Flat	95554
Myrtletown	95501
Nadeau	90001
Napa	94558-59

	ZIP
	94581
For specific Napa Zip Codes call (707) 255-1791, or your local postmaster.	
Napa Junction	94590
Naples (Part of Long Beach)	90803
Nashville	95623
National City	91950*
	91951†
Navajo (Part of San Diego)	92119
Naval Air Facility	92243
Naval Air Station (Alameda County)	94501
Naval Air Station (Kings County)	93245
Naval Amphibious Base	92155
Naval Base (Part of Port Hueneme)	93043
Naval Regional Medical Center	92055
Naval Weapons Station (Contra Costa County)	94520
Naval Weapons Station (Orange County)	90740
Navarro	95463
Navelencia	93654
Nebo	92311
Nebo Center	92311
Needles	92363
Nelson	95958
Nestor (Part of San Diego)	92153
Nevada City	95959
New Almaden	95042
Newark	94560
New Auberry	93602
Newberry Springs	92365
Newburg	95540
Newbury Park	91319†
	91320*
Newcastle	95658
New Cuyama	93254
Newell	96134
Newhall	91321*
	91322†
Newhall Ranch (Part of Santa Clarita)	91350
New Helvetia (Part of Sacramento)	95815
Newman	95360
New Monterey (Part of Monterey)	93940
New Park Mall (Part of Newark)	94560
New Pine Creek	97635
Newport Beach	92657-63
For specific Newport Beach Zip Codes call (714) 640-8720, or your local postmaster.	
Newport Center Fashion Island (Part of Newport Beach)	92660
Newport Heights (Part of Newport Beach)	92663
Newport Island (Part of Newport Beach)	92663
Newtown (El Dorado County)	95667
Newtown (Nevada County)	95959
Newville	95963
Nicasio	94946
Nice	95464
Nichols	94565
Nicolaus	95659
Nigger Hill	95667
Nightingale	92561
Niguel Terrace (Part of Laguna Niguel)	92677
Niland	92257
Niles (Part of Fremont)	94536
Niles Junction (Part of Fremont)	94536
Nimshew	95954
Nipinnawassee	93601
Nipomo	93444
Nipton	92364
Nob Hill (Part of San Francisco)	94108
Noe Valley (Part of San Francisco)	94114
No Mirage	92259
Norco	91760
Nord	95926
Norden	95724
Normal Heights (Part of San Diego)	92116

	ZIP
North (Part of Los Angeles)	91342
North Auburn	95603
North Beach (Part of San Francisco)	94133
North Belridge	93429
North Berkeley (Part of Berkeley)	94709
North Bloomfield	95959
North Clairemont (Part of San Diego)	92117
North Columbia	95959
North County Fair (Part of Escondido)	92025
Northcrest (Part of Crescent City)	95531
North Downey (Part of Downey)	90240
Northeast Modesto (Part of Modesto)	95355
North Edwards	93523
North El Monte	91006
North Elsinore (Part of Lake Elsinore)	92530
Northern California Women's Facility	95213
North Fair Oaks	94025
North Fork	93643
North Gardena	90247
North Glendale (Part of Glendale)	91202*
	91222†
North Highlands	95660
North Hills (Part of Los Angeles)	91343
North Hollywood	91601-03
	91605-06
	91609-10
	91615-16
For specific North Hollywood Zip Codes call (818) 503-0695, or your local postmaster.	
North Inglewood (Part of Inglewood)	90302
North Island Naval Air Station	92135
North Lakeport	95453
North Loma Linda (Part of Loma Linda)	92354
North Long Beach (Part of Long Beach)	90805
North Modesto (Part of Modesto)	95356
North Oakland (Part of Oakland)	94609
North Oaks	91350
North Palm Springs	92258
North Park (Part of San Diego)	92104
North Redondo Beach (Part of Redondo Beach)	90278
North Richmond	94804
Northridge	91324-28
For specific Northridge Zip Codes call (818) 349-4475, or your local postmaster.	
Northridge Center (Part of Salinas)	93906
Northridge Fashion Center (Part of Los Angeles)	91324
North Sacramento (Part of Sacramento)	95815
North San Juan	95960
North Shore	92254
North Torrance (Part of Torrance)	90504
North Valley Plaza (Part of Chico)	95926
North Whittier	91746
North Whittier Heights	91745
Norwalk	90650-52
For specific Norwalk Zip Codes call (310) 868-3247, or your local postmaster.	
Norwalk Manor (Part of Norwalk)	90650
Novato	94945
	94947-49
For specific Novato Zip Codes call (415) 897-3171, or your local postmaster.	
Noyo	95437
Nubieber	96068
Nuevo	92567
Nummi (Part of Fremont)	94538
Nut Tree (Part of Vacaville)	95696
Nyland Acres	93030

	ZIP
Oak Bottom	96095
Oakdale	95361
Oak Glen (Part of Yucaipa)	92399
Oak Grove (Butte County)	95966
Oak Grove (San Diego County)	92536
Oak Grove (San Mateo County)	94025
Oakhills	93907
Oakhurst	93644
Oak Knoll Hills (Part of Cupertino)	95014
Oak Knolls	93455
Oakland	94601-07
	94609-10
	94612-19
	94621-61
For specific Oakland Zip Codes call (510) 251-3300, or your local postmaster.	
Oakley	94561
Oakmont (Part of Santa Rosa)	95409
Oak Park (Sacramento County)	95817
Oak Park (San Luis Obispo County)	93446
Oak Park (Ventura County)	91301
Oak Park Estates	95249
Oakridge (Part of Stockton)	95207
Oakridge Mall (Part of San Jose)	95123
Oak Run	96069
Oaks (Part of Arroyo Grande)	93420
Oaks, The (Part of Thousand Oaks)	91360
Oak Shores	93426
Oak View	93022
Oakville	94562
Oakwood (Part of Los Angeles)	90004
Oasis	89010
O'Brien	96070
Occidental (Sonoma County)	95465
Ocean Beach (Part of San Diego)	92107
Oceano	93445
Ocean Park (Part of Santa Monica)	90405*
	90409†
Oceanside	92049-58
For specific Oceanside Zip Codes call (619) 433-8711, or your local postmaster.	
Ocean View (Orange County)	92647
Ocean View (San Francisco County)	94112
Ocean View (Sonoma County)	94923
Ockenden	93664
Ocotillo	92259
Ocotillo Wells	92004
Odd Fellows Park	95446
Oildale	93308
Ojai	93023*
	93024†
Olancha	93549
Old Fort Jim	95667
Old Gilroy	95020
Old Hopland	95449
Old Mammoth (Part of Mammoth Lakes)	93546
Old River	93309
Old San Diego (Part of San Diego)	92110
Old Station	96071
Old Town (Madera County)	93643
Old Town (Riverside County)	92593
Old Towne (Part of Tehachapi)	93582
Oleander	93725
Olema	94950
Oleum	94572
Olinda (Orange County)	92621
Olinda (Shasta County)	96007
Olive (Part of Orange)	92665
Olivehurst	95961
Olivenhain (Part of Encinitas)	92024
Olympia	95018

	ZIP
Olympic (Part of Beverly Hills)	90212
Olympic Valley	96146
Omo Ranch	95684
O'Neals	93645
One Hundred Palms	92274
Ono	96047
Ontario	91758
	91761-62
	91764
	91798
For specific Ontario Zip Codes call (909) 983-1873, or your local postmaster.	
Ontario Mail Facility (Part of Ontario)	91761
Onyx	93255
Opal Cliffs	95062
Ophir	95603
Orange	92613
	92664-69
For specific Orange Zip Codes call (714) 997-1255, or your local postmaster.	
Orange Center (Part of Riverside)	92501
Orange Cove	93646
Orangefair Mall (Part of Fullerton)	92632
Orange Glen (Part of Escondido)	92027
Orange Heights (Part of Upland)	91786
Orangehurst (Part of Fullerton)	92633
Orange Park Acres	92669
Orangevale	95662
Orangewood (Part of Pasadena)	91115
Orcutt	93455
Ord	93941
Ordbend	95943
Oregon City	95965
Oregon House	95962
Orick	95555
Orinda	94563
Orinda Village (Part of Orinda)	94563
Orland	95963
Orleans	95556
Ormand	92509
Oro Fino	96032
Oro Grande	92368
Oro Loma	93622
Orosi	93647
Oroville	95965-66
For specific Oroville Zip Codes call (916) 533-4515, or your local postmaster.	
Oroville East	95965
Osbourne (Part of Los Angeles)	90028
Otay (Part of Chula Vista)	91911
Otay Mesa	92153†
	92154*
Otterbein	91748
Outingdale	95684
Oval (Part of Visalia)	93291
Oxnard	93030-35
For specific Oxnard Zip Codes call (805) 485-6722, or your local postmaster.	
Oxnard Beach	93035
Pabrico (Part of Union City)	94587
Pachappa	92506
Pacheco	94553
Pacific (Part of Long Beach)	90806
Pacifica	94044*
	94045†
Pacific Beach (Part of San Diego)	92109
Pacific Gardens	95204
Pacific Grove	93950
Pacific Grove Acres (Part of Pacific Grove)	93950
Pacific House	95726
Pacific Manor (Humboldt County)	95521
Pacific Manor (San Mateo County)	94044
Pacific Missile Test Center-Point Mugu	93042
Pacific Palisades (Part of Los Angeles)	90272
Pacific Shores	95531
Pacific Valley	93920

	ZIP
Pacoima	91331-34
For specific Pacoima Zip Codes call (818) 896-7491, or your local postmaster.	
Paddison Square (Part of Norwalk)	90652
Paicines	95043
Paintersville	95615
Pajaro	95076
Pala	92059
Pala Indian Reservation	92059
Pala Mesa Village	92028
Palermo	95968
Palm City (Part of Palm Desert)	92211
Palmdale	93550-52
	93590-91
For specific Palmdale Zip Codes call (805) 266-2800, or your local postmaster.	
Palmdale East	93550
	93552
	93591
For specific Palmdale East Zip Codes call (805) 266-2800, or your local postmaster.	
Palm Desert	92211
	92255
	92260-61
For specific Palm Desert Zip Codes call (619) 568-5803, or your local postmaster.	
Palm Desert Country	92211
Palm Desert Town Center (Part of Palm Desert)	92260
Palmer Creek	95540
Palms (Part of Los Angeles)	90034
Palm Springs	92262-64
	92292
For specific Palm Springs Zip Codes call (619) 325-9631, or your local postmaster.	
Palm Springs Mall (Part of Palm Springs)	92262
Palo Alto	94301-10
For specific Palo Alto Zip Codes call (415) 321-4310, or your local postmaster.	
Palo Cedro	96073
Paloma	95252
Palomar Mountain	92060
Palomar Park	94062
Palos Verdes Estates	90274
Palos Verdes Peninsula	90274-75
For specific Palos Verdes Peninsula Zip Codes call (310) 377-6833, or your local postmaster.	
Palo Verde	92266
Palo Vista (Part of Vista)	92083
Panoche	95043
Panorama City (Part of Los Angeles)	91402*
	91412†
Panorama Heights (Orange County)	92705
Panorama Heights (Tulare County)	93260
Panorama Mall (Part of Los Angeles)	91402
Pappas	93640
Paradise (Butte County)	95967†
	95969*
Paradise (Stanislaus County)	95351
	95358
For specific Paradise Zip Codes call (209) 523-8326, or your local postmaster.	
Paradise Cay (Part of Tiburon)	94920
Paradise Estates	93514
Paradise Hills (Part of San Diego)	92139
Paradise Park	95060
Paraiso Springs	93960
Paramount	90723
Parchers Camp	93514
Park (Part of Berkeley)	94702
Park Central (Part of Alameda)	94501
Parker Dam	92267
Parkfield	93451
Parkmoor (Part of San Jose)	95128
Parksdale	93637
Parkside (Part of San Francisco)	94116

	ZIP
Park Siding (Part of Petaluma)	94952
Park Village	92328
Parkway	95823
Parkway Plaza (Part of El Cajon)	92020
Parkway-South Sacramento	95823
Parkwood	93637
Parlier	93648
Pasadena	91101-07
	91109-17
For specific Pasadena Zip Codes call (818) 304-7183, or your local postmaster.	
Pasatiempo	95060
Paskenta	96074
Paso Robles	93446*
	93447†
Patata (Part of South Gate)	90280
Patrick Creek	95543
Patricks Point	95570
Patterson (Stanislaus County)	95363
Patterson (Tulare County)	93291
Patton	92369
Patton Village	96113
Pauma Indian Reservation	92061
Pauma Valley	92061
Paxton	95971
Paynes Creek	96075
Paynesville	96120
Peanut	96041
Pearblossom	93553
Peardale	95945
Pearland (Part of Palmdale)	93550
Pearsonville	93527
Pebble Beach	93953
Pechanga Indian Reservation	92590
Pecwan	95546
Pedley	92509
Pedro Valley (Part of Pacifica)	94044
Pelican Bay State Prison	95531
Peninsula Center (Part of Rolling Hills Estates)	90274
Peninsula Village	96137
Penngrove	94951
Pennington	95953
Penn Valley	95946
Penryn	95663
Pentz	95965
Pepperwood	95565
Peralta Hills	92667
Perkins	95826*
	95827†
Perris	92570-72
For specific Perris Zip Codes call (909) 657-2396, or your local postmaster.	
Perry (Part of Whittier)	90603
Pescadero	94060
Petaluma	94952-55
	94975
	94999
For specific Petaluma Zip Codes call (707) 778-5340, or your local postmaster.	
Peters	95236
Petrolia	95558
Phelan	92329†
	92371*
Phillipsville	95559
Philo	95466
Phoenix Lake-Cedar Ridge	95370
Phoenix Lake Country Club Estates	95370
Pico (Part of Pico Rivera)	90660
Pico Heights (Part of Los Angeles)	90006
Pico Rivera	90660-62
For specific Pico Rivera Zip Codes call (310) 942-7008, or your local postmaster.	
Piedmont	94611
	94620
For specific Piedmont Zip Codes call (510) 251-3130, or your local postmaster.	
Piedra	93649
Pierce Lake Estates	93644
Piercy	95587
Pierpoint Springs	93208
Pike	95960
Pilot Hill	95664

	ZIP
Pine Cove (Riverside County)	92549
Pine Cove (Trinity County)	96052
Pinecrest	95364
Pinedale (Part of Fresno)	93650
Pine Flat (Fresno County)	93649
Pine Flat (Tulare County)	93207
Pine Grove (Amador County)	95665
Pine Grove (Lake County)	95426
Pine Grove (Mendocino County)	95437
Pine Grove (Shasta County)	96079
Pine Hills (Humboldt County)	95503
Pine Hills (San Diego County)	92036
Pinehurst	93641
Pine Mountain Club	93222
Pine Mountain Lake	95321
Pineridge	93602
Pine Street (Part of San Francisco)	94109
Pine Valley	91962
Pinnacles	95043
Pinole	94564
Pinon Hills	92372
Pinon Pines Estates	93225
Pinyon Crest	92262
Pinyon Pines	92561
Pioneer	95666
Pioneer Point	93562
Pioneertown	92268
Piru	93040
Pismo Beach	93448†
	93449*
Pittsburg	94565
Pittville	96056
Pixley	93256
Placentia	92670
Placerville	95667
Plainsburg	95333
Plainview	93267
Planada	95365
Planehaven	95652
Plantation	95421
Plaster City	92243
Platina	96076
Playa (Part of Laguna Beach)	92652
Playa Del Rey (Part of Los Angeles)	90293*
	90296†
Playa Vista (Part of Los Angeles)	90094
Playmor (Part of Chula Vista)	91911
Plaza (Los Angeles County)	91102
Plaza (Orange County)	92666
Plaza (Santa Clara County)	94086
Plaza Camino Real (Part of Carlsbad)	92008
Plaza Center (Part of Ontario)	91762
Plaza Pasadena (Part of Pasadena)	91101
Pleasant Grove	95668
Pleasant Hill	94523
Pleasanton	94566
	94588
For specific Pleasanton Zip Codes call (510) 846-5631, or your local postmaster.	
Pleasant Valley	95667
Pleasant View	93260
Plymouth	95669
Poinsettia Tract	94565
Point Arena	95468
Point Dume	90264†
	90265*
Point Loma (Part of San Diego)	92106
Point Pleasant	95758
Point Reyes Station	94956
Point Richmond (Part of Richmond)	94807
Poker Flat	95228
Pollock Pines	95726
Pomona	91766-69
For specific Pomona Zip Codes call (909) 623-4476, or your local postmaster.	
Pond	93280
Ponderosa Sky Ranch	96075
Pondosa	96057
Pope Valley	94567

	ZIP
Poplar	93258
Port Chicago	94520
Port Costa	94569
Porter Ranch	91326*
	91327†
Porterville	93257*
	93258†
Porterville Development Center	93257
Porterville West (Part of Porterville)	93257
Port Hueneme	93041*
	93044†
Port Kenyon	95536
Portola	96122
Portola Hills	92679
Portola Valley	94028
Port San Luis	93424
Portuguese Bend (Part of Rancho Palos Verdes)	90274
Posey	93260
Poso Park	93260
Postal Avenue (Part of Moreno Valley)	92556†
	92557*
Post Office Annex (Part of Burlingame)	94010
Potrero (San Diego County)	91963
Potrero (San Francisco County)	94110
Potter Valley	95469
Poway	92064*
	92074†
Power Tract	93283
Pozo	93453
Prather	93651
Prattville	95923
Presidential Heights (Part of San Clemente)	92672
Preston Heights (Part of Arcata)	95521
Preuss (Part of Los Angeles)	90035
Priest Valley	93210
Princeton (Colusa County)	95970
Princeton (San Mateo County)	94019
Proberta	96078
Project City	96079
Promenade Mall (Part of Los Angeles)	91367
Prosser Lakeview Estates	96161
Prunedale	93907
Pudding Creek	95437
Puente Junction (Part of City of Industry)	91744
Puerco Beach (Part of Malibu)	90265
Pulga	95965
Pumpkin Center	93309
Quail Valley	92587
Quaking Aspen	93265
Quartz Hill	93551
Quincy	95971
Quincy-East Quincy	95971
Quintette	95634
Quito (Part of Saratoga)	95070
Rackerby	95972
Radec	92543
Rafael Village (Part of Novato)	94949
Rail Road Flat	95248
Rainbow	92028
Raisin	93652
Ralph	95370
Ramirez (Part of Los Angeles)	90037
Ramona	92065
Ramona Acres	93432
Ramona Woods	95006
Ramos Village	95336
Rancheria	95449
Ranch House	92055
Ranchita	92066
Rancho Bernardo (Part of San Diego)	92128
Rancho Buena	96022
Rancho California (Part of Temecula)	92590
Rancho Cordova	95741-42
	95670
For specific Rancho Cordova Zip Codes call (916) 574-3060, or your local postmaster.	
Rancho Cucamonga	91729-30

	ZIP
	91739
For specific Rancho Cucamonga Zip Codes call (909) 987-4641, or your local postmaster.	
Rancho Del Mar	94590
Rancho Del Rey (Part of Chula Vista)	91909†
	91911*
Rancho Los Amigos (Part of Downey)	90242
Rancho Mirage	92270
Rancho Murieta	95683
Rancho Palos Verdes	90274
Rancho Park (Part of Los Angeles)	90064
Rancho Penasquitos (Part of San Diego)	92129
Rancho Rinconada	95014
Rancho San Diego	91941
Rancho Santa Fe	92067
Rancho Santa Margarita	92688
Randall Island	95615
Randolph	96126
Randsburg	93554
Ravendale	96123
Ravenswood (Part of East Palo Alto)	94303
Rawhide	95370
Rawson	96080
Raymond	93653
Raynor Park (Part of Sunnyvale)	94087
Red Bank	96080
Red Bluff	96080
Redcrest	95569
Redding	96001-03
	96049
	96099
For specific Redding Zip Codes call (916) 223-7502, or your local postmaster.	
Red Hill	92705
Redlands	92373-75
For specific Redlands Zip Codes call (714) 793-2171, or your local postmaster.	
Red Mountain	93558
Redondo Beach	90277-78
For specific Redondo Beach Zip Codes call (310) 376-2472, or your local postmaster.	
Reds Meadow	93546
Red Top	95340
Redway	95560
Redwood City	94059
	94061-65
For specific Redwood City Zip Codes call (415) 368-4181, or your local postmaster.	
Redwood Estates	95044
Redwood Grove	95006
Redwood Lodge	95437
Redwood Retreat	95020
Redwood Terrace	94020
Redwood Valley	95470
Reedley	93654
Relief	95959
Represa	95630
Requa	95548
Rescue	95672
Reseda	91335-37
For specific Reseda Zip Codes call (818) 342-6111, or your local postmaster.	
Rheem (Part of San Pablo)	94801
Rheem Valley (Part of Moraga)	94570
Rialto	92376-77
For specific Rialto Zip Codes call (909) 875-1522, or your local postmaster.	
Rice	92280
Richardson Springs	95973
Richfield	96021
Richgrove	93261
Richmond	94801-02
	94804-05
	94807-08
For specific Richmond Zip Codes call (510) 232-9707, or your local postmaster.	
Richmond (Part of San Francisco)	94118
Richvale	95974
Ridgecrest	93555*
	93556†

	ZIP
Rimcrest (Part of Palm Springs)	92264
Rimforest	92378
Rimpau (Part of Los Angeles)	90019
Rimrock	92268
Rincon	92061
Rincon Center (Part of San Francisco)	94119
Rincon Indian Reservation	92025
Rincon Valley (Part of Santa Rosa)	95409
Rio Bonito	95917
Rio Bravo	93306
Rio Dell (Humboldt County)	95562
Rio Dell (Sonoma County)	95436
Rio del Mar	95003
Rio Linda	95673
Rio Nido	95471
Rio Oso	95674
Rio Vista	94571
Ripley	92272
Ripon	95366
Ripperdan	93637
Ritter Ranch	93551
Rivera (Part of Pico Rivera)	90660
Riverbank	95367
Riverbank Army Ammunition Plant	95367
Riverdale	93656
River Kern	93238
River Oaks	95045
River Pines	95675
River Road (Part of Modesto)	95351
Riverroad Estates	93637
Riverside	92501-17
	92519
For specific Riverside Zip Codes call (909) 788-4600, or your local postmaster.	
Riverside (Part of Newport Beach)	92659†
	92663*
Riverside Grove	95006
Riverside Park	95528
Riverside Plaza (Part of Riverside)	92506
Rivertown (Part of Antioch)	94509
Riverview	92040
Riverview Farms	92040
Riviera Cliff	95204
Roads End	93238
Robbins	95676
Robertsville (Part of San Jose)	95118
Robinsons Corner	95965
Robles Del Rio	93924
Rob Roy Junction	95003
Rockaway Beach (Part of Pacifica)	94044
Rock Creek	95965
Rock Crest	95980
Rock Haven	93664
Rocking Horse Ranchos (Part of Rancho Palos Verdes)	90731
Rocklin	95677
	95765
For specific Rocklin Zip Codes call (916) 624-2400, or your local postmaster.	
Rockport	95488
Rockridge (Part of Oakland)	94618
Rockville	94585
Rodeo	94572
Rodgers Flat	95980
Rogina Heights	95482
Rohnert Park	94927*
	94928†
Rohnerville	95540
Rolinda	93706
Rolling Hills (Los Angeles County)	90274
Rolling Hills (Madera County)	93637
Rolling Hills (Riverside County)	92539
Rolling Hills Estates (Los Angeles County)	90274
Rolling Hills Estates (San Luis Obispo County)	93401
Rolling Hills Plaza (Part of Torrance)	90505

	ZIP
Rolling Hills Riviera (Part of Rancho Palos Verdes)	90731
Rollingwood	94806
Romie Lane (Part of Salinas)	93901
Romoland	92585
Roosevelt Corner	93534
Roosevelt Terrace	94590
Rosamond	93560
Rose Bowl (Part of Pasadena)	91103
Rosedale	93308
Roseland	95407
Rosemead	91770
Rosemead Square (Part of Rosemead)	91770
Rosemont (Sacramento County)	95826
Rosemont (San Diego County)	92065
Roseville	95661
	95678
	95747
For specific Roseville Zip Codes call (916) 782-1203, or your local postmaster.	
Rosewood (Part of Eureka)	95503
Ross	94957
Ross Corner	92222
Rossmoor	90720
Rossmoor Business Center (Part of Seal Beach)	90740
Rossmoor Highlands (Part of Los Alamitos)	90720
Rough And Ready	95975
Round Hill Country Club	94507
Round Mountain	96084
Round Valley	93514
Round Valley Indian Reservation	95428
Rovana	93514
Rowland (Part of City of Industry)	91743
Rowland Heights	91748
Rubidoux	92509
Rucker	95020
Rumsey	95679
Running Springs	92382
Rupert	95901
Russell (Part of Hayward)	94541
Russian River Terrace	95436
Ruth	95526
Rutherford	94573
Ryde	95680
Sabre City	95678
Sacramento	94203-99
	95801-66
For specific Sacramento Zip Codes call (916) 263-7181, or your local postmaster.	
Sacramento Area Mail Processing Center	95798-99
For specific Sacramento Area Mail Processing Center Zip Codes call (916) 373-8100, or your local postmaster.	
Sacramento South	95820
Sage	92544
Sage Valley	96113
St. Bernard	96061
St. Francis Heights (Part of Daly City)	94015
St. Helena	94574
St. James Park (Part of San Jose)	95113
St. Johns	93286
St. Marys College (Part of Moraga)	94575
St. Matthew (Part of San Mateo)	94401
	94405
For specific St. Matthew Zip Codes call (415) 343-5618, or your local postmaster.	
Salida	95368
Salinas	93901-15
For specific Salinas Zip Codes call (408) 422-8687, or your local postmaster.	
Salinas Resort	95451
Salmon Creek	94923
Salton City	92275
Salton Sea Beach	92274
Saltus	92304
Salvador (Part of Napa)	94558
Salyer	95563

*Area Zip Code   †Post Office Boxes

* Area Zip Code   † Post Office Boxes

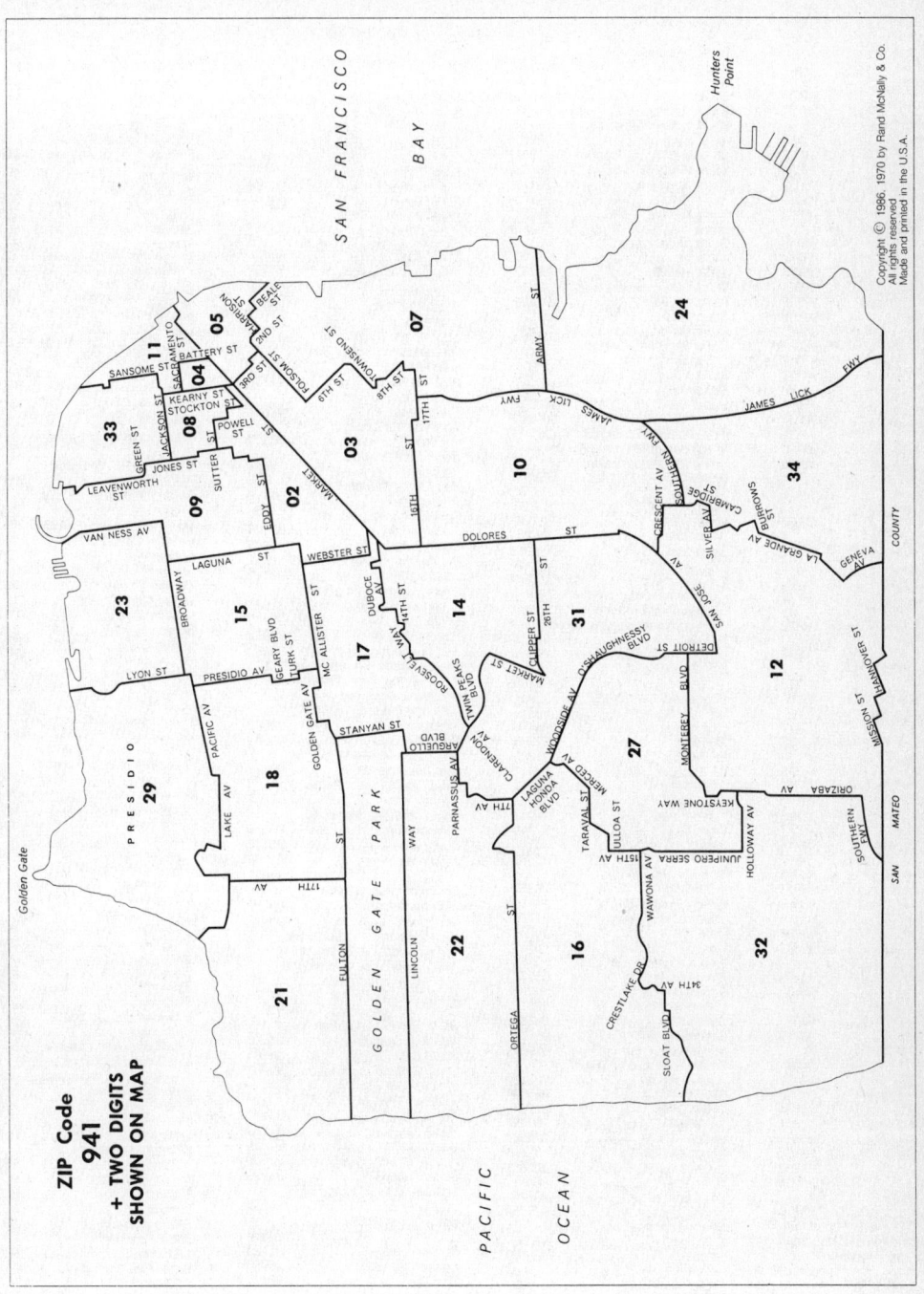

ZIP Code
941
+ TWO DIGITS
SHOWN ON MAP

	ZIP
	92173*
Saranap	94595
Saratoga	95070*
	95071†
Saratoga Springs	95493
Sather Gate (Part of Berkeley)	94704
Saticoy (Part of Ventura)	93004*
	93007†
Sattley	96124
Saugus (Part of Santa Clarita)	91350
Sausalito	94965*
	94966†
Saviers (Part of Oxnard)	93033
Sawyers Bar	96027
Scenic Brook Estates	95370
Scenic Center (Part of Modesto)	95355
Scheideck	93252
Schellville	95476
Scotia	95565
Scotland	92358
Scott Bar	96085
Scotts Valley	95066*
	95067†
Seacliff	95003
Seahaven	94937
Seal Beach	90740
Seal Beach Naval Weapons Station	90740
Seal Cove	94038
Searles Valley	93562
Seaside	93955
Sebastiani (Part of Sonoma)	95476
Sebastopol (Nevada County)	95960
Sebastopol (Sonoma County)	95472*
	95473†
Sedco Hills	92530
Seeley	92273
Seiad Valley	96086
Selby	94525
Selma	93662
Seneca	95923
Sepulveda (Part of Los Angeles)	91343
Sequoia Crest	93265
Sequoia Mall (Part of Visalia)	93277
Sequoia National Park	93262
Serena Park	93013
Serene Lakes	95728
Serra (Part of Dana Point)	92624
Serra Mesa (Part of San Diego)	92123
Serramonte (Part of Daly City)	94015
Serramonte Center (Part of Daly City)	94015
Sespe	93015
Seven Oaks	92305
Seven Pines	93526
Seville	93291
Shadow Hills	95461
Shady Glen	95713
Shafter	93263
Shandon	93461
Sharon Heights (Part of Menlo Park)	94025
Sharpe Army Depot	95330
Sharp Park (Part of Pacifica)	94044
Shasta	96087
Shasta Forest Village	96088
Shaver Lake	93664
Shaver Lake Heights	93664
Shaver Lake Point	93664
Shaw City (Part of Fresno)	93704
Sheepranch	95250
Sheldon	95624
Shell Beach (Part of Pismo Beach)	93449
Shelter Cove (Humboldt County)	95589
Shelter Cove (San Mateo County)	94044
Sheridan	95681
Sherman Oaks (Part of Los Angeles)	91403
	91413
	91423
For specific Sherman Oaks Zip Codes call (818) 908-6912, or your local postmaster.	
Sherman Oaks Galleria (Part of Los Angeles)	91403

	ZIP
Sherwood (Part of Salinas)	93906
Sherwood Forest	94803
Sherwood Mall (Part of Stockton)	95207
Shingle Springs	95682
Shingletown	96088
Shinn (Part of Fremont)	94536
Shively	95565
Shore Acres	94565
Short Acres (Part of Hanford)	93230
Shoshone	92384
Sierra (Part of Fresno)	93703
Sierra Army Depot	96113
Sierra Brooks	96118
Sierra Cedars	93664
Sierra City	96125
Sierra Conservation Center	95327
Sierra Heights	93247
Sierra Lake Estates	93644
Sierra Madre	91024*
	91025†
Sierra Pines	89439
Sierra Sky Park (Part of Fresno)	93722
Sierra Village No.1	95346
Sierraville	96126
Signal Hill	90804
	90806-07
For specific Signal Hill Zip Codes call (310) 428-6454, or your local postmaster.	
Silverado	92676
Silver City	93271
Silver Fork	95720
Silver Lake	95666
Silver Strand	93035
Simi Valley	93062-63
	93065
	93093
For specific Simi Valley Zip Codes call (805) 526-1331, or your local postmaster.	
Simmler	93453
Simms (Marin County)	94901
Simms (San Joaquin County)	95366
Sisquoc	93454
Sites	95979
Skaggs Island	95476
Skyforest	92385
Skyhigh	95223
Skyline East	92311
Skyline North	92311
Sky Londa (Part of Woodside)	94062
Sky Valley	92241
Slawson (Part of Pico Rivera)	90662
Sleepy Hollow (Marin County)	94960
Sleepy Hollow (San Bernardino County)	91710
Slide Inn	95335
Sloat	96103
Sloughhouse	95683
Smartville	95977
Smiley Heights (Part of Redlands)	92373
Smiley Park	92382
Smithflat	95667
Smith River	95567
Smoke Tree (Part of Palm Springs)	92262
Snelling	95369
Snow Creek	92282
Snowline	95709
Soboba Hot Springs	92583
Soboba Indian Reservation	92583
Soda Bay	95451
Soda Springs	95728
Solana Beach	92075
Solano Mall (Part of Fairfield)	94533
Soledad	93960
Solemint (Part of Santa Clarita)	91350
Solvang	93463*
	93464†
Somerset	95684
Somesbar	95568
Somis	93066
Sonoma	95476
Sonoma Vista	95476
Sonora	95370
Sonora Junction	93517

	ZIP
Soquel	95073
Sorensen (Part of Hayward)	94544
Sorensens	96120
Sorrento Valley (Part of San Diego)	92191
Soto (Part of Huntington Park)	90255
Soulsbyville	95372
South (Part of Los Angeles)	90061
South Alhambra (Part of Alhambra)	91803
South Bakersfield (Part of Bakersfield)	93384
South Belridge	93251
South Berkeley (Part of Berkeley)	94703
South Coast Plaza (Part of Costa Mesa)	92626
South Corona (Part of Corona)	91718
South Dos Palos	93665
South Downey (Part of Downey)	90242
Southeastern (Part of San Diego)	92113
South El Monte	91733
South Fontana (Part of Fontana)	92337
South Fork (Humboldt County)	95569
South Fork (Madera County)	93643
South Fork (Mariposa County)	95318
South Gardena (Part of Gardena)	90248
South Gate	90280
South Hills (Part of West Covina)	91791
South Laguna (Part of Laguna Beach)	92677
South Lake	93240
South Lake Tahoe	96150-58
For specific South Lake Tahoe Zip Codes call (916) 544-2208, or your local postmaster.	
Southland Shopping Center (Part of Hayward)	94545
South Leggett	95585
South Los Angeles (Part of Los Angeles)	90061
South Main (Part of Santa Ana)	92707
South Modesto (Part of Modesto)	95350
South Oroville	95965
South Pasadena	91030*
	91031†
Southport (Part of West Sacramento)	95691
South San Francisco	94080-83
For specific South San Francisco Zip Codes call (415) 588-2855, or your local postmaster.	
South San Gabriel	91770
South San Jose Hills	91744
South San Leandro (Part of San Leandro)	94578
South Santa Rosa	95401
South Shafter	93263
South Shore Shopping Center (Part of Alameda)	94501
South Taft	93268
South Whittier	90605
South Whittier Heights	90605
South Yuba City	95991
Spanish Flat (El Dorado County)	95633
Spanish Flat (Napa County)	94558
Spanish Hills	91720
Spanish Ranch	95956
Spaulding	96130
Spicer City	93206
Spreckels	93962
Spring Creek Tract	96158
Springfield	95370
Spring Garden	95971
Spring Hill (Part of Grass Valley)	95945
Springstowne (Part of Vallejo)	94591

	ZIP
Spring Valley	91976-79
For specific Spring Valley Zip Codes call (619) 670-9815, or your local postmaster.	
Spring Valley Lake (Part of Apple Valley)	92392
Springville	93265
Spruce Point	95503
Spurgeon	92701*
	92702†
Squaw Valley	93675
Squirrel Mountain Valley	93240
Stadium (Part of Anaheim)	92825
Stafford	95565
Stallion Springs	93561
Stamoules	93640
Standard	95373
Standish	96128
Stanford	94305
Stanford Shopping Center (Part of Palo Alto)	94304
Stanton	90680
Starlight	93514
Starlite Pines	96088
State Capitol (Part of Sacramento)	95814
Stateline (Part of South Lake Tahoe)	96157
State Street (Part of Huntington Park)	90255
Steele Park	94558
Steinbeck (Part of Salinas)	93901
Stent	95370
Stephens (Part of Santa Fe Springs)	90670
Sterling Park (Part of Daly City)	94017
Stevenson Ranch (Part of Santa Clarita)	91381
Stevinson	95374
Stewarts Point	95480
Stewart Springs	96094
Stine Station (Part of Bakersfield)	93309
Stinson Beach	94970
Stirling City	95978
Stockdale (Part of Bakersfield)	93309
Stockton	95201-19
	95267-69
For specific Stockton Zip Codes call (209) 983-6317, or your local postmaster.	
Stonegate (Part of Portola Valley)	94028
Stonehurst (Part of Oakland)	94603
Stone Lagoon	95570
Stoneman (Part of Alhambra)	91801
Stonestown (Part of San Francisco)	94132
Stonewood Shopping Center (Part of Downey)	90241
Stonyford	95979
Storrie	95980
Stovepipe Wells	92328
Stratford	93266
Strathmore	93267
Strawberry (El Dorado County)	95720
Strawberry (Marin County)	94941
Strawberry (Tuolumne County)	95375
Strawberry Valley	95981
Stuart	92054
Studebaker (Part of Norwalk)	90650
Studio City (Part of Los Angeles)	91604*
	91614†
Suburban Acres	96080
Sugarloaf	92386
Sugarloaf Mountain Park	93260
Sugar Pine (Madera County)	93644
Sugar Pine (Tuolumne County)	95383
Suisun City	94585
Sulphur Springs	93060
Sultana	93666
Summer Home	95336
Summerhome Park	95436
Summerland	93067
Summit	92345
Summit City	96089
Sumner Hill	93637

* Area Zip Code   **† Post Office Boxes**

	ZIP
Sun City	92585-87

For specific Sun City Zip Codes call (909) 679-1737, or your local postmaster.

	ZIP
Sunfair	92252
Sunkist (Part of Anaheim)	92806
Sunland	91040*
	91041†
Sunny Brae (Part of Arcata)	95521
Sunnybrook	95640
Sunny Hills (Part of Fullerton)	92635
Sunnymead (Part of Moreno Valley)	92551
Sunnyside (Fresno County)	93727
Sunnyside (Placer County)	96145
Sunnyside (San Diego County)	91902
Sunnyside-Tahoe City	96145
Sunnyslope (Butte County)	95914
Sunnyslope (Riverside County)	92509
Sunnyvale	94086-91

For specific Sunnyvale Zip Codes call (408) 732-0121, or your local postmaster.

	ZIP
Sunnyvale Town Center (Part of Sunnyvale)	94086
Sunny Vista (Part of Chula Vista)	91910
Sunol	94586
Sunrise Mall	95610
Sunrise Vista	95451
Sunset (Humboldt County)	95521
Sunset (San Francisco County)	94122
	94172

For specific Sunset Zip Codes call (415) 759-1707, or your local postmaster.

	ZIP
Sunset Beach (Orange County)	90742
Sunset Beach (Santa Cruz County)	95076
Sunset Cliffs (Part of San Diego)	92107
Sunset Hills	91745
Sunset Terrace	93402
Sunset Tract	93022
Sunset View	95945
Sunset Whitney Ranch (Part of Rocklin)	95677
Sunshine Homes	91350
Sunshine Summit	92536
Sun Valley	91352*
	91353†
Sunvalley (Part of Concord)	94520
Sun Village (Part of Palmdale)	93550
Surf	93436
Surfside (Part of Seal Beach)	90743
Susana Knolls (Part of Simi Valley)	93063
Susanville	96130
Sutter	95982
Sutter Creek	95685
Sutter Hill	95685
Sutter Island	95615
Sutter Street (Part of San Francisco)	94104
Swall Meadows	93514
Swanton	95017
Sweet Brier	96017
Sweetwater	95451
Sycamore (Colusa County)	95957
Sycamore (Contra Costa County)	94526
Sylmar (Part of Los Angeles)	91342
Sylvia Park	90290
Table Bluff	95551
Taft	93268
Taft Heights	93268
Tahoe City	96145
Tahoe Keys (Part of South Lake Tahoe)	96154
Tahoe Paradise (Part of South Lake Tahoe)	96155
Tahoe Pines	96141
Tahoe Valley (Part of South Lake Tahoe)	96158
Tahoe Vista	96148
Tahoma	96142

	ZIP
Talica (Part of Oceanside)	92054
Talmage	95481
Tarnal	94974
Tamalpais-Homestead Valley	94941
Tamalpais Valley	94941
Tamarack	95223
Tanforan (Part of South San Francisco)	94080
Tanforan Park (Part of San Bruno)	94066
Tangair	93437
Tanglewood	95018
Tara Hills	94564
Tarpey (Part of Fresno)	93727
Tarzana	91356*
	91357†
Tassajara Hot Springs	93924
Taurusa	93291
Taylorsville	95983
Tecate	91980
Tecnor	96058
Tecopa	92389
Tecopa Hot Springs	92389
Tehachapi	93561
	93581-82

For specific Tehachapi Zip Codes call (805) 822-3276, or your local postmaster.

	ZIP
Tehama	96090
Temecula	92589-93

For specific Temecula Zip Codes call (909) 699-1121, or your local postmaster.

	ZIP
Temelec	95476
Temple City	91780
Templeton	93465
Tennant	96058
Tent City (Part of Coronado)	92118
Terminal Annex (Part of Los Angeles)	90054
Terminous	95240
Termo	96132
Terra Bella	93270
Terra Linda (Part of San Rafael)	94903
Textile (Part of Los Angeles)	90015
The Falls	93604
The Forks (Madera County)	93604
The Forks (Mendocino County)	95482
The Geysers	95425
The Hermitage	95585
The Oaks	95945
The Pines	93604
Thermal	92274
Thermalito	95965
The Sea Ranch	95497
Thomas Mountain	92561
Thornton	95686
Thousand Oaks	91358-60

For specific Thousand Oaks Zip Codes call (805) 497-8661, or your local postmaster.

	ZIP
Thousand Palms	92276
Three Arch Bay (Part of Dana Point)	92677
Three Point	93532
Three Rivers	93271
Three Rocks	93608
Tiburon	94920
Tierra Buena	95991
Tierra del Sol	91905
Tionesta	96134
Tipton	93272
Tivy Valley	93657
Tobin	95965
Tocaloma	94950
Todd Valley	95631
Todos Santos (Part of Concord)	94522
Tollhouse	93667
Toluca Lake (Part of Los Angeles)	91610
Tomales	94971
Toms Place	93514
Tonyville	93247
Tooleville	93221
Topanga	90290
Topanga Beach (Part of Malibu)	90265
Topanga Oaks	90290
Topanga Park	90290
Topanga Plaza (Part of Los Angeles)	91303
Topaz	96133

	ZIP
Top of the World (Part of Laguna Beach)	92651
Tormey	94525
Torrance	90501-10

For specific Torrance Zip Codes call (310) 222-5900, or your local postmaster.

	ZIP
Torres-Martinez Indian Reservation	92274
Torrey Pines Homes (Part of San Diego)	92037
Tower (Part of Fresno)	93728
Town and Country (Riverside County)	92551
Town and Country (Sacramento County)	95821
Town Center (Los Angeles County)	93550
Town Center (Tulare County)	93291
Town Center Corte Madera (Part of Corte Madera)	94925
Town Square (Part of Palmdale)	93550
Trabuco Canyon	92678†
	92679*
Trabuco Highlands	92691
Tracy	95376-78

For specific Tracy Zip Codes call (209) 835-4774, or your local postmaster.

	ZIP
Trade Center	90831*
	90832†
Tranquillity	93668
Traver	93673
Tres Pinos	95075
Trevarno (Part of Livermore)	94550
Trigo	93637
Trimmer	93657
Trinidad	95570
Trinity Alps	96052
Trinity Center	96091
Trinity Village	95527
Triple R Estates	93257
Trona	93562*
	93592†
Tropico (Part of Glendale)	91204-05
	91208

For specific Tropico Zip Codes call (818) 502-3251, or your local postmaster.

	ZIP
Tropico (Kern County)	93560
Trowbridge	95659
Truckee	96160-62

For specific Truckee Zip Codes call (916) 587-3442, or your local postmaster.

	ZIP
Tujunga	91042*
	91043†
Tulare	93274*
	93275†
Tulelake	96134
Tule River Indian Reservation	93257
Tunitas	94019
Tuolumne	95379
Tuolumne Meadows	95389
Tupman	93276
Turlock	95380-82

For specific Turlock Zip Codes call (209) 632-3801, or your local postmaster.

	ZIP
Turner	95336
Tustin	92680*
	92681†
Tustin Foothills	92680
Tustin Marine Corps Air Station	92710
Tuttle	95340
Tuttletown	95370
Tuxedo Country Club Estates	95204
Tuxedo Park (Part of Stockton)	95204
T.V. Bell (Part of Merced)	95340
Twain	95984
Twain Harte	95383
Twentynine Palms	92277-78

For specific Twentynine Palms Zip Codes call (619) 367-3501, or your local postmaster.

	ZIP
Twentynine Palms Base	92278
Twentynine Palms Marine Corps Base	92278
Twentytwo Mile House	93637
Twin Bridges	95735
Twin Creeks	95120

	ZIP
Twin Lakes (Lake County)	95457
Twin Lakes (Mono County)	93517
Twin Lakes (Santa Cruz County)	95060
Twin Oaks	92069
Twin Peaks	92391
Two Rock Coast Guard Station	94952
Tyler Mall (Part of Riverside)	92503
Ukiah	95482
Ulmar (Part of Livermore)	94550
Union (Part of Napa)	94558
Union City	94587
Union Hill	95945
Universal City (Part of Los Angeles)	91608
University (University of California) (Santa Barbara County)	93106-07

For specific University Zip Codes call (805) 564-2266, or your local postmaster.

	ZIP
University (Part of Santa Ana)	92716
University City (Part of San Diego)	92122
University of California-Davis	95616
University of Santa Clara (Part of Santa Clara)	95050
University Towne Centre (Part of San Diego)	92122
Upland	91784-86

For specific Upland Zip Codes call (714) 981-2824, or your local postmaster.

	ZIP
Upper Lake	95485
Uptown (Part of San Bernardino)	92405*
	92406†
Vaca (Part of Vacaville)	95687
Vacation	95446
Vacaville	95687-88
	95696

For specific Vacaville Zip Codes call (707) 448-2030, or your local postmaster.

	ZIP
Valencia	91354-55
	91385

For specific Valencia Zip Codes call (805) 254-1684, or your local postmaster.

	ZIP
Valinda	91744
Valla (Part of Santa Fe Springs)	90670
Vallco Fashion Park (Part of Cupertino)	95014
Vallecito	95251
Vallecitos Town Center (Part of San Marcos)	92069
Vallejo	94589-92

For specific Vallejo Zip Codes call (707) 642-4441, or your local postmaster.

	ZIP
Vallemar (Part of Pacifica)	94044
Valle Vista (Alameda County)	94541
Valle Vista (Riverside County)	92544
Valley Acres	93268
Valley Center	92082
Valley Estates	93283
Valley Fair (Part of San Jose)	95128
Valley Ford	94972
Valley Home	95384
Valley Lake Ranchos	93637
Valley of Enchantment	92325
Valley of the Moon	92325
Valley Plaza (Imperial County)	92243
Valley Plaza (Kern County)	93304
Valley Plaza (Los Angeles County)	91606
Valley Springs	95252
Valley View Park	92325
Valley Village (Part of Los Angeles)	91607
Valona	94525
Val Verde Park	91350
Valyermo	93563
Vandenberg Air Force Base	93437
Vandenberg Village	93436
Van Nuys (Part of Los Angeles)	91401

* **Area Zip Code**　　† **Post Office Boxes**

	ZIP
	91404-11
For specific Van Nuys Zip Codes call (818) 908-6608, or your local postmaster.	
Vanowen (Part of Los Angeles)	91405
Vasona (Part of Los Gatos)	95030
Venice (Part of Los Angeles)	90291*
	90294†
Ventucopa	93252
Ventu Park (Part of Thousand Oaks)	91320
Ventura	93001-09
For specific Ventura Zip Codes call (805) 643-5457, or your local postmaster.	
Verdemont	92402
Verdi	89439
Verdugo City (Part of Glendale)	91046
Verdugo Viejo	91206-08
	91226
For specific Verdugo Viejo Zip Codes call (213) 586-1467, or your local postmaster.	
Vermont (Part of Los Angeles)	90029
Vernalis	95385
Vernon	90058
Vernon Landing	95659
Verona	95659
Veteran Heights	94508
Veterans Administration	90073
Veterans Bureau Hospital (Part of Palo Alto)	94304
Veterans Home (Part of Yountville)	94599
Veterans Hospital (Part of Los Angeles)	91343
Victor	95253
Victoria Court (Part of Santa Barbara)	93101
Victoria Park (Part of Carson)	90746
Victorville	92392-94
For specific Victorville Zip Codes call (619) 245-7723, or your local postmaster.	
Victory Center (Part of Los Angeles)	91609
Vidal	92280
Vidal Junction	92280
Viejas Indian Reservation	91901
View Park	90043
View Park-Windsor Hills	90043
Viking (Part of Long Beach)	90808
Village (Los Angeles County)	90024
Village (Santa Clara County)	95071
Villa Grande	95486
Villa Park	92667
Villa Verona	95965
Vina	96092
Vincent	91722
Vineburg	95487
Vine Hill	94553
Vintage Faire Mall (Part of Modesto)	95356
Vinton	96135
Vinvale (Part of South Gate)	90280
Viola	96088
Virginia Colony	93021
Virner	95634
Visalia	93277-79
	93291-92
For specific Visalia Zip Codes call (209) 732-8073, or your local postmaster.	
Visalia Mall (Part of Visalia)	93277
Visitacion (Part of San Francisco)	94134
Vista	92083-85
For specific Vista Zip Codes call (619) 726-0772, or your local postmaster.	
Vista Del Mar (Part of San Clemente)	92672
Vista del Morro	93402
Vista Grande (Madera County)	93637
Vista Grande (San Mateo County)	94014

	ZIP
Vista La Mesa (Part of La Mesa)	91941
Vista Park	93307
Volcano	95689
Volcanoville	95634
Volta	93635
Vorden	95690
Waddington	95536
Wagner (Part of Los Angeles)	90047
Wagy Flats	93240
Walerga	95660
Walker (Los Angeles County)	90201
Walker (Mono County)	96107
Walker Landing	95690
Wallace	95254
Walnut	91788†
	91789*
Walnut Creek	94593-98
For specific Walnut Creek Zip Codes call (510) 935-2611, or your local postmaster.	
Walnut Creek West	94596
Walnut Grove	95690
Walnut Heights	94596
Walnut Park	90255
Walteria (Part of Torrance)	90505
Warm Springs (Part of Fremont)	94539
Warner Ranch (Part of Moreno Valley)	92551
Warner Springs	92086
Wasco	93280
Washington (Part of Los Angeles)	90011
Washington (Part of Pasadena)	91114
Washington (Nevada County)	95986
Washington Manor (Part of San Leandro)	94579
Waterford	95386
Waterloo	95215
Waterman Gardens (Part of San Bernardino)	92410
Watson (Part of Carson)	90745
Watsonville	95076*
	95077†
Watsonville Junction	95076
Watts (Part of Los Angeles)	90002
Watts Valley	93667
Waukena	93282
Waverly Heights (Part of Thousand Oaks)	91360
Wawona	95389
Weaverville	96093
Webster Street (Part of Alameda)	94501
Weed	96094
Weedpatch	93241
Weimar	95736
Weitchpec	95546
Weldon	93283
Wendel	96136
Weott	95571
West Adams (Part of Los Angeles)	90016
West Arcadia (Part of Arcadia)	91006
West Athens	90247
West Bishop	93514
West Butte	95953
West Carson	90502
Westchester (Part of Los Angeles)	90045
West Compton	90220
West Covina	91790-93
For specific West Covina Zip Codes call (818) 962-8611, or your local postmaster.	
West Covina Fashion Plaza (Part of West Covina)	91790
Westend	93562
Western Pacific Mole (Part of Oakland)	94607
Western Village	93501
West Escondido (Part of Escondido)	92029
West Garden Grove (Part of Garden Grove)	92645
Westgate (Part of San Jose)	95117
Westgate Mall (Part of San Jose)	95129
West Guernewood	95446

	ZIP
Westhaven (Fresno County)	93245
Westhaven (Humboldt County)	95570
Westhaven-Moonstone	95570
West Hills	91307*
	91308†
West Hollywood	90069
Westlake	94014
Westlake Shopping Center (Part of Daly City)	94015
Westlake Village (Los Angeles County)	91361
Westlake Village (Ventura County)	91361
West Lane (Part of Stockton)	95208
Westley	95387
West Los Angeles (Part of Los Angeles)	90025
West Menlo Park	94025
Westminster	92683*
	92684†
Westminster Mall (Part of Westminster)	92683
West Modesto (Part of Modesto)	95351
Westmont	90044
Westmorland	92281
West Palm Springs	92282
West Parlier (Part of Parlier)	93648
West Point	95255
Westport	95488
West Portal (Part of San Francisco)	94127
	94169
For specific West Portal Zip Codes call (415) 759-1811, or your local postmaster.	
West Puente Valley	91744
West Sacramento	95691
West Saticoy (Part of Ventura)	93004
Westside (Part of San Bernardino)	92411
Westside Pavilion (Part of Los Angeles)	90064
Westvern (Part of Los Angeles)	90062
West Whittier	90606
West Whittier-Los Nietos	90606
Westwood (Lassen County)	96137
Westwood (Los Angeles County)	90024
Westwood Manor	96001
Westwood Village (Humboldt County)	95521
Westwood Village (Los Angeles County)	90024
Wheatland	95692
Wheeler Ridge	93301
Wherry Housing	93523
Whiskeytown	96095
Whispering Pines (Lake County)	95461
Whispering Pines (San Diego County)	92036
White Hall	95726
White Oak (Part of Los Angeles)	91416
White Pines	95223
White River	93257
White Rock	95630
Whitethorn	95589
White Water	92282
Whitewood (Part of Whittier)	90603
Whitley Gardens	93446
Whitlow	95554
Whitmore	96096
Whitmore Hot Springs	93546
Whitner Heights (Part of Parlier)	93648
Whittier	90601-10
For specific Whittier Zip Codes call (310) 696-9921, or your local postmaster.	
Whittier Quad Shopping Center (Part of Whittier)	90605
Whittwood Mall (Part of Whittier)	90603
Wiest	92227
Wilbur Springs	95987
Wilcox (Part of Los Angeles)	90038
Wildflower	93662

	ZIP
Wildomar	92595
Wildwood (Santa Cruz County)	95006
Wildwood (Trinity County)	96076
Wilfred	95401
Wilkerson	93514
Willaura Estates	95949
Williams	95987
William Taft (Part of San Diego)	92117
Willits	95490
Willowbrook	90222
Willow Creek (Humboldt County)	95573
Willow Creek (Plumas County)	96020
Willow Glen (Part of San Jose)	95125
Willow Ranch	96108
Willows	95988
Willow Springs (Kern County)	93560
Willow Springs (Mono County)	93517
Willow Springs (Tuolumne County)	95372
Will Rogers (Part of Santa Monica)	90402*
	90408†
Wilmar (Part of Rosemead)	91770
Wilmington (Part of Los Angeles)	90744*
	90748†
Wilmington Park (Part of Los Angeles)	90744
Wilseyville	95257
Wilsona	93535
Wilson Acres	96080
Wilsona Gardens	93534
Wilsonia	93633
Wilton (Sacramento County)	95693
Winchester	92596
Windsor	95492
Windsor Hills	90052
Windy Acres	93283
Winnetka (Part of Los Angeles)	91306*
	91396†
Winter Gardens	92040
Winterhaven	92283
Winters	95694
Wintersburg (Part of Huntington Beach)	92647
Winterwarm	92028
Winton	95388
Wise (Part of El Segundo)	90245
Wiseburn (Part of Hawthorne)	90250
Wishon	93669
Witch Creek	92065
Witter Springs	95493
Wofford Heights	93285
Wolf	95603
Wonderland	96003
Wonder Valley	93649
Woodacre	94973
Woodbridge	95258
Woodcrest	92504
Woodfords	96120
Woodlake	93286
Woodland	95695
	95776
For specific Woodland Zip Codes call (916) 662-5976, or your local postmaster.	
Woodland Hills	91364-67
For specific Woodland Hills Zip Codes call (818) 347-4056, or your local postmaster.	
Woodleaf	95925
Woodruff Avenue (Part of Bellflower)	90706
Woodside	94062
Woodside Glens (Part of Woodside)	94062
Woodson Bridge Estates	96021
Woodville	93258
Woodward Park (Part of Fresno)	93710
	93720
	93729
For specific Woodward Park Zip Codes call (209) 435-2767, or your local postmaster.	
Woody	93287
Workman (Part of South Gate)	90280

* **Area Zip Code**   † **Post Office Boxes**

	ZIP
Worldway Postal Center (Part of Los Angeles)	90009
Wrights Lake	95720
Wrightwood	92397
Wyandotte	95965
Wynola	92070
Wyntoon	96091
Yale (Part of Hemet)	92544
Yankee Hill	95965
Yankee Jims	95631
Yerba Buena Island (Part of San Francisco)	94130
Yermo	92398

	ZIP
Yettem	93670
Ygnacio Valley (Part of Walnut Creek)	94598
Yolanda (Part of San Anselmo)	94960
Yolo	95697
Yorba (Part of Pomona)	91767
Yorba Linda	92686-87
For specific Yorba Linda Zip Codes call (714) 528-7601, or your local postmaster.	
York (Part of Los Angeles)	90050

	ZIP
Yorkville	95494
Yosemite Forks	93644
Yosemite Lakes	93614
Yosemite Lodge	95389
Yosemite National Park	95389
Yosemite West	95389
Yountville	94599
Yreka	96097
Yuba City	95991-93
For specific Yuba City Zip Codes call (916) 673-9153, or your local postmaster.	

	ZIP
Yuba City Farm Labor Center	95991
Yucaipa	92399
Yucca Valley	92284*
	92286†
Yurok Indian Reservation	95546
Zamora	95698
Zayante	95018
Zenia	95595

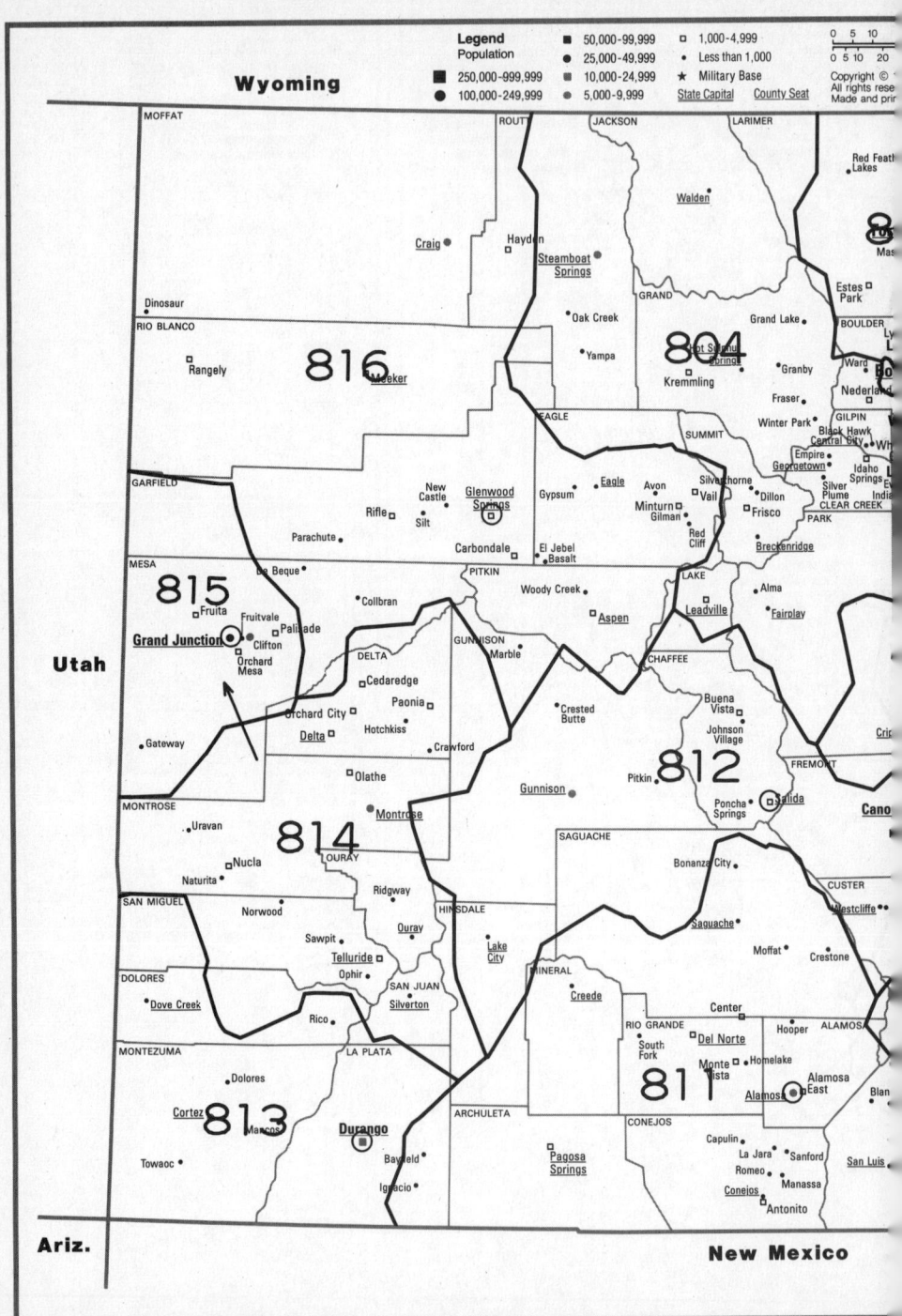

Legend
Population
■ 250,000-999,999
● 100,000-249,999
■ 50,000-99,999
● 25,000-49,999
■ 10,000-24,999
● 5,000-9,999
□ 1,000-4,999
· Less than 1,000
★ Military Base
State Capital   County Seat

0 5 10
0 5 10   20

Wyoming

MOFFAT
ROUT
JACKSON
LARIMER

Red Feath
· Lakes

Walden

· Craig
Hayden
Steamboat
Springs

GRAND

Estes
Park □
BOULDER

Dinosaur
· Oak Creek
Grand Lake ·
· Granby
Ward ·
Nederland ·

RIO BLANCO

· Rangely
Meeker

816

· Yampa
Kremmling

Fraser ·

Winter Park ·

GILPIN
Black Hawk
Central City
Empire
Georgetown
Idaho
Springs
Indi
CLEAR CREEK

EAGLE

804

Silverthorne ·
· Vail
Minturn ·
Gilman
Dillon ·
Frisco ·

GARFIELD
New
Castle
Glenwood
Springs
Gypsum
· Eagle
Avon ·

Silver
Plume

· Rifle
Silt
Red
Cliff

PARK
Breckenridge

Parachute ·
Carbondale
El Jebel
Basalt
LAKE

· De Beque
PITKIN
Woody Creek ·
Alma ·
Fairplay

MESA

815
· Fruita
Fruitvale
Collbran ·
· Aspen
Leadville
CHAFFEE

Grand Junction ⊙
Palisade
Clifton
Orchard
Mesa
DELTA
GUNNISON
Marble ·

· Cedaredge
Paonia ·
Crested
Butte
Buena
Vista ·

Orchard City ·
Hotchkiss
Johnson
Village

· Gateway
Delta
· Crawford
Gunnison ·
Pitkin ·

812
FREMONT

· Olathe

MONTROSE
· Uravan
Montrose
SAGUACHE
Poncha
Springs
Salida ⊙
Cano

814
Bonanza City ·

· Nucla
OURAY

Ridgway ·
CUSTER

Naturita ·
HINSDALE
Saguache ·
Westcliffe ·

SAN MIGUEL
Norwood ·
Ouray
Lake
City
Moffat ·
Crestone ·

Sawpit ·
Telluride
Ophir ·
MINERAL

DOLORES
SAN JUAN
Creede
Center
· Dove Creek
Silverton
RIO GRANDE

MONTEZUMA
Rico ·
LA PLATA
South
Fork
· Del Norte
Hooper ·
ALAMOSA

· Dolores
Monte
Vista
Homelake ·
Alamosa
East

813
811
Alamosa ⊙
Blan

Cortez ⊙
Mancos
ARCHULETA
CONEJOS
Capulin ·
La Jara ·
Sanford ·
San Luis

Towaoc ·
Durango ⊙
Bayfield ·
Pagosa
Springs
Romeo ·
Manassa

Ignacio ·
Conejos ·
Antonito ·

Ariz.
New Mexico

Utah

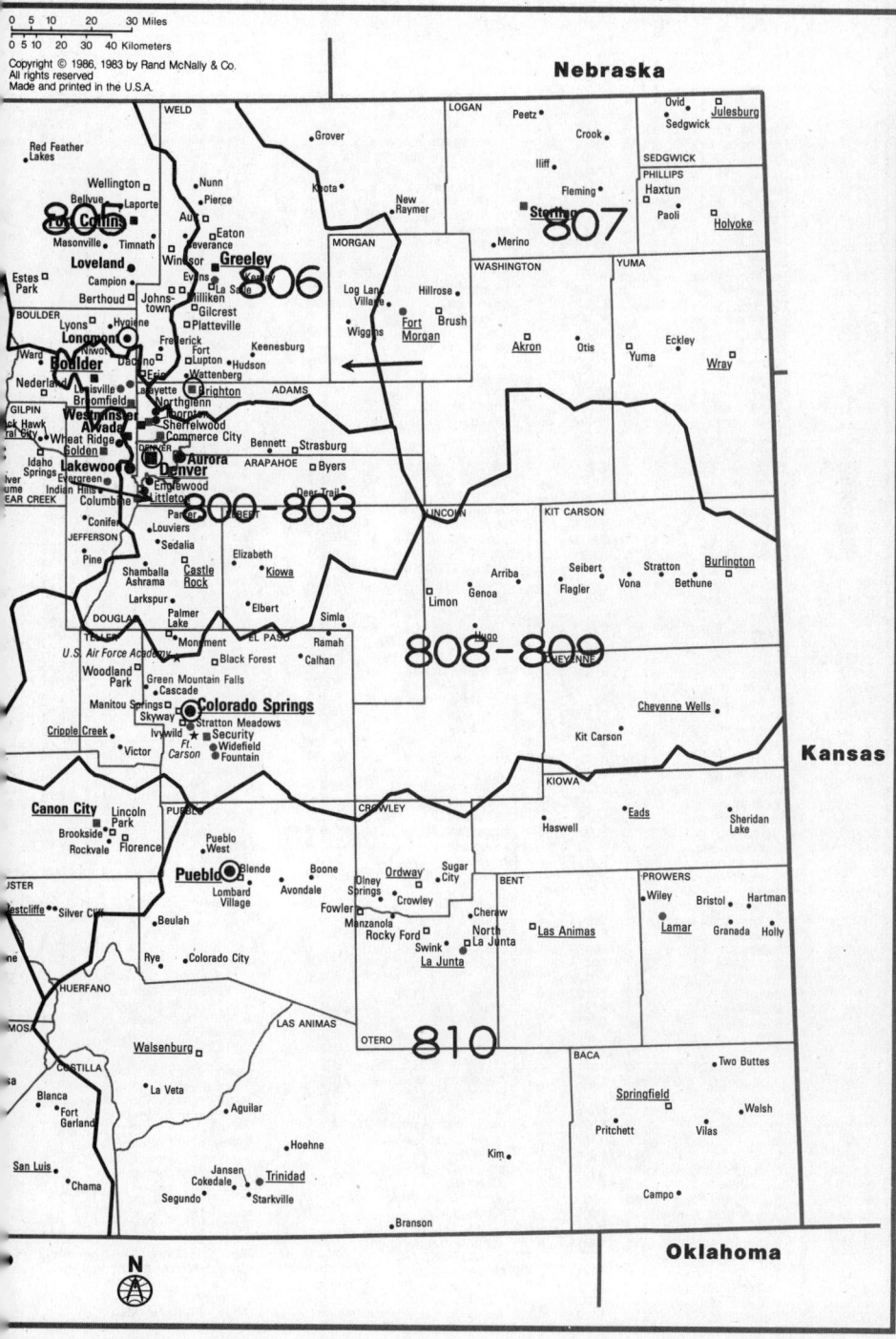

0 5 10   20   30 Miles

0 5 10   20   30   40 Kilometers

Nebraska

Kansas

Oklahoma

N

Name	ZIP
Acres Green	80124
Adams	80022
Adams City (Part of Commerce City)	80022
Agate	80101
Aguilar	81020
Airport Mail Facility (Part of Denver)	80207
Akron	80720
Alameda (Part of Lakewood)	80215
Alamosa	81101
Alamosa East	81101
Alcott (Part of Denver)	80212
Allenspark	80510
Allison	81137
Alma	80420
Almont	81210
Alpine (Chaffee County)	81236
Alpine (Rio Grande County)	81154
Altura (Part of Aurora)	80011
Altura Annex (Part of Aurora)	80011
American City	80427
Ames	81426
Amherst	80721
Andersonville (Part of Fort Collins)	80521
Angel Acres	80433
Antares (Part of Colorado Springs)	80909
Antelope Hills	81230
Antlers	81650
Anton	80801
Antonito	81120
Apache City	81089
Apex	80403
Appleton	81501
Applewood	80401
Applewood Village (Part of Wheat Ridge)	80033
Arabian Acres	80816
Arapahoe	80802
Arapahoe East (Part of Greenwood Village)	80112
Arboles	81121
Arickaree	80812
Aristocrat Ranchettes	80621
Arlington	81021
Aroya	80862
Arriba	80804
Arriola	81323
Arvada	80001-06

For specific Arvada Zip Codes call (303) 421-2200, or your local postmaster.

Name	ZIP
Aspen	81611-12

For specific Aspen Zip Codes call (303) 925-7523, or your local postmaster.

Name	ZIP
Aspen (Part of Fort Collins)	80527
Aspen-Gerbaz	81611
Aspen Park	80433
Association Camp	80511
Atwood	80722
Ault	80610
Aurora	80010-19, 80040-47

For specific Aurora Zip Codes call (303) 364-9215, or your local postmaster.

Name	ZIP
Aurora Mall (Part of Aurora)	80012
Austin (Part of Orchard City)	81410
Avon	81620
Avondale	81022
Bailey	80421
Bakersville	80476
Baldwin	81230
Balltown	81228
Barnesville	80624
Barr	80601
Bartlett	81090
Barton	81041
Basalt	81621
Battlement Mesa	81636
Baxterville	81132
Bayfield	81122
Beacon Hill	80860
Bear Valley (Part of Denver)	80227, 80232, 80235-36

For specific Bear Valley Zip Codes call (303) 986-6808, or your local postmaster.

Name	ZIP
Bear Valley Shopping Center (Part of Denver)	80227
Beaver Ridge	80440
Bedrock	81411
Beecher Island	80758
Belle Plain (Part of Pueblo)	81001
Bellvue	80512
Belmar (Part of Lakewood)	80226
Belmont (Part of Pueblo)	81001
Bendemeer Valley	80439
Bennett	80102
Bergen Park	80439
Berthoud (Larimer County)	80513
Berthoud (Weld County)	80513
Berthoud Falls	80438
Berthoud Pass	80452
Bethune	80805
Beulah	81023
Beverly Heights	80401
Beverly Hills	80104
Big Bend	81092
Big Elk Meadows	80540
Black Forest	80908
Black Hawk	80422
Blanca	81123
Blende	81006
Blue Mountain	81610
Blue Mountain Estates	80403
Blue Ridge	80424
Blue River	80424
Blue Valley	80452
Bonanza	81155
Boncarbo	81024
Bond	80423
Bondad	81301
Boone	81025
Boulder	80301-08

For specific Boulder Zip Codes call (303) 938-1100, or your local postmaster.

Name	ZIP
Boulder Heights	80302
Boulder Mail Handling Facility (Part of Boulder)	80501
Bountiful	81140
Bovina	80818
Bowie	81428
Bow Mar	80123
Boxelder Estates	80521
Boyero	80806
Bracewell	80631
Brandon	81026
Branson	81027
Breckenridge	80424
Breen	81326
Brewster	81226
Briargate (Part of Colorado Springs)	80920
Brigadoon Glen	80501
Briggsdale	80611
Brighton	80601
Bristol	81028
Broadmoor (Part of Colorado Springs)	80906
Broadway Estates	80120
Broken Arrow Acres	80433
Brook Forest	80439
Brook Forest Estates	80439
Brookridge	80120
Brookside	81212
Brookvale	80439
Broomfield	80020-21

For specific Broomfield Zip Codes call (303) 466-1711, or your local postmaster.

Name	ZIP
Brownlee	80480
Brownsville	80026
Brush	80723
Buckeye	80549
Buckingham (Part of Fort Collins)	80521
Buckingham Square (Part of Aurora)	80012
Buda	80513
Buena Vista	81211
Buena Vista Correctional Facility	81211
Buffalo Creek	80425
Buffalo Park Estate	80439
Buford	81641
Burdett	80720
Burland Ranchettes	80470
Burlington	80807
Burns	80426
Burnt Mill	81005
Byers	80103
Caddoa	81044

Name	ZIP
Cadet	80841
Cahone	81320
Calhan	80808
Camp Bird	81427
Camp George West	80401
Campion	80537
Campo	81029
Canfield	80026
Canon	81120
Canon City	81212-15, 81246

For specific Canon City Zip Codes call (719) 275-6877, or your local postmaster.

Name	ZIP
Capitol Hill (Part of Denver)	80218
Capulin	81124
Carbondale	81623
Cardiff	81601
Carr	80612
Cascade	80809
Cascade-Chipita Park	80809
Castle Rock	80104
Castlewood (Arapahoe County)	80120
Castlewood (Douglas County)	80116
Cattle Creek	81623
Cedar Cove	80537
Cedaredge	81413
Center	81125
Centerville	81236
Central City	80427
Chaddsford (Part of Aurora)	80014
Chama	81126
Chambers Square (Part of Aurora)	80011
Chapel Hills	80907
Chatfield Estates	80123
Chautauqua (Part of Boulder)	80302
Cheraw	81030
Cherry Creek (Part of Denver)	80206
Cherry Creek Shopping Center (Part of Denver)	80206
Cherry Hills Crest	80120
Cherry Hills Manor	80120
Cherry Hills Village	80110
Cherry Knolls	80120
Cherry Park	80110
Cherry Valley	80116
Cherrywood Village	80120
Cheyenne Canon (Part of Colorado Springs)	80906
Cheyenne Wells	80810
Chimney Rock	81127
Chipita Park	80809
Chivington	81036
Chromo	81128
Chula Vista	80403
Cimarron	81220
Cimarron Hills	80906
Cinderella City (Part of Englewood)	80110
Citadel, The (Part of Colorado Springs)	80909
Clark	80428
Clark Farms (Part of Parker)	80134
Clifton	81520
Climax	80429
Coal Creek	81221
Coaldale	81222
Coalmont	80430
Cokedale	81032
Collbran	81624
College Heights (Part of Durango)	81301
Colona	81401
Colorado City (El Paso County)	80904
Colorado City (Pueblo County)	81019
Colorado Mountain Estates	80816
Colorado Sierra	80403
Colorado Springs	80901-70

For specific Colorado Springs Zip Codes call (719) 570-5377, or your local postmaster.

Name	ZIP
Colorado Technical College	80907
Columbine (Jefferson County)	80123
Columbine (Routt County)	80428
Columbine Hills	80120
Columbine Knolls South	80123

Name	ZIP
Columbine Manor	80123
Columbine Valley	80123
Commerce City	80022*
	80037†
Como	80432
Conejos	81129
Conifer	80433
Conifer Mountain	80433
Conifer Park	80433
Cope	80812
Copper Mountain	80443
Copper Spur	80423
Cornelia	81054
Cornish	80611
Coronado	80229
Cortez	81321
Cory (Part of Orchard City)	81414
Cotopaxi	81223
Country Acres	80534
Country Club Estates	80521
Country Club Park	80303
Cowdrey	80434
Cozy Corner	80234
Cragmor (Part of Colorado Springs)	80907
Craig	81625*
	81626†
Cranor Acres (Part of Gunnison)	81230
Crawford	81415
Creede	81130
Crescent	80403
Crested Butte	81224*
	81225†
Crested Butte South	81224
Crestmoor (Part of Glendale)	80222
Crestone	81131
Crestview Village	80403
Crestwoods	80424
Crews	80911
Cripple Creek	80813
Crisman	80302
Crook	80726
Crossroads Mall (Part of Boulder)	80301
Crowley	81033
Crystola	80863
Cuchara	81055
Cuerna Verde	81069
Dacono	80514
Dailey	80728
De Beque	81630
Deckers	80135
Deer Creek Valley Ranchos	80470
Deer Park	80467
Deer Trail	80105
Delhi	81059
Del Norte	81132
Delta	81416

Name	ZIP
Denver	80201-14
	80216-25
	80227
	80229
	80231
	80233-95

For specific Denver Zip Codes call (303) 297-6000, or your local postmaster.

COLLEGES & UNIVERSITIES

Name	ZIP
Metropolitan State College of Denver	80217
Regis University	80221
University of Colorado at Denver	80217
University of Colorado Health Sciences Center	80262
University of Denver	80208

FINANCIAL INSTITUTIONS

Name	ZIP
Bank of Cherry Creek, N.A.	80206
Bank One-Denver	80202
Colorado National Bank	80202
Colorado State Bank of Denver	80202
Affiliated National Bank-Denver	80202
First Federal Savings Bank of Colorado	80202
First Interstate Bank of Denver, N.A.	80270
First National Bank of Southeast Denver	80210

* Area Zip Code † Post Office Boxes

	ZIP
Guaranty Bank & Trust Company	80202
Mountain States Bank	80218
Norwest Bank-Denver, National Association	80274

HOSPITALS

	ZIP
Denver Health and Hospitals	80204
Porter Memorial Hospital	80210
Presbyterian-St. Luke's Medical Center	80203
Rose Medical Center	80220
St. Anthony Hospital Central	80204
St. Joseph Hospital	80218
University Hospital	80262
Veterans Affairs Medical Center	80220

HOTELS/MOTELS

	ZIP
Brown Palace Hotel	80202
Embassy Suites-Downtown	80202
Hyatt Regency Denver	80202
Marriott City Center	80202
Oxford Hotel	80202
Radisson Hotel Denver	80202
Warwick Hotel	80203
Westin Hotel, Tabor Center	80202

MILITARY INSTALLATIONS

	ZIP
Defense Finance and Accounting Service	80297
Denver Merchandise Mart	80216
Derby	80022
Derby Junction	80426
Devine	81001
Dillon	80435
Dinosaur	81610
Divide	80814
Dolores	81323
Dome Rock	80441
Dorey Lakes	80403
Dotsero	81637
Dove Creek	81324
Downieville	80436
Downtown (Part of Colorado Springs)	80903
Downtown (Part of Englewood)	80110
Downtown (Part of Loveland)	80537
Doyleville	81239
Drake	80515
Drakes (Part of Fort Collins)	80521
Dream House Acres	80120
Dry Creek Basin	81431
Dumont	80436
Dupont	80024
Durango	81301*
	81302†
Durango West	81301
Dyke	81147
Eads	81036
Eagle	81631
Eagle-Vail	81620
Eastlake (Adams County)	80614
Eastlake (Pueblo County)	81004
Eastonville	80831
East Portal	80474
Eastridge (Part of Aurora)	80014
East Weston	81091
Eastwood (Part of Pueblo)	81001
Eaton	80615
Echo Lake	80452
Eckert (Part of Orchard City)	81418
Eckley	80727
Eden	81003
Edgemont (Part of Lakewood)	80401
Edgewater	80214
Edison	80864
Edith	81128
Edler	81073
Edwards	81632
Egnar	81325
Elba	80720
Elbert	80106
Eldora	80466
Eldorado Springs	80025
Elephant Park	80439
Eleven Mile Village	80827
Elizabeth	80107
El Jebel	81628

	ZIP
Elk Creek Acres	80470
Elk Creek Highlands	80421
Elkdale	80478
Elkhorn Acres	80470
Elk Springs	81633
Elkton	80860
Ellicott	80808
El Moro	81082
El Rancho	80401
El Vado	80302
Elwell	80534
Emma	81621
Empire	80438
Englewood	80110-12
	80150-55
For specific Englewood Zip Codes call (303) 761-0474, or your local postmaster.	
Erie	80516
Erie Air Park (Part of Erie)	80516
Escalante Forks	81416
Espinosa	81141
Estes Park	80517
Estrella	81101
Evans	80620
Evanston	80530
Evergreen	80439
Evergreen Highlands	80439
Ever Green Hills	80439
Evergreen Meadows	80439
Evergreen Meadows West	80439
Evergreen Park Estate	80439
Evergreen West	80439
Fairplay	80440
Fairview	81069
Fairview Estates	80123
Fairway Estates	80521
Falcon	80908
Falcon Estates	80920
Falfa	81301
Fall Creek	81430
Farisita	81089
Farmers	80631
Federal Correctional Institution	80110
Federal Heights	80221
Fenders	80465
Ferncliff	80510
Firestone	80520
First View	80810
Flagler	80815
Fleming	80728
Fletcher (Part of Aurora)	80010
Flintwood Hills	80116
Florence	81226
Florissant	80816
Florissant Heights	80816
Fondis	80106
Foothills Fashion Mall (Part of Fort Collins)	80525
Forest Hills	80403
Fort Carson	80913
Fort Collins	80521-27
For specific Fort Collins Zip Codes call (303) 225-4100, or your local postmaster.	
Fort Garland	81133
Fort Logan (Part of Sheridan)	80236
Fort Lupton	80621
Fort Lyon	81038
Fort Morgan	80701
	80705
For specific Fort Morgan Zip Codes call (303) 867-7111, or your local postmaster.	
Fountain	80817
Fountain Valley School	80911
Fowler	81039
Fox Creek	81120
Foxton	80441
Franktown	80116
Fraser	80442
Frederick	80530
Friendship Ranch	80470
Frisco	80443
Fruita	81521
Fruitvale	81504
Fulton Heights (Part of Pueblo)	81003
Galeton	80622
Garcia	81134
Garden City	80631
Gardner	81040
Garfield	81227
Gateway (Arapahoe County)	80014
Gateway (Douglas County)	80126

	ZIP
Gateway (Mesa County)	81522
Gato	81147
Gaynor Lakes	80501
Gem Village	81122
Genesee	80401
Genoa	80818
Georgetown	80444
Gilcrest	80623
Gill	80624
Gilman	81645
Glade Park	81523
Glen Comfort	80515
Glendale	80222
Glendevey	82063
Gleneagle	80132
Glen Eden	80428
Glenelk	80470
Glen Haven	80532
Glen Isle	80421
Glen Park (Part of Palmer Lake)	80133
Glenwood Springs	81601*
	81602†
Goat Hill	81006
Golden	80401-03
For specific Golden Zip Codes call (303) 278-8537, or your local postmaster.	
Golden Mail Handling Unit (Part of Golden)	80401
Goldfield	80860
Gold Hill	80302
Goodnight	81005
Goodrich	80653
Gould	80480
Granada	81041
Granby	80446
Grand Junction	81501-06
For specific Grand Junction Zip Codes call (303) 244-3400, or your local postmaster.	
Grand Lake	80447
Grand Mesa	81413
Grandview	81301
Grandview Estates	80134
Granite	81228
Grant	80448
Gray's Mary Greenwood	81069
Great Divide	81625
Greeley	80631-34
For specific Greeley Zip Codes call (303) 353-0398, or your local postmaster.	
Greeley Mall (Part of Greeley)	80631
Green Gables (Part of Lakewood)	80232
Greenhorn	81019
Greenland	80118
Green Mountain (Part of Lakewood)	80228
Green Mountain Camp	80498
Green Mountain Estates (Part of Lakewood)	80228
Green Mountain Falls	80819
Green Mountain Village (Part of Lakewood)	80228
Green Towers	81069
Green Valley Acres	80433
Greenway Park	80020
Greenwood (Custer County)	81253
Greenwood (Pueblo County)	81069
Greenwood Village	80111
Greystone	81640
Greystone Lodge	80439
Grover	80729
Guadalupe	81129
Guffey	80820
Gulnare	81042
Gunbarrel	80501
Gunbarrel Estates	80501
Gunbarrel Greens	80301
Gunnison	81230
Gypsum	81637
Hahns Peak	80428
Hale	80735
Halfway House	81220
Hamilton	81638
Hanover	80909
Happy Canyon	80104
Hardin	80644
Harmony (Part of Fort Collins)	
Harris Park (Adams County)	80036
Harris Park (Park County)	80470
Hartman	81043

	ZIP
Hartsel	80449
Hasty	81044
Haswell	81045
Hawley	81067
Haxtun	80731
Hayden	81639
Hazeltine Heights	80640
Heather Ridge (Part of Aurora)	80014
Heatherwood	80301
Heeney	80498
Henderson	80640
Hereford	80732
Heritage Dells	80401
Heritage Place	80110
Hermosa	81301
Herzman Mesa	80439
Hesperus	81326
Hiawatha	82901
Hidden Valley	80439
Hideaway Park (Part of Winter Park)	80482
High Chateau Ranches	80816
Highland Acres	80631
Highland Hills	80634
Highland Lake	80651
Highland Lakes	80814
Highland Park	80470
Highland Pines	80470
Highlands (Part of Denver)	80211
Highlands Ranch	80126
High-Mar (Part of Boulder)	80303
Hi-Land Acres	80601
Hill N' Park	80631
Hillrose	80733
Hillside	81232
Hilltop	80134
Hiwan Hills	80439
Hoehne	81046
Hoffman Heights (Part of Aurora)	80012
Holiday Acres	81147
Holiday Hills	80863
Holland Park (Part of Colorado Springs)	80907
Holly	81047
Holyoke	80734
Homelake	81135
Hooper	81136
Hotchkiss	81419
Hot Sulphur Springs	80451
Howard	81233
Howells (Part of Littleton)	80120
Hoyt	80654
Hudson	80642
Hugo	80821
Husted	80840
Hyde	80743
Hygiene	80533
Hyland Hills	80439
Hyland Knolls	80634
Idaho Springs	80452
Idalia	80735
Idledale	80453
Ignacio	81137
Iliff	80736
Ilse	81212
Indian Creek	80816
Indian Creek Ranch	80135
Indian Head	81239
Indian Hills	80454
Indian Springs Village	80470
Indian Tree (Part of Arvada)	80006
Ione	80621
Irondale	80022
Ivywild (Part of Colorado Springs)	80906
Jacks Cabin	81210
Jamestown	80455
Jansen	81082
Jaroso	81138
Jefferson	80456
Jefferson Heights	80456
Joes	80822
Johnson Village	81211
Johnstown	80534
Juanita	81147
Julesburg	80737
Kahler	80513
Karval	80823
Kearns	81147
Keenesburg	80643
Kelim	80537
Kelker (Part of Colorado Springs)	80906
Kellytown	80125
Ken Caryl	80127

* Area Zip Code   † Post Office Boxes

	ZIP
Ken Caryl (census designated place)	80123
Keota	80729
Kersey	80644
Keystone	80435
Kim	81049
Kingsborough (Part of Aurora)	80017
Kingsborough South (Part of Aurora)	80012
Kings Corner	80537
Kiowa	80117
Kipling Hills	80123
Kipling Villas	80123
Kirk	80824
Kit Carson	80825
Kittredge	80457
Kline	81326
Knaus	80634
Knob Hill (Part of Colorado Springs)	80910
Koen	81041
Kornman	81052
Kremmling	80459
Kuhlmann Heights	80403
Kutch	80832
Lafayette	80026
La Garita	81132
Laird	80758
La Jara	81140
La Junta	81050
La Junta Gardens (Part of La Junta)	81050
Lakeborough	80235
Lake City	81235
Lake George	80827
Lakeside	80212
Lake View	80403
Lakewood	80226
Lamar	81052
La Montana Mesa	80816
Laporte	80535
La Posta	81301
Lariat (Part of Monte Vista)	81144
Larkspur	80118
La Salle	81054
Las Animas	81054
Lasauses	81151
Las Mesitas	81120
Last Chance	80757
La Valley	81152
La Veta	81055
Lawson	80452
Lay	81625
Lazear	81420
Leadville	80461
Leadville North	80461
Leawood	80123
Lebanon	81323
Leisure Living	80516
Lewis	81327
Leyden	80403
Liberty Bell Village	81435
Lime	81005
Limon	80828
Lincoln Park	81212
Lindon	80740
Littleton	80120-27
	80160-62
For specific Littleton Zip Codes call (303) 798-2461, or your local postmaster.	
Livengood Hills	80134
Livermore	80536
Lobatos	81120
Lochbuie	80601
Lochwood (Part of Lakewood)	80232
Log Lane Village	80705
Loma	81524
Loma Linda	81301
Lombard Village	81006
Lone Pine Estates	80465
Lone Star	80743
Lonetree	81147
Longmont	80501-04
For specific Longmont Zip Codes call (303) 776-2135, or your local postmaster.	
Longview	80441
Lookout Mountain	80401
Loretto Heights (Part of Denver)	80236
Los Fuertes	81152
Louisville	80027
Louviers	80131

	ZIP
Loveland	80537-39
For specific Loveland Zip Codes call (303) 667-0344, or your local postmaster.	
Loveland Heights	80515
Lubers	81057
Lucerne	80646
Ludlow	81082
Lyons	80540
Lyons Park Estates	80540
McClave	81057
McClellands (Part of Fort Collins)	80521
McCoy (Chaffee County)	81201
McCoy (Eagle County)	80463
Mack	81525
Mad Creek	80487
Madison Hill (Part of Westminster)	80030
Madrid	81082
Magnolia	80466
Maher	81421
Mail Handling Center (Part of Englewood)	80111
Manassa	81141
Mancos	81328
Mandalay Gardens	80021
Manitou Springs	80829
Manzanola	81058
Marble	81623
Marshall	80302
Marshdale Park	80439
Marvel	81329
Mary Jane	80480
Maryvale	80442
Mason Corner	80631
Masonic Park	81154
Masonville	80541
Massadona	81610
Masters	80649
Matheson	80830
Maxeyville	81144
Maybell	81640
Mayday	81326
Maysville	81201
May Valley	81052
Mead	80542
Meadow Brook Heights	80120
Meadowood (Part of Aurora)	80013
Medina Plaza	81091
Meeker	81641
Meeker Park	80510
Meredith	81642
Merino	80741
Mesa (Mesa County)	81643
Mesa (Pueblo County)	81006
Mesa Lakes	81643
Mesa Verde National Park	81330
Mesita	81152
Messex	80741
Milliken	80543
Milner	80487
Mineral Hot Springs	81143
Minnequa (Part of Pueblo)	81004
Minnequa Heights (Part of Pueblo)	81004
Minturn	81645
Mirage	81143
Mission Viejo (Part of Aurora)	80013
Model	81059
Moffat	81143
Mogote	81120
Molina	81646
Montbello (Part of Denver)	80239
Montclair (Part of Denver)	80220
Monte Vista	81144
Monte Vista Estates	80104
Montezuma	80435
Montrose	81401*
	81402†
Monument	80132
Monument Lake Park	81091
Moore Dale	80421
Morgan	81140
Morrison	80465
Mosca	81146
Mountain View (Jefferson County)	80212
Mountain View (Larimer County)	80521
Mountain View Acres	81101
Mountain View Lakes	80470
Mount Crested Butte	81225
Mount Massive Lakes	80461
Mount Princeton Hot Springs	81236
Mount Vernon Club Place	80401

	ZIP
Mutual	81089
Nast	81642
Nathrop	81236
Naturita	81422
Nederland	80466
Nevadaville	80427
New Castle	81647
New Raymer	80742
Nighthawk	80135
Nine Mile Corner	80026
Niwot	80544
Nob Hill	80122
North Avondale	81022
North Cherry Creek Valley	80231
North Delta	81416
North End (Part of Colorado Springs)	80907
Northglenn	80233
Northglenn Mall (Part of Northglenn)	80234
North La Junta (Part of La Junta)	81050
North Pecos	80221
North Pole	80809
North Valley Shopping Center (Part of Thornton)	80229
North Washington Heights	80229
North Yard (Part of Denver)	80221
Norwood	81423
Nucla	81424
Numa	81063
Nunn	80648
Nutria	81147
Oak Creek	80467
Oak Grove	81401
Oehlmann Park	80433
Ohio	81237
Olathe	81425
Olney Springs	81062
Olympus Heights	80515
Ophir	81426
Orchard	80649
Orchard City	81410
Orchard Mesa	81501
Ordway	81063
Ormandale	81005
Ortiz	81120
Otis	80743
Ouray	81427
Ovid	80744
Oxford	81137
Pactolus	80403
Padroni	80745
Pagosa Springs	81147
	81157
For specific Pagosa Springs Zip Codes call (303) 264-5440, or your local postmaster.	
Paisaje	81120
Palisade	81526
Palmer Lake	80133
Palos Verdes	80123
Palos Verdes East	80110
Pandora	81435
Panorama Heights	80401
Panoview Park (Part of Gunnison)	81230
Paoli	80746
Paonia	81428
Parachute	81635
Paradox	81429
Paragon Estates	80303
Park Center	81212
Park City	80420
Parker	80134
Park Hill (Part of Denver)	80207
Park Vista Estates	80908
Parlin	81239
Parshall	80468
Peaceful Valley	80540
Peagreen	81416
Peak Seven West	80424
Peckham	80645
Peetz	80747
Penitentiary (Part of Canon City)	81212
Penrose	81240
Peyton	80831
Pheasant Run (Part of Aurora)	80015
Phippsburg	80469
Piedra	81147
Pierce	80650
Pine	80470
Pinebrook Hills	80302
Pinecliffe	80471

	ZIP
Pine Crest (Part of Palmer Lake)	80133
Pinehaven	81055
Pine Hills	80132
Pine Junction	80470
Pine Nook	80135
Pine Park Estates	80465
Pinewood Springs	80540
Pinnacle Park	80631
Pinon	81008
Pinon Acres	81301
Pinon Canyon	81059
Pitkin	81241
Placerville	81430
Plateau City	81624
Platner	80743
Platoro	81144
Platteville	80651
Plaza	81132
Pleasant Valley (Part of Colorado Springs)	80904
Pleasant View (Jefferson County)	80401
Pleasant View (Montezuma County)	81331
Poncha Springs	81242
Ponderosa	80424
Ponderosa Hills	80134
Ponderosa Park	80107
Poudre Park	80521
Powderhorn	81243
Powder Wash	82901
Pritchett	81064
Proctor	80736
Prospect Heights	81212
Prospect Valley	80643
Prowers	81052
Pryor	81065
Pueblo	81001-08
For specific Pueblo Zip Codes call (719) 544-0132, or your local postmaster.	
Pueblo Army Depot	81001
Pueblo Dam	81003
Pueblo Mall (Part of Pueblo)	81008
Pueblo West	81007
Punkin Center	80821
Quincy (Part of Aurora)	80015
Radium	80423
Ragged Mountain	81434
Rainbow Valley	80814
Ramah	80832
Rand	80473
Rangely	81648
Rangeview Estates (Boulder County)	80501
Range View Estates (Weld County)	80631
Rattlesnake Buttes	81089
Raymond	80540
Read	81416
Red Cliff	81649
Red Feather Lakes	80545
Redlands	81503
Redmesa	81326
Red Rock Ranch	80132
Redstone	81623
Redvale	81431
Red Wing	81066
Rezago	81082
Richfield	81140
Rico	81332
Ridgeview Hills	80122
Ridgway	81432
Rifle	81650
Rinn	80501
Rio Blanco	81650
Riverside	80540
Roberta	81050
Rockrimmon (Part of Colorado Springs)	80919
Rockvale	81244
Rocky Ford	81067
Rocky Mountain Arsenal	80022
Rogers Mesa	81419
Roggen	80652
Roland Valley	80470
Rollinsville	80474
Romeo	81148
Rosedale (Jefferson County)	80439
Rosedale (Weld County)	80631
Rosita	81252
Roswell (Part of Colorado Springs)	80907
Rowena	80455
Roxborough Park	80125
Royal Gorge	81246

* Area Zip Code **† Post Office Boxes**

	ZIP
Royal Ranch	80421
Ruedi	81621
Rulison	81635
Rush	80833
Russell Gulch	80427
Russelville	80116
Rustic	80512
Rye	81069
Rye Ranchettes	81069
Sable (Part of Aurora)	80011
Saguache	81149
Saint Charles Mesa	81006
St. Elmo	81236
St. Petersburg	80728
Salida	81201
Salina	80302
Salt Creek (Part of Pueblo)	81006
San Acacio	81151
San Antonio	81120
Sandown (Part of Denver)	80216
Sanford	81151
Sangre De Cristo Ranches	81133
San Isabel	81069
San Juan	81082
San Luis	81152
San Pablo	81152
Santa Fe (Denver County)	80204
Santa Fe (Pueblo County)	81003
Sapinero	81247
Sarcillo	81091
Sarcillo Canon	81091
Sargents	81248
Sargents School	81144
Sawpit	81430
Security	80911
Security-Widefield	80911
Sedalia	80135
Sedgwick	80749
Segundo	81082
Seibert	80834
Semper	80021
Severance	80546
Shadow Mountain (Grand County)	80447
Shadow Mountain (Jefferson County)	80433
Shadows North	80424
Shaffers Crossing	80433
Shamballa Ashrama	80135
Shaw Heights	80030
Shaw Heights Mesa	80030
Shawnee	80475
Sheridan	80110
Sheridan Lake	81071
Sherrelwood	80221
Sherrelwood Estates	80221
Silt	81652
Silver Cliff	81249
Silver Creek	80446
Silver Heights	80104
Silver Plume	80476
Silver Shekel	80424
Silver Springs	80470
Silver Spruce	80301
Silverthorne	80498
Silverton	81433
Simla	80835
Singleton	80475
Skyland	81224
Skyland Village (Part of Westminster)	80030
Skyline	80222
Sky Village	80465
Skyway (El Paso County)	80906
Skyway (Mesa County)	81643
Skyway Estates (Part of Colorado Springs)	80906
Skyway Park (Part of Colorado Springs)	80906
Slater	81653
Slick Rock	81333
Smeltertown	81201
Smith Hill	80403
Smoky Hill (Part of Aurora)	80015
Snowmass	81654
Snowmass Village	81615
Snow Mountain Ranch	80446
Snyder	80750
Somerset	81434
South Canon (Part of Canon City)	81212
South Denver (Part of Denver)	80209

	ZIP
Southern Ute Indian Reservation	81137
South Fork	81154
Southglenn	80122
South Park City (Part of Fairplay)	80440
South Platte	80441
South Roggen	80652
Southwind	80120
Southwood	80120
Spanish Peaks	81055
Spanish Village	80631
Sparks	82901
Sphinx Park	80470
Spivak (Part of Lakewood)	80214
Springfield	81073
Spring Valley	80814
Sprucedale	80439
Stanley Park	80439
Starkville	81074
Steamboat Plaza (Part of Steamboat Springs)	80488
Steamboat Springs	80477
	80487-88
For specific Steamboat Springs Zip Codes call (303) 879-3556, or your local postmaster.	
Steamboat Village (Part of Steamboat Springs)	80487
Stem Beach	81005
Sterling	80751
Stockyards (Part of Denver)	80216
Stonegate (Part of Parker)	80134
Stoneham	80754
Stoner	81323
Stonewall	81091
Stonington	81075
Strasburg	80136
Stratmoor	80906
Stratmoor Hills	80906
Stratton	80836
Stratton Meadows (Part of Colorado Springs)	80906
Stratton Park (Part of Colorado Springs)	80907
Stringtown	80461
Stroh Ranch	80134
Sugar City	81076
Sugarloaf	80302
Sullivan (Part of Denver)	80231
Summit Cove	80435
Summitville	81132
Sunbeam	81640
Sunnyside (Boulder County)	80466
Sunnyside (Denver County)	80211
Sunnyside (La Plata County)	81301
Sunnyslopes	80020
Sunset (Part of Pueblo)	81005
Sunshine	80302
Superior	80027
Surrey Ridge	80104
Sutank	81623
Swallows	81003
Swede Corners	81149
Sweetwater	81637
Swink	81077
Swissvale	81201
Switzerland Village	80470
Tabernash	80478
Tallahassee School	81212
Tamarron (El Paso County)	80919
Tamarron (La Plata County)	81301
Tanglewood Acres	81252
Tarryall	80827
Taylor Park	81210
Telluride	81435
Templeton (Part of Colorado Springs)	80936
Ten Mile Vista	80424
Tennyson Heights (Part of Fort Collins)	80521
Terminal Annex (Part of Denver)	80217
Texas Creek	81223
Thatcher	81059
The Meadows	80127
The Mesa	80904
The Pinery	80134
The Shadows	80424

	ZIP
The Springs	80906
Thomasville	81642
Thornton	80229
Thurman	80801
Tiffany	81137
Timbers (Part of Aurora)	80014
Timnath	80547
Timpas	81050
Tincup	81210
Tiny Town	80465
Tolland	80474
Toltec	81089
Tomichi Heights (Part of Gunnison)	81230
Toponas	80479
Tordal Estates	80424
Torres (Las Animas County)	81091
Torres (Rio Grande County)	81144
Towaoc	81334
Towner	81071
Tranquil Acres	80863
Trimble	81301
Trinchera	81081
Trinidad	81082
Troutdale	80439
Trout Haven	80814
Trout Lake	81426
Truckton	80864
Trujillo	81147
Trumbull	80135
Twin Crossing	81301
Twin Forks	80454
Twin Lakes	81251
Twin Rock	80816
Twin Spruce	80403
Two Buttes	81084
Tyrone	81059
Unaweep	81527
Uncompahgre	81401
Union	80750
Union Stockyards (Part of Denver)	80216
United States Air Force Academy	80840*
	80841†
University (Part of Boulder)	80309
University Hills Mall (Part of Denver)	80222
University Park (Part of Denver)	80210
	80250
For specific University Park Zip Codes call (303) 759-5759, or your local postmaster.	
Upper San Juan River	81147
Uravan	81422
Ute Heights	81201
Ute Mountain Indian Reservation	81334
Uteyville	81064
Vail	81657*
	81658†
Valdez	81082
Vallecito	81122
Valley of Blue	80424
Vancorum	81422
Velasquez Plaza	81091
Venetian Village (Part of Colorado Springs)	80907
Vernon	80755
Victor	80860
Viejo San Acacio	81151
Vigil	81091
Vilas	81087
Village East (Part of Aurora)	80012
Village Seven (Part of Colorado Springs)	80917
Villa Grove	81155
Villa Italia Center (Part of Lakewood)	80226
Villegreen	81049
Vineland	81001
Virginia Dale	80548
Vista Grande (Part of Colorado Springs)	80918
Vista Verde	80120
Vollmar	80621
Vona	80861
Vroman	81067
Waconda Hills	80132
Wagner Manor	80302

	ZIP
Wagon Wheel Gap	81154
Wahatoya	81055
Wah Keeney Park	80439
Wahketa Village	80701
Walden	80480
Wallstreet	80302
Walnut Hills	80112
Walsenburg	81089
Walsh	81090
Waltonia	80515
Walts Corner	81027
Wamble Park	80433
Wamble Valley	80433
Wandcrest Park	80470
Ward	80481
Waterton	80125
Watkins	80137
Wattenberg	80621
Waverly	81101
Welby	80229
Weldona	80653
Wellington	80549
Wellshire (Part of Denver)	80222
Wellsville	81201
West (Part of Greeley)	80634
Westcliffe	81252
West End (Part of Colorado Springs)	80904
Western Hills	80221
West Farm	81052
Westland Center (Part of Lakewood)	80215
Westminster	80030-31
	80035-36
For specific Westminster Zip Codes call (303) 429-0340, or your local postmaster.	
Westminster East	80221
Westminster Mall (Part of Westminster)	80030
Weston	81091
Westridge	80634
West Vail (Part of Vail)	81657
Westwood (Part of Denver)	80219
Westwood Lake	80863
Wetmore	81253
Wheat Ridge	80033*
	80034†
Wheeler	80403
White Pine	81248
Whitewater	81527
Widefield	80911
Wiggins	80654
Wild Horse (Cheyenne County)	80862
Wild Horse (Pueblo County)	81001
Wiley	81092
Willard	80741
Williamsburg (Fremont County)	81226
Williamsburg (Jefferson County)	80127
Willis Heights	80501
Willowbrook	80465
Willow Creek	80110
Willow Gulch	81423
Wilmot	80439
Wilson Lake Estates	80816
Windsor	80550
Windsor Gardens (Part of Denver)	80231
Winter Park	80482
Wolcott	81655
Wondervu	80403
Woodglen (Part of Thornton)	80233
Woodland Acres	81069
Woodland Park	80863*
	80866
Woodmar Village	80123
Woodmoor	80908
Woodrow	80757
Woody Creek	81656
Wray	80758
Yampa	80483
Yellow Jacket	81335
Yoder	80864
Yorkborough (Part of Thornton)	80229
Yuma	80759
Yuma Camp Of The Rockies (Part of Estes Park)	80511

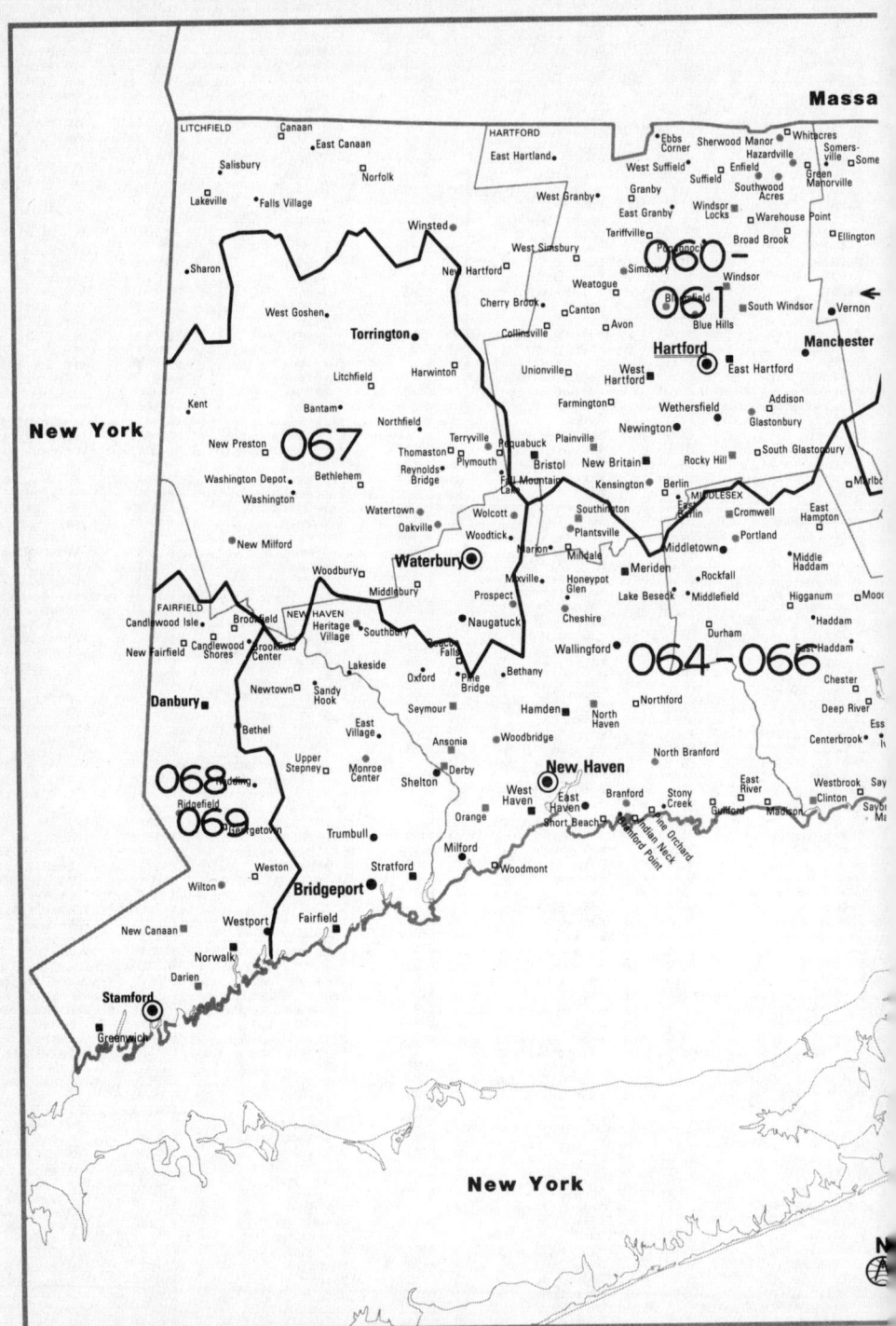

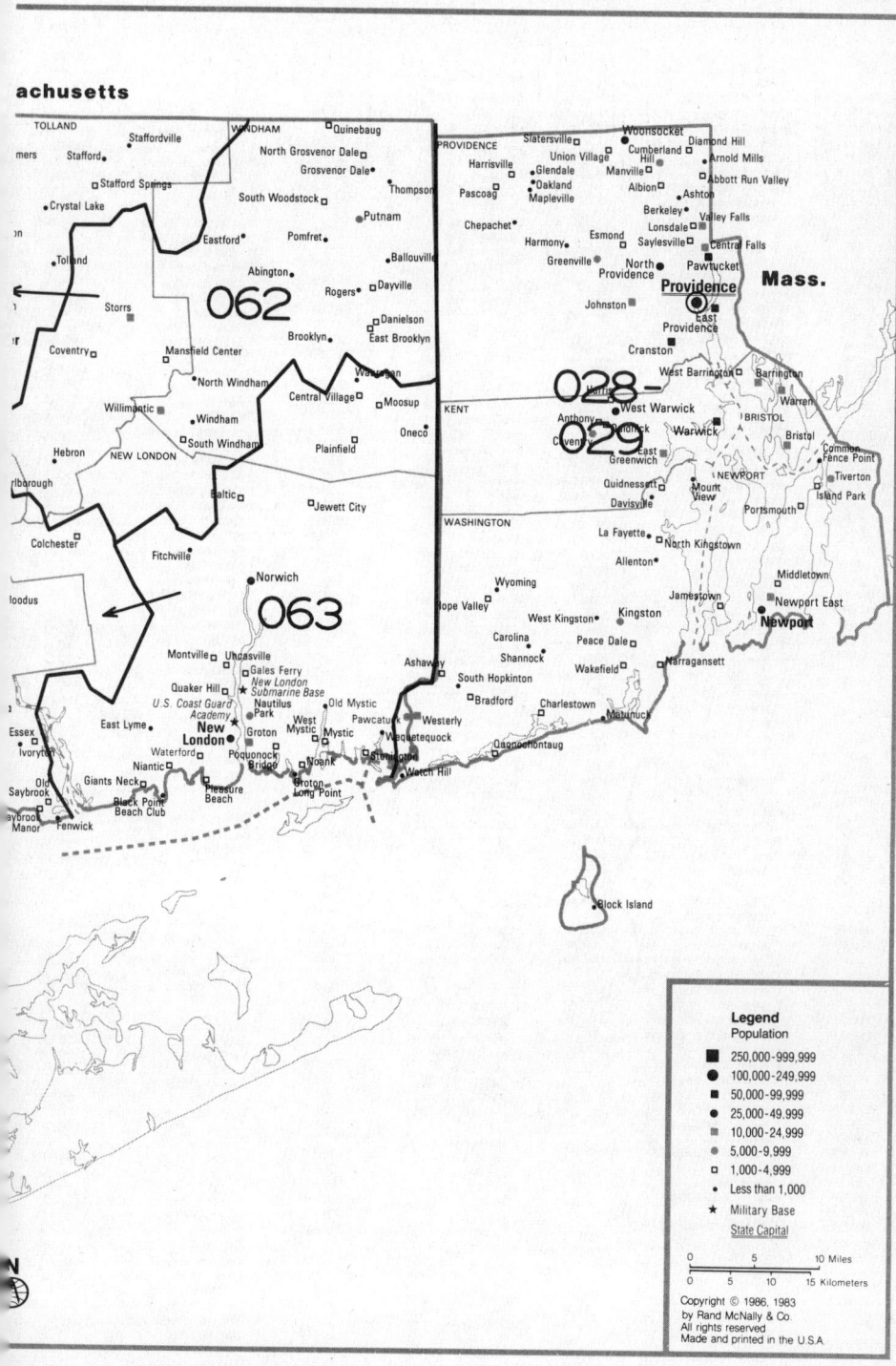

achusetts

TOLLAND
Staffordville
Stafford
Stafford Springs
Crystal Lake
Toland
Storrs
Coventry
Mansfield Center
Hebron
Marlborough
Colchester
oodus

WINDHAM
North Grosvenor Dale
Grosvenor Dale
South Woodstock
Eastford
Abington
Rogers
Dayville
Danielson
Brooklyn
East Brooklyn
North Windham
Willimantic
Windham
Moosup
South Windham
Plainfield
Oneco
Baltic
Jewett City
Fitchville

062

Quinebaug
Thompson
Putnam
Pomfret
Ballouville
Central Village
Waterman
NEW LONDON

PROVIDENCE
Slatersville
Harrisville
Pascoag
Chepachet
Harmony
Greenville
Johnston
KENT
Anthony
Coventry
East Greenwich
Quidnessett
Davisville
WASHINGTON
La Fayette
Allenton
Wyoming
Hope Valley
West Kingston
Carolina
Shannock
South Hopkinton
Bradford
Charlestown

Woonsocket
Diamond Hill
Cumberland Hill
Arnold Mills
Union Village
Glendale
Manville
Abbott Run Valley
Oakland
Mapleville
Albion
Ashton
Berkeley
Valley Falls
Lonsdale
Esmond
Saylesville
Central Falls
North Providence
Pawtucket
Providence
East Providence
Cranston
West Barrington
Barrington
West Warwick
Warren
Warwick
BRISTOL
Bristol
Common Fence Point
NEWPORT
Tiverton
Mount View
Island Park
Portsmouth
North Kingstown
Middletown
Jamestown
Newport East
Kingston
Newport
Peace Dale
Wakefield
Narragansett
Matunuck

Mass.

Providence

028–029

Norwich

063

Montville
Uncasville
Gales Ferry
Quaker Hill
New London
Submarine Base
U.S. Coast Guard Academy
Nautilus Park
Old Mystic
East Lyme
West Mystic
Mystic
Ashaway
Pawcatuck
Westerly
Wequetequock
Niantic
Waterford
Poquonock Bridge
Noank
Stonington
Watch Hill
Qoonochontaug
Giants Neck
Black Point Beach Club
Pleasure Beach
Groton Long Point
Essex
Ivoryton
Old Saybrook
aybrook Manor
Fenwick
New London
Groton

Block Island

	ZIP
Abington	06230
Addison	06033
Agua Vista (Part of Danbury)	06810
Aljen Heights	06339
Allerton Farms (Part of Naugatuck)	06770
Allingtown (Part of West Haven)	06516
Almyville	06354
Alpine	06810
Amenia Union	06069
Amesville	06031
Amity (Part of New Haven)	06524
Amston	06231
Andover	06232
Andover (Town)	06232
Ansonia	06401
Ansonia (Town)	06401
Ashford	06278
Ashford (Town)	06250
Ashford Lake	06250
Aspetuck	06880
Attawan Beach	06357
Attawaugan	06241
Atwoodville	06250
Avery Heights	06776
Avery Hill	06339
Avon	06001
Avon (Town)	06001
Baileyville	06455
Bakersville	06057
Ballouville	06233
Ball Pond	06812
Baltic	06330
Banksville	06830
Bantam	06750
Barkhamsted (Town)	06063
Barnum (Part of Bridgeport)	06605
Barry Square (Part of Hartford)	06134
Bartlett Corners	06375
Bayview (Part of Milford)	06460
Beacon Falls	06403
Beacon Falls (Town)	06403
Beardsley (Part of Bridgeport)	06606
Beaverbrook (Part of Danbury)	06810
Beckettville (Part of Danbury)	06810
Bedlam Corner	06256
Bel Aire Estates	06355
Belden (Part of Norwalk)	06850
Belle Haven	06830
Bell Island (Part of Norwalk)	06853
Belltown (Part of Stamford)	06906
Berkshire	06482
Berkshire Estates	06488
Berkshire Shopping Center (Part of Danbury)	06810
Berlin	06037
Berlin (Town)	06037
Beseck Lake	06455
Bethany	06524
Bethany (Town)	06524
Bethel (Town)	06801
Bethel	06801
Bethlehem	06751
Bethlehem (Town)	06751
Birch Groves	06776
Birch Hill	06757
Birch Meadow	06479
Birch Mountain	06040
Birchwood	06095
Birdland	06082
Bishop	06374
Bishops Corner	06137
Bissell	06074
Black Point	06357
Black Point Beach Club	06357
Bloomfield	06002
Bloomfield (Town)	06002
Blue Hills (Hartford County) (Bloomfield Township)	06002
Blue Hills (Hartford County) (Hartford Township)	06132
Boardman Manor	06776
Boardmans Bridge	06776
Bolton	06043
Bolton (Town)	06043
Bolton Center	06040

	ZIP
Bonny Brook	06776
Borough (Part of Groton)	06340
Botsford	06404
Boulder Lake	06413
Bozrah (Town)	06334
Bozrah	06334
Branchville	06829
Brandy Hill	06277
Branford	06405
Branford (Town)	06405
Branford Hills	06405
Branhaven Shopping Center	06405
Brendan Heights	06078
Bretton Heights (Part of Middletown)	06457
Bridgeport	06601-10
	06650
For specific Bridgeport Zip Codes call (203) 332-5337, or your local postmaster.
Bridgeport (Town)	06604
Bridgewater	06752
Bridgewater (Town)	06752
Brighton Beach	06371
Bristol	06010*
	06011†
Bristol Terrace (Part of Naugatuck)	06770
Broad Brook	06016
Bromica	06757
Brookfield	06804
Brookfield (Town)	06804
Brookfield Center	06804
Brooklyn	06234
Brooklyn (Town)	06234
Brook Valley (Part of Naugatuck)	06770
Bruce Park	06830
Brush Island	06820
Buckingham	06033
Buckland	06040
Buckland Hills Mall	06040
Bucks Corners	06073
Bulls Bridge	06785
Bunker Hill (Part of Waterbury)	06708
Burlington	06013
Burlington (Town)	06085
Burnside	06108
Burr Hill	06419
Burrville (Part of Torrington)	06790
Burwells Beach (Part of Milford)	06460
Byram	06830
Camp Bethel	06438
Camptown (Part of Derby)	06418
Canaan	06018
Canaan (Town)	06031
Candleset Cove	06776
Candlewood Hill	06441
Candlewood Hills	06810
Candlewood Isle	06812
Candlewood Knolls	06810
Candlewood Lake Club	06804
Candlewood Lake Estates	06784
Candlewood Orchards	06804
Candlewood Point	06776
Candlewood Shores	06804
Candlewood Springs	06776
Candlewood Trails	06776
Cannondale	06897
Canterbury	06331
Canterbury (Town)	06331
Canton	06019
Canton (Town)	06019
Canton Center	06020
Carl Robinson Correctional Institution	06082
Carmel Hill	06751
Castle Hill	02891
Cedar Beach (Part of Milford)	06460
Cedar Heights (Part of Danbury)	06810
Cedarhurst	06482
Cedar Knolls	06776
Cedar Lake (Part of Bristol)	06010
Cedar Land	06488
Center	06611
Centerbrook	06409
Center Groton	06340
Center Hill	06057
Centerville	06518
Centerville-Mount Carmel	06518
Central (Part of Hartford)	06103

	ZIP
Central Commons (Part of Bridgeport)	06607
Central Manchester	06040
Central Village	06332
Chaffeeville	06268
Chalkers Beach	06475
Chaplin	06235
Chaplin (Town)	06235
Chapman Beach	06498
Charcoal Ridge	06812
Cherry Brook	06020
Cherry Hill	06796
Cherrywood	06479
Cheshire	06410
Cheshire (Town)	06410
Chester	06412
Chester (Town)	06412
Chickahominy	06830
Chippens Hill (Part of Bristol)	06010
Christy Hill Estates	06335
Church Hill	06794
Churchwood	06357
Clam Island	06405
Clarks Corner	06256
Clarks Falls	06359
Clarksville	02891
Clearview Heights	06076
Clinton (Town)	06413
Clinton	06413
Clinton Beach	06413
Clintonville	06473
Cobalt	06414
Codfish Hill	06801
Colburn Hill	06076
Colchester	06415
Colchester (Town)	06415
Colebrook	06021
Colebrook River	06021
Collinsville	06022
Colonial Manor	06360
Columbia	06237
Columbia (Town)	06237
Compo Beach	06880
Compo Hill	06880
Conantville	06226
Congamond Lakes	06093
Connecticut Correctional Center (New Haven County)	06410
Connecticut Correctional Institution (Hartford County)	06082
Connecticut Correctional Institution (Tolland County)	06071
Connecticut Post Mall (Part of Milford)	06460
Conning Towers	06340
Conning Towers-Nautilus Park	06340
Copaco Shopping Center	06002
Cornwall	06753
Cornwall (Town)	06753
Cornwall Bridge	06754
Cornwall Center	06796
Cornwall Hollow	06031
Cos Cob	06807
Cottage Grove	06002
Coventry	06238
Coventry (Town)	06238
Cranbury (Part of Norwalk)	06851
Cranska Village	06354
Crescent Beach	06357
Cromwell (Town)	06416
Cromwell	06416
Cromwell Hills	06416
Crystal Lake	06029
Daleville	06279
Damascus	06405
Danbury	06810-11
	06813
For specific Danbury Zip Codes call (203) 748-1230, or your local postmaster.
Danbury Fair Mall (Part of Danbury)	06810
Danbury Quarter	06098
Danbury Shopping Center (Part of Danbury)	06810
Danielson	06239
Darien (Town)	06820
Darien	06820
Dayville	06241
Deep River	06417

	ZIP
	06419
For specific Deep River Zip Codes call (203) 526-5970, or your local postmaster.
Deep River (Town)	06417
Deer Island	06758
Deer Run Shores	06784
Derby	06418
Derby (Town)	06418
Derby Junction (Part of Derby)	06418
Derby Neck (Part of Derby)	06418
Devil's Backbone	06751
Devon (Part of Milford)	06460
Diamond Lake	06033
Dibble Hill	06796
Dickerman's Corner	06479
Doanville	06384
Dodgingtown	06470
Dolphin Gardens	06340
Double Beach	06405
Dowd's Corner	06019
Downersville	02891
Drakeville (Part of Torrington)	06790
Durham	06422
Durham (Town)	06422
Durham Center	06422
Eagleville	06268
East Berlin	06023
East Bristol (Part of Bristol)	06010
East Brooklyn	06239
East Canaan	06024
East Cornwall	06759
East Derby (Part of Derby)	06418
East End (Part of Waterbury)	06705
Eastern Point (Part of Groton)	06340
East Farmington Heights	06032
East Farms (Part of Waterbury)	06705
Eastford	06242
Eastford (Town)	06242
East Glastonbury	06025
East Granby	06026
East Granby (Town)	06026
East Great Plain (Part of Norwich)	06360
East Haddam	06423
East Haddam (Town)	06423
East Haddam Landing	06423
East Hampton	06424
East Hampton (Town)	06424
East Hampton Center	06424
East Hartford (Town)	06108
East Hartford	06108
	06118
	06128
	06138
For specific East Hartford Zip Codes call (203) 528-6529, or your local postmaster.
East Hartland	06027
East Haven (Town)	06512
East Haven	06512
East Hill	06019
East Killingly	06243
East Litchfield	06759
East Lyme	06333
East Lyme (Town)	06333
East Morris	06763
East Mountain (Part of Waterbury)	06706
East New London (Part of New London)	06320
East Norwalk (Part of Norwalk)	06601
Easton	06612
Easton (Town)	06612
East Plymouth	06786
East Port Chester	06830
East Putnam	06260
East River	06443
East Thompson	06277
East Village	06468
East Wallingford	06492
East Willington	06279
East Windsor (Town)	06016
East Windsor	06088
East Windsor Hill	06028
East Woodstock	06244
Ebbs Corner	06093
Edgewood (Hartford County)	06010

* Area Zip Code   † Post Office Boxes

	ZIP
Edgewood (Tolland County)	06076
Ekonk	06354
Ekonk Hill	06384
Ellington	06029
Ellington (Town)	06029
Elliot	06259
Ellsworth	06069
Elm Hill	06111
Elmville	06241
Elmwood	06133
Elys Ferry	06371
Enders Island	06378
Enfield	06082*
	06083†
Enfield Square	06082
Enfield Street	06082
Essex	06426
Essex (Town)	06426
Ethel Acres	06351
Ettadore Park (Part of Milford)	06460
Fabyan	06255
Fairfield	06430-32
For specific Fairfield Zip Codes call (203) 255-4591, or your local postmaster.	
Fairfield Hills Hospital	06470
Fairground (Part of Norwich)	06360
Fair Haven (Part of New Haven)	06513
Fair Lawn (Part of Waterbury)	06705
Fairmount (Part of Waterbury)	06706
Fairy Lake	06370
Fall Mountain (Part of Bristol)	06010
Fall Mountain Lake	06786
Falls Switch (Part of Norwich)	06360
Falls Village	06031
Farmington	06032*
	06034†
Farmington (Town)	06032
Far View Beach (Part of Milford)	06460
Federal (Part of New Haven)	06510
Federal Correctional Institution	06810
Fenwick	06475
Fenwood	06475
Ferris Estates	06776
Ferry Point	06475
Ferry View Heights	06335
Field Crest Estates	06355
Firetown	06070
Five City Plaza Shopping Center	06032
Five Points (Fairfield County)	06896
Five Points (Hartford County)	06035
Flanders	06757
Flax Hill (Part of Norwalk)	06850
Floral Park	06475
Floydville	06035
Forbes Village	06108
Forest Glen	06475
Forest Heights (Part of Milford)	06460
Forest Hills	06489
Forest Park	06248
Forestville (Part of Bristol)	06010
Fort Hill	06776
Fort Trumbull Beach (Part of Milford)	06460
Fox Den	06001
Foxon	06512
Franklin	06254
Franklin (Town)	06254
Franklin Square (Part of Norwich)	06360
Furnace Hollow	06076
Gales Ferry	06335
Gallows Hill	06896
Gaylordsville	06755
Georgetown (Fairfield County)	06829
Georgetown (Hartford County)	06479
Germantown (Part of Danbury)	06810
Giants Neck	06357
Giants Neck Heights	06357
Gildersleeve	06480
Gilead	06248

	ZIP
Gilman	06336
Glasgo	06337
Glastonbury	06033
Glastonbury (Town)	06033
Glen	06896
Glenbrook (Part of Stamford)	06906
Glenville	06830
Golden Spur	06385
Good Hill (Litchfield County) (Kent Township)	06757
Good Hill (Litchfield County) (Woodbury Township)	06798
Good Hill (New Haven County)	06478
Goodrich Heights	06416
Goodsell Point	06405
Goshen	06756
Goshen (Town)	06756
Goshen	06385
Goshen Hills	06249
Governor's Hill	06478
Granby	06035
Granby (Town)	06035
Granite Bay	06405
Grappaville	06750
Grassy Hill (Litchfield County)	06798
Grassy Hill (New London County)	06371
Grassy Plain	06801
Great Hammock	06475
Great Harbor	06437
Great Meadows	06810
Greenfield Hill	06430
Greenhaven Shores	02891
Green Manorville	06082
Greens Farms	06436
Greenville (Part of Norwich)	06360
Greenwich	06830-36
For specific Greenwich Zip Codes call (203) 869-3737, or your local postmaster.	
Greystone	06786
Griswold (Town)	06351
Griswoldville	06109
Grosvenor Dale	06246
Groton	06340
Groton (Town)	06340
Groton Heights (Part of Groton)	06340
Groton Lake Shores	06357
Groton Long Point	06340
Grove Beach	06413
Gugliotti	06479
Guilford	06437
Guilford (Town)	06437
Guilford Lake	06437
Gurleyville	06268
Haddam	06438
Haddam (Town)	06438
Haddam Neck	06424
Hadlyme	06439
Hale Court	06880
Hallville	06365
Hamburg	06371
Hamden	06514
	06517-18
For specific Hamden Zip Codes call (203) 782-7114, or your local postmaster.	
Hamden (Town)	06514
Hamden Plaza	06514
Hampton	06247
Hampton (Town)	06247
Hank Hills	06268
Hanover	06350
Happyland	06365
Harborview (Fairfield County)	06853
Harbor View (Middlesex County)	06413
Harrisons	06375
Harrisville	06281
Hartford	06101-06
	06112-15
	06120-26
	06132
	06134
	06140-99
For specific Hartford Zip Codes call (203) 524-6004, or your local postmaster.	
Hartford (Town)	06101
Hartland (Town)	06027
Harwinton	06791

	ZIP
Harwinton (Town)	06790
Hawks Nest Beach	06371
Hawleyville	06440
Hawthorne Terrace (Part of Danbury)	06810
Hayden	06095
Hayestown (Part of Danbury)	06810
Hazardville	06082
Headquarters	06759
Hebron	06248
Hebron (Town)	06248
Heritage Village	06488
Hidden Lake	06441
Higganum	06441
Highland Park	06040
Hi-Ho Shopping Mall (Part of Bridgeport)	06604
Hillside (Part of Bridgeport)	06610
Hitchcock Lake	06716
Holiday Homes (Part of Colchester)	06415
Hollywyle Park	06810
Holy Apostles College	06416
Honeypot Glen	06410
Hopeville (New Haven County)	06706
Hopeville (New London County)	06351
Horton Park (Part of Naugatuck)	06770
Hotchkissville	06798
Huckleberry Hill	06001
Hungary Hill	06377
Huntington (Part of Shelton)	06484
Hydeville	06075
I-91 Exit 8 Mall (Part of New Haven)	06515
Indian Cove	06437
Indian Neck	06405
Ivoryton	06442
Jericho Hill	06371
Jewett City	06351
Jordan Village	06385
Kelseytown	06413
Kensington	06037
Kent	06757
Kent (Town)	06757
Kent Furnace	06757
Kenyonville	06282
Kilby (Part of New Haven)	06519
Killingly (Town)	06239
Killingly Center	06241
Killingworth	06419
Killingworth (Town)	06419
Kings Corner	06088
Knollcrest	06810
Knollwood	06475
Lake Bashan	06423
Lake Beseck	06455
Lake Bungee	06282
Lake Garda	06013
Lake Hayward	06415
Lake Plymouth	06782
Lake Pocotopaug	06424
Lakeside (Litchfield County)	06758
Lakeside (New Haven County)	06488
Lakeview Terrace	06076
Lakeville	06039
Lakewood (Part of Waterbury)	06704
Lattins Landing (Part of Danbury)	06810
Laurel (Part of Middletown)	06457
Laurel Beach (Part of Milford)	06460
Laurel Hill (Part of Norwich)	06360
Laysville	06371
Lebanon	06249
Lebanon (Town)	06249
Ledyard	06339
Ledyard (Town)	06339
Leesville	06469
Leetes Island	06437
Leffingwell	06360
Liberty Hill	06249
Lime Rock	06039
Lisbon	06351
Lisbon (Town)	06351
Litchfield	06759
Litchfield (Town)	06759
Little Boston	06875
Little City	06441

	ZIP
Long Hill (Fairfield County)	06611
Long Hill (Middlesex County)	06457
Long Hill (New Haven County)	06704
Long Hill (New London County)	06340
Long Ridge (Part of Stamford)	06901
Lordship	06497
Lords Point	06378
Lydallville	06040
Lyme	06371
Lyme (Town)	06371
Lyons Plains	06880
Macedonia	06757
Madison	06443
Madison (Town)	06443
Manchester (Town)	06040
Manchester	06040
	06045
For specific Manchester Zip Codes call (203) 6453-2735, or your local postmaster.	
Manchester Green	06040
Mansfield (Town)	06250
Mansfield Center	06250
Mansfield City	06268
Mansfield Depot	06251
Mansfield Four Corners	06268
Mansfield Hollow	06250
Maple Hill	06111
Maplewood (Part of Derby)	06418
Marble Dale	06777
Margerie Manor (Part of Danbury)	06810
Marion	06444
Marlborough	06447
Marlborough (Town)	06447
Maromas (Part of Middletown)	06457
Mashantucket Pequot Indian Reservation	06339
Mashapaug	06076
Mason Island	06355
Massapeag	06382
Mayberry Village	06108
Mechanicsville	06277
Melrose	06049
Melville Village	06430
Meriden	06450-51
For specific Meriden Zip Codes call (203) 235-5755, or your local postmaster.	
Meriden Square (Part of Meriden)	06450
Merrow	06251
Mianus	06807
Middle Beach	06443
Middlebury	06762
Middlebury (Town)	06762
Middlefield	06455
Middlefield (Town)	06455
Middle Haddam	06456
Middletown	06457
Middletown (Town)	06460
Midway	06340
Milbrook	06830
Milford	06460
Milford (Town)	06460
Milford Lawns (Part of Milford)	06460
Millbrook	06518
Milldale	06467
Millington	06423
Mill Plain (Part of Danbury)	06810
Millville (Part of Naugatuck)	06770
Milton	06759
Mixville	06410
Mohegan	06382
Momauguin	06512
Monroe	06468
Monroe (Town)	06468
Monroe Center	06468
Montowese	06473
Montville	06353
Montville (Town)	06353
Montville Manor	06370
Moodus	06469
Moosup	06354
Morningside (Part of Milford)	06460
Morris	06763
Morris (Town)	06763
Morris Cove	06512
Mount Carmel	06518

	ZIP
Mount Hope	06250
Murphy Road Annex (Part of Hartford)	06114
Murray	06430
Myrtle Beach (Part of Milford)	06460
Mystic	06355
Naugatuck	06770
Naugatuck (Town)	06770
Naugatuck Gardens (Part of Milford)	06460
Naugatuck Valley Mall (Part of Waterbury)	06705
Nautilus Park	06340
Nepaug	06057
Newberry Corner (Part of Torrington)	06790
New Britain	06050-53
For specific New Britain Zip Codes call (203) 223-3681, or your local postmaster.	
New Canaan (Town)	06840
New Canaan	06840
Newent	06351
New Fairfield	06812
New Fairfield (Town)	06810
Newfield	06607
Newfield Heights (Part of Middletown)	06457
Newhallville (Part of New Haven)	06511
New Hartford	06057
New Hartford (Town)	06057
New Haven	06501-11
	06513
	06515
	06519-21
	06530-36
For specific New Haven Zip Codes call (203) 782-7203, or your local postmaster.	
New Haven (Town)	06501
Newington (Town)	06131
Newington	06111*
	06131†
Newington Junction	06111
New London	06320
New London (Town)	06320
New London Submarine Base	06349
New Milford	06776
New Milford (Town)	06776
New Preston	06777
New Preston-Marble Dale	06777
Newtown	06470
Newtown (Town)	06470
New Village	06374
Niantic	06357
Nichols	06611
Noank	06340
Noble (Part of Bridgeport)	06608
Norfolk	06058
Norfolk (Town)	06058
Noroton	06820
Noroton Heights	06820
North Ashford	06282
North Bloomfield	06002
North Branford	06471
North Branford (Town)	06471
North Bridgeport (Part of Bridgeport)	06601
North Canaan (Town)	06018
North Canton	06059
North Cornwall	06796
North End (Part of Waterbury)	06704
North Farms	06471
Northfield	06778
Northford	06472
North Franklin	06254
North Glenwood	06335
North Granby	06060
North Grosvenor Dale	06255
North Guilford	06437
North Haven (Town)	06473
North Haven	06473
North Kent	06757
North Madison	06443
North Mianus	06807
North Plain	06423
North Sterling	06377
North Stonington	06359
North Stonington (Town)	06359
North Thompsonville	06082
Northville	06776
North Westchester	06474
North Wilton	06897
North Windham	06256

	ZIP
Norwalk	06850-56
For specific Norwalk Zip Codes call (203) 838-4881, or your local postmaster.	
Norwich	06360
Norwich (Town)	06360
Norwich Hospital	06365
Norwichtown (Part of Norwich)	06360
Nut Plains	06437
Oakdale	06370
Oakdale Heights	06370
Oakdale Manor	06488
Oakland Gardens	06032
Oakville	06779
Oakwood Acres	06812
Occum (Part of Norwich)	06360
Old Greenwich	06870
Old Lyme	06371
Old Lyme (Town)	06371
Old Lyme Shores	06371
Old Mystic	06372
Old Saybrook	06475
Old Saybrook (Town)	06475
Old Saybrook Shopping Center	06475
Old State House (Part of Hartford)	06123
Oneco	06373
Orange (Town)	06477
Orange	06477
Orcutts	06076
Oronoke (Part of Waterbury)	06708
Oronoque	06497
Oswegatchie	06385
Overlook (Part of Waterbury)	06710
Owenoke	06880
Oxford	06478
Oxford (Town)	06478
Ox Hill (Part of Norwich)	06360
Oxoboxo Lake	06370
Pachaug	06351
Palestine	06470
Palmertown	06353
Paradise Green	06497
Parcel Post (Part of Milford)	06460
Parkville (Part of Hartford)	06106
Pavilion at Buckland Hills, The	06040
Pawcatuck	06379
Pemberwick	06830
Pequabuck	06781
Perkins Corner	06226
Phoenixville	06235
Pine Bridge	06403
Pine Grove (Litchfield County)	06031
Pine Grove (New London County)	06357
Pine Meadow	06061
Pine Orchard	06405
Pine Rock Park (Part of Shelton)	06484
Plainfield	06374
Plainfield (Town)	06374
Plainville (Town)	06062
Plainville	06062
Plantsville	06479
Platts Mills (Part of Waterbury)	06706
Plaza (Part of Waterbury)	06704
Pleasant Acres (Part of Danbury)	06810
Pleasant Valley	06063
Pleasure Beach	06385
Plymouth	06782
Plymouth (Town)	06782
Point Beach (Part of Milford)	06460
Point O'Woods	06376
Pomfret	06258
Pomfret (Town)	06258
Pomfret Center	06259
Pomfret Landing	06259
Pond Point (Part of Milford)	06460
Ponset	06441
Pootatuck Park	06482
Poquetanuck	06365
Poquonock	06064
Poquonock Bridge	06340
Portland (Town)	06480
Portland	06480
Presidential	06082
Preston	06365
Preston (Town)	06365

	ZIP
Prospect (Town)	06712
Prospect	06712
Prospect Beach (Part of West Haven)	06516
Puddle Town	06022
Putnam	06260
Putnam (Town)	06260
Putnam Heights	06260
Putney	06497
Quaddick	06277
Quaker Farms	06478
Quaker Hill	06375
Quarryville	06040
Quebec	06239
Quinebaug	06262
Quinnipiac	06492
Rawson	06247
Redding (Town)	06875
Redding	06875
Redding Ridge	06876
Reynolds Bridge	06787
Ridgebury	06877
Ridgefield	06877
Ridgefield (Town)	06877
Ridgeway (Part of Stamford)	06905
Ridgewood	06413
Ridgewood Park	06385
Rising Corner	06093
Rivercliff (Part of Milford)	06460
River Glen	06032
Riverside (Fairfield County) (Greenwich Township)	06878
Riverside (Fairfield County) (Newtown Township)	06482
Riverside (Hartford County)	06022
Riverside (New Haven County)	06478
Riversville	06830
Riverton	06065
Robertsville	06065
Rockfall	06481
Rock Ridge	06830
Rocky Hill	06067
Rocky Hill	06067
Rogers	06263
Round Hill	06830
Rowayton (Part of Norwalk)	06853
Roxbury	06783
Roxbury (Town)	06783
Roxbury Falls	06783
Sachem Head	06437
Salem	06420
Salem (Town)	06420
Salisbury	06068
Salisbury (Town)	06068
Samp Mortar	06430
Sandy Beach	06758
Sandy Hook	06482
Sanfordtown	06896
Saugatuck	06880
Saugatuck Shores	06880
Saunders Point	06357
Savin Rock (Part of West Haven)	06516
Saybrook Manor	06475
Saybrook Point	06475
Scantic	06088
Scitico	06082
Scotland	06264
Scotland (Town)	06264
Seaview Beach	06443
Secret Lake	06001
Seymour (Town)	06483
Seymour	06483
Shady Rest	06482
Shailerville	06438
Sharon	06069
Sharon (Town)	06069
Sharon Valley	06069
Shelton	06484
Shelton (Town)	06484
Sherman	06784
Sherman (Town)	06784
Sherman Corner	06256
Sherwood Manor	06082
Shippan Point (Part of Stamford)	06902
Short Beach	06405
Silver Beach (Part of Milford)	06460
Silver Lane	06138
Simsbury	06070
Simsbury (Town)	06070
Skiff Mountain	06757

	ZIP
Somers	06071
Somers (Town)	06071
Somersville	06072
Sound View	06371
South Britain	06487
Southbury	06488
Southbury (Town)	06488
South Canaan	06031
South Coventry	06238
South Ellsworth	06069
South End (Fairfield County)	06902
South End (New Haven County)	06512
South Farms (Part of Middletown)	06457
South Glastonbury	06073
South Glenwoods	06335
Southington	06489
Southington (Town)	06489
South Kent	06785
South Killingly	06239
South Lyme	06376
South Manchester	06040
South Meriden (Part of Meriden)	06451
South Norfolk	06058
South Norwalk (Part of Norwalk)	06854
Southport	06490
South Wethersfield	06109
South Willington	06265
South Windham	06266
South Windsor	06074
South Windsor (Town)	06074
Southwood Acres	06082
South Woodstock	06267
Sport Hill	06612
Sprague (Town)	06330
Springdale (Part of Stamford)	06907
Spring Hill	06268
Spring Lake Village	06489
Stafford	06075
Stafford (Town)	06075
Stafford Springs	06076
Staffordville	06077
Stamford	06901-12
For specific Stamford Zip Codes call (203) 326-2158, or your local postmaster.	
Stamford Town Center (Part of Stamford)	06901
Stanwich	06830
State Line	06076
Station A (Part of Hartford)	06126
Sterling	06377
Sterling (Town)	06377
Sterling Hill	06354
Stetson Corner	06234
Stevenson	06491
Stonington	06378
Stonington (Town)	06378
Stony Corners	06001
Stony Creek	06405
Storrs	06268
Straitsville (Part of Naugatuck)	06770
Stratfield	06432
Stratford (Town)	06497
Stratford	06497
Stratmore Farms	06492
Suburban Enfield Mall	06082
Suffield	06078
Suffield (Town)	06078
Summer Hill	06492
Sunrise Hill	06525
Taconic	06079
Taft Station (Part of Norwich)	06360
Taftville (Part of Norwich)	06380
Talcott Village	06032
Talcottville	06066
Talmadge Hill	06840
Tariffville	06081
Terminal (Part of New Haven)	06511
Terryville	06786
Thamesville (Part of Norwich)	06360
Thomaston	06787
Thomaston (Town)	06787
Thompson	06277
Thompson (Town)	06277
Titicus	06877
Tokeneke	06820
Tolland	06084
Tolland (Town)	06084

* Area Zip Code   **† Post Office Boxes**

	ZIP		ZIP		ZIP		ZIP
Torringford (Part of Torrington)	06790	Washington Green	06793	West Hartford	06107	Wheeler Farms (Part of Milford)	06460
Torrington (Town)	06790	Washington Hill	06059		06110	Whigville	06013
Torrington	06790	Washington Square (Part of Norwich)	06360		06117	Whipstick	06877
Town Hill	06057	Waterbury	06701-10		06119	Whitacres	06082
Town Plot Hill (Part of Waterbury)	06708		06720-26		06127	White Sands Beach	06371
Trails Corner	06340	For specific Waterbury Zip Codes call (203) 574-6553, or your local postmaster.			06133	Whitneyville	06517
Trumbull (Town)	06612				06137	Wildermere Beach (Part of Milford)	06460
Trumbull	06611	Waterbury (Town)	06701	For specific West Hartford Zip Codes call (203) 231-2871, or your local postmaster.		Williams Crossing	06249
Trumbull Shopping Center	06611	Waterbury Plaza Shopping Center (Part of Waterbury)	06704	West Hartland	06091	Willimantic	06226
Trumbull Shopping Park	06611	Waterford	06385	West Haven	06516	Willington (Town)	06279
Turn of River (Part of Stamford)	06901	Waterford (Town)	06385	West Haven (Town)	06516	Willington Hill	06279
Turnpike	06066	Waterside (Part of Stamford)	06901	West Lakes	06437	Willow Point	06388
Twin Lakes	06079	Watertown	06795	West Mystic	06388	Wilsonville	06255
Tyler Lake Heights	06756	Watertown (Town)	06795	West Norfolk	06058	Wilton	06897
Uncasville	06382	Waterville (Part of Waterbury)	06704	West Norwalk (Part of Norwalk)	06851	Wilton (Town)	06897
Uncasville-Oxoboro Valley	06382	Wauregan	06387	Weston	06883	Winchester (Town)	06094
Union	06076	Wauwecus Hill (Part of Norwich)	06360	Weston (Town)	06880	Winchester Center	06094
Union (Town)	06076	Weatogue	06089	Westport	06880*	Windham	06280
Union City (Part of Naugatuck)	06770	Webster Square Shopping Center	06037		06881†	Windham (Town)	06280
Unionville	06085	Weekeempee	06798	West Putnam Avenue	06830	Winding Lanes	06001
Unity Plaza (Part of Hartford)	06140	Welles Village	06033	West Redding	06896	Windsor	06095
Upper Stepney	06468	Wells Quarter Village	06109	West Shore (Part of West Haven)	06516	Windsor (Town)	06095
Vernon (Town)	06066	Wequetequock	02891	West Side (Part of Norwich)	06360	Windsor Locks (Town)	06096
Vernon	06066	Wesleyan (Part of Middletown)	06457	West Side Hill (Part of Waterbury)	06708	Windsor Locks	06096
Vernon Center	06066	West Ashford	06250	West Simsbury	06092	Windsorville	06016
Versailles	06383	West Avon	06001	West Stafford	06076	Winnipauk (Part of Norwalk)	06851
Versailles Station	06383	West Bantam	06750	West Suffield	06093	Winsted	06098
Village Hill	06249	Westbrook	06498	West Thompson	06255	Winthrop	06417
Voluntown (Town)	06384	Westbrook (Town)	06498	West Torrington (Part of Torrington)	06790	Wolcott	06716
Voluntown	06384	Westchester	06415	Westview Acres	06478	Wolcott (Town)	06716
Wailacks Point (Part of Stamford)	06902	West Cornwall	06796	Westville (Part of New Haven)	06515	Woodbridge (Town)	06525
Wallingford (Town)	06492	West End (Part of Bristol)	06010	West Wauregan	06387	Woodbridge	06525
Wallingford	06492	Westfarms	06032	West Willington	06279	Woodbury	06798
Wallingford Center	06492	West Farms Village (Part of New Britain)	06050	Westwood Park (Part of Norwich)	06360	Woodbury (Town)	06798
Walnut Beach (Part of Milford)	06460	Westfield (Part of Middletown)	06457	West Woods	06069	Woodlake	06798
Walnut Hill	06333	Westford	06076	West Woodstock	06281	Woodmont	06460
Walnut Tree Hill	06482	West Goshen	06756	Wethersfield (Town)	06129	Woodstock	06281
Wamphassuc Point	06378	West Granby	06090	Wethersfield	06109*	Woodstock (Town)	06281
Wapping	06074	West Hartford (Town)	06107		06129†	Woodstock Valley	06282
Warren	06754			Wethersfield Shopping Center	06109	Woodtick	06716
Warren (Town)	06753					Woodville	06777
Warrenville	06278					Yale (Part of New Haven)	06520
Washington (Town)	06793					Yalesville	06492
Washington Depot	06793-94					Yantic (Part of Norwich)	06389
For specific Washington Depot Zip Codes call (203) 868-7474, or your local postmaster.						Zoar	06482

***** Area Zip Code   † Post Office Boxes**

	ZIP		ZIP		ZIP		ZIP
Adams Crossroads	19950	Capitol Park	19901	Edgehill Acres (Part of Dover)	19901	Hilltop Manor	19809
Adamsville	19950	Cardiff	19810			Hitchens Crossroads	19956
Afton	19810	Carlisle Village	19904	Edgemoor	19809	Hockessin	19707
Alapocas	19803	Carrcroft	19803	Edgemoor (census designated place)	19802	Holiday Acres	19939
Albertson Park	19808	Carrcroft Crest	19803	Edgemoor Gardens	19802	Hollandsville	19943
Analine Village	19703	Carter	19901	Edgemoor Terrace	19802	Holletts Corners	19938
Andrewville	19950	Castle Hills	19720	Edgewater Acres	19975	Holloway Terrace	19720
Anglesey	19807	Catalina Gardens (Part of Newark)	19711	Edgewood Hills	19802	Holly Oak (New Castle County)	19809
Angola	19958	Cave Colony	19968	Edwardsville	19943	Holly Oak (Sussex County)	19973
Angola Beach	19951	Cedar Beach	19963	Ellendale	19941		
Angola by the Bay	19958	Cedarbrook Acres	19977	Elmhurst	19804	Holly Oak Terrace	19809
Anne Acres	19971	Cedar Heights	19804	Elsmere	19805	Hollyville	19951
Arden	19803	Centerville	19807	Elsmere Junction (Part of Elsmere)	19805	Houston	19954
Ardencroft	19810	Chalfonte	19810			Huntley	19901
Ardentown	19810	Channin	19803	English Village	19711	Hyde Park	19808
Argos Corner	19963	Chapel Hill	19711	Evergreen Acres	19963	Idella	19804
Arundel	19808	Chatham	19810	Fairfax	19803	Indian Beach	19971
Ashbourne Hills	19703	Chelsea Estates	19720	Fairfield Farms	19901	Indian Field	19810
Ashland	19807	Cherokee Woods	19713	Fairmount	19951	Indian River Acres	19939
Ashley	19804	Chestnut Hill Estates	19713	Fairwinds	19701	Iron Hill Apartments	19702
Atlanta	19933	Chestnut Knoll	19963	Farmington	19942	Ivy Ridge	19720
Atlanta Estates	19973	Cheswold	19936	Faulkland	19808	Jefferson Farms	19720
Augustine Beach	19731	Christiana	19702	Faulkland Heights	19808	Jimtown	19958
Avalon	19808	Christiana Acres	19720	Faulkwoods	19808	Johnson	19975
Bacon	19940	Clarksville	19970	Federal (Part of Newark)	19711	Johnstown	19950
Bakers Choice	19946	Claymont	19703	Felton	19943	Jones Crossroads	19956
Baldton (Part of New Castle)	19720	Clayton	19938	Felton Heights	19943	Keen-Wik	19975
		Clearfield	19703	Felton Manor	19943	Kenilworth	19703
Bayard	19945	Cleland Heights	19805	Fenwick Island	19944	Kenmore Park	19973
Bay Berry Dunes	19930	Clifton Park Manor	19802	Fieldsboro	19734	Kent Acres	19901
Bay View Beach	19709	Cocked Hat	19933	Fireside Park	19713	Kenton	19955
Bay View Park	19930	College Park (Part of Newark)	19711	Flemings Corner	19952	Kiamensi	19804
Bayville	19975			Flemings Landing	19734	Kirkwood	19708
Bay Vista	19971	Collins Park	19720	Forest Brook Glen	19804	Kitts Hummock	19901
Bear	19701	Colmar Manor	19977	Forest Hills Park	19803	Klair Estates	19808
Beaver Brook Apartments	19720	Colonial Heights	19805	Four Seasons	19702	Kynlyn Apartments	19809
Beaverdam Heights	19973	Colonial Park	19805	Foxhall Courtside	19904	Lake Pines	19956
Bellefonte	19809	Columbia	19940	Fox Hollow	19958	Lamatan	19711
Bellemoor	19804	Concord	19973	Frankford	19945	Lancashire	19810
Bellevue Manor	19809	Concord Mall	19803	Frederica	19946	Lancaster Court	19805
Belltown	19958	Concord Manor	19803	Galewood	19803	Lancaster Village	19805
Belmont Hall	19977	Cool Spring	19968	Garfield Park	19720	Laurel	19956
Belvedere	19804	Cooper Farm	19808	Gateway Farms	19707	Lebanon	19901
Bestfield	19804	Cottonpatch Hill	19930	Georgetown	19947	Leedom Estates	19720
Bethany Beach	19930	Country Club Estates	19963	Ginns Corner	19734	Leipsic	19901
Bethany Dunes	19930	Coventry	19720	Glasgow	19711	Lewes	19958
Bethany Village	19930	Coverdale Crossroads	19933	Glasgow Court	19702	Lewes Beach (Part of Lewes)	19958
Bethel	19931	Covered Bridge Farms	19711	Glasgow Pines	19702		
Big Mills Bridge	19956	Covey Creek	19958	Glen Berne Estates	19804	Liftwood	19803
Big Oak Corners	19977	Cragmere	19809	Glendale	19711	Limestone Acres	19808
Big Pine	19950	Cragmere Woods	19809	Glenville	19804	Limestone Gardens	19808
Big Stone Beach	19963	Craigs Mill	19973	Goldey Beacom College	19808	Lincoln	19960
Binns Village (Part of Newark)	19711	Cranston Heights	19808	Gordon Heights	19802	Lindenmere	19809
		Crossgates (Part of Dover)	19904	Gordy Estates	19804	Little Creek	19961
Birchwood Park	19711			Granogue	19807	Little Heaven	19946
Blackbird	19734	Cross Keys	19966	Gravel Hill	19947	Llangollen Estates	19720
Blackiston	19938	Dagsboro	19939	Graylyn Crest	19803	London Village	19962
Blackwater Village	19939	Darley Woods	19810	Green Acres	19803	Long Neck	19966
Blades	19973	Dartmouth Woods	19810	Green Bank	19808	Longview Farms	19810
Blue Hen Mall (Part of Dover)	19901	Deerhurst	19803	Greenbriar	19720	Lowe	19956
		Delaney Corner	19938	Greenshire	19703	Lowes Crossroads	19966
Blue Rock Manor	19803	Delaplane Manor	19711	Greentree	19703	Lumbrook (Part of Newark)	19711
Bowers	19946	Delaware City	19706	Greenview	19901		
Bowers Beach	19946	Delaware Correctional Center	19977	Greenville (Kent County)	19952	Lynch Heights	19963
Boxwood	19804			Greenville (New Castle County)	19807	Lyndalia	19804
Brack-Ex	19805	Delaware Heights	19807			Lynnfield	19803
Brandywine	19810	Del Haven Estates	19962	Greenville Place	19807	Lynnfield	19711
Brandywine Estates	19703	Delmar	19940	Greenwood	19950	McClellandville	19711
Brandywine Springs Manor	19808	Del Park Manor	19808	Gulls Nest	19930	McDaniel Heights	19803
		Devon	19810	Gumboro	19945	Magnolia	19962
Brandywood	19810	Devonshire	19810	Guyencourt	19807	Manor	19720
Breezewood (Kent County)	19943	Dewey Beach	19971	Gwinhurst	19809	Manor Park	19720
		Diamond Acres	19939	Hall Estates	19963	Manor Park Apartments	19720
Breezewood (New Castle County)	19713	Dobbinsville (Part of New Castle)	19720	Hamilton Park	19720	Maplecrest	19808
				Hanbys Corner	19810	Marabou Meadows	19702
Brenford	19977	Dover	19901-05	Harbeson	19951	Marshallton	19808
Briar Park	19904	For specific Dover Zip Codes call (302) 734-5821, or your local postmaster.		Hardscrabble	19973	Marvels Crossroads	19952
Bridgeville	19933			Harmony Hills	19711	Marydel	19964
Broadacres	19973			Harrington	19952	Mastens Corner	19943
Broad Creek	19956	Dover Air Force Base Housing Annex	19901	Hartly	19953	Mayfair (Part of Dover)	19904
Broadkill Beach	19968			Hayden Park	19804	Mayfield	19803
Brookbend	19713	Dover Base Housing	19901	Hearns Crossroads	19956	Mayview Manor	19720
Brookdale Heights	19934	Doverbrook Gardens	19901	Hearns Mill	19973	Meadowbrook	19804
Brookhaven	19711	Dover Mall (Part of Dover)	19901	Heather Woods	19702	Meadowbrook Acres	19962
Brookland Terrace	19805	Downs Chapel	19938	Henlopen Acres	19971	Meadowood	19711
Brookside	19713	Drummond North	19711	Henry Clay	19807	Mechanicsville	19711
Brookview Apartments	19703	Dublin Hill	19933	Hickman	21629	Meeting House Hill	19711
Brownsville	19952	Dunleith	19801	Hickory Hill	19966	Melody Meadows	19702
Bull Pine Corners	19947	Dunlinden Acres	19808	Hickory Ridge	19977	Middleford	19973
Bunting	19975	Dupont Manor	19901	Highland Acres (Kent County)	19901	Middlesex Beach	19930
Buttonwood (Part of New Castle)	19720	Du Ross Heights	19720			Middletown	19709
		Dutch Acres	19958	Highland Acres (Sussex County)	19958	Midvale	19720
Camden	19934	Eastman Heights	19963			Midway	19971
Camden-Wyoming (Part of Wyoming)	19934	Eastover Hills (Part of Dover)	19901	Highland West	19808	Milford	19963
				High Point Park	19946	Milford Cross Roads	19711
Cannon	19933	Eberton	19901	Hillcrest	19809	Millpond Acres	19958
Canterbury	19943	Eden Park	19720	Hillside Acres	19943	Millsboro	19966
Capitol Green (Part of Dover)	19901	Edge Hill (Part of Dover)	19901	Hillside Heights	19711	Millville	19970
						Milton	19968

	ZIP
Minquadale	19720
Mispillion Light	19963
Mission	19966
Montchanin	19710
Monterey Farms	19720
Morris Estates (Part of Dover)	19901
Mount Cuba	19807
Mount Pleasant	19709
Naamans Gardens	19810
Naamans Manor	19810
Naamans Trailer Park	19703
Nanticoke Acres	19973
Nassau	19969
Newark	19702
	19711-15
For specific Newark Zip Codes call (302) 737-5770, or your local postmaster.	
New Castle	19720
New Castle Manor (Part of New Castle)	19720
Newkirk Estates	19711
Newport	19804
Newport Heights	19804
Northcrest	19810
North Hills	19809
North Ridge	19703
North Seaford Heights	19973
Northshire	19810
North Shores (Kent County)	19963
North Shores (Sussex County) (mail Milton)	19968
North Shores (Sussex County) (mail Rehoboth Beach)	19971
North Shores (Sussex County) (mail Seaford)	19711
North Star	19711
Northwest Dover Heights (Part of Dover)	19904
Northwood	19803
Oak Forest Estates	19953
Oak Grove (Kent County)	19901
Oak Grove (New Castle County)	19805
Oak Grove (Sussex County)	19973
Oak Hill	19805
Oak Lane Manor	19803
Oakley	19941
Oakmont	19720
Oak Orchard	19966
Ocean View	19970
Ocean Village	19930
Odessa	19730
Ogletown	19711
Old Furnace	19947
Omar	19945
Orchard Acres	19943
Overview Gardens	19720
Owens	19950
Owls Nest Estates	19807
Palm Springs Manor	19711
Paris Villa	19962
Pembrey	19803
Penarth	19803
Penn Acres	19720
Pennrock	19809
Penny Hill	19809
Pepper	19956
Pepperbox	19956
Perry Park	19810

	ZIP
Perth	19803
Petersburg	19979
Pickering Beach	19901
Pine Creek	19711
Pinetown	19958
Pine Tree Corners	19734
Piney Grove	19947
Pleasant Hill	19804
Pleasanton Acres	19901
Pleasantville	19720
Plymouth	19943
Polly Drummond	19711
Polly Drummond Hill	19711
Porter	19701
Port Mahon	19901
Port Penn	19731
Portsville	19956
Primehook Beach	19963
Quakertown	19958
Radnor Green	19703
Radnor Woods	19703
Rambleton Acres	19720
Ramblewood	19810
Redden	19947
Redden Crossroads	19947
Red Lion	19701
Reeves Crossing	19943
Rehoboth Beach	19971
Reliance	19973
Richardson Park	19805
Rising Sun	19934
Rising Sun-Lebanon	19901
Riverdale	19966
Riverside Gardens	19703
Riverview (Kent County)	19962
Riverview (Sussex County)	19966
Robscott Manor	19713
Rockland	19732
Rodney Square (Part of Wilmington)	19801
Rodney Village	19901
Rodric Village	19901
Rogers Haven	19970
Rogers Manor (Part of New Castle)	19720
Rolling Hills	19804
Rolling Park	19703
Rosedale Beach	19966
Rose Gate	19720
Rose Hill	19720
Rose Hill Gardens	19720
Roselle	19805
Roseville Park	19711
Roxana	19945
Rutherford	19711
St. Georges	19733
Sandtown	19943
Sandy Brae	19958
Scottfield	19711
Scotts Corner	19933
Seabreeze	19971
Sea Del Estates	19930
Seaford	19973
Seaford Heights	19973
Sedgley Farms	19807
Seeneytown	19938
Selbyville	19975
Shady Lane	19901
Shaft Ox Corner	19966
Sharpley	19803
Shawnee Acres	19963
Shawtown (Part of New Castle)	19720

	ZIP
Shell Bridge	19956
Shellburne	19803
Sherwood (Part of Dover)	19904
Sherwood Acres	19945
Sherwood Park	19808
Shipley Heights	19803
Shortly	19947
Silverbrook	19805
Silver Lake Shores	19971
Silverside Heights	19809
Silview	19804
Simonds Gardens	19720
Slaughter Beach	19963
Smyrna	19977
Smyrna Landing (Part of Smyrna)	19977
Snug Harbor	19973
South Bethany	19930
South Bowers	19963
South Dover Acres (Part of Dover)	19901
Spruance City	19977
Stanton	19804
Star Hill	19901
Staytonville	19952
Stockdale	19703
Stockley	19947
Stockton	19720
Stoneybrook Apartments	19703
Stratford	19720
Summit Bridge	19709
Surrey Park	19803
Sussex Correctional Institution	19947
Sussex Shores	19930
Swain Acres	19947
Swann Keys	19975
Swanwyck	19720
Swanwyck Estates	19720
Swanwyck Gardens	19720
Sycamore	19956
Sycamore Gardens	19711
Talleyville	19803
Tanglewood	19713
Tarleton	19803
Taylor Estates	19901
Taylors Bridge	19734
The Beeches (Part of Dover)	19904
The Cedars	19808
The Island	19973
The Timbers	19803
Thomas Landing	19734
Thompsonville	19963
Tidbury Manor	19901
Todd Estates	19713
Towne Point (Part of Dover)	19901
Townsend	19734
Tuxedo Park	19804
Twin Eagle Farms	19938
Tybrook	19808
Union Street (Part of Wilmington)	19805
Valley Run	19810
Van Dyke Village (Part of New Castle)	19720
Varlano	19702
Vernon	19952
Village of Drummond Hill	19711
Village of Garrisons Lake	19977
Village of Windhover	19702
Villa Monterey	19809

	ZIP
Viola	19979
Voshells Cove	19901
Ward	19940
Warwick	19966
Washington Heights	19971
Washington Park (Part of New Castle)	19720
Webb Manor	19963
Webster Farms	19803
Wedgewood Acres	19720
Weisman Acres	19963
Wellington Woods	19702
Welshire	19803
West Beach	19939
Westfield	19804
West Haven	19807
West Meadow	19711
Westover Hills	19807
West Park	19807
Westview	19804
Westwood Manor	19810
Whaleys Corners	19956
Whaleys Crossroads	19956
Whiteleysburg	19943
White Oak Farms (Part of Dover)	19901
Whitesville	19940
Widener University / Delaware Campus	19803
Williamsville (Kent County)	19954
Williamsville (Sussex County)	19975
Willow Grove	19934
Willow Run	19805
Wilmington	19801-99
For specific Wilmington Zip Codes call (302) 323-3783, or your local postmaster.	
Wilmington College	19720
Wilmington Manor	19720
Wilmington Manor Gardens	19720
Wilmont	19810
Windermere	19804
Windsor Hills	19803
Windy Bush	19810
Windy Hills	19711
Winterthur	19735
Woodbine	19803
Woodbrook (Kent County)	19901
Woodbrook (New Castle County)	19803
Woodcrest (Kent County)	19904
Woodcrest (New Castle County)	19804
Wooddale	19807
Woodenhawk	19950
Woodland (New Castle County)	19805
Woodland (Sussex County)	19973
Woodland Beach	19977
Woodshade	19702
Woods Haven	19963
Woodside	19980
Woodside East	19980
Woodside Hills	19809
Woods Manor	19901
Workmans Corners	19947
Wyoming	19934
York Beach (Part of South Bethany)	19930
Yorklyn	19736

* Area Zip Code † Post Office Boxes

Parts of Washington	ZIP
Anacostia	20020
Barnaby Terrace	20032
Benjamin Franklin	20004
Benning	20019
Blue Plains	20032
Bolling Air Force Base	20336
Brightwood	20011
Brightwood Park	20011
Brookland	20017
Calvert	20007
Cardinal	20017
Central	20005
Chillum	20011
City Delivery Annex	20012
Cleveland Park	20008
Colonial Village	20012
Columbia Heights	20009-10
For specific Columbia Heights Zip Codes call (202) 682-9595, or your local postmaster.	
Congress Heights	20032
Congress Park	20032
Customs House	20018
Douglas Dwellings	20020
Eagle	20016
Eckington	20002
Fairfax Village	20020
Farragut	20033
Fort Davis	20020
Fort Lincoln	20018
Fort McNair	20319
Friendship	20007-08
For specific Friendship Zip Codes call (202) 682-9595, or your local postmaster.	
Friendship Heights	20088
F Street	20004
Garfield Heights	20020
Georgetown	20007
Glover Park	20007
Good Hope	20020
Hillcrest	20020
Hoya	20007
Kalorama	20009
Kendall Green	20002
Knox Hill Dwellings	20020
Lamond	20011
Le Droit Park	20001
L'Enfant Plaza	20024
Les Champs	20037
McLean Gardens	20016
Manor Park	20011
Marlow Heights Shopping Center	20002
Martin Luther King, Jr.	20043
Mid City	20005
Mount Pleasant	20010
National Capitol	20013
Naval Research Laboratory	20375
Naylor Gardens	20020
Northeast	20002
Northwest	20015
Palisades	20016
Park View	20010
Petworth	20011
Philatelic Sales Division	20265
Randle	20020
Saint Elizabeth	20032
Shepherd	20032
Southeast	20003
Southwest	20003
Spring Valley	20016
State Department	20520
Techworld	20091
Temple Heights	20009
Tenleytown	20016
Terra Cotta	20011
The Palisades	20016
T Street	20009
Twentieth Street	20036
Twining	20020
U.S. Naval Station	20374
Walter Reed	20012
Ward Place	20036-37
For specific Ward Place Zip Codes call (202) 682-9595, or your local postmaster.	
Washington	20001-91
	20101-04
	20201-99
	20301-72
	20501-99
For specific Washington Zip Codes call (202) 682-9595, or your local postmaster.	

COLLEGES & UNIVERSITIES	ZIP
American University	20016
Catholic University of America	20064
Gallaudet University	20002
Georgetown University	20057
George Washington University	20052
Howard University	20059
University of the District of Columbia	20008

FINANCIAL INSTITUTIONS	ZIP
American Security Bank, N.A.	20013
Citizen's Bank of Washington, National Association	20005
Columbia First Bank, F.S.B.	20005
Crestar Bank, N.A.	20005
First Union National Bank	20005
Home Federal Savings Bank	20015
Independence Federal Savings Bank	20036
Industrial Bank of Washington	20011
Nationsbank of D.C., N.A.	20006
Oba Federal Savings & Loan Association	20004
Riggs National Bank of Washington, D.C.	20005
Signet Bank, N.A.	20036
Washington Federal Savings Bank	20016

GOVERNMENT OFFICES	ZIP
ACTION	20525
Administrative Committee of the Federal Register	20408
Administrative Conference of the United States	20037
Administrative Office of the United States Courts	20544
Advisory Commission on Intergovernmental Relations	20575
Advisory Council on Historic Preservation	20004
African Development Foundation	20005
Agency for International Development	20523
American Battle Monuments Commission	20314
Appalachian Regional Commission	20235
Architect of the Capitol	20515
Architectural and Transportation Access Barriers Compliance Board	20004
Board for International Broadcasting	20036
Bureau of Alcohol, Tobacco and Firearms	22043
Bureau of Engraving and Printing	20228
Bureau of Prisons	20534
Central Intelligence Agency	20505
Citizens' Stamp Advisory Committee	20260
Commission of Fine Arts	20001
Commission on Civil Rights	20425
Committee for the Implementation of Textile Agreements	20230
Committee on Foreign Investment in the United States	20220
Commodity Futures Trading Commission	20581
Congressional Budget Office	20515
Coordinating Council on Juvenile Justice and Delinquency Prevention	20531
Council of Economic Advisors	20500
Council on Environmental Quality	20503
Defense Intelligence Agency	20340

	ZIP
Defense Investigative Service	20324
Defense Legal Services Agency	20301
Defense Mapping Agency	22031
Defense Nuclear Agency	20305
Defense Security Assistance Agency	20301
Delaware River Basin Commission	20240
Department of Agriculture	20250
Department of Commerce	20230
Department of Defense	20301
Department of Education	20202
Department of Energy	20585
Department of Health and Human Services	20201
Department of Housing and Urban Development	20410
Department of Justice	20530
Department of Labor	20210
Department of State	20520
Department of the Air Force	20330
Department of the Army	20310
Department of the Interior	20240
Department of the Navy	20350
Department of the Treasury	20220
Department of Transportation	20590
Department of Veterans Affairs	20420
Development Coordination Committee	20523
Drug Enforcement Administration	20537
Endangered Species Committee	20240
Environmental Protection Agency	20460
Equal Employment Opportunity Commission	20507
Export Administration Review Board	20230
Export-Import Bank of the United States	20571
Federal Aviation Administration	20591
Federal Bureau of Investigation	20535
Federal Communications Commission	20554
Federal Deposit Insurance Corporation	20429
Federal Election Commission	20463
Federal Emergency Management Agency	20472
Federal Financial Institutions Examination Council	20037
Federal Financing Bank	20220
Federal Highway Administration	20590
Federal Housing Finance Board	20006
Federal Interagency Committee on Education	20202
Federal Judicial Center	20002
Federal Labor Relations Authority	20424
Federal Library and Information Center Committee	20540
Federal Maritime Commission	20573
Federal Mediation and Conciliation Service	20427
Federal Mine Safety and Health Review Commission	20006
Federal Property Resources Service	20405
Federal Railroad Administration	20590
Federal Reserve System	20551
Federal Supply Service	20406
Federal Trade Commission	20580
Financial Management Service	20227
Foreign Claims Settlement Commission of the United States	20579

	ZIP
Franklin Delano Roosevelt Memorial Commission	20515
Gallaudet University	20002
General Accounting Office	20548
General Services Administration	20405
Government Printing Office	20401
Graduate School, U.S. Department of Agriculture	20250
Harry S. Truman Scholarship Foundation	20006
Health Care Financing Administration	20201
House of Representatives	20515
Howard University	20059
Immigration and Naturalization Service	20536
Indian Arts and Crafts Board	20240
Industrial College of the Armed Forces	20319
Information Resources Management College	20319
Information Resources Management Service	20405
Information Security Oversight Office	20006
Institute of Museum Service	20506
Interagency Committee on Employment of People with Disabilities	20507
Inter-American Defense Board	20441
Inter-American Development Bank	20577
Internal Revenue Service	20224
International Bank for Reconstruction and Development	20433
International Boundary Commission, United States and Canada	20037
International Finance Corporation	20433
International Joint Commission-United States and Canada	20440
International Monetary and Financial Policies	20220
International Monetary Fund	20431
Interstate Commerce Commission	20423
Japan-United States Friendship Commission	20004
Joint Board for the Enrollment of Actuaries	20220
Legal Services Corporation	20002
Library of Congress	20540
Mailers Technical Advisory Committee	20260
Marine Mammal Commission	20009
Maritime Administration	20590
Merit Systems Protection Board	20419
Migratory Bird Conservation Commission	20240
National Aeronautics and Space Administration	20546
National Archives and Records Administration	20408
National Archives Trust Fund Board	20408
National Capital Planning Commission	20576
National Commission on Libraries and Information Science	20005
National Council on Disability	20591
National Credit Union Administration	20456
National Defense University	20319
National Endowment for the Arts	20506
National Endowment for the Humanities	20506
National Energy Information Center	20585
National Highway Traffic Safety Administration	20590

* **Area Zip Code**   † **Post Office Boxes**

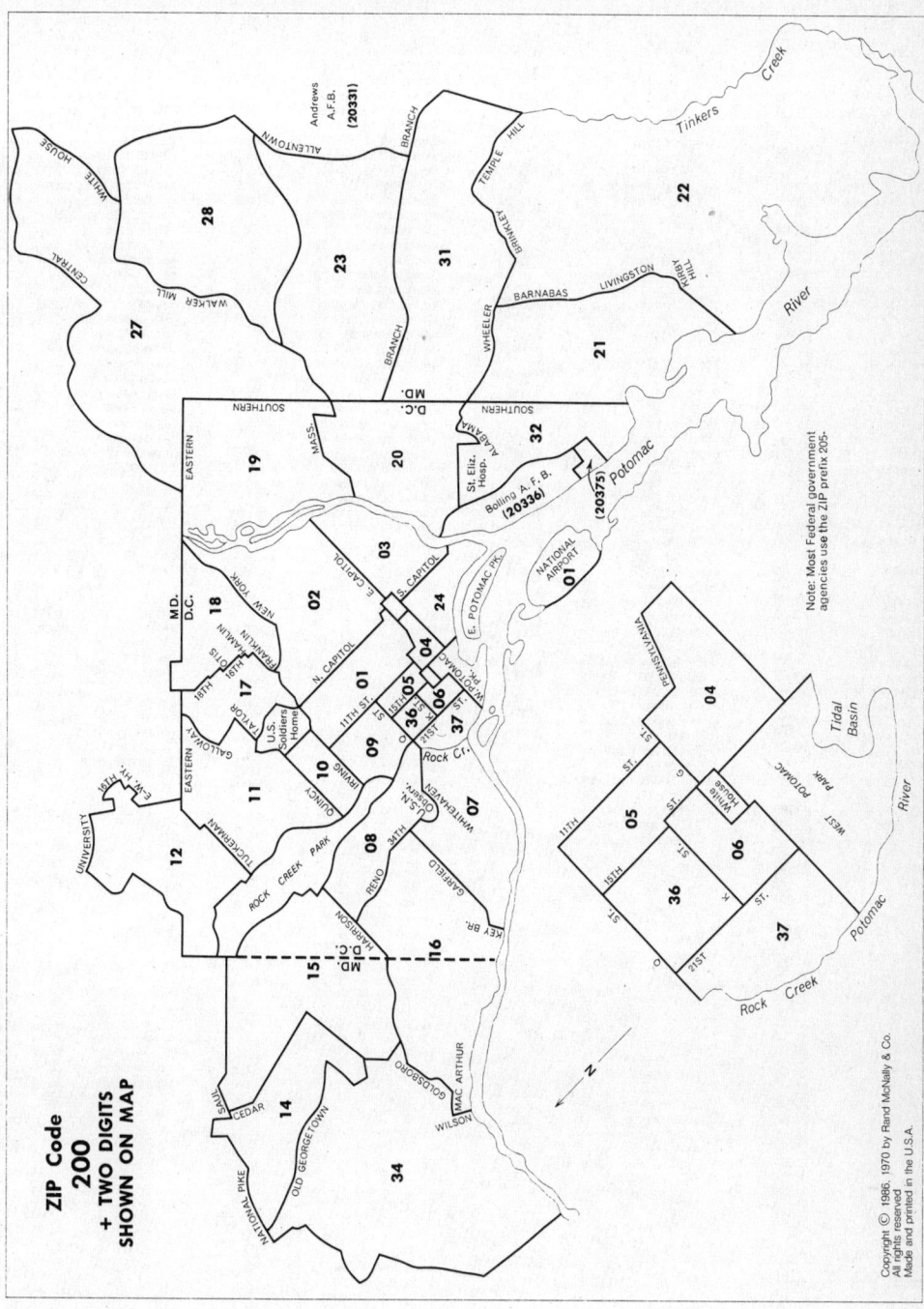

ZIP Code
200
+ TWO DIGITS
SHOWN ON MAP

Note: Most Federal government agencies use the ZIP prefix 205-

	ZIP
National Historical Publications and Records Commission	20408
National Labor Relations Board	20570
National Mediation Board	20572
National Oceanic and Atmospheric Administration	20230
National Park Foundation	20036
National Railroad Passenger Corporation (AMTRAK)	20002
National Science Foundation	20550
National Security Council	20506
National Transportation Safety Board	20594
National War College	20319
Nuclear Regulatory Commission	20555
Occupational Safety and Health Review Commission	20036
Office of Administration	20503
Office of Aviation Information Management	20591
Office of Emergency Transportation	20590
Office of Hazardous Materials Transportion	20590
Office of Human Development Services	20447
Office of Management and Budget	20503
Office of Personnel Management	20415
Office of Pipeline Safety	20590
Office of Policy Development	20500
Office of Science and Technology Policy	20500
Office of Technology Assessment	20510
Office of the United States Trade Representative	20506
Office of the Vice President of the United States	20501
Organization of American States	20006
Overseas Private Investment Corporation	20527
Panama Canal Commission	20006
Peace Corps	20526
Pennsylvania Avenue Development Corporation	20004

	ZIP
Pension Benefit Guaranty Corporation	20006
Permanent Committee for the Oliver Wendell Holmes Devise	20540
Postal Rate Commission	20268
President's Committee on Employment of People with Disabilities	20004
President's Council on Integrity and Efficiency	20503
President's Foreign Intelligence Advisory Board	20500
President's Intelligence Oversight Board	20500
Public Buildings Service	20405
Railroad Retirement Board	20036
Regulatory Information Service Center	20006
Research and Special Programs Administration	20590
Saint Lawrence Seaway Development Corporation	20590
Securities and Exchange Commission	20549
Selective Service System	20435
Senate	20510
Small Business Administration	20416
Smithsonian Institution	20560
Strategic Defense Initiative Organization	20301
Supreme Court of the United States	20543
Susquehanna River Basin Commission	20001
Tennessee Valley Authority	20444
Textile Trade Policy Group	20506
Trade and Development Agency	20523
Trade Policy Committee	20506
United States Arms Control and Disarmament Agency	20451
United States Botanic Garden	20024
United States Coast Guard	20593
United States Customs Service	20229
United States Information Agency	20547
United States International Development Cooperation Agency	20523

	ZIP
United States International Trade Commission	20436
United States Marine Corps	20380
United States National Central Bureau- International Criminal Police Organization	20530
United States Office of the Special Counsel	20036
United States Postal Service	20260
United States Savings Bond Division	20226
United States Secret Service	20223
United States Sentencing Commission	20002
United States Tax Court	20217
Urban Mass Transportation Administration	20590
Veterans Day National Committee	20420
White House Commission on Presidential Scholars	20202
White House Office	20500

HOSPITALS

	ZIP
District of Columbia General Hospital	20003
Georgetown University Hospital	20007
George Washington University Hospital	20037
Greater Southeast Community Hospital	20032
Howard University Hospital	20060
Providence Hospital	20017
Sibley Memorial Hospital	20016
Veterans Affairs Medical Center	20422
Walter Reed Army Medical Center	20307
Washington Hospital Center	20010

HOTELS/MOTELS

	ZIP
Hay-Adams Hotel	20006
Hyatt Regency Washington-On Capitol Hill	20001
Jefferson Hotel	20036
J.W. Marriott Hotel	20004

	ZIP
Ramada Inn-Downtown	20005
Sheraton Washington Hotel	20008
Stouffer Mayflower Hotel	20036
Watergate Hotel	20037
Wyndham Bristol Hotel	20037

MILITARY INSTALLATIONS

	ZIP
Armed Forces Institute of Pathology	20307
Bolling Air Force Base	20332
Coast Guard Headquarters, Washington D.C.	20593
Comptroller and Supply Department, Naval District, Washington Navy Yard	20374
Fort Lesley J. McNair	20319
Marine Barracks	20390
Marine Corps Headquarters, Navy Annex	20380
Military District of Washington D.C., Headquarters	20319
Naval Research Laboratory	20375
Naval Security Station	20390
United States Property and Fiscal Office, Washington D.C.	20315
Walter Reed Medical Center	20307
Washington General Mail Facility (Part of Washington)	20066
Washington Highlands (Part of Washington)	20032
Washington Square (Part of Washington)	20036
Watergate (Part of Washington)	20037
Wesley Heights (Part of Washington)	20016
West End (Part of Washington)	20037
Woodley Park (Part of Washington)	20008
Woodley Road (Part of Washington)	20008
Woodridge (Part of Washington)	20018

---

* **Area Zip Code**   † **Post Office Boxes**

	ZIP
Aberdeen	33437
Abe Springs	32424
Acline	33950
Adams Beach	32347
Adamsville (Hillsborough County)	33534
Adamsville (Sumter County)	34785
Airport Siding (Part of Jacksonville)	32229
Alachua	32615
Aladdin City	33187
Alamana	32168
Alderman Park (Part of Jacksonville)	32211
Alford	32420
Allandale	32119
Allanton	32404
Allapattah (Part of Miami)	33142*
	33242†
Allentown	32570
Alliance	32448
Alligator Point	32327
Aloma (Part of Winter Park)	32792
Alpine Heights	32433
Altamonte Mall (Part of Altamonte Springs)	32701
Altamonte Springs	32701
	32714-16
For specific Altamonte Springs Zip Codes call (407) 682-3977, or your local postmaster.	
Altha	32421
Alton	32066
Altoona	32702
Alturas	33820
Alumni Village (Part of Tallahassee)	32310
Alva	33920
Amelia City	32034
Amelia Island Plantation	32034
American Beach	32034
Anclote	34691
Andalusia	32110
Andover	33169
For specific Andover Zip Codes call (305) 470-0327, or your local postmaster.	
Andover Golf Estates	33169
Andover Lake Estates	33169
	33179
For specific Andover Lake Estates Zip Codes call (305) 470-0327, or your local postmaster.	
Andrews	32046
Angel City	32952
Angler Park	33037
Angus Valley	33544
Anna Maria	34216
Anthony	32617
Antioch	33565
Apalachee Correctional Institution	32324
Apalachee Ridge (Part of Tallahassee)	32301
Apalachicola	32320*
	32329†
Apollo Beach	33572
Apopka	32703-04
	32712
For specific Apopka Zip Codes call (407) 886-2951, or your local postmaster.	
Aquarina	32951
Araquey	32095
Arbor Hills (Part of Tallahassee)	32308
Arcadia	33821
Archer	32618
Argyle	32422
Aripeka	34679
Arlington (Part of Jacksonville)	32211
	32239
	32277
For specific Arlington Zip Codes call (904) 744-5222, or your local postmaster.	
Arlington Hills (Part of Jacksonville)	32211
Arlingwood (Part of Jacksonville)	32211
Armstrong	32033
Arran	32327
Arredondo	32608
Asbury Lake	32043

	ZIP
Ashton	34771
Ashville	32331
Astatula	34705
Astor	32102
Astor Park	32102
Astronaut Trail (Part of Titusville)	32782
Athena	32347
Atlantic Beach	32233
Atlantic Boulevard (Part of Coral Springs)	33071*
	33077†
Atlantic Boulevard Estates (Part of Jacksonville)	32225
Atlantic Heights (Part of Miami Beach)	33139
Atlantis	33462
Auburn	32536
Auburndale	33823
Aucilla	32344
Audubon	32952
Aurantia	32754
Autumn Woods	34683
Avalon Beach	32583
Aventura	33160
	33180
	33280
For specific Aventura Zip Codes call (305) 931-7682, or your local postmaster.	
Aventura Mall	33180
Avenues, The (Part of Jacksonville)	32256
Avondale (Part of Jacksonville)	32205
Avon Park	33825
Avon Park Air Force Base	33825
Avon Park Correctional Institution	33825
Avon Park Estates	33825
Avon Park Lakes	33825
Azalea Park	32807
Babson Park	33827
Bagdad	32530
Bahia Oaks	34474
Bahia Shores (Part of St. Pete Beach)	33706
Baker	32531
Baker Correctional Institution	32072
Baker Settlement	32464
Bakersville	32092
Bal-Alex Estates	32561
Baldwin	32234
Bal Harbour	33154
Bal Harbour Shops (Part of Bal Harbour)	33154
Ballantine Manor	34243
Ballast Point (Part of Tampa)	33611
Balm	33503
Bamboo	34748
Barberville	32105
Bardin	32177
Bardmoor	34641
Bare Beach	33440
Barefoot Bay	32976
Barrineau Park	32577
Barry University (Part of Miami Shores)	33161
Barth	32531
Bartow	33830*
	33831†
Bascom	32423
Basinger	34972
Baskin	34644
	34648
For specific Baskin Zip Codes call (813) 584-2191, or your local postmaster.	
Bassville Park	34788
Basswood Estates	34972
Baum	32308
Bay Acres	34229
Bayard (Part of Jacksonville)	32258
Bay Crest Park	33615
Bay Grove	32439
Bay Harbor Islands	33154
Bayhead (Bay County)	32466
Bay Head (Pasco County)	33525
Bay Hill	32819
Bay Lake	34736
Bayonet Point	34667
Bayou George	32405
Bay Pines	33504
Bay Point (Bay County)	32411
Bay Point (Dade County)	33137
Bayport	34607

	ZIP
Bayridge	32703
Bayshore	33917
Bayshore Gardens	34207
Bayshore Manor	33917
Bay Springs	32568
Bayview	32401
Bay Vista (Dade County)	33181
Bay Vista (Pinellas County)	33712
Bayway (Part of St. Petersburg)	33715
Baywood	32140
Baywood Village	34683
Beach (Part of Vero Beach)	32963*
	32964†
Beach Haven	32507
Beach Highlands	32459
Beach Park (Part of Tampa)	33609
	33629
For specific Beach Park Zip Codes call (813) 877-0717, or your local postmaster.	
Beachville	32071
Beachwood (Part of Jacksonville)	32246
Beacon Beach	32403
Beacon Groves	34683
Beacon Hill	32456
Beacon Hills (Part of Jacksonville)	32225
Beacon Lakes	34691
Beacon Light (Part of Lighthouse Point)	33064
Beacon Square	34691
Bealsville	33567
Bean City	33440
Bear Creek	32401
Bear Lake	32703
Bearss Plaza	33612
Beauclere Gardens (Part of Jacksonville)	32257
Beaver Creek	32531
Becker	32097
Beckhamtown	32640
Beeghly Heights (Part of Jacksonville)	32218
Bee Ridge	34233
Bel-Air (Part of Sanford)	32771
Belair Beach	32408
Bell	32619
Bellair	32073
Bellair-Meadowbrook Terrace	32073
Bellair Plaza (Part of Daytona Beach)	32118
Belleair	34616
Belleair Beach	34634
Belleair Bluffs	34640
Belleair Shore	34634
Belle Glade	33430
Belle Glade Camp	33430
Belle Isle	32809
Belleview	34420-21
For specific Belleview Zip Codes call (904) 245-8777, or your local postmaster.	
Belleview Heights	34420
Bellview	32506
	32526
For specific Bellview Zip Codes call (904) 941-1000, or your local postmaster.	
Bellwood	32780
Belvedere Homes	33409
Benbow	33440
Bennett	32466
Bent Tree Village	34241
Ben White Raceway (Part of Orlando)	32810
Beresford	32720
Berkshire Estates	34241
Berry	33868
Berrydale	32565
Bertha	32792
Bethany	34251
Bethel	32327
Bethlehem	32425
Bethune Beach	32169
Betmar Acres	33541
Betton Hills (Part of Tallahassee)	32312
Beulah (Escambia County)	32526
Beulah (Orange County)	34787
Beverly Beach	32136

	ZIP
Beverly Hills	34464-65
For specific Beverly Hills Zip Codes call (904) 746-3076, or your local postmaster.	
Beverly Hills (Part of Jacksonville)	32208
Beverly Terrace	34234
Bevilles Corner	33513
Big Bayou (Part of St. Petersburg)	33705*
	33739†
Big Coppitt Key	33040
Big Cypress Seminole Indian Reservation	33440
Big Pine Key	33043
Big Scrub	32179
Biltmore (Part of Jacksonville)	32205
Biltmore Beach	32408
Bird Key (Part of Sarasota)	34236
Biscayne Gardens	33168
Biscayne One (Part of Miami)	33111†
	33131*
Biscayne Park	33161
Biscayne Plaza Shopping Center (Part of Miami)	33138
Biscayne St. Thomas College	33054
Bithlo	32807
Black Creek	32439
Black Jacks	32680
Blackman	32531
Black Rock	32097
Bland	32615
Blanton	33525
Blichton	34482
Bloomingdale	33594
Blountstown	32424
Bloxham	32310
Blue Gulf Beach	32459
Blue Lake	32720
Blue Mountain Beach	32459
Blue Springs	34797
Bluff Springs	32535
Boardman	32633
Boca Del Mar	33433
Boca Grande	33921
Boca Pointe	33433
Boca Raton	33427-29
	33431-34
	33481
	33486-87
	33496-98
For specific Boca Raton Zip Codes call (407) 994-2700, or your local postmaster.	
Boca West	33434
Bogia	32568
Bokeelia	33922
Bonaventure	33326
Bonifay	32425
Bonita Beach	33923
Bonita Shores	33923
Bonita Springs	33923*
	33959†
Bonnie Loch	33064
Bookertown	32771
Bostwick	32007
Boulougne	32046
Bowden (Part of Jacksonville)	32216
Bowling Green	33834
Boyd	32347
Boyette	33547
Boynton Beach	33424-26
	33435-37
For specific Boynton Beach Zip Codes call (407) 738-5220, or your local postmaster.	
Boynton Beach Mall (Part of Boynton Beach)	33426
Boys Ranch	32060
Braden Castle (Part of Bradenton)	34208
Braden River	34201-03
	34208
For specific Braden River Zip Codes call (813) 758-6797, or your local postmaster.	
Bradenton	34201-10
	34280-82
For specific Bradenton Zip Codes call (813) 746-4195, or your local postmaster.	
Bradenton Beach	34217
Bradfordville	32312
Bradley	33835

*Area Zip Code   † Post Office Boxes

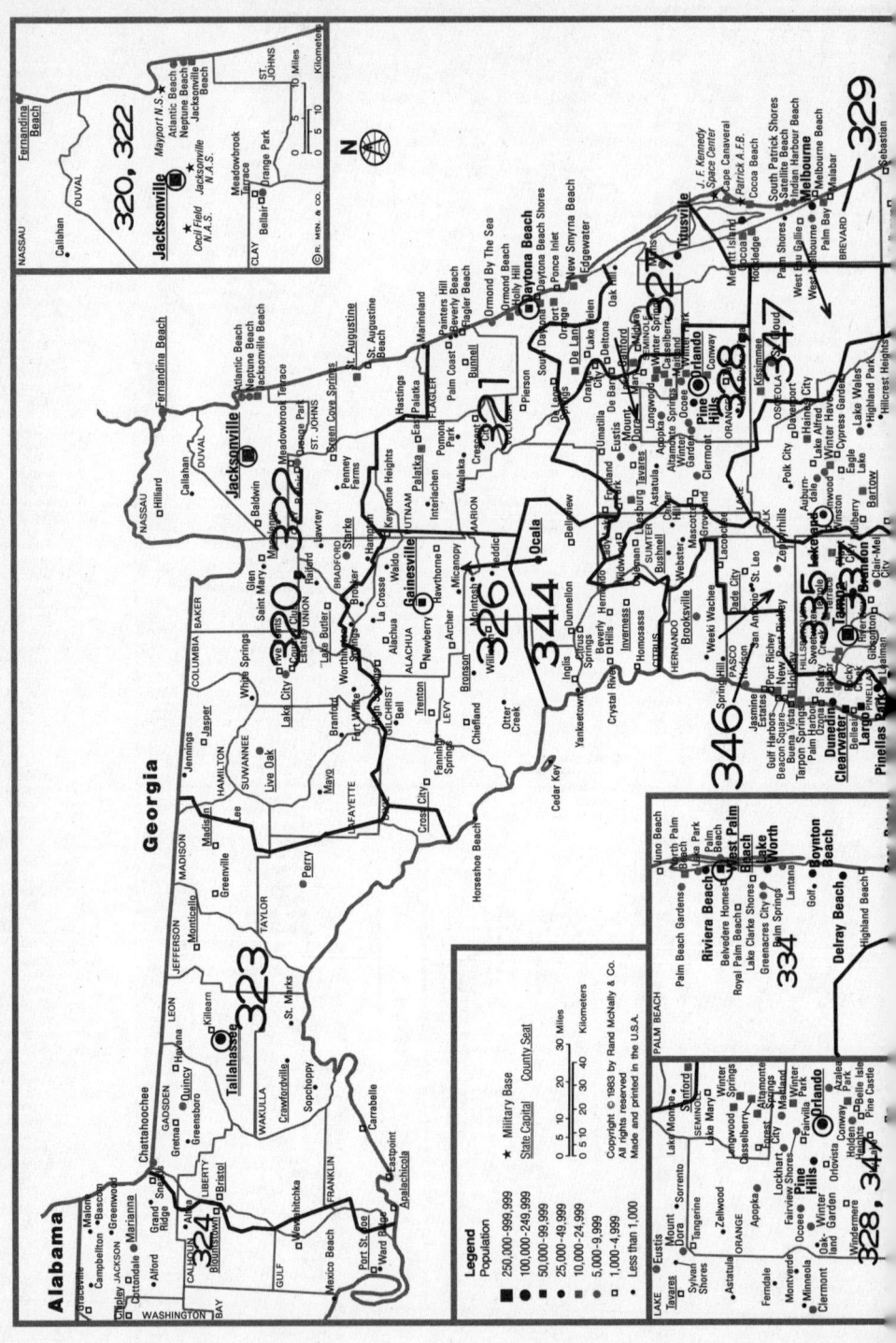

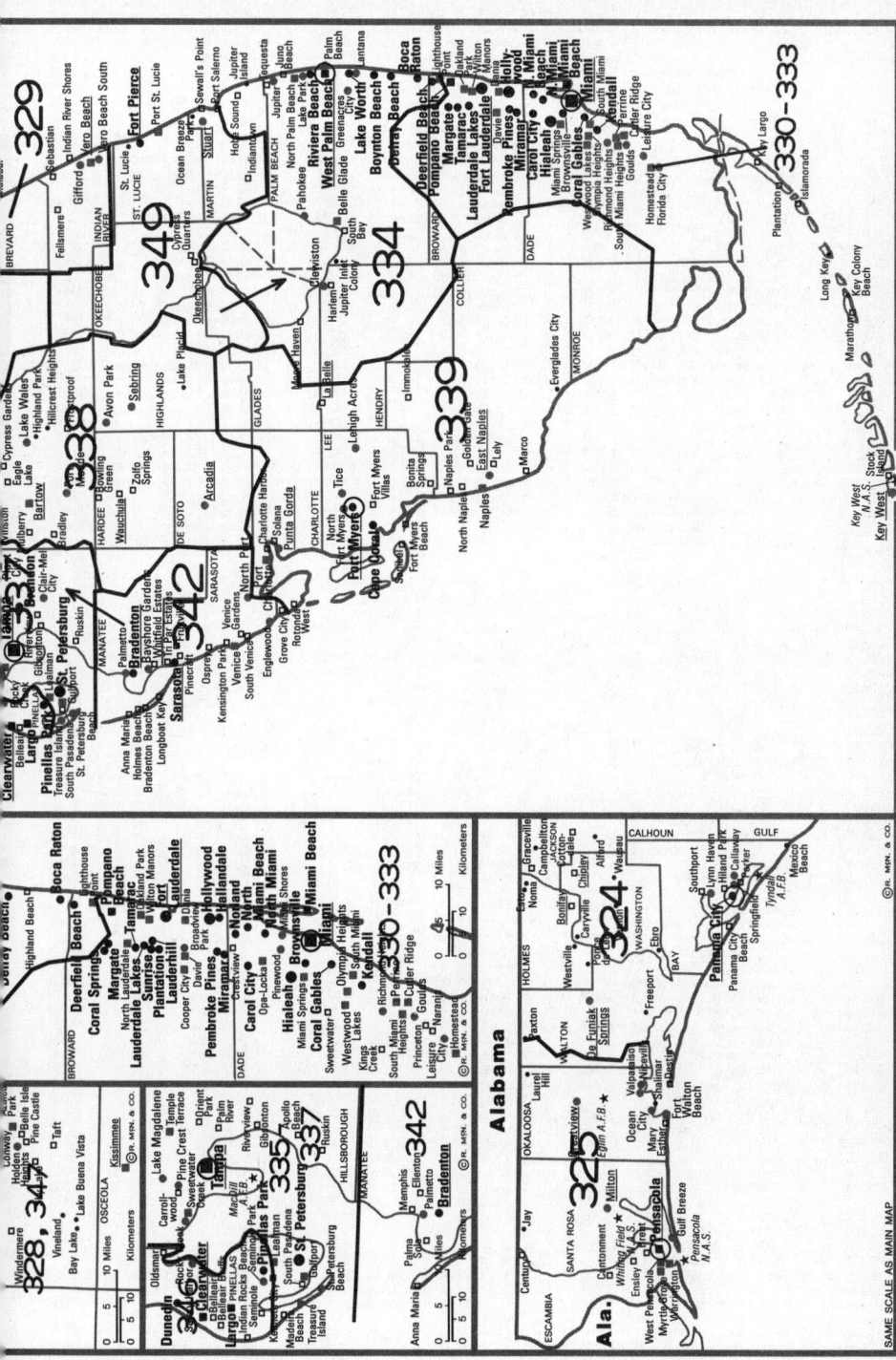

	ZIP
Bradshaw Acres	34711
Brandon	33509-11
For specific Brandon Zip Codes call (813) 689-1616, or your local postmaster.	
Branford	32008
Brannonville	32401
Bratt	32535
Brent	32503
	32505
For specific Brent Zip Codes call (904) 433-0065, or your local postmaster.	
Brentwood (Duval County)	32206
Brentwood (Sarasota County)	34232
Bright (Part of Hialeah)	33013
Brighton	34972
Brighton Seminole Indian Reservation	33471
Briny Breezes	33435
Bristol	32321
Britton Plaza (Part of Tampa)	33611
Broadview Park	33317
Broadview-Pompano Park	33068
Broadwater (Part of St. Petersburg)	33711
Brock Crossroad	32463
Bronson	32621
Brooker	32622
Brooklyn (Part of Jacksonville)	32204
Brookridge	34613
Brooksville	34601-05
	34609-14
For specific Brooksville Zip Codes call (904) 799-4441, or your local postmaster.	
Browardale	33311
Broward Correctional Institution	33024
Broward Mall (Part of Plantation)	33388
Brownsdale	32565
Brownsville (Dade County)	33142
Brownsville (Escambia County)	32505
Browntown	32440
Brownville	33821
Bruce	32455
Bruceville	34488
Bryant	33439
Bryceville	32009
Brynwood	33912
Buccaneer Estates	33054
Buchanan	33890
Buckhead Ridge	34974
Buckhorn	32358
Buckingham	33905
Buckingham West	32601
Buena Ventura Lakes	34743
Buena Vista (Dade County)	33137
Buena Vista (Jackson County)	32460
Buena Vista (Orange County)	32830
Buena Vista (Pasco County)	34691
Buffalo	32189
Bunche Park	33054
Bunker (DeSoto County)	33821
Bunker (Walton County)	32459
Bunnell	32110
Burbank	32134
Burnett's Lake (Part of Alachua)	32615
Bushnell	33513
Butler Beach	32084
Byrneville	32535
Calhoun Correctional Institution	32424
Callahan	32011
Callaway	32404
Camellia Gardens	32809
Camelot Park (Part of Tallahassee)	32301
Cameron City	32771
Campbell	34746
Campbellton	32426
Camps Mine	34601
Campton	32567
Campville	32640
Canaan	32771
Canal Point	33438
Candler	32111
Cannon Town	32531
Canoe Creek	34990

	ZIP
Cantonment	32533
Cape Canaveral	32920
Cape Coral	33904
	33909-10
	33914-15
	33990-91
For specific Cape Coral Zip Codes call (813) 772-5515, or your local postmaster.	
Cape Coral Central (Part of Cape Coral)	33915
Cape Haze	33946
Capital Hills (Part of Tallahassee)	32308
Capitola	32311
Capps	32336
Capri Isle (Part of Treasure Island)	33706
Captiva	33924
Carleton	32640
Carl Fisher (Part of Miami Beach)	33139
Carlson	33538
Carlton Village	32159
Carol City	33055-56
For specific Carol City Zip Codes call (305) 620-0390, or your local postmaster.	
Carr	32421
Carrabelle	32322
Carrabelle Beach	32322
Carraway	32177
Carrollwood	33618
	33624
	33688
For specific Carrollwood Zip Codes call (813) 961-2962, or your local postmaster.	
Carrollwood Village	33618
	33624
For specific Carrollwood Village Zip Codes call (813) 961-2962, or your local postmaster.	
Carters Corner	33823
Carver (Part of Jacksonville)	32209
Carver Manor (Part of Jacksonville)	32209
Carver Ranches	33023
Caryville	32427
Casa Bianco	32344
Casey Key	34275
Cason Inglis Acres	34449
Cassadaga	32706
Casselberry	32707-08
	32718-19
	32730
For specific Casselberry Zip Codes call (407) 339-5919, or your local postmaster.	
Cassia	32726
Causeway Isles (Part of St. Petersburg)	33707
Cedar Creek	34488
Cedar Grove	32401
	32405
For specific Cedar Grove Zip Codes call (904) 747-4840, or your local postmaster.	
Cedar Hammock	34207
Cedar Hills (Part of Jacksonville)	32210
Cedar Hills Estates (Part of Jacksonville)	32210
Cedar Key	32625
Cedar Lake Estates	34428
Cedar Point (Part of Jacksonville)	32226
Cedar Shores (Part of Ocala)	34471
Center Hill	33514
Centerville (Part of Tallahassee)	32308
	32312
	32317
For specific Centerville Zip Codes call (904) 385-0824, or your local postmaster.	
Central Florida Reception Center	32862
Central Plaza (Part of St. Petersburg)	33713
Central Shopping Plaza (Part of Miami)	33126
Century	32535
Century Village (census designated place)	33417
Century Village	33434
Cerrogordo	32464

	ZIP
Chain O'Lakes	32767
Chaires	32311
Charlotte Beach	33927
Charlotte Harbor	33980
Charlotte Park	33950
Chaseville (Part of Jacksonville)	32276
Chason	32421
Chassahowitzka	34447
Chatmar	34432
Chattahoochee	32324
Cherry Lake (Madison County)	32340
Cherry Lake (Sumter County)	32159
Chester	32097
Chestnut Hill Ranches	34482
Chiefland	32626
Chipley	32428
Chipola	32421
Chipola Terrace	32448
Choctaw	32459
Choctaw Beach	32439
Chokoloskee	33925
Christina	33813
Christmas	32709
Chuluota	32766
Chumuckla	32571
Cinco Bayou	32548
Cisky Park	34748
Citra	32113
Citronelle	34433
Citrus (Part of Inverness)	34450
Citrus Center	33471
Citrus Park	33624
Citrus Springs	34433
City of Sunrise	33313
	33323-24
	33338
	33345
	33351
For specific City of Sunrise Zip Codes call (305) 748-8675, or your local postmaster.	
Clair-Mel City	33619
Clarcona	32710
Clark	32643
Clarksville	32430
Clear Springs (Okaloosa County)	32567
Clear Springs (Walton County)	32567
Clearwater	34615-30
For specific Clearwater Zip Codes call (813) 464-2900, or your local postmaster.	
Clearwater Beach (Part of Clearwater)	34630
Clearwater Coast Guard Air Station	34622
Clearwater Mall (Part of Clearwater)	34624
Clermont	34711*
	34712†
Cleveland	33982
Cleveland Street (Part of Clearwater)	34615
Clewiston	33440
Clifton (Part of Jacksonville)	32211
Clinton Heights	33525
Cloud Lake	33406
Cluster Springs	32433
Coastland Center (Part of Naples)	33940
Cobbtown	32565
Cocoa	32922-24
	32926-27
For specific Cocoa Zip Codes call (407) 636-6565, or your local postmaster.	
Cocoa Beach	32931*
	32932†
Cocoa West	32922
Coconut	33923
Coconut Creek	33063
	33066
	33073
For specific Coconut Creek Zip Codes call (305) 974-6080, or your local postmaster.	
Coconut Grove (Part of Miami)	33133*
	33233†
Cody	32344
Colee (Part of Fort Lauderdale)	33301*
	33303†
Coleman	33521

	ZIP
College Park (Duval County)	32209
College Park (Marion County)	34474
College Park (Orange County)	32804
College Point	32444
Collier City (Part of Pompano Beach)	33069
Collier Manor-Cresthaven	33064
Colonial Gables	34232
Colonial Hills	34652
Colonial Manor (Part of Jacksonville)	32207
Colonial Plaza Mall (Part of Orlando)	32803
Colonialtown (Part of Orlando)	32803
Columbia	32055
Combee Settlement	33805
Commerce (Part of Tampa)	33602
Compass Lake	32420
Compass Lake Hills	32420
Conch Key	33050
Concord	32333
Concord Shopping Plaza	33165
Conner	34488
Connersville	33830
Conway	32806
	32812
For specific Conway Zip Codes call (407) 240-9496, or your local postmaster.	
Cooks Hammock	32066
Cooper City	33328
Copeland	33926
Copeland Settlement	32609
Coquina Key (Part of St. Petersburg)	33705
Cora	32565
Coral Cove	34231
Coral Gables	33114
	33133-34
For specific Coral Gables Zip Codes call (305) 445-8842, or your local postmaster.	
Coral Gardens	34997
Coral Ridge Mall (Part of Fort Lauderdale)	33306*
	33339†
Coral Springs	33065
	33067
	33075-76
For specific Coral Springs Zip Codes call (305) 752-7640, or your local postmaster.	
Coral Square (Part of Coral Springs)	33071
Coral Terrace	33144
	33156
For specific Coral Terrace Zip Codes call (305) 470-0327, or your local postmaster.	
Coral Way Village	33155
Coralwood Mall (Part of Cape Coral)	33904
Cordova (Part of Pensacola)	32503
Cordova Lakes (Part of Bradenton)	34209
Cordova Mall (Part of Pensacola)	32504
Corkscrew	33934
Corley Island	34748
Cornwell	33857
Coronet	33566
Corry Station Naval Training Center	32511
Cortez	34215
Cortez Road (Part of Bradenton)	34210
Cottage Hill	32533
Cottondale	32431
Cotton Plant	34474
Country Club	33015
Country Club Acres	33484
Country Club Estates (Columbia County)	32055
Country Club Estates (Polk County)	33805
Country Club Manor (Part of Sanford)	32771
Country Club Trail	33436-37
For specific Country Club Trail Zip Codes call (407) 732-6689, or your local postmaster.	
Countryside (Marion County)	34481

* Area Zip Code † Post Office Boxes

	ZIP		ZIP		ZIP		ZIP
Countryside (Pinellas County)	34621		33328-32	Dowling Park	32060		32940
Countryside Mall (Part of Clearwater)	34621	For specific Davie Zip Codes call (305) 474-2557, or your local postmaster.		Downtown (Part of Boca Raton)	33429	For specific Eau Gallie Zip Codes call (407) 254-3433, or your local postmaster.	
Countryway	33635				33432		
Courtenay	32952	Davis Islands (Part of Tampa)	33606	For specific Downtown Zip Codes call (407) 395-4733, or your local postmaster.		Ebb	32331
Cove (Part of Panama City)	32401	Day	32013			Ebro	32437
Cox	32424	Daytona Beach	32114-29	Downtown (Part of Boynton Beach)	33435	Edgar	32149
Coytown (Part of Orlando)	32803	For specific Daytona Beach Zip Codes call (904) 274-3500, or your local postmaster.		Downtown (Part of Daytona Beach)	32115	Edgewater (Dade County)	33137
Crackertown (Part of Inglis)	34449	Daytona Beach Shores	32116	Downtown (Part of Fort Myers)	33901	Edgewater (Volusia County)	32132
Crandall	32097	Daytona Highbridge Estates	32114	Downtown (Part of Fort Pierce)	34950		32141
Crawford	32009	Daytona Mall (Part of Daytona Beach)	32114	Downtown (Part of Jacksonville)	32202	For specific Edgewater Zip Codes call (904) 428-6656, or your local postmaster.	
Crawfordville	32326†	Daytona Park Estates	32720	Downtown (Part of Longwood)	32750	Edgewater Gulf Beach (Part of Panama City Beach)	32407
	32327†	De Bary	32713	Downtown (Part of Milton)	32570	Edgewood	32809
Crescent Beach (Sarasota County)	34242	Deerfield Beach	33441-43	Downtown (Part of Naples)	33939†		32839
Crescent Beach (St. Johns County)	32086	For specific Deerfield Beach Zip Codes call (305) 427-3600, or your local postmaster.			33940*	For specific Edgewood Zip Codes call (904) 765-1530, or your local postmaster.	
Crescent City	32112	Deerfield Lakes	32011	Downtown (Part of Orlando)	32801	Edgewood Manor (Part of Jacksonville)	32209
Crescent Shores Heights	32157	Deerfield Mall (Part of Deerfield Beach)	33442	Downtown (Part of Pensacola)	32501	Edison	33547
Crestview	32536	Deering Bay	33158	Downtown (Part of Tampa)	33601†	Edison Center (Part of Miami)	33150*
	32539	Deerland	32536		33602*		33151†
For specific Crestview Zip Codes call (904) 682-2634, or your local postmaster.		Deer Park	32901	Downtown (Part of West Palm Beach)	33401	Edison Mall (Part of Fort Myers)	33901
Crewsville	33890	Deer Point	32405	Drayton Island	32139	Eglin Air Force Base (Okaloosa County)	32542
Crooked Lake Park	33853	Deerwood (Part of Jacksonville)	32256	Dreamworld (Part of Sanford)	32771	Eglin Village	32544
Croom-A-Coochee	33597	De Funiak Springs	32433	Drew Park (Part of Tampa)	33614	Egypt Lake	33614
Cross City	32628	Dekle Beach	32347	Drifton	32344	El Chico	33040
Cross City Correctional Institution	32628	De Land	32720-21	Dr. M. L. King, Jr.	33147	Elder Springs	32773
Cross County Mall	33409		32723-24	Druid Hills	32751	Electra	32179
Cross Creek	32640	For specific De Land Zip Codes call (904) 734-7600, or your local postmaster.		Duck Key	33050	Elfers	34680
Crossroads	33709-10	De Land Highlands	32720	Duette	33834	El Jobean	33927
	33743	De Land Southwest	32720	Dundee	33838	Elkton	32033
For specific Crossroads Zip Codes call (813) 343-1277, or your local postmaster.		De Leon Springs	32130	Dune Allen Beach	32459	Ellaville (Jackson County)	32426
Crows Bluff	32720	Delespine	32927	Dunedin	34697†	Ellaville (Suwannee County)	32060
Crystal Beach	34681	Dellwood (Jackson County)	32442		34698*	Ellenton	34222
Crystal Lake (Polk County)	33801*	Dellwood (Leon County)	32303	Dunedin Isles (Part of Dunedin)	34698	Ellinor Village (Part of Ormond Beach)	32175
	33803†	Delray Beach	33444-47	Dunnellon	34430-34	Ellison Acres	32168
Crystal Lake (Washington County)	32409		33483-84	For specific Dunnellon Zip Codes call (904) 489-4224, or your local postmaster.		Ellisville	32055
Crystal River	34423	For specific Delray Beach Zip Codes call (407) 276-6047, or your local postmaster.		Dupont	32110	Elzey	32683
	34428-29	Delray Beach Mall (Part of Delray Beach)	33483	Dupont Center	32086	Eloise	33880
For specific Crystal River Zip Codes call (904) 795-2030, or your local postmaster.		Delray Garden Estates	33484	Durant	33530	Eloise Woods	33884
Crystal Springs	33524	Del Rio	33617	Durham	32424	El Portal	33138
Cudjoe	33042	Deltona	32725	Duval (Part of Jacksonville)	32218		33150
Cudjoe Key	33044		32728	Dyal	32011	For specific El Portal Zip Codes call (305) 754-2524, or your local postmaster.	
Cunningham Acres	33541		32738	Eagle Lake	33839	Elsi De Monde Heights	32448
Curlew	34683	For specific Deltona Zip Codes call (407) 574-6363, or your local postmaster.		Eagle Ridge	33912	Elwood Park	34208
Curtis Mill	32358	Del Tura	33903	Eagles Nest	33852	Empire Point (Part of Jacksonville)	32207
Cutler	33157-58	Denaud	33935	Earleton	32631	Emporia	32180
For specific Cutler Zip Codes call (305) 233-6859, or your local postmaster.		Denver	32112	East Avenue (Part of Sarasota)	34237	Englewood	34223-24
Cutler Ridge	33157	De Soto Acres	34235	Eastbrook	32792		34295
	33189-90	De Soto City	33870	Eastern Shores (Part of North Miami Beach)	33160	For specific Englewood Zip Codes call (813) 474-3547, or your local postmaster.	
For specific Cutler Ridge Zip Codes call (305) 233-6859, or your local postmaster.		DeSoto Correctional Institution	33821	Eastgate (Leon County)	32308	Englewood (Part of Jacksonville)	32207
Cutler Ridge Mall	33189	Desoto Lakes	34235	Eastgate (Orange County)	32792	Englewood Beach	34223
Cypress (Broward County)	33060	DeSoto Square	34205	East Hill (Part of Pensacola)	32503	Englewood Isles	34223
Cypress (Jackson County)	32432	Destin	32540†	East Lake	33610	English Estates	32730
Cypress Creek	33850		32541*	East Lake Harris Estates	34705	Enon	32568
Cypress Gardens	33884	Devils Garden	33440	East Lake-Orient Park	33610	Ensley	32514
Cypress Lake	33919	Dickerson City	32583		33619		32534
Cypress Lake Estates	33919	Dills	32344	For specific East Lake-Orient Park Zip Codes call (813) 464-2900, or your local postmaster.		For specific Ensley Zip Codes call (904) 478-7114, or your local postmaster.	
Cypress Lakes	33417	Dinsmore (Part of Jacksonville)	32219	Eastlake Square	33610	Enterprise	32725
Cypress Point	32131	Diplomat Mall (Part of Hallandale)	33009	Eastlake Weir	32133	Eppes Heights (Part of Tallahassee)	32304
Cypress Quarters	34972	Dirego Park	32405	East Lake Woodlands	34677	Eridu	32331
Cypress Trace	33907	Dixie Heights	32962	East Milton	32583	Erin Park	33872
Cyprus Village	33014	Dixieland (Part of Lakeland)	33803	East Naples	33962	Errol Estates	32712
Dade City	33525*	Dixie Ranch Acres	34972	East Orlando Estates	32822	Escambia Farms	32531
	33526†	Dixie Village (Part of Orlando)	32806	East Palatka	32131	Espanola	32110
Dade City North	33525	Doctor Phillips	32819	Eastpoint	32328	Esperenza	32131
Dade Correctional Institution	33034	Doctors Inlet	32030	East Port Plaza (Part of Port St. Lucie)	34952	Estero	33928
Dadeland Mall	33156	Dogtown	32351	East Rockland Key	33040	Estiffanulga	32321
Dalkeith	32465	Dogwood Estates	34601	East Side (Part of Altamonte Springs)	32701	Esto	32425
Dallas	34491	Dogwood Heights	32446	East Silver Springs Shores	32179	Eucheeanna	32433
Dames Point (Part of Jacksonville)	32226	Dogwood Lake Estates	32425	East Tampa	33619	Euclid (Part of St. Petersburg)	33704*
Dania	33004	Dona Vista	32784	East Williston	32696		33734†
Danks Corner	34491	Doral	33178	Eaton Park	33840	Eureka	32134
Darby	33525	Dorcas	32539	Eatonville	32751	Eustis	32726*
Darlington	32464	Douglas City	32351	Eau Gallie	32934-36		32727†
Davenport	33837	Douglas Crossroads	32455			Eva	33809
Davie	33312	Dover	33527			Evans Village	32808
	33314	Dover Shores (Part of Orlando)	32806				
	33325-26						

* Area Zip Code   **† Post Office Boxes**

	ZIP
Everglades City	33929
Evergreen (Martin County)	34990
Evergreen (Nassau County)	32097
Evinston	32633
Facil	32096
Factory Outlet World-Orlando (Part of Orlando)	32819
Fairbanks	32601
Fairfield	32634
Fair Meadows (Part of Tallahassee)	32304
Fairmont (Part of St. Petersburg)	33711
Fairview Shores	32804
Fairvilla	32804
Fairway Village	33624
Fairyland	32952
Falls, The	33176
Falmouth	32060
Fanlew	32344
Fanning Springs	32680
Fashion Mall, The (Part of Plantation)	33324
Favorita	32110
Feather Sound	34622
Federal Correctional Institute (Jackson County)	32446
Federal Correctional Institution (Leon County)	32301
Federal Point	32131
Fedhaven	33854
Felda	33930
Fellowship	34482
Fellsmere	32948
Fenholloway	32347
Fernandina Beach	32034*
	32035†
Ferndale	34729
Fern Park	32730
Ferry Pass	32504
	32514
For specific Ferry Pass Zip Codes call (904) 477-1707, or your local postmaster.	
Festus	32344
Fiddlesticks	33912
Fidelis	32565
Fiesta Key	33001
Fifty Seventh Avenue	34202
	34207
For specific Fifty Seventh Avenue Zip Codes call (813) 755-8087, or your local postmaster.	
Fisher Island (Part of Miami Beach)	33139
Fisherman's Cove	34997
Fishermans Road	32767
Fish Lake	34744
Five Points (Brevard County)	32922
Five Points (Columbia County)	32055
Five Points (Washington County)	32427
Flagami (Part of Miami)	33126
Flagler (Dade County)	33128-32
	33136
For specific Flagler Zip Codes call (305) 294-2557, or your local postmaster.	
Flagler (Monroe County)	33040
	33045
For specific Flagler Zip Codes call (305) 371-2911, or your local postmaster.	
Flagler Beach	32136
Flagler Estates	32145
Flagler-Tamiami (Part of Miami)	33126
	33144
For specific Flagler-Tamiami Zip Codes call (305) 261-5102, or your local postmaster.	
Flamingo	33034
Flamingo Bay	33956
Flamingo Plaza (Part of Hialeah)	33010
Flemington	32686
Fletcher	33612*
	33695†
Florahome	32140
Floral Bluff (Part of Jacksonville)	32211
Floral City	34436

	ZIP
Floral Park	33462
Florence Lake	33881
Florence Villa (Part of Winter Haven)	33881
	33885
For specific Florence Villa Zip Codes call (813) 293-8423, or your local postmaster.	
Florida A and M University (Part of Tallahassee)	32307
Florida City	33034
Florida Correctional Institution	32663
Florida Gardens	33460
Florida International University	33199
Floridana Beach	32951
Florida Ridge	32962
Florida State Prison	32091
Florida State University (Part of Tallahassee)	32313
Florosa	32569
Flowersville	32567
Fluffy Landing	32439
Footman	32952
Forest City	32714
Forest Heights (Part of Tallahassee)	32303
Forest Hills (Hillsborough County)	33612
	33682
For specific Forest Hills Zip Codes call (813) 935-8054, or your local postmaster.	
Forest Hills (Lake County)	32720
Forest Hills (Pasco County)	34690
Forest Hills (Volusia County)	32174
Forest Island Park	33908
Forest Lakes (Pinellas County)	34677
Forest Lakes (Sarasota County)	34232
Forest Lakes Park	32179
Forest Ridge Village (Part of Fernandina Beach)	32034
Formosa (Part of Orlando)	32804
Fort Basinger	34972
Fort Caroline Club Estates (Part of Jacksonville)	32276
Fort Drum	34972
Fort George Island (Part of Jacksonville)	32226
Fort Green	33834
Fort Green Springs	33834
Fort King Acres	33541
Fort Lauderdale	33301-94
For specific Fort Lauderdale Zip Codes call (305) 527-2074, or your local postmaster.	
COLLEGES & UNIVERSITIES	
Nova University	33314
FINANCIAL INSTITUTIONS	
NationsBank of Florida, N.A.	33301
Sun Bank/South Florida, N.A.	33301
HOSPITALS	
Broward General Medical Center	33316
Florida Medical Center Hospital	33313
Holy Cross Hospital	33308
North Ridge Medical Center	33334
HOTELS/MOTELS	
Best Western Oceanside Inn	33316
Best Western Marina Inn & Yacht Harbor	33316
Days Inn Downtown	33312
Crown Sterling Suites	33316
Travel Lodge Fort Lauderdale Executive Airport	33309
Holiday Inn Lauderdale-by-the-Sea	33308
Holiday Inn North	33309
Holiday Inn West	33319
Howard Johnson Lauderdale-by-the Sea	33308
Howard Johnson Beach Resort	33308

	ZIP
Howard Johnson Ocean's Edge Resort	33304
Marriott Harbor Beach Resort	33316
Marriott North	33309
Westin	33334
MILITARY INSTALLATIONS	
Naval Surface Warfare Center, Fort Lauderdale	33315
Fort Lonesome	33547
Fort McCoy	32134
Fort Meade	33841
Fort Myers	33901-03
	33905-08
	33911-13
	33916-19
For specific Fort Myers Zip Codes call (813) 334-2117, or your local postmaster.	
Fort Myers Beach	33931*
	33932†
Fort Myers Shores	33905
Fort Myers Villas	33912
Fort Ogden	33842
Fort Pierce	34945-51
	34954
	34979-82
For specific Fort Pierce Zip Codes call (407) 461-2460, or your local postmaster.	
Fort Pierce Beach (Part of Fort Pierce)	34949
Fort Pierce North	34946-47
For specific Fort Pierce North Zip Codes call (407) 461-8014, or your local postmaster.	
Fort Pierce Shores	34949
Fort Pierce South	34981-82
For specific Fort Pierce South Zip Codes call (407) 461-2460, or your local postmaster.	
Fort Taylor (Part of Key West)	33040
Fort Union	32060
Fort Walton Beach	32547-49
For specific Fort Walton Beach Zip Codes call (904) 243-2311, or your local postmaster.	
Fort White	32038
Forty Ninth Street (Part of Gulfport)	33707
Fountain	32438
Four Mile Village	32459
Fowler Bluff	32626
Foxcroft (Part of Tallahassee)	32308
Fox Town	33809
Francis	32177
Franklin Park	33916
Franklintown	32034
Freeport	32439
Frink	32430
Frontenac	32927
Frostproof	33843
Fruit Cove	32259
Fruitland	32112
Fruitland Park	34731
Fruitville	34232
Fuller Heights	33860
Fussels Corner	33823
Gainesville	32601-14
	32641
	32653
For specific Gainesville Zip Codes call (904) 334-1863, or your local postmaster.	
Gainesville Mall (Part of Gainesville)	32601
Galleria at Fort Lauderdale, The (Part of Fort Lauderdale)	33304
Galliver	32564
Galloway	33809
Galt City	32583
Galt Ocean Mile (Part of Fort Lauderdale)	33308
Gandy	33702
Garden City (Duval County)	32218
Garden City (Okaloosa County)	32536
Garden Grove Estates	34609
Gardens, The (Part of Palm Beach Gardens)	33410
Gardenville	33534
Gardner	33890
Gaskin	32433

	ZIP
Gateway (Part of Fort Lauderdale)	33338
Gateway Center (Part of Jacksonville)	32208
Gateway Mall (Part of St. Petersburg)	33702*
	33742†
Gator Creek Estates	34241
General Mail Facility (Part of Jacksonville)	32203
Geneva	32732
Georgetown (Madison County)	32340
Georgetown (Putnam County)	32139
Georgiana	32952
Gibson	32333
Gibsonia	33809
Gibsonton	33534
Gifford	32960-61
	32967
For specific Gifford Zip Codes call (407) 567-5206, or your local postmaster.	
Gilberts Mill	32428
Gillette	34221
Gilmore (Part of Jacksonville)	32276
Gladeview	33147
	33150
For specific Gladeview Zip Codes call (305) 836-9710, or your local postmaster.	
Glencoe (Volusia County)	32168
Glendale (Leon County)	32303
Glendale (Walton County)	32433
Glen Oaks (Part of Sarasota)	34232
Glen Ridge	33406
Glen Saint Mary	32040
Glenvar Heights	33143
	33155
For specific Glenvar Heights Zip Codes call (305) 661-8101, or your local postmaster.	
Glenwood (Nassau County)	32097
Glenwood (Volusia County)	32722
Glory	32351
Glynlea Park (Part of Jacksonville)	32216
Golden Beach	33160
Golden Gate (Collier County)	33999
Golden Gate (Martin County)	34997
Golden Gate Estates	33964
	33999
For specific Golden Gate Estates Zip Codes call (813) 262-5411, or your local postmaster.	
Golden Glades	33055
Golden Hills	34482
Golden Isles (Part of Hallandale)	33009
Golden Lakes	33411
Goldenrod	32733
Golden Shores	33160
Golfview	33406
Golfview Park	33853
Gomez	33455
Gonzalez	32560
Goodbys (Part of Jacksonville)	32257
Good Hope	32531
Goodland	33933
Gopher Ridge	32145
Gordon	32433
Gordon Chapel	32640
Gordonville	33830
Gotha	34734
Goulding	32501
Goulds	33170
Governor's Square Mall (Part of Tallahassee)	32301
Graceville	32440
Graham	32042
Grahamsville	34488
Grand Crossing (Part of Jacksonville)	32209
Grandin	32138
Grand Island	32735
Grand Park (Part of Jacksonville)	32209
Grand Ridge	32442
Grandview	32131
Grangers Mill	32055

* Area Zip Code   *† Post Office Boxes*

	ZIP
Grant	32949
Grassy Key	33050
Gratigny (Part of North Miami)	33168
Grayton Beach	32459
Greater Northdale	33624
Greenacres	33463
Greenbriar	32771
Green Cove Springs	32043
Greenhead	32428
Green Hills	32438
Greenland (Part of Jacksonville)	32256
	32258

For specific Greenland Zip Codes call (904) 642-2066, or your local postmaster.

	ZIP
Greensboro	32330
Greenville	32331
Greenwood (Jackson County)	32443
Greenwood (Santa Rosa County)	32565
Grenelefe	33844
Gretna	32332
Griffin	33801
Gross	32097
Grove City	34224
Groveland	34736
Grove Park (Alachua County)	32640
Grove Park (Duval County)	32216
Grove Park (Polk County)	33801
Gulf Beach	32507
Gulf Beach Heights	32507
Gulf Breeze	32561-62
	32566

For specific Gulf Breeze Zip Codes call (904) 932-2662, or your local postmaster.

	ZIP
Gulf City	33570
Gulf Gate East	34231
	34276

For specific Gulf Gate East Zip Codes call (813) 924-8116, or your local postmaster.

	ZIP
Gulf Gate Estates	34231
Gulf Gate Mall	34231
Gulf Hammock	32639
Gulf Harbors	34652
Gulf Pines	32459
Gulfport	33707*
	33737†
Gulf Resort Beach (Part of Panama City Beach)	32407
Gulf Stream	33483
Hague	32601
Haines City	33844*
	33845†
Hainesworth	32615
Hallandale	33008*
	33009†
Hamilton (Part of Pompano Beach)	33072
Hammock	32137
Hammocks	33196
Hampton	32044
Hamptons at Boca Raton	33434
Hanson	32340
Harbinwood Estates	32303
Harbor Bluffs	34640
Harbor Oaks	32127
Harbor Shores	34748
Harbor View (Charlotte County)	33980
Harborview (Duval County)	32209
Harbour Heights	33983
Hardaway	32324
Hardeetown (Part of Chiefland)	32626
Hardin Heights	32324
Harlem	33440
Harmony Heights	34946
Harold	32563
Harshaw (Part of St. Petersburg)	33713
Hastings	32145
Hatchbend	32008
Havana	32333
Haverhill	33413
	33417

For specific Haverhill Zip Codes call (407) 697-2040, or your local postmaster.

	ZIP
Hawthorne (Alachua County)	32640
Hawthorne (Lake County)	34748

	ZIP
Heathrow	32746
Hedges	32097
Heilbronn	32091
Henderson Creek	33961
Hendry Correctional Institution	33934
Heritage Estates	32960
Hernando	34442
Hernando Beach	34607
Hernando City Heights	34442
Hernando Ridge	33525
Herndon (Part of Orlando)	32803
Hero	32097
Hesperides	33853
Hialeah	33010-17

For specific Hialeah Zip Codes call (305) 888-6491, or your local postmaster.

	ZIP
Hialeah Gardens	33010
Hialeah Lakes	33014-15

For specific Hialeah Lakes Zip Codes call (305) 821-6881, or your local postmaster.

	ZIP
Hiawasee	32808
Hibernia	32043
Hibiscus	32757
Hickory Hill	32464
Hidden Lake Villas (Part of Sanford)	32773
Hidden Oaks	33173
Hidden River	34240
Highland	32058
Highland Beach	33487
Highland City	33846
Highland Lakes	34684
Highland Park (Franklin County)	32320
Highland Park (Polk County)	33853
Highland Park (Seminole County)	32771
Highlands (Part of Jacksonville)	32218
Highlands Lakes	33825
Highlands Park Estates	33852
Highland View	32456
High Point (Hernando County)	34613
High Point (Palm Beach County)	33484
Highpoint (Pinellas County)	34620
High Springs	32643
Highway Park	33852
Hiland Park	32405
Hildreth	32008
Hillcrest Heights	33827
Hilldale (Part of Tampa)	33614*
	33684†
Hilliard	32046
Hill N Dale	34602
Hillsboro Beach	33062*
	33072†
Hillsborough Correctional Institution	33569
Hinson	32333
Hinson Crossroads	32427
Hobe Sound	33455*
	33475†
Hog Valley	32134
Holden Heights	32805
Holder	34445
Holiday	34690-91

For specific Holiday Zip Codes call (813) 942-3621, or your local postmaster.

	ZIP
Holiday Harbor (Part of Jacksonville)	32224
Holiday Heights	33037
Holiday Manor	33844
Holland Crossroads	32425
Holley	32561
Holliday Hill (Part of Jacksonville)	32216
Hollister	32147
Holly Ford (Part of Jacksonville)	32218
Holly Hill	32117
Holly Hills (Part of Tallahassee)	32303
Holly Point (Part of Orange Park)	32073
Hollywood	33019-29
	33081
	33083-84

For specific Hollywood Zip Codes call (305) 527-2074, or your local postmaster.

	ZIP
Hollywood Beach	32413

	ZIP
Hollywood Beach Gardens (Part of Hollywood)	33021
Hollywood Fashion Center (Part of Hollywood)	33023
Hollywood Hills (Part of Hollywood)	33021*
	33081†
Hollywood Mall (Part of Hollywood)	33021
Hollywood Seminole Indian Reservation	33024
Holmes Beach	34218
Holmes Correctional Institution	32425
Holmes Valley	32462
Holopaw	32901
Holt	32564
Homeland	33847
Homestead	33030-35
	33039
	33090-92

For specific Homestead Zip Codes call (305) 247-2641, or your local postmaster.

	ZIP
Homestead Air Force Base	33039
Homestead Ridge	32308
Homosassa	34446
	34448
	34487

For specific Homosassa Zip Codes call (904) 628-2396, or your local postmaster.

	ZIP
Homosassa Springs	34447
Honeyville	32465
Hooker Point (Hendry County)	33440
Hooker Point (Hillsborough County)	33605
Hopewell (Hillsborough County)	33566
Hopewell (Madison County)	32340
Horseshoe Beach	32648
Hosford	32334
Houston	32060
Howard	33176
Howard Creek	32465
Howey-in-the-Hills	34737
Hudson	34667
Hull	33821
Hunt Club	32703
Huntington	32112
Huntington Estates	32303
Huntington Woods (Part of Tallahassee)	32303
Hurlburt Field	32544
Hutchinson Island South	34949
Hyde Grove (Part of Jacksonville)	32210
Hyde Park (Duval County)	32210
Hyde Park (Hillsborough County)	33606
	33609

For specific Hyde Park Zip Codes call (813) 253-3140, or your local postmaster.

	ZIP
Hyde Park (Wakulla County)	32327
Hypoluxo	33462
Iddo	32331
Immokalee	33934
Imperial Lakes	33860
Imperial Point	34644
Indialantic	32903
Indian Bluff	32466
Indian Bluff Island	34683
Indian Creek	33154
Indian Harbour Beach	32937
Indian Head Acres (Part of Tallahassee)	32301
Indian Hills (Part of Cocoa)	32922
Indian Lake Estates	33855
Indian Mound Village	32771
Indianola	32952
Indian Pass	32456
Indian River City (Part of Titusville)	32780
Indian River Correctional Institution	32968
Indian River Estates	34982
Indian River Shores	32963
Indian Rocks Beach	34634-35

For specific Indian Rocks Beach Zip Codes call (813) 595-5575, or your local postmaster.

	ZIP
Indian Shores	34635

	ZIP
Indiantown	34956
Indian Wells	34746
Indrio	34946
Inglis	34449
Inlet Beach	32413
Innerarity Point	32507
Innisbrook	34684
Interbay (Part of Tampa)	33611*
	33681†
Intercession City	33848
Interlachen	32148
Inverness	34450-53

For specific Inverness Zip Codes call (904) 726-2757, or your local postmaster.

	ZIP
Inverrary (Part of Lauderhill)	33319
Inwood (Jackson County)	32460
Inwood (Polk County)	33881
Iona	33908
Irvine	32686
Islamorada	33036
Island Estates (Part of Clearwater)	34630
Island Grove	32654
Islandia	33131
Isleboro (Part of New Smyrna Beach)	32168
Isle of Palms (Duval County)	32250
Isle of Palms (Pinellas County)	33706
Isle Of Palms South (Part of Jacksonville)	32250
Isles of Capri	33962
Isleworth	34786
Istachatta	34636
Istokpoga Shores	33857
Ivan	32327
Ives Estates	33162
Izagora	32427
Jacksonville	32201-32
	32234-47
	32254-59
	32267
	32276-77

For specific Jacksonville Zip Codes call (904) 359-2711, or your local postmaster.

	ZIP
Jacksonville Air Transfer Office (Part of Jacksonville)	32229
Jacksonville Beach	32240†
	32250*
Jacksonville Heights (Part of Jacksonville)	32210
Jacob City	32431
Jamaica Bay	33912
Jan Phyl Village	33880
Jarrott	32344
Jasmine Estates	34668
Jasper	32052
Jay	32565
Jena	32359
Jennings	32053
Jensen Beach	34957*
	34958†
Jerome	33926
Jessamine	33525
John's Lake	34787
Johnson	32640
Johnson's Corner	32767
Jonathan's Landing	33477
Jonesville	32669
Judson	32693
Julington Forest (Part of Jacksonville)	32258
June Park	32901
Jungle (Part of St. Petersburg)	33710
Juniper	32330
Juno Beach	33408
Jupiter	33458
	33468-69
	33477-78

For specific Jupiter Zip Codes call (407) 746-3620, or your local postmaster.

	ZIP
Jupiter Inlet Beach Colony	33469
Jupiter Island	33455
Kathleen	33849
Keaton Beach	32347
Kenansville	34739
Kendale Lakes	33175
	33183

For specific Kendale Lakes Zip Codes call (305) 235-7511, or your local postmaster.

	ZIP
Kendale Lakes Mall	33183

---

* Area Zip Code   † Post Office Boxes

	ZIP
Kendall	33156
	33173
	33176
	33183
	33256
For specific Kendall Zip Codes call (305) 235-7511, or your local postmaster.	
Kendall Green	33064
Kendall Lakes West	33193
Kendall Town & Country	33183
Kendrick	34475
Kennedy Space Center	32815
Kenneth City	33709
Kensington Park	34235
Kerr City	32134
Keuka	32148
Key Biscayne	33149
Key Colony Beach	33051
Key Largo	33037
Key Largo Park	33037
Key Largo Village	33037
Keystone Heights	32656
Keystone Islands (Part of North Miami)	33181
Keysville	33547
Key West	33040-41
	33045
For specific Key West Zip Codes call (305) 294-2557, or your local postmaster.	
Key West Naval Air Station	33040
Killarney	34740
Killearn Acres	32308
Killearn Estates (Part of Tallahassee)	32308
Killearn Lakes	32312
Kinard	32449
Kincaid Hills	32601
Kings Bay	33158
Kings Ferry	32046
Kingsley Lake	32091
Kingsley Village	32091
Kings Point	33484
Kings Road (Part of Jacksonville)	32254
Kingswood Manor	32804
Kissimmee	34741-47
	34758-59
For specific Kissimmee Zip Codes call (407) 846-3121, or your local postmaster.	
Kissimmee Park	34772
Knights	33565
Korona	32110
Kossuthville	33823
Kynesville	32431
La Belle	33935
Lackawana Estates	32640
Lacoochee	33537
La Crosse	32658
Lady Lake	32158†
	32159*
La Gorce Island (Part of Miami Beach)	33141
La Grange	32796
Laguna Beach	32413
Lake Alfred	33850
Lake Ashby Shores	32168
Lake Bird	32347
Lake Brantley	32750
Lakebreeze	32303
Lake Bryant	32179
Lake Buena Vista	32830
Lake Butler	32054
Lake Cain Hills	32805
Lake Charm (Part of Oviedo)	32765
Lake City	32024-25
	32055-56
For specific Lake City Zip Codes call (904) 752-3373, or your local postmaster.	
Lake Clarke Shores	33406
Lake Como	32157
Lake Correctional Institution	34711
Lake Crescent Estates	32112
Lake Forest (Broward County)	33023
Lake Forest (Duval County)	32208
Lake Forest Hills (Part of Jacksonville)	32208
Lake Frances (Part of Tavares)	32778
Lake Garfield	33830
Lake Geneva	32160

	ZIP
Lake Hamilton	33851
Lake Harbor	33459
Lake Harris Shores	32778
Lake Haven Estates	33872
Lake Helen	32744
Lake Jem	32745
Lake Joanna	32726
Lake Josephine	33872
Lake Kathryn Heights	32720
Lakeland	33801-13
For specific Lakeland Zip Codes call (813) 683-6245, or your local postmaster.	
Lakeland Highlands	33813
Lakeland Mall (Part of Lakeland)	33801
Lakeland Square (Part of Lakeland)	33809
Lake Letta	33825
Lake Lindsey	34601
Lake Lorraine	32579
Lake Lotela	33825
Lake Lucerne	33055-56
	33169
For specific Lake Lucerne Zip Codes call (305) 470-0327, or your local postmaster.	
Lake Lucina (Part of Jacksonville)	32211
Lake Mack Park	32720
Lake Magdalene	33612-13
For specific Lake Magdalene Zip Codes call (813) 877-0746, or your local postmaster.	
Lake Marian Highlands	34739
Lake Mary	32746*
	32795†
Lake Mendelin Estates	32703
Lake Miona Heights	34785
Lake Monroe	32747
Lakemont	33825
Lake Mystic	32321
Lake of the Hills	33853
Lake Panasoffkee	33538
Lake Park	33403
Lake Pasadena Heights	33525
Lake Placid	33852*
	33862†
Lakeport	33471
Lake Sarasota	34241
Lake Saunders	32757
Lakes by the Bay	33157
	33189-90
For specific Lakes by the Bay Zip Codes call (305) 233-6859, or your local postmaster.	
Lake Shore (Part of Jacksonville)	32210*
	32238†
Lakeshore Mall	33870
Lakeside	32073
Lakeside Green	33417
Lakeside Hills	32140
Lakes Mall (Part of Lauderdale Lakes)	33319
Lake St. George	34684
Lake Wales	33853
	33859
	33867
For specific Lake Wales Zip Codes call (813) 676-2531, or your local postmaster.	
Lake Weir	32179
Lake Winnott	32640
Lakewood (Duval County)	32207
Lakewood (Walton County)	32433
Lakewood Heights (Part of Tallahassee)	32311
Lakewood Park	34951
Lakewood Village	32303
Lake Worth	33460-67
For specific Lake Worth Zip Codes call (407) 964-1102, or your local postmaster.	
Lamont	32336
Lamplighter (Part of Gainesville)	32609
Lam Smith Crossroads	32425
Lanark Village	32323
Land O'Lakes	34639
Lane (Part of Jacksonville)	32254
Lantana	33462*
	33465†
Lantana Homes	33463
Largo	34640-49
For specific Largo Zip Codes call (813) 584-2191, or your local postmaster.	

	ZIP
Largo Mall (Part of Largo)	34641
Larkin Fish Camp	32321
Lauderdale-by-the-Sea	33308
Lauderdale Lakes	33309
	33311
	33313
	33319
For specific Lauderdale Lakes Zip Codes call (305) 527-2077, or your local postmaster.	
Lauderhill	33313
	33319
	33351
For specific Lauderhill Zip Codes call (305) 587-2450, or your local postmaster.	
Lauderhill Mall (Part of Lauderhill)	33313
Laurel	34272
Laurel Grove (Part of Orange Park)	32073
Laurel Hill	32567
Laurel Park (Escambia County)	32505
Laurel Park (Orange County)	32809
Lawtey	32058
Lazy Lagoon	33982
Lazy Lake	33305
Lealman	33714
Lebanon	34431
Lecanto	34460-61
For specific Lecanto Zip Codes call (904) 746-2424, or your local postmaster.	
Lee	32059
Lee Cypress	33926
Leesburg	34748-49
	34788-89
For specific Leesburg Zip Codes call (904) 787-3679, or your local postmaster.	
Lehigh (Part of Tallahassee)	32301
Lehigh Acres	33936
	33970-71
For specific Lehigh Acres Zip Codes call (813) 369-2159, or your local postmaster.	
Leisure City	33033
Leisure Lakes	33852
Lely	33961
Lemon Bluff	32764
Lemon City (Part of Miami)	33137
	33187
For specific Lemon City Zip Codes call (305) 576-0404, or your local postmaster.	
Lemon Grove	33873
Leon (Part of Tallahassee)	32303*
	32315†
Leonards	32424
Leonia	32464
Leonton	32344
Lessie	32046
Liberty	32433
Liberty City (Part of Miami)	33142
Liberty Square (Part of Miami)	33147
Lido Key (Part of Sarasota)	34239
Lighthouse Point (Broward County)	33064*
	33074†
Lighthouse Point (Martin County)	34994
Lily	33865
Limestone (Hardee County)	33865
Limestone (Jefferson County)	32344
Limona	33510
Lincoln City	32091
Lincoln Estates (Part of Gainesville)	32601
Lincoln Road Mall (Part of Miami Beach)	33139
Linden	33597
Lindgren Acres	33186
Lisbon	34788
Lithia	33547
Little Acres	34736
Little Gasparilla	33946
Little Havana (Part of Miami)	33125
Little Hollywood	32976
Little Lake City	32619

	ZIP
Little River (Part of Miami)	33138*
	33238†
Little River Springs	32071
Little Torch Key	33042
Live Oak (Suwannee County)	32060
Live Oak (Washington County)	32462
Live Oak Island	32327
Lloyd	32337
Lochloosa	32662
Lochmoor	33903
Lochmoor Waterway Estates	33903
Lock Arbor (Part of Sanford)	32773
Lockhart	32810
Londonderry (Part of Orlando)	32808
Longboat Key	34228
Long Key	33001
Longwood (Okaloosa County)	32579
Longwood (Seminole County)	32750
	32752
	32779
	32791
For specific Longwood Zip Codes call (407) 682-7559, or your local postmaster.	
Lorida	33857
Lotus	32952
Loughman	33858
Lovedale	32423
Lovett	32331
Lovewood	32431
Lowell	32663
Lower Clay Landing	32626
Lower Grand Lagoon	32401
Lower Matecumbe Key	33036
Loxahatchee	33470
Lucerne Avenue (Part of Lake Worth)	33460
Lucerne Park (Part of Winter Haven)	33881
Ludiam (Part of Miami)	33155*
	33255†
Lullwater Beach (Part of Panama City Beach)	32407
Lulu	32061
Lumberton	33540
Lundy	32177
Luraville	32060
Lutz	33549
Lynne	34488
Lynn Haven	32444
Mabel	33514
Mabry Manor (Part of Tallahassee)	32310
McAlpin	32062
Macclenny	32063
Macclenny II	32063
MacDill Air Force Base	33608†
	33621*
McDavid	32568
Macedonia	32424
McGregor	33919
McIntosh	32664
McKinnon	32568
McLellen	32570
McMeekin	32640
Madeira Beach	33708*
	33738†
Madison	32340*
	32341†
Magnolia Beach	32408
Magnolia Gardens (Part of Jacksonville)	32209
Magnolia Springs	32043
Mainland (Part of Ormond Beach)	32174
Mainlands Center (Part of Pinellas Park)	34666
Maitland	32751
	32794
For specific Maitland Zip Codes call (407) 647-5505, or your local postmaster.	
Malabar	32950
Malone	32445
Manalapan	33462
Manasota	34260
Manasota Key	34223
Manatee (Part of Bradenton)	34208
Mandarin (Part of Jacksonville)	32223*

* Area Zip Code   **† Post Office Boxes**

	ZIP
	32241†
Mango	33550
Mango (census designated place)	33584
Mango Hills	33584
Mangonia Park	33407
Marathon	33050
Marathon Shores	33052
Maravilla (Part of Fort Pierce)	34982
Marco	33937*
	33969†
Margate	33063
	33068
For specific Margate Zip Codes call (305) 974-6080, or your local postmaster.	
Marianna	32446-48
For specific Marianna Zip Codes call (904) 482-4951, or your local postmaster.	
Marietta (Part of Jacksonville)	32220
Marineland	32086
Mariner Mall	32505
Mariner Sands	34997
Marion Correctional Institution	32663
Marion Oaks	34473
Market Square Mall (Part of Jacksonville)	32207
Martel	34475
Martin	32617
Martin Correctional Institution and Work Camp	34956
Martin Downs	34990
Mary Esther	32569
Masaryktown	34609
Mascotte	34753
Matlacha	33909
Maxcy Quarters	33843
Maximo Moorings (Part of St. Petersburg)	33711
Maxville (Part of Jacksonville)	32234
Mayfair in the Grove (Part of Miami)	33133
Mayo	32066
Mayo Correctional Institution	32066
Mayo Junction	32066
Mayport (Part of Jacksonville)	32233*
	32267†
Mayport Naval Station	32227*
	32228†
Meadowbrook	32808
Meadowbrook Terrace	32073
Meadowlawn (Part of St. Petersburg)	33702
Meadowlea on the River	32713
Meadow Wood	32824
Mecca	32771
Medart	32327
Medley	33178
Medulla	33811
Melbourne	32901-02
	32904
	32934-36
	32940-41
For specific Melbourne Zip Codes call (407) 254-3433, or your local postmaster.	
Melbourne Beach	32951
Melbourne Shores	32951
Melbourne Square Mall (Part of Melbourne)	32904
Melbourne Village	32904
Melody Hills (Part of Tallahassee)	32308
Melrose	32666
Melrose Park (Broward County)	33312
Melrose Park (Columbia County)	32055
Memphis	34221
Memphis Heights	34221
Merritt Island	32952-54
For specific Merritt Island Zip Codes call (407) 453-1366, or your local postmaster.	
Merritt Square Mall	32952
Metro Mall (Part of Fort Myers)	33916
Mexico Beach	32410
Miami	33101-02
	33111
	33116
	33122-38
	33140-47
	33150-99
	33201-65
	33269-99
For specific Miami Zip Codes call (305) 470-0327, or your local postmaster.	
COLLEGES & UNIVERSITIES	
Barry University	33161
FINANCIAL INSTITUTIONS	
American Savings of Florida, F.S.B.	33169
Barnett Bank of South Florida, N.A.	33131
Capital Bank	33131
Chase Federal Bank, F.S.B.	33156
Citizens Federal Bank	33131
City National Bank of Florida	33130
Coconut Grove Bank	33133
Continental National Bank of Miami	33135
Coral Gables Federal Savings & Loan Association	33156
County National Bank of South Florida	33137
Dadeland Bank	33156
Eagle National Bank of Miami	33132
Intercontinental Bank	33131
Northern Trust Bank of Florida, N.A.	33131
Ocean Bank	33126
Pacific National Bank	33131
Republic National Bank of Miami	33126
Safra Republic Bank	33180
Sun Bank/Miami, N.A.	33131
Terrabank, N.A.	33145
Totalbank	33145
United National Bank	33130
HOSPITALS	
Aventura Hospital & Medical Center	33180
Baptist Hospital of Miami	33176
Cedars Medical Center	33136
Golden Glades Regional Medical Center	33169
Jackson Memorial Hospital	33136
Mercy Hospital	33133
North Shore Medical Center	33150
South Miami Hospital	33143
Veterans Affairs Medical Center	33125
HOTELS/MOTELS	
Hyatt Regency Miami	33131
Miami Airport Hilton & Marina	33126
Radisson Mart Plaza Hotel	33126
MILITARY INSTALLATIONS	
7th Coast Guard District, Miami	33131
Miami Beach	33109
	33119
	33139
For specific Miami Beach Zip Codes call (305) 672-8793, or your local postmaster.	
Miami Coast Guard Station	33054
Miami Gardens	33023
Miami Gardens-Utopia-Carver	33023
Miami Lakes	33014
Miami Shores	33138*
	33153†
Miami Springs	33166*
	33266†
Micanopy	32667
Micco	32958
Micco (census designated place)	32976
Miccosukee	32309
Miccosukee Hills (Part of Tallahassee)	32308
Miccosukee Indian Reservation	33440
Middle (Part of Lake Mary)	32799
Middleburg	32050†
	32068*
Mid Florida Lakes	34788
Mid Town Plaza (Part of Sarasota)	34239
Midway (Broward County)	33322
Midway (Gadsden County)	32343
Midway (Hillsborough County)	33565
Midway (Seminole County)	32771
Millcreek	32092
Millers Ferry	32462
Milligan	32537
Millview	32506
Millville (Part of Panama City)	32401
Milton	32570-72
	32583
For specific Milton Zip Codes call (904) 623-3807, or your local postmaster.	
Mi-Lu Estates	32159
Mims	32754
Mineral Springs	32565
Minneola	34755
Miracle City Mall (Part of Titusville)	32780
Miracle Mile (Part of Fort Myers)	33901
Miramar	33023
	33025
	33027
	33029
For specific Miramar Zip Codes call (305) 436-7200, or your local postmaster.	
Miramar Beach	32541
Miramar Terrace (Part of Jacksonville)	32207
Mission Bay	33428
Mission City	32168
Mission Hills (Part of Clearwater)	34619
Mobile Gardens	34224
Moffitt	33890
Molino	32577
Molino Crossroads	32577
Monroes Corner	34491
Montbrook	32696
Montclair	34748
Monteocha	32609
Monterey (Part of Jacksonville)	32211
Monticello	32344*
	32345†
Montverde	34756
Monument Lakes (Part of Jacksonville)	32225
Moon Lake Estates	34654
Moore Haven	33471
Moreland Park	34785
Morningside (Part of Miami)	33137
Morningside Park	32809
Morrison Bluff	32102
Morriston	32668
Morse Shores	33905
Mosley Hall	32331
Moss Bluff	32179
Moss Town	33537
Mossy Head	32434
Moultrie	32086
Mountain Park	34601
Mount Carmel	32565
Mount Dora	32757
Mount Pleasant	32352
Mount Plymouth	32776
Mount Royal	32193
Mulberry	33860
Munson	32570
Murat Hills (Part of Tallahassee)	32304
Murdock	33938
Murray Hill (Part of Jacksonville)	32205
	32236
	32254
For specific Murray Hill Zip Codes call (904) 781-2651, or your local postmaster.	
Myakka City	34251
Myakka Head	33865
Myakka Valley Ranchos	34241
Myrtis	32055
Myrtle Grove	32506*
	32516†
Nalcrest	33856
Naples	33939-42
	33961-64
For specific Naples Zip Codes call (813) 262-5411, or your local postmaster.	
Naples Manor	33961
Naples Park	33963
Naranja	33032-33
For specific Naranja Zip Codes call (305) 247-2641, or your local postmaster.	
Narcoossee	34771
Nash	32336
Nashua	32189
Nassau Village	32011
Nassau Village-Ratliff	32011
Nassauville	32034
National Gardens	32174
Naval Air Station	32508
Naval Coastal Systems Lab	32407
Naval Regional Medical Clinic	33040
Naval Training Center Annex	32824
Navarre	32566
Navy Point	32507
Neptune Beach	32266
Neptune Shores	34744
New Berlin (Part of Jacksonville)	32226
Newberry	32669
Newburn	32060
New Eden	34771
New Harmony	32433
New Hope (Holmes County)	32464
New Hope (Washington County)	32462
Newmans Lake Homesites	32601
Newport (Monroe County)	33037
Newport (Wakulla County)	32327
New Port Richey	34652-56
For specific New Port Richey Zip Codes call (813) 849-4333, or your local postmaster.	
New Port Richey East	34653
New River	33301*
	33302†
New River Correctional Institution	32083
New Smyrna Beach	32168-70
For specific New Smyrna Beach Zip Codes call (904) 427-1377, or your local postmaster.	
New Zion	33865
Niceville	32578*
	32588†
Nichols	33863
Nobles (Part of Pensacola)	32504
	32514
For specific Nobles Zip Codes call (904) 434-9137, or your local postmaster.	
Nobleton	34661
Nocatee	33864
Nokomis	34274†
	34275*
Noma	32452
Norland	33169*
	33269†
Normandy (Dade County)	33141
Normandy (Duval County)	32205
Normandy Mall (Part of Jacksonville)	32254
Normandy Manor (Part of Jacksonville)	32221
Normandy Village (Part of Jacksonville)	32210
North Andrews Gardens	33309
	33334
For specific North Andrews Gardens Zip Codes call (305) 568-1323, or your local postmaster.	
North Babcock (Part of Melbourne)	32901
North Bay Village	33141
North Beach	32095
North Biscayne (Part of North Miami)	33161
North Brooksville	34601
Northcliffe	32561
Northcrest	32703
Northdale	33624

*** Area Zip Code** **† Post Office Boxes**

	ZIP
North De Land	32720
Northeast Florida State Hospital	32063
North Florida Reception Center	32054
North Fort Myers	33903
	33917
For specific North Fort Myers Zip Codes call (813) 656-6075, or your local postmaster.	
North Jacksonville (Part of Jacksonville)	32218
	32226
For specific North Jacksonville Zip Codes call (904) 359-2711, or your local postmaster.	
North Key Largo	33037
North La Belle	33935
North Lauderdale	33068
North Meadowbrook Terrace	32073
North Miami	32073
	33161
	33168
	33261
For specific North Miami Zip Codes call (305) 470-0327, or your local postmaster.	
North Miami Beach	33160
	33162
	33179
	33181
For specific North Miami Beach Zip Codes call (305) 944-5339, or your local postmaster.	
North Naples	33963
North Oak Hill (Part of Jacksonville)	32210
North Palm Beach	33408
North Port	34287
North Redington Beach	33708
North River Shores	34994
North Sarasota	34234
North Shore (Part of Jacksonville)	32208
North Side (Part of Panama City)	32406
Northside Shopping Center	33147
Northwood (Part of West Palm Beach)	33407
Northwood Centre (Part of Tallahassee)	32303
Northwood Pines (Part of Gainesville)	32605
Northwood Plaza (Part of Clearwater)	34621
Norwood (Part of Jacksonville)	32208
Nubbin Ridge	32531
Nutall Rise	32336
Oak	34479
Oakbrook (Part of Ocala)	34470
Oak Crest (Alachua County)	32640
Oakcrest (Marion County)	34479
Oakdale	32448
Oak Forest	34436
Oak Grove (Escambia County)	32568
Oak Grove (Gadsden County)	32324
Oak Grove (Gulf County)	32456
Oak Grove (Hardee County)	33873
Oak Grove (Lake County)	32159
Oak Grove (Okaloosa County)	32531
Oak Grove (Sumter County)	33597
Oak Harbor (Part of Jacksonville)	32233
Oak Haven (Part of Jacksonville)	32211
Oak Hill	32759
Oak Hill Park (Part of Jacksonville)	32244
Oakhurst	34646
Oakland	34760
Oakland Park (Broward County)	33306-10
	33334
For specific Oakland Park Zip Codes call (305) 527-2012, or your local postmaster.	
Oakland Park (Lake County)	32757
Oakland Shores	32751
Oak Ridge	32809

	ZIP
	32839
For specific Oak Ridge Zip Codes call (305) 470-0327, or your local postmaster.	
Oak Run	34481
Oak Street (Part of Kissimmee)	34741
	34746-47
For specific Oak Street Zip Codes call (407) 846-6375, or your local postmaster.	
Oak Terrace	33860
Oakwood	34488
Oakwood Hills	32433
Oakwood Villa (Part of Jacksonville)	32211
O'Brien	32037
Ocala	34470-82
For specific Ocala Zip Codes call (904) 629-7146, or your local postmaster.	
Ocala Highlands (Part of Ocala)	34471
Ocala Highlands Estates	34482
Ocala Park Ranch	34482
Ocala Ridge	34474
Ocala Waterway	34474
Ocala West	34474-75
For specific Ocala West Zip Codes call (904) 237-3777, or your local postmaster.	
Ocean Breeze Park	34957
Ocean City	32547-48
For specific Ocean City Zip Codes call (904) 243-2311, or your local postmaster.	
Ocean Reef Club	33037
Ocean Ridge	33435
Ocean View (Part of Miami Beach)	33140
Oceanway (Part of Jacksonville)	32218
Ocheesee	32442
Ochopee	33943
Ocoee	34761
Odessa	33556
Ojus	33163†
	33180*
Okahumpka	34762
Okaloosa Correctional Institution	32539
Okaloosa Island	32548
Okeechobee	34972-74
For specific Okeechobee Zip Codes call (813) 763-3616, or your local postmaster.	
Oklawaha	32179
Old Fernandina (Part of Fernandina Beach)	32034
Old Myakka	34240
Oldsmar	34677
Old Town	32680
Olga	33905
Olustee	32072
Olympia Heights	33165
	33174-75
	33184-85
For specific Olympia Heights Zip Codes call (305) 226-7522, or your local postmaster.	
Omni International of Miami (Part of Miami)	33132
Ona	33865
Oneco	34203
O'Neil	32034
On Top of the World	34481
Opa-Locka	33054-56
For specific Opa-Locka Zip Codes call (305) 681-7489, or your local postmaster.	
Opa-Locka North	33054
Open Air (Part of St. Petersburg)	33701
	33731-32
For specific Open Air Zip Codes call (813) 823-7558, or your local postmaster.	
Orange	32321
Orange Bend	34788
Orange Blossom (Part of Orlando)	32805
Orange Blossom Estates	33872
Orange Blossom Gardens	32159
Orange Blossom Hills	34491
Orange Blossom Hills South	32159
Orange Blossom Mall (Part of Fort Pierce)	34947
Orange City	32763*

	ZIP
Orange City Hills	32774†
Orange City Terrace	32763
Orangedale (Polk County)	32763
Orangedale (St. Johns County)	33809
	32092
Orange Harbor	33905
Orange Heights	32640
Orange Hill	32428
Orange Home	34785
Orange Lake	32681
Orange Mills	32131
Orange Park	32065
	32067
	32073
For specific Orange Park Zip Codes call (904) 264-6721, or your local postmaster.	
Orange River Hills	33905
Orange Springs	32182
Orchid	32960
Orient Park	33619
Oriole Beach	32561
Orlando	32801-72
For specific Orlando Zip Codes call (407) 850-6200, or your local postmaster.	

COLLEGES & UNIVERSITIES

	ZIP
University of Central Florida	32816

FINANCIAL INSTITUTIONS

	ZIP
Sun Bank, National Association	32801

HOSPITALS

	ZIP
Florida Hospital Medical Center	32803
Lucerne Medical Center	32801
Orlando Regional Medical Center	32806

HOTELS/MOTELS

	ZIP
Ramada Hotel Resort-Florida Center	32819
Sheraton World Resort	32821

MILITARY INSTALLATIONS

	ZIP
Naval Research Laboratory, Underwater Sound Reference Detachment	32856
Naval Training Center, Orlando	32813
Navy and Marine Corps Reserve Center, Orlando	32803
Orlando Fashion Square (Part of Orlando)	32803
Orlo Vista	32811
	32835
For specific Orlo Vista Zip Codes call (407) 293-6410, or your local postmaster.	
Ormond Beach	32174-76
For specific Ormond Beach Zip Codes call (904) 677-0333, or your local postmaster.	
Ormond By The Sea	32174
Ortega (Part of Jacksonville)	32210
Ortega Farms (Part of Jacksonville)	32210
Ortega Forest (Part of Jacksonville)	32210
Ortega Hills (Part of Jacksonville)	32244
Ortega Terrace (Part of Jacksonville)	32210
Osceola Heights (Part of Tallahassee)	32301
Osprey	34229
Osteen	32764
Otter Creek	32683
Overstreet	32453
Oviedo	32765-66
For specific Oviedo Zip Codes call (407) 365-3343, or your local postmaster.	
Owens	33821
Oxford	34484
Ozello	34429
Ozona	34660
Pace	32571
Paddock Mall (Part of Ocala)	34474

	ZIP
Page Park	33907
Page Park-Pine Manor	33907
Pahokee	33476
Painters Hill	32136
Paisley	32767
Palatka	32177*
	32178†
Palma Ceia (Part of Tampa)	33609
	33629
	33690
For specific Palma Ceia Zip Codes call (813) 831-7963, or your local postmaster.	
Palma Sola	34209*
	34280†
Palma Sola Park	34209
Palm Bay	32905-10
For specific Palm Bay Zip Codes call (407) 723-8838, or your local postmaster.	
Palm Beach	33480
Palm Beach Gardens	33410
	33418
	33420
For specific Palm Beach Gardens Zip Codes call (407) 622-1447, or your local postmaster.	
Palm Beach Mall (Part of West Palm Beach)	33401
Palm Beach Shores	33404
Palm City	34990
Palm Coast	32135
	32137
	32142
	32164
For specific Palm Coast Zip Codes call (904) 445-1325, or your local postmaster.	
Palm Coast Plaza (Part of West Palm Beach)	33405
Palmdale	33944
Palmetto	34220*
	34221†
Palmetto Estates	33157
Palm Grove Colony	34607
Palm Harbor	34682-85
For specific Palm Harbor Zip Codes call (813) 784-3203, or your local postmaster.	
Palm Plaza	34233
Palm River (Collier County)	33942
Palm River (Hillsborough County)	33619
Palm River-Clair Mel	33619
Palm Shores	32935
	32940
For specific Palm Shores Zip Codes call (407) 254-3433, or your local postmaster.	
Palm Springs	33460
Palm Springs Mile Shopping Center (Part of Hialeah)	33012
Palm Springs North	33015
Palm Valley	32082
Palm View	34221
Palm Village (Part of Hialeah)	33012
Panacea	32346
Panacea Park	32346
Panacoochee Retreats	33538
Panama City	32401-09
	32411-17
For specific Panama City Zip Codes call (904) 785-5280, or your local postmaster.	
Panama City Beach	32407-08
	32411
	32413
	32417
For specific Panama City Beach Zip Codes call (904) 234-9011, or your local postmaster.	
Panama City General Mail Facility (Part of Panama City)	32412
Panama City Mall (Part of Panama City)	32405
Panama Park (Part of Jacksonville)	32208
Paola	32771
Paradise Bay	34210
Paradise Beach	32506
Paradise Heights	32703
Paradise Island (Part of Treasure Island)	33706

* **Area Zip Code**   † **Post Office Boxes**

	ZIP
Paradise Palms (Part of Boca Raton)	33486
Paradise Park	34946
Paradise Point (Part of Crystal River)	34429
Park Avenue (Part of Tallahassee)	32302
Parker	32404
Parkland	33060
Parkside (Part of Tallahassee)	32303
Parmalee	34251
Parramore	32423
Parrish	34219
Pasadena Shores	33525
Pass-a-Grille Beach (Part of St. Pete Beach)	33706*
	33741†
Patersonville	32131
Patrick Air Force Base	32925
Paxton	32538
Peaceful Acres	34431
Peace River Shores	33982
Peach Orchard	32618
Pecan Park (Part of Jacksonville)	32218
Pedro	34491
Pelican Bay	33940
Pelican Lake	33438
Pembroke Lakes Mall (Part of Pembroke Pines)	33024
Pembroke Park	33009
	33023
For specific Pembroke Park Zip Codes call (305) 457-8456, or your local postmaster.	
Pembroke Pines	33019-20
	33022-29
	33084
For specific Pembroke Pines Zip Codes call (305) 432-8331, or your local postmaster.	
Peniel	32177
Peninsula (Hillsborough County)	33609*
	33679†
Peninsula (Volusia County)	32118
Penney Farms	32079
Pennsuco	33010
Pensacola	32501-26
	32534
	32573-76
	32581-82
	32589-98
For specific Pensacola Zip Codes call (904) 434-9184, or your local postmaster.	
Pensacola Beach	32561
Pensacola Heights (Part of Pensacola)	32503
Pensacola Naval Air Station	32508
Peppertree Bay	34231
Perdido Bay	32507
Perrine	33157*
	33257†
Perry	32347
Pettis Springs	32331
Pheasant Walk	33487
Phillipi Gardens	34231
Pickettville (Part of Jacksonville)	32205
Picnic	33547
Picolata	32092
Piedmont (Leon County)	32312
Piedmont (Orange County)	32703
Pierce	33860
Pierson	32180
Pine Castle	32809
	32839
For specific Pine Castle Zip Codes call (407) 855-3010, or your local postmaster.	
Pinecraft	34239*
	34278†
Pinecrest	33547
Pineda	32935
Pine Dale	33860
Pine Forest	32506
Pine Grove (Osceola County)	34771
Pine Grove (Suwannee County)	32060
Pine Hill Estates	32601
Pine Hills (Lake County)	32726
Pine Hills (Orange County)	32808

	ZIP
	32818
For specific Pine Hills Zip Codes call (407) 293-3274, or your local postmaster.	
Pine Hills Center	32808
Pine Island (Calhoun County)	32424
Pine Island (Hernando County)	34607
Pine Island Center	33945
Pine Island Ridge (Broward County)	33324
Pine Island Ridge (Lee County)	33922
Pine Island Ridge Plaza (Part of Davie)	33324
Pine Lakes	32726
Pineland	33945
Pineland Gardens (Part of Jacksonville)	32216
Pine Level	34221
Pinellas Park	34664-66
For specific Pinellas Park Zip Codes call (813) 546-0007, or your local postmaster.	
Pinellas Square (Part of Pinellas Park)	34665
Pine Log	32437
Pine Manor	33907
Pineola	34436
Pine Ridge	33940
Pine Ridge Country Estates	34465
Pine Run	34481
Pine Shores	34231
Pinesville	32618
Pinetta	32350
Pineville	32568
Pinewood	33168
Pinewood Park	33147
	33150
For specific Pinewood Park Zip Codes call (305) 836-9710, or your local postmaster.	
Pinland	32347
Pipers Landing	34990
Pirate Harbor	33955
Pirates Wood	32097
Pittman (Holmes County)	32427
Pittman (Lake County)	32702
Placida	33946-47
For specific Placida Zip Codes call (813) 697-1511, or your local postmaster.	
Placid Lakes	33852
Plantation (Broward County)	33317-18
	33322-24
For specific Plantation Zip Codes call (305) 587-2450, or your local postmaster.	
Plantation (Monroe County)	33036
Plantation (Sarasota County)	34293
Plant City	33564-67
For specific Plant City Zip Codes call (813) 752-4111, or your local postmaster.	
Playland Estates (Part of Hollywood)	33021
Playland Isles	33312
Pleasant Grove (Escambia County)	32507
Pleasant Grove (Hillsborough County)	33530
Pleasant Grove (Walton County)	32567
Pleasant Ridge	32433
Plummer (Part of Jacksonville)	32219
Plymouth	32768
Poinciana	33467
Poinciana Park	32962
Poinciana Place	34758-59
For specific Poinciana Place Zip Codes call (407) 846-3121, or your local postmaster.	
Poinciana Village	33942
Point Baker	32570
Point Brittany (Part of St. Petersburg)	33715
Point O' Rocks	34242
Point Washington	32454
Polk City	33868
Polk Correctional Institution	33868
Polly Town (Part of Jacksonville)	32218

	ZIP
Pomona Park	32181
Pompano Beach	33060-69
	33071-77
For specific Pompano Beach Zip Codes call your local postmaster.	
Pompano Beach Highlands	33064
Pompano Park	33319
Pompano Square (Part of Pompano Beach)	33062
Ponce de Leon	32455
Ponce Inlet	32127
Ponte Vedra	32082
Ponte Vedra Beach	32004†
	32082*
Poplar Head	32425
Port Charlotte	33948-49
	33952-54
	33980-81
For specific Port Charlotte Zip Codes call (813) 625-6011, or your local postmaster.	
Port Charlotte Town Center	33948
Port Everglades (Part of Fort Lauderdale)	33316
Port Hatchineha	33844
Port La Belle	33935
Portland	32439
Port Malabar (Part of Palm Bay)	32905
Port Mayaca	33438
Port Orange	32129
Port Richey	34667-74
For specific Port Richey Zip Codes call (813) 849-1233, or your local postmaster.	
Port Salerno	34992
Port Sewall	34996
Port St. Joe	32456
Port St. John	32927
Port St. Lucie	34952-53
	34983-88
For specific Port St. Lucie Zip Codes call (407) 335-2772, or your local postmaster.	
Port St. Lucie-River Park	34983
Port Tampa City (Part of Tampa)	33616
Pottsburg (Part of Jacksonville)	32216
	32245-46
For specific Pottsburg Zip Codes call (904) 642-2066, or your local postmaster.	
Powell	34609
Pretty Bayou	32401
Princeton	33032*
	33092†
Produce (Part of Tampa)	33610*
	33680†
Progress Village	33619
Prospect	33309
Prospect Road (Part of Oakland Park)	33309
Prosperity	32464
Providence (Polk County)	33809
Providence (Union County)	32054
Pumpkin Center	34797
Punta Gorda	33950-51
	33955
	33982-83
For specific Punta Gorda Zip Codes call (813) 639-3395, or your local postmaster.	
Punta Gorda Isles (Part of Punta Gorda)	33950
Punta Rassa	33908
Putnam Hall	32185
Quail Heights	33157
	33170
	33187
	33189-90
	33197
For specific Quail Heights Zip Codes call (305) 233-6859, or your local postmaster.	
Queens Cove	34947
Quincy	32351*
	32353†
Raccoon Key	33040
Raiford	32083
Rainbow Lakes (Marion County)	34431
Rainbow Lakes (Palm Beach County)	33437
Rainbow Springs	34432

	ZIP
Raleigh	32696
Ramblewood (Part of Sanford)	32773
Ramrod Key	33042
Ratliff	32011
Ravenna Park	32771
Recruit Training Command	32893
Red Bay	32455
Reddick	32686
Red Head	32437
Redington Beach	33708
Redington Shores	33708
Redland	33031
Red Level	34428
Regal Oaks	34744
Regal Park	34475
Regency (Part of Jacksonville)	32211
Regency Park (Part of Jacksonville)	32225
Regency Square Mall (Part of Jacksonville)	32225
Resota Beach	32409
Rex	32640
Ribault Manor (Part of Jacksonville)	32208
Rice Creek	32177
Rich Bay	32333
Richey Lakes	34653
Richland	33540
Richloam	33597
Richmond Heights	33176
Richter Crossroads	32440
Ridge Harbor	33982
Ridge Manor	33525
Ridgeway	33903
Ridgewood	32065
Ridgewood Estates	34232
Ridge Wood Heights	34231
Rio	34957
Riomar (Part of Vero Beach)	32963
Riverdale (Hernando County)	33525
Riverdale (St. Johns County)	32095
River Forest (Part of Jacksonville)	32211
Riverhaven Village	34447
River Isles (Part of Bradenton)	34208
Riverland	33312
River Park	34983
River Retreats	34431
Riverside (Dade County)	33135
Riverside (Duval County)	32204
River Trails	33917
Riverview (Duval County)	32208
Riverview (Hillsborough County)	33569
Riviera Beach	33404*
	33419†
Robin Hill	32701
Robinson Heights	32667
Robinwood	32808
	32818
For specific Robinwood Zip Codes call (407) 293-3274, or your local postmaster.	
Rochelle	32601
Rock Bluff	32321
Rockdale	33157
Rock Harbor	33037
Rock Hill (Okaloosa County)	32531
Rock Hill (Walton County)	32433
Rock Hill (Washington County)	32428
Rockledge	32955*
	32956†
Rocksprings (Marion County)	34431
Rock Springs (Orange County)	32703
Rocky Creek	33615
Rocky Point	32608
Roeville	32583
Ro-Len Lake Gardens (Part of Hallandale)	33009
Rolling Acres	34602
Rolling Hills (Duval County)	32221
Rolling Hills (Marion County)	34474
Rolling Hills (Polk County)	33860
Rolling Ranches	34431
Romeo	34432

	ZIP
Roosevelt Mall (Part of Jacksonville)	32210
Rosedale	32324
Roseland	32957
Rosewood	32625
Rotonda	33946
Rotonda West	33946
Round Lake	32420
Royal	34785
Royal Gardens Estates	34209
Royal Palm Beach	33411
Royal Palm Village	33908
Royals Cross Roads	32464
Royal Terrace (Part of Jacksonville)	32209
Rubonia	34221
Runnymeade	32303
Ruskin	33570-71
	33573
For specific Ruskin Zip Codes call (813) 645-1820, or your local postmaster.	
Russell	32043
Rutland	33538
Sabal Palm Estates	33068
Saddlebunch Keys	33040
Saddle Creek	34241
Safety Harbor	34695
St. Andrews (Part of Panama City)	32401
St. Armands (Part of Sarasota)	34236
St. Augustine	32084-86
	32092
	32095
For specific St. Augustine Zip Codes call (904) 829-8716, or your local postmaster.	
St. Augustine Beach	32086
St. Augustine Shores	32086
St. Augustine South	32086
St. Catherine	33513
St. Cloud	34769-73
For specific St. Cloud Zip Codes call (407) 892-3779, or your local postmaster.	
St. George Island	32328
Saint James	32358
St. James City	33956
Saint Joe Beach	32456
St. Johns Park (Duval County)	32210
St. Johns Park (Flagler County)	32110
St. Johns River Estates (Putnam County)	32189
Saint Johns River Estates (Seminole County)	32771
Saint Josephs	32771
St. Leo	33574
St. Lucie	34946
St. Marks	32355
St. Nicholas (Part of Jacksonville)	32207
St. Pete Beach	33706
	33715
	33736
For specific St. Pete Beach Zip Codes call (813) 367-2261, or your local postmaster.	
St. Petersburg	33701-84
For specific St. Petersburg Zip Codes call (813) 323-6516, or your local postmaster.	
St. Teresa	32358
Saint Vincent de Paul Regional Seminary	33436
Salem	32356
Salt Springs	32134
Samoset	34208
Sample Square (Part of Pompano Beach)	33064
Sampson City	32091
Samsula	32168
Samsula-Spruce Creek	32168
San Antonio	33576
San Blas	32456
San Carlos Park	33912
Sandalfoot Cove	33428
Sandalwood (Part of Jacksonville)	32246
Sand Cut	33438
Sanderson	32087
Sandestin	32541
Sand Lake (Part of Orlando)	32819
	32821

	ZIP
	32836-37
For specific Sand Lake Zip Codes call (407) 351-9037, or your local postmaster.	
Sandlefoot Cove	33428
	33433
For specific Sandlefoot Cove Zip Codes call (407) 479-0650, or your local postmaster.	
Sandy	34251
Sandy Point	32008
Sanford	32771-73
For specific Sanford Zip Codes call (407) 322-2892, or your local postmaster.	
Sanibel	33957
San Jose (Part of Jacksonville)	32217
San Marco (Part of Jacksonville)	32207
San Mateo (Duval County)	32218
San Mateo (Putnam County)	32187
San Souci (Part of Jacksonville)	32216
San Souci Estates (Part of North Miami)	33181
San Souci Lakes	33917
Sans Souci	33982
Santa Fe	32615
Santa Monica	32413
Santa Rosa Beach	32459
Santa Rosa Mall (Part of Mary Esther)	32569
Santos	34474
Sarabay Acres	34229
Sarasota	34230-43
	34276-78
For specific Sarasota Zip Codes call (813) 361-6830, or your local postmaster.	
Sarasota Heights (Part of Sarasota)	34239
Sarasota Main Plaza (Part of Sarasota)	34236
Sarasota Springs	34232
Sarasota Square Mall	34238
Saratoga	32189
Sarno Plaza (Part of Melbourne)	32935
Sasafrass Acres	32038
Satellite Beach	32937
Satsuma	32189
Saufley Field	32509
Sawdust	32351
Sawgrass	32082
Sawgrass Mills (Part of City of Sunrise)	33323
Scenic Heights (Part of Tallahassee)	32303
Scotland	32333
Scott Lake	33056
Scotts Ferry	32424
Scottsmoor	32775
Seaglades	32507
Seagrove Beach	32459
Sea Ranch Lakes	33062
Searstown Mall (Part of Titusville)	32780
Seascape	32541
Seaside	32459
Sebastian	32958
	32976-78
For specific Sebastian Zip Codes call (407) 589-4397, or your local postmaster.	
Sebastian Highlands (Part of Sebastian)	32958
Sebring	33870-72
For specific Sebring Zip Codes call (813) 382-1151, or your local postmaster.	
Sebring Country Estates	33870
Sebring Hills	33872
Sebring Hills South	33870
Sebring Ridge	33870
Sebring Shores	33870
Seffner	33584
Seminole (Okaloosa County)	32564
Seminole (Pinellas County)	34642
Seminole Heights (Part of Tampa)	33603*
	33673†
Seminole Mall (Part of Seminole)	34642
Seminole Manor (Leon County)	32310

	ZIP
Seminole Manor (Palm Beach County)	33460
Seminole Park	34647
Seminole Plaza (Part of Casselberry)	32707
Seven Springs	34655
Seville	32190
Sewall's Point	34996
Shadeville	32327
Shadow Run	33569
Shady	34474
Shady Grove (Jackson County)	32442
Shady Grove (Taylor County)	32357
Shalimar	32579
Shamrock	32628
Shangri La	33584
Shannon Forest (Part of Tallahassee)	32308
Shannon Woods	32607
Sharpes	32959
Shawnee	33440
Shell Point	32327
Shenandoah (Part of Miami)	33245*
	33245†
Sheridan Plaza (Part of Hollywood)	33021
Sherman	34974
Sherwood Forest (Duval County)	32208
Sherwood Forest (Osceola County)	34746
Sherwood Park (Part of Delray Beach)	33445
Shockley Heights	32702
Shockley Hills	32702
Shore Acres (Part of St. Petersburg)	33705
Siesta Key	34242
Siesta Lago	34746
Silver Beach Heights	32784
Silver Lake	34788
Silver Sands (Part of Panama City Beach)	32407
Silver Springs	34488-89
For specific Silver Springs Zip Codes call (904) 687-4480, or your local postmaster.	
Silver Springs	32536
Silver Springs Shores	34472
Simmons Point	32346
Singer Island (Part of Riviera Beach)	33404
Sink Creek	32448
Sirmans	32331
Skycrest (Part of Clearwater)	34615
Sky Lake	32809
Skylake Mall	33162
Skyland Meadows	34442
Skyline Hills (Part of Lady Lake)	32159
Slavia	32765
Slones Ridge	34736
Snapper Creek	33116
	33176
	33186
	33196
For specific Snapper Creek Zip Codes call (305) 274-9050, or your local postmaster.	
Sneads	32460
Snell Isle (Part of St. Petersburg)	33705
Snow Hill	32765
Socrum	33809
Solana	33950
Sopchoppy	32358
Sorrento	32776
Sorrento Shores	34229
Sorrento Shores South	34275
South Apopka	32703
South Bay	33493
South Beach (Dade County)	33139
South Beach (Indian River County)	32963
Southboro (Part of West Palm Beach)	33405
South Bradenton	34205
South Brooksville	34601
South Clermont	34711
South Clinton Heights	33525
South Daytona	32121
Southeast Arcadia	33821

	ZIP
South Florida Mail Processing Center (Part of Pembroke Pines)	33082
Southgate	34239*
	34277†
South Gate Plaza (Part of Sarasota)	34239
South Gate Ridge	34233
South Jacksonville (Part of Jacksonville)	32207*
	32247†
South Merritt Estates	32952
South Miami	33143
	33155
	33243
For specific South Miami Zip Codes call (305) 661-1734, or your local postmaster.	
South Miami Heights	33157
South Mulberry	33860
South Palm Beach	33480
South Pasadena	33707
South Patrick Shores	32937
South Pine Lakes	32726
Southpoint (Part of Jacksonville)	32256
South Ponte Vedra Beach	32082
Southport (Bay County)	32409
South Port (Osceola County)	34746
South Punta Gorda Heights	33955
South Sarasota	34231
Southside (Part of Fort Lauderdale)	33315-16
	33335
For specific Southside Zip Codes call (305) 761-1194, or your local postmaster.	
Southside (Part of Lakeland)	33807
	33811
	33813
For specific Southside Zip Codes call (305) 761-1194, or your local postmaster.	
Southside Estates (Part of Jacksonville)	32216
South Trail	34231
South Venice	34293
South Weeki Wachee	34606
Southwood	32809
Sparr	32192
Spring Creek	32327
Springfield (Bay County)	32401
Springfield (Duval County)	32206
Spring Glen (Part of Jacksonville)	32207
Springhead	33566
Spring Hill	34606-08
For specific Spring Hill Zip Codes call (904) 683-3634, or your local postmaster.	
Springhill	32071
Spring Lake (Hernando County)	34602
Spring Lake (Highlands County)	33870
Spring Oaks (Part of Altamonte Springs)	32714
Springside	32177
Springs Plaza (Part of Longwood)	32779
Spruce Creek	32119
Spuds	32033
Starke	32091
State Capitol (Part of Tallahassee)	32399
State Line	32426
Steinhatchee	32359
Stetson University (Part of De Land)	32720
Stock Island	33040
Stuart	34994-97
For specific Stuart Zip Codes call (407) 287-2171, or your local postmaster.	
Stucky Still	34736
Sugar Loaf Shores	33044
Sugar Mill (Hillsborough County)	33624
Sugar Mill (Volusia County)	32168
Sugarmill Woods (Citrus County)	34446
Sulphur Springs (Part of Tampa)	33604*
	33674†
Sumatra	32335

* Area Zip Code *† Post Office Boxes*

	ZIP
Summerbrooke (Part of Tallahassee)	32312
Summerfield	34491-92
For specific Summerfield Zip Codes call (904) 245-2784, or your local postmaster.	
Summerfield	33569
Summer Haven	32086
Summerland Key	33042
Summer Place	32960
Summerport Beach	34786
Sumner	32625
Sumter Correctional Institution	33513
Sumterville	33585
Sun City	33586
Sun City Center	33571†
	33573*
Suncoast Estates	33917
Sun Haven	34231
Suniland	33156
Sunlake	32735
Sunland Estates	32771
Sunland Gardens	34947
Sunniland (Collier County)	33934
Sunniland (Dade County)	33156
Sun 'n Lake Acres	33852
Sun 'n Lake Estates	33852
Sun 'n Lakes	33870
Sunny Breeze Harbour	33821
Sunny Hills	32428
Sunny Isles	33160
Sunnyland	34233
Sunnyside (Bay County)	32461
Sunnyside (Lake County)	34748
Sun Ray Homes	33843
Sunrise (Part of Fort Lauderdale)	33304
Sunset	33143
	33183
For specific Sunset Zip Codes call (305) 596-6752, or your local postmaster.	
Sunset Harbor	34491
Sunset Islands (Part of Miami Beach)	33140
Sunshine Mall (Part of Clearwater)	34616
Suntree	32940
Sun Valley	33437
Surf	32346
Surfside	33154
Suwannee	32692
Suwannee Gardens	32680
Suwannee River Park Estates	32060
Suwannee Springs	32060
Suwannee Valley	32055
Svea	32567
Sweet Gum Head	32464
Sweetwater (Dade County)	33172
	33174
For specific Sweetwater Zip Codes call (305) 477-6708, or your local postmaster.	
Sweetwater (Liberty County)	32321
Sweetwater Creek	33615
Sweetwater Oaks	32750
Switzerland	32043
Sycamore	32351
Sydney	33587
Sylvania	32462
Sylvan Shores (Highlands County)	33852
Sylvan Shores (Lake County)	32757
Taft	32824
Talisman Estates	33525
Tallahassee	32301-04
	32306-08
	32310-17
	32399
For specific Tallahassee Zip Codes call (904) 877-4189, or your local postmaster.	
Tallahassee Mall (Part of Tallahassee)	32303
Tallevast	34270
Talleyrand (Part of Jacksonville)	32206
Tamarac	33319-21
For specific Tamarac Zip Codes call (305) 722-6080, or your local postmaster.	
Tamiami	33175
	33182

	ZIP
	33184
For specific Tamiami Zip Codes call (305) 261-5102, or your local postmaster.	
Tamiami (Part of Miami)	33144
Tampa	33601-97
For specific Tampa Zip Codes call (813) 877-0717, or your local postmaster.	
COLLEGES & UNIVERSITIES	
Tampa College	33614
University of South Florida	33620
University of Tampa	33606
FINANCIAL INSTITUTIONS	
Bank of Tampa	33603
Barnett Bank of Tampa	33602
Bay Financial Savings Bank, F.S.B.	33615
Central Bank of Tampa	33609
NationsBank of Florida, N.A.	33602
Sun Bank of Tampa Bay	33602
HOSPITALS	
James A. Haley Veterans Hospitals	33612
St. Joseph's Hospital	33607
Tampa General Hospital	33601
University Community Hospital	33613
HOTELS/MOTELS	
Days Inn Conference Center	33602
Embassy Suite Hotel	33609
Marriott, Tampa Airport	33607
Marriott, Westshore Hotel	33607
Tampa Airport Hilton at Metrocenter	33607
MILITARY INSTALLATIONS	
MacDill Air Force Base	33608
Marine Corps Reserve Training Center, Tampa	33611
Tampa Bay Center (Part of Tampa)	33607
Tangelo Park	32819
Tangerine	32777
Tang-O-Mar Beach	32541
Tarpon Lake Village	34685
Tarpon Springs	34688†
	34689*
Tarpon Woods	34685
Tarrytown	33597
Tavares	32778
Tavernier	33070
Taylor	32087
Taylor Creek	34974
Tee and Green Estates	33982
Telogia	32360
Temple Terrace	33617*
	33687†
Tenille	32356
Tequesta	33469
Terra Ceia	34250
The Forest	33908
The Fountains	33467
The Hamptons	33434
The Landings (Lee County)	33919
The Landings (Sarasota County)	34231
The Meadows (Clay County)	32065
The Meadows (Lake County)	32702
The Meadows (Sarasota County)	34235
Theressa	32091
The Vineyards	33999
Thomas City	32344
Thompson Estates	32778
Thonotosassa	33592
Three Rivers	32322
Three Rivers Estates	32038
Tice	33905
Tierra Verde	33715
Tiger Point	32561
Tildenville	34787
Timberline Estates	34461
Timber Pines	34606
Timberwood Estates	34785
Tisonia (Part of Jacksonville)	32218
Titusville	32780-83

	ZIP
	32796
For specific Titusville Zip Codes call (407) 267-4826, or your local postmaster.	
Tocoi	32033
Tommytown (Part of Dade City)	33525
Tomoka Estates	32174
Torchlite	34711
Torrey	33834
Tower Shops (Part of Davie)	33314
Town and Country Plaza	32505
Town and River Estates	33919
Town Center At Boca Raton (Part of Boca Raton)	33431
Town & Country Center	33183
Towne Mall (Part of Plantation)	33317
Town 'n' Country	33615
	33635
For specific Town 'n' Country Zip Codes call (813) 877-0717, or your local postmaster.	
Town Park Estates	33165
	33174
For specific Town Park Estates Zip Codes call (305) 226-7522, or your local postmaster.	
Trailer Estates	34281
Trailer Haven (Part of Melbourne)	32901
Trapnell	33567
Treasure Island (Dade County)	33141
Treasure Island (Lake County)	34788
Treasure Island (Pinellas County)	33706
Trenton	32693
Triangle Acres	32757
Trilby	33593
Tri Par Estates	34234
Tropic	32952*
	32965†
Tropical Acres	33569
Tropical Farms	34990
Tropical Gulf Acres	33955
Tropical Shores Manor	32778
Tropic Palms (Part of Delray Beach)	33444
Tropic Vista	33469
Truckland	33908
Turkey Creek	33567
Turner River	33943
Turquoise Beach	32459
Tuscanooga	34736
Tuskawilla (Part of Winter Springs)	32708
Twin City Mall (Part of North Palm Beach)	33408
Two Egg	32423
Tyndall Air Force Base	32403
Tyrone Square (Part of St. Petersburg)	33710
Uleta	33164
Umatilla	32784
Union Correctional Institution	32083
Union Park	32817
	32825
For specific Union Park Zip Codes call (407) 282-1421, or your local postmaster.	
University (Part of Gainesville)	32603*
	32604†
University Mall (Broward County)	33024
University Mall (Escambia County)	32504
University Mall (Hillsborough County)	33612
University Of Miami (Part of Coral Gables)	33124
University of South Florida	33620
University of Tampa (Part of Tampa)	33606
University of West Florida	32514
University Park (Duval County)	32211
University Park (Orange County)	32817
University Plaza	33612
University West	33612-13
For specific University West Zip Codes call (813) 935-8054, or your local postmaster.	

	ZIP
Upper Grand Lagoon	32407*
	32411†
U.S. Air Force Hospital	32542
Useppa Island	33924
Valdez	32713
Valkaria	32905
Valparaiso	32580
Valrico	33594
Vamo	34231
Venetia (Part of Jacksonville)	32210
Venetian Islands (Part of Miami Beach)	33139
Venetian Isles (Pinellas County)	33705
Venetian Isles (Santa Rosa County)	32561
Venetia Terrace (Part of Jacksonville)	32244
Venice	34284-85
For specific Venice Zip Codes call (813) 485-2881, or your local postmaster.	
Venice Acres	34292
Venice East	34293
Venice Gardens	34293
Venus	33960
Verdie	32009
Vermont Heights	32033
Verna	34251
Vernon	32462
Vero Beach	32960-68
For specific Vero Beach Zip Codes call (407) 567-5206, or your local postmaster.	
Vero Beach Highlands	32962
Vero Beach South	32960
	32962
	32966
	32968
For specific Vero Beach South Zip Codes call (407) 567-5206, or your local postmaster.	
Vero Lake Estates	32967
Vero Shores	32962
Vicksburg	32401
Viera	32940
Vilano Beach	32095
Vilas	32334
Village (Part of Deerfield Beach)	33442
Village Green (Brevard County)	32955
Village Green (Manatee County)	34209
Village of Golf	33436
Village of Pine Run	32174
Villages of Oriole	33446
Villas	33912
Villa Sabine	32561
Villa Tasso	32578
Vina del Mar (Part of St. Pete Beach)	33706
Virginia Gardens	33166
Volusia	32102
Volusia Mall (Part of Daytona Beach)	32114
Wabasso	32970
Wacahotta	32667
Waccasassa Lake	32693
Wacissa	32361
Wadesboro	32308
Wahneta	33880
Wahoo	33513
Wakulla	32327
Wakulla Gardens	32327
Wakulla Springs	32305
Waldo	32694
Wallace	32571
Walnut Hill	32568
Walsingham	34644
Walton	34957
Wannee	32619
Ward Ridge	32456
Warm Mineral Springs	34287
Warrington	32507
Washington Lake Estates (Part of Jacksonville)	32218
Washington Park	33311
Washington Shores (Part of Orlando)	32805
Waters Lake	32693
Watertown	32055
Waterway Estates	33903
Wauchula	33873
Wauchula Hills	33873
Waukeenah	32344
Wausau	32463
Waverly	33877

* Area Zip Code   † Post Office Boxes

	ZIP		ZIP		ZIP		ZIP
Waverly Hills (Part of Tallahassee)	32312	West Lantana (Part of Lantana)	33462	Whitfield	34243		33481†
Weathersfield	32714	West Little River	33147*	Whitfield Estates	34243	Woodland Drives (Part of Tallahassee)	32301
Webster	33597		33150†	Whiting Field	32570	Woodlawn (Bay County)	32407
Weeki Wachee	34606	West Melbourne	32904	Whitney	34748	Woodlawn (Pinellas County)	33704
Weeki Wachee Acres	34606	West Miami	33144	Whitney Beach (Part of Longboat Key)	34228	Woodlawn (St. Johns County)	32095
Weeki Wachee Gardens	34607		33155	Wilbur-By-The-Sea	32127	Woodlawn Beach	32561
Weirsdale	32195	For specific West Miami Zip Codes call (305) 385-1366, or your local postmaster.		Wilcox	32693	Wood Memorial Hospital	33821
Wekiva Springs	32750			Wildwood	34785	Woodmont (Part of Tamarac)	33321
Wekiwa Acres	32703	Weston	33326	Williamsburg	32821*	Woods	32321
Welaka	32193	West Palm Beach	33401-07		32823†	Woods and Lakes	32179
Welcome	33547		33409-20	Williams Point	32959	Woodville	32362
Wellborn	32094	For specific West Palm Beach Zip Codes call (407) 697-1933, or your local postmaster.		Willis Landing	32465	Woodward Avenue (Part of Tallahassee)	32304*
Wellington	33414			Williston	32696		32316†
Wesconnett (Part of Jacksonville)	32244	West Palmetto Park (Part of Boca Raton)	33427†	Williston Highlands	32696	Worthington Springs	32697
Wesley Chapel	33543-44		33486*	Willow Oak	33860	Wright	32547
For specific Wesley Chapel Zip Codes call (813) 782-2013, or your local postmaster.		West Panama City Beach (Part of Panama City Beach)	32413	Wilson Corner	33597	Wulfert (Part of Sanibel)	33957
				Wilson Neck	32097	Wynnehaven Beach	32569
Wesley Manor	32223	West Park	33614	Wilton Manors	33305-06	Wynwood (Dade County)	33127
West Atlantic	33071*	West Pensacola	32505		33311	Wynwood (Seminole County)	32771
	33077†	Westridge	33433		33334	Yacht Club Colony	33917
West Bay	32413	West Samoset	34208	For specific Wilton Manors Zip Codes call (305) 527-2077, or your local postmaster.		Yalaha	34797
West Bradenton	34209	West Scenic Park	33853			Yankeetown	34498
Westchester	33144	West Shore Plaza (Part of Tampa)	33609	Wimauma	33598	Ybor City (Part of Tampa)	33605*
	33155	West Tampa (Part of Tampa)	33607*	Windermere	34786		33675†
	33165		33677†	Winding Lakes	33428	Yeehaw Junction	34972
	33174	West Town Corners (Part of Altamonte Springs)	32714	Windsor	32601	Yellow Pine	32340
For specific Westchester Zip Codes call (305) 445-8841, or your local postmaster.		Westview	33168	Winfield	32055	Yelvington	32131
		Westville	32464	Winston	33801	York	34474
West Dade	33196	Westwood (Duval County)	32244		33803	Youmans	33566
West De Land	32720	Westwood (Orange County)	32808	For specific Winston Zip Codes call (813) 688-5572, or your local postmaster.		Youngstown	32466
West End (Broward County)	33326	Westwood Acres	34474			Yukon (Part of Jacksonville)	32244
West End (Calhoun County)	32424	Westwood Lakes	33165	Winston (Polk County)	33803	Yulee	32097
West End (Jackson County)	32446	Wewahitchka	32465	Winter Beach	32971	Yulee Heights	32097
Western Acres	33903	Whiskey Creek	33919	Winter Garden	34777†	Yulee Woods	32097
West Farm	32340	Whispering Pines (Madison County)	32340		34787*	Zellwood	32798
West Frostproof	33843	Whispering Pines (Okeechobee County)	34972	Winter Haven	33880-85	Zephyrhills	33539-44
Westgate (Manatee County)	34205	Whispering Pines (Putnam County)	32139	For specific Winter Haven Zip Codes call (813) 294-4157, or your local postmaster.		For specific Zephyrhills Zip Codes call (813) 782-2013, or your local postmaster.
Westgate (Palm Beach County)	33409	Whisper Walk	33496	Winter Haven Mall (Part of Winter Haven)	33880	Zephyrhills Correctional Institution	33539
Westgate-Belvedere Homes	33409	White City (Gulf County)	32465	Winter Park	32789-90	Zephyrhills North	33540
West Holly Hill	32117	White City (St. Lucie County)	34981		32792-93	Zephyrhills South	33540-41
West Hollywood (Part of Pembroke Pines)	33023*	Whitehouse (Part of Jacksonville)	32220	For specific Winter Park Zip Codes call (407) 647-3621, or your local postmaster.		For specific Zephyrhills South Zip Codes call (813) 782-2013, or your local postmaster.
	33083†	White Springs (Hamilton County)	32096	Winter Park Estates	32792	Zephyrhills West	33541
West Jacksonville (Part of Jacksonville)	32205	White Springs (Liberty County)	32321	Winter Park Mall (Part of Winter Park)	32789	Zolfo Springs	33890
West Kendall	33296			Winter Springs	32708*	Zuber	34475
Westland Mall (Part of Hialeah)	33012				32719†		
Westland Promenade (Part of Hialeah)	33014			Wiscon	34609		
				Woodland (Part of Boca Raton)	33431*		

	ZIP
Aaron	30450
Abac	31794
Abba	31750
Abbeville	31001
Abbott	30207
Abbottsford	30240
Aberdeen (Part of Peachtree City)	30269
Acree	31791
Acworth	30101*
	30102†
Adairsville	30103
Adams Park (Fulton County)	30311
Adams Park (Twiggs County)	31020
Adamsville (Part of Atlanta)	30331
Adasburg	30673
Adel	31620
Adgateville	31038
Adrian	31002
Agnes	30817
Agnes Scott College (Part of Decatur)	30030
Agricola	30820
Ailey	30410
Air Line	30516
Airport Mail Facility (Part of Atlanta)	30320
Akin	30415
Alamo	30411
Alapaha	31622
Albany	30239
	31701-08
For specific Albany Zip Codes call (912) 435-2725, or your local postmaster.	
Albion Acres	30906
Alcovy	30209
Alcovy Shores	31064
Aldora	30204
Alexander	30456
Alfords	31791
Aline	30420
Allendale (Gwinnett County)	30245
Allendale (Muscogee County)	31909
Allenhurst	31301
Allentown	31003
Allenville	31639
Allenwood	31061
Allie	30222
Alma	31510
Almon	30209
Almond Park (Part of Atlanta)	30318
Alpharetta	30201-02
	30239
For specific Alpharetta Zip Codes call (404) 475-7235, or your local postmaster.	
Alpine	30731
Alps Road (Part of Athens)	30604
Alston	30412
Altamaha	30453
Alta Vista (Part of Columbus)	31907
Altman	30467
Alto	30510
Alto Park	30165
Alvaton	30218
Amboy	31714
Ambrose	31512
Americus	31709
Amity	30817
Amos Mill	35967
Amsterdam	31734
Anderson City	31744
Andersonville	31711
Andrew Wood (Part of Columbus)	31903
Anguilla	31525
Ansley	30828
Ansley Estates	30274
Anthony Terrace (Part of Macon)	31206
Antioch (Polk County)	30125
Antioch (Troup County)	30240
Aonia	30673
Apalachee	30650
Apple Valley	30529
Appling	30802
Arabi	31712
Aragon	30104
Aragon Park	30901
Arcade	30549

	ZIP
Arch City	30701
Arco	31520
Arcola	30415
Ardick	31331
Ardmore	31329
Ardsley Park (Part of Savannah)	31405
Argyle	31623
Arkwright	31204
Arlington	31713
Arlington Park (Part of Macon)	31204
Armstrong State College	31406
Armuchee	30105
Arnco Mills	30263
Arnoldsville	30619
Arp	31783
Arrowhead Village	30236
Ascalon	30738
Ashburn	31714
Ashford Park	30319
Ashintilly	31331
Ashland	30521
Athens	30601-13
For specific Athens Zip Codes call (706) 613-2695, or your local postmaster.	
Atkinson	31543
Atlanta	30301-94
	31119-56
For specific Atlanta Zip Codes call (404) 765-7261, or your local postmaster.	

COLLEGES & UNIVERSITIES

	ZIP
Clark Atlanta University	30314
Emory University	30322
Georgia Institute of Technology	30332
Georgia State University	30303
Morris Brown College	30314
Oglethorpe University	30319
Spelman College	30314

FINANCIAL INSTITUTIONS

	ZIP
Bank South, National Association	30303
Citizens Trust Bank	30303
First Union National Bank of Georgia	30303
The Prudential Bank and Trust Company	30328
Southern Federal Savings Association of Georgia	30308
SouthTrust Bank of Florida, N.A.	30303
Trust Company Bank	30303
Wachovia Bank of Georgia, National Association	30303

HOSPITALS

	ZIP
Crawford Long Hospital of Emory University	30365
Emory University Hospital	30322
Georgia Baptist Medical Center	30312
Grady Memorial Hospital	30335
West Paces Medical Center	30327
Northside Hospital	30342
Piedmont Hospital	30309
Saint Joseph's Hospital of Atlanta	30342

HOTELS/MOTELS

	ZIP
Atlanta Hilton & Towers	30303
Atlanta Renaissance	30308
Holiday Inn at Lenox	30326
Lanier Plaza Hotel & Country Club	30324
Marriott Perimeter Center	30346
Omni Hotel at CNN Center	30335
Ramada Hotel Dunwoody	30338
Ritz-Carlton Atlanta	30303
Sheraton Inn Atlanta Airport	30344
Westin Peachtree Plaza	30303
Wyndham Garden Buckhead	30326
Wyndham Garden Midtown	30309

MILITARY INSTALLATIONS

	ZIP
United States Army Engineer Division, South Atlantic Division	30335

	ZIP
United States Property and Fiscal Office for Georgia	30316
Atlanta Naval Air Station	30060
Attapulgus	31715
Attapulgus Station	31715
Attica	30607
Auburn	30203
Audubon	30735
Augusta	30901-19
For specific Augusta Zip Codes call (706) 724-4826, or your local postmaster.	
Aumond Heights	30909
Aumond Place	30909
Auraria	30534
Austell	30001
Autreyville	31768
Autumn Forest	30236
Avallon	30328
Avalon (Chatham County)	31419
Avalon (Stephens County)	30557
Avans	30752
Avants	30411
Avera	30803
Avert Acres	31705
Avery	30115
Avondale (Bibb County)	31206
Avondale (McDuffie County)	30814
Avondale (Muscogee County)	31903
Avondale Estates	30002
Avondale Heights (Part of Columbus)	31903
Avondale Park (Part of Savannah)	31404
Axson	31624
Ayersville	30577
Azalea Park (Part of Macon)	31204
Babcock	31737
Bachlott	31553
Baconton	31716
Bainbridge	31717
Bairdstown	30669
Baker Village (Part of Columbus)	31903
Baldwin	30511
Baldwin Park (Part of Savannah)	31401
Baldwinville	31812
Ball Ground (Cherokee County)	30107
Ball Ground (Murray County)	30705
Baltimore (Part of Washington)	30673
Banning	30185
Bannockburn	31639
Barksdale	31082
Barnesville	30204
Barnett	30821
Barnett Shoals	30605
Barney	31625
Barneyville	31647
Barnhill	30457
Barnsley	30145
Barrett Parkway (Part of Kennesaw)	30144
Barretts	31602
Barrettsville	30534
Barrow Heights	30680
Bartletts Ferry	31808
Barton Village	30906
Bartonwoods	30307
Bartow	30413
Barwick	31720
Bascom	30467
Bass Crossroads	30230
Batesville	30523
Bath	30805
Battery Point	31404
Battle Forest (Part of Decatur)	30034
Baughs Crossroads	31833
Baxley	31513
Bay	31756
Bay Branch	30467
Bayview	31316
Beach	31554
Beachton	31792
Beacon Heights	30650
Beallwood (Part of Columbus)	31904
Beaulieu	31406
Beaumount	30736
Beaverdale	30721

	ZIP
Bedingfield (Part of Macon)	31206
Beechwood Shopping Center (Part of Athens)	30606
Belair	30907
Belair Hills Estates	30909
Belfast	31324
Bellemeade	30906
Bellton (Part of Lula)	30554
Bellville	30414
Bellville Bluff	31331
Belmont (DeKalb County)	30086
Belmont (Hall County)	30507
Belmont Hills Shopping Center (Part of Smyrna)	30080
Belvedere	30032
Belvedere Park	30032
Belvedere Plaza	30032
Belvins Acres	30736
Bemiss	31602
Benedict	30125
Benevolence	31740
Ben Hill (Part of Atlanta)	30331*
	31131†
Benning Hills (Part of Columbus)	31903
Bentley Place	30741
Benton	30165
Bent Tree	30143
Berckman Hills	30909
Berckman Village	30909
Berkeley Lane	30136
Berkshire Woods (Part of Savannah)	31419
Berlin	31722
Berner	31029
Berryton	30747
Berzelia	30814
Bethany	31762
Bethel (Jasper County)	31064
Bethel (Randolph County)	31740
Bethesda (Chatham County)	31406
Bethesda (Greene County)	30669
Bethesda (Gwinnett County)	30245
Bethlehem	30620
Between	30656
Beulah (Hancock County)	31087
Beulah (Lincoln County)	30668
Beulah (Paulding County)	30153
Beulah Heights (Part of Atlanta)	30312
Beverly Hills	30741
Bexton	30259
Bibb City	31904
Bibb Mills	31029
Bickley	31554
Big Canoe	30143
Big Creek	30131
Big Springs	30240
Billarp	30187
Bingville (Part of Savannah)	31405
Birdie	30223
Birmingham	30201
Bishop	30621
Blackjack	30276
Blackshear	31516
Blackshear Place	30507
Blacksville	30253
Blackville	30457
Blackwells	30066
Blackwood	30701
Blaine	30175
Blairsville	30512
Blair Village (Part of Atlanta)	30354
Blakely	31723
Blandford	31326
Bland Villa	31015
Blandy (Part of Milledgeville)	31061
Blitchton	31308
Bloomfield Gardens (Part of Macon)	31206
Bloomingdale	31302
Blount	31029
Blowing Springs	30725
Blue Ridge	30513
Blue Spring	30736
Blue Springs (Dougherty County)	31707
Blue Springs (Screven County)	30446
Bluffton	31724
Blun	30401
Blundale	30401

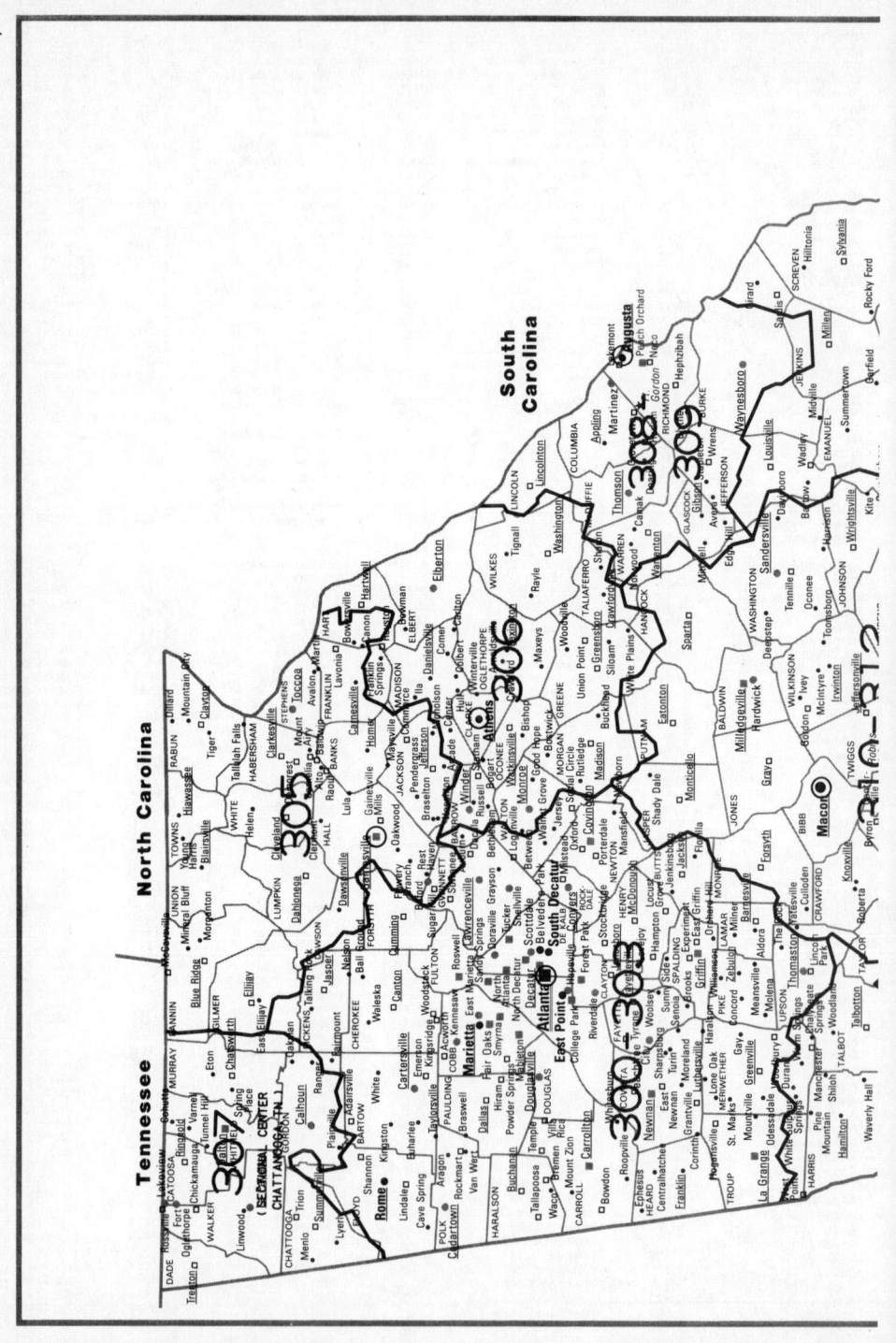

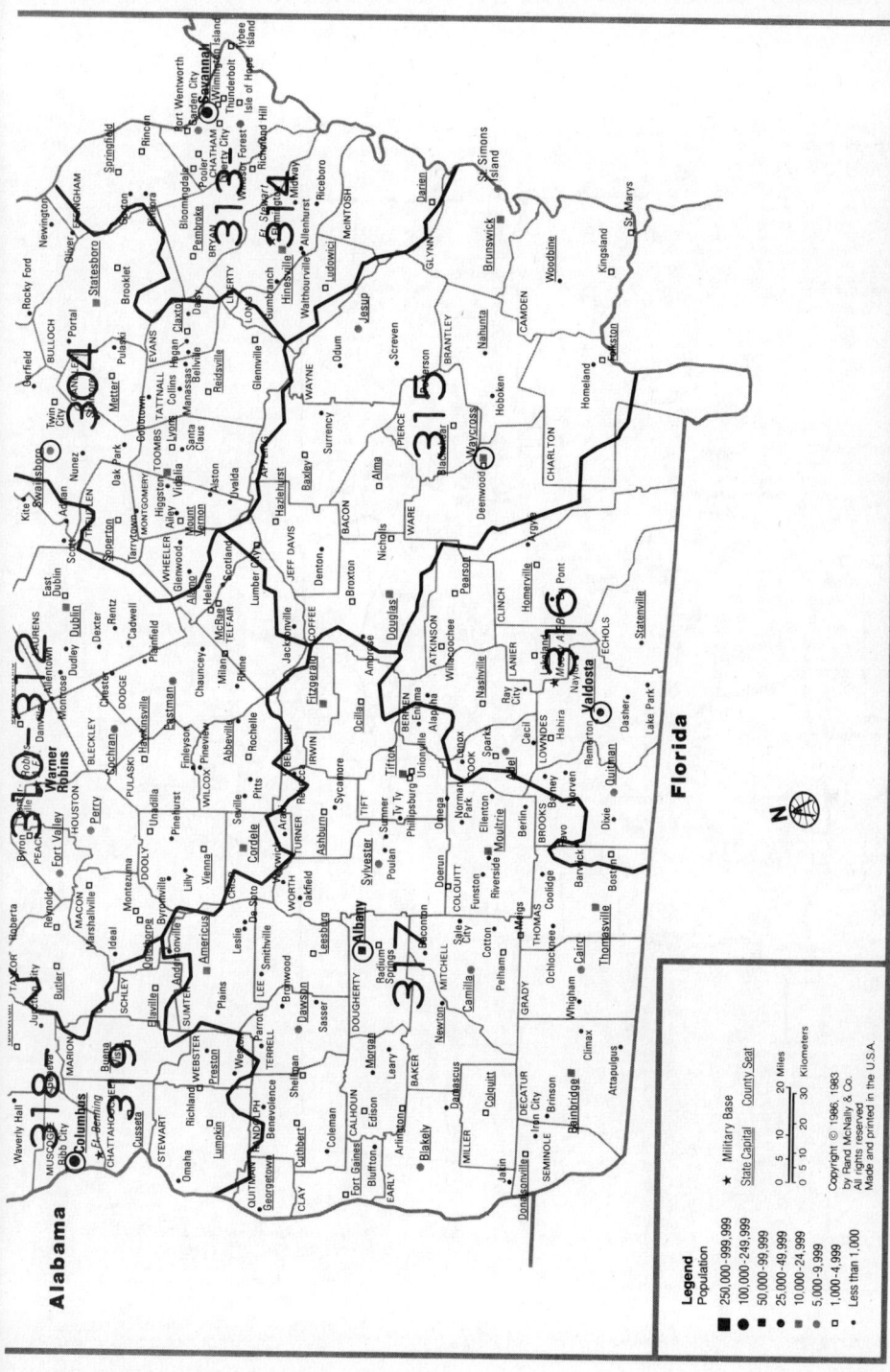

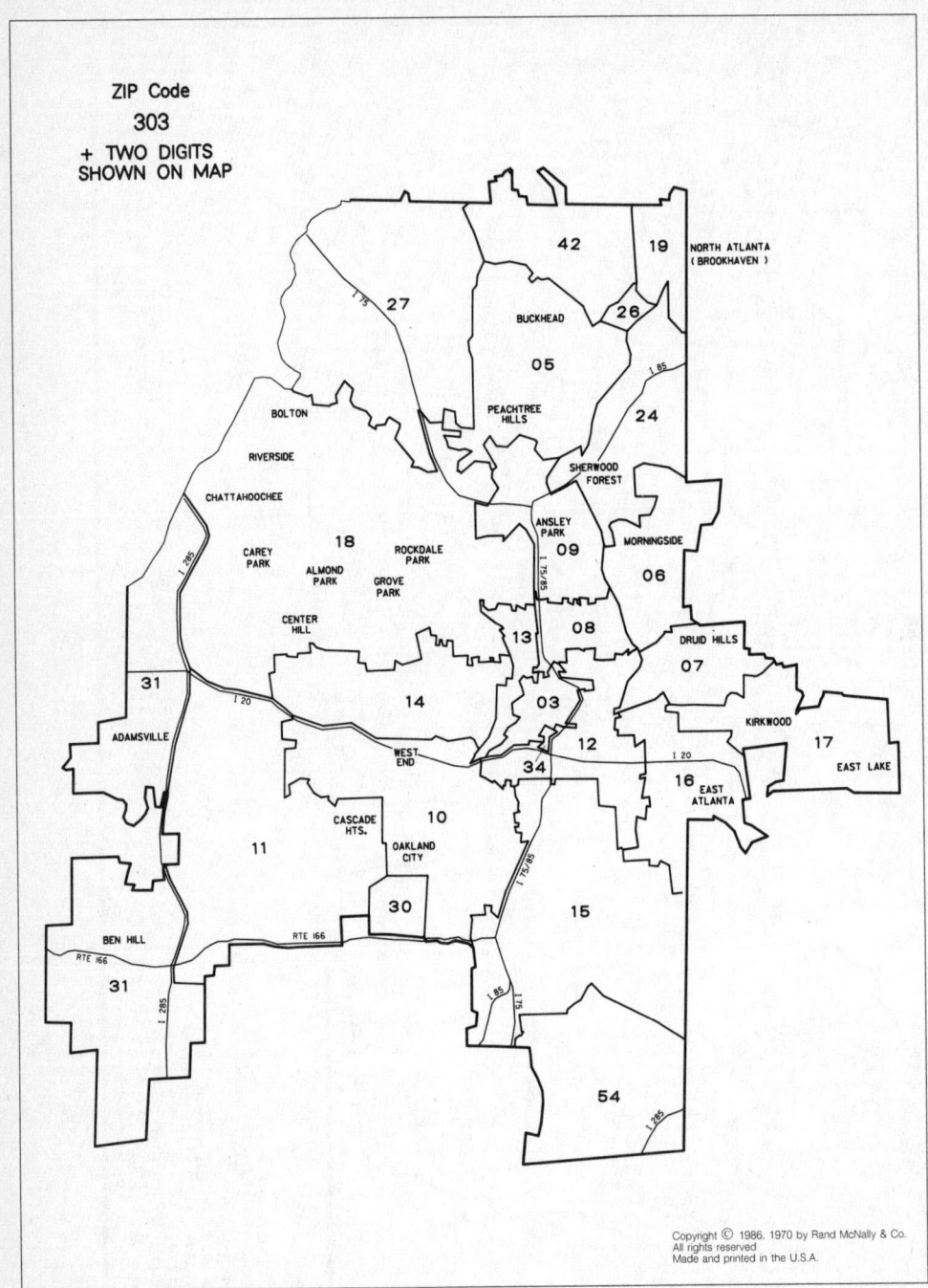

ZIP Code
303
+ TWO DIGITS
SHOWN ON MAP

42

19   NORTH ATLANTA
(BROOKHAVEN)

27

BUCKHEAD

26

05

I 85

PEACHTREE
HILLS

24

BOLTON

RIVERSIDE

CHATTAHOOCHEE

SHERWOOD
FOREST

ANSLEY
PARK

MORNINGSIDE

18

ROCKDALE
PARK

09

CAREY
PARK

ALMOND
PARK

GROVE
PARK

06

I 285

CENTER
HILL

08

DRUID HILLS

13

31

07

I 20

14

KIRKWOOD

ADAMSVILLE

03

17

WEST
END

12

34

EAST LAKE

I 20

16   EAST
ATLANTA

CASCADE
HTS.

10

11

OAKLAND
CITY

30

15

BEN HILL

RTE 166

RTE 166

RTE 166

31

I 285

I 75/85

54

I 285

I 85   I 75

	ZIP		ZIP		ZIP		ZIP
Blythe	30805	Brownsville	30133	Carsonville	31006	Chelsea	30731
Bogart	30622	Browntown	31543	Cartecay	30540	Chennault	30668
Bold Spring	30656	Brownwood	30650	Carter Acres (Part of		Cherokee (Part of Macon)	31204
Bolingbroke	31004	Broxton	31519	Columbus)	31903	Cherokee Forest	30188
Bolton (Part of Atlanta)	30318	Brunswick	31520-21	Carters	30705	Cherrylog	30522
Bona Bella	31406		31523-25	Carters Grove	30660	Cheshire Bridge (Part of	
Bonair	30907	For specific Brunswick Zip		Cartersville	30120	Atlanta)	30324
Bonaire	31005	Codes call (912) 265-6186, or		Carver Heights (Part of		Chestatee	30130
Bonanza	30236	your local postmaster.		Columbus)	31906	Chester	31012
Bond	30633	Brynwood	30909	Carver Village (Part of		Chestnutflat	30728
Boneville	30806	Buchanan	30113	Savannah)	31401	Chestnut Mountain	30502
Booker Washington		Buckhead (Fulton County)	30339	Cary	31014	Chickamauga	30707
Heights (Part of		Buckhead (Morgan		Cascade Heights (Part of		Chickasawhatchee	31742
Columbus)	31909	County)	30625	Atlanta)	30311	Chicopee	30507
Boozeville	30147	Bucktown	30108	Cascade Hills (Part of		China Hill	31077
Boston	31626	Budapest	30176	Columbus)	31904	Chippewa Terrace (Part of	
Bostwick	30623	Buena Vista	31803	Cash	30701	Savannah)	31406
Bowden Hills (Part of		Buffington	30114	Cassandra	30707	Choestoe	30512
Macon)	31201	Buford	30518-19	Cassville	30123	Chubbtown	30124
Bowdon	30108	For specific Buford Zip Codes		Castle Park (Part of		Chula	31733
Bowdon Junction	30109	call (404) 945-9275, or your		Valdosta)	31604	Cinderella Hills	30736
Bowens Mill	31750	local postmaster.		Castlewood (Part of		Cisco	30708
Bowersville	30516	Bullard	31020	Columbus)	31907	Civic Center (Part of	
Bowman	30624	Bulloch Crossroads	31816	Cataula	31804	Atlanta)	30308
Box Springs	31801	Bumphead	31806	Catlett	30728	Clarkdale	30020
Boyd Highlands	30736	Bunker Hill	30512	Cave Spring	30124	Clarke Dale	30605
Boydville	30577	Burning Bush	30736	Cecil	31627	Clarkesville	30523
Boykin	31737	Burnside	31406	Cedar Creek	30274	Clarksboro	30607
Boynton	30736	Burnside Island	31406	Cedar Creek Park	30605	Clarkston	30021
Boys Estate	31523	Burroughs	31405	Cedar Crossing	30436	Clarkview (Part of Macon)	31204
Bradley	31032	Burwell	30117	Cedar Grove (Chatham		Claxton	30417
Branchville	31730	Bushnell	31533	County)	31419	Clayfields	31054
Brantley	31803	Butler (Dougherty County)	31705	Cedar Grove (DeKalb		Clayton	30525
Braselton	30517	Butler (Taylor County)	31006	County)	30027	Clearview (Part of	
Braswell	30153	Butler Manor	30905	Cedar Grove (Fulton		Savannah)	31401
Bremen	30110	Butts	30442	County)	30213	Clem	30116
Brent	31029	Byers Crossroads	30185	Cedar Grove (Laurens		Clermont	30527
Brentwood (Dougherty		Byne Crossroads	31763	County)	31021	Cleveland	30528
County)	31707	Byromville	31007	Cedar Grove (Walker		Cliftondale	30337
Brentwood (Wayne		Byron	31008	County)	30707	Climax	31734
County)	31555	Cabaniss	31029	Cedar Hammock	31406	Clinchfield	31013
Brest	31716	Cadley	30821	Cedar Hills (Part of		Clinton	31032
Brewton	31021	Cadwell	31009	Columbus)	31907	Cloudland	30731
Briarcliff (Part of Atlanta)	30329	Cagle	30143	Cedar Point	31332	Cloverdale	30738
Briarwood (Chatham		Cairo	31728	Cedar Springs	31732	Clubview Heights (Part of	
County)	31408	Caleb	30058	Cedartown	30125	Columbus)	31906
Briarwood (Columbia		Calhoun	30701-03	Celeste	30673	Clyattville	31601
County)	30907	For specific Calhoun Zip Codes		Cenchat	30707	Clyo	31303
Briarwood (Fulton County)	30344	call (706) 629-3053, or your		Centennial	30663	Coal Mountain	30130
Briarwood (Rockdale		local postmaster.		Center (Bartow County)	30120	Coastal Correctional	
County)	30207	Callaway	30660	Center (Jackson County)	30601	Institution	31408
Briar Wood Estates	30068	Calvary	31729	Center (Toombs County)	30474	Cobb	31735
Brick Store	30279	Camak	30807	Center Hill (Colquitt		Cobb Centre Mall (Part of	
Bridgeboro	31705	Carnellia Terrace (Part of		County)	31768	Smyrna)	30080
Bridgeman Heights	31201	Savannah)	31404	Center Hill (Fulton County)	30318	Cobbtown	30420
Brighton	31794	Camelot (Clarke County)	30606	Center Point	30179	Cochran	31014
Brighton Woods (Part of		Camelot (Clayton County)	30236	Centerpost	30728	Coffee	31551
Pooler)	31322	Cameron	30467	Centerville (Elbert County)	30635	Coffee Bluff Plantation	
Brinson	31725	Camilla	31730	Centerville (Gwinnett		(Part of Savannah)	31419
Brisbon	31324	Campania	30814	County)	30058	Cogdell	31634
Bristol	31518	Campbellton	30213	Centerville (Houston		Cohutta	30710
Bristol Forest (Part of		Campton	30655	County)	31028	Cohutta Springs	30711
Macon)	31201	Campus (Part of Athens)	30605	Centerville (Talbot County)	31812	Colbert	30628
Bristol Woods	30208	Canal Lake	30512	Central City (Part of		Cole City	30752
Broad	30668	Candler	30507	Atlanta)	30303	Coleman	31736
Broadhurst	31545	Candler-McAfee	30032	Central City Retail (Part of		Colemans Lake	30441
Broadview (Part of		Cannon Crossing	30742	Atlanta)	30302	Colesburg	31569
Atlanta)	30324	Cannon Gate	30907	Centralhatchee	30217	College (Part of Fort	
Brockton	30549	Cannonville	30240	Central Junction (Part of		Valley)	31030
Bronco	30728	Canon	30520	Garden City)	31408	College Heights	
Bronwood	31726	Canoochee	30471	Century	31763	(Dougherty County)	31705
Brookfield	31727	Canton	30114-15	Chalybeate Springs	31816	College Heights	
Brookfield West	30907	For specific Canton Zip Codes		Chamberlain	30728	(Muscogee County)	31906
Brookhaven (Bibb County)	31206	call (404) 345-6318, or your		Chamblee	30341	College Park	30337
Brookhaven (DeKalb		local postmaster.		Chambliss	31709	Collins	30421
County)	30319	Canton Plaza (Part of		Chapel Hill	30134	Collinsville	30058
Brookhaven (Muscogee		Marietta)	30066	Chappel	30257	Colomokee	31723
County)	31906	Capel	31728	Charing	31058	Colonial Oaks (Part of	
Brooklet	30415	Capitol Hill (Part of		Charles (Stewart County)	31815	Savannah)	31419
Brooklyn	31825	Atlanta)	30334	Charles (Toombs County)	30474	Colonial Place	31705
Brooks	30205	Captola	30467	Charleston South	30906	Colonial Village (Part of	
Brookstone (Cobb		Carbondale	30721	Charlotteville	30473	Savannah)	31406
County)	30101	Carey Park (Part of		Charter Oaks (Part of		Colony Park	30909
Brookstone (Muscogee		Atlanta)	30318	Columbus)	31909	Colquitt	31737
County)	31904	Carl	30203	Chaserville	31647	Columbia Heights	30907
Brookstore Place	30342	Carlton	30627	Chastain	31738	Columbus	31829
Brooksville	31740	Carmichael Crossroads	30115	Chatham City (Part of			31901-09
Brookton	30506	Carnegie	31740	Garden City)	31408		31995
Brookvale Estates	30736	Carnes Creek	30577	Chatham Villa (Part of		For specific Columbus Zip	
Brookview	31406	Carnesville	30521	Garden City)	31408	Codes call (706) 563-0100, or	
Brookwood (Forsyth		Carnigan	31319	Chatsworth	30705	your local postmaster.	
County)	30202	Carns Mill	30175	Chattahoochee (Part of		Columbus Heights (Part of	
Brookwood (Laurens		Caroline Park (Part of		Atlanta)	30318	Macon)	31204
County)	31021	Columbus)	31904	Chattahoochee Plantation	30067	Columbus Square (Part of	
Brookwood (Richmond		Carrollton	30116-18	Chattanooga Valley	30725	Columbus)	31906
County)	30909	For specific Carrollton Zip		Chatterton	31554	Colwell	30541
Browndale	31036	Codes call (404) 834-4491, or		Chattoogaville	30730	Comer	30629
Browns (Baldwin County)	31061	your local postmaster.		Chauncey	31011	Commerce	30529
Browns (Dade County)	30752	Carrs	31087	Checkero	30525		

* Area Zip Code   **† Post Office Boxes**

	ZIP
Concord (Jasper County)	31064
Concord (Pike County)	30206
Concord (Schley County)	31806
Concord (Sumter County)	31709
Coney	31015
Conley	30027
Constitution	30316
Conyers	30207-08
For specific Conyers Zip Codes call (404) 483-8378, or your local postmaster.	
Cooksville	30230
Cooktown	31737
Coolidge	31738
Cool Spring	31771
Cooper Creek Park (Part of Columbus)	31907
Cooper Heights	30707
Coopers	31031
Coosa	30165
Copeland	31077
Cordele	31015
Corinth	30230
Cornelia	30531
Cotton	31739
Cotton Hill	31767
Council	31631
Country Club Estates	31520
Country Club Hills (Part of Augusta)	30904
Country Park	30906
Country Place	30809
Country Side (Part of Savannah)	31406
County Line (Barrow County)	30680
County Line (DeKalb County)	30032
Court Square (Part of Dublin)	31021
Covena	30401
Coverdale	31714
Covington	30209
Covington Mills (Part of Covington)	30209
Cox	31331
Coxs Crossing	30321
Crabapple	30201
Crandall	30711
Craneeater	30701
Cravey	31060
Crawford	30630
Crawfordville	30631
Crescent	31304
Crest	30286
Cresthill	31406
Crest Hill Gardens (Part of Savannah)	31406
Crestview	31713
Crestwell Heights	31204
Crosland	31771
Cross Keys (Part of Macon)	31201
Crossroads (Hart County)	30516
Crossroads (Liberty County)	31323
Crossroads at Stewart Lakewood, The (Part of Atlanta)	30315
Cruse	30245
Crystal Springs (Bibb County)	31201
Crystal Springs (Floyd County)	30105
Crystal Valley (Part of Columbus)	31907
Culloden	31016
Culverton	31087
Cumberland	30339
Cumming	30130-31
For specific Cumming Zip Codes call (404) 887-5777, or your local postmaster.	
Curryville	30701
Curtis	30513
Cusseta	31805
Custer Terrace (Part of Columbus)	31905
Cuthbert	31740
Cypress Mills	31520
Dacula	30211
Daffin Heights (Part of Savannah)	31404
Dahlonega	30533
Daisy	30423
Dakota	31714
Dallas	30132
Dallas Heights	30906
Dallondale	30741

	ZIP
Dalton	30719-22
For specific Dalton Zip Codes call (706) 278-7450, or your local postmaster.	
Damascus (Early County)	31741
Damascus (Gordon County)	30701
Dames Ferry	31046
Danburg	30668
Daniel	31324
Daniel Springs	30669
Danielsville	30633
Danville	31017
Darien	31305
Dasher	31601
Davisboro	31018
Davis Crossroads	30707
Dawesville	31792
Dawnville	30721
Dawson	31742
Dawsonville	30534
Days Crossroads	31751
Dearing	30808
Decatur	30030-37
	30089
For specific Decatur Zip Codes call (404) 378-8857, or your local postmaster.	
Deenwood	31503
Deepstep	31082
Deer Run	30208
Deerwood Forest	30906
Deerwood Park	30032
Delhi	30668
Dellwood	30401
DeLowe (Part of East Point)	30344
Demorest	30535
Denmark	30415
Dennis	31024
Denton	31532
Denver	30217
Deptford (Part of Savannah)	31404
De Soto	31743
De Soto Park	30161
Desser	31745
Devereux	31087
Dewberry	30741
Dewy Rose	30634
Dexter	31019
Dial	30513
Dialtown	30267
Diamond Hill	30628
Dickey	31746
Digbey	30205
Dillard	30537
Dillon	31792
Dinglewood (Part of Columbus)	31906
Dixie (Brooks County)	31629
Dixie (Newton County)	30209
Dixie Heights (Part of Albany)	31705
Dixie Union	31503
Dobbins Air Force Base	30060
Dock Junction	31520
Doctortown	31545
Doerun	31744
Doles	31791
Donald	31316
Donalsonville	31745
Donegal	30458
Donovan	31096
Doogan	30708
Dooling	31063
Doraville	30340
Dorchester (Liberty County)	31320
Dorchester (Richmond County)	30909
Dot	30108
Double Branches	30817
Doublegate	31707
Double Run	31072
Dougherty	30534
Douglas	31533
Douglasville	30133-35
For specific Douglasville Zip Codes call (404) 765-7261, or your local postmaster.	
Dove Creek	30635
Dover	30424
Doverel	31742
Downs	31018
Downtown (Part of Atlanta)	30301
Downtown (Part of Columbus)	31901

	ZIP
Doyle	31803
Drakes Still	31745
Draketown	30179
Dranesville	31803
Drayton	31092
Dresden	30263
Drew	30130
Druid Hills	30333
Dry Branch (Jenkins County)	30822
Dry Branch (Twiggs County)	31020
Dry Pond	30529
Dublin	31021*
	31040†
Dubois	31014
Ducktown	30130
Dudley	31022
Due West	30064
Duffee	31730
Dugdown	30113
Duluth	30136
Dumas	31824
Dunaire	30032
Duncan Park	37412
Dunwoody	30338
Du Pont	31630
Durand	31830
Dutch Island	31406
Eagle Cliff	30725
Eagle Grove	30520
Eason	31792
East Albany (Part of Albany)	31701
Eastanollee	30538
East Armuchee	30728
East Athens	30683
East Atlanta (Part of Atlanta)	30316
East Boundary	30901
East Boynton	30736
East Columbus	31907
East Dublin	31021
East Edgewood (Part of Columbus)	31907
East Ellijay	30539
East Griffin	30223
East Highlands (Part of Columbus)	31901
East Juliette	31046
East Lake (Part of Decatur)	30030
Eastman	31023
East Marietta	30062
East Meadow	30605
East Newnan	30263
East Point	30344
East Savannah (Part of Savannah)	31404
East Side (Part of Dalton)	30719
East Town (Part of Albany)	31705
East Trion (Part of Trion)	30753
Eastview	30901
Eastville	30621
Eastwood	30316
Eastwood (Part of Atlanta)	30317
Eatonton	31024
Ebernezer	30279
Echeconnee	31008
Echota	30701
Eden	31307
Edge Hill	30810
Edgemoor East	30236
Edgemoor West	30236
Edgewater (Part of Savannah)	31406
Edgewater Park (Part of Savannah)	31406
Edgewood (Columbia County)	30907
Edgewood (Muscogee County)	31907
Edison	31746
Edith	31631
Ednaville	30517
Egypt	31329
Elberta	31093
Elberton	30635
Elder	30677
Eldora	31308
Eldorado	31794
Eldorendo	31737
Eleanor Village	31705
Elim	31316
Elizabeth (Part of Marietta)	30060
Elko	31025
Ellabell	31308
Ella Gap	30540

	ZIP
Ellaville	31806
Ellenton	31747
Ellenwood	30049
Ellerslie	31807
Ellijay	30540
Elliotts Bluff	31558
Ellwood	30805
Elmodel	31770
Elza	30453
Embry Hills	30341
Emerson	30137
Emerson Park	31503
Emit	30458
Emma	30534
Emmalane	30442
Emory University	30322
Empire	31014
Englewood (Part of Columbus)	31907
Enigma	31749
Enon Grove	30217
Enterprise	30627
Ephesus	30217
Epworth	30541
Epworth Acres	31522
Eric	30411
Esom Hill	30138
Etna	30125
Eton	30724
Euharlee	30120
Eulonia	31331
Evans	30809
Evansville	30240
Everett	31525
Everett Springs	30105
Evergreen	31707
Excelsior	30439
Executive Park	30347
Experiment	30212
Faceville	31717
Fairburn	30213
Fairchild	31745
Fairfax	31552
Fairfield (Part of Savannah)	31404
Fairlawn Acres (Part of Fort Oglethorpe)	30741
Fairmount	30139
Fair Oaks	30060
Fairplay (Douglas County)	30187
Fairplay (Morgan County)	30663
Fairview (Franklin County)	30553
Fairview (Habersham County)	30535
Fairview (Jackson County)	30567
Fairview (Walker County)	30741
Fairway Oaks (Part of Savannah)	31406
Fairway Village	30906
Fancy Hall	31324
Fantasy Hills	30725
Fargo	31631
Farmdale	30467
Farmers High	30117
Farmington	30638
Farmville	30701
Farrar	31085
Fashion	30705
Faulkner	30107
Fayetteville	30214
	30232
For specific Fayetteville Zip Codes call (404) 461-7878, or your local postmaster.	
Federal Reserve (Part of Atlanta)	30303
Federal Station (Part of Albany)	31702
Fellwood Homes (Part of Savannah)	31401
Felton	30140
Fernwood (Part of Savannah)	31404
Ficklin	30673
Ficklings Mill	31006
Fidele	30735
Fife	30213
Fincherville	30233
Findlay	31070
Finleyson	31071
Fish Creek	30125
Fitzgerald	31750
Fitzgerald Cotton Mill	31750
Fitzpatrick	31044
Five Forks (Gwinnett County)	30245
Five Forks (Thomas County)	31626
Fivemile Still	31634

	ZIP
Five Points (Fulton County)	30303
Five Points (Lowndes County)	31601
Five Points (Macon County)	31063
Five Points (Marion County)	31803
Five Points (Randolph County)	31786
Five Points (Taylor County)	31006
Five Points (Treutlen County)	30457
Five Springs	30721
Flat Rock (Muscogee County)	31907
Flat Rock (Putnam County)	31024
Flat Shoals	30516
Fleetwood (Part of Savannah)	31404
Fleming	31309
Fleming Heights	30906
Flemington	31313
Flint	31716
Flint Hill	31826
Flint River	31711
Flint River Estates	30236
Flintside	31735
Flintstone	30725
Flintwood	30274
Flippen	30253
Floral Hill	30668
Florence	31821
Flovilla	30216
Flowery Branch	30542
Floyd	30059
Floyd Springs	30105
Folkston	31537
Folsom	30103
Forest Estates	30909
Forest Hills (Muscogee County)	31907
Forest Hills (Richmond County)	30909
Forest Lake (Part of Macon)	31210
Forest Park (Clayton County)	30050* / 30051†
Forest Park (Dougherty County)	31701
Forest Park (Richmond County)	30904
Forest River Farms (Part of Savannah)	31406
Forrest Hills (Part of Savannah)	31404
Forsyth	31029
Fort Benning	31905
Fort Benning South	31905
Fort Gaines	31751
Fort Gillem	30050
Fort Gordon	30905
Fort Lamar	30633
Fort McAllister	31324
Fort Oglethorpe	30742
Fort Screven (Part of Tybee Island)	31328
Fortson (Part of Columbus)	31808
Fortsonia	30635
Fort Stewart	31313-14
For specific Fort Stewart Zip Codes call (912) 368-3380, or your local postmaster.	
Fort Valley	31030
Foster Hills	30736
Fosters Mills	30161
Four Points (Part of Albany)	31705
Four Seasons	30207
Fowlstown	31752
Fox (Part of Rome)	30161
Foxboro	31602
Frances Hollow	30207
Franklin	30217
Franklin Springs	30639
Franklinton	31020
Frazier	31014
Free Home	30115
Friendship (Polk County)	30125
Friendship (Sumter County)	31709
Frolona	30217
Fruitland	31630
Fry	30555
Fullwood Springs	30125

	ZIP
Funston	31753
Furniture City	30001
Gabbettville	30240
Gaddistown	30572
Gaillard	31078
Gaines Community	30605
Gaines School	30605
Gainesville	30501-07
For specific Gainesville Zip Codes call (404) 532-3138, or your local postmaster.	
Gainesville Mills	30501
Galloway	30513
Garden Acres Estates (Part of Pooler)	31322
Garden City	31408
Garden Lakes	30165
Garden Valley	31041
Gardi	31545
Gardner (Part of Oconee)	31067
Garfield	30425
Garland	30533
Garnersville	31767
Garretta	31021
Gasco (Part of Atlanta)	30301
Gates City (Part of Atlanta)	30312
Gateway (Part of Thomasville)	31792
Gay	30218
Geneva	31810
Gentian (Part of Columbus)	31907
Georgetown (Chatham County)	31405
Georgetown (Quitman County)	31754
Georgetown Estates	30906
Georgia Diagnostic and Classification	30233
Georgia Pacific Sru (Part of Atlanta)	30303
Georgia Southern (Part of Statesboro)	30458
Georgia Southwestern College (Part of Americus)	31709
Georgia State Prison	30453
Georgia Training and Development Center	30519
Georgia University (Part of Athens)	30612
Germany	30525
Gibson	30810
Gill	30668
Gillis Springs	30457
Gillsville	30543
Girard	30426
Gladesville	31064
Gladys	31622
Glasgow	31626
Gleason Heights (Part of Pooler)	31322
Glencliff	32286
Glen Haven	30032
Glenloch	30217
Glenloch Village (Part of Peachtree City)	30269
Glenmore	31503
Glenn	30217
Glenn Hills	30906
Glennville	30427
Glenridge (Part of Atlanta)	30342
Glenwood (Floyd County)	30165
Glenwood (Wheeler County)	30428
Glenwood Hills	30032
Glory	31622
Gloster	30245
Glynn Haven	31522
Goat Town	31082
Gobblers Hill	31805
Gober	30107
Godfrey	30650
Godwinsville	31023
Goggins	30204
Golden Isle	31410
Goldmine	30520
Goldsboro	31014
Goldson	31006
Goodes	30268
Good Hope	30641
Goolsby	31064
Gordon	31031
Gordon Springs	30740
Gordonston (Part of Savannah)	31404
Gordy	31791
Gore	30747

	ZIP
Goss	30635
Gough	30811
Graball	30668
Gracewood	30812
Grady	30153
Graham	31513
Grandview	30143
Grange	30434
Granite Hill	31087
Grantville	30220
Gratis	30655
Graves	31742
Gray	31032
Gray Hill	31833
Graymont (Part of Twin City)	30471
Grays	31404
Grayson	30221
Graysville	30726
Great Southwest Industrial Park (Part of Atlanta)	30336
Green Acres (Catoosa County)	30741
Green Acres (Chatham County)	31404
Green Acres (Clarke County)	30605
Green Acres Estate (Part of Dublin)	31021
Greenbriar (Part of Atlanta)	30331
Green Island Hills (Part of Columbus)	31904
Greenough	31716
Greensboro	30642
Greens Cut	30906
Greenville	30222
Greenway (Emanuel County)	30441
Greenway (Fulton County)	30075
Greenwood (Henry County)	30253
Greenwood (Lanier County)	31649
Greenwood (Mitchell County)	31730
Greenwood Forest	31649
Gregorys Mill	30711
Gresham Park	30316
Gresham Road (Part of Marietta)	30067
Greshamville	30650
Gresston	31023
Griffin	30223* / 30224†
Grimball Park	31406
Griswoldville	31201
Grizzletown	30101
Grooverville	31626
Grovania	31036
Groveland (Bryan County)	31321
Groveland (Chatham County)	31405
Grove Park (Chatham County)	31406
Grove Park (Fulton County)	30318
Grove Point	31405
Grovetown	30813
Gumbranch	31313
Gumlog (Towns County)	30582
Gum Log (Union County)	30512
Gumlong	30553
Guysie	31510
Guyton	31312
Habersham	30544
Haddock	31033
Hagan	30429
Haggards Crossroads	30633
Hahira	31632
Halcyondale	30467
Hale Gap	30752
Halfmoon Landing	31320
Halls	30145
Halls Crossing	31018
Hallwood	31024
Halycon Bluff	31401
Hamilton	31811
Hammett	31078
Hampton	30228
Handy	30263
Haney	30124
Hannah	30187
Hannahs Mill	30286
Hannatown	31717
Hansell	31765
Hapeville	30354
Haralson	30229
Harbins	30620

	ZIP
Harbor Creek	31410
Hard Cash	30634
Hardwick	31034
Hardwicke	31324
Harlem	30814
Harmony	31024
Harmony Church	31905
Harp	30214
Harper Mill (Part of Lake City)	30260
Harrietts Bluff	31569
Harrington	31522
Harrisburg	30747
Harris City	30222
Harrison	31035
Harrisonville	30230
Harrock Hall	31406
Hartford	31036
Harts	30810
Hartsfield (Colquitt County)	31756
Hartsfield (Fulton County)	31123
Hartwell	30643
Harvest	30523
Haskins Crossing	31022
Hassier Mill	30740
Hatcher	31754
Hatcher's Store	30830
Hatley	31015
Hawkinsville	31036
Haylow	31630
Hayneville	31036
Hayston	30255
Hazlehurst	31539
Head River	30731
Heardville	30130
Hebardville	31503
Helen	30545
Helena	31037
Hemp	30560
Henderson	31025
Hentown	31723
Hephzibah	30815
Herndon	30441
Herod	31742
Hiawassee	30546
Hickory Bluff	31565
Hickory Flat (Banks County)	30554
Hickory Flat (Cherokee County)	30115
Hickory Level	30116
Hickory Ridge (Part of Macon)	31204
Hickox	31553
Hicks Circle	30207
Hidden Acres	30207
Hidden Lake (Part of Savannah)	31419
Higdon	30541
Higgston	30410
Highfalls	30233
Highgate	30909
Highland Circle (Part of Macon)	31211
Highland Heights	31709
Highland Mills	30223
Highland Park (Part of Savannah)	31406
Highland Pines (Part of Columbus)	31909
High Point (Newton County)	30209
High Point (Walker County)	30707
High Shoals	30645
Hightower	30130
Hill City	30735
Hillcrest	30240
Hillcrest Heights (Part of Macon)	31204
Hillman	30631
Hillsboro	31038
Hillsdale	31794
Hillside (Part of La Grange)	30240
Hilltonia	30467
Hilton	31723
Hilton Heights (Part of Columbus)	31906
Hinesville	31313-14
For specific Hinesville Zip Codes call (912) 876-3978, or your local postmaster.	
Hinkles	30738
Hinsonton	31765
Hinton	30143
Hiram	30141
Hi Roc Shores	30207

* Area Zip Code   † Post Office Boxes

	ZIP
Hobby	31714
Hoboken	31542
Hogansville	30230
Hoggard Mill	31770
Hog Hammock	31327
Holbrook	30130
Holcomb Bridge (Part of Roswell)	30076
Holland	30730
Hollingsworth	30510
Hollis	31778
Hollonville	30292
Holly Hills (Part of Columbus)	31906
Holly Springs (Cherokee County)	30142
Holly Springs (Jackson County)	30558
Hollywood	30523
Holt	31798
Homeland	31537
Homer	30547
Homerville	31634
Honey Creek	30208
Hooker	30752
Hopeful	31730
Hopeulikit	30458
Hopewell (Cherokee County)	30115
Hopewell (Harris County)	31822
Horns	31078
Hornsby	30901
Horseleg Estates	30165
Hortense	31543
Hoschton	30548
Houston Avenue (Part of Macon)	31206
Houston Lake	31047
Houston Mall (Part of Warner Robins)	31093
Howard	31039
Howell	31636
Howell Mill (Part of Atlanta)	30325
Howells Transfer (Part of Atlanta)	30301
Howell Tower (Part of Atlanta)	30318
Huber	31201
Hubert	30415
Huffer	31533
Hughland	30438
Hulett	30116
Hull	30646
Hunter	30467
Hunters Point (Part of Columbus)	31909
Huntington	31709
Hunts Corner	30701
Hurst	30560
Hutchins	30630
Ideal	31041
Ila	30647
Imlac	30293
Imperial	31024
Inaha	31790
Indian Hills	30236
Indianola	31602
Indian Springs (Butts County)	30216
Indian Springs (Catoosa County)	30736
Industrial (Part of Atlanta)	30336
Industrial City	30705
Ingleside (Part of Macon)	31204
Inman	30232
Iron City	31759
Irondale	30236
Irwins Crossroads	31089
Irwinton	31042
Irwinville	31760
Isabella	31791
Islandwood	31410
Isle of Hope	31406
Isle of Hope-Dutch Island	31406
Ivey	31031
Ivy Log	30512
Jackson	30233
Jacksons Crossroads	30668
Jacksons Store	30668
Jacksonville (Telfair County)	31544
Jacksonville (Towns County)	30582
Jake	30182
Jakin	31761
Jamaica Estates	30907
James	31032
Jamestown	31503

	ZIP
Jarrell	31006
Jasper	30143
Jay Bird Springs	31011
Jefferson	30549
Jeffersonville	31044
Jekyll Island	31527
Jenkinsburg	30234
Jersey	30235
Jerusalem (Camden County)	31568
Jerusalem (Pickens County)	30143
Jesup	31545
Jewell	31045
Jewtown	31522
Jinks	31717
Johnson Corner	30436
Johnson Crossroads	31822
Johnstonville	30204
Jolly	30292
Jones	31323
Jones Acres	31201
Jonesboro	30236*
	30237†
Jones Creek	30512
Jones Crossroads	31822
Jonesville	30108
Jordan	30411
Jordan City (Part of Columbus)	31904
Jot Em Down Store	31516
Joy Lake	30260
Juliette	31046
Junction City	31812
Juniper	31801
Juno	30534
Kansas	30182
Kathleen	31047
Keith	30755
Keithsburg	30114
Keller	31324
Kelley Hill	31905
Kelleytown	30253
Kelly	31085
Kemp	30401
Kenilworth	30909
Kennesaw	30144
Kensington	30707
Kensington Park (Part of Savannah)	31405
Kenwood (Fayette County)	30214
Kenwood (Muscogee County)	31909
Keysville	30816
Kibbee	30474
Kiker	30540
Kildare	30446
Killarney	31761
Kimbrough	31825
Kinderlou	31601
Kings	30209
Kings Bay	31547
Kings Bay Base	31547
Kingsboro	31811
Kingsland	31547
Kingsridge	30188
Kingston (Bartow County)	30145
Kingston (Muscogee County)	31904
Kingston (Richmond County)	30909
Kings Wood (Chatham County)	31401
Kingswood (Clarke County)	30606
Kings Wood (Richmond County)	30904
Kirkland (Atkinson County)	31642
Kirkland (Jeff Davis County)	31539
Kirkwood (Colquitt County)	31768
Kirkwood (Muscogee County)	31904
Kite	31049
Klondike (DeKalb County)	30058
Klondike (Houston County)	31036
Knott	30240
Knoxville	31050
Kramer	31001
La Crosse	31806
La Fayette	30728
Lafayette Plaza (Part of Albany)	31707

	ZIP
La Grange	30240-41
For specific La Grange Zip Codes call (706) 882-1851, or your local postmaster.	
Lake	30125
Lake Arrowhead	30183
Lake Capri Estates	30058
Lake Cindy	30228
Lake City	30260
Lake Creek	30125
Lake Hills	30263
Lake Howard	30728
Lake Jodeco	30236
Lakeland	31635
Lake Lanier Islands	30518
Lake Lucerne	30247
Lakemont (Rabun County)	30552
Lakemont (Richmond County)	30901
Lake Park	31636
Lakeshore Estates (Part of Gainesville)	30501
Lakeshore Mall (Part of Gainesville)	30501
Lakeside Hills (Part of Macon)	31201
Lakeside Park	31406
Lake Talmadge	30228
Lake Tara	30236
Lakeview (Bleckley County)	31014
Lakeview (Catoosa County)	30741
Lakeview (Peach County)	31030
Lakeview Estates	30207
Lakewood (Clarke County)	30605
Lakewood (Fulton County)	30315
Lakewood Heights (Part of Atlanta)	30315
Lamar	31709
Lamara Heights (Part of Savannah)	31405
Lamarville (Part of Savannah)	31405
Landrum	30534
Lanier	31321
Laroche Park (Part of Savannah)	31404
Lashley	31005
Lathemtown	30115
Laurel Hills (Part of Columbus)	31904
Lavender	30165
La Vista	30329
Lavonia	30553
Lawrenceville	30243-46
For specific Lawrenceville Zip Codes call (404) 963-7118, or your local postmaster.	
Lax	31774
Leaf	30528
Leafmore	30033
Leah	30802
Leary	31762
Leathersville	30817
Lebanon	30146
Lee (Part of Lake City)	30260
Lee Correctional Institution	31763
Leefield	30415
Lee Pope	31030
Leesburg	31763
Lees Crossing (Part of La Grange)	30240
Lees Mill	30214
Leland	30059
Leliaton	31650
Lena	30101
Lenox	31637
Lenox Square (Part of Atlanta)	30326
Leslie	31764
Lewis	30467
Lewis Corner	30701
Lewiston	30809
Lexington	30648
Lexsy	30401
Liberty	30678
Liberty City (Part of Savannah)	31405
Liberty Hill	30257
Lifsey	30295
Lilburn	39226†
	30247*
Lilly	31051
Lillypond	30701
Limestone	31014
Lincoln Hills (Part of Columbus)	31909

	ZIP
Lincoln Park	30286
Lincolnton	30817
Lindale	30147
Lindbergh Plaza (Part of Atlanta)	30324
Lindsey Creek (Part of Columbus)	31907
Lindsley Park (Part of Macon)	31206
Linesville	30631
Linton	31087
Linwood	30728
Lions Gate	30327
Listonia	31015
Lithia Springs	30057
Lithonia	30038
	30058
For specific Lithonia Zip Codes call (404) 482-6554, or your local postmaster.	
Little Five Points (Part of Atlanta)	30307
Little Hope	31745
Little Miami	31601
Livingston	30161
Lizella	31052
Loco	30817
Locust Grove	30248
Loftin	31816
Loganville	30249
Lollie	31021
Lone Oak	30230
Long Cane	30240
Lookout Mountain	30750
Lorane	31201
Lorenzo	31329
Lorwood (Part of Savannah)	31406
Lost Mountain	30073
Lothair	30457
Lotts	31519
Louise	30230
Louisville	30434
Louvale	31814
Lovejoy	30250
Lovett	31021
Loving	30560
Lowell	30116
Lowndes Correctional Institution	31602
Lowry	30214
Lucile	31723
Lucius	30522
Ludowici	31316
Ludville	30175
Ludville	30248
Luella	30554
Lula	30554
Lulaton	31553
Lumber City	31549
Lumpkin	31815
Lundberg	30673
Luthersville	30251
Luvdale	31701
Luxomni	30247
Lyerly	30730
Lyn Hills (Part of Columbus)	31909
Lynhurst	31406
Lynmore Estates (Part of Macon)	31206
Lynn	31717
Lynnwood	30741
Lyons	30436
Lytle	30707
Mableton (Cobb County)	30059
McAfee	30032
McBean	30906
McCaysville	30555
McCollum	30263
McDaniels	30701
McDonald Acres	30741
McDonough	30253
Macedonia (Cherokee County)	30115
Macedonia (Towns County)	30546
McElroys Mill	30249
McGregor	30410
Machen	31064
McIntosh	31320
McIntosh Mill Village	30263
McIntyre	31054
McKinnon	31545
Macland	30073
Macon	31201-12
For specific Macon Zip Codes call (912) 752-8424, or your local postmaster.	

* Area Zip Code   † Post Office Boxes

Name	ZIP	Name	ZIP	Name	ZIP	Name	ZIP
Macon Correctional Center	31201	Mill Creek Estates	30506	Mountville	30261	Northlake	30345
Macon Mall (Part of Macon)	31206	Milledgeville	31061	Mount Zion	30150	Northridge (Part of Conyers)	30207
McPherson	30132	Millen	30442	Moxley	30477	North Roswell (Part of Roswell)	30075
McRae	31055	Millers Mill	30281	Mulberry	30680	North Side (Fulton County)	30305
McWhorter	30134	Millhaven	30467	Mulberry Grove	31804	Northside (Houston County)	31093
Madison	30650	Millwood	31552	Mulberry Heights (Part of Albany)	31705	North West Point	31833
Madola	30541	Milner	30257	Mulberry Street (Part of Macon)	31201	Norton Acres	30906
Madras	30263	Milstead	30207	Munnerlyn	30830	Norwood	30821
Madray Springs	31545	Mineola	31602	Murphy	31738	Note	31024
Magby Gap	30752	Mineral Bluff	30559	Murray Hills	30909	Nuberg	30634
Magnet	30208	Minish	30646	Murrays Crossroads	31806	Nunez	30448
Magnolia (Chatham County)	31406	Minnesota	31744	Murrayville	30564	Oakdale (Chatham County)	31405
Magnolia (Fulton County)	30318	Mission Ridge (Part of Rossville)	30741	Musella	31066	Oakdale (Cobb County)	30080
Magruder	30441	Mitchell (Dodge County)	31023	Myrtle Grove	31324	Oakfield	31772
Mallorysville	30668	Mitchell (Glascock County)	30820	Mystic	31769	Oak Forest (Chatham County)	31404
Manassas	30438	Mize	30577	Nahunta	31553	Oak Forest (Clayton County)	30236
Manchester	31816	Mizell	31006	Nails Creek	30521	Oak Grove (Carroll County)	30117
Manningtown	31545	Mock Road (Part of Albany)	31705	Nance Springs	30721	Oak Grove (Cherokee County)	30102
Manor	31550	Modoc	30401	Nankipooh (Part of Columbus)	31909	Oak Grove (DeKalb County)	30033
Mansfield	30255	Molena	30258	Naomi	30728	Oak Grove (Troup County)	31822
Manta	31805	Moncrief	32301	Nashville	31639	Oakhaven	31707
Marblehill	30148	Moniac	31646	National Hills	30904	Oak Hill (Gilmer County)	30540
Maretts	30553	Monroe	30655-56	Naylor	31641	Oak Hill (Newton County)	30209
Margret	30572	For specific Monroe Zip Codes call (404) 267-5254, or your local postmaster.		Neal	30206	Oakhurst (Part of Savannah)	31406
Maridale Estates (Part of Columbus)	31904			Nebo	30132	Oakland	30218
Marietta	30007	Montclair	30907	Needmore	31631	Oakland City (Part of Atlanta)	30301
	30060-68	Monteith (Part of Port Wentworth)	31407	Neese	30646	Oakland Heights	30120
For specific Marietta Zip Codes call (404) 424-0140, or your local postmaster.		Montevideo	30635	Nelson	30151	Oakland Park (Chatham County)	31404
Marietta Campground	30062	Montezuma	31063	Nevils	31321	Oakland Park (Muscogee County)	31903
Marine Corps Supply Center	31704	Montgomery (Chatham County)	31406	Newark	31792	Oaklawn	30263
Marion	31020	Montgomery Correctional Institution	30445	Newborn	30262	Oakleaf Plantation	30067
Marketplace at North DeKalb (Part of Decatur)	30033	Monticello (Jasper County)	31064	New Branch	30436	Oakman	30732
Marlborough	30236	Monticello (Richmond County)	30906	New Elm	31768	Oak Mountain	31826
Marlow	31312	Montreal	30033	New England	30752	Oak Park	30401
Marshallville	31057	Montrose	31065	New Era	31709	Oakwood	30566
Mars Hill	30101	Moody Air Force Base	31601	New Georgia	30132	Oasis	30513
Martech (Part of Atlanta)	30318	Moody Field	31601	New Holland	30501	Oatland Island	31410
Martin	30557	Moons	30725	New Home	30752	Ocee	30202
Martinez	30907	Moores	31021	New Hope (Gilmer County)	30540	Ochillee	31905
Massee	31620	Mora	31650	New Hope (Gwinnett County)	30245	Ochlocknee	31773
Matt	30130	Moreland	30259	New Hope (Lincoln County)	30817	Ochwalkee	30428
Matthews	30818	Morgan (Calhoun County)	31766	New Hope (Paulding County)	30132	Ocilla	31774
Mattox	31537	Morgan (Haralson County)	30110	Newington	30446	Oconee	31067
Mauk	31058	Morganton	30560	Newnan	30263-65	Oconee Heights	30607
Maura Estates	30906	Morganville	30757	For specific Newnan Zip Codes call (404) 253-2725, or your local postmaster.		Odessadale	30222
Maxeys	30671	Morningside (Fulton County)	30324			Odum	31555
Maxim	30817	Morningside (Muscogee County)	31909	New Point	31780	Offerman	31556
Maxwell	31085	Morningside Hills	30501	New Salem	30547	Ogeechee	30467
Mayday	31636	Morris	31767	Newton	31770	Ogeechee Farms	31405
Mayfair (Part of Savannah)	31406	Morris Brown (Part of Atlanta)	30314	Newtown (Fulton County)	30202	Ogeechee Road	31405
Mayfield	31087	Morris Estates	30376	New Town (Gordon County)	30701	Ogeecheeton (Part of Savannah)	31401
Mayhaw	31723	Morris Siding (Part of Atlanta)	30301	New Town (Wilkes County)	30673	Oglethorpe (Chatham County)	31406
Maysville	30558	Morrow	30260	New York (Part of Aragon)	30153	Oglethorpe (Macon County)	31068
Meadowbrook (Part of Macon)	31204	Mortons	31405	Neyami	31763	Oglethorpe Mall (Part of Savannah)	31406
Meadow Grove	30906	Morven	31638	Nicholasville	31713	Oglethorpe Park (Part of Savannah)	31406
Meansville	30256	Mossy Creek	30528	Nicholls	31554	Oglethorpe University	30319
Mechanicsville	30340	Moultrie	31768*	Nicholson	30565	Ogletree Woods (Part of Columbus)	31909
Meeks	31049		31776†	Nickelsville	30701	Ohoopee	30436
Meigs	31765	Mountainbrook (Part of Pine Mountain)	31822	Nicklesville	31042	Okefenokee	31503
Meinhard (Part of Port Wentworth)	31407	Mountain City	30562	Nickleville	31797	Ola	30253
Meldrim	31318	Mountain Hill	31811	Nickville	30634	Old Damascus	31741
Melrose	31636	Mountain Park (Fulton County)	30075	Noah's Station	30818	Old National (Part of Atlanta)	30349
Mendes	30427	Mountain Park (Gwinnett County)	30087	Noble	30728	Old South	30236
Menlo	30731	Mountaintown	30540	Noonday	30066	Olive Branch	31827
Mercer University (Part of Macon)	31204	Mountain View (Clayton County)	30321	Norcross	30071	Oliver	30449
Meridian	31319	Mountain View (Walker County)	30741		30091-93	Olney	31308
Merrillville	31738	Mount Airy	30563	For specific Norcross Zip Codes call (404) 448-2241, or your local postmaster.		Omaha	31821
Mershon	31551	Mount Berry	30149			Omega	31775
Mesena	30819	Mount Bethel	30060	Norman	30668	Oostanaula	30701
Metasville	30673	Mount Carmel	30728	Norman Park	31771	Ophir	30107
Metcalf	31792	Mount Olivet	30643	Normantown	30474	Orange	30115
Metter	30439	Mount Pleasant (Banks County)	30547	Norris	30828	Orchard Hill	30266
Mica	30107	Mount Pleasant (Wayne County)	31543	Norristown	30447	Orchard Hills	30741
Middleton	30635	Mount Vernon (Montgomery County)	30445	North Atlanta	30319	Orianna (Laurens County)	31002
Midland (Part of Columbus)	31820	Mount Vernon (Walton County)	* 30655	North Canton	30114	Orianna (Treutlen County)	30457
Midtown (Part of Atlanta)	30309	Mount Vernon (Whitfield County)	30740	North Decatur	30033	Orland	30457
Midville	30441			North Druid Hills	30033		
Midway (Catoosa County)	30741			North Dublin (Part of Dublin)	31021		
Midway (Clinch County)	31634			North Elberton	30635		
Midway (Liberty County)	31320			Northgate (Part of Columbus)	31907		
Midway (Tattnall County)	30427			North Highland (Part of Atlanta)	30306		
Midway-Hardwick	31061			North Highlands (Part of Columbus)	31904		
Milan	31060			North High Shoals	30645		
Miles Park	30906						
Milford	31762						
Mill Creek	30740						

* Area Zip Code   † Post Office Boxes

	ZIP
Ormewood (Part of Atlanta)	30312
Oscarville	30506
Osierfield	31750
Other	30132
Ottawa Estates (Part of Bloomingdale)	31302
Owen	31516
Owensboro	31079
Owltown	30512
Oxford	30267
Pace	30209
Pachitta	31740
Padena	30560
Palalto	31064
Palmetto (Fulton County)	30268
Palmetto (Oglethorpe County)	30627
Palmyra	31763
Pancras	31061
Panhandle	31076
Pannell	30655
Panola	30058
Pantertown	30559
Panthersville	30032
Paoli	30629
Paradise Park (Chatham County)	31406
Paradise Park (Wayne County)	31545
Paradise Valley	30607
Parhams	30521
Parkchester (Part of Columbus)	31906
Park City (Part of Fort Oglethorpe)	30741
Parkers	30467
Parkersburg	31406
Parkerville	31744
Park Hill (Part of Gainesville)	30501
Parkwood (Part of Savannah)	31404
Parrott	31777
Pateville	31015
Patillo	30233
Patten	31626
Patterson	31557
Pavo	31778
Payne (Bibb County)	31201
Payne (Cherokee County)	30102
Peach Orchard	30906
Peachtree Center (Part of Atlanta)	30343
Peachtree City	30269
Peachtree Hills (Part of Atlanta)	30305
Peachtree Mall (Part of Columbus)	31909
Pearly	31021
Pearson	31642
Pebble City	31784
Pedenville	30206
Pelham	31779
Pembroke	31321
Pendergrass	30567
Pendley Hills	30032
Penfield	30669
Penia	31015
Pennick	31525
Pennington	30650
Pennville	30747
Peoples Still	31797
Pepperton (Part of Jackson)	30233
Perkins	30822
Perry	31069
Persimmon	30525
Petross	30474
Phelps	30720
Phillips	30907
Phillipsburg	31794
Philomath	30660
Phinizy	30802
Phipps Plaza (Part of Atlanta)	30326
Phoenix	31024
Pickard	30286
Piedmont (Jasper County)	31064
Piedmont (Lamar County)	30204
Pierceville	37317
Pineboro	31768
Pine Chapel	30701
Pine Gardens (Part of Savannah)	31404
Pine Grove	31513
Pine Harbor	31331
Pine Hill (Part of Columbus)	31903

	ZIP
Pinehurst (Dooly County)	31070
Pinehurst (Henry County)	30281
Pine Lake	30072
Pineland	31631
Pine Log	30171
Pine Mountain (DeKalb County)	30058
Pine Mountain (Harris County)	31822
Pine Mountain (Rabun County)	29664
Pine Mountain Valley	31823
Pineora	31312
Pine Park	31728
Pine Valley (Cook County)	31620
Pine Valley (Richmond County)	30904
Pineview	31071
Pinewood Shores	30207
Piney Bluff	31565
Piney Grove	31808
Pin Point	31406
Pinson	30161
Pio Nono (Part of Macon)	31206
Pirkle Woods	30130
Pitts	31072
Pittsburg	30084
Plainfield	31073
Plains	31780
Plainview (Franklin County)	30521
Plainview (Whitfield County)	30720
Plainville	30733
Planter	30646
Pleasant Hill (Fulton County)	30337
Pleasant Hill (Gwinnett County)	30136
Pleasant Hill (Talbot County)	31836
Pleasant Hill (Terrell County)	31742
Pleasant Valley (Bartow County)	30103
Pleasant Valley (Dooly County)	31092
Pocataligo	30633
Pointe South	30236
Point Peter	30627
Pollards Corner	30802
Pomona	30223
Pond Spring	30707
Pooler	31322
Pope City	31079
Popes Ferry	31046
Poplar Springs (Haralson County)	30113
Poplar Springs (Oconee County)	30677
Portal	30450
Porter	31014
Porterdale	30270
Porter Springs	30533
Portland	30104
Port Royal	31324
Port Wentworth	31407
Port Wentworth Junction (Part of Port Wentworth)	31407
Postell	31201
Potterville	31076
Poulan	31781
Powder Springs	30073
Powell Place	31701
Powelton	31087
Powers Lake	30327
Powersville	31008
Prather	30673
Prattsburg	31827
Presley	30546
Preston	31824
Pretoria	31701
Price	30506
Pridgen	31519
Primrose	30222
Princeton (Part of Athens)	30601
Pringle	31096
Prior	30125
Pritchetts	31744
Privette Heights	30060
Prospect	31064
Pulaski	30451
Pumpkin Center	30814
Putnam	31803
Putney	31782
Pyles Marsh	31525
Pyne	30240
Queensland	31750

	ZIP
Quitman	31643
Rabbit Hill	31324
Rabun Gap	30568
Race Pond	31537
Radium Springs	31702
Raines	31015
Raleigh	30293
Ramhurst	30705
Randall	31815
Ranger	30734
Raoul	30510
Raulerson (Brantley County)	31557
Raulerson (Pierce County)	31557
Ravenwood	30907
Raybon	31553
Ray City	31645
Rayle	30660
Raymond	30265
Raytown	30631
Rebecca	31783
Rebie	31012
Recovery	32324
Redan	30074
Redbud	30701
Red Clay	30710
Red Hill (Franklin County)	30521
Red Hill (Stewart County)	31825
Red Lane	30501
Red Oak	30272
Red Rock (Paulding County)	30101
Red Rock (Worth County)	31791
Red Stone	30549
Red Store Crossroads	31770
Reed Creek	30643
Reese	30828
Reeves	30701
Regency Mall (Part of Augusta)	30904
Register	30452
Rehoboth	30033
Reidsboro	30292
Reidsville	30453
Reka	31321
Relay	30125
Remerton	31601
Renfroe	31805
Reno	31728
Rentz	31075
Reo	30740
Resaca	30735
Resseaus Crossroads	31024
Rest Haven	30518
Retreat	31323
Rex	30273
Reynolds	31076
Reynoldsville	31745
Rhine	31077
Riceboro	31323
Richfield (Part of Savannah)	31405
Richland	31825
Richmond Hill	31324
Richwood	31092
Rico	30268
Riddleville	31018
Ridgefield Heights (Part of Columbus)	31907
Ridgeville	31331
Ridgewood	30909
Rincon	31326
Ringgold	30736
Rio	30223
Rio Vista (Chatham County)	31406
Rio Vista (Dougherty County)	31705
Rising Fawn	30738
Riverdale	30274
	30296
For specific Riverdale Zip Codes call (404) 997-5566, or your local postmaster.	
Riverland Terrace (Part of Columbus)	31903
River Oaks	31410
River Road	31707
Rivers End (Part of Savannah)	31406
Riverside (Bibb County)	31204
Riverside (Colquitt County)	31768
Riverside (Floyd County)	30161
Riverside (Fulton County)	30318
Rivertown	30213
Riverturn	31745
Riverview (Part of Macon)	31204
Rivoli (Part of Macon)	31210

	ZIP
Roanoke Acres	31750
Roberta	31078
Robertstown	30545
Robertsville	30707
Robins Air Force Base	31098
Robinson	30669
Rochelle	31079
Rock Branch	30635
Rock Chapel	30058
Rockdale (Part of Atlanta)	30318
Rock Hill	31723
Rockingham	31510
Rockledge	30454
Rockmart	30153
Rock Spring	30739
Rockville	31024
Rocky Creek	30701
Rocky Face	30740
Rocky Ford	30455
Rocky Mount	30251
Rocky Plains	30209
Roddy	31014
Rogers	30529
Rogers Correctional Institution	30453
Rolling Green	30207
Rolling Meadows	30905
Rome	30161-65
For specific Rome Zip Codes call (706) 232-1073, or your local postmaster.	
Roopville	30170
Roosterville	30170
Roper	31539
Ropers Crossroads	30809
Roscoe	30263
Rosebud	30249
Rosedale	30701
Rose Dhu	31406
Rose Hill (Chatham County)	31406
Rose Hill (Pike County)	30256
Rose Hill Heights (Part of Columbus)	31904
Rosemont	30802
Rosemont Park	30161
Rosier	30434
Rossignol Hill (Part of Garden City)	31408
Rossville	30741
Roswell	30075-77
For specific Roswell Zip Codes call (404) 993-6778, or your local postmaster.	
Round Oak	31038
Roundtop	30540
Rover	30292
Rowena	31713
Roxanna	30132
Royston	30662
Ruckersville	30635
Rudden	31024
Rupert	31081
Russell	30680
Russellville	31016
Rutledge	30663
Rydal	30171
Ryo	30139
Saginaw	31554
St. Charles	30259
St. Clair	30816
St. George	31646
St. Marks	30230
St. Marys	31558
St. Marys Hills (Part of Columbus)	31906
St. Simons Island	31522
Sale City	31784
Salem Arms	30906
Sanborn	31705
Sandalwood	31701
Sand Bed	31047
Sandersville	31082
Sandfly	31406
Sand Hill (Brooks County)	31778
Sand Hill (Carroll County)	30180
Sand Hill (Muscogee County)	31905
Sand Hills	30904
Sandtown	30673
Sandy Cross (Franklin County)	30662
Sandy Cross (Oglethorpe County)	30627
Sandy Plains	30075
Sandy Springs	30328
Sanford (Madison County)	30646
Sanford (Stewart County)	31815

	ZIP
Sangrena Woods (Part of Pooler)	31322
Santa Claus	30436
Sapelo Island	31327
Sapp	31014
Sardis	30456
Sargent	30275
Sasser	31785
Satolah	30525
Sautee-Nacoochee	30571
Savannah	31401-99
For specific Savannah Zip Codes call (912) 236-7851, or your local postmaster.	
Savannah Gardens (Part of Savannah)	31404
Sawdust	30814
Sawhatchee	31723
Scarboro	30442
Scarbrough Cross Roads	30049
Scarlet	31569
Schatulga (Part of Columbus)	31820
Schlatterville	31501
Schley	31768
Scotland	31083
Scott	31002
Scottdale	30079
Scottsboro	31061
Screven	31560
Screven Fork	31320
Screvens Point	31410
Seabrook	31320
Seagraves	30646
Sea Island	31561
Sea Palms	31522
Sells	30548
Seney	30104
Senoia	30276
Sessoms	31554
Seville	31084
Shady Dale	31085
Shake Rag	30174
Shannon	30172
Sharon	30664
Sharon Park (Part of Garden City)	31408
Sharpe	30728
Sharphagen	31745
Sharpsburg	30277
Sharps Spur	30410
Sharp Top	30114
Shawnee	31329
Sheffield	30909
Shell Bluff	30830
Shellman	31786
Shellman Bluff	31331
Shelly	31778
Shenandoah	30265
Sheppards	30467
Sherwood (Clayton County)	30236
Sherwood (Richmond County)	30904
Sherwood Forest (Bibb County)	31206
Sherwood Forest (Coweta County)	30263
Sherwood Forest (DeKalb County)	30032
Sherwood Forest (Floyd County)	30161
Shields Crossroads	30707
Shiloh (Harris County)	31826
Shiloh (Lowndes County)	31634
Shiloh (Madison County)	30633
Shiloh (Sumter County)	31709
Shingler	31781
Shirley Hills (Part of Macon)	31211
Shirley Park (Part of Savannah)	31404
Shoal Creek	30553
Shoals	30820
Shurlington (Part of Macon)	31211
Sigsbee	31744
Silco	31537
Silica Hills	31705
Silk Hope	31401
Silk Mills	30635
Siloam	30665
Silver City	30506
Silver Creek	30173
Silver Crest	30906
Silver Pines	31206
Simpson	30217
Six Mile	30165
Skidaway Island	31411

	ZIP
Skipperton	31206
Skyland	30319
Skyland Terrace (Part of Savannah)	31401
Sky Valley	30525
Smarr	31086
Smiths Crossroads (Harris County)	31823
Smiths Crossroads (Troup County)	30240
Smithsonia	30628
Smithville	31787
Smyrna	30080-82
For specific Smyrna Zip Codes call (404) 436-5246, or your local postmaster.	
Snake Nation	30513
Snapfinger	30058
Snapping Shoals	30209
Snead	30809
Snellville	30278
Snipesville	31532
Snow Spring	31091
Snug Harbor Estates	30504
Soapstick	30701
Social Circle	30279
Sofkee	31206
Somerset Park (Part of Savannah)	31419
Sonoraville	30701
Soperton	30457
South Augusta	30901
South Base (Part of Warner Robins)	31098
South Cobb	30001
Southdale	30906
South Decatur	30034
South DeKalb Mall	30034
Southern Tech (Part of Marietta)	30062
Southgate Villa	30906
South Glen	30236
Southlake Mall (Part of Morrow)	30260
Southland	30906
South Macon (Part of Macon)	31206
South Moultrie (Part of Moultrie)	31768
South Nellieville	30901
South Newport	31323
Southover (Part of Savannah)	31405
South Pooler	31322
Southside (Part of Savannah)	31419
Spalding	31063
Spanish Trace	30906
Spann	31096
Sparks	31647
Sparta	31087
Spence	31779
Spencer Hills	30741
Split Silk	30249
Spout Spring Crossroads	30542
Spring Bluff	31565
Springfield	31329
Spring Hill (Chatham County)	31404
Spring Hill (Wheeler County)	30411
Spring Lake (Part of Columbus)	31909
Spring Place	30705
Springvale	31767
Springvale Station	31767
Spring Valley (Part of Columbus)	31909
Springview Acres (Part of Gainesville)	30501
Staley Heights (Part of Savannah)	31405
Stanleys Store	30436
Stanton Woods	30208
Stapleton	30823
Stark	30233
Starr	30207
Starrs Mill	30214
Starrsville	30209
State College	31404
Statenville	31648
State Sanitarium	31061
Statesboro	30458-60
For specific Statesboro Zip Codes call (912) 764-3223, or your local postmaster.	
Statham	30666
Staunton	31637
Steadham Store	31717

	ZIP
Steadman	30176
Steam Mill	31745
Steffen Wood Estates (Part of Pooler)	31322
Stellaville	30833
Stephens	30667
Stephensville	30752
Sterling	31525
Stevens Pottery	31031
Stewart	30209
Stewart Town	30752
Stilesboro	30120
Stillmore	30464
Stillwell	31329
Stilson	30415
Stockbridge	30281
Stockton	31649
Stockwood	30188
Stone Mountain	30086-88
For specific Stone Mountain Zip Codes call (404) 469-4544, or your local postmaster.	
Stone Mountain	30083
Stonewall (Part of Union City)	30349
Stoney Point	30170
Stovall (Habersham County)	30531
Stovall (Meriwether County)	30222
Stratford (Part of Atlanta)	30311
Strouds	31016
Stuckey	30428
Subligna	30747
Suches	30572
Sudie	30132
Sugar Hill (Gwinnett County)	30518
Sugar Hill (Hall County)	30507
Sugartown	30755
Sugar Valley	30746
Sulphur Springs	30738
Sulphur Springs Station	35967
Sumach	30705
Summertown	30466
Summerville	30747
Summit (Part of Twin City)	30471
Sumner	31789
Sumter	31709
Sunbury	31320
Sunny Acres	31701
Sunnydale Acres (Part of Macon)	31201
Sunny Side (Spalding County)	30284
Sunnyside (Ware County)	31501
Sunset	31768
Sunset Heights (Part of Gainesville)	30501
Sunset Park (Part of Savannah)	31404
Sunset Village	30286
Sunshine Acres (Part of Columbus)	31909
Sunsweet	31794
Surrency	31563
Sutalee	30184
Suttles Mill	30728
Suttons Corner	31724
Suwanee	30174
Swainsboro	30401
Swan Lake	30281
Swords	30625
Sybert	30817
Sycamore	31790
Sylvan Hills (Part of Atlanta)	30310
Sylvania	30467
Sylvester	31791
Tails Creek	30540
Talahi Island	31410
Talbotton	31827
Talking Rock	30175
Tallapoosa	30176
Tallulah Falls	30573
Tallulah Lodge	30573
Talmo	30575
Talona	30175
Tanglewood (Clarke County)	30606
Tanglewood (Richmond County)	30909
Tarboro	31568
Tarrytown	30470
Tarver	31631
Tarversville	31020
Tate	30177
Tate City	30525

	ZIP
Tatumsville (Part of Savannah)	31405
Tax	31826
Taylorsville	30178
Tazewell	31803
Teloga	30747
Temperance	31077
Temple	30179
Temple Grove	30711
Tennga	30751
Tennille	31089
Terrace Manor	30906
Terrell	31789
Texas	30217
Thalmann	31525
The Hill (Part of Augusta)	30904
The Landings	31411
The Rock	30285
Thomasboro	30455
Thomaston	30286
Thomasville (Fulton County)	30315
Thomasville (Thomas County)	31792*
	31799†
Thomas Woods	30906
Thompson	31601
Thompsonville	30738
Thomson	30824
Thornhedge	30274
Thornton Estates	30236
Thrift	30442
Thunderbolt	31404
Thurmock	30567
Thurston	30642
Thyatira	30549
Ticknor	31744
Tifton	31793†
	31794*
Tiger	30576
Tignall	30668
Tilton	30720
Timothy Estates	30606
Tippettville	31092
Tison	30427
Titus	30546
Toccoa	30577
	30598
For specific Toccoa Zip Codes call (706) 886-4058, or your local postmaster.	
Toccoa Falls	30598
Toco Hills	30329
Toledo	31646
Tom	31049
Toms Creek	30557
Toney Valley (Part of Decatur)	30032
Toomsboro	31090
Topeka Junction	30285
Town and Country	30815
Town and Country Acres	31707
Town and Country Shopping Center (Part of Marietta)	30060
Towns	31055
Townsend	31331
Traders Hill	31537
Tranquilla Woods (Part of Savannah)	31419
Trans	30728
Travisville	31634
Tremont (Crisp County)	31015
Tremont (Richmond County)	30907
Tremont Park (Part of Savannah)	31405
Trenton	30752
Trice	30286
Trickum	30755
Trimble	30230
Trion	30753
Troutman	31740
Trudie	31557
Tucker	30084*
	30085†
Tugaloo (Part of Tallulah Falls)	30573
Tulakes (Part of Columbus)	31904
Tunnel Hill	30755
Turin	30289
Turner City (Part of Albany)	31705
Turners Corner	30528
Turners Rock	31406
Turnerville	30580
Tusculum	31329
Tuxedo (Part of Atlanta)	30342

* Area Zip Code *† Post Office Boxes*

	ZIP
Twin City	30471
Twin Lakes	31636
Tybee Island	31328
Tyler	31064
Tyrone (Fayette County)	30290
Tyrone (Wilkes County)	30673
Ty Ty	31795
Tyus	30108
Unadilla	31091
Underground (Part of Atlanta)	31135
Union (Marion County)	31803
Union (Paulding County)	30179
Union (Quitman County)	31767
Union (Stewart County)	31821
Unionburg	31794
Union City	30291
Union Hill	30201
Union Point	30669
	30671

For specific Union Point Zip Codes call (706) 486-2508, or your local postmaster.

	ZIP
Unionville (Bibb County)	31204
Unionville (Tift County)	31794
Unity	30521
University Heights	30605
Upatoi (Part of Columbus)	31829
Upton	31533
Uptonville	31537
Uvalda	30473
Vada	31734
Valdosta	31601-04

For specific Valdosta Zip Codes call (912) 242-8201, or your local postmaster.

	ZIP
Valley Forge	30906
Valley View	30725
Valona	31332
Vanceville	31794
Vandiver Heights	30066
Vanna	30662
Vans Valley	30161
Van Wert	30153
Varnell	30756
Vaughn	30223
Veal	30108
Veazey	30642
Vega	30256
Veribest	30627
Vernonburg	31406
Vernon View	31406
Vesta	30627
Veterans Hospital (Part of Augusta)	30909
Victoria	30188
Victory	30108
Victory Heights (Part of Savannah)	31404
Vidalia	30474
Vidette	30434
Vienna	31092
View	30531
Villanow	30728
Villa Rica	30180
Vineland	30909
Vineville (Part of Macon)	31204
Vinings (Cobb County)	30339
Vinson Village (Part of Macon)	31206
Vista-Grove	30033
Vulcan	30738
Waco	30182
Wadley	30477
Wagon Wheel	31647
Wahoo	30533
Walden	31206
Waleska	30183
Walker Correctional Institution	30739

	ZIP
Walker Park	30655
Walkersville	31516
Wallace	31036
Wallaceville	30707
Walls Crossing	31806
Walnut Grove (Walker County)	30728
Walnut Grove (Walton County)	30209
Walnut Square (Part of Dalton)	30720
Walthourville	31333
Ware Correctional Institution	31503
Waresboro	31564
Wares Crossroads	30240
Waresville	30217
Waring	30720
Warm Springs	31830
Warner Robins	31088
	31093
	31095
	31098-99

For specific Warner Robins Zip Codes call (912) 922-3121, or your local postmaster.

	ZIP
Warren Terrace	30741
Warrenton	30828
Warsaw	30202
Warthen	31094
Warwick	31796
Washington	30673
Waterloo	31733
Waterport	30249
Waters	30467
Watkinsville	30677
Waverly (Camden County)	31565
Waverly (Richmond County)	30909
Waverly Hall	31831
Waverly Heights (Part of Macon)	31206
Waverly Park	30741
Wax	30104
Wayback	31746
Waycross	31501-03

For specific Waycross Zip Codes call (912) 283-2822, or your local postmaster.

	ZIP
Wayne Correctional Institution	31555
Waynesboro	30830
Waynesville	31566
Wayside	31032
Webb	30201
Weber	31639
Welcome	30263
Welcome Hill	30753
Wenona	31015
Weracoba Heights (Part of Columbus)	31906
Wesley (Emanuel County)	30401
Wesley (Taylor County)	31812
Wesleyan College (Part of Macon)	31201
Wesleyan Estates	31204
Wesleyan Woods (Part of Macon)	31210
West Augusta	30901
West Bainbridge (Part of Bainbridge)	31717
West Brow	30738
West Crossing	30176
West Dublin (Part of Dublin)	31021
West End (Floyd County)	30165
West End (Fulton County)	30310
Westgate (Part of Albany)	31707

	ZIP
Westgate Mall (Part of Macon)	31206
Westgate Park	30607
West Georgia College (Part of Carrollton)	30118
West Green	31567
Westhampton	30907
West Hills	30907
Westmont	30907
Westoak	30062
Weston	31832
West Point	31833
West Rome (Part of Rome)	30164
West Savannah (Part of Savannah)	31401
Westside (Catoosa County)	30741
Westside (Hall County)	30501
West Valdosta	31601
West Vidalia (Part of Vidalia)	30474
Westwick	30909
Westwood	31750
Wexwood	30274
Wheat Hill (Part of Garden City)	31408
Wheeler Heights	31201
Whigham	31797
Whistleville	30680
Whitaker	31543
White	30184
White Bluff (Part of Savannah)	31406
White City	30187
White Hall	30605
Whitehouse	30253
Whitemarsh Island	31404
White Oak	31568
White Plains	30678
Whitesburg	30185
Whitestone	30175
White Sulphur Springs	31822
Whitesville	31833
Whitworth	30553
Wilbanks Store	30711
Wildwood	30757
Wiley	30581
Willacoochee	31650
Willard	31024
Williamsburg Manor (Part of Savannah)	31419
Williamson	30292
Williams Plaza (Part of Warner Robins)	31093
Wilmington Island	31410
Wilmington Park	31410
Wilshire (Part of Savannah)	31419
Wilshire Estates (Part of Savannah)	31419
Wilsons Church	30558
Wilsonville	31554
Wimberly on the Marsh	31406
Wimbish Wood (Part of Macon)	31210
Winchester	31057
Winchester Hills	30207
Winder	30680
Windermere	30904
Windsor	30249
Windsor Estates	30263
Windsor Forest (Chatham County)	31419
Windsor Forest (Richmond County)	30904
Windsor Park (Lowndes County)	31601

	ZIP
Windsor Park (Muscogee County)	31909
Windward (Part of Savannah)	31419
Windy Ridge	30559
Winfield	30824
Winokur	31537
Winona Park	31503
Winship Gardens (Part of Macon)	31204
Winston	30187
Winterville	30683
Withers	31630
Woodbine	31569
Woodbury	30293
Woodcliff	30467
Woodgate	30909
Woodlake	30906
Woodlake Landing	30274
Woodland	31836
Woodland Hills (Laurens County)	31021
Woodland Hills (Walker County)	30741
Woodlawn (Part of Savannah)	31406
Woodlawn Estates (Part of Columbus)	31907
Woodlawn Terrace (Part of Garden City)	31406
Woodridge Estates	31410
Woods Grove	30582
Wood Station	30736
Woodstock	30188
Woodville (Chatham County)	31401
Woodville (Greene County)	30669
Woolsey	30214
Wooster	30218
Wormsloe	31406
Worth	31714
Worthville	30233
Wray	31798
Wrayswood	30677
Wrens	30833
Wright Landing	30236
Wright Square (Part of Savannah)	31401
Wrightsville	31096
Wymberly	31406
Wynngate	30907
Wynnton (Part of Columbus)	31906
Yahoola	30533
Yates	30263
Yatesville	31097
Yellow Bluff Fishing Village	31320
Yeomans	31742
Yonah	30510
Yonkers	31014
Yorktown (Part of Columbus)	31907
Yorkville	30132
Youngcane	30512
Young Harris	30582
Youngs	30125
Youngstown	30512
Youth	30249
Zaidee	30457
Zebina	30833
Zebulon	30295
Zeigler	30467
Zenith	31078
Zetella	30223
Zetto	31751
Zingara	30207

	ZIP
Ahualoa	96727
Ahuimanu	96744
Aiea	96701
Aiea Heights	96701
Aiea Shopping Center	96701
Aikahi	96734
Aina Haina	96821*
	96824†
Akasaki Camp	96774
Alabama Village	96784
Alewa Heights (Part of Honolulu)	96819
Aliamanu	96818
Amauulu Camps	96720
Anahola	96703
Andrade Camp	96783
Barbers Point Housing	96862
Barbers Point Naval Air Station	96762
Brigham Young University-Hawaii	96762
Camp 106	96727
Camp H.M. Smith Marine Corps Base	96861
Captain Cook	96704
Chinatown (Part of Honolulu)	96817
Chin Chuck	96710
Coconut Grove	96734
Coral Gardens	96744
Crestview	96797
Downtown (Part of Hilo)	96720
Downtown (Part of Honolulu)	96813
Downtown (Part of Lahaina)	96767
Dowsett Highlands (Part of Honolulu)	96817
Eight and One-half Mile Camp	96749
Eightmile Camp	96749
Eleele	96705
Elevenmile Homestead	96760
Ewa	96706
Ewa Beach	96706-07

For specific Ewa Beach Zip Codes call (808) 689-5033, or your local postmaster.

	ZIP
Ewa Gentry	96706
Fernandez Village	96706
Ford Island	96818
Fort Shafter	96819
Foster Village	96818
Glenwood	96771
Haaheo	96720
Haena	96714
Haiku	96708
Haiku-Pauwela	96708
Haina	96727
Hakalau	96710
Halaula	96755
Halawa (Hawaii County)	96755
Halawa (Honolulu County)	96701
Halawa (Maui County)	96748
Halawa Heights	96701
Halawa Hills	96701
Haleiwa	96712
Halepalaoa Landing	96763
Haliimaile	96768
Hamoa	96713
Hana	96713
Hanalei	96714
Hanamaulu	96715
Hanapepe	96716
Hanapepe Heights	96716
Haou	96713
Happy Valley	96793
Hauula	96717
Hawaiian Beaches	96778
Hawaiian Ocean View	96704
Hawaiian Paradise Park	96778
Hawaiian Village (Part of Honolulu)	96813
Hawaii Kai (Part of Honolulu)	96825
Hawaii National Park	96718
Hawaii State Hospital	96744
Hawi	96719
Heeia	96744
Hickam Air Force Base	96818
Hickam Housing	96818
Highway Village	96728
Hilo	96720*
	96721†
Hoaeae	96797
Hokamahoe House Lot	96764
Holualoa	96725
Honalo	96750
Honaunau	96726

	ZIP
Honaunau-Napoopoo	96726
Honohina	96710
Honokaa	96727
Honokahua	96761
Honokai Hale	96707
Honokohau	96725
Honokowai	96761
Honolulu	**96801-39**
	96860

For specific Honolulu Zip Codes call (808) 423-3990, or your local postmaster.

COLLEGES & UNIVERSITIES

	ZIP
Chaminade University of Honolulu	96816
Hawaii Pacific College	96813
University of Hawaii at Manoa	96822

FINANCIAL INSTITUTIONS

	ZIP
American Savings Bank, F.S.B.	96813
Bank of Hawaii	96813
Central Pacific Bank	96813
City Bank	96813
First Federal Savings & Loan Association of America	96813
First Hawaiian Bank	96813
Hawaii National Bank	96817
International Savings & Loan Association, Ltd.	96813
Liberty Bank	96817
Pioneer Federal Savings Bank	96813
Territorial Savings & Loan Association	96813

HOSPITALS

	ZIP
Kuakini Medical Center	96817
Queen's Medical Center	96813
Tripler Army Medical Center	96859

HOTELS/MOTELS

	ZIP
Alana Waikiki	96815
Ambassador Hotel of Waikiki	96815
Best Western WaikikiTower	96815
Breakers	96815
Colony Surf Hotel	96815
Coral Reef Hotel	96815
Halekulani Hotel	96815
Hawaiiana Hotel	96815
Hawaiian Monarch	96815
Hawaiian Regent	96815
Hawaiian Waikiki Beach Hotel	96815
Hilton Hawaiian Village	96815
Holiday Inn-Honolulu Airport	96819
Hyatt Regency Waikiki	96815
Ilikai	96815
Ilima Hotel	96815
Kahala Hilton	96816
Miramar at Waikiki	96815
New Otani Kaimana Beach Hotel	96815
Outrigger Coral Seas	96815
Outrigger East	96815
Outrigger Malia	96815
Outrigger Prince Kuhio	96815
Outrigger Surf	96815
Outrigger West	96815
Pacific Beach Hotel	96815
Pagoda Hotel	96814
Park Shore Hotel	96815
Royal Hawaiian Hotel	96815
Sheraton Princess Kaiulani Hotel	96815
Sheraton-Waikiki	96815
Waikiki Beachcomber	96815
Waikikian On The Beach	96815
Honomakau	96755
Honomu	96728
Honouliuli	96706
Honuapo	96772
Hookena	96704
Hoolehua	96729
Hoopuloa	96726
Huehue	96725
Huelo	96708
Iroquois Point	96706
Iwasaki Camp	96760
Iwilei (Part of Honolulu)	96817

	ZIP
Kaaawa	96730
Kaahumanu Center	96732
Kaalaea	96744
Kaalawai	96821
Kaanapali	96761
Kaapahu	96776
Kaapoko Homesteads	96781
Kaauhuhu Homesteads	96719
Kaawanui Village	96769
Kahakuloa	96793
Kahala Mall	96816
Kahaluu (Hawaii County)	96725
Kahaluu (Honolulu County)	96744
Kahaluu-Keauhou	96725
Kahana (Honolulu County)	96717
Kahana (Maui County)	96761
Kahei Homesteads	96719
Kahua	96755
Kahuku (Hawaii County)	96772
Kahuku (Honolulu County)	96731
Kahului	96732*
	96733†
Kaiaakea	96773
Kaieie Homesteads	96781
Kailua (Honolulu County)	96734
Kailua (Maui County)	96708
Kailua Kona	96739-40
	96745

For specific Kailua Kona Zip Codes call (808) 329-1927, or your local postmaster.

	ZIP
Kai Malino	96704
Kaimu	96778
Kaimuki (Part of Honolulu)	96816
Kainaliu	96750
Kainalu	96748
Kaiwiki	96720
Kalae	96757
Kalaheo	96741
Kalamaula	96748
Kalaoa	96740
Kalaoa Homesteads	96725
Kalapana	96778
Kalauao	96701
Kalaupapa	96742
Kalepolepo	96753
Kalihi (Part of Honolulu)	96819
Kalihi Kai (Part of Honolulu)	96818
Kalihi Shopping Center (Part of Honolulu)	96819
Kalihiwai	96754
Kaluaaha	96748
Kamaili	96778
Kamalo	96748
Kamehameha Heights (Part of Honolulu)	96819
Kamiloloa	96748
Kamooloa	96791
Kamuela	96743
Kaneohe	96744
Kaneohe Station	96863
Kaniahiku Village	96778
Kapaa	96746
Kapaau	96755
Kapahulu (Part of Honolulu)	96815
Kapaia	96766
Kapaka	96747
Kapalama (Part of Honolulu)	96817
Kapalua	96761
Kapehu	96780
Kapoho	96778
Kapulena	96727
Kaumakani	96747
Kaumalapau	96763
Kaumana	96720
Kaunakakai	96748
Kaupakalua	96708
Kaupo	96713
Kawaihae	96743
Kawaihua	96746
Kawailoa	96712
Kawailoa Beach	96712
Kawainui	96783
Kawela (Honolulu County)	96731
Kawela (Maui County)	96748
Keaau	96749
Keaau Camp	96749
Keaau Ranch	96749
Kealakehe Homesteads	96740
Kealakekua	96750
Kealia	96751
Keanae	96708
Keauhou	96740
Keaukaha	96720
Keawakapu	96753

	ZIP
Keehia	96774
Keei	96726
Kehena	96778
Kekaha	96752
Kelawea	96761
Keokea (Hawaii County)	96704
Keokea (Maui County)	96790
Keolu Hills	96734
Kihei	96753
Kilauea	96754
Kilauea Military Camp	96718
Kilauea Settlement	96785
Kipahulu	96713
Kipu (Kauai County)	96766
Kipu (Maui County)	96757
Koali	96713
Koele	96763
Kokee	96752
Kokohahi	96744
Kokomo	96708
Kolekole Beach Park	96710
Kolo	96704
Koloa	96756
Kualapuu	96757
Kualoa	96730
Kuhio Village	96743
Kuhua	96761
Kukaiau	96776
Kukui	96771
Kukuihaele	96727
Kukuiula	96756
Kukui Village	96774
Kula	96790
Kumukumu	96703
Kunia	96759
Kupolo	96766
Kurtistown	96760
Lahaina	96761*
	96767†
Lahaina Shopping Center	96761
Laie	96762
Lalakoa	96763
Lanai City	96763
Lanikai	96734
Lanikai Heights	96734
Laupahoehoe	96764
Laupahoehoe Point	96764
Lawai	96765
Lihue	96766
Lihue Shopping Center	96766
Lower Paia	96779
Lower Village	96706
Lualualei	96792
Lualualei Homesteads	96792
Maalaea	96793
McGerrow Village	96784
McGrew Point	96701
Maili	96792
Makaha	96792
Makaha Valley	96792
Makakilo City	96706
Makapala	96755
Makawao	96768
Makaweli	96769
Makena	96753
Makiki	96822-23
	96826

For specific Makiki Zip Codes call (808) 423-3990, or your local postmaster.

	ZIP
Makiki Heights (Part of Honolulu)	96822
Mana	96752
Mark Twain Estates	96772
Maulua	96780
Maunalani Heights (Part of Honolulu)	96816
Maunaloa	96770
Maunalua	96816
Maunawili	96734
Mililani Town	96789
Milolii	96726
Milo Village	96774
Moanalua (Part of Honolulu)	96819
Moiliili (Part of Honolulu)	96814
Mokuleia	96791
Momilani Estates	96782
Mountain View	96771
Muolea	96713
Naalehu	96772
Nanakuli	96792
Napili	96761
Napili-Honokowai	96761
Napoopoo	96704
Naval Communication Station	96786
Navy Cantonment (Part of Honolulu)	96818

* Area Zip Code   † Post Office Boxes

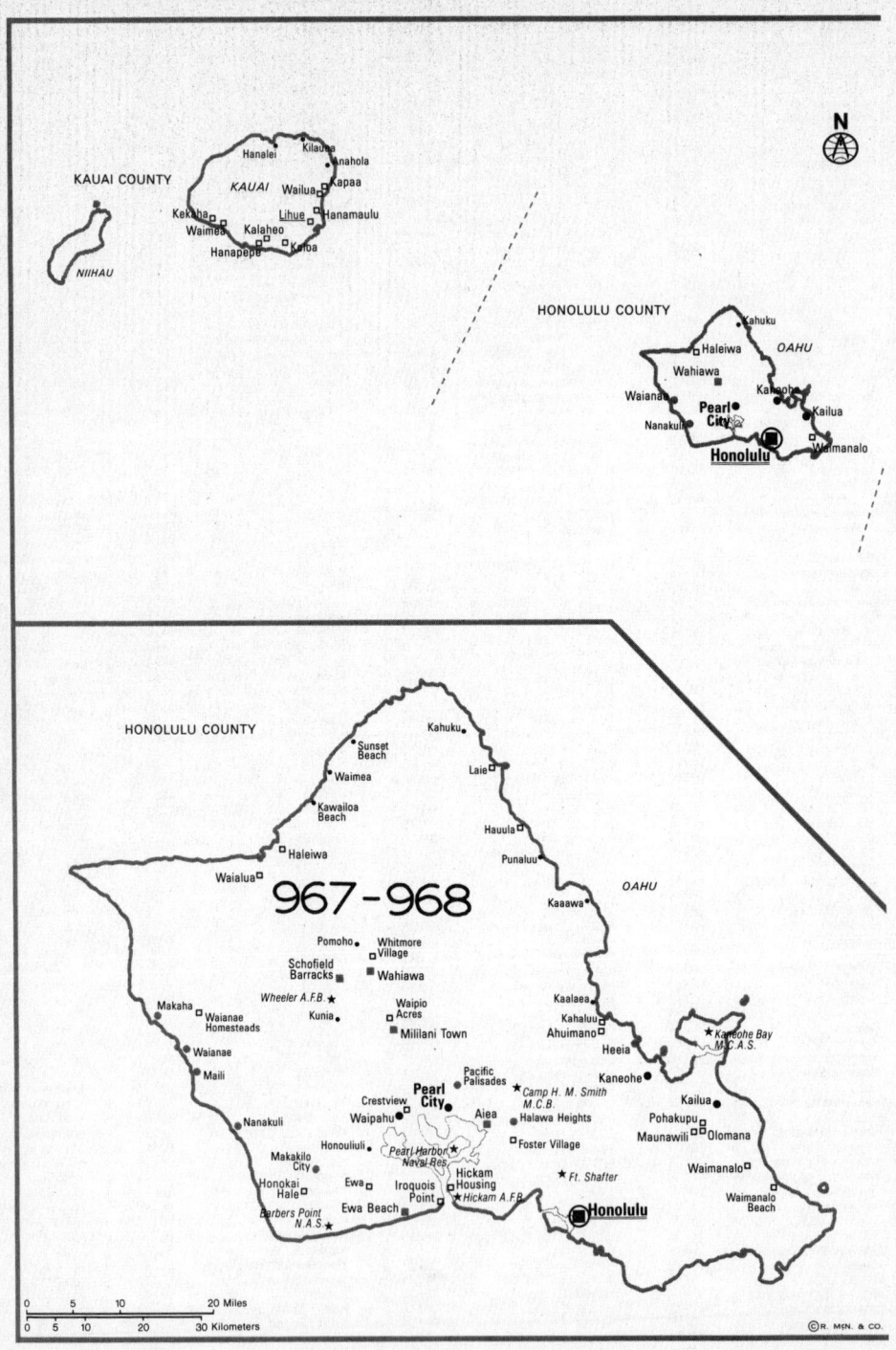

N

KAUAI COUNTY

KAUAI

Hanalei
Kilauea
Anahola
Wailua
Kapaa
Kekaha
Lihue
Hanamaulu
Waimea
Kalaheo
Hanapepe
Koloa

NIIHAU

HONOLULU COUNTY

OAHU

Kahuku
Haleiwa
Wahiawa
Kaneohe
Waianae
Pearl City
Kailua
Nanakuli
Honolulu
Waimanalo

HONOLULU COUNTY

967-968

Kahuku
Sunset Beach
Waimea
Laie
Kawailoa Beach
Hauula
Haleiwa
Punaluu
Waialua
OAHU
Kaaawa
Pomoho
Whitmore Village
Schofield Barracks
Wahiawa
Wheeler A.F.B.
Kunia
Waipio Acres
Makaha
Waianae Homesteads
Mililani Town
Kaalaea
Waianae
Kahaluu
Ahuimano
Maili
Heeia
Kaneohe Bay M.C.A.S.
Pacific Palisades
Kaneohe
Nanakuli
Pearl City
Camp H. M. Smith M.C.B.
Kailua
Crestview
Aiea
Pohakupu
Waipahu
Halawa Heights
Maunawili
Olomana
Honouliuli
Foster Village
Makakilo City
Pearl Harbor Naval Res.
Hickam Housing
Ft. Shafter
Waimanalo
Honokai Hale
Ewa
Iroquois Point
Hickam A.F.B.
Waimanalo Beach
Barbers Point N.A.S.
Ewa Beach
Honolulu

0   5   10   20 Miles
0 5 10   20   30 Kilometers

© R. M‡N. & CO.

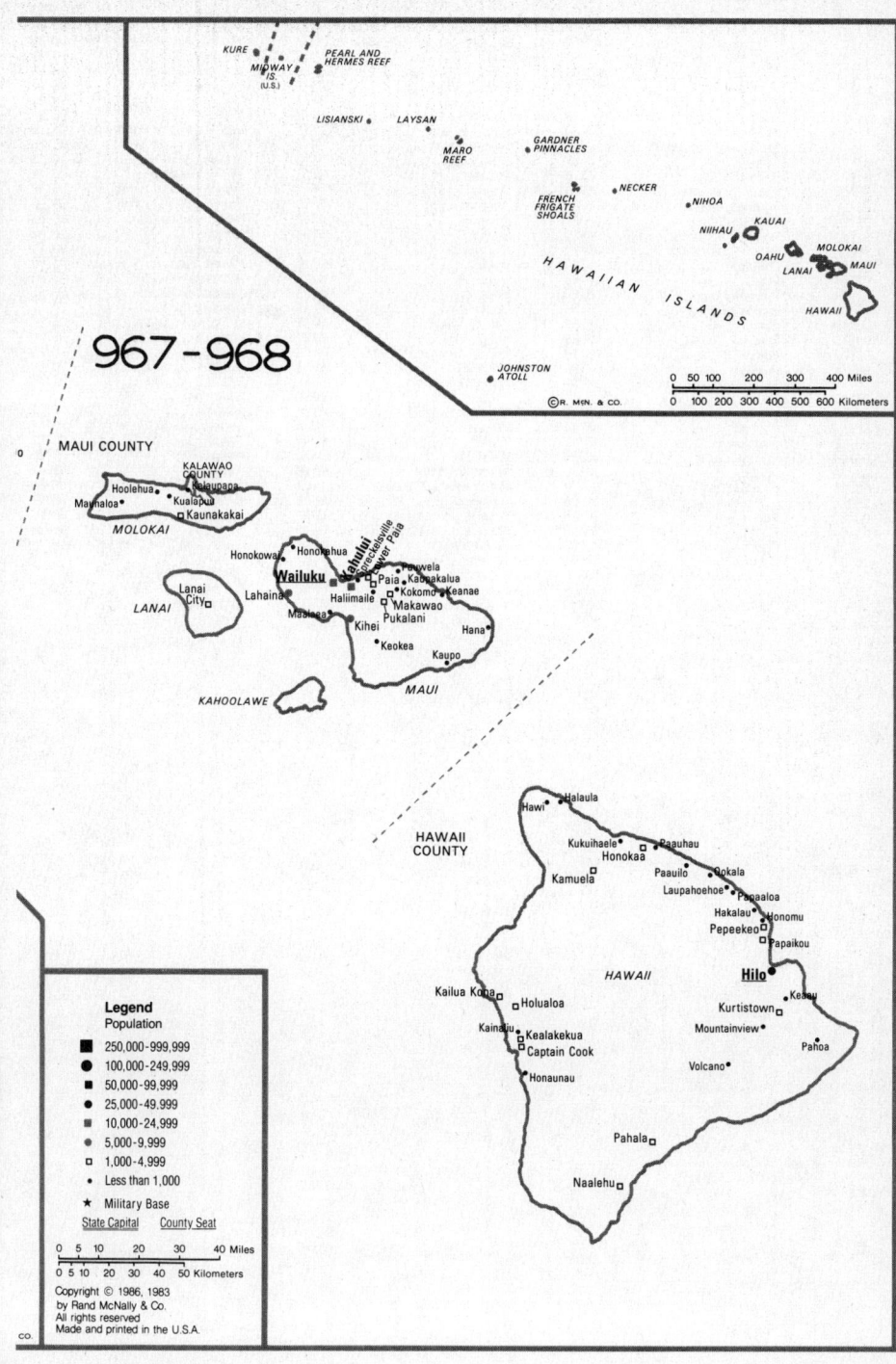

KURE
MIDWAY
IS.
(U.S.)
PEARL AND
HERMES REEF

LISIANSKI • LAYSAN

MARO
REEF

GARDNER
PINNACLES

FRENCH
FRIGATE
SHOALS
NECKER

NIHOA

NIIHAU
KAUAI

OAHU
LANAI
MOLOKAI
MAUI

H A W A I I A N   I S L A N D S

HAWAII

JOHNSTON
ATOLL

©R. MⁿN. & CO.

0 50 100   200   300   400 Miles

0   100 200 300 400 500 600 Kilometers

967-968

MAUI COUNTY

KALAWAO
COUNTY
Hoolehua • • Kalaupapa
• Kualapuu
Maunaloa • • Kaunakakai

MOLOKAI

Honokowai •
Honokahua •
Kahului
Brickskalsville
Lower Paia
Puuwela
Paia • Kaupakalua
Kokomo • Keanae

Wailuku
Lanai
City
LANAI
Lahaina •
Maalaea •
Haliimaile
Makawao
Pukalani
Kihei •
Keokea •
Hana

Kaupo
MAUI

KAHOOLAWE

HAWAII
COUNTY

Hawi • • Halaula

Kukuihaele • • Paauhau
Honokaa •
Kamuela • Paauilo • • Ookala
Laupahoehoe • • Papaaloa
Hakalau • • Honomu
Pepeekeo • • Papaikou

HAWAII

Kailua Kona • • Holualoa

Kainaliu •
Kealakekua
Captain Cook •
Honaunau •

Hilo
Keaau •
Kurtistown •
Mountainview •
Pahoa •

Volcano •

Pahala •

Naalehu •

	ZIP		ZIP		ZIP		ZIP
Navy Terminal (Part of Honolulu)	96818	Pauwela	96708	Puuwai	96769	Waiau View Estates	96782
Nawiliwili	96766	Pearl City	96782	Renton Village	96706	Waiawa Correctional	
Newtown Estates	96701	Pearl City Heights	96782	Royal Hawaiian (Part of		Facility	96782
Nine Miles	96749	Pearl Harbor Naval		Honolulu)	96815	Waiehu	96793
Ninole	96773	Reservation	96860	St. Louis Heights (Part of		Waiehu Village	96793
Niulii	96755	Pearl Harbor Naval Supply		Honolulu)	96816	Waihee	96793
Niumalu	96766	Center	96860	Schofield Barracks	96786	Waihee-Waiehue	96793
Niu Valley (Part of		Pepeekeo	96783	Spanish Village B	96784	Waikane	96744
Honolulu)	96821	Pepeekeo Mill	96783	Spreckelsville	96779	Waikapu	96793
Niu Valley Shopping		Pihana	96793	Submarine Base	96818	Waikele	96797
Center (Part of		Piihonua	96720	Sunset Beach	96712	Waikiki (Part of Honolulu)	96815
Honolulu)	96821	Pohakea Homesteads	96776	Tantalus (Part of		Waikoloa	96738
Niu Village	96774	Pohakupu	96734	Honolulu)	96822	Wailea	96710
Numila	96705	Pohoiki	96778	Tenney	96706	Wailea-Makena	96753
Olinda	96768	Poipu	96756	Timber Town (Part of		Wailua (Kauai County)	96746
Olomana	96734	Pomoho	96786	Honolulu)	96826	Wailua (Maui County)	96708
Olowalu	96761	Port Allen	96705	Ualapue	96748	Wailua Homesteads	96746
Omao	96756	Portlock	96825	Ulumalu	96708	Wailuku	96793
Omapio	96790	Prince Kuhio Plaza	96720	Ulupalakua	96790	Wailupe	96821
Onomea	96781	Princeville	96722	Umikoa	96776	Waimalu	96701
Ookala	96774	Puako	96743	Union Mill	96719	Waimanalo	96795
Opihikao	96778	Pualaea Homestead	96764	University	96822	Waimanalo Beach	96795
Orpheum Village	96779	Pua Loke	96766	Upolu Point	96719	Waimea (Honolulu	
Paauhau	96775	Puhi	96766	Varona Village	96706	County)	96712
Paauhau Mauka	96727	Pukalani	96788	Village Park	96797	Waimea (Kauai County)	96796
Paauilo	96776	Pukoo	96748	Village Seven	96705	Wainaku	96720
Pacific Heights (Part of		Pulehu	96790	Volcano	96785	Wainee	96761
Honolulu)	96817	Punaluu (Hawaii County)	96777	Wahiawa (Honolulu		Wainiha	96714
Pacific Palisades	96782	Punaluu (Honolulu		County)	96786	Waiohinu	96772
Pahala	96777	County)	96717	Wahiawa (Kauai County)	96705	Waipahu	96797
Pahoa	96778	Puohala Village	96744	Waiahole	96744	Waipio (Hawaii County)	96727
Pahoehoe	96704	Pupukea	96712	Waiaka	96743	Waipio (Honolulu County)	96797
Paia	96779	Puuanahulu	96725	Waiakea	96720	Waipio Acres	96786
Palama (Part of Honolulu)	96817	Puueo	96720	Waiakea Camps	96720	Waipouli	96746
Palani Junction	96725	Pu'uhonua o Honaunau		Waialae-Kahala (Part of		Waipunalei Homesteads	96764
Panaewa	96720	National Historical Park	96726	Honolulu)	96816	Wharf	96761
Papa	96704	Puu Hue	96719	Waialua (Honolulu County)	96791	Wheeler Air Force Base	96854
Papaaloa	96780	Puuiki	96713	Waialua (Maui County)	96748	Whitmore Village	96786
Papaikou	96781	Puunene	96784	Waialua Mill	96791	Wilhelmina Rise (Part of	
Paukaa	96720	Puunoa	96761	Waianae (Honolulu		Honolulu)	96816
Paukukalo	96793	Puunui (Part of Honolulu)	96819	County)	96792	Woodlawn (Part of	
Paumalu	96712	Puuohala	96793	Waianae Homesteads	96792	Honolulu)	96822
		Puu Waawaa	96740	Waiau	96782	Wood Valley	96777

Place	ZIP
Aberdeen	83210
Acequia	83350
Ahsahka	83520
Alameda (Part of Pocatello)	83201
Albion	83311
Aldape Heights (Part of Boise)	83701
Algoma	83860
Almo	83312
Alpha	83611
Alton	83254
American Falls	83211
Ammon	83404
Anderson Dam	83647
Annis	83442
Apple Valley	83660
Arbon	83212
Arbon Valley	83203
Archer	83440
Arco	83213
Argora	83423
Arimo	83214
Artesian City	83344
Ashton	83420
Athol	83801
Atlanta	83601
Atomic City	83215
Avery	83802
Avon	83823
Baker	83467
Bancroft	83217
Banida	83263
Banks	83602
Bannock (Part of Pocatello)	83204
Basalt	83218
Basin	83346
Bates	83422
Bayview	83803
Beachs Corner	83401
Bear	83612
Bellevue	83313
Belmont	83801
Bench	83241
Benewah	83861
Bennington	83254
Berger	83301
Bern	83220
Big Creek	83677
Big Little Acres	83338
Big Springs (Part of Island Park)	83433
Blackfoot	83221
Black Lake	83861
Blackrock	83245
Blaine	83843
Blanchard	83804
Bliss	83314
Bloomington	83223
Boise	83701-88
For specific Boise Zip Codes call (208) 383-4211, or your local postmaster.	
Boise Airport (Part of Boise)	83715
Boise Town Square (Part of Boise)	83701
Boles	83522
Bone	83427
Bonners Ferry	83805
Borah (Part of Boise)	83702
Bovill	83806
Bowmont	83686
Box Canyon (Part of Island Park)	83429
Bradley (Part of Kellogg)	83837
Bridge	83342
Bruneau	83604
Bruneau Valley	83604
Buhl	83316
Buist	83243
Bunn	83873
Burgdorf	83638
Burke	83873
Burley	83318
Burmah	83349
Burton	83440
Butler Bay	83861
Butte City	83213
Cabinet	83811
Cache	83452
Calder	83808
Caldwell	83605*
	83606†
Caldwell Labor Camp	83605
Cambridge (Bannock County)	83234

Place	ZIP
Cambridge (Washington County)	83610
Cameron	83537
Cardiff	83546
Care-Free Estates	83318
Carey	83320
Careywood	83809
Carlin Bay	83833
Carmen	83462
Cascade	83611
Castleford	83321
Cataldo	83810
Cathedral Pines	83340
Cavendish	83537
Central	83217
Central Cove	83676
Challis	83226
Chapin	83455
Chatcolet	83851
Cherry Creek	83252
Cherry Lane (Part of Boise)	83705
Chester	83421
Chesterfield	83217
Chilco	83801
Chubbuck	83202
Churchill	83318
Clagstone	83856
Clark Fork	83811
Clarkia	83812
Clawson	83452
Clayton	83227
Clearwater	83539
Clementsville	83436
Cleveland	83263
Cliffs	97910
Clifton	83228
Clover	83316
Coats	83350
Cobalt	83229
Cocolalla	83813
Coeur d'Alene	83814-16
For specific Coeur d'Alene Zip Codes call (208) 773-4922, or your local postmaster.	
Coeur d'Alene Indian Reservation	83851
Colburn	83865
Cole Village (Part of Boise)	83704
Collister (Part of Boise)	83703
Coltman	83401
Columbus Park (Part of Boise)	83705
Conda	83230
Conkling Park	83876
Conner	83342
Coolin	83821
Cooperville	83554
Corral	83322
Cotterel	83323
Cottonwood	83522
Council	83612
Country Club Mall (Part of Idaho Falls)	83401
Country Club Manor (Part of Boise)	83705
Country Club Terrace (Part of Boise)	83705
Craigmont	83523
Crescent	83537
Crouch	83622
Crystal	83672
Culdesac	83524
Culver	83865
Cuprum	83612
Curry	83328
Dalton Gardens	83814
Daniels	83252
Darlington	83255
David Taylor Research Center, Acoustic Research Detachment	83803
Davis Acres (Part of Garden City)	83704
Dayton	83232
Deary	83823
Declo	83323
Deep Creek (Oneida County)	83252
Deep Creek (Twin Falls County)	83316
Delta	83873
Dent	83544
Denton (Part of Boise)	83704
Denver	83530
Desmet	83824
Dietrich	83324
Dingle	83233

Place	ZIP
Dixie	83525
Doles	83605
Donnelly	83615
Dover	83825
Downey	83234
Driggs	83422
Drummond	83420
Dubois	83423
Duck Valley Indian Reservation	89832
Dudley	83810
Eagle (Ada County)	83616
Eagle (Shoshone County)	83874
Eagle Rock (Part of Idaho Falls)	83402
Easley Hot Springs	83340
East Hope	83836
East Kamiah	83536
East Lewiston (Part of Lewiston)	83501
Eastport	83826
Eaton	83672
Echo Beach	83858
Eddiville	83814
Eden	83325
Edgemere	83856
Edmonds	83440
Egin	83445
Elba	83326
Elk City	83525
Elk River	83827
Ellis	83235
Elmira	83862
Emida	83861
Emmett	83617
Enaville	83839
Enkraft	83350
Enrose	83605
Evergreen	83654
Excelsior Beach	83858
Fairfield	83327
Fairview (Franklin County)	83263
Fairview (Twin Falls County)	83316
Fall Creek (Elmore County)	83647
Fall Creek (Idaho County)	83530
Falls City	83338
Featherville	83647
Felt	83424
Fenn	83531
Ferdinand	83526
Fernan Lake Village	83814
Fernwood	83830
Filer	83328
Firth	83236
Fish Haven	83287
Florence	83542
Fort Hall (Bannock County)	83203
Fort Hall (Bingham County)	83203
Fort Hall Indian Reservation	83203
Fox Creek	83455
Franklin (Ada County)	83704
Franklin (Franklin County)	83237
Franklin Park (Part of Boise)	83704
Fraser	83544
Freedom	83120
Frisco	83873
Fruitland	83619
Fruitvale	83620
Galena	83340
Gannett	83313
Gardena	83629
Garden City	83714
Garden Valley	83622
Garfield	83442
Garwood	83835
Gem	83873
Genesee	83832
Geneva	83238
Georgetown	83239
Gibbonsville	83463
Gibson	83221
Gibson City (Part of Pinehurst)	83850
Gifford	83541
Glendale	83263
Glengary	83864
Glenns Ferry	83623
Glenwood (Clearwater County)	83544
Glenwood (Idaho County)	83536
Golden	83530
Gooding	83330
Goodrich	83612

Place	ZIP
Goshen	83274
Grace	83241
Grand Teton Mall (Part of Idaho Falls)	83401
Grandview (Bingham County)	83210
Grand View (Owyhee County)	83624
Grangemont	83544
Grangeville	83530
Granite	83801
Grant	83442
Grasmere	83604
Gray	83285
Greencreek	83533
Greenleaf	83626
Greenwood	83335
Greer	83544
Gross	83657
Groveland	83221
Gwenford	83252
Hagerman	83332
Hailey	83333
Hamer	83425
Hammett	83627
Hampton	83857
Hansen	83334
Harpster	83539
Harrison	83833
Harvard	83834
Hatch	83217
Hatwai	83501
Hauser	83854
Havens	83221
Hayden	83835
Hayden Lake	83835
Hazelton	83335
Headquarters	83534
Heglar	83211
Heise	83443
Helmer	83823
Heman	83445
Henry	83230
Heyburn	83336
Hibbard	83440
Highlands (Part of Boise)	83702
Hill City	83337
Hillview (Part of Ammon)	83401
Holbrook	83243
Hollister	83301
Home Acres (Part of Boise)	83704
Homedale	83628
Honeysuckle Hills	83835
Hop (Part of Greenleaf)	83626
Hope	83836
Hornet	83612
Horseshoe Bend	83629
Hot Spring Landing	83333
Hot Springs	83604
Howe	83244
Hoyt	83802
Huckleberry Bay	83821
Huetter	83854
Hulen Meadows	83340
Humphrey	83446
Hunt	83325
Huston	83630
Idaho City	83631
Idaho Falls	83401-06
For specific Idaho Falls Zip Codes call (208) 523-3650, or your local postmaster.	
Idaho Maximum Security Institution	83701
Idahome	83323
Idmon	83423
Indian Cove	83627
Indian Hills (Part of Pocatello)	83204
Indian Valley	83632
Inkom	83245
Iona	83427
Irwin	83428
Island Park	83429
Jackson	83350
Jacques	83524
Jamestown	83274
Jerome	83338
Joel	83843
Johnny Creek (Part of Pocatello)	83204
Jonathan	83672
Joseph	83522
Judge Town	83546
Juliaetta	83535
Juniper	84336
Kamiah	83536

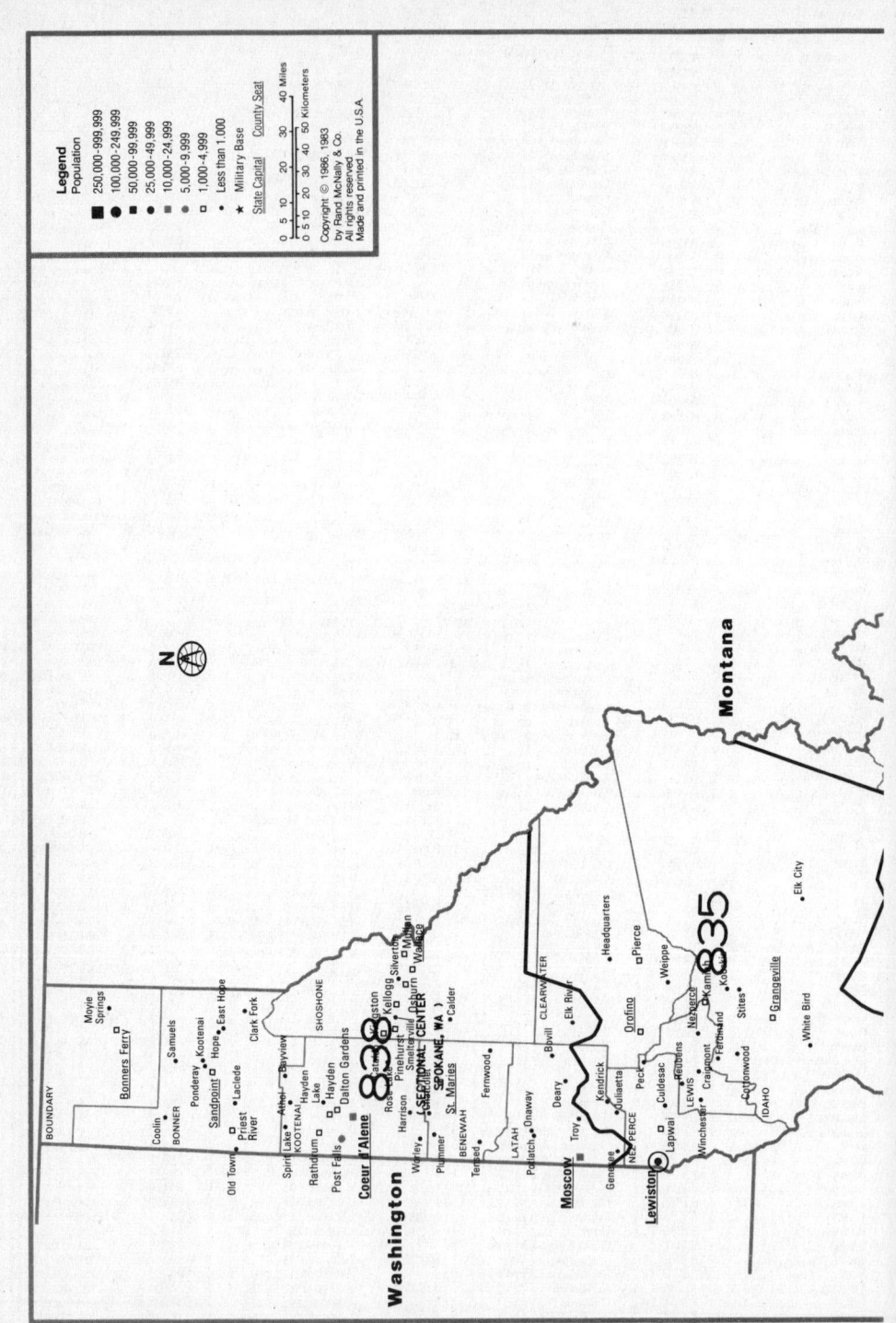

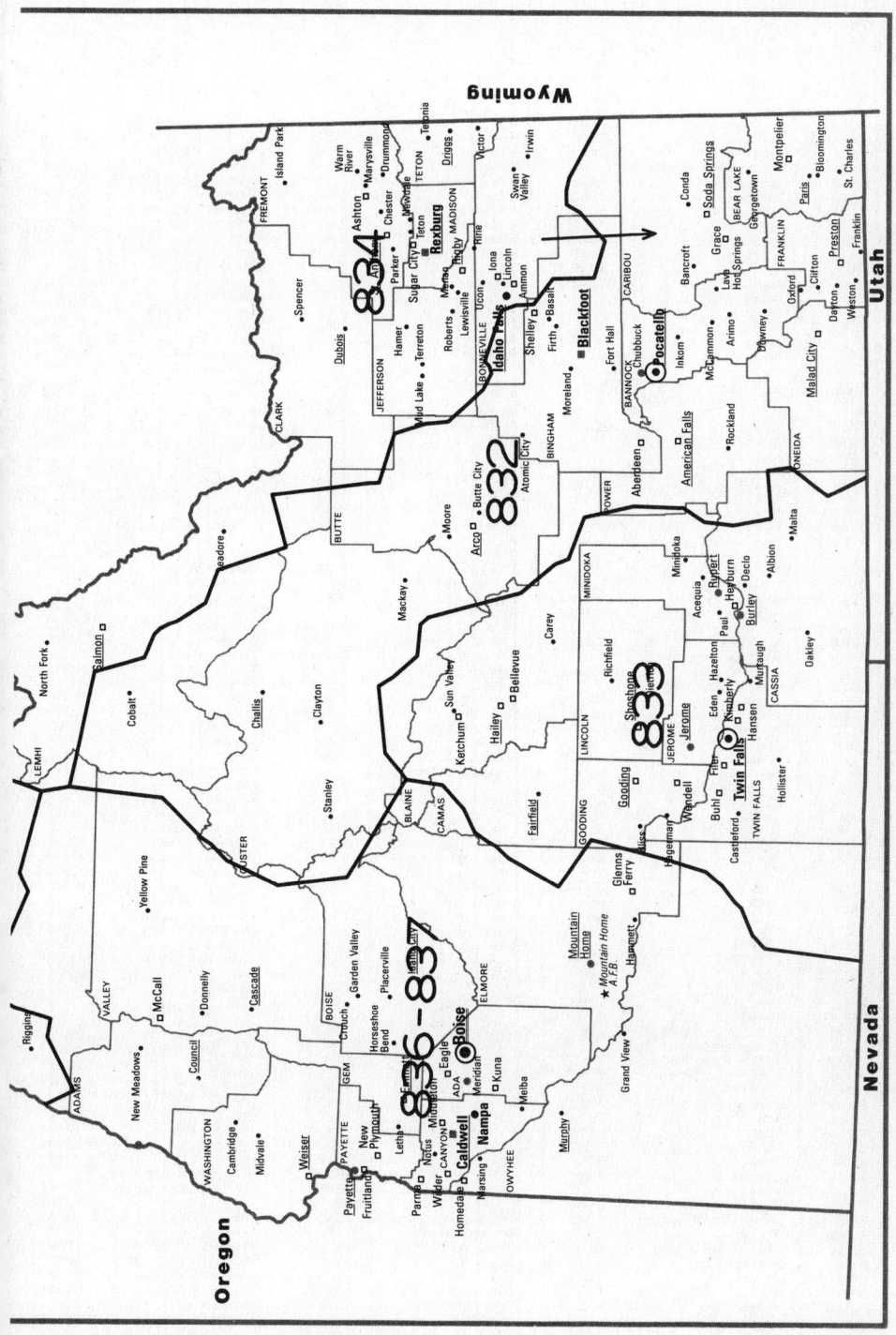

	ZIP
Karcher Mall (Part of Nampa)	83651
Kellogg	83837
Kendrick	83537
Ketchum	83340
Keuterville	83538
Kidder	83539
Kilgore	83423
Kimball	83236
Kimberly	83341
King Hill	83633
Kings Corner	83686
Kingston	83839
Knowlton Heights	83605
Kooskia	83539
Kootenai	83840
Kuna	83634
Labelle	83442
Laclede	83841
Lake Creek	83876
Lake Fork	83635
Lakeview	83803
Lamb Creek	83856
Lamont	83420
Lanark	83260
Lancaster Terrace (Part of Boise)	83702
Lane	83810
Lapwai	83540
Lardo (Part of McCall)	83638
Last Chance Resort (Part of Island Park)	83429
Lava Hot Springs	83246
Leadore	83464
Leland	83537
Lemhi	83465
Lenore	83541
Leslie	83255
Letha	83636
Lewiston	83501
Lewiston Orchards (Part of Lewiston)	83501
Lewisville	83431
Liberty	83260
Lidy Hot Springs	83423
Lincoln	83401
Linrose	83286
Lone Pine	83464
Lorenzo	83442
Lost River (Butte County)	83255
Lost River (Custer County)	83255
Lowell	83539
Lower Stanley	83278
Lowman	83637
Lucile	83542
Lund	83217
Lyman	83440
McArthur	83847
McCall	83638
McCammon	83250
Mace	83873
McGuires (Part of Post Falls)	83854
Mackay	83251
Macks Inn (Part of Island Park)	83433
Magic City	83313
Magic Resort	83352
Malad City	83252
Malta	83342
Mapleton	83263
Marble Creek	83808
Marion	83346
Marley (Part of Richfield)	83349
Marshcenter	83234
Marsing	83639
Marysville	83420
May	83253
Meadow Creek	83805
Meadows	83654
Meadowville	83276
Medimont	83842
Melba	83641
Menan	83434
Meridian	83642*
	83680†
Mesa	83643
Mica	83814
Midas	83864
Middleton	83644
Midvale	83645
Midway	83651
Miller Creek Settlement	89832
Milltown	83861
Milo	83401
Minidoka	83343
Minkcreek	83263
Mohler	83523

	ZIP
Montana Junction (Part of Pocatello)	83201
Monteview	83435
Montour	83617
Montpelier	83254
Moore	83255
Mora	83634
Moravia	83805
Moreland	83256
Morgans Alley (Part of Lewiston)	83501
Moscow	83843
Mountain Home	83647
Mountain Home Air Force Base	83648
Mountain View (Part of Boise)	83704
Mount Idaho	83530
Moyie Springs	83845
Mud Lake	83450
Mullan	83846
Murphy	83650
Murray	83874
Murtaugh	83344
Myrtle	83535
Naf	83342
Nampa	83651-53
	83686-87
For specific Nampa Zip Codes call (208) 466-8938, or your local postmaster.	
Naples	83847
Naval Administration Unit, Idaho Falls	83401
Neeley	83211
New Centerville	83631
Newdale	83436
New Meadows	83654
New Plymouth	83655
New Sweden	83402
Nezperce	83543
Nez Perce Indian Reservation	83540
Niter	83241
Nordman	83848
Norland	83343
North Fork	83466
North Idaho Correctional Institution	83522
North Lewiston (Part of Lewiston)	83501
North Shoshone	83352
Northside (Ada County)	83702
Northside (Gem County)	83617
Notus	83656
Nounan	83254
Nuclear Power Training Unit, Idaho Falls	83401
Oakley	83346
Obsidian	83340
Ola	83657
Old Town	83822
Onaway	83855
Oreana	83650
Orofino	83544
Orogrande	83525
Osburn	83849
Osgood	83402
Outlet Bay	83856
Ovid	83260
Oxford	83263
Page	83868
Palisades	83437
Palmetto (Part of Eagle)	83616
Palouse Empire Mall (Part of Moscow)	83843
Paradise Hot Springs	83647
Paris	83261
Park	83823
Parker	83438
Parma	83660
Patterson	83253
Paul	83347
Payette	83661
Pearl	83616
Peck	83545
Pedee (Part of Chatcolet)	83851
Pegram	83254
Pella	83318
Picabo	83348
Pierce	83546
Pine	83647
Pinehurst (Adams County)	83654
Pinehurst (Shoshone County)	83850
Pine Ridge	83612
Pine Ridge Mall (Part of Pocatello)	83201
Pingree	83262

	ZIP
Pinto Point	83821
Pioneerville	83631
Placerville	83666
Plano	83440
Pleasantview	83252
Plummer	83851
Pocatello	83201-02
	83204-06
For specific Pocatello Zip Codes call (208) 233-0800, or your local postmaster.	
Polaris (Part of Osburn)	83849
Pollock	83547
Ponderay	83852
Ponds Resort (Part of Island Park)	83429
Porthill	83853
Post Falls	83854
Potlatch	83855
Potlatch Junction	83855
Prairie	83647
Preston	83263
Prichard	83873
Priest River	83856
Princeton	83857
Raft River	83211
Ramsdell (Part of Chatcolet)	83851
Rathdrum	83858
Raymond	83114
Redfish Lake	83278
Red River Hot Springs	83525
Reno	83423
Reubens	83548
Rexburg	83440
Reynolds	83650
Richfield	83349
Riddle	83604
Rigby	83442
Riggins	83549
Ririe	83443
Riverdale	83263
Riverside (Bingham County)	83221
Riverside (Canyon County)	83605
Riverside (Clearwater County)	83544
Roberts	83444
Robin	83214
Rock Creek	83334
Rockford	83221
Rockford Bay	83814
Rockland	83271
Rocky Bar	83647
Rocky Point (Benewah County)	83851
Rocky Point (Bonner County)	83821
Rogerson	83302
Rose	83221
Roseberry	83615
Rose Lake	83810
Roseworth	83321
Roswell	83660
Roy	83271
Rupert	83350
Sagle	83860
St. Anthony	83445
St. Charles	83272
St. Joe	83861
St. John	83252
St. Leon	83401
St. Maries	83861
Salem	83440
Salmon	83467
Samaria	83252
Samuels	83862
Sanders	83870
Sandpoint	83864
Sandy Shores Addition	83821
Santa	83866
Selle	83864
Setters	83876
Sharon	83260
Shelley	83274
Shelton	83401
Sherwood Beach	83821
Shoshone	83352
Shoup	83469
Silver City	83650
Silver Creek Plunge	83602
Silver Sands Beach	83858
Silverton	83867
Skyline (Part of Idaho Falls)	83402
Slate Creek	83554
Slickpoo	83524
Small	83423

	ZIP
Smelter Heights (Part of Kellogg)	83837
Smelterville	83868
Smiths Ferry	83611
Soda Springs	83276
Soldier	83327
Soldiers Home (Part of Boise)	83704
South Boise (Part of Boise)	83706
South Gate Plaza (Part of Lewiston)	83501
South Park (Part of Pocatello)	83204
Southside (Part of Boise)	83706
Southwick	83537
Spalding	83551
Spencer	83446
Spirit Lake	83869
Springdale	83318
Springfield	83277
Squirrel	83420
Standrod	83342
Stanley	83278
Star	83669
Starkey	83620
Starrhs Ferry	83318
State Line	83854
Sterling	83210
Stites	83552
Stoddard	83686
Stone	83252
Sugar City	83448
Sunbeam	83278
Sunnydell	83440
Sunnyside	83864
Sunnyslope	83605
Sun Valley	83353-54
For specific Sun Valley Zip Codes call (208) 622-5265, or your local postmaster.	
Swan Falls	83634
Swanlake	83281
Swan Valley	83449
Sweet	83670
Sweetwater	83540
Syringa	83539
Taber	83221
Talache	83860
Tamarack	83612
Taylor	83401
Teakean	83541
Tendoy	83468
Tenmile	83642
Tensed	83870
Terreton	83450
Teton	83451
Tetonia	83452
Thatcher	83283
Thomas	83221
Thomas Junction	83221
Thornton	83440
Three Creek	83301
Topaz	83246
Transfer (Part of Lewiston)	83501
Treasureton	83263
Trestle Creek	83836
Triumph	83333
Troy	83871
Turner Bay	83833
Tuttle	83314
Twin Falls	83301*
	83303†
Twin Groves	83445
Twin Lakes	83858
Twinlow	83858
Tyhee	83201
Ucon	83454
Unity	83318
University (Part of Moscow)	83843
Ustick	83713
Valley View Heights (Part of Lewiston)	83501
Victor	83455
View	83318
Viola	83872
Virginia	83234
Waha	83501
Wallace	83873
Wapello	83221
Wardboro	83254
Wardner	83837
Warm Lake	83611
Warm River	83420
Warren	83671
Washoe	83661
Wayan	83276

* Area Zip Code   **† Post Office Boxes**

	ZIP		ZIP		ZIP		ZIP
Webb	83540	Westmond	83860	Whitney (Franklin County)	83263	Wolverine	83236
Weippe	83553	Westmoreland (Part of		Wilder	83676	Woodland	83536
Weiser	83672	Boise)	83704	Wilford	83445	Woodland Park	83873
Weitz	83605	West Mountain	83611	Winchester	83555	Woodruff	83252
Wendell	83355	Weston	83286	Winder	83263	Woodville	83274
Westgate Acres (Part of		Whiskeyjack	83864	Winona	83539	Worley	83876
Boise)	83704	White Bird	83554	Wolf Lodge	83814	Yellow Pine	83677
Westlake	83526	Whitney (Ada County)	83705				

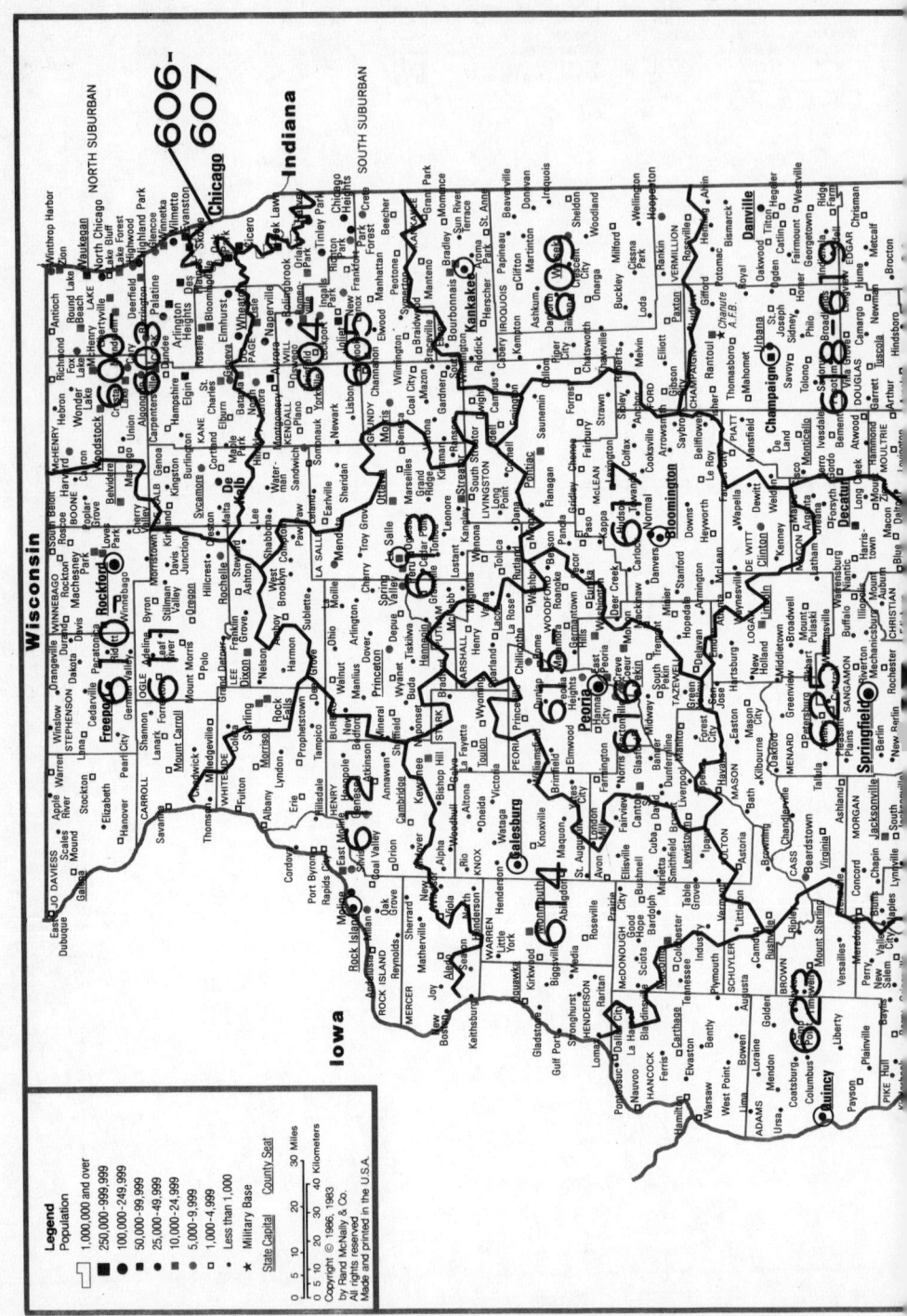

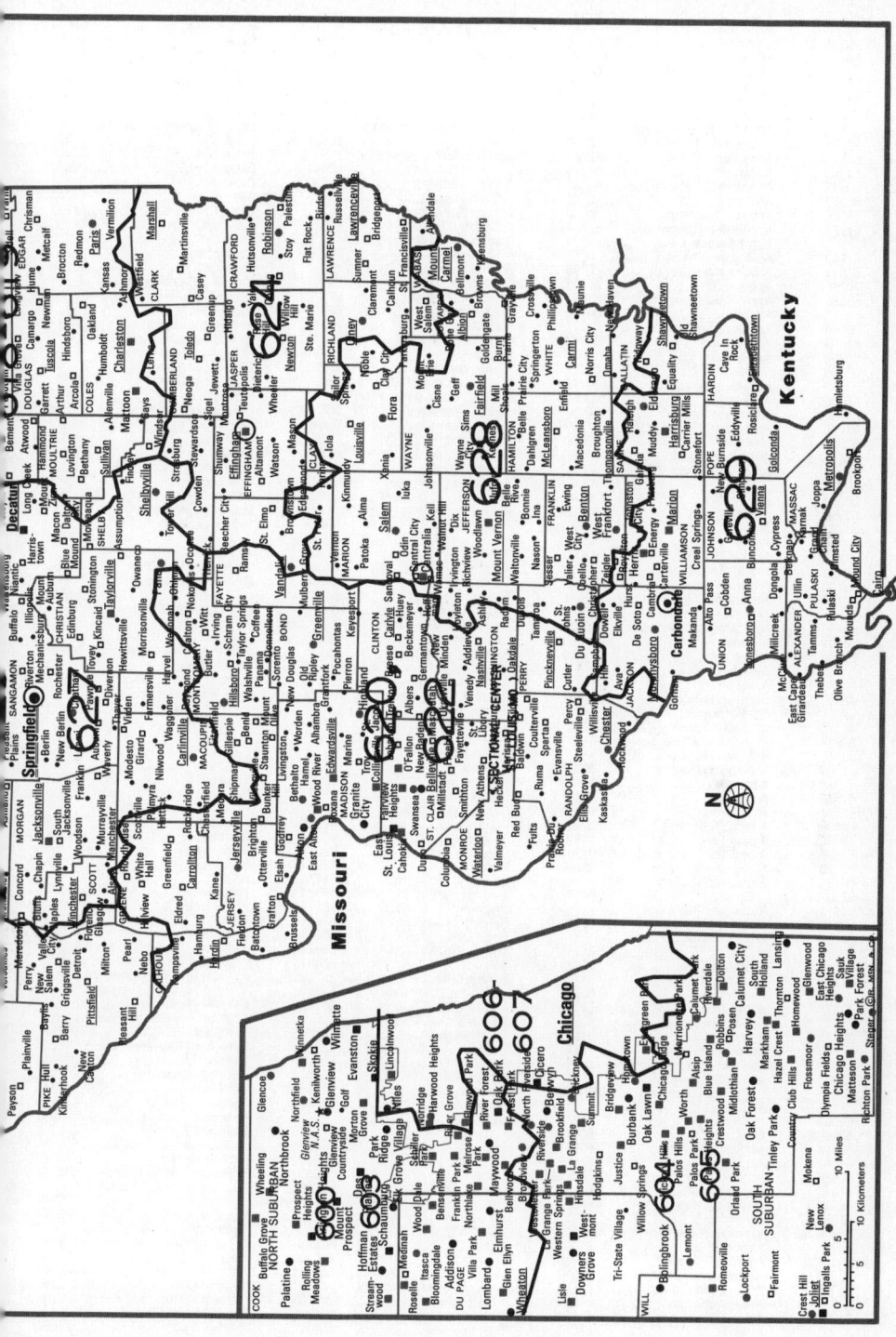

	ZIP
Abingdon	61410
Abington (Township)	61476
Acacia Acres	60525
Acme Station (Part of Bartonville)	61607
Adair	61411
Adams (Adams County)	62347
Adams (La Salle County) (Township)	60531
Adams Corner	62410
Addieville	62214
Addison (Township)	60101
Addison	60101
Adeline	61047
Aden	62895
Adrian	62310
Aero Estates	60564
Aetna (Coles County)	61938
Aetna (Logan County) (Township)	61749
Afolkey	61018
Afton (Township)	60115
Agnew	61081
Air Mail Center Ohare (Part of Chicago)	60666
Airport	61074
Airport Heights	61607
Akin	62805
Akron (Township)	61559
Alan Dale	62035
Alba (Township)	61235
Albany	61230
Albany (Township)	61230
Albers	62215
Albion	62806
Alden	60001
Alden (Township)	60001
Aldridge	62998
Aledo	61231
Alexander	62601
Alexis	61412
Algonquin	60102
Algonquin (Township)	60102
Algonquin Shores	60102
Algonquin Trails (Part of Mount Prospect)	60056
Alhambra	62001
Alhambra (Township)	62001
Allen (La Salle County) (Township)	60470
Allen (Mason County)	62682
Allen (Whiteside County)	61071
Allendale	62410
Allen Grove (Township)	62682
Allens Corners	60140
Allentown	61568
Allenville	61951
Allerton	61810
Allin (Township)	61774
Allison (Township)	62439
Alma	62807
Alma (Township)	62807
Almora	60123
Almora Heights	60123
Alorton	62207
Alpha	61413
Alsey	62610
Alsip	60658
Alsip Woods (Part of Alsip)	60658
Alta	61614
Altamont (Effingham County)	62411
Altamont (Madison County)	62035
Alto (Township)	60553
Alton	62002
Alton (Township)	62002
Altona	61414
Alton Square (Part of Alton)	62002
Alto Pass	62905
Altorf	60914
Alvin	61811
Alworth	61088
Amboy	61310
Amboy (Township)	61310
Amenia	61856
America	62996
Americana Village (Part of Glendale Heights)	60139
Ames	62277
Amity (Township)	61319
Anchor	61720
Anchor (Township)	61720
Anchorage (Part of Glenview)	60026
Ancient Tree (Part of Northbrook)	60062
Ancona	61311

	ZIP
Andalusia	61232
Andalusia (Township)	61232
Anderman Acres	60544
Anderson (Township)	62441
Anderson Lake	61501
Andover	61233
Andover (Township)	61233
Andres	60468
Andrew	62707
Anna	62906
Anna Mental Health and Developmental Center	62906
Annapolis	62413
Annawan	61234
Annawan (Township)	61234
Antioch	60002
Antioch (Township)	60002
Appanoose (Township)	62354
Apple Canyon Lake	61001
Applegate (Part of Schaumburg)	60194
Apple River	61001
Apple River (Township)	61001
Appleton	61428
Appletree (Part of Country Club Hills)	60477
Apple Valley (Part of Glenview)	60025
Appoloosa West	60119
Aptakisic	60069
Arboretum East	60137
Arboretum Villages (Part of Lisle)	60532
Arboretum West	60137
Arbor Trails (Part of Park Forest)	60466
Arbury Hills	60448
Arcadia	62650
Archer	62707
Archie	61876
Arcola	61910
Arcola (Township)	61910
Arenzville	62611
Arenzville (Township)	62611
Argenta	62501
Argo (Part of Summit)	60501
Argo Fay	61053
Argyle	61011
Arispie (Township)	61368
Arlington	61312
Arlington Heights	60004-06
For specific Arlington Heights Zip Codes call (708) 253-7456, or your local postmaster.	
Arlington Ridge (Part of Arlington Heights)	60004
Armington	61721
Armstrong	61812
Arnold	62650
Aroma (Township)	60901
Aroma Park	60910
Aroma Park Northwest	60901
Arrington (Township)	62886
Arrowhead (DuPage County)	60187
Arrowhead (Kankakee County)	60914
Arrowhead (McDonough County)	61455
Arrowhead Hills	60543
Arrowsmith (Township)	61772
Arrowsmith	61722
Arrow Wood	62035
Artesia (Township)	60918
Arthur	61911
Asbury (Township)	62871
Ashburn (Part of Chicago)	60652
Ash Grove (Iroquois County) (Township)	60953
Ash Grove (Shelby County) (Township)	61957
Ashkum	60911
Ashkum (Township)	60911
Ashland	62612
Ashland (Township)	62612
Ashley	62808
Ashley (Township)	62808
Ashmore	61912
Ashmore (Township)	61912
Ashton	61006
Ashton (Township)	61006
Assumption	62510
Assumption (Township)	62510
Astoria	61501
Astoria (Township)	61501
Athens	62613
Athensville	62082
Athensville (Township)	62082
Atkinson	61235
Atkinson (Township)	61235

	ZIP
Atlanta	61723
Atlanta (Township)	61723
Atlas	62370
Atlas (Township)	62370
Atlee Ogles	62223
Atrium (Part of Elmhurst)	60126
Atterbury	62675
Attila	62974
Atwater	62511
Atwood	61913
Atwood Heights (Part of Alsip)	60658
Auburn (Clark County) (Township)	62441
Auburn (Sangamon County)	62615
Auburn (Sangamon County) (Township)	62615
Auburn Park (Part of Chicago)	60620
Auburn Woods (Part of Palatine)	60067
Audubon (Township)	62075
Augsburg	62885
Augusta	62311
Augusta (Township)	62311
Aurora	60504-07
For specific Aurora Zip Codes call (708) 897-2221, or your local postmaster.	
Aurora (Township)	60505
Austin (Cook County)	60644
Austin (Macon County) (Township)	62573
Austin View	60463
Aux Sable (Township)	60447
Ava	62907
Avalon Park (Part of Chicago)	60619
Avena	62458
Avena (Township)	62458
Avery Hill	62223
Aviston	62216
Avoca (Township)	61739
Avon (Fulton County)	61415
Avon (Lake County) (Township)	60030
Avondale (Part of Chicago)	60641
Ayers (Township)	61816
Babcock	61244
Babson (Part of St. Charles)	60174
Babylon	61415
Baden Baden (Part of Pierron)	62273
Bader	62624
Baileyville	61007
Bainbridge (Township)	62639
Baker	60531
Baker Lake	60010
Bakerville	62864
Balcom	62906
Bald Bluff (Township)	61476
Bald Hill (Township)	62883
Baldwin	62217
Baldwin Beach	62644
Bales Lake	60948
Ball (Township)	62629
Ballou	60481
Banner (Effingham County) (Township)	62461
Banner (Fulton County)	61520
Banner (Fulton County) (Township)	61520
Bannister	62881
Bannockburn	60015
Barclay	62561
Bardolph	61416
Bargerville	62960
Barnett (De Witt County) (Township)	61727
Barnett (Montgomery County)	62056
Barnhill	62809
Barnhill (Township)	62809
Barr (Macoupin County) (Township)	62674
Barr (Sangamon County)	62613
Barren (Township)	62812
Barrington	60010*
	60011†
Barrington Center (Part of Barrington Hills)	60010
Barrington Highlands	60010
Barrington Hills	60010
Barrington Square (Part of Hoffman Estates)	60195
Barrington Woods	60074
Barrow	62082

	ZIP
Barry	62312
Barry (Township)	62312
Barstow	61236
Bartelso	62218
Bartlett	60103
Bartonville	61607
Basco	62313
Base (Part of Rantoul)	61866
Batavia	60510
Batavia (Township)	60510
Batavia Highlands (Part of Batavia)	60510
Batchtown	62006
Bates	62670
Batestown	61832
Bath	62617
Bath (Township)	62617
Bay City	62938
Bayle	62080
Baylestown	62033
Baylis	62314
Bay View Gardens	61611
Beach Park	60085
Beacon Hill (Part of Chicago Heights)	60411
Bear Creek (Christian County) (Township)	62556
Bear Creek (Hancock County) (Township)	62313
Beardstown	62618
Beardstown (Township)	62618
Bear Grove (Township)	62471
Bearsdale	62526
Beason	62512
Beau Bien (Part of Lisle)	60532
Beaucoup	62263
Beaucoup (Township)	62263
Beaver (Township)	60931
Beaver Creek (Bond County)	62246
Beaver Creek (Hamilton County) (Township)	62887
Beaver Valley (Boone County)	61008
Beaver Valley (Cook County)	60462
Beaverville	60912
Beaverville (Township)	60912
Beckemeyer	62219
Bedford (Pike County)	62361
Bedford (Wayne County) (Township)	62823
Bedford Park	60638
Beecher	60401
Beecher City	62414
Beechville	62006
Beecreek	62361
Beh Lake Estates	61038
Bel Air Gardens (Part of Glenview)	60025
Belgium	61883
Belgium Row	61858
Belknap	62908
Bellair	62449
Belle Prairie (Township)	61731
Belle Prairie City	62828
Belle Rive	62810
Belleview	62045
Belleville	62220-23
For specific Belleville Zip Codes call (618) 233-0390, or your local postmaster.	
Belleville (Township)	62221
Bellevue	61604
Bellflower	61724
Bellflower (Township)	61724
Belmont	62811
Bell Plain (Township)	61541
Bell Ridge	61944
Belltown	62092
Bellwood	60104
Bellwood (Part of Glenview)	60025
Bel-Mar Estates	61008
Belmont (DuPage County)	60515
Belmont (Iroquois County) (Township)	60970
Belmont Acres	60970
Belmont Road (Part of Downers Grove)	60515
Belmont Village	62035
Beltrees	62022
Belvidere	61008
Belvidere (Township)	61008
Belvidere Mall (Part of Waukegan)	60085
Bement	61813
Bement (Township)	61813
Benedale Green (Part of Lisle)	60532

Name	ZIP	Name	ZIP	Name	ZIP	Name	ZIP
Benevolent Heights	62220	Black Hawk Springs	60545	Bourbon	61953	Brookfield (La Salle County) (Township)	60470
Benld	62009	Blackstone	61313	Bourbon (Township)	61953		
Bennington (Edwards County)	62476	Blaine	61065	Bourbonnais	60914	Brook Forest (Part of Oak Brook)	60521
Bennington (Marshall County) (Township)	61369	Blair (Clay County) (Township)	62858	Bourbonnais (Township)	60914	Brookforest North	60435
Bensenville	60106	Blair (Livingston County)	60961	Bowdre (Township)	61910	Brookhaven	61277
Benson	61516	Blair (Randolph County)	62286	Bowen	62316	Brookhaven Manor (Part of Darien)	60561
Bentley	62321	Blairsville (Hamilton County)	62859	Bowes	60123	Brookhill	60048
Benton	62812	Blairsville (Williamson County)	62918	Bowlesville (Township)	62984	Brooklyn (Lee County) (Township)	61318
Benton (Franklin County) (Township)	62812	Blandinsville	61420	Bowling (Township)	61264		
Benton (Lake County) (Township)	60096	Blandinsville (Township)	61420	Bowling Green (Township)	62422	Brooklyn (Schuyler County)	62367
Benton City Park	62812	Blissville (Township)	62894	Boyd	62830	Brooklyn (Schuyler County) (Township)	62367
Ben Town	61701	Block	61877	Boyleston	62837	Brookport	62910
Bent Tree Village (Part of Elgin)	60120	Blodgett (Part of Highland Park)	60035	Boynton (Township)	61734	Brooks	62040
Benwick (Part of Schaumburg)	60194	Bloom (Township)	60411	Braceville	60407	Brookside (Clinton County) (Township)	62801
Berdan	62016	Bloomfield (Adams County)	62338	Braceville (Township)	60407	Brookside (Kane County)	60175
Bergen	53525	Bloomfield (Edgar County)	61924	Bradbury	62468	Brooks Isle	61061
Berger (Part of Dolton)	60419	Bloomfield (Johnson County)	62995	Bradford (Lee County) (Township)	61006	Brookview	61614
Berkeley	60163	Bloomingdale	60108	Bradford (Stark County)	61421	Brookville	61064
Berkland Heights	61341	Bloomingdale (Township)	60108	Bradfordton	62707	Brookville (Township)	61064
Berlin (Bureau County) (Township)	61312	Bloomingdale Court (Part of Bloomingdale)	60108	Bradley (Grundy County)	60450	Brookwood (Part of Prospect Heights)	60070
Berlin (Sangamon County)	62670	Bloomington	61701-04	Bradley (Jackson County) (Township)	62907	Brookwood (Part of Rolling Meadows)	60008
Bernadotte	61441	For specific Bloomington Zip Codes call (309) 663-8484, or your local postmaster.		Bradley (Kankakee County)	60915	Brookwood (Kane County)	60174
Bernadotte (Township)	61441			Braeside (Part of Highland Park)	60035	Brookwood Estates (Part of Wood Dale)	60191
Bernice (Part of Lansing)	60438	Bloomington City (Township)	61701	Braidwood	60408	Brothers	61858
Berreman (Township)	61053	Bloomington Heights	61701	Brainerd (Part of Chicago)	60620	Broughton (Hamilton County)	62817
Berry (Sangamon County)	62563	Blossom Hill (Part of Cary)	60013	Branding	62013		
Berry (Wayne County) (Township)	62850	Blount (Township)	61832	Brandywine	60181	Broughton (Livingston County) (Township)	60934
Berryville (Richland County)	62419	Blue Fountain	62035	Branigar Estates	60007	Brouillets Creek (Township)	61924
Berryville (Union County)	62952	Blue Island	60406	Breckenridge	62563	Brown (Township)	61845
Bertinetti Lake	62568	Blue Island Junction (Part of Blue Island)	60406	Breeds	61520	Brownfield	62938
Berwick	61417			Breese	62230	Browning (Franklin County) (Township)	62812
Berwick (Township)	61417	Blue Island Junction (Part of Chicago)	60617	Breese (Township)	62230		
Berwyn	60402	Blue Mound (Macon County)	62513	Bremen (Cook County) (Township)	60426	Browning (Schuyler County)	62624
Berwyn (Township)	60402			Bremen (Randolph County)	62233	Browning (Schuyler County) (Township)	62624
Bethalto	62010	Blue Mound (Macon County) (Township)	62514	Brementowne Mall (Part of Tinley Park)	60477	Browns	62818
Bethany	61914	Blue Mound (McLean County) (Township)	61730	Brenton (Township)	60959	Brownstown	62418
Bethel (McDonough County) (Township)	61415	Blue Point	62401	Brentwood (Part of Des Plaines)	60016	Brownsville	62821
Bethel (Morgan County)	62628	Blue Ridge	61854	Brentwood Estates	60074	Brownwood	61747
Bethel (Vermilion County)	61870	Blue Ridge (Township)	61854	Brereton	61520	Brubaker	62807
Bethlehem	62411	Bluff City (Fayette County)	62471	Brettwood (Part of Decatur)	62526	Bruce (La Salle County) (Township)	61364
Beulah Heights (Part of Eldorado)	62930	Bluff City (Schuyler County)	62624	Briar Bluff	61240	Bruce (Moultrie County)	61951
Be-Ver Kreek	61008	Bluffdale (Greene County) (Township)	62027	Briarbrook Village (Part of Wheaton)	60187	Brunning	60441
Beverly	62312			Briarcliffe (Part of Wheaton)	60187	Brunswick	62534
Beverly (Township)	62312	Bluffdale (Henderson County)	61437	Briarcliffe Knolls (Part of Wheaton)	60187	Brushy (Township)	62935
Beverly Hills (Part of Chicago)	60642	Bluff Hall	62360	Briarcliff Estates (Part of Bourbonnais)	60914	Brushy Mound (Township)	62033
Beverly Manor (Part of Washington)	61571	Bluffs	62621	Briarwick	61938	Brussels	62013
Beyers Lake Addition	62557	Bluffside	62236	Briarwood	61107	Bryant	61519
Bible Grove	62858	Bluff Springs	62622	Briarwoods Estates (Part of Deerfield)	60015	Bryce	60953
Bible Grove (Township)	62858	Bluff Springs (Township)	62622	Briarwood Trace	62901	Bryn Mawr (Part of Chicago)	60649
Biddleborn	62257	Bluff View Park (Part of Caseyville)	62232	Brickman Manor (Part of Mount Prospect)	60056	Buck (Township)	61944
Big Bay	62960	Bluford	62814	Brickyard, The (Part of Chicago)	60635	Buckeye (Township)	61013
Big Foot	60033	Blyton	61477	Bridgelane	61265	Buckhart (Christian County) (Township)	62531
Big Grove (Township)	60541	Boaz	62956	Bridgeport	62417		
Biggs	62633	Boden	61281	Bridgeport (Township)	62417	Buckhart (Sangamon County)	62545
Biggsville	61418	Bogan's (Part of Effingham)	62401	Bridgeview	60455	Buckheart (Township)	61563
Biggsville (Township)	61418	Bogota	62448	Bridgeway Addition (Part of Moline)	61265	Buckhorn	62353
Big Hollow	60041	Bohleysville	62260	Bridle Creek Estates	60175	Buckhorn (Township)	62375
Big Mound (Township)	62837	Bois d'Arc (Township)	62533	Brierwood	60175	Buckingham	60917
Bigneck	62349	Boles	62909	Bright Oaks (Part of Cary)	60013	Buckley	60918
Big Rock	60511	Bolingbrook	60440	Brighton	62012	Buckner	62819
Big Rock (Township)	60511	Boling Green (Part of Bolingbrook)	60440	Brighton (Township)	62012	Bucks	61745
Big Spring (Township)	62447	Bolivia	62545	Brighton Park (Part of Chicago)	60632	Buda	61314
Billett	62439	Bolo (Township)	62808	Brimfield	61517	Budd	61313
Bingham	62011	Bolton	61032	Brimfield (Township)	61517	Buena Vista (Saline County)	62946
Binghampton	61310	Bond (Township)	62439	Brisbane	60451	Buena Vista (Schuyler County) (Township)	62681
Binney	62074	Bondville	61815	Bristol	60512		
Bird (Township)	62630	Bone Gap	62815	Bristol (Township)	60512	Buena Vista (Stephenson County)	61032
Birds	62415	Bonfield	60913	Bristol Lake	60560		
Birkbeck	61727	Bongard	61864	Bristol Ridge	60560	Buffalo (Ogle County) (Township)	61064
Birmingham	62367	Bonnie	62816	Broadlands	61816		
Birmingham (Township)	62367	Bonnie Brea	60441	Broadmoor	61421	Buffalo (Sangamon County)	62515
Bishop (Effingham County) (Township)	62424	Bonpas (Township)	62419	Broadview	60153	Buffalo Grove (Cook County)	60089
Bishop (Mason County)	61532	Bonus (Township)	61038	Broadway (Part of Rockford)	61106	Buffalo Grove (Ogle County)	61064
Bishop Hill	61419	Boody	62514	Broadwell	62634	Buffalo Hart	62515
Bishop Quarter Lane (Part of Oak Park)	60301	Boone (Township)	61012	Broadwell (Township)	62634	Buffalo Hart (Township)	62515
Bismarck	61814	Boos	62448	Brocton	61917	Buffalo Prairie	61237
Bissell	62707	Booster Station	62269	Brooke Estates (Part of Highland Park)	60035	Buffalo Prairie (Township)	61237
Black	62806	Borton	61917	Brookeridge	60515	Bull Creek	60048
Blackberry (Township)	60119	Boskydell	62901	Brookfield (Cook County)	60513	Bullock Addition	61241
Blackberry Heights	60538	Boulder	62283			Bull Valley	60098
Blackberry Woods	60554	Boulder Hill	60538				
Blackhawk (Township)	61264	Boulevard Manor (Part of Cicero)	60650				
Blackhawk Heights (Part of Clarendon Hills)	60514						
Blackhawk Island	61102						

*Area Zip Code   †Post Office Boxes

	ZIP
Bulpitt	62517
Buncombe	62912
Bungay	62887
Bunker Hill (Township)	62014
Bunker Hill (Township) ...	62014
Bunkum (Part of Fairview Heights)	62208
Bunsenville	61846
Burbank	60459
Burches	60914
Bureau	61315
Bureau (Township)	61379
Burgess (Bond County) (Township)	62275
Burgess (Mercer County)	61231
Burksville (Monroe County)	62298
Burlington	60109
Burlington (Township)	60109
Burnham	60633
Burnham Mill (Part of Elgin)	60123
Burns (Township)	61443
Burnside (Cook County)	60617
Burnside (Hancock County)	62318
Burnside's Lakewood (Part of Richton Park)	60466
Burnt Prairie	62820
Burnt Prairie (Township)	62821
Burritt (Township)	61088
Burr Oak (Part of Blue Island)	60406
Burr Oaks (Part of Joliet)	60435
Burrowsville	61929
Burr Ridge	60521
Burt	61721
Burton (Adams County)	62301
Burton (Adams County) (Township)	62301
Burton (McHenry County) (Township)	60081
Burtons Bridge	60050
Burtonview	62656
Bush (Jackson County)	62901
Bush (Williamson County)	62924
Bushnell	61422
Bushnell (Township)	61422
Bushton	61920
Butler (Montgomery County)	62015
Butler (Vermilion County) (Township)	62015
Butler Grove (Township)	62015
Butterfield	60148
Butterfield West	60137
Button (Township)	60960
Buysse Addition	61240
Buzzville	62644
Byron	61010
Byron (Township)	61010
Byron Hills (Ogle County)	61010
Byron Hills (Rock Island County)	61275
Cabery	60919
Cable	61281
Cache	62913
Cadiz	62931
Cadwell	61911
Cahokia (Macoupin County) (Township) ...	62023
Cahokia (St. Clair County)	62206
Cairo	62914
Caledonia	61011
Caledonia (Township)...	61011
Calhoun	62419
Calumet	60429
Calumet (Township)	60406
Calumet City	60409
Calumet Harbor (Part of Chicago)	60633
Calumet Park	60643
Calvin	62827
Camargo	61919
Camargo (Township)	61919
Cambria	62915
Cambridge	61238
Cambridge (Township)...	61238
Cambridge (Part of Libertyville)	60048
Camden	62319
Camden (Township)	62319
Camelot	62401
Cameo Terrace (Part of Wheeling)	60090
Cameron	61423
Campbell Hill	62916
Campbells Island	61244
Camp Epworth	61038
Camp Ground	62864

	ZIP
Camp Grove	61424
Camp Logan	60099
Camp Point	62320
Camp Point (Township)	62320
Campton (Township)	60183
Campus	60920
Campus Walk (Part of Elgin)	60120
Camridge West (Part of Mundelein)	60060
Candlewood Estates	61853
Canoe Creek (Township)	61257
Canteen (Township)	62204
Canterbury Lane (Part of Glenview)	60025
Canterbury Shopping Center (Part of Markham)	60426
Canton	61520
Canton (Township)	61520
Cantrall	62625
Capital (Township)	62707
Capitol (Part of Springfield)	62701
Capri Gardens	60074
Capri Village	60074
Capron	61012
Carbon (Part of O'Fallon)	62269
Carbon Cliff	61239
Carbondale	62901-03
For specific Carbondale Zip Codes call (618) 457-3800, or your local postmaster.	
Carbon Hill	60416
Cardiff	60420
Carlinville (Township)	62626
Carlinville	62626
Carlock	61725
Carlsburg	62069
Carlyle	62231
Carlyle (Township)	62231
Carlysle (Part of Schaumburg)	60194
Carman	61425
Carman (Township)	61425
Carmi	62821
Carmi (Township)	62821
Carol Stream	60188
	60197-99
For specific Carol Stream Zip Codes call (708) 260-5137, or your local postmaster.	
Carpenter	62205
Carpentersville	60110
Carriage Creek (Part of Richton Park)	60466
Carriage Park	60543
Carriage Way Court	60074
Carrier Mills	62917
Carrier Mills (Township)	62917
Carrigan (Clinton County)	62231
Carrigan (Marion County) (Township)	62875
Carroll (Township)	61870
Carroll Addition (Champaign County)	61801
Carroll Addition (Ford County)	60936
Carrollton	62016
Carrollton (Township)	62016
Carrollwood (Part of Wood River)	62095
Carson (Township)	62080
Carterville	62918
Carthage	62321
Carthage (Township)	62321
Carthage Lake	61425
Cartter	62853
Cartwright (Township)	62677
Cary	60013
Casey	62420
Casey (Township)	62420
Caseyville	62232
Caseyville (Township)...	62232
Casner (Jefferson County) (Township)	62898
Casner (Macon County)	62552
Cass (Township)	61477
Castellean Lower	61021
Castellean Upper	61021
Castleton	61426
Catatoga	60123
Catatoga 2	60123
Catlin	61817
Catlin (Township)	61817
Cave (Township)	62890
Cave In Rock	62919
Cayuga	61764
Cazenovia	61545
Cazenovia (Township) ..	61545

	ZIP
Cedar (Township)	61410
Cedar Glen	60543
Cedar Grove	62959
Cedar Island	60020
Cedar Meadows	62269
Cedar Park	62040
Cedar Point	61316
Cedar Run (Part of Wheeling)	60090
Cedarville	61013
Centaur Estate	61008
Center Hill	61053
Centerville (Calhoun County)	62036
Centerville (Knox County)	61485
Centerville (Macoupin County)	62685
Centerville (Piatt County)	61854
Centerville (White County)	62821
Central (Township)	62246
Central City (Grundy County)	60407
Central City (Marion County)	62801
Centralia	62801
Centralia (Township)	62801
Central Park	61832
Central Street (Part of Evanston)	60201
Centre of Park Forest, The (Part of Park Forest)	60466
Centreville (Township)	62207
Centreville	62207
Century Oaks (Part of Elgin)	60123
Century Oaks West (Part of Elgin)	60123
Cerro Gordo	61818
Cerro Gordo (Township)	61818
Chadwick	61014
Chalfin Bridge	62244
Chalmers (Township) ...	61455
Chambersburg	62323
Chambersburg (Township)	62323
Chambord (Part of Oak Brook)	60521
Champaign	61820-26
For specific Champaign Zip Codes call (217) 373-6000, or your local postmaster.	
Champaign City (Township)	61820
Champlin	61739
Chana	61015
Chandlerville	62627
Chandlerville (Township)	62627
Channahon (Township)	60410
Channahon	60410
Channel Lake	60002
Chantilly (Part of Highland Park)	60035
Chapin	62628
Chapman	62032
Charleston	61920
Charleston (Township) ...	61920
Charlestowne Mall (Part of St. Charles)	60174
Charlotte	60921
Charlotte (Township)	60921
Charlotte Hills	62274
Charter Grove	60178
Chasco	62923
Chateau Terrace	62221
Chatham (Township)	62629
Chatham (Cook County)	60619
Chatham (Sangamon County)	62629
Chatham Manor (Part of Buffalo Grove)	60089
Chatsworth	60921
Chatsworth (Township)	60921
Chatton	62346
Chauncey	62466
Chautauqua	62028
Chautauqua Park (Mason County)	62644
Chautauqua Park (Menard County)	62675
Chebanse	60922
Chebanse (Township) ...	60927
Checkrow	61415
Chelsea Cove (Part of Wheeling)	60090
Cheltenham (Part of Chicago)	60649
Chemung	60033
Chemung (Township) ...	60033
Cheneys Grove (Township)	61770

	ZIP
Cheneyville	60942
Chenoa	61726
Chenoa (Township)	61726
Chenot Place	62221
Cherry	61317
Cherry Grove-Shannon (Township)	61046
Cherry Hill	60431
Cherry Hills (Champaign County)	61821
Cherry Hills (Kane County)	60506
Cherry Point	61924
Cherryvale Mall (Part of Cherry Valley)	61112
Cherry Valley (Township)	61016
Cherry Valley	61016
Cherrywood (Christian County)	62568
Cherrywood (Will County)	60440
Chester (Logan County) (Township)	62656
Chester (Randolph County)	62233
Chesterfield (Cook County)	60619
Chesterfield (Macoupin County)	62630
Chesterfield (Macoupin County) (Township) ...	62630
Chesterville	61911
Chestline	62314
Chestnut (Knox County) (Township)	61544
Chestnut (Logan County)	62518
Chestnut Street (Part of Chicago)	60610
Chicago	60601-41
	60643-49
	60651-57
	60659-64
	60680-91
	60701
	60799
For specific Chicago Zip Codes call (312) 765-3585, or your local postmaster.	

COLLEGES & UNIVERSITIES

	ZIP
Chicago State University	60628
Columbia College	60605
De Paul University	60604
DeVry Institute of Technology-Chicago...	60618
Illinois Institute of Technology	60616
John Marshall Law School	60604
Keller Graduate School of Management	60606
Loyola University of Chicago	60611
Moody Bible Institute	60610
Mundelein College	60660
North Park College & Theological Seminary	60625
Northeastern Illinois University	60625
Roosevelt University	60605
Rush University	60612
Saint Xavier College	60655
School of the Art Institute of Chicago	60603
University of Chicago	60637
University of Illinois at Chicago	60680

FINANCIAL INSTITUTIONS

	ZIP
Amalgamated Bank of Chicago	60603
American National Bank and Trust Company of Chicago	60690
Associated Bank Chicago	60601
Avondale Federal Savings Bank	60602
Bank of Commerce & Industry	60631
Bell Federal Savings & Loan Association	60603
Belmont National Bank of Chicago	60657
Beverly Bank	60643
Boulevard Bank, N.A.	60611
Calumet Federal Savings & Loan	60617
Central Federal Savings & Loan Association of Chicago	60657

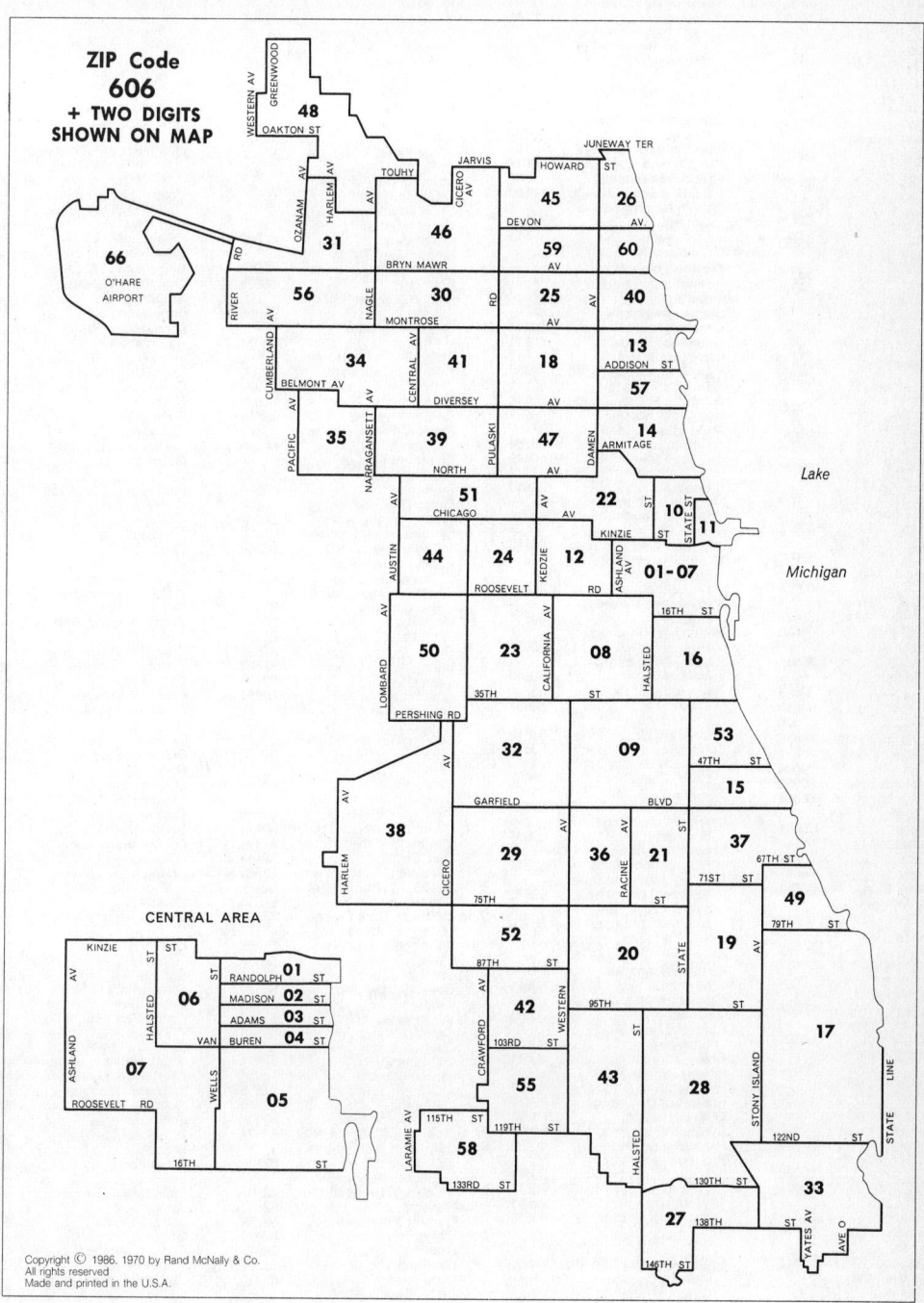

ZIP Code
606
+ TWO DIGITS
SHOWN ON MAP

CENTRAL AREA

	ZIP
Chesterfield Federal Savings & Loan Association	60643
Chicago City Bank & Trust Company	60621
The Chicago-Tokyo Bank	60602
Cole Taylor Bank	60607
Colonial Bank	60634
Columbia National Bank of Chicago	60656
Commercial National Bank of Chicago	60625
Continental Bank, National Association	60697
Cosmopolitan Bank and Trust	60610
Cragin Federal Bank for Savings	60639
Damen Federal Bank for Savings	60609
Devon Bank	60645
Drexel National Bank	60616
Fidelity Federal Savings Bank	60641
First Commercial Bank	60626
First Cook Community Bank	60659
First Savings Bank of Hegewisch	60633
First National Bank of Chicago	60670
First National Bank of Evergreen Park	60638
First National Bank of Lincolnwood	60659
First Security Federal Savings Bank	60622
First State Bank of Chicago	60656
Harris Trust and Savings Bank	60603
Heritage Pullman Bank & Trust Company	60628
Hoyne Savings Bank	60630
Hyde Park Bank & Trust Company	60615
Independence Bank of Chicago	60619
Irving Federal Bank for Savings	60618
Jefferson State Bank	60630
Lake Shore National Bank	60611
Lakeside Bank	60604
LaSalle Bank-Lake View	60657
LaSalle National Bank	60603
LaSalle Northwest National Bank	60641
Liberty Federal Savings Bank	60659
Liberty Bank for Savings	60647
Lincoln National Bank	60613
Lincoln Park Savings Bank	60613
Madison Bank & Trust Company	60606
Manufacturer's Bank	60622
Marquette National Bank	60636
Merchandise National Bank of Chicago	60654
Michigan Avenue National Bank of Chicago	60602
Mid-City National Bank of Chicago	60607
Midwest Bank and Trust Company	60604
Midwest Securities Trust Company	60605
Mount Greenwood Bank	60655
National Security Bank of Chicago	60622
NBD Chicago Bank	60601
Northern Trust Bank/O'Hare, N.A.	60631
Northern Trust Company	60675
Northwestern Savings & Loan Association	60647
Park National Bank and Trust Company of Chicago	60618
Peterson Bank	60659
Pioneer Bank & Trust Company	60639
River Valley Savings Bank, F.S.B.	60606
St. Paul Federal Bank for Savings	60635
Seaway National Bank of Chicago	60619

	ZIP
Second Federal Savings & Loan Association of Chicago	60623
Security Federal Savings & Loan Association of Chicago	60622
South Chicago Bank	60617
South Shore Bank of Chicago	60649
Standard Federal Bank for Savings	60632
Steel City National Bank of Chicago	60617
LaSalle Talman Bank, F.S.B.	60503
Uptown National Bank of Chicago	60640

HOSPITALS

	ZIP
Chicago Osteopathic Hospital and Medical Center	60615
Children's Memorial Hospital	60614
Columbus Hospital	60614
Cook County Hospital	60612
Edgewater Medical Center	60660
EHS Trinity Hospital	60617
Grant Hospital of Chicago	60614
Holy Cross Hospital	60629
Illinois Masonic Medical Center	60657
Jackson Park Hospital	60649
Louis A. Weiss Memorial Hospital	60640
Mercy Hospital and Medical Center	60616
Michael Reese Hospital & Medical Center	60616
Mount Sinai Hospital Medical Center of Chicago	60608
Northwestern Memorial Hospital	60611
Our Lady of Resurrection Medical Center	60634
Ravenswood Hospital Medical Center	60640
Resurrection Medical Center	60631
Rush-Presbyterian-St. Luke's Medical Center	60612
St. Elizabeth's Hospital	60622
St. Joseph Hospital and Health Care Center	60657
St. Mary of Nazareth Hospital Center	60622
University of Chicago Hospitals	60637
University of Illinois Hospital and Clinics	60612
Veterans Affairs Lakeside Medical Center	60611
Veterans Affairs West Side Medical Center	60612

HOTELS/MOTELS

	ZIP
Chicago Downtown Marriott	60611
Chicago Hilton and Towers	60605
Congress Hotel of Chicago	60605
Drake Chicago	60611
Holiday Inn-Mart Plaza	60654
Hyatt Regency Chicago	60601
Knickerbocker Chicago	60611
O'Hare Hilton	60666
O'Hare Marriott Hotel	60631
Palmer House Hilton	60603
Park Hyatt on Water Tower Square	60611
Ritz-Carlton	60611
Tremont	60611
Westin Hotel Chicago	60611

MILITARY INSTALLATIONS

	ZIP
Illinois Air National Guard, FB6121, Chicago O'Hare International Airport	60666
United States Army Engineer District Chicago	60606
928th Airlift Group, O'Hare Air Reserve Forces Facility	60666
Chicago Bulk Mail Center (Part of Forest Park)	60799

	ZIP
Chicago Heights	60411
Chicago Lawn (Part of Chicago)	60629
Chicago - Read Mental Health Center	60634
Chicago Ridge	60415
Chicago Ridge Mall (Part of Chicago Ridge)	60415
Chicken Bristle	61953
Chili	62380
Chili (Township)	62380
Chillicothe	61523
Chillicothe (Township)	61523
Chilon Chalet (Part of Chicago Heights)	60411
China (Township)	61310
Chinatown (Part of Maryville)	62062
Chippendale (Part of Barrington)	60010
Chippewa	60658
Chippewa Ridge (Part of Alsip)	60658
Chittenden (Part of Gurnee)	60031
Chittyville (Part of Herrin)	62948
Chouteau (Township)	62040
Chrisman	61924
Christopher	62822
Christy (Township)	62466
Churchill (Part of Hoffman Estates)	60195
Churchville (Part of Bensenville)	60126
Cicero	60650
Cicero (Township)	60650
Cimic (Part of Divernon)	62530
Cincinnati (Pike County) (Township)	62343
Cincinnati (Tazewell County) (Township)	61554
Cinnamon Creek (Part of Bolingbrook)	60440
Circle Drive	61364
Circle Park	62565
Cisco	61830
Cisne	62823
Cissna Park	60924
Citation Lake Estates	60062
City Park (Part of Taylorville)	62568
Claburn (Part of Chicago)	60617
Clank	62988
Clare	60111
Claremont	62421
Claremont (Township)	62421
Clarence	60960
Clarendon Hills	60514
Clarion (Township)	61330
Clark Center	62441
Clarksburg	62565
Clarksburg (Township)	62565
Clarksdale	62556
Clarksville (Clark County)	62441
Clarksville (McLean County)	61753
Clarmin	62257
Clay City	62824
Clay City (Township)	62824
Claypool	60450
Clays Prairie	61944
Clayton (Adams County)	62324
Clayton (Adams County) (Township)	62324
Clayton (Woodford County) (Township)	61516
Claytonville	60926
Clearing	60638
Clear Lake (Cass County)	62622
Clear Lake (Sangamon County)	62707
Clear Lake (Sangamon County) (Township)	62707
Cleburne	62865
Clement (Township)	62252
Clements	62638
Cleone	62442
Cleveland	61241
Clifton	60927
Clifton Terrace (Part of Godfrey)	62035
Clifty Heights	62959
Clinch	62832
Clinton (De Witt County)	61727
Clinton (DeKalb County) (Township)	60556
Clintonia (Township)	61727
Clover (Township)	61490
Cloverdale (DuPage County)	60103

	ZIP
Cloverdale (Tazewell County)	61611
Cloverleaf (Madison County)	62060
Cloverleaf (Rock Island County)	61265
Clybourn (Part of Chicago)	60610
Clyde (Cook County)	60650
Clyde (Whiteside County) (Township)	61270
Coach Homes of. Willow Bend (Part of Rolling Meadows)	60008
Coach Light Manor (Part of Mount Prospect)	60056
Coal City	60416
Coal Hollow	61356
Coalton	62075
Coal Valley	61240
Coal Valley (Township)	61240
Coatsburg	62325
Cobblestone	60025
Cobblewood (Part of Northbrook)	60062
Cobden	62920
Coe (Township)	61275
Coello	62825
Coffeen	62017
Colby Point	60050
Colchester	62326
Colchester (Township)	62326
Coldbrook	61423
Coldbrook (Township)	61401
Cold Spring (Township)	62571
Colehour (Part of Chicago)	60617
Coleman	60177
Coles	61928
Coleta	61017
Colfax (Champaign County) (Township)	61851
Colfax (McLean County)	61728
College Hills Mall (Part of Normal)	61761
College Park (Part of Elgin)	60123
College View	60441
Collins (Will County)	60544
Collins (Winnebago County)	61080
Collinsville	62234
Collinsville (Township)	62234
Collison	61831
Colmar	62367
Coloma (Township)	61071
Colona	61241
Colona (Township)	61241
Colonial Gardens (Part of Machesney Park)	61115
Colonial Manor (Part of Mount Prospect)	60056
Colonial Ridge	60016
Colonial Village (Madison County)	62035
Colonial Village (Will County)	60440
Colonial Village (Winnebago County)	61108
Colony Grove	61853
Colony Park (Part of Carol Stream)	60188
Colony Point (Part of Deerfield)	60015
Colp	62921
Columbia	62236
Columbia Village	61801
Columbus	62328
Columbus (Township)	62320
Colusa	62329
Colvin Park	60145
Como	61081
Compromise (Township)	61862
Compton	61318
Compton Pines	60175
Conant	62274
Concord (Adams County) (Township)	62324
Concord (Bureau County) (Township)	61361
Concord (Iroquois County) (Township)	60945
Concord (Morgan County)	62631
Condit (Township)	61840
Confidence	62418
Congerville	61729
Congress Park (Part of Brookfield)	60513
Conlogue	61944
Conover	60560

	ZIP
Conrad	62036
Continental Village (Part of Waukegan)	60085
Cooks Mills	61931
Cooksville	61730
Cooper (Township)	62563
Cooperstown	62353
Cooperstown (Township)	62353
Copley (Township)	61485
Cora	62280
Coral	60152
Coral (Township)	60180
Coral Gable (Part of O'Fallon)	62269
Cordova	61242
Cordova (Township)	61242
Corinth	62890
Cornell	61319
Corneville	62935
Cornland	62519
Cornwall (Township)	61235
Cortese	60901
Cortland	60112
Cortland (Township)	60112
Corwin (Township)	62666
Costin (Part of Bloomington)	61701
Cottage (Township)	62946
Cottagegrove	62930
Cottage Hills	62018
Cotton Hill (Township)	62563
Cottonwood (Cumberland County) (Township)	62468
Cottonwood (Gallatin County)	62871
Coulterville	62237
Council Hill	61075
Council Hill (Township)	61075
Council Hill Station	61075
Country Acres (La Salle County)	61360
Country Acres (St. Clair County)	62220
Country Aire (Jefferson County)	62864
Country Aire (Kane County)	60120
Country Club	61938
Country Club Acres	62626
Country Club Heights	61938
Country Club Hills	60478
Country Club Manor (Part of Country Club Hills)	60477
Country Club Place	62223
Country Club Terrace	62220
Country Courts	61265
Country Estates	61254
Country Fair (Part of Champaign)	61821
Country Gardens (Part of Prospect Heights)	60070
Country Heights (Part of Mount Vernon)	62864
Country Knolls (Kane County)	60123
Country Knolls (Knox County)	61410
Country Lake	60563
Country Lake Estates	62613
Country Manor (Coles County)	61938
Country Manor (Effingham County)	62401
Country Manor (Henry County)	61254
Country Orchard	61938
Countryside (Cook County)	60525
Countryside (Kane County)	60560
Countryside (Kendall County)	60560
Countryside (Lake County)	60047
Countryside Estates	60922
Countryside Lake	60060
Countryside Manor	60048
Country Squire (Part of Urbana)	61801
Country Squire Estates	61032
Countryview Estates (Kane County)	60118
Country View Estates (Will County)	60565
Covel	61701
Coventry (Part of Crystal Lake)	60014
Coventry East (Part of Crystal Lake)	60014

	ZIP
Coventry West (Part of Crystal Lake)	60014
Covington	62271
Covington (Township)	62271
Covington Manor	60089
Cow Bell Lane	62274
Cowden	62422
Cowling	62863
Crab Orchard	62959
Crab Orchard Estates	62901
Cragin (Part of Chicago)	60639
Cragin Junction (Part of Chicago)	60639
Craig Manor (Part of Des Plaines)	60016
Crainville	62918
Cramers	61529
Crane Creek (Township)	62633
Cravat	62801
Crawford Countryside (Part of Matteson)	60443
Creal Springs	62922
Creek (Township)	61750
Creekside (Part of Matteson)	60443
Creekside (Part of Rolling Meadows)	60008
Creekwood	60439
Crenshaw	62959
Crescent (Township)	60953
Crescent City	60928
Cress Creek (Part of Naperville)	60563
Crest Haven (Part of Fairview Heights)	62221
Crest Hill	60435
Creston	60113
Crestview	60970
Crestview Terrace (Part of Fairfield)	62837
Crestwood	60445
Crestwood Estates	62959
Crete	60417
Crete (Township)	60417
Creve Coeur	61610
Cricket Hill (Part of Matteson)	60443
Crisp	62895
Crittenden (Township)	61880
Crocketts Estates	60041
Crook (Township)	62859
Crooked Creek (Cumberland County) (Township)	62428
Crooked Creek (Jasper County) (Township)	62432
Crooked Lake	60046
Crooked Lake Oaks	60046
Cropsey	61731
Cropsey (Township)	61731
Cross County Mall (Part of Mattoon)	61938
Crossroads (Johnson County)	62995
Crossroads (St. Clair County)	62232
Crossroad Terrace (Part of Fairview Heights)	62232
Crossville	62827
Crouch (Township)	62895
Crown Estates (Part of Elmhurst)	60126
Cruger	61530
Cruger (Township)	61530
Crystal Gardens (Part of Crystal Lake)	60014
Crystal Lake (Jersey County)	62012
Crystal Lake (Madison County)	62035
Crystal Lake (McHenry County)	60012
	60014
	60039
For specific Crystal Lake Zip Codes call (815) 459-0140, or your local postmaster.	
Crystal Lake Estates	60014
Crystal Lawns	60435
Crystal Manor (Part of Crystal Lake)	60014
Crystal Point Mall (Part of Crystal Lake)	60014
Crystal Vista (Part of Crystal Lake)	60014
Cuba (Fulton County)	61427
Cuba (Lake County) (Township)	60010
Cullom	60929

	ZIP
Cumberland (Part of Des Plaines)	60016
Cumberland Green (Part of St. Charles)	60174
Cumberland Heights (Part of Fairfield)	62837
Cumberland Highlands (Part of Des Plaines)	60016
Cunningham (Township)	61801
Cunningham Courts (Part of Palatine)	60067
Curran	62670
Curran (Township)	62670
Custer (Township)	60481
Custer Park	60481
Cutler	62238
Cypress	62923
Cypress Gardens	62901
D'Adrian Gardens	62035
Daggetts	61053
Dahinda	61428
Dahlgren	62828
Dahlgren (Township)	62828
Dailey	61862
Dakota	61018
Dakota (Township)	61018
Dale (Hamilton County)	62829
Dale (McLean County) (Township)	61772
Dale Valley	61853
Dallasania	62917
Dallas City	62330
Dallas City (Township)	62330
Dalton City	61925
Dalzell	61320
Damiansville	62215
Dana	61321
Danada North (Part of Wheaton)	60187
Danada West (Part of Wheaton)	60187
Danforth	60930
Danforth (Township)	60930
Danvers	61732
Danvers (Township)	61732
Danville	61832*
	61834†
Danville (Township)	61832
Danville Junction (Part of Danville)	61832
Danway	61341
Darien	60561
Darmstadt	62255
Darrow	60966
Darwin	62477
Darwin (Township)	62477
Davis	61019
Davis Junction	61020
Dawson (McLean County) (Township)	61737
Dawson (Sangamon County)	62520
Dawson Park	60953
Daysville	61061
Dayton	61350
Dayton (Township)	61350
Dearborn Heights (Part of Oak Lawn)	60453
Decatur	62521-26
For specific Decatur Zip Codes call (217) 428-4474, or your local postmaster.	
Decker (Township)	62868
Decorra	61480
Deep Lake	60046
Deep Spring Woods	60097
Deep Woods (Part of Mundelein)	60060
Deerbrook Mall (Part of Deerfield)	60015
Deer Creek	61733
Deer Creek (Township)	61733
Deerfield (Fulton County) (Township)	61431
Deerfield (Lake County)	60015
Deerfield (Lake County) (Township)	60035
Deer Grove	61243
Deering (Part of Chicago)	60610
Deering City	62896
Deer Lake	60010
Dee Road (Part of Park Ridge)	60068
Deer Park (La Salle County) (Township)	61348
Deer Park (Lake County)	60010
Deer Plain	62013
Deer Run	60175
Deerwood Estates	62471
Degognia (Township)	62950

	ZIP
De Kalb	60115
De Kalb (Township)	60115
Delafield	62859
De Land	61839
Delavan	61734
Delavan (Township)	61734
Del-Bar	61520
Delhi	62052
Dellwood Highlands	60441
Del Mar Woods	60015
DeLong	61436
Del Rey	60968
Delwood	62946
Dement (Township)	61068
Denison (Township)	62460
Denmark	62238
Denning (Township)	62896
Dennison	62423
Denny	62832
Denver (Hancock County)	62321
Denver (Richland County) (Township)	62868
Depue	61322
Derby (Ford County)	60936
Derby (Saline County)	62947
Derinda (Township)	61028
Derinda Center	61028
Derry (Township)	62312
Deselm	60950
De Soto	62924
De Soto (Township)	62924
Des Plaines	60016-19
For specific Des Plaines Zip Codes call (708) 827-5591, or your local postmaster.	
Des Plaines Manor (Part of Des Plaines)	60016
Des Plaines Terrace (Part of Des Plaines)	60016
Detroit	62332
Detroit (Township)	62332
Devereux Heights (Part of Springfield)	62707
Devonshire (Part of Des Plaines)	60018
Dewey	61840
Dewitt	61735
De Witt (Township)	61735
Dewmaine	62918
Dexter	62411
Diamond	60416
Diamond City	62859
Diamond Lake	60060
Diamond Town	62274
Dieterich	62424
Dillon	61568
Dillon (Township)	61568
Dillsburg	61866
Dimmick (Township)	61301
Diona	62428
Disco	61450
Diswood	62988
Divernon	62530
Divernon (Township)	62530
Divide	62889
Division Street (Part of Chicago)	60651
Dix (Ford County) (Township)	60933
Dix (Jefferson County)	62830
Dixmoor	60406
Dixon	61021
Dixon (Township)	61021
Dixon Springs	62943
Dobbins Downs	61801
Dodds (Township)	62864
Doddsville	61452
Dollville	62571
Dolson (Township)	61944
Dolton	60419
Dongola	62926
Donnellson	62019
Donovan	60931
Dora (Township)	61925
Dorans	61938
Dorchester	62033
Dorchester (Township)	62009
Dorr (Township)	60098
Dorris Heights (Part of Harrisburg)	62946
Dorsey	62021
Douglas (Clark County) (Township)	62441
Douglas (Effingham County) (Township)	62401
Douglas (Iroquois County) (Township)	60938
Douglas (Knox County)	61572
Douglas (St. Clair County)	62243

* Area Zip Code   † Post Office Boxes

	ZIP		ZIP		ZIP		ZIP
Douglas Park	61081	East Cape Girardeau	62957	Elam Lake	61951	Enfield	62835
Dover	61323	East Carondelet	62240	Elba (Gallatin County)	62871	Enfield (Township)	62835
Dover (Township)	61356	East Clinton	61252	Elba (Knox County)		Engelmann (Township)	62258
Dow	62022	East Dubuque	61025	(Township)	61489	England Heights	62901
Dowell	62927	East Dundee	60118	Elba Center	61572	Englewood (Part of	
Downers Fairview (Part of		East Eldorado (Township)	62930	Elbridge	61944	Chicago)	60621
Downers Grove)	60515	Eastern (Township)	62812	Elbridge (Township)	61944	English (Township)	62052
Downers Grove	60515-17	East Fork (Clinton County)		Elburn	60119	Enion	62644
For specific Downers Grove Zip		(Township)	62283	Elco	62929	Enos	62626
Codes call (708) 969-2001, or		East Fork (Montgomery		El Dara	62312	Enright	61738
your local postmaster.		County) (Township)	62017	Eldena	61324	Enterprise	62823
Downers Grove		East Fulton	61252	Elderville	62313	Eola	60519
(Township)	60559	East Galena (Township)	61036	Eldorado (McDonough		Eppards Point (Township)	61764
Downers Grove Estates	60515	East Galesburg	61430	County) (Township)	61411	Epworth	62821
Downey (Part of North		Eastgate	62881	Eldorado (Saline County)	62930	Equality	62934
Chicago)	60064	East Gillespie	62033	Eldred	62027	Equality (Township)	62934
Downs	61736	East Grove (Township)	61349	Eleanor	61453	Erie	61250
Downs (Township)	61736	East Hannibal	62343	Eleroy	61027	Erie (Township)	61250
Downtown (Part of		East Hardin	62031	Elgin	60120-23	Erienna (Township)	60450
Bloomington)	61701	East Hazel Crest	60429	For specific Elgin Zip Codes		Erin (Township)	61027
Downtown (Part of		East Keokuk (Part of		call (708) 741-0725, or your		Erontenac	60118
Carbondale)	62901	Hamilton)	62341	local postmaster.		Esmen (Township)	60460
Downtown (Part of Des		Eastland Mall (Part of		Elgin Estates	60123	Esmond	60129
Plaines)	60016	Bloomington)	61701	Eliza	61272	Essex (Kankakee County)	60935
Downtown (Part of Glen		East Lincoln (Township)	62656	Eliza (Township)	61272	Essex (Kankakee County)	
Ellyn)	60137	East Loon Lake	60002	Elizabeth	61028	(Township)	60935
Downtown (Part of La		East Lynn	60932	Elizabeth (Township)	61028	(Stark County)	
Salle)	61301	East Meadowbrook	62067	Elizabethtown	62931	Essex (Township)	61491
Downtown (Part of		East Meadowview (Part of		Elk (Township)	62932	Estate Lane (Part of	
Northbrook)	60062	Bradley)	60915	Elk Grove (Township)	60007	Glenview)	60025
Downtown (Part of		East Moline	61244	Elk Grove Village	60007*	Etherton	62966
Rockford)	61101	East Nelson (Township)	61951		60009†	Eubanks	62301
Downtown (Part of		East Newbern	62022	Elkhart	62634	Euclid Lake (Part of	
Springfield)	62701	East Oakland (Township)	61943	Elkhart (Township)	62634	Mount Prospect)	60056
Downtown (Part of		Easton	62633	Elkhorn (Township)	62353	Eureka	61530
Quincy)	62301	East Peoria	61611	Elkhorn Grove (Township)	61051	Evans	61377
Drake	62092	East River	60964	Elk Prairie (Township)	62816	Evans (Township)	61377
Dresden Acres	60450	East Rockford (Part of		Elk Ridge Villa (Part of		Evanston	60201-04
Drexel (Part of Cicero)	60650	Rockford)	61110	Mount Prospect)	60056	For specific Evanston Zip	
Drivers	62898	East Side (Cook County)	60617	Elkton	62268	Codes call (708) 328-6201, or	
Druce Lake	60046	East Side (Kankakee		Elkville	62932	your local postmaster.	
Drummer (Township)	60936	County)	60954	Ellery	62833	Evansville	62242
Drury (Township)	52761	East St. Louis	62201-08	Ellington	62301	Evarts	61067
Dry Grove (Township)	61732	For specific East St. Louis Zip		Ellington (Township)	62301	Evergreen Park	60642
Dry Point (Township)	62422	Codes call (618) 875-0200, or		Elliott	60933	Evergreen Plaza (Part of	
Dubois	62831	your local postmaster.		Elliottstown	62424	Evergreen Park)	60642
Du Bois (Township)	62831	East Wenona	61377	Ellis	61865	Ewing	62836
Duck Lake Woods	60041	Eastwood Manor	60050	Ellis Grove	62241	Ewing (Township)	62836
Dudley	61944	Eaton	62454	Ellison	61478	Exeter	62621
Dudleyville	62246	Eberle	62424	Ellisville	61431	Exline	60901
Duncan (Mercer County)		Echo Lake	60047	Ellisville (Township)	61431	Expo Park (Part of	
(Township)	61231	Eckard	62644	Ellsworth	61737	Hoffman Estates)	60192
Duncan (Stark County)	61559	Eddyville	62928	Elwood Greens	60135	Eylar	61769
Duncans Mills	61542	Edelstein	61526	Elm Estates (Part of		Ezra	62896
Duncanville	62454	Eden (La Salle County)		Elmhurst)	60126	Factory Outlet Mall (Part	
Dundas	62425	(Township)	61370	Elm Grove (Township)	61554	of Kankakee)	60901
Dundee	60118	Eden (Peoria County)	61536	Elmhurst	60126	Fairbanks	61937
Dundee (Township)	60118	Eden (Randolph County)	62286	Elmira	61483	Fairbury	61739
Dunfermline	61524	Eden Park	62933	Elmira (Township)	61483	Fair City	62952
Dunham (Township)	60033	Edford (Township)	61254	Elmore	61451	Fairdale	60146
Dunhurst (Part of		Edgar	61924	El Morro (Part of Oak		Fairfield (Bureau County)	
Wheeling)	60090	Edgar (Township)	60118	Forest)	60452	(Township)	61283
Dunkel	62557	Edgebrook (Cook County)	60646	Elm River (Township)	62842	Fairfield (Lake County)	60047
Dunlap	61525	Edgebrook (DeKalb		Elmwood	61529	Fairfield (Wayne County)	62837
Dunlap Lake (Part of		County)	60178	Elmwood (Township)	61529	Fairfield Heights	61032
Edwardsville)	62025	Edgemont (Part of East		Elmwood Park	60635	Fair Grange	61920
Dunleith (Township)	61025	St. Louis)	62203	El Paso	61738	Fair Haven	61014
Dunn	61951	Edgewater Beach	62231	El Paso (Township)	61738	Fairhaven (Township)	61014
Dunning (Part of Chicago)	60634	Edgewood (Champaign		El-Rancho	60901	Fairland	61956
Du Page (Township)	60441	County)	61801	Elsah	62028	Fairman	62882
Dupo	62239	Edgewood (Effingham		Elsah (Township)	62028	Fairmont	60441
Du Quoin	62832	County)	62426	Elsdon (Part of Chicago)	60632	Fairmont City	62201
Durand	61024	Edgewood (Woodford		El Sierra (Part of Downers		Fairmount (Madison	
Durand (Township)	61024	County)	61530	Grove)	60515	County)	62002
Durham	62330	Edgewood Heights	61008	Elva	60115	Fairmount (Massac	
Durham (Township)	62330	Edgington	61284	Elvaston	62334	County)	62960
Durley Camp	62246	Edgington (Township)	61284	Elvira	62912	Fairmount (Pike County)	
Dutch Creek Woodlands	60050	Edinburg	62531	El Vista (Cook County)	60452	(Township)	62314
Dutch Hollow (Part of		Edison Park (Part of		El Vista (Peoria County)	61604	Fairmount (Vermilion	
Belleville)	62221	Chicago)	60631	Elwin	62532	County)	61841
Duvall	62565	Edison Square (Part of		Elwood (Vermilion County)		Fair Oaks (Cook County)	60103
Dwight	60420	Waukegan)	60085	(Township)	61870	Fair Oaks (DuPage	
Dwight (Township)	60420	Edwards	61528	Elwood (Will County)	60421	County)	60185
Dwight Correctional		Edwardsville	62025	Embarrass (Township)	61949	Fair Oaks (Kane County)	60175
Center	60420	Edwardsville (Township)	62025	Emden	62635	Fairview (Christian	
Dykersburg	62987	Edwardsville Junction		Emerald Green (Part of		County)	62568
Eagarville	62023	(Part of Edwardsville)	62025	Warrenville)	60555	Fairview (Cook County)	60176
Eagle (Township)	61364	Effingham	62401	Emerald Park	60050	Fairview (Fulton County)	61432
Eagle Creek (Township)	62934	Effner	60966	Emerald Terrace	62223	Fairview (Fulton County)	
Eagle Heights	60123	Egan	61047	Emerson	61081	(Township)	61432
Eagle Lake	60401	Egyptian Hills	62922	Emerson City	62883	Fairview (St. Clair County)	62232
Eagle Park	62060	Egyptian Shores	62922	Eminence (Township)	61721	Fairview Addition	62930
Eagle Point (Township)	61064	Eight Mile Prairie	62918	Emington	60934	Fairview Avenue (Part of	
Eagle Point Bay	62939	Eighty-Seventh Street		Emma	62834	Downers Grove)	60515
Earl (Township)	60518	(Part of Chicago)	60619	Emma (Township)	62834	Fairview Gardens (Part of	
Earl Estates	60554	Eighty-Third Street (Part of		Emmet (Township)	61455	Mount Prospect)	60056
Earlville	60518	Chicago)	60617	Empire (Township)	61752	Fairview Heights	62208
East Alton	62024	Eiker Addition	61448	Empire Hills	60175	Fairway	61401
East Bend (Township)	61840	Eileen (Part of Coal City)	60416	Enchanted Forest	61604	Fairway Estates (Cook	
East Brooklyn	60474	Ela (Township)	60047	Energy	62933	County)	60462

	ZIP		ZIP		ZIP		ZIP
Fairway Estates (DuPage County)	60187	Flora (Boone County) (Township)	61008	Fox River Bluffs 2	60118	Garden of Eden	60954
Fall Creek	62360	Flora (Clay County)	62839	Fox River Commons (Part of Aurora)	60540	Garden Plain	61252
Fall Creek (Township)	62360	Floraville	62298	Fox River Estates	60174	Garden Plain (Township)	61252
Fall Creek (Township)	61350	Florence (Pike County)	62363	Fox River Gardens	60560	Garden Prairie	61038
Falmouth	62448	Florence (Stephenson County)	61032	Fox River Grove	60021	Garden Quarter (Part of Elgin)	60123
Fancher	62444	Florence (Stephenson County) (Township)	61032	Fox River Heights	60174	Gardner (Grundy County)	60424
Fancy Creek (Township)	62684	Florence (Will County) (Township)	60481	Fox River Valley Gardens	60010	Gardner (Sangamon County) (Township)	62677
Fancy Prairie	62613	Florid	61327	Fox Valley Center (Part of Aurora)	60504	Gards Point	62863
Fandon	62326	Flossmoor	60422	Fox Valley East (Part of Aurora)	60505	Garfield (Grundy County) (Township)	60424
Fargo	62375	Flossmoor Highlands (Part of Flossmoor)	60422	Fox Valley Mail Processing Center	60598† 60599*	Garfield (La Salle County)	61377
Farina	62838	Flowerfield Acres (Part of Lombard)	60148	Fox Valley Villages (Part of Aurora)	60505	Garfield Park (Part of Chicago)	60624
Farmer City	61842	Floyd (Township)	61423	Frankfort (Franklin County) (Township)	62896	Garland	61917
Farmers (Township)	61482	Fondulac (Tazewell County) (Township)	61611	Frankfort (Will County) (Township)	60423	Garrett	61913
Farmersville	62533	Fon-Du-Lac (Will County)	60544	Frankfort (Will County)	60423	Garrett (Township)	61913
Farmingdale (DuPage County)	60561	Foosland	61845	Frankfort Heights (Part of West Frankfort)	62840	Gary Gardens	60188
Farmingdale (Sangamon County)	62677	Ford City Shopping Center (Part of Chicago)	60652	Frankfort Square	60423	Gas Light Village	60450
Farmingdale South (Part of Darien)	60561	Fordham (Part of Chicago)	60619	Franklin (DeKalb County) (Township)	60146	Gateway Yard (Part of East St. Louis)	62207
Farmingdale Terrace (Part of Darien)	60561	Ford Heights	60411	Franklin (Morgan County)	62638	Gays	61928
Farmingdale Village (Part of Darien)	60561	Forest Acres	62201	Franklin Grove	61031	Geff	62842
Farmington (Township)	61531	Forest City	61532	Franklin Park	60131	Genesee (Township)	61270
Farmington (Kane County)	60174	Forest City (Township)	61532	Franklin Square	60423	Geneseo	61254
Farmington (Lake County)	60047	Forest Estates	60067	Franklinville	60098	Geneseo (Township)	61254
Farmington (Coles County)	62440	Forest Gardens	60084	Frederick	62639	Geneseo Hills	61254
Farmington (Fulton County)	61531	Forest Glen (Part of Chicago)	60630	Frederick (Township)	62639	Geneva	60134
Farm Ridge (Township)	61325	Foresthaven	60045	Freeburg	62243	Geneva (Township)	60134
Farmsted (Part of Naperville)	60565	Forest Heights (Part of Chicago Heights)	60411	Freeburg (Township)	62243	Genoa	60135
Farnsworth (Part of Waukegan)	60088	Forest Hill (Part of Chicago)	60652	Freedom (Carroll County) (Township)	61046	Genoa (Township)	60135
Farrington (Township)	62814	Forest Hills Estates	62471	Freedom (La Salle County) (Township)	61350	Gent City	62959
Farrow	61605	Forest Homes	62018	Freeman Spur	62841	Gentry Acres	62918
Fayette (Greene County)	62044	Forest Lake	60047	Freeport	61032	Georgetown (Township)	61846
Fayette (Livingston County) (Township)	61775	Forest Manor	60441	Freeport (Township)	61032	Georgetown (Carroll County)	61046
Fayetteville	62258	Forest Park	60130	Fremont (Township)	60060	Georgetown (McDonough County)	61455
Fayetteville (Township)	62258	Forest River	60056	Fremont Center	60060	Georgetown (Vermilion County)	61846
Fayville	62990	Forest View	60402	Fremont Junction (Part of Hanover Park)	60103	Gerald	61812
Federal Penitentiary	62959	Forest View Hills (Part of Oak Forest)	60452	Frenchman's Cove (Part of Arlington Heights)	60004	Gerlaw	61435
Feehanville (Part of Mount Prospect)	60056	Forman	62908	French Village (Part of Fairview Heights)	62208	German (Township)	62421
Felix (Township)	60416	Forrest	61741	Frentress Lake	61025	Germantown	62245
Felker (Part of Washington)	61571	Forrest (Township)	61741	Friends Creek (Township)	62501	Germantown (Township)	62245
Fenton	61251	Forrestal Village (Part of North Chicago)	60088	Friendsville	62863	Germantown	61548
Fenton (Township)	61251	Forreston	61030	Frisco	62836	Germantown Hills	61548
Fergestown	62959	Forreston (Township)	61030	Frog City	62913	German Valley	61039
Fernway (Part of Orland Park)	60462	Forsyth	62535	Frogtown (Clinton County)	62231	Germanville (Township)	60921
Ferrel	61944	Fort Dearborn	60610-11	Frogtown (Washington County)	62271	Gibson City	60936
Ferrin	62231	For specific Fort Dearborn Zip Codes call (312) 644-7603, or your local postmaster.		Frontenac	60563	Gibsonia	62954
Ferris	62336			Frontenac Place	62035	Gifford	61847
Fiatt	61433	Fort Gage	62241	Frost	62901	Gila	62445
Ficklin	61953	Fort Russell (Township)	62010	Fruit	62025	Gilberts	60136
Fiday View	60435	Foss Acres (Part of Waukegan)	60088	Fruitland	61265	Gilchrist	61486
Fidelity	62030	Foster (Madison County) (Township)	62002	Fry's Wheatland View	60565	Gilead	62006
Fidelity (Township)	62030	Foster (Marion County) (Township)	62807	Fulton	61252	Gillespie	62033
Field (Township)	62889	Fosterburg	62002	Fulton (Township)	61252	Gillespie (Township)	62033
Fieldcrest (Part of Oak Forest)	60452	Foster Pond	62298	Fults	62244	Gillespie Lakes	62033
Fieldon	62031	Fountain	62295	Funkhouser	62401	Gillum	61701
Fields West	61821	Fountain Bluff (Township)	62950	Funks Grove	61754	Gilman	60938
Fifty-Fifth Street (Part of Chicago)	60615	Fountain Creek	60942	Funks Grove (Township)	61754	Gilmer (Township)	62328
Fifty-Ninth Street (Part of Chicago)	60637	Fountain Creek (Township)	60942	Future City	62914	Gilmore	62443
Fifty-Seventh Street (Part of Chicago)	60637	Fountain Gap	62236	Fyre Lake	61281	Gilmore Lake	62236
Fillmore	62032	Fountain Green	62321	Gages Lake	60030	Gilson	61436
Fillmore (Township)	62032	Fountain Green (Township)	62321	Galatia	62935	Ginger Creek (Part of Oak Brook)	60521
Filson	61910	Four Lakes	60532	Galatia (Township)	62935	Ginger Hill (Part of Milan)	61264
Findlay	62534	Four Mile (Township)	62895	Gale	62990	Girard	62640
Finley Square Mall (Part of Downers Grove)	60515	Fowler	62338	Galena	61036	Girard (Township)	62640
Finney Heights	62801	Fox (Jasper County) (Township)	62448	Galena Oaks	61028	Givins (Part of Chicago)	60620
First Pommier	60964	Fox (Kendall County)	60560	Galesburg	61401* 61402†	Gladstone	61437
Fisher	61843	Fox (Kendall County) (Township)	60560	Galesburg City (Township)	61401	Gladstone (Township)	61437
Fishhook	62314	Fox Chase (Part of St. Charles)	60174	Galesville	61854	Gladstone Commons (Part of Mount Prospect)	60056
Fithian	61844	Foxcroft	60137	Gallagher	62450	Gladstone Park (Part of Chicago)	60630
Five Islands Park	60177	Foxfield	60175	Galnipper Place	62047	Glasford	61533
Flag Center	61068	Fox Lake	60020	Galt	61037	Glasgow	62694
Flagg	61068	Fox Lake Hills	60046	Galton	61910	Glass Works (Part of Alton)	62002
Flagg (Township)	61068	Fox Lake Vista	60081	Galva	61434	Glen (Part of Glen Carbon)	62034
Flamingo Estates	62286	Fox Lawn	60560	Galva (Township)	61434	Glen Acres (Part of Rosemont)	60018
Flanagan	61740	Fox Point (Part of Barrington)	60010	Ganeer (Township)	60954	Glenarm	62536
Flannigan (Township)	62890	Fox Ridge (Part of South Elgin)	60177	Ganntown	62943	Glen Arms	60041
Flat Branch (Township)	62550			Garber	60936	Glenavon	61724
Flat Rock	62427			Gardena (Part of East Peoria)	61611	Glenayre (Part of Glenview)	60025
Flatville	61878			Garden Heights	62946	Glenayre Gardens (Part of Glenview)	60025
Flat Woods	62985			Garden Hill (Township)	62899	Glenbard South	60532
Fletcher	61730			Garden Hills (Part of Champaign)	61821	Glenbrook Countryside	60062
Flickerville	60914			Garden Homes	60655	Glenburn	61858
Flint (Township)	62340					Glen Carbon	62034
						Glencoe	60022
						Glendale (Pope County)	62985

* Area Zip Code   † Post Office Boxes

	ZIP		ZIP		ZIP		ZIP
Glendale (Rock Island County)	61282	Grandwood Park	60031	Grover (Township)	62837	Harmony (McHenry County)	60140
Glendale Gardens (Part of Wood River)	62024	Grange	61872	Grupe	62401	Harmony Village (Part of Wheeling)	60090
Glendale Heights	60139	Granite City	62040	Guilford	61036	Harp (Township)	61727
Glen Ellyn	60137*	Granite City (Township)	62040	Guilford (Township)	61028	Harper	61030
	60138†	Grant (Lake County) (Township)	60041	Gulf Port	52601	Harpster	61845
Glen Ellyn Countryside	60137	Grant (Vermilion County) (Township)	60942	Gurnee	60031	Harris (Fulton County) (Township)	61459
Glen Ellyn Woods	60137	Grantfork	62249	Gurnee Mills (Part of Gurnee)	60031	Harris (Piatt County)	61842
Glengarry (Part of Geneva)	60134	Grant Park	60940	Guthrie	60936	Harrisburg	62946
Glen Hill (Part of Glendale Heights)	60139	Grantsburg	62943	Hadley	62312	Harrisburg (Township)	62946
Glenn	62280	Granville	61326	Hadley (Township)	62312	Harrison (Jackson County)	62966
Glennshire (Part of Lake Zurich)	60047	Granville (Township)	61326	Haegers Bend	60102	Harrison (Winnebago County)	61072
Glen Oak	60137	Grape Creek	61832	Hafer	62918	Harrison (Winnebago County) (Township)	61072
Glen Park	60551	Grass Lake	60002	Hagaman	62630	Harrisonville (Grundy County)	60416
Glen Ridge (Part of Matteson)	60443	Gray (Township)	62844	Hagarstown	62247	Harrisonville (Monroe County)	62295
Glenshire (Part of Glenview)	60025	Grayland (Part of Chicago)	60641	Hagener (Township)	62618	Harristown	62537
Glenview (Cook County)	60025	Graymont	61743	Hahnaman	61243	Harristown (Township)	62537
Glen View (St. Clair County)	62269	Graymoor (Part of Olympia Fields)	60461	Hahnaman (Township)	61283	Harter (Township)	62839
Glenview Countryside	60025	Grayslake	60030	Haines (Township)	62853	Hartford	62048
Glenview Estates	60025	Grays Siding	61858	Hainesville	60030	Hartland	60098
Glenview Naval Air Station	60026	Grayville	62844	Haldane	61030	Hartland (Township)	60098
Glenview Terrace (Part of Glenview)	60025	Green Acres (McDonough County)	61455	Hale (Township)	61462	Hartsburg	62643
Glenview Woodlands	60025	Green Acres (Sangamon County)	62707	Half Day	60069	Harvard	60033
Glenwood	60425	Greenbriar (Part of New Lenox)	60451	Hall (Township)	61362	Harvard Hills	61571
Glenwood Estates (Part of Glenwood)	60425	Greenbriar Addition	62918	Hallidayboro	62932	Harvel	62538
Glenwood Plaza (Part of Glenwood)	60425	Greenbrook Country (Part of Hanover Park)	60103	Hallock (Iroquois County)	60973	Harvel (Township)	62538
Godfrey	62035	Greenbush	61415	Hallock (Peoria County) (Township)	61526	Harvey	60426
Godfrey (Township)	62035	Greenbush (Township)	61415	Hallville	61727	Harwood (Township)	61847
Godley	60407	Greene (Mercer County) (Township)	61486	Halsey Village (Part of Waukegan)	60088	Harwood Heights	60656
Golconda	62938	Greene (Woodford County) (Township)	61516	Halsted Street (Part of Chicago)	60608	Hastings	61810
Gold (Township)	61344	Greenfield (Greene County)	62044	Hamburg (Bond County)	62262	Hatcher Woods	60450
Golden	62339	Greenfield (Grundy County) (Township)	60474	Hamburg (Calhoun County)	62045	Havana	62644
Golden Acres	60025	Green Garden (Township)	60423	Hamel	62046	Havana (Township)	62644
Golden Eagle	62036	Greenleaf Hills	61842	Hamel (Township)	62046	Haw Creek (Township)	61458
Golden Gardens (Part of Centreville)	62206	Green Meadows (Cook County)	60103	Hamilton (Hancock County)	62341	Hawthorn Center (Part of Vernon Hills)	60061
Goldengate	62843	Green Meadows (Kane County)	60510	Hamilton (Lee County) (Township)	61349	Hawthorne (Part of Cicero)	60650
Golden Highridge (Part of Des Plaines)	60016	Green Oak	61356	Hamlet	61231	Hawthorne (Part of Chicago)	60623
Golden Lilly	62914	Green Oaks	60048	Hamletsburg	62944	Hawthorne (White County) (Township)	62821
Golden Manor (Part of Des Plaines)	60016	Greenpond	62361	Hammond	61929	Hawthorn Woods	60047
Gold Hill (Township)	62984	Green River	61241	Hampshire	60140	Hawthrone Hills	62864
Golena Knolls	61523	Green Rock	61241	Hampshire (Township)	60140	Hayes	61953
Golf	60029	Greentree (Part of Libertyville)	60048	Hampshire Manor (Part of Hampshire)	60140	Hayford (Part of Chicago)	60652
Golf Mill Center (Part of Niles)	60714	Greenup	62428	Hampton	61256	Haymarket (Part of Chicago)	60606
Golfview Hills	60521	Greenup (Township)	62428	Hampton (Township)	61256	Haypress	62027
Goode (Township)	62884	Green Valley (DuPage County)	60148	Hampton Court (Part of Country Club Hills)	60477	Hazel Crest	60429
Goodenow	60401	Green Valley (Tazewell County)	61534	Hancock (Township)	62321	Hazelcrest Highlands (Part of Hazel Crest)	60429
Goodfarm (Township)	60424	Greenview	62642	Hanna (Township)	61254	Hazel Dell	62428
Goodfield	61742	Greenville (Bond County)	62246	Hanna City	61536	Hazelgreen (Part of Alsip)	60482
Good Hope	61438	Greenville (Bureau County) (Township)	61376	Hannon (Part of Taylorville)	62568	Hazelhurst	61064
Goodings Grove	60441	Greenwich	60901	Hanover (Cook County) (Township)	60103	Hazelwood	61254
Goodrich	60913	Greenwood (Christian County) (Township)	62546	Hanover (Jo Daviess County)	61041	Hazelwood Heights	61254
Goodwine	60939	Greenwood (McHenry County)	60098	Hanover (Jo Daviess County) (Township)	61041	Hazelwood West	61254
Goofy Ridge	61567	Greenwood (McHenry County) (Township)	60098	Hanover Highlands (Part of Hanover Park)	60103	Headyville	62424
Goose Creek (Township)	61839	Greenwood Acres	61840	Hanover Park	60103	Healy (Part of Chicago)	60639
Goose Lake (Township)	60444	Greenwood Meadows	62035	Hanover Park-Ontarioville (Part of Hanover Park)	60103	Heapsville	61425
Gordons	62454	Greer	60973	Hanover Square (Part of Hanover Park)	60103	Heartville	62401
Goreville	62939	Gresham (Part of Chicago)	60620	Hanson	62080	Heathercrest (Part of Northbrook)	60062
Gorham	62940	Gridley	61744	Hanson Park (Part of Chicago)	60639	Heatherfield	60450
Goshen (Township)	61483	Gridley (Township)	61744	Happy Hills	60175	Heatherlea	60074
Gossett	62869	Grigg	62278	Happy Hollow Lake	61428	Heathsville	62427
Grafton (Jersey County)	62037	Griggsville	62340	Harbor Dell	62035	Hebron	60034
Grafton (McHenry County) (Township)	60142	Griggsville (Township)	62340	Harbor Estates	60010	Hebron (Township)	60034
Graham Correctional Center	62049	Grimes Addition	61081	Harco	62945	Hecker	62248
Grand Chain	62941	Grimsby	62940	Hardin (Calhoun County)	62047	Hegeler	61832
Grand Crossing (Part of Chicago)	60619	Grinnell	62908	Hardin (Pike County) (Township)	62355	Hegewisch (Part of Chicago)	60633
Grand Detour	61021	Grisham (Township)	62077	Harding	60518	Helena	62466
Grand Detour (Township)	61021	Griswold	60929	Hardinville	62449	Helmar	60541
Grand Prairie (Township)	62898	Gromers Woods	60120	Harlem (Stephenson County) (Township)	61032	Helvetia (Township)	62249
Grand Rapids (Township)	61325	Gross	62931	Harlem (Winnebago County)	61111	Heman	62573
Grand Ridge	61325	Grove (Township)	62448	Harlem (Winnebago County) (Township)	61111	Henderson	61439
Grand Tower	62942	Grove, The (Part of Downers Grove)	60516	Harlem Avenue (Part of Berwyn)	60402	Henderson (Township)	61439
Grand Tower (Township)	62942	Grove City	62531	Harlem-Irving Plaza (Part of Chicago)	60634	Henderson	62033
Grandview (Carroll County)	61285	Groveland (La Salle County) (Township)	61358	Harmon	61042	Henderson Grove	61401
Grandview (Edgar County)	61944	Groveland (Tazewell County)	61535	Harmon (Township)	61042	Hendryx Manor	61614
Grandview (Edgar County) (Township)	61944	Groveland (Tazewell County) (Township)	61535	Harmony (Hancock County) (Township)	62321	Hennepin	61327
Grandview (Sangamon County)	62702			Harmony (Jefferson County)	62864	Hennepin (Township)	61327
Grandview (Woodford County)	61611					Henning	61848
Grandville (Township)	62481					Henry	61537
						Henry (Township)	61537
						Hensley (Township)	61820
						Henton	62565
						Herald	62845
						Heralds Prairie (Township)	62869
						Herbert	60145
						Herborn	62465

	ZIP		ZIP		ZIP		ZIP
Heritage (Part of Moline)	61265	Hodgkins	60525	Huey	62252	Ingleside	60041
Heritage Estates (Part of		Hoffman	62250	Hugh's Addition	62684	Ingleside Shores	60041
Bourbonnais)	60914	Hoffman Estates	60194-95	Hugo	61953	Ingraham	62434
Hermon	61458	For specific Hoffman Estates		Hull	62343	Ingram Hill	62946
Hermosa (Part of		Zip Codes call (708) 885-6510,		Humboldt	61931	International Village (Cook	
Chicago)	60639	or your local postmaster.		Humboldt (Township)	61931	County)	60194
Herod	62947	Hoffmann Edition	60924	Hume (Edgar County)	61932	International Village	
Herrick	62431	Holbrook	60411	Hume (Whiteside County)		(DuPage County)	60148
Herrick (Township)	62431	Holcomb	61043	(Township)	61071	International Village (Will	
Herrin	62948	Holden	62832	Humm Wye	62938	County)	60440
Herscher	60941	Holder	61736	Humrick	61870	Inverness	60067
Hersman	62353	Holiday Hills	60050	Hunt City	62480	Inverness on the Ponds	
Hervey City	62549	Holiday Shores	62025	Hunt City (Township)	62480	(Part of Inverness)	60067
Hettick	62649	Holland	62414	Hunter (Boone County)	61011	Iola	62847
Heworth	61745	Holland (Township)	62414	Hunter (Edgar County)	61944	Ipava	61441
Hickory (Township)	62624	Hollandia	62221	Hunter (Edgar County)		Irene	61016
Hickory Falls	60097	Hollenback	60450	(Township)	61944	Irishtown (Township)	62253
Hickory Grove	62301	Hollendale (Part of South		Hunter Trail (Part of Oak		Irondale (Part of Chicago)	60617
Hickory Hill (Township)	62895	Holland)	60473	Brook)	60521	Iroquois	60945
Hickory Hills (Cook		Holliday	62414	Huntington (Part of		Iroquois (Township)	60928
County)	60457	Hollis (Township)	61607	Naperville)	60540	Irving	62051
Hickory Hills (Piatt		Hollowayville	61356	Huntington Commons		Irving (Township)	62051
County)	61884	Hollydale (Part of		(Part of Mount		Irving Park (Part of	
Hickory Hollow	60118	Homewood)	60430	Prospect)	60056	Chicago)	60641
Hickory Point (Macon		Hollywood (Part of		Huntington Park (Part of		Irvington	62848
County) (Township)	62526	Brookfield)	60513	Elgin)	60120	Irvington (Township)	62848
Hickory Point (Shelby		Hollywood Heights	62232	Huntinton Park	62035	Irwin	60901
County)	62565	Hollywood Ridge (Part of		Huntley	60142	Isabel (Edgar County)	61943
Hickoryville	63673	Wheeling)	60090	Huntsville	62344	Isabel (Fulton County)	
Hicks	62947	Holmes Center	61523	Huntsville (Township)	62344	(Township)	61542
Hidalgo	62432	Homberg	62938	Hurlbut (Township)	62634	Island Grove (Jasper	
Hidden Creek	60074	Home Gardens (Part of		Hurricane (Township)	62080	County)	62467
Hidden Hills	61455	Danville)	61832	Hurst	62949	Island Grove (Sangamon	
Higginsville	61865	Homer (Champaign		Hutchins Park	61103	County) (Township)	62677
High Knob	60187	County)	61849	Hutsonville	62433	Island Lake	60042
High Lake	60185	Homer (Will County)		Hutsonville (Township)	62433	Itasca	60143
Highland (Grundy County)		(Township)	60441	Hutton	61920	Itasca Ranchettes	60143
(Township)	60437	Homerican Villas (Part of		Hutton (Township)	61920	Iuka	62849
Highland (Madison		Des Plaines)	60016	Hyde Park (Part of		Iuka (Township)	62849
County)	62249	Homestead (Part of		Chicago)	60615	Ivanhoe (Cook County)	60627
Highlander	62901	O'Fallon)	62269		60653	Ivanhoe (Lake County)	60060
Highland Haven	60123	Hometown	60456	For specific Hyde Park Zip		Ivanhoe (Will County)	60440
Highland Hills	60148	Homewood (Cook		Codes call (312) 924-9221, or		Ivanhoe Estates	61801
Highland Lake	60030	County)	60430	your local postmaster.		Ivesdale	61851
Highland Park (Lake		Homewood (Rock Island		Idaville Corner	60924	Ivy Glen (Part of Aurora)	60506
County)	60035	County)	61265	Ideal	61285	Ivy Heights (Part of Wood	
Highland Park (Marion		Homewood Acres	60430	Idlewild	60030	River)	62024
County)	62881	Homewood Shores (Part		Idlewood	62864	Jackson (Effingham	
Highlands (Cook County)	60411	of Homewood)	60430	Iliana	47982	County) (Township)	62401
Highlands (DuPage		Homewood Terrace (Part		Illiana Heights	60954	Jackson (Will County)	
County)	60521	of Homewood)	60430	Illini (Township)	62573	(Township)	60421
Highlands-Clarks	60543	Honegger	61741	Illinois Center (Part of		Jackson Park (Part of	
Highland Shores	60097	Honey Bend	62056	Marion)	62959	Chicago)	60637
Highlawn (Part of		Honey Creek (Adams		Illinois City	61259	Jacksonville	62650*
Riverdale)	60627	County) (Township)	62325	Illinois River Correctional			62651†
High Meadows	61607	Honey Creek (Crawford		Center	61520	Jacksonville Correctional	
High Point (Part of		County) (Township)	62427	Illinois Veterans Home		Center	62650
Hoffman Estates)	60195	Honey Creek (Ogle		(Part of Quincy)	62301	Jacob	62950
Highview Estates	60514	County)	61015	Illiopolis	62539	Jalapa	62054
Highway Village (Part of		Honey Point (Township)	62056	Illiopolis (Township)	62539	Jamaica	61841
East Peoria)	61611	Hononegah Heights	61073	Imbs	62240	Jamaica (Township)	61841
Highwood (Lake County)	60040	Hoodville	62859	Imperial	60048	Jamesburg	61865
Highwood (St. Clair		Hookdale	62284	Ina	62846	Jamestown (Clinton	
County)	62221	Hoopeston	60942	Independence (Pike		County)	62275
Highwood Terrace (Part of		Hoopole	61258	County)	62363	Jamestown (Perry County)	62238
Belleville)	62221	Hoosier (Township)	62858	Independence (Saline		Janesville	62435
Hilcrest	62089	Hope (La Salle County)		County) (Township)	62946	Jarvis (Township)	62294
Hildreth	61876	(Township)	61334	Indian Creek (Lake		Jasper (Township)	62837
Hill Correctional Center	61401	Hope (Vermilion County)	61812	County)	60060	Jefferson (Cook County)	60630
Hillcrest (Calhoun County)	62045	Hopedale	61747	Indian Creek (White		Jefferson (Stephenson	
Hillcrest (Christian County)	62568	Hopedale (Township)	61747	County) (Township)	62869	County) (Township)	61062
Hillcrest (Cook County)	60439	Hopewell	61565	Indian Grove (Township)	61739	Jefferson Square Mall	
Hillcrest (Douglas County)	61953	Hopewell (Township)	61540	Indian Head Park	60525	(Part of Joliet)	60435
Hillcrest (Henry County)	61254	Hop Hollow	62035	Indian Hill (Cook County)	60093	Jeffries	62951
Hillcrest (Ogle County)	61068	Hopkins (Township)	61081	Indian Hill (DuPage		Jeiseyville	62568
Hildale Villages (Part of		Hopkins Park	60944	County)	60563	Jenkins	61727
Hoffman Estates)	60195	Hopper	61480	Indian Hills (Cook County)	60411	Jerome	62704
Hillerman	62941	Horace	61924	Indian Hills (Jo Daviess		Jersey (Township)	62052
Hillery	61832	Horatio Gardens	60069	County)	61025	Jerseyville	62052
Hillsboro	62049	Hord	62858	Indian Oaks (Kankakee		Jewett	62436
Hillsboro (Township)	62049	Hornsby	62056	County)	60914	Jimtown	61872
Hillsdale	61257	Horseshoe	62934	Indian Oaks (Will County)	60440	Johannisburg	62214
Hillside (Cook County)	60162	Houston (Adams County)		Indianola	61850	Johannisburg (Township)	62214
Hillside (Kankakee		(Township)	62339	Indian Point (Knox		Johnsburg	60050
County)	60901	Houston (Randolph		County) (Township)	61410	Johnson (Christian	
Hillside Manor	60901	County)	62286	Indian Point (Lake County)	60002	County) (Township)	62568
Hill Top	62675	Howardton	62942	Indian Point (Menard		Johnson (Clark County)	
Hilview	62050	Howe (Part of Depue)	61322	County)	62613	(Township)	62420
Hillyard (Township)	62676	Howe Terrace	60010	Indian Prairie (Township)	62823	Johnsonville	62850
Himrod	61883	Hoyleton	62803	Indian Ridge (McHenry		Johnston City	62951
Hinckley	60520	Hoyleton (Township)	62803	County)	60097	Johnstown	62440
Hindsboro	61930	Hubbard Woods (Cook		Indian Ridge (Piatt		Joliet	60431-36
Hinsdale	60521*	County)	60093	County)	61884	For specific Joliet Zip Codes	
	60522†	Hubbard Woods (Marion		Indiantown (Township)	61421	call (815) 741-7813, or your	
Hinswood (Part of Darien)	60561	County)	62801	Indian Trail Estates	60015	local postmaster.	
Hire (Township)	62326	Hubly	62642	Industrial Park	62864	Jonathan Creek	
Hitt	61051	Hudgens	62959	Industry	61440	(Township)	61911
Hittle (Township)	61721	Hudson	61748	Industry (Township)	61440	Jones (Coles County)	61938
Hodgetown	62865	Hudson (Township)	61748	Ingalls Park	60431	Jones (Cook County)	60452
		Huegely	62803	Ingalton	60185	Jonesboro	62952

* Area Zip Code   **† Post Office Boxes**

	ZIP		ZIP		ZIP		ZIP
Jones Ridge	62280	Kings Cove (Part of		Lake Fork	62541	Lane	61750
Jonesville	61348	Deerfield)	60015	Lake Fork (Township)	62548	Lanesville	62515
Joppa	62953	Kings Island (Part of Fox		Lake Holiday	60548	Lanesville (Township)	62515
Jordan (Township)	61081	Lake)	60020	Lakehurst Shopping		Langleyville	62568
Joshua (Township)	61432	Kings Park (Part of		Center (Part of		Lansing	60438
Joslin	61257	Bolingbrook)	60440	Waukegan)	60085	Laona (Township)	61024
Joy	61260	Kingston (Adams County)	62312	Lake in the Hills	60102	La Place	61936
Joywood Farms Estates	60228	Kingston (DeKalb County)	60145	Lake in the Woods	60515	La Prairie (Adams County)	62346
Jubilee (Township)	61559	Kingston (DeKalb County)		Lake Iroquois	60948	La Prairie (Marshall	
Junction	62954	(Township)	60145	Lake Ka-Ho	62069	County) (Township)	61523
Junction City	62882	Kingston Mines	61539	Lake Killarney	60013	La Prairie Center	61565
Justice	60458	Kingswood	60175	Lake Lancelot	61547	Larchland	61462
Kampsville	62053	Kinkaid (Township)	62907	Lakeland Hills (Jackson		Larkdale (Lake County)	60084
Kane	62054	Kinmundy	62854	County)	62901	Larkdale (Macon County)	62521
Kane (Township)	62054	Kinmundy (Township)	62854	Lakeland Hills (St. Clair		Larkinsburg (Township)	62426
Kaneville	60144	Kinsman	60437	County)	62221	La Rose	61541
Kaneville (Township)	60144	Kirkland	60146	Lakeland Park (Part of		La Salle	61301
Kangley	61364	Kirksville	61951	McHenry)	60050	La Salle (Township)	61301
Kankakee	60901	Kirkwood	61447	Lake Lawrence	47591	Latham	62543
Kankakee (Township)	60901	Kishwaukee Glen	61109	Lake Louise	61010	Latona	62479
Kankakee Valley	60964	Klein Acres (Part of		Lake Lynwood (Cook		Laura	61451
Kansas (Edgar County)	61933	Rantoul)	61866	County)	60411	La Vergne (Part of	
Kansas (Edgar County)		Klendworth Addition	61250	Lake Lynwood (Henry		Berwyn)	60402
(Township)	61933	Klondike (Alexander		County)	61262	Lawndale (Logan County)	61751
Kansas (Woodford		County)	62914	Lake Mantero	60950	Lawndale (McLean	
County) (Township)	61725	Klondike (Lake County)	60002	Lake Marie	60002	County) (Township)	61728
Kappa	61738	Klondyke	62466	Lake Marion	60110	Lawn Ridge	61526
Karbers Ridge	62955	Knapp's Noll	61072	Lake Mattoon	62447	Lawrence (Lawrence	
Karnak	62956	Knight Prairie (Township)	62859	Lakemoor	60050	County) (Township)	62439
Kasbeer	61328	Knollcrest (Part of Hazel		Lake Oakland	61943	Lawrence (McHenry	
Kaskaskia (Fayette		Crest)	60429	Lake of the Winds (Part		County)	60033
County) (Township)	62892	Knollwood (Christian		of Wheeling)	60090	Lawrenceville	62439
Kaskaskia (Randolph		County)	62568	Lake of the Woods		Layton	62681
County)	63673	Knollwood (Lake County)	60044	(Champaign County)	61820	Leaf River	61047
Kaskaskia Heights	62217	Knollwood (Lake County;		Lake of the Woods		Leaf River (Township)	61047
Kaskaskia River	62231	Part of Lake Zurich)	60047	(Peoria County)	61525	Leaverton Park	62451
Kaufman	62001	Knollwood (Sangamon		Lake Pana	62557	Lebanon	62254
Kedron	62934	County)	62684	Lake Park	61821	Lebanon (Township)	62254
Kedzie (Part of Chicago)	60623	Knottingham (Part of		Lake Park Estates	60067	Leclaire (Part of	
Kedzie Grace (Part of		Downers Grove)	60515	Lake Park Forest	60067	Edwardsville)	62025
Chicago)	60618	Knox (Township)	61448	Lake Petersburg	62675	Ledford	62946
Keene (Township)	62349	Knoxville	61448	Lake Piasa	62012	Lee (Brown County)	
Keenes	62851	Kortcamp (Part of Schram		Lake Ranier	62626	(Township)	62375
Keeneyville	60172	City)	62049	Lake Sara	62401	Lee (Fulton County)	
Keensburg	62852	Kraft Addition	62812	Lakeshore Acres	62231	(Township)	61470
Keith (Township)	62878	Kriegh Addition	61448	Lakeside Knolls	62049	Lee (Lee County)	60530
Keithsburg	61442	Kristal Lake Ranch	61032	Lakeside Villas (Part of		Lee Center	61331
Keithsburg (Township)	61442	Kuhn	62025	Wheeling)	60090	Lee Center (Township)	61331
Kell	62853	La Clede	62426	Lake Summerset	61019	Leech (Township)	62833
Kellar Lake	60924	La Clede (Township)	62426	Lake Tacoma	62901	Leeds	61377
Kellerville	62324	Lacon	61540	Lake Tara Estates	60118	Leef (Township)	62249
Kelleyville (Part of		Lacon (Township)	61540	Lake Thunderbird	61560	Leepertown (Township)	61315
Westville)	61883	La Crosse	61450	Lakeview (Part of		Leesburg	61501
Kelly (Township)	61412	Ladd	61329	Chicago)	60613	Leesville	60964
Kemp	61910	Laenna (Township)	62548	Lakeview Acres	62234	Lehigh	60901
Kemper	62063	Lafayette (Coles County)		Lakeview Estate	62881	Leisure Lea	60543
Kempton	60946	(Township)	61938	Lakeview Estates		Leisure Village (Part of	
Kendall (Township)	60560	Lafayette (Ogle County)		(Jefferson County)	62864	Fox Lake)	60020
Kendall Hills	62024	(Township)	61006	Lake View Estates		Leland	60531
Keneddy	61080	Lafayette (Randolph		(Williamson County)	62958	Leland Grove	62704
Kenilwicke	60067	County)	63673	Lakeview Heights (Part of		Leland Lake	62650
Kenilworth	60043	La Fayette (Stark County)	61449	Fairfield)	62837	Lemont	60439
Kenney	61749	La Fontaine (Part of		Lake Villa	60046	Lemont (Township)	60439
Ken Rock	61109	Glenview)	60025	Lake Villa (Township)	60046	Le Moyne (Part of	
Kensington (Part of		Lafox	60147	Lake Wildwood	61336	Chicago)	60638
Chicago)	60628	Lagrange (Bond County)		Lake Williamson	62626	Lena	61048
Kensington Junction (Part		(Township)	62019	Lakewood (Cook County)	60466	Lenox (Township)	61462
of Chicago)	60628	La Grange (Brown		Lakewood (DuPage		Lenzburg	62255
Kent	61044	County)	62378	County)	60185	Lenzburg (Township)	62257
Kent (Township)	61044	La Grange (Cook County)	60525	Lakewood (Madison		Leonard	60938
Kenton (Part of Chicago)	60644	La Grange Highlands	60525	County)	62035	Leon Corners	61277
Kentucky	61944	La Grange Park	60525	Lakewood (McHenry		Leonore	61332
Kenwood (Champaign		La Grange Road (Part of		County)	60014	L'Erable	60927
County)	61821	La Grange)	60525	Lakewood (Shelby		Lerna	62440
Kenwood (Cook County)	60615	Laguna Woods	60462	County)	62438	Le Roy (Boone County)	
Keptown	62411	La Harpe	61450	Lakewood (Shelby		(Township)	61012
Kernan	61364	La Harpe (Township)	61450	County) (Township)	62438	Le Roy (McLean County)	61752
Kerr (Township)	61847	La Hogue	60938	Lakewood Park	62901	Levan (Township)	62966
Kerton (Township)	62644	Lake	62283	Lakewood Shores	60481	Levee (Township)	62343
Kewanee	61443	Lake (Township)	62801	Lakewood Village (Part of		Leverett	61821
Kewanee (Township)	61443	Lake Barrington	60010	Carpentersville)	60110	Lewistown	61542
Keyesport	62253	Lake Bluff	60044	Lake Zurich	60047	Lewistown (Township)	61542
Keyesport Landing	62253	Lake Boulevard Addition	61832	Lamard (Township)	62842	Lewood	60544
Key West (Part of Niles)	60016	Lake Bracken	61401	Lamb	62919	Lexington	61753
Kickapoo	61528	Lake Briarwood	60004	Lambert	60439	Lexington (Township)	61753
Kickapoo (Township)	61528	Lake Camelot	61547	La Moille	61330	Leyden (Township)	60131
Kidd	62277	Lake Carlinville	62626	La Moille (Township)	61349	Liberty	62347
Kidley	61924	Lake Catherine	60002	Lamoine (Township)	61415	Liberty (Township)	62347
Kilbourne	62655	Lake Centralia	62801	Lamotte (Township)	62451	Liberty (Effingham	
Kilbourne (Township)	62655	Lake Charleston	61920	Lamplighter (Part of		County) (Township)	62414
Kildeer	60047	Lake Charlotte	60174	Towanda)	61776	Liberty (Saline County)	62946
Kimberly Heights	60477	Lake City	61937	Lanark	61046	Liberty Acres	60048
Kincaid	62540	Lakecrest (Montgomery		Lancaster (Stephenson		Liberty Lake (Part of	
Kinderhook	62345	County)	62049	County) (Township)	61032	Libertyville)	60048
Kinderhook (Township)	62345	Lake Crest (Williamson		Lancaster (Wabash		Liberty Park	60559
King (Township)	62546	County)	62922	County)	62855	Libertyville	60048*
Kingdom	61021	Lake Estates	62959	Landers (Part of Chicago)	60652		60092†
Kingman	62463	Lake Forest	60045	Landes	62466	Libertyville (Township)	60048
Kings	61045	Lake Forest Estates (Part		Landings, The (Part of		Lick	62629
		of Belleville)	62221	Lansing)	60438	Lick Creek	62912

	ZIP
Licking (Township)	62449
Lidice (Part of Crest Hill)	60435
Lightsville	61047
Lilac Circle Homes (Part of Lombard)	60148
Lilly	61755
Lily Cache	60544
Lily Cache Acres	60544
Lily Lake	60151
Lilymoor	60050
Lima	62348
Lima (Township)	62348
Limerick	61349
Limestone (Kankakee County) (Township)	60901
Limestone (Peoria County) (Township)	61604
Limestone (Peoria County)	61607
Lincoln (Logan County)	62656
Lincoln (Ogle County) (Township)	61064
Lincoln Addition (Part of Wood River)	62095
Lincoln Correctional Center	62656
Lincoln Developmental Center	62656
Lincoln Estates	60423
Lincoln Gardens (Part of Alton)	62002
Lincoln Highway (Part of Olympia Fields)	60461
Lincoln Hills	60137
Lincoln Mall (Part of Matteson)	60443
Lincoln Park (Part of Chicago)	60614
	60657
For specific Lincoln Park Zip Codes call (312) 525-5959, or your local postmaster.	
Lincolnshire (Lake County)	60069
Lincolnshire (Will County)	60417
Lincolnshire Fields	61821
Lincolnwood	60645
	60659
For specific Lincolnwood Zip Codes call (312) 463-1210, or your local postmaster.	
Lincolnwood Hills	60451
Lincolnwood Town Center (Part of Lincolnwood)	60645
Lindenhurst	60046
Lindenhurst Estates (Part of Lindenhurst)	60046
Lindenwood	61049
Linder (Township)	62016
Linn (Wabash County)	62410
Linn (Woodford County) (Township)	61570
Linrose Heights	62216
Lintner	61929
Lioncrest (Part of Richton Park)	60466
Lis	62448
Lisbon	60541
Lisbon (Township)	60541
Lisbon Center	60541
Lisle	60532
Lisle (Township)	60532
Litchfield (Kankakee County)	60954
Litchfield (Montgomery County)	62056
Literberry	62660
Little America	61542
Little Indian	62691
Little Mackinaw (Township)	61759
Little Rock	60545
Little Rock (Township)	60545
Little Swan Lake	61415
Littleton	61452
Littleton (Township)	61452
Little York	61453
Lively Grove	62268
Lively Grove (Township)	62268
Liverpool	61543
Liverpool (Township)	61543
Livingston (Clark County)	62441
Livingston (Madison County)	62058
Loami	62661
Loami (Township)	62661
Loch Lomond (Part of Mundelein)	60060
Lockhaven	62035
Lockport	60441*
	60446†

	ZIP
Lockport (Township)	60441
Locust (Township)	62555
Loda	60948
Loda (Township)	60948
Lodemia	61739
Lodge	61856
Logan (Edgar County)	61924
Logan (Franklin County)	62856
Logan (Peoria County) (Township)	61536
Logan Correctional Center	62656
Logan Square (Part of Chicago)	60647
Log Cabin Camp	60954
Lomax	61454
Lomax (Township)	61454
Lombard	60148
Lombardville	61421
London Mills	61544
Lone Grove (Township)	62880
Lone Tree	61368
Long Branch (Mason County)	62644
Long Branch (Saline County) (Township)	62935
Long Creek	62521
Long Creek (Township)	62521
Long Grove	60047
Long Lake	60041
Long Meadow (Part of Downers Grove)	60515
Long Point	61333
Long Point (Township)	61333
Longshadow	60175
Longview	61852
Longwood Farms (Part of Chicago Heights)	60411
Longwood Manor	60563
Loogootee	62857
Looking Glass (Township)	62265
Lookout Point	60097
Loon Lake	60002
Loop (Part of Chicago)	60601-05
For specific Loop Zip Codes call (312) 427-4225, or your local postmaster.	
Loraine (Adams County)	62349
Loraine (Henry County) (Township)	61277
Loran	61062
Loran (Township)	61062
Lords' Park Manor (Part of Elgin)	60120
Lorenzo	60481
Loretto	60460
Lorraine Park (Part of Wheaton)	60187
Lostant	61334
Lost Lake	61070
Lost Nation	61021
Lotus	61845
Lotus Woods	60081
Lou Del	62298
Loudon (Township)	62414
Louis Joliet Mall (Part of Joliet)	60435
Louisville	62858
Louisville (Township)	62858
Love (Township)	61870
Lovejoy (Iroquois County) (Township)	60973
Lovejoy (St. Clair County)	62059
Loves Park	61111
	61130-32
For specific Loves Park Zip Codes call (815) 877-7071, or your local postmaster.	
Lovington	61937
Lovington (Township)	61937
Lowder	62662
Lowe (Township)	61911
Lowell	61370
Lowpoint	61545
Loxa	61938
Lucas (Township)	62424
Ludlow	60949
Ludlow (Township)	60949
Lukin (Township)	62417
Lumaghi Heights	62234
Luther	62664
Lyman (Township)	60962
Lynchburg (Township)	62617
Lyndon	61261
Lyndon (Township)	61261
Lynn (Henry County) (Township)	61262
Lynn (Knox County) (Township)	61414
Lynn Center	61262
Lynn Gardens	60901

	ZIP
Lynnville (Morgan County)	62650
Lynnville (Ogle County) (Township)	61049
Lynnwood (Cook County)	60411
Lynnwood (Kendall County)	60543
Lynnwood (La Salle County)	61354
Lynwood	60411
Lyons	60534
Lyons (Township)	60525
Lyons (Part of Belgium)	61883
McCall	62321
McClellan (Township)	62894
McClure	62957
McClusky	62052
McConnell	61050
McCook	60525
McCormick	62987
McCullom Lake	60050
McCully	61764
McDowell	61764
Macedonia	62860
McGirr	60556
McHenry	60050*
	60051†
McHenry Shores (Part of McHenry)	60050
Machesney Park	61115
Machesney Park Mall (Part of Machesney Park)	61111
MacIntoch	61364
McIntosh	60123
McKee (Township)	62347
McKeen	62441
McKendree (Township)	61832
Mackinaw (Township)	61755
Mackinaw	61755
Mackler Heights (Part of Chicago Heights)	60411
McLean	61754
McLeansboro	62859
McLeansboro (Township)	62859
McNabb	61335
Macomb	61455
Macomb (Township)	61438
Macomb City (Township)	61455
Macon (Bureau County) (Township)	61314
Macon (Macon County)	62544
Macoupin	62676
McQueen	60185
McVey	62640
Madison (Madison County)	62060
Madison (Richland County) (Township)	62450
Madonnaville	62298
Maeystown	62256
Magnet	61938
Magnolia	61336
Magnolia (Township)	61336
Mahomet	61853
Mahomet (Township)	61853
Maine (Cook County) (Township)	60016
Maine (Grundy County) (Township)	60444
Main Post Office (Part of Chicago)	60607
Main Street (Part of Evanston)	60202
Makanda	62958
Makanda (Township)	62958
Malden	61337
Malibu Village	62901
Mallard West (Part of Schaumburg)	60194
Malone (Township)	61534
Malta	60150
Malta (Township)	60150
Malvern	61270
Manchester (Boone County) (Township)	61011
Manchester (Scott County)	62663
Manhattan	60442
Manhattan (Township)	60442
Manito	61546
Manito (Township)	61546
Manlius (Bureau County)	61338
Manlius (Bureau County) (Township)	61338
Manlius (La Salle County) (Township)	61360
Mannheim (Part of Franklin Park)	60131
Mannon	61272
Mansfield	61854

	ZIP
Manteno	60950
Manteno (Township)	60950
Manville	61319
Maplebrook (Part of Naperville)	60565
Maple Grove	62476
Maple Lane	61081
Maple Park	60151
Maple Point	62428
Maples Mill	61542
Mapleton	61547
Maplewood (Cook County)	60647
Maplewood (St. Clair County)	62206
Maplewood Estates	61520
Maquon	61458
Maquon (Township)	61458
Marblehead	62301
Marcelline	62376
Marcoe	62864
Mardell Manor	61607
Marengo	60152
Marengo (Township)	60152
Marietta	61459
Marigold	62242
Marina Terrace	60543
Marina Village	60543
Marine	62061
Marine (Township)	62061
Marion (Lee County) (Township)	61310
Marion (Ogle County) (Township)	61015
Marion (Williamson County)	62959
Marion Circle	60554
Marion Country Club	62959
Marion Hills (Part of Darien)	60561
Marissa	62257
Marissa (Township)	62257
Mark	61340
Market Place (Part of Champaign)	61820
Markham (Cook County)	60426
Markham (Morgan County)	62628
Markham City (Part of Bluford)	62814
Marley (Edgar County)	61944
Marley (Will County)	60448
Marlow	62872
Marnico Village	62650
Maroa	61756
Maroa (Township)	61756
Marquette Heights	61554
Marrowbone (Township)	61914
Mars (Part of Chicago)	60639
Marseilles	61341
Marshall	62441
Marshall (Township)	62441
Marston	61279
Martin (Crawford County) (Township)	62454
Martin (McLean County) (Township)	61728
Martinsburg	62363
Martinsburg (Township)	62363
Martinsville	62442
Martinsville (Township)	62442
Martinton	60951
Martinton (Township)	60951
Mary Crest (Part of Country Club Hills)	60477
Marydale	62231
Marydale Manor (Part of Dolton)	60419
Maryland	61064
Maryland (Township)	61007
Mary Meadows	60175
Maryville	62062
Mascoutah	62258
Mascoutah (Township)	62258
Mason	62443
Mason (Township)	62443
Mason City (Township)	62664
Mason City	62664
Massbach	61028
Massilon (Township)	62883
Matanzas Beach	62644
Matherville	61263
Matteson	60443
Mattoon	61938
Mattoon (Township)	61938
Maud	62863
Maunie	62861
Maxwell (Township)	62661
May (Christian County) (Township)	62567

*** Area Zip Code** **† Post Office Boxes**

	ZIP
May (Lee County) (Township)	61367
Mayberry (Township)	62817
Mayfair (Cook County)	60630
Mayfair (Tazewell County)	61550
Mayfield (Township)	60178
Maynard Lake	61821
Mays	61944
Maysville	62340
Maytown	61310
Mayview	61801
Maywood	60153
Mazon	60444
Mazon (Township)	60444
Meacham (Township)	62854
Meadowbrook (Madison County)	62010
Meadowbrook (McDonough County)	61455
Meadowbrook East (Part of Wheeling)	60090
Meadowbrook West (Part of Wheeling)	60090
Meadowdale (Part of Carpentersville)	60110
Meadowdale Shopping Center (Part of Carpentersville)	60110
Meadow Heights (Part of Collinsville)	62234
Meadow Knolls (Part of Schaumburg)	60194
Meadowlake	61821
Meadows	61726
Meadowview (Kane County)	60175
Meadowview (Kankakee County)	60901
Mechanicsburg	62545
Mechanicsburg (Township)	62545
Medalist Park (Part of Palatine)	60067
Media	61460
Media (Township)	61460
Medina (Township)	61523
Medinah	60157
Medinah on the Lake (Part of Bloomingdale)	60108
Medora	62063
Meeks	61846
Meersman	61244
Melrose (Adams County) (Township)	62301
Melrose (Clark County)	62478
Melrose (Clark County) (Township)	62478
Melrose Park	60160-61
	60164

For specific Melrose Park Zip Codes call (708) 343-2150, or your local postmaster.

	ZIP
Melville (Part of Godfrey)	62035
Melvin	60952
Menard	62259
Mendon	62351
Mendon (Township)	62351
Mendota	61342
Mendota (Township)	61342
Menominee (Township)	61025
Menominee	61025
Meppen	62013
Mercer (Township)	61231
Mercer Street (Part of Decatur)	62522
Merchandise Mart (Part of Chicago)	60654
Meredosia	62665
Meriden	61342
Meriden (Township)	61342
Meridian (Township)	62283
Meridian Heights (Part of Mounds)	62964
Mermet	62908
Merna	61758
Merriam	62837
Merrimac	62295
Merrionette Park	60655
Merritt	62650
Merry Oaks	61244
Mesa Lake	62855
Metamora	61548
Metamora (Township)	61548
Metcalf	61940
Metropolis	62960
Mettawa	60048
Meyer (Adams County)	62379
Meyer (Kankakee County)	60901
Meyerbrook	60545

	ZIP
Meyers Bay (Part of Fox Lake)	60050
Michael	62065
Middlebury (Part of Barrington Hills)	60010
Middle Creek (Hancock County)	62321
Middlecreek (Kane County)	60175
Middlefork (Township)	61865
Middle Grove	61531
Middleport (Township)	60970
Middlesworth	62565
Middletown	62666
Midland City	61727
Midland Hills	62958
Midlothian	60445
Midway (Madison County)	62067
Midway (Massac County)	62960
Midway (Tazewell County)	61554
Midway (Vermilion County)	61883
Midwest (Part of Chicago)	60612
Midwest Club (Part of Oak Brook)	60521
Milam (Township)	62544
Milan (DeKalb County) (Township)	60550
Milan (Rock Island County)	61264
Mildred	62707
Miles Station	62012
Milford	60953
Milford (Township)	60953
Milks Grove (Township)	60941
Millbrook (Kendall County)	60536
Millbrook (Peoria County) (Township)	61451
Millburn	60083
Millcreek	62961
Milledgeville	61051
Miller (Township)	61360
Miller Addition	61250
Miller City	62962
Miller Lake	62864
Millersburg	61231
Millersburg (Township)	61260
Millersville	62557
Miller Woods	60411
Millhurst	60545
Millington	60537
Mills (Township)	62246
Mill Shoals	62862
Mill Shoals (Township)	62862
Mill Spring	62035
Millstadt	62260
Millstadt (Township)	62260
Milmine	61855
Milo (Township)	61421
Milo	61421
Milton (DuPage County) (Township)	60187
Milton (Pike County)	62352
Mindale	62319
Mineral	61344
Mineral (Township)	61344
Mineral Springs	61081
Minier	61759
Minonk	61760
Minonk (Township)	61760
Minooka	60447
Missal	61364
Mission (Township)	60551
Mission Hills	60062
Mississippi (Township)	62022
Missouri (Township)	62353
Mitchell	62040
Mitchellsville	62917
Mitchie	62295
Mobet Meadows	61275
Mobile City	61401
Moccasin	62411
Moccasin (Township)	62411
Mode	62444
Modena	61491
Modesto	62667
Modoc	62261
Moecherville	60504
Mohawk (Part of Bensenville)	60106
Mokena	60448
Moline	61265*
	61266†
Momence	60954
Momence (Township)	60954
Mona (Township)	60964
Monee	60449
Monee (Township)	60449
Money Creek (Township)	61753
Monica	61559

	ZIP
Monmouth	61462
Monmouth (Township)	61462
Monroe (Township)	61052
Monroe Center	61052
Monroe City	62298
Mont	62025
Montague Forest	60123
Mont Clare (Part of Chicago)	60639
Montebello (Township)	62341
Monterey	61520
Monterey Village (Part of University Park)	60466
Montezuma	62361
Montezuma (Township)	62361
Montgomery (Crawford County) (Township)	62427
Montgomery (Kane County)	60538
Montgomery (Woodford County) (Township)	61733
Monticello	61856
Monticello (Township)	61856
Montmorency (Township)	61071
Montrose	62445
Moon Lake Village (Part of Hoffman Estates)	60195
Moonshine	62442
Moores Prairie (Township)	62810
Mooseheart	60539
Moraine Valley Facility (Part of Bridgeview)	60455
Morea	62451
Morehaven	61073
Morgan (Township)	61943
Morgan Park (Part of Chicago)	60643
Morgan's Gate	60067
Moriah	62420
Moro	62067
Moro (Township)	62361
Morris	60450
Morris (Township)	60450
Morris Hills (Part of Collinsville)	62234
Morrison	61270
Morrisonville	62546
Morristown	61274
Morseville	61085
Morton	61550
Morton (Township)	61550
Morton Grove	60053
Morton Park (Part of Cicero)	60650
Moser Highlands (Part of Naperville)	60540
Mosquito (Township)	62547
Mossville	61552
Mound (Effingham County) (Township)	62411
Mound (McDonough County) (Township)	61455
Mound City	62963
Mounds	62964
Mountain (Township)	62946
Mountain Glen	62920
Mount Auburn	62547
Mount Auburn (Township)	62547
Mount Carbon	62966
Mount Carmel	62863
Mount Carroll	61053
Mount Carroll (Township)	61053
Mount Clair	62035
Mount Clare	62033
Mount Erie	62446
Mount Erie (Township)	62446
Mount Greenwood (Part of Chicago)	60655
	60658

For specific Mount Greenwood Zip Codes call (312) 238-1477, or your local postmaster.

	ZIP
Mount Hope (Township)	61754
Mount Joy	61723
Mount Morris	61054
Mount Morris (Township)	61054
Mount Olive	62069
Mount Olive (Township)	62069
Mount Palatine	61334
Mount Pleasant (Union County)	62912
Mount Pleasant (Whiteside County) (Township)	61270
Mount Prospect	60056
Mount Prospect Gardens (Part of Mount Prospect)	60056
Mount Prospect Plaza (Part of Mount Prospect)	60056

	ZIP
Mount Pulaski	62548
Mount Pulaski (Township)	62548
Mount Sterling	62353
Mount Sterling (Township)	62353
Mount Vernon	62864
Mount Vernon (Township)	62864
Mount Zion	62549
Mount Zion (Township)	62549
Moweaqua	62550
Moweaqua (Township)	62550
Mozier	62070
Mozier Landing	62045
Mt. Vernon	61025
Muddy	62965
Mulberry Grove	62262
Mulberry Grove (Township)	62262
Mulkeytown	62865
Muncie	61857
Mundelein	60060
Mundelein Ridge Estates (Part of Mundelein)	60060
Munson (Township)	61238
Munster	61364
Murdock	61941
Murdock (Township)	61941
Murphy Acres	60435
Murphysboro	62966
Murphysboro (Township)	62966
Murrayville	62668
Myers Lake	62568
Mylith Park	60050
Myrtle	61047
Naausay (Township)	60560
Nachusa	61057
Nachusa (Township)	61057
Nameoki (Township)	62040
Nameoki	62040
Nantucket Cove (Part of Schaumburg)	60194
Naperville	60563-67

For specific Naperville Zip Codes call (708) 717-2662, or your local postmaster.

	ZIP
Naperville (Township)	60540
Naplate	61350
Naples	62665
Nashua (Township)	61061
Nashville	62263
Nashville (Township)	62263
Nason	62866
Natalie Estates (Part of Oak Forest)	60452
National Stock Yards	62071
Natrona	62682
Nauvoo	62354
Nauvoo (Township)	62354
Navajo Hills (Part of Palos Heights)	60463
Neadmore	62442
Nebo	62355
Nebraska (Township)	61740
Neelys	62621
Nekoma	61490
Nelson	61058
Nelson (Township)	61058
Neoga (Township)	62447
Neoga	62447
Neponset	61345
Neponset (Township)	61345
Nerska (Part of Chicago)	60632
Nettle Creek (Township)	60541
Neunert	62950
Nevada (Township)	60460
Nevins	61944
Newark	60541
New Athens	62264
New Athens (Township)	62264
New Baden	62265
New Bedford	61346
New Berlin	62670
New Berlin (Township)	62670
Newbern	62022
New Blossom Hill (Part of Cary)	60013
New Boston	61272
New Boston (Township)	61272
Newburg (Macon County)	62501
Newburg (Pike County) (Township)	62363
New Burnside	62967
Newby	61938
New Camp	62921
New Canton	62356
Newcastle	62987
New Century Town (Part of Vernon Hills)	60060
New City	62563
New Columbia	62943

* **Area Zip Code** † **Post Office Boxes**

	ZIP
Ossami Lake (Part of Morton)	61550
Oswego	60543
Oswego (Township)	60543
Otego (Township)	62418
Ottawa	61350
Ottawa (Township)	61350
Otter Creek (Jersey County) (Township)	62052
Otter Creek (La Salle County) (Township)	61364
Otterville	62037
Otto	60922
Otto (Township)	60922
Otto Mall (Part of Chicago Heights)	60411
Ottville	61362
Outter Creek	62031
Owaneco	62555
Owego (Township)	61764
Owen (Township)	61103
Oxford (Township)	61413
Oxville	62621
Ozark	62972
Pacesetter Park (Part of South Holland)	60473
Paderborn	62298
Padua	61737
Painesville	62948
Palatine	60067
	60074
	60078
	60094-95
For specific Palatine Zip Codes call (708) 590-8000, or your local postmaster.	
Palatine (Township)	60067
Palermo	61876
Palestine (Crawford County)	62451
Palestine (Woodford County) (Township)	61771
Palmer	62556
Palmyra (Lee County)	61021
Palmyra (Lee County) (Township)	61021
Palmyra (Macoupin County)	62674
Paloma	62359
Palos (Township)	60464
Palos Gardens	60463
Palos Heights	60463
Palos Hills	60465
Palos Park	60464
Palos Westgate (Part of Palos Heights)	60463
Palsgrove	61053
Pam Anne Estates	60025
Pana	62557
Pana (Township)	62557
Panama	62077
Pankeyville	62946
Panola	61738
Panola (Township)	61738
Panther Creek (Township)	62627
Papineau	60956
Papineau (Township)	60956
Paradise	61938
Paradise (Township)	61938
Paradise Acres	62918
Paris	61944
Paris (Township)	61944
Park City	60085
Parker (Clark County) (Township)	62474
Parker (Johnson County)	62922
Parkersburg	62452
Parkfield Terrace	62206
Park Forest	60466
Park Hills (Part of Effingham)	62401
Parkhome (Part of Cicero)	60650
Park Lane	60964
Park Manor (Part of Chicago)	60619
Park Meadows (Part of Rolling Meadows)	60008
Park Ridge	60068
Parkville	61872
Parkway (Part of North Riverside)	60546
Parkwood (Part of Elgin)	60120
Parkwood Village (Part of Elgin)	60120
Parnell	61842
Parrish	62890
Parrish Addition	62930
Partridge (Township)	61545
Partridge Hill (Part of Hoffman Estates)	60195

	ZIP
Passport	62868
Patoka	62875
Patoka (Township)	62875
Patterson	62078
Patterson (Township)	62078
Patterson Heights	62035
Patterson Springs	61919
Patton (Ford County) (Township)	60957
Patton (Wabash County)	62863
Pattonsburg	61369
Paulton	62959
Pavillion	60560
Pawnee	62558
Pawnee (Township)	62558
Paw Paw (DeKalb County) (Township)	60518
Paw Paw (Lee County)	61353
Paxton	60957
Paynes Point	61015
Payson	62360
Payson (Township)	62360
Peach Orchard (Township)	60952
Pea Ridge (Township)	62375
Pearl	62361
Pearl (Township)	62361
Pearl City	61062
Pebble Beach	60450
Pecan Grove	62031
Pecatonica	61063
Pecatonica (Township)	61063
Peerless	60544
Pekin	61554*
	61555†
Pekin Heights (Part of Pekin)	61554
Pekin Mall (Part of Pekin)	61554
Pella (Township)	60959
Pembroke (Township)	60964
Pendleton (Township)	62810
Penfield	61862
Penn (Shelby County) (Township)	62550
Penn (Stark County) (Township)	61421
Pennsylvania (Township)	62664
Penny Oaks (Part of Macomb)	61455
Penrose	61081
Peoria	61601-07
	61612-56
For specific Peoria Zip Codes call (309) 671-8813, or your local postmaster.	
Peoria City (Township)	61601
Peoria Heights	61614
Peotone	60468
Peotone (Township)	60468
Pepper Tree	60067
Pequot (Part of Coal City)	60416
Percy	62272
Perdueville	60957
Perks	62973
Perry	62362
Perry (Township)	62362
Perryton (Township)	61279
Perryville	61016
Persifer (Township)	61436
Peru	61354
Peru (Township)	61354
Peru Mall (Part of Peru)	61354
Pesotum	61863
Pesotum (Township)	61863
Peters (Part of Glen Carbon)	62034
Petersburg (Menard County)	62675
Petersburg (St. Clair County)	62269
Peters Creek	62931
Peterson Avenue (Part of Chicago)	60646
Petite Lake	60002
Petrolia	62417
Petty (Township)	62466
Pharoah's Gardens	62932
Pheasant Creek (Part of Northbrook)	60062
Pheasant Hollow	60187
Pheasant Meadows	60401
Pheasant Ridge	60544
Pheasant Ridge (Part of Mokena)	60448
Phelps	62240
Phenix (Township)	61254
Philadelphia	62612
Philadelphia (Township)	62612
Philippe (Part of Rolling Meadows)	60008

	ZIP
Phillips (Township)	62827
Phillipstown	62827
Philo	61864
Philo (Township)	61864
Phinney	61801
Phoenix	60426
Piasa (Jersey County) (Township)	62012
Piasa (Macoupin County)	62079
Piasa Hills	62035
Picadilly Terrace	60514
Pickaway (Township)	61914
Pierce (Township)	60151
Pierceburg	62449
Pierron	62273
Pierson	61929
Piety Hill	61348
Pigeon Grove (Township)	60924
Pike (Livingston County) (Township)	61726
Pike (Pike County)	62370
Pilot (Kankakee County) (Township)	60941
Pilot (Vermilion County) (Township)	61831
Pilot Grove (Township)	62318
Pilot Knob (Township)	62263
Pilsen (Part of Chicago)	60608
Pinckneyville	62274
Pine Creek (Township)	61064
Pinecrest	60435
Pine Grove	60450
Pinelands	60174
Pine Meadow (Part of Bolingbrook)	60440
Pine Ridge	61254
Pine Rock (Township)	61015
Pingree Grove	60140
Pinkstaff	62439
Pin Oak (Township)	62025
Pioneer Acres	61025
Pioneer Terrace	60115
Piopolis	62859
Piper City	60959
Pisgah	62650
Pistakee Bay	60050
Pistakee Heights (Part of Fox Lake)	60050
Pistakee Highlands (McHenry County)	60050
Pistakee Hills	60050
Pistaqua Heights	60050
Pitchin	60924
Pitman (Township)	62572
Pittsburg (Fayette County)	62471
Pittsburg (Williamson County)	62974
Pittsfield	62363
Pittsfield (Township)	62363
Pittwood	60970
Pixley (Township)	62868
Plainfield	60544
Plainfield (Township)	60544
Plainfield Acres	60544
Plainview	62676
Plainville	62365
Plano	60545
Plato (Township)	60123
Plato Center	60170
Plattville	60560
Playfield (Part of Crestwood)	60445
Plaza (Part of Belleville)	62223
Pleasant (Township)	61441
Pleasant Dale (Part of Burr Ridge)	60525
Pleasantdale Estates	60439
Pleasant Grove (Coles County) (Township)	62440
Pleasant Grove (Johnson County)	62912
Pleasant Hill (DuPage County)	60188
Pleasant Hill (Jackson County)	62901
Pleasant Hill (McLean County)	61753
Pleasant Hill (Pike County)	62366
Pleasant Hill (Pike County) (Township)	62366
Pleasant Hills	60172
Pleasant Mound	62284
Pleasant Mound (Township)	62284
Pleasant Plains	62677
Pleasant Ridge (Livingston County) (Township)	61741
Pleasant Ridge (Madison County)	62234

	ZIP
Pleasant Run (Part of Wheeling)	60090
Pleasant Vale (Township)	62356
Pleasant Valley (Township)	61085
Pleasant View (Macon County) (Township)	62513
Pleasant View (Schuyler County)	62681
Plumfield	62896
Plum Grove Countryside (Part of Rolling Meadows)	60008
Plum Grove Estates	60067
Plum Grove Hills (Part of Rolling Meadows)	60008
Plum Grove Village (Part of Rolling Meadows)	60008
Plum Grove Woods	60067
Plum Hill	62263
Plum Hill (Township)	62214
Plum Hollow	61021
Plymouth	62367
Plymouth Farms (Part of Vernon Hills)	60060
Poag	62025
Pocahontas	62275
Poe	62278
Point Pleasant (Township)	61473
Point West (Part of Lombard)	60148
Polk (Township)	62626
Polo	61064
Pomona	62975
Pomona (Township)	62975
Pond	62995
Pontiac	61764
Pontiac (Township)	61764
Pontiac (Part of Fairview Heights)	62232
Pontiac Correctional Center	61764
Pontiac Station (Part of Fairview Heights)	62208
Pontoon Beach	62040
Pontoosuc	62330
Pontoosuc (Township)	62330
Pope (Township)	62875
Poplar City	62633
Poplar Grove (Boone County)	61065
Poplar Grove (Boone County) (Township)	61065
Poplar Grove (Rock Island County)	61244
Port Byron	61275
Port Byron (Township)	61275
Port Jackson	62427
Portland (Township)	61277
Portland	61277
Port Ridge (Part of Lockport)	60441
Posen (Cook County)	60469
Posen (Washington County)	62263
Posey	62231
Post Oak	62418
Potomac	61865
Pottawatawi Highlands (Part of Tinley Park)	60477
Pottstown	61614
Powder Creek	62223
Powder Mill Woods	62220
Powellton	62358
Prairie (Crawford County) (Township)	62442
Prairie (Edgar County) (Township)	61924
Prairie (Hancock County) (Township)	62321
Prairie (Randolph County) (Township)	62278
Prairie (Shelby County) (Township)	62463
Prairie Center	61350
Prairie City	61470
Prairie City (Township)	61470
Prairie Court (Part of Oak Park)	60301
Prairie Creek (Township)	62635
Prairie Du Long (Township)	62243
Prairie du Pont	62240
Prairie Du Rocher	62277
Prairie Estates	62675
Prairie Green (DuPage County)	60187
Prairie Green (Iroquois County) (Township)	60942
Prairie Grove	60050
Prairie Home	62550

* Area Zip Code   † Post Office Boxes

	ZIP
Prairie Ridge (Part of Hoffman Estates)	60195
Prairieton (Township)	62550
Prairietown	62097
Prairie View	60069
Prairieville	61021
Preemption	61276
Preemption (Township)	61276
Prentice	62612
Presswood Hills	62274
Prestbury	60506
Preston (Randolph County)	62242
Preston (Richland County) (Township)	62450
Preston Heights	60431
Prestwick	60423
Prickett (Part of Edwardsville)	62025
Princeton	61356
Princeton (Township)	61356
Princeville	61559
Princeville (Township)	61559
Proctor	60936
Prophetstown	61277
Prophetstown (Township)	61277
Prospect	61866
Prospect Heights	60070
Prospect Meadows (Part of Mount Prospect)	60056
Prospect Park (Part of Fairview Heights)	62208
Providence	61368
Provincetown (Part of Country Club Hills)	60477
Proving Ground	61074
Proviso (Township)	60160
Prudential Plaza (Part of Chicago)	60601
Pruett	62458
Pujol	63673
Pulaski	62976
Pulleys Mill	62939
Pullman (Part of Chicago)	60628
Pullman Junction (Part of Chicago)	60617
Putman (Township)	61427
Putnam	61560
Quarry (Township)	62037
Quatoga	62035
Quincy	62301-06
For specific Quincy Zip Codes call (217) 224-4950, or your local postmaster.	
Quincy Mall (Part of Quincy)	62301
Quiver (Township)	62644
Quiver Beach	62644
Raccoon (Township)	62801
Racine Avenue (Part of Chicago)	60628
Raddle	62950
Radford	62550
Radnor (Township)	61525
Radom	62876
Rainbow Hills	60174
Rakers Addition	62216
Raleigh	62977
Raleigh (Township)	62977
Ramona Place	62035
Ramsey	62080
Ramsey (Township)	62080
Randhurst (Part of Mount Prospect)	60056
Randolph	61745
Randolph (Township)	61745
Randolph Street (Part of Chicago)	60601
Range	62864
Rankin	60960
Ransom	60470
Ransom Ridge Estates (Part of Park Ridge)	60068
Rantoul	61866
Rantoul (Township)	61866
Rapatee	61544
Rapids City	61278
Rardin	61920
Raritan	61471
Raritan (Township)	61471
Rasmussen Addition	60936
Raven	61924
Ravenswood (Part of Chicago)	60625
Ravinia (Part of Highland Park)	60035
Ravinia Park (Part of Highland Park)	60035
Rawalts	61520
Rawlins (Township)	61036

	ZIP
Ray	62681
Raymond (Champaign County) (Township)	61852
Raymond (Montgomery County)	62560
Raymond (Montgomery County) (Township)	62560
Reader	62630
Reading	61311
Reading (Township)	61311
Rector (Township)	62930
Red Bud	62278
Reddick	60961
Redmon	61949
Red Oak	61032
Red Oak Terrace (Part of Highland Park)	60035
Reed (Township)	60408
Reed City	61547
Reeds Station	62924
Rees	62638
Reevesville	62943
Regency Grove	60515
Regency Terrace (Part of Bloomingdale)	60108
Reilly	60960
Reily Lake	62241
Rellswood Hills	61008
Renault	62279
Renchville	61523
Rend City	62812
Reno	62246
Rentchler	62221
Reseda (Part of Palatine)	60067
Resthaven	60481
Reynolds (Lee County) (Township)	61006
Reynolds (Rock Island County)	61279
Reynoldsburg	62991
Reynoldsville	62952
Rice (Jo Daviess County) (Township)	61036
Rice (Perry County)	62274
Rice Lake	61401
Rich (Township)	60471
Richards	60450
Richardson	60151
Richardson Estates	61801
Richfield	62365
Richfield (Township)	62365
Richland (La Salle County) (Township)	61334
Richland (Marshall County) (Township)	61570
Richland (Sangamon County)	62677
Richland (Shelby County) (Township)	62465
Richland Grove (Township)	61281
Richmond	60071
Richmond (Township)	60071
Richmond Estates (Part of Oak Forest)	60452
Richton (Part of Richton Park)	60466
Richton Park	60471
Richview	62877
Richview (Township)	62877
Richwood (Township)	62031
Richwoods (Crawford County)	62451
Richwoods (Peoria County) (Township)	61614
Ricks (Township)	62546
Ridge (Township)	62565
Ridgecrest	60450
Ridge Farm	61870
Ridgefield	60012
Ridgeland (Township)	60968
Ridgemoor (Part of Willowbrook)	60521
Ridge Prairie Heights (Part of O'Fallon)	62269
Ridgeville	60955
Ridgewood (Part of Western Springs)	60558
Ridgewood East	60452
Ridgewood West (Part of Oak Forest)	60452
Ridgway	62979
Ridgway (Township)	62979
Ridott	61067
Ridott (Township)	61067
Rieuf's Meadows	61341
Riffel	62858
Riggston	62694
Riley (Township)	61038
Riley Center	60152

	ZIP
Rinard	62878
Ring Neck	60543
Ringwood	60072
Rio	61472
Rio (Township)	61472
Ripley	62353
Ripley (Township)	62353
Rising Sun	62821
Ritchason Addition	62896
Ritchie	60481
Riverair	62035
Rivercrest Center (Part of Crestwood)	60607
Riverdale (Cook County)	60627
Riverdale (Winnebago County)	61073
River Forest	60305
River Forest (Township)	60305
River Glen	60010
River Grange Lakes	60175
River Grove	60171
River Heights (Part of Danville)	61832
River Isle	60954
River Oaks Center (Part of Calumet City)	60409
River Reach	61008
River Ridge	60560
Riverside (Adams County) (Township)	62301
Riverside (Cook County)	60546
Riverside (Cook County) (Township)	60546
Riverside Island (Part of Fox Lake)	60020
Riverside Lawns	60546
Riverside Park	60050
Riverton	62561
Riverview (Carroll County)	61285
Riverview (Lee County)	61021
Riverview (Whiteside County)	61071
Riverview Heights	60543
Riverwoods	60015
Rivoli (Township)	61465
Roaches	62898
Roachtown	62260
Roanoke	61561
Roanoke (Township)	61561
Robbins	60472
Robbs	62985
Robein (Part of East Peoria)	61611
Roberts (Ford County)	60962
Roberts (Marshall County) (Township)	61375
Roberts Park (Part of Bridgeview)	60453
Robin Hill (Part of Joliet)	60435
Robinson	62454
Robinson (Township)	62454
Robinson Correctional Center	62454
Rob Roy Country Club (Part of Prospect Heights)	60070
Roby	62545
Rochelle	61068
Rochester	62563
Rochester (Township)	62563
Rochester	62863
Rock	62938
Rockbridge	62081
Rockbridge (Township)	62081
Rock City	61070
Rock Creek (Adams County)	62301
Rock Creek (Hancock County) (Township)	62321
Rock Creek (Hardin County)	62919
Rock Creek-Lima (Township)	61046
Rockdale	60436
Rock Falls	61071
Rockford	61101-10
	61112-14
	61125-26
For specific Rockford Zip Codes call (815) 229-4811, or your local postmaster.	
Rockford (Township)	61101
Rockgate Estates	62035
Rock Grove	61070
Rock Grove (Township)	61070
Rock Island	61201-04
For specific Rock Island Zip Codes call (309) 793-7200, or your local postmaster.	
Rock Island Arsenal	61299

	ZIP
Rockport	62370
Rock River Terrace	61010
Rock Run (Township)	61019
Rockton	61072
Rockton (Township)	61072
Rockvale (Township)	61061
Rock Vale Heights	61010
Rockville (Township)	60950
Rockwell (Part of La Salle)	61301
Rockwood	62280
Rocky Run (Township)	62373
Rodden	61041
Rogers (Township)	60946
Rogers Park (Part of Chicago)	60626
	60660
For specific Rogers Park Zip Codes call (312) 508-1200, or your local postmaster.	
Rolling Acres (Champaign County)	61866
Rolling Acres (Peoria County)	61614
Rolling Green	61938
Rolling Hills (Clinton County)	62293
Rolling Hills (Piatt County)	61884
Rolling Meadows (Cook County)	60008
Rolling Meadows (McDonough County)	61455
Rollo	60518
Rome (Jefferson County) (Township)	62830
Rome (Peoria County)	61562
Rome Heights	61523
Romeoville	60441
Romine (Township)	62849
Rondout	60044
Roodhouse	62082
Roodhouse (Township)	62082
Rooks Creek (Township)	61764
Rooney Heights	60435
Roosevelt Road (Part of Chicago)	60607
Roots	62277
Root Spring	60013
Ropers Landing	62938
Rosamond	62083
Rosamond (Township)	62083
Roscoe	61073
Roscoe (Township)	61073
Rose (Township)	62565
Rosebud	62938
Rosecrans	60083
Rosedale	62031
Rosedale (Township)	62031
Rosefield (Township)	61529
Rose Hill (Cook County)	60640
Rose Hill (DuPage County)	60515
Rose Hill (Jasper County)	62432
Rose Lake (Part of Fairmont City)	62201
Roseland (Part of Chicago)	60628
Rose Lawn (Part of Chicago)	60628
Roselle	60172
Rosemont (Cook County)	60018
Rosemont (St. Clair County)	62204
Roseville	61473
Roseville (Township)	61473
Rosewood	62024
Rosewood Heights	62024
Rosiclare	62982
Roslyn	62462
Ross (Edgar County) (Township)	61924
Ross (Pike County) (Township)	62366
Ross (Vermilion County) (Township)	60963
Rossville	60963
Round Barn (Part of Champaign)	61821
Round Grove (Livingston County) (Township)	60420
Round Grove (Whiteside County)	61270
Round Knob	62960
Round Lake	60073
Round Lake Beach	60073
Round Lake Heights	60073
Round Lake Park	60073
Round Prairie	62823
Rountree (Township)	62094
Rowe	61764
Roxana	62084

* Area Zip Code   † Post Office Boxes

* Area Zip Code   **† Post Office Boxes**

	ZIP		ZIP		ZIP		ZIP
South Mounds (Part of Mounds)	62964	Sterling (Township)	61081	Summit Heights	62089	Terminal Junction (Part of Rock Island)	61201
South Muddy (Township)	62448	Sterling	61081	Summum	61501	Terra Cotta	60014
South Oak Park (Part of Oak Park)	60304	Sterling Place (Part of Caseyville)	62232	Sumner (Kankakee County) (Township)	60940	Terre Haute	61454
South Ottawa (Township)	61350	Steuben (Township)	61565	Sumner (Lawrence County)	62466	Terre Haute (Township)	61454
South Otter (Township)	62674	Stevenson (Township)	62881	Sumner (Warren County) (Township)	61453	Teutopolis	62467
South Palmyra (Township)	62674	Steward	60553	Sumpter (Township)	62248	Teutopolis (Township)	62467
Southpark Mall (Part of Moline)	61265	Stewardson	62463	Sunbeam	61231	Texas (Township)	61727
South Pekin	61564	Stickney	60402	Sunbury	61313	Texas City	62930
Southport	61517	Stickney (Township)	60402	Sunbury (Township)	61313	Texico	62889
South Rock Island (Township)	61201	Stillman Valley	61084	Sunfield	62832	Thackeray	62859
South Rome	61523	Stillmeadow	60119	Sunny Acres (Champaign County)	61853	Thawville	60968
South Ross (Township)	61848	Stillwell	62380	Sunny Acres (Kankakee County)	60950	Thayer	62689
South Roxana	62087	Stiritz	62896	Sunny Crest	60430	Thebes	62990
South Shore (Part of Chicago)	60649	Stites (Township)	62059	Sunnydale	61021	Thebes Junction (Part of Thebes)	62990
South Twigg (Township)	62817	Stockland (Township)	60967	Sunny Hill	61273	The Burg	61318
South Waukegan (Part of North Chicago)	60064	Stockland	60967	Sunny Hill Estates	61273	The Clusters (Part of Bolingbrook)	60440
Southwest (Township)	62466	Stockton	61085	Sunny Hills Estates	60515	The Covered Bridges (Part of Carol Stream)	60188
South Wheatland (Township)	62532	Stockton (Township)	61085	Sunnyland (Tazewell County)	61571	The Fairway of Country Lakes (Part of Naperville)	60563
South Wilmington	60474	Stock Yards (Part of Chicago)	60609	Sunny Land (Will County)	60435	The Greens of Woodgate (Part of Matteson)	60443
Space Valley	60521	Stolletown	62231	Sunnyside (McHenry County)	60050	The Grove Shopping Center (Part of Elk Grove Village)	60007
Spanish Court (Part of Highland Park)	60035	Stone	62931	Sunnyside (Williamson County)	62948	The Knolls	60175
Spankey	62031	Stone Church	62214	Sunnyside Acres	62531	The Laurels (Part of Justice)	60458
Sparks Hill	62931	Stonefort (Township)	62987	Sun Prairie Seed	61873	The Ledges	61073
Sparland	61565	Stonefort	62987	Sun Ridge (Part of Hoffman Estates)	60195	The Meadows	60532
Sparta (Knox County) (Township)	61488	Stonehenge	60178	Sunrise Ridge (Part of Romeoville)	60441	The Old Farm	61821
Sparta (Randolph County)	62286	Stonelake (Part of Woodstock)	60098	Sun River Terrace	60964	Third Lake	60046
Spaulding (Cook County)	60120	Stone Park	60165	Sunset Acres (Lake County)	60048	Thomas	61283
Spaulding (Sangamon County)	62561	Stoneyville	61350	Sunset Acres (Stephenson County)	61032	Thomasboro	61878
Speer	61479	Stonington	62567	Sunset Harbor	62959	Thomas Eddition	61364
Spencer	60451	Stonington (Township)	62567	Sunset Hills (Part of Roselle)	60172	Thomasville	62533
Spencer Heights	62964	Stony Island Avenue (Part of Chicago)	60649	Sunset Lake	62640	Thompson (Township)	61001
Spillertown	62959	Stookey (Township)	62221	Sunset Trailer Park (Part of Glenview)	60025	Thompson Addition	61241
Spin Lake	61732	Storeyland	62035	Sutter	62373	Thompsonville	62890
Sportsman Lake	62881	Storybrook	60512	Sutton	60010	Thomson	61285
Spring (Township)	61008	Stoy	62464	Sutton Point (Part of Northbrook)	60062	Thornhill (Part of Carol Stream)	60187
Spring Arbor Lake	62901	Strasburg	62465	Swan (Township)	61473	Thornton	60476
Spring Bay (Township)	61611	Stratford	61064	Swan Creek	61473	Thornton (Township)	60476
Spring Bay	61611	Stratford Hills (Part of Elmhurst)	60126	Swansea	62221	Thornton Junction (Part of South Holland)	60473
Spring Creek (Township)	62355	Stratford Park	61821	Swanwick	62237	Thornwilde (Part of Warrenville)	60555
Springerton	62887	Stratford Square (Part of Bloomingdale)	60108	Swedona	61262	Thunderbird Lake	62012
Springfield	62701-94	Stratton (Edgar County) (Township)	61944	Sweetwater	62642	Tice	62675
For specific Springfield Zip Codes call (217) 788-7200, or your local postmaster.		Stratton (Jefferson County)	62814	Swiss Valley (Part of Crete)	60417	Ticona	61370
Springfield (Township)	62702	Strawberry Hill	61270	Swissville (Part of Dixon)	61021	Tierra Grande (Part of Country Club Hills)	60477
Spring Garden	62846	Strawn	61775	Swygert	61764	Tilden	62292
Spring Garden (Township)	62846	Streamwood	60107	Sycamore	60178	Tilton	61833
Spring Grove (McHenry County)	60081	Streator	61364	Sycamore (Township)	60178	Timber (Township)	61533
Spring Grove (Warren County) (Township)	61412	Streator Junction (Part of Eureka)	61530	Sylvan Hill	60462	Timberbrook	61254
Springhaven	62035	Stringtown	62450	Sylvan Lake	60060	Timbercrest (Part of Schaumburg)	60194
Spring Hill	61250	Stronghurst	61480	Symerton	60481	Timber Lake (Carroll County)	61053
Spring Hill Mall (Part of Dundee)	60118	Stronghurst (Township)	61480	Symmes (Township)	61944	Timber Lake (Lake County)	60010
Spring Lake (Champaign County)	61853	Stubblefield	62246	Table Grove	61482	Timberlake Estate	62568
Spring Lake (Tazewell County)	61546	Sublette	61367	Tabor	61778	Timberlake Estates	60521
Spring Lake (Tazewell County) (Township)	61546	Sublette (Township)	61367	Taggert Woods	62626	Timberlake Village (Part of Mount Prospect)	60056
Spring Point (Township)	62462	Suburban Estates	60515	Talkington (Township)	62692	Timber Lane	61008
Spring Valley	61362	Suburban Heights	62801	Tall Trees (Part of Glenview)	60025	Timberline	60435
Squaw Grove (Township)	60520	Suez (Township)	61412	Tallula	62688	Timber Ridge (Cook County)	60457
Squaw Prairie Estate	61008	Sugar Brook (Part of Bolingbrook)	60440	Tamalco	62253	Timber Ridge (DuPage County)	60190
Stable	62918	Sugar Creek (Township)	62293	Tamalco (Township)	62253	Timber Terrace	60115
Stainfield	60545	Sugar Grove (Kane County)	60554	Tamarac (Part of Flossmoor)	60422	Timber Trails (Part of Oak Brook)	60521
Staley	61821	Sugar Grove (Kane County) (Township)	60554	Tamaroa	62888	Timber View (mail Urbana)	61801
Standard	61363	Sugar Grove (Mercer County)	61231	Tamms	62988	Timberview (mail Mahomet)	61853
Standard City	62686	Sugar Island	60922	Tampico	61283	Time	62363
Stanford (Clay County) (Township)	62824	Sugar Loaf (Township)	62240	Tampico (Township)	61283	Timewell	62375
Stanford (McLean County)	61774	Sugar Loaf	62240	Tanbark (Part of Tinley Park)	60477	Timothy	62428
Stanton (Township)	61873	Sullivan (Township)	61951	Tanglewood (Part of Hanover Park)	60103	Tinley Park	60477
Stanton Point	60041	Sullivan (Livingston County) (Township)	60929	Tate (Township)	62935	Tinley Terrace (Part of Tinley Park)	60477
Stark	61559	Sullivan (Moultrie County)	61951	Tatumville	62988	Tioga	62351
Starks	60140	Sullivant (Township)	61773	Taylor (Township)	61021	Tipton	62298
Starnes	62707	Summerdale (Part of Chicago)	60640	Taylor Ridge	61284	Tiskilwa	61368
State Line	62423	Summerfield	62289	Taylor Springs	62089	Todds Mill	62263
State Park Place	62201	Summerhill (Cook County; Part of Northbrook)	60062	Taylorville	62568	Todds Point	61914
State Street (Part of Chicago)	60628	Summer Hill (Cook County; Part of Elgin)	60120	Taylorville (Township)	62568	Todds Point (Township)	61914
Staunton	62088	Summer Hill (Pike County)	62363	Taylorville Correctional Center	62568	Toledo	62468
Staunton (Township)	62088	Summerlakes (Part of Warrenville)	60555	Techny	60082	Tolono	61880
Stavanger	61360	Summersville (Part of Mount Vernon)	62864	Teheran	62664	Tolono (Township)	61880
Steel City	62812	Summerville	62063	Temple Hill	62938	Toluca	61369
Steeleville	62288	Summit (Cook County)	60501	Tenerelli	60511	Tomahawk Bluff	61301
Steeple Run	60540	Summit (Effingham County) (Township)	62461	Tennessee	62374		
Steger	60475	Summit-Argo (Part of Summit)	60501	Tennessee (Township)	62374		
Stelle	60919						

Name	ZIP
Tompkins (Township)	61447
Toms Prairie	62837
Tonica	61370
Tonti	62881
Tonti (Township)	62881
Topeka	61567
Toronto	62707
Toulon	61483
Toulon (Township)	61483
Tovey	62570
Towanda	61776
Towanda (Township)	61776
Tower Hill	62571
Tower Hill (Township)	62571
Tower Lakes	60010
Town and Country	62901
Towne Oaks	61535
Tradewinds	60115
Trago Lake	62839
Tremont	61568
Tremont (Township)	61568
Tremont (Madison County)	62035
Tremont (Tazewell County)	61568
Trenton	62293
Trilla	62469
Trimble	62454
Triple Lance Heights	62901
Tri-State Village	60521
Triumph	61371
Triumvera	60025
Trivoli	61569
Trivoli (Township)	61569
Trout Valley (Part of Cary)	60013
Trowbridge	62447
Troxel	60151
Troy (Madison County)	62294
Troy (Will County) (Township)	60435
Troy Grove	61372
Troy Grove (Township)	61372
Tru Lock Acres	61455
Trumbull	62821
Truro (Township)	61489
Tullamore (Part of Mundelein)	60060
Tunbridge (Township)	61749
Tunnel Hill	62991
Turnberry	60014
Tuscola	61953
Tuscola (Township)	61953
Twelvemile Corner	61318
Twenty-Second Street (Part of Chicago)	60616
Twenty-Seventh Street (Part of Chicago)	60616
Twenty-Third Street (Part of Chicago)	60616
Twigg (Township)	62829
Twilight Terrace	62221
Twin City (Part of Champaign)	61801
Twin Creek Acres	61010
Twin Lakes	62294
Twin Oaks (Part of Joliet)	60435
Tyrone (Township)	62822
Udina	60123
Ulah	61238
Ullin	62992
Union (Cumberland County) (Township)	62428
Union (Effingham County) (Township)	62424
Union (Fulton County) (Township)	61415
Union (Livingston County) (Township)	60460
Union (Logan County)	62635
Union (McHenry County)	60180
Union Center	62428
Union Grove	61270
Union Grove (Township)	61270
Union Hill (Kankakee County)	60969
Union Hill (St. Clair County)	62232
Union Stock Yards (Part of Chicago)	60609
Uniontown	61572
Unionville (Massac County)	62910
Unionville (Vermilion County)	61883
Unionville (Whiteside County)	61270
Unity (Alexander County)	62993
Unity (Piatt County) (Township)	61913
University (Part of Urbana)	61801
University Heights (Part of Charleston)	61920
University Mall (Part of Carbondale)	62901
University Park	60466
Upper Alton (Part of Alton)	62002
Uptown (Part of Chicago)	60640
Urbain	62822
Urban (Part of Taylorville)	62568
Urbana	61801
Urbana (Township)	61801
Urbandale	62914
Ursa	62376
Ursa (Township)	62376
Ustick (Township)	61270
Utica	61373
Utica (Township)	61373
Vale Vue Acres	62650
Valier	62891
Valley (Township)	61491
Valley City	62340
Valley Lo (Part of Glenview)	60025
Valley View (DeKalb County)	60145
Valley View (DuPage County)	60137
Valley View (Kane County)	60174
Valley View (Tazewell County)	61611
Valmeyer	62295
Van Burensburg	62032
Van Buren Street (Part of Chicago)	60601
Vance (Township)	61841
Vandalia	62471
Vandalia (Township)	62471
Vandalia Correctional Center	62471
Van Orin	61374
Varna	61375
Velma	62568
Venedy	62214
Venedy (Township)	62214
Venetian Village (Lake County)	60046
Venice	62090
Venice (Township)	62090
Venice Crossing (Part of Venice)	62090
Vera	62080
Vergennes	62994
Vergennes (Township)	62994
Vermilion (Edgar County)	61955
Vermilion (La Salle County) (Township)	61370
Vermilion Grove	61870
Vermilion Heights	61832
Vermilionville	61370
Vermilion Estates	61764
Vermont	61484
Vermont (Township)	61484
Vernon (Lake County) (Township)	60069
Vernon (Marion County)	62892
Vernon Hills	60061
Verona	60479
Versailles	62378
Versailles (Township)	62378
Versailles-on-the-Lake (Part of Schaumburg)	60194
Veterans Administration Medical Center	60064
Vets Row	61523
Vevay Park	62420
Vicic (Part of East Peoria)	61611
Victor (Township)	60556
Victoria	61485
Victoria (Township)	61485
Vienna (Grundy County) (Township)	60479
Vienna (Johnson County)	62995
Village Crossing Shopping Center (Part of Skokie)	60076
Village Mall (Part of Danville)	61832
Village Square	60515
Villa Grove	61956
Villa Grove Junction (Part of Villa Grove)	61956
Villa Hills	62223
Villa Marie	62035
Villa Park	60181
Villa Ridge	62996
Villas Salceda (Part of Northbrook)	60062
Villa Verde (Part of Buffalo Grove)	60090
Villa West	60462
Villa Westbrook (Part of Macomb)	61455
Vincennes Trail	60954
Vinegar Hill (Township)	61036
Viola (Lee County) (Township)	61318
Viola (Mercer County)	61486
Virden	62690
Virden (Township)	62690
Virgil	60182
Virgil (Township)	60182
Virginia	62691
Virginia (Township)	62691
Volo	60073
Vonachen Knolls	61523
Von Glenn Acres	61010
Voorhies	61813
Vulcan (Part of East Carondelet)	62240
Wabash (Township)	62441
Wacker (Carroll County)	61053
Wacker (Kendall County)	60560
Waddams (Township)	61050
Waddams Grove	61048
Wade (Clinton County) (Township)	62231
Wade (Jasper County) (Township)	62448
Wadsworth	60083
Waggoner	62572
Wakefield	62448
Waldo (Township)	61744
Walker (Township)	62373
Walkerville	62050
Walkerville (Township)	62050
Wall (Township)	60948
Wallace (Township)	61350
Wallingford	60442
Walnut	61376
Walnut (Township)	61376
Walnut Grove (Knox County) (Township)	61414
Walnut Grove (McDonough County)	61470
Walnut Grove (McDonough County) (Township)	61438
Walnut Hill	62893
Walnut Park	62231
Walnut Prairie	62477
Walpole	62817
Walsh	62297
Walshville	62091
Walshville (Township)	62091
Waltham	61373
Waltham (Township)	61373
Walton	61021
Waltonville	62894
Wamac	62801
Wanda	62025
Wanlock	61231
Wapella	61777
Wapella (Township)	61777
Wards Grove (Township)	61048
Ware	62952
Warner	61273
Warren (Jo Daviess County)	61087
Warren (Jo Daviess County) (Township)	61087
Warren (Lake County) (Township)	60031
Warren G. Murray Developmental Center	62801
Warrenhurst (Part of Warrenville)	60555
Warren Park (Part of Cicero)	60650
Warrensburg	62573
Warrenville	60555
Warsaw	62379
Warsaw (Township)	62379
Wartburg	62298
Wartrace	62943
Wasco	60183
Washburn	61570
Washington (Carroll County) (Township)	61074
Washington (Tazewell County)	61571
Washington (Tazewell County) (Township)	61571
Washington (Will County) (Township)	60401
Washington Heights (Part of Chicago)	60628
Washington Park	62204
Washington Square Mall (Part of Homewood)	60430
Wasson	62930
Wataga	61488
Waterford (DuPage County)	60521
Waterford (Fulton County) (Township)	61542
Waterloo	62298
Waterman	60556
Water Tower Place (Part of Chicago)	60611
Watertown (Part of East Moline)	61244
Watervalley	62920
Watseka	60970
Watson	62473
Watson (Township)	62473
Wauconda	60084
Wauconda (Township)	60084
Waukegan	60079
	60085-87
For specific Waukegan Zip Codes call (708) 662-6800, or your local postmaster.	
Wauponsee (Township)	60450
Waverly	62692
Waycinden Park	60016
Wayne (Township)	60185
Wayne	60184
Wayne Center	60185
Wayne City	62895
Waynesville	61778
Waynesville (Township)	61778
Weathersfield (Part of Schaumburg)	60194
Weaver	62423
Webber (Township)	62814
Webster	62321
Webster Park (Part of Spring Valley)	61362
Wedgewood Estates	62293
Wedron	60557
Weedman	61842
Wee-Ma-Tuk Hills	61427
Weldon	61882
Welge	62288
Weller (Township)	61238
Wellington	60973
Wellington Heights	60435
Wells	62871
Wendelin	62448
Wenona	61377
Wenonah	62075
Wentworth Avenue (Part of Calumet City)	60409
Wesley (Tazewell County)	61611
Wesley (Will County) (Township)	60481
West (Effingham County) (Township)	62458
West (McLean County) (Township)	61722
Westaway	60504
Westbrook	61853
Westbrook Estates (Part of O'Fallon)	62269
West Brooklyn	61378
West Brook Village (Part of Macomb)	61455
Westbury (Part of Bolingbrook)	60440
Westchester	60154
West Chicago	60185*
	60186†
West City	62812
West Clinton Estates	62265
Westdale Gardens	60126
West Deerfield (Township)	60015
West End	62890
Western (Township)	61273
Western Illinois Correctional Center	62353
Western Knolls	62707
Western Mound (Township)	62630
Western Springs	60558
Westervelt	62574
Westfield (Township)	62474
Westfield (Part of Joliet)	60435
Westfield (Bureau County) (Township)	61312
Westfield (Clark County)	62474
West Frankfort	62896
West Frankfort Lake	62896
West Galena (Township)	61036
Westgate	62959
West Glen (Part of Peoria)	61614
West Glenview	60025
West Hallock	61526
West Jersey	61483
West Jersey (Township)	61483

	ZIP
West Kankakee (Part of Kankakee)	60901
West Lake (Crawford County)	62454
Westlake (DuPage County)	60139
West Lake Forest (Part of Lake Forest)	60045
West Liberty	62475
West Lincoln (Township)	62656
West Meadowview (Part of Kankakee)	60901
West Miltmore	60046
Westmont	60559
Westmore (Part of Lombard)	60148
Weston	61726
West Peoria	61604
West Peoria (Township)	61604
West Point (Hancock County)	62380
West Point (Morgan County)	62650
West Point (Stephenson County) (Township)	61048
Westport (Knox County)	61401
Westport (Lawrence County)	47591
West Pullman (Part of Chicago)	60628
Westridge (Cook County)	60070
West Ridge (Douglas County)	61953
West Salem	62476
West Sandford	61944
West Twenty-Second St. (Part of Chicago)	60650
West Union	62477
Westville	61883
Westwood (Part of Addison)	60101
West York	62478
Wetaug	62926
Wethersfield (Township)	61277
Wetzel	61944
Wheatfield (Township)	62231
Wheatland (Bureau County) (Township)	61368
Wheatland (Fayette County) (Township)	62418
Wheatland (Will County) (Township)	60544
Wheaton	60187*
	60189†
Wheaton Center (Part of Wheaton)	60187
Wheeler	62479
Wheeling	60090
Wheeling (Township)	60090
Whiskey Corners	60071
Whiskey Creek	60185
Whispering Hills	60050
Whispering Oaks (Part of Lake Forest)	60045
Whitaker	60940
Whiteash	62959
White City	62069
White Cliffs	62035
Whitefield	61537
Whitefield (Township)	61537
Whitehall (Cook County)	60056
White Hall (Greene County)	62092
White Hall (Greene County) (Township)	62092
White Heath	61884
White Oak (Township)	61725
White Oaks	61021
White Oaks Bay	60097
White Oaks Mall (Part of Springfield)	62704
White Pigeon	61270
White Pines	60106
White Post	62093
White Rock (Township)	61045
White Rock (Lee County)	61021
White Rock (Ogle County)	61015

	ZIP
Whites Addition	61244
Whitford Place	62035
Whitley (Township)	61928
Whitmore (Township)	62501
Whittington	62897
Wichert	60964
Wicker Park (Part of Chicago)	60622
Wickmore	62035
Wideview	60175
Wiesbrook	62918
W. I. Junction (Part of Chicago)	60621
Wilbern	61570
Wilberton (Township)	62885
Wilbur Heights	61821
Wilcox (Clay County)	62824
Wilcox (Hancock County) (Township)	62379
Wildrose	60174
Wildwood (Cook County)	60628
Wildwood (Kane County)	60504
Wildwood (Lake County; mail Grayslake)	60030
Wildwood (Lake County; mail Spring Grove)	60081
Wildwood Addition (Part of Moline)	61265
Wildwood Valley	60123
Will (Township)	60468
Willard (Alexander County)	62962
Willard (St. Clair County)	62269
Willeys	62568
Williams (Township)	62693
Williamsburg	61937
Williamsfield	61489
Williamson	62088
Williams Park	60084
Williams Place	62035
Williamsville	62693
Willisville	62997
Willow	61085
Willoway (Part of Naperville)	60540
Willoway Manor (Part of Willowbrook)	60521
Willow Branch (Township)	61830
Willowbrook (DuPage County)	60521
Willowbrook (Kendall County)	60512
Willowbrook (Will County)	60417
Willow Brooke	61080
Willow Creek (Township)	60530
Willow Estates (DeKalb County)	60135
Willow Estates (Iroquois County)	60912
Willow Hill	62480
Willow Hill (Township)	62480
Willow's East (Part of Glenview)	60025
Willow Springs	60480
Willow Wood (Part of Palatine)	60067
Wilmette	60091
Wilmington	60481
Wilmington (Township)	60481
Wilshire Bluffs Estate	61008
Wilson (Township)	61777
Wilson Avenue (Part of Chicago)	60640
Wilson Heights	62234
Wilsonville	62093
Wilton (Township)	60442
Wilton Center	60442
Winchester	62694
Winden Oak	60119
Windham Manor (Part of Northbrook)	60062
Windings	60175
Windsor	61957
Windsor (Township)	61957
Windsor Estates West (Part of Mount Prospect)	60056

	ZIP
Windsor Park (Champaign County)	61801
Windsor Park (Cook County)	60649
Windsor Square (Part of Peoria)	61614
Wine Hill	62288
Winfield	60190
Winfield (Township)	60185
Wing	61741
Winkle	62237
Winnebago	61088
Winnebago (Township)	61088
Winneshiek	61032
Winnetka	60093
Winslow	61089
Winslow (Township)	61089
Winston Hills (Part of Woodridge)	60515
Winston Park (Part of Palatine)	60067
Winston Park Northwest (Part of Palatine)	60067
Winston Park South (Part of Country Club Hills)	60477
Winston Plaza Shopping Center (Part of Melrose Park)	60160
Winston Village (Part of Bolingbrook)	60440
Winston Woods (Part of Bolingbrook)	60440
Winterrowd	62424
Winthrop Harbor	60096
Wireton (Part of Blue Island)	60406
Witt	62094
Witt (Township)	62094
Woburn	62246
Wolf Lake	62998
Womac	62626
Wonder Lake	60097
Wonder View	60097
Wonder Woods	60097
Woodbine (Township)	61085
Woodbine (Township)	61085
Woodborough (Part of Homewood)	60430
Woodburn	62014
Woodbury	62445
Woodbury (Township)	62445
Wood Dale (DuPage County)	60191
Wooddale (Peoria County)	61607
Wooded Shores	60097
Woodfield (Part of Schaumburg)	60173
Woodford	61516
Woodford Heights	61548
Woodgate	60178
Wood Hill (Part of University Park)	60466
Woodhill Estates	61038
Woodhull	61490
Woodland (Carroll County) (Township)	61053
Woodland (Fulton County) (Township)	61501
Woodland (Iroquois County)	60974
Woodland (Kankakee County)	60954
Woodland Addition	61350
Woodland Heights (Part of Streamwood)	60103
Woodland Hills (Part of Batavia)	60510
Woodland Lake	61817
Woodland Shores	61021
Woodlawn (Cook County)	60637
Woodlawn (Jefferson County)	62898
Woodlawn Heights	61081
Woodmere (Part of Libertyville)	60048
Woodridge	60517
Wood River	62095

	ZIP
Wood River (Township)	62095
Woodruff (Part of Chicago)	60619
Woods Edge	61801
Woodside (Township)	62703
Woodside Estates (Part of Oak Brook)	60521
Woodson	62665
Woodstock (McHenry County)	60098
Woodstock (Schuyler County) (Township)	62681
Woodview Manor (Part of Prospect Heights)	60070
Woodville (Township)	62027
Woodworth	60953
Woody	62016
Woodyard (Edgar County)	61924
Woodyard (Fayette County)	62885
Wooster Lake	60041
Woosung	61091
Woosung (Township)	61091
Worden	62097
Worth (Cook County)	60482
Worth (Cook County) (Township)	60482
Worth (Woodford County) (Township)	61548
Wrights	62098
Wrights (Township)	62098
Wrights Corner	62414
Wyanet	61379
Wyanet (Township)	61379
Wynoose	62868
Wyoming (Lee County) (Township)	61353
Wyoming (Stark County)	61491
Wysox (Township)	61051
Wythe (Township)	62373
Xenia	62899
Xenia (Township)	62899
Yale	62481
Yankee Ridge	61801
Yantisville	62534
Yard Center (Part of Dolton)	60419
Yates (Township)	61726
Yates City	61572
Yatesville	62612
Yellowhead (Township)	60940
Yeoward Addition	61071
York (Carroll County) (Township)	61285
York (Clark County)	62477
York (Clark County) (Township)	62477
York (DuPage County) (Township)	60181
York Center	60148
Yorkfield	60126
Yorkshire Woods (Part of Oak Brook)	60521
Yorktown (Bureau County)	61283
Yorktown (Henry County) (Township)	61277
Yorktown Shopping Center (Part of Lombard)	60148
Yorkville	60560
Young America (Township)	61940
Young Hickory (Township)	61544
Youngstown	61473
Zanesville (Township)	62572
Zearing	61337
Zeigler	62999
Zenith	62899
Zif	62824
Zion (Carroll County)	61074
Zion (Lake County)	60099
Zion (Lake County) (Township)	60099
Zuma (Township)	61257
Zurich Heights (Part of Lake Zurich)	60047

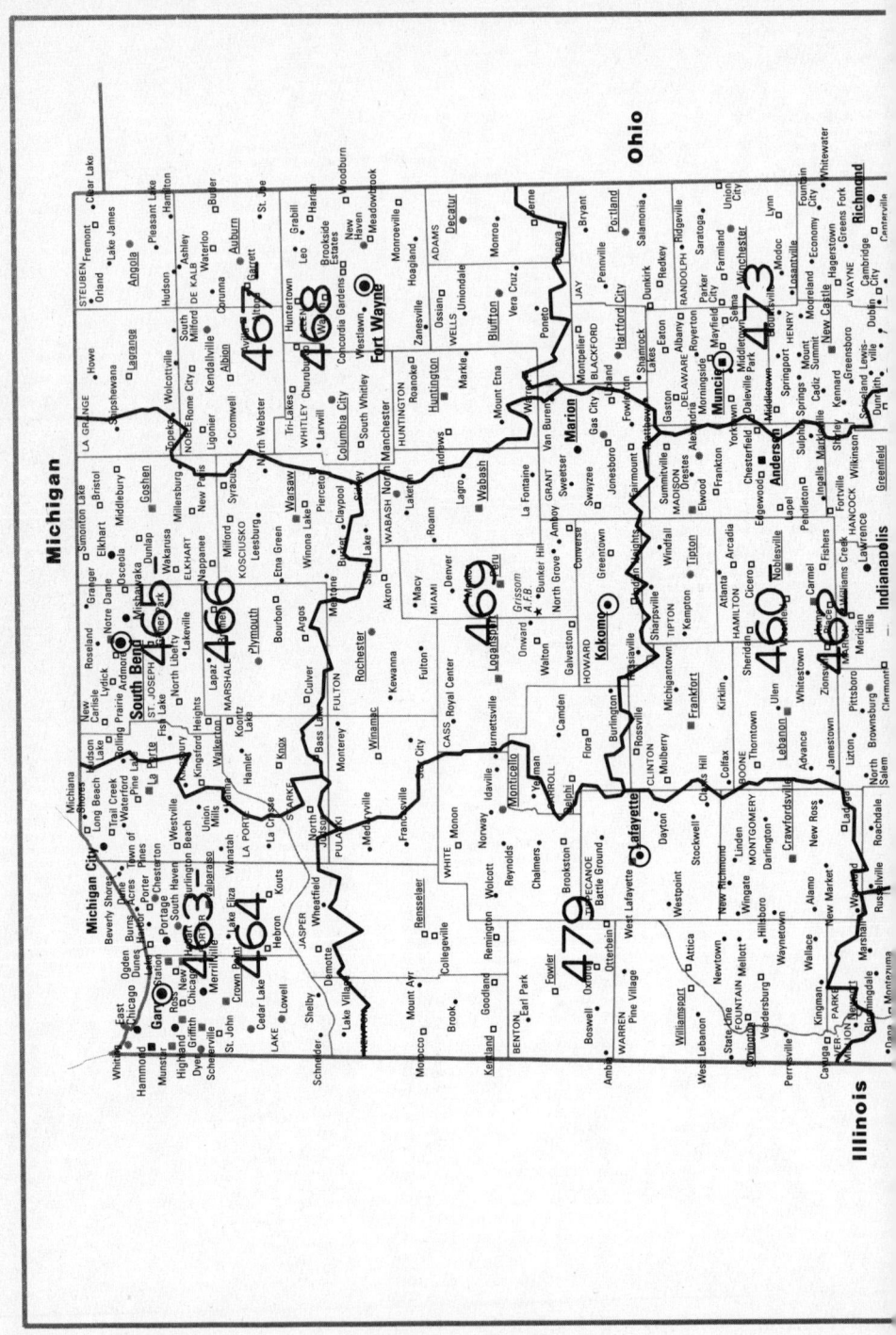

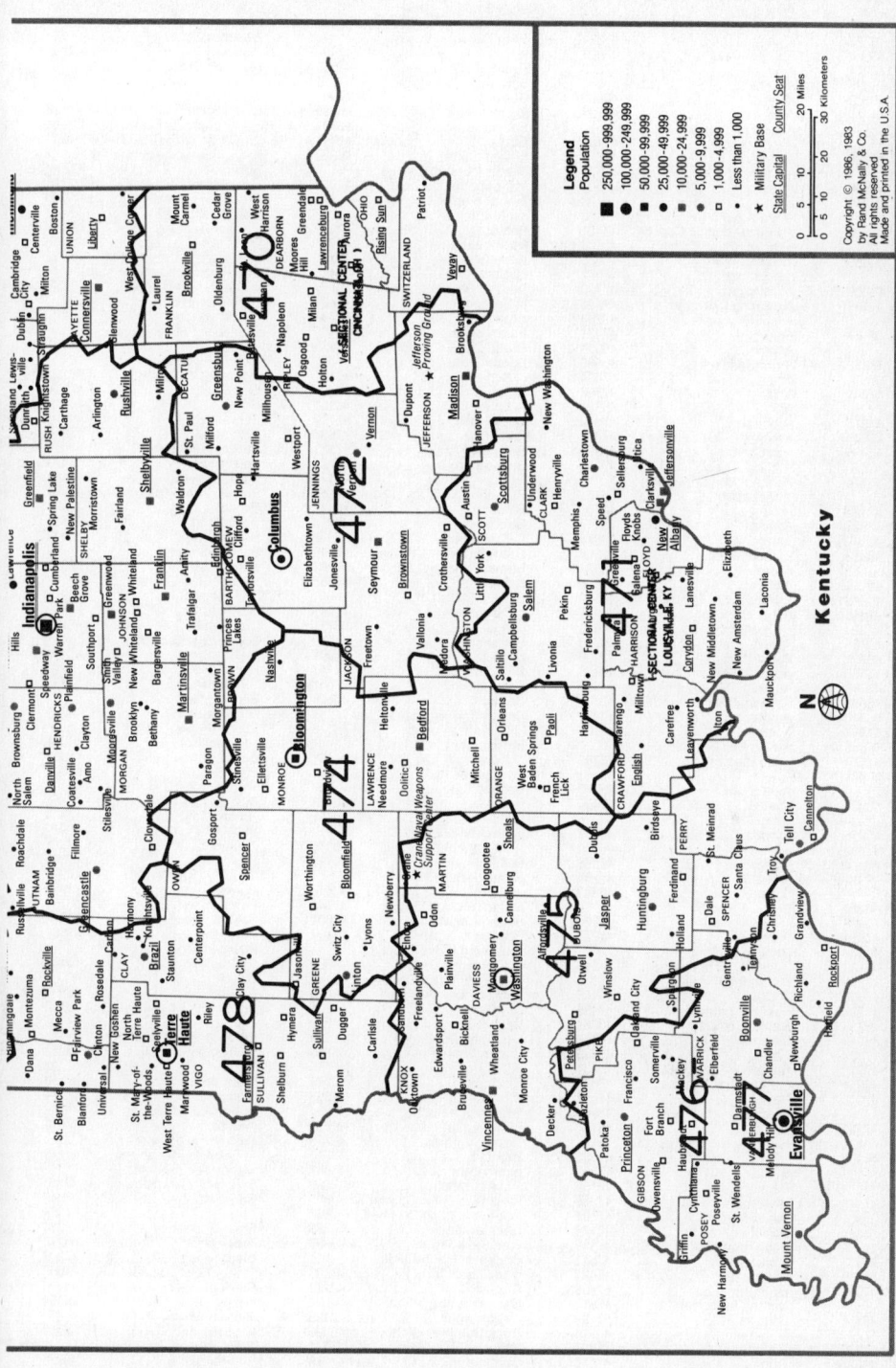

Name	ZIP
Abbey Dell	47469
Aberdeen	47040
Abington	47330
Abington (Township)	47330
Aboite	46783
Aboite (Township)	46804
Acme	47274
Acton (Part of Indianapolis)	46259
Adams (Allen County) (Township)	46774
Adams (Carroll County) (Township)	47960
Adams (Cass County) (Township)	46988
Adams (Decatur County)	47240
Adams (Decatur County) (Township)	47272
Adams (Hamilton County) (Township)	46069
Adams (Madison County) (Township)	46056
Adams (Morgan County)	46151
Adams (Morgan County) (Township)	46151
Adams (Parke County) (Township)	47872
Adams (Ripley County) (Township)	47041
Adams (Warren County) (Township)	47975
Adamsboro	46947
Adams Lake	46795
Adams Mill	46920
Addison (Township)	46176
Addmore (Part of Clarksville)	47129
Ade	47922
Advance	46102
Ainsworth	46342
Air Mail Field (Part of Indianapolis)	46251
Akron	46910
Alamo	47916
Albany	47320
Albion	46701
Albion (Township)	46701
Aldine	46366
Alert	47283
Alexandria	46001
Alfont	46040
Alford	47567
Alfordsville	47553
Algers	47567
Alida	46391
Allen (Miami County) (Township)	46951
Allen (Noble County) (Township)	46755
Allendale	47802
Allens Acres	46077
Allensville	47011
Allisonville (Part of Indianapolis)	46250
Allman	46158
Alma Lake	47834
Alpine	47331
Alquina	47331
Alta	47854
Alto	46902
Alton	47137
Altona	46738
Alvarado	46742
Amber Valley	47803
Ambia	47917
Amboy	46911
Americus	47905
Ames (Part of Crawfordsville)	47933
Amity	46131
Amo	46103
Anderson (Madison County)	46011-18
For specific Anderson Zip Codes call (317) 643-3356, or your local postmaster.	
Anderson (Madison County) (Township)	46016
Anderson (Perry County) (Township)	47586
Anderson (Rush County) (Township)	46156
Anderson (Warrick County) (Township)	47630
Andersonville	47024
Andrews	46702
Angola	46703
Annandale Estates	47448
Annapolis	47832

Name	ZIP
Anoka	46947
Ansley Acres	46804
Anthony	47302
Antioch	46041
Antiville	47371
Apache Acres	47805
Arba	47355
Arcadia	46030
Arcana	46952
Arcola	46704
Arctic Springs (Part of Jeffersonville)	47130
Arda	47567
Ardmore	46628
Argos	46501
Ari	46723
Ar'les Acres	46060
Arlington (Monroe County)	47401
Arlington (Rush County)	46104
Arlington Park	46835
Armiesburg	47862
Armstrong	47720
Armstrong (Township)	47720
Armuth Acres	47203
Arney	47431
Aroma	46031
Arrowhead Park	46580
Art	47834
Arthur	47598
Artic	46721
Ashboro	47840
Asherville	47834
Ash Grove	47920
Ashland (Henry County)	47362
Ashland (Morgan County) (Township)	46151
Ashley	46705
Athens	46912
Atherton	47874
Atkinsonville	47868
Atlanta	46031
Attica	47918
Atwood	46502
Aubbeenaubbee (Township)	46975
Auburn	46706
Auburn Junction	46706
Augusta (Marion County)	46268
Augusta (Pike County)	47598
Aultshire (Part of Muncie)	47302
Aurora	47001
Austin	47102
Avalon Hills (Part of Indianapolis)	46250
Avery	46041
Avilla	46710
Avoca	47420
Avon	46234
Avondale	46952
Ayr	46550
Ayrshire	47598
Azalia	47232
Babcock	46383
Bacon (Part of Indianapolis)	46220
Baileys Corner	47978
Bainbridge (Dubois County) (Township)	47546
Bainbridge (Putnam County)	46105
Baker (Township)	47433
Bakers Corners	46069
Bakertown	46701
Balbec	47369
Baldwin Heights (Part of Princeton)	47670
Bandon	47514
Banquo	46940
Banta	46106
Bar-Barry Heights (Part of West Lafayette)	47906
Barbee	46562
Bargersville	46106
Barkley (Township)	47978
Barnaby Acres	47201
Barnard	46172
Barr (Township)	47519
Barrick Corner	47841
Bartlettsville	47421
Bartley	47805
Barton (Township)	47613
Bartonia	47390
Bass Lake	46534
Batesville	47006
Bath	47010
Bath (Township)	47010
Battle Ground	47920
Baugh City	47610
Baugo (Township)	46514

Name	ZIP
Bayfield	46562
Beal	47591
Bean Blossom (Brown County)	46160
Bean Blossom (Monroe County) (Township)	47429
Bear Branch	47018
Bearcreek (Township)	47326
Beard	46041
Beardstown	46996
Bear Lake	46701
Beatrice	46341
Beattys Corner	46360
Beaver (Newton County) (Township)	47963
Beaver (Pulaski County) (Township)	46996
Beaver City	47922
Becks Grove	47235
Becks Mill	47167
Bedford	47421
Bedford Heights (Part of Bedford)	47421
Beecamp	47250
Beech Brook	46176
Beech Creek (Township)	47459
Beech Grove (Marion County)	46107
Beech Grove (Morgan County)	46151
Beechwood	47137
Bee Ridge	47834
Bell Center	47925
Bellefountain	47371
Belle Union	46120
Belleview	47250
Belleville	46118
Bellmore	47830
Bell Rohr Park	46538
Belmont (Brown County)	47448
Belmont (Henry County)	47362
Belshaw	46356
Ben Davis (Part of Indianapolis)	46241
Bengal	46131
Benham	47042
Bennetts	46901
Bennettsville	47143
Bennington	47011
Benton	46526
Benton (Elkhart County) (Township)	46526
Benton (Monroe County) (Township)	47401
Bentonville	47322
Benwood	47834
Berlien	46703
Berne	46711
Berwick Manor (Part of Shelbyville)	46176
Bethany	46111
Bethel (Posey County) (Township)	47616
Bethel (Wayne County)	47341
Bethel Village	47201
Bethlehem (Township)	47104
Bethlehem (Cass County) (Township)	46988
Bethlehem (Clark County)	47104
Between-the-Lakes Park	46538
Beverly Shores	46301
Bicknell	47512
Big Creek (Township)	47929
Bigger (Township)	47265
Big Lake	46725
Big Springs	46069
Billingsville	47353
Billtown	47834
Billville	47834
Bippus	46713
Birdseye	47513
Birmingham	46951
Black (Township)	47620
Blackhawk (Allen County)	46815
Blackhawk (Vigo County)	47866
Blackhawk Beach	46383
Blackhawk Forest	46805
Blackiston Heights (Part of Clarksville)	47129
Blackiston Mill	47129
Blackiston Village (Part of Clarksville)	47129
Black Oak (Part of Gary)	46406
Blaine	47371
Blairsville	47638
Blanford	47831
Blocher	47138
Bloomfield (Greene County)	47424

Name	ZIP
Bloomfield (Lagrange County) (Township)	46761
Bloomfield (Spencer County)	47611
Bloomingdale	47832
Blooming Grove	47012
Blooming Grove (Township)	47012
Bloomingport	47355
Bloomington	47401-08
For specific Bloomington Zip Codes call (812) 334-4030, or your local postmaster.	
Blountsville	47354
Blue Creek (Adams County) (Township)	46772
Blue Creek (Franklin County)	47041
Blue Lake	46723
Blue Ridge	46176
Blue River (Hancock County) (Township)	46140
Blue River (Harrison County) (Township)	47115
Blue River (Henry County) (Township)	47360
Blue River (Johnson County) (Township)	46124
Bluff Point	47371
Bluffs	46151
Bluffton	46714
Bobtown	47274
Bogard (Township)	47568
Boggstown	46110
Bogle Corner	47438
Bolivar (Township)	47970
Bonnell	47022
Bonnenburger	47130
Bono	47446
Bono (Township)	47446
Boon (Township)	47601
Boone (Cass County) (Township)	46978
Boone (Crawford County) (Township)	47137
Boone (Dubois County) (Township)	47546
Boone (Harrison County) (Township)	47135
Boone (Madison County) (Township)	46036
Boone (Porter County) (Township)	46341
Boone Grove	46302
Boonville	47601
Borden	47106
Boston	47324
Boston (Township)	47324
Boswell	47921
Boundary	47371
Bourbon	46504
Bourbon (Township)	46504
Bowers	47940
Bowerstown	46750
Bowling Green	47833
Bowman	47567
Bowman Acres (Part of Greenfield)	46140
Boxley	46069
Boyleston	46057
Bracken	46750
Bradford	47107
Bradford Village (Part of Marion)	46952
Bradley	47611
Bramble	47553
Branchville	47514
Branchville Training Center	47586
Brandywine (Hancock County) (Township)	46140
Brandywine (Shelby County) (Township)	46126
Braytown	47043
Brazil	47834
Brazil (Township)	47834
Breezewood	46952
Breezewood Park	47302
Breezy Point	47960
Bremen	46506
Brems	46534
Brendan Wood (Part of Lebanon)	46052
Brendonwood (Part of Indianapolis)	46226
Brent Wood (Part of Shelbyville)	46176
Bretzville	47542
Brewersville	47265

	ZIP
Brewington Woods	47302
Briarwood	46157
Brice	47371
Brick Chapel	46135
Bridgeport (Part of Indianapolis)	46231
Bridgeton	47836
Brierwood Hills	46804
Bright	47025
Brighton	46746
Brightwood (Part of Indianapolis)	46218
Brimfield	46720
Brinckley	47340
Bringhurst	46913
Bristol	46507
Bristow	47515
Broadlands	47805
Broad Ripple (Part of Indianapolis)	46220
Broadview (Grant County)	46952
Broadview (Lawrence County)	47421
Broadview (Monroe County)	47401
Bromer	47452
Brook	47922
Brookfield	46126
Brook Haven	46952
Brook Knoll (Part of Bedford)	47421
Brooklyn	46111
Brookmoor	46158
Brooks	46060
Brooksburg	47250
Brookside Estates (Allen County)	46805
Brookside Estates (Vigo County)	47802
Brookston	47923
Brook Trails	46637
Brookville	47012
Brookville (Township)	47012
Brookville Heights	46163
Brookwood (Part of Warsaw)	46580
Broom Hill	47106
Brown (Hancock County) (Township)	47384
Brown (Hendricks County) (Township)	46112
Brown (Montgomery County) (Township)	47933
Brown (Morgan County) (Township)	46158
Brown (Ripley County) (Township)	47250
Brown (Washington County) (Township)	47108
Brownsburg	46112
Browns Crossing	46151
Brownstown (Crawford County)	47118
Brownstown (Jackson County) (Township)	47220
Brownstown (Jackson County)	47220
Browns Valley	47933
Brownsville	47325
Brownsville (Township)	47325
Bruce Lake	46939
Bruceville	47516
Brummitt Acres	46304
Brunswick (Lake County)	46303
Brunswick (Part of Gary)	46406
Brushy Prairie	46761
Bryant	47326
Bryantsburg	47250
Bryantsville	47446
Buck Creek (Hancock County) (Township)	46140
Buck Creek (Tippecanoe County)	47924
Buckeye	46792
Buckskin	47647
Bucktown	47838
Bud	46131
Buddha	47421
Buena Vista	47024
Buffalo	47925
Buffaloville	47550
Buffington (Part of Gary)	46406
Bufkin	47620
Bugtown	47633
Bullocktown	47601
Bunker Hill (Fayette County)	47331
Bunker Hill (Knox County)	47591
Bunker Hill (Miami County)	46914

	ZIP
Bunker Hill (Washington County)	47167
Burdick	46304
Burglen Hills (Part of Tell City)	47586
Burket	46508
Burlington	46915
Burlington (Township)	46915
Burlington Beach	46383
Burnett	47805
Burnettsville	47926
Burney	47222
Burns City	47553
Burns Harbor	46304
Burnsville	47201
Burr Oak (Marshall County)	46511
Burr Oak (Noble County)	46701
Burrows	46916
Busseron	47561
Busseron (Township)	47561
Butler (De Kalb County)	46721
Butler (De Kalb County) (Township)	46763
Butler (Franklin County) (Township)	47006
Butler (Miami County) (Township)	46970
Butler Center	46738
Butlerville	47223
Byrneville	47122
Byron	46371
Caborn	47620
Cadiz	47362
Caesar Creek (Township)	47018
Cagle Mill	47868
Cain (Township)	47949
Cairo	47906
Cale	47581
California (Township)	46534
Calumet (Township)	46402
Calvertville	47424
Cambria	46041
Cambridge City	47327
Camby (Part of Indianapolis)	46113
Camden	46917
Cammack	47302
Campbell (Jennings County) (Township)	47023
Campbell (Warrick County) (Township)	47610
Campbellsburg	47108
Campbelltown	47598
Canaan	47224
Candleglo Village	46176
Candle Light Village (Part of Columbus)	47201
Cannelburg	47519
Cannelton	47520
Cannelton Heights (Part of Cannelton)	47520
Canton	47167
Carbon	47837
Carbondale	47993
Cardonia	47834
Carefree	47137
Carey (Part of Noblesville)	46060
Carlisle	47838
Carlos City	47355
Carmel	46032-33
For specific Carmel Zip Codes call (317) 846-1566, or your local postmaster.	
Carp	47460
Carpenter (Township)	47977
Carpentersville	46172
Carr (Clark County) (Township)	47143
Carr (Jackson County) (Township)	47260
Carriage Estates (Bartholomew County)	47201
Carriage Estates (Hancock County)	46163
Carrollton	46913
Carrollton (Township)	46929
Carter (Township)	47523
Cartersburg	46114
Carthage	46115
Carwood	47106
Cascade Heights (Part of Bloomington)	47401
Cass (Clay County) (Township)	47868
Cass (Dubois County) (Township)	47541
Cass (Greene County) (Township)	47449

	ZIP
Cass (La Porte County) (Township)	46390
Cass (Ohio County) (Township)	47040
Cass (Pulaski County) (Township)	47957
Cass (Sullivan County)	47882
Cass (Sullivan County) (Township)	47882
Cass (White County) (Township)	47960
Cassville	46901
Castleton	46250
Castleton Square (Part of Castleton)	46250
Cataract	47460
Cates	47952
Catlin	47872
Cato	47598
Cavanaugh (Part of Gary)	46406
Cayuga	47928
Cedar Canyons	46825
Cedar Creek (Allen County) (Township)	46741
Cedar Creek (De Kalb County)	46738
Cedar Creek (Lake County) (Township)	46356
Cedar Grove	47016
Cedar Lake	46303
Cedar Point	47960
Cedar Shores	46741
Cedarville	46741
Celestine	47521
Cemar Estates	47805
Cementville (Part of Jeffersonville)	47129
Centenary	47842
Centennial (Allen County)	46808
Centennial (Fountain County)	47952
Center (Benton County) (Township)	47944
Center (Boone County) (Township)	46052
Center (Clinton County) (Township)	46041
Center (Dearborn County) (Township)	47001
Center (Delaware County) (Township)	47302
Center (Gibson County) (Township)	47649
Center (Grant County) (Township)	46952
Center (Greene County) (Township)	47424
Center (Hancock County) (Township)	46140
Center (Hendricks County) (Township)	46122
Center (Howard County)	46902
Center (Howard County) (Township)	46902
Center (Jay County)	47371
Center (Jennings County) (Township)	47265
Center (La Porte County) (Township)	46350
Center (Lake County) (Township)	46307
Center (Marion County) (Township)	46204
Center (Marshall County) (Township)	46563
Center (Martin County) (Township)	47553
Center (Porter County) (Township)	46383
Center (Posey County) (Township)	47620
Center (Ripley County) (Township)	47037
Center (Rush County) (Township)	46148
Center (Starke County) (Township)	46534
Center (Union County) (Township)	47353
Center (Vanderburgh County) (Township)	47710
Center (Warrick County)	47601
Center (Wayne County) (Township)	47330
Centerpoint	47840
Center Square	47043
Centerton	46151
Center Valley	46158

	ZIP
Centerville (Spencer County)	47611
Centerville (Wayne County)	47330
Central	47110
Central Barren	47161
Centre (Township)	46614
Century Consumer Mall (Part of Merrillville)	46410
Ceylon	46740
Chain O'Lakes	46628
Chalmers	47929
Chambersburg	47454
Champlin Meadows (Part of Martinsville)	46151
Chandler	47610
Chapel Bluff (Part of Columbus)	47201
Chapel Hill (Marion County)	46224
Chapelhill (Monroe County)	47436
Chapel Manor (Part of Merrillville)	46410
Charlemac Village (Part of Indianapolis)	46259
Charlestown	47111
Charlestown (Township)	47111
Charle Sumac Estates (Part of Indianapolis)	46259
Charlottesville	46117
Chase	47921
Chelsea	47138
Cherokee Terrace	47130
Cherry Grove	47933
Chester (Wabash County) (Township)	46962
Chester (Wayne County)	47374
Chester (Wells County) (Township)	46781
Chesterfield	46017
Chesterton (Hamilton County)	46280
Chesterton (Porter County)	46304
Chesterville	47032
Chestnut Hill (Part of Chesterton)	46304
Chestnut Ridge	47274
Chicago Avenue (Part of East Chicago)	46312
Chili	46926
China	47250
Chippewa	46613-14
For specific Chippewa Zip Codes call (219) 282-8500, or your local postmaster.	
Chrisney	47611
Christiansburg	47201
Christmas Lake Village (Part of Santa Claus)	47579
Churubusco	46723
Cicero (Hamilton County)	46034
Cicero (Tipton County) (Township)	46031
Cicero Heights	46072
Cincinnati	47424
Circle City (Part of Indianapolis)	46202
Circle Park	46742
Circleville	46173
Clare	46060
Clark (Johnson County) (Township)	46142
Clark (Montgomery County) (Township)	47954
Clark (Perry County) (Township)	47515
Clarksburg	47225
Clarks Hill	47930
Clarks Landing	46742
Clarksville (Clark County)	47129
Clarksville (Hamilton County)	46060
Clay (Bartholomew County) (Township)	47201
Clay (Carroll County) (Township)	46923
Clay (Cass County) (Township)	46947
Clay (Dearborn County) (Township)	47032
Clay (Decatur County) (Township)	47240
Clay (Hamilton County) (Township)	46032-33
For specific Clay Zip Codes call (317) 846-1566, or your local postmaster.	

Place	ZIP	Place	ZIP	Place	ZIP	Place	ZIP
Clay (Hendricks County) (Township)	46121	College Hill (Part of Logansport)	46947	Crestwood (Part of Fort Wayne)	46804	Denham	46925
Clay (Howard County) (Township)	46901	College Mall (Part of Bloomington)	47407	Crete	47355	Denmark	47427
Clay (Kosciusko County) (Township)	46580	College Meadows	46240	Crisman (Part of Portage)	46368	Denver	46926
Clay (Lagrange County) (Township)	46761	Collegeville	47978	Critchfield	46142	Depauw	47115
Clay (Miami County) (Township)	46914	Collett	47371	Crocker (Part of Portage)	46383	Deputy	47230
Clay (Morgan County) (Township)	46111	Collins	46725	Crompton Hill	47842	Derby	47525
Clay (Owen County) (Township)	47460	Coloma	47872	Cromwell	46732	Desoto	47302
Clay (Pike County) (Township)	47640	Colonial Hills	47630	Crooked Lake	46703	Devon Park (Part of Muncie)	47304
Clay (Spencer County) (Township)	47579	Colonial Park	47802	Cross Plains	47017	Devonshire (Part of Lawrence)	46226
Clay (St. Joseph County) (Township)	46637	Colonial Village	46040	Crothersville	47229	Dewey (Township)	46348
Clay (Wayne County) (Township)	47345	Columbia (Dubois County) (Township)	47527	Crown Center	46157	Diamond	47874
Clay City (Clay County)	47841	Columbia (Fayette County)	47331	Crown Colony	46816	Diamond Lake	46794
Clay City (Spencer County)	47550	Columbia (Fayette County) (Township)	47331	Crown Point	46307	Diamond Valley (Part of Evansville)	47710
Claypool	46510	Columbia (Gibson County) (Township)	47660	Crows Nest	46208	Dick Johnson (Township)	47834
Claysville	47108	Columbia (Jennings County) (Township)	47265	Crumley Crossing	47336	Dike (Part of Princeton)	47670
Clayton	46118	Columbia (Whitley County) (Township)	46725	Crump Estates (Part of Columbus)	47201	Dillman	46792
Clear Creek (Huntington County) (Township)	46750	Columbia City	46725	Crumstown	46554	Dillsboro	47018
Clear Creek (Monroe County)	47426	Columbus	47201-03	Crystal	47527	Diplomat Plaza (Part of Fort Wayne)	46806
Clear Creek (Monroe County) (Township)	47401	For specific Columbus Zip Codes call (812) 378-2089, or your local postmaster.		Cuba (Allen County)	46741	Disko	46982
Clear Lake (Township)	46737	Commercial Place (Part of Greencastle)	46135	Cuba (Bartholomew County)	46124	Dixon	46773
Clear Lake	46737	Commiskey	47227	Cuba (Owen County)	47460	Doans	47424
Clear Spring (Jackson County)	47220	Como	47371	Culver	46511	Dodd	47587
Clearspring (Lagrange County) (Township)	46571	Concord (De Kalb County)	46706	Culver Military Academy (Part of Culver)	46511	Dodds Bridge	47849
Clermont	46234	Concord (De Kalb County) (Township)	46785	Cumback	47501	Dogwood	47135
Clermont Heights	46112	Concord (Elkhart County) (Township)	46514	Cumberland	46229	Dolan	47401
Cleveland (Elkhart County) (Township)	46514	Concord (Tippecanoe County)	47905	Cunot	46120	Domestic	46714
Cleveland (Hancock County)	46140	Concordia Gardens (Part of Fort Wayne)	46825	Curby	47118	Donaldson	46513
Cleveland (Whitley County) (Township)	46787	Connersville	47331	Curry (Township)	47879	Dongola	47660
Clifford	47226	Connersville (Township)	47331	Curryville (Adams County)	46731	Doolittle Mills	47118
Clifty (Township)	47246	Continental Camp	47616	Curryville (Sullivan County)	47879	Door Village	46350
Clifty Village	47203	Converse	46919	Curtisville	46036	Dover (Boone County)	46052
Clinton (Boone County) (Township)	46052	Cook (Part of Cedar Lake)	46303	Cutler	46920	Dover (Dearborn County)	47022
Clinton (Cass County) (Township)	46947	Cool Spring (Township)	46360	Cuzco	47432	Dover Hill	47581
Clinton (Decatur County) (Township)	47240	Coolwood Acres	46383	Cyclone	46041	Dovers View	46072
Clinton (Elkhart County) (Township)	46526	Cope	46151	Cynthiana	47612	Dowden Acres	47802
Clinton (La Porte County) (Township)	46382	Coppess Corner	46772	Cypress	47712	Downtown (Part of Gary)	46402
Clinton (Putnam County) (Township)	46135	Cordry Lake	46164	Dabney	47023	Downtown (Part of Kokomo)	46901
Clinton (Vermillion County)	47842	Corn Brook	47203	Daggett	47427	Downtown (Part of Lafayette)	47902
Clinton (Vermillion County) (Township)	47842	Cornettsville	47568	Daisy Hill	47106	Downtown (Part of Muncie)	47305
Clinton Falls	46135	Correct	47042	Dale	47523	Dreamwold Heights	46637
Cloud Crest Hills	47448	Correctional Industrial Complex	46064	Daleville	47334	Dresden	47453
Cloverdale	46120	Cortland	47228	Dallas (Township)	46702	Dresser	47885
Cloverdale (Township)	46120	Corunna	46730	Dalton	47346	Drexel Gardens (Part of Indianapolis)	46241
Cloverland	47834	Cory	47846	Dalton (Township)	47346	Driftwood (Township)	47281
Clover Village	46126	Corydon	47112	Dana	47847	Dublin	47335
Clunette	46538	Cosperville	46794	Danville	46122	Dubois	47527
Clymers	46947	Cottage Grove	47353	Darlington	47940	Dubois Crossroads	47527
Coal Bluff	47874	Cotton (Township)	47011	Darmstadt	47711	Duck Creek (Township)	46036
Coal City	47427	Country Club Gardens	46804	Darrough Chapel	46901	Dudley (Township)	47387
Coal Creek (Fountain County)	47932	Country Club Heights	46011	Davis (Fountain County) (Township)	47918	Dudleytown	47274
Coal Creek (Montgomery County) (Township)	47994	Country Club Meadows (Part of Evansville)	47710	Davis (La Porte County)	46360	Duff	47542
Coalmont	47845	Countryside Estates	46805	Davis (Starke County) (Township)	46532	Dugger	47848
Coatesville	46121	Country Terrace	47302	Daylight	47711	Dundee	46001
Cochran (Part of Aurora)	47001	Country Village	47303	Dayton	47941	Dune Acres	46304
Coe	47598	Courter	46970	Dayville	47630	Dune Acres Station (Part of Dune Acres)	46304
Coesse	46725	Coveyville	47421	Deacon	46994	Duneland Beach	46360
Coesse Corners	46725	Covington	47932	De Camp Gardens	46516	Dunfee	46818
Coffey	47448	Covington Dells	46804	Decatur (Adams County)	46733	Dunkirk (Cass County)	46947
Cofield Corner	47040	Covington Plaza (Part of Fort Wayne)	46804	Decatur (Marion County) (Township)	46241	Dunkirk (Jay County)	47336
Colburn	47931	Cowan	47302	Decker	47524	Dunlap	46514
Colburn Acres	46536	Coxville	47874	Decker (Township)	47524	Dunlapsville	47353
Cold Springs (Dearborn County)	47032	Craig (Township)	47043	Deedsville	46921	Dunn	47944
Cold Springs (Steuben County)	46742	Craig Highlands	46060	Deep River	46342	Dunnington	47944
Colfax (Clinton County)	46035	Craigville	46731	Deer Creek (Carroll County)	46917	Dunns Bridge	46380
Colfax (Newton County) (Township)	46349	Crandall	47114	Deer Creek (Carroll County) (Township)	46923	Dunreith	47337
Collamer	46787	Crane	47522	Deer Creek (Cass County) (Township)	46932	Dupont	47231
College Corner	47371	Crane Naval Depot	47522	Deer Creek (Miami County) (Township)	46959	Durbin	46060
		Crane Naval Weapons Support Center	47522	Deerfield (Bartholomew County)	47201	Dutch Town (Part of Garrett)	46738
		Crawfordsville	47933	Deerfield (Randolph County)	47380	Dyer	46311
		Cree Lake	46755	Deerfield (Vigo County)	47802	Eagle (Township)	46077
		Crest Manor (Part of South Bend)	46614	Deer Park	46310	Eagle Creek (Lake County) (Township)	46341
		Crestmoor (Part of Shelbyville)	46176	Deers Mills	47989	Eagle Creek (Marion County)	46214
		Creston	46356	De Gonia	47601	Eagledale Plaza Shopping Center (Part of Indianapolis)	46222
		Crestview	46383	Delaware (Delaware County) (Township)	47320	Eagle Hollow	47250
		Crestview Heights	46158	Delaware (Hamilton County) (Township)	46060	Eagletown	46074
				Delaware (Ripley County)	47037	Eagle Village	46077
				Delaware (Ripley County) (Township)	47037	Eaglewood Estates	46077
				Delong	46922	Earle	47711
				Delp	47905	Earlham (Part of Richmond)	47374
				Delphi	46923	Earl Park	47942
				Deming	46034	East Cedar Lake (Part of Cedar Lake)	46303
				Democrat (Township)	46920	East Chicago	46312
				Demotte	46310	East Clifford	47203

* **Area Zip Code**   † **Post Office Boxes**

	ZIP		ZIP		ZIP		ZIP
East Columbus (Part of Columbus)	47201	Englewood (Part of Bedford)	47421	Fisher's Woodland	46060	Franklin (Pulaski County) (Township)	46996
East Enterprise	47019	English	47118	Fish Lake (La Porte County)	46574	Franklin (Putnam County) (Township)	46172
Eastern Heights (Part of Bloomington)	47401	English Lake	46366	Fish Lake (Lagrange County)	46761	Franklin (Randolph County) (Township)	47380
Eastgate (Bartholomew County)	47201	Enochsburg	47240	Five Points (Marion County)	46239	Franklin (Ripley County) (Township)	47031
Eastgate (Clark County)	47130	Enos	47963	Five Points (Morgan County)	46158	Franklin (Washington County) (Township)	47167
East Gate (Hancock County)	46040	Enos Corners	47660	Five Points (Whitley County)	46725	Franklin (Wayne County)	47346
Eastgate (Marion County)	46219	Epsom	47568	Flat Rock (Bartholomew County) (Township)	47201	Franklin (Wayne County) (Township)	47341
Eastgate Consumer Mall (Part of Indianapolis)	46219	Epworth Forest	46555	Flat Rock (Shelby County)	47234	Franklin Hills (Part of Tell City)	47586
East Glenn	47803	Erie	46970	Flat Rock Park	47201	Frankton	46044
Eastland Gardens (Part of Fort Wayne)	46816	Erie (Township)	46970	Flat Rock Park North (Part of Columbus)	47201	Fredericksburg	47120
Eastland Mall (Part of Evansville)	47715	Ervin (Township)	46929	Fleming	47274	Fredonia	47137
East Monticello	47960	Etna (Kosciusko County) (Township)	46524	Fletcher	46939	Freedom	47431
East Mount Carmel	47665	Etna (Whitley County)	46725	Flint	46703	Freeland Park	47944
East Oolitic	47421	Etna Green	46524	Flintwood (Part of Columbus)	47201	Freelandville	47535
East Park (Part of Frankfort)	46041	Etna-Troy (Township)	46764	Flora (Carroll County)	46929	Freeman	47460
Eastridge Manor	47203	Eugene	47928	Flora (Miami County)	46970	Freeport	46161
East Shelburn (Part of Shelburn)	47879	Eugene (Township)	47928	Florence	47020	Freetown	47235
East Shoals (Part of Shoals)	47581	Eureka	47635	Florida (Madison County)	46011	Fremont (Township)	46737
East Union	46031	Evanston	47531	Florida (Parke County) (Township)	47874	Fremont	46737
Eastwich (Part of Lafayette)	47901	Evansville	47701-37	Floyd (Township)	46121	French (Adams County) (Township)	46714
Eaton	47338	For specific Evansville Zip Codes call (812) 429-3400, or your local postmaster.		Floyds Knobs	47119	French (Ohio County)	47001
Echo Heights (Part of Muncie)	47302			Folsomville	47614	French Lake	47802
Eckerty	47116	Evergreen Acres (Part of Clarksville)	47129	Fontanet	47851	French Lick	47432
Economy	47339	Everroad Park East (Part of Columbus)	47203	Foraker	46526	French Lick (Township)	47432
Eddy	46795	Everroad Park West (Part of Columbus)	47203	Foresman	47922	Frenchtown	47115
Eden (Hancock County)	46140	Everton	47331	Forest	46039	Friendship	47021
Eden (Lagrange County) (Township)	46571	Ewing (Part of Brownstown)	47220	Forest (Township)	46039	Friendswood	46113
Edgerton	46797	Fair Acres (Part of Salem)	47167	Forest Hill	47240	Fritchton	47591
Edgewater	46383	Fairbanks (Township)	47849	Forest Park (Part of Columbus)	47201	Fritz Corner	47585
Edgewood (Bartholomew County)	47201	Fairbanks	47849	Forest Park Beach	46742	Fruitdale	46160
Edgewood (La Porte County)	46360	Fairfield (De Kalb County) (Township)	46730	Forest Park Heights	47401	Fugit (Township)	47240
Edgewood (Lawrence County)	47421	Fairfield (Franklin County) (Township)	47012	Forest Park North (Part of Columbus)	47201	Fulda	47536
Edgewood (Madison County)	46011	Fairfield (Tippecanoe County) (Township)	47904	Forest Ridge (Allen County)	46804	Fulton (Fountain County) (Township)	47932
Edgewood (Marion County)	46227	Fairfield Center	46730	Forest Ridge (Grant County)	46952	Fulton (Fulton County)	46931
Edgewood Park	46818	Fair Grounds (Part of Indianapolis)	46205	Forest Ridge Estates	46804	Furnace	47424
Edinburgh	46124	Fairland	46126	Forrest Hills	46036	Furnessville	46304
Edison Park (Part of South Bend)	46615	Fairlawn (Part of Columbus)	47201	Fort Branch	47648	Gadsden	46052
Edna Mills	46065	Fairmount	46928	Fort Ritner	47430	Galena (Floyd County)	47119
Edwardsport	47528	Fairmount (Township)	46928	Fortville	46040	Galena (La Porte County) (Township)	46371
Edwardsville	47150	Fair Oaks	47943	Fort Wayne	46801-99	Galveston	46932
Eel (Township)	46947	Fairplay (Township)	47465	For specific Fort Wayne Zip Codes call (219) 427-7311, or your local postmaster.		Gambill	47848
Eel River (Allen County) (Township)	46723	Fairview	47331			Gar Creek	46774
Eel River (Hendricks County) (Township)	46165	Fairview (Township)	47331	Foster	47932	Garden Acres (Boone County)	46071
Effner	60966	Fairview (Randolph County)	47373	Fountain	47918	Garden Acres (Monroe County)	47401
Ege	46763	Fairview (Switzerland County)	47011	Fountain City	47341	Garden City	47201
Ehrmandale	47805	Fairview Park	47842	Fountain Park (Jasper County)	47977	Garfield (Part of Indianapolis)	46203
Ekin	46031	Fairwood Hills (Part of Indianapolis)	46256	Fountain Park (Steuben County)	46742	Garrett	46738
Elberfeld	47613	Fall Creek (Hamilton County) (Township)	46064	Fountain Square (Part of Indianapolis)	46203	Gary	46401-11
El Dorado	46142	Fall Creek (Henry County) (Township)	47356	Fountaintown	46130	For specific Gary Zip Codes call (219) 886-8011, or your local postmaster.	
Elizabeth	47117	Fall Creek (Madison County) (Township)	46011	Fowler	47944		
Elizabethtown	47232	Falmouth	46127	Fowlerton	46930	Gasburg	46158
Elizaville	46052	Farlen	47562	Foxglen	46060	Gas City	46933
Elkhart (Elkhart County)	46514-17	Farmers	47431	Fox Hill	46113	Gaston	47342
For specific Elkhart Zip Codes call (219) 293-5502, or your local postmaster.		Farmersburg	47850	Fox Lake	46703	Gatchel	47586
		Farmers Retreat	47018	Fox Ridge	46135	Gatesville	46164
Elkhart (Elkhart County) (Township)	46526	Farmersville	47620	Francesville	47946	Gateway Shopping Center (Part of Richmond)	47374
Elkhart (Noble County) (Township)	46794	Farmland	47340	Francisco	47649	Gatewood (Part of Muncie)	47304
Elkinsville	47448	Farrabee	47167	Frankfort	46041	Gaynorsville	47240
Elettsville	47429	Farrville	46952	Franklin (De Kalb County) (Township)	46721	Geetingsville	46041
Ellis	47848	Fayette (Boone County)	46052	Franklin (Floyd County) (Township)	47117	Gem	46140
Elliston	47424	Fayette (Vigo County) (Township)	47885	Franklin (Grant County) (Township)	46952	Geneva (Adams County)	46740
Elmdale	47933	Fayetteville	47421	Franklin (Harrison County) (Township)	47136	Geneva (Jennings County) (Township)	47273
Elmira	46761	Federal (Part of Indianapolis)	46204	Franklin (Hendricks County) (Township)	46180	Geneva (Shelby County)	47234
Elmore (Township)	47529	Fenn Haven	47586	Franklin (Henry County) (Township)	47352	Gentryville	47537
Elmwood (Part of Peru)	46970	Ferdinand	47532	Franklin (Johnson County)	46131	Georgetown (Allen County)	46741
Elnora	47529	Ferdinand (Township)	47532	Franklin (Johnson County) (Township)	46131	Georgetown (Cass County)	46947
Elrod	47018	Ferguson Hill	47885	Franklin (Kosciusko County) (Township)	46910	Georgetown (Floyd County)	47122
Elston	47905	Fewell Rhoades	46151	Franklin (Marion County) (Township)	46239	Georgetown (Floyd County) (Township)	47122
Elwood	46036	Fiat	47326	Franklin (Montgomery County) (Township)	47940	Georgetown (Randolph County)	47340
Elwren	47401	Fickle	46041	Franklin (Owen County) (Township)	47431	Georgetown (St. Joseph County)	46635
Eminence	46125	Fields	46158			Georgia	47446
Emison	47561	Fifteenth Avenue (Part of Gary)	46407			Georgia Heights (Part of Merrillville)	46410
Emma	46571	Fillmore	46128			Gerald	47520
Emporia	46056	Fincastle	46172			German (Bartholomew County) (Township)	47201
Enchanted Hills	46732	Finley (Township)	47170				
		Finly	46129				
		Fishers	46038				
		Fishersburg	46051				

	ZIP
German (Marshall County) (Township)	46506
German (St. Joseph County) (Township)	46628
German (Vanderburgh County) (Township)	47712
Germantown	47272
Gessie	47974
Gibson (Township)	47170
Gifford	47978
Gilboa (Township)	47944
Gilead	46951
Gill (Township)	47861
Gillam (Township)	46392
Gilman	46001
Gilmer Park	46624
Gilmour	47438
Gingrich	47960
Gings	46173
Giro	47640
Glen Aire	47803
Glenbrook Square (Part of Fort Wayne)	46805
Glendale	47558
Glendale Center (Part of Indianapolis)	46220
Glendale Lake	46952
Glen Eden	46703
Glenhall	47992
Glenns Valley (Part of Indianapolis)	46217
Glen Park East (Part of Gary)	46409
Glenview	47203
Glenwood	46133
Glenwood Acres	47620
Glenwood Park (Part of Fort Wayne)	46805
Glezen	47567
Gnaw Bone	47448
Goblesville	46750
Goff	46952
Golden Acres	46815
Golden Hill	47960
Golden Lake	46779
Goldsmith	46045
Golfview Estates	47130
Goodland	47948
Goose Lake	46725
Goshen (Elkhart County)	46526*
	46527†
Goshen (Scott County)	47170
Gospel Grove	47803
Gosport	47433
Gowdy	46173
Grabill	46741
Graceland Heights (Part of Hagerstown)	47346
Grafton	47620
Graham (Township)	47230
Graham Valley	47601
Graham Woods	46304
Grammer	47236
Grandview (Monroe County)	47401
Grandview (Spencer County)	47615
Grandview Lake	47201
Grandview Village	47150
Granger	46530
Grant (Benton County) (Township)	47944
Grant (De Kalb County) (Township)	46793
Grant (Greene County) (Township)	47465
Grant (Newton County) (Township)	47948
Grant City	47384
Grantsburg	47123
Granville	47338
Grass (Township)	47611
Grass Creek	46935
Grasselli (Part of East Chicago)	46312
Grassy Fork (Township)	47274
Gravel Beach	46747
Gravelton	46542
Grayford	47265
Graysville	47852
Green (Grant County) (Township)	46928
Green (Hancock County) (Township)	46040
Green (Madison County) (Township)	46048
Green (Marshall County) (Township)	46501

	ZIP
Green (Morgan County) (Township)	46151
Green (Noble County) (Township)	46763
Green (Randolph County) (Township)	47368
Green (Wayne County) (Township)	47393
Green Acres	46410
Greenbriar (Marion County)	46260
Greenbriar (Putnam County)	46135
Greenbrier	47601
Greencastle	46135
Greencastle (Township)	46135
Green Center	46701
Greendale (Allen County)	46805
Greendale (Dearborn County)	47025
Greene (Jay County) (Township)	47371
Greene (Parke County) (Township)	47989
Greene (St. Joseph County) (Township)	46614
Greenfield (Hancock County)	46140
Greenfield (Lagrange County) (Township)	46746
Greenfield (Orange County) (Township)	47118
Greenfield Estates	46952
Greenfield Mills	46746
Greenhill	47970
Greenleaf Manor (Part of Elkhart)	46514
Green Meadows (Shelby County)	46126
Green Meadows (Tippecanoe County)	47906
Greenoak	46975
Greensboro	47344
Greensboro (Township)	47344
Greensburg	47240
Greensfork (Randolph County) (Township)	47335
Greens Fork (Wayne County)	47345
Greentown	46936
Green Tree Mall (Part of Clarksville)	47129
Greenvalley	46060
Greenview	46815
Greenville	47124
Greenville (Township)	47124
Greenville	46781
Greenwood (Johnson County)	46142-43
For specific Greenwood Zip Codes call (317) 881-2323, or your local postmaster.	
Greenwood (Lagrange County)	46795
Greenwood Park Mall (Part of Greenwood)	46142
Greer (Township)	47613
Gregg (Township)	46157
Greybrook Lake	47868
Griffin	47616
Griffith	46319
Grissom Air Force Base	46971
Groomsville	46049
Groveland	46105
Grovertown	46531
Guilford (Dearborn County)	47022
Guilford (Hendricks County) (Township)	46168
Guion	47872
Gulivoire Park	46624
Gurley Corner	47038
Guthrie	47421
Guthrie (Township)	47467
Guy	46936
Gwynneville	46144
Hacienda Village	46805
Hackleman	46928
Haddon (Township)	47838
Hadley	46121
Hagerstown	47346
Halbert (Township)	47581
Haleysbury	47281
Hall (Dubois County) (Township)	47546
Hall (Morgan County)	46157
Halteman Village (Part of Muncie)	47304
Hamblen (Township)	46164

	ZIP
Hamburg (Clark County)	47172
Hamburg (Franklin County)	47036
Hamilton (Clinton County)	46058
Hamilton (Delaware County) (Township)	47302
Hamilton (Jackson County) (Township)	47274
Hamilton (Madison County)	46011
Hamilton (Steuben County)	46742
Hamilton (Sullivan County) (Township)	47882
Hamilton Park	47302
Hamilton Village	47303
Hamlet	46532
Hammond	46320-27
For specific Hammond Zip Codes call (219) 932-1519, or your local postmaster.	
Hammond (Township)	47615
Hamor Heights	47203
Hancock	47115
Handy	47401
Hanfield	46952
Hanging Grove (Township)	47978
Hangman Crossing	47274
Hanna	46340
Hanna (Township)	46340
Hanover (Jefferson County)	47243
Hanover (Jefferson County) (Township)	47243
Hanover (Lake County) (Township)	46303
Hanover (Shelby County) (Township)	46161
Hanover Beach	47243
Happy Hollow Heights (Part of West Lafayette)	47906
Harbison (Township)	47527
Harbor (Part of East Chicago)	46312
Hardinsburg (Dearborn County)	47025
Hardinsburg (Washington County)	47125
Hardscrabble	46051
Harlan	46743
Harmony (Clay County)	47853
Harmony (Posey County) (Township)	47631
Harmony (Union County) (Township)	47331
Harper	47283
Harris (Township)	46530
Harrisburg	47331
Harris City	47240
Harrison (Bartholomew County) (Township)	47201
Harrison (Blackford County) (Township)	47359
Harrison (Boone County) (Township)	46052
Harrison (Cass County) (Township)	46947
Harrison (Clay County) (Township)	47841
Harrison (Daviess County) (Township)	47501
Harrison (Dearborn County) (Township)	47060
Harrison (Delaware County) (Township)	47302
Harrison (Elkhart County) (Township)	46526
Harrison (Fayette County) (Township)	47331
Harrison (Harrison County) (Township)	47122
Harrison (Henry County) (Township)	47384
Harrison (Howard County) (Township)	46979
Harrison (Knox County) (Township)	47591
Harrison (Kosciusko County) (Township)	46502
Harrison (Miami County) (Township)	46911
Harrison (Morgan County) (Township)	46151
Harrison (Owen County) (Township)	47433
Harrison (Pulaski County) (Township)	46939

	ZIP
Harrison (Spencer County) (Township)	47532
Harrison (Union County) (Township)	47353
Harrison (Vigo County) (Township)	47807
Harrison (Wayne County) (Township)	47327
Harrison (Wells County) (Township)	46714
Harrison Hills (Part of Columbus)	47201
Harrison Lake	47201
Harristown	47167
Harrisville	47390
Harrodsburg	47434
Hart (Township)	47619
Hartford (Adams County) (Township)	46740
Hartford (Ohio County)	47001
Hartford City	47348
Hartford Place (Part of Columbus)	47201
Hartleyville	47421
Hartsdale (Part of Schererville)	46375
Hartsville	47244
Harveysburg	47952
Hashtown	47424
Haskells	46390
Hastings	46542
Hatfield	47617
Haubstadt	47639
Haw Creek (Township)	47246
Hawthorne Hills	46307
Hayden	47245
Haymond	47006
Haysville	47546
Hazelrigg	46052
Hazelwood (Allen County)	46805
Hazelwood (Hendricks County)	46118
Hazelwood (Shelby County)	46176
Hazleton	47640
Headlee	47960
Heath	47905
Heather Heights (Part of Columbus)	47201
Heather Hills (Part of Indianapolis)	46229
Heaton Lake	46514
Hebron	46341
Hedrick	47993
Heilman	47523
Helmcrest (Part of Fortville)	46040
Helmer	46747
Helmsburg	47435
Helt (Township)	47847
Heltonville	47436
Hemlock	46937
Hemlock Lakes	47952
Henderson	46173
Hendricks (Johnson County)	46142
Hendricks (Shelby County) (Township)	46176
Hendricksville	47459
Henry (Fulton County) (Township)	46910
Henry (Henry County) (Township)	47362
Henryville	47126
Hensley (Township)	46181
Herbst	46952
Heritage Lake	46128
Herr	46052
Hessen Cassel	46806
Hesston	46350
Hessville (Part of Hammond)	46323
Heth (Township)	47110
Heusler	47712
Hibbard	46511
Hibernia	47111
Hibernia Mills	47933
Hickory Grove (Township)	47984
Hickory Hills	46952
Hidden Valley	47025
Hideaway Lake	47952
Highbanks	46555
High Lake	46701
Highland (Franklin County) (Township)	47012
Highland (Greene County) (Township)	47424
Highland (Lake County)	46322

	ZIP
Highland (Vanderburgh County)	47710
Highland (Vermillion County)	47854
Highland (Vermillion County) (Township)	47974
Highland Meadows	46952
Highland Village (Part of Bloomington)	47401
Highwoods (Part of Indianapolis)	46222
Hiker Trace (Part of Columbus)	47201
Hildebrand Village	46176
Hill and Dale (Part of Sellersburg)	47172
Hillcrest (Bartholomew County)	47201
Hillcrest (Harrison County)	47112
Hillcrest (Porter County)	46383
Hillcrest Circle (Part of Bedford)	47421
Hillendale	47006
Hillham	47432
Hillisburg	46046
Hills And Dales	47383
Hillsboro (Fountain County)	47949
Hillsboro (Henry County)	47362
Hillsdale (Vanderburgh County)	47711
Hillsdale (Vermillion County)	47854
Hillview Estates	47201
Hindostan Falls	47581
Hindustan	47401
Hitchcock	47167
Hi-View (Part of South Bend)	46624
Hoagland	46745
Hobart	46342
Hobart (Township)	46342
Hobbieville	47462
Hobbs	46047
Hoffman Lake	46580
Hogan (Township)	47001
Hogtown	47140
Holaday Hills and Dales	46032
Holiday Lakes	46738
Holiday Park	46902
Holland	47541
Hollandsburg	47872
Hollybrook Lake	47433
Holly Hills	47802
Holton	47023
Home Corner	46952
Homecroft	46227
Home Place	46240
Homer	46146
Homestead (Part of Greendale)	47025
Honey Creek (Henry County)	47356
Honey Creek (Howard County) (Township)	46979
Honey Creek (Vigo County) (Township)	47802
Honey Creek (White County) (Township)	47980
Honeyville	46571
Hoosier Acres (Part of Bloomington)	47401
Hoosier Highlands	47868
Hoosierville	47834
Hoover	46947
Hope	47246
Hopewell (De Kalb County)	46706
Hopewell (Johnson County)	46131
Horace	47240
Horton	46069
Houston	47235
Hovey	47620
Howard (Howard County) (Township)	46901
Howard (Parke County)	47952
Howard (Parke County) (Township)	47859
Howard (Washington County) (Township)	47167
Howe	46746
Howell (Part of Evansville)	47712
Howesville	47438
Hubbell	47427
Hubbells Corner	47041
Hudson (La Porte County) (Township)	46552
Hudson (Steuben County)	46747

	ZIP
Hudson Lake	46552
Hudsonville	47558
Huff (Township)	47615
Huffman	47588
Hull Addition	46072
Hunter (Part of Indianapolis)	46239
Huntersville (Part of Batesville)	47006
Huntertown	46748
Huntingburg	47542
Huntington (Township)	46750
Huntington	46750
Huntsville (Madison County)	46064
Huntsville (Randolph County)	47358
Huron	47437
Hyde Park	47302
Hymera	47855
Hyndsdale	46151
Idaho (Part of Terre Haute)	47802
Idaville	47950
Ijamsville	46962
Imperial Gardens	46815
Imperial Hills (Part of Greenwood)	46227
Independence	47918
Independence Hill (Part of Merrillville)	46410
Indiana Army Ammunition Plant	47111
Indiana Beach	47960
Indiana Oaks	47172
Indianapolis	46201-90

For specific Indianapolis Zip Codes call (317) 464-6150, or your local postmaster.

COLLEGES & UNIVERSITIES

	ZIP
Butler University	46208
Indiana University-Purdue University at Indianapolis	46202
Marian College	46222
University of Indianapolis	46227

FINANCIAL INSTITUTIONS

	ZIP
Bank One, Indianapolis, N.A.	46277
First of America Bank-Indiana	46224
Huntington National Bank of Indiana	46204
INB National Bank	46266
National City Bank, Indiana	46255
Peoples Bank & Trust Company	46204
Union Federal Savings Bank of Indianapolis	46204

HOSPITALS

	ZIP
Community Hospitals of Indianapolis	46219
Indiana University Medical Center	46202
Methodist Hospital of Indianapolis	46202
Richard L. Roudebush Veterans Affairs Medical Center	46202
St. Vincent Hospital and Health Care Center	46032
William N. Wishard Memorial Hospital	46202

HOTELS/MOTELS

	ZIP
Adam's Mark Indianapolis	46241
Airport Hilton Inn	46241
Canterbury Hotel	46225
Embassy Suites Downtown	46204
Holiday Inn-Southeast	46203
Indianapolis Hilton	46204
Marriott Hotel	46219
Radisson Suite Hotel-Indianapolis	46240

MILITARY INSTALLATIONS

	ZIP
Naval Air Warfare Center	46219
United States Property and Fiscal Office for Indiana	46241
United States Property and Fiscal Office, Camp Atterbury	46241

	ZIP
Indianapolis Union Stock Yards (Part of Indianapolis)	46241
Indiana State Farm	46135
Indiana State Reformatory	46064
Indiana State University Evansville Campus	47712
Indian Creek (Lawrence County) (Township)	47421
Indian Creek (Monroe County) (Township)	47401
Indian Creek (Pulaski County) (Township)	46985
Indian Creek Settlement	47512
Indianhead Lake	46122
Indian Heights	46902
Indian Hills	47201
Indian Lake (De Kalb County)	46730
Indian Lake (Marion County)	46226
Indianola	46795
Indian Springs	47581
Indian Village (Noble County)	46732
Indian Village (St. Joseph County)	46637
Industry (Part of Muncie)	47302
Ingalls	46048
Inglefield (Part of Darmstadt)	47618
Innisdale	46001
Inverness	46703
Inwood	46563
Iona	47591
Ireland	47545
Ironton	47581
Iroquois (Township)	47922
Irvington (Part of Indianapolis)	46219
Irvington Plaza Shopping Center (Part of Indianapolis)	46219
Island Park (Kosciusko County)	46580
Island Park (Steuben County)	46742
Iva	47564
Ivanhoe (Part of Indianapolis)	46219
Ivy Hills (Part of Indianapolis)	46220
Jackson (Allen County) (Township)	46773
Jackson (Bartholomew County) (Township)	47274
Jackson (Blackford County) (Township)	47348
Jackson (Boone County) (Township)	46147
Jackson (Brown County) (Township)	47448
Jackson (Carroll County) (Township)	46917
Jackson (Cass County) (Township)	46932
Jackson (Clay County) (Township)	47834
Jackson (Clinton County) (Township)	46041
Jackson (De Kalb County) (Township)	46706
Jackson (Dearborn County) (Township)	47041
Jackson (Decatur County) (Township)	47283
Jackson (Dubois County) (Township)	47542
Jackson (Elkhart County) (Township)	46553
Jackson (Fayette County) (Township)	47331
Jackson (Fountain County) (Township)	47949
Jackson (Greene County) (Township)	47462
Jackson (Hamilton County) (Township)	47030
Jackson (Hancock County) (Township)	46140
Jackson (Harrison County) (Township)	47161
Jackson (Howard County) (Township)	46936
Jackson (Huntington County) (Township)	46783
Jackson (Jackson County) (Township)	47274

	ZIP
Jackson (Jay County) (Township)	47326
Jackson (Kosciusko County) (Township)	46566
Jackson (Madison County) (Township)	46011
Jackson (Miami County) (Township)	46919
Jackson (Morgan County) (Township)	46160
Jackson (Newton County) (Township)	47963
Jackson (Orange County) (Township)	47432
Jackson (Owen County) (Township)	46120
Jackson (Parke County) (Township)	47837
Jackson (Porter County) (Township)	46304
Jackson (Putnam County) (Township)	46172
Jackson (Randolph County) (Township)	47390
Jackson (Ripley County) (Township)	47034
Jackson (Rush County) (Township)	46115
Jackson (Shelby County) (Township)	46176
Jackson (Spencer County) (Township)	47537
Jackson (Starke County) (Township)	46534
Jackson (Steuben County) (Township)	46703
Jackson (Sullivan County) (Township)	47855
Jackson (Tippecanoe County) (Township)	47901
Jackson (Washington County) (Township)	47165
Jackson (Wayne County) (Township)	47327
Jackson (Wells County) (Township)	46991
Jackson (White County) (Township)	47926
Jacksonburg	47327
Jackson Hill	47879
Jackson Park	47302
Jacksons	46072
Jacksonville	47842
Jalapa	46952
Jamestown (Boone County)	46147
Jamestown (Steuben County)	46737
Jamestown (Steuben County) (Township)	46737
Jasonville	47438
Jasper	47546*
	47547†
Jay City	47326
Jefferson (Adams County) (Township)	46711
Jefferson (Allen County) (Township)	46773
Jefferson (Boone County) (Township)	46071
Jefferson (Carroll County) (Township)	46923
Jefferson (Cass County) (Township)	46978
Jefferson (Clinton County) (Township)	46041
Jefferson (Dubois County) (Township)	47513
Jefferson (Elkhart County) (Township)	46526
Jefferson (Grant County) (Township)	46989
Jefferson (Greene County) (Township)	47471
Jefferson (Henry County) (Township)	47388
Jefferson (Huntington County) (Township)	46792
Jefferson (Jay County) (Township)	47371
Jefferson (Kosciusko County) (Township)	46550
Jefferson (Miami County) (Township)	46970
Jefferson (Morgan County) (Township)	46151
Jefferson (Newton County) (Township)	47951
Jefferson (Noble County) (Township)	46701

* Area Zip Code   † Post Office Boxes

	ZIP
Jefferson (Owen County) (Township)	47427
Jefferson (Pike County) (Township)	47564
Jefferson (Pulaski County) (Township)	46996
Jefferson (Putnam County) (Township)	46120
Jefferson (Sullivan County) (Township)	47838
Jefferson (Switzerland County) (Township)	47043
Jefferson (Tipton County) (Township)	46072
Jefferson (Washington County) (Township)	47108
Jefferson (Wayne County) (Township)	47346
Jefferson (Wells County) (Township)	46777
Jefferson (Whitley County) (Township)	46725
Jefferson Proving Ground	47250
Jeffersonville	47129-31
For specific Jeffersonville Zip Codes call (812) 284-4834, or your local postmaster.	
Jennings (Crawford County) (Township)	47137
Jennings (Fayette County) (Township)	47331
Jennings (Owen County) (Township)	46120
Jennings (Scott County) (Township)	47102
Jericho	47848
Jerome	46936
Jessups	47874
Jewell Village	47201
Jimtown	46514
Jockey	47637
Johnsburg	47542
Johnson (Clinton County) (Township)	46041
Johnson (Crawford County) (Township)	47116
Johnson (Gibson County)	47665
Johnson (Gibson County) (Township)	47639
Johnson (Knox County) (Township)	47591
Johnson (La Porte County) (Township)	46574
Johnson (Lagrange County) (Township)	46796
Johnson (Ripley County) (Township)	47042
Johnson (Scott County) (Township)	47230
Johnsonville	47993
Johnstown (Greene County)	47471
Johnstown (Knox County)	47512
Jolietville	46069
Jonesboro	46938
Jonestown	47842
Jonesville	47247
Joppa	46158
Jordan (Jasper County) (Township)	47978
Jordan (Owen County)	47868
Jordan (Warren County) (Township)	47993
Judah	47421
Judson (Howard County)	46901
Judson (Parke County)	47856
Judyville	47993
Julietta (Part of Indianapolis)	46239
Junction (Part of Peru)	46970
Kalorama Park	46538
Kankakee (Jasper County) (Township)	46374
Kankakee (La Porte County) (Township)	46371
Karwick (Part of Michigan City)	46360
Kasson	47712
Keener (Township)	46310
Kellerville	47527
Kelso (Township)	47022
Kempton	46049
Kendallville	46755
Kennard	47351
Kent (Jefferson County)	47250
Kent (Warren County) (Township)	47982
Kentland	47951

	ZIP
Kentwood (Part of Frankfort)	46041
Kenwood	47885
Kersey	46310
Kewanna	46939
Keyser (Township)	46738
Keystone	46759
Kilmore	46041
Kimmell	46760
Kinder	46106
Kingman	47952
Kingsbury	46345
Kingsford Heights	46346
Kingsland	46777
Kingston	47240
Kingswood Terra	47802
Kirkland (Township)	46733
Kirklin	46050
Kirklin (Township)	46050
Kirkpatrick	47955
Kirksville	47401
Kirkville	47649
Kitchell	47353
Klemmes Corner	47012
Klondyke (Parke County)	47862
Klondyke (Vermillion County)	47842
Knapp Lake	46732
Knight (Township)	47711
Knighthood Grove	46176
Knighthood Village	46176
Knight Ridge	47401
Knightstown	46148
Knightstown Lake	46148
Knightsville	47857
Kniman	46392
Knob Hill	47711
Knox (Jay County) (Township)	47336
Knox (Starke County)	46534
Kokomo	46901-04
For specific Kokomo Zip Codes call (317) 455-8300, or your local postmaster.	
Koleen	47439
Koontz Lake	46574
Kossuth	47167
Kouts	46347
Kramer	47918
Kreitsburg	46311
Kriete Corners	47274
Kurtz	47249
Kyana	47575
Kyle	47001
Laconia	47135
La Crosse	46348
Ladoga	47954
Lafayette (Allen County) (Township)	46783
Lafayette (Floyd County) (Township)	47119
Lafayette (Madison County) (Township)	46011
Lafayette (Owen County) (Township)	47460
Lafayette (Tippecanoe County)	47901-05
For specific Lafayette Zip Codes call (317) 448-9245, or your local postmaster.	
Lafayette Square (Part of Indianapolis)	46254
La Fontaine	46940
Lagrange	46761
Lagro	46941
Lagro (Township)	46941
Lake (Allen County) (Township)	46818
Lake (Kosciusko County) (Township)	46982
Lake (Newton County) (Township)	46349
Lake Bodona	46158
Lake Bruce	46939
Lake Cicott	46942
Lakecrest (Part of Noblesville)	46060
Lake Dalecarlia	46356
Lake Dilldear	47018
Lake Edgewood	46151
Lake Eliza	46383
Lake Everett	46808
Lake Front (Part of Whiting)	46394
Lake Hart	46158
Lake Hills	46375
Lake Holiday	47933
Lake James	46703

	ZIP
Lakeland (Part of Michigan City)	46360
Lake Latonka	46511
Lake Lincoln	47552
Lake Manitou	46975
Lake Maxine	47456
Lake McCoy	47240
Lake Mohee	47348
Lake Noji	47802
Lake of the Woods	46506
Lake Park	46552
Lakeside	46795
Lakeside Park (Part of Warsaw)	46580
Lakes of the Four Seasons	46307
Lake Station	46405
Lake Sullivan	47882
Laketon	46943
Lakeview (Franklin County)	47024
Lakeview (Lagrange County)	46795
Lake View (Porter County)	46383
Lakeview Estates	47802
Lake Village	46349
Lakeville	46536
Lake Wood (Grant County)	46952
Lakewood (Vigo County)	47802
Lakewood (White County)	47960
Lakewood Hills (Part of Evansville)	47711
Lalumiere	46350
Lamar	47550
Lamb	47043
Lamb Lake	46181
Lamong	46069
Lamplighter	46060
Lancaster (Huntington County)	46750
Lancaster (Huntington County) (Township)	46750
Lancaster (Jefferson County)	47250
Lancaster (Jefferson County) (Township)	47250
Lancaster (Wells County) (Township)	46714
Lancaster Park	47401
Landess	46944
Lane (Township)	47637
Lanesville	47136
Lantana Estate (Part of Shelbyville)	46176
Lantern Park	47302
Laotto	46763
Lapaz	46537
La Paz Junction	46563
Lapel	46051
La Porte	46350-52
For specific La Porte Zip Codes call (219) 362-9514, or your local postmaster.	
Larimer Hill	47885
Larwill	46764
Lasalle Square (Part of South Bend)	46601
Laud	46725
Laughery (Township)	47006
Lauramie (Township)	47930
Laurel	47024
Laurel (Township)	47024
Lawndale (Part of Evansville)	47715
Lawrence	46226
Lawrence (Township)	46226
Lawrenceburg	47025
Lawrenceburg (Township)	47025
Lawrenceport	47446
Lawrenceville	47041
Lawton	46996
Laynecrest (Part of Muncie)	47304
Leases Corner	46950
Leavenworth	47137
Lebanon	46052
Lee	47978
Leesburg	46538
Leesville	47421
Leininger Acres	46072
Leipsic	47452
Leisure	46036
Leiters Ford	46945
Lena	47834
Leo	46765
Leopold	47551
Leopold (Township)	47551
Leota	47170

	ZIP
Leroy	46355
Letts	47240
Letts Corner	47240
Lewis (Clay County) (Township)	47438
Lewis (Vigo County)	47858
Lewisburg	46970
Lewis Creek	47234
Lewisville (Henry County)	47352
Lewisville (Morgan County)	46120
Lexington (Carroll County)	46920
Lexington (Scott County)	47138
Lexington (Scott County) (Township)	47138
Liber	47371
Liberty (Carroll County) (Township)	46916
Liberty (Crawford County) (Township)	47140
Liberty (Delaware County) (Township)	47383
Liberty (Fulton County) (Township)	46931
Liberty (Grant County) (Township)	46952
Liberty (Hendricks County) (Township)	46118
Liberty (Henry County) (Township)	47362
Liberty (Howard County) (Township)	46901
Liberty (Parke County) (Township)	47952
Liberty (Porter County) (Township)	46383
Liberty (Shelby County) (Township)	46182
Liberty (St. Joseph County) (Township)	46554
Liberty (Tipton County) (Township)	46068
Liberty (Union County)	47353
Liberty (Union County) (Township)	47353
Liberty (Wabash County) (Township)	46940
Liberty (Warren County) (Township)	47918
Liberty (Wells County) (Township)	46766
Liberty (White County) (Township)	47925
Liberty Center	46766
Liberty Hills	46804
Liberty Mills	46946
Liberty Park	46307
Libertyville	47885
Licking (Township)	47348
Liggett	47885
Ligonier	46767
Lilly Dale	47586
Lima (Township)	46746
Limberlost Hills	47803
Limedale	46135
Lincoln (Cass County)	46994
Lincoln (Hendricks County) (Township)	46112
Lincoln (La Porte County) (Township)	46365
Lincoln (Newton County) (Township)	46310
Lincoln (St. Joseph County) (Township)	46574
Lincoln (White County) (Township)	47950
Lincoln City	47552
Lincoln Heights (Clark County)	47129
Lincoln Heights (Madison County)	46001
Lincoln Hills	46383
Lincoln Park (Part of Clarksville)	47129
Lincoln Village (Part of Merrillville)	46410
Lincolnville	46992
Linden	47955
Linden Park (Part of Muncie)	47303
Lindenwood (Part of Indianapolis)	46227
Linkville	46563
Linn Grove	46769
Linnsburg	47933
Linton (Greene County)	47441
Linton (Vigo County) (Township)	47802

	ZIP
Linwood (Madison County)	46001
Linwood (Marion County)	46201
Lippe	47620
Lisbon	46755
Little	47567
Little Acres	47274
Little Point	46180
Little Saint Louis	47115
Little York	47139
Liverpool (Part of Lake Station)	46408
Livonia	47108
Lizton	46149
Locke	46550
Locke (Township)	46550
Lockhart (Township)	47585
Lockport	47926
Lodi	47952
Logan	47060
Logan (Dearborn County) (Township)	47060
Logan (Fountain County) (Township)	47918
Logan (Pike County) (Township)	47567
Logansport	46947
Logansport State Hospital	46947
Lomax	46374
London	46126
London Heights	46126
Long Acres	46176
Long Beach	46360
Long Lake	46962
Long Lake Island	46383
Longview Beach	47130
Loogootee	47553
Lookout	47041
Loon Lake	46725
Lorane	46725
Loree	46914
Losantville	47354
Lost Creek (Township)	47803
Lost River (Township)	47432
Lottaville (Part of Merrillville)	46410
Lotus	47353
Lovett	47265
Lovett (Township)	47265
Lowell (Bartholomew County)	47201
Lowell (Lake County)	46356*
	46399†
Lower Sunset Park	47960
Loyal	46975
Luce (Township)	47617
Lucerne	46950
Ludwig Park (Part of Fort Wayne)	46825
Lukens Lake	46974
Luray	47386
Luther	46787
Lutheran Lake	47274
Lydick	46628
Lyford	47874
Lynn (Posey County) (Township)	47620
Lynn (Randolph County)	47355
Lynnhurst (Part of Indianapolis)	46241
Lynnville	47619
Lyons	47443
Lyonsville	47331
McBride Heights	47130
McCarthy Addition (Part of Alexandria)	46001
McCarty	46142
McClellan (Township)	47963
Mc Col Place (Part of Salem)	47167
McCool (Part of Portage)	46368
McCordsville	46055
McCoysburg	47978
McCutchanville	47711
McDaniel	46151
Mace	47933
Mac-Fair-Mar	46947
McGrawsville	46911
Mackey	47654
McKinley	47108
McKinley Town and Country Shopping Center (Part of Mishawaka)	46545
McNatts	47359
Macy	46951
Madison (Allen County) (Township)	46773

	ZIP
Madison (Carroll County) (Township)	46923
Madison (Clinton County) (Township)	46058
Madison (Daviess County) (Township)	47562
Madison (Dubois County) (Township)	47546
Madison (Jay County) (Township)	45846
Madison (Jefferson County)	47250
Madison (Jefferson County) (Township)	47250
Madison (Montgomery County) (Township)	47933
Madison (Morgan County) (Township)	46158
Madison (Pike County) (Township)	47567
Madison (Putnam County) (Township)	46135
Madison (St. Joseph County) (Township)	46614
Madison (Tipton County) (Township)	46072
Madison (Washington County) (Township)	47108
Madison State Hospital	47250
Magley	46733
Magnet	47555
Mahalasville	46151
Mahon	46750
Majenica	46750
Malden	46383
Malott Park (Part of Indianapolis)	46205
Maltersville	47542
Manchester	47001
Manchester (Township)	47001
Manhattan	46135
Manilla	46150
Manor Woods	46804
Mansfield	47872
Manson	46041
Manville	47250
Maplecrest Shopping Center (Part of Kokomo)	46902
Maple Lane	46635
Maples	46806
Mapleton (Part of Indianapolis)	46208
Maple Valley	46117
Maplewood (Hendricks County)	46122
Maplewood (Vigo County)	47885
Maplewood Park	46805
Marco	47443
Marengo	47140
Mariah Hill	47556
Marietta	46176
Marineland Gardens	46567
Marion (Allen County) (Township)	46745
Marion (Boone County) (Township)	46069
Marion (Decatur County) (Township)	47261
Marion (Dubois County) (Township)	47546
Marion (Grant County)	46952-53
For specific Marion Zip Codes call (317) 668-8191, or your local postmaster.	
Marion (Hendricks County) (Township)	46122
Marion (Jasper County) (Township)	47978
Marion (Jennings County) (Township)	47270
Marion (Lawrence County) (Township)	47446
Marion (Owen County) (Township)	47455
Marion (Pike County) (Township)	47590
Marion (Putnam County) (Township)	46128
Marion (Shelby County)	46176
Marion (Shelby County) (Township)	46176
Marion Heights	47885
Marion Manor (Part of Valparaiso)	46383
Markland	47020
Markland Mall (Part of Kokomo)	46902
Markle	46770

	ZIP
Markleville	46056
Marlin Hills	47401
Marquette Farm	47805
Marquette Mall (Part of Michigan City)	46360
Marrs (Township)	47620
Marrs Center	47620
Marshall (Lawrence County) (Township)	47421
Marshall (Parke County)	47859
Marshfield	47993
Mars Hill (Part of Indianapolis)	46241
Marshtown	46939
Martin Heights (Part of Salem)	47167
Martinsburg	47165
Martinsville	46151
Martz	47841
Maryland	47802
Marysville (Clark County)	47141
Marysville (Pike County)	47598
Marywood	47802
Matlock Heights (Part of Bloomington)	47401
Matthews	46957
Mattix Corner	46041
Mauckport	47142
Maumee (Township)	46797
Mauzy	46173
Max	46052
Maxinkuckee	46511
Maxville	47340
Maxwell (Hancock County)	46154
Maxwell (Morgan County)	46151
Mayfield (Part of Muncie)	47302
Maynard (Part of Munster)	46321
Mays	46155
Maysville	47501
Maywood (Part of Indianapolis)	46241
M-Dee Acres	46550
Meadowbrook (Allen County)	46774
Meadowbrook (Tippecanoe County)	47901
Meadowood (Elkhart County)	46514
Meadowood (Marion County)	46224
Meadowood Estates	46036
Meadows (Part of Terre Haute)	47803
Meadows Shopping Center (Part of Indianapolis)	46205
Meadowview	46947
Mead Village (Part of Columbus)	47201
Mecca	47860
Mechanicsburg (Boone County)	46050
Mechanicsburg (Henry County)	47356
Medaryville	47957
Medford	47302
Medina (Township)	47970
Medora	47260
Meiks	46176
Mellott	47958
Melody Acres (Part of Warsaw)	46580
Melody Hill	47711
Meltzer	46176
Memphis	47143
Mentone	46539
Mentor	47513
Meridian Hills	46260
Merom	47861
Merriam	46701
Merrillville	46410*
	46411†
Metamora (Township)	47030
Metamora	47030
Metea	46950
Metz	46703
Mexico	46958
Miami (Cass County) (Township)	46947
Miami (Miami County)	46959
Miami Bend	46947
Miami Trails Addition	46614
Michaelsville	46952
Michiana Shores	49117
Michigan (Clinton County) (Township)	46057
Michigan (La Porte County) (Township)	46360

	ZIP
Michigan City	46360*
	46361†
Michigantown	46057
Mickleyville (Part of Indianapolis)	46241
Middle (Township)	46167
Middleboro	47374
Middlebury	46540
Middlebury (Township)	46540
Middlefork (Clinton County)	46041
Middlefork (Jefferson County)	47231
Middletown (Henry County)	47356
Middletown (Shelby County)	46182
Middletown Park	47302
Midland	47445
Midway (Elkhart County)	46526
Midway (Jefferson County)	47250
Midway (Spencer County)	47601
Midwest (Part of Portage)	46368
Mier	46919
Mifflin	47118
Milan (Allen County) (Township)	46797
Milan (Ripley County)	47031
Milan Center	46774
Milford (Decatur County)	47240
Milford (Kosciusko County)	46542
Milford (Lagrange County) (Township)	46795
Milford Junction	46542
Mill (Township)	46933
Mill Creek (Fountain County) (Township)	47952
Mill Creek (Hamilton County)	46060
Mill Creek (La Porte County)	46365
Milledgeville	46052
Miller (Dearborn County) (Township)	47025
Miller (Lake County)	46403
Millersburg (Elkhart County)	46543
Millersburg (Hamilton County)	46030
Millersburg (Orange County)	47454
Millersburg (Warrick County)	47610
Millersville (Part of Lawrence)	46226
Mill Grove (Blackford County)	47348
Millgrove (Steuben County) (Township)	46776
Millhousen	47261
Milligan	47872
Milltown	47145
Millville	47362
Milners Corner	46140
Milo	46991
Milroy (Jasper County) (Township)	47978
Milroy (Rush County)	46156
Milton (Jefferson County) (Township)	47250
Milton (Ohio County)	47018
Milton (Wayne County)	47357
Mineral	47424
Mineral Springs	46538
Mishawaka	46544-46
For specific Mishawaka Zip Codes call (219) 255-9691, or your local postmaster.	
Mitchell	47446
Mitchellville (Part of Indianapolis)	46201
Mitcheltree (Township)	47581
Mixerville	47010
Moberly	47115
Modesto	47401
Modoc	47358
Mohawk	46140
Mongo	46771
Monitor	47905
Monmouth	46733
Monon	47959
Monon (Township)	47959
Monoquet	46580
Monroe (Adams County)	46772
Monroe (Adams County) (Township)	46711

	ZIP
Monroe (Allen County) (Township)	46773
Monroe (Carroll County) (Township)	46929
Monroe (Clark County) (Township)	47126
Monroe (Delaware County) (Township)	47302
Monroe (Grant County) (Township)	46952
Monroe (Howard County) (Township)	46979
Monroe (Jefferson County) (Township)	47250
Monroe (Kosciusko County) (Township)	46580
Monroe (Madison County) (Township)	46001
Monroe (Morgan County) (Township)	46157
Monroe (Pike County) (Township)	47584
Monroe (Pulaski County) (Township)	46996
Monroe (Putnam County) (Township)	46135
Monroe (Randolph County) (Township)	47368
Monroe (Tippecanoe County)	47901
Monroe (Washington County) (Township)	47167
Monroe City	47557
Monroe Manor	46350
Monroeville	46773
Monrovia	46157
Montclair	46149
Monterey	46960
Monterey Village (Part of Noblesville)	46060
Montezuma	47862
Montgomery (Daviess County)	47558
Montgomery (Gibson County) (Township)	47665
Montgomery (Jennings County) (Township)	47230
Montgomery (Owen County) (Township)	47460
Monticello	47960
Montmorenci	47962
Montpelier	47359
Moonlight Bay	46779
Moonville	46001
Moore	46721
Moorefield (Marion County)	46222
Moorefield (Switzerland County)	47250
Mooreland	47360
Moores Hill	47032
Mooresville	46158
Moral (Township)	46126
Moran	46041
Morgan (Harrison County) (Township)	47164
Morgan (Owen County) (Township)	47868
Morgan (Porter County) (Township)	46383
Morgan Park (Part of Chesterton)	46304
Morgantown	46160
Morningside (Part of Muncie)	47302
Morocco	47963
Morris	47033
Morristown	46161
Morton	46135
Moscow	46156
Mott Station	47161
Mound (Township)	47932
Mounds Mall (Part of Anderson)	46013
Mount Auburn (Shelby County)	46124
Mount Auburn (Wayne County)	47327
Mount Ayr	47964
Mount Carmel (Franklin County)	47012
Mount Carmel (Washington County)	47108
Mount Comfort	46140
Mount Etna	46750
Mount Healthy	47201
Mount Meridian	46135
Mount Olympus	47640
Mount Pisgah	46761

	ZIP
Mount Pleasant (Delaware County)	47302
Mount Pleasant (Delaware County) (Township)	47396
Mount Pleasant (Johnson County)	46131
Mount Pleasant (Martin County)	47553
Mount Pleasant (Perry County)	47520
Mounts	47665
Mount Sinai	47032
Mount Sterling	47043
Mount Summit	47361
Mount Vernon	47620
Mount Zion	46792
Mud Center (Part of Evansville)	47712
Mudlavia Springs	47918
Mulberry	46058
Mull	47394
Muncie	47302-08
For specific Muncie Zip Codes call (317) 286-9600, or your local postmaster.	
Muncie Mall (Part of Muncie)	47303
Munster	46321
Muren	47598
Murray	46714
Nabb	47147
Napoleon	47034
Nappanee	46550
Nashville	47448
Navilleton	47119
Nead	46970
Nebraska	47262
Needham	46162
Needham (Township)	46126
Needmore (Brown County)	47448
Needmore (Lawrence County)	47421
Negangards Corner	47031
Nevada	46068
Nevada Mills	46703
Nevins (Township)	47851
New Albany	47150*
	47151†
New Alsace	47022
New Amsterdam	47110
Newark	47459
New Augusta (Part of Indianapolis)	46268
New Bellsville	47201
Newbern	47201
Newberry	47449
New Boston (Harrison County)	47117
New Boston (Spencer County)	47531
New Britton	46060
New Brunswick	46052
Newburgh	47629*
	47630†
New Burlington	47302
Newbury (Township)	46565
New Carlisle	46552
Newcastle (Fulton County) (Township)	46975
New Castle (Henry County)	47362
New Chicago	46342
New Columbus	46011
New Corydon	47326
New Durham (Township)	46350
New Elizabethtown	47274
New Elliott	46319
New Fairfield	47012
New Farmington	47274
New Frankfort	47170
New Garden (Township)	47374
New Goshen	47863
New Harmony	47631
New Haven	46774
New Hope	47601
Newland	47978
New Lebanon	47864
New Lisbon (Henry County)	47366
New Lisbon (Randolph County)	47390
New London	46979
New Marion	47023
New Market	47965
New Maysville	46172
New Middletown	47160
New Mount Pleasant	47371
New Palestine	46163

	ZIP
New Paris	46553
New Philadelphia	47167
New Pittsburg	47390
New Point	47263
Newport	47966
New Richmond	47967
New Ross	47968
New Salem	46173
New Salisbury	47161
New Santa Fe	46970
Newton (Township)	47978
Newtonville	47615
Newtown	47969
New Trenton	47035
Newville	46721
Newville (Township)	46721
New Washington	47162
New Waverly	46961
New Whiteland	46184
New Winchester	46122
Nibbyville	46507
Niles (Township)	47338
Nine Mile	46809
Nineveh	46164
Nineveh (Township)	46164
Nisbet	47639
Noble (Cass County) (Township)	46947
Noble (Jay County) (Township)	47371
Noble (La Porte County) (Township)	46382
Noble (Noble County) (Township)	46796
Noble (Rush County) (Township)	46173
Noble (Shelby County) (Township)	47234
Noble (Wabash County) (Township)	46992
Noblesville	46060
Noblesville (Township)	46060
Noblitt Falls (Part of Columbus)	47201
Nora (Part of Indianapolis)	46240
Nora Plaza (Part of Indianapolis)	46240
Norland Park	46706
Normal	46986
Norman	47264
Normanda	46072
Normandy Addition (Part of Muncie)	47302
Norristown	47234
North (Lake County) (Township)	46312
North (Marshall County) (Township)	46506
Northaven (Part of Jeffersonville)	47130
North Bend (Township)	46534
Northcliff	47201
North Columbus (Part of Columbus)	47201
Northcrest Shopping Center (Part of Fort Wayne)	46805
North Crows Nest	46208
North Delphi	46923
Northeast (Township)	47452
Northern Meadows	46077
Northfield	46077
Northfield Village (Part of Lebanon)	46052
North Gate	47201
North Grove	46911
North Harbor (Part of Noblesville)	46060
North Hayden	46356
North Judson	46366
North Liberty	46554
North Madison (Part of Madison)	47250
North Manchester	46962
North Oaks	46714
North Ogilville	47201
North Park (Bartholomew County)	47280
North Park (Vanderburgh County)	47710
North Park Mall (Part of Marion)	46952
North Ridge Village	46240
North Salem	46165
North Terre Haute	47805
North Vernon	47265
North Webster	46555
Northwest (Township)	47469

	ZIP
Northwood (Elkhart County)	46550
Northwood (Putnam County)	46135
Northwood (Vigo County)	47805
Northwood Hills	46033
North Wood Park	46383
Norton	47432
Nortonsburg	47201
Norway	47960
Norwood Addition (Part of Muncie)	47304
Notre Dame	46556
Nottingham	47359
Nottingham (Township)	47359
Nulltown	47331
Numa	47874
Nyesville	47872
Nyona Lake	46951
Oakcrest	47201
Oakdale (Part of Peru)	46970
Oakford	46965
Oak Forest	47012
Oak Grove (Benton County) (Township)	47971
Oak Grove (Starke County)	46511
Oak Grove (Vigo County)	47802
Oak Hill	47660
Oakland City	47660
Oaklandon (Part of Lawrence)	46226
Oaklawn Terrace (Part of Jeffersonville)	47130
Oak Park	47130
Oaktown	47561
Oakville	47367
Oakwood	46742
Oakwood Commons	46952
Oakwood Park	46567
Oakwood Shores	46742
Oatsville	47567
Ober	46534
Occident	46115
Ockley	46923
Odell	47918
Odon	47562
Ogden	46148
Ogden Dunes	46368
Ogilville	47201
Ohio (Bartholomew County) (Township)	47201
Ohio (Crawford County) (Township)	47137
Ohio (Spencer County) (Township)	47635
Ohio (Warrick County) (Township)	47610
Ohio Falls (Part of Clarksville)	47129
Oil (Township)	47576
Old Bargersville	46106
Old Bath	47012
Oldenburg	47036
Old Milan	47031
Old Otto	47162
Old Pekin (Part of Pekin)	47165
Old St. Louis	47246
Old Stone	47630
Old Tip Town	46570
Oldtown (Part of Lawrenceburg)	47025
Old Watson (Part of Jeffersonville)	47130
Olean	47042
Olive (Elkhart County) (Township)	46573
Olive (St. Joseph County) (Township)	46552
Oliver	47620
Olive Street (Part of South Bend)	46619
Omega	46030
Ontario	46746
Onward	46967
Oolitic	47451
Ora	46968
Orange (Fayette County)	47331
Orange (Fayette County) (Township)	47331
Orange (Noble County) (Township)	46755
Orange (Rush County) (Township)	46173
Orangeville	47452
Orangeville (Township)	47542
Orchard Heights Addition	46624
Orchard Park	46280

* Area Zip Code   *† Post Office Boxes*

	ZIP
Oregon (Clark County) (Township)	47141
Oregon (Starke County) (Township)	46574
Oregon Heights (Part of Hobart)	46405
Orestes	46063
Oriole	47551
Orland	46776
Orleans	47452
Orleans (Township)	47452
Orleans Southwest	46902
Ormas	46725
Osborn Landing	46580
Osceola	46561
Osgood	47037
Osolo (Township)	46514
Ossian	46777
Oswego	46538
Otis	46367
Otisco	47163
Otsego (Township)	46742
Otterbein	47970
Otter Creek (Ripley County) (Township)	47023
Otter Creek (Vigo County) (Township)	47805
Otter Lake	46703
Otter Village	47023
Otto	47162
Otwell	47564
Owasco	46065
Owen (Clark County) (Township)	47111
Owen (Clinton County) (Township)	46041
Owen (Jackson County) (Township)	47220
Owen (Warrick County) (Township)	47614
Owensburg	47453
Owensville	47665
Oxford	47971
Packertown	46510
Paint Mill Lake	47802
Palestine (Franklin County)	47012
Palestine (Kosciusko County)	46539
Palmer	46307
Palmyra (Harrison County)	47164
Palmyra (Knox County) (Township)	47591
Paoli	47454
Paoli (Township)	47454
Papakeechie Lake	46567
Paradise	47630
Paradise Lakes	46151
Paragon	46166
Paris	47230
Paris Crossing	47270
Parish Grove (Township)	47944
Park	47424
Parker City	47368
Parkersburg	47954
Parkers Settlement	47638
Park Fletcher	46241*
	46242†
Park Forest Estates (Part of Columbus)	47201
Parkmor (Part of Elkhart)	46514
Park Ridge (Part of Bloomington)	47401
Parkside (Part of Columbus)	47201
Park View Heights (Part of Peru)	46970
Parkway Hills	46804
Parkwood	47129
Parr	47978
Pate	47040
Patoka (Crawford County) (Township)	47175
Patoka (Dubois County) (Township)	47542
Patoka (Gibson County)	47666
Patoka (Gibson County) (Township)	47670
Patoka (Pike County) (Township)	47598
Patricksburg	47455
Patriot	47038
Patronville	47635
Patton	47960
Patton Hill	47421
Patton Lake	46151
Paw Paw (Township)	46974
Paxton	47865
Paynesville	47243

	ZIP
Peabody	46725
Pearsontown	46120
Pecksburg	46118
Peerless	47421
Pekin	47165
Pelzer	47601
Pence	47973
Pendleton	46064
Penn (Jay County) (Township)	47369
Penn (Parke County) (Township)	47832
Penn (St. Joseph County) (Township)	46544
Penn Meadows	46544
Penn Park	46742
Penntown	47041
Pennville (Jay County)	47369
Pennville (Wayne County)	47327
Peoga	46181
Peoria (Franklin County)	45056
Peoria (Miami County)	46970
Peppertown	47030
Perkinsville	46011
Perry (Allen County) (Township)	46748
Perry (Boone County) (Township)	46052
Perry (Clay County) (Township)	47846
Perry (Clinton County) (Township)	46041
Perry (Delaware County) (Township)	47302
Perry (Lawrence County) (Township)	47462
Perry (Marion County) (Township)	46227
Perry (Martin County) (Township)	47553
Perry (Miami County) (Township)	46974
Perry (Monroe County) (Township)	47401
Perry (Noble County) (Township)	46767
Perry (Tippecanoe County) (Township)	47901
Perry (Vanderburgh County) (Township)	47712
Perry (Wayne County) (Township)	47339
Perry Crossing	47172
Perry Manor (Part of Indianapolis)	46227
Perrysburg	46951
Perrysville	47974
Pershing (Jackson County) (Township)	47235
Pershing (Wayne County)	47370
Perth	47837
Peru	46970
Peru (Township)	46970
Petersburg	47567
Peterson	46733
Peters Switch	47274
Petersville	47201
Petroleum	46778
Pettit	47905
Pheasant Run	46819
Philadelphia	46140
Philomath	47325
Phlox	46936
Pickard	46050
Pierce (Township)	47167
Pierceton	46562
Pierceville	47039
Pierre Moran (Part of Elkhart)	46514
Pierson (Township)	47802
Pigeon (Vanderburgh County) (Township)	47708
Pigeon (Warrick County) (Township)	47523
Pike (Boone County)	46052
Pike (Jay County) (Township)	47371
Pike (Marion County) (Township)	46254
Pike (Ohio County) (Township)	47011
Pike (Warren County) (Township)	47991
Pikes Peak	47201
Pikeville	47590
Pilot Knob	47145
Pimento	47866
Pine (Benton County) (Township)	47970

	ZIP
Pine (Porter County) (Township)	46360
Pine (Warren County) (Township)	47975
Pine Grove Estates	47006
Pine Lake	46350
Pine Valley	47454
Pine Village	47975
Pinhook (La Porte County)	46350
Pinhook (Lawrence County)	47421
Pinola	46350
Pipe Creek (Madison County) (Township)	46036
Pipe Creek (Miami County) (Township)	46914
Pittsboro	46167
Pittsburg	46923
Plain (Township)	46538
Plainfield	46168
Plainville	47568
Plano	46151
Plato	46761
Plattsburg	47281
Pleasant (Allen County) (Township)	46798
Pleasant (Grant County) (Township)	46952
Pleasant (Johnson County) (Township)	46131
Pleasant (La Porte County) (Township)	46350
Pleasant (Porter County) (Township)	46347
Pleasant (Steuben County) (Township)	46703
Pleasant (Switzerland County)	47224
Pleasant (Switzerland County) (Township)	47224
Pleasant (Wabash County) (Township)	46962
Pleasant Gardens	46171
Pleasant Lake	46779
Pleasant Mills	46780
Pleasant Plain	46792
Pleasant Run (Township)	47436
Pleasant Valley	46544
Pleasant View	46126
Pleasant View Village	46124
Pleasantville	47838
Pleasure Valley	46182
Plevna	46901
Plummer	47424
Plum Tree	46792
Plymouth	46563
Poe	46819
Point (Township)	47620
Point Commerce	47471
Point Idalaw	47468
Point Isabel	46928
Poland	47868
Polk (Huntington County) (Township)	46750
Polk (Marshall County) (Township)	46574
Polk (Monroe County) (Township)	47436
Polk (Washington County) (Township)	47165
Poneto	46781
Pontiac	47837
Pony Express (Part of Evansville)	47710
Popcorn	47462
Portage (Portage County)	46368
Portage (Portage County) (Township)	46368
Portage (St. Joseph County) (Township)	46601
Porter	46304
Porter (Township)	46383
Portersville	47546
Port Fulton (Part of Jeffersonville)	47130
Portland	47371
Portland Mills	46135
Posey (Clay County) (Township)	47834
Posey (Fayette County) (Township)	47331
Posey (Franklin County) (Township)	47024
Posey (Harrison County) (Township)	47117
Posey (Rush County) (Township)	46104
Posey (Switzerland County) (Township)	47038

	ZIP
Posey (Washington County) (Township)	47120
Poseyville	47633
Pottawattomie Park	46360
Pottersville	47460
Powers	47371
Prairie (Henry County) (Township)	47360
Prairie (Kosciusko County) (Township)	46580
Prairie (La Porte County) (Township)	46340
Prairie (Tipton County) (Township)	46049
Prairie (Warren County) (Township)	47921
Prairie (White County) (Township)	47923
Prairie City	47834
Prairie Creek	47869
Prairie Creek (Township)	47869
Prairieton	47870
Prairieton (Township)	47870
Prather	46151
Preble	46782
Preble (Township)	46733
Prescott	46176
Presidential Village	46803
Pretty Lake	46795
Prince Hall Plaza (Part of Marion)	46952
Princes Lakes	46164
Princeton (Gibson County)	47670
Princeton (White County) (Township)	47995
Progress	47302
Progress Acres	47805
Prospect	47469
Providence	46106
Publico (Part of New Albany)	47150
Puckett	46952
Pulaski	46996
Pumpkin Center	47170
Purcell	47591
Purdue University	47906
Purdue University North Central Campus	46391
Putnamville	46170
Pyrmont	46923
Quail Meadows Estates (Part of Batesville)	47006
Queensville	47265
Quercus Grove	47040
Quincy	47456
Raber	46725
Raccoon (Parke County) (Township)	47874
Raccoon (Putnam County)	46172
Radioville	47957
Radley	46938
Radnor	46923
Raglesville	47562
Ragsdale	47573
Railroad (Township)	46374
Rainbow (Part of Indianapolis)	46222
Rainsville	47918
Raleigh	46173
Ramsey	47166
Randolph (Ohio County) (Township)	47040
Randolph (Tippecanoe County) (Township)	47981
Raub	47976
Ravenswood (Part of Indianapolis)	46240
Ravinamy	47906
Ray (Franklin County) (Township)	47036
Ray (Morgan County) (Township)	46166
Ray (Steuben County)	46737
Raymond	47010
Rays Crossing	46176
Raysville	46148
Reception Diagnostic Center	46168
Red Bridge	46911
Red Bush	47630
Redding (Township)	47274
Reddington	47274
Redkey	47373
Redmond Park	46567
Reed Station	47302
Reelsville	46171
Reeve (Township)	47553
Rego	47125

	ZIP		ZIP		ZIP		ZIP
Reiffsburg	46714	Roble Woods	46383	St. Joe	46785	Scott (Steuben County)	
Remington	47977	Rob Roy	47918	St. John (Lake County)	46373	(Township)	46703
Reno	46121	Rochester	46975	St. John (Lake County)		Scott (Vanderburgh	
Rensselaer	47978	Rochester (Township)	46975	(Township)	46373	County) (Township)	47711
Reo	47635	Rock Creek (Bartholomew		St. John (Warrick County)	47613	Scott City	47879
Republican (Township)	47138	County) (Township)	47232	St. Johns (De Kalb		Scottsburg (Pike County)	47660
Reserve (Township)	47862	Rock Creek (Carroll		County)	46738	Scottsburg (Scott County)	47170
Retreat	47229	County) (Township)	46923	St. Joseph (Allen County)		Scottsdale Mall (Part of	
Rexville	47250	Rock Creek (Huntington		(Township)	46805	South Bend)	46612
Reynolds	47980	County)	46750	St. Joseph (Vanderburgh		Scottsville	47106
Riceville	47513	Rock Creek (Huntington		County)	47720	Searcy Crossroads	47038
Richey Park (Township)	47960	County) (Township)	46750	St. Leon	47060	Sedalia	46067
Rich Grove (Township)	46996	Rockcreek (Wells County)		St. Louis Crossing	47201	Sedan	46793
Richland (Benton County)		(Township)	46714	St. Marks (Dubois County)	47575	Seelyville	47878
(Township)	47942	Rockdale	47060	St. Marks (Perry County)	47586	Sellersburg	47172
Richland (De Kalb		Rockfield	46977	St. Mary-of-the-Woods	47876	Sellers Lake	46562
County) (Township)	46730	Rockford (Jackson		St. Marys (Adams County)		Selma	47383
Richland (Fountain		County)	47274	(Township)	46733	Selvin	47523
County) (Township)	47969	Rockford (Wells County)	46714	St. Marys (Floyd County)	47119	Servia	46980
Richland (Fulton County)		Rock Island (Part of		St. Marys (St. Joseph		Sevastopol	46510
(Township)	46975	Indianapolis)	46268	County)	46556	Seward (Township)	46510
Richland (Grant County)		Rock Lake	46910	St. Maurice	47240	Sexton	46173
(Township)	46952	Rocklane	46142	St. Meinrad	47577	Seymour	47274
Richland (Greene County)		Rockport	47635	St. Omer	47272	Shadeland (Grant County)	46952
(Township)	47424	Rockville	47872	St. Paul	47272	Shadeland (Tippecanoe	
Richland (Jay County)		Rockville Training Center	47872	St. Peters	47012	County)	47905
(Township)	47373	Rocky Fork Lake	47834	St. Philip	47620	Shady Hills	46952
Richland (Madison		Rocky Ripple	46208	St. Thomas	47591	Shady Hills Estates	46952
County) (Township)	46011	Roland	47469	St. Wendel	47720	Shady Lawn	46307
Richland (Miami County)		Roll	47348	Salamonia	47381	Shady Nook	46795
(Township)	46970	Rolling Acres	47601	Salamonie (Township)	46792	Shady Side (Part of Burns	
Richland (Monroe County)		Rolling Hill Estates (Part of		Salem (Delaware County)		Harbor)	46304
(Township)	47429	Schererville)	46410	(Township)	47334	Shaffer Woods	47303
Richland (Rush County)	46173	Rolling Hills (Allen County)	46804	Salem (Jay County)	47390	Shamrock Lakes	47348
Richland (Rush County)		Rolling Hills (Clark		Salem (Pulaski County)		Shannondale	47933
(Township)	46173	County)	47111	(Township)	47946	Sharon	46929
Richland (Spencer		Rolling Hills (Grant		Salem (Steuben County)		Sharpsville	46068
County)	47634	County)	46952	(Township)	46747	Shawnee (Township)	47987
Richland (Steuben		Rolling Prairie	46371	Salem (Washington		Shawswick (Township)	47421
County) (Township)	46703	Rolling Ridge (Part of		County)	47167	Shawville	47805
Richland (Whitley County)		Shelbyville)	46176	Salem Center	46747	Sheddfield (Part of	
(Township)	46764	Rollins	47581	Salem Heights	46350	Hammond)	46320
Richmond	47374*	Rome	47574	Saline City	47840	Sheffield (Township)	47901
	47375†	Rome City	46784	Salt Creek (Decatur		Sheffield Woods (Part of	
Richmond Square (Part of		Romney	47981	County) (Township)	47240	Indianapolis)	46229
Richmond)	47374	Romona	47460	Salt Creek (Franklin		Shelburn	47879
Richmond State Hospital	47374	Root (Township)	46733	County) (Township)	47024	Shelburne	46151
Richvalley	46992	Roseburg (Grant County)	46952	Salt Creek (Jackson		Shelby (Jefferson County)	
Riddle	47118	Roseburg (Union County)	47353	County) (Township)	47235	(Township)	47250
Ridgemede (Part of		Rosedale	47874	Salt Creek (Monroe		Shelby (Lake County)	46377
Bloomington)	47401	Rosedale Hills (Part of		County) (Township)	47401	Shelby (Ripley County)	
Ridgeport	47424	Indianapolis)	46227	Salt Creek Commons	46383	(Township)	47250
Ridgeview (Part of Peru)	46970	Rose Hill Gardens	47805	Saltillo	47108	Shelby (Shelby County)	
Ridgeview Heights	46806	Rose-Hulman Institute of		Saluda	47243	(Township)	46176
Ridgeville	47380	Technology	47803	Saluda (Township)	47243	Shelby (Tippecanoe	
Ridgeway	46809	Roseland	46637	Samaria	46181	County) (Township)	47906
Ridinger Lake	46562	Roselawn	46372	Sandborn	47578	Shelbyville	46176
Rigdon	46036	Rosewood	47117	Sand Creek (Bartholomew		Shepardsville	47880
Riley	47871	Ross (Clinton County)		County) (Township)	47232	Sheridan (Hamilton	
Riley (Township)	47871	(Township)	46041	Sand Creek (Decatur		County)	46069
Rileysburg	47932	Ross (Lake County)		County) (Township)	47283	Sheridan (La Porte	
Riley Village (Part of		(Township)	46410	Sand Creek (Jennings		County)	46360
Shelbyville)	46176	Ross (Lake County)	46408	County) (Township)	47265	Sherwood Forest (Part of	
Ripley (Montgomery		Rosston	46077	Sandcut	47805	Indianapolis)	46240
County) (Township)	47933	Rosstown	47201	Sanders	47401	Shideler	47338
Ripley (Pulaski County)	46996	Rossville	46065	Sandford	47877	Shields	47274
Ripley (Rush County)		Roth Park	47960	Sand Ridge	47635	Shiloh Village	47201
(Township)	46115	Round Grove (Township)	47923	Sandusky	47240	Shipshewana	46565
Rising Sun	47040	Round Lake	46755	Sandy Beach	47960	Shirkieville	47885
Risse (Part of Frankfort)	46041	Royal Center	46978	Sandy Hook (Part of		Shirley	47384
Rivare	46733	Royal Oaks	46815	Columbus)	47201	Shoals	47581
River City (Part of		Royalton	46077	Sandytown	47842	Shoe Lake	46538
Evansville)	47714	Royal View	47201	San Jacinto	47223	Shore Acres (Part of	
River Falls Mall (Part of		Royer Lake	46761	San Pierre	46374	Indianapolis)	46201
Clarksville)	47129	Royerton	47302	Santa Claus	47579	Shoreland Hills	46360
River Forest	46011	Royerton Park	47303	Santa Fe	46970	Siberia	47515
Riverhaven	46802	Royville	46845	Saratoga	47382	Sidney	46566
River Ridge	47111	Rugby	47246	Sardinia	47283	Silver Creek (Township)	47172
Riverside (Clark County)	47129-30	Rural	47246	Savah	47620	Silver Hills (Part of New	
For specific Riverside Zip		Rushville	46173	Scenic Heights	47586	Albany)	47150
Codes call (317) 762-3360, or		Rushville (Township)	46173	Scenic Hill	47553	Silver Lake	46982
your local postmaster.		Russell (Township)	46172	Schaefer Lake	47246	Silver Lakes Estates	47129
Riverside (Fountain		Russell Lake	46077	Schererville	46375	Silverville	47470
County)	47918	Russellville	46175	Schneider	46376	Silverwood	47952
Riverton	47861	Russels Point	46742	Schnellville	47580	Simonton Lake	46514
River Vale	47446	Russiaville	46979	Scipio (Allen County)		Sims (Bartholomew	
Riverview	47849	Rustic Hills	47630	(Township)	45813	County)	47201
Riverview Acres	47201	Rutherford (Township)	47553	Scipio (Franklin County)	45053	Sims (Grant County)	46983
Riverwood	46060	Rutland	46563	Scipio (Jennings County)	47273	Sims (Grant County)	
Riviera Plaza (Part of Fort		Ryan Place	47620	Scipio (La Porte County)		(Township)	46983
Wayne)	46815	Rykers Ridge	47250	(Township)	46350	Sitka	47960
Roachdale	46172	Saddle Lake	46733	Scircleville	46041	Skelton (Township)	47637
Roann	46974	Sagers Lake	46383	Scotchtown	47848	Skinner Lake	46701
Roanoke	46783	Sagunay Lake	46371	Scotland	47457	Sleepy Hollow	46182
Robb (Township)	47633	St. Anthony	47575	Scott (Kosciusko County)		Sleeth	46923
Robertsdale (Part of		St. Bernice	47875	(Township)	46550	Sloan	47993
Hammond)	46394	St. Croix	47576	Scott (Lagrange County)	46565	Smartsburg	47933
Robinson (Township)	47638	St. Henry	47532	Scott (Montgomery		Smedley	47108
Robinwood	47803	St. James	47639	County) (Township)	47933		

	ZIP		ZIP		ZIP		ZIP
Smith (Greene County) (Township)	47471	Springfield (Lagrange County) (Township)	46771	Sugar Creek (Shelby County) (Township)	46110	Timbercrest (Allen County)	46804
Smith (Posey County) (Township)	47612	Springfield (La Porte County) (Township)	46360	Sugar Creek (Vigo County) (Township)	47885	Timbercrest (Cass County)	46947
Smith (Whitley County) (Township)	46723	Springfield (Posey County)	47620	Sugar Ridge (Township)	47840	Timberhurst	46795
Smithfield (De Kalb County) (Township)	46793	Spring Grove	47374	Sullivan	47882	Tiosa	46975
Smithfield (Delaware County)	47383	Spring Grove Heights (Part of Spring Grove)	47374	Sulphur	47174	Tippecanoe (Carroll County) (Township)	46923
Smithland	46176	Spring Hill	46208	Sulphur Springs	47388	Tippecanoe (Kosciusko County) (Township)	46555
Smithson	47980	Spring Hill Estates	47802	Suman	46383	Tippecanoe (Marshall County)	46570
Smith Valley	46142	Spring Lake	46140	Sumava Resorts	46379	Tippecanoe (Marshall County) (Township)	46570
Smithville	47458	Springport	47386	Summit Grove	47842	Tippecanoe (Pulaski County) (Township)	46960
Smyrna	47250	Springtown	46122	Summit Ridge (Part of Fort Wayne)	46805	Tippecanoe (Tippecanoe County) (Township)	47906
Smyrna (Township)	47250	Spring Valley Estates	47802	Summitville	46070	Tippecanoe Mall (Part of Lafayette)	47905
Snow Hill	47394	Springville (La Porte County)	46350	Sundown Manor	46158	Tipton (Cass County) (Township)	46994
Solitude	47620	Springville (Lawrence County)	47462	Sunman	47041	Tipton (Tipton County)	46072
Solsberry	47459	Springwood	47805	Sunnybrook Acres	46805	Tipton Park (Part of Columbus)	47201
Somerset	46984	Spurgeon	47584	Sunnymeadow	46815	Toad Hop	47885
Somerville	47683	Spurgeons Corner	47235	Sunnymede (Allen County)	46803	Tobin (Township)	47574
South Bend	46601-80	Stacer	47639	Sunnymede (Wabash County)	46992	Tobinsport	47587
For specific South Bend Zip Codes call (219) 282-8400, or your local postmaster.		Stafford (De Kalb County) (Township)	46721	Sunnymede Woods	46803	Tocsin	46777
South Bethany	47201	Stafford (Greene County) (Township)	47578	Sunny Slopes	47401	Toledo	46750
South Boston	47167	Stampers Creek (Township)	47454	Sunset Acres	46514	Tolleston (Part of Gary)	46404
South Calumet Avenue (Part of Hammond)	46324	Stanford	47463	Sunset Parkway (Part of Seymour)	47274	Toll Gate Heights	46714
South Center	46532	Star City	46985	Sunset Village	47111	Tomahawk Village (Part of Indianapolis)	46224
Southeast (Township)	47140	Stardust Village	46060	Sunshine Gardens (Part of Indianapolis)	46217	Topeka	46571
Southeast Grove	46341	Starlight	47106	Sunview	46040	Toto	46534
Southeast Manor	46126	State Line (Vigo County)	47885	Surprise	47274	Townley	46773
South Edgewood (Part of Edgewood)	46011	State Line (Warren County)	47982	Sussex Woods (Part of Hobart)	46342	Town of Pines	46360
South Gate (Franklin County)	47060	Staunton	47881	Swan	46763	Tracy	46532
Southgate (La Porte County)	46360	Stavetown	47012	Swan (Township)	46763	Traders Point (Part of Indianapolis)	46278
South Harbor (Part of Noblesville)	46060	Stearleyville	47834	Swanington	47944	Trafalgar	46181
South Haven	46383	Steele (Township)	47501	Swayzee	46986	Trail Creek	46360
South Lake	47885	Steen (Township)	47597	Sweetser	46987	Travisville	46714
Southlake Mall (Part of Merrillville)	46410	Steinbarger Lake	46784	Sweetwater Lake	46164	Treaty	46992
South Marion (Part of Marion)	46952	Steinmeir Estates (Part of Indianapolis)	46250	Switz City	47465	Tremont	46304
South Milford	46786	Stendal	47585	Sycamore	46936	Trenton	47348
Southmoor (Part of Merrillville)	46410	Sterling (Crawford County) (Township)	47118	Sycamore Hills	46036	Trevlac	47448
South Mud Lake	46951	Sterling (Fountain County)	47987	Sycamore Knolls	47802	Trier Ridge Park	46806
South Park	46567	Steuben (Steuben County) (Township)	46705	Sycamore Park	47885	Tri-Lakes	46725
South Peru (Part of Peru)	46970	Steuben (Warren County) (Township)	47993	Sylvan Hills	46952	Trilobi Hills (Part of Lawrence)	46226
Southport	46217	Steubenville	46705	Sylvania	47832	Trinity	47326
South Raub	47905	Stevenson	47610	Sylvan Manor	46383	Trinity Springs	47581
South Salem	47390	Stewart	47993	Syndicate	47842	Troy (Township)	47588
Southwest Mall (Part of Fort Wayne)	46816	Stewartsville	47633	Syracuse	46567	Troy (De Kalb County) (Township)	46721
South Wanatah	46390	Stilesville	46180	Tab	47917	Troy (Fountain County) (Township)	47932
South Washington	47501	Stillwell	46351	Tabertown (Part of Seelyville)	47878	Troy (Perry County)	47588
Southwest	46526	Stinesville	47464	Talbot	47984	Tudor	47201
South Whitley	46787	Stockdale	46974	Tall Timbers	46952	Tulip	47424
Southwick Village	46816	Stockton (Township)	47441	Talma	46975	Tunker	46787
Southwood (La Porte County)	46360	Stockwell	47983	Tampico	47220	Tunnel Hill	47118
Southwood (Vigo County)	47802	Stone	47394	Tangier	47952	Tunnelton	47467
Spades	47041	Stonebluff	47987	Tanglewood (Part of New Haven)	46774	Turkey Creek (Township)	46567
Sparksville	47260	Stoneburner Landing	46580	Taswell	47175	Turkey Creek Meadows (Part of Merrillville)	46410
Sparta (Dearborn County)	47032	Stonecrest	46952	Taylor (Greene County) (Township)	47424	Turkey Track	46151
Sparta (Dearborn County) (Township)	47032	Stonegate Square (Part of Newburgh)	47630	Taylor (Harrison County) (Township)	47117	Turman (Township)	47882
Sparta (Noble County) (Township)	46760	Stone Head	47448	Taylor (Howard County) (Township)	46901	Turner	47834
Spartanburg	47355	Stones Crossing	46142	Taylor (Owen County) (Township)	47460	Twelve Mile	46988
Spearsville	46181	Stoney Creek (Henry County) (Township)	47360	Taylors	47905	Twelve Points (Part of Terre Haute)	47804
Speed	47172	Stoney Creek (Randolph County) (Township)	47368	Taylorsville	47280	Twin Branch (Part of Mishawaka)	46544
Speedway	46224	Stonington	47446	Tecumseh	47885	Twin Brooks (Part of Indianapolis)	46227
Speedway SuperCenter (Part of Speedway)	46224	Stony Creek (Township)	46051	Teegarden	46574	Twin Crest	47201
Speicher	46992	Stony Lonesome	47201	Tee Lake	46350	Twin Lakes	46563
Spelterville	47805	Stony Ridge	46538	Tefft	46380	Twin Oaks Lake	46160
Spencer (De Kalb County) (Township)	46788	Story	47448	Tell City	47586	Tyner	46572
Spencer (Harrison County) (Township)	47115	Straughn	47387	Temple	47118	Ulen	46052
Spencer (Jennings County) (Township)	47265	Strawtown	46600	Templeton	47986	Underwood	47177
Spencer (Owen County)	47460	Stringtown (Boone County)	46052	Tennyson	47637	Underwood Meadows	46036
Spencerville	46788	Stringtown (Hancock County)	46140	Terhune	46069	Union (Adams County) (Township)	46733
Spiceland	47385	Stroh	46789	Terrace Bay	47960	Union (Benton County) (Township)	47944
Spiceland (Township)	47385	Sugar Creek (Boone County) (Township)	46071	Terrace Lake (Part of Columbus)	47201	Union (Boone County) (Township)	46069
Spice Valley (Township)	47437	Sugar Creek (Clinton County) (Township)	46050	Terre Haute	47801-08	Union (Clark County) (Township)	47143
Spraytown	47274	Sugar Creek (Hancock County) (Township)	46163	For specific Terre Haute Zip Codes call (812) 231-9414, or your local postmaster.		Union (Clinton County) (Township)	46041
Springersville	47325	Sugar Creek (Montgomery County) (Township)	46035	Tetersburg	46072	Union (Crawford County) (Township)	47123
Springfield (Allen County) (Township)	46743	Sugar Creek (Parke County) (Township)	47859	Texas (Part of Aurora)	47001	Union (De Kalb County) (Township)	46706
Springfield (Franklin County) (Township)	45056	Sugar Creek (Shelby County)	46126	Thayer	46381		

(continued)

Thayer ... 46381
The Hamlet ... 47303
Thomas Lake ... 46135
Thomaston ... 46390
Thorncreek (Township) ... 46725
Thornhope ... 46985
Thorntown ... 46071
Thurman ... 46774
Tilden ... 46122
Tillman ... 46773

	ZIP		ZIP		ZIP		ZIP
Union (Delaware County) (Township)	47302	Vanada Camps	47630	Wallace	47988	Washington (Morgan County) (Township)	46151
Union (Elkhart County) (Township)	46550	Van Bibber Lake	46135	Wallen	46806	Washington (Newton County) (Township)	47922
Union (Fulton County) (Township)	46939	Van Buren (Brown County) (Township)	47448	Wall Lake	46776	Washington (Noble County) (Township)	46760
Union (Gibson County) (Township)	47648	Van Buren (Clay County) (Township)	47837	Walnut (Marshall County)	46501	Washington (Owen County) (Township)	47460
Union (Hendricks County) (Township)	46149	Van Buren (Daviess County) (Township)	47553	Walnut (Marshall County) (Township)	46501	Washington (Parke County) (Township)	47859
Union (Howard County) (Township)	46936	Van Buren (Fountain County) (Township)	47932	Walnut (Montgomery County) (Township)	47933	Washington (Pike County) (Township)	47567
Union (Huntington County) (Township)	46750	Van Buren (Grant County) (Township)	46991	Walnut Gardens	47960	Washington (Porter County) (Township)	46383
Union (Jasper County) (Township)	47943	Van Buren (Grant County)	46991	Walnut Grove	46030	Washington (Putnam County) (Township)	46171
Union (Johnson County) (Township)	46106	Van Buren (Kosciusko County) (Township)	46542	Walnut Heights	47421	Washington (Randolph County) (Township)	47394
Union (La Porte County) (Township)	46346	Van Buren (Lagrange County) (Township)	46540	Walnut Ridge (Clark County)	47130	Washington (Ripley County) (Township)	47031
Union (Madison County) (Township)	46017	Van Buren (Madison County) (Township)	46070	Walnut Ridge (Jennings County)	47265	Washington (Rush County) (Township)	46127
Union (Marshall County) (Township)	46511	Van Buren (Monroe County) (Township)	47401	Walton	46994	Washington (Shelby County) (Township)	46176
Union (Miami County) (Township)	46921	Van Buren (Pulaski County) (Township)	46985	Waltz (Township)	46992	Washington (Starke County) (Township)	46534
Union (Montgomery County) (Township)	47933	Van Buren (Shelby County) (Township)	46176	Wanamaker (Part of Indianapolis)	46239	Washington (Tippecanoe County) (Township)	47924
Union (Ohio County) (Township)	47001	Van Buren Park	47401	Wanatah	46390	Washington (Warren County) (Township)	47993
Union (Parke County) (Township)	47872	Vandalia	47460	Ward (Township)	47380	Washington (Washington County) (Township)	47167
Union (Perry County) (Township)	47555	Vanmeter Park	46996	Warren (Clinton County) (Township)	46039	Washington (Wayne County) (Township)	47357
Union (Pike County)	47640	Vawter Park	46567	Warren (Huntington County)	46792	Washington (Whitley County) (Township)	46725
Union (Porter County) (Township)	46342	Veale (Township)	47501	Warren (Huntington County) (Township)	46713	Washington Center	46725
Union (Randolph County) (Township)	47355	Veedersburg	47987	Warren (Marion County) (Township)	46219	Washington Place (Part of Indianapolis)	46219
Union (Rush County) (Township)	46173	Velpen	47590	Warren (Putnam County) (Township)	46135	Washington Square (Part of Indianapolis)	46229
Union (Shelby County) (Township)	46150	Vera Cruz	46714	Warren (St. Joseph County) (Township)	46552	Washington Square Mall (Part of Evansville)	47715
Union (St. Joseph County) (Township)	46536	Vermillion (Township)	47966	Warren (Warren County) (Township)	47918	Washington Trails (Part of Indianapolis)	46229
Union (Tippecanoe County) (Township)	47901	Vermillion Acres	47885	Warren Park	46219	Waterford	46360
Union (Union County) (Township)	47003	Vermont	46901	Warrenton	47639	Waterford Mills	46526
Union (Vanderburgh County) (Township)	47712	Verne	47591	Warrington	46186	Waterloo (De Kalb County)	46793
Union (Wells County) (Township)	46777	Vernon (Hancock County) (Township)	46040	Warsaw	46580*	Waterloo (Fayette County)	47331
Union (White County) (Township)	47960	Vernon (Jackson County) (Township)	47229		46581†	Waterloo (Fayette County) (Township)	47331
Union (Whitley County) (Township)	46725	Vernon (Jennings County)	47282	Washington (Adams County) (Township)	46733	Waterswolde	46825
Union City	47390	Vernon (Jennings County) (Township)	47282	Washington (Allen County) (Township)	46808	Wathen Heights	47130
Uniondale	46791	Vernon (Wabash County)	46940	Washington (Blackford County) (Township)	47348	Watson	47130
Union Mills	46382	Vernon (Washington County) (Township)	47108	Washington (Boone County) (Township)	46071	Waugh	46075
Unionport	47340	Versailles	47042	Washington (Brown County) (Township)	47448	Wauhob Lake	46383
Uniontown (Jackson County)	47229	Veterans Administration Medical Center (Part of Marion)	46952	Washington (Carroll County) (Township)	46947	Waveland	47989
Uniontown (Perry County)	47515	Vevay	47043	Washington (Cass County) (Township)	46994	Waverly	46151
Unionville (New Unionville)	47401	Vicksburg	47441	Washington (Clark County) (Township)	47162	Waverly Woods	46151
Unionville	47468	Victor	47401	Washington (Clay County) (Township)	47833	Wawaka	46794
Universal	47884	Vienna	47170	Washington (Clinton County) (Township)	46041	Wawpecong	46901
University Heights (Delaware County)	47303	Vienna (Township)	47170	Washington (Daviess County)	47501	Waymansville	47201
University Heights (Marion County)	46227	Vigo (Township)	47512	Washington (Daviess County) (Township)	47501	Wayne (Allen County) (Township)	46806
University Park Mall (Part of Mishawaka)	46545	Vilas	47460	Washington (Dearborn County) (Township)	47001	Wayne (Bartholomew County) (Township)	47201
Upland	46989	Vincennes (Township)	47591	Washington (Decatur County) (Township)	47240	Wayne (Fulton County) (Township)	46939
Upper Long Lake	46701	Vincennes	47591	Washington (Delaware County) (Township)	47342	Wayne (Hamilton County) (Township)	46060
Upper Sunset Park	47960	Virgie	47978	Washington (Elkhart County) (Township)	46507	Wayne (Henry County) (Township)	46148
Upton	47620	Vistula	46507	Washington (Gibson County) (Township)	47640	Wayne (Huntington County) (Township)	46940
Urbana	46990	Volga	47250	Washington (Grant County) (Township)	46952	Wayne (Jay County) (Township)	47371
Urbandale	46902	Wabash (Adams County) (Township)	46740	Washington (Greene County) (Township)	47443	Wayne (Kosciusko County) (Township)	46590
Urmeyville	46131	Wabash (Fountain County) (Township)	47932	Washington (Hamilton County) (Township)	46074	Wayne (Marion County) (Township)	46241
Utah (Part of Aurora)	47001	Wabash (Gibson County) (Township)	47665	Washington (Harrison County) (Township)	47110	Wayne (Montgomery County) (Township)	47990
Utica	47130	Wabash (Jay County) (Township)	47326	Washington (Hendricks County) (Township)	46122	Wayne (Noble County) (Township)	46755
Utica (Township)	47130	Wabash (Parke County) (Township)	47860	Washington (Jackson County) (Township)	47274	Wayne (Owen County) (Township)	47433
Valeene	47125	Wabash (Tippecanoe County) (Township)	47906	Washington (Knox County) (Township)	47516	Wayne (Randolph County) (Township)	47390
Valentine	46761	Wabash (Wabash County)	46992	Washington (Kosciusko County) (Township)	46562	Wayne (Starke County) (Township)	46366
Valley Acres	46952	Wabash Shores (Part of West Lafayette)	47906	Washington (La Porte County) (Township)	46350	Wayne (Tippecanoe County) (Township)	47992
Valley Brook (Marion County)	46229	Wabash Valley Correctional Institute	47838	Washington (Marion County) (Township)	46220	Wayne (Wayne County) (Township)	47374
Valley Brook (Wabash County)	46992	Wadena	47944	Washington (Miami County) (Township)	46970	Wayne Center	46755
Valley City	47110	Wadesville	47638	Washington (Monroe County) (Township)	47401	Waynedale (Part of Fort Wayne)	46809
Valley Mills (Part of Indianapolis)	46241	Wakarusa	46573			Waynesburg	47244
Valley View Hills	46514	Wakefield Village	46755				
Vallonia	47281	Wakeland	46166				
Vallyd Acres	46816	Wake Robin Fields	46304				
Valparaiso	46383*	Walden	46805				
	46384†	Waldron	46182				
Van (Part of Logansport)	46947	Waldron Lake	46794				
		Walesboro	47201				
		Walford Manor	47130				
		Walker (Jasper County) (Township)	47978				
		Walker (Rush County) (Township)	46146				
		Walker Park	46538				
		Walkerton	46574				
		Walkerville (Part of Shelbyville)	46176				

	ZIP		ZIP		ZIP		ZIP
Waynesville	47201	West Point (Howard		Wilkinson	46186	Woodland Park (Lagrange	
Waynetown	47990	County)	46901	Williams (Adams County)	46733	County)	46795
Wea (Township)	47901	Westpoint (Tippecanoe		Williams (Lawrence		Woodland Trace (Part of	
Webster (Harrison		County)	47992	County)	47470	Carmel)	46032
County) (Township)	47112	West Point (White County)		Williamsburg	47393	Woodlawn Heights	46011
Webster (Wayne County)	47392	(Township)	47980	Williams Creek	46240	Woodridge	47803
Webster (Wayne County)		Westport	47283	Williamsport	47993	Woodruff	46795
(Township)	47392	Westport Addition	47302	Williamstown	47240	Woodruff Place (Part of	
Wegan	47220	Westside (Part of Aurora)	47001	Willisville	47567	Indianapolis)	46201
Wehmeir	47201	West Terre Haute	47885	Willow Branch	46187	Woodville	46304
Weisburg	47041	Westville	46391	Willowbrook Estates	46151	Woodville Hills	47401
Wellington Heights (Part		Westville Correctional		Willow Creek (Part of		Wooster (Kosciusko	
of Shelbyville)	46176	Center	46391	Portage)	46368	County)	46562
Wells	46970	West Wabash (Part of		Willow Valley	47581	Wooster (Scott County)	47138
Wellsboro	46382	Evansville)	47712	Wills (Township)	46371	Worth (Township)	46075
Wellsburg	46714	Westwood	47362	Wilmington (Dearborn		Worthington	47471
West (Township)	46563	Wey Lake	47834	County)	47001	Wright (Township)	47441
Westacres	47302	Wheatfield	46392	Wilmington (De Kalb		Wrights Corners	47001
West Atherton	47874	Wheatfield (Township)	46392	County) (Township)	46721	Wyatt	46595
West Baden Springs	47469	Wheatland	47597	Wilmot	46562	Wynnedale	46208
West Brook Acres (Part of		Wheatonville	47613	Wilshire (Part of Frankfort)	46041	Yankeetown	47630
Batesville)	47006	Wheeler	46393	Wilson (Clark County)	47106	Yeddo	47952
West Brook Downs	47401	Wheeling (Carroll County)	46929	Wilson (Porter County)	46368	Yellowbanks	46555
Westchester (Jay County)	47371	Wheeling (Delaware		Wilson (Shelby County)	46176	Yellow Creek Lake	46510
Westchester (Porter		County)	47342	Wilson Lake	46725	Yeoman	47997
County) (Township)	46304	Whiskey Run (Township)	47145	Winamac	46996	Yockey	47446
West College Corner	47003	Whitaker	46166	Winchester	47394	Yoder	46798
West Creek (Township)	46356	Whitcomb	47012	Windemere Lake	47885	York (Benton County)	
West Elwood	46036	Whitcomb Heights	47885	Windfall	46076	(Township)	47942
Western Acres (Part of		White Cloud	47112	Windom	47581	York (Dearborn County)	
Chesterton)	46304	Whitehall	47401	Windsor	47368	(Township)	47022
Western Hills (Part of		Whiteland	46184	Windsor Village (Part of		York (Elkhart County)	
Mount Vernon)	47620	Whiteoak	47598	Indianapolis)	46219	(Township)	46507
Westfield	46074	White Post (Township)	47957	Winfield	46307	York (Noble County)	
West Fork	47118	White Ridge	46952	Winfield (Township)	46307	(Township)	46701
West Franklin	47620	White River (Gibson		Wingate	47994	York (Steuben County)	46737
West Harrison	47060	County) (Township)	47666	Winona	46534	York (Steuben County)	
West Haven	46580	White River (Hamilton		Winona Lake	46590	(Township)	46703
West Hill	46383	County) (Township)	46031	Winslow	47598	York (Switzerland County)	
West Indianapolis (Part of		White River (Johnson		Winthrop	47918	(Township)	47020
Indianapolis)	46221	County) (Township)	46142	Wirt	47250	Yorktown	47396
West Lafayette	47906-07	White River (Randolph		Wirt Station	47250	Yorkville	47022
	47996	County) (Township)	47394	Witmer Manor	46795	Young	46158
For specific West Lafayette Zip		White River Bluffs (Part of		Witts	47353	Young America	46998
Codes call (317) 448-9245, or		Bedford)	47421	Wolcott	47995	Youngs Corner	47012
your local postmaster.		Whites Crossing	47441	Wolcottville	46795	Youngs Creek	47454
Westland	46140	Whitestown	46075	Wolff	46151	Youngstown	47802
Westlawn	46804	Whitesville	47933	Wolflake	46796	Youngstown Acres	47802
West Lebanon	47991	Whitewater (Franklin		Wonder Lake	47802	Youngstown Meadows	47802
West Liberty	46936	County) (Township)	47060	Wood (Township)	47106	Youngstown Shopping	
West Middleton	46995	Whitewater (Wayne		Woodbridge (Part of		Center (Part of	
Westmoor (Part of Fort		County)	47374	Bloomington)	47407	Jeffersonville)	47130
Wayne)	46804	Whitfield	47553	Woodburn	46797	Yountsville	47933
West Muncie (Part of		Whiting	46394	Woodbury	46055	Yule Estates (Part of	
Yorktown)	47396	Wickliffe	47116	Woodcrest	46151	Alexandria)	46001
West Newton (Part of		Widner (Township)	47561	Woodgate	47802	Zanesville	46799
Indianapolis)	46183	Wilbur	46151	Woodgate East	47802	Zelma	47264
West Noblesville (Part of		Wildcat (Township)	46076	Woodland	46619	Zenas	47223
Noblesville)	46060	Wilders	46348	Woodland Heights	46952	Zionsville	46077
West Peru (Part of Peru)	46970	Wildwood	46952	Woodland Lake	46160	Zoar	47585
West Petersburg (Part of		Wildwood Lake	47454	Woodland Park (Delaware		Zulu	46773
Petersburg)	47567	Wilfred	47879	County)	47302		
Westphalia	47596						

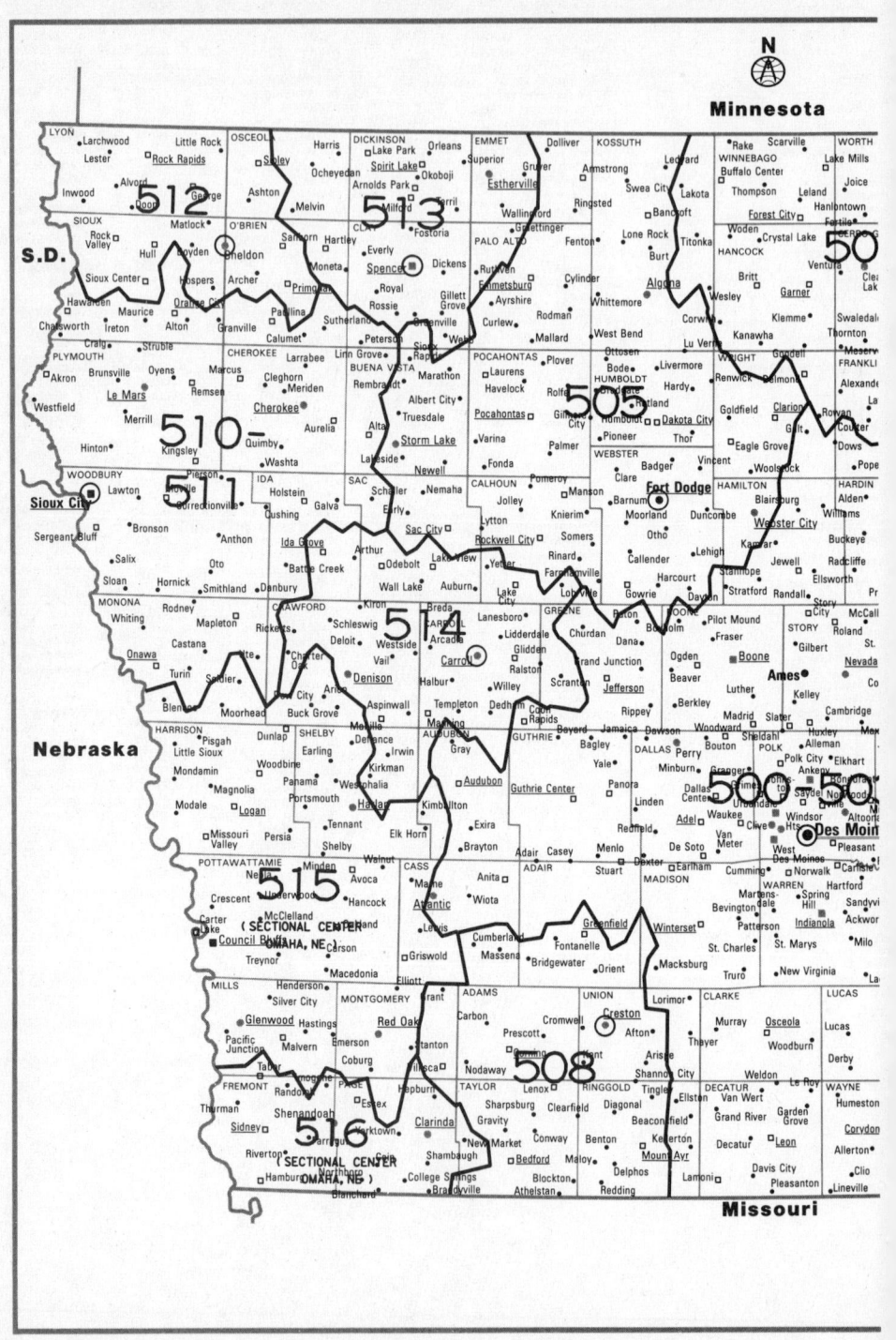

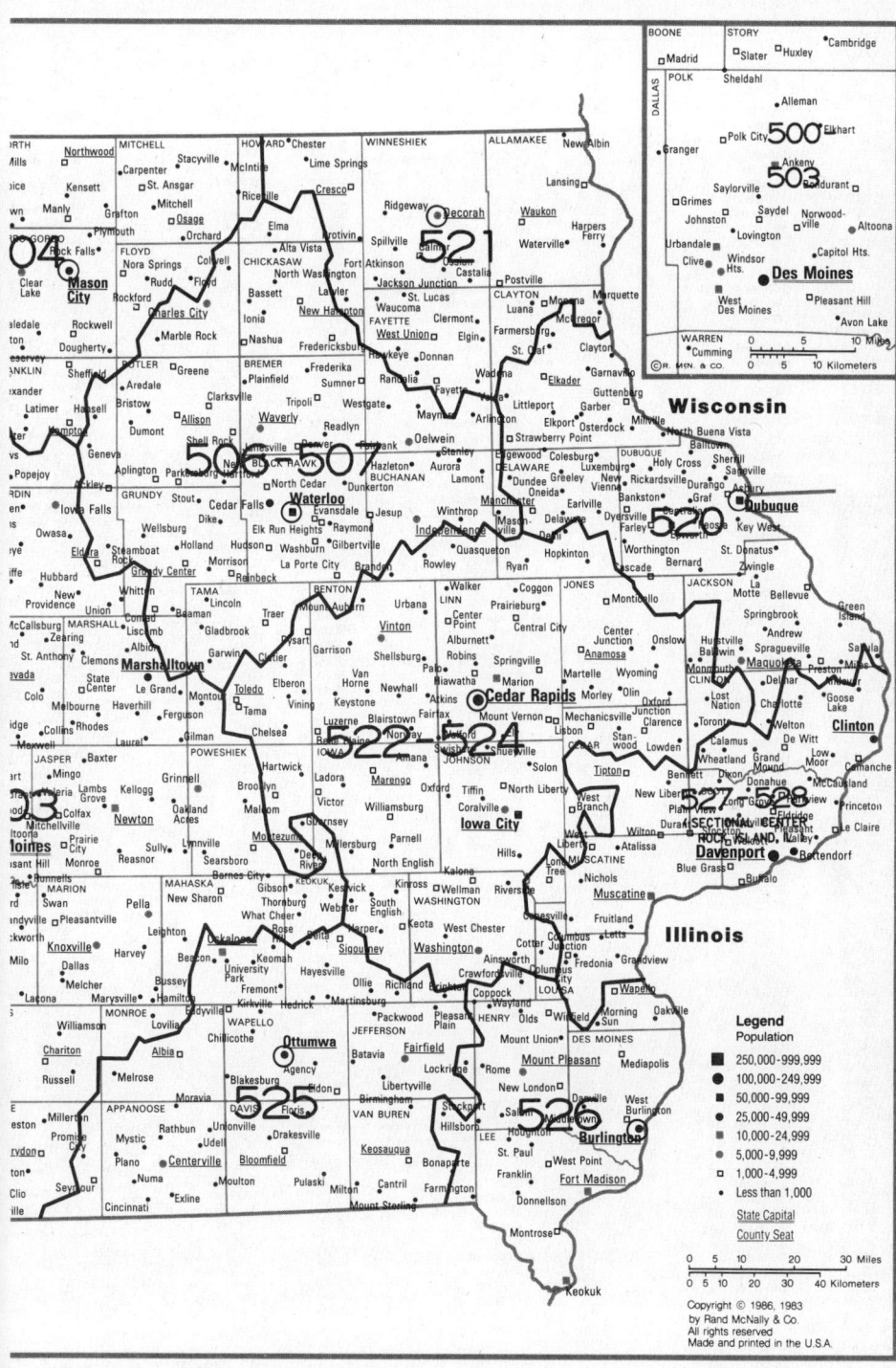

Legend
Population
■ 250,000-999,999
● 100,000-249,999
● 50,000-99,999
• 25,000-49,999
□ 10,000-24,999
□ 5,000-9,999
□ 1,000-4,999
• Less than 1,000
State Capital
County Seat

	ZIP
Abingdon	52533
Ackley	50601
Ackworth	50001
Adair	50002
Adaza	50050
Adel	50003
Afton	50830
Agency	52530
Ainsworth	52201
Akron	51001
Albert City	50510
Albia	52531
Albion	50005
Alburnett	52202
Alden	50006
Alexander	50420
Algona	50511
Alleman	50007
Allendorf	51330
Allerton	50008
Allison	50602
Alpha	52130
Alta	51002
Alta Vista	50603
Alton	51003
Altoona	50009
Alvord	51230
Amana	52203
Amber	52205
Amboy	50208
Ames	50010-14
For specific Ames Zip Codes call (515) 292-2098, or your local postmaster.	
Anamosa	52205
Anderson	51652
Andover	52701
Andrew	52030
Anita	50020
Ankeny	50021
Anthon	51004
Aplington	50604
Arcadia	51430
Archer	51231
Aredale	50605
Argyle	52619
Arion	51520
Arispe	50831
Arlington	50606
Armstrong	50514
Arnolds Park	51331
Artesian	50677
Arthur	51431
Asbury	52002
Ashton	51232
Aspinwall	51432
Atalissa	52720
Athelstan	50836
Atkins	52206
Atlantic	50022
Attica	50138
Auburn	51433
Audubon	50025
Augusta	52658
Aurelia	51005
Aureola	50653
Aurora	50607
Austinville	50608
Avery	52531
Avoca	51521
Avon	50047
Avon Lake	50047
Ayrshire	50515
Badger	50516
Bagley	50026
Baldwin	52207
Balltown	52073
Bancroft	50517
Bangor	50258
Bankston	52045
Barnes City	50027
Barnum	50518
Barrett Superette	50164
Bartlett	51654
Bassett	50645
Batavia	52533
Battle Creek	51006
Baxter	50028
Bayard	50029
Beacon	52534
Beaconsfield	50030
Beaman	50609
Beaver	50031
Beaverdale (Part of Des Moines)	50310
Beaverdale Heights	52655
Beckwith	52556
Bedford	50833
Beebeetown	51546

	ZIP
Beech	50225
Bel Air Beach	50588
Belknap	52537
Belle Plaine	52208
Bellevue	52031
Belmond	50421
Beloit	51240
Bennett	52721
Benton	50835
Bentonsport	52565
Berkley	50220
Bernard	52032
Bertram	52401
Berwick	50032
Bethlehem	50238
Bettendorf	52722
Bevington	50033
Big Mound	52630
Big Rock	52745
Bingham	51601
Birmingham	52535
Bladensburg	52501
Blairsburg	50034
Blairstown	52209
Blakesburg	52536
Blanchard	51630
Blencoe	51523
Blockton	50836
Bloomfield	52537
Blue Grass	52726
Bluff Park (Part of Montrose)	52639
Bluffton	52101
Bode	50519
Bolan	50448
Bonair	52155
Bonaparte	52620
Bondurant	50035
Boone	50036
Booneville	50038
Botna	51454
Bouton	50039
Boxholm	50040
Boyd	50659
Boyden	51234
Boyer	51448
Braddyville	51631
Bradford	50041
Bradgate	50520
Brainard	52141
Brandon	52210
Brayton	50042
Brazil	52574
Breda	51436
Bremer	50677
Bridgewater	50837
Brighton	52540
Bristow	50611
Britt	50423
Bronson	51007
Brooklyn	52211
Brooks	50841
Brunsville	51008
Brushy	50532
Bryant	52727
Bryantsburg	52641
Buchanan	52772
Buckcreek	50674
Buckeye	50043
Buck Grove	51528
Buckingham	50612
Buffalo	52728
Buffalo Center	50424
Buffalo Heights	52728
Burchinal	50469
Burlington	52601
Burnside	50521
Burr Oak	52131
Burt	50522
Bussey	50044
Cairo	52738
Calamus	52729
Calhoun	51555
California Junction	51555
Callender	50523
Calmar	52132
Calumet	51009
Camanche	52730
Cambria	50060
Cambridge	50046
Camp Dodge	50111
Canby	50048
Canton	52309
Cantril	52542
Capitol Heights	50317
Capitol Square (Part of Des Moines)	50393
Carbon	50839
Carl	50841

	ZIP
Carlisle	50047
Carmel	51247
Carnarvon	51450
Carnes	51003
Carney	50021
Carnforth	52347
Carpenter	50426
Carroll	51401
Carson	51525
Carter Lake	51510
Cartersville	50469
Cascade	52033
Casey	50048
Casino Beach	50588
Castalia	52133
Castana	51010
Cedar	52543
Cedar Bluff	52772
Cedar Falls	50613
Cedar Rapids	52401-11
For specific Cedar Rapids Zip Codes call (319) 399-2900, or your local postmaster.	
Cedar Valley	52358
Cedar View	50616
Centerdale	52776
Center Grove (Part of Dubuque)	52003
Center Junction	52212
Center Point	52213
Centerville (Appanoose County)	52544
Centerville (Boone County)	50036
Central (Part of Davenport)	52801
Central City	52214
Central College (Part of Pella)	50219
Central Heights (Part of Mason City)	50401
Centralia	52068
Chapin	50427
Chariton	50049
Charles City	50616
Charleston	52619
Charlotte	52731
Charter Oak	51439
Chatsworth	51011
Chelsea	52215
Cherokee	51012
Chester	52134
Chickasaw	50645
Chillicothe	52548
Church	52151
Churchville	50211
Churdan	50050
Cincinnati	52549
Clare	50524
Clarence	52216
Clarinda	51632
Clarion	50525
Clarkdale	52544
Clarksville	50619
Clayton	52049
Clayton Center	52043
Clearfield	50840
Clear Lake	50428
Cleghorn	51014
Clemons	50051
Clermont	52135
Cleves	50601
Climbing Hill	51015
Clinton	52732*
	52733†
Clio	50052
Clive	50325
Cloverdale	51249
Cloverhills (Part of West Des Moines)	50265
Clutier	52217
Coalville	50501
Coburg	51566
Coggon	52218
Coin	51636
Colesburg	52035
Colfax	50054
College Springs	51637
College Square (Part of Cedar Falls)	50613
Collins	50055
Colo	50056
Colonial Village (Part of West Des Moines)	50266
Columbia	50057
Columbus City	52737
Columbus Junction	52738
Colwell	50620

	ZIP
Commerce (Part of West Des Moines)	50265
Conesville	52739
Confidence	52569
Conger	50240
Conover	52132
Conrad	50621
Conroy	52220
Conway	50833
Cool	50125
Coon Rapids	50058
Cooper	50059
Coppock	52654
Coralville	52241
Corley	51537
Cornelia	50525
Cornell	50585
Corning	50841
Correctionville	51016
Corwith	50430
Corydon	50060
Cosgrove	52322
Cotter	52738
Cottonville	52054
Coulter	50431
Council Bluffs	51501-03
For specific Council Bluffs Zip Codes call (712) 325-0630, or your local postmaster.	
Covington	52324
Craig	51017
Crandalls Lodge	51360
Cranston	52754
Crawfordsville	52621
Crescent	51526
Cresco	52136
Creston	50801
Crestwood (Part of Windsor Heights)	50311
Crocker	50226
Cromwell	50842
Crossroads Center (Part of Waterloo)	50702
Crossroads Mall (Part of Fort Dodge)	50501
Croton	52626
Crystal Lake	50432
Cumberland	50843
Cumming	50061
Curlew	50527
Cushing	51018
Cylinder	50528
Dahlonega	52501
Dakota City	50529
Dallas (Part of Melcher)	50062
Dallas Center	50063
Dana	50064
Danbury	51019
Danville	52623
Darbyville	52544
Davenport	52801-09
For specific Davenport Zip Codes call (319) 322-5991, or your local postmaster.	
Davis City	50065
Dawson	50066
Dayton	50530
Daytonville	52356
Dean	52572
Decatur	50067
Decorah	52101
Dedham	51440
Deep River	52222
Defiance	51527
Delaware	52036
Delhi	52223
Delmar	52037
Deloit	51441
Delphos	50860
Delta	52550
Denison	51442
Denmark	52624
Denver	50622
Depew	50528
Derby	50068
Des Moines	50301-95
For specific Des Moines Zip Codes call (515) 283-7500, or your local postmaster.	
De Soto	50069
Dewar	50623
Dewey	50853
De Witt	52742
Dexter	50070
Diagonal	50845
Dickens	51333
Dike	50624
Dillon	50158
Dinsdale	50669

* Area Zip Code   † Post Office Boxes

Place	ZIP	Place	ZIP	Place	ZIP	Place	ZIP
Dixon	52745	Fairmount Park (Part of Council Bluffs)	51503	Grand (Part of Des Moines)	50309	Holiday Lake	52211
Dodge Park (Part of Council Bluffs)	51501	Fairport	52761	Grand Junction	50107	Holland	50642
Dodgeville	52650	Fairview	52205	Grand Mound	52751	Holly Springs	51026
Dolliver	50531	Fanslers	50115	Grand River	50108	Holmes	50525
Donahue	52746	Farley	52046	Grandview	52752	Holstein	51025
Donnan	52142	Farlin	50077	Granger	50109	Holy Cross	52053
Donnellson	52625	Farmersburg	52047	Granger Homesteads	50109	Homer	50595
Doon	51235	Farmington	52626	Granite	52241	Homestead	52236
Dorchester	52140	Farnhamville	50538	Grant	50847	Honey Creek	51542
Douds	52551	Farragut	51639	Grant Wood (Part of Bettendorf)	52722	Hopeville	50174
Dougherty	50433	Farrar	50161	Granville	51022	Hopkinton	52237
Douglas	52175	Farson	52563	Gravity	50848	Hornick	51026
Dow City	51528	Faulkner	50601	Gray	50110	Horton	50677
Downey	52358	Fayette	52142	Greeley	52050	Hospers	51238
Downtown (Part of Cedar Rapids)	52401	Fenton	50539	Green Castle	50054	Houghton	52631
Dows	50071	Ferguson	50078	Greene	50636	Hubbard	50122
Drakesville	52552	Fern	50665	Greenfield	50849	Hudson	50643
Dubuque	52001-04	Fernald	50201	Greenfield Plaza	50315	Hull	51239
For specific Dubuque Zip Codes call (319) 582-3674, or your local postmaster.		Fertile	50434	Green Island	52064	Humboldt	50548
Duck Creek Plaza (Part of Bettendorf)	52722	Festina	52144	Green Mountain	50637	Humeston	50123
Dumont	50625	Fillmore	52033	Greenville	51343	Huntington	51334
Dunbar	50158	Finchford	50647	Greenwood Acres	50021	Hurstville	52060
Duncan	50423	First Street (Part of Cedar Rapids)	52407	Grimes	50111	Hutchins	50423
Duncombe	50532	Fiscus	50025	Grinnell	50112	Huxley	50124
Dundee	52038	Five Points	52073	Griswold	51535	Iconium	52571
Dunkerton	50626	Flagler	50138	Grundy Center	50638	Ida Grove	51445
Dunlap	51529	Florenceville	52136	Gruver	51344	Imogene	51645
Durango	52039	Floris	52560	Guernsey	50172	Independence	50644
Durant	52747	Floyd	50435	Gunder	52162	Indian Creek (Part of Marion)	52302
Durham	50119	Folletts	52730	Guss	50857	Indianola	50125
Dutchtown	52057	Fonda	50540	Guthrie Center	50115	Industry	50540
Dyersville	52040	Fontanelle	50846	Guttenberg	52052	Inwood	51240
Dysart	52224	Forbush	52544	Halbur	51444	Ionia	50645
Eagle Center	50701	Forest City	50436	Hale	52230	Iowa Army Ammunition Plant	52638
Eagle Grove	50533	Fort Atkinson	52144	Hamburg	51640	Iowa Center	50161
Eagle Point (Part of Dubuque)	52001	Fort Dodge	50501	Hamill	52625	Iowa City	52240
Earlham	50072	Fort Dodge Junction (Part of Fort Dodge)	50501	Hamilton	50116		52242-46
Earling	51530	Fort Madison	52627	Hamlin	50117	For specific Iowa City Zip Codes call (319) 354-1560, or your local postmaster.	
Earlville	52041	Fostoria	51340	Hampton	50441	Iowa Falls	50126
Early	50535	Four Corners	52635	Hancock	51536	Iowa State University (Part of Ames)	50011-13
East Amana	52203	Franklin	52625	Hanford	50401	For specific Iowa State University Zip Codes call (515) 292-2098, or your local postmaster.	
East Des Moines (Part of Des Moines)	50309	Frankville	52162	Hanley	50240		
East Fourteenth Street (Part of Des Moines)	50316	Fraser	50036	Hanlontown	50444	Ira	50127
East Pleasant Plain	52540	Fredericksburg	50630	Hanover	51002	Ireton	51027
Eddyville	52553	Frederika	50631	Hansell	50640	Ironhills	52060
Edgewood	52042	Fredonia	52738	Harcourt	50544	Irving	52208
Edgewood Park (Part of Bettendorf)	52722	Freeman	50401	Hardy	50545	Irvington	50560
Edna	51246	Freeport	52101	Harlan	51537	Irwin	51446
Egralharve	51360	Fremont	52561		51593	Ivy	50009
Elberon	52225	Froelich	52047	For specific Harlan Zip Codes call (712) 755-5812, or your local postmaster.		Jackson Junction	52150
Eldon	52554	Fruitland	52749			Jacksonville	51537
Eldora	50627	Fulton	52060	Harper	52231	Jamaica	50128
Eldorado	52175	Galesburg	50232	Harpers Ferry	52146	James	51108
Eldridge	52748	Galland	52639	Harris	51345	Jamison	50210
Elgin	52141	Galt	50101	Harrisburg	52620	Janesville	50647
Elkader	52043	Galva	51020	Hartford	50118	Jefferson	50129
Elkhart	50073	Gambrill	52756	Hartley	51346	Jerico	50659
Elk Horn	51531	Garber	52048	Hartwick	52232	Jerome	52544
Elkport	52044	Garden City	50102	Harvard	50008	Jesup	50648
Elk Run Heights	50701	Garden Grove	50103	Harvey	50119	Jewell	50130
Elliott	51532	Gardiner	50039	Haskins	52201	Joetown	52247
Ellston	50074	Garnavillo	52049	Hastings	51540	Johnston	50131
Ellsworth	50075	Garner	50438	Hauntown	52732	Johnston Station (Part of Johnston)	50131
Elma	50628	Garrison	52229	Havelock	50546	Joice	50446
Elon	52170	Garwin	50632	Haven	52339	Jolley	50551
Elrick	52653	Gaza	51245	Haverhill	50120	Jordan	50036
Elvira	52732	Geneva	50633	Hawarden	51023	Julien	52003
Elwood	52226	George	51237	Hawkeye	52147	Juniata	50588
Ely	52227	Georgetown	52531	Hawleyville	51632	Kalo	50569
Emeline	52207	Germantown	51046	Hawthorne	51566	Kalona	52247
Emerson	51533	German Valley	50480	Hayesville	52562	Kamrar	50132
Emery	50401	Germanville	52540	Hayfield	50438	Kanawha	50447
Emmetsburg	50536	Giard	52157	Hazleton	50641	Kellerton	50133
Enterprise	50073	Gibson	50104	Hedrick	52563	Kelley	50134
Epworth	52045	Gifford	50259	Henderson	51541	Kellogg	50135
Essex	51638	Gilbert	50105	Hepburn	51632	Kendallville	52136
Estherville	51334	Gilbertville	50634	Herndon	50128	Kennedy Mall (Part of Dubuque)	52001
Evans	52577	Gillett Grove	51341	Herrold	50111	Kensett	50448
Evansdale	50707	Gilman	50106	Hesper	52101	Kent	50850
Evanston	50532	Gilmore City	50541	Hiawatha	52233	Keokuk	52632
Evergreen	52804	Gladbrook	50635	Hickman Road (Part of Urbandale)	50322	Keomah Village	52577
Everly	51338	Glasgow	52556	High	52203	Keosauqua	52565
Ewart	50171	Glendale Acres	51503	Highland Center	52501	Keota	52248
Exira	50076	Glendon	50164	Highland Park (Part of Des Moines)	50313	Kesley	50649
Exline	52555	Glenwood	51534	Highlandville	52149	Keswick	50136
Fairbank	50629	Glidden	51443	High Point	50103	Keystone	52249
Fairfax	52228	Goddard	50054	Highview	50595	Key West	52003
Fairfield	52556	Goldfield	50542	Hills	52235	Kilbourn	50137
Fair Ground (Part of Dubuque)	52002	Goodell	50439	Hillsboro	52630	Killduff	50137
		Goose Lake	52750	Hinton	51024	Kimballton	51543
		Gowrie	50543	Hiteman	52531		
		Grace Hill	52353	Hobarton	50511		
		Graettinger	51342	Hocking	52531		
		Graf	52073	Holbrook	52325		
		Grafton	50440				

* **Area Zip Code**   † **Post Office Boxes**

	ZIP
Kingsley	51028
Kingston	52637
Kinross	52250
Kirkman	51447
Kirkville	52566
Kiron	51448
Klemme	50449
Klinger	50668
Knierim	50552
Knittel	50668
Knoke	50553
Knoxville	50138
Knoxville Estates	50138
Konigsmark	52401
Kossuth	52637
Koszta	52208
Lacelle	50213
Lacey	50207
Lacona	50139
Ladora	52251
La Fayette	52202
Lake Canyada	52804
Lake City	51449
Lake Mills	50450
Lake Park	51347
Lakeside	50588
Lake View	51450
Lakewood	50211
Lakota	50451
Lambs Grove	50208
Lamoille	50158
Lamoni	50140
Lamont	50650
La Motte	52054
Lanesboro	51451
Langdon	51301
Langworthy	52252
Lansing	52151
Lanyon	50544
La Porte City	50651
Larchwood	51241
Larrabee	51029
Latimer	50452
Laurel	50141
Laurens	50554
Lawler	52154
Lawn Hill	50206
Lawton	51030
Leando	52551
Lebanon (Sioux County)	51250
Lebanon (Van Buren County)	52565
Le Claire	52753
Ledyard	50556
Leeds (Part of Sioux City)	51108
Le Grand	50142
Lehigh	50557
Leighton	50143
Leland	50453
Le Mars	51031
Lenox	50851
Leon	50144
Le Roy	50123
Lester	51242
Letts	52754
Lewis	51544
Liberty	50210
Liberty Center	50145
Libertyville	52567
Lidderdale	51452
Lime City	52778
Lime Springs	52155
Linby	52580
Lincoln	50652
Lincoln Center	50841
Lindale Mall (Part of Cedar Rapids)	52402
Linden	50146
Lineville	50147
Linn Grove	51033
Linwood (Part of Buffalo)	52805
Lisbon	52253
Liscomb	50148
Little Cedar	50454
Littleport	52055
Little Rock	51243
Little Sioux	51545
Littleton	50648
Little Turkey	52154
Livermore	50558
Livingston	52549
Lockridge	52635
Logan	51546
Logansport	50036
Lohrville	51453
Lone Rock	50559
Lone Tree	52755
Long Grove	52756
Lorah	50022

	ZIP
Lorimor	50149
Lost Nation	52254
Lourdes	50628
Loveland	51555
Lovilia	50150
Lovington	50322
Lowden	52255
Lowell	52645
Low Moor	52757
Luana	52156
Lucas	50151
Lundstrom Heights	50021
Luther	50152
Luther Manor (Part of Bettendorf)	52722
Luton	51052
Lu Verne	50560
Luxemburg	52056
Luzerne	52257
Lyman	51535
Lynnville	50153
Lyons (Clinton County)	52732
Lyons (Linn County)	52302
Lytton	50561
McCallsburg	50154
McCausland	52758
McClelland	51548
Macedonia	51549
McGregor	52157
McIntire	50455
Macksburg	50155
McNally	51027
Macy	50601
Madison (Part of Council Bluffs)	51503
Madrid	50156
Magnolia	51550
Maine	52571
Malcom	50157
Mallard	50562
Mall of the Bluffs (Part of Council Bluffs)	51503
Malone	52742
Maloy	50852
Malvern	51551
Manawa (Part of Council Bluffs)	51501
Manchester	52057
Manilla	51454
Manly	50456
Manning	51455
Manson	50563
Maple Heights	50616
Maple Hill	50514
Maple River	51401
Mapleton	51034
Maquoketa	52060
Marathon	50565
Marble Rock	50653
Marcus	51035
Marengo	52301
Marietta	50158
Marion	52302
Mark	52537
Marne	51552
Marquette	52158
Marquisville	50313
Marsh	52659
Marshalltown	50158
Marshalltown Mall (Part of Marshalltown)	50158
Martelle	52305
Martensdale	50160
Martinsburg	52568
Martinstown	52575
Marysville	50116
Mason City	50401*
	50402†
Masonville	50654
Massena	50853
Massey	52003
Massillon	52255
Matlock	51244
Maurice	51036
Maxwell	50161
May City	51349
Maynard	50655
Maysville	52773
Mechanicsville	52306
Mederville	52043
Mediapolis	52637
Medora	50125
Melbourne	50162
Melcher	50163
Melrose	52569
Meltonville	50472
Melvin	51350
Menlo	50164
Meriden	51037

	ZIP
Merle Hay Mall (Part of Des Moines)	50310
Meroa	50461
Merrill	51038
Meservey	50457
Methodist Camp	51360
Meyer	50455
Middle	52307
Middleburg	51041
Middletown	52638
Midlands Mall (Part of Council Bluffs)	51503
Midvale	50124
Midway (Floyd County)	50616
Midway (Linn County)	52302
Miles	52064
Milford	51351
Miller	50438
Millersburg	52308
Millerton	50165
Millnerville	51062
Millville	52052
Milo	50166
Milton	52570
Minburn	50167
Minden	51553
Mineola	51554
Mineral Ridge	50036
Minerva	50005
Mingo	50168
Missouri Valley	51555
Mitchell	50461
Mitchellville	50169
Modale	51556
Moingona	50036
Mona	50472
Mondamin	51557
Moneta	51346
Monmouth	52309
Monona	52159
Monroe	50170
Monteith	50115
Monterey	52537
Montezuma	50171
Montgomery	51360
Monti	52218
Monticello	52310
Montour	50173
Montpelier	52759
Montrose	52639
Mooar	52632
Moorhead	51558
Moorland	50566
Moran	50276
Moravia	52571
Morley	52312
Morningside (Part of Sioux City)	51106
Morning Sun	52640
Morrison	50657
Morse	52240
Morton Mills	50864
Moscow	52760
Moulton	52572
Mount Auburn	52313
Mount Ayr	50854
Mount Carmel	51401
Mount Etna	50841
Mount Joy	52804
Mount Pleasant	52641
Mount Sterling	52573
Mount Union	52644
Mount Vernon	52314
Mount Zion	52565
Moville	51039
Munterville	52536
Murphy	50677
Murray	50174
Muscatine	52761
Muscatine Mall (Part of Muscatine)	52761
Mystic	52574
Napier	50014
Nashua	50658
Nashville	52060
Nemaha	50567
Neola	51559
Nevada	50201
Nevinville	50801
New Albin	52160
New Boston	52619
Newburg	50112
Newell	50568
New Era	52761
Newhall	52315
New Hampton	50659
New Hartford	50660
New Haven	50461
Newkirk	51238

	ZIP
New Liberty	52765
New London	52645
New Market	51646
New Providence	50206
New Sharon	50207
Newton	50208
New Vienna	52065
New Virginia	50210
Nichols	52766
Noble	52641
Nodaway	50857
Nora Springs	50458
Nora Springs Junction (Part of Nora Springs)	50458
Northboro	51647
North Branch	50002
North Buena Vista	52066
North Central Correctional Facility	50579
Northeast (Part of Cedar Rapids)	52402
North English	52316
North Grand Mall (Part of Ames)	50010
North Liberty	52317
Northpark Mall (Part of Davenport)	52806
North Side (Part of Sioux City)	51104
North Wall Lake (Part of Wall Lake)	51466
North Washington	50661
Northwest (Linn County)	52405
Northwest (Scott County)	52804
Northwood	50459
Norwalk	50211
Norway	52318
Norwich	51601
Norwood	50151
Norwoodville	50317
Numa	52575
Nyman	51566
Oakdale (Part of Coralville)	52319
Oakland	51560
Oakland Acres	50112
Oakland Mills	52641
Oakley	50049
Oakville	52646
Oakwood	50653
Oasis	52358
Ocheyedan	51354
Odebolt	51458
Oelwein	50662
Ogden	50212
Okoboji	51355
Old Balltown	52073
Olds	52647
Old Town	51351
Olin	52320
Olivet	50143
Ollie	52576
Onawa	51040
Oneida	52057
Onslow	52321
Ontario (Part of Ames)	50014
Oralabor	50021
Oran	50664
Orange (Part of Waterloo)	50701
Orange City	51041
Orchard	50460
Orient	50858
Orilla	50061
Orleans	51360
Osage	50461
Osborne	52043
Osceola	50213
Osgood	50536
Oskaloosa	52577
Ossian	52161
Osterdock	52035
Otho	50569
Otley	50214
Oto	51044
Otranto	50472
Otter Creek	52079
Otterville	50644
Ottosen	50570
Ottumwa	52501
Ottumwa Junction (Part of Ottumwa)	52501
Owasa	50126
Oxford	52322
Oxford Junction	52323
Oxford Mills	52323
Oyens	51045
Pacific Junction	51561
Packard	50619
Packwood	52580

	ZIP		ZIP		ZIP		ZIP
Painted Rocks	50214	Rembrandt	50576	Scranton	51462	Struble	51057
Palmer	50571	Remsen	51050	Searsboro	50242	Stuart	50250
Palm Grove	50501	Renwick	50577	Sedan	52544	Suburban Heights	52556
Palmyra	50047	Rhodes	50234	Selma	52588	Sully	50251
Palo	52324	Riceville	50466	Seneca	50539	Sulphur Springs	50588
Panama	51562	Richards	50579	Seney	51031	Summerset	50125
Panora	50216	Richland	52585	Sergeant Bluff	51054	Summitville	52632
Panorama Park	52722	Richmond	52247	Sewal	50060	Sumner	50674
Paralta	52336	Rickardsville	52073	Sexton	50483	Sunbury	52778
Paris (Davis County)	52552	Ricketts	51460	Seymour	52590	Sunshine	52544
Paris (Linn County)	52214	Ridgeport	50036	Shaffton	52730	Superior	51363
Parkersburg	50665	Ridgeway	52165	Shambaugh	51651	Sutherland	51058
Park Hills	50214	Rinard	50587	Shannon City	50861	Sutliff	52253
Park View	52748	Ringsted	50578	Sharon Center	52240	Swaledale	50477
Parnell	52325	Rippey	50235	Sharpsburg	50862	Swan	50252
Paton	50217	Rising Sun	50317	Shawondasse	52003	Swea City	50590
Patterson	50218	Ritter	51201	Sheffield	50475	Swedesburg	52652
Paullina	51046	Riverdale	52722	Shelby	51570	Sweetland Center	52761
Payne	51640	River Heights	52240	Sheldahl	50243	Swisher	52338
Pekin	52580	River Junction	52755	Sheldon	51201	Tabor	51653
Pella	50219	Riverside (Washington		Shell Rock	50670	Taintor	50253
Peoria	50219	County)	52327	Shellsburg	52332	Talleyrand	52248
Peosta	52068	Riverside (Woodbury		Shenandoah	51601	Tama	52339
Percival	51648	County)	51109		51693	Tara	50501
Perkins	51239	River Sioux	51545	For specific Shenandoah Zip		Teeds Grove	52771
Perlee	52556	Riverton	51650	Codes call (712) 246-2703, or		Templar Park	51360
Perry	50220	Riverview Release Center	50208	your local postmaster.		Templeton	51463
Pershing	50138	Roberts	50569	Sheridan	50157	Ten Mile	52727
Persia	51563	Robertson	50601	Sherrill	52073	Tennant	51574
Peru	50222	Robins	52328	Sherwood	50579	Tenville	50864
Petersburg	52040	Robinson	52330	Shipley	50201	Tenville Junction	50864
Peterson	51047	Rochester	52772	Shueyville	52404	Terril	51364
Petersville	52731	Rock Creek	50461	Siam	50833	Thayer	50254
Pierceville	52565	Rockdale (Part of		Sibley	51249	Thirty	52544
Pierson	51048	Dubuque)	52003	Sidney	51652	Thompson	50478
Pilot Grove	52648	Rock Falls	50467	Sigourney	52591	Thor	50591
Pilot Mound	50223	Rockford	50468	Silver City	51571	Thornburg	50255
Pioneer	50541	Rock Rapids	51246	Sinclair	50665	Thornton	50479
Piper	50579	Rock Valley	51247	Sioux Center	51250	Thorpe	52057
Pisgah	51564	Rockwell	50469	Sioux City	51101-11	Thurman	51654
Pittsburg	52565	Rockwell City	50579	For specific Sioux City Zip		Ticonic	51010
Pitzer	50072	Rodman	50580	Codes call (712) 277-6411, or		Tiffin	52340
Plainfield	50666	Rodney	51051	your local postmaster.		Timberland Heights (Part	
Plain View	52773	Roelyn	50566	Sioux Rapids	50585	of Ames)	50014
Plano	52581	Roland	50236	Six Mile	52732	Tingley	50863
Plaza Hills (Part of		Rolfe	50581	Slater	50244	Tipton	52772
Windsor Heights)	50311	Rome	52642	Slifer	50543	Titonka	50480
Pleasantgrove	52645	Rose Hill	52586	Sloan	51055	Toddville	52341
Pleasant Hill	50317	Roselle	51401	Smithland	51056	Toeterville	50481
Pleasanton	50065	Ross	50025	Soldier	51572	Toledo	52342
Pleasant Plain	52540	Rossie	51357	Solon	52333	Toolesboro	52653
Pleasant Prairie	52761	Rossville	52159	Somers	50586	Toronto	52343
Pleasant Valley	52767	Rowan	50470	South Amana	52334	Tracy	50256
Pleasantville	50225	Rowley	52329	South Des Moines (Part of		Traer	50675
Plover	50573	Royal	51357	Des Moines)	50315	Trenton	52641
Plymouth	50464	Rubio	52585	South English	52335	Treynor	51575
Pocahontas	50574	Rudd	50471	Southern Hills Mall (Part of		Triboji Beach	51360
Polk City	50226	Runnells	50237	Sioux City)	51106	Tripoli	50676
Pomeroy	50575	Russell	50238	South Muscatine (Part of		Troy	52537
Popejoy	50227	Ruthven	51358	Muscatine)	52761	Troy Mills	52344
Portland	50401	Rutland	50582	South Ottumwa (Part of		Truax	52553
Portsmouth	51565	Ryan	52330	Ottumwa)	52501	Truesdale	50592
Postville	52162	Sabula	52070	Southridge Mall (Part of		Truro	50257
Powersville	50636	Sac and Fox Indian		Des Moines)	50315	Turin	51059
Prairieburg	52219	Reservation	52339	Spaulding	50801	Turkey River	52052
Prairie City	50228	Sac City	50583	Spencer	51301	Twin View Heights	52333
Prairie Grove	52655	Sageville	52001	Sperry	52650	Udell	52593
Prescott	50859	St. Ansgar	50472	Spillville	52168	Ulmer	51450
Preston	52069	St. Anthony	50239	Spirit Lake	51360	Underwood	51576
Primghar	51245	St. Benedict	50511	Spragueville	52074	Union	50258
Primrose	52625	St. Catherines	52003	Springbrook	52075	Union Center	51031
Princeton	52768	St. Charles	50240	Springdale	52358	Union Mills	50207
Prole	50229	St. Donatus	52071	Spring Grove	52601	Unionville	52594
Promise City	52583	St. Joseph	50519	Spring Hill	50125	University Heights	52240
Prospect Hill (Part of		St. Lucas	52166	Springville	52336	University Park	52595
Burlington)	52601	St. Marys	50241	Spruce Hills Village (Part		University Place (Part of	
Protivin	52163	St. Olaf	52072	of Bettendorf)	52722	Des Moines)	50311
Pulaski	52584	St. Paul	52657	Stacyville	50476	Urbana	52345
Quarry	50158	Salem	52649	Stanhope	50246	Urbandale	50322
Quasqueton	52326	Salina	52556	Stanley	50671	Ute	51060
Quimby	51049	Salix	51052	Stanton	51573	Utica	52651
Radcliffe	50230	Sanborn	51248	Stanwood	52337	Vail	51465
Rake	50465	Sand Springs	52237	Stanzel	50849	Valeria	50054
Ralston	51459	Sandusky	52632	State Center	50247	Valley West Mall (Part of	
Randalia	52164	Sandyville	50001	Steamboat Rock	50672	West Des Moines)	50266
Randall	50231	Santiago	50169	Stennett	51566	Van Cleve	50162
Randolph	51649	Saratoga	52155	Sterling	52070	Vandalia	50228
Rands	50579	Saude	52154	Stiles	52537	Van Horne	52346
Rathbun	52544	Savannah	52537	Stilson	50423	Van Meter	50261
Raymar	50701	Sawyer	52627	Stockport	52651	Van Wert	50262
Raymond	50667	Saydel	50313	Stockton	52769	Varina	50593
Readlyn	50668	Saylorville	50313	Stone City	52205	Ventura	50482
Reasnor	50232	Scarville	50473	Storm Lake	50588	Vernon	52565
Redding	50860	Schaller	51053	Story City	50248	Vernon Springs	52136
Redfield	50233	Schleswig	51461	Stout	50673	Vernon View	52401
Red Line	51447	Schley	52136	Strahan	51540	Veterans Administration	
Red Oak	51566	Sciola	50864	Stratford	50249	Medical Center (Part of	
Red Rock Lakeview	50138	Scotch Grove	52331	Strawberry Point	52076	Knoxville)	50138
Reinbeck	50669	Scotch Ridge	50047	Stringtown	50851	Victor	52347

	ZIP		ZIP		ZIP		ZIP
Villisca	50864	Waupeton	52073	West Le Mars	51031	Williamstown	52247
Vincennes	52619	Waverly	50677	West Liberty	52776	Wilton	52778
Vincent	50594	Wayland	52654	West Okoboji	51351	Windham	52322
Vining	52348	Webb	51366	Weston	51576	Windsor Heights	50311
Vinton	52349	Webster (Keokuk County)	52355	Westphalia	51578	Winfield	52659
Viola	52350	Webster (Madison		West Point	52656	Winnebago Heights	50401
Volga	52077	County)	50273	Westside	51467	Winterset	50273
Volney	52159	Webster City	50595	West Spencer	51338	Winthrop	50682
Voorhies	50643	Welch Avenue (Part of		West Storm Lake (Part of		Wiota	50274
Wadena	52169	Ames)	50014	Storm Lake)	50588	Wiscotta	50233
Wahpeton	51351	Weldon	50264	West Suburban (Part of		Woden	50484
Walcott	52773	Wellman	52356	Des Moines)	50325	Wood	52042
Wales	51533	Wellsburg	50680	West Union	52175	Woodbine	51579
Walford	52351	Welton	52774	Westwood	52641	Woodburn	50275
Walker	52352	Wesley	50483	Wever	52658	Woodland	50103
Wallingford	51365	West Ackley (Part of		What Cheer	50268	Woodward	50276
Wall Lake	51466	Ackley)	50601	Wheatland	52777	Woodward State Hospital-	
Walnut	51577	West Amana	52203	White Oak	50073	School	50276
Walnut City	52574	West Bend	50597	Whiting	51063	Woolstock	50599
Wapello	52653	West Branch	52358	Whittemore	50598	Worthington	52078
Ware	50546	West Broadway (Part of		Whitten	50269	Wright	52577
Washburn	50706	Council Bluffs)	51501	Whittier	52336	Wyman	52621
Washington	52353	West Burlington	52655	Wichita	50115	Wyoming	52362
Washta	51061	West Chester	52359	Wick	50240	Yale	50277
Waterloo	50701-07	Westdale Mall (Part of		Wildwood Camp	52756	Yarmouth	52660
For specific Waterloo Zip Codes		Cedar Rapids)	52404	Willey	51401	Yetter	51433
call (319) 291-7400, or your		West Des Moines	50265-66	William Penn College (Part		Yorktown	51656
local postmaster.		For specific West Des Moines		of Oskaloosa)	52577	Zaneta	50643
Waterville	52170	Zip Codes call (515) 255-7410,		Williams	50271	Zearing	50278
Watkins	52354	or your local postmaster.		Williamsburg	52361	Zion	50858
Waubeek	52214	Western College	52404	Williamson (Adams		Zook Spur	50156
Waucoma	52171	Westfield	51062	County)	50859	Zwingle	52079
Waukee	50263	Westgate	50681	Williamson (Lucas			
Waukon	52172	West Grove	52538	County)	50272		
Waukon Junction	52146						

	ZIP		ZIP		ZIP		ZIP
Abbyville	67510	Belleville	66935	Caney	67333	Cunningham	67035
Abilene	67410	Belmont	67068	Canton	67428	Cunningham Highlands	
Ada	67414	Beloit	67420	Capaldo	66762	(Part of Overland Park)	66204
Adams	67128	Belpre	67519	Carbondale	66414	Curranville	66756
Admire	66830	Belvidere	67015	Carlton	67429	Dalton	67152
Agenda	66930	Belvue	66407	Carlyle	66749	Damar	67632
Aggieville Shopping		Bendena	66008	Carneiro	67425	Danville	67036
Center (Part of		Benedict	66714	Carona	66773	Dartmouth	67530
Manhattan)	66502	Bennington	67422	Cassoday	66842	Dearing	67340
Agra	67621	Bentley	67016	Castleton	67501	Deerfield	67838
Agricola	66871	Benton	67017	Catharine	67627	De Graff	66840
Akron	67156	Bern	66408	Cato	66711	Delano (Part of Wichita)	67209
Alamota	67839	Berryton	66409	Cave	67952	Delavan	67449
Albert	67511	Berwick	66534	Cawker City	67430	Delia	66418
Alden	67512	Beulah	66743	Cedar (Johnson County)	66018	Delphos	67436
Alexander	67513	Beverly	67423	Cedar (Smith County)	67628	Denison	66419
Aliceville	66093	Big Bow	67855	Cedar Bluffs	67749	Denmark	67455
Allen	66833	Big Springs	66050	Cedar Point	66843	Dennis	67341
Alma	66401	Bird City	67731	Cedar Vale	67024	Densmore	67645
Almena	67622	Birmingham	66436	Centerville	66014	Denton	66017
Altamont	67330	Bismarck Grove (Part of		Centralia	66415	Denton-McWorter Addition	67101
Alta Vista	66834	Lawrence)	66044	Centropolis	66067	Derby	67037
Alton	67623	Bison	67520	Chanute	66720	Dermot	67954
Altoona	66710	Black Wolf	67490	Chapman	67431	De Soto	66018
Americus	66835	Blaine	66549	Charleston	67853	Detroit	67410
Ames	66901	Blair	66090	Chase	67524	Devon	66701
Amy	67850	Blakeman	67730	Chautauqua	67334	Dexter	67038
Andale	67001	Bloom	67865	Cheney	67025	Diamond Springs	66838
Andover	67002	Bloomington (Butler		Cherokee	66724	Dighton	67839
Angelus	67738	County)	67010	Cherryvale	67335	Dillwyn	67557
Angola	67337	Bloomington (Osborne		Chetopa	67336	Dispatch	67430
Anna	66701	County)	67473	Chicopee	66762	Dodge City	67801
Anness	67106	Blue Mound	66010	Child's Acres	67101	Doniphan	66002
Anson	67152	Blue Rapids	66411	Chiles	66071	Dorrance	67634
Antelope	66858	Blue Valley (Part of		Chisholm (Part of Wichita)	67213	Douglass	67039
Anthony	67003	Overland Park)	66213	Cicero	67152	Dover	66420
Antioch	66083	Bluff City	67018	Cimarron	67835	Downs	67437
Antonino	67601	Bogue	67625	Circleville	66416	Downtown (Part of	
Arcadia	66711	Boicourt	66075	Civic Center (Part of		Topeka)	66601†
Argentine (Part of Kansas		Bolton	67301	Kansas City)	66101		66603*
City)	66106	Bonita	66061	Claflin	67525	Downtown (Part of	
Argonia	67004	Bonner Springs	66012	Clare	66061	Wichita)	67201-03
Arkansas City	67005	Bonnie Brae (Part of		Claudell	67628	For specific Downtown Zip	
Arlington	67514	Wichita)	67207	Clay Center	67432	Codes call (316) 262-6245, or	
Arma	66712	Bonnie Ridge	67401	Clayton	67629	your local postmaster.	
Armourdale (Part of		Boyle	66088	Clearfield	66025	Dresden	67635
Kansas City)	66105	Brainerd	67154	Clearview City	66019	Drury	67022
Arnold	67515	Brazilton	66743	Clearwater	67026	Dubuque	67634
Arrington	66436	Bremen	66412	Clements	66843	Duluth	66521
Arthur Heights (Part of Bel		Brenham	67059	Clifton	66937	Dundee	67530
Aire)	67220	Brenner Heights (Part of		Climax	67137	Dunkirk	66762
Arvonia	66523	Kansas City)	66104	Clinton	66046	Dunlap	66846
Asherville	67420	Brewster	67732	Clonmel	67149	Duquoin	67058
Ash Grove	67481	Bridgeport	67416	Clyde	66938	Durham	67438
Ashland (Clark County)	67831	Bronson	66716	Coalvale	66711	Dwight	66849
Ashland (Riley County)	66502	Brookhaven Estates	67230	Coats	67028	Earlton	66720
Ashton	67051	Brookridge (Part of		Codell	67630	East Bank (Part of Iola)	66749
Assaria	67416	Overland Park)	66212	Coffeyville	67337	Eastborough	67206-07
Atchison	66002		66282	Colby	67701	For specific Eastborough Zip	
Atchison Mall (Part of		For specific Brookridge Zip		Coldwater	67029	Codes call (316) 685-1426, or	
Atchison)	66002	Codes call (913) 831-5302, or		Collyer	67631	your local postmaster.	
Athol	66932	your local postmaster.		Colony	66015	East Forbes	66620
Atlanta	67008	Brookville	67425	Columbus	66725	Eastgate Shopping Center	
Attica	67009	Brookwood Shopping		Colwich	67030	(Part of Wichita)	67207
Atwood	67730	Center (Part of Topeka)	66614	Concordia	66901	Easton	66020
Aubry	66085	Brownell	67521	Conway	67460	Eastshore	66861
Auburn	66402	Browns Spur	67068	Conway Springs	67031	Edgerton	66021
Augusta	67010	Buckeye	67410	Coolidge	67836	Edmond	67636
Aulne	66861	Bucklin	67834	Copeland	67837	Edna	67342
Aurora	67417	Bucyrus	66013	Corbin (Montgomery		Edson	67733
Aurora Park (Part of Bel		Buffalo	66717	County)	67335	Edwardsville	66113
Aire)	67220	Buhler	67522	Corbin (Sumner County)	67032	Effingham	66023
Axtell	66403	Bunker Hill	67626	Corinth Shopping		Elbing	67041
Baileyville	66404	Burden	67019	Center (Part of Prairie		El Dorado	67042
Bala	66531	Burdett	67523	Village)	66208	El Dorado Honor Camp	67042
Baldwin City	66006	Burdick	66838	Corning	66417	Elgin	67361
Bancroft	66428	Burlingame	66413	Corporate Hills (Part of		Elk City	67344
Barclay	66523	Burlington	66839	Wichita)	67207	Elk Falls	67345
Barker (Part of Kansas		Burns	66840	Corwin	67061	Elkhart	67950
City)	66104	Burr Oak	66936	Cottonwood Falls	66845	Ellinwood	67526
Barnard	67418	Burrton	67020	Council Grove	66846	Ellis	67637
Barnes	66933	Busby	67349	Countryside	66202	Ellsworth	67439
Bartlett	67332	Bush City	66032	County Acres (Part of		Elmdale	66850
Basehor	66007	Bushong	66833	Wichita)	67212	Elmhurst (Part of Overland	
Bassett	66749	Bushton	67427	Courtland	66939	Park)	66204
Bavaria	67401	Buxton	66736	Covert	67651	Elmo	67451
Baxter Springs	66713	Byers	67021	Cow Town (Part of		Elmont	66618
Bayard	66039	Cairo	67035	Wichita)	67203	Elsmore	66732
Bazaar	66845	Caldwell	67022	Coyville	66727	Elwood	66024
Bazine	67516	Calista	67035	Craig	66215	Elyria	67460
Beagle	66064	Callahan (Part of Wichita)	67209	Crestline	66728	Emmeram	67671
Beardsley	67730	Calvert	67622	Croweburg	66756	Emmett	66422
Beattie	66406	Cambridge	67023	Cruppers Corner	67501	Empire City (Part of	
Beaumont	67012	Camp Forsyth	66442	Cuba	66940	Galena)	66739
Beaver	67525	Camp Funston	66442	Cullen Village (Part of		Empire Junction (Part of	
Beeler	67518	Camp Naish	66111	Topeka)	66619	Galena)	66739
Bel Aire	67220	Campus	67748	Cullison	67124	Emporia	66801
Bellaire	66952	Camp Whiteside	66442	Culver	67484	Englevale	66756
Belle Plaine	67013	Canada	66861	Cummings	66016	Englewood	67840

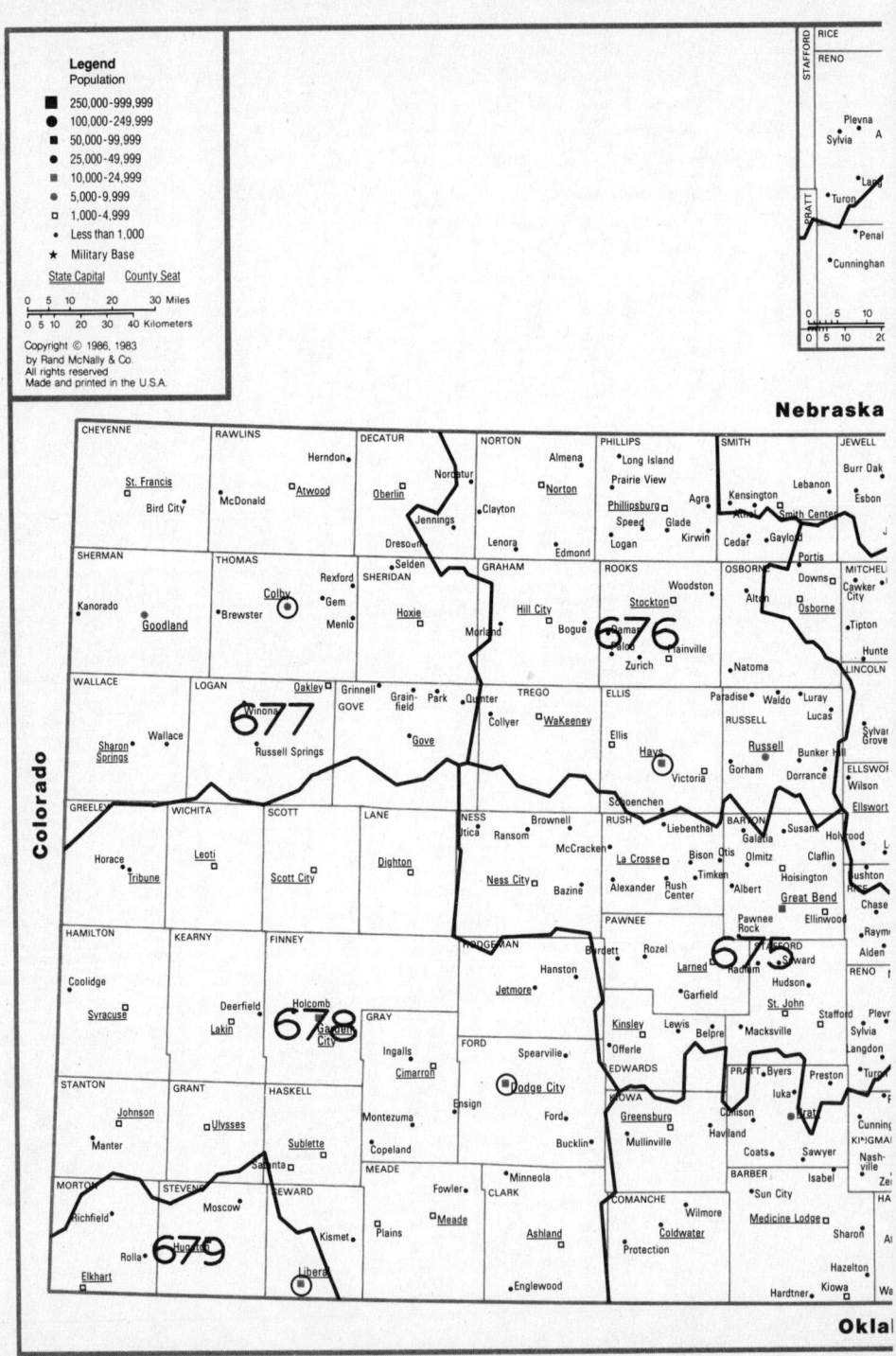

Legend
Population

- ■ 250,000 - 999,999
- ● 100,000 - 249,999
- ▪ 50,000 - 99,999
- • 25,000 - 49,999
- ▪ 10,000 - 24,999
- • 5,000 - 9,999
- □ 1,000 - 4,999
- • Less than 1,000
- ★ Military Base

State Capital   County Seat

0 5 10   20   30 Miles
0 5 10 20   40 Kilometers

Nebraska

Oklahoma

Sterling McPHERSON Moundridge MARION JACKSON Effingham PLATTE
Nickerson HARVEY Peabody Circleville ATCHISON
Willowbrook Buhler North Newton Walton Holton Easton Ft. Leavenworth CLAY
Hutchinson South Newton Elbing Denison JEFFERSON Nortonville Winchester Lansing Leavenworth
675 Hutchinson Halstead Whitewater Mayetta Valley Falls MISSOURI
Abbyville Partridge Sedgwick Hoyt Ozawkie Meriden LEAVENWORTH WYANDOTTE Bonner Springs
Arlington Haven Bentley SHAWNEE Perry McLouth Tonganoxie Basehor JACKSON
Langdon Valley Center Park City Kechi Silver Lake Topeka Linwood Merriam Kansas City
Pretty Mount Hope Maize Bel Aire Lecompton Shawnee Mission Overland Park
Prairie Andale River- Andover DOUGLAS De Soto Lenexa Olathe
Penalosa KINGMAN Garden view East- Lawrence Eudora JOHNSON Leawood
Wichita Plain borough Auburn Overland Park
Kingman Cheney Goddard Midland Pk. Oaklawn OSAGE Carbondale Gardner
670-6 Sedgwick Sunset Baldwin CASS
Haysville Park Rose Scranton Overbrook City Spring Hill
Clearwater Hill Burlingame
Norwich Viola Derby SUMNER Mulvane

N

ka

Webber REPUBLIC Narka Mahaska MARSHALL Summerfield NEMAHA Bern BROWN Reserve White Cloud
Republic WASHINGTON Hollenberg Oketo Morrill Hamlin
Formoso Munden Haddam Hanover Beattie Axtell Seneca Oneida Fairview Hiawatha Highland
Mankato Cuba Morrowville Marysville Robinson DONIPHAN Troy Wathena
669 Courtland Agenda Frankfort Centralia Powhattan Willis Severance Denton Elwood
Jewell Greenleaf Barnes Goff Wetmore Netawaka Whiting Muscotah Atchison
Randall Jamestown Clyde Linn Waterville Blue Rapids Corning Horton Lancaster
Glen Elder Scottsville Concordia Vining Palmer RILEY Havens- Soldier Circleville ATCHISON Effingham
Beloit CLOUD Aurora Clifton Green Randolph ville Onaga JACKSON Denison JEFFERSON Easton Leavenworth
Simpson Glasco Miltonvale CLAY Olsburg **664-** Mayetta Holton LEAVENWORTH Lansing
OTTAWA Oakhill Clay Center Leonardville Delia Hoyt Winchester Basehor
Minneapolis Wakefield Riley **666** Louisville Belvue Ozawkie McLouth Tonganoxie WYANDOTTE
Barnard Longford Milford St. George Wamego Rossville Meriden Perry Bonner Springs Kansas City
Tescott DICKINSON Manhattan Ogden McFarland Maple Hill SHAWNEE Silver Lake Linwood Shawnee Overland
Bennington Manchester Chapman GEARY Ft. Riley Pasixco Willard Topeka Lecompton Eudora JOHNSON Park
674 Solomon Abilene Junction City Alma Auburn Lawrence De Soto Olathe **660**
Salina New Enterprise WABAUNSEE Alta Vista Eldridge OSAGE Carbondale DOUGLAS Baldwin Gardner
Brookville Cambria White Dwight Scranton City
Smolan Gypsum City Parkerville LYON Harveyville Burlingame FRANKLIN Wells- MIAMI Spring
Kanopolis Assaria Carlton Hope Latimer Allen Osage City ville Hill
Lorraine Marquette Lindsborg Herington Council Grove Bushong Lyndon Ottawa   Quenemo Ottawa Louisburg Paola
Geneseo Ramona MORRIS Wilsey Dunlap Melvern Princeton Rantoul Osawatomie
Little River Windom Galva Tampa Lost Springs Reading Olivet Williamsburg Richmond Lane **662** Fontana
McPHERSON Durham CHASE Americus Lebo Waverly ANDERSON Greeley LINN La
Raymond Lyons Canton Lehigh Lincolnville Strong City Emporia Neosho Coffey Garnett Parker Cygne
Sterling Inman Moundridge MARION Elmdale **668** Rapids Hartford Pleasanton
Nickerson Willow- Hillsboro Florence Cedar Matfield Madison Burlington Westphalia Mound City
brook Butler North Goessel Point Green Colony Kincaid Blue Mound Prescott
Hutchinson Hesston Newton Walton Burns GREENWOOD Gridley Le Roy Elm Fulton
South Burrton Elbing Cassoday Virgil WOODSON ALLEN Mildred Mapleton BOURBON
Abbyville Hutchinson HARVEY BUTLER Hamilton Neosho Gas Bronson
Partridge Halstead Sedgwick Whitewater Yates Center Falls Iola La Union- Fort
Mount Potwin El Dorado Toronto Humboldt Harpe town Redfield Scott
Arlington Haven Hope Bentley Valley Center Climax WILSON Buffalo Elsmore
Pretty SEDGWICK Park Towanda Severy Benedict Altoona St. Paul **667** Arcadia
Penalosa Prairie Garden Plain Maize Kechi City Andover Augusta Leon Fredonia Earlton Hepler Mulberry
Kingman Colwich Wichita McConnell Fall Coyville NEOSHO Erie Walnut Arma Girard
KINGMAN Cheney Goddard Haysville A.F.B. Rose Hill Latham River Benedict Thayer Galesburg CRAWFORD Frontenac
Norwich Clearwater Douglass ELK Howard Neodesha McCune Cherokee Pittsburg
Spivey Viola Derby COWLEY Atlanta Moline Elk City Altamont Weir Scammon
670-672 Conway Mulvane Udall Burden Cambridge Elk Falls MONTGOMERY LABETTE CHEROKEE West Mineral
Harper Danville Wellington Oxford Grenola Cherryvale Parsons Mound Columbus
Attica Argonia May- Winfield Dexter CHAUTAUQUA Elk City Liberty Valley Labette Weir
Freeport field Sedan Independence Edna Altamont Oswego Riverton
Anthony Bluff City South Geuda Springs Cedar Peru Havana **673** Bartlett Chetopa Baxter Galena
Waldron Caldwell Haven Arkansas City Vale Chautauqua Niotaze Caney Tyro Coffeyville Treece Springs

lahoma

	ZIP		ZIP		ZIP		ZIP
Ensign	67841	Grandview Plaza	66441	Hunter	67452	Kickapoo Indian	
Enterprise	67441	Grantville	66429	Huron	66041	Reservation	66439
Erie	66733	Great Bend	67530	Huscher	66901	Kimball	66733
Esbon	66941	Greeley	66033	Hutchinson	67501-04	Kimeo	66943
Eskridge	66423	Green	67447	For specific Hutchinson Zip		Kincaid	66039
Eudora	66025	Greenbush	66743	Codes call (316) 662-1295, or		Kingman	67068
Eureka	67045	Greenleaf	66943	your local postmaster.		Kingsdown	67858
Eureka City Lake	67045	Greensburg	67054	Hutchinson Mall (Part of		Kinsley	67547
Everest	66424	Greenwich	67055	Hutchinson)	67501	Kiowa	67070
Fairfax (Part of Kansas		Greenwich Heights	67207	Idana	67432	Kipp	67401
City)	66115	Grenola	67346	Imes	66079	Kirkwood	66762
Fairmount	66048	Gretna	67661	Independence	67301	Kiro	66539
Fairport	67665	Gridley	66852	Indian Creek (Part of		Kirwin	67644
Fairview	66425	Grigston	67871	Overland Park)	66207	Kismet	67859
Fairway	66205	Grinnell	67738	Indian Ridge	66512	Labette	67356
Fall Leaf	66052	Gross	66711	Indian Springs Shopping		La Crosse	67548
Fall River	67047	Grove	66539	Center (Part of Kansas		La Cygne	66040
Falun	67442	Groveland	67546	City)	66102	Lafontaine	66736
Fanning	66087	Gypsum	67448	Indian Valley	66608	La Harpe	66751
Farlington	66734	Hackney	67156	Indian Village	67337	Lake Chaparral	66056
Farlinville	66014	Haddam	66944	Industry	67410	Lake City	67071
Farmington	66023	Haggard	67835	Ingalls	67853	Lake Kahola	66846
Faulkner	67336	Half Mound	66088	Inman	67546	Lake of the Forest (Part	
Federal Penitentiary	66048	Halford	67701	Iola	66749	of Bonner Springs)	66012
Fellsburg	67552	Hallowell	66725	Ionia	66949	Lake Quivira	66106
Fleming	66762	Halls Summit	66871	Iowa Indian Reservation	66094	Lake Shore (Ellsworth	
Floral	67156	Halstead	67056	Iowa Point	66035	County)	67454
Florence	66851	Hamilton	66853	Isabel	67065	Lake Shore (Jefferson	
Flush	66535	Hamlin	66434	Iuka	67066	County)	66070
Fontana	66026	Hammond	66701	Jacobs Creek Landing	66854	Lakeshore (Shawnee	
Ford	67842	Hanover	66945	Jamestown	66948	County)	66605
Forest Hills (Part of		Hanston	67849	Jarbalo	66048	Lakeside Acres Addition	67208
Wichita)	67206	Hardtner	67057	Jayhawk (Part of		Lakeside Village	66070
Forest Lake (Part of		Harlan	67641	Lawrence)	66046	Lakeview Heights	67230
Edwardsville)	66113	Harper	67058	Jefferson	67301	Lake Wabaunsee	66401
Formoso	66942	Harris	66032	Jennings	67643	Lakewood Hills	66070
Fort Dodge	67843	Hartford	66854	Jetmore	67854	Lakin	67860
Fort Leavenworth	66027	Harveyville	66431	Jewell	66949	Lamont	66855
Fort Riley	66442	Haskell (Part of Lawrence)	66044	Johnson	67855	Lancaster	66041
Fort Riley-Camp Whiteside	66442	Havana	67347	Junction City	66441	Lane	66042
Fort Riley North	66442	Haven	67543	Juniata	67423	Langdon	67583
Fort Scott	66701	Havensville	66432	Kackley	66948	Langley	67464
Fostoria (Osage County)	66413	Haverhill	67010	Kalloch	67337	Lanham	68415
Fostoria (Pottawatomie		Haviland	67059	Kalvesta	67856	Lansing	66043
County)	66426	Hays	67601	Kanona	67749	Larkinburg	66436
Four Corners	66537	Haysville	67060	Kanopolis	67454	Larned	67550
Fowler	67844	Hazelton	67061	Kanorado	67741	Larned State Hospital	67550
Fox Town	66756	Healy	67850			Latham	67072
Frankfort	66427	Hedville	67401	**Kansas City**	66101-19	Latimer	67449
Franklin	66735	Heizer	67530	For specific Kansas City Zip		Lawrence	66044-47
Frederick	67444	Hepler	66746	Codes call (913) 573-2600, or			66049
Fredonia	66736	Herington	67449	your local postmaster.		For specific Lawrence Zip	
Freeport	67049	Heritage Hills	66002			Codes call (913) 843-1681, or	
Friend	67871	Herkimer	66508	*COLLEGES & UNIVERSITIES*		your local postmaster.	
Frontenac	66763	Herndon	67739	University of Kansas		Lawton	66781
Fulton	66738	Hesper	66025	Medical Center	66103	Leavenworth	66048
Furley	67147	Hessdale	66401			Leawood	66206
Gage Center (Part of		Hesston	67062	*FINANCIAL INSTITUTIONS*			66211
Topeka)	66604	Hewins	67024	Brotherhood Bank and		For specific Leawood Zip	
Galatia	67565	Hiattville	66701	Trust Company	66101	Codes call (913) 648-1163, or	
Galena	66739	Hiawatha	66434	Citizens Bank & Trust of		your local postmaster.	
Galesburg	66740	Hickok	67880	Kansas City	66103	Lebanon	66952
Galva	67443	Hickory Acres	66512	Home State Bank of		Lebo	66856
Garden City	67846	Hicrest (Part of Topeka)	66605	Kansas City, Kansas	66101	Lecompton	66050
Garden Plain	67050	Hidden Lakes (Part of		Inter-State Federal		Lehigh	67073
Gardner	66030	Wichita)	67212	Savings and Loan		Le Loup	66091
Gardner Lake	66030	Highland	66035	Association of Kansas		Lenape	66052
Garfield	67529	Highland Park (Part of		City	66101	Lenexa	66210
Garland	66741	Topeka)	66605	Security Bank of Kansas			66214-15
Garnett	66032	Hill City	67642	City	66101		66219-20
Gas	66742	Hillcrest Shopping Center					66227
Gaylord	67638	(Part of Lawrence)	66044	*HOSPITALS*			66285
Gem	67734	Hillsboro	67063	Bethany Medical Center	66102	For specific Lenexa Zip Codes	
General Mail Facility (Part		Hillsdale	66036	Providence Medical		call (913) 888-5234, or your	
of Wichita)	67209	Hillside (Part of Wichita)	67208	Center	66112	local postmaster.	
Geneseo	67444	Hitschmann	67525	University of Kansas		Lenexa Plaza (Part of	
Geuda Springs	67051	Hoge	66086	Hospital	66160	Lenexa)	66215
Girard	66743	Hoisington	67544			Lenora	67645
Glade	67639	Holcomb	67851	*HOTELS/MOTELS*		Leon	67074
Glasco	67445	Holland	67410	Best Western Flamingo		Leona	66532
Glendale	67425	Hollenberg	66946	Motel	66102	Leonardville	66449
Glen Elder	67446	Holliday (Part of Shawnee)	66218	Best Western Inn	66103	Leoti	67861
Glen Park (Part of Kansas		Holliday Square Shopping		LaQuinta Motor Inn	66215	Leoville	67757
City)	66102	Center (Part of Topeka)	66611			Le Roy	66857
Glenville (Part of Wichita)	67217	Holton	66436			Levant	67743
Goddard	67052	Holyrood	67450	Kansas State Penitentiary	66043	Lewis	67552
Goessel	67053	Home	66438	Kansas State University of		Liberal	67901-05
Goff	66428	Homewood	66095	Agriculture and Applied		For specific Liberal Zip Codes	
Golden Belt Spur (Part of		Hope	67451	Science	66506	call (316) 624-4031, or your	
Salina)	67401	Hopewell	67557	Keats	66502	local postmaster.	
Goodland	67735	Horace	67879	Kechi	67067	Liberty	67351
Goodrich	66072	Horton	66439	Keene	66423	Liebenthal	67553
Gorham	67640	Howard	67349	Kellogg	67156	Lillis	66544
Gove	67736	Hoxie	67740	Kelly	66538	Lincoln	67455
Grainfield	67737	Hoyt	66440	Kendall	67857	Lincolnville	66858
Granada	66550	Hudson	67545	Kennekuk	66439	Lindsborg	67456
Grand Summit	67023	Hugoton	67951	Kenneth	66223	Linn	66953
Grandview (Part of		Humboldt	66748	Kensington	66951	Linn Valley Lakes	66040
Bonner Springs)	66012	Hunnewell	67140	Kickapoo	66048	Linwood	66052

* Area Zip Code   † Post Office Boxes

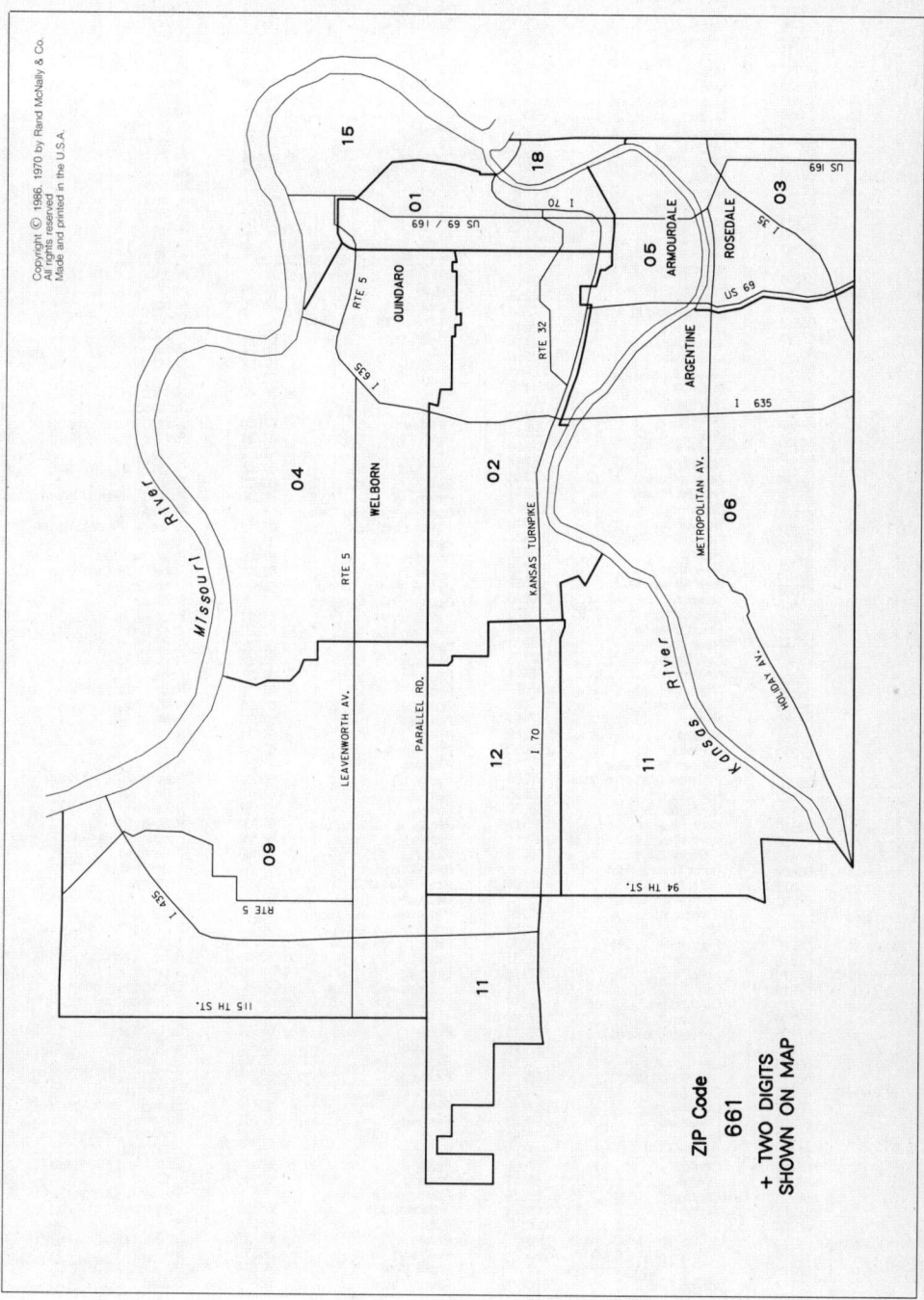

ZIP Code
661
+ TWO DIGITS
SHOWN ON MAP

	ZIP
Little River	67457
Logan	67646
Lone Elm	66039
Lone Star	66046
Longford	67458
Long Island	67647
Longton	67352
Loretta	67520
Lorraine	67459
Lost Springs	66859
Louisburg	66053
Louisville	66450
Lovewell	66942
Lowell	66713
Lowemont	66020
Lucas	67648
Ludell	67744
Luray	67649
Lydia	67861
Lyndon	66451
Lyons	67554
McConnell Air Force Base	67221
McCracken	67556
McCune	66753
McDonald	67745
McFarland	66501
Mackie	66725
Macksville	67557
McLouth	66054
McPherson	67460
Madison	66860
Mahaska	66955
Maize	67101
Manchester	67410
Manhattan	66502
Mankato	66956
Manning	67871
Manter	67862
Maple City	67102
Maple Hill	66507
Mapleton	66754
Marienthal	67863
Marietta	66518
Marion	66861
Marion County Lake	66861
Marmaton	66701
Marquette	67464
Marysville	66508
Matfield Green	66862
Mayetta	66509
Mayfield	67103
Meade	67864
Mecca Acres	67230
Medicine Lodge	67104
Medina	66073
Medora	67502
Melrose	67336
Melvern	66510
Menlo	67753
Mentor	67465
Mercier	66439
Meriden	66512
Merriam	66202
Metcalf South Shopping Center (Part of Overland Park)	66212
Michigan	66528
Midland (Part of Wichita)	67216
Midland Park	67216
Midway (Kingman County)	67111
Midway (Rawlins County)	67739
Milan	67105
Milberger	67665
Mildred	66039
Milford	66514
Millbrook (Part of Wichita)	67212
Miller	66868
Milton	67106
Miltonvale	67466
Mingo	67701
Minneapolis	67467
Minneola	67865
Mission	66201†
	66205*
Mission Hills	66205
Mission Shopping Center (Part of Mission)	66222
Mission Woods	66205
Mitchell	67554
Modoc	67863
Moline	67353
Monmouth	66753
Monrovia	66023
Montana	67356
Montara	66619
Montezuma	67867
Monticello (Part of Shawnee)	66218
Mont Ida	66091

	ZIP
Montrose	66956
Monument	67747
Moran	66755
Moray	66087
Morehead	66776
Morganville	67468
Morland	67650
Morrill	66515
Morrowville	66958
Morse	66061
Moscow	67952
Mound City	66056
Moundridge	67107
Mound Valley	67354
Mount Hope	67108
Mount Vernon	67025
Mulberry	66756
Mullinville	67109
Mulvane	67110
Muncie (Part of Kansas City)	66111
Munden	66959
Munger (Part of Wichita)	67208
Munjor	67601
Murdock	67111
Muscotah	66058
Narka	66960
Nashville	67112
Natoma	67651
Navarre	67469
Neal	66863
Nekoma	67559
Neodesha	66757
Neosho Falls	66758
Neosho Rapids	66864
Ness City	67560
Netawaka	66516
Neuchatel	66521
Neutral	66725
New Albany	66759
New Almelo	67652
Newbury	66526
New Cambria	67470
New Lancaster	66040
Newman	66073
New Salem	67156
Newton	67114
Nickerson	67561
Nicodemus	67625
Niles	67480
Niotaze	67355
Norcatur	67653
Normandie Shopping Center (Part of Wichita)	67206
Northbranch	66936
Northern Hills	66608
North Newton	67117
North Osage City (Part of Osage City)	66523
North Topeka (Part of Topeka)	66608
North Wichita (Part of Wichita)	67204
Norton	67654
Nortonville	66060
Norway	66961
Norwich	67118
Oakhill	67472
Oakland (Part of Topeka)	66616
Oaklawn	67216
Oaklawn-Sunview	67216
Oakley	67748
Oak Park Mall (Part of Overland Park)	66214
Oak Valley	67352
Oberlin	67749
Ocheltree	66083
Odin	67562
Offerle	67563
Ogallah	67656
Ogden	66517
Oketo	66518
Olathe	66051
	66061-63
For specific Olathe Zip Codes call (913) 782-3410, or your local postmaster.	
Olathe East	66062-63
For specific Olathe East Zip Codes call (913) 764-0375, or your local postmaster.	
Olivet	66856
Olmitz	67564
Olpe	66865
Olsburg	66520
Onaga	66521
Oneida	66522
Opolis	66760

	ZIP
Orchard Park (Part of Parsons)	67357
Osage City	66523
Osawatomie	66064
Osborne	67473
Oskaloosa	66066
Ost	67108
Oswego	67356
Otego	66936
Otis	67565
Ottawa	66067
Ottumwa	66839
Overbrook	66524
Overland Park	66204
	66207
	66209-14
	66221
	66223-24
For specific Overland Park Zip Codes call (913) 831-5302, or your local postmaster.	
Oxford	67119
Ozawkie	66070
Packers (Part of Kansas City)	66105
Padonia	66434
Page City	67764
Palco	67657
Palmer	66962
Paola	66071
Paradise	67658
Park	67751
Park City	67219
Park East	67208
Parker	66072
Parkerville	66846
Parklane Shopping Center (Part of Wichita)	67218
Parsons	67357
Partridge	67566
Patterson	67020
Pauline (Part of Topeka)	66619
Pawnee Plaza Mall (Part of Wichita)	67211
Pawnee Rock	67567
Paxico	66526
Peabody	66866
Pearl	67431
Peck	67120
Peck Addition	66605
Penalosa	67035
Pence	67871
Pen Dennis	67874
Penokee	67659
Peoria	66067
Perry	66073
Perth	67152
Peru	67360
Petrolia	66720
Pfeifer	67660
Phillipsburg	67661
Pickrell Corner	67010
Piedmont	67122
Pierceville	67868
Pilsen	66861
Piper	66109
Piqua	66761
Pittsburg	66762-63
For specific Pittsburg Zip Codes call (316) 231-6000, or your local postmaster.	
Plains	67869
Plainville	67663
Pleasant Grove	66046
Pleasanton	66075
Plevna	67568
Plymell	67846
Plymouth	66801
Polk	66743
Pomona	66076
Portis	67474
Portland	67140
Potawatomi Indian Reservation	66439
Potter	66077
Potwin	67123
Powhattan	66527
Prairie View	67664
Prairie Village	66208
Prairie Village Shopping Center (Part of Prairie Village)	66208
Pratt	67124
Prescott	66767
Preston	67583
Pretty Prairie	67570
Princeton	66078
Prospect	67042
Prospect Park	67215

	ZIP
Protection	67127
Purcell	66041
Quenemo	66528
Quincy	66870
Quinter	67752
Radium	67550
Radley	66762
Rago	67128
Ramona	67475
Ranch Mart Shopping Center (Part of Leawood)	66206
Randall	66963
Randolph	66554
Ransom	67572
Rantoul	66079
Raymond	67573
Reading	66868
Reager	67654
Redel	66085
Redfield	66769
Redwing	67544
Reece	67045
Reno	66086
Republic	66964
Reserve	66434
Rexford	67753
Rice	66901
Richfield	67953
Richland	66409
Richmond	66080
Richter	66067
Riley	66531
Ringer (Part of Wichita)	67212
Ringo	66743
River City (Part of Wichita)	67216
Riverdale	67152
Riverside (Part of Wichita)	67203
Riverton	66770
Riverview	67204
Robert L. Roberts (Part of Kansas City)	66104
Robinson	66532
Rock	67131
Rock Creek	66512
Rocky Ford	66502
Roeland Park	66205
Rolla	67954
Rolling Hills (Part of Wichita)	67212
Rome	67152
Roper	66714
Rosalia	67132
Rose	66783
Rosedale (Part of Kansas City)	66103
Rose Hill	67133
Roseland	66773
Rosewood (Part of Parsons)	67357
Rossville	66533
Roxbury	67476
Rozel	67574
Ruleton	67735
Rush Center	67575
Russell	67665
Russell Springs	67755
Sabetha	66534
Sac and Fox Indian Reservation	66434
Saffordville	66801
St. Benedict	66538
St. Francis	67756
St. George	66535
St. John	67576
St. Joseph	66938
St. Leo	67112
St. Mark	67030
St. Marys (Pottawatomie County)	66536
Saint Marys (Sedgwick County)	67050
St. Mary's College (Part of Leavenworth)	66048
St. Pats	66002
St. Paul	66771
St. Peter	67650
St. Theresa	67861
Salina	67401*
	67402†
	67410
Sand Spring	67550
Sanford	67550
Sarcoxie	66052
Satanta	67870
Saunders	67862
Savonburg	66772
Sawyer	67134
Saxman	67579
Scammon	66773

	ZIP
Scandia	66966
Schoenchen	67667
Schulte	67215
Scipio	66032
Scott City	67871
Scottsville	67420
Scranton	66537
Sedan	67361
Sedgwick	67135
Seguin	67740
Selden	67757
Selkirk	67861
Selma	66039
Seneca	66538
Severance	66087
Severy	67137
Seward	67577
Shady Bend	67455
Shady Brook	67449
Shallow Water	67871
Sharon	67138
Sharon Springs	67758
Sharpe	66871
Shaw	66733
Shawnee	66203
	66216-18
	66226

For specific Shawnee Zip
Codes call (913) 831-5302, or
your local postmaster.

Shawnee Mission	66201-85

For specific Shawnee Mission
Zip Codes call (913) 831-5302,
or your local postmaster.

	ZIP
Sherman	67356
Sherwin	66725
Sherwood Estates	66604
Shields	67874
Silverdale	67005
Silver Lake	66539
Simpson	67478
Sitka	67831
Skiddy	66872
Skidmore	66773
Smith Center	66967
Smolan	67479
Soldier	66540
Solomon	67480
Somerset	66071
South Dodge (Part of Dodge City)	67801
Southeast (Part of Wichita)	67218
Southgate Shopping Center (Part of Liberal)	67901
South Haven	67140
South Hoisington	67544
South Hutchinson	67505
South Mound	67357
South Radley	66762
South Seneca Gardens (Part of Wichita)	67217
Sparks	66035
Spearville	67876
Speed	67661
Spivey	67142
Springdale (Leavenworth County)	66020
Springdale (Sedgwick County)	67230
Spring Grove (Part of Galena)	66739
Spring Hill	66083
Stafford	67578
Stanley	66221
	66223-24

For specific Stanley Zip Codes
call (913) 897-2432, or your
local postmaster.

Stanton	66064

	ZIP
Stark	66775
State House (Part of Topeka)	66612
Sterling	67579
Stilwell	66085
Stippville	66725
Stockton	67669
Stony Point (Part of Kansas City)	66111
Strauss	66753
Strawn	66839
Strong City	66869
Studley	67759
Stull	66050
Stuttgart	67670
Sublette	67877
Suburban Heights (Part of Independence)	67301
Sugar Valley	66056
Summerfield	66541
Sun City	67143
Sunnydale	67147
Sunset Park (Part of Haysville)	67060
Suppesville	67106
Susank	67544
Sweetbriar Shopping Center (Part of Wichita)	67204
Sycamore	67363
Sylvan Grove	67481
Sylvia	67581
Syracuse	67878
Talmage	67482
Talmo	66935
Tampa	67483
Tanglewood Lake	66040
Tasco	67740
Tecumseh	66542
Terra Heights (Part of Topeka)	66609
Tescott	67484
Thayer	66776
The Dell (Part of Wichita)	67209
Thompsonville	66073
Timken	67582
Tipton	67485
Tonganoxie	66086
Topeka	66601-86

For specific Topeka Zip Codes
call (913) 295-9100, or your
local postmaster.

	ZIP
Toronto	66777
Towanda	67144
Tower Grove (Part of Overland Park)	66204
Towne East Square (Part of Wichita)	67207
Towne West Square (Part of Wichita)	67209
Trading Post	66075
Traer	67749
Travel Air	67206
Treece	66778
Trego Center	67672
Tribune	67879
Trousdale	67059
Troy	66087
Turck	66725
Turkville	67663
Turner (Part of Kansas City)	66106
Turon	67583
Twin Lakes Shopping Center (Part of Wichita)	67203
Tyro	67364
Udall	67146
Ulysses	67880
Union Stock Yards (Part of Wichita)	67219
Uniontown	66779

	ZIP
University (Crawford County)	66762
University (Douglas County)	66044
Urbana	66720
Utica	67584
Valeda	67337
Valencia	66604
Valley Center	67147
Valley Falls	66088
Varner	67068
Vassar	66543
Venango	67464
Verdi	67480
Vermillion	66544
Vernon	66783
Vesper	67455
Veterans' Administration Hospital (Part of Topeka)	66622
Victoria	67671
Vilas	66720
Village Square, The (Part of Dodge City)	67801
Vine Creek	67458
Vining	66937
Vinland	66006
Viola	67149
Virgil	66870
Vliets	66544
Voda	67631
Wabaunsee	66547
Waco	67120
Wagon Wheel Ranch	67010
Wagstaff	66071
Wakarusa	66546
WaKeeney	67672
Wakefield	67487
Waldo	67673
Waldron	67150
Walker	67674
Wallace	67761
Walnut	66780
Walton	67151
Wamego	66547
Washburn University (Part of Topeka)	66621
Washington	66968
Waterloo	67111
Waterville	66548
Wathena	66090
Watson	66542
Wauneta	67024
Waverly	66871
Wayne	66930
Wayside	67301
Wea	66013
Webber	66970
Webster	67669
Wego-Waco	67216
Weir	66781
Welborn (Part of Kansas City)	66104
Welda	66091
Wellington	67152
Wells	67488
Wellsford	67059
Wellsville	66092
Weskan	67762
Wesleyan (Part of Salina)	67401
Westboro (Part of Topeka)	66604
West Coffeyville	67337
Westfall	67455
Westlink Shopping Center (Part of Wichita)	67212
Westlink Village (Part of Wichita)	67212
West Mineral	66782

	ZIP
Westmoreland	66549
Westphalia	66093
Westport (Part of Wichita)	67217
West Ridge Mall (Part of Topeka)	66604
West Shore	66512
Westway Shopping Center (Part of Wichita)	67217
Westwood	66205
Westwood Hills	66205
Wetmore	66550
Wheaton	66551
Wheatridge Addition (Part of Wichita)	67212
Wheeler	67756
White Church (Part of Kansas City)	66109
White City	66872
White Cloud	66094
White Lakes Mall (Part of Topeka)	66611
Whitewater	67154
Whiting	66552
Wichita	67201-20
	67223-78

For specific Wichita Zip Codes
call (316) 946-4511, or your
local postmaster.

	ZIP
Wichita State University (Part of Wichita)	67208
Wilburton	67950
Wilder Junction	66018
Willard	66604
Williamsburg	66095
Williamstown	66073
Willis	66435
Willowbrook	67501
Willowdale	67142
Wilmore	67155
Wilmot	67131
Wilroads Gardens	67801
Wilsey	66873
Wilson	67490
Winchester	66097
Windom	67491
Windsor Park	67207
Windthorst	67876
Winfield	67156
Winfield State Hospital and Training Center	67156
Winifred	66427
Winona	67764
Winway (Part of Parsons)	67357
Wolcott (Part of Kansas City)	66109
Womer	66952
Wonsevu	66840
Woodbine	67492
Woodruff	67661
Woods	67951
Woodston	67675
Worden	66006
Wright	67882
Wyandotte West	66111-12

For specific Wyandotte West
Zip Codes call (913) 334-5858,
or your local postmaster.

	ZIP
Xenia	66716
Yaggy	67501
Yale	66762
Yates Center	66783
Yocemento	67601
Yoder	67585
Zarah (Part of Shawnee)	66218
Zeandale	66502
Zenda	67159
Zenith	67578
Zook	67550
Zurich	67676

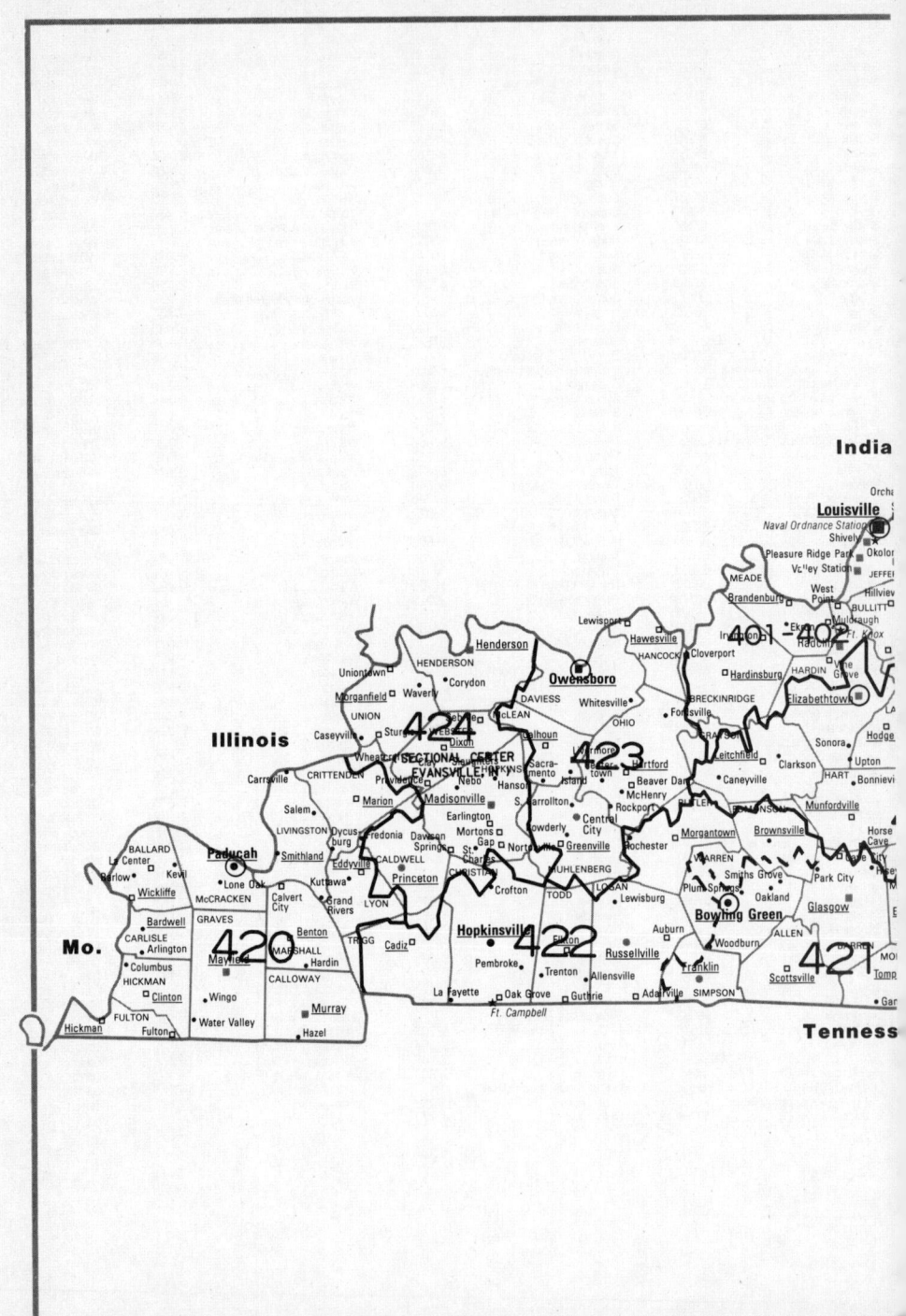

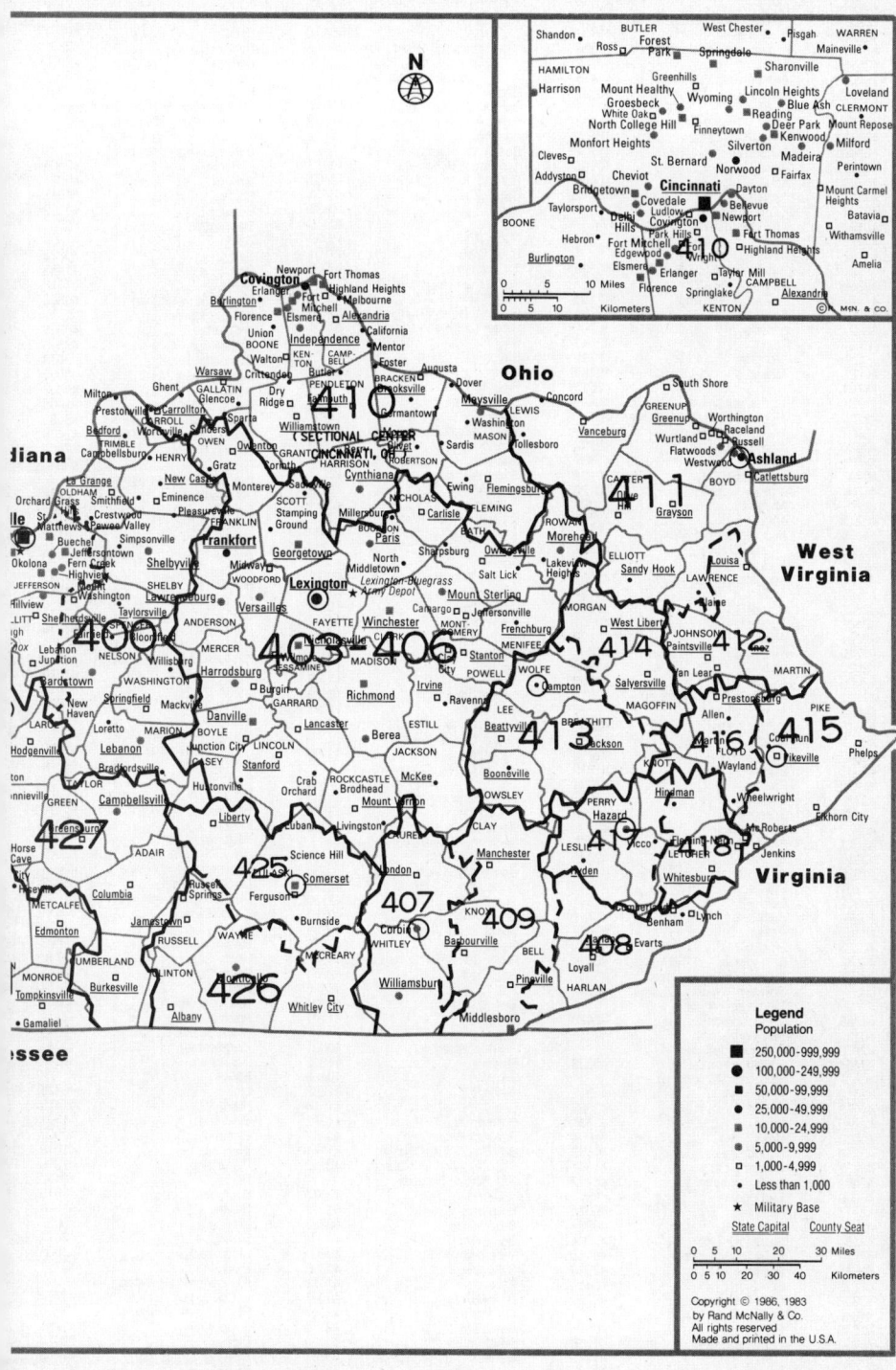

Legend

Population

Symbol	Population
■	250,000-999,999
●	100,000-249,999
▪	50,000-99,999
●	25,000-49,999
□	10,000-24,999
▫	5,000-9,999
□	1,000-4,999
•	Less than 1,000
★	Military Base

State Capital   County Seat

0 5 10   20   30 Miles

0 5 10   20   30   40 Kilometers

	ZIP		ZIP		ZIP		ZIP
Aaron	42601	Armstrong Hill	41164	Barrier	42633	Bengal	42718
Abbott	40006	Arnett	41314	Barr Street (Part of		Benham	40807
Abegall	41044	Arnold	42349	Lexington)	40501	Benito	40849
Aberdeen	42201	Arnold Ridge Estates (Part			40507	Bennettstown	42236
Absher	42728	of Frankfort)	40601		40584-96	Benson	40601
Access	41164	Arrington Corner	42348	For specific Barr Street Zip		Bent	42501
Acorn	42510	Artemus	40903	Codes call (606) 254-6156, or		Benton	42025
Acorn Village (Part of		Arthurmable	41465	your local postmaster.		Bentwoods	40601
Henderson)	42420	Artville	40387	Barterville	40311	Berea	40403-04
Acton	42718	Arvel	40447	Barthell	42647	For specific Berea Zip Codes	
Acup	41751	Ary	41712	Barwick	41306	call (606) 986-3941, or your	
Adaburg	42347	Ashbyburg	42456	Bascom	41171	local postmaster.	
Adair	42348	Ashcamp	41512	Bashford Manor Mall (Part		Berea College (Part of	
Adairville	42202	Asher	40803	of West Buechel)	40218	Berea)	40404
Adams	41230	Ashers Fork	40962	Baskett	42402	Berkley	42021
Adamson	41517	Ashland	41101-05	Bass	42733	Berlin	41043
Add	41224	For specific Ashland Zip Codes		Bath	41836	Bernice	40932
Addison	40143	call (606) 327-2121, or your		Battle	40040	Bernstadt	40741
Adeline	41129	local postmaster.		Battle Run	41039	Berry	41003
Aden	41142	Ashland Park (Part of		Battletown	40104	Berrytown	40223
Adolphus	42120	Lexington)	40502	Baughman	40906	Bethanna	41465
Aetnaville	42368	Ashland Town Center		Baughman Heights (Part		Bethany	41313
Aflex	41514	(Part of Ashland)	41101	of Danville)	40422	Bethel (Bath County)	40306
Ages	40801	Ashlock	42768	Baxter (Harlan County)	40806	Bethel (Jessamine	
Ages-Brookside	40801	Ashville	40291	Baxter (Jefferson County)	40204	County)	40356
Air Mail Facility-Standiford		Askin	42343	Bayfork	42122	Bethelridge	42516
Field (Amf-Sdf) (Part of		Atchison	42718	Bayou	42081	Bethesda	42633
Louisville)	40221	Athens (Part of Lexington)	40509	Bays	41310	Bethlehem	40007
Airport Gardens	41701		40515	Bays Branch	41216	Betsey	42633
Airview Estates	42701	For specific Athens Zip Codes		Bealers Knob	42371	Betsy Layne	41605
Akersville	42133	call (606) 231-6700, or your		Beals	42451	Beulah (Hickman County)	42039
Albany	42602	local postmaster.		Bear Branch	41714	Beulah (Hopkins County)	42408
Alberta	40370	Athertonville	42748	Beartown	41164	Beulah Heights	42607
Alcalde	42501	Athol	41307	Bearville	41740	Beverly	40913
Alcorn	40447	Atkinstown	40434	Bear Wallow	42127	Beverly Hills (Part of	
Alexandria	41001	Atoka	40422	Beattyville	41311	Danville)	40422
Algonquin Manor (Part of		Atwood	41063	Beaumont	42124	Bevier	42337
Louisville)	40211	Auburn	42206	Beaumont Park (Part of		Bevinsville	41606
Alhambra	41055	Audobon Acres (Part of		Lexington)	40504	Bewleyville	40146
Aliceton	40328	Owensboro)	42301	Beauty	41203	Biddle	40324
Allais (Part of Hazard)	41701	Audubon Park	40213	Beaver	41604	Big Bear Creek	42025
Allegre	42203	Augusta	41002	Beaver Bottom	41522	Big Bone	41091
Allen	41601	Ault	41164	Beaver Dam	42320	Big Branch	41522
Allendale	42782	Aurora	42048	Beaverlick	41094	Big Clifty	42712
Allen Springs	42122	Austerlitz	40361	Becknerville	40391	Big Creek	40914
Allensville	42204	Austin	42123	Beckton	42141	Big Eddy	40601
Allock	41710	Auxier	41602	Beda	42347	Big Fork	41777
Almo	42020	Avawam	41713	Bedford	40006	Biggs	41524
Almo Heights	42020	Avoca	40223	Beech	41306	Bighill	40405
Alonzo	42120	Avon (Part of Lexington)	40516	Beech Bottom	42539	Big Laurel	40808
Alpha	42603	Avondale (Part of		Beechburg	41093	Big Rock	41777
Alphoretta	41619	Paducah)	42001	Beech Creek	42321	Big Sandy Junction (Part	
Alpine	42519	Axtel	40143	Beech Grove (Bullitt		of Catlettsburg)	41129
Alton	40342	Azalea Hills	42420	County)	40150	Big Spring	40106
Alton Station	40342	Bachelors Rest	41040	Beech Grove (Carter		Bigstone	41171
Altro	41306	Backusburg	42054	County)	41143	Big Woods	40387
Alumbaugh	40336	Bagdad	40003	Beech Grove (McLean		Bimble	40915
Alum Springs	40440	Bailey Creek	40828	County)	42322	Birdie	40342
Alva	40863	Baileys Switch	40906	Beechland	42256	Birdsville	42081
Alvaton	42122	Bainbridge	42215	Beechmont (Jefferson		Birk City	42301
Amandaville	42711	Baizetown	42349	County)	40214	Birmingham	42044
Amba	41635	Baker Branch	41263	Beechmont (Muhlenberg		Black Bottom	40828
Amburgey	41801	Bakerton	42711	County)	42323	Blackburn Correctional	
Ammie	40962	Bald Hill	41041	Beechville	42129	Complex	40511
Ammons	40170	Baldrock	40741	Beechwood	40359	Blackey	41804
Amos	42153	Baldwin	40475	Beechwood Village	40207	Blackford	42403
Anchorage	40223	Ballard	40342	Beechy	41175	Black Gnat	42718
	40245	Ballardsville	40014	Beefhide	41537	Black Gold	42285
For specific Anchorage Zip		Balltown (Nelson County)	40051	Beelerton	42041	Black Jack	42134
Codes call (502) 245-5791, or		Balltown (Whitley County)	40769	Bee Lick	40419	Black Mountain	40847
your local postmaster.		Balmoral (Part of		Bee Spring	42207	Black Rock	42754
Anco	41759	Henderson)	42420	Beetle	41143	Black Snake	40845
Andyville	40157	Baltimore	42066	Bel-Air (Part of		Blackwater	40741
Anna	42270	Bancroft (Jefferson		Winchester)	40391	Bladeston	41004
Anneta	42754	County)	40222	Belcher	41513	Blaine	41124
Annville	40402	Bancroft (Muhlenberg		Belcourt	42456	Blair	40823
Ano	42510	County)	42345	Belcraft	41858	Blairs Mills	41472
Ansel	42553	Bandana	42022	Belfry	41514	Blair Town	41501
Anthoston	42420	Bandy	42567	Belknap	41342	Blanche	40902
Antioch	41003	Bank Lick	41094	Belknap Beach	40059	Blanchet	41010
Antioch Shores	42519	Banner	41603	Bell City (Elliott County)	41171	Blandville	42026
Anton	42431	Baptist	41301	Bell City (Graves County)	42040	Blaze	41472
Apex	42464	Barbourmeade	40222	Bell County Forestry		Bledsoe	40810
Aqua Shores	40065	Barbourville	40906	Camp	40977	Blevins	41124
Arat	42717	Barcreek	40972	Bellefonte	41101	Blincoe	40037
Arch	42724	Bardo	40831	Bellemeade	40222	Blood	42071
Argillite	41121	Bardstown	40004	Bellepoint (Part of		Bloomfield	40008
Argo	41568	Bardstown Junction	40165	Frankfort)	40601	Bloomingdale	40391
Argyle	42516	Bardwell	42023	Belleview	41005	Bloomington (Grayson	
Arista	42718	Barefoot	40311	Bellevue	41073	County)	42754
Arjay	40902	Bark Camp	40701	Bellewood	40207	Bloomington (Magoffin	
Arkansas	41649	Barlow	42024	Bell Farm	42647	County)	41465
Arkansas Creek	41649	Barnesburg	42501	Bells Run	42378	Bloss	40456
Arkle	40734	Barnetts Creek	41256	Belltown	40033	Blowing Spring	42743
Arlington (Carlisle County)	42021	Barnrock	41219	Bellview (Part of Frankfort)	40601	Bluebank	41041
Arlington (Madison		Barnsley	42431	Belmont (Bullitt County)	40150	Blue Diamond	41719
County)	40475	Barnyard	40935	Belmont (Harrison County)	41031	Blue Grass (Part of	
Arlington Heights (Part of		Barrallton	40165	Belton	42324	Lexington)	40503
Frankfort)	40601	Barren River	42101	Ben Bow	41230		

* Area Zip Code   **† Post Office Boxes**

	ZIP
....	40523-24

For specific Blue Grass Zip Codes call (606) 271-3281, or your local postmaster.

	ZIP
Bluegrass Estates (Part of Danville)	40422
Blue Heron	42647
Bluehole	40962
Blue John	42519
Blue Level	42274
Blue Lick Springs	40311
Blue Moon	41655
Blue Ridge Manor	40223
Blue River	41607
Blue Spring	42211
Bluestone	40351
Blue Water Estates	42211
Bluff Boom	42743
Bluff City	42420
Board Tree	41528
Boatwright	42071
Boaz	42027
Bobs Creek	40815
Bobs Fork	41714
Bobtown	40403
Bohon	40330
Boiling Spring	42101
Boldman	41501
Boles	42167
Boltsfork	41168
Bolyn	41630
Bon	40769
Bon Air Hills	40601
Bonanza	41653
Bon Ayr	42160
Bond	40407
Bondurant	42050
Bondville	40372
Boneyville	40484
Bon Haven (Part of Winchester)	40391
Bonnie Brae	40065
Bonnieville	42713
Bonnyman	41719
Booker	40069
Boone	40403
Boone Aire	41042
Boone Heights	40906
Boonesboro	40475
Boonesborough	40475
Booneville	41314
Boons Camp	41204
Bordley	42404
Boreing	40740
Borowick Farms	40031
Boston (Butler County)	42268
Boston (Nelson County)	40107
Boston (Pendleton County)	41006
Botland	40004
Botto	40944
Bourbon Downs (Part of Bardstown)	40004
Bourbon Furnace	40360
Bourne	40444
Bow	42714
Bowen	40309
Bowling Green	42101-04

For specific Bowling Green Zip Codes call (502) 782-4202, or your local postmaster.

	ZIP
Boyce	42122
Boyd	41003
Boyds Crossing	42782
Boydsville	42079
Boydtown	40324
Bracht	41030
Bracktown (Part of Lexington)	40510
Bradford	41043
Bradfordsville	40009
Bradley	41465
Bradshaw	40434
Brady (Part of Morehead)	40351
Brainard	41465
Bramlett	42743
Brandenburg	40108
Brandenburg Station	40108
Brandy	40351
Brandykeg	41653
Brassfield	40385
Braxton	40330
Breadens Creek	40927
Breckinridge	41031
Breckinridge Center	42437
Breeding	42715
Bremen	42325
Brentsville	40361

	ZIP
Brentwood (Part of Madisonville)	42431
Brewers	42025
Briartown (Part of Springfield)	40069
Briarwood	40222
Briarwood Manor (Part of Bowling Green)	42103
Bridgeport	40601
Bridge Street (Part of Paducah)	42003
Bridgeville	41004
Briensburg	42025
Brighton (Part of Lexington)	40505
Brightshade	40962
Brinegar	41164
Brinkley	41805
Bristow	42101
Britmart	42220
Broadbent Subdivision	42211
Broad Bottom	41501
Broad Fields	40207
Broad Ford	42726
Broadview Manor	40601
Broadway	42207
Broadwell	41031
Brodhead	40409
Broeck Pointe	40201
Bromley (Kenton County)	41016
Bromley (Owen County)	41086
Bromo	40456
Bronston	42518
Brookhaven (Part of Lexington)	40503
Brooklyn	42209
Brooks	40109
Brookside	40801
Brooksville	41004
Broughtentown	40419
Browder	42326
Browning	42274
Browning Corner	41040
Brownsboro	40014
Brownsboro Farm	40222
Brownsboro Village	40207
Browns Crossroads	42602
Browns Fork	41720
Browns Grove	42071
Browns Valley	42376
Brownsville (Edmonson County)	42210
Brownsville (Fulton County)	42050
Brownwood Manor	42303
Bruin	41125
Brushart	41144
Brush Grove	40040
Brutus	40972
Bryan	42629
Bryants Store	40921
Bryantsville	40410
Buchanan	41129
Buckettown	40475
Buckeye	40444
Buck Grove	40117
Buckhorn	41721
Buckingham	41636
Buckner	40010
Buechel	40218
	40228

For specific Buechel Zip Codes call (502) 454-1881, or your local postmaster.

	ZIP
Buel	42327
Buena Vista (Garrard County)	40444
Buena Vista (Harrison County)	41031
Buena Vista (Lewis County)	41179
Buena Vista (Marshall County)	42044
Buffalo (Larue County)	42716
Buffalo (Trigg County)	42211
Buford	42376
Bug	42602
Bugtussle	42140
Bulan	41722
Bull Creek	41653
Bullittsville	41005
Burdick	42718
Burdine (Part of Jenkins)	41517
Burfield	41653
Burgin	40310
Burke	41171
Burkes Spring	40037
Burkesville	42717
Burkhart	41342

	ZIP
Burk Hollow	40769
Burkshire Terrace	40214
Burlington	41005
Burna	42028
Burnaugh	41129
Burnetta	42544
Burning Fork (Magoffin County)	41465
Burning Fork (Pike County)	41501
Burning Springs	40962
Burnside	42519
Burnwell	41518
Burr	40456
Burton	41612
Burtonville	41189
Bush	40724
Bushtown	40330
Buskirk (Morgan County)	41406
Buskirk (Pike County)	41544
Busseyville	41230
Busy	41723
Butler (Franklin County)	40601
Butler (Pendleton County)	41006
Butterfly	41719
Buttimer Hill (Part of Frankfort)	40601
Buttonsberry	42350
Bybee	40385
Bypro	41612
Cabell	42633
Cabot	42343
Caddo	41040
Cadentown (Part of Lexington)	40505
Cadiz	42211
Cains Store	42544
Cairo	42420
Caldwell Manor (Part of Danville)	40422
Caleast	42475
Caledonia	42211
Calf Creek	41224
Calhoun	42327
California	41007
Calla	40336
Callaway	40977
Calloway	40456
Calvary	40033
Calvert City	42029
Calvin	40813
Camargo	40353
Cambridge	40220
Cambridge Shores	42044
Campbellsburg	40011
Campbellsville	42718*
	42719†
Camp Dick Robinson	40444
Camp Dix	41127
Camp Grounds	40701
Camp Kennedy	40444
Camp Nelson	40444
Camp Nelson (rural)	40356
Camp Pleasant	40601
Camp Springs	41059
Camp Taylor (Part of Louisville)	40213
Campton	41301
Canada	41519
Canby	41010
Cane Creek	40741
Cane Valley	42720
Caney	41472
Caneyville	42721
Canmer	42722
Cannel City	41408
Cannon	40923
Cannonsburg	41102*
	41105†
Canoe	41339
Canton	42212
Canton Heights Estates	42211
Canyon Falls	41311
Capital Estates	40601
Capito	40965
Carbondale	42408
Carbon Glow	41832
Carcassonne	41804
Cardinal Hill	40004
Cardinal Hills (Part of Frankfort)	40601
Cardinal Valley (Part of Lexington)	40503
Cardwell	40330
Carlisle	40311
Carntown	41006
Carpenter	40906
Carr Creek	41847
Carrie	41725

	ZIP
Carrollton	41008
Carrsville	42081
Carter	41128
Carthage	41007
Cartwright	42602
Carver	41409
Cary	40977
Casey Creek	42728
Caseyville	42459
Cash	42784
Casky	42240
Catalpa	41129
Catawba	41040
Cat Creek	40380
Catlettsburg	41129
Causey	41777
Cave City	42127
Cavehill	42274
Cave Ridge	42129
Cave Spring	42265
Cawood	40815
Cayce	42041
Cecil	42001
Cecilia	42724
Cedar Bluff	42445
Cedar Brook	41031
Cedar Flats	42129
Cedar Grove	42220
Cedar Hill Heights	42518
Cedar Knoll Galleria (Part of Ashland)	41101
Cedar Run Creek	40601
Cedar Spring	42160
Cedar Springs	42164
Cedarville	40456
Center	42214
Centerfield	40014
Center Point	42167
Center Ridge	42071
Centertown	42328
Centerview	42145
Centerville	40324
Central Avenue (Part of Paducah)	42001
Central City	42330
Ceralvo	42369
Cerulean	42215
Chad	40823
Chalybeate	42171
Chambers	42348
Chance	42728
Chandlers Chapel	42206
Chandlerville	41257
Chapel Hill	42120
Chaplin	40012
Chapman	41230
Chappell	40816
Charleston	42408
Charleswood	40229
Charley	41230
Charters	41179
Chatham	41002
Chavies	41727
Chenault	40170
Chenoa	40977
Chenowee	41339
Cherokee (Jefferson County)	40205
	40225

For specific Cherokee Zip Codes call (606) 638-4840, or your local postmaster.

	ZIP
Cherokee (Lawrence County)	41180
Cherry	42071
Cherrywood Village	40207
Chesnutburg	40962
Chestnut Gap	41314
Chestnut Grove	40065
Chevrolet	40831
Chevy Chase (Part of Lexington)	40502
Chicken Bristle	40484
Chilesburg (Part of Lexington)	40509
Chloe	41501
Choateville	40601
Christianburg	40065
Christine	42728
Christopher	41701
Church Hill	42240
Cinda	41728
Cinderella Estates	40229
Cisco	41410
Cisselville	40069
Clabber Bottom	40324
Clare	42134
Clarence	42567
Clark	40023

Name	ZIP	Name	ZIP	Name	ZIP	Name	ZIP
Clark Hill	41164	Consolation	40003	Crocus	42728	Dekoven	42459
Clarksburg	41179	Constance	41009	Crofton	42217	Delafield (Part of Bowling	
Clarkson	42726	Constantine	40114	Croley	42031	Green)	42101
Clark Street (Part of		Conway	40417	Cromona	41810	Delaplain	40324
Paducah)	42001	Cooktown	42123	Cromwell	42333	Delaware	42373
Claryville	41001	Coolbrook	40601	Cropper	40057	Delia	41097
Claxton	42408	Cool Springs	42320	Crossgate	40222	Delmer	42544
Clay	42404	Cooper	42633	Cross Keys	40065	Delphia	41735
Clay City	40312	Co-Operative	42647	Crossland	42049	Delta	42633
Clayhole	41317	Cooperstown	42276	Crown	41811	Delville	40011
Clay Lick	40337	Coopersville	42611	Crowtown (Part of		Delvinta	41311
Claymour	42220	Copebranch	41339	Princeton)	42445	Dema	41859
Claypool	42103	Copland	41369	Crummies	40815	Democrat	41858
Claysville	41031	Copperfield	40223	Crutchfield	42041	De Mossville	41033
Clay Village	40065	Coral Hill	42141	Crystal	40420	Demplytown	40014
Clear Creek Springs	40977	Coral Ridge	40118	Crystal Lake	40031	Denney	42633
Clearfield	40313	Corbin	40701*	Cuba	42066	Dennis	42276
Cleaton	42332		40702†	Cubage	40856	Denniston	40316
Clementsville	42539	Cordell	41124	Cub Run	42729	Denton	41132
Clemons	41719	Cordia	41701	Culver	41211	Denver	41215
Cleopatra	42327	Cordova	41010	Culvertown	40051	Depoy	42345
Clermont	40110	Corey	41142	Cumberland	40823	Derby Hills	40383
Cliff (Part of		Corinth (Grant County)	41010	Cumberland City	42602	Dermont	42303
Prestonsburg)	41653	Corinth (Logan County)	42276	Cumberland College (Part		Desda	42601
Clifford	41230	Cork	42129	of Williamsburg)	40769	Devon	41042
Clifton	40383	Corn Creek	40006	Cumberlane Estates (Part		Devondale (Part of	
Clifty	42216	Corners	40146	of Campbellsville)	42718	Graymoor-Devondale)	40222
Climax	40456	Cornette	40729	Cumminsville	41004	Dewdrop	41171
Clinton	42031	Cornettsville	41731	Cundiff	42728	Dewitt	40930
Clintonville	40361	Cornishville	40330	Cunningham	42035	Dexter	42036
Clio	40769	Corydon	42406	Cupio	40177	Dexterville	42261
Closplint	40927	Costelow	42276	Curdsville (Daviess		Diablock	41701
Clover Bottom	40447	Cote	40828	County)	42334	Diamond	42404
Cloverdale (Part of		Cottageville	41179	Curdsville (Mercer County)	40330	Dice	41736
Frankfort)	40601	Cottle	41472	Curt	41339	Dietz Acres	40121
Clover-Darby	40927	Cottonburg	40475	Custer	40115	Dillon	40865
Cloverport	40111	Country Club Estates	40475	Cutshin	41732	Dimple	42261
Clovertown	40831	Country Club Heights		Cutuno	41465	Dingus	41417
Cloyds Landing	42752	(Franklin County)	40601	Cuzick	40475	Dione	40823
Clutts	40823	Country Club Heights		Cyclone	42166	Dishman Springs	40906
Coakley	42743	(Mason County)	41056	Cynthiana	41031	Disputanta	40456
Coalgood	40818	Country Lane Estates	40601	Dabney	42501	Dix Fork	41564
Coal Run	41501	Country Manor	40065	Dabolt	40421	Dixie (Henderson County)	42406
Coalton	41168	Countryside	40059	Dahl	42501	Dixie (Kenton County)	41017
Cobb	42445	Country Village	40014	Daisy	41733	Dixie Bend	42558
Cobhill	40415	Counts Crossroads	41164	Dal	40769	Dixie Manor Shopping	
Coburg	42743	Covedale	41179	Dalesburg (Breathitt		Center	40258
Codyville (Part of		Covington	41011-18	County)	41314	Dixie Plantation (Part of	
Hardinsburg)	40143	For specific Covington Zip		Dalesburg (Fleming		Lexington)	40505
Cofer	42129	Codes call (606) 261-4425, or		County)	41041	Dixon	42409
Colby Hills	40391	your local postmaster.		Dalton	42445	Dix River Estates	40484
Coldiron	40819	Cowan	41039	Dan (Menifee County)	40387	Dixville	40330
Cold Spring	41076	Cow Creek (Estill County)	40472	Dan (Ohio County)	42349	Dizney	40825
Cold Spring-Highland		Cowcreek (Owsley		Dana	41615	Dobson	41228
Heights (Part of		County)	41314	Danby	42276	Dock	41653
Highland Heights)	41076	Cox Bend	42519	Daniel Boone	42442	Doddy	42164
Coldstream	40202	Coxs Creek	40013	Daniels Creek	41265	Doe Creek	40336
Coldwater	42071	Coxton	40831	Danleytown	41144	Doe Valley Estates	40108
Coleman	41553	Crab Orchard	40419	Dant	40037	Dogtown	42025
Colemansville	41003	Cracker	41649	Danville	40422*	Dog Walk (Lincoln	
Colesburg	40150	Crailhope	42214		40423†	County)	40409
Coletown (Part of		Craintown	41041	Darfork	41701	Dogwalk (Ohio County)	42766
Lexington)	40515	Crane Nest	40906	Darkmont	40828	Dogwood	42051
Colfax	41049	Cranks	40820	Davella	41214	Donaldson	42211
College (Part of Berea)	40403	Cranston	40351	David	41616	Donansburg	42743
College Farm	41501	Crawford	41719	Davis	40370	Donerail (Part of	
College Heights (Part of		Crayne	42033	Davisburg	40977	Lexington)	40511
Bowling Green)	42101	Craynor	41614	Davis Cross Roads	42268	Dongola	41858
College Hill	40385	Creal	42764	Davison Station	42361	Dorton	41520
College Park (Part of		Creekmore	42649	Davisport	41262	Dorton Branch	40977
Frankfort)	40601	Creekside	40222	Davistown (Garrard		Do Stop	42721
Collins	41501	Creekville	40962	County)	40444	Dot	42202
Collista	41222	Creelsboro	42629	Davistown (Woodford		Douglas	41560
Colmar	40965	Crenshaw	40071	County)	40347	Douglass Hills	40243
Colonial Terrace	40222	Crescent Hill (Part of		Dawson Springs	42408	Dover	41034
Colony (Part of Frankfort)	40601	Louisville)	40206	Day	41858	Downtown (Part of	
Colson	41858	Crescent Park	41017	Dayhoit	40824	Bowling Green)	42101
Columbia	42728	Crescent Springs	41017	Daylight	42408	Downtown (Part of	
Columbus	42032	Cressmont	41311	Daysboro	41332	Louisville)	40201
Colville	41031	Crest	42701	Daysville	42276		40203
Combs	41729	Crestmoor (Part of		Dayton	41074	For specific Downtown Zip	
Comer	42327	Bowling Green)	42101	Deane	41812	Codes call (502) 587-8546, or	
Concord (Fleming County)	41041	Creston	42539	Deatsville	40013	your local postmaster.	
Concord (Lewis County)	41131	Crestview	41076	Debord	41214		
Concord (McCracken		Crestview Hills	41017	Decker	42721	Doylesville	40475
County)	42001	Crestview Hills Mall (Part		DeCoursey (Part of Taylor		Dozier Heights	42431
Concord (Pendleton		of Crestview Hills)	41017	Mill)	41015	Draffenville	42025
County)	41040	Crestwood (Fayette		Decoy	41339	Draffin	41521
Concordia	40157	County)	40503	Dee Acres	42366	Drake	42128
Conder	41514	Crestwood (Franklin		Deep Springs (Part of		Drakesboro	42337
Confederate	42038	County)	40601	Lexington)	40505	Draper (Part of Evarts)	40828
Confederate Estates	40056	Crestwood (Oldham		Deepwood (Part of		Drennon Springs	40011
Confluence	41730	County)	40014	Hopkinsville)	42240	Dressen (Part of Harlan)	40831
Congleton (Lee County)	41311	Creswell	42411	Deer Lick	42256	Dreyfus	40426
Congleton (McLean		Crider	42445	Defeated Creek	41833	Drift	41619
County)	42327	Crittenden	41030	Defiance	41760	Dripping Spring	42171
Conley	41465	Crix	40313	Defoe	40017	Drip Rock	40336
Connersville	41031	Croakes	40069	Defries	42722	Dr. Martin Luther King Jr.	
Conoloway	42726	Crockett	41413	Dehart	41472	(Part of Louisville)	40211*
							40251†

	ZIP		ZIP		ZIP		ZIP
Druid Hills	40207	Elizaville	41037	Fairview (Fleming County)	41039	Flippin	42167
Drum	42501	Elkatawa	41339	Fairview (Kenton County)	41015	Floral	42348
Dry Creek	41862	Elk Creek	40023	Fairview (Lyon County)	42038	Florence	41022†
Dry Fork (Barren County)	42155	Elkfork	41421	Fairview (Whitley County)	40769		41042*
Dry Fork (Pike County)	41561	Elk Horn	42733	Fairview Heights (Part of		Florence Mall (Part of	
Dryhill	41749	Elkhorn City	41522	Frankfort)	40601	Florence)	41042
Dry Ridge	41035	Elk Lake Shores	40359	Fairview Hill	41146	Florence Square (Part of	
Dublin	42039	Elkton	42220	Fairway (Part of		Florence)	41042
Dubre	42731	Ella	42728	Lexington)	40502	Florress	41472
Duckers	40347	Ellington	42752	Falcon	41426	Flournoy	42437
Duckrun	40769	Elliottville	40317	Fall Rock	40932	Floyd	42567
Duco	41465	Ellisburg	40437	Fallsburg	41230	Floydsburg	40014
Duff	42754	Elliston (Grant County)	41035	Falls of Rough	40119	Fogertown	40936
Duganville	40330	Elliston (Madison County)	40475	Falmouth	41040	Folsom	41035
Dukedom	42085	Ellisville	40311	Fancy Farm	42039	Folsomdale	42051
Dukes	42348	Ellmitch	42343	Fannin	41171	Fonde	40940
Dulaney	42445	Ellwood	41538	Fariston	40741	Fonthill	42642
Duluth	40403	Elmburg	40057	Farler	41774	Foraker	41465
Dunbar	42219	Elmer Davis Lake	40359	Farmdale	40601	Ford	40320
Duncan (Casey County)	40442	Elmrock	41640	Farmers	40351	Fords Branch	41526
Duncan (Mercer County)	40330	Elmville	40601	Farmers Mill	40831	Fordsville	42343
Dundee	42338	Elna	41219	Farmersville	42445	Forest Grove	40391
Dunham (Part of Jenkins)	41537	Elsie	41422	Farmington	42040	Forest Hills (Jefferson	
Dunlap	41524	Elsinore	40601	Farraday	41855	County)	40299
Dunleary	41522	Elsmere	41018	Farristown	40403	Forest Hills (McCracken	
Dunmor	42339	Elswick	41538	Faubush	42532	County)	42003
Dunnville	42528	Elva	42082	Faulconer	40422	Forest Hills (Pike County)	41527
Dunraven	41754	Elys	40939	Faxon	42071	Forest Hills (Taylor	
Durbin	41129	Emanuel	40734	Faye	41171	County)	42718
Durbintown	41003	Emerson	41135	Fayette Mall (Part of		Forks of Elkhorn	40601
Duval	40324	Eminence	40019	Lexington)	40503	Forkton	42167
Dwale	41621	Emlyn	40730	Faywood	40383	Forrest Park (Part of	
Dwarf	41739	Emma	41653	Fearisville	41179	Winchester)	40391
Dycusburg	42037	Emmalena	41740	Fearsville	42240	Fort Campbell	42223
Dyer	40115	Empire	42442	Feathersburg	42733	Fort Campbell North	42223
Dykes	42501	Endicott	41626	Federal Correctional		Fort Knox	40121
Eadsville	42633	End of Line	41667	Institution (Boyd		Fort Mitchell	41017
Eagle Creek	41098	Engle	41727	County)	41102	Fort Spring (Part of	
Eagle Hill	41046	English	41008	Federal Correctional		Lexington)	40510
Eagle Station	41083	Ennis	42337	Institution (Fayette			40513
Earlington	42410	Ensor	42366	County)	40511	For specific Fort Spring Zip	
East Bernstadt	40729	Enterprise	41164	Fedscreek	41524	Codes call (606) 231-6700, or	
Easterday	41008	Eolia	40826	Feliciana	42085	your local postmaster.	
Eastern	41622	Epleys	42276	Felty	40962	Fort Thomas	41075
East Fork	42129	Epperson	42003	Fentress Lookout	40119	Fort Wright	41011
East Hickman	40356	Epson	41465	Fenwick (Part of		Foster	41043
East Jenkins (Part of		Epworth	41189	Lexington)	40516	Fount	40999
Jenkins)	41537	Equality	42328	Ferguson (Logan County)	40276	Fountain Run	42133
Eastland	40004	Eriline	40962	Ferguson (Pulaski County)	42533	Fourmile	40939
Eastland Park (Fayette		Erlanger	41018	Ferguson Creek (Part of		Four Oaks	41040
County)	40505	Ermine	41815	Pikeville)	41501	Fourseam	41701
Eastland Park (Warren		Erose	40970	Fern Creek	40291	Fox	40336
County)	42104	Essie	40827	Ferndale	40977	Fox Chase	40165
Eastland Shopping Center		Estesburg	40489	Fernleaf	41034	Fox Creek	40342
(Part of Lexington)	40505	Estill	41627	Ferrells Creek	41513	Foxport	41093
East McDowell	41647	Esto	42642	Fiddle Bow	42408	Foxtown	40447
Easton	42343	Ethridge	41095	Fielden	41177	Frakes	40940
East Pineville	40977	Etna	42567	Fillmore	41323	Frances	42064
East Point	41216	Etoile	42131	Fincastle	40222	Francisville	41048
East Union	40311	Etterwood	40324	Finchville	40022	Frankfort	40601-04
East View	42732	Etty	41572	Finley	42736	For specific Frankfort Zip	
Eastwood	40018	Eubank	42567	Finley Addition	42420	Codes call (502) 223-3447, or	
Ebenezer (Mercer County)	40372	Eunice	42728	Finney	42141	your local postmaster.	
Ebenezer (Monroe		Evanston	41340	Firebrick	41137	Franklin	42134*
County)	42167	Evarts	40828	Firmantown	40383		42135†
Ebenezer (Muhlenberg		Eveleigh	42754	Fisherville	40023	Franklin Cross Roads	42724
County)	42337	Ever	41465	Fishtrap	41557	Franklinton	40057
Echo	42154	Everett	42256	Fiskburg	41033	Frazer	42618
Echols	42320	Evergreen	40601	Fisty	41743	Fraziertown	40056
Echo Point	42518	Eversole	41314	Fitch	41164	Fredericktown	40069
Echo Valley	40031	Ewing	41039	Fitchburg	40472	Fredonia	42411
Eddyville	42038	Ewingford	40006	Five Forks	41230	Fredville	41465
Eddyville Shores	42038	Ewington	40353	Fivemile	41339	Freeburn	41528
Edenton	40475	Exie	42743	Fixer	41397	Freedom (Barren County)	42157
Edgewater	41534	Ezel	41425	Flag Fork	40601	Freedom (Russell County)	42629
Edgewood (Franklin		Faber	42701	Flag Spring	41007	Free Union	42409
County)	40601	Fagan	40322	Flaherty	40175	Fremont	42003
Edgewood (Jefferson		Fairbanks (Graves		Flat	41301	Frenchburg	40322
County)	40213	County)	42079	Flat Fork	41427	Fresh Meadows	40824
Edgewood (Kenton		Fairbanks (Owen County)	40359	Flatgap	41219	Friendly Hills	40219
County)	41017	Fairdale	40118	Flat Lick	40935	Frisby	42633
Edgewood (Nelson		Fairdealing	42025	Flat Rock (Caldwell		Fritz	41465
County)	40004	Fairfield (Breckinridge		County)	42411	Frogtown	40033
Edmonton	42129	County)	40144	Flat Rock (McCreary		Frogue	42714
Edna	41419	Fairfield (Nelson County)	40020	County)	42653	Frontier Village (Part of	
Edwards	42256	Fairland	42602	Flat Rock (Rockcastle		Henderson)	42420
Eglon	40447	Fairmeade	40207	County)	40460	Frozen Creek	41339
Egypt	40430	Fairmont (Jefferson		Flat Rock (Simpson		Fruit Hill	42217
Eighty Eight	42130	County)	40291	County)	42170	Fry	42743
Ekron	40117	Fairmont (Webster		Flatwoods	41139	Fryer	42445
Elamton	41472	County)	42404	Fleming (Part of Fleming-		Fuget	41266
Elba	42327	Fairplay	42735	Neon)	41840	Fulgham	42031
Elcomb	40831	Fairview (Anderson		Fleming-Neon	41840	Fulton	42041
Eldridge	41149	County)	40342	Flemingsburg	41041	Fultz	41143
Eli	42642	Fairview (Boyd County)	41101	Flemingsburg Junction	41041	Funston	42634
Elihu	42501	Fairview (Christian		Flener	42261	Furnace	40472
Elizabeth Station	40361	County)	42221	Flingsville	41030	Fusonia	41774
Elizabethtown	42701*	Fairview (Edmonson		Flint Springs	42349	Future City	42053
	42702†	County)	42210	Flintville	41348	Gabbard	41364

Name	ZIP	Name	ZIP	Name	ZIP	Name	ZIP
Gabe	42743	Goddard	41093	Gregoryville	41143	Hayes	41040
Gadberry	42735	Goering	42348	Gresham	42743	Haynesville	42368
Gaffey Heights	40121	Goffs Corner	40391	Grethel	41631	Hays	42171
Gage	42056	Goforth	41040	Grider	42717	Hays Crossing	40351
Gainesville	42164	Goins	40763	Griderville	42127	Hayward	41173
Gainesway (Part of		Goldbug	40769	Griffin	42640	Haywood	42141
Lexington)	40502	Gold City	42134	Griffith	42301	Hazard	41701*
Gallup	41230	Golden Ash	40831	Griffytown	40243		41702†
Galveston	41635	Golden Pond	42211	Grigsby	41722	Hazel	42049
Gamaliel	42140	Golo	42054	Grove Center	42437	Hazel Green	41332
Gapcreek	42603	Goochtown	42567	Grundy	42501	Hazel Patch	40729
Gap in Knob	40165	Goodluck	42129	Guage	41339	Head of Grassy	41135
Gapville	41433	Goodnight	42127	Gubser Mill	41007	Headquarters	40311
Gardenside (Part of		Goodwater	42501	Guerrant	41339	Hearin	42404
Lexington)	40504	Goody	41514	Guffie	42327	Heath	42086
	40533	Goose Creek	40222	Gullett	41465	Hebbardsville	42420
	40544	Goose Rock	40944	Gulnare	41501	Hebron	41048
For specific Gardenside Zip		Gordon	41819	Gulston	40830	Hebron Estates	40165
Codes call (606) 278-6425, or		Gordon Ford	41472	Gum Sulphur	40419	Hecla	42410
your local postmaster.		Gordonsville	42276	Gum Tree	42167	Hector	40962
Garden Springs (Part of		Goshen	40026	Gunlock	41632	Hedgeville	40444
Lexington)	40504	Gotts	42103	Guston	40142	Heekin	41097
Garden Village	41501	Grab	42743	Guthrie	42234	Heenon	41545
Gardnersville	41033	Grace	40962	Guy	42101	Heflin	42347
Garfield	40140	Gracey	42232	Gwinn Island	40422	Hegira	42717
Garlin	42728	Gradyville	42742	Gypsy	41438	Heidelberg	41333
Garner (Boyd County)	41168	Graefenburg	40601	Habit	42366	Heidrick	40949
Garner (Knott County)	41817	Graham	42344	Haddix	41331	Heiner	41722
Garrard	40941	Graham Hill	42420	Hadensville	42234	Helechawa	41332
Garrett (Floyd County)	41630	Grahamville	42086	Hadley	42101	Helena	41055
Garrett (Meade County)	40117	Grahn	41142	Hager	41465	Hellier	41534
Garrettsburg	42236	Gra-Mor	40004	Hagerhill	41222	Helton	40840
Garrison	41141	Grancer	42287	Hail	42501	Hemp Ridge	40076
Garvin Ridge	41164	Grand Rivers	42045	Halcom	41171	Henderson	42420
Gascon	42129	Grandview (Part of		Haldeman	40329	Hendricks	41465
Gaskill (Part of Jenkins)	41537	Tompkinsville)	42167	Halfway	42150	Hendron	42001
Gasper	42206	Grandview Heights (Part		Halifax	42164	Henrietta	41269
Gates	40351	of Frankfort)	40601	Hall (Jessamine County)	40356	Henry Clay (Fayette	
Gatewood	42348	Grange City	41049	Hall (Knott County)	41840	County)	40502*
Gatliff	40769	Grangertown	42459	Hallie	41821		40522†
Gatun	40806	Grants Lick	41001	Halls Gap	40489	Henry Clay (Pike County)	41542
Gausdale	40906	Grant Wood Hills	42420	Halls Store	42276	Henryville	40311
Gaybourn	40383	Grapevine	42431	Halo	41606	Henshaw	42437
Gays Creek	41745	Grassy Creek	41332	Hamlin	42046	Hensley (Breckinridge	
Geddes	42134	Grassy Lick	40353	Hammackville	42286	County)	40146
General Mail Facility (Part		Gratz	40327	Hammond	41269	Hensley (Clay County)	40962
of Owensboro)	42304	Gravel Switch	40328	Hammonville	42757	Herbert	42368
Geneva (Henderson		Gray	40734	Hampton	42047	Herd	40435
County)	42406	Gray Hawk	40434	Hampton Manor (Part of		Heritage Village (Part of	
Geneva (Lincoln County)	40437	Graymoor (Part of		Winchester)	40391	Campbellsville)	42718
Gentrys Mill	42728	Graymoor-Devondale)	40222	Handshoe	41640	Hermitage Hills (Part of	
Georgetown (Harlan		Graymoor-Devondale	40222	Hanly	40356	Lexington)	40505
County)	40843	Grays Branch	41144	Hannah	41124	Hermon	42234
Georgetown (Scott		Grays Knob	40829	Hansford	40456	Herndon	42236
County)	40324	Grayson	41143	Hanson	42413	Herron Hill	41189
Germantown (Bracken		Grayson Springs	42726	Happy	41746	Heselton	41179
County)	41044	Graysville	40146	Happy Acre	42642	Hesler	40359
Germantown (Jefferson		Greasy Creek	41562	Happy Landing	40403	Hestand	42151
County)	40217	Great Crossing	40324	Harbor Village	40324	Hi Acres (Part of	
Gertrude	41004	Greear	41472	Hardburly	41747	Lexington)	40505
Gesling	41128	Green	41164	Hardin	42048	Hickman	42050
Gest	40057	Green Acres (Boyle		Hardinsburg	40143	Hickory	42051
Gethsemane	40051	County)	40422	Hardin Springs	42783	Hickory Flat	42134
Ghent	41045	Green Acres (Fayette		Hardmoney	42003	Hickory Grove	
Gibbs	40906	County)	40511	Hardshell	41348	(Cumberland County)	42752
Gifford	41465	Greenbriar (Daviess		Hardwick	42618	Hickory Grove (McCreary	
Gilbertsville	42044	County)	42303	Hardy	41531	County)	42638
Gillem Branch	41219	Greenbriar (Marion		Hardyville	42746	Hickory Hill	40222
Gilley	41819	County)	40033	Hare	40729	Hickory Hill (Part of	
Gillmore	41301	Greenbriar (Oldham		Hargett	40336	Frankfort)	40601
Gilpin	42539	County)	40031	Harlan	40831	Hidalgo	42633
Gilreath	42635	Greenbrier	40489	Harlan Crossroads	42167	Hide-A-Way Hills	40359
Gilstrap	42349	Greencastle	42270	Harlan Gas	40831	High Bridge	40390
Gimlet	41164	Greendale (Part of		Harmony	40359	High Falls	41301
Girdler	40943	Lexington)	40511	Harmony Lake Estates	40059	Highgrove	40013
Girkin	42101	Green Fields Estates	40391	Harmony Village	40059	High Knob	40402
Gishton	42325	Green Grove	42714	Harned	40144	Highland (Lincoln County)	40484
Glasgow	42141*	Green Hall	41328	Harold	41635	Highland (Simpson	
	42142†	Green Hill (Jackson		Harper	41465	County)	42134
Gleanings	40052	County)	40402	Harreldsville	42256	Highland Heights	41076
Glenarm	40014	Greenhill (Warren County)	42103	Harrington Mill Estates	40065	Highland Park (Jefferson	
Glencoe	41046	Green Hills	42728	Harris	41179	County)	40209
Glendale	42740	Greenland Park	40065	Harris Grove	42071	Highland Park (Whitley	
Glendale Junction	42740	Greenmount	40741	Harrisonville	40076	County)	40769
Glen Dean	40119	Green Road	40946	Harrodsburg	40330	Highlands (Fayette	
Glengary	40118	Greensburg	42743	Harrods Creek	40027	County)	40511
Glensboro	40342	Green Spring	40222	Harrods Hills (Part of		Highlands (Jefferson	
Glens Fork	42741	Greenup	41144	Lexington)	40513	County)	40206
Glen Springs	41179	Greenview	41042	Hart	40741	High Plains	40106
Glenview (Jefferson		Greenville	42345	Hartford	42347	High Point	42086
County)	40025	Greenwood (McCreary		Hartley	41572	Highsplint	40828
Glenview (Shelby County)	40065	County)	42634	Harveyton	41719	Hightop	40741
Glenview Hills	40222	Greenwood (Pendleton		Harvy	42025	Highview (Jefferson	
Glenview Manor	40222	County)	41006	Haskinsville	42743	County)	40228
Glenville	42376	Greenwood (Warren		Hatcher	42718	Highview (Ohio County)	42320
Glenwood	41230	County)	42104	Hatfield	41514	Highway	42602
Glo	41666	Greenwood Mall (Part of		Hatton	40601	Hignite	40965
Globe	41164	Bowling Green)	42104	Hawesville	42348	Hi Hat	41636
Glomawr	41701	Gregory	42633	Hawkeegan Point	40601		

	ZIP		ZIP		ZIP		ZIP
Hikes Point (Part of Louisville)	40220*	Humble	42642	Jarvis	40906	Kentucky Oaks Mall (Part of Paducah)	42001
	40250†	Hummel	40492	Jason	41714	Kentucky State Reformatory	40032
Hilda	40351	Hunnewell	41121	Jasper Bend	42519	Kenvir	40847
Hillcrest	40475	Hunt	40391	Jeff	41751	Kenwood (Part of Louisville)	40214
Hillendale	41095	Hunter	41641	Jeffersontown	40229	Kerby Knob	40441
Hill-N-Dale	40065	Hunter Hill	40258		40269	Kernie	41465
Hill Ridge	40299	Hunters Hollow	40229		40299	Kessinger	42765
Hills and Dales	40222	Hunters Trace	40216	For specific Jeffersontown Zip Codes call (502) 266-5844, or your local postmaster.		Keswick	40769
Hillsboro	41049	Huntersville	42602	Jeffersonville	40337	Kettle	42752
Hillsdale	42134	Hunter Town	40383	Jeffrey	42157	Kettlecamp	41522
Hillside	42330	Hunting Creek (Part of Hopkinsville)	42240	Jellico	40769	Kettle Island	40958
Hill Top (Fleming County)	41039	Huntington Woods	40601	Jellico Creek	40769	Kevil	42053
Hilltop (Grant County)	41097	Huntsville	42251	Jenkins	41537	Keysburg	42204
Hilltop (Logan County)	42202	Hurley	40447	Jenkinsville	40040	Keyser Heights	41501
Hill Top (McCreary County)	42647	Hurricane Hills	40107	Jenson	40977	Kidder	42518
Hillview (Bullitt County)	40229	Hurstbourne	40222	Jeptha	41472	Kidds Crossing	42611
Hillview (Edmonson County)	42207	Hurstbourne Acres	40220	Jeremiah	41826	Kidds Store	40437
Hima	40951	Hustonville	40437	Jericho (Henry County)	40068	Kiddville	40353
Himyar	40906	Hutch	40965	Jericho (Larue County)	42748	Kildav	40828
Hinda Heights (Part of Lexington)	40502	Hutchison	40361	Jerico	42256	Kilgore	41168
Hindman	41822	Hyattsville	40444	Jessietown	40033	Kimbrell	40336
Hinkle	40953	Hyden	41749	Jetson	42252	Kimper	41539
Hinkleville	42056	Hydro	42171	Jett	40601	Kinchloes Bluff	42330
Hinton	41010	Iberia	42726	Jetts Creek	41314	Kingbee	42516
Hinton Hills	40143	Ibex	41164	Jewell City	42456	Kings Creek	41858
Hippo	41653	Ice	41858	Jimtown (Fayette County)	40505	Kings Forest	40165
Hiram	40823	Ida	42602	Jimtown (Washington County)	40069	Kingsley	40205
Hisel	40447	Ida May	41311	Jinks	40336	Kings Mountain	40442
Hiseville	42152	Idle Hour (Part of Lexington)	40502	Job	41224	Kingston (Fayette County)	40505
Hislope	42544	Idlewild	41005	Jock	42207	Kingston (Madison County)	40403
Hitchins	41146	Ilsley	42408	Johnetta	40460	Kingswood	40144
Hite	41649	Independence	41051	Johns Creek	41265	Kinniconick	41179
Hitesville	42437	Index (Part of West Liberty)	41472	Johnsontown	40272	Kino	42141
Hobson	42718	Indian Fields	40391	Johnsport (Part of Campbellsville)	42718	Kirbyton	42023
Hode	41267	Indian Hills (Carroll County)	41008	Johns Run	41143	Kirk	40143
Hodgenville	42748	Indian Hills (Christian County)	42240	Johnsville	41043	Kirkmansville	42220
Hogue	42553	Indian Hills (Franklin County)	40601	Jonancy	41538	Kirksey	42054
Holbrook	41097	Indian Hills (Hardin County)	42701	Jonesville (Grant County)	41052	Kirksville	40475
Holiday Hills (Part of Lexington)	40504	Indian Hills (Jefferson County)	40207	Jonesville (Hart County)	42757	Kirkwood	40372
Holifield	42088	Indian Hills (Russell County)	42642	Joppa	42728	Kirkwood Springs	42408
Holland	42153	Indian Hills (Scott County)	40324	Jordan	42050	Kite	41828
Holliday	41474	Indian Hills (Warren County)	42103	Josephine	40370	Kitts	40831
Hollonville	41301	Indian Hills Cherokee Section	40207	Joy	42047	Knifley	42728
Holloway Hills	40420	Indian Lake	42348	Judio	42752	Knob Lick	42154
Hollow Bill	42256	Indian Trail Square	42219	Judson	40444	Knottsville	42366
Hollow Creek	40228	Inez	41224	Judy	40334	Knowlton	40380
Hollybush	41823	Ingle	42536	Judyville	40311	Knoxfork	40906
Hollyhill	42635	Ingleside	42053	Julien	42232	Knoxville	41097
Hollyvilla	40118	Ingram	40955	Julip	40769	Kodak	41773
Holmes Mill	40843	Insco	42276	Jumbo	40484	Kona	41829
Holt	42332	Insko	41443	Junction City	40440	Korea	40387
Holy Cross	40037	Inverness Estates (Part of Frankfort)	40601	Juniper Hill (Part of Frankfort)	40601	Kragon	41339
Homer	42276	Iron Hill (Carter County)	41143	Justell	41605	Krypton	41754
Homestead	40383	Iron Hill (Lyon County)	42055	Justice	42256	Kuttawa	42055
Honaker	41639	Ironville	41102	Justiceville	41501	Kyrock	42285
Honeybee	42634	Ironworks Estates	40324	Kaler	42051	Labascus	42539
Honey Fork	41513	Iroquois (Part of Louisville)	40209	Kaliopi	41749	La Center	42056
Honey Grove	42240		40214	Kansas	42069	Lacey	41465
Honeysuckle Estates	40342	For specific Iroquois Zip Codes call (502) 368-8911, or your local postmaster.		Karlus	42629	Lacie	40075
Hooktown	41031	Iroquois Heights	40214	Katharyn	40177	Lackey	41643
Hootentown	40391	Irvine	40336	Kavanaugh	41129	Lacon	42726
Hope	40334	Irvington	40146	Kayjay	40906	Laden	40865
Hopeful Heights	41042	Irvins Store	42642	Keaton	41226	La Fayette	42254
Hopewell (Greenup County)	41163	Island	42350	Keavy	40737	La Grange	40031
Hopewell (Jefferson County)	40299	Island City	41338	Keefer	41010	Lair	41031
Hopkinsville	42240*	Isom	41824	Keene	40339	Lake	40741
	42241†	Isonville	41149	Keeneland	40223	Lake Carnico	40311
For specific Hopkinsville Zip Codes call (502) 886-5259, or your local postmaster.		Iuka	42045	Kehoe	41141	Lake City	42045
Hopson	42445	Ivel	41642	Keith	40846	Lake Dreamland	40216
Horntown	42642	Ivis	41822	Kelat	41003	Lake Louisvilla	40014
Horse Branch	42349	Ivor	41007	Kellacey	41472	Lakeside Park	41017
Horse Cave	42749	Ivy Grove	40939	Kelly	42240	Lakeview (Part of Fort Wright)	41011
Horton	42320	Ivyton	41444	Kellyville	42728	Lakeview Heights	40351
Hoskinston	40844	Jabez	42532	Keltner	42761	Lakeview-Mt. Tabor (Part of Lexington)	40502
Houston	41314	Jackhorn	41825	Ken Acres	40065	Lakeview-Woodspoint (Part of Lexington)	40509
Houston Acres	40220	Jackson	41339	Kenawood (Part of Lexington)	40505	Lakeville	41465
Hovious Ridge	42728	Jacksonville (Bourbon County)	40361	Kendall Springs	40360	Lakeway Shore	42071
Howard Mills	40334	Jacksonville (Shelby County)	40003	Kennianna	42046	Lakewood Acres (Part of Lexington)	40502
Howardstown	40028	Jackstown	40311	Keno	42558	Lamasco	42038
Howel	42262	Jacktown	40009	Kensee	40769	Lamb	42155
Howe Valley	42724	Jacobs	41150	Kenshores	42046	Lambric	41340
Hubble	40444	Jamboree	41536	Kentenia	40873	Lamero	40341
Hubbs	40921	Jamestown	42629	Kenton	41053	Lamont (McCracken County)	42053
Huddy	41535			Kenton Hills (Part of Covington)	41011	Lamont (Perry County)	41727
Hudgins	42782			Kentontown	41064	Lancaster	40444
Hudson	40145			Kenton Vale	41015	Lancelot Estates	40324
Hueys Corners	41091			Kentucky Correctional Institution for Women	40056	Lancer (Part of Prestonsburg)	41653
Hueysville	41640			Kentucky Dam Village	42044	Landsaw	41301
Huff	42250			Kentucky Heights	41166	Langdon Place	40222
Hulen	40845			Kentucky Mills (Part of Jeffersontown)	40299		

* Area Zip Code   **† Post Office Boxes**

	ZIP
Langley	41645
Langnau	40741
Lanhamtown	42539
Lansdowne (Part of Lexington)	40502
Larkslane	41817
Latonia (Part of Covington)	41015
Latonia Lakes	41015
Laura	41250
Laurel Creek	40962
Laurel Fork	40940
Laurel Ridge	42259
Lawhorn Hill	42539
Lawrenceburg	40342
Lawrenceville	41010
Lawson	41339
Lawton	41164
Layman	40819
Leafdale	42748
Leander	41228
Leatha	41465
Leatherwood	41731
Lebanon	40033
Lebanon Junction	40150
Leburn	41831
Leckieville	41514
Lecta	42141
Ledbetter	42058
Ledocio	41230
Lee City	41342
Leeco	41343
Leesburg	41031
Lees Lick	41031
LeGrande	42749
Leighton	40336
Leitchfield	42754*
	42755†
Leitchfield Crossing (Part of Munfordville)	42765
Lejunior	40849
Lemon	42327
Lenarue	40818
Lenore	40013
Lenox	41447
Lenoxburg	41040
Leon	41143
Lerose	41344
Lesbas	40741
Leslie	42717
Letcher	41832
Levee	40337
Level Green	40456
Levi	41314
Levias	42064
Lewisburg (Logan County)	42256
Lewisburg (Mason County)	41056
Lewisport	42351
Lexington	40501-96
For specific Lexington Zip Codes call (606) 231-6700, or your local postmaster.	
Lexington-Bluegrass Army Depot (Headquarters) (Fayette County)	40511
Lexington-Bluegrass Army Depot (Madison County)	40475
Lexington Mall (Part of Lexington)	40502
Liberty (Casey County)	42539
Liberty (Webster County)	42409
Liberty (Whitley County)	40769
Liberty Heights (Fayette County)	40505
Liberty Heights (Nicholas County)	40311
Liberty Road	41472
Lick Branch	41472
Lickburg	41465
Lick Creek	41540
Lick Fork	40313
Licking River	41472
Lickskillet (Logan County)	42265
Lickskillet (Meade County)	40175
Lida	40741
Liggett	40831
Ligon	41604
Liletown	42743
Lily	40740
Limaburg	41005
Limestone	41164
Limestone Springs	40165
Limeville	41175
Lincoln	40962
Lincolnshire	40220
Lindseyville	42257

	ZIP
Linefork	41833
Linton	42211
Linwood (Grayson County)	42726
Linwood (Hart County)	42757
Lionilli	41537
Lisletown	40391
Lisman	42404
Litsey	40069
Littcarr	41834
Little	41339
Little Barren	42743
Little Bear Creek	42044
Little Creek	40902
Little Cypress	42029
Little Dixie	41501
Little Georgetown (Part of Lexington)	40513
Little Hickman	40356
Little Mount	40071
Little Needmore	40422
Little Rock	40311
Little Sandy	41171
Little Tar Springs	42348
Little Texas (Part of Lexington)	40513
Littleton	40962
Littrell	42752
Livermore	42352
Livia	42327
Livingston	40445
Lloyd	41156
Load	41144
Lockards Creek	40941
Lockport	40036
Lockwood Estates	40014
Locust	41008
Locust Grove (Clark County)	40391
Locust Grove (Pendleton County)	41040
Locust Hill	40144
Lodiburg	40146
Logana	40356
Logansport	42261
Logantown	40484
Log Lick	40391
Log Mountain	40977
Logville	41465
Lola	42059
Lombard	40380
London	40741-45
For specific London Zip Codes call (606) 864-2251, or your local postmaster.	
Lone	41347
Lone Oak	42003
Lone Star	42713
Lone Way Acres	42718
Long Fork	41572
Longlick	40379
Long Ridge	40359
Long Run	40245
Long View	42701
Longview Estates	40422
Lookout	41542
Loradale (Part of Lexington)	40505
Loretto	40037
Lost Creek	41348
Lot	40769
Lothair (Part of Hazard)	41701
Lotus	40013
Louden	40769
Louellen	40828
Louisa	41230
Louisville	40201-99
For specific Louisville Zip Codes call (502) 454-1650, or your local postmaster.	

COLLEGES & UNIVERSITIES

	ZIP
Spalding University	40203
University of Louisville	40292

FINANCIAL INSTITUTIONS

	ZIP
Cumberland Federal Savings Bank	40202
Great Financial Federal	40202
Liberty National Bank and Trust Company of Kentucky	40202
National City Bank, Kentucky	40202
PNC Bank, Kentucky, Inc.	40202
Mid-America Bank of Louisville and Trust Company	40202

	ZIP
Republic Bank & Trust Company	40202
Stock Yards Bank & Trust Company	40206

HOSPITALS

	ZIP
Audubon Regional Medical Center	40217
Baptist Hospital East	40207
Jewish Hospital	40202
Methodist Evangelical Hospital	40202
Saints Mary and Elizabeth Hospital	40215
Suburban Medical Center	40207
University of Louisville Hospital	40202
Veterans Affairs Medical Center-Louisville	40206

HOTELS/MOTELS

	ZIP
Brown-a Camberley Hotel	40202
Galt House Hotel	40202
Hyatt Regency Louisville	40202
Ramada Inn Brownsboro East	40207
Seelbach Hotel	40202

MILITARY INSTALLATIONS

	ZIP
Kentucky Air National Guard, FB6161, Standiford Field	40213
Naval Surface Warfare Center, Crane Division/Naval Ordinance Station, Louisville	40214
United States Army Engineer District, Louisville	40201

	ZIP
Lovelaceville	42060
Lovely	41231
Lowell	40461
Lower Kings Addition	41175
Lower Pompey	41501
Lowes	42061
Lowmansville	41232
Loyall	40854
Lucas	42156
Lucastown	41855
Lucky Fork	41364
Lucky Stop (Part of Jeffersonville)	40337
Ludlow	41016
Luner	40456
Lusby's Mill	40359
Luther Luckett Correctional Complex	40031
Luzerne	42345
Lykins	41465
Lynch	40855
Lyndale	40391
Lyndon	40222
	40241-42
	40252
For specific Lyndon Zip Codes call (502) 425-4547, or your local postmaster.	
Lynn	41144
Lynn City	42372
Lynn Grove	42071
Lynnview	40213
Lynnville	42063
Lyons	40051
Lytten	41171
Mac	42718
McAfee	40330
McAndrews	41543
McBrayer	40342
McCarr	41544
McClure	41250
McCombs	41545
McCreary	40444
McDaniels	40152
McDowell	41647
Macedonia (Christian County)	42217
Macedonia (Jackson County)	40447
Maceo	42355
McGowan	42445
McHenry	42354
McKee	40447
McKinney	40448
McKinneysburg	41040
Mackville	40040
McQuady	40153
McRoberts	41835

	ZIP
McVeigh	41546
McVille	41005
McWhorter	40741
Madison Hills (Part of Richmond)	40475
Madisonville	42431
Madrid	42754
Magan	42343
Maggard	41465
Magnolia	42757
Magoffin	41465
Majestic	41547
Major	41314
Malaga	41301
Mallard Point	40324
Mallie	41836
Mall in St. Matthews, The (Part of St. Matthews)	40207
Malone	41451
Maloneton	41175
Mammoth Cave	42259
Manchester	40962
Mangum	42516
Manila	41238
Manitou	42436
Mannington	42217
Mannsville	42758
Manor Creek	40222
Man O' War Place (Part of Lexington)	40509
Manse	40461
Manton (Floyd County)	41649
Manton (Washington County)	40037
Maple Grove	42211
Maple Mount	42356
Maplesville	40741
Marcellus	40444
Marcum	40962
Marcus	41003
Maretburg	40456
Mariba	40345
Marion	42064
Mark	42501
Marksbury	40444
Marlowe	41858
Marrowbone	42759
Marshall (Marshall County)	42044
Marshall (Mason County)	41056
Marshallville	41452
Marshes Siding	42631
Martha	41159
Martin	41649
Martinsville	42159
Mary	41301
Mary Alice	40964
Marydell	40751
Maryhill Estates	40207
Mashfork	41465
Mason (Grant County)	41054
Mason (Magoffin County)	41465
Masonic Home (Part of Louisville)	40041
Masonville	42376
Massac	42001
Matanzas	42328
Matlock	42104
Matthew	41472
Mattingly	40111
Mattoon	42064
Mattoxtown (Part of Lexington)	40505
Maud	40069
Maulden	40486
Mavity	41129
Maxine	42776
Maxwell	42376
Mayfield	42066
Mayflower	41501
Mayking	41837
Maynard	42164
Mayo	40330
Mayo Village (Part of Pikeville)	41501
Mays Lick	41055
Maysville	41056
Maytown	41472
Maywood	40484
Mazie	41160
Meador	42164
Meadowbrook (Clark County)	40391
Meadowbrook (Shelby County)	40065
Meadowbrook Farm	40223
Meadow Creek	40759
Meadowrun	40065
Meadows (Fayette County)	40505

Place	ZIP	Place	ZIP	Place	ZIP	Place	ZIP
Meadows (Franklin County)	40601	Monica	41362	Mulberry	40065	Nicholson (Kenton County)	41051
Meadowthorpe (Part of Lexington)	40511	Monica Gardens	40065	Muldraugh	40155	Nicholson (Trigg County)	42215
Meadow Vale	40222	Monitor	40006	Mulfordtown	42459	Nickell	41332
Meadowview Estates	40220	Monkeys Eyebrow	42056	Mullikin Junction	42028	Nigh	41524
Meads	41101	Monroe	42746	Mullins	40456	Nina	40444
Meally	41234	Montclair (Fayette County)	40502	Mummie	40486	Nineteen	42320
Means	40346	Montclair (Shelby County)	40067	Munfordville	42765	Ninevah	40342
Medora	40272	Monterey	40359	Murl	42633	Nippa	41240
Meece	42501	Montgomery	42211	Murphyfork	41332	Noble	41317
Meeting Creek	42732	Montgomerys Mill	42743	Murphysville	41056	Nobob	42166
Melber	42069	Monticello	42633	Murray	42071	No Creek	42347
Melbourne	41059	Monticello Estates (Part of Lexington)	40503	Murray Hill	40222	Noctor	41357
Meldrum	40965	Montpelier	42729	Muses Mills	41065	Node	42214
Mell	42743	Montrose (Part of Lexington)	40516	Music	41168	Noetown (Part of Middlesboro)	40965
Melody Lake	40051	Montrose Park (Part of Frankfort)	40601	Myers	40311	Nolansburg	40870
Melvin	41650	Mooleyville	40143	Myra	41549	Nolin	42776
Memphis Junction	42101	Moon	41457	Mystic	40146	Nolin Lake Estates	42726
Mentor	41007	Moon Lake Estates	40324	Nada	40380	Nonesuch	40383
Meredith	42754	Moorefield	40350	Nancy	42544	Nonnel	42337
Merewood (Part of Versailles)	40383	Moore Hill	40701	Naomi	42544	Nora	42602
Meridian	41006	Moores Creek	40402	Napfor	41754	Norbourne Estates	40207
Merrick Place (Part of Lexington)	40502	Moores Ferry	40371	Naples	41102	Norfleet	42544
Merrimac	40009	Mooresville	40069	Napoleon	41046	Normal (Part of Ashland)	41101
Merrittstown	42240	Moorland	40223	Narrows	42358	Normandy	40071
Merry Oaks	42171	Moorman	42357	Narvel	42602	North Corbin	40701
Mershons	40729	Moranburg	41056	Nashtown	41189	Northfield	40222
Meshack	42167	Morehead	40351	Natlee	41010	North Irvine	40336
Meta	41501	Moreland	40437	Natural Bridge	40376	North Middletown	40357
Mexico	42064	Morgan	41040	Nazareth	40048	Northpoint Training Center	40310
Midas	41640	Morganfield	42437	Neafus	42766	Northtown	42749
Middleburg	42541	Morgantown	42261	Neave	41040	Norton Branch	41168
Middlesboro	40965	Morning Glory	41031	Nebo (Hopkins County)	42441	Nortonville	42442
Middlesboro Mall (Part of Middlesboro)	40965	Morning View	41063	Nebo (Muhlenberg County)	42345	Norwood (Jefferson County)	40222
Middleton	42134	Morrill	40455	Ned	41317	Norwood (Pulaski County)	42553
Middleton Heights (Part of Shelbyville)	40065	Morris Fork	41314	Needmore (Boyle County)	40422	Nuckols	42352
Middletown (Jefferson County)	40243* 40253†	Mortiner Station	42202	Needmore (Butler County)	42261	Nugent Cross Roads	40383
		Mortons Gap	42440	Needmore (Caldwell County)	42445	Nugym	40902
Middletown (Madison County)	40403	Mortonsville	40383	Nelse	41550	Number One	42633
Midland (Bath County)	40371	Moscow	42031	Nelson	42330	Oakbrook	41042
Midland (Muhlenberg County)	42325	Moseleyville	42301	Nelsonville	40107	Oakdale (Breathitt County)	41339
Midway (Calloway County)	42049	Mossy Bottom	41501	Neon (Part of Fleming-Neon)	41840	Oakdale (Jefferson County)	40215
Midway (Crittenden County)	42064	Motley	42103	Neon Junction	41840	Oakdale (McCracken County)	42003
Midway (Meade County)	40142	Mount Aerial	42128	Neosheo	42134	Oak Forest	42164
Midway (Woodford County)	40347	Mountain Ash	40769	Nepton	41039	Oak Grove (Christian County)	42262
Milburn	42070	Mountain Top	41164	Nerinx	40049	Oak Grove (Ohio County)	42333
Mildred	40447	Mountain Valley	41385	Nero	41265	Oak Hill (Hopkins County)	42442
Milford	41061	Mount Auburn	41006	Netty	41465	Oak Hill (Pulaski County)	42501
Millard	41562	Mount Carmel (Fleming County)	41041	Nevada	40330	Oakland	42159
Mill Creek	41055	Mount Carmel (Hopkins County)	42464	Nevelsville	42653	Oakland Mills	40311
Milledgeville	40437	Mount Eden	40046	Nevin	40342	Oaklawn Estates	41222
Miller (Fulton County)	42050	Mount Gilead (Green County)	42743	Nevisdale	40754	Oak Level	42025
Miller (Nicholas County)	40311	Mount Gilead (Monroe County)	42167	New	40359	Oakley	40729
Millersburg	40348	Mount Hermon	42157	New Allen	41601	Oak Ridge (Edmonson County)	42207
Millers Creek	40472	Mount Lebanon	40356	Newburg	40213	Oak Ridge (Kenton County)	41051
Millerstown	42726	Mount Olive (Casey County)	42539		40218-19	Oaks (Bell County)	40856
Million	40475	Mount Olive (Lee County)	41311	For specific Newburg Zip Codes call (502) 454-1650, or your local postmaster.		Oaks (McCracken County)	42003
Mill Pond	40962	Mount Olivet	41064	Newby	40475	Oaks (Ohio County)	42343
Millport	42372	Mount Pisgah	42633	New Camp	41503	Oakton	42031
Mills	40970	Mount Pleasant (Ohio County)	42333	New Castle	40050	Oakville	42263
Millseat	41101	Mount Pleasant (Trimble County)	40006	New Columbus	41010	Oakwood (Part of Lexington)	40511
Mill Springs	42632	Mount Salem	40437	Newcombe	41149	O'Bannon	40223
Millstone	41838	Mount Sherman	42764	New Concord	42076	Oddville	41031
Milltown (Adair County)	42761	Mount Sterling	40353	New Cypress (Hickman County)	42031	Odessa	40360
Milltown (Nicholas County)	40350	Mount Tabor (Larue County)	42716	New Cypress (Muhlenberg County)	42345	Offutt	41237
Millville	40601	Mount Tabor (Todd County)	42220	Newfound	40972	Ogle	40962
Millwood	42762	Mount Union	42120	Newfoundland	41171	Oil City	42141
Milner	40383	Mount Vernon (Rockcastle County)	40456	Newgarden	40121	Oil Springs	41238
Milo	41262	Mount Vernon (Scott County)	40324	New Haven	40051	Oil Valley	42633
Milton	40045	Mount Victor	42104	New Hope	40052	Okolona	40219
Mima	41457	Mount Victory	42501	New Liberty	40355		40229
Minerva	41062	Mount Washington	40047	Newman	42301		40259
Minnie	41651	Mount Zion (Allen County)	42164	New Market	40033	For specific Okolona Zip Codes call (502) 966-8049, or your local postmaster.	
Minor Lane Heights	40219	Mount Zion (Grant County)	41035	Newport	41071-76		
Minorsville	40379			For specific Newport Zip Codes call (606) 291-5250, or your local postmaster.		Olaton	42361
Mintonville	42539	Mount Zion (Pulaski County)	42553	Newport Shopping Center (Part of Newport)	41071	Olcott	40977
Miracle	40856	Mousie	41839	New Providence	42049	Old Brownsboro Place	40222
Mistletoe	41351	Moutardier	42754	New Roe	42120	Old Christianburg	40003
Mitchell Hill (Part of Madisonville)	42431	Mouthcard	41548	New Salem	40437	Old Flat Lick	40935
Mitchellsburg	40452	Moxley	40363	Newstead	42240	Oldham Acres	40059
Mize	41352	Mozelle	40858	Newt	42743	Old Landing	41358
Moberly	40475	Mud Camp	42717	Newtown	40324	Old Olga	42629
Mockingbird Valley	40207	Muddy Ford	40324	New Zion (Jackson County)	40447	Old Orchard	40447
Moct	41385	Mud Lick	42167	New Zion (Scott County)	40324	Old Pine Grove	40391
Modoc	42714	Muir (Part of Lexington)	40516	Niagara	42420	Old Stephensburg	42781
Molus	40819			Nicholasville	40340† 40356*	Old Taylor Place	40026
Monford	42252			Nichols (Bullitt County)	40177	Oldtown	41163
				Nichols (Hickman County)	42031	Old Volney	42265
						Olga	42629

Place	ZIP
Olin	40447
Olive	42025
Olive Branch (Fleming County)	41041
Olive Branch (Shelby County)	40065
Olive Hill	41164
Ollie	42259
Olmstead	42265
Olney	42408
Olympia	40358
Olympia Springs	40358
Omaha	41843
Oneida	40972
Oneonta	41007
Ono	42642
Onton	42455
Open Gates (Part of Lexington)	40503
Ophir	41459
Orangeburg	41056
Orchard Grass Hills	40014
Ordinary	41171
Oregon	40372
Orkney	41647
Orlando	40460
Orr	41180
Ortiz	42455
Orville	40057
Osborn	41635
Oscaloosa	41858
Oscar	42056
Otia	42167
Ottawa	40409
Ottenheim	40489
Otter Pond	42445
Oven Fork	40861
Overlook (Part of Eddyville)	42038
Ovesen Heights	42748
Owensboro	42301-04
For specific Owensboro Zip Codes call (502) 684-2301, or your local postmaster.	
Owensboro East (Part of Owensboro)	42303
Owensboro West (Part of Owensboro)	42301
Owenton	40359
Owingsville	40360
Owsley	41501
Oxford	40324
Oxmoor Center (Part of Louisville)	40222
Ozark	42728
Pactolus	41143
Paddock Place	40383
Paducah	42001-03
For specific Paducah Zip Codes call (502) 444-7272, or your local postmaster.	
Paint Lick	40461
Paintsville	41240
Palestine	41091
Palma	42025
Palmer	40336
Panama	41472
Panco	40972
Panola	40385
Panorama Shores	42071
Panther	42376
Paragon Park (Part of Henderson)	42420
Paris	40361*
	40362†
Park City	42160
Parkers Lake	42634
Park Hills (Fayette County)	40502
Park Hills (Kenton County)	41011
Park Hills (Rowan County)	40351
Park Lake	41093
Parkland (Part of Louisville)	40211
Parksville	40464
Parkview Shores No. 1	42164
Parkview Shores No. 2	42164
Parkway Village	40207
Parmleysville	42640
Parnell	42633
Parrot	40465
Partridge	40862
Partridge Run (Part of Henderson)	42420
Pascal	42746
Patesville	42348
Pathfork	40863
Patrick	41230
Patsey	40380

Place	ZIP
Pauley (Part of Pikeville)	41501
Paw Paw	41551
Paxton	41385
Payne Gap	41537
Paynes Depot	40324
Payneville	40157
Payton	41332
Peabody	40914
Peach Grove	41006
Peach Orchard	41230
Peak	40324
Peaks Mill	40601
Pea Ridge (Scott County)	40379
Pea Ridge (Todd County)	42220
Pearl	40940
Pearman	42726
Peasticks	40360
Pebble	40360
Pebworth	41314
Peden Mill	42134
Peedee	42236
Pelfrey	40313
Pellville	42364
Pellyton	42728
Pembroke	42266
Pence	41313
Pendleton	40055
Penile	40272
Penny (Calloway County)	42071
Penny (Pike County)	41501
Pennyrile Mall (Part of Hopkinsville)	42240
Penrod	42365
Peonia	42726
Peoples	40467
Perry Park	40363
Perryville	40468
Persimmon Grove	41001
Persimon	42167
Petersburg	41080
Petersville	41179
Petra	41004
Petrie	42348
Petroleum	42120
Petros	42274
Pettit	42301
Pewee Valley	40056
Peytona	40065
Peyton Creek	41501
Peytonsburg	42768
Peytons Store	40437
Peytontown	40475
Phelps	41553
Phillipsburg	42736
Philpot	42366
Phyllis	41554
Pickett	42761
Pickway (Part of Lexington)	40503
Pierce	42743
Pig	42171
Pigeon	41501
Pigeonroost	40962
Pike View	42757
Pikeville	41501*
	41502†
Pilgrim	41250
Pilot Oak	42085
Pilot View	40391
Pinchem (Clark County)	40391
Pinchem (Todd County)	42234
Pinckard	40383
Pinckneyville	42078
Pine Bluffs	42046
Pine Grove (Clark County)	40391
Pine Grove (Laurel County)	40740
Pine Hill	40456
Pine Knob	42721
Pine Knot	42635
Pine Meadows (Part of Lexington)	40504
Pine Mountain	40810
Piner	41063
Pine Ridge	41360
Pine Top	41843
Pineville	40977
Piney Fork	42064
Piney Grove	42501
Pink	40356
Pinnacle	41358
Pinson	41543
Pinsonfork	41555
Pioneer	41005
Pioneer Village	40165
Pippa Passes	41844
Piqua	41064
Pisgah	40383
Piso	41501

Place	ZIP
Pitts	40472
Pittsburg	40755
Plainview (Part of Jeffersontown)	40224
Plank	40978
Plano	42104
Plantation	40222
Plato	42501
Pleasant Grove Hill	42240
Pleasant Hill (Butler County)	42273
Pleasant Hill (Mercer County)	40330
Pleasant Hill (Pendleton County)	41006
Pleasant Home	40359
Pleasant Ridge	42376
Pleasant Valley (Nicholas County)	41039
Pleasant Valley (Pike County)	41501
Pleasant View	40769
Pleasure Ridge Park	40258*
	40268†
Pleasureville (Fleming County)	41093
Pleasureville (Henry County)	40057
Plum	40361
Plummers Landing	41081
Plummers Mill	41093
Plum Springs	42101
Plumville	41056
Plymouth Village	40207
Poindexter	41031
Pointer	42544
Point Leavell	40444
Point Pleasant	42718
Polksville	40371
Polkville	42159
Polly	41858
Pomeroyton	40365
Pomp	41472
Ponderosa	42726
Pondsville	42171
Pongo	40456
Poole	42444
Poortown	40356
Pope	42128
Poplar	41128
Poplar Corner	40033
Poplar Flat	41189
Poplar Grove (Fleming County)	41041
Poplar Grove (McLean County)	42372
Poplar Grove (Owen County)	41046
Poplar Highlands	41169
Poplar Hills	40213
Poplar Plains	41041
Poplarville	42501
Porter	40370
Portland (Adair County)	42761
Portland (Jefferson County)	40212
Portland (Pendleton County)	41033
Port Royal	40058
Portsmouth	41339
Possum Trot	42029
Potters	41230
Potters Fork	41537
Pottsville (Graves County)	42051
Pottsville (Washington County)	40069
Powderly	42367
Powells Creek	41501
Powersburg	42633
Powersville	41004
Prairie Village	40272
Prater	41164
Pratt	42455
Preachersville	40419
Premium	41845
Prentiss	42320
Presidential	40004
Press	41339
Preston	40366
Preston Estates	41240
Prestonia (Part of Louisville)	40213
Prestonsburg	41653
Prestonville	41008
Price	41636
Prices Mill	42134
Pricetown (Casey County)	42539
Pricetown (Fayette County)	40509

Place	ZIP
Priceville	42765
Pride	42404
Primrose	41362
Princess	41102
Princeton	42445
Printer	41655
Pritchardsville	42141
Privett	40486
Proctor	41311
Prospect	40059
Prosperity	42207
Providence (Jessamine County)	40503
Providence (Knox County)	40906
Providence (Simpson County)	42134
Providence (Trimble County)	40011
Providence (Webster County)	42450
Provo	42267
Pruden	37851
Pryorsburg	42066
Pryse	40471
Public	42501
Pueblo	42633
Pulaski	42567
Pumpkin Center	42445
Puncheon	41828
Purdy	42728
Putney	40865
Pyles	42058
Pyramid	41653
Quail	40409
Quality	42268
Quicksand	41363
Quincy	41166
Quinton	42518
Rabbit Hash	41005
Rabbit Ridge	42441
Raccoon	41557
Raceland	41169
Radcliff	40159†
	40160*
Radcliff (Part of Lexington)	40505
Ragland	42053
Railton	42171
Randolph	42129
Ransom	41531
Rapids	42134
Raven	41861
Ravenna	40472
Raymond	40176
Raywick	40060
Ready	42721
Rectorville	41056
Redbud	40828
Redbush	41219
Red Cross	42160
Redfox	41847
Red Hill (Allen County)	42164
Red Hill (Daviess County)	42376
Redhouse	40475
Red Lick	42129
Red River	42202
Redwine	41477
Reed	42451
Reeds Crossing	40475
Reedville	41143
Reedyville	42275
Regina	41559
Region	42275
Reidland	42003
Reid Village	40353
Relief	41472
Rella	40902
Renaker	41003
Render	42320
Renfro Valley	40473
Renfrow	42349
Repton	42064
Revelo	42638
Rex	42746
Rexville	41332
Reynolds Station	42368
Reynoldsville	42374
Rhea	40806
Rheber	42528
Rhoda	42210
Rhodelia	40161
Ribolt	41189
Rice Station	40336
Ricetown	41364
Riceville (Fulton County)	42041
Riceville (Johnson County)	41258
Richardson	41230
Richardsville	42270
Richelieu	42206

	ZIP
Richland	42431
Richlawn	40207
Richmond	40475*
	40476†
Richmond Mall (Part of Richmond)	40475
Rich Pond	42104
Richwood	41094
Ridgeview Estates (Part of Frankfort)	40601
Ridgeview Heights (Part of Independence)	41051
Ridgeway	40849
Riley	40328
Rileyville	40927
Rineyville	40162
Ringgold	42501
Ringos Mills	41049
Rio Vista (Part of Loyall)	40854
Risner	41649
Ritchie	41701
Ritner	42633
Rivals	40071
River	41254
River Bluff	40059
Riverfront (Part of Louisville)	40270
River Oaks	42765
River Park (Part of Lexington)	40502
River Ridge	40828
Riverside	42270
Riverside Gardens	40216
Riverview	42003
Riverview Estates (Part of Harrodsburg)	40330
Riverwood	40207
Road Junction	41522
Roaring Spring	42211
Roark	40979
Robards	42452
Robinson	41031
Robinson Creek	41560
Robinsville	40475
Robinswood	40207
Robinwood Estates (Part of Lexington)	40503
Rob Roy	42320
Rochester	42273
Rockbridge	42167
Rockcastle	42211
Rockdale (Boyd County)	41102
Rockdale (Owen County)	40359
Rockfield	42274
Rock Haven	40175
Rockholds	40759
Rockhouse	41561
Rockland	42101
Rockport	42369
Rock Springs	42406
Rockybranch	42640
Rocky Hill (Barren County)	42141
Rocky Hill (Edmonson County)	42163
Rodburn	40351
Roederer Farm Center	40031
Roff	40178
Rogers	41365
Rogers Chapel	40380
Rogers Gap	40324
Rolling Acres (Part of Frankfort)	40601
Rolling Fields	40207
Rolling Hills	40222
Rollington (Part of Pewee Valley)	40056
Rome	42301
Romine	42718
Rookwood (Part of Lexington)	40505
Roscoe	41171
Rose Crossroads	42629
Rosefork	41301
Rose Hill (Carter County)	41164
Rose Hill (Mercer County)	40330
Rose Terrace	40121
Rosetta	40146
Roseville (Barren County)	42141
Roseville (Hancock County)	42368
Rosewood	42345
Rosine	42370
Ross	41059
Rossland	40734
Rosslyn	40380
Rosspoint	40806
Rothwell	40322
Roundhill (Edmonson County)	42275

	ZIP
Round Hill (Madison County)	40475
Roundstone	40456
Rouse (Part of Covington)	41014
Rousseau	41366
Routt	40299
Rowdy	41367
Rowena	42629
Rowland	40484
Rowletts	42772
Roxana	41848
Royalton	41464
Royrader	40402
Royville	42642
Ruckerville	40391
Ruddels Mills	40361
Ruin	41171
Rumsey	42371
Rural	41514
Rush	41168
Russell	41169
Russell Heights (Part of Russell)	41169
Russell Springs	42642
Russellville	42276
Ruth	42501
Rutherford	40927
Rutland	41031
Ryan	41093
Ryland	41015
Ryland Heights	41015
Sacramento	42372
Sadieville	40370
Sadler	42754
St. Catharine	40061
St. Charles	42453
St. Dennis	40216
St. Elmo	42266
St. Francis	40062
St. Helens	41368
St. John	42701
St. Johns	42001
St. Joseph (Daviess County)	42373
St. Joseph (Marion County)	40060
St. Mary	40063
St. Matthews	40206-07
	40222
	40257
For specific St. Matthews Zip Codes call (502) 454-1650, or your local postmaster.	
St. Paul (Grayson County)	42754
St. Paul (Lewis County)	41170
St. Regis Park	40220
St. Vincent	42437
Saldee	41369
Salem (Livingston County)	42078
Salem (Russell County)	42642
Salleeton	40033
Salmons	42134
Saloma	42718
Salt Gum	40935
Salt Lick	40371
Salt River (Part of Shepherdsville)	40165
Salt Well	40311
Salvisa	40372
Salyersville	41465
Sample	40143
Samuels	40013
Sandefur Crossing	42320
Sanders	41083
Sandgap	40481
Sand Hill (Estill County)	40336
Sand Hill (Harlan County)	40823
Sand Hill (Warren County)	42101
Sand Springs (Jackson County)	40447
Sand Springs (Rockcastle County)	40456
Sandy	42325
Sandy Hook	41171
Sano	42728
Sarah	41171
Saratoga	42445
Sardis	41056
Sassafras	41759
Sassafras Ridge	42050
Sasser	40741
Saul	40981
Savage	42602
Savage Branch	41129
Savoy	40769
Savoyard	42749
Sawyer	42643
Saxton	40769
Saylor	40840

	ZIP
Scale	42025
Scalf	40982
Schley	42202
Schochoh	42202
Schultztown	42320
Schweizer	42134
Science Hill	42553
Scottown	42320
Scottsburg	42445
Scotts Station	40065
Scottsville	42164
Scoville	41314
Scranton	40322
Scuddy	41760
Seatonville	40299
Seaville	40078
Sebastians Branch	41314
Sebree	42455
Seco	41849
Sedalia	42079
Segal	42210
Seitz	41466
Select	42333
Seminary	42602
Seminary Village (Part of Louisville)	40207
Semiway	42371
Seneca Gardens	40205
Senterville	41522
Se Ree	40164
Sergent	41858
Settle	42164
Settlers Point	40059
Seventy Six	42602
Sewell	41385
Sewellton	42629
Sextons Creek	40983
Seymour	42749
Shadeland (Part of Lexington)	40502
Shady Grove (Crittenden County)	42064
Shady Grove (McCracken County)	42003
Shady Grove (Metcalfe County)	42214
Shady Nook	41031
Shafter	42501
Sha Lawn Village	42718
Shannon	41055
Sharer	42235
Sharkey	40351
Sharon	41002
Sharondale	41514
Sharon Grove	42280
Sharpe	42025
Sharpsburg	40374
Sharpsville	40330
Shawhan	40361
Shawnee (Part of Louisville)	40212
Shawnee Estates (Part of Bowling Green)	42104
Shearer Valley	42633
Shelbiana	41562
Shelby (Part of Louisville)	40217
Shelby City (Part of Junction City)	40422
Shelby Gap	41563
Shelbyville	40065*
	40066†
Shepherdsville	40165
Shepola	42544
Sherburne	41041
Sheridan	42064
Sherman	41035
Sherwood Shores	42044
Shetland	40383
Shields	40849
Shiloh	42071
Shipley	42602
Shively	40216*
	40256†
Shopville	42554
Shore Acres	40601
Short Creek	42721
Short Town	40828
Shoulderblade	41339
Shreve	42343
Shrewsbury	42721
Sibert	40962
Sidell	40962
Sideview	40353
Sideway	41164
Sidney	41564
Siler (Knox County)	40701
Siler (Whitley County)	40763
Silerville	42649
Silica	41164

	ZIP
Siloam	41175
Silver City	42261
Silver Creek	40403
Silver Grove	41085
Silverhill	41467
Silver Lake Farm (Part of Frankfort)	40601
Simmons	42354
Simpson	41301
Simpsonville	40067
Sims Fork	40902
Sinai	40342
Sinking Fork	42240
Sirocco	40108
Sitka	41255
Sizerock	41762
Skillman	42348
Skinnersburg	40379
Skycrest (Part of Lexington)	40504
Skylight	40026
Skyline	41821
Slade	40376
Slat	42633
Slate Lick	40403
Slater	42087
Slate Valley	40360
Slaughters	42456
Slavans	42653
Slemp	41763
Slickford	42633
Slick Rock	42141
Sligo	40055
Sloans Valley	42555
Smilax	41764
Smile	40351
Smith	40815
Smithfield	40068
Smithland	42081
Smith Mills	42457
Smiths Creek	41164
Smiths Grove	42171
Smith Town	42647
Smithview	42721
Smithwood	42076
Smoky Valley	41164
Smyrna	40219
Snell	42501
Snow	42602
Snow Hill	40065
Soft Shell	41831
Soldier	41173
Somerset	42501-02
	42564
For specific Somerset Zip Codes call (606) 678-5712, or your local postmaster.	
Sonora	42776
Sorgho	42301
South	42754
South Buffalo	42716
South Campbellsville (Part of Campbellsville)	42718
South Carrollton	42374
Southdown	41815
South Elkhorn (Part of Lexington)	40503
Southern Hills (Part of Richmond)	40475
South Fork (Lincoln County)	40437
Southfork (Owsley County)	41314
Southgate	41071
South Higginsport	41002
South Highlands	42066
South Hill	42261
South Irvine	40336
Southland (Part of Lexington)	40503
South Marshall	42025
South Park	40118
South Park View	40219
Southport (Part of Lexington)	40503
South Portsmouth	41174
South Ripley	41034
South Shore	41175
South Shores	40065
South Union	42283
Southville	40065
South Wallins	40873
South Williamson	41503
Southwire	42348
Spa	42256
Spann	42633
Sparksville	42728
Sparta	41086
Spears	40502

	ZIP
Speck	42728
Speedwell	40475
Speight	41572
Spence (Part of Newport)	41071
Spencer	40353
Spider	41843
Spindletop	40324
Spiro	40456
Spottsville	42458
Spring Creek	40962
Springfield	40069
Spring Grove	42437
Springhill (Hickman County)	42031
Springhill (Nelson County)	40004
Springhill (Warren County)	42101
Spring Hill Estates	40601
Springlake	41015
Springlee	40207
Spring Lick	42779
Spring Mill	40228
Spring Station	40347
Spring Valley	40222
Sprout	40350
Spruce Pine	40874
Sprule	40906
Spurlington	42718
Spurlock	40972
Squib	42501
Squiresville	40359
Stab	42557
Stacy Fork	41472
Staffordsburg	41051
Staffordsville	41256
Stambaugh	41257
Stamping Ground	40379
Stanfill	40831
Stanford	40484
Stanley	42375
Stanton	40380
Stanville	41659
Stark	41164
Star Mills	42740
Stateland (Part of Richmond)	40475
State Line	42050
Static	42602
Station Camp	40336
Station No. 1 (Part of Tompkinsville)	42167
Stay	41364
Stearns (McCreary County)	42647
Steele	41566
Steff	42780
Stella (Calloway County)	42071
Stella (Magoffin County)	41465
Stephens	41177
Stephensburg	42781
Stephensport	40170
Stepstone	40360
Steubenville	42648
Stewart	40330
Stewartsville	41097
Stiles	40028
Stillwater	41301
Stinnett	40868
Stinnettsville	40146
Stinson	41143
Stockholm	42259
Stone	41567
Stonegate	40383
Stone Hedge Estates	40324
Stonestreet	40272
Stonewall (Bracken County)	41004
Stonewall (Scott County)	40370
Stonewall Estates (Fayette County)	40503
Stonewall Estates (Franklin County)	40601
Stoney Fork	40988
Stoney Point	41034
Stony Fork Junction (Part of Middlesboro)	40965
Stop	42633
Stopover	41568
Stormking	41701
Stovall	42160
Straight Creek	40977
Strait Creek	41132
Strathmoor Gardens	40205
Strathmoor Manor	40205
Strathmoor Village	40205
Straw	42259
Strawberry	42501
Stricklett	41179
Stringtown (Anderson County)	40342

	ZIP
Stringtown (Boone County)	41040
Stringtown (Fleming County)	41049
Stringtown (Grant County)	41003
Stringtown (Lawrence County)	41230
Stringtown (Madison County)	40475
Stringtown (Magoffin County)	41465
Stringtown (McLean County)	42372
Stringtown (Mercer County)	40330
Stringtown (Muhlenberg County)	42372
Strunk	42649
Stubblefield	42088
Sturgeon	41314
Sturgis	42459
Sublett	41465
Sublimity City	40741
Subtle	42129
Sudith	40371
Sugar Creek	41095
Sugar Grove	42261
Sugar Hill	42501
Sugartit	41042
Sullivan	42460
Sulphur	40070
Sulphur Lick	42166
Sulphur Springs	42358
Sulphur Well (Jessamine County)	40356
Sulphur Well (Metcalfe County)	42129
Summer Shade	42166
Summersville	42782
Summit (Boyd County)	41102
Summit (Hardin County)	42783
Summit Hills Heights (Part of Edgewood)	41017
Sumpter	42633
Sunfish	42284
Sunny Acres (Part of Taylor Mill)	41015
Sunnybrook	42633
Sunny Corner	42348
Sunnydale	42358
Sunnyside	42101
Sunrise	41031
Sunset	41049
Sunshine (Greenup County)	41175
Sunshine (Harlan County)	40831
Susie	42633
Sussex Estates	40356
Suterville	40379
Sutherland	42376
Sutton	41562
Suwanee	42055
Swallowfield	40601
Swamp Branch	41258
Swampton	41465
Swanee Shores	41097
Swan Lake	40906
Swanpond	40906
Sweeden	42285
Sweeneyville	42718
Sweet Owen	40359
Switzer	40601
Sycamore	40223
Sycamore Estates	40383
Sylvandell	41031
Sylvania	40258
Symbol	40729
Symsonia	42082
Tabernacle	42220
Tablow	40330
Tacky Town	40988
Taffy	42347
Taft	41314
Talbert	41377
Talcum	41722
Tallega	41378
Talmage	40330
Tanbark	42752
Tanglewood (Part of Frankfort)	40601
Tanksley	40962
Tanner	42748
Tar Fork	40111
Tar Hill	42754
Tarryon No 1	42055
Tates Creek Estates	40356
Tateville	42558
Tatham Springs	40078
Tattersail Trails Estates	40701

	ZIP
Tatumsville	42044
Taulbee	41385
Taylor Mill	41015
Taylor Mines	42320
Taylorsport	41048
Taylors Store	42049
Taylorsville	40071
Teaberry	41660
Tedders	40906
Teddy	42539
Teetersville	40831
Teges	40972
Temperance	42134
Temple Hill	42141
Ten Broeck	40222
Ten Spot	40828
Teresita	40359
Terrapin	40330
Terryville	41159
Texas	40069
Texola	40471
Thealka	41240
The Colony (Fayette County)	40504
The Colony (Woodford County)	40383
Thelma	41260
The Moors	42044
The Ridge	41171
Thistleton Heights (Part of Frankfort)	40601
Thixton	40291
Thomas	41626
Thompsonville	40069
Thorn Hill (Franklin County)	40601
Thornhill (Jefferson County)	40222
Thornton	41855
Thorobred East Subdivision No. 2	42301
Thousandsticks	41766
Threeforks (Martin County)	41261
Three Forks (Warren County)	42159
Threelinks	40456
Three Mile	41144
Three Point	40815
Three Springs (Hart County)	42746
Three Springs (Warren County)	42104
Thruston	42301
Thurlow	42743
Tierra Linda (Part of Frankfort)	40601
Tierra Linda III (Part of Frankfort)	40601
Tilden	42409
Tilford	42721
Tiline	42083
Tilton	41041
Timber Lake	42518
Timberwood Lake Shores	41010
Tina	41740
Tinsley	40977
Tiny Town	42234
Tiptop	41409
Todds Point	40065
Toddville	40444
Toler	41569
Toliver	41332
Tollesboro	41189
Tolliver Town	41810
Tolu	42084
Tomahawk	41262
Tompkinsville	42167
Tonieville	42748
Toonerville	41548
Topmost	41862
Topton	40741
Torrent	41396
Totz	40870
Toulouse	41723
Touristville	42633
Tousey	40119
Town and Country (Daviess County)	42301
Town and Country (Logan County)	42276
Towne Mall (Part of Elizabethtown)	42701
Towne Square Mall (Part of Owensboro)	42301
Tracy	42133
Trailwood Lakes	40003
Tram	41663
Trammel	42164

	ZIP
Trapp	40391
Trappist	40051
Travellers Rest	41314
Treasure Island	40229
Tremont	40873
Trent	41301
Trenton	42286
Tress Shop	42220
Tribbey	41722
Tribune	42064
Tri City	42040
Trigg Furnace	42211
Trimble	42544
Trinity	41179
Trisler	42343
Trosper	40995
Troublesome	41712
Troy	40383
Tuckertown	42159
Tuggleville	40845
Tunnel Hill	42701
Turfland Mall (Part of Lexington)	40504
Turkey	41314
Turkey Creek	41570
Turkey Foot	40370
Turkeytown	40419
Turners Station	40075
Turnersville	40484
Turnertown (Butler County)	42268
Turnertown (Simpson County)	42134
Tutor Key	41263
Tuttle	40741
Tway (Part of Harlan)	40831
Twentysix	41472
Twila	40873
Twin Lakes	41091
Twin Oaks (Part of Lexington)	40503
Two Creeks	40601
Tyewhoppety	42216
Tyner	40486
Typo	41771
Tyrone	40342
Ula	42501
Ulvah	41731
Ulysses	41264
Union	41091
Union City	40475
Union Hall	40472
Union Mills	40356
Union Ridge	42365
Union Star	40171
Uniontown	42461
University Estates	42701
University Heights (Part of Hopkinsville)	42240
Uno	42749
Upchurch	42602
Upper Kings Addition	41175
Upper Tygart	41164
Upton	42784
Urban	40962
Utica	42376
Utility	42348
Uttingertown (Part of Lexington)	40516
Vada	41311
Valeria	41301
Valley Downs	40272
Valley Gardens	40258
Valley Hill	40069
Valley Oak	42501
Valley Station	40272
Valley View (Bracken County)	41002
Valley View (Madison County)	40475
Valley Village	40272
Van	41858
Vanarsdell	40330
Vanceburg	41179
Vancleve	41385
Vanderburg	42409
Vandetta	42413
Vanhook	42501
Van Lear	41265
Van Voorhis Manor	40121
Vanzant	40119
Varilla	40813
Varney	41571
Veech	40022
Venters	41522
Verda	40828
Verna Hills	40391
Verne	40769
Vernon	42151

Name	ZIP	Name	ZIP	Name	ZIP	Name	ZIP
Verona	41092	Weaverton (Part of Henderson)	42420	White Mills	42788	Wittensville	41274
Versailles	40383	Webbs	42743	White Oak (Garrard County)	40444	Witt Springs	40336
Vertrees	42785	Webbs Cross Roads	42642	White Oak (Morgan County)	41474	Wofford	40769
Vest	41772	Webbville	41180	White Oak Junction	42647	Wolf	41164
Vester	42728	Weberstown	42364	White Plains (Allen County)	42164	Wolf Coal	41339
Vicco	41773	Webster	40176	White Plains (Hopkins County)	42464	Wolf Creek	40104
Victory	40729	Wedonia	41055	Whitepost	41514	Wolfpit	41522
Village Center (Part of Harlan)	40831	Weeksbury	41667	White Run	42349	Wolverine	41339
Villa Hills	41016	Weir	42345	Whitesburg	41858	Wonder	41626
Vincent	41386	Welborn	42501	White Sulphur (Caldwell County)	42411	Wonnie	41465
Vine Grove	40175	Welchs Creek	42287	White Sulphur (Scott County)	40324	Woodbine	40771
Vineyard	40356	Welcome	42261	Whitesville	42378	Woodburn	42170
Viola	42051	Weldon	40108	White Tower	41051	Woodbury	42288
Viper	41774	Wellhope	40456	White Villa	41063	Woodford Village (Part of Versailles)	40383
Virden	40312	Wellington (Jefferson County)	40205	Whitewood	42743	Woodlake	40601
Virgie	41572	Wellington (Menifee County)	40387	Whitfield	40047	Woodland Estates	41240
Visalia	41015	Wellington Place (Part of Bardstown)	40004	Whitley City	42653	Woodland Hills	40243
Volga	41266	Wells	42330	Wiborg	42653	Woodland Park (Part of Hazard)	41701
Vortex	41301	Wellsburg	41043	Wickliffe	42087	Woodlands (Part of Frankfort)	40601
Wabaco	41701	Wells Landing	40422	Wicks Well	42431	Woodlawn (Campbell County)	41071
Wabash	42713	Wendover	41775	Widecreek	41391	Woodlawn (McCracken County)	42003
Wabd	40456	Wentz	41731	Wilbur	41124	Woodlawn (Nelson County)	40004
Waco	40385	Wesco	42431	Wild Cat	40962	Woodlawn-Oakdale	42003
Waddy	40076	Wesleyan Park (Part of Winchester)	40391	Wilder	41071	Woodlawn Park (Anderson County)	40342
Wadesboro	42048	Wesleyville	41164	Wilder	41076	Woodlawn Park (Jefferson County)	40207
Wagersville	40336	Westbend	40312	For specific Wilder Zip Codes call (606) 291-5250, or your local postmaster.		Woodman	41568
Wago	42602	West Brook	42240	Wilderness Road	42259	Woods	41653
Wait	42603	West Buechel	42218	Wildie	40492	Woodsbend	41472
Wakefield	40071	West Clifty	42754	Wildwood	40223	Woodson Bend	42518
Walden	40701	West Danville (Part of Danville)	40422	Wilhurst	41385	Woodsonville	42765
Waldo	41632	Western	42050	Willailla	40409	Woodstock	42501
Wales	41572	Western Kentucky Correctional Complex	42038	Willard	41181	Woodville	42086
Walker	40997	Western State Hospital	42240	Williams	41474	Wooleyville	42718
Walkertown (Part of Hazard)	41701	West Fairview	41101	Williamsburg	40769	Woollum	40999
Wallaceton	40461	West Future City	42053	Williamsport	41271	Wooton	41776
Wallingford	41093	West Garrett	41630	Williamstown	41097	Worthington	41183
Wallins Creek	40873	Westgate (Part of Frankfort)	40601	Willisburg	40078	Worthington Hills	40223
Wallonia	42211	West Irvine	40336	Willow (Bracken County)	41004	Worthville	41098
Walltown	40489	West Liberty	41472	Willow (Lee County)	41358	Wray Gap	42633
Walnut Grove (Allen County)	42120	West Louisville	42377	Willowcrest	40601	Wrights	42718
Walnut Grove (Caldwell County)	42411	Weston	40311	Willow Grove	41043	Wrightsburg	42327
Walnut Grove (Marshall County)	42025	West Paducah	42086	Willow Shade	42169	Wrigley	41477
Walnut Grove (Pulaski County)	42563	Westplains	42051	Willowtown	42718	Wurtland	41144
Walsh	41175	West Point	40177	Willow Tree	40472	Wyett	41171
Waltersville	40312	Westport	40077	Wilmore	40390	Wyman	42327
Walton	41094	West Prestonsburg (Part of Prestonsburg)	41668	Wilson	42406	Yaden	40769
Waltz	40351	West Russell (Part of Flatwoods)	41169	Wilsonville (Boyle County)	40422	Yancey	40831
Wanamaker	42455	West Somerset (Part of Somerset)	42564	Wilsonville (Spencer County)	40023	Yatesville	41230
Waneta	40488	West Van Lear	41268	Wilstacy	41339	Yeaddiss	41777
Warbranch	40874	Westview	40178	Wilton	40771	Yeager	41501
Warco	41645	Westwood (Boyd County)	41101	Winburn Estates (Part of Lexington)	40511	Yeaman	42361
War Creek	41339	Westwood (Jefferson County)	40222	Winchester	40391*	Yellow Rock	41311
Warfield	41267	Westwood Park (Part of Frankfort)	40601		40392†	Yelvington	42355
Warnock	41144	Wheatcroft	42463	Wind Cave	40494	Yerkes	41778
Warren	40906	Wheatley	40389	Winding Falls	40207	Yesse	42164
Warsaw	41095	Wheel	42061	Windsor	42565	Yocum	41472
Washington (Part of Maysville)	41096	Wheeler	40906	Windy	42655	York	41175
Wasioto	40977	Wheelersburg	41465	Windy Hill	42349	Yosemite	42566
Watauga	42602	Wheelwright	41669	Windy Hills	40207	Younger Creek	42701
Watch	40701	Whick	41390	Windyville	42210	Youngs Creek	40701
Waterford	40071	Whipps Millgate	40223	Wingo	42088	Yuma	42733
Watergap	41653	Whitaker (Floyd County)	41216	Winifred	41219	Zachariah	41396
Waterloo	41005	Whitaker (Letcher County)	41849	Winlow Park	42064	Zag	41472
Water Valley	42085	Whitco	41858	Winston	40495	Zandale (Part of Lexington)	40503
Waterview	42786	White City (Hopkins County)	42464	Winston Park (Part of Taylor Mill)	41015	Zebulon	41501
Watkinsville	40379	White City (Larue County)	42748	Winwright	41501	Zelda	41129
Watterson Park	40213	White Hall	40475	Wiscoal	41759	Zion (Henderson County)	42420
Watterson Park	40218	Whitehouse	41269	Wisconsin	41759	Zion (Todd County)	42234
For specific Watterson Park Zip Codes call (502) 454-1650, or your local postmaster.		White Lily	42501	Wisdom	42129	Zion Hill	40347
Watts	41348			Wisemantown	40336	Zion Station	41035
Waverly	42462			Wises Landing	40006	Zoe	41397
Waverly Hills	40272			Wiswell	42071	Zoneton (Part of Pioneer Village)	40165
Wax	42726					Zula	42603
Wayland	41666						
Waynesburg	40489						

* Area Zip Code † Post Office Boxes

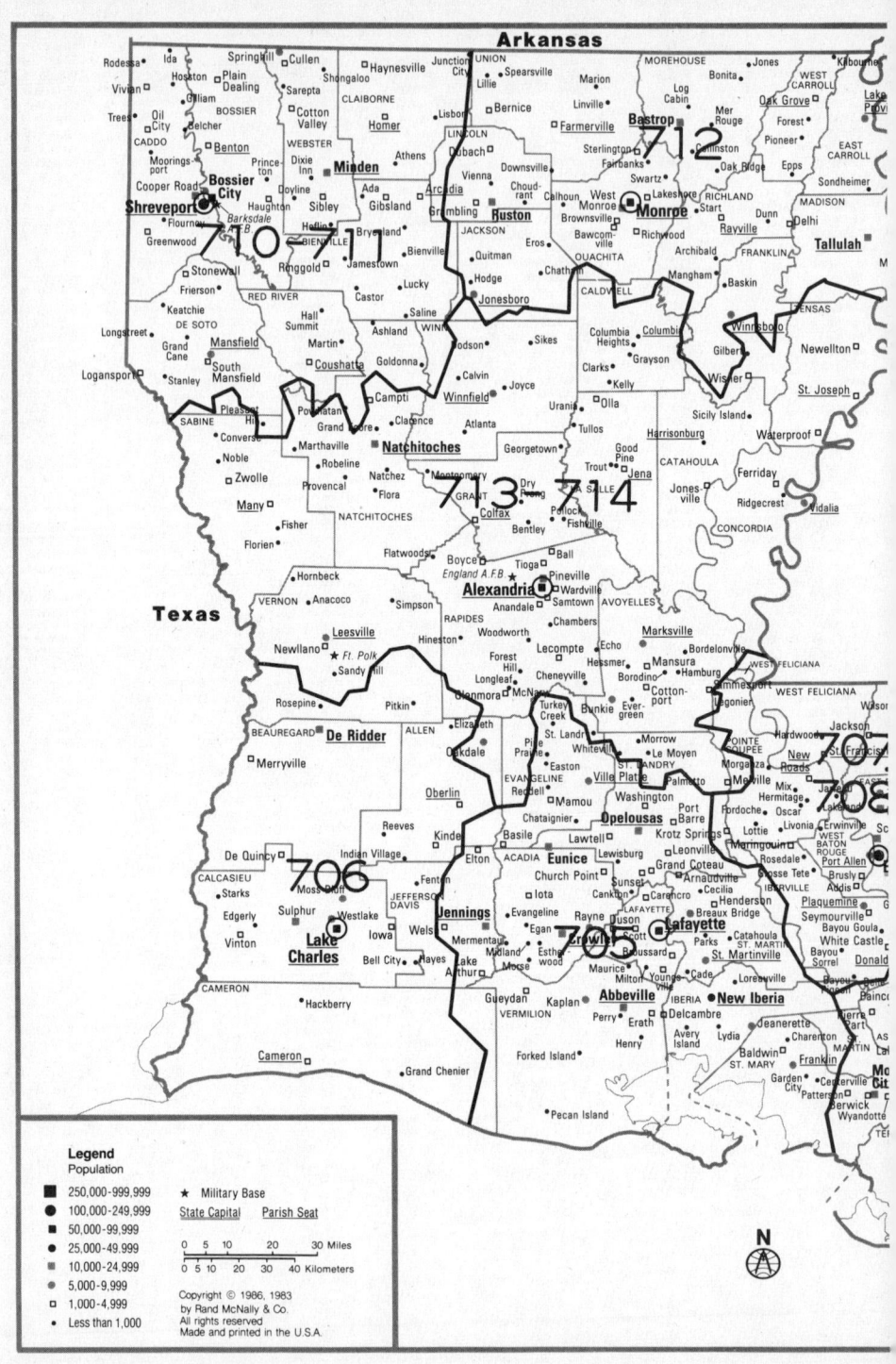

Arkansas

Texas

710
711
712
713
714
706
705
707
708
709

Rodessa Ida Springhill Cullen Haynesville Junction UNION Spearsville Marion MOREHOUSE Bonita Jones Kilbourne
Vivian Plain Dealing Shongaloo City Lillie Linville Log Cabin Oak Grove Forest WEST CARROLL Lake Prov
Trees Oil City Hosston CLAIBORNE Bernice Sterlington Mer Rouge Collinston Pioneer Epps EAST CARROLL
Moorings port Belcher Cotton Valley Lisbon LINCOLN Dubach Downsville West Monroe Swartz Oak Ridge Sondheimer
CADDO Prince ton BOSSIER Homer Athens Vienna Choud rant Calhoun Brownsville Richwood RICHLAND Start Dunn Delhi MADISON Tallulah
Cooper Road Benton WEBSTER Dixie Inn Minden Arcadia Grambling Ruston Monroe Archibald FRANKLIN
Bossier City Haughton Doyline Sibley Ada Gibsland JACKSON Quitman Eros Mangham Baskin
Shreveport Barksdale A.F.B. Heflin Bryceland Bienville Hodge CALDWELL TENSAS Winnsboro Newellton
Greenwood BIENVILLE Jamestown Lucky Castor Saline Columbia Heights Columbia Gilbert Wisner St. Joseph
Stonewall RED RIVER Ringgold Jonesboro Clarks Grayson Sicily Island Waterproof
Frierson Hall Summit Ashland WINN Sikes Urania Kelly Harrisonburg
Keatchie DE SOTO Martin Goldonna Calvin Joyce Olla Good Pine Ferriday
Longstreet Grand Cane Mansfield Coushatta Winnfield Tullos Trout Jena CATAHOULA Ridgecrest Vidalia
Logansport South Mansfield Stanley Campti Clarence Atlanta Georgetown GRANT Pollock Fishville Jones ville CONCORDIA
Pleasant Hill Powhatan Natchitoches Montgomery Dry Prong LA SALLE Bentley Ball
Converse Marthaville Natchez Flora Colfax Tioga Pineville
Noble Robeline RAPIDES Boyce England A.F.B. Alexandria Wardville Samtown AVOYELLES Marksville
Zwolle Provencal NATCHITOCHES Flatwoods Anandale Chambers
Many Fisher VERNON Woodworth Lecompte Echo Mansura Hamburg WEST FELICIANA
Florien Hornbeck Anacoco Simpson Hineston Forest Hill Cheneyville Borodino New Roads
Leesville Woodworth Hessmer Bordelonville POINTE COUPEE
Newllano Ft. Polk Sandy Hill Longleaf Cotton port Evergreen Lettsworth Livonia
Rosepine Pitkin Glenmora McNary Turkey Creek Bunkie Morrow Le Moyen Fordoche
BEAUREGARD De Ridder ALLEN Elizabeth Oakdale Pine Prairie Whiteville ST. LANDRY Palmetto Melville Mix Livonia WEST BATON ROUGE
Merryville Oberlin Reddell Mamou Washington Port Barre Oscar Erwinville
Reeves Kinder Chataignier Opelousas Krotz Springs Lottie IBERVILLE Port Allen
De Quincy Indian Village Elton Basile Lawtell EVANGELINE Leonville Rosedale Grosse Tete Plaquemine
CALCASIEU Starks Fenton ACADIA Eunice Church Point Sunset Grand Coteau Arnaudville Cecilia Seymourville
Edgerly Sulphur Westlake Iota Carencro Henderson St. Gabriel
Vinton Lake Charles Iowa Welsh Jennings Midland Mermentau Rayne Scott Lafayette Breaux Bridge Catahoula ST. MARTIN Bayou Goula White Castle
Bell City Hayes Lake Arthur Estherwood Crowley Duson Youngsville Cade St. Martinville Loreauville Donald
CAMERON Gueydan Kaplan Abbeville Milton Maurice New Iberia Jeanerette Charenton
Hackberry VERMILION Perry Erath IBERIA Delcambre Baldwin Franklin
Cameron Forked Island Henry Avery Island Lydia ST. MARY Garden City Patterson Berwick

N

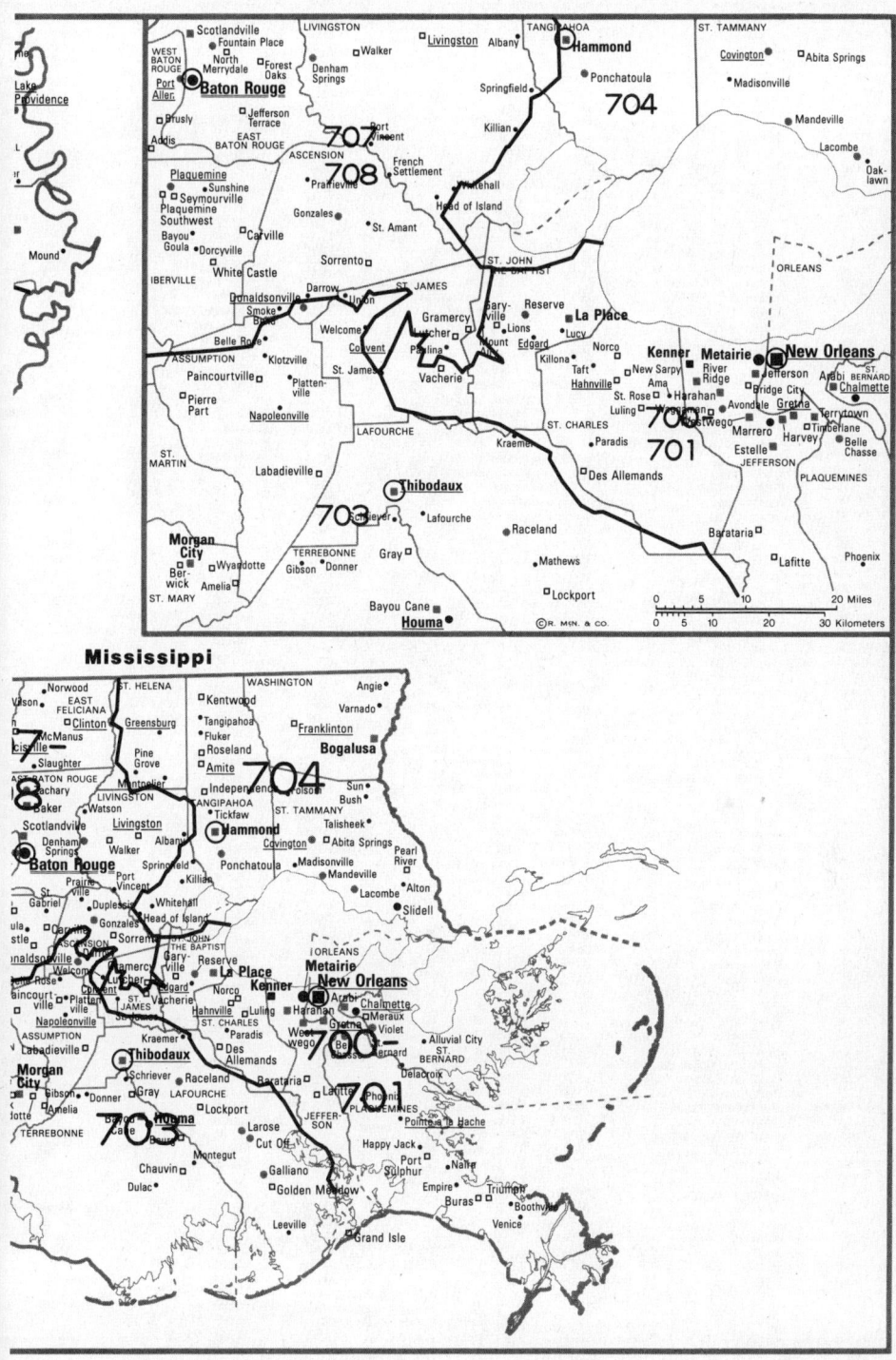

	ZIP
Abbeville	70510*
	70511†
Abby Plantation	70301
Aben	70346
Abington	71052
Abita Springs	70420
Acadia	70301
Acadia Academy	70535
Acme	71316
Acy	70774
Ada	71080
Addis	70710
Adeline	70544
Adner	71037
Advance (Part of Hodge)	71247
Afton	71282
Aimwell	71401
Airline Park	70003
Airview Terrace (Part of Alexandria)	71301
Ajax	71450
Akers	70421
Albania	70544
Albany	70711
Alberta	71016
Alco	71446
Alden Bridge	71006
Alexandria	71301-15
For specific Alexandria Zip Codes call (318) 484-4637, or your local postmaster.	
Alexandria Mall (Part of Alexandria)	71301
Alfalfa	71409
Alfords	70720
Algiers (Part of New Orleans)	70114
Alice B	70538
Alice C	70538
Allemand	70360
Allen	71469
Allendale	70767
Alliance	70037
Allon	70760
Alluvial City	70085
Aloha	71417
Aloysia	70788
Alsen	70807
Alto	71269
Alton	70458
Alvin Callender	70037
Ama	70031
Amelia	70340
Amite	70422
Anacoco	71403
Anandale	71301
Andrew	70548
Andrew Guillot Subdivision	70301
Angelina	70076
Angie	70426
Annadale	70788
Ansley	71270
Antioch (Claiborne Parish)	71040
Antioch (Lincoln Parish)	71275
Antonia	71467
Antonio	70767
Antrim	71064
Arabi	70032
Ararat	70601
Arbroth	70720
Arcadia	71001
Archibald	71218
Archie	71343
Arcola	70456
Ardoyne	70360
Argo	71343
Argyle	70360
Arizona	71040
Arklatex (Part of Mooringsport)	71060
Arlington	70808
Armistead	71019
Arnaudville	70512
Ashland (Natchitoches Parish)	71002
Ashland (Terrebonne Parish)	70360
Ashley	71282
Ashton	70538
Athens	71003
Atlanta	71404
Attakapas Landing	70390
Audubon (Part of Baton Rouge)	70806
Audubon Terrace	70808
Augusta (Iberville Parish)	70788
Augusta (Plaquemines Parish)	70037
Avalon	70392

	ZIP
Avandale	71366
Avery Island	70513
Avondale	70094
Aycock	71001
Azucena	71375
Bagdad	71417
Bains	70775
Baker	70704†
	70714*
Baldwin	70514
Ball	71405
Bancroft	70653
Bankers	70582
Banks	70807
Banks Springs	71418
Baptist	70403
Barataria	70036
Barber Spur	70586
Bardel	71269
Barnet Springs (Part of Ruston)	71270
Barron	71328
Barton	70346
Basile	70515
Baskin	71219
Baskinton	71219
Bastrop	71220*
	71221†
Batchelor	70715
Baton Rouge	70801-98
For specific Baton Rouge Zip Codes call (504) 763-3700, or your local postmaster.	
Batree	70090
Bawcomville	71291
Bayou Barbary	70754
Bayou Blue	70360
Bayou Cane	70359
Bayou Chicot	70586
Bayou Crab	70390
Bayou Current	71353
Bayou Gauche	70030
Bayou Goula	70716
Bayou Pigeon	70764
Bayou Sale	70538
Bayou Sorrel	70764
Baywood	70739
Beach Grove	71277
Beachview (Part of Kenner)	70065
Bear Creek	71008
Bear Skin	71266
Beaver	71463
Bee Bayou	71269
Beech Springs	71247
Beekman	71220
Beggs	71322
Bel	70658
Belah	71371
Belair	70040
Belair Cove	70586
Belcher	71004
Bell City	70630
Belle Amie	70345
Belle Chasse	70037
Belledeau	71341
Belle Place	70552
Belle Point	70084
Belle River	70339
Belle Rose	70341
Belle Terre (Assumption Parish)	70346
Belle Terre (Iberville Parish)	70764
Belleview	70570
Bellevue (Bossier Parish)	71037
Bellevue (Caldwell Parish)	71418
Bellfontaine	70815
Bell Helene	70734
Bellwood	71468
Belmont (Sabine Parish)	71406
Belmont (St. James Parish)	70743
Belmont (West Baton Rouge Parish)	70767
Benson	71419
Bentley	71407
Benton	71006
Bermuda	71456
Bernice	71222
Bertie	70390
Bertrandville (Assumption Parish)	70390
Bertrandville (Plaquemines Parish)	70040
Berwick	70342
Bethany	71007
Bienville	71008
Big Bend	71318
Big Branch	70445

	ZIP
Big Cane	71356
Big Creek	71219
Big Island	71328
Big Woods	70668
Billeaud	70518
Bissonnet	70003
Bivens	70653
Blackburn	71038
Black Hawk	71373
Blade	71342
Blanchard	71009
Blanche	71433
Blanks	70717
Blankston	71202
Blond	70435
Bluff Creek	70722
Bob Acres	70560
Bodcau	71037
Bodoc	71329
Bogalusa	70427-29
For specific Bogalusa Zip Codes call (504) 735-5921, or your local postmaster.	
Bohemia	70082
Bolden	71358
Boleyn	71450
Bolinger	71064
Bolivar	70444
Bonaire	70808
Bond	71463
Bonfouca	70458
Bonita	71223
Bon Marche Mall (Part of Baton Rouge)	70806
Bon Secour	70086
Book	71343
Boone's Corner	70605
Boothville	70038
Boothville-Venice	70038
Bordelonville	71320
Borgne Mouth	70092
Borodino	71355
Bosco	71202
Boscoville	70570
Bossier City	71111-13
	71171-72
For specific Bossier City Zip Codes call (318) 746-1481, or your local postmaster.	
Boston	70533
Boudreaux Canal	70344
Bourg	70343
Boutte	70039
Boyce	71409
Braithwaite	70040
Branch	70516
Breard (Part of Monroe)	71203
Breaux Bridge	70517
Breezy Hill	71467
Brewton's Mill	71031
Bridge City	70094
Brignac	70737
Bristol	70584
Brittany	70718
Broadmoor (Lafayette Parish)	70501
Broadmoor (Orleans Parish)	70125
Broadmoor (Terrebonne Parish)	70360
Broadview (Part of Baton Rouge)	70815
Brooks	70760
Brouillette	71351
Broussard	70518
Brown	71016
Brownell	71295
Brownfields	70811
Brown Heights	70714
Brownlee	71111
Brownsville-Bawcomville	71291
Brownville (Caldwell Parish)	71418
Brownville (Ouachita Parish)	71291
Brule	70372
Brule Guillot	70301
Bruly La Croix	70788
Bruly Saint Martin	70341
Brusle Saint Vincent	70390
Brusly	70719
Bryant (Part of New Iberia)	70560
Bryceland	71014
Buckeye	71328
Buckner	71269
Bueche	70720
Buhler	70663
Bull Run	70395
Bunkie	71322

	ZIP
Buras	70041
Buras-Triumph	70041
Burkplace	71016
Burr Ferry	71403
Burroughs	71418
Burwood	70091
Burton Lane	70086
Bush	70431
Bushes	71295
Bywater (Part of New Orleans)	70117
Caddo (Part of Oil City)	71061
Caddo Station	71082
Cade	70519
Cadeville	71238
Caernarvon	70040
Caffery	70538
Calcasieu (Allen Parish)	71433
Calcasieu (Rapides Parish)	71433
Calhoun	71225
Calumet	70392
Calvin	71410
Camelia Gardens (Part of Alexandria)	71301
Cameron	70631
Camp Beauregard	71301
Camperdown	70538
Campti	71411
Cancienne	70390
Canebrake	71334
Caney	71446
Cankton	70584
Cannonburg	70788
Capitan	70592
Capitol (Part of Baton Rouge)	70804
Caplis	71111
Carencro	70520
Carlisle	70042
Carlton	71225
Carlyss	70663
Carmel	71052
Caroline	70552
Carrollton (Part of New Orleans)	70118
Carrollton Central Plaza (Part of New Orleans)	70118
Carrolwood	70068
Carterville	71064
Carthage Bluff Landing	70462
Cartwright	71227
Carville	70721
Caspiana	71115
Castle Village	71301
Castor	71016
Catahoula	70582
Catherine	70716
Cat Island	71418
Catuna	71052
Cavett	71004
Cecile	71105
Cecilia	70521
Cedar Crest	70816
Cedar Glen	70811
Cedar Grove (Assumption Parish)	70372
Cedar Grove (Caddo Parish)	71106
Cedar Grove (Plaquemines Parish)	70037
Cedarton	71227
Centenary (Part of Shreveport)	71104
Center Point	71323
Centerville (Evangeline Parish)	71367
Centerville (St. Mary Parish)	70522
Central (East Baton Rouge Parish)	70818
Central (St. James Parish)	70723
Central (Terrebonne Parish)	70360
Chacahoula	70395
Chackbay	70301
Chalmette	70043*
	70044†
Chalmette Vista	70043
Chamale Cove (Part of Slidell)	70460
Chamberlin	70767
Chambers	71346
Chandler Park (Part of Alexandria)	71301
Charenton	70523
Charles Park (Part of Alexandria)	71301
Charlotte	70560
Chase	71324

	ZIP		ZIP		ZIP		ZIP
Chataignier	70524	Coteau Holmes	70582	Downsville	71234	Evans	70639
Chateau Village (Part of		Coteau Rodaire	70512	Downtown (Part of		Evelyn	71052
Kenner)	70065	Cotton Plant	71435	Alexandria)	71309	Evergreen (Avoyelles	
Chatham	71226	Cottonport	71327	Downtown (Part of Baton		Parish)	71333
Chatman Town	70090	Cotton Valley	71018	Rouge)	70821	Evergreen (Webster	
Chauvin	70344	Couchwood	71018	Downtown (Part of		Parish)	71055
Chef Menteur (Part of		Coulon Plantation	70301	Monroe)	71201	Evergreen Fashion Square	70808
New Orleans)	70126	Country Club Subdivision	70301	Downtown (Part of		Extension	71239
Cheneyville	71325	Coushatta	71019	Morgan City)	70380	Fairbanks	71240
Cheniere	71291	Covington	70433-35	Downtown (Part of		Fairlane	70360
Cherokee Court	70123	For specific Covington Zip		Shreveport)	71101	Fairmont	71417
Cherokee Village (Part of		Codes call (504) 892-2421, or		Doyle (Part of Livingston)	70754	Fairview	71373
Alexandria)	71301	your local postmaster.		Doyline	71023	Farmer Spur (Part of	
Cherry Grove	70655	Covington Country Club		Drew (Calcasieu Parish)	70605	Vienna)	71270
Chesbrough	70444	Estates	70433	Drew (Ouachita Parish)	71291	Farmerville	71241
Chestnut	71070	Cow Island	70510	Drusilla (Part of Baton		Faubourg	70589
Chickama	71346	Cravens	70656	Rouge)	70809	Federal Correctional	
Chickasaw	71263	Creedmoor	70085	Dry Creek	70637	Institution	71463
Chinchuba	70448	Creole	70632	Dry Prong	71423	Felixville	70722
Chipola	70441	Crescent (Iberville Parish)	70764	Dubach	71235	Fellowship	71371
Chitimacha Indian		Crescent (Terrebonne		Dubberly	71024	Fenris	70554
Reservation	70523	Parish)	70360	Duckroost	70774	Fenton	70640
Chloe	70647	Creston	71020	Dufresne	70070	Ferriday	71334
Choctaw (Iberville Parish)	70767	Crew Lake	71269	Dukedale	71006	Ferry Lake	71061
Choctaw (Lafourche		Crews	71454	Dulac	70353	Fields	70653
Parish)	70301	Crichton	71019	Dunbarton	71334	Fifth Ward	71351
Chopin	71447	Cross-Road	71435	Dunn	71232	Fillmore	71037
Choudrant	71227	Crossroads (Lincoln		Duplessis	70728	Fisher	71426
Choupique (Lafourche		Parish)	71235	Dupont (Avoyelles Parish)	71329	Fishville	71467
Parish)	70301	Cross Roads (Red River		Dupont (Pointe Coupee		Fiske	71263
Choupique (St. Mary		Parish)	71019	Parish)	70783	Five Forks	71483
Parish)	70538	Crowley	70526*	Duson	70529	Flat Creek	71479
Chula	70372		70527†	Dutch Town	70734	Flatwoods	71427
Church Point	70525	Crown Point	70072	Dykesville	71038	Flora	71428
Church Spur	70390	Crowville	71230	Easleyville	70441	Florence	70538
Cinclare	70767	Crozier	70360	Eastgate Plaza (Part of		Florien	71429
Cindy Park	70075	Cullen	71021	Shreveport)	71108	Florrissant	70085
Claiborne (Ouachita		Curry	71483	East Hammond (Part of		Flournoy	71109
Parish)	71291	Curtis	71112	Hammond)	70401	Floyd	71266
Claiborne (St. Tammany		Cut Off	70345	East Hodge	71247	Fluker	70436
Parish)	70433	Cypremort	70538	East Louisiana State		Foley (Allen Parish)	70655
Claibourne Gardens	70094	Cypress (Natchitoches		Hospital	70748	Foley (Assumption Parish)	70390
Clare	71429	Parish)	71420	Easton	70586	Folsom	70437
Clarence	71414	Cypress (Ouachita Parish)	71291	East Point	71025	Fondale	71201
Clarks	71415	Cypress Gardens (St.		East Side (Part of Lake		Forbing	71106
Clay	71270	Bernard Parish)	70075	Charles)	70615	Fordoche	70732
Clayton	71326	Cypress Gardens		Eastside Columbia	71418	Foreman	70815
Clayton Junction (Part of		(Terrebonne Parish)	70360	Eastwood	71037	Forest	71242
Clayton)	71326	Cypress Island	70582	Ebenezer	70526	Forest Glen	70445
Clearview Shopping		Daigleville (Part of Houma)	70360	Echo	71330	Forest Hill	71430
Center	70002	Dalcour	70040	Eden	71371	Forest Oaks	70815
Clearwater	71325	Danville	71008	Eden Isle	70458	Forest Park	71291
Clifton (Rapides Parish)	71455	D'Arbonne	71227	Edgard	70049	Forked Island	70510
Clifton (Washington		Darlington	70441	Edgefield	71019	Forksville	71225
Parish)	70438	Darnell	71266	Edgerly	70668	Fort De Russy	71351
Clinton	70722	Darrow	70725	Edna	70648	Fort Jesup	71449
Clio	70449	Daspit	70560	Effie	71331	Fort Necessity	71243
Clotilda	70394	Davant	70046	Egan	70531	Fort Polk	71459
Cloutierville	71416	Dean	71260	Elam	71378	Fort Polk North	71459
Clovelly Farms	70345	Dean Chapel	71291	Elba	71353	Fort Polk South	71459
Cocodrie	70344	De Broeck Landing	71106	Eliza	70764	Fosters (Part of Bossier	
Cocoville	71350	Deerford	70791	Elizabeth	70638	City)	71111
Coker	71052	Deer Park	71373	Ellendale	70360	Fosters Canal	70083
Coleman	71282	Dehlco	71269	Ellis	70526	Foules	71326
Colfax	71417	Delacroix (St. Bernard		Ellsworth	70360	Fourborge	70586
Colgrade	71483	Parish)	70085	Elmer (Lafourche Parish)	70301	Four Corners	70538
College (Part of		Delacroix (St. Martin		Elmer (Rapides Parish)	71424	Four Forks (Caddo Parish)	71046
Hammond)	70401	Parish)	70582	Elmfield	70390	Four Forks (Richland	
Collinsburg	71064	Del Bueno Park	70075	Elm Grove	71051	Parish)	71259
Collinston	71229	Delcambre	70528	Elm Hall	70390	Fowler	71240
Colonial Heights	71109	Delhi	71232	Elm Hall Junction	70390	Francis Place	70075
Colquitt	71038	Delta	71233	Elm Park	70775	Franklin	70538
Columbia (Caldwell		Delta Farms	70374	Elmwood	70123	Franklinton	70438
Parish)	71418	Denham Springs	70726*	Elton	70532	Fred	70791
Columbia (St. John the			70727†	Empire	70050	Freetown (Assumption	
Baptist Parish)	70049	Dennis Mills	70726	Encalade	70083	Parish)	70390
Columbia Heights	71418	Denson	70449	Energy Center (Part of		Freetown (St. Mary Parish)	70538
Commerce Park (Part of		Dent Terrace	70808	Lafayette)	70598	French Settlement	70733
Baton Rouge)	70810	De Quincy	70633	England Air Force Base	71303	Frenier	70068
Como	71295	De Ridder	70634	Englewood	71282	Friendship	71008
Concession	70037	Derry	71416	English Turn	70040	Frierson	71027
Concord	71263	Des Allemands	70030	Enola	70390	Frisco	70755
Constance Beach	70631	De Selle	71301	Enon	70438	Frogmore	71334
Consuella	71375	Dess	71429	Enterprise (Catahoula		Frost	70754
Contreras	70085	Destrehan	70047	Parish)	71425	Frost Town	71234
Convent	70723	Devalls	70767	Enterprise (Iberia Parish)	70544	Fryeburg	71039
Converse	71419	Deville	71328	Eola	71322	Fullerton	70642
Conway	71260	Dewdrop	71220	Epps	71237	Fulton	70657
Coon	70715	Diamond	70083	Erath	70533	Funston	71049
Cooper Road	71107	Dixie	71107	Eros	71238	Gaars Mill	71422
Coopers	71446	Dixie Acres	71280	Erwinville	70729	Gahagan	71019
Copenhagen	71418	Dixie Gardens	71105	Essen Heights	70808	Galbraith	71447
Cora	71444	Dixie Inn	71055	Estelle	70072	Galion	71223
Corbin (Part of Walker)	70785	Dixon Correctional		Esther	70510	Galliano	70354
Corey	71202	Institute	70748	Estherwood	70534	Galva	70421
Corinth	71235	Dodson	71422	Ethel	70730	Galvez	70769
Cornerview	70737	Donaldsonville	70346	Eunice	70535	Gandy Spur	71429
Cornor	39669	Donner	70352	Eureka	71234	Gansville	71422
Cortana Mall (Part of		Dorcyville	70788	Eva	71354	Garden City	70540
Baton Rouge)	70815	Douglas	71227	Evangeline	70537	Gardere	70810

	ZIP		ZIP		ZIP		ZIP
Gardner	71431	Gueydan	70542	Hollywood (Terrebonne Parish)	70360	Jonesville	71343
Garland	71322	Gulf Outport (Part of New Orleans)	70146	Hollywood (West Feliciana Parish)	70775	Jordan Hill	71483
Garyville	70051	Gullett	70422			Joyce	71440
Gassoway	71254	Gum Ridge	71264	Holmwood	70647	Junction	70653
Gateway (Part of Baton Rouge)	70835	Gurley	70730	Holum	71435	Junction City	71749
Gayles	71105	Haaswood	70452	Home Place	70083	Kadesh	71454
Ged	70668	Hackberry	70645	Homer	71040	Kahns	70767
Geismar	70734	Hacketts Corner	70630	Hopedale	70085	Kaplan	70548
Gentilly (Part of New Orleans)	70122	Hackley	70438	Hope Villa	70808	Katy	70538
Georgetown	71432	Hagewood	71457	Hornbeck	71439	Keatchie	71046
Georgeville	70443	Hahnville	70057	Horse Bluff Landing	70462	Kedron	70422
Georgia	70390	Haile	71260	Hosston	71043	Keithville	71047
Getty Camp	70091	Haire	70548	Hotwells	71409	Kelly	71441
Gheens	70355	Half Way (Assumption Parish)	70346	Houltonville	70447	Kellys	71270
Gibbstown	70630	Halfway (Red River Parish)	71019	Houma	70360-64	Kendale	70062
Gibsland	71028	Hall Summit	71034	For specific Houma Zip Codes call (504) 868-3800, or your local postmaster.		Kendrick's Ferry	71336
Gibson	70356	Hamburg	71339			Kenilworth	70085
Gilark	71055	Hammet	71373	Howard	71105	Kenmore	70757
Gilbert	71336	Hammond	70401-04	Hubertville (Part of Jeanerette)	70544	Kennedy Heights	70094
Gilleyville	71269	For specific Hammond Zip Codes call (504) 345-6014, or your local postmaster.		Hudson	71422	Kenner	70062-65
Gilliam	71029			Hughes	71006	For specific Kenner Zip Codes call (504) 469-1506, or your local postmaster.	
Gillis	70611	Hanna	71019	Humphreys	70356		
Girard	71269	Hanson City (Part of Kenner)	70062	Hundley	70535	Kenner Junction (Part of Kenner)	70062
Glade	71343	Happy Jack	70083	Hunter	71052	Kentwood	70444
Glencoe	70538	Harahan	70123	Huntington (Part of Shreveport)	71129	Kickapoo	71030
Glen Dale	70049	Hardwood	70775	Huron	70512	Kilbourne	71253
Glenmora	71433	Hargis	71454	Hurricane	71003	Killian	70462
Glenwild	70342	Hargrove	70633	Husser	70442	Killona	70066
Glenwood	70390	Harlem (Plaquemines Parish)	70046	Hutton	71446	Kinder	70648
Gloria	70037	Harlem (Vermilion Parish)	70510	Hyde (Part of Simmesport)	71369	King Hill	71019
Gloster	71030	Harmon	71036	Hymel	70090	Kingston	71032
Glynn	70736	Harrisonburg	71340	Iberville	70776	Kingsville	71360
Godchaux	70394	Harvey	70058*	Ida	71044	Kiroli Woods	71291
Godchaux Community	70068		70059†	Idlewild (St. Mary Parish)	70392	Kisatchie	71468
Gold Dust	71322	Hathaway	70532	Idlewild (Terrebonne Parish)	70364	Kleinpeter	70808
Golden Meadow	70357	Haughton	71037	Ikes	70634	Klondyke	70343
Golden Star Plantation	70090	Hawthorne	71446	Independence	70443	Klotzville	70341
Goldman	71375	Hayes	70646	Indian Bayou	70578	Kolin	71360
Goldonna	71031	Haynesville	71038	Indian Mound	70739	Kolter (Part of Keatchie)	71046
Goldridge	70788	Hazelwood	70577	Indian Village (Allen Parish)	70648	Koran	71037
Gonzales	70707†	Head of Island	70449	Indian Village (Ouachita Parish)	71225	Kraemer	70371
	70737*	Hearn Island	71418	Industrial (Part of Shreveport)	71107	Krotz Springs	70750
Goodbee	70433	Hebert	71418	Ingleside	70390	Kurthwood	71443
Good Hope	70079	Hecker	70647	Innis	70747	Laark	71250
Good Pine	71342	Heflin	71039	Inniswold	70809	Labadieville	70372
Goodwill	71263	Helena	71366	International Trade Mart (Part of New Orleans)	70130	Labarre	70751
Goodwood	71353	Henderson	70517	Intracoastal City	70510	Lacamp	71444
Gordon	71038	Henfer Park	70123	Iota	70543	Lacassine	70650
Gorum	71434	Henry	70533	Iowa	70647	Lachute	71115
Goudeau	71333	Hermitage	70749	Irish Bend	70538	Lacombe	70445
Gouldsboro (Part of Gretna)	70053	Hessmer	71341	Irma	71457	Lacour	70715
Grambling	71245	Hester	70743	Ironton	70083	Lafayette	70501-09
Gramercy	70052	Hewes	70762	Isabel	70427		70593-98
Grand Bayou	71052	Hickory (Avoyelles Parish)	71327	Isle Labbe	70582	For specific Lafayette Zip Codes call (318) 269-4800, or your local postmaster.	
Grandbois	70343	Hickory (St. Tammany Parish)	70452	Istrouma (Part of Baton Rouge)	70805		
Grand Caillou	70360	Hickory Grove	71328	Ivan	71006	Lafayette Square (Part of New Orleans)	70130
Grand Cane	71032	Hickory Valley	71473	Jackson	70748	Lafayette Woods	70360
Grand Chenier	70643	Hicks	71446	Jackson Road	70748	Lafitte	70067
Grand Coteau	70541	Hico	71235	Jacoby	70753	Lafourche	70301
Grand Ecore	71457	Higginbotham	71525	Jamestown	71045	Lagan	70086
Grand Isle	70358	Highland Acres	70123	Janie	71447	Lagonda	70380
Grand Lake	70605	Highland Park (Part of Monroe)	71201	Jarreau	70749	Lake	70769
Grand Point	70763	Highland Park (Part of West Monroe)	71291	Jay	70374	Lake Arthur	70549
Grand Prairie	70589	Highland Park (Terrebonne Parish)	70360	Jeanerette	70544	Lake Bruin	71366
Grand River	70764	Highland Park Heights	70808	Jean Lafitte	70067	Lake Charles	70601-16
Grangeville	70422	Highland Road	70808	Jefferson (Part of Lafayette)	70501*	For specific Lake Charles Zip Codes call (318) 439-3631, or your local postmaster.	
Grant	70644	Highway Park (Part of Kenner)	70065		70502†		
Gray	70359	Hi-Land	70092	Jefferson (Jefferson Parish)	70121	Lake End	71019
Gray Point	70586	Hillaryville	70725	Jefferson Island	70560	Lake Forest (Part of New Orleans)	70127
Grayson	71435	Hillsdale	70422	Jefferson Terrace	70808	Lake Judge Perez	70083
Green Acres (Concordia Parish)	71373	Hilltop	71268	Jena	71342	Lakeland	70752
Green Acres (East Baton Rouge Parish)	70811	Hilly	71235	Jennings	70546	Lake Providence	71254
Green Acres (St. Charles Parish)	70030	Hineston	71438	Jesuit Bend	70037	Lakeshore	71201
Green Gables	71360	Hobart	70769	Jewella (Part of Shreveport)	71109	Lakeside (Cameron Parish)	70542
Greenlaw	70444	Hodge	71247	Jigger	71249	Lakeside (Rapides Parish)	71360
Green Lawn (Part of Kenner)	70065	Hohen Solms	70788	Johnson (St. John the Baptist Parish)	70049	Lakeside Shopping Center	70002
Green Lawn Terrace (Part of Kenner)	70065	Holden	70744	Johnson (St. Mary Parish)	70538	Lakeview (Caddo Parish)	71107
Greensburg	70441	Holiday Park	70502	Johnson Ridge	70301	Lakeview (Natchitoches Parish)	71456
Greenwell Springs	70739	Holloway	71328	Johnson's Bayou	70631	Lakeview (Orleans Parish)	70124
Greenwood (Caddo Parish)	71033	Holly	71032	Johnson Street	70001	Lamar	71232
Greenwood (St. Mary Parish)	70380	Holly Beach	70631	Jones	71250	Lamourie	71346
Greenwood (Terrebonne Parish)	70356	Hollybrook	71254	Jonesboro	71251	Lampman (Part of Abbeville)	70510
Greenwood Park	71108	Holly Grove	71378	Jonesburg	71269	Landay Gautreaux Subdivision	70301
Gretna	70053-54	Holly Ridge (Richland Parish)	71269	Jones Park (Part of Kenner)	70065	Lapine	71291
	70056	Holly Ridge (Tensas Parish)	71375			La Place	70068*
For specific Gretna Zip Codes call (504) 362-5610, or your local postmaster.		Hollywood (Calcasieu Parish)	70663				70069†
						Laran	71765
Grosse Tete	70740					La Reusitte	70037
						Larose	70373

* Area Zip Code   † Post Office Boxes

	ZIP
La Rosen (Part of Shreveport)	71118
Larto	71343
Latanier	71346
Laurel Grove	70301
Laurel Hill	39669
Laurel Lea	70808
Laurel Ridge	70788
Laurel Valley Plantation	70301
Lawhon	71045
Lawtell	70550
Lazy Acres	70360
Leander	71438
Lebeau	71345
Le Blanc	70651
Le Bleu	70615
Lecompte	71346
Lee Bayou	71326
Lee Heights	71360
Lees Creek	70427
Lees Landing	70454
Leesville	71446*
	71496†
Leeville	70357
Legonier	70753
Leighton	70301
Leland	71368
Leleux	70560
Lemannville	70346
Le Moyen	71356
Lena	71447
Leonville	70551
Leroy	70555
Leton	71072
Lettsworth	70753
Levert	70582
Levins	71334
Lewisburg (St. Landry Parish)	70525
Lewisburg (St. Tammany Parish)	70448
Lewiston	70444
Lewistown	70394
Liberty	71225
Liberty Hill	71008
Libuse	71348
Liddieville	71295
Lillie	71256
Linda Lee	70726
Lindsay	70748
Link	70516
Linton	71006
Linville	71260
Linwood	70514
Lions	70068
Lisbon	71048
Lismore	71343
Litroe	71260
Little Caillou	70344
Little Creek	71371
Little Prairie	70769
Little Texas	70390
Live Oak	70037
Live Oak Hills	70447
Live Oak Manor	70094
Liverpool	70441
Livingston	70754
Livonia	70755
Lobdell	70767
Lockhart	71277
Lockport	70374
Lockport Heights	70374
Locust Ridge	71366
Logansport	71049
Log Cabin	71220
Logtown	71201
Lonepine	71367
Lone Star (Iberville Parish)	70788
Lone Star (St. Charles Parish)	70070
Longbridge (Avoyelles Parish)	71327
Long Bridge (Lafayette Parish)	70501
Longlake	71418
Longleaf	71448
Long Straw	71227
Longstreet	71049
Longview	71295
Longville	70652
Longwood (Caddo Parish)	71060
Longwood (East Baton Rouge Parish)	70780
Loranger	70446
Loreauville	70552
Lorelein	71336
Lottie	70756
Louisiana Army Ammunition Plant	71102

	ZIP
Louisiana Correctional and Industrial School	70633
Louisiana Correctional Institute for Women	70776
Louisiana Tech (Part of Ruston)	71272
Louisville (Part of Monroe)	71207
Lower Bonne Idee	71264
Lower Texas	70390
Loyds Bridge	71325
Lozes	70560
Lucas	71105
Lucky	71008
Lucy	70049
Ludington (Part of De Ridder)	70634
Ludvine	70374
Lukeville	70719
Lula	71052
Luling	70070
Luna	71291
Lunita	70661
Lutcher	70071
Lydia	70569
Lynbrook (Part of Shreveport)	71106
Lyons Point	70526
MacArthur Village (Part of Alexandria)	71301
McBride	70360
McCall	70346
McClendon	70438
McCrea	70715
McDade	71051
McDonoghville (Part of Gretna)	70053
McGinty	71250
McIlhenny	70513
McIntyre	71055
McKneeley	70732
McLeod	70374
McManus	70748
McNary	71433
McNeely	71417
McNeese University (Part of Lake Charles)	70609
Madewood	70390
Madisonville	70447
Magda	71301
Magnolia (Assumption Parish)	70341
Magnolia (East Baton Rouge Parish)	70739
Magnolia (Livingston Parish)	70744
Magnolia (Natchitoches Parish)	71456
Magnolia (Plaquemines Parish)	70083
Magnolia (Terrebonne Parish)	70360
Magnolia Park	71417
Magnolia Woods (Part of Baton Rouge)	70808
Maitland	71326
Major (Part of New Roads)	70760
Mallard Junction	70647
Mamou	70554
Manchester	70647
Mandalay	70360
Mandeville	70448
	70470-71
For specific Mandeville Zip Codes call (504) 626-8147, or your local postmaster.	
Mangham	71259
Manifest	71343
Mansfield	71052
Mansura	71350
Many	71449
Maplewood (Part of Sulphur)	70663
Marcel	70560
Marco	71447
Maringouin	70757
Marion	71260
Marksville	71351
Marrero	70072*
	70073†
Marsalis	71003
Mars Hill	71404
Marthaville	71450
Martin	71019
Martin Park (Part of Alexandria)	71301
Mason	71295
Mathews	70375
Maurepas	70449
Maurice	70555

	ZIP
Maxie	70526
Mayfair (Part of Baton Rouge)	70808
Mayna	71343
Meadowbrook	70056
Meadow Park Heights	71108
Meaux	70510
Mechanicsville (Part of Houma)	70360
Meeker	71346
Melder	71451
Melrose	71452
Melville	71353
Meraux	70075
Mermentau	70556
Mer Rouge	71261
Merrydale	70812
Merryville	70653
Messick	71019
Metairie	70001-11
	70033
	70055
For specific Metairie Zip Codes call (504) 831-7750, or your local postmaster.	
Methvin	71019
Michoud (Part of New Orleans)	70129
Mid City (Part of New Orleans)	70119
Midland	70559
Midway (Bossier Parish)	71006
Midway (La Salle Parish)	71342
Midway (Rapides Parish)	71430
Midway (St. Mary Parish)	70538
Midway (Webster Parish)	71071
Milldale	70791
Millerton	71038
Millerville (Acadia Parish)	70543
Millerville (East Baton Rouge Parish)	70815
Millikin	71254
Milly Plantation	70764
Milton	70558
Mimosa Park	70070
Minden	71055-58
For specific Minden Zip Codes call (318) 377-1757, or your local postmaster.	
Mineral Springs (Lincoln Parish)	71235
Mineral Springs (Ouachita Parish)	71225
Minerva	70360
Minorca	71334
Mira	71059
Mire	70578
Mitchell	71419
Mittie	70654
Mix	70760
Modeste	70376
Moisant Airport (Part of Kenner)	70141
Moncla	71351
Monette Ferry	71447
Monroe	71201-13
For specific Monroe Zip Codes call (318) 387-6161, or your local postmaster.	
Montcalm	71275
Montegut	70377
Monterey	71354
Montgomery	71454
Monticello (East Baton Rouge Parish)	70815
Monticello (East Carroll Parish)	71254
Montpelier	70422
Montrose	71457
Montz	70068
Mooringsport	71060
Mora	71455
Morbihan	70560
Moreauville	71355
Moreland	71301
Morgan City	70380*
	70381†
Morganza	70759
Morningside (Part of Shreveport)	71108
Morrisonville	70764
Morrow	71356
Morse	70559
Morvant	70301
Morville	71373
Moss Bluff	70611
Moss Lake	70663
Mossville	70663
Mot	71064
Mound	71282

	ZIP
Mount Airy	70076
Mount Carmel	71429
Mount Hermon	70450
Mount Lebanon	71028
Mount Moriah	71226
Mount Olive	71268
Mount Sinai	71038
Mount Union	71277
Mount Zion (Lincoln Parish)	71235
Mount Zion (Winn Parish)	71454
Mowata	70535
Mudville	71432
Mulberry	70360
Myrtle Grove (Iberville Parish)	70764
Myrtle Grove (Plaquemines Parish)	70083
Naborton	71052
Nairn	70041
Naomi	70037
Napoleonville	70390
Napoleonville Junction (Part of Thibodaux)	70301
Naquin	70301
Natalbany	70451
Natchez	71456
Natchitoches	71457*
	71458†
Neal Landing	70462
Nebo	71342
Negreet	71460
Nesser	70815
Newellton	71357
New Era	71354
Newhope	71266
New Iberia	70560*
	70562†
New Light (Richland Parish)	71259
Newlight (Tensas Parish)	71357
New Llano	71461
New Orleans	70101-90
For specific New Orleans Zip Codes call (504) 589-1111, or your local postmaster.	

COLLEGES & UNIVERSITIES

Dillard University	70122
Louisiana State University Medical Center	70112
Loyola University	70118
New Orleans Baptist Theological Seminary	70126
Southern University at New Orleans	70126
Tulane University of Louisiana	70118
University of New Orleans	70148
Xavier University	70125

FINANCIAL INSTITUTIONS

Alerion Bank, Inc.	70130
Fidelity Homestead Association	70112
Fifth District Savings & Loan Association	70114
First National Bank of Commerce	70112
Hibernia National Bank	70130
Oak Tree Federal Savings Bank	70130
Whitney National Bank	70130

HOSPITALS

Ochsner Foundation Hospital	70121
Southern Baptist Hospital	70115
Touro Infirmary	70115
Tulane University Hospital and Clinics	70112
Veterans Affairs Medical Center	70146

HOTELS/MOTELS

Holiday Inn Crowne Plaza	70130
Hotel Marie Antoinette	70130
Hyatt Regency New Orleans at Superdome	70140
Le Meridien New Orleans	70130
New Orleans Hilton Riverside	70140
Omni Royal Orleans	70140
Royal Sonesta Hotel	70140
Sheraton New Orleans Hotel	70130
Westin Canal Place	70130

* Area Zip Code   † Post Office Boxes

	ZIP
MILITARY INSTALLATIONS	
Louisiana Air National Guard, FB6171, New Orleans Naval Air Station	70143
MTMC Gulf Outport	70146
Naval Support Activity	70142
Supervisor of Shipbuilding, Conversion and Repair, New Orleans	70142
United States Army Engineer District, New Orleans	70160
United States Property and Fiscal Office for Louisiana	70146
8th Coast Guard District, New Orleans	70130
8th Marine Corps District	70142
926th Fighter Group, New Orleans Naval Air Station (AFRES)	70143
New Orleans Centre (Part of New Orleans)	70112
New Roads	70760
New Rockdale	71052
New Sarpy	70078
Newton	70601
New Verda	71404
Nibletts Bluff	70668
Nicholas	70560
Nicholls University (Part of Thibodaux)	70301
Nickel	71465
Ninock	71051
Noble	71462
Noles Landing	71073
Norah	70374
Norco	70079
Normandy Park	70094
Norris Springs	71368
Northeast Louisiana University (Part of Monroe)	71209
Northgate Mall (Part of Lafayette)	70501
North Hodge	71247
North Merrydale	70812
North Monroe	71201
North Plaquemine (Part of Plaquemine)	70764
North Shore	70458
North Shore Beach	70458
North Slidell (Part of Slidell)	70458
Northwestern (Part of Natchitoches)	71457
Norton Shop	71072
Norwood	70761
Notleyville	70512
Notnac	71357
Numa	70560
Nunez	70548
Oakdale	71463
Oak Forest	70356
Oak Grove (Ascension Parish)	70769
Oak Grove (Cameron Parish)	70643
Oak Grove (Grant Parish)	71417
Oak Grove (Lincoln Parish)	71275
Oak Grove (Sabine Parish)	71419
Oak Grove (West Carroll Parish)	71263
Oak Hills Place	70808
Oakland	71260
Oaklawn (St. Mary Parish)	70538
Oaklawn (St. Tammany Parish)	70445
Oakley	70390
Oak Manor	70815
Oaknolia	70777
Oak Ridge	71264
Oaks	71038
Oakshire Manor	70364
Oakville	70037
Oakwood Center (Part of Gretna)	70053
Oberlin	70655
Oil Center (Part of Lafayette)	70501
Oil City	71061
Okaloosa	71238
Old Athens	71003
Oldfield	70785

	ZIP
Old Hammond (Part of Baton Rouge)	70815-19
For specific Old Hammond Zip Codes call (504) 273-2567, or your local postmaster.	
Old Jefferson	70816
Old Lafitte	70067
Old Shongaloo	71072
Olive Branch	70777
Oliver (Part of Hammond)	70401
Olivier	70560
Olla	71465
Ollie	70037
Omega	71276
Opelousas	70570*
	70571†
Orange Grove Plantation	70301
Oretta	70633
Oscar	70762
Ossun	70583
Ostrica	70041
Otis	71466
Ouachita City	71280
Oubre (Part of Loreauville)	70552
Oxford (De Soto Parish)	71052
Oxford (St. Mary Parish)	70538
Pace	71055
Packton	71483
Paincourtville	70391
Palmetto	71358
Palo Alto	70346
Panchoville	70532
Panola	71254
Paradis	70080
Paradise	71360
Paradise Manor	70123
Parhams	71343
Park Manor	70003
Parks	70582
Parkside Manor	70123
Park Vista (Part of Opelousas)	70570
Patoutville	70544
Patterson	70392
Paulina	70763
Pearl River	70452
Peason	71429
Pecan Grove	70094
Pecaniere	70512
Pecan Island	70548
Pecan Place	70764
Peck	71368
Pelican	71063
Perkins	70633
Perry	70575
Perryville	71220
Phoenix	70042
Pickering	71446
Pierre Bossier Mall (Part of Bossier City)	71112
Pierre Part	70339
Pierre Part Settlement	70339
Pilottown	70081
Pine	70438
Pine Coupee	71427
Pine Grove (Ouachita Parish)	71201
Pine Grove (St. Helena Parish)	70453
Pine Island	70532
Pine Oak Terrace (Part of Shreveport)	71108
Pine Prairie	70576
Pineville	71360*
	71361†
Pioneer	71266
Pitkin	70656
Pitreville	70525
Plain Dealing	71064
Plains	70791
Plainview	70427
Plaisance	70570
Plantation Acres (Part of Alexandria)	71301
Plaquemine	70764*
	70765†
Plaquemine Southwest (Part of Plaquemine)	70764
Plattenville	70393
Plaucheville	71362
Plaza, The (Part of New Orleans)	70127
Pleasant Hill (Bienville Parish)	71028
Pleasant Hill (Sabine Parish)	71065
Pleasant Hills	70811
Pleasant Valley	71234
Plettenberg	70775
Point	71234

	ZIP
Point Au Chien	70377
Point Blue	70586
Pointe a la Hache	70082
Pointe Coupee	70760
Point Pleasant	71220
Poland	71301
Pollock	71467
Ponchatoula	70454
Ponchatoula Beach	70454
Pontchartrain Beach (Part of New Orleans)	70122
Poole	71051
Poplar Grove	70767
Portage	70512
Port Allen	70767
Port Barre	70577
Port Barrow (Part of Donaldsonville)	70346
Port Eads	70091
Porters Curve	70450
Porterville	71071
Port Fourchon	70357
Port Gardner	70791
Port Hickey	70791
Port Manchac	70421
Port of West Saint Mary	70538
Port Sulphur	70083
Port Vincent	70726
Potash	70083
Pot Cove	70586
Poufette	70560
Powhatan	71066
Poydras	70085
Prairie Ronde	70570
Prairieville	70769
Pratt	71028
Presque Isle	70363
Pride	70770
Prien	70605
Prien Lake Mall (Part of Lake Charles)	70601
Princeton	71067
Promised Land	70040
Prospect (Grant Parish)	71423
Prospect (St. Charles Parish)	70078
Provencal	71468
Providence	70062
Puckett	70791
Pumpkin Center	70403
Punkin Center	71247
Quaid	71343
Quimby	71282
Quitman	71268
Raceland	70394
Ragley	70657
Ramah	70757
Rambin	71063
Randolph	71256
Rapides	71409
Ratliff	71390
Rattan	71429
Rayne	70578
Rayville	71269
Readhimer	71070
Red Chute	71037
Reddell	70580
Red Gum	71334
Redland (Bossier Parish)	71064
Redland (Evangeline Parish)	70554
Red Oaks	70815
Reeves	70658
Reggio	70085
Reids	70656
Remy	70763
Reserve	70084
Rhinehart	71363
Rhymes	71269
Riceville	70542
Richard	70525
Richardson	70438
Richmond	71282
Richohoc	70538
Richwood	71201
Rideau Settlement	71358
Ridge	70578
Ridgecrest	71334
Ridgewood	70739
Rienzi Plantation	70301
Ringgold	71068
Rio	70427
Risinger Woods	71107
Riverlands	70068
River Ridge	70123
Riverton	71418
Riverwood	70433
Roanoke	70581
Robeline	71469
Robert	70455

	ZIP
Robson	71105
Rock	71447
Rock Hill	71423
Rocky Branch	71241
Rocky Mount	71064
Rodessa	71069
Rogers	71342
Romeville	70723
Roosevelt	71276
Rosa	71345
Rosedale (Assumption Parish)	70390
Rosedale (Iberville Parish)	70772
Rosefield	71435
Roseland	70456
Rosepine	70659
Rougon	70773
Rousseau	70394
Roxana	71301
Roy	71016
Ruby	71365
Rum Center	71256
Ruple	71038
Rural Park	70123
Ruston	71270-73
For specific Ruston Zip Codes call (318) 255-3791, or your local postmaster.	
Ruth	70517
Rynella	70560
Sadie	71260
Sadou	70529
Sailes	71028
St. Amant	70774
St. Benedict	70457
St. Bernard	70085
St. Bernard Grove	70075
St. Charles	70301
St. Clair	70040
St. Claude Heights	70032
St. Elmo	70725
St. Francisville	70775
St. Gabriel	70776
St. Genevieve	71373
St. Gertrude	70435
St. James	70086
St. Joe	70452
St. John	70301
St. Joseph	71366
St. Landry	71367
St. Martinville	70582
St. Maurice	71471
St. Rosalie	70037
St. Rose	70087
St. Tammany	70445
St. Thomas	70390
Saline	71070
Samstown	70788
Samtown	71301
Sandy Hill	71446
Sardis (Sabine Parish)	71419
Sardis (Winn Parish)	71483
Sarepta	71071
Satsuma	70754
Savoy	70535
Scarsdale	70040
Schriever	70395
Scotlandville	70807
Scott	70583
Searcy	71371
Sebastapol	70085
Sellers	70079
Selma	71432
Sentell	71107
Serena	71343
Seymourville	70764
Shadyside	70538
Shamrock	71469
Sharon	71235
Sharon Hills	70811
Sharp	71447
Shaw	71373
Shelburn	71254
Shelton	71220
Shenandoah	70816
Sherburne	70750
Sheridan	70438
Sherwood	71435
Shiloh (Tangipahoa Parish)	70422
Shiloh (Union Parish)	71222
Shongaloo	71072
Shreve City Shopping Center (Part of Shreveport)	71105
Shreveport	71101-10
	71115-66
For specific Shreveport Zip Codes call (318) 677-2334, or your local postmaster.	
Shrewsbury	70121

* Area Zip Code   **† Post Office Boxes**

	ZIP
Shuteston	70570
Sibley (Lincoln Parish)	71227
Sibley (Webster Parish)	71073
Sicard (Part of Monroe)	71201
Sicily Island	71368
Siegle	71291
Sieper	71472
Sikes	71473
Sikes Ferry	71072
Silverwood	70546
Simmesport	71369
Simms	71467
Simpson	71474
Simsboro	71275
Singer	70660
Siracusaville	70380
Slacks	70757
Slagle	71475
Slaughter	70777
Slidell	70458-61
For specific Slidell Zip Codes call (504) 643-5338, or your local postmaster.	
Sligo	71112
Smithfield	70767
Smith Ridge	70344
Smoke Bend	70346
Socola	70083
Soileau	70655
Somerset	71357
Sondheimer	71276
Soniat	70788
Sorrell	70544
Sorrento	70778
South Acres	70663
South Bend	70538
Southdown	70360
Southeast (Part of Baton Rouge)	70808
Southeast Louisiana Hospital	70448
Southern	70813
Southfield (Part of Shreveport)	71105
South Fort Trailer Park	71459
South Kenner	70094
South Lafourche	70357
South Mansfield	71052
South Park (Caddo Parish)	71118
South Park (Rapides Parish)	71301
South Park Mall (Part of Shreveport)	71118
South Pass	70091
Southport	70121
South Sherwood (Part of Baton Rouge)	70816
Southside (Part of Lafayette)	70503
South Vacherie	70090
Southwestern University (Part of Lafayette)	70504
Spaulding	71441
Spearsville	71277
Spencer	71280
Spillman	70748
Splane Place (Part of West Monroe)	71291
Spokane	71334
Springcreek	70444
Springfield	70462
Spring Hill (Jackson Parish)	71251
Springhill (Washington Parish)	70438
Springhill (Webster Parish)	71075
Spring Ridge (Caddo Parish)	71047
Spring Ridge (Sabine Parish)	71065
Springville (Livingston Parish)	70754
Springville (Red River Parish)	71019
Standard	71465
Stanley	71049
Star	71037
Starhill	70748
Staring (Part of Baton Rouge)	70801
Starks	70661
Start	71279

	ZIP
State Line	70438
Stella	70040
Stephensville	70380
Sterlington	71280
Stevensdale	70815
Stevenson	71220
Stonewall	71078
Stoney Point	70438
Stonypoint	70739
Stumpf's Westside Shopping Center (Part of Gretna)	70053
Sugarcreek	71001
Sugartown	70662
Sulphur	70663*
	70664†
Summerfield	71079
Summer Grove (Part of Shreveport)	71118
Summerville	71465
Sun	70463
Sunnybrook	70814
Sunny Hill	70438
Sunrise	70767
Sunset	70584
Sunshine	70780
Sun Spur	71232
Supreme	70390
Susan Park (Part of Kenner)	70062
Swampers	71295
Swartz	71281
Sweet Lake	70630
Swords	70525
Taconey	71373
Taft	70057
Talisheek	70464
Talla Bena	71276
Tallulah	71282-84
For specific Tallulah Zip Codes call (318) 574-0295, or your local postmaster.	
Tangipahoa	70465
Tanglewood (East Baton Rouge Parish)	70811
Tanglewood (Rapides Parish)	71301
Tannehill	71422
Tate Cove	70586
Taylor	71080
Taylor Hill	71447
Taylortown (Bossier Parish)	71051
Taylortown (Union Parish)	71277
Tchefuncte Estates	70433
Temple	71474
Tendal	71282
Terry	71263
Terrytown	70053
Theriot	70397
The Rock	71417
Thibodaux	70301-10
For specific Thibodaux Zip Codes call (504) 447-3737, or your local postmaster.	
Thomas	70438
Thomastown	71282
Thornwell	70549
Three Oaks	70032
Three Rivers Heights	70447
Tickfaw	70466
Tidewater Camp	70091
Tigerville	70049
Timberlane	70053
Timber Trails	71360
Tioga	71477
Toca	70085
Toomey	70668
Topsy	70601
Torbert	70781
Toro	71429
Torras	70753
Tower Park (Part of Leesville)	71446
Town and Country	71201
Transylvania	71286
Trees	71082
Tremont	71227
Trenton	71052
Trinity (Catahoula Parish)	71343
Trinity (Iberville Parish)	70772
Triumph	70041
Tropical Bend	70050

	ZIP
Trout	71371
Truxno	71260
Tullos	71479
Tunica	70782
Turkey Creek	70585
Turnerville (Part of Plaquemine)	70764
Twin Oaks	71223
Uncle Sam	70792
Union	70723
Union Church	71268
Union Hill (Rapides Parish)	71433
Union Hill (Winn Parish)	71483
Union Landing	70754
Union Springs	71419
Unionville	71235
University (Part of Baton Rouge)	70803
Upland	71220
Upstream	70123
Uptown (Part of New Orleans)	70115
Urania	71480
Utility	71343
Vacherie	70090
Valmar	70075
Valverda	70757
Vanceville	71111
Varnado	70467
Vatican	70520
Vaughn	71220
Velma	70422
Venice	70091
Ventress	70783
Verda	71481
Verdun	70754
Verdunville	70538
Vernon	71270
Verret	70085
Veterans Administration Hospital (Part of Shreveport)	71101
Vick	71331
Vidalia	71373
Vidrine	70586
Vienna	71270
Vieux Carre (Part of New Orleans)	70112
Village East	70360
Village St. George	70808
Ville Platte	70586
Vincent Landing	70663
Vincent Park	70075
Vinton	70668
Violet	70092
Vista Village Regional Shopping Center (Part of Opelousas)	70570
Vivian	71082
Vixen	71418
Voorhies	71355
Vowells Mill	71469
Wade Correctional Center	71038
Wadesboro	70454
Waggaman	70094
Wakefield	70784
Waldheim	70435
Walker (Jackson Parish)	71251
Walker (Livingston Parish)	70785
Wallace	70049
Wallace Ridge	71343
Walls	70720
Walters	71343
Ward	71463
Warden	71232
Wardview	71064
Wardville (Morehouse Parish)	71220
Wardville (Rapides Parish)	71360
Warnerton	70438
Warsaw Landing	70462
Washington	70589
Waterloo	70783
Waterproof (Tensas Parish)	71375
Waterproof (Terrebonne Parish)	70360
Watson	70786
Waverly	71232
Waxia	70589
Weil	71301
Welcome	70086
Weldon	71222

	ZIP
Welsh	70591
Wemple	71052
Westdale	71105
Western Kraft	71411
West Ferriday	71334
Westfield	70390
Westlake	70669
Westminster	70809
West Monroe	71291-94
For specific West Monroe Zip Codes call (318) 387-8821, or your local postmaster.	
Weston	71251
Westover	70767
West Pointe a la Hache	70083
Westport	70656
Westside (Part of Alexandria)	71301
West Slidell (Part of Slidell)	70460
Westwego	70094*
	70096†
Weyanoke	70787
Whatley Landing	71371
Wheeling	71454
White	70301
White Castle	70788
Whitehall (La Salle Parish)	71342
Whitehall (Livingston Parish)	70449
White Hall (St. James Parish)	70723
White Hills	70714
White Sulphur Springs	71371
Whiteville	71322
Whittington	71301
Wickland Terrace	70815
Wickliffe	70783
Wildsville	71377
Wildwood (Assumption Parish)	70390
Wildwood (East Baton Rouge Parish)	70808
Willhite	71234
Williams	71105
Williana	71423
Willow Glen	71301
Wills Point	70040
Wilmer	70444
Wilshire Park	71301
Wilson	70789
Wilsona	71366
Wilson Point	71301
Wilton Subdivision	71107
Winnfield	71483
Winnsboro	71295
Wisner	71378
Womack (Jackson Parish)	71226
Womack (Red River Parish)	71068
Woodardville	71068
Woodhaven	70466
Woodland	70083
Woodlawn (Part of Baton Rouge)	70816-17
For specific Woodlawn Zip Codes call (504) 752-8994, or your local postmaster.	
Woodlawn (Assumption Parish)	70390
Woodlawn (Jefferson Davis Parish)	70647
Woodlawn (Plaquemines Parish)	70040
Woodlawn (Terrebonne Parish)	70360
Woodside	71353
Woodville	71270
Woodworth	71485
Wyandotte	70380
Wyatt	71251
Yellow Pine	71073
Youngsville	70592
Zachary	70791
Zebedee	71269
Zenoria	71371
Zion	71432
Zion City (Part of Baton Rouge)	70811
Zwolle	71486
Zylks	71069

* Area Zip Code   † Post Office Boxes

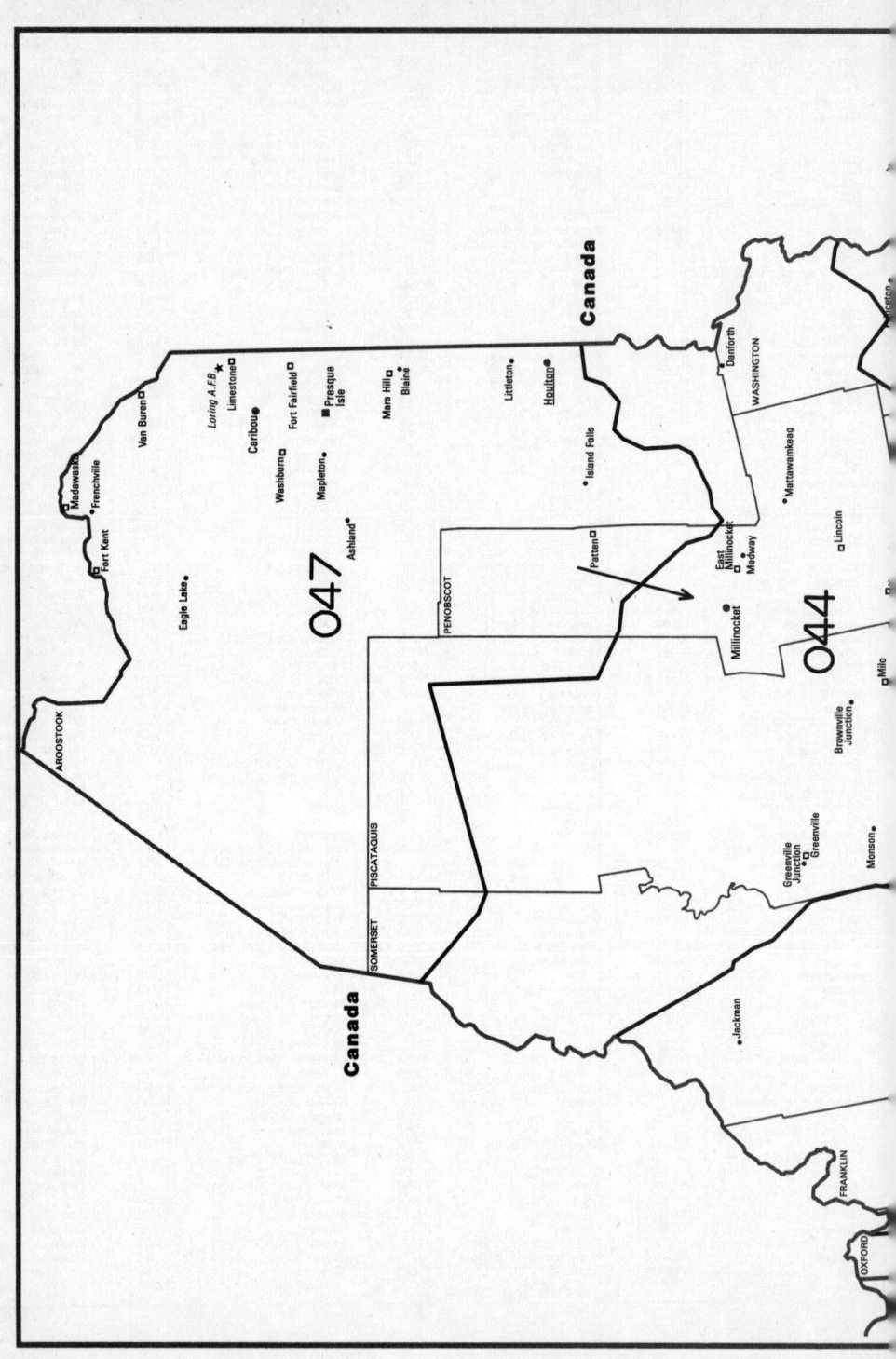

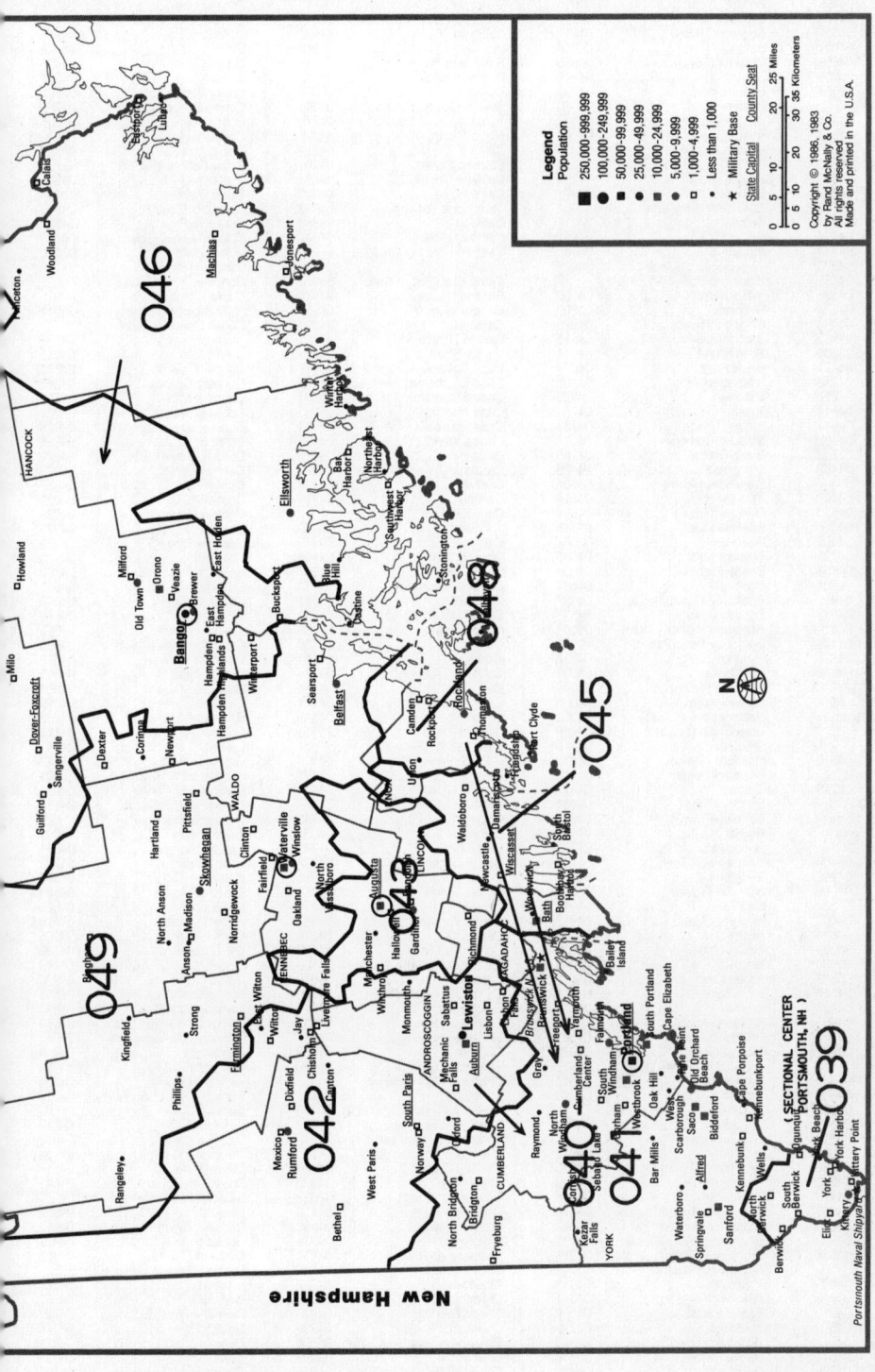

	ZIP
Abbot (Town)	04406
Abbotts Mill	04219
Abbot Village	04406
Acadia Terrace	04785
Acton	04001
Acton (Town)	04001
Addison	04606
Addison (Town)	04606
Admiralty Village	03904
Airport Mall (Part of Bangor)	04401
Albion	04910
Albion (Town)	04910
Alexander	04619
Alexander (Town)	04619
Alfred	04002
Alfred (Town)	04002
Alfred Mills	04002
Allagash	04774
Allagash (Town)	04774
Allens Mills	04938
Alna	04535
Alna (Town)	04535
Alna Center	04535
Alton (Town)	04468
Amherst	04605
Amherst (Town)	04605
Amity (Town)	04471
Andover	04216
Andover (Town)	04216
Anson	04911
Anson (Town)	04911
Appleton	04862
Appleton (Town)	04862
Argyle (Town)	04468
Aroostook Farm (Part of Presque Isle)	04769
Arrowsic (Town)	04530
Arundel (Town)	04046
Ashdale	04565
Ashland	04732
Ashland (Town)	04732
Ashville	04607
Athens	04912
Athens (Town)	04912
Atkinson (Town)	04426
Atkinson Corner	04426
Atkinson Mills	04426
Atlantic	04608
Auburn	04210-12
For specific Auburn Zip Codes call (207) 786-0604, or your local postmaster.	
Auburn Mall (Part of Auburn)	04210
Auburn Plains (Part of Auburn)	04210
Augusta	04330-38
For specific Augusta Zip Codes call (207) 622-6114, or your local postmaster.	
Aurora	04408
Aurora (Town)	04408
Avon (Town)	04966
Back Narrows	04537
Bailey Island	04003
Baileyville (Town)	04694
Baker Corner	04082
Balch Pond	03830
Bald Head	03907
Baldwin (Town)	04024
Bancroft	04497
Bancroft (Town)	04497
Bangor	04401*
	04402†
Bangor Mall (Part of Bangor)	04401
Bar Harbor	04609
Bar Harbor (Town)	04609
Baring	04619
Baring (Town)	04619
Bar Mills	04004
Barrett (Part of Caribou)	04736
Bartlett Mills	04043
Basin Mills	04473
Bass Harbor	04653
Batchelders Crossing	04350
Bath	04530
Bay Point	04548
Bayside (Hancock County)	04605
Bayside (Waldo County)	04915
Bayview (Part of Saco)	04072
Bayville	04536
Beals	04611
Beals (Town)	04611
Beans Corner	04225
Beaver Cove (Town)	04441
Beaver Dam	03901

	ZIP
Beddington (Town)	04622
Beech Ridge	03909
Belfast	04915
Belgrade	04917
Belgrade (Town)	04917
Belgrade Lakes	04918
Belmont (Town)	04915
Belmont Corner	04915
Benedicta	04733
Benton	04910
Benton (Town)	04910
Benton Falls	04901
Benton Station	04937
Bernard	04612
Berry Mills	04224
Berwick	03901
Berwick (Town)	03901
Bethel	04217
Bethel (Town)	04217
Biddeford	04005*
	04007†
Biddeford Pool (Part of Biddeford)	04006
Bingham	04920
Bingham (Town)	04920
Birch Harbor	04613
Birch Island	04011
Black Point	04074
Blackstrap	04105
Blackwell	04950
Blaine	04734
Blaine (Town)	04734
Blaisdell Corners	04027
Blake Corner	04250
Blanchard	04406
Blanchard (Town)	04406
Blue Hill	04614
Blue Hill (Town)	04614
Blue Hill Falls	04615
Blue Point	04074
Bolsters Mills	04040
Bonny Eagle	04093
Boothbay	04537
Boothbay (Town)	04537
Boothbay Harbor	04538
Boothbay Harbor (Town)	04538
Boothbay Park (Part of Saco)	04072
Bowdoin	04008
Bowdoin (Town)	04008
Bowdoinham	04008
Bowdoinham (Town)	04008
Bowerbank (Town)	04426
Bradford	04410
Bradford (Town)	04410
Bradford Center	04410
Bradley	04411
Bradley (Town)	04411
Bremen (Town)	04551
Brewer	04412
Bridgewater	04735
Bridgewater (Town)	04735
Bridgton	04009
Bridgton (Town)	04009
Brighton	04912
Brighton (Town)	04912
Bristol	04539
Bristol (Town)	04539
Brixham	03909
Broad Cove	04572
Brookhaven	04062
Brooklin	04616
Brooklin (Town)	04616
Brooks	04921
Brooks (Town)	04921
Brooksville (Town)	04617
Brooksville	04617
Brookton	04413
Brown Corner (Aroostook County)	04750
Brown Corner (Waldo County)	04915
Brownfield	04010
Brownfield (Town)	04010
Brownville	04414
Brownville (Town)	04414
Brownville Junction	04415
Brunswick	04011
Brunswick (Town)	04011
Brunswick Naval Air Station	04011
Brunswick Station	04011
Bryant Pond	04219
Buckfield	04220
Buckfield (Town)	04220
Bucks Harbor	04618
Bucksport	04416
Bucksport (Town)	04416
Bunganuc Landing	04011

	ZIP
Bunkers Harbor	04613
Burkettville	04574
Burlington	04417
Burlington (Town)	04417
Burnham	04922
Burnham (Town)	04922
Burnt Meadow Pond	04041
Bustins Island	04013
Buxton (Town)	04093
Buxton Center	04093
Byron	04275
Byron (Town)	04275
Calais	04619
Caldwel Corner	04281
Caldwell Corner	04281
Cambridge	04923
Cambridge (Town)	04923
Camden	04843
Camden (Town)	04843
Campbell (Part of Presque Isle)	04769
Camp Ellis (Part of Saco)	04072
Canaan	04924
Canaan (Town)	04924
Canton	04221
Canton (Town)	04221
Canton Point	04221
Cape Cottage	04107
Cape Elizabeth (Town)	04107
Cape Elizabeth	04107
Cape Neddick	03902
Cape Porpoise	04014
Capitol Island	04538
Caratunk	04925
Caratunk (Town)	04925
Cardville	04418
Caribou	04736
Caribou Road (Part of Presque Isle)	04769
Carmel	04419
Carmel (Town)	04419
Carrabassett	04947
Carrabassett Valley (Town)	04947
Carroll	04487
Carroll (Town)	04487
Carson	04786
Carthage	04224
Carthage (Town)	04224
Cary	04471
Cary (Town)	04471
Casco	04015
Casco (Town)	04015
Cash Corner (Part of South Portland)	04106
Castine	04421
Castine (Town)	04421
Castle Hill (Town)	04757
Caswell (Town)	04750
Cathance	04086
Cedar Grove	04342
Center Lebanon	04027
Center Lovell	04016
Center Minot	04258
Center Montville	04941
Center Vassalboro	04989
Centerville	04623
Centerville (Town)	04623
Central Aroostook (Town)	04760
Central Hancock (Town)	04640
Central Somerset (Town)	04920
Chamberlain	04541
Chapman	04757
Chapman (Town)	04757
Charleston	04422
Charleston (Town)	04422
Charleston Correctional Facility	04422
Charlotte (Town)	04666
Chases Pond	03909
Chebeague Island	04017
Chelsea	04330
Chelsea (Town)	04345
Cherryfield	04622
Cherryfield (Town)	04622
Chester	04458
Chester (Town)	04458
Chesterville	04938
Chesterville (Town)	04938
Chesuncook	04441
Chicopee	04038
China	04926
China (Town)	04926
Chisholm	04239
Christmas Cove	04568
Cider Hill	03909
City Point (Part of Belfast)	04915
Clapboard Island	04105
Clark Island	04859

	ZIP
Clarks Mill	04042
Clay Hill	03902
Clayton Lake	04737
Cliff Island (Part of Portland)	04019
Clifton	04428
Clifton (Town)	04428
Clinton	04927
Clinton (Town)	04927
Cobbs Bridge	04260
Coburn Gore	04936
Codyville (Town)	04490
Colby	04736
Colby College (Part of Waterville)	04901
Coles Corner	04496
Columbia (Town)	04623
Columbia Falls	04623
Columbia Falls (Town)	04623
Concordville	03910
Connor (Town)	04736
Convene	04091
Cooks Corner (Cumberland County)	04011
Cooks Corner (Waldo County)	04987
Cooks Mills	04015
Cooper (Town)	04638
Coopers Corner	04046
Coopers Mills	04341
Coplin (Town)	04982
Corea	04624
Corinna	04928
Corinna (Town)	04928
Corinna Center	04928
Corinth (Town)	04427
Cornish	04020
Cornish (Town)	04020
Cornville	04976
Cornville (Town)	04976
Costigan	04423
Cote Corner	04750
Country Living	04073
Cousins Island	04096
Coventry North	04048
Cranberry Isles	04625
Cranberry Isles (Town)	04625
Crawford (Town)	04619
Crescent Lake	04015
Criehaven (Town)	04851
Crockett Corner	04069
Crossman Corner	04252
Crouseville	04738
Crystal	04747
Crystal (Town)	04747
Cumberland (Town)	04021
Cumberland Center	04021
Cumberland Foreside	04110
Cumberland Mills (Part of Westbrook)	04092
Cundys Harbor	04011
Curtis Corner	04263
Cushing	04563
Cushing (Town)	04563
Cutler	04626
Cutler (Town)	04626
Cutts Island	03905
Cyr (Town)	04785
Daigle	04743
Dallas (Town)	04970
Damariscotta	04543
Damariscotta (Town)	04543
Damariscotta Mills	04553
Damariscotta-Newcastle	04543
Damascus	04419
Danforth	04424
Danforth (Town)	04424
Danville (Part of Auburn)	04223
Danville Corner (Part of Auburn)	04210
Dark Harbor	04848
Davenport Cove	04424
Davis Island	04556
Days Ferry	04579
Dayton (Town)	04005
Deblois	04622
Deblois (Town)	04622
Dedham	04429
Dedham (Town)	04429
Deering (Part of Presque Isle)	04769
Deer Isle	04627
Deer Isle (Town)	04627
Delano Park	04106
Denmark	04022
Denmark (Town)	04022
Dennistown (Town)	04945
Dennysville	04628
Dennysville (Town)	04628

* Area Zip Code   † Post Office Boxes

	ZIP
Hunts Corner	04217
Hutchins Corner	04942
Indian Island	04468
Indian Point	04660
Indian River	04606
Indian Township Indian Reservation	04668
Industrial (Part of Presque Isle)	04769
Industry (Town)	04938
Ingall's Hill	04009
Intervale	04260
Irish Settlement	04424
Island Falls	04747
Island Falls (Town)	04747
Isle au Haut	04645
Isle Au Haut (Town)	04645
Isle of Springs	04549
Islesboro	04848
Islesboro (Town)	04848
Islesford	04646
Jackman	04945
Jackman (Town)	04945
Jackson	04921
Jackson (Town)	04921
Jackson Corners	04921
Jacksonville	04630
Jay	04239
Jay (Town)	04239
Jefferson	04348
Jefferson (Town)	04348
Jemtland	04783
Jonesboro	04648
Jonesboro (Town)	04648
Jones Corner	04354
Jonesport	04649
Jonesport (Town)	04649
Kalers Corner	04572
Keegan	04785
Kelleyland	04694
Kendalls Corner (Part of Belfast)	04915
Kenduskeag	04450
Kenduskeag (Town)	04450
Kennebago Lake	04970
Kennebec	04654
Kennebunk	04043
Kennebunk (Town)	04043
Kennebunk Beach	04043
Kennebunk Landing	04043
Kennebunk Lower Village	04046
Kennebunkport	04046
Kennebunkport (Town)	04046
Kennedy Terrace	04785
Kents Hill	04349
Kezar Falls	04047
Kingfield	04947
Kingfield (Town)	04947
Kingman	04451
Kingman (Town)	04451
Kingsbury (Town)	04942
Kinney Shores (Part of Saco)	04072
Kittery	03904
Kittery (Town)	03904
Kittery Point	03905
Knights Landing	04414
Knightville (Part of South Portland)	04106
Knowles Corner	04780
Knox (Town)	04986
Knox Center	04986
Knox Corner	04986
Knox Station	04986
Kokadjo	04441
Lagrange	04453
Lagrange (Town)	04453
Lake Arrowhead Estates	04061
Lake City	04843
Lake Moxie	04985
Lake View (Town)	04463
Lakeville (Town)	04487
Lakewood	04976
Lambert Lake	04454
Lamoine (Town)	04605
Lamoine	04605
Lamoine Beach	04605
Lamoine Corner	04605
Larone	04937
Larrabee	04655
Lawry	04547
Lebanon (Town)	04027
Lee	04455
Lee (Town)	04455
Leeds (Town)	04263
Leeds	04263
Leeds Junction	04263
Levant	04456
Levant (Town)	04456

	ZIP
Lewiston	04240-43
For specific Lewiston Zip Codes call (207) 783-8551, or your local postmaster.	
Lewiston Junction (Part of Auburn)	04210
Lewiston Lower (Part of Lewiston)	04240
Lewiston Mall (Part of Lewiston)	04240
Lewiston Upper (Part of Lewiston)	04240
Libby Hill (Part of Gardiner)	04345
Liberty	04949
Liberty (Town)	04949
Lille	04746
Lily Bay	04441
Limerick	04048
Limerick (Town)	04048
Limerick Mills	04048
Limestone	04750
Limington	04049
Limington (Town)	04049
Lincoln (Oxford County) (Town)	03579
Lincoln (Penobscot County)	04457
Lincoln (Penobscot County) (Town)	04457
Lincoln Center	04458
Lincoln Mills	04928
Lincolnville	04849
Lincolnville (Town)	04849
Lincolnville Center	04850
Linekin	04544
Linneus	04730
Linneus (Town)	04730
Lisbon	04250
Lisbon (Town)	04250
Lisbon Center	04251
Lisbon Falls	04252
Litchfield	04350
Litchfield (Town)	04350
Litchfield Corners	04350
Litchfield Plains	04350
Little Deer Isle	04650
Little Falls	04082
Little Falls-South Windham	04082
Littlefield (Part of Auburn)	04210
Littlefield Corner (Part of Auburn)	04210
Little Machias	04626
Littleton	04730
Littleton (Town)	04730
Livermore	04253
Livermore (Town)	04253
Livermore Falls	04254
Livermore Falls (Town)	04254
Locke Mills	04255
Long Beach (Cumberland County)	04075
Long Beach (York County)	03910
Longcove	04857
Long Island	04050
Lookout	04645
Loring Air Force Base	04751
Lovell	04051
Lovell (Town)	04051
Lowell	04433
Lowell (Town)	04433
Lower Dennysville	04628
Lubec	04652
Lubec (Town)	04652
Lucerne-In-Maine	04429
Ludlow	04730
Ludlow (Town)	04730
Lyman (Town)	04005
Lynchville	04231
McFarlands Corner	04941
Machias	04654
Machias (Town)	04654
Machiasport	04655
Machiasport (Town)	04655
Mackworth Island	04105
Mackworth Point	04105
MacMahan	04548
Macwahoc	04451
Macwahoc (Town)	04451
Madawaska	04756
Madawaska (Town)	04756
Madawaska Lake	04783
Madison	04950
Madison (Town)	04950
Madrid	04966
Madrid (Town)	04966
Magalloway (Town)	03579

	ZIP
Maine Mall (Part of South Portland)	04106
Mainstream	04942
Mallison Falls	04082
Manchester	04351
Manchester (Town)	04351
Manset	04656
Maple Grove	04742
Mapleton	04757
Mapleton (Town)	04757
Maplewood	04095
Mariaville	04605
Mariaville (Town)	04605
Marion	04628
Marlboro	04605
Marrtown	04548
Marshfield	04654
Marshfield (Town)	04654
Mars Hill	04758
Mars Hill (Town)	04758
Mars Hill-Blaine	04758
Marshville	04643
Marston Corner (Part of Auburn)	04210
Martin	04547
Martinsville	04860
Masardis	04759
Masardis (Town)	04759
Mason Bay	04649
Mast Landing	04032
Matinicus	04851
Matinicus Isle (Town)	04851
Mattawamkeag	04459
Mattawamkeag (Town)	04459
Maxfield (Town)	04453
Mayberry Hill	04015
Mayville	04217
Mechanic Falls (Town)	04256
Mechanic Falls	04256
Meddybemps	04657
Meddybemps (Town)	04657
Medford	04453
Medford (Town)	04453
Medford Center	04453
Medomak	04551
Medway	04460
Medway (Town)	04460
Melvin Heights	04843
Mercer	04957
Mercer (Town)	04957
Merepoint	04053
Merrill (Town)	04780
Mexico	04257
Mexico (Town)	04257
Middledam	04216
Middle Intervale	04217
Milbridge	04658
Milbridge (Town)	04658
Milford	04461
Milford (Town)	04461
Milliken Mills	04064
Millinocket (Town)	04462
Millinocket	04462
Milltown (Part of Calais)	04619
Milo	04463
Milo (Town)	04463
Milton	04219
Milton (Town)	04219
Minot	04258
Minot (Town)	04258
Minturn	04659
Molunkus	04451
Monarda	04776
Monhegan	04852
Monhegan (Town)	04852
Monmouth	04259
Monmouth (Town)	04259
Monroe	04951
Monroe (Town)	04951
Monroe Center	04951
Monson	04464
Monson (Town)	04464
Monticello	04760
Monticello (Town)	04760
Montsweag	04578
Montville (Town)	04941
Moody	04054
Moody Beach	04054
Moosehead	04442
Moose River	04945
Moose River (Town)	04945
Moro (Town)	04780
Morrill	04952
Morrill (Town)	04952
Morris Corner	04750
Morse Corners	04928
Moscow (Town)	04920
Moscow	04920
Mount Chase (Town)	04765

	ZIP
Mount Desert	04660
Mount Desert (Town)	04660
Mount Pisgah	04538
Mount Vernon	04352
Mount Vernon (Town)	04352
Murphy Corner	04578
Muscongus	04551
Muscongus Bay	04555
Naples	04055
Naples (Town)	04055
Nashville (Town)	04732
Naskeag	04616
Naval Air Station	04011
Naval Communications Unit	04630
Naval Shipyard	03801
Nequasset	04579
Newagen	04552
New Auburn (Part of Auburn)	04210
Newburgh	04444
Newburgh (Town)	04444
New Canada (Town)	04743
Newcastle	04553
Newcastle (Town)	04553
Newfield	04056
Newfield (Town)	04056
New Gloucester	04260
New Gloucester (Town)	04260
Newhall	04062
New Harbor	04554
New Limerick	04761
New Limerick (Town)	04761
Newport	04953
Newport (Town)	04953
New Portland	04954
New Portland (Town)	04954
Newry	04261
Newry (Town)	04261
New Sharon	04955
New Sharon (Town)	04955
New Sweden	04762
New Sweden (Town)	04762
Newtown (Part of Biddeford)	04005
New Vineyard	04956
New Vineyard (Town)	04956
Nicolin (Part of Ellsworth)	04605
Nobleboro	04555
Nobleboro (Town)	04555
Norridgewock	04957
Norridgewock (Town)	04957
North Alfred	04002
North Amity	04471
North Anson	04958
North Auburn (Part of Auburn)	04210
North Augusta (Part of Augusta)	04330
North Baldwin	04024
North Bancroft	04424
North Bangor (Part of Bangor)	04401
North Bath (Part of Bath)	04530
North Belgrade	04963
North Berwick	03906
North Berwick (Town)	03906
North Blue Hill	04614
North Bradford	04410
North Bridgton	04057
North Brooklin	04661
North Brooksville	04617
North Buckfield	04220
North Castine	04472
North Chesterville	04938
North Cutler	04630
North Dixmont	04932
North East Carry	04478
Northeast Harbor	04662
Northeast Piscataquis (Town)	04462
Northeast Somerset (Town)	04920
North Edgecomb	04556
North Ellsworth (Part of Ellsworth)	04605
Northern Maine Junction	04401
North Fairfield	04937
North Falmouth	04105
Northfield	04654
Northfield (Town)	04654
North Franklin (Town)	04936
North Fryeburg	04058
North Gorham	04075
North Gray	04039
North Guilford	04443
North Harpswell	04079
North Haven	04853
North Haven (Town)	04853

	ZIP
North Hermon	04401
North Hill	04220
North Islesboro	04848
North Jay	04262
North Lamoine	04605
North Lebanon	04027
North Leeds	04263
North Limington	04049
North Livermore	04254
North Lovell	04231
North Lubec	04652
North Lyndon (Part of Caribou)	04736
North Monmouth	04265
North Monroe	04951
North Newcastle	04553
North New Portland	04961
North Norway	04268
North Orland	04429
North Orrington	04474
North Oxford (Town)	03579
North Palermo	04354
North Paris	04289
North Parsonsfield	04047
North Penobscot (Hancock County)	04476
North Penobscot (Penobscot County) (Town)	04462
North Perry	04667
Northport (Town)	04849
Northport	04849
North Pownal	04069
North Raymond	04274
North Scarborough	04074
North Searsmont	04973
North Searsport	04974
North Sebago	04029
North Sedgwick	04676
North Shapleigh	04060
North Sullivan	04664
North Turner	04266
North Vassalboro	04962
North Wade	04786
North Waldoboro	04572
North Warren	04864
North Washington (Town)	04686
North Waterboro	04061
North Waterford	04267
North Wayne	04284
Northwest Aroostook	04770
Northwest Aroostook (Town)	04788
Northwest Bethel	04217
Northwest Hancock (Town)	04408
Northwest Piscataquis (Town)	04441
Northwest Somerset (Town)	04945
North Whitefield	04353
North Windsor	04361
North Woodstock	04219
North Yarmouth (Town)	04021
Norumbega	04617
Norway	04268
Norway (Town)	04268
Norway Center	04268
Norway Lake	04268
Number Four	04051
Oakfield	04763
Oakfield (Town)	04763
Oak Hill (Androscoggin County)	04273
Oak Hill (Cumberland County)	04074
Oakland	04963
Oakland (Town)	04963
Oak Point	04605
Oak Ridge (Part of Biddeford)	04005
Oak Terrace	03904
Ocean Park	04063
Ocean Point	04544
Oceanview Harbor	04074
Oceanville	04681
Ogontz	04478
Ogunquit (Town)	03907
Ogunquit	03907
Olamon	04467
Olde Mill Brook	04074
Old Orchard Beach (Town)	04064
Old Orchard Beach	04064
Old Town	04468
Onawa	04443
Oquossoc	04964
Orffs Corner	04572
Orient	04471

	ZIP
Orient (Town)	04471
Orland	04472
Orland (Town)	04472
Orono (Town)	04473
Orono	04473
Orrington	04474
Orrington (Town)	04474
Orrington Center	04474
Orrs Island	04066
Osborn (Town)	04605
Otis	04605
Otis (Town)	04605
Otisfield	04270
Otisfield (Town)	04270
Otter Creek	04665
Owls Head	04854
Owls Head (Town)	04854
Oxbow	04764
Oxbow (Town)	04764
Oxford	04270
Oxford (Town)	04270
Paine Corner	04281
Palermo	04354
Palermo (Town)	04354
Palmyra	04965
Palmyra (Town)	04965
Paris	04271
Paris (Town)	04271
Parker Head	04562
Parkman	04443
Parkman (Town)	04443
Parsonsfield	04048
Parsonsfield (Town)	04028
Passadumkeag	04475
Passadumkeag (Town)	04475
Passamaquoddy Indian Township (Town)	04668
Passamaquoddy Pleasant Point Indian Reservation (Town)	04667
Patten	04765
Patten (Town)	04765
Peabbles Cove	04107
Peaks Island (Part of Portland)	04108
Pea Ridge	04458
Pejepscot	04086
Pelton Hill (Part of Augusta)	04330
Pemaquid	04558
Pemaquid Beach	04554
Pemaquid Harbor	04558
Pemaquid Point	04554
Pembroke	04666
Pembroke (Town)	04666
Penley's Corner (Part of Auburn)	04210
Penobscot	04476
Penobscot (Town)	04476
Penobscot Indian Island Reservation	04468
Perham	04766
Perham (Town)	04766
Perkins (Town)	04357
Perry (Town)	04667
Perry (Aroostook County)	04769
Perry (Washington County)	04667
Perrys Corner	04048
Peru	04290
Peru (Town)	04290
Peter Dana Point	04668
Phair (Part of Presque Isle)	04769
Phillips	04966
Phillips (Town)	04966
Phippsburg	04562
Phippsburg (Town)	04562
Pigeon Hill	04658
Pike Corner	04015
Pine Cliff	04576
Pine Hill	03902
Pine Park	04064
Pine Point	04074
Pittsfield	04967
Pittsfield (Town)	04967
Pittston	04345
Pittston (Town)	04345
Pittston Farm	04478
Plaisted	04739
Plantation Number Fourteen (Town)	04628
Plantation Number Twenty-one (Town)	04668
Pleasant Beach	04858
Pleasantdale (Part of South Portland)	04106
Pleasant Hill (mail Freeport)	04032

	ZIP
Pleasant Hill (mail Portland)	04105
Pleasant Hill (mail Scarborough)	04074
Pleasant Lake	04619
Pleasant Point	04563
Pleasant Point Indian Reservation	04667
Pleasant Pond	04925
Pleasant Ridge (Town)	04920
Pleasantville	04864
Plummer Island	04074
Plymouth	04969
Plymouth (Town)	04969
Poland	04273
Poland (Town)	04273
Poland Spring	04274
Pond Cove	04107
Poors Mills (Part of Belfast)	04915
Popham Beach	04562
Portage	04768
Portage Lake (Town)	04768
Port Clyde	04855
Porter	04068
Porter (Town)	04068
Porterfield	04047
Porter Landing	04032
Portland	04101-04
	04109
	04112
For specific Portland Zip Codes call (207) 871-8411, or your local postmaster.	
Portsmouth Naval Shipyard	03801
Pownal	04069
Pownal (Town)	04069
Pownal Center	04069
Pratt Corner	04281
Prentiss	04487
Prentiss (Town)	04487
Presque Isle	04769
Prides Corner (Part of Westbrook)	04092
Princeton	04668
Princeton (Town)	04668
Promenade Mall (Part of Lewiston)	04240
Promised Land	04273
Prospect	04981
Prospect (Town)	04981
Prospect Ferry	04981
Prospect Harbor	04669
Prouts Neck	04074
Pulpit Harbor	04853
Pumpkin Valley	04009
Quimby	04770
Quoddy Village (Part of Eastport)	04631
Randolph (Town)	04346
Randolph	04346
Rangeley	04970
Rangeley (Town)	04970
Raymond	04071
Raymond (Town)	04071
Rayville	04270
Razorville	04574
Reach	04627
Readfield (Town)	04355
Readfield	04355
Red Beach (Part of Calais)	04619
Redding	04292
Reed (Town)	04497
Reeds	04966
Richmond	04357
Richmond (Town)	04357
Richmond Mill	04284
Richville	04075
Ridlonville	04257
Rileys	04239
Ripley	04930
Ripley (Town)	04930
Ripley	04643
Riverside	04330
Riverview (Part of Presque Isle)	04769
Robbinston	04671
Robbinston (Town)	04671
Robinhood	04530
Robinson	04758
Robinson Corner	04240
Robyville	04450
Rockland	04841
Rockport	04856
Rockport (Town)	04856
Rockville	04841
Rockwood	04478

	ZIP
Rogers Corners	04987
Rome	04957
Rome (Town)	04957
Roque Bluffs	04654
Roque Bluffs (Town)	04654
Ross Corner	04087
Round Pond	04564
Roxbury	04275
Roxbury (Town)	04275
Royal Corner (Part of Auburn)	04210
Rumford	04276
Rumford (Town)	04276
Rumford Center	04278
Rumford Corner	04219
Rumford Junction (Part of Auburn)	04210
Rumford Point	04279
Sabattus	04280
Sabattus (Town)	04280
Sabbathday Lake	04274
Saco	04072
St. Agatha	04772
St. Agatha (Town)	04772
St. Albans	04971
St. Albans (Town)	04971
St. David	04773
St. Francis	04774
St. Francis (Town)	04774
St. Francis College (Part of Biddeford)	04005
St. George	04857
St. George (Town)	04857
St. John	04743
St. John (Town)	04743
St. Josephs College	04062
Salem	04983
Salmon Falls	04004
Salsbury Cove	04672
Sanderson Corners	04349
Sandhill Corner	04341
Sandy Beach	04401
Sandy Creek	04009
Sandy Point	04972
Sandy River (Town)	04970
Sandy River Beach	04649
Sanford	04073
Sanford (Town)	04073
Sangerville	04479
Sangerville (Town)	04479
Sargentville	04673
Saunders (Part of Presque Isle)	04769
Scarboro Beach	04074
Scarborough	04074
Scarborough (Town)	04074
Scituate	03909
Scotland	03909
Scott (Part of Presque Isle)	04769
Scribners Mill	04040
Seabury	03909
Seal Cove	04674
Seal Harbor	04675
Searsmont	04973
Searsmont (Town)	04973
Searsport	04974
Searsport (Town)	04974
Seawall	04656
Sebago (Town)	04029
Sebago Lake	04075
Sebasco	04565
Sebasco Estates	04565
Sebec	04481
Sebec (Town)	04481
Sebec Corners	04426
Sebec Lake	04482
Seboeis	04448
Seboeis (Town)	04448
Seboomook	04478
Seboomook Lake (Town)	04478
Sedgwick	04676
Sedgwick (Town)	04676
Shady Nook	03830
Shaker Village	04274
Shapleigh	04076
Shapleigh (Town)	04076
Shaw Mills	04075
Shawmut	04975
Sheepscot	04578
Sheridan	04775
Sherman	04776
Sherman (Town)	04776
Sherman Mills	04776
Shermans Corner	04949
Sherman Station	04777
Shin Pond	04765
Shirley (Town)	04485

	ZIP
Shirley Mills	04485
Sidney	04330
Sidney (Town)	04330
Silver Ridge	04776
Simonton Corners	04843
Simpson Corners	04932
Sinclair	04779
Skillings Corner	04210
Skowhegan	04976
Skowhegan (Town)	04976
Slab City (Oxford County)	04231
Slab City (Waldo County)	04849
Small Point	04567
Smithfield	04978
Smithfield (Town)	04978
Smithville	04680
Smyrna (Town)	04780
Smyrna Center	04780
Smyrna Mills	04780
Soldier Pond	04781
Solon	04979
Solon (Town)	04979
Somerville	04341
Somerville (Town)	04341
Sorrento	04677
Sorrento (Town)	04677
Sound	04660
South Acton	04027
South Addison	04606
South Andover	04216
South Arm	04216
South Aroostook (Town)	04730
South Bancroft	04424
South Berwick	03908
South Berwick (Town)	03908
South Blue Hill	04615
South Brewer (Part of Brewer)	04412
South Bridgton	04009
South Bristol	04568
South Bristol (Town)	04568
South Buxton	04038
South Casco	04077
South China	04358
South Corinth	04427
South Deer Isle	04681
South Dover	04426
South Durham	04032
Southeast Piscataquis (Town)	04463
South Eliot	03903
South Exeter	04928
South Franklin (Town)	04224
South Freeport	04078
South Gardiner (Part of Gardiner)	04359
South Gorham	04038
South Gouldsboro	04607
South Gray	04039
South Hancock	04605
South Harpswell	04079
South Hiram	04041
South Hollis	04042
South Hope	04862
South Jefferson	04553
South Lagrange	04453
South Lebanon	04027
South Levant	04456
South Lewiston (Part of Lewiston)	04240
South Liberty	04949
South Limington	04048
South Lincoln	04457
South Livermore	04254
South Lubec	04652
South Monmouth	04259
South Montville	04949
South Newcastle	04556
South Orland	04472
South Orrington	04474
South Oxford (Town)	04267
South Paris	04281
South Parsonsfield	04048
South Penobscot	04476
Southport	04576
Southport (Town)	04576
South Portland	04106*
	04116†
South Princeton	04668
South Rangeley	04964
South Rumford	04276
South Sanford	04073
South Side	03909
South Surry	04684
South Thomaston	04858
South Thomaston (Town)	04858
South Trescott	04652
South Union	04864
South Waldoboro	04572

	ZIP
South Warren	04864
South Waterford	04081
South West Bend	04252
Southwest Harbor	04679
Southwest Harbor (Town)	04679
Southwest Harbor Coast Guard Base	04679
South Windham	04082
South Windsor	04363
South Woodstock	04289
South Woodville	04458
Spears Corner	04345
Spragueville (Part of Presque Isle)	04769
Springfield	04487
Springfield (Town)	04487
Springvale	04083
Spruce Head	04859
Spruce Head Island	04859
Spruce Point	04538
Spruce Shores	04544
Squa Pan	04732
Square Lake (Town)	04743
Squirrel Island	04570
Stacyville	04782
Stacyville (Town)	04782
Standish	04084
Standish (Town)	04084
Starboard	04618
Starks	04911
Starks (Town)	04911
State Road	04769
Stebbins	04742
Steep Falls	04085
Stetson	04488
Stetson (Town)	04488
Steuben	04680
Steuben (Town)	04680
Stevens Corner	03830
Stevensville	04742
Stickney Corner	04574
Stillwater (Part of Old Town)	04489
Stockholm	04783
Stockholm (Town)	04783
Stockton Springs	04981
Stockton Springs (Town)	04981
Stoneham (Town)	04231
Stonington	04681
Stonington (Town)	04681
Stover Corner	04617
Stow	04058
Stow (Town)	04058
Stratton	04982
Stricklands	04263
Strong	04983
Strong (Town)	04983
Sullivan	04664
Sullivan (Town)	04664
Summerhaven (Part of Augusta)	04330
Sumner (Town)	04292
Sunset	04683
Sunshine	04627
Surfside	04064
Surry	04684
Surry (Town)	04684
Sutton Island	04662
Swans Island	04685
Swans Island (Town)	04685
Swanville	04915
Swanville (Town)	04915
Sweden (Aroostook County)	04762
Sweden (Oxford County) (Town)	04040
Tacoma	04350
Tainter Corner	04224
Tallwood	04355
Talmadge (Town)	04492
Tatnic	03906
Temple	04984
Temple (Town)	04984
Temple Heights	04915
Tenants Harbor	04860
The Forks (Town)	04985
The Kingdom	04941
The Ridge	04009
Thomaston	04861
Thomaston (Town)	04861
Thompson's Point	04055
Thorndike	04986
Thorndike (Town)	04986
Thorndike Center	04986
Thornton Heights (Part of South Portland)	04106
Todds Corner	04930
Topsfield	04490
Topsfield (Town)	04490

	ZIP
Topsham	04086
Topsham (Town)	04086
Tory Hill	04038
Town Farm Hill	04040
Town Hill	04609
Town House Corners	04046
Tracy Corners	04606
Trainor Corner	04345
Trap Corner	04289
Tremont (Town)	04653
Trenton	04605
Trenton (Town)	04605
Trevett	04571
Troutdale	04985
Troy	04987
Troy (Town)	04987
Troy Center	04987
Turbats Creek	04046
Turner	04282
Turner (Town)	04282
Turner Center	04283
Turnpike Mall (Part of Augusta)	04330
Twelve Corners	04254
Twombly (Town)	04417
Union	04862
Union (Town)	04862
Unionville	04622
Unity (Kennebec County) (Town)	04988
Unity (Waldo County)	04988
Unity (Waldo County) (Town)	04988
University Bookstore	04473
Upper Abbot	04406
Upper Frenchville	04784
Upper Gloucester	04260
Upton	04261
Upton (Town)	04261
Van Buren	04785
Van Buren (Town)	04785
Vanceboro	04491
Vanceboro (Town)	04491
Vassalboro	04989
Vassalborough (Town)	04989
Veazie (Town)	04401
Veazie	04401
Verona	04416
Verona (Town)	04416
Vienna	04360
Vienna (Town)	04360
Viking Village	04217
Vinalhaven	04863
Vinalhaven (Town)	04863
Wade (Town)	04786
Waite	04492
Waite (Town)	04492
Waites Landing	04105
Waldo	04915
Waldo (Town)	04915
Waldoboro	04572
Waldoboro (Town)	04572
Wales (Town)	04280
Wales Corner	04280
Walkers Mill	04217
Wallagrass	04781
Wallagrass (Town)	04781
Walnut Hill	04021
Walpole	04573
Waltham	04605
Waltham (Town)	04605
Wards Cove	04075
Wardtown	04032
Warren (Town)	04864
Warren	04864
Washburn	04786
Washburn (Town)	04786
Washburn Junction (Part of Presque Isle)	04769
Washington	04574
Washington (Town)	04574
Waterboro	04087
Waterboro (Town)	04087
Waterboro Center	04030
Waterford	04088
Waterford (Town)	04088
Waterman Beach	04858
Water Street (Part of Augusta)	04330
Waterville	04901*
	04903†
Waverly	04967
Wayne	04284
Wayne (Town)	04284
Webster	04473
Webster (Town)	04487
Webster Corner	04252
Weeks Mills	04361
Welchville	04270

	ZIP
Welcomes Corner (Part of Auburn)	04210
Weld	04285
Weld (Town)	04285
Wellington	04942
Wellington (Town)	04942
Wells	04090
Wells (Town)	04090
Wells Beach	04090
Wells Branch	04090
Wesley	04686
Wesley (Town)	04686
West Appleton	04949
West Athens	04912
West Auburn (Part of Auburn)	04210
West Baldwin	04091
West Bath (Town)	04530
West Bethel	04286
West Boothbay Harbor	04575
West Bowdoin	04287
West Bridgton	04009
Westbrook	04092*
	04098†
West Brooklin	04616
West Brooksville	04617
West Buxton	04093
West Central Franklin (Town)	04285
West Charleston	04422
West Corinth	04427
West Cumberland	04021
West Denmark	04010
West Durham	04069
West Ellsworth (Part of Ellsworth)	04605
West End (Part of Portland)	04102
West Enfield	04493
West Falmouth	04105
West Farmington	04992
Westfield	04787
Westfield (Town)	04787
West Forks	04985
West Forks (Town)	04985
West Franklin	04634
West Fryeburg	04037
West Gardiner (Town)	04345
West Georgetown	04548
West Gorham	04038
West Gouldsboro	04607
West Gray	04039
West Harpswell	04079
West Harrington	04643
West Hollis	04042
West Jonesport	04649
West Kennebunk	04094
West Lebanon	04027
West Leeds	04263
West Levant	04456
West Lovell	04051
West Lubec	04652
Westmanland (Town)	04783
West Mills	04938
West Minot	04288
West Mount Vernon	04352
West Newfield	04095
West Old Town (Part of Old Town)	04468
Weston	04424
Weston (Town)	04424
West Paris	04289
West Paris (Town)	04289
West Pembroke	04666
West Penobscot	04476
West Peru	04290
Westpoint	04565
West Poland	04291
Westport	04578
Westport (Town)	04578
West Princeton	04668
West Rockport	04865
West Scarborough	04070
West Seboois	04462
West Southport	04576
West Stonington	04681
West Sullivan	04664
West Sumner	04292
West Surry	04605
West Tremont	04690
West Trenton	04605
West Waldoboro	04572
West Washington	04341
West Winterport	04496
Whitefield	04353
Whitefield (Town)	04353
White Rock	04038
Whites Corner	04260
Whiting	04691

* Area Zip Code   **† Post Office Boxes**

	ZIP		ZIP		ZIP		ZIP
Whiting (Town)	04691	Windham Hill	04062	Winthrop	04364	Worthley Pond	04290
Whitney (Town)	04487	Windsor	04363	Winthrop (Town)	04364	Wyman (Franklin County)	
Whitneyville	04692	Windsor (Town)	04363	Winthrop Center	04364	(Town)	04982
Whitneyville (Town)	04692	Winkumpaugh Corners		Wiscasset	04578	Wyman (Washington	
Wildes District	04046	(Part of Ellsworth)	04605	Wiscasset (Town)	04578	County)	04658
Wildwood Park	04110	Winn	04495	Wonsqueak Harbor	04613	Wytopitlock	04497
Wiley's Corner	04861	Winn (Town)	04495	Woodfords (Part of		Yarmouth	04096
Williamsburg	04414	Winnecook	04922	Portland)	04103	Yarmouth (Town)	04096
Willimantic	04443	Winnegance	04530	Woodland (Aroostook		York	03909
Willimantic (Town)	04443	Winslow	04901	County) (Town)	04736	York (Town)	03909
Wilson Corner (Part of		Winslow (Town)	04901	Woodland (Washington		York Beach	03910
Ellsworth)	04605	Winslows Mills	04572	County)	04694	York Cliffs	03902
Wilsons Mills	03579	Winter Harbor	04693	Woodmans Mills	04973	York Harbor	03911
Wilton	04294	Winter Harbor (Town)	04693	Woodstock (Town)	04219	York Heights	03909
Wilton (Town)	04294	Winterport	04496	Woodville (Town)	04458	Youngs Corner (Part of	
Windham (Town)	04062	Winterport (Town)	04496	Woolwich	04579	Auburn)	04210
Windham	04062	Winterville	04788	Woolwich (Town)	04579	Youngtown	04850
Windham Center	04062	Winterville (Town)	04788				

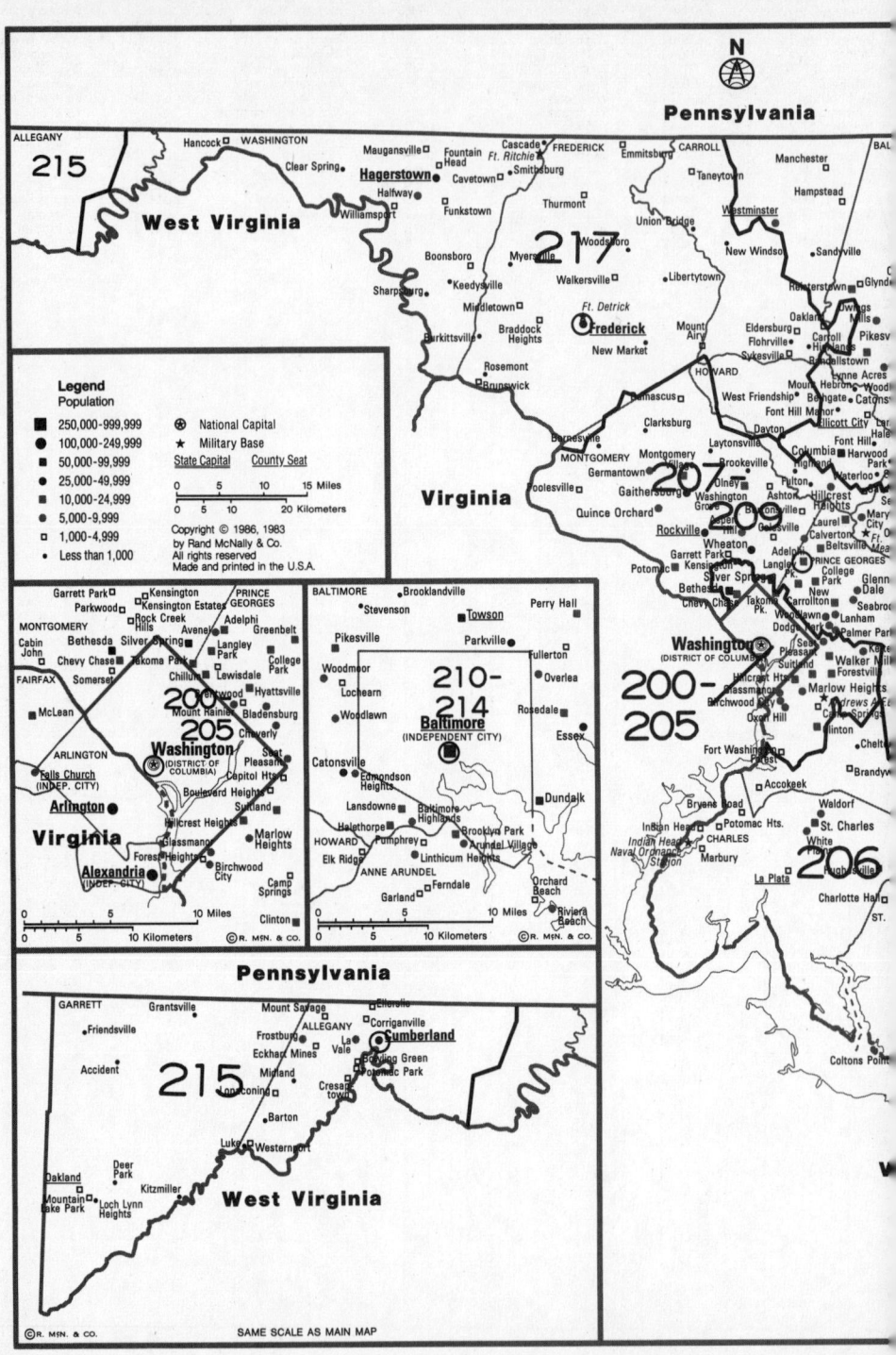

Legend
Population
■ 250,000-999,999
● 100,000-249,999
● 50,000-99,999
● 25,000-49,999
■ 10,000-24,999
□ 5,000-9,999
□ 1,000-4,999
• Less than 1,000

⊛ National Capital
★ Military Base
State Capital   County Seat

0   5   10   15 Miles
0   5   10   20 Kilometers

Copyright © 1986, 1983
by Rand McNally & Co.
All rights reserved
Made and printed in the U.S.A.

SAME SCALE AS MAIN MAP

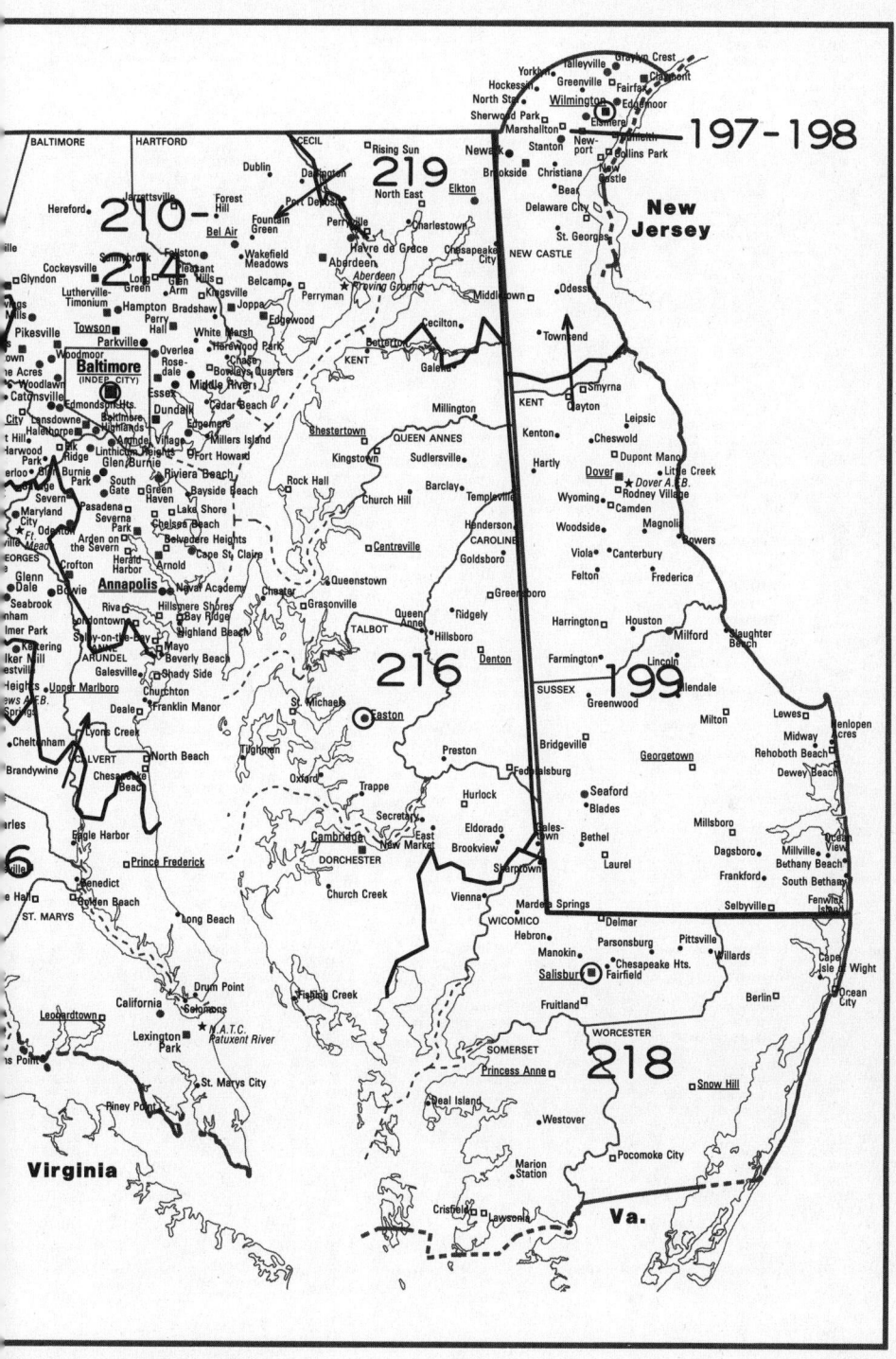

	ZIP
Abell	20606
Aberdeen	21001
Aberdeen Proving Ground	21005
Abingdon	21009
Academy Heights	21228
Academy Junction	21113
Accident	21520
Accokeek	20607
Accokeek Acres	20607
Accokeek Groves	20607
Acco Park	20607
Adamstown	21710
Adams Woods	20783
Adelina	20678
Adelphi	20783
Adelphi Hills	20783
Adelphi Manor	20783
Ady	21154
Aero Acres	21220
Aikin (Part of Perryville)	21903
Airey	21613
Albantown	21074
Albeth Heights	21163
Aldino	21001
Alesia	21107
Allanwood	20906
Allegany	21532
Allegany Grove	21502
Allen	21810
Allenford	21042
Allens Fresh	20632
Allenwood	21801
Allenwood Acres	20748
Allview	21045
Allview Estates	21046
Alpha	21104
Alpine Beach	21122
Altamont	21561
Alta Vista	20817
Alta Vista Gardens	20814
Alta Vista Terrace	20814
Amberly	21401
Amberly of Kings Court	21237
Amber Meadows (Part of Bowie)	20716
Amcelle	21502
Amcelle Acres	21502
American Cities	21044
American Corners	21632
Ammendale	20705
Anchorage (Part of Annapolis)	21403
Ancient Oak	20878
Ancient Oak North	20878
Andersontown	21629
Andover Estates	20692
Andrew Hills	20748
Andrews	21626
Andrews Air Force Base	20331
Andrews Air Force Base Hospital	20331
Andrews Estates	20746
Andrews Manor	20746
Annapolis	21401-05
For specific Annapolis Zip Codes call (301) 263-9292, or your local postmaster.	
Annapolis Junction	20701
Annapolis Rock	21797
Anneslie	21212
Antietam	21782
Apple Green	20754
Apple Grove	20744
Appleton Acres	21921
Appliance Park-East (Part of Baltimore)	21045
Appolds	21778
Aquasco	20608
Aragona Village	20744
Arbutus	21227
Arden-on-the-Severn	21032
Ardmore	20785
Ardwick	20785
Argonne Hills	20755
Argyle Park	20901
Arlington (Part of Baltimore)	21215
Armagh	21204
Arnold	21012
Arnold Heights	20746
Arnoldtown	21718
Arrowhead (Howard County)	21046
Arrow Head (Montgomery County)	20879
Arrowood	20817
Arundel Gardens	21225
Arundel Hills	21090
Arundel on the Bay	21403

	ZIP
Arundel Plaza	21146
Arundel View	21054
Arundel Village	21225
Asbury Methodist Home (Part of Gaithersburg)	20877
Ashburton	20817
Asher Glade	21531
Ashland	21030
Ashton	20861
Ashton Pond	20861
Ashton-Sandy Springs	20861
Asleigh	20817
Aspen Hill	20906
Aspen Hill Park	20853
Aspen Knolls	20853
Athol	21837
Atholton	21045
Atholton Manor	21045
Augusta	21758
Aurora Hills	21108
Auth Village	20746
Autrey Park (Part of Rockville)	20850
Autumn Hill	21043
Avalon Shores	20764
Avenue	20609
Avilton	21539
Avondale Grove	20782
Ayrlawn	20814
Back Bay Beach	20778
Back River Highlands	21221
Baden	20613
Bainbridge Naval Training Center	21904
Bakersville	21713
Bald Eagle	20613
Baldwin	21013
Baldwin Hill	21108
Baldwin Hills South	21032
Ballard	20735
Ballard Gardens	21220
Ballenger Creek	21701
Baltimore	21201-86
For specific Baltimore Zip Codes call (301) 347-4430, or your local postmaster.	
COLLEGES & UNIVERSITIES	
College of Notre Dame of Maryland	21210
Coppin State College	21216
Johns Hopkins University	21218
Loyola College	21210
Maryland Institute College of Art	21217
University of Maryland at Baltimore	21201
FINANCIAL INSTITUTIONS	
American National Savings Association, F.A.	21201
Arundel Federal Savings Bank	21225
Atlantic Federal Savings Bank	21204
Baltimore County Savings Bank, F.S.B.	21236
Bank of Baltimore	21202
Bradford Federal Savings Bank	21212
Carrollton Bank	21201
Chase Bank of Maryland	21202
Citibank (Maryland), N.A.	21202
Fairfax Savings, F.S.B.	21202
First National Bank of Maryland	21201
Hamilton Federal Savings & Loan Association	21214
Harbor Federal Savings Bank	21230
Leeds Federal Savings & Loan Association	21229
Loyola Federal Savings Bank	21201
Maryland National Bank	21202
Mercantile-Safe Deposit & Trust Company	21201
NationsBank of Maryland, N.A.	21201
Provident Bank of Maryland	21202
Rosedale Federal Savings & Loan Association	21206
Signet Bank/Maryland	21202

	ZIP
HOSPITALS	
Francis Scott Key Medical Center	21224
Franklin Square Hospital Center	21237
Good Samaritan Hospital of Maryland	21239
Greater Baltimore Medical Center	21204
Harbor Hospital Center	21225
Johns Hopkins Hospital	21287
Levindale Hebrew Geriatric Center and Hospital	21215
Liberty Medical Center	21215
Mercy Medical Center	21202
St. Agnes Hospital of The City of Baltimore	21229
St. Joseph Hospital	21204
Sinai Hospital of Balitimore	21215
Union Memorial Hospital	21218
University of Maryland Medical System	21201
Veterans Affairs Medical Center	21201
HOTELS/MOTELS	
Baltimore Marriott Inner Harbor	21201
Baltimore Ramada Inner Harbor	21201
Brookshire Inner Harbor Suite Hotel	21202
Cross Keys Inn	21210
Holiday Inn-Inner Harbor	21201
Holiday Inn-Moravia Road	21206
Hyatt Regency Baltimore Inner Harbor	21202
Omni Inner Harbor Hotel	21201
Radisson Plaza Lord Baltimore	21201
Sheraton Inner Harbor Hotel	21201
Sheraton Baltimore North	21204
Society Hill Hopkins Hotel	21218
Tremont Hotel	21202
Tremont Plaza	21202
MILITARY INSTALLATIONS	
Air Force Publications Distribution Center	21220
Coast Guard Yard, Curtis Bay	21226
Maryland Air National Guard, FB6191, Martin State Airport	21220
MTMC Baltimore Outport	21222
United States Army Engineer District, Baltimore	21203
United States Army Publications Distribution Center	21220
Baltimore Corner	21640
Baltimore Highlands	21227
Banks O'Dee	20664
Bannockburn	20814
Bannockburn Estates	20817
Bannockburn Heights	20817
Barclay	21607
Barefoot Acres	20619
Bar Harbor	21122
Bark Hill	21791
Barksdale	21921
Barnaby Manor	20744
Barnaby Run Estates	20745
Barnaby Village	20745
Bar Neck	21671
Barnes Corner	21917
Barnesville	20838
Barnesville (Sellman)	20842
Barrelville	21545
Barstow	20610
Bartholows	21771
Barton	21521
Bartonsville	21701
Battery Park	20814
Battle Grove	21222
Bayberry	21012
Bay City	21666
Bay Highlands	21403
Baynesville	21204
Bay Ridge	21403
Bayside Beach	21122
Bay View (Part of Baltimore)	21224

	ZIP
Bay View (Cecil County)	21901
Bay View Estates	21919
Beachville	20684
Beachwood Forest	21122
Beachwood Grove	21122
Beachwood on the Burley	21401
Beacon Heights	20737
Beacon Hill	21401
Beale Manor	21403
Beall Estates	20716
Beallsville	20839
Beantown	20601
Bear Creek Junction	21222
Beaufort Park	20759
Beauty Beach	21061
Beauvue	20650
Beaver Creek	21740
Beaver Dam	21851
Beaver Dam Estates	20785
Beaver Heights	20743
Beckleysville	21074
Bedford	20708
Bedfordshire	20854
Bel Air (Allegany County)	21502
Bel Air (Harford County)	21014-15
For specific Bel Air Zip Codes call (410) 838-6262, or your local postmaster.	
Belair (Prince George's County)	20715
Bel Air Acres (Charles County)	20601
Bel Air Acres (Harford County)	21014
Belair Buckingham (Part of Bowie)	20715
Belair Chapel Forge (Part of Bowie)	20715
Belair Foxhill (Part of Bowie)	20715
Belair Heather Hills (Part of Bowie)	20715
Belair Idlewild (Part of Bowie)	20715
Belair Kenilworth (Part of Bowie)	20715
Belair Longridge (Part of Bowie)	20715
Bel Air North	21050
Belair Overbrook (Part of Bowie)	20715
Belair Rockledge (Part of Bowie)	20715
Belair Shopping Center (Part of Bowie)	20715
Belair Somerset (Part of Bowie)	20715
Bel Air South	21015
Belair Tulip Grove (Part of Bowie)	20715
Belair White Hall (Part of Bowie)	20715
Belair Yorktown (Part of Bowie)	20715
Bel Alton	20611
Belcamp	21017
Belhaven	21122
Belleair Estates	20744
Belle Farm Estates	21208
Bellefonte	20735
Belle Grove	21766
Bellemead	20784
Belleview Estates	21146
Bellevue	21662
Bellevue Estates	20607
Bells Mill Village	20854
Belmar	21206
Bel Pre Estates	20906
Bel Pre Park	20906
Bel Pre Woods	20853
Beltsville	20704*
	20705†
Beltsville	20705
Beltsville Heights	20705
Beltway Plaza (Part of Greenbelt)	20770
Belvedere Heights	21012
Bembe Beach	21403
Benedict	20612
Benevola	21713
Bennsville	20603
Ben Oaks	21146
Benson	21018
Bentley Springs	21120
Bentons Pleasure	21619
Berkley	21034
Berkshire	20746
Berlin	21811
Berrett	21784

* Area Zip Code   **† Post Office Boxes**

Name	ZIP
Berry	20603
Berrywood	21146
Berwyn (Part of College Park)	20740
Berwyn Heights	20740
Bestgate	21401
Bethany Manor	21042
Bethel (Carroll County)	21048
Bethel (Cecil County)	21915
Bethel (Frederick County)	21702
Bethel (Garrett County)	21550
Bethesda	20813-14
	20816-17
	20824
	20827
For specific Bethesda Zip Codes call (301) 652-7401, or your local postmaster.	
Bethgate	21043
Bethlehem	21609
Betterton	21610
Beulah	21643
Beverly Beach	21106
Beverly Farms	20854
Big Pines	20850
Big Pool	21711
Big Spring	21722
Bigwoods	21678
Billingsley Forest	20640
Birchwood City	20745
Birchwood Gardens	20708
Birdlawn	20744
Bird River Beach	21220
Birdsville	20776
Birmingham Estates	20705
Birmingham Terrace	20705
Bishop	21813
Bishops Head	21672
Bishopville	21813
Bitter Sweet	21403
Bittinger	21522
Bivalve	21814
Black Horse	21161
Blackrock Estates	20874
Blacks Corner	21157
Blackwater	21622
Bladensburg	20710
Bladenwoods (Part of Bladensburg)	20710
Blair	20910
Blenheim	21131
Bloomfield	21702
Blooming Rose Settlement	21531
Bloomington	21523
Bloomsbury	21228
Blossom Hills	21122
Blueball	21921
Blueberry Hills	20855
Blue Hill (Part of Hancock)	21750
Blue Mount	21111
Blue Mountain (Frederick County)	21788
Blue Mountain (Washington County)	21783
Blue Ridge Manor	20902
Blue Ridge View	21157
Blythedale	21903
Bolivar Heights	21769
Bolton	20601
Bond Mill Park	20707
Bonds	20607
Bon Haven	21401
Bonnie Acres	21043
Bonnie Brae	21784
Bonnie Brook	21613
Bonnie Knob (Part of Woodsboro)	21798
Bonnie Ridge	21209
Boonsboro	21713
Borden Shaft	21532
Boring	21020
Boulevard Heights	20743
Boulevard Park on the Magothy	21122
Bowens	20678
Bowie	20715-21
For specific Bowie Zip Codes call (301) 464-0707, or your local postmaster.	
Bowie State University	20715
Bowleys Quarters	21220
Bowling Green	21502
Bowlings Alley	20622
Boxhill North	21009
Boxiron	21829
Boxwood Village (Part of Greenbelt)	20770
Boyds	20841
Boyer Mill Heights	21774
Bozman	21612
Bradbury Heights	20743
Bradbury Park	20746
Braddock	21702
Braddock Estates (Part of Frostburg)	21532
Braddock Heights	21714
Bradley Farms	20854
Bradley Hills	20817
Bradley Hills Grove	20817
Bradley Woods	20817
Bradshaw	21021
Brady	21502
Braebrook Village	20770
Branchville (Part of College Park)	20740
Brandwine Farms	21047
Brandywine	20613
Brandywine Country	20772
Brandywine Heights	20613
Breathedsville	21740
Breezewood Farms	21163
Breezy Point	20732
Breezy Point Beach	21221
Brentwood	20722
Breton Beach	20650
Briarcrest Heights	21755
Briarwood (Charles County)	20601
Briarwood (Prince George's County)	20708
Briddletown	21811
Bridewell	20794
Bridgeport (Frederick County)	21787
Bridgeport (Washington County)	21742
Bridgetown	21636
Bright Oaks	21015
Brighton (Baltimore County)	21244
Brighton (Montgomery County)	20833
Brightview Woods	21108
Brightwood Acres	21740
Brinkleigh	21042
Brinkleigh Manor	21042
Brinkley Manor	20748
Brinklow	20862
Bristol	20711
Broad Creek	21160
Broadmoor	21030
Broad Run	21718
Broadview	20748
Broadview Acres	21701
Broadwater Estates	20744
Broadwater Point	20733
Broadwood Manor (Part of Rockville)	20851
Brock Bridge	20708
Brock Hall	20772
Brock Hall Estates	20772
Brock Hall Gardens	20772
Brock Hall Manor	20772
Brookdale	20815
Brookdale Heights	21801
Brooke-Jane Manor	20735
Brooke Manor	20745
Brookemanor Estates	20853
Brookeville	20833
Brook Hill	21702
Brooklandville	21093
Brooklyn (Part of Baltimore)	21225
Brooklyn-Curtis Bay	21225-26
For specific Brooklyn-Curtis Bay Zip Codes call (410) 789-3020, or your local postmaster.	
Brooklyn Park	21225
Brookmead	20874
Brookmead North	20874
Brookmont	20816
Brookside Forest	20901
Brookside Manor	20782
Brookview	21659
Brookville Knolls	20833
Brookwood	20772
Brookwood Estates	20695
Broomes Island	20615
Browns Corner	21617
Brownsville (Queen Anne's County)	21617
Brownsville (Washington County)	21715
Browns Woods Villa	21401
Bruceville (Carroll County)	21757
Bruceville (Talbot County)	21673
Brunswick	21716
Bryans Road	20616
Bryantown (Charles County)	20617
Bryantown (Queen Anne's County)	21658
Bryant Square	21044
Bryant Woods	21044
Buckeystown	21717
Buckingham View	21157
Buck Lodge	20783
Bucktown	21613
Budds Creek	20659
Buena Vista	20678
Buffalo Run	21531
Burgundy Estates (Part of Rockville)	20851
Burgundy Knolls (Part of Rockville)	20850
Burgundy Village (Part of Rockville)	20850
Burkittsville	21718
Burning Tree Estates	20817
Burning Tree Manor	20817
Burns Corner (Part of Aberdeen)	21001
Burnt Mills	20901
Burnt Mills Hills	20901
Burnt Mills Knolls	20901
Burnt Mills Manor	20901
Burnt Mills Village	20901
Burrisville	21617
Burrsville	21629
Burtner	21713
Burtonsville	20866
Bush	21009
Bushs Corner	21132
Bushwood	20618
Butler	21023
Butlertown	21678
Buttercup Estates	21794
Buttonwood Beach	21919
Byford Knolls	20895
Bynum	21050
Bynum Ridge	21050
Byrdtown	21817
Cabin Creek	21643
Cabin John	20818
Cabin John-Brookmont	20816
Cabin John Park	20818
Cactus Hill	20607
Cadillac Homes	21060
California	20619
Callaway	20620
Caltor Manor	20744
Calvary	21028
Calvert (Part of Baltimore)	21202
Calvert (Cecil County)	21901
Calvert Beach	20685
Calvert Beach-Long Beach	20685
Calvert Manor	20607
Calverton	20705
Cambria	21131
Cambridge	21613
Cambridge Estates	20735
Camden (Part of Baltimore)	21230
Camden (Wicomico County)	21810
Camelback Village	20832
Camelot (Harford County)	21015
Camelot (Prince George's County)	20769
Camotop	20854
Campbell	21813
Campbelltown	21813
Camp Springs	20748
Camp Springs Forest	20748
Campus Hills	21286
Canal	21904
Candlewood Park	20855
Cannon Acres	21613
Canton (Part of Baltimore)	21224
Cape Anne	20733
Cape Arthur	21146
Cape Estate	21012
Cape Isle of Wight	21842
Cape Loch Haven	21037
Cape May Beach	21221
Cape St. Claire	21401
Cape St. John	21401
Capital Estates	20695
Capitol Heights	20731
	20743
	20791
For specific Capitol Heights Zip Codes call (301) 336-5650, or your local postmaster.	
Capitol Hills	21061
Capitol Plaza (Part of Landover Hills)	20784
Capitol View Park	20910
Capri Estate	21012
Captains Hill	21842
Carderock Springs	20817
Cardiff	21024
Carea	21161
Carleton East	20706
Carlos	21532
Carlson Spring	20747
Carmichael	21658
Carmody Hills	20743
Carmody Hills-Pepper Mill Village	20743
Carney	21234
Carney Grove	21234
Carney Heights	21234
Carole Highlands	20783
Carpenter Point	21903
Carroll (Part of Baltimore)	21229
Carroll County Trails	21048
Carroll Heights (Part of Hagerstown)	21740
Carroll Highlands	21784
Carroll Island	21220
Carroll Knolls	20910
Carroll Manor (Part of Takoma Park)	20912
Carrollton	21784
Carrollton Manor	21146
Carrollwood	21220
Carrollwood Estate	21771
Carsins Run	21001
Carsondale	20706
Carter Hill (Part of Rockville)	20850
Carvel Beach	21226
Carver Heights	20653
Cascade	21719
Cashell Estates	20855
Casselman	21536
Castle Marina	21619
Castleton	21034
Catchpenny	21856
Catoctin	21716
Catoctin Furnace	21788
Catoctin View	21771
Catonsville	21228
Catonsville Heights	21228
Catonsville Manor	21207
Cavalier Country	20754
Cavetown	21720
Cayots	21915
Cearfoss	21740
Cecilton	21913
Cedar Acres	21044
Cedar Beach	21221
Cedar Grove	20876
Cedar Grove Beach	21631
Cedar Hall	21851
Cedar Haven	20608
Cedar Heights	20743
Cedarhurst (Anne Arundel County)	20764
Cedarhurst (Carroll County)	21048
Cedarhurst Acres	21830
Cedarhurst-on-the-Bay	20764
Cedar Lawn	21740
Cedarmere	21117
Cedar Park (Part of Annapolis)	21401
Cedar Spring	21015
Cedartown	21863
Cedarville	20613
Centennial	21042
Centennial Estates	21042
Center Court	20879
Centerville	21754
Centreville	21617
Ceresville	21701
Chadwick Manor	21244
Chalfone Manor	21228
Chalk Point	20778
Champ	21853
Chance	21816
Chaney	20754
Chaneyville	20736
Chaneyville Farm Estates	20736
Chapel	21601
Chapel Gate	21113
Chapel Hill	20744
Chapel Hill Estates	20610
Chapel Oaks	20743
Chapelview	20621
Chaptico	20621
Charles Manor	21047
Charlesmont	21222

* Area Zip Code   † Post Office Boxes

	ZIP		ZIP		ZIP		ZIP
Charlestown (Allegany County)	21539	Claremont (Part of Baltimore)	21223	Connecticut Avenue Hills	20902	Darcy Manor	20746
Charlestown (Cecil County)	21914	Clarksburg	20871	Connecticut Avenue Park	20906	Dares Beach	20678
Charlestown Manor Beach	21901	Clarks Landing	20636	Connecticut Gardens	20902	Dargan	21782
Charlesville	21702	Clarksville	21029	Conowingo	21918	Darleigh Manor	21236
Charlotte Hall	20622	Clarksville Ridge	21029	Conowingo Village	21034	Darlington	21034
Charlton	21722	Clarysville	21532	Contee	20708	Darnestown	20874
Charred Oak Estates	20817	Clayton Manor	21085	Cooksville	21723	Darryl Gardens	21162
Chartley	21136	Clearfield	21157	Cooperstown	21023	Daugherty Town	21817
Chartridge	21146	Clear Spring	21722	Coopstown	21050	Davidsonville	21035
Chartwell	21146	Clearview	21040	Copenhaver	20854	Dawson	26726
Chase	21027	Clearview Manor	20745	Copperville (Carroll County)	21787	Dawsonville	20841
Chateau Valley	21042	Clearview Village	21122			Day	21797
Chatham	20783	Clearwater Beach	21226	Copperville (Talbot County)	21601	Daysville	21793
Chattolanee	21117	Clements	20624	Coral Hills	20743	Dayton	21036
Chelsea Beach	21122	Clifford (Part of Baltimore)	21230	Corbett (Baltimore County)	21111	Deale	20751
Chelsea Woods (Part of Greenbelt)	20770	Cliffs City	21620			Deale Beach	20751
Cheltenham	20623	Clifton	21702	Corbett (Washington County)	21740	Deal Island	21821
Cheltenham Forest	20735	Clifton-East End (Part of Baltimore)	21213	Cordova	21625	Deanwood Park	20743
Chelten Park	20735	Clifton on the Potomac	20664	Cornersville	21613	Decatur Heights (Part of Bladensburg)	20710
Cherry Hill (Cecil County)	21921	Clifton Park	20901	Cornfield Harbor	20687	Deep Creek	21012
Cherry Hill (Harford County)	21154	Clinton	20735	Corriganville	21524	Deep Creek Lake	21541
Cherry Hill (Prince George's County)	20705	Clinton Acres	20613	Costen	21851	Deep Landing Estates	20639
		Clinton Estates	20735	Cottage City	20722	Deerfield (Harford County)	21034
Cherry Hill (Part of College Park)	20740	Clinton Gardens	20735	Country Club Acres	21550	Deerfield (Montgomery County)	20817
Cherrywalk	21830	Clinton Grove	20735	Country Club Estate	21060	Deerfield Run	20708
Chesaco Park	21237	Clinton Hills	20735	Country Club Manor	21060	Deer Harbour	21801
Chesapeake Beach	20732	Clinton Park	20735	Country Club Park	21093	Deer Park (Garrett County)	21550
Chesapeake City	21915	Clinton Vista	20735	Country Club Village	20814		
Chesapeake Estates	21666	Clinton Woods	20735	Country Place	20866	Deer Park (Montgomery County)	20877
Chesapeake Heights	21801	Clopper	20878	Country Road Estates	20754		
Chesapeake Isle	21901	Cloverfields	21666	Courthouse (Part of Rockville)	20850	Deer Park (Prince George's County)	20748
Chesapeake Landing	21620	Clover Hill	21702	Courtleigh	21133	Deer Park Estates	21048
Chesapeake Ranch Estates	20657	Cloverlea	21106	Cove	21520	Deer Park Heights	20748
Chesapeake Terrace	21222	Cloverly	20904	Coventry	21234	Deers Head	21801
Cheshaven	21919	Club of Stedwick	20879	Cove Point	20657	Defense Heights (Baltimore County)	21222
Chester	21619	Clubside	20879	Covers Corner	21776		
Chesterfield	21032	Clydesdale Acres	21048	Cowentown	21921	Defense Heights (Prince George's County)	20784
Chesterfield Gardens	21122	Cobb Island	20625	Coxby Estates	21037		
Chester Harbor	21620	Cockeysville	21030-31	Cox Creek Acres	21619	Delight	21117
Chester River Beach	21638	For specific Cockeysville Zip Codes call (410) 771-0780, or your local postmaster.		Crabtree	21561	Delmar	21875
Chestertown	21620			Craigtown	21904	Delmont	21144
Chesterville	21651			Cranberry	21157	Den Lee Acres	20735
Chesterville Forest	21651	Cohasset	20814	Crapo	21626	Dennings	21776
Chestnut Grove (Frederick County)	21701	Cohill Estates	21750	Creagerstown	21788	Dennis Grove Apartments	20745
		Cokesburg	21851	Crellin	21550	Denton	21629
Chestnut Grove (Washington County)	21756	Cokesbury	21904	Cremona	20659	Dentsville	20646
		Cold Spring Estates	20854	Cresaptown	21502	Derwood	20855
Chestnut Hill (Baltimore County)	21286	Coleman	21678	Cresaptown-Bel Air	21502	Detmold	21539
		Colesville	20904-05	Crescendo	21676	Detour	21757
Chestnut Hill (Harford County)	21050	For specific Colesville Zip Codes call (301) 384-0656, or your local postmaster.		Cresthaven	20903	Devonshire Forest	21093
				Crestleigh	21042	Diamond Farms (Part of Gaithersburg)	20878
Chestnut Hill (Howard County)	21043			Crestview	20814		
Chestnut Hill Estates	21043	Colesville Farm Estates	20904	Crestview Manor	20735	Dickerson	20842
Chestnut Hills	20705	Colesville Gardens	20904	Crestwood (Anne Arundel County)	21090	Discovery-Spring Garden	21793
Chestnut Ridge (Baltimore County)	21117	Colesville Manor	20904			District Heights	20747*
		Colesville Park	20904	Crestwood (Wicomico County)	21801		20753†
Chestnut Ridge (Prince George's County)	20737	College (Part of Westminster)	21157	Crestwood Acres	21040	Dodge Park	20785
		College Estates (Part of Frederick)	21702	Creswell	21015	Dogwood Flats	21521
Cheverly	20785			Crisfield	21817	Dogwood Hills	21286
Cheverly Manor	20785	College Gardens (Part of Rockville)	20850	Crisp (Part of Baltimore)	21225	Dominion	21619
Chevy Chase	20815			Criswold Manor	21029	Doncaster	20640
Chevy Chase Lake	20815	College Heights Estates	20783	Crocheron	21627	Doncaster Village	21234
Chevy Chase Manor	20815	College Park	20740*	Crofton	21114	Donleigh	21046
Chevy Chase Section Five	20815		20741†	Cromwood	21234	Donnybrook	21204
Chevy Chase Section Three	20815	College Park Woods (Part of College Park)	20740	Croom	20772	Dorceytown	21771
				Crosby	21661	Dorchester Estates	20735
Chevy Chase Terrace	20815	College View	20902	Crowder	21043	Dorrs Corner	21108
Chevy Chase View	20895	Colmar Manor	20722	Crownsville	21032	Dorsey	21227
Chevy Chase Village	20815	Colonial Acres (Cecil County)	21921	Crownsville Hospital Center	21032	Dorseys Regard	20879
Chewsville	21721					Doubs	21710
Chicamuxen	20640	Colonial Acres (Harford County)	21014	Croydon Park (Part of Rockville)	20850	Dowell	20629
Childs	21916					Downsville	21795
Chillum	20783	Colonial Gardens	21228	Crumpton	21628	Drayden	20630
Chillum Estates	20783	Colonial Park (Baltimore County)	21207	Crystal Beach	21919	Dresden Green	20706
Chillum Heights	20783			Cub Hill	21234	Drexel Woods	21228
Chillum Manor	20783	Colonial Park (Washington County)	21740	Cuckhold Creek	20664	Druid (Part of Baltimore)	21217
Chingville	20620			Cumberland	21501-05	Drumcliff	20636
Choptank	21655	Colonial Village	21208	For specific Cumberland Zip Codes call (301) 722-8190, or your local postmaster.		Drumeldra Hills	20904
Christs Rock	21613	Colony Heights	21502			Drum Point	20657
Church Creek	21622	Colony Ridge	21113			Drury	20711
Church Hill (Frederick County)	21773	Colora	21917	Curtis Bay (Part of Baltimore)	21225	Drybranch	21161
		Coltons Point	20626			Dry Run	21722
Church Hill (Queen Anne's County)	21623	Columbia	21044-46	Cypress Creek	21146	Dublin	21034
		For specific Columbia Zip Codes call (410) 381-0121, or your local postmaster.		Dailsville	21613	Dufief	20878
Churchill Town Sector	20874			Daisy	21797	Dulaney Village	21204
Churchton	20733			Dalton	21045	Dulls Corner	21401
Churchville	21028	Columbia Beach	20764	Damascus	20872	Dumbarton	21208
Cinnamon Ridge	20772	Columbia Hills	21043	Dameron	20628	Dumbarton Heights	21208
Cissel Farms	20777	Columbia Park	20785	Dames Quarter	21820	Dunbrook	21122
Claggettsville	20872	Compton	20627	Dam No. 4	21782	Dundalk	21222
Claiborne	21624	Comus	20842	Daniel	21797	Dundalk Shopping Center	21222
		Concord	21632	Daniels Park (Part of College Park)	20740	Dundalk-Sparrows Point	21222
		Congressional Forest Estates	20817			Dundee Village	21220
				Danville	21557	Dunkirk	20754
		Connecticut Avenue Estates	20902	Danwood	21801	Dunlaney Village	21093
						Dunloggin	21042

	ZIP
Dunwood	21085
Dupont Heights	20746
Dynard	20621
Eagle Harbor	20608
Eakles Mills	21756
Earleigh Heights	21146
Earleville	21919
Earlton	21078
East Columbia Park	20785
Eastfield	21222
East Fort Foote Village	20744
East Meadow	20745
East New Market	21631
Easton	21601
Easton Point	21601
Eastover Knolls	20745
East Park Village	21061
Eastpines	20737
Eastpoint	21222
Eastpoint Mall	21224
Eastport (Part of Annapolis)	21403
East Riverdale	20737
East Springbrook	20904
Eastview (Carroll County)	21048
Eastview (Frederick County)	21702
Eastview Estates	21048
Eckhart Mines	21528
Eden	21822
Eder	21921
Edesville	21661
Edgemere	21221
Edgemont (Frederick County)	21702
Edgemont (Washington County)	21783
Edgemoor	20814
Edgewater	21037
Edgewater Beach	21037
Edgewater Village	21040
Edgewood (Frederick County)	21702
Edgewood (Harford County)	21040
Edgewood (Montgomery County)	20814
Edgewood Arsenal	21040
Edgewood Meadows	21040
Edmondson Ridge	21228
Edmonson Heights	21207
Edmonston	20781
Ednor	20905
Ednor Acres	20904
Elberon	20854
Elder Hill	21531
Eldersburg	21784
Eldorado	21659
Elioak	21044
Elk Mills	21920
Elkmore	21921
Elk Neck	21901
Elk Ranch Park	21921
Elkridge	21227
Elkton	21921*
	21922†
Elkton Heights (Part of Elkton)	21921
Elktonia	21401
Elkton Landing (Part of Elkton)	21921
Elkwood Estates	21921
Ellerslie	21529
Ellerton	21773
Ellicott City	21041-43
For specific Ellicott City Zip Codes call (410) 465-0440, or your local postmaster.	
Ellicott Mills (Baltimore County)	21228
Ellicott Mills (Howard County)	21043
Elliott	21869
Elmwood	21206
Elvaton Acres	21108
Elvatone Town	21061
Elwood	21643
Emmitsburg	21727
Emmorton	21009
Emory Grove (Baltimore County)	21071
Emory Grove (Montgomery County)	20877
Emory Hills	21048
Engles Mill	21520
Englewood	20785
English Manor	20853
English Village	20814
Enterprise Estates	20721

	ZIP
Enterprise Shopping Center	20706
Epping Forest	21401
Ernstville	21711
Essex	21221
Estonian Estates	20772
Etchison	20882
Eudowood	21204
Eutaw Forest	20603
Evanston	20747
Evergreen Estates	21146
Evergreen Hills	21048
Evergreen Overlook	20745
Evergreen Park	21221
Evergreen Valley Estates	21042
Evitts Creek	21502
Ewell	21824
Ewingville	21620
Fahrney Keedy Memorial Home	21713
Fairbank	21671
Fairfield (Part of Baltimore)	21226
Fairfield (Carroll County)	21157
Fairfield Knolls	20747
Fairgreen	20772
Fairgreen Acres	21740
Fair Haven	20754
Fairhaven on the Bay	20754
Fair Hill	21921
Fairidge	20879
Fairknoll	20905
Fairland	20904
Fairland Acres	20866
Fairland Heights	20904
Fairlee	21620
Fairmont	21014
Fairmount	21871
Fairmount Heights	20743
Fair Play	21733
Fairview (Anne Arundel County) (mobile home park)	20707
Fairview (Anne Arundel County)	21122
Fairview (Washington County)	21722
Fairview Estates	20904
Fairway	21015
Fairway Hills	20812
Fairway Island	20879
Fallsmont	21047
Fallston	21047
Family Estates	20743
Farmington (Cecil County)	21911
Farmington (Montgomery County)	20815
Farmsbrook	21702
Faulkner	20632
Faulkner Ridge	21044
Fawsett Farms	20854
Feagaville	21702
Federal Hill	21084
Federalsburg	21632
Felicity Cove	20764
Fellowship Forest	21204
Ferdinand Heights	21061
Ferndale	21061
Fernglen Manor	21061
Fernwood (Montgomery County)	20817
Fernwood (Prince George's County)	20737
Fernwood (Prince George's County) (mobile home park)	20743
Fiddlersburg	21740
Figgs Landing	21863
Finksburg	21048
Finzel	21532
Fishing Creek	21634
Fleishman Village	20746
Flickersville	21756
Flintstone	21530
Flohrville	21784
Florence	21797
Flower Valley	20853
Flower Valley Estates	20853
Fontana Village	21237
Font Hill	21042
Font Hill Manor	21042
Forest Estates	20910
Forest Glen	20910
Forest Greens	21001
Forest Heights	20745
Forest Hill	21050
Forest Knolls (Montgomery County)	20901
Forest Knolls (Prince George's County)	20744

	ZIP
Forest Lake	21050
Forest Lawn	21014
Forest Manor	20747
Forest Oaks	21784
Forest Park	20705
Forestville	20747
Forestville Estates	20747
Forge Acres	21128
Forge Heights	21128
Fork	21051
Forrest Hall	20659
Fort Foote Estates	20747
Fort Foote Village	20744
Fort George G. Meade	20755
Fort Howard	21052
Fort Meade	20755
Fort Ritchie	21719
Fort Sumner	20816
Fort Washington	20744*
	20749†
Fort Washington Estates	20744
Fort Washington Forest	20744
Foundry Siding (Part of Westernport)	21562
Fountaindale	21769
Fountain Green	21015
Fountain Green Heights	21015
Fountain Head	21742
Fountain Mills	21770
Fountain Rock (Part of Walkersville)	21793
Fountain Valley	21157
Four Locks	21722
Four Seasons Estates	21113
Four Winds	21204
Fowblesburg	21155
Fowlers Concord	20747
Fox Chapel	20876
Fox Chapel North	20876
Fox Chase	21061
Foxhall	20906
Foxhall Estates	21035
Fox Hills	20854
Fox Hills West	20854
Foxley Manor	21620
Fox Rest	20708
Fox Rest South	20708
Foxridge	21078
Fox Run Estates	20735
Foxville	21780
Franklin (Part of Baltimore)	21223
Franklin Manor Beach	20733
Franklin Manor on-the-Bay	20733
Franklin Park	20852
Franklin Square	20744
Franklinville (Baltimore County)	21087
Franklinville (Frederick County)	21788
Frederick	21701-05
For specific Frederick Zip Codes call (301) 662-2131, or your local postmaster.	
Frederick Junction	21701
Frederick Shopping Center (Part of Frederick)	21701
Frederick Towne Mall (Part of Frederick)	21702
Frederick Village	21228
Freedom Forest	21784
Freeland	21053
Free State Mall (Part of Bowie)	20715
Frenchtown (Part of Perryville)	21903
Friendly	20744
Friendly Farms	20744
Friends Creek	21727
Friendship (Anne Arundel County)	20758
Friendship (Frederick County)	21791
Friendship (Worcester County)	21811
Friendship Heights	20813
Friendship Park	21740
Friendsville	21531
Frizzelburg	21158
Frostburg	21532
Frostown	21769
Fruitland	21826
Fullerton	21236
Fulton	20759
Fulton Junction (Part of Baltimore)	21217
Funkstown	21734
Furnace Branch	21061
Gaither	21784

	ZIP
Gaithersburg	20877-79
	20882-86
	20898
For specific Gaithersburg Zip Codes call (301) 948-1894, or your local postmaster.	
Galena	21635
Galestown	19973
Galesville	20765
Gallant Green	20601
Gamber	21048
Gambrills	21054
Gannon	21562
Gapland	21736
Garfield	21783
Garland	21061
Garrett Forest	20906
Garrett Park	20896
Garrett Park Estates	20895
Garretts Mill	21758
Garrison	21055
Gatts Corner	21106
Gayfields	20906
George Island Landing	21864
Georgetown (Anne Arundel County)	20794
Georgetown (Cecil County)	21930
Georgetown (Kent County) (mail Chestertown)	21620
Georgetown (Kent County) (mail Georgetown)	21930
Georgetown Estates	20852
Georgetown Village	20812
Georgian Forest	20902
Germantown (Montgomery County)	20874-76
For specific Germantown Zip Codes call (301) 428-3839, or your local postmaster.	
Germantown (Worcester County)	21811
Germantown Estates	20874
Germantown Park	20874
Germantown View	20874
Gibson Island	21056
Gibson Manor	21015
Gilmore	21532
Gingerville Manor Estates	21037
Girdletree	21829
Gist	21784
Glade Towne (Part of Walkersville)	21793
Gladstone Acres	21034
Glassmanor	20745
Glazewood Manor (Part of Takoma Park)	20912
Glebe Heights	21037
Glenallen	20902
Glenarden	20706
Glen Arm	21057
Glen Brook	21042
Glenbrook Knolls	20814
Glenbrook Village	20814
Glen Burnie	21060-61
For specific Glen Burnie Zip Codes call (410) 766-8880, or your local postmaster.	
Glen Burnie Mall	21061
Glen Burnie Park	21061
Glencoe (Baltimore County)	21152
Glencoe (Kent County)	21645
Glen Cove	20816
Glendale (Baltimore County)	21204
Glendale (Wicomico County)	21801
Glen Echo	20812
Glen Echo Heights	20816
Glenelg	21737
Glen Ellen	21286
Glen Elyn	21047
Glen Farms	21921
Glen Gardens	21060
Glen Hills	20850
Glen Isle	21401
Glen Kyle	19711
Glenmar (Baltimore County)	21220
Glenmar (Howard County)	21043
Glen Mar Park	20814
Glen Mary Heights (Part of Elkton)	21921
Glenmont (Baltimore County)	21239

	ZIP
Glenmont (Montgomery County)	20902
Glenmont Park	20906
Glenmore	21061
Glen Morris	21136
Glenn Dale	20769
Glenn Dale Heights	20769
Glenn Heights	21078
Glen Oaks	20854
Glenora Hills (Part of Rockville)	20850
Glen Park	20854
Glen Ridge	20784
Glenside Park	21234
Glenville	21034
Glen Westover	19711
Glen Willows	20743
Glenwood (Harford County)	21014
Glenwood (Howard County)	21738
Glenwood Estates	21738
Glenwood Park	20706
Glover Acres	21157
Glymont	20640
Glyndon	21071
Goddard	20770
Goddard Space Flight Center	20770
Golden Beach	20659
Golden Hill	21622
Golden Ring	21237
Golden Ring Mall	21237
Goldsboro	21636
Golf Club Shores	21811
Golts	21637
Good Acres	21740
Good Hope	20905
Goodwill	21851
Gorman	26720
Gortner	21550
Goshen	20879
Goshen Estates	20879
Gotts	21032
Govans (Part of Baltimore)	21212
Governors Run	20676
Graceham	21788
Graceton	21160
Grahamtown	21532
Granby Woods	20855
Grand Bel Manor	20906
Grandview	21784
Granite	21163
Grantsville	21536
Grasonville	21638
Gratitude	21661
Gray Haven	21222
Gray Manor	21222
Gray Rock	21042
Grayton	20662
Greater Capitol Heights	20743
Greater Upper Marlboro	20772
Great Mills	20634
Green Acres (Harford County)	21085
Green Acres (Montgomery County)	20817
Greenbelt	20768†
	20770*
Greenberry Hills	21740
Greenbriar	21713
Greenbrier (Part of Greenbelt)	20770
Greendale Estates	21047
Greenfield	20735
Greenfield Mills	21710
Green Glade	21561
Green Haven	21122
Green Hill	21856
Green Hill Acres	21742
Green Meadows (Charles County)	20640
Green Meadows (Prince George's County)	20782
Greenmount (Part of Hampstead)	21074
Green Ridge (Allegany County)	21766
Green Ridge (Baltimore County)	21093
Greenridge (Harford County)	21015
Greensboro	21639
Greensburg	21783
Green Spring Hills	21085
Greentop Manor	21030
Greentree (Anne Arundel County)	21061

	ZIP
Greentree (Montgomery County)	20879
Green Tree Manor	20817
Greenvale Village	21783
Green Valley	21771
Greenview Knolls	20653
Greenwich Forest	20814
Greenwood Acres	21401
Greenwood Farms	20777
Greenwood Forest	20706
Gregg Neck	21635
Greystone Manor (Part of Hagerstown)	21740
Grimesville	21053
Grosstown	20637
Grove	21655
Grove Hill	21702
Guilford	20794
Guilford Manor	21225
Gum Springs	20868
Gum Springs Farm	20868
Gunners Lake Village	20874
Gunpowder (Baltimore County)	21021
Gunpowder (Harford County)	21010
Gunpowder Estates	21128
Gwenlee Estates	21738
Gwynn	21042
Gwynn Acres	21042
Gwynnbrook	21117
Gwynn Oak (Part of Baltimore)	21207
	21244
For specific Gwynn Oak Zip Codes call (410) 944-9300, or your local postmaster.	
Hack Point	21919
Hacks Point Acre	21919
Hagerstown	21740-42
For specific Hagerstown Zip Codes call (301) 797-8100, or your local postmaster.	
Halethorpe	21227
Halfway	21740
Halfway Manor	21740
Hallett Heights	21863
Halley Estates	21695
Halpine Village	20852
Hambleton Estates	21140
Hamilton (Part of Baltimore)	21214
Hamilton Park (Part of Hagerstown)	21740
Hamlet North	20855
Hammondell Heights	21108
Hammond Park	20723
Hampden (Part of Baltimore)	21211
Hampshire Knolls	20783
Hampstead	21074
Hampton	21286
Hampton Gardens	21286
Hance Point	21901
Hancock	21750
Hanesville	21678
Hanover (Anne Arundel County)	21076
Hanover (Howard County)	21076
Hanson Valley View	20748
Hansonville	21702
Harbor View (Anne Arundel County)	21037
Harborview (Queen Anne's County)	21619
Hardesty Estates	21035
Harewood	21220
Harewood Park	21220
Harford Estates	21050
Harford Farms	21234
Harford Furnace	21015
Harford Hills	21234
Harford Mall (Part of Bel Air)	21014
Harford Park	21234
Harford Square	21040
Harmans	21077
Harmony (Caroline County)	21655
Harmony (Frederick County)	21769
Harmony Grove	21701
Harmony Hall	20744
Harmony Hills	20906
Harness Woods	21403
Harney	21787
Harpers Choice	21044
Harpers Corner	20659
Harpers Mill	21108

	ZIP
Harris Heights	21061
Harrison Ferry	21643
Harrisonville	21133
Harrisville (Carroll County)	21771
Harrisville (Cecil County)	21917
Harundale	21060
Harundale Mall	21061
Harvest Hills	21047
Harwood (Anne Arundel County)	20776
Har-Wood (Howard County)	21227
Harwood Estates	20748
Harwood Park	21227
Havenwood Hills	21783
Haverhill	21234
Havre de Grace	21078
Havre de Grace Heights	21078
Hawbottom	21769
Hawkeye	21631
Hayes Landing	21811
Hazelhurst	21561
Hazelmoor	21919
Head of the Creek	21856
Hearn Bailey Farm	21801
Heather Heights	21784
Heather Hill Apartments	20748
Hebbville	21244
Hebron	21830
Helen	20635
Helen Estates	20635
Henderson	21640
Henryton	21080
Herald Harbor	21032
Herald Square	21244
Hereford	21111
Heritage Farm	20854
Heritage Harbor	21401
Heritage Hills	21061
Heritage Walk	20852
Hermanville	20653
Hermitage Park	20906
Hernwood Heights	21133
Herrington Manor	21550
Hickman	21629
Hickory	21014
Hickory Hills (Part of Bel Air)	21014
Hickory Ridge	21044
Hicksburg	21631
Hidden Point	21401
High Bridge	20720
High Bridge Estates	20720
Highfield (Montgomery County)	20879
Highfield (Washington County)	21719
Highland (Frederick County)	21773
Highland (Howard County)	20777
Highland Beach	21403
Highland Park (Prince George's County)	20743
Highland Park (Worcester County)	21811
Highlands	20854
Highlands of Olney	20832
Highland Stone	20854
Highlandtown (Part of Baltimore)	21224
High Point (Anne Arundel County)	21122
High Point (Montgomery County)	20814
Highpoint Heights	20705
High Point Manor	21050
High Ridge	20723
High Ridge Park	20723
High View	21771
High-View Estates (Carroll County)	21074
Highview Estates (Howard County)	21042
Highview on the Bay	20779
Hillandale	20903
Hillandale Forest	20907
Hillandale Heights	20903
Hillcrest (Anne Arundel County)	21225
Hill Crest (Montgomery County)	20912
Hillcrest (Prince George's County)	20748
Hillcrest Estates	20748
Hillcrest Heights (Howard County)	20723
Hillcrest Heights (Prince George's County)	20748
Hillcrest Terrace	20748

	ZIP
Hillendale Shopping Center	21204
Hillmead	20817
Hillmeade	20769
Hillmeade Manor	20769
Hillsboro	21641
Hillsborough	20707
Hillside	21157
Hillsmere Estates	21403
Hillsmere Shores	21403
Hills Point	21613
Hill Top	20693
Hillwood Manor	20783
Hobbs	21629
Hoffman	21532
Holabird (Part of Baltimore)	21224
Holbrook	21133
Holiday Acres	21783
Holiday Beach	20732
Holiday Hills	21044
Holiday Park	20906
Holland Cliff Shores	20639
Holland Heights	21801
Hollaway Estates	20772
Hollinsworth Manor (Part of Elkton)	21921
Holly Beach	21221
Holly Gaf. Acres	20636
Holly Hall Terrace	21921
Holly Hill Harbor	21037
Holly Lake Estates	21801
Holly Spring	20747
Holly Tree	20601
Hollywood (Prince George's County)	20740
Hollywood (St. Mary's County)	20636
Hollywood Beach	21915
Hollywood Estates (Part of College Park)	20740
Hollywood Park	20904
Hollywood Shores	20636
Holmehurst	20720
Home Acres	20705
Homecrest	20906
Homestead Estates	20904
Homewood (Allegany County)	21502
Homewood (Montgomery County)	20895
Honga	21622
Hood College (Part of Frederick)	21701
Hoods Mill	21723
Hoopersville	21634
Hope Hill	21701
Hopewell	21817
Hopkins Mead	21029
Horizon Run	20877
Houcksville	21074
Howard Heights	21042
Howardville	21208
Hoyes	21531
Hudson	21613
Hughesville	20637
Hungerford Towne (Part of Rockville)	20852
Hunt Club Estates (Charles County)	20601
Hunt Club Estates (Howard County)	21227
Hunt Crest Estates	21286
Hunters Harbor	21122
Hunters Hill	21093
Hunters Ridge	20610
Huntersville	20659
Hunting Hills	20639
Hunting Lodge	21234
Hunting Park	21801
Huntington Terrace	20814
Huntingtown	20639
Huntsmoor	21227
Huntsville	20785
Hunt Valley	21030-31
For specific Hunt Valley Zip Codes call (410) 771-0780, or your local postmaster.	
Hunt Valley Mall	21030
Hurlock	21643
Hurry	20621
Hutton	21550
Huyett	21740
Hyattstown	20871
Hyattsville	20780-89
For specific Hyattsville Zip Codes call (301) 699-8905, or your local postmaster.	

Name	ZIP
Hyde Park (Baltimore County)	21221
Hyde Park (Wicomico County)	21801
Hydes	21082
Hynesboro	20706
Hynson	21632
Idlewild	20764
Idlewylde	21204
Ijamsville	21754
Ilchester	21043
Imperial Gardens	21133
Indian Creek Estates	20622
Indian Head	20640
Indian Head Manor	20616
Indian Head Naval Ordnance Station	20640
Indian Queen Estates	20744
Indian River Estates	20659
Indian Springs (Frederick County)	21702
Indian Springs (Washington County)	21711
Indiantown	21863
Ingleside	21644
Inverness	21222
Inverness Forest	20854
Inverness Woods	20854
Iron Hill	19711
Ironshire	21811
Ironsides	20643
Isabella Park	20783
Island Creek	20685
Island View Beach	21221
Issue	20645
Iverson Mall	20748
Ivy Hills	21043
Ivytown	21601
Jackson	21903
Jacksonville (Baltimore County)	21131
Jacksonville (Somerset County)	21817
Jacktown	21613
Jacobsville	21122
James	21613
Jarrettsville	21084
Jefferson	21755
Jefferson Heights (Prince George's County)	20743
Jefferson Heights (Washington County)	21740
Jennings	21536
Jersey Heights	21801
Jerusalem (Baltimore County)	21087
Jerusalem (Frederick County)	21773
Jerusalem (Montgomery County)	20837
Jessup	20794
Jesterville	21814
Jewell	20754
Johnsontown	21620
Johnsville (Carroll County)	21784
Johnsville (Frederick County)	21791
Jones	21146
Jonestown	21655
Joppa	21085
Joppa Heights	21234
Joppatowne	21085
Joppa View	21128
Josenhans Corner	21221
Joyce Acres	21012
Kalma Ridge	21032
Kalmia	21015
Kalmia Farms	21036
Kalten Acres	21158
Kastle Estates	20735
Kaywood Gardens (Part of Mount Rainier)	20712
Keedysville	21756
Keeler Glade	21531
Keifer	25434
Kemp Mill Estates	20902
Kemp Mill Farms	20902
Kempton	26292
Kemptown	21770
Ken Gar	20895
Kennedyville	21645
Kensington	20895
Kensington Estates	20895
Kensington Heights	20902
Kensington View	20895
Kent Island Estates	21666
Kentland	20785
Kentmore Park	21645
Kentmorr	21666
Kent Village	20785
Kenwood (Baltimore County)	21236
Kenwood (Montgomery County)	20815
Kenwood Beach	20676
Kerby Hills	20744
Kettering	20772
Kettering Estate Park	20772
Keymar	21757
Keysers Ridge	21536
Keystone Manor	20747
Keysville	21757
Kilbirnie Estates	21801
Kilbourn Estates	20748
Kilmarock	20912
Kimberly Gardens	20708
Kings Contrivance	21045
Kings County	21087
Kings Creek Estate	20772
Kingsford	20721
Kings Grove	21529
Kings Manor	20695
Kings Park	21233
Kings Ransom	21113
Kings Ridge	21234
Kingston	21871
Kingston Manor	20772
Kingstown	21620
Kingsville	21087
Kingwood Common	21244
Kirkham	21601
Kirkwood	20782
Kitzmiller	21538
Klej Grange	21851
Knettishall	21204
Knollview	21043
Knollwood (Baltimore County)	21204
Knollwood (Prince George's County)	20783
Knoxville	21758
Ladiesburg	21759
Lakeland (Anne Arundel County)	21146
Lakeland (Prince George's County)	20740
Lake Linganore	21774
Lake Normandy Estates	20854
Lake Roland	21209
Lake Shore	21122
Lakeside Manor	21801
Lakeside Park	21740
Lakeside Terrace	20817
Lakeside Vista	21085
Lakesville	21622
Lakeview (Howard County)	20723
Lakeview (Montgomery County)	20817
Lakewood	21801
Lakewood Estates (Calvert County)	20754
Lakewood Estates (Montgomery County)	20850
Lancaster	20603
Land-O-Lakes	20636
Landon Woods	20817
Landover	20785
Landover Estates	20784
Landover Hills	20789
Landover Knolls	20785
Landover Park (Part of Cheverly)	20785
Lane Beach	20650
Langley Park	20783
Lanham	20703†
Lanham	20706*
Lanham Heights	20706
Lanham-Seabrook	20706
Lanham Woods	20706
Lansdowne	21227
Lansdowne-Baltimore Highlands	21227
Lantz	21780
Lapidum	21078
La Plata	20646
Lappans	21733
Larchmont Knolls	20895
Largo	20772
Largo/Kettering	20775
Largo Knolls	20772
Laurel	20707-09 / 20723-26
Laurel Acres	21122
Laurel Brook	21047
Laureldale	21234
Laurel Grove	20659
Laurel Pines	20708
Laurel Shopping Center (Part of Laurel)	20707
Laurel Wood	20708
La Vale	21502
Lawndale Acres	21048
Lawsonia	21817
Layhill	20906
Layhill Gardens	20906
Layhill Village	20906
Laytonia	20877
Laytonsville	20879
Lees Woods	21014
Legion Avenue (Part of Annapolis)	21401
Le Gore	21757
Leisure World	20906
Leitersburg	21742
Leon	20711
Leonardtown	20650
Leslie	21901
Level	21078
Lewis Corner	21811
Lewisdale	20783
Lewis Heights	20783
Lewis Spring Manor	20735
Lewistown (Frederick County)	21701
Lewistown (Talbot County)	21625
Lexington Park	20653
Liberty Grove	21918
Liberty Manor	21244
Libertytown (Frederick County)	21762
Libertytown (Worcester County)	21811
Lime Kiln	21701
Linchester	21655
Lincoln Avenue	21740
Lincoln Heights (Part of Salisbury)	21801
Lincoln Manor	21102
Lincoln Park (Part of Rockville)	20850
Lindamoor on the Severn	21401
Linden	20907
Linden Chapel Hills	21036
Lineboro	21088
Linganore-Bartonsville	21701
Linhigh	21236
Linkwood	21835
Linsey Acres	20748
Linsted on the Severn	21146
Linthicum	21090
Linthicum Heights	21090
Linthicum Hills	21090
Linthicum Oaks	21090
Linwood (Carroll County)	21764
Linwood (Howard County)	21043
Linwood Village	21122
Lipins Corner	21122
Lisbon	21765
Little Orleans	21766
Little Washington	20747
Livingston Grove	20607
Llandaff	21601
Lloyds	21613
Loartown	21532
Lochearn	21207
Loch Haven	21234
Loch Hill	21212
Loch Lynn Heights	21550
Loch Raven	21234
Loch Raven Heights	21234
Loch Raven Village	21234
Locust Grove (Allegany County)	21502
Locust Grove (Kent County)	21645
Locust Grove (Washington County)	21779
Locust Grove Beach	20732
Locust Grove Station	21788
Locust Hill Estates	20814
Locust Valley	21769
Lodgecliffe	21613
Lodge Forest	21222
Lonaconing	21539
Londontown	21037
Londontowne	21037
London Woods	20743
Lone Oak	20814
Long	21502
Long Bar Harbor	21009
Long Beach	20685
Long Corner	21771
Longfellow	21043
Longfield Estates	20747
Long Green	21092
Long Meadow (Carroll County)	21784
Long Meadow (Washington County)	21740
Long Meadow Estates	20814
Long Meadow Shopping Center (Part of Hagerstown)	21740
Long Meadow West	21208
Long Point	21122
Long Reach	21045
Longview Beach	20618
Longwood	20817
Longwoods	21601
Lord	21532
Lord Calvert Estates	20736
Loreley	21162
Loretta Heights	21401
Lothian	20711
Louisville	21048
Lou Mar Estates	21009
Love Point	21666
Loveville	20656
Lower Magothy Beach	21146
Lower Marlboro	20736
Loyola (Part of Baltimore)	21210
Lucas Heights	21502
Luke	21540
Lusby	20657
Lusby Crossroads	21401
Lute	20906
Lutherville	21093
Lutherville-Timonium	21093* / 21094†
Lutz Hill	21237
Luxmanor	20852
Lynch	21646
Lynch Point	21222
Lynnbrook (Anne Arundel County)	21225
Lynnbrook (Charles County)	20601
Lynne Acres	21244
Lyons Creek (Anne Arundel County)	20711
Lyons Creek (Calvert County)	20754
Lyons Homes	21222
Mac Alpine	21042
McCahill Estates	20707
McCanns Corner	21154
McComas Beach	21550
McCoole	26726
McDaniel	21647
Mc Daniel City	20603
Mac Donald Farms	20736
McDonogh	21208
Mc Donogh Park	21133
Maceys Corner	21146
McHenry	21541
McKaig	21701
McKay Beach	20650
Mc Kendree	20879
McKenney Hills	20910
McKinleyville	21661
McKinstrys Mill	21791
Maddox	20621
Madison	21648
Madonna	21084
Madonna Manor	21084
Magnolia	21085
Magnolia Springs	20784
Magothy Beach	21122
Magothy Park Beach	21122
Mago Vista Beach	21012
Magruder Landing	20613
Main Street (Part of Salisbury)	21801
Malcolm	20601
Mall in Columbia, The	21044
Malvern	21204
Manchester	21102
Manchester Estates	20746
Manhattan Woods	21146
Manokin (Somerset County)	21836
Manokin (Wicomico County)	21801
Manor	21111
Manor Lake	20853
Manor Park	20853
Manor View	21057
Manor Woods	20853
Maple Crest (Baltimore County)	21220

For specific Laurel Zip Codes call (301) 498-1400, or your local postmaster.

* Area Zip Code   † Post Office Boxes

	ZIP		ZIP		ZIP		ZIP
Maplecrest (Carroll County)	21157	Middleton Valley	20748	Mount Washington (Part of Baltimore)	21209	North Linthicum	21090
Maple Park	21801	Middletown (Baltimore County)	21053	Mount Westley	21863	North Ocean City (Part of Ocean City)	21842
Maple Plains	21801	Middletown (Frederick County)	21769	Mount Zion	21649	North Point	21222
Mapleside (Part of Cumberland)	21502	Middletown Heights	21769	Mount Zoar	21918	North Point Village	21222
Maple View	21157	Midland	21542	Mousetown	21713	North Potomac	20878
Mapleville	21713	Midlothian	21543	Muirkirk	20705	North Potomac Vista	20745
Maplewood (Howard County)	21042	Milford	21207	Mulberry Hills	21401	Northridge Manor	21740
Maplewood (Montgomery County)	20814	Milford Mill	21244	Murray Hills	20745	North Roblee Acres	20772
Maplewood (Prince George's County)	20744	Milford Park	21117	Myersdale (Part of Hancock)	21750	North Sherwood Forest	20904
Marbury	20658	Milford Ridge	21244	Myersville	21773	Northshire	21222
Mardela Springs	21837	Millbrook (Part of Laurel)	20707	Nanjemoy	20662	North Shore	21122
Margate	21060	Mill Creek South	20855	Nanticoke	21840	North Springbrook	20904
Mariners	21817	Mill Creek Towne	20707	Narrows	21638	North Wellham	21061
Marion Station	21838	Mill Creek Towne East	20855	Narrows Park	21502	Northwest Park (Montgomery County; mail Bethesda)	20814
Market Center (Part of Baltimore)	21201	Miller	21532	National Naval Medical Center	20814	
Marley	21060	Millers	21107	Naval Academy	21402	Northwest Park (Montgomery and Prince George's Counties; mail Silver Spring)	20903
Marley Heights	21061	Millers Island	21219	Naval Air Facility	20390	
Marley Station	21061	Millersville	21108	Naval Ordnance Station	20640	
Marling Farms	21619	Mill Green	21154	Naval Surface Weapons Center	20903	Northwood (Part of Baltimore)	21239
Marlow Heights	20748	Millington	21651	Naylor	20772	Northwood Park	20901
Marlton	20772	Millison Plaza	20653	Neavitt	21652	Northwood Village	20901
Marlywood	21286	Mill Point	20621	Needwood Estates	20855	Norwood Corner	20906
Marriottsville	21104	Mill Point Shores	20621	Neeld Estates	20639	Norwood Estates	20905
Mars Estates	21221	Millrace	21108	Neelsville	20876	Notch Cliff	21057
Marshall Hall	20616	Mill Run	21562	Neilwood	20852	Nottingham	21236
Marshalls Corner	20646	Mills Choice	20879	New Addition	21758	Nottingham Woods	21236
Marston	21776	Millwood	20743	Newark	21841	Oak Acres	21701
Martin's Additions	20815	Millwood Towne	20743	New Birmingham Manor	20866	Oak Court	21401
Martinsburg	20842	Mimosa Cove	20751	Newburg	20664	Oakcrest	20707
Martins Woods (Part of New Carrollton)	20706	Minefield	21154	New Carrollton	20784	Oakcrest Towers	20743
Marwood	21061	Mitchell Manor	21550	Newcomb	21653	Oakdale	20853
Marydel	21649	Mitchellville	20706	New Germany	21536	Oak Estates	20622
Maryland City	20724	Mitchellville (Part of Bowie)	20717	New Hampshire Estates	20903	Oak Forest	21228
Maryland Correctional Institution for Women	20794	Mondawmin/Metro Plaza (Part of Baltimore)	21215	New Hampshire Gardens (Part of Takoma Park)	20912	Oak Hollow	21122
Maryland Correctional Pre-Release System	20794	Monie	21853	Newhope	21874	Oakhurst	20866
Maryland Line	21105	Monkton	21111	New London	21771	Oakington	21078
Maryland Park	20743	Monrovia	21770	New Mark Commons (Part of Rockville)	20850	Oakland (Baltimore County)	21053
Maryland Point	20662	Montego (Part of Ocean City)	21842	New Market (Frederick County)	21774	Oakland (Carroll County)	21784
Marymount	20814	Montevideo (Anne Arundel County)	21076	New Market (St. Mary's County)	20622	Oakland (Garrett County)	21550
Maryvale (Part of Rockville)	20850	Montevideo (Howard County)	20794	New Market View	21771	Oakland (Prince George's County)	20747
Marywood	21014	Montgomery Knolls	21043	New Midway	21775	Oakland Acres	20622
Masons Beach	20751	Montgomery Square	20854	New Orchard Estates	20772	Oakland Mills	21045
Mason Springs	20640	Montgomery Village	20879	Newport	20622	Oakland Park	21133
Massey	21650	Montgomery White Oak	20904	Newport Hills	20895	Oakland Terrace	20895
Mattapex	21666	Montpelier	20708*	Newton	21655	Oaklawn	20744
Mattapony (Part of Bladensburg)	20710		20709†	Newton Village	20781	Oakleigh	21234
Matthews	21601	Montpelier Woods	20708	Newtown (Charles County)	20646	Oakleigh Forest	21146
Maugansville	21767	Montrose	20852	Newtown (Kent County)	21678	Oakleigh Manor	21234
Mayberry	21158	Monumental	21227	Newtown (Talbot County)	21625	Oakley	20609
Maydale	20868	Mooresfield	20759	New Valley	21918	Oaklyn Manor	21085
Mayfield (Anne Arundel County)	21113	Morantown	21532	New Windsor	21776	Oakmont	20814
Mayfield (Howard County)	21043	Morgan	21797	Nikep	21539	Oak Orchard	20735
Mayo	21106	Morgantown	20664	Nob Hill (Howard County)	21042	Oak Park (Baltimore County)	21227
Mays Chapel	21093	Morganza	20660	Nob Hill (Montgomery County)	20903	Oak Park (Garrett County)	21550
Mays Chapel Village	21093	Morningside	20746	Nomira Heights (Part of Elkton)	21921	Oak Ridge	21740
Meadowbrook (Part of Bowie)	20715	Moscow	21521	Norbeck	20906	Oak Springs	20868
Meadowbrook Estates	20876	Mount Aetna	21740	Normandy Heights	21043	Oak Summit	21234
Meadowcliff	21057	Mountain	21085	Normans	21666	Oak View	20903
Meadowland	21093	Mountaindale	21788	Norris Corner	21009	Oakville (Somerset County)	21853
Meadowood	20904	Mountain Lake Park	21550	Norrisville	21161	Oakville (St. Mary's County)	20659
Meadowood of Davidsonville	21035	Mountain View	21157	Northampton (Baltimore County)	21093	Oakwood	21918
Meadowvale Manor (Part of Havre de Grace)	21078	Mountain View Estates	20878	Northampton (Prince George's County)	20772	Oakwood Knolls	20817
Meadowview Park	21921	Mountain Wood	21122	North Barnaby	20745	Ocean City	21842
Mechanicsville	20659	Mount Airy	21771	North Beach	20714	Ocean City Harbor	21842
Medford	21776	Mount Briar	21756	North Beach Park	20714	Ocean Pines	21811
Melitota	21620	Mount Carmel	21122	North Bethesda	20814	Odenton	21113
Mellwood Hills	20772	Mount Clare (Part of Baltimore)	21223	North Branch	21502	Odenton Gardens	21113
Melody Acres	20622	Mount De Sales	21228	North Brentwood	20722	Odenton Heights	21113
Melrose	21102	Mount Harmony	20736	North Chevy Chase	20815	Odenton Park	21113
Melson	21875	Mount Hebron	21042	North College Park (Part of College Park)	20740	Odyssey	20736
Merchants (Part of Baltimore)	21201	Mount Hermon	21801	North Deale	20751	Oella	21228
Merrimack Park	20817	Mount Hope (Part of Baltimore)	21215	North East	21901	Old Country Estates	21146
Merritt Heights	21801	Mount Lena	21713	Northeast Heights	21901	Olde Colonial Woods	20832
Merrymount	21244	Mount Olive	21771	North Englewood	20785	Olde Fort Village	20744
Michigan Park Hills	20782	Mount Pleasant (Frederick County)	21701	Northern (Part of Hagerstown)	21740	Olde Towne Village (Part of District Heights)	20747
Middleborough	21221	Mount Pleasant (Washington County)	21713	North Forestville	20747	Old Farm	20852
Middlebrook	20876	Mount Pleasant (Wicomico County)	21874	North Fort Foote Village	20744	Old Field (Dorchester County)	21622
Middleburg	21757	Mount Pleasant Beach	21122	North Glade	21561	Oldfield (Frederick County)	21791
Middlepoint	21773	Mount Rainier	20712	North Indian Head Estates	20616	Old Field (Montgomery County)	20854
Middle River	21220	Mount Saint Mary's College	21727	North Junction (Part of Hagerstown)	21740	Old Fort Hills	20744
Middlesex	21221	Mount Savage	21545	North Kensington	20902	Old Glory Beach	21060
Middlesex Shopping Center	21221	Mount Vernon	21853	North Laurel	20723	Old Salem Village	20904
		Mount Victoria	20661	North Laurel Park	20723	Old Severna Park	21146
		Mountview	21104			Oldtown	21555
		Mountville	21701			Olive	21758

* Area Zip Code   **† Post Office Boxes**

	ZIP		ZIP		ZIP		ZIP
Oliver Beach	21220	Perry Hall Manor	21128	Poplar Springs	21771	Redford Estates	20744
Olivet	20657	Perry Hall Shopping		Port Covington (Part of		Red Hill	20658
Olivet Hill	21637	Center	21128	Baltimore)	21230	Redhouse	21550
Olney	20830*	Perry Hall Village	21128	Port Deposit	21904	Redland	20855
	20832†	Perryman	21130	Porters Park	21221	Red Point	21901
Olney	20832	Perry Point	21902	Porterstown	21756	Reeder Development (Part	
Olney Mills	20832	Perrys Corner	21638	Port Herman	21915	of Frederick)	21701
Olney Square	20832	Perry View	21128	Port Republic	20676	Reese	21157
Orangeville (Part of		Perryville	21903	Port Tobacco	20677	Reese Manor	21048
Baltimore)	21224	Perrywood Estates	20866	Port Tobacco Riviera	20677	Regal Estates	20754
Oraville	20659	Perry Wright	20640	Potomac	20854	Regency Estates	20852
Orchard Beach	21226	Petersburg	21643	Potomac Commons	20854	Regent Park	20854
Orchard Hills (Baltimore		Petersville	21758	Potomac Falls Estates	20854	Regent Square (Part of	
County)	21093	Pfeiffer Corners	21045	Potomac Green	20854	Rockville)	20850
Orchard Hills (Washington		Pheasant Run	20708	Potomac Heights (Charles		Rehobeth	21857
County)	21742	Phoenix	21131	County)	20640	Reid	21740
Oregon	21030	Picketts Corner	21797	Potomac Heights		Reids Grove	21659
Oriole	21853	Pike (Part of Rockville)	20852	(Washington County)	21740	Reisterstown	21136
Otter Point	21009	Pikesville	21208	Potomac Hills	20854	Reisterstown Road Plaza	
Overlea	21206	Pilot Town	21918	Potomac Park	21502	(Part of Baltimore)	21270
Owen Brown	21045	Pindell	20711	Potomac Ranch	20854	Relay	21227
Owings	20736	Pine Cliff	21701	Potomac Shores (Charles		Reliance	19973
Owings Beach	20751	Pinecrest (Part of Takoma		County)	20677	Rest Haven	20751
Owings Mills	21117	Park)	20912	Potomac Shores (St.		Revell	21012
Owings Wood (Part of		Pinedale	21128	Mary's County)	20650	Revere Park	21234
North Beach)	20714	Pinefield	20601	Potomac View	20664	Reynolds	21521
Oxford	21654	Pine Grove	21801	Potomac View Estates	20854	Rhodesdale	21659
Oxon Hill	20745*	Pine Grove Village	21122	Potomac Village	20854	Rhodes Point	21824
	20750†	Pine Hill Estates	20601	Potomac Vista	20745	Riawakin Acres	21830
Oxon Hill-Glassmanor	20745	Pinehurst Estates	20744	Potomac Woods (Part of		Richards Oak	21917
Oxon Hill Village	20745	Pinehurst on the Bay	21122	Rockville)	20854	Ricmar	21801
Oxon Run Hills	20748	Pine Knoll	21157	Pot Spring	21093	Riderwood	21139
Oyster Harbor	21401	Pine Knoll Terrace	21801	Powder Mill Estates	20783	Riderwood Hills	21139
Padonia	21030	Pineleigh	21286	Powder Mill Village	20705	Ridge	20680
Pagetts Corner	20748	Pine Orchard Meadows	21042	Powellville	21852	Ridge Lake	21042
Paint Branch Estates	20904	Pine Ridge	21234	Powhatan Beach	21122	Ridgeleigh	21234
Paint Branch Farm	20904	Pinesburg	21795	Powhattan Mill	21207	Ridgely	21660
Palmer Park	20785	Pines on the Severn	21012	Prathertown	20879	Ridgeview	21077
Palmers Corner	20744	Pinewiff Beach	21037	Presidential Park	20783	Ridgeville (Part of Mount	
Palmetto	21853	Pinewood Hill	20744	Presidential Towers	20783	Airy)	21771
Paradise	21228	Piney Glen Farms	20854	Presley Manor	20784	Ridgeway	21144
Paradise Beach	21122	Piney Grove	21766	Preston	21655	Ridgeway Estates	20743
Paramount	21740	Piney Point	20674	Preston Manor	21009	Ridgley Park	21784
Paramount Manor	21740	Pinto	21556	Price	21656	Riding Woods	21122
Paris	20736	Pioneer City	21144	Priceville	21152	Riggins Corner	21622
Parkertown	21811	Piscataway	20607	Prince Frederick	20678	Ringgold	21740
Parker Wharf	20685	Piscataway Bay	20744	Princess Anne	21853	Rio Vista	21663
Park Hall (St. Mary's		Piscataway Estates	20744	Princeton	20746	Ripley	20646
County)	20667	Piscataway Hills	20744	Principio Furnace	21903	Ripplewood	21244
Park Hall (Washington		Pisgah	20640	Prophecy	20744	Rippling Ridge	21061
County)	21713	Pittsville	21850	Prospect Knolls	20720	Rising Sun	21911
Parkhead	21711	Plainfield	21801	Prospect Walk	21044	Rison	20658
Parkhurst Manor	21801	Plane Number Four	21771	Providence (Baltimore		Ritchie	20747
Parkland	20746	Pleasant Fields	20874	County)	21286	Ritchie Heights	20747
Parkland Apartments	20746	Pleasant Grove (Baltimore		Providence (Cecil County)	21921	Ritchie Manor	20747
Parkland Terrace	20746	County)	21136	Public Landing	21863	Riva	21140
Park Mills	21710	Pleasant Grove (Frederick		Pumphrey	21225	Rivendell	21146
Park Overlook	20855	County)	21771	Puncheon Landing	21851	River Bend	20744
Parkridge	20878	Pleasant Hill (Baltimore		Putnam	21050	River Bend Estates	20744
Parkside	20814	County)	21117	Putty Hill	21236	River Club Estates	21037
Parkside Estates	20855	Pleasant Hill (Cecil		Pylesville	21132	Riverdale (Anne Arundel	
Parkton	21120	County)	21921	Quail Ridge	21227	County)	21146
Parktowne	21234	Pleasant Hills	21087	Quail Run	20879	Riverdale (Prince	
Parkview	20735	Pleasant Ridge	21797	Quaint Acres	20904	George's County)	20737*
Parkville	21234	Pleasant Springs	20613	Quaker Neck Landing	21620		20738†
Park West	21061	Pleasant Valley (Allegany		Quantico	21856	Riverdale Heights	20737
Parkwood	20814	County)	21502	Queen Anne	21657	Riverdale Hills	20737
Parole	21401	Pleasant Valley (Carroll		Queen Anne Colony	21666	River Falls	20854
Parsonsburg	21849	County)	21158	Queens Chapel Manor		River Forest	20744
Partridge Place	20879	Pleasant Valley		(Part of Hyattsville)	20782	River Meadows	21045
Pasadena	21122	(Washington County)	21783	Queenstown (Prince		River Ridge Estates	20745
Patapsco	21048	Pleasant View (Frederick		George's County)	20712	Riverside	20662
Patterson (Part of		County)	21710	Queenstown (Queen		River Springs	20609
Baltimore)	21231	Pleasant View (Howard		Anne's County)	21658	Riverton	21837
Patuxent	21113	County)	21043	Queenswood	20772	Riverview Manor	21401
Patuxent Beach	20619	Pleasantville	21061	Quince Orchard	20878	Riverview Village (Part of	
Patuxent Institution	20794	Pleasant Walk	21773	Quincy Manor	20784	Indian Head)	20640
Patuxent Manor	21035	Plumgar	20876	Rabbit Town	21869	Riverwood	21035
Patuxent Naval Air Test		Plum Point	20639	Radiant Valley	20784	Riviera Beach	21122
Center	20670	Pocomoke City	21851	Ramblewood Village	20735	Riviera Isle	21122
Patuxent Palisades	20754	Pointer Ridge (Part of		Ramgate	20744	Robbins	21626
Patuxent Park	20653	Bowie)	20716	Rancheigh (Baltimore		Roberts	21623
Patuxent River	20670	Point Lookout	20687	County)	21209	Roberts Glen	20854
Peach Orchard Heights	20866	Point of Rocks	21777	Rancheigh (Part of		Robinson	21146
Peachwood	20905	Point of Rocks Estates	21777	Baltimore)	21209	Robinwood	21740
Peacock Corners	21651	Point Pleasant	21060	Randalia	21915	Roblee Acres	20772
Pearl	21701	Pomfret	20675	Randallstown	21133	Rockawalking Village	21801
Pectonville	21711	Pomona	21620	Randle Cliff Beach	20732	Rockaway Beach	21221
Pendennis Mount	21401	Pomonkey	20640	Randolph Farms	20852	Rock Creek Forest	20815
Peninsula General		Ponder Cove	21037	Randolph Hills	20852	Rock Creek Gardens	20815
Hospital (Part of		Pondsville	21783	Random Heights	21157	Rock Creek Highlands	20895
Salisbury)	21801	Pooks Hill	20814	Raspeburg (Part of		Rock Creek Hills	20895
Pen Mar	21719	Poole	21034	Baltimore)	21206	Rock Creek Manor	20853
Pen-Mar Shopping Center	20747	Poolesville	20837	Rawlings	21557	Rock Creek Palisades	20895
Penn Mary Junction (Part		Popes Creek	20664	Rawlings Heights	21557	Rock Creek Village	20853
of Baltimore)	21224	Poplar Grove	21154	Raynor Heights	21090	Rockcrest (Part of	
Pepper Mill Village	20743	Poplar Hill	20613	Rayville	21120	Rockville)	20851
Perry Hall	21128	Poplar Hill Estates	20735	Red Coat Woods	20854	Rockdale	21244
Perry Hall Estates	21236	Poplar Knob	21788	Reddings Corner	21678		

Place	ZIP	Place	ZIP	Place	ZIP	Place	ZIP
Rock Hall (Frederick County)	21790	Ruxton	21286	Shady Side	20764	Southerland	20601
Rock Hall (Kent County)	21661	Ryceville	20659	Shallmar	21538	Southern Garden Apartments	20032
Rock Hill Beach	21122	Sabillasville	21780	Shane	21161	South Fort Foote Village	20744
Rockland (Howard County)	21043	Sackertown	21817	Sharewood Acres	20794	South Gate	21061
Rockland (Montgomery County)	20850	St. Andrews Estates	20619	Sharonville	21122	South Haven	21401
Rockland Run	21209	St. Anthony's	21727	Sharon Woods	20879	South Kensington	20895
Rock Point	20682	St. Aubins Heights (Part of Easton)	21601	Sharperville	20601	Southland Hills	21204
Rock Run	21078	St. Augustine	21915	Sharpsburg	21782	South Laurel	20708
Rockshire (Part of Rockville)	20850	St. Charles	20601	Sharpstown	21661	South Lawn	20745
Rockshire Square (Part of Rockville)	20850	St. Charles Town Center	20603	Sharptown	21861	South Layhill	20906
Rockshire Village (Part of Rockville)	20850	St. Clement Shores	20650	Shavox	21801	South Piscataway	20607
Rockview Beach	21122	St. Denis	21227	Shawsville	21161	South River Park	21037
Rockville	20847-59	St. George Island	21674	Shawsville Acres	21161	South Salisbury (Part of Salisbury)	21801
For specific Rockville Zip Codes call (301) 424-2600, or your local postmaster.		St. Georges	21071	Shelltown	21838	South Tantallon	20744
Rockville Estates (Part of Rockville)	20850	St. George's Park	20690	Shervettes Corner	21784	Southview	20745
Rockwell	21228	St. Helena	21222	Sherwood (Kent County)	21635	South Woodside Park	20910
Rocky Gorge Estates	20707	St. Inigoes	20684	Sherwood (Talbot County)	21665	Sparks	21152
Rocky Ridge	21778	St. James (Washington County)	21781	Sherwood Forest (Anne Arundel County)	21405	Sparks Glencoe	21152
Rocky Springs	21702	St. James (Worcester County)	21851	Sherwood Forest (Montgomery County)	20904	Sparrows Point	21219
Rodgers Forge	21204	St. Jeromes	20628	Sherwood Forest (Prince George's County)	20772	Spaulding Heights	20747
Rogers Heights	20781	St. Johns Manor	21042	Sherwood Manor (Prince George's County)	20715	Spence	21863
Rohrersville	21779	St. Johns Village	21042	Sherwood Manor (Wicomico County)	21801	Spencerville	20868
Rohrersville (Trego)	21756	St. Leonard	20685	Shetland Hills	21093	Spielman	21733
Roland Park (Part of Baltimore)	21210	St. Margarets	21401	Shiloh (Charles County)	20664	Spoolsville	21769
Rolling Acres (Prince George's County)	20623	St. Margarets Farm	21401	Shiloh (Dorchester County)	21643	Springbrook (Baltimore County)	21133
Rolling Acres (St. Mary's County)	20622	St. Mark's	21758	Shipley	21090	Springbrook (Montgomery County)	20904
Rolling Green	21028	St. Martins	21811	Shookstown	21702	Springbrook Forest	20902
Rolling Hills (Anne Arundel County)	21401	St. Marys City	20686	Shore Acres	21012	Springbrook Manor	20904
Rolling Hills (Carroll County)	21784	St. Michaels	21663	Shoreham Beach	21037	Springbrook Village	20904
Rolling Knolls	21401	St. Stephen	21853	Shoreland	21061	Springdale (Baltimore County)	21030
Rolling Ridge (Carroll County)	21157	Salem	21869	Shorwood Estates	21637	Springdale (Prince George's County)	20706
Rolling Ridge (Howard County)	21043	Salisbury	21801-03	Showell	21862	Springdale Gardens	20706
Rolling Ridge (Prince George's County)	20743	For specific Salisbury Zip Codes call (410) 742-9261, or your local postmaster.		Sierra Manor	21801	Springfield	20814
Rolling Terrace	20912	Salisbury Mall (Part of Salisbury)	21801	Silesia	20744	Spring Gap	21560
Rolling Terrace Estates	20912	Samples Manor	21782	Sillery Bay	21122	Spring Garden Estates	21793
Rollingwood	20815	Sams Creek	21776	Siloam	21822	Spring Grove	21837
Rollins Park (Part of Rockville)	20852	Sanders Park	21122	Silver Gate Village	21236	Spring Hill	21830
Rolphs	21620	Sandgates	20659	Silver Hill	20746	Springhill Acres	21801
Romancoke	21666	Sand Spring	21531	Silver Hill Park	20746	Springhill Lake (Part of Greenbelt)	20770
Rosaryville	20772	Sandy Acres	21613	Silver Meadow	21128	Springlake	20817
Rosaryville Estates	20772	Sandy Bottom	21620	Silver Rock (Part of Rockville)	20850	Spring Meadow	21084
Rosecroft	20748	Sandy Hook	21758	Silver Run	21158	Spring Mills	21157
Rosecroft Park	20744	Sandy Spring	20860	Silver Sands	21060	Spring Valley	21740
Rosedale	21237	Sandy Spring Estates	20707	Silver Spring	20901-18	Squires Woods	20744
Rosedale Estates	20744	Sandy Spring Meadows	20860	For specific Silver Spring Zip Codes call (301) 588-2926, or your local postmaster.		Stablersville	21161
Rosedale Park	20815	Sandyville	21048	Silver Valley	20746	Stafford	21034
Rose Haven	20714	Sang Run	21541	Simpsonville	21150	Stanbrook	21222
Rose Hill Estates	20817	Sanmar	21713	Sinepuxent	21811	Stansbury Estates	21220
Rosemary Hills	20910	Sansbury Park	20747	Singerly	21916	Stansbury Manor	21220
Rosemont (Baltimore County)	21225	Santa Fe Acres	21801	Skidmore	21401	Starkeys Corner	21623
Rosemont (Frederick County)	21758	Santo Domingo	21837	Skipton	21625	Starr	21617
Rosemont (Montgomery County)	20877	Sassafras	21637	Skyline	20746	Stemmer's Run	21220
Rose Valley Estates	20744	Satyr Hill	21234	Skyline Additions	20746	Stepney	21001
Rossville	21237	Saunders Point	21037	Sky Valley	21561	Steuart Level	21037
Round Acres	21047	Savage	20763	Slabtown	21545	Stevenson	21153
Round Bay	21146	Savage-Guilford	20763	Sligo Park Knolls	20901	Stevensville	21666
Round Hill	21702	Scaggsville	20723	Smallwood	21157	Stevensville South	21666
Roundtop	21750	Scarboro (Harford County)	21154	Smithsburg	21783	Stewartown	20879
Rover Mill Estates	21794	Scarboro (Worcester County)	21863	Smithville (Caroline County)	21632	Stillmeadows	21144
Rowlandsville	21918	Schnaders Shores	21122	Smithville (Dorchester County)	21669	Still Pond	21667
Roxboro (Part of Rockville)	20850	Schultz	20735	Smoketown	21713	Stockton	21864
Roxbury Correctional Institution	21740	Scientists Cliffs	20676	Smugglers Cove	21146	Stonecrest Hill	21043
Royal Beach	21122	Scotland (Montgomery County)	20854	Snowden Manor	21157	Stonegate	20905
Royal Oak (Talbot County)	21662	Scotland (St. Mary's County)	20687	Snowden Oaks	20708	Stone Haven	21060
Royal Oak (Wicomico County)	21856	Scotland Beach	20687	Snow Hill	21863	Stoneleigh	21212
Rugby Hall	21012	Seabrook	20706	Snow Hill Manor	20708	Stoneybrook Estates	20906
Ruhl	21053	Seabrook Acres	20706	Snug Harbor (Anne Arundel County)	20764	Stony Beach	21226
Rumbley	21871	Seabrook Park Estates	20706	Snug Harbor (Worcester County)	21811	Stony Run	21076
Rumsey Island	21085	Seat Pleasant	20743	Snydersburg	21074	Stratford	21093
Running Brook	21044	Sebring	21045	Social Security Administration	21207	Strathmore At Bel Pre	20906
Rustic Acres	21801	Secretary	21664	Society Hill	20650	Strathmore Estates	20906
Rusty Acres	20866	Security	21740	Sollers Homes	21222	Stratton Woods	20817
Ruthsburg	21617	Security Square Mall	21207	Sollers Point	21222	Strawberry Hills Estates	20616
Rutledge	21047	Selassie Villa	20764	Solley Heights	21060	Strawbridge Estates	21784
		Selby-on-the-Bay	21037	Solomons	20688	Strawleigh	21702
		Selbysport	21531	Somerset	20815	Street	21154
		Seneca	20837	Sonoma	20814	Stronghold	20842
		Seneca Park	20876	South (Part of Baltimore)	21230	Suburban Acres	21801
		Sequioa	20868	Southampton	20653	Suburbia	21060
		Severn	21144	South Cheverly Forest	20784	Sudbrook Park	21202
		Severna Forest	21146	South Cumberland (Part of Cumberland)	21502	Sudlersville	21668
		Severna Park	21146	Southdown Shores	21037	Sugarland	20837
		Severn Grove	21401	Southeast (Part of Baltimore)	21281	Sugarloaf Estates	21710
		Severn Heights	21146			Suitland	20746*
		Severnside	21401			Suitland	20752†
		Sewell	21009			Suitland-Silver Hill	20746
		Sewells Orchard	21045			Sullivan Heights	21157
		Shad Point	21801			Summerhill (Anne Arundel County)	21032
		Shady Dale	20659			Summerhill (Montgomery County)	20837
		Shady Oaks	20778			Summit Farms	21237

* Area Zip Code   † Post Office Boxes

	ZIP
Summit Park	21209
Sumner	20816
Sunair (Part of Salisbury)	21801
Sunderland	20689
Sunny Acres	20747
Sunnybrook	21131
Sunnybrook Hills	21131
Sunny Isle of Kent	21666
Sunrise	20744
Sunrise Beach	21032
Sunset Acres	21740
Sunset Beach	21122
Sunset Heights	21801
Sunset Hills	21702
Sunset Knoll	21122
Sunshine	20833
Sunshine Acres	20639
Sun Valley	21060
Surratt Gardens	20735
Susquehanna Hills	21078
Sussex Square	21108
Sutton Acres	20677
Swallow Falls	21550
Swan Creek	21078
Swanton	21561
Sweet Air	21013
Sweetser Heights	21090
Sycamore Acres	20853
Sycamore Heights	21742
Sykesville	21784
Sylmar	21911
Sylvan Grove	21740
Sylvan View	21122
Table Rock	26720
Takoma Park	20912
Tall Timbers	20690
Tammany Manor	21795
Tanager Forest	21108
Taneytown	21787
Tanglewood	21401
Tantallon	20744
Tantallon North	20744
Tantallon on the Potomac	20744
Tantallon Square	20744
Tanterra	20833
Tanyard	21655
Tarquin Village	20735
Taylor Mill Village	21801
Taylors Island	21669
Taylorsville	21771
Taylorville	21811
Temple Heights	20748*
	20757†
Temple Hills Park	20748
Templeton Estates	20737
Templeton Manor	20737
Templeville	21670
Temple Woods	20744
Terrace Gardens	21012
Terrace View Estates	21225
Texas	21030
Thayerville	21550
The Colony	20874
The Crest of Wickford	20852
The Downs	21401
The Glen	20854
The Hamlet	20815
The Highlands	21061
The Lakes	21030
The Meadows	20736
The Oaks (Calvert County)	20639
The Oaks (Howard County)	21043
Theodore	21911
The Orchards	21043
The Pines	20772
The Points	20879
Thomas	21613
Thomas Choice	20879
Thomas Run	21015
Thomas Town	21629
Thompson Corner	20659
Thompsontown	21631
Thomson Estates	21921
Thornleigh	21139
Thornwood Knoll	20744
Thorwood Park	21234
Thunder Hill	21045
Thurmont	21788
Thurston	20842
Tilden Woods	20852
Tilghman	21671
Tilghmanton	21713
Timber Grove	21117
Timber Ridge (Anne Arundel County)	21076
Timber Ridge (Carroll County)	21157

	ZIP
Timberview	21227
Timonium	21093
Tintop Hill	20650
Tobytown	20854
Todd Village	21048
Toddville	21672
Tolchester Beach	21620
Tollgate	21117
Tompkinsville	20664
Tonytank	21801
Tower Acres	20723
Tower Garden on the Bay	21666
Town Creek	25434
Town Creek Estates	20619
Town Creek Manor	20653
Town Crest	20855
Towne and Country North	21030
Towne Center	20708
Town Point	21915
Townshend	20613
Townsontown Centre	21286
Towson	21204
	21285-86
For specific Towson Zip Codes call (410) 823-0510, or your local postmaster.	
Towson Estates	21204
Towson Marketplace	21204
Towson Park	21286
Towson Town Center	21204
Tracys Landing	20779
Trappe (St. Mary's County)	20628
Trappe (Talbot County)	21673
Trappe (Worcester County)	21811
Trappe Station	21654
Travilah	20850
Treetops	21122
Trengall Acres	21740
Trent Hall	20659
Trenton	21155
Trescher Heights	21502
Triple Lakes	21502
Troutville	21798
Truman Heights	20748
Tulip Hill (Frederick County)	21702
Tulip Hill (Montgomery County)	20816
Tunis Mills	21601
Turkey Neck	21561
Turkey Point (Anne Arundel County)	21037
Turkey Point (Baltimore County)	21221
Turnbull Estates	21037
Turners Station	21222
Tuscarora	21790
Tuxedo (Part of Cheverly)	20785
Tuxedo Colony	20785
Twinbrook (Part of Rockville)	20851
Twinbrook Estates	20601
Twin Brook Forest (Part of Rockville)	20851
Twinbrook Park (Part of Rockville)	20851
Twin Harbors	21012
Tyaskin	21865
Tydings on the Bay	21401
Tylerton	21866
Tyrone	21158
Ulmsted Acres	21012
Ulmsted Estate	21012
Ulmsted Gardens	21012
Ulmsted Point	21012
Union Bridge	21791
Union Corner	21636
Union Mills	21158
Uniontown	21158
Unionville (Frederick County)	21791
Unionville (Talbot County)	21601
Unionville (Worcester County)	21851
Unity	20833
University City	20783
University Gardens	20783
University Hills	20783
University Park	20784
Upperco	21155
Upper Crossroads	21047
Upper Fairmount	21867
Upper Falls	21156
Upper Ferry Estates	21801
Upper Hill	21867
Upper Homewood	21502

	ZIP
Upper Marlboro	20772-75
For specific Upper Marlboro Zip Codes call (301) 627-4330, or your local postmaster.	
Urbana	21701
Utica	21788
Vale	21015
Vale Summit	21532
Valley Crest	21093
Valley Lee	20692
Valley Mede	21042
Valley Stream Estates	20866
Valley View (Howard County)	21043
Valley View (Prince George's County)	20744
Valleywood (Baltimore County)	21093
Valleywood (Wicomico County)	21801
Van Bibber	21040
Van Bibber Manor	21040
Van Lear Manor	21795
Vansville	20705
Venice on the Bay	21122
Venton	21853
Vernon	21161
Veterans Administration Medical Center	21902
Victory Villa	21220
Vienna	21869
Viers Mill	20906
View More Acres	21701
Villa Cresta	21234
Village of Vanderway	21234
Villages of Montpelier	20708
Villa Heights	20784
Villa Monticello	21723
Villa Nova	21207
Villa Toscano	21122
Villa Verdi	21054
Waggaman Heights	20748
Wakefield (Baltimore County)	21093
Wakefield (Carroll County)	21776
Wakefield Meadows	21014
Walbrook (Part of Baltimore)	21216
Waldon Woods	20735
Waldorf	20601-04
For specific Waldorf Zip Codes call (301) 645-5231, or your local postmaster.	
Walker Hill	20707
Walker Mill	20743
Walker Mill Estates	20743
Walkersville	21793
Wallington Estates	20747
Wallville	20685
Walnut Hill	20877
Walnut Ridge	21157
Walnut Woods	20852
Walston	21849
Walter Heights	20748
Wango	21801
Warburton Oaks	20744
Wards Chapel	21133
Warfield Estates	21738
Warfieldsburg	21157
Warington Hills (Part of Indian Head)	20640
Warlinda	20646
Warren	21030
Warwick	21912
Washington Grove	20880
Waterbury	21032
Waterloo	21227
Wateroak Point	21122
Watersville	21771
Waterview	21840
Watkins Glen	20854
Waverly (Part of Baltimore)	21218
Wayside	20664
Webster Village	21078
Weems Creek	21401
Weisburg	21161
Welcome	20693
Wellington Estates	20707
Wenona	21870
Wesley	21626
Wesmond (Part of Poolesville)	20837
West Baltimore (Part of Baltimore)	21227
West Beach (Part of Chesapeake Beach)	20732
West Bethesda	20817
Westboro	20814

	ZIP
West Bowie (Part of Bowie)	20719
Westchester (Baltimore County)	21228
Westchester (Montgomery County)	20902
Westchester Estates	20748
Westchester Park (Part of College Park)	20740
West Denton	21629
West Edmondale	21229
West Elkridge	21227
West End (Part of Annapolis)	21401
West End Park (Part of Rockville)	20850
Westerlea	21228
Westernport	21562
Western Shores Estates	20676
West Friendship	21794
Westgate	20816
West Gate Woods	20706
West Hills (Baltimore County)	21207
West Hills (Frederick County)	21702
West Hyattsville (Part of Hyattsville)	20782
Westlake	21801
West Lanham Estates	20784
West Lanham Hills	20784
West Laurel	20707
West Laurel Acres	20707
West Liberty	21161
West Magothy Manor	21012
Westminster (Carroll County)	21157-58
For specific Westminster Zip Codes call (410) 848-4780, or your local postmaster.	
Westminster (Part of Randolph Hills)	20852
Westminster South	21157
Westmore (Part of Rockville)	20850
Westmoreland Hills	20816
West Nottingham	21917
West Ocean City	21842
Westover	21871
Westowne	21229
Westphalia Estates	20772
Westphalia Woods	20772
West River	20778
West Severna Park	21146
West Shady Side	20764
West Shore	21106
West Twin River Beach	21220
Westview	21801
Westview Mall	21228
Westview Park	21228
West View Shores	21919
West Vindex	21538
Westwood	20613
Westwood Estates (Charles County)	20601
Westwood Estates (Prince George's County)	20623
Wetipquin	21856
Weverton	21758
Wexford	21012
Whaleysville	21872
Wheaton	20902
Wheaton Crest	20902
Wheaton Forest	20902
Wheaton-Glenmont	20902
Wheaton Hills	20902
Wheaton Plaza Regional Center	20902
Wheaton Woods	20853
Whetstone	20879
Whipporwill Estates	21122
Whiskey Bottom	20723
Whiteburg	21863
White Crystal Beach	21919
Whitefield Knolls	20706
Whitefield Woods	20706
White Flint	20895
White Flint Park	20895
Whiteford	21160
White Hall (Baltimore County)	21161
Whitehall (Prince George's County)	20607
Whitehall Beach	21401
Whitehall Manor	20814
Whitehaven	21856
Whitehouse Heights	20785
White Landing	20613
Whiteleysburg	21639

	ZIP		ZIP		ZIP		ZIP
White Marsh	21162	Williamsport	21795	Wingates Point	21675	Woodlawn Heights	21061
White Oak	20904	Williams Wharf	20685	Winsor Hills	20854	Woodmont	20815
White Oak Manor	20904	Williston	21629	Winterest	20854	Woodmoor (Baltimore	
White Oak Park	20904	Willoughby Beach	21040	Wisperren Oaks	21701	County)	21207
White Oak Shopping		Willow Beach Colony	20732	Wittman	21676	Woodmoor (Montgomery	
Center	20904	Willowbrook (Montgomery		Wolfsville	21773	County)	20901
White Oak Tower	20904	County)	20854	Wolverton Park	20735	Woodmoor (Washington	
White Plains	20695	Willowbrook (Prince		Woodacres	20816	County)	21740
White Point Beach	20650	George's County)	20783	Woodberry Forest	20748	Woodmore	20716
White Rock	21702	Willow Lake	20708	Woodbine	21797	Wood Point	21740
White Sands	20657	Wilson	21722	Woodbrook	21212	Woodsboro	21798
Whiton	21863	Wilson Hills	20906	Woodburn	20817	Woods Corner	20748
Wicomico	20622	Wilson Point	21220	Wood Creek	21045	Woodside	20901
Wicomico Beach	20664	Wiltondale	21204	Woodcroft	21234	Woodside Park	20901
Wilburn Estates	20743	Wilton Farm Acres	21043	Woodensburg	21136	Woodstock	21163
Wilde Lake	21044	Winchester on the Severn	21401	Woodfield	20882	Woodville	21771
Wildercroft	20737	Winchester Park	21157	Woodford	21044	Woolford	21677
Wild Rose Shores	21403	Windbrook	20735	Woodhaven	20817	Worthington	21043
Wild Wood Beach	21221	Windham Manor		Woodhaven Park	20646	Worthington Heights	21014
Wildwood Estates	20735	(Montgomery County)	20904	Woodland	21532	Worton	21678
Wildwood Hills	20817	Windham Manor		Woodland Acres	20619	Wrights Crossing	21532
Wildwood Manor	20817	(Wicomico County)	21801	Woodland Point	20664	Wye Mills	21679
Wildwoods	21133	Winding Brook Village	21921	Woodlands	21133	Wyngate	20814
Wilelinor Estates	21037	Windmere Acres	20763	Woodlane	20748	Wynne Wood	21227
Willards	21874	Windsor	21244	Woodlark	20784	Yarrowsburg	21758
Willerburn Acres	20854	Windsor Estates	21717	Woodlawn (Baltimore		Yellow Springs	21702
Williamsburg	21643	Windsor Terrace	21207	County)	21207	Yorkshire Knolls	20743
Williamsburg Estates	20772	Winfield (Carroll County)	21157	Woodlawn (Cecil County)	21904	Zion	21901
Williamsburg Gardens	20854	Winfield (Howard County)	21044	Woodlawn (Prince		Zittlestown	21713
Williamsburg Village	20832	Winfield Heights	21157	George's County)	20784		
Williamsbury	21208	Wingate	21675				

	ZIP
Aberdeen (Part of Boston)	02135
Abington	02351
Abington (Town)	02351
Acapesket	02536
Accord	02018
Acoaxet	02801
Acton	01720
Acton (Town)	01720
Acton Center	01720
Acushnet	02743
Acushnet (Town)	02743
Adams	01220
Adams (Town)	01220
Adamsdale	02760
Adams Shore (Part of Quincy)	02169
Adamsville	01340
Agawam	01001
Agawam Beach	02571
Agawam Shopping Center (Part of Agawam)	01001
Airport Mail Facility (Part of Boston)	02109
Aldenville (Part of Chicopee)	01013
Alford	01230
Alford (Town)	01230
Allendale (Part of Pittsfield)	01201
Allendale Shopping Center (Part of Pittsfield)	01201
Allerton	02045
Allston (Part of Boston)	02134
Amesbury	01913
Amesbury (Town)	01913
Amesbury Center	01913
Amherst	01002-04
For specific Amherst Zip Codes call (413) 549-0523, or your local postmaster.	
Amrita	02534
Andover	01810
Andover (Town)	01810
Annisquam (Part of Gloucester)	01930
Antassawamock Beach	02739
Apponagansett Village	02748
Arlington	02174
Arlington (Town)	02174
Arlington Heights	02175
Armory (Part of Springfield)	01101
Army Materials and Mechanics Research Center (Part of Watertown)	02172
Arsenal Mall (Part of Watertown)	02172
Ashburnham	01430
Ashburnham (Town)	01430
Ashby	01431
Ashby (Town)	01431
Ashdod	02332
Ashfield	01330
Ashfield (Town)	01330
Ashland	01721
Ashland (Town)	01721
Ashley Falls	01222
Ashley Heights	02717
Ashmont (Part of Boston)	02124
Assinippi	02339
Assonet	02702
Assonet Bay Shores	02702
Assumption College (Part of Worcester)	01609
Astor (Part of Boston)	02123
Athol	01331
Athol (Town)	01331
Athol Junction (Part of Springfield)	01101
Atlantic (Part of Quincy)	02169
Attleboro	02703
Attleboro Falls	02763
Auburn	01501
Auburn (Town)	01501
Auburndale (Part of Newton)	02166
Auburn Shopping Mall	01501
Avon	02322
Avon (Town)	02322
Ayer	01432-33
For specific Ayer Zip Codes call (508) 772-2083, or your local postmaster.	
Ayer (Town)	01432
Ayers Village (Part of Haverhill)	01830
Babson Park	02157

	ZIP
Back Bay Annex (Part of Boston)	02115
Bakers Grove	01473
Bakers Island (Part of Salem)	01970
Baldwinville	01436
Ballardvale	01810
Bancroft	01243
Baptist Corner	01370
Barkerville (Part of Pittsfield)	01201
Barnstable	02630
Barre	01005
Barre (Town)	01005
Barre Plains	01606
Barrowsville	02766
Bass Point	01908
Bass River	02664
Bass Rocks (Part of Gloucester)	01930
Bay State (Part of Northampton)	01060
Bay State Correctional Center	02056
Baystate West Shopping Center (Part of Springfield)	01103
Bayview (Bristol County)	02748
Bayview (Essex County)	01930
Beach (Part of Revere)	02151
Beachmont (Part of Revere)	02151
Beach Point	02652
Beachwood	01262
Beacon Hill (Part of Boston)	02108
Beaver Brook (Middlesex County)	02154
Beaver Brook (Worcester County)	01602
Becket	01223
Becket (Town)	01223
Becket Center	01011
Bedford (Town)	01730
Bedford	01730
Bedford Springs	01730
Beechwood	02025
Belcher Square	01230
Belchertown	01007
Belchertown (Town)	01007
Belchertown State School	01007
Bellingham	02019
Bellingham (Town)	02019
Bell Rock (Part of Malden)	02148
Belmont	02178
Belmont (Town)	02178
Belvidere (Part of Lowell)	01852
Bennetts Corner	02379
Berkley	02779
Berkley (Town)	02779
Berkshire	01224
Berkshire Heights	01230
Berlin	01503
Berlin (Town)	01503
Bernardston	01337
Bernardston (Town)	01337
Beverly	01915
Beverly Cove (Part of Beverly)	01915
Beverly Farms (Part of Beverly)	01915
Beverly Junction (Part of Beverly)	01915
Big Pond	01029
Billerica	01821*
	01822†
Birch Island	01570
Blackinton (Part of North Adams)	01247
Black Rock	02025
Blackstone	01504
Blackstone (Town)	01504
Blandford	01008
Blandford (Town)	01008
Bleachery (Part of Lowell)	01852
Bleachery (Part of Waltham)	02154
Bliss Corner	02748
Blissville	01364
Bloomingdale (Part of Worcester)	01604
Blue Hills	02186
Blush Hollow	01243
Bolton	01740
Bolton (Town)	01740
Bondsville	01009
Boston	02101-17
	02123
	02127-28
	02133
	02163
	02199
	02201-22
For specific Boston Zip Codes call (617) 451-9922, or your local postmaster.	

COLLEGES & UNIVERSITIES

Berklee College of Music	02215
Boston University	02215
Emerson College	02116
Massachusetts College of Art	02215
Massachusetts College of Pharmacy and Allied Health Sciences	02115
Northeastern University	02115
School of the Museum of Fine Arts	02115
Suffolk University	02114
University of Massachusetts at Boston	02125
Wentworth Institute of Technology	02115

FINANCIAL INSTITUTIONS

BayBank Boston, N.A.	02110
Boston Safe Deposit and Trust Company	02108
Brown Brothers Harriman & Company	02109
East Boston Savings Bank	02128
First National Bank of Boston	02110
Fleet Bank of Massachussets, N.A.	02106
Greater Boston Bank (A Cooperative Bank)	02135
Grove Bank	02146
Hibernia Savings Bank	02110
Hyde Park Savings Bank	02136
Massachusetts Company, Inc.	02110
Neworld Bank	02110
Shawmut Bank, N.A.	02211
South Boston Savings Bank	02127
State Street Bank and Trust Company	02110
United States Trust Company	02108

HOSPITALS

Beth Israel Hospital	02215
Boston City Hospital	02118
Boston University Medical Center-University Hospital	02118
Brigham and Women's Hospital	02115
Carney Hospital	02124
Children's Hospital	02115
Faulkner Hospital	02130
Hebrew Rehabilitation Center for Aged	02131
Lemuel Shattuck Hospital	02130
Massachusetts General Hospital	02114
New England Deaconess Hospital	02215
New England Medical Center	02111
St. Elizabeth's Hospital of Boston	02135
Spaulding Rehabilitation Hospital	02114
Veterans Affairs Medical Center	02130

HOTELS/MOTELS

Boston Park Plaza Hotel & Towers	02116
Le Meridien Boston	02110
Ritz-Carlton, Boston	02117
Sheraton-Boston Hotel & Towers	02199
Westin Hotel, Copley Place	02116

MILITARY INSTALLATIONS

Army Materials Technology Laboratory	02172
Coast Guard Support Center, Boston	02109
Naval Air Station, South Weymouth	02190
Naval Recruiting District, Boston	02210
Supervisor of Shipbuilding, Conversion and Repair, Boston	02210
United States Army Engineer Division, New England	02254

	ZIP
Boston College (Part of Newton)	02167
Boston University (Part of Boston)	02215
Bourne	02532
Bourne (Town)	02532
Bourne	02532
Bournedale	02532
Boxborough	01719
Boxborough (Town)	01719
Boxford	01921
Boxford (Town)	01921
Boylston	01505
Boylston (Town)	01505
Bradford (Part of Haverhill)	01830
Bradstreet	01038
Braintree	02184*
	02185†
Braintree Highlands	02184
Braleys	02717
Bramanville	01527
Brant Rock	02020
Brayton Point	02725
Brewster	02631
Brewster (Town)	02631
Briarwood Beach	02571
Bridgewater	02324
Bridgewater (Town)	02324
Brier Neck (Part of Gloucester)	01930
Brigadoon Village	01949
Briggsville	01247
Brighton (Part of Boston)	02135
Brightside (Part of Holyoke)	01040
Brightwood (Part of Springfield)	01107
Brimfield	01010
Brimfield (Town)	01010
Brittan Square (Part of Worcester)	01605
Broadway (Part of Malden)	02148
Brockton	02401-05
For specific Brockton Zip Codes call (508) 559-1800, or your local postmaster.	
Brookfield	01506
Brookfield (Town)	01506
Brookline	02146
Brookline (Town)	02146
Brookline Hill	02146
Brookline Village	02147
Brooks Place	02379
Brookville	02343
Brownell Corner	02790
Browns Point	01950
Brushwood (Part of Franklin)	02038
Bryantville	02327
Buckland	01338
Buckland (Town)	01338
Buena Vista Shores	02346
Buffington Corner	02725
Buffumville	01540
Bullardville	01475
Burlington	01803
Burlington (Town)	01803
Burlington Mall	01803
Burncoat (Part of Worcester)	01606
Buzzards Bay	02532
Byfield	01922
Cabot (Part of Newton)	02158
Cambridge	02138-42
	02238
For specific Cambridge Zip Codes call (617) 876-0620, or your local postmaster.	
Campello	02403-04
For specific Campello Zip Codes call (508) 559-1824, or your local postmaster.	
Campground Landing	02651
Camp Grounds	01564
Canterbury Estates	02563
Canton	02021

*** Area Zip Code** **† Post Office Boxes**

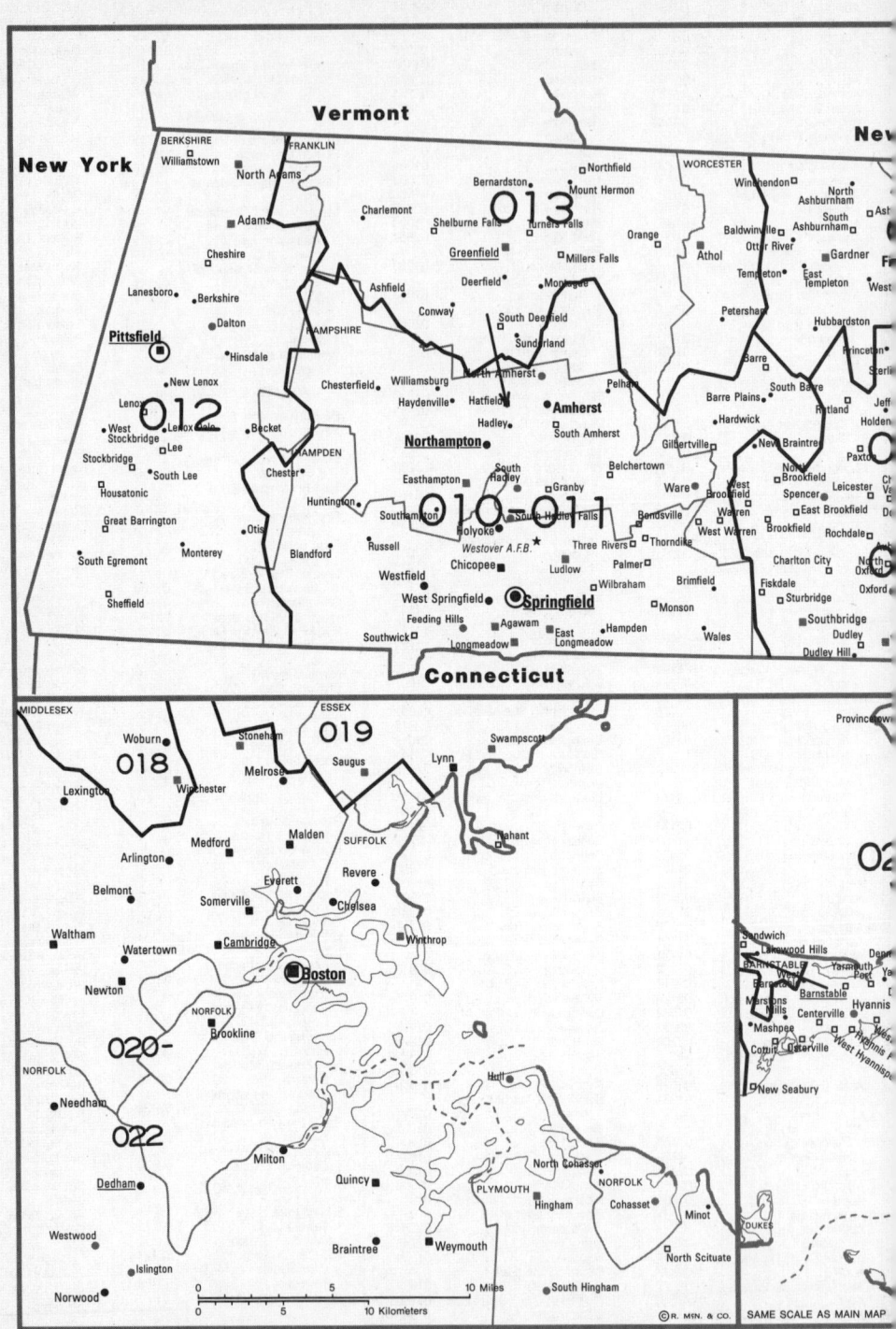

SAME SCALE AS MAIN MAP

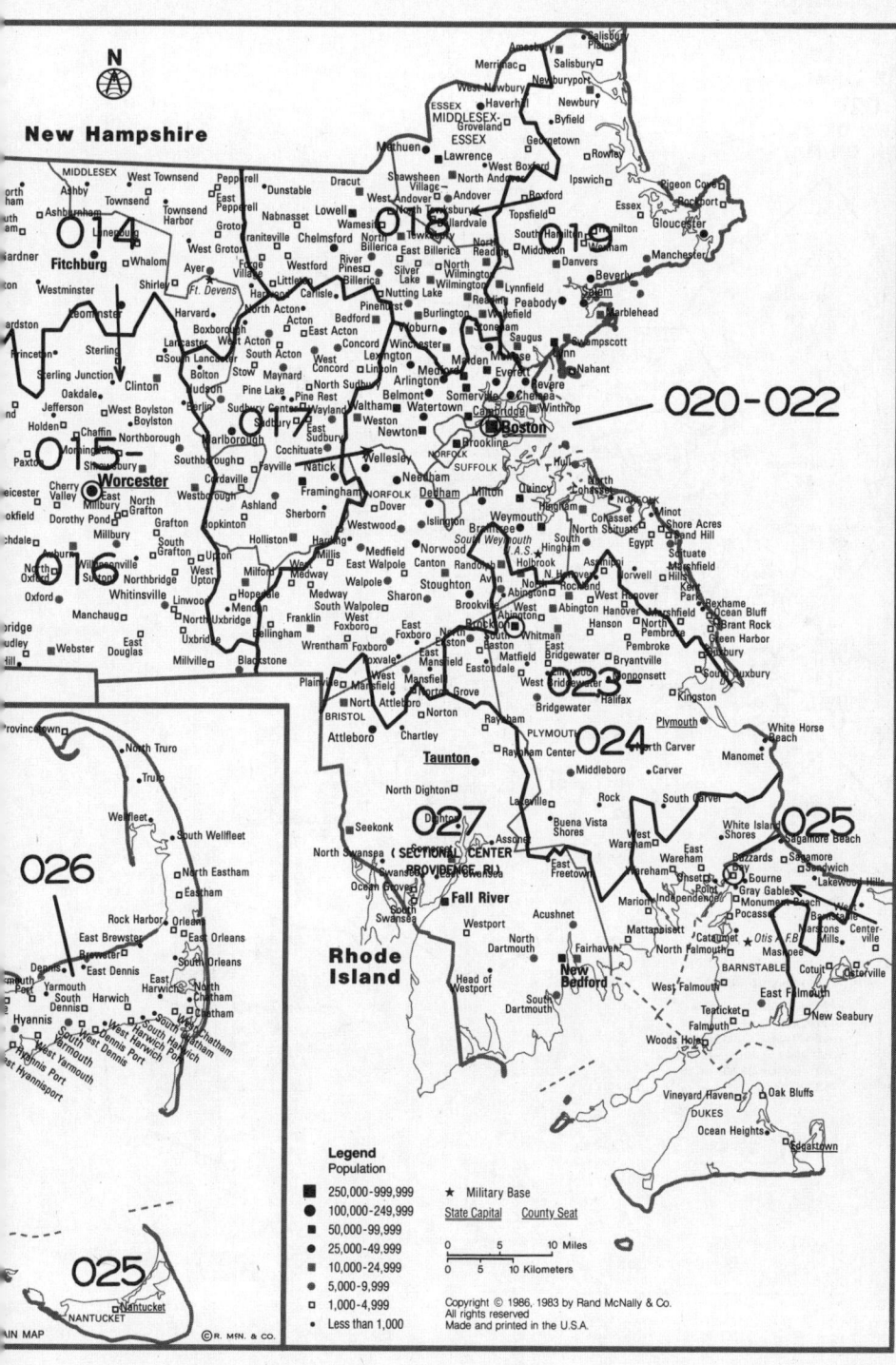

N

New Hampshire

014

015-

016

Fitchburg

Worcester

018

019

020-022

023

024

Boston

Taunton

027

026

SECTIONAL CENTER
(PROVIDENCE, RI)

Fall River

New Bedford

Rhode Island

025

025

NANTUCKET

AIN MAP

Legend
Population

■ 250,000–999,999
● 100,000–249,999
■ 50,000–99,999
● 25,000–49,999
● 10,000–24,999
● 5,000–9,999
□ 1,000–4,999
• Less than 1,000

★ Military Base
State Capital   County Seat

0   5   10 Miles
0   5   10 Kilometers

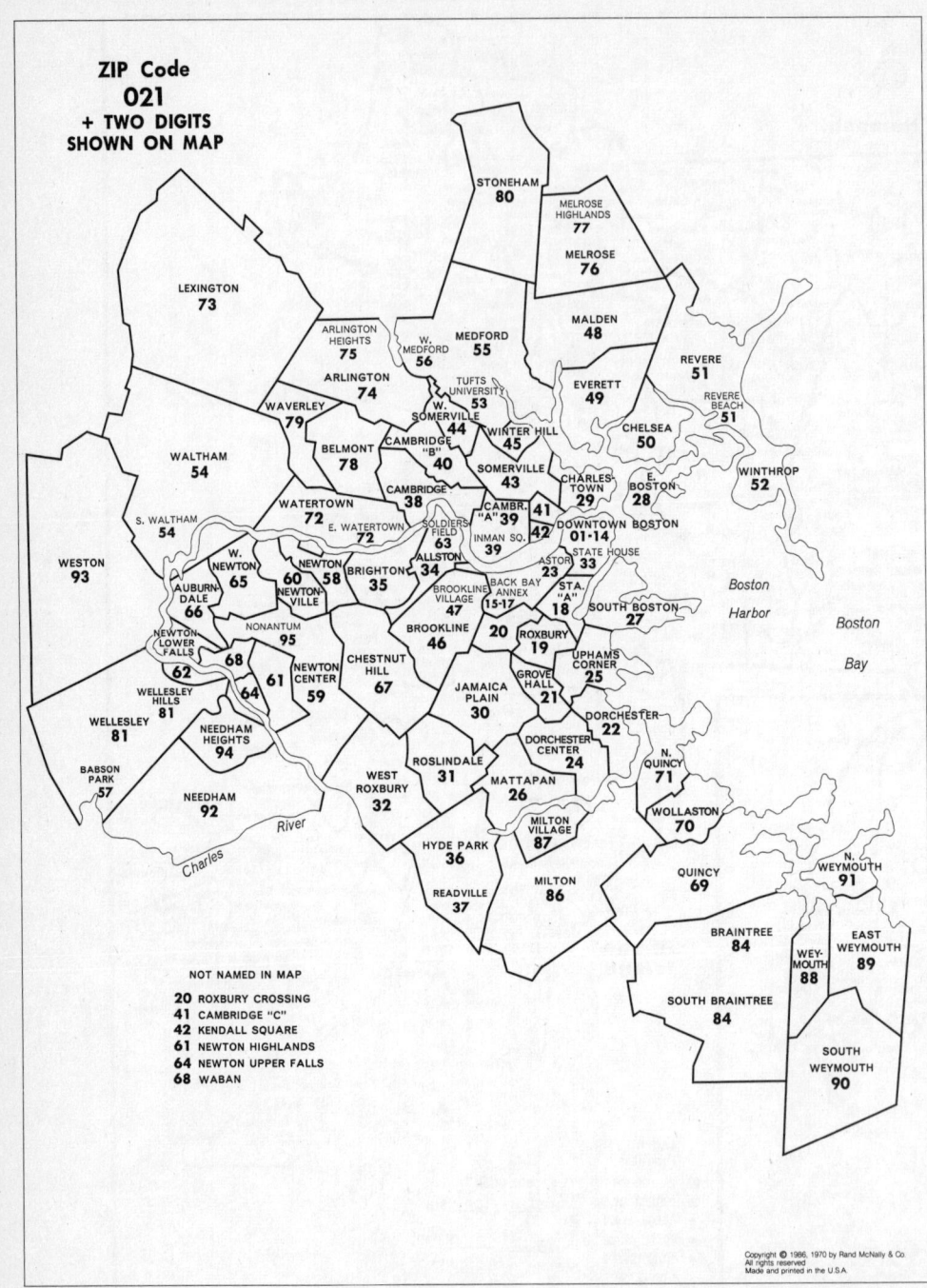

ZIP Code
021
+ TWO DIGITS
SHOWN ON MAP

STONEHAM
80

MELROSE
HIGHLANDS
77

MELROSE
76

LEXINGTON
73

ARLINGTON
HEIGHTS
75

W.
MEDFORD
56

MEDFORD
55

MALDEN
48

REVERE
51

ARLINGTON
74

TUFTS
UNIVERSITY
53

EVERETT
49

REVERE
BEACH
51

WAVERLEY
79

W.
SOMERVILLE
44

WINTER HILL
45

CHELSEA
50

WINTHROP
52

WALTHAM
54

BELMONT
78

CAMBRIDGE
"B"
40

SOMERVILLE
43

CHARLES-
TOWN
29

E
BOSTON
28

S. WALTHAM
54

WATERTOWN
72

CAMBRIDGE
38

CAMBR.
"A" 39

CAMBR.
41
42

DOWNTOWN BOSTON
01-14

WESTON
93

E. WATERTOWN
72

SOLDIERS
FIELD
63

INMAN SQ.
39

STATE HOUSE

ASTOR
23

STA.
33

W.
NEWTON
65

NEWTON
58

ALLSTON
34

BACK BAY
ANNEX
15-17

STA.
"A"
18

SOUTH BOSTON
27

Boston
Harbor

Boston

AUBURN-
DALE
66

NEWTON-
VILLE

BRIGHTON
35

BROOKLINE
VILLAGE
47

Bay

NONANTUM
95

BROOKLINE
46

ROXBURY
20

ROXBURY
19

NEWTON
LOWER
FALLS
62

68

61

NEWTON
CENTER
59

CHESTNUT
HILL
67

UPHAMS
CORNER
25

WELLESLEY
HILLS
81

64

JAMAICA
PLAIN
30

GROVE
HALL
21

DORCHESTER
22

WELLESLEY
81

NEEDHAM
HEIGHTS
94

N.
QUINCY
71

BABSON
PARK
57

NEEDHAM
92

ROSLINDALE
31

DORCHESTER
CENTER
24

WEST
ROXBURY
32

MATTAPAN
26

WOLLASTON
70

Charles River

MILTON
VILLAGE
87

QUINCY
69

N.
WEYMOUTH
91

HYDE PARK
36

MILTON
86

READVILLE
37

BRAINTREE
84

WEY-
MOUTH
88

EAST
WEYMOUTH
89

SOUTH BRAINTREE
84

SOUTH
WEYMOUTH
90

NOT NAMED IN MAP

20 ROXBURY CROSSING
41 CAMBRIDGE "C"
42 KENDALL SQUARE
61 NEWTON HIGHLANDS
64 NEWTON UPPER FALLS
68 WABAN

	ZIP		ZIP		ZIP		ZIP
Canton (Town)	02021	Cole Corner	02043	Dunstable	01827	Elmdale	01569
Canton Junction	02021	College Hill (Part of		Dunstable (Town)	01827	Elm Grove	01340
Cape Cod Mall (Part of		Worcester)	01610	Duxbury	02331*	Elm Square	02379
Barnstable)	02601	Collinsville	01826		02332†	Elmwood (Hampden	
Carletonville (Part of		Colonial Park	01570	Duxbury (Town)	02332	County)	01040
Salem)	01970	Colonial Station (Part of		Dwight	01007	Elmwood (Plymouth	
Carlisle	01741	Springfield)	01103	Eagleville	01364	County)	02337
Carlisle (Town)	01741	Colrain	01340	East Acton	01720	Endicott	02026
Carver	02330	Colrain (Town)	01340	East Arlington	02174	Erving	01344
Carver (Town)	02330	Coltsville (Part of		East Billerica	01821	Erving (Town)	01344
Castle Hill (Part of Salem)	01970	Pittsfield)	01201	East Blackstone	01504	Essex	01929
Cataumet	02534	Columbus Park (Part of		East Boston (Part of		Essex (Town)	01929
Cathedral (Part of Boston)	02118	Worcester)	01603	Boston)	02128	Essex (Part of Boston)	02112
Cedar Bushes	02345	Cominsville	01542	East Boxford	01921	Everett	02149
Cedarville	02532	Concord	01742	East Braintree	02184	Factory Hollow	01002
Center (Middlesex		Concord (Town)	01742	East Brewster	02631	Fairfield Mall (Part of	
County)	01801	Congamond	01077	East Bridgewater	02333	Chicopee)	01020
Center (Plymouth County)	02360	Conomo	01929	East Bridgewater (Town)	02333	Fairhaven	02719
Centerville (Barnstable		Conway	01341	East Brimfield	01010	Fairhaven (Town)	02719
County)	02632	Conway (Town)	01341	East Brookfield	01515	Fairlawn	01545
	02634	Cooks Brook Beach	02651	East Brookfield (Town)	01515	Fairmount (Part of Boston)	02136
	02636	Cooleyville	01355	East Cambridge (Part of		Fairview (Part of	
For specific Centerville Zip		Copley Place (Part of		Cambridge)	02141	Chicopee)	01020
Codes call (508) 775-2062, or		Boston)	02116	East Carver	02355	Fall River	02720-24
your local postmaster.		Cordaville	01772	East Charlemont	01370	For specific Fall River Zip	
Centerville (Essex County)	01915	Cotley (Part of Taunton)	02780	East Chelmsford	01824	Codes call (508) 675-7438, or	
Central Massachusetts		Cottage Hill	02152	East Dedham	02026	your local postmaster.	
Mail Processing Center	01546	Cottage Park	02152	East Deerfield	01342	Falls	01075
Central Village	02790	Cotuit (Part of Barnstable)	02635	East Dennis	02641	Falmouth	02540*
Centralville (Part of Lowell)	01850	Country View Estates		East Douglas	01516		02541†
Chadwick Square (Part of		(Part of Franklin)	02038	East Fairhaven	02719	Falmouth (Town)	02540
Worcester)	01605	Court Park	02152	East Falmouth	02536	Falmouth Heights	02540
Chaffin	01520	Coury Heights	02743	Eastfield Mall (Part of		Farley	01344
Chandler Hill (Part of		Cow Yard	02748	Springfield)	01129	Farm Hill	02180
Worcester)	01609	Craigville (Part of		East Foxboro	02035	Farnams	01225
Chapel Hill Estates	02359	Barnstable)	02636	East Freetown	02717	Farnumsville	01560
Chappaquiddick Island	02539	Craigville Beach (Part of		East Gloucester (Part of		Faulkner (Part of Malden)	02148
Chappaquoit	02574	Barnstable)	02636	Gloucester)	01930	Fayville	01745
Charlemont	01339	Crescent Beach		East Greenfield	01301	Federal (Part of	
Charlemont (Town)	01339	(Plymouth County)	02739	Eastham	02642	Worcester)	01601
Charles River Grove	02019	Crescent Beach (Suffolk		Eastham (Town)	02642	Feeding Hills	01030
Charles Street (Part of		County)	02151	Easthampton	01027	Felchville	01760
Boston)	02114	Crescent Mills	01050	Easthampton (Town)	01027	Fellsway (Part of Medford)	02155
Charlestown (Part of		Crooks Corner	02019	East Harwich	02645	Fentonville	01069
Boston)	02129	Cummaquid	02637	East Holliston	01746	Fields Corner (Part of	
Charlton	01507	Cummington	01026	East Junction (Part of		Boston)	02122
Charlton (Town)	01507	Cummington (Town)	01026	Attleboro)	02703	Fieldston	02065
Charlton City	01508	Cushman	01002	East Lee	01238	Findlen	02026
Charlton Depot	01509	Cuttyhunk	02713	East Leverett	01054	First Cliff	02066
Chartley	02712	Dalton	01226*	East Longmeadow	01028	Fiskdale	01518
Chaseville	01571		01227†	East Longmeadow (Town)	01028	Fitchburg	01420
Chatham	02633	Danvers	01923	East Lynn (Part of Lynn)	01904	Five Corners	02356
Chatham (Town)	02633	Danvers (Town)	01923	East Mansfield	02031	Flint (Part of Fall River)	02723
Chelmsford	01824	Danversport	01923	East Marion	02738	Florence (Part of	
Chelmsford (Town)	01824	Dartmouth	02714	East Middleboro	02346	Northampton)	01060
Chelsea	02150	Dartmouth (Town)	02714	East Millbury	01527	Florida	01343
Cherry Brook	02193	Davisville	02536	East Milton	02186	Florida (Town)	01343
Cherry Valley	01611	Dawson	01520	East Northfield	01360	Forbes Park	02019
Cheshire	01225	Dedham	02026*	Easton	02334	Fore River (Part of	
Cheshire (Town)	01225		02027†	Easton (Town)	02334	Quincy)	02169
Cheshire Harbor	01220	Dedham Mall	02026	Eastondale	02375	Forestdale	02644
Chester	01011	Deerfield	01342	East Orleans	02643	Forestdale Estates	02359
Chester (Town)	01011	Deerfield (Town)	01342	East Otis	01029	Forest Hills (Part of	
Chester Center	01011	Deer Island (Part of		East Pembroke	02359	Boston)	02130
Chesterfield	01012	Boston)	02152	East Pepperell	01463	Forest Lake	01069
Chesterfield (Town)	01012	Dennis	02638	East Princeton	01541	Forest Park (Part of	
Chestnut Hill (Part of		Dennis (Town)	02638	East Sandwich	02537	Springfield)	01108
Newton)	02167	Dennis Port	02639	East Saugus	01906	Forest River (Part of	
Chicopee	01013-22	Devenscrest	01432	East Springfield (Part of		Salem)	01970
For specific Chicopee Zip		Devereux	01945	Springfield)	01101	Forge Village	01886
Codes call (413) 592-9451, or		Dighton	02715	East Sudbury	01776	Fort Banks (U.S. Army,	
your local postmaster.		Dighton (Town)	02715	East Swansea	02777	inactive)	02152
Chicopee Center (Part of		Division Street (Part of		East Taunton (Part of		Fort Bellingham	02019
Chicopee)	01020	New Bedford)	02744	Taunton)	02718	Fort Devens	01433
Chilmark	02535	Dodge	01507	East Templeton	01438	Fort Heath	02152
Chilmark (Town)	02535	Dorchester	02121-22	Eastview Park (Part of		Fort Point (Part of Boston)	02205
Chiltonville	02360		02124-25	Waltham)	02154	Foundry Village	01340
Churchill Shores	02346	For specific Dorchester Zip		East Village	01570	Foxboro	02035
City Mills	02056	Codes call (617) 288-1219, or		Eastville	02557	Foxborough (Town)	02035
City Point (Part of Boston)	02127	your local postmaster.		East Walpole	02032	Foxvale	02035
Clarendon Hills (Part of		Dorchester Center (Part of		East Wareham	02538	Framingham	01701
Boston)	02131	Boston)	02124	East Watertown (Part of		Framingham (Town)	01701
Clarksburg (Town)	01247	Dorchester Lower Mills		Watertown)	02172	Framingham Center	01701
Clayton	06018	(Part of Boston)	02124	East Weymouth	02189	Franklin	02038
Clematis Brook (Part of		Dorothy Manor	01527	East Windsor	01270	Franklin Park (Part of	
Waltham)	02154	Dorothy Pond	01527	East Woburn (Part of		Revere)	02151
Clevelandtown	02539	Douglas	01516	Woburn)	01801	Freetown (Town)	02702
Clicquot	02054	Douglas (Town)	01516	Eddyville	02346	Fresh Pond (Part of	
Clifton	01945	Dover	02030	Edgartown	02539	Cambridge)	02138
Cliftondale	01906	Dover (Town)	02030	Edgartown (Town)	02539	Freshwater Cove (Part of	
Clinton (Town)	01510	Downtown (Part of Lowell)	01852	Edgemere	01545	Gloucester)	01930
Clinton	01510	Dracut	01826	Edgewater Estates	02359	Fuller Shores	02346
Cochesett	02379	Dracut (Town)	01826	Edgeworth (Part of		Furnace Pond Colony	02359
Cochituate	01778	Drury	01343	Malden)	02148	Furnace Village	02334
Cohasset	02025	Drury Square	01501	Egleston Square (Part of		Galleria at Worcester	
Cohasset (Town)	02025	Dry Pond	02072	Boston)	02116	Center (Part of	
Cohasset Army		Dudley	01571	Egremont (Town)	01252	Worcester)	01608
Ammunition Activity	02043	Dudley (Town)	01571	Egypt	02066	Gardner	01440
Cold Spring	01253	Dudley Hill	01570	Ellisville	02532	Gay Head	02535

* Area Zip Code   **† Post Office Boxes**

	ZIP		ZIP		ZIP		ZIP
Gay Head (Town)	02535	Harvard Square (Part of		Ipswich	01938	Linwood	01525
Georgetown	01833	Cambridge)	02138	Ipswich (Town)	01938	Lithia	01032
Georgetown (Town)	01833	Harwich	02645	Island Creek	02332	Little Acres	02327
Germantown (Part of		Harwich (Town)	02645	Islington	02090	Little Harbor Beach	02571
Quincy)	02169	Harwich Port	02646	Jamaica Plain (Part of		Little Nahant	01908
Gilbertville	01031	Harwood	01460	Boston)	02130	Little Neck (Bristol	
Gill (Town)	01376	Hasncom Air Force Base	01731	Jefferson	01522	County)	02777
Gillett Corner	01077	Hastings	02193	Jefferson Shores	02532	Little Neck (Essex	
Gleasondale	01775	Hatchville	02536	Jeffries Point (Part of		County)	01938
Glendale	01229	Hatfield	01038	Boston)	02128	Little River (Part of	
Glen Echo	02072	Hatfield (Town)	01038	John Fitzgerald Kennedy		Westfield)	01085
Glen Grove	01508	Hathorne	01937	(Part of Boston)	02114	Littleton	01460
Glen Grove Annex	01508	Haverhill	01830-32	John W. Mc Cormack		Littleton (Town)	01460
Glenridge	02030	For specific Haverhill Zip Codes		(Part of Boston)	02109	Lobsterville	02535
Gloucester	01930*	call (508) 373-5643, or your		Katama	02539	Lockerville	01760
	01931†	local postmaster.		Kearney Square (Part of		Locks Village	01072
Goodrichville	01462	Hawley	01339	Lowell)	01852	Long Beach	01930
Goshen	01032	Hawley (Town)	01339	Kempton Croft	02747	Long Hill Acres	02359
Goshen (Town)	01032	Haydenville	01039	Kendal Green	02193	Long Island Hospital (Part	
Gosnold (Town)	02713	Head of Westport	02790	Kendall Square (Part of		of Boston)	02169
Goss Heights	01050	Heath	01346	Cambridge)	02142	Longmeadow	01106
Goulding Village	01331	Heath (Town)	01346	Kenmore (Part of Boston)	02215	Longmeadow (Town)	01106
Grafton	01519	Heaven Heights	02717	Kent Park	02050	Long Plain	02743
Grafton (Town)	01519	Hebronville (Part of		Kenwood	01826	Long Pond Village	02532
Granby	01033	Attleboro)	02703	Killdeer Island	01570	Longwood	02146
Granby (Town)	01033	Hemlocks	02346	Kingsbury Beach	02642	Loudville	01027
Graniteville	01886	Hickory Hills Lake	01462	Kings Forest	01921	Lovell Corners	02188
Granville	01034	Hicksville	02747	Kingston	02364	Lowell	01850-54
Granville (Town)	01034	Highland (Part of		Kingston (Town)	02364	For specific Lowell Zip Codes	
Granville Center	01034	Springfield)	01109	Knightville	01050	call (508) 934-0500, or your	
Gray Gables	02532	Highland Lake	02056	Knollmere	02719	local postmaster.	
Great Barrington	01230	Highland Park (Part of		Konkapot	01244	Lower Mills (Part of	
Great Barrington (Town)	01230	Holyoke)	01040	Lafayette Place (Part of		Boston)	02126
Great Brook Valley (Part		Highlands (Hampden		Boston)	02111	Lower Village	01775
of Worcester)	01605	County)	01040	Lagoon Heights	02557	Ludlow (Hampden	
Greenbush	02040	Highlands (Middlesex		Lake Attitash	01913	County) (Town)	01056
Greendale (Part of		County)	01851	Lake Forest Park	01760	Ludlow (Hampden	
Worcester)	01606	Hillcrest Acres	02790	Lake Hiawatha	02019	County)	01056
Greenfield	01301*	Hilltop Acres	02346	Lake Mattawa	01364	Ludlow (Worcester	
	01302†	Hingham	02043	Lake Pleasant	01347	County)	01603
Greenfield Center	01301	Hingham (Town)	02043	Lakeside (Bristol County)	02790	Lunds Corner (Part of	
Green Harbor	02041	Hingham Center	02043	Lakeside (Plymouth		New Bedford)	02745
Green Harbor-Cedar Crest	02041	Hinsdale	01235	County)	02346	Lunenburg	01462
Greenlodge	02026	Hinsdale (Town)	01235	Lake Street	02174	Lunenburg (Town)	01462
Green Ridge Park	01226	Hinsdale Estates	02019	Lakeview (Middlesex		Lynn	01901-05
Greenview Estates	02035	Hodges Village	01540	County)	02154	For specific Lynn Zip Codes	
Greenville	01542	Holbrook	02343	Lake View (Worcester		call (617) 586-9000, or your	
Greenwood	01880	Holbrook (Town)	02343	County)	01604	local postmaster.	
Greenwood Manor		Holden	01520	Lakeview Heights	02717	Lynnfield	01940
Estates	02359	Holden (Town)	01520	Lakeview Terrace (Part of		Lynnfield (Town)	01940
Greylock (Part of North		Holland	01521	Pittsfield)	01201	Lynnhurst	01906
Adams)	01247	Holland (Town)	01521	Lakeville	02347	Lyonsville	01340
Griswoldville	01340	Holliston	01746	Lakeville (Town)	02346	Madaket	02554
Grosvenor Corner (Part of		Holliston (Town)	01746	Lakewood (Part of		Magnolia (Part of	
Methuen)	01844	Holly Woods	02739	Pittsfield)	01201	Gloucester)	01930
Groton	01450	Holyoke	01040*	Lakewood Hills	02537	Mahkeenac Heights	01240
Groton (Town)	01450		01041†	Lakewood Park	01473	Main Street	02532
Grove Hall (Part of		Holyoke Mall at Ingleside		Lambs Grove	01562	Main Street Station (Part	
Boston)	02121	(Part of Holyoke)	01040	Lancaster	01523	of Worcester)	01601
Groveland	01834	Hoosac Tunnel	01367	Lancaster (Town)	01523	Malden	02148
Groveland (Town)	01834	Hopedale	01747	Lanesboro	01237	Manchaug	01526
Hadley	01035	Hopedale (Town)	01747	Lanesborough (Town)	01237	Manchester	01944
Hadley (Town)	01035	Hopkinton	01748	Lanesville (Part of		Manchester (Town)	01944
Halfway Pond	02532	Hopkinton (Town)	01748	Gloucester)	01930	Manleys Corner	02379
Halifax	02338	Horseneck Beach	02790	Lane Village	01430	Manomet	02345
Halifax (Town)	02338	Hortonville	02777	Larrywaug	01262	Manomet Beach	02345
Halifax Beach	02338	Houghs Neck (Part of		Laurel Park (Part of		Manomet Bluffs	02345
Hamilton	01936	Quincy)	02169	Northampton)	01060	Mansfield	02048
Hamilton (Town)	01936	Houghtonville	01247	Lawrence	01840-43	Mansfield (Town)	02048
Hamilton (Part of		Housatonic	01236	For specific Lawrence Zip		Maple Park (Part of	
Worcester)	01604	Hovey's Corner	01463	Codes call (508) 691-4500, or		Methuen)	01844
Hamilton Beach	02571	Howe	01949	your local postmaster.		Maplewood (Middlesex	
Hampden	01036	Hubbardston	01452	Le Count Hollow	02663	County)	02148
Hampden (Town)	01036	Hubbardston (Town)	01452	Lee	01238	Maplewood (Worcester	
Hampshire Mall	01035	Huckleberry Corner	02576	Lee (Town)	01238	County)	01536
Hampton Mills	01027	Huckleberry Shores	02346	Leeds (Part of		Mara Vista	02536
Hancock	01237	Hudson (Town)	01749	Northampton)	01053	Marblehead	01945
Hancock (Town)	01237	Hudson	01749	Leicester	01524	Marblehead (Town)	01945
Hancock Village	02146	Hull	02045	Leicester (Town)	01524	Marblehead Neck	01945
Hanover	02339	Hull (Town)	02045	Leino Park	01473	Marion	02738
Hanover (Town)	02339	Humarock	02047	Lenox	01240	Marion (Town)	02738
Hanover Center	02339	Huntington	01050	Lenox (Town)	01240	Marlboro	01833
Hanover Street (Part of		Huntington (Town)	01050	Lenox Dale	01242	Marlborough	01752
Boston)	02113	Hyannis (Part of		Leominster	01453	Marshfield	02050
Hanson	02341	Barnstable)	02601	Leverett	01054	Marshfield (Town)	02050
Hanson (Town)	02341	Hyannis Port (Part of		Leverett (Town)	01054	Marshfield Hills	02051
Happy Hills	02019	Barnstable)	02647	Lexington	02173	Marstons Mills (Part of	
Harbor Beach	02739	Hyde Park	02136*	Lexington (Town)	02173	Barnstable)	02648
Harbour Mall (Part of Fall			02137†	Leyden (Town)	01301	Mashnee Island	02532
River)	02721	Idlewell	02188	Liberty Tree Mall	01923	Mashpee	02649
Harding	02052	Idlewood	02747	Lincoln	01773	Mashpee (Town)	02649
Hardwick	01037	Indian Mound Beach	02532	Lincoln (Town)	01773	Masons Corner	02717
Hardwick (Town)	01037	Indian Orchard (Part of		Lincoln Center	01773	Massachusetts	
Harrubs Corner	02367	Springfield)	01151	Lincoln Mall Station (Part		Correctional Institution	
Harthaven	02557	Indian Shore	02346	of Worcester)	01605	(Middlesex County)	01701
Hartsville	01230	Ingleside (Part of Holyoke)	01040	Lincoln Square (Part of		Massachusetts	
Harvard	01451	Inman Square (Part of		Worcester)	01601	Correctional Institution	
Harvard (Town)	01451	Cambridge)	02139	Linden (Part of Malden)	02148	(Norfolk County)	02071
		Interlaken	01266	Lindenwood	02180		

* Area Zip Code   † Post Office Boxes

	ZIP
Massachusetts Correctional Institution (Plymouth County)	02366
Massachusetts Institute of Technology (Part of Cambridge)	02139
Matfield	02379
Mattapan (Part of Boston)	02126
Mattapoisett	02739
Mattapoisett (Town)	02739
Maynard	01754
Maynard (Town)	01754
Mayo Beach	02667
Medfield	02052
Medfield (Town)	02052
Medford	02153†
	02155*
Medway	02053
Medway (Town)	02053
Meeting House Hill (Part of Boston)	02122
Megansett	02556
Melrose	02176-77
For specific Melrose Zip Codes call (617) 665-0182, or your local postmaster.	
Melrose Highlands (Part of Melrose)	02177
Menauhant	02536
Mendon	01756
Mendon (Town)	01756
Menemsha	02552
Merrick	01089
Merrimac	01860
Merrimac (Town)	01860
Merrimack College	01845
Merrimacport	01860
Merrymount (Part of Quincy)	02169
Methuen	01844
Methuen Mall (Part of Methuen)	01844
Middleboro	02346
Middleborough (Town)	02346
Middlefield	01243
Middlefield (Town)	01243
Middleton	01949
Middleton (Town)	01949
Midland	02019
Mile Oak Center	01095
Milford	01757
Milford (Town)	01757
Millbury	01527
Millbury (Town)	01527
Millers Falls	01349
Millerville	01504
Millis	02054
Millis (Town)	02054
Millis-Clicquot	02054
Mill River	01244
Millville	01529
Millville (Town)	01529
Millville Center	01529
Milton	02186
Milton (Town)	02186
Milton Center	02186
Milton Village	02187
Minot	02055
Mirror Lake	02093
Mishaum Point	02748
Monomoy	02554
Monponsett	02350
Monroe (Town)	01350
Monroe Bridge	01350
Monson	01057
Monson (Town)	01057
Montague	01351
Montague (Town)	01351
Montague City	01376
Montello (Part of Brockton)	02403
	02405
For specific Montello Zip Codes call (508) 559-1823, or your local postmaster.	
Monterey	01245
Monterey (Town)	01245
Montgomery	01085
Montgomery (Town)	01085
Montserrat (Part of Beverly)	01915
Montville	01255
Monument Beach	02553
Moores Corner	01054
Morningdale	01505
Morrills	02062
Morseville	01760
Mount Auburn (Part of Watertown)	02172
Mount Bowdoin (Part of Boston)	02121
Mount Hermon	01354
Mount Pleasant (Part of New Bedford)	02745
Mount Saint James (Part of Worcester)	01610
Mount Tom	01027
Mount Washington	12517
Mount Washington (Town)	12517
Myricks	02718
Mystic Grove	01507
Mystic Wharf (Part of Boston)	02109
Nabnasset	01886
Nahant	01908
Nahant (Town)	01908
Nantucket	02554*
	02584†
Nantucket (Town)	02554
Nashaquitsa	02535
Natick	01760
Natick (Town)	01760
Natick Development Center	01760
Natick Laboratories	01760
Natick Mall	01760
Needham	02192
	02194
For specific Needham Zip Codes call (617) 444-0128, or your local postmaster.	
Needham (Town)	02192
Needham Heights	02194
Nelsons Grove	02346
Nelsons Shores	02346
Neponset (Part of Boston)	02122
New Ashford	01237
New Ashford (Town)	01237
New Bedford	02740-42
	02744-46
For specific New Bedford Zip Codes call (508) 996-8523, or your local postmaster.	
New Boston	01255
New Braintree	01531
New Braintree (Town)	01531
Newbury	01951
Newbury (Town)	01950
Newburyport	01950-51
For specific Newburyport Zip Codes call (508) 462-4403, or your local postmaster.	
New England Shopping Center	01906
New Lenox	01240
New Marlboro	01230
New Marlborough (Town)	01230
New Salem	01355
New Salem (Town)	01355
New Seabury	02649
Newton	02158-62
	02164-66
	02168
	02195
For specific Newton Zip Codes call (617) 527-8529, or your local postmaster.	
Newton Center (Part of Newton)	02159
Newton Highlands (Part of Newton)	02161
Newton Lower Falls (Part of Newton)	02162
Newton Upper Falls (Part of Newton)	02164
Newtonville (Part of Newton)	02160
New Town	02258
New Village	01588
Nobska Beach	02571
Nonantum (Part of Newton)	02195
Nonquitt	02748
Noquochoke	02790
Norfolk	02056
Norfolk (Town)	02056
North (Part of New Bedford)	02746
North Abington	02351
North Acton	01720
North Adams	01247
North Adams Junction (Part of Pittsfield)	01201
North Amherst	01059
Northampton	01060-61
For specific Northampton Zip Codes call (413) 584-0960, or your local postmaster.	
North Andover	01845
North Andover (Town)	01845
North Andover Center	01845
North Ashburnham	01430
North Attleboro	02760-61
	02763
For specific North Attleboro Zip Codes call (508) 699-7556, or your local postmaster.	
North Attleborough (Town)	02760
North Bellingham	02019
North Beverly (Part of Beverly)	01915
North Billerica	01862
North Blandford	01008
Northborough	01532
Northborough (Town)	01532
Northbridge	01534
Northbridge (Town)	01534
Northbridge Center	01588
North Brighton (Part of Boston)	02135
North Brookfield	01535
North Brookfield (Town)	01535
North Cambridge (Part of Cambridge)	02138
North Carver	02355
North Chatham	02650
North Chelmsford	01863
North Chester	01050
North Cohasset	02025
North Dartmouth	02747
North Dartmouth Mall	02747
North Dighton	02764
North Duxbury	02332
North Eastham	02651
North Easton	02356
North Egremont	01252
Northey Point (Part of Salem)	01970
North Falmouth	02556
Northfield	01360
Northfield (Town)	01360
Northgate Shopping Center (Part of Revere)	02151
North Grafton	01536
North Hadley	01035
North Hancock	01267
North Hanover	02339
North Harwich	02645
North Hatfield	01066
North Lancaster	01523
North Leominster (Part of Leominster)	01453
North Leverett	01054
North Littleton	01460
North Marshfield	02059
North Middleboro	02346
North Milford	01757
North Natick	01760
North New Salem	01364
North Orange	01364
North Otis	01253
North Oxford	01537
North Pembroke	02358
North Pepperell	01463
North Plymouth	02360
North Plympton	02364
North Quincy (Part of Quincy)	02171
North Randolph	02368
North Reading	01864
North Reading (Town)	01864
North Rehoboth	02769
North Rutland	01543
North Salem (Part of Salem)	01970
North Saugus	01906
North Scituate	02060
North Seekonk	02771
Northshore Shopping Center (Part of Peabody)	01960
North Sommerville (Part of Somerville)	02143
North Stoughton	02072
North Sudbury	01776
North Swansea	02777
North Tewksbury	01876
North Tisbury	02568
North Truro	02652
North Uxbridge	01538
North Waltham (Part of Waltham)	02154
Northwest Harwich	02645
North Weymouth	02191
North Wilmington	01887
North Woburn (Part of Woburn)	01801
North Worcester (Part of Worcester)	01606
Norton	02766
Norton (Town)	02766
Norton Grove	02766
Norwell	02061
Norwell (Town)	02161
Norwood	02062
Norwood (Town)	02062
Norwood Central	02062
Nutting Lake	01865
Oak Bluffs (Town)	02557
Oak Bluffs	02557
Oakdale (Hampden County)	01040
Oakdale (Norfolk County)	02026
Oakdale (Worcester County)	01583
Oak Grove (Part of Malden)	02148
Oakham	01068
Oakham (Town)	01068
Oak Island (Part of Revere)	02151
Oakland Vale	01906
Ocean Bluff	02065
Ocean Bluff-Brant Rock	02020
Ocean Grove	02777
Ocean Heights	02539
Ocean Spray	02152
Old City	01474
Old Common	01527
Old Furnace	01031
Oldham Pines	02359
Oldham Village	02359
Old Silver Beach	02556
Old Sturbridge Village	01566
Onset	02558
Orange	01364
Orange (Town)	01364
Orchard Street (Part of New Bedford)	02740
Orient Heights (Part of Boston)	02128
Orleans	02653
Orleans (Town)	02653
Osceola	01254
Osterville (Part of Barnstable)	02655
Otis	01253
Otis (Town)	01253
Otis Air Force Base	02542
Otter River	01436
Overbrook	02181
Oxford	01540
Oxford (Town)	01540
Oyster Harbors (Part of Barnstable)	02655
Packard Heights	01331
Padanaram Village	02748
Pages Beach	01430
Painting Island	02738
Pakachoag	01501
Palmer	01069
Palmer (Town)	01069
Park Street (Part of Medford)	02155
Parkwood Beach	02571
Patuisset	02559
Pawtucketville (Part of Lowell)	01854
Paxton	01612
Paxton (Town)	01612
Payson Park (Part of Watertown)	02172
Peabody	01960*
	01961†
Pelham	01002
Pelham (Town)	01002
Pembroke	02359
Pembroke (Town)	02359
Pembroke Heights	02358
Pepperell	01463
Pepperell (Town)	01463
Perryville	02769
Peru	01235
Peru (Town)	01235
Petersham	01366
Petersham (Town)	01366
Phelps Mills (Part of Peabody)	01960
Phillipston	01331
Phillipston (Town)	01331
Phillipston Four Corners	01331
Pierceville	02576
Piety Corner (Part of Waltham)	02154

*** Area Zip Code** **† Post Office Boxes**

	ZIP
Pigeon Cove	01966
Pilgrim Heights	02652
Pilgrim Pines Estates	02327
Pilgrim Village	02019
Pine Bluffs	02346
Pinefield	01938
Pine Grove (Part of Northampton)	01060
Pinehurst	01866
Pinehurst Beach	02571
Pine Island	01951
Pine Island Lake	01060
Pine Lake	01776
Pine Point (Part of Springfield)	01101
Pine Rest	01776
Piney Point Beach	02738
Pingryville	01460
Pittsfield	01201-03
For specific Pittsfield Zip Codes call (413) 442-6961, or your local postmaster.	
Plainfield	01070
Plainfield (Town)	01070
Plainville (Hampshire County)	01002
Plainville (Norfolk County)	02762
Plainville (Norfolk County) (Town)	02762
Pleasant Lake	02645
Plimptonville	02081
Plumbush	01951
Plum Island (Part of Newburyport)	01950
Plummer Corner	01588
Plymouth	02360-62
For specific Plymouth Zip Codes call (508) 746-0058, or your local postmaster.	
Plympton	02367
Plympton (Town)	02367
Pocasset	02559
Pocomo	02554
Podunk	01515
Point Independence	02532
Point of Pines (Part of Revere)	02151
Point Pleasant	01570
Point Shirley	02152
Polpis	02554
Pomponotto Pines	02333
Ponakin Mill	01523
Pond Village	02652
Pondville (Norfolk County)	02093
Pondville (Plymouth County)	02532
Pondville (Worcester County)	01501
Pontoosuc Gardens (Part of Pittsfield)	01201
Pope Beach	02719
Popponesset Beach	02649
Porter Square (Part of Cambridge)	02140
Potoosuc Lake	01237
Pratt Corner	01072
Precinct	02346
Prentice Gardens	01588
Prides Crossing (Part of Beverly)	01965
Princeton	01541
Princeton (Town)	01541
Priscilla Beach	02360
Provincetown	02657
Provincetown (Town)	02657
Provincetown Wharf	02657
Prudential Center (Part of Boston)	02199
Quaise	02554
Queen Lake	01331
Quidnet	02554
Quincy	02169-71
For specific Quincy Zip Codes call (617) 328-5544, or your local postmaster.	
Quincy Adams (Part of Quincy)	02169
Quincy Center (Part of Quincy)	02169
Quincy Point (Part of Quincy)	02169
Quinsigamond Village (Part of Worcester)	01607
Quissett	02540
Rakeville	02019
Randolph	02368
Randolph (Town)	02368
Raynham	02767
Raynham (Town)	02767

	ZIP
Raynham Center	02768
Reading	01867
Reading (Town)	01867
Readville (Part of Boston)	02137
Redstone Shopping Center	02180
Rehoboth	02769
Rehoboth (Town)	02769
Renfrew	01220
Reservoir	02146
Revere	02151
Revere Beach (Part of Revere)	02151
Rexhame	02050
Rice Square (Part of Worcester)	01604
Richmond	01254
Richmond (Town)	01254
Richmond Furnace	01254
Rings Island	01950
Rio Vista	01862
Risingdale	01230
Riverdale (Essex County)	01930
Riverdale (Norfolk County)	02026
Riverdale (Worcester County)	01534
Rivermoor	02066
River Pines	01821
Riverside (Essex County)	01830
Riverside (Franklin County)	01376
Riverside (Hampden County)	01040
Riverside (Plymouth County)	02558
Riverview (Essex County)	01930
Riverview (Middlesex County)	02154
Roberts (Part of Waltham)	02154
Rochdale	01542
Rochester	02770
Rochester (Town)	02770
Rock	02346
Rockdale	01236
Rock Harbor	02653
Rockland	02370
Rockland (Town)	02370
Rockport	01966
Rockport (Town)	01966
Rocks Village (Part of Haverhill)	01830
Rock Valley (Part of Holyoke)	01040
Rockville	02054
Rocky Hill	01757
Rolling Acres Estates	01886
Roosterville	01255
Roslindale (Part of Boston)	02131
Rowe	01367
Rowe (Town)	01367
Rowley	01969
Rowley (Town)	01969
Roxbury	02118-20
For specific Roxbury Zip Codes call (617) 654-5768, or your local postmaster.	
Roxbury Crossing (Part of Boston)	02120
Royalston	01368
Royalston (Town)	01368
Russell	01071
Russell (Town)	01071
Russellville	01085
Rutland	01543
Rutland (Town)	01543
Saconesset Hills	02540
Sagamore	02561
Sagamore Beach	02562
Sagamore Highlands	02562
Salem	01970*
	01971†
Salem Neck (Part of Salem)	01970
Salem State College (Part of Salem)	01970
Salisbury	01952
Salisbury (Town)	01950
Salisbury Beach	01952
Salisbury Heights (Part of Worcester)	01609
Salisbury Plains	01950
Salters Point	02748
Sandersdale	01550
Sand Hill	02066
Sandisfield	01255
Sandisfield (Town)	01255
Sandwich	02563
Sandwich (Town)	02563

	ZIP
Sandy Beach (Norfolk County)	02025
Sandy Beach (Worcester County)	01543
Santuit (Part of Barnstable)	02635
Sassaquin (Part of New Bedford)	02745
Saugus	01906
Saugus (Town)	01906
Saugus Center	01906
Saundersville	01560
Savin Hill (Part of Boston)	02125
Savoy	01256
Savoy (Town)	01256
Saxonville	01701
Scituate	02066
Scituate (Town)	02066
Scorton Shores	02537
Scott Hill Acres	02019
Searstown Mall (Part of Leominster)	01453
Searsville	01096
Sea View	02050
Second Cliff	02066
Seekonk	02771
Seekonk (Town)	02771
Segreganset	02715
Shaker Village	01451
Sharon	02067
Sharon (Town)	02067
Sharon Heights	02067
Shattuckville	01369
Shawkemo	02554
Shawsheen Heights	01810
Shawsheen Village	01810
Sheffield	01257
Sheffield (Town)	01257
Shelburne	01370
Shelburne (Town)	01370
Shelburne Falls	01370
Sheldonville	02070
Shell Beach	02739
Shepardville	02762
Sherborn	01770
Sherborn (Town)	01770
Sherwood Forest (Berkshire County)	01223
Sherwood Forest (Bristol County)	02743
Shimmo	02554
Shirley	01464
Shirley (Town)	01464
Shirley Center	01464
Shoppers World	01701
Shore Acres (Bristol County)	02748
Shore Acres (Plymouth County)	02066
Shrewsbury	01545
Shrewsbury (Town)	01545
Shutesbury	01072
Shutesbury (Town)	01072
Siasconset	02564
Silver Beach	02565
Silver Hill	02193
Silver Lake (Middlesex County)	01887
Silver Lake (Plymouth County)	02360
Silver Shell Beach	02719
Silver Spring Beach	02651
Simon's Rock College of Bard	01230
Sippewisset	02540
Sixteen Acres (Part of Springfield)	01101
Smith Highlands (Part of Chicopee)	01020
Smith Mills	02747
Smiths Ferry (Part of Holyoke)	01040
Smoke Rise Heights	02777
Snug Harbor	02332
Soldiers Field (Part of Boston)	02163
Somerset	02725-26
For specific Somerset Zip Codes call (508) 673-7746, or your local postmaster.	
Somerset Centre	02725
Somerville	02143-45
For specific Somerville Zip Codes call (617) 666-0745, or your local postmaster.	
South (Part of Fall River)	02724
South Acton	01720
South Amherst	01002
Southampton	01073

	ZIP
Southampton (Town)	01073
South Ashburnham	01466
South Ashfield	01330
South Athol	01331
South Attleboro (Part of Attleboro)	02703
South Barre	01074
South Bellingham	02019
South Berlin	01503
South Billerica	01730
South Bolton	01740
Southborough	01772
Southborough (Town)	01772
South Boston (Part of Boston)	02127
South Braintree	02184
Southbridge	01550
Southbridge (Town)	01550
South Byfield	01922
South Carver	02366
South Charlton	01507
South Chatham	02659
South Chelmsford	01824
South Dartmouth	02748
South Deerfield	01373
South Dennis	02660
South Duxbury	02332
Southeastern Correctional Center	02324
South Easton	02375
South Egremont	01258
Southfield	01259
South Foxboro	02035
South Framingham	01701
South Georgetown	01833
South Grafton	01560
South Groveland	01834
South Hadley	01075
South Hadley (Town)	01075
South Hadley Falls	01075
South Hamilton	01982
South Hanover	02339
South Harwich	02661
South Hingham	02043
South Lakeville	02346
South Lancaster	01561
South Lawrence (Part of Lawrence)	01842
South Lee	01260
South Lowell	01876
South Lynnfield	01940
South Mashpee	02649
South Middleboro	02346
South Milford	01747
South Natick	01760
South Orleans	02662
South Peabody (Part of Peabody)	01960
South Postal Annex (Part of Boston)	02109
South Quincy (Part of Quincy)	02169
South Rehoboth	02769
South Royalston	01331
South Salem (Part of Salem)	01970
South Sandisfield	01255
South Sandwich	02563
South Shore Plaza	02184
South Springfield (Part of Springfield)	01101
South Stoughton	02072
South Sutton	01516
South Swansea	02777
South Truro	02666
South Uxbridge	01569
Southville	01772
South Walpole	02071
South Waltham (Part of Waltham)	02154
South Wareham	02571
South Wellfleet	02663
South Westport	02790
South Weymouth	02190
South Weymouth Naval Air Station	02190
Southwick	01077
Southwick (Town)	01077
South Williamstown	01267
South Wilmington (Part of Woburn)	01801
South Worthington	01050
South Yarmouth	02664
Spencer	01562
Spencer (Town)	01562
Spindleville	01747
Springdale (Part of Holyoke)	01040

*Area Zip Code †Post Office Boxes

	ZIP
Springdale Mall (Part of Springfield)	01101
Springfield	01101-05
	01107-09
	01118-44
	01152
For specific Springfield Zip Codes call (413) 731-0396, or your local postmaster.	
Springfield Plaza (Part of Springfield)	01104
Squantum (Part of Quincy)	02171
Standish (Part of Taunton)	02780
Staples Shore	02346
State House (Part of Boston)	02133
State Line	01266
Sterling	01564
Sterling (Town)	01564
Sterling Junction	01564
Stetson Road	02359
Stevens Corner	01201
Still River	01467
Stockbridge	01262
Stockbridge (Town)	01262
Stoneham	02180
Stoneham (Town)	02180
Stoneville (Franklin County)	01344
Stoneville (Worcester County)	01501
Stony Brook	02193
Stoughton	02072
Stoughton (Town)	02072
Stow	01775
Stow (Town)	01775
Sturbridge	01566
Sturbridge (Town)	01566
Sudbury	01776
Sudbury (Town)	01776
Sudbury Center	01776
Summit (Part of Worcester)	01606
Sunderland	01375
Sunderland (Town)	01375
Sunderland (Part of Worcester)	01604
Sunken Meadow Beach	02651
Sunnyside	01571
Surfside	02554
Sutton	01527
Sutton (Town)	01527
Swampscott	01907
Swampscott (Town)	01907
Swansea	02777
Swansea (Town)	02777
Swansea Center	02777
Sweets Corner	01267
Swift River	01026
Swifts Beach	02571
Symmes Corner	01890
Tafts Corner	01562
Tahanto Beach	02559
Tapleyville	01923
Tatnuck (Part of Worcester)	01602
Taunton	02718†
	02780*
Teaticket	02536
Templeton	01468
Templeton (Town)	01468
Tewksbury	01876
Tewksbury (Town)	01876
Tewksbury Hospital	01876
Texas	01537
The Green	02346
The Pines	01866
Thomastown	02346
Thorndike	01079
Three Rivers	01080
Thumpertown Beach	02651
Tihonet	02571
Tinkertown	02332
Tinkhamtown	02739
Tisbury (Town)	02568
Tobeys Island	02553
Tolland	01034
Tolland (Town)	01034
Tonset	02653
Topsfield	01983
Topsfield (Town)	01983
Touisset	02777
Town Crest Village	01225
Town Hall	02341
Townsend	01469
Townsend (Town)	01469
Townsend Harbor	01469

	ZIP
Tozier Corner (Part of Methuen)	01844
Tri-Town Shopping Center	02021
Truro	02666
Truro (Town)	02666
Tufts University (Part of Medford)	02153
Tully	01331
Turkey Hill Shores	01543
Turners Falls	01376
Turnpike	01545
Twin City Plaza (Part of Fitchburg)	01420
Tyngsboro	01879
Tyngsborough (Town)	01879
Tyringham	01264
Tyringham (Town)	01264
Union Market (Part of Watertown)	02172
Union Point	01570
Unionville (Norfolk County)	02038
Unionville (Worcester County)	01520
University Park (Part of Worcester)	01605
Uphams Corner (Part of Boston)	02125
Upton	01568
Upton (Town)	01568
Upton-West Upton	01568
Uxbridge	01569
Uxbridge (Town)	01569
Vallersville	02532
Valley View	02019
Van Deusenville	01236
Varnumtown	01826
Veterans Administration Hospital (Part of Boston)	02130
Victory Hill (Part of Pittsfield)	01201
Village	02053
Village Mall, The	02021
Village of Nagog Woods	01718
Vineyard Haven	02568
Vineyard Highlands	02557
Waban (Part of Newton)	02168
Wachusett (Part of Fitchburg)	01420
Wakeby	02563
Wakefield	01880
Wakefield (Town)	01880
Wakefield Center	01880
Wakefield Junction	01880
Wales	01081
Wales (Town)	01081
Wallis Street (Part of Peabody)	01960
Walnut Hill (Part of Woburn)	01801
Walpole	02081
Walpole (Town)	02081
Walpole Mall, The	02032
Waltham	02154
Waltham Highlands (Part of Waltham)	02154
Wamesit	01876
Wampun Corner	02093
Wapping	01342
Waquoit	02536
Ward Hill (Part of Haverhill)	01830
Ware	01082
Ware (Town)	01082
Wareham	02571
Wareham (Town)	02571
Warren	01083
Warren (Town)	01083
Warren Terrace	02359
Warrentown	02346
Warwick	01378
Warwick (Town)	01378
Washington	01223
Washington (Town)	01223
Watertown	02172
Waterville (Plymouth County)	02346
Waterville (Worcester County)	01475
Watuppa (Part of Fall River)	02721
Wauwinet	02554
Waverley	02179
Wawela Park	01570
Wayland	01778
Wayland (Town)	01778
Wayside Inn	01776

	ZIP
Webster	01570-71
For specific Webster Zip Codes call (508) 943-0809, or your local postmaster.	
Webster Square (Part of Worcester)	01603
Wedgemere	01890
Weir Village (Part of Taunton)	02780
Wellesley	02181
Wellesley (Town)	02181
Wellesley Farms	02181
Wellesley Fells	02181
Wellesley Hills	02181
Wellfleet	02667
Wellfleet (Town)	02667
Wellington (Part of Medford)	02155
Wellville	01430
Wendell	01379
Wendell (Town)	01379
Wendell Depot	01380
Wenham	01984
Wenham (Town)	01984
West Abington	02351
West Acton	01720
West Andover	01810
West Auburn	01501
West Barnstable (Part of Barnstable)	02668
West Becket	01238
West Bedford	01730
West Berlin	01503
West Billerica	01862
Westborough	01581
Westborough (Town)	01581
West Boxford	01885
West Boylston	01583
West Boylston (Town)	01583
West Bridgewater	02379
West Bridgewater (Town)	02379
West Brimfield	01069
West Brookfield	01585
West Brookfield (Town)	01585
West Cambridge (Part of Cambridge)	02138
West Chatham	02669
West Chelmsford	01863
Westchester (Part of Worcester)	01605
West Chesterfield	01084
West Chop	02573
West Concord	01742
West Cummington	01026
Westdale	02333
West Deerfield	01342
West Dennis	02670
West Dudley	01550
West Duxbury	02332
West Falmouth	02574
West Farms (Part of Northampton)	01060
Westfield	01085*
	01086†
West Fitchburg (Part of Fitchburg)	01420
Westford	01886
Westford (Town)	01886
West Foxboro	02035
Westgate Mall (Part of Brockton)	02401
West Gloucester (Part of Gloucester)	01930
West Granville	01034
West Groton	01472
Westhampton	01027
Westhampton (Town)	01027
West Hanover	02339
West Harwich	02671
West Hatfield	01088
West Hawley	01339
West Hingham	02043
West Hyannisport	02672
Westlands	01824
West Leominster (Part of Leominster)	01453
West Leyden	01337
West Lynn (Part of Lynn)	01905
West Manchester	01944
West Mansfield	02048
West Medford (Part of Medford)	02156
West Medway	02053
West Millbury	01586
Westminster	01473
Westminster (Town)	01473
West Natick	01760
West New Boston	01255
West Newbury	01985

	ZIP
West Newbury (Town)	01985
West Newton (Part of Newton)	02165
Weston	02193
Weston (Town)	02193
West Otis	01245
Westover Air Force Base	01022
West Peabody (Part of Peabody)	01960
West Pelham	01002
Westport (Town)	02790
Westport	02790
Westport Factory	02790
Westport Point	02791
West Quincy (Part of Quincy)	02169
West Roxbury (Part of Boston)	02132
West Royalston	01331
West Side (Part of Worcester)	01602
West Somerville (Part of Somerville)	02144
West Springfield	01089*
	01090†
West Sterling	01564
West Stockbridge	01266
West Stockbridge (Town)	01266
West Stockbridge Center	01266
West Stoughton	02072
West Sutton	01527
West Tatnuck (Part of Worcester)	01602
West Tisbury	02575
West Tisbury (Town)	02575
West Townsend	01474
West Upton	01568
Westview (Part of Franklin)	02038
Westville (Part of Taunton)	02780
West Walpole	02081
West Wareham	02576
West Warren	01092
West Watertown (Part of Watertown)	02172
West Whately	01039
West Wind Shores	02532
Westwood	02090
Westwood (Town)	02090
West Worthington	01098
West Wrentham	02070
West Yarmouth	02673
Wethersfield	02019
Weweantic	02571
Weymouth	02188-91
For specific Weymouth Zip Codes call (617) 337-1412, or your local postmaster.	
Weymouth Heights	02188
Weymouth Landing	02188
Whalom	01420
Whately (Town)	01093
Whately (East Whately)	01373
Whately	01093
Wheelockville	01569
Wheelwright	01094
White City	01747
White City Shopping Center	01545
White Horse Beach	02381
White Island Shores	02538
White Oaks	01267
Whitinsville	01588
Whitman	02382
Whitman (Town)	02382
Whittenton (Part of Taunton)	02780
Wigginsville (Part of Lowell)	01850
Wilbraham	01095
Wilbraham (Town)	01095
Wilkinsonville	01527
Williamsburg	01096
Williamsburg (Town)	01096
Williamstown	01267
Williamstown (Town)	01267
Williamsville (Berkshire County)	01236
Williamsville (Worcester County)	01452
Wilmington	01887
Wilmington (Town)	01887
Wilson (Part of Gloucester)	01930
Winchendon	01475
Winchendon (Town)	01475
Winchendon Springs	01477
Winchester	01890
Winchester (Town)	01890

*** Area Zip Code   † Post Office Boxes**

	ZIP		ZIP		ZIP		ZIP
Winchester Highlands....	01890	Woburn	01801	Woronoco...............	01097	Yankee Orchards (Part of	
Windsor................	01270	Wollaston (Part of Quincy)	02170	Woronoco Heights.......	01097	Pittsfield)..............	01201
Windsor (Town)	01270	Woodland Park..........	01501	Worthington	01098	Yarmouth	02675
Winmere	01803	Woods Hole............	02543	Worthington (Town)......	01098	Yarmouth (Town)	02675
Winnecunnet	02766	Woods Hole Coast Guard		Worthington Center	01098	Yarmouth Port...........	02675
Winslows	02062	Base	02543	Wrentham...............	02093	Zoar	01367
Winter Hill (Part of		Woodville	01784	Wrentham (Town)	02093	Zylonite	01220
Somerville)	02145	Worcester	01601-55	Wyben	01085		
Winthrop	02152	For specific Worcester Zip		Wyoming (Part of			
Winthrop (Town).........	02152	Codes call (508) 795-3666, or		Melrose)	02176		
Winthrop Highlands......	02152	your local postmaster.					

	ZIP
Abscota	49029
Ackerson Lake	49201
Acme	49610
Acme (Township)	49610
Ada	49301
Ada (Township)	49301
Adair	48064
Adams (Arenac County) (Township)	48659
Adams (Hillsdale County) (Township)	49262
Adams (Houghton County) (Township)	49963
Adams Park	49097
Adamsville	49112
Addison (Lenawee County)	49220
Addison (Oakland County) (Township)	48367
Adrian	49221
Adrian (Township)	49221
Advance	49712
Aetna (Mecosta County) (Township)	49336
Aetna (Missaukee County) (Township)	48632
Aetna (Newaygo County)	49412
Afton	49705
Agate	49967
Agnew	49460
Ahmeek	49901
Airport Forest	48625
Akron	48701
Akron (Township)	48701
Alabaster	48763
Alabaster (Township)	48763
Alaiedon (Township)	48854
Alamo	49009
Alamo (Township)	49009
Alanson	49706
Alaska	49302
Alba	49611
Albee (Township)	48655
Albert (Township)	49756
Alberta	49946
Albion	49224
Albion (Calhoun County) (Township)	49224
Albion (Houghton County)	49913
Alcona	48740
Alcona (Township)	48721
Alden	49612
Algansee (Township)	49082
Alger	48610
Algoma (Township)	49341
Algonac	48001
All Bright Shores	48612
Allegan	49010
Allegan (Township)	49010
Allen	49227
Allen (Township)	49227
Allendale (Clare County)	48625
Allendale (Ottawa County)	49401
Allendale (Ottawa County) (Township)	49401
Allen Park	48101
Allenton	48002
Allenville	49760
Allis (Township)	49765
Allouez	49805
Allouez (Township)	49805
Alma	48801
Almeda Beach	48653
Almena	49079
Almena (Township)	49079
Almer (Township)	48723
Almira (Township)	49630
Almont	48003
Almont (Township)	48003
Aloha	49721
Aloha (Township)	49721
Alpena	49707
Alpena (Township)	49707
Alpena Junction (Part of Alpena)	49707
Alpha	49902
Alpine	49321
Alpine (Township)	49321
Alston	49958
Alto	49302
Altona	49336
Alverno	49721
Amador	48422
Amasa	49903
Amber (Township)	49431
Amble	49329
Amboy (Township)	49232
Anchorville	48004
Andersonville	48350

	ZIP
Andrews	49104
Ann Arbor	48103-09
	48113
For specific Ann Arbor Zip Codes call (313) 665-1100, or your local postmaster.	
Ann Arbor (Township)	48105
Antioch (Township)	49688
Antoine (Part of Iron Mountain)	49801
Antrim (Antrim County)	49659
Antrim (Shiawassee County) (Township)	48418
Antwerp (Township)	49065
Anvil Location	49911
Aplin Beach	48706
Applegate	48401
Arbela (Township)	48746
Arborland Consumer Mall (Part of Ann Arbor)	48104
Arbutus Beach	49735
Arcade (Part of Ann Arbor)	48106
Arcadia (Lenawee County)	49613
Arcadia (Lapeer County) (Township)	48412
Arcadia (Manistee County)	49613
Arcada (Manistee County) (Township)	48801
Arenac (Township)	48749
Argentine	48451
Argentine (Township)	48451
Argyle	48410
Argyle (Township)	48410
Arlington (Township)	49013
Armada	48005
Armada (Township)	48005
Armstrong Corners	49079
Arnheim	49958
Arnold	49819
Artesia Beach	48656
Arthur (Township)	48617
Arvon (Township)	49962
Ash (Township)	48117
Ashland (Township)	49327
Ashland Center	49327
Ashley	48806
Ashmore	48767
Ashton	49655
Askel	49958
Assyria	49021
Assyria (Township)	49021
Athens	49011
Athens (Township)	49011
Atlanta	49709
Atlantic Mine	49905
Atlas	48411
Atlas (Township)	48438
Attica	48412
Attica (Township)	48412
Atwood	49729
Auburn	48611
Auburn Hills	48321†
	48326*
Au Gres	48703
Au Gres (Township)	48703
Augusta (Kalamazoo County)	49012
Augusta (Washtenaw County) (Township)	48191
Aura	49946
Aurelius	48854
Aurelius (Township)	48854
Aurora (Part of Ironwood)	49938
Au Sable (Iosco County)	48750
Au Sable (Iosco County) (Township)	48750
Au Sable (Roscommon County) (Township)	48653
Au Sable River Park	48656
Austin (Hillsdale County)	49232
Austin (Marquette County)	49841
Austin (Mecosta County) (Township)	49346
Austin (Sanilac County) (Township)	48475
Austin Center	48475
Austin Lake (Part of Portage)	49081
Au Train	49806
Au Train (Township)	49806
Auvinen Corner	49938
Avalon Beach	48161
Averill	48640
Avery (Township)	49709
Avoca	48006
Avondale	49631
Azalia	48110
Bach	48759

	ZIP
Backus (Township)	48656
Backus Beach	48762
Bad Axe	48413
Bagley (Menominee County)	49821
Bagley (Otsego County) (Township)	49735
Baie de Wasai	49783
Bailey	49303
Bainbridge (Township)	49022
Bainbridge Center	49022
Bakertown	49107
Baldwin (Delta County) (Township)	49872
Baldwin (Iosco County) (Township)	48770
Baldwin (Lake County)	49304
Baltic	49905
Baltimore (Barry County) (Township)	49058
Baltimore (Ontonagon County)	49912
Banat	49821
Bancroft	48414
Banfield	49017
Bangor (Bay County) (Township)	48706
Bangor (Van Buren County)	49013
Bangor (Van Buren County) (Township)	49103
Bankers	49242
Banks (Township)	49729
Banksons Lake	49065
Bannister	48807
Baraga	49908
Baraga (Township)	49908
Barbeau	49710
Barker Creek	49690
Bark River	49807
Bark River (Township)	49807
Bar Lake	49660
Barnard	49720
Barnes Lake-Millers Lake	48421
Baroda	49101
Baroda (Township)	49101
Barron Lake	49120
Barry (Township)	49060
Barryton	49305
Barton (Township)	49338
Barton City	48705
Barton Hills	48105
Barton Lake	49097
Base Line Lake	49055
Bass Lake	49449
Batavia	49036
Batavia (Township)	49036
Batavia Center	49036
Bates (Grand Traverse County)	49690
Bates (Iron County) (Township)	49935
Bath	48808
Bath (Township)	48808
Battle Creek	49015-18
For specific Battle Creek Zip Codes call (616) 965-3280, or your local postmaster.	
Bauer	49426
Baw Beese Lake	49242
Bay (Township)	49712
Bay City	48706-08
For specific Bay City Zip Codes call (517) 895-5555, or your local postmaster.	
Bay de Noc (Township)	49878
Bay Mills (Township)	49715
Bay Mills	49715
Bay Mills Indian Reservation	49715
Bay Port	48720
Bayshore	49711
Bay View	49770
Beachwood	48654
Beacon	49814
Beacon Hill	49905
Beadle Lake	49017
Beal City	48858
Bear Creek (Township)	49770
Bearinger (Township)	49759
Bear Lake (Hillsdale County)	49242
Bear Lake (Kalkaska County) (Township)	49646
Bear Lake (Manistee County)	49614
Bear Lake (Manistee County) (Township)	49614
Beaugrand (Township)	49721

	ZIP
Beaver (Bay County) (Township)	48611
Beaver (Newaygo County) (Township)	49309
Beaver Creek (Township)	48653
Beaverdam	49464
Beaver Grove	49855
Beaverton	48612
Beaverton (Township)	48612
Bedford (Calhoun County)	49020
Bedford (Calhoun County) (Township)	49017
Bedford (Monroe County) (Township)	48182
Beebe	48847
Beecher	48458
Beechwood (Iron County)	49909
Beechwood (Ottawa County)	49423
Belding	48809
Belknap (Township)	49743
Bell	49707
Bellaire	49615
Belleville	48111*
	48112†
Bellevue	49021
Bellevue (Township)	49021
Bell Oak	48892
Belmont	49306
Belsay (Part of Burton)	48503
Belvedere	49720
Belvidere (Township)	48886
Bendon	49643
Bengal (Township)	48879
Bennington	48867
Bennington (Township)	48867
Benona (Township)	49455
Bentheim	49419
Bentley (Bay County)	48613
Bentley (Gladwin County) (Township)	48652
Bentleys Corners	49245
Benton (Berrien County) (Township)	49022
Benton (Cheboygan County) (Township)	49721
Benton (Eaton County) (Township)	48876
Benton Harbor	49022*
	49023†
Benton Heights	49022
Benzonia	49616
Benzonia (Township)	49616
Bergland	49910
Bergland (Township)	49910
Berkley	48072
Berlamont	49026
Berlin (Ionia County) (Township)	48846
Berlin (Monroe County) (Township)	48166
Berlin (St. Clair County) (Township)	48002
Berne	48755
Berrien (Township)	49102
Berrien Center	49102
Berrien Springs	49103
Bertrand	49120
Bertrand (Township)	49120
Berville	48002
Bessemer	49911
Bessemer (Township)	49959
Bete Grise	49950
Bethany	48880
Bethany Beach	49125
Bethel (Township)	49028
Betzer	49271
Beulah	49617
Beverly Hills (Marquette County)	49866
Beverly Hills (Oakland County)	48009
Big Bay	49808
Big Creek (Township)	48647
Biggs Settlement	48647
Big Prairie (Township)	49349
Big Rapids	49307
Big Rapids (Township)	49307
Big Rock	49709
Billings (Township)	48612
Bingham (Clinton County) (Township)	48879
Bingham (Huron County) (Township)	48475
Bingham (Leelanau County) (Township)	49684
Bingham Farms	48025
Birch Beach	48450

***** Area Zip Code   † Post Office Boxes

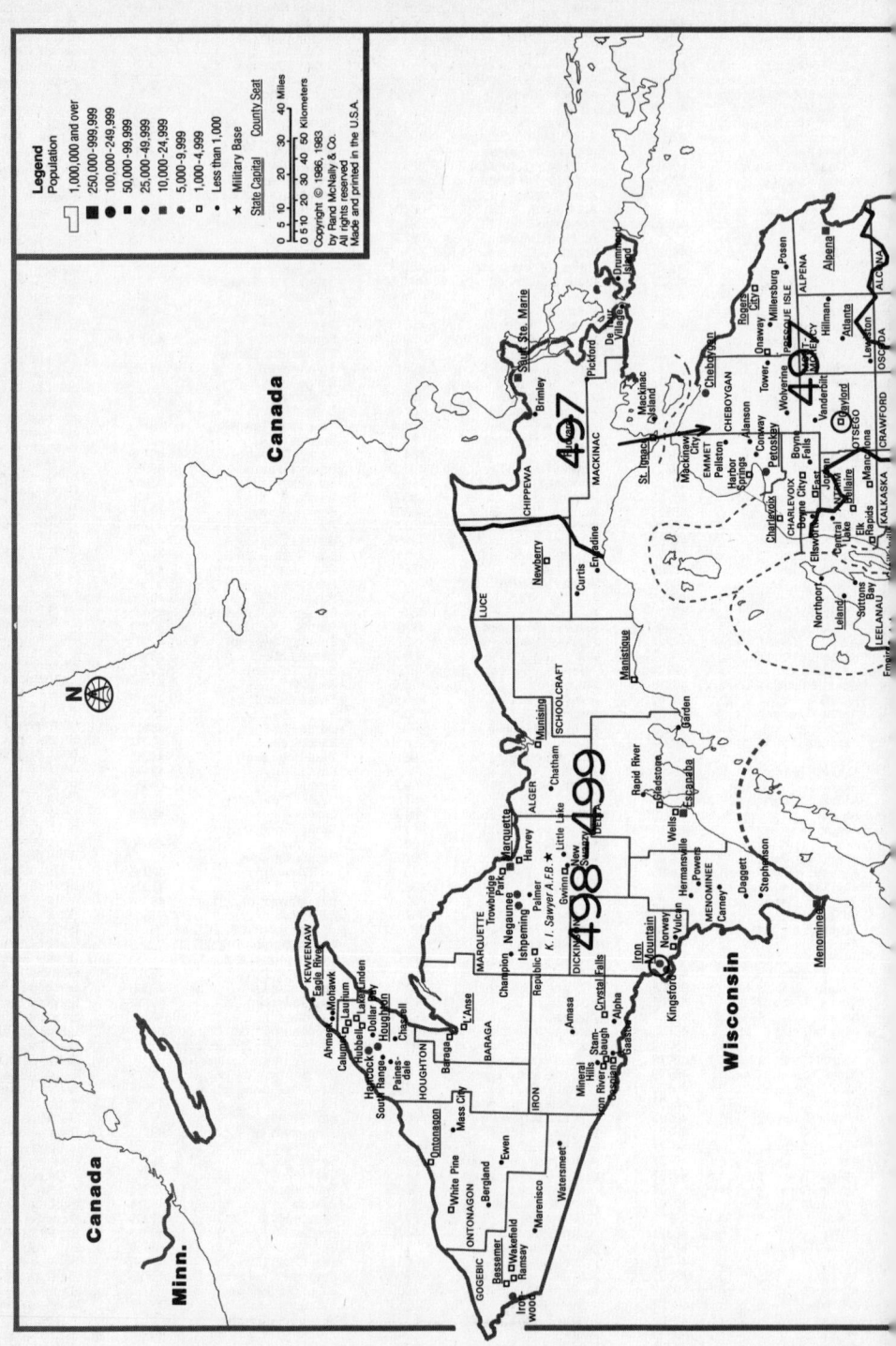

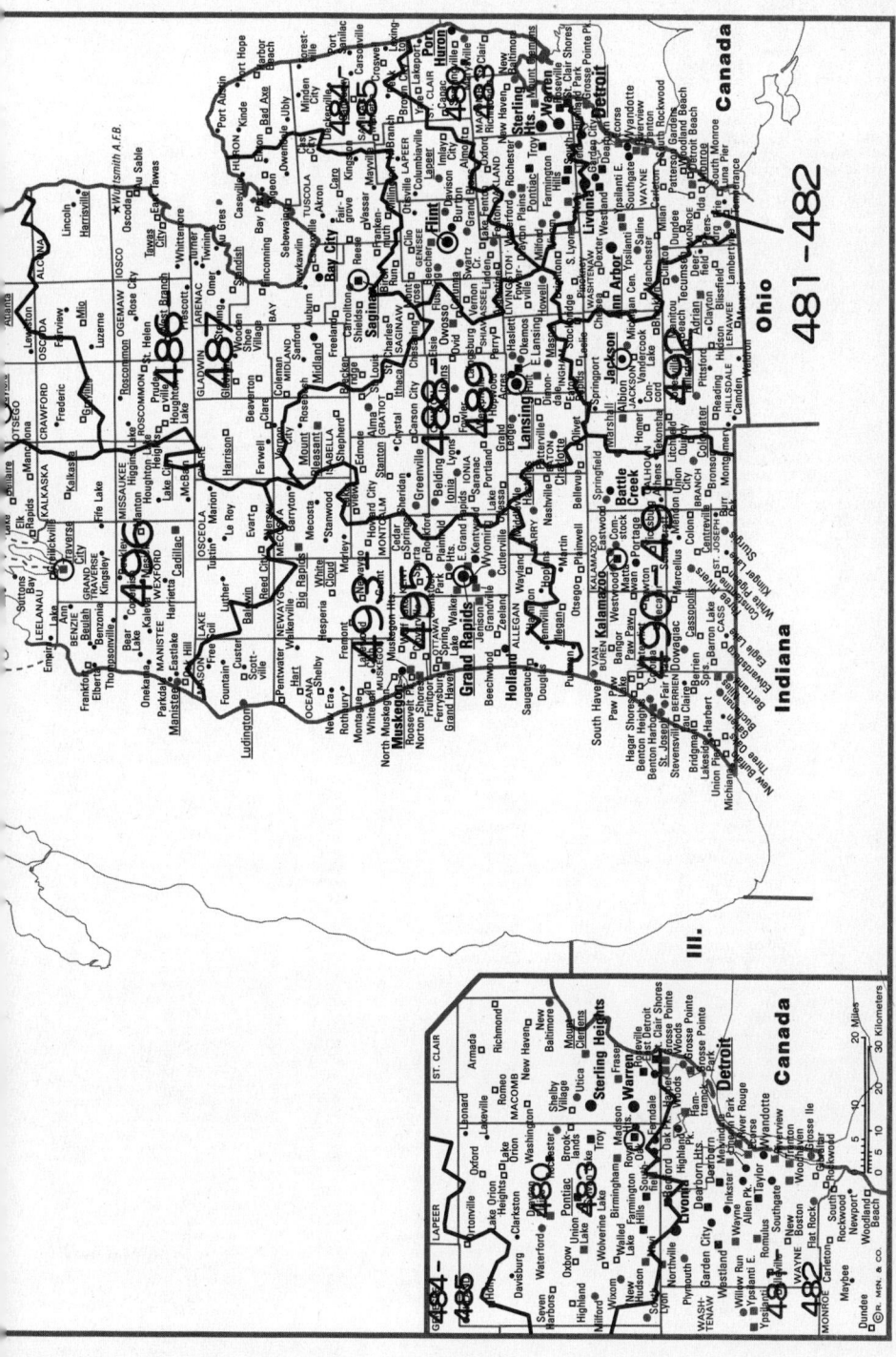

Place	ZIP
Birch Creek	49858
Birch Run	48415
Birch Run (Township)	48415
Birchwood (Berrien County)	49115
Birchwood (Cheboygan County)	49721
Birmingham	48009-12
For specific Birmingham Zip Codes call (810) 646-4331, or your local postmaster.	
Birmingham Farms	48010
Bismarck (Township)	49779
Bitely	49309
Black Lake Bluffs	49765
Blackman (Township)	49202
Black River	48721
Black River Harbor	49938
Blaine (Benzie County) (Township)	49635
Blaine (St. Clair County)	48032
Blair (Township)	49684
Blanchard	49310
Blaney Park	49836
Blendon (Township)	49426
Bliss	49755
Bliss (Township)	49755
Blissfield	49228
Blissfield (Township)	49228
Bloomer (Township)	48811
Bloomfield (Huron County) (Township)	48468
Bloomfield (Missaukee County) (Township)	49651
Bloomfield (Oakland County) (Township)	48302
Bloomfield Glens	48322
Bloomfield Hills	48301-04
For specific Bloomfield Hills Zip Codes call (313) 697-7030, or your local postmaster.	
Bloomfield Hills North	48302
Bloomfield Township	48301-02
For specific Bloomfield Township Zip Codes call (810) 642-7030, or your local postmaster.	
Bloomfield Town Square	48302
Bloomfield Village	48301
Bloomingdale	49026
Bloomingdale (Township)	49026
Blue Jacket	49913
Blue Lake (Kalkaska County) (Township)	49646
Blue Lake (Muskegon County) (Township)	49461
Blue Water Beach	48450
Bluff Beach	49099
Blumfield (Township)	48757
Blumfield Corners	48757
Boardman (Township)	49680
Bohemia (Township)	49965
Boichott Acres	48906
Bois Blanc (Township)	49775
Bolles Harbor	48161
Bombay	48642
Boon	49618
Boon (Township)	49618
Bootjack	49945
Borculo	49464
Boston (Houghton County)	49930
Boston (Ionia County) (Township)	48881
Bostwick Lake	49341
Bourret (Township)	48610
Bowens Mills	49333
Bowne (Township)	49302
Boyne City	49712
Boyne Falls	49713
Boyne Valley (Township)	49713
Bradley	49311
Brady (Kalamazoo County) (Township)	49097
Brady (Saginaw County) (Township)	48649
Brampton	49837
Brampton (Township)	49837
Branch	49402
Branch (Township)	49458
Brandon (Township)	48462
Brandywine Lake	49055
Brant	48614
Brant (Township)	48614
Brassar	49783
Bravo	49408
Breckenridge	48615
Breedsville	49027
Breen (Township)	49834
Breezy Beach	49099
Breitung (Township)	49876
Brent Creek	48433
Brethren	49619
Bretton Woods	48917
Brevort	49760
Brevort (Township)	49760
Briarwood (Part of Ann Arbor)	48108
Bridgehampton (Township)	48419
Bridgeport	48722
Bridgeport (Township)	48722
Bridgeton	49327
Bridgeton (Township)	49327
Bridgeville	48879
Bridgewater	48115
Bridgewater (Township)	48158
Bridgman	49106
Brightmoor (Part of Detroit)	48223
Brighton	48116
Brighton (Township)	48116
Briley (Township)	49709
Brimley	49715
Brinton	48632
Bristol	49688
Britton	49229
Broad Acres	48035
Brockway	48097
Brockway (Township)	48097
Brohman	49312
Bronson	49028
Bronson (Township)	49028
Brookfield (Eaton County)	48813
Brookfield (Eaton County) (Township)	48813
Brookfield (Huron County) (Township)	48754
Brooklyn	49230
Brooks (Township)	49337
Brookside	49412
Brookville	48170
Broomfield (Township)	49340
Brown (Township)	49660
Brown City	48416
Brownlee Park	49017
Brownstown (Township)	48134
Brownsville	49031
Brownwood Lake	49079
Bruce (Chippewa County) (Township)	49783
Bruce (Macomb County) (Township)	48065
Bruce Crossing	49912
Bruningville	49779
Brunswick	49313
Brutus	49716
Buchanan	49107
Buchanan (Township)	49107
Buckeye (Township)	48624
Buckley	49620
Bucks Corners	49449
Buel (Township)	48422
Buena Vista	48601
Buena Vista (Township)	48601
Bullock Creek	48642
Bumbletown	49805
Bunker Hill	49251
Bunker Hill (Township)	49251
Bunny Run	48362
Burdell (Township)	49688
Burdickville	49664
Burgess	49720
Burleigh (Township)	48770
Burley Corner	49017
Burlington (Calhoun County)	49029
Burlington (Calhoun County) (Township)	49029
Burlington (Lapeer County) (Township)	48727
Burnips	49314
Burns (Township)	48418
Burnside (Township)	48416
Burr Oak	49030
Burr Oak (Township)	49030
Burt (Alger County) (Township)	49839
Burt (Cheboygan County) (Township)	49721
Burt (Saginaw County) (Township)	48417
Burtchville (Township)	48059
Burt Lake	49717
Burton (Genesee County)	48509
Burton (Shiawassee County)	48867
Burton-Northeast (Part of Burton)	48509
Burton-Southeast (Part of Burton)	48529
Bushnell (Township)	48884
Butler (Township)	49082
Butman (Township)	48624
Butterfield (Township)	48632
Butternut	48811
Byron (Kent County) (Township)	49315
Byron (Shiawassee County)	48418
Byron Center	49315
Cadillac	49601
Cadmus	49231
Cady	48035
Calcite (Part of Rogers City)	49779
Calderwood	49967
Caldwell (Township)	49651
Caledonia (Alcona County) (Township)	48762
Caledonia (Kent County)	49316
Caledonia (Kent County) (Township)	49316
Caledonia (Shiawassee County) (Township)	48817
California	49255
California (Township)	49255
Calumet	49913
Calumet (Township)	49913
Calvin (Township)	49031
Calvin Center	49031
Cambria	49242
Cambria (Township)	49242
Cambridge (Township)	49265
Cambridge Junction	49230
Camden	49232
Camden (Township)	49232
Campbell (Township)	48815
Campbells Corner	48367
Campbells Corners	48661
Camp Grayling	49739
Canada Corners	49318
Canada Creek Ranch	49709
Canada Shores	49036
Canal (Part of Sault Ste. Marie)	49783
Canandaigua	49235
Canfield Beach	49765
Cannon (Township)	49341
Cannonsburg	49317
Canton	48187-88
For specific Canton Zip Codes call (313) 459-1012, or your local postmaster.	
Canton (Township)	48184
Capac	48014
Caribou Lake	49725
Carland	48831
Carleton	48117
Carlisle	49508
Carlshend	49885
Carlton (Township)	49058
Carlton Center	49325
Carmel (Township)	48813
Carney	49812
Caro	48723
Carp Lake (Emmett County)	49718
Carp Lake (Emmett County) (Township)	49718
Carp Lake (Ontonagon County) (Township)	49953
Carrollton	48724
Carrollton (Township)	48724
Carr Settlement	49402
Carson City	48811
Carsonville	48419
Cascade	49506
Cascade (Township)	49506
Casco (Allegan County) (Township)	49090
Casco (St. Clair County) (Township)	48064
Case (Township)	49759
Caseville	48725
Caseville (Township)	48725
Cash	48471
Casnovia	49318
Casnovia (Township)	49318
Caspian	49915
Cass City	48726
Cassidy Lake Technical School	48118
Cassopolis	49031
Castle Park	49423
Castleton (Township)	49073
Cathro	49707
Cato (Township)	48850
Cedar (Leelanau County)	49621
Cedar (Osceola County) (Township)	49631
Cedar Bluff	49090
Cedar Creek (Barry County)	49046
Cedar Creek (Muskegon County) (Township)	49457
Cedar Creek (Wexford County) (Township)	49663
Cedar Lake (Montcalm County)	48812
Cedar Lake (Van Buren County)	49067
Cedar River	49813
Cedar Springs	49319
Cedarville (Mackinac County)	49719
Cedarville (Menominee County) (Township)	49813
Cement City	49233
Centennial Heights	49913
Center (Township)	49769
Center Line	48015
Centerville (Township)	49621
Central	49950
Central Lake	49622
Central Lake (Township)	49622
Centreville	49032
Ceresco	49033
Chamberlains	49067
Champion	49814
Champion (Township)	49814
Chandler (Charlevoix County) (Township)	49712
Chandler (Huron County) (Township)	48731
Channing	49815
Chapin	48841
Chapin (Township)	48841
Charleston (Kalamazoo County) (Township)	49053
Charleston (Sanilac County)	48456
Charlevoix	49720
Charlevoix (Township)	49720
Charlotte	48813
Charlton (Township)	49751
Chase	49623
Chase (Township)	49623
Chassell	49916
Chassell (Township)	49916
Chatham	49816
Chatham Corners (Part of Chatham)	49816
Chauncey	49306
Cheboygan	49721
Chelsea	48118
Cherry Beach	48039
Cherry Bend	49684
Cherry Grove (Township)	49601
Cherry Hill	48187
Cherry Island (Part of Rockwood)	48173
Cherryland Mall (Part of Traverse City)	49686
Cherry Valley (Township)	49623
Chesaning	48616
Chesaning (Township)	48616
Cheshire (Township)	49010
Cheshire Center	49010
Chester	48813
Chester (Township)	48813
Chester (Otsego County) (Township)	49735
Chester (Ottawa County) (Township)	49403
Chesterfield	48051
Chesterfield (Township)	48051
Chestonia (Township)	49611
Chicagon Lake	49920
Chicora	49010
Chief Lake	49645
Chikaming (Township)	49116
China (Township)	48054
Chippewa (Chippewa County) (Township)	49790
Chippewa (Isabella County) (Township)	48858
Chippewa (Mecosta County) (Township)	49320
Chippewa Lake	49320
Chippewa Vista	49305
Chocolay (Township)	49855
Christie Lake	49064
Christmas	49862
Churchill (Muskegon County)	49441

	ZIP
Churchill (Ogemaw County) (Township)	48661
Circle Pine Center	49046
Cisco Lake	49969
Clam Lake (Township)	49601
Clam River	49615
Clam Union (Township)	48632
Clare	48617
Clarence (Township)	49224
Clarendon	49245
Clarendon (Township)	49245
Clarion	49713
Clark (Township)	49719
Clarklake	49234
Clarkston	48346-48
For specific Clarkston Zip Codes call (810) 625-0032, or your local postmaster.	
Clarksville	48815
Clawson	48017
Clay (Township)	48001
Claybanks (Township)	49452
Clayton (Arenac County) (Township)	48659
Clayton (Genesee County) (Township)	48473
Clayton (Lenawee County)	49235
Clear Lake	48661
Clearwater (Township)	49676
Clement (Township)	48610
Cleon (Township)	49625
Cleveland (Township)	49664
Clifford	48727
Climax	49034
Climax (Township)	49034
Clinton (Lenawee County)	49236
Clinton (Lenawee County) (Township)	49236
Clinton (Macomb County)	48035-36
	48038
For specific Clinton Zip Codes call (810) 465-1936, or your local postmaster.	
Clinton (Oscoda County) (Township)	48619
Clinton Village	48906
Clio	48420
Cloverdale	49035
Cloverville	49444
Clyde (Allegan County) (Township)	49408
Clyde (Oakland County)	48356
Clyde (St. Clair County) (Township)	48049
Coats Grove	49058
Coddes Beach	49765
Cody (Part of Flint)	48507
Coe	48880
Coe (Township)	48880
Cohoctah	48816
Cohoctah (Township)	48816
Cohoctah Center	48816
Cold Springs (Township)	49646
Coldwater (Branch County)	49036
Coldwater (Branch County) (Township)	49036
Coldwater (Isabella County) (Township)	48632
Coleman	48618
Colfax (Benzie County) (Township)	49683
Colfax (Huron County) (Township)	48413
Colfax (Mecosta County) (Township)	49307
Colfax (Oceana County) (Township)	49459
Colfax (Wexford County) (Township)	49663
College Park (Part of Detroit)	48221
College Town	48706
Colling	48767
Collins	48851
Coloma	49038
Coloma (Township)	49038
Colon (Township)	49040
Colon	49040
Columbia (Jackson County) (Township)	49230
Columbia (Tuscola County) (Township)	48767
Columbia (Van Buren County) (Township)	49056
Columbiaville	48421
Columbus (Luce County) (Township)	49853
Columbus (St. Clair County) (Township)	48063
Colwood	48767
Comins	48619
Comins (Township)	48621
Commerce	48387
Commerce (Township)	48382
Comstock	49041
Comstock (Township)	49041
Comstock Northwest	49041
Comstock Park	49321
Concord	49237
Concord (Township)	49237
Condit	49245
Cone	48160
Conklin	49403
Connorville	49968
Constantine	49042
Constantine (Township)	49042
Convis (Township)	49017
Conway (Emmet County)	49722
Conway (Livingston County) (Township)	48836
Cooks	49817
Cooks Corners	48809
Cooper (Township)	49004
Cooper Center	49004
Coopersville	49404
Copemish	49625
Copenhagen	49854
Copper City	49917
Copper Harbor	49918
Coral	49322
Corey	49093
Corinne	49838
Cornell	49818
Cornell (Township)	49818
Corrections Camp Program	49240
Corunna	48817
Corwith (Township)	49795
Coryell Islands	49719
Cottage Grove	48653
Cottage Park	49724
Cottrellville (Township)	48039
Court (Part of Kalamazoo)	49007
Courtland (Township)	49341
Courtland Center (Part of Burton)	48509
Covert	49043
Covert (Township)	49043
Covington	49919
Covington (Township)	49919
Cranbrook (Part of Bloomfield Hills)	48303
Crescent Lake Estates	48327
Crisp	49423
Crockery (Township)	49448
Crofton	49680
Crooked Lake (Barry County)	49046
Crooked Lake (Livingston County)	48116
Crossroads, The (Part of Portage)	49002
Cross Village	49723
Cross Village (Township)	49723
Croswell	48422
Croton	49337
Croton (Township)	49337
Croton Heights	49337
Crump	48634
Crystal (Montcalm County)	48818
Crystal (Montcalm County) (Township)	48818
Crystal (Oceana County) (Township)	49420
Crystal Beach	49036
Crystal Falls (Iron County) (Township)	49920
Crystal Falls (Iron County)	49920
Crystal Lake (Township)	49635
Crystal Valley	49420
Cumber	48475
Cumming (Township)	48635
Cunard	49847
Curran	48728
Curtis (Alcona County) (Township)	48737
Curtis (Mackinac County)	49820
Curtisville	48761
Custer (Antrim County) (Township)	49659
Custer (Mason County)	49405
Custer (Mason County) (Township)	49405
Custer (Sanilac County) (Township)	48471
Cutlerville	49508
Dafter	49724
Dafter (Township)	49724
Daggett	49821
Daggett (Township)	49821
Dailey	49031
Dallas (Township)	48835
Dalton	49445
Dalton (Township)	49445
Damon	48654
Danby (Township)	48890
Danish Landing	49738
Dansville	48819
Darragh	49646
Davis	48094
Davisburg	48350
Davison	48423
Davison (Township)	48423
Day (Township)	48852
Dayton (Berrien County)	49113
Dayton (Newaygo County) (Township)	49412
Dayton (Tuscola County) (Township)	48744
Dayton Center	49412
Dearborn	48120-21
	48128
For specific Dearborn Zip Codes call (313) 337-4711, or your local postmaster.	
Dearborn Heights	48125
	48127
For specific Dearborn Heights Zip Codes call (313) 278-2567, or your local postmaster.	
Decatur	49045
Decatur (Township)	49045
Decker	48426
Deckerville	48427
Deep River (Township)	48659
Deerfield (Isabella County) (Township)	48858
Deerfield (Lapeer County) (Township)	48421
Deerfield (Lenawee County)	49238
Deerfield (Lenawee County) (Township)	49238
Deerfield (Livingston County) (Township)	48451
Deerfield (Mecosta County) (Township)	49336
Deerfield Center (Isabella County)	48858
Deerfield Center (Livingston County)	48451
Deer Park	49868
Deerton	49822
Deford	48729
Dehoco	48175
Delano	48703
Delaware (Township)	48456
Delhi (Township)	48842
Delray (Part of Detroit)	48217
Delta (Township)	48917
Delta Mills	48917
Delton	49046
Delwin	48858
Denmark (Township)	48758
Denton (Roscommon County) (Township)	48651
Denton (Wayne County)	48111
Denver (Isabella County) (Township)	48858
Denver (Newaygo County) (Township)	49421
Derby	49127
Detour (Township)	49725
De Tour Village	49725
Detroit	48201-17
	48219
	48221-24
	48226-28
	48231-35
	48238
	48242-44
For specific Detroit Zip Codes call (313) 271-6544, or your local postmaster.	
COLLEGES & UNIVERSITIES	
Marygrove College	48221
University of Detroit Mercy	48219
FINANCIAL INSTITUTIONS	
Comerica Bank	48243
Detroit Savings Bank, F.S.B.	48226
First Federal of Michigan	48226
First of America Bank-Southeast Michigan, N.A.	48226
NBD Bank, National Association	48226
HOSPITALS	
Children's Hospital of Michigan	48201
Detroit Receiving Hospital and University Health Center	48201
Detroit Riverview Hospital	48214
Grace Hospital	48235
Harper Hospital	48201
Henry Ford Hospital	48202
Holy Cross Hospital	48234
Hutzel Hospital	48201
North Detroit General Hospital	48212
St. John Hospital and Medical Center	48236
Sinai Hospital	48235
HOTELS/MOTELS	
Detroit Airport Marriott	48242
Radisson Hotel Pontchartrain	48226
Westin Hotel	48243
MILITARY INSTALLATIONS	
Coast Guard Base, Detroit	48207
Detroit Marine Terminal, Inc.	48218
United States Army Engineer District, Detroit	48231
United States Army Engineer District, Detroit Area Office	48209
Detroit Beach	48161
Detroit River (Part of Detroit)	48222
Devereaux	49224
Devils Lake	49253
De Witt	48820
De Witt (Township)	48820
Dexter	48130
Dexter (Township)	48169
Diamond Lake	49349
Diamond Shores	49031
Diamond Springs	49419
Dice Corners	48640
Dickson (Township)	49619
Diffin	49891
Dighton	49688
Dimondale	48821
Diorite	49814
Disco	48315
Dixboro	48105
Dodgeville	49921
Dollar Bay	49922
Dollar Settlement	49715
Dollarville	49868
Dolph	49632
Donaldson	49783
Donken	49965
Donoghue Beach	48706
Doriva Beach	49721
Dorr	49323
Dorr (Township)	49323
Doster	49080
Doughertys Corners	49009
Douglas	49406
Douglass (Township)	48888
Dover (Lake County) (Township)	49656
Dover (Lenawee County) (Township)	49235
Dover (Otsego County) (Township)	49738
Dowagiac	49047
Dowling	49050
Downington	48427
Downtown (Part of Flint)	48502
Downtown (Part of Lansing)	48924
Downtown (Part of Midland)	48640
Doyle (Township)	49840
Drayton Plains	48330
Drenthe	49464
Drummond (Township)	49726
Drummond Island	49726
Dryburg	49780
Dryden	48428
Dryden (Township)	48428
Dublin	49689

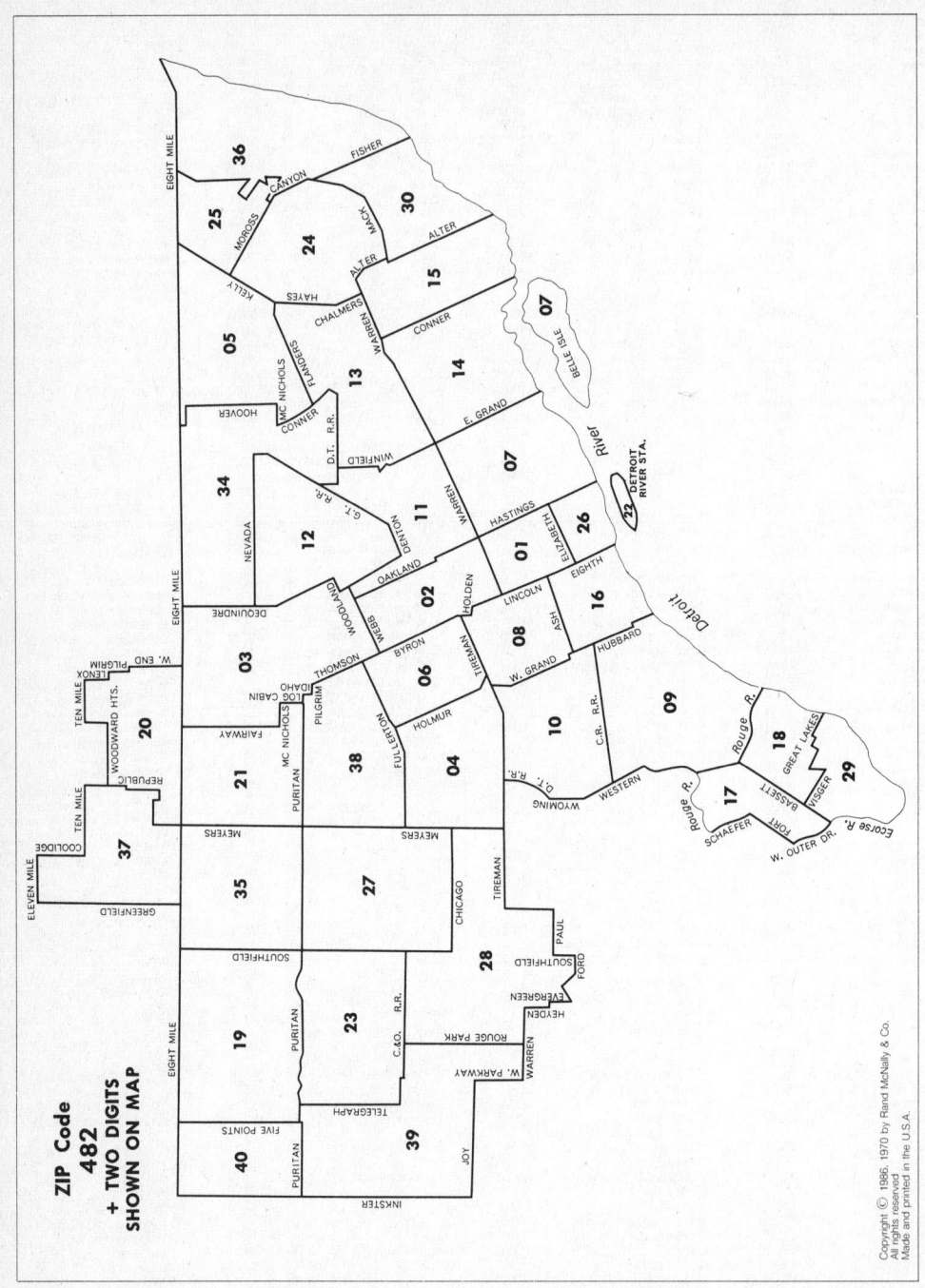

ZIP Code
482
+ TWO DIGITS
SHOWN ON MAP

Place	ZIP
Duck Lake (Allegan County)	49055
Duck Lake (Calhoun County)	49224
Duel	48640
Duffield	48473
Dukes	49885
Duncan (Township)	48131
Dundee	48131
Dundee (Township)	48131
Dunham Lake	48092
Dunningville	49010
Duplain	48879
Duplain (Township)	48831
Durand	48429
Dutton	49316
Dwight (Township)	48445
Eagle	48822
Eagle (Township)	48822
Eagle Harbor	49950
Eagle Harbor (Township)	49950
Eagle Lake (Cass County)	49112
Eagle Lake (Van Buren County)	49079
Eagle Point	49031
Eagle River	49924
East Bay (Township)	49686
Eastbrook Mall (Part of Grand Rapids)	49523
East China (Township)	48054
East Cooper	49004
East Dayton	48723
Eastgate Shopping Center (Part of Roseville)	48066
East Gilead	49028
East Grand Rapids	49506
East Houghton (Part of Houghton)	49931
East Jordan	49727
East Kingsford	49801
Eastlake	49626
Eastland Center (Part of Harper Woods)	48225
East Lansing	48823-26

For specific East Lansing Zip Codes call (517) 351-3205, or your local postmaster.

Place	ZIP
East Leroy	49051
Eastmanville	49404
Easton (Ionia County) (Township)	48846
Easton (Shiawassee County)	48867
East Paris (Part of Kentwood)	49508
Eastpointe	48021
Eastport	49627
East Rockwood	48173
East Saugatuck	49419
East Sebewa	48890
East Side (Part of Saginaw)	48601
East Tawas	48730
Eastview	48065
Eastwood	49001
Eaton (Township)	48813
Eaton Rapids	48827
Eaton Rapids (Township)	48827
Eau Claire	49111
Eben Junction	49825
Echo (Township)	49622
Eckerman	49728
Eckford	49245
Eckford (Township)	49245
Ecorse	48229
Eden (Ingham County)	48854
Eden (Lake County) (Township)	49644
Eden (Mason County) (Township)	49454
Edenville (Township)	48620
Edenville	48620
Edgemont Park	48917
Edgerton	49341
Edmore	48829
Edwards (Township)	48661
Edwardsburg	49112
Edwards Corners	49067
Egelston (Township)	49442
Eight Point Lake	48632
Elba (Gratiot County) (Township)	48807
Elba (Lapeer County)	48446
Elba (Lapeer County) (Township)	48446
Elberta	49628
Elbridge (Township)	49459
Elizabeth Lake Estates	48327

Place	ZIP
Elk (Lake County) (Township)	49644
Elk (Sanilac County) (Township)	48466
Elkland (Township)	48726
Elk Rapids	49629
Elk Rapids (Township)	49629
Elkton	48731
Ellington (Township)	48723
Ellis (Township)	49705
Ellsworth (Antrim County)	49729
Ellsworth (Lake County) (Township)	49656
Elmdale	48815
Elmer (Oscoda County) (Township)	48647
Elmer (Sanilac County) (Township)	48471
Elm Hall	48830
Elmira	49730
Elmira (Township)	49730
Elm River (Township)	49965
Elmwood (Leelanau County) (Township)	49684
Elmwood (Tuscola County) (Township)	48726
Elo	49958
Eloise (Part of Westland)	48185
Elsie	48831
Elwell	48832
Ely (Township)	49814
Emerson (Township)	48615
Emmett (Calhoun County) (Township)	49017
Emmett (St. Clair County)	48022
Emmett (St. Clair County) (Township)	48022
Empire	49630
Empire (Township)	49630
Engadine	49827
Ensign	49878
Ensign (Township)	49878
Ensley (Township)	49329
Ensley Center	49343
Enterprise (Township)	49667
Entrican	48888
Epoufette	49762
Epsilon	49770
Erie	48133
Erie (Township)	48133
Erwin (Township)	49938
Escanaba	49829
Escanaba (Township)	49829
Essex (Township)	48879
Essexville	48732
Estey	48652
Estral Beach	48166
Eureka (Clinton County)	48833
Eureka (Montcalm County) (Township)	48838
Evangeline (Township)	49712
Evans	49319
Evans Lake	49287
Evart	49631
Evart (Township)	49631
Eveline (Township)	49727
Everett (Township)	49349
Evergreen (Montcalm County) (Township)	48884
Evergreen (Sanilac County) (Township)	48426
Evergreen Acres	48161
Evergreen Shores	49781
Ewen	49925
Ewing (Township)	49880
Excelsior (Township)	49646
Exeter (Township)	48159
Eyedywild Beach	49735
Fabius (Township)	49093
Factoryville	49066
Fairbanks (Township)	49817
Fairfax	49040
Fairfield (Lenawee County)	49221
Fairfield (Lenawee County) (Township)	49221
Fairfield (Shiawassee County) (Township)	48831
Fairgrove	48733
Fairgrove (Township)	48733
Fairhaven (Huron County) (Township)	48720
Fair Haven (St. Clair County)	48023
Fairlane Town Center (Part of Dearborn)	48126
Fair Plain (Berrien County)	49022
Fairplain (Montcalm County) (Township)	48838

Place	ZIP
Fairplain Plaza	49022
Fairport	49817
Fairview	48621
Fairview Heights	48197
Faithorn	49892
Faithorn (Township)	49892
Falmouth	49632
Fargo	48006
Farmers Creek	48455
Farmington	48331-36

For specific Farmington Zip Codes call (810) 553-3910, or your local postmaster.

Place	ZIP
Farmington Hills	48331-34

For specific Farmington Hills Zip Codes call (810) 553-3910, or your local postmaster.

Place	ZIP
Farrandville	48420
Farwell	48622
Fawn River	49091
Fawn River (Township)	49091
Fayette (Delta County)	49817
Fayette (Hillsdale County) (Township)	49250
Federal (Part of Saginaw)	48606
Federal Correctional Institution	48160
Felch	49831
Felch (Township)	49831
Felch Mountain	49801
Fenkell (Part of Detroit)	48238
Fennville	49408
Fenton	48430
Fenton (Township)	48430
Fenwick	48834
Ferndale	48220
Ferris (Township)	48891
Ferry	49455
Ferry (Township)	49455
Ferrysburg	49409
Fibre	49780
Fife Lake	49633
Fife Lake (Township)	49633
Filer (Township)	49660
Filer City	49634
Filion	48432
Fillmore (Township)	49423
Filmore	49423
Findley	49030
Fisher (Part of Wyoming)	49509
Fisher Building (Part of Detroit)	48211
Fisherville	48611
Fitchburg	49285
Five Lakes	48446
Five Points	48867
Flat Rock (Delta County)	49837
Flat Rock (Wayne County)	48134
Flint	48501-07
Flint	48531-32

For specific Flint Zip Codes call (810) 257-1574, or your local postmaster.

Place	ZIP
Flint (Township)	48532
Florence (Township)	49042
Florida	49913
Flowerfield	49093
Flowerfield (Township)	49093
Floyd	48640
Flushing	48433
Flushing (Township)	48433
Flynn (Township)	48453
Foote Site Village	48750
Ford Lake	49410
Ford River (Township)	49829
Ford River (Hyde)	49807
Ford River	49829
Forest (Cheboygan County) (Township)	49792
Forest (Genesee County) (Township)	48463
Forest (Missaukee County) (Township)	49651
Forester	48419
Forester (Township)	48419
Forest Grove	49426
Forest Grove Station	49426
Forest Hill	48801
Forest Hills	49506
Forest Home (Township)	49615
Forest Lake	49862
Forestville	48434
Fork	49305
Forsyth (Township)	49833
Fort Dearborn (Part of Dearborn)	48124
Fort Gratiot (Township)	48059
Fortune Lake	49920
Foster	48661

Place	ZIP
Foster City	49834
Fosters	48415
Fostoria	48435
Fountain	49410
Fountain Park	49266
Four Mile Corner	49868
Fowler	48835
Fowlerville	48836
Fox	49813
Fox Creek (Part of Detroit)	48215
Francisco	49240
Frandor Shopping Center (Part of Lansing)	48912
Frankenlust (Township)	48706
Frankenmuth	48734
Frankenmuth (Township)	48734
Frankentrost	48601
Frankfort	49635
Franklin (Clare County) (Township)	48625
Franklin (Houghton County) (Township)	49930
Franklin (Lenawee County) (Township)	49287
Franklin (Oakland County)	48025
Franklin Mine	49930
Fraser (Bay County) (Township)	48634
Fraser (Macomb County)	48026
Freda	49905
Frederic	49733
Frederic (Township)	49733
Fredonia (Township)	49068
Freedom (Township)	48158
Freeland	48623
Freeman (Township)	48632
Freeport	49325
Free Soil	49411
Free Soil (Township)	49411
Freiburger	48475
Fremont (Isabella County) (Township)	49310
Fremont (Newaygo County)	49412
Fremont (Saginaw County) (Township)	48655
Fremont (Sanilac County) (Township)	48097
Fremont (Tuscola County) (Township)	48744
French Landing (Part of Romulus)	48174
Frenchtown (Marquette County)	49849
Frenchtown (Monroe County) (Township)	48161
French Town (Oceana County)	49449
Friendship (Township)	49740
Frontier	49239
Frost (Township)	48625
Frost Corners	48875
Fruitland (Township)	49461
Fruitport	49415
Fruitport (Township)	49415
Fruitport Siding (Part of Norton Shores)	49444
Fulton (Gratiot County) (Township)	48871
Fulton (Kalamazoo County)	49052
Fulton (Keweenaw County)	49950
Fulton Center	48871
Gaastra	49927
Gagetown	48735
Gaines (Genesee County)	48436
Gaines (Genesee County) (Township)	48436
Gaines (Kent County) (Township)	49508
Galesburg	49053
Galien	49113
Galien (Township)	49113
Ganges	49408
Ganges (Township)	49408
Garden	49835
Garden (Township)	49835
Garden City	48135*
	48136†
Garden Corners	49817
Gardendale	48059
Gardenville	49783
Gardner	49821
Garfield (Bay County) (Township)	48634
Garfield (Clare County) (Township)	49684

* Area Zip Code   † Post Office Boxes

	ZIP
Garfield (Grand Traverse County) (Township) ...	49684
Garfield (Kalkaska County) (Township) ...	49633
Garfield (Mackinac County) (Township) ...	49827
Garfield (Newaygo County) (Township) ...	49337
Garnet	49762
Garth	49878
Gay	49945
Gaylord	49735
General Post Office (Part of Detroit)	48233
Genesee	48437
Genesee (Township)	48437
Geneva (Midland County) (Township)	48618
Geneva (Van Buren County) (Township) ...	49056
Genoa (Township)	48116
Georgetown (Township)	49426
Gera	48734
Germfask	49836
Germfask (Township)	49836
Gerrish (Township)	48653
Gibraltar	48173
Gibson (Allegan County)	49423
Gibson (Bay County) (Township)	48613
Gilbo Corners	49679
Gilchrist	49762
Gilead	49028
Gilead (Township)	49028
Gilford	48736
Gilford (Township)	48736
Gilmore (Benzie County) (Township)	49628
Gilmore (Isabella County) (Township)	48622
Gingellville	48359
Girard	49036
Girard (Township)	49036
Gladstone	49837
Gladwin	48624
Gladwin (Township)	48624
Glen Arbor	49636
Glen Arbor (Township)	49636
Glencoe Hills Apartments (Part of Ann Arbor)	48108
Glendale	49079
Glendora	49107
Glen Haven	49621
Glenn	49416
Glenn Haven Shores	49090
Glennie	48737
Glenn Shores	49090
Glenside (Part of Norton Shores)	49441
Glenwood	49047
Gobles	49055
Goetzville	49736
Golden (Township)	49436
Golfcrest	48161
Goodar (Township)	48761
Goodells	48027
Good Hart	49737
Goodison	48306
Goodland (Township)	48444
Goodrich	48438
Goodwell (Township)	49349
Gordon Beach	49129
Gordonville	48640
Gore (Township)	48468
Gotts Corners	48725
Gould City	49838
Gourley (Township)	49812
Gowen	49326
Graafschap	49423
Grace	49759
Graham Lake	49017
Grand Beach	49117
Grand Blanc	48439
Grand Blanc (Township)	48439
Grand Haven	49417
Grand Haven (Township)	49417
Grand Island (Township)	49862
Grand Junction	49056
Grand Ledge	48837
Grand Marais	49839
Grand Rapids	49501-88
For specific Grand Rapids Zip Codes call (616) 776-1415, or your local postmaster.	
Grand Rapids (Township)	49505
Grand River (Part of Detroit)	48208
Grand Shelby (Part of Detroit)	48216

	ZIP
Grand View Acres	48167
Grand View Beach (Cheboygan County)	49749
Grandview Beach (Monroe County)	48145
Grandville	49418*
	49468†
Grant (Cheboygan County) (Township)	49721
Grant (Clare County) (Township)	48617
Grant (Grand Traverse County) (Township)	49643
Grant (Huron County) (Township)	48726
Grant (Iosco County) (Township)	48763
Grant (Keweenaw County) (Township)	49918
Grant (Mason County) (Township)	49411
Grant (Mecosta County) (Township)	49307
Grant (Newaygo County) (Township)	49327
Grant (Newaygo County) (Township)	49327
Grant (Oceana County) (Township)	49452
Grant (St. Clair County) (Township)	48032
Grant Center	49307
Grape	48161
Grass Lake (Gladwin County)	48624
Grass Lake (Jackson County)	49240
Grass Lake (Jackson County) (Township) ...	49240
Grassmere	48731
Gratiot (Part of Detroit)	48207
Grattan	48809
Grattan (Township)	48809
Gravel Lake	49065
Grawn	49637
Grayling	49738
Grayling (Township)	49738
Greater Galesburg	49053
Great Lake Beach	48450
Great Lakes Bible College	48917
Great Western (Part of Crystal Falls)	49920
Greeley	49753
Green (Alpena County) (Township)	49753
Green (Mecosta County) (Township)	49338
Green (Ontonagon County)	49953
Greenbush (Alcona County)	48738
Greenbush (Alcona County) (Township)	48738
Greenbush (Clinton County) (Township)	48833
Greendale (Township)	48883
Greenfield Village (Part of Dearborn)	48124
Green Lake (Allegan County)	49316
Green Lake (Grand Traverse County) (Township)	49643
Greenland	49929
Greenland (Township)	49929
Greenleaf (Township)	48726
Greenmead (Part of Livonia)	48153
Green Oak (Township) ...	48116
Green River	49659
Green Road (Part of Ann Arbor)	48113
Greenville	48838
Greenwood (Clare County) (Township)	48625
Greenwood (Marquette County)	49849
Greenwood (Oceana County) (Township) ...	49412
Greenwood (Ogemaw County)	48610
Greenwood (Oscoda County) (Township)	49756
Greenwood (St. Clair County) (Township)	48006
Greenwood (Wexford County) (Township)	49663
Gregory	48137
Greilickville	49684
Gresham	48813

	ZIP
Grim (Township)	48652
Grind Stone City	48467
Groos	49837
Gros Cap	49781
Grosse Ile	48138
Grosse Ile (Township)	48138
Grosse Pointe	48230
	48236
For specific Grosse Pointe Zip Codes call (313) 884-1640, or your local postmaster.	
Grosse Pointe (Township)	48236
Grosse Pointe Farms	48230
Grosse Pointe Park	48230
Grosse Pointe Shores	48230
Grosse Pointe Woods	48230
Grosvenor	49228
Grout (Township)	48624
Groveland (Township)	48462
Gulliver	49840
Gull Lake	49083
Gunplain (Township)	49080
Gustin (Township)	48740
Gwinn	49841
Hadley	48440
Hadley (Township)	48455
Hagar (Township)	49038
Hagar Shores	49039
Hagensville	49779
Hagerman Lake	49935
Haight (Township)	49912
Hale	48739
Halfway Corners	48441
Hamburg	48139
Hamburg (Township)	48169
Hamilton (Allegan County)	49419
Hamilton (Clare County) (Township)	48625
Hamilton (Gratiot County) (Township)	48847
Hamilton (Van Buren County) (Township)	49045
Hamlin (Eaton County) (Township)	48827
Hamlin (Mason County) (Township)	49431
Hammond Bay	49759
Hampton (Township)	48732
Hampton Village Centre (Part of Rochester Hills)	48308
Hamtramck	48212
Hancock	49930
Hancock (Township)	49930
Handy (Township)	48836
Hannah	49649
Hannahville Indian Community	49896
Hanover (Jackson County)	49241
Hanover (Jackson County) (Township) ...	49241
Hanover (Wexford County) (Township)	49620
Harbert	49115
Harbor Beach	48441
Harbor Point	49740
Harbor Springs	49740
Harbor View	49777
Hardwood	49807
Haring (Township)	49601
Harlan	49625
Harlow	49423
Harper (Part of Detroit)...	48213
Harper Woods	48225
Harrietta	49638
Harris	49845
Harris (Township)	49845
Harrisburg	49451
Harrison (Clare County)	48625
Harrison (Macomb County) (Township) ...	48045
Harrison Beach	49854
Harrison Township	48045
Harrisville	48740
Harrisville (Township)	48740
Harsens Island	48028
Hart	49420
Hart (Township)	49420
Hartford	49057
Hartford (Township)	49057
Hartland	48353
Hartland (Township)	48353
Hartwick (Township)	49631
Harvard	49319
Harvey	49855
Haslett	48840
Hastings	49058
Hastings (Township)	49058
Hatton (Township)	48625

	ZIP
Hautala Corner	49938
Hawes (Township)	48742
Hawkhead	49416
Hawkins	49677
Hawks	49743
Hay (Township)	48624
Hayes (Charlevoix County) (Township) ...	49720
Hayes (Clare County) (Township)	48625
Hayes (Otsego County) (Township)	49735
Haynes (Township)	48742
Hazelhurst Camp	49115
Hazel Park	48030
Hazelton (Township)	48433
Heath (Township)	49419
Hebron (Township)	49755
Helena (Township)	49612
Hell	48169
Helmer	49853
Helps	49873
Hemans	48426
Hematite (Township)	49903
Hemlock	48626
Henderson (Shiawassee County)	48841
Henderson (Wexford County) (Township) ...	49601
Hendricks (Township)	49762
Henrietta (Township)	49259
Henry Street (Part of Norton Shores)	49441
Herman	49946
Hermansville	49847
Herron	49744
Hersey	49639
Hersey (Township)	49639
Hesperia	49421
Hessel	49745
Hetherton	49751
Hiawatha (Township)	49854
Hickory Corners	49060
Higgins (Township)	48653
Higgins Lake	48627
Highland	48356-57
For specific Highland Zip Codes call (810) 887-2211, or your local postmaster.	
Highland (Township)	49665
Highland Lakes	48167
Highland Park (Kalamazoo County)	49083
Highland Park (Wayne County)	48203
Highway	49913
Hi Hill Villa	48360
Hill (Township)	48739
Hillcrest	49938
Hillcrest Orchard	48145
Hilliards	49328
Hillman	49746
Hillman (Township)	49746
Hillsdale	49242
Hillsdale (Township)	49242
Hinchman	49103
Hinton (Township)	48850
Hockaday	48624
Hodunk	49094
Holland (Missaukee County) (Township)	48632
Holland (Ottawa County)	49422-24
For specific Holland Zip Codes call (616) 396-5201, or your local postmaster.	
Holland (Ottawa County) (Township)	49423
Holloway	49229
Holly	48442
Holly (Township)	48442
Holmes (Township)	49821
Holt	48842
Holton	49425
Holton (Township)	49425
Home (Montcalm County) (Township)	48829
Home (Newaygo County) (Township)	49309
Home Acres (Part of Wyoming)	49508
Homer (Calhoun County)	49245
Homer (Calhoun County) (Township)	49245
Homer (Midland County) (Township)	48640
Homestead (Benzie County) (Township) ...	49640
Homestead (Chippewa County)	49783

	ZIP		ZIP		ZIP		ZIP
Hongore Bay	49765	Ironwood	49938	Killarney Beach	48706	Lakeview (Berrien County)	49129
Honor	49640	Ironwood (Township)	49938	Killmaster	48740	Lakeview (Calhoun	
Hooper	49080	Irving	49058	Kilmanagh	48759	County)	49015
Hope (Barry County)		Irving (Township)	49058	Kimball (Township)	48074	Lakeview (Montcalm	
(Township)	49058	Isabella (Delta County)	49878	Kincheloe	48788	County)	48850
Hope (Midland County)	48628	Isabella (Isabella County)		Kinde	48445	Lakeview Square (Part of	
Hope (Midland County)		(Township)	48628	Kinderhook	49036	Battle Creek)	49017
(Township)	48628	Isabella Indian Reservation	48858	Kinderhook (Township)	49036	Lakeville	48366
Hopkins	49328	Isadore	49621	King Arthur's Court	48906	Lakewood (Kalamazoo	
Hopkins (Township)	49328	Ishpeming	49849	Kingsford	49801	County)	49002
Hopkinsburg	49328	Ishpeming (Township)	49849	Kingsley	49649	Lakewood (Monroe	
Hopwood Acres	48912	Ithaca	48847	Kings Mill	48461.	County)	48157
Horr	48893	Iva	48626	Kingston	48741	Lakewood Club	49457
Horton (Jackson County)	49246	Ivanrest (Part of		Kingston (Township)	48729	Lamar (Part of Wyoming)	49509
Horton (Ogemaw County)		Grandville)	49418	Kinneville	48827	Lamb	48027
(Township)	48661	Jackson	49201-04	Kinross	49752	Lambertville	48144
Houghton (Houghton		For specific Jackson Zip Codes		Kinross (Township)	49752	Lamont	49430
County)	49931	call (517) 789-2400, or your		Kinross Correctional		Lamotte (Township)	48426
Houghton (Keweenaw		local postmaster.		Facility	49788	Lanewood (Part of	
County) (Township)	49924	Jacobsville	49945	Kipling	49837	Chelsea)	48118
Houghton Lake	48629	Jam	48637	K. I. Sawyer Air Force		Langston	48888
Houghton Lake Heights	48630	James (Township)	48609	Base	49843	L'Anse	49946
Houghton Point	48629	Jamestown	49427	Kissipee	49751	L'Anse (Township)	49946
Howard (Township)	49120	Jamestown (Township)	49426	Kiva	49891	L'Anse Indian Reservation	55401
Howard City	49329	Jasper (Lenawee County)	49248	Klacking (Township)	48654	Lansing	48901-33
Howardsville	49067	Jasper (Midland County)		Klinger Lake	49091	For specific Lansing Zip Codes	
Howell	48843*	(Township)	48880	Klingville	49916	call (517) 337-8711, or your	
	48844†	Jeddo	48032	Klondike	49421	local postmaster.	
Hoxeyville	49601	Jefferson (Cass County)		Kneeland	46647	Lansing (Township)	48912
Hubbard Lake	49747	(Township)	49112	Knollwood Park	49203	Lapeer	48446
Hubbardston	48845	Jefferson (Hillsdale		Kochville (Township)	48604	Lapeer (Township)	48446
Hubbell	49934	County) (Township)	49266	Koehler (Township)	49705	Laporte	48623
Hudson (Charlevoix		Jefferson (Jackson		Koss	49887	Larkin (Township)	48642
County) (Township)	49730	County)	49230	Koylton (Township)	48741	Larson Beach	48762
Hudson (Lenawee		Jefferson (Wayne County)	48214	Krakow (Township)	49776	La Salle	48145
County)	49247	Jenison	49428*	La Branch	49873	La Salle (Township)	48145
Hudson (Lenawee			49429†	Lacey	49021	La Salle Gardens	48341
County) (Township)	49247	Jennings	49651	Lachine	49753	Lathrup Village	48076
Hudson (Mackinac		Jericho Corners	49090	Lac La Belle	49950	Laurel Park Place (Part of	
County) (Township)	49762	Jerome (Hillsdale County)	49249	Lacota	49063	Livonia)	48152
Hudsonville	49426	Jerome (Midland County)		Lafayette (Township)	48662	Laurium	49913
Hulbert	49748	(Township)	48657	Lagoon Beach	48706	Lawrence	49064
Hulbert (Township)	49748	Jessieville (Part of		La Grange	49031	Lawrence (Township)	49064
Humboldt (Township)	49814	Ironwood)	49938	La Grange (Township)	49031	Lawson	49885
Hume (Township)	48467	Johannesburg	49751	Laing	48472	Lawton	49065
Hunters Creek	48446	Johnstown (Township)	49050	Laingsburg	48848	Layton Corners	48118
Huntington Woods	48070	Jones	49061	Laird (Township)	49952	Leaton	48858
Huron (Huron County)		Jonesfield (Township)	48637	Lake (Benzie County)		Leavitt (Township)	49459
(Township)	48467	Jonesville	49250	(Township)	49640	Lebanon (Township)	48845
Huron (Wayne County)		Joppa	49051	Lake (Berrien County)		Ledyard (Part of Grand	
(Township)	48164	Jordan (Township)	49729	(Township)	49106	Rapids)	49523
Huron Gardens	48341	Joyfield (Benzie County)		Lake (Clare County)	48632	Lee (Allegan County)	
Huronia Heights	48450	(Township)	49616	Lake (Huron County)		(Township)	49450
Huron Mountain	49808	Joyfield (Wayne County)	48228	(Township)	48725	Lee (Calhoun County)	
Hurontown	49931	Juddville	48817	Lake (Lake County)		(Township)	49068
Huron Valley Men's		Jugville	49349	(Township)	49304	Lee (Midland County)	
Facility	48197	Juhl	48453	Lake (Macomb County)		(Township)	48640
Huron Valley Women's		Juniata	48744	(Township)	48236	Lee Center	49076
Facility	48197	Juniata (Township)	48768	Lake (Menominee County)		Leelanau (Township)	49670
Hylas	49807	Kaiserville	48137	(Township)	49821	Leighton (Township)	49316
Ida	48140	Kalamazoo	49001-09	Lake (Missaukee County)		Leisure	49090
Ida (Township)	48140	For specific Kalamazoo Zip		(Township)	49651	Leland	49654
Idlewild	49642	Codes call (616) 388-7211, or		Lake (Roscommon		Leland (Township)	49654
Imlay (Township)	48444	your local postmaster.		County) (Township)	48629	Lemon Park	49097
Imlay City	48444	Kalamazoo (Township)	49004	Lake Angeline (Part of		Lennon	48449
Imperial Heights	49861	Kalamo	49096	Ishpeming)	49849	Lennon Green Estates	48449
Ina	49688	Kalamo (Township)	49096	Lake Angelus	48326	Lenox (Township)	48050
Independence (Township)	48346	Kaleva	49645	Lake Ann	49650	Leonard	48367
Indianfield (Part of		Kalkaska	49646	Lake City	49651	Leoni	49201
Portage)	49081	Kalkaska (Township)	49646	Lake Fenton	48430	Leoni (Township)	49201
Indianfields (Township)	48723	Karlin	49643	Lakefield (Luce County)		Leonidas	49066
Indian Lake	49047	Kasson (Township)	49664	(Township)	49853	Leonidas (Township)	49066
Indian River	49749	Kawkawlin	48631	Lakefield (Saginaw		Leroy (Calhoun County)	
Indiantown	48601	Kawkawlin (Township)	48631	County) (Township)	48637	(Township)	49051
Ingalls	49848	Kearney (Township)	49615	Lake George	48633	Leroy (Ingham County)	
Ingallston (Township)	49893	Kearsarge	49942	Lakeland	48143	(Township)	48892
Ingersoll (Township)	48623	Keego Harbor	48320	Lake Lansing	48840	Le Roy (Osceola County)	49655
Ingham (Township)	48819	Keeler	49057	Lake Leelanau	49653	Le Roy (Osceola County)	
Ingleside	49755	Keeler (Township)	49057	Lake Linden	49945	(Township)	49655
Inkster	48141	Keene (Township)	48881	Lake Margrethe	49738	Les Cheneaux Club	49719
Inland (Township)	49643	Kegomic	49770	Lake Mine	49948	Leslie	49251
Inland Corners	49643	Kellogg	49010	Lake Nepessing	48446	Leslie (Township)	49251
Interior (Township)	49967	Kelloggsville (Part of		Lake Odessa	48849	Level Park	49017
Interlochen	49643	Kentwood)	49508	Lake Orion	48359-62	Level Park-Oak Park	49017
Inverness (Township)	49721	Kellys Corners	49451	For specific Lake Orion Zip		Levering	49755
Inwood (Township)	49817	Kelsey Lake	49031	Codes call (810) 693-8368, or		Lewiston	49756
Ionia	48846	Kendall	49062	your local postmaster.		Lewisville	48468
Ionia (Township)	48846	Kenockee (Township)	48006	Lake Orion Heights	48361*	Lexington	48450
Ionia Maximum		Kensington (Part of			48362†	Lexington (Township)	48450
Correctional Facility	48846	Detroit)	48224	Lake Pleasant	48412	Lexington Heights	48450
Ionia Temporary Facility	48846	Kent City	49330	Lakeport	48059	Liberty (Jackson County)	49233
Iosco (Township)	48836	Kenton	49943	Lake Roland	49968	Liberty (Jackson County)	
Ira (Township)	48023	Kentwood	49508	Lakeside (Berrien County)	49116	(Township)	49234
Iron Mountain	49801*	Kerby	48817	Lakeside (Huron County)	48467	Liberty (Washtenaw	
	49802†	Kessington	49112	Lakeside (Macomb		County)	48107
Iron River	49935	Kewadin	49648	County)	48313	Liberty (Wexford County)	
Iron River (Township)	49935	Keweenaw Bay	49908	Lakeside Landing	48430	(Township)	49663
Irons	49644	Keystone	49686	Laketon (Township)	49445	Liberty Corners	48144
Ironton	49720	Kibbie Corners	49090	Laketown (Township)	49423	Lilley (Township)	49309

	ZIP
Lima (Township)	48118
Lima Center	48130
Lime Island	49736
Limestone	49816
Limestone (Township)	49816
Lincoln (Alcona County)	48742
Lincoln (Arenac County) (Township)	48658
Lincoln (Berrien County) (Township)	49127
Lincoln (Clare County) (Township)	48633
Lincoln (Huron County) (Township)	48432
Lincoln (Isabella County) (Township)	48883
Lincoln (Midland County) (Township)	48640
Lincoln (Newaygo County) (Township)	49349
Lincoln (Osceola County) (Township)	49677
Lincoln Park (Muskegon County)	49441
Lincoln Park (Wayne County)	48146
Linden	48451
Linden Hills	49042
Linkville	48755
Linwood (Bay County)	48634
Linwood (Wayne County)	48206
Linwood Beach	48634
Lisbon	49403
Liske	49743
Litchfield	49252
Litchfield (Township)	49252
Littlefield (Township)	49706
Little Lake	49833
Little Point Sable	49455
Little Traverse (Township)	49740
Livernois (Part of Detroit)	48210
Livingston (Township)	49735
Livonia	48150-54
For specific Livonia Zip Codes call (313) 425-8050, or your local postmaster.	
Livonia Mall (Part of Livonia)	48152
Loch Alpine	48103
Locke (Township)	48895
Lockport (Township)	49032
Lodi (Kalkaska County)	49646
Lodi (Washtenaw County) (Township)	48103
Logan (Mason County) (Township)	49402
Logan (Ogemaw County) (Township)	48756
London (Township)	48159
Long Lake (Clare County)	48625
Long Lake (Grand Traverse County) (Township)	49684
Long Lake (Ionia County)	48865
Long Lake (Iosco County)	48743
Long Lake Shores	48323
Long Point	49721
Long Rapids (Township)	49753
Longrie	49887
Loomis	48617
Loretto	49852
Lost Lake Woods	48762
Loud (Township)	48619
Lovells	49738
Lovells (Township)	49738
Lowell	49331
Lowell (Township)	49331
Lucas	49657
Ludington	49431
Lulu	48140
Lum	48412
Luna Pier	48157
Lupton	48635
Luther	49656
Luzerne	48636
Lyndon (Township)	48118
Lynn (Township)	48097
Lyon (Oakland County) (Township)	48167
Lyon (Roscommon County) (Township)	48653
Lyon Lake	49068
Lyons	48851
Lyons (Township)	48851
Mable	49690
Macatawa	49434
McBain	49657
McBrides	48852
McCords	49302

	ZIP
McDonald	49013
McFarlands	49880
McGregor	48427
McIntyre Landing	49738
McIvor	48748
Mackinac Island	49757
Mackinaw (Township)	49701
Mackinaw City	49701
McKinley (Emmet County) (Township)	49769
McKinley (Huron County) (Township)	48755
McKinley (Oscoda County)	48647
McLean	49412
McLeods Corner	49868
McMillan (Luce County)	49853
McMillan (Luce County) (Township)	49868
McMillan (Ontonagon County) (Township)	49925
McMillan Corner	49853
Macomb	48042
	48044
For specific Macomb Zip Codes call (810) 465-1936, or your local postmaster.	
Macomb (Township)	48042
Macomb Mall (Part of Roseville)	48066
Macon	49236
Macon (Township)	49236
Madison (Township)	49221
Madison Center (Part of Madison Heights)	48071
Madison Heights	48071
Mancelona	49659
Mancelona (Township)	49659
Manchester	48158
Manchester (Township)	48158
Manistee	49660
Manistee (Township)	49660
Manistique	49854
Manistique (Township)	49854
Manitou Beach (Lenawee County)	49253
Manitou Beach (Presque Isle County)	49779
Manitou Beach-Devils Lake	49253
Manlius (Township)	49408
Manning	49721
Mansfield (Township)	49920
Mansfield	49881
Manton	49663
Maple (Part of Dearborn)	48126
Maple City	49664
Maple Forest (Township)	49738
Maple Grove (Barry County)	49073
Maple Grove (Barry County) (Township)	49073
Maple Grove (Manistee County) (Township)	49645
Maple Grove (Saginaw County) (Township)	48460
Maple Grove Corners	49090
Maple Hill	49339
Maple Lake (Part of Paw Paw)	49079
Maple Rapids	48853
Maple Ridge (Alpena County) (Township)	49707
Maple Ridge (Arenac County)	48766
Maple Ridge (Delta County) (Township)	49880
Maple River (Township)	49716
Mapleton (Grand Traverse County)	49686
Mapleton (Midland County)	48640
Maple Valley (Montcalm County) (Township)	49347
Maple Valley (Roscommon County)	48656
Maple Valley (Sanilac County) (Township)	48416
Marathon (Township)	48421
Marcellus	49067
Marcellus (Township)	49067
Marengo	49224
Marengo (Township)	49224
Marenisco	49947
Marenisco (Township)	49947
Marilla (Township)	49625
Marine City	48039
Marion (Charlevoix County) (Township)	49720

	ZIP
Marion (Livingston County) (Township)	48843
Marion (Osceola County)	49665
Marion (Osceola County) (Township)	49665
Marion (Saginaw County) (Township)	48614
Marion (Sanilac County) (Township)	48426
Marion Springs	48614
Markey (Township)	48629
Marlette	48453
Marlette (Township)	48453
Marne	49435
Marquette (Mackinac County) (Township)	49774
Marquette (Marquette County)	49855
Marquette (Marquette County) (Township)	49855
Marshall	49068
Marshall (Township)	49068
Martin	49070
Martin (Township)	49070
Martiny (Township)	49342
Marysville	48040
Mason (Arenac County) (Township)	48766
Mason (Cass County) (Township)	49112
Mason (Houghton County)	49930
Mason (Ingham County)	48854
Masonville (Township)	49878
Mass City	49948
Mastodon (Township)	49902
Matchwood (Township)	49925
Matherton	48845
Mathias (Township)	49891
Mattawan	49071
Matteson (Township)	49028
Matteson Lake	49028
Max Myers Addition	49120
Maybee	48159
Mayfield (Grand Traverse County)	49666
Mayfield (Grand Traverse County) (Township)	49649
Mayfield (Lapeer County) (Township)	48446
Mayflower	49913
Mayville	48744
Maywood	49878
Meade (Huron County) (Township)	48432
Meade (Macomb County)	48048
Meade (Mason County) (Township)	49411
Meads Landing	48629
Mears	49436
Meauwataka	49601
Mecosta	49332
Mecosta (Township)	49346
Medina	49247
Medina (Township)	49247
Melita	48659
Mellen (Township)	49848
Melrose (Township)	49796
Melstrand	49884
Melvin	48454
Melvindale	48122
Memphis	48041
Mendon	49072
Mendon (Township)	49072
Menominee	49858
Menominee (Township)	49858
Menonaqua Beach	49740
Mentha	49055
Mentor (Cheboygan County) (Township)	49799
Mentor (Oscoda County) (Township)	48647
Meredith	48624
Meridian (Township)	48823
Meridian Mall	48864
Merrill (Newaygo County) (Township)	49309
Merrill (Saginaw County)	48637
Merriman	49801
Merritt (Bay County) (Township)	48747
Merritt (Missaukee County)	49667
Merriweather	49947
Merson	49010
Mesick	49668
Metamora	48455
Metamora (Township)	48455
Metropolitan	49801

	ZIP
Metropolitan Airport (Part of Romulus)	48242-44
For specific Metropolitan Airport Zip Codes call (313) 955-2200, or your local postmaster.	
Metropolitan Airport South Terminal (Part of Romulus)	48242-44
For specific Metropolitan Airport South Terminal Zip Codes call (313) 955-2200, or your local postmaster.	
Metz	49776
Metz (Township)	49776
Meyer (Township)	49847
Miami Park	49090
Michiana	49117
Michigamme	49861
Michigamme (Township)	49861
Michigan Center	49254
Michigan Reformatory	48846
Michigan State University	48824
Michigan State University Residence Halls	48825
Michigan Training Unit	48846
Middlebelt (Part of Romulus)	48174
Middle Branch (Township)	49665
Middlebury (Township)	48866
Middleton	48856
Middletown	48817
Middle Village	49737
Middleville	49333
Midland	48640-42
For specific Midland Zip Codes call (517) 631-6580, or your local postmaster.	
Midland (Township)	48642
Midland Park	49060
Mikado	48745
Mikado (Township)	48745
Milan (Monroe County) (Township)	48160
Milan (Washtenaw County)	48160
Milford	48380-81
For specific Milford Zip Codes call (810) 684-0775, or your local postmaster.	
Milford (Township)	48381
Millbrook	49334
Millbrook (Township)	49334
Millburg	49022
Millecoquins	49827
Millen (Township)	48705
Millersburg	49759
Millett	48917
Milleville Beach	48173
Mill Grove	49010
Millington	48746
Millington (Township)	48746
Mill Lake	49055
Mills (Houghton County)	49934
Mills (Midland County) (Township)	48652
Mills (Ogemaw County) (Township)	48756
Mills (Sanilac County)	48427
Millville	48285
Milnes	49250
Milton (Antrim County) (Township)	49648
Milton (Cass County) (Township)	49120
Minards Mill	49269
Minden (Township)	48456
Minden City	48456
Mineral Hills	49935
Minor Beach	49854
Mio	48647
Missaukee Park	49651
Mitchell (Township)	48728
M & M Plaza (Part of Menominee)	49858
Moddersville	48632
Moffatt (Township)	48610
Mohawk	49950
Moline	49335
Moltke (Township)	49779
Monitor (Township)	48706
Monongahela Location	49920
Monroe (Monroe County)	48161
Monroe (Monroe County) (Township)	48161
Monroe (Newaygo County) (Township)	49349
Monroe Center	49637
Montague	49437
Montague (Township)	49437

	ZIP
Montcalm (Township)	48838
Monterey (Township)	49010
Monterey Center	49010
Montgomery	49255
Montmorency (Township)	49746
Montrose	48457
Montrose (Township)	48457
Moore (Township)	48471
Moore Park	49093
Moorestown	49651
Mooreville	48160
Moorland	49451
Moorland (Township)	49451
Moran	49760
Moran (Township)	49781
Morenci	49256
Morgan	49073
Morgan Corners	49017
Morley	49336
Morrice	48857
Morseville	48415
Morton (Township)	49332
Moscow	49257
Moscow (Township)	49257
Mosherville	49258
Mosherville Station	49250
Motley	49952
Mott Park (Part of Flint)	48504
Mottville	49099
Mottville (Township)	49099
Mound Spring	49091
Mountain Beach	49460
Mount Clemens	48043-46
For specific Mount Clemens Zip Codes call (810) 465-1936, or your local postmaster.	
Mount Clemens Southeast	48043
Mount Elliott (Part of Detroit)	48234
Mount Forest	48650
Mount Forest (Township)	48650
Mount Haley (Township)	48637
Mount Morris	48458
Mount Morris (Township)	48458
Mount Pleasant (Allegan County)	49090
Mount Pleasant (Isabella County)	48804†
	48858*
Mount Vernon	48306
Mueller (Township)	49840
Muir	48860
Mullet Lake	49761
Mullett (Township)	49791
Mulliken	48861
Mundy (Township)	48507
Munger	48747
Munising	49862
Munising (Township)	49895
Munith	49259
Munro (Township)	49755
Munson	49256
Muskegon	49440-45
For specific Muskegon Zip Codes call (616) 722-7292, or your local postmaster.	
Muskegon (Township)	49445
Muskegon Heights	49444
Muskegon Mall (Part of Muskegon)	49440
Mussey (Township)	48014
Muttonville (Part of Richmond)	48062
Nadeau	49863
Nadeau (Township)	49863
Nagel Corner	49743
Nahma	49864
Nahma (Township)	49864
Napoleon	49261
Napoleon (Township)	49261
Nashville	49073
Nathan	49821
National (Part of Crystal Falls)	49920
National City	48748
National Mine	49865
Naubinway	49762
Nazareth (Part of Kalamazoo)	49074
Needmore	48813
Neeley	49080
Negaunee	49866
Negaunee (Township)	49866
Nelson (Kent County) (Township)	49343
Nelson (Saginaw County)	48626
Nessen City	49683
Nester (Township)	48624
Nestoria	49861
New Allouez	49901
Newark (Gratiot County) (Township)	48847
Newark (Oakland County)	48442
Newaygo	49337
New Baltimore	48047
Newberg (Township)	49061
Newberry	49868
New Boston	48164
New Bristol Location	49920
New Buffalo	49117
New Buffalo (Township)	49117
New Era	49446
Newfield (Township)	49421
New Greenleaf	48726
New Haven (Gratiot County) (Township)	48889
New Haven (Macomb County)	48048
New Haven (Shiawassee County) (Township)	48867
New Holland	49423
New Hudson	48165
Newkirk (Township)	49656
Newland	49660
New Lothrop	48460
Newport	48166
New Richmond	49408
New Salem	49315
New Swanzy	49841
Newton (Calhoun County) (Township)	49017
Newton (Mackinac County) (Township)	49838
New Troy	49119
Nicholsville	49067
Niles	49120
Niles (Township)	49120
Nirvana	49623
Nisula	49952
Noble (Township)	49028
Noordeloos	49423
Norman (Township)	49689
North Adams	49262
North Allis (Township)	49765
North Bay City	48706
North Bell	48815
North Blendon	49426
North Bradley	48618
North Branch (Township)	48461
North Branch	48461
North Dorr	49323
Northeast (Genesee County)	48509
Northeast (Wayne County)	48152
North End (Part of Detroit)	48202
North Epworth	49431
Northfield (Township)	48189
Northgate	49505
North Kent Mall	49505
North Lake (Lapeer County)	48464
North Lake (Marquette County)	49849
North Lake (Van Buren County)	49055
North Lakeport	48059
Northland	49869
Northland Shopping Center (Part of Southfield)	48075
North Manitou	49654
North Morenci	49256
North Muskegon	49445
North Paynesville	49912
North Plains (Township)	48845
Northport	49670
Northport Point	49670
North Shade (Township)	48856
North Shores	48145
North Side (Part of Flint)	48505
North Star	48862
North Star (Township)	48862
North Street	48049
Northview	49505
Northville (Kent County)	49505
Northville (Wayne County)	48167
Northville (Wayne County) (Township)	48167
Northville Commons	48167
Northville Regional Psychiatric Hospital	48167
Northwest (Part of Grand Rapids)	49504
Northwestern (Part of Detroit)	48204
North Wheeler	48662
Northwood	49004
Norton Shores	49441
Norvell	49263
Norvell (Township)	49263
Norwalk	49660
Norway	49870
Norway (Township)	49892
Norwich (Missaukee County) (Township)	49651
Norwich (Newaygo County) (Township)	49307
Norwood	49720
Norwood (Township)	49720
Nottawa (Township)	49075
Nottawa (Isabella County) (Township)	48858
Nottawa (St. Joseph County)	49075
Novesta (Township)	48729
Novi	48374-77
For specific Novi Zip Codes call (810) 349-2100, or your local postmaster.	
Novi (Township)	48375
Novi I & II (Part of Novi)	48374
Nunda (Township)	49799
Nunica	49448
Oakfield (Township)	48838
Oak Grove (Livingston County)	48863
Oak Grove (Otsego County)	49735
Oak Grove (Roscommon County)	48653
Oak Hill	49660
Oakhurst	48701
Oakland (Allegan County)	49419
Oakland (Oakland County) (Township)	48363
Oakley	48649
Oak Manor	49120
Oak Park (Calhoun County)	49017
Oak Park (Oakland County)	48237
Oaks Correctional Facility	49626
Oak Shade Park	49230
Oakville	48160
Oakwood (Oakland County)	48371
Oakwood (St. Joseph County)	49099
Oakwood (Wayne County)	48122
Oceola (Township)	48843
Ocqueoc	49759
Ocqueoc (Township)	49759
Oden	49764
Odessa (Township)	48849
Odgers Location	49920
Ogden (Township)	49228
Ogden Center	49228
Ogemaw (Township)	48661
Ogemaw Springs	48661
Oil City	48883
Okemos	48805†
	48864*
Old Mission	49673
Old Redford (Part of Detroit)	48219
Olive (Clinton County) (Township)	48879
Olive (Ottawa County) (Township)	49460
Olive Center	49423
Olive Hills	49460
Oliver (Huron County) (Township)	48731
Oliver (Kalkaska County) (Township)	49646
Olivet (Eaton County)	49076
Olson	48640
Omena	49674
Omer	48749
Onaway	49765
Oneida (Township)	48837
Onekama	49675
Onekama (Township)	49675
Onondaga	49264
Onondaga (Township)	49264
Onota (Township)	49822
Onsted	49265
Ontonagon	49953
Ontonagon (Township)	49953
Ontwa (Township)	49112
Orange (Ionia County) (Township)	48846
Orange (Kalkaska County) (Township)	49646
Orangeville	49080
Orangeville (Township)	49080
Orchard Beach	49721
Orchard Lake	48323-24
For specific Orchard Lake Zip Codes call (810) 626-9873, or your local postmaster.	
Orchard Park (Part of Battle Creek)	49017
Oregon (Township)	48446
Orient (Township)	49679
Orion	48360-62
For specific Orion Zip Codes call (810) 693-8368, or your local postmaster.	
Orleans	48865
Orleans (Township)	48865
Oronoko (Township)	49103
Ortonville	48462
Osceola (Houghton County)	49913
Osceola (Houghton County) (Township)	49913
Osceola (Osceola County) (Township)	49631
Oscoda	48750
Oscoda (Township)	48750
Oscoda Indian Mission	48745
Oshtemo	49077
Oshtemo (Township)	49077
Osier	49878
Oskar	49931
Osseo	49266
Ossineke	49766
Ossineke (Township)	49747
Otisco (Township)	48809
Otisville	48463
Otsego	49078
Otsego (Township)	49078
Otsego Lake	49735
Otsego Lake (Township)	49735
Ottawa Beach	49423
Ottawa Center	49404
Ottawa Lake	49267
Otterburn (Part of Swartz Creek)	48473
Otter Lake	48464
Otto (Township)	49421
Overisel	49423
Overisel (Township)	49423
Ovid (Branch County) (Township)	49036
Ovid (Clinton County)	48866
Ovid (Clinton County) (Township)	48866
Owasippe	49457
Owendale	48754
Owosso	48867
Owosso (Township)	48867
Owosso Junction (Part of Owosso)	48867
Oxford	48370-71
For specific Oxford Zip Codes call (810) 628-2557, or your local postmaster.	
Oxford (Township)	48371
Ozark	49760
Paavola	49930
Painesdale	49955
Paka Plaza (Part of Jackson)	49202
Palestine	49887
Palisades Park	49043
Palmer	49871
Palms	48465
Palmyra	49268
Palmyra (Township)	49268
Palo	48870
Paradise (Chippewa County)	49768
Paradise (Grand Traverse County) (Township)	49649
Parchment	49004
Paris (Huron County) (Township)	48470
Paris (Mecosta County)	49338
Parisville	48470
Park (Ottawa County) (Township)	49423
Park (St. Joseph County) (Township)	49093
Parkdale	49660
Parkers Corners	48836
Park Grove (Part of Detroit)	48205
Park Lake	48808
Park Plaza (Part of Lincoln Park)	48146
Park Shore Resort	49031
Parkville	49093
Parma	49269
Parma (Township)	49224

*** Area Zip Code** **† Post Office Boxes**

	ZIP
Parnell	49301
Parshallville	48430
Partello	49076
Patterson Gardens	48161
Patterson Lake	48169
Paulding	49912
Pavilion (Township)	49088
Paw Paw	49079
Paw Paw (Township)	49079
Paw Paw Lake	49038
Payment	49783
Paynesville	49912
Peacock	49644
Peacock (Township)	49644
Peaine (Township)	49782
Pearl	49408
Pearl Beach (Branch County)	49036
Pearl Beach (St. Clair County)	48001
Pearl Grange	49022
Peck	48466
Pelkie	49958
Pellston	49769
Peninsula (Township)	49686
Penn	49031
Penn (Township)	49031
Pennellwood	49103
Pennfield	49017
Pennfield (Township)	49017
Penobscot	48226-28
For specific Penobscot Zip Codes call (313) 965-1331, or your local postmaster.	
Pentland (Township)	49868
Pentoga	49920
Pentwater	49449
Pentwater (Township)	49449
Pequaming	49946
Pere Marquette (Township)	49431
Perkins	49872
Perrinton	48871
Perronville	49873
Perry	48872
Perry (Township)	48872
Perry Acres	48360
Perry Lake Heights	48462
Peshawbestown	49682
Peters	48039
Petersburg	49270
Petoskey	49770
Pewabic	49930
Pewamo	48873
Phillipsville	49805
Phoenix (Keweenaw County)	49950
Phoenix (Oakland County)	48342
Phoenix Correctional Facility	48170
Pickford	49774
Pickford (Township)	49774
Pier Cove	49090
Pierport	49614
Pierson	49339
Pierson (Township)	49339
Pigeon	48755
Pinckney	48169
Pinconning	48650
Pinconning (Township)	48650
Pine (Township)	48888
Pine Bluffs	48653
Pine Creek	49051
Pine Grove	49055
Pine Grove (Township)	49055
Pine River (Arenac County)	48658
Pine River (Gratiot County) (Township)	48801
Pine Run	48420
Pine Stump Junction	49868
Piney Woods	48625
Pinnebog	48445
Pinora (Township)	49677
Pioneer (Township)	49651
Pipestone (Township)	49111
Pittsburg	48867
Pittsfield (Township)	48108
Pittsford	49271
Pittsford (Township)	49271
Plainfield (Iosco County) (Township)	48739
Plainfield (Kent County) (Township)	49321
Plainfield (Livingston County)	48137
Plainfield Heights	49505
Plainwell	49080
Platte (Township)	49640

	ZIP
Pleasant Lake (Hillsdale County)	49266
Pleasant Lake (Jackson County)	49272
Pleasant Lake (Washtenaw County)	48158
Pleasanton (Township)	49614
Pleasant Plains (Township)	49304
Pleasant Ridge	48069
Pleasant Valley	48880
Pleasant View (Township)	49740
Plymouth (Gogebic County)	49968
Plymouth (Wayne County)	48170
Plymouth (Wayne County) (Township)	48170
Plymouth Township	48170
Pogy	49639
Point Au Gres	48703
Pointe Aux Barques	48467
Pointe Aux Barques (Township)	48467
Pointe aux Peaux Farms	48166
Pointe aux Pins	49775
Point Nipigon	49721
Pokagon	49047
Pokagon (Township)	49047
Polkton (Township)	49404
Pomona	49625
Pompeii	48874
Ponchartrain Shores	49781
Ponshewaing	49706
Pontiac	48340-43
For specific Pontiac Zip Codes call (810) 338-4511, or your local postmaster.	
Portage (Houghton County) (Township)	49921
Portage (Kalamazoo County)	49081
Portage (Mackinac County) (Township)	49820
Portage Entry	49916
Portage Lake	48169
Port Austin	48467
Port Austin (Township)	48467
Port Austin Air Force Station	48467
Porter (Cass County) (Township)	49042
Porter (Midland County) (Township)	48615
Porter (Van Buren County) (Township)	49065
Port Gypsum (Part of Tawas City)	48763
Port Hope	48468
Port Huron	48059-61
For specific Port Huron Zip Codes call (810) 984-4121, or your local postmaster.	
Port Huron (Township)	48060
Portland (Ionia County)	48875
Portland (Ionia County) (Township)	48875
Port Sanilac	48469
Port Sheldon	49460
Port Sheldon (Township)	49460
Portsmouth (Township)	48708
Posen	49776
Posen (Township)	49776
Poseyville	48640
Potters Lake	48423
Potterville	48876
Powell (Township)	49808
Powers	49874
Prairie Ronde (Township)	49087
Prairieville	49046
Prairieville (Township)	49080
Prattville	49273
Prescott	48756
Presque Isle	49777
Presque Isle (Township)	49777
Princeton	49841
Prosper	49632
Prudenville	48651
Pulaski	49241
Pulaski (Township)	49241
Pulawski (Township)	49776
Pullman	49450
Putnam (Township)	48169
Quanicassee	48733
Quarry	48720
Quimby	49058
Quincy (Branch County)	49082
Quincy (Branch County) (Township)	49082

	ZIP
Quincy (Houghton County) (Township)	49930
Quincy Mine	49930
Quinnesec	49876
Rabbit Bay	49945
Rabbits Back	49781
Raber	49736
Raber (Township)	49736
Raco	49778
Rainy Beach	49765
Raisin (Township)	49221
Raisinville (Township)	48161
Ralph	49877
Rambaultown	49913
Ramsay	49959
Ranch Acres	49456
Randall Lake	49036
Randville	49801
Rankin	48473
Ransom	49266
Ransom (Township)	49266
Rapid City	49676
Rapid River (Delta County)	49878
Rapid River (Kalkaska County) (Township)	49659
Rapson	48413
Rathbone	48615
Rattle Run	48079
Ravenna	49451
Ravenna (Township)	49451
Ravenswood	48917
Ray (Branch County)	46737
Ray (Macomb County) (Township)	48096
Ray Center	48096
Raymond Corners	49656
Reading	49274
Reading (Township)	49274
Readmond (Township)	49723
Redding (Township)	48625
Redford	48239-40
For specific Redford Zip Codes call (313) 937-0360, or your local postmaster.	
Redford A	48240
Redman	48468
Red Oak	49756
Red Park	49660
Redridge	49931
Reed City	49677
Reeder (Township)	49651
Reeds Lake (Part of East Grand Rapids)	49506
Reeman	49412
Reese	48757
Regional Shopping Center	48043
Remus	49340
Renaissance Center (Part of Detroit)	48243
Reno (Township)	48770
Republic	49879
Republic (Township)	49879
Rescue	48735
Resort (Township)	49770
Rexton	49762
Reynolds (Township)	49329
Rhodes	48652
Rich	48744
Richfield (Genesee County) (Township)	48423
Richfield (Roscommon County) (Township)	48656
Richfield Center	48423
Richland	49083
Richland (Kalamazoo County) (Township)	49083
Richland (Missaukee County) (Township)	49657
Richland (Montcalm County) (Township)	48891
Richland (Ogemaw County) (Township)	48756
Richland (Saginaw County) (Township)	48626
Richmond (Macomb County)	48062
Richmond (Macomb County) (Township)	48062
Richmond (Marquette County) (Township)	49871
Richmond (Osceola County) (Township)	49677
Richmondville	48427
Richville	48758
Ridgeway	49275
Ridgeway (Township)	49275
Riga	49276
Riga (Township)	49276

	ZIP
Riley (Clinton County) (Township)	48820
Riley (St. Clair County) (Township)	48041
Riley Center	48041
Ripley	49930
Riverdale	48877
River Rouge	48218
Riverside (Berrien County)	49084
Riverside (Missaukee County) (Township)	49657
Riverside Correctional Facility	48846
Riverton (Township)	49454
Riverview	48192
Rives (Township)	49277
Rives Junction	49277
Roberts Corners	49868
Roberts Landing	48001
Robin Glen-Indiantown	48601
Robinson (Township)	49460
Rochester	48306-09
For specific Rochester Zip Codes call (810) 651-8551, or your local postmaster.	
Rochester Hills	48306-07
	48309
For specific Rochester Hills Zip Codes call (810) 651-8551, or your local postmaster.	
Rock	49880
Rockford	49341
Rockland	49960
Rockland (Township)	49960
Rock River (Township)	49825
Rockwood	48173
Rodney	49342
Rogers (Township)	49779
Rogers City	49779
Roger's Plaza (Part of Wyoming)	49509
Rolland (Township)	49310
Rollin	49278
Rollin (Township)	49278
Rome (Township)	49221
Rome Center	49221
Romeo	48065
Romulus	48174
Ronald (Township)	48846
Rondo	49799
Roosevelt Park	49441
Roscommon	48653
Roscommon (Township)	48653
Rose (Oakland County) (Township)	48442
Rose (Ogemaw County) (Township)	48654
Roseburg	48097
Rosebush	48878
Rose Center	48442
Rose City	48654
Rosedale	49783
Rose Island	48759
Rose Lake (Township)	49655
Roseville	48066
Roseville Plaza (Part of Roseville)	48066
Ross (Township)	49012
Rothbury	49452
Round Lake (Lenawee County)	49253
Round Lake (Mason County)	49410
Rousseau	49948
Rowes Corner	48158
Roxand (Township)	48837
Royal Oak	48067-68
	48073
For specific Royal Oak Zip Codes call (810) 546-7108, or your local postmaster.	
Royal Oak (Township)	48220
Royal Oak Beach	49721
Royalton (Township)	49085
Rubicon (Township)	48468
Ruby	48027
Rudyard	49780
Rudyard (Township)	49780
Rumely	49826
Rush (Township)	48841
Rush Lake	48169
Rusk	49464
Russell Island	48001
Russellville	48423
Rust	49746
Rust (Township)	49746
Ruth	48470
Rutland (Township)	49058
Ryan	48637

	ZIP
Sac Bay	49817
Saddle Lake	49056
Sage (Township)	48624
Saginaw	48601-09
For specific Saginaw Zip Codes call (517) 771-5725, or your local postmaster.	
Saginaw (Township)	48603
Saginaw Township North	48603
Saginaw Township South	48603
Saginaw Valley State University	48604
Sagola	49881
Sagola (Township)	49881
St. Anthony	48182
St. Charles	48655
St. Charles (Township)	48655
St. Clair	48079
St. Clair (Township)	48079
St. Clair Shores	48080-82
For specific St. Clair Shores Zip Codes call (810) 775-5050, or your local postmaster.	
St. Helen	48656
St. Ignace	49781
St. Ignace (Township)	49781
St. Jacques	49878
St. James	49782
St. James (Township)	49782
St. Johns	48879
Saint John's Provincial Seminary	48170
St. Joseph	49085
St. Joseph (Township)	49022
St. Louis	48880
St. Marys Lake	49017
St. Nicholas	49880
Salem (Allegan County) (Township)	49314
Salem (Washtenaw County) (Township)	48178
Salem (Washtenaw County)	48175
Saline	48176
Saline (Township)	49236
Salisbury (Part of Ishpeming)	49849
Samaria	48177
Sanborn (Township)	49766
Sand Beach (Township)	48441
Sand Creek	49279
Sand Lake (Iosco County)	48748
Sand Lake (Kent County)	49343
Sand Lake Corners	49265
Sand River	49822
Sands	49841
Sands (Township)	49841
Sandstone (Township)	49201
Sandusky	48471
Sandy Beach	49091
Sanford	48657
Sanilac (Township)	48469
San Souci Beach	49036
Santiago	48765
Saranac	48881
Sauble (Township)	49402
Saugatuck	49453
Saugatuck (Township)	49453
Sault Ste. Marie	49783
Sault Ste. Marie Air Force Station	49783
Sault Ste. Marie Indian Reservation	49783
Sawyer	49125
Sawyer Lake	49815
Schaffer	49807
Schoolcraft (Houghton County) (Township)	49934
Schoolcraft (Kalamazoo County)	49087
Schoolcraft (Kalamazoo County) (Township)	49087
Schuck Island	48759
Schultz	49058
Scio (Township)	48130
Sciota (Township)	48848
Scipio (Township)	49250
Scott Correctional Facility	48170
Scottdale	49085
Scott Lake	49927
Scotts	49088
Scottville	49454
Sears	49679
Sears Lincoln Park Shopping Center (Part of Lincoln Park)	48146
Sebewa	48875
Sebewa Center	48875
Sebewaing	48759

	ZIP
Sebewaing (Township)	48759
Secord (Township)	48624
Seidler Corners	48611
Selfridge Air Force Base	48045
Selkirk	48661
Selma (Township)	49601
Seneca	49280
Seneca (Township)	49280
Seneca Location	49950
Seney	49883
Seney (Township)	49883
Senter	49922
Seven Harbors	48356
Seven-Mile & Mack Shopping Center (Part of Detroit)	48236
Seven Oaks (Part of Detroit)	48235
Seville (Township)	48832
Seymour Square (Part of Grand Rapids)	49510
Shabbona	48426
Shady Shores	48635
Shadyside	49266
Shafer Location	49920
Shaftsburg	48882
Shanghai Corners	49111
Sharon (Township)	48158
Sharon Hollow	48158
Sharps Corners	48653
Shawnee Shores	49036
Shelby (Macomb County)	48315-16
For specific Shelby Zip Codes call (810) 731-9412, or your local postmaster.	
Shelby (Oceana County)	49455
Shelby (Oceana County) (Township)	49455
Shelbyville	49344
Sheldon	48111
Shepardsville	48866
Shepherd	48883
Sheridan (Calhoun County) (Township)	49224
Sheridan (Clare County) (Township)	48617
Sheridan (Huron County) (Township)	48413
Sheridan (Mason County) (Township)	49410
Sheridan (Mecosta County) (Township)	49305
Sheridan (Montcalm County)	48884
Sheridan (Newaygo County) (Township)	49412
Sherman (Gladwin County) (Township)	48624
Sherman (Huron County) (Township)	48456
Sherman (Iosco County) (Township)	48748
Sherman (Isabella County) (Township)	48632
Sherman (Keweenaw County) (Township)	49945
Sherman (Mason County) (Township)	49410
Sherman (Newaygo County) (Township)	49412
Sherman (Osceola County) (Township)	49688
Sherman (St. Joseph County) (Township)	49091
Sherman (Wexford County)	49668
Sherman City	48632
Sherwood	49089
Sherwood (Township)	49089
Sherwood Corners	48647
Shiawassee (Township)	48429
Shiawasseetown	48429
Shields	48609
Shiloh	48865
Shingleton	49884
Shoreham	49085
Shore Line Junction (Part of Hancock)	49930
Shorewood Hills	49125
Shorewood-Tower Hills-Harbert	49115
Sibley (Part of Trenton)	48183
Sidnaw	49961
Sidney	48885
Sidney (Township)	48885
Sid Town	48750
Sigel (Township)	48441
Silver City	49953
Silver Creek (Township)	49047

	ZIP
Silverwood	48760
Simar	49948
Sims (Township)	48703
Sister Lakes	49047
Sitka	49412
Six Lakes	48886
Skandia	49885
Skandia (Township)	49885
Skanee	49962
Skeels	48624
Skidway Lake	48756
Slagle (Township)	49638
Slapneck	49816
Sleepy Hollow	49912
Slocum	49451
Smith Corners	49420
Smiths Creek	48074
Smyrna	48887
Snover	48472
Snyderville	48063
Sodus	49126
Sodus (Township)	49126
Sokol Camp	49117
Solon (Kent County) (Township)	49319
Solon (Leelanau County)	49621
Solon (Leelanau County) (Township)	49621
Somerset	49281
Somerset (Township)	49281
Somerset Center	49282
Somerset Collection, The (Part of Troy)	48084
Sonoma	49017
Soo (Township)	49783
South Arm (Township)	49727
South Blendon	49426
South Boardman	49680
South Branch (Crawford County) (Township)	48653
South Branch (Ogemaw County)	48761
South Branch (Wexford County) (Township)	49601
South Butler	49082
Southfield	48034-37
	48075-76
	48086
For specific Southfield Zip Codes call (810) 357-3310, or your local postmaster.	
Southfield (Township)	48009
South Flint Plaza (Part of Flint)	48507
Southgate	48195
Southgate Shopping Center (Part of Southgate)	48192
South Gull Lake	49083
South Haven	49090
South Haven (Township)	49090
South Ionia	48846
Southland Center (Part of Taylor)	48180
Southland Mall (Part of Portage)	49081
South Lyon	48178
South Manitou	49654
South Monroe	48161
South Monterey	49010
South Range	49963
South Riley	48820
South Rockwood	48179
Spalding	49886
Spalding (Township)	49886
Sparlingville	48074
Sparr	49735
Sparta	49345
Sparta (Township)	49345
Spaulding (Township)	48655
Speaker (Township)	48454
Spencer (Kalkaska County)	49646
Spencer (Kent County) (Township)	49326
Spinks Corners	49022
Spratt	49753
Spring Arbor	49283
Spring Arbor (Township)	49283
Spring Beach	49031
Springdale (Township)	49683
Springfield (Calhoun County)	49015
Springfield (Kalkaska County) (Township)	49680
Springfield (Oakland County)	48346
Springfield (Oakland County) (Township)	48346

	ZIP
Springfield Place (Part of Battle Creek)	49015
Spring Grove	49416
Spring Lake	49456
Spring Lake (Township)	49456
Springport	49284
Springport (Township)	49284
Springvale (Township)	49770
Springville (Lenawee County)	49265
Springville (Wexford County) (Township)	49668
Springwells (Part of Detroit)	48209
Spruce	48762
Spurr (Township)	49861
Stalwart	49789
Stambaugh	49964
Stambaugh (Township)	49935
Standale (Part of Walker)	49504
Standish	48658
Standish (Township)	48658
Stannard (Township)	49912
Stanton (Houghton County) (Township)	49931
Stanton (Montcalm County)	48888
Stanwood	49346
Star (Township)	49611
Star Corners (Manistee County)	49660
Star Corners (Menominee County)	49887
Starville	48039
Steamburg	49242
Stephenson	49887
Stephenson (Township)	49887
Sterling	48659
Sterling Heights	48310-14
For specific Sterling Heights Zip Codes call (810) 268-2880, or your local postmaster.	
Steuben	49854
Stevensville	49127
Stockbridge	49285
Stockbridge (Township)	49285
Stonington	49878
Stony Creek	48197
Stony Lake	49455
Stony Point	48166
Strasburg	48161
Strathmoor (Part of Detroit)	48227
Strawberry Point	49456
Stronach	49660
Stronach (Township)	49660
Strongs	49790
Strongs Corners	49790
Stuart Lake	49068
Sturgeon Point	48740
Sturgeon River	49864
Sturgis	49091
Sturgis (Township)	49091
Sugar Island (Township)	49783
Sugar Rapids	48624
Sullivan	49451
Sullivan (Township)	49451
Summerfield (Clare County) (Township)	48625
Summerfield (Monroe County) (Township)	49270
Summit (Jackson County) (Township)	49203
Summit (Mason County) (Township)	49431
Summit City	49649
Summit Heights	48629
Summit Place	48328
Sumner	48889
Sumner (Township)	48889
Sumnerville	49120
Sumpter (Township)	48111
Sun	49327
Sunfield	48890
Sunfield (Township)	48890
Sunrise Heights	49015
Sunset Beach	49230
Superior (Chippewa County) (Township)	49715
Superior (Washtenaw County) (Township)	48197
Surrey (Township)	48622
Suttons Bay	49682
Suttons Bay (Township)	49682
Swains Lake	49237
Swan Creek (Township)	48655
Swanson	49821
Swartz Creek	48473
Swedetown	49913

* Area Zip Code   **† Post Office Boxes**

	ZIP
Sweetwater (Township)	49304
Sylvan (Osceola County) (Township)	49631
Sylvan (Washtenaw County) (Township)	48118
Sylvan Center	48118
Sylvan Lake	48320
Sylvester	49332
Talbot	49821
Tallmadge	49504
Tallmadge (Township)	49504
Tallman	49410
Tamarack	49913
Tapiola	49916
Tawas (Township)	48763
Tawas Centre	48730
Tawas City	48763*
	48764†
Taylor	48180
Taymouth (Township)	48417
Teapot Dome	49079
Tecumseh	49286
Tecumseh (Township)	49286
Tekonsha	49092
Tekonsha (Township)	49092
Teleford (Part of Dearborn Heights)	48128
Tel-Twelve Mall (Part of Southfield)	48034
Temperance	48182
Temple	48625
Texas (Township)	49009
Texas Corners	49009
The Fingerboard Corner	49705
The Heights	49230
Theodore	49801
Thetford (Township)	48420
Thomas (Oakland County)	48371
Thomas (Saginaw County) (Township)	48609
Thomaston	49968
Thompson	49854
Thompson (Township)	49854
Thompsonville	49683
Thornapple (Township)	49333
Thornville	48455
Three Lakes	49861
Three Mile Lake	49079
Three Oaks	49128
Three Oaks (Township)	49128
Three Rivers	49093
Thunder Mountain	49038
Tilden (Township)	49849
Tipton	49287
Tittabawassee (Township)	48623
Tobacco (Township)	48612
Tobico Beach	48706
Tobin Location	49920
Tobins Harbor	55605
Toivola	49965
Tompkins	49277
Tompkins (Township)	49277
Topaz	49925
Topinabee	49791
Toquin	49057
Torch Lake (Antrim County)	49627
Torch Lake (Antrim County) (Township)	49648
Torch Lake (Houghton County) (Township)	49934
Torch River	49676
Towar Gardens	48823
Tower	49792
Tower Hill	49125
Town Corners	49446
Traunik	49890
Traverse Bay	49945
Traverse City	49684-86
For specific Traverse City Zip Codes call (616) 946-9616, or your local postmaster.	
Tremaine Corners	48846
Trenary	49891
Trent	49303
Trenton	48183
Triangle Park	48653
Trimountain	49905
Trolley (Part of Detroit)	48231-35
For specific Trolley Zip Codes call (313) 965-1719, or your local postmaster.	
Trombly	49880
Trout Creek	49967
Trout Lake	49793
Trout Lake (Township)	49793
Trowbridge (Allegan County) (Township)	49010

	ZIP
Trowbridge (Ingham County)	48823
Trowbridge Park	49855
Troy	48007
	48083-84
	48098-99
For specific Troy Zip Codes call (810) 689-6262, or your local postmaster.	
Troy (Township)	49309
Trufant	49347
Turin (Township)	49880
Turk Lake	48838
Turner	48765
Turner (Township)	48765
Turner Shores	49116
Tuscarora (Township)	49749
Tuscola	48769
Tuscola (Township)	48769
Tustin	49688
Twelve Corners	49022
Twining	48766
Twin Lake	49457
Twin Lakes (Cass County)	49047
Twin Lakes (Houghton County)	49965
Two Rivers	48858
Tyre	48475
Tyrone (Kent County) (Township)	49330
Tyrone (Livingston County) (Township)	48430
Tyrone Lake	48430
Ubly	48475
Unadilla	48137
Unadilla (Township)	48137
Union (Branch County) (Township)	49094
Union (Cass County)	49130
Union (Grand Traverse County) (Township)	49633
Union (Isabella County) (Township)	48858
Union City	49094
Union Lake	48386*
	48387†
Union Pier	49129
Unionville	48767
Universal Mall (Part of Warren)	48092
Upjohn (Part of Portage)	49081
Upper Peninsula Mail Processing Center	49801*
	49802†
Urbandale (Part of Battle Creek)	49017
Utica	48315-18
For specific Utica Zip Codes call (810) 731-9412, or your local postmaster.	
Valley (Township)	49010
Valley Center	48416
Valley Farms	48906
Van	49755
Van Buren (Township)	48111
Vandalia	49095
Vanderbilt	49795
Vandercook Lake	49203
Van Meer	49884
Vantown	48892
Vassar	48768
Vassar (Township)	48768
Venice (Township)	48817
Vergennes (Township)	49331
Vermontville	49096
Vermontville (Township)	49096
Vernon (Isabella County) (Township)	48617
Vernon (Shiawassee County)	48476
Vernon (Shiawassee County) (Township)	48429
Vernon City	48617
Verona (Calhoun County)	49017
Verona (Gogebic County)	49968
Verona (Huron County)	48413
Verona (Huron County) (Township)	48413
Verona Park	49017
Vestaburg	48891
Veterans Administration Hospital (Part of Iron Mountain)	49801
Vevay (Township)	48854
Vickery Landing	49050
Vickeryville	48884
Vicksburg	49097
Victor (Township)	48848
Victoria	49960

	ZIP
Victory (Township)	49454
Vienna (Genesee County) (Township)	48420
Vienna (Montmorency County) (Township)	49751
Virginia Park	49423
Vogel Center	49657
Volinia	49045
Volinia (Township)	49045
Volney	49309
Vriesland	49464
Vulcan	49892
Wabaningo	49463
Wacousta	48837
Wadhams	48074
Wagarville	48624
Wahjamega	48723
Wainola	49948
Wakefield	49968
Wakefield (Township)	49968
Wakelee	49067
Wakeshma (Township)	49052
Waldenburg	48044
Waldron	49288
Wales (Township)	48027
Walhalla	49458
Walker (Cheboygan County) (Township)	49705
Walker (Kent County)	49504
Walkers Point	49721
Walkerville	49459
Wallace	49893
Walled Lake	48390*
	48391†
Wallin	49683
Wall Lake	49046
Walloon Lake	49796
Walnut Lake	48301
Walnut Point	49068
Walters	48346
Walton (Township)	49076
Waltz	48164
Wardcliff	48823
Warner (Township)	49730
Warren	48089-93
For specific Warren Zip Codes call (810) 751-4900, or your local postmaster.	
Warren (Township)	48618
Wasepi	49032
Washington (Gratiot County) (Township)	48806
Washington (Macomb County)	48094-95
For specific Washington Zip Codes call (810) 781-4251, or your local postmaster.	
Washington (Sanilac County) (Township)	48401
Washington Harbor	55605
Washington Heights (Part of Battle Creek)	49017
Waterford	48327-29
For specific Waterford Zip Codes call (810) 623-0020, or your local postmaster.	
Waterloo	49240
Waterloo (Township)	49240
Watermill Lake	49642
Waters	49797
Watersmeet	49969
Watersmeet (Township)	49969
Watertown (Clinton County) (Township)	48820
Watertown (Sanilac County)	48471
Watertown (Sanilac County) (Township)	48471
Watertown (Tuscola County) (Township)	48435
Watervale	49613
Watervliet	49098
Watervliet (Township)	49098
Watrousville	48768
Watson	49078
Watson (Township)	49078
Watson Corners	49078
Wattles Park	49017
Watton	49970
Waucedah	49892
Waucedah (Township)	49892
Waverly (Cheboygan County) (Township)	49765
Waverly (Eaton County)	48917
Waverly (Van Buren County) (Township)	49079
Wawatam (Township)	49701
Wawatam Beach (Part of Mackinaw City)	49701

	ZIP
Wayland	49348
Wayland (Township)	49348
Wayne (Cass County) (Township)	49047
Wayne (Wayne County)	48184
Weadlock	49755
Weale	48720
Weare (Township)	49420
Webber (Township)	49304
Webberville	48892
Webster (Township)	48130
Weesaw (Township)	49128
Weidman	48893
Welcome Corners	49058
Weldon (Township)	49683
Wellington (Township)	49753
Wells	49894
Wells (Township)	49894
Wells (Marquette County) (Township)	49818
Wells (Tuscola County) (Township)	48723
Wellston	49689
Wellsville	49228
Wenona Beach	48706
Wequetonsing	49740
West Bloomfield	48322-25
For specific West Bloomfield Zip Codes call (810) 626-9873, or your local postmaster.	
West Bloomfield Township	48323-24
For specific West Bloomfield Township Zip Codes call (810) 626-9873, or your local postmaster.	
West Branch (Dickinson County) (Township)	49877
West Branch (Marquette County) (Township)	49885
West Branch (Missaukee County) (Township)	49667
West Branch (Ogemaw County)	48661
West Branch (Ogemaw County) (Township)	48661
Westchester Village	48301
Western Wayne Correctional Facility	48170
West Ishpeming	49849
Westland	48185
Westland Center (Part of Westland)	48185
West Leroy	49051
West Millbrook	49310
West Monroe	48161
West Olive	49460
Weston	49289
Westphalia	48894
Westphalia (Township)	48894
West Sebewa	48875
West Side (Part of Saginaw)	48603
West Traverse (Township)	49740
Westville	48888
West Willow	48198
West Windsor	48813
Westwood	49006
	49009
	49019
For specific Westwood Zip Codes call (616) 343-2560, or your local postmaster.	
Westwood Heights	48504
Wetmore	49895
Wetzel	49659
Wexford (Township)	49668
Wheatfield (Township)	48895
Wheatland (Hillsdale County) (Township)	49220
Wheatland (Mecosta County) (Township)	49340
Wheatland (Sanilac County) (Township)	48427
Wheeler	48662
Wheeler (Township)	48662
White	49952
White Cloud	49349
Whitefish (Township)	49728
Whitefish Point	49768
Whiteford (Township)	49267
Whiteford Center	49267
Whitehall	49461
Whitehall (Township)	49461
White Lake	48383
White Lake (Township)	48383
White Oak (Township)	49285
White Pigeon	49099
White Pigeon (Township)	49099
White Pine	49971

*Area Zip Code †Post Office Boxes

	ZIP		ZIP		ZIP		ZIP
White River (Township)	49437	Wilson (Charlevoix		Woodard Lake	48834	Wurtsmith Air Force Base	48753
Whites Beach	48658	County) (Township)	49729	Woodbridge (Township)	49242	Wyandotte	48192
Whitewater (Township)	49690	Wilson (Menominee		Woodbury	48849	Wyman	49310
Whitmore Lake	48189	County)	49896	Wooden Shoe Village	48624	Wyoming	49509
Whitney (Township)	48765	Windemere	48917	Woodhaven	48183	Wyoming Park (Part of	
Whittaker	48190	Windsor (Township)	48821	Woodhull (Township)	48872	Wyoming)	49509
Whittemore	48770	Winegars	48624	Woodland	48897	Yale (Gogebic County)	49911
Wickware	48726	Winfield (Township)	48850	Woodland (Township)	48897	Yale (St. Clair County)	48097
Wilber (Township)	48730	Winn	48896	Woodland (Part of		Yankee Springs	
Wilcox (Township)	49349	Winona	49965	Kentwood)	49508	(Township)	49333
Wildwood (Cheboygan		Winsor (Township)	48755	Woodland Beach	48161	Yates (Township)	49642
County)	49706	Winterfield (Township)	49665	Woodland Lake	48116	Yellow Jacket	49913
Wildwood (Manistee		Winters	49878	Woodland Mall (Part of		York (Township)	48160
County)	49614	Winthrop Junction (Part of		Kentwood)	49512	Yorkville	49083
Willard	48611	Ishpeming)	49849	Woodland Park	49309	Ypsilanti	48197-98
Williams (Township)	48611	Wise (Township)	48618	Woods Corner	48622	For specific Ypsilanti Zip Codes	
Williamsburg	49690	Wisner	48701	Wood Spur	49953	call (313) 482-6905, or your	
Williamston	48895	Wisner (Township)	48733	Woodstock (Township)	49220	local postmaster.	
Williamston (Township)	48895	Witch Lake	49879	Woodville	49349	Ypsilanti Regional	
Williamsville (Cass		Wixom	48393	Wooster	49412	Psychiatric Hospital	48197
County)	49095	Wolf Lake (Jackson		Worth (Arenac County)	48650	Yuba	49690
Williamsville (Livingston		County)	49201	Worth (Sanilac County)		Yuma	49668
County)	48137	Wolf Lake (Muskegon		(Township)	48422	Zeba	49946
Willis	48191	County)	49442	Wright (Hillsdale County)		Zeeland	49464
Willow	48164	Wolverine	49799	(Township)	49271	Zeeland (Township)	49464
Willwalk	49783	Wolverine Lake	48390	Wright (Ottawa County)	49403	Zilwaukee	48604
Wilmot (Cheboygan		Wonderland Mall (Part of		Wright (Ottawa County)		Zilwaukee (Township)	48604
County) (Township)	49799	Livonia)	48150	(Township)	49403	Zutphen	49426
Wilmot (Tuscola County)	48729						
Wilson (Alpena County)							
(Township)	49707						

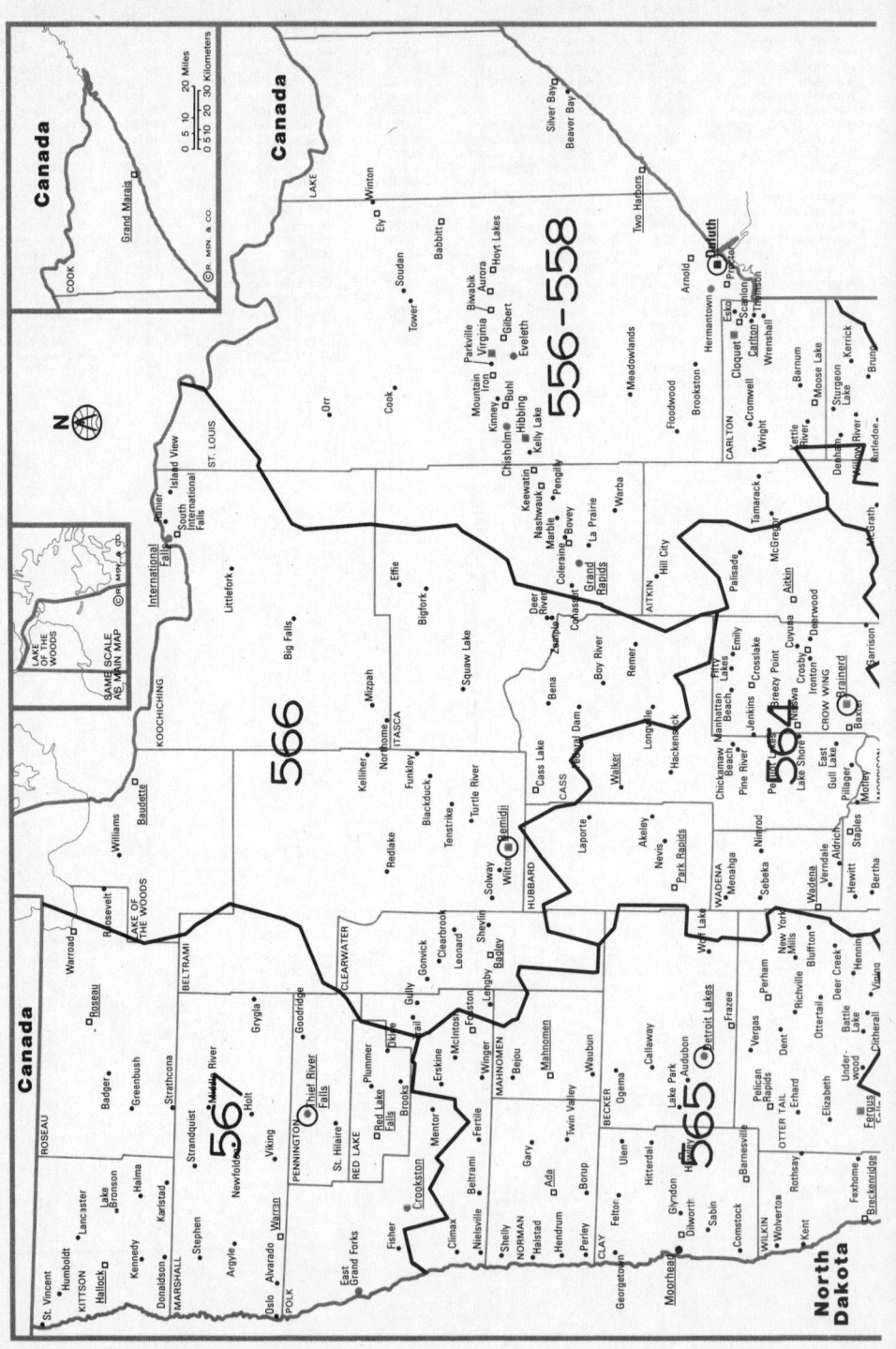

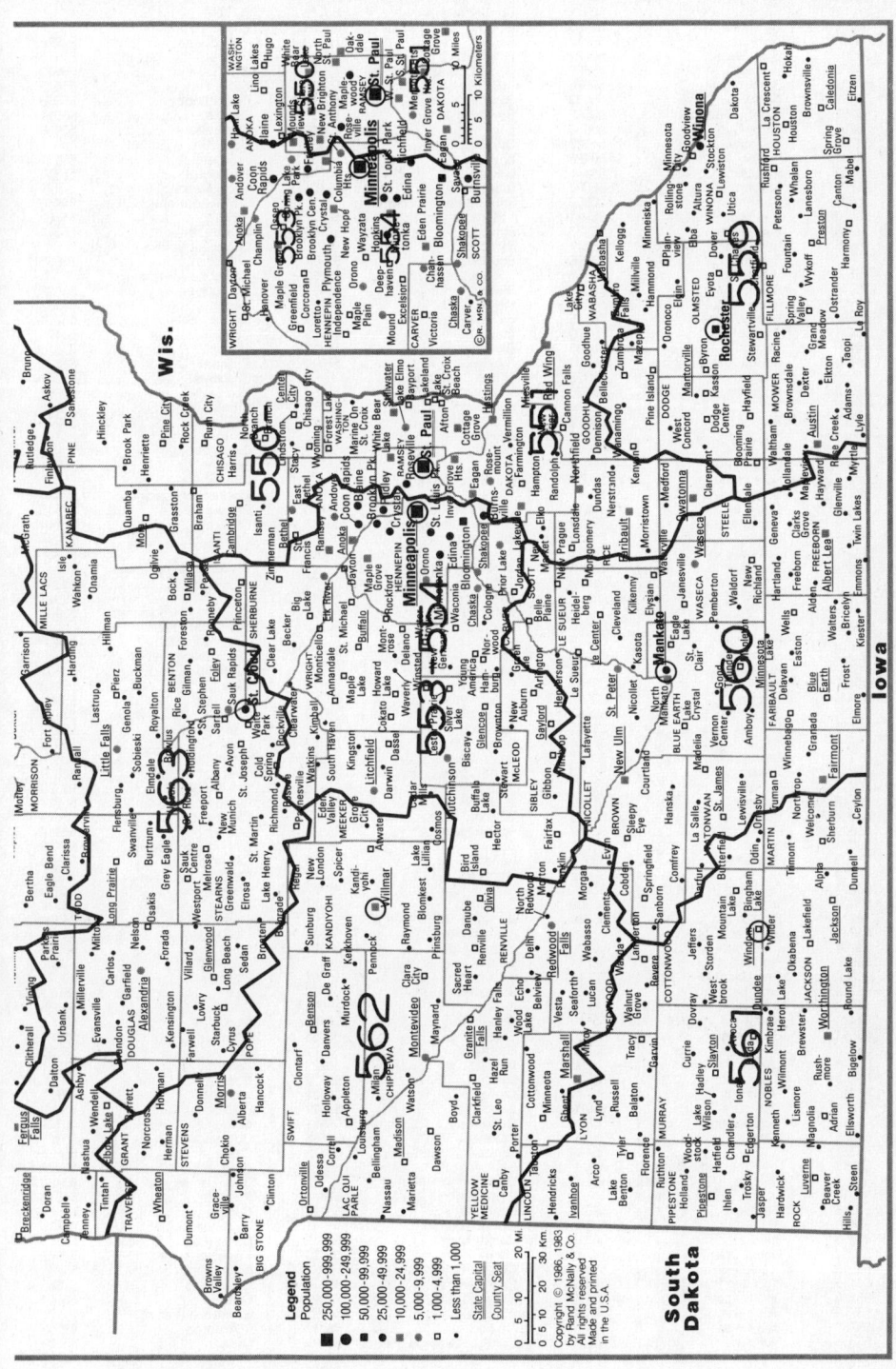

Wis.

Iowa

South
Dakota

Legend
Population
250,000-999,999
100,000-249,999
50,000-99,999
25,000-49,999
10,000-24,999
5,000-9,999
1,000-4,999
Less than 1,000
State Capital
County Seat

	ZIP
Ada	56510
Adams	55909
Adolph (Part of Hermantown)	55701
Adrian	56110
Afton	55001
Ah-Gwah-Ching	56430
Aitkin	56431
Akeley	56433
Albany	56307
Alberta	56207
Albert Lea	56007
Albertville	55301
Albion Center	55302
Alborn	55702
Alden	56009
Aldrich	56434
Alexandria	56308
Alida	56676
Allen Junction (Part of Hoyt Lakes)	55750
Alma City	56048
Almelund	55002
Almora	56551
Alpha	56111
Altura	55910
Alvarado	56710
Alvwood	56630
Amboy	56010
Amherst	55922
Amiret	56175
Amor	56515
Andover	55304
Andree	55006
Andyville	55912
Angle Inlet	56711
Angora	55703
Angus	56712
Annandale	55302
Anoka	55303-04
For specific Anoka Zip Codes call (612) 421-1114, or your local postmaster.	
Antlers Park (Part of Lakeville)	55044
Apache Mall (Part of Rochester)	55902
Apache Plaza (Part of St. Anthony)	55421
Appleton	56208
Apple Valley	55124
Arco	56113
Arcturus (Part of Taconite)	55786
Arden Hills	55112
Arendahl	55962
Argonne (Part of Lakeville)	55044
Argyle	56713
Arlington	55307
Armstrong	56009
Arnesen	56673
Arnold	55803
Arthyde	56350
Artichoke Lake	56227
Ashby	56309
Ashcreek	56173
Ash Lake	55771
Askov	55704
Aspelund	55946
Assumption	55338
Atkinson	55718
Atwater	56209
Atwood (Part of Edina)	55424
Audubon	56511
Augusta	55318
Aure	56676
Aurora	55705
Austin	55912
Austin Acres	55912
Auto Club (Part of Bloomington)	55420
Automba	55757
Averill	56547
Avoca	56114
Avon	56310
Babbitt	55706
Backus	56435
Badger	56714
Bagley	56621
Baker	56513
Balaton	56115
Bald Eagle	55110
Balkan	55719
Ball Bluff	55752
Ball Club	56636
Balmoral	56515
Bancroft	56007
Barden (Part of Shakopee)	55379
Barnesville	56514

	ZIP
Barnum	55707
Barr	55992
Barrett	56311
Barrows	56401
Barry	56210
Bass Brook	55721
Bassett	55602
Basswood	56576
Basswood Grove	55033
Battle Lake	56515
Battle River	56630
Baudette	56623
Baxter	56425
Bay Lake	56444
Bayport	55003
Bayview	56359
Beardsley	56211
Bear River	55723
Bear Valley	55041
Beauford	56065
Beaulieu	56557
Beaver	55910
Beaver Bay	55601
Beaver Creek	56116
Beaver Falls	56270
Bechyn	56283
Becida	56601
Becker	55308
Beckville	55355
Bejou	56516
Belgrade	56312
Bellaire	55110
Bellechester	55027
Belle Creek	55009
Belle Plaine	56011
Belle Prairie	56345
Belleriver	56319
Bellingham	56212
Beltrami	56517
Belview	56214
Bemidji	56601-19
For specific Bemidji Zip Codes call (218) 751-5600, or your local postmaster.	
Bena	56626
Benedict	56436
Bennettville	56431
Benson	56215
Bergen	56101
Bergville	56661
Bernadotte	56054
Berne	55985
Berner	56644
Berning Mill	55376
Beroun	55063
Bertha	56437
Bethany	55910
Bethel	55005
Big Bend City	56262
Bigelow	56117
Big Falls	56627
Bigfork	56628
Big Island (Part of Orono)	55331
Big Lake	55309
Big Spring	55939
Big Stone City (Part of Ortonville)	56278
Big Woods	56744
Bingham Lake	56118
Birch Beach	56686
Birchdale	56629
Birchwood Village	55110
Bird Island	55310
Biscay	55336
Biwabik	55708
Bixby	55917
Blackberry	55744
Blackduck	56630
Black Hammer	55974
Blaine	55434
For specific Blaine Zip Codes call (612) 784-1029, or your local postmaster.	
Blakeley	56011
Blomford	55040
Blomkest	56216
Bloom Dale (Part of Bloomington)	55431
Blooming Prairie	55917
Bloomington	55420
Blue Earth	56013
Blue Grass	56477
Bluffton	56518
Bock	56313
Bodum	55040
Boisberg	56296
Bois Fort	55772
Bombay	55946

	ZIP
Bonanza Grove	56211
Bongards	55368
Bonnie Glen	55013
Border	56629
Borup	56519
Bovey	55709
Bovey-Coleraine (Part of Bovey)	55709
Bowlus	56314
Bowstring	56631
Boyd	56218
Boy River	56632
Bradford	55040
Braham	55006
Brainerd	56401
Brainerd Regional Human Services Center	56401
Branch	55056
Brandon	56315
Bratsberg	55971
Breckenridge	56520
Breezy Point	56472
Bremen	55957
Brennyville	56329
Brevik	56655
Brewster	56119
Bricelyn	56014
Bridge Court (Part of Anoka)	55303
Bridgeman	56473
Bridgewater	55021
Brimson	55602
Bristol	55939
Britt	55710
Brookdale Shopping Center (Part of Brooklyn Center)	55430
Brooklyn (Part of Hibbing)	55746
Brooklyn Center	55428-30
For specific Brooklyn Center Zip Codes call (612) 566-8700, or your local postmaster.	
Brooklyn Park	55445
Brook Park	55007
Brooks	56715
Brookston	55711
Brooten	56316
Browerville	56438
Brownsdale	55918
Browns Valley	56219
Brownsville	55919
Brownton	55312
Bruno	55712
Brunswick	55051
Brush Creek	56014
Brushvale	56520
Buckman	56317
Buffalo	55313
Buffalo Lake	55314
Buhl	55713
Bunde	56222
Burchard	56115
Burnett	55727
Burnsville	55337
Burnsville Center (Part of Burnsville)	55337
Burr	56220
Burschville (Part of Corcoran)	55357
Burtrum	56318
Butler	56567
Butterfield	56120
Butternut	56055
Buyck	55771
Bygland	56721
Byron	55920
Cable	56301
Caledonia	55921
Callaway	56521
Calumet	55716
Cambria	56073
Cambridge	55008
Camden Place (Part of Minneapolis)	55412
Campbell	56522
Camp Lacupolis	55041
Camp Ripley	56345
Canby	56220
Cannon City	55021
Cannon Falls	55009
Cannon Lake	55021
Canton	55922
Canyon	55717
Cardigan Junction (Part of Shoreview)	55112
Caribou	56735
Carimona	55965
Carlisle	56537
Carlos	56319

	ZIP
Carlton	55718
Carp	56623
Carver	55315
Cashtown (Part of Ortonville)	56278
Casino	56473
Cass Lake	56633
Castle Danger	55616
Castle Rock	55010
Cedar	55011
Cedar Beach	55960
Cedar Grove (Part of Eagan)	55111
Cedar Mills	55350
Cedar Riverside (Part of Minneapolis)	55440
Celina	55723
Center City	55012
Centerville (Anoka County)	55038
Centerville (Winona County)	55987
Central	56481
Central Lakes	55734
Ceylon	56121
Champlin	55316
Chandler	56122
Chanhassen	55317
Charlesville	56583
Chaska	55318
Chatfield	55923
Cherry	55751
Cherry Grove	55975
Chester	55904
Chicago Bay	55606
Chickamaw Beach	56474
Chisago City	55013
Chisholm	55719
Choice	55954
Chokio	56221
Chowens Corner (Part of Deephaven)	55391
Circle Pines	55014
City (Part of Rochester)	55904
City Center (Part of Minneapolis)	55402
Civic Center (Part of Duluth)	55802
Clara City	56222
Claremont	55924
Clarissa	56440
Clarkfield	56223
Clarks Grove	56016
Clearbrook	56634
Clear Lake	55319
Clearwater	55320
Clements	56224
Clementson	56623
Cleveland	56017
Cliff (Part of Lilydale)	55118
Climax	56523
Clinton	56225
Clinton Falls	55060
Clitherall	56524
Clontarf	56226
Cloquet	55720
Clotho	56347
Cloverdale	55037
Cloverton	55072
Clyde	55979
Coates	55068
Cobden	56085
Cohasset	55721
Coin	56358
Cokato	55321
Colby (Part of Hoyt Lakes)	55750
Cold Spring	56320
Coleraine	55722
Collegeville	56321
Collis	56236
Cologne	55322
Columbia Heights	55421
Comfrey	56019
Commerce (Part of Minneapolis)	55415
Como (Part of St. Paul)	55108
Comstock	56525
Conception	55945
Concord	55985
Conger	56020
Constance (Part of Andover)	55303
Cook	55723
Cooley	55769
Coon Creek (Part of Coon Rapids)	55433
Coon Lake Beach (Part of East Bethel)	55092

Name	ZIP	Name	ZIP	Name	ZIP	Name	ZIP
Coon Rapids	55433	Duelm	56329	Erie	56725	Gemmell	56660
	55448	Duluth	55801-16	Erskine	56535	Geneva	56035
For specific Coon Rapids Zip Codes call (612) 755-1150, or your local postmaster.		For specific Duluth Zip Codes call (218) 723-2590, or your local postmaster.		Esden	56444	Genoa (Olmsted County)	55920
				Esko	55733	Genoa (St. Louis County)	55734
				Essig	56030	Genola	56364
Copas	55073	Duluth International		Estes Brook	56357	Gentilly	56716
Corcoran	55357	Airport, 4787th Air Base		Etna	55975	Georgetown	56546
Cordova	56057	Group	55814	Etter	55089	Georgeville	56312
Cormorant	56572	Dumfries	55981	Euclid	56722	Gheen	55771
Corning	55912	Dumont	56236	Evan	56266	Gheen Corner	55771
Correll	56227	Dundas	55019	Evansville	56326	Ghent	56239
Corvuso	56228	Dundee	56126	Eveleth	55734	Gibbon	55335
Cosmos	56228	Dunnell	56127	Everdell	56520	Giese	55735
Cottage Grove	55016	Dunvilla	56572	Evergreen	56544	Gilbert	55741
Cotton	55724	Duquette	55729	Excelsior	55331	Gilfillan	56283
Cottonwood	56229	Duxbury	55072	Eyota	55934	Gilman	56333
Courtland	56021	Eagan	55120-23	Fairbanks	55602	Gladstone (Part of	
Cove	56359	For specific Eagan Zip Codes call (612) 454-1049, or your local postmaster.		Fairfax	55332	Maplewood)	55109
Craigville	56639			Fairhaven	55382	Glen	56431
Crane Lake	55725			Fairmont	56031	Glencoe	55336
Credit River	55372	Eagle Bend	56446	Faith	56584	Glendale	55771
Croftville	55604	Eagle Lake	56024	Falcon Heights	55108	Glendorado	55371
Cromwell	55726	East Beaver Bay	55601	Faribault	55021	Glen Lake (Part of	
Crookston	56716	East Bethel	55005	Farming	56368	Minnetonka)	55345
Crosby	56441	East Chain	56031	Farmington	55024	Glenville	56036
Crosby Beach	56444	East Cottage Grove (Part		Farris	56633	Glenwood	56334
Crosslake	56442	of Cottage Grove)	55016	Farwell	56327	Glenwood Junction (Part	
Crown	55070	Eastern Heights (Part of		Federal Correctional		of Golden Valley)	55427
Crow River	56243	St. Paul)	55119	Institution	55072	Glory	56431
Crow Wing	56401	East Grand Forks	56721	Federal Dam	56641	Gloster (Part of	
Crystal	55422	East Gull Lake	56401	Felton	56536	Maplewood)	55109
Crystal Bay (Part of		East Hastings (Part of		Fergus Falls	56537*	Gluek	56260
Orono)	55323	Hastings)	55033		56538†	Glyndon	56547
Crystal Shopping Center		East Lake	55760	Fernando	55385	Godahl	56081
(Part of Crystal)	55428	East Lake Francis Shores	55040	Fertile	56540	Golden Hill	55901
Culver	55727	Easton	56025	Fifty Lakes	56448	Golden Hills (Part of St.	
Cummingsville	55923	East Prairieville	55021	Fillmore	55990	Louis Park)	55416
Currie	56123	Eastside (Part of		Finland	55603	Golden Valley	55426
Cushing	56443	Minneapolis)	55418	Finland Air Force Station,		Gonvick	56644
Cusson	55771	East Union	55315	756th Radar Squadron	55603	Goodhue	55027
Cutler	56431	Ebro	56621	Finlayson	55735	Goodland	55742
Cuyuna	56444	Echo	56237	Fisher	56723	Goodridge	56725
Cyrus	56323	Echols	56081	Flensburg	56328	Good Thunder	56037
Dakota	55925	Eddsville	55310	Fletcher	55369	Goodview	55987
Dalbo	55017	Eden	55927	Flintwood Hills (Part of		Gordon	56036
Dale	56549	Eden Prairie	55344	Ramsey)	55303	Gotha	55322
Dalton	56324		55344-47	Flom	56541	Graceton	56686
Danube	56230	For specific Eden Prairie Zip Codes call (612) 942-5266, or your local postmaster.		Floodwood	55736	Graceville	56240
Danvers	56231			Florence	56170	Granada	56039
Darfur	56022			Florenton	55792	Grand Falls	56627
Darling	56345	Eden Prairie Center (Part		Florian	56758	Grand Marais	55604
Darwin	55324	of Eden Prairie)	55344	Foley	56329	Grand Meadow	55936
Dassel	55325	Eden Valley	55329	Fond du Lac Indian		Grand Portage	55605
Dawson	56232	Edgerton	56128	Reservation	55720	Grand Portage Indian	
Day (Anoka County)	55006	Edgewood	55008	Forada	56308	Reservation	55605
Dayton (Anoka County)	55303	Edina	55410	Forbes	55738	Grand Rapids	55730†
Dayton (Hennepin			55416	Fordson (Part of Eagan)	55121		55744*
County)	55327		55424	Forest City	55355	Grand View Heights	56753
Daytons Bluff (Part of St.			55435-36	Forest Grove	56660	Grandy	55029
Paul)	55106	For specific Edina Zip Codes call (612) 920-5226, or your local postmaster.		Forest Lake	55025	Granger	55939
Debs	56676			Forest Mills	55992	Granite Falls	56241
Deephaven	55391			Foreston	56330	Grass Lake	55006
Deer Creek	56527	Effie	56639	Fork	56744	Grasston	55030
Deer Creek Indian		Eidswold	55020	Fort Ripley	56449	Grattan	56661
Reservation	56639	Eitzen	55931	Fort Snelling	55111	Greaney	55771
Deerfield	55049	Elba	55910	Fosston	56542	Greenbush	56726
Deer River	56636	Elbow Lake	56531	Fossum	56584	Greenfield	55357
Deerwood	56444	Eldes Corner	55810	Fountain	55935	Green Isle	55338
De Graff	56233	Eldred	56523	Four Corners	55811	Greenland	56028
Delano	55328	Elgin	55932	Fourtown	56727	Greenleaf	55355
Delavan	56023	Elizabeth	56533	Foxhome	56543	Greenleafton	55965
Delft	56101	Elkland	55021	Fox Lake	56181	Green Valley	56258
Delhi	56283	Elko	55020	Franconia	55074	Greenwald	56335
Dell	56013	Elk River	55330	Franklin (Renville County)	55333	Greenwood	55331
Dellwood	55110	Elkton	55933	Franklin (St. Louis County)	55792	Grey Eagle	56336
Denham	55728	Ellendale	56026	Franklin Avenue (Part of		Grogan	56081
Dennison	55018	Ellsworth	56129	Minneapolis)	55404	Groningen	55072
Dent	56528	Elmdale	56314	Frazee	56544	Grove City	56243
Detroit Lakes	56501*	Elmer	55765	Freeborn	56032	Grove Lake	56316
	56502†	Elmore	56027	Freeburg	55921	Grygla	56727
Dexter	55926	Elmwood (Part of St.		Freedhem	56345	Guckeen	56013
Diamond Lake (Part of		Louis Park)	55416	Freeport	56331	Gully	56646
Minneapolis)	55419	Elrosa	56325	Fremont	55979	Gutches Grove	56347
Dilworth	56529	Elway (Part of St. Paul)	55116	French Lake	55302	Guthrie	56461
Dinkytown (Part of		Ely	55731	French River	55804	Hackensack	56452
Minneapolis)	55414	Ely Lake	55734	Fridley	55432	Hackett	56623
Dodge Center	55927	Elysian	56028	Friesland	55037	Hader	55992
Donaldson	56720	Embarrass	55732	Frontenac	55026	Hadley	56151
Donnelly	56235	Emco (Part of Hoyt		Frost	56033	Hagan	56262
Dora Lake	56661	Lakes)	55750	Fulda	56131	Hallock	56728
Doran	56522	Emily	56447	Funkley	56630	Halma	56729
Dorothy	56750	Emmons	56029	Garden City	56034	Halstad	56548
Dorset	56470	Empire	55024	Garfield	56332	Hamburg	55339
Douglas	55960	Enfield	55362	Garrison	56450	Hamel	55340
Douglas Lodge	56460	Englund	56758	Garvin	56132	Hamilton	55975
Dover	55929	Erdahl	56531	Gary	56545	Ham Lake	55304
Dovray	56125	Erhard	56534	Gatzke	56724	Hammond	55991
Downer	56514	Ericksonville	56359	Gaylord	55334	Hampton	55031
Dresbach	55947	Ericsburg	56649	Gem Lake	55110	Hancock	56244

* **Area Zip Code**   † **Post Office Boxes**

Name	ZIP	Name	ZIP	Name	ZIP	Name	ZIP
Hanley Falls	56245	Huntersville	56464	Knife River	55609	Little Falls	56345
Hanover	55341	Huntley	56047	Knollwood Mall (Part of		Littlefork	56653
Hanska	56041	Husby Spur (Part of		St. Louis Park)	55426	Little Marais	55614
Happyland	56653	Arden Hills)	55112	Komensky	55350	Little Pine	56431
Harding	56364	Hutchinson	55350	Kragnes	56560	Little Rock (Beltrami	
Hardwick	56134	Hydes Lake	55322	Kroschel	55037	County)	56671
Har-Mar Mall (Part of		Ideal Corners	56472	Lac qui Parle	56265	Little Rock (Morrison	
Roseville)	55113	Idington	55703	La Crescent	55947	County)	56373
Harmony	55939	Ihlen	56140	Lafayette	56054	Little Sauk	56347
Harnell Park	55779	Illgen City	55614	Lagoona Beach	56278	Little Swan (Part of	
Harris	55032	Imogene	56039	Lake Benton	56149	Hibbing)	55746
Hart	55971	Independence (Hennepin		Lake Bronson	56734	Local	56501
Hartland	56042	County)	55359	Lake Center	56511	Lockhart	56510
Hassan	55374	Independence (St. Louis		Lake City	55041	Loman	56654
Hassman	56431	County)	55727	Lake Crystal	56055	London	56061
Hastings	55033	Indus	56629	Lake Elmo	55042	Long Beach	56334
Hasty	55320	Industrial (Part of St. Paul)	55104	Lake Eunice	56501	Long Lake	55356
Hatfield	56164	Inger	56636	Lakefield	56150	Long Point	56686
Havana	56060	Inguadona	56655	Lake George	56458	Long Prairie	56347
Hawick	56246	International Falls	56649	Lake Henry	56362	Long Siding	55371
Hawley	56549	Inver Grove Heights	55076-77	Lake Hubert	56459	Longville	56655
Hay Creek	55066	For specific Inver Grove Heights		Lake Itasca	56460	Lonsdale	55046
Haydenville	56256	Zip Codes call (612) 451-1243,		Lakeland	55043	Loop (Part of Minneapolis)	55402
Hayfield	55940	or your local postmaster.		Lakeland Shores	55043	Loretto	55357
Haypoint	55748	Iona	56141	Lake Lillian	56253	Loring (Part of	
Hayward	56043	Iron	55751	Lake Netta (Part of Ham		Minneapolis)	55403
Hazel Run	56247	Ironhub	56431	Lake)	55303	Louisburg	56254
Hazelwood	55057	Ironton	56455	Lake Nichols	55717	Louriston	56260
Heatwole	55350	Isabella	55607	Lake Park	56554	Lower Sioux Indian	
Hector	55342	Isanti	55040	Lake Sarah (Part of		Reservation	56270
Heiberg	56584	Island Lake	56667	Greenfield)	55357	Lowry	56349
Heidelberg	56071	Island Park (Part of		Lake Shore	56401	Lucan	56255
Heinola	56567	Mound)	55364	Lake Shore Park (Part of		Lude	56686
Henderson	56044	Island View	56649	White Bear Lake)	55110	Lutsen	55612
Hendricks	56136	Isle	56342	Lakeside (Renville County)	55314	Luverne	56156
Hendrum	56550	Ivanhoe	56142	Lakeside (St. Louis		Luxemburg	56301
Henning	56551	Iverson	55718	County)	55804	Lydia	55352
Henriette	55036	Jackson	56143	Lake St. Croix Beach	55043	Lyle	55953
Henrytown	55939	Jacobson	55752	Lake Street (Part of		Lynd	56157
Herman	56248	Jacobs Prairie	56320	Minneapolis)	55408	Lyndale (Part of	
Hermantown	55810	Jakeville	56329	Lakeville	55044	Independence)	55359
Heron Lake	56137	Jameson	56649	Lake Wilson	56151	Lynwood (Part of Hibbing)	55746
Hewitt	56453	Janesville	56048	Lamberton	56152	Mabel	55954
Hiawatha Spur (Part of		Jarretts	55957	Lamoille	55987	McCauleyville	56553
Eagan)	55111	Jasper	56144	Lamson	55325	McGrath	56350
Hibbing	55746-47	Jeffers	56145	Lancaster	56735	McGregor	55760
For specific Hibbing Zip Codes		Jenkins	56456	Landfall	55128	McHugh	56501
call (218) 263-4086, or your		Jennie	55325	Lanesboro	55949	McIntosh	56556
local postmaster.		Jessenland	56044	Langdon (Part of Cottage		McKee (Part of Eagan)	55121
Hidden Creek (Part of		Jessie Lake	56637	Grove)	55016	McKinley	55761
Andover)	55303	Johnsburg	55909	Lansing	55950	Madelia	56062
High Forest	55976	Johnson	56236	Laporte	56461	Madison	56256
Highland (Fillmore County)	55986	Johnsville (Part of Blaine)	55434	La Prairie	55744	Madison East (Part of	
Highland (Hennepin		Jonathan (Part of Chaska)	55318	Larsmont	55616	Mankato)	56001
County)	55411	Jordan	55352	La Salle	56056	Madison Lake	56063
Highland (Lake County)	55616	Judson	56055	Lastrup	56344	Magnolia	56158
Highland (Wright County)	55349	Kabekona	56461	Lauderdale	55108	Mahkonce	56557
High Landing	56725	Kabetogama	56669	Lavinia	55746	Mahnomen	56557
Highland Park (Part of St.		Kanaranzi	56110	Lawler	55760	Mahtomedi	55115
Paul)	55116	Kandi Mall Shopping		Lawndale	56579	Mahtowa	55762
Hill City	55748	Center (Part of Willmar)	56201	Lax Lake	55614	Maine	56586
Hillman	56338	Kandiyohi	56251	Leader	56466	Maine Prairie	55353
Hills	56138	Karlstad	56732	Leaf Lake	56551	Makinen	55763
Hilltop	55421	Kasota	56050	Leaf Valley	56332	Mall (Part of Fairmont)	56031
Hillview	56477	Kasson	55944	Leavenworth	56085	Mall of America (Part of	
Hinckley	55037	Katrine	56444	Le Center	56057	Bloomington)	55420
Hines	56647	Keewatin	55753	Leech Lake Indian		Malmo	56431
Hitterdal	56552	Kelliher	56650	Reservation	56633	Manannah	56243
Hoffman	56339	Kellogg	55945	Leetonia (Part of Hibbing)	55746	Manchester	56064
Hoffmans Corners (Part of		Kelly Lake (Part of		Le Hillier	56001	Manhattan Beach	56463
Gem Lake)	55110	Hibbing)	55754	Lengby	56651	Manitou	56629
Hokah	55941	Kelsey	55724	Lenora	55922	Mankato	56001-03
Holdingford	56340	Kennedy	56733	Leonard	56652	For specific Mankato Zip Codes	
Holland	56139	Kenneth	56147	Leonidas	55734	call (507) 625-1781, or your	
Hollandale	56045	Kensington	56343	Leota	56153	local postmaster.	
Holloway	56249	Kent	56553	Lerdal	56007	Mansfield	56009
Hollywood	55388	Kenwood (Hennepin		Le Roy	55951	Mantorville	55955
Holmes City	56341	County)	55403	Lester Prairie	55354	Maple	55387
Holt	56738	Kenwood (St. Louis		Le Sueur	56058	Maple Bay	56736
Holyoke	55749	County)	55811	Lewis Lake	55006	Maple Grove	55369
Homer	55942	Kenyon	55946	Lewiston	55952	Maple Hill	55604
Hoot Lake (Part of Fergus		Kerkhoven	56252	Lewisville	56060	Maple Island	56045
Falls)	56537	Kerr (Part of Hibbing)	55746	Lexington (Anoka County)	55112	Maple Lake	55358
Hope	56046	Kerrick	55756	Lexington (Le Sueur		Maple Plain	55359
Hopkins	55305	Kettle River	55757	County)	56057	Mapleton	56065
	55343	Kiester	56051	Libby	55760	Mapleview	55912
	55345	Kilkenny	56052	Lilydale	55118	Maplewood	55119
For specific Hopkins Zip Codes		Kimball	55353	Lime Creek	56131	Maplewood Mall (Part of	
call (612) 935-8606, or your		Kimberly	56431	Lincoln	56443	Maplewood)	55109
local postmaster.		Kinbrae	56126	Linden Grove	55723	Marble	55764
Hopper (Part of Mountain		Kingsdale	55072	Lindford	56653	Marcell	56657
Iron)	55792	Kings Park	55960	Lindstrom	55045	Margie	56658
Houston	55943	Kingston	55325	Lino Lakes	55126	Marietta	56257
Hovland	55606	Kinmount	55771	Linwood	55005	Marine On St. Croix	55047
Howard Lake	55349	Kinney	55758	Lismore	56155	Marion	55901
Hoyt Lakes	55750	Kitzville (Part of Hibbing)	55746	Litchfield	55355	Markham	55763
Hubbard	56470	Kjellberg Park	55362	Litomysl	56060	Markville	55072
Hugo	55038	Klossner	56053	Little Canada	55117	Marshall	56258
Humboldt	56731	Knapp	55321	Little Chicago	55057	Martin Lake	55079

	ZIP
Marty	55353
Marysburg	56063
Marystown	55379
Matawan	56072
Mattson	56728
Max	56659
Mayer	55360
Mayhew	56379
Mayhew Lake	56379
Maynard	56260
Mayville	55912
Mazeppa	55956
M&D Junction (Part of White Bear Lake)	55110
Meadowlands	55765
Medford	55049
Medicine Lake	55441
Meire Grove	56352
Melby	56326
Melrose	56352
Melrude	55766
Menahga	56464
Mendota	55150
Mendota Heights	55118
Mentor	56736
Meriden	56067
Merrifield	56465
Merton	55060
Mesaba (Part of Hoyt Lakes)	55750
Middle River	56737
Midway (Becker County)	56464
Midway (Ramsey County)	55104
Midway (St. Louis County)	55792
Midway Center (Part of St. Paul)	55104
Micsville	55009
Milaca	56353
Milan	56262
Mille Lacs Indian Reservation	56359
Miller Hill (Part of Duluth)	55811
Miller Hill Mall (Part of Duluth)	55811
Millersburg	55021
Millerville	56315
Millville	55957
Milroy	56263
Miltona	56354
Mineral Center	55605

Minneapolis 55401-70
.... 55480
For specific Minneapolis Zip Codes call (612) 452-3800, or your local postmaster.

COLLEGES & UNIVERSITIES

	ZIP
Augsburg College	55454
North Central Bible College	55404
University of Minnesota-Twin Cities	55455

FINANCIAL INSTITUTIONS

	ZIP
Firstar Bank of Minnesota, N.A.	55417
First Bank, N.A.	55402
IDS Trust	55440
Investors Savings Bank, F.S.B.	55402
National City Bank of Minneapolis	55402
Norwest Bank Minnesota, National Association	55479
TCF Bank Minnesota, F.S.B.	55402

HOSPITALS

	ZIP
Abbott-Northwestern Hospital	55407
Fairview Riverside Medical Center	55454
Fairview Southdale Hospital	55435
Hennepin County Medical Center	55415
University of Minnesota Hospital and Clinic	55455
Veterans Affairs Medical Center	55417

HOTELS/MOTELS

	ZIP
Hyatt Regency Minneapolis-Nicollet Mall	55403
Marquette	55402
Sheraton Park Place Hotel	55416

	ZIP
MILITARY INSTALLATIONS	
934th Mission Support Squadron, Minneapolis-St. Paul Air Reserve Base	55450
Minnehaha (Part of Minneapolis)	55406
Minneiska	55910
Minneota	56264
Minnesota City	55959
Minnesota Lake	56068
Minnesota Transfer (Part of St. Paul)	55114
Minnetonka	55345
Minnetonka Beach	55361
Minnetonka Mills (Part of Minnetonka)	55305
Minnetrista	55364
Minnewawa	55760
Mizpah	56660
Moland	55946
Money Creek	55943
Montevideo	56265
Montgomery	56069
Monticello	55362*
	55365†
Montrose	55363
Moorhead	56560*
	56561†
Moose Lake	55767
Moose Lake State Hospital	55767
Mora	55051
Morgan	56266
Morgan Park (Part of Duluth)	55808
Morningside (Part of Edina)	55424
Morrill	56329
Morris	56267
Morristown	55052
Morton	56270
Moscow	55912
Motley	56466
Mound	55364
Mounds View	55112
Mountain Iron	55768
Mountain Lake	56159
Mount Royal (Part of Duluth)	55803
Munger	55806
Murdock	56271
Murphy City	55603
Muskoda	56549
Myrtle	56036
Nashua	56565
Nashwauk	55769
Nassau	56272
Navarre (Part of Orono)	55392
Naytahwaush	56566
Nebish	56667
Nelson	56355
Nerstrand	55053
Nett Lake	55772
Nett Lake Indian Reservation	55772
Nevis	56467
New Auburn	55366
New Brighton	55112
Newburg	55954
Newfolden	56738
New Germany	55367
New Hartford	55925
New Hope	55427
Newhouse	55954
New London	56273
New Market	55054
New Munich	56356
Newport	55055
New Prague	56071
New Richland	56072
New Rome	55307
Newry	56045
New Trier	55031
New Ulm	56073
New York Mills	56567
Nickerson	55797
Nicollet	56074
Nicols (Part of Eagan)	55121
Nicolville	55912
Nielsville	56568
Nimrod	56478
Nininger	55033
Nisswa	56468
Nodine	55925
Nokomis (Part of Minneapolis)	55417

	ZIP
Nopeming	55810
Norcross	56274
Normandale (Part of Edina)	55439
Norseland	56082
North Benton	56329
North Branch	55056
Northcote	56728
Northdale (Part of Coon Rapids)	55433
North Douglas (Part of Crystal)	55422
Northfield	55057
North Mankato	56003
North Oaks	55127
Northome	56661
North Prairie	56314
North Redwood	56283
Northrop	56075
Northside (Part of Albert Lea)	56007
North St. Paul	55109
Northtown Mall (Part of Blaine)	55434
Northwest Terminal (Part of Minneapolis)	55418
Norway Lake	56289
Norwood	55368*
	55383†
Nowthen	55303
Noyes	56740
Oak Center	55041
Oakdale	55128
Oakhill	56347
Oak Island	56741
Oak Knoll (Part of Minnetonka)	55305
Oakland	56076
Oak Park (Anoka County)	55434
Oak Park (Benton County)	56357
Oak Park Heights	55082
Oakport	56560
Oak Ridge	55910
Odessa	56276
Odin	56160
Ogema	56569
Ogilvie	56358
Okabena	56161
Oklee	56742
Old Frontenac	55041
Olga	56646
Olivia	56277
Onamia	56359
Onigum	56484
Opole	56340
Orchard Lake (Part of Lakeville)	55044
Org	56187
Orleans	56735
Ormsby	56162
Orono	55323
Oronoco	55960
Orr	55771
Orrock	55309
Ortonville	56278
Osage	56570
Osakis	56360
Oshawa	56082
Oslo (Dodge County)	55940
Oslo (Marshall County)	56744
Oslund	56680
Osseo	55311
	55369
For specific Osseo Zip Codes call (612) 425-2843, or your local postmaster.	
Ostrander	55961
Otisco	56077
Otisville	55073
Otrey	56278
Otsego	55301
Ottawa	56058
Otter Creek	55718
Ottertail	56571
Outing	56662
Owatonna	55060
Oxlip	55040
Oylen	56481
Padua	56378
Palisade	56469
Palmdale	55084
Palmers	55804
Palo	55705
Parent	56329
Parkers Prairie	56361
Park Rapids	56470
Park View (Part of Crookston)	56716

	ZIP
Parkville (Part of Mountain Iron)	55773
Payne	55765
Paynesville	56362
Pease	56363
Pelican Rapids	56572
Pelland	56649
Pemberton	56078
Pencer	56751
Pengilly	55775
Pennington	56663
Pennock	56279
Pequaywan Lake	55801
Pequot Lakes	56472
Perham	56573
Perkins	55943
Perley	56574
Petersburg	56143
Peterson	55962
Petran	56043
Phelps	55586
Philbrook	56466
Pickwick	55987
Pierz	56364
Pigeon River	55605
Pike Lake	55811
Pillager	56473
Pillsbury	56382
Pilot Grove	56027
Pilot Mound	55923
Pine Bend (Dakota County)	55068
Pine Bend (Mahnomen County)	56651
Pine Brook	55008
Pine Center	56401
Pine City	55063
Pinecreek	56751
Pine Island	55963
Pine River	56474
Pine Springs	55115
Pineville	55705
Pinewood	56664
Pioneer (Part of St. Paul)	55101
Pipestone	56164
Pitt	56623
Plainview	55964
Plato	55370
Pleasant Grove	55976
Pleasant Lake	56301
Plummer	56748
Plymouth	55441-42
	55446-47
For specific Plymouth Zip Codes call (612) 559-2148, or your local postmaster.	
Point Douglas	55033
Ponemah	56666
Ponsford	56575
Poplar	56479
Popple Creek	56379
Port Cargill (Part of Savage)	55378
Porter	56280
Post Town	55920
Potsdam	55932
Powderhorn (Part of Minneapolis)	55407
Prairie Island Indian Reservation	55089
Prairieville	55021
Pratt	55060
Predmore	55934
Preston	55965
Priam	56282
Princeton	55371
Prinsburg	56281
Prior Lake	55372
Proctor	55810
Prosit	55702
Prosper	55954
Pulaski Lake Shores	55313
Puposky	56667
Quamba	55007
Racine	55967
Radium	56762
Rainy Junction (Part of Virginia)	55792
Ramey	56329
Ramsey (Anoka County)	55303
Ramsey (Mower County)	55912
Randall	56475
Randolph	55065
Ranier	56668
Rapidan	56001
Rassat	55313
Rauch	55771
Ray	56669
Raymond	56282

* **Area Zip Code**   † **Post Office Boxes**

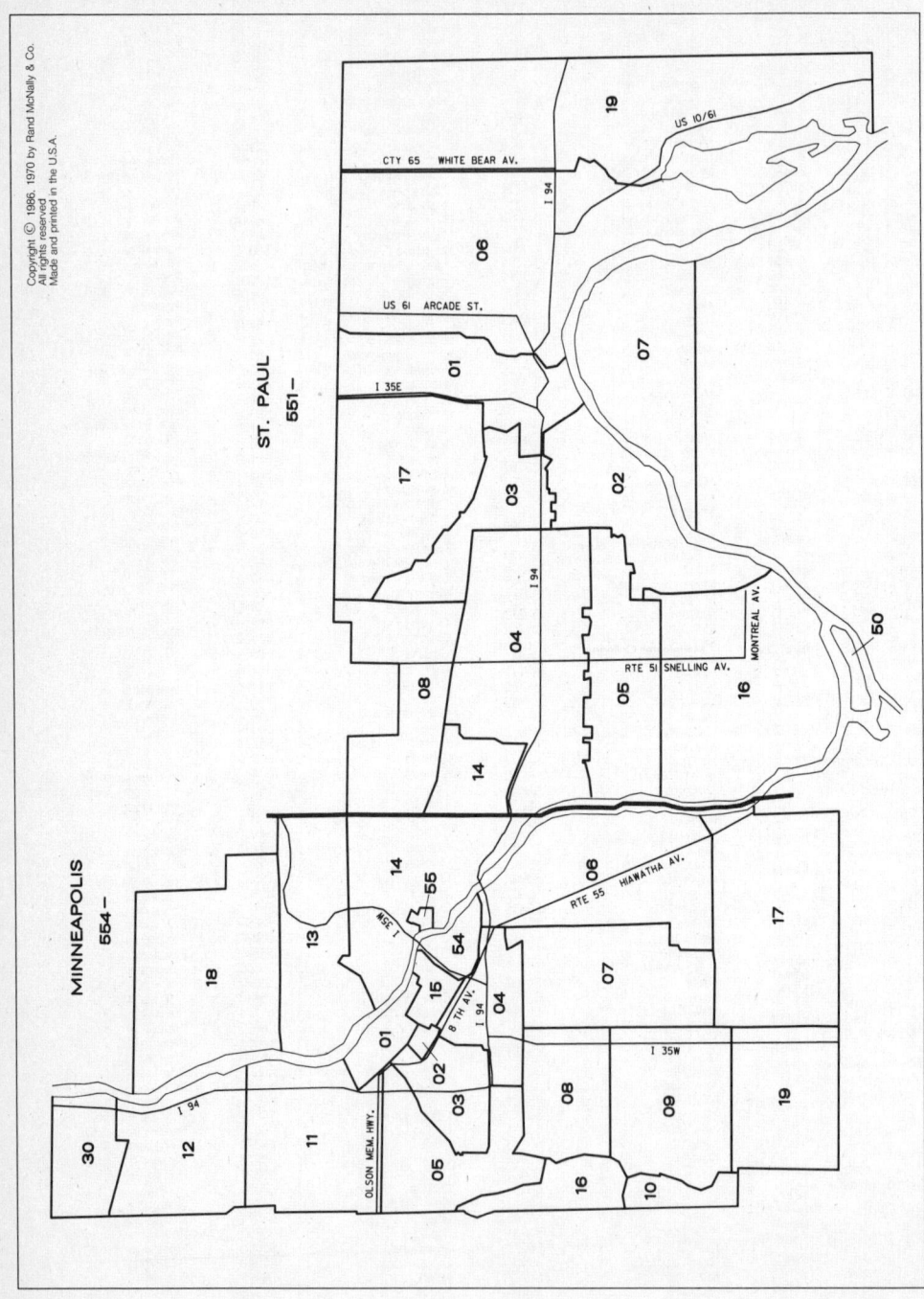

ST. PAUL
551—

MINNEAPOLIS
554—

	ZIP		ZIP		ZIP		ZIP
Reading	56165	St. Anna	56310	St. Wendel	56310	Spring Lake (Itasca	
Reads Landing	55968	St. Anthony (Hennepin		Salem Corners	55920	County)	56680
Redby	56670	County)	55418	Salol	56756	Spring Lake Park	55432
Redlake	56671	St. Anthony (Stearns		Sanborn	56083	Spring Park	55384
Red Lake Falls	56750	County)	56307	Sandstone	55072	Springsteel Island	56763
Red Lake Indian		St. Augusta	56301	Santiago	55377	Springvale	55080
Reservation	56671	Saint Benedict	56071	Saratoga	55972	Spring Valley	55975
Red Rock	55605	St. Bonifacius	55375	Sargeant	55973	Spruce Center	56354
Red Top	56342	St. Charles	55972	Sartell	56377	Squaw Lake	56681
Red Wing	55066	St. Clair (Blue Earth		Sauk Centre	56378	Stacy	55078†
Redwood Falls	56283	County)	56080	Sauk Rapids	56379		55079*
Reformatory (Part of St.		St. Clair (Ramsey County)	55116	Saum	56674	Stanchfield	55080
Cloud)	56301	St. Cloud	56301-04	Savage	55378	Stanley	55008
Regal	56312	For specific St. Cloud Zip		Sawyer	55780	Stanton	55018
Remer	56672	Codes call (612) 251-8220, or		Scandia	55073	Staples	56479
Reno	55919	your local postmaster.		Scandia Valley	56443	Starbuck	56381
Renville	56284	St. Croix Junction (Part of		Scanlon	55720	Stark	55032
Revere	56166	Hastings)	55033	Schley	56633	Steele Center	55060
Rice	56367	St. Francis (Anoka		Schroeder	55613	Steelton (Part of Duluth)	55808
Riceford	55954	County)	55070	Scotts Corner	55718	Steen	56173
Rice Street (Part of St.		St. Francis (Stearns		Seaforth	56287	Stephen	56757
Paul)	55117	County)	56331	Searles	56084	Sterling Center	56010
Richfield	55423	St. George	56073	Sebeka	56477	Stewart (Lake County)	55616
Richfield Hub Shopping		St. Henry	56057	Section Thirty	55731	Stewart (McLeod County)	55385
Center (Part of		St. Hilaire	56754	Sedan	56380	Stewartville	55976
Richfield)	55423	St. James	56081	Seven-Hi Shopping Center		Stillwater	55082*
Richmond	56368	St. Joseph	56374	(Part of Minnetonka)	55345		55083†
Rich Valley (Part of		St. Killian	56185	Shafer	55074	Stockholm	55321
Rosemount)	55075	St. Leo	56264	Shakopee	55379	Stockton	55988
Richville	56576	St. Louis Park	55426	Shaw	55717	Storden	56174
Richwood	56577	St. Martin	56376	Sheffield Mill (Part of		Strandquist	56758
Ridgedale Shopping		St. Mary's Point	55043	Faribault)	55021	Strathcona	56759
Center (Part of		St. Mathias	56449	Sheldon	55921	Strout	55355
Minnetonka)	55343	St. Michael	55376	Shelly	56581	Stubbs Bay (Part of	
Ridgeway	55943	St. Nicholas	55389	Sherack	56722	Orono)	55356
Rindal	56540	St. Patrick	56071	Sherburn	56171	Sturgeon	55703
Riverside (Part of				Sheshebee	55760	Sturgeon Lake	55783
Minneapolis)	55454	**St. Paul**	55101-28	Shevlin	56676	Sugar Loaf (Part of	
Riverside Heights	56013		55164-89	Shieldsville	55021	Winona)	55987
Riverton	56455	For specific St. Paul Zip Codes		Shooks	56661	Summit	55917
Riverview (Part of St.		call (612) 452-3800, or your		Shoreham	56501	Sunburg	56289
Paul)	55107	local postmaster.		Shoreview	55126	Sundal	56545
Robbin	58225			Shorewood	55331	Sunfish Lake	55118
Robbinsdale	55422	COLLEGES & UNIVERSITIES		Shotley	56650	Sunrise	55056
Robinson	55731	Bethel College	55112	Shovel Lake	55785	Svea	56216
Rochert	56578	College of St. Catherine	55105	Side Lake	55781	Sveadahl	56081
Rochester	55901-06	Macalester College	55105	Signal Hills Shopping		Swanburg	56474
For specific Rochester Zip		Metropolitan State		Center (Part of West St.		Swan River	55784
Codes call (507) 287-1240, or		University	55101	Paul)	55118	Swanville	56382
your local postmaster.		William Mitchell College of		Silica	55746	Swatara	55785
Rock Creek	55067	Law	55105	Silo	55952	Swift	56682
Rock Dell	55920			Silver Bay	55614	Swift Falls	56215
Rockford	55373	FINANCIAL INSTITUTIONS		Silver Creek (Lake		Sylvan	56473
Rockville	56369	American National Bank &		County)	55616	Syre	56584
Rogers	55374	Trust Company	55101	Silver Creek (Wright		Tabor	56712
Rollag	56549	Commercial State Bank of		County)	55380	Taconite	55786
Rollingstone	55969	Minnesota	55102	Silverdale	55771	Taconite Harbor	55613
Rollins	55602	Eastern Heights State		Silver Lake	55381	Talmoon	56637
Ronneby	56329	Bank of St. Paul	55119	Simpson	55901	Tamarack	55787
Roosevelt	56673	Firstar Bank of Minnesota,		Sioux Valley	51347	Taopi	55977
Roscoe (Goodhue		N.A.	55116	Skibo	55750	Taunton	56291
County)	55983	Liberty State Bank	55104	Skyburg	55946	Tawney	55954
Roscoe (Stearns County)	56371	Midway National Bank of		Skyline	56001	Taylors Falls	55084
Roseau	56751	St. Paul	55104	Slayton	56172	Tenney	56583
Rose City	56446			Sleepy Eye	56085	Tenstrike	56683
Rose Creek	55970	HOSPITALS		Sletten	56556	Terrace	56380
Roseland	56216	Healtheast Bethesda		Smiths Mill	56048	Terrebonne	56750
Rosemount	55068	Lutheran Hospital	55103	Snellman	56570	The Arches	55952
Rosen	56212	St. Paul-Ramsey Medical		Sobieski	56345	Theilman	55978
Rosendale	56243	Center	55101	Soderville (Part of Ham		Thief River Falls	56701
Roseport (Part of Inver				Lake)	55304	Third Crow Wing Lake	56467
Grove Heights)	55075	HOTELS/MOTELS		Sogn	55018	Thompson Grove (Part of	
Roseville	55113	Holiday Inn St. Paul/East	55119	Solway	56678	Cottage Grove)	55016
Rosewood	56701	Ramada Hotel St. Paul	55119	Soudan	55782	Thompson Heights (Part	
Ross	56751	Saint Paul	55102	South Bend	56001	of Coon Rapids)	55433
Rossburg	56431			South Branch	56081	Thompson Heights	
Rothsay	56579	MILITARY INSTALLATIONS		Southdale (Part of Edina)	55435	Shopping Center (Part	
Round Lake	56167	Fort Snelling	55111	Southdale Shopping		of Coon Rapids)	55433
Round Prairie	56347	Minnesota Air National		Center (Part of Edina)	55435	Thompson Park (Part of	
Rowena	56293	Guard, FB6231,		South Haven	55382	Coon Rapids)	55433
Royalton	56373	Minneapolis-St.Paul		South International Falls		Thompson Riverview	
Roy Lake	56557	International Airport	55111	(Part of International		Terrace (Part of Coon	
Ruby Junction (Part of		Twin Cities Army		Falls)	56679	Rapids)	55433
Hibbing)	55746	Ammunition Plant		South Minneapolis (Part of		Thomson	55718
Rush City	55069	(Caretaker Status)	55112	Minneapolis)	55408	Thor	56431
Rushford	55971	United States Army		South St. Paul	55075-77	Thorhult	56727
Rushford Village	55962	Engineer District, St.		For specific South St. Paul Zip		Tintah	56583
Rushmore	56168	Paul	55101	Codes call (612) 451-1243, or		Toad Lake	56544
Rush Point	55080	United States Army		your local postmaster.		Tofte	55615
Rush River	56058	Transportation Office,		Southtown Center (Part of		Togo	55788
Ruskin	55021	Minneapolis-St. Paul		Bloomington)	55420	Toimi	55602
Russell	56169	Area	55111	Spafford	56187	Toivola	55789
Rustad	56560			Spectacle Lake	55008	Tonka Bay	55331
Ruthton	56170	St. Paul Park	55071	Spicer	56288	Tower	55790
Rutledge	55778	St. Peter	56082	Springfield	56087	Tracy	56175
Sabin	56580	St. Rosa	56331	Spring Grove	55974	Traffic (Part of	
Sacred Heart	56285	St. Stephen	56375	Spring Hill	56352	Minneapolis)	55403
Saga Hill (Part of Orono)	55323	St. Thomas	56058	Spring Lake (Isanti		Trail	56684
Saginaw	55779	St. Vincent	56755	County)	55056	Trails End	55604

* Area Zip Code   † Post Office Boxes

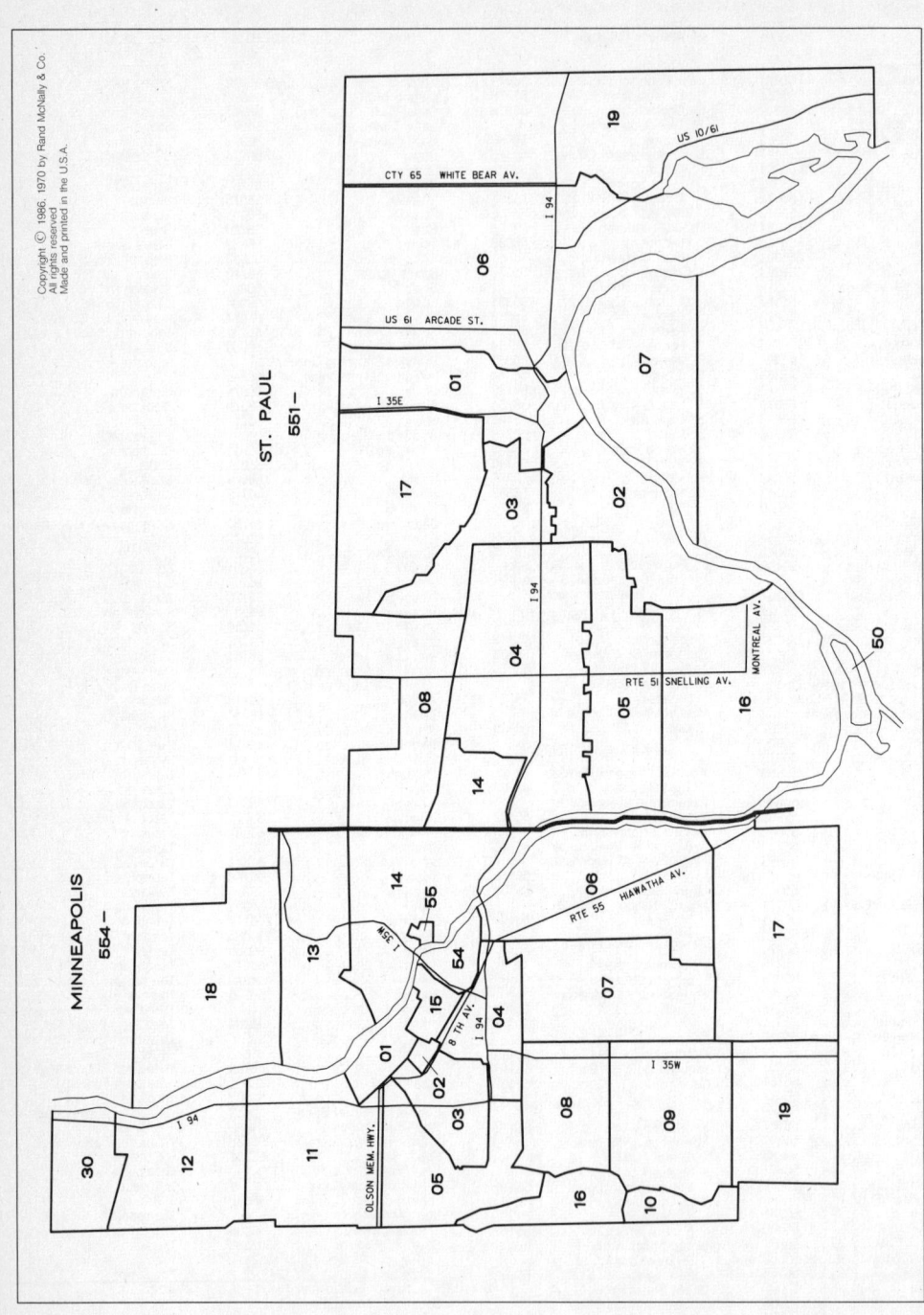

ST. PAUL
551—

MINNEAPOLIS
554—

19

US 10/61

CTY 65 WHITE BEAR AV.

I 94

06

US 61 ARCADE ST.

01

I 35E

07

17

03

02

I 94

MONTREAL AV.

50

RTE 51 SNELLING AV.

04

08

05

18

14

06

RTE 55 HIAWATHA AV.

14

55

13

MSS I

54

17

18

15

8 TH AV.

04

07

01

I 94

02

30

12

11

OLSON MEM. HWY.

03

05

08

09

19

I 35W

I 94

16

10

	ZIP		ZIP		ZIP		ZIP
Traverse	56082		55792*	Wendell	56590	Winger	56592
Trimont	56176	Vista	56077	West Albany	55957	Winnebago (Faribault	
Trommald	56441	Wabasha	55981	West Albion	55302	County)	56098
Trosky	56177	Wabasso	56293	Westbrook	56183	Winnebago (Houston	
Troy	55972	Wabedo	56655	Westbury	56501	County)	55921
Truman	56088	Waconia	55387	West Concord	55985	Winnipeg Junction	56549
Turtle River	56601	Wacouta	55066	West Duluth (Part of		Winona	55987
Twig	55791	Wadena	56482	Duluth)	55807	Winsted	55395
Twin Cities (Part of		Wahkon	56386	West End (Part of St.		Winthrop	55396
Richfield)	55111	Waite Park	56387	Paul)	55102	Winton	55796
Twin Lakes	56089	Walbo	55008	West Lake Francis Shores	55040	Wirock	56141
Twin Valley	56584	Waldo	55616	West Lynn	55350	Wirt	56688
Two Harbors	55616	Waldorf	56091	West Newton	55945	Withrow	55082
Two Inlets	56470	Wales	55616	West Point	55008	Witoka	55987
Tyler	56178	Walker	56484	Westport	56385	Wolf	55751
Ulen	56585	Walnut Grove	56180	West Rock	55063	Wolf Lake	56593
Underwood	56586	Walters	56092	West St. Paul	55118	Wolford	56441
Union Hill	56071	Waltham	55982	West Union	56389	Wolverton	56594
University (Part of		Wanamingo	55983	West Virginia (Part of		Woodbury	55125
Minneapolis)	55414	Wanda	56294	Mountain Iron)	55792	Wood Lake	56297
Upper Sioux Indian		Wannaska	56761	Whalan	55986	Woodland (Hennepin	
Reservation	56241	Warba	55793	Wheatland	56069	County)	55391
Upsala	56384	Ward Springs	56336	Wheaton	56296	Woodland (Kanabec	
Uptown (Part of St. Paul)	55102	Warman	55051	Wheeler's Point	56623	County)	56342
Urbank	56361	Warren	56762	Whipholt	56484	Woodland (St. Louis	
U.S. Air Force	55814	Warroad	56763	White Bear Beach	55110	County)	55803
Utica	55979	Warsaw	55087	White Bear Lake	55110	Woodland Park	56551
Vadnais Heights	55127	Waseca	56093	White Earth	56591	Woodland Terrace (Part of	
Valley Ridge (Part of		Washington	55975	White Earth Indian		Andover)	55303
Burnsville)	55378	Wasioja	55927	Reservation	56591	Woodstock	56186
Valley West Shopping		Waskish	56685	Whiteface	55766	Worthington	56187
Center (Part of		Wastedo	55009	White Rock	55009	Wrenshall	55797
Bloomington)	55420	Waterford	55057	Whyte	55616	Wright	55798
Vasa	55089	Watertown	55388	Wig Wam Bay	56359	Wrightstown	56453
Verdi	56179	Waterville	56096	Wilbert	56121	Wyattville	55952
Vergas	56587	Watkins	55389	Wilder	56101	Wykoff	55990
Vermillion	55085	Watson	56295	Wildwood	56661	Wylie	56750
Vermillion Dam	55771	Waubun	56589	Wilkinson	56633	Wyman (Part of Hoyt	
Verndale	56481	Waverly	55390	Willernie	55090	Lakes)	55750
Vernon Center	56090	Wawina	55736	Williams	56686	Wyoming	55092
Veseli	55046	Wayzata	55391	Willmar	56201	Yorktown (Part of Edina)	55435
Vesta	56292	Wayzata Boulevard (Part		Willmar State Hospital	56201	Young America	55394†
Victoria	55386	of St. Louis Park)	55416	Willow Creek	56010		55397*
Viking	56760	Wealthwood	56431	Willow River	55795	Yucatan	55943
Village North Shopping		Weaver	55910	Wilmington	55921	Zemple	56636
Center (Part of		Weber	55056	Wilmont	56185	Zerkel	56621
Brooklyn Park)	55429	Webster	55088	Wilno	56142	Zim	55799
Villard	56385	Wegdahl	56265	Wilpen (Part of Hibbing)	55746	Zimmerman	55398
Vineland	56359	Welch	55089	Wilson	55987	Zumbra Heights (Part of	
Vining	56588	Welcome	56181	Wilton (Beltrami County)	56687	Victoria)	55386
Viola	55934	Wells	56097	Wilton (Waseca County)	56093	Zumbro Falls	55991
Virginia	55777†	Weme	56634	Windom	56101	Zumbrota	55992

* Area Zip Code   **† Post Office Boxes**

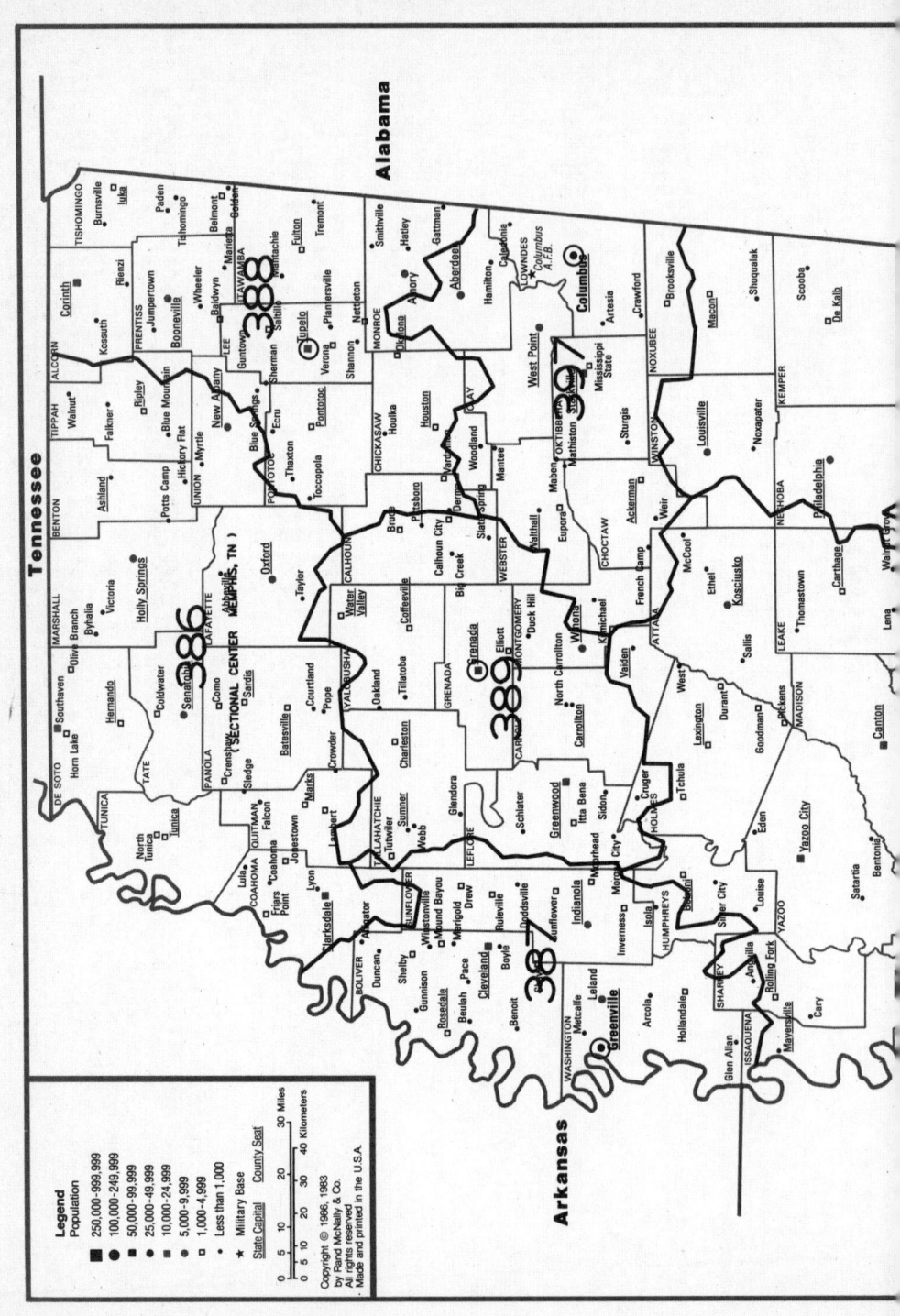

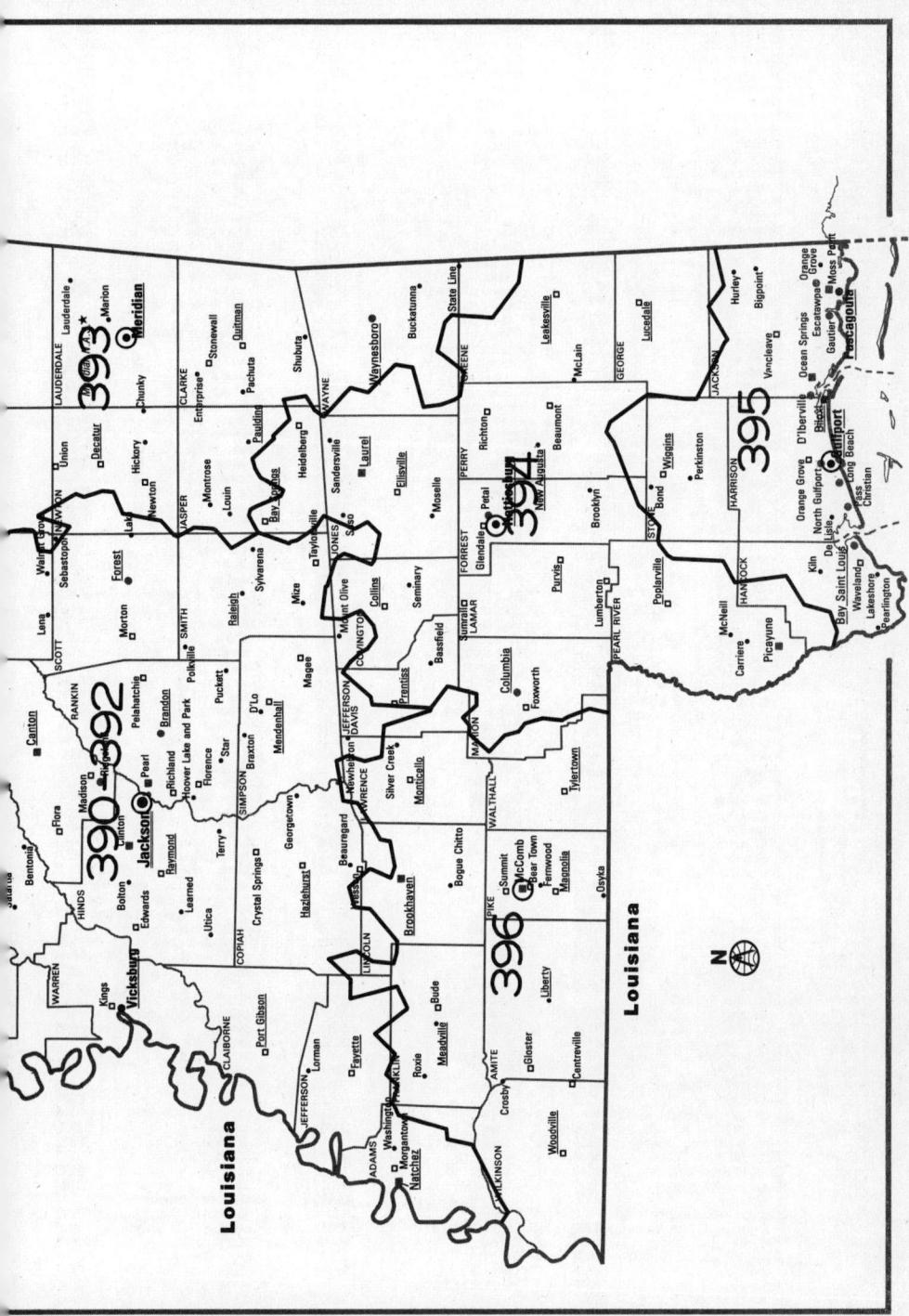

Name	ZIP
Abbeville	38601
Abbott	39773
Aberdeen	39730
Ackerman	39735
Acona	39095
Adams	39175
Adaton	39759
Addie	38744
Agricola	39452
A H Mccoy Federal Bldg (Part of Jackson)	39269
Airey	39574
Albin	38966
Alcorn State University	39096
Algoma	38820
Allen	39083
Alligator	38720
Alpine	38849
Altitude	38829
Alva	38925
Amory	38821
Anchor	39776
Anchorage	39194
Anding	39040
Anguilla	38721
Anse	39073
Ansley	39558
Antioch	39440
Apple Ridge (Part of Jackson)	39204
Arcola	38722
Ariel	39638
Arkabutla	38602
Arlington (Lincoln County)	39629
Arlington (Neshoba County)	39350
Arm	39663
Arnold Line	39402
Artesia	39736
Ashland	38603
Askew	38621
Athens	39730
Atlanta	39776
Atway	38635
Auburn (Lee County)	38801
Auburn (Lincoln County)	39666
Austin	38676
Avalon	38912
Avera	39451
Avon	38723
Bailey	39320
Baird	38751
Baker	38652
Bald Hill	38652
Baldwyn	38824
Ballard	39046
Ballardsville	38801
Ballentine	38621
Ball Ground	39156
Baltzer	38732
Banks	38664
Banner	38913
Barlow	39083
Barnes	39051
Barnesville	38109
Barnett	39347
Barr	38668
Barrontown	39465
Bartahatchie	39740
Barth	39470
Barto	39648
Barton (George County)	39452
Barton (Marshall County)	38017
Basic	39330
Basin	39452
Bassfield	39421
Batesville	38606
Batson	39401
Battlefield (Hinds County)	39204
Battle Field (Newton County)	39325
Battles	39362
Baugh	38669
Baxter	39338
Baxterville	39455
Bayland	39194
Bay Saint Louis	39520-22
	39529

For specific Bay Saint Louis Zip Codes call (601) 467-5788, or your local postmaster.

Name	ZIP
Bayside Park	39520
Bay Springs	39422
Beacon Hill	38652
Beans Ferry	38843
Bear Town	39648
Beasley	39755
Beatline	39350
Beatrice	39330
Beatty	39176
Beaumont	39423
Beauregard	39191
Becker	38825
Beech Springs	38866
Beechwood	39645
Beelake	39169
Belden	38826
Belen	38609
Bellefontaine	39737
Belle Isle	39572
Belleville	39462
Bellewood	38754
Bells School	39759
Belmont	38827
Belzoni	39038
Benjoe	39456
Benndale	39456
Benoit	38725
Benson	39437
Bentley	39751
Bent Oak	39701
Benton	39039
Bentonia	39040
Benwood	38922
Berclair	38941
Berwick	39645
Bethany	38849
Betheden	39339
Bethel	39345
Bethlehem (Marshall County)	38659
Bethlehem (Pontotoc County)	38863
Bethsaida	39350
Bett	38618
Beulah (Bolivar County)	38726
Beulah (Newton County)	39337
Beulah Hubbard	39337
Bewelcome	39638
Bexley	39452
Bigbee	38821
Bigbee Valley	39738
Big Creek	38914
Biggersville	38834
Big Level	39573
Bigpoint	39581
Billups	39701
Biloxi	39530-35

For specific Biloxi Zip Codes call (601) 432-0311, or your local postmaster.

Name	ZIP
Binford	39730
Binnsville	39358
Birmingham Ridge	38828
Bissell	38801
Black Bayou Junction	38928
Black Hawk	38923
Blackjack	39759
Blackland	38829
Blackwater (Kemper County)	39326
Blackwater (Lafayette County)	38685
Blaine	38778
Blair	38849
Blakely	39180
Blanton	39159
Bloody Springs	38827
Bloomfield (Kemper County)	39328
Bloomfield (Neshoba County)	39350
Blue Hills	39144
Blue Lake	38737
Blue Mountain	38610
Blue Springs	38828
Bluff Springs (Kemper County)	39328
Bluff Springs (Panola County)	38666
Bobo (Coahoma County)	38614
Bobo (Quitman County)	38646
Boggan Bend	38849
Bogue Chitto (Kemper County)	39350
Bogue Chitto (Lincoln County)	39629
Boice	39367
Bolatusha	39160
Bolivar	38725
Bolton	39041
Bond (Neshoba County)	39350
Bond (Stone County)	39577
Bon Homme	39401
Bonita (Part of Meridian)	39301
Boon	39339
Boone	38614
Booneville	38829
Bothwell	39476
Bounds Crossroads	35582
Bourbon	38756
Bovina	39180
Bowdre	38664
Bowling Green	39063
Bowman	38618
Boyer	38751
Boyette	39160
Boyle	38730
Bradley	39759
Branch	39117
Brandon	39042-43
	39047

For specific Brandon Zip Codes call (601) 825-2552, or your local postmaster.

Name	ZIP
Branyan	38828
Brasfield	39096
Braxton	39044
Brazil	38963
Brewer (Clarke County)	39355
Brewer (Lee County)	38868
Brewer (Perry County)	39476
Bright	38632
Bristers Store	39641
Brockton (Part of Meridian)	39301
Brody	38603
Brookhaven	39601
Brook Hollow	39212
Brooklyn	39425
Brooks	38737
Brooksville	39739
Brownfield	38683
Browning	38930
Brownsville	39041
Brown Town	39452
Brozville	39095
Bruce	38915
Brunswick	39180
Bryant	38922
Buchannan	38863
Buckatunna	39322
Buckhorn	38864
Bude	39630
Buena Vista (Chickasaw County)	38851
Buena Vista (Tippah County)	38663
Buena Vista Lakes	38632
Bunker Hill	39429
Bunkley	39653
Burgess	38655
Burns	39153
Burnside	39350
Burnsville	38833
Burrell	38628
Burtons	38829
Bush	39149
Busy Corner	39638
Butler	39169
Byhalia	38611
Byram	39272
Cadamy	38876
Cadaretta	38929
Caesar	39466
Caile	38754
Cairo	38873
Caledonia	39740
Calhoun (Jones County)	39440
Calhoun (Newton County)	39345
Calhoun City	38916
Calyx	39361
Cambridge	38601
Camden	39045
Cameron	39146
Cameta	39159
Campbell (Part of Ripley)	38663
Canaan	38603
Candlestick (Part of Jackson)	39212
Candlestick Park (Part of Jackson)	39212
Cannonsburg	39120
Canton	39046
Cardsville	38858
Carlisle	39086
Carlos	39191
Carmack	39176
Carmichael (Clarke County)	39360
Carmichael (Perry County)	39423
Carnes	39455
Carolina	38858
Carpenter	39086
Carriere	39426
Carrollton	38917
Carson	39427
Carter	39194
Carterville (Part of Petal)	39465
Carthage	39051
Cary	39054
Cascilla	38920
Caseyville	39191
Cato	39042
Cayce	38017
Cayuga	39175
Cedarbluff	39741
Cedar Hill (Madison County)	39071
Cedar Hill (Montgomery County)	38925
Cedars	39180
Cedarview	38654
Center (Attala County)	39090
Center (Union County)	38652
Center Hill	39307
Center Ridge (Newton County)	39337
Center Ridge (Smith County)	39168
Center Ridge (Winston County)	39339
Centerville	38855
Central Academy	38606
Centralgrove	38858
Centreville	39631
Chalybeate	38683
Champion Hill	39066
Chapel Hill	39175
Charleston	38921
Chatawa	39632
Chatham	38731
Cheraw	39483
Cherrycreek	38828
Chester	39735
Chesterville	38801
Chicora	39322
Chiwapa	38863
Choctaw (Bolivar County)	38773
Choctaw (Jones County)	39440
Chulahoma	38635
Chunky	39323
Church Hill	39120
Clack	38664
Clara	39324
Claremont	38614
Clarksburg	39117
Clarksdale	38614
Clarkson	39752
Clay	38843
Clayrysville	38663
Clayton	38626
Clayton Village	39759
Claytown	39339
Clem	39474
Cleo	39440
Clermont Harbor	39558
Cleveland (Bolivar County)	38732-33

For specific Cleveland Zip Codes call (601) 843-4031, or your local postmaster.

Name	ZIP
Cleveland (Kemper County)	39328
Clifton	39074
Cliftonville	39739
Clinton	39056*
	39060†
Cloverdale	39120
Clover Hill	38645
Cloverleaf Mall (Part of Hattiesburg)	39401
Coahoma	38617
Coats	39119
Cobbs	39601
Cobbville	39046
Cockrum	38632
Coffeeville	38922
Cohay	39153
Coila	38923
Colby	39194
Coldwater (Neshoba County)	39350
Coldwater (Tate County)	38618
Coles	39633
College (Part of Columbus)	39701
College Hill	38655
College Hill Sta	38655
Collins	39428
Collinsville	39325
Colonial (Part of Jackson)	39211
Colony Town	38941
Colsub (Part of Amory)	38821
Columbia	39429

* Area Zip Code   † Post Office Boxes

	ZIP
Columbus	39701-05
For specific Columbus Zip Codes call (601) 328-6171, or your local postmaster.	
Columbus Air Force Base	39701
Commerce	38664
Como	38619
Concord	38652
Conehatta	39057
Conway	39051
Cooksville	39341
Cooperville	39117
Coosa	39051
Corinth	38834
Cornersville	38633
Corrona	38849
Cotton Plant	38610
Cottonville	38618
Counts	38614
County Line	39362
Courthouse (Part of Gulfport)	39501
Courtland	38620
Cowart	38921
Coxburg	39095
Coxs Ferry	39041
Coy	39354
Craigside	38930
Craig Springs	39769
Crandall	39355
Crane Creek	39573
Cranfield	39661
Crawford	39743
Crenshaw	38621
Crockett	38668
Crosby	39633
Crossgates (Part of Brandon)	39042
Crossroad	39051
Crossroads (George County)	39452
Crossroads (Neshoba County)	39350
Crossroads (Pearl River County)	39470
Cross Roads (Rankin County)	39145
Cross Roads (Tishomingo County)	38852
Crossroads (Washington County)	38703
Crotts	39437
Crowder	38622
Cruger	38924
Crupp	39194
Crystal Springs	39059
Cuba	38834
Cub Lake	38632
Cuevas	39571
Cumberland	39750
Curtis Station	38606
Cybur	39466
Cynthia	39206
Dahomey	38725
Daisy-Vestry	39573
Daleville	39326
Damascus (Kemper County)	39328
Damascus (Scott County)	39189
Dancy	39751
Daniel	39151
Darbun	39643
Darden	38650
Darling	38623
Darlove	38748
Darracott	39730
Darrington	39633
Davenport	38614
Davis	39046
Days	38641
Deans Corner	38641
Deasonville	39179
Decatur	39327
Deemer	39350
Deemer Station	39320
Deep Creek	39425
Deerbrook	39739
Deeson	38740
De Kalb	39328
De Lay	38655
De Lisle	39571
Delta	38621
Delta City	39061
Delta Drive (Part of Jackson)	39213
Delta State University (Part of Cleveland)	38733
Denham	39367
Denmark	38655

	ZIP
Dennis	38838
Dennis Settlement	39092
Dentontown	38916
Dentville	39086
Deovolente	39038
Derby	39470
Derma	38839
De Soto	39360
Deweese	39350
Dexter	39667
Diamondhead	39525
D'Iberville	39532
Dinsmore	39341
Divide	39654
Dixie	39401
Dixie Pine	39401
Dixon	39350
D'Lo	39062
Doddsville	38736
Doloroso	39669
Donegal	39669
Doolittle	39345
Dorsey	38843
Doskie	38852
Dossville	39051
Dover (Neshoba County)	39365
Dover (Yazoo County)	39040
Dowdville	39350
Downtown (Part of Gulfport)	39501
Downtown (Part of Jackson)	39201
	39205
	39207
	39215
	39225
For specific Downtown Zip Codes call (601) 968-0520, or your local postmaster.	
Downtown (Part of Tupelo)	38801
Downtown (Part of Vicksburg)	39181
Drew	38737
Dry Creek	39428
Dubard	38901
Dubbs	38626
Dublin	38739
Duck Hill	38925
Duffee	39337
Dumas	38625
Duncan	38740
Dundee	38626
Dunleith	38756
Durant	39063
Dwiggins	38737
Dwyer	38778
Eagle Lake	39180
Earlygrove	38642
East Aberdeen	39730
Eastabuchie	39436
Eastfork	39664
East Heights (Part of Tupelo)	38801
East Hillsboro	39074
Eastlawn (Part of Pascagoula)	39569
East Lincoln	39601
East Moss Point (Part of Moss Point)	39563
Eastport	38852
East Side	39476
East Tupelo (Part of Tupelo)	38801
Eatonville	39401
Ebenezer	39095
Ecru	38841
Eddiceton	39647
Eden	39194
Edgewater Mall (Part of Biloxi)	39532
Edinburg	39051
Edwards	39066
Eggville	38801
Egremont	39159
Egypt (Chickasaw County)	38860
Egypt (Holmes County)	38924
Electric Mills	39358
Elizabeth	38756
Ellard	38915
Elliott	38926
Ellistown	38838
Ellisville	39437
Ellisville Junction	39437
Elsie	38878
Elton (Part of Jackson)	39212
Elwood	39355
Eminence	39479

	ZIP
Emory	39095
Endville	38828
Energy	39301
Enid	38927
Enon	39641
Enondale	39352
Enterprise (Amite County)	39645
Enterprise (Clarke County)	39330
Enterprise (Lincoln County)	39601
Enterprise (Union County)	38650
Enzor	39301
Errata	39440
Erwin	38744
Escatawpa	39552
Eset	39362
Eskridge	38925
Essex	38623
Estes	39339
Estesmill	39051
Estill	38748
Ethel	39067
Etta	38627
Eucutta	39360
Eudora	38632
Eunice	38638
Eupora	39744
Eureka Springs	38620
Evansville (Tate County)	38618
Evansville (Tunica County)	38676
Everett	39114
Evergreen	38843
Expose	39429
Fairfield	38828
Fairground	39350
Fairhaven	38654
Fairhill	39361
Fairlane (Part of Columbus)	39701
Fair Oaks Springs	39601
Fair River	39601
Fairview (Itawamba County)	38847
Fairview (Sunflower County)	38751
Falcon	38628
Falkner	38629
Fame	39744
Fannin	39042
Farmhaven	39046
Farmington	38834
Farrell	38630
Fayette	39069
Fenton	39571
Fentress	39735
Fenwick	39120
Fernwood	39635
Fikestown	39092
Fitler	39070
Fitzhugh	38737
Flora	39071
Florence	39073
Flowerdale (Part of Tupelo)	38801
Floweree	39156
Flowood	39208
Floyd	38603
Fondren (Part of Jackson)	39216
Fontainebleau	39564
Fords Creek	39470
Fordyke	39039
Forest	39074
Forestdale	39365
Forest Grove	39051
Forest Hill (Part of Jackson)	39212
Forkville	39117
Fort Adams	39669
Fort Stephens	39320
Four Corners	39090
Four Mile	39038
Foxworth	39483
Franklin	39661
Frankstown	38824
Freeny	39051
Freerun	39194
Freetrade	39051
Freeze Corner	38632
French Camp	39745
French Store	39073
Friars Point	38631
Friendship (Lincoln County)	39601
Friendship (Pontotoc County)	38841
Frog Island	38801
Frostbridge	39367
Fruitland Park	39577
Fugate	39039

	ZIP
Fulton	38843
Furrs	38863
Futheyville	38901
Gallman	39077
Gandsi	39479
Garden City	39661
Garlandville	39345
Gaston	38865
Gatesville	39059
Gatewood	38922
Gattman	38844
Gault	38655
Gautier	39553
Geeslin Corner	38901
Geeville	38829
Geneill	38756
General Mail Facility (Part of Jackson)	39205
Georgetown	39078
Gholson	39354
Gibson	39730
Gift	38834
Giles	39358
Gill	39051
Gillsburg	39657
Gitano	39168
Glade	39440
Glancy	39083
Glen	38846
Glen Allan	38744
Glendale	39401
Glendora	38928
Glenfield (Part of New Albany)	38652
Glenville	38619
Glenwild	38901
Gloster	39638
Glover	38680
Gluckstadt	39110
Golden	38847
Golden Grove	39365
Goldfield	38737
Gooden Lake	39038
Good Hope (Leake County)	39094
Good Hope (Neshoba County)	39350
Good Hope (Perry County)	39476
Goodman	39079
Goodwater	39366
Goodyear (Part of Picayune)	39466
Gore Springs	38929
Goshen Springs	39042
Goss	39429
Grace	38745
Grady	39744
Graham	38824
Grand Gulf	39150
Grange	39140
Grange Hall	39180
Grapeland	38725
Gravel Hill	38930
Graves	38828
Gravestown	38663
Greenbrier Park	39466
Greenfield	39042
Greenfield Addition (Part of Greenville)	38701
Green Grove	38767
Greenland	39365
Greenville	38701-04
For specific Greenville Zip Codes call (601) 335-4523, or your local postmaster.	
Greenville Mall (Part of Greenville)	38701
Greenville North (Part of Greenville)	38701
Greenwood (Itawamba County)	38843
Greenwood (Leflore County)	38930
Greenwood Springs	38848
Grenada	38901*
	38902†
Griffith	39741
Gulde	39042
Gulf Hills	39564
Gulf Hills Country Club	39564
Gulf Park Estates	39564
Gulfport	39501-07
For specific Gulfport Zip Codes call (601) 831-5400, or your local postmaster.	
Gum Grove	39169
Gums	38922
Gum Springs	39074

* Area Zip Code   † Post Office Boxes

	ZIP		ZIP		ZIP		ZIP
Gunnison	38746	Houlka	38850	Lackey	39730	Louin	39338
Guntown	38849	House	39365	Lafayette Springs	38655	Louise	39097
Gwin (Part of Tchula)	39169	Houston	38851	Lake	39092	Louisville	39339
Gwinville	39140	Howard	39095	Lake Center	38659	Love	38632
Hale	39360	Howell	39452	Lake City (Prentiss		Loyd	38878
Halltown	38849	Howison	39574	County)	38829	Loyd Star	39601
Hamburg	39661	Hoy	39440	Lake City (Yazoo County)	39194	Lucas	39474
Hamilton	39746	Hub	38429	Lake Como	39422	Lucedale	39452
Hampton	38744	Hubbard	39066	Lake Cormorant	38641	Lucern	39365
Handle	39339	Hudsonville	38635	Lakeland (Part of		Lucien	39601
Handsboro (Part of		Humber	38614	Richland)	39218	Luckney	39208
Gulfport)	39501	Huntsville	39745	Lake of Hills	38632	Ludlow	39098
Handy Corner	38654	Hurley	39555	Lakeshore	39558	Lula	38644
Hard Cash	39038	Hurricane	38863	Lake View	38680	Lumberton	39455
Hardy	38901	Hurricane Creek	39301	Lamar	38642	Lurand	38614
Harleston	39452	Hushpuckena	38774	Lamar Park	39401	Lux	39401
Harmontown	38619	Improve	39429	Lambert	38643	Lyman	39503
Harmony	39355	Increase	39301	Lamkin	39166	Lynchburg	38109
Harperville	39080	Inda	39573	Lamont	38755	Lynn Creek	39739
Harriston	39081	Independence (Scott		Lampton	39429	Lynville	39354
Harrisville	39082	County)	39117	Landon	39503	Lyon	38645
Harvey (Part of Petal)	39465	Independence (Tate		Langford	39042	Maben	39750
Hathorn	39429	County)	38638	Langsdale	39360	McAdams	39107
Hatley	38821	Indian Hills	38866	Larue	39565	McBride	39144
Hattiesburg	39401-07	Indianola	38751	Latimer	39565	McCall Creek	39647
For specific Hattiesburg Zip		Indian Springs	39401	Latonia	39452	McCallum	39401
Codes call (601) 268-0888, or		Industrial	39466	Lauderdale	39335	McCarley	38943
your local postmaster.		Ingomar	38652	Laurel	39440-42	McComb	39648
Hayes Crossing	38666	Ingrams Mill	38611	For specific Laurel Zip Codes		McCondy	38854
Hays	39057	Inverness	38753	call (601) 425-1408, or your		McCool	39108
Hazel	39092	Isola	38754	local postmaster.		McCrary	39701
Hazlehurst	39083	Itta Bena	38941	Laurelhill	39350	McCutcheon	38722
Heads	38756	Iuka	38852	Lawrence	39336	Mc Donald (Leake	
Heathman	38751	Jacinto	38865	Laws Hill	38685	County)	39094
Hebron (Jefferson Davis		Jack	39175	Leaf	39456	McDonald (Neshoba	
County)	39140	Jackson	39201-98	Leakesville	39451	County)	39365
Hebron (Jones County)	39168	For specific Jackson Zip Codes		Learned	39154	Macedonia (Forrest	
Heidelberg	39439	call (601) 968-0572, or your		Lebanon (Hinds County)	39154	County)	39401
Helena	39581	local postmaster.		Lebanon (Marshall		Macedonia (Lee County)	38801
Helm	38756	Jackson Mall (Part of		County)	38659	Macedonia (Union	
Henderson's Point (Part of		Jackson)	39213	Lee Donald	39366	County)	38650
Pass Christian)	39571	Jackson Square (Part of		Leedy	38833	Macel	38950
Hendrix	39747	Jackson)	39204	Leesburg	39117	McElveen	39666
Henleyfield	39426	Jackson State University		Leesdale	39661	McHenry	39561
Herbert Springs	39325	(Part of Jackson)	39217	Leeville	39401	McLain	39456
Hermanville	39086	Jago	38671	Lefleur (Part of Jackson)	39211	McLaurin	39401
Hernando	38632	Jaketown	39038	Leflore	38940	McLaurin Heights (Part of	
Hero	39345	James	38748	Leigh Mall (Part of		Pearl)	39208
Hesterville	39192	Jamestown	39483	Columbus)	39701	McLeod	39341
Heucks Retreat	39191	Janice	39425	Leland	38756	McMillan	39339
Hickory	39332	Jayess	39641	Lemon	39074	McNair	39069
Hickory Flat	38633	Jeannette	39120	Lena	39094	McNeal	39338
Hideaway Hills	38666	Jeff Davis	39180	Lessley	39669	McNeill	39457
Hidi	39166	Jefferson	38917	Le Tourneau	39180	Macon	39341
Higgins	39482	Jeffries	38626	Leverett	38920	McSwain	39476
High Hill	39350	Jenkins	39437	Lewisburg	38654	McVille	39090
Highlandale	38952	Jericho	38824	Lexie	39667	Madden	39109
High Point	39339	Johns	39042	Lexington	39095	Madison	39110*
Hightown	38834	Johnson	39437	Liberty (Amite County)	39645		39130†
Hillhouse	38720	Johnston	39666	Liberty (Kemper County)	39328	Madisonville	39046
Hillman	39451	Jonathan	39451	Lightsey	39440	Magee	39111
Hillsboro	39087	Jonestown (Coahoma		Lillian	39074	Magnolia	39652
Hillsdale	39470	County)	38639	Linn	38736	Mahned	39462
Hinchcliff	38646	Jonestown (Yazoo		Linwood (Neshoba		Main (Part of Meridian)	39302
Hinkle	38865	County)	39194	County)	39365	Malone	38685
Hintonville	39423	Jug Fork	38828	Linwood (Yazoo County)	39179	Malvina	38769
Hinze	39108	Jumpertown	38829	Little Creek	39423	Mannassa	39355
Hiram	38963	Junction City	39355	Little Italy	39092	Mantachie	38855
Hiwannee	39367	Kalem	39117	Little Rock	39337	Mantee	39751
Hobo Station	38829	Keirn	38924	Little Texas	38676	Marcella	39169
Hohenlinden	39751	Kellis Store	39354	Little Yazoo	39040	Marianna	38635
Holcomb	38940	Kelona	39366	Litton	38773	Marie	38751
Holcut	38852	Kendrick	38834	Lizana	39503	Marietta	38856
Hollandale	38748	Keownville	38652	Lobdell	38726	Marion	39342
Hollis	38878	Kewanee	39364	Lobutcha	39108	Maris Town (Part of	
Holly Bluff	39088	Key Field (Part of		Loch Leven	39669	Canton)	39046
Holly Grove	38954	Meridian)	39301	Locke Station	38606	Markette	38655
Holly Ridge	38749	Kilmichael	39747	Lockhart	39335	Markham	38761
Holly Springs	38634†	Kiln	39556	Lodi (Humphreys County)	39166	Marks	38646
	38635*	King and Anderson	38614	Lodi (Montgomery		Mars Hill	39666
Hollywood	38676	Kings	39180	County)	39767	Martin	39325
Holmesville	39648	Kingston	39120	Lombardy	38774	Martin Bluff	39553
Holts Spur	38833	Kinlock	38751	Long	38756	Martinsville	39083
Homewood	39074	Kipling	39661	Long Beach	39560	Martintown	38652
Homochitto	39638	Kirby	39661	Longino	39350	Martinville	39114
Honey Island	39038	Kirkville	38843	Long Lake (Coahoma		Marydell	39051
Hoover Lake and Park	39073	Kittrell	39423	County)	38617	Mashulaville	39341
Hope	39350	Klem	39074	Long Lake (Warren		Matherville	39360
Hopedale	39113	Klondike	39320	County)	39180	Mathiston	39752
Hopewell (Benton County)	38611	Knobtown	39362	Longshot	38773	Mattson	38758
Hopewell (Copiah County)	39059	Knoxo	39667	Longtown	38665	Maxie	39425
Hopoca	39051	Knoxville	39661	Longview (Oktibbeha		Maybank	39401
Horn Lake	38637	Kokomo	39643	County)	39759	Maybell	39437
Horseshoe (Holmes		Kola	39428	Longview (Pontotoc		Mayersville	39113
County)	39169	Kolola Springs	39740	County)	38863	Mayhew	39753
Horse Shoe (Scott		Kosciusko	39090	Looxahoma	38668	Mayton	39042
County)	39189	Kossuth	38834	Lorena	39074	Maywood	38654
Hortontown	38863	Kroolo (Part of Moss		Lorenzen	39159	Meadville	39653
Hot Coffee	39428	Point)	39563	Lorman	39096	Mechanicsburg	39040

	ZIP
Meehan	39301
Meeks	38924
Melba	39482
Meltonville	39046
Memphis	38680
Mendenhall	39114
Meridian	39301-07

For specific Meridian Zip Codes call (601) 693-2581, or your local postmaster.

	ZIP
Meridian Naval Air Station	39309
Meridian Station	39309
Merigold	38759
Merit	39114
Merrill	39452
Mesa	39667
Metcalfe	38760
Metrocenter (Part of Jackson)	39209
Meyers	39401
Michigan City	38647
Midnight	39115
Midway (Copiah County)	39191
Midway (Hinds County)	39170
Midway (Leake County)	39051
Midway (Scott County)	39074
Midway (Tishomingo County)	38852
Midway (Yazoo County)	39039
Mileston	39169
Millard	39470
Mill Creek (Jones County)	39440
Mill Creek (Pearl River County)	39426
Mill Creek (Rankin County)	39042
Millcreek (Winston County)	39339
Mill Creek Cabin Area	38852
Miller	38654
Millington	39358
Millsaps College (Part of Jackson)	39210
Mill Town (Part of Canton)	39046
Mimms	38606
Mineral Wells	38648
Mingo	38873
Minter City	38944
Missionary	39356
Mississippi Choctaw Indian Reservation	39350
Mississippi City (Part of Gulfport)	39501
Mississippi College (Part of Clinton)	39058
Mississippi State	39762
Mississippi Valley State University	38941
Mitchell	38663
Mize	39116
Money	38945
Monroe	39653
Monterey	39073
Monte Vista	39744
Montgomery	39191
Monticello	39654
Montpelier	39754
Montrose	39338
Moon	38662
Moores Mill	38838
Mooreville	38857
Moorhead	38761
Morgan City	38946
Morgans	39170
Morgantown (Adams County)	39120
Morgantown (Marion County)	39484
Morgantown (Oktibbeha County)	39769
Morning Star	39066
Morriston	39401
Morton	39117
Moscow	39328
Moselle	39459
Moss	39460
Moss Point	39562-63

For specific Moss Point Zip Codes call (601) 475-3951, or your local postmaster.

	ZIP
Mossy Lake	38959
Mound Bayou	38762
Mound City (Bolivar County)	38726
Mound City (Union County)	38828
Mount Carmel	39474
Mount Nebo	39328

	ZIP
Mount Olive (Covington County)	39119
Mount Olive (Franklin County)	39653
Mount Olive (Jones County)	39440
Mount Pleasant (Itawamba County)	38876
Mount Pleasant (Marshall County)	38649
Mount Vernon	38801
Mount Zion	39111
Movella	39452
Muldon	39730
Mullins Store	38655
Murphy	38748
Murry	38663
Muskegon	39092
Myrick	39440
Myrleville	39039
Myrtle	38650
Nancy	39366
Nason	38940
Natchez	39120-22

For specific Natchez Zip Codes call (601) 442-4361, or your local postmaster.

	ZIP
National Cemetery (Part of Vicksburg)	39180
Necaise	39573
Neely	39461
Nellieburg	39307
Nesbit	38651
Neshoba	39365
Nettleton	38858
Nevada	39041
New Albany	38652
New Augusta	39462
New Byram	39212
New Canaan	38603
New Fitler	39070
New Garden	38618
New Harmony	38828
New Hebron	39140
New Hope	39702
Newman	39066
Newmans	39180
Newmans Grove	39154
Newport (Attala County)	39160
Newport (DeSoto County)	38641
New Salem	38843
New Sight	39601
New Site	38859
Newton	39345
New Town	38668
New Wren	39730
Nichols	38959
Nicholson	39463
Nida	39169
Nitta Yuma	38763
Nixon (Humphreys County)	39115
Nixon (Pontotoc County)	38863
Nod	39039
Nola	39665
Norfield	39629
Norfolk	38641
Norris	39074
North (Hinds County)	39206
North (Lauderdale County)	39305
North Bay (Part of D'Iberville)	39532
North Bend	39350
North Carrollton	38947
North Crossroads	38852
North Greenville (Part of Greenville)	38701
North Gulfport	39503
North Haven	38652
North Long Beach (Part of Long Beach)	39560
Northpark Mall (Part of Ridgeland)	39157
North Tunica	38676
Northwest Junior College (Part of Senatobia)	38668
Norton	38663
Noxapater	39346
Oak Bowery	39437
Oak Grove (Holmes County)	39169
Oak Grove (Jones County)	39437
Oak Grove (Lamar County)	39401
Oak Grove (Perry County)	39423
Oakland (Itawamba County)	38843
Oakland (Pike County)	39666

	ZIP
Oakland (Yalobusha County)	38948
Oakley	39154
Oak Ridge	39180
Oak Vale	39656
Obadiah	39320
Ocean Springs	39564-66

For specific Ocean Springs Zip Codes call (601) 875-4431, or your local postmaster.

	ZIP
Ocobla	39350
Ofahoma	39051
Oil City	39040
Okahola	39475
Oklahoma	38917
Okolona	38860
Oktoc	39759
Old Cairo	38829
Old Dominion	38946
Oldenburg	39661
Oldham	38852
Old Hamilton	39746
Old Houlka	38850
Old Red Star	39601
Old Union	38868
Olive Branch	38654
Oloh	39482
Oma	39654
Omega	39169
Onward	39159
Ora	39428
Orange	39347
Orange Grove (Harrison County)	39503
Orange Grove (Jackson County)	39581
Orange Hill	39041
O'Reilly	38730
Orwood	38655
Osborn	39759
Osborne Creek	38829
Osyka	39657
Ovett	39464
Owens Wells	39095
Oxberry	38940
Oxford (Amite County)	39638
Oxford (Lafayette County)	38655
Ozona	39426
Pace	38764
Pachuta	39347
Paden	38873
Palmer	39401
Palmetto	38801
Panther Burn	38765
Parchman	38738
Parham	38848
Paris	38949
Parks	38652
Parksplace	38619
Pascagoula	39567-69

For specific Pascagoula Zip Codes call (601) 762-5722, or your local postmaster.

	ZIP
Pascagoula River Estates	39456
Pass Christian	39571
Patosi	39194
Pattison	39144
Paul	38920
Paulding	39348
Paulette	39341
Paynes	38920
Pearl (Rankin County)	39208
Pearl (Simpson County)	39073
Pearl City (Part of Pearl)	39208
Pearlington	39572
Pearl River	39350
Pearson	39208
Pecan	39581
Pecan Grove	39437
Pelahatchie	39145
Penantly	39356
Pendorff	39440
Penns Station	39743
Penton	38664
Peoples	38663
Peoria	39645
Percy	38748
Perdue	39337
Perkinston	39573
Perrytown	39633
Perth	39069
Perthshire	38746
Petal	39465
Peteet	38946
Peyton	39144
Pheba	39755
Philadelphia	39350
Philipp	38950

	ZIP
Phillipstown	38954
Phoenix	39040
Piave	39476
Picayune	39466
Pickens	39146
Pickwick	39483
Pierce Crossroads	39194
Piggtown	39094
Piketown	39074
Pinckneyville	39669
Pinebluff	39751
Pinebur	39429
Pinedale	38627
Pine Flat (Lafayette County)	38965
Pine Flat (Tishomingo County)	38852
Pine Grove (Benton County)	38633
Pine Grove (Lamar County)	39475
Pine Grove (Lee County)	38868
Pine Grove (Tippah County)	38829
Pine Ridge (Adams County)	39120
Pine Ridge (Lamar County)	39475
Pine Springs	39301
Pine Valley	38965
Pineview	39440
Pineville	39074
Piney Woods	39148
Pinola	39149
Pisgah (Greene County)	39452
Pisgah (Prentiss County)	38865
Pisgah (Rankin County)	39042
Pistol Ridge	39455
Pittman	39483
Pittsboro	38951
Plainview (Part of Richland)	39218
Plantersville	38862
Plattsburg	39350
Pleasant Grove	38657
Pleasant Hill (Copiah County)	39668
Pleasant Hill (DeSoto County)	38651
Pleasant Hill (Union County)	38652
Pleasant Ridge (Jones County)	39440
Pleasant Ridge (Union County)	38625
Plum Point	38671
Pluto	39169
Poagville	38618
Pocahontas	39072
Pokal	39140
Polfrey	39564
Polkville	39117
Pollock	38751
Pond	39669
Ponta	39301
Pontotoc	38863
Poolville	38650
Pope	38658
Poplar Corners	38680
Poplar Creek	39747
Poplar Springs (Holmes County)	39063
Poplar Springs (Montgomery County)	39747
Poplar Springs (Newton County)	39345
Poplarville	39470
Porterville	39352
Port Gibson	39150
Posey Mound	38623
Post	39325
Potts Camp	38659
Powell	38626
Powers	39440
Prairie	39756
Prairie Point	39341
Prentiss	39474
Presidential Hills (Part of Jackson)	39213
Preston	39354
Pricedale	39666
Prichard	38676
Prince Chapel	39354
Priscilla	38701
Prismatic	39320
Progress (Jefferson Davis County)	39474
Progress (Perry County)	39423
Progress (Pike County)	39648

* Area Zip Code   † Post Office Boxes

	ZIP		ZIP		ZIP		ZIP
Prospect	39057	Sabino	38646	Smiths	39066	Thomastown	39171
Puckett	39151	Sabougla	38916	Smithville	38870	Thomasville	39073
Pulaski	39152	St. Ann	39051	Smyrna (Attala County)	39090	Thompson	39664
Pumpkin Center	38652	St. Martin	39533	Smyrna (Copiah County)	39083	Thompsonville	39059
Purvis	39475	Salem (Leake County)	39189	Snell	39301	Thorn	38851
Pyland	38851	Salem (Walthall County)	39667	Snow Lake Shores	38603	Thornton	39169
Quentin	39647	Sallis	39160	Somerville	38944	Thrashers	38829
Quincy	38848	Saltillo	38866	Sonora	38851	Three Rivers	39581
Quitman	39355	Sanatorium	39112	Sontag	39665	Thyatira	38668
Quito	38941	Sandersville	39477	Soso	39480	Tibbee	39773
Quofaloma	39169	Sand Hill (Copiah County)	39191	South Amory (Part of		Tibbs	38670
Rainey	39459	Sand Hill (Greene County)	39476	Amory)	38821	Tie Plant	38901
Raleigh	39153	Sand Hill (Jones County)	39437	Southaven	38671	Tilden	38843
Ramsey Springs	39573	Sandhill (Rankin County)	39161	Southern (Part of		Tillatoba	38961
Randolph	38864	Sandpoint	39153	Hattiesburg)	39401	Tillman	39150
Rankin	39042	Sandtown	39350	South McComb (Part of		Tilton	39654
Ratliff	38855	Sandy Hook	39478	McComb)	39648	Tinsley	39173
Rawls Springs	39401	Sanford	39479	South Mississipi		Tiplersville	38674
Raworth	39117	Sapa	39744	Correctional Institution	39451	Tippah	38603
Raymond	39154	Sarah	38665	Spanish Fort	39088	Tippo	38962
Raytown	39046	Saratoga	39111	Sparta	39776	Tishomingo	38873
Red Banks	38661	Sardis (Copiah County)	39083	Splinter	38673	Toccopola	38874
Redbone	39180	Sardis (Panola County)	38666	Splunge	38848	Tocowa	38620
Reddoch	39168	Sarepta	38864	Spring Cottage	39429	Tomnolen	39744
Red Lick	39096	Sartinsville	39641	Spring Creek	39350	Toomsuba	39364
Redstar	39191	Satartia	39162	Springdale	38965	Topeka	39641
Redwater	39051	Saucier	39574	Springdale Lakes	38650	Topisaw	39662
Redwood	39156	Saukum	39633	Spring Hill (Benton		Topton	39301
Reedtown	39175	Savage	38665	County)	38647	Touchstone	39044
Reform	39757	Savannah	39470	Springhill (Jones County)	39440	Tougaloo (Part of	
Refuge	38701	Savannah Grove (Part of		Spring Hill (Lafayette		Jackson)	39174
Reid	38951	Meridian)	39301	County)	38655	Townsend	39352
Remus	39051	Savoy	39301	Spring Hill (Neshoba		Tralake	38756
Rena Lara	38767	Schamberville	39325	County)	39350	Trapp	39350
Renfroe	39051	Schlater	38952	Springville	38863	Traxler	39111
Renova	38732	Schley	39140	Stallo	39350	Trebloc	38875
Revive	39045	Scobey	38953	Stampley	39069	Tremont	38876
Rexburg	38756	Scooba	39358	Standing Pine	39051	Triangle (Part of Biloxi)	39534
Rexford	39073	Scotland	39040	Stanton	39120	Tribbett	38756
Rhodes	39476	Scott	38772	Star	39167	Trinity (DeSoto County)	38632
Riceville	39573	Sebastopol	39359	Starkville	39759	Trinity (Lowndes County)	39743
Rich	38662	Sellers	39573	State Line	39362	Troy	38863
Richardson	39466	Sels Prairie	39360	Steele	39074	Truitt	39146
Richland (Holmes County)	39079	Seminary	39479	Steens	39766	Tucker	39350
Richland (Humphreys		Senatobia	38668	Steiner	38773	Tuckers Crossing	39440
County)	39166	Senatobia Lakes	38668	Stewart	39767	Tula	38675
Richland (Rankin County)	39218	Seneca	39455	Stokes	39046	Tunica	38676
Richmond	38801	Sessums	39759	Stoneville	38776	Tupelo	38801-03
Richton	39476	Seven Springs	39154	Stonewall (Clarke County)	39363	For specific Tupelo Zip Codes	
Ridgeland	39157*	Shackleford	39169	Stonewall (DeSoto		call (601) 791-8401, or your	
	39158†	Shady Grove (Copiah		County)	38611	local postmaster.	
Rienzi	38865	County)	39083	Stonewall (Holmes		Turnbull	39669
Ripley	38663	Shady Grove (Jones		County)	39169	Turnerville	39338
Rising Sun	38954	County)	39440	Stovall	38614	Turon	38870
Riverton (Part of		Shannon	38868	Straight Bayou	38721	Tuscola	39094
Clarksdale)	38614	Sharkey	38921	Stratton	39365	Tutwiler	38963
Riverview Estates	39456	Sharon (Jones County)	39440	Strayhorn	38665	Twin	39478
Robbs	38864	Sharon (Madison County)	39163	Strengthford	39440	Twin Lakes	38680
Roberts	39336	Sharpsburg	39146	Strickland	38834	Tylertown	39667
Robinson Gin	38632	Shaw	38773	Stringer	39481	Tyro	38668
Robinsonville	38664	Shelby	38774	Stringtown	38725	Union (Jones County)	39437
Robinwood	39654	Shellmound	38930	Stronghope	39191	Union (Lee County)	38862
Rock Creek	39365	Shelton	39459	Strongs	39730	Union (Newton County)	39365
Rock Hill (Alcorn County)	38834	Sheppard Town	38946	Sturgis	39769	Union (Simpson County)	39149
Rock Hill (Forrest County)	39475	Sherard	38669	Sucarnochee	39352	Union Church	39668
Rock Hill (Oktibbeha		Sherman	38869	Success	39574	Union Hall	39601
County)	39759	Sherwood	39752	Sumbax	39483	Unity	38849
Rock Hill (Panola County)	38666	Sherwood Forest	39042	Summerland	39168	University (Part of Oxford)	38677
Rock Hill (Rankin County)	39042	Shiloh (Itawamba County)	38855	Summit	39666	University Medical Center	
Rockport	39083	Shiloh (Rankin County)	39145	Sumner	38957	(Part of Jackson)	39216
Rocky Springs	39086	Shipman	39452	Sumrall	39482	University of Mississippi	38677
Rodney	39096	Shivers	39149	Sunflower (Prentiss		Usrytown	39074
Roebuck	38954	Shoccoe	39046	County)	38829	Utica	39175
Rogerslacy	39477	Shoreline Park	39576	Sunflower (Sunflower		Utica Junior College	39175
Rolling Fork	39159	Shrock	39079	County)	38778	Vaiden	39176
Rome	38768	Shubuta	39360	Sunnycrest	38901	Valewood	38744
Roseacres	38617	Shucktown	39301	Sunnyside	38944	Valley	39194
Rosebloom	38920	Shuford	38620	Sunrise (Forrest County)	39401	Valley Hill	38917
Rosebud	39189	Shuqualak	39361	Sunrise (Leake County)	39051	Valley Park	39177
Rosedale	38769	Sibley	39165	Suqualena	39301	Value (Part of Brandon)	39042
Rose Hill	39356	Sibleyton	39747	Swan Lake	38958	Van Buren	38858
Rosella	39654	Sidon	38954	Sweatman	38925	Vance	38964
Rosemary	39170	Signal	39180	Swiftown	38959	Vancleavee	39565
Rosetta	39633	Silver City	39166	Swiftwater	38701	Van Vleet	38877
Rough Edge	38863	Silver Creek	39663	Sylvarena	39153	Vardaman	38878
Roundaway	38614	Silver Run	39573	Symonds	38769	Vaughan	39179
Roundlake	38740	Singleton	39051	Tallula	39159	Vaughn	39601
Rounsaville	39452	Singleton Settlement	39074	Talowah	39455	Velma	38965
Roxie	39661	Skene	38730	Tatum	39638	Vernal	39452
Ruby	38950	Skuna	38915	Taylor	38673	Vernon (Madison County)	39339
Rudyard	38617	Skyline	38801	Taylorsville	39168	Vernon (Winston County)	39339
Ruleville	38771	Slate Spring	38955	Tchula	39169	Verona	38879
Runnelstown	39401	Slayden	38642	Teasdale	38927	Vickland	39159
Rural Hill	39108	Sledge	38670	Ted	38338	Vicksburg	39180-82
Russell	39301	Sloan	39046	Teoc	38917	For specific Vicksburg Zip	
Russellville	39162	Smith (Covington County)	39428	Terry	39170	Codes call (601) 636-1071, or	
Russum	39096	Smith (Lauderdale		Thaxton	38871	your local postmaster.	
Ruth	39662	County)	39364	Theadville	39355	Victoria	38679
Ryan	38843	Smithdale	39664	Theo	38683	Vidalia	39571

	ZIP		ZIP		ZIP		ZIP
Village Fair Mall (Part of Meridian)	39301	Watson (Forrest County)	39401	Wheeler	38880	Winborn	38633
Vimville	39301	Watson (Marshall County)	38611	Whistler	39367	Winchester	39367
Virlilia	39046	Wautubbee	39330	White Apple	39661	Windsor Park	39564
Vossburg	39366	Waveland	39576	Whitebluff	39483	Wingate (Part of New Augusta)	39462
Waco	38753	Waxhaw	38746	White Cap	39638	Winona	38967
Waddell	39741	Way	39046	Whitehead	38928	Winstonville	38781
Wade (Jackson County)	39581	Waynesboro	39367	White Oak	39111	Winterville	38782
Wade (Sunflower County)	38737	Wayside	38780	Whites (Clay County)	39773	Wolf Springs	39301
Wahalak	39358	Weathersby	39114	Whites (Rankin County)	39073	Woodburn	38751
Wakefield	38618	Webb	38966	Whitesand (Jefferson Davis County)	39140	Woodland (Chickasaw County)	39776
Wakeland	38930	Weir	39772	White Sand (Pearl River County)	39470	Woodland (Pontotoc County)	38863
Waldrup	39422	Wells (Part of Caledonia)	39740	Whites Crossing	39577	Woodland Lake	38632
Wallerville	38652	Wells Town	39455	Whitfield (Jones County)	39464	Woodville	39669
Wallhill	38618	Wenasoga	38834	Whitfield (Rankin County)	39193	Woodwards	39367
Walls	38680	Wesson	39191	Whitney	38737	Woolmarket	39532
Walnut (Quitman County)	38964	West (Holmes County)	39192	Whitten Town	38663	Wortham	39574
Walnut (Tippah County)	38683	West (Lauderdale County)	39305	Whynot	39301	Wren	39730
Walnut Grove (Coahoma County)	38767	West Biloxi (Part of Biloxi)	39531	Wickware	39345	Wright	38746
Walnut Grove (Leake County)	39189	West Days	38641	Wiggins (Leake County)	39051	Wyatte	38668
		West Gulfport	39501	Wiggins (Stone County)	39577	Yazoo City	39194
Walters	39437	West Hattiesburg	39401	Wilco Estates	38632	Yocona	38655
Waltersville	39180	West Hill	39063	Wildwood	38930	Yokena	39180
Walthall	39771	West Jackson (Part of Jackson)	39207	Wilkinson	39669	Youngs	38922
Wanilla	39654	Westland (Part of Jackson)	39209	Willet	38748	Zama	39090
Wardwell	38878	West Lincoln	39601	Williamsburg	39428	Zemuly	39160
Warrenton	39180	West Marks	38646	Williamsville (Attala County)	39090	Zero	39301
Warsaw	38611	West Point	39773			Zetus	39601
Washington	39190	West Poplarville	39470	Williamsville (Neshoba County)	39350	Zieglerville	39039
Waterford	38685	Westside	39150	Willowood	39212	Zion	38863
Water Oak	39367	West Union	38650	Willows	39150	Zumbro	38732
Water Valley	38965	Westville	39114				

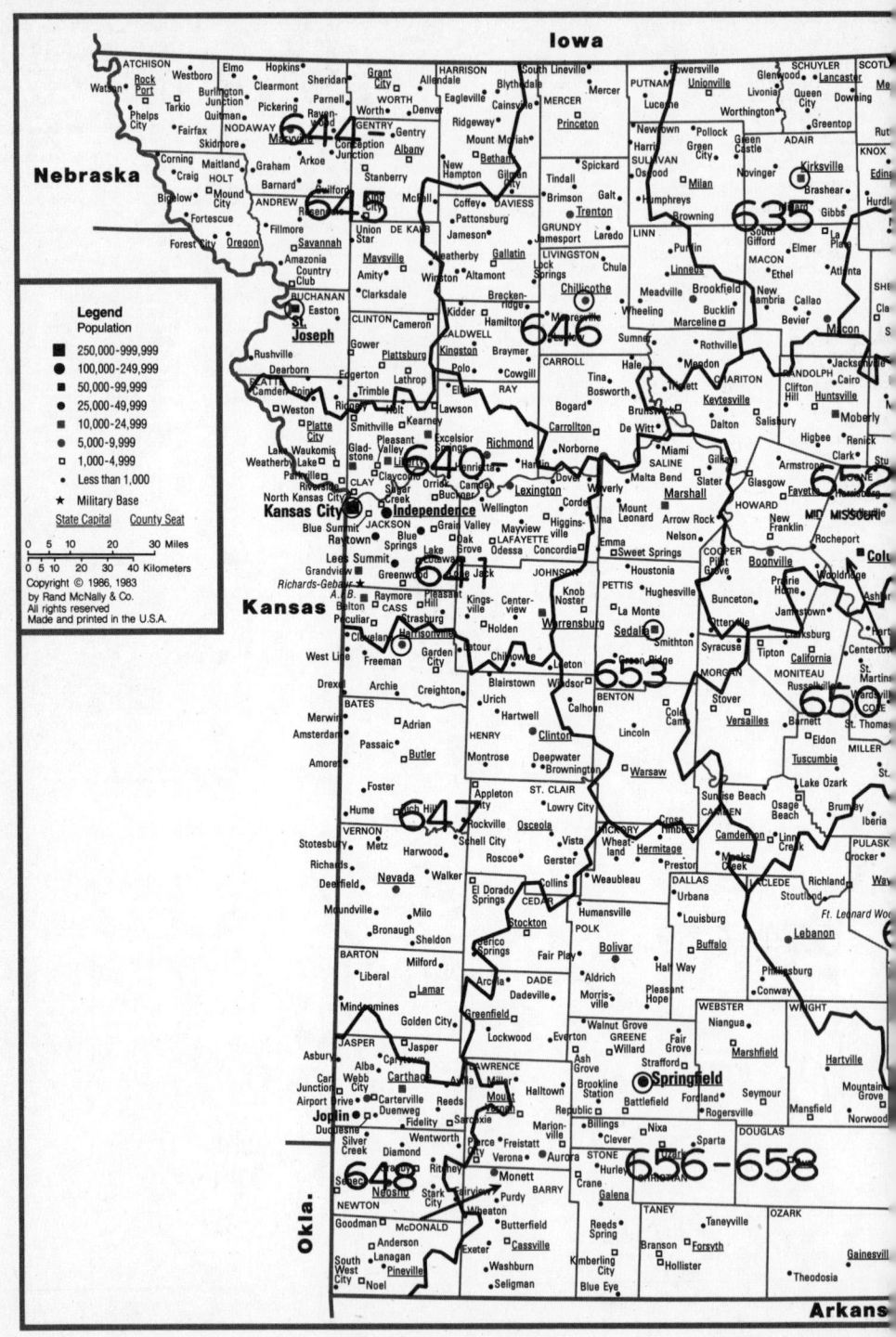

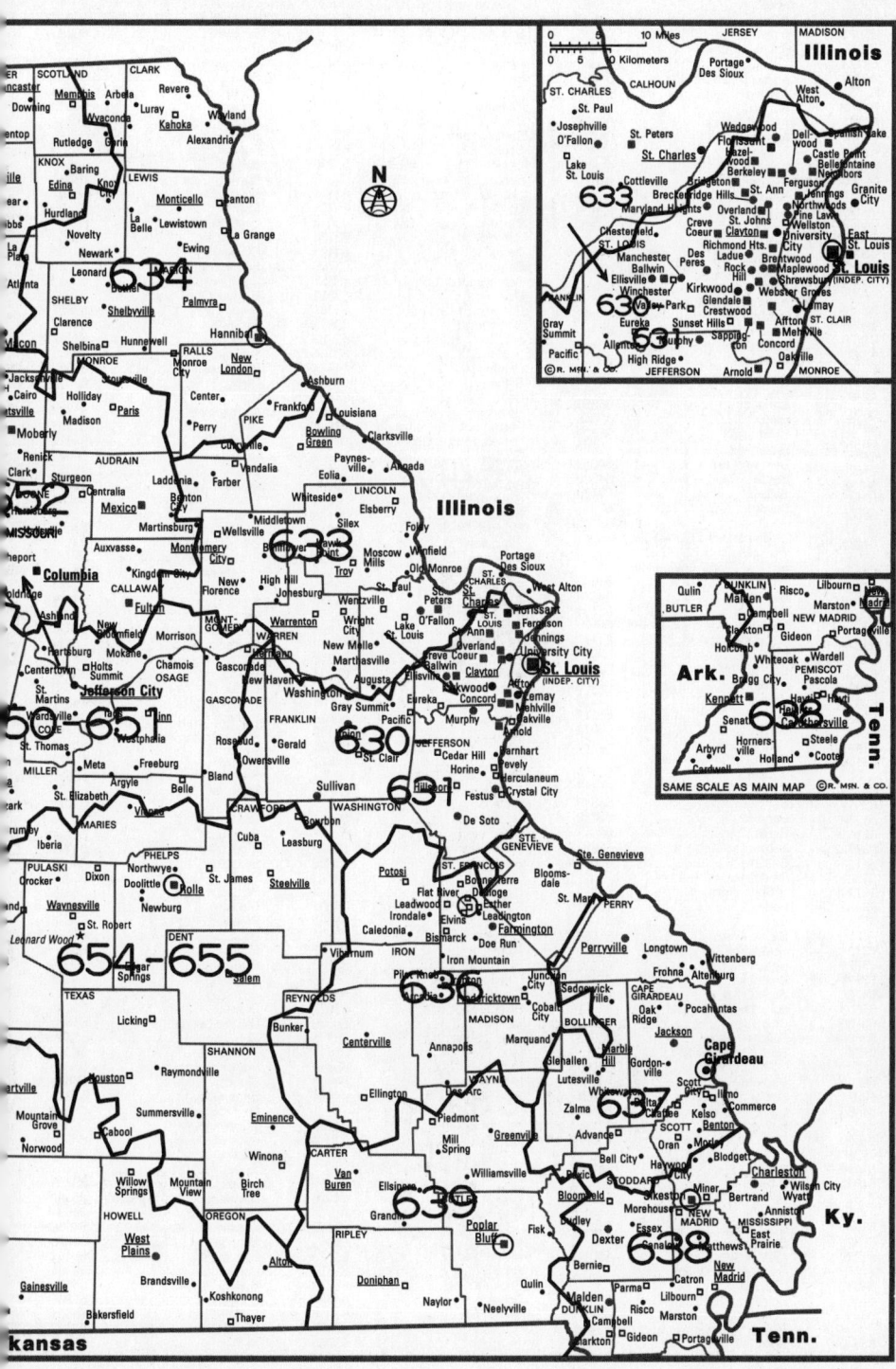

	ZIP		ZIP		ZIP		ZIP
Aaron	64720	Athens	63465	Belvidere (Part of		Bonne Terre	63628
Abesville	65656	Atherton	64050	Grandview)	64030	Bonnots Mill	65016
Abo	65536	Atlanta	63530	Bem	65066	Boonesboro	65250
Acorn Corner	63877	Atlas	64836	Ben Avis (Part of		Boonville	65233
Acornridge	63960	Atwater Terrace	63136	Ferguson)	63135	Bosky Dell (Part of	
Adair	63533	Auburn	63343	Benbow	63440	Lanagan)	64831
Adrian	64720	Augusta	63332	Benbush	63141	Boss	65440
Advance	63730	Aullville	64037	Bendavis	65433	Boston	64759
Affton	63123	Aurora	65605	Benjamin	63435	Bosworth	64623
Agency	64401	Aurora Springs	65026	Bennett Springs	65536	Boulder City	64844
Aid	63825	Austin	64725	Bentley Farms	63088	Bourbon	65441
Airline Acres	63834	Auxvasse	65231	Benton	63736	Bowen	65360
Airport Drive	64801	Ava	65608	Benton City	65232	Bowers Mill	64848
Akers	65560	Avalon	64621	Benton Park (Part of St.		Bowling Green	63334
Alanthus	64489	Avenue City	64505	Louis)	63104	Boydsville	65251
Alba	64830	Avert	63825	Bentonville	65355	Boynton	63556
Albany (Gentry County)	64402	Avery	65355	Berger	63014	Boys Ranch	65617
Albany (Ray County)	64077	Avilla	64833	Berkeley	63134	Boys Town	65559
Aldrich	65601	Avon	63640	Berlin	64463	Bracken	65706
Alexandria	63430	Avondale	64117	Bermott	65706	Bradfield	65705
Alfalfa Center	63834	Axtell	63552	Bernheimer	63357	Bradleyville	65614
Algonquin (Part of		Azen	63432	Bernie	63822	Braggadocio	63826
Webster Groves)	63119	Babbtown	65085	Berryman	65565	Bragg City	63827
Allbright	63655	Bacon	65046	Bertrand	63823	Braley	64477
Allendale	64420	Baden (Part of St. Louis)	63147	Berwick	65723	Branch	65786
Allenton	63001	Baderville	63862	Bessville	63764	Brandon	65360
Allenville	63740	Bado	65689	Bethany	64424	Brandsville	65688
Alley Spring	65466	Bagnell	65026	Bethel	63434	Branson	65615*
All Saints Village	63376	Bahner	65350	Bethlehem	64861		65616†
Alma	64001	Baker	63846	Bethpage	64867	Branson West	65737
Almartha	65773	Bakersfield	65609	Beulah (Madison County)	63636	Brashear	63533
Almon	65732	Bakersville	63827	Beulah (Phelps County)	65436	Brasher	63877
Alpha	64652	Baldwin Lake	64080	Beverly	64079	Braymer	64624
Altamont	64620	Baldwin Park	64080	Beverly Hills	63121	Brays	65486
Altenburg	63732	Ballard	64730	Bevier	63532	Brazeau	63737
Altheim	63141	Ballwin	63011	Biblegrove	63531	Brazil	63664
Alton	65606		63021-22	Biehle	63775	Brazito	65101
Altona	64720	For specific Ballwin Zip Codes		Bigelow	64437	Breckenridge	64625
Amazonia	64421	call (314) 227-8720, or your		Big Lake	64437	Breckenridge Hills	63114
Americus	65069	local postmaster.		Big Piney	65550	Breen Acres (Part of	
Amity	64422	Bancroft	64642	Big River Mills	63628	Kansas City)	64152
Amoret	64722	Banner	63623	Bigspring	63363	Brentwood	63144
Amsterdam	64723	Bannister	65786	Billings	65610	Brewer	63775
Amy	65626	Bannister Mall (Part of		Billingsville	65233	Briar	63931
Anabel	63431	Kansas City)	64137	Billmore	65690	Brickeys	63627
Anaconda	63077	Bardley	63935	Birch Tree	65438	Bridgeton	63044
Anderson	64831	Baring	63531	Birds Corners	63846	Bridgeton Terrace (Part of	
Annada	63330	Barnard	64423	Birds Point	63834	Bridgeton)	63044
Annapolis	63620	Barnesville	63530	Birdtown	65637	Bridlecroft	64083
Anniston	63820	Barnett	65011	Birmingham	64161	Brighton	65617
Anson	52626	Barnhart	63012	Bismarck	63624	Brimson	64642
Anthonies Mill	65441	Barretts	63122	Bixby	65439	Brinktown	65443
Antioch (Clark County)	63445	Barry (Part of Kansas		Black	63625	Briscoe	63379
Antioch (Clay County)	64119	City)	64155	Blackburn	65321	Bristow	64772
Antioch Center (Part of		Bartlett	65438	Blackjack (St. Clair		Brixey	65618
Kansas City)	64119	Barwick	64649	County)	65785	Broadway (Part of St.	
Antonia	63052	Baryties	63626	Black Jack (St. Louis		Louis)	63147
Anutt	65540	Bates City	64011	County)	63031	Brock	63555
Apache Flats	65101	Batesville	63932	Black Walnut	63301	Bronaugh	64728
Apple Creek	63775	Battlefield	65619	Blackwater	65322	Brookdale	63141
Appleton City	64724	Battlefield Mall (Part of		Blackwell	63626	Brookfield	64628
Aquilla	63825	Springfield)	65804	Blairstown	64726	Brooking Park	65301
Arab	63733	Baxter	65681	Bland	65014	Brookline Station	65619
Arbela	63432	Bay	65041	Blendville (Part of Joplin)	64801	Brooklyn	64481
Arbor	63740	Baydy Peak	65065	Bliss	63626	Brooklyn Heights	64836
Arbor Terrace (Part of		Bayshore (Part of Arnold)	63010	Blodgett	63824	Broseley	63932
Northwoods)	63121	Beach	65632	Blomeyer	63740	Brownbranch	65608
Arbyrd	63821	Beaman	65350	Bloomfield	63825	Brownfield	65556
Arcadia	63621	Bean Lake	64484	Blooming Rose	65436	Browning	64630
Archie	64725	Bearcreek	65649	Bloomington	63532	Brownington	64740
Arcola	65603	Bearfield	65201	Bloomsdale	63627	Browns	65202
Ardeola	63730	Beaufort	63013	Blosser	65339	Browns Spring	65610
Arditta	63626	Beckville (Part of		Blue Branch	65355	Brownwood	63738
Ardmore	65247	Piedmont)	63957	Blue Eye	65611	Brumley	65017
Argo	65441	Bedford	64643	Blue Lick	65350	Bruner	65620
Argyle	65001	Bedison	64434	Blue Mound	64638	Brunot	63636
Arkmo	63821	Belews Creek	63050	Blue Ridge	64424	Brunswick	65236
Arkoe	64468	Belgique	63775	Blue Ridge Mall (Part of		Brushcreek	65536
Arley	64060	Belgrade	63622	Kansas City)	64133	Brushyknob	65608
Arlington	65550	Bellair	65237	Blue Springs	64013-15	Buck Donic	63829
Armstrong	65230	Bellamy	64784	For specific Blue Springs Zip		Buckhart	65638
Arnold	63010	Bella Villa	63125	Codes call (816) 229-6900, or		Buckhorn (Madison	
Aroma	64844	Bell City	63735	your local postmaster.		County)	63655
Arroll	65571	Belle	65013	Blue Vue (Part of Kansas		Buckhorn (Pulaski County)	65583
Arrowhead Beach (Part of		Belle Center	64801	City)	64133	Bucklin	64631
Lake Ozark)	65049	Bellefontaine (St. Louis		Bluffton	65069	Buckner	64016
Arrowhead Lake Estates	65326	County)	63017	Blythedale	64426	Bucoda	63876
Arrow Rock	65320	Bellefontaine (Washington		Boaz	65631	Bucyrus	65444
Arthur	64779	County)	63630	Boekerton	63873	Buell	63361
Asbury	64832	Bellefontaine Neighbors	63137	Bogard	64622	Buffalo	65622
Ashburn	63433	Bellerive	63121	Bois D'Arc	65612	Buffington	63846
Asherville	63960	Bellerive Estates	63141	Bolckow	64427	Bullion	63501
Ash Grove	65604	Belleview	63623	Boles	63055	Bunceton	65237
Ash Hill	63940	Belleville	64801	Bolivar	65613	Bunker	63629
Ashland	65010	Bellflower	63333	Bona	65601	Bunker Hill	65257
Ashley	63334	Bel-Nor	63133	Bonanza	64650	Burbank	63944
Ashley Creek	65555	Bel-Ridge	63133	Bongor Lake Estate	65202	Burdett	64720
Ashton	63453	Belton	64012	Bonham	65605	Burfordville	63739
Aspenhoff	63357			Bona		Burgess	64769

Place	ZIP
Burke City	63135
Burksville	63434
Burlington Junction	64428
Burnham	65793
Burns	65613
Burr	72478
Burton	65248
Burtville	65336
Butcher	65774
Butler	64730
Butler Hill Estates	63128
Butterfield	65623
Butts	65441
Bynumville	65281
Byrnes Mill	63051
Byron	65013
Cabanne (Part of St. Louis)	63112
Cabool	65689
Caddo	65706
Cadet	63630
Cainsville	64632
Cairo	65239
Caledonia	63631
Calhoun	65323
California	65018
Callao	63534
Calm	63942
Calton Mill	65769
Calumet	63336
Calverton Park	63136
Calwood	65251
Cambridge	65330
Camden	64017
Camden Point	64018
Camdenton	65020
Cameron	64429
Campbell	63933
Campbellton	63068
Camp Clark	64772
Canaan	65014
Canalou	63828
Cane Hill	65635
Caney Creek	63771
Cannon Mines	63630
Canton	63435
Cantwell (Part of Desloge)	63601
Cape Fair	65624
Cape Girardeau	63701-03

For specific Cape Girardeau Zip Codes call (314) 335-5501, or your local postmaster.

Place	ZIP
Capital Mall (Part of Jefferson City)	65109
Capitol Hill	63136
Caplinger Mills	65607
Cappeln	63348
Capps	65082
Cardwell	63829
Carl Junction	64834
Carlow	64648
Carmack	64402
Carola	63961
Carondelet (Part of St. Louis)	63111
Carr (Part of Florissant)	63031
Carrington	65251
Carr Lane	72616
Carrollton	64633
Carsonville	63121
Carterville	64835
Carthage	64836
Caruth	63857
Caruthersville	63830
Carytown	64836
Cascade	63632
Case	65041
Cash	63534
Cassel Addition	65785
Cassidy	65714
Cassville	65625
Castle Point	63136
Castle Rock (Part of Joplin)	64801
Castlewood	63011
Catawba	64624
Catawissa	63015
Catherine Place	63645
Cato	65605
Catron	63833
Caulfield	65626
Cave	63379
Cave Hill	65041
Caverna	72739
Cave Spring	65770
Cawood	64427
Cedar City (Part of Jefferson City)	65022
Cedarcreek	65627

Place	ZIP
Cedar Gap	65746
Cedar Hill	63016
Cedar Hill Lakes	63016
Cedar Lake (Boone County)	65201
Cedar Lake (Jefferson County)	63070
Cedar Ridge	65590
Cedar Springs	64744
Cedar Valley	63901
Cedarville	64756
Celt	65764
Center	63436
Center Square (Part of Kansas City)	64196
Centertown	65023
Centerview	64019
Centerville	63633
Central (Jackson County)	64142
Central (Madison County)	63645
Central City	64801
Centralia	65240
Central Missouri Correctional Center	65101
Centropolis (Part of Kansas City)	64126
Chadwick	65629
Chaffee	63740
Chain of Rocks	63369
Chain-O-Lakes	65625
Chambersburg	63445
Chamois	65024
Champ	63042
Champion	65717
Champion City	63056
Chandler	64060
Channel	63877
Chapel Hill	64011
Chapel Hills	65785
Chariton	63565
Charity	65644
Charlack	63114
Charles Nagel (Part of St. Louis)	63115
Charleston	63834
Charteroak	63833
Cherokee Pass	63645
Cherry Box	63451
Cherry Valley Estates	65804
Cherryville	65446
Chesapeake	65712
Chesterfield	63005-06
	63017

For specific Chesterfield Zip Codes call (314) 532-3482, or your local postmaster.

Place	ZIP
Chestnutridge	65630
Chicopee	63965
Chilhowee	64733
Chillicothe	64601
Chilton	63965
Chitwood (Part of Joplin)	64801
Chloride	63646
Chouteau (Part of St. Louis)	63110
Chula	64635
Circle City	63846
Civic Center (Part of Kansas City)	64106
Civil Bend	64670
Clapper	63456
Clara	65483
Clarence	63437
Clark	65243
Clark City	63445
Clarksburg	65025
Clarksdale	64430
Clarkson Valley	63017
Clarksville	63336
Clarkton	63837
Claryville	63775
Claycomo	64119
Claysvil	65039
Clayton	63105
Clear Creek	65276
Clearmont	64431
Clear Spring	63965
Clear Springs	65793
Clearview	65202
Clearwater	63670
Cleavesville	65014
Cleveland	64734
Clever	65631
Cliff Village	64801
Clifton City	65348
Clifton Hill	65244
Climax Springs	65324
Clines Island	63846
Clinton	64735

Place	ZIP
Cliquot	65640
Clover Bottom	63090
Cloverdale	65590
Clubb	63934
Clyde	64432
Coal	64735
Coal Hill	64744
Coatsville	63535
Cobalt City	63645
Cody	65742
Coffey	64636
Coffeyton	65441
Coffman	63670
Coldspring	65717
Cold Springs	65355
Coldwater	63964
Cole Camp	65325
Cole Camp Junction	65325
College Mound	65247
Collins	64738
Coloma	64622
Colony	63563
Columbia	65201-05
	65299

For specific Columbia Zip Codes call (314) 876-7829, or your local postmaster.

Place	ZIP
Columbia Mall (Part of Columbia)	65203
Columbus	64019
Commerce	63742
Commerce Tower (Part of Kansas City)	64199
Commercial (Part of Springfield)	65803
Competition	65470
Conception	64433
Conception Junction	64434
Conclay (Part of Ladue)	63124
Concord (Callaway County)	65231
Concord (St. Louis County)	63128
Concord Hill	63357
Concordia	64020
Connelsville	63559
Conran	63838
Converse	64465
Conway	65632
Cook Station	65449
Cool Valley	63135
Cooper Hill	65014
Cooter	63839
Cora	63556
Corder	64021
Cornelia	64093
Corning	64435
Cornwall	63645
Corridon	63633
Corry	65635
Corsicana	65734
Corso	63377
Corticelli	65074
Cosby	64436
Cossville	64849
Cottage Farm	63050
Cottleville	63338
Cotton Plant	63855
Cottonwood Point	63877
Couch	65690
Coulstone	65542
Country Club (Andrew County)	64505
Country Club (Jackson County)	64113
Country Club Hills	63136
Country Club Plaza (Part of Kansas City)	64112
Country Lake Woods	63011
Country Life Acres	63131
Countryside (Part of Kansas City)	64152
Courtney (Part of Sugar Creek)	64050
Courtois	65565
Cowgill	64637
Coy	64831
Crabbs	65746
Craig	64437
Crane	65633
Creighton	64739
Crescent	63025
Crescent Hill	64720
Crescent Lake (Part of Excelsior Springs)	64024
Crestwood	63126
Crestwood Plaza (Part of Crestwood)	63126
Cretcher	65351

Place	ZIP
Creve Coeur	63141
Crider	65790
Crites Corner	63937
Crocker	65452
Cross Keys	63031
Cross Keys Shopping Center (Part of Florissant)	63033
Cross Roads (Douglas County)	65608
Cross Roads (Ozark County)	65637
Cross Timbers	65634
Crosstown	63775
Cross Way	65706
Crowder	63801
Crown	65706
Cruise Mill	63626
Crump	63785
Crystal City	63019
Crystal Lake Park	63131
Crystal Lakes	64024
Cuba	65453
Cunningham	64681
Curdton	63960
Cureall	65790
Currentview	63935
Curryville	63339
Custer	65501
Cyclone	64856
Cyrene	63334
Dadeville	65635
Daisy	63743
Daleview	64446
Dalton	65246
Damascus	64776
Dameron	63343
Damsel (Part of Osage Beach)	65065
Danby	63627
Danforth	63559
Danville	63361
Dardenne	63366
Dardenne Prairie	63366
Darien	65560
Daris Crossing	63601
Darksville	65259
Darlington	64438
Daugherty	64701
Davis (Lincoln County)	63379
Davis (St. Francois County)	63601
Davis Store	63932
Davisville	65456
Dawn	64638
Dawson	65711
Dawsonville	64428
Dawt	65760
Dayton	64747
Daytown	63653
Daytown (rural)	63601
Dearborn	64439
Decaturville	65536
Deckard-Y	65690
Dederick	64744
Deepwater	64740
Deerfield	64741
Deering	63840
Deer Land	63857
Deer Park	65201
Deer Ridge	63447
Deer Run	63965
Defiance	63341
Deicke	63025
De Kalb	64440
De Lassus	63640
Delaware	65438
Delbridge	63664
Dell Junction	65355
Dellwood	63136
Delmar	64735
Delmo	63801
Delta	63744
Dennis Acres	64801
Denton (Johnson County)	64040
Denton (Pemiscot County)	63877
Denver	64441
Derby	63601
Des Arc	63636
Desloge	63601
De Soto	63020
Des Peres	63131
Dessa	64850
Detmold	63068
Devils Elbow	65457
De Witt	64639
Dexter	63841
Diamond	64840
Dickens	65759

	ZIP		ZIP		ZIP		ZIP
Diehlstadt	63834	Elkhorn	64077	Farmersville	64683	Fruitland (Cape Girardeau	
Diggins	65636	Elkhurst	65201	Farmington	63640	County)	63755
Dikeland	64083	Elkland	65644	Farmington Correctional		Fruitland (Greene County)	65648
Dillard	65456	Elk Prairie	65401	Center	63640	Fulton	65251
Dillon	65401	Elk Springs	64854	Farrar	63746	Gaines	64735
Dissen	63068	Elkton	65650	Farrenberg	63869	Gainesville	65655
Dittmer	63023	Ellington	63638	Faucett	64448	Galena	65656
Dixie	65063	Ellis	64772	Fayette	65248	Galesburg	64855
Dixon	65459	Ellis Prairie	65444	Fayetteville	64093	Gallatin	64640
Dockery	64085	Ellisville	63011	Federal (Part of Park Hills)	63601	Galloway (Part of	
Doc Long Estates	65355	Ellsinore	63937	Fee Fee	63141	Springfield)	65804
Doe Run	63637	Elm	64061	Femme Osage	63332	Galmey	65779
Dogwood (Douglas		Elmdale Village (Part of		Fenton	63026	Galt	64641
County)	65746	St. Johns)	63114	Ferguson	63135	Gamburg	63955
Dogwood (Mississippi		Elmer	63538	Fern Ridge	63141	Game	63830
County)	63845	Elmira	64062	Fernview Estates	63141	Gamma	63333
Dolly Siding (Part of		Elmo	64445	Ferrelview	64163	Garden City	64747
Bonne Terre)	63628	Elmont	63080	Fertile	63630	Gardenview	63033
Dongola	63730	Elmwood	65321	Festus	63028	Garfield	65690
Doniphan	63935	Elsberry	63343	Fidelity	64836	Garland	64735
Doolittle	65401	Elsey	65633	Field (Part of St. Louis)	63108	Garrison	65657
Dora	65637	Elston	65101	Filley	64744	Garwood	63957
Dorena	63845	Elvins (Part of Park Hills)	63601	Fillmore	64449	Gasconade	65036
Doss	65560	Elwood	65802	Fisk	63940	Gascondy	65013
Dotham	64446	Ely	63461	Flag Springs (Andrew		Gashland (Part of Kansas	
Dove	65536	Emden	63439	County)	64494	City)	64155
Dover (Lafayette County)	64022	Emerald Beach	65658	Flag Springs (Phelps		Gateway Drive (Part of	
Dover (Lewis County)	63448	Emerson	63454	County)	65559	Joplin)	64801
Downing	63536	Eminence	65466	Flat	65550	Gateway South	65201
Drake	65066	Emma	65327	Flat River (Part of Park		Gatewood	63942
Dresden	65301	Empire Prairie	64463	Hills)	63601	Gaynor	64475
Drexel	64742	Englewood (Boone		Flatwood	65466	Gazette	63359
Dripping Spring	65202	County)	65010	Fleming	64077	Geneva	72438
Drury	65638	Englewood (Jackson		Flemington	65650	Gentry	64453
Dudenville	64748	County)	64052	Fletcher	63030	Gentryville (Douglas	
Dudley	63936	Enon (Moniteau County)	65074	Flinthill	63346	County)	65608
Duenweg	64841	Enon (St. Charles County)	65385	Flordell Hills	63136	Gentryville (Gentry	
Dugginsville	65761	Enyart	64453	Florence (Buchanan		County)	64402
Duke	65461	Eolia	63344	County)	64504	Georgetown (Boone	
Duncans Bridge	63437	Epworth	63469	Florence (Morgan County)	65329	County)	65203
Duncans Point	65324	Erie	64843	Florida	65283	Georgetown (Pettis	
Dundee	63090	Ernestville	64020	Florissant	63031-34	County)	65301
Dunksburg	65351	Essex	63846	For specific Florissant Zip		Gerald	63037
Dunlap	64683	Estes	63359	Codes call (314) 837-1810, or		Germantown	64770
Dunn	65711	Esther (Part of Park Hills)	63601	your local postmaster.		Gerster	64776
Dunnegan	65640	Estill	65274	Floyd	64077	Gibbs	63540
Duquesne	64801	Ethel	63539	Flucom	63020	Gibson	63847
Durham	63438	Ethlyn	63369	Foil	65755	Gideon	63848
Dutchtown	63745	Etlah	63014	Foley	63347	Gilbert	63855
Dutzow	63342	Etterville	65031	Folk	65085	Gilliam	65330
Dye	64098	Eudora	65645	Foose	65622	Gilman City	64642
Dykes	65444	Eugene	65032	Forbes	64473	Gilmore	63385
Eagle Rock	65641	Eunice	65468	Ford City	64463	Ginger Blue	64854
Eagleville	64442	Eureka	63025	Fordland	65652	Gipsy	63750
Easley	65203	Evans	65608	Forest City	64451	Girdner	65608
East Bonne Terre	63628	Evansville (Buchanan		Forest Green	65281	Gladden	65560
East End	63623	County)	64507	Forest Hills	65355	Gladstone	64118-19
East Hills Mall (Part of St.		Evansville (Monroe		Foristell	63348	For specific Gladstone Zip	
Joseph)	64506	County)	65270	Forker	64651	Codes call (816) 436-1850, or	
East Independence (Part		Eve	64741	Forkners Hill	65632	your local postmaster.	
of Independence)	64056	Eveningshade	65552	Forrest Mill	64859	Glasgow	65254
East Kirkwood (Part of		Everett	64725	Forsyth	65653	Glasgow Village	63137
Kirkwood)	63122	Eversonville	64688	Fortescue	64452	Glenaire	64068
East Leavenworth	64079	Everton	65646	Fort Henry	65259	Glenallen	63751
East Lynne	64743	Ewing	63440	Fort Leonard Wood	65473	Glencoe	63038
East Mexico (Part of		Excello	65247	Fortuna	65034	Glendale (Putnam County)	63551
Mexico)	65265	Excelsior	65084	Fort Zumwalt	63366	Glendale (St. Louis	
Easton	64443	Excelsior Estates	64062	Foster	64745	County)	63122
East Prairie	63845	Excelsior Springs	64024	Fountain Grove	64659	Glen Echo Park	63121
East Purdy	65734	Excelsior Springs Junction	64077	Fox Creek	63069	Glennon	63764
Eastwood	63965	Executive Park (Part of		Fox Haven	64083	Glennonville	63933
Ebenezer	65803	Kansas City)	64120	Foxwood Springs	64083	Glen Park	63070
Ebo	63664	Exeter	65647	Frailie	63848	Glensted	65084
Eccles	65261	Fagus	63938	Frankclay	63644	Glenstone (Part of	
Echo Valley	65065	Fairdealing	63939	Frankenstein	65016	Springfield)	65804
Economy	63530	Fairfax	64446	Frankford	63441	Glenwood	63541
Ectonville	64089	Fairgrounds (Part of St.		Franklin	65250	Glenwood Junction (Part	
Edgar Springs	65462	Louis)	63107	Franks	65459	of Glenwood)	63541
Edge Acres	65785	Fair Grove	65648	Frazier	64401	Glidewell	65803
Edgehill	63625	Fair Haven	64750	Fredericksburg	65061	Glover	63646
Edgerton	64444	Fairleigh (Part of St.		Fredericktown	63645	Gobler	63849
Edgerton Junction	64439	Joseph)	64506	Fredville	64850	Golden	65658
Edgewater Beach	65653	Fairmont	63474	Freeburg	65035	Golden City	64748
Edgewood	63334	Fairmount (Part of		Freedom (Camden		Golden Oak (Part of	
Edina	63537	Independence)	64053	County)	65052	Kansas City)	64117
Edinburg	64683	Fair Play	65649	Freedom (Osage County)	65024	Goldman	63050
Edmonson	65338	Fairport	64447	Freeman	64746	Goldsberry	63539
Edmundson	63134	Fairview (Newton County)	64842	Freistatt	65654	Gooch Mill	65068
Edwards	65326	Fairview (Taney County)	65744	Fremont	63941	Goodhope	65608
Egypt Grove	65626	Fairview (Texas County)	65689	Fremont Hills	65721	Goodland	63623
Egypt Mills	63701	Fairview Acres (Part of		French Village	63036	Goodman	64843
El Chaparral	65201	Park Hills)	63601	Friedheim	63747	Goodson	65659
Eldon	65026	Falcon	65470	Friendly Valley	63775	Gordonville	63752
El Dorado Springs	64744	Fanchon	65788	Frisbee	63852	Gorin	63543
Eldridge	65463	Fanning	65453	Frisco	63846	Goshen	64673
Elgin	63434	Farber	63345	Fristoe	65355	Gospel Ridge (Part of St.	
Elijah	65626	Farewell	64487	Frohna	63748	Robert)	65583
Elk Creek	65464	Farley	64028	Frontenac	63131	Gower	64454
Elkhead	65753	Farmer	63339			Graff	65660

Name	ZIP	Name	ZIP	Name	ZIP	Name	ZIP
Graham	64455	Hartwell	64788	Hoover	64079	Jarvis	63050
Grain Valley	64029	Hartzell	63848	Hope	65024	Jasper	64755
Granby	64844	Harvester	63302	Hopewell (Warren County)	63357	Jaudon	64012
Grand Center	63534	Harviell	63945	Hopewell (Washington County)	63660	Jawdea	64083
Grand Falls	64801	Harwood	64750	Hopkins	64461	Jaywye	63873
Grandin	63943	Haseltine	65802	Horine	63070	Jedburg	63011
Grand Pass	65339	Hassard	63456	Hornersville	63855	Jefferson City	65101-10
Grandview (Benton County)	65355	Hastain	65326	Hornet	64865	For specific Jefferson City Zip Codes call (314) 636-4186, or your local postmaster.	
Grandview (Jackson County)	64030	Hatfield	64458	Hortense	64735	Jefferson Memorial (Part of St. Louis)	63102
Granger	63442	Hatton	65231	Horton	64751	Je-Ke-Ki	65326
Graniteville	63650	Havenhurst	64856	House Creek	63965	Jenkins	65605
Grant (Part of Grantwood Village)	63123	Hawkeye	65452	House Springs	63051	Jennings	63136
Grant City	64456	Hawk Point	63349	Houston	65483	Jerico	65746
Grantwood Village	63123	Hayden	65459	Houstonia	65333	Jerico Springs	64756
Granville	65275	Hayes Park (Part of Sibley)	64088	Houston Lake	64152	Jerk Tail	65667
Grassy	63753	Hayti	63851	Howards Ridge	65655	Jerome	65529
Gravelhill	63739	Hayti Heights	63851	Howardville	63869	Jesse M. Donaldson (Part of Kansas City)	64195
Gravelton	63655	Hayward	63873	Howell	63303	Jewett	63260
Gravois (Part of St. Louis)	63116	Haywood City	63736	Howes Mill	65560	J&G Junction (Part of Joplin)	64801
Gravois Mills	65037	Hazelgreen	65556	H. S. Jewell (Part of Springfield)	65802	Johnson City	64724
Grayridge	63850	Hazel Run	63628	Hudson	64724	Johnstown (Bates County)	64770
Grayson	64492	Hazelwood	63042	Huggins	65484	Johnstown (Jasper County)	64835
Grays Point	65707	Heatonville	65707	Hughesville	65334	Jonesburg	63351
Gray Summit	63039	Hebron	65775	Hugo	65052	Joplin	64801-04
Graysville	63551	Hecla	64653	Humansville	65674	For specific Joplin Zip Codes call (417) 623-6176, or your local postmaster.	
Green Acres	64801	Hedge City	63460	Hume	64752		
Green Bay Terrace	65079	Helena	64459	Humphreys	64646	Jordan	65634
Greenbrier	63730	Helm	65459	Hunnewell	63443	Jordan W Chambers (Part of St. Louis)	63106
Green Castle	63544	Heman Park (Part of University City)	63130	Hunter	63943	Josephville	63385
Green City	63545	Hematite	63047	Hunters Mill	63664	Judge	65051
Greendale	63133	Hemple	64490	Hunterville	63846	Junction City	63645
Greenfield	65661	Henderson	65742	Huntingdale	64735	Junland	63901
Green Forest	63901	Hendrickson	63967	Huntington	63456	Kahoka	63445
Green Grove	63559	Henley	65040	Huntleigh	63131	Kaiser	65047
Green Lawn	63462	Henrietta	64036	Huntsdale	65203	Kampville	63301
Green-Mar	63026	Henry's Acres	65338	Huntsville	65259	Kampville Beach	63301
Green Mound Ridge	65669	Henry Winfield Wheeler (Part of St. Louis)	63101	Hurdland	63547	Kampville Court	63301
Green Mountain	65711	Herbs	65338	Hurley	65675	Kansas City	64101-99
Green Oaks	63936	Herculaneum	63048	Hurlingen	64443	For specific Kansas City Zip Codes call (816) 842-2800, or your local postmaster.	
Green Ridge	65332	Hercules	65614	Huron	65613		
Greensburg	63531	Heritage Hills	64083	Hurricane	63764	Karr's	65355
Greenstreet	63013	Hermann	65041	Hurricane Deck	65079	Kaseyville	63534
Greentop	63546	Hermitage	65668	Hurryville	63640	Kearney	64060
Green Trail	63026	Hermondale	63877	Hutton Valley	65793	Keener Cave	63967
Greenville (Clay County)	64060	Hickman Mills (Part of Kansas City)	64134	Iantha	64759	Keenland	64083
Greenville (Wayne County)	63944	Hickory Creek	64683	Iatan	64098	Keethtown	65486
Greenwood	64034	Hickory Hill	65040	Iberia	65486	Keightley's Beach	65355
Greer	65606	Higbee	65257	Iconium	64776	Kellerville	63469
Gregory	63435	Higdon	63645	Idalia	63825	Kelso	63758
Gregory Heights	65202	Higginsville	64037	Idlewild	63960	Keltner	65720
Gretna	65616	High Gate	65559	Ike	65737	Kendricktown	64836
Grimmet	65775	High Hill	63350	Ilasco	63401	Kennett	63857
Grisham	63764	Highland	63775	Illmo (Part of Scott City)	63780	Kenoma	64759
Grogan	65464	Highlandville	65669	Imperial	63052	Keota	63532
Grover	63400	Highley Heights (Part of Desloge)	63601	Independence	64050-58	Kerr	64429
Grovespring	65662	High Point	65042	For specific Independence Zip Codes call (816) 836-1440, or your local postmaster.		Kersey Coates (Part of Kansas City)	64105
Grubville	63041	High Ridge	63049	Independence Center (Part of Independence)	64057	Ketterman	64790
Guilford	64457	Hilda	65680	Indian Creek	63456	Kewanee	63860
Gumbo	63601	Hill City	65625	Indian Ford	65582	Keys Summit	63122
Gunn City	64760	Hillhouse Addition (Part of Richland)	65556	Indian Grove	65236	Keysville	65565
Guthrie	65063	Hilliard	63901	Indian Hills (Part of Kansas City)	64114	Keytesville	65261
Hagers Grove	63437	Hillsboro	63050	Indian Lake	65453	Kidder	64649
Hahatonka	65020	Hillsdale	63133	Indian Point	65616	Kiel	63068
Hahn	63764	Hill Top	63935	Indian Springs	64783	Killarney Shores	63650
Hailey	65605	Hinch	65441	Ink	65466	Kilwinning	63555
Hale	64643	Hinton	65202	Ionia	65335	Kimberling City	65686
Half Rock	64679	Hiram	63947	Irena	64456	Kimberling Hills (Part of Kimberling City)	65686
Half Way	65663	Hitt	63555	Irondale	63648	Kimble	65542
Halls	64504	Hoberg	65712	Iron Gates	64801	Kime	63944
Hallsville	65255	Hobson	65560	Iron Mountain	63650	Kimmswick	63053
Halltown	65664	Hocomo	65626	Iron Mountain Lake	63624	Kinder	63960
Hamilton	64644	Hodge	64096	Ironton	63650	Kinderpost	65542
Hammond	65762	Hoene Spring	63025	Irwin	64759	Kinfolks Ridge	63830
Hams Prairie	65251	Hoffman Junction	63628	Isabella	65676	King City	64463
Hancock	65452	Holcomb	63852	Isadora	64456	Kingdom City	65262
Handy	63941	Holden	64040	Ishmael	63664	Kings Lake	63347
Hanley Hills	63133	Holiday Shores	65326	Ives	63936	Kings Point	65682
Hannibal	63401	Holland	63853	Jack	65560	Kingston	64650
Hannon	64762	Holliday	65258	Jacket	65745	Kingsville	64061
Happy Hollow	63630	Holliday Landing	63944	Jacks Fork	65466	Kingsway Mall (Part of Sikeston)	63801
Hardeman	65340	Hollister	65672	Jackson (Benton County)	65355	Kinloch	63140
Hardenville	65666	Hollow	63069	Jackson (Cape Girardeau County)	63755	Kinsey	63627
Hardin	64035	Hollywood	63821	Jacksonville	65260	Kirbyville	65679
Harg	65201	Holman	65757	Jadwin	65501	Kirksville	63501
Harper	64776	Holmes Park (Part of Kansas City)	64131	James Crews (Part of Kansas City)	64127	Kirkwood	63122
Harris	64645	Holstein	63357	Jameson	64647	Kirschner (Part of St. Joseph)	64504
Harrisburg	65256	Holt	64048	Jamesport	64648		
Harrisonville	64701	Holts Summit	65043	Jamestown	65046		
Harry S. Truman (Part of Independence)	64055	Homestead	64024	Jamesville	65631		
Hart	64865	Homestown	63879	Jane	64856		
Hartford	63565	Honey Creek	65101	Japan	63080		
Hartsburg	65039	Hooker	65550				
Hartshorn	65479						
Hartville	65667						

* Area Zip Code † Post Office Boxes

	ZIP		ZIP		ZIP		ZIP
Kissee Mills	65680	Lawson	64062	Lowndes	63951	Maryville Gardens (Part of	
Kliever	65018	Leadington	63601	Lowry City	64763	St. Louis)	63111
Knobby	65326	Lead Mine	65764	Low Wassie	65588	Maryville University of St.	
Knob Lick	63651	Leadwood	63653	Lucas	64788	Louis	63141
Knob Noster	65336	Leann	65605	Lucas and Hunt Village	63121	Masters	65649
Knobtown (Part of Kansas		Leasburg	65535	Lucerne	64655	Matson	63341
City)	64138	Leawood	64801	Ludlow	64656	Mattese	63129
Knolls	65065	Lebanon	65536	Luebbering	63061	Matthews	63867
Knox City	63446	Lebo	65775	Lulu	65606	Maud	63437
Knoxville	64084	Lecoma	65540	Luna	65655	Maupin	63061
Kodiak	64485	Leeds (Part of Kansas		Lupus	65046	Mayesburg	64788
Koeltztown	65048	City)	64129	Luray	63453	Mayfield	63662
Koenig	65013	Leemon	63755	Lutesville (Part of Marble		Maysville	64469
Koshkonong	65692	Leeper	63957	Hill)	63764	Mayview	64071
Krakow	63090	Lees Summit	64063-64	Luystown	65016	Maywood	63454
Kurreville	63766		64081-82	Lynchburg	65543	McCord Bend	65656
Labadie	63055	*For specific Lees Summit Zip*		Lyon	63068	Meacham Park (Part of	
La Belle	63447	*Codes call (816) 524-0199, or*		Mc Allister Springs	65333	Kirkwood)	63122
Lac du Bois	63141	*your local postmaster.*		McBaine	65203	Meadowbrook Acres	64083
Laclede	63549	Leesville	64735	McBride	63776	Meadowbrook Downs	
La Crosse	64735	Leeton	64761	McCarty	63830	(Part of Overland)	63114
Lacyville	64720	Lemay	63125	McClurg	65701	Meadowbrook West	65203
Laddonia	63352	Lemons	63565	McCracken	65753	Meadville	64659
La Due (Henry County)	64735	Lenox	65541	McCurry	64438	Mecca	64492
Ladue (St. Louis County)	63124	Lentner	63450	McDowell	65769	Medford	64040
Laflin	63760	Leonard	63451	Macedonia	65401	Medill	63445
La Forge	63869	Leon Mercer Jordan (Part		McFall	64657	Medoc	64855
Lagonda	63558	of Kansas City)	64128	McGee	63763	Mehlville	63129
La Grange	63448	Leopold	63760	McGirk	65055	Meinert	65682
Laguna Beach (Part of		Leora	63825	Machens	63373	Melbourne	64642
Osage Beach)	65065	Leota	63626	McKenna Villa	65326	Melrose	63069
Lake Adelle	63016	Leslie	63056	Mackenzie	63123	Memphis	63555
Lake Annette	64746	Lesterville	63654	McKinley	65705	Mendon	64660
Lake Arrowhead	63060	Levasy	64066	McKittrick	65056	Menfro	63765
Lake City (Part of		Lewis	64735	Macks Camp	65355	Mentor	65742
Independence)	64016	Lewis and Clark Village	64484	Macks Creek	65786	Mercer	64661
Lake Contrary	64504	Lewistown	63452	McMullin	63801	Mercyville	63538
Lake Creek	65325	Lexington	64067	McNatt	64867	Merriam Woods	65653
Lake Forest Estates	63670	Liberal	64762	Macomb	65702	Merritt	65720
Lake Junction (Part of		Liberty (Callaway County)	65063	Macon	63552	Merwin	64723
Webster Groves)	63119	Liberty (Clay County)	64068	Madison	65263	Mesler	63772
Lake Kah-Tan-Da	63775	Libertyville	63640	Madisonville	63436	Meta	65058
Lakeland	65026	Lick	65233	Madry	65605	Metro North Mall (Part of	
Lake Lotawana	64086	Licking	65542	Magnolia	64040	Kansas City)	64155
Lake Mykee Town	65043	Liguori	63057	Main City	64742	Metz	64765
Lakenan	63468	Lilbourn	63862	Maitland	64466	Mexico	65265
Lake of the Woods		Lilly	64477	Majorville	65355	Miami	65344
(Boone County)	65201	Lincoln	65338	Makalu Estates	65065	Miami Station	64633
Lake-of-the-Woods		Lindbergh	65202	Malden	63863	Michelles Corner	65444
(Grundy County)	64683	Linden	65742	Malta Bend	65339	Micola	63877
Lake Ozark	65049	Lindenlure Lake	65742	Mammoth	65655	Middle Brook	63656
Lake Sherwood	63357	Lindley	64652	Manchester	63011	Middle Grove	65263
Lakeshire	63125	Lingo	64631	Mandeville	64622	Middletown	63359
Lakeside (Benton County)	65338	Linkville (Part of Kansas		Manes	65711	Mid Rivers Mall (Part of	
Lakeside (Boone County)	65256	City)	64152	Mano	65625	St. Peters)	63376
Lakeside (Jasper County)	64801	Linn	65051	Mansfield	65704	Midvale	65571
Lakeside (Miller County)	65026	Linn Creek	65052	Many Springs	65606	Midway	65202
Lake Spring	65532	Linneus	64653	Mapaville	63065	Mike	64658
Lake St. Louis	63367	Lisbon	65254	Maplegrove	64748	Milan	63556
Lake Tapawingo	64015	Lisle	64742	Maples	65542	Mildred	65679
Lake Tekakwitha	63069	Lithium	63775	Maplewood (Cass		Milford	64766
Lake Timberline	63628	Little Blue (Part of Kansas		County)	64083	Millard	63501
Lake Valle	63020	City)	64133	Maplewood (St. Louis		Millcreek	63645
Lakeview (Cass County)	64083	Little Village (Part of		County)	63143	Miller	65707
Lakeview (Miller County)	65026	Kansas City)	64118	Marble Hill	63764	Millersburg	65251
Lakeview Heights	65338	Livonia	63551	Marceline	64658	Millersville	63766
Lake Viking	64640	Lock Springs	64654	March	65644	Mill Grove	64673
Lake Ware	63020	Lockview Estates	65785	Marco	63870	Millheim	63775
Lake Waukomis	64152	Lockwood	65682	Margona Village (Part of		Mill Spring	63952
Lake Wauwanoka	63050	Locust Hill	63460	St. Johns)	63114	Millville	64085
Lake Winnebago	64034	Lodi	63950	Marion	65023	Millwood	63377
Lake Wittona	64683	Logan	65705	Marionville	65705	Milo	64767
Lakewood	65201	Lohman	65053	Mark Twain Mall (Part of		Milton (Atchison County)	64446
Lamar	64759	Loma Linda	63901	St. Charles)	63301	Milton (Randolph County)	65270
Lamar Heights	64759	Lonedell	63060	Marlborough	63123	Mincy	65679
Lambert	63736	Lone Elm (Cooper		Marling	63359	Mindenmines	64769
Lamine	65233	County)	65237	Marquand	63655	Mine La Motte	63645
La Monte	65337	Lone Elm (Jasper County)	64801	Marshall	65340	Mineola	63361
Lampe	65681	Lone Hill	63901	Marshall Junction	65340	Miner	63801
Lanagan	64847	Lone Jack	64070	Marshfield	65706	Mineral Point	63660
Lancaster	63548	Lone Star	63862	Marston	63866	Mineral Spring	65625
Lanes Prairie	65013	Lone Tree	64701	Marthasville	63357	Mineville (Part of Kansas	
Langdon	64446	Long Beach	65616	Martin City	64145-47	City)	64161
Lanton	65775	Long Lane	65590	*For specific Martin City Zip*		Mingo	63960
La Plata	63549	Longrun	65761	*Codes call (816) 943-0531, or*		Minimum	63961
Laquey	65534	Longtown	63775	*your local postmaster.*		Minnith	63673
Laredo	64652	Longview	64138-39	Martinsburg	65264	Mint Hill	65024
Larimore	63138	*For specific Longview Zip*		Martinstown	63565	Mirabile	64671
La Russell	64848	*Codes call (816) 353-0538, or*		Martinsville	64467	Missionary Acres	63944
Latham	65050	*your local postmaster.*		Marvel Cave Park	65616	Missouri City	64072
Lathrop	64465	Longwood	64861	Marvin	65084	Missouri Eastern	
La Tour	64760	Longwood	65340	Marvin Terrace (Part of St.		Correctional Center	63069
Latty	63664	Loose Creek	65054	Johns)	63114	Missouri Training Center	
Laurel Heights (Part of		Loughboro	63601	Mayden	63624	for Men	65270
Raytown)	64133	Louisburg	65685	Maryknoll	63369	Mitchell	65201
Laurie	65038	Louisiana	63353	Maryland Heights	63043	Moberly	65270
La Valle	63833	Louisville	63334	Marys Home	65032	Modena	64673
Lawrenceburg	65646	Lowground	63559	Maryville	64468	Mokane	65059
Lawrenceton	63627					Moline Acres	63136

***Area Zip Code   †Post Office Boxes**

	ZIP		ZIP		ZIP		ZIP
Molino	65265	New Melle	63365	Olathia	65704	Parkway (Jackson	
Monark Springs	64850	New Offenburg	63661	Old Appleton	63770	County)	64129-30
Monegaw Springs	64776	New Piper	64788	Old Bland	65014	For specific Parkway Zip Codes	
Monett	65708	New Point	64473	Old Chilhowee	64733	call (816) 861-8993, or your	
Monkey Run	63401	Newport	64759	Olden	65789	local postmaster.	
Monroe City	63456	New Santa Fe (Part of		Oldfield	65720	Parma	63870
Montague	65669	Kansas City)	64145	Old Fredonia	65355	Parnell	64475
Montague Hill	65340	New Survey	63877	Oldham	65010	Pasadena Hills	63121
Montevallo	64767	Newtonia	64853	Old Linn Creek	65052	Pasadena Park	63121
Montgomery City	63361	Newtown	64667	Old Merritt	65720	Pascola	63871
Monticello	63457	New Truxton	63381	Old Mines	63630	Passaic	64777
Montier	65546	New Wells	63732	Old Monroe	63369	Passo	65355
Montreal	65591	New Woolam	65066	Old Orchard (Part of		Patterson	63956
Montrose	64770	New York	64644	Webster Groves)	63119	Patton	63662
Montserrat	65336	Niangua	65713	Old Post Office (Part of		Patton Junction	63662
Moody	65777	Niangua Junction	65713	St. Louis)	63169	Pattonsburg	64670
Mooresville	64664	Nichols (Part of		Old Success	65570	Paulding	63821
Mora	65345	Springfield)	65802	Old Woollam	65066	Paulina Hills	63010
Morehouse	63868	Nind	63501	Olean	65064	Paydown	65582
Morgan	65632	Ninnescah Park	64740	Olive (Dallas County)	65648	Paynesville	63371
Morgan Heights	64836	Nishnabotna	64482	Olive (Part of St. Louis)	63101	Peace Valley	65788
Morley	63767	Nixa	65714	Olivette	63132	Peach Orchard	63848
Morrison	65061	Noble	65715	Olivewood	64083	Peaksville	63465
Morrisville	65710	Nodaway	64421	Olney	63370	Pea Ridge	63080
Morse Mill	63066	Noel	64854	Olympia	64744	Pebble Acres	63141
Morton	64085	Norborne	64668	Olympian Village	63020	Peculiar	64078
Mosby	64073	Normandy	63121	Omaha	63565	Peerless Park	63088
Moscow Mills	63362	Normandy Shopping		Ongo	65753	Peers	63357
Moselle	63084	Center (Part of		Opolis	66760	Pendleton	63383
Mosher	63670	Northwoods)	63121	Oran	63771	Penermon	63846
Mound City	64470	Norris	64726	Orange	65605	Pennsboro	65752
Moundville	64771	North Boonville	65274	Orchard Farm	63301	Pennville	63545
Mountain	65772	North County	63137-38	Orchard Lakes	63141	Peoria	63622
Mountain Grove	65711	For specific North County Zip		Orearville	65349	Pepsin	64844
Mountain View	65548	Codes call (314) 869-0433, or		Oregon	64473	Perkins	63774
Mount Airy	65259	your local postmaster.		Oriole	63701	Perrin	64477
Mount Freedom	63050	Northeast (Part of Kansas		Orla	65536	Perry	63462
Mount Hope	63077	City)	64123	Oronogo	64855	Perryville	63775
Mount Hulda	65325	Northern Heights (Part of		Orrick	64077	Pershing	65061
Mount Leonard	65339	Kansas City)	64152	Orrsburg	64475	Peru	64730
Mount Moriah	64665	North Kansas City	64116	Osage	65101	Peruque	63301
Mount Pleasant	65026	Northland Shopping		Osage Beach	65065	Petersburg	65250
Mount Shira	64854	Center (Part of		Osage Bend	65101	Petersville	63055
Mount Sterling	65062	Jennings)	63136	Osage Bluff	65101	Pevely	63070
Mount Vernon	65712	North Lilbourn	63862	Osage Hill (Part of		Phelps	64848
Mount Zion (Douglas		Northmoor	64152	Kirkwood)	63122	Phelps City	64482
County)	65608	North Noel (Part of Noel)	64854	Osborn	64474	Philadelphia	63463
Mount Zion (Henry		North Park Mall (Part of		Oscar	65542	Phillipsburg	65722
County)	64740	Joplin)	64801	Osceola	64776	Pickering	64476
Mulberry (Barton County)	66756	North Patton	63662	Osgood	64641	Piedmont	63957
Mulberry (Bates County)	64722	North Salem	63566	Osiris	64756	Pierce City	65723
Mullendike	64083	North Shores	65355	Oskaloosa	64762	Pierpont	65201
Munsell	65588	Northview	65706	Otterville	65348	Pierre Laclede (Part of St.	
Murphy	63026	North Wardell	63879	Otto	63052	Louis)	63108
Murry	65255	Northwest Plaza (Part of		Overland	63114	Pilot Grove	65276
Musicks Ferry	63034	St. Ann)	63074	Overton	65233	Pilot Knob	63663
Musselfork	65261	Northwood Acres	64152	Owens	65717	Pinckney	63357
Myrtle	65778	Northwoods	63121	Owensville	65066	Pine	63935
Mystic	63545	Northwye	65401	Owls Bend	65466	Pine Cove	65324
Napier	64451	Norwood	65717	Owsley	65332	Pine Crest	65571
Napoleon	64074	Norwood Court	63121	Oxford	64475	Pine Lawn	63120
Napton	65340	Nottinghill	65762	Oxly	63955	Pineville	64856
Nashua (Part of Kansas		Novelty	63460	Oyer	64744	Piney Park	63077
City)	64155	Novinger	63559	Ozark	65721	Pinhook	63845
Nashville	64855	Number Eight	63532	Ozark Beach	65653	Pioneer	65734
Naylor	63953	Nyhart	64730	Ozark Correctional Center	65652	Piper	64770
Nebo	65470	Nyssa	63932	Ozark Springs	65583	Pisgah	65237
Neck City	64849	Oak	64422	Ozark View	63122	Pittsburg	65724
Neelys	63755	Oak Grove (Franklin		Pacific	63069	Pittsville	64040
Neelyville	63954	County)	63080	Pack	64854	Plad	65764
Neeper	63445	Oak Grove (Jackson		Pagedale	63133	Plato	65552
Neier	63084	County)	64075	Painton	63772	Platte City	64079
Nelson	65347	Oak Grove Heights	65801	Palace	65552	Platte Woods	64151
Nelsonville	63440	Oak Hill	65453	Palisades	63011	Plattin	63028
Nemo	65724	Oakland (Laclede County)	65536	Palmer	63664	Plattsburg	64477
Neola	65661	Oakland (St. Louis		Palmyra	63461	Plaza (Part of Kansas	
Neosho	64850	County)	63122	Palopinto	65338	City)	64112
Netherlands	63851	Oakland Park	64870	Papin	63020	Plaza Shopping Center	
Nettleton	64644	Oak Leaf	65065	Papinsville	64780	(Part of Springfield)	65804
Nevada	64772	Oak Ridge	63769	Paradise	64089	Pleasant Gap	64730
Newark	63458	Oaks	64118	Paradise Point	65355	Pleasant Green	65276
New Bloomfield	65063	Oakside	65548	Paris	65275	Pleasant Grove	65068
New Boston	63557	Oakton	64759	Paris Springs	65646	Pleasant Hill	64080
Newburg	65550	Oakview	64118	Parkcrest Village (Part of		Pleasant Hope	65725
New Cambria	63558	Oakville	63129	Springfield)	65807	Pleasant Ridge (Barry	
New Florence	63363	Oakwood (Clay County)	64116	Parkdale (Jefferson		County)	65769
New Frankfort	65349	Oakwood (Marion County)	63401	County)	63049	Pleasant Ridge (Bates	
New Franklin	65274	Oakwood Park	64116	Parkdale (Platte County)	64152	County)	64780
New Hamburg	63736	Oasis	63347	Parker Lake	63775	Pleasant Valley (Clay	
New Hampton	64471	Oates	63625	Parkers Park	63347	County)	64068
New Harmony	63339	Ocie	65761	Park Forest (Part of		Pleasant Valley (Jasper	
New Hartford	63364	Octa	63876	Kansas City)	64152	County)	64836
New Haven	63068	Odessa	64076	Park Hills	63601	Plevna	63464
New Hope	63343	Odin	65667	Parkville	64152	Plew	64848
New Lebanon	65237	O'Fallon	63366	Parkway (Franklin County)	63077	Plymouth	64624
New Liberty	65588	Ogborn	63640			Pocahontas	63779
New London	63459	Oglesville	63961			Point Lookout	65726
New Madrid	63869	Ohio	64763			Point Pleasant	63873
New Market	64439	Okete	63379			Polk	65727

	ZIP
Pollock	63560
Polo	64671
Pomona	65789
Pom-o-sa Heights	65355
Ponce de Leon	65728
Pond	63038
Pondfork	65762
Pontiac	65729
Pony Express (Part of St. Joseph)	64503
Poplar	65355
Poplar Bluff	63901*
	63902†
Portage Des Sioux	63373
Portageville	63873
Port Hudson	63068
Portland	65067
Possumwalk	64428
Post Oak	64761
Potosi	63664
Pottersville	65790
Powe	63822
Powell	65730
Powersite	65731
Powersville	64672
Poynor	63935
Prairie City	64780
Prairie Hill	65281
Prairie Home	65068
Prairie Meadows Estate	65201
Prathersville (Boone County)	65202
Prathersville (Clay County)	64024
Pratt	63935
Prescott	65483
Preston (Hickory County)	65732
Preston (Jasper County)	64836
Princeton	64673
Principia	63131
Prospect	65713
Prospect Hill (Part of Riverview)	63137
Prosperity	64801
Protem	65733
Pulaski	63935
Pulaskifield	65708
Pumpkin Center	64423
Purcell	64857
Purdin	64674
Purdy	65734
Pure Air	63559
Purina Farm	63039
Purman	63935
Purvis	65079
Puxico	63960
Pyletown	63841
Pyrmont	65078
Quarles	64735
Queen City	63561
Quincy	65735
Quitman	64487
Qulin	63961
Racine	64858
Racket	64735
Racola	63630
Rader (Maries County)	65582
Rader (Webster County)	65713
Ralls	63401
Randles	63740
Randolph	64161
Ravanna	64673
Ravena (Part of Pleasant Valley)	64068
Ravena Gardens (Part of Pleasant Valley)	64068
Ravenwood	64479
Raymondville	65555
Raymore	64083
Raytown	64133
Rayville	64084
Rea	64480
Readsville	65067
Rector	65560
Redbird	65014
Red Bridge (Part of Kansas City)	64131
Redford	63665
Redings Mill	64801
Redman	63431
Red Oak	64848
Red Top	65757
Reeds	64859
Reeds Spring	65737
Reform	65077
Regal	64624
Reger	63556
Renick	65278
Rensselaer	63401
Renz Correctional Center	65022

	ZIP
Republic	65738
Rescue	64848
Revere	63465
Reynolds	63666
Rhineland	65069
Rhyse	65560
Richards	64778
Richards-Gebaur Air Force Base	64147
Rich Fountain	65035
Rich Hill	64779
Richland	65556
Richmond	64085
Richmond Heights	63117
Richville (Douglas County)	65637
Richville (Holt County)	64473
Richwoods	63071
Ridgedale	65739
Ridgely	64444
Ridgeway	64481
Ridgley	65647
Riggs	65284
Rimby	65659
Ripley (Part of Independence)	64056
Risco	63874
Rise Branch	65324
Ritchey	64844
River Aux Vases	63670
River Bend Estates	63017
Rivermines (Part of Park Hills)	63601
River Roads Mall (Part of Jennings)	63136
Riverside (Dunklin County)	63829
Riverside (Platte County)	64150
Riverside Inn	64854
Riverton	65606
Riverview	63137
Rives	63875
Roach	65787
Roads	64668
Roanoke	65230
Roanridge (Part of Kansas City)	64152
Robertson	63042
Robertsville	63072
Robinwood East	63141
Robinwood West	63141
Roby	65557
Rocheport	65279
Rochester	64459
Rockaway Beach	65740
Rockbridge	65741
Rockbridge Estate	65201
Rock Hill	63124
Rockingham	64035
Rock Port	64482
Rock Springs	63601
Rockview	63740
Rockville	64780
Rocky Comfort	64861
Rocky Mount	65072
Rocky Ridge	63670
Rogersville	65742
Rolla	65401
Rolling Hills	64083
Rombauer	63962
Rome	65608
Rondo	65650
Roosterville (Part of Liberty)	64068
Rosati	65559
Roscoe	64781
Rosebud	63091
Rosedale (Part of St. Louis)	63112
Roseland	65323
Roselle	63650
Rosendale	64483
Rothville	64676
Roubidoux	65444
Round Grove	65707
Round Spring	65466
Rover	65775
Rowena	65240
Royal	65559
Royal Heights (Part of Joplin)	64801
Royal Oak	65606
Ruble	63638
Rucker	65243
Rueter	65744
Running Deer	65065
Rush Hill	65280
Rush Tower	63028
Rushville	64484
Russ	65536
Russellville (Cole County)	65074

	ZIP
Russellville (Ray County)	64035
Rutledge	63563
Sabula	63620
Saco	63645
Sac Valley Estates	65785
Safe	65559
Sage Hill	65605
Saginaw	64864
St. Albans	63073
St. Ann	63074
St. Ann Shopping Center	63074
St. Anthony	65486
St. Catharine	65486
St. Charles	63301-04
For specific St. Charles Zip Codes call (314) 724-4810, or your local postmaster.	
St. Clair	63077
St. Clement	63334
St. Cloud	65441
St. Elizabeth	65075
St. Francisville	63430
St. Francois (Part of Fairview Acres)	63601
Ste. Genevieve	63670
St. George (St. Louis County)	63125
St. George (Wright County)	65667
St. James	65559
St. Johns	63114
St. Johns Station (Part of St. Johns)	63114
St. Joseph	64501-08
For specific St. Joseph Zip Codes call (816) 364-3503, or your local postmaster.	
St. Joseph Stock Yards (Part of St. Joseph)	64501
St. Louis	63101-88
For specific St. Louis Zip Codes call (314) 534-2841, or your local postmaster.	

COLLEGES & UNIVERSITIES

	ZIP
Harris-Stowe State College	63103
Maryville University-St. Louis	63141
St. Louis University	63103
University of Missouri-St. Louis	63121
Washington University	63130
Webster University	63119

FINANCIAL INSTITUTIONS

	ZIP
Boatmen's National Bank of St. Louis	63101
Cass Bank & Trust Company	63101
Citizens National Bank of Greater St. Louis	63143
Commerce Bank of St. Louis, National Association	63105
Heartland Savings Bank, F.S.B.	63101
Home Federal Savings Bank of Missouri	63141
Jefferson Bank & Trust Company	63103
Lemay Bank and Trust Company	63125
Magna Bank of Missouri	63101
Mark Twain Bank	63101
Mercantile Bank of St. Louis, National Association	63101
Pulaski Bank, a Savings Bank	63141
Southern Commercial Bank	63111
South Side National Bank in St. Louis	63116
Southwest Bank of St. Louis	63110
United Missouri Bank of St. Louis, National Association	63102
United Postal Savings Association	63122

HOSPITALS

	ZIP
Barnes Hospital	63110
Christian Hospital Northeast	63136
Deaconess Hospital	63139
Deaconess West	63131

	ZIP
Jewish Hospital of St. Louis	63110
Lutheran Medical Center	63118
St. Anthony's Medical Center	63128
St. John's Mercy Medical Center	63141
St. Mary's Health Center	63117
Veterans Affairs Medical Center	63125

HOTELS/MOTELS

	ZIP
Frontenac Hilton	63131
Harley of St. Louis	63045
Holiday Inn Southwest	63127
Marriott Pavilion	63102
Radisson Hotel Clayton	63105
Sheraton Westport Inn	63146
Stouffer Concourse Hotel	63134

MILITARY INSTALLATIONS

	ZIP
Aviation Systems Command	63120
Coast Guard Base, St. Louis	63111
Defense Mapping Agency, Aerospace Center, Installation One	63118
Defense Mapping Agency, Aerospace Center, Installation Two	63125
United States Army Aviation Troop Command	63120
United States Army Engineer District, St. Louis	63103
United States Army Publications Distribution Center	63114
United States Army Reserve Personnel Center	63132

	ZIP
St. Louis Centre (Part of St. Louis)	63102
St. Louis Galleria (Part of Richmond Heights)	63117
St. Luke	65632
St. Martins	65101
St. Mary	63673
St. Patrick	63466
St. Paul	63366
St. Peters	63376
St. Robert	65583
St. Thomas	65076
Salcedo	63801
Salem	65560
Saline	64632
Saline City	65349
Salisbury	65281
Salt Springs	65340
Samford	63877
Sampsel	64601
Sampson	65713
San Antonio	64443
Sandhills	63563
Sandstone	64767
Sandy Hook	65046
Santa Fe	65282
Santa Rosa	64670
Sapp	65203
Sappington	63126-28
For specific Sappington Zip Codes call (314) 843-6310, or your local postmaster.	
Saratoga	64854
Sarcoxie	64862
Sarvis Point	65746
Savannah	64485
Saverton	63467
Saxton	64507
Schell City	64783
Schlatitz	63730
Schluersburg	63332
Schofield	65663
Scholten	65605
Schubert	65101
Schuermann Heights (Part of Woodson Terrace)	63114
Scobeville	63857
Scopus	63764
Scotland	64836
Scotsdale	63051
Scott City	63780
Scotts Corner	63352
Scrivner	65074
Scrub Ridge	63873
Seaton	65560

	ZIP
Sedalia	65301*
	65302†
Sedgewickville	63781
Seligman	65745
Sellers	63457
Selma	63028
Selmore	65721
Selsa (Part of Independence)	64057
Senate Grove	63068
Senath	63876
Seneca	64865
Sequoita (Part of Springfield)	65804
Sereno	63775
Seymour	65746
Shackelford	65340
Shade	63851
Shady Dell	63901
Shady Grove (Christian County)	65753
Shady Grove (Pulaski County)	65583
Shady Slope	65065
Shamrock	63361
Shannondale (Chariton County)	65281
Shannondale (Shannon County)	65560
Sharon	65349
Shaw	65202
Shawnee Mound	64733
Shawneetown	63755
Shearwood	64648
Sheffield (Part of Kansas City)	64125
Shelbina	63468
Shelby	64674
Shelbyville	63469
Sheldon	64784
Shell Knob	65747
Sheridan	64486
Sherrill	65542
Shibboleth	63630
Shibleys Point	63559
Shirley	63664
Shoal Creek Drive	64801
Shoal Creek Estates	64801
Shook	63963
Short Bend	65560
Shoveltown	63031
Shrewsbury	63119
Sibley	64088
Sigsbee	63434
Sikeston	63801
Silex	63377
Silica	63028
Siloam Springs	65775
Silva	63964
Silver Creek	64801
Silver Dollar City	65616
Silver Lake (Cass County)	64083
Silver Lake (Perry County)	63775
Silver Mine	63645
Simcoe	64861
Simmons	65689
Sinsabaugh	63953
Sitze Store	63753
Skidmore	64487
Slabtown	65542
Slagle	65613
Slater	65349
Sleeper	65536
Sligo	65560
Smallett	65608
Smelter Hill (Part of Joplin)	64801
Smithfield	64834
Smithton	65350
Smithville	64089
Smoky Hollow	65560
Sni Mills	64075
Snow Hollow Lake	63656
Snyder	65286
Solo	65564
Souder	65773
Soulard (Part of St. Louis)	63157
South Carrollton (Part of Carrollton)	64633
South Cedar City (Part of Cedar City)	65022
South County Center	63129
Southeast (Part of Kansas City)	64132
Southeast Missouri Mental Health Center	63640
Southern Hills	65301
South Fork	65776

	ZIP
Southgate Shopping Center (Part of Springfield)	65804
South Gifford	63549
South Greenfield	65752
South Lee (Part of Lees Summit)	64081
South Liberty (Part of Liberty)	64068
South Lineville	50147
South Mall (Part of Warrensburg)	64093
South Point (Part of Washington)	63090
South Saint Joseph (Part of St. Joseph)	64504
South Shore	63301
South Side (Part of Springfield)	65806
South Troost (Part of Kansas City)	64131
South Troy	63379
South Van Buren	63965
Southwest (Part of St. Louis)	63139
South West City	64863
Spalding	63401
Spanish Lake	63138
Sparta	65753
Speed	65233
Spencerburg	63339
Sperry	63501
Spickard	64679
Splitlog	64843
Spokane	65754
Sprague	64779
Spring Bluff	63080
Spring City	64801
Spring Creek	65461
Springfield	65801-10
For specific Springfield Zip Codes call (417) 864-0101, or your local postmaster.	
Spring Garden	65032
Springhill	64601
Spring Lake	63501
Springtown	63660
Spring Valley (Camden County)	65065
Spring Valley (McDonald County)	64854
Sprott	63670
Spruce	64730
Spurgeon	64850
Squires	65755
Stahl	63559
Stanberry	64489
Stanhope	65339
Stanley	63851
Stanton	63079
Star City	65734
Stark	63353
Stark City	64866
Starkenburg	65069
State Correctional Pre-release Center	65081
Steedman	65077
Steele	63877
Steeles	63935
Steelville	65565
Steffenville	63470
Steinmetz	65254
Stella	64867
Stephens (Boone County)	65202
Stephens (Callaway County)	65201
Stet	64680
Stewartsville	64490
Stillings	64079
Stinson	65707
Stockton	65785
Stockton Hills	65785
Stockyards (Part of Kansas City)	64101-02
For specific Stockyards Zip Codes call (816) 221-1165, or your local postmaster.	
Stockyards (Part of St. Joseph)	64504
Stone Hill	65560
Stoneridge	65737
Stony Hill	63068
Stotesbury	64752
Stotts City	65756
Stoutland	65567
Stoutsville	65283
Stover	65078
Strafford	65757
Strain	63080

	ZIP
Strasburg	64090
Stringtown (Butler County)	63901
Stringtown (Cole County)	65053
Stringtown (Jasper County)	64834
Stults	65737
Stultz	65464
Sturdivant	63782
Sturgeon	65284
Sturges	64601
Sublette	63546
Success	65570
Sue City	63549
Sugar Creek	64054
Sugar Lake	64484
Sugartree	64668
Sullivan	63080
Sulphur Springs	63083
Sumach	63852
Summerfield	65013
Summerset Lake	63020
Summersville	65571
Summit	63660
Summit Shopping Center (Part of Lees Summit)	64081
Sumner	64681
Sundown	65761
Sunland Hills	63031
Sunlight	63622
Sunny Slope (Part of Kansas City)	64110
Sunnyvale (Part of Joplin)	64801
Sunrise	63855
Sunrise Beach	65079
Sunrise Lake	63020
Sunset Hills	63127
Sutherland	65360
Swan	65759
Swedeborg	65572
Sweden	65608
Sweet Springs	65351
Sweetwater (Newton County)	64850
Sweetwater (Reynolds County)	63638
Swift	63851
Swinton	63730
Swiss	65041
Sycamore	65758
Sycamore Hills	63114
Sycamore Valley	65355
Syenite	63651
Sylvania	65682
Syracuse	65354
Taberville	64780
Table Rock	65616
Taitsville	64671
Tallapoosa	63878
Taneyville	65759
Tanner	63801
Tan Tar Estates	65065
Tanyard	64801
Taos (Buchanan County)	64448
Taos (Cole County)	65101
Tara	63123
Tarkio	64491
Tarrants	63334
Tarsney Lakes	64075
Taskee	63967
Tauria	65737
Taylor	63471
Tea	63091
Teal Bend	65355
Tebbetts	65080
Tecumseh	65760
Tempo	63141
Ten Brook (Part of Arnold)	63010
Tenmile	63552
Ten Mile Corner	64784
Teresita	65573
Terre DuLac	63628
Thayer	65791
The Landing	63456
Theodosia	65761
Thomas Hill	65244
Thomasville	65438
Thompson	65285
Thornfield	65762
Thorpe	65644
Thox Rock	65550
Thrush	64735
Tiff	63674
Tiffany Springs (Part of Kansas City)	64152
Tiff City	64868
Tiffin	64744
Tightwad	64735
Tillman	63730
Tilsit	63755

	ZIP
Timber	65560
Times Beach	63025
Tina	64682
Tindall	64683
Tinkerville	63857
Tin Town	65622
Tipperary	63559
Tipton	65081
Tipton Ford	64801
Tip Top (Benton County)	65355
Tip Top (Iron County)	63621
Toga	63730
Toledo	65755
Tolona	63452
Torch	63953
Tower Grove (Part of St. Louis)	63163
Town and Country	63131
Town Pavilion (Part of Kansas City)	64105
Tracy	64079
Trask	65548
Treloar	63378
Trenton	64683
Trimble	64492
Triplett	65286
Troutt	63664
Troy	63379
Truesdail	63383
Truman Corners (Part of Grandview)	64030
Truxton	63381
Tuckahoe	64801
Tucker	63942
Tuckers Corner	64849
Tunas	65764
Turners	65765
Turnerville	65548
Turney	64493
Turtle	65560
Tuscumbia	65082
Tuxedo Park (Part of Webster Groves)	63119
Twelve Mile	63645
Twin	65355
Twin Bridges	65536
Twin Oaks	63011
Twin Springs	63079
Tyler	63877
Tyrone	65483
Udall	65766
Ulman	65083
Umber	65785
Umberland	65785
Umber View	65785
Umber View Heights	65785
Union (Franklin County)	63084
Union (Ray County)	64062
Union City	65610
Union Star	64494
Uniontown	63783
Unionville	63565
Unity Village	64064
University City	63130
Uplands Park	63121
Upton	65552
Urbana	65767
Urbandale (Part of Moberly)	65270
Urich	64788
Useful	65051
Utica	64686
Vale (Part of Kansas City)	64138
Valles Mines	63087
Valley City	65336
Valley Park	63088
Valley View (Benton County)	65355
Valley View (Ste. Genevieve County)	63627
Valley Water Mills	65803
Van	65613
Van Buren	63965
Vance	65713
Vancleve	65058
Vandalia	63382
Vandiver	65265
Vanduser	63784
Vanzant	65768
Vastus	63954
Velda Village	63133
Velda Village Hills	63121
Vera	63334
Verdella	64762
Verona	65769
Verona Hills (Part of Kansas City)	64145
Versailles	65084

	ZIP		ZIP		ZIP		ZIP
Veterans Hospital (Part of Kansas City)	64128	Waverly	64096	Wheeling	64688	Winona	65588
Vibbard	64062	Wayland	63472	Whispering Hills	63141	Winston	64689
Viburnum	65566	Wayne	65772	Whispering Pines	65401	Winthrop	64484
Vichy	65580	Waynesville	65583	Whitakerville	65355	Wisdom	65355
Victoria	63020	Weatherby	64497	White Branch	65355	Wishart	65710
Vida	65401	Weatherby Lake	64152	White Church	65789	Withers Mill	63401
Vienna	65582	Weaubleau	65774	White City	65020	Wittenberg	63786
Vigus	63042	Webb City	64870	White Cloud	65779	Wolf Island	63881
Village of Charlack	63114	Weber Hill	63051	White Hall Fields (Part of Liberty)	64068	Womack	63645
Village of Four Seasons	65049	Webster Groves	63119	Whiteman Air Force Base	65305	Woodbine Heights (Part of Kirkwood)	63122
Villa Heights (Part of Joplin)	64801	Webster Park (Part of Webster Groves)	63119	Whiteoak	63880	Woodcliffe	65804
Villa Ridge	63089	Wedgewood	63031	Whiteside	63387	Woodland	63461
Vineland	63020	Wedgewood Green	63031	Whitesville	64480	Woodland Park	65026
Vinita Park	63114	Weingarten	63670	Whitewater	63785	Woodland Shores	65355
Vinita Terrace	63114	Wela	64865	Whiting	63845	Woodlandville	65279
Vinson	63841	Weldon Spring	63301	Whitman	65286	Woodlawn	65263
Viola	65747	Weldon Spring Heights	63301	Wien	63558	Woodridge	63033
Virgil City	64744	Wellington	64097	Wilbur Park	63123	Woodruff	64098
Virginia	64730	Wellston (St. Louis County)	63112	Wilcox	64468	Woods Heights	64024
Vista	64789	Wellston (Part of St. Louis)	63112	Wilderness	63941	Woodson Terrace	63134
Vulcan	63675	Wellsville	63384	Wildwood	64424	Woodville	65247
Waco	64869	Wentworth	64873	Wildwood Estates	65804	Woolam	65014
Wagoner	65785	Wentzville	63385	Wildwood Lake (Part of Raytown)	64133	Wooldridge	65287
Wainwright	65043	Wesco	65586	Wilhelmina	63933	Worland	64752
Wakenda	64687	West Alton	63386	Willard	65781	Worlds of Fun (Part of Kansas City)	64161
Waldo (Part of Kansas City)	64114	West Aurora†	65026	William M Chick (Part of Kansas City)	64124	Wornall	64113*
Waldron	64092	Westboro	64498	Williamsburg	63388		64114†
Walker	64790	Westbrooke	65201	Williamstown	63473	Worth	64499
Wallace	64439	West County Center (Part of Des Peres)	63131	Williamsville	63967	Wortham	63601
Wall Street	65590	West Ely	63401	Willmathsville	63546	Worthington	63567
Walnut Grove	65770	West Eminence	65466	Willow Brook	64448	Wright City	63390
Walnut Shade	65771	Western Missouri Correctional Center	64429	Willow Springs	65793	Wyaconda	63474
Wanamaker	65340	West Hermondale	63877	Wilson City	63882	Wyatt	63882
Wanda	64866	West Line	64734	Wilton	65039	Wyatt Park (Part of St. Joseph)	64507
Wappapello	63966	Weston	64098	Winchester (Clark County)	63435	Wyeth	64483
Wardell	63879	West Park Mall (Part of Cape Girardeau)	63701	Winchester (St. Louis County)	63011	Yacht Club Harbor	65065
Ward Parkway Center (Part of Kansas City)	64114	Westphalia	65085	Winchester Gap	65536	Yancy Mills	65401
Wardsville	65101	West Plains	65775	Windsor	65360	Yarrow	63501
Ware	63050	Westport (Part of Kansas City)	64111	Windsor Springs (Part of Kirkwood)	63122	Yates	65257
Warren	63456	West Quincy	63471	Windyville	65783	Yonkerville	65723
Warrensburg	64093	Westview	64850	Winfield	63389	Youngstown	63559
Warrenton	63383	Westville	64658	Winigan	63566	Yount	63775
Warsaw	65355	Westwood	63131	Winnwood (Part of Kansas City)	64117	Yukon	65589
Warson Woods	63122	Wet Glaize	65567	Winnwood Gardens (Part of Kansas City)	64117	Zalma	63787
Washburn	65772	Wheatland	65779	Winnwood Lake (Part of Kansas City)	64117	Zanoni	65784
Washington	63090	Wheaton	64874			Zell	63670
Washington Center	64467	Wheelerville	65605			Zion	63645
Wasola	65773					Zion Hill	65559
Waterloo	64097					Zora	65078
Watson	64496						

Name	ZIP	Name	ZIP	Name	ZIP	Name	ZIP
Absarokee	59001	Buxton (Part of Butte)	59750	Drummond	59832	Greenfield	59436
Acton	59002	Bynum	59419	Dublin Gulch (Part of Butte)	59701	Greenough	59836
Adel	59421	Camas	59845	Dunkirk	59474	Gregson (Part of Butte)	59748
Agawam	59422	Camas Prairie	59859	Dupuyer	59432	Greycliff	59033
Agency	59831	Cameron	59720	Durant (Part of Butte)	59748	Hackney (Part of Butte)	59748
Alberton	59820	Canyon Creek	59633	Dutton	59433	Half Moon	59912
Albion	59311	Canyon Ferry	59601	Eagleton	59520	Hall	59837
Alder	59710	Capitol	57724	East Butte (Part of Butte)	59701	Hamilton	59840
Alhambra	59634	Cardwell	59721	East Glacier Park	59434	Hammond	59332
Alloy (Part of Butte)	59701	Carlyle	59353	East Helena	59635	Hammond Valley	59327
Alpine	59071	Carter	59420	East Missoula (Part of Missoula)	59801	Happyis Inn	59923
Alzada	59311	Cartersville	59347	Ekalaka	59324	Happy Valley	59937
Amazon	59632	Cascade	59421	Elkhorn Hot Springs	59746	Hardin	59034
Amsterdam	59741	Castle Rock	59327	Elliston	59728	Hardy	59421
Anaconda	59711	Castner Falls	59421	Elmdale	59213	Harlem	59526
Anceney	59741	Cat Creek	59017	Elmo	59915	Harlowton	59036
Andes	59218	Centennial (Part of Billings)	59108	Emigrant	59027	Harrison	59735
Angela	59312	Centerville (Cascade County)	59472	Enid	59243	Hathaway	59333
Antelope	59211	Centerville (Silver Bow County)	59701	Ennis	59729	Haugan	59842
Apgar	59936	Central Park	59714	Epsie	59317	Havre	59501
Argenta	59725	Champion (Part of Anaconda)	59722	Essex	59916	Havre North	59501
Arlee	59821	Chapman	59537	Ethridge	59435	Hays	59527
Armington	59412	Charles M. Russell (Part of Great Falls)	59405	Eureka	59917	Heart Butte	59448
Ashland	59003	Charlo	59824	Evaro	59801	Heath	59457
Ashuelot	59443	Charlos Heights	59840	Evergreen	59901	Hedgesville	59078
Augusta	59410	Checkerboard	59053	Everson	59430	Helena	59601-24
Avon	59713	Chester	59522	Fairfield	59436	For specific Helena Zip Codes call (406) 443-3304, or your local postmaster.	
Babb	59411	Chico Hot Springs	59065	Fairview	59221		
Bainville	59212	Chinook	59523	Fallon	59326	Helena Valley Northeast	59601
Baker	59313	Choteau	59422	Farmington	59422	Helena Valley Northwest	59601
Ballantine	59006	Christina	59451	Feely (Part of Butte)	59727	Helena Valley Southeast	59601
Bannack	59725	Church Hill	59741	Ferdig	59466	Helena Valley West Central	59601
Basin	59631	Circle	59215	Fergus	59451	Helena West Side	59601
Bearcreek	59007	Clancy	59634	Findon	59053	Hellgate (Part of Missoula)	59802
Bearmouth	59832	Clinton	59825	Finley Point	59860	Helmville	59843
Bear Spring	59430	Clyde Park	59018	First Creek	59538	Heron	59844
Beaverton	59261	Coalridge	59219	First Electronic Combat Range Group - Detachment 1	59501	Herron Park	59501
Beehive	59061	Coalwood	59351	Fishtail	59028	Hesper	59106
Belfry	59008	Cobden	59872	Flathead Indian Reservation	59831	Highwood	59450
Belgrade	59714	Coffee Creek	59424	Flatwillow	59087	Hilger	59451
Belknap	59874	Cohagen	59322	Flaxville	59222	Hingham	59528
Belle Creek	59317	Colorado Gulch	59601	Floral Park (Part of Butte)	59701	Hinsdale	59241
Belmont	59046	Colstrip	59323	Florence	59833	Hobson	59452
Belt	59412	Columbia Falls	59912	Floweree	59440	Hodges	59353
Beltower	59324	Columbia Gardens (Part of Butte)	59701	Forestgrove	59441	Hogeland	59529
Benchland	59462	Columbia Heights	59912	Forest Park	59330	Holiday Village (Part of Great Falls)	59405
Benteen	59031	Columbus	59019	Forsyth	59327	Holter Dam	59648
Biddle	59314	Comanche	59015	Fort Belknap	59526	Homestead	59242
Big Arm	59910	Condon	59826	Fort Belknap Indian Reservation	59526	Hopp	59520
Bigfork	59911	Conner	59827	Fort Benton	59442	Hot Springs	59845
Bighorn	59010	Conrad	59425	Fortine	59918	Howard	59327
Big Sandy	59520	Cooke City	59020	Fort Keogh	59301	Hughesville	59463
Big Sky	59716	Coram	59913	Fort Kipp	59213	Hungry Horse	59919
Big Timber	59011	Corbin	59638	Fort Peck	59223	Huntley	59037
Billings	59101-08	Corvallis	59828	Fort Peck Indian Reservation	59255	Huson	59846
For specific Billings Zip Codes call (406) 657-5709, or your local postmaster.		Corwin Springs	59021	Fort Shaw	59443	Hysham	59038
		Crackerville (Part of Anaconda)	59711	Four Buttes	59263	Iliad	59520
Billings Heights	59105	Craig	59648	Fourchette	59538	Ingomar	59039
Birch Creek Colony	59486	Crane	59217	Four Corners	59466	Inverness	59530
Birney	59012	Creston	59902	Frazer	59225	Ismay	59336
Black Eagle	59414	Crow Agency	59022	Frenchtown	59834	Jackson	59736
Blackfeet Indian Reservation	59417	Crow Indian Reservation	59022	Froid	59226	Janney (Part of Butte)	59701
Blackfoot	59417	Crow Rock	59301	Fromberg	59029	Jardine	59030
Bloomfield	59315	Culbertson	59218	Galata	59444	Jeffers	59729
Blossburg	59728	Cushman	59046	Galen (Part of Anaconda)	59722	Jefferson City	59638
Bonner	59823	Custer	59024	Gallatin Gateway	59730	Jefferson Island	59721
Bonner-West Riverside	59801	Cut Bank	59427	Gardiner	59030	Jellison Place	59085
Boulder	59632	Dagmar	59219	Garland	59301	Joliet	59041
Box Elder	59521	Danvers	59457	Garneill	59445	Joplin	59531
Boyd	59013	Darby	59829	Garrison	59731	Jordan	59337
Boyes	59316	Dawson (Part of Butte)	59748	Garryowen	59031	Judith Gap	59453
Bozeman	59771-73	Dayton	59914	Georgetown (Part of Anaconda)	59711	Kalispell	59901-04
	59715	Dearborn	59648	Geraldine	59446	For specific Kalispell Zip Codes call (406) 755-6450, or your local postmaster.	
For specific Bozeman Zip Codes call (406) 586-1508, or your local postmaster.		De Borgia	59830	Geyser	59447		
		Decker	59025	Gibson Flats	59401	Kenilworth	59520
Bozeman	59715	Deerfield Colony	59457	Gildford	59525	Kevin	59454
Bozeman Hot Springs	59715	Deer Lodge	59722	Gilt Edge	59457	Kicking Horse	59864
Brady	59416	Del Bonita	59427	Glacier Colony	59427	Kila	59920
Brandenberg	59301	Dell	59724	Glasgow	59230	Kingsbury Colony	59486
Brandon	59749	Delphia	59073	Glasgow Air Base	59231	Kinsey	59338
Bridger (Carbon County)	59014	Dempsey	59722	Glen	59732	Kiowa	59417
Bridger (Gallatin County)	59722	Denton	59430	Glendive	59330	Kirby	59016
Broadus	59317	Dentons Point (Part of Anaconda)	59711	Glentana	59240	Klein	59072
Broadview	59015	Devon	59474	Goldcreek	59733	Kolin	59451
Brock Creek	59731	Dewey	59727	Golden Ridge	59436	Kremlin	59532
Brockton	59213	Dillon	59725	Goldstone	59540	Lake McDonald	59921
Brockway	59214	Divide (Part of Butte)	59727	Grace (Part of Butte)	59759	Lakeside	59922
Brooks	59457	Dixon	59831	Grant	59725	Lakeview	59739
Brown (Part of Anaconda)	59711	Dodson	59524	Grantsdale	59835	Lambert	59243
Brown Addition	59472	Donald (Part of Butte)	59759	Grass Range	59032	Lame Deer	59043
Browning	59417	Dover	59479	Great Falls	59401-06	Landusky	59524
Brusett	59318	Dovetail	59087	For specific Great Falls Zip Codes call (406) 761-4894, or your local postmaster.		Larslan	59244
Buffalo	59418	Downtown (Part of Billings)	59101			LaSalle	59912
Busby	59016					Last Chance (Part of Helena)	59601
Butte	59701-03					Laurel	59044
	59750					Laurin	59749
For specific Butte Zip Codes call (406) 494-2107, or your local postmaster.						Lavina	59046

* Area Zip Code   † Post Office Boxes

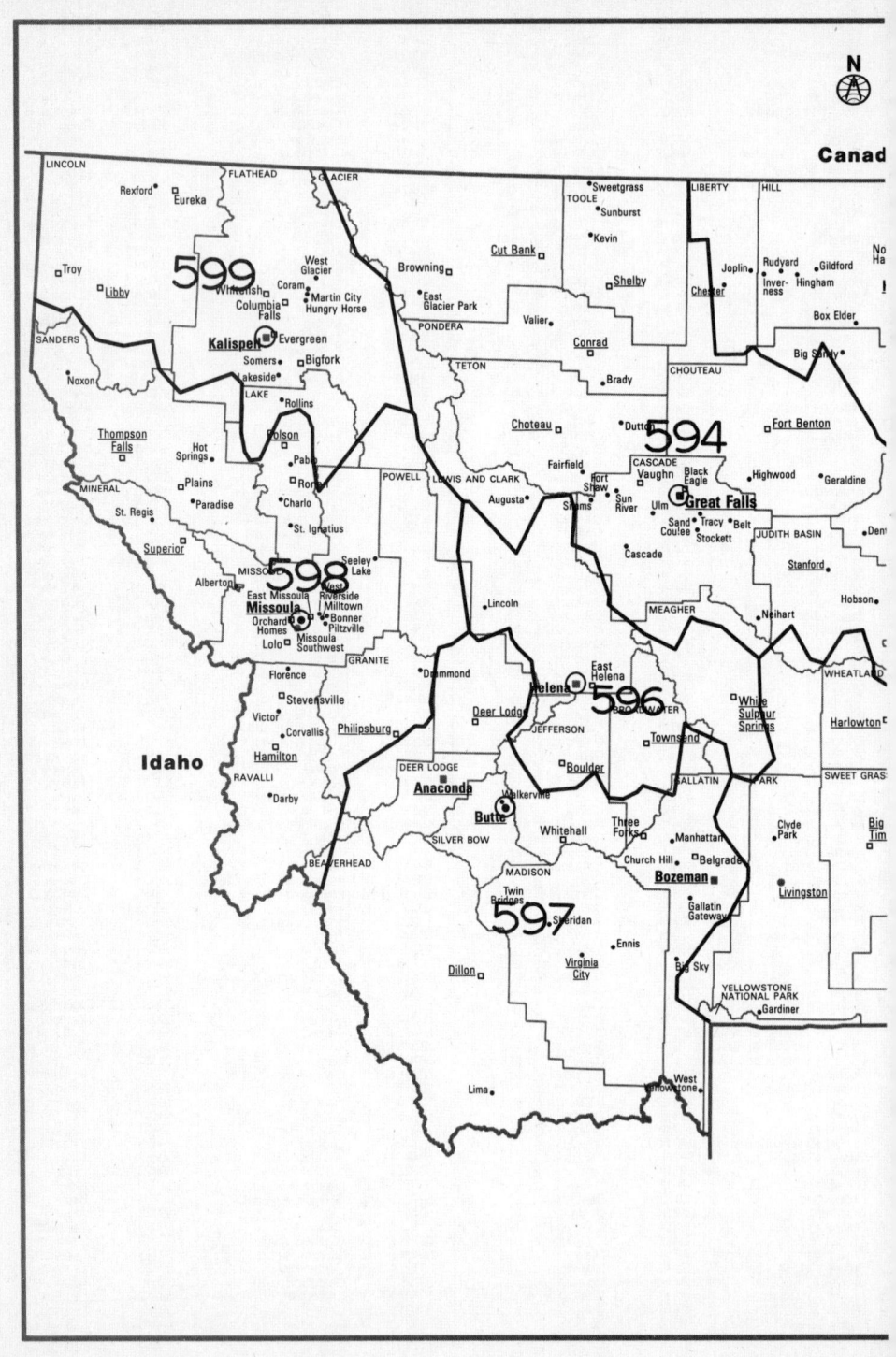

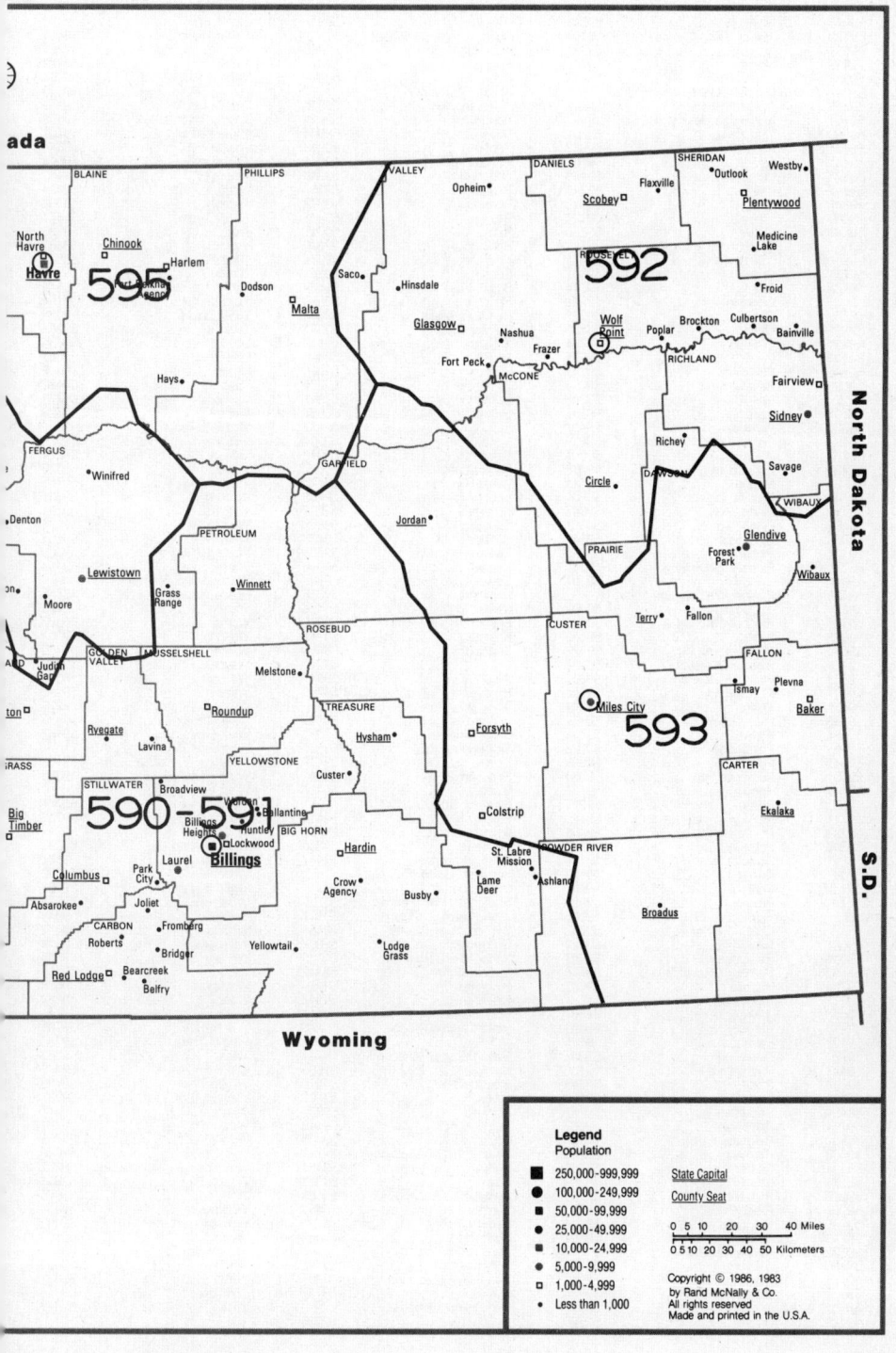

ada

BLAINE PHILLIPS VALLEY DANIELS SHERIDAN Westby

North
Havre
Chinook Harlem
Havre **595**

Opheim Scobey Flaxville Outlook Plentywood

Medicine
Lake

592

Dodson Saco Hinsdale Froid

Malta Glasgow Nashua Wolf Brockton Culbertson
Point Poplar Bainville

Frazer

Hays Fort Peck McCONE RICHLAND Fairview

Sidney

Richey Savage

FERGUS Winifred GARFIELD Circle DAWSON WIBAUX

Denton PETROLEUM Jordan Glendive

Lewistown Winnett PRAIRIE Forest Wibaux
Park

Grass Terry Fallon
Range
Moore ROSEBUD CUSTER FALLON

Judith GOLDEN MUSSELSHELL Melstone Ismay Plevna
Gap VALLEY
ton Roundup L.TREASURE Miles City Baker

Ryegate Hysham Forsyth **593**
Lavina
RASS YELLOWSTONE Custer CARTER

STILLWATER Broadview
Big Watford Ballantine Colstrip Ekalaka
Timber **590-591** Huntley BIG HORN
Billings POWDER RIVER
Heights Lockwood Hardin
Columbus Park Laurel **Billings** St. Labre Ashland
City Mission
Absarokee Joliet Crow Busby Lame Broadus
Agency Deer
CARBON Fromberg
Roberts Lodge
Bridger Yellowtail Grass
Red Lodge Bearcreek
Belfry

North Dakota

S.D.

Wyoming

Legend
Population

◼ 250,000-999,999 State Capital
● 100,000-249,999 County Seat
▪ 50,000-99,999
● 25,000-49,999 0 5 10 20 30 40 Miles
▪ 10,000-24,999 0 5 10 20 30 40 50 Kilometers
● 5,000-9,999
□ 1,000-4,999 Copyright © 1986, 1983
• Less than 1,000 by Rand McNally & Co.
All rights reserved
Made and printed in the U.S.A.

	ZIP		ZIP		ZIP		ZIP
Lebo	59053	New Rockport Colony	59422	Roberts	59070	Sun River	59483
Ledger	59456	Niarada	59852	Rocker (Part of Butte)	59701	Sunset	59836
Lennep	59053	Nibbe	59088	Rockport Colony	59467	Superior	59872
Lewistown	59457	Nickwall	59201	Rock Springs (Rosebud		Swan Lake	59911
Libby	59923	Nine Mile	59846	County)	59312	Sweetgrass	59484
Lima	59739	Nissler (Part of Butte)	59701	Rock Springs (Sheridan		Swiftcurrent	59411
Limestone	59061	Nohle	59221	County)	59258	Tampico	59230
Lincoln	59639	Norris	59745	Rockvale	59041	Tarkio	59872
Lindsay	59339	North Browning	59417	Rocky Boy	59521	Teigen	59084
Livingston	59047	Northern Cheyenne Indian		Rocky Boys Indian		Terry	59349
Lloyd	59535	Reservation	59043	Reservation	59521	The Pines	59859
Lockwood	59101	Northridge Heights (Part		Rollins	59931	Thompson Falls	59873
Lodge Grass	59050	of Kalispell)	59901	Ronan	59864	Three Forks	59752
Lodge Pole	59524	Noxon	59853	Roosville	59917	Toston	59643
Logan	59741	Nye	59061	Roscoe	59071	Townsend	59644
Lohman	59523	Oilmont	59466	Rosebud	59347	Tracy	59472
Lolo	59847	Olive	59343	Rossfork	59457	Trego	59934
Lolo Hot Springs	59847	Ollie	59313	Roundup	59072	Trident	59752
Loma	59460	Olney	59927	Roy	59471	Trout Creek	59874
Lonepine	59848	Opheim	59250	Ruby	59710	Troy	59935
Loring	59537	Opportunity (Part of		Rudyard	59540	Truly	59485
Lost Creek (Part of		Anaconda)	59711	Ryegate	59074	Turah	59825
Anaconda)	59711	Orchard Homes	59801	Saco	59261	Turner	59542
Lothair	59474	Ossette	59244	Sage Creek	59522	Turner Colony	59542
Lower Sun River (Part of		Oswego	59201	St. Ignatius	59865	Twin Bridges	59754
Great Falls)	59401	Otter	59062	St. Labre Mission	59004	Twin Creeks	59823
Lustre	59225	Outlook	59252	St. Marie	59231	Twodot	59085
Luther	59051	Ovando	59854	St. Mary	59417	Ulm	59485
McAllister	59740	Pablo	59855	St. Peter	59421	Unionville	59601
McCabe	59245	Paradise	59856	St. Regis	59866	Utica	59452
McClellans Creek	59635	Park City	59063	St. Xavier	59075	Valier	59486
McGlone Heights (Part of		Park Grove	59248	Salmon Prairie	59911	Vandalia	59273
Butte)	59701	Peerless	59253	Saltese	59867	Varney	59729
McLeod	59052	Pendroy	59467	Sand Coulee	59472	Vaughn	59487
McQueen (Part of Butte)	59701	Perma	59859	Sand Creek	59201	Victor	59875
Madoc	59222	Petrolia	59087	Sanders	59076	Vida	59274
Maiden	59457	Philipsburg	59858	Sand Springs	59077	Virgelle	59520
Maiden Rock (Part of		Piegan	59411	Santa Rita	59473	Virginia City	59755
Butte)	59743	Piltzville	59801	Sapphire Village	59452	Volborg	59351
Malmstrom Air Force		Pine Creek	59047	Savage	59262	Volt	59201
Base	59402	Pinegrove	59801	Savoy	59526	Wagner	59538
Malta	59538	Pinesdale	59841	Scobey	59263	Walkerville	59701
Manchester	59404	Pinnacle	59916	Seaver Park	59601	Wan-i-gan	59065
Manhattan	59741	Pioneer (Silver Bow		Sedan	59086	Ware	59457
Many Glacier Hotel	59411	County)	59701	Seeley Lake	59868	Warmsprings (Part of	
Marion	59925	Pioneer (Yellowstone		Shawmut	59078	Anaconda)	59756
Marsh	59326	County)	59102	Shelby	59474	Warren	82423
Martin City	59926	Pioneer Junction	59923	Shepherd	59079	Warrick	59520
Martinsdale	59053	Plains	59859	Sheridan	59749	Washoe	59007
Marysville	59640	Pleasant Prairie	59222	Shonkin	59450	Waterloo	59759
Maudlow	59714	Pleasant Valley	59925	Sidney	59270	Wayne	59412
Maxville	59858	Pleasant View	59330	Silesia	59041	Webster	59313
Medicine Lake	59247	Plentywood	59254	Silver Bow (Part of Butte)	59750	Weldon	59215
Medicine Springs	59827	Plevna	59344	Silver Bow Park (Part of		Westby	59275
Melrose (Part of Butte)	59743	Plum Creek	59457	Butte)	59701	West Glacier	59936
Melstone	59054	Polaris	59746	Silver Gate	59081	West Lewistown	59457
Melville	59055	Polebridge	59928	Silver Star	59751	West Park Plaza (Part of	
Mildred	59341	Polson	59860	Simms	59477	Billings)	59102
Miles City	59301	Pompeys Pillar	59064	Simpson	59501	West Riverside	59801
Milford Colony	59648	Pony	59747	Sipple	59464	West Valley (Part of	
Mill Creek (Part of		Poplar	59255	Sleeping Buffalo	59261	Anaconda)	59711
Anaconda)	59711	Portage	59440	Smelter Hill	59414	West Yellowstone	59758
Miller Colony	59422	Post Creek	59865	Somers	59932	Whately	59248
Mill Iron	59324	Potomac	59823	Sonnette	59348	Wheeler	59230
Milltown	59851	Powderville	59345	South Browning	59417	Whitefish	59937
Miner	59027	Power	59468	Southern Cross (Part of		Whitehall	59759
Missoula	59801-07	Pray	59065	Anaconda)	59711	White Haven	59923
For specific Missoula Zip Codes		Proctor	59929	Southgate Mall (Part of		Whitepine	59874
call (406) 329-2200, or your		Pryor	59066	Missoula)	59801	White Sulphur Springs	59645
local postmaster.		Quinn (Part of Butte)	59743	Spring Creek Colony	59457	Whitetail	59276
Missoula Southwest	59801	Racetrack	59722	Springdale	59082	Whitewater	59544
Mizpah	59301	Radersburg	59641	Springdale Colony	59645	Whitlash	59545
Moccasin	59462	Ramsay (Part of Butte)	59748	Square Butte	59442	Wibaux	59353
Moffit Canyon	59715	Rapelje	59067	Stanford	59479	Wickes	59638
Moiese	59824	Rattlesnake (Part of		Stark	59846	Willard	59354
Molt	59057	Missoula)	59801	Starr School	59417	Williamsburg (Part of	
Mona	59213	Ravalli	59863	State Capitol (Part of		Butte)	59701
Monarch	59463	Ravenna	59825	Helena)	59601	Willow Creek	59760
Monida	59739	Raymond	59256	Staton (Part of Anaconda)	59711	Wilsall	59086
Montague	59442	Raynesford	59469	Stemple	59633	Windham	59479
Montana City	59634	Red Bluff	59745	Stevensville	59870	Winifred	59489
Montanapolis Springs	59065	Red Lodge	59068	Stockett	59480	Winnett	59087
Moore	59464	Redstone	59257	Stone	59837	Winston	59647
Morel (Part of Anaconda)	59711	Reedpoint	59069	Straw	59418	Wisdom	59761
Morgan	59537	Regina	59538	Stryker	59933	Wise River	59762
Mosby	59058	Reserve	59258	Stuart (Part of Anaconda)	59711	Wolf Creek	59648
Moulton	59451	Rexford	59930	Suffolk	59451	Wolf Point	59201
Mount Ellis	59715	Richey	59259	Sula	59871	Woods Bay	59911
Muddy	59016	Richland	59260	Sumatra	59083	Woodside	59875
Musselshell	59059	Ridgelawn	59270	Summit	59434	Woodworth	59836
Myers	59038	Ridgway	59332	Summit Valley	59721	Worden	59088
Nashua	59248	Rimini	59601	Sunburst	59482	Wyola	59089
Navajo	59222	Rimrock Mall (Part of		Sunnyside (Part of		Yaak Valley	59935
Neihart	59465	Billings)	59102	Anaconda)	59711	Yellowtail	59035
Nevada City	59755	Ringling	59642	Sun Prairie (Cascade		York	59601
New Chicago	59832	Rising Sun	59434	County)	59487	Zortman	59546
Newcomb (Part of Butte)	59701	Riverside	59840	Sun Prairie (Phillips		Zurich	59547
New Miami Colony	59425	Rivulet	59820	County)	59538		

	ZIP		ZIP		ZIP		ZIP
Abie	68001	Breslau	68765	Dawson	68337	Gothenburg	69138
Adams	68301	Brewster	68821	Daykin	68338	Grafton	68365
Agnew	68428	Bridgeport	69336	Debolt (Part of Omaha)	68152	Grainton	69169
Ainsworth	69210	Briggs	68122	Decatur	68020	Grand Island	68801-03
Air Mail Facility (Part of Omaha)	68119	Bristow	68719	Denman	68956	For specific Grand Island Zip Codes call (308) 385-6581, or your local postmaster.	
Air Park West	68524	Broadwater	69125	Denton	68339	Grand Island Mall (Part of Grand Island)	68801
Akron	68620	Brock	68320	Deshler	68340	Grant	69140
Albion	68620	Broken Bow	68822	De Soto	68023	Greeley	68842
Alda	68810	Brownlee	69166	Deweese	68934	Green Meadows	68164
Alexandria	68303	Brownson	69162	De Witt	68341	Greenwood	68366
Allen	68710	Brownville	68321	Dickens	69132	Gresham	68367
Alliance	69301	Brule	69127	Diller	68342	Gretna	68028
Alma	68920	Bruning	68322	Dix	69133	Gross	68719
Almeria	68879	Bruno	68014	Dixon	68732	Grover	68405
Aloys	68788	Brunswick	68720	Dodge	68633	Guide Rock	68942
Altona	68787	Burchard	68323	Doniphan	68832	Gurley	69141
Alvo	68304	Burkett (Part of Grand Island)	68801	Dorchester	68343	Hadar	68738
Amelia	68711	Burr	68324	Douglas	68344	Haig	69357
Ames	68621	Burress	68354	Downtown (Part of Omaha)	68101	Haigler	69030
Ames Avenue	68110-11	Burton	68778	Du Bois	68345	Hallam	68368
For specific Ames Avenue Zip Codes call (402) 451-7737, or your local postmaster.		Burwell	68823	Dunbar	68346	Halsey	69142
Amherst	68812	Bushnell	69128	Duncan	68634	Hamlet	69031
Angora	69331	Butte	68722	Dunning	68833	Hampton	68843
Angus	68961	Byron	68325	Dwight	68635	Hansen	68901
Anoka	68722	Cadams	68978	Eagle	68347	Harbine	68377
Anselmo	68813	Cairo	68824	Eddyville	68834	Hardy	68943
Ansley	68814	Callaway	68825	Edgar	68935	Harrisburg	69345
Antioch	69340	Cambridge	69022	Edison	68936	Harrison	69346
Arapahoe	68922	Campbell	68932	Elba	68835	Hartington	68739
Arcadia	68815	Carleton	68326	Elgin	68636	Harvard	68944
Archer	68816	Carroll	68723	Eli	69201	Hastings	68901*
Arlington	68002	Cedar Bluffs	68015	Elk City	68064		68902†
Arnold	69120	Cedar Creek	68016	Elk Creek	68348	Havelock (Part of Lincoln)	68529
Arthur	69121	Cedar Rapids	68627	Elkhorn	68022	Havens	68628
Ashby	69333	Center	68724	Ellis	68310	Hayes Center	69032
Ashland	68003	Central City	68826	Ellsworth	69340	Hay Springs	69347
Ashton	68817	Ceresco	68017	Elm Creek	68836	Hazard	68844
Assumption	68955	Chadron	69337	Elmwood	68349	Heartwell	68945
Aten	68730	Chalco	68046	Elmwood Park	68105-06	Hebron	68370
Atkinson	68713	Chambers	68725	For specific Elmwood Park Zip Codes call (402) 551-7531, or your local postmaster.		Hemingford	69348
Atlanta	68923	Champion	69023	Elsie	69134	Henderson	68371
Auburn	68305	Chapman	68827	Elsmere	69135	Hendley	68946
Aurora	68818	Chappell	69129	Elwood	68937	Henry	69349
Autumn Hills (Part of Omaha)	68134	Cheneys	68526	Elyria	68837	Herman	68029
Avoca	68307	Chester	68327	Emerald	68528	Hershey	69143
Axtell	68924	Clarks	68628	Emerson	68733	Hickman	68372
Ayr	68925	Clarkson	68629	Emmet	68734	Hideaway Acres	68730
Bancroft	68004	Clatonia	68328	Enders	69027	Hildreth	68947
Barada	68355	Clay Center	68933	Endicott	68350	Hillerage	69361
Barneston	68309	Clearwater	68726	Enola	68701	Holbrook	68948
Bartlett	68622	Clinton	69343	Ericson	68637	Holdrege	68949
Bartley	69020	Cody	69211	Ericson Lake	68637	Holland	68372
Bassett	68714	Coleridge	68727	Eustis	69028	Hollinger	68967
Battle Creek	68715	College View (Part of Lincoln)	68506	Ewing	68735	Holmesville	68374
Bayard	69334	Colon	68018	Exeter	68351	Holstein	68950
Bazile Mills	68729	Colton	69162	Fairbury	68352	Homer	68030
Beatrice	68310	Columbus	68601-02	Fairfield	68938	Hooper	68031
Beaver City	68926	For specific Columbus Zip Codes call (402) 564-3208, or your local postmaster.		Fairmont	68354	Hordville	68846
Beaver Crossing	68313	Comstock	68828	Falls City	68355	Hoskins	68740
Bee	68314	Concord	68728	Farnam	69029	Howe	68305
Beemer	68716	Conestoga Mall (Part of Grand Island)	68803	Farwell	68838	Howells	68641
Belden	68717	Constance	68730	Filley	68357	Hubbard	68741
Belgrade	68623	Cook	68329	Firth	68358	Hubbell	68375
Bellevue	68005	Cordova	68330	Florence (Part of Omaha)	68112	Humboldt	68376
Bellwood	68624	Cornlea	68642	Fontanelle	68044	Humphrey	68642
Belvidere	68315	Cortland	68331	Fordyce	68736	Huntley	68951
Benedict	68316	Cotesfield	68829	Fort Calhoun	68023	Hyannis	69350
Benkelman	69021	Cowles	68930	Fort Robinson	69339	Imperial	69033
Bennet	68317	Cozad	69130	Foster	68737	Imperial Mall (Part of Hastings)	68901
Bennington	68007	Crab Orchard	68332	Franklin	68939	Inavale	68952
Benson (Part of Omaha)	68104	Craig	68019	Fremont	68025	Indianola	69034
Berea	69301	Crawford	69339	Friend	68359	Indian Village (Part of Lincoln)	68502
Bertrand	68927	Creighton	68729	Fullerton	68638		68542
Berwyn	68819	Creston	68631	Funk	68940	For specific Indian Village Zip Codes call (402) 473-1622, or your local postmaster.	
Bethany (Part of Lincoln)	68505	Crete	68333	Gandy	69163	Inglewood	68025
Bignell	69151	Crofton	68730	Garland	68360	Inland	68954
Big Springs	69122	Crookston	69212	Garrison	68632	Inman	68742
Bingham	69335	Crossroads Mall (Part of Omaha)	68114	Gates	68822	Irvington	68134
Bixby	68979	Crowell	68057	Gateway Shopping Center (Part of Lincoln)	68505	Ithaca	68033
Bladen	68928	Crown Point (Part of Omaha)	68122	Geneva	68361	Jacinto	69133
Blair	68008	Culbertson	69024	Genoa	68640	Jackson	68743
Bloomfield	68718	Curtis	69025	Gering	69341	Jamison	68759
Bloomington	68929	Cushing	68873	Gibbon	68840	Jansen	68377
Blue Hill	68930	Dakota City	68731	Gilead	68362	Johnson	68378
Blue River Lodge	68333	Dalton	69131	Giltner	68841	Johnson Lake	68937
Blue Springs	68318	Dana College	68008	Gladstone	68352	Johnstown	69214
Boelus	68820	Danbury	69026	Glen	69339	Julian	68379
Boone	68625	Dannebrog	68831	Glenover (Part of Beatrice)	68310	Juniata	68955
Bostwick	68978	Darr	69130	Glenvil	68941	Kearney	68847*
Bow Valley	68739	Davenport	68335	Glenwood Park	68847		68848†
Boys Town	68010	Davey	68336	Goehner	68364	Keene	68924
Bradshaw	68319	David City	68632	Good Samaritan Village (Part of Hastings)	68901	Kenesaw	68956
Brady	69123			Gordon	69343		
Brainard	68626						
Brandon	69140						

* Area Zip Code   † Post Office Boxes

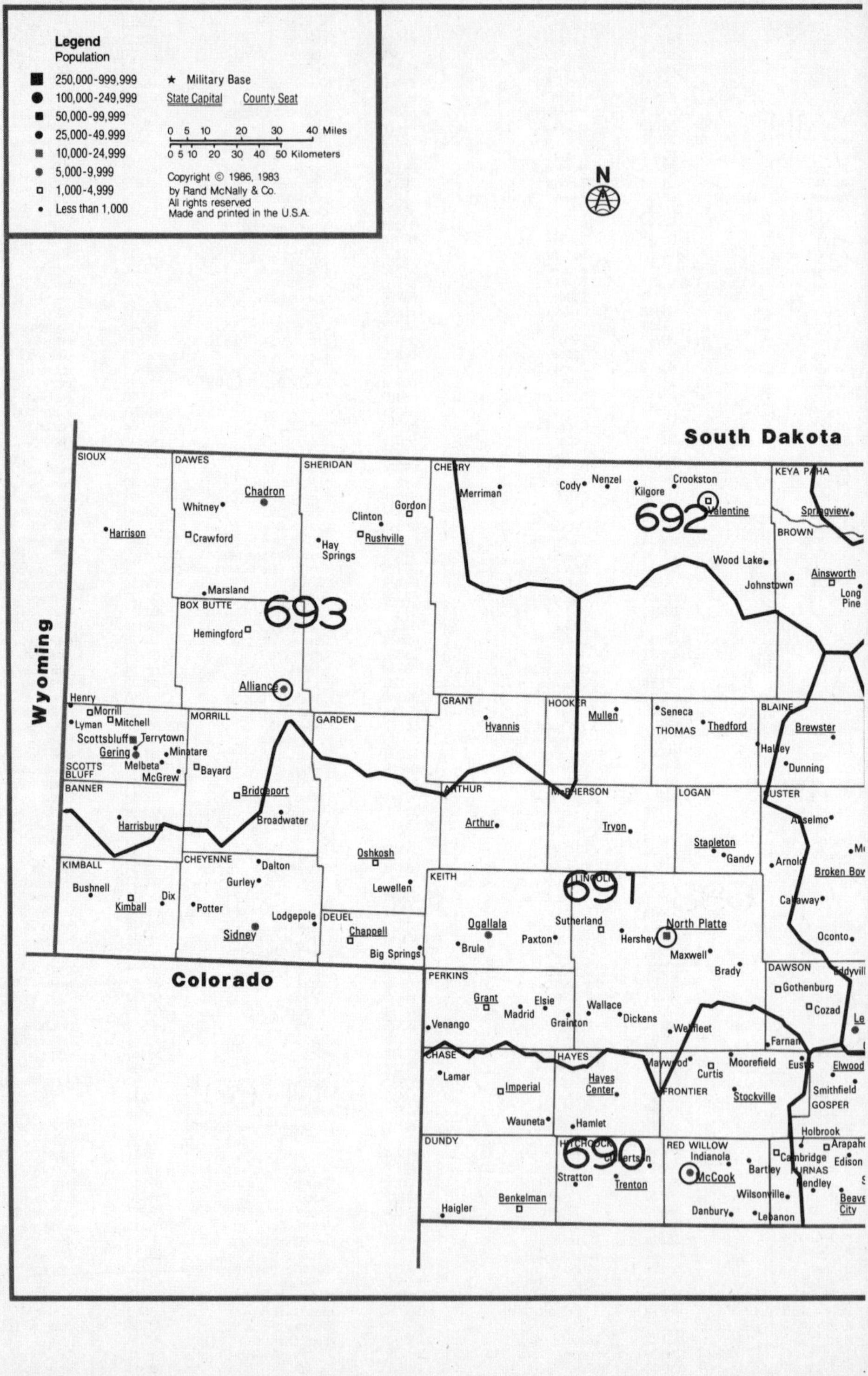

Legend
Population

■ 250,000-999,999
● 100,000-249,999
■ 50,000-99,999
● 25,000-49,999
■ 10,000-24,999
● 5,000-9,999
□ 1,000-4,999
• Less than 1,000

★ Military Base
State Capital   County Seat

0 5 10   20   30   40 Miles
0 5 10 20 30 40 50 Kilometers

Copyright © 1986, 1983
by Rand McNally & Co.
All rights reserved
Made and printed in the U.S.A.

N

South Dakota

Wyoming

Colorado

SIOUX

DAWES

SHERIDAN

CHERRY

KEYA PAHA

Chadron
Whitney
Harrison
Crawford

Marsland

BOX BUTTE

Hemingford

Clinton
Gordon
Hay
Springs
Rushville

Merriman
Cody   Nenzel
Kilgore
Crookston
Valentine

692

Springview
BROWN
Wood Lake
Ainsworth
Johnstown
Long
Pine

693

Alliance

Henry
Morrill
Lyman   Mitchell
Scottsbluff   Terrytown
Gering   Minatare
Melbeta
SCOTTS   McGrew
BLUFF
BANNER

MORRILL

GARDEN

Hyannis

GRANT

HOOKER
Mullen

Seneca
THOMAS   Thedford
Halsey
Dunning

BLAINE

Brewster

Bayard
Bridgeport
Broadwater

Harrisburg

KIMBALL

CHEYENNE
Dalton
Gurley
Bushnell
Dix
Kimball   Potter
Lodgepole
Sidney

Oshkosh

Lewellen

DEUEL
Chappell
Big Springs

ARTHUR

Arthur

McPHERSON

Tryon

LOGAN

Stapleton
Gandy

CUSTER
Anselmo
Arnold   Broken Bow
Callaway
Oconto

KEITH

691

Ogallala
Brule
Sutherland
Paxton   Hershey
North Platte
Maxwell
Brady

LINCOLN

DAWSON
Gothenburg
Cozad

Colorado

PERKINS

Grant
Venango   Madrid
Elsie
Grainton
Wallace
Dickens
Wellfleet
Farnam

CHASE
Lamar
Imperial
Wauneta

HAYES
Hayes
Center
Hamlet

Maywood
Curtis
FRONTIER
Moorefield
Stockville
Eustis   Elwood

Smithfield
GOSPER

Holbrook
Arapahoe

DUNDY
Haigler
Benkelman
HITCHCOCK
Stratton
Trenton
Culbertson

690

RED WILLOW
Indianola
McCook
Wilsonville
Danbury   Lebanon

Cambridge   Edison
Bartley   FURNAS
Hendley

Beaver
City

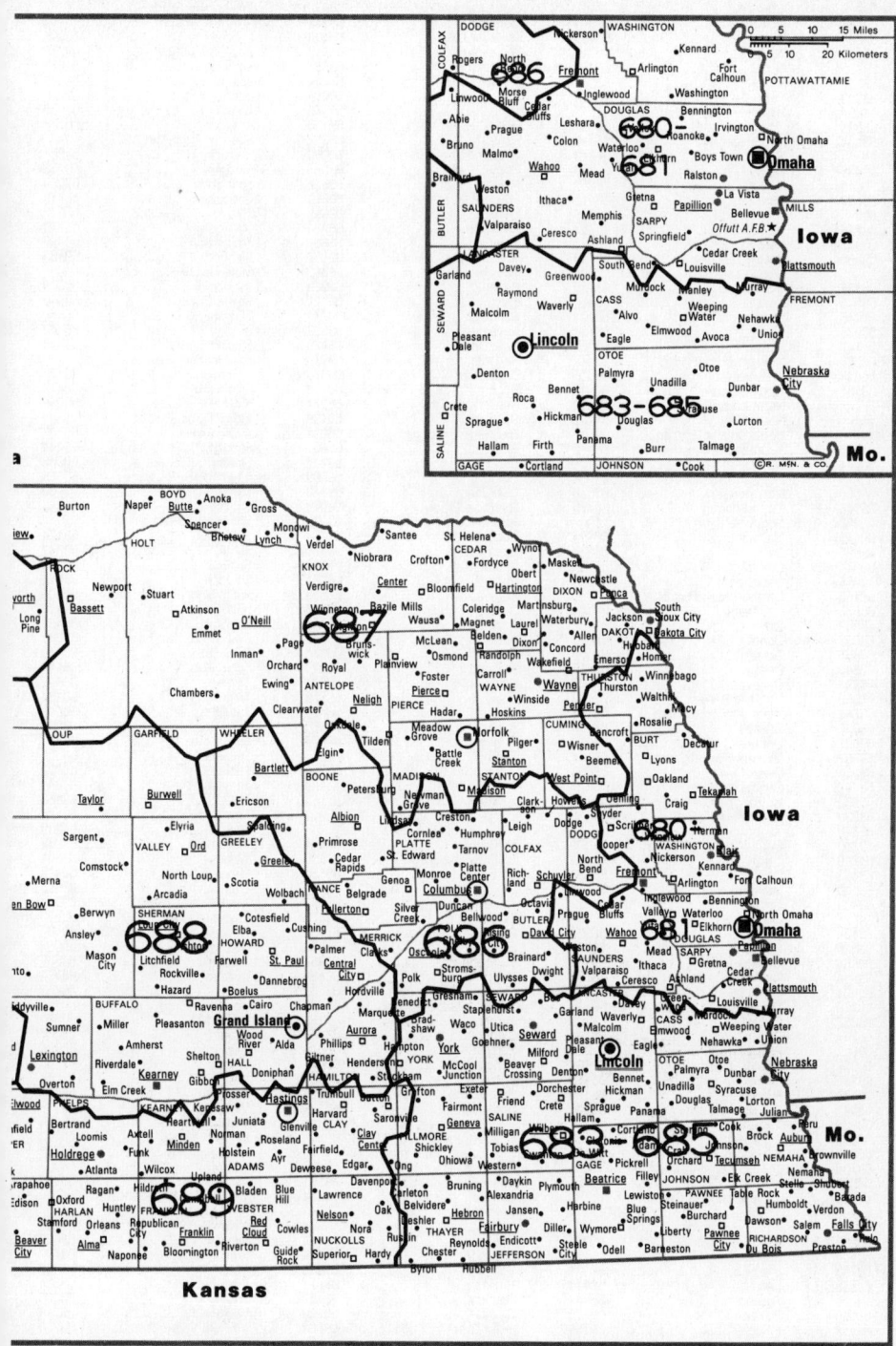

	ZIP		ZIP		ZIP		ZIP
Kennard	68034	Mount Michael	68022	Pilger	68768	South Omaha (Part of Omaha)	68107
Keystone	69144	Mullen	69152	Plainview	68769	Southroads Shopping	
Kilgore	69216	Murdock	68407	Platte Center	68653	Center (Part of	
Kimball	69145	Murphy	68865	Plattsmouth	68048	Bellevue)	68005
King Lake	68064	Murray	68409	Pleasant Dale	68423	South Sioux City	68776
Kingsley	69153	Mynard	68048	Pleasant Hill	68343	South Yankton	57078
Knievels Corner	68735	Naper	68755	Pleasanton	68866	Spalding	68665
Kohles Acres	68730	Naponee	68960	Plymouth	68424	Sparks	69220
Kramer	68333	Nashville	68112	Polk	68654	Sparta	68783
Kronborg	68854	Nebraska Center For		Ponca	68770	Spencer	68777
Kuesters Lake	68801	Women	68467	Potter	69156	Spencer Park (Part of	
Lake Forest Estates	68134	Nebraska City	68410	Powell	68352	Hastings)	68901
Lakeside	69351	Nehawka	68413	Prague	68050	Sprague	68438
Lamar	69035	Neligh	68756	Prairie Home	68527	Springfield	68059
Lanham	68415	Nelson	68961	Precept	68977	Springview	68778
La Platte	68123	Nemaha	68414	Preston	68355	Stamford	68977
Laurel	68745	Nenzel	69219	Primrose	68655	Stanton	68779
La Vista	68128	Newcastle	68757	Princeton	68404	Staplehurst	68439
Lawrence	68957	Newman Grove	68758	Prosser	68868	Stapleton	69163
Lebanon	69036	Newport	68759	Purdum	69157	State House (Part of	
Lee Valley (Part of		Nickerson	68044	Raeville	68652	Lincoln)	68509
Omaha)	68134	Niobrara	68760	Ragan	68969	Steele City	68440
Leigh	68643	Nora	68961	Ralston	68127	Steinauer	68441
Lemoyne	69146	Norfolk	68701*	Randolph	68771	Stella	68442
Leshara	68035		68702†	Ravenna	68869	Sterling	68443
Lewellen	69147	Norman	68963	Raymond	68428	Still Meadow (Part of	
Lewiston	68380	North Auburn (Part of		Red Cloud	68970	Omaha)	68122
Lexington	68850	Auburn)	68305	Redington	69336	Stockham	68818
Liberty	68381	North Bend	68649	Regency (Part of Omaha)	68114	Stockville	69042
Lincoln	68501-88	North Loup	68859	Republican City	68971	Stock Yards (Part of	
For specific Lincoln Zip Codes		North Oaks	68122	Reynolds	68429	Omaha)	68107
call (402) 473-1695, or your		North Omaha (Part of		Richfield	68054	Strang	68444
local postmaster.		Omaha)	68112	Richland	68601	Stratton	69043
Lindsay	68644	North Platte	69101*	Ringgold	69167	Stromsburg	68666
Lindy	68718		69103†	Rising City	68658	Stuart	68780
Linwood	68036	Northport	69336	Riverdale	68870	Sumner	68878
Lisco	69148	North Shore	68776	Riverside Lakes	68069	Sunnyslope (Part of	
Litchfield	68852	Northwest (Part of		Riverton	68972	Omaha)	68134
Lodgepole	69149	Omaha)	68134	Roanoke (Part of Omaha)	68134	Sunol	69149
Loma	68626	Oak	68964	Roca	68430	Superior	68978
Long Pine	69217	Oakdale	68761	Rockford	68310	Surprise	68667
Loomis	68958	Oakland	68045	Rockville	68871	Sutherland	69165
Lorenzo	69162	Oakview Mall (Part of		Rogers	68659	Sutton	68979
Loretto	68620	Omaha)	68144	Rosalie	68055	Swanton	68445
Lorton	68382	Obert	68757	Roscoe	69153	Swedeburg	68066
Louisville	68037	Oconto	68860	Rose	68772	Syracuse	68446
Loup City	68853	Octavia	68650	Roseland	68973	Table Rock	68447
Lowell	68840	Odell	68415	Rosemont	68930	Talmage	68448
Lushton	68371	Odessa	68861	Rosenburg	68644	Tamora	68434
Lyman	69352	Offutt AFB West	68113	Royal	68773	Tarnov	68642
Lynch	68746	Offutt Air Force Base	68113	Rulo	68431	Taylor	68879
Lyons	68038	Ogallala	69153	Rushville	69360	Tecumseh	68450
McCook	69001	Ohiowa	68416	Ruskin	68974	Tekamah	68061
McCool Junction	68401	Old Mill (Part of Omaha)	68134	Sac and Fox Indian		Telbasta	68002
McGrew	69353	Olean	68633	Reservation	68355	Terrytown	69341
McLean	68747	Omaha	68101-64	Saddle Creek	68131-32	Thayer	68460
Macon	68939	For specific Omaha Zip Codes		For specific Saddle Creek Zip		Thedford	69166
Macy	68039	call (402) 348-2861, or your		Codes call (402) 551-0692, or		Thompson	68352
Madison	68748	local postmaster.		your local postmaster.		Thurston	68062
Madrid	69150	Omaha Indian Reservation	68039	St. Bernard	68644	Tilden	68781
Magnet	68749	O'Neill	68763	St. Columbans	68056	Tobias	68453
Malcolm	68402	Ong	68452	St. Edward	68660	Touhy	68065
Malmo	68040	Orchard	68764	St. Helena	68774	Trenton	69044
Manley	68403	Ord	68862	St. James	68792	Trumbull	68980
Maple Hills (Part of		Orleans	68966	St. Libory	68872	Tryon	69167
Omaha)	68134	Orum	68008	St. Mary	68432	Uehling	68063
Marion	69026	Osceola	68651	St. Paul	68873	Ulysses	68669
Marquette	68854	Oshkosh	69154	St. Stephens	68957	Unadilla	68454
Marsland	69354	Osmond	68765	Salem	68433	Union	68455
Martell	68404	Otoe	68417	Santee	68760	University Place (Part of	
Martinsburg	68770	Overton	68863	Santee Indian Reservation	68760	Lincoln)	68504
Mascot	68967	Oxford	68967	Sarben	69155	Upland	68981
Maskell	68751	Page	68766	Sargent	68874	Utica	68456
Mason City	68855	Palisade	69040	Saronville	68975	Valentine	69201
Max	69037	Palmer	68864	Schaupps	68817	Valley	68064
Maxwell	69151	Palmyra	68418	Schuyler	68661	Valparaiso	68065
Maywood	69038	Panama	68419	Scotia	68875	Venango	69168
Mead	68041	Papillion	68046	Scottsbluff	69361-63	Venice	68069
Meadow Grove	68752	Papillion-La Vista (Part of		For specific Scottsbluff Zip		Verdel	68760
Melbeta	69355	Papillion)	68128	Codes call (308) 635-1121, or		Verdigre	68783
Memphis	68042		68133	your local postmaster.		Verdon	68457
Menominee	68736		68138-39	Scribner	68057	Vesta	68450
Merna	68856		68157	Seneca	69161	Veterans' Administration	
Merriman	69218	For specific Papillion-La Vista		Seward	68434	Hospital (Part of	
Milford	68405	Zip Codes call (402) 348-2861,		Seymour Park (Part of		Omaha)	68105
Millard (Part of Omaha)	68137	or your local postmaster.		Ralston)	68127	Virginia	68458
Miller	68858	Parks	69041	Shelby	68662	Wabash	68407
Milligan	68406	Parkview (Part of Grand		Shelton	68876	Waco	68460
Mills	68753	Island)	68801	Shickley	68436	Wagners Lake	68601
Milton	68858	Paul	68410	Sholes	68771	Wahoo	68066
Minatare	69356	Pauline	68941	Shubert	68437	Wakefield	68784
Minden	68959	Pawnee City	68420	Sidney	69162	Walkers Valley View	68730
Mitchell	69357	Paxton	69155	Silver Creek	68663	Wallace	69169
Monowi	68746	Pender	68047	Skyline	68022	Walthill	68067
Monroe	68647	Peru	68421	Smithfield	68976	Walton	68461
Monterey	68788	Petersburg	68652	Snyder	68664	Wann	68003
Moorefield	69039	Phillips	68865	South Bend	68058	Washington	68068
Morrill	69358	Pickrell	68422	South Minden (Part of		Waterbury	68785
Morse Bluff	68648	Pierce	68767	Minden)	68959		

	ZIP		ZIP		ZIP		ZIP
Waterloo	68069	Weston	68070	Willis	68743	Wood Lake	69221
Wauneta	69045	West Point	68788	Willow Island	69171	Woodland Park	68701
Wausa	68786	Westroads (Part of		Wilsonville	69046	Wood River	68883
Waverly	68462	Omaha)	68114	Winnebago	68071	Worms	68872
Wayne	68787	Westwood Plaza (Part of		Winnebago Indian		Wymore	68466
Wayside	69337	Omaha)	68144	Reservation	68071	Wynot	68792
Weeping Water	68463	Whiteclay	69365	Winnetoon	68789	York	68467
Weissert	68880	Whitman	69366	Winside	68790	Yossem's Paradise Valley	
Wellfleet	69170	Whitney	69367	Winslow	68072	(Part of Omaha)	68134
Western	68464	Wilber	68465	Wisner	68791	Yutan	68073
Westerville	68881	Wilcox	68982	Wolbach	68882		
West Omaha (Part of							
Omaha)	68114						

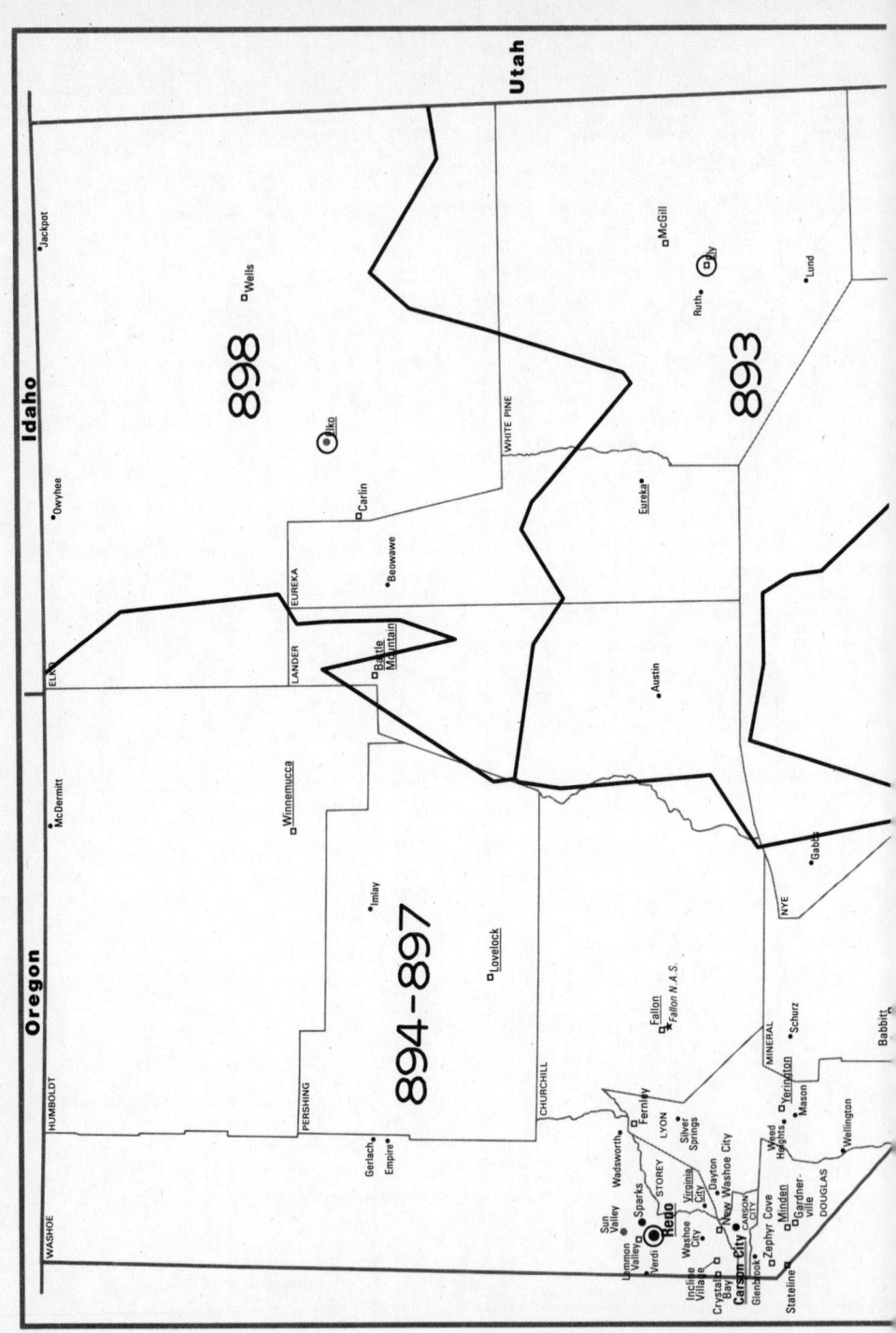

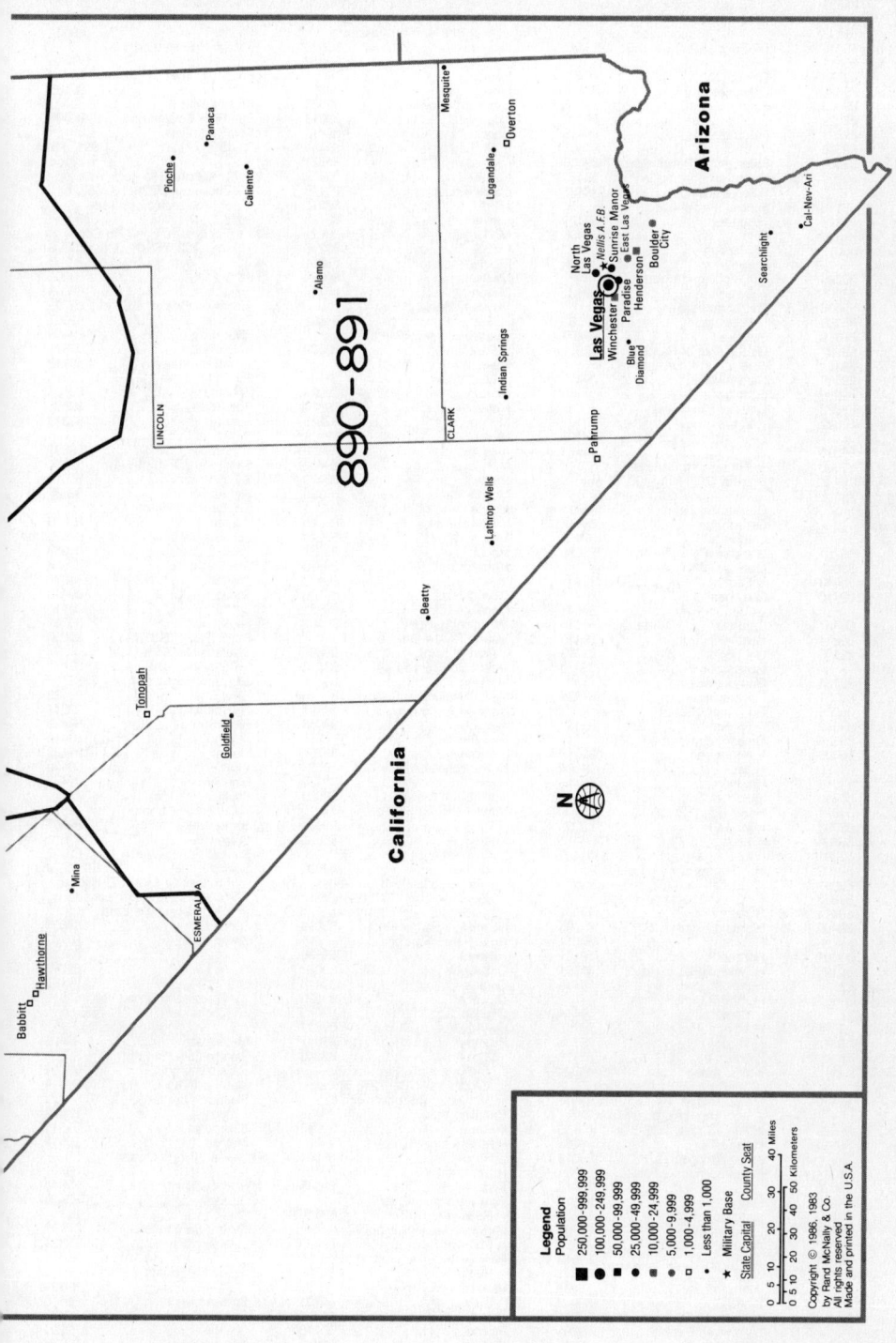

Arizona

Mesquite

Panaca

Overton

Pioche

Logandale

Caliente

North Las Vegas
Nellis A.F.B.
Sunrise Manor
Winchester
East Las Vegas
Paradise
Henderson
Boulder City

890-891

Alamo

Las Vegas

Blue Diamond

Cal-Nev-Ari

Searchlight

LINCOLN

Indian Springs

CLARK

Pahrump

Lathrop Wells

California

Beatty

Tonopah

N

Goldfield

Mina

ESMERALDA

Babbitt
Hawthorne

Legend
Population

■ 250,000-999,999
● 100,000-249,999
■ 50,000-99,999
● 25,000-49,999
● 10,000-24,999
□ 5,000-9,999
• 1,000-4,999
• Less than 1,000
★ Military Base

State Capital   County Seat

0 5 10   20   30   40 Miles
0 5 10 20 30 40 50 Kilometers

Copyright © 1986, 1983
by Rand McNally & Co.
All rights reserved
Made and printed in the U.S.A.

	ZIP		ZIP		ZIP		ZIP
Alamo	89001	Elgin	89008	Las Vegas	89101-85	Preston	89301
Amargosa Valley	89020	Elko	89801-03		89193-99	Pyramid Lake Indian	
Arthur	89833	For specific Elko Zip Codes call		For specific Las Vegas Zip		Reservation	89424
Ash Springs	89017	(702) 738-6444, or your local		Codes call (702) 361-9450, or		Quail Ridge	89403
Atlanta	89043	postmaster.		your local postmaster.		Rachel	89001
Austin	89310	Elk Point	89448	Laughlin	89028*	Raleigh Heights (Part of	
Baker	89311	Ely	89301		89029†	Reno)	89506
Basalt	93512	Empire	89405	Lawton	89503	Rancho Estates	89410
Battle Mountain	89820	Enterprise	89118	Lee	89801	Rancho Haven	89506
Beatty	89003	Etna	89008	Lemmon Valley	89506	Rancho Vista	89403
Belmont	89022	Eureka	89316	Lida	89013	Red Rock Estates	89506
Beowawe	89821	Fallon	89406*	Lincoln Park	89413	Red Rock Vista	89108
Black Springs	89506		89407†	Lockwood	89434		89128-31
Blue Diamond	89004	Fallon Indian Reservation	89406	Logandale	89021		89134
Bluffs (Part of Elko)	89801	Fallon Naval Air Station	89406	Lovelock	89419	For specific Red Rock Vista Zip	
Bonanza (Part of Las		Fallon Station	89406	Lower Kingsbury	89449	Codes call (702) 256-7580, or	
Vegas)	89106	Federal (Part of Las		Lund	89317	your local postmaster.	
	89127	Vegas)	89101	Luning	89420	Reno	89501-70
For specific Bonanza Zip Codes		Fernley	89408	McDermitt	89421	For specific Reno Zip Codes	
call (702) 385-8933, or your		Fish Spring	89410	McGill	89318	call (702) 788-0600, or your	
local postmaster.		Flanigan	89506	Majors Place	89301	local postmaster.	
Border Town	89506	Fort McDermitt Indian		Manhattan	89022	Reno Park	89506
Boulder City	89005*	Reservation	89421	Mason	89447	Rhyolite	89003
	89006†	Fort Mojave Indian		Mayberry-Highland Park		Ridgeview Estates	89705
Boulevard Mall, The	89109	Reservation	92363	(Part of Reno)	89501	Riverside	89007
Buckeye	89410	Gabbs	89409	Meadowood Mall (Part of		River Village	89403
Bunkerville	89007	Galena (Part of Reno)	89511	Reno)	89502	Rixie's	89820
Cactus Springs	89101	Galena Forest Estates	89511	Meadows, The (Part of		Round Hill Village	89448
Caliente	89008	Gardnerville	89410	Las Vegas)	89107	Round Mountain	89045
Cal Nev Ari	89039	Gardnerville Ranchos	89410	Mercury	89023	Rowland	83604
Carlin	89822	Garside (Part of Las		Mesquite	89024	Ruby Valley	89833
Carlin Conservation Camp	89822	Vegas)	89102	Metropolis	89835	Ruth	89319
Carlton Square (Part of			89107	Midas	89414	Sagecrest Complex (Part	
North Las Vegas)	89030		89126	Mill City	89418	of Elko)	89801
Carp	89008	For specific Garside Zip Codes		Mina	89422	Sage Hills 2 (Part of Elko)	89801
Carson City	89701-21	call (702) 871-1499, or your		Minden	89423	Sandy Valley	89019
For specific Carson City Zip		local postmaster.		Moapa	89025	San Jacinto	89825
Codes call (702) 887-7000, or		Genoa	89411	Moapa River Indian		Satalite Hills (Part of	
your local postmaster.		Gerlach	89412	Reservation	89025	Sparks)	89436
Carson Meadows (Part of		Glenbrook	89413	Moapa Valley	89040	Schurz	89427
Carson City)	89701	Glendale (Clark County)	89025	Mogul	89523	Scotty's Junction	89013
Carvers	89045	Glendale (Washoe		Montello	89830	Searchlight	89046
Caselton	89043	County)	89431	Mottsville	89410	Shafter	89835
Centerville	89410	Golconda	89414	Moundhouse	89706	Sheridan	89410
Chaparral Ridge (Part of		Golden Valley	89501	Mountain City	89831	Sheridan Acres	89410
Elko)	89801	Goldfield	89013	Mountain Springs	89101	Shoshone	89301
Charleston	89801	Gold Hill	89440	Mountain View Estates		Sierra (Part of Reno)	89506
Charleston Park	89108	Gold Point	89013	(Part of Elko)	89801	Silverada Mall (Part of	
Charleston Plaza (Part of		Goodsprings	89019	Mount Montgomery	93512	Reno)	89431
Las Vegas)	89104	Goshute Indian		Mustang	89434	Silverado Heights	89705
Cherry Creek	89301	Reservation	84034	Naval Ammunition Depot	89415	Silver City	89428
Clover Hills (Part of Elko)	89801	Greenbrae (Part of		Nellis Air Force Base	89191	Silverpeak	89047
Coaldale	89049	Sparks)	89431	Nelson	89046	Silver Springs	89429
Cobre	89835	Green Valley (Part of		New Empire (Part of		Skyland	89448
Cold Springs	89406	Henderson)	89014	Carson City)	89701	Sloan	89103
Contact	89825	Halleck	89824	New Washoe City	89701	Smith	89430
Cottonwood Cove	89046	Hawthorne	89415*	Nixon	89424	Smith Valley	89430
Country Lane Estates	89410		89416†	North Battle Mountain	89820	Southern Nevada	
Crescent Valley	89821	Hazen	89408	North 7 Estates (Part of		Correctional Center	89019
Crystal Bay	89402	Henderson	89009	Elko)	89801	Southgate	89801
Currant	89301		89011-12	North Fork	89801	South Hills	89501
Currie	89301		89014-16	North Las Vegas	89030-31	Spanish Springs Valley	89436
Dayton	89403	For specific Henderson Zip			89036	Sparks	89431-36
Deep Creek	89801	Codes call (702) 565-8388, or		For specific North Las Vegas		For specific Sparks Zip Codes	
Deeth	89823	your local postmaster.		Zip Codes call (702) 642-6384,		call (702) 359-1161, or your	
Denio	89404	Hidden Valley	89502	or your local postmaster.		local postmaster.	
Dixie Valley	89406	Highland Estates	89705	Northridge (Part of Elko)	89801	Spring Creek	89801
Downtown (Part of Las		Hiko	89017	North Valley (Part of		Spring Valley	89103
Vegas)	89101	Horizon Hills	89501	Reno)	89506		89113
	89125	Huffakers (Part of Reno)	89501	Oasis	89835		89117
For specific Downtown Zip		Humboldt	89418	Oreana	89419		89180
Codes call (702) 361-9212, or		Humboldt Conservation		Orovada	89425	For specific Spring Valley Zip	
your local postmaster.		Camp	89445	Overton	89040	Codes call (702) 871-7555, or	
Downtown (Part of Reno)	89501	Huntridge (Part of Las		Owyhee	89832	your local postmaster.	
	89504-05	Vegas)	89104	Pahrump	89041	Stagecoach	89429
For specific Downtown Zip		Imlay	89418		89048	Stanton Park (Part of	
Codes call (702) 786-5523, or		Incline Village	89450-52	For specific Pahrump Zip		Carson City)	89701
your local postmaster.		For specific Incline Village Zip		Codes call (702) 727-5308, or		Stateline (Clark County)	89019
Dresslerville	89410	Codes call (702) 831-0382, or		your local postmaster.		Stateline (Douglas	
Duck Valley Indian		your local postmaster.		Palomino Valley	89433	County)	89449
Reservation	89832	Incline Village-Crystal Bay	89450	Panaca	89042	Steamboat	89511
Duckwater	89314	Indian Hills	89705	Panther Valley (Part of		Steptoe	89318
Duckwater Indian		Indian Springs	89018	Reno)	89501	Stewart (Part of Carson	
Reservation	89314	Indian Springs Air Force		Paradise	89109	City)	89701
Dunphy	89820	Auxiliary Field	89018	Paradise Hill	89445	Stewarts Point	89040
Dyer	89010	Ione	89310	Paradise Valley (Clark		Stillwater	89406
East Elko (Part of Elko)	89802	Jackpot	89825	County)	89119	Strip Station	89114
East Ely (Part of Ely)	89315	Jacks Valley	89705	Paradise Valley (Humboldt		Summit Lake Indian	
Eastland Hills (Part of		Jarbidge	89826	County)	89426	Reservation	89404
Elko)	89801	Jean	89019	Park Lane Center (Part of		Suncrest (Part of Elko)	89801
East Las Vegas	89121-22	Jiggs	89801	Reno)	89502	Sundance Estates (Part of	
	89160	Johnson Lane	89423	Park Terrace (Part of		Elko)	89801
For specific East Las Vegas Zip		Kingsbury	89449	Carson City)	89701	Sunrise Manor	89110
Codes call (702) 456-1654, or		Kingston	89310	Patrick	89434	Sun Valley	89433
your local postmaster.		Lake Mead Base	89191	Pinenut	89410	Sutcliffe	89501
Echo Bay	89040	Lakeridge	89448	Pioche	89043	Tahoe Village	89449
Edgewood	89449	Lake Village	89449	Pittman (Part of		Te-Moak Indian	
Elburz	89824	Lamoille	89828	Henderson)	89015	Reservation	89801
Eldorado Lakes	89403	Lane	89301	Pleasant Valley	89511	Tempiute	89001

* Area Zip Code   *† Post Office Boxes*

	ZIP		ZIP		ZIP		ZIP
Thomas Creek Estates...	89501	Upper Kingsbury	89449	Washington (Part of		Westwood Village	89423
Thousand Springs	89835	Ursine	89043	Reno).................	89503*	Willow Beach............	89005
Timberline Estates (Part of		Valmy...................	89438	....	89513†	Winchester	89101
Carson City)	89703	Verdi....................	89439	Washoe City	89701	Winnemucca	89445*
Tonopah	89049	Virginia City	89440	Washoe Indian		....	89446†
Topaz Junction	89410	Vista (Part of Sparks)	89436	Reservation	89410	Yerington	89447
Topaz Lake	89410	Vya	96104	Weed Heights	89447	Yerington Indian	
Topaz Ranch Estates	89444	Wabuska.................	89447	Wellington..............	89444	Reservation	89447
Tracy-Clark..............	89434	Wadsworth..............	89442	Wells	89835	Yomba Indian Reservation	89310
Tuscarora	89834	Walker Lake.............	89415	Wendover...............	89883	Zephyr Cove	89448
Tyrolean Village	89450	Walker River Indian		Westland Mall (Part of Las		Zephyr Cove-Round Hill	
Unionville	89418	Reservation	89427	Vegas)	89102	Village	89448
University (Part of Reno)	89507	Warm Springs	89049	West Reno (Part of Reno)	89509		

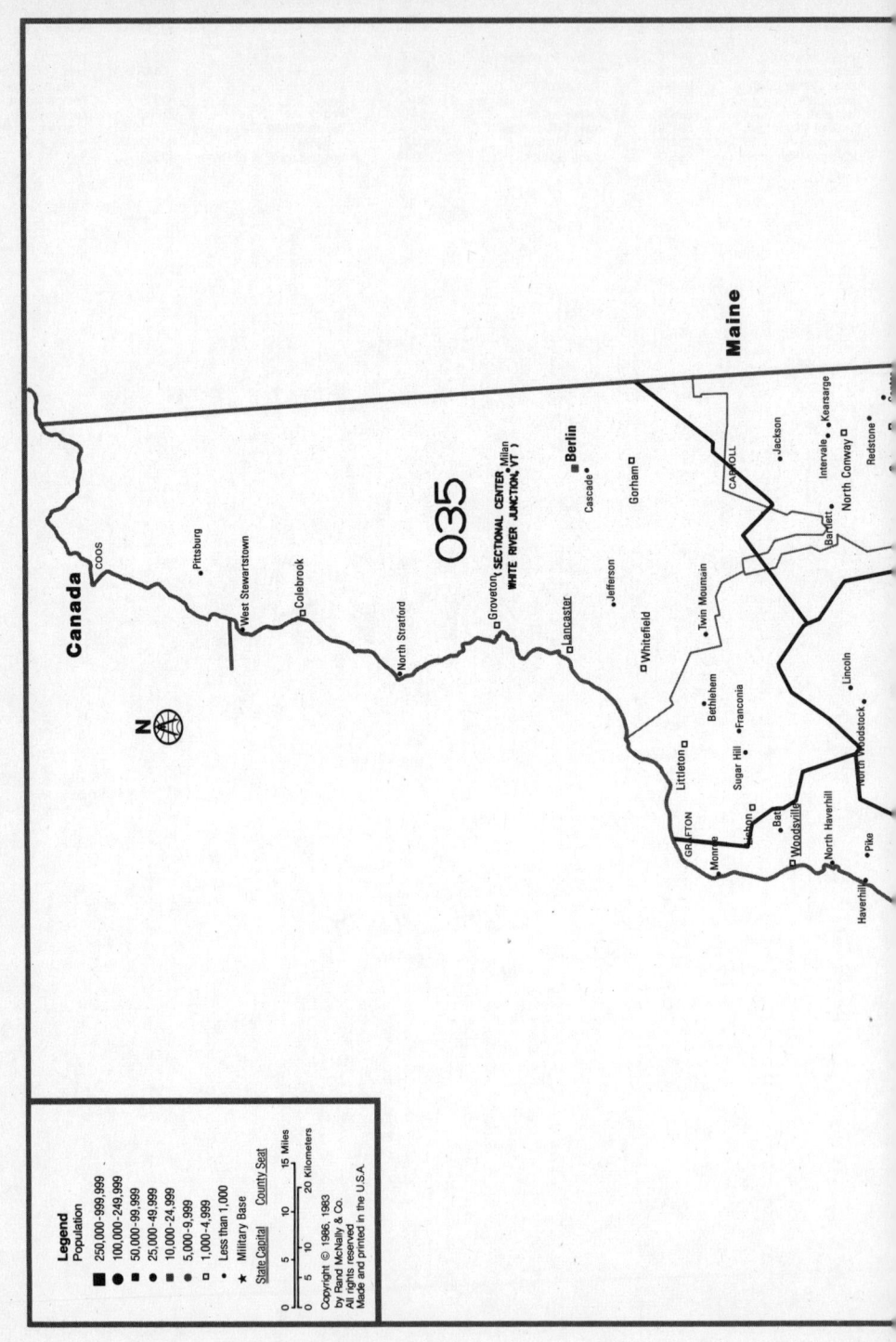

Maine

035

Canada

COOS

Pittsburg

West Stewartstown

Colebrook

North Stratford

Groveton

SECTIONAL CENTER
WHITE RIVER JUNCTION, VT)

Milan

Berlin

Cascade

Gorham

Lancaster

Jefferson

Whitefield

Twin Mountain

Bethlehem

Franconia

Sugar Hill

Littleton

GRAFTON

Monroe

Lisbon

Bath

Woodsville

North Haverhill

Pike

Haverhill

Lincoln

North Woodstock

CARROLL

Jackson

Intervale   Kearsarge

North Conway   Redstone

Bartlett

N

Legend
Population
■ 250,000-999,999
● 100,000-249,999
■ 50,000-99,999
• 25,000-49,999
■ 10,000-24,999
• 5,000-9,999
□ 1,000-4,999
• Less than 1,000
★ Military Base

State Capital   County Seat

0   5   10   15 Miles
0   5   10   20 Kilometers

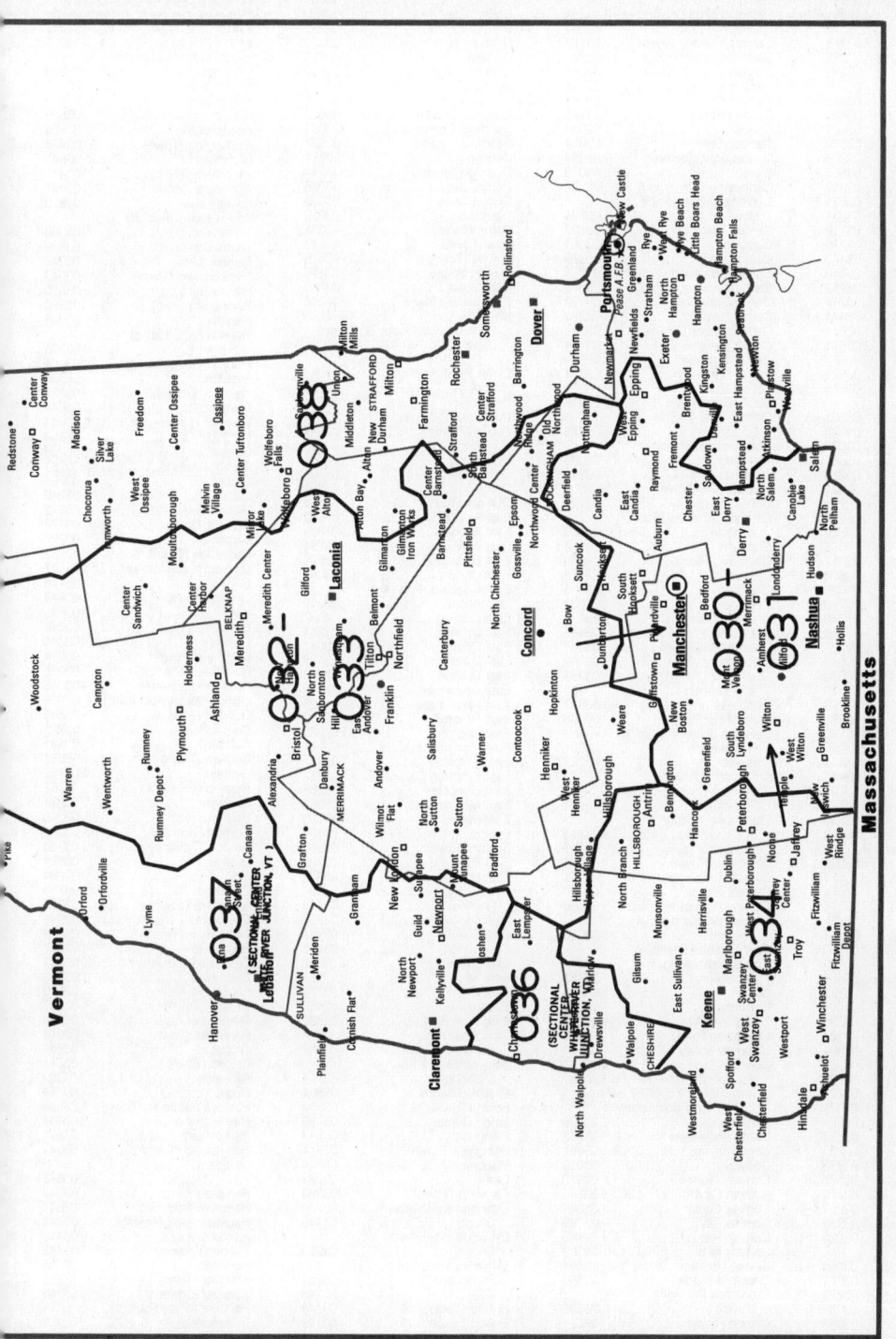

Place	ZIP
Ackerman's Trailer Park	03079
Acworth	03601
Acworth (Town)	03601
Albany	03818
Albany (Town)	03818
Alexandria	03222
Alexandria (Town)	03222
Allenstown	03275
Allenstown (Town)	03275
Alstead	03602
Alstead (Town)	03602
Alstead Center	03602
Alton	03809
Alton (Town)	03809
Alton Bay	03810
Amherst	03031
Amherst (Town)	03031
Andover	03216
Andover (Town)	03216
Antrim	03440
Antrim (Town)	03440
Ashland	03217
Ashland (Town)	03217
Ashuelot	03441
Atkinson	03811
Atkinson (Town)	03811
Atkinson and Gilmanton Academy (Town)	03579
Atkinson Heights	03811
Atlantic Heights (Part of Portsmouth)	03801
Auburn	03032
Auburn (Town)	03032
Baboosic Lake	03031
Bagley	03278
Bank Village	03071
Barnstead	03218
Barnstead (Town)	03218
Barrington	03825
Barrington (Town)	03825
Bartlett	03812
Bartlett (Town)	03812
Base	03595
Bath	03740
Bath (Town)	03740
Beans (Town)	03595
Beans Island	03077
Beans Purchase (Town)	03581
Beaver Lake	03038
Bedford	03110
Bedford (Town)	03110
Beebe River	03223
Belmont	03220
Belmont (Town)	03220
Bennington	03442
Bennington (Town)	03442
Benton	03785
Benton (Town)	03785
Berlin	03570
Berlin Mills (Part of Berlin)	03570
Bersum Gardens (Part of Portsmouth)	03801
Bethlehem	03574
Bethlehem (Town)	03574
Bethlehem Junction	03598
Birch Hill	03855
Blair	03264
Blais Park (Part of Berlin)	03570
Blodgett Landing	03255
Bonds Corner	03458
Boscawen	03301
Boscawen (Town)	03301
Bow	03304
Bow (Town)	03304
Bow Center	03304
Bowkerville	03465
Box Corner	03220
Bradford	03221
Bradford (Town)	03221
Bradford Center	03221
Brentwood	03833
Brentwood (Town)	03833
Brentwood Corners	03833
Bretton Woods	03575
Bridgewater	03222
Bridgewater (Town)	03222
Bristol	03222
Bristol (Town)	03222
Broad Acres (Part of Nashua)	03060
Brookfield	03872
Brookfield (Town)	03872
Brookline	03033
Brookline (Town)	03033
Brook Village North (Part of Nashua)	03060
Bungy	03576
Burkehaven	03782
Cambridge (Town)	03588

Place	ZIP
Camp Hedding	03042
Campton	03223
Campton (Town)	03223
Campton Hollow	03264
Campton Lower Village	03223
Campton Upper Village	03223
Canaan	03741
Canaan (Town)	03741
Canaan Center	03741
Canaan Street	03741
Candia	03034
Candia (Town)	03034
Candia Four Corners	03034
Canobie Lake	03079
Canterbury (Town)	03224
Canterbury (Merrimack County)	03224
Carroll (Town)	03595
Cascade	03581
Cedar Pond	03570
Center Barnstead	03225
Center Conway	03813
Center Effingham	03882
Center Harbor	03226
Center Harbor (Town)	03226
Center Haverhill	03774
Center Ossipee	03814
Center Sandwich	03227
Center Strafford	03815
Center Tuftonboro	03816
Central Park (Part of Somersworth)	03878
Chandlers Purchase (Town)	03595
Charlestown	03603
Charlestown (Town)	03603
Chase Village	03281
Chateau Richelieu (Part of Nashua)	03060
Chatham	04058
Chatham (Town)	04058
Cheever	03266
Chesham	03455
Chester	03036
Chester (Town)	03036
Chesterfield	03443
Chesterfield (Town)	03443
Chichester	03263
Chichester (Town)	03263
Chicks Corner	03259
Chocorua	03817
Christian Hollow	03608
Christian Shore (Part of Portsmouth)	03801
Cilleyville	03265
Claremont	03743
Claremont Center (Part of Claremont)	03743
Claremont Junction (Part of Claremont)	03743
Clarks Landing	03226
Clarksville (Town)	03576
Clinton Grove	03281
Clinton Village	03440
Clovelly (Part of Nashua)	03060
Coburn Woods (Part of Nashua)	03060
Cold Regions Research and Engineering Laboratory	03755
Cold River	03608
Colebrook	03576
Colebrook (Town)	03576
Columbia (Town)	03576
Columbia Valley	03576
Concord	03301-03
For specific Concord Zip Codes call (603) 225-5536, or your local postmaster.	
Contoocook	03229
Contoocook Lake	03452
Converseville	03461
Conway	03818
Conway (Town)	03818
Cornish (Town)	03745
Cornish Center	05089
Cornish City	05089
Cornish Flat	03746
Cornish Mills	05089
Cotton Mountain	03894
Crawford Notch	03595
Crawfords Purchase (Town)	03595
Cricket Corner	03031
Croydon	03773
Croydon (Town)	03773
Croydon Flat	03773
Crystal	03570
Cushman	03598

Place	ZIP
Cutts (Town)	03595
Dalton	03598
Dalton (Town)	03598
Danbury	03230
Danbury (Town)	03230
Danville	03819
Danville (Town)	03819
Davisville	03229
Deerfield	03037
Deerfield (Town)	03037
Deerfield Center	03037
Deerfield Parade	03037
Deering	03244
Deering (Town)	03244
Derry	03038
Derry (Town)	03038
Derry	03038
Derry Village	03038
Dixs (Town)	03576
Dixville (Town)	03576
Dixville Notch	03576
Dorchester	03266
Dorchester (Town)	03266
Dover	03820-21
For specific Dover Zip Codes call (603) 742-4040, or your local postmaster.	
Dover Point (Part of Dover)	03820
Drewsville	03604
Dublin	03444
Dublin (Town)	03444
Dummer (Town)	03588
Dunbarton	03301
Dunbarton (Town)	03301
Durham	03824
Durham (Town)	03824
East Alstead	03602
East Alton	03809
East Andover	03231
East Barrington	03825
East Candia	03040
East Concord (Part of Concord)	03301
East Conway	04037
East Deering	03244
East Derry	03041
East Dummer	03588
East Grafton	03240
East Grantham	03753
East Hampstead	03826
East Haverhill	03780
East Hebron	03232
East Holderness	03217
East Kingston	03827
East Kingston (Town)	03827
East Lempster	03605
East Merrimack	03054
East Milford	03055
Easton	03580
Easton (Town)	03580
East Plainfield	03766
East Rindge	03461
East Rochester (Part of Rochester)	03868
East Sandwich	03226
East Sullivan	03445
East Sutton	03278
East Swanzey	03446
East Tilton	03252
East Unity	03773
Eastview	03450
East Wakefield	03830
East Washington	03244
East Westmoreland	03467
East Wilder (Part of Lebanon)	03784
East Wolfeboro	03894
Eaton (Town)	03832
Eaton Center	03832
Effingham	03814
Effingham (Town)	03814
Effingham Falls	03814
Elkins	03233
Ellsworth (Town)	03264
Elmwood (Hillsborough County)	03449
Elmwood (Merrimack County)	03230
Elwyn Park (Part of Portsmouth)	03801
Enfield	03748
Enfield (Town)	03748
Enfield Center	03749
Epping	03042
Epping (Town)	03042
Epsom	03234
Epsom (Town)	03234
Errol	03579

Place	ZIP
Errol (Town)	03579
Ervings (Town)	03576
Etna	03750
Exeter	03833
Exeter (Town)	03833
Exeter Hampton Mobile Village	03833
Exeter Villa	03833
Exeter West	03833
Fabyan	03595
Farmington	03835
Farmington (Town)	03835
Fitzwilliam	03447
Fitzwilliam (Town)	03447
Fitzwilliam Depot	03447
Forest Lake	03470
Forest Ridge (Part of Nashua)	03060
Foyes Corner	03870
Francestown	03043
Francestown (Town)	03043
Franconia	03580
Franconia (Town)	03580
Franklin	03235
Franklin Falls (Part of Franklin)	03235
Franklin Pierce College	03461
Freedom	03836
Freedom (Town)	03836
Fremont	03044
Fremont (Town)	03044
Gardners Grove	03252
Gaza	03269
Georges Mills	03751
Gerrish	03301
Gilford	03246
Gilford (Town)	03246
Gilmans Corner	03777
Gilmanton	03237
Gilmanton (Town)	03237
Gilmanton Iron Works	03837
Gilsum	03448
Gilsum (Town)	03448
Glen	03838
Glencliff	03238
Glendale	03246
Glenmere Village	03824
Goffstown	03045
Goffstown (Town)	03045
Gonic (Part of Rochester)	03839
Goodrich Falls	03846
Goose Hollow	03223
Gorham	03581
Gorham (Town)	03581
Goshen	03752
Goshen (Town)	03752
Gossville	03234
Grafton	03240
Grafton (Town)	03240
Grafton Center	03240
Grange	03584
Granite	03864
Grantham	03753
Grantham (Town)	03753
Grasmere	03045
Great Boars Head	03842
Greenfield	03047
Greenfield (Town)	03047
Greenland	03840
Greenland (Town)	03840
Greens (Town)	03581
Greenville	03048
Greenville (Town)	03048
Groton	03241
Groton (Town)	03241
Groveton	03582
Guild	03754
Hadleys Purchase (Town)	03595
Hale's (Town)	03845
Hampstead	03841
Hampstead (Town)	03841
Hampton	03842*
	03843†
Hampton Beach	03842
Hampton Falls	03844
Hampton Falls (Town)	03844
Hancock	03449
Hancock (Town)	03449
Hanover	03755
Hanover (Town)	03755
Hanover Center	03750
Hanover Street (Part of Manchester)	03101
Happy Corner	03592
Happy Valley	03458
Harrisville	03450
Harrisville (Town)	03450
Hart's Location (Town)	03812

	ZIP		ZIP		ZIP		ZIP
Hastings	03257	Louisburg Square (Part of		New Boston Air Force		Peterborough	03458
Haverhill	03765	Nashua)	03060	Tracking Station	03031	Pheasant Lane Mall (Part	
Haverhill (Town)	03765	Low and Burbanks		Newbury	03255	of Nashua)	03063
Hayes (Rockingham		(Town)	03581	Newbury (Town)	03255	Pickpocket Woods	03833
County)	03833	Lower Bartlett	03845	New Castle (Town)	03854	Piermont	03779
Hayes (Strafford County)	03867	Lower Gilmanton	03263	New Castle	03854	Piermont (Town)	03779
Hebron	03241	Lower Village (Cheshire		New Durham	03855	Pike	03780
Hebron (Town)	03241	County)	03448	New Durham (Town)	03855	Pinardville	03045
Hedding	03042	Lower Village (Merrimack		Newfields	03856	Pine Brook Estates	03833
Hell Hollow	03746	County)	03278	Newfields (Town)	03856	Pinecrest	03833
Henniker	03242	Lyman (Town)	03585	New Hampton	03256	Pine Valley	03086
Henniker (Town)	03242	Lyme	03768	New Hampton (Town)	03256	Pinkhams (Town)	03581
High Bridge	03071	Lyme (Town)	03768	Newington (Town)	03801	Pittsburg	03592
Hill	03243	Lyme Center	03769	New Ipswich	03071	Pittsburg (Town)	03592
Hill (Town)	03243	Lyndeborough	03082	New Ipswich (Town)	03071	Pittsfield	03263
Hill Center	03243	Lyndeborough (Town)	03082	New London	03257	Pittsfield (Town)	03263
Hillsboro	03244	Madbury	03820	New London (Town)	03257	Plaice Cove	03842
Hillsborough (Town)	03244	Madbury (Town)	03820	Newmarket	03857	Plainfield	03781
Hillsborough Center	03244	Madison	03849	Newmarket (Town)	03857	Plainfield (Town)	03781
Hillsborough Lower Village	03244	Madison (Town)	03849	Newport	03773	Plaistow	03865
Hillsborough Upper Village	03244	Mall at Rockingham Park,		Newport (Town)	03773	Plaistow (Town)	03865
Hinsdale	03451	The	03079	New Rye	03275	Plymouth	03264
Hinsdale (Town)	03451	Mall of New Hampshire,		Newton	03858	Plymouth (Town)	03264
Holderness	03245	The (Part of		Newton (Town)	03858	Ponemah	03055
Holderness (Town)	03245	Manchester)	03103	Newton Junction	03859	Portsmouth	03801-04
Hollis	03049	Manchester	03101-05	Noone	03458	For specific Portsmouth Zip	
Hollis (Town)	03049		03108-09	North Barnstead	03225	Codes call (603) 431-1300, or	
Hooksett	03106	For specific Manchester Zip		North Beach	03842	your local postmaster.	
Hooksett (Town)	03106	Codes call (603) 644-4111, or		North Branch	03440	Portsmouth Plains (Part of	
Hopkinton	03229	your local postmaster.		North Brookline	03055	Portsmouth)	03801
Hopkinton (Town)	03229	Maplehaven (Part of		North Charlestown	03603	Potter Place	03265
Horses Corner	03263	Portsmouth)	03801	North Chatham	04058	Puckershire (Part of	
Hudson	03051	Maplewood	03281	North Chichester	03263	Claremont)	03743
Hudson (Town)	03051	Marlborough	03455	North Conway	03860	Quaker City	03603
Hudson Center	03051	Marlborough (Town)	03455	North Danville	03819	Quincy	03266
Intervale	03845	Marlow	03456	Northfield	03276	Quintown	03777
Jackson	03846	Marlow (Town)	03456	Northfield (Town)	03276	Rand	03461
Jackson (Town)	03846	Marshall Corner	03833	North Grantham	03766	Randolph	03570
Jady Hill	03833	Marshall Farms	03833	North Groton	03266	Randolph (Town)	03570
Jaffrey	03452	Martin	03106	North Hampton	03862	Raymond	03077
Jaffrey (Town)	03452	Martins (Town)	03581	North Hampton (Town)	03862	Raymond (Town)	03077
Jaffrey Center	03452	Mascoma (Part of		North Hampton Center	03862	Redstone	03813
Jefferson	03583	Lebanon)	03748	North Haverhill	03774	Reeds Ferry	03054
Jefferson (Town)	03583	Mason	03048	North Holderness	03264	Richardson	03055
Jones Corner	03461	Mason (Town)	03048	North Londonderry	03053	Richmond	03470
Joslin (Part of Keene)	03431	Meadowbrook (Part of		North Newport	03773	Richmond (Town)	03470
Kearsarge	03847	Portsmouth)	03801	North Pelham	03076	Rindge	03461
Keene	03431	Meadows	03587	North Pembroke	03301	Rindge (Town)	03461
Kelleys Corner	03263	Melrose Corner (Part of		North Richmond	03470	Rivercrest	03755
Kellyville	03743	Rochester)	03867	North Salem	03073	Riverdale	03045
Kelwyn Park (Part of		Melvin Mills	03278	North Sanbornton	03269	Riverhill (Part of Concord)	03301
Somersworth)	03878	Melvin Village	03850	North Sandwich	03259	Riverside	03874
Kensington	03827	Meredith	03253	North Stratford	03590	Riverside Plaza (Part of	
Kensington (Town)	03827	Meredith (Town)	03253	North Sutton	03260	Keene)	03431
Kidderville	03576	Meredith Center	03246	North Swanzey	03431	Robinson Corner	03240
Kilkenny (Town)	03584	Meriden	03770	Northumberland	05905	Roby	03278
Kingston	03848	Merrimack	03054	Northumberland (Town)	05905	Rochester	03836
Kingston (Town)	03848	Merrimack (Town)	03054	North Village	03458		03866-68
Laconia	03246*	Middleton (Town)	03887	North Walpole	03609	For specific Rochester Zip	
	03247†	Middleton Corners	03887	North Wilmot	03230	Codes call (603) 332-1433, or	
Lakeport (Part of Laconia)	03246	Milan	03588	North Wolfeboro	03894	your local postmaster.	
Lancaster	03584	Milan (Town)	03588	Northwood	03261	Rockwold	03245
Lancaster (Town)	03584	Milford	03055	Northwood (Town)	03261	Rollinsford	03869
Landaff (Town)	03585	Milford (Town)	03055	Northwood Center	03261	Rollinsford (Town)	03869
Landaff Center	03585	Mill Hollow	03602	Northwood Narrows	03261	Roxbury (Town)	03431
Langdon	03602	Millsfield (Town)	03579	Northwood Ridge	03261	Royal Crest Estates (Part	
Langdon (Town)	03602	Mill Village (Cheshire		North Woodstock	03262	of Nashua)	03060
Langs Corner	03870	County)	03464	Nottingham	03290	Rumney	03266
Laskey Corner	03887	Mill Village (Sullivan		Nottingham (Town)	03290	Rumney (Town)	03266
Laurel Lake	03447	County)	03781	Noyes Terrace	03079	Rumney Depot	03266
Leavitts Hill	03037	Millville Lake	03079	Nuttings Beach	03222	Ryder Corner	03773
Lebanon	03756†	Milton	03851	Odell (Town)	03582	Rye	03870
	03766*	Milton (Town)	03851	Onway Lake	03077	Rye (Town)	03870
Lee	03824	Milton Mills	03852	Orange	03741	Rye Beach	03871
Lee (Town)	03824	Mirror Lake	03853	Orange (Town)	03741	Rye North Beach	03870
Lempster	03606	Monroe	03771	Orford	03777	Sachem Village (Part of	
Lempster (Town)	03606	Monroe (Town)	03771	Orford (Town)	03777	Lebanon)	03784
Lincoln	03251	Mont Vernon	03057	Orfordville	03777	Salem	03079
Lincoln (Town)	03251	Mont Vernon (Town)	03057	Ossipee	03864	Salem (Town)	03079
Lincoln Park (Part of		Moultonboro	03254	Ossipee (Town)	03864	Salem Depot	03079
Nashua)	03060	Moultonborough (Town)	03254	Pages Corner	03301	Salisbury	03268
Lisbon	03585	Moultonborough Falls	03254	Pannaway Manor (Part of		Salisbury (Town)	03268
Lisbon (Town)	03585	Moultonville	03814	Portsmouth)	03801	Salisbury Heights	03268
Litchfield	03051	Mountain View Estates		Parker Hill	03585	Sanbornton	03269
Litchfield (Town)	03051	(Part of Nashua)	03060	Park Hill	03467	Sanbornton (Town)	03269
Little Boars Head	03862	Mount Sunapee	03772	Partridge Lake	03561	Sanbornville	03872
Little Island Pond	03076	Mount Washington	03589	Passaconaway	03818	Sandown	03873
Littleton	03561	Munsonville	03457	Pearls Corner	03301	Sandown (Town)	03873
Littleton (Town)	03561	Nashua	03060-63	Pelham	03076	Sandwich	03227
Livermore (Town)	03251	For specific Nashua Zip Codes		Pelham (Town)	03076	Sandwich (Town)	03227
Livermore Falls	03264	call (603) 882-2646, or your		Pembroke (Town)	03275	Sargents Purchase (Town)	03589
Lochmere	03252	local postmaster.		Penacook (Part of		Sawyers (Part of Dover)	03820
Lockehaven	03748	Nashua Mall (Part of		Concord)	03303	Scotland	03470
Londonderry (Town)	03053	Nashua)	03063	Pendleton Beach (Part of		Seabrook	03874
Londonderry (Rockingham		Nelson	03457	Laconia)	03246	Seabrook (Town)	03874
County)	03053	Nelson (Town)	03457	Pequawket	03875	Seabrook Beach	03874
Loudon	03301	New Boston	03070	Percy	03582	Second College (Town)	03576
Loudon (Town)	03301	New Boston (Town)	03070	Peterborough	03458	Severance	03032
Loudon Center	03301			Peterborough (Town)	03458	Sharon	03458

* **Area Zip Code**   † **Post Office Boxes**

	ZIP		ZIP		ZIP		ZIP
Sharon (Town)	03458	Stoddard	03464	Walpole	03608	West Lebanon (Part of	
Shelburne (Town)	03581	Stoddard (Town)	03464	Walpole (Town)	03608	Lebanon)	03784
Sherwood Forest	03833	Strafford	03884	Warner	03278	West Milan	03570
Shirley Hill	03045	Strafford (Town)	03884	Warner (Town)	03278	Westmoreland	03467
Short Falls	03234	Stratford	03590	Warren	03279	Westmoreland (Town)	03467
Silver Lake	03875	Stratford (Town)	03590	Warren (Town)	03279	West Nottingham	03291
Simoneau Plaza (Part of		Stratham	03885	Washington	03280	West Ossipee	03890
Nashua)	03060	Stratham (Town)	03885	Washington (Town)	03280	West Peterborough	03468
Smiths Point	03246	Strawberry Banke (Part of		Waterloo	03278	West Plymouth	03264
Smithtown	03874	Portsmouth)	03801	Water Village	03864	Westport	03469
Smithville	03071	Success (Town)	03570	Waterville Estates	03223	West Rindge	03461
Snowville	03849	Sugar Hill	03585	Waterville Valley	03215	West Rumney	03266
Snumshire	03603	Sugar Hill (Town)	03585	Waterville Valley (Town)	03215	West Rye	03870
Somersworth	03878	Sullivan	03431	Wawbeek	03853	West Salisbury	03216
Soo Nipi	03257	Sullivan (Town)	03431	Weare	03281	West Springfield	03284
South Acworth	03607	Sunapee	03782	Weare (Town)	03281	West Stewartstown	03597
South Barnstead	03225	Sunapee (Town)	03782	Webster	03301	West Swanzey	03469
South Brookline	03033	Suncook	03275	Webster (Town)	03301	West Thornton	03285
South Charlestown	03603	Surry	03431	Webster Lake (Part of		West Unity	03743
South Chatham	04037	Surry (Town)	03431	Franklin)	03235	Westville	03865
South Conway	03813	Sutton	03221	Webster Place (Part of		West Wilton	03086
South Cornish	05089	Sutton (Town)	03221	Franklin)	03235	West Windham	03087
South Danville	03819	Swanzey (Town)	03431	Weirs Beach (Part of		Whiteface	03259
South Deerfield	03037	Swanzey Center	03431	Laconia)	03246	Whitefield	03598
South Effingham	03882	Swiftwater	03785	Wendell	03782	Whitefield (Town)	03598
South Hampton	03827	Tamworth	03886	Wentworth (Coos County)		Whittier	03890
South Hampton (Town)	03827	Tamworth (Town)	03886	(Town)	03579	Willey House	03812
South Hooksett	03106	Temple	03084	Wentworth (Grafton		Wilmot	03287
South Keene (Part of		Temple (Town)	03084	County)	03282	Wilmot (Town)	03287
Keene)	03431	The Glen	03592	Wentworth (Grafton		Wilmot Flat	03287
South Kingston	03848	Thomas	03461	County) (Town)	03282	Wilton (Hillsborough	
South Lee	03824	Thompson and Meserves		Wentworth Acres (Part of		County)	03086
South Lyndeboro	03082	Purchase (Town)	03595	Portsmouth)	03801	Wilton (Hillsborough	
South Merrimack	03060	Thornton	03223	Wentworth By The Sea	03854	County) (Town)	03086
South Milford	03055	Thornton (Town)	03223	West Alton	03246	Wilton Center	03086
South Newbury	03272	Thorntons Ferry	03054	West Andover	03265	Winchester	03470
South Pittsfield	03263	Tilton	03276	West Barrington	03825	Winchester (Town)	03470
South Stoddard	03464	Tilton (Town)	03276	West Campton	03223	Windham	03087
South Sutton	03273	Tilton-Northfield	03276	West Canaan	03741	Windham (Town)	03087
South Tamworth	03883	Tinkerville	03585	West Center Harbor	03217	Windham Depot	03087
South Weare	03281	Trapshire	03603	West Chesterfield	03466	Windsor (Town)	03244
South Wolfeboro	03894	Troy	03465	West Claremont (Part of		Winnisquam	03289
Spofford	03462	Troy (Town)	03465	Claremont)	03743	Winona	03217
Spofford Lake	03462	Tuftonboro	03864	West Deering	03440	Wolfeboro	03894
Springfield	03284	Tuftonboro (Town)	03864	West Dummer	03570	Wolfeboro (Town)	03894
Springfield (Town)	03284	Twin Mountain	03595	West Epping	03042	Wolfeboro Center	03894
Squantum	03452	Union	03887	West Franklin (Part of		Wolfeboro Falls	03896
Stark	03582	Unity	03603	Franklin)	03235	Wonalancet	03897
Stark (Town)	03582	Unity (Town)	03603	West Gonic (Part of		Woodman	03830
State Line	03447	Upper Kidderville	03576	Rochester)	03839	Woodmere	03452
Stewartstown	03576	Wadley Falls	03824	West Hampstead	03841	Woodstock	03293
Stewartstown (Town)	03576	Wakefield	03872	West Henniker	03242	Woodstock (Town)	03293
Stewartstown Hollow	03576	Wakefield (Town)	03872	West Hopkinton	03229	Woodsville	03785
Stinson Lake	03274	Wallis Sands	03870				

	ZIP
Aberdeen (Township)	07747
Absecon	08201
Absecon Heights	08201
Absecon Highlands	08201
Academy Estates	07981
Ackors Corner	08534
A Country Place	08701
Adams	08902
Adamston	08723
Adelphia	07710
Agasote	08618
Ajax Park	08618
Albion	08009
Albion Place (Part of Clifton)	07013
Aldene (Part of Roselle)	07203
Aldine	08318
Aldrich Estates	07731
Alexandria (Township)	08848
Allaire	07727
Allamuchy	07820
Allamuchy (Township)	07820
Allamuchy-Panther Valley	07820
Allendale	07401
Allenhurst	07711
Allentown	08501
Allenwood	08720
Allerton	08833
Alloway	08001
Alloway (Township)	08001
Allwood (Part of Clifton)	07012
Almolind	08096
Almonesson	08096
Alpha	08865
Alphano	07838
Alpine	07620
Amber Terrace (Part of Pine Hill)	08021
Amon Heights	08110
Ampere (Part of East Orange)	07017
Ancora	08037
Anderson	07882
Andover	07821
Andover (Township)	07860
Andover Junction (Part of Andover)	07821
Andrews	08081
Anglesea (Part of North Wildwood)	08260
Annandale	08801
Anthony	08826
Applegarth	08512
Apple Hill	08002
Apshawa	07405
Arbor	08854
Arbors	08857
Arcola (Part of Paramus)	07652
Ardena	07728
Arlington (Part of Kearny)	07032
Arneys Mount	08068
Arneytown	08501
Arrowhead Park	08723
Arrowhead Village	08723
Asbury	08802
Asbury Gardens	07753
Asbury Park	07712
Ashland	08043
Atco	08004
Atlantic City	08401*
	08404†
Atlantic Highlands	07716
Atlantis	08087
Atsion	08088
Auburn	08085
Audubon	08106
Audubon Park	08106
Augusta	07822
Aura	08028
Avalon	08202
Avenel	07001
Avis Mills	08098
Avon By The Sea	07717
Avondale	07110
Awosting	07421
Babbitt	07047
Bacons Neck	08302
Bakersville (Atlantic County)	08225
Bakersville (Mercer County)	08638
Baldwins Corner	08534
Baleville	07860
Baltusrol	07081
Bamber Lake	08731
Baptistown	08803
Barbertown	08825
Barclay Farm	08002
Bargaintown	08221

	ZIP
Barkers Corner	07838
Barley Sheaf	08822
Barlow	08002
Barnegat	08005
Barnegat (Township)	08005
Barnegat Beach	08758
Barnegat Light	08006
Barnegat Pines	08731
Barnsboro	08080
Barrington	08007
Barrington Manor (Part of Barrington)	08033
Bartley	07836
Basking Ridge	07920
Bassett Park	07801
Bass River (Township)	08224
Bates Mill	08037
Batesville	08002
Batsto	08037
Battentown (Part of Swedesboro)	08085
Bay Harbor Estates	08723
Bay Head	08742
Bay Head Junction (Part of Bay Head)	08742
Bayonne	07002
Bay Shore West	08204
Bay Side (Cumberland County)	08302
Bay Side (Ocean County)	08050
Bayview Heights	08753
Bayview Shores	08738
Bayville	08721
Bayville Park	08721
Bayway (Part of Elizabeth)	07202
Baywood	08723
Beach Creek (Part of North Wildwood)	08260
Beach Glen	07866
Beach Haven	08008
Beach Haven Crest	08008
Beach Haven Gardens	08008
Beach Haven Heights	08008
Beach Haven Terrace	08008
Beach Haven West	08050
Beach View	08005
Beachwood	08722
Beattyestown	07840
Beaufort (Part of Roseland)	07068
Beaver Dam	08070
Beaver Lake	07416
Beckerville	08733
Beckett	08085
Bedminster	07921
Bedminster (Township)	07921
Beechwood Heights	07876
Beemerville	07461
Beesleys Point	08223
Belcher Creek	07480
Belcoville	08330
Belford	07718
Belle Mead	08502
Belleplain	08270
Belleville	07109
Belleville (Township)	07109
Belleville Annex (Part of Newark)	07109
Bellmawr	08031*
	08099†
Bellmawr Park (Part of Bellmawr)	08030
Bells Crossing (Part of Glen Gardner)	08826
Bells Lake	08012
Bellview	08077
Bellwood Park (Part of Bellmawr)	08030
Belmar	07719
Belmar Gardens	07719
Belvidere	07823
Belwood Park	07109
Bennett	08204
Bennetts Mills	08527
Bergen (Part of Jersey City)	07304
Bergenfield	07621
Bergenline (Part of Union City)	07087
Bergen Mall (Part of Paramus)	07652
Bergen Point (Part of Bayonne)	07002
Berkeley (Township)	08721
Berkeley Heights	07922
Berkeley Heights (Township)	07922
Berkeley Shore Estates	08721
Berlin	08009

	ZIP
Berlin (Township)	08091
Berlin Estates	08009
Berlin Heights (Part of Berlin)	08009
Bernards (Township)	07920
Bernardsville	07924
Bertrand Island (Part of Mount Arlington)	07856
Bethlehem (Township)	08802
Betsytown (Part of Elizabeth)	07201
Beverly	08010
Billingsport (Part of Paulsboro)	08066
Birches	08012
Birches West	08071
Birch Hills	07981
Birchwood Lakes	08055
Birchwood Park	08723
Birmingham	08011
Bishops	08009
Bivalve	08349
Black Horse Pike Shopping Center (Part of Audubon)	08106
Blackwells Mills	08873
Blackwood	08012
Blackwood Terrace	08096
Blairstown	07825
Blairstown (Township)	07825
Blawenburg	08504
Blenheim	08012
Bloomfield	07003
Bloomfield (Township)	07003
Bloomfield Terrace	08816
Bloomingdale (Morris County)	07457
Bloomingdale (Passaic County)	07403
Bloomsbury	08804
Blue Anchor	08037
Blue Bell	08344
Blue Star Shopping Center (Part of Watchung)	07060
Bogota	07603
Bon Air	08110
Bonhamton	08817
Boonton	07005
Boonton (Township)	07005
Bordentown	08505
Bordentown (Township)	08505
Bossert Estates	08505
Bound Brook (Camden County)	08002
Bound Brook (Somerset County)	08805
Bowman Manor	08251
Braddock	08037
Bradley Beach	07720
Bradley Gardens	08876
Bradley Park	07753
Braeburn Heights	08638
Braeburn Park	08638
Brainards	08865
Brainy Boro (Part of Metuchen)	08840
Branchburg (Township)	08876
Branchport (Part of Long Branch)	07740
Branchville	07826
Brant Beach	08008
Brass Castle	07882
Breton Woods	08723
Brick	08723-24
For specific Brick Zip Codes call (908) 477-0100, or your local postmaster.	
Brick (Township)	08723
Brick Church (Part of East Orange)	07018
Bricksboro	08332
Bridgeboro	08075
Bridgeport	08014
Bridgeton	08302
Bridgeton Junction (Part of Bridgeton)	08302
Bridgeville	07823
Bridgewater	08807
Bridgewater (Township)	08807
Brielle	08730
Brigadoon	08096
Brigantine	08203
Brighton Beach	08008
Broad Lane	08094
Broad Street Annex (Part of Newark)	07102
Broadway	08808

	ZIP
Brookdale (Camden County)	08002
Brookdale (Essex County)	07003
Brookfields	08002
Brooklawn	08030
Brookmeade	08002
Brookside	07926
Brook Tree	08520
Brook Valley (Part of Kinnelon)	07405
Brookville (Hunterdon County)	08559
Brookville (Ocean County)	08005
Brookwood	08527
Brotmanville	08302
Browns Mills	08015
Browntown	08857
Brunswick Acres	08852
Brunswick Gardens	08857
Brunswick Shopping Center (Part of New Brunswick)	08902
Brunswick Square	08816
Brush Hollow	08053
Buckingham Village	08080
Buckshutem	08332
Budd Lake	07828
Buddtown	08088
Buena	08310
Buena Vista (Township)	08360
Bulltown	08215
Bunker Hill	08080
Bunnvale	07830
Burcliff Farms	08638
Burleigh	08210
Burlington	08016
Burlington (Township)	08016
Burnt Mills	07921
Bustleton	08016
Butler	07405
Butler Park	07882
Butlers Park	07882
Butterworth Farms	07801
Buttzville	07829
Byram (Hunterdon County)	08559
Byram (Sussex County) (Township)	07821
Byram Cove (Part of Hopatcong)	07843
Caldwell	07006*
	07007†
Caldwell Borough (Township)	07006
Califon	07830
Callahans	07849
Cambridge	08075
Cambridge Park	08053
Camden	08101-05
For specific Camden Zip Codes call (609) 757-0330, or your local postmaster.	
Camp Tecumseh	08867
Candlewood	08701
Canton	08079
Cape Breton	08723
Cape May	08204
Cape May Court House	08210
Cape May Point	08212
Capitol Hill	08010
Cardiff	08232
Carlls Corner	08302
Carlstadt	07072
Carlton Hill (Part of Rutherford)	07073
Carmel	08332
Carmerville	07719
Carneys Point (Township)	08069
Carneys Point	08069
Carpenterville	08865
Carteret	07008
Cassville	08527
Castle Point (Part of Hoboken)	07030
Cecil	08094
Cedar Beach (Monmouth County)	07758
Cedar Beach (Ocean County)	08721
Cedar Bonnet Island	08050
Cedar Bridge Manor	08723
Cedar Brook	08018
Cedar Crest Manor	08069
Cedar Croft	08723
Cedar Glen Homes East	08757
Cedar Glen Lakes	08759
Cedar Glen West	08733
Cedar Grove (Cape May County)	08210

*** Area Zip Code** **† Post Office Boxes**

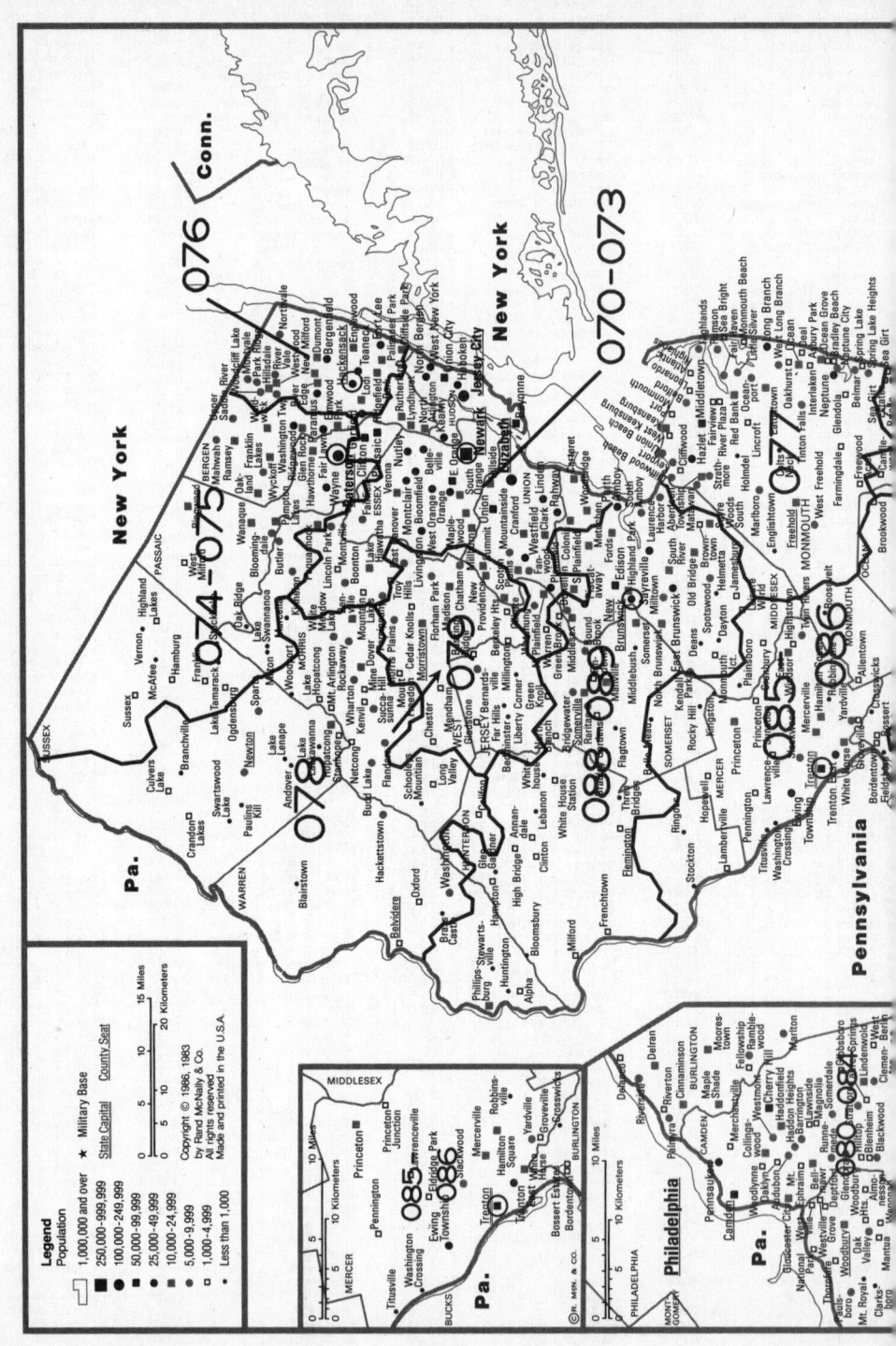

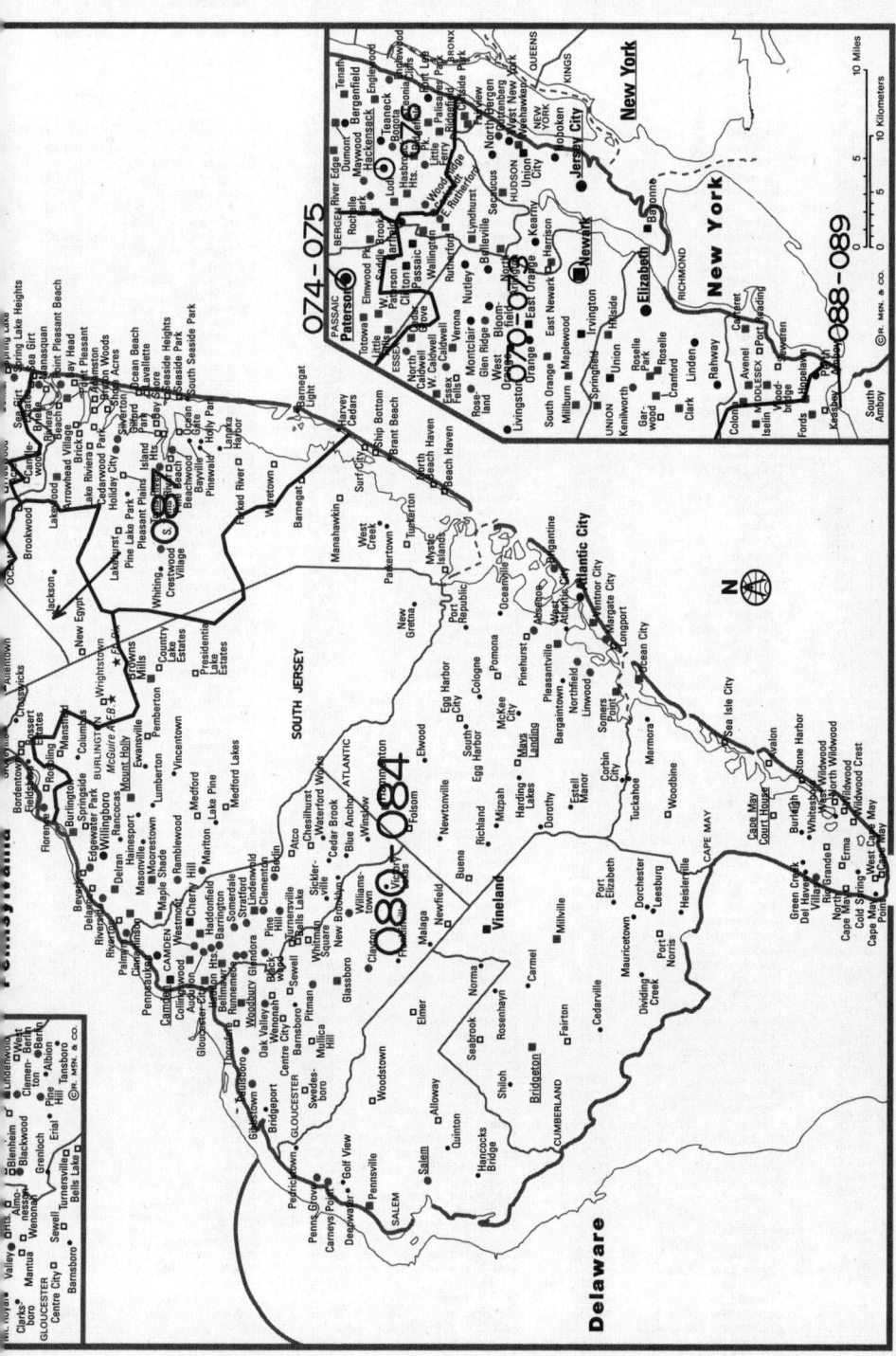

SOUTH JERSEY

074 – 075

070 – 073

088 – 089

080 – 084

New York

New York

Jersey City

Newark

Elizabeth

Paterson

PASSAIC

ESSEX

HUDSON

UNION

MIDDLESEX

RICHMOND

KINGS

QUEENS

BRONX

Pennsylvania

Delaware

ATLANTIC

BURLINGTON

OCEAN

CAMDEN

GLOUCESTER

SALEM

CUMBERLAND

CAPE MAY

Atlantic City

Vineland

Bridgeton

Camden

Salem

Woodstown

McGuire A.F.B.

N

10 Miles

10 Kilometers

© R. MςN. & CO.

Name	ZIP
Cedar Grove (Essex County)	07009
Cedar Grove (Essex County) (Township)	07009
Cedar Heights	08801
Cedar Knolls	07927
Cedar Lake	07834
Cedar Ridge	08857
Cedar Run	08092
Cedarville (Cumberland County)	08311
Cedarville (Salem County)	08098
Cedarwood Park	08723
Centennial Lake	08053
Center (Part of Trenton)	08608
Center Grove	07869
Center Square	08085
Centerton (Burlington County)	08054
Centerton (Salem County)	08318
Centerville (Mercer County)	08534
Centerville (Somerset County)	08853
Central (Part of East Orange)	07018
Central Park	08070
Centre City	08051
Centre Grove	08332
Ceramics	08817
Chadwick Beach	08739
Chairville	08055
Chambersburg (Part of Trenton)	08611
Chambers Corner	08060
Changewater	07831
Chapel Heights	08080
Charlotteburg	07435
Charlton Village	07747
Chatham	07928
Chatham (Township)	07928
Chatsworth	08019
Cheesequake	08857
Cheesequake Estates	07747
Cherry Hill	08002-03
	08034
For specific Cherry Hill Zip Codes call (609) 424-4324, or your local postmaster.	
Cherry Hill (Township)	08002
Cherry Hill Estates	08002
Cherry Quay	08723
Cherry Ridge	08002
Cherry Valley	08002
Cherryville	08822
Cherrywood	08012
Chesilhurst	08089
Chester	07930
Chester (Township)	07930
Chesterfield	08650
Chesterfield (Township)	08650
Chestnut	07083
Chewalla Park	08619
Chews Landing	08012
Chrome (Part of Carteret)	07008
Churchtown	08070
Cinnaminson	08077
Cinnaminson (Township)	08077
City of Orange (Township)	07050
Clark	07066
Clark (Township)	07066
Clarksboro	08020
Clarksburg	08510
Clarks Landing (Part of Point Pleasant)	08742
Clarktown	08330
Clayton	08312
Claytons Corner	07746
Clayville (Part of Vineland)	08360
Clearbrook Park	08831
Clear View Lake	07860
Clementon	08021
Clermont (Burlington County)	08060
Clermont (Cape May County)	08210
Cliffdale Park	07865
Cliff Park (Part of Cliffside Park)	07010
Cliffside Park	07010
Cliffwood	07721
Cliffwood Beach (Middlesex County)	08879
Cliffwood Beach (Monmouth County)	07735
Cliffwood Lake	07460

Name	ZIP
Clifton	07011-15
For specific Clifton Zip Codes call (201) 472-7900, or your local postmaster.	
Clinton	08809
Clinton (Township)	08801
Clinton Hill (Part of Newark)	07108
Closter	07624
Cloverdale (Camden County)	08030
Cloverdale (Cumberland County)	08332
Cloverhill	08822
Clover Hill at Holmdel	07733
Clover Leaf Lakes	08330
Coffins Corner	08026
Cohansey	08302
Cokesbury	08833
Cold Indian Springs	07712
Cold Spring	08204
Colesville	07461
Collings Lakes	08094
Collingswood	08108
Collingwood Park	07727
Collinsville	07960
Cologne	08213
Colonia	07067
Colonial Arms	08527
Colonial Manor	08096
Colonial Park	08520
Colonial Terrace	07712
Colts Neck	07722
Colts Neck (Township)	07722
Columbia	07832
Columbia Lakes	08002
Columbus	08022
Colwick	08002
Commercial (Township)	08349
Concordia	08512
Congressional Estates	08002
Conklintown (Part of Ringwood)	07465
Conovertown	08201
Constable Hook (Part of Bayonne)	07002
Constable Junction (Part of Bayonne)	07002
Convent Station	07961
Cookstown	08511
Coontown	07060
Cooper Park Village	08002
Cooper Village	08096
Copper Hill	08551
Corbin City	08270
Cornish	07823
Country Farms	07733
Country Lake Estates	08015
Country Manor	08857
Country Woods	07733
Coytesville (Part of Fort Lee)	07024
Cozy Lake	07438
Cragmere Park	07430
Cranberry Lake	07821
Cranbury (Township)	08512
Cranbury	08512
Cranbury Manor	08512
Crandon Lakes	07860
Cranford	07016
Cranford (Township)	07016
Cranford Junction	07016
Creamridge	08514
Crescent Heights	08068
Crescent Park (Part of Bellmawr)	08030
Cresskill	07626
Crestmoor	07853
Creston	08619
Crestwood Village	08759
Cropwell	08053
Cross Keys	08080
Crossroads	08055
Crosswicks	08515
Croton	08822
Crowfoot	08004
Crystal Lake (Bergen County)	07436
Crystal Lake (Ocean County)	08721
Culvers Lake	07826
Cumberland	08332
Cumberland Mall (Part of Vineland)	08360
Cuthbert Manor	08108
Cyn-Wyd	08016
Da Costa (Part of Hammonton)	08037
Danceys Corner	08069

Name	ZIP
Daretown	08318
Darlington Heights	08088
Darts Mills	08822
Davis	08514
Davis Bridge	07946
Dayton	08810
Deacons	08060
Deal	07723
Deal Park	07723
Deans	08852
Deauville Beach	08739
De Cou Village	08610
Deepwater	08023
Deerfield (Township)	08352
Deerfield Park	08087
Deerfield Street	08313
Deer Park	08002
Deer Trail Lake	07460
Delair	08110
Delanco	08075
Delanco (Township)	08075
Delaware (Part of Clifton)	07014
Delaware (Hunterdon County) (Township)	08822
Delaware (Warren County)	07833
Delaware Gardens	08110
Delaware Park	08865
Delcrest	08075
Del Haven	08251
Delmont	08314
Delran	08075
Delran (Township)	08075
Delwood	08002
Demarest	07627
Dennis (Township)	08214
Dennisville	08214
Denville	07834
Denville (Township)	07834
Deptford	08096
Deptford (Township)	08096
Deptford Mall	08096
Deptford Terrace	08097
Devonshire	08215
Dias Creek	08210
Dicktown	08081
Dividing Creek	08315
Doddtown (Part of East Orange)	07017
Dolphin (Part of Northfield)	08225
Dorchester	08316
Dorothy	08317
Dover	07801*
	07802†
Dover (Township)	08753
Dover Hills	07801
Dover Shores	08753
Dover Walk	08753
Downe (Township)	08315
Downer	08094
Downs Farms	08002
Downtown (Part of Trenton)	08608
Drakestown	07840
Drew University (Part of Madison)	07940
Dumont	07628
Dunbarton	08004
Dundee (Part of Passaic)	07055
Dunellen	08812
Dunham's Corner	08816
Dunham Siding	07047
Dunns Mills	08505
Durham	08817
Durham Park	08854
Dutch Neck	08550
Dutchtown	08802
Eagleswood (Township)	08092
Earle	07722
East (Part of Paterson)	07514
Eastampton (Township)	08060
East Amwell (Township)	08551
East Berlin	08009
East Bound Brook (Part of Middlesex)	08846
East Bridgeton (Part of Bridgeton)	08302
East Brunswick	08816
East Brunswick (Township)	08816
East Burlington (Part of Burlington)	08016
East Camden (Part of Camden)	08105
East Freehold	07728
East Greenwich (Township)	08020
East Hanover	07936
East Hanover (Township)	07936

Name	ZIP
East Keansburg	07734
East Long Branch (Part of Long Branch)	07740
East Millstone	08873
East Newark	07029
East Orange	07017-19
For specific East Orange Zip Codes call (201) 673-5555, or your local postmaster.	
East Pennsauken	08110
East Riverton	08077
East Rutherford	07073
East Side (Part of Bridgeton)	08302
East Spotswood	08857
East Trenton Heights	08638
East Vineland (Part of Vineland)	08360
East Wenonah	08090
East Windsor	08520
East Windsor (Township)	08520
East Woodbury	08096
Eatontown	07724
Echelon	08043
Echo Lake	07435
Edgar	07095
Edgebrook (Part of New Brunswick)	08901
Edgewater	07020
Edgewater Park	08010
Edgewater Park (Township)	08010
Edgewater Park Estates	08016
Edgewood	08210
Edgewood Park	08527
Edinburg	08691
Edison	08817-20
For specific Edison Zip Codes call (908) 287-4311, or your local postmaster.	
Egg Harbor (Township)	08221
Egg Harbor City	08215
Eilers Corner	08520
Elberon (Part of Long Branch)	07740
Elberon Park	07755
Eldora	08270
Eldridge Park	08638
Eldridges Hill	08098
Elizabeth	07201-02
	07206-08
For specific Elizabeth Zip Codes call (908) 352-8400, or your local postmaster.	
Elizabethport (Part of Elizabeth)	07206
Elk (Township)	08028
Elks Terrace	08079
Ellisburg	08002
Ellisdale	08501
Elm	08037
Elmer	08318
Elmora (Part of Elizabeth)	07202
Elmwood Park	07407
Elsinboro (Township)	08079
Elsmere (Part of Glassboro)	08028
Elwood	08217
Elwood-Magnolia	08217
Emerson	07630
Emmelville	08330
Englewood	07631-32
For specific Englewood Zip Codes call (201) 568-0086, or your local postmaster.	
Englewood Cliffs	07632
English Creek	08330
Englishtown	07726
Erial	08081
Erlton	08002
Erma	08204
Erma Park	08204
Ernston (Part of Sayreville)	08859
Erskine (Part of Ringwood)	07456
Erskine Lakes (Part of Ringwood)	07456
Essex Fells	07021
Essex Green Mall	07052
Estell Manor	08319
Estelville (Part of Estell Manor)	08319
Estling Lake	07834
Etra	08520
Everett	07735
Everittstown	08867
Evesboro	08053
Evesham (Township)	08053
Ewan	08025

	ZIP		ZIP		ZIP		ZIP
Ewansville	08060	Forty-third Street (Part of		Golf Hill	07876	Hanover Neck	07936
Ewing	08618	Union City)	07087	Golf Manor	08069	Harbourton	08530
Ewing (Township)	08618	Fostertown	08060	Golf View	08069	Harding (Township)	07940
Ewing Park	08638	Foster Village (Part of		Gordon Lakes	07405	Harding Lakes	08330
Ewingville	08638	Bergenfield)	07621	Goshen	08218	Hardingville	08343
Extonville	08501	Foul Rift	07823	Gouldtown	08302	Hardistonville (Part of	
Fairfield (Cumberland		Four Bridges	07853	Grandin	08801	Hamburg)	07419
County) (Township)	08320	Foxborough Village	08857	Granton Junction	07047	Hardwick (Township)	07825
Fairfield (Essex County)	07004	Fox Chase	08088	Grasselli (Part of Linden)	07036	Hardyston (Township)	07460
Fairfield (Essex County)		Fox Hills (Part of Mountain		Grassy Sound	08260	Harfield	08527
(Township)	07004	Lakes)	07046	Gravel Hill	07726	Harker Village	08096
Fairfield (Monmouth		Fox Hollow Woods	08002	Great Meadows	07838	Harlingen	08502
County)	07728	Francis Mills	08527	Great Meadows-Vienna	07838	Harmersville	08079
Fair Haven	07704	Frankford (Township)	07826	Great Notch	07424	Harmony (Township)	08865
Fair Lawn	07410	Franklin (Gloucester		Green (Township)	07821	Harmony (Monmouth	
Fairmount	07830	County) (Township)	08322	Green Acres	08618	County)	07748
Fairton	08320	Franklin (Hunterdon		Green Bank	08215	Harmony (Ocean County)	08527
Fairview (Bergen County)	07022	County) (Township)	08822	Green Brook (Township)	08812	Harmony (Warren County)	08865
Fairview (Burlington		Franklin (Somerset		Green Brook	08812	Harrington Park	07640
County; Medford		County) (Township)	08873	Green Creek	08219	Harrison (Gloucester	
Township)	08075	Franklin (Sussex County)	07416	Green Curve Heights	08638	County) (Township)	08062
Fairview (Burlington		Franklin (Warren County)		Greendell	07839	Harrison (Hudson County)	07029
County; Delran		(Township)	08808	Greenfield	08230	Harrison Mountain Lake	
Township)	08055	Franklin Lakes	07417	Greenfield Heights	08096	(Part of Ringwood)	07456
Fairview (Gloucester		Franklin Park	08823	Greenfields Village	08096	Harrisonville (Gloucester	
County)	08080	Franklinville	08322	Green Grove	07712	County)	08039
Fairview (Hudson County)	07047	Frazier Park	08008	Green Haven	08002	Harrisonville (Salem	
Fairview (Monmouth		Fredon (Township)	07860	Green Hills	08876	County)	08079
County)	07701	Free Acres	07922	Green Hut Park	07801	Hartford	08057
Falcon Courts North	08562	Freehold	07728	Green Island	08753	Harvey Cedars	08008
Fanwood	07023	Freehold (Township)	07728	Green Knoll	08876	Hasbrouck Heights	07604
Far Hills	07931	Freewood Acres	07727	Greenland (Part of		Haskell (Part of Wanaque)	07420
Farmersville	07830	Frelinghuysen (Township)	07821	Magnolia)	08049	Haven Beach	08008
Farmingdale	07727	Frenchtown	08825	Green Pond	07435	Haworth	07641
Farmington	08232	Freneau (Part of		Green Pond Junction		Hawthorne	07506*
Farrington Lake Heights	08816	Matawan)	07747	(Part of Kinnelon)	07405		07507†
Fashion Center, The (Part		Friendship (Carneys Point		Greensand	08817	Hazen	07823
of Paramus)	07652	Township)	08069	Greens Bridge (Part of		Hazlet	07730
Fawn Lakes	08050	Friendship (Upper		Phillipsburg)	08865	Hazlet (Township)	07730
Fayson Lakes (Part of		Piltsgrove Township)	08343	Green Village	07935	Head Of River (Part of	
Kinnelon)	07405	Fries Mill	08322	Greenville (Hudson		Estell Manor)	08270
Fellowship	08057	Galilee (Part of Monmouth		County)	07305	Headquarters	08557
Fenwick	08098	Beach)	07750	Greenville (Ocean County)	08701	Heathcote	08528
Fernwood Terrace	08618	Galloping Hill	07920	Greenville (Salem County)	08318	Heather Hills	07439
Ferrell	08343	Galloway (Township)	08213	Greenwich	08323	Hedding	08505
Ferry Road Manor	08628	Gandys Beach	08345	Greenwich (Township)	08323	Heislerville	08324
Fieldsboro	08505	Garden City	08096	Greenwich (Gloucester		Helmetta	08828
Fieldstone	07920	Gardendale	08079	County) (Township)	08027	Helmetta Park	08828
Finderne	08807	Garden Lake (Part of		Greenwich (Warren		Hensfoot	08827
Finesville	08865	Lindenwold)	08021	County) (Township)	08886	Herbertsville	08723
Firthtown (Part of		Gardens (Part of Ocean		Greenwich Pier	08323	Heritage Village	08053
Phillipsburg)	08865	City)	08226	Greenwood Park	08071	Herman	08215
Fish House	08110	Gardens of Pleasant		Grenloch	08032	Herwood	08002
Fish House Junction	08110	Plains	08753	Grenloch Terrace	08032	Hesstown	08332
Fishing Creek	08204	Garden State (Part of		Greystone Park	07950	Hewitt	07421
Five Corners (Part of		Paramus)	07652	Griggstown	08540	Heyden	07095
Jersey City)	07308	Garden State Plaza (Part		Grove	07003	Hibernia	07842
Five Points (Salem		of Paramus)	07652	Grove Chapel (Part of		Hibernia Junction (Part of	
County)	08067	Gardenville	08096	Vineland)	08344	Rockaway)	07866
Five Points (Sussex		Gardenville Center	08096	Grovers Mill	08550	Hickory Acres	08520
County)	07860	Garfield	07026	Groveville	08620	Hickory Tree	07928
Flagtown	08821	Garwood	07027	Gum Tree Corner	08302	Hickstown	08012
Flanders	07836	Genasco	08861	Guttenberg	07093	Higbee Town	08201
Flatbrookville	07832	General Lafayette (Part of		Hackensack	07601*	High Bridge	08829
Flemington	08822	Jersey City)	07309		07602†	High Crest Lake	07480
Flemington Junction	08822	Georgetown	08022	Hackettstown	07840	Highland Beach (Part of	
Floral Hill	07928	Georgetowne	08053	Haddon (Township)	08108	Sea Bright)	07760
Florence (Part of		Georgia	07728	Haddonfield	08033	Highland Lakes	07422
Roebling) (Burlington		Germania	08215	Haddon Heights	08035	Highland Park (Camden	
County)	08554	Germania Gardens	08213	Haddon Hills	08033	County)	08012
Florence (Burlington		Gibbsboro	08026	Haddon Leigh	08033	Highland Park (Part of	
County)	08518	Gibbstown	08027	Haddontowne	08002	Gloucester City)	
Florence (Burlington		Giffordtown	08057	Hainesburg	07832	(Camden County)	08030
County) (Township)	08518	Gilford Park	08753	Haines Corner	08620	Highland Park (Middlesex	
Florence (Camden		Gillespie (Part of		Hainesport	08036	County)	08904
County)	08009	Sayreville)	08872	Hainesport (Township)	08036	Highlands	07732
Florence-Roebling	08518	Gillette	07933	Hainesville	07826	High Point (Part of Harvey	
Florham Park	07932	Gilman Lake	08343	Haledon	07508*	Cedars)	08008
Folsom	08037	Glacier Hills	07950		07538†	High Point Manor	08857
Ford Estates	08096	Gladstone	07934	Haleyville	08349	Highs Beach	08210
Ford Landing	08065	Glassboro	08028	Halsey	07860	Hightstown	08520
Fords	08863	Glasser (Part of		Hamburg	07419	Hightstown Heights	08520
Forest Grove	08360	Hopatcong)	07837	Hamden	08801	Highview Park	08736
Forest Hill (Camden		Glen Cove	08721	Hamilton (Atlantic County)		Hillcrest (Camden County)	08109
County)	08002	Glendale (Camden		(Township)	08330	Hillcrest (Passaic County)	07502
Forest Hill (Ocean County)	08721	County)	08043	Hamilton (Mercer County)		Hillcrest (Warren County)	08865
Forked River	08731	Glendale (Mercer County)	08618	(Township)	08619	Hilliard	08050
Forked River Beach	08731	Glendola	07719	Hamilton (Monmouth		Hillsborough (Township)	08853
Forrest Lake Estates	08328	Glendora	08029	County)	07753	Hillsdale	07642
Fort Dix	08640	Glen Gardner	08826	Hamilton Square	08690	Hillsdale Manor (Part of	
Fort Elfsborg	08079	Glen Oaks	08021	Hammond Heights	08090	Hillsdale)	07642
Fortescue	08321	Glen Ridge	07028	Hammonton	08037	Hillside (Township)	07205
Fort Hancock	07732	Glen Rock	07452	Hampton (Hunterdon		Hillside	07205
Fort Lee	07024	Glenside	08070	County)	08827	Hilltop	08012
Fort Mercer (Part of		Glenview	08002	Hampton (Sussex County)		Hilltop Terrace	08816
National Park)	08063	Glenwood	07418	(Township)	07860	Hilltown	07885
Fort Mott	08079	Gloucester (Township)	08012	Hancocks Bridge	08038	Hillwood Lakes	08638
Fort Plains	07728	Gloucester City	08030	Hanover	07981	Hilton (Part of Atlantic	
		Godfrey Manor	08723	Hanover (Township)	07981	Highlands)	07716

Place	ZIP
Hinchman	08002
Hi-Nella	08083
Hoboken	07030
Hoffmans	07830
Hoffner	08518
Ho Ho Kus	07423
Holgate	08008
Holiday City	08753
Holiday City at Berkeley	08757
Holiday City-Berkeley	08753
Holiday City-Dover	08753
Holiday City South	08757
Holiday City West	08757
Holiday Heights	08757
Holiday on the Bay	08753
Holland	08848
Holland (Township)	08848
Holly Brook	08060
Holly Crest	08723
Holly Hills	08060
Holly Park	08721
Holmansville	08527
Holmdel	07733
Holmdel (Township)	07733
Holmdel Village	07733
Holmeson	08526
Homes Mills	08514
Homestead	07047
Homestead Park	07933
Homestead Run	08753
Homestead Village	07920
Hootens Hollow	08002
Hoot Owl Estates	08055
Hoover Village	08302
Hopatcong	07843
Hopatcong Heights (Part of Hopatcong)	07843
Hopatcong Hills (Part of Hopatcong)	07843
Hope	07844
Hope (Township)	07844
Hopelawn	08861
Hopewell (Cumberland County) (Township)	08302
Hopewell (Mercer County)	08525
Hopewell (Mercer County) (Township)	08560
Hornerstown	08514
Howell (Township)	07727
Howell	07731
Howell (rural)	07728
Hudson City (Part of Jersey City)	07307
Hudson Heights	07047
Hudson Shopping Plaza (Part of Jersey City)	07304
Hughesville	08848
Huntington	08865
Huntsburg	07860
Hunt Tract	08002
Hurdtown	07885
Hurffville	08080
Hutchinson	08865
Hutchinson Mills	08619
Hyson	08527
Ideal Beach	07734
Imlaystown (Nelsonville)	08501
Imlaystown	08526
Immaculate Conception Seminary	07430
Imperial Manor	08002
Independence (Township)	07840
Independence Corner	07461
Indian Lake	07834
Indian Mills	08088
Industrial-Hillside	07205
Interlaken	07712
Interlaken Estates	07712
Interstate Shopping Center (Part of Ramsey)	07446
Iona	08322
Ironbound (Part of Newark)	07105
Ironia	07845
Iron Rock	08109
Irven Heights	08638
Irvington	07111
Irvington (Township)	07111
Iselin	08830
Island Beach	08752
Island Heights	08732
Ivystone Farms	08004
Ivywood	08077
Jackson (Camden County)	08004
Jackson (Ocean County)	08527
Jackson (Ocean County) (Township)	08527

Place	ZIP
Jackson Avenue (Part of Jersey City)	07305
Jacksonburg	07825
Jackson Estates	08527
Jacksons Mills	08527
Jacksonville (Burlington County)	08505
Jacksonville (Morris County)	07035
Jacobstown	08562
Jamesburg	08831
Janvier	08322
Jefferson (Gloucester County)	08062
Jefferson (Morris County) (Township)	07849
Jeffrey Lane Estates	08721
Jenkins	08019
Jericho	08096
Jersey City	07301-11
For specific Jersey City Zip Codes call (201) 915-7033, or your local postmaster.	
Jerseyville	07728
Jobstown	08041
Johnsonburg	07846
Jones Island	08311
Jordantown	08109
Journal Square (Part of Jersey City)	07306
Juliustown	08042
Jutland	08827
Kampfe Lake (Part of Bloomingdale)	07403
Karrsville	07865
Kay Gardens	08067
Keansburg	07734
Kearny	07031-32
For specific Kearny Zip Codes call (201) 991-3700, or your local postmaster.	
Kearny Junction (Part of Kearny)	07032
Keasbey	08832
Keasbey Heights	08832
Kemah Lake	07860
Kendall Park	08824
Kenilworth	07033
Kenvil	07847
Kenwood	08002
Keswick Grove	08759
Keyport	07735
Kingfisher Cove	08723
Kings Hill	08002
Kingsland	07071
Kingston	08528
Kingston Estates	08002
Kingsway Village	08002
Kingswood	08002
Kingwood (Township)	08825
Kinkora	08505
Kinnelon	07405
Kirbys Mill	08055
Kirkwood	08043
Kitchell Lake	07480
Kittatinny Lake	07826
Klinesville	08822
Knollwood	08002
Knowlton	07832
Knowlton (Township)	07832
Kresson	08053
Lacey (Township)	08731
Lafayette	07848
Lafayette (Township)	07848
La Gorce Square	08016
Lake	08344
Lake Arrowhead	07834
Lake Como (Part of Spring Lake Heights)	07762
Lake Denmark	07801
Lake Forest	07849
Lake Grinnell	07871
Lake Hiawatha	07034
Lake Hopatcong	07849
Lakehurst	08733
Lakehurst Naval Air Station	08733
Lake Iliff	07860
Lake Intervale	07005
Lake Lackawanna	07874
Lakeland	08012
Lake Lenape	07860
Lake Lookover	07421
Lake Neepaulin	07461
Lake Nelson	08854
Lake Owassa	07860
Lake Pine	08053
Lakeridge	07747
Lake Riviera	08723

Place	ZIP
Lake Rogerine (Part of Mount Arlington)	07856
Lake Shawnee	07885
Lakeside	07421
Lakeside Park	08610
Lake Stockholm	07460
Lake Swannanoa	07438
Lake Tamarack	07460
Lake Telemark	07866
Lakeview (Burlington County)	08060
Lakeview (Monmouth County)	08501
Lake Villa Estates	08009
Lakewood (Township)	08701
Lakewood	08701
Lambertville	08530
Lambs Terrace	08081
Lamington	07921
Landing	07850
Landisville (Part of Buena)	08326
Land of Pines	08701
Landsdown	08801
Lanes Mills	08701
Lanoka Harbor	08734
Lanoka Harbor Estates	08734
Larger Cross Roads	07921
Larison's Corner	08551
Larrabees	08701
Laurel Acres	08723
Laureldale	08330
Laurel Harbor	08734
Laurel Hill	08021
Laurel Homes	08861
Laurelhurst	08723
Laurel Lake (Part of Millville)	08332
Laurel Manor (Camden County)	08021
Laurel Manor (Ocean County)	08723
Laurel Springs	08021
Laurel Springs Gardens	08021
Laurelton Acres	08723
Laurelton Heights	08723
Laurelton Park	08723
Laurence Harbor	08879
Lavallette	08735
Lawnside	08045
Lawrence (Cumberland County) (Township)	08311
Lawrence (Mercer County) (Township)	08638
Lawrence Brook	08816
Lawrenceville	08648
Layton	07851
Lebanon	08833
Lebanon (Township)	07830
Lebanon Lake Estates	08015
Lebanon Park	08088
Ledgewood	07852
Ledgewood Mall	07852
Leeds Point	08220
Leektown	08215
Leesburg	08327
Leisure Knoll	08733
Leisuretowne	08088
Leisure Village	08701
Leisure Village East	08753
Leisure Village West	08733
Leisure Village West-Pine Lake Park	08753
Lenola	08057
Leonardo	07737
Leonia	07605
Lewisville	08638
Liberty (Township)	07863
Liberty Corner	07938
Libertyville	07461
Lincoln	08062
Lincoln Park	07035
Lincroft	07738
Linden	07036
Linden Junction (Part of Linden)	07036
Lindenwold	08021
Lindy's Lake	07405
Linvale	08551
Linwood	08221
Little Egg Harbor (Township)	08087
Little Falls (Township)	07424
Little Falls	07424
Little Falls (Part of Totowa)	07512
Little Ferry	07643
Little Ferry (Part of Ridgefield Park)	07660

Place	ZIP
Little Ferry Junction (Part of Ridgefield Park)	07657
Little Rocky Hill	08540
Little Silver	07739
Little Silver Point (Part of Little Silver)	07739
Littleton (Part of Morris Plains)	07950
Little York	08834
Livingston (Township)	07039
Livingston	07039
Livingston Mall	07039
Loch Arbour	07711
Locktown	08822
Locust	07760
Locust Corner	08512
Lodi	07644
Logan (Township)	08014
Lommasons Glen	07823
London Terrace	08859
Long Beach	08008
Long Beach (Township)	08008
Long Branch	07740
Long Bridge	07838
Long Hill	07928
Long Hill (Township)	07946
Longport	08403
Long Valley	07853
Longwood Lake	07438
Lopatcong (Township)	08865
Lorillard Beach (Part of Union Beach)	07735
Lorraine (Part of Roselle Park)	07204
Louden	08004
Loveladies	08008
Lower (Township)	08204
Lower Alloways Creek (Township)	08038
Lower Bank	08215
Lower Berkshire Valley	07885
Lower Harmony	08865
Lower Longwood Lake	07438
Lower Montville	07045
Lower Squankum	07731
Lower Valley (Part of Califon)	07830
Low Moor (Part of Sea Bright)	07760
Lows Hollow	08886
Lozier Park (Part of Oradell)	07649
Lucaston (Part of Lindenwold)	08009
Lumberton	08048
Lumberton (Township)	08048
Lyndhurst (Township)	07071
Lyndhurst	07071
Lynn Oaks	07067
Lyons	07920
Lyons (Veterans Administration Medical Center)	07939
Lyonsville	07005
McAfee	07428
McCoys Corner	07461
McDonoughs (Part of South Amboy)	08879
McGuire Air Force Base	08641
McKee City	08232
Macopin	07405
Madison	07940
Madison Park	08859
Madisonville	07920
Magnolia (Burlington County)	08068
Magnolia (Camden County)	08049
Mahoneyville	08070
Mahwah	07430
	07495
For specific Mahwah Zip Codes call (201) 529-3366, or your local postmaster.	
Mahwah (Township)	07430
Main Avenue (Cumberland County)	08360
Main Avenue (Passaic County)	07011
Malaga	08328
Malapardis	07981
Mall at Short Hills, The	07078
Manahawkin	08050
Manalapan	07726
Manalapan (Township)	07726
Manasquan	08736
Manasquan Park	08736
Manasquan Shores	08736
Manchester (Township)	08759

*****　Area Zip Code　　†　Post Office Boxes**

	ZIP
Northfield (Atlantic County)	08225
Northfield (Essex County)	07039
North Hackensack (Part of River Edge)	07661
North Haledon	07508
North Hanover (Township)	08562
North Hawthorne (Part of Hawthorne)	07507
North Highlands Beach	08251
North Long Branch (Part of Long Branch)	07740
North Merchantville (Part of Merchantville)	08109
North Middletown	07758
Northmont (Part of Mount Ephraim)	08059
North Plainfield	07060
North Port Norris	08349
North Stelton	08854
Northvale	07647
North Vineland (Part of Vineland)	08360
North Wildwood	08260
North Woodbury (Part of Woodbury)	08096
Norton	08827
Nortonville	08085
Norwood	07648
Nottingham	08619
Nugentown	08087
Nutley	07110
Nutley (Township)	07110
Oak Dale	08060
Oak Glen	07731
Oak Hill	07748
Oakhurst	07755
Oakland	07436
Oaklyn	08107
Oak Ridge (Ocean County)	08753
Oak Ridge (Passaic County)	07438
Oak Ridge Lake	07438
Oak Shades	07747
Oak Tree (Middlesex County)	08817
Oak Tree (Ocean County)	08527
Oak Valley	08090
Oakview	08096
Oakwood	08055
Oakwood Beach	08079
Oakwood Park (Part of New Providence)	07974
Ocean (Monmouth County) (Township)	07755
Ocean (Ocean County) (Township)	08758
Ocean Acres	08050
Ocean Beach	08735
Ocean City	08226
Ocean City Gardens	08226
Ocean County Mall	08753
Ocean Gate	08740
Ocean Grove	07756
Ocean Heights (Part of Linwood)	08221
Oceanport	07757
Ocean View	08230
Oceanville	08231
Ogdensburg	07439
Old Bridge	08857
Old Bridge (Township)	08857
Old Charleston Woods	08002
Old Forge Village	07960
Old Manor	07730
Oldmans (Township)	08067
Old Orchard	08002
Old Tappan	07675
Oldwick	08858
Olivet	08318
Oradell	07649
Orange	07050*
	07051†
Orchard Center	08302
Orchard View	08016
Orston (Part of Audubon)	08106
Ortley Beach	08751
Osage	08043
Osbornsville	08723
Othello	08302
Outcalt	08831
Outwater (Part of Garfield)	07026
Overbrook (Camden County)	08021
Overbrook (Essex County)	07009
Owens	07461
Oxford	07863
Oxford (Township)	07863

	ZIP
Oyster Creek	08220
Packanack Lake	07470
Pahaquarry (Township)	07832
Palatine	08318
Palermo	08223
Palisade (Part of Fort Lee)	07024
Palisades Park	07650
Palmer Square (Part of Princeton)	08540
Palmyra (Burlington County)	08065
Palmyra (Hunterdon County)	08867
Pamrapo (Part of Bayonne)	07002
Pancoast	08310
Panther Lake	07821
Paradise Lakes	08001
Paramus	07652*
	07653†
Paramus Park (Part of Paramus)	07652
Park (Part of Paterson)	07513
Park Avenue	07087
Parker	07853
Parkertown	08087
Park Ridge	07656
Park Ridge Farms	08505
Parkside	08865
Park Village	07016
Parkway Pines	08701
Parkway Village	08628
Parlin (Part of Sayreville)	08859
Parry	08077
Parsippany (Part of Parsippany-Troy Hills)	07054
Parsippany (Part of Mountain Lakes)	07046
Parsippany-Troy Hills	07005
Parsippany-Troy Hills (Township)	07054
Pasadena	08759
Passaic	07055
Passaic Junction	07663
Passaic Park (Part of Passaic)	07055
Paterson	07501-05
	07509-10
	07513-33
	07543-44
For specific Paterson Zip Codes call (201) 977-4738, or your local postmaster.	
Patricks Corner	08816
Pattenburg	08802
Paulina	07825
Paulins Kill	07860
Paulsboro	08066
Peahala Park	08008
Peapack (Part of Gladstone)	07977
Pedricktown	08067
Peermont (Part of Avalon)	08202
Pelican Island	08751
Pellet Pond	07480
Pellettown	07822
Pemberton	08068
Pemberton (Township)	08015
Pemberton Heights	08068
Penbryn	08009
Penekum	08021
Pennington	08534
Pennsauken (Township)	08110
Pennsauken (shopping center)	08110
Penns Beach	08070
Penns Grove	08069
Penns Neck	08540
Pennsville	08070
Pennsville (Township)	08070
Penny Pot (Part of Folsom)	08037
Penton	08079
Penwell	07865
Peppermill Farms	08002
Pequannock	07440
Pequannock (Township)	07440
Pequest	07863
Perrineville	08535
Perth Amboy	08861*
	08862†
Petersburg	08270
Philips Mills	07734
Phillipsburg	08865
Phoenix	08817
Picatinny Arsenal	07806
Pierces Point	08210
Piersonville	08620

	ZIP
Pilesgrove (Township)	08093
Pine Acres (Part of Woodbury Heights)	08090
Pine Beach	08741
Pine Brook (Monmouth County)	07724
Pine Brook (Morris County)	07058
Pine Brook (Somerset County)	08502
Pine Cliff Lake	07480
Pine Grove	08053
Pine Hill	08021
Pinehurst	08201
Pine Lake Park	08753
Pine Ridge	08857
Pine Ridge at Crestwood	08759
Pines Lake	07470
Pine Terrace	08753
Pinetree Village	08857
Pine Valley	08021
Pinewald	08721
Pinewold Village	08016
Piscataway	08854*
	08855†
Pitman	08071
Pittsgrove	08318
Pittsgrove (Township)	08347
Pittstown	08867
Plainfield	07060-63
For specific Plainfield Zip Codes call (908) 756-5200, or your local postmaster.	
Plainsboro	08536
Plainsboro (Township)	08536
Plainville	08502
Plauderville (Part of Garfield)	07026
Plaza (Part of Secaucus)	07094
Plaza Park	08016
Pleasant Gardens	08527
Pleasant Grove (Morris County)	07853
Pleasant Grove (Ocean County)	08527
Pleasant Hill	07876
Pleasant Mills	08037
Pleasant Plains (Morris County)	07980
Pleasant Plains (Ocean County)	08753
Pleasant Run (Burlington County)	08077
Pleasant Run (Hunterdon County)	08822
Pleasant Terrace	08314
Pleasant Valley	07882
Pleasant View	08502
Pleasantville (Atlantic County)	08232
Pleasantville (Cumberland County)	08360
Pleasure Bay (Part of Long Branch)	07740
Pluckemin	07978
Plumbsock	07461
Plumsted (Township)	08533
Pohatcong (Township)	08804
Pointers	08079
Point Pleasant	08742
Point Pleasant Beach	08742
Point Pleasant Manor	08723
Polkville	07832
Pomona	08240
Pompton Junction (Part of Pompton Lakes)	07442
Pompton Lakes	07442
Pompton Plains	07444
Porchtown	08344
Port-au-Peck (Part of Oceanport)	07757
Port Colden	07882
Port Elizabeth	08348
Portertown	08098
Port Johnson (Part of Bayonne)	07002
Port Monmouth	07758
Port Morris	07850
Port Murray	07865
Port Norris	08349
Port Reading	07064
Port Reading Junction (Part of Manville)	08835
Port Republic	08241
Port Warren	08886
Possumtown	08854
Post Brook Farms Lake	07480
Potter	08817
Potterstown	08833

	ZIP
Pottersville	07979
Powerville	07005
Prallsville (Part of Stockton)	08559
Presidential Lakes Estates	08015
Princeton	08540-43
For specific Princeton Zip Codes call (609) 452-9044, or your local postmaster.	
Princeton Ivy East	08520
Princeton Junction	08550
Princeton North	08540
Prospect Heights	08638
Prospect Highlands	08638
Prospect Park (Mercer County)	08638
Prospect Park (Passaic County)	07508
Prospect Plains	08512
Prospect Point	07849
Prospertown	08514
Pullentown	08501
Quaker Gardens	08619
Quakertown	08868
Quarryville	07461
Quinton	08072
Quinton (Township)	08072
Racoon Island	07849
Radburn (Part of Fair Lawn)	07410
Rahway	07065-67
For specific Rahway Zip Codes call (908) 388-1110, or your local postmaster.	
Rainbow Lakes	07834
Raines Corner	08069
Ralston	07945
Ramblewood	08054
Ramsey	07446
Ramseysburg	07832
Rancocas	08073
Rancocas Heights	08060
Rancocas Woods	08060
Randolph	07869
Randolph (Township)	07970
Raritan (Hunterdon County) (Township)	08822
Raritan (Somerset County)	08869
Raven Rock	08559
Readington	08870
Readington (Township)	08870
Reaville	08822
Rebel Hill	07920
Red Bank (Monmouth County)	07701-04
For specific Red Bank Zip Codes call (908) 741-9200, or your local postmaster.	
Red Bank (Gloucester County)	08063
Red Lion	08088
Reed Crossing (Part of Berlin)	08009
Reeds Beach	08210
Reevytown (Part of Tinton Falls)	07753
Repaupo	08066
Retreat	08088
Richard Mine	07885
Richland	08350
Richwood	08074
Rider College	08648
Ridgefield	07657
Ridgefield Park	07660
Ridgeway	08733
Ridgewood	07450*
	07451†
Ridgewood Junction (Part of Glen Rock)	07452
Riegel Ridge	08848
Riegelsville	08848
Ringoes	08551
Ringwood	07456
Rio Grande	08242
Ritz (Part of Garfield)	07026
River Bank	08741
Riverdale	07457
River Edge	07661
River Edge Manor (Part of New Milford)	07646
Riverfront Plaza (Part of Newark)	07102
River Plaza	07701
River Road (Part of Fair Lawn)	07410
Riverside (Township)	08075
Riverside	08075
Riverside Park	08075

* Area Zip Code　　**† Post Office Boxes**

	ZIP
Riverside Square (Part of Hackensack)	07601
River Street (Part of Paterson)	07524
Riverton	08076-77
For specific Riverton Zip Codes call (609) 829-0575, or your local postmaster.	
River Vale (Township)	07675
River Vale	07675
Riverview Manor	08854
Riverwood	08753
Riviera Beach	08723
Roadstown	08302
Robbinsville	08691
Robertsville (census designated place)	07746
	07751
For specific Robertsville Zip Codes call (908) 462-2980, or your local postmaster.	
Robertsville	07726
Robin Hood Homes	08010
Robins Estates	08527
Rochelle Park	07662-63
For specific Rochelle Park Zip Codes call (201) 843-2692, or your local postmaster.	
Rockaway	07866
Rockaway (Township)	07866
Rockaway Neck	07054
Rockaway Valley	07005
Rockleigh	07647
Rockport	07840
Rock Ridge Lake	07834
Rocktown	08551
Rocky Hill	08553
Roebling	08554
Roosevelt	08555
Roosevelt City	08759
Roosevelt Park (Part of Millville)	08332
Rosedale (Part of Hammonton)	08037
Rosegate	08857
Rose Hill Heights	08865
Roseland	07068
Roselle	07203
Roselle Park	07204
Rosemont (Hunterdon County)	08556
Rosemont (Mercer County)	08619
Rosenhayn	08352
Roseville (Part of Newark)	07107
Ross Corner	07822
Rossmoor	08831
Rowe Street	07003
Roxbury	08865
Roxbury (Township)	07876
Rudeville	07419
Rumson	07760
Runnemede	08078
Runyon	08857
Russia	07438
Rutgers Village (Part of New Brunswick)	08901
Rutherford	07070-75
For specific Rutherford Zip Codes call (201) 933-1213, or your local postmaster.	
Saddle Brook (Township)	07663
Saddle Brook	07663
Saddle River	07458
St. Cloud	07052
St. Josephs Village (Part of Rockleigh)	07647
Salem	08079
Salem Hills	08701
Salina	08080
Sand Brook	08559
Sand Hills (Edison Township)	08861
Sand Hills (Woodbridge Township)	08852
Sands Point (Part of Oceanport)	07757
Sandy Point	08723
Sandyston (Township)	07851
Saxton Falls	07874
Sayres Neck	08311
Sayreville	08871†
	08872*
Sayre Woods (Part of Sayreville)	08859
Sayre Woods South	08857
Schellengers Landing (Part of Cape May)	08204
Schooleys Mountian	07870

	ZIP
Scobeyville	07724
Scotch Bonnet	08210
Scotch Plains (Township)	07076
Scotch Plains	07076
Scudders Falls	08628
Scullville	08330
Seaboard (Part of Kearny)	07032
Sea Breeze	08302
Sea Bright	07760
Seabrook	08302
Sea Girt	08750
Sea Girt Estates	08750
Sea Isle City	08243
Seaside Heights	08751
Seaside Park	08752
Seaview Park	08201
Seaview Square Mall	07712
Seaville	08230
Secaucus	07094*
	07096†
Sedgefield	07950
Sergeantsville	08557
Seven Stars	08701
Sewaren	07077
Sewell	08080
Shady Lake	07480
Shafto Corners (Part of Tinton Falls)	07727
Shamong (Township)	08088
Shark River Hills	07753
Shark River Manor	07719
Sharptown	08098
Shaw Crest	08260
Shelter Cove	08753
Sherbrook Estates	08520
Sherwood on the Green	08096
Sherwood West	08066
Shiloh	08353
Shimer Manor	08865
Ship Bottom	08008
Shippenport	07850
Shirley	08318
Shongum	07970
Shore Acres	08723
Shore Crest	07067
Shore Mall (Part of Pleasantville)	08232
Short Hills	07078
Shrewsbury	07702
Shrewsbury (Township)	07724
Shrewsbury Road	08501
Sicklerville	08081
Sidney	08867
Siloam	07728
Silver Bay	08753
Silver Lake (Essex County)	07109
Silver Lake (Warren County)	07825
Silver Ridge	08753
Silver Ridge Park	08757
Silver Ridge Park West	08757
Silver Springs	07850
Silverton	08753
Sim Place	08005
Singac	07424
Sinnickson Landing	08079
Six Points	08302
Skillman	08558
Skylands (Part of Ringwood)	07456
Sky Line Lake (Part of Ringwood)	07465
Slackwoods	08638
Sloop Creek Estates	08721
Sloping Hills	07920
Smithburg	07728
Smiths Mills	07405
Smith Tract	08008
Smithville (Atlantic County)	08201
Smithville (Burlington County)	08060
Smoke Rise (Part of Kinnelon)	07405
Snow Hill (Part of Lawnside)	08045
Society Hill	08857
Society Hill (Part of Cedar Ridge)	08817
Soho	07109
Somerdale	08083
Somerset (Mercer County)	08628
Somerset (Somerset County)	08873-75
For specific Somerset Zip Codes call (908) 873-8600, or your local postmaster.	
Somers Point	08244

	ZIP
Somerville	08876-77
For specific Somerville Zip Codes call (908) 725-0570, or your local postmaster.	
South (Part of Newark)	07114
South Amboy	08879
Southampton (Township)	08088
Southard	08701
South Belmar	07719
South Bound Brook (Middlesex County)	08846
South Bound Brook (Somerset County)	08880
South Branch	08876
South Brunswick	08540
South Brunswick (Township)	08852
South Camden (Part of Camden)	08104
South Dennis	08245
South Egg Harbor	08215
Southern State 1 & 2	08314
South Glassboro (Part of Glassboro)	08028
South Hackensack (Township)	07606
South Hackensack	07606
South Harrison (Township)	08039
South Kearny (Part of Kearny)	07032
South Lakewood	08701
South Livingston	07039
South Mantoloking	08738
South Merchantville (Part of Merchantville)	08109
South Ogdensburg (Part of Ogdensburg)	07439
South Orange	07079
South Orange Village (Township)	07079
South Paterson (Part of Paterson)	07503
South Pemberton (Part of Pemberton)	08068
South Penns Grove	08069
South Plainfield	07080
South River	08882
South Seaside Park	08752
South Seaville	08246
South Toms River	08757
South Vineland (Part of Vineland)	08360
South Westville (Part of Westville)	08093
Southwest Vinland (Part of Vineland)	08360
Southwind	08527
Southwood	08857
South Woodstown (Part of Woodstown)	08098
Sparta	07871
Sparta (Township)	07871
Sparta Junction	07871
Sparta Lake	07871
Sperry Springs (Part of Hopatcong)	07843
Spotswood	08884
Spray Beach	08008
Springdale (Camden County)	08002
Springdale (Sussex County)	07860
Springfield (Burlington County) (Township)	08041
Springfield (Union County) (Township)	07081
Springfield (Union County)	07081
Spring Gardens	08618
Spring Lake	07762
Spring Lake Heights	07762
Spring Mills	08848
Springside	08016
Springtown (Cumberland County)	08302
Springtown (Warren County)	08865
Springville	08057
Squire Village	08753
Stafford (Township)	08050
Staffordville	08092
Stanhope	07874
Stanton	08885
Stanton Station	08822
Stanwick	08057
Stanwick Glen	08057
Star Cross	08322
State Hospital	08625
Staten Island Junction	07016
Steelmantown	08270

	ZIP
Steelmanville	08221
Stephensburg	07865
Stevens	08016
Stewartsville	08886
Still Valley	08865
Stillwater	07875
Stillwater (Township)	07875
Stirling	07980
Stockholm	07460
Stockton	08559
Stockton State College	08240
Stone Harbor	08247
Stone House	07946
Stone Tavern	08514
Stonetown (Part of Ringwood)	07465
Stoney Brook Estates	08096
Stony Hill	07922
Stoutsburg	08525
Stow Creek (Township)	08302
Stow Creek Landing	08302
Stratford	08084
Strathmere	08248
Strathmore	07747
Styertowne Shopping Center (Part of Clifton)	07012
Suburban	07701
Succasunna	07876
Succasunna-Kenvil	07876
Summerfield	07823
Summit	07901*
	07902†
Summit Avenue (Part of Union City)	07087
Sunbury	08068
Sunnyside	08801
Sunrise Beach	08731
Sunrise Park	07876
Sunset Hills	08540
Surf City	08008
Sussex	07461
Sutton Park	07836
Swainton	08210
Swartswood	07877
Swartswood Lake	07860
Swedesboro	08085
Sweet Briar	07733
Sweetwater	08037
Sykesville	08562
Sylvan Glen	08505
Sylvan Lake	08016
Tabernacle	08088
Tabernacle (Township)	08088
Tanglewood Farms	07733
Tanners Corner	08816
Tansboro	08004
Taunton Lakes	08053
Taurus (Part of West New York)	07093
Tavistock	08033
Taylortown	07005
Teabo	07885
Teaneck (Township)	07666
Teaneck	07666
Tenafly	07670
Tennent	07763
Teterboro	07608
Tewksbury (Township)	08833
The Acres (Part of Glassboro)	08028
The Dunes	08008
The Orchards	08619
Thompson Beach	08324
Thorofare	08086
Three Bridges	08887
Timber Lakes	08094
Timbuctoo	08060
Tinton Falls	07724
Titusville	08560
Toms River	08753-57
For specific Toms River Zip Codes call (908) 349-0710, or your local postmaster.	
Totowa	07511†
	07512*
Towaco	07082
Town Bank	08204
Town Brook	07748
Town Center	07052
Town Estates	08016
Townley	07083
Townsbury	07863
Townsends Inlet (Part of Sea Isle City)	08243
Tranquility	07879
Tremley (Part of Linden)	07036
Tremley Point (Part of Linden)	07036

Place	ZIP
Abbott	87747
Abeytas	87006
Abiquiu	87510
Abo	87036
Abuelo	87732
Academy (Part of Albuquerque)	87109
Acoma	87049
Acoma Indian Reservation	87031
Acomita	87034
Acomita Lake	87034
Adelino	87031
Adobe Acres	87105
Agua Fria (Santa Fe County)	87501
Air Mail Facility (Part of Albuquerque)	87119
Alameda	87113
	87114

For specific Alameda Zip Codes call (505) 245-9610, or your local postmaster.

Place	ZIP
Alamito	87831
Alamo	87825
Alamogordo	88310-11

For specific Alamogordo Zip Codes call (505) 437-9390, or your local postmaster.

Place	ZIP
Alamo Navajo Indian Reservation	87825
Albert	87733
Albuquerque	87101-23
	87125-54
	87176-99

For specific Albuquerque Zip Codes call (505) 245-9578, or your local postmaster.

Place	ZIP
Alcalde	87511
Algodones	87001
Alire	87518
Allison	87301
Alma	88039
Alpine Village	88345
Alto	88312
Alto Crest (Part of Ruidoso)	88345
Amalia	87512
Ambrosia Lake	87020
Amistad	88410
Anaconda	87020
Ancho	88301
Angel Fire	87710
Angostura (Dona Ana County)	87940
Angostura (Taos County)	87579
Angus	88316
Animas	88020
Animas Valley Mall (Part of Farmington)	87401
Anthony	88021
Anton Chico	87711
Apache Creek	87830
Apache Park	88345
Apodaca	87527
Arabela	88351
Aragon	87820
Arch	88130
Arenas Valley	88022
Arkansas Junction	88240
Armijo	87105
Arrey	87930
Arroyo del Agua	87012
Arroyo Hondo	87513
Arroyo Seco	87514
Artesia	88210*
	88211†
Artesia Camp	88347
Atoka	88210
Atrisco (Part of Albuquerque)	87105
Aurora (Mora County)	87734
Aurora (San Miguel County)	87583
Aztec	87410
Bacaville (Part of Belen)	87002
Bard	88411
Barelas (Part of Albuquerque)	87102
Barranca	87510
Bayard	88023
Becenti	87313
Beclabito	87420
Belen	87002
Bell Ranch	88441
Bellview	88111
Bennett	88252
Bent	88314
Berino	88024
Bernal	87569
Bernalillo	87004
Bernardo	87006
Beulah	87745
Bibo	87055
Bingham	87815
Bisti	87401
Black Forest (Part of Ruidoso)	88345
Black Lake	87734
Black River Village	88220
Black Rock	87327
Blanchard	87569
Blanco	87412
Blanco Trading Post	87037
Bloomfield	87413
Bluewater (Cibola County)	87005
Bluewater (Lincoln County)	88351
Boles	88311
Boles Acres	88311
Bonito	88341
Bosque	87006
Bosque Farms	87068
Boys Ranch	87002
Brazos	87551
Bread Springs	87301
Brimhall	87310
Broadmoor (Part of Roswell)	88201
Broadview	88112
Broadview Acres	87020
Buckeye	88260
Buckhorn	88025
Buena Vista	87712
Bueyeros	88412
Burnham	87401
Butterfield Park	88001
Caballo	87931
Cameron	88120
Campus (Part of Socorro)	87801
Canada de los Alamos	87501
Canjilon	87515
Cannon Air Force Base	88103
Canon	87571
Canoncito (Bernalillo County; rural)	87008
Canoncito (Bernalillo County; Canoncito Indian Reservation)	87026
Canoncito (Rio Arriba County)	87527
Canoncito (San Miguel County)	87745
Canoncito (Santa Fe County)	87505
Canoncito Indian Reservation	87026
Canones	87516
Canon Plaza	87581
Canova	87582
Canyon	87024
Canyoncito	87535
Capitan	88316
Caprock	88213
Capulin	88414
Carlsbad	88220*
	88221†
Carlsbad North	88220
Carnuel	87112
Carrizo	88345
Carrizozo	88301
Carson	87517
Casa Blanca	87007
Causey	88113
Cebolla	87518
Cedar Creek	88345
Cedar Crest	87008
Cedar Grove	87056
Cedar Hill	87410
Cedarvale	87009
Cedro Village	87059
Central	88026
Central New Mexico Correctional Facility	87031
Cerrillos	87010
Cerro	87519
Chacon	87713
Chama	87520
Chamberino	88027
Chamisal	87521
Chamita	87566
Chaparral	88021
Chapelle	87569
Chaperito	87701
Chelwood Park (Part of Albuquerque)	87112
Chical	87031
Chi Chil Tah	87326
Chili	87537
Chilili	87059
Chimayo	87522
Chippeway Park	88317
Chloride	87943
Chupadero	87501
Church Rock	87311
Cimarron	87714
Claunch	87011
Clayton	88415
Cleveland	87715
Cliff	88028
Clines Corners	87070
Cloud Country Estates	88317
Cloudcroft	88317
Cloverdale	88020
Clovis	88101*
	88102†
Cochiti Indian Reservation	87041
Cochiti Lake	87083
Cochiti Pueblo	87072
Colonias	88435
Columbine	87556
Columbus	88029
Conchas Dam	88416
Continental Divide	87312
Contreras	87028
Coolidge	87312
Corazon	87701
Cordova	87523
Corona	88318
Coronado (Part of Santa Fe)	87501-02

For specific Coronado Zip Codes call (505) 438-8452, or your local postmaster.

Place	ZIP
Coronado Center (Part of Albuquerque)	87110
Corrales	87048
Coruco	87560
Costilla	87524
Cotton City	88020
Counselor	87018
Country Club Estates (Bernalillo County)	87114
Country Club Estates (Lincoln County)	88345
Country Club Heights (Part of Ruidoso)	88345
Cowles	87573
Coyote	87012
Cree Meadows Heights (Part of Ruidoso)	88345
Crossroads	88114
Crownpoint	87313
Cruzville	87830
Crystal	87328
Cuba	87013
Cubero	87014
Cuchillo	87932
Cuervo	88417
Cundiyo	87522
Cuyamungue	87501
Dahlia	87711
Dalies	87031
Dalton Pass	87313
Datil	87821
Del Norte (Part of Ruidoso)	88345
Deming	88030*
	88031†
Derry	87933
Des Moines	88418
De Vargas Shopping Center (Part of Santa Fe)	87501
Dexter	88230
Dilia	87724
Dixon	87527
Dog Canyon Estates	88310
Domingo	87052
Dona Ana	88032
Dora	88115
Downtown (Part of Albuquerque)	87103
Dulce	87528
Dunken	88344
Duran	88319
Dusty	87943
Eagle Nest	87718
East Grand Plains	88201
East Pecos	87552
Edgewood	87015
El Ancon	87560
El Cerrito	87583
El Cerro	87031
Eldorado (Part of Albuquerque)	87111
Eldorado at Santa Fe	87505
El Duende	87537
Elephant Butte	87935
Elephant Butte Estates	87935
El Gauche	87566
El Guique	87566
Elida	88116
Elk	88339
Elkins	88201
El Llanito	87004
El Llano (Rio Arriba County)	87532
El Llano (San Miguel County)	87701
El Morro	87034
El Portero	87522
El Porvenir	87731
El Prado	87529
El Pueblo	87560
El Rancho	87532
El Rancho Loma Linda	87579
El Renz-O-Ranch	87718
El Rincon de los Trujillos	87522
El Rito	87530
El Turquillo	87722
El Vado	87575
El Valle	87521
Embudo	87531
Emplazado	87745
Enchanted Hills (Part of Ruidoso)	88345
Encinal	87014
Encino	88321
Engele	87935
Ensenada	87575
Escabosa	87059
Escondida	87801
Espanola	87532
Estaca	87566
Estancia	87016
Eunice	88231
Fairacres	88033
Fairview (Part of Espanola)	87533
Farley	88422
Farmington	87401-02
	87499

For specific Farmington Zip Codes call (505) 325-5047, or your local postmaster.

Place	ZIP
Faywood	88034
Faywood Hot Springs	88034
Fence Lake	87315
Field	88124
Fierro	88041
First Plaza (Part of Albuquerque)	87102
Five Points	87105
	87121

For specific Five Points Zip Codes call (505) 245-9640, or your local postmaster.

Place	ZIP
Flora Vista	87415
Florida	87801
Floyd	88118
Flume Canyon (Part of Ruidoso)	88345
Flying H	88344
Folsom	88419
Forest Heights (Part of Ruidoso)	88345
Forest Park	87008
Forrest	88427
Fort Bliss	79916
Fort Stanton	88323
Fort Sumner	88119
Fort Wingate	87316
Fort Wingate Depot Activity	87301
French Corners	87747
Fruitland	87416
Gabaldon	87701
Galisteo	87010
Gallegos	88426
Gallina	87017
Gallina Plaza	87017
Gallinas	87731
Gallup	87301-05

For specific Gallup Zip Codes call (505) 863-3491, or your local postmaster.

Place	ZIP
Gamerco	87317
Garanbuio	87568
Garfield	87936
Garita	88421
Garrison	88132
Gascon	87742
Gavilan	87029
Gila	88038
Gila Hot Springs	88061
Gladstone	88422

* Area Zip Code   † Post Office Boxes

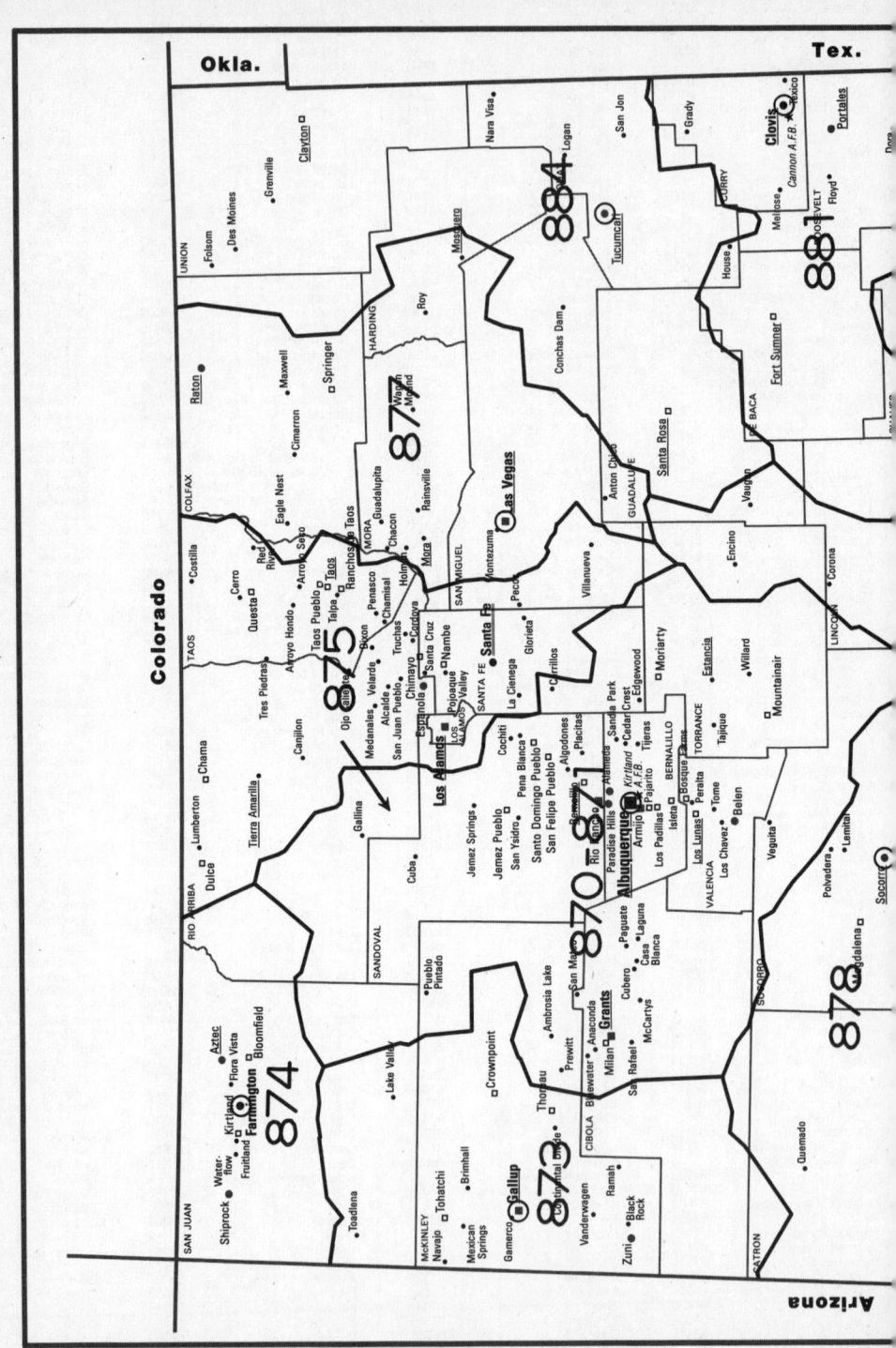

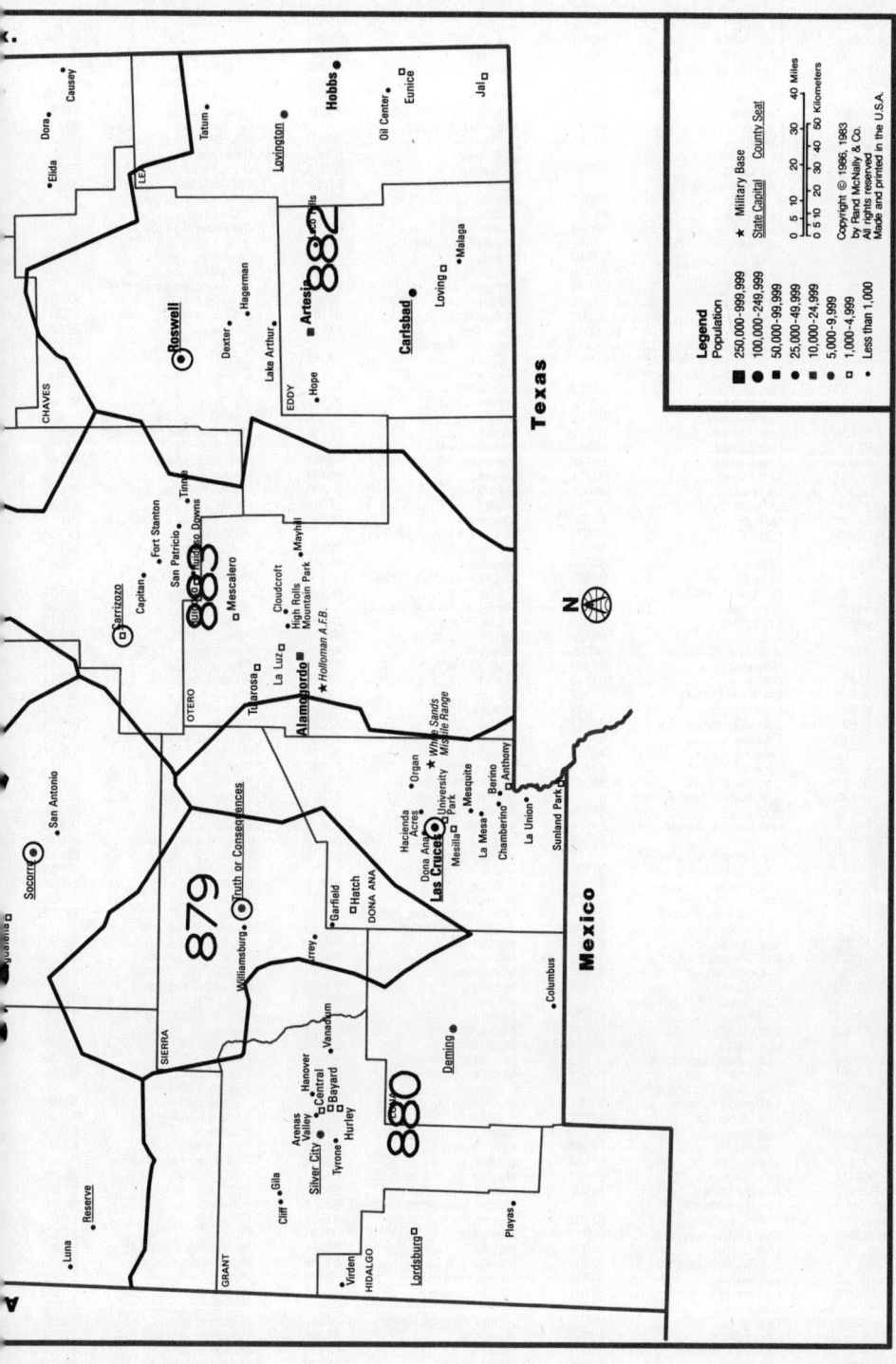

Legend
Population
■ 250,000-999,999
● 100,000-249,999
● 50,000-99,999
■ 25,000-49,999
■ 10,000-24,999
□ 5,000-9,999
□ 1,000-4,999
• Less than 1,000

★ Military Base
State Capital County Seat

0 5 10   20   30   40 Miles
0 5 10 20 30 40 50 Kilometers

Copyright © 1986, 1983
by Rand McNally & Co.
All rights reserved
Made and printed in the U.S.A.

Texas

Mexico

N

882

883

879

880

Hobbs
Eunice
Jal
Causey
Dora
Elida
Tatum
Lovington
Oil Center
Malaga
Roswell
Hagerman
Dexter
Lake Arthur
Loving
Carlsbad
Artesia
Hope
CHAVES
EDDY
LEA
Tinnie
Ruidoso Downs
Fort Stanton
San Patricio
Capitan
Carrizozo
Mescalero
Cloudcroft
High Rolls
Mountain Park
Mayhill
La Luz
Tularosa
Alamogordo
Holloman A.F.B.
OTERO
White Sands
Missile Range
Organ
San Antonio
Socorro
Truth or Consequences
Williamsburg
Hacienda
Acres
Dona Ana
University
Park
Mesilla
Las Cruces
La Mesa
Mesquite
Chamberino
Berino
Anthony
Sunland Park
La Union
Garfield
Hatch
DONA ANA
Arrey
SIERRA
Vanadium
Deming
Columbus
Hanover
Central
Bayard
Silver City
Hurley
Tyrone
Arenas
Valley
Cliff
Gila
Reserve
Luna
GRANT
Virden
HIDALGO
Lordsburg
Playas

	ZIP
Glencoe	88324
Glen Grove (Part of Ruidoso)	88345
Glenrio	88423
Glenwood	88039
Glorieta	87535
Gobernador	87412
Golden	87047
Golondrinas	87712
Gonzales Ranch	87560
Grady	88120
Gran Quivira	87036
Grants	87020
Greenfield	88230
Green Meadows (Part of Ruidoso)	88345
Grenville	88424
Grier	88101
Guachupangue	87532
Guadalupita	87722
Hachita	88040
Hacienda Acres	88001
Hagerman	88232
Hamilton Terrace (Part of Ruidoso)	88345
Hanover	88041
Happy Valley	88220
Hatch	87937
Hayden	88410
Hernandez	87537
Highland (Part of Albuquerque)	87108
High Rolls	88325
Hill	88005
Hillburn City	88260
Hillsboro	88042
Hobbies	87059
Hobbs	88240*
	88241†
Hoffman Town (Part of Albuquerque)	87112
Holiday Acres (Part of Ruidoso)	88345
Hollene	88101
Holloman Air Force Base	88330
Hollywood (Part of Ruidoso)	88345
Holman	87723
Hondo	88336
Hooverville	88416
Hope	88250
Horse Springs	87821
Hospah	87313
Hot Springs	87731
Hot Springs Landing	87935
House	88121
Humble City	88240
Hurley	88043
Hyde Park Estates	87501
Idlewild	87718
Ilfeld	87538
Indian Hills (Part of Ruidoso)	88345
Isleta	87022
Isleta Indian Reservation	87022
Iyanbito	87316
Jacona	87501
Jaconita	87501
Jal	88252
Jarales	87023
Jemez Indian Reservation	87024
Jemez Pueblo	87024
Jemez Springs	87025
Jicarilla Apache Indian Reservation	87528
Jordan	88427
Kenna	88122
Kingston	88042
Kingswood (Part of Ruidoso)	88345
Kirtland	87417
Kirtland Air Force Base	87115
	87118

For specific Kirtland Air Force Base Zip Codes call (505) 245-9605, or your local postmaster.

	ZIP
Knowles	88240
La Bolsa	87531
La Cienega	87501
La Constancia	87002
La Cueva (Mora County)	87712
La Cueva (Santa Fe County)	87535
La Fraqua	87568
Laguna	87026
Laguna Indian Reservation	87026
Lagunita	87560
La Huerta	88220
La Jara	87027

	ZIP
La Joya (Santa Fe County)	87535
La Joya (Socorro County)	87028
La Junta	87531
Lake Arthur	88253
Lake Valley	87313
Lake View Pines	87718
Lakewood	88254
La Ladera	87031
La Loma	87724
La Luz	88337
Lama	87556
La Madera (Rio Arriba County)	87539
La Madera (Sandoval County)	87047
La Manga	87701
La Mesa	88044
La Mesilla	87532
Lamy	87540
La Plata	87418
La Puebla	87532
La Puente	87575
Las Cruces	88001
	88003-06

For specific Las Cruces Zip Codes call (505) 524-2841, or your local postmaster.

	ZIP
Las Mochas	87579
Las Nutrias	87062
Las Palomas	87942
Las Placitas	87530
Las Tablas	87541
Las Tusas	87745
Las Vegas	87701
La Union	88021
La Vilita	87511
Ledoux	87725
Lemitar	87823
Levy	87752
Leyba	87560
Lincoln	88338
Linda Vista (Part of Roswell)	88201
Lindrith	87029
Lingo	88123
Little Walnut Village	88061
Littlewater	87461
Llano	87543
Llano del Medio	87724
Llano Largo	87553
Llano Quemado	87557
Llaves	87027
Loco Hills	88255
Logan	88426
Lordsburg	88045
Los Alamos (Los Alamos County)	87544
Los Alamos (San Miguel County)	87745
Los Candelarias (Part of Albuquerque)	87107
Los Chavez	87002
Los Cordovas	87571
Los Duranes (Part of Albuquerque)	87104
Los Febres	87734
Los Griegos (Part of Albuquerque)	87107
Los Huevos	87734
Los Lentes (Part of Los Lunas)	87031
Los Luceros	87511
Los Lunas	87031
Los Lunas Correctional Center	87031
Los Lunas Hospital and Training School	87031
Los Montoyas	87701
Los Ojos	87551
Los Pachecos	87522
Los Padillas	87105
Los Pinos	87120
Los Ranchos	87101
Los Ranchos de Albuquerque	87107
Lost Lodge	88317
Los Trujillos	87002
Los Trujillos-Gabaldon	87002
Los Vigiles	87701
Lourdes	87701
Lovato	87568
Loving	88256
Lovington	88260
Lower La Posada	87552
Lower Nutria	87327
Lower Pueblo	87560
Lower Ranchito	87581
Lower Rociada	87742

	ZIP
Lower San Francisco Plaza	87830
Lucero	87736
Lucy	87063
Luis Lopez	87801
Lumberton	87547
Luna	87824
Lyden	87582
McAlister	88427
McCartys (Cibola County)	87049
McCartys (Harding County)	88430
McDonald	88262
McGaffey	87316
Macimiliano Luna	87701
McIntosh	87032
Madrid	87010
Maes	87701
Magdalena	87825
Malaga	88263
Maljamar	88264
Mangas	87821
Mangas Springs	88061
Manuelitas	87745
Manuelito	87319
Manzano (Bernalillo County)	87112
Manzano (Torrance County)	87036
Mariano Lake	87301
Maxwell	87728
Mayhill	88339
Meadow Lake	87031
Medanales	87548
Melrose	88124
Mentmore	87319
Mesa Poleo	87012
Mescalero	88340
Mescalero Apache Indian Reservation	88340
Mesilla	88046
Mesilla Park (Part of Las Cruces)	88047
Mesilla Valley Mall (Part of Las Cruces)	88001
Mesita	87026
Mesquite	88048
Mexican Springs	87320
Miami	87729
Midway	88201
Milagro	88321
Milan	87021
Mills	87730
Milnesand	88125
Mimbres	88049
Mimbres Hot Springs	88041
Mineral Hill	87701
Mission Park	87031
Mogollon	88039
Monero	87547
Monte Aplanado	87732
Monte Verde (Part of Angel Fire)	87718
Montezuma	87731
Montgomery Plaza Mall (Part of Albuquerque)	87110
Monticello	87939
Montoya	88401
Monument	88265
Moqino	87040
Mora	87732
Moriarty	87035
Mosquero	87733
Mountainair	87036
Mountain Park	88325
Mountain View (Bernalillo County)	87105
Mountain View (Chaves County)	88201
Mount Dora	88429
Mule Creek	88051
Nadine	88240
Nageezi	87037
Nambe	87501
Nambe Indian Reservation	87501
Nambe Pueblo	87501
Nara Visa	88430
Naschitti	87325
Navajo	87328
Navajo Dam	87419
Navajo Estates	87375
Navajo Indian Reservation	86515
Navajo Wingate Village	87311
Newcomb	87455
Newkirk	88431
New Laguna	87038
New York	87014
Nogal	88341
North Acomita Village	87034

	ZIP
North Carmen	87732
North Hurley	88043
North San Ysidro	87538
North Valley	87107
	87109

For specific North Valley Zip Codes call (505) 245-9665, or your local postmaster.

	ZIP
Nutrias	87575
Ocate	87734
Oil Center	88266
Ojito (Rio Arriba County)	87029
Ojito (Taos County)	87521
Ojitos Frios	87701
Ojo Amarillo	87417
Ojo Caliente (Cibola County)	87327
Ojo Caliente (Taos County)	87549
Ojo Feliz	87735
Ojo Sarco	87550
Old Albuquerque (Part of Albuquerque)	87104
Old Picacho	88033
Omega	87829
Organ	88052
Orogrande	88342
Oscuro	88301
Otis	88220
Paguate	87040
Pajarito (Bernalillo County)	87105
Pajarito (Santa Fe County)	87532
Paradise Hills	87114
Park Springs	87701
Pastura	88435
Paxton Springs	87020
Pecos	87552
Pena Blanca	87041
Penasco	87553
Penasco Blanco	87742
Pendaries	87742
Penitentiary of New Mexico	87501
Pep	88126
Peralta	87042
Perea	87316
Pescado	87327
Petaca	87554
Philadelphia	87014
Philmont	87714
Picacho	88343
Picuris	87553
Picuris Indian Reservation	87553
Pie Town	87827
Pilar	87571
Pine	87552
Pinedale	87301
Pinehill	87357
Pine View	87579
Pineywoods Estates	88317
Pinon	88344
Pinos Altos	88053
Pinoswells	87009
Pintada	88435
Placita	87579
Placitas (Dona Ana County)	87937
Placitas (Rio Arriba County)	87515
Placitas (Sandoval County)	87043
Placitas (Sierra County)	87939
Playas	88009
Plaza Blanca	87563
Pleasant Hill	88135
Pleasanton	88039
Pojoaque Indian Reservation	87501
Pojoaque Valley	87501
Polvadera	87828
Ponderosa	87044
Ponderosa Heights (Part of Ruidoso)	88345
Ponderosa Pines	87059
Portales	88130
Pot Creek	87571
Potrero	87522
Prairie Dog Trading Post	87013
Prairieview	88260
Prewitt	87045
Progresso	87063
Pueblito	87566
Pueblitos	87002
Pueblo of Acoma	87034
Pueblo Pintado	87013
Puerto de Luna	88432
Punta de Agua	87036
Quarris Acres	88317
Quarteles	87532

	ZIP		ZIP		ZIP		ZIP
Quay	88433	Sandia Knolls	87047	Sile	87041	Twin Forks Estates	88317
Queen	88220	Sandia Park	87047	Silver Acres	87061	Twin Lakes	87301
Quemado	87829	Sandia Pueblo	87004	Silver City	88061*	Two Gray Hills	87325
Questa	87556	San Felipe Indian			88062†	Two Wells	87326
Radium Springs	88054	Reservation	87004	Sipapu	87579	Tyrone	88065
Rainsville	87736	San Felipe Pueblo	87001	Sixteen Springs	88317	University (Bernalillo	
Ramah	87321	San Fidel	87049	Skyline-Ganipa	87034	County)	87106
Ramah Navajo Indian		San Francisco	87006	Smith Lake	87365	University (Roosevelt	
Reservation	87327	San Francisco Plaza	87830	Socorro	87801	County)	88130
Ramon	88136	San Geronimo	87701	Sofia	88424	University Park	88003
Ranchito	87571	San Ignacio	87745	Soham	87565	Upper Anton Chico	87711
Ranchitos	87532	San Ildefonso Indian		Solano	87746	Upper Dilia	87724
Rancho Grande Estates	87830	Reservation	87502	Sombrillo	87532	Upper Pueblo	87560
Ranchos de Taos	87557	San Ildefonso Pueblo	87501	South Carmen	87725	Upper Rociada	87742
Ranchos Lake Conchas	88416	San Jon	88434	Southern New Mexico		Uptown (Part of	
Ranchvale	88101	San Jose (Bernalillo		Correctional Facility	88004	Albuquerque)	87110
Raton	87740	County)	87102	South San Ysidro	87565	Ute Mountain Indian	
Red Hill	87829	San Jose (Rio Arriba		South Springs Acres	88201	Reservation	81334
Red River	87558	County)	87537	South Valley	87102	Ute Park	87749
Redrock (Grant County)	88055	San Jose (San Miguel		Spencerville	87410	Vadito	87579
Red Rock (McKinley		County)	87565	Springer	87747	Vado	88072
County)	87420	San Juan (Grant County)	88041	Springstead	87311	Valdez	87580
Regina	87046	San Juan (Rio Arriba		Squirrel Springs	87325	Valencia	87031
Rehoboth	87322	County)	87566	Standing Rock	87313	Vallecitos	87581
Rencona	87562	San Juan (San Miguel		Stanley	87056	Vallecitos de los Indios	87025
Reserve	87830	County)	87565	Star Lake	87013	Valle Escondido	87571
Ribera	87560	San Juan Indian		Stead	88438	Valmora	87750
Rincon	87940	Reservation	87566	Sumner Lake State Park	88119	Val Verde	87718
Rinconada	87531	San Juan Pueblo	87566	Sunland Park	88063	Vanadium	88023
Rincon Montoso	87745	San Lorenzo	88041	Sunshine	88030	Vanderwagen	87326
Rio Chiquito	87522	San Mateo	87020	Sunspot	88349	Vaughn	88353
Rio Communities	87002	San Miguel (Dona Ana		Sun Valley	88312	Veguita	87062
Rio Grande Estates	87002	County)	88058	Taiban	88134	Velarde	87582
Rio Lucio	87553	San Miguel (Rio Arriba		Tajique	87057	Ventero	87512
Rio Puerco	87064	County)	81120	Talpa	87557	Vermejo Park	87740
Rio Rancho	87124	San Miguel (San Miguel		Taos	87571	Villa Linda Mall (Part of	
Rio West Mall (Part of		County)	87560	Taos Indian Reservation	87571	Santa Fe)	87505
Gallup)	87301	Sanostee	87461	Taos Pueblo	87571	Villa Madonna	88312
Rito de las Sillas	87064	San Pablo	87701	Taos Ski Valley	87525	Villanueva	87583
Riverside (Eddy County)	88210	San Patricio	88348	Tatum	88267	Virden	85534
Riverside (Lincoln County)	88201	San Pedro	87532	Tecolote	87701	Volcano Cliffs (Part of	
Robin Hood Park	88317	San Rafael (Cibola		Tecolotito	87711	Albuquerque)	87120
Rociada	87742	County)	87051	Tererro	87573	Wagon Mound	87752
Rock Canyon	87935	San Rafael (San Miguel		Tesuque	87574	Walker (Part of Roswell)	88201
Rock Springs	87301	County)	88439	Tesuque Indian		Waterfall	88317
Rodarte	87553	San Sebastian	87501	Reservation	87574	Waterflow	87421
Rodeo	88056	Santa Ana Indian		Tesuque Pueblo	87501	Watrous	87753
Rodey	87937	Reservation	87004	Texico	88135	Weed	88354
Rogers	88132	Santa Ana Pueblo	87004	Thoreau	87323	Western New Mexico	
Romeroville	87701	Santa Clara Indian		Three Rivers	88352	Correctional Facility	87020
Rosebud	88410	Reservation	87532	Tierra Amarilla	87575	Westgate Heights (Part of	
Roswell	88201*	Santa Clara Pueblo	87532	Tierra Monte	87742	Albuquerque)	87105
	88202†	Santa Cruz	87567	Tijeras	87059	West Las Vegas (Part of	
Roswell Mall (Part of		Santa Fe	87501-06	Timberon	88350	Las Vegas)	87701
Roswell)	88201	For specific Santa Fe Zip		Tinian	87401	White Horse	87013
Rowe	87562	Codes call (505) 988-6351, or		Tinnie	88351	White Lakes	87056
Roy	87743	your local postmaster.		Tiptonville	87753	White Oaks	88301
Ruidoso	88345	Santa Rosa	88435	Toadlena	87324	White Rock (Los Alamos	
Ruidoso Downs	88346	Santa Teresa	88008	Tocito	87461	County)	87544
Rutheron	87563	Santo Domingo Indian		Tohatchi	87325	White Rock (San Juan	
Sabinal	87006	Reservation	87052	Tohlakai	87301	County)	87313
Sabinoso	87746	Santo Domingo Pueblo	87052	Tolar	88134	White Sands	88002
Sacramento	88347	Santo Nino	87567	Tome	87060	White Sands Missile	
St. Vrain	88133	Santo Tomas	88044	Tome-Adelino	87060	Range	88002
Salem	87941	San Ysidro	87053	T-O Ranch	87740	Whites City	88268
San Acacia	87831	Sapello	87745	Torreon (Sandoval		White Signal	88061
San Antonio (Bernalillo		Seama	87014	County)	87013	Willard	87063
County)	87008	Seboyeta	87055	Torreon (Torrance County)	87061	Williams Acres	87301
San Antonio (San Miguel		Sedan	88436	Tortugas	88047	Williamsburg	87942
County)	87701	Sedillo Hill	87059	Totavi	87544	Willow Creek	88039
San Antonio (Socorro		Sena	87568	Trampas	87576	Winrock Center (Part of	
County)	87832	Seneca	88437	Trechado	87315	Albuquerque)	87110
San Antonio de Padua del		Separ	88045	Trementina	88439	Winston	87943
Rancho	87501	Serafina	87569	Tres Piedras	87577	Wyoming Mall, The (Part	
San Antonito (Bernalillo		Servilleta Plaza	87539	Tres Ritos	87579	of Albuquerque)	87112
County)	87047	Seton Village	87501	Truchas	87578	Yah-Ta-Hey	87375
San Antonito (Socorro		Seven Lakes	87313	Trujillo	87701	Yeso	88136
County)	87832	Seven Rivers	88254	Truth or Consequences	87901	Youngsville	87064
Sanchez	87746	Seven Springs	87025	Tse Bonito	86515	Zamora	87059
San Cristobal	87564	Shady Brook	87571	Tucumcari	88401	Zia Indian Reservation	87053
Sandia	87047	Sheep Springs	87364	Tularosa	88352	Zia Pueblo	87053
Sandia Base	87115	Shiprock	87420	Turley	87412	Zuni	87327
Sandia Heights	87004	Sierra Vista	88312	Turn	87002	Zuni Indian Reservation	87327
Sandia Indian Reservation	87004	Sierra Vista Estates	87008				

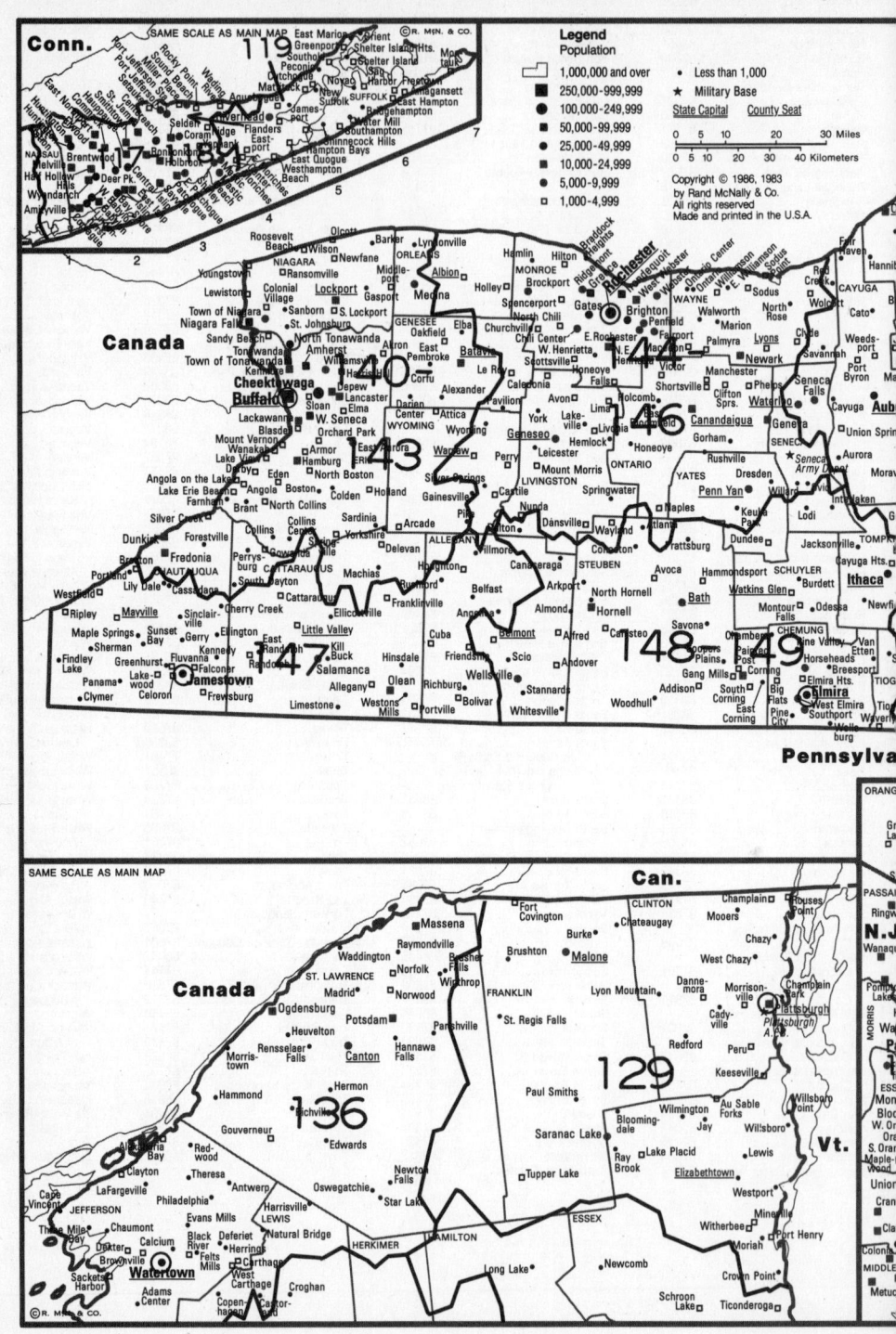

	ZIP		ZIP		ZIP		ZIP
Abbotts	14727	Amblerville	13843	Athens	12015	Barneveld	13304
Academy (Albany County)	12208	Amboy (Onondaga County)	13031	Athens (Town)	12015	Barnum Island	11558
Academy (Ontario County)	14424	Amboy (Oswego County) (Town)	13493	Athol	12810	Barre (Town)	14411
Accord	12404	Amboy Center	13493	Athol Springs	14010	Barre Center	14411
Acidalia	12760	Amchir (Part of Middletown)	10940	Atlanta	14808	Barrington (Town)	14837
Acra	12405	Amenia	12501	Atlantic (Part of New York)	10307	Barrytown	12507
Adams	13605	Amenia (Town)	12501	Atlantic Beach	11509	Barryville	12719
Adams (Town)	13605	Amenia Union	12501	Atlantique	11706	Bartlett	13440
Adams Basin	14410	Ames	13317	Attica	14011	Bartlett Corners	14468
Adams Center	13606	Amherst	14226	Attica (Town)	14011	Bartlett Hollow	13775
Adams Corners	10579	Amherst (Town)	14226	Attica Center	14011	Barton	13734
Adams Cove	13634	Amity (Allegany County) (Town)	14813	Attica Correctional Facility	14011	Barton (Town)	13734
Adamsville	12827	Amity (Orange County)	10990	Attlebury	12581	Basket	12760
Addison	14801	Amity Harbor	11701	Atwater	13081	Basom	14013
Addison (Town)	14801	Amityville	11701	Atwell	13338	Batavia	14020*
Addison Hill	16920	Amsdell Heights	14075	Atwood	12484		14021†
Adelphi (Part of New York)	11238	Amsterdam	12010	Auburn	13021*	Batchellerville	12134
Adirondack	12808	Amsterdam (Town)	12010		13022†	Bates	12469
Adrian	14823	Ancram	12502	Audubon (Part of New York)	10032	Bath	14810
Afton	13730	Ancram (Town)	12502	Augusta	13425	Bath (Town)	14810
Afton (Town)	13730	Ancramdale	12503	Augusta (Town)	13425	Bath Beach (Part of New York)	11214
Afton Lake	13730	Andes	13731	Aurelius (Town)	13034	Battenville	12834
Airmont	10901	Andes (Town)	13731	Auriesville	12016	Battery Park City (Part of New York)	10007
Airmont Heights (Part of Airmont)	10901	Andover	14806	Aurora (Cayuga County)	13026	Baxter Estates	11050
Akins Corners	12563	Andover (Town)	14806	Aurora (Erie County) (Town)	14052	Bay (Part of New York)	11235
Akron	14001	Andrea Park Estates	10598	Aurora Tract	13088	Bayberry	13088
Alabama	14003	Angelica	14709	Au Sable (Town)	12944	Bayberry Dunes	11772
Alabama (Town)	14003	Angelica (Town)	14709	Au Sable Chasm	12944	Bayberry Park (Part of New Rochelle)	10804
Albany	12201-60	Angola	14006	Au Sable Forks	12912	Bayberry Shopping Center	13088
For specific Albany Zip Codes call (518) 452-2499, or your local postmaster.		Angola on the Lake	14006	Austerlitz	12017	Baychester (Part of New York)	10469
Albany Medical Center (Part of Albany)	12208	Annandale-on-Hudson	12504	Austerlitz (Town)	12017	Bay Park	11518
Albertson	11507	Annsville (Oneida County) (Town)	13471	Ava	13303	Bay Point	11963
Albia (Part of Troy)	12180	Annsville (Westchester County)	10566	Ava (Town)	13303	Bayport	11705
Albion	14411	Ansonia (Part of New York)	10023	Averill Park	12018	Bay Ridge (Part of New York)	11220
Albion (Orleans County) (Town)	14411	Antwerp	13608	Avoca	14809	Bay Shore	11706
Albion (Oswego County) (Town)	13302	Antwerp (Town)	13608	Avoca (Town)	14809	Bay Shores	13110
Albion Correctional Facility	14411	Apalachin	13732	Avon	14414	Bayside (Part of New York)	11360
Alcove	12007	Apex	13783	Avon (Town)	14414	Bay Terrace (Queens County)	11360
Alden	14004	Appleton	14008	Axeville	14726	Bay Terrace (Richmond County)	10306
Alden (Town)	14004	Apulia	13159	Babcock Hill	13318	Bay View (Erie County)	14075
Alden Bend	12910	Apulia Station	13020	Babcock Lake	12138	Bayview (Suffolk County)	11971
Alden Center	14004	Aquebogue	11931	Babylon	11702	Bayville	11709
Alden Manor	11003	Aqueduct	12308	Babylon (Town)	11702	Baywood	11706
Alder Creek	13301	Aquetuck	12143	Bacon Hill	12871	Beach Hampton	11930
Alexander	14005	Arcade	14009	Baggs Corner	13601	Beach Ridge	14120
Alexander (Town)	14005	Arcade (Town)	14009	Bainbridge	13733	Beach Shopping Center (Part of Peekskill)	10566
Alexander Corners	13650	Arcade Junction (Part of Arcade)	14009	Bainbridge (Town)	13733	Beachville	14807
Alexander Shopping Center (Part of Yonkers)	10710	Arcadia (Town)	14513	Baiting Hollow	11933	Beacon	12508
Alexandria (Town)	13607	Archdale	12834	Bakers Mills	12811	Beacon Hill	12508
Alexandria Bay	13607	Archville	10510	Bakerstand	14101	Beantown	14859
Alfred	14802	Arden	10910	Balcom	14138	Bear Mountain	10911
Alfred (Town)	14802	Ardonia	12515	Balcom Beach	14777	Bearsville	12409
Alfred Station	14803	Ardsley	10502	Bald Mountain	12834	Beaver Brook	12764
Allaben	12480	Ardsley-on-Hudson (Part of Irvington)	10503	Baldwin (Chemung County) (Town)	14861	Beaverdam Lake-Salisbury Mills	12553
Allard Corners	12586	Argusville	13459	Baldwin (Nassau County)	11510	Beaver Dams	14812
Allegany	14706	Argyle	12809	Baldwin Harbor	11510	Beaver Falls	13305
Allegany (Town)	14706	Argyle (Town)	12809	Baldwin Heights (Part of Olean)	14760	Beaverkill	12758
Allegany Indian Reservation (Town)	14081	Arietta (Town)	12139	Baldwin Place	10505	Beaver Meadow	13832
Allegany Indian Reservation	14081	Arkport	14807	Baldwin Place Shopping Center	10505	Beaver River	13367
Allen (Town)	14709	Arkville	12406	Baldwinsville	13027	Beckers Corners	12158
Allen Center	14735	Arkwright (Town)	14718	Ballina	13035	Becks Grove (Part of Rome)	13308
Allens Hill	14469	Arlington	12603	Ballston (Town)	12019	Bedell	12430
Allentown	14707	Arlyn Oaks	11758	Ballston Center	12020	Bedford (Chemung County) (Town)	10506
Allenwood	11021	Armonk	10504	Ballston Lake	12019	Bedford (Kings County)	11210
Allerton (Part of New York)	10467	Armor	14075	Ballston Spa	12020	Bedford (Westchester County)	10506
Alligerville	12440	Arnolds Mill	12037	Balltown	14062	Bedford Hills	10507
Alloway	14489	Arrochar (Part of New York)	10305	Balmat	13609	Bedford Hills Correctional Facility	10507
Alma	14708	Arthur Manor (Part of Scarsdale)	10583	Balmville	12550	Bedford-Stuyvesant (Part of New York)	11233
Alma (Town)	14708	Arthursburg	12533	Baltimore	13141	Beecher Corners	12442
Almond	14804	Arverne (Part of New York)	11692	Bangall (Dutchess County)	12506	Beechertown	13697
Almond (Town)	14804	Asharoken	11768	Bangall (Onondaga County)	13112	Beech Hill (Part of Yonkers)	10710
Aloquin	14561	Ashford	14731	Bangor	12966	Beechhurst (Part of New York)	11357
Alpine	14805	Ashford (Town)	14171	Bangor (Town)	12966	Beechmont (Part of New Rochelle)	10804
Alplaus	12008	Ashford Hollow	14171	Bangor Station	12966	Beechmont Woods (Part of New Rochelle)	10804
Alps	12018	Ashland (Chemung County) (Town)	14894	Bank Plaza	11566	Beechwood (Part of Rochester)	14609
Alsen	12415	Ashland (Greene County)	12407	Barberville	12018	Beehive Crossing	12090
Altamont (Albany County)	12009	Ashland (Greene County) (Town)	12407	Barcelona	14787	Beekman	12533
Altamont (Franklin County) (Town)	12986	Ashokan	12481	Barclay Heights (Part of Saugerties)	12477	Beekman (Town)	12570
Altay	14837	Ashville	14710	Bardonia	10954	Beekman Corners	13459
Altmar	13302	Ashville Bay	14710	Bare Hill Correctional Facility	12953	Beekmantown	12901
Alton	14413	Ashwood	14098	Barker (Broome County) (Town)	13746		
Altona	12910	Aspenwood	12065	Barker (Niagara County)	14012		
Altona (Town)	12910	Aspinwall Corners	13650	Barkers Grove	12154		
Amagansett	11930	Assembly Point	12845	Barkersville	12850		
Amawalk	10501	Association Island	13651	Barkertown	14836		
Amber	13110	Astoria (Part of New York)	11102	Barnegat	12603		
				Barnerville	12092		
				Barnes Corners	13626		
				Barnes Hole	11930		

	ZIP
Beekmantown (Town)	12901
Beixedon Estates	11971
Belair Road (Part of New York)	10305
Belcher	12865
Belcoda	14546
Belden	13787
Belfast	14711
Belfast (Town)	14711
Belfort	13327
Belgium	13027
Belle Isle	13209
Bellerose (Nassau County)	11426
Bellerose (Queens County)	11426
Bellerose Terrace	11426
Belle Terre	11777
Belleview	14712
Belleville	13611
Bellevue (Erie County)	14225
Bellevue (Schenectady County)	12306
Bellevue Gardens	12151
Bellmont (Town)	12917
Bellmont Center	12920
Bellmore	11710
Bellona (rural)	14527
Bellona	14415
Bellow Corners	14171
Bellport	11713
Bellvale	10912
Bellville	14717
Belmont	14813
Belvidere	14813
Bemis Heights	12170
Bemus Point	14712
Benedict Beach	14464
Bennett Bridge	13302
Bennettsburg	14818
Bennettsville	13733
Bennington	14011
Bennington (Town)	14011
Benson	12134
Benson (Town)	12134
Benson Mines	13690
Benton (Town)	14527
Benton Center	14527
Berea	12549
Bergen	14416
Bergen (Town)	14416
Bergen Beach	14847
Bergen Park	11746
Bergholtz	14304
Berkshire (Town)	13736
Berkshire (Fulton County)	12078
Berkshire (Onondaga County)	13066
Berkshire (Tioga County)	13736
Berkshire Terrace	10512
Berlin	12022
Berlin (Town)	12022
Berne	12023
Berne (Town)	12023
Bernhards Bay	13028
Berryville	12068
Berwyn	13084
Best	12018
Bethany	14054
Bethany (Town)	14054
Bethel (Dutchess County)	12567
Bethel (Sullivan County)	12720
Bethel (Sullivan County) (Town)	12720
Bethel Corners	13111
Bethel Grove	14850
Bethford	14219
Bethlehem (Town)	12054
Bethlehem Center	12077
Bethlehem Heights	12161
Bethpage	11714
Beukendaal	12302
Beverly Inn Corners	13315
Bible School Park (Part of Johnson City)	13737
Bidwell (Part of Buffalo)	14222
Big Brook	13486
Big Flats	14814
Big Flats (Town)	14814
Big Flats Airport	14814
Big Fresh Pond	11968
Big H Shopping Center	11743
Big Indian	12410
Big Island	10924
Big Moose	13331
Big Tree	14219
Big Wolf Lake	12986
Billings	12510
Billington Bay	13030
Billington Heights	14052
Biltmore Shores	11758

	ZIP
Bingham Mills	12526
Binghamton	13901-05
For specific Binghamton Zip Codes call (607) 773-2142, or your local postmaster.	
Binghamton (Town)	13902
Binghamton Plaza (Part of Binghamton)	13901
Bingley	13035
Binnewater	12401
Birchwood Estates	12184
Birdsall	14709
Birdsall (Town)	14709
Bishopville	14807
Black Brook	12912
Black Brook (Town)	12912
Black Creek	14714
Blackmans Corners	12959
Black River	13612
Black Rock (Part of Buffalo)	14207
Blackwatch Hills	14450
Blakeley	14052
Blasdell	14219
Blauvelt	10913
Bleecker	12078
Bleecker (Town)	12078
Blenheim (Town)	12131
Bliss	14024
Blockville	14710
Blodgett Mills	13738
Bloomfield (Ontario County)	14443
Bloomfield (Richmond County)	10314
Bloomingburg	12721
Bloomingdale	12913
Blooming Grove	10914
Blooming Grove (Town)	10914
Bloomington	12411
Bloomville	13739
Blossvale	13308
Blue Mountain	12477
Blue Mountain Lake	12812
Blue Point	11715
Blue Ridge	12534
Blue Stores	12526
Bluff Point	14478
Blythebourne (Part of New York)	11219
Boardmanville (Part of Olean)	14760
Boerum Hill (Part of New York)	11201
Boght Corners	12047
Bohemia	11716
Boiceville	12412
Bolivar	14715
Bolivar (Town)	14715
Bolton	12824
Bolton (Town)	12824
Bolton Landing	12814
Bolts Corners	13147
Bombay	12914
Bombay (Town)	12914
Bon Air Heights (Part of Suffern)	10901
Bonney	13464
Bonni Castle	14590
Bonnie Crest (Part of New Rochelle)	10804
Bonny Lee Estates	12184
Boonville	13309
Boonville (Town)	13309
Borden	14801
Border City (Ontario County)	14456
Border City (Seneca County)	14456
Borodino	13152
Borough Hall (Part of New York)	11424
Boston	14025
Boston (Town)	14025
Boston Corners	12546
Botanical (Part of New York)	10458
Bouckville	13310
Boughton Hill	14564
Boulevard (Part of New York)	10459
Boulevard Mall	14226
Boultons Beach (Part of Sackets Harbor)	13685
Bouquet	12936
Bournes Beach	14787
Bovina (Town)	13740
Bovina Center	13740
Bowen	14772
Bowens Corners	13069

	ZIP
Bowerstown	13326
Bowling Green (Part of New York)	10004
Bowmansville	14026
Boylston (Town)	13083
Boyntonville	12090
Boysen Bay	13039
Braddock Heights	14612
Bradford	14815
Bradford (Town)	14815
Bradley	12754
Braeside	12123
Brainard	12024
Brainards Corners	13315
Brainardsville	12915
Braman Corners	12053
Bramans Corners	12186
Bramanville	12092
Brambler Ridge	14450
Branchport	14418
Brandon (Town)	12966
Brandon Center	12966
Brandreth	12847
Brant	14027
Brant (Town)	14027
Brantingham	13312
Brant Lake	12815
Brasher (Town)	13613
Brasher Center	13613
Brasher Falls	13613
Brasher Falls-Winthrop	13613
Brasie Corners	13642
Breakabeen	12122
Breesport	14816
Breezy Point (Part of New York)	11697
Brentwood	11717
Brevoort (Part of New York)	11216
Brewerton	13029
Brewster	10509
Brewster Heights	10509
Brewster Hill	10509
Briarcliff Manor	10510
Briar Park	11793
Bridge (Part of Niagara Falls)	14305
Bridgehampton	11932
Bridgeport	13030
Bridgeville	12701
Bridgewater	13313
Bridgewater (Town)	13313
Brier Hill	13614
Brighton (Franklin County) (Town)	12970
Brighton (Kings County)	11235
Brighton (Monroe County) (Town)	14610
Brighton (Monroe County)	14610
Brighton (Otsego County)	13439
Brighton Beach (Part of New York)	11235
Brightside	13436
Brightwaters	11718
Brinckerhoff	12524
Brisben	13830
Briscoe	12783
Bristol	14469
Bristol (Town)	14469
Bristol Center	14424
Bristol Springs	14512
Broadacres	13905
Broadalbin	12025
Broadalbin (Town)	12025
Broad Channel (Part of New York)	11693
Broadway (Part of New York)	11106
Broadway Mall	11801
Brockport	14420
Brockville	14411
Brocton	14716
Brodhead	12494

	ZIP
Bronx	10401-75

For specific Bronx Zip Codes call (718) 960-5020, or your local postmaster.

COLLEGES & UNIVERSITIES

	ZIP
City University of New York-Lehman College	10468
Fordham University	10458
Manhattan College	10471
State University of New York Maritime College	10465

FINANCIAL INSTITUTIONS

	ZIP
North Side Savings Bank	10463
City and Suburban Federal Savings Bank	10467

HOSPITALS

	ZIP
Bronx Municipal Hospital Center	10461
Bronx-Lebanon Hospital Center	10457
Bronx Psychiatric Center	10461
Lincoln Medical and Mental Health Center	10451
Montefiore Medical Center	10467
North Central Bronx Hospital	10467
Our Lady of Mercy Medical Center	10466
St. Barnabas Hospital	10457
Veterans Affairs Medical Center	10468

	ZIP
Bronxville	10708
Bronxville Heights (Part of Yonkers)	10708
Brookdale	13668
Brookfield	13314
Brookfield (Town)	13314
Brookhaven	11719
Brookhaven (Town)	11719

	ZIP
Brooklyn	11201-56
	13775

For specific Brooklyn Zip Codes call (212) 967-8585, or your local postmaster.

COLLEGES & UNIVERSITIES

	ZIP
Brooklyn Law School	11201
City University of New York-Brooklyn College	11210
City University of New York-Medgar Evers College	11225
City University of New York-New York City Technical College	11201
Long Island University-Brooklyn Campus	11201
Polytechnic University	11201
Pratt Institute	11205
St. Francis College	11201
State University of New York Health Science Center at Brooklyn	11203

FINANCIAL INSTITUTIONS

	ZIP
Bay Ridge Federal Savings Bank	11209
Brooklyn Federal Savings Bank	11201
Crossland Federal Savings Bank	11201
Dime Savings Bank of Williamsburgh	11211
East New York Savings Bank	11207
Flatbush Federal Savings & Loan Association	11210
Green Point Savings Bank	11222
Hamilton Federal Savings, F.A.	11209
Home Savings Bank of America, F.S.B.	11237
Independence Savings Bank	11201

HOSPITALS

	ZIP
Brookdale Hospital Medical Center	11212
Brooklyn Hospital Center	11201
Catholic Medical Center of Brooklyn and Queens	11213
Coney Island Hospital	11235
Interfaith Medical Center	11238
Kingsbrook Jewish Medical Center	11203
Kings County Hospital Center	11203
Long Island College Hospital	11201
Lutheran Medical Center	11220
Maimonides Medical Center	11219
Methodist Hospital	11215
University Hospital of Brooklyn-State University of New York Health Sciences Center at Brooklyn	11203

*** Area Zip Code** **† Post Office Boxes**

	ZIP
Veterans Affairs Medical Center	11209
Victory Memorial Hospital	11228
Woodhull Medical and Mental Health Center	11206
Wyckoff Heights Medical Center	11237

MILITARY INSTALLATIONS

	ZIP
Coast Guard Supply Center, Brooklyn	11232
Fort Hamilton and New York Area Command	11252
Supervisor of Shipbuilding, Conversion and Repair, Brooklyn	11251

	ZIP
Brooks Avenue Station (Part of Rochester)	14624
Brooksburg	12496
Brooks Grove	14510
Brooktondale	14817
Brookview	12026
Brookville	11545
Brookville Park	11751
Broome (Town)	12122
Broome Center	12076
Broughton Park	13760
Browns Bridge	3625
Browns Hollow	13317
Brownsville (Kings County)	11212
Brownsville (Ontario County)	14564
Brownville	13615
Brownville (Town)	13615
Bruceville	12440
Brunswick (Town)	12180
Brushton	12916
Brutus (Town)	13166
Bruynswick	12589
Bryant (Part of New York)	10036
Bryn Mawr Park (Part of Yonkers)	10701
Buchanan	10511
Buckingham Estates	10989
Buckleyville	12037
Bucks Bridge	3660
Buckton	13697
Buel	13317
Buellville	13104
Buena Vista	14823
Buffalo	14201-16
	14220
	14222-23
	14240
	14263-73

For specific Buffalo Zip Codes call (716) 846-2538, or your local postmaster.

	ZIP
Buffalo Creek (Part of Buffalo)	14224
Buffalo Junction (Part of Buffalo)	14201
Buffalo Lake (Part of Buffalo)	14222
Bull Hill	13324
Bulls Head (Monroe County)	14611
Bulls Head (Richmond County)	10314
Bullville	10915
Bundys	13126
Burden Lake	12018
Burdett	14818
Burgoyne	12871
Burke	12917
Burke (Town)	12917
Burke Center	12917
Burlingham	12722
Burlington	13315
Burlington (Town)	13315
Burlington Flats	13315
Burnhams (Part of Cassadaga)	14718
Burns	14807
Burns (Town)	14807
Burnside	12543
Burns-Whitney Estates	12110
Burnt Hills	12027
Burnwood	13756
Burrs Mills	13601
Burt	14028
Burtonsville	12066
Bushes Landing	13367
Bushnell Basin	14534
Bushnellsville	12480
Bush Terminal (Part of New York)	11232

	ZIP
Bushville (Genesee County)	14020
Bushville (Sullivan County)	12701
Bushwick (Part of New York)	11221
Buskirk	12028
Busti	14701
Busti (Town)	14701
Butler (Town)	14590
Butler Center	14590
Butlerville	10519
Butterfield (Part of Utica)	13503
Butternut Grove	12776
Butternuts (Town)	13776
Byersville	14517
Byrden	12526
Byron	14422
Byron (Town)	14422
Cabinhill	13752
Cadiz	14737
Cadosia	13783
Cadyville	12918
Cahoonzie	12780
Cairo	12413
Cairo (Town)	12413
Calcium	13616
Calcutta	12064
Caldor Shopping Center (Part of Port Chester)	10573
Caledonia	14423
Caledonia (Town)	14423
Calico Colony	12065
Callicoon	12723
Callicoon (Town)	12791
Callicoon Center	12724
Calverton	11933
Cambria (Town)	14094
Cambria Heights (Part of New York)	11411
Cambridge	12816
Cambridge (Town)	12816
Camden	13316
Camden (Town)	13316
Cameron	14819
Cameron (Town)	14819
Cameron Mills	14820
Camillus	13031
Camillus (Town)	13031
Camillus Plaza	13031
Campbell	14821
Campbell (Town)	14821
Campbell Hall	10916
Camp Hemlock	12721
Camp Hill (Part of Pomona)	10970
Camps Mills	13601
Campville	13760
Camroden	13440
Canaan	12029
Canaan (Town)	12029
Canaan Center	12029
Canada Lake	12032
Canadice	14560
Canadice (Town)	14560
Canajoharie	13317
Canajoharie (Town)	13317
Canal Street (Part of New York)	10013
Canandaigua	14424-25

For specific Canandaigua Zip Codes call (716) 394-1500, or your local postmaster.

	ZIP
Canarsie (Part of New York)	11236
Canaseraga	14822
Canastota	13032
Canawaugus	14423
Candor	13743
Candor (Town)	13743
Caneadea	14717
Caneadea (Town)	14717
Canisteo	14823
Canisteo (Town)	14823
Cannon Corners	12959
Canoe Place	11946
Canoga	13148
Canterbury Hill (Part of Rome)	13440
Canterbury Woods	13116
Canton	13617
Canton (Town)	13617
Cape Vincent	13618
Cape Vincent (Town)	13618
Capitol (Part of Albany)	12224
Capitol Annex (Part of Albany)	12225
Capitol Hills	10950
Cardiff	13084
Carle Place	11514
Carle Terrace	12449

	ZIP
Carlisle	12031
Carlisle (Town)	12031
Carlisle Center	12035
Carlisle Gardens	14094
Carlton	14411
Carlton (Town)	14411
Carman	12303
Carmel	10512
Carmel (Town)	10512
Carmel Park Estates	10512
Carnegie	14075
Caroga (Town)	12032
Caroga Lake	12032
Caroline	14817
Caroline (Town)	14817
Caroline Center	14817
Carousel Center (Part of Syracuse)	13290
Carroll (Town)	14738
Carroll Gardens (Part of New York)	11231
Carrollton	14748
Carrollton (Town)	14753
Carson	14823
Carthage	13619
Cascade	13118
Case	13084
Casowasco	13118
Cassadaga	14718
Cassville	13318
Castile	14427
Castile (Town)	14427
Castile Center	14427
Castle (Part of New Rochelle)	10801
Castle Creek	13744
Castle Hill (Part of New York)	10462
Castle Point	12511
Castleton Corners (Part of New York)	10314
Castleton on Hudson	12033
Castorland	13620
Catatonk	13827
Catharine	14869
Catharine (Town)	14869
Cathedral (Part of New York)	10025
Catlin (Town)	14812
Cato	13033
Cato (Town)	13033
Caton	14830
Caton (Town)	14830
Catskill	12414
Catskill (Town)	12414
Cattaraugus	14719
Cattaraugus Indian Reservation	14081
Cattaraugus Indian Reservation (Town)	14081
Cattown	13337
Caughdenoy	13036
Cayuga	13034
Cayuga Correctional Facility	13118
Cayuga Heights	14850
Cayuta	14824
Cayuta (Town)	14824
Cayutaville	14805
Caywood	14860
Cazenovia	13035
Cazenovia (Town)	13035
Cecil Park (Part of Yonkers)	10707
Cedar Cliff	12542
Cedarcrest	14487
Cedar Flats	10980
Cedar Hill	12158
Cedarhurst	11516
Cedar Knolls (Part of Yonkers)	10708
Cedarvale	13215
Cedarville	13357
Celoron	14720
Cementon	12415
Centenary	10956
Center Avenue (Part of East Rockaway)	11518
Center Brunswick	12180
Centereach	11720
Center Falls	12834
Centerfield	14424
Center Lisle	13797
Center Moriches	11934
Centerport (Cayuga County)	13166
Centerport (Suffolk County)	11721
Centerville (Allegany County)	14029

	ZIP
Centerville (Allegany County) (Town)	14029
Centerville (Delaware County)	13756
Center White Creek	12057
Central (Part of New York)	11435
Central Bridge	12035
Centralia	14782
Central Islip	11722
Central Nyack	10960
Central Parcel Post (Part of New York)	10011
Central Park	14214-15

For specific Central Park Zip Codes call (716) 834-3215, or your local postmaster.

	ZIP
Central Park Shopping Center (Part of Buffalo)	14214
Central Square	13036
Central Valley	10917
Centre Island	11771
Centre Village	13787
Centuck (Part of Yonkers)	10710
Ceres	14721
Chadwicks	13319
Chaffee	14030
Chamberlain Corners	13660
Chambers	14812
Champion	13619
Champion (Town)	13619
Champion Huddle	13619
Champlain	12919
Champlain (Town)	12919
Champlain Park	12901
Chapel Hill Estates	10598
Chapin	14424
Chappaqua	10514
Charleston (Montgomery County) (Town)	12066
Charleston (Richmond County)	10301
Charleston Four Corners	12166
Charlotte (Chautauqua County) (Town)	14782
Charlotte (Monroe County)	14612
Charlotte Center	14782
Charlotteville	12036
Charlton	12019
Charlton (Town)	12019
Charwood Manor	12065
Chase Lake	13343
Chase Mills	13621
Chaseville	12116
Chasm Falls	12953
Chateaugay	12920
Chateaugay (Town)	12920
Chatham	12037
Chatham (Town)	12037
Chatham Center	12184
Chaumont	13622
Chauncey (Part of Dobbs Ferry)	10502
Chautauqua	14722
Chautauqua (Town)	14722
Chautauqua Mall (Part of Lakewood)	14750
Chazy	12921
Chazy (Town)	12921
Chazy Lake	12935
Chazy Landing	12921
Chedwel	14712
Cheektowaga (Town)	14225
Cheektowaga	14225
Cheektowaga Northwest	14225
Cheektowaga Southwest	14227
Chelsea (Dutchess County)	12512
Chelsea (Richmond County)	10314
Chemung	14825
Chemung (Town)	14825
Chemung Center	14825
Chenango (Town)	13745
Chenango Bridge	13745
Chenango Forks	13746
Chenango Lake	13815
Cheneys Point	14710
Cheningo	13158
Cherokee (Part of New York)	10028
Cherry Creek	14723
Cherry Creek (Town)	14723
Cherry Grove	11782
Cherry Lane (Part of Fredonia)	14063
Cherry Plain	12040
Cherrytown	12446
Cherry Valley	13320
Cherry Valley (Town)	13320
Cherry Valley Junction	12043

* Area Zip Code   † Post Office Boxes

Name	ZIP
Cheshire	14424
Chester (Orange County)	10918
Chester (Orange County) (Town)	10918
Chester (Warren County) (Town)	12860
Chesterfield (Town)	12944
Chester Heights (Part of Yonkers)	10701
Chester Hill Park (Part of Mount Vernon)	10550
Chestertown	12817
Chestnut Hill	13088
Chestnut Ridge (Niagara County)	14094
Chestnut Ridge (Rockland County)	10952
Cheviot	12526
Chichester	12416
Childs	14411
Childwold	12922
Chili (Town)	14428
Chili Center	14624
Chilson	12883
Chinatown (Part of New York)	10013
Chipmonk	14706
Chippewa Bay	13623
Chittenango	13037
Chittenango Falls	13035
Choconut Center	13905
Church Street (Part of New York)	10007
Churchtown	12521
Churchville (Monroe County)	14428
Churchville (Oneida County)	13478
Churubusco	12923
Cicero	13039
Cicero (Town)	13039
Cicero Center	13041
Cincinnatus	13040
Cincinnatus (Town)	13040
Circleville	10919
City Island (Part of New York)	10464
Clairemont Farms	13088
Clare (Town)	13684
Claremont Park (Part of New York)	10457
Clarence	14031
Clarence (Town)	14031
Clarence Center	14032
Clarendon	14429
Clarendon (Town)	14429
Clark Heights	12569
Clark Mills	13321
Clarksburg	14057
Clarks Corners	14747
Clarks Mills	12834
Clarkson	14430
Clarkson (Town)	14430
Clarkstown (Town)	10956
Clarksville (Albany County)	12041
Clarksville (Allegany County) (Town)	14786
Claryville	12725
Clason Point (Part of New York)	10473
Classon (Part of New York)	11238
Claverack	12513
Claverack (Town)	12513
Claverack-Red Mills	12513
Clay	13041
Clay (Town)	13041
Clayburg	12981
Clayton	13624
Clayton (Town)	13624
Clayville	13322
Clear Creek	14726
Clearfield	14221
Clemons	12819
Clermont	12526
Clermont (Town)	12526
Cleveland	13042
Cleveland Hill	14225
Cleverdale	12820
Cliff Haven	12901
Clifford	13069
Cliffside	12116
Clifton (Monroe County)	14428
Clifton (Richmond County)	10304
Clifton (St. Lawrence County) (Town)	13666
Clifton Gardens	12065
Clifton Heights	14085
Clifton Knolls	12065
Clifton Park	12065
Clifton Park (Town)	12065
Clifton Park Center	12065
Clifton Springs	14432
Climax	12042
Clinton (Clinton County) (Town)	12923
Clinton (Dutchess County) (Town)	12514
Clinton (Oneida County)	13323
Clinton Corners	12514
Clintondale	12515
Clinton Heights	12144
Clinton Hollow	12578
Clinton Park	12144
Clintonville	12924
Clockville	13043
Clough Corners	13862
Clove	12043
Clover Bank	14075
Cloverville	12430
Clyde	14433
Clymer	14724
Clymer (Town)	14724
Cobb	11976
Cobble Hill (Part of New York)	11201
Cobleskill	12043
Cobleskill (Town)	12043
Cochecton	12726
Cochecton (Town)	12726
Cochecton Center	12727
Coeymans	12045
Coeymans (Town)	12045
Coeymans Hollow	12046
Coffins Mills	13670
Cohocton	14826
Cohocton (Town)	14826
Cohoes	12047
Cokertown	12571
Colchester	13856
Colchester (Town)	13755
Cold Brook (Herkimer County)	13324
Coldbrook (Schenectady County)	12303
Colden	14033
Colden (Town)	14033
Coldenham	12549
Coldspring (Cattaraugus County) (Town)	14783
Cold Spring (Putnam County)	10516
Cold Spring Harbor	11724
Cold Springs (Onondaga County)	13027
Cold Springs (Steuben County)	14810
Cold Spring Terrace	11743
Coldwater	14624
Colemans Mills	13492
Colesville (Town)	13787
Colgate (Part of Hamilton)	13346
Collabar	12549
Collamer	13057
College (Part of New York)	10030
College Park	12571
College Point (Part of New York)	11356
Colliersville	13747
Collingwood	13084
Collingwood Estates	14174
Collins	14034
Collins (Town)	14034
Collins Center	14035
Collins Correctional Facility	14079
Collins Landing	13607
Collinsville	13433
Colonial Acres	12077
Colonial Green	12188
Colonial Heights (Dutchess County)	12603
Colonial Heights (Westchester County)	10708
Colonial Park (Part of New York)	10039
Colonial Springs	11798
Colonial Village (Part of Niagara Falls)	14304
Colonie (Town)	12212
Colonie	12212
Colonie Center	12205
Colosse	13131
Colton	13625
Colton (Town)	13625
Columbia (Town)	13357
Columbia Center	13357
Columbia University (Part of New York)	10025
Columbia University Extension	10926
Columbiaville	12050
Columbus	13411
Columbus (Town)	13411
Columbus Circle (Part of New York)	10023
Colvin Elmwood (Part of Syracuse)	13207
Commack	11725
Commack Corners Shopping Center	11725
Comstock	12821
Comstock Tract	13027
Concord (Erie County) (Town)	14141
Concord (Richmond County)	10304
Conesus	14435
Conesus (Town)	14435
Conesville	12076
Conesville (Town)	12076
Conewango	14726
Conewango (Town)	14726
Conewango Valley	14726
Coney Island (Part of New York)	11224
Conger Corners	13480
Congers	10920
Conifer	12986
Conklin	13748
Conklin (Town)	13748
Conklin Forks	13903
Conklingville	12835
Connelly	12417
Connelly Park	14710
Conquest	13140
Conquest (Town)	13140
Constable	12926
Constable (Town)	12926
Constableville	13325
Constantia	13044
Constantia (Town)	13044
Constantia Center	13028
Continental Village	10566
Cook Corners	13625
Cooksburg	12469
Cooks Falls	12776
Cookville	14036
Coolidge Beach	14172
Coonrod (Part of Rome)	13440
Co-op City (Part of New York)	10475
Cooper (Part of New York)	10003
Coopers Plains	14827
Cooperstown	13326
Cooperstown Junction	12116
Coopersville (Clinton County)	12919
Coopersville (Livingston County)	14517
Copake	12516
Copake (Town)	12516
Copake Falls	12517
Copake Lake	12521
Copenhagen	13626
Copiague	11726
Coram	11727
Coram Hill	11763
Corbett	13755
Corbettsville	13749
Coreys	12986
Corfu	14036
Corinth	12822
Corinth (Town)	12822
Cornell (Part of New York)	10473
Corners (Part of Cayuga Heights)	14850
Corning	14830
Corning (Town)	14830
Corning Manor	14830
Cornwall	12518
Cornwall (Town)	12518
Cornwall on Hudson	12520
Cornwallville	12418
Corona-A (Part of New York)	11368
Corona-Elmhurst (Part of New York)	11373
Cortland	13045
Cortlandt (Town)	10520
Cortlandville (Town)	13045
Cortland West	13045
Cosmos Heights	13045
Cossayuna	12823
Coss Corners	14810
Cottage	14138
Cottage City	14424
Cottage Park	14750
Cottam Hill	12590
Cottekill	12419
Cottonwood Point	14435
Council Meadows	12027
Country Knolls	12151
Country Knolls (census designated place)	12019
Country Knolls South	12065
Country Life Press (Part of Garden City)	11530
Country Ridge Estates	10573
County Line	14098
Cove Neck	11771
Coventry	13778
Coventry (Town)	13778
Coventryville	13733
Covert	14847
Covert (Town)	14847
Coveytown Corners	12917
Covington	14525
Covington (Town)	14525
Cowlesville	14037
Coxsackie	12051
Coxsackie (Town)	12051
Coxsackie Correctional Facility	12192
Crafts	10512
Cragsmoor	12420
Craigville	10918
Crains Mills	13158
Cranberry Creek	12117
Cranberry Lake	12927
Crandall Corners	12154
Cranes Corners	13340
Cranesville	12010
Cranford (Part of New York)	10470
Crary Mills	13617
Craryville	12521
Craterclub	12936
Crawford (Town)	12566
Creek Locks	12411
Crescent	12188
Crescent Beach (Monroe County)	14612
Crescent Beach (Richmond County)	10301
Crescent Estates	12065
Crescent Estates North	12065
Crestview Heights	13760
Crestwood (Part of Yonkers)	10710
Crestwood (Part of Tuckahoe)	10707
Crestwood Gardens (Part of Yonkers)	10710
Crittenden	14038
Crocketts	13156
Crofts Corners	10579
Croghan	13327
Croghan (Town)	13327
Crompond	10517
Cropseyville	12052
Cross Country Shopping Center (Part of Yonkers)	10704
Crossgates Mall	12203
Cross River	10518
Cross Roads Estates	10598
Croton	14864
Crotona Park (Part of New York)	10460
Croton Falls	10519
Croton Heights	10598
Croton-on-Hudson	10520
Crotonville	10562
Crown Heights	12603
Crown Point	12928
Crown Point (Town)	12928
Crown Point Center	12928
Crown Village	11762
Crugers	10521
Crum Creek	13452
Crystal Brook	11766
Crystal Dale	13367
Crystal Lake (Albany County)	12147
Crystal Lake (Cattaraugus County)	14060
Cuba	14727
Cuba (Town)	14727
Cuddebackville	12729
Cullen	13439
Cumberland Head	12901
Cummingsville	14437
Curriers	14009
Curry	12765
Currytown	12166

Name	ZIP	Name	ZIP	Name	ZIP	Name	ZIP
Curtis	14821	Dexterville	13069	East Atlantic Beach	11509	East Pembroke	14056
Cutchogue	11935	Diamond Point	12824	East Aurora	14052	East Penfield	14450
Cutting	14724	Diana (Town)	13648	East Avon	14414	East Pharsalia	13758
Cuyler	13050	Dibbletown	13308	East Bay	14590	East Pitcairn	13648
Cuyler (Town)	13050	Dickersonville	14131	East Beekmantown	12901	East Pittstown	12028
Cuyler Hill	13050	Dickinson (Broome		East Bend Park	12603	East Poestenkill	12018
Cuylerville	14481	County) (Town)	13905	East Berkshire	13736	Eastport	11941
Cypress Hills (Part of New		Dickinson (Franklin		East Berne	12059	East Quogue	11942
York)	11208	County) (Town)	12930	East Bethany	14054	East Randolph	14730
Dadville	13367	Dickinson Center	12930	East Bloomfield (Town)	14443	East Ripley	14775
Dag Hammarskjold (Part		Dick Urban	14043	East Bloomfield (Part of		East River	13056
of New York)	10017	Dimmick Corners	12831	Bloomfield)	14443	East Rochester	14445
Dahlia	12758	Dineharts	14810	East Branch	13756	East Rochester (Town)	14445
Dairyland	12435	Divine Corners	12759	East Brentwood	11717	East Rockaway	11518
Dale	14039	Dix (Town)	14891	East Buffalo	14225	East Rodman	13601
Dalton	14836	Dix Hills	11746	East Buskirk	12028	East Salamanca (Part of	
Damascus	13865	Dobbs Ferry	10522	East Campbell	14870	Salamanca)	14779
Danby	14850	Dolgeville	13329	East Cayuga Heights	14850	East Schodack	12063
Danby (Town)	14850	Dongan Hills (Part of New		East Chatham	12060	East Schuyler	13340
Dannemora	12929	York)	10304	Eastchester (Town)	10709	East Seneca	14224
Dannemora (Town)	12929	Doraville	13813	East Chester (Orange		East Setauket	11733
Dansville (Livingston		Doris Park	13044	County)	10918	East Shelby	14103
County)	14437	Dorloo	12043	Eastchester (Westchester		East Shoreham	11786
Dansville (Steuben		Dormansville	12055	County)	10709	East Side (Broome	
County) (Town)	14807	Dorwood Park	14131	East Cobleskill	12157	County)	13904
Danube (Town)	13365	Douglass	12944	East Coldenham	12550	East Side (Erie County)	14206
Darien	14040	Douglaston (Part of New		East Concord	14055	Eastside (Suffolk County)	11937
Darien (Town)	14040	York)	11363	East Corning	14830	East Sidney	13775
Darien Center	14040	Dover (Town)	12522	East De Kalb	13630	East Springfield	13333
Darrowsville	12817	Dover Furnace	12522	East Durham	12423	East Steamburg	14886
Davenport	13750	Dover Plains	12522	East Eden	14057	East Stone Arabia	13428
Davenport (Town)	13750	Downstate Correctional		East Elmhurst (Part of		East Syracuse	13057
Davenport Center	13751	Facility	12524	New York)	11369	East Taghkanic	12502
Davis Park	11772	Downsville	13755	Eastern Hills Mall	14221	East Varick	14541
Daws	14020	Downtown (Part of Elmira)	14901	Eastern New York		East Vestal	13902
Day (Town)	12835	Downtown (Part of		Correctional Facility	12458	East Victor	14564
Days Rock	13407	Rochester)	14603	East Farmingdale	11735	East View	10595
Dayton	14041	Downtown (Part of		East Fishkill (Town)	12533	East Watertown	13601
Dayton (Town)	14041	Syracuse)	13201	East Floyd	13354	East Wawarsing	12489
Daytonville	13480	Doyle	14206	East Frankfort	13340	East White Plains (Part of	
Deansboro	13328	Dreiser Loop (Part of New		East Freetown	13055	Harrison)	10604
Debruce	12758	York)	10475	East Gaines	14411	East Williamson	14449
Decatur	12197	Dresden (Washington		East Galway	12850	East Williston	11596
Decatur (Town)	12197	County) (Town)	12887	East Genoa	13092	East Windham	12439
Deck	13407	Dresden (Yates County)	14441	East Glenville	12302	East Windsor	13865
Deckertown	12758	Dresden Station	12887	East Greenbush	12061	East Winfield	13491
Deerfield (Town)	13503	Dresserville	13118	East Greenbush (Town)	12061	Eastwood (Part of	
Deerland	12847	Drews Corner	13694	East Greenlawn	11731	Syracuse)	13206
Deerpark (Orange County)		Dryden	13053	East Greenwich	12826	East Worcester	12064
(Town)	12729	Dryden (Town)	13053	East Half Hollow Hills	11746	Eaton	13334
Deer Park (Suffolk		Duane (Town)	12953	East Hampton	11937	Eaton (Town)	13334
County)	11729	Duane Center	12953	East Hampton (Town)	11937	Eatons Neck	11768
Deer River	13627	Duanesburg	12056	East Hampton North	11937	Eavesport	12490
Deferiet	13628	Duanesburg (Town)	12056	East Hartford	12832	Ebenezer	14224
Defreestville	12144	Dublin	14433	East Hebron	12865	Ebenezer Junction	14224
Degrasse	13684	Dugway	13131	East Herkimer	13350	Echota (Part of Niagara	
De Kalb	13630	Dunbar	13865	East Hill	14850	Falls)	14302
De Kalb (Town)	13630	Dundee	14837	East Hills	11576	Eddy	13617
De Kalb Junction	13630	Dunewood	11706	East Hillsdale	12529	Eddyville (Cattaraugus	
De Lancey	13752	Dunham Hollow	12018	East Homer	13056	County)	14755
Delanson	12053	Dunham Manor	13492	East Hoosick	12090	Eddyville (Ulster County)	12401
Delaware (Albany County)	12209	Dunkirk	14048	East Hounsfield	13601	Eden	14057
Delaware (Sullivan		Dunkirk (Town)	14048	East Huntington	11743	Eden (Town)	14057
County) (Town)	12723	Dunnsville	12009	East Irvington	10533	Edenville	10990
Delevan	14042	Dunraven	12455	East Islip	11730	Edgemere (Part of New	
Delhi	13753	Dunsbach Ferry	12047	East Ithaca	14850	York)	11691
Delhi (Town)	13753	Dunwoodie (Part of		East Jewett	12424	Edgemont	10583
Delmar	12054	Yonkers)	10701	East Kingston	12401	Edgewater Beach	13308
Delphi Falls	13051	Dunwoody Heights (Part		East Koy	14536	Edgewater Park	13669
Delray	14224	of Yonkers)	10701	East Lake Ronkonkoma	11779	Edgewood (Greene	
Dempster Beach	13126	Durham	12422	East Lansing	14852	County)	12450
Demster	13126	Durham (Town)	12422	East Leon	14719	Edgewood (Suffolk	
Denmark	13631	Durhamville	13054	East Line	12020	County)	11717
Denmark (Town)	13631	Durkeetown	12828	East Marion	11939	Edgewood Garden	13164
Dennies Hollow	12117	Durlandville	10924	East Martinsburg	13367	Edinburg	12134
Denning	12725	Dutchess Junction	12508	East Masonville	13839	Edinburg (Town)	12134
Denning (Town)	12725	Dutch Flats	14167	East Massapequa	11758	Edmeston	13335
Dennison Corners	13407	Dutch Meadows	12065	East Mattituck	11952	Edmeston (Town)	13335
Denton	10958	Dwaar Kill	12566	East McDonough	13830	Edson	13865
Denton Hills	11721	Dyke	14830	East Meadow	11554	Edwards	13635
Denver	12421	Dykemans	10509	East Meredith	13757	Edwards (Town)	13635
Depauville	13632	Dyker Heights (Part of		East Middletown	10940	Edwards Hill	12811
Depew	14043	New York)	11228	Eastmor	12180	Edwards Park	12029
De Peyster	13633	Eagle	14009	East Moriches	11940	Edwardsville	13646
De Peyster (Town)	13633	Eagle (Town)	14009	East Nassau	12062	Egbertville (Part of New	
Deposit	13754	Eagle Bay	13331	East Neck	11743	York)	10306
Deposit (Town)	13754	Eagle Bridge	12057	East New York (Part of		Eggertsville	14226
Derby	14047	Eagle Center	14024	New York)	11207	Egypt	14450
Dering Harbor	11964	Eagle Harbor	14442	East Nichols	13812	Einstein (Part of New	
DeRuyter	13052	Eagle Lake	12883	East Northport	11731	York)	10475
DeRuyter (Town)	13052	Eagle Mills	12180	East Norwich	11732	Elayne Meadows	12188
Deuels Corners	14127	Eagle Point	14454	East Olean (Part of Olean)	14760	Elba	14058
Devereux	14731	Eagle Village	13104	Easton (Town)	12834	Elba (Town)	14058
Devon	11930	Eagleville	12873	East Otto	14729	Elbridge	13060
Dewey (Part of Rochester)	14613	Earlton	12058	East Otto (Town)	14729	Elbridge (Town)	13060
Dewey Bridge	12827	Earlville (Franklin County)	12920	East Palermo	13036	Eldred	12732
De Witt	13214	Earlville (Madison County)	13332	East Palmyra	14444	Elizabethtown	12932
De Witt (Town)	13214	East (Part of Yonkers)	10704	East Park	12538	Elizabethtown (Town)	12932
Dewittville	14728	East Amherst	14051	East Part	13697	Elizaville	12523
Dexter	13634	East Arcade	14009	East Patchogue	11772	Elka Park	12427

	ZIP
Elk Brook	12776
Elk Creek	12155
Elkdale	14779
Ellenburg	12933
Ellenburg (Town)	12933
Ellenburg Center	12934
Ellenburg Depot	12935
Ellenville	12428
Ellery (Town)	14756
Ellery Center	14712
Ellicott (Chautauqua County) (Town)	14733
Ellicott (Erie County)	14127
Ellicott (Part of Buffalo) (Erie County)	14203-05
For specific Ellicott Zip Codes call (716) 856-4603, or your local postmaster.	
Ellicottville	14731
Ellicottville (Town)	14731
Ellington	14732
Ellington (Town)	14732
Ellisburg	13636
Ellisburg (Town)	13636
Ellis Hollow	14850
Ellistown	14892
Elma	14059
Elma (Town)	14059
Elmdale	13642
Elm Grove	13808
Elmhurst	14701
Elmhurst-A (Part of New York)	11373
Elmira	14901-25
For specific Elmira Zip Codes call (607) 737-5100, or your local postmaster.	
Elmira (Town)	14902
Elmira Heights	14903
Elmira Heights North	14903
Elmont	11003
Elm Park (Part of New York)	10303
Elmsford	10523
Elm Valley	14895
Elmwood (Part of Syracuse)	13207
Elnora	12065
Elsmere	12054
Eltingville (Part of New York)	10312
Elton	14042
Elton Station	14042
Elwood	11731
Elwood Farms	11731
Embogcht	12414
Emerson	13140
Emerson Hill (Part of New York)	10301
Emeryville	13642
Eminence	12175
Emmons	13820
Empeyville	13316
Empire State (Part of New York)	10001
Empire State Plaza (Part of Albany)	12220
Endicott	13760-61
	13763
For specific Endicott Zip Codes call (607) 748-8207, or your local postmaster.	
Endwell	13762
Enfield	14850
Enfield (Town)	14850
Ensenore	13118
Ephratah	13339
Ephratah (Town)	13339
Erieville	13061
Erin	14838
Erin (Town)	14838
Erwin (Town)	14870
Erwins	14870
Escarpment	14092
Esopus	12429
Esopus (Town)	12429
Esperance	12066
Esperance (Town)	12066
Esplanade (Part of New York)	10469
Essex	12936
Essex (Town)	12936
Etna	13062
Euclid	13041
Evans (Town)	14006
Evans Center	14006
Evans Mills	13637
Exeter (Town)	13315
Exeter Center	13315
F (Part of Buffalo)	14212

	ZIP
Fabius	13063
Fabius (Town)	13063
Factory Village	12020
Factoryville	12928
Fairdale	13074
Fairfield	13336
Fairfield (Town)	13336
Fairfield Farms	13066
Fairfield Gardens	12205
Fair Harbor	11706
Fair Haven	13064
Fairlawn Estates	12110
Fairmount	13219
Fairmount (census designated place)	13031
	13219
For specific Fairmount Zip Codes call (315) 468-4795, or your local postmaster.	
Fairmount Fair Mall	13219
Fair Oaks	10940
Fairport	14450
Fairview (Allegany County)	14060
Fairview (Dutchess County)	12601
Fairview (Westchester County)	10603
Fairview (Wyoming County)	14427
Falconer	14733
Falcon Manor	14304
Falconwood	14072
Falls (Part of Niagara Falls)	14303
Fallsburg	12733
Fallsburg (Town)	12733
Fancher	14452
Fargo	14036
Farleys Point	13160
Farmers Mills	10512
Farmersville (Town)	14060
Farmersville Center	14737
Farmersville Station	14060
Farmingdale	11735
Farmington	14425
Farmington (Town)	14425
Farmingville	11738
Farnham	14061
Farragut (Part of New York)	11203
Far Rockaway	11601-97
For specific Far Rockaway Zip Codes call (718) 327-7700, or your local postmaster.	
HOSPITALS	
Peninsula Hospital Center	11691
St. John's Episcopal Hospital-South Shore	11691
MILITARY INSTALLATIONS	
Fort Tilden	11695
Fawn Ridge	13027
Fayette	13065
Fayette (Town)	13065
Fayetteville	13066
Federal (Part of Rochester)	14614
Federal Correctional Institution	10963
Federal Reserve (Part of New York)	10045
Felts Mills	13638
Fenimore	12801
Fenner (Town)	13035
Fenton (Town)	13833
Ferenbaugh	14830
Fergusons Corners	14456
Fergusonville	12155
Ferndale	12734
Fernwood (Oswego County)	13142
Fernwood (Sullivan County)	12760
Ferry Village	14072
Feura Bush	12067
Fieldston (Part of New York)	10463
Filer Corners	13808
Fillmore	14735
Finchville	10940
Findley Lake	14736
Fine	13639
Fine (Town)	13639
Fineview	13640
Finger Lakes Manor (Part of Canandaigua)	14424
Fink Basin	13365
Finnegans Corners	10924

	ZIP
Fire Island Pines	11782
Firthcliffe Heights	12584
Fish Creek (Lewis County)	13325
Fish Creek (Ulster County)	12477
Fish Creek Landing	13308
Fishers	14453
Fishers Island	06390
Fishers Landing	13641
Fisherville	14903
Fish House	12025
Fishkill	12524
Fishkill (Town)	12524
Fishkill Plains	12590
Fishs Eddy	13774
Five Corners (Madison County)	13421
Five Corners (Oneida County)	13480
Fivemile Point	13795
Five Points	14456
Five Town Plaza	11598
Flackville	13669
Flanders	11901
Flatbrook	12029
Flatbush (Kings County)	11226
Flatbush (Ulster County)	12477
Flat Creek (Montgomery County)	13317
Flat Creek (Schoharie County)	12076
Fleetwood (Part of Mount Vernon)	10552
Fleischmanns	12430
Fleming	13021
Fleming (Town)	13021
Flemingville	13827
Flint	14561
Floral Park	11001-05
For specific Floral Park Zip Codes call (516) 354-3297, or your local postmaster.	
Florence	13316
Florence (Town)	13316
Florida (Montgomery County) (Town)	12010
Florida (Orange County)	10921
Floridaville	13033
Flowerfield Estates (Part of Lake Grove)	11755
Flower Hill	11050
Flowers	13865
Floyd	13440
Floyd (Town)	13440
Flushing	11301-88
For specific Flushing Zip Codes call (718) 321-5340, or your local postmaster.	
COLLEGES & UNIVERSITIES	
City University of New York-Queens College	11367
FINANCIAL INSTITUTIONS	
Asia Bank, N.A.	11354
Flushing Savings Bank	11354
Queens County Savings Bank	11354
HOSPITALS	
Booth Memorial Medical Center	11355
Elmhurst Hospital Center	11373
Flushing Hospital Medical Center	11355
LaGuardia Hospital	11375
HOTELS/MOTELS	
Best Western Midway Hotel	11368
Metropole Hotel	11368
Pan American Motor Inn	11373
MILITARY INSTALLATIONS	
Fort Totten	11359
Fluvanna	14701
Fly Creek	13337
Flying Point	11976
Fly Summit	12834
Fonda	12068
Foots Corners	14435
Fordham (Part of New York)	10458
Forest	12935
Forestburgh	12777
Forestburgh (Town)	12701
Forest Glen (Part of Hamburg)	14075

	ZIP
Forest Hills (Part of New York)	11375
Forest Home	14850
Forest Knolls (Part of New Rochelle)	10804
Forest Lawn	14580
Forest Park (Chautauqua County)	14787
Forest Park (Dutchess County)	12572
Forestport	13338
Forestport (Town)	13338
Forestport Station	13338
Forestville	14062
Forge Hollow	13328
Forks	14225
Forsonville	10524
Forsyth	14775
Fort Ann	12827
Fort Ann (Town)	12827
Fort Covington	12937
Fort Covington (Town)	12937
Fort Covington Center	12937
Fort Drum	13612
Fort Edward	12828
Fort Edward (Town)	12828
Fort George (Part of New York)	10040
Fort Herkimer	13407
Fort Hunter (Albany County)	12303
Fort Hunter (Montgomery County)	12069
Fort Jackson	12965
Fort Johnson	12070
Fort Miller	12828
Fort Montgomery	10922
Fort Niagara Beach	14174
Fort Orange (Part of Albany)	12206
Fort Plain	13339
Fort Salonga	11768
Fortsville	12831
Fort Washington (Part of New York)	10032
Foster	13827
Fosterdale	12726
Fosterville	13021
Foster-Wheeler Junction (Part of Dansville)	14437
Fourth Lake	12846
Fowler	13642
Fowler (Town)	13642
Fowlersville	13433
Fowlerville	14423
Fox Hill	12134
Fox Meadows (Part of Scarsdale)	10583
Frankfort	13340
Frankfort (Town)	13340
Frankfort Center	13340
Franklin	13775
Franklin (Delaware County) (Town)	13775
Franklin (Franklin County) (Town)	12913
Franklin Correctional Facility	12953
Franklin D. Roosevelt (Part of New York)	10022
Franklin Park	13057
Franklin Springs	13341
Franklin Square	11010
Franklinton	12122
Franklinville	14737
Franklinville (Town)	14737
Franks Corner	13045
Fraser	13753
Fredonia	14063
Freedom	14065
Freedom (Town)	14065
Freedom Plains	12569
Freehold	12431
Freeman	14801
Freeport	11520
Freetown (Cortland County) (Town)	13803
Freetown (Suffolk County)	11937
Freetown Corners	13803
Freeville	13068
Fremont (Steuben County) (Town)	14807
Fremont (Sullivan County) (Town)	12736
Fremont Center	12736
Fremont Heights	13057
Fremont Hills	13057
French Creek (Town)	14724
Frenchville	13486
French Woods	13783

* Area Zip Code   † Post Office Boxes

	ZIP
Fresh Meadows (Part of New York)	11365
Fresh Pond (Part of New York)	11385
Frewsburg	14738
Friend	14527
Friendship	14739
Friendship (Town)	14739
Friends Point	12836
Frontenac	13624
Fruitland	14519
Fruit Valley	13126
Fullerville	13642
Fulmer Valley	14806
Fulton (Oswego County)	13069
Fulton (Schoharie County) (Town)	12122
Fultonham	12071
Fultonville	12072
Furnace Brook	10925
Furnaceville	14519
Furnace Woods	10566
Furniss	13126
Fyler Settlement	13082
Gabriels	12939
Gaines	14411
Gaines (Town)	14411
Gainesville	14066
Gainesville (Town)	14066
Galatia	13803
Gale	12973
Galen (Town)	14433
Galeville (Onondaga County)	13088
Galeville (Ulster County)	12589
Gallatin	12567
Gallatin (Town)	12567
Galleria at Crystal Run	10940
Galleria of White Plains (Part of White Plains)	10601
Gallupville	12073
Galway	12074
Galway (Town)	12074
Galway Lake	12025
Ganahgote	12525
Gang Mills	14870
Gansevoort	12831
Garbutt	14546
Garden City	11530
Garden City Park	11040
Garden City South	11530
Garden Park Estates	12203
Gardenville	14224
Gardiner	12525
Gardiner (Town)	12525
Gardiner Manor Mall	11706
Gardiners Bay Estates	11939
Gardnersville	12043
Gardnertown	12550
Garfield	12168
Garland	14420
Garnerville (Part of West Haverstraw)	10923
Garnet Lake	12843
Garoga	12095
Garrattsville	13342
Garrison	10524
Garrison Four Corners	10524
Garwoods	14822
Gaskill	13827
Gasport	14067
Gates (Town)	14624
Gates	14624
Gates Center	14611
Gates-North Gates	14626
Gayhead	12533
Gay Ridge Estates	10598
Gayville	13044
Geddes (Town)	13209
Gedney (Part of White Plains)	10605
Geers Corners	13648
Genegantslet	13778
Genesee (Town)	14754
Genesee Falls (Town)	14536
Geneseo	14454
Geneseo (Town)	14454
Geneva	14456
Geneva (Town)	14456
Genoa	13071
Genoa (Town)	13071
Georgetown (Madison County)	13072
Georgetown (Madison County) (Town)	13072
Georgetown (Monroe County)	14450
Georgetown Square (Part of Williamsville)	14221
Georgtown Station	13334

	ZIP
German	13040
German (Town)	13040
German Flatts (Town)	13407
Germantown	12526
Germantown (Town)	12526
Germantown (Part of Port Jervis)	12771
German Village	14617
Germonds	10956
Gerry	14740
Gerry (Town)	14740
Getzville	14068
Geyser Crest	12866
Ghent	12075
Ghent (Town)	12075
Gibson (Nassau County)	11580
Gibson (Steuben County)	14830
Gifford	12056
Gilbert Mills	13135
Gilbertsville	13776
Gilboa	12076
Gilboa (Town)	12076
Gilgo Beach	11702
Gilmantown	12190
Gimbels Number One	11581
Glasco	12432
Glass Lake	12018
Glen	12072
Glen (Town)	12072
Glen Aubrey	13777
Glen Castle	13901
Glenclyffe	10524
Glenco Mills	12534
Glen Cove	11542
Glendale (Lewis County)	13343
Glendale (Queens County)	11385
Glendale Manor (Part of Rome)	13440
Glenerie	12477
Glenfield	13343
Glenford	12433
Glenham	12527
Glen Haven (Monroe County)	14617
Glenhaven (Oneida County)	13492
Glen Head	11545
Glen Island	12814
Glen Lake	12801
Glenmark	14516
Glenmont	12077
Glen Oaks (Part of New York)	11004
Glenora	14837
Glen Park	13601
Glenridge	12148
Glens Falls	12801
Glens Falls North	12801
Glen Spey	12737
Glen Street (Part of Sea Cliff)	11579
Glenville (Schenectady County) (Town)	12302
Glenville (Westchester County)	10591
Glen Wild	12738
Glenwood (Erie County)	14069
Glenwood (Westchester County)	10701
Glenwood Landing	11547
Gloversville	12078
Godeffroy	12739
Golden Glow Heights	14905
Goldens Bridge	10526
Goodman Street (Part of Rochester)	14607
Goodyears Corners	13081
Goose Bay Estates	11971
Goose Island	12809
Gordon Heights	11727
Gorham	14461
Gorham (Town)	14461
Goshen	10924
Goshen (Town)	10924
Goshen Hills	10924
Gothicville	12197
Goulds	12760
Goulds Mill	13368
Gouverneur	13642
Gouverneur (Town)	13642
Governors Island (Part of New York)	10004
Gowanda	14070
Gracie (Cortland County)	13045
Gracie (New York County)	10028
Grafton	12082
Grafton (Town)	12082
Graham Hill	10537
Grahamsville	12740

	ZIP
Granby (Town)	13069
Granby Center	13069
Grand Central (Part of New York)	10017
Grand Gorge	12434
Grand Island	14072
Grand Island (Town)	14072
Grand Station (Part of New York)	11103
Grand View Beach	14612
Grand View Heights	14612
Grand View-on-Hudson	10960
Grandview Park	13692
Grandyle Village	14072
Granger (Town)	14735
Grangerville	12871
Granite	12446
Granite Springs	10527
Graniteville (Part of New York)	10301
Grant	13324
Grant Avenue (Part of Auburn)	13021
Grant Hollow	12121
Grant Park	11557
Granville	12832
Granville (Town)	12832
Grapeville	12042
Graphite	12836
Grassy Point	10980
Gravesend (Part of New York)	11223
Gravesville	13431
Gray	13324
Graymoor	10524
Gray Oaks (Part of Yonkers)	10703
Great Bend	13643
Great Kills (Part of New York)	10308
Great Neck	11020-27
For specific Great Neck Zip Codes call (516) 482-5010, or your local postmaster.	
Great Neck Estates	11021
Great Neck Plaza	11020
Great River	11739
Great South Bay (Part of Lindenhurst)	11702
Great Valley	14741
Great Valley (Town)	14741
Greece (Monroe County) (Town)	14616
	14626
For specific Greece Zip Codes call (716) 663-3321, or your local postmaster.	
Greece (Ridgemont) (Monroe County)	14626
Greece (Monroe County)	14616
Greeley Square (Part of New York)	10001
Green Acres (Part of Fredonia)	14063
Green Acres Mall (Part of Valley Stream)	11581
Greenburgh (Town)	10591
Green Corners	12010
Green Crest	14063
Greendale	12534
Greene	13778
Greene (Town)	13778
Greene Correctional Facility	12051
Greenfield (Town)	12833
Greenfield Center	12833
Greenfield Park	12435
Greenhaven (Part of Rye)	10580
Green Haven Correctional Facility	12570
Greenhurst	14742
Green Island	12183
Green Island (Town)	12183
Greenlawn	11740
Greenpoint (Part of New York)	11222
Greenport (Columbia County) (Town)	12534
Greenport (Suffolk County)	11944
Greenport West	11944
Green River	12529
Greenvale	11548
Greenville (Greene County)	12083
Greenville (Greene County) (Town)	12083
Greenville (Orange County) (Town)	12771

	ZIP
Greenville (Westchester County)	10583
Greenville Center	12083
Greenway (Part of Rome)	13440
Greenwich	12834
Greenwich (Town)	12834
Greenwood	14839
Greenwood (Town)	14839
Greenwood Lake	10925
Gregorytown	13755
Greig	13345
Greig (Town)	13345
Greigsville	14533
Greigsville Station	14533
Grenell	13624
Greycourt (Part of Chester)	10918
Greystone	10701*
	10702†
Gridleyville	13864
Grindstone	13624
Grooms Corners	12148
Grossinger	12734
Groton	13073
Groton (Town)	13073
Groton City	13073
Grove (Town)	14884
Groveland	14462
Groveland (Town)	14462
Grover	14226
Grover Hills	12956
Grovernor Corners	12035
Groveville	12508
Grymes Hill (Part of New York)	10301
Guilderland	12084
Guilderland (Town)	12084
Guilderland Center	12085
Guilderland Gardens	12203
Guilford	13780
Guilford (Town)	13780
Guilford Center	13780
Gulf Summit	13865
Gunther Park (Part of Yonkers)	10708
Gurn Spring	12831
Guymard	12739
Gypsum	14432
Hadley	12835
Hadley (Town)	12835
Hadley Bay	14785
Hagaman	12086
Hagedorns Mills	12074
Hagerman	11713
Hague	12836
Hague (Town)	12836
Hailesboro	13645
Haines Falls	12436
Halcott (Town)	12430
Halcott Center	12430
Halcottsville	12438
Hales Eddy	13783
Halesite	11743
Half Acre	13021
Half Hollow Hills	11746
Halfmoon	12188
Halfmoon (Town)	12188
Halfway	13060
Halfway House Corners	13660
Hall	14463
Hallow	13413
Halls Corners (Seneca County)	14847
Halls Corners (Wyoming County)	14569
Hallsport	14895
Hallsville	13339
Halsey (Part of New York)	11233
Halseys (Part of Plattsburgh)	12901
Halsey Valley	14883
Hambletville	13754
Hamburg (Erie County)	14075
Hamburg (Erie County) (Town)	14075
Hamburg (Greene County)	12414
Hamburg-on-the-Lake	14075
Hamden	13782
Hamden (Town)	13782
Hamilton	13346
Hamilton (Town)	13346
Hamilton Beach (Part of New York)	11414
Hamilton Center	13346
Hamilton College	13323
Hamilton Grange (Part of New York)	10031
Hamilton Park (Part of New York)	10301

	ZIP
Hamlet	14138
Hamlin	14464
Hamlin (Town)	14464
Hammertown	12567
Hammond	13646
Hammond (Town)	13646
Hammondsport	14840
Hampshire	14855
Hampton	12837
Hampton (Town)	12837
Hampton Bays (Suffolk County)	11946
Hamptonburgh (Town)	10916
Hampton Manor	12144
Hampton Park	11968
Hancock	13783
Hancock (Town)	13783
Hankins	12741
Hannacroix	12087
Hannawa Falls	13647
Hannibal	13074
Hannibal (Town)	13074
Hannibal Center	13074
Hanover (Town)	14136
Hanover Hill	14136
Harbor Acres (Part of Sands Point)	11050
Harbor Heights Park	11743
Harbor Hills	11023
Harbor Isle	11558
Hardenburgh (Town)	12455
Hardys	14066
Harford	13784
Harford (Town)	13784
Harford Mills	13835
Harkness	12972
Harlem (Part of New York)	10030
Harlemville	12075
Harmon Park	12302
Harmony (Town)	14767
Harmony Corners	12020
Harpersfield	13786
Harpersfield (Town)	13786
Harpursville	13787
Harriet	14223
Harrietstown (Town)	12983
Harriman	10926
Harris	12742
Harrisburg (Cattaraugus County)	14753
Harrisburg (Lewis County) (Town)	13367
Harrisburg (Warren County)	12878
Harris Corners	14145
Harris Hill	14221
Harrison	10528
Harrison (Town)	10528
Harrisville	13648
Harrower	12010
Hartfield	14728
Hartford	12838
Hartford (Town)	12838
Hartland	14067
Hartland (Town)	14067
Hartmans Corners	12009
Hartsdale	10530
Harts Hill	13492
Hartson Point	14487
Hartsville	14843
Hartsville (Town)	14843
Hartwick	13348
Hartwick (Town)	13348
Hartwick Seminary	13349
Hartwood	12729
Harvard	13756
Hasbrouck	12788
Haskell Flats	14727
Haskinville	14826
Hastings	13076
Hastings (Town)	13076
Hastings Center	13036
Hastings-on-Hudson	10706
Hatch's Corner	13684
Hauppauge	11760
	11788

For specific Hauppauge Zip Codes call (516) 360-7208, or your local postmaster.

	ZIP
Haven	12790
Haverstraw	10927
Haverstraw (Town)	10927
Haviland	12538
Hawkeye	12912
Hawkins Corner	13440
Hawkinsville	13309
Hawleys	13856
Hawleyton	13903
Hawthorne	10532
Hawthorne Hill	12309

	ZIP
Hawthorne Park	14787
Hawversville	12122
Hay Beach Point	11964
Haydenville	14760
Hayt Corners	14521
Hazel	12758
Head of the Harbor	11780
Heathcote (Part of Scarsdale)	10801
Heathcote (Part of New Rochelle)	10583
Heatherwood North	11733
Heatherwood South	11720
Heath Grove	13110
Heavenly Valley	12466
Hebron (Town)	12832
Hecla	13490
Hector	14841
Hector (Town)	14841
Hedgesville	14801
Helena	13649
Hell Gate (Part of New York)	10029
Helmuth	14079
Hemlock	14466
Hempstead	11550*
	11551†
Hempstead Gardens	11552
Hemstreet Park	12118
Henderson	13650
Henderson (Town)	13650
Henderson Harbor	13651
Hendy Creek	14871
Henrietta	14467
Henrietta (Town)	14467
Hensonville	12439
Heritage (Part of Schenectady)	12303
Heritage Hills	12020
Heritage Knolls	12020
Herkimer	13350
Herkimer (Town)	13350
Hermitage (Steuben County)	14810
Hermitage (Wyoming County)	14066
Hermon	13652
Hermon (Town)	13652
Herrick Grove	13622
Herricks	11040
Herrings	13619
Hertel (Part of Buffalo)	14216
Herthum Heights	13492
Hervey Street	12418
Hessville	13339
Heuvelton	13654
Hewittville	13668
Hewlett	11557
Hewlett Bay Park	11557
Hewlett Harbor	11557
Hewlett Neck	11598
Hickeys Corners (Part of Saratoga Springs)	12866
Hickorybush	12401
Hickory Grove	13126
Hicks	14859
Hicksville	11801-02
	11805

For specific Hicksville Zip Codes call (516) 933-2476, or your local postmaster.

	ZIP
Higgins	14065
Higgins Bay	12108
Higginsville	13054
High Bank	12981
High Bridge (Bronx County)	10452
High Bridge (Onondaga County)	13066
High Falls	12440
High Flats	13625
Highland (Sullivan County) (Town)	12732
Highland (Ulster County)	12528
Highland Falls	10928
Highland Lake	12743
Highland Mills	10930
Highland-on-the-Lake	14047
Highlands (Town)	10928
Highlawn (Part of New York)	11223
High Mills	12027
Highmount	12441
High View	12721
High Woods	12477
Hiler	14223
Hillburn	10931
Hillcrest (Broome County)	13901
Hillcrest (Rockland County)	10977

	ZIP
Hiller Heights	13041
Hillis	12603
Hillsboro	13316
Hillsdale	12529
Hillsdale (Town)	12529
Hillside (Part of New York)	10469
Hillside Heights	11040
Hillside Lake	12590
Hillside Manor	11040
Hillside Park (Part of Johnstown)	12095
Hillview	12144
Hilton	14468
Himrod	14842
Hinckley	13352
Hinckleyville	14559
Hindsburg	14411
Hinmans Corners	13905
Hinmansville	13135
Hinsdale	14743
Hinsdale (Town)	14743
Hoag Corners	12062
Hobart	13788
Hoboken	13411
Hoffmans	12302
Hoffmeister	13353
Hogansburg	13655
Hogtown	12827
Holbrook	11741
Holcomb (Part of Bloomfield)	14469
Holcombville	12853
Holiday Manor (Part of Geneva)	14456
Holland	14080
Holland (Town)	14080
Holland Cove	14589
Holland Patent	13354
Holley	14470
Hollis (Part of New York)	11423
Hollis Court (Part of New York)	11429
Holliswood (Part of New York)	11352
Hollowville	12530
Hollywood	12922
Holmes	12531
Holmesville	13843
Holton Beach	14847
Holtsville	11742
Homecrest (Part of New York)	11229
Homer	13077
Homer (Town)	13077
Homer Hill (Part of Olean)	14760
Homestead Park (Part of New Rochelle)	10801
Homestead Village	11727
Homewood	13066
Homewood Park	14225
Honeoye	14471
Honeoye Falls	14472
Honest Hill	14470
Honeywell Corners	12025
Honk Hill	12458
Honnedaga Lake	13338
Hoosick	12089
Hoosick (Town)	12089
Hoosick Falls	12090
Hoosick Junction	12133
Hope (Town)	12134
Hope Falls	12134
Hope Farm	12545
Hope Valley	12134
Hopewell (Town)	14424
Hopewell Center	14424
Hopewell Junction	12533
Hopkinton	12965
Hopkinton (Town)	12965
Horace Harding (Part of New York)	11362
Horicon (Town)	12815
Hornby	14812
Hornby (Town)	14812
Hornell	14843
Hornellsville (Town)	14807
Horseheads	14844†
	14845*
Horseheads (Town)	14845
Horseheads North	14845
Horton	12776
Horton Estates	10587
Hortonville	12745
Hospital (Part of Binghamton)	13904
Houghton	14744
Hounsfield (Town)	13685
Housevile	13473
Housons Corners	12122
Howard (Town)	14809

	ZIP
Howard (New York County)	10013
Howard (Steuben County)	14809
Howard Beach (Part of New York)	11414
Howardville	13302
Howells	10932
Howes Cave	12092
Howlett Hill	13031
Hub (Part of New York)	10455
Hubbardsville	13355
Hubbardtown	13743
Hudson	12534
Hudson Falls	12839
Hudson Upper (Part of Hudson)	12534
Hughsonville	12537
Huguenot (Orange County)	12746
Huguenot (Richmond County)	10301
Huguenot Park (Part of New Rochelle)	10801
Hulberton	14470
Huletts Landing	12841
Hullsville	13827
Hume	14745
Hume (Town)	14745
Humphrey (Town)	14741
Humphrey Center	14741
Hungerford Corners	13650
Hunt	14846
Hunter	12442
Hunter (Town)	12442
Hunter Lake	12768
Huntersland	12122
Huntington (Town)	11743
Huntington	11743
Huntington Bay	11743
Huntington Beach	11721
Huntington Square	11731
Huntington Station	11746
Huntingtonville	13601
Hunts Corners (Cortland County)	13803
Hunts Corners (Erie County)	14031
Hunts Corners (Sullivan County)	12764
Hurd Corners	12564
Hurley	12443
Hurley (Town)	12443
Hurleyville	12747
Huron (Town)	14590
Hyde Park	12538
Hyde Park (Town)	12538
Hyde Park	13326
Hylan Shopping Plaza (Part of New York)	10306
Hyndsville	12043
Idle Hour	11769
Idlewood	14085
Ilion	13357
Imperial Plaza (Part of Wappingers Falls)	12590
Inavale	14739
Independence	14806
Independence (Town)	14806
Index	13326
Indian Castle	13365
Indian Cove	13118
Indian Falls	14036
Indian Kettles	12836
Indian Lake	12842
Indian Lake (Town)	12842
Indian Park	10925
Indian River	13327
Indian Springs	13027
Indian Village	13120
Industry	14474
Ingham Mills	13365
Ingleside	14512
Ingraham	12992
Inlet	13360
Inlet (Town)	13360
Inman	12989
Inter County Shopping Center	11758
Interlaken	14847
Interlaken Beach	14847
International Junction	14223
Inwood (Nassau County)	11696
Inwood (New York County)	10034
Ionia (Onondaga County)	13112
Ionia (Ontario County)	14475
Ira	13033
Ira (Town)	13033
Ira Station	13033
Ireland Corners	12525

* Area Zip Code   † Post Office Boxes

	ZIP
Leicester (Town)	14481
LeMarr Estates	12184
Lenox (Town)	13032
Lenox Furnace	13032
Lenox Hill (Part of New York)	10021
Lenox Park	14456
Leon	14751
Leon (Town)	14751
Leonardsville	13364
Leonta	13775
Le Ray (Town)	13637
Le Roy	14482
Le Roy (Town)	14482
Le Roy Island	14590
Levanna	13026
Levant	14733
Levittown	11756
Lewbeach	12753
Lewis (Essex County)	12950
Lewis (Essex County) (Town)	12950
Lewis (Lewis County) (Town)	13489
Lewisboro (Town)	10590
Lewiston	14092
Lewiston (Town)	14092
Lewiston Heights (Part of Lewiston)	14092
Lewiston Manor	13224
Lexington	12452
Lexington (Town)	12452
Leyden (Town)	13433
Liberty	12754
Liberty (Town)	12754
Liberty Gardens (Part of Rome)	13440
Libertypole	14437
Lido Beach	11561
Lily Dale	14752
Lima	14485
Lima (Town)	14485
Lime Lake	14042
Lime Lake-Machias	14042
Limerick	13657
Lime Rock	14482
Limestone	14753
Limestreet	12414
Lincklaen	13052
Lincklaen (Town)	13052
Lincoln (Madison County) (Town)	13043
Lincoln (Wayne County)	14502
Lincolndale	10540
Lincoln Park (Erie County)	14223
Lincoln Park (Monroe County)	14611
Lincoln Park (Ulster County)	12401
Lincolnshire	13760
Lincolnton (Part of New York)	10037
Lindbergh Court (Part of Colonie)	12205
Linden	14054
Linden Acres	12571
Linden Hill (Part of New York)	11354
Lindenhurst	11757
Lindley	14858
Lindley (Town)	14858
Linlithgo	12526
Linwood	14486
Lisbon	13658
Lisbon (Town)	13658
Lisle	13797
Lisle (Town)	13797
Litchfield (Town)	13456
Lithgow	12545
Little America	13144
Little Bow	13642
Little Britain	12575
Little Canada	14054
Little Falls	13365
Little Falls (Town)	13407
Little Falls Park (Part of Wappingers Falls)	12590
Little France	13036
Little Genesee	14754
Little Neck (Part of New York)	11363
Little Plains	11731
Little Ram Island	11964
Little Utica	13135
Little Valley	14755
Little Valley (Town)	14755
Littleville	14424
Little York (Cortland County)	13087

	ZIP
Little York (Orange County)	10969
Liverpool	13088-90
For specific Liverpool Zip Codes call (315) 451-3060, or your local postmaster.	
Livingston	12541
Livingston (Town)	12541
Livingston (Part of New York)	11201
Livingston Manor	12758
Livingstonville	12122
Livonia	14487
Livonia (Town)	14487
Livonia Center	14488
Lloyd (Town)	12528
Lloyd Harbor	11743
Lochada Lake	12719
Loch Muller	12857
Loch Sheldrake	12759
Lock Berlin	14489
Locke	13092
Locke (Town)	13092
Lockport	14094*
	14095†
Locksley Park	14075
Lockwood	14859
Locust Grove (Lewis County)	13309
Locust Grove (Nassau County)	11791
Locust Manor (Part of New York)	11431
Locust Point (Part of New York)	10465
Locust Valley	11560
Lodi	14860
Lodi (Town)	14860
Lodi Center	14860
Lodi Point	14860
Logan	14818
Logtown	12771
Lomala	12533
Lombard	14775
Lomond Shore	14476
Lomontville	12401
London Terrace (Part of New York)	10011
Lonelyville	11706
Long Beach	11561
Long Branch	13088
Long Branch Manor	13088
Long Bridge	13153
Long Eddy	12760
Long Island City	11101-06
For specific Long Island City Zip Codes call (718) 321-5340, or your local postmaster.	
FINANCIAL INSTITUTIONS	
Astoria Federal Savings & Loan Association	11103
Financial Federal Savings & Loan Association	11104
HOSPITALS	
Long Island Jewish Medical Center	11042
Long Island University Southampton College	11968
Long Lake	12847
Long Lake (Town)	12847
Long Ridge Mall	14626
Long View	14710
Longwood (Part of New York)	10459
Loomis	12754
Loomises	14710
Loon Lake	12989
Loon Lake Junction	12989
Lordville	13783
Lorenz Park	12534
Lorings	13045
Lorraine	13659
Lorraine (Town)	13659
Lost Valley	12010
Loudonville	12211
Louisville	13662
Louisville (Town)	13662
Lounsberry	13812
Lower Chateaugay Lake	12920
Lower Cincinnatus	13040
Lower Genegantslet Corner	13778
Lower Melville	11747
Lower Oswegatchie	13670
Lower Rotterdam	12306
Lower South Bay	13041
Low Hampton	05743

	ZIP
Lowman	14861
Lowville	13367
Lowville (Town)	13367
Ludingtonville	12531
Ludlow (Part of Yonkers)	10705
Ludlowville	14882
Lumberland (Town)	12770
Luther	12061
Lutheranville	12064
Lycoming	13093
Lyell (Part of Rochester)	14606
Lykers	12166
Lyme (Town)	13693
Lynbrook	11563
Lyncourt	13208
Lyndon (Cattaraugus County) (Town)	14737
Lyndon (Onondaga County)	13066
Lyndonville	14098
Lynelle Meadows	13088
Lyon Mountain	12952
	12955
For specific Lyon Mountain Zip Codes call (518) 735-4747, or your local postmaster.	
Lyons	14489
Lyons (Town)	14489
Lyonsdale	13368
Lyonsdale (Town)	13368
Lyons Falls	13368
Lyonsville	12404
Lysander	13094
Lysander (Town)	13094
Mabbettsville	12545
McClure	13754
McConnellsville	13401
MacDonnell Heights	12603
McDonough	13801
McDonough (Town)	13801
MacDougall	14541
Macedon	14502
Macedon (Town)	14502
Macedon Center	14502
McGraw	13101
McGrawville	14777
Machias (Town)	14101
Machias	14101
McKeever	13338
Mackey	12076
McKinley	13428
McKinstry Hollow	14042
McKown Park	12203
McKownville	12203
McKownville Estates	12203
McLaughlin Acres	10541
McLean	13102
McMasters Corners	13201
McNalls	14067
Macomb (Town)	13642
McPherson Point	14487
Madison	13402
Madison (Town)	13402
Madison Park	11731
Madison Square (Part of New York)	10010
Madrid	13660
Madrid (Town)	13660
Magnolia	14757
Mahopac	10541
Mahopac Falls	10542
Mahopac Hills	10541
Mahopac Point	10541
Mahopac Ridge	10541
Maidstone Park	11937
Maine	13802
Maine (Town)	13802
Main Settlement	14770
Main Village (Part of Williamsville)	14221
Malden Bridge	12115
Malden on Hudson	12453
Mall	11706
Mall at Greeceridge Center, The	14626
Mall at New Rochelle, The (Part of New Rochelle)	10801
Mallory	13103
Malone	12953
Malone (Town)	12953
Malta	12020
Malta (Town)	12020
Malta Ridge	12020
Maltaville	12020
Maltbie Heights	14070
Malverne	11565
Malvic Manor	13088
Mamakating (Town)	12790
Mamakating Park	12790
Mamaroneck	10543

	ZIP
Mamaroneck (Town)	10543
Manchester	14504
Manchester (Town)	14504
Manchester Bridge	12603
Mandana	13152
Manhasset	11030
Manhasset Hills	11040
Manhattan	10001-99
	10101-99
	10201-82
For specific Manhattan Zip Codes call (212) 967-8585, or your local postmaster.	
Manhattan Park (Part of White Plains)	10601
Manhattanville (Part of New York)	10027
Manhattanville College (Part of Harrison)	10577
Manheim (Town)	13329
Manheim Center	13365
Manitou	10524
Manitou Beach	14468
Manlius	13104
Manlius (Town)	13104
Manlius Center	13066
Mannetto Hills	11747
Manning	14470
Mannsville	13661
Mannville	12189
Manny Corners	12010
Manor	13413
Manorhaven	11050
Manorkill	12076
Manors	11507
Manorville (Suffolk County)	11949
Manorville (Ulster County)	12477
Mansfield (Town)	14755
Maple Bay	14710
Maplecrest	12454
Mapledale	12406
Maple Grove (Hamilton County)	12134
Maple Grove (Otsego County)	13808
Maple Hill	12401
Maplehurst	14743
Maples	14755
Maple Springs	14756
Mapleton	13021
Mapletown	13317
Maple Valley	13488
Mapleview	13107
Maplewood (Albany County)	12189
Maplewood (Sullivan County)	12701
Marathon	13803
Marathon (Town)	13803
Marble Hill (Part of New York)	10463
Marbletown	12401
Marbletown (Town)	12401
Marbletown	14513
Marcellus	13108
Marcellus (Town)	13108
Marcellus Falls	13108
Marcy (Kings County)	11206
Marcy (Oneida County) (Town)	13503
Marcy Correctional Facility	13403
Marengo	14433
Margaretville	12455
Mariaville	12137
Marietta	13110
Marilla	14102
Marilla (Town)	14102
Marine Hospital (Part of New York)	10301
Mariners Harbor (Part of New York)	10303
Marion	14505
Marion (Town)	14505
Mariposa	13155
Markhams	14070
Marlboro	12542
Marlborough (Town)	12542
Marshall (Allegany County)	14711
Marshall (Oneida County) (Town)	13328
Marshfield	14091
Marshland Heights	13760
Marshville (Montgomery County)	13317
Marshville (St. Lawrence County)	13652
Martindale Depot	12521
Martinsburg	13404

* Area Zip Code   † Post Office Boxes

	ZIP
Martinsburg (Town)	13404
Martisco	13108
Martville	13111
Maryknoll	10545
Maryland	12116
Maryland (Town)	12116
Marymount (Part of Tarrytown)	10591
Masonville	13804
Masonville (Town)	13804
Maspeth (Part of New York)	11378
Massapequa	11758
Massapequa Park	11762
Massawepie	12986
Massena	13662
Massena (Town)	13662
Massena Center	13662
Massena Springs (Part of Massena)	13662
Masten Lake	12790
Mastic	11950
Mastic Beach	11951
Matinecock	11560
Matteawan (Part of Beacon)	12508
Mattituck	11952
Mattydale	13211
Maybrook	12543
Mayfair	12302
Mayfair Shopping Center	11725
Mayfield	12117
Mayfield (Town)	12117
Mayville	14757
Maywood (Albany County)	12205
Maywood (Suffolk County)	11701
Meacham	11003
Meadowbrook	12550
Meadowdale	12009
Meadow Hill	12550
Meadow Lane Estates	12184
Meadowmere Park	11598
Meadow Run (Part of Hamburg)	14075
Meadows	14420
Meads	12498
Meads Creek	14870
Mechanicville	12118
Mecklenburg	14863
Meco	12078
Medford	11763
Medina	14103
Medusa	12120
Medway	12042
Melcourt (Part of New York)	10451
Mellenville	12544
Melrose	12121
Melrose Park	13021
Melville	11747
Memphis	13112
Menands	12204
Mendon	14506
Mendon (Town)	14506
Mendon Center	14472
Mendon Farms	14506
Menteth Point	14424
Mentz (Town)	13140
Meredith	13753
Meredith (Town)	13753
Meridale	13806
Meridian	13113
Merillon Avenue (Part of Garden City)	11530
Merrick	11566
Merrickville	13839
Merriewold	12701
Merriewold Lake	10950
Merrifield	13147
Merrill	12955
Merrillsville	13421
Merrilville	12986
Merriweather Campus (Part of Brookville)	11548
Mertensia	14564
Messengerville	13803
Metropolitan (Part of New York)	11206
Mettacahonts	12404
Mews	11507
Mexico	13114
Mexico (Town)	13114
Middle Bridge	13730
Middleburgh	12122
Middleburgh (Town)	12122
Middlebury (Town)	14591
Middle Falls	12848
Middlefield	13450
Middlefield (Town)	13450

	ZIP
Middlefield Center	13320
Middle Granville	12849
Middle Grove	12850
Middle Hope	12550
Middle Island	11953
Middleport (Madison County)	13346
Middleport (Niagara County)	14105
Middlesex	14507
Middlesex (Town)	14507
Middletown	10940-41
For specific Middletown Zip Codes call (914) 343-1496, or your local postmaster.	
Middletown (Town)	12455
Middletown Psychiatric Center (Part of Middletown)	10940
Middle Village (Part of New York)	11379
Middleville (Herkimer County)	13406
Middleville (Suffolk County)	11768
Mid-Island Mall	11801
Midland Beach (Part of New York)	10306
Mid-Orange Correctional Facility	10990
Mid-State Correctional Facility	13403
Midtown (Part of New York)	10018
Midtown Plaza (Part of Rochester)	14604
Midway	14864
Midwood (Part of New York)	11230
Milan (Town)	12571
Mileses	12741
Milford	13807
Milford (Town)	13807
Milford Center	13820
Mill Brook (Bronx County)	10454
Millbrook (Dutchess County)	12545
Millen Bay	13618
Miller Place	11764
Millers	14098
Millers Mills	13491
Millersport	14051
Millerton	12546
Millertown	12094
Mill Grove	14770
Mill Hook	12404
Mill Neck	11765
Mill Point	12010
Millport	14864
Millsburgh	10933
Mills Mills	14735
Millville	14103
Millwood	10546
Milo (Town)	14527
Milo Center	14527
Milton	12020
Milton (Saratoga County) (Town)	12020
Milton (Saratoga County)	12020
Milton (Ulster County)	12547
Milton Point (Part of Rye)	10580
Mina	14781
Mina (Town)	14781
Minaville	12010
Minden (Town)	13339
Mindenville	13339
Mineola	11501
Mineral Springs	12043
Minerva	12851
Minerva (Town)	12851
Minetto	13115
Minetto (Town)	13115
Mineville	12956
Mineville-Witherbee	12956
Minisink (Town)	10998
Minisink Ford	12719
Minklers Corners	13662
Minoa	13116
Mitchellsville	14810
Model City	14107
Modena	12548
Moffitsville	12981
Mohawk (Herkimer County)	13407
Mohawk (Montgomery County) (Town)	12068
Mohawk Hill	13309
Mohawk Mall	12304
Mohawk View	12110
Mohawk Village	12303

	ZIP
Mohegan Heights (Part of Yonkers)	10708
Mohegan Lake	10547
Mohonk Lake	12561
Moira	12957
Moira (Town)	12957
Mombaccus	12446
Mongaup	12780
Mongaup Valley	12762
Monroe	10950
Monroe (Town)	10950
Monsey	10952
Monsey Heights	10952
Montague (Town)	13367
Montario Point	13661
Montauk	11954
Montauk Beach	11954
Montclair Colony	11964
Montebello	10901
Monterey	14812
Monterey Estates	10989
Montezuma	13117
Montezuma (Town)	13117
Montgomery	12549
Montgomery (Town)	12549
Monticello	12701
Montour (Town)	14865
Montour Falls	14865
Montrose	10548
Montville	13118
Moody	12986
Mooers	12958
Mooers (Town)	12958
Mooers Forks	12959
Moores Mill	12569
Moorhouse Corner	12037
Moose River	13433
Moravia	13118
Moravia (Town)	13118
Moreau (Town)	12801
Morehouse (Town)	13324
Morehouseville	13324
Moreland	14812
Morey Park	12123
Morgan (Part of New York)	10001
Morgan Hill	12401
Morganville	14143
Moriah	12960
Moriah (Town)	12960
Moriah Center	12961
Moriches	11955
Morley	13617
Morningside (Part of New York)	10026
Morris	13808
Morris (Town)	13808
Morrisania (Part of New York)	10456
Morris Heights (Part of New York)	10453
Morrison Heights	12549
Morrisonville	12962
Morris Park (Part of New York)	10461
Morristown	13664
Morristown (Town)	13664
Morrisville	13408
Morrisville Station	13408
Morsston	12758
Morton (Monroe County)	14464
Morton (Orleans County)	14508
Mosherville	12074
Mosholu (Part of New York)	10467
Mosquito Point	12468
Mott Haven (Part of New York)	10454
Mottville	13119
Mountain Dale	12763
Mountain Lodge	10950
Mountain View (Franklin County)	12969
Mountain View (Rensselaer County)	12180
Mountain View East	10989
Mountainville	10953
Mount Carmel (Part of New York)	10458
Mount Eve	10924
Mount Hope	10940
Mount Hope (Town)	10940
Mount Hope (Part of Hastings-on-Hudson)	10706
Mount Ivy	10970
Mount Kisco	10549
Mount Kisco (Town)	10549
Mount Loretto (Part of New York)	10309
Mount Marion	12456

	ZIP
Mount McGregor Correctional Facility	12866
Mount Merion Park	12456
Mount Morris	14510
Mount Morris (Town)	14510
Mount Pleasant (Oswego County)	13069
Mount Pleasant (Ulster County)	12457
Mount Pleasant (Westchester County) (Town)	10591
Mount Prosper	12790
Mount Ross	12567
Mount Sinai	11766
Mount Tremper	12457
Mount Upton	13809
Mount Vernon	10550-53
For specific Mount Vernon Zip Codes call (914) 668-9699, or your local postmaster.	
Mount Vernon	14075
Mount View Acres	12184
Mount View Estates	12184
Mount Vision	13810
Mud Mills	14513
Muitzeskill	12156
Mumford	14511
Mungers Corners	13069
Municipal Building (Part of New York)	11201
Munnsville	13409
Munsey Park	11030
Munsons Corners	13045
Murdochs Crossing	14098
Murdock Woods	10583
Murray	14470
Murray (Town)	14470
Murray Hill (New York County)	10016
Murray Hill (Queens County)	11354
Murray Hill (Westchester County)	10583
Murray Isle	13624
Muttontown	11791
Myers	14882
Myers Corner	12590
Myers Grove	12739
Nanticoke	13802
Nanticoke (Town)	13803
Nanuet	10954
Nanuet Mall	10954
Napanoch	12458
Napeaque	11930
Naples	14512
Naples (Town)	14512
Napoli	14755
Napoli (Town)	14755
Narrowsburg	12764
Nashville	14062
Nassau	12123
Nassau (Town)	12123
Nassau Lake	12123
Nassau Mall	11756
Nassau Shores	11758
Natural Bridge	13665
Natural Dam	13642
Naumburg	13620
Nauraushaun	10965
Navarino	13108
Nazareth College of Rochester	14610
Nedrow	13120
Neiam (Part of New York)	11212
Nelliston	13410
Nelson	13035
Nelson (Town)	13035
Nelsonville	10516
Nepera Park (Part of Yonkers)	10710
Neponsit (Part of New York)	11694
Nepperhan (Part of Yonkers)	10703
Nesconset	11767
Neversink	12765
Neversink (Town)	12765
New Albion	14719
New Albion (Town)	14719
Newark	14513
Newark Valley	13811
Newark Valley (Town)	13811
New Baltimore	12124
New Baltimore (Town)	12124
New Berlin	13411
New Berlin (Town)	13411
New Berlin Junction	13733
New Bremen	13367
New Bremen (Town)	13367

* Area Zip Code   † Post Office Boxes

* Area Zip Code   † Post Office Boxes

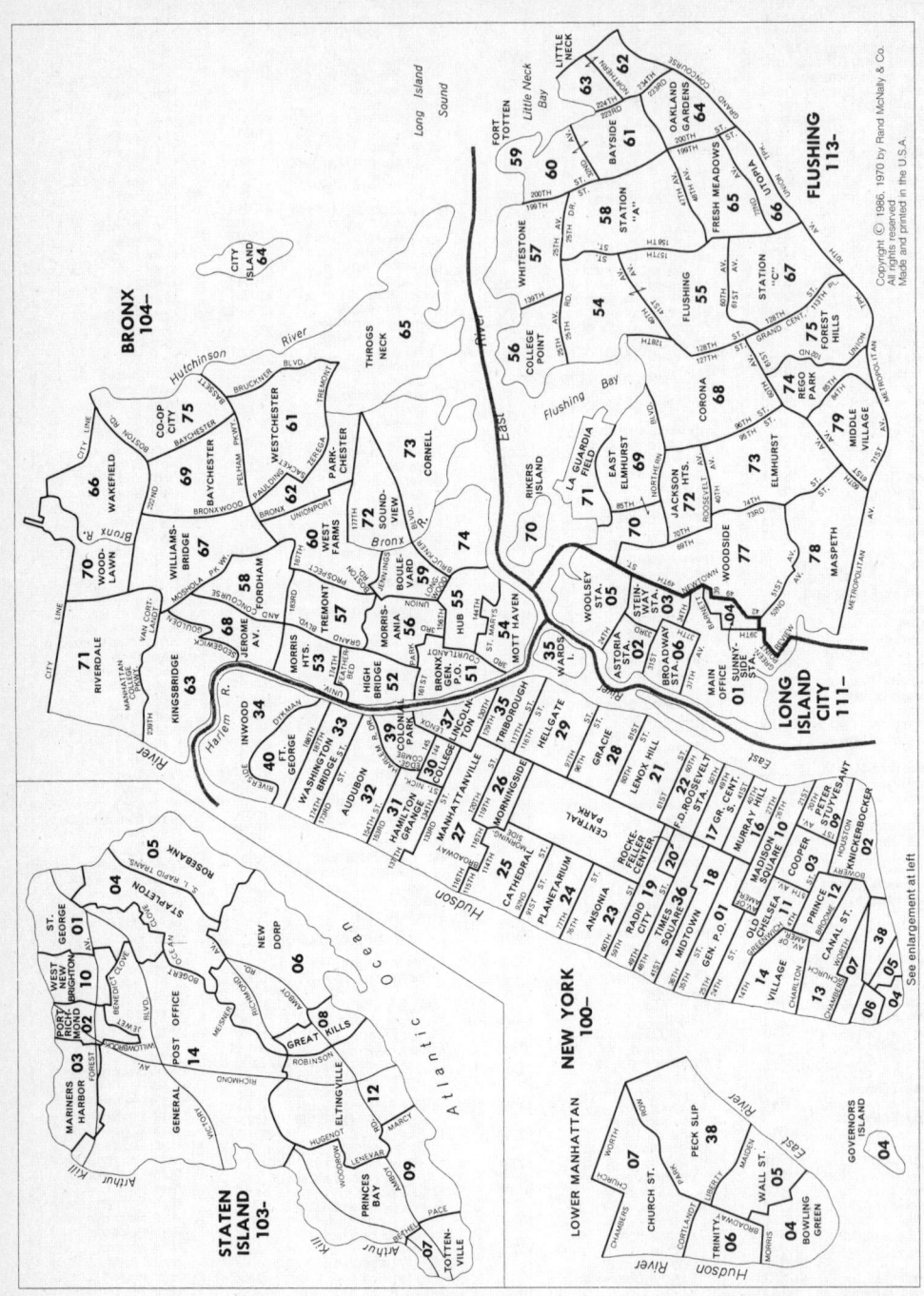

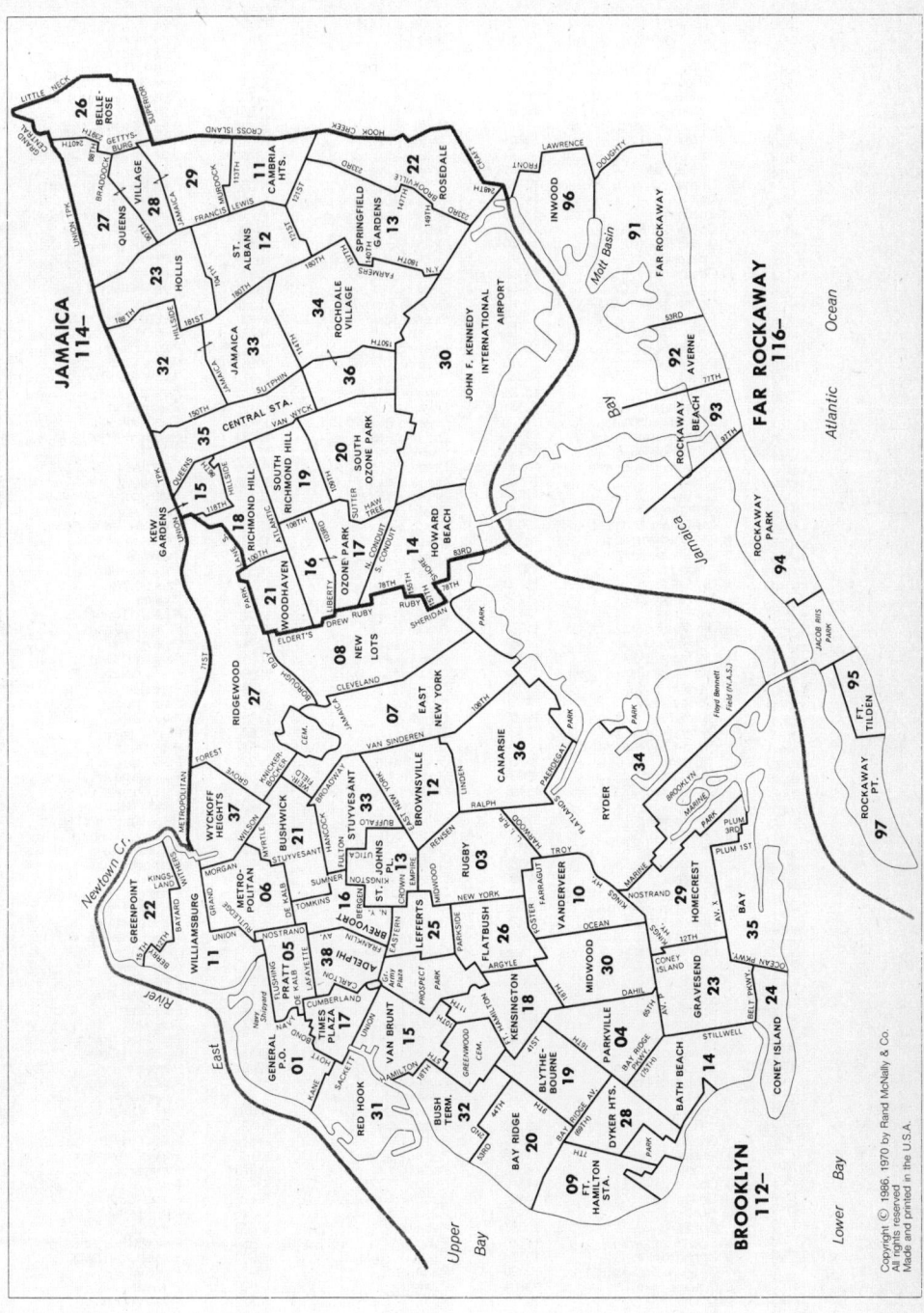

JAMAICA 114—

26 BELLE-ROSE
LITTLE NECK
GRAND CENTRAL PKWY
240TH
SUPERIOR
CROSS ISLAND
GETTYS-BURG
BRADDOCK
249TH
27 QUEENS VILLAGE
28 VILLAGE
29
HOOK CREEK
CAMBRIA HTS.
133TD
121ST
11
22 ROSEDALE
LAWRENCE
FRONT
DOUGHTY
FRANCIS LEWIS
JAMAICA
12 ST. ALBANS
 FARMERS
SPRINGFIELD GARDENS 13
23RD
140TH
MOORING
OWEGO
147TH
96 INWOOD
96
FAR ROCKAWAY
91
23 HOLLIS
FARMERS
191ST
34 ROCHDALE VILLAGE
180TH
MOTT
Basin
FAR ROCKAWAY 116—

184TH
188TH
HILLSIDE
181ST
32
33 JAMAICA
36
30 JOHN F. KENNEDY INTERNATIONAL AIRPORT
Bay
53RD
92 AVERNE
35 CENTRAL STA.
150TH
SUTPHIN
VAN WYCK
18 RICHMOND HILL
19 SOUTH RICHMOND HILL
20 SOUTH OZONE PARK
ROCKAWAY BEACH 93
77TH
88TH
FAR ROCKAWAY
77TH
15 KEW GARDENS
18
116TH
21 WOODHAVEN
16 OZONE PARK
17
SUTTER
HAW TREE
14 HOWARD BEACH
N. CONDUIT
83RD
ROCKAWAY PARK 94
Jamaica

27 RIDGEWOOD
CEM.
ELDERT'S
DREW RUBY
08 NEW LOTS
SHERIDAN
PARK
Floyd Bennett Field (N.A.S.)
JACOB RIIS PARK
95 FT. TILDEN

Atlantic Ocean

CLEVELAND
07 EAST NEW YORK
116TH
VAN SINDEREN
34 RYDER
BROOKLYN MARINE PARK
37 WYCKOFF HEIGHTS
FOREST
JAMAICA
CEM.
06
21 BUSHWICK
33 STUYVESANT
12 BROWNSVILLE
36 CANARSIE
FLATLANDS
PARK
ROCKAWAY PT. 97
PLUM 3RD

Newtown Cr.
22 GREENPOINT
METRO-POLITAN
11 WILLIAMSBURG
05 PRATT
38 ADELPHI
17 TIMES PLAZA
16 BREVOORT
25 LEFFERTS
13 ST. JOHNS PL.
03 RUGBY
26 FLATBUSH
10 VANDERVEER
29 HOMECREST
35 BAY
PLUM 1ST

01 GENERAL P.O.
31 RED HOOK
15 VAN BRUNT
32 BUSH TERM.
20 BAY RIDGE
19 BLYTHE-BOURNE
18 KENSINGTON
04 PARKVILLE
28 DYKER HTS.
30 MIDWOOD
23 GRAVESEND
14 BATH BEACH
24 CONEY ISLAND

East River
Upper Bay
09 FT. HAMILTON STA.

BROOKLYN 112—

Lower Bay

Place	ZIP
North Java	14113
North Jay	12941
North Kortright	13739
North Lansing	14852
North Lawrence	12967
North Lindenhurst	11757
North Litchfield	13340
North Lynbrook	11563
North Manlius	13082
North Massapequa	11758
North Merrick	11566
North New Hyde Park	11040
North Norwich	13814
North Norwich (Town)	13814
North Olean (Part of Olean)	14760
North Patchogue	11772
North Pembroke	14020
North Petersburg	12138
North Pharsalia	13844
North Pitcher	13124
North Pole	12946
Northport	11768
North River	12856
North Rockville Centre	11570
North Rose	14516
North Rush	14543
North Russell	13617
North Salem	10560
North Salem (Town)	10560
North Sanford	13754
North Sea	11968
North Selden	11784
North Settlement	12496
North Shore Beach	11778
North Side (Erie County)	14207
Northside (Steuben County)	14830
North Smithtown	11787
North Spencer	14883
North Stephentown	12168
North Stockholm	13668
North Syracuse	13212
North Tarrytown	10591
North Tonawanda	14120
Northtown Plaza	14226
Northumberland	12871
Northumberland (Town)	12871
North Valley Stream	11580
North Victory	13111
Northview Gardens	14094
Northville (Fulton County)	12134
Northville (Suffolk County)	11901
North Wantagh	11793
North Waverly	14892
Northway Mall, The	12205
Northway Plaza	12801
North Western	13486
Northwest Harbor	11937
Northwest Ithaca	14850
North White Plains	10603
North Wilmurt	13438
North Wilna	13608
North Winfield	13491
North Wolcott	14590
Northwood	12188
North Woodmere	11581
Norton Hill	12135
Norway	13416
Norway (Town)	13416
Norwich	13815
Norwich (Town)	13815
Norwich Corners	13456
Norwood	13668
Nostrand (Part of New York)	11235
Nottingham Estates	14094
Noxon	12603
Noyack	11963
Number Forty (Part of New York)	10001
Number Four	13367
Nunda	14517
Nunda (Town)	14517
Nyack	10960
Oak Beach	11702
Oakdale	11769
Oakdale Mall (Part of Johnson City)	13790
Oakfield	14125
Oakfield (Town)	14125
Oak Hill	12460
Oakland	14517
Oakland Gardens (Part of New York)	11364
Oak Orchard	14103
Oak Point (Bronx County)	10455
Oak Point (St. Lawrence County)	13646

Place	ZIP
Oak Ridge (Montgomery County)	12066
Oakridge (Onondaga County)	13088
Oaks Corners	14518
Oaksville	13337
Oakwood (Cayuga County)	13021
Oakwood (Richmond County)	10301
Oakwood Beach (Part of New York)	10301
Oakwood Heights (Part of New York)	10301
Oburnburg	12767
Obi	14715
Occanum	13865
Ocean Bay Park	11706
Ocean Beach	11770
Oceanside	11572
Odessa	14869
Ogden (Bronx County)	10452
Ogden (Monroe County) (Town)	14559
Ogden Center	14559
Ogdensburg	13669
O'Hara Corners	12083
Ohio	13324
Ohio (Town)	13324
Ohioville	12561
Oil Springs Indian Reservation	14081
Oil Springs Indian Reservation (Town)	14081
Olcott	14126
Old Bethpage	11804
Old Brookville	11545
Old Central Bridge	12035
Old Chatham	12136
Old Chelsa (Part of New York)	10011
Old Field	11733
Old Field South	11790
Old Forge	13420
Old Mastic	11951
Old Orchard Point	14487
Old Stony Brook	11790
Old Village (Part of Great Neck)	11023
Old Westbury	11568
Olean	14760
Olean (Town)	14760
Olean Center Mall (Part of Olean)	14760
Olive (Town)	12461
Olivebridge	12461
Oliverea	12410
Olmstedville	12857
Omar	13607
Omi	12075
Onativia	13084
Onchiota	12989
One Hundred Thirty Eight (Part of New York)	10001
Oneida	13421
Oneida Castle	13421
Oneida Correctional Facility	13440
Oneonta	13820
Oneonta (Town)	13861
Onesquethaw	12067
Oniontown	12522
Onleys Station	10940
Onondaga	13215
Onondaga (Town)	13215
Onondaga Indian Reservation	13120
Onondaga Indian Reservation (Town)	13120
Ontario	14519
Ontario (Town)	14519
Ontario Center	14520
Ontario on the Lake	14519
Onteo Beach	14464
Onteora Park	12485
Oot Park	13057
Open Meadows	14710
Oppenheim	13329
Oppenheim (Town)	13329
Oquaga Lake	13754
Oramel	14711
Oran	13125
Orange (Town)	14812
Orangeburg	10962
Orange Lake	12550
Orangeport	14067
Orangetown (Town)	10960
Orangeville (Town)	14569
Orangeville Center	14011
Orangeville Corners	14167

Place	ZIP
Orchard Knoll	14845
Orchard Park	14127
Orchard Park (Town)	14127
Orchard Village	13031
Oregon	11952
Orient	11957
Orienta (Part of Mamaroneck)	10543
Oriental Park	14712
Orient Point	11957
Oriskany	13424
Oriskany Falls	13425
Orlando	14755
Orleans (Jefferson County) (Town)	13656
Orleans (Ontario County)	14432
Orleans Four Corners	13656
Orwell	13426
Orwell (Town)	13426
Oscawana Corners	10579
Oscawana Lake	10579
Osceola	13316
Osceola (Town)	13316
Ossian (Town)	14437
Ossian Center	14437
Ossining	10562
Ossining (Town)	10562
Oswegatchie	13670
Oswegatchie (Town)	13654
Oswego	13126
Oswego (Town)	13126
Oswego Bitter	13031
Oswego Center	13126
Otego	13825
Otego (Town)	13825
Otisco	13159
Otisco (Town)	13159
Otisco Valley	13110
Otisville	10963
Otisville Correctional Facility	10963
Otsego (Town)	13337
Otselic	13072
Otselic (Town)	13072
Otselic Center	13072
Otter Creek	13343
Otter Lake	13338
Ott Meadows	13088
Otto	14766
Otto (Town)	14766
Ouaquaga	13826
Overlook	12822
Ovid	14521
Ovid (Town)	14521
Ovid Center	14847
Ovington (Part of New York)	11220
Owasco	13130
Owasco (Town)	13130
Owego	13827
Owego (Town)	13827
Owens Mills	14825
Owls Head	12969
Oxbow	13671
Oxford (Chenaugo County)	13830
Oxford (Chenaugo County) (Town)	13830
Oxford (Orange County)	10918
Oyster Bay	11771
Oyster Bay (Town)	11771
Oyster Bay Cove	11771
Ozone Park (Part of New York)	11416
Pacama	12401
Pace University Pleasantville-Briarcliff Campus	10570
Paddlefords	14424
Paddy Hill	13615
Paines Hollow	13407
Painted Post	14870
Palatine (Town)	13428
Palatine Bridge	13428
Palentown	12446
Palenville	12463
Palermo	13069
Palermo (Town)	13069
Palisades	10964
Palmyra	14522
Palmyra (Town)	14522
Pamelia (Town)	13637
Pamelia	13637
Panama	14767
Panorama	14625
Panther Lake	13028
Pantigo	11937
Paradise Hill	12051
Paradox	12858
Parcells Corner	14062

Place	ZIP
Paris	13429
Paris (Town)	13429
Parish	13131
Parish (Town)	13131
Parishville	13672
Parishville (Town)	13672
Parishville Center	13676
Paris Station	13456
Parkchester (Part of New York)	10462
Park Hill (Onondaga County)	13057
Park Hill (Westchester County)	10705
Parkside (Part of New York)	11375
Park Slope (Part of New York)	11215
Parkston	12758
Parksville	12768
Park Terrace	13903
Parkville (Part of New York)	11204
Parkway (Part of New York)	10462
Parma	14468
Parma Center	14468
Parma Corners	14559
Parson Farms	13031
Pastime Park	14456
Pataukunk	12446
Patchin (Part of New York)	10011
Patchinville	14572
Patchogue	11772
Patchogue Highlands	11772
Patria	12187
Patroon (Part of Albany)	12204
Patterson	12563
Patterson (Town)	12563
Pattersonville	12137
Paul Smiths	12970
Pavilion	14525
Pavilion (Town)	14525
Pavilion Center	14525
Pawling	12564
Pawling (Town)	12564
Payne Beach	14468
Peabrook	12760
Peach Lake	10509
Peakville	13756
Pearl Creek	14591
Pearl River	10965
Peas Eddy	13783
Peasleeville	12985
Peat Corners	13036
Pebble Beach	14480
Peck Slip (Part of New York)	10038
Peconic	11958
Peekskill	10566
Pekin	14132
Pelham	10803
Pelham (Town)	10803
Pelham Manor	10803
Pelham Parkway (Part of New York)	10462
Pellets Island	10958
Pembroke	14036
Pembroke (Town)	14036
Penataquit	11706
Pendleton	14094
Pendleton (Town)	14094
Pendleton Center	14094
Penfield	14526
Penfield (Town)	14526
Pennellville	13132
Penn Yan	14527
Peoria	14525
Perch River	13601
Perinton (Town)	14450
Perkinsville	14529
Perry	14530
Perry (Town)	14530
Perry Center	14530
Perry City	14886
Perrysburg	14129
Perrysburg (Town)	14129
Perrys Mills	12919
Perryville	13133
Persia (Town)	14070
Perth	12010
Perth (Town)	12010
Peru (Clinton County) (Town)	12972
Peru (Clinton County)	12972
Peru (Onondaga County)	13112
Peruville	13073
Peterboro	13134
Petersburg	12138

	ZIP		ZIP		ZIP		ZIP
Petersburg (Town)	12138	Plainview Shopping		Port Kent	12975	Queens Village (Part of	
Peter Stuyvesant (Part of		Center	11803	Portland	14769	New York)	11428
New York)	10009	Plainville	13137	Portland (Town)	14769	Quigley Park	14710
Peth	14741	Plandome	11030	Portlandville	13834	Quinneville	13746
Petries Corners	13367	Plandome Heights	11030	Port Leyden	13433	Quioque	11978
Petrolia	14895	Plandome Manor	11030	Port Richmond (Part of		Quogue	11959
Pharsalia (Town)	13758	Planetarium (Part of New		New York)	10302	Raceville	05764
Phelps	14532	York)	10024	Portville	14770	Radio City (Part of New	
Phelps (Town)	14532	Plato	14171	Portville (Town)	14770	York)	10019
Philadelphia	13673	Platte Clove	12427	Port Washington	11050	Radison	13027
Philadelphia (Town)	13673	Plattekill	12568	Port Washington North	11050	Rainbow Lake	12976
Philipse Manor (Part of		Plattekill (Town)	12568	Post Corners	12057	Ralmar Park	12302
North Tarrytown)	10591	Platten	14098	Post Creek	14812	Ramapo	10931
Philipstown (Town)	10516	Plattsburgh	12901	Potsdam	13676	Ramapo (Town)	10931
Phillipsburg	10940	Plattsburgh (Town)	12918	Potsdam (Town)	13676	Ram Island	11964
Phillips Creek	14813	Plattsburgh Air Force		Potter	14527	Rampasture	11946
Phillips Mills	14712	Base	12903	Potter (Town)	14527	Randall	12072
Phillipsport	12769	Plattsburgh West	12962	Potter Hollow	12469	Randallsville	13346
Philmont	12565	Plaza (Part of New York)	11101	Pottersville	12860	Randolph	14772
Phoenicia	12464	Pleasantbrook	13320	Poughkeepsie	12601-03	Randolph (Town)	14772
Phoenix	13135	Pleasantdale	12182	For specific Poughkeepsie Zip		Ransomville	14131
Phoenix Mills	13326	Pleasant Plains (Dutchess		Codes call (914) 452-3421, or		Rapids	14094
Picketts Corners	12981	County)	12580	your local postmaster.		Raquette Lake	13436
Pickettsville	13672	Pleasant Plains (Richmond		Poughkeepsie (Town)	12602	Rathbone	14801
Piercefield	12973	County)	10309	Poughquag	12570	Rathbone (Town)	14801
Piercefield (Town)	12973	Pleasant Point	13126	Pound Ridge	10576	Ravena	12143
Pierces Corner	13642	Pleasantside	10566	Pound Ridge (Town)	10576	Ravenwood (Part of	
Pierceville	13334	Pleasant Valley	12569	Pratt (Part of New York)	11205	Colonie)	12205
Piermont	10968	Pleasant Valley (Town)	12569	Pratt Corners	13087	Rawson	14727
Pierrepont	13617	Pleasant Valley (Oneida		Prattsburg (Town)	14873	Ray Brook	12977
Pierrepont (Town)	13617	County)	13480	Prattsburgh	14873	Raymertown	12180
Pierrepont Manor	13674	Pleasant Valley (Steuben		Pratts Hollow	13434	Raymondville	13678
Pierstown	13326	County)	14810	Prattsville	12468	Rayville	12136
Piffard	14533	Pleasantville	10570-72	Prattsville (Town)	12468	Reading (Town)	14876
Pike	14130	For specific Pleasantville Zip		Preble	13141	Reading Center	14876
Pike (Town)	14130	Codes call (914) 769-1517, or		Preble (Town)	13141	Reber	12996
Pike Five Corners	14024	your local postmaster.		Prendergast Point	14757	Red Creek (Suffolk	
Pilgrim (Part of New York)	10461	Plessis	13675	Presho	14858	County)	11946
Pilgrim Corners (Part of		Plymouth	13832	Preston	13830	Red Creek (Wayne	
Middletown)	10940	Plymouth (Town)	13832	Preston (Town)	13830	County)	13143
Pilgrimport	14489	Pocantico Hills	10591	Preston Hollow	12469	Redfalls	12468
Pillar Point	13634	Poestenkill	12140	Prince (Part of New York)	10012	Redfield	13437
Pilot Knob	12844	Poestenkill (Town)	12140	Princes Bay (Part of New		Redfield (Town)	13437
Pinckney (Town)	13626	Point Au Rouche	12901	York)	10309	Redford	12978
Pindars Corners	13860	Point Breeze	14477	Princetown	12056	Red Hook	12571
Pine (Part of Albany)	12203	Point Chautauqua	14728	Princetown (Town)	12056	Red Hook (Town)	12571
Pine Aire	11706	Point Lookout	11569	Progress	12078	Red Hook (Part of New	
Pinebrook (Part of New		Point O'Woods	11706	Prospect	13435	York)	11231
Rochelle)	10804	Point Peninsula	13693	Prospect Heights	12144	Red House (Town)	14779
Pinebrook Heights (Part of		Point Pleasant	14622	Prospect Hill	12188	Red Mills (Columbia	
New Rochelle)	10804	Point Rochester	14512	Prospect Park West (Part		County)	12513
Pine Bush	12566	Point Rock	13471	of New York)	11215	Red Mills (St. Lawrence	
Pine City	14871	Point Stockholm	14742	Providence (Town)	12850	County)	13669
Pine Grove (Lewis		Point Vivian	13607	Pulaski	13142	Red Oaks Mill	12603
County)	13343	Poland (Chautauqua		Pulteney	14874	Red Rock (Columbia	
Pine Grove (Schoharie		County) (Town)	14747	Pulteney (Town)	14874	County)	12060
County)	12122	Poland (Herkimer County)	13431	Pultneyville	14538	Red Rock (Onondaga	
Pinegrove Park	12205	Poland Center	14747	Pulvers	12075	County)	13027
Pine Hill (Erie County)	14225	Polkville	13101	Pulvers Corners	12567	Redwood (Jefferson	
Pine Hill (Oneida County)	13471	Pomfret (Town)	14063	Pumpkin Hill	14422	County)	13679
Pine Hill (Ulster County)	12465	Pomona	10970	Pumpkin Hollow	12529	Redwood (Suffolk County)	11963
Pinehill Estates	12303	Pomona Heights (Part of		Purchase (Part of		Reeds Corner	14437
Pinehurst	14085	Pomona)	10901	Harrison)	10577	Reeds Corners	14437
Pine Island	10969	Pomonok (Part of New		Purdys	10578	Reeves Park	11901
Pine Knolls	13760	York)	11365	Purdys Mills	12910	Rego Park (Part of New	
Pine Lake	12032	Pompey	13138	Purling	12470	York)	11374
Pine Meadows	13302	Pompey (Town)	13138	Putnam (Town)	12861	Reidsville	12186
Pine Neck	11963	Pompey Center	13104	Putnam Lake	10509	Remsen	13438
Pine Plains	12567	Ponck Hockie (Part of		Putnam Station	12861	Remsen (Town)	13438
Pine Plains (Town)	12567	Kingston)	12401	Putnam Valley	10579	Remsenburg	11960
Pine Ridge	12203	Pond Eddy	12770	Putnam Valley (Town)	10579	Remsenburg-Speonk	11960
Pine Ridge Estates	10573	Ponquogue	11946	Pyramid Mall Ithaca (Part		Rensselaer	12144
Pine Valley (Chemung		Poolville	13432	of Lansing)	14850	Rensselaer Falls	13680
County)	14872	Poospatuck Indian		Pyrites	13677	Rensselaerville	12147
Pine Valley (Suffolk		Reservation (Town)	11950	Quackenbush Hill	14830	Rensselaerville (Town)	12147
County)	11901	Poospatuck Indian		Quackenkill	12052	Residence Park (Part of	
Pineville (Delaware		Reservation	11950	Quail (Part of Albany)	12206	New Rochelle)	10805
County)	13856	Pope Mills	13654	Quaker Basin	13052	Retsof	14539
Pineville (Oswego County)	13302	Poplar Beach	14541	Quaker Hill	12564	Rexford	12148
Pinewood Estates	12303	Poplar Ridge	13139	Quaker Ridge (Part of		Rexville	14877
Pine Woods	13310	Poquott	11733	New Rochelle)	10801	Reydon Shores	11971
Pioneer	12020	Portage	14846	Quaker Springs	12871	Reynoldsville	14818
Piseco	12139	Portage (Town)	14846	Quaker Street	12141	Rheims	14840
Pitcairn	13648	Portageville	14536	Quarry Heights	10603	Rhinebeck	12572
Pitcairn (Town)	13648	Port Authority (Part of		Quarryville	12477	Rhinebeck (Town)	12572
Pitcher	13136	New York)	10011	Queechy	12029	Rhinecliff	12574
Pitcher (Town)	13136	Port Byron	13140	Queens	11001-06	Ricard	13302
Pitcher Hill	13212	Port Chester	10573		11101-06	Rice Grove	13110
Pitt (Part of New York)	10002	Port Crane	13833		11301-86	Riceville (Cattaraugus	
Pittsfield	13411	Port Dickinson	13901		11401-36	County)	14171
Pittsfield (Town)	13411	Porter (Town)	14131		11601-97	Riceville (Fulton County)	12078
Pittsford	14534	Porter Center	14131	For specific Queens Zip Codes		Riceville Station	14171
Pittsford (Town)	14534	Porter Corners	12859	call (718) 321-5000, or your		Richburg	14774
Pittstown	12094	Porterville	14052	local postmaster.		Richfield	13439
Pittstown (Town)	12094	Port Ewen	12466	Queensbridge (Part of		Richfield (Town)	13439
Place Corners	12431	Port Gibson	14537	New York)	11101	Richfield Springs	13439
Plainedge	11714	Port Henry	12974	Queensbury	12801	Richford	13835
Plainfield (Town)	13491	Port Jefferson	11777	Queensbury (Town)	12801	Richford (Town)	13835
Plainfield Center	13491	Port Jefferson Station	11776	Queen's Center (Part of		Richland	13144
Plainview	11803	Port Jervis	12771	New York)	11373	Richland (Town)	13144

	ZIP
Richmond	10301-14
For specific Richmond Zip Codes call (718) 816-2700, or your local postmaster.	
Richmond (Town)	14471
Richmond Hill (Part of New York)	11418
Richmond Valley (Part of New York)	10307
Richmondville	12149
Richmondville (Town)	12149
Richs Corners	14411
Richville	13681
Riders Mills	12024
Ridge (Livingston County)	14510
Ridge (Suffolk County)	11961
Ridgebury	10973
Ridgelea Heights	14094
Ridge Mills (Part of Rome)	13440
Ridgemont Plaza	14626
Ridgeway	14103
Ridgeway (Town)	14103
Ridgeway (Part of White Plains)	10601
Ridgewood (Niagara County)	14094
Ridgewood (Oneida County)	13501
Ridgewood (Queens County)	11385
Rifton	12471
Riga (Town)	14428
Rigney Bluff	14612
Riley Cove	12020
Ringdahl Court (Part of Rome)	13440
Rio	12780
Riparius	12862
Ripley	14775
Ripley (Town)	14775
Rippleton	13035
Risingville	14820
River (Part of Rochester)	14627
Riverdale (Part of New York)	10471
Riverhead	11901
Riverhead (Town)	11901
Riverside (Broome County)	13795
Riverside (Erie County)	14207
Riverside (Otsego County)	13838
Riverside (Saratoga County)	12118
Riverside (Steuben County)	14830
Riverside (Suffolk County)	11901
Riverside Estates	11901
Riverside Mall (Part of Utica)	13502
Riverside Manors	14172
Riverside Park	12401
Riverview	12981
Riverview Correctional Facility	13669
Roanoke	14143
Robbins Rest	11770
Roberts Corner	13650
Rochdale	12603
Rochdale Village (Part of New York)	11434
Rochelle Heights (Part of New Rochelle)	10801
Rochelle Park (Part of New Rochelle)	10801
Rochester	14601-92
For specific Rochester Zip Codes call (716) 272-8090, or your local postmaster.	
Rochester (Town)	12404
Rockaway Beach (Part of New York)	11693
Rockaway Park (Part of New York)	11694
Rockaway Point (Part of New York)	11697
Rock City (Cattaraugus County)	14760
Rock City (Dutchess County)	12571
Rock City Falls	12863
Rock Cut	13078
Rockdale	13809
Rockefeller Center (Part of New York)	10020
Rock Glen	14550
Rock Hill	12775
Rockhurst	12801
Rockland	12776
Rockland (Rockland County)	10962

	ZIP
Rockland (Sullivan County)	12776
Rockland Lake	10989
Rockland Psychiatric Center	10962
Rock Stream	14878
Rock Tavern	12575
Rockton	12010
Rock Valley	12760
Rockville (Allegany County)	14711
Rockville (Orange County)	10940
Rockville Centre	11570*
	11571†
Rockville Lake	14711
Rockwells Mills	13843
Rockwood	12095
Rocky Point (Clinton County)	12901
Rocky Point (Suffolk County)	11778
Rodman	13682
Rodman (Town)	13682
Roe Park	10566
Roesslevile	12205
Rolling Acres	14559
Rolling Hills (Monroe County)	14450
Rolling Hills (Nassau County)	11507
Rolling Meadows	12401
Romanoff	10512
Rombout Ridge	12603
Rome	13440†
	13442*
Romulus	14541
Romulus (Town)	14541
Rondaxe	13420
Rondout (Part of Kingston)	12401
Ronkonkoma	11779
Ronkonkoma West	11779
Roosa Gap	12721
Roosevelt	11575
Roosevelt Beach	14172
Roosevelt Field (Part of Garden City)	11530
Rooseveltown	13683
Root (Town)	12166
Roscoe	12776
Rose	14542
Rose (Town)	14542
Rosebank (Part of New York)	10305
Roseboom	13450
Roseboom (Town)	13450
Rosecrans Park	12123
Rosedale (Part of New York)	11422
Rose Grove	11968
Rose Hill	13110
Rosemont Park (Part of Rensselaer)	12144
Rosendale	12472
Rosendale (Town)	12472
Roseton	12550
Rosiere	13618
Roslyn	11576
Roslyn Estates	11576
Roslyn Harbor	11576
Roslyn Heights	11577
Rossburg	14776
Ross Corners	13850
Rossie	13646
Rossie (Town)	13646
Rossman	12173
Ross Mill	14733
Rosstown	14871
Rossville (Part of New York)	10309
Rotterdam	12303
Rotterdam (Town)	12303
Rotterdam Junction	12150
Rotterdam Square Mall (Part of Schenectady)	12306
Round Lake	12151
Roundout Harbor	12466
Round Top	12473
Rouses Point	12979
Roxbury	12474
Roxbury (Town)	12474
Roxbury (Part of New York)	11697
Royalton	14067
Royalton (Town)	14067
Ruby	12475
Ruby Corner	13646
Rugby (Part of New York)	11203
Rumsey Ridge	14092
Rural Grove	12166

	ZIP
Rural Hill	13650
Rush	14543
Rush (Town)	14543
Rushford	14777
Rushford (Town)	14777
Rushford Lake	14717
Rushville	14544
Russell	13684
Russell (Town)	13684
Russell Gardens	11021
Russia	13431
Russia (Town)	13431
Rutland (Town)	13638
Rutland Center	13601
Ryder (Part of New York)	11234
Rye	10580
Rye (Town)	10573
Rye Brook	10573
Rye Hills	10573
Sabael	12864
Sabattis	12847
Sabbath Day Point	12874
Sacandaga	12134
Sackets Harbor	13685
Sacketts Lake	12701
Saddle Rock	11023
Saddle Rock Estates	11021
Sagaponack	11962
Sages Cottages	11944
Sagetown	14871
Sag Harbor	11963
Sailors Snug Harbor (Part of New York)	10301
St. Albans (Part of New York)	11412
St. Andrew	12586
St. Armand (Town)	12913
St. Bonaventure	14778
St. George (Part of New York)	10301
St. Huberts	12943
St. James	11780
St. James Heights	11780
St. John Fisher College	14618
St. Johnsburg	14302
St. Johns Place (Part of New York)	11213
St. Johnsville	13452
St. Johnsville (Town)	13452
St. Josephs	12701
St. Lawrence Park	13607
St. Mary's Park (Part of New York)	10455
St. Regis Falls	12980
St. Regis Indian Reservation	13655
St. Regis Indian Reservation (Town)	13655
St. Remy	12401
Saintsville	13116
Salamanca	14779
Salamanca (Town)	14779
Salem	12865
Salem (Town)	12865
Salem Center	10578
Salina (Town)	13088
Salina	13208
Salisbury	13365
Salisbury (Town)	13365
Salisbury	11801
Salisbury Center	13454
Salisbury Mills	12577
Salmon River	12901
Saltaire	11706
Salt Point	12578
Salt Springville	13320
Sammonsville	12095
Samsondale (Part of West Haverstraw)	10993
Samsonville	12481
Sanborn	14132
Sandford Boulevard (Part of Mount Vernon)	10550
Sandfordville	13676
Sand Hill (Erie County)	14001
Sand Hill (Montgomery County)	13339
Sand Lake	12153
Sand Lake (Town)	12153
Sand Ridge	13132
Sands Point	11050
Sandusky	14133
Sandy Beach	14072
Sandy Creek	13145
Sandy Creek (Town)	13145
Sandy Harbour Beach	14464
Sanford (Town)	13754
Sangerfield	13455
Sangerfield (Town)	13455
Sanitaria Springs	13833

	ZIP
San Remo	11754
Santa Clara	12980
Santa Clara (Town)	12980
Santapoque	11707
Saranac	12981
Saranac (Town)	12981
Saranac Inn	12982
Saranac Lake	12982-83
For specific Saranac Lake Zip Codes call (518) 891-4390, or your local postmaster.	
Saratoga (Town)	12871
Saratoga Springs	12866
Sardinia	14134
Sardinia (Town)	14134
Saugerties	12477
Saugerties (Town)	12477
Saugerties South	12477
Sauquoit	13456
Savannah	13146
Savannah (Town)	13146
Savona	14879
Sawkill	12401
Sawyers Corners	13021
Saxon Park	11706
Sayville	11782
Scarborough (Part of Briarcliff Manor)	10510
Scarsdale	10583
Scarsdale (Town)	10583
Schaghticoke	12154
Schaghticoke (Town)	12154
Schaghticoke Hill	12154
Schenectady	12301-08
For specific Schenectady Zip Codes call (518) 395-5400, or your local postmaster.	
Schenevus	12155
Schermerhorn Corners	14747
Schodack (Town)	12033
Schodack Center	12033
Schodack Landing	12156
Schoharie	12157
Schoharie (Town)	12157
Schonowe	12306
Schroeppel (Town)	13135
Schroon (Town)	12870
Schroon Lake	12870
Schultzville	12572
Schuluski Estates	12188
Schuyler (Town)	13340
Schuyler Falls	12985
Schuyler Falls (Town)	12985
Schuyler Lake	13457
Schuylerville	12871
Scio	14880
Scio (Town)	14880
Sciota	12992
Scipio (Town)	13147
Scipio Center	13147
Scipioville	13147
Sconondoa	13421
Scotchbush (Fulton County)	13452
Scotch Bush (Montgomery County)	12010
Scotchtown	10940
Scotia	12302
Scott	13077
Scott (Town)	13077
Scottsburg	14545
Scottsville	14546
Scranton	14075
Scriba (Town)	13126
Scriba Center	13126
Sea Breeze	14617
Sea Cliff	11579
Seaford	11783
Seager	12406
Searingtown	11507
Searsburg	14886
Sears Corners	10509
Searsville	12549
Seaview	11770
Second Milo	14527
Seeley Creek	14871
Selden	11784
Selkirk	12158
Selkirk Beach	13142
Sellecks Corners	13625
Sempronius	13118
Sempronius (Town)	13118
Seneca	14561
Seneca Army Depot	14541
Seneca Castle	14547
Seneca Falls	13148
Seneca Falls (Town)	13148
Seneca Hill	13126
Seneca Knolls	13209
Seneca Mall (Erie County)	14224

* **Area Zip Code** † **Post Office Boxes**

	ZIP		ZIP		ZIP		ZIP
Seneca Mall (Onondaga County)	13088	Silver Lake Village	10940	South Bethlehem	12161	South Setauket	11733
Seneca Point	14512	Silver Springs	14550	South Bloomfield	14469	South Shore Mall	11706
Sennett	13021	Simmons Island (Part of Cohoes)	12047	South Bolivar	14715	South Side (Chemung County)	14904
Sennett (Town)	13021	Simpsonville	12155	South Bombay	12957	South Side (Erie County)	14220
Sentinel Heights	13078	Sinclairville	14782	South Bradford	14879	South Sodus	14489
Setauket	11733	Sissonville	13676	South Bristol	14512	South St. Johnsville	13339
Setauket-East Setauket	11733	Skaneateles	13152	South Bristol (Town)	14512	South Stockton	14782
Settlers Hill	10509	Skaneateles (Town)	13152	South Brookfield	13485	South Stony Brook	11790
Seven Hills	10512	Skaneateles Falls	13153	South Buffalo (Part of Buffalo)	14210	South Trenton	13304
Seventh Day Hollow	13072	Skaneateles Junction	13060	South Butler	13154	South Utica (Part of Utica)	13501
Severance	12872	Skerry	12966	South Byron	14557	South Valley (Cattaraugus County) (Town)	14779
Seward	12043	Skinnerville	13697	South Cairo	12482	South Valley (Otsego County)	13320
Seward (Town)	12043	Sky Meadow Farms	10573	South Cambridge	12028	South Valley Stream	11581
Shackport	13757	Slab City (Cortland County)	13141	South Canisteo	14823	South Vandalia	14706
Shadigee	14098	Slab City (St. Lawrence County)	13676	South Centereach	11720	South Vestal	13850
Shady	12409	Slate Hill	10973	South Chili	14546	Southview (Part of Binghamton)	13903
Shandaken	12480	Slaterville Springs	14881	South Colton	13687	South Wales	14139
Shandaken (Town)	12480	Sleightsburg	12401	South Columbia	13439	South Warsaw	14569
Shandelee	12758	Slingerlands	12159	South Corinth	12822	South Westbury	11590
Sharon	13459	Sloan	14225	South Corning	14830	South Westerlo	12163
Sharon (Town)	13459	Sloansville	12160	South Cortland	13045	Southwest Oswego	13126
Sharon Springs	13459	Sloatsburg	10974	South Danby	13864	Southwood	13078
Shawangunk (Town)	12589	Slyboro	12832	South Dansville	14807	South Worcester	12197
Shawnee	14132	Smallwood	12778	South Dayton	14138	Spackenkill	12603
Sheds	13122	Smartville	13083	South Dover	12522	Spafford	13077
Shekomeko	12546	Smithboro	13840	South Durham	12405	Spafford (Town)	13077
Shelby	14103	Smith Corners	13407	Southeast (Town)	10509	Sparkill	10976
Shelby (Town)	14103	Smithfield (Dutchess County)	12501	Southeast Owasco	13118	Sparkle Lake	10598
Shelby Basin	14103	Smithfield (Madison County) (Town)	13134	South Edmeston	13466	Sparrow Bush	12780
Shelby Center	14103	Smith Haven Mall (Part of Lake Grove)	11755	South Edwards	13635	Sparta (Livingston County) (Town)	14437
Sheldon	14145	Smiths Basin	12827	South Fallsburg	12779	Sparta (Westchester County)	10562
Sheldon (Town)	14145	Smiths Corner	12120	South Farmingdale	11735	Spawn Hollow	12161
Sheldrake	14521	Smiths Mills	14062	Southfields	10975	Speculator	12164
Sheldrake Springs	14847	Smithtown (Town)	11787	South Floral Park	11001	Speedsville	13736
Shelter Island	11964	Smithtown (Part of Village of the Branch)	11787	South Flushing (Part of New York)	11365	Speigletown	12182
Shelter Island (Town)	11964	Smithtown	11787	Southgate Plaza	14224	Spencer	14883
Shelter Island Heights	11965	Smithtown Branch	11787	Southgate Shopping Center (Part of Massapequa Park)	11762	Spencer (Town)	14883
Shenandoah	12533	Smithtown Pines	11787	South Gilboa	12167	Spencerport	14559
Shenorock	10587	Smithtown Shopping Center	11787	South Glens Falls	12803	Spencer Settlement	13440
Sherburne	13460	Smith Valley	14805	South Granville	12832	Spencertown	12165
Sherburne (Town)	13460	Smithville (Chenango County) (Town)	13778	South Greece	14626	Speonk	11972
Sheridan	14135	Smithville (Jefferson County)	13605	South Hamilton	13332	Split Rock	13031
Sheridan (Town)	14135	Smithville Center	13778	South Hannibal	13074	Spragueville	13642
Sheridan Park (Part of Geneva)	14456	Smithville Flats	13841	South Hartford (Otsego County)	13810	Sprakers	12166
Sherman	14781	Smyrna	13464	South Hartford (Washington County)	12838	Spring Brook	14140
Sherman (Town)	14781	Smyrna (Town)	13464	South Haven	11719	Spring Creek (Part of New York)	11239
Sherman Park	10594	Snooks Corners	12010	South Hempstead	11550	Springfield (Town)	13468
Shermerhorn Landing	13646	Snufftown	10924	South Highland	10524	Springfield Center	13468
Sherrill	13461	Snyder	14226	South Hill	14850	Springfield Gardens (Part of New York)	11413
Sherwood Forest	12065	Snyder Crossing	13116	South Holbrook	11741	Spring Glen	12483
Sherwood Knolls	13031	Snyders Corners	12180	South Horicon	12815	Spring Lake	13140
Sherwood Park	12144	Snyders Lake	12180	South Hornell	14843	Spring Mills	14897
Shinhopple	13755	Sodom (Putnam County)	10509	South Huntington	11746	Springport (Town)	13160
Shinnecock Hills	11946	Sodom (Warren County)	12853	South Ilion	13357	Springs	11937
Shinnecock Indian Reservation (Town)	11968	Sodus	14551	South Jamesport	11970	Springtown	12561
Shinnecock Indian Reservation	11968	Sodus (Town)	14551	South Jefferson	12167	Springvale	13815
Shirewood	12065	Sodus Center	14554	South Jewett	12442	Spring Valley (Rockland County)	10977
Shirley	11967	Sodus Point	14555	South Kortright	13842	Spring Valley (Westchester County)	10562
Shokan	12481	Solon	13055	South Lake	10512	Springville (Erie County)	14141
Sholam	12458	Solon (Town)	13055	South Lebanon	13332	Springville (Suffolk County)	11946
Shongo	16923	Solsville	13465	South Lima	14558	Springwater	14560
Shooktown (Part of Lockport)	14094	Solvay	13209	South Livonia	14487	Springwater (Town)	14560
Shoppingtown Mall	13214	Solvay	13209	South Lockport	14094	Springwood Village	12538
Shore Acres (Chautauqua County)	14712	Somers	10589	South Millbrook	12545	Sprout Brook	13317
Shore Acres (Monroe County)	14468	Somers (Town)	10589	South New Berlin	13843	Spruceton	12492
Shore Acres (Suffolk County)	11952	Somerset	14012	South Newstead	14001	Spuyten Duyvil (Part of New York)	10463
Shore Acres (Westchester County)	10543	Somerset (Town)	14012	South Nineveh	13787	Squiretown	11946
Shoreham	11786	Somerset Lake	13783	South Nyack	10960	Staatsburg	12580
Shore Haven	14787	Somerville	13642	Southold	11971	Stacy Basin	13054
Shorelands	14728	Sonora	14879	Southold (Town)	11971	Stadium (Part of New York)	10452
Shore Oaks	13126	Sonyea	14556	South Olean (Part of Olean)	14760	Stafford	14143
Shorewood	11721	Sound Beach	11789	South Onondaga	13120	Stafford (Town)	14143
Shortsville	14548	Soundview (Part of New York)	10472	South Otselic	13155	Stamford	12167
Short Tract	14735	South (Part of Yonkers)	10705	South Owego	13827	Stamford (Town)	12167
Shrub Oak	10588	South Addison	14801	South Oxford	13830	Standish	12952
Shumla	14063	South Alabama	14013	South Ozone Park (Part of New York)	11420	Stanford (Town)	12581
Shushan	12873	South Albion	13302	South Park (Part of Buffalo)	14220	Stanford Heights	12301
Shutter Corners	12157	South Amenia	12592	South Plainedge	11758	Stanfordville	12581
Shutts Corners	12043	Southampton	11968*	South Plymouth	13844	Stanley	14561
Sibleyville	14472		11969†	South Pole (Part of New York)	10090	Stanley Manor	13031
Sidney	13838	Southampton	11968	Southport	14904	Stannards	14895
Sidney (Town)	13838	Southampton College	11946	Southport (Town)	14904	Stanwix (Part of Rome)	13440
Sidney Center	13839	South Amsterdam (Part of Amsterdam)	12010	South Richmond Hill (Part of New York)	11419	Stanwix Heights (Part of Rome)	13440
Siena	12211	South Apalachin	13732	South Ripley	14775	Stanwood	10549
Sillimans Corners	14030	South Argyle	12809	South Russell	13684	Stapleton (Part of New York)	10304
Silver Bay	12874	South Bay	13032	South Rutland	13688		
Silver Creek	14136	South Bay Shopping Center	11702	South Salem	10590		
Silver Lake (Orange County)	10940	South Bay Village	12827	South Schodack	12162		
Silver Lake (Wyoming County)	14549			South Schroon	12870		

* Area Zip Code   **† Post Office Boxes**

	ZIP
Starbuckville	12817
Stark (Town)	13339
Starkey	14837
Starkey (Town)	14837
Starks Knob	12871
Starkville	13339
Star Lake	13690
State Bridge	13054
State Line	14775
Staten Island	**10301-14**

For specific Staten Island Zip Codes call (718) 816-2700, or your local postmaster.

COLLEGES & UNIVERSITIES

City University of New York-College of Staten Island	10301
Wagner College	10301

FINANCIAL INSTITUTIONS

Gateway State Bank	10304
Northfield Savings Bank	10314
Richmond County Savings Bank	10310
Staten Island Savings Bank	10304

HOSPITALS

St. Vincent's Medical Center of Richmond	10310
Staten Island University Hospital	10305

Staten Island Mall (Part of New York)	10314
State School	10990
State University (Part of Old Westbury)	11568
State University of New York (Part of Albany)	12203
State University of New York at Binghamton	13901
State University of New York at Stony Brook	11794
Steamburg	14783
Steam Valley	14760
Stears Corners	13659
Steelton	14219
Steinway (Part of New York)	11103
Stella	13905
Stella Niagara	14144
Stephens Mills	14843
Stephentown	12168
Stephentown (Town)	12168
Stephentown Center	12168
Sterling	13156
Sterling (Town)	13156
Sterling Forest	10979
Sterling Valley	13156
Stetsonville	13415
Steuben (Town)	13354
Steuben Valley	13354
Stever Mill	12025
Stewart Air Force Base	12550
	12533

For specific Stewart Air Force Base Zip Codes call (914) 564-2100, or your local postmaster.

Stewart Manor	11530
Stilesville	13754
Stillman Village	12138
Stillwater (Town)	12170
Stillwater (Chautauqua County)	14701
Stillwater (Putnam County)	10541
Stillwater (Saratoga County)	12170
Stillwater Hill	10562
Stirling	11944
Stissing	12581
Stittville	13469
Stockbridge	13409
Stockbridge (Town)	13409
Stockholm (Town)	13697
Stockholm Center	13697
Stockport (Columbia County)	12534
Stockport (Columbia County) (Town)	12534
Stockport (Delware County)	13783
Stockport Station	12534
Stockton	14784
Stockton (Town)	14784
Stockwell	13480
Stokes	13363
Stone Arabia	13339
Stone Church	14416

	ZIP
Stonedam	16923
Stone Gate	10950
Stone Mills	13656
Stone Ridge (Montgomery County)	12072
Stone Ridge (Ulster County)	12484
Stony Brook	11790
Stony Creek	12878
Stony Creek (Town)	12878
Stony Creek Estates	12065
Stony Hollow	12401
Stony Point	10980
Stony Point (Town)	10980
Stormville	12582
Stottville	12172
Stow	14785
Straits Corners	13827
Stratford	13470
Stratford (Town)	13470
Strathmore	11030
Streeters Corners	14094
Streetroad	12883
Strykersville	14145
Stuyvesant	12173
Stuyvesant (Town)	12173
Stuyvesant (Part of New York)	11233
Stuyvesant Falls	12174
Suffern	10901
Suffern Park	10901
Sugarbush	12989
Sugar Loaf	10981
Sugartown	14741
Sullivan	13037
Sullivan (Town)	13037
Sullivanville	14845
Summerhill	13092
Summerhill (Town)	13092
Summit	12175
Summit (Town)	12175
Summit Park	10977
Summit Park Mall (Part of Niagara Falls)	14304
Summitville	12781
Sun	12917
Sundown	12782
Sun Haven (Part of New Rochelle)	10801
Sunmount (Part of Tupper Lake)	12986
Sunny Side (Chautauqua County)	14701
Sunnyside (Columbia County)	12106
Sunnyside (Queens County)	11104
Sunrise Mall	11758
Sunrise Terrace	13902
Sunset (Part of New York)	11220
Sunset Bay Hanover Township	14081
Sunset Bay Ellery Township	14712
Sunset Beach	14172
Sunset City Shopping Center	11703
Sunset Manor	13492
Surprise	12176
Svahn Manor	10989
Swain	14884
Swan Lake	12783
Swartwood	14889
Swastika	12985
Swazy Acres	12188
Sweden (Town)	14420
Sweden Center	14420
Sweet Meadows	12401
Swenson Drive (Part of Wappingers Falls)	12590
Swifts Mills	14001
Swormville	14051
Sycaway	12180
Sylvan Beach	13157
Sylvan Lake	12533
Syosset	11791
Syracuse	13201-90

For specific Syracuse Zip Codes call (315) 452-3486, or your local postmaster.

Taberg	13471
Tabor Corners	14572
Taborton	12153
Taconic Correctional Facility	10507
Taconic Lake	12138
Taghkanic	12502
Taghkanic (Town)	12502
Talcottville	13309
Talcville	13635

	ZIP
Tallman (Part of Airmont)	10982
Tanglewood Hills	11727
Tannersville	12485
Tappan	10983
Tarrytown	10591
Tarrytown Heights (Part of Tarrytown)	10591
Taunton	13219
Taylor	13040
Taylor (Town)	13040
Taylor Center	13040
Teall (Part of Syracuse)	13217
Teboville	12953
Ten Mile River	12764
Tennanah	12776
Tennanah Lake	12776
Terminal (Part of New York)	10301
Terrace Park	13669
Terry's Corners	14067
Terryville	11776
Texas	13114
Texas Valley	13803
Thayer Corners	12917
The Bridges	14477
The Forge	12920
The Forks	14030
The Glen	12885
The Hook	12809
The Narrows	14737
Thendara	13472
Theresa	13691
Theresa (Town)	13691
The Terrace	11050
The Vly	12484
Thiells	10984
Thomaston	11021
Thompson (Ontario County)	14489
Thompson (Sullivan County) (Town)	12701
Thompson Ridge	10985
Thompsons Lake	12009
Thompsonville	12784
Thomson	12834
Thornton	14723
Thornton Grove	13152
Thornton Heights	13152
Thornwood	10594
Thousand Island Park	13692
Three Mile Bay	13693
Three Rivers	13041
Throg's Neck (Part of New York)	10465
Throop (Town)	13021
Throopsville	13021
Thruway Mall	14225
Thurman (Town)	12885
Thurston	14821
Thurston (Town)	14821
Thurston Road (Part of Rochester)	14619
Tiana	11946
Tiana Shores	11942
Ticonderoga	12883
Ticonderoga (Town)	12883
Tillson	12486
Times Plaza (Part of New York)	11217
Times Square (Part of New York)	10036
Timothy Heights	12569
Tinkertown	14803
Tioga (Town)	13845
Tioga Center	13845
Tioga Terrace	13732
Tiona	13811
Titusville	12603
Tivoli	12583
Toddsville	13326
Toddville	10566
Todt Hill (Part of New York)	10301
Toll Gate Corner	14770
Tomhannock	12185
Tomkins Cove	10986
Tompkins (Town)	13754
Tompkins Corners	14845
Tompkins Square (Part of New York)	10009
Tompkinsville (Part of New York)	10301
Tonawanda	14150*
	14151†
Tonawanda (Town)	14150
Tonawanda (census designated place)	14223
Tonawanda Indian Reservation (Erie County) (Town)	14150

	ZIP
Tonawanda Indian Reservation (Genesee County) (Town)	14150
Tonawanda Indian Reservation (Genesee County)	14150
Tonawanda Junction	14223
Torrey (Town)	14441
Tottenville (Part of New York)	10307
Towerville Corners	14701
Towlesville	14810
Town (Part of Newburgh)	12550
Towners	12531
Town Line	14086
Town Pump	14559
Townsend	14891
Townsendville	14847
Tracy Creek	13850
Trainsmeadow (Part of New York)	11370
Transitown	14221
Travis (Part of New York)	10301
Travis Corners	10524
Treadwell	13846
Tremont (Part of New York)	10457
Trenton (Town)	13304
Trenton Assembly Park	13304
Trenton Falls	13304
Triangle	13778
Triangle (Town)	13778
Triangle Lake	12122
Tribes Hill	12177
Triborough (Part of New York)	10035
Triphammer Mall (Part of Lansing)	14852
Tripoli	12827
Troupsburg	14885
Troupsburg (Town)	14885
Troutburg	14464
Trout Creek	13847
Trout River	12926
Troy	12180-83

For specific Troy Zip Codes call (518) 272-7300, or your local postmaster.

Truesdale Lake	10590
Trumansburg	14886
Trumbulls Corners	14867
Truthville	12854
Truxton	13158
Truxton (Town)	13158
Tuckahoe (Suffolk County)	11968
Tuckahoe (Westchester County)	10707
Tucker Heights	12019
Tucker Terrace	13662
Tudor (Part of New York)	10017
Tully	13159
Tully (Town)	13159
Tunnel	13848
Tupper Lake	12986
Turin	13473
Turin (Town)	13473
Turnwood	12758
Tuscan	12197
Tuscarora (Livingston County)	14510
Tuscarora (Steuben County) (Town)	14801
Tuscarora Indian Reservation (Town)	14094
Tuscarora Indian Reservation	14094
Tusten (Town)	12764
Tuthill	12525
Tuxedo (Town)	10987
Tuxedo Park	10987
Twelve Corners	14618
Twilight Park	12436
Twin Lakes Village	10590
Twin Orchards	13850
Tyner	13830
Tyre	13148
Tyre (Town)	13148
Tyrone	14887
Tyrone (Town)	14887
Ulster (Town)	12401
Ulster Heights	12428
Ulster Landing	12477
Ulster Park	12487
Ulsterville	12566
Ulysses (Town)	14886
Unadilla	13849
Unadilla (Town)	13849
Unadilla Forks	13491

* Area Zip Code   **† Post Office Boxes**

	ZIP		ZIP		ZIP		ZIP
Underwood	12964	Varna	14850	Wall Street (Part of New		Wesley Hills	10901
Union (Town)	13760	Varysburg	14167	York)	10005	West Almond	14804
Union	13760	Vaughs Corners	12839	Walton	13856	West Almond (Town)	14804
	13763	Vega	12455	Walton (Town)	13856	West Amboy	13167
For specific Union Zip Codes		Venice	13147	Walton Park	10950	West Babylon	11704
call (607) 785-1181, or your		Venice (Town)	13147	Walt Whitman Mall	11746		11707
local postmaster.		Venice Center	13147	Walworth	14568	For specific West Babylon Zip
Union Center	13760	Verbank	12585	Walworth (Town)	14568	Codes call (516) 587-4707, or
Uniondale	11553	Verbank Village	12585	Wampsville	13163	your local postmaster.
Union Falls	12912	Verdoy	12110	Wanakah	14075	West Bainbridge	13733
Union Hill	14563	Vermilion	13114	Wanakena	13695	West Bangor	12966
Union Mills	12025	Vermontville	12989	Wantagh	11793	West Barre	14411
Union Shopping Center		Vernon	13476	Wappinger (Town)	12590	West Batavia	14020
(Part of Endicott)	13760	Vernon (Town)	13476	Wappingers Falls	12590	West Bay Shore	11706
Union Springs	13160	Vernon Center	13477	Ward (Town)	14880	West Bellport	11772
Union Vale (Town)	12585	Vernon Valley	11768	Wards Island (Part of New		West Berne	12023
Union Valley	13052	Verona	13478	York)	10035	West Bethany	14054
Unionville (Albany County)	12054	Verona (Town)	13478	Warners	13164	West Bloomfield	14585
Unionville (Ontario		Verona Beach	13162	Warnerville	12187	West Bloomfield (Town)	14585
County)	14532	Verona Mills	13440	Warren	13439	West Branch	13303
Unionville (Orange		Verplanck	10596	Warren (Town)	13439	West Brentwood	11717
County)	10988	Versailles	14168	Warrensburg	12885	Westbrookville	12785
Unionville (St. Lawrence		Vesper	13159	Warrensburg (Town)	12885	West Burlington	13482
County)	13676	Vestal	13850*	Warrens Corners	14094	Westbury (Cayuga
United Nations New York			13851†	Warsaw	14569	County)	13143
(Part of New York)	10017	Vestal Center	13850	Warsaw (Town)	14569	Westbury (Nassau
University (Part of		Vestal Gardens	13850	Warwick	10990	County)	11590
Syracuse)	13210	Veteran (Chemung		Warwick (Town)	10990	West Bush	12078
University Gardens	11020	County) (Town)	14864	Washington (Town)	12545	West Cameron	14819
University Heights (Part of		Veteran (Ulster County)	12477	Washington Bridge (Part		West Camp	12490
New York)	10452	Veterans Administration		of New York)	10033	West Candor	13743
Upper Benson	12134	Facility	14020	Washington Heights	10940	West Carthage	13619
Upper Brookville	11545	Veterans Administration		Washington Lake	12550	West Caton	14830
Upper Grand View	10960	Hospital	14215	Washington Mills	13479	West Charlton	12010
Upper Hollowville	12530	Veterans Hospital (Part of		Washingtonville	10992	West Chazy	12992
Upper Jay	12987	Syracuse)	13210	Wassaic	12592	West Chenango	13905
Upper Lisle	13862	Victor	14564	Waterboro	14747	Westchester (Part of New
Upper Little York	13087	Victor (Town)	14564	Waterburg	14886	York)	10461
Upper Little York Lake	13141	Victoria	14710	Waterford	12188	Westchester Heights (Part
Upper Mongaup	12737	Victory	13033	Waterford (Town)	12188	of New York)	10461
Upper Nyack	10960	Victory (Town)	13033	Water Island	11772	West Chili	14514
Upper Red Hook	12571	Victory Mills	12884	Waterloo	13165	West Clarksville	14786
Upper St. Regis	12945	Victory Park (Part of New		Waterloo (Town)	13165	West Colesville	13904
Upper Union	12309	Rochelle)	10804	Waterman Corners	14728	West Conesville	12076
Upperville	13464	Vienna	13308	Water Mill	11976	West Copake	12593
Upton Lake	12514	Vienna (Town)	13308	Waterport	14571	West Corners	13760
Uptonville (Part of		Viewmonte	12526	Waterside Park	11768	West Coxsackie (Part of
Rochester)	14617	Village (New York County)	10014	Watertown	13601-03	Coxsackie)	12192
Uptown (Part of Kingston)	12401	Village (Niagara County)	14094	For specific Watertown Zip		Westdale	13483
Urbana (Town)	14840	Village Green (Onondaga		Codes call (315) 786-5900, or		West Danby	14896
U.S. Cadet Corps	10997	County)	13027	your local postmaster.		West Davenport	13860
Ushers	12151	Village Green (Saratoga		Watertown Junction (Part		West Dryden	13068
U.S. Military Academy	10996	County)	12065	of Watertown)	13601	West Durham	12422
Utica	13501-05	Village of the Branch	11787	Watervale	13104	West Eaton	13484
For specific Utica Zip Codes		Villenova (Town)	14138	Water Valley	14075	West Edmeston	13485
call (315) 738-5354, or your		Vincent	14424	Waterville	13480	West Elmira	14905
local postmaster.		Vine Valley	14507	Watervliet	12189	West End	13820
Utopia (Part of New York)	11366	Vintonton	12187	Watkins Glen	14891	West Endicott	13760
Vail Mills	12025	Viola	10952	Watson	13367	Westerlea	13031
Vails Gate	12584	Viola Park	10952	Watson (Town)	13367	Westerleigh (Part of New
Vail's Grove	10509	Virgil	13045	Watsonville	12122	York)	10314
Valatie	12184	Virgil (Town)	13045	Wattlesburg	14775	Westerlo	12193
Valcour	12972	Vischer Ferry	12148	Watts Flats	14710	Westerlo (Town)	12193
Valhalla	10595	Vista	06840	Wautoma Beach	14468	Western (Town)	13486
Valley Cottage	10989	Voak	14527	Wave Crest (Part of New		Western Lights Shopping
Valley Falls	12185	Volney	13069	York)	11691	Center (Part of
Valley Mills	13409	Volney (Town)	13069	Waverly (Franklin County)		Syracuse)	13219
Valley Pond Estates	10536	Volusia	14787	(Town)	12980	Western Pine Knolls	12203
Valley Stream	11580-82	Voorheesville	12186	Waverly (Tioga County)	14892	Westernville	13486
For specific Valley Stream Zip		Vukote	14710	Wawarsing	12489	West Exeter	13487
Codes call (516) 825-2220, or		Waccabuc	10597	Wawarsing (Town)	12489	West Falls	14170
your local postmaster.		Waddington	13694	Wawayanda (Town)	10973	West Farms (Part of New
Valley View Manor (Part		Waddington (Town)	13694	Wayland	14572	York)	10460
of Rome)	13440	Wadhams	12990	Wayland (Town)	14572	Westfield	14787
Vallonia Springs	13813	Wadhams Park	13669	Wayne (Schuyler County)	14893	Westfield (Town)	14787
Valois	14888	Wading River	11792	Wayne (Steuben County)		Westford	13488
Van Brunt (Part of New		Wainscott	11975	(Town)	14840	Westford (Town)	13488
York)	11215	Waits	13827	Wayne Center	14489	West Fort Ann	12827
Van Buren (Town)	13027	Wakefield (Part of New		Webb (Town)	13420	West Fort Salonga	11768
Van Buren Bay	14048	York)	10466	Webbs Mills	14871	West Frankfort	13340
Van Buren Point	14166	Walden (Erie County)	14225	Webster	14580	West Fulton	12194
Van Burenville	10940	Walden (Orange County)	12586	Webster (Town)	14580	West Gaines	14411
Van Cortlandtville	10566	Walden Galleria (Part of		Webster Crossing	14584	West Galway	12010
Van Cott (Part of New		Buffalo)	14225	Websters Corners	14127	Westgate	14624
York)	10467	Wales (Town)	14139	Wedgewood	14891	West Genesee Terrace	13031
Vandalia	14706	Wales Center	14169	Weedsport	13166	West Ghent	12075
Van Del (Part of		Wales Hollow	14139	Wegatchie	13608	West Gilgo Beach	11702
Kenmore)	14217	Walesville	13492	Welcome	13810	West Glens Falls	12801
Van Deusenville	13317	Walker	14468	Wells	12190	West Glenville	12010
Vandever (Part of New		Walker Lane	12801	Wells (Town)	12190	West Greece	14626
York)	11210	Walker Valley	12588	Wells Bridge	13859	West Greenwood	14839
Van Etten	14889	Wallace	14809	Wellsburg	14894	West Groton	13073
Van Etten (Town)	14889	Wallington	14551	Wellsville	14895	Westhampton	11977
Van Fleet	16920	Wallins Corner	12010	Wellsville (Town)	14895	Westhampton Beach	11978
Van Hornesville	13475	Wallkill (Orange County)		Weltonville	13811	West Harpersfield	13786
Van Nest (Part of New		(Town)	10919	Wende Correctional		West Haverstraw	10993
York)	10462	Wallkill (Ulster County)	12589	Facility	14004	West Hebron	12865
Van Schaick Island (Part		Wallkill Correctional		Wendelville	14120	West Hempstead	11552
of Cohoes)	12047	Facility	12589	Wesley	14070	West Henrietta	14586
Varick (Town)	14541	Walloomsac	12090	Wesley Chapel	10901	West Hill	12301

* Area Zip Code   **† Post Office Boxes**

Location	ZIP
West Hills	11743
West Hoosick	12028
West Huntington	11743
West Hurley	12491
West Islip	11795
West Jewett	12444
West Kendall	14476
West Kill	12492
West Latham	12110
West Laurens	13796
Westlawn	12203
West Lebanon	12195
West Lee	13363
West Leyden	13489
West Lowville	13367
West Mahopac	10541
West Martinsburg	13367
Westmere	12203
West Meredith	13757
West Middleburg	12122
West Middlebury	14054
West Milton	12020
Westminster Park	13607
West Monroe	13167
West Monroe (Town)	13167
Westmore Estates	12203
Westmoreland	13490
Westmoreland (Town)	13490
Westmoreland	11965
West Newark	13811
West New Brighton (Part of New York)	10310
West Newburgh (Part of Newburgh)	12550
West Nyack (census designated place)	10960
	10994
For specific West Nyack Zip Codes call (914) 358-0121, or your local postmaster.	
West Nyack	10994
Weston	14837
West Oneonta	13861
Westons Mills	14788
Westover	13790
West Park	12493
West Pawling	12564
West Perrysburg	14129
West Perth	12010
West Phoenix	13135
West Pierrepont	13617
West Point	10996*
	10997†
Westport	12993
Westport (Town)	12993
West Portland	14787
West Potsdam	13676
West Ridge (Part of Rochester)	14615
West Ronkonkoma	11779
West Rush	14543
West Salamanca (Part of Salamanca)	14779
West Sand Lake	12196
West Saugerties	12477
West Sayville	11796
West Schuyler	13502
West Seneca	14224
West Seneca (Town)	14224
West Shelby	14103
West Shokan	12494
West Side (Chemung County)	14905
West Side (Erie County)	14213
West Slaterville	14881
West Smithtown	11787
West Somerset	14008
West Sparta (Town)	14437
West Stephentown	12168
West St. James	11787
West Stockholm	13696
West Taghkanic	12502
West Tiana	11946
Westtown	10998
West Turin (Town)	13325
West Union (Town)	14877
West Utica (Part of Utica)	13501
Westvale	13219
West Valley	14171
West Valley Falls (Part of Valley Falls)	12185
Westview (Broome County)	13905
Westview (Livingston County)	14437
West Village (Part of New York)	10014
Westville (Franklin County)	12926
Westville (Franklin County) (Town)	12926
Westville (Otsego County)	12155
Westville Center	12926
West Walworth	14502
West Waterford (Part of Waterford)	12188
West Webster	14580
West Windsor	13865
West Winfield	13491
West Yaphank	11980
Wethersfield (Town)	14569
Wethersfield Springs	14569
Wevertown	12886
Whaley Lake	12531
Whallonsburg	12994
Wheatfield (Town)	14150
Wheatland (Town)	14546
Wheatley (Part of Old Westbury)	11568
Wheatley Heights	11798
Wheatville	14013
Wheeler	14810
Wheeler (Town)	14810
Wheeler Estates	12019
Wheelers	14469
Wheelerville	12032
Whig Corners	13326
Whippleville	12995
Whippoorwill	10504
White Bay	13650
White Creek	12057
White Creek (Town)	12057
White Fathers	12989
Whitehall	12887
Whitehall (Town)	12887
White Lake (Oneida County)	13494
White Lake (Sullivan County)	12786
Whitelaw	13032
White Plains	10601-07
For specific White Plains Zip Codes call (914) 287-2500, or your local postmaster.	
Whiteport	12401
Whitesboro	13492
Whites Store	13843
Whitestone (Part of New York)	11357
Whitestone Shopping Center (Part of New York)	11357
Whitestone (Town)	13492
White Sulphur Springs	12787
Whitesville	14897
Whitfield	12404
Whitman	13804
Whitney Country	14450
Whitney Farms	14450
Whitney Highlands	14450
Whitney Point	13862
Wiccopee	12533
Wickham Knolls	10990
Wickham Village	10990
Wilbur (Part of Kingston)	12401
Wildwood	11792
Wileyville	14877
Willard	14588
Willet	13863
Willet (Town)	13863
Williams Bridge (Part of New York)	10467
Williamsburg (Part of New York)	11211
Williams Grove	13110
Williams Lake	12472
Williamson	14589
Williamson (Town)	14589
Williamstown	13493
Williamstown (Town)	13493
Williamsville	14221
Willing (Town)	14895
Williston Park	11596
Willoughby	14741
Willow	12495
Willow Brook (Chautauqua County)	14712
Willowbrook (Richmond County)	10301
Willow Brook Estates	12303
Willow Brook Park	12302
Willowemac	12758
Willow Glen (Saratoga County)	12118
Willow Glen (Tompkins County)	13053
Willow Grove	13140
Willow Point	13850
Willow Ridge Estates	14150
Willsboro	12996
Willsboro (Town)	12996
Willsboro Point	12996
Willseyville	13864
Wilmington	12997
Wilmington (Town)	12997
Wilna (Town)	13619
Wilson	14172
Wilson (Town)	14172
Wilton	12866
Wilton (Town)	12866
Winchester	14224
Winderest Park	13031
Windham	12496
Windham (Town)	12496
Windham Ridge	12496
Winding Ways	13152
Windmill Farms	10504
Windom	14219
Windsor	13865
Windsor (Town)	13865
Windsor Beach	14617
Winebrook Hills	12852
Winfield (Town)	13491
Wingdale	12594
Winona Lake	12550
Winthrop	13697
Wirt (Town)	14774
Wiscoy	14536
Wisner	10990
Witherbee	12998
Wittenberg	12409
Wolcott	14590
Wolcott (Town)	14590
Wolcottsburg	14032
Wolcottsville	14001
Woodberry Hills	13413
Woodbourne	12788
Woodbury (Nassau County)	11797
Woodbury (Orange County) (Town)	10930
Woodbury Falls	10930
Woodcliff Park	11933
Woodgate	13494
Wood Haven (Part of New York)	11421
Woodhull	14898
Woodhull (Town)	14898
Woodinville	12564
Woodland	12464
Woodland Hills	12065
Woodlands	10607
Woodlawn (Bronx County)	10470
Woodlawn (Chautauqua County)	14710
Woodlawn Beach	14219
Woodmere	11598
Woodridge	12789
Woodrow (Part of New York)	10309
Woodruff Heights	12302
Woodsburgh	11598
Woods Corners	13815
Woods Falls	12910
Woodside (Part of New York)	11377
Woods Mill	13608
Woods Mills	12918
Woodstock	12498
Woodstock (Town)	12498
Woodsville	14437
Woodville (Jefferson County)	13650
Woodville (Ontario County)	14512
Wooglin	14728
Woolsey (Part of New York)	11105
Worcester	12197
Worcester (Town)	12197
Worley Heights	10950
Worth	13659
Worth (Town)	13659
Worthington (Part of White Plains)	10607
Wright (Town)	12073
Wright Park Manor (Part of Rome)	13440
Wrights Corners (Niagara County)	14094
Wrights Corners (Onondaga County)	13135
Wurtemburg	12572
Wurtsboro	12790
Wurtsboro Hills	12790
Wyandanch	11798
Wyatts	12302
Wycoff Heights (Part of New York)	11237
Wykagyl (Part of New Rochelle)	10804
Wykagyl Park (Part of New Rochelle)	10804
Wynantskill	12198
Wyomanock	12168
Wyoming	14591
Yaddo	12866
Yagerville	12458
Yaleville	13668
Yankee Lake	12790
Yaphank	11980
Yates (Town)	14098
Yates Center	14098
Yatesville	14527
Yonkers	10701-05
	10710
For specific Yonkers Zip Codes call (914) 378-3600, or your local postmaster.	
York	14592
York (Town)	14592
York Corners	14895
Yorkshire	14173
Yorkshire (Town)	14173
Yorktown	10598
Yorktown (Town)	10598
Yorktown Heights	10598
Yorkville	13495
Yosts	12068
Young Hickory	14885
Youngstown	14174
Youngstown Estates	14174
Youngsville	12791
Yulan	12792
Zena	12498
Zoar	13682

	ZIP
Aarons Corner	27053
Abbottsburg	28320
Aberdeen	28315
Abner	27356
Abshers	28635
Acme	28456
Acorn Hill	27979
Acorn Woods	28079
Acre	27865
Addie	28779
Addor	28315
Adoniram	24598
Advance	27006
Advent Crossroads	28601
Afton	27589
Aho	28607
Ahoskie	27910
Ai	27583
Airboro (Part of Goldsboro)	27530
Airlie	27850
Airport (Part of Charlotte)	28219
Alamance	27201
Alamance Correctional Center	27253
Alamance Square (Part of Greensboro)	27406
Alarka	28713
Albemarle	28001*
	28002†
Albemarle Beach	27970
Albertson	28508
Albrittons	28501
Alert	27589
Alexander	28701
Alexander Correctional Center	28681
Alexander Mills	28043
Alexis	28006
Alfordsville	28383
Allen	28212
Allen Grove	27839
Allen Jay (Part of High Point)	27263
Allens Crossroads	28174
Allensville	27573
All Healing Springs	28681
Alliance	28509
Alligator	27925
Allison	27326
Allreds	27356
Alma	28364
Almond	28702
Alspaugh (Part of Winston-Salem)	27105
Altamahaw	27202
Altamahaw-Ossipee	27202
Altamont	28657
Altan	28112
Altapass	28777
Amantha	28679
Amerotron Mill (Part of Red Springs)	28377
AMF (Part of Greensboro)	27425
Amity	27013
Amity Gardens (Part of Charlotte)	28205
Ammon	28337
Anderson (Caswell County)	27215
Anderson (Dare County)	27949
Anderson Creek	28323
Anderson Crossroads	27850
Andrews	28901
Angier	27501
Anson Correctional Center	28135
Ansonville	28007
Antioch (Brunswick County)	28422
Antioch (Hoke County)	28377
Antioch (Madison County)	28753
Apex	27502
Appie	27888
Apple Grove	28643
Aquadale	28128
Aquone	28703
Arabia	28376
Arapahoe	28510
Ararat	27007
Arba	28580
Arcadia	27292
Archdale	27263
Archer	27520
Arcola	27589
Arden	28704
Ardmore (Part of Winston-Salem)	27103
Ardulusa	28301
Argura	28783

	ZIP
Arlington	28642
Armour	28456
Arnold	27292
Arran Hills	28304
Arrowhead Beach	27932
Arrowhead Place	28025
Arrowood (Part of Charlotte)	28241
Artesia	28442
Asbury	27330
Ash	28420
Asheboro	27203*
	27204†
Asheville	28801-16
For specific Asheville Zip Codes call (704) 257-4112, or your local postmaster.	
Asheville Mall, The (Part of Asheville)	28805
Ashford	28752
Ash Hill	27007
Ashland (Ashe County)	28615
Ashland (Bertie County)	27957
Ashland (Caswell County)	27320
Ashland (Rockingham County)	27320
Ashley Heights	28315
Ashton	28425
Ashton Forrest	28304
Ashwood	28571
Askewville	27983
Askin	28527
Aspen	27850
Atkinson	28421
Atlantic	28511
Atlantic Beach	28512
Atlantic Christian College (Part of Wilson)	27893
Auburn	27610
Audubon (Part of Wilmington)	28403
Aulander	27805
Aurelian Springs	27850
Aurora	27806
Austin	28621
Autryville	28318
Avalon Valley	27253
Avent Ferry Road (Part of Raleigh)	27606
Aventon	27891
Averasboro	28334
Avery Correctional Center	28657
Avery Creek	28704
Avery Shores	27974
Avon	27915
Axtell	27563
Ayden	28513
Aydlett	27916
Ayersville	27027
Azalea (Buncombe County)	28805
Azalea (New Hanover County)	28403†
	28406*
Bachelor	28532
Badin	28009
Bagley	27542
Bahama	27503
Bailey	27807
Bailey Town	27052
Baker Rhyne Apartments	28152
Bakers	28110
Bakersville	28705
Bald Creek	28714
Bald Head Island	28461
Bald Mountain	28714
Baldwin (Ashe County)	28694
Baldwin (Moore County)	27341
Baldwin Woods (Part of Whiteville)	28472
Balfour	28739
Ballantree	28803
Ballard	27840
Ballards Crossroad	27834
Ballew Store	28714
Balm	28604
Balsam	28707
Balsam Grove	28708
Baltic	28398
Baltimore	28434
Bamboo	28605
Bandana	28705
Bandy	28609
Banks Creek	28714
Banner Elk	28604
Bannertown	27030
Banoak	28168
Barber	27008
Barclaysville	27501

	ZIP
Barco	27917
Barham	27587
Barium Springs	28010
Barker Heights	28792
Barkers Creek	28789
Barker Ten Mile	28358
Barnard	28753
Barnardsville	28709
Barnesfield	28570
Barnesville	28319
Barrett	28623
Barriers Mill	28124
Bass Crossroads	27882
Basstown	28328
Bat Cave	28710
Batchelor Crossroads	27882
Bath	27808
Baton	28630
Battleboro	27809
Battleground (Part of Greensboro)	27438
Bay	27925
Bayboro	28515
Bayleaf	27615
Baynes	27302
Bayshore	28405
Baytree	27613
Bayview	27808
Beach Spring	27944
Bear Creek (Chatham County)	27207
Bear Creek (Onslow County)	28539
Beard	28301
Bear Grass	27892
Bearpond	27536
Bear Poplar	28125
Bearskin	28328
Bearwallow	28735
Beatties Ford	28216
Beaufort	28516
Beaufort Heights	27889
Beaver Creek	28694
Beaverdam (Buncombe County)	28715
Beaver Dam (Cleveland County)	28152
Beaver Dam (Columbus County)	28431
Beaverdam (Cumberland County)	28318
Beaverdam (Halifax County)	27823
Beaverdam (Haywood County)	28716
Beckwith	27865
Beech	28787
Beech Bottom	28657
Beechbrook (Part of Belmont)	28012
Beech Creek	28604
Beechertown	28781
Beech Mountain	28604
Beechwood Shores	27958
Bee Log	28714
Beesons Crossroads	27284
Belair	28306
Belcross	27921
Belews Creek	27009
Belfast	27530
Belgrade	28555
Belhaven	27810
Bellarthur	27811
Belle Mead	28601
Bellemont	27216
Bell Island	27929
Bells Cross Roads	28166
Bells Fork (Onslow County)	28546
Bells Fork (Pitt County)	27858
Belltown	27565
Bell View	28906
Belmont (Gaston County)	28012
Belmont (Halifax County)	27870
Belmont Abbey College	28012
Belva	28753
Belvedere	27834
Belvidere	27919
Belville	28451
Belvoir	27834
Belwood	28090
Benham	28621
Bennett	27208
Benson	27504
Bent Creek	28806
Benton Heights (Part of Monroe)	28110
Bentons Crossroad	28110
Berea	27565

	ZIP
Berkeley (Part of Goldsboro)	27534
Bertha	27965
Bertie (Part of Windsor)	27983
Bessemer (Part of Greensboro)	27405
Bessemer City	28016
Bests	28551
Beta	28779
Bethabara (Part of Winston-Salem)	27106
Bethania	27010
Bethany	27320
Bethel (Caswell County)	27311
Bethel (Columbus County)	28432
Bethel (Haywood County)	28716
Bethel (Hoke County)	28376
Bethel (Perquimans County)	27944
Bethel (Pitt County)	27812
Bethel Hill	27573
Bethesda (Davidson County)	27292
Bethesda (Durham County)	27703
Bethlehem (Alexander County)	28601
Bethlehem (Hertford County)	27922
Bettie	28516
Beulah (Hyde County)	27875
Beulah (Polk County)	28756
Beulahtown	27542
Beulaville	28518
Beverly Woods (Part of Charlotte)	28210
Bexley (Part of Wilmington)	28412
Biddleville (Part of Charlotte)	28216
Big Cove	28719
Biggs Park (Part of Lumberton)	28358
Big Laurel	28753
Big Lick	28129
Big Pine	28753
Big Ridge (Carteret County)	28570
Big Ridge (Jackson County)	28736
Biltmore (Part of Asheville)	28813
Biltmore Forest	28803
Birchwood	27215
Bird Cage	28431
Birdtown	28719
Biscoe	27209
Bishops Cross	27860
Bixby	27006
Blackburn	28658
Black Creek	27813
Black Jack	27858
Blackman	27524
Black Mountain	28711
Black Mountain Sanatorium	28711
Blackwell	27311
Blackwood	27514
Bladenboro	28320
Bladenboro North (Part of Bladenboro)	28320
Bladen Correctional Center	28337
Bladen Springs	28434
Blaine	27239
Blanch	27212
Blantyre	28768
Blevins Crossroads	28675
Blevins Store	27017
Blizzards Crossroads	28365
Bloomingdale	28369
Blossomtown	28734
Blounts Creek	27814
Blowing Rock	28605
Blue Ridge (Buncombe County)	28711
Blue Ridge (Henderson County)	28792
Blue Ridge Mall (Part of Hendersonville)	28792
Bluff	28743
Boardman	28438
Boat Club Road	28012
Bobbitt	27544
Boddies Pond	27856
Boger City	28092
Bogue	28570
Boiling Spring Lakes	28461
Boiling Springs (Cherokee County)	28906

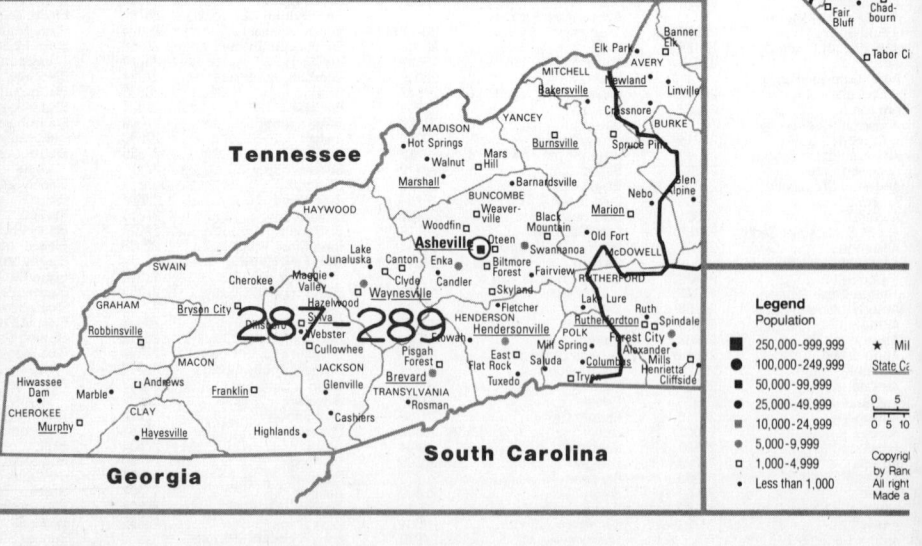

Virg...

Tenn.

ASHE   ALLEGHANY   SURRY

Lansing   Sparta   Toast   Mount Airy   STOKES   ROCKINGHAM   Eden   CASWELL   Milton   PERSON
Jefferson   Bannertown   Danbury   Mayodan   Stoneville   Ruffin   Yanceyville   Roxboro   GRA...
West Jefferson   WILKES   Dobson   Pilot Mountain   Pinnacle   Pine Hall   Madison   Wentworth   Reidsville   Butner
WATAUGA   McGrady   State Road   Elkin   King   Walnut Cove   FORSYTH   ALAMANCE   ORANGE   Roug...
Boone   Mulberry   Hays   Fairplains   Jonesville   Rural Hall   Walkertown   Summerfield   Ossipee   Haw River   Mebane   Hillsborough   DURHAM
Blowing Rock   Millers Creek   Roaring River   Arlington   East Bend   Pfafftown   Kernersville   Oak Ridge   GUILFORD   Burlington   Gibsonville   Elon College   Graham   Saxapahaw   Chapel Hill   Durham   Gorman

286

Newland   Linville   North Wilkesboro   Yadkinville   Lewisville   James-town   High Point   Archdale   Pleasant Garden   CHATHAM   Carrboro   Parkwood

20-274   Greensboro   Winston-Salem

280-282   283   28...-289

Legend
Population
■ 250,000-999,999
● 100,000-249,999
● 50,000-99,999
○ 25,000-49,999
○ 10,000-24,999
○ 5,000-9,999
□ 1,000-4,999
· Less than 1,000

★ Mil...
State Ca...

South Carolina

Tennessee

Georgia

Asheville

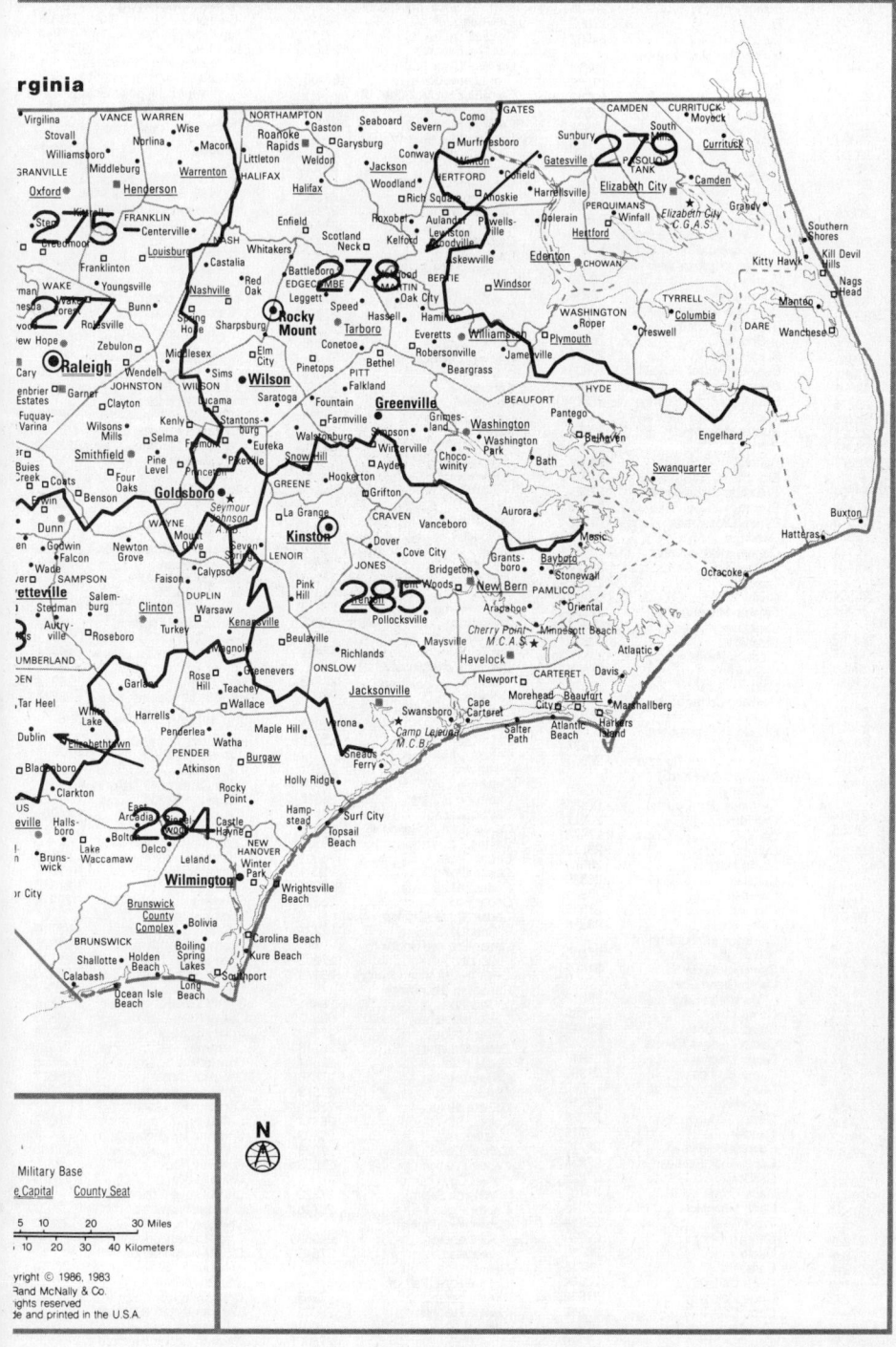

rginia

275

277

278

279

285

284

N

Military Base
e Capital   County Seat

5   10   20   30 Miles
10   20   30   40 Kilometers

	ZIP
Boiling Springs (Cleveland County)	28017
Bolivia	28422
Bolton	28423
Bolyston Creek	28768
Bon Air (Part of Winston-Salem)	27105
Bonaparte Landing	28459
Bonham Heights (Part of Morehead City)	28557
Bonlee	27213
Bonnerton	27806
Bonnetsville	28328
Bonnie Doone	28303
Bonsal	27562
Boomer	28606
Boone	28607
Boones Crossroads	27845
Boone Trail	27552
Boonford	28705
Boonville	27011
Bordeaux (Part of Fayetteville)	28304
Bostian Heights	28023
Bostic	28018
Bostwood Estates	28025
Botany Woods	28805
Bottom	27030
Boulevard (Part of Eden)	27288
Bowdens	28398
Bowditch	28714
Bowmore	28376
Boyles Chapel	27021
Bracey	28383
Bradfords Cross Roads	28677
Braggtown (Part of Durham)	27704
Branon	27055
Brantleys Grove	27910
Brasstown	28902
Braswell	28431
Brendletown	28734
Brentwood (Cumberland County)	28304
Brentwood (Wake County)	27604
Brettonwood	28311
Brevard	28712
Briarwood Terrace	28147
Brices Crossroads	28458
Brickhaven	27559
Bricks	27891
Brickton	28732
Bridgersville	27852
Bridgeton	28519
Brief	28107
Briertown	28781
Brigand Bay	27920
Brightwood (Part of Greensboro)	27214
Brindle Town	28655
Brinkleyville (Hertford County)	27910
Brinkleyville (Lee County)	27823
British Acres	27215
Broad Acres	27253
Broad Creek	28570
Broadway	27505
Brocks	28574
Brogden	27530
Brook Cove	27052
Brookdale	28792
Brookford	28601
Brookhaven	27612
Brookland Manor	28792
Brooks Cross Roads	27020
Brooksdale	27573
Brookside (Part of Goldsboro)	27530
Brookston	27536
Brook Valley	27858
Broughton Hospital	28655
Browns Summit	27214
Brown Town (Part of Belmont)	28012
Brownwood	28684
Bruce	27834
Brunswick	28424
Brutonville	27229
Bryantown	27869
Bryantville Park	27818
Bryson City	28713
Buckhorn	27243
Buckhorn Cross Roads	27542
Buckland	27937
Bucklesberry	28551
Buckner	28754
Buck Shoals	27020
Buena Vista	27983
Buffalo Cove	28645

	ZIP
Bug Hill	28455
Buie	28377
Buies Creek	27506
Buladean	28705
Bullhead	27863
Bullock	27507
Buncombe Correctional Center	28814
Bunn	27508
Bunnlevel	28323
Bunyan	27889
Burbage Crossroads	27808
Burden	27805
Burgaw	28425
Burgess	27944
Burke Chapel	28601
Burkemont	28655
Burlington	27215-17

For specific Burlington Zip Codes call (910) 227-4293, or your local postmaster.

	ZIP
Burney	28399
Burningtown	28734
Burnsville (Anson County)	28135
Burnsville (Yancey County)	28714
Burnt Mills	27976
Busbee (Part of Asheville)	28803
Bushy Fork	27541
Busick (Guilford County)	27214
Busick (Yancey County)	28714
Butlers Crossroads	28328
Butner	27509
Butters	28324
Buxton	27920
Buzzards Crossroads	27924
Bynum	27228
Byrum Crossroads	27980
Cabarrus	28107
Cabarrus Correctional Center	28124
Cabin	28572
Cairo	28119
Cajah's Mountain	28645
Calabash	28467
Calahaln	27028
Caldwell (Mecklenburg County)	28078
Caldwell (Orange County)	27572
Caldwell Correctional Center	28638
Caledonia Correctional Center	27887
California (Dare County)	27954
California (Hertford County)	27986
California (Pitt County)	27828
Callisons	28571
Cal-Vel	27573
Calvert	28712
Calvin Heights	28570
Calypso	28325
Camden	27921
Camelot	27529
Cameron	28326
Cameron Village (Part of Raleigh)	27605
Campbell Creek	27806
Camp Glenn (Part of Morehead City)	28557
Camp Leach	27889
Camp Lejeune	28542
Camp Lejeune Central	28542
Camp MacKall	28347
Camp Springs	27320
Camp Sutton (Part of Monroe)	28110
Cana	27028
Candler	28715
Candler Heights	28715
Candlewick Estates	27834
Candor	27229
Cane Creek	28167
Cane Mountain	27349
Cane River	28714
Cannon Ferry	27980
Canto	28716
Canton	28716
Cape Carteret	28584
Cape Colony	27932
Cape Fear	27562
Capella	27021
Capelsie	27229
Carbonton	27330
Carmel (Part of Charlotte)	28226
....	28247
....	28270

	ZIP
....	28277

For specific Carmel Zip Codes call (704) 541-7851, or your local postmaster.

	ZIP
Caroleen	28019
Carolina	27217
Carolina Beach	28428
Carolina Circle Mall (Part of Greensboro)	27405
Carolina East Mall (Part of Greenville)	27834
Carolina Forest	27371
Carolina Mall (Part of Concord)	28025
Carolina Pines	28303
Carolina Place (Part of Charlotte)	28134
Carolina Trace	27330
Carolina Village	28792
Carova Beach	27927
Carpenter	27560
Carpenter Bottom	28657
Carr	27302
Carrboro	27510
Carr Creek	27330
Carroll	28398
Carter	27938
Carteret Correctional Center	28570
Cartersville	28466
Carthage	28327
Cartoogechaye	28734
Carvers	28434
Cary	27511-13
	27518-19

For specific Cary Zip Codes call (919) 831-3661, or your local postmaster.

	ZIP
Cary Towne Center (Part of Cary)	27511
Casar	28020
Cashiers	28717
Cason Old Field	28170
Castalia	27816
Castle Hayne	28429
Castoria	27888
Casville	27326
Caswell Beach	28461
Caswell Correctional Center	27379
Catawba	28609
Catawba Correctional Center	28658
Catawba Heights	28012
Catawba Mall (Part of Hickory)	28601
Catherine Lake	28574
Catherine Square	28518
Cat Square	28168
Ca-Vel (Part of Roxboro)	27573
Cayton	28527
Cedar Creek	28301
Cedar Croft	28081
Cedar Falls	27230
Cedar Fork	28518
Cedar Grove (Orange County)	27231
Cedar Grove (Randolph County)	27203
Cedar Hill (Anson County)	28170
Cedar Hill (Brunswick County)	28451
Cedar Island	28520
Cedar Lodge	27360
Cedar Mountain	28718
Cedar Point	28584
Cedarrock	27816
Ceffo	27573
Celeste Hinkle	28677
Celo	28714
Celotex	28333
Center (Davie County)	27028
Center (Yadkin County)	27055
Center City (Part of Winston-Salem)	27120
Center Pigeon	28716
Centerview (Part of Kannapolis)	28083
Centerville	27549
Central	28677
Central Falls (Part of Asheboro)	27203
Central Heights	28025
Century	27601*
	27602†
Cerro Gordo	28430
Chadbourn	28431
Chadwick Acres	28460
Chalybeate Springs	27526

	ZIP
Champion	28624
Chantilly (Camden County)	27921
Chantilly (Mecklenburg County)	28205
Chapanoke	27944
Chapel Hill	27514-16

For specific Chapel Hill Zip Codes call (919) 942-4179, or your local postmaster.

	ZIP
Charity	28458
Charles	28677
Charlotte	28201-99
	28256-99

For specific Charlotte Zip Codes call (704) 393-4555, or your local postmaster.

COLLEGES & UNIVERSITIES

Johnson C. Smith University	28216
Queens College	28274
University of North Carolina at Charlotte	28223

FINANCIAL INSTITUTIONS

Central Carolina Bank and Trust Company	28235
First Federal Savings & Loan Association of Charlotte	28202
First Union National Bank of North Carolina	28288
Home Federal Savings & Loan Association	28202
NationsBank of North Carolina, N.A.	28255

HOSPITALS

Carolinas Medical Center	28203
Mercy Hospital	28207
Presbyterian Hospital	28204

HOTELS/MOTELS

Adam's Mark Charlotte	28204
Guest Quarters Suite Hotel	28211
Holiday Inn-Woodlawn	28217
Park Hotel	28211
Ramada Inn-Central	28217

MILITARY INSTALLATIONS

Naval and Marine Corps Reserve Center, Charlotte	28256
North Carolina Air National Guard, FB6331, Morris Field	28208

Charlotte Correctional Center	28208
Chatham	27514
Cheeks	27316
Cherokee	28719
Cherokee Indian Reservation	28719
Cherry	27928
Cherryfield	28712
Cherry Grove	28430
Cherry Lane	28627
Cherry Oaks	27858
Cherry Point	28533
Cherry Springs	28762
Cherryville	28021
Chesterfield	28655
Chestnut Dale	28657
Chestnut Grove	27021
Chestnut Hill (Ashe County)	28617
Chestnut Hill (Henderson County)	28735
Chimney Rock	28720
China Grove	28023
China Grove Cotton Mill Village	28023
Chinquapin	28521
Chip (Craven County)	28586
Chip (Montgomery County)	27306
Choco Village	27817
Chocowinity	27817
Chowan Beach (Chowan County)	27932
Chowan Beach (Hertford County)	27855
Chublake	27573
Church Crossroads	27871
Churchill	27551

* Area Zip Code   † Post Office Boxes

	ZIP
Churchland	27292
Cid	27292
Cisco	27980
City View (Part of Winston-Salem)	27101
Claremont	28610
Clarendon	28432
Clark	28562
Clarkton	28433
Clarrissa	28705
Clay	27565
Clayroot	28513
Clayton	27520
Clear Creek	28212
Clear Run	28441
Clegg	27560
Clemmons	27012
Clemont	28318
Cleveland	27013
Cleveland Correctional Center	28152
Cleveland Springs	28150
Clifdale	28304
Cliffside	28024
Clifton	28693
Climax	27233
Clinchfield	28752
Clingman	28670
Clinton	28328
Cloverdale (Part of Garner)	27529
Clover Garden	27217
Cloverleaf	28304
Club Pines	27834
Clyde	28721
Coakley	27886
Coalville	28901
Coats	27521
Coats Cross Roads	27504
Cobb Town	27829
Cofield	27922
Cognac	28363
Coinjock	27923
Cokesbury (Harnett County)	27526
Cokesbury (Vance County)	27536
Cold Springs	28025
Cold Water	28025
Cole Park	27514
Cole Park Plaza (Part of Chapel Hill)	27514
Colerain	27924
Coleridge	27316
Colewood Acres	27604
Colfax	27235
Colington	27948
College (Part of Durham)	27708
College Downs	28213
College Lakes	28301
College Park (Cabarrus County)	28075
College Park (Guilford County)	27403
College Park (Richmond County)	28345
Collettsville	28611
Collinstown	24171
Colly	28448
Colon	27330
Colonial Heights (Beaufort County)	27889
Colonial Heights (Wake County)	27603
Colony Park (Part of Durham)	27705
Columbia	27925
Columbia Heights (Part of Winston-Salem)	27107
Columbus	28722
Columbus Correctional Center	28424
Comfort	28522
Commodore Peninsula	28115
Como	27818
Concord (Cabarrus County)	28025-27
For specific Concord Zip Codes call (704) 786-3161, or your local postmaster.	
Concord (Duplin County)	28453
Concord (Person County)	27573
Concord (Rutherford County)	28018
Concord (Sampson County)	28382
Conetoe	27819
Congleton	27871
Connarista	27805

	ZIP
Connelly Springs	28612
Conover	28613
Conway	27820
Cooksville	28168
Cooktown	28705
Cooleemee	27014
Cool Spring	27013
Cool Springs	27330
Cooper Estates	27253
Copeland	27017
Coral Bay	28557
Corapeake	27926
Corbett	27302
Cordova	28330
Core Creek	28516
Core Point	27814
Corinth (Chatham County)	27559
Corinth (Nash County)	27856
Corinth (Rutherford County)	28040
Cornatzer	27028
Cornelius	28031
Cornwall	27565
Corolla	27927
Correll Park	28146
Corriher Heights	28023
Costin	28421
Cotswold Mall (Part of Charlotte)	28211
Cottonade	28303
Cotton Grove	27292
Cottonville	28128
Council	28434
Country Club Estates	28472
Country Hills	27529
Country Homes Estates	27258
Courtney	27055
Cove City	28523
Cove Creek	28786
Covington	27306
Cowee	28734
Cox Crossing	27858
Coxville	28513
Cozart	27522
Crab Point	28557
Crabtree	28721
Crabtree Valley Mall (Part of Raleigh)	27612
Craggy	28804
Craggy Correctional Center	28802
Cramerton	28032
Cranberry	28614
Cranberry Gap	28657
Crater Park	28213
Creedmoor	27522
Creeksville	27820
Cremo	27924
Crescent	28138
Crestmont	28601
Creston	28615
Crestview	27344
Creswell	27928
Cricket	28659
Crisp	27852
Croatan	28562
Cross Landing	27925
Cross Mill	28752
Crossnore	28616
Cross Road	27030
Crossroads Plaza (Part of Cary)	27602
Crossway	28352
Crosswinds	27615
Crouse	28033
Crowders	28052
Crowells	27839
Crumpler	28617
Crump Town (Part of Wagram)	28396
Cruso	28716
Crusoe Island	28472
Crutchfield Crossroads	27344
Crystal Park	28306
Culberson	28903
Culbreth	27565
Cullasaja	28741
Cullowhee	28723
Cumberland	28331
Cumnock	27237
Cunningham	27343
Currie	28435
Currituck	27929
Currituck Correctional Center	27956
Currytown	27292
Cutshalltown	28753
Cycle	27020

	ZIP
Cypress Creek (Columbus County)	28472
Cypress Creek (Duplin County)	28466
Cyrus	28540
Dabney	27536
Dallas	28034
Dalton	27043
Dana	28724
Danbury	27016
Danieltown	28043
Dan River Shores	27016
Dan Valley	27048
Darby	28624
Darden	27846
Dark Ridge	28622
Darlington	27839
Davenport Forks	27970
Davidson	28036
Davidson Correctional Center	27292
Davidson River	28768
Davie Correctional Center	27028
Davie Crossroads	27028
Davis	28524
Davistown (Edgecombe County)	27864
Davistown (McDowell County)	28762
Dawson Crossroads	27823
Day Book	28740
Days Crossroads	27839
Deep Creek	28133
Deep Gap	28618
Deep River (Part of High Point)	27265
Deep Run	28525
Deerfield	28607
Deerwood	28532
Dehart	28635
Delco	28436
Delight	28090
Dellview	28021
Dellwood	28786
Delway	28458
Democrat	28787
Dennis	27052
Dennys Store	27573
Denton	27239
Denver	28037
Deppe	28555
Derby	28338
Derita (Part of Charlotte)	28213
Devonshire	28081
Devotion	27017
Dewey Pier	27925
Dexter	27565
Dickens Park	28570
Dickerson	27565
Diggs	28379
Dillard	27025
Dillsboro	28725
Dilworth (Part of Charlotte)	28203
Dixon	28445
Dixon Crossroad	28590
Dixon Crossroads	28213
Dobbersville	28365
Dobbins Heights	28345
Dobson	27017
Dockery	28635
Dodgetown	27025
Dodsons Crossroads	27278
Dogwood Acres (Durham County)	27704
Dogwood Acres (Randolph County)	27203
Dogwood Park	28027
Don Lee Heights	28532
Donnaha	27050
Doolie	28115
Dortches	27801
Dosier	27040
Dothan	29569
Double Shoals	28090
Douglas Crossroads	27889
Dover (Cleveland County)	28150
Dover (Craven County)	28526
Downtown (Part of Asheville)	28802
Downtown (Part of Boone)	28607
Downtown (Part of Charlotte)	28202-04
	28206
For specific Downtown Zip Codes call (704) 393-4555, or your local postmaster.	
Downtown (Part of Salisbury)	28145
Draco	28645

	ZIP
Drake	27809
Drake Park	28304
Draper (Part of Eden)	27288
Draughn	27891
Drewry	27553
Drexel	28619
Druid Hills (Part of Hendersonville)	28739
Drum Hill	27937
Drums Crossroads	28609
Dry Creek	27229
Duan	28658
Duart	28384
Dublin	28332
Duck	27949
Dudley	28333
Dudley Heights (Part of Greensboro)	27401
Dudley Shoals	28630
Duff Creek	28464
Duffies	28377
Duke (Part of Durham)	27706
Dulah	28463
Dula Springs	28787
Duncan	27526
Dundarrach	28386
Dunn	28334*
	28335†
Dunn Crossroads	27822
Dunns Rock	28712
Dunns Store	27874
Duplin Correctional Center	28349
Dupree Crossroads	27829
Durants Neck	27930
Durham	27701-22
For specific Durham Zip Codes call (919) 683-1976, or your local postmaster.	
Dutchess Downs	27529
Dysartville	28761
Eagle	27020
Eagle Rock	27523
Eagle's Nest	28570
Eagle Springs	27242
Eagletown	27869
Earl	28038
Earley	27910
Earpsboro	27597
Easonburg	27801
Easons Crossroads	27938
East Arcadia	28456
East Bend	27018
East Carolina University (Part of Greenville)	27834
Eastcrest Ridge	28025
East Durham (Part of Durham)	27703
Eastern Correctional Center	28554
East Fayetteville	28301
East Flat Rock	28726
East Franklin (Part of Franklin)	28734
East Lake	27953
Eastland Mall (Part of Charlotte)	28212
East Laport	28723
East Laurinburg	28352
East Lumberton (Part of Lumberton)	28358
East Marion	28752
East Monbo	28677
Easton (Part of Winston-Salem)	27107
Eastover (Cumberland County)	28301
Eastover (Mecklenburg County)	28207
Eastridge (Part of Gastonia)	28054
Eastridge Mall (Part of Gastonia)	28053
East Rockingham	28379
East Rocky Mount (Part of Rocky Mount)	27801
East Side Park (Richmond County)	28379
East Side Park (Robeson County)	28340
East Spencer	28039
East Tabor	28463
Eastway (Part of Charlotte)	28205
East Wilmington (Part of Wilmington)	28405
Eastwood	28327
Ebenezer	28906
Echo	28383
Echo Heights	27603

	ZIP		ZIP		ZIP		ZIP
Eckerd Contract-Concord		Erect	27341	Five Forks (Rowan		Frazier Crossroads	27557
(Part of Concord)	28027	Ernul	28527	County)	28023	Fraziers Crossroads	27910
Eck Reece	28642	Ervintown	28574	Five Forks (Warren		Frederick	27817
Eden	27288*	Erwin	28339	County)	27551	Freedom (Part of	
	27289†	Erwin Heights (Part of		Five Point (Part of		Charlotte)	28208
Edenhouse	27957	Thomasville)	27360	Raleigh)	27608	Freedom Mall (Part of	
Edenton	27932	Essex	27844	Five Points (Beaufort		Charlotte)	28208
Edgar	27350	Estatoe	28777	County)	27889	Freeland	28420
Edgemont	28645	Estelle	27305	Five Points (Columbus		Freeman	28423
Edgewood Acres	28016	Ether	27247	County)	28431	Fremont	27830
Edmonds	28623	Etowah	28729	Five Points (Hoke County)	28376	Friendly Acres	28027
Edneyville	28727	Eufola	28677	Five Points (Richmond		Friendly Shoppnig Center	
Edward	27821	Eure	27935	County)	28379	(Part of Greensboro)	27404
Edwards Crossroads		Eureka	27830	Flat Branch (Gates		Friendship (Cherokee	
(Alleghany County)	28675	Eureka Springs	28301	County)	27938	County)	28906
Edwards Crossroads		Eutaw (Part of		Flat Branch (Harnett		Friendship (Duplin County)	28398
(Nash County)	27882	Fayetteville)	28303	County)	27546	Friendship (Guilford	
Edwards Crossroads		Evansdale	27893	Flat Creek	28787	County)	27410
(Northampton County)	27820	Everetts	27825	Flat Rock (Henderson		Friendship (Wake County)	27502
Edwards Fork	27874	Everetts Crossroads	27865	County)	28731	Friendship (Yadkin	
Efland	27243	Evergreen (Beaufort		Flat Rock (Stokes County)	27043	County)	27018
Ela	28713	County)	27817	Flat Rock (Surry County)	27030	Frisco	27936
Elams	23845	Evergreen (Columbus		Flats	28781	Frog Level	27834
Elberon	27589	County)	28438	Flat Shoals	27019	Frog Pond	28129
Eldorado	27371	Evergreen Estates	28304	Flat Springs	28622	Frogsboro	27314
Eleanors Crossroads	27937	Exum	28420	Flay	28021	Fruitland	28792
Eleazer	27371	Exway	27306	Fleetwood	28626	Frying Pan Landing	27925
Elf	28904	Fair Bluff	28439	Fleetwood Acres	28052	Fulchers Landing	28460
Eliah	28451	Fairfield (Hyde County)	27826	Fletcher	28732	Fullers	27360
Eli Whitney	27253	Fairfield (Union County)	28103	Flint Hill (Montgomery		Fulp	27052
Elizabeth (Part of		Fair Field Estate	28150	County)	27371	Funston	28479
Charlotte)	28204	Fairfield Harbour	28560	Flint Hill (Randolph		Fuquay Springs (Part of	
Elizabeth City	27906-09	Fairfield Sapphire Valley	28774	County)	27350	Fuquay-Varina)	27526
For specific Elizabeth City Zip		Fair Grove	27360	Flint Hill (Yadkin County)	27018	Fuquay-Varina	27526
Codes call (919) 338-3869, or		Fairlane	28303	Florence	28556	Furches	28644
your local postmaster.		Fairmont	28340	Florence Town	27302	Furnitureland (Part of High	
Elizabeth City Coast		Fairmont Junction	28383	Flowes Store	28025	Point)	27264
Guard Air Station	27909	Fairplains	28659	Floytan Crossroads	27536	Galatia	27876
Elizabeth Heights	27893	Fairport	27544	Folkstone	28445	Gales Creek	28570
Elizabethtown	28337	Fairview (Buncombe		Folly	27979	Galloway Crossroads	27858
Elkin	28621	County)	28730	Fontana Dam	28733	Gallup Acres	28304
Elk Mountain (Part of		Fairview (Orange County)	27278	Footsville	27055	Gamble Hill	28016
Woodfin)	28804	Fairview (Rockingham		Forbes	28740	Gamewell	28645
Elk Park	28622	County)	27288	Forestburg	27944	Garden Homes (Part of	
Elk Valley	28604	Fairview (Union County)	28110	Forest City	28043	Greensboro)	27408
Ellenboro	28040	Fairview Cross Roads	27017	Forest Hills (Cumberland		Gardnerville	28513
Ellendale (Alexander		Fairview Park	28636	County)	28303	Gardner Webb College	
County)	28681	Fairway Hills	28786	Forest Hills (Forsyth		(Part of Boiling Springs)	28017
Ellendale (Wake County)	27545	Faison	28341	County)	27105	Garland	28441
Eller	27107	Faisons	27876	Forest Hills (Gaston		Garner	27529
Ellerbe	28338	Faith	28041	County)	28120	Garysburg	27831
Ellerbe Grove	28379	Falcon	28342	Forest Hills (New Hanover		Gaston	27832
Ellijay	28734	Falkland	27827	County)	28403	Gaston Correctional	
Elliott	28393	Fall Creek	27018	Forest Hills (Rockingham		Center	28034
Ellis Crossroads	28144	Falling Creek	28501	County)	27320	Gastonia	28051-56
Ellis Store	27983	Falling Creek Estates	28601	Forest Oaks	27406	For specific Gastonia Zip	
Elm City	27822	Falls	27609	Forest Ridge	28152	Codes call (704) 867-6311, or	
Elm Grove (Bertie County)	27924	Fallston	28042	Forestville (Anson County)	28091	your local postmaster.	
Elm Grove (Lenoir		Far Away Place	28025	Forestville (Wake County)	27587	Gaston Mall (Part of	
County)	28501	Farmer	27203	Fork Church	27028	Gastonia)	28054
Elmore	28352	Farmington	27028	Fort Barnwell	28526	Gates	27937
Elmwood	28677	Farmville (Chatham		Fort Bragg	28307	Gates Correctional Center	27938
Elon College	27244	County)	27330	Fort Caswell	28461	Gates Four	28306
Elroy	27534	Farmville (Pitt County)	27828	Fort Junction	28307	Gatesville	27938
Embro	27551	Faro	27883	Fort Landing	27925	Gateway	28789
Emerald Gardens	28304	Farrington	27514	Fort Macon Coast Guard		Gause Landing	28469
Emerald Isle	28594	Faust	28754	Base	28512	Gay	28779
Emerald Village	27610	Fayblock (Part of		Fort Point	27817	Gaylord	27808
Emerson (Bladen County)	28433	Fayetteville)	28301	Foscoe	28604	Gela	27582
Emerson (Columbus		Fayetteville	28301-06	Foster Creek	28753	Gentry Store	27573
County)	28463		28309-14	Fountain (Duplin County)	28521	George	27897
Emerywood (Part of High		For specific Fayetteville Zip		Fountain (Pitt County)	27829	Georgetown (Buncombe	
Point)	27262	Codes call (910) 486-2311, or		Fountain Hill	28133	County)	28806
Emit	27557	your local postmaster.		Four Oaks	27524	Georgetown (Davidson	
Emma	28806	Fayetteville North (Part of		Four Seasons (Part of		County)	27284
Enderly Park (Part of		Fayetteville)	28311	Hendersonville)	28739	Georgetown (Lenoir	
Charlotte)	28208	Fearrington	27312	Four Seasons Town		County)	28501
Endy	28001	Fearrington Post	27312	Centre (Part of		Georgeville	28025
Enfield	27823	Federal Building (Part of		Greensboro)	27407	Germanton	27019
Engelhard	27824	Elizabeth City)	27909	Fourway	28538	Germantown	27875
Englewood (Part of Rocky		Federal Correctional		Foxcroft East (Part of		Gerton	28735
Mount)	27801	Institution	27509	Charlotte)	28226	Gethsemane	27891
English Woods	28025	Feezor	27292	Fox Fire (Cumberland		Gibson	28343
Enka	28728	Feltonville	27502	County)	28303	Gibsontown	28716
Enka Village	28728	Ferguson	28624	Foxfire (Moore County)	27281	Gibsonville	27249
Ennice	28623	Ferncliff Estates	28025	Foxwood Acres	28025	Giddensville	28341
Eno	27278	Fibreville (Part of Canton)	28716	Francisco	27053	Gilkey	28139
Enochville	28023	Fields	28551	Francis Mill	27805	Gill	27536
Enola	28655	Fines Creek	28721	Francktown	28574	Gillburg	27536
Enon	27018	Finger	28124	Frank	28657	Glade Valley	28627
Eno Valley (Part of		Fires Creek	28904	Franklin (Macon County)	28734	Glady	28715
Durham)	27712	First Union (Part of		Franklin (Rowan County)	28144	Glass (Part of Kannapolis)	28081
Enterprise (Davidson		Charlotte)	28202	Franklin Correctional		Glen Alpine	28628
County)	27292	Fisher Park (Part of		Center	27508	Glen Ayre	28705
Enterprise (Warren		Greensboro)	27401	Franklin Grove	28713	Glenbrook	28304
County)	27850	Fisher Town	28081	Franklin Street (Part of		Glencoe	27217
Ephesus	27028	Fitch	27379	Chapel Hill)	27514	Glendale Acres (Part of	
Epsom	27536	Five Forks (Person		Franklinton	27525	Fayetteville)	28304
Erastus	28723	County)	27573	Franklinville	27248	Glendale Springs	28629

	ZIP
Glendon	27251
Glenhaven	28304
Glen Lennox (Part of Chapel Hill)	27514
Glenn	27705
Glenola	27263
Glen Raven	27215
Glenview	27823
Glenville	28736
Glenwood (Guilford County)	27403
Glenwood (McDowell County)	28737
Glenwood (Richmond County)	28379
Globe	28645
Gloucester	28528
Gneiss	28734
Goat Neck	27925
Godwin	28344
Golden Forest	27604
Golden Gate (Part of Greensboro)	27405
Gold Hill (Rockingham County)	27025
Gold Hill (Rowan County)	28071
Gold Mine	28741
Gold Point	27871
Goldrock	27891
Goldsboro	27530-34

For specific Goldsboro Zip Codes call (919) 734-3521, or your local postmaster.

Goldston	27252
Gold Valley Crossroads	27557
Goodsonville	28092
Goose Creek	27974
Gooseneck	28456
Goose Pond	27924
Gordonton	27541
Gordontown	27292
Gorman	27704
Goshen	28697
Governors Island	28713
Grace (Part of Asheville)	28814
Grace Chapel	28630
Gradys	28365
Graham	27253
Graingers	28501
Grandfather	28646
Grandview	28906
Grandview Heights (Part of Boone)	28607
Grandy	27939
Granite Falls	28630
Granite Quarry	28072
Grantham	27530
Granthams	28560
Grantsboro	28529
Grape Creek	28906
Grapevine	28753
Graphite	28762
Grassy Creek (Ashe County)	28631
Grassy Creek (Mitchell County)	28777
Grays Chapel	27248
Grayson	28632
Great Neck Landing	28539
Green Acres (Alamance County)	27217
Green Acres (Gaston County)	28012
Green Acres (Wake County)	27603
Green Acres Park	28025
Greenbrier Estates	27603
Greene Correctional Center	28554
Greene Cove	28705
Greenevers	28458
Green Farm	27834
Greenfield	27932
Greenhill (Haywood County)	28716
Green Hill (Rutherford County)	28139
Greenlee	28762
Green Level (Alamance County)	27217
Green Level (Wake County)	27502
Greenmountain	28740
Greenriver	28722
Greensboro	27401-55

For specific Greensboro Zip Codes call (910) 370-9291, or your local postmaster.

Greens Creek	28779

	ZIP
Green Valley	28615
Greenville	27834-36
	27858

For specific Greenville Zip Codes call (919) 752-2153, or your local postmaster.

Greenwood Homes (Part of Fayetteville)	28303
Gregory	27973
Gregory Crossroads (Bertie County)	27957
Gregory Crossroads (Onslow County)	28574
Greystone	27536
Griffins Crossroads	27312
Grifton	28530
Grimesdale	28792
Grimesland	27837
Grissettown	28470
Grissom	27522
Grist	28431
Grove Hill	27551
Grovemont	28778
Grove Park (Part of Charlotte)	28215
Grover	28073
Grovestone	28778
Growers Crossroads	27924
Guide	28463
Guideway	28463
Guilford (Part of Greensboro)	27409
Guilford College (Part of Greensboro)	27410
Guilford Correctional Center	27301
Guilford Hills (Part of Greensboro)	27408
Gulf	27256
Gull Rock	27824
Gumberry	27838
Gumbranch	28540
Gum Neck	27925
Gum Springs	27312
Guntertown	28753
Gupton	27549
Guthrie	27284
Guyton	28320
Haddocks Crossroads	28590
Hairtown	28302
Half Hell	28422
Half Moon	28540
Halifax	27839
Halifax Correctional Institution	27839
Hallsboro	28442
Halls Ferry Junction	28127
Halls Mills	28649
Halls Store	28385
Hallsville	28518
Hamer	27212
Hamilton	27840
Hamilton Lakes (Part of Greensboro)	27410
Hamlet	28345
Hampstead	28443
Hamptonville	27020
Hamrick	28714
Hancheys Store	28466
Hancock	27932
Handy	27239
Hanes Mall (Part of Winston-Salem)	27103
	27130

For specific Hanes Mall Zip Codes call (910) 760-9818, or your local postmaster.

Hanrahans	28530
Happy Valley (Buncombe County)	28805
Happy Valley (Caldwell County)	28645
Harbinger	27941
Harbor Island (Part of Wrightsville Beach)	28480
Hardees Cross Road	27504
Hardins	28034
Hare	28627
Hargetts Cross Roads	28574
Harkers Island	28531
Harlem Heights	28170
Harlowe	28570
Harmony	28634
Harper's Crossroads	27207
Harrells	28444
Harrellsville	27942
Harrelsonville	28472
Harris (Moore County)	28327
Harris (Rutherford County)	28074

	ZIP
Harrisburg	28075
Harrisburg Estates	28075
Harris Crossroads (Franklin County)	27596
Harris Crossroads (Vance County)	27536
Harris Landing	27932
Harrison Cross Roads	27320
Hartland	28645
Hartman	27016
Hartsease	27886
Harveytown	28501
Hassell	27841
Hastings Corner	27921
Hasty	28352
Hatteras	27943
Havelock	28532
Havelock Station (Part of Havelock)	28532
Haw Branch (Moore County)	27330
Haw Branch (Onslow County)	28574
Haw Creek (Part of Asheville)	28805
Hawfields	27302
Hawk	28705
Haw River	27258
Haws Run	28454
Hayesville	28904
Haymount (Part of Fayetteville)	28305
Hayne	28318
Hays	28635
Hayti (Part of Durham)	27701
Haywood	27559
Haywood Road (Part of Asheville)	28806
Hazelwood	28738
Hazelwood Park	27864
Healing Springs	27239
Heathsville	27823
Heaton	28622
Hedrick Grove	27292
Helens Crossroads	28513
Helton	28631
Hemby Acres	28079
Hemby Bridge	28079
Henderson	27536
Henderson Correctional Center	28739
Hendersonville	28739
	28792-93

For specific Hendersonville Zip Codes call (704) 692-2547, or your local postmaster.

Hendersonville	28739
Hendrix Estates	28147
Henrico	27842
Henrietta	28076
Henry	28168
Henry River	28602
Hepco	28721
Heritage Hill	27516
Heritage Square (Part of Durham)	27707
Heritage Woods	28025
Herrings Crossroads (Duplin County)	28508
Herrings Crossroads (Greene County)	27888
Hertford	27944
Hester	27581
Hesters Store	27541
Hestertown	28358
Hewitt	28781
Hexlena	27805
Hibbs Acres	28570
Hickmans Crossroads	28470
Hickory	28601-03

For specific Hickory Zip Codes call (704) 328-5503, or your local postmaster.

Hickory Crossroads	27919
Hickory Grove (Cumberland County)	28304
Hickory Grove (Gaston County)	28056
Hickory Grove (Mecklenburg County)	28215
Hickory Knoll	28734
Hickory Point	27806
Hickory Rock	27549
Hicks Crossroads (Mecklenburg County)	28078
Hicks Crossroads (Vance County)	27565
Hiddenite	28636
Higdonville	28734

	ZIP
Higgins	28714
High Crossroads	27807
Highfalls	27259
High Hampton	28717
Highland Park	28345
Highland Park West (Part of Greensboro)	27407
Highlands	28741
High Point	27260-65

For specific High Point Zip Codes call (910) 884-8344, or your local postmaster.

High Rock	27239
High Shoals	28077
Highsmiths	28382
Hightowers	27379
Hildebran	28637
Hillcrest (Hoke County)	28376
Hill Crest (Moore County)	28327
Hilliardston	27856
Hillsborough	27278
Hills Crossroads	27839
Hillsdale (Davie County)	27006
Hillsdale (Guilford County)	27405
Hillsville	27350
Hilltop (Guilford County)	27417
Hilltop (Lincoln County)	28092
Hilltop Acres	28570
Hill View	28580
Hines Crossroad	27834
Hinsons Crossroads	28439
Hiwassee Dam	28906
Hobbsville	27946
Hobbton	28366
Hobgood	27843
Hobucken	28537
Hodges Gap	28607
Hodman	27028
Hoffman	28347
Hog Island	28394
Ho-Ho Village	28570
Holden Beach	28462
Holdens Cross Roads	27893
Holiday Island	27944
Holiday Shores	27371
Holland	27526
Hollemans Crossroads	27562
Hollis	28040
Hollister	27844
Holly Grove (Davidson County)	27292
Holly Grove (Gates County)	27926
Holly Hill Mall (Part of Burlington)	27215
Holly Ridge	28445
Holly Springs (Macon County)	28734
Holly Springs (Wake County)	27540
Hollyville	28515
Hollywood	28304
Hollywood Crossroads	27858
Homestead (Part of Charlotte)	28214
Homestead Heights (Part of Durham)	27704
Honey Hill	28442
Honey Island	28420
Honey Town	28379
Honolulu	28530
Hood Swamp	27534
Hookerton	28538
Hooper Hill	28451
Hoopers Creek	28732
Hootentown	27889
Hopedale	27217
Hope Mills	28348
Hope Valley (Part of Durham)	27707
Hopewell (Rutherford County)	28040
Hopewell (Wayne County)	28565
Hopkins	27597
Horner	27565
Horse Shoe	28742
Hosiery Mill	28170
Hoskins (Part of Charlotte)	28208
Hothouse	28906
Hot Springs	28743
Houston	28112
Houstonville	28634
Howland Parkway	28516
Hubert	28539
Hudson	28638
Hudsons Crossroads	27858
Huffmantown	28574
Hughes	28657
Hugo	28530

	ZIP		ZIP		ZIP		ZIP
Hulls Crossroads	28168	Johnsons Corner	27976	Kornegay	28508	Lenoir	28645
Huntdale	28740	Johnsontown (Davidson		Kure Beach	28449	Lenoir Mall (Part of Lenoir)	28645
Hunters Bridge	27865	County)	27360	Kyle	28781	Lenoir Rhyne (Part of	
Huntersville	28078	Johnsontown (Sampson		Laboratory	28092	Hickory)	28601
Hunting Creek	28659	County)	28328	Lackey Hill	28713	Letitia	28906
Hunts	27882	Johnsonville (Cherokee		Lackey Town	28762	Level Cross (Randolph	
Huntsboro	27565	County)	28906	Ladonia	27030	County)	27317
Huntsville (Rockingham		Johnsonville (Harnett		Lafayette	28304	Level Cross (Surry	
County)	27025	County)	28326	Lagoon	28448	County)	27017
Huntsville (Yadkin County)	27028	Johnston Correctional		La Grange (Cumberland		Levels	27925
Hurdle Mills	27541	Center	27577	County)	28303	Lewis	27565
Husk	28639	Johnstown	28021	La Grange (Lenoir		Lewisburg	28714
Hyatt Creek	28786	John Umstead Hospital	27509	County)	28551	Lewiston Woodville	27849
Hyde Park Estates	28216	Jonas Ridge	28641	Lakecrest	28301	Lewisville	27023
Hymans	28562	Jonathan	28786	Lakedale (Part of		Lexington	27292*
Icard	28666	Jones	27311	Fayetteville)	28306		27293†
Icaria	27980	Jonesboro Heights (Part		Lake Daniel (Part of		Lexington Plaza (Part of	
Ida	28351	of Sanford)	27330	Greensboro)	27408	Lexington)	27292
Idlewild (Ashe County)	28694	Jones Chapel	27545	Lake Ellsworth	27834	Liberia	27589
Idlewild (Mecklenburg		Jonestown	28572	Lake Gaston Estates	27551	Liberty (Cherokee County)	37391
County)	28212	Jonesville	28642	Lake Glenwood	27858	Liberty (Randolph County)	27298
Idlewild Annex (Part of		Joppa	27919	Lake in the Pine	27371	Liberty (Rowan County)	28071
Charlotte)	28227	Joyceton (Part of Hudson)	28638	Lake Junaluska	28745	Liberty Hill	27306
Ijames Crossroads	27028	Joyland (Part of Durham)	27703	Lake Landing	27824	Liddell	28578
Independence (Part of		Joyners Crossroads	27801	Lake Lure	28746	Light Oak	28150
Charlotte)	28212	Joynes	28685	Lake Lynn	28306	Liledown	28681
Independence Mall (Part		Jubilee	27299	Lake Montonia	28086	Lilesville	28091
of Wilmington)	28403	Jugtown	28715	Lakemont Park	28601	Lillington	27546
Index	28694	Julian	27283	Lakeside (Forsyth County)	27105	Lilly	27976
Indian Beach	28557	Juno	28806	Lakeside (Stanly County)	28001	Lincoln Correctional	
Indian Hills	28789	Jupiter	28787	Lake Toxaway	28747	Center	28092
Indian Springs	28578	Justice	27549	Lakeview (Alamance		Lincolnton	28092*
Indian Town	27973	Kalmia	28777	County)	27215		28093†
Indian Trail	28079	Kannapolis	28081-83	Lakeview (Davidson		Lindell	27883
Indian Valley	27217	For specific Kannapolis Zip		County)	27299	Linden	28356
Inez	27589	Codes call (704) 938-1129, or		Lakeview (Moore County)	28350	Lindley Park (Part of	
Ingalls	28657	your local postmaster.		Lakeview Estates		Greensboro)	27403
Ingleside	27549	Kappa	27028	(Alamance County)	27215	Lineberry	27233
Ingold	28446	Kapps Mill	27017	Lakeview Estates		Linville	28646
Institute	28551	Katesville	27525	(Henderson County)	28792	Linville Falls	28647
Intelligence	27025	Keene	27707	Lake View Park	27870	Linwood	27299
Iotla	28734	Keener	28328	Lake Waccamaw	28450	Lisbon	28434
Iredell Correctional Center	28677	Kelford	27847	Lakewood (Cabarrus		Little Creek	28754
Iris Gardens	28306	Kellersville	28604	County)	28025	Littlefield	28513
Ironduff	28786	Kellogs Fork	27979	Lakewood (Henderson		Little Horse Creek	28643
Irongate	28306	Kellum	28540	County)	28739	Little Mountain	28761
Ironhill	28463	Kellumtown	28539	Lambert	28163	Little Pinecreek	28753
Iron Station	28080	Kelly	28448	Lambs Corner	27921	Little Richmond	28621
Irving Park (Part of		Kenansville	28349	Lamm	27893	Little River (Alexander	
Greensboro)	27408	Kendale Shopping Center		Lamms Crossroads	27882	County)	28681
Isenhour	28127	(Part of Sanford)	27330	Lancaster Crossroads	27816	Little River (Transylvania	
Island View Shores	27808	Kenilworth (Part of		Landis	28088	County)	28766
Isle of Pines	28115	Asheville)	28805	Langley Store	27801	Little Switzerland	28749
Ita	27823	Kenly	27542	Lansdowne (Part of		Littleton	27850
Ivanhoe	28447	Kenmure	28731	Charlotte)	28226	Livingstons Quarters	28351
Ivy	28754	Kennebec	27592	Lansing	28643	Lizard Lick	27591
Ivy Hills	28786	Kennells Beach	28529	Lanvale	28451	Lizzie	28580
Jackson	27845	Kentwood	28081	Lasker	27848	Lloyd Crossroads	27942
Jackson Hamlet	28315	Kernersville	27284*	Last Chance	27824	Loafers Glory	28705
Jackson Hill	27239		27285†	Latham Town (Part of		Lobelia	28394
Jackson Line	28713	Kerr	28444	Greensboro)	27407	Lochlommond	28304
Jackson Park (Part of		Kershaw	28571	Lattimore	28089	Locust	28097
Kannapolis)	28081	Keys Crossroads	27946	Lauada	28713	Locust Grove	28740
Jackson Park (Part of		Kikers	28133	Laurel	28753	Locust Hill	27320
Concord)	28027	Kilby Island	27808	Laurel Hill (Buncombe		Loftins Crossroads	28501
Jacksons Creek	27239	Kill Devil Hills	27948	County)	28715	Logan	28139
Jacksons Crossroads		Kimesville	27298	Laurel Hill (Scotland		Lola	28520
(Duplin County)	28518	King	27021	County)	28351	Lomax	28669
Jacksons Crossroads		King Charles (Part of		Laurel Hills	27612	Lone Hickory	27055
(Lenoir County)	28501	Raleigh)	27610	Laurel Park	28739	Long Acres (Part of	
Jackson Springs	27281	Kingsboro	27801	Laurel Springs	28644	Jacksonville)	28546
Jacksons Store	28518	Kings Creek	28645	Laurinburg	28352*	Longcreek	28457
Jacksontown	27556	Kings Crossroads			28353†	Longisland	28609
Jacksonville	28540-41	(Guilford County)	27284	Lawndale (Cleveland		Long John Mountain	
	28546	Kings Crossroads (Pitt		County)	28090	Estates	28739
For specific Jacksonville Zip		County)	27829	Lawndale (Guilford		Longleaf	28570
Codes call (910) 346-4135, or		Kings Forest	28147	County)	27408	Long Leaf Park (Part of	
your local postmaster.		Kings Mountain	28086	Lawrence	27886	Wilmington)	28403
Jacktown	28752	Kingstown	28150	Lawsonville (Rockingham		Long Pine	28170
Jakesville	27292	King Whites Fork	27843	County)	27320	Long Ridge	28754
James City	28560	Kinston	28501-03	Lawsonville (Stokes		Long Shoals	28092
Jamestown	27282	For specific Kinston Zip Codes		County)	27022	Longs Store	27573
Jamesville	27846	call (919) 527-6123, or your		Laytown	28645	Longtown (Burke County)	28761
Janeiro	28510	local postmaster.		Leaksville (Part of Eden)	27288	Longtown (Yadkin	
Jarman Forks	28574	Kinton Fork	27565	Leaman	27325	County)	27011
Jarvisburg	27947	Kipling	27543	Leasburg	27291	Long View (Bladen	
Jason	28551	Kirbys Crossing	27851	Leatherman	28734	County)	28448
Jasper	28562	Kirkwood (Part of		Ledbetter	28379	Longview (Catawba	
Jefferson	28640	Greensboro)	27408	Ledger	28705	County)	28602
Jefferson Park	28379	Kittrell	27544	Leechville	27810	Longview (Cumberland	
Jenkins Heights (Part of		Kitty Fork	28328	Lee's Ridge	28806	County)	28301
Gastonia)	28052	Kitty Hawk	27949	Leewood Acres	28092	Longwood	28452
Jenny Lind	28551	Knightdale	27545	Leggett	27886	Longwood Park	28345
Jericho	27379	Knob Hill	28379	Leicester	28748	Loray	28677
Jerome	28399	Knollwood (Part of		Leland	28451	Louisburg	27549
Jerusalem	27028	Southern Pines)	28387	Lemon Springs	28355	Love Field	28779
Joe	28743	Knotts Island	27950	Lennon Crossroads	28422	Lovejoy	27371
Johns	28352	Kona	28705	Lennons Crossroads	28438	Love Valley	28677
Johnson Crossroad	27501	Kornbow	28303	Lennoxville	28516	Lowell	28098

Place	ZIP
Lowes Grove	27713
Lowesville	28164
Lowgap	27024
Lowland	28552
Luart	27546
Lucama	27851
Lucia	28120
Luck	28743
Lumber Bridge	28357
Lumberton	28358*
	28359†
Luther	28715
Lyman	28521
Lynchs Corner	27909
Lynn	28750
Lynndale	27858
Lynnwood Jr. Estate	28025
Lynwood Lakes	27406
Mabel	28698
McAdenville	28101
McAdoo Heights (Part of Greensboro)	27405
McArthers Crossroads	28352
Macclesfield	27852
McConnell (Beaufort County)	27814
McConnell (Moore County)	27325
McCray	27215
McCullen	28328
McCullers	27603
Mc Cutcheon Field	28545
McDade	27231
McDaniel	28382
McDonald	28340
McDowell Correctional Center	28752
Macedonia (Wake County)	27606
Macedonia (Washington County)	27962
McFarlan	28102
MacGee Crossroads	27501
McGehees Mill	27343
McGinnis Crossroads	28722
McGowans Crossroads	27858
McGrady	28649
Machpelah	28080
Mackeys	27970
Macks Village	27526
McLamb Crossroads	28366
McLeansville	27301
Maco	28451
Macon	27551
Madison	27025
Maggie Valley	28751
Magnolia (Burke County)	28655
Magnolia (Duplin County)	28453
Maiden	28650
Maine	27028
Main Street (Part of Garner)	27529
Makatoka	28420
Makleyville	27875
Malmo	28451
Malpass Corner	28425
Maltby	28905
Malvern Hills (Part of Asheville)	28806
Mamers	27552
Mamie	27966
Manchester (Part of Spring Lake)	28390
Mangum	27306
Manly	28387
Manns Harbor	27953
Manor Station	27103-04
	27114

For specific Manor Station Zip Codes call (910) 760-4131, or your local postmaster.

Place	ZIP
Mansfield	28557
Mansfield Park	28557
Manson	27553
Manteo	27954
Maple	27956
Maple Cypress	28530
Maple Hill	28454
Maple Springs	28665
Mapleton	27855
Mapleville	27549
Maplewood (Part of Rockingham)	28379
Marble	28905
Marcus	27281
Maready	28521
Margaretsville	27853
Maribel	28515
Marietta	28362
Marion	28752
Mariposa	28164
Marlboro	27828
Marler	27020
Marlwood Acres (Part of Charlotte)	28212
Mar-Mac	27530
Mar-Man	28532
Marshall	28753
Marshallberg	28553
Mars Hill	28754
Marshville	28103
Marston	28363
Martel Village (Part of Woodfin)	28804
Martin Correctional Center	27892
Martins Creek	28906
Marvin	28173
Marys Grove	28086
Mashoes	27953
Masonboro	28403
Masons Crossroads	28343
Mason Store	27546
Masontown	28581
Massapoag (Part of Lincolnton)	28092
Mast	28692
Mathews Crossroads	27816
Matkins	27249
Matney	28604
Matthews	28105*
	28106†
Maury	28554
Mavaton	27932
Maxton	28364
Mayfair	28304
Mayfield	27326
Mayhew	28115
Mayodan	27027
Maysville	28555
Mazeppa	28115
Meadow (Johnston County)	27504
Meadow (Stokes County)	27052
Meadowood	28379
Meadowood Lakes	27302
Meadow Summit (Part of Eden)	27288
Meadow Wood	28304
Meat Camp	28607
Mebane	27302
Mecklenburg Correctional Center	28078
Medfield	27607
Melanchton	27298
Melrose	28773
Melville	27302
Melvin Hill	28722
Menola	27910
Meredith College (Part of Raleigh)	27601
Merrimon	28516
Merritt	28556
Merry Hill	27957
Merry Oaks	27559
Mesic	28515
Metcalf	28150
Method (Part of Raleigh)	27606
Methodist College	28311
Mewborns Crossroads	28501
Micaville	28755
Micro	27555
Middleburg	27556
Middle Fork	28712
Middlesex	27557
Middletown	27824
Midland	28107
Midpine	28086
Midway (Alexander County)	28636
Midway (Beaufort County)	27808
Midway (Bertie County)	27957
Midway (Brunswick County)	28422
Midway (Cabarrus County)	28081
Midway (Richmond County)	28379
Midway (Rockingham County)	27320
Midway Park	28544
Midwood (Part of Charlotte)	28205
Milburnie	27604
Mildred	27886
Miles	27302
Millboro	27248
Mill Branch	28420
Millbridge	28147
Millbrook (Part of Raleigh)	27658
Mill Creek (Ashe County)	28684
Mill Creek (Brunswick County)	28479
Mill Creek (Carteret County)	28570
Mill Crossroads	27932
Millennium Church	27805
Millers Creek	28651
Millersville	28681
Millingport	28001
Mill Spring	28756
Mills River	28742
Milltown	28771
Milton	27305
Milwaukee	27854
Mimosa Shores	27889
Mineral Springs (Anson County)	28135
Mineral Springs (Union County)	28108
Mingo	28334
Minneapolis	28652
Minnesott Beach	28510
Minpro	28777
Mint Hill	28227
Mintons Store	27897
Mintonsville	27946
Mintz	28382
Minuet	28209-10

For specific Minuet Zip Codes call (704) 522-6414, or your local postmaster.

Place	ZIP
Mirror Lake	28741
Misenheimer	28109
Mitchells Fork	27946
Mitchell Village	28557
Mitcheners Crossroads	27525
Mocksville	27028
Moffitt Hill	28762
Mollie	28432
Moltonville	28328
Momeyer	27856
Moncure	27559
Monks Crossroads	28366
Monroe	28110-12

For specific Monroe Zip Codes call (704) 289-4507, or your local postmaster.

Place	ZIP
Monroe Mall (Part of Monroe)	28110
Monroetown (Moore County)	28374
Monroetown (Rockingham County)	27320
Montague	28435
Montclair	28304
Montezuma	28653
Montgomery Correctional Center	27371
Monticello	27214
Montreat	28757
Montrose	28376
Moores Beach	27810
Mooresboro	28114
Moores School House	27542
Moores Springs	27053
Mooresville	28115
Mooresville Junction (Part of Mooresville)	28115
Moravian Falls	28654
Mordecai (Part of Raleigh)	27604
Morehead City	28557
Morgans Corner	27909
Morganton	28655*
	28680†
Morgantown	27215
Moriah	27572
Morlan Park	28146
Morning Star	28716
Morris Landing	28445
Morrisville	27560
Mortimer	28645
Morven	28119
Moss	28127
Moss Hill	28501
Mother Vineyard	27954
Motleta	27203
Mountain Home	28758
Mountain Island	28120
Mountain Park	28676
Mountain Valley	28790
Mountain View (Buncombe County)	28704
Mountain View (Catawba County)	28601
Mountain View (Gaston County)	28086
Mountain View (Orange County)	27278
Mountain View (Stokes County)	27021
Mount Airy	27030
Mount Carmel	27306
Mount Carmel Acres	28806
Mount Energy	27522
Mount Gilead (Avery County)	28622
Mount Gilead (Cabarrus County)	28025
Mount Gilead (Montgomery County)	27306
Mount Gould	27957
Mount Herman	28638
Mount Holly	28120
Mount Mourne	28123
Mount Olive (Bladen County)	28337
Mount Olive (Columbus County)	28472
Mount Olive (Hyde County)	27810
Mount Olive (Stokes County)	27021
Mount Olive (Wayne County)	28365
Mount Pleasant (Avery County)	28657
Mount Pleasant (Cabarrus County)	28124
Mount Pleasant (Cherokee County)	28906
Mount Pleasant (Moore County)	28326
Mount Pleasant (Nash County)	27807
Mount Pleasant (Richmond County)	28338
Mount Pleasant (Yadkin County)	27011
Mount Sterling	37821
Mount Tabor (Forsyth County)	27106
Mount Tabor (Washington County)	27928
Mount Tirzah	27583
Mount Ulla	28125
Mount Vernon (Rowan County)	27013
Mount Vernon (Rutherford County)	28139
Mount Vernon Springs	27344
Mount Zion (Part of Greensboro)	27406
Moxley	28635
Moyock	27958
Mt. Mitchell	28083
Mt. Pleasant	27592
Muddy Cross	27946
Mulberry	28659
Murdocksville	28374
Murfreesboro	27855
Murphey	28458
Murphy	28906
Murray Hills	28081
Murrays Mills	28609
Murraysville	28405
Murray Town	28425
Musgraves Crossroads	27863
Myers Park (Part of Charlotte)	28207
Myrick Estates	27850
Myrtle Grove	28403
Nags Head	27959
Nahunta	27863
Nakina	28455
Nantahala	28781
Naples	28760
Nash Correctional Institution	27856
Nashville	27856
Nathans Creek	28617
Naval Hospital	28542
Navassa	28404
Nebo (McDowell County)	28761
Nebo (Yadkin County)	27011
Nebraska	27824
Needmore (Rowan County)	27054
Needmore (Swain County)	28713
Neel Estates	28147
Nelson	27560
Neuse	27661
Neuse Crossroads	27661
Neuse Forest (census designated place)	28562
Neuse Forest	28560

* Area Zip Code   † Post Office Boxes

	ZIP
Neverson	27880
New Bern	28560-64
For specific New Bern Zip Codes call (919) 638-6111, or your local postmaster.	
New Bern Junction (Part of Wilmington)	28405
New Bethel	27572
Newbold (Part of Fayetteville)	28301
New Bridge (Part of Woodfin)	28804
Newdale	28714
Newell	28126
Newfound	28748
New Hanover Correctional Center	28401
New Haven	28675
New Hill	27562
New Holland	27885
New Hope (Chatham County)	27559
New Hope (Franklin County)	27549
New Hope (Iredell County)	28689
New Hope (Orange County)	27514
New Hope (Randolph County)	27239
New Hope (Wake County)	27604
New Hope (Wayne County)	27534
New Hope (Wilson County)	27893
New House	28150
Newland	28657
New Lands	27925
New Leaksville	27288
Newlife	28635
New London	28127
New Market	27350
Newport	28570
New River Marine Corps Air Station	28540
New River Plaza (Part of Jacksonville)	28540
New Salem	28103
Newsom	27239
Newton	28658
Newton Grove	28366
Newton Park	27893
Newtons Crossroads	28478
Newtowne Plaza (Part of Statesville)	28677
Niagara	28387
Nixons Beach	27932
Nixonton	27909
Nobles Cross Roads	28525
Nocarva	27551
Nocho Park (Part of Greensboro)	27406
Norfleet	27874
Norlina	27563
Norman	28367
Norrington Crossroads	27546
North (Part of Winston-Salem)	27105
North Albemarle (Part of Albemarle)	28001
North Asheboro (Part of Asheboro)	27203
North Belmont (Part of Belmont)	28012
North Brevard	28712
North Burlington (Part of Burlington)	27215
North Charlotte (Part of Charlotte)	28225
North Chase (Part of Wilmington)	28405
North Concord (Part of Concord)	28025
North Cooleemee (Part of Cooleemee)	27014
North Cove	28752
North Durham (Part of Durham)	27712
North Elkin	28621
Northgate (Part of Durham)	27701
Northgate Mall (Part of Durham)	27701
North Harbor	28516
North Harlowe	28532
North Henderson (Part of Henderson)	27536
North Hickory	28601
North Hills Mall & Plaza (Part of Raleigh)	27609

	ZIP
	27614
	27619
For specific North Hills Mall & Plaza Zip Codes call (919) 781-0410, or your local postmaster.	
Northlakes	28630
North Lumberton (Part of Lumberton)	28358
Northmoor	28601
North Point (Part of Winston-Salem)	27106
North Raeford	28376
North Ridge (Part of Raleigh)	27615
North River	28516
North River Corner	28516
North Roxboro (Part of Roxboro)	27573
Northside (Granville County)	27564
Northside (Wilson County)	27822
North Topsail Beach	28445
North Tryon (Part of Charlotte)	28213
	28215
	28262
	28269
For specific North Tryon Zip Codes call (704) 393-4555, or your local postmaster.	
Northview	27330
Northwest	28451
Northwest Cabarrus Woods	28081
North Wilkesboro	28659
North Winston (Part of Winston-Salem)	27105
Northwoods (Part of Jacksonville)	28540
Norton (Jackson County)	28723
Norton (Macon County)	28763
Norwood (Rockingham County)	27320
Norwood (Stanly County)	28128
Norwood Beach	28128
Norwood Hollow	28604
Oakboro	28129
Oak City	27857
Oak Crest (Part of Fayetteville)	28301
Oakdale (Guilford County)	27282
Oakdale (Iredell County)	28677
Oak Forest	28803
Oak Grove (Brunswick County)	28462
Oak Grove (Cleveland County)	28086
Oak Grove (Guilford County)	27406
Oak Grove (Macon County)	28734
Oak Grove (Surry County)	27030
Oak Hill (Burke County)	28655
Oak Hill (Caldwell County)	28645
Oakhurst (Part of Charlotte)	28205
Oak Island	28465
Oakland (Nash County)	27882
Oakland (Rutherford County)	28160
Oakley (Part of Asheville)	28803
Oak Park (Buncombe County)	28704
Oak Park (Cherokee County)	28906
Oak Ridge	27310
Oak Ridge Park	28379
Oaks	28560
Oaksmith Acres	28557
Oakview (Part of High Point)	27265
Oak Villa	27986
Oakville	27589
Oakwillow	27910
Oakwood (Part of Greensboro)	27407
Oakwood Acres	27292
Occoneechee	27278
Ocean	28570
Ocean Isle Beach	28469
Ocracoke	27960
Odom Correctional Institution	27845
Ogburn (Part of Winston-Salem)	27105
Ogden	28405
Ogreeta	28906
Oine	27563
Okeewemee	27371

	ZIP
Okisko	27909
Old Bethlehem	27589
Old Dock	28472
Olde Farm	28390
Old Farm	28025
Old Ford	27889
Old Fort	28762
Old Fort Shores	28117
Old Hundred	28351
Old Providence (Part of Charlotte)	28226
Old Sparta	27852
Old Spring Hope	27882
Oldtown (Part of Winston-Salem)	27106
Old Trap	27974
Olin	28660
Olive Branch	28103
Olive Crossroads	28573
Olivehill	27573
Olivers Crossroads	28658
Olivia	28368
Olympia	28560
Olyphic	28463
Onvil	27306
Ophir	27371
Ora Mill	28150
Orange Correctional Center	27278
Orange Grove	27278
Oregon Hill	27326
Oriental	28571
Ormondsville	28513
Orrum	28369
Osborne	28345
Osceola	27214
Osgood	27330
Osmond	27291
Ossipee	27244
Oswalt	28166
Oteen	28805
Othello	28694
Otto	28763
Otway	28516
Outlaws Bridge	28508
Overhills Park	28390
Oxford	27565
Oxford Park	28610
Pacolet Valley	28782
Pactolus	27834
Padgett	28454
Paint Fork	28754
Paint Rock	28743
Pala Alto	28555
Palestine	28001
Palmerville	28127
Palmyra	27859
Pamlico	28571
Pamlico Beach	27810
Pantego	27860
Panther Creek	28721
Paradise Point	28012
Parkersburg	28441
Parkers Fork	27926
Park Road (Part of Charlotte)	28209
Parks Crossroads	27316
Park Spring	27315
Parkstone (Part of Charlotte)	28210
Parkstown	28551
Parkton	28371
Parktown	27589
Park View (Part of Kinston)	28501
Parkville	27944
Parkway Forest (Part of Asheville)	28805
Parkwood (Cabarrus County)	28027
Parkwood (Durham County)	27713
Parkwood (Moore County)	28327
Parkwood (Wilson County)	27893
Parmele	27861
Parrott Fork	28501
Parsonville	28665
Paschall	27589
Pates	28372
Patetown	27534
Patterson	28661
Patterson Grove	28086
Patterson Springs	28152
Pauls Crossing	28137
Paw Creek (Part of Charlotte)	28130
Paynes Tavern	27573
Peace Haven Estates	27104
Peachland	28133

	ZIP
Peachtree	28906
Peacock Crossing	28431
Pearce Crossroads	27597
Pea Ridge (Polk County)	28756
Pea Ridge (Yadkin County)	27020
Pecan Grove	27874
Peden	28672
Pee Dee	27306
Pekin	27306
Peletier	28584
Pelham	27311
Pembroke	28372
Pender Correctional Center	28425
Pender Crossroad	27822
Penderlea	28478
Pendleton	27862
Penland	28765
Penrose	28766
Pensacola	28714
Perch	27043
Perfection	28523
Perkinsville (Part of Boone)	28607
Perry's Beach	27924
Perrytown	27924
Peru	28460
Petersburg (Madison County)	28753
Petersburg (Onslow County)	28574
Petersville	27292
Pettys Shore	27922
Pfafftown	27040
Philadelphia	27974
Philadelphus	28377
Phillips Cross Roads	28585
Phoenix	28451
Piedmont Crescent Country Club	27253
Piedmont Heights (Part of Greensboro)	27403
Pierceville	27976
Pigeon Roost	28740
Pike Crossroads	27863
Pike Road	27860
Pikeville	27863
Pilands Crossroads	27922
Pilot (Davidson County)	27360
Pilot (Franklin County)	27597
Pilot Mountain	27041
Pinebluff	28373
Pine Crest	27808
Pinecrest Acres	28301
Pinecroft (Part of Greensboro)	27407
Pine Hall	27042
Pine Haven	27239
Pine Hill (Hoke County)	28315
Pine Hill (Surry County)	27011
Pinehurst	28374
Pinehurst Park	27529
Pine Knoll (Part of Hope Mills)	28348
Pine Knoll Shores	28557
Pine Lakes	27030
Pine Level	27568
Pinelog	28472
Pineola	28662
Pine Ridge (Cabarrus County)	28201
Pine Ridge (Franklin County)	27597
Pine Ridge (Surry County)	27030
Pine Ridge (Washington County)	27970
Pinetops	27864
Pinetown	27865
Pine Valley	28403
Pine View	27330
Pineville	28134
Piney Creek	28663
Piney Green (rural Sampson County)	28328
Piney Green (Part of Camp Lejeune)	28544
Piney Green (census designated place)	28540
Piney Grove (Brunswick County)	28422
Piney Grove (Craven County)	28532
Piney Grove (Orange County)	27278
Piney Ridge	28328
Pin Hook	28466
Pink Hill	28572
Pinkney	27830

	ZIP
Pinnacle	27043
Pireway	28463
Pisgah Forest	28768
Pisgah View (Part of Asheville)	28806
Pittmans Store	27891
Pittsboro	27312
Plainview	28383
Plateau	28658
Plaza (Guilford County)	27429
Plaza (Mecklenburg County)	28299
Plaza, The (Part of Greenville)	27858
Pleasant Acres	28301
Pleasant Garden	27313
Pleasant Gardens	28752
Pleasant Grove (Alamance County)	27217
Pleasant Grove (Buncombe County)	28787
Pleasant Grove (Caswell County)	27379
Pleasant Grove (Duplin County)	28365
Pleasant Grove (Northampton County)	27831
Pleasant Grove (Washington County)	27970
Pleasant Hill (Jones County)	28572
Pleasant Hill (Northampton County)	27866
Pleasant Hill (Wilkes County)	28621
Pleasant Plains	27910
Pleasant View	27925
Pleasantville	27025
Plott Farm Addition	28716
Plumtree	28664
Plyler	28001
Plymouth	27962
Pocomoke	27525
Point Caswell	28421
Point Harbor	27964
Pole Creek	28715
Polks Landing	27514
Polkton	28135
Polkville	28136
Pollocksville	28573
Pomona (Part of Greensboro)	27407
Ponderosa (Cumberland County)	28303
Ponderosa (Harnett County)	28334
Ponzer	27810
Pooletown	28137
Poor Town	27910
Pope Air Force Base	28308
Poplar	28740
Poplar Branch	27965
Poplar Grove	28341
Poplar Springs	27021
Poplar Tent	28027
Porter	28128
Portsmouth	27960
Postell	28906
Potecasi	27867
Pot Neck	28551
Potters Curve	28431
Potters Hill	28572
Pottertown	28684
Powell Crossroads	27946
Powells Point	27966
Powells Store	27326
Powellsville	27967
Powhatan	27520
Prentiss	28734
Prestonville	27025
Price	27048
Price Creek	28714
Princeton	27569
Princeville	27886
Proctors Corner	27910
Proctorville	28375
Propst Crossroads	28601
Prospect	28462
Prospect Hill	27314
Prosper	28436
Providence (Caswell County)	27315
Providence (Granville County)	27565
Providence (McDowell County)	28752
Providence (Mecklenburg County)	28105

	ZIP
Providence Square (Part of Charlotte)	28211
Proximity (Part of Greensboro)	27405
Pumpkin Center (Lincoln County)	28092
Pumpkin Center (Onslow County)	28540
Pumpkintown	28779
Pungo	27860
Pungo Stores	27810
Purlear	28665
Purley	27379
Purnell	27587
Purvis	28383
Putnam	28327
Pyatte	28657
Quail Corners (Part of Charlotte)	28210
Quail Ridge (Craven County)	28532
Quail Ridge (Cumberland County)	28306
Quail Ridge (Lee County)	27330
Qualla	28789
Quebec	28747
Queen	27371
Quick	27326
Quinerly	28530
Quinns Store	28518
Quitsna	27983
Rabbit Corner	27909
Radical	28649
Radio Island	28516
Raeford	28376
Raemon	28364
Rainbow Springs	28734
Raleigh	27601-76
For specific Raleigh Zip Codes call (919) 831-3661, or your local postmaster.	
Rama Woods	28025
Ramseur	27316
Ramseytown	28714
Randleman	27317
Randolph (Mecklenburg County)	28211
Randolph (Pitt County)	27834
Randolph Correctional Center	27203
Randolph Mall (Part of Asheboro)	27203
Ranger	28906
Rangewood	27603
Rankin (Guilford County)	27405
Rankin (Pender County)	28421
Ranlo	28054
Ransomville	27810
Rawls	27526
Rayconda	28304
Raynham	28383
Rebel Acres	27604
Red Banks	28364
Redbug	28442
Red Cross (Randolph County)	27233
Red Cross (Stanly County)	28129
Reddies River	28696
Red Hill (Bladen County)	28433
Red Hill (Edgecombe County)	27891
Red Hill (Mitchell County)	28705
Redland	27006
Red Oak (Nash County)	27868
Red Oak (Pitt County)	27834
Red Springs	28377
Reeds Cross Roads	27292
Reedy Creek	27292
Reelsboro	28560
Reepsville	28168
Reese	28692
Reeves Ferry	28455
Regal	28906
Regan	28420
Register	28458
Rehoboth	27845
Reidsville	27320-23
For specific Reidsville Zip Codes call (910) 342-0391, or your local postmaster.	
Relief	28740
Rena	27020
Rennert	28386
Renston	28513
Republican	27983
Rest Haven	27808
Revolution (Part of Greensboro)	27405

	ZIP
Rex (Gaston County)	28054
Rex (Robeson County)	28378
Reynolda (Part of Winston-Salem)	27109
Reynolda Park (Part of Winston-Salem)	27107
Rheasville	27870
Rhems	28562
Rhems Landing	28562
Rhodes	27805
Rhodes-Rhyne	28092
Rhodhiss	28667
Rhodo	28901
Rhoney	28602
Rhyne Crossroads	28425
Riceville	28805
Richardson	28320
Richfield	28137
Richlands	28574
Richmond Hill (Alamance County)	27215
Richmond Hill (Yadkin County)	27011
Richmond Mills	28351
Rich Square	27869
Rico	28472
Riddle	27973
Ridgecrest	28770
Ridge Haven	27591
Ridge Run	28025
Ridgeville	27314
Ridgeway	27570
Ridgewood	28379
Riegelwood	28456
Riley	27596
Rimer	28025
Ringwood	27823
River Acres	27889
River Bend	28562
Riverdale	28560
River Hills	27858
Rivermont	28501
River Neck	27925
River Road	27889
Riverside (rural Craven County)	28530
Riverside (Part of New Bern) (Craven County)	28560
Riverside (Yancey County)	28714
Riverton	27932
Roanoke Rapids	27870
Roaring Creek	28657
Roaring Gap	28668
Roaring River	28669
Robbins	27325
Robbinsville	28771
Roberdel	28379
Roberdo	27306
Roberson Store	27892
Robersonville	27871
Roberta Mill	28027
Robeson Correctional Center	28358
Robin Hood Forest	27545
Robinson's	28570
Robinwood (Part of Gastonia)	28056
Rock Creek	27349
Rockdale (Part of Belwood)	28090
Rockefeller Estates	28326
Rockfish	28376
Rockford	27011
Rock Hill	28025
Rockingham	28379
Rockingham Correctional Center	27320
Rockingham Lake	27320
Rock Ridge	27893
Rockwell	28138
Rockwell Park (Part of Charlotte)	28213
Rocky Cross	27557
Rocky Ford	27544
Rockyhock	27932
Rocky Mount	27801-04
For specific Rocky Mount Zip Codes call (919) 977-3123, or your local postmaster.	
Rocky Pass	28761
Rocky Point	28457
Rocky River	28025
Rocky Springs	28636
Rodanthe	27968
Roduco	27969
Rolesville	27571
Rollingwood	28301
Rominger	28604
Ronda	28670

	ZIP
Rooks	28421
Roper	27970
Rose Bay	27885
Roseboro	28382
Roseborough	28646
Rosebud (Stokes County)	27052
Rosebud (Wilson County)	27822
Rose Hill (Duplin County)	28458
Rose Hill (Warren County)	27553
Roseland (Columbus County)	28432
Roseland (Lincoln County)	28092
Roseland (Moore County)	28315
Rosemary Park	28079
Rosemead	27924
Rosemont (Part of Winston-Salem)	27107
Roseneath	27874
Roseville	27573
Rosewood	27530
Rosindale	28434
Rosman	28772
Ross Store	27052
Rougemont	27572
Roughedge	28112
Round Peak	27030
Roundtree	28513
Rowan Correctional Center	28145
Rowan Mill	28147
Rowes Corner	28560
Rowland	28383
Roxboro	27573
Roxobel	27872
Royal	27806
Royal Oaks (Part of Kannapolis)	28083
Royal Pines	28704
Royster	28451
Rudd	27214
Ruffin	27326
Rural Hall	27045
Ruskin	28399
Russtown	28420
Ruth	28139
Rutherford College	28671
Rutherford Correctional Center	28043
Rutherfordton	28139
Rutherwood	28607
Ryland	27980
Saddle Mountain	28623
Saddletree	28358
Sadler	27320
St. Helena	28425
St. John	27910
St. Johns	27932
St. Lewis	27852
St. Martin	28001
St. Pauls	28384
St. Stephens	28601
Salem (Burke County)	28655
Salem (Forsyth County)	27108
Salem (Lincoln County)	28092
Salem (Nash County)	27891
Salem (Randolph County)	27317
Salem (Surry County)	27030
Salemburg	28385
Salisbury	28144-47
For specific Salisbury Zip Codes call (704) 636-0231, or your local postmaster.	
Salter Path	28575
Salty Shores	28570
Saluda	28773
Salvo	27972
Samarcand	27242
Samaria	27557
Sampson Correctional Center	28328
Sanderling	27948
Sand Hill (Buncombe County)	28806
Sandhill (Pamlico County)	28560
Sandhill Acres	27229
Sands	28607
Sandy Bottom	28501
Sandy Bottoms	28352
Sandy Creek	28451
Sandy Cross (Gates County)	27946
Sandy Cross (Nash County)	27856
Sandy Cross (Rockingham County)	27320
Sandy Grove (Davidson County)	27292
Sandy Grove (Hoke County)	28376

	ZIP
Sandymush (Buncombe County)	28753
Sandy Mush (Rutherford County)	28043
Sandy Plain (Columbus County)	28463
Sandy Plain (Duplin County)	28572
Sandy Plains	28782
Sandy Ridge (Guilford County)	27235
Sandy Ridge (Stokes County)	27046
Sandy Ridge Correctional Center	27265
Sanford	27330*
	27331†
Santeetlah	28771
Sapona	28301
Sapphire	28774
Saratoga	27873
Sardis Village (Part of Charlotte)	28270
Sarecta	28349
Sarecta Junction	28349
Sarvis Heights	28052
Sassers Mill	28526
Satterwhite	27565
Saulston	27534
Saunook	28786
Savannah	28779
Saw	28023
Sawmills	28630
Saxapahaw	27340
Sayles Village (Part of Asheville)	28803
Scaly Mountain	28775
Schley	27278
Scholl	28345
Schrams Beach	27810
Scotch Grove	28352
Scotland Correctional Center	28396
Scotland Neck	27874
Scotsdale (Cumberland County)	28304
Scotsdale (Scotland County)	28352
Scott Acres	27302
Scott Park (Part of Greensboro)	27401
Scotts (Iredell County)	28699
Scotts (Wilson County)	27851
Scotts Hill	28405
Scotts Store (Duplin County)	28365
Scotts Store (Pamlico County)	28560
Scottville	28672
Scranton	27875
Scuffleton	28513
Scuppernong	27928
Seaboard	27876
Seabreeze	28403
Seagate	28403
Seagate IV	28516
Seagrove	27341
Sealevel	28577
Seaside	28468
Sedalia	27342
Sedgefield (Guilford County)	27407
Sedgefield (Mecklenburg County)	28203
Sedgefield Lakes	27407
Sedgefield Park	27407
Sedge Garden	27105
Selica	28712
Selma	27576
Selwin	27946
Selwyn Park (Part of Charlotte)	28209
Seminole	27505
Semora	27343
Senia	28657
Seven Devils	28604
Seven Lakes	27376
Seven Paths	27549
Seven Springs	28578
Severn	27877
Seversville (Part of Charlotte)	28208
Sevier	28752
Seward	27040
Seymour Johnson Air Force Base	27531
Shacktown	27055
Shadey Oaks Acres	28150
Shady Banks	27889

	ZIP
Shady Brook (Part of Kannapolis)	28081
Shady Forest	28467
Shady Grove	28501
Shale Brick	27360
Shallotte	28459
Shallotte Point	28470
Shallowell	27330
Shanghai (Cleveland County)	28150
Shanghai (Sampson County)	28458
Shankletown	28027
Shannon	28386
Shannon Plaza (Part of Durham)	27707*
	27717†
Sharon (Camden County)	27976
Sharon (Iredell County)	28677
Sharonbrook (Part of Charlotte)	28210
Sharp Point	27829
Sharpsburg	27878
Shatley Springs	28617
Shawboro	27973
Shaw Heights	28303
Sheffield	27028
Shelby	28150-52
For specific Shelby Zip Codes call (704) 487-4324, or your local postmaster.	
Shell Rock Landing	28539
Shelmerdine	28513
Shelter Neck	28425
Shelton	27311
Shelton Town	27030
Shepard (Part of Durham)	27707
Shepherds	28115
Sherrills Ford (Catawba County)	28673
Sherron Acres (Part of Durham)	27703
Sherwood	28692
Sherwood Forest (Buncombe County)	28778
Sherwood Forest (Part of Asheville) (Buncombe County)	28805
Sherwood Forest (Forsyth County)	27104
Sherwood Forest (Transylvania County)	28712
Sherwood Forrest	27983
Sherwood Park	28306
Sherwood Terrace	28712
Sherwood Village (Part of High Point)	27260
Shields Commissary	27874
Shiloh (Buncombe County)	28803
Shiloh (Camden County)	27974
Shiloh (Rutherford County)	28043
Shines Crossroads	28580
Shingle Hollow	28139
Shinnville	28115
Shoal	27043
Shoofly	27581
Shooting Creek	28904
Shopton	28210
Short Off	28741
Shotwell	27545
Shuffletown	28214
Shulls Mills	28607
Shupings Mill	28138
Sidestown	28027
Sidney (Beaufort County)	27810
Sidney (Columbus County)	28472
Signal Hill Mall (Part of Statesville)	28677
Sign Pine	27980
Siler City	27344
Silk Hope	27344
Siloam	27047
Silver City	28376
Silverdale	28539
Silver Hill (Davidson County)	27292
Silver Hill (Pamlico County)	28560
Silver Lake	28403
Silverstone	28698
Silver Valley	27292
Simpson	27879
Sims	27880
Sioux	28740
Sivey Town	28462
Six Forks	27615
Skibo	28304

	ZIP
Skinnersville	27970
Skyco	27954
Skycrest Village	27604
Skyland	28776
Skyline	28394
Skyway Terrace	28364
Sladesville	27875
Slatestone Hills	27889
Sligo	27958
Sloan	28466
Slocomb	28356
Slocum	27824
Small	27806
Small Cross Roads	27932
Smallwood (Part of Washington)	27889
Smethport	28694
Smith Creek	28480
Smith Crossing	28442
Smithfield	27577
Smith Grove	27028
Smithtown (Beaufort County)	27810
Smithtown (Perquimans County)	27944
Smithtown (Yadkin County)	27018
Smyre	28054
Smyrna	28579
Sneads Ferry	28460
Sneads Grove	28352
Snow Camp	27349
Snowden	27958
Snow Hill (Chowan County)	27980
Snow Hill (Greene County)	28580
Snow Hill (Sampson County)	28382
Snug Harbor	27944
Soapstone Mountain	27355
Sodom	28753
Somerset (Chowan County)	27932
Somerset (Person County)	27573
Somerset Hills	27604
Sophia	27350
Soul City	27553
Sound Side (Dare County)	27959
Sound Side (Tyrrell County)	27925
South Albemarle (Part of Albemarle)	28001
South Aulander	27805
South Belmont (Part of Belmont)	28012
South Creek	27806
Southern Correctional Center	27311
Southern Hills	28025
Southern Pines	28387*
	28388†
Southern Shores (Dare County)	27949
Southern Shores (Perquimans County)	27944
South Fork (Part of Winston-Salem)	27104
South Gastonia	28052
Southgate	28304
South Henderson	27536
South Hills Elizabethtown	28337
South Hills Mall and Plaza (Part of Cary)	27606
South Hills Outlet Mall (Part of Cary)	27511
South Hominy	28715
South Lexington (Part of Lexington)	27292
South Lumberton (Part of Lumberton)	28358
South Mills	27976
Southmont	27351
Southpark Shopping Center (Part of Charlotte)	28211
Southport	28461
South River	28516
South Rocky Mount (Part of Rocky Mount)	27801
South Rosemary	27870
South Salisbury	28147
Southside (Henderson County)	28739
Southside (Lincoln County)	28092
South Square (Part of Durham)	27707
South Tunis	27986

	ZIP
South Wadesboro	28170
South Weldon	27890
Southwest	28540
South Whiteville (Part of Whiteville)	28472
Southwood	28501
Southwood Apartments	28304
Sparta	28675
Spear	28657
Speed	27881
Speedwell	28723
Speights Bridge	27888
Spencer	28159
Spencer Mountain	28056
Spences Corner	27921
Spies	27325
Spindale	28160
Spivey's Corner	28334
Spokane	27341
Spot	27966
Spout Springs	28326
Spray (Part of Eden)	27288
Spring Creek	28743
Springfield	28635
Springfield Mills	28351
Spring Garden	28562
Spring Hill	27874
Spring Hope	27882
Spring Lake	28390
Spring Road (Part of Hickory)	28601
Spring Valley (Guilford County)	27406
Spring Valley (Mecklenburg County)	28210
Springwood (Part of Belmont)	28052
Spruce Pine	28777
Stackhouse	28753
Stacy	28581
Stag Park	28425
Staley	27355
Stallings	28105
Stamey Branch	28657
Stanfield	28163
Stanhope	27882
Stanley	28164
Stanleyville	27045
Stantonsburg	27883
Star	27356
Starmount (Part of Charlotte)	28224
Starmount Forest (Part of Greensboro)	27403
Startown	28658
State Road	28676
Statesville	28677*
	28687†
State University (Part of Raleigh)	27607
Stecoah	28771
Stedman	28391
Steeds	27341
Steen Town	28345
Stella	28582
Stem	27581
Sterling (Part of Charlotte)	28134
Stevens Mill	27530
Stocksville	28787
Stokes	27884
Stokes Correctional Center	27052
Stokesdale	27357
Stokestown	28513
Stonebridge	27613
Stonehaven (Part of Charlotte)	28211
Stoneville	27048
Stonewall	28583
Stoneybrook	28147
Stoneycrest	28739
Stoney Knob	28787
Stonycreek	27244
Stony Fork (Buncombe County)	28715
Stony Fork (Watauga County)	28618
Stony Hill	27587
Stony Knoll	27017
Stony Point	28678
Storys	27935
Stotts Cross Roads	27880
Stouts	28110
Stovall	27582
Straits	28516
Stratford	28675
Strickland Cross Roads	27882
Stubbs	28150
Stumpy Point	27978

	ZIP		ZIP		ZIP		ZIP
Sturgills	28643	Thelma	27850		27284	Walnut Cove	27052
Sugar Grove	28679	Thomasboro	28470	For specific Union Cross Zip		Walnut Creek (Madison	
Sugar Hill	28752	Thomas Landing	28445	Codes call (910) 993-3812, or		County)	28753
Sugarloaf Shores	27371	Thomas Valley	28789	your local postmaster.		Walnut Creek (Wayne	
Sugar Mountain	28604	Thomasville	27360*	Union Grove (Davidson		County)	27534
Sugar Town	28135		27361†	County)	27292	Walstonburg	27888
Sulphur Springs	27030	Three Mile	28657	Union Grove (Iredell		Wananish (Part of Lake	
Summerfield	27358	Thruway Shopping Center		County)	28689	Waccamaw)	28450
Summerhaven	28778	(Part of Winston-Salem)	27103	Union Hill	27018	Wanchese	27981
Summer Hill	28303	Thurman	28560	Union Mills	28167	Warbler	27826
Summerlins Crossroads	28365	Thurmond	28683	Union Ridge	27215	Wards	28431
Summit (Guilford County)	27405	Tillery	27887	Unionville	28110	Wards Corner	28425
Summit (Halifax County)	27850	Timberlake	27583	University Estates		Wards Store	27891
Summit (Wilkes County)	28665	Timberlyne (Part of		(Cumberland County)	28301	Wardville	27979
Sunbury	27979	Chapel Hill)	27516	University Estates		Warne	28909
Sunny Point Military		Timber Ridge	28081	(Rockingham County)	27320	Warren Plains	27589
Ocean Terminal (U.S.		Timothy	28334	University Mall and Plaza		Warrensville	28693
Army)	28471	Tin City	28466	(Part of Chapel Hill)	27514	Warrenton	27589
Sunnyside (Burke County)	28655	Tiny Oak Fork	27885	University of North		Warren Wilson College	28778
Sunny Side (Dare County)	27954	Tipton Hill	28740	Carolina-Charlotte	28223	Warrior	28645
Sunnyside (Forsyth		Toast	27049	University of North		Warsaw	28398
County)	27107	Tobaccoville	27050	Carolina (Part of		Washburn	28150
Sunnyside (Gaston		Tobemory	28384	Wilmington)	28403	Washburn Store	28018
County)	28016	Todd	28684		28407	Washington	27889
Sunny Side (Halifax		Todds Crossroads	27983	For specific University of North		Washington Correctional	
County)	27850	Toddy	27828	Carolina Zip Codes call (910)		Center	27928
Sunny View	28756	Toecane	28705	721-6056, or your local		Washington Forks	28560
Sunset Beach	28468	Tolarsville	28384	postmaster.		Washington Park	27889
Sunset Harbor	28422	Toledo	28740	University Park (Part of		Watauga	28734
Sunset Hills (Catawba		Toluca	28090	Charlotte)	28297	Watauga Correctional	
County)	28601	Tomahawk	28444	Upchurch	27502	Center	28607
Sunset Hills (Guilford		Tomotla	28905	Upton	28645	Waterlily	27923
County)	27403	Toms Creek	28752	Upward	28731	Waterville	37821
Sunset Hills (Rockingham		Topia	28672	Uwharie	27371	Watha	28471
County)	27288	Topnot	27379	Valdese	28690	Watson Crossroads	27542
Sunshine	28018	Topsail Beach	28445	Vale	28168	Watts Crossroads	28025
Supply	28462	Topton	28781	Valhalla (Chowan County)	27932	Waughtown (Part of	
Surf City	28445	Town and Country Woods	27030	Valhalla (Polk County)	28782	Winston-Salem)	27107
Surl	27583	Town Creek (Brunswick		Valle Crucis	28691		27117
Sutherlands	28615	County)	28451	Valley	28657		27127
Sutton Park (Part of		Town Creek (Wilson		Valley Hill	28739	For specific Waughtown Zip	
Monroe)	28110	County)	27822	Valley Hills Mall (Part of		Codes call (910) 784-9801, or	
Suttons Corner	28337	Town Forest	28739	Hickory)	28601	your local postmaster.	
Suttontown	28341	Town Mountain Estates	28804	Vanceboro	28586	Waverly	28754
Swain	27970	Townsville	27584	Vance Correctional Center	27536	Waves	27982
Swainsville	28152	Tradingford	28146	Vandemere	28587	Waxhaw	28173
Swancreek	28642	Tramway	27330	Vander	28301	Waycross	28453
Swann	27330	Tranquility	28081	Vannoy	28696	Wayne Correctional	
Swannanoa	28778	Trap	27924	Varnamtown	28462	Center	27533
Swanns	27330	Traphill	28685	Vashti	28636	Waynesville	28786
Swanquarter	27885	Travis	27925	Vass	28394	Wayside	28376
Swansboro	28584	Trayton Woods	28025	Vaughan	27586	Weaversford	28617
Sweet Gum	28771	Tree Haven	28739	Vein Mountain	28752	Weaverville	28787
Swepsonville	27359	Trenholm Woods	28739	Venable	28803	Webster	28788
Swindell's Fork	27885	Trenton	28585	Venters	28513	Weddington	28173
Swiss	28714	Trent Woods	28562	Vernon Park Mall (Part of		Wedgewood Lakes	27958
Sylva	28779	Triangle (Lincoln County)	28164	Kinston)	28501	Weeksville	27909
Tabor City	28463	Triangle (Wake County)	27709	Verona	28540	Wehutty	37391
Talleys Crossing	27284	Trinity (Randolph County)	27370	Vests	28906	Welcome	27374
Tanglewood	28306	Trinity (Union County)	28112	Vicksboro	27536	Weldon	27890
Tapoco	28780	Triple Springs	27573	Vienna	27040	Wellons Village (Part of	
Tarawa Terrace	28543	Triplett	28618	Viewmont (Part of		Durham)	27703
Tarboro	27886	Trotville	27946	Hickory)	28601	Wells	28304
Tar Corner	27976	Troutman	28166	Vilas	28692	Welmar Heights	28304
Tar Heel (Bladen County)	28392	Troy	27371	Villa Heights (Part of		Wendell	27591
Tarheel (Gates County)	27935	Trust	28743	Charlotte)	28205	Wenona	27860
Tar Landing	28540	Tryon (Gaston County)	28016	Vinegar Hill	28463	Wentworth	27375
Tar River	27565	Tryon (Polk County)	28782	Vineland Park	28306	Wesleyan College	27804
Tarrytown Mall (Part of		Tryon Mall (Part of		Vinton Woods	28034	Wesley Chapel	28110
Rocky Mount)	27804	Charlotte)	28213	Violet	28906	Wesley Heights (Part of	
Tate Street (Part of		Tuckasegee	28783	Virgilina	24598	Charlotte)	28208
Greensboro)	27403	Tuckerdale	28643	Vista	28443	Wesser	28713
Taylor Cross Roads	27856	Tungsten	27536	Vixen	28714	West	28398
Taylors Bridge	28328	Tunis	27986	Volunteer	27043	West Asheville (Part of	
Taylors Corners	28585	Turkey	28393	Waccamaw	28420	Asheville)	28816
Taylors Store (Bertie		Turkey Knob	28675	Waco	28169	West Brook (Part of	
County)	27957	Turlington	28334	Wade	28395	Kannapolis)	28081
Taylors Store (Nash		Turnersburg	28688	Wade Mills (Part of		West Canton	28716
County)	27856	Turners Crossroads	27853	Wadesboro)	28170	Westchester Mall (Part of	
Taylorsville	28681	Turnpike	28715	Wadesboro	28170	High Point)	27262
Taylorsville Beach	28681	Tuscarora	28562	Wades Point	27810	Westcliff	28147
Taylortown	28374	Tuscarora Beach	27986	Wadeville	27306	West Concord (Part of	
Teachey	28464	Tusk	28579	Wagoner	28640	Concord)	28027
Teer	27516	Tuskeegee	28771	Wagram	28396	West Cramerton (Part of	
Temple Point	28532	Tusquitee	28904	Wake Crossroads	27604	Cramerton)	28032
Temple's	28570	Tuxedo	28784	Wakefield	27597	West Durham (Part of	
Terrace Gardens (Part of		Twin Lake (Part of Sunset		Wake Forest	27587*	Durham)	27705
Hendersonville)	28739	Beach)	28468		27588†	West Edgecombe	27801
Terra Ceia	27860	Twin Oaks	28675	Wakelon	27924	Westend (Guilford	
Terra Cotta (Part of		Tyner	27980	Wakulla	28397	County)	27262
Greensboro)	27407	Tyro	27292	Walkers Crossroads	27587	West End (Moore County)	27376
Terrell	28682	Ulah	27203	Walkertown (Forsyth		Western Prong	28472
Texaco Beach	27974	Unaka	28906	County)	27051	Westerwood (Part of	
Texana	28906	Union (Hertford County)	27910	Walkertown (Harnett		Greensboro)	27403
Texas	27974	Union (Macon County)	28734	County)	28356	Westfield	27053
Thankful	28606	Union (Rutherford County)	28139	Wallace	28466	West Gastonia (Part of	
The Black Cat	28516	Union Cross	27107	Walla Watta	27865	Gastonia)	28052
The Borough	28435			Wallburg	27373	Westhaven	27834
The Bottom	27924			Walnut	28753		

	ZIP		ZIP		ZIP		ZIP
West Highlands (Part of Winston-Salem)	27104	White Oak (Gates County)	27935	Williston	28589	Woodford	28684
West Jefferson	28694	White Oak (Guilford County)	27405	Willits	28779	Woodington	28501
West Lumberton (Part of Lumberton)	28358	White Oak (Halifax County)	27823	Wil-Lotta Acres	28025	Woodland	27897
West Marion	28752	White Oak (Nash County)	27856	Willow	27946	Woodland Acres	27892
West Market Street (Part of Greensboro)	27402	White Oaks Acres	27893	Willow Green	28513	Woodland Hills	28804
Westminster	28139	White Oaks Acres West	27893	Willow Spring	27592	Woodlawn (Alamance County)	27302
Westmont (Part of Asheboro)	27203	White Pines	27049	Wilmar	28586	Woodlawn (McDowell County)	28752
Westmore	27341	White Plains (Hyde County)	27824	Wil-Mar Park (Part of Concord)	28025	Woodlea	28304
West New Bern (Part of New Bern)	28562	White Plains (Surry County)	27031	Wilmington	28401-12	Woodleaf	27054
Westover (Wake County)	27606	Whitepost	27808	For specific Wilmington Zip Codes call (910) 313-3250, or your local postmaster.		Woodrow (Craven County)	28560
Westover (Washington County)	27962	Whiterock	28753	Wilmington Beach	28428	Woodrow (Haywood County)	28716
West Philadelphia	27209	White's Beach	27924	Wilmore (Part of Charlotte)	28203	Woodrun	27306
Westport	28037	Whites Chapel Church	27292	Wilmot	28789	Woodsdale	27573
Westridge (Part of Rocky Mount)	27801	Whites Crossroads	27924	Wilshire Park (Part of Asheville)	28806	Woodside	28081
West Rockingham	28379	White Stocking	28425	Wilson	27893-96	Woodside Hills	28715
West Rocky Mount (Part of Rocky Mount)	27801	Whiteston	27919	For specific Wilson Zip Codes call (919) 237-4161, or your local postmaster.		Woodville (Bertie County)	27849
Westry	27801	White Store	28133	Wilsons Mills	27593	Woodville (Perquimans County)	27944
West Salem (Part of Winston-Salem)	27101	Whiteville	28472	Wilsonville	27502	Woodville (Surry County)	27030
Westside	28023	Whitfield Crossroads	28578	Wilton	27525	Woodworth	27536
Wests Mill	28734	Whitley Heights	27520	Wind Blow	27281	Wootens Crossroads (Columbus County)	28433
West Smithfield	27577	Whitnel (Part of Lenoir)	28645	Windemere	28405	Wootens Crossroads (Greene County)	27888
West Statesville (Part of Statesville)	28677	Whitsett	27377	Windom	28714	Wootens Crossroads (Lenoir County)	28501
West Trade Street (Part of Charlotte)	28202	Whittier	28789	Windsor	27983	Worley	28753
Westview (Part of Winston-Salem)	27114	Whitt Town	27573	Windsors Cross Roads	27020	Worthingtons Crossroads	27858
Westwood (Scotland County)	28352	Whortonville	28556	Windy Gap	28659	Worthville	27317
Westwood (Surry County)	27049	Whynot	27341	Winfall	27985	Wrightsboro	28401
West Yanceyville	27379	Wilbanks	27822	Wing	28705	Wrightsville	28480
Wexford	28213	Wilbar	28696	Wingate	28174	Wrightsville Beach	28480
Whalebone (Part of Nags Head)	27959	Wilbon	27526	Winnabow	28479	Yadkin	28144
Whaley	28622	Wilbourns Store	24598	Winstead Crossroads	27822	Yadkin Correctional Center	27055
Wharton	27889	Wilders Grove	27604	Winsteadville	27810	Yadkin Valley	28645
Whichard	27884	Wildwood (Carteret County)	28557	Winston-Salem	27101-30	Yadkinville	27055
Whichard Beach	27817	Wildwood (Henderson County)	28732	For specific Winston-Salem Zip Codes call (910) 721-6056, or your local postmaster.		Yamacraw	28435
Whispering Pines	28327	Wildwood Estate	28570	Wintergreen	28523	Yanceyville	27379
Whitakers	27891	Wilgrove (Part of Charlotte)	28212	Winterville	28590	Yancy Correctional Center	28714
White Cross	27516	Wilkerson Cross Roads	27542	Winton	27986	Yaupon Beach	28461
Whitehall Shores	27921	Wilkesboro	28697	Wise	27594	Yeatsville	27808
Whitehead	28695	Wilkes Mall (Part of Wilkesboro)	28697	Wise Forks	28526	Yellow Creek	28771
White Hill	27330	Wilkinson	27860	Witherspoon Crossroads	28610	Yeopim	27932
Whitehouse	28167	Willard	28478	Wittys Crossroads	27320	Yorick	28399
Whitehurst	27871	Willeyton	27937	Wolf Creek	37317	Yorkmont Park (Part of Charlotte)	28217
Whitehurst Park	28025	Williams	28472	Wolf Laurel	28754	Yorkwood	28052
White Lake	28337	Williamsboro	27536	Wolf Mountain	28783	Youngsville	27596
White Oak (Bladen County)	28399	Williamsburg (Iredell County)	28634	Wood	27549	Zebulon	27597
		Williamsburg (Rockingham County)	27320	Woodard (Bertie County)	27983	Zephyr	28621
		Williamson Crossroads	28431	Woodard (Wilson County)	27893	Zionville	28698
		Williamston	27892	Woodburn	28451	Zirconia	28790
		Willis Landing	28539	Wood Crest	28570		
				Wood Dale	28401		
				Woodfin	28804		

	ZIP		ZIP		ZIP		ZIP
Abercrombie	58001	Brooks Addition	58703	Durbin	58059	Glenwood Estates	58501
Absaraka	58002	Brooktree Park	58042	Dwight	58075	Glover	58474
Acres A-Plenty	58504	Buchanan	58420	Eagle Bend Estates	58301	Golden Valley	58541
Adams	58210	Bucyrus	58639	Eastdale	58601	Goldfines Shopping	
Adrian	58472	Buffalo	58011	East Dunseith	58329	Center (Part of Grand	
Agate	58310	Buffalo Springs	58623	East Fairview	59221	Forks)	58201
Akra	58220	Burke Addition	58201	Eastside Estates	58701	Golva	58632
Alamo	58830	Burlington	58722	East Valley City	58072	Goodrich	58444
Alexander	58831	Burnstad	58495	Eckelson	58432	Gorham	58627
Alfred	58411	Burt	58646	Eckman	58760	Grace City	58445
Alice	58003	Butte	58723	Edgeley	58433	Grafton	58237
Alkabo	58845	Buttzville	58054	Edinburg	58227	Grandberg	58102
Almont	58520	Buxton	58218	Edmore	58330	Grand Forks	58201-08
Alpha	58654	Caledonia	58219	Edmunds	58476	For specific Grand Forks Zip	
Alsen	58311	Calio	58352	Egeland	58331	Codes call (701) 775-5329, or	
Ambrose	58833	Calvin	58323	El Dorado Acres	58601	your local postmaster.	
Amenia	58004	C and L Estates	58504	Eldridge	58401	Grand Forks (census	
Amidon	58620	Cando	58324	Elgin	58533	designated place)	58205
Anamoose	58710	Cannon Ball	58528	Ellendale	58436	Grand Forks Air Force	
Anderson Acres	58504	Carbury	58783	Elliott	58033	Base	58201
Aneta	58212	Carlsbad	58504	Embden	58079	Grandin	58038
Anselm	58068	Carolville	58801	Emerado	58228	Grand Prairie Estates	58501
Antler	58711	Carpio	58725	Emmet	58540	Grand Rapids	58458
Appam	58830	Carrington	58421	Emrick	58422	Grandview	58801
Apple Creek Country Club	58501	Carson	58529	Enderlin	58027	Grano	58750
Apple Creek Estates	58558	Cartwright	58838	Englevale	58033	Granville	58741
Apple Valley	58558	Cashel	58225	Epping	58843	Grassy Butte	58634
Ardoch	58213	Casselton	58012	Erie	58029	Great Bend	58039
Arena	58412	Cathay	58422	Esmond	58332	Green Acres Estates	58501
Argusville	58005	Cavalier	58220	Evergreen	58051	Greene	58787
Arnegard	58835	Cayuga	58013	Faiman's Sunrise Addition	58504	Greenvale	58601
Arthur	58006	Center	58530	Fairdale	58229	Grenora	58845
Arvilla	58214	Chaffee	58014	Fairfield	58627	Guelph	58474
Ashley	58413	Charbonneau	58831	Fairmount	58030	Guthrie	58736
Ashlund Estates	58504	Charlson	58763	Falconer Estates	58504	Gwinner	58040
Auburn	58237	Chaseley	58423	Falkirk	58577	Hague	58542
Aurelia	58734	Chrisan	58102	Fargo	58102-09	Halliday	58636
Ayr	58007	Christine	58015	For specific Fargo Zip Codes		Hallson	58220
Backoo	58282	Churchs Ferry	58325	call (701) 241-6100, or your		Hamar	58380
Baker	58386	Circle K Estates	58501	local postmaster.		Hamberg	58337
Baldwin	58521	City View Heights	58504	Fessenden	58438	Hamilton	58238
Balfour	58712	Cleveland	58424	Fillmore	58332	Hamlet	58795
Balta	58313	Clifford	58016	Fingal	58031	Hampden	58338
Bantry	58713	Clyde	58352	Finley	58230	Hankinson	58041
Bar-D Estates	58504	Cogswell	58017	Finley Air Force Station,		Hanks	58856
Barks Spur	58331	Coleharbor	58531	785th Radar Squadron	58230	Hanks Corner	58220
Barlow	58421	Colfax	58018	Flasher	58535	Hannaford	58448
Barney	58008	Colgan	58844	Flaxton	58737	Hannah	58239
Bartlett	58344	Colgate	58046	Flora	58348	Hannover	58563
Barton	58384	Columbia Mall (Part of		Fonda	58366	Hansboro	58339
Bathgate	58216	Grand Forks)	58201	Forbes	58439	Happy Valley	58701
Battleground Addition	58703	Columbus	58727	Fordville	58231	Harlow	58346
Battleview	58773	Concrete	58220	Forest River (Cass		Hartland	58725
Bayshore	58072	Conway	58233	County)	58102	Harvey	58341
Beach	58621	Cooperstown	58425	Forest River (Walsh		Harwood	58042
Belcourt	58316	Corinth	58830	County)	58233	Hastings	58049
Belden	58784	Coteau	58721	Forest River Colony	58231	Hatton	58240
Belfield	58622	Coulee	58746	Forman	58032	Havana	58043
Benedict	58716	Country Acres	58047	Fort Berthold Indian		Havelock	58647
Bentley	58562	Country-Side Addition	58201	Reservation	58763	Hay Creek	58501
Berea	58072	Courtenay	58426	Fort Buford	58853	Hay Creek Pines	58501
Bergen	58792	Crary	58327	Fort Clark	58530	Haynes	58639
Berlin	58415	Crested Butte Addition	58501	Fort Ransom	58033	Hazelton	58544
Berthold	58718	Crete	58040	Fort Rice	58537	Hazen	58545
Berwick	58788	Crosby	58730	Fort Totten	58335	Heaton	58450
Beulah	58523	Crystal	58222	Fortuna	58844	Hebron	58638
Big Bend	58531	Crystal Springs	58467	Fortuna Air Force Station,		Heil	58533
Binford	58416	Cuba	58072	780th Radar Squadron	59275	Heimdal	58341
Bisbee	58317	Cummings	58223	Fort Yates	58538	Hensel	58241
Bismarck	58501-07	Dahlen	58224	Four Bears Village	58763	Hensler	58530
For specific Bismarck Zip		Dakota Boys Ranch	58703	Four K's Estates	58501	Heritage Hills Estates	58102
Codes call (701) 221-6517, or		Dakota Square (Part of		Foxholm	58718	Hesper	58348
your local postmaster.		Minot)	58701	Fox Island	58504	Hettinger	58639
Blabon	58046	Davenport	58021	Fradet	58047	Hickson	58047
Blacktail Lake	58801	Dawson	58428	Frazier (Part of		Hi-Land Heights	58801
Blaisdell	58718	Dazey	58429	Wimbledon)	58492	Hillcrest Acres	58501
Blanchard	58009	Decker	58601	Fredonia	58440	Hillsboro	58045
Bluffview Estates	58504	Deering	58731	Fried	58401	Holiday Colony	58701
Bonetrail	58801	De Lamere	58060	Frison	58301	Holmes	58275
Bordulac	58421	Denbigh	58788	Frontier	58104	Home on the Range for	
Bottineau	58318	Denhoff	58430	Fryburg	58622	Boys	58654
Bowbells	58721	Des Lacs	58733	Fullerton	58441	Honeyford	58235
Bowdon	58418	Devils Lake	58301	Gackle	58442	Hoople	58243
Bowesmont	58225	Devils Lake Sioux Indian		Galchutt	58075	Hope	58046
Bowman	58623	Reservation	58335	Galesburg	58035	Horace	58047
Braddock	58524	Dickey	58431	Gardar	58227	Horseshoe Bend	58102
Brampton	58017	Dickinson	58601*	Gardena	58739	Huff	58537
Brantford	58356		58602†	Gardner	58036	Hull	58542
Breen's Addition	58501	Dodge	58625	Garrison	58540	Hunter	58048
Breien	58570	Donnybrook	58734	Garske	58382	Hurdsfield	58451
Brekke Addition	58701	Douglas	58735	Gascoyne	58653	Hutterite Colony	58458
Bremen	58319	Doyon	58328	Geneseo	58053	Imperial Manor	58701
Brentwood Estates	58501	Drake	58736	Gilby	58235	Imperial Valley	58504
Briardale	58504	Drayton	58225	Gladstone	58630	Inkster	58244
Briarwood	58104	Dresden	58249	Glasser	58504	Jamestown	58401*
Bridgeview Addition	58701	Driscoll	58532	Glasston	58236		58402†
Brinsmade	58320	Dunn Center	58626	Glenburn	58740	Jessie	58452
Brocket	58321	Dunning	58760	Glenfield	58443	Jewett Landing	58072
Brookfield Estates	58501	Dunseith	58329	Glen Ullin	58631	Jiran	58504

* Area Zip Code   † Post Office Boxes

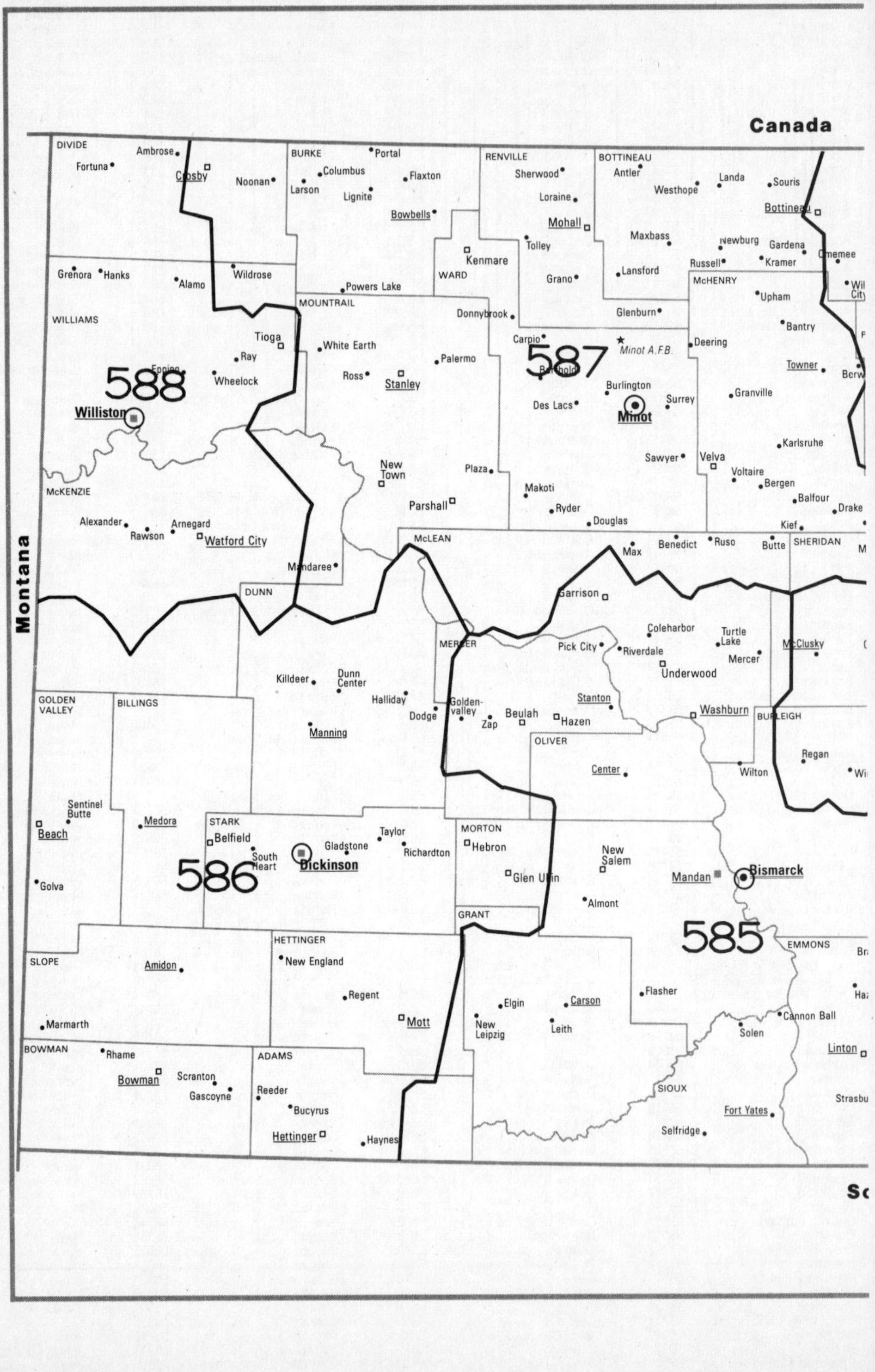

Canada

Montana

DIVIDE
Ambrose
Fortuna
Crosby
Noonan

BURKE
Columbus
Larson
Lignite
Portal
Flaxton
Bowbells

RENVILLE
Sherwood
Loraine
Mohall
Tolley
Grano

BOTTINEAU
Antler
Westhope
Maxbass
Russell
Lansford
Landa
Souris
Bottineau
Newburg
Kramer
Gardena
Omemee

Kenmare
WARD
Donnybrook
Glenburn

McHENRY
Upham
Wil
City
Bantry

Grenora Hanks
Alamo Wildrose
Powers Lake
MOUNTRAIL

WILLIAMS
Tioga
Ray
Wheelock

588
Epping
Williston

White Earth
Ross Stanley
Palermo

Carpio
587
Minot A.F.B.
Burlington
Des Lacs
Minot
Surrey
Deering
Granville
Towner
Berw

McKENZIE
Alexander
Rawson Arnegard
Watford City
Mandaree

New
Town
Parshall
Plaza
Makoti
Ryder
Douglas

Sawyer
Velva
Voltaire
Bergen
Karlsruhe
Balfour
Drake
Kief

McLEAN
Max Benedict Ruso Butte SHERIDAN M

DUNN
Garrison

MERCER
Pick City
Riverdale
Coleharbor
Turtle
Lake
Underwood
Mercer
McClusky

GOLDEN
VALLEY
BILLINGS
Killdeer
Dunn
Center
Halliday
Dodge
Golden-
valley
Beulah
Zap Hazen
Stanton
OLIVER
Center
Washburn
BURLEIGH
Regan
Wilton
Wil

Manning

Sentinel
Butte
Beach
Medora
STARK
Belfield
South
Heart
Gladstone
Taylor
Richardton
Dickinson
MORTON
Hebron
Glen Ullin
New
Salem
Almont
Mandan
Bismarck

Golva

GRANT

586

585
EMMONS
Bra
Ha

SLOPE
Amidon
HETTINGER
New England
Regent
Mott
New
Leipzig
Elgin Carson
Leith
Flasher
Cannon Ball
Solen
Linton
Strasbu

Marmarth
BOWMAN
Rhame
Bowman
Scranton
Gascoyne
ADAMS
Reeder
Bucyrus
Hettinger
Haynes
SIOUX
Fort Yates
Selfridge

So

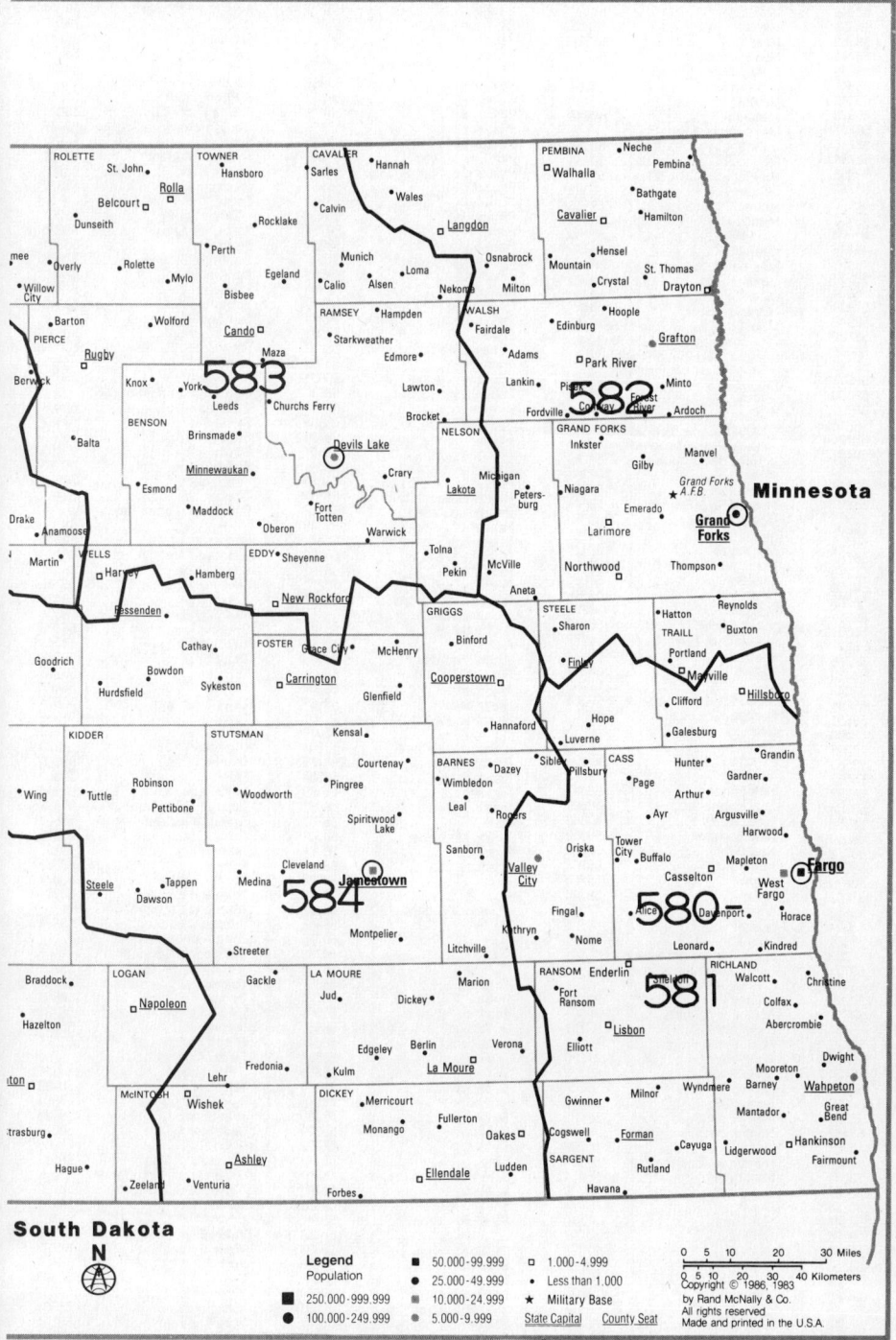

ROLETTE
St. John
Rolla
Belcourt
Dunseith

mee
Overly
Willow City
Rolette
Mylo

Barton
Wolford

PIERCE
Rugby

Berwick
Knox
York
Leeds
Churchs Ferry

Balta
BENSON
Brinsmade

Esmond
Maddock
Oberon

Drake
Anamoose

Martin
WELLS
Harvey
Hamberg

Goodrich
Cathay
FOSTER
Grace City
McHenry

Bowdon
Carrington

Hurdsfield
Sykeston
Glenfield

KIDDER
STUTSMAN
Kensal

Wing
Tuttle
Robinson
Pettibone
Woodworth
Pingree
Courtenay
Sanborn

Cleveland
Steele
Tappen
Medina
Jamestown
584
Dawson

Streeter
Montpelier
Litchville

Braddock
LOGAN
Gackle
LA MOURE
Jud
Dickey
Marion
Napoleon

Hazelton
Fort Ransom

Edgeley
Berlin
Verona
ton
Fredonia
Kulm
Lehr
La Moure

McINTOSH
Wishek
DICKEY
Merricourt
Gwinner
Milnor
strasburg
Monango
Fullerton
Oakes
Cogswell
Forman
Hague
Ashley
Zeeland
Venturia
Ellendale
Ludden
SARGENT
Rutland
Forbes
Havana

TOWNER
Hansboro
Perth
Rocklake
Egeland
Bisbee
Cando
Maza

RAMSEY
Hampden
Starkweather
Edmore
Lawton
Brocket
NELSON

Munich
Calio
Alsen
Loma
Nekoma
Milton

583

Devils Lake
Minnewaukan
Crary
Fort Totten
Warwick

EDDY
Sheyenne
New Rockford

Fessenden

Binford
GRIGGS
Cooperstown
Finley
Hannaford
Hope
Luverne

BARNES
Dazey
Sibley
Pillsbury
Wimbledon
Leal
Rogers

Spiritwood Lake

Valley City
Fingal
Kathryn
Nome

RANSOM
Enderlin
Walcott
Lisbon
Elliott

CAVALIER
Sarles
Hannah
Wales
Langdon
Osnabrock
Calvin

PEMBINA
Neche
Walhalla
Pembina
Bathgate
Cavalier
Hamilton
Mountain
Hensel
St. Thomas
Crystal
Drayton

WALSH
Fairdale
Hoople
Edinburg
Grafton
Adams
Park River
Lankin
Minto
582
Conway
Forest River
Fordville
Ardoch

GRAND FORKS
Inkster
Gilby
Manvel
Michigan
Petersburg
Niagara
Lakota
Larimore
Emerado
Grand Forks A.F.B.
Grand Forks

Tolna
Pekin
McVille
Aneta
Northwood
Thompson

STEELE
Sharon
TRAILL
Hatton
Buxton
Reynolds
Portland
Mayville
Clifford
Hillsboro
Galesburg
Grandin

CASS
Hunter
Gardner
Page
Arthur
Ayr
Argusville
Harwood
Tower City
Buffalo
Mapleton
Fargo
Casselton
West Fargo
580
Alice
Davenport
Horace
Leonard
Kindred

RICHLAND
Colfax
581
Abercrombie
Dwight
Mooreton
Wyndmere
Barney
Wahpeton
Mantador
Great Bend
Cayuga
Lidgerwood
Hankinson
Fairmount

Minnesota

South Dakota
N

Legend
Population
■ 50.000-99.999   □ 1.000-4.999
● 25.000-49.999   • Less than 1.000
■ 250.000-999.999 ★ Military Base
● 100.000-249.999 ● 5.000-9.999
■ 10.000-24.999   State Capital   County Seat

0 5 10   20   30 Miles
0 5 10 20   30   40 Kilometers

Name	ZIP	Name	ZIP	Name	ZIP	Name	ZIP
Johnsons Corner	58847	Marshall	58644	Park Manor (Part of Grand Forks)	58201	Shields	58569
Johnstown	58235	Martin	58758	Park River	58270	Shryock	58801
Joliette	58271	Max	58759	Parshall	58770	Sibley	58429
Juanita	58443	Maxbass	58760	Patterson Lake	58601	Sibley Island Estates	58504
Jud	58454	Mayville	58257	Pekin	58361	Silva	58368
Judson	58563	Maza	58324	Pembina	58271	Simcoe	58741
Karlsruhe	58744	Meadowbrook	58701	Penn	58362	Sims	58520
Kathryn	58049	Meadow View (Part of Bismarck)	58504	Perth	58363	Sioux Village	58538
Keene	58847	Medina	58467	Petersburg	58272	Sisseton Indian Reservation	57262
Kelso	58045	Medora	58645	Pettibone	58475	Skyline Estates	58501
Kelvin	58329	Mee's Country Home Estates	58558	Pheasant Lake	58436	Sleepy Hollow	58047
Kempton	58267	Mekinock	58258	Picardville	58463	Solen	58570
Kenaston	58746	Melville	58421	Pick City	58545	Sorenson Addition	58701
Kenmare	58746	Menoken	58558	Pillsbury	58065	Souris	58783
Kensal	58455	Mercer	58559	Pingree	58476	Southam	58327
Kief	58747	Merricourt	58433	Pisek	58273	South Forks Plaza (Part of Grand Forks)	58201
Killdeer	58640	Michigan	58259	Pitcher Park	58301	South Heart	58655
Kindred	58051	Millarton	58472	Plaza	58771	Southview	58801
Kings Court	58703	Mills	58504	Pleasant Lake	58368	Southview Estates	58601
Kintyre	58549	Milnor	58060	Ponderosa Riverside Village	58501	Spiritwood	58481
Kirkwood Plaza (Part of Bismarck)	58504	Milton	58260	Porcupine	58568	Spiritwood Lake	58401
Kloten	58254	Minnewaukan	58351	Portal	58772	Spring Brook	58843
KMK Estates	58501	Minot	58701-03	Portland	58274	Standing Rock Indian Reservation	58538
Knox	58343	For specific Minot Zip Codes call (701) 852-3296, or your local postmaster.		Powell	58201	Stanley	58784
Kongsberg	58792			Powers Lake	58773	Stanton	58571
Kralicek	58601	Minot Air Force Base	58704-05	Prairie Rose	58104	Starkweather	58377
Kramer	58748	For specific Minot Air Force Base Zip Codes call (701) 727-4887, or your local postmaster.		Prairie View Acres	58501	State Hospital (Part of Jamestown)	58401
Kubishta	58601			Price	58530	Steele	58482
Kulm	58456	Minot Air Force Station, 786th Radar Squadron	58759	Prosper	58042	Sterling	58572
Lake Jessie	58801	Minto	58261	Raleigh	58564	Stirum	58069
Lake Metigoshe	58318	Mirror Lake	58639	Raub	58779	Strasburg	58573
Lake Park	58801	Missouri River Estates	58504	Raulston	58801	Straubville	58017
Lake Side Estate	58401	Moffit	58560	Rawson	58831	Streeter	58483
Lake Tschida	58533	Mohall	58761	Ray	58849	Stromquist (Part of Devils Lake)	58301
Lake Williams	58478	Monango	58471	Raymond Lee	58801	Strong	58301
Lakewood Park	58301	Montpelier	58472	Red Willow Lake	58416	Sunnyside Addition	58102
Lakota	58344	Mooreton	58061	Reeder	58649	Sunny Slope	58701
Lamoine Addition	58201	Mott	58646	Regan	58477	Surrey	58785
Lamoure	58458	Mountain	58262	Regent	58650	Sutton	58484
Landa	58783	Mount Carmel	58249	Reile's Acres	58102	Swansonville	58504
Langdon	58249	Mouse River Park	58787	Reynolds	58275	Sykeston	58486
Lankin	58250	Mr. B's	58501	Rhame	58651	Taft	58045
Lansford	58750	Munich	58352	Richards West (Part of Grand Forks)	58201	Tagus	58718
Larimore	58251	Mylo	58353	Richardton	58652	Talbotts	58703
Lark	58535	Nanson	58366	Ridgeview Acres	58504	Tappen	58487
Larson	58727	Napoleon	58561	Rio Vista Heights	58801	Tatley Meadows	58504
Lawton	58345	Nash	58237	River Bend	58047	Taylor	58656
Leal	58479	Neche	58265	Riverdale	58565	Temvik	58552
Leeds	58346	Nekoma	58355	Riverside (Part of West Fargo)	58078	Thompson	58278
Lefor	58641	Newburg	58762	River View Acres	58504	Thorne	58366
Lehigh	58601	New England	58647	Robinson	58478	Tilden	58351
Lehr	58460	New Hradec	58601	Rocklake	58365	Timber Lake Place	58504
Leisure World Estates	58504	New Leipzig	58562	Rogers	58479	Tioga	58852
Leith	58551	New Rockford	58356	Rolette	58366	TJ Ranch Estates	58501
Leonard	58052	New Salem	58563	Rolla	58367	Tokio	58379
Leroy	58282	New Town	58763	Rolling Meadows	58501	Tolley	58787
Lewis and Clark Estates	58504	Niagara	58266	Roseglen	58775	Tolna	58380
Leyden	58282	Niobe	58746	Roshau	58601	Tower City	58071
Lidgerwood	58053	Nome	58062	Ross	58776	Town and Country	58801
Lignite	58752	Noonan	58765	Roth	58783	Town and Country Estates	58504
Lincoln	58501	Norma	58746	Round Hill Estates	58102	Town And Country Shopping Center (Part of Minot)	58701
Lincoln Valley	58430	North Dakota Penitentiary	58501	Rugby	58368	Towner	58788
Linha Addition	58703	North Dakota State University (Part of Fargo)	58105	Ruso	58778	Trenton	58853
Linton	58552	North Forty Estates	58501	Russell	58762	Trestle Valley	58701
Lisbon	58054	Northgate	58737	Ruthville	58703	Trotters	58657
Litchville	58461	North Grand Forks	58203	Rutland	58067	Turtle Lake	58575
Little Ponderosa	58703	North Lemmon	57638	Ryder	58779	Turtle Mountain Indian Reservation	58316
Logan	58311	North River	58102	Sabot's First	58501	Tuttle	58488
Loma	58718	North Star Acres	58501	St. Anthony	58566	Twin Butte	58504
Lone Tree	58718	North Valley City	58072	St. Benedict	58047	Twin Buttes	58636
Loraine	58761	Northwood (Cass County)	58102	St. Gertrude	58564	Underwood	58576
Lostwood	58784	Northwood (Grand Forks County)	58267	St. John	58369	Union	58269
Lucca	58027	Northwood Estates	58501	St. Michael	58370	University of Mary	58501
Ludden	58474	Nortonville	58454	St. Thomas	58276	University of North Dakota (Part of Grand Forks)	58202
Lunds Valley	58784	Norwich	58768	Sanborn	58480	Upham	58789
Luverne	58056	Oakes	58474	San Haven	58329	Urbana	58841
Lynchburg	58059	Oak Ridge	58270	Sanish	58763	Valley City	58072
McCanna	58251	Oakwood	58237	Sarles	58372	Velva	58790
Mcclusky	58463	Oberon	58357	Sawdwood	58270	Venturia	58489
Mcgregor	58755	Olga	58249	Sawyer	58781	Verona	58490
Mchenry	58464	Omemee	58384	Scenic East	58801	Veseleyville	58237
Mckenzie	58553	Oriska	58063	Schefield	58647	Vista South	58504
McLeod	58057	Orr	58244	Scranton	58653	Vohs Dapplegrey	58801
McVille	58254	Orrin	58359	Secluded Acres	58504	Voltaire	58792
Maddock	58348	Osnabrock	58269	Selfridge	58568	Voss	58261
Maida	58255	Overly	58360	Selz	58341	Wabek	58771
Makoti	58756	Oxbow	58047	Sentinel Butte	58654	Wahpeton	58074†
Mandan	58554	Page	58064	Shamrock Acres	58501		58075*
Mandaree	58757	Palermo	58769	Sharon	58277	Walcott	58077
Manfred	58465	Palm Beach	58601	Sheldon	58068		
Manitou	58776			Shell Valley	58316		
Manning	58642			Shepard	58425		
Mantador	58058			Sherwood	58782		
Manvel	58256			Sheyenne	58374		
Mapes	58344			Sheyenne Valley Addition	58072		
Mapleton	58059						
Marion	58466						
Marmarth	58643						

* Area Zip Code   † Post Office Boxes

	ZIP		ZIP		ZIP		ZIP
Wales	58281	West Fargo	58078	Whitman	58259	Wolford	58385
Walhalla	58282	Westfield	58542	Wild Rice	58047	Wolseth	58740
Walum	58448	West Heart Estates	58504	Wildrose	58795	Woodland	58051
Warren	58021	Westhope	58793	Williston	58801*	Woods	58052
Warsaw	58261	West Industrial Park	58601		58802†	Woodworth	58496
Warwick	58381	West Jamestown	58401	Williston Park	58801	Wutzke	58501
Washburn	58577	West Oakwood	58237	Willow City	58384	Wyndmere	58081
Watford City	58854	West Town	58401	Wilton	58579	York	58386
Webster	58382	Westwood on the River	58501	Wimbledon	58492	Ypsilanti	58497
Welle	58501	Wheatland	58079	Windsor	58424	Zahl	58856
Wellsburg	58341	Wheelock	58849	Wing	58494	Zap	58580
West Acres Estates	58801	White Earth	58794	Wishek	58495	Zeeland	58581
Westbrook	58047	White Shield	58540				

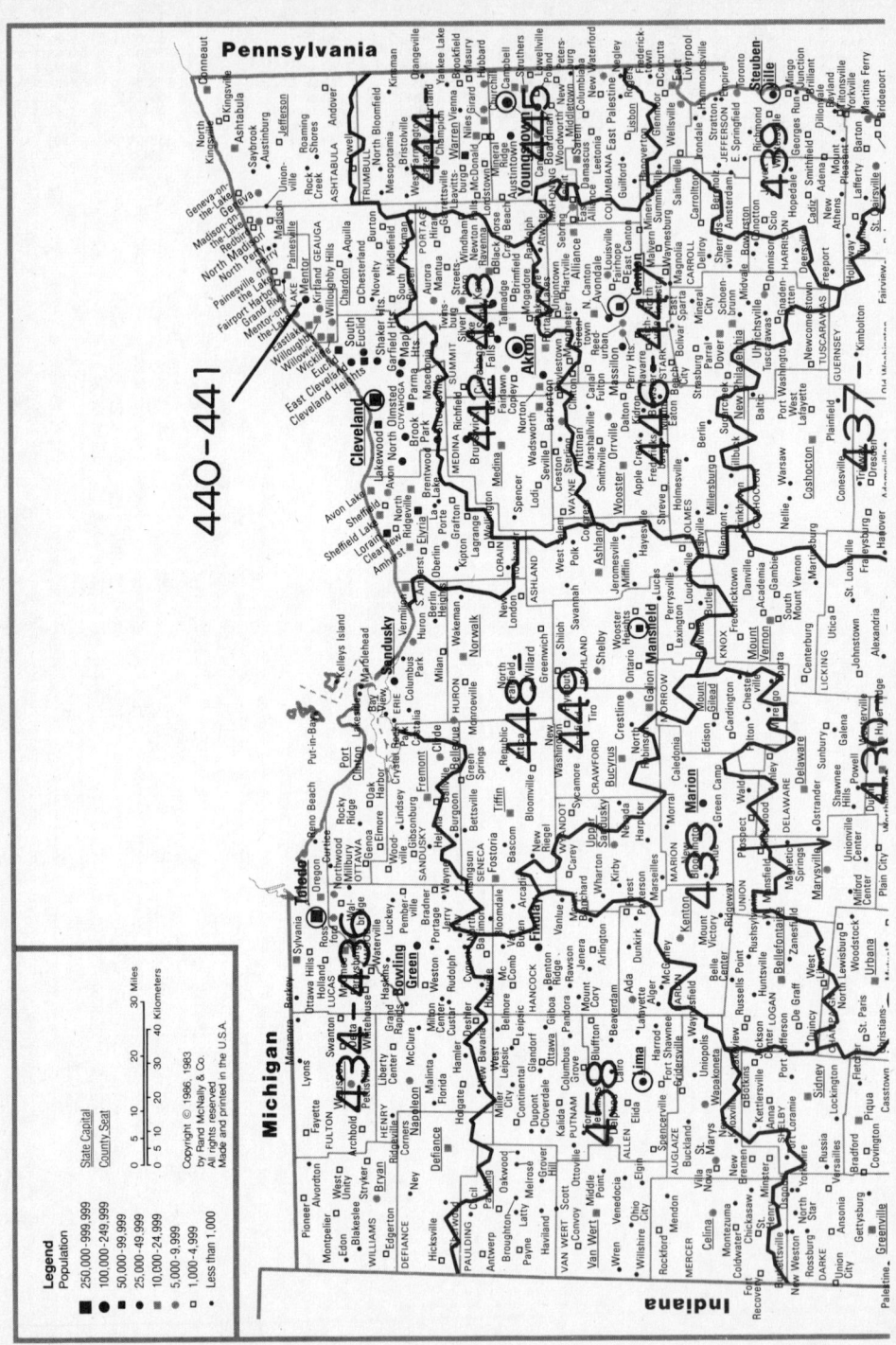

Legend
Population
■ 250,000–999,999
● 100,000–249,999
● 50,000–99,999
● 25,000–49,999
● 10,000–24,999
● 5,000–9,999
● 1,000–4,999
· Less than 1,000

● State Capital
□ County Seat

0   5   10   20   30 Miles
0 5 10   20   30   40 Kilometers

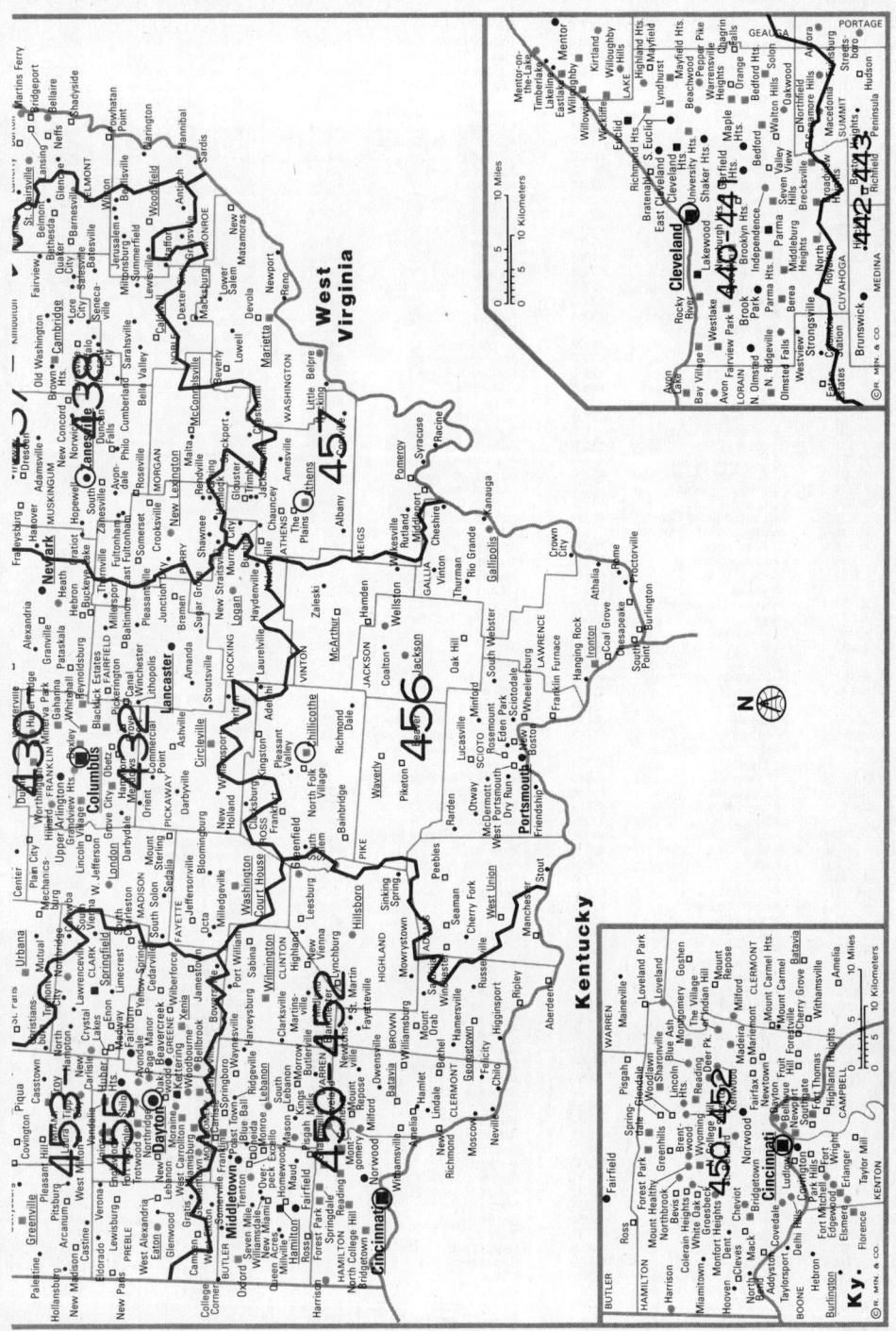

	ZIP
Abanaka	45874
Abbottsville	45304
Aberdeen	45101
Academia	43050
Acme	44281
Ada	45810
Adams (Champaign County) (Township)	43070
Adams (Clinton County) (Township)	45177
Adams (Coshocton County) (Township)	43832
Adams (Darke County) (Township)	45308
Adams (Defiance County) (Township)	43512
Adams (Guernsey County) (Township)	43725
Adams (Monroe County) (Township)	43914
Adams (Muskingum County) (Township)	43821
Adams (Seneca County) (Township)	44867
Adams (Washington County) (Township)	45744
Adams Mills	43821
Adamsville (Gallia County)	45614
Adamsville (Muskingum County)	43802
Adario	44837
Addison	45631
Addison (Township)	45631
Addyston	45001
Adelphi	43101
Adena	43901
Adrian	44801
Africa	43021
Afton	45103
Aid	45645
Aid (Township)	45645
Ainger	43543
Air Mail Facility (Franklin County)	43236
Air Mail Facility (Montgomery County)	45490
Air Material Command	45433
Airport (Cuyahoga County)	44181
Airport (Franklin County)	43219
Airway	45431
Airway	45437
For specific Airway Zip Codes call (513) 227-1231, or your local postmaster.	
Akron	44301-72
For specific Akron Zip Codes call (216) 996-9905, or your local postmaster.	
Albany	45710
Al Bar Meadows (Part of The Village of Indian Hill)	45243
Albion	44287
Alcony	45373
Alexander (Township)	45701
Alexanders (Part of Independence)	44131
Alexandersville (Part of West Carrollton)	45449
Alexandria	43001
Alexis Place (Part of Toledo)	43612
Alfred	45723
Alger	45812
Alikanna	43952
Alledonia	43902
Allen (Darke County) (Township)	45362
Allen (Hancock County) (Township)	45889
Allen (Ottawa County) (Township)	43412
Allen (Union County) (Township)	43070
Allen Center	43040
Allensburg	45133
Allensville	45651
Allentown (Allen County)	45807
Allentown (Scioto County)	45694
Alliance	44601
Alma	45690
Alpha	45301
Alpine Village (Part of Valley Hi)	43360
Alta	44903
Altamont Hills	43938
Altamont Park (Part of Mingo Junction)	43938
Alton	43119

	ZIP
Alvada	44802
Alvordton	43501
Amanda (Allen County) (Township)	45807
Amanda (Fairfield County) (Township)	43102
Amanda (Fairfield County)	43102
Amanda (Hancock County) (Township)	45867
Amberley	45213
Amberly	43227
Amboy (Ashtabula County)	44030
Amboy (Fulton County) (Township)	43540
Amelia	45102
American (Township)	45807
Ames (Township)	45711
Amesville	45711
Amherst	44001
Amherst (Township)	44001
Amity (Hamilton County)	45236
Amity (Knox County)	43050
Amity (Madison County)	43064
Amity (Montgomery County)	45309
Amlin	43002
Amlin Heights	45385
Amsden	44803
Amsterdam (Jefferson County)	43903
Amsterdam (Licking County)	43076
Anderson (Hamilton County) (Township)	45230
Anderson (Hamilton County)	45255
Anderson (Ross County)	45601
Anderson Ferry (Part of Cincinnati)	45238
Andersonville	45601
Andis	45645
Andover	44003
Andover (Township)	44003
Angle	45631
Ankenytown	43019
Anlo	45344
Anna	45302
Annapolis	43910
Ansonia	45303
Antioch	43793
Antiquity	45771
Antrim (Guernsey County)	43773
Antrim (Wyandot County) (Township)	43323
Antwerp	45813
Apple Creek	44606
Apple Grove	45771
Appleton	43031
Aquilla	44024
Arabia	45659
Arcadia	44804
Arcanum	45304
Archbold	43502
Archer (Township)	43986
Archers Fork	45767
Arion	45652
Arkoe	45661
Arlington (Hancock County)	45814
Arlington (Montgomery County)	45309
Arlington Heights	45215
Armstrongs Mills	43933
Arnheim	45121
Arnold (Miami County)	45383
Arnold (Union County)	43064
Arrow Head (Part of Xenia)	45385
Artanna	43022
Arthur	43512
Ashland	44805
Ashley	43003
Ashley Corner	45694
Ash Ridge	45121
Ashtabula	44004
Ashtabula (Township)	44004
Ashville	43103
Assumption	43558
Athalia	45669
Athens (Athens County)	45701
Athens (Athens County) (Township)	45701
Athens (Harrison County) (Township)	43981
Atlanta	43145
Atlas	43713
Attica	44807
Attica Junction	44807
Atwater	44201

	ZIP
Atwater (Township)	44201
Atwater Center	44201
Auburn (Butler County)	45013
Auburn (Crawford County) (Township)	44887
Auburn (Geauga County) (Township)	44255
Auburn (Tuscarawas County) (Township)	44681
Auburn Center (Crawford County)	44875
Auburn Center (Geauga County)	44022
Auburn Corners	44021
Augersburg	44266
Auglaize (Allen County) (Township)	45850
Auglaize (Paulding County) (Township)	43512
Augusta	44607
Augusta (Township)	44607
Ault	43947
Aultman	44630
Aurelius (Township)	45746
Aurora	44202
Aurora East	44240
Aurora Meadows	44202
Ausdale Ave. (Part of Mansfield)	44906
Austin	45628
Austinburg	44010
Austinburg (Township)	44010
Austintown (Township)	44515
Austintown	44512
Austintown Plaza	44515
Austin Village (Part of Warren)	44481
Autumn Acres	45239
Ava	43711
Avalon (Butler County)	45042
Avalon (Perry County)	43107
Avalon Heights (Part of Lebanon)	45036
Avenue at Tower City Center, The (Part of Cleveland)	44113
Avon	44011
Avondale (Belmont County)	43947
Avondale (Hamilton County)	45229
Avondale (Licking County)	43076
Avondale (Logan County)	43331
Avondale (Montgomery County)	45404
Avondale (Muskingum County)	43777
Avondale (Stark County)	44708
Avon Lake	44012
Avon Park (Part of Girard)	44420
Axtel	44089
Ayersville	43512
Bachman	45309
Badgertown	43719
Bailey Lakes	44805
Baileys Mills	43713
Bainbridge (Geauga County)	44023
Bainbridge (Geauga County) (Township)	44023
Bainbridge (Ross County)	45612
Bainbridge Center	44022
Bairdstown	45872
Bakersville	43803
Ballville	43420
Ballville (Township)	43420
Baltic	43804
Baltimore	43105
Bangs	43050
Bannock	43972
Bantam	45103
Barberton	44203
Bardwell	45154
Barlow	45712
Barlow (Township)	45712
Barnesburg	45239
Barnesville	43713
Barnhill	44663
Barretts Mills	45612
Barrs Mills	44681
Bartles	45659
Bartlett	45713
Bartley Estates	45414
Bartlow (Township)	43516
Barton	43905
Bartramville	45669
Bascom	44809
Bashan	45743
Bass Lake	44024
Batavia (Township)	45103

	ZIP
Batavia	45103
Batemantown	43019
Batesville	43773
Bath (Allen County) (Township)	45801
Bath (Greene County) (Township)	45324
Bath (Summit County)	44210
Bath (Summit County) (Township)	44210
Battlesburg	44626
Baughman (Township)	44667
Bay (Township)	43452
Bayard	44657
Bay Bridge	44870
Bays	43462
Bay View	44870
Bay Village	44140
Bazetta	44410
Bazetta (Township)	44410
Beach City	44608
Beachland (Part of Cleveland)	44119
Beachwood	44122
Beachwood Place (Part of Beachwood)	44122
Beacon Hill	45241
Beallsville	43716
Beals (Part of Pickerington)	43147
Beamsville	45303
Bear Creek	45657
Bearfield (Township)	43730
Beartown	44622
Beatty	45506
Beaumont	45701
Beaver (Mahoning County) (Township)	44408
Beaver (Noble County) (Township)	43773
Beaver (Pike County)	45613
Beaver (Pike County) (Township)	45690
Beavercreek	45430-32
For specific Beavercreek Zip Codes call (513) 426-6644, or your local postmaster.	
Beavercreek (Township)	45401
Beaverdam	45808
Beaver Park (Part of Lorain)	44053
Beavertown (Montgomery County)	45429
Beavertown (Washington County)	45767
Becker Highlands (Part of Steubenville)	43952
Beckett Ridge	45069
Becks Mills	44654
Bedford (Coshocton County) (Township)	43812
Bedford (Cuyahoga County)	44146
Bedford (Meigs County) (Township)	45769
Bedford Heights	44128
Beebe	45778
Beechcrest	44240
Beechview Estates (Part of Cincinnati)	45201
Beechwold (Part of Columbus)	43214
Beechwood (Jefferson County)	43952
Beechwood (Preble County)	45064
Beechwood (Stark County)	44601
Beechwood Trails	43062
Belden	44044
Belfast (Clermont County)	45122
Belfast (Highland County)	45133
Belfort	44641
Bellaire	43906
Bellaire Gardens	43302
Bellbrook	45305
Belle Center	43310
Bellefontaine	43311
Bellepoint	43015
Belle Valley	43717
Belle Vernon	44882
Belleview Heights (Preble County)	45347
Belleview Heights (Ross County)	45601
Bellevue	44811
Bellview	45305
Bellview Estates	45305
Bellview Heights	43906

	ZIP		ZIP		ZIP		ZIP
Bellville	44813	Bishopville	45732	Boston Heights	44236	Brookfield (Noble County)	
Belmont (Allen County)	45801	Bismarck	44811	Boston Mill	44264	(Township)	43732
Belmont (Belmont County)	43718	Blachleyville	44691	Botkins	45306	Brookfield (Trumbull	
Belmont (Butler County)	45015	Black Creek (Township)	45882	Boudes Ferry	45121	County)	44403
Belmont Meadows (Part		Blackfork	45656	Boughtonville	44890	Brookfield (Trumbull	
of Springfield)	45505	Black Fork Junction	45656	Bourneville	45617	County) (Township)	44403
Belmont Park	44420	Black Horse	44266	Bowerston	44695	Brookhill	45224
Belmont Ridge	43983	Blacklick	43004	Bowersville	45307	Brook Hollow	45324
Belmore	45815	Blacklick Estates	43227	Bowling Green (Licking		Brooklyn	44144
Beloit	44609	Black Run	43830	County) (Township)	43076	Brooklyn Heights	44131
Belpre	45714	Blacktop	43780	Bowling Green (Marion		Brook Park	44142
Belpre (Township)	45714	Bladen	45623	County) (Township)	43332	Brookside (Belmont	
Belvedere	43952	Bladensburg	43005	Bowling Green (Wood		County)	43912
Bennington (Licking		Blaine	43909	County)	43402	Brookside (Scioto County)	45652
County) (Township)	43011	Blainesville	43950	Bowlusville	43078	Brookside Estates	43085
Bennington (Morrow		Blairmont	43901	Boydsville	43912	Brookview	43912
County) (Township)	43334	Blakeslee	43505	Braceville	44444	Brookville	45309
Bentley (Part of		Blanchard (Hancock		Braceville (Township)	44444	Brookwood (Part of	
Lowellville)	44436	County) (Township)	45816	Braceville Ridge	44444	Amberley)	45237
Bentleyville	44022	Blanchard (Hardin County)	45836	Bradbury	45760	Broughton	45879
Benton (Crawford County)	44882	Blanchard (Hardin County)		Bradford	45308	Brown (Carroll County)	
Benton (Hocking County)		(Township)	45836	Bradley	43917	(Township)	44644
(Township)	43152	Blanchard (Putnam		Bradner	43406	Brown (Darke County)	
Benton (Holmes County)	44654	County) (Township)	45875	Bradrick	45619	(Township)	45303
Benton (Monroe County)		Blanches Addition	43062	Brady (Township)	43570	Brown (Delaware County)	
(Township)	45767	Blanchester	45107	Brady Lake	44211	(Township)	43015
Benton (Ottawa County)		Blendon (Township)	43081	Brady Lake Addition	44211	Brown (Franklin County)	
(Township)	43432	Blissfield	43805	Bradyville	45144	(Township)	43026
Benton (Paulding County)		Bloom (Fairfield County)		Braffettsville	45347	Brown (Knox County)	
(Township)	45880	(Township)	43136	Brailey	43558	(Township)	43014
Benton (Pike County)		Bloom (Morgan County)		Branch Hill	45140	Brown (Miami County)	
(Township)	45690	(Township)	43756	Brandon	43050	(Township)	45317
Benton Ridge	45816	Bloom (Scioto County)		Brandt	45371	Brown (Paulding County)	
Bentonville	45105	(Township)	45682	Brandywine	44820	(Township)	45873
Berea	44017	Bloom (Seneca County)		Bratenahl	44108	Brown (Vinton County)	
Berea (Part of Middleburg		(Township)	44818	Bratton (Township)	45660	(Township)	45654
Heights)	44130	Bloom (Wood County)		Brecksville	44141	Brown Heights	43725
Bergholz	43908	(Township)	44817	Brecon	45242	Brownhelm	44089
Berkey	43504	Bloom Center	43318	Bremen	43107	Brownhelm (Township)	44001
Berkley Heights (Part of		Bloomdale	44817	Brentwood (Hamilton		Brownstown	45171
Kettering)	45429	Bloomer	45318	County)	45231	Brownsville (Licking	
Berkshire	43074	Bloomfield (Columbiana		Brentwood (Jefferson		County)	43721
Berkshire (Township)	43074	County)	43920	County)	43952	Brownsville (Monroe	
Berlin (Delaware County)		Bloomfield (Jackson		Brentwood (Lake County)	44060	County)	45767
(Township)	43015	County) (Township)	45640	Brentwood Estates	43952	Brownsville (Ross County)	45601
Berlin (Erie County)		Bloomfield (Logan		Brentwood Lake	44044	Brunersburg	43512
(Township)	44814	County) (Township)	43333	Brewster	44613	Bruno	43076
Berlin (Holmes County)	44610	Bloomfield (Morrow		Briarwood Beach	44215	Brunswick	44212
Berlin (Holmes County)		County)	43011	Brice	43109	Brunswick Hills	
(Township)	44610	Bloomfield (Muskingum		Brice Road Square (Part		(Township)	44280
Berlin (Knox County)		County)	43762	of Columbus)	43068	Brush Creek (Adams	
(Township)	43019	Bloomfield (Trumbull		Briceton	45879	County) (Township)	45650
Berlin (Mahoning County)		County) (Township)	44450	Bridgeport (Belmont		Brushcreek (Highland	
(Township)	44401	Bloomfield (Washington		County)	43912	County) (Township)	45172
Berlin Center	44401	County)	45734	Bridgeport (Hardin		Brush Creek (Jefferson	
Berlin Heights	44814	Bloomingburg	43106	County)	45843	County) (Township)	43945
Berlinville	44814	Bloomingdale	43910	Bridgetown	45211	Brush Creek (Muskingum	
Bern (Township)	45770	Blooming Grove (Morrow		Bridgeville	43701	County) (Township)	43777
Berne (Township)	43155	County)	44833	Bridgewater (Township)	43543	Brush Creek (Scioto	
Bernice	43832	Blooming Grove (Richland		Bridgewater Center	43543	County) (Township)	45657
Berryman	45805	County) (Township)	44878	Brier Hill (Part of		Brush Ridge	43302
Berrysville	45133	Bloomington	45169	Youngstown)	44510	Bryan	43506
Berwick	44853	Bloomingville	44870	Brigglesville	43731	Buchanan	45690
Bessemer	45764	Bloom Junction	45682	Briggs (Cuyahoga County)	44134	Buchtel	45716
Bethany	45042	Bloomville	44818	Briggs (Washington		Buck (Township)	43326
Bethel (Clark County)		Blue Ash	45242	County)	45714	Buckeye	43701
(Township)	45344	Blue Ball	45005	Briggsdale	43223	Buckeye Lake	43008
Bethel (Clermont County)	45106	Blue Bell	43772	Brighton (Clark County)	45369	Buckeye Road (Part of	
Bethel (Miami County)		Bluebird Beach (Part of		Brighton (Hamilton		Cleveland)	44102
(Township)	45371	Vermilion)	44089	County)	45214	Buckeyeville	43725
Bethel (Monroe County)		Blue Creek (Adams		Brighton (Lorain County)	44090	Buckhorn	45694
(Township)	45745	County)	45616	Brighton (Lorain County)		Buckingham	43730
Bethel (Pike County)	45661	Blue Creek (Paulding		(Township)	44090	Buckland	45819
Bethesda	43719	County) (Township)	45886	Brightwood	44663	Bucks (Township)	43824
Bethlehem (Coshocton		Blue Rock	43720	Brilliant	43913	Buckskin (Township)	45647
County) (Township)	43812	Blue Rock (Township)	43720	Brimfield	44240	Bucyrus	44820
Bethlehem (Richland		Blue Valley Acres	43130	Brimfield (Township)	44240	Bucyrus (Township)	44820
County)	44875	Bluffton	45817	Brinkhaven	43006	Buena Vista (Butler	
Bethlehem (Stark County)		Boardman	44512	Bristol (Morgan County)		County)	45042
(Township)	44662	Boardman (Township)	44512	(Township)	43756	Buena Vista (Fayette	
Bettsville	44815	Boardman Plaza	44512	Bristol (Perry County)	43764	County)	43160
Beulah Beach	44089	Bobo	45613	Bristol (Trumbull County)		Buena Vista (Hocking	
Beverly	45715	Boden	43762	(Township)	44402	County)	43149
Beverly Gardens	45431	Bokes Creek (Township)	43358	Bristol Village (Part of		Buena Vista (Scioto	
Bevis	45239	Bolindale	44484	Waverly)	45690	County)	45684
Bexley	43209	Bolivar	44612	Bristolville	44402	Buffalo (Guernsey County)	43722
Bidwell	45614	Bolton	44601	Broadacre	43910	Buffalo (Noble County)	
Big Island	43302	Bond Hill (Part of		Broadview Acres (Clark		(Township)	43772
Big Island (Township)	43302	Cincinnati)	45237	County)	45504	Buford	45110
Biglick (Township)	44802	Boneta	44256	Broadview Acres		Bulah	44047
Big Plain	43140	Bonn	45788	(Muskingum County)	43701	Bulaville	45631
Big Prairie	44611	Bono	43445	Broadview Heights	44147	Bulk Mail Center (Part of	
Big Rock	45613	Bookwalter	43128	Broadway	43007	Sharonville)	45235
Big Run	45724	Booth (Lucas County)	43618	Broadwell	45778	Bunker Hill (Butler County)	45013
Big Spring (Township)	44853	Booth (Tuscarawas		Brock	45380	Bunker Hill (Holmes	
Big Springs	43347	County)	43832	Brokaw	43787	County)	44654
Birds Run	43749	Borromeo College of Ohio	44092	Brokensword	44820	Burbank	44214
Birmingham (Erie County)	44816	Boston (Highland County)	45133	Brokes	45672	Burghill	44404
Birmingham (Guernsey		Boston (Summit County)		Bronson (Township)	44857	Burgoon	43407
County)	43749	(Township)	44264			Burkettsville	45310

* Area Zip Code   **† Post Office Boxes**

	ZIP
Burkhart	43754
Burlingham	45776
Burlington (Fulton County)	43502
Burlington (Lawrence County)	45680
Burlington (Licking County) (Township)	43027
Burnetts Corners	44691
Burnet Woods (Part of Cincinnati)	45220
Burr Oak	45732
Burr Oaks	43143
Burton	44021
Burton (Township)	44021
Burton City	44667
Burton Lake	44021
Burton Station	44062
Burtonville	45177
Busch (Part of Columbus)	43226
Busenbark (Part of Trenton)	45011
Bushnell	44030
Businessburg	43933
Business Corners	43542
Butler (Columbiana County) (Township)	44460
Butler (Darke County) (Township)	45346
Butler (Knox County) (Township)	43843
Butler (Mercer County) (Township)	45828
Butler (Montgomery County) (Township)	45337
Butler (Richland County)	44822
Butler (Richland County) (Township)	44837
Butlerville	45162
Byers Junction	45692
Byesville	43723
Byhalia	43344
Byington	45646
Byrd (Township)	45115
Byron	45385
Cable	43009
Cadiz	43907
Cadiz (Township)	43907
Cadiz Junction	43976
Cadmus	45658
Caesars Creek (Township)	45385
Cain Heights (Part of East Liverpool)	43920
Cairo (Allen County)	45820
Cairo (Stark County)	44721
Calais	43773
Calcutta	43920
Caldwell	43724
Caledonia	43314
California (Clark County)	45503
California (Hamilton County)	45228
Calla	44406
Cambridge (Township)	43725
Cambridge	43725
Cambridge Mental Health and Development Center	43725
Camden (Lorain County) (Township)	44049
Camden (Preble County)	45311
Cameron	43914
Campbell	44405
Campbellsport	44266
Campbellstown	45320
Camp Creek (Pike County) (Township)	45671
Camp Creek (Stark County)	44662
Camp Dennison	45111
Camp Ground	43130
Camp Luther (Part of North Kingsville)	44068
Campus (Part of Cincinnati)	45221
Canaan (Athens County) (Township)	45701
Canaan (Madison County) (Township)	43064
Canaan (Morrow County) (Township)	43320
Canaan (Wayne County)	44217
Canaan (Wayne County) (Township)	44217
Canaanville	45701
Canal Fulton	44614
Canal Lewisville	43812
Canal Winchester	43110
Candle Lite Estates (Part of Warren)	44484

	ZIP
Canfield	44406
Canfield (Township)	44406
Cannelville	43777
Cannons Creek	45659
Cannons Mills	43920
Canton	44701-35
For specific Canton Zip Codes call (216) 438-6432, or your local postmaster.	
Canton Centre (Part of Canton)	44708
Canyon Park	44429
Captina	43933
Carbondale	45717
Carbon Hill	43111
Cardinal Lake	44085
Cardington	43315
Cardington (Township)	43315
Carey	43316
Carlisle (Lorain County) (Township)	44035
Carlisle (Noble County)	43724
Carlisle (Warren County)	45005
Carmel	45133
Caroline	44807
Carpenter	45710
Carriage	45502
Carroll (Fairfield County)	43112
Carroll (Ottawa County) (Township)	43449
Carrollton	44615
Carrothers	44807
Carryall (Township)	45813
Carthage (Athens County) (Township)	45735
Carthage (Hamilton County)	45216
Carthagena	45822
Carysville	45317
Cass (Hancock County) (Township)	44804
Cass (Muskingum County) (Township)	43821
Cass (Richland County) (Township)	44878
Cassell	43725
Cassella	45883
Cassinelli Square (Part of Springdale)	45246
Casstown	45312
Castalia	44824
Castine	45304
Catawba (Champaign County)	43044
Catawba (Clark County)	43010
Catawba Island	43452
Catawba Island (Township)	43452
Causeway Manor	44003
Cavallo	43843
Cavett	45891
Caywood	45750
Cecil	45821
Cedar Center Plaza (Part of University Heights)	44125
Cedarhill	43102
Cedar Mills	45616
Cedar Point (Part of Sandusky)	44870
Cedar Valley	44214
Cedarville	45314
Cedarville (Township)	45314
Cedron	45121
Celeryville	44890
Celina	45822
Centenary	45631
Center (Carroll County) (Township)	44615
Center (Columbiana County) (Township)	44432
Center (Guernsey County)	43725
Center (Guernsey County) (Township)	43725
Center (Mercer County) (Township)	45822
Center (Monroe County) (Township)	43793
Center (Morgan County) (Township)	45715
Center (Noble County) (Township)	43724
Center (Williams County) (Township)	43506
Center (Wood County) (Township)	43402
Centerburg	43011
Centerfield	45123
Centerpoint	45656
Center Station	45659
Centerton	44890

	ZIP
Center Village	43021
Centerville (Belmont County)	43718
Centerville (Brown County)	45154
Centerville (Marion County)	43342
Centerville (Montgomery County)	45441
	45458-59
For specific Centerville Zip Codes call (513) 433-1213, or your local postmaster.	
Centerville (Wayne County)	44676
Central (Part of Toledo)	43604
Central College (Part of Westerville)	43081
Cessna (Township)	43326
Ceylon	44839
Chagrin Falls	44022-23
For specific Chagrin Falls Zip Codes call (216) 247-6452, or your local postmaster.	
Chagrin Falls Annex	44023
Chagrin Falls Park	44022
Chagrin Harbor (Part of Eastlake)	44094
Chalfants	43739
Chambersburg (Columbiana County)	44657
Chambersburg (Gallia County)	45631
Champion (Township)	44481
Champion Heights	44481
Chandler	43910
Chandlersville	43727
Chapel Hill Shopping Center (Part of Akron)	44310
Chapmans	45692
Chardon	44024
Chardon (Township)	44024
Charity Rotch (Part of Massillon)	44646
Charlestown	44266
Charlestown (Township)	44266
Charloe	45873
Charm	44617
Chase	45710
Chasetown	45118
Chaseville	43772
Chaska Beach (Part of Huron)	44839
Chateau Estates	45502
Chateau Ridge (Part of Marion)	43302
Chatfield	44825
Chatfield (Township)	44825
Chatham (Chatham County) (Township)	44275
Chatham (Licking County)	43055
Chatham (Medina County)	44256
Chattanooga	45882
Chauncey	45719
Chautauqua	45342
Cherokee	43324
Cherry Fork	45618
Cherry Grove (Clermont County)	45230
Cherry Grove (Hamilton County)	45230
Cherry Grove Plaza	45230
Cherry Valley	44003
Cherry Valley (Township)	44003
Chesapeake	45619
Cheshire (Delaware County)	43021
Cheshire (Gallia County)	45620
Cheshire (Gallia County) (Township)	45620
Chesswood Acres	45239
Chester (Clinton County) (Township)	45177
Chester (Geauga County) (Township)	44026
Chester (Meigs County)	45720
Chester (Meigs County) (Township)	45720
Chester (Morrow County) (Township)	43338
Chester (Wayne County) (Township)	44691
Chester Center	44026
Chesterfield (Township)	43567
Chesterhill	43728
Chesterland	44026
Chesterville	43317
Cheviot	45211
Cheviot Hills	45502
Chevy Chase	44833

	ZIP
Chickasaw	45826
Chickwan	43901
Chili	43824
Chillicothe	45601
Chillicothe Correctional Institute	45601
Chillicothe Manor	45601
Chilo	45112
Chipman	45805
Chippewa (Township)	44230
Chippewa Lake	44215
Chippewa Lake Park	44215
Chocktou Lake	43140
Christiansburg	45389
Christopher Columbus (Part of Columbus)	43215
Chuckery	43029
Churchill	44505
Churchills (Part of Sylvania)	43560
Churchtown	45750
Cincinnati	45201-75
For specific Cincinnati Zip Codes call (513) 684-5571, or your local postmaster.	

COLLEGES & UNIVERSITIES

God's Bible School and College	45210
University of Cincinnati	45221
Xavier University	45207

FINANCIAL INSTITUTIONS

Centennial Savings Bank	45205
Century Bank	45209
Fidelity Federal Savings Bank	45202
Fifth Third Bank	45263
First Financial Savings Association, F.A.	45243
Franklin Savings & Loan Company	45202
Huntington National Bank	45202
North Side Bank & Trust Company	45223
Oak Hills Savings & Loan Company, F.A.	45248
PNC Bank	45202
Provident Bank	45202
Star Bank, N.A., Cincinnati	45202
Suburban Federal Savings Bank	45242
Winton Savings & Loan Company	45247

HOSPITALS

Bethesda North Hospital	45242
Bethesda Oak Hospital	45206
Children's Hospital Medical Center	45229
Christ Hospital	45219
Deaconess Hospital	45219
Drake Center	45216
Good Samaritan Hospital	45220
Jewish Hospital of Cincinnati	45229
Providence Hospital	45239
St. Francis-St. George Hospital	45238
University of Cincinnati Hospital	45267
Veterans Affairs Medical Center	45220

HOTELS/MOTELS

Clarion Hotel	45202
Hampshire House Hotel	45246
Harley of Cincinnati	45236
Holiday Inn-Cincinnati	45241
Hyatt Regency Cincinnati-Saks Fifth Avenue Center	45202
Omni Netherland Plaza	45202
Ramada Hotel Northeast-Blue Ash	45242
Vernon Manor Hotel	45219

MILITARY INSTALLATIONS

United States Army Engineer District, Ohio River Division, Laboratory	45201
Circle Green	43908
Circle Hill (Athens County)	45764
Circle Hill (Miami County)	45308
Circleville (Township)	43113
Circleville	43113

***** Area Zip Code   † Post Office Boxes

	ZIP
Circleville Bible College	43113
City View Heights	45013
Claiborne	43344
Claibourne (Township)	43344
Claridon (Geauga County)	44024
Claridon (Geauga County) (Township)	44024
Claridon (Marion County)	43314
Claridon (Marion County) (Township)	43314
Clarington	43915
Clark (Brown County) (Township)	45130
Clark (Clinton County) (Township)	45146
Clark (Coshocton County)	43812
Clark (Coshocton County) (Township)	43844
Clark (Holmes County) (Township)	43804
Clark Corners (Ashtabula County)	44030
Clark Corners (Medina County)	44281
Clarksburg (Belmont County)	43960
Clarksburg (Ross County)	43115
Clarksfield	44889
Clarksfield (Township)	44889
Clarks Lake	43143
Clarkson	44455
Clarkstown	45648
Clarksville (Clinton County)	45113
Clarksville (Perry County)	43748
Clay (Auglaize County) (Township)	45895
Clay (Gallia County) (Township)	45631
Clay (Highland County) (Township)	45171
Clay (Jackson County)	45656
Clay (Knox County) (Township)	43080
Clay (Montgomery County) (Township)	45354
Clay (Muskingum County) (Township)	43777
Clay (Ottawa County) (Township)	43430
Clay (Scioto County) (Township)	45662
Clay (Tuscarawas County) (Township)	44629
Clay Center	43408
Clay Lick	43055
Claysville	43725
Clayton (Adams County)	45144
Clayton (Miami County)	45318
Clayton (Montgomery County)	45315
Clayton (Perry County) (Township)	43764
Clear Creek (Ashland County) (Township)	44874
Clearcreek (Fairfield County) (Township)	43102
Clear Creek (Warren County) (Township)	45066
Clearport	43130
Clearview (Athens County)	45701
Clearview (Lorain County)	44055
Clearview (Stark County)	44646
Clermontville	45157
Clertoma (Part of Milford)	45150
Cleveland	44101-06
	44108-15
	44117-32
	44134-35
	44142-44
	44181-99

For specific Cleveland Zip
Codes call (216) 443-4444, or
your local postmaster.

COLLEGES & UNIVERSITIES

	ZIP
Case Western Reserve University	44106
Cleveland State University	44115
Dyke College	44115
John Carroll University	44118
Ursuline College	44124

FINANCIAL INSTITUTIONS

	ZIP
Bank One, Cleveland, N.A.	44114
Charter One Bank, F.S.B.	44114
Home Federal Savings Bank, Northern Ohio	44113
National City Bank	44114
Ohio Savings Bank	44114
Security Federal Savings & Loan Association of Cleveland	44115
Society National Bank	44114
Third Federal Savings & Loan Association of Cleveland	44105
Transohio Federal Savings Bank	44114

HOSPITALS

	ZIP
Cleveland Clinic Hospital	44195
Deaconess Hospital of Cleveland	44109
Fairview General Hospital	44111
Meridia Huron Hospital	44112
Mt. Sinai Medical Center	44106
St. Vincent Charity Hospital	44115
University Hospitals of Cleveland	44106
Veterans Affairs Medical Center	44106

HOTELS/MOTELS

	ZIP
Cleveland South Hilton Inn	44131
Sheraton Airport Hotel	44135

	ZIP
Cleveland Heights	44118
Cleves	45002
Clifton (Greene County)	45316
Clifton (Hamilton County)	45219
Clifton Farms (Part of Middletown)	45044
Climax	43320
Clinton (Franklin County) (Township)	43224
Clinton (Fulton County) (Township)	43567
Clinton (Knox County) (Township)	43050
Clinton (Seneca County) (Township)	44883
Clinton (Shelby County) (Township)	45365
Clinton (Summit County)	44216
Clinton (Vinton County) (Township)	45634
Clinton (Wayne County) (Township)	44676
Clintonville (Part of Columbus)	43202
Clipper Mills	45631
Cloverdale	45827
Cloverhill	43764
Cluff	45244
Clyde	43410
Coach Lite Village	43528
Coal (Jackson County) (Township)	45621
Coal (Perry County) (Township)	43766
Coalburg	44425
Coal Grove	45638
Coalport (Part of Newcomerstown)	43832
Coal Ridge	43711
Coal Run	45721
Coalton	45621
Coddingville	44256
Coffee Corners	44062
Coitsville (Township)	44436
Coitsville Center	44505
Colby	43410
Cold Springs	45502
Coldwater	45828
Colebrook	44076
Colebrook (Township)	44076
Colerain	43916
Colerain (Township)	43916
Colerain (Hamilton County) (Township)	45251
Colerain (Ross County) (Township)	45644
Colerain Heights	45239
Coles Park	45663
Coletown	45331
College (Township)	43022
College Corner	45003
College Hill (Guernsey County)	43725
College Hill (Hamilton County)	45224
College Hill Junction (Part of Cincinnati)	45224
College Hills	45324

	ZIP
Collins	44826
Collinsville	45004
Collinwood (Part of Cleveland)	44110
Colonial Hills (Part of Worthington)	43085
Colony Square (Part of Zanesville)	43701
Colton	43510
Columbia (Hamilton County) (Township)	45243
Columbia (Lorain County) (Township)	44028
Columbia (Meigs County) (Township)	45710
Columbia (Stark County)	44646
Columbia (Tuscarawas County)	44622
Columbia (Williams County)	43518
Columbia Center (Licking County)	43062
Columbia Center (Lorain County)	44028
Columbia Hills Corners	44028
Columbiana	44408
Columbia Station	44028
Columbus	43201-40

For specific Columbus Zip
Codes call (614) 469-4200, or
your local postmaster.

COLLEGES & UNIVERSITIES

	ZIP
Capital University	43209
Columbus College of Art and Design	43215
DeVry Institute of Technology-Columbus	43209
Ohio Dominican College	43219
Ohio State University	43210

FINANCIAL INSTITUTIONS

	ZIP
Bank One, Columbus, N.A.	43271
Fifth Third Bank of Columbus	43215
Household Bank, F.S.B.	43231
Huntington National Bank	43215
National City Bank, Columbus	43251
Society National Bank	43215
Star Bank City Center	43215
State Savings Bank	43215

HOSPITALS

	ZIP
Children's Hospital	43205
Columbus Community Hospital	43207
Doctors Hospital	43201
Grant Medical Center	43215
Mount Carmel Health Center	43222
Ohio State University Hospitals	43210
Riverside Methodist Hospital	43214

HOTELS/MOTELS

	ZIP
Columbus Marriott/North	43229
Harley of Columbus	43229
Holiday Inn Crowne Plaza	43215
Hyatt Regency Columbus	43215
Parke University Hotel	43202

MILITARY INSTALLATIONS

	ZIP
Defense Construction Supply Center	43215
Rickenbacker Air National Guard Base	43217

	ZIP
Columbus Circle (Part of Ashland)	44805
Columbus City Center (Part of Columbus)	43215
Columbus Grove	45830
Columbus Mall (Part of Columbus)	43229
Columbus Park	44870
Comet	44216
Commercial Point	43116
Compton Park	45231
Compton Woods (Part of Wyoming)	45215
Conant	45887
Concept	45807
Concord (Champaign County) (Township)	43072
Concord (Delaware County) (Township)	43015

	ZIP
Concord (Fayette County) (Township)	43160
Concord (Highland County) (Township)	45697
Concord (Lake County)	44060
Concord (Lake County) (Township)	44077
Concord (Licking County)	43031
Concord (Miami County) (Township)	43373
Concord (Ross County) (Township)	45628
Condit	43074
Conesville	43811
Congo	43730
Congress (Morrow County) (Township)	43338
Congress (Wayne County)	44287
Congress (Wayne County) (Township)	44287
Congress Lake	44632
Conneaut	44030
Conneaut Harbor (Part of Conneaut)	44030
Connett	45764
Connor	43943
Conotton	44695
Conover	45317
Constitution	45750
Continental	45831
Converse	45887
Convoy	45832
Conway Addition	43731
Cook	43143
Cool Ridge Heights (Part of Mansfield)	44905
Coolville	45723
Coonville	45654
Cooperdale	43821
Coopersville	45657
Copley	44321
Copley (Township)	44321
Copley Center	44321
Corinth	44417
Cork	44041
Corner	45714
Cornersburg (Part of Youngstown)	44511
Cornerville	45773
Corning	43730
Correctional Reception Center	43146
Corryville (Hamilton County)	45219-20

For specific Corryville Zip
Codes call (513) 751-1176, or
your local postmaster.

	ZIP
Corryville (Lawrence County)	45619
Cortland	44410
Cortsville	45368
Corwin	45068
Coryville	45638
Coshocton	43812
Cottage Grove	44319
Country Acres	45324
Country Acres (Part of Beavercreek)	45430
Country Club Estates (Part of Steubenville)	43952
Country Club Hills	45801
Country Estates	45371
Country Fair Station (Part of Canton)	44708
Cove	45640
Covedale	45238
Coventry (Township)	44319
Covington	45318
Cozaddale	45122
Crabapple	43950
Craig Beach	44429
Craigton	44676
Cranberry (Township)	44854
Cranberry Prairie	45883
Crandenbrook	43551
Crane (Paulding County) (Township)	45821
Crane (Wyandot County) (Township)	43351
Cranwood (Part of Cleveland)	44128
Crawford (Coshocton County) (Township)	43804
Crawford (Wyandot County)	43316
Crawford (Wyandot County) (Township)	43316
Crawford Corners	44254
Cream City (Part of Irondale)	43932

	ZIP		ZIP		ZIP		ZIP
Creola	45622	Deerfield (Portage County) (Township)	44411	Dover (Tuscarawas County) (Township)	44622	East Lewistown	44408
Crescent	43950					East Liberty (Delaware County)	43074
Crescent Gardens	44646	Deerfield (Ross County) (Township)	43115	Dover (Union County) (Township)	43040		
Crescentville (Part of Sharonville)	45241	Deerfield (Warren County) (Township)	45040	Dowling	43551	East Liberty (Logan County)	43319
Crestline	44827	Deerfield (Morgan County) (Township)	43758	Downtown (Part of Akron)	44308	East Liberty (Summit County)	44319
Creston	44217			Doylestown	44230		
Crestwood Hills (Part of Vandalia)	45377	Deering	45638	Drakes	43730	East Liverpool	43920
		Deer Park	45236	Drakesburg	44288	East Mansfield	44905
Cridersville	45806	Deersville	44693	Dresden	43821	East Mecca	44410
Crissey	43528	Defiance	43512	Drexel	45427	East Millersport	43046
Cromers	44883	Defiance (Township)	43512	Driftwood (Ashtabula County)	44041	East Millfield	45761
Crooked Tree	45727	Defiance Junction (Part of Defiance)	43512			East Monroe	45135
Crooksville	43731			Driftwood (Lake County)	44041	East Norwalk	44857
Crosby (Township)	45030	DeForest	44484	Drinkle	43102	East Norwood (Hamilton County)	45212
Cross Creek (Township)	43952	De Graff	43318	Dry Run (Hamilton County)	45244		
Crossenville	43107	Dekalb	44887			East Norwood (Washington County)	45750
Crosstown	45176	Delaware (Defiance County) (Township)	43556	Dry Run (Scioto County)	45663		
Crosswick	45068			Dublin	43016-17	Easton	44270
Croton	43013	Delaware (Delaware County)	43015	For specific Dublin Zip Codes call (614) 889-0763, or your local postmaster.		East Orwell (Part of Orwell)	44076
Crown City	45623					East Over	45011
Crystal Lake	44003	Delaware (Delaware County) (Township)	43015	Dublin (Township)	45882	East Palestine	44413
Crystal Lakes	45341			Dublin Village Center (Part of Dublin)	43017	East Plains (Part of Middletown)	45044
Crystal Rock Park	44870	Delaware (Hancock County) (Township)	45897				
Crystal Springs	44614			Duchouquet (Township)	45895	East Richland	43950
Cuba	45114	Delhi (Township)	45238	Dudley (Hardin County) (Township)	43326	East Rochester	44625
Cumberland	43732	Delhi	45238			East Side (Part of Youngstown)	44506
Cumminsville (Part of Cincinnati)	45223	Delhi Hills	45238	Dudley (Noble County)	43724		
		Delightful	44470	Dueber (Part of Canton)	44706	East Sparta	44626
Curtice	43412	Delisle	45304	Duffy	43946	East Springfield	43925
Custar	43511	Dellroy	44620	Dull	45874	East Toledo (Part of Toledo)	43605
Cutler	45724	Delmont	43130	Dumontville	43130		
Cuyahoga Falls	44221-24	Delphi	45833	Dunbridge	43414	East Townsend	44826
For specific Cuyahoga Falls Zip Codes call (216) 945-5807, or your local postmaster.		Delphos	45833	Duncan Falls	43734	East Trumbull	44084
		Delta	43515	Dundas	45634	East Union (Noble County)	43779
Cuyahoga Heights	44127	Denmark (Ashtabula County) (Township)	44047	Dundee	44624		
Cygnet	43413			Dungannon (Columbiana County)	44423	East Union (Wayne County) (Township)	44606
Cynthian (Township)	45845	Denmark (Morrow County)	43320				
Cynthiana	45624	Denmark Center	44047	Dungannon (Noble County)	45721	East View (Jefferson County)	43938
Dabel (Part of Dayton)	45420	Dennison	44621				
Dadsville	45381	Densons	43533	Dunglen	43917	Eastview (Montgomery County)	45431
Dailyville	45690	Dent	45211	Dunham (Township)	45784		
Dale	43787	Denver	45690	Dunkinsville	45660	Eastwood	45154
Dallas (Township)	44849	Derby	43117	Dunkirk	45836	Eastwood Mall (Part of Niles)	44446
Dallasburg	45140	Derwent	43733	Dunlap	45239		
Dalton	44618	Deshler	43516	Dupont	45837	Eaton (Lorain County) (Township)	44035
Dalzell	45745	Deunquat	44882	Durbin (Clark County)	45502		
Daman Park	45044	Devil Town	44691	Durbin (Mercer County)	45822	Eaton (Preble County)	45320
Damascus (Henry County) (Township)	43534	Devola	45750	Duval	43137	Eaton Estates	44044
		Deweyville	45858	Dyesville	45769	Eber	43160
Damascus (Mahoning County)	44619	Dexter	45741	Eagle (Brown County) (Township)	45171	Echo	43940
		Dexter City	45727			Echo Glen Lake	44233
Danbury (Township)	43452	Deyarmonville	43917	Eagle (Hancock County) (Township)	45881	Eckmansville	45697
Danville (Highland County)	45133	Dialton	45502			Eden (Licking County) (Township)	43071
Danville (Knox County)	43014	Diamond	44412	Eagle (Vinton County) (Township)	43152		
Danville (Meigs County)	45741	Dicken	43138			Eden (Seneca County) (Township)	44845
Darby (Madison County) (Township)	43064	Dilles Bottom	43947	Eagle Beach	43452		
		Dillon Falls	43701	Eagle City	45504	Eden (Wyandot County) (Township)	44849
Darby (Pickaway County) (Township)	43146	Dillonvale (Hamilton County)	45236	Eagle Point Colony (Part of Rossford)	43460		
				Eagleport	43756	Eden Park (Hamilton County)	45202
Darby (Union County) (Township)	43064	Dillonvale (Jefferson County)	43917	Eagleville (Ashtabula County)	44047		
						Eden Park (Scioto County)	45662
Darbydale	43123	Dilworth	44417	Eagleville (Wood County)	44817	Edenton	45122
Darbyville	43136	Dinsmore (Township)	45306	East (Township)	44427	Edenville	44849
Darlington (Muskingum County)	43701	Dixie	43782	East Akron (Part of Akron)	44305	Edgefield (Fayette County)	43128
		Dixie Heights (Butler County)	45042	East Alliance	44601		
Darlington (Richland County)	44813			East Ashtabula (Part of Ashtabula)	44004	Edgefield (Stark County)	44709
		Dixie Heights (Montgomery County)	45414			Edgemont	45216
Darrowville (Part of Stow)	44224			East Bass Lake	44024	Edgerton	43517
Darrtown	45056	Dixon (Preble County) (Township)	45320	East Batavia Heights	45103	Edgewater (Part of Lakewood)	44107
Dart	45773			East Cadiz	43907		
Darwin	45769	Dixon (Van Wert County)	45832	East Cambridge (Part of Cambridge)	43725	Edgewater Beach	43076
Davisville	45692	Dixonville	43920			Edgewater Park	43227
Dawn	45303	Doanville	45764	East Canton	44730	Edgewood	44004
Dawson	45333	Dobbston	45678	East Carlisle	44035	Edgewood Estates	45805
Day Heights	45150	Dodds	45036	East Claridon	44033	Edinburg	44272
Dayton	45401-90	Dodgeville	44085	East Clayton	45764	Edinburg (Township)	44272
For specific Dayton Zip Codes call (513) 227-1231, or your local postmaster.		Dodson (Highland County) (Township)	45142	East Cleveland	44112	Edison	43320
				East Conneaut (Part of Conneaut)	44030	Edmunds	45682
Dayton View (Part of Dayton)	45406	Dodson (Montgomery County)	45309			Edon	43518
				East Cumminsville (Part of Cincinnati)	45223	Egypt (Auglaize County)	45865
Dean Dale (Part of Mingo Junction)	43938	Dodsonville	45142			Egypt (Belmont County)	43713
		Dola	45835	East Danville	45133	Eifort	45682
Deavertown	43731	Dolly Varden	45368	East End (Columbiana County)	43920	Eileen Gardens	45238
Decatur (Brown County)	45115	Donald L Marrs (Part of Cincinnati)	45258			Elba	45746
Decatur (Lawrence County) (Township)	45659			East End (Hamilton County)	45226	Elberta Beach (Part of Vermilion)	44089
		Doneys (Part of Whitehall)	43213				
Decatur (Washington County) (Township)	45742	Donnelsville	45319	East Fairfield	44408	Eldean	45373
		Donnersville	43950	East Fultonham	43735	Eldon	43773
Decaturville	45712	Dorcas	45771	Eastgate Shopping Center (Part of Mayfield Heights)	44125	Eldorado (Butler County)	45044
Decrow Corners	43031	Dornbusch	45239			Eldorado (Preble County)	45321
Dee	44824	Dorset	44032			Elery	43535
Deep Run	43935	Dorset (Township)	44032	East Goshen	44609	Elgin	45838
Deer Creek (Madison County) (Township)	43140	Dover (Athens County) (Township)	45761	East Greenville	44666	Elida	45807
				Eastlake	44094	Elizabeth (Lawrence County) (Township)	45659
Deer Creek (Pickaway County) (Township)	43164	Dover (Fulton County) (Township)	43567	Eastland Mall (Part of Columbus)	43232		
						Elizabeth (Miami County) (Township)	45312
Deerfield (Portage County)	44411	Dover (Tuscarawas County)	44622	East Lawn	43447		

	ZIP		ZIP		ZIP		ZIP
Elizabethtown (Hamilton County)	45052	Fairfield (Madison County) (Township)	43162	Five Points (Greene County)	45324	Franklin (Harrison County) (Township)	44699
Elizabethtown (Warren County)	45005	Fairfield (Tuscarawas County) (Township)	44678	Five Points (Mahoning County)	44452	Franklin (Jackson County) (Township)	45640
Elk (Noble County) (Township)	45745	Fairfield (Washington County) (Township)	45724	Five Points (Pickaway County)	43143	Franklin (Licking County) (Township)	43055
Elk (Vinton County) (Township)	45651	Fairfield Beach	43076	Five Points (Summit County)	44302	Franklin (Mercer County) (Township)	45866
Elkrun (Township)	44415	Fairground Acres	45107	Five Points (Trumbull County)	44404	Franklin (Monroe County) (Township)	43754
Elkton	44415	Fairhaven	45003				
Ellerton	45342	Fairhope	44641	Five Points (Warren County)	45066	Franklin (Morrow County) (Township)	43338
Ellet (Part of Akron)	44312	Fairlawn	44313	Flatiron (Perry County)	43731	Franklin (Portage County) (Township)	44240
Elliot	43728			Flat Iron (Warren County)	45005		
Elliottville	45701	For specific Fairlawn Zip Codes call (216) 864-6409, or your local postmaster.		Flatrock (Henry County) (Township)	43545	Franklin (Richland County) (Township)	44875
Ellis	43701						
Ellisonville	45638	Fairlawn Heights	44484	Flat Rock (Seneca County)	44828	Franklin (Ross County) (Township)	45601
Elliston	43432	Fairmount (Part of Cincinnati)	45214	Fleatown	43055	Franklin (Shelby County) (Township)	45363
Elisberry	45101	Fair Oaks	45102	Fleetwood Addition	43040		
Ellsworth	44416	Fairplay (Butler County)	45014	Fleming	45729	Franklin (Summit County) (Township)	44216
Ellsworth (Township)	44416	Fairplay (Jefferson County)	43910	Fletcher	45326		
Elm Acres	44646	Fairpoint	43927	Flint	43085	Franklin (Tuscarawas County) (Township)	44680
Elm Grove	45661	Fairport Harbor	44077	Florence (Belmont County)	43935	Franklin (Warren County)	45005
Elmira	43502	Fairview (Guernsey and Belmont Counties)	43736	Florence (Erie County)	44814	Franklin (Warren County) (Township)	45005
Elmore	43416						
Elmville	45133	Fairview (Guernsey County)	43772	Florence (Erie County) (Township)	44814	Franklin (Wayne County) (Township)	44627
Elmwood Place	45216						
Elroy	45303	Fairview (Highland County)	45133	Florence (Noble County)	43724	Franklin Furnace	45629
Elton	44662			Florence (Williams County) (Township)	43518	Franklin Park Mall (Part of Toledo)	43623
Elyria	44035-39	Fairview Heights (Jefferson County)	43964				
For specific Elyria Zip Codes call (216) 323-7400, or your local postmaster.		Fairview Heights (Washington County)	45750	Florida	43545	Franklin Square	44431
				Flushing	43977	Frazeysburg	43822
Emerald (Adams County)	45697	Fairview Lanes	44870	Flushing (Township)	43977	Frederick (Miami County)	45371
Emerald (Paulding County) (Township)	45879	Fairview Park	44126	Fly	45730	Frederick (Scioto County)	45694
		Fairway Terrace	45341	Footville	44084	Fredericksburg	44627
Emerson	43917	Fairway View Estates	45805	Foraker	45812	Fredericksdale	43779
Emerson Heights (Part of Marietta)	45750	Fairwind Acres (Part of Montgomery)	45242	Forest	45843	Fredericktown (Columbiana County)	43920
Emery Chapel	45502	Falls (Hocking County) (Township)	43138	Forestdale	45638		
Empire	43926			Forest Fair Mall (Part of Forest Park)	45240	Fredericktown (Knox County)	43019
Enchanted Hills	45133	Falls (Muskingum County) (Township)	43701	Forest Hills	45502	Fredonia	43023
England Station	44805			Forest Hills Estates	45230	Freeburg	44669
Englewood	45322	Fallsburg	43822	Forest Park (Hamilton County)	45240	Freedom (Henry County) (Township)	43545
English Woods (Part of Cincinnati)	45225	Fallsbury (Township)	43822				
Enoch (Township)	43724	Fargo	43074	Forest Park (Montgomery County)	45405	Freedom (Portage County)	44288
Enon	45323	Farmdale	44417	Forest Park Plaza	45405		
Enterprise (Hocking County)	43138	Farmer	43520	Forest View	43952	Freedom (Portage County) (Township)	44288
Enterprise (Preble County)	45381	Farmer (Township)	43520	Forestville	45230	Freedom (Wood County) (Township)	43450
Epworth	44903	Farmers	45146	Fort Jefferson	45331		
Epworth Heights	45140	Farmerstown	43804	Fort Jennings	45844	Freeport	43973
Era	43143	Farmersville	45325	Fort Loramie	45845	Freeport (Township)	43973
Erastus	45822	Farmington (Belmont County)	43912	Fort McKinley	45426	Fremont	43420
Erhart	44256			Fort Meigs Place	43551	Frenchtown (Darke County)	45380
Erie (Township)	43439	Farmington (Trumbull County) (Township)	44491	Fort Miami Addition (Part of Maumee)	43537		
Erieview (Part of Cleveland)	44199			Fort Recovery	45846	Frenchtown (Seneca County)	43316
Eris	43078	Farnham (Part of Conneaut)	44030	Fort Scott Camps	45030	Fresno	43824
Erlin	43420	Farrington	45373	Fort Seneca	44883	Friendship	45630
Espyville	43302	Fashion Heights	45238	Fort Shawnee	45806	Frischkorn Heights	43968
Essex	43344	Fawcett	45616	Fort Steuben Mall (Part of Steubenville)	43952	Frontier Park	45239
Etna	43018	Fayette (Fulton County)	43521			Frontier Town	44514
Etna (Township)	43018	Fayette (Lawrence County) (Township)	45680	Foster	45039	Frost	45723
Euclid	44117			Fosterville (Part of Youngstown)	44511	Fruitdale	45123
Euclid Heights (Part of Middletown)	45044	Fayetteville	45118	Fostoria	44830	Fruit Hill	45230
		Fay Gardens	45140	Fountain Park	43084	Fryburg (Auglaize County)	45895
Euclid Square Mall (Part of Euclid)	44132	Fearing (Township)	45788	Fountain Square	45201†	Fryburg (Holmes County)	44654
		Federal Reserve (Part of Cleveland)	44101		45202*	Frys Corners	45331
Eureka	44408			Fowler	44418	Frytown	45418
Evansport	43519	Feed Springs	44683	Fowler (Township)	44418	Fulda	43724
Evanston (Part of Cincinnati)	45207	Feesburg	45119	Fowlers Mill	44024	Fulton (Fulton County) (Township)	43558
Evansville	44440	Felicity	45120	Fox (Carroll County) (Township)	43945	Fulton (Morrow County)	43321
Evendale	45241	Fernald	45030			Fultonham	43738
Everett	44264	Fernbank (Part of Cincinnati)	45233	Fox (Pickaway County) (Township)	43113	Funk	44691
Evergreen (Gallia County)	45614	Fernell Heights	45244	Foxboro Manor (Part of Vandalia)	45377	Fursville	43062
Evergreen (Washington County)	45750	Fernwood	43952	Foxborough Commons	44870	Gabels Corner	43420
		Ferry (Erie County)	44870	Fox Chase	43502	Gage	45658
Ewing	43138	Ferry (Greene County)	45068	Fox Hollow	43542	Gageville	44048
Ewington	45686	Fields Terrace	45619	Frank	44811	Gahanna	43230
Excello	45044	Filburns Island	45865	Frankfort	45628	Galatea	45872
Fairborn	45324	Fincastle	45171	Franklin (Adams County)	45660	Galaxy Acres	45239
Fairbrondt	44833	Findlater Garden (Part of Cincinnati)	45232			Galena	43021
Fairdale	43725			Franklin (Brown County) (Township)	45121	Galion	44833
Fairfax (Hamilton County)	45227	Findlay	45840†			Gallia	45658
Fairfax (Highland County)	45133		45839†	Franklin (Clermont County) (Township)	45120	Gallipolis	45631
Fairfield (Butler County)	45014	Findlay Village Mall (Part of Findlay)	45840			Gallipolis (Township)	45631
Fairfield (Butler County) (Township)	45014			Franklin (Columbiana County) (Township)	43962	Galloway	43119
		Findley Gardens	43964			Gambier	43022
Fairfield (Columbiana County) (Township)	44408	Finneytown	45224	Franklin (Coshocton County) (Township)	43811	Ganges	44875
		Fire Brick	45656			Gano	45241
Fairfield (Greene County)	45324	Fireside	44811	Franklin (Darke County) (Township)	45304	Garden	45735
Fairfield (Highland County) (Township)	45135	Firestone Park (Part of Akron)	44301			Garden Acres (Clark County)	45503
		Fishack	43452	Franklin (Franklin County) (Township)	43204		
Fairfield (Huron County) (Township)	44855	Fitchville	44851			Garden Acres (Jefferson County)	43952
		Fitchville (Township)	44851	Franklin (Fulton County) (Township)	43502		
Fairfield (Jefferson County)	43944	Five Forks	43945			Garden City	45694
		Five Mile	45154				

	ZIP		ZIP		ZIP		ZIP
Garden Hill Top (Part of Cincinnati)	45232	Glenwood	45381	Great Western Shopping Center (Part of Columbus)	43213	Guysville	45735
Garden Isle	44254	Glenwood Acres	44087			Gypsum	43433
Garden Terrace (Part of Steubenville)	43952	Gloria Glens Park	44215	Green (Adams County) (Township)	45684	Hackney	45715
Garfield	44460	Glouster	45732			Hagan Addition	43901
Garfield Heights	44125	Glynwood	45885	Green (Ashland County) (Township)	44842	Hageman Junction	45036
Garrettsville	44231	Gnadenhutten	44629			Hale (Township)	43340
Gaslight Village	45122	Goes	45387	Green (Brown County) (Township)	45154	Hallock	43506
Gasper (Township)	45320	Golden Corners	45214			Hallsville	45633
Gates Mills	44040	Golden Gate Shopping Center (Part of Mayfield Heights)	44124	Green (Clark County) (Township)	45502	Hambden	44024
Gath	45171					Hambden (Township)	44024
Gavers	44432	Goldsboro	45692	Green (Clinton County) (Township)	45159	Hamburg (Fairfield County)	43130
Geauga Lake (Part of Aurora)	44202	Golf Manor	45237	Green (Fayette County) (Township)	45135	Hamburg (Preble County)	45321
Geeburg	44406	Golfway Acres	45239			Hamden	45634
Geneva (Ashtabula County)	44041	Gomer	45809	Green (Gallia County) (Township)	45658	Hamer (Township)	45133
		Good Hope (Fayette County)	43160			Hamersville	45130
Geneva (Ashtabula County) (Township)	44041	Good Hope (Hocking County) (Township)	43149	Green (Hamilton County) (Township)	45211	Hametown (Part of Norton)	44203
Geneva (Fairfield County)	43107	Goodland Acres	44688	Green (Harrison County) (Township)	43976	Hamilton (Butler County)	45011-13
Geneva-on-the-Lake	44041	Goodyear Heights (Part of Akron)	44305				45015-18
Genntown	45036			Green (Hocking County) (Township)	43138	For specific Hamilton Zip Codes call (513) 867-8877, or your local postmaster.	
Genoa (Delaware County) (Township)	43081	Goose Run	45732				
Genoa (Ottawa County)	43430	Gordon	45329	Green (Mahoning County) (Township)	44406	Hamilton (Franklin County) (Township)	43137
Genung Corners	44057	Gore	43138				
Georges Run	43938	Gorham (Township)	43521	Green (Monroe County) (Township)	43793	Hamilton (Jackson County) (Township)	45656
Georgesville	43123	Goshen (Auglaize County) (Township)	43331	Green (Ross County) (Township)	45644	Hamilton (Lawrence County) (Township)	45638
Georgetown	45121						
Gepharts	45694	Goshen (Belmont County) (Township)	43719	Green (Scioto County) (Township)	45629	Hamilton (Warren County) (Township)	45039
Gerald	43545						
German (Auglaize County) (Township)	45869	Goshen (Champaign County) (Township)	43044	Green (Shelby County) (Township)	45365	Hamilton Meadows	43207
				Green (Summit County)	44720	Hamler	43524
German (Clark County) (Township)	45504	Goshen (Clermont County)	45122	Green (Wayne County) (Township)	44667	Hamlet	45102
						Hamley Run	45701
German (Fulton County) (Township)	43502	Goshen (Clermont County) (Township)	45122	Green Acres	45042	Hammansburg	43413
		Goshen (Hardin County) (Township)	43326	Greenbush (Brown County)	45154	Hammondsville	43930
German (Harrison County) (Township)	43976					Hampton Woods	45502
		Goshen (Mahoning County) (Township)	44460	Greenbush (Preble County)	45064	Hanersville	45631
German (Montgomery County) (Township)	45327					Hanging Rock	45638
		Goshen (Tuscarawas County)	44663	Green Camp	43322	Hanley Village	44904
Germano	43986			Green Camp (Township)	43322	Hanna Hills	44266
Germantown (Montgomery County)	45327	Goshen (Tuscarawas County) (Township)	44663	Greencastle	43112	Hannibal	43931
		Gould Park	43230	Green Creek (Township)	43410	Hanover (Township)	43055
Germantown (Washington County)	45745	Goulds	43938	Greendale	43138	Hanover	43055
		Graceland Shopping Center (Part of Columbus)	43214	Greene (Township)	44450	Hanover (Ashland County) (Township)	44842
German Village (Part of Columbus)	43206			Greenfield (Fairfield County) (Township)	43130	Hanover (Butler County) (Township)	45013
Getaway	45619	Grafton	44044	Greenfield (Gallia County) (Township)	45658	
Gettysburg (Darke County)	45328	Grafton (Township)	44044			Hanover (Columbiana County) (Township)	44625
		Grand (Township)	45843	Greenfield (Highland County)	45123	
Gettysburg (Preble County)	45347	Grand Prairie (Township)	43302			Hanover (Harrison County)	43988
		Grand Rapids	43522	Greenfield (Huron County) (Township)	44855	Hanoverton	44423
Geyer	45895	Grand Rapids (Township)	43522			Hanville Corners	44855
Ghent	44333	Grand River	44045	Greenfield Village	45224	Happy Hollow	44626
Gibisonville	43149	Grandview (Hamilton County)	45002	Greenford	44422	Harbor (Part of Ashtabula)	44004
Gibson (Guernsey County)	43778			Green Hills (Greene County)	45324	Harbor Hills	43025
		Grandview (Washington County)	45767	Greenhills (Hamilton County)	45218	Harbor Point	45822
Gibson (Mercer County) (Township)	45846					Harbor View	43434
		Grandview (Washington County) (Township)	45767	Greenland	43115	Hardin	45365
Gibsonburg	43431			Greenlex	43302	Harding (Township)	43558
Gilbert	43701	Grandview Estates (Delaware County)	43015	Green Meadows	45323	Hardy (Township)	44654
Gilboa	45875			Greensburg (Putnam County) (Township)	45875	Harewood Acres	45236
Gilead (Township)	43338	Grandview Estates (Marion County)	43302			Harlan (Township)	45162
Gillivan	43140			Greensburg (Summit County)	44232	Harlan Park (Part of Middletown)	45042
Gilmore	43837	Grandview Heights (Champaign County)	43072			
Ginghamsburg	45371			Green Springs	44836	Harlem	43021
Girard	44420	Grandview Heights (Franklin County)	43212	Greens Run	45732	Harlem (Township)	43021
Girton	43457			Greens Store	45640	Harlem Springs	44631
Gist Settlement	45159	Grandview Homes (Part of Lima)	45804	Greentown	44630	Harmar (Part of Marietta)	45750
Givens	45690			Greenview	45415	Harmon	44662
Glade	45613	Grange Hall	43143	Greenville	45331	Harmons Landing	45885
Gladstone	45314	Granger	44256	Greenville (Township)	45331	Harmony	45502
Glandorf	45848	Granger (Township)	44256	Greenwich	44837	Harmony (Clark County) (Township)	45502
Glasgow (Columbiana County)	43968	Grants	45843	Greenwich (Township)	44837	
		Granville (Licking County)	43023	Greer	44628	Harmony (Morrow County) (Township)	43315
Glasgow (Tuscarawas County)	43837	Granville (Licking County) (Township)	43023	Grelton	43523	
				Griffith (Part of North Bend)	45052	Harper	43311
Glass Rock	43739	Granville (Mercer County) (Township)	45883			Harpersfield	44041
Glenbrook Acres	45305			Griggs	44047	Harpersfield (Township)	44041
Glencoe (Belmont County)	43928	Granville South	43023	Grimms Bridge	43920	Harpster	43323
Glencoe (Hamilton County)	45231	Grape Grove	45335	Groesbeck	45239	Harriett (Guernsey County)	43725
		Gratiot	43740	Groton (Township)	44839	
Glendale	45246	Gratis	45330	Grove City	43123	Harriett (Highland County)	45133
Glendwell (Part of Steubenville)	43952	Gratis (Township)	45330	Grover Hill	45849	Harriettsville	45745
		Graysville	45734	Guerne	44691	Harris (Ottawa County) (Township)	43416
Glen Este	45103	Graytown	43432	Guernsey	43749	
Glenford	43739	Greasy Ridge	45678	Guilford (Columbiana County)	44432	Harris (Ross County) (Township)	45612
Glengary Heights	43081	Greater State Road Shopping Center (Part of Cuyahoga Falls)	44223			Harrisburg (Franklin County)	43126
Glen Karn	45332			Guilford (Medina County) (Township)	44273	
Glenmary (Part of Fairfield)	45246					Harrisburg (Gallia County)	45614
		Great Lakes Mall (Part of Mentor)	44060	Gunnerville	45335	Harrisburg (Stark County)	44641
Glenmont	44628			Gurneyville	45177	Harrison (Carroll County) (Township)	44615
Glenmoor	43920	Great Northern Mall (Part of North Olmsted)	44070	Gustavus	44417	
Glenmore	45874			Gustavus (Township)	44417	Harrison (Champaign County) (Township)	43357
Glenns Run	43935	Great Southern Shopping Center (Part of Columbus)	43207	Gutman	45895	
Glen Robbins	43943			Guyan (Township)	45623	Harrison (Darke County) (Township)	45346
Glen Roy	45692					
Glenwillow	44139					Harrison (Gallia County) (Township)	45631

	ZIP
Harrison (Hamilton County)	45030
Harrison (Hamilton County) (Township)	45030
Harrison (Henry County) (Township)	43545
Harrison (Knox County) (Township)	43022
Harrison (Licking County) (Township)	43033
Harrison (Logan County) (Township)	43311
Harrison (Montgomery County) (Township)	45415
Harrison (Muskingum County) (Township)	43771
Harrison (Paulding County) (Township)	45880
Harrison (Perry County) (Township)	43731
Harrison (Pickaway County) (Township)	43103
Harrison (Preble County) (Township)	45338
Harrison (Ross County) (Township)	45601
Harrison (Scioto County) (Township)	45653
Harrison (Van Wert County) (Township)	45891
Harrison (Vinton County) (Township)	45647
Harrison Furnace	45662
Harrison Mills	45682
Harrisonville	45769
Harrisville (Harrison County)	43974
Harrisville (Medina County) (Township)	44214
Harrod	45850
Harshasville	45660
Hartford (Licking County) (Township)	43013
Hartford (Trumbull County)	44424
Hartford (Trumbull County) (Township)	44424
Hartland	44826
Hartland (Township)	44857
Hartland Center	44826
Hartleyville	45732
Hartsgrove	44085
Hartsgrove (Township)	44085
Hartshorn	45734
Hartville	44632
Hartwell (Part of Cincinnati)	45216
Harveysburg	45032
Haskins	43525
Hasting Hill	45662
Hatch	45661
Hatton	43457
Havana	44890
Havens Corners	43004
Havensport	43112
Haven View	45373
Haverhill	45636
Haviland	45851
Hayden	43002
Haydenville	43127
Hayes Colony (Part of Delaware)	43015
Hayes Corners	44062
Hayesville	44838
Haynes	43135
Hazelwood (Part of Blue Ash)	45242
Heath	43056
Heatherdowns (Part of Toledo)	43614
Hebbardsville	45701
Hebron	43025
Hecla	45638
Hegemans Landing	45865
Heidelburg Beach	44089
Helena	43435
Helmick	43844
Hemlock	43730
Hemlock Grove	45769
Hempstead (Part of Kettering)	45429
Hendrysburg	43713
Henley	45652
Henrietta (Township)	44889
Henry (Township)	45872
Hepburn	43326
Heritage	45805
Heritage Hills	44087
Heritage Park	44212
Hessville	43431

	ZIP
Hickman	43055
Hicksville	43526
Hicksville (Township)	43526
Hide-A-Way Hills	43107
Higginsport	45131
Highland (Defiance County) (Township)	43512
Highland (Highland County)	45132
Highland (Muskingum County) (Township)	43762
Highland Heights	44124
Highland Hills	44122
Highland Holliday	45133
Highland Park (Hamilton County)	45238
Highland Park (Mercer County)	45822
Highland Park (Scioto County)	45629
Highland Park (Stark County)	44646
Highlands (Part of Springfield)	45503
Highland Terrace	43950
Highlandtown	43945
Highland Trails	45133
Highpoint	45242
High Water	43055
Hill Addition (Part of East Liverpool)	43920
Hill And Hollow (Part of Oxford)	45056
Hillcrest (Columbiana County)	43968
Hillcrest (Warren County)	45036
Hill Crest (Wayne County)	44691
Hillcrest (Williams County)	43543
Hill Grove	45390
Hilliar (Township)	43011
Hilliard	43026
Hills and Dales (Montgomery County)	45429
Hills and Dales (Stark County)	44708
Hillsboro (Highland County)	45133
Hillsboro (Jefferson County)	43938
Hilltop (Franklin County)	43204
Hilltop (Trumbull County)	44437
Hilltop Acres (Part of Wyoming)	45215
Hinckley	44233
Hinckley (Township)	44233
Hiram	44234
Hiram (Township)	44234
Hiram Rapids	44234
Hiramsburg	43732
Hitchcock	45656
Hoadley	45658
Hoagland	45133
Hoaglin (Township)	45891
Hobson	45760
Hocking (Township)	43130
Hocking Correctional Facility	45764
Hockingport	45739
Hoke	45383
Holden	45896
Holgate	43527
Holiday Acres	45236
Holiday Hills	45502
Holiday Lakes	44890
Holiday Valley	45324
Holland	43528
Hollansburg	45332
Hollister	45732
Holloway	43985
Hollowtown	45171
Holman-Stonybrook Shopping Center (Part of Loveland)	45140
Holmes (Township)	44820
Holmesville	44633
Home Acres (Butler County)	45044
Home Acres (Miami County)	45373
Homedale (Part of Columbus)	43085
Home Orchards (Part of Springfield)	45503
Homer (Licking County)	43027
Homer (Medina County) (Township)	44235
Homer (Morgan County) (Township)	45732
Homerville	44235
Homeside	43950

	ZIP
Homeville	44870
Homewood (Part of Hamilton)	45015
Homeworth	44634
Honeytown	44691
Hooker	43130
Hooksburg	43787
Hooring	45766
Hooven	45033
Hopedale	43976
Hopetown	45601
Hopewell (Jefferson County)	43943
Hopewell (Licking County) (Township)	43740
Hopewell (Mercer County) (Township)	45822
Hopewell (Muskingum County)	43746
Hopewell (Muskinghum County) (Township)	43746
Hopewell (Perry County) (Township)	43739
Hopewell (Seneca County) (Township)	44809
Hopkinsville	45039
Horatio	45331
Horns Mill	43130
Hoskinsville	43724
Houck Meadows (Part of Enon)	45502
Houcktown	45814
Houston	45333
Howard	43028
Howard (Township)	43028
Howenstein	44626
Howland (Township)	44484
Howland Center	44484
Hoytville	43529
Hubbard	44425
Hubbard (Township)	44425
Huber Heights	45424
Huber Ridge	43081
Huber South	45439
Hudson	44236
Hudson (Township)	44236
Hue	45622
Hughes	45042
Hulington	45106
Humboldt	45612
Hume	45806
Hunt	43050
Hunter	43719
Hunterdon	45732
Huntington (Brown County) (Township)	45101
Huntington (Gallia County) (Township)	45686
Huntington (Lorain County)	44090
Huntington (Lorain County) (Township)	44090
Huntington (Ross County) (Township)	45601
Huntington Hills	43147
Huntington Park (Part of Aberdeen)	45101
Hunting Valley	44022
Huntsburg	44046
Huntsburg (Township)	44046
Hunts Corners	44811
Huntsville (Butler County)	45042
Huntsville (Logan County)	43324
Hurford	43901
Huron	44839
Huron (Township)	44839
Hustead	45502
Hyatts	43065
Hyde Park (Hamilton County)	45208
Hyde Park (Montgomery County)	45429
Hyde Park Plaza (Part of Cincinnati)	45209
Iberia	43325
Idaho	45661
Idlewild (Part of Cincinnati)	45201
Iler	44830
Ilesboro	43138
Immergrun (Part of Oregon)	43618
Independence (Cuyahoga County)	44131
Independence (Defiance County)	43512
Independence (Washington County) (Township)	45767
Indian Camp	43725

	ZIP
Indian Knolls (Part of Milford)	45150
Indian Ridge	45231
Indianview	45147
Ingle Mann (Part of New Paris)	45347
Ingomar	45381
Ink	44883
Ira	44333
Iradale	44313
Irondale (Jefferson County)	43932
Irondale (Muskingum County)	43821
Ironspot	43777
Ironton	45638
Irvington	45414
Irwin	43029
Island Creek (Township)	43964
Island View	43331
Isle Saint George	43436
Isleta	43845
Israel (Township)	45003
Ithaca	45304
Ivorydale (Part of St. Bernard)	45217
Ivorydale Junction (Part of St. Bernard)	45217
Jackson (Allen County) (Township)	45854
Jackson (Ashland County) (Township)	44287
Jackson (Auglaize County) (Township)	45865
Jackson (Brown County) (Township)	45697
Jackson (Champaign County) (Township)	45389
Jackson (Clermont County) (Township)	45145
Jackson (Coshocton County) (Township)	43812
Jackson (Crawford County) (Township)	44827
Jackson (Darke County) (Township)	45390
Jackson (Franklin County) (Township)	43123
Jackson (Guernsey County) (Township)	43723
Jackson (Hancock County) (Township)	45814
Jackson (Hardin County) (Township)	45843
Jackson (Highland County) (Township)	45133
Jackson (Jackson County)	45640
Jackson (Jackson County) (Township)	45640
Jackson (Knox County) (Township)	43005
Jackson (Mahoning County) (Township)	44451
Jackson (Monroe County) (Township)	45730
Jackson (Montgomery County) (Township)	45325
Jackson (Muskingum County) (Township)	43822
Jackson (Noble County) (Township)	45727
Jackson (Paulding County) (Township)	45855
Jackson (Perry County) (Township)	43748
Jackson (Pickaway County) (Township)	43113
Jackson (Pike County) (Township)	45690
Jackson (Preble County) (Township)	45320
Jackson (Putnam County) (Township)	45844
Jackson (Richland County) (Township)	44875
Jackson (Sandusky County) (Township)	43407
Jackson (Seneca County) (Township)	44830
Jackson (Shelby County) (Township)	45334
Jackson (Stark County) (Township)	44646
Jackson (Union County) (Township)	43344
Jackson (Van Wert County) (Township)	45863
Jackson (Vinton County) (Township)	45651

	ZIP		ZIP		ZIP		ZIP
Jackson (Wood County) (Township)	43529	Jerry City	43437	Kings Creek	43078	Lakeside (Licking County)	43008
Jackson (Wyandot County) (Township)	45843	Jersey	43062	Kingsdale Center (Part of Columbus)	43221	Lakeside (Ottawa County)	43440
Jackson Belden (Part of Canton)	44718	Jersey (Township)	43062	Kingsgate	45231	Lakeside-Marblehead (Part of Marblehead)	43440
Jacksonburg	45067	Jerusalem (Lucas County) (Township)	43412	Kingsgate Mall (Part of Mansfield)	44901	Lake Slagle	44720
Jackson Center (Mahoning County)	44451	Jerusalem (Monroe County)	43747	Kings Mills	45034	Lake Sylvan	45369
Jackson Center (Shelby County)	45334	Jesse C Owens (Part of Cleveland)	44104	Kingston (Delaware County) (Township)	43074	Lake View (Knox County)	43019
Jackson Heights (Jackson County)	45640	Jewell	43530	Kingston (Ross County)	45644	Lakeview (Logan County)	43331
Jackson Heights (Jefferson County)	43943	Jewett	43986	Kingsville	44048	Lakeview Heights	45690
Jackson Lake	44656	Jobs	45732	Kingsville (Township)	44048	Lakeville (Ashtabula County)	44030
Jacksontown	43030	Joetown	43758	Kingsville On-the-Lake (Part of North Kingsville)	44068	Lakeville (Holmes County)	44638
Jacksonville (Adams County)	45660	Johnson (Township)	43072	Kingsway	43420	Lake Waynoka	45171
Jacksonville (Athens County)	45740	Johnsons Corners (Part of Barberton)	44203	Kinnickinnick	45601	Lakewood	44107
Jacksonville (Clark County)	45502	Johnston (Trumbull County)	44417	Kinsman (Belmont County)	43950	Lakota Hills	45069
Jacktown	45042	Johnston (Trumbull County) (Township)	44417	Kinsman (Trumbull County)	44428	Lamira	43718
Jacobsburg	43933	Johnston (Tuscarawas County)	44622	Kinsman (Trumbull County) (Township)	44428	Lancaster	43130
Jaite (Part of Brecksville)	44141	Johnstown	43031	Kiousville	43143	Landeck	45833
Jamestown	45335	Johnsville (Part of New Lebanon)	45345	Kipling	43750	Landen	45040
Jasper (Fayette County) (Township)	43128	Jonesboro (Clinton County)	45146	Kipton	44049	Langsville	45741
Jasper (Pike County)	45642	Jonesboro (Fayette County)	43160	Kirby	43330	Lanier (Township)	45381
Jasper Mills	43160	Jonestown	45894	Kirkersville	43033	Lansing	43934
Jays	45331	Jordanville	44432	Kirkpatrick	43302	LaPorte	44035
Jefferson (Adams County) (Township)	45684	Joy	43728	Kirkwood (Belmont County) (Township)	43713	Lapperel	45660
Jefferson (Ashtabula County)	44047	Joyce Avenue (Part of Columbus)	43219	Kirkwood (Shelby County)	45365	La Rue	43332
Jefferson (Ashtabula County) (Township)	44047	Jug Run	43917	Kirkwood Heights	43912	Latcha	43447
Jefferson (Brown County) (Township)	45168	Jumbo	43326	Kirtland	44094	Latham	45646
Jefferson (Clinton County) (Township)	45148	Jump	43326	Kirtland Hills	44060	Latimer	44428
Jefferson (Coshocton County) (Township)	43844	Junction	43512	Kitchen	45656	Lattasburg	44287
Jefferson (Crawford County) (Township)	44827	Junction City	43748	Kitts Hill	45645	Lattaville	45628
Jefferson (Fairfield County)	43112	Junior Furnace	45629	Kiwanis Lake	44065	Latty	45855
Jefferson (Fayette County) (Township)	43128	Justus	44662	Klondike	44410	Latty (Township)	45849
Jefferson (Franklin County) (Township)	43004	Kalida	45853	Knockemstiff	45601	Laura	45337
Jefferson (Greene County) (Township)	45335	Kamms (Part of Cleveland)	44111	Knollwood (Part of Beavercreek)	45432	Laurel (Clermont County)	45157
Jefferson (Guernsey County) (Township)	43755	Kanauga	45631	Knollwood Village	43113	Laurel (Hocking County) (Township)	43149
Jefferson (Jackson County) (Township)	45656	Kansas	44841	Knox (Columbiana County) (Township)	44634	Laurel Creek	44212
Jefferson (Knox County) (Township)	44628	Karen Woods	45502	Knox (Guernsey County) (Township)	43725	Laurel Ridge	44721
Jefferson (Logan County) (Township)	43311	Kay	45005	Knox (Holmes County) (Township)	44638	Laurelville	43135
Jefferson (Madison County) (Township)	43162	Keays (Part of Middletown)	45044	Knox (Jefferson County) (Township)	43964	Lawco Lake	45659
Jefferson (Mercer County) (Township)	45822	Keene	43828	Knox (Vinton County) (Township)	45710	Lawndale (Part of Massillon)	44646
Jefferson (Montgomery County) (Township)	45345	Keene (Township)	43828	Knoxville	43964	Lawrence (Lawrence County)	45659
Jefferson (Muskingum County) (Township)	43821	Keist Manor	43130	Kolmont	43938	Lawrence (Lawrence County) (Township)	45645
Jefferson (Noble County) (Township)	43724	Keith	43724	Kossuth	45887	Lawrence (Stark County) (Township)	44614
Jefferson (Preble County) (Township)	45347	Kelleys Island	43438	Kunkle	43531	Lawrence (Tuscarawas County) (Township)	44612
Jefferson (Richland County) (Township)	44813	Kellogg Corners	44410	Kyger	45620	Lawrence (Washington County) (Township)	45750
Jefferson (Ross County) (Township)	45601	Kelloggsville	44030	La Belle View (Part of Steubenville)	43952	Lawrenceville	45502
Jefferson (Scioto County) (Township)	45648	Kemp	45806	Lacarne	43439	Lawshe	45660
Jefferson (Tuscarawas County) (Township)	43840	Kendall Heights	44646	La Croft	43920	Layhigh	45013
Jefferson (Wayne County)	44691	Kenmore (Part of Akron)	44314	Lafayette (Allen County)	45854	Layland	44637
Jefferson (Williams County) (Township)	43543	Kennard	43009	Lafayette (Coshocton County) (Township)	43845	Layman	45724
Jefferson Estates	43113	Kennedy Heights (Part of Cincinnati)	45213	Lafayette (Madison County)	43140	Leaper	45631
Jefferson Heights	43938	Kennonsburg	43773	Lafayette (Medina County)	44256	Leavittsburg	44430
Jeffersonville	43128	Keno	45743	Lafayette (Medina County) (Township)	44256	Leavittsville	44614
Jelloway	43014	Kenridge (Part of Blue Ash)	45242	Lafferty	43951	Lebanon (Meigs County) (Township)	45770
Jenera	45841	Kensington	44427	Lagonda (Part of Springfield)	45503	Lebanon (Monroe County)	45745
Jenkins Addition	43701	Kensington Park	45305	Lagrange (Township)	44050	Lebanon (Warren County)	45036
Jennings (Putnam County) (Township)	45844	Kent	44240	La Grange (Lawrence County)	45638	Lebanon Correctional Institution	45036
Jennings (Van Wert County) (Township)	45894	Kenton	43326	Lagrange (Lorain County)	44050	Lecta	45678
Jep	45659	Kenwood (Hamilton County)	45236	Laings	43752	Lee (Athens County) (Township)	45710
Jericho	45042	Kenwood (Harrison County)	43901	Lake (Ashland County) (Township)	44628	Lee (Carroll County) (Township)	44615
Jerome	43064	Kenwood (Lucas County)	43606	Lake (Logan County) (Township)	43311	Lee (Cuyahoga County)	44120
Jerome (Township)	43064	Kenwood Heights (Part of Springfield)	45505	Lake (Stark County) (Township)	44720	Lee (Monroe County) (Township)	43946
Jeromesville	44840	Kenwood Knolls	45236	Lake (Wood County) (Township)	43447	Leesburg (Highland County)	45135
		Kenwood Mall	45236	Lake Cable	44718	Leesburg (Union County) (Township)	43040
		Kenwood Towne Center	45236	Lake Darby	43204	Lees Creek	45138
		Kerr	45643	Lake Fork	44840	Leesville (Carroll County)	44639
		Kessler	45383	Lakeline	44094	Leesville (Crawford County)	44827
		Kettering	45429	Lake Lorelei	45118	Leetonia	44431
		Kettlersville	45336	Lake Lucerne	44022	Lehmkuhl Landing	45865
		Key	43933	Lake Milton	44429	Leipsic	45856
		Kidron	44636	Lakemore	44250	Leipsic Junction (Part of Leipsic)	45856
		Kieferville	45831	Lake of the Woods	43021	Leistville	43113
		Kilbourne	43032	Lake O'Springs	44718	Lemert	44882
		Kile	43064	Lake Seneca	43543	Lemon (Township)	45050
		Kilgore	43988	Lakeside (Butler County)	45042	Lemoyne	43441
		Killbuck	44637	Lakeside (Fairfield County)	43046	Lena	45317
		Killbuck (Township)	44637			Lenox	44047
		Kilvert	45778			Lenox (Township)	44047
		Kimball	44847			Leo	45640
		Kimberly	45764			Leon	44003
		Kimbolton	43749			Leonardsburg	43015
		Kingman	45177			Lerado	45176
		King Mines	43755			Leroy (Township)	44077
		Kings Corners	44904			Le Sourdsville	45042

Name	ZIP
Lester	44256
Letart (Township)	45771
Letart Falls	45771
Levanna	45167
Lewis (Township)	45121
Lewis Addition	43952
Lewisburg	45338
Lewis Center	43035
Lewistown	43333
Lewisville	43754
Lexington (Richland County)	44904
Lexington (Stark County)	44601
Lexington (Stark County) (Township)	44601
Liberty (Adams County) (Township)	45693
Liberty (Butler County) (Township)	45011
Liberty (Clinton County) (Township)	45177
Liberty (Crawford County) (Township)	44881
Liberty (Darke County) (Township)	45352
Liberty (Delaware County) (Township)	43065
Liberty (Fairfield County) (Township)	43105
Liberty (Guernsey County) (Township)	43725
Liberty (Hancock County) (Township)	45840
Liberty (Hardin County) (Township)	45810
Liberty (Henry County) (Township)	43532
Liberty (Highland County) (Township)	45133
Liberty (Jackson County) (Township)	45640
Liberty (Knox County) (Township)	43050
Liberty (Licking County) (Township)	43031
Liberty (Logan County) (Township)	43357
Liberty (Mercer County) (Township)	45882
Liberty (Montgomery County)	45418
Liberty (Putnam County) (Township)	45856
Liberty (Ross County) (Township)	45647
Liberty (Seneca County) (Township)	44841
Liberty (Trumbull County) (Township)	44420
Liberty (Union County) (Township)	43040
Liberty (Van Wert County) (Township)	45891
Liberty (Washington County) (Township)	45745
Liberty (Wood County) (Township)	43462
Liberty Center	43532
Liberty Plaza	44505
Lick (Township)	45640
Licking (Licking County) (Township)	43076
Licking (Muskingum County) (Township)	43830
Licking View	43701
Liebs Island	43046
Lightsville	45362
Lilly Chapel	43160
Lima	45801-07
For specific Lima Zip Codes call (419) 224-5801, or your local postmaster.	
Lima (Township)	43073
Limaville	44640
Lime City	43551
Limecrest	45502
Limerick	45601
Limestone	43432
Limestone City	45506
Lincoln (Morrow County) (Township)	43321
Lincoln (Richland County)	44905
Lincoln Heights (Hamilton County)	45215
Lincoln Heights (Jefferson County)	43952
Lincoln Heights (Richland County)	44903
Lincoln Knolls Plaza (Part of Youngstown)	44505
Lincoln Village	43228
Lindair Estates	45502
Lindale	45102
Linden Station (Part of Columbus)	43211
Lindentree	44656
Lindenwald (Part of Hamilton)	45015
Lindsey	43442
Lindsley-Gay	44003
Linndale	44135
Linneman	45804
Linnville (Lawrence County)	45696
Linnville (Licking County)	43076
Linton (Township)	43836
Linwood (Part of Cincinnati)	45226
Linworth	43085
Lippincotts	43078
Lisbon (Clark County)	45368
Lisbon (Columbiana County)	44432
Lisman	45659
Litchfield	44253
Litchfield (Township)	44253
Lithopolis	43136
Little Farms	43228
Little Hocking	45742
Little Sandusky	43323
Little Walnut	43113
Little Washington	44903
Little York	45414
Liverpool (Columbiana County) (Township)	43920
Liverpool (Medina County) (Township)	44280
Livingston (Part of Columbus)	43227
Lloydsville	43950
Lock	43011
Lockbourne	43137
Lockington	45356
Lockland	45215
Lock Two	45869
Lockville	43112
Lockwood	44450
Lockwood Corners	44319
Locust Corner	45245
Locust Grove (Adams County)	45660
Locust Grove (Butler County)	45042
Locust Grove (Mahoning County)	44460
Locust Lake	45102
Locust Point	43449
Locust Ridge	45176
Lodi (Athens County) (Township)	45735
Lodi (Medina County)	44254
Logan (Auglaize County) (Township)	45887
Logan (Hocking County)	43138
Logan Elm Village	43113
Logansville	43318
Logtown	44432
Lombardsville	45652
London (Madison County)	43140
London (Richland County)	44875
London Correctional Institution	43140
Londonderry (Guernsey County)	43973
Londonderry (Guernsey County) (Township)	43973
Londonderry (Ross County)	45647
Long	45331
Long Beach	43449
Long Bottom	45743
Long Lake	44638
Long Run	43917
Longs Crossing	44431
Longstreth	45764
Longview Heights (Part of Athens)	45701
Longvue (Part of Marietta)	45750
Loomis	43718
Lorain	44052-55
For specific Lorain Zip Codes call (216) 244-4221, or your local postmaster.	
Loramie (Township)	45363
Lordstown	44481
Lore City	43755
Lostcreek (Township)	45312
Lost Creek Addition	45804
Lottridge	45723
Louden (Adams County)	45660
Louden (Tuscarawas County)	44622
Loudon (Carroll County) (Township)	44615
Loudon (Seneca County) (Township)	44830
Loudonville	44842
Louisville (Adams County)	45660
Louisville (Stark County)	44641
Loveland	45140
Loveland Park	45140
Lovell	43351
Lowellville	44436
Lowell	45744
Lowellville Junction (Part of Lowellville)	44436
Lower Salem	45745
Loyal Oak (Part of Norton)	44203
Lucas	44843
Lucasburg	43723
Lucasville	45648
Lucerne	43019
Luckey	43443
Ludington	43730
Ludlow (Township)	45734
Ludlow Falls	45339
Lugbill Addition (Part of Archbold)	43502
Lumberton	45177
Luray	43025
Lush Addition	43302
Lykens	44818
Lykens (Township)	44818
Lyme (Township)	44811
Lynchburg (Columbiana County)	44427
Lynchburg (Highland County)	45142
Lyndhurst	44124
Lyndhurst-Mayfield Heights (Part of Mayfield Heights)	44124
Lyndon	45681
Lynn (Township)	43326
Lynns Corners	44406
Lynx	45650
Lyons	43533
Lyra	45694
Lytle	45068
McArthur (Logan County) (Township)	43324
McArthur (Vinton County)	45651
McCance	44627
Mc Cappin Mill	45133
McCartyville	45302
McClainville	43906
McClimansville	43143
McClintocksburg	44444
McClure	43534
McComb	45858
McConnelsville	43756
McCracken Corners	44460
McCuneville	43782
McCutchenville	44844
McDermott	45652
McDonald (Hardin County) (Township)	43326
McDonald (Trumbull County)	44437
McDonaldsville	44720
Macedon	45828
Macedonia	44056
McGill	45880
McGonigle	45013
Mc Gough	43050
McGuffey	45859
McGuffey Heights (Part of Youngstown)	44505
McIntyre	43910
Mack	45211
McKay	44842
McKean (Township)	43055
McKinley Heights	44446
Mack North	45211
Macksburg	45746
Mack South	45211
Mackstown	43081
McLean (Township)	45845
McLuney	43731
McMorran	43311
Macon	45697
McZena	44638
Madeira	45243
Madison (Butler County) (Township)	45042
Madison (Clark County) (Township)	45368
Madison (Columbiana County) (Township)	43968
Madison (Fairfield County) (Township)	43130
Madison (Fayette County) (Township)	43160
Madison (Franklin County) (Township)	43125
Madison (Guernsey County) (Township)	43773
Madison (Hancock County) (Township)	45814
Madison (Highland County) (Township)	45123
Madison (Jackson County) (Township)	45656
Madison (Lake County)	44057
Madison (Lake County) (Township)	44057
Madison (Licking County) (Township)	43055
Madison (Montgomery County) (Township)	45426
Madison (Muskingum County) (Township)	43821
Madison (Perry County) (Township)	43760
Madison (Pickaway County) (Township)	43103
Madison (Richland County) (Township)	44903
Madison (Sandusky County) (Township)	43435
Madison (Scioto County) (Township)	45653
Madison (Vinton County) (Township)	45698
Madison (Williams County) (Township)	43554
Madisonburg	44691
Madison Correctional Institution	43140
Madison Hill	44691
Madison Lake Area	43140
Madison Mills	43143
Madison-on-the-Lake	44057
Madisonville (Part of Cincinnati)	45227
Mad River (Champaign County) (Township)	43083
Mad River (Clark County) (Township)	45324
Mad River (Montgomery County) (Township)	45424
Magnetic Springs	43036
Magnolia	44643
Mahoning	44231
Maineville	45039
Mainsville	43764
Malaga	43757
Malaga (Township)	43757
Malinta	43535
Mallet Creek	44256
Malta	43758
Malta (Township)	43758
Malvern	44644
Manchester (Adams County)	45144
Manchester (Adams County) (Township)	45144
Manchester (Morgan County) (Township)	43756
Manchester (Summit County)	44216
Mandale	45827
Manhattan (Part of Steubenville)	43952
Mannhassett Village (Part of Mason)	45040
Mansfield	44901-07
For specific Mansfield Zip Codes call (419) 755-4621, or your local postmaster.	
Mantua	44255
Mantua (Township)	44255
Mantua Center	44255
Mantua Corners	44255
Maple Corner	45385
Maple Grove (Geauga County)	44231
Maple Grove (Ross County)	45601
Maple Grove (Seneca County)	44883
Maple Heights (Cuyahoga County)	44137
Maple Heights (Noble County)	43724
Maple Lake	43944
Maple Park	45040
Maple Ridge	44601

	ZIP
Mapleshade (Part of Gallipolis)	45631
Mapleton	44730
Maple Valley (Part of Akron)	44320
Maplewood	45340
Marathon	45145
Marble Cliff	43212
Marble Furnace	45660
Marblehead	43440
Marchand	44720
Marcy	43110
Marengo	43334
Margaretta (Township)	44824
Maria Stein	45860
Mariemont	45227
Marietta	45750
Marietta (Township)	45750
Marion (Allen County) (Township)	45833
Marion (Clinton County) (Township)	45107
Marion (Fayette County) (Township)	43145
Marion (Hancock County) (Township)	45840
Marion (Hardin County) (Township)	45812
Marion (Henry County) (Township)	43524
Marion (Hocking County) (Township)	43138
Marion (Marion County)	43302†
	43301*
Marion (Marion County) (Township)	43302
Marion (Mercer County) (Township)	45883
Marion (Morgan County) (Township)	43728
Marion (Noble County) (Township)	43788
Marion (Pike County) (Township)	45613
Marion Correctional Institution	43302
Marion East	43302
Mark (Township)	43556
Mark Center	43536
Marlain Acres	45231
Marlboro (Delaware County) (Township)	43015
Marlboro (Stark County)	44601
Marlboro (Stark County) (Township)	44601
Marne	43055
Marquis	44406
Marr	43789
Marseilles	43351
Marseilles (Township)	43351
Marshall	45133
Marshall (Township)	45133
Marshallville	44645
Martel	43335
Martin	43445
Martinsburg	43037
Martins Ferry	43935
Martinsville	45146
Mary Ann (Township)	43055
Marysville	43040
Mason (Lawrence County) (Township)	45696
Mason (Warren County)	45040
Mason Heights (Part of Mason)	45040
Massie (Township)	45032
Massieville	45601
Massillon	44646-48
For specific Massillon Zip Codes call (216) 837-8323, or your local postmaster.	
Massillon State Hospital	44646
Masury	44438
Matville	43146
Maud	45069
Maumee	43537
Maustown	45011
Maximo	44650
Maxville	43748
Mayfield (Butler County)	45044
Mayfield (Cuyahoga County)	44143
Mayfield Heights	44124
Mayflower Village (Part of Massillon)	44647
May Hill	45679
Maynard	43937
Maysville (Allen County)	45810
Maysville (Wayne County)	44606

	ZIP
Mead (Township)	43947
Meade	45644
Meadowbrook	43701
Meadowbrook Lake (Part of Stow)	44224
Meadow Lawn (Part of Middletown)	45044
Mecca	44410
Mecca (Township)	44410
Mechanic (Township)	43804
Mechanicsburg (Champaign County)	43044
Mechanicsburg (Crawford County)	44887
Mechanicsburg (Monroe County)	43793
Mechanicsburg (Wayne County)	44691
Mechanicstown	44651
Mechanicsville	44041
Medina	44256*
	44258†
Medway	45341
Meeker	43302
Meigs (Adams County) (Township)	45660
Meigs (Morgan County)	43756
Meigs (Muskingum County) (Township)	43727
Meigsville (Township)	43756
Melbern	43506
Mellett Mall (Part of Canton)	44708
Melmore	44845
Melrose	45861
Melvin	45177
Memphis	45135
Mendon	45862
Mentor	44060*
	44061†
Mentor Headlands (Part of Mentor)	44060
Mentor-on-the-Lake	44060
Mercer	45862
Mercerville	45631
Mermill	43451
Mesopotamia	44439
Mesopotamia (Township)	44439
Metamora	43540
Metham	43844
Methodist Theological School of Ohio	43015
Metzger	45601
Mexico	44882
Meyers Lake	44730
Miami (Clermont County) (Township)	45147
Miami (Greene County) (Township)	45387
Miami (Hamilton County)	45041
Miami (Hamilton County) (Township)	45002
Miami (Logan County) (Township)	43343
Miami (Montgomery County) (Township)	45342
Miami Heights	45002
Miamisburg	45342*
	45343†
Miami Shores (Part of Moraine)	45439
Miamitown	45041
Miami Township (Part of Centerville)	45475
Miami University (Part of Oxford)	45056
Miami Valley Center Mall (Part of Piqua)	45356
Miami Villa (Part of Huber Heights)	45424
Miamiville	45147
Michael Manor	45371
Mid City (Part of Dayton)	45402
Middle Bass	43446
Middleboro	45152
Middlebourne	43773
Middlebranch	44652
Middleburg (Jefferson County)	43903
Middleburg (Logan County)	43336
Middleburg (Noble County)	43724
Middleburg Heights	44130
Middleburg (Knox County) (Township)	43019
Middlebury (Van Wert County)	45832
Middlefield	44062
Middlefield (Township)	44062

	ZIP
Middle Point	45863
Middleport	45760
Middleton (Columbiana County)	44408
Middleton (Columbiana County) (Township)	44455
Middleton (Jackson County)	45692
Middleton (Wood County) (Township)	43525
Middleton Corner	45385
Middletown (Butler County)	45042-44
For specific Middletown Zip Codes call (513) 422-6316, or your local postmaster.	
Middletown (Champaign County)	43009
Middletown (Crawford County)	44833
Midland	45148
Midpark (Part of Parma Heights)	44130
Midtown (Part of Zanesville)	43701
Midvale	44653
Midway	43950
Midway Mall (Part of Elyria)	44035
Mifflin (Ashland County)	44805
Mifflin (Ashland County) (Township)	44805
Mifflin (Franklin County) (Township)	43230
Mifflin (Pike County) (Township)	45646
Mifflin (Richland County) (Township)	44843
Mifflin (Wyandot County) (Township)	43351
Milan	44846
Milan (Township)	44846
Milford (Butler County) (Township)	45004
Milford (Clermont County)	45150
Milford (Defiance County) (Township)	43526
Milford (Knox County) (Township)	43011
Milford Center	43045
Mill (Township)	44683
Millbrook	44691
Millbury	43447
Mill Creek (Coshocton County) (Township)	44654
Millcreek (Union County) (Township)	43040
Mill Creek (Williams County) (Township)	43501
Milledgeville	43142
Miller (Knox County) (Township)	43050
Miller (Lawrence County) (Township)	45623
Miller City	45864
Millers	45383
Millersburg	44654
Millersport	43046
Miller Station	43976
Millerstown	43072
Millersville	43435
Millertown	43730
Millfield	45761
Milligan	43731
Millport (Columbiana County)	44427
Millport (Pickaway County)	43103
Millville (Butler County)	45013
Millville (Mahoning County)	44460
Millwood (Guernsey County) (Township)	43773
Millwood (Knox County)	43028
Milton (Ashland County) (Township)	44805
Milton (Jackson County) (Township)	45692
Milton (Mahoning County) (Township)	44429
Milton (Wayne County) (Township)	44270
Milton (Wood County) (Township)	43441
Milton Center	43541
Miltonsburg	43793
Miltonville	45042
Mineral	45766
Mineral City	44656
Mineral Ridge	44440
Minersville	45769
Minerva	44657

	ZIP
Minerva Park	43229
Mineyahta on-The-Bay	43440
Minford	45653
Mingo	43047
Mingo Junction	43938
Minster	45865
Misco (Morgan County)	43731
Misco (Perry County)	43731
Mishler	44260
Mississinawa (Township)	45390
Mitiwanga	44839
Mizer Addition	43832
Modest	45122
Modoc	45732
Moffit Heights	44646
Moffitt	45816
Mogadore	44260
Mohawk	43844
Mohawk Lake	44883
Mohican (Township)	44840
Mohicanville	44840
Moline	43465
Momeneetown (Part of Oregon)	43616
Monclova	43542
Monclova (Township)	43542
Monclova Gardens (Part of Maumee)	43537
Monday Creek (Township)	43138
Monfort Heights	45239
Monfort Heights East	45239
Monfort Heights South	45239
Monnette	43302
Monroe (Adams County) (Township)	45144
Monroe (Allen County) (Township)	45807
Monroe (Ashtabula County) (Township)	44030
Monroe (Butler County)	45050
Monroe (Carroll County) (Township)	44620
Monroe (Clermont County) (Township)	45148
Monroe (Coshocton County) (Township)	43844
Monroe (Darke County) (Township)	45358
Monroe (Guernsey County) (Township)	43749
Monroe (Harrison County) (Township)	44695
Monroe (Henry County) (Township)	43535
Monroe (Holmes County) (Township)	44654
Monroe (Knox County) (Township)	43050
Monroe (Licking County) (Township)	43031
Monroe (Logan County) (Township)	43360
Monroe (Madison County) (Township)	43140
Monroe (Miami County) (Township)	45371
Monroe (Muskingum County) (Township)	43762
Monroe (Perry County) (Township)	43730
Monroe (Pickaway County) (Township)	43143
Monroe (Preble County) (Township)	45338
Monroe (Putnam County) (Township)	45831
Monroe (Richland County) (Township)	44843
Monroe Center	44030
Monroe Mills	43028
Monroeville (Huron County)	44847
Monroeville (Jefferson County)	43945
Monterey (Clermont County)	45103
Monterey (Putnam County) (Township)	45833
Montezuma	45866
Montgomery (Ashland County) (Township)	44805
Montgomery (Hamilton County)	45242
Montgomery (Marion County) (Township)	43332
Montgomery (Wood County) (Township)	43466
Montgomery Heights (Part of Montgomery)	45242
Monticello	45887

* Area Zip Code   † Post Office Boxes

Place	ZIP
Montpelier	43543
Montra	45302
Montrose	44333
Montrose-Ghent	44333
Montville (Geauga County)	44064
Montville (Geauga County) (Township)	44064
Montville (Medina County) (Township)	44256
Moorefield (Clark County) (Township)	45502
Moorefield (Harrison County) (Harrison County)	43907
Moorefield (Township)	43907
Moores Fork	45107
Moores Junction	43731
Mooresville	45601
Moraine	45439
Moreland	44691
Moreland Hills	44022
Morgan (Ashtabula County) (Township)	44084
Morgan (Butler County) (Township)	45053
Morgan (Gallia County) (Township)	45686
Morgan (Knox County) (Township)	43050
Morgan (Morgan County) (Township)	43756
Morgan (Scioto County) (Township)	45648
Morgan Center	45686
Morgandale	44481
Morgan Place (Part of Englewood)	45322
Morgansville	43758
Morgantown (Mahoning County)	44514
Morgantown (Pike County)	45612
Morges	44688
Morning Sun	45311
Morning View Court (Part of Orrville)	44667
Morral	43337
Morris (Township)	43019
Morris Apartments	45414
Morristown (Athens County)	45761
Morristown (Belmont County)	43759
Morrisville	45146
Morrow	45152
Moscow	45153
Moss Run	45750
Moulton	45895
Moulton (Township)	45895
Moultrie	44657
Moundbuilders (Part of Newark)	43055
Moundsville	43724
Mount Adams (Part of Cincinnati)	45202
Mount Air	43085
Mount Airy (Part of Cincinnati)	45223
Mount Auburn (Part of Cincinnati)	45219
Mount Blanchard	45867
Mount Carmel (Clermont County)	45244
Mount Carmel (Sandusky County)	43410
Mount Carmel Heights	45244
Mount Cory	45868
Mount Eaton	44659
Mount Ephraim	43779
Mount Everett (Part of Marietta)	45750
Mount Forest Trails	45244
Mount Gilead	43338
Mount Healthy	45231
Mount Healthy Heights	45231
Mount Holly (Clermont County)	45102
Mount Holly (Warren County)	45068
Mount Hope	44660
Mount Jefferson	45333
Mount Joy	45657
Mount Liberty	43048
Mount Lookout (Part of Cincinnati)	45226
Mount Olive	45106
Mount Orab	45154
Mount Perry	43760
Mount Pisgah	45157

Place	ZIP
Mount Pleasant (Hocking County)	43138
Mount Pleasant (Jefferson County)	43939
Mount Pleasant (Jefferson County) (Township)	43939
Mount Pleasant (Sandusky County)	44811
Mount Pleasant (Stark County)	44720
Mount Repose	45140
Mount Sterling	43143
Mount St. Joseph	45051
Mount Union (Part of Alliance)	44601
Mount Vernon	43050
Mount Vernon Avenue (Part of Columbus)	43203
Mount Victory	43340
Mount View	45133
Mountville	45732
Mount Washington (Part of Cincinnati)	45230
Mowrystown	45155
Moxahala	43761
Moxahala Park	43701
Mudsock (Franklin County)	43026
Mudsock (Gallia County)	45658
Muhlenberg (Township)	43146
Mulberry	45150
Mule Town	45653
Muncie Hollow	43420
Munroe Falls	44262
Munson (Township)	44024
Munson Hill	44004
Murdock	45140
Murlin Heights	45414
Murray City	43144
Museville	43720
Muskingum (Muskingum County) (Township)	43830
Muskingum (Washington County) (Township)	45744
Mutual	43044
Myersville	44685
Myrtle Brook	45140
Myrtle Village	45140
Naceville	45646
Nankin	44848
Napoleon	43545
Napoleon (Township)	43545
Nashport	43830
Nashville (Darke County)	45331
Nashville (Holmes County)	44661
Nashville (Miami County)	45373
National Road	43025
Navarre	44662
Neapolis	43547
Neave (Township)	45331
Needmore	45833
Neel	45167
Neelysville	43756
Neffs	43940
Negley	44441
Nellie	43844
Nelson	44231
Nelson (Township)	44231
Nelsonville	45764
Neptune	45822
Nettle Lake	43543
Nevada	44849
Neville	45156
New Albany (Franklin County)	43054
New Albany (Mahoning County)	44460
New Alexander	44625
New Alexandria	43938
New Antioch	45177
Newark	43055-58
For specific Newark Zip Codes call (614) 345-4021, or your local postmaster.	
Newark Air Force Station	43057
Ne Waterworks (Part of Canton)	44705
New Athens	43981
New Baltimore (Hamilton County)	45030
New Baltimore (Stark County)	44601
New Bavaria	43548
New Bedford	43804
Newbery (Township)	45318
New Bloomington	43341
New Boston	45662
New Bremen	45869
New Buffalo	44406

Place	ZIP
Newburg (Part of Cleveland)	44105
Newburgh Heights	44105
New Burlington	45231
Newbury	44065
Newbury (Township)	44065
New California	43064
New Carlisle	45344
New Castle (Belmont County)	43716
Newcastle (Coshocton County)	43843
Newcastle (Coshooton County) (Township)	43843
New Castle (Lawrence County)	45638
New Cleveland	45875
Newcomerstown	43832
New Concord	43762
New Cumberland	44656
New Dover	43040
Newell	43941
Newell Run	45768
New England	45778
Newfain	45660
New Floodwood	45764
New Franklin	44657
New Garden	44423
New Germany (Part of Beavercreek)	45431
New Guilford	43843
New Hagerstown	44695
New Hampshire	45870
New Harmony	45154
New Harrisburg	44615
New Harrison	45331
New Haven (Hamilton County)	45030
New Haven (Huron County)	44850
New Haven (Huron County) (Township)	44850
New Holland	43145
Newhope (Brown County)	45121
New Hope (Preble County)	45320
New Jasper	45385
New Jasper (Township)	45385
New Jerusalem	43311
New Knoxville	45871
New Lebanon	45345
New Lexington (Perry County)	43764
New Lexington (Preble County)	45381
New Liberty	44413
New London	44851
New London (Township)	44851
New Lyme	44085
New Lyme (Township)	44085
New Madison	45346
Newman	44646
New Market	45133
New Market (Township)	45133
Newmarket Station (Part of Canton)	44702
New Marshfield	45766
New Martinsburg	45123
New Matamoras	45767
New Miami	45011
New Middletown	44442
New Moorefield	45502
New Moscow	43812
New Palestine	45157
New Paris	45347
New Petersburg	45123
New Philadelphia	44663
New Pittsburg	44691
New Pittsburgh	44865
New Plymouth	45654
New Plymouth Heights	45629
Newport (Madison County)	43140
Newport (Shelby County)	45845
Newport (Tuscarawas County)	44683
Newport (Washington County)	45768
Newport (Washington County) (Township)	45768
New Princeton	43844
New Reading	43783
New Richland	43310
New Richmond	45157
New Riegel	44853
New Rochester	43450
New Rome	43228
New Rumley	43984
New Salem	43148
New Salisbury	43930

Place	ZIP
New Somerset	43964
New Springfield	44443
New Stark	45897
New Straitsville	43766
New Strasburg	43102
Newton (Licking County) (Township)	43055
Newton (Miami County) (Township)	45339
Newton (Muskingum County) (Township)	43735
Newton (Pike County) (Township)	45661
Newton (Trumbull County) (Township)	44444
Newton Falls	44444
Newtonsville	45158
Newtown (Hamilton County)	45244-45
For specific Newtown Zip Codes call (513) 561-5853, or your local postmaster.	
Newtown (Jefferson County)	43917
Newtowne Mall (Part of New Philadelphia)	44663
New Vienna	45159
Newville	44864
New Washington	44854
New Waterford	44445
New Weston	45348
New Westville	47374
New Winchester	44820
Ney	43549
Nicholsville	45106
Nile (Township)	45630
Niles	44446
Nimishillen (Township)	44641
Nimisila	44216
Nipgen	45612
Noble (Auglaize County) (Township)	45885
Noble (Cuyahoga County)	44132
Noble (Defiance County) (Township)	43512
Noble (Noble County) (Township)	43724
Normandy Heights	45015
Norris	45383
North (Township)	43988
North Akron (Part of Akron)	44310
Northampton (Township)	44221
North Auburn	44887
North Baltimore	45872
North Bend	45052
North Benton (Mahoning County)	44449
North Benton (Portage County)	44449
North Berne	43130
North Bloomfield (Morrow County) (Township)	44833
North Bloomfield (Trumbull County)	44450
North Brewster (Part of Brewster)	44613
North Bristol	44402
Northbrook	45231
North Canton	44720
North Clippinger (Part of The Village of Indian Hill)	45243
North College Hill	45231
North Condit	43074
North Creek	45831
North Dayton (Darke County)	45390
North Dayton (Montgomery County)	45404
Northeast (Part of Columbus)	43231
North Eaton	44044
North Fairfield	44855
North Feesburg	45130
Northfield	44067
Northfield Center	44067
Northfield Center (Township)	44067
North Findlay	45840
North Fork Village	45601
Northgate	45251
North Georgetown	44665
North Greenfield	43358
North Hampton	45349
North Hill (Part of Akron)	44310
North Hills Estates	45224
North Houston	45333
North Industry	44707
North Jackson	44451

* Area Zip Code   † Post Office Boxes

	ZIP
North Kenova (Part of South Point)	45680
North Kingsville	44068
Northland (Part of Columbus)	43229
Northland Mall (Part of Columbus)	43229
North Lawrence	44666
North Lewisburg	43060
North Liberty	44822
North Lima	44452
North Madison	44057
North Monroeville	44847
Northmoor	45315
North Moreland (Part of Portsmouth)	45662
North Mount Vernon	43050
North Olmsted	44070
North Perry	44081
North Randall	44128
North Richmond	44003
Northridge (Clark County)	45502
Northridge (Montgomery County)	45414
North Ridgeville	44039
North Robinson	44856
North Royalton	44133
North Sagamore Heights	45236
North Salem	43749
North Side (Part of Youngstown)	44504
North Star	45350
North Towne Square Mall (Part of Toledo)	43612
North Uniontown	45133
Northup	45658
Northview	45322
Northwest (Franklin County)	43220
Northwest (Williams County) (Township)	43518
Northwest Plaza (Part of Dayton)	45405
Northwood (Logan County)	43310
Northwood (Wood County)	43619
North Woodbury	44813
North Zanesville	43701
Norton (Delaware County)	43356
Norton (Summit County)	44203
Norwalk	44857
Norwalk (Township)	44857
Norwich (Franklin County) (Township)	43026
Norwich (Huron County) (Township)	44890
Norwich (Muskingum County)	43767
Norwood (Hamilton County)	45212
Norwood (Washington County)	45750
Norwood Heights (Part of Cincinnati)	45212
Nottingham (Cuyahoga County)	44110
Nottingham (Harrison County) (Township)	43907
Nova	44859
Novelty	44072
Oakdale (Athens County)	45732
Oakdale (Montgomery County)	45429
Oakdale (Stark County)	44646
Oakfield (Perry County)	43731
Oakfield (Trumbull County)	44450
Oak Grove (Clark County)	45502
Oak Grove (Washington County)	45750
Oak Harbor	43449
Oak Hill	45656
Oakland (Butler County)	45050
Oakland (Clinton County)	45177
Oakland (Fairfield County)	43102
Oakland Park	43224
Oakley (Part of Cincinnati)	45209
Oakmont	43920
Oak Park	43907
Oak Run (Township)	43143
Oak Shade	43567
Oakview	45805
Oakwood (Cuyahoga County)	44146
Oakwood (Montgomery County)	45419
Oakwood (Paulding County)	45873
Oberlin	44074

	ZIP
Oberlin Beach	44839
Obetz	43207
Oceola	44860
Oco	43950
O'Connor Landing	43310
Octa	43160
Ogden	45177
Ogontz	44814
Ohio (Clermont County) (Township)	45157
Ohio (Gallia County) (Township)	45623
Ohio (Monroe County) (Township)	43931
Ohio City	45874
Ohio Furnace	45638
Ohio Reformatory for Women	43040
Ohio Soldiers and Sailors Home	44870
Ohio State Reformatory	44901
Ohio State University-Lima Campus	45804
Okeana	45053
Okolona	43550
Old Fort	44861
Old Gore	43138
Old Mill Creek	44212
Old Plymouth Heights	45629
Old Straitsville	43766
Oldtown	45385
Old Washington	43768
Old West End (Part of Toledo)	43610
Olena	44857
Olentangy	44820
Olive (Meigs County) (Township)	45743
Olive (Noble County) (Township)	43724
Olive Branch	45103
Olive Green (Delaware County)	43074
Olive Green (Noble County)	43724
Oliver (Township)	45693
Olivesburg	44805
Olivett	43713
Olmsted (Township)	44138
Olmsted Falls	44138
Olszeski	43917
Omega	45690
Oneida (Butler County)	45042
Oneida (Carroll County)	44644
Ontario	44862
Opperman	43732
Oran	45365
Orange (Ashland County) (Township)	44805
Orange (Carroll County) (Township)	44639
Orange (Coshocton County)	43832
Orange (Cuyahoga County)	44022
Orange (Delaware County) (Township)	43021
Orange (Hancock County) (Township)	45817
Orange (Meigs County) (Township)	45723
Orange (Shelby County) (Township)	45365
Orangeville	44453
Orbiston	45732
Orchard Beach	44089
Orchard Island	43331
Orchard Park Heights	44904
Oregon	43605
	43616
	43613
For specific Oregon Zip Codes call (419) 693-5033, or your local postmaster.	
Oregonia	45054
Oreville	43766
Orient	43146
Orient Correctional Institution	43146
Orland	45654
Orrville	44667
Orwell	44076
Orwell (Township)	44076
Osage	43964
Osgood	45351
Osnaburg (Township)	44730
Ostrander	43061
Otsego	43762
Ottawa	45875
Ottawa (Township)	45875

	ZIP
Ottawa Hills	43606
Otterbein Home	45036
Ottokee	43567
Ottoville	45876
Otway	45657
Outville	43062
Overlook	45431
Overlook Court	43906
Overlook Hills	43952
Overlook Homes	45431
Overlook-Page Manor	45431
Overpeck	45055
Over The Rhine (Part of Cincinnati)	45210
Overton	44691
Owens Hill	43701
Owensville	45160
Oxford (Butler County)	45056
Oxford (Butler County) (Township)	45056
Oxford (Coshocton County) (Township)	43845
Oxford (Delaware County) (Township)	43003
Oxford (Erie County) (Township)	44870
Oxford (Guernsey County) (Township)	43773
Oxford (Tuscarawas County) (Township)	43832
Ozark	43716
Padanaram	44003
Padua	45846
Page Manor	45431
Pagetown	43334
Pageville	45710
Painesville	44077
Painesville (Township)	44077
Painesville on the Lake	44077
Painesville Shopping Center (Part of Painesville)	44077
Paint (Fayette County) (Township)	43106
Paint (Highland County) (Township)	45612
Paint (Holmes County) (Township)	44690
Paint (Madison County) (Township)	43140
Paint (Ross County) (Township)	45612
Paint (Wayne County) (Township)	44659
Painters Creek	45304
Paintersville	45335
Paint Valley	45654
Palermo	44615
Palestine	45352
Palmer (Putnam County) (Township)	45831
Palmer (Washington County) (Township)	43787
Palmyra (Knox County)	43019
Palmyra (Portage County)	44412
Palmyra (Portage County) (Township)	44412
Palos	45732
Pancoastburg	43160
Pandora	45877
Pansy	45107
Paradise	44406
Paradise Hill	44805
Paris (Portage County)	44266
Paris (Portage County) (Township)	44266
Paris (Stark County)	44669
Paris (Stark County) (Township)	44669
Paris (Union County) (Township)	43040
Parkdale (Hamilton County)	45218
Parkdale (Jefferson County)	43952
Parkertown	44824
Park Layne (Clark County)	45344
Park Layne (Montgomery County)	45431
Parkman	44080
Parkman (Township)	44080
Park Place (Part of Wyoming)	45215
Park Ridge Acres	45506
Parkview (Part of Fairview Park)	41126
Parkview Heights	45224
Parlett	43907
Parma	44129
Parma (Part of Cleveland)	44130

	ZIP
Parma Heights	44130
Parmatown Mall (Part of Parma)	44129
Parral	44622
Parrott	43160
Pasadena (Part of Kettering)	45429
Pasco	45365
Pataskala	43062
Patmos	44460
Patriot	45658
Patterson (Darke County) (Township)	45388
Patterson (Hardin County)	45843
Pattersonville	44657
Pattin Addition (Part of Marietta)	45750
Pattonville	45640
Paulding	45879
Paulding (Township)	45879
Paul Laurence Dunbar (Part of Dayton)	45417
Pavonia	44903
Pawnee	44254
Paxton (Township)	45612
Payne	45880
Peacock Acres	45502
Pearlbrook (Part of Cleveland)	44109
Pease (Township)	43935
Pebble (Township)	45690
Pedro	45659
Peebles	45660
Pee Pee (Township)	45690
Pekin (Carroll County)	44657
Pekin (Jefferson County)	43952
Pekin (Warren County)	45036
Pemberton	45353
Pemberville	43450
Penfield	44052
Penfield (Township)	44090
Peniel	45658
Peninsula	44264
Penn (Highland County) (Township)	45135
Penn (Morgan County) (Township)	43787
Pennsville	43770
Penn View	44003
Peoli	43832
Peoria (Butler County)	45056
Peoria (Union County)	43067
Pepper Pike	44124
Perintown	45150
Perkins (Township)	44870
Perry (Allen County) (Township)	45806
Perry (Ashland County) (Township)	44866
Perry (Brown County) (Township)	45118
Perry (Carroll County) (Township)	43988
Perry (Columbiana County) (Township)	44460
Perry (Coshocton County) (Township)	43843
Perry (Fayette County) (Township)	45135
Perry (Franklin County) (Township)	43017
Perry (Gallia County) (Township)	45658
Perry (Hocking County) (Township)	43135
Perry (Lake County)	44081
Perry (Lake County) (Township)	44081
Perry (Lawrence County) (Township)	45638
Perry (Licking County) (Township)	43055
Perry (Logan County) (Township)	43319
Perry (Monroe County) (Township)	43793
Perry (Montgomery County) (Township)	45309
Perry (Morrow County) (Township)	44904
Perry (Muskingum County) (Township)	43701
Perry (Pickaway County) (Township)	43145
Perry (Pike County) (Township)	45616
Perry (Putnam County) (Township)	45837
Perry (Richland County) (Township)	44813

	ZIP
Perry (Shelby County) (Township)	45353
Perry (Stark County) (Township)	44708
Perry (Tuscarawas County) (Township)	44699
Perry (Wood County) (Township)	44817
Perry Addition	45648
Perry Heights	44646
Perrysburg	43551*
	43552†
Perrysburg Heights	43551
Perrysville (Ashland County)	44864
Perrysville (Carroll County)	43988
Perryton	43822
Peru (Huron County)	44857
Peru (Huron County) (Township)	44847
Peru (Morrow County) (Township)	43334
Petersburg (Carroll County)	44615
Petersburg (Jackson County)	45640
Petersburg (Mahoning County)	44454
Petrea	45640
Petroleum	44438
Pettisville	43553
Pfeiffer Station	43326
Phalanx	44470
Pharisburg	43040
Phillippstown (Part of Columbus)	43201
Phillipsburg	45354
Philo	43771
Philothea	45828
Phoneton	45371
Pickaway (Township)	43113
Pickaway Correctional Institution	43146
Pickerington	43147
Pickrelltown	43357
Piedmont	43983
Pierce (Township)	45245
Pierpont	44082
Pierpont (Township)	44082
Pigeon Creek	44321
Pigeon Run	44646
Pike (Brown County) (Township)	45176
Pike (Clark County) (Township)	45502
Pike (Coshocton County) (Township)	43822
Pike (Fulton County) (Township)	43515
Pike (Knox County) (Township)	44822
Pike (Madison County) (Township)	43029
Pike (Perry County) (Township)	43764
Pike (Stark County) (Township)	44626
Piketon	45661
Pikeville	45331
Pine Grove	45638
Pinehurst	45750
Pine Valley (Part of Dillonvale)	43917
Piney Fork	43941
Pink	45630
Pinkerman	45682
Pioneer	43554
Piqua	45356
Piqua East Mall (Part of Piqua)	45356
Pisgah	45069
Pitchin	45502
Pitsburg	45358
Pitt (Township)	43323
Pittlime (Part of Norton)	44203
Pittsburgh Junction	43986
Pittsfield	44090
Pittsfield (Township)	44090
Placid Meadows	45238
Plain (Franklin County) (Township)	43081
Plain (Stark County) (Township)	44708
Plain (Wayne County) (Township)	44691
Plain (Wood County) (Township)	43402
Plain City	43064
Plainfield	43836
Plain View	43793

	ZIP
Plankton	44882
Planktown	44878
Plantation Acres	45224
Plants	45771
Plantsville	43728
Plattsburg	43568
Plattsville	45365
Playhouse Square (Part of Cleveland)	44115
Pleasant (Brown County) (Township)	45121
Pleasant (Clark County) (Township)	43010
Pleasant (Fairfield County) (Township)	43130
Pleasant (Franklin County) (Township)	43123
Pleasant (Hancock County) (Township)	45858
Pleasant (Hardin County) (Township)	43326
Pleasant (Henry County) (Township)	43527
Pleasant (Knox County) (Township)	43050
Pleasant (Logan County) (Township)	43318
Pleasant (Madison County) (Township)	43143
Pleasant (Marion County) (Township)	43302
Pleasant (Perry County) (Township)	43731
Pleasant (Putnam County) (Township)	45830
Pleasant (Seneca County) (Township)	44861
Pleasant (Van Wert County) (Township)	45891
Pleasant Bend	43548
Pleasant City	43772
Pleasant Corners	43123
Pleasant Grove (Belmont County)	43901
Pleasant Grove (Muskingum County)	43701
Pleasant Heights (Columbiana County)	43920
Pleasant Heights (Jefferson County)	43952
Pleasant Hill (Athens County)	45701
Pleasant Hill (Jefferson County)	43952
Pleasant Hill (Miami County)	45359
Pleasant Hills	45231
Pleasant Home	44287
Pleasant Lea	43130
Pleasant Plain	45162
Pleasant Ridge (Part of Cincinnati)	45213
Pleasant Run	45231
Pleasant Run Farms	45240
Pleasant Valley (Coshocton County)	43812
Pleasant Valley (Pike County)	45661
Pleasant Valley (Ross County)	45601
Pleasant Valley (Vinton County)	45601
Pleasant View (Fayette County)	43128
Pleasant View (Stark County)	44705
Pleasantville	43148
Plumwood	43140
Plymouth (Ashtabula County) (Township)	44004
Plymouth (Ashtabula County)	44004
Plymouth (Richland County)	44865
Plymouth (Richland County) (Township)	44865
Plymouth Center	44004
Poast Town	45042
Poetown	45130
Point (Part of Columbus)	43223
Point Isabel	45153
Point Place (Part of Toledo)	43611
Point Pleasant	45153
Point Rock	45710
Poland	44514
Poland (Township)	44514
Poland Center	44436
Polaris (Part of Columbus)	43240
Polk (Ashland County)	44866

	ZIP
Polk (Crawford County) (Township)	44833
Pomeroy	45769
Pond Run	45684
Poplargrove	45660
Portage (Hancock County) (Township)	45872
Portage (Ottawa County) (Township)	43452
Portage (Wood County)	43451
Portage (Wood County) (Township)	43451
Portage Lakes	44319
Port Clinton	43452
Porter (Delaware County) (Township)	43074
Porter (Gallia County)	45614
Porter (Scioto County) (Township)	45694
Porterfield	45714
Portersville	43730
Port Homer	43964
Port Jefferson	45360
Portland	45770
Portsmouth	45662-63
For specific Portsmouth Zip Codes call (614) 353-2070, or your local postmaster.	
Port Union	45015
Port Washington	43837
Port William	45164
Possum Woods	45506
Post Town	45042
Post Town Heights	45042
Potsdam	45361
Pottery Additon	43952
Powell	43065
Powellsville	45629
Powhatan Point	43942
Prairie (Franklin County) (Township)	43119
Prairie (Holmes County) (Township)	44633
Prairie Meadows	43812
Pratts Fork	45776
Prattsville	45651
Prentiss	45856
Preston Addition	45648
Price Hill (Part of Cincinnati)	45205
Pricetown (Highland County)	45133
Pricetown (Trumbull County)	44429
Pride	45601
Princeton	45015
Proctor	44266
Proctorville	45669
Prospect	43342
Prospect (Township)	43342
Prout	44870
Providence (Township)	43504
Provident	43950
Provincial Point	45244
Public Square (Part of Cleveland)	44114
Pulaski	43506
Pulaski (Township)	43506
Pulaskiville	43338
Pulse	45118
Pultney (Township)	43906
Puritas Park (Part of Cleveland)	44135
Purity	43071
Pusheta (Township)	45895
Put-in-Bay	43456
Put-in-Bay (Township)	43456
Putnam Place (Part of Marietta)	45750
Pymatuning Shores	44003
Pyrmont	45309
Pyro	45656
Quaker City	43773
Qualey	45724
Queen Acres	45013
Quincy	43343
Raccoon (Township)	45685
Racine	45771
Radcliff	45670
Radford Road	45701
Radio Heights	43920
Radnor	43066
Radnor (Township)	43066
Ragersville	44681
Rainsboro	45165
Ra-Mar Estates	45502
Ramsey	43917
Ranchwood	44870
Randall Park Mall (Part of North Randall)	44128

	ZIP
Randolph (Montgomery County) (Township)	45322
Randolph (Portage County)	44265
Randolph (Portage County) (Township)	44265
Range	43143
Range (Township)	43143
Ransom	45381
Rarden	45671
Rarden (Township)	45671
Rathbone (Delaware County)	43015
Rathbone (Washington County)	45750
Rathbone Heights (Part of Marietta)	45750
Ravenna	44266
Ravenna (Township)	44266
Ravenna Army Ammunition Plant	44266
Rawson	45881
Ray	45672
Rayland	43943
Raymond	43067
Rays Corners	44047
Reading (Columbiana County)	44634
Reading (Hamilton County)	45215
Reading (Perry County) (Township)	45783
Recovery (Township)	45846
Red Bank (Part of Fairfax)	45227
Redbird	44057
Redbush	45742
Red Coach Farm (Part of Centerville)	45429
Redfield	43764
Red Fox	44240
Redhaw	44866
Red Lion	45005
Redoak	45167
Red River	45308
Redtown	45732
Reed (Township)	44807
Reedsburg	44691
Reedsmills	43910
Reedsville	45772
Reedtown	44807
Reedurban	44710
Reese Station	43207
Reesville	45166
Reform	43055
Rehoboth	43764
Reily	45056
Reily (Township)	45056
Reinersville	43756
Reminderville	44202
Remington	45140
Remsen Corners	44256
Rendville	43730
Reno	45773
Reno Beach	43412
Rensselaer Park	45216
Republic	44867
Resaca	43140
Residence Park (Part of Dayton)	45417
Revenge	43130
Reynoldsburg	43068
Reynolds Corner (Part of Toledo)	43615
	43617
	43635
For specific Reynolds Corner Zip Codes call (419) 841-1375, or your local postmaster.	
Rialto	45069
Rice (Putnam County)	45831
Rice (Sandusky County) (Township)	43420
Riceland	44667
Richfield (Henry County) (Township)	43516
Richfield (Lucas County) (Township)	43504
Richfield (Summit County)	44286
Richfield (Summit County) (Township)	44286
Richfield Center	43504
Richfield Heights (Part of Richfield)	44286
Rich Hill (Knox County)	43011
Rich Hill (Muskingum County) (Township)	43727
Richland (Allen County) (Township)	45817
Richland (Belmont County) (Township)	43950

	ZIP		ZIP		ZIP		ZIP
Richland (Clinton County) (Township)	45169	Rochester	44090	Rush (Tuscarawas County) (Township)	44683	Saltair	45106
Richland (Darke County) (Township)	45380	Rochester (Township)	44090	Rush Creek (Fairfield County) (Township)	43107	Salt Creek (Hocking County) (Township)	43135
Richland (Defiance County) (Township)	43512	Rochester Place (Part of Northwood)	43618	Rushcreek (Logan County) (Township)	43347	Salt Creek (Holmes County) (Township)	44660
Richland (Fairfield County) (Township)	43150	Rockbridge	43149	Rushmore	45844	Salt Creek (Muskingum County) (Township)	43727
Richland (Guernsey County) (Township)	43780	Rock Camp (Columbiana County)	44432	Rush Run	43943	Salt Creek (Pickaway County) (Township)	43113
Richland (Holmes County) (Township)	44628	Rock Camp (Lawrence County)	45675	Rushsylvania	43347	Salt Creek (Wayne County) (Township)	44627
Richland (Logan County) (Township)	43310	Rock Creek	44084	Rushtown	45652	Saltillo	43777
Richland (Marion County) (Township)	43302	Rockdale	45015	Rushville	43150	Salt Lick (Township)	43782
Richland (Montgomery County)	45431	Rockford	45882	Russell (Geauga County) (Township)	44072	Salt Rock (Township)	43337
Richland (Vinton County) (Township)	45651	Rockhill	43977	Russell (Highland County)	45133	Salt Run	43943
Richland (Wyandot County) (Township)	43359	Rockland (Part of Belpre)	45714	Russell Center	44072	Samantha	45135
Richland Mall (Part of Ontario)	44906	Rock Mills	43160	Russell Heights	43968	Sand Beach	43449
Richmond (Ashtabula County) (Township)	44032	Rockport	45830	Russells	43701	Sand Hill (Erie County)	44870
Richmond (Huron County) (Township)	44890	Rock Way	45504	Russells Point	43348	Sand Hill (Scioto County)	45694
Richmond (Jefferson County)	43944	Rockwood (Erie County)	44824	Russellville	45168	Sand Hill (Washington County)	45773
Richmond Center	44003	Rockwood (Lawrence County)	45619	Russia (Lorain County) (Township)	44074	Sand Ridge	45761
Richmond Dale	45673	Rocky Fall Estates	45133	Russia (Shelby County)	45363	Sandrun	45764
Richmond Heights	44143	Rockyhill	45640	Rustic Hills	44256	Sandusky (Crawford County) (Township)	44887
Richmond Mall (Part of Richmond Heights)	44143	Rocky Point	45502	Rutland	45775	Sandusky (Erie County)	44870*
Richville	44706	Rocky Ridge	43458	Rutland (Township)	45775		44871†
Richwood	43344	Rocky River	44116	Rye Beach (Part of Huron)	44839	Sandusky (Richland County) (Township)	44827
Rickard Acres	45005	Rodney	45631	Sabina	45169	Sandusky (Sandusky County) (Township)	43420
Rickenbacker Air Force Base	43217	Rogers	44455	Sagamore Hills	44067	Sandusky South	44870
Ridge (Van Wert County) (Township)	45891	Rokeby Lock	43756	Sagamore Hills (Township)	44067	Sandy (Stark County) (Township)	44688
Ridge (Wyandot County) (Township)	43316	Rolandus	45771	Sahara Sands	44646	Sandy (Tuscarawas County) (Township)	44656
Ridgefield (Township)	44847	Rollersville	43431	St. Albans (Township)	43062	Sandy Beach	45885
Ridgeland	45640	Rolling Acres (Part of Akron)	44322	St. Anthony	45844	Sandy Springs	45684
Ridgeton	44820	Rolling Mill Park	45044	St. Bernard	45216-17	Sandyville	44671
Ridgeville (Henry County) (Township)	43555	Rome (Ashtabula County)	44085	For specific St. Bernard Zip Codes call (513) 242-3773, or your local postmaster.		San Margherita	43204
Ridgeville (Warren County)	45036	Rome (Ashtabula County) (Township)	44085	St. Charles	45013	Santa Fe	45895
Ridgeville Corners	43555	Rome (Athens County) (Township)	45723	St. Clair (Butler County) (Township)	45011	Santoy	43730
Ridgeway	43345	Rome (Lawrence County)	45669	St. Clair (Columbiana County) (Township)	43920	Sarahsville	43779
Ridgewood (Allen County)	43701	Rome (Lawrence County) (Township)	45669	St. Clairsville	43950	Sardinia	45171
Ridgewood (Muskingum County)	43821	Rome (Richland County)	44878	St. Henry	45883	Sardis	43946
Ridgewood Heights	45427	Rome Station	44085	St. Joe	43906	Savannah	44874
Rigrish	45662	Romohr Acres	45244	St. Johns	45884	Saville Estates	45431
Riley (Putnam County) (Township)	45877	Rootstown	44272	St. Joseph (Mercer County)	45846	Savona	45331
Riley (Sandusky County) (Township)	43420	Rootstown (Township)	44272	St. Joseph (Portage County)	44201	Sawyerwood	44312
Rimer	45830	Rose (Township)	44643	St. Joseph (Williams County) (Township)	43517	Saybrook	44004
Rinard Mills	45734	Rosedale	43029	St. Louisville	43071	Saybrook (Township)	44004
Ringgold (Morgan County)	43758	Rose Farm	43731	St. Martin	45118	Saybrook-on-the-Lake	44004
Ringgold (Pickaway County)	43113	Rose Heights (Part of Steubenville)	43952	St. Marys	45885	Saylor Park (Part of Cincinnati)	45233
Rio Grande	45674	Rose Hill	45348	St. Marys (Township)	45885	Sayre	43731
Ripley (Brown County)	45167	Roseland	44906	St. Paris	43072	Scenic Hills	43162
Ripley (Holmes County) (Township)	44676	Roselawn (Part of Cincinnati)	45237	St. Pauls	45103	Schauers Acres	45341
Ripley (Huron County) (Township)	44837	Roselms	45849	St. Peters	45846	Schley	45768
Risingsun	43457	Rosemont	44451	St. Rosa	45886	Schoenbrunn	44663
Rittman	44270	Rosemount	45662	St. Sebastian	45826	Schooleys	45601
River Corners	44275	Roseville	43777	St. Stephens	44807	Schrader	45601
Riverdale	45661	Rosewood	43070	St. Wendelin	45883	Schumm	45898
Riveredge (Township)	44135	Roslyn (Part of Kettering)	45429	Salem (Auglaize County) (Township)	45887	Scio	43988
Riverlea	43085	Ross (Butler County)	45061	Salem (Champaign County) (Township)	43078	Scioto (Delaware County) (Township)	43061
Riverside (Montgomery County)	45424	Ross (Butler County) (Township)	45061	Salem (Columbiana County)	44460	Scioto (Jackson County) (Township)	45640
Riverside (Shelby County)	45365	Ross (Greene County) (Township)	45153	Salem (Columbiana County) (Township)	44431	Scioto (Pickaway County) (Township)	43103
Riverside Park	44683	Ross (Jefferson County) (Township)	43944	Salem (Highland County) (Township)	45133	Scioto (Pike County) (Township)	45687
River Styx	44256	Rossburg	45362	Salem (Jefferson County) (Township)	43944	Scioto (Ross County) (Township)	45601
River Valley Mall (Part of Lancaster)	43130	Rossford	43460	Salem (Meigs County) (Township)	45741	Sciotodale	45662
Riverview (Belmont County)	43906	Rossmoyne	45236	Salem (Monroe County) (Township)	43915	Scioto Furnace	45677
Riverview (Washington County)	45750	Rossville (Part of Hamilton)	45013	Salem (Muskingum County) (Township)	43802	Sciotoville (Part of Portsmouth)	45662
Rix Mills	43762	Roswell	44663	Salem (Ottawa County) (Township)	43449	Scipio (Butler County)	45053
Roachester	45152	Round Bottom	43915	Salem (Shelby County) (Township)	45365	Scipio (Meigs County) (Township)	45710
Roads	45640	Roundhead	43346	Salem (Tuscarawas County) (Township)	43832	Scipio (Seneca County) (Township)	44867
Roaming Rock Shores	44085	Roundhead (Township)	43346	Salem (Warren County) (Township)	45152	Scotch Ridge	43450
Roaming Shores	44085	Rousculp	45806	Salem (Washington County) (Township)	45745	Scott (Adams County) (Township)	45679
Roanoke	44683	Rowsburg	44866	Salem (Wyandot County) (Township)	43351	Scott (Brown County) (Township)	45121
Robertsville	44670	Roxabell	45628	Salem Center	45741	Scott (Marion County) (Township)	43302
Robins	43723	Roxanna	45068	Salem Heights	44460	Scott (Sandusky County) (Township)	43435
Robtown	43103	Roxbury	43787	Salesville	43778	Scott (Van Wert County)	45886
Robyville	43901	Royalton (Fairfield County)	43130	Saline (Township)	43932	Scottown	45678
		Royalton (Fulton County) (Township)	43533	Salineville	43945	Scotts Crossing	45833
		Royersville	45638	Salisbury (Township)	45769	Scotty's Beauty Beach	45822
		Rubyville	45662			Scroggsfield	44615
		Rudolph	43462			Scrub Ridge	45616
		Ruggles	44837			Seal (Pike County) (Township)	45661
		Ruggles (Township)	44851			Seal (Wyandot County)	44849
		Ruggles Beach	44839				
		Rumley (Harrison County) (Township)	43986				
		Rumley (Shelby County)	45302				
		Rural	45120				
		Ruraldale	43720				
		Rush (Champaign County) (Township)	43084				
		Rush (Scioto County) (Township)	45652				

	ZIP		ZIP		ZIP		ZIP
Seaman	45679	Sherman (Huron County)		Southern Hills (Part of		Springfield (Gallia County)	
Seasons Four	45140	(Township)	44847	Kettering)	45409	(Township)	45614
Sebring	44672	Sherman (Richland		Southern Knoll (Part of		Springfield (Hamilton	
Secedar Corners	44425	County)	44906	Oxford)	45056	County) (Township)	45239
Sedalia	43151	Sherman (Summit County)	44203	Southern Ohio		Springfield (Jefferson	
Sedamsville (Part of		Sherritts	45688	Correctional Facility	45648	County) (Township)	43903
Cincinnati)	45238	Sherrodsville	44675	Southern Park Mall	44513	Springfield (Lucas County)	
Seilcrest Acres	45140	Sherwood (Defiance		South Euclid	44121	(Township)	43528
Sellers Point	43046	County)	43556	South Excello	45042	Springfield (Mahoning	
Selma	45368	Sherwood (Hamilton		Southfield Park (Part of		County) (Township)	44442
Seneca (Monroe County)		County)	45230	Columbus)	43201	Springfield (Muskingum	
(Township)	43754	Sherwood Park	45805	Southgate (Part of		County) (Township)	43701
Seneca (Noble County)		Shillings Mill	44429	Springfield)	45506	Springfield (Richland	
(Township)	43779	Shiloh (Clermont County)	45122	Southgate Acres	44870	County) (Township)	44906
Seneca (Seneca County)		Shiloh (Montgomery		Southgate Shopping		Springfield (Ross County)	
(Township)	44853	County)	45415	Center (Part of Newark)	43056	(Township)	45601
Senecaville	43780	Shiloh (Richland County)	44878	Southgate U.S.A. (Part of		Springfield (Summit	
Senior	45152	Shinrock	44839	Maple Heights)	44137	County) (Township)	44312
Sentinel	44032	Shore (Part of Euclid)	44123	South Highlands (Part of		Springfield (Williams	
Seven Hills (Cuyahoga		Shoregate Shopping		Middletown)	45042	County) (Township)	43557
County)	44131	Center (Part of		South Hill Park	43528	Springhills	43318
Seven Hills (Hamilton		Willowick)	44095	Southington (Township)	44470	Spring Meadows	45231
County)	45231	Short Creek (Township)	43901	Southington	44470	Spring Mill	44903
Seven Mile	45062	Short Creek	43989	South Kingman	45177	Spring Mountain	43844
Seventeen	44629	Shreve	44676	Southland Shopping		Springvale	45140
Severance Town Center		Sidney	45365	Center (Cuyahoga		Spring Valley (Greene	
(Part of Cleveland		Signal	44432	County)	44130	County) (Township)	45370
Heights)	44118	Silica	43560	Southland Shopping		Spring Valley (Greene	
Seville	44273	Silver Creek (Greene		Center (Lucas County)	43614	County)	45370
Seward	43533	County) (Township)	45335	South Lebanon	45065	Spring Valley (Lorain	
Sewellsville	43713	Silver Creek (Medina		South Logan (Part of		County)	44035
Shade	45776	County)	44281	Logan)	43138	Spring Valley (Lucas	
Shademore	45244	Silver Lake	44221	South Lorain (Part of		County)	43528
Shadeville	43137	Silverton	45236	Lorain)	44055	Springville (Seneca	
Shady Bend	43832	Simons	44093	South Madison	44057	County)	43316
Shady Glen	43964	Singing Hills	45449	South Middletown	45044	Springville (Wayne	
Shady Grove	45324	Sinking Spring	45172	South Milford (Part of		County)	44676
Shadyside (Belmont		Sitka	45750	Milford)	45150	Springwood	45056
County)	43947	Six Corners	43526	South Moor Shores	45885	Squirrel Town	45684
Shadyside (Columbiana		Skyline Acres	45231	South Mount Vernon	43050	Stafford	43786
County)	43920	Skypark	45281	South Newbury	44021	Standardsburg	44847
Shaker Crossing (Part of		Skyview Acres	43968	South Olive	43724	Standley	43527
Kettering)	45429	Slabtown	45801	South Park (Allen County)	45804	Stanleyville	45788
Shaker Heights	44120	Slate Mills	45601	South Park (Cuyahoga		Stanwood	44662
Shalersville (Township)	44266	Slaters	43724	County)	44131	Starbucktown	45177
Shalersville	44255	Sligo	45177	South Park (Wyandot		Starlight Plaza (Part of	
Shandon	45063	Slocums	45662	County)	43351	Sylvania)	43560
Shane	43944	Smith (Belmont County)		South Perry	43135	Starr (Township)	45764
Shanesville (Part of		(Township)	43718	South Plymouth	43160	Starr	45654
Sugarcreek)	44681	Smith (Mahoning County)		South Point	45680	Starrs Corners	44406
Shannon	43821	(Township)	44672	Southridge	45505	State Road (Part of	
Sharon (Franklin County)		Smith Corners	44515	South Russell	44022	Cuyahoga Falls)	44223
(Township)	43085	Smithfield (Township)	43948	South Salem	45681	Staunton (Fayette County)	43160
Sharon (Medina County)		Smithfield	43948	South Shore Acres	45885	Staunton (Miami County)	45373
(Township)	44274	Smithfield (railroad station)	43943	South Shore Park (Part of		Staunton (Miami County)	
Sharon (Noble County)		Smithville (Wayne County)	44677	Oregon)	43618	(Township)	45373
(Township)	43724	Smithville (Wyandot		South Side (Mahoning		Steam Corners	44904
Sharon (Noble County)		County)	43351	County)	44507	Steinersville	43942
(Township)	43724	Smyrna	43973	South Side (Tuscarawas		Stella	45622
Sharon (Richland County)		Snodes	44609	County)	44663	Stelvideo	45331
(Township)	44875	Snowville	45710	South Solon	43153	Sterling (Brown County)	
Sharon Center	44274	Snyder Terrace (Part of		South Vienna	45369	(Township)	45154
Sharon Hills	43085	Springfield)	45504	South Webster	45682	Sterling (Wayne County)	44276
Sharon Park (Allen		Snyderville	45502	Southwest (Part of		Sterling Heights	45005
County)	45805	Soaptown	44440	Mansfield)	44907	Steuben	44847
Sharon Park (Butler		Socialville	45050	South West Hubbard	44425	Steubenville	43952
County)	45013	Soldiers Home	44870	Southwood	45805	Steubenville (Township)	43952
Sharonville	45241*	Solon	44139	South Woodbury	43334	Stewart	45778
	45262†	Somerdale	44678	Southworth	45833	Stewartsville	43960
Sharon West	44438	Somerford (Township)	43044	Southwyck Shopping		Stillwater	44679
Sharpeye	45331	Somers (Township)	45311	Center (Part of Toledo)	43614	Stillwell	44637
Sharpsburg	45777	Somerset (Belmont		South Zanesville	43701	Stiversville	45770
Shartz Road	45005	County) (Township)	43713	Spargursville	45612	Stock (Harrison County)	
Shauck	43349	Somerset (Perry County)	43783	Sparta	43350	(Township)	43988
Shawnee (Allen County)		Somersville	43067	Speaker's Addition	43952	Stock (Noble County)	
(Township)	45805	Somerton	43713	Speidel	43719	(Township)	43724
Shawnee (Perry County)	43782	Somerville	45064	Spencer (Allen County)		Stockdale	45683
Shawnee Hills (Delaware		Sonora	43701	(Township)	45887	Stockham	45694
County)	43065	South Amherst	44001	Spencer (Guernsey		Stockport	43787
Shawnee Hills (Greene		South Arlington (Part of		County) (Township)	43732	Stockton (Part of Fairfield)	45014
County)	45335	Akron)	44306	Spencer (Lucas County)		Stock Yards (Part of	
Shawnee Meadows	45806	South Bay	43019	(Township)	43528	Cincinnati)	45225
Shawtown	45858	South Bloomfield (Morrow		Spencer (Medina County)	44275	Stokes (Logan County)	
Shawville (Part of North		County) (Township)	43050	Spencer (Medina County)		(Township)	43331
Ridgeville)	44035	South Bloomfield		(Township)	44275	Stokes (Madison County)	
Shay	45767	(Pickaway County)	43103	Spencerville	45887	(Township)	43153
Sheffield (Ashtabula		South Bloomingville	43152	Spokane	44402	Stone	43720
County) (Township)	44048	South Boy	43019	Spreading Oaks	45701	Stone Creek	43840
Sheffield (Lorain County)		Southbrook	45409	Spreng	44840	Stonelick (Township)	45103
(Township)	44054	South Brooklyn (Part of		Sprigg (Township)	45144	Stonelick	45103
Sheffield (Lorain County)	44054	Cleveland)	44109	Springboro	45066	Stony Lake	44615
Sheffield Lake	44054	South Canal	44444	Springbrook	43464	Stony Prairie	43420
Shelby	44875	South Charleston	45368	Springcreek (Township)	45356	Stony Ridge	43463
Shelby Junction (Part of		South Columbus (Part of		Springdale	45246	Stonyrill	45005
Shelby)	44875	Columbus)	43207	Springfield (Clark County)	45501-06	Storms	45612
Shell Beach	43076	South Condit	43074	For specific Springfield Zip		Stout	45684
Shenandoah	44837	Southdale (Part of		Codes call (513) 323-6496, or		Stoutsville	43154
Shepard (Part of		Kettering)	45429	your local postmaster.		Stovertown	43701
Columbus)	43219	Southeastern Coporational		Springfield (Clark County)		Stow	44224
Shepherdstown	43950	Institution	43130	(Township)	45505	Strasburg	44680
Sheridan	45680						

	ZIP
Stratford	43015
Stratton	43961
Streetsboro	44241
Stringtown (Athens County)	45701
Stringtown (Brown County)	45167
Stringtown (Clermont County)	45120
Stringtown (Muskingum County)	43701
Stringtown (Perry County)	43731
Strongs Ridge	44811
Strongsville	44136
Struthers	44471
Stryker	43557
Stuart Manor	43952
Suffield (Township)	44260
Suffield	44260
Sugar Bush Knolls	44240
Sugar Creek (Allen County) (Township)	45807
Sugar Creek (Athens County)	45701
Sugar Creek (Greene County) (Township)	45305
Sugar Creek (Putnam County) (Township)	45830
Sugar Creek (Stark County) (Township)	44662
Sugarcreek (Tuscarawas County)	44681
Sugar Creek (Tuscarawas County) (Township)	44681
Sugar Creek (Wayne County) (Township)	44618
Sugar Grove (Crawford County)	44820
Sugar Grove (Fairfield County)	43155
Sugar Grove (Jefferson County)	43964
Sugar Grove (Miami County)	45318
Sugar Grove (Scioto County)	45663
Sugar Grove Hill	45506
Sugar Ridge	43402
Sugar Tree Ridge	45133
Sugar Valley	45320
Sullivan	44880
Sullivan (Township)	44880
Sulphurgrove (Part of Huber Heights)	45424
Sulphur Springs (Crawford County)	44881
Sulphur Springs (Perry County)	43782
Summerfield	43788
Summerford	43140
Summerside	45244
Summerside Estates	45244
Summit (Hamilton County)	45238
Summit (Monroe County) (Township)	43754
Summit (Ross County)	45601
Summit (Trumbull County)	44420
Summithill	45601
Summit Mall (Part of Fairlawn)	44333
Summit Station	43073
Summitville	43962
Sumner	45720
Sunbury (Delaware County)	43074
Sunbury (Montgomery County)	45327
Sundale	43767
Sunfish (Township)	45661
Sunny Acres	43952
Sunnyland	45502
Sunny Meade	43725
Sunnyside Beach (Part of Vermilion)	44089
Sunsbury (Township)	43716
Sunset Beach	44429
Sunset Heights	43912
Sunset Point	44077
Sunshine	45684
Sunshine Park	43952
Sun Valley Estates	45505
Superior (Township)	43543
Surrey Hill	44484
Sutton (Township)	45771
Swan (Township)	45622
Swan Creek (Township)	43558
Swanders	45369
Swanktown	45309
Swanton (Fulton County)	43558

	ZIP
Swanton (Lucas County) (Township)	43558
Swickards Additions	43952
Swifton Commons (Part of Cincinnati)	45237
Switzerland (Township)	43942
Sybene	45680
Sycamore (Hamilton County) (Township)	45242
Sycamore (Hamilton County)	45242
Sycamore (Wyandot County)	44882
Sycamore (Wyandot County) (Township)	44882
Sycamore Valley	43789
Sychar Road	43050
Sylvania (Township)	43560
Sylvania	43560
Symmes (Butler County)	45014
Symmes (Hamilton County) (Township)	45242
Symmes (Lawrence County) (Township)	45688
Syracuse	45779
Taborville	44022
Tacoma	43713
Taft	45236
Tallmadge	44278
Tama	45822
Tarlton	43156
Tate (Township)	45106
Tatmans	43730
Tawawa	45365
Taylor (Franklin County)	43230
Taylor (Union County) (Township)	43344
Taylor Creek (Township)	43326
Taylorsburg	45315
Taylors Creek	45239
Taylorsville	45133
Taylortown (Jefferson County)	43964
Taylortown (Richland County)	44875
Tedrow	43567
Teegarden	44432
Temperanceville	43713
Ten Hills	45805
Tennyson	45661
Terrace Park	45174
Terre Haute	43078
Terry Acres	45324
Texas (Crawford County) (Township)	44882
Texas (Henry County)	43532
Thackery	43078
Thatcher	43113
The Avenue	44438
The Bend	43512
The Eastern	43908
Thelma City	44601
The Plains	45780
The Village of Indian Hill	45243
Thompson (Delaware County) (Township)	43066
Thompson (Geauga County)	44086
Thompson (Geauga County) (Township)	44086
Thompson (Seneca County) (Township)	44828
Thorn (Township)	43076
Thornville	43076
Thorny Acres	45042
Three Locks	45601
Thrifton	45123
Thurman	45685
Thurston	43157
Tiffany Acres	45502
Tiffin (Adams County) (Township)	45693
Tiffin (Defiance County) (Township)	43512
Tiffin (Seneca County)	44883
Tiltonsville	43963
Timberlake	44094
Timberview	43040
Tinny	43435
Tipp City	45371
Tippecanoe	44699
Tipton	45851
Tiro	44887
Tiverton (Township)	43006
Tiverton	43006
Toboso	43055
Tod (Township)	44882
Todds	43728
Toledo	43601-15
	43617

	ZIP
	43620-99
For specific Toledo Zip Codes call (419) 245-6951, or your local postmaster.	
Toledo Dock (Part of Oregon)	43618
Toledo Great Eastern Shopping Center (Part of Northwood)	43616
Toledo Miracle Mile Shopping Center (Part of Toledo)	43613
Tom Corwin	45692
Tomlison Addition	45648
Tontogany	43565
Torch	45781
Toronto	43964
Town and Country Estates	45429
Town and Country Shopping Center (Part of Whitehall)	43213
Townsend (Huron County) (Township)	44826
Townsend (Sandusky County) (Township)	43464
Townview	45427
Townwood	45856
Tradersville	43044
Trail	44624
Trail Run	43946
Tranquility	45679
Traschel	43302
Trebein (Part of Beavercreek)	45434
Tremont City	45372
Trenton (Butler County)	45067
Trenton (Delaware County) (Township)	43021
Triadelphia	43758
Tri-County Mall (Part of Springdale)	45246
Trimble	45782
Trimble (Township)	45782
Trinway	43842
Tri-Village (Part of Columbus)	43212
Trotwood	45426
Trowbridge	43432
Troy (Ashland County) (Township)	44859
Troy (Athens County) (Township)	45723
Troy (Delaware County) (Township)	43015
Troy (Geauga County) (Township)	44021
Troy (Miami County)	45373
Troy (Morrow County) (Township)	44901
Troy (Richland County) (Township)	44904
Troy (Wood County) (Township)	43443
Truetown	45761
Trumbull	44041
Trumbull (Township)	44041
Truro	43068
Truro (Township)	43068
Tuckaho	44003
Tucson	45601
Tully (Marion County) (Township)	43314
Tully (Van Wert County) (Township)	45832
Tunnel	45750
Tunnel Hill	43844
Tuppers Plains	45783
Turnpike Interchange	44444
Turpin Hills	45244
Turtle Creek (Shelby County) (Township)	45365
Turtle Creek (Warren County) (Township)	45036
Tuscalum (Part of Cincinnati)	45226
Tuscarawas (Coshocton County) (Township)	43812
Tuscarawas (Stark County) (Township)	44646
Tuscarawas (Tuscarawas County)	44682
Twain	44212
Twenty Mile Stand	45140
Twightwee	45140
Twin (Darke County) (Township)	45304
Twin (Preble County) (Township)	45381

	ZIP
Twin (Ross County) (Township)	45617
Twin Lakes (Allen County)	45804
Twin Lakes (Portage County)	44240
Twinsburg	44087
Twinsburg (Township)	44087
Twinsburg Heights	44087
Twin Valley	45662
Two Hundred Ten Row	45701
Tymochtee (Township)	44882
Tymochtee	43351
Tyndall	43812
Uhrichsville	44683
Union (Athens County)	45766
Union (Auglaize County) (Township)	45895
Union (Belmont County) (Township)	43759
Union (Brown County) (Township)	45167
Union (Butler County) (Township)	45069
Union (Carroll County) (Township)	44615
Union (Champaign County) (Township)	43009
Union (Clermont County) (Township)	45245
Union (Clinton County) (Township)	45177
Union (Fayette County) (Township)	43160
Union (Hancock County) (Township)	45881
Union (Highland County) (Township)	45133
Union (Knox County) (Township)	43014
Union (Lawrence County) (Township)	45619
Union (Licking County) (Township)	43025
Union (Logan County) (Township)	43311
Union (Madison County) (Township)	43140
Union (Mercer County) (Township)	45862
Union (Miami County) (Township)	45383
Union (Montgomery County)	45322
Union (Morgan County) (Township)	43758
Union (Muskingum County) (Township)	43762
Union (Pike County) (Township)	45648
Union (Putnam County) (Township)	45844
Union (Ross County) (Township)	45628
Union (Scioto County) (Township)	45652
Union (Tuscarawas County) (Township)	44621
Union (Union County) (Township)	43045
Union (Van Wert County) (Township)	45891
Union (Warren County) (Township)	45036
Union City	45390
Union Furnace	43158
Union Landing Siding	45638
Union Plains	45154
Unionport	43966
Union Station	43025
Uniontown (Belmont County)	43950
Uniontown (Stark County)	44685
Unionvale	43907
Unionville (Ashtabula County)	44088
Unionville (Morgan County)	43756
Unionville (Washington County)	45750
Unionville Center	43077
Uniopolis	45888
Unity (Adams County)	45693
Unity (Columbiana County)	44413
Unity (Columbiana County) (Township)	44413
University (Part of Columbus)	43210
University Center (Part of Cleveland)	44106

	ZIP
University Heights (Allen County)	45804
University Heights (Cuyahoga County)	44118
University View	43212
Upland Heights	43943
Upper (Township)	45645
Upper Arlington (Butler County)	45042
Upper Arlington (Franklin County)	43221
Upper Five Mile	45154
Upper Fox Hollow	45502
Upper Lowell	45744
Upper Sandusky	43351
Urbana	43078
Urbana (Township)	43078
Urbancrest	43123
Utica (Licking County)	43080
Utica (Warren County)	45036
Utopia	45121
Valley (Columbiana County)	44460
Valley (Guernsey County) (Township)	43772
Valley (Scioto County) (Township)	45648
Valley City	44280
Valley City Station	44280
Valley Crossing (Part of Columbus)	43207
Valleydale (Part of Cincinnati)	45216
Valley Forge	44212
Valley Glen	43938
Valley Hi	43360
Valley View (Cuyahoga County)	44131
Valleyview (Franklin County)	43204
Valley View (Jefferson County)	43910
Valley View (Scioto County)	45662
Valley View Estates	44403
Valley View Heights	45244
Valley View Village	43701
Valleywood (Part of Beavercreek)	45430
Vanatta	43055
Van Buren (Darke County) (Township)	45304
Van Buren (Hancock County)	45889
Van Buren (Hancock County) (Township)	45897
Vanburen (Licking County)	43055
Van Buren (Putnam County) (Township)	45856
Van Buren (Shelby County) (Township)	45336
Vandalia	45377
Vanlue	45890
Van Wert	45891
Vaughan (Part of Evendale)	45241
Vaughnsville	45893
Vega	45685
Venedocia	45894
Venice (Erie County)	44870
Venice (Seneca County) (Township)	44807
Venice Heights	44484
Vera Cruz	45118
Vermilion	44089
Vermilion (Township)	44089
Vermilion-on-the-Lake (Part of Vermilion)	44089
Vermillion (Township)	44805
Vernon (Clinton County) (Township)	45113
Vernon (Crawford County) (Township)	44827
Vernon (Lawrence County)	45659
Vernon (Richland County)	44875
Vernon (Scioto County) (Township)	45694
Vernon (Trumbull County)	44428
Vernon (Trumbull County) (Township)	44428
Vernon Heights (Part of Marion)	43302
Verona	45378
Versailles	45380
Vesuvius	45659
Veterans Administration	45428
Veterans Administration Medical Center	45601

	ZIP
Veto	45714
Vickery	43464
Vicksville	45732
Vienna	44473
Vienna (Township)	44473
Vienna Center	44473
Vigo	45601
Viking Village	45244
Villa	45503
Villa Nova	45885
Vincent (Lorain County)	44035
Vincent (Washington County)	45784
Vinton	45686
Vinton (Township)	45670
Violet (Township)	43147
Virginia (Township)	43811
Vo-Ash Lake	44615
Volunteer Bay	44089
Vore Ridge	45780
Wabash (Darke County) (Township)	45380
Wabash (Mercer County)	45822
Wacker Heights	43130
Waco	44707
Wade	45767
Wadsworth	44281
Wadsworth (Township)	44281
Waggoner Place	43551
Wagram	43062
Wahlsburg	45121
Wainwright (Jackson County)	45692
Wainwright (Tuscarawas County)	44663
Waite Hill	44094
Wakatomika	43821
Wakefield (Darke County)	45331
Wakefield (Pike County)	45687
Wakeman	44889
Wakeman (Township)	44889
Walbridge	43465
Waldo	43356
Waldo (Township)	43356
Walhonding (Coshocton County)	43843
Walhonding (Guernsey County)	43772
Wallace Heights	43964
Walnut (Fairfield County) (Township)	43046
Walnut (Gallia County) (Township)	45658
Walnut (Pickaway County) (Township)	43103
Walnut Creek	44687
Walnut Creek (Township)	44687
Walnut Grove	43358
Walnut Hills (Hamilton County)	45206
Walnut Hills (Jackson County)	45640
Walnut Hills (Stark County)	44646
Walnutrun	43140
Walton Hills	44146
Wamsley	45657
Wapakoneta	45895
Ward (Township)	43144
Wardwood Acres	45239
Warner	45745
Warnock	43967
Warren (Belmont County) (Township)	43713
Warren (Jefferson County) (Township)	43943
Warren (Trumbull County)	44481-85
For specific Warren Zip Codes call (216) 392-1571, or your local postmaster.	
Warren (Trumbull County) (Township)	44430
Warren (Tuscarawas County) (Township)	44656
Warren (Washington County) (Township)	45750
Warren Correctional Institution	45036
Warrensburg	43061
Warrensville Heights	44122
Warrenton	43943
Warsaw	43844
Warwick (Summit County)	44216
Warwick (Tuscarawas County) (Township)	44663
Washington (Auglaize County) (Township)	45871
Washington (Belmont County) (Township)	43716

	ZIP
Washington (Brown County) (Township)	45171
Washington (Carroll County) (Township)	44615
Washington (Clermont County) (Township)	45153
Washington (Clinton County) (Township)	45114
Washington (Columbiana County) (Township)	43945
Washington (Coshocton County) (Township)	43842
Washington (Darke County) (Township)	47390
Washington (Defiance County) (Township)	43549
Washington (Franklin County) (Township)	43017
Washington (Guernsey County) (Township)	43749
Washington (Hancock County) (Township)	45830
Washington (Hardin County) (Township)	45835
Washington (Harrison County) (Township)	44699
Washington (Henry County) (Township)	43532
Washington (Highland County) (Township)	45133
Washington (Hocking County) (Township)	43138
Washington (Holmes County) (Township)	44638
Washington (Jackson County) (Township)	45692
Washington (Lawrence County) (Township)	45656
Washington (Licking County) (Township)	43080
Washington (Logan County) (Township)	43348
Washington (Lucas County) (Township)	43612
Washington (Mercer County) (Township)	45828
Washington (Miami County) (Township)	45356
Washington (Monroe County) (Township)	45734
Washington (Montgomery County) (Township)	45459
Washington (Morrow County) (Township)	43338
Washington (Muskingum County) (Township)	43701
Washington (Paulding County) (Township)	45859
Washington (Pickaway County) (Township)	43113
Washington (Preble County) (Township)	45320
Washington (Richland County) (Township)	44906
Washington (Sandusky County) (Township)	43442
Washington (Scioto County) (Township)	45663
Washington (Shelby County) (Township)	45365
Washington (Stark County) (Township)	44601
Washington (Tuscarawas County) (Township)	43832
Washington (Union County) (Township)	43344
Washington (Van Wert County) (Township)	45833
Washington (Warren County) (Township)	45054
Washington (Wood County) (Township)	43565
Washington Court House	43160
Washingtonville	44490
Waterford (Knox County)	43019
Waterford (Washington County)	45786
Waterford (Washington County) (Township)	45786
Waterloo (Athens County) (Township)	45766
Waterloo (Fairfield County)	43110
Waterloo (Lawrence County)	45688
Watertown	45787
Watertown (Township)	45787
Waterville	43566
Waterville (Township)	43566
Watkins	43040
Wattsville	44615

	ZIP
Wauseon	43567
Waverly	45690
Waverly Gables	45690
Way	45734
Wayland	44285
Wayne (Adams County) (Township)	45618
Wayne (Ashtabula County)	44093
Wayne (Ashtabula County) (Township)	44093
Wayne (Auglaize County) (Township)	45896
Wayne (Belmont County) (Township)	43747
Wayne (Butler County) (Township)	45042
Wayne (Champaign County) (Township)	43009
Wayne (Clermont County) (Township)	45122
Wayne (Clinton County) (Township)	45138
Wayne (Columbiana County) (Township)	44432
Wayne (Darke County) (Township)	45380
Wayne (Fayette County) (Township)	45123
Wayne (Jefferson County) (Township)	43910
Wayne (Knox County) (Township)	43019
Wayne (Monroe County) (Township)	45734
Wayne (Muskingum County) (Township)	43701
Wayne (Noble County) (Township)	43773
Wayne (Pickaway County) (Township)	43113
Wayne (Tuscarawas County) (Township)	44624
Wayne (Warren County) (Township)	45068
Wayne (Wayne County) (Township)	44691
Wayne (Wood County) (Township)	43466
Wayne Lakes	45331
Waynesburg (Crawford County)	44887
Waynesburg (Stark County)	44688
Waynesfield	45896
Waynesville	45068
Weathersfield (Township)	44420
Weaver Station	45331
Webb Heights	43947
Webb Summit	43138
Webster (Darke County)	45309
Webster (Wood County) (Township)	43450
Wegee	43947
Welcome	44637
Weller (Township)	44903
Wellington	44090
Wellington (Township)	44090
Wellington Park	45231
Wellman	45068
Wells (Township)	43913
Wellston	45692
Wellsville	43968
Welshfield	44021
Welshtown	45769
Wengerlawn	45309
Wernert (Part of Toledo)	43613
Wesley (Township)	45713
Wesleyan Woods (Part of Delaware)	43015
West (Township)	44625
West Akron (Part of Akron)	44307
West Alexandria	45381
West Andover	44003
West Bass Lake	44024
West Bedford	43844
West Bellaire (Part of Bellaire)	43906
West Berlin	43015
Westboro	45148
West Brookfield (Part of Massillon)	44646
West Carlisle (Coshocton County)	43822
West Carlisle (Lorain County)	44035
West Carrollton	45449
West Charleston	45371
West Chesapeake	45619

* Area Zip Code   † Post Office Boxes

	ZIP		ZIP		ZIP		ZIP
West Chester (Butler County)	45069*	West Unity	43570	Williamstown	45897	Woodville Gardens	43616
	45071††	Westview	44028	Williston	43468	Woodville Mall (Part of	
West Chester		Westville (Champaign		Willoughby	44094-95	Northwood)	43619
(Tuscarawas County)	44699	County)	43083	For specific Willoughby Zip		Woodworth	44512
West Clarksfield	44889	Westville (Columbiana		Codes call (216) 942-9420, or		Woodworth Corners	44473
West Covington	45318	County)	44609	your local postmaster.		Wooster	44691
West Elkton	45070	Westville Lake	44609	Willoughby Hills	44092	Wooster (Township)	44691
West End (Part of		West Warren (Part of		Willow (Part of Cleveland)	44127	Wooster Heights	44903
Ashtabula)	44004	Warren)	44485	Willow (Part of Cuyahoga		Worstville	45880
West Enon Estates	45323	West Wheeling	43906	Heights)	44125	Worthington (Franklin	
Westerly Park	45805	West Williamsfield	44093	Willow Brook Heights	44721	County)	43085
Western Hills	45238	Westwood (Hamilton		Willowcrest	44452	Worthington (Richland	
Western Hills Plaza (Part		County)	45211	Willowdale Lake	44720	County) (Township)	44822
of Cincinnati)	45211	Westwood (Jefferson		Willowdell	45380	Wren	45899
Western Reserve Estates	44236	County)	43952	Willow Grove	43906	Wright Brothers (Part of	
Westerville	43081-82	Westwood (Wayne		Willowick	44094	Oakwood)	45409
	43086	County)	44691	Willow Lakes	44701	Wright-Patterson Air Force	
For specific Westerville Zip		Westwood Estates (Part		Willowville	45103	Base	45433
Codes call (614) 882-2243, or		of Steubenville)	43952	Willow Wood	45696	Wrightsville (Adams	
your local postmaster.		West Woodville	45107	Wills (Township)	43755	County)	45144
West Fairport (Part of		West Worthington	43234-35	Wills Creek	43811	Wrightsville (Franklin	
Grand River)	44045	For specific West Worthington		Willshire	45898	County)	43123
West Farmington	44491	Zip Codes call (614) 793-8789,		Willshire (Township)	45898	Wrightview (Part of	
Westfield (Columbiana		or your local postmaster.		Wilmington	45177	Fairborn)	45324
County)	43920	Wetzel	45863	Wilmot	44689	Wyandot	44849
Westfield (Medina County)		Weymouth	44256	Wilshire	45122	Wyoming	45215
(Township)	44251	Wharton	43359	Wilshire Heights	45005	Wyoming Meadows	45231
Westfield (Morrow		Wheat Ridge	45693	Wilson (Clinton County)		Xavier (Part of Cincinnati)	45207
County)	43003	Wheelersburg	45694	(Township)	45169	Xenia	45385
Westfield (Morrow		Wheeling (Belmont		Wilson (Monroe County)	43716	Xenia (Township)	45385
County) (Township)	43003	County) (Township)	43927	Wiltondale	45224	Yale (Ottawa County)	43468
Westfield Center	44251	Wheeling (Guernsey		Winameg	43515	Yale (Portage County)	44411
West Florence	45320	County) (Township)	43749	Winchester (Adams		Yankeeburg	45768
Westgate Mall (Part of		Whetstone (Township)	44820	County)	45697	Yankee Hills	44403
Fairview Park)	44126	Whigville	43788	Winchester (Admas		Yankee Lake	44403
Westgate Village		Whipple	45788	County) (Township)	45697	Yankeetown	45130
Shopping Center (Part		Whisler	45644	Winchester (Jackson		Yatesville	43106
of Toledo)	43606	White Cottage	43791	County)	45640	Yellowbud	45601
West Hill	44403	White Eyes (Township)	43824	Windfall Heights	44256	Yellow Creek (Columbiana	
Westhope	43516	White Hall (Athens		Windham	44288	County) (Township)	43968
West Independence	44802	County)	45701	Windham (Township)	44288	Yellow Creek (Jefferson	
West Jefferson (Madison		Whitehall (Franklin		Windor Park (Part of		County)	43968
County)	43162	County)	43213	Xenia)	45385	Yellow Springs	45387
West Jefferson (Williams		Whitehouse	43571	Windsor	44099	Yellowtown	43731
County)	43543	White Oak (Brown		Windsor (Township)	44099	Yelverton	43326
West Lafayette	43845	County)	45154	Windsor (Lawrence		Yoder	45806
Westlake	44145	Whiteoak (Fayette		County) (Township)	45678	York (Athens County)	
West Lakeville (Part of		County)	43143	Windsor (Morgan County)		(Township)	45764
Conneaut)	44030	White Oak (Hamilton		(Township)	43787	York (Belmont County)	
West Lancaster	43128	County)	45239	Windsor (Richland		(Township)	43942
Westland (Township)	43725	Whiteoak (Highland		County)	44903	York (Darke County)	
West Lebanon	44618	County) (Township)	45133	Windsor (Warren County)	45162	(Township)	45380
West Leipsic	45856	White Oak East	45239	Windsor Mills	44099	York (Fulton County)	
West Liberty (Crawford		White Oak Meadows	45239	Windy Acres	45502	(Township)	43515
County)	44887	White Oaks (Part of		Winesburg	44690	York (Jefferson County)	43901
West Liberty (Logan		Steubenville)	43952	Winfield	44622	York (Medina County)	
County)	43357	White Oak Valley	45121	Wingett Run	45789	(Township)	44256
West Liberty (Morrow		White Oak West	45239	Wingston	43462	York (Morgan County)	
County)	43334	White Pond	44321	Winona	44493	(Township)	43731
West Lodi	44811	White's Landing	43464	Winterdale (Part of		York (Sandusky County)	
West Logan	43138	White Sulphur	43061	Wintersville)	43952	(Township)	44811
West Manchester	45382	Whitetree (Part of		Winterhaven	45305	York (Tuscarawas County)	
West Mansfield	43358	Cincinnati)	45236	Winterset	43755	(Township)	44663
West Marietta (Part of		Whitewater	45002	Wintersville	43952	York (Union County)	
Marietta)	45750	Whitewater (Township)	45002	Wintondale	45231	(Township)	43067
West Marysville (Part of		Whitfield	45342	Winton Place (Part of		York (Van Wert County)	
Marysville)	43040	Wick	44093	Cincinnati)	45232	(Township)	45874
West Mecca	44410	Wickliffe (Lake County)	44092	Winton Place (Part of St.		York Center	43067
West Middletown	45042	Wickliffe (Mahoning		Bernard)	45216	Yorkshire	45388
West Millgrove	43467	County)	44515	Winton Terrace (Part of		Yorkshire Estates	43302
West Milton	45383	Widowville	44805	Cincinnati)	45232	Yorkville	43971
Westminster	45850	Wiggonsville	45106	Wisterman	45831	Young Hickory	43732
Westmoor	44833	Wightmans Grove	43420	Withamsville	45245	Youngs	45657
West Newton	45850	Wilberforce	45384	Wolf	43832	Youngs Corners	44256
Weston	43569	Wildare	44410	Wolfhurst	43912	Youngstown	44501-15
Weston (Township)	43569	Wildbrook Acres	45231	Wolf Run	43970	For specific Youngstown Zip	
West Park (Cuyahoga		Wildwood (Part of		Woodbourne	45459	Codes call (216) 744-6805, or	
County)	44111	Middletown)	45042	Woodbourne-Hyde Park	45429	your local postmaster.	
West Park (Hancock		Wilgus	45696	Woodhaven	45005	Youngsville	45679
County)	45840	Wilkesville	45695	Woodington	45331	Zahns Corners	45690
West Park (Jefferson		Wilkesville (Township)	45695	Woodlawn (Hamilton		Zaleski	45698
County)	43952	Wilkins Corners	43055	County)	45215	Zane (Township)	43336
West Park (Stark County)	44646	Wilkshire Hills	44612	Woodlawn (Miami County)	45373	Zane Addition	45601
West Point (Columbiana		Willard	44890	Woodlawn Village	45373	Zanesfield	43360
County)	44492	Willetsville	45133	Woodmere	44122	Zanesville	43701-02
West Point (Morrow		Williamsburg	45176	Woodridge Plaza (Part of		For specific Zanesville Zip	
County)	44833	Williamsburg (Township)	45176	Fairfield)	45014	Codes call (614) 455-2802, or	
West Portsmouth	45663	Williams Center	43506	Woods	45056	your local postmaster.	
West Richfield (Part of		Williams Corner	45103	Woodsdale	45067	Zenz City	45846
Richfield)	44286	Williamsdale	45011	Woodsfield	43793	Zimmer Estates	45431
West Rushville	43163	Williamsfield	44093	Woodside	43406	Zimmerman (Part of	
West Salem	44287	Williamsfield (Township)	44093	Woodstock	43084	Beavercreek)	45434
West Side (Part of		Williamsport (Columbiana		Woodville (Clermont		Ziontown	43076
Youngstown)	44509	County)	44432	County)	45122	Zoar (Tuscarawas County)	44697
West Sonora	45338	Williamsport (Morrow		Woodville (Sandusky		Zoar (Warren County)	45152
West Toledo (Part of		County)	43338	County)	43469	Zoarville	44656
Toledo)	43612	Williamsport (Pickaway		Woodville (Sandusky		Zone	43521
West Union	45693	County)	43164	County) (Township)	43469		

	ZIP		ZIP		ZIP		ZIP
Achille	74720	Bethel Acres	74801	Caney Ridge	74471	Connerville	74836
Acme	73082	Big Cabin	74332	Canton	73724	Conser	74937
Ada	74820*	Big Cedar	74939	Canute	73626	Cookietown	73562
	74821†	Big Spring	74883	Capitol Hill (Part of		Cookson	74427
Adair	74330	Billings	74630	Oklahoma City)	73109	Cooperton	73564
Adams	73901	Binger	73009	Capron	73725	Copan	74022
Adamson	74547	Bison	73720	Cardin	74335	Corbett	73051
Addington	73520	Bixby	74008	Carleton	73772	Cordell	73632
Afton	74331	Blackburn	74058	Carmen	73726	Corinne	74735
Agawam	73067	Blackgum	74962	Carnegie	73015	Corn	73024
Agra	74824	Blackwell	74631	Carney	74832	Cornish	73456
Ahloso	74820	Blair	73526	Carpenter	73644	Corum	73529
Ahpeatone	73572	Blanchard	73010	Carriage Hills (Part of		Cottonwood	74538
Akins	74955	Blanco	74528	Lawton)	73501	Council Hill	74428
Albany	74721	Blocker	74529	Carrier	73727	Countyline	73025
Albert	73001	Blue	74701	Carson	74850	Courtney	73456
Albion	74521	Bluejacket	74333	Carter (Beckham County)	73627	Covington	73730
Alderson	74522	Bluff	74759	Carter (Cherokee County)	74451	Cowden	73632
Aledo	73654	Boatman	74361	Cartersville	74941	Coweta	74429
Alex	73002	Boehler	74727	Cartwright	74731	Cowlington	74941
Alfalfa	73015	Boggy Depot	74525	Cashion	73016	Cox City	73082
Aline	73716	Bois D'Arc	74601	Castle	74833	Coyle	73027
Allen	74825	Boise City	73933	Catale	74332	Cravens	74563
Allison	74730	Bokchito	74726	Catoosa	74015	Crawford	73638
Alluwe	74048	Bokhoma	74740	Cedar Crest	74352	Creosote	74743
Alma	73533	Bokoshe	74930	Cedar Ridge (Part of		Crescent	73028
Altus	73521-23	Boley	74829	Cleveland)	74020	Criner	73080
For specific Altus Zip Codes		Bond	74426	Cedar Valley	73044	Cromwell	74837
call (405) 482-3339, or your		Boone	73006	Cement	73017	Crossbow (Part of Tulsa)	74146
local postmaster.		Boss	74745	Center	74820	Crossroads Mall (Part of	
Alva	73717	Boswell	74727	Center City (Part of		Oklahoma City)	73149
Amber	73004	Boulevard (Part of		Oklahoma City)	73101†	Crowder	74430
Ames	73718	Norman)	73069		73102*	Crystal	74555
Amorita	73719	Bowden	74107	Centerview	74801	Crystal Lakes	73718
Anadarko	73005	Bowlegs	74830	Centrahoma	74534	Cumberland	73446
Antioch	73035	Bowlin Spring	74016	Centralia	74301	Curchece	74020
Antlers	74523	Bowring	74009	Central Mall (Part of		Curt's Shopping Center	
Apache	73006	Box	74962	Lawton)	73501	(Part of Muskogee)	74403
Apperson	74633	Boynton	74422	Ceres	74651	Cushing	74023
Apple	74760	Braden	74959	Cerrogordo	74740	Custer City	73639
Arapaho	73620	Bradley	73011	Cestos	73859	Cyril	73029
Arcadia	73007	Brady	73098	Chandler	74834	Dacoma	73731
Ardmore	73401-03	Braggs	74423	Chase	74401	Daisy	74540
For specific Ardmore Zip Codes		Braman	74632	Chattanooga	73528	Dale	74851
call (405) 223-8383, or your		Bray	73012	Checotah	74426	Damon	74578
local postmaster.		Breckenridge	73701	Chelsea	74016	Darwin	74523
Arkoma	74901	Brent	74955	Cherokee	73728	Davenport	74026
Arlington	74864	Briartown	74455	Cherry Tree	74960	Davidson	73530
Armstrong	74729	Bridgeport	73047	Chester	73838	Davis	73030
Arnett (Ellis County)	73832	Briggs	74464	Chewey	74964	Dawson (Part of Tulsa)	74115
Arnett (Harmon County)	73550	Brinkman	73673	Cheyenne	73628	Deer Creek	74636
Arpelar	74548	Bristow	74010	Chickasha	73018*	Degnan	74578
Artillery Village	73503	Britton (Part of Oklahoma			73023†	Delaware	74027
Asher	74826	City)	73114	Childers	74027	Del City	73115
Ashland	74570	Brock	73401	Chilli	74578	Delhi	73662
Atoka	74525	Broken Arrow	74011-14	Chilocco	74647	Dempsey	73628
Atwood	74827	For specific Broken Arrow Zip		Chitwood	73067	Dennis	74301
Avant	74001	Codes call (918) 258-6626, or		Choctaw	73020	Depew	74028
Avard	73717	your local postmaster.		Chouteau	74337	Depot	74501
Avery	74023	Broken Bow	74728	Christie	74965	Devol	73531
Bache	74526	Bromide	74530	Cimarron (Part of		Dewar	74431
Bacone (Part of		Brooken	74462	Oklahoma City)	73111	Dewey	74029
Muskogee)	74401	Brooksville	74873	Cimarron City	73028	Dibble	73031
Bailey	73055	Brown	74701	Cisco	74745	Dickson	73401
Baker	73950	Broxton	73006	Citra	74825	Dighton	74437
Baldhill	74447	Brush Hill	74426	Claremore	74017*	Dillard	73463
Balko	73931	Brushy	74955		74018†	Dill City	73641
Ballard	74964	Bryant	74880	Clarita	74535	Disney	74340
Banner (Part of El Reno)	73036	Buffalo (Harper County)	73834	Clarksville	74454	Dixon	74884
Banty	74723	Buffalo (McCurtain		Clayton	74536	Donaldson (Part of Tulsa)	74104
Barber	74471	County)	74963	Clayton Lake	74536	Dotyville	74354
Barnsdall	74002	Bunch	74931	Clear Lake	73849	Dougherty	73032
Baron	74965	Burbank	74633	Clearview	74835	Douglas	73733
Bartlesville	74003-06	Burlington	73722	Clebit	74728	Dover	73734
For specific Bartlesville Zip		Burmah	73659	Clemscot	73437	Dow	74501
Codes call (918) 336-0947, or		Burneyville	73430	Cleora	74331	Doyle	73039
your local postmaster.		Burns Flat	73624	Cleo Springs	73729	Drake	73086
Battiest	74722	Burwell	74754	Cleveland	74020	Driftwood	73728
Baugh	74020	Bushyhead	74016	Clinton	73601	Drumb	74578
Baum	73401	Butler	73625	Clothier (Part of Oklahoma		Drummond	73735
Beachton	71945	Butner	74884	City)	73160	Drumright	74030
Bearden	74859	Byars	74831	Cloud Chief	73632	Duke	73532
Beaver	73932	Byng	74820	Cloudy	74562	Dunbar	73448
Bee	74748	Byron	73722	Clyde	73759	Duncan	73533-34
Beggs	74421	Cache	73527	Coalgate	74538		73575
Beland	74401	Caddo	74729	Coalton	74437	For specific Duncan Zip Codes	
Bell	74960	Cairo	74538	Cobb	74701	call (405) 255-7226, or your	
Bellemont	74864	Calera	74730	Cogar	73059	local postmaster.	
Belvin	74563	Calhoun	74956	Colbert	74733	Dunjee Park (Part of	
Belzoni	74523	Calida	74020	Colcord	74338	Oklahoma City)	73084
Bengal	74966	Calumet	73014	Cole	73010	Durant	74701*
Bennington	74723	Calvin	74531	Coleman	73432		74702†
Bentley	74525	Camargo	73835	College (Part of Stillwater)	74074	Durham	73642
Berlin	73662	Cambria	74578	Collinsville	74021	Durwood (Part of	
Bernice	74331	Cameron	74932	Colony	73021	Dickson)	73401
Bessie	73622	Cameron University (Part		Comanche	73529	Dustin	74839
Bethany	73008	of Lawton)	73505	Commerce	74339	Eagle City	73658
Bethel (Comanche		Camp Houston	73842	Concho (Part of El Reno)	73022	Eagletown	74734
County)	73501	Canadian	74425	Conner Correctional		Eakly	73033
Bethel (McCurtain County)	74724	Caney	74533	Center	74035	Earl	73447

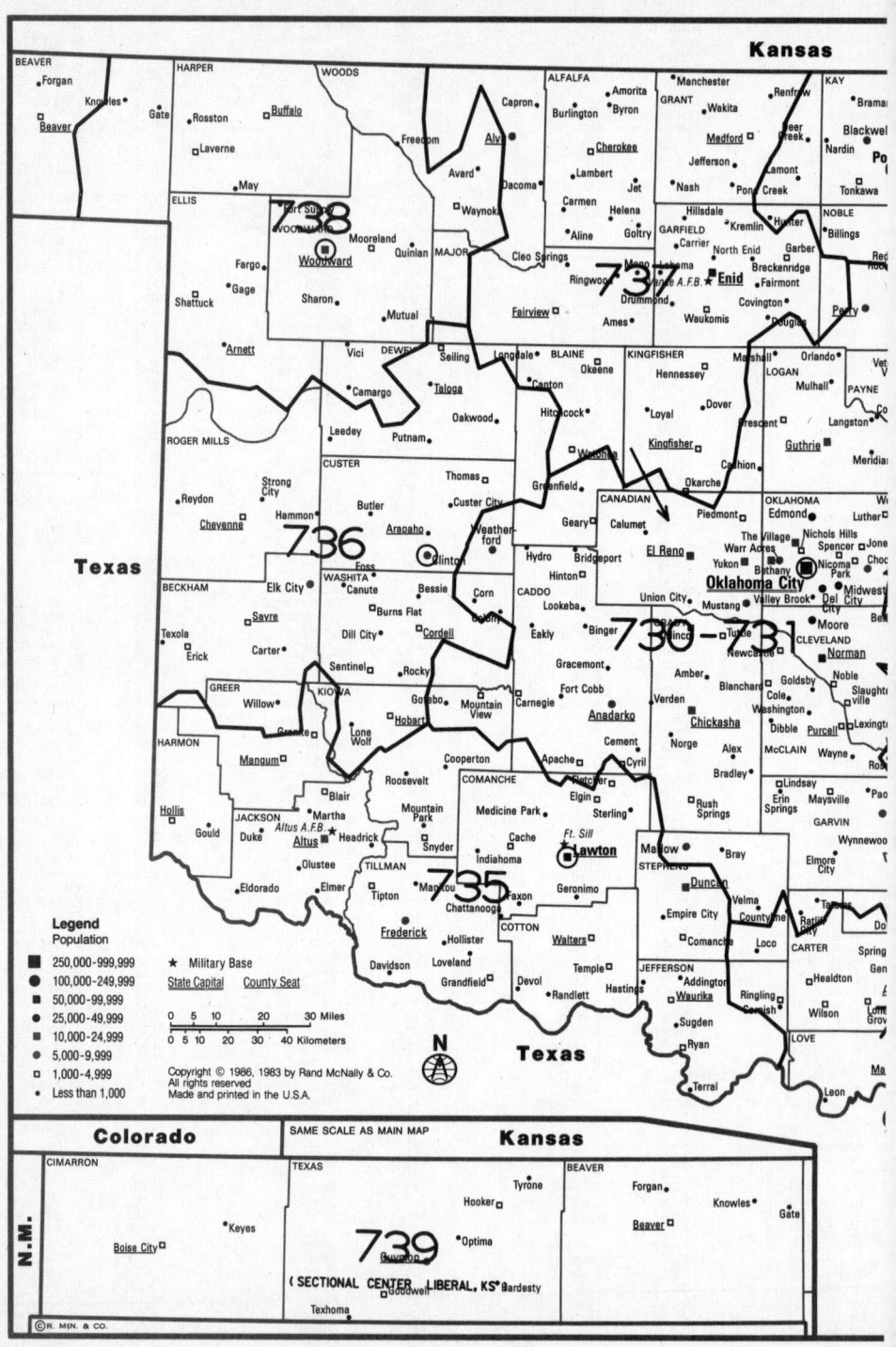

Kansas

BEAVER
Forgan
Knowles
Gate
Beaver

HARPER
Rosston
Buffalo
Laverne
May

WOODS
Freedom
Capron
Alva
Avard
Dacoma
Waynoka

ALFALFA
Amorita
Burlington
Byron
Cherokee
Lambert
Jet
Carmen
Helena
Aline
Goltry

GRANT
Manchester
Wakita
Medford
Jefferson
Nash
Pond Creek

KAY
Renfrow
Deer Creek
Lamont
Tonkawa

Bramar
Blackwell
Nardin
Tonkawa

ELLIS
Fort Supply
WOODWARD
Woodward
Fargo
Gage
Shattuck
Arnett

Mooreland
Quinlan
Sharon
Mutual

MAJOR
Cleo Springs
Ringwood
Fairview

GARFIELD
Carrier
North Enid
Kremlin
Enid
Drummond
Fairmont
Covington
Douglas
Waukomis
Ames

NOBLE
Billings
Red
Perry

733

ROGER MILLS
Reydon
Cheyenne
Strong City
Hammon

DEWEY
Seiling
Longdale
Camargo
Taloga
Canton
Leedey
Putnam
Oakwood

CUSTER
Thomas
Custer City
Butler
Arapaho
Clinton
Foss

BLAINE
Okeene
Hitchcock
Greenfield

KINGFISHER
Hennessey
Loyal
Dover
Kingfisher
Okarche

LOGAN
Marshall
Crescent
Guthrie
Langston
Cashion

Orlando
Mulhall

PAYNE
Meridian

CANADIAN
Geary
Calumet
El Reno
Piedmont

OKLAHOMA
Edmond
The Village
Warr Acres
Nichols Hills
Spencer
Yukon
Bethany
Oklahoma City
Nicoma Park

Luther
Jones
Choc

736

Weatherford
Hydro
Bridgeport
Hinton

Texas

BECKHAM
Texola
Erick
Elk City
Sayre
Carter

WASHITA
Canute
Burns Flat
Dill City
Cordell
Sentinel
Rocky

CADDO
Lookeba
Eakly
Colony
Corn
Bessie

Union City
Mustang
Valley Brook
Moore
Newcastle
Tuttle

730-731

CLEVELAND
Norman
Noble
Goldsby
Slaughterville

GREER
Willow
Granite

KIOWA
Hobart
Gotebo
Mountain View
Lone Wolf

Gracemont
Fort Cobb
Carnegie
Anadarko
Cement
Apache

Verden
Amber
Blanchard
Washington
Cole
Chickasha
Dibble
Purcell
Lexington

McCLAIN
Norge
Alex
Bradley

HARMON
Hollis
Gould

Mangum

JACKSON
Martha
Duke
Altus A.F.B.
Altus
Olustee
Eldorado
Elmer

Blair
Mountain Park
Roosevelt
Cooperton
Snyder

COMANCHE
Medicine Park
Cache
Ft. Sill
Lawton
Indiahoma
Geronimo

Fletcher
Elgin
Sterling

Rush Springs
Marlow
Bray

Lindsay
Erin
Maysville

GARVIN
Elmore City
Wynnewood

STEPHENS
Duncan
Velma
Comanche
Loco

735

TILLMAN
Manitou
Tipton
Chattanooga
Faxon

COTTON
Frederick
Hollister
Walters

JEFFERSON
Addington
Waurika
Sugden

CARTER
Rattan City
Healdton
Wilson

Spring
Gen

Davidson
Loveland
Grandfield
Devol
Randlett
Temple
Hastings

Ringling
Cornish

LOVE
Ryan
Leon
Terral
Ma

Texas

N

Legend
Population
■ 250,000-999,999
● 100,000-249,999
● 50,000-99,999
■ 25,000-49,999
■ 10,000-24,999
• 5,000-9,999
□ 1,000-4,999
• Less than 1,000

★ Military Base
State Capital   County Seat

0 5 10   20   30 Miles
0 5 10 20 30 40 Kilometers

Copyright © 1986, 1983 by Rand McNally & Co.
All rights reserved
Made and printed in the U.S.A.

Colorado   SAME SCALE AS MAIN MAP   Kansas

N.M.

CIMARRON
Keyes
Boise City

TEXAS
Hooker
Optima
Guymon
Goodwell
Hardesty
Texhoma

739
(SECTIONAL CENTER   LIBERAL, KS)

Tyrone

BEAVER
Forgan
Beaver
Knowles
Gate

©R. McN. & CO.

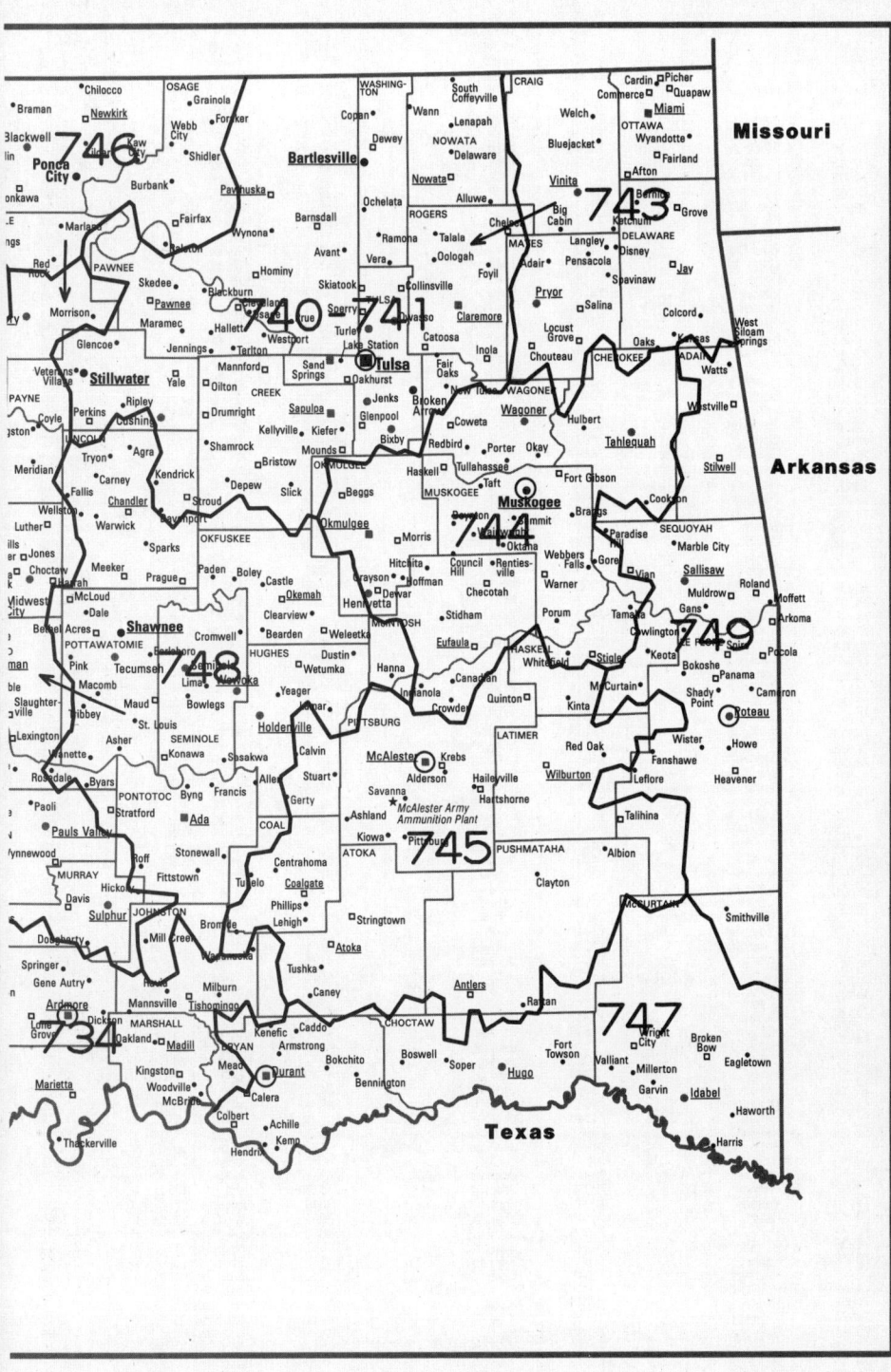

	ZIP
Earlsboro	74840
Eastborough	74014
Eastern Oklahoma A&M College	74578
Eastern State Hospital	74301
East Jessie	74871
Eastland Mall (Part of Tulsa)	74134
Eastside (Custer County)	73096
East Side (Tulsa County)	74134
East Side (Washington County)	74006
Eddy	74643
Edgewater Park	73006
Edmond	73003
	73013
	73034
	73083
For specific Edmond Zip Codes call (405) 341-1502, or your local postmaster.	
Edna	74010
Eighty Ninth Street (Part of Oklahoma City)	73159
Eldon	74464
Eldorado	73537
Elgin	73538
Elk City	73644*
	73648†
Elmer	73539
Elmore City	73035
Elmwood	73932
El Reno	73036
Emerson Center	73572
Emet	73450
Empire City	73533
Empy	74020
Enid	73701-06
For specific Enid Zip Codes call (405) 237-4331, or your local postmaster.	
Enos	73439
Enterprise	74561
Enville	73448
Erick	73645
Erin Springs	73052
Ethel	74523
Etowah	73068
Etta	74471
Eucha	74342
Euchee Creek (Part of Sand Springs)	74063
Eufaula	74432
Eva	73939
Ewing (Part of Clinton)	73601
Fairfax	74637
Fairland	74343
Fairmont	73736
Fair Oaks	74015
Fairview	73737
Falconhead	73430
Falfa	74571
Fallis	74881
Fame	74432
Fanshawe	74935
Fargo	73840
Farley (Part of Oklahoma City)	73107
Farmers Hill	74736
Farris	74542
Faxon	73540
Fay	73646
Featherston	74561
Federal Correctional Institution	73036
Felker	74764
Felt	73937
Fillmore	73432
Finley	74543
First National Bank (Part of Oklahoma City)	73102
Fisher (Part of Sand Springs)	74063
Fittstown	74842
Fitzhugh	74843
Fletcher	73541
Floris	73938
Folsom	73432
Fontana Shopping Center (Part of Tulsa)	74145
Foraker	74652
Forest Hill	74937
Forest Park	73121
Forgan	73938
Forney	74743
Forrester	74937
Fort Cobb	73038
Fort Coffee	74959
Fort Gibson	74434

	ZIP
Fort Reno (Part of El Reno)	73036
Fort Sill	73503
Fort Supply	73841
Fort Towson	74735
Foss	73647
Foster	73039
Four Corners	74437
Fox	73435
Foyil	74031
Francis	74844
Frederick	73542
Freedom	73842
French Market (Part of Oklahoma City)	73116
Friendship	73521
Frisco	74871
Frogville	74743
Gaar Corner	74820
Gage	73843
Gans	74936
Garber	73738
Garden Grove	74801
Garland	74462
Garvin	74736
Gate	73844
Gay	74743
Geary	73040
Gene Autry	73436
Georgetown	74434
Geronimo	73543
Gerty	74531
Gibson	74467
Gideon	74464
Gilcrease (Part of Tulsa)	74127
Gilmore	74953
Glencoe	74032
Glendale	74940
Glenpool	74033
Glover	74728
Golden	74737
Goldsby	73093
Goltry	73739
Goodland	74743
Goodwater	74740
Goodwell	73939
Gore	74435
Gotebo	73041
Gould	73544
Gowen	74545
Gracemont	73042
Grady	73569
Graham	73437
Grainola	74652
Grandfield	73546
Grand Lake Towne	74301
Granite	73547
Grant	74738
Gray Horse	74637
Grayson	74437
Greasy	74931
Greenfield	73043
Green Pastures (Part of Oklahoma City)	73084
Green Valley Estates	74962
Greenville	73448
Greenwood	74523
Griggs	73949
Grimes	73628
Grove	74344
Guthrie	73044
Guymon	73942
Haileyville	74546
Hall Addition (Part of Sand Springs)	74063
Hallett	74034
Hall Park	73069
Hammon	73650
Hanna	74845
Hanson	74955
Happyland	74820
Harden City	74871
Hardesty	73944
Harmon	73832
Harrah	73045
Harris	74740
Harrison	74955
Hartshorne	74547
Haskell	74436
Hastings	73548
Haw Creek	74939
Hawley	73761
Haworth	74740
Hayward	73730
Haywood	74548
Headrick	73549
Healdton	73438
Heavener	74937
Hefner (Part of Oklahoma City)	73162

	ZIP
Helena	73741
Hendrix	74741
Hennepin	73046
Hennessey	73742
Henryetta	74437
Heritage Hills	73507
Heritage Park Mall (Part of Midwest City)	73110
Hess	73539
Hester	73554
Hewitt (Part of Wilson)	73463
Hext	73645
Hickory	74865
Hicks Addition (Part of Spencer)	73084
Hill	74932
Hillsdale	73743
Hillsdale Free Will Baptist College	73160
Hill Top	74570
Hinton	73047
Hissom Memorial Center	74063
Hitchcock	73744
Hitchita	74438
Hobart	73651
Hockerville	74363
Hodgen	74939
Hodge Podge (Part of Tulsa)	74105
Hoffman	74437
Holdenville	74848
Holley Creek	74728
Hollis	73550
Hollister	73551
Homer	74820
Homestead	73763
Hominy	74035
Honobia	74549
Hontubby	74937
Hooker	73945
Hoot Owl	74365
Hopeton	73746
Hough	73942
Howard C. McLeod Correctional Center	74542
Howe	74940
Hoyt	74440
Hugo	74743
Hulbert	74441
Hulen	73572
Humphreys	73521
Hunter	74640
Hyde Park (Part of Muskogee)	74401
Hydro	73048
Idabel	74745
Independence	74937
Indiahoma	73552
Indian Meadows	74464
Indianola	74442
Ingalls	74074
Ingersoll	73728
Inola	74036
Iona	73086
Iron Stob Corner	74736
Irving	73565
Isabella	73747
Jackson	74723
Jacktown	74855
Jamestown	74080
Jay	74346
Jefferson	73759
Jenks	74037
Jennings	74038
Jesse	74871
Jet	73749
Jimtown	73430
Joburn	74556
Joe Harp Correctional Center	73051
John H. Lilley Correctional Center	74829
Johnson	74801
Jollyville	73030
Jones	73049
Joy	73098
Juby's	74020
Jumbo	74557
Kansas	74347
Karen Park (Part of Midwest City)	73110
Katie	73035
Kaw City	74641
Keefeton	74401
Keetonville	74017
Kellond	74523
Kellyville (Creek County)	74039
Kellyville (Ottawa County)	74370
Kemp	74747
Kendrick	74079

	ZIP
Kenefic	74748
Kensington Center (Part of Tulsa)	74103
Kent	74759
Kenton	73946
Kenwood	74365
Keota	74941
Ketchum	74349
Keyes	73947
Kiamichi	74574
Kiefer	74041
Kildare	74601
Kingfisher	73750
Kingston	73439
Kinta	74552
Kiowa	74553
Knowles	73847
Konawa	74849
Kosoma	74557
Krebs	74554
Kremlin	73753
Kulli	74745
Kusa	74437
Lacey	73742
Lahoma	73754
Lake Aluma	73121
Lake Creek	73547
Lake Hiwasse	73007
Lake Humphreys	73055
Lakeside Village	73538
Lake Station (Part of Sand Springs)	74127
Lake Valley	73041
Lake West	74727
Lamar	74850
Lambert	73728
La Mesa (Part of Enid)	73701
Lamont	74643
Lane	74555
Langley	74350
Langston	73050
Lark	73439
Last Chance	74859
Latta	74820
Laverne	73848
Lawrence Creek	74044
Lawton	73501-02
	73505-07
For specific Lawton Zip Codes call (405) 353-1500, or your local postmaster.	
Leach	74364
Leader	74825
Leander	74020
Lebanon	73440
Leedey	73654
Leflore	74942
Lehigh	74556
Leisure Square (Part of Tulsa)	74112
Lenapah	74042
Lenna	74432
Lenora	73667
Leon	73441
Leonard	74043
Lequire	74943
Leroy	74020
Lewisville	74552
Lexington	73051
Lexington Assessment and Recption Center	73051
Liberty (Bryan County)	74741
Liberty (Sequoyah County)	74948
Liberty (Tulsa County)	74101
Lighthouse (Part of Tulsa)	74136
Lima	74884
Limestone (Latimer County)	74578
Limestone (Rogers County)	74017
Lincolnville	74363
Lindsay	73052
Little	74868
Little Chief	74637
Little City	73446
Little Ponderosa	67901
Loco	73442
Locust Grove	74352
Logan	73849
Lona	74552
Lone Grove	73443
Lone Oak	74948
Lone Wolf	73655
Long	74948
Longdale	73755
Longtown	74561
Lookeba	73053
Lotsee	74063
Loveland	73553

* Area Zip Code   † Post Office Boxes

	ZIP
Lovell	73028
Loving	74937
Loyal	73756
Lucien	73757
Lugert	73655
Lula	74825
Luther	73054
Lutie	74578
Lynn Addition	74056
Lyons	74960
McAlester	74501*
	74502†
McAlester Army Ammunition Plant	74501
MacArthur Park (Part of Lawton)	73507
McBride	73439
McCord	74637
McCurtain	74944
McKey	74962
Mack H. Alford Correctional Center	74569
McKiddyville	73051
McKnight	73550
McLain	74401
McLoud	74851
McMillan	73446
Macomb	74852
McWillie	73716
Madill	73446
Maguire (Part of Slaughterville)	73068
Manard	74434
Manchester	73758
Mangum	73554
Manitou	73555
Mannford	74044
Mannsville	73447
Maple	74948
Maramec	74045
Marble City	74945
Marietta	73448
Marland	74644
Marlow	73055
Marshall	73056
Martha	73556
Martin	74401
Martin Luther King (Part of Oklahoma City)	73111
Mason	74859
Matoy	74729
Maud	74854
Maxwell	74820
May	73851
Mayfield	73656
May Ridge (Part of Oklahoma City)	73119
Maysville	73057
Mazie	74353
Mead	73449
Medford	73759
Medicine Park	73557
Meeker	74855
Meers	73558
Mehan	74074
Mellette	74432
Melvin	74441
Meno	73760
Meridian (Logan County)	73058
Meridian (Stephens County)	73529
Merritt	73644
Messer	74743
Miami	74354*
	74355†
Micawber	74882
Middleberg	73010
Midlothian	74834
Midway	74538
Midwest City	73110
Milburn	73450
Milfay	74046
Mill Creek	74856
Miller	74557
Millerton	74750
Milo	73401
Milton	74944
Minco	73059
Moffett	74946
Monroe	74947
Montclair Addition (Part of Heavener)	74937
Moodys	74444
Moon	74740
Moore	73160
Mooreland	73852
Moorewood	73650
Morris	74445
Morrison	73061
Mound Grove	74764

	ZIP
Mounds	74047
Mountain Park	73559
Mountain View	73062
Mount Herman	74728
Mount Zion	74736
Moyers	74557
Mudsand	74759
Muldrow	74948
Mule Barn (Part of Cleveland)	74101
Mulhall	73063
Murphy	74352
Muse	74949
Muskogee	74401-03
For specific Muskogee Zip Codes call (918) 682-7832, or your local postmaster.	
Mustang	73064
Mutual	73853
Nani-Chito	74957
Narcissa	74354
Nardin	74646
Nash	73761
Nashoba	74558
Natura	74421
Navina	73044
Nebo	73086
Needmore	73068
Neff	74953
Nelagony	74056
Newalla (Part of Oklahoma City)	74857
Newcastle	73065
Newkirk	74647
New Liberty	73662
New Lima	74884
New Oberlin	74727
Newport	73401
New Tulsa	74429
Nichols Hills	73116
Nicoma Park	73066
Nicut	74948
Nida	74748
Ninnekah	73067
Noble	73068
Nobletown	74884
Non	74531
Norge	73018
Norman	73069-72
For specific Norman Zip Codes call (405) 321-2484, or your local postmaster.	
Norris	74563
Northeast (Part of Tulsa)	74112
	74115-17
	74158
For specific Northeast Zip Codes call (918) 835-9506, or your local postmaster.	
North Enid	73701
North McAlester (Part of McAlester)	74501
North Miami	74358
Northside (Part of Tulsa)	74106
Northwest (Part of Oklahoma City)	73106*
	73146†
Nowata	74048
Nuyaka	74447
Oak Grove (Murray County)	73032
Oak Grove (Pawnee County)	74020
Oak Grove (Payne County)	74030
Oak Hill	74728
Oakhurst	74050
Oakland	73446
Oakman	74820
Oak Park (Part of Bartlesville)	74003
Oaks	74359
Oakwood	73658
Oberlin	74727
Ochelata	74051
Octavia	74957
Oglesby	74061
Oil Center	74820
Oil City	73463
Oilton	74052
Okarche	73762
Okay	74446
Okeene	73763
Okemah	74859
Okesa	74003
Okfuskee	74859

	ZIP
Oklahoma City	73101-89
For specific Oklahoma City Zip Codes call (405) 278-6122, or your local postmaster.	
COLLEGES & UNIVERSITIES	
Oklahoma Christian College	73136
Oklahoma City University	73106
University of Oklahoma Health Sciences Center	73190
FINANCIAL INSTITUTIONS	
Bank of Oklahoma, National Association	73124
Bank One	73101
Boatman's First National Bank of Oklahoma	73102
Guaranty Bank & Trust Company	73127
Liberty Bank and Trust Company of Oklahoma City, N.A.	73102
Local Federal Bank, F.S.B.	73116
Midfirst Bank, S.S.B.	73118
Oklahoma Bank	73108
HOSPITALS	
Baptist Medical Center of Oklahoma	73112
Mercy Health Center	73120
Southwest Medical Center of Oklahoma	73109
St. Anthony Hospital	73101
Veterans Affairs Medical Center	73104
HOTELS/MOTELS	
Embassy Suites	73108
Hilton Inn Northwest	73112
Radison Inn	73108
Waterford Hotel	73118
MILITARY INSTALLATIONS	
Oklahoma Air National Guard, FB6562, Will Rogers Airport	73179
Oklahoma City Air Force Material Command, Tinker Air Force Base	73145
United States Property and Fiscal Office for Oklahoma	73111
Oklahoma State Penitentiary	74501
Okmulgee	74447
Oktaha	74450
Oleta	74735
Olive	74030
Olney	74538
Olustee	73560
Omega	73764
Oneta	74012
Oologah	74053
Optima	73945
Ord	74738
Orienta	73737
Orlando	73073
Orr	73456
Osage	74054
Osage Hills Estates (Part of Sand Springs)	74063
Osage Indian Reservation	74056
Oscar	73561
Ouachita Correctional Center	74939
Overbrook	73453
Owasso	74055
Paden	74860
Page	74939
Panama	74951
Panola	74559
Paoli	73074
Paradise Hill	74955
Paradise View	74337
Park Hill	74451
Parkland	74824
Park Lane (Part of Lawton)	73501
Patterson	74578
Pauls Valley	73075
Pawhuska	74056
Pawnee	74058
Paw Paw	74948
Payne	73052
Payson	74855
Pearson	74826
Pearsonia	74056

	ZIP
Peckham	74647
Peggs	74452
Penn Square Mall (Part of Oklahoma City)	73118
Penn 89th (Part of Oklahoma City)	73159
Pensacola	74301
Peoria	74363
Perkins	74059
Pernell	73076
Perry	73077
Pershing	74002
Peterman Ridge	74020
Petersburg	73456
Petros	74937
Pettit	74451
Pettit Bay	74451
Pharoah	74862
Phillips	74538
Picher	74360
Pickens	74752
Pickett	74820
Piedmont	73078
Pierce	74426
Piney	74960
Pink	74873
Pin Oaks Acres	74337
Pittsburg	74560
Platter	74753
Pleasant Hill	74740
Plunkettville	74963
Pocasset	73079
Pocola	74902
Pollard	74740
Ponca City	74601-04
For specific Ponca City Zip Codes call (405) 762-2485, or your local postmaster.	
Pond Creek	73766
Pontotoc	74820
Pooleville	73458
Porter	74454
Porter Hill	73538
Porum	74455
Poteau	74953
Powell	73439
Prague	74864
Prattville (Part of Sand Springs)	74063
Preston	74456
Proctor	74457
Prue	74060
Pruitt City	73081
Pryor	74361*
	74362†
Pumpkin Center (Comanche County)	73501
Pumpkin Center (Okmulgee County)	74445
Purcell	73080
Purdy	73052
Putnam	73659
Pyramid Corners	74333
Quail Creek (Part of Oklahoma City)	73120
Quail Springs Mall (Part of Oklahoma City)	73134
Qualls	74451
Quapaw	74363
Quay	74085
Quinlan	73852
Quinton	74561
Rabornville	74020
Raiford	74432
Ralston	74650
Ramona	74061
Ranchwood Manor (Part of Oklahoma City)	73160
Randlett	73562
Ratliff City	73081
Rattan	74562
Ravia	73455
Reagan	73460
Reck	73463
Redbird	74458
Red Hill	74941
Red Horse (Part of Midwest City)	73110
Redland	74948
Red Oak	74563
Red Rock	74651
Reed	73554
Regal (Part of Lawton)	73501
Reichert	74937
Remus	74801
Renfrow	73759
Reno Meridian (Part of Oklahoma City)	73137
Rentiesville	74459
Retrop	73627

* Area Zip Code   **† Post Office Boxes**

Name	ZIP	Name	ZIP	Name	ZIP	Name	ZIP
Reydon	73660	Soper	74759	Teresita	74364	Warner	74469
Rhea	73654	Southard	73770	Terlton	74081	Warr Acres	73132
Richards Spur	73538	South Coffeyville	74072	Terral	73569	Warren	73526
Richland	73099	South East (Part of		Texanna	74426	Warwick	74834
Richville	74501	Oklahoma City)	73129*	Texhoma	73949	Washington	73093
Rigsby	74020		73143†	Texola	73668	Washita	73094
Ringling	73456	Southeast (Part of Tulsa)	74145	Thackerville	73459	Waterloo	73034
Ringold	74754		74147	Thirty-Fourth Street (Part		Watonga	73772
Ringwood	73768		74158	of Woodward)	73801	Watova	74048
Ripley	74062	For specific Southeast Zip		Thirty Ninth Street (Part of		Watson	74963
Roberta	74701	Codes call (918) 627-2886, or		Oklahoma City)	73112	Watts	74964
Rock Island	74932	your local postmaster.		Thomas	73669	Wauhillau	74960
Rocky	73661	Southroads Mall (Part of		Ti	74528	Waukomis	73773
Rocky Mountain	74960	Tulsa)	74135	Tiawah	74017	Waurika	73573
Rocky Point	74467	Southside (Part of Tulsa)	74105	Timber Brook	74014	Wayne	73095
Roff	74865		74136-37	Timberlane	74020	Waynoka	73860
Roland	74954		74170	Tiner	74728	Weatherford	73096
Roll	73628	For specific Southside Zip		Tipton	73570	Webb	73835
Roosevelt	73564	Codes call (918) 492-4035, or		Tishomingo	73460	Webb City	74652
Rose	74364	your local postmaster.		Titanic	74960	Webbers Falls	74470
Rosedale	74831	Southwest (Part of		Tom	74740	Welch	74369
Rosston	73855	Oklahoma City)	73119*	Tonkawa	74653	Weleetka	74880
Rossville	74881		73144†	Topsy	74366	Welling	74471
Rubottom	73463	Sparks	74869	Tribbey	74852	Wellston	74881
Rufe	74755	Spaulding	74848	Trousdale	74878	Welty	74882
Rush Springs	73082	Spavinaw	74366	Troy	74856	Wes	74020
Russell	73554	Speer	74743	Trusty Unit	74501	West Nichols Hills (Part of	
Russellville	74561	Spelter City	74437	Tryon	74875	Oklahoma City)	73116
Russett	73447	Spencer	73084	Tucker	74959	West Park (Part of	
Ryan	73565	Spencerville	74760	Tullahassee	74466	Oklahoma City)	73123
Sacred Heart	74849	Sperry	74073	Tulsa	74101-70	Westport	74020
Sageeyah	74017	Spiro	74959	For specific Tulsa Zip Codes		Westside (Part of	
St. Louis	74866	Sportsmen Acres	74361	call (918) 599-6965, or your		Oklahoma City)	73127
Salem	74437	Springer	73458	local postmaster.		West Siloam Springs	72761
Salina	74365	Springlake Park (Part of		Tulsa Promenade (Part of		West Tulsa (Part of Tulsa)	74107
Sallisaw	74955	Oklahoma City)	73111	Tulsa)	74135	Westville	74965
Salt Fork	74640	Stafford	73601	Tupelo	74572	Wetumka	74883
Sams Point	74501	Stanley	74536	Turley	74156	Wewoka	74884
Sandbluff	74759	Stapp	74939	Turner	73430	Wheatland (Part of	
Sand Point	73449	Star	74941	Turpin	73950	Oklahoma City)	73097
Sand Springs	74063	State Capitol (Part of		Tushka	74525	Wheeless	73933
Sansbois	74552	Oklahoma City)	73105	Tuskahoma	74574	Whippoorwill	74056
Sapulpa	74066*	Stealy	73080	Tuskegee	74010	White Bead	73075
	74067†	Stecker	73006	Tussy	73088	White Eagle	74601
Sardis	74536	Steedman	74825	Tuttle	73089	Whitefield	74472
Sasakwa	74867	Steel Junction	74728	Tuxedo (Part of		White Oak (Cherokee	
Savanna	74565	Steen (Part of Enid)	73701	Bartlesville)	74003	County)	74451
Sawyer	74756	Sterling	73567	Twin Hills	74447	White Oak (Craig County)	74301
Sayre	73662	Stidham	74461	Twin Oaks	74368	Whitesboro	74577
Schulter	74460	Stigler	74462	Tyler	73446	Whittier (Part of Tulsa)	74150
Scipio	74501	Stillwater	74074-76	Tyrone	73951	Wichita Mountains Estates	73501
Scraper	74464	For specific Stillwater Zip Codes		Unger	74727	Wilburton	74578
Scullin	73086	call (405) 377-3867, or your		Union (Cleveland County)	73070	Wildcat Point	74451
Scullyville	74959	local postmaster.		Union (Tulsa County)	74012	Wild Horse	74035
Seiling	73663	Stilwell	74960	Union City	73090	Williams	74932
Selman	73834	Stockyards (Part of		Union Valley	74871	William S. Key	
Seminole	74818*	Oklahoma City)	73108	University (Garfield		Correctional Center	73841
	74868†	Stonebluff	74436	County)	73701	Willis	73439
Sentinel	73664	Stonewall	74871	University (Pottawatomie		Willow	73673
Sequoyah	74017	Stony Point (Adair		County)	74801	Wilson (Carter County)	73463
Seward	73044	County)	74960	University of Science		Wilson (Okmulgee	
Shady Grove (Pawnee		Stony Point (Le Flore		and Arts (Part of		County)	74437
County)	74112	County)	74959	Chickasha)	73018	Winchester	74421
Shady Grove (Sequoyah		Story	73057	Uptown Shopping Center		Winganon	74016
County)	74954	Straight	73942	(Part of Midwest City)	73110	Wister	74966
Shady Point	74956	Strang	74367	Utica	74726	Wolco	74002
Shamrock	74068	Stratford	74872	Utica Square (Part of		Wolf	74854
Sharon	73857	Stringtown	74569	Tulsa)	74152	Woodford	73458
Shartel (Part of Oklahoma		Strong City	73628	Valley Brook	73149	Woodland Hills Mall (Part	
City)	73118	Stroud	74079	Valley Park	74017	of Tulsa)	74133
Sha-To-She	74020	Stuart	74570	Valliant	74764	Woodland View (Part of	
Shattuck	73858	Sugden	73573	Vamoosa	74849	Tulsa)	74145
Shawnee	74801*	Sullivan Village (Part of		Vance Air Force Base	73701	Woodlawn Park	73008
	74802†	Lawton)	73501	Vanoss	74820	Woods	73020
Shay	73439	Sulphur	73086	Velma	73091	Woodville	73439
Shepherd Mall (Part of		Summerfield	74966	Vera	74082	Woodward	73801*
Oklahoma City)	73107	Summit	74401	Verden	73092		73802†
Sheridan (Comanche		Sumner	73077	Verdigris	74017	Woody Chapel	73095
County)	73505	Sungate (Part of Lawton)	73501	Vernon	74845	Wright City	74766
Sheridan (Tulsa County)	74135	Sunkist	74727	Vian	74962	Wyandotte	74370
Sherwood	74728	Sunray	73529	Vici	73859	Wybark	74401
Shidler	74652	Sweetwater	73666	Victory	73560	Wye	74852
Shinewell	74740	Swink	74761	Village	73120	Wynnewood	73098
Short	72955	Tabler	73018	Vinco	74059	Wynona	74084
Shults	74745	Tablerville	74734	Vinita	74301	Yale	74085
Sickles	73053	Taft	74463	Vinson	73571	Yanush	74574
Silo	74701	Tahlequah	74464*	Virgil	74756	Yarnaby	74741
Silver City	74038		74465†	Vista	74849	Yeager	74848
Skedee	74058	Tahona	74932	Vivian	74432	Yewed	73728
Skiatook	74070	Tailholt	74471	Wade	74723	Yost Lake	74032
Slapout	73848	Talala	74080	Wagoner	74467*	Yuba	74721
Slaughterville	73051	Talihina	74571		74477†	Yukon	73085*
Slick	74071	Tallant	74002	Wainwright	74468		73099†
Smith Village	73115	Taloga	73667	Wakita	73771	Zafra	71945
Smithville	74957	Tamaha	74462	Wallville	73052	Zena	74346
Snow	74567	Tangier	73801	Walters	73572	Zincville	66713
Snyder	73566	Tatums	73087	Wanette	74878	Zion	74960
Sobol	74735	Taylor	73562	Wann	74083	Zoe	74939
Sooner Fashion Mall (Part		Tecumseh	74873	Wapanucka	73461		
of Norman)	73072	Temple	73568	Wardville	74576		

Place	ZIP	Place	ZIP
Acorn Park (Part of Eugene)	97402	Bingham Springs	97810
Ada	97493	Birkenfeld	97016
Adair Village	97330	Blachly	97412
Adams	97810	Black Butte Ranch	97759
Adel	97620	Blaine	97108
Adrian	97901	Blalock	97812
Agate Beach (Part of Newport)	97365	Blodgett	97326
Agency Lake	97624	Blooming	97113
Agness	97406	Blue River	97413
Aims	97019	Bly	97622
Airlie	97361	Boardman	97818
Ajax	97823	Bolton (Part of West Linn)	97068
Albany	97321	Bonanza	97623
Albany Yard (Part of Albany)	97321	Bonneville	97014
Alder Creek	97055	Bonny Slope	97229
Aldrich Point	97103	Boring	97009
Alfalfa	97701	Boyd	97021
Alicel	97824	Boyer	97347
Alkali Lake	97758	Bradwood	97016
Allegany	97407	Breitenbush	97342
Alston	97048	Brickerville	97453
Aloha	97006	Bridal Veil	97010
Alpine	97456	Bridge	97458
Alsea	97324	Bridgeport (Baker County)	97819
Altamont	97603	Bridgeport (Polk County)	97338
Alvadore	97409	Brighton	97136
Amity	97101	Brightwood	97011
Anchor	97410	Broadacres	97002
Andrews	97720	Broadbent	97414
Anlauf	97428	Brockway	97496
Annex	83672	Brogan	97903
Antelope	97001	Brookings	97415
Apiary	97048	Brooklyn (Part of Portland)	97242
Applegate	97530	Brooks	97305
Arago	97458	Brothers	97712
Arch Cape	97102	Brownlee	97840
Arleta	97206	Brownsboro	97524
Arlington	97812	Brownsmead	97016
Arock	97902	Brownsville	97327
Ashland	97520	Bryant (Part of Lake Oswego)	97035
Ashwood	97711	Buchanan	97720
Astoria	97103	Buena Vista	97351
Astoria Coast Guard Base	97103	Bullrun	97055
Athena	97813	Bunker Hill	97420
Aumsville	97325	Burlington	97231
Aurora	97002	Burns	97720
Austin	97817	Burnside	97103
Austin Junction	97817	Burns Junction	97910
Avon (Part of Rainier)	97048	Burns Paiute Indian Reservation	97720
Azalea	97410	Burnt Woods	97326
Bakeoven	97037	Butte Falls	97522
Baker City	97814	Butteville	97002
Ballston	97378	Buxton	97109
Bandon	97411	Cages	97739
Banks	97106	Cairo	97914
Barlow	97013	Calapooya	97386
Barton	97022	Camas Valley	97416
Barview (Coos County)	97420	Camp Clatsop	97146
Barview (Tillamook County)	97136	Camp Polk	97759
Basque	89421	Camp Sherman	97730
Bates	97817	Camp Twelve	97391
Battin	97266	Campus Station (Part of Corvallis)	97331
Bay City	97107	Canaan	97054
Bay Park	97420	Canary	97493
Bayshore	97394	Canby	97013
Bayside Garden	97131	Canemah (Part of Oregon City)	97045
Bayview	97394	Cannon Beach	97110
Beatty	97621	Cannon Beach Junction	97138
Beaver	97108	Canyon City	97820
Beavercreek	97004	Canyonville	97417
Beaver Homes	97048	Cape Meares	97141
Beaver Marsh	97731	Capitol Hill (Part of Portland)	97219
Beaver Springs	97048	Carlton	97111
Beaverton	97005-08, 97075-76	Carnation (Part of Forest Grove)	97116
For specific Beaverton Zip Codes call (503) 646-3196, or your local postmaster.		Carpenterville	97415
Beaverton Mall (Part of Beaverton)	97005	Carson	97834
Belknap Springs	97413	Carus	97045
Belleview (Part of Ashland)	97520	Carver	97015
Bellevue	97128	Cascade Gorge	97536
Bellfountain	97456	Cascade Locks	97014
Bend	97701-09	Cascade Summit	97425
For specific Bend Zip Codes call (503) 388-1971, or your local postmaster.		Cascadia	97329
Berlin	97355	Cave Junction	97523
Bethany	97123	Cayuse	97821
Bethel Heights	97304	Cecil	97843
Beulah	97911	Cedar Dale	97038
Beverly Beach	97365	Cedar Hills	97225
Biggs	97065	Cedarhurst Park	97023
		Cedar Mill	97291
		Celilo	97058
		Centennial	97236
		Central (Part of Portland)	97204

Place	ZIP	Place	ZIP
Central Point (Clackamas County)	97045	Deschutes Junction	97701
Central Point (Jackson County)	97502	Deschutes River Woods	97701
Central Point West	97502	Detroit	97342
Chapman	97056	Dever	97321
Charleston	97420	Dew Valley	97411
Charlestown	97838	Dexter	97431
Chemult	97731	Diamond	97722
Chenoweth	97058	Diamond Lake	97731
Cherry Grove	97119	Diamond Lake Junction	97731
Cherry Heights	97058	Dickey Prairie	97038
Cherryville	97055	Dillard	97432
Cheshire	97419	Dilley	97116
Chiloquin	97624	Dixie	97907
Chitwood	97391	Dixonville	97470
Christmas Valley	97641	Dodge	97023
Chutes (Part of Portland)	97202	Dodson	97014
Clackamas	97015	Dolph Corner	97338
Clackamas Heights	97045	Donald	97020
Clarkes	97004	Dora	97458
Clarno	97830	Dorena	97434
Clatskanie	97016	Dover	97055
Clatskanie Heights	97016	Downing	97016
Clear Lake	97303	Downtown (Part of Bend)	97701
Clifton	97016	Drain	97435
Cloverdale (Deschutes County)	97756	Draperville	97321
Cloverdale (Lane County)	97426	Drew	97484
Cloverdale (Tillamook County)	97112	Drewsey	97904
Clow Corner	97338	Dufur	97021
Coaledo	97420	Dukes Valley	97031
Coburg	97408	Dundee	97115
College Hill (Part of Eugene)	97405	Dunes City	97439
Colton	97017	Durham	97223
Columbia City	97018	Durkee	97905
Concord	97222	Eagle Creek	97022
Condon	97823	Eagle Point	97524
Cook (Part of Lake Oswego)	97034	East Gardiner	97467
Coos Bay	97420	East Gresham (Part of Gresham)	97030
Cooston	97459	East Lake	97739
Coquille	97423	East Parkrose	97230
Corbett	97019	East Portland (Part of Portland)	97214-15, 97232
Cornelius	97113	For specific East Portland Zip Codes call (503) 234-7269, or your local postmaster.	
Cornelius Pass	97231	Eastside (Part of Coos Bay)	97420
Coronado Shores	97388	Eastwood (Part of Roseburg)	97470
Corvallis	97330-33, 97339	Echo	97826
For specific Corvallis Zip Codes call (503) 758-1412, or your local postmaster.		Echo Dell	97045
Cottage Grove	97424	Eckman Lake	97394
Cottrell	97009	Eddyville	97343
Courtrock	97864	Elgarose	97470
Cove	97824	Elgin	97827
Cove Orchard	97148	Elk City	97391
Crabtree	97335	Elkhead	97499
Crane	97732	Elkhorn	97358
Crater Lake	97604	Elk Lake	97701
Crawfordsville	97336	Elkton	97436
Crescent	97733	Ellendale	97338
Crescent Lake	97425	Ellingson Mill	97884
Crescent Lake Junction	97425	Elliott Prairie	97071
Creston (Part of Portland)	97206	Elmira	97437
Creswell	97426	Elsie	97138
Crooked River Ranch	97760	Elwood	97017
Crow	97405	Emerald Heights (Part of Astoria)	97103
Crowfoot	97355	Empire (Part of Coos Bay)	97420
Culp Creek	97427	Endersby	97058
Culver	97734	Englewood	97420
Currinsville	97023	Enterprise	97828
Curtin	97428	Errol Heights (Part of Portland)	97266
Cutler City (Part of Lincoln City)	97367	Estacada	97023
Dairy	97625	Eugene	97401-05, 97408, 97440
Dale	97880	For specific Eugene Zip Codes call (503) 341-3611, or your local postmaster.	
Daley	97702	Fairfield	97026
Dallas	97338	Fair Oaks (Clackamas County)	97222
Damascus	97009	Fairoaks (Douglas County)	97479
Damascus Heights	97009	Fairview (Coos County)	97423
Dammasch State Hospital	97070	Fairview (Multnomah County)	97024
Danebo (Part of Eugene)	97402	Fairview (Tillamook County)	97141
Danner	97910	Falcon Heights	97601
Days Creek	97429	Fall Creek	97438
Dayton	97114	Falls City	97344
Dayville	97825	Fargo	97002
Deadwood	97430	Faubion	97049
Dee	97031	Fayetteville	97377
Deer Island	97054	Federal Correctional Institution	97378
De Lake (Part of Lincoln City)	97367		
Delena	97016		
Dellwood	97420		
Delmoor	97146		
Denmark	97450		
Depoe Bay	97341		

* Area Zip Code   † Post Office Boxes

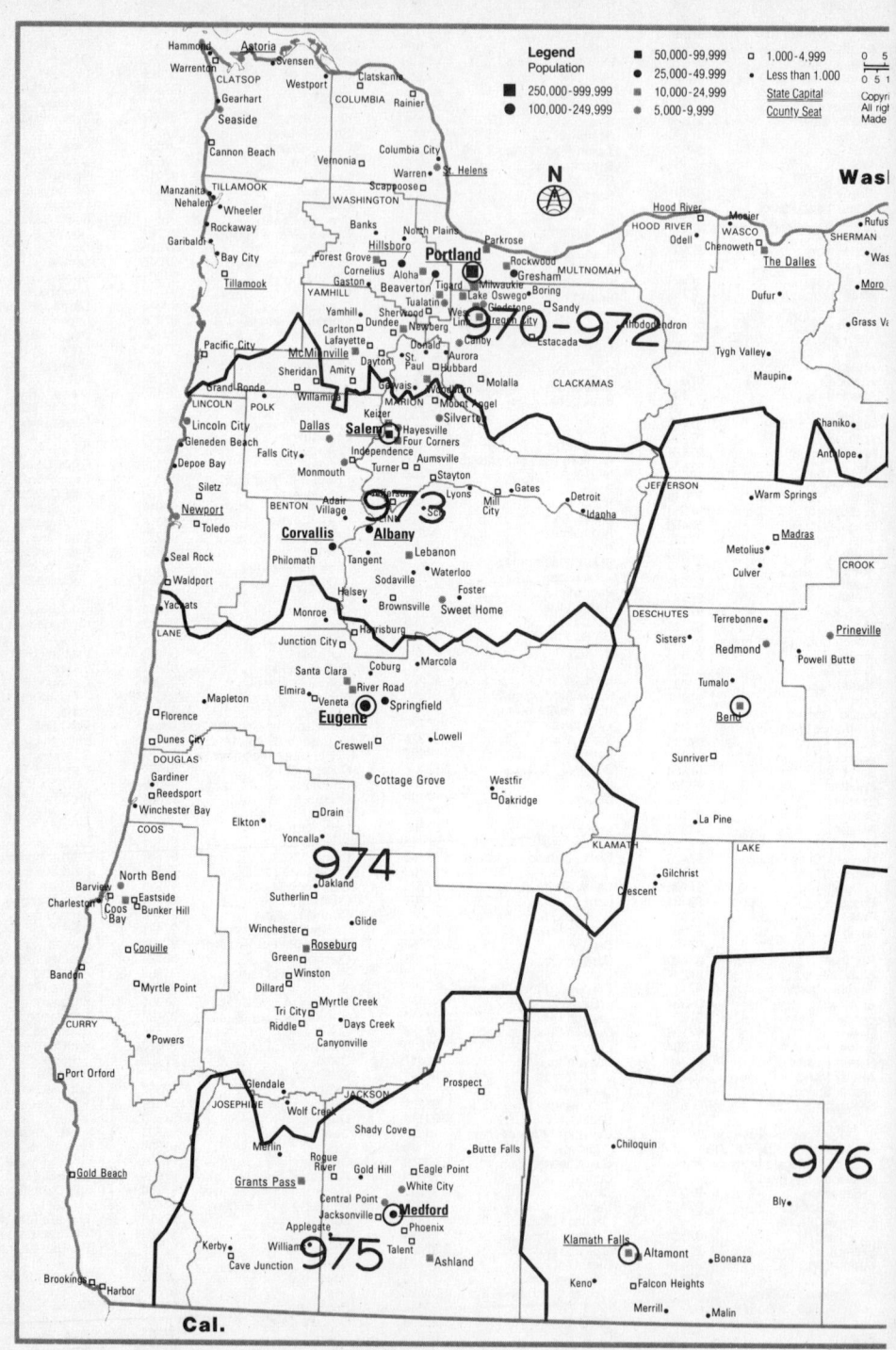

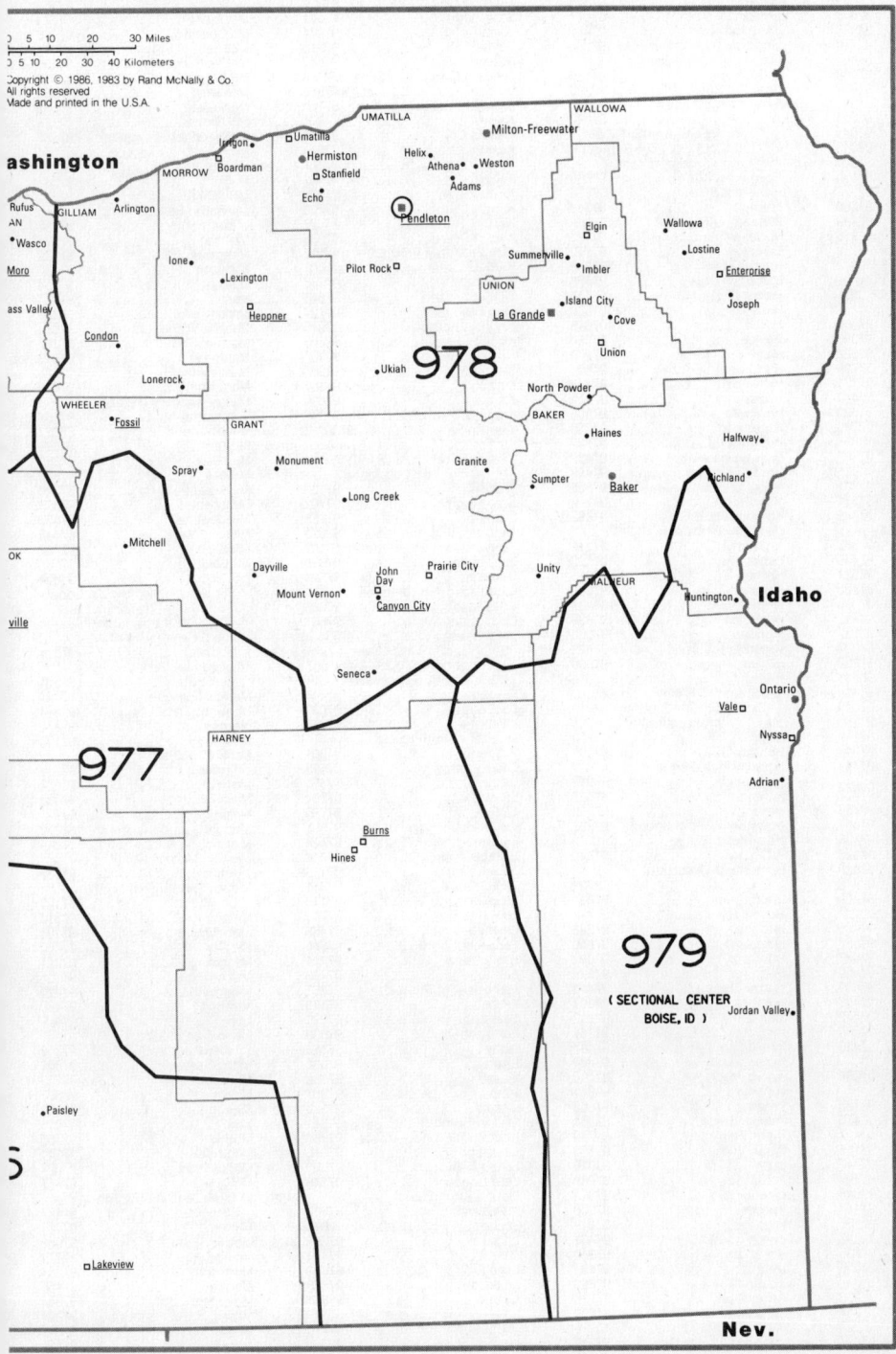

0 5 10   20   30 Miles
0 5 10   20   30   40 Kilometers

ashington

978

977

979

(SECTIONAL CENTER
BOISE, ID)

Idaho

Nev.

WASHINGTON

UMATILLA

Irrigon
Umatilla
Hermiston
Boardman
Stanfield
Echo

Helix
Athena
Weston
Adams

Milton-Freewater

WALLOWA

Rufus
AN
Wasco
Moro
ass Valley

GILLIAM
Arlington

Pendleton

Elgin
Summerville
Imbler

Wallowa
Lostine
Enterprise
Joseph

Condon

Ione
Lexington
Pilot Rock

UNION
Island City
La Grande
Cove
Union

Heppner

Lonerock

Ukiah

North Powder

WHEELER
Fossil

GRANT

BAKER

Haines

Halfway

Spray

Monument

Granite

Sumpter
Baker
ichland

Long Creek

OK

Mitchell

Dayville

John
Day
Prairie City

Unity

MALHEUR

Huntington

ville

Mount Vernon
Canyon City

Seneca

Ontario

HARNEY

Vale
Nyssa

Adrian

Burns
Hines

Jordan Valley

Paisley

Lakeview

Place	ZIP
Fern Corner	97338
Fern Hill (Clatsop County)	97103
Fern Hill (Columbia County)	97048
Ferns	97338
Fields (Harney County)	97710
Fields (Lane County)	97463
Finn Rock	97488
Fir Grove	97404
Fir Villa	97338
Firwood	97055
Fishers Corner	97045
Fishers Mill	97045
Fish Lake Resort	97524
Five Corners	97630
Flora	97828
Floras Lake	97450
Florence	97439
Forest Grove	97116
Forest Park (Part of Portland)	97209-10
For specific Forest Park Zip Codes call (503) 223-6906, or your local postmaster.	
Forfar	97366
Fort Hill	97396
Fort Klamath	97626
Fort Rock	97735
Fort Stevens	97121
Fortune Branch	97442
Fossil	97830
Foster	97345
Four Corners (Jackson County)	97502
Four Corners (Marion County)	97301
Fox	97831
Franklin	97448
Freewater (Part of Milton-Freewater)	97862
Frenchglen	97736
Friend	97021
Fruitdale	97526
Fruitvale	97365
Gales Creek	97117
Galice	97532
Garden Home	97223
Garden Home-Whitford	97223
Gardiner	97441
Gardiner Ridge	97415
Garfield	97023
Garibaldi	97118
Gaston	97119
Gates	97346
Gateway	97741
Gateway Mall (Part of Springfield)	97477
Gaylord	97458
Gazley	97457
Gearhart	97138
George	97023
Gervais	97026
Gibbon	97810
Gilbert	97266
Gilchrist	97737
Gillespie Corners	97405
Gilliams	97338
Gladstone	97027
Glasgow	97459
Glenada	97439
Glenbrook	97456
Glendale	97442
Gleneden Beach	97388
Glengary	97470
Glenmorrie (Part of Lake Oswego)	97034
Glenwood (Clatsop County)	97146
Glenwood (Lane County)	97403
Glenwood (Washington County)	97116
Glide	97443
Globe	97490
Goble	97048
Gold Beach	97444
Gold Hill	97525
Gooseberry	97843
Goshen	97405
Government Camp	97028
Grande Ronde Indian Reservation	97396
Grand Ronde	97347
Grand Ronde Agency	97347
Granite	97877
Grants Pass	97526-27
For specific Grants Pass Zip Codes call (503) 479-7526, or your local postmaster.	
Grass Valley	97029

Place	ZIP
Green	97470
Green Acres	97420
Greenberry	97333
Greenhorn	97877
Greenleaf	97430
Greenville (Linn County)	97386
Greenville (Washington County)	97116
Greenway (Part of Tigard)	97223
Gresham	97030
	97080
For specific Gresham Zip Codes call (503) 665-3114, or your local postmaster.	
Haines	97833
Halfway	97834
Halsey	97348
Hammond (Part of Warrenton)	97121
Hampton	97712
Happy Valley	97236
Harbeck-Fruitdale	97526
Harbor	97415
Hardman	97836
Harlan	97343
Harney	97720
Harper	97906
Harriman	97601
Harrisburg	97446
Hauser	97459
Hayesville	97303
Hazelwood	97230
Hebo	97122
Heceta Beach	97439
Heceta Junction	97439
Helix	97835
Helvetia	97123
Hemlock (Lane County)	97492
Hemlock (Tillamook County)	97112
Henley	97603
Henrice	97045
Heppner	97836
Hereford	97837
Hermiston	97838
Highland	97004
Hildebrand	97623
Hilgard	97850
Hillsboro	97123-24
For specific Hillsboro Zip Codes call (503) 294-2308, or your local postmaster.	
Hines	97738
Hobsonville	97107
Holladay Park (Part of Portland)	97212
Holland	97523
Holley	97386
Hollywood (Part of Salem)	97303
Homestead (Baker County)	97840
Homestead (Deschutes County)	97702
Hood River	97031
Horton	97412
Hoskins	97326
Hot Lake	97850
Hubbard	97032
Hugo	97526
Hunter Creek	97444
Huntington	97907
Idanha	97350
Idaville	97141
Idleyld Park	97447
Illahe	97406
Illinois Valley	97523
Imbler	97841
Imnaha	97842
Independence	97351
Indian Ford	97759
Indian Village	97720
Inglis	97016
Interlachen	97060
Ione	97843
Ironside	97908
Irrigon	97844
Irving	97402
Island City	97850
Ivy Station	97103
Izee	97820
Jacksonville	97530
Jamieson	97909
Jantzen Beach Center (Part of Portland)	97217
Jasper	97438
Jeffers Garden	97103
Jefferson	97352
Jennings Lodge	97267
Jewell	97138

Place	ZIP
Jimtown	97834
John Day	97845
Johnson City	97222
Jonesboro	97911
Jordan	97374
Jordan Valley	97910
Joseph	97846
Junction City	97448
Juntura	97911
Kahneeta Hot Springs	97761
Kamela	97801
Kansas City	97116
Keating	97814
Keizer	97307
Kellogg	97462
Kelso	97009
Kendall	97206
Keno	97627
Kent	97033
Kenton (Part of Portland)	97217
Kerby	97531
Kernville	97367
Kimberly	97848
King City	97224
Kingman Kolony	97913
Kingsley Field	97603
Kingston	97383
Kings Valley	97361
Kinton	97007
Kinzua	97830
Kiwanda Beach	97149
Klamath Falls	97601-03
For specific Klamath Falls Zip Codes call (503) 884-9226, or your local postmaster.	
Knappa	97103
Knoll Heights	97702
Lacomb	97355
Ladd Hill	97070
Lafayette	97127
La Grande	97850
Lakecreek	97524
Lake Grove (Part of Lake Oswego)	97035
Lake of the Woods	97601
Lake Oswego	97034-35
For specific Lake Oswego Zip Codes call (503) 294-2308, or your local postmaster.	
Lakeside	97449
Lakeview	97630
Lancaster	97448
Lancaster Mall (Part of Salem)	97301
Langell Valley	97623
Langlois	97450
Langrell	97834
La Pine	97739
Larwood	97374
Latham	97424
Latourell Falls	97014
Laurel	97123
Laurel Grove	97411
Laurelwood	97119
Lawen	97740
Leaburg	97489
Lebanon	97355
Lee's Camp	97141
Leland	97497
Lents (Part of Portland)	97266
Leona	97435
Lewisburg	97330
Lexington	97839
Libby	97420
Liberal	97038
Liberty	97386
Lime	97907
Lincoln	97520
Lincoln Beach	97341
Lincoln City	97367
Lindbergh	97048
Little Albany	97390
Little Sweden	97346
Lloyd Center (Part of Portland)	97232
Locoda	97016
Logsden	97357
London	97424
Lone Elder	97013
Lonerock	97823
Long Creek	97856
Lookingglass (Douglas County)	97470
Looking Glass (Union County)	97827
Lorane	97451
Lorella	97623
Lostine	97857
Lowell	97452

Place	ZIP
Lower Logan	97045
Lynch (Part of Portland)	97236
Lyons	97358
McCoy	97371
Mc Dermitt	97910
McEwen	97877
McKee Bridge	97530
Mc Kenzie Bridge	97413
McKinley	97458
Macksburg	97013
McMinnville	97128
McNary (Part of Umatilla)	97882
McNulty	97051
Madras	97741
Malin	97632
Mall 205 (Part of Portland)	97216
Manhattan Beach (Part of Rockaway)	97136
Manning	97125
Manzanita	97130
Mapleton	97453
Marcola	97454
Marion	97359
Marion Forks	97350
Marlene Village	97005
Marquam	97362
Marshland	97016
Martin Manor	97225
Marylhurst	97036
Mason Additions (Part of Prineville)	97754
Maupin	97037
Mayger	97016
May Park	97850
Mayville	97830
Maywood Park	97220
Meacham	97859
Meadowbrook	97038
Meadow View	97448
Meda	97112
Medford	97501
	97504
For specific Medford Zip Codes call (503) 776-1326, or your local postmaster.	
Medford Center (Part of Medford)	97504
Medford Mall (Part of Medford)	97504
Medical Springs	97814
Mehama	97384
Melrose	97470
Melville	97103
Menlo Park (Part of Portland)	97230
Merlin	97532
Merrill	97633
Metolius	97741
Metzger	97223
Midland	97634
Midway (Multnomah County)	97233
Midway (Washington County)	97123
Mikkalo	97812
Miles Crossing	97103
Mill City	97360
Millersburg	97321
Millican	97701
Millington	97420
Millwood	97486
Milo	97429
Milton (Part of Milton-Freewater)	97862
Milton-Freewater	97862
Milwaukie	97222
Minam	97827
Mission	97801
Mist	97016
Mitchell	97750
Modeville	97351
Modoc Point	97624
Mohawk	97477
Mohawk Junction (Part of Springfield)	97477
Mohler	97131
Molalla	97038
Monitor	97071
Monmouth	97361
Monroe	97456
Monument	97864
Moody	97391
Morgan	97843
Moro	97039
Mosier	97040
Mountaindale	97113
Mount Angel	97362
Mount Hebron	97801
Mount Hood	97041

	ZIP		ZIP		ZIP		ZIP
Mount Hood-Parkdale	97041	Palestine	97321	Riley	97758	Sherwood	97140
Mount Hood Village	97049	Paradise Park	97023	Ritter	97872	Shorewood	97459
Mount Pleasant (Part of Oregon City)	97045	Parkdale	97041	Riverdale (Part of Portland)	97219	Shutter Creek Correctional Institution	97459
Mount Vernon	97865	Parker	97351	Rivergrove	97035	Siletz	97380
Mulino	97042	Parkersburg	97411	River Road	97404	Siltcoos	97493
Mulloy	97140	Park Place	97045	Riverside (Linn County)	97321	Silver Lake	97638
Multnomah (Part of Portland)	97219	Parkrose (Part of Portland)	97230	Riverside (Malheur County)	97917	Silverton	97381
Murphy	97533	Patterson Junction	97844	Riverside (Umatilla County)	97801	Silvies	97720
Myrick	97810	Paulina	97751	Riverton	97423	Simnasho	97761
Myrtle Creek	97457	Pedee	97361	Riverview (Columbia County)	97064	Sisters	97759
Myrtle Point	97458	Peel	97443	Riverview (Lane County)	97448	Sitkum	97548
Narrows (Harney County)	97721	Pendair Heights (Part of Pendleton)	97801	Roans Estate	97739	Six Corners (Part of Sherwood)	97140
Narrows (Linn County)	97386	Pendleton	97801	Roaring Springs Ranch	97736	Sixes	97476
Nashville	97326	Pendleton Junction (Part of Pendleton)	97801	Robinwood (Part of West Linn)	97068	Skelley	97499
Natal	97064	Peoria	97377	Rockaway	97136	Smithfield	97338
Neahkahnie	97131	Perry	97850	Rock Creek (Baker County)	97833	Snake River Correctional Institution	97914
Nedonna	97136	Perrydale	97101	Rock Creek (Gilliam County)	97812	Sodaville	97355
Needy	97013	Philomath	97370	Rockcreek (Washington County)	97225	Southbeach	97366
Nehalem	97131	Phoenix	97535	Rockford	97031	Southgate (Part of Portland)	97266
Nelscott (Part of Lincoln City)	97367	Piedmont (Part of Portland)	97211	Rockie Four Corners	97375	South Junction	97037
Neotsu	97364	Pigeon Point	97420	Rock Point	97525	South Lebanon	97355
Nesika Beach	97444	Pike	97148	Rockville	97910	South Scappoose	97056
Neskowin	97149	Pilot Rock	97868	Rockwood	97233	Southside (Part of Eugene)	97405
Netarts	97143	Pine	97834	Rocky Point	97601	Spicer	97355
Newberg	97132	Pine Grove (Hood River County)	97031	Rogue River	97537	Sprague River	97639
New Bridge	97870	Pine Grove (Wasco County)	97037	Rogue Valley Mall (Part of Medford)	97501	Spray	97874
New Era	97013	Pinehurst	97520	Rome	97910	Springbrook	97132
New Hope	97527	Pine Ridge	97624	Roseburg	97470	Springdale	97060
New Idanha	97350	Pioneer (Part of Portland)	97204	Roseburg North	97470	Springfield	97477-78
New Pine Creek	97635	Pistol River	97444	Rose City Park (Part of Portland)	97213		94782
Newport	97365	Pittsburg	97064	Rose Lodge	97372	For specific Springfield Zip Codes call (503) 747-3383, or your local postmaster.	
Newton Creek	97470	Plainview (Deschutes County)	97701	Rosemont	97068		
Nimrod	97488	Plainview (Linn County)	97377	Rowena	97058	Springwater	97023
Ninety One	97013	Pleasant Hill	97455	Roy	97106	Stafford	97068
Nonpareil	97479	Pleasant Valley (Baker County)	97814	Ruch	97530	Staleys Junction	97109
North Albany	97321	Pleasant Valley (Josephine County)	97532	Rufus	97050	Stanfield	97875
North Bend	97459	Pleasant Valley (Tillamook County)	97141	Ruggs	97836	Starkey	97850
North Bend Coast Guard Air Station	97459	Plush	97637	Rural Dell	97032	Starvout	97410
North Fork	97467	Pocahontas	97814	Russellville (Part of Portland)	97216	Stayton	97383
North Howell	97381	Polk Station	97338	Rye Valley	97907	Steamboat	97447
North Plains	97133	Pondosa	97814	Saginaw	97424	Stewart Lennox Addition	97601
North Powder	97867	Pony Village (Part of North Bend)	97459	St. Benedict	97373	Stimson Mill	97119
North Roseburg (Part of Roseburg)	97470	Porter Creek	97481	St. Helens	97051	Sublimity	97385
North Santiam	97325	Portland	97201-99	St. Johns (Part of Portland)	97203	Summer Lake	97640
North Springfield	97477	For specific Portland Zip Codes call (503) 294-2308, or your local postmaster.		St. Louis	97026	Summer Lake Hot Springs	97636
North Umpqua Village	97447			St. Paul	97137	Summerville	97876
Norway	97460	Port Orford	97465	Salem	97301-06	Summit	97326
Norwood	97062	Post	97752		97308-09	Sumner	97420
Noti	97461	Powell Butte	97753	For specific Salem Zip Codes call (503) 370-4700, or your local postmaster.		Sumpter	97877
Nottingham	97702	Powellhurst	97236			Sunnycrest	97132
Nyssa	97913	Powellhurst-Centennial	97236	Salmon Harbor	97467	Sunnydale	97435
Nyssa Heights	97913	Powers	97466	Salt Creek	97338	Sunnyside (Clackamas County)	97015
Oak Grove (Clackamas County)	97268	Prairie City	97869	Sams Valley	97525	Sunnyside (Umatilla County)	97862
Oak Grove (Hood River County)	97031	Pratum	97301	Sand Lake	97112	Sunny Valley	97497
Oak Hills	97225	Prescott	97048	Sandy	97055	Sunriver	97707
Oakland	97462	Princeton	97721	San Marine	97498	Sunset (Part of West Linn)	97068
Oakridge	97463	Prineville	97754	Santa Clara	97404	Sunset Beach	97146
Oak Springs	97037	Prineville Southeast (Part of Prineville)	97754	Santiam Terrace	97355	Sunset Hills (Part of Seaside)	97138
Oakville	97377	Pringle Park Plaza (Part of Salem)	97301	Saunders Lake	97459	Suntex Valley	97758
Oakway Mall (Part of Eugene)	97401	Progress	97008	Scappoose	97056	Suplee	97751
Oatfield	97222	Prospect	97536	Scholls	97123	Surf Pines	97146
O'Brien	97534	Prosper	97411	Scio	97374	Surprise Valley	97457
Oceanlake (Part of Lincoln City)	97367	Quartz Mountain	97630	Scofield	97109	Sutherlin	97479
Oceanside	97134	Quinaby	97303	Scottsburg	97473	Suver	97361
Odell	97044	Quincy	97016	Scotts Mills	97375	Suver Junction	97361
Odessa	97601	Quines Creek	97442	Seal Rock	97376	Svensen	97103
Oklahoma Hill	97016	Rainbow	97413	Seaside	97138	Swedetown	97016
Old Colton	97017	Rainier	97048	Seekseequa	97761	Sweet Home	97386
Old Town	97462	Raleigh Hills	97225	Seghers	97119	Swisshome	97480
Olene	97601	Ramsey	97701	Sellwood (Part of Portland)	97202	Sylvan (Part of Portland)	97221
Olex	97812	Ramsey Hall	97021	Sellwood Moreland (Part of Portland)	97202	Table Rock	97501
Olney	97103	Randolph	97411	Selma	97538	Taft (Part of Lincoln City)	97367
Ontario	97914	Redland	97045	Seneca	97873	Takilma	97523
Ophir	97464	Redmond	97756	Service Creek	97830	Talbot	97352
Ordnance	97838	Redwood	97526	Shadowood	97068	Talent	97540
Oregon City	97045	Reedsport	97467	Shady Cove	97539	Tallman	97355
Orenco	97123	Remote	97458	Shady Dell	97038	Tangent	97389
Oretech (Part of Klamath Falls)	97601	Reston	97470	Shaniko	97057	Taylorville	97016
Oretown	97112	Rhododendron	97049	Shasta Plaza (Part of Klamath Falls)	97603	Telocaset	97883
Orient	97030	Rice Hill	97462	Shaw	97325	Tenmile	97481
Orleans	97321	Richardson	97490	Shedd	97377	Terrebonne	97760
Otis	97368	Richland	97870	Shelburn	97374	Thatcher	97116
Otter Rock	97369	Richmond	97874	Sheridan	97378	The Dalles	97058
Outlook	97045	Rickreall	97371			Thornhollow	97810
Owyhee	97913	Riddle	97469			Three Lynx	97023
Oxbow	97840	Rieth	97801			Three Rivers	97701
Pacific City	97135					Thurston (Part of Springfield)	97482
Page (Part of Albany)....	97321					Tide	97480
Paisley	97636					Tidewater	97390

* Area Zip Code   † Post Office Boxes

	ZIP		ZIP		ZIP		ZIP
Tiernan	97453	Union	97883	Warren	97053	Wilderville	97543
Tierra Del Mar	97112	Union Creek	97536	Warrendale	97014	Wildwood	97049
Tigard	97223-24	Union Gap	97462	Warrenton	97146	Wilhoit	97038
	97281	Union Mills	97042	Wasco	97065	Willakenzie (Part of	
For specific Tigard Zip Codes		Union Point	97327	Washington Park Zoo		Eugene)	97401
call (503) 639-1730, or your		Unionvale	97114	Railway (Part of		Willamette (Part of West	
local postmaster.		Unity (Baker County)	97884	Portland)	97221	Linn)	97068
Tillamook	97141	Unity (Lane County)	97438	Washington Square (Part		Willamette City (Part of	
Tiller	97484	University (Lane County)	97403	of Portland)	97223	Oakridge)	97463
Tillican	97701	University (Multnomah		Waterloo	97355	Willamina	97396
Timber	97144	County)	97207	Watseco	97136	Willbridge (Part of	
Timber Grove	97004	Upper Highland	97004	Weatherby	97905	Portland)	97231
Timberline Lodge	97028	Upper Hood River Valley	97044	Wecoma Beach (Part of		Williams	97544
Toketee Falls	97447	Upper Soda	97345	Lincoln City)	97367	Willowcreek	97918
Toledo	97391	Vale	97918	Wedderburn	97491	Willowdale	97741
Tollgate	97886	Valley Falls	97630	Welches	97067	Willsburg Junction (Part of	
Tolovana Park	97145	Valley Junction	97396	Wemme	97067	Milwaukie)	97222
Tongue Point Village	97103	Valley River Center (Part		Western Evangelical		Wilson Beach	97141
Top	97864	of Eugene)	97401	Seminary	97045	Wilsonville	97070
Tophill	97109	Valley View	97321	Westfall	97920	Wimer	97537
Town Center (Part of		Valsetz	97380	Westfir	97492	Winchester	97495
Portland)	97229	Van	97904	West Haven-Sylvan	97225	Winchester Bay	97467
Trail	97541	Vaughn	97487	West Lake (Clatsop		Windmaster Corner	97031
Trask	97141	Veneta	97487	County)	97146	Winema Beach	97112
Treharne	97064	Verboort	97116	Westlake (Lane County)	97493	Wingville	97814
Trent	97431	Vermont Hills	97219	West Linn	97068	Winston	97496
Triangle Lake	97412	Vernonia	97064	Weston	97886	Winterville	97411
Tri-City	97457	Vida	97488	Westport	97016	Witch Hazel	97123
Trout Creek (Harney		Viola	97023	West Salem (Part of		Wocus	97601
County)	97710	Vista (Part of Salem)	97302	Salem)	97304	Wolf Creek	97497
Trout Creek (Hood River		Waconda	97026	West Scio	97374	Women's Release Unit	97301
County)	97041	Wagontire	97738	West Side (Lake County)	97630	Wonder	97543
Troutdale	97060	Wagon Trail Ranch	97739	West Side (Lane County)	97402	Woodburn	97071
Troy	97828	Wakonda Beach	97394	West Slope	97225	Woods	97112
Tualatin	97062	Walden	97424	West Stayton	97325	Woodson	97016
Tumalo	97701	Waldport	97394	West St. Helens (Part of		Wood Village	97060
Turner	97392	Walker	97426	St. Helens)	97051	Worden	97601
Twelve Mile	97030	Wallowa	97885	West Union	97123	Wren	97326
Twickenham	97750	Wallowa Lake Resort	97846	Wetmore	97830	Wyeth	97014
Twin Rocks	97136	Walterville	97489	Weyerhaeuser Townsite	97601	Yachats	97498
Twomile	97411	Walton	97490	Wheeler	97147	Yamhill	97148
Tygh Valley	97063	Wamic	97063	Wheeler Heights (Part of		Yankton	97051
Ukiah	97880	Wapato	97119	Wheeler)	97147	Yaquina	97365
Umapine	97862	Wapinitia	97037	Whiskey Hill	97032	Yoder	97032
Umatilla	97882	Warm Springs	97761	White City	97503	Yoncalla	97499
Umatilla Indian		Warm Springs Indian		Whiteson	97101	Yonna	97623
Reservation	97801	Reservation	97761	Wilbur	97494	Zigzag	97049
Umpqua	97486						

	ZIP
Aaronsburg	16820
Abbott (Township)	16922
Abbottstown	17301
Aberdeen	18444
Abington (Lackawanna County) (Township)	18471
Abington (Montgomery County)	19001
Abington (Montgomery County) (Township)	19001
Abrahamsville	12723
Abrams	19406
Academia	17082
Academy Corners	16928
Academy Gardens (Part of Philadelphia)	19114
Acahela	18610
Accomac	17406
Ackermanville	18010
Acme	15610
Acmetonia	15024
Acosta	15520
Adah	15410
Adams (Armstrong County)	16028
Adams (Butler County) (Township)	16046
Adams (Cambria County) (Township)	15955
Adams (Snyder County) (Township)	17813
Adams (Somerset County)	15541
Adamsburg	15611
Adams Corners	16057
Adamsdale	17972
Adams Hill	15642
Adamstown	19501
Adamsville	16110
Addingham	19026
Addison	15411
Addison (Township)	15540
Adelaide	15425
Admire	17364
Adrian	16210
Adrian Furnace	15801
Advance	15732
Africa	17236
Afton Village	18034
Ahrensville	16301
Aiden Lair	19025
Aiken	16744
Airville	17302
Airydale	17060
Ajax	16323
Akeley	16345
Akersville	15536
Akron	17501
Aladdin	15682
Alameda Park	16001
Alaska	15825
Alba	16910
Albany (Berks County)	19529
Albany (Berks County) (Township)	19529
Albany (Bradford County) (Township)	18833
Albany (Fayette County)	15417
Albert	18707
Albidale	19006
Albion (Erie County)	16401
Albion (Jefferson County)	15767
Albrightsville	18210
Alburtis	18011
Alcoa Center	15068
Aldan	19018
Alden	18634
Aldenville	18401
Alderson (Part of Harveys Lake)	18618
Aldham	19460
Aleppo (Allegheny County) (Township)	15143
Aleppo (Greene County)	15310
Aleppo (Greene County) (Township)	15310
Alexander Springs	17004
Alexandria	16611
Alfarata	17841
Alford	18826
Alicia (Fayette County)	15417
Alicia (Greene County)	15338
Alinda	17040
Aline	17853
Aliquippa	15001
Allandale	17011
Allegany (Township)	16923
Allegheny (Allegheny County)	15212
Allegheny (Blair County) (Township)	16635

	ZIP
Allegheny (Butler County) (Township)	16049
Allegheny (Cambria County) (Township)	15940
Allegheny (Somerset County) (Township)	15538
Allegheny (Venango County) (Township)	16341
Allegheny (Westmoreland County) (Township)	15613
Allegheny Acres	15024
Allegheny Center Mall (Part of Pittsburgh)	15212
Allegheny College (Part of Meadville)	16335
Allegheny Furnace (Part of Altoona)	16602
Allegheny Springs	16371
Alleghenyville	19540
Allemans	16639
Allen (Cumberland County)	17007
Allen (Northampton County) (Township)	18067
Allen Crest	18052
Allen Lane (Part of Philadelphia)	19119
Allenport (Huntingdon County)	17066
Allenport (Washington County)	15412
Allens Mills	15851
Allensville	17002
Allentown	18101-95
For specific Allentown Zip Codes call (215) 821-8450, or your local postmaster.	
Allenvale	15501
Allenwood	17810
Allis Hollow	18837
Allison (Clinton County) (Township)	17751
Allison (Fayette County)	15413
Allison Heights	15413
Allison Park	15101
Allport (Cambria County)	15714
Allport (Clearfield County)	16821
Almaden	16680
Almedia	17815
Almont	18960
Alpha (Part of Windgap)	18091
Alpine	17339
Alsace (Township)	19606
Alsace Manor	19560
Alta Manor (Part of Altoona)	16601
Altamont	17931
Altenwald	17268
Althom	16351
Alton	19380
Alton Park (Part of Allentown)	18103
Altoona	16601-03
For specific Altoona Zip Codes call (814) 944-4505, or your local postmaster.	
Alum Bank	15521
Alum Rock	16373
Aluta	18064
Alverda	15710
Alverton	15612
Amaranth	17267
Amasa	18433
Ambau	17362
Amberson	17210
Ambler	19002
Ambler Highlands	19034
Ambridge	15003
Ambridge Heights	15003
Ambrose	15759
Amend	15401
American Philatelic Society Building (Part of State College)	16803
Amesville	16651
Amity (Berks County) (Township)	19518
Amity (Bucks County)	18036
Amity (Erie County) (Township)	16438
Amity (Washington County)	15311
Amity Gardens	19518
Amity Hall	17020
Amsbry	16641
Amsterdam	16127
Amwell (Township)	15301
Analomink	18320
Ancient Oaks	18062
Ancient Oaks West	18062

	ZIP
Andalusia	19020
Anderson	17044
Andersonburg	17047
Andersontown	17055
Andreas	18211
Andrews Bridge	17509
Andrews Plan	15001
Andrews Settlement	16923
Angelica	19540
Angels	18445
Angora (Part of Philadelphia)	19143
Anita	15711
Ankeny	15547
Annaline Village	19061
Annin (Township)	16743
Annisville	16049
Annville	17003
Annville (Township)	17003
Anselma	19425
Ansonia	16901
Ansonville	16656
Antes Fort	17720
Anthony (Lycoming County) (Township)	17728
Anthony (Montour County) (Township)	17772
Anthracite (Part of Cornwall)	17016
Antis (Township)	16617
Antrim (Franklin County) (Township)	17225
Antrim (Tioga County)	16901
Apolacon (Township)	18830
Apollo	15613
Appenzell	18360
Applebachsville	18951
Appletree Hill	19007
Appleville	19380
Applewold	16201
Aquashicola	18012
Aqueduct	17020
Aquetong	18938
Ararat	18465
Ararat (Township)	18465
Arbor	17356
Arbuckle	16438
Arcadia (Indiana County)	15712
Arcadia (Lancaster County)	17563
Archbald	18403
Arch Rock	17059
Arch Spring	16686
Arcola	19420
Ardara	15615
Arden	15301
Ardenheim	16652
Arden Mines	15301
Ardmore	19003
Ardmore Manor	19003
Ardmore Park	19003
Ardsley	19038
Arendtsville	17303
Arensberg	15433
Argentine	16040
Argus	18960
Aristes	17920
Arlingham	19031
Arlingham Hills	19031
Arlington (Allegheny County)	15137
Arlington (Wayne County)	18436
Arlington Heights	18360
Arlington Knolls	18052
Armagh (Indiana County)	15920
Armagh (Mifflin County) (Township)	17063
Armbrust	15616
Armenia (Township)	16947
Armstrong (Indiana County) (Township)	15774
Armstrong (Lycoming County) (Township)	17701
Arndts	18038
Arnold	15068
Arnold City	15012
Arnot	16911
Arnots Addition (Part of St. Clair)	17970
Arona	15617
Aronimink	19026
Arrowhead Lake	18347
Arsenal (Part of Pittsburgh)	15201
Artemas	17211
Arundel Village	19044
Arwin Acres	17036
Asaph	16901
Asbury (Columbia County)	17859
Asbury (Erie County)	16509

	ZIP
Ashcom	15537
Asherton	17801
Ashfield	18212
Ashland (Clarion County) (Township)	16232
Ashland (Clearfield County)	16666
Ashland (Schuylkill County)	17921
Ashley	18706
Ashtola	15963
Ashville	16613
Askam	18706
Aspers	17304
Aspinwall	15215
Aston	19014
Aston (Township)	19014
Asylum (Township)	18848
Atco	12764
Atglen	19310
Athens (Bradford County)	18810
Athens (Bradford County) (Township)	18810
Athens (Crawford County) (Township)	16404
Athol	19519
Atkinsons Mills	17051
Atlantic (Clearfield County)	16651
Atlantic (Crawford County)	16111
Atlantic (Westmoreland County)	15671
Atlas	17851
Atlasburg	15004
Atwood	16249
Auburn (Schuylkill County)	17922
Auburn (Susquehanna County) (Township)	18630
Auburn Center	18623
Auburn Four Corners	18630
Audenried	18201
Audubon	19407
Aughwick	17066
Augustaville	17801
Aultman	15713
Austin	16720
Austinburg	16928
Austinville	16914
Avalon	15202
Avella	15312
Avella Highlands	15312
Avis	17721
Avoca	18641
Avon	17042
Avondale	19311
Avondale Knolls	19086
Avon Heights	17042
Avonia	16415
Avonmore	15618
Axemann	16823
Ayr (Township)	17233
Bachmanville	17033
Baden	15005
Baederwood	19046
Bagdad	15656
Baggaley	15650
Baidland	15063
Bailey	17074
Baileys Corner	16926
Baileyville	16865
Bainbridge	17502
Bair	17405
Bairdford	15006
Bairdstown	15717
Bakers Summit	16614
Baker Station	13390
Bakerstown	15007
Bakerstown Station	15044
Bakersville	15501
Bala	19004
Bala-Cynwyd	19004
Bala-Cynwyd Shopping Center	19004
Bald Eagle (Blair County)	16686
Bald Eagle (Clinton County) (Township)	17751
Bald Hill (Clearfield County)	16850
Bald Hill (Greene County)	15349
Baldwin (Allegheny County)	15227
Baldwin (Allegheny County) (Township)	15234
Baldwin (Delaware County)	19013
Balliettsville	18037
Balls Eddy	18461
Balls Mills	17728
Balltown	16347
Bally	19503

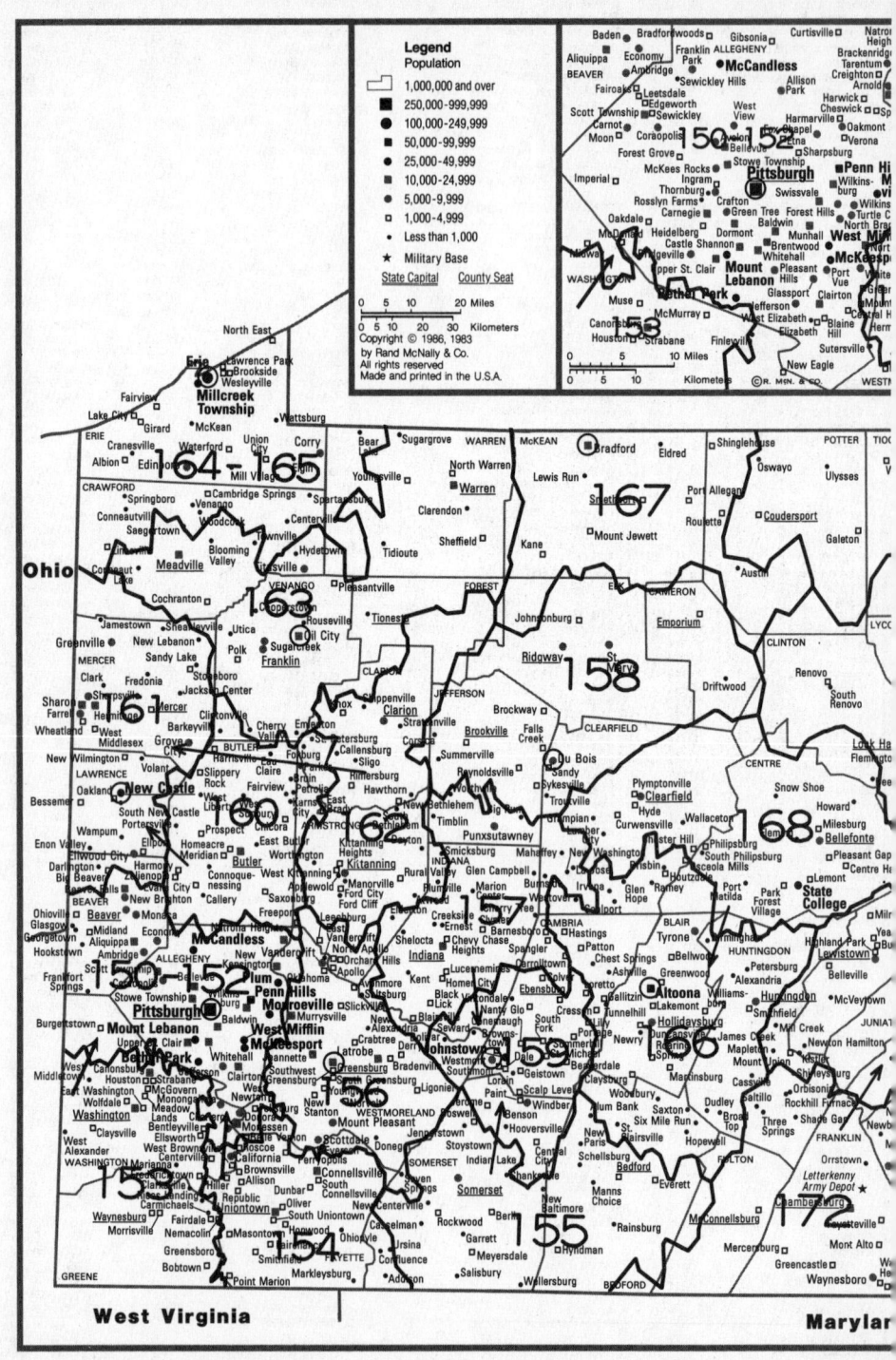

Legend
Population

☐ 1,000,000 and over
■ 250,000-999,999
● 100,000-249,999
● 50,000-99,999
• 25,000-49,999
■ 10,000-24,999
□ 5,000-9,999
□ 1,000-4,999
• Less than 1,000
★ Military Base
State Capital   County Seat

0   5   10   20 Miles
0 5 10   20   30 Kilometers
Copyright © 1986, 1983
by Rand McNally & Co.
All rights reserved
Made and printed in the U.S.A.

West Virginia

Maryland

Ohio

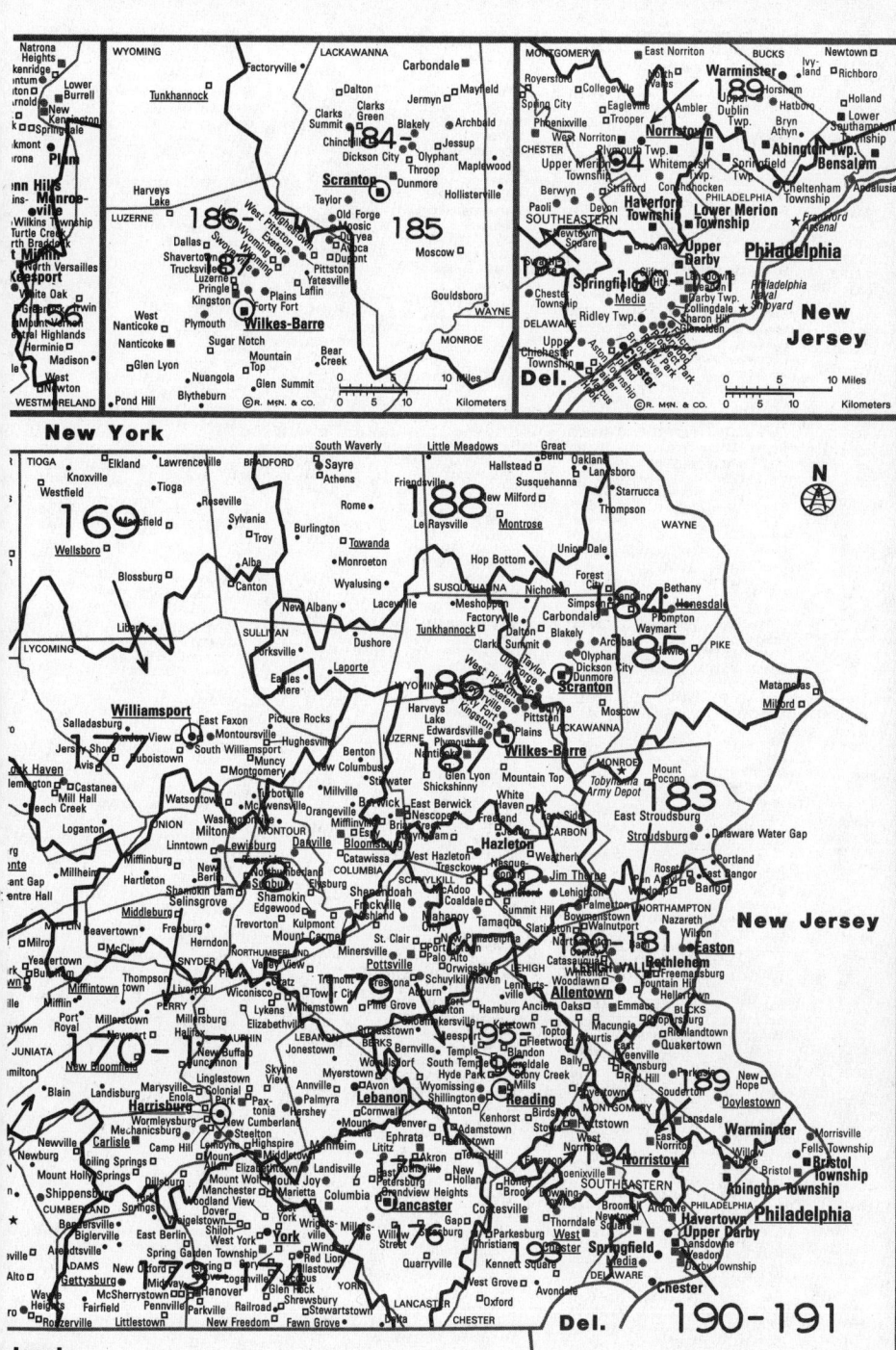

	ZIP		ZIP		ZIP		ZIP
Balsinger	15401	Beaver (Jefferson County)		Belsena Mills	16661	Betz	16661
Banbury Crossing	17036	(Township)	15864	Belton	16117	Betzwood	19401
Bando	15501	Beaver (Snyder County)		Beltzhoover (Part of		Beulah	16661
Banetown	15301	(Township)	17813	Pittsburgh)	15210	Beverly Estates	17601
Baney Settlement	16830	Beaver Acres	15136	Ben Avon (Allegheny		Beverly Heights	17046
Bangor	18013	Beaver Brook	18201	County)	15202	Beverly Hills (Blair County)	16601
Banian Junction	16661	Beaver Center	16435	Ben Avon (Indiana		Beverly Hills (Delaware	
Banks (Carbon County)		Beaverdale (Cambria		County)	15701	County)	19082
(Township)	18254	County)	15921	Ben Avon Heights	15202	Beyer	16211
Banks (Indiana County)		Beaverdale		Bencetown	15734	Biddle	15692
(Township)	15742	(Northumberland		Bendersville	17306	Biesecker Gap	17268
Banksville (Part of		County)	17851	Bendertown	17859	Big Beaver	15010
Pittsburgh)	15216	Beaverdale-Lloydell	15921	Benedicts	17315	Big Cove Tannery	17212
Banner Ridge	15757	Beaver Dam	16407	Benedicts	17315	Biggertown	17774
Bannerville	17841	Beaver Falls	15010	Benezett	15821	Bigler	16825
Banning	15428	Beaver Lake	17758	Benezette (Township)	15821	Bigler (Township)	16661
Baptist Bible College and		Beaver Meadows	18216	Benfer	17812	Biglerville	17307
Seminary	18411	Beaver Springs	17812	Benjamin (Part of		Big Mine Run	17921
Barbours	17701	Beavertown (Blair County)	16662	Perkasie)	18944	Bigmount	17315
Bard	15534	Beavertown (Snyder		Benner (Township)	16823	Big Pond	16914
Baresville	17331	County)	17813	Bensalem	19020-21	Big Run	15715
Bareville	17540	Beavertown (York County)	17019	For specific Bensalem Zip		Big Shanty	16738
Barkeyville	16038	Beaver Valley	16640	Codes call (215) 639-5050, or		Bimber Corners	16351
Barlow	17325	Beccaria	16616	your local postmaster.		Bingen	18015
Barnards	16222	Beccaria (Township)	16627	Bens Creek	15938	Bingham (McKean	
Barnes (Cambria County)	15737	Bechtelsville	19505	Benson	15935	County)	16726
Barnes (Jefferson County)	15825	Beckersville	19540	Bentley Creek	14894	Bingham (Potter County)	
Barnes (Warren County)	16347	Becks	17901	Bentleyville	15314	(Township)	16923
Barnesboro	15714	Bedford	15522	Benton (Columbia County)	17814	Bingham Center	16923
Barneston	19344	Bedford (Township)	15522	Benton (Columbia County)		Binnstown (Part of	
Barnesville	18214	Bedminster	18910	(Township)	17814	Centerville)	15417
Barnett (Forest County)		Bedminster (Township)	18910	Benton (Lackawanna		Bino	17225
(Township)	15828	Beech Creek	16822	County) (Township)	18420	Birchardville	18801
Barnett (Jefferson County)		Beech Creek (Township)	16822	Benvenue	17020	Birchrunville	19421
(Township)	15860	Beecherstown	17307	Benzinger (Township)	15857	Birch Valley	19058
Barnettstown	16634	Beech Flats	17724	Bergey	19438	Birchwood Lakes	18328
Barneytown	17052	Beech Glen	17758	Berkeley Hills	15237	Birdell	19344
Barnitz	17013	Beech Grove (Elk County)	15822	Berkley	19605	Bird in Hand	17505
Barnsley	19363	Beech Grove (Lycoming		Berkleys Mill	15552	Birdsboro	19508
Barr (Township)	15762	County)	17771	Berkshire Heights (Part of		Birdville	17052
Barree	16611	Beechton	15824	Wyomissing)	19610	Birmingham (Chester	
Barree (Township)	16669	Beechview (Part of		Berkshire Mall (Part of		County)	19380
Barren Hill	19444	Pittsburgh)	15216	Wyomissing)	19610	Birmingham (Chester	
Barret Plan	15001	Beechwood	15834	Berlin (Somerset County)	15530	County) (Township)	19380
Barrett (Clearfield County)	16830	Beechwood Park	19014	Berlin (Wayne County)		Birmingham (Delaware	
Barrett (Monroe County)		Beechwoods	15840	(Township)	18431	County) (Township)	19317
(Township)	18342	Beeman	16946	Berlin Junction	17350	Birmingham (Huntingdon	
Barronvale	15557	Beersville	18067	Berlinsville	18088	County)	16686
Barr Slope	15734	Beesons	15445	Bermudian	17019	Bishop	15057
Barville	17084	Beham	15376	Bern (Township)	19605	Bitner	15431
Barry (Township)	17921	Bela	16049	Berne	19526	Bittersville	17366
Barry Heights (Part of		Belair	17601	Bernharts	19605	Bitumen	17778
Norristown)	19401	Belair Park	17601	Bernice	18632	Bixler	17047
Bart	17503	Belardley	19007	Bernville	19506	Black (Bradford County)	18848
Bart (Township)	17562	Belden	15522	Berrysburg	17005	Black (Somerset County)	
Barto	19504	Belfast (Fulton County)		Berrytown	16925	(Township)	15557
Bartonsville	18321	(Township)	17238	Berwick (Adams County)		Black Ash	16327
Bartville	17509	Belfast (Northampton		(Township)	17316	Black Bear (Part of St.	
Basket	19547	County)	18064	Berwick (Columbia		Lawrence)	19606
Bassards Corners	18038	Belfast Junction	18040	County)	18603	Blackburn (Part of	
Bastress (Township)	17701	Belfry	19401	Berwinsdale	16656	Trafford)	15085
Bath	18014	Belknap	16222	Berwyn	19312	Black Creek (Township)	18246
Bath Addition	19007	Bell (Clearfield County)		Besco	15322	Black Diamond (Part of	
Bath Manor	19007	(Township)	15757	Bessemer (Allegheny		Monongahela)	15063
Bauerstown	15209	Bell (Jefferson County)		County)	15104	Blackfield	15542
Baumgardner	17584	(Township)	15767	Bessemer (Lawrence		Blackhawk	15010
Baumstown	19508	Bell (Westmoreland		County)	16112	Blackhorse (Chester	
Bausman	17504	County) (Township)	15613	Bessemer (Westmoreland		County)	19365
Bavington	15019	Bell Acres	15143	County) (Township)	15666	Black Horse (Delaware	
Baxter	15829	Bella Vista	17754	Best (Part of West Mifflin)	15122	County)	19063
Beachdale	15530	Belle Bridge (Part of		Best Station	18080	Black Horse (Montgomery	
Beach Haven	18601	Lincoln)	15037	Bethany	18431	County)	19401
Beach Lake	18405	Bellefield (Part of		Bethayres	19006	Blacklick (Cambria	
Beachly	15424	Pittsburgh)	15213	Bethel (Armstrong		County) (Township)	15943
Beadling	15241	Bellefonte	16823	County) (Township)	16226	Black Lick (Indiana	
Beale (Township)	17082	Bellegrove	17003	Bethel (Berks County)	19507	County)	15716
Beallsville	15313	Bellemont	17562	Bethel (Berks County)		Black Lick (Indiana	
Beans Cove	15535	Belle Valley	16509	(Township)	19507	County) (Township)	15717
Bear Creek	18602	Belle Vernon	15012	Bethel (Delaware County)		Blacklog	17243
Bear Creek (Township)	18602	Belleville	17004	(Township)	19061	Blackman	18702
Bear Creek Lake	18229	Bellevue	15202	Bethel (Fulton County)		Black Ridge	15235
Bear Gap	17824	Bell Mountain (Part of		(Township)	17267	Blackrock	21088
Bear Lake	16402	Dickson City)	18508	Bethel (Lebanon County)		Blacktown	16137
Bear Rocks	15610	Bell Point	15613	(Township)	17026	Black Walnut	18623
Beartown (Franklin		Bells Camp	16727	Bethel (Mercer County)	16159	Blackwell	16938
County)	17268	Bells Landing	15757	Bethel (Westmoreland		Blain	17006
Beartown (Lancaster		Bells Mills	15767	County)	15658	Blain City	16627
County)	17555	Belltown (Elk County)	15860	Bethelboro	15401	Blaine (Township)	15365
Bear Valley	17866	Belltown (Mifflin County)	17841	Bethel Park	15102	Blaine Hill	15037
Beatty	15650	Bellview	15301	Bethesda	17532	Blainesburg (Part of West	
Beaufort Farms	17110	Bellwood	16617	Bethlehem (Clearfield		Brownsville)	15417
Beaumont	18618	Belmar (Allegheny		County)	15757	Blainsport	17569
Beaver (Beaver County)	15009	County)	15206	Bethlehem (Northampton		Blair (Township)	16635
Beaver (Clarion County)		Belmar (Venango County)	16323	County)	18015-18	Blairs Corners	16232
(Township)	16232	Belmar Park	16101	For specific Bethlehem Zip		Blairs Mills	17213
Beaver (Columbia County)		Belmont	15904	Codes call (215) 866-0911, or		Blairsville	15717
(Township)	17815	Belmont Corner	18453	your local postmaster.		Blairtown	15370
Beaver (Crawford County)		Belmont Hills	19020	Bethlehem (Northampton		Blakely	18447
(Township)	16406	Belmont Terrace	19406	County) (Township)	18017	Blakeslee	18610
		Belsano	15922	Bethton	18964		
				Betula	16749		

	ZIP
Blanchard (Allegheny County)	15084
Blanchard (Centre County)	16826
Blanco	16249
Blandburg	16619
Blandon	19510
Blanket Hill	16201
Blawnox	15238
Bloom (Township)	16838
Bloomfield (Allegheny County)	15224
Bloomfield (Bedford County) (Township)	16664
Bloomfield (Crawford County) (Township)	16438
Bloomingdale (Carbon County)	18250
Bloomingdale (Lancaster County)	17601
Bloomingdale (Luzerne County)	18655
Blooming Glen	18911
Blooming Grove (Pike County)	18428
Blooming Grove (Pike County) (Township)	18464
Blooming Grove (York County)	17331
Bloomington (Clearfield County)	16833
Bloomington (Lackawanna County)	18444
Blooming Valley	16335
Bloomsburg	17815
Bloomsdale Gardens	19058
Bloserville	17241
Bloss (Township)	16911
Blossburg	16912
Blosser Hill	15474
Blossom Hill	17601
Blossom Valley	17601
Blough	15936
Blue Ball	17506
Blue Bell	19422
Blue Heron Pond	18328
Blue Hill	17870
Blue Jay	16347
Blue Knob	15946
Blue Ridge	19058
Blue Ridge Summit	17214
Bluff	15341
Blythe (Township)	17930
Blytheburn	18707
Blythedale	15018
Blythewood	18901
Boaba	18428
Boalsburg	16827
Boardman	16863
Bobbys Corners (Part of Hermitage)	16159
Bobtown	15315
Bocktown	15001
Bodines	17722
Boeckel Landing	17302
Boggs (Armstrong County) (Township)	16259
Boggs (Centre County) (Township)	16823
Boggs (Clearfield County) (Township)	16878
Boggsville	16055
Bohemia	18428
Bohrmans Mill	17972
Boiling Springs	17007
Bolde Point	18428
Bolivar	15923
Bolivar Run	16701
Boltz	15954
Bon Air (Cambria County)	15902
Bon Aire (Delaware County)	19083
Bon Aire	16001
Bondsville	19335
Bonnair	17327
Bonneauville	17325
Bonnie Brook	16001
Bonus	16049
Boone	15926
Booneville	17747
Booths Corner	19061
Boothwyn	19061
Boothwyn Highlands	19061
Boot Jack	15853
Boquet	15644
Bordnersville	17038
Borland Manor	15317
Bortondale	19063
Boston	15135
Boston Run	17948

	ZIP
Boswell	15531
Boulevard (Part of Philadelphia)	19149
Bourne	18850
Bovard (Butler County)	16020
Bovard (Westmoreland County)	15619
Bowdertown	15724
Bower	15757
Bower Hill (Allegheny County)	15106
Bower Hill (Washington County)	15367
Bowers	19511
Bowie	16133
Bowling Green	19063
Bowman Addition	17331
Bowman Heights	17201
Bowmans	17948
Bowmansdale	17008
Bowmans Store	17329
Bowmanstown	18030
Bowmansville	17507
Bowood	15478
Boyce	15241
Boyds Mills	18443
Boydstown	16025
Boydtown	17872
Boyers	16020
Boyers Junction	19522
Boyertown	19512
Boynton	15532
Brackenridge	15014
Brackney	18812
Bradbury Plan	15001
Braddock (Allegheny County)	15104
Braddock (Washington County)	15301
Braddock Hills	15221
Braden Plan	15322
Bradenville	15620
Bradford (Clearfield County) (Township)	16881
Bradford (McKean County)	16701
Bradford (McKean County) (Township)	16701
Bradford Hills	19335
Bradford Park (Part of Economy)	15005
Bradfordwoods	15015
Bradley Junction	15931
Bradleytown	16317
Brady (Butler County) (Township)	16057
Brady (Clarion County) (Township)	16248
Brady (Clearfield County) (Township)	15848
Brady (Clearfield County)	15801
Brady (Huntingdon County) (Township)	17002
Brady (Lycoming County) (Township)	17752
Bradys Bend	16028
Bradys Bend (Township)	16028
Braeburn (Part of Lower Burrell)	15068
Braintrim (Township)	18623
Braman	18417
Bramcote	19464
Branch (Township)	17901
Branch Dale	17923
Branchton	16021
Branchville	16426
Brandamore	19316
Brandon	16374
Brandonville	17967
Brandt	18847
Brandtsville	17055
Brandy Camp	15822
Brandywine Hills	19380
Brandywine Homes	19320
Brandywine Manor	19343
Brandywine Summit	19342
Brandywine Village	19406
Bratton (Township)	17044
Brave	15316
Braznell	15442
Breakneck	15425
Brecknock (Berks County) (Township)	19540
Brecknock (Lancaster County) (Township)	17517
Breezewood	15533
Breezy Corner	19522
Breinigsville	18031
Brenizer	15717
Brent	16156

	ZIP
Brentwood	15227
Breslau	18702
Bressler	17113
Bressler-Enhaut-Oberlin	17113
Bretonville	16656
Briarbrook	18707
Briarcliff	19036
Briar Creek	18603
Briar Creek (Township)	18603
Briar Hill (Armstrong County)	16201
Briar Hill (Wayne County)	18438
Brick Church	16226
Brickerville	17543
Brick Tavern	18951
Bridesburg (Part of Philadelphia)	19137
Bridgeburg	16210
Bridgeport (Adams County)	17307
Bridgeport (Carbon County)	18661
Bridgeport (Clearfield County)	16833
Bridgeport (Lancaster County)	17602
Bridgeport (Montgomery County)	19405
Bridgeport (Perry County)	17040
Bridgeport (Westmoreland County)	15666
Bridgeton (Bucks County) (Township)	18972
Bridgeton (York County)	17321
Bridgetown	19047
Bridge Valley	18925
Bridgeville	15017
Bridgewater (Beaver County)	15009
Bridgewater (Bucks County)	19020
Bridgewater (Susquehanna County) (Township)	18801
Bridgewater Farms	19014
Brier Hill	15415
Briggsville	18635
Brighton (Township)	15009
Brightwood (Part of Bethel Park)	15102
Brilhart	17404
Brinker	16001
Brinkerton	15601
Brintons	19380
Brisbin	16620
Briscoe Springs	16127
Bristol	19007
Bristol (Township)	19021
Bristoria	15337
Brittany Farms	18914
Brittany Farms-Highlands	18914
Britton Run	16434
Broad Acres	16127
Broad Axe	19002
Broad Ford	15425
Broadlawn Highlands	15241
Broad Street (Part of Hazleton)	18201
Broad Top (Bedford County) (Township)	16679
Broad Top (Huntingdon County)	16621
Broadview	15084
Broadway	18655
Broadway Manor	19007
Brock	15362
Brockport	15823
Brockton	17925
Brockway	15824
Brodbecks	17329
Brodhead	18017
Brodheadsville	18322
Brogue	17309
Brogueville	17322
Brokenstraw (Township)	16340
Brommerstown	17922
Brookdale (Cambria County)	15942
Brookdale (Susquehanna County)	18822
Brookes Mill	16635
Brookfield (Township)	16950
Brookhaven	19015
Brookland	16948
Brookline (Allegheny County)	15226
Brookline (Delaware County)	19083
Brooklyn	18813
Brooklyn (Township)	18813

	ZIP
Brookside (Cumberland County)	17257
Brookside (Erie County)	16510
Brookside (Lycoming County)	17771
Brookside (Schuylkill County)	17963
Brookside (York County)	17315
Brookside Farms	15241
Brookside Villa	18101
Brookston	16347
Brookthorpe Hills	19008
Brookville	15825
Brookwater Park	19426
Broomall	19008
Brothersvalley (Township)	15530
Brotherton	15530
Broughton	15236
Brown (Lycoming County) (Township)	17727
Brown (Mifflin County) (Township)	17084
Brownbacks	19475
Browndale	18421
Brownfield	15416
Brown Hill	16403
Browns (Part of Avoca)	18641
Brownsburg	18938
Brownsdale	16053
Browns Mill	17201
Brownstown (Armstrong County)	15630
Brownstown (Cambria County)	15906
Brownstown (Fayette County)	15438
Brownstown (Lancaster County)	17508
Brownsville (Berks County)	19565
Brownsville (Fayette County)	15417
Brownsville (Fayette County) (Township)	15417
Brownsville (Franklin County)	17222
Brownsville (Schuylkill County)	17976
Brownsville Junction	15417
Browntown (Bradford County)	18853
Browntown (Luzerne County)	18640
Bruin	16022
Brunnerville	17543
Brunot Island (Part of Pittsburgh)	15233
Brush Creek (Township)	15536
Brushtown (Adams County)	17331
Brushtown (Cumberland County)	17241
Brush Valley	15720
Brush Valley (Township)	15720
Brushville	18847
Bryan (Armstrong County)	16222
Bryan (Fayette County)	15428
Bryan Hill Manor	15701
Bryan Mills	17737
Bryansville	17314
Bryant	15101
Bryn Athyn	19009
Bryn Gweled	18966
Bryn Mawr (Allegheny County)	15241
Bryn Mawr (Montgomery County)	19010
Brysonia	17307
Bucher	16661
Buck (Lancaster County)	17566
Buck (Luzerne County) (Township)	18610
Buckeye	15666
Buck Hill Falls	18323
Buckhorn (Cambria County)	16613
Buckhorn (Columbia County)	17815
Buckingham (Bucks County)	18912
Buckingham (Bucks County) (Township)	18912
Buckingham (Wayne County) (Township)	18437
Buckingham Valley	18938
Buckland Valley Farms	18977
Buckman Village (Part of Chester)	19013
Buckmanville	18938

	ZIP		ZIP		ZIP		ZIP
Buck Mountain (Carbon County)	18255		16003†	Canoe Camp	16933	Cedarbrook Mall	19095
Buck Mountain (Schuylkill County)	18214	Butler (Butler County) (Township)	16001	Canoe Creek	16648	Cedar Cliff Manor	17011
Buck Run (Chester County)	19320	Butler (Luzerne County) (Township)	18222	Canoe Ridge	15772	Cedar Heights	19428
Buck Run (Indiana County)	15728	Butler (Schuylkill County) (Township)	17921	Canonsburg	15317	Cedar Hollow	19355
Buck Run (Schuylkill County)	17901	Butler Junction	16229	Canton (Bradford County)	17724	Cedar Knoll	19320
Buckstown	15563	Butler Mall	16001	Canton (Bradford County) (Township)	17724	Cedar Lane	17519
Bucksville	18930	Buttonwood (Luzerne County)	18702	Canton (Washington County) (Township)	15301	Cedar Ledge	17724
Bucktown	19464	Buttonwood (Lycoming County)	17771	Capital City Plaza	17011	Cedar Ridge	17350
Buck Valley	17267	Buttonwood Glen	18901	Caprivi	17013	Cedar Run	17727
Buell Corners	16434	Buttonwood Manor	18901	Carbon (Huntingdon County) (Township)	16678	Cedars	19423
Buena Vista (Allegheny County)	15018	Butztown	18017	Carbon (Mercer County)	16154	Cedar Springs	17751
Buena Vista (Butler County)	16025	Buyerstown	17535	Carbon (Westmoreland County)	15601	Cedar Top	19607
Buena Vista (Fayette County)	15486	Buzzingtown	15642	Carbon Center	16001	Cedarville	19464
Buena Vista (Franklin County)	17268	Byberry (Part of Philadelphia)	19116	Carbondale	18407	Cementon	18052
Buena Vista (Lancaster County)	17527	Bycot	18928	Carbondale (Township)	18407	Centennial (Adams County)	17331
Buena Vista Springs	17268	Byers	19480	Cardale	15420	Centennial (Centre County)	16870
Buffalo (Butler County) (Township)	16055	Byersdale	15005	Cardiff	15943	Centennial Hills	18974
Buffalo (Perry County) (Township)	17045	Byrnedale	15827	Cardington	19082	Center (Allegheny County)	15239
Buffalo (Union County) (Township)	17837	Byrnsville	17927	Carlisle	17013	Center (Beaver County) (Township)	15001
Buffalo (Washington County)	15301	Byromtown	16239	Carlisle Barracks	17013	Center (Butler County) (Township)	16001
Buffalo (Washington County) (Township)	15323	Bywood	19082	Carlisle Springs	17013	Center (Greene County) (Township)	15359
Buffalo Cross Roads	17837	Bywood Heights	19082	Carlson	16735	Center (Indiana County) (Township)	15748
Buffalo Mills	15534	Cabot	16023	Carlton	16311	Center (Juniata County)	17059
Buffalo Run	16870	Cacoossing	19608	Carlton Heights	17252	Center (Perry County)	17062
Buffalo Springs	17042	Cadis	18837	Carmichaels	15320	Center Bridge	18938
Buffalo Valley	16262	Cadogan	16212	Carnegie	15106	Center City (Part of Williamsport)	17701
Buffington (Fayette County)	15468	Cadogan (Township)	16212	Carnot	15108	Center Hill	16201
Buffington (Indiana County) (Township)	15961	Caernarvon (Berks County) (Township)	19543	Carnot-Moon	15108	Center Mills	17304
Buhl (Part of Sharon)	16146	Caernarvon (Lancaster County) (Township)	17555	Carnwath	16861	Center Moreland	18657
Buhls	16033	Cains	17527	Carol Acres	17036	Centerport	19516
Bulger	15019	Cairnbrook	15924	Carpenter Corners	16153	Center Road	16424
Bullion	16374	Calder Square (Part of State College)	16805	Carpenter Town (Lackawanna County)	18414	Center Square	19422
Bullis Mills	16731	Caldwell	17745	Carpentertown (Westmoreland County)	15666	Centertown	16127
Bullskin (Township)	15666	Caledonia (Elk County)	15868	Carriage Hill	19067	Center Union	16652
Bully Hill	16323	Caledonia (Franklin County)	17222	Carrick (Part of Pittsburgh)	15210	Center Valley	18034
Bunches	17070	California (Bucks County)	18951	Carrier (Part of Summerville)	15864	Centerville (Bedford County)	15522
Bungalow Park	18104	California (Washington County)	15419	Carroll (Clinton County)	17747	Centerville (Bradford County)	14894
Bunker Hill (Cumberland County)	17055	Calkins	18443	Carroll (Perry County) (Township)	17090	Centerville (Crawford County)	16404
Bunker Hill (Lebanon County)	17046	Callapoose	18444	Carroll (Washington County) (Township)	15063	Centerville (Lancaster County)	17602
Bunkertown	17049	Callensburg	16213	Carroll (York County) (Township)	17019	Centerville (Perry County)	17045
Bunola	15020	Callery	16024	Carroll Park (Columbia County)	17815	Centerville (Washington County)	15417
Burbank	16749	Callimont	15552	Carroll Park (Montgomery County)	19151	Centerville (York County)	17327
Burd Coleman Village (Part of Cornwall)	17016	Caln	19320	Carrolltown	15722	Central (Allegheny County)	15132
Burgettstown	15021	Caln (Township)	19320	Carroll Valley	17320	Central (Columbia County)	17814
Burholme (Part of Philadelphia)	19111	Calumet	15621	Carson (Part of Pittsburgh)	15203	Central (Washington County)	15301
Burlington	18814	Calumet-Norvelt	15621	Carsontown	17776	Central (Westmoreland County)	15688
Burlington (Township)	18848	Calvert	17771	Carson Valley	16635	Central City (Centre County)	16853
Burnham	17009	Calvert Hills (Part of Altoona)	16601	Carsonville	17032	Central City (Somerset County)	15926
Burning Well	16735	Calvin	16622	Carter Camp	16922	Central Highlands	15037
Burnside (Centre County) (Township)	16845	Camargo	17566	Cartwright	15823	Centralia	17927
Burnside (Clearfield County)	15721	Cambra	18611	Carver Court	19320	Central Manor	17582
Burnside (Clearfield County) (Township)	16692	Cambria (Township)	15931	Carversville	18913	Central Oak Heights	17886
Burnside (Northumberland County)	17872	Cambria City (Part of Johnstown)	15906	Carverton	18644	Central Square Greens	19401
Burnstown	16117	Cambridge (Chester County)	19344	Casanova	16860	Centre (Berks County) (Township)	19541
Burnt Cabins	17215	Cambridge (Crawford County) (Township)	16403	Cascade (Township)	17771	Centre (Perry County)	17047
Burnwood	18465	Cambridge Springs	16403	Cashtown	17310	Centre (Perry County) (Township)	17068
Burrell (Armstrong County) (Township)	16226	Cameron	15834	Cass (Huntingdon County) (Township)	16623	Centre (Snyder County) (Township)	17842
Burrell (Indiana County) (Township)	15717	Cammal	17723	Cass (Schuylkill County) (Township)	17901	Centre Hall	16828
Burson Plan	15322	Camp Akiba	18352	Cassandra	15925	Centre Hill	16828
Bursonville	18077	Campbelltown (Lebanon County)	17010	Casselman	15557	Century	15417
Burtville	16743	Campbelltown (McKean County)	16735	Cassville	16623	Century III Mall (Part of West Mifflin)	15123
Bushkill (Northampton County) (Township)	18064	Camp Bnai Brith	18461	Castanea	17726	Ceres (Township)	16748
Bushkill (Pike County)	18324	Camp Curtin (Part of Harrisburg)	17110	Castanea (Township)	17726	Cessna	15522
Bushkill Center	18064	Camp Hill	17001†	Caste Village (Part of Whitehall)	15236	Cetronia	18104
Bush Patch (Part of Old Forge)	18518		17011*	Castle Garden	15832	Ceylon	15320
Bustleton (Part of Philadelphia)	19115	Camp Hill Shopping Mall (Part of Camp Hill)	17011	Castle Rock	19073	Chadds Ford	19317
Bute	15489	Camp Indian Run	19344	Castle Shannon	15234	Chadville	15401
Butler (Adams County) (Township)	17307	Camp Jo-Ann	15668	Castle Valley	18914	Chain	17960
Butler (Butler County)	16001*	Camp Perry	16114	Castlewood	16101	Chain Bridge	18940
		Camp Starlight	18461	Castor (Part of Philadelphia)	19149	Chaintown	15428
		Camptown	18815	Cataract	16871	Chalfant	15112
		Camp Westmont	18449	Catasauqua	18032	Chalfont	18914
		Canaan	18472	Catawissa	17820	Chalkhill	15421
		Canaan (Township)	18472	Catawissa (Township)	17820	Challenge	15823
		Canadensis	18325	Catharine (Township)	16693	Chalybeate	15522
		Canadohta Lake	16438	Cavettsville	15085	Chambersburg	17201
		Canal (Township)	16314	Ceasetown	18612	Chambers Hill	17111
		Canan	16602	Cecil	15321	Chambers Mill	15301
		Candor	15019	Cecil (Township)	15057	Chambersville	15723
		Cannelton	16115	Cecil-Bishop	15057		
		Canoe (Township)	15772	Cedarbrook	19095		
				Cedarbrook Hills	19095		

	ZIP
Champion (Fayette County)	15622
Champion (Westmoreland County)	15622
Chanceford (Township)	17309
Chandlers Valley	16312
Chaneysville	15535
Chapel	18070
Chapel Downs	15024
Chapel Valley	15001
Chapman (Clinton County) (Township)	17760
Chapman (Lehigh County)	18106
Chapman (Northampton County)	18014
Chapman (Snyder County)	17864
Chapman (Snyder County) (Township)	17864
Chapman Lake	18433
Chapmanville	16354
Charleroi	15022
Charleston (Mercer County)	16148
Charleston (Tioga County) (Township)	16901
Charlestown	19460
Charlestown (Township)	19460
Charlestown	17236
Charlesville	15522
Charlottsville	16686
Charlton (Clinton County)	17745
Charlton (Dauphin County)	17111
Charmian	17214
Charming Forge	19551
Charteroak	16669
Charter Oaks	16509
Chartiers (Greene County)	15322
Chartiers (Washington County) (Township)	15342
Chase	18708
Chatham (Chester County)	19318
Chatham (Tioga County) (Township)	16935
Chatham Park	19083
Chatham Village	19083
Chatwood	19380
Checkerville	16925
Chelsea	19013
Chelten Avenue (Part of Philadelphia)	19144
Cheltenham	19012
Cheltenham (Township)	19012
Cheltenham Shopping Center	19095
Cheltenham Square	19150
Cherokee Ranch	19560
Cherry (Butler County) (Township)	16057
Cherry (Sullivan County) (Township)	18614
Cherry City	15223
Cherry Flats	16917
Cherry Grove (Huntingdon County)	17264
Cherry Grove (Warren County)	16313
Cherry Grove (Warren County) (Township)	16313
Cherry Hill (Erie County)	16401
Cherryhill (Indiana County) (Township)	15765
Cherry Hill (Lancaster County)	17563
Cherry Hill (Northampton County)	18064
Cherry Hill (York County)	17070
Cherry Lane	15613
Cherry Ridge (Township)	18431
Cherry Run	17885
Cherrytown	16657
Cherry Tree (Indiana County)	15724
Cherry Tree (Venango County)	16354
Cherrytree (Venango County) (Township)	16354
Cherry Valley (Butler County)	16373
Cherry Valley (Washington County)	15021
Cherryville (Northampton County)	18035
Cherryville (Schuylkill County)	17966
Chest (Cambria County) (Township)	16668

	ZIP
Chest (Clearfield County) (Township)	15753
Chester	19013-16
For specific Chester Zip Codes call (215) 876-1613, or your local postmaster.	
Chesterbrook	19087
Chesterfield	16627
Chester Heights	19017
Chester Hill	16866
Chester Plaza	19014
Chester Springs	19425
Chester Township	19013
Chester Valley Knoll	19355
Chesterville	19350
Chestnut Grove	16838
Chestnut Hill (Erie County)	16509
Chestnut Hill (Lancaster County)	17512
Chestnut Hill (Lehigh County)	18036
Chestnuthill (Monroe County) (Township)	18331
Chestnut Hill (Northampton County)	18042
Chestnut Hill (Philadelphia County)	19118
Chestnut Level	17566
Chestnut Ridge (Fayette County)	15422
Chestnut Ridge (Lancaster County)	17603
Chestnut View	17603
Chest Springs	16624
Cheswick	15024
Chevy Chase Heights	15701
Chewton	16157
Cheyney	19319
Chickasaw	16259
Chicora	16025
Childs	18407
Chillisquaque	17850
Chinchilla	18410
Chippewa (Township)	15010
Choconut	18812
Choconut (Township)	18818
Christiana	17509
Christian Springs	18064
Christmans	18229
Chrome	19362
Chrystal	16748
Church Hill (Fayette County)	15458
Church Hill (Forest County)	16353
Church Hill (Franklin County)	17236
Church Hill (Mifflin County)	17084
Church Hills	17082
Churchill	15235
Churchill Plan	16117
Churchill Valley	15235
Churchtown	17555
Churchville (Bedford County)	16667
Churchville (Bucks County)	18966
Churchville (Clarion County)	16255
Circleville	15642
Cisna Run	17047
Cito	17233
City View	17044
Clair Manor	15012
Clairton	15025
Clairton Junction (Part of West Mifflin)	15122
Clamtown	18252
Clappertown	16693
Clapp Farm	16301
Clara (Township)	16748
Clarence	16829
Clarendon	16313
Clarendon Heights	16313
Claridge	15623
Clarington	15828
Clarion	16214
Clarion (Township)	16258
Clark	16113
Clark Manor	15001
Clarksburg	15725
Clarks Green	18411
Clarks Mills	16114
Clarks Summit	18411
Clarks Summit State Hospital	18501
Clarkstown	17756
Clarksville	15322
Clarksville Hill	15322

	ZIP
Claussville	18069
Clay (Butler County) (Township)	16061
Clay (Huntingdon County) (Township)	17264
Clay (Lancaster County)	17522
Clay (Lancaster County) (Township)	17578
Clay Hill	17201
Claylick	17236
Claypoole Heights	15701
Claysburg	16625
Claysville	15323
Clayton	19503
Claytonia	16057
Clearbrook Village	19040
Clearfield (Butler County) (Township)	16034
Clearfield (Cambria County) (Township)	16668
Clearfield (Clearfield County)	16830
Clearfield (Northampton County)	18064
Clear Ridge (Bedford County)	15537
Clear Ridge (Fulton County)	17229
Clear Run	15801
Clear Spring	17019
Clearview	17601
Clearview Estates (Beaver County)	15001
Clearview Estates (Cumberland County)	17011
Clearview Mall	16001
Clearview Manor	18101
Clearville	15535
Cleona	17042
Clermont	16740
Cleveland (Township)	17820
Cleversburg	17257
Cliff Mine	15108
Clifford (Snyder County)	17870
Clifford (Susquehanna County)	18413
Clifford (Susquehanna County) (Township)	18413
Clifton (Dauphin County)	17057
Clifton (Lackawanna County) (Township)	18424
Clifton (Lackawanna County)	18424
Clifton Heights	19018
Climax (Armstrong County)	16242
Climax (Clarion County)	16242
Climax (Indiana County)	15944
Clinton (Allegheny County)	15026
Clinton (Armstrong County)	16229
Clinton (Butler County)	16055
Clinton (Butler County) (Township)	16059
Clinton (Fayette County)	15469
Clinton (Lycoming County) (Township)	17752
Clinton (Venango County) (Township)	16373
Clinton (Wayne County) (Township)	18472
Clinton (Wyoming County) (Township)	18419
Clintondale	17751
Clintonville	16372
Cloe	15767
Clonmell	19390
Clover (Township)	15829
Clover Creek	16662
Cloverdale Park	18915
Clover Hill	15423
Clover Run	15757
Clune	15727
Cly	17370
Clyde	15944
Clymer (Indiana County)	15728
Clymer (Tioga County) (Township)	16943
Coal (Township)	17872
Coal Bluff	15332
Coal Cabin Beach	17314
Coal Castle	17901
Coal Center	15423
Coal City	16374
Coaldale (Dauphin County)	17048
Coaldale (Schuylkill County)	18218
Coal Glen	15824

	ZIP
Coal Hill	16301
Coal Hollow	15846
Coalmont	16678
Coalport (Carbon County)	18229
Coalport (Clearfield County)	16627
Coal Run (Clearfield County)	16666
Coal Run (Northumberland County)	17872
Coal Run (Somerset County)	15552
Coaltown (Butler County)	16057
Coaltown (Lawrence County)	16101
Coatesville	19320
Cobalt Ridge	19058
Cobblerville	17241
Cobbs Corners	16434
Cobham	16351
Coburn (Blair County)	16601
Coburn (Centre County)	16832
Cocalico	17517
Cochran Acres	15001
Cochrans Mills	16226
Cochranton	16314
Cochranville	19330
Cocolamus	17014
Codorus	17311
Codorus (Township)	17327
Coffeetown (Lebanon County)	17078
Coffeetown (Lehigh County)	18069
Coffeetown (Northampton County)	18042
Cogan House (Township)	17771
Cogan Station	17728
Cokeburg	15324
Cokeburg Junction	15331
Cold Point	19462
Cold Run	19508
Cold Spring (Lebanon County) (Township)	17028
Cold Spring (Wayne County)	18431
Cold Spring (York County)	17360
Cold Spring Park	19464
Cold Springs Crossing	19426
Colebrook (Clinton County) (Township)	17734
Colebrook (Lebanon County)	17015
Colebrookdale	19512
Colebrookdale (Township)	19512
Colegrove	16749
Coleman	15541
Colemanville	17565
Colerain (Bedford County) (Township)	15522
Colerain (Huntingdon County)	16683
Colerain (Lancaster County) (Township)	17536
Coles	17948
Colesburg	16915
Coles Creek	17814
Colesville	18015
Coleville (Centre County)	16823
Coleville (McKean County)	16749
Colfax	16652
College (Township)	16801
College Heights	19605
College Hill (Part of Beaver Falls)	15010
College Manor	18612
College Misericordia	18612
College Park (Montgomery County)	19031
College Park (Union County)	17837
College View Heights	18016
Collegeville	19426
Colley (Township)	18614
Collier (Allegheny County) (Township)	15106
Collier (Fayette County)	15401
Collingdale	19023
Collins	17566
Collinsburg	15089
Collinsville	17302
Collinswood Acres	15317
Collomsville	17701
Colmar	18915
Colona (Part of Monaca)	15061
Colonial Crest	17111
Colonial Hills (Berks County)	19608

	ZIP
Colonial Hills (Mifflin County)	17044
Colonial Manor	17603
Colonial Park (Dauphin County)	17109
Colonial Park (Delaware County)	19064
Colonial Park (Lancaster County)	17540
Colonial Park (Northumberland County)	17847
Colonial Village (Chester County)	19087
Colonial Village (Venango County)	16301
Colony Park	19608
Columbia (Bradford County) (Township)	16914
Columbia (Lancaster County)	17512
Columbia Cross Roads	16914
Columbus	16405
Columbus (Township)	16405
Colver	15927
Colwyn	19023
Comly	17772
Commerce (Part of Philadelphia)	19108
Commodore	15729
Compass	17527
Conashaugh Lake	18337
Concord (Butler County) (Township)	16025
Concord (Delaware County) (Township)	19331
Concord (Erie County) (Township)	16407
Concord (Franklin County)	17217
Concord (Westmoreland County)	15012
Concord Park	19047
Concordville	19331
Conemaugh (Cambria County) (Township)	15902
Conemaugh (Indiana County) (Township)	15725
Conemaugh (Somerset County) (Township)	15935
Conestoga (Chester County)	19520
Conestoga (Lancaster County)	17516
Conestoga (Lancaster County) (Township)	17516
Conestoga Woods	17602
Coneville	16915
Conewago (Adams County) (Township)	17331
Conewago (Dauphin County) (Township)	17022
Conewago (York County) (Township)	17404
Conewago Heights	17345
Conewango (Township)	16365
Confluence	15424
Congo	19504
Congruity	15601
Conifer	15864
Connaughton	19428
Conneaut (Crawford County) (Township)	16424
Conneaut (Erie County) (Township)	16401
Conneaut Lake	16316
Conneaut Lake Park	16316
Conneaut Lakeshore	16316
Conneautville	16406
Connellsville	15425
Connellsville (Township)	15425
Connersville	17851
Connerton	17935
Connoquenessing	16027
Connoquenessing (Township)	16053
Conoy (Township)	17502
Conrad	16720
Conshohocken	19428
Continental (Part of Philadelphia)	19106
Conway	15027
Conyngham (Columbia County) (Township)	17851
Conyngham (Luzerne County)	18219
Conyngham (Luzerne County) (Township)	18655
Cook (Township)	15687
Cooke (Township)	17241
Cookport	15729

	ZIP
Cooks	16674
Cooksburg	16217
Cookseytown	18707
Cooks Mill	15545
Cooks Run	17778
Coolbaugh (Township)	18466
Coolbaughs	18324
Coolspring (Fayette County)	15445
Coolspring (Jefferson County)	15730
Coolspring (Mercer County) (Township)	16137
Cool Valley (Washington County)	15317
Cool Valley (Westmoreland County)	15601
Coon Hunter	17842
Coon Island	15376
Coontown	16735
Cooper (Clearfield County) (Township)	16839
Cooper (Montour County) (Township)	17821
Coopersburg	18036
Cooper Settlement	16834
Cooperstown (Butler County)	16059
Cooperstown (Venango County)	16317
Cooperstown (Westmoreland County)	15650
Coopersville	17509
Copella	18014
Copesville	19380
Coplay	18037
Coppersdale (Part of Johnstown)	15906
Coral	15731
Coraopolis	15108
Coraopolis Heights	15108
Corinne	19380
Cork Lane	18640
Corliss (Part of Pittsburgh)	15204
Corner Ketch	19335
Corner Store	19460
Corning	18092
Cornish	15478
Cornog	19343
Cornplanter (Township)	16301
Cornpropst Mills	16652
Cornwall	17016
Cornwall Center (Part of Cornwall)	17016
Cornwells Heights-Eddington	19020
Corry	16407
Corsica	15829
Cortez	18436
Corwins Corners	16701
Corydon (Township)	16701
Coryville	16731
Costello	16720
Cosytown	17225
Coterell Lake	18470
Cottage	16669
Cottage Grove	16105
Cottage Hill	16242
Cottageville	18901
Cotton Town	16625
Couchtown	17047
Coudersport	16915
Coulters	15028
Council Crest	18201
Country Club Estates (Armstrong County)	16201
Country Club Estates (Lancaster County)	17601
Country Club Estates (Montgomery County)	19444
Country Club Heights	17601
Country Gardens	17540
Country Hills	15642
Countryside	17011
County Line	18966
County Line Park	18914
Coupon	16629
Court at King of Prussia, The	19406
Courtdale	18704
Courtney	15029
Cove	17020
Covedale	16693
Cove Gap	17236
Coventryville	19464
Coverdale (Part of Bethel Park)	15102
Coveville	18325
Coveytown	18614

	ZIP
Covington (Clearfield County) (Township)	16836
Covington (Lackawanna County) (Township)	18424
Covington (Tioga County)	16917
Covington (Tioga County) (Township)	16917
Covode	15767
Cowan	17844
Cowanesque	16918
Cowansburg	15642
Cowanshannock (Township)	16249
Cowans Village	17224
Cowansville	16218
Cowden	15057
Coxeville	18216
Coy	15748
Coy Junction	15748
Coyleville	16034
Crabapple	15380
Crabtree	15624
Crabtree Hollow	19053
Crackersport	18104
Crafton	15205
Craig	18414
Craigheads	17013
Craigs	17948
Craigs Meadow	18301
Craigsville	16262
Craley	17312
Cramer	15954
Cramer Heights (Part of Latrobe)	15650
Cranberry (Butler County) (Township)	16046
Cranberry (Luzerne County)	18201
Cranberry (Venango County)	16319
Cranberry (Venango County) (Township)	16319
Cranberry Mall	16319
Cranberry Ridge	18201
Cranesville	16410
Crates	16240
Crawford (Township)	17740
Crawfordtown	15733
Creamery	19430
Creamton	18421
Creekside	15732
Creighton	15030
Crenshaw	15824
Crescent (Township)	15046
Crescentdale (Part of Wampum)	16157
Crescent Heights	15427
Crescent Lake (Monroe County)	18332
Crescent Lake (Pike County)	18337
Cresco	18326
Cresmont Farms	19335
Cress	17268
Cresson	16630
Cresson (Township)	16630
Cressona	17929
Crestmont (Clinton County)	17745
Crestmont (Montgomery County)	19090
Crestmont Village	15001
Crestview	19040
Crestwood (Berks County)	19606
Crestwood (Lackawanna County)	18444
Creswell	17516
Crete	15701
Criders Corners	16046
Crimson Maple	18837
Croft	16830
Cromby	19460
Cromwell (Township)	17264
Crookham	15332
Crosby	16724
Cross Creek	15021
Cross Creek (Township)	15312
Cross Fork	17729
Crossgrove	17841
Crossingville	16412
Cross Keys (Adams County)	17350
Cross Keys (Blair County)	16635
Cross Keys (Bucks County)	18901
Cross Keys (Juniata County)	17021
Crossroads (Northampton County)	18014

	ZIP
Cross Roads (York County)	17322
Crosswicks	19046
Crown	16220
Crown Meadows	15238
Croydon	19021
Croydon Acres	19021
Croydon Heights	19021
Croydon Manor	19021
Croyle (Township)	15956
Crozer Park Gardens (Part of Chester)	19013
Crucible	15325
Crum Creek Manor	19013
Crum Lynne	19022
Crum Lynne (Part of Ridley Park)	19078
Crystal	15439
Crystal Lake	18407
Crystal Spring	15536
Crystal Springs	16353
Cuba Mills	17059
Cuddy	15031
Cuddy Hill	15031
Culbertson	17201
Cullen Manor	17888
Culmerville	15084
Culp	16601
Cumberland (Adams County) (Township)	17325
Cumberland (Greene County) (Township)	15320
Cumberland Park	17011
Cumberland Valley (Township)	15522
Cumberland Village	15320
Cumbola	17930
Cummings (Township)	17776
Cumminstown	17013
Cumru (Township)	19540
Cupola	19344
Curley Hill	18901
Curllsville	16221
Curren Terrace (Part of Norristown)	19401
Curry Run	15757
Curryville	16631
Curtin	16841
Curtin (Township)	16841
Curtis Hills	19095
Curtis Park (Part of Sharon Hill)	19079
Curtisville	15032
Curwensville	16833
Cush Creek	15712
Cussewago (Township)	16433
Custards	16314
Custer City	16725
Custis Woods	19038
Cyclone	16726
Cymbria	15714
Cypher	16650
Daggett	16936
Dagus	15846
Daguscahonda	15853
Dagus Mines	15831
Dahoga	15870
Daisytown (Cambria County)	15902
Daisytown (Washington County)	15427
Dale (Cambria County)	15902
Dale (Clearfield County)	16881
Dale Summit	16823
Daleville (Chester County)	19330
Daleville (Lackawanna County)	18424
Dalevue	16801
Daley	15924
Dallas	18612
Dallas (Township)	18612
Dallas City	16701
Dallastown	17313
Dalmatia	17017
Dalton	18414
Damascus	18415
Damascus (Township)	18415
Danboro	18916
Danielsville	18038
Dannersville	18067
Danville	17821
Danville State Hospital	17821
Darby	19023
Darby (Township)	19036
Darby Township (census designated place)	19036
Darlington (Beaver County)	16115
Darlington (Beaver County) (Township)	16115

	ZIP
Darlington (Delaware County)	19063
Darlington (Westmoreland County)	15658
Darlington Corners	19380
Darragh	15625
Darthmouth Farms	17036
Dauberville	19517
Daugherty (Township)	15066
Dauphin	17018
Davidsburg	17315
Davidson (Township)	17758
Davidson Heights	15001
Davidsville	15928
Davis Grove	19044
Davistown (Fayette County)	15446
Davistown (Greene County)	15349
Dawson	15428
Dawson Manor	19040
Dawson Ridge	15009
Dawson Run	16370
Day	16258
Daylesford	19312
Dayton (Armstrong County)	16222
Dayton (Dauphin County)	17098
Deal	15552
Dean	16636
Dean (Township)	16636
Deanville	16242
Dearth	15401
Decatur (Clearfield County) (Township)	16666
Decatur (Mifflin County) (Township)	17841
Deckard	16314
Deckers Point	15759
Deckertown	18446
Deegan	16020
Deemers Cross Roads	15851
Deemston	15333
Deep Dale East	19058
Deep Dale West	19058
Deep Run	18944
Deep Valley	15352
Deer Creek (Township)	16145
Deerfield (Tioga County) (Township)	16928
Deerfield (Warren County) (Township)	16351
Deer Lake (Fayette County)	15421
Deer Lake (Schuylkill County)	17961
Deer Mt. Lake	18355
Deer Park	18938
Defiance	16633
Degolia	16701
Deiblers Station	17821
Delabole	18072
De Lancey	15733
Delano	18220
Delano (Township)	18220
Delaware (Juniata County) (Township)	17094
Delaware (Mercer County) (Township)	16124
Delaware (Northumberland County) (Township)	17777
Delaware (Pike County) (Township)	18328
Delaware Grove	16124
Delaware Run	17777
Delaware Valley College (Part of New Britain)	18901
Delaware Water Gap	18327
Dellville	17020
Delmar (Township)	16901
Delmont	15626
Delphi	19473
Delps	18038
Delroy	17406
Delta	17314
Delta Manor	18017
Dempseytown	16317
Denbeau Heights (Part of Centerville)	15417
Denbo (Part of Centerville)	15429
Denholm	17059
Denison	15601
Dennison (Township)	18661
Dennys Corners	16335
Dennys Mill	16023
Dents Run	15832
Denver	17517
Deodate	17022
Deringer	18241
Derrick City	16727

	ZIP
Derrs	17814
Derry (Dauphin County) (Township)	17033
Derry (Mifflin County) (Township)	17099
Derry (Montour County) (Township)	17821
Derry (Westmoreland County)	15627
Derry (Westmoreland County) (Township)	15627
Derwood Park	19094
Derwyn	19004
Deshon Manor	16001
Desire	15851
Detters Mill	17315
De Turksville	17963
Devault	19432
Devon	19333
Devon-Berwyn	19312
Dewart	17730
Dewey Heights	18052
De Young	16728
Diamond	16354
Diamondtown	17851
Diamondville	15728
Dice	17844
Dickerson Run	15430
Dickinson	17241
Dickinson (Township)	17065
Dicksonburg	16406
Dickson City	18519
Dieners Hall	17901
Dilliner	15327
Dillinger	18049
Dillingersville	18092
Dillontown	18417
Dillsburg	17019
Dilltown	15929
Dilworthtown	19380
Dime	15690
Dimeling	16830
Dimmsville	17094
Dimock	18816
Dimock (Township)	18816
Dimock Corners	18430
Dingman (Township)	18337
Dingmans Ferry	18328
Dipple Manor	18201
Distant	16223
District (Township)	19512
Divide	17814
Dividing Ridge	15530
Dixon	18657
Dixonville	15734
D&M Junction	17019
Doe Run	19320
Dogtown (Columbia County)	17815
Dogtown (Luzerne County)	18655
Dogtown (Snyder County)	17870
Dogwood Acres	18966
Dogwood Hollow	19053
Dolington	18940
Dombach Manor	17601
Donaldson	17981
Donaldsons Crossroads	15317
Donation	16652
Donegal (Butler County) (Township)	16025
Donegal (Washington County) (Township)	15323
Donegal (Westmoreland County)	15628
Donegal (Westmoreland County) (Township)	15628
Donegal Heights	17552
Donegal Springs	17552
Donerville	17603
Donnally Mills	17062
Donnelly	15612
Donnellytown	17013
Donohoe	15650
Donora	15033
Dooleyville	17851
Dora (Greene County)	15338
Dora (Jefferson County)	15767
Dormont	15216
Dorneyville	18104
Dornsife	17823
Dorothy	15650
Dorrance	18707
Dorrance (Township)	18707
Dorset	17960
Dorseyville	15238
Dott	17267
Dotters Corners	18058
Doubling Gap	17241

	ZIP
Douglass (Berks County) (Township)	19464
Douglass (Montgomery County) (Township)	19525
Douglassville	19518
Doutyville	17872
Dover	17315
Dover (Township)	17315
Down East	19355
Downey	15530
Downieville	16059
Downingtown	19335
Downtown (Part of Erie)	16501-02
	16507
	16512
For specific Downtown Zip Codes call (814) 454-6486, or your local postmaster.	
Downtown (Part of Lancaster)	17603*
	17608†
Downtown (Part of New Castle)	16103
Downtown (Part of Reading)	19603
Downtown (Part of Scranton)	18501
Downtown (Part of Uniontown)	15401
Doylesburg	17219
Doyles Mills	17058
Doylestown	18901
Doylestown (Township)	18901
Drake	16156
Drakes Mills	16403
Draketown (Clinton County)	17751
Draketown (Somerset County)	15424
Drane	16666
Draper	16901
Drauckers	15848
Dravosburg	15034
Dreher (Township)	18445
Drehersville	17961
Drennen (Part of Murrysville)	15068
Dresher	19025
Drexelbrook	19026
Drexel Heights	18067
Drexel Hill	19026
Drexel Hills (Part of New Cumberland)	17070
Drexeline Shopping Center	19026
Drexlewood	19610
Drifting	16834
Drifton	18221
Driftwood	15832
Drinker	18444
Dromgold	17090
Druid Hills (Part of Dallas)	18708
Drummond	15823
Drumore	17518
Drumore (Township)	17563
Drums	18222
Drury Run	17764
Dry Hill	15425
Dry Run	17220
Dry Tavern	15357
Dry Valley Crossroads	17889
Dryville	19539
Dublin (Bucks County)	18917
Dublin (Fulton County) (Township)	17223
Dublin (Huntingdon County) (Township)	17239
Dublin Mills	17229
Du Bois	15801
Duboistown	17701
Dudley	16634
Duffield	17201
Duhring	16239
Duke Center	16729
Dumas	15424
Dunbar	15431
Dunbar (Township)	15431
Duncan (Township)	16901
Duncan Circle	15009
Duncannon	17020
Duncansville	16635
Duncott	17901
Dundaff	18407
Dundore	17864
Dungarvin	16877
Dunkard	15327
Dunkard (Township)	15327
Dunkelbergers	17872
Dunlap Creek Village	15475
Dunlevy	15432

	ZIP
Dunlo	15930
Dunmore	18512
Dunningsville	15330
Dunningtown (Part of Murrysville)	15632
Dunns Eddy	16371
Dunnstable (Township)	17745
Dunnstown	17745
Dupont	18641
Duquesne	15110
Duquesne Heights (Part of Pittsburgh)	15211
Duquesne Wharf (Part of Duquesne)	15110
Durham	18039
Durham (Township)	18039
Durham Furnace	18930
Durlach	17522
Durrell	18848
Duryea	18642
Dushore	18614
Dutch Hill (Clarion County)	16049
Dutch Hill (Fayette County)	15450
Dutch Hill (Mercer County)	16148
Dutch Settlement	15946
Dutchtown (Cambria County)	15938
Dutchtown (Franklin County)	17236
Dutton Mill	19380
Dyberry (Township)	18431
Dysart	16636
Eagle Foundry	16657
Eaglehurst	16505
Eagle Point	19530
Eagle Rock	16301
Eagles Mere	17731
Eagles Mere Park (Part of Eagles Mere)	17731
Eagleville (Centre County)	16826
Eagleville (Montgomery County)	19408
Earl (Berks County) (Township)	19512
Earl (Lancaster County) (Township)	17557
Earlington	18918
Earlston	15537
Earlville	19519
Earnest	19401
Earnestville	16666
East Allen (Township)	18067
East Altoona	16601
East Ararat	18470
East Athens	18810
East Bangor	18013
East Benton	18414
East Berlin	17316
East Berwick	18603
East Bethlehem (Township)	15322
East Bradford (Township)	19380
East Brady	16028
East Branch	16434
East Brandywine (Township)	19335
East Brook	16101
East Brunswick (Township)	17960
East Buffalo (Township)	17837
East Butler	16029
East Caln (Township)	19341
East Cameron (Township)	17872
East Canton	17724
East Carnegie (Part of Pittsburgh)	15230
East Carroll (Township)	15722
East Chilisquaque (Township)	17847
East Cocalico (Township)	17517
East Conemaugh	15909
East Connellsville	15425
East Coventry (Township)	19457
East Deer (Township)	15030
East Donegal (Township)	17547
East Drumore (Township)	17566
East Du Bois (Part of Du Bois)	15801
East Earl	17519
East Earl (Township)	17519
East End (Blair County)	16602
East End (Luzerne County)	18702
East Fairfield (Township)	16314
East Fallowfield (Chester County) (Township)	19320
East Fallowfield (Crawford County) (Township)	16111

	ZIP		ZIP		ZIP		ZIP
East Falls (Part of Philadelphia)	19129	East Sharon	16748	Edgmont (Township)	19028	Elm	17521
East Finley	15377	East Sharpsburg	16673	Edie	15501	Elmdale	18436
East Finley (Township)	15377	East Side	18661	Edinboro	16412	Elmer	16950
East Fork (Township)	16720	East Smethport	16730	Edinburg	16116	Elmhurst	18416
East Franklin (Township)	16201	East Smithfield	18817	Edison	18901	Elmhurst (Township)	18416
East Fredericktown	15450	East Springfield	16411	Edisonville	17579	Elmo	16232
East Freedom	16637	East St. Clair (Township)	15559	Edmon	15630	Elmora	15737
East Germantown (Part of Philadelphia)	19138	East Stroudsburg	18301	Edwardsville	18704	Elmwood (Philadelphia County)	19142
East Goshen (Township)	19380	East Taylor (Township)	15909	Effort	18330	Elmwood (York County)	17403
East Greenville	18041	East Texas	18046	Egypt (Clearfield County)	16881	Elmwood Terrace (Bucks County)	19057
East Hanover (Dauphin County) (Township)	17028	East Titusville	16354	Egypt (Jefferson County)	15824	Elmwood Terrace (Lackawanna County)	18444
East Hanover (Lebanon County) (Township)	17003	East Towanda	18848	Egypt (Lehigh County)	18052	Elora	16057
East Hempfield (Township)	17603	Easttown (Township)	19312	Egypt Corners	16323	Elrama	15038
East Herrick	18853	Easttown Woods	19312	Ehrenfeld	15956	Elroy	18964
East Hickory	16321	East Troy	16947	Eichelbergertown	16650	Elstie	16613
East Hills	15904	East Union (Township)	18248	Eidenau	16037	Elstonville	17545
East Honesdale (Part of Honesdale)	18431	East Uniontown	15401	Eighty Four	15330	Elton	15934
East Hopewell (Township)	17322	Eastvale	15010	Ekastown	16055	Elverson	19520
East Huntingdon (Township)	15679	East Vandergrift	15629	Elam	19342	Elwood Park	15301
East Kane	16735	East View	15370	Elberta	16601	Elwyn	19063
East Keating (Township)	17778	Eastville	17747	Elbon	15823	Elwyn Terrace	17545
East Kendall	17356	East Vincent (Township)	19475	Elbrook	17268	Elysburg	17824
East Kittanning	16201	East Washington	15301	Elco	15434	Emanuelsville	18014
East Lackawannock (Township)	16137	East Waterford	17021	Elder (Township)	16646	Emblem (Part of White Oak)	15131
East Lampeter (Township)	17602	East Weissport	18235	Elders Ridge	15681	Embreeville	19320
Eastland	19362	East Wheatfield (Township)	15920	Eldersville	15036	Embreeville State Hospital	19320
Eastland Hills (Franklin County)	17268	East Whiteland (Township)	19355	Elderton	15736	Emeigh	15738
Eastland Hills (Lancaster County)	17602	Eastwicks (Part of Philadelphia)	19153	El-Do-Lake	18058	Emerald	18080
Eastland Marketplace	15137	East William Penn	17976	Eldora (Lancaster County)	17563	Emerickville	15825
East Lansdowne	19050	Eastwood (Allegheny County)	15235	Eldora (Washington County)	15063	Emigsville	17318
East Lawn	18064	Eastwood (Westmoreland County)	15601	Eldorado (Blair County)	16602	Emilie	19057
Eastlawn Gardens	18064	East Yoe	17356	Eldorado (Butler County)	16049	Emlenton	16373
East Lawrence	16929	East York	17402	Eldred (Jefferson County) (Township)	15860	Emmaus	18049
East Lemon	18657	Eaton (Township)	18657	Eldred (Lycoming County) (Township)	17754	Emmaville	15536
East Lenox	18470	Eatonville	18657	Eldred (McKean County)	16731	Emporium	15834
East Lewisburg	17847	Eau Claire	16030	Eldred (McKean County) (Township)	16731	Emsworth	15202
East Liberty (Part of Pittsburgh)	15206	Ebenezer	17046	Eldred (Monroe County) (Township)	18058	Endeavor	16322
East Mahoning (Township)	15759	Ebensburg	15931	Eldred (Schuylkill County) (Township)	17964	Enders	17032
East Manchester (Township)	17347	Eberlys Mill	17011	Eldred (Warren County) (Township)	16420	Energy	16101
East Marianna	15445	Ebervale	18223	Eldredsville	18616	Enfield	19075
East Marlborough (Township)	19348	Echo (Armstrong County)	16222	Eleven Mile	16923	Engleside (Part of Lancaster)	17602
East McKeesport	15035	Echo (Cambria County)	15942	Elfinwild	15101	Engles Lake	18370
East Mead (Township)	16335	Echo Lake	18301	Elgin	16413	Englesville	19512
East Millsboro	15433	Echo Valley (Delaware County)	19073	Elim	15905	Englewood	17931
East Mines (Part of St. Clair)	17970	Echo Valley (Schuylkill County)	17981	Elimsport	17810	English Center	17776
Eastmont (Allegheny County)	15235	Eckenrode Mill	16668	Elizabeth (Allegheny County)	15037	Enhaut	17113
Eastmont (York County)	17315	Eckley	18255	Elizabeth (Allegheny County) (Township)	15018	Enid	16691
East Nantmeal (Township)	19421	Eckville	19529	Elizabeth (Lancaster County) (Township)	17543	Enlow	15126
East New Castle	16101	Economy	15005	Elizabethtown	17022	Ennisville	16652
East Newport	17074	Eddington	19020	Elizabethville	17023	Enola	17025
East Norriton	19401	Eddington Gardens	19020	Elk (Chester County) (Township)	19351	Enon	15377
East Norriton (Township)	19401	Eddystone	19013	Elk (Clarion County) (Township)	16232	Enon Valley	16120
East Norwegian (Township)	17901	Eddyville	16242	Elk (Tioga County) (Township)	16921	Enterline	17032
East Nottingham (Township)	19363	Edelman	18064	Elk (Warren County) (Township)	16345	Enterprise (Mercer County)	16127
East Oakmont (Part of Plum)	15239	Eden (Clearfield County)	16836	Elk City	16232	Enterprise (Warren County)	16354
Easton (Clarion County)	16255	Eden (Lancaster County)	17601	Elk Creek (Township)	16401	Entierville	17241
Easton (Northampton County)	18040	Eden (Lancaster County) (Township)	17566	Elkdale (Chester County)	19352	Entriken	16657
	18042-45	Edenborn	15458	Elkdale (Susquehanna County)	18470	Ephrata	17522
For specific Easton Zip Codes call (215) 252-9987, or your local postmaster.		Edenburg	19526	Elk Grove	17814	Ephrata (Township)	17522
		Edendale	16666	Elkins Park	19027	Equinunk	18417
East Oreland	19075	Eden Heights	17601	Elk Lake (Susquehanna County)	18801	Ercildoun	19320
East Penn (Township)	18235	Edenton	19330	Elk Lake (Wayne County)	18472	Erdenheim	19118
East Pennsboro (Township)	17025	Edenville	17201	Elkland (Sullivan County) (Township)	18616	Erdman	17048
East Petersburg	17520	Edgebrook (Part of Pittsburgh)	15226	Elkland (Tioga County)	16920	Erhard	16861
East Pike	15701	Edgecliff (Part of Lower Burrell)	15068	Elk Lick (Township)	15558	Erie	16501-65
East Pikeland (Township)	19460	Edgegrove	17331	Elk Run Junction (Part of Punxsutawney)	15767	For specific Erie Zip Codes call (814) 898-7317, or your local postmaster.	
East Pittsburgh	15112	Edge Hill	19038	Elkview	19390	
Eastpoint	17765	Edgely	19007	Ellen Gowan	17976	Erie Heights (Part of Erie)	16508
East Prospect	17317	Edgemere	18328	Ellenton	17724	Eriton	15801
East Providence (Township)	15533	Edgemont (Dauphin County)	17109	Ellerslie	19020	Erlen	19126
East Riverside	15433	Edgemont (Delaware County)	19028	Eliger Park	19034	Erly	17024
East Rochester	15074	Edgemont (Northampton County)	18088	Elliott (Part of Pittsburgh)	15205	Ernest	15739
East Rockhill (Township)	18944	Edgewater Terrace	15650	Elliott Heights (Part of Bethlehem)	18015	Erney	17315
East Run	15759	Edgewood (Allegheny County)	15218	Elliott Mills	16057	Erwinna	18920
East Rush	18801	Edgewood (Indiana County)	15701	Elliottsburg	17024	Eshbach	19505
East Salem	17059	Edgewood (Northumberland County)	17872	Elliottson	17013	Eshcol	17062
East Saxton	16678	Edgewood Grove (Part of Somerset)	15501	Elliottsville	15437	Esplen (Part of Pittsburgh)	15204
		Edgewood Park (Bucks County)	19067	Ellisburg	16923	Espy	17815
		Edgewood Park (Delaware County)	19008	Ellport	16117	Espyville	16424
		Edgeworth	15143	Ellsworth	15331	Espyville Station	16424
				Ellwood City	16117	Essington	19029
						Estella	18616
						Esterly (Part of St. Lawrence)	19606
						Estherton	17110
						Etna	15223
						Etters	17319
						Euclid	16001
						Eulalia (Township)	16915
						Eureka	15479
						Evansburg	19426
						Evans City	16033

	ZIP
Evans Falls	18657
Evans Manor	15401
Evanston	15625
Evansville (Berks County)	19522
Evansville (Columbia County)	18603
Evendale	17086
Everett	15537
Evergreen	18833
Evergreen Park	18052
Everhartville	17074
Everson	15631
Ewalt (Part of Pittsburgh)	15212
Ewings Mill	15765
Ewingsville	15106
Excelsior	17825
Exchange	17821
Exeter (Berks County) (Township)	19606
Exeter (Luzerne County)	18643
Exeter (Luzerne County) (Township)	18643
Exeter (Wyoming County) (Township)	18615
Exmoor	17963
Experiment (Part of Jefferson)	15230
Export	15632
Exton	19341
Exton Square Mall	19341
Eyers Grove	17846
Eynon (Part of Archbald)	18403
Factoryville (Northampton County)	18013
Factoryville (Wyoming County)	18419
Faggs Manor	19330
Fagleysville	19525
Fagundus	16351
Fair Acres	17070
Fairbank	15435
Fairbrook	16865
Fairchance	15436
Fairdale (Greene County)	15320
Fairdale (Susquehanna County)	18801
Fairfield (Adams County)	17320
Fairfield (Crawford County) (Township)	16314
Fairfield (Erie County)	16510
Fairfield (Lycoming County) (Township)	17754
Fairfield (Washington County)	15345
Fairfield (Westmoreland County) (Township)	15923
Fair Grounds	15344
Fairhaven Heights	15137
Fairhill (Bucks County)	19440
Fairhill (Philadelphia County)	19133
Fairhope (Fayette County)	15012
Fairhope (Somerset County)	15538
Fairhope (Somerset County) (Township)	15538
Fairland	17543
Fairlawn	17728
Fairless	19030
Fairless Hills	19030
Fairmont	15642
Fairmount (Lancaster County)	17566
Fairmount (Luzerne County) (Township)	17814
Fairmount (Philadelphia County)	19121
Fairmount (Wayne County)	18462
Fairmount City	16224
Fairmount Springs	17814
Fair Oaks (Allegheny County)	15003
Fairoaks (Montgomery County)	19044
Fairplay	17325
Fairview (Beaver County)	15052
Fairview (Blair County)	16601
Fairview (Butler County)	16050
Fairview (Butler County) (Township)	16025
Fairview (Clearfield County)	16858
Fairview (Elk County)	15846
Fairview (Erie County)	16415
Fairview (Erie County) (Township)	16415
Fairview (Franklin County)	17268
Fairview (Jefferson County)	15767

	ZIP
Fairview (Luzerne County) (Township)	18707
Fairview (Mercer County)	16124
Fairview (Mercer County) (Township)	16137
Fairview (Mifflin County)	17044
Fairview (Northumberland County)	17872
Fairview (York County) (Township)	17070
Fairview Drive	17331
Fairview-Ferndale	17872
Fairview Heights (Allegheny County)	15238
Fairview Heights (Berks County)	19533
Fairview Heights (Luzerne County)	18707
Fairview Heights (McKean County)	16701
Fairview Hills	18707
Fairview Knolls	18042
Fairview Park (Chester County)	19380
Fairview Park (Luzerne County)	18707
Fairview Park (York County)	17070
Fairview Village	19409
Fairville (Chester County)	19317
Fairville (Union County)	17837
Fairway Park	17603
Fairways of Brookside	18062
Falconcrest	19380
Fall Brook	16939
Fallentimber	16639
Falling Spring (Franklin County)	17201
Falling Spring (Perry County)	17040
Fallowfield (Township)	15022
Falls (Bucks County) (Township)	19054
Falls (Wyoming County)	18615
Falls (Wyoming County) (Township)	18615
Falls Creek	15840
Fallsdale	18431
Fallsington	19054
Fallston	15066
Falmouth	17502
Fannett (Township)	17220
Fannettsburg	17221
Faraday Park	19070
Farmbrook	19007
Farmdale	17552
Farmers	17364
Farmers Mills	16875
Farmers Valley (Bradford County)	16947
Farmers Valley (McKean County)	16749
Farmersville (Lancaster County)	17522
Farmersville (Northampton County)	18045
Farming Ridge	19606
Farmington (Berks County)	19539
Farmington (Clarion County) (Township)	16233
Farmington (Fayette County)	15437
Farmington (Lehigh County)	18103
Farmington (Tioga County) (Township)	16946
Farmington (Warren County) (Township)	16345
Farmington Hill	16946
Farquhar Estates	17403
Farragut	17754
Farrandsville	17734
Farrell	16121
Farview	19607
Farwell	17764
Fassett	16925
Faunce	16863
Fawn (Allegheny County) (Township)	15084
Fawn (York County) (Township)	17321
Fawn Grove	17321
Faxon	17701
Fayette (Juniata County) (Township)	17049
Fayette (Lawrence County)	16156
Fayette City	15438
Fayetteville	17222

	ZIP
Fayfield	17402
Fay Terrace	18125
Fearnot	17968
Feasterville	19047
Feasterville-Trevose	19047
Federal	15071
Federal Correctional Institution (McKean County)	16701
Federal Correctional Institution (Schuylkill County)	17954
Federal Penitentiary	17837
Federal Prison Camp	17752
Federal Reserve (Part of Pittsburgh)	15230
Federal Square (Part of Harrisburg)	17108
Fell (Township)	18421
Fellsburg	15012
Fellwick	19034
Felton	17322
Feltonville	19013
Fenelton	16034
Ferguson (Centre County) (Township)	16801
Ferguson (Clearfield County) (Township)	15757
Ferguson (Fayette County)	15431
Fergusonville	19007
Fermanagh (Township)	17059
Fern	16319
Fern Brook	18612
Ferndale (Bucks County)	18921
Ferndale (Cambria County)	15905
Ferndale (Northumberland County)	17872
Ferndale (Schuylkill County)	17985
Fern Glen	18241
Fern Hill	19380
Fernridge	18610
Fern Village	19040
Fernville	17815
Fernway	16063
Fernwood (Clearfield County)	16680
Fernwood (Delaware County)	19050
Ferrellton	15563
Fertigs	16364
Fertility	17602
Fetterville	17555
Fiddle Lake	18465
Fiddlers Green	15946
Fidelity (Part of Philadelphia)	19109
Fifficktown	15956
Fiketown	15459
Filbert	15435
Fillmore	16823
Finch Hill	18407
Findlay (Township)	15026
Findley (Township)	16137
Finland	18073
Finleyville (Bedford County)	16679
Finleyville (Washington County)	15332
Fireside Terrace (Part of York)	17404
Fisher (Clarion County)	16225
Fisher (Washington County)	15063
Fisherdale	17824
Fisher Heights	16001
Fishers Corner	19013
Fishers Ferry	17801
Fishertown (Bedford County)	15539
Fishertown (Cambria County)	15956
Fisherville (Chester County)	19335
Fisherville (Dauphin County)	17032
Fishing Creek (Township)	17859
Fiske	16639
Fitch Corner	18615
Fitz Henry	15479
Five Corners	16404
Five Forks	17268
Five Points (Adams County)	17350
Five Points (Beaver County)	15001
Five Points (Berks County)	19606

	ZIP
Five Points (Butler County)	16061
Five Points (Chester County)	19348
Five Points (Clearfield County)	15753
Five Points (Erie County)	16509
Five Points (Indiana County)	15732
Five Points (Luzerne County)	18249
Five Points (Mercer County)	16133
Five Points (Mercer County)	16150
Five Points (Northumberland County)	17772
Five Points (Venango County)	16342
Five Points (Westmoreland County)	15601
Fivepointville	17517
Fizzleburg	16143
Flat Rock (Centre County)	16870
Flat Rock (Fayette County)	15459
Flatwoods	15486
Fleetville	18420
Fleetwing Estates	19057
Fleetwood	19522
Fleming	16835
Flemington	17745
Flicksville	18050
Flinton	16640
Flintville	17042
Floradale	17307
Floreffe (Part of Jefferson)	15025
Florence	15021
Florida Park	19073
Florin (Part of Mount Joy)	17552
Flourtown	19031
Flourtown Gardens	19031
Flying Hills	19607
FM Corners (Part of Hermitage)	16148
Fogelsville	18051
Folcroft	19032
Foleys Siding (Part of Castle Shannon)	15234
Folsom	19033
Folstown	18707
Fombell	16123
Font	19335
Fontana	17042
Footedale	15468
Foot of Ten	16635
Forbes Road	15633
Force	15841
Ford City	16226
Ford Cliff	16228
Fordham	15767
Ford View	16226
Fordville	17364
Fordyce	15370
Forest	16879
Forest Castle (Part of Exeter)	18643
Forest City	18421
Forest Grove (Allegheny County)	15108
Forest Grove (Bucks County)	18922
Foresthill (Union County)	17844
Forest Hill (York County)	17356
Forest Hills (Allegheny County)	15221
Forest Hills (Lancaster County)	17540
Forest Inn	18235
Forest Lake	18801
Forest Lake (Township)	18801
Forest Park (Bucks County)	18914
Forest Park (Luzerne County)	18702
Forestville (Butler County)	16035
Forestville (Chester County)	19390
Forestville (Schuylkill County)	17901
Forge	16686
Forks (Columbia County)	17859
Forks (Northampton County) (Township)	18040
Forks (Sullivan County) (Township)	18614
Forks Church	15656
Forkston	18629
Forkston (Township)	18629

Name	ZIP	Name	ZIP	Name	ZIP	Name	ZIP
Forksville	18616	Franklin (Luzerne County) (Township)	18640	Frutcheys	18301	Georgeville	15759
Forsythia Gate	19056	Franklin (Lycoming		Fryburg	18326	German (Township)	15458
Fort Allen Plan	15601	County) (Township)	17742	Frystown	17067	German Corners	18053
Fortenia	18431	Franklin (Snyder County)		Fuhrmans Mill	17331	Germania	16922
Fort Fetter	16648	(Township)	17861	Fulmor Heights	19040	Germans	18235
Fort Hill (Somerset		Franklin (Susquehanna		Fulton (Township)	17563	Germansville	18053
County)	15540	County) (Township)	18801	Fulton Run	15701	Germantown (Adams	
Fort Hill (Westmoreland		Franklin (Venango		Furlong	18925	County)	17340
County)	15687	County)	16323	Furnace Hill (Fayette		Germantown (Franklin	
Fort Hunter	17110	Franklin (York County)		County)	15431	County)	17222
Fort Indiantown Gap	17003	(Township)	17019	Furnace Hill (Mercer		Germantown (Philadelphia	
Fort Littleton	17223	Franklin Center (Delaware		County)	16159	County)	19144
Fort Loudon	17224	County)	19063	Furnace Run	16201	Germantown (Pike	
Fortney	17339	Franklin Center (Erie		Furniss	17563	County)	18428
Fort Roberston	17047	County)	16412	Gabby Heights	15301	Germany (Township)	17340
Fortuna	18915	Franklindale	18832	Gabelsville	19512	Geryville	18073
Fort Washington	19034	Franklin Farms	15301	Gahagen	15926	Getty Heights	15701
Forty Fort	18704	Franklin Forks	18801	Gaibleton	15747	Gettysburg	17325
Forward (Allegheny		Franklin Hill	18822	Gaines	16921	Ghennes Heights	15063
County) (Township)	15063	Franklin Millo (Part of		Gaines (Township)	16921	Ghent	18850
Forward (Butler County)		Philadelphia)	19154	Galeton	16922	Giant Oaks	15317
(Township)	16033	Franklin Mills (Part of		Galilee	18415	Gibbon Glade	15440
Forwardstown	15531	Philadelphia)	19154	Gallagher (Township)	17745	Gibbs Hill	16735
Fossilville	15534	Franklin Park	15143	Gallagherville	19335	Gibraltar	19508
Foster (Indiana County)	15681	Franklin Pike Corners	16335	Gallatin	15063	Gibson (Cameron County)	
Foster (Luzerne County)		Franklintown	17323	Gallery at Market East,		(Township)	15832
(Township)	18224	Franklinville	16683	The (Part of		Gibson (Susquehanna	
Foster (McKean County)		Frankstown	16648	Philadelphia)	19107	County)	18820
(Township)	16701	Frankstown (Township)	16648	Gallitzin	16641	Gibson (Susquehanna	
Foster (Schuylkill County)		Frazer (Allegheny County)		Gallitzin (Township)	16641	County) (Township)	18842
(Township)	17901	(Township)	15084	Galloway (Part of		Gibson (Washington	
Foster Brook	16701	Frazer (Chester County)	19355	Sugarcreek)	16323	County)	15314
Fostoria	16686	Frederick	19435	Gamble (Township)	17771	Gibsonia	15044
Foundryville	18603	Fredericksburg		Ganister	16693	Gibsonton	15012
Fountain	17938	(Armstrong County)	16041	Gans	15439	Gifford	16732
Fountain Dale	17320	Fredericksburg (Blair		Gap	17527	Gilbert	18331
Fountain Hill	18015	County)	16625	Gapsville	15533	Gilberton	17934
Fountain House Corners	16433	Fredericksburg (Crawford		Garards Fort	15334	Gilbertsville	19525
Fountain Springs	17921	County)	16335	Gardeau	16720	Gilfoyle	16239
Fountainville	18923	Fredericksburg (Lebanon		Garden City (Allegheny		Gillespie	15438
Fourth Avenue (Part of		County)	17026	County)	15146	Gillett	16925
Pittsburgh)	15222	Fredericksville	19539	Garden City (Delaware		Gillingham	16836
Foustown	17404	Fredericktown	15333	County)	19013	Gillintown	16874
Foustwell	15935	Fredericktown Hill	15333	Gardendale	19061	Gilmore (Fayette County)	15478
Fowler Heights	15701	Fredericktown-Millsboro	15333	Garden Hills	17603	Gilmore (Greene County)	
Fowlersville	18603	Fredonia	16124	Garden View (Lycoming		(Township)	15352
Fox (Elk County)		Freeburg	17827	County)	17701	Gilmore (McKean County)	16727
(Township)	15846	Freedom (Adams County)		Garden View (Mifflin		Gilmore (Washington	
Fox (Sullivan County)		(Township)	17307	County)	17084	County)	15057
(Township)	17724	Freedom (Beaver County)	15042	Gardenville	18926	Gilpin (Township)	15656
Foxburg (Clarion County)	16036	Freedom (Blair County)		Gardners	17324	Ginger Hill	15332
Foxburg (Jefferson		(Township)	16637	Garfield	19506	Ginter	16651
County)	15767	Freehold (Township)	16402	Gargol	17337	Ginther	18252
Fox Chapel	15238	Freeland	18224	Garland	16416	Gipsy	15741
Fox Chase (Lancaster		Freemansburg	18017	Garmantown	15714	Girard (Clearfield County)	
County)	17601	Freemansburg Heights	18017	Garrett	15542	(Township)	16836
Fox Chase (Philadelphia		Freemansville	19607	Garrett Hill	19010	Girard (Erie County)	16417
County)	19111	Freeport (Armstrong		Garretts Run	16201	Girard (Erie County)	
Fox Chase Manor	19027	County)	16229	Garrison	15352	(Township)	16417
Foxcroft (Delaware		Freeport (Erie County)	16428	Gas Center	15954	Girard Avenue (Part of	
County)	19008	Freeport (Greene County)		Gaskill (Township)	15767	Philadelphia)	19122
Foxcroft (Montgomery		(Township)	15352	Gastonville	15336	Girardville	17935
County)	19046	Freeport Junction (Part of		Gastown	15774	Girty	15686
Fox Hill (Franklin County)	17268	Freeport)	16229	Gatchellville	17352	Gitts Run	17331
Fox Hill (Luzerne County)	18702	French Creek (Mercer		Gates	15410	Gladden	15057
Fox Run	16046	County) (Township)	16311	Gatesburg	16877	Gladden Heights	15057
Foxton Lake	18847	Frenchcreek (Venango		Gateway Center (Part of		Glade (Somerset County)	15530
Foxtown	15639	County) (Township)	16323	Pittsburgh)	15222	Glade (Warren County)	
Foxtown Hill	18360	Frenchs Corners	16210	Gateway Shopping Center		(Township)	16365
Frackville	17931	Frenchtown	16327	(Part of Edwardsville)	18704	Glade (Warren County)	16365
Frailey (Township)	17981	Frenchville	16836	Gauff Hill	18017	Glade City	15552
Francis Mine	15021	Freysville	17356	Gayly	15126	Glades	17402
Franconia	18924	Fricks	18927	Gaysport (Part of		Gladhill	17320
Franconia (Township)	18924	Fricks Lock	19464	Holidaysburg)	16648	Gladstone (Part of	
Frankford (Part of		Friedens (Lehigh County)	18080	Gay Street (Part of West		Lansdowne)	19050
Philadelphia)	19124	Friedens (Somerset		Chester)	19380	Gladwyne	19035
Frankfort Springs	15050	County)	15541	Gearhartville	16866	Glasgow (Beaver County)	15059
Franklin (Adams County)		Friedensburg	17933	Geeseytown	16648	Glasgow (Cambria	
(Township)	17307	Friedensville	18017	Geiger	15501	County)	16644
Franklin (Beaver County)		Friendship Heights	15467	Geigertown	19523	Glasgow (Montgomery	
(Township)	16123	Friendship Village	19320	Geistown	15904	County)	19464
Franklin (Bradford County)		Friendsville	18818	Gelatt	18825	Glass City	16866
(Township)	18848	Friesville	16625	General Warren Village	19355	Glassmere	15030
Franklin (Butler County)		Frisbie	17961	Genesee	16923	Glassport	15045
(Township)	16052	Frisco	16117	Genesee (Township)	16923	Glassworks	15338
Franklin (Cambria County)	15909	Fritztown	19608	Geneva	16316	Glatfelter	17360
Franklin (Carbon County)		Frogtown (Armstrong		Geneva Hill	15010	Gleason	17724
(Township)	18235	County)	16028	Georges (Township)	15401	Gleasonton	17760
Franklin (Chester County)		Frogtown (Clarion County)	16224	George School (Part of		Glen Acres	19380
(Township)	19350	Frogtown (Huntingdon		Newtown)	18940	Glen Ashton Farms	19020
Franklin (Columbia		County)	16877	Georgetown (Adams		Glenburn	18414
County) (Township)	17820	Frogtown (York County)	17070	County)	17340	Glenburn (Township)	18414
Franklin (Erie County)		Froman	15332	Georgetown (Armstrong		Glen Campbell	15742
(Township)	16412	Frostburg	15740	County)	15656	Glen Carbon	17901
Franklin (Fayette County)		Frugality	16639	Georgetown (Beaver		Glencoe	15538
(Township)	15486	Fruitville (Lancaster		County)	15043	Glendale (Allegheny	
Franklin (Greene County)		County)	17601	Georgetown (Luzerne		County)	15106
(Township)	15370	Fruitville (Montgomery		County)	18702	Glendale (Luzerne	
Franklin (Huntingdon		County)	19473	Georgetown		County)	18641
County) (Township)	16865			(Northampton County)	18064		

	ZIP
Glendale Gardens (Part of Glenolden)	19036
Glendale Manor	18701
Glendon (Northampton County)	18042
Glendon (Schuylkill County)	17948
Glen Dower	17901
Glen Eden	16033
Glenfield	15143
Glen Forney	17268
Glen Gormely	15071
Glenhall	19380
Glen Hazel	15870
Glen Hope	16645
Glenhurst (Part of Bryn Athyn)	19009
Gleniron	17845
Glenloch	19380
Glen Lyon	18617
Glenmar Gardens	16509
Glen Mawr	17737
Glen Mills	19342
Glenmoore (Chester County)	19343
Glen Moore (Lancaster County)	17601
Glenolden	19036
Glen Oley Farms	19606
Glen Richey	16837
Glen Riddle	19037
Glen Riddle-Lima	19037
Glen Rock	17327
Glen Rose	19320
Glen Roy	19362
Glenruadh	16505
Glen Savage	15538
Glenshaw	15116
Glenside	19038
Glenside Gardens	19038
Glenside Heights	19038
Glen Summit	18707
Glenville	17329
Glenwillard	15046
Glenwood (Allegheny County)	15207
Glenwood (Dauphin County)	17109
Glenwood (Erie County)	16509
Glenwood (Mifflin County)	17044
Glenwood (Susquehanna County)	18446
Glenworth	17901
Glosser View	17701
Glyde	15301
Glyndon	16434
Gnatstown	17331
Goat Hill	15301
Godfrey	15656
Goheenville	16259
Gold	16923
Golden Hill	18623
Golden Key Lake	18337
Goldenridge	19057
Golden Rod Farms	16830
Golden Triangle (Part of Pittsburgh)	15222
Goodhope	17055
Good Hope Farms	17055
Good Intent	15323
Goodmans Corners	16364
Goods Corner	15901
Good Spring	17981
Goodtown	15530
Goodville (Juniata County)	17094
Goodville (Lancaster County)	17528
Goodyear	17324
Goosetown	19320
Gordon	17936
Gordonville	17529
Goshen	16830
Goshen (Township)	16830
Goshen	17563
Goshenville	19380
Gosser Hill	15656
Gottshalls	17872
Gouglersville	19608
Gouldsboro	18424
Gourley	15061
Gowen	18241
Gowen City	17828
Gracedale	18707
Graceton	15748
Graceville	15537
Gracey	17228
Gradwohl Terrace	18017
Gradyville	19039
Grafton	15717
Graham	16866

	ZIP
Graham (Township)	16858
Grampian	16838
Grampian Hills (Part of Williamsport)	17701
Grand Valley	16420
Grandview (Armstrong County)	16201
Grandview (Elk County)	15857
Grandview (Indiana County)	15701
Grandview (Washington County)	15063
Grandview Heights	17601
Grandview Park (Elk County)	15857
Grand View Park (Montgomery County)	19426
Grange	15767
Grange Center	16433
Grangeville	17331
Granite	17325
Grant (Elk County)	15821
Grant (Indiana County) (Township)	15759
Grant City	16051
Grantham	17027
Grantley	17403
Grant Street (Part of Pittsburgh)	15219
Grantville	17028
Granville (Bradford County) (Township)	16926
Granville (Mifflin County)	17029
Granville (Mifflin County) (Township)	17044
Granville Center	16926
Granville Summit	16926
Grapeville	15634
Grassflat	16839
Grassmere Park	17814
Grassy (Part of Olyphant)	18447
Graterford	19426
Gratz	17030
Gratztown	15089
Gravity	18436
Gray (Clearfield County)	16881
Gray (Greene County) (Township)	15337
Gray (Somerset County)	15544
Graydon	17322
Grays	15717
Grays Landing	15461
Graysville (Greene County)	15337
Graysville (Huntingdon County)	16865
Grazier	15935
Grazierville	16686
Greason	17013
Great Belt	16001
Great Bend	18821
Great Bend (Township)	18822
Greater Point Marion	15474
Great Southern Shopping Center (Part of Bridgeville)	15017
Greble	17067
Greece City	16025
Greeley	18425
Green (Forest County) (Township)	16353
Green (Indiana County) (Township)	15724
Greenawalds	18104
Greenbrae	16201
Green Briar	15825
Greenbrier (Centre County)	16875
Greenbrier (Dauphin County)	17036
Greenbrier (Northumberland County)	17867
Greenbrook	19007
Greenburr	17747
Greencastle	17225
Green Circle	18451
Greencrest Park	16125
Greendale	16735
Greendown Acres	16635
Greene (Beaver County) (Township)	15050
Greene (Clinton County) (Township)	17747
Greene (Erie County) (Township)	16509
Greene (Franklin County) (Township)	17254
Greene (Greene County) (Township)	15320

	ZIP
Greene (Lancaster County)	17518
Greene (Mercer County) (Township)	16134
Greene (Pike County) (Township)	18426
Greenfield (Allegheny County)	15207
Greenfield (Blair County) (Township)	16625
Greenfield (Cambria County)	16613
Greenfield (Erie County) (Township)	16428
Greenfield (Lackawanna County) (Township)	18407
Greenfield (Mercer County)	16137
Greenfields (Berks County)	19605
Green Fields (Dauphin County)	17098
Green Garden	15001
Green Grove (Centre County)	16875
Green Grove (Lackawanna County)	18447
Green Hill	19380
Green Hills (Berks County)	19607
Green Hills (Delaware County)	19079
Green Hills (Washington County)	15301
Green Lane	18054
Green Lane Farms	17011
Greenlawn Park	19007
Greenmount	17325
Greenock	15047
Green Park	17031
Green Point	17038
Green Ridge (Delaware County)	19014
Green Ridge (Lackawanna County)	18509
Green Ridge (Luzerne County)	18201
Greenridge (Westmoreland County)	15642
Greensboro	15338
Greensburg	15601
Greens Landing	18810
Greenspring	17241
Green Springs	17331
Greentown	18426
Green Tree (Allegheny County)	15242
Green Tree (Chester County)	19355
Green Valley	15825
Green Village	17201
Greenville (Clearfield County)	16838
Greenville (Mercer County)	16125
Greenville (Somerset County) (Township)	15552
Greenville East	16125
Greenwald	15670
Greenwich (Berks County) (Township)	19530
Greenwich (Cambria County)	15714
Greenwood (Blair County)	16602
Greenwood (Clearfield County) (Township)	15757
Greenwood (Columbia County)	17846
Greenwood (Columbia County) (Township)	17859
Greenwood (Crawford County) (Township)	16316
Greenwood (Franklin County)	17222
Greenwood (Juniata County) (Township)	17094
Greenwood (Perry County) (Township)	17062
Greenwood Hills	17057
Greenwood Village	16001
Gregg (Allegheny County)	15071
Gregg (Centre County) (Township)	16875
Gregg (Union County) (Township)	17810
Gregory (Part of Larksville)	18704
Grenoble	18974
Gresham	16354
Greshville	19512

	ZIP
Gretna	15301
Grey Nuns	19067
Grier City	18214
Griesemersville	19512
Griffiths	16735
Grill	19607
Grimesville	17701
Grimms Crossroads	17356
Grimville	19530
Grindstone	15442
Grindstone-Rowes Run	15442
Gringo	15001
Grisemore	15728
Groffdale	17557
Grovania	17821
Grove (Cameron County) (Township)	15861
Grove (Chester County)	19380
Grove Chapel	15701
Grove City	16127
Grover	17735
Groveton	15108
Grugan (Township)	17745
Gruversville	18036
Gruvertown	18013
Guenot Settlement	16836
Guernsey	17307
Guffey (McKean County)	16740
Guffey (Westmoreland County)	15642
Guilford	17201
Guilford (Township)	17201
Guilford Hills	17201
Guilford Springs	17201
Guitonville	16239
Guldens	17325
Gulich (Township)	16680
Gulph	19406
Gulph Mills	19428
Gump	15362
Gum Tree	19320
Guth	18104
Guthriesville	19335
Guthsville	18069
Guys Mills	16327
Gwynedd	19436
Gwynedd Square	19446
Gwynedd Valley	19437
Haafsville	18031
Habrenfield Hills	18612
Hackelbernie (Part of Jim Thorpe)	18229
Hackett	15367
Haddenville	15401
Haddock	18201
Hadley	16130
Hagersville	18944
Hahnstown	17522
Hahntown	15642
Haines (Township)	16882
Haines Acres	17402
Haleeka	17728
Halfmoon (Township)	16877
Halford Hills	19401
Halfville	17543
Halfway	17042
Halfway House	19464
Halifax	17032
Halifax (Township)	17032
Hallowell	17044
Halls	17756
Hallstead	18822
Hallston	16057
Hallton	15860
Hallwood	18621
Halsey	16735
Hamburg	19526
Hametown	17327
Hamilton (Adams County) (Township)	17316
Hamilton (Franklin County) (Township)	17201
Hamilton (Jefferson County)	15744
Hamilton (McKean County) (Township)	16735
Hamilton (Monroe County) (Township)	18354
Hamilton (Northumberland County)	17801
Hamilton (Tioga County) (Township)	16912
Hamiltonban (Township)	17325
Hamilton Heights	17201
Hamilton Mall (Part of Allentown)	18101
Hamilton Park	17603
Hamlin (Lebanon County)	17026
Hamlin (McKean County) (Township)	16733

	ZIP		ZIP		ZIP		ZIP
Hamlin (Wayne County)	18427	Harrison Valley	16927	Helen Mills	15823	Hicksville	15618
Hammersley Fork	17764	Harrisonville	17228	Helfenstein	17939	Hidden Valley	
Hammett	16510	Harristown	17562	Helixville	15559	(Montgomery County)	19406
Hammond	16946	Harrisville	16038	Hellam	17406	Hidden Valley (Somerset	
Hammondville	15666	Harrity	18235	Hellam (Township)	17368	County)	15502
Hamorton	19348	Harrow	18942	Hellertown	18055	Hidden Valley Estates	18062
Hampden (Berks County)	19604	Harshaville	15026	Helvetia	15848	Higgins Corner	16040
Hampden (Cumberland		Hartfield	16930	Hemlock (Columbia		Highcliff	15229
County) (Township)	17055	Hartleton	17829	County) (Township)	17815	Highfield	16001
Hampden Heights (Part of		Hartley (Township)	17835	Hemlock (Warren County)	16365	High House	15478
Reading)	19604	Hartranft	19401	Hemlock Grove (Pike		Highland (Adams County)	
Hampshire Heights	15601	Hartstown	16131	County)	18426	(Township)	17325
Hampton (Adams County)	17350	Hartsville	18974	Hemlock Grove (Sullivan		Highland (Part of	
Hampton (Allegheny		Harveys Lake	18618	County)	17758	McCandless Township)	
County) (Township)	15101	Harveyville	18655	Hempfield (Mercer		(Allegheny County)	15237
Hampton Station	16301	Harwick	15049	County) (Township)	16125	Highland (Part of	
Hampton Township	15101	Harwood	18201	Hempfield (Westmoreland		Pittsburgh) (Allegheny	
Hancock	19539	Hasentab's	16635	County) (Township)	15601	County)	15206
Haneyville	17745	Hasson Heights	16301	Hempfield Manor	15601	Highland (Beaver County)	15010
Hankey Farms	15071	Hastings	16646	Henderson (Clearfield		Highland (Chester County)	
Hanlin	15021	Hatboro	19040	County)	16651	(Township)	19320
Hannah	16870	Hatfield (Fayette County)	15401	Henderson (Huntingdon		Highland (Clarion County)	
Hannahstown	16023	Hatfield (Montgomery		County) (Township)	16652	(Township)	16214
Hannastown	15635	County)	19440	Henderson (Jefferson		Highland (Elk County)	
Hannaville	16314	Hatfield (Montgomery		County) (Township)	15767	(Township)	16735
Hann Hill (Part of		County) (Township)	19440	Henderson (Mercer		Highland (Luzerne	
Hermitage)	16159	Hauto (Part of		County)	16153	County)	18224
Hanover (Beaver County)		Nesquehoning)	18240	Henderson Park	19406	Highland (Westmoreland	
(Township)	15050	Haverford (Delaware		Hendersonville (Butler		County)	15633
Hanover (Lehigh County)		County) (Township)	19083	County)	16046	Highland Acres	17602
(Township)	18103	Haverford (Montgomery		Hendersonville		Highland Corners	16735
Hanover (Luzerne County)		County)	19041	(Washington County)	15339	Highland Meadows	15037
(Township)	18702	Havertown	19083	Hendricks	18979	Highland Park (Bucks	
Hanover (Luzerne County)	18634	Hawkeye	15683	Henningsville	18011	County)	18960
Hanover (Northampton		Hawk Run	16840	Henrietta	16662	Highland Park	
County)	18017	Hawksville	17566	Henry Clay (Township)	15459	(Cumberland County)	17011
Hanover (Northampton		Hawley	18428	Henrys Bend	16301	Highland Park (Delaware	
County) (Township)	18017	Hawleywood	18428	Henrys Mill	16347	County)	19082
Hanover (Washington		Hawstone	17044	Henryville	18332	Highland Park (Erie	
County) (Township)	15021	Hawthorn	16230	Hensel	17566	County)	16506
Hanover (York County)	17331	Haycock (Township)	18951	Hensingerville	18011	Highland Park (Mifflin	
Hanoverdale	17036	Haydentown	15478	Hepburn (Township)	17728	County)	17044
Hanover Green	18702	Hayesville	19363	Hepburn Heights	17728	Highland Park	
Hanover Heights	19464	Hayfield (Township)	16433	Hepburnia	16838	(Northampton County)	18042
Hanover Hills	17036	Haymaker	16731	Hepburnville	17728	Highland Woods	18701
Hanover Junction	17360	Hays (Allegheny County)	15230	Hephzibah	19320	High Meadows	19063
Happy Valley (Part of		Hays (Fayette County)	15401	Hepler	17941	Highmount	17406
Exeter)	18643	Hays Grove	17241	Herbert	15435	High Park	19040
Harbor	16101	Hays Mill	15552	Hercules (Part of		High Rock	17302
Harborcreek	16421	Haysville (Allegheny		Stockertown)	18083	Highspire	17034
Harborcreek (Township)	16421	County)	15143	Hereford	18056	Highville	17516
Harding	18643	Haysville (Butler County)	16041	Hereford (Township)	18056	Hileman Heights (Part of	
Hardy Hill	15431	Hayti	19320	Heritage Hills	16117	Altoona)	16602
Harford	18823	Hazel Hurst	16733	Herman	16039	Hillchurch (Berks County)	19512
Harford (Township)	18823	Hazel Kirk	15063	Herminie	15637	Hill Church (Washington	
Harford Heights	15642	Hazelwood (Part of		Hermitage	16148	County)	15317
Harkness	16914	Pittsburgh)	15207	Hermitage Towne Plaza		Hill City	16319
Harlan	15829	Hazen (Beaver County)	16123	(Part of Hermitage)	16146	Hillcrest (Allegheny	
Harlansburg	16101	Hazen (Jefferson County)	15825	Herndon	17830	County)	15102
Harleigh	18225	Hazle (Township)	18201	Hero	15341	Hillcrest (Beaver County)	15001
Harlem	18062	Hazlebrook	18201	Herrick (Bradford County)		Hill Crest (Fayette County)	15425
Harleysville	19438	Hazleton	18201	(Township)	18853	Hill Crest (Montgomery	
Harmar (Township)	15024	Hazle Village (Part of		Herrick (Susquehanna		County)	19126
Harmar Heights	15024	Hazleton)	18201	County) (Township)	18430	Hillcrest (York County)	17403
Harmarville	15238	Hazzard (Part of		Herrick Center	18430	Hillcroft	17403
Harmonsburg	16422	Monongahela)	15063	Herrick Corner	18430	Hilldale	18702
Harmonville	19428	Heacock Meadows	19067	Herrickville	18853	Hiller	15444
Harmony (Beaver County)		Headlee Heights	15334	Hershey	17033	Hilliards	16040
(Township)	15003	Heart Lake	18801	Hershey Heights	17331	Hillman	15767
Harmony (Butler County)	16037	Heath (Township)	15860	Heshbon	15717	Hillsboro	15963
Harmony (Clearfield		Heathville	15864	Heshbon Park	17701	Hills Creek Lake	16901
County)	16692	Hebe	17830	Hessdale	17560	Hillsdale	15746
Harmony (Forest County)		Heberlig	17241	Hesston	16647	Hillsgrove	18619
(Township)	16370	Hebron (Lebanon County)	17042	Hetlerville	18635	Hillsgrove (Township)	18619
Harmony (Jefferson		Hebron (Potter County)		Hettesheimer Corners	18636	Hillside (Lehigh County)	18069
County)	15767	(Township)	16915	Hiawatha	18462	Hillside (Luzerne County)	18708
Harmony (Susquehanna		Hebron Center	16915	Hibbs	15443	Hillside (Schuylkill County)	17901
County) (Township)	18847	Heckscherville	17901	Hickernell	16435	Hillside (Westmoreland	
Harmony Grove	17315	Hecktown	18017	Hickman	15071	County)	15627
Harmony Hill	19335	Hecla	17960	Hickory (Forest County)		Hillside Junction (Part of	
Harmony Junction	16037	Hector (Township)	16948	(Township)	16322	Moosic)	18507
Harmony Township	15003	Hegarty Crossroads	16627	Hickory (Lawrence		Hills Terrace	17948
Harmonyville	19464	Hegins	17938	County) (Township)	16105	Hillsview	15658
Harnedsville	15424	Hegins (Township)	17938	Hickory (Washington		Hillsville	16132
Harpers	18088	Heidelberg (Allegheny		County)	15340	Hilltop	18951
Harper Tavern	17003	County)	15106	Hickory Corners (Mercer		Hill Top Acres (Armstrong	
Harper Village	15001	Heidelberg (Berks County)		County)	16146	County)	16226
Harris (Township)	16827	(Township)	19567	Hickory Corners		Hilltop Acres (Lancaster	
Harris Acres	16801	Heidelberg (Lebanon		(Northumberland		County)	17603
Harrisburg	17101-30	County) (Township)	17088	County)	17017	Hilltown (Adams County)	17307
For specific Harrisburg Zip		Heidelberg (Lehigh		Hickory Grove	18847	Hilltown (Bucks County)	18927
Codes call (717) 257-2150, or		County) (Township)	18053	Hickory Heights	16101	Hilltown (Bucks County)	
your local postmaster.		Heidelberg (York County)		Hickoryhill	19363	(Township)	18911
Harrison (Allegheny		(Township)	17362	Hickory Hills	19067	Hillville	16041
County) (Township)	15065	Heidersburg	17372	Hickory Run Forest	18229	Hilton	17315
Harrison (Bedford County)		Heilmandale	17046	Hickorytown (Cumberland		Hines Corners	18449
(Township)	15534	Heilwood	15745	County)	17013	Hinkle	18947
Harrison (Potter County)		Heise Run	16901	Hickorytown (Montgomery		Hinkletown	17522
(Township)	16927	Heistersburg	15433	County)	19401	Hinkson Corner	19086
Harrison City	15636	Helen Furnace	16214	Hickox	16923	Hiyasota	15935

	ZIP
Hoadleys	18431
Hoban Heights	18657
Hobart	17331
Hobbie	18660
Hoblitzell	15545
Hockersville	17241
Hoenerstown	17036
Hoffer	17864
Hoffmansville	19435
Hogestown	17055
Hog Island	19029
Hoguetown	16630
Hokendauqua	18052
Hokes	17327
Holbrook	15341
Holicong	18928
Holiday Hills	18106
Holiday Park (Part of Plum)	15239
Holiday Pocono	18210
Holland	18966
Hollenback (Township)	18660
Hollentown	16639
Hollers Hill	18201
Holley Heights	17404
Holliday	16935
Hollidaysburg	16648
Hollinger	17603
Hollisterville	18444
Hollsopple	15935
Hollywood (Clearfield County)	15849
Hollywood (Luzerne County)	18201
Hollywood (Montgomery County)	19027
Hollywood Heights	17403
Holmes	19043
Holmesburg (Part of Philadelphia)	19136
Holt	15001
Holtwood	17532
Homans Corner	16678
Home	15747
Homeacre	16001
Homeacre-Lyndora	16045
Home Camp	15856
Homeland	17601
Home Park	18052
Homer (Township)	16915
Homer City	15748
Homer Gap	16601
Homestead	15120
Homesville	17921
Hometown	18252
Homets Ferry	18853
Homeville	19330
Homewood (Allegheny County)	15208
Homewood (Beaver County)	15010
Homewood (York County)	17019
Honeoye	16748
Honesdale	18431
Honey Brook	19344
Honeybrook (Township)	19344
Honey Creek	17084
Honey Grove	17035
Honey Pot (Part of Nanticoke)	18634
Hooker	16041
Hookstown	15050
Hoover	15458
Hooverhurst	15742
Hooversville	15936
Hop Bottom	18824
Hopeland	17533
Hope Mills	16137
Hopewell (Beaver County) (Township)	15001
Hopewell (Bedford County)	16650
Hopewell (Bedford County) (Township)	16650
Hopewell (Chester County)	19363
Hopewell (Cumberland County) (Township)	17240
Hopewell (Huntingdon County) (Township)	16657
Hopewell (Washington County) (Township)	15301
Hopewell (York County) (Township)	17363
Hoppenville	18073
Hopwood	15445
Horatio	15767
Hormtown	15851
Horn Brook	18848
Hornby	16428

	ZIP
Hornerstown (Part of Johnstown)	15902
Horning (Part of Baldwin)	15236
Horseshoe Heights	17602
Horsham	19044
Horsham (Township)	19044
Horton (Township)	15823
Hosensack	18092
Hosensock	18214
Hospital (Part of Norristown)	19401
Host	19567
Hostetter	15638
Hottelville	16239
Houserville	16801
Houston	15342
Houston City	18641
Houtzdale	16651
Hovey (Township)	16049
Howard	16841
Howard (Township)	16841
Howard Siding	15834
Howe (Forest County) (Township)	16239
Howe (Jefferson County)	15825
Howe (Perry County) (Township)	17074
Howellville	19312
Howersville	18088
Howertown	18067
Hoytdale (Part of Big Beaver)	16157
Hoytville	16938
Hublersburg	16823
Hubley (Township)	17968
Huckenberry	16849
Hudson (Clearfield County)	16866
Hudson (Luzerne County)	18702
Hudsondale	18255
Huefner	16235
Huey	16248
Huffs Church	18011
Hughes Park	19406
Hughestown	18640
Hughesville	17737
Hughs	18621
Hulltown	15428
Hulmeville	19047
Humboldt	18201
Hummelstown	17036
Hummels Wharf	17831
Humphreys	15601
Humphreyville	19320
Hungerford (Part of Shrewsbury)	17361
Hungry Hollow	15656
Hunker	15639
Hunlock (Township)	18621
Hunlock Creek	18621
Hunlock Gardens	18621
Hunter	17872
Hunter Hill	19462
Hunters Run	17324
Hunterstown	17325
Huntersville	17756
Huntingdon	16652
Huntingdon Furnace	16686
Huntingdon Heights	15642
Huntingdon Manor	17540
Huntingdon Valley	19006
Hunting Park (Part of Philadelphia)	19140
Huntington (Adams County) (Township)	17372
Huntington (Luzerne County) (Township)	18655
Huntington Mills	18622
Huntley	15832
Huntsdale	17013
Huntsville	18612
Husband	15501
Huston (Blair County) (Township)	16693
Huston (Centre County) (Township)	16844
Huston (Clearfield County) (Township)	15849
Huston Run	15332
Hustontown	17229
Hutchins	16740
Hutchinson (Fayette County)	15401
Hutchinson (Westmoreland County)	15640
Hyde	16843
Hyde Park (Berks County)	19605
Hyde Park (Lackawanna County)	18504

	ZIP
Hyde Park (Westmoreland County)	15641
Hydetown	16328
Hyde Villa	19605
Hyndman	15545
Hynemansville	18066
Hyner	17738
Icedale	19344
Ickesburg	17037
Idaho	15774
Idamar	15734
Idaville	17337
Idetown (Part of Harveys Lake)	18612
Idlewood (Part of Crafton)	15205
Imler	16655
Imlertown	15522
Immaculata	19345
Imperial	15126
Imperial-Enlow	15126
Independence	15001
Independence (Beaver County) (Township)	15001
Independence (Snyder County)	17864
Independence (Washington County)	15312
Independence (Washington County) (Township)	15312
Indiana (Allegheny County) (Township)	15051
Indiana (Indiana County)	15701
Indian Creek (Bucks County)	19057
Indian Creek (Cumberland County)	17055
Indian Crossing	16731
Indian Head (Erie County)	16441
Indian Head (Fayette County)	15446
Indian Hills	16201
Indian King	19380
Indian Lake (Luzerne County)	18661
Indian Lake (Somerset County)	15926
Indianland	18088
Indian Mountain Lake	18210
Indianola	15051
Indian Orchard	18431
Indian Springs Estates	15701
Industry (Allegheny County)	15018
Industry (Beaver County)	15052
Inez	16915
Ingleby	16882
Inglenook	17032
Inglesmith	17211
Ingomar	15237
Ingram	15205
Inkerman	18640
Intercourse	17534
Iola	17846
Iona	17042
Irishtown (Adams County)	17350
Irishtown (Clearfield County)	16838
Irishtown (McKean County)	16738
Irishtown (Mercer County)	16137
Iron Bridge	15666
Iron Springs	17320
Ironton	18037
Ironville (Blair County)	16686
Ironville (Lancaster County)	17512
Irvine	16329
Irving	17963
Irvona	16656
Irwin (Venango County) (Township)	16038
Irwin (Westmoreland County)	15642
Isabella	15447
Iselin	15681
Iselin Heights	15801
Island Lake	18462
Island Park	17801
Ithan	19085
Iva	17562
Ivarea	16410
Ivyland	18974
Ivy Mills (Part of Chester Heights)	19342
Ivy Ridge (Part of Philadelphia)	19101
Ivywood (Butler County)	16056
Ivywood (Pike County)	18451
Jacks Creek	17044

	ZIP
Jacks Mountain	17320
Jackson (Butler County) (Township)	16063
Jackson (Cambria County) (Township)	15909
Jackson (Columbia County) (Township)	17814
Jackson (Dauphin County) (Township)	17032
Jackson (Greene County) (Township)	15341
Jackson (Huntingdon County) (Township)	16669
Jackson (Lebanon County) (Township)	17042
Jackson (Luzerne County) (Township)	18708
Jackson (Lycoming County) (Township)	17765
Jackson (Mercer County) (Township)	16133
Jackson (Monroe County) (Township)	18352
Jackson (Northumberland County) (Township)	17830
Jackson (Perry County) (Township)	17006
Jackson (Snyder County) (Township)	17889
Jackson (Susquehanna County)	18825
Jackson (Susquehanna County) (Township)	18825
Jackson (Tioga County) (Township)	16936
Jackson (Venango County) (Township)	16317
Jackson (York County) (Township)	17362
Jackson Center	16133
Jackson Corner	16652
Jackson Crossing	16365
Jackson Knolls Gardens	16101
Jackson Summit	16936
Jackson Valley	18830
Jacksonville (Centre County)	16841
Jacksonville (Lehigh County)	18066
Jacksonville (Northampton County)	18014
Jacksonwald	19606
Jacksville	16057
Jacktown	15642
Jacktown Acres	15642
Jacobs Creek	15448
Jacobs Mills	17331
Jacobus	17407
Jalappa	19526
James City	16734
James Creek	16657
Jamestown (Cambria County)	15946
Jamestown (Carbon County)	18235
Jamestown (Mercer County)	16134
Jamesville	18014
Jamison (Bucks County)	18929
Jamison (Fayette County)	15401
Jamison (Forest County)	16370
Jamison City	17814
Japan	18224
Jarrettown	19025
Jay (Township)	15868
Jeanesville	18201
Jeannette	15644
Jeddo	18224
Jednota	17057
Jefferis Crossing	15401
Jefferson (Allegheny County)	15025
Jefferson (Berks County) (Township)	19506
Jefferson (Butler County) (Township)	16056
Jefferson (Dauphin County) (Township)	17032
Jefferson (Fayette County) (Township)	15442
Jefferson (Greene County)	15344
Jefferson (Greene County) (Township)	15344
Jefferson (Lackawanna County) (Township)	18436
Jefferson (Mercer County) (Township)	16148
Jefferson (Schuylkill County)	17922

	ZIP
Jefferson (Somerset County) (Township)	15501
Jefferson (Washington County)	15312
Jefferson (Washington County) (Township)	15021
Jefferson Center	16056
Jeffersonville	19403
Jenkins (Township)	18640
Jenkins Corner	17563
Jenkintown	19046
Jenkintown Manor	19027
Jenks (Township)	16239
Jenner (Township)	15546
Jenners	15546
Jenners Crossroads	15531
Jennerstown	15547
Jennersville	19390
Jenningsville	18629
Jericho	15861
Jericho Mills	17059
Jermyn	18433
Jerome	15937
Jersey Mills	17739
Jersey Shore	17740
Jerseytown	17815
Jerusalem Corners	16341
Jessup (Lackawanna County)	18434
Jessup (Susquehanna County) (Township)	18801
Jim Thorpe	18229
Jimtown	15501
Joanna	19543
Joanna Heights	19543
Jobs Corners	16936
Joffre	15053
Johnsonburg (Elk County)	15845
Johnsonburg (Indiana County)	15772
Johnsons Corner	19317
Johnstown (Cambria County)	15901-15
For specific Johnstown Zip Codes call (814) 533-4935, or your local postmaster.	
Johnstown (Union County)	17844
Johnsville	18974
John Wanamaker (Part of Philadelphia)	19107
Jo Jo	16735
Joliett	17981
Joller	16674
Jollytown	15352
Jonas	18058
Jonathan Point	18210
Jones (Township)	15870
Jones Mills	15646
Jones Terrace	18042
Jonestown (Columbia County)	17859
Jonestown (Lebanon County)	17038
Jonestown (Schuylkill County)	17901
Jonestown (Washington County)	15022
Jordan (Clearfield County) (Township)	16656
Jordan (Lehigh County)	18053
Jordan (Lycoming County) (Township)	17774
Jordan (Northumberland County) (Township)	17830
Jordan Valley	18053
Josephine	15750
Joyce	16101
Jugtown (Bucks County)	18972
Jugtown (Franklin County)	17268
Julian	16844
Jumonville	15445
Juneau	15751
Junedale	18230
June Meadows	19006
Junewood	19055
Juniata (Bedford County) (Township)	15550
Juniata (Blair County) (Township)	16635
Juniata (Blair County)	16601
Juniata (Fayette County)	15431
Juniata (Huntingdon County) (Township)	16652
Juniata (Perry County) (Township)	17074
Juniata Gap	16601
Juniata Terrace	17044
Just A Farm	19006
Justus	18411
Kaiserville	18630
Kammerer	15330
Kane	16735
Kanesholm	16735
Kaneville	16301
Kantner	15548
Kantz	17870
Kaolin	19374
Kapp Heights	17857
Karns City	16041
Karthaus	16845
Karthaus (Township)	16845
Kaseville	17821
Kasiesville	17236
Kaska	17959
Kasson	16749
Kauffman	17201
Kaybrook Manor	18101
Kaylor	16025
Kaywood	16827
Kearney	16679
Kearsarge	16509
Keating (Clinton County)	17778
Keating (McKean County) (Township)	16749
Keating (Potter County) (Township)	16720
Keating Summit	16720
Kecksburg	15666
Kedron Park	19070
Keelersburg	18657
Keelersville	18944
Keeneyville	16935
Keepville	16401
Keewaydin	16836
Keffer	17981
Keifertown	15683
Keisters	16057
Keisterville	15449
Kelayres	18231
Kellersburg	16259
Kellers Church	18944
Kellersville	18360
Kellettville	16353
Kelly (Armstrong County)	16226
Kelly (Union County) (Township)	17837
Kelly Crossroads	17837
Kelly Point	17837
Kellytown (Clearfield County)	16863
Kellytown (Tioga County)	16933
Kelton	19346
Kemblesville	19347
Kempton	19529
Kendall (Beaver County)	15043
Kendall (York County)	17356
Kendrick	16651
Kenhorst	19607
Kenilworth	19464
Kenmar	17701
Kenmawr	15136
Kennard	16125
Kennedy (Allegheny County) (Township)	15136
Kennedy (Tioga County)	16901
Kennedy Mill	16051
Kennedy's Corner	15001
Kennedy Township	15136
Kennells Mills	15545
Kennerdell	16374
Kennett (Township)	19348
Kennett Square	19348
Kenny Row	15468
Kensington (Part of Philadelphia)	19125
Kensington Heights	17201
Kent	15752
Kenwick Village	17601
Kenwood (Bucks County)	19007
Kenwood (Indiana County)	15728
Kepner	17960
Kepple Hill	15690
Kepples Corner	16025
Kernsville	18069
Kernville (Part of Johnstown)	15901
Kerr	16830
Kerrmoor	16833
Kerrs Corners	16127
Kerrsville	17013
Kerrtown	16335
Kersey	15846
Kesslerville	18064
Keys	17322
Keyser Valley (Part of Scranton)	18504
Keystone (Luzerne County)	18702
Keystone (Somerset County)	15552
Keystone (Westmoreland County)	15637
Khedive	15320
Kidder (Township)	18624
Kilbuck	15233
Kilbuck (Township)	15143
Kilgore	16153
Killam Park	18451
Killinger	17061
Kimberton	19442
Kimbles	18428
Kimmel (Bedford County) (Township)	16655
Kimmel (Somerset County)	15557
Kimmelton	15563
Kim Plan	15642
Kinderhook	17512
Kindts Corner	19555
King	16655
King (Township)	16655
King of Prussia	19406
King of Prussia Plaza	19406
Kingsdale	17340
Kingsessing (Part of Philadelphia)	19143
Kingsley (Forest County) (Township)	16353
Kingsley (Susquehanna County)	18826
Kings Manor	19406
Kingston (Luzerne County)	18704
Kingston (Luzerne County) (Township)	18708
Kingston (Westmoreland County)	15650
Kingston-Forty Fort (Part of Kingston)	18704
Kingsville	15864
Kingswood Park	19007
Kingview	15683
Kingwood	15551
Kinlock (Part of Lower Burrell)	15068
Kinney	16923
Kinport	15724
Kintersburg	15728
Kintigh Plan	15601
Kintnersville	18930
Kinzers	17535
Kipps Run	17821
Kirby	15370
Kirbyville	19522
Kirks Bridge	19362
Kirks Mills	19362
Kirkwood	17536
Kirwan Heights	15017
Kiser Corners	16353
Kishacoquillas	17004
Kiskimere	15690
Kiskiminetas (Township)	15613
Kis-Lyn	18222
Kissel Hill	17543
Kissimmee	17842
Kissingers Mill	16248
Kistler (Mifflin County)	17066
Kistler (Perry County)	17047
Kitches Corners	16125
Kittanning	16201
Kittanning (Township)	16226
Kittanning (Part of Applewold)	16201
Kittanning Heights	16201
Kladder Station	16648
Klahr	16625
Klecknersville	18014
Kleinfeltersville	17039
Kline (Township)	18237
Klines Corner	19539
Klines Grove	17801
Klinesville (Berks County)	19534
Klinesville (Lancaster County)	17512
Kline Village (Part of Harrisburg)	17104
Klingerstown	17941
Klondike	16738
Klondyke	17044
Knapp	16901
Knauers	19540
Knauertown	19464
Kneedler	19446
Knepper	17268
Knightsville	17052
Knobsville	17233
Knobville	17063
Knoebel's Grove	17824
Knousetown	17062
Knowltonwood	19065
Knox (Beaver County)	16117
Knox (Clarion County)	16232
Knox (Clarion County) (Township)	16235
Knox (Clearfield County) (Township)	16863
Knox (Jefferson County) (Township)	15825
Knox Dale	15847
Knoxlyn	17325
Knox Run	16858
Knoxville (Allegheny County)	15210
Knoxville (Fayette County)	15417
Knoxville (Tioga County)	16928
Koonsville	18655
Koppel	16136
Korn Krest	18702
Kossuth	16331
Kralltown	17316
Kratzerville	17870
Krayn	15963
Kreamer	17833
Kregar	15622
Kreidersville	18067
Kremis	16125
Kresgeville	18333
Kreutz Creek	17406
Kricktown	19608
Krings	15904
Krocksville	18104
Krumsville	19534
Kuhn	15501
Kuhnsville	18103
Kuhntown	15341
Kulp	17820
Kulpmont	17834
Kulps Corner	18944
Kulpsville	19443
Kulptown	19518
Kunkle	18612
Kunkletown	18058
Kushequa	16735
Kutztown (Berks County)	19530
Kutztown (Lebanon County)	17067
Kylers Corners	15846
Kylertown	16847
Kyleville	17302
La Anna	18326
La Belle	15450
Laboratory	15301
Labott	17364
Lacey Park	18974
Laceyville	18623
Lack (Township)	17021
Lackawannock (Township)	16137
Lackawaxen	18435
Lackawaxen (Township)	18425
Lacock	15301
Laddsburg	18833
Lafayette	16738
Lafayette (Township)	16738
Lafayette College (Part of Easton)	18042
Lafayette Hill	19444
Lafayetteville	16664
Laflin	18705
La Gonda	15301
Lahaska	18931
Lairds Crossing	16262
Lairdsville	17742
La Jose	15753
Lake (Luzerne County) (Township)	18621
Lake (Mercer County) (Township)	16153
Lake (Wayne County) (Township)	18436
Lake Ariel	18436
Lake Carey	18657
Lake City	16423
Lake Como	18437
Lake Donegal	15610
Lake Harmony	18624
Lake Heritage	17325
Lake Idlewild	18470
Lakeland	18436
Lake Lynn	15451
Lake Meade	17316
Lake Monroe	18335
Lakemont	16602
Lake Naomi	18350
Lake Pleasant	16438
Lake Quinn	18472
Lake Sheridan	18446
Lakeside (Bucks County)	19053

	ZIP
Lakeside (Susquehanna County)	18834
Lake Stonycreek	15541
Laketon Heights	15235
Lakeview	18847
Lakeview Heights	17111
Lakeville	18438
Lake Waynewood	18436
Lake Wesauking	18848
Lake Winola	18625
Lakewood (Erie County)	16505
Lakewood (Wayne County)	18439
Lakewood Park	16101
Lake Wynonah	17972
Lamar	16848
Lamar (Township)	17751
Lamartine	16375
Lamberton	15458
Lambertsville	15563
Lambs Creek	16933
Lamonaville	16239
Lamont	16735
Lamonts Corners (Part of Hermitage)	16150
La Mott	19012
Lampeter	17537
Lanark	18034
Lancaster (Butler County) (Township)	16037
Lancaster (Lancaster County)	17601-08
For specific Lancaster Zip Codes call (717) 665-4199, or your local postmaster.	
Lancaster (Lancaster County) (Township)	17603
Lancaster Avenue (Part of Philadelphia)	19104
Lancaster Bible College	17601
Lancaster Junction	17545
Landenberg	19350
Lander	16345
Landingville	17942
Landisburg	17040
Landis Farms	17601
Landis Store	19512
Landis Valley	17604
Landisville	17538
Landreth Manor	19007
Landstreet	15935
Lanesboro	18827
Lanes Mills	15824
Laneville (Part of Freeport)	16229
Langdon	17763
Langdondale	16650
Langeloth	15054
Langhorne	19047
Langhorne Gardens	19047
Langhorne Manor	19047
Langhorne Terrace	19047
Lansdale	19446
Lansdowne	19050
Lansdowne Park Gardens (Part of Collingdale)	19023
Lanse	16849
Lansford	18232
Lantz Corners	16740
Lapidea Hills	19013
La Plume	18440
La Plume (Township)	18440
Laporte	18626
Laporte (Township)	17758
Larabee	16731
Lardintown	16055
Large (Part of Jefferson)	15025
Larimer (Somerset County) (Township)	15552
Larimer (Westmoreland County)	15647
Larke	16693
Larksville	18704
Larrys Creek	17740
Larryville	17740
Larue	17327
Lashley	17267
Lathrop (Township)	18446
Latimore	17372
Latimore (Township)	17372
Latrobe	15650
Lattimer Mines	18234
Laughlin Junction (Part of Pittsburgh)	15207
Laughlintown	15655
Laurel (Cumberland County)	17324
Laurel (York County)	17322
Laurel Bend	19007
Laureldale	19605
Laurel Falls	15552

	ZIP
Laurel Gardens	15229
Laurel Hill (Fayette County)	15431
Laurel Hill (Washington County)	15057
Laurel Lake (Luzerne County)	18707
Laurel Lake (Susquehanna County)	18812
Laurel Mountain	15655
Laurel Park	17845
Laurel Ridge	15009
Laurel Run	18702
Laurelton	17835
Laurelville (Fayette County)	15666
Laurelville (Lancaster County)	17557
Laurys Station	18059
Lausanne (Township)	18255
Lavansville	15501
Lavelle	17943
Laverock	19118
Lawn	17041
Lawnherst	18045
Lawnton	17111
Lawrence (Clearfield County) (Township)	16830
Lawrence (Tioga County) (Township)	16946
Lawrence (Washington County)	15055
Lawrence Park (Delaware County)	19008
Lawrence Park (Erie County) (Township)	16511
Lawrence Park (Erie County)	16511
Lawrenceville (Allegheny County)	15201
Lawrenceville (Lackawanna County)	18642
Lawrenceville (Tioga County)	16929
Lawsonham	16248
Lawson Heights	15650
Lawsville Center	18801
Lawton	18828
Layfield	19525
Layton	15473
Leacock	17540
Leacock (Township)	17572
Leacock-Leola-Bareville	17540
Leaders Heights	17403
Leaf Park	17603
Leaman Place	17562
Leamersville	16635
Learn Settlement	15729
Leasuresville	16055
Leather Corner Post	18069
Leatherwood	16242
Lebanon (Lebanon County)	17042
	17046
For specific Lebanon Zip Codes call (717) 274-2594, or your local postmaster.	
Lebanon (Wayne County) (Township)	18431
Lebanon Plaza	17042
Lebanon South	17042
Lebo	17040
Le Boeuf (Township)	16441
Le Boeuf Gardens	16441
Leck Kill	17836
Leckrone	15454
Lecontes Mills	16850
Lederach	19450
Ledgedale	18463
Lee	18617
Leechburg	15656
Leech Hill	16943
Leedom Estates	19078
Leedom Gardens	19078
Lee Mine	18634
Lee Park	18702
Leeper	16233
Leesburg	16156
Leesburg Station	16156
Lees Cross Roads	17257
Leesport	19533
Leet (Township)	15143
Leetonia	17727
Leetsdale	15056
Lehigh (Carbon County) (Township)	18255
Lehigh (Lackawanna County)	18424
Lehigh (Lackawanna County) (Township)	18424

	ZIP
Lehigh (Northampton County) (Township)	18088
Lehigh (Wayne County) (Township)	18424
Lehigh Furnace	18080
Lehigh Gap (Carbon County)	18071
Lehigh Gap (Lehigh County)	18080
Lehighton	18235
Lehigh University (Part of Bethlehem)	18015
Lehigh Valley General Mail Facility	18001-02
For specific Lehigh Valley General Mail Facility Zip Codes call (215) 882-3256, or your local postmaster.	
Lehigh Valley Mall	18052
Lehman (Luzerne County)	18627
Lehman (Luzerne County) (Township)	18612
Lehman (Pike County) (Township)	18324
Lehman (York County)	17362
Leibeyville	17960
Leidy (Township)	17764
Leinbachs	19605
Leisenring	15455
Leith	15401
Leith-Hatfield	15401
Leithsville	18055
Lemasters	17231
Lemon (Township)	18657
Lemon	18657
Lemont	16851
Lemont Furnace	15456
Lemoyne	17043
Lenape	19380
Lenape Heights	16226
Lenhartsville	19534
Lenker Manor	17109
Lenkerville	17061
Lenni	19052
Lenni Heights	19037
Lennox Park (Part of Trainer)	19015
Lenover	19365
Lenox (Township)	18446
Lenoxville	18441
Lenwood Heights	17236
Leola	17540
Leolyn	17765
Leona	16914
Leopard	19312
Leopard Lakes	19312
Le Raysville	18829
Leroy	17743
Leroy (Township)	17724
Lester	19029
Letort	17582
Letterkenny (Township)	17244
Letterkenny Army Depot	17201
Level Corner	17744
Level Green	15085
Levittown	19054-59
For specific Levittown Zip Codes call (215) 949-3131, or your local postmaster.	
Levittown Center	19054
Levittown Shopping Center (Part of Tullytown)	19055
Levittown-Tullytown	19007
Lewis (Lycoming County) (Township)	17771
Lewis (Northumberland County) (Township)	17772
Lewis (Union County) (Township)	17880
Lewisberry	17339
Lewisburg	17837
Lewis Run	16738
Lewistown (Mifflin County)	17044
Lewistown (Schuylkill County)	18252
Lewistown Junction	17044
Lewisville (Chester County)	19351
Lewisville (Indiana County)	15725
Lexington	17543
Liberty (Adams County) (Township)	17320
Liberty (Allegheny County)	15133
Liberty (Bedford County) (Township)	16678
Liberty (Centre County) (Township)	16841
Liberty (McKean County) (Township)	16743

	ZIP
Liberty (McKean County)	16743
Liberty (Mercer County) (Township)	16127
Liberty (Montour County) (Township)	17821
Liberty (Susquehanna County) (Township)	18801
Liberty (Tioga County)	16930
Liberty (Tioga County) (Township)	16930
Liberty Corners	18848
Liberty Square	17518
Library	15129
Lickdale	17038
Licking (Township)	16049
Licking Creek (Township)	17228
Lickingville	16332
Lightner	17404
Light Street	17839
Ligonier	15658
Ligonier (Township)	15658
Lilly	15938
Lillyville	16117
Lima	19037
Limehill	18853
Limekiln	19535
Limeport	18060
Limerick	19468
Limerick (Township)	19468
Lime Ridge	17815
Lime Rock	17543
Limestone	16234
Limestone (Clarion County) (Township)	16234
Limestone (Lycoming County) (Township)	17740
Limestone (Montour County) (Township)	17821
Limestone (Union County) (Township)	17844
Limestone (Warren County) (Township)	16351
Limestoneville	17847
Lime Valley	17584
Limeville	17527
Lincoln (Allegheny County)	15037
Lincoln (Bedford County) (Township)	15521
Lincoln (Huntingdon County) (Township)	16657
Lincoln (Lancaster County)	17522
Lincoln (Somerset County) (Township)	15501
Lincoln Acres	15642
Lincoln Beach	15068
Lincoln Colliery	17963
Lincoln Falls	18616
Lincoln Heights (Berks County)	19508
Lincoln Heights (Westmoreland County)	15644
Lincoln Hill	15301
Lincoln Park (Allegheny County)	15235
Lincoln Park (Berks County)	19609
Lincoln Park (Delaware County)	19079
Lincoln Place (Part of Pittsburgh)	15207
Lincoln Terrace	18042
Lincoln University	19352
Lincolnville	16404
Lincolnway	17404
Linconia	19047
Linden (Lycoming County)	17744
Linden (Washington County)	15317
Linden Hall	16828
Lindenhurst	19067
Linds Crossing	16648
Lindsey (Part of Punxsutawney)	15767
Line Lexington	18932
Line Mountain	17941
Linesville	16424
Linfield	19468
Linglestown	17112
Linhart	15145
Linn	15442
Linntown	17837
Linville Circle (Part of Lancaster)	17602
Linwood	19061
Linwood Park	19061
Linwood Terrace	19061
Lionville	19353
Lionville-Marchwood	19341

* Area Zip Code   † Post Office Boxes

	ZIP
Lippincott	15370
Lisbon	16373
Lisburn	17055
Listie	15549
Listonburg	15424
Litchfield	18810
Litchfield (Township)	18810
Lithia Springs	17857
Lithia Valley (Part of Factoryville)	18419
Lititz	17543
Little Beaver (Township)	16120
Little Britain (Township)	19363
Little Chicago	15320
Little Cooley	16404
Little Corners	16335
Little Gap	18058
Little Hickory	16353
Little Hope	16428
Little Italy	18956
Little Kansas	17051
Little Mahanoy (Township)	17823
Little Marsh	16950
Little Meadows	18830
Littlestown	17340
Little Summit	15431
Littletown	15748
Little Washington	19335
Live Easy	15320
Liverpool	17045
Liverpool (Township)	17045
Livonia	16872
Llandrilla	19004
Llanfair	15930
Llewellyn	17944
Llewelyn Corners	18602
Lloydell	15921
Lloydesville	15650
Llyswen (Part of Altoona)	16602
Loag	19520
Lobachsville	19547
Lochiel	17837
Lochvale	15742
Locke Mills	17063
Lock Haven	17745
Lockport (Clinton County)	17745
Lockport (Mifflin County)	17044
Lockport (Westmoreland County)	15923
Locksley	19342
Lockview	15022
Locust (Columbia County) (Township)	17820
Locust (Indiana County)	15771
Locustdale	17945
Locust Gap	17840
Locust Grove (Centre County)	16875
Locust Grove (York County)	17402
Locust Grove Gardens	17402
Locust Hill	15474
Locust Lakes Village	18347
Locust Point	17055
Locust Run	17094
Locust Summit	17840
Locust Valley (Lehigh County)	18036
Locust Valley (Schuylkill County)	18214
Lofty	18201
Logan (Blair County) (Township)	16601
Logan (Clinton County) (Township)	17747
Logan (Huntingdon County) (Township)	16669
Logan (Indiana County)	15742
Logan (Philadelphia County)	19141
Logan Mills	17747
Logans Ferry (Part of Plum)	15239
Logans Ferry Heights (Part of Plum)	15239
Logan Square (Part of Norristown)	19401
Loganton	17747
Loganville	17342
Log Pile	15301
London	16127
London Britain (Township)	19350
Londonderry (Bedford County) (Township)	15545
Londonderry (Chester County) (Township)	19330
Londonderry (Dauphin County) (Township)	17057
London Grove	19348
London Grove (Township)	19390

	ZIP
Lone Pine	15301
Long Acre Park (Part of Yeadon)	19050
Long Branch	15423
Long Bridge	15658
Longbrook	17758
Longfellow	17044
Longlevel	17368
Long Pond	18334
Long Run	18235
Longs Crossroad	16668
Longsdale	15939
Longsdorf	17241
Longstown	17402
Longswamp	19539
Longswamp (Township)	19539
Longview (Part of Bethel Park)	15102
Longwood Gardens	19348
Lookabough Corners	15656
Lookout	18417
Loomis Park	18702
Loop	16648
Lopez	18628
Lorain	15902
Lorane	19606
Lorberry	17963
Lords Valley	18428
Lorenton	16938
Loretto	15940
Loretto Road	15931
Loshs Run	17020
Lost Creek	17946
Lottsville	16402
Loux Corner	18927
Lovedale	15037
Lovejoy	15729
Lovell	16407
Lovelton	18629
Lovely	15521
Lover	15022
Lowber (Fayette County)	15438
Lowber (Westmoreland County)	15660
Lowe Lake	18470
Lower Allen	17011
Lower Allen (Township)	17011
Lower Alsace (Township)	19606
Lower Askam	18706
Lower Augusta (Township)	17801
Lower Brownville	17976
Lower Burrell	15068
Lower Chanceford (Township)	17302
Lower Chichester (Township)	19061
Lower Frankford (Township)	17013
Lower Frederick (Township)	19492
Lower Gwynedd (Township)	19437
Lower Heidelberg (Township)	19604
Lower Longswamp	19539
Lower Macungie (Township)	18062
Lower Mahanoy (Township)	17017
Lower Makefield (Township)	19067
Lower Merion (Township)	19003
Lower Mifflin (Township)	17241
Lower Milford (Township)	18036
Lower Moreland (Township)	19006
Lower Mount Bethel (Township)	18063
Lower Nazareth (Township)	18017
Lower Orchard	19058
Lower Oxford (Township)	19363
Lower Paxton	17109
Lower Paxton (Township)	17109
Lower Peanut	15480
Lower Pottsgrove (Township)	19464
Lower Providence (Township)	19401
Lower Sagon	17877
Lower Salford (Township)	19438
Lower Saucon (Township)	18015
Lower Southampton (Township)	19047
Lower Swatara (Township)	17057
Lower Towamensing (Township)	18071
Lower Turkeyfoot (Township)	15424

	ZIP
Lower Tyrone (Township)	15428
Lower Windsor (Township)	17368
Lower Yoder (Township)	15905
Lowhill (Lehigh County) (Township)	18069
Low Hill (Washington County)	15417
Lowville	16442
Loyalhanna	15661
Loyalhanna (Township)	15681
Loyalhanna Woodlands No. 1	15681
Loyalsock (Township)	17701
Loyalsockville	17754
Loyalton	17048
Loyalville	18612
Loysburg	16659
Loysville	17047
Lucernemines	15754
Lucinda	16235
Luciusboro	15748
Lucknow	17110
Lucky	17322
Lucon	19473
Lucy Crossing (Part of Glendon)	18042
Lucy Furnace	17066
Ludlow	16333
Ludwigs Corner	19343
Luke Fidler	17872
Lumber (Township)	15834
Lumber City (Clearfield County)	16833
Lumber City (Mifflin County)	17084
Lumberville	18933
Lundys Lane	16401
Lungerville	17774
Lurgan	17232
Lurgan (Township)	17232
Luthersburg	15848
Luthers Mills	18848
Lutzville	15537
Luxor	15662
Luzerne	15433
Luzerne (Township)	15417
Luzerne	18709
Lycippus	15650
Lycoming (Township)	17728
Lykens	17048
Lykens (Township)	17048
Lyleville	16627
Lynch	16347
Lynchville	15857
Lyndell	19354
Lyndon	17602
Lyndora	16045
Lynn (Lehigh County) (Township)	19529
Lynn (Susquehanna County)	18844
Lynnewood	19150
Lynnewood Gardens	19012
Lynnport	18066
Lynnville	18066
Lynnwood (Fayette County)	15012
Lynnwood (Luzerne County)	18702
Lynnwood-Pricedale	15012
Lyon Station	19536
Lyon Valley	18066
Mable	17921
Mable Hill	15327
McAdoo	18237
McAdoo Heights	18237
McAlevys Fort	16652
McAlisters Crossroads	15086
McAlisterville	17049
MacArthur (Part of Aliquippa)	15001
McCalmont (Township)	15711
McCandless (Township)	15237
McCandless Township (census designated place)	15237
McCartney	16661
McCauley	16651
McChesneytown	15650
McChesneytown-Loyalhanna	15620
McClarran	15650
McCleary	15050
McClellan	17032
McClellandtown	15458
McClellan Heights	17403
McClintock	16301
McClure (Fayette County)	15666
McClure (Snyder County)	17841

	ZIP
McConnellsburg	17233
Mcconnells Mills	15301
McConnellstown	16660
McCoysville	17058
McCracken	15380
McCrea	17241
Mccullochs Mills	17035
McCullough	15636
McDonald	15057
Macdonaldton	15530
Macedonia (Bradford County)	18848
Macedonia (Juniata County)	17059
McElhattan	17748
McEwensville	17749
Mcgarey	15825
McGees Mills	15757
McGillstown	17003
McGovern	15342
McGrann	16236
McGregor	16222
McHenry (Township)	17723
McIlhaney	18322
McIntyre (Indiana County)	15756
McIntyre (Lycoming County) (Township)	17763
McKean	16426
McKean (Township)	16426
McKeansburg	17960
McKee	16637
McKee Half Falls	17853
McKeesport	15130-35
For specific McKeesport Zip Codes call (412) 672-9721, or your local postmaster.	
McKees Rocks	15136
Mackeyville	17750
McKinley	19027
McKinley Hill (Part of Point Marion)	15474
McKinney	17240
McKnight	15237
McKnightstown	17343
McLane	16426
McMurray	15317
McNett (Township)	17765
McPherron	15753
McSherrystown	17344
Macungie	18062
McVeytown	17051
McVille	16229
Maddensville	17229
Madera	16661
Madison (Armstrong County) (Township)	16259
Madison (Clarion County) (Township)	16248
Madison (Columbia County) (Township)	17846
Madison (Lackawanna County) (Township)	18444
Madison (Westmoreland County)	15663
Madisonburg	16852
Madisonville	18444
Madley	15534
Magee	16351
Magill Heights	15024
Magnolia Gardens	19007
Magnolia Hill	19007
Mahaffey	15757
Mahanoy (Township)	17976
Mahanoy City	17948
Mahanoy Plane (Part of Gilberton)	17949
Mahoning (Armstrong County)	16259
Mahoning (Armstrong County) (Township)	16242
Mahoning (Carbon County) (Township)	18235
Mahoning (Lawrence County) (Township)	16132
Mahoning (Montour County) (Township)	17821
Mahoning Manor	17847
Mahoningtown (Part of New Castle)	16102
Maiden Creek	19510
Maidencreek (Township)	19605
Main (Township)	17815
Mainesburg	16932
Mainland	19451
Mainsville	17257
Mainville	17815
Maitland	17044
Maizeville (Part of Gilberton)	17934
Majeriks Corners	16441

* Area Zip Code   **† Post Office Boxes**

	ZIP
Malden Place (Part of Centerville)	15417
Malta	17017
Malvern	19355
Mammoth	15664
Mamont	15632
Manada Gap	17112
Manatawny	19547
Manayunk (Part of Philadelphia)	19127
Manchester (Allegheny County)	15233
Manchester (Wayne County) (Township)	18417
Manchester (York County)	17345
Manchester (York County) (Township)	17402
Mandata	17830
Manhattan	16921
Manheim (Lancaster County)	17545
Manheim (Lancaster County) (Township)	17601
Manheim (York County) (Township)	17329
Manifold	15301
Manito	15650
Mann (Township)	17211
Mannitto	15670
Manns Choice	15550
Mannsville	17024
Manoa	19083
Manor (Armstrong County) (Township)	16226
Manor (Indiana County)	15765
Manor (Lancaster County) (Township)	17603
Manor (Westmoreland County)	15665
Manor Hill	16652
Manor Hills (Part of Yeadon)	19050
Manor Ridge	17603
Manorville	16238
Manown	15063
Mansfield	16933
Mansville	15658
Mantz	18252
Maple Beach	19007
Mapledale	16323
Maple Glen (Montgomery County)	19002
Maple Glen (Washington County)	15417
Maple Grove (Berks County)	18011
Maple Grove (Chester County)	19363
Maple Grove (Clarion County)	16248
Maple Grove (Fayette County)	15622
Maple Grove Park	19540
Maple Hill (Lycoming County)	17752
Maple Hill (Montgomery County)	19422
Maple Hill (Schuylkill County)	17976
Maple Hills	17319
Maple Hollow	16635
Maplelake	18444
Maple Manor	18201
Maple Ridge	15935
Maple Shade (Bucks County)	19021
Maple Shade (Venango County)	16319
Mapleton Depot	17052
Mapletown	15338
Maplewood	18436
Maplewood Heights	18612
Maplewood Park	19018
Maplewood Terrace	15601
Marble	16334
Marble City	16650
Marble Hall	19444
Marcel Lake Estates	18328
Marchand	15758
Marchwood	19341
Marcus Hook	19061
Marengo	16877
Margaret	16201
Margaretta Furnace	17406
Margo Gardens	19007
Marguerite	15650
Maria	16664
Marianna	15345
Mariann Estates	16254
Mariasville	16373

	ZIP
Marienville	16239
Marietta	17547
Marion (Beaver County) (Township)	15066
Marion (Berks County) (Township)	19567
Marion (Butler County) (Township)	16020
Marion (Centre County) (Township)	16841
Marion (Franklin County)	17235
Marion Acres	17888
Marion Center	15759
Marion Heights	17832
Marion Hill	15066
Mark Acres	15642
Markelsville	17074
Markes	17236
Market Square (Part of Philadelphia)	19118
Market Street (Part of West Chester)	19380
Markle	15613
Markleton	15551
Markleysburg	15459
Markton	15764
Markvue Manor	15642
Marlboro	19348
Marlborough (Township)	18084
Mar Lin	17951
Marple (Township)	19008
Marron	16833
Mars	16046
Marsh	15920
Marshall (Township)	15086
Marshall Heights	15716
Marshalls Creek	18335
Marshall Terrace	19061
Marshallton (Chester County)	19380
Marshallton (Northumberland County)	17872
Marshbrook	18414
Marshburg	16738
Marsh Hill	17771
Marshlands	16921
Marsh Run	17070
Marshview	18848
Marshwood (Part of Olyphant)	18434
Marsteller	15760
Marstown	17963
Martha Furnace	16870
Martic (Township)	17565
Martic Forge	17565
Marticville	17565
Martin	15460
Martindale (Cambria County)	15946
Martindale (Lancaster County)	17549
Martinsburg	16662
Martins Corner	19320
Martins Creek	18063
Martinsville	17366
Martzville	18603
Marvel Gardens	19094
Marvindale	16749
Marwood	16023
Mary D	17952
Marysville (Bedford County)	16678
Marysville (Perry County)	17053
Marywood College (Part of Scranton)	18509
Mascot	17572
Mason-Dixon	17225
Masontown	15461
Masseyburg	16669
Mastersonville	17545
Mast Hope	18435
Matamoras (Dauphin County)	17032
Matamoras (Pike County)	18336
Mather	15346
Mattawana	17054
Mattey Plan	15012
Matthews Run	16371
Mattie	15537
Mausdale	17821
Maxatawny	19538
Maxatawny (Township)	19538
Maxwell	15450
Mayberry (Township)	17821
Mayburg	16347
Mayfair (Part of Philadelphia)	19136
Mayfield	18433
Mayfield East	17405

	ZIP
Mayport	16240
Maysville (Armstrong County)	15618
Maysville (Mercer County)	16125
Maysville (Northumberland County)	17866
Maytown (Lancaster County)	17550
Maytown (York County)	17339
Mayview	15017
Mayville	16105
Maze	17094
Mazeppa	17837
McKimm	16117
Mead (Township)	16313
Meade Heights	17057
Meadia Heights	17602
Meadowbrook (Fayette County)	15401
Meadowbrook (Montgomery County)	19046
Meadowbrook Manor	19341
Meadow Gap	17243
Meadow Lands	15347
Meadowood	16045
Meadowview Estates	17540
Meadville	16335
Mechanicsburg	17055
Mechanics Grove	17566
Mechanicsville (Bucks County)	18934
Mechanicsville (Clarion County)	16214
Mechanicsville (Lancaster County)	17545
Mechanicsville (Lehigh County)	18104
Mechanicsville (Montour County)	17821
Mechanicsville (Schuylkill County)	17901
Meckesville	18210
Mecks Corner	17068
Media	19063-65
For specific Media Zip Codes call (215) 566-3196, or your local postmaster.	
Media Annex (Part of Media)	19063
Medix Run	15868
Meeker	18612
Megargee	19320
Mehoopany	18629
Mehoopany (Township)	18629
Meiser	17842
Meiserville	17853
Melcroft	15462
Mellingertown	15666
Mellwood Manor	15068
Melrose	18847
Melrose Park	19012
Menallen (Adams County) (Township)	17304
Menallen (Fayette County) (Township)	15468
Mench	15537
Mendenhall	19357
Mendon	15679
Menges Mills	17346
Menno	17004
Menno (Township)	17004
Mentcle	15761
Mercer (Butler County) (Township)	16038
Mercer (Mercer County)	16137
Mercersburg	17236
Mercur	18854
Meredith	16249
Meridian	16001
Merion Park	19066
Merion Square	19035
Merion Station	19066
Meriwether Farms	19380
Merlin	19460
Mermaid Estates	19401
Merrian	17851
Merrittstown	15463
Merryall	18853
Mertztown	19539
Merwinsburg	18330
Meshoppen	18630
Meshoppen (Township)	18630
Messiah College	17027
Messmore	15458
Metal	17224
Metal (Township)	17224
Metzler	15557
Mexico	17056
Meyersdale	15552
Meyersville	18104

	ZIP
Middleburg (Luzerne County)	18661
Middleburg (Snyder County)	17842
Middlebury (Township)	16935
Middlebury Center	16935
Middle Churches	15666
Middle City (Part of Philadelphia)	19103
Middle Creek (Snyder County)	17813
Middlecreek (Snyder County) (Township)	17833
Middlecreek (Somerset County) (Township)	15557
Middle Lancaster	16037
Middle Paxton (Township)	17018
Middleport	17953
Middlesex (Butler County) (Township)	16059
Middlesex (Cumberland County)	17013
Middlesex (Cumberland County) (Township)	17013
Middle Smithfield (Township)	18301
Middle Spring	17257
Middle Taylor (Township)	15906
Middleton	15757
Middletown (Bucks County) (Township)	19056
Middletown (Dauphin County)	17057
Middletown (Delaware County) (Township)	19037
Middletown (Huntingdon County)	16678
Middletown (McKean County)	16749
Middletown (Northampton County)	18017
Middletown (Susquehanna County) (Township)	18818
Middletown (Westmoreland County)	15601
Middletown Center	18818
Middletown Heights	19063
Midland (Beaver County)	15059
Midland (Washington County)	15342
Midvale	18705
Midvale Manor	19608
Midvalley	17888
Midway (Adams County)	17331
Midway (Lebanon County)	17042
Midway (Washington County)	15060
Midway (Westmoreland County)	15601
Mifflin (Columbia County) (Township)	18631
Mifflin (Dauphin County) (Township)	17061
Mifflin (Juniata County)	17058
Mifflin (Lycoming County) (Township)	17740
Mifflinburg	17844
Mifflintown	17059
Mifflinville	18631
Milan	18831
Milanville	18443
Mildred	18632
Mile Run	17801
Miles (Township)	16872
Milesburg	16853
Milford (Bucks County) (Township)	18968
Milford (Juniata County) (Township)	17062
Milford (Pike County)	18337
Milford (Pike County) (Township)	18337
Milford (Somerset County)	15557
Milford (Somerset County) (Township)	15557
Milford Manor	19067
Milford Square	18935
Milfred Terrace	15348
Militia Hill	19034
Millardsville	17067
Millbach	17073
Millbank	15658
Millbourne	19082
Millbrook (Centre County)	16801
Millbrook (Mercer County)	16133
Mill Brook (Pike County)	18426
Millburn	16137
Mill City	18414
Millcreek (Clarion County) (Township)	16225

Place	ZIP
Millcreek (Erie County)	16505-06
	16509
For specific Millcreek Zip Codes call (814) 898-7317, or your local postmaster.	
Mill Creek (Huntingdon County)	17060
Millcreek (Lebanon County) (Township)	17073
Mill Creek (Lycoming County) (Township)	17756
Mill Creek (Mercer County) (Township)	16145
Mill Creek (Schuylkill County)	17901
Mill Creek Falls	19007
Millcreek Mall	16509
Milledgeville	16311
Miller (Huntingdon County) (Township)	16652
Miller (Perry County) (Township)	17094
Miller Heights	18017
Miller Manor	18067
Miller Run	15936
Millersburg	17061
Miller Shaft	15946
Millers Station	16403
Millerstown (Allegheny County)	15084
Millerstown (Blair County)	16662
Millerstown (Clarion County)	16334
Millerstown (Perry County)	17062
Millersville	17551
Millerton	16936
Millertown (Columbia County)	17815
Millertown (Fayette County)	15446
Mill Grove	17820
Mill Hall	17751
Millheim	16854
Milligantown	15068
Millmont	17845
Millport (Lancaster County)	17540
Millport (Potter County)	16748
Millrift	18340
Mill Run (Blair County)	16601
Mill Run (Clearfield County)	15849
Mill Run (Fayette County)	15464
Mills	16937
Millsboro	15348
Millstone (Township)	15860
Milltown (Allegheny County)	15147
Milltown (Bradford County)	18840
Milltown (Chester County)	19380
Millvale	15209
Millview	18616
Mill Village	16427
Millville	17846
Millway	17543
Milwood	15627
Milmont Park	19033
Milnesville	18239
Milnor	17225
Milroy	17063
Milton (Armstrong County)	16222
Milton (Northumberland County)	17847
Milton Grove	17552
Milwaukee	18411
Mina	16915
Mineral (Township)	16342
Mineral Point	15942
Mineral Springs	16855
Miners Mills (Part of Wilkes-Barre)	18705
Miners Village (Part of Cornwall)	17016
Minersville (Cambria County)	15906
Minersville (Schuylkill County)	17954
Minesite (Part of Allentown)	18103
Mingo	19468
Mingoville	16856
Minisink Hills	18341
Minister	16347
Minnequa	17724
Minooka (Part of Scranton)	18507
Miola	16214
Miquon	19452
Miquon Hills	19452
Mission Hill	17601
Mitchell Park (Part of Hatboro)	19040
Mix Run	15832
Mocanaqua	18655
Moc-A-Tek Lake	18436
Mocking Bird Hill	15642
Modena	19358
Moffit Sterling	15327
Mogees	19401
Mohns Hill	19608
Mohnton	19540
Mohrsville	19541
Molino	17961
Molltown	19522
Monaca	15061
Monaghan (Township)	17404
Monarch	15431
Monessen	15062
Mongul	17257
Moninger	15342
Moniteau	16061
Monocacy Station	19542
Monongahela (Greene County) (Township)	15338
Monongahela (Washington County)	15063
Monroe (Bedford County) (Township)	15535
Monroe (Bradford County) (Township)	18848
Monroe (Clarion County)	16232
Monroe (Clarion County) (Township)	16232
Monroe (Cumberland County) (Township)	17055
Monroe (Juniata County) (Township)	17086
Monroe (Snyder County) (Township)	17831
Monroe (Wyoming County) (Township)	18657
Monroe Heights (Part of Monroeville)	15146
Monroeton	18832
Monroeville	15146
Monroeville Mall (Part of Monroeville)	15146
Mont Alto	17237
Montandon	17850
Mont Clare	19453
Montdale	18447
Montello	19608
Monterey (Berks County)	19530
Monterey (Franklin County)	17214
Monterey (Lancaster County)	17540
Montgomery (Franklin County) (Township)	17236
Montgomery (Indiana County) (Township)	15724
Montgomery (Lycoming County)	17752
Montgomery (Montgomery County) (Township)	18936
Montgomery Ferry	17074
Montgomery Square	18936
Montgomeryville	18936
Montmorenci	15853
Montour (Allegheny County)	15244
Montour (Columbia County) (Township)	17815
Montoursville	17754
Montrose (Berks County)	19607
Montrose (Susquehanna County)	18801
Montrose Hill	15238
Montsera	17013
Monument	16822
Moon	15108
Moon (Township)	15108
Moon Crest	15108
Moon Run	15136
Moore (Township)	18014
Mooredale	17013
Mooresburg	17821
Moores Corners	16057
Moorestown	18014
Moorheadville	16428
Moosic	18507
Moosic Lake	18416
Morado (Part of Beaver Falls)	15010
Morann	16663
Moravia	16157
Moravian (Part of Bethlehem)	18018
Mordansville	17815
Morea	17948
Moreland (Township)	17756
Moreland Farms	19040
Moreland Manor	19040
Morewood	19040
Morgan (Allegheny County)	15064
Morgan (Fayette County)	15456
Morgan (rural) (Fayette County)	15425
Morgan (Greene County) (Township)	15344
Morgan Hill	15031
Morgans Hill	18042
Morgantown	19543
Morningside (Part of Pittsburgh)	15206
Morrellville (Part of Johnstown)	15906
Morris (Clearfield County) (Township)	16858
Morris (Greene County) (Township)	15364
Morris (Huntingdon County) (Township)	16611
Morris (Tioga County)	16938
Morris (Tioga County) (Township)	16938
Morris (Washington County) (Township)	15329
Morris Crossroads	15451
Morrisdale	16858
Morris Run	16939
Morrisville (Bucks County)	19067
Morrisville (Greene County)	15370
Morrows Corner	16210
Morstein	19380
Morton	19070
Mortonville	19320
Morwood	18969
Morysville	19512
Moscow	18444
Moselem	19526
Moselem Springs	19522
Mosgrove	16259
Moshannon (Cambria County)	15938
Moshannon (Centre County)	16859
Mosherville	16925
Mosiertown	16433
Mosserville	18066
Mostoller	15563
Mottarns Mill	15771
Moudy Hill	15946
Moulstown	17331
Mount Aetna	19544
Mountaindale (Cambria County)	16639
Mountain Dale (Dauphin County)	17110
Mountain Grove	17815
Mountainhome	18342
Mountain Lake	18848
Mountain Top (Lancaster County)	17555
Mountain Top (Luzerne County)	18707
Mountain Valley Lake	17921
Mount Airy (Lancaster County)	17578
Mount Airy (Philadelphia County)	19119
Mount Airy Terrace	18708
Mount Allen	17055
Mount Alton	16738
Mount Bethel	18343
Mount Braddock	15465
Mount Carbon	17901
Mount Carmel	17851
Mount Carmel (Township)	17851
Mount Chestnut	16001
Mount Chestnut Springs	16001
Mount Cobb	18436
Mount Eagle	16841
Mount Etna	16693
Mount Gretna	17064
Mount Gretna Heights	17064
Mount Holly Springs	17065
Mount Hope (Adams County)	17320
Mount Hope (Lancaster County)	17545
Mount Independence	15456
Mount Jackson	16102
Mount Jewett	16740
Mount Joy (Adams County) (Township)	17340
Mount Joy (Clearfield County)	16830
Mount Joy (Lancaster County)	17552
Mount Joy (Lancaster County) (Township)	17022
Mount Joy (Westmoreland County)	15666
Mount Laffee	17901
Mount Laurel	18201
Mount Lebanon (Township)	15228
Mount Lebanon	15228
Mount Misery	17350
Mount Morris	15349
Mount Nebo (Allegheny County)	15143
Mount Nebo (Lancaster County)	17565
Mount Nebo (Westmoreland County)	15683
Mount Oliver	15210
Mount Patrick	17045
Mount Penn	19606
Mount Pleasant (Adams County)	17331
Mount Pleasant (Adams County) (Township)	17325
Mount Pleasant (Berks County)	19506
Mount Pleasant (Columbia County) (Township)	17815
Mount Pleasant (Delaware County)	19087
Mount Pleasant (Lebanon County)	17042
Mount Pleasant (Mifflin County)	17063
Mount Pleasant (Northampton County)	18013
Mount Pleasant (Northumberland County)	17801
Mount Pleasant (Perry County)	17006
Mount Pleasant (Schuylkill County)	17901
Mount Pleasant (Tioga County)	16938
Mount Pleasant (Washington County) (Township)	15340
Mount Pleasant (Wayne County) (Township)	18472
Mount Pleasant (Westmoreland County)	15666
Mount Pleasant (Westmoreland County) (Township)	15666
Mount Pleasant (York County)	17019
Mount Pleasant Mills	17853
Mount Pocono	18344
Mountrock (Cumberland County)	17013
Mount Rock (Franklin County)	17257
Mount Royal	17315
Mount Sterling	15461
Mount Tabor	17324
Mount Troy	15212
Mount Union (Franklin County)	17222
Mount Union (Huntingdon County)	17066
Mount Vernon (Allegheny County)	15135
Mount Vernon (Chester County)	19363
Mount Vernon (Lancaster County)	17527
Mount Vernon (Westmoreland County)	15601
Mountville	17554
Mount Washington (Part of Pittsburgh)	15211
Mount Wilson	17042
Mount Wolf	17347
Mount Zion (Cumberland County)	17055
Mount Zion (Cumberland County)	17013
Mount Zion (Lebanon County)	17046
Mount Zion (Luzerne County)	18643
Mount Zion (Monroe County)	18301
Mount Zion (York County)	17402
Moween	15681

	ZIP		ZIP		ZIP		ZIP
Mowersville	17257	Neshaminy	18976	New Lebanon	16145	Niles	16323
Mowry	17921	Neshaminy Falls	19047	New Lexington	15557	Niles Valley	16935
Moxham (Part of		Neshaminy Hills	19047	Newlin (Chester County)		Ninepoints	17509
Johnstown)	15902	Neshaminy Valley	19020	(Township)	19380	Nine Row	15927
Moyer	15425	Neshaminy Woods	19047	Newlin (Columbia County)	17820	Nineveh (Clarion County)	16232
Moylan	19065	Neshannock	16105	New London	19360	Nineveh (Greene County)	15353
Mozart	18925	Neshannock (Township)	16105	New London (Township)	19360	Nippenose (Township)	17720
Mt Pocahontas	18210	Neshannock Falls	16156	New London	16351	Nisbet	17759
Muddy Creek (Township)	16051	Nesquehoning	18240	Newlonsburg (Part of		Nittany	16841
Muddy Creek Forks	17302	Nether Providence		Murrysville)	15668	Niverton	15558
Muhlenberg (Berks		(Township)	19086	New Mahoning	18235	Nixon	16001
County) (Township)	19560	Nether Providence		Newmanstown	17073	Noble	19046
Muhlenberg (Luzerne		Township	19013	Newmansville	16353	Noblestown	15071
County)	18621	Neville (Township)	15225	New Market	17070	Nockamixon (Township)	18930
Muhlenberg Park	19605	Neville Island	15225	New Milford	18834	Noll Acres	17055
Muir	17957	New Albany	18833	New Milford (Township)	18834	Nolo	15765
Mullertown	17331	New Alexandria	15670	New Millport	16861	Nook	17058
Mumbauersville	18073	New Athens	16248	New Mines	17923	Nordmont	17758
Mummasburg	17325	New Baltimore (Somerset		New Oxford	17350	Normal Square	18235
Muncy	17756	County)	15553	New Paris	15554	Normalville	15469
Muncy (Township)	17756	New Baltimore (York		New Park	17352	Norristown	19401-04
Muncy Creek (Township)	17756	County)	17331	New Philadelphia	17959	For specific Norristown Zip	
Muncy Valley	17758	New Beaver	16141	Newport (Lawrence		Codes call (215) 275-9780, or	
Munderf	15825	New Bedford	16140	County)	16157	your local postmaster.	
Mundys Corner	15909	New Berlin	17855	Newport (Luzerne County)		Norrisville	16406
Munhall	15120	New Berlinville	19545	(Township)	18634	North Abington	
Munson	16860	Newberry (Lycoming		Newport (Perry County)	17074	(Township)	18414
Munster	15940	County)	17701	Newportville	19056	Northampton (Bucks	
Munster (Township)	15931	Newberry (York County)		Newportville Terrace	19020	County) (Township)	18954
Murdock	15501	(Township)	17370	New Providence	17560	Northampton	
Murrell	17522	Newberrytown	17319	New Richmond	16327	(Northampton County)	18067
Murrinsville	16020	New Bethlehem	16242	New Ringgold	17960	Northampton (Somerset	
Murry Hill	15317	New Bloomfield	17068	Newry	16665	County) (Township)	15538
Murrysville	15668	Newboro	15435	New Salem (Armstrong		Northampton Hills	18966
Muse	15350	New Boston	17948	County)	16240	North Annville (Township)	17038
Mustard	15037	New Bridgeville	17356	New Salem (Fayette		North Apollo	15673
Mutual	15601	New Brighton	15066	County)	15468	North Bangor	18013
Myersburg	18854	New Britain	18901	New Salem-Buffington	15468	North Barnesboro (Part of	
Myerstown (Cumberland		New Britain (Township)	18914	New Schaefferstown	19506	Barnesboro)	15714
County)	17324	New Buena Vista	15550	New Sewickley		North Beaver (Township)	16102
Myerstown (Lebanon		New Buffalo	17069	(Township)	15074	North Belle Vernon	15012
County)	17067	Newburg (Blair County)	16601	New Sheffield	15001	North Bend	17760
Mylo Park	15931	Newburg (Cumberland		Newside	18080	North Bessemer	15235
Myobeach	18630	County)	17240	New Smithville	19530	North Bethlehem	
Myoma	16046	Newburg (Northampton		New Stanton	15672	(Township)	15360
Myrtle	16748	County)	18017	New Street	17901	North Bingham	16941
Mystic Park	16404	Newburg Homes	18045	New Texas (Allegheny		North Braddock	15104
Naces Corner	18927	New Castle	16101-08	County)	15239	North Branch (Township)	18629
Naceville	18960	For specific New Castle Zip		New Texas (Lancaster		Northbrook	19380
Nadine	15147	Codes call (412) 656-7214, or		County)	17563	Northbrook Hills	17601
Naginey	17063	your local postmaster.		Newton (Township)	18411	North Buffalo (Township)	16201
Nansen	16735	New Castle (Township)	17970	Newtonburg	15757	North Butler	16001
Nanticoke	18634	New Castle Northwest	16105	Newton Hamilton	17075	North Catasauqua	18032
Nantmeal Village	19343	New Centerville	15557	Newton Lake	18407	North Centre (Township)	18603
Nanty Glo	15943	Newchester	17350	Newtown (Bucks County)	18940	North Charleroi	15022
Naomi	15438	New Columbia	17856	Newtown (Bucks County)		North Codorus (Township)	17362
Napier (Township)	15559	New Columbus (Carbon		(Township)	18940	North Cornwall	17016
Napierville	17522	County)	18240	New Town (Centre		North Cornwall (Township)	17042
Narberth	19072	New Columbus (Luzerne		County)	16666	North Coventry	
Narbrook Park (Part of		County)	17878	Newtown (Clearfield		(Township)	19464
Narberth)	19072	Newcomer	15401	County)	16878	North East	16428
Narrows Creek	15801	New Cumberland	17070	Newtown (Delaware		North East (Township)	16428
Narrows Shopping Center		New Cumberland Army		County) (Township)	19073	Northeast Madison	
(Part of Edwardsville)	18704	Depot	17070	Newtown (Greene		(Township)	17047
Narrowsville	18972	New Danville	17603	County)	15327	North Edinburg	16116
Narvon	17555	New Derry	15671	Newtown (Lancaster		North End (Part of Wilkes-	
Nashua	16101	New Eagle	15067	County)	17512	Barre)	18705
Nashville (Indiana County)	15771	Newell	15466	Newtown (Lehigh County)	18031	Northern Lights Shopping	
Nashville (York County)	17362	New England	18252	Newtown (Luzerne		Center (Part of	
Nassau Village	19078	New Enterprise	16664	County)	18706	Economy)	15005
Natalie	17851	New Era	18833	Mowtown Grant	18940	North Essington	19029
Natrona	15065	Newfield (Allegheny		Newtown Square	19073	North Fayette (Township)	15071
Natrona Heights	15065	County)	15147	New Tripoli	18066	North Fork	16950
Nauvoo	16938	Newfield (Potter County)	16948	New Vernon	16145	North Franklin (Township)	15301
Naval Air Development		New Florence	15944	New Vernon (Township)	16145	North Fredericktown	15333
Center	18974	Newfoundland	18445	Newville (Bucks County)	18914	North Freedom	16240
Nazareth	18064	New Franklin	17201	Newville (Cumberland		North Hanover Mall (Part	
Nealmont	16686	New Freedom	17349	County)	17241	of Hanover)	17331
Neason Hill	16335	New Freeport	15352	Newville (Lancaster		North Heidelberg	
Neath	18829	New Galena	18914	County)	17023	(Township)	19506
Nebo	15622	New Galilee	16141	New Virginia (Part of		North Hills (Montgomery	
Nectarine	16038	New Garden	19374	Hermitage)	16146	County)	19038
Ned	15352	New Garden (Township)	19350	New Washington	15757	North Hills	
Needful	16881	New Geneva	15467	New Wilmington	16142	(Northumberland	
Needmore	17238	New Germantown	17071	Niagara	18453	County)	17847
Neelyton	17239	New Germany	15946	Niantic	19504	North Hills Village	15237
Neffs	18065	New Grass Manor	18612	Nicetown (Part of		North Hopewell	
Neffs Mills	16669	New Grenada	16674	Philadelphia)	19140	(Township)	17322
Neffsville	17601*	New Hamburg	16124	Nichola	16262	North Huntingdon	
	17606†	New Hanover	19525	Nicholson (Fayette		(Township)	15642
Neiffer	19473	New Hanover (Township)	19525	County) (Township)	15461	North Irwin	15642
Neiltown	16341	New Hanover Square	19435	Nicholson (Wyoming		North Jackson	18847
Neiman	17327	Newhard	18080	County)	18446	North Lebanon	
Nellie	15486	New Holland	17557	Nicholson (Wyoming		(Township)	17046
Nelson	16940	New Hope	18938	County) (Township)	18446	North Liberty	16127
Nelson (Township)	16940	New Ireland	16438	Nickel Mines	17562	North Londonderry	
Nemacolin	15351	New Jerusalem	19522	Nickleville	16373	(Township)	17078
Nemanie	18451	New Kensington	15068	Nicklin	16323	North Mahoning	
Nescopeck	18635	New Kingstown	17072	Nicktown	15762	(Township)	15758
Nescopeck (Township)	18635	Newkirk	18252	Nilan	15474		

* Area Zip Code   † Post Office Boxes

	ZIP
Parker (Armstrong County)	16049
Parker (Butler County) (Township)	16049
Parker Ford	19457
Parkers Glen	18458
Parkersville	19380
Parkesburg	19365
Park Forest Village	16803
Park Gate	16117
Park Heights	17331
Parkhill	15945
Park Hills (Centre County)	16803
Park Hills (York County)	17331
Parkland	19047
Park Manor	19607
Park Meadows	15642
Park Place	17948
Parks (Township)	15690
Parkside	19015
Parkside Courts	18104
Parkside Manor (Part of Parkside)	19015
Parkstown (Cambria County)	15902
Parkstown (Lawrence County)	16101
Parktown Estates	19067
Park View	15215
Parkview Gardens	18052
Park View Heights (Part of Bellefonte)	16823
Parkville	17331
Parkway Center (Part of Green Tree)	15220
Park Way Manor	18104
Parkwood	15774
Parnassus (Part of New Kensington)	15068
Parryville	18244
Parsonville (Butler County)	16050
Parsonville (Clearfield County)	16651
Parvin	17751
Paschall (Part of Philadelphia)	19142
Passer	18036
Patchinville	15724
Patterson (Township)	15010
Patterson Grove	18655
Patterson Heights	15010
Patterson Hill (Part of Lincoln)	15037
Pattersons Mill	15312
Patterson Township	15010
Pattersonville	17967
Patton (Cambria County)	16668
Patton (Centre County) (Township)	16803
Patton (Washington County)	15301
Pattonville	16226
Paulton	15613
Paupack (Pike County)	18451
Paupack (Wayne County) (Township)	18428
Paupack Gardens	18451
Pavia	16655
Pavia (Township)	16655
Paxinos	17860
Paxtang	17111
Paxtang Manor	17111
Paxton	17017
Paxtonia	17111
Paxtonville	17861
Peacedale	19363
Peach Bottom (Lancaster County)	17563
Peach Bottom (York County) (Township)	17314
Peach Bottom Village	17563
Peach Glen	17324
Pealertown	17859
Peanut (Lawrence County)	16116
Peanut (Westmoreland County)	15627
Pearl	16342
Pebble Hill	18901
Pecan	16342
Pechin	15431
Pecks Pond	18328
Peckville (Part of Blakely)	18452
Pemberton	16683
Pen Argyl	18072
Penarth	19004
Penbrook	17103
Penbryn	17765
Pendle Hill	19086
Penfield	15849

	ZIP
Penllyn	19422
Pen Mar	17268
Penn (Berks County) (Township)	19506
Penn (Butler County) (Township)	16001
Penn (Centre County) (Township)	16832
Penn (Chester County) (Township)	19390
Penn (Clearfield County) (Township)	16838
Penn (Cumberland County) (Township)	17257
Penn (Huntingdon County) (Township)	16647
Penn (Lancaster County) (Township)	17545
Penn (Lycoming County) (Township)	17737
Penn (Perry County) (Township)	17020
Penn (Snyder County) (Township)	17870
Penn (Westmoreland County)	15675
Penn (Westmoreland County) (Township)	15636
Penn (York County) (Township)	17331
Penn Allen	18064
Pennbrook (Part of Lansdale)	19446
Penn Center (Part of Philadelphia)	19102
Penncraft	15433
Penndel	19047
Pennersville	17268
Penn Estates	18301
Pennfield	19007
Penn Five	16666
Penn Forest (Township)	18210
Penn Glyn (Part of Irwin)	15642
Penn Hall	16875
Penn Heights (Part of Hanover)	17331
Penn Hill	17563
Penn Hills	15235
Penn Hills (Township)	15235
Penn Hills Shopping Center	15235
Pennhurst Center	19475
Penn Lake Park	18661
Pennline	16424
Penn Pines	19018
Penn Pitt	15338
Penn Rose Park	17601
Penn Run	15765
Pennsburg	18073
Pennsbury (Township)	19317
Pennsbury Heights	19067
Pennsbury Village	15205
Penns Creek	17862
Pennsdale	17756
Pennside (Berks County)	19606
Pennside (Erie County)	16401
Penns Park	18943
Penn Square Village	19401
Pennsville (Fayette County)	15425
Pennsville (Northampton County)	18067
Penns Woods	15642
Pennsylvania Furnace	16865
Pennvale	17701
Penn Valley	19072
Penn Valley Terrace	19047
Penn Village (Part of Pottstown)	19464
Pennville	17331
Penn Wood	15537
Pennwyn	19607
Penn Wynne	19151
Penobscot	18707
Penowa	15312
Penryn	17564
Pequea	17565
Pequea (Township)	17584
Percy	15456
Perdix	17020
Perkasie	18944
Perkiomen (Township)	19426
Perkiomen Heights	18073
Perkiomen Junction	19460
Perkiomen Village	19426
Perkiomenville	18074
Perrine Corners	16153
Perry (Armstrong County) (Township)	16041

	ZIP
Perry (Berks County) (Township)	19526
Perry (Clarion County) (Township)	16049
Perry (Fayette County) (Township)	15473
Perry (Greene County) (Township)	15349
Perry (Jefferson County) (Township)	15767
Perry (Lawrence County) (Township)	16117
Perry (Mercer County) (Township)	16130
Perry (Snyder County) (Township)	17853
Perryopolis	15473
Perry Square (Part of Erie)	16507
Perrysville	15237
Perryville (Clarion County)	16049
Perryville (Lycoming County)	17728
Perryville (Westmoreland County)	15618
Perulack	17021
Peters (Franklin County) (Township)	17236
Peters (Washington County) (Township)	15317
Petersburg	16669
Peters Corner	18934
Petersville	18067
Petrolia	16050
Pettis Corners	16335
Pheasant Hill	17601
Pheasant Ridge	18901
Philadelphia	19101-60
For specific Philadelphia Zip Codes call (215) 895-9000, or your local postmaster.	

COLLEGES & UNIVERSITIES

	ZIP
Chestnut Hill College	19118
Drexel University	19104
Hahnemann University	19102
Holy Family College	19114
LaSalle University	19141
Philadelphia College of Pharmacy and Science	19104
Philadelphia College of Textiles and Science	19144
St. Joseph's University	19131
Temple University	19122
University of Pennsylvania	19104
University of the Arts	19102

FINANCIAL INSTITUTIONS

	ZIP
Beneficial Mutual Savings Bank	19107
Brown Brothers Harriman & Company	19102
Cheltenham Bank	19111
Fidelity Federal Savings & Loan Association	19135
Fox Chase Federal Savings Bank	19111
Frankford Bank	19124
Prime Bank	19111
Roxborough-Manayunk Federal Savings Bank	19128
Third Federal Savings Bank	19124

HOSPITALS

	ZIP
Albert Einstein Medical Center	19141
Children's Hospital of Philadelphia	19104
Episcopal Hospital	19125
Frankford Hospital of the City of Philadelphia	19114
Germantown Hospital and Medical Center	19144
Graduate Health Systems Parkview Hospital	19124
Graduate Hospital	19146
Hahnemann University Hospital	19102
Hospital of the University of Pennsylvania	19104
Lankenau Hospital	19096
Methodist Hospital	19148
Nazareth Hospital	19152
Pennsylvania Hospital	19107
Presbyterian Medical Center of Philadelphia	19104
Temple University Hospital	19140
Thomas Jefferson University Hospital	19107

	ZIP
Veterans Affairs Medical Center	19104

HOTELS/MOTELS

	ZIP
Barclay Hotel	19103
Four Seasons Hotel Philadelphia	19103
Holiday Inn-Independence Mall	19106
Latham	19103
Philadelphia Airport Marriott	19153
Warwick	19103
Wyndham Franklin Plaza Hotel	19103

MILITARY INSTALLATIONS

	ZIP
Defense Industrial Supply Center	19111
Defense Mapping Agency, Combat Support Center	19120
Defense Personnel Support Center	19101
Fort Mifflin Distribution Center, U.S. Army Corps. of Engineers	19153
Naval Regional Medical Clinic	19145
Naval Station, Philadelphia	19112
Philadelphia Naval Shipyard	19112

	ZIP
Philipsburg (Centre County)	16866
Philipsburg (Washington County)	15419
Phillips (Fayette County)	15401
Phillips (Tioga County)	16918
Phillipston	16248
Phillipsville (Chester County)	19320
Phillipsville (Erie County)	16442
Philmont	19006
Philson	15552
Phoenix Park	17901
Phoenixville	19460
Piatt (Township)	17740
Picture Rocks	17762
Pierce (Part of Jefferson)	15025
Pierceville	17327
Pigeon	16239
Pike (Berks County) (Township)	19547
Pike (Bradford County) (Township)	18829
Pike (Clearfield County) (Township)	16833
Pike (Potter County) (Township)	16922
Pikeland	19425
Pike Mine	15417
Pikes Creek	18621
Pikes Peak	15765
Piketown	17112
Pikeville	19547
Pilgrim Gardens	19026
Pilgrimham	16232
Pillow	17080
Pilltown	15531
Pine (Allegheny County) (Township)	15090
Pine (Armstrong County) (Township)	16259
Pine (Clearfield County) (Township)	15849
Pine (Clinton County)	17748
Pine (Columbia County) (Township)	17846
Pine (Crawford County) (Township)	16424
Pine (Indiana County) (Township)	15957
Pine (Lycoming County) (Township)	16938
Pine (Mercer County) (Township)	16127
Pine Bank	15352
Pine Beach	18428
Pinebrook	17011
Pine City	16254
Pine Creek (Clinton County) (Township)	17721
Pinecreek (Jefferson County)	15825
Pine Creek (Jefferson County) (Township)	15825
Pinecroft	16601
Pinedale (Part of Deer Lake)	17961

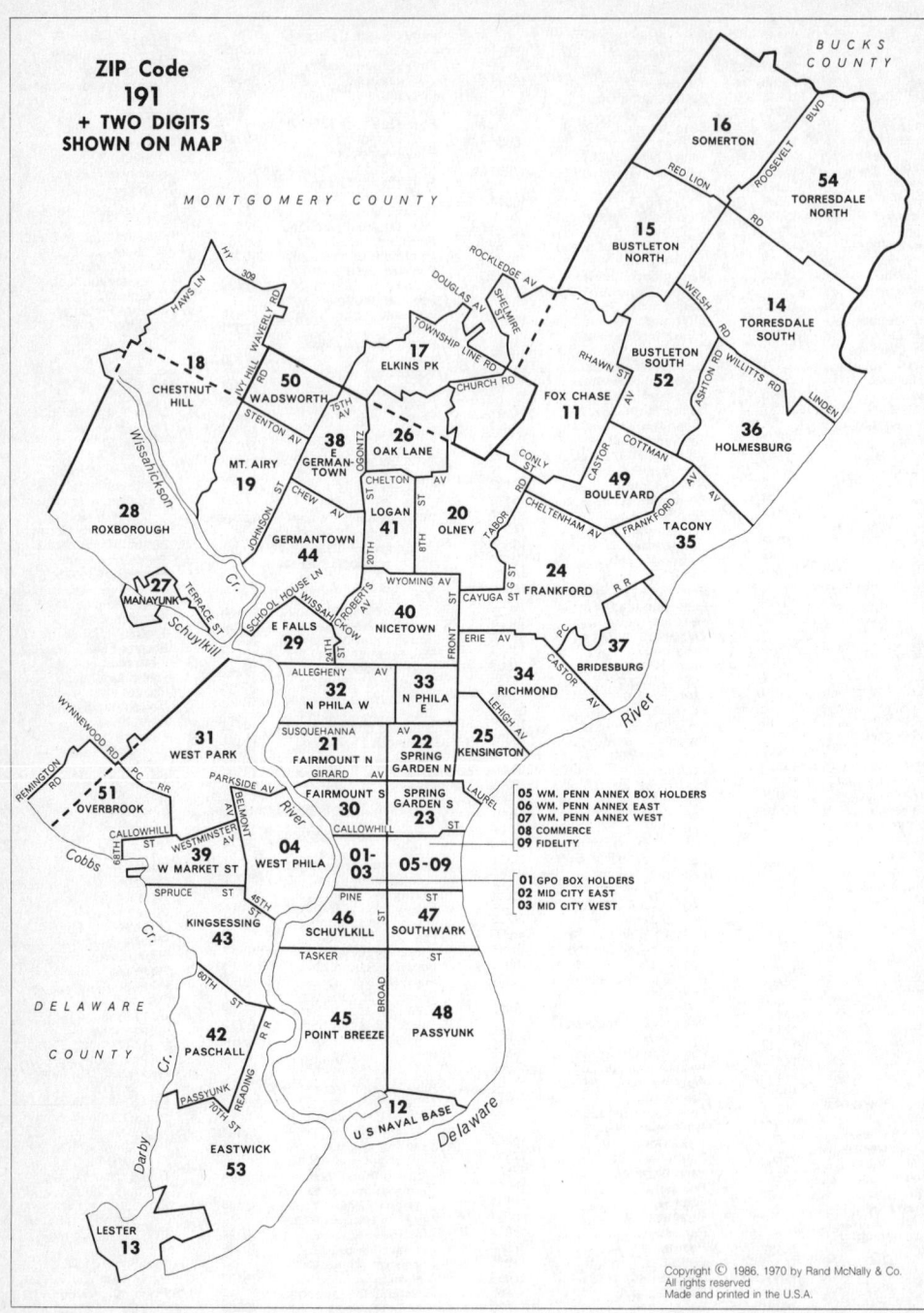

ZIP Code
191
+ TWO DIGITS
SHOWN ON MAP

BUCKS COUNTY

MONTGOMERY COUNTY

16 SOMERTON

54 TORRESDALE NORTH

15 BUSTLETON NORTH

14 TORRESDALE SOUTH

18 CHESTNUT HILL

50 WADSWORTH

17 ELKINS PK

11 FOX CHASE

52 BUSTLETON SOUTH

36 HOLMESBURG

38 E GERMANTOWN

26 OAK LANE

49 BOULEVARD

19 MT. AIRY

28 ROXBOROUGH

41 LOGAN

20 OLNEY

35 TACONY

44 GERMANTOWN

24 FRANKFORD

27 MANAYUNK

29 E FALLS

40 NICETOWN

37 BRIDESBURG

31 WEST PARK

32 N PHILA W

33 N PHILA E

34 RICHMOND

51 OVERBROOK

21 FAIRMOUNT N

22 SPRING GARDEN N

25 KENSINGTON

39 W MARKET ST

30 FAIRMOUNT S

23 SPRING GARDEN S

04 WEST PHILA

01-03

05-09

43 KINGSESSING

46 SCHUYLKILL

47 SOUTHWARK

42 PASCHALL

45 POINT BREEZE

48 PASSYUNK

DELAWARE COUNTY

12 U S NAVAL BASE

53 EASTWICK

13 LESTER

05 WM. PENN ANNEX BOX HOLDERS
06 WM. PENN ANNEX EAST
07 WM. PENN ANNEX WEST
08 COMMERCE
09 FIDELITY

01 GPO BOX HOLDERS
02 MID CITY EAST
03 MID CITY WEST

	ZIP
Pine Flats	15728
Pine Forge	19548
Pine Glen (Centre County)	16845
Pine Glen (Mifflin County)	17044
Pine Grove (Perry County)	17047
Pine Grove (Schuylkill County)	17963
Pine Grove (Schuylkill County) (Township)	17963
Pine Grove (Susquehanna County)	18446
Pinegrove (Venango County) (Township)	16301
Pine Grove (Warren County) (Township)	16345
Pine Grove Furnace	17324
Pine Grove Mills	16868
Pine Hill (Armstrong County)	16201
Pine Hill (Schuylkill County)	17901
Pine Ridge	19063
Pine Run (Bucks County)	18901
Pine Run (Lycoming County)	17744
Pine Summit	17846
Pine Swamp	19520
Pinetown	17339
Pinetree (Part of Scottdale)	15683
Pine Valley	14055
Pine Valley Estates	18901
Pine View	18707
Pineville (Bucks County)	18946
Pineville (Warren County)	16420
Pinewood	19054
Piney	16214
Piney (Township)	16255
Piney Fork	15129
Pinola	17257
Pipersville	18947
Pitcairn	15140
Pitman	17964
Pitt Gas	15322
Pittock	15136
Pitts	16901
Pittsburgh	**15201-90**
For specific Pittsburgh Zip Codes call (412) 359-7860, or your local postmaster.	

COLLEGES & UNIVERSITIES

	ZIP
Carlow College	15213
Carnegie Mellon University	15213
Duquesne University	15282
La Roche College	15237
Point Park College	15222
University of Pittsburgh	15260

FINANCIAL INSTITUTIONS

	ZIP
Allegheny Valley Bank of Pittsburgh	15201
Bell Federal Savings & Loan Association of Bellevue	15202
Dollar Bank, A Federal Savings Bank	15222
Fayette Bank	15203
First Home Savings Bank	15203
Great American Federal Savings & Loan Association	15236
Integra Bank/Pittsburgh	15278
North Side Deposit Bank	15212
Pittsburgh Home Savings Bank	15222
PNC Bank	15265
West View Savings Bank	15237

HOSPITALS

	ZIP
Allegheny General Hospital	15212
Magee-Womens Hospital	15213
Mercy Hospital of Pittsburgh	15219
Montefiore Hospital	15213
North Hills Passavant Hospital	15237
Presbyterian-University Hospital	15213
St. Clair Hospital	15243
St. Francis Medical Center	15201
St. Margaret Memorial Hospital	15215
Shadyside Hospital	15232
Veterans Affairs Medical Center	15240
Western Pennsylvania Hospital	15224

	ZIP
HOTELS/MOTELS	
Holiday Inn Pittsburgh Airport	15231
Best Western Parkway Center Inn	15220
Days Inn	15216
Harley of Pittsburgh	15235
Hyatt Pittsburgh at Chatham Center	15219
Pittsburgh Green Tree Marriott	15205
Sheraton Hotel at Station Square	15219

MILITARY INSTALLATIONS

	ZIP
911th Airlift Group, Greater Pittsburgh International Airport, (AFRES)	15231
Hays Army Ammunition Plant	15207
Pennsylvania Air National Guard, FB6381, Greater Pittsburgh International Airport	15231
United States Army Engineer District, Pittsburgh	15222
Charles E. Kelley Support Facility, Maintenance Division, Neville Island	15225

	ZIP
Pittsburgh Valley	17516
Pittsfield	16340
Pittsfield (Township)	16340
Pittston	18640-44
For specific Pittston Zip Codes call (717) 654-3313, or your local postmaster.	
Pittston Junction (Part of Wilkes-Barre)	18705
Pittsville	16374
Plainfield (Cumberland County)	17081
Plainfield (Northampton County) (Township)	18064
Plain Grove (Township)	16156
Plains	18705
Plains (Township)	18705
Plainsville	18705
Plainview	17325
Planebrook	19355
Plank	16938
Platea	16417
Plateau Heights	16335
Plattsville	16646
Plaza (Part of Butler)	16001
Plaza Heights (Part of Hanover)	17331
Pleasant (Township)	16365
Pleasant Acres	17044
Pleasant Corners	18235
Pleasant Gap	16823
Pleasant Grove (Lancaster County)	17563
Pleasant Grove (Washington County)	15323
Pleasant Hall	17246
Pleasant Hill (Cambria County)	15738
Pleasant Hill (rural) (Clearfield County)	16839
Pleasant Hill (Clearfield County)	16866
Pleasant Hill (Delaware County)	19063
Pleasant Hill (Fayette County)	15425
Pleasant Hill (Indiana County)	15701
Pleasant Hill (Lawrence County)	16123
Pleasant Hill (Lebanon County)	17042
Pleasant Hill (York County)	17331
Pleasant Hills (Allegheny County)	15236
Pleasant Hills (Dauphin County)	17112
Pleasant Mount	18453
Pleasant Union	15552
Pleasant Unity	15676
Pleasant Valley (Blair County)	16602
Pleasant Valley (Bucks County)	18951
Pleasant Valley (Fayette County)	15425

	ZIP
Pleasant Valley (Lancaster County)	17604
Pleasant Valley (Potter County) (Township)	16743
Pleasant Valley (Schuylkill County)	17963
Pleasant Valley (Westmoreland County)	15642
Pleasant Valley Estates	18058
Pleasant View (Armstrong County)	15690
Pleasant View (Franklin County)	17201
Pleasantview (Juniata County)	17082
Pleasant View (York County)	17356
Pleasantville	16341
Pleasureville	17402
Pleasureville Heights	17402
Plowville	19540
Plum	15239
Plum (Township)	16354
Plumbridge	19056
Plumbsock	15329
Plumcreek (Township)	15774
Plumer	16301
Plum Run	17238
Plumsock	19073
Plumstead (Township)	18923
Plumsteadville	18949
Plumville	16246
Plunketts Creek (Township)	17701
Plymouth (Luzerne County)	18651
Plymouth (Luzerne County) (Township)	18651
Plymouth (Montgomery County) (Township)	19401
Plymouth Junction (Part of Larksville)	18651
Plymouth Meeting	19462
Plymouth Meeting Mall	19462
Plymouth Valley	19401
Plymptonville	16830
Pocahontas	15552
Pocono (Township)	18372
Pocono Country Place	18466
Pocono Farms	18466
Pocono Farms East	18466
Pocono Heights	18301
Pocono Lake	18347
Pocono Lake Preserve	18348
Pocono Manor	18349
Pocono Mt. Lake Forest	18328
Pocono Mtn Lake Estate	18661
Pocono Park	18360
Pocono Pines	18350
Pocono Summit	18346
Pocono Summit Estates	18346
Pocopson	19366
Pocopson (Township)	19366
Pogue	17264
Point (Bedford County)	15559
Point (Northumberland County) (Township)	17857
Point Breeze (Part of Penn Hills)	15147
Point Breeze (Part of Pittsburgh)	15208
Point Breeze (Northumberland County)	17872
Point Breeze (Part of Philadelphia)	19145
Point Marion	15474
Point Phillip	18014
Point Pleasant	18950
Point Ridge Farms	17011
Point View	16693
Poland	15327
Polk (Jefferson County) (Township)	15825
Polk (Monroe County) (Township)	18333
Polk (Venango County)	16342
Polktown	17268
Polk Valley	18055
Pomeroy	19367
Pomeroy Heights	19320
Pond Bank	17201
Pond Creek	18661
Pond Eddy	12770
Pond Hill	18660
Pont	16401
Poplar Grove (Fayette County)	15425
Poplar Grove (Lancaster County)	17543

	ZIP
Porkey	16347
Portage (Cambria County)	15946
Portage (Cambria County) (Township)	15946
Portage (Cameron County) (Township)	15834
Portage (Potter County) (Township)	16720
Port Allegany	16743
Port Ann	17882
Port Barnett	15825
Port Blanchard	18640
Port Carbon	17965
Port Clinton	19549
Porter (Clarion County) (Township)	16242
Porter (Clinton County) (Township)	17751
Porter (Huntingdon County) (Township)	16611
Porter (Jefferson County)	15767
Porter (Jefferson County) (Township)	15767
Porter (Lycoming County) (Township)	17740
Porter (Pike County) (Township)	18301
Porter (Schuylkill County) (Township)	17980
Porters Sideling	17354
Portersville	16051
Port Griffith	18640
Port Indian	19401
Port Jenkins	18661
Port Kennedy	19406
Portland	18351
Portland Mills	15853
Port Matilda	16870
Port Providence	19453
Port Royal (Juniata County)	17082
Port Royal (Westmoreland County)	15012
Port Trevorton	17864
Port Vue	15133
Possum Hollow (Part of New Beaver)	16157
Potetown	16673
Potosi	17327
Potter (Beaver County) (Township)	15061
Potter (Centre County) (Township)	16828
Potter Brook	16950
Pottersdale	16871
Potters Mills	16875
Potterville	18837
Pottsgrove (Montgomery County)	19464
Potts Grove (Northumberland County)	17865
Pottstown	19464-65
For specific Pottstown Zip Codes call (215) 323-2100, or your local postmaster.	
Pottstown Landing	19464
Pottsville	17901
Powder Mill Village	15677
Powder Valley	18092
Powell	18832
Powells Valley	17032
Powys	17728
Poyntelle	18454
Prentisvale	16731
Prescott	17042
Prescottville	15851
President	16353
President (Township)	16353
Presidential Heights (Allegheny County)	15237
Presidential Heights (Franklin County)	17201
Presque Isle	16505
Presto	15142
Preston (Luzerne County)	18706
Preston (Wayne County) (Township)	18455
Preston Hill	17935
Preston Park	18455
Pretoria	15935
Price (Township)	18301
Priceburg (Part of Dickson City)	18519
Pricedale	15072
Pricetown	19522
Priceville	18417
Primos	19018
Primos-Secane	19018

	ZIP
Primrose (Schuylkill County)	17901
Primrose (Washington County)	15057
Princeton	16101
Pringle	18704
Pritchard	18621
Pritchards Corner	16150
Prittstown	15666
Proctor	17701
Progress	17109
Prompton	18456
Prospect (Butler County)	16052
Prospect (Cambria County)	15901
Prospect Gardens	17602
Prospect Heights	18017
Prospect Park (Cameron County)	15834
Prospect Park (Delaware County)	19076
Prospectville	19002
Prosperity	15329
Providence (Township)	17560
Providence Downe	19063
Providence Square	19426
Provins Works	15461
Pughtown	19464
Puite	17110
Pulaski (Beaver County) (Township)	15066
Pulaski (Lawrence County)	16143
Pulaski (Lawrence County) (Township)	16143
Punxsutawney	15767
Purcell	15535
Purchase Line	15729
Puritan (Cambria County)	15946
Puritan (Fayette County)	15458
Putnam (Township)	16917
Putneyville	16242
Puttstown	16678
Puzzletown	16635
Pyles Mills	16117
Pymatuning (Township)	16154
Pyrra	16226
Quakake	18245
Quaker Hills (Part of Millersville)	17551
Quaker Lake	18812
Quakertown	18951
Quaker Valley	17307
Quarryville	17566
Quecreek	15555
Queen (Bedford County)	16670
Queen (Forest County)	16351
Queen City	17820
Queens Grant	19067
Queens Run	17745
Queenstown	16041
Quemahoning (Township)	15563
Quentin	17083
Quicks Bend	18846
Quicktown	18444
Quiggleville	17728
Quincy	17247
Quincy (Township)	17268
Quincy Hollow	19057
Raccoon (Township)	15001
Radebaugh	15601
Radnor (Township)	19087
Rahns	19426
Railroad	17355
Raineytown	15428
Rainsburg	15522
Ralph	15443
Ralpho (Township)	17872
Ralphton	15563
Ralston	17763
Ramblewood	16865
Ramey	16671
Ramona	17067
Ramsay Terrace (Part of Mount Pleasant)	15666
Ramsaytown	15825
Ramsey	17740
Ranavilla	17011
Randolph (Township)	16327
Rankin	15104
Ranshaw	17866
Ransom	18653
Ransom (Township)	18411
Rapho (Township)	17545
Rasler Run	15469
Rasleytown	18072
Rasselas	15870
Rathbun	15857
Rathmel	15851
Rattigan	16025

	ZIP
Raubsville	18042
Rauchtown	17740
Rauschs	17960
Raven Creek	17814
Raven Run	17946
Ravine	17966
Rawlinsville	17532
Rayburn (Township)	16201
Raymilton	16342
Raymond	16923
Rayne (Township)	15747
Raytown	15742
Rea	15356
Reade (Township)	16619
Reading	19601-12
For specific Reading Zip Codes call (215) 689-4404, or your local postmaster.	
Reading (Township)	17350
Reading Mines	15563
Reagantown	15679
Reamstown	17567
Reamstown Heights	17567
Rebel Hill	19406
Rebersburg	16872
Rebuck	17867
Rector	15677
Redbank (Armstrong County) (Township)	16240
Redbank (Clarion County) (Township)	16224
Red Bank (Union County)	17844
Redbird	15946
Red Bridge	17201
Redclyffe	16239
Red Cross	17823
Redds Mill	15022
Red Gate Farms	18901
Red Hill (Blair County)	16601
Red Hill (Montgomery County)	18076
Redington	18055
Red Lion (Berks County)	18062
Red Lion (Chester County)	19348
Red Lion (York County)	17356
Red Mill	15840
Red Oak	18436
Red Rock (Luzerne County)	17814
Red Rock (McKean County)	16727
Red Rose Gate	19056
Redrun	17517
Redstone	15438
Redstone (Township)	15442
Redstone Junction	15472
Reduction	15479
Reeceville	19335
Reed (Dauphin County) (Township)	17032
Reed (Northumberland County)	17860
Reeder	18938
Reeders	18352
Reeds Gap	17035
Reeds Road	19335
Reedsville	17084
Reels Corners	15926
Reemersville	18426
Reese	16648
Reesedale	16210
Reevesdale	18252
Reflection Lakes	18417
Refton	17568
Regency Park (Part of Plum)	15239
Register	18611
Rehrersburg	19550
Reidsburg	16214
Reiffton	19606
Reightown	16686
Reilly (Township)	17923
Reillys	16668
Reinerton	17980
Reinerton-Orwin-Muir	17980
Reinholds	17569
Reinoeldville	17046
Reistville	17067
Reitz (Jefferson County)	15824
Reitz (Somerset County)	15924
Relay	17313
Reliance	18964
Rembrant	15728
Renfrew	16053
Rennerdale	15106
Reno (Part of Sugarcreek)	16343
Renovo	17764
Renton (Part of Plum)	15239
Republic	15475

	ZIP
Reserve (Township)	15212
Reservoir	16648
Retort	16677
Revere	18953
Revloc	15948
Rew	16744
Reward	17062
Rexford	16921
Rexis	15961
Rexmont (Part of Cornwall)	17085
Rextown	16080
Reyburn	18655
Reynolds	18252
Reynoldsdale	15554
Reynolds Heights	16125
Reynoldsville	15851
Rheems	17570
Ribot	16669
Rice (Township)	18707
Rices Landing	15357
Riceville	16432
Richards Grove	17774
Richardsville	15825
Richboro	18954
Richboro Manor	18954
Richeyville (Part of Centerville)	15358
Richfield	17086
Rich Hill (Bucks County)	18951
Richhill (Greene County) (Township)	15380
Rich Hill (Washington County)	15347
Richland (Allegheny County) (Township)	15044
Richland (Bucks County) (Township)	18951
Richland (Cambria County) (Township)	15904
Richland (Cambria County)	16636
Richland (Clarion County) (Township)	16049
Richland (Lebanon County)	17087
Richland (Venango County) (Township)	16373
Richlandtown	18955
Richmond (Berks County) (Township)	19530
Richmond (Crawford County) (Township)	16327
Richmond (Northampton County)	18013
Richmond (Philadelphia County)	19134
Richmond (Tioga County) (Township)	16933
Richmondale	18421
Richmond Furnace	17224
Richvale	17213
Riddlesburg	16672
Riddlewood	19063
Ridgebury (Township)	16914
Ridge Valley	18960
Ridgeview	17112
Ridgeville	17821
Ridgewood (Berks County)	19508
Ridgewood (Luzerne County)	18705
Ridgewood Farm	19380
Ridgway	15853
Ridgway (Township)	15853
Ridley (Township)	19033
Ridley Farms	19070
Ridley Gardens	19043
Ridley Park (Cumberland County)	17011
Ridley Park (Delaware County)	19078
Riegelsville	18077
Rienze	18853
Rife	17061
Riggles Gap	16601
Riggs	18850
Rillton	15678
Rimer	16259
Rimersburg	16248
Rinely	17363
Ringdale	18614
Ringertown (Part of Murrysville)	15632
Ringgold	15770
Ringgold (Township)	15770
Ringing Hill	19464
Ringing Rock Park	19464
Ringtown (Berks County)	19539

	ZIP
Ringtown (Schuylkill County)	17967
Rising Sun	18080
Riterville	16738
Ritzie Village	17112
River Hill	15063
Riverside (Cambria County)	15905
Riverside (Lackawanna County)	18403
Riverside (Northumberland County)	17868
Riverton	18013
River View (Armstrong County)	15690
Riverview (Clearfield County)	16830
River View (Washington County)	15067
Riverview Acres	18080
Riverview Heights	17011
River View Park	19605
Rixford	16745
Roadside	17268
Roaring Branch	17765
Roaring Brook (Township)	18444
Roaring Brook Estates	18444
Roaring Creek	17820
Roaring Creek (Township)	17820
Roaring Spring	16673
Robb	15944
Robert Bruce West (Part of Hatboro)	19040
Robert Morris College	15108
Robertsdale	16674
Robertsville	15767
Robeson (Township)	19508
Robeson Crossing	19508
Robeson Extension	16693
Robesonia	19551
Robindale Heights	15954
Robin Hood Lakes	18058
Robinson (Allegheny County) (Township)	15136
Robinson (Indiana County)	15949
Robinson (Lawrence County)	16132
Robinson (Washington County) (Township)	15057
Rocherty	17042
Rochester	15074
Rochester (Township)	15074
Rochester Mills	15771
Rock	17963
Rockdale (Bucks County)	19007
Rockdale (Crawford County) (Township)	16403
Rockdale (Delaware County)	19014
Rockdale (Jefferson County)	15840
Rockdale (Lehigh County)	18080
Rockdale Acres	16403
Rockefeller (Township)	17801
Rock Glen	18246
Rock Hill (Bucks County)	18960
Rockhill (Lancaster County)	17516
Rockhill Furnace	17249
Rockingham	15924
Rock Lake	18453
Rockland (Berks County) (Township)	19522
Rockland (Venango County)	16374
Rockland (Venango County) (Township)	16374
Rockledge	19111
Rockport	18255
Rockrimmin Ridge	17540
Rock Run	19320
Rockspring	16865
Rockton	15856
Rockton Station	15856
Rocktown	15688
Rockview	16823
Rockville (Armstrong County)	16226
Rockville (Cambria County)	15956
Rockville (Chester County)	19344
Rockville (Clarion County)	16242
Rockville (Dauphin County)	17110
Rockville (Juniata County)	17059
Rockville (Mifflin County)	17004
Rockville (Northampton County)	18038

	ZIP
Rockwood (Lebanon County)	17046
Rockwood (Somerset County)	15557
Rock Works	15461
Rocky Forest	18623
Rocky Grove (Part of Sugarcreek)	16323
Rocky Hill	19380
Rocky Valley	18036
Roedersville	17963
Rogers Mills	15469
Rogers Stop	15022
Rogerstown	15425
Rogersville	15359
Rogertown	16313
Rohrerstown	17603*
	17607†
Rohrsburg	17859
Rolling Glen	19341
Rolling Hills (Berks County)	19607
Rolling Hills (Lehigh County)	18052
Rolling Meadows	15370
Romansville	19320
Romar	15943
Rome (Bradford County)	18837
Rome (Bradford County) (Township)	18850
Rome (Crawford County) (Township)	16354
Romney	15446
Ronco	15476
Ronks	17572
Rook (Part of Green Tree)	15220
Roosevelt Mall (Part of Philadelphia)	19149
Roots Crossing	16686
Rosas	12770
Roscoe	15477
Rose (Township)	15825
Roseann	17063
Rosebud	16627
Roseburg	17074
Rosecrans	17747
Rosedale (Allegheny County)	15147
Rosedale (Bucks County)	18981
Rosedale (Chester County)	19317
Rosedale (Fayette County)	15401
Roseglen	17020
Rosehill (Part of Philadelphia)	19140
Rose Hollow	19067
Rosemont (Delaware County)	19010
Rosemont (Montgomery County)	19010
Rose Point	16101
Roses	16239
Roseto	18013
Rose Valley (Delaware County)	19063
Rose Valley (Montgomery County)	19002
Rose Valley Acres	19063
Roseville (Jefferson County)	15825
Roseville (Tioga County)	16933
Rosewood Gardens	18974
Roslyn (Chester County)	19380
Roslyn (Montgomery County)	19001
Ross (Allegheny County) (Township)	15237
Ross (Luzerne County) (Township)	18656
Ross (Monroe County) (Township)	18353
Ross Common	18353
Rossford	16226
Rossiter	15772
Rossland	18350
Rosslyn Farms	15106
Rossmere	17601
Rossmoyne	17011
Ross Park Mall	15237
Ross Park Malls (Part of Pittsburgh)	15237
Ross Siding	17723
Rosston	16226
Ross Township	15237
Rossville	17358
Rostraver (Township)	15012
Rote	17751
Rothsville	17543
Rough and Ready	17941

	ZIP
Roulette	16746
Roulette (Township)	16746
Round Knob	16679
Round Top	17325
Roundtown	17404
Rouseville	16344
Rouzerville	17250
Rowes Run	15442
Rowland	18457
Rowland Park	19012
Rowles	15757
Roxborough (Part of Philadelphia)	19128
Roxbury (Cambria County)	15905
Roxbury (Cumberland County)	17055
Roxbury (Franklin County)	17251
Roxbury (Somerset County)	15530
Royal	18446
Royalton	17057
Royer	16693
Royersford	19468
Roystone	16347
Roytown	15501
Rozel Park	18966
Ruble	15478
Ruchsville	18037
Rudytown	17070
Ruff Creek	15329
Ruffs Dale	15679
Ruggles	18636
Rummel	15963
Rummerfield	18853
Rundell	16406
Runville	16823
Rupert	17815
Ruppsville	18106
Rural Ridge	15075
Rural Valley	16249
Ruscombmanor (Township)	19522
Rush (Centre County) (Township)	16866
Rush (Dauphin County) (Township)	17980
Rush (Northumberland County) (Township)	17821
Rush (Schuylkill County) (Township)	18252
Rush (Susquehanna County)	18801
Rush (Susquehanna County) (Township)	18801
Rushland	18956
Rushtown	17821
Rushville	18839
Russell	16345
Russell Hill	18657
Russellton	15076
Russellville (Chester County)	19363
Russellville (Huntingdon County)	16657
Rutan	15341
Rutherford	17111
Rutherford Park	17036
Ruthford	15955
Ruthfred Acres (Part of Bethel Park)	15102
Rutland (Township)	16933
Rutledge	19070
Rutledgedale	18469
Ryan (Township)	18214
Ryans Corner	18940
Rydal	19046
Ryde	17051
Rye (Perry County) (Township)	17053
Rye (York County)	17313
Ryerson Station	15380
Ryot	15521
Rywal Park	19020
Sabinsville	16943
Sabula	15801
Sackett	16735
Saco (Bradford County)	18848
Saco (Lackawanna County)	18436
Sacramento	17968
Saddle Brook	18101
Saddlebrook Village I and II	19565
Sadlers Corner	16301
Sadsbury (Chester County) (Township)	19369
Sadsbury (Crawford County) (Township)	16316

	ZIP
Sadsbury (Lancaster County) (Township)	17509
Sadsburyville	19369
Saegersville	18053
Saegertown	16433
Safe Harbor	17516
Sagamore (Armstrong County)	16250
Sagamore (Fayette County)	15446
Sagamore Hills	18101
Saginaw	17347
Sagon	17872
St. Augustine	16636
St. Benedict	15773
St. Boniface	16675
St. Charles	16242
St. Clair (Allegheny County)	15210
St. Clair (Schuylkill County)	17970
St. Clair (Westmoreland County)	15601
St. Clair (Westmoreland County) (Township)	15954
St. Clairsville	16667
St. Davids	19087
St. George	16374
St. Johns	18247
St. Joseph	18818
St. Lawrence (Berks County)	19606
St. Lawrence (Cambria County)	16668
St. Leonard	18940
St. Marys	15857
St. Michael	15951
St. Michael-Sidman	15951
St. Nicholas	17948
St. Paul	15552
St. Peters	19470
St. Petersburg	16054
St. Thomas	17252
St. Thomas (Township)	17252
St. Vincent Seminary	15650
St. Vincent Shaft	15650
Salco	15530
Salem (Clarion County) (Township)	16232
Salem (Clearfield County)	15801
Salem (Franklin County)	17201
Salem (Luzerne County) (Township)	18603
Salem (Mercer County)	16125
Salem (Mercer County) (Township)	16125
Salem (Snyder County)	17870
Salem (Wayne County) (Township)	18444
Salem (Westmoreland County) (Township)	15601
Salem Harbor	19020
Salemville	16664
Salford	18957
Salford (Township)	18969
Salford Heights	19438
Salfordville	18958
Salida (Part of Baldwin)	15227
Salina	15680
Salisbury (Lancaster County) (Township)	17535
Salisbury (Lehigh County) (Township)	18103
Salisbury (Somerset County)	15558
Salisbury Heights	17527
Salix	15952
Salix-Beauty Line Park	15952
Salladasburg	17740
Salona	17767
Saltillo	17253
Saltlick (Township)	15469
Saltsburg	15681
Salunga	17538
Salunga-Landisville	17538
Saluvia	17228
Sample Run (Part of Clymer)	15728
Sampson	15063
Sanatoga	19464
Sanatoga Park	19464
Sanbourn	16651
Sandbeach	17033
Sand Hill (Lebanon County)	17046
Sandhill (Monroe County)	18354
Sand Hill (Westmoreland County)	15666
Sand Patch	15552
Sand Springs	18222

	ZIP
Sandts Eddy	18040
Sandy	15801
Sandy (Township)	15801
Sandy Bank	19063
Sandy Creek (Allegheny County)	15147
Sandy Creek (Mercer County) (Township)	16130
Sandycreek (Venango County) (Township)	16323
Sandy Hill	19401
Sandy Hollow	16248
Sandy Lake	16145
Sandy Lake (Township)	16145
Sandy Plains	15322
Sandy Ridge	16677
Sandy Ridge Acres	18901
Sandy Run (Bucks County)	19067
Sandy Run (Greene County)	15338
Sandy Run (Luzerne County)	18224
Sandy Shore	18428
Sandy Valley	15851
Sandyville	18324
Sanford	16340
Sankertown	16630
Sarah Furnace	16248
Sardis (Part of Murrysville)	15668
Sartwell	16731
Sarver	16055
Sarverville	16055
Sassamansville	19472
Satterfield	18614
Satterfield Junction	18614
Saucon Acres	18034
Saulsburg	16652
Saville	17074
Saville (Township)	17037
Sawtown	16301
Sawyer City	16701
Saxonburg	16056
Saxton	16678
Saybrook	16347
Saylorsburg	18353
Sayre	18840
Scalp Level	15963
Scammells Corner	19067
Scandia	16345
Scanlan Hill	15938
Scenery Hill	15360
Schaefferstown	17088
Schellsburg	15559
Schenkel	19464
Schenley	15682
Schenley Heights (Part of Pittsburgh)	15219
Scherersville	18104
Schlusser	17013
Schnecksville	18078
Schoeneck (Lancaster County)	17578
Schoeneck (Northampton County)	18064
Schoenersville	18103
Schoentown (Part of Port Carbon)	17965
Schofer	19530
Schollard	16137
School Lane	17603
School Lane Hills	17604
School Valley Farms	17520
Schubert	19507
Schultzville (Berks County)	19504
Schultzville (Lackawanna County)	18411
Schuster Heights	16229
Schuyler	17772
Schuylkill (Chester County) (Township)	19460
Schuylkill (Philadelphia County)	19146
Schuylkill (Schuylkill County) (Township)	17952
Schuylkill Haven	17972
Schuylkill Hills	19401
Schwenksville	19473
Sciota	18354
Sconnelltown	19380
Scotch Hill	16233
Scotch Hollow	16666
Scotia (Part of Jefferson)	15025
Scotland	17254
Scotrun	18355
Scott (Allegheny County) (Township)	15106
Scott (Columbia County) (Township)	17815

	ZIP		ZIP		ZIP		ZIP
Scott (Lackawanna County) (Township)	18447	Sharon (Potter County) (Township)	16748	Shoaf	15478	Slovan	15078
Scott (Lawrence County) (Township)	16101	Sharon Center	16748	Shocks Mills	17547	Slovene National Benefit Society	16120
Scott (Wayne County) (Township)	18462	Sharon Hill	19079	Shoemaker	15946	Smallwood (Part of California)	15423
Scott Center	18462	Sharon Park (Part of Sharon Hill)	19079	Shoemakers (Monroe County)	18301	Smethport	16749
Scottdale	15683	Sharpsburg (Allegheny County)	15215	Shoemakers (Schuylkill County)	17948	Smicksburg	16256
Scott Haven	15083	Sharpsburg (Huntingdon County)	17002	Shoemakersville	19555	Smiley	15478
Scottsville	15001	Sharps Hill	15215	Shohola	18458	Smith (Indiana County)	15717
Scott Township	15106	Sharpsville	16150	Shohola (Township)	18458	Smith (Washington County) (Township)	15021
Scranton	18501-05	Sharrertown	15427	Shope Gardens	17057	Smith Bridge	15380
	18508-15	Shartlesville	19554	Shorbes Hill	17331	Smithdale	15089
For specific Scranton Zip Codes call (717) 969-5100, or your local postmaster.		Shavertown (Delaware County)	19061	Shortsville	16935	Smithfield (Bradford County) (Township)	18831
Scrubgrass (Township)	16373	Shavertown (Luzerne County)	18708	Shrader	17084	Smithfield (Fayette County)	15478
Scullton	15557	Shawanese (Part of Harveys Lake)	18654	Shrewsbury (Lycoming County) (Township)	17737	Smithfield (Huntingdon County) (Township)	16652
Scyoc	17021	Shaw Mines	15552	Shrewsbury (Sullivan County) (Township)	17758	Smithfield (Huntingdon County)	16652
Seamentown	15729	Shawmut	15823	Shrewsbury (York County)	17361	Smithfield (Monroe County) (Township)	18335
Seanor	15953	Shawnee on Delaware	18356	Shrewsbury (York County) (Township)	17327	Smith Gardens	17345
Searights	15401	Shawtown	15642	Shumans	17815	Smithland	16242
Sebring	16930	Shawville	16873	Shunk	17768	Smithmill	16680
Secane	19018	Shay	16226	Sickles Corner	16601	Smithport	15742
Seek (Part of Coaldale)	18218	Sheakleyville	16151	Siddonsburg	17019	Smiths	17362
Seelyville	18431	Shearersburg	15613	Sidman	15955	Smiths Corner	18950
Seemsville	18067	Sheatown	18634	Siegfried (Part of Northampton)	18067	Smiths Corners	16374
Seger	15627	Sheffield	16347	Sigel	15860	Smiths Ferry (Part of Ohioville)	15059
Seidersville	18015	Sheffield (Township)	16347	Siglerville	17063	Smithton	15479
Seipstown	18031	Sheffield Heights	15001	Sigmund	18092	Smithtown	15947
Seisholtzville	18062	Sheffield Terrace	15001	Silkworth	18621	Smithville	17560
Seitzland	17327	Sheffield Village	19401	Silvara	18623	Smock	15480
Seitzville	17360	Shehawken	18462	Silver Creek	17959	Smokerun	16681
Selea	17264	Shellsville	17028	Silverdale	18962	Smoketown (Bucks County)	18951
Selinsgrove	17870	Shelly	18951	Silver Ford Heights	17066	Smoketown (Franklin County)	17222
Sellersville	18960	Shellytown	16693	Silver Lake (Bucks County)	18940	Smoketown (Lancaster County)	17576
Seltzer	17974	Shelocta	15774	Silver Lake (Susquehanna County)	18812	Smullton	16872
Seminole	16253	Shelvey	15846	Silver Lake (Susquehanna County) (Township)	18812	Smyerstown	15772
Seneca	16346	Shenandoah	17976	Silver Lake (Wayne County)	18469	Smyrna	17509
Seneca Valley	15642	Shenandoah Heights	17976	Silver Lake (York County)	17339	Snake Spring (Township)	15537
Sereno	17846	Shenandoah Junction	17949	Silver Spring (Cumberland County) (Township)	17055	Snedekerville	16914
Sergeant	16735	Shenango (Lawrence County) (Township)	16101	Silver Spring (Lancaster County)	17575	Snively Corners	16232
Sergeant (Township)	16740	Shenango (Mercer County)	16125	Silverville	16055	Snowball Gate	19056
Seven Fields	16046	Shenango (Mercer County) (Township)	16159	Simmonstown	17527	Snowden	15129
Seven Hills	18837	Shenango Valley Mall (Part of Hermitage)	16148	Simpson	18407	Snowdenville	19475
Seven Pines	17082	Shenks Ferry	17309	Singersville	17018	Snow Shoe	16874
Sevenpoints	17801	Shepherd Hills	18101	Sinking Spring	19608	Snow Shoe (Township)	16829
Seven Springs	15622	Shepherdstown	17055	Sinking Valley	16686	Snyder (Blair County) (Township)	16686
Seven Stars (Adams County)	17325	Sheppton	18248	Sinnemahoning	15861	Snyder (Jefferson County) (Township)	15824
Seven Stars (Juniata County)	17062	Sheraden (Part of Pittsburgh)	15204	Sinsheim	17362	Snyder Corner	17356
Seven Valleys	17360	Sheridan (Lebanon County)	17073	Sipesville	15561	Snyders	17960
Seward	15954	Sheridan (Schuylkill County)	17980	Siqusca	19376	Snydersburg	16235
Sewickley (Allegheny County)	15143	Sherman	18847	Sitka	15431	Snydersville	18360
Sewickley (Westmoreland County) (Township)	15637	Shermans Dale	17090	Siverly (Part of Oil City)	16301	Snydertown (Centre County)	16841
Sewickley Heights	15143	Shermansville	16316	Six Mile Run	16679	Snydertown (Northumberland County)	17877
Sewickley Hills	15143	Sherrett	16218	Six Points	16049		
Seybertown	16028	Sherwood Acres	15061	Sizerville	15834	Snydertown (Westmoreland County)	15620
Seyfert	19508	Sheshequin	18850	Skelp	16601	Snyderville	16222
Shade (Township)	15926	Sheshequin (Township)	18848	Skeltontown	16403	Social Island	17201
Shade Gap	17255	Shetters Grove	17405	Skidmore	16101	Soho (Part of Pittsburgh)	15219
Shadeland	16435	Shickshinny	18655	Ski Haven Lake Estates	18326	Soldier	15851
Shades Glen	18661	Shieldsburg	15670	Skinners Eddy	18623	Solebury	18963
Shade Valley	17213	Shillington	19607	Skippack	19474	Solebury (Township)	18963
Shadle	17853	Shiloh (Clearfield County)	16881	Skippack (Township)	19474	Somerset (Somerset County)	15501
Shado-wood Village	15701	Shiloh (York County)	17404	Skyline Heights	17402	Somerset (Somerset County) (Township)	15501
Shady Acres	17834	Shiloh East	17405	Skyline View	17112	Somerset (Washington County) (Township)	15330
Shady Grove	17256	Shimerville	18049	Skytop	18357	Somers Lane	16929
Shady Plain	15613	Shimpstown	17236	Sky View	18426	Somerton (Part of Philadelphia)	19116
Shadyside (Part of Pittsburgh)	15232	Shindle	17841	Slab	17302	Somerville	16028
Shaffer	15801	Shinglehouse	16748	Slabtown	17268	Sonestown	17770
Shaffers Corner	15401	Shingletown	16801	Slackwater	17551	Sonman	15946
Shaffersville	16652	Shintown	17764	Slatedale	18079	Soradoville	17841
Shaft (Schuylkill County)	17976	Shipmans Eddy	16365	Slatefield	18038	Soudersburg	17577
Shaft (Somerset County)	15530	Shippen (Cameron County) (Township)	15834	Slateford	18343	Souderton	18964
Shafton	15642	Shippen (Tioga County) (Township)	16901	Slate Hill	17314	Soukesburg	15956
Shaler (Township)	15116	Shippensburg	17257	Slate Lick	16229	South Abington (Township)	18410
Shamokin	17872	Shippensburg (Township)	17257	Slate Run	17769	South Altoona (Part of Altoona)	16602
Shamokin (Township)	17860	Shippensburg University of Pennsylvania	17257	Slate Valley	18038		
Shamokin Dam	17876	Shippenville	16254	Slateville	19529	Southampton (Bedford County) (Township)	15535
Shamrock (Fayette County)	15401	Shippingport	15077	Slatington	17080		
Shamrock (Somerset County)	15557	Ships Parts Control Center, United States Navy	17055	Slickport	16646	Southampton (Bucks County)	18966
Shamrock Station	15539	Shiremanstown	17011	Slickville	15684		
Shaner	15642	Shirks Corner	19473	Sligo	16255		
Shanesville	15512	Shirley (Township)	17066	Slippery Rock (Butler County)	16057		
Shankles (Part of Du Bois)	15801	Shirleysburg	17260	Slippery Rock (Butler County) (Township)	16057		
Shanksville	15560			Slippery Rock (Lawrence County) (Township)	16101		
Shankweilers	18069			Slippery Rock Park	16057		
Shannondale	16240			Slocum (Township)	18660		
Shannon Heights	15147			Slocum Corners	18660		
Shanor Heights	16001						
Shanor-Northvue	16001						
Sharon (Mercer County)	16146						

	ZIP		ZIP		ZIP		ZIP
Southampton (Cumberland County) (Township)	17257	South Versailles (Township)	15028	Spring Garden (Lancaster County)	17535	Star Junction	15482
Southampton (Franklin County) (Township)	17244	Southview	15361	Spring Garden (Philadelphia County)	19122	Starkville	18657
Southampton (Somerset County) (Township)	15552	Southwark (Part of Philadelphia)	19147	Spring Garden (Union County)	17810	Starlight	18461
South Annville (Township)	17042	South Waverly	14892	Spring Garden (Westmoreland County)	15666	Starners Station	17324
South Auburn	18630	Southwest (Warren County) (Township)	16354	Spring Garden (York County) (Township)	17403	Starr (Forest County)	16353
South Beaver (Township)	16115	Southwest (Westmoreland County)	15685	Spring Garden (York County)	17403	Starr (Warren County)	16420
South Bend	15686	Southwest Greensburg	15601	Spring Glen	17978	Starrucca	18462
South Bend (Township)	15774	Southwest Madison (Township)	17047	Spring Grove	17362	Starview	17347
South Bethlehem	16242	South Whitehall (Township)	18104	Spring Hill (Allegheny County)	15212	Starview Heights	17402
South Bradford	16701	South Williamsport	17701	Springhill (Bradford County)	18853	State College	16801-05
South Buffalo (Township)	16229	South Woodbury (Township)	16664	Spring Hill (Cambria County)	15946	For specific State College Zip Codes call (814) 238-2435, or your local postmaster.	
South Canaan	18459	Southwood Hills	17403	Spring Hill (Delaware County)	19018	State Correctional Institution at Dallas	18612
South Canaan (Township)	18472	Spaces Corners	16201	Springhill (Fayette County) (Township)	15478	State Correctional Institution at Greensburg	15601
South Carnegie	15106	Spangenberg Lake	18436	Springhill (Greene County) (Township)	15352	State Correctional Institution at Retreat	18621
South Centre (Township)	17815	Spangler	15775	Springhope	15559	State Correctional Institution (Lycoming County)	17756
South Clarksville	15322	Spangsville	19512	Spring House	19477	State Correctional Institution (Montgomery County)	19426
South Coatesville	19320	Sparta (Crawford County) (Township)	16434	Springhouse Farms	18104	State Correction Institution	17011
South Connellsville	15425	Sparta (Washington County)	15329	Spring Meadow	15554	State Hill (Berks County)	19608
South Coventry (Township)	19464	Spartansburg	16434	Spring Meadows	19565	State Hill (Chester County)	17527
South Creek (Township)	16925	Spears Grove	17021	Spring Mill	19428	State Line (Bedford County)	15545
Southdale	18655	Speedwell	17543	Spring Mills	16875	Stateline (Erie County)	16428
South Duquesne (Part of Duquesne)	15110	Speers	15012	Springmont	19609	State Line (Franklin County)	17263
Southeastern	19397-99	Spike Island	16666	Spring Mount (Huntingdon County)	16877	Station #5	16506
For specific Southeastern Zip Codes call (215) 964-6448, or your local postmaster.		Spillway Lake	15473	Spring Mount (Montgomery County)	19478	Steamburg	16424
South Easton (Part of Easton)	18042	Spindley City	16641	Spring Run	17262	Steam Valley	17771
South Eaton	18657	Spinnerstown	18968	Springs	15562	Steel City	18015
South Enola	17025	Spinners Point	18464	Springtown (Bucks County)	18081	Steelstown	17003
South Erie (Part of Erie)	16508	Split Rock	18624	Springtown (Franklin County)	17221	Steelton	17113
South Fayette (Township)	15064	Sporting Hill (Cumberland County)	17055	Springtown (Luzerne County)	18707	Steelville	19370
South Fork	15956	Sporting Hill (Lancaster County)	17545	Springtown (Northumberland County)	17777	Steene	18472
South Franklin (Township)	15301	Sportsburg	15767	Springvale	17356	Steinbachs Corner	18847
South Gibson	18842	Spraggs	15362	Spring Valley (Berks County)	19560	Steinsburg	18951
South Greensburg	15601	Sprankle Mills	15776	Spring Valley (Bucks County)	18901	Steinsville	15529
South Hanover (Township)	17033	Spring (Berks County) (Township)	19609	Spring Valley (Clearfield County)	16878	Stemlersville	18235
South Heidelberg (Township)	19565	Spring (Centre County) (Township)	16823	Spring Valley (Northampton County)	18015	Sterling (Township)	18445
South Heights	15081	Spring (Crawford County) (Township)	16435	Spring Valley Farms	18901	Sterling (Clearfield County)	16651
South Hermitage	17555	Spring (Perry County) (Township)	17040	Springville (Township)	18844	Sterling (Wayne County)	18463
South Hills (Allegheny County)	15216	Spring (Snyder County) (Township)	17812	Springville	16342	Sterling Run	15832
South Hills (Mifflin County)	17044	Spring Bank	16872	Springville (Cumberland County)	17007	Sterlingworth	18104
South Hills Village	15241	Springboro	16435	Springville (Lancaster County)	17535	Sterrettania	16415
South Huntingdon (Township)	15089	Spring Brook (Township)	18444	Springville (Susquehanna County)	18844	Stetlersville	18069
South Lakemont	16602	Spring Church	15686	Sproul	16682	Steuben (Township)	16404
Southland 4 Seasons Centre (Part of Pleasant Hills)	15236	Spring City	19475	Spruce Creek	16683	Stevens (Bradford County) (Township)	18854
South Lebanon (Township)	17042	Spring Creek (Elk County) (Township)	15853	Spruce Creek (Township)	16683	Stevens (Lancaster County)	17578
South Londonderry (Township)	17010	Spring Creek (Lehigh County)	18011	Spruce Hill	17082	Stevens Point	18847
South Mahoning (Township)	15747	Spring Creek (Warren County)	16436	Spruce Hill (Township)	17082	Stevenstown	17019
South Manheim (Township)	17972	Spring Creek (Warren County) (Township)	16436	Sprucetown	15474	Stevensville	18845
South Media	19063	Springdale	15144	Spry	17403	Stewardson (Township)	17729
South Middleton (Township)	17007	Springdale (Township)	15049	Squab Hollow	15846	Stewart (Township)	15470
Southmont	15905	Springdell	19320	Square Corner	17325	Stewart Run	16341
South Montrose	18843	Springettsbury (Township)	17402	Squirrel Hill (Part of Pittsburgh)	15217	Stewartstown	17363
South Mountain	17261	Springetts Manor-Yorklyn	17402	Stack Town	17502	Stewartsville	15642
South Mountain Restoration Center	17261	Springfield (Bradford County)	16914	Stafore Estates	18017	Stickney	16701
South New Castle	16101	Springfield (Bradford County) (Township)	18831	Stahlstown	15687	Sticks	17329
South Newton (Township)	17266	Springfield (Bucks County) (Township)	18951	Stairville	18660	Stiefler Corner	16670
South Park (Township)	15129	Springfield (Cumberland County)	17241	Stalker	12741	Stier	18013
South Philipsburg	16866	Springfield (Delaware County) (Township)	19064	Standard (Part of Mount Pleasant)	15666	Stifflertown	15724
South Pottstown	19464	Springfield (Delaware County)	19064	Standard Shaft	15666	Stiles	18052
South Pymatuning (Township)	16150	Springfield (Erie County) (Township)	16443	Standing Stone	18854	Stiles Hill	16943
South Renovo	17764	Springfield (Fayette County) (Township)	15464	Standing Stone (Township)	18853	Still Creek	18252
South Rockwood	15557	Springfield (Huntingdon County) (Township)	17264	Stanhope	17963	Stillwater	17878
South Shenango (Township)	16134	Springfield (Mercer County) (Township)	16137	Stanley	15801	Stillwater Lake Estates	18346
South Side (Allegheny County)	15203	Springfield (Montgomery County) (Township)	19118	Stanleys Corner	16301	Stiltz	17327
South Side (Butler County)	16001	Springfield (York County) (Township)	17327	Stanton	15825	Stines Corner	18066
South Side (Lackawanna County)	18505	Springfield Falls	16137	Stanton Heights (Allegheny County)	15201	Stobo	15061
Southside (Northampton County)	18015	Springfield Mall	19064	Stanton Heights (Westmoreland County)	15672	Stockdale	15483
South Sterling	18460	Spring Garden (Bucks County)	18940	Stanwood Gardens	19020	Stockertown	18083
South Strabane (Township)	15301			Star Brick	16365	Stockton	18201
South Tamaqua	18252			Starford	15777	Stockton Number Eight	18201
South Temple	19560					Stockton Number Seven	18201
South Towanda	18848					Stockton Number Six	18201
South Union (Township)	15401					Stoddartsville	18610
South Uniontown	15401					Stokesdale	16901
						Stoneboro	16153
						Stone Church	18343
						Stone Glen	17018
						Stoneham	16313
						Stone Hill	17516
						Stone House	16258
						Stonehurst	19006
						Stonerstown	16678
						Stonersville	19508
						Stonetown	19508
						Stonevilla	15601
						Stoneybreak	17267

* Area Zip Code   **† Post Office Boxes**

	ZIP		ZIP		ZIP		ZIP
Stonington	17801	Summerhill (Lancaster		Swengel	17880	Thompson No. 1	15475
Stonybrook	17402	County)	19362	Swiftwater (Part of		Thompson No. 2	15468
Stonybrook Heights	17402	Summerson	15821	Middleburg)	18370	Thompsontown (Clearfield	
Stonybrook-Wilshire	17402	Summersville	18822	Swineford (Part of		County)	15753
Stonycreek (Cambria		Summerville	15864	Middleburg)	17842	Thompsontown (Juniata	
County) (Township)	15904	Summit (Butler County)		Swissdale	17745	County)	17094
Stonycreek (Somerset		(Township)	16001	Swissmont	15857	Thompsonville	15317
County) (Township)	15541	Summit (Cambria County)	16630	Swissvale	15218	Thornburg	15205
Stony Creek Mills	19606	Summit (Crawford		Switzer	18066	Thornbury (Chester	
Stonyfork	16901	County) (Township)	16316	Swoyersville	18704	County) (Township)	19395
Stony Point (Bucks		Summit (Erie County)		Sybertsville	18251	Thornbury (Delaware	
County)	18930	(Township)	16509	Sycamore	15364	County) (Township)	19373
Stony Point (Crawford		Summit (McKean County)	16701	Sygan	15017	Thorndale	19372
County)	16316	Summit (Potter County)		Sygan Hill	15017	Thorndale Heights	19335
Stony Point (Franklin		(Township)	16720	Sykesville	15865	Thornhurst	18424
County)	17262	Summit (Somerset		Sylmar	19362	Thornridge	19054
Stony Point (Greene		County) (Township)	15552	Sylvan	17236	Thornton	19373
County)	15344	Summit Grove Camp (Part		Sylvan Crest	15061	Thornwood	15683
Stony Run	19557	of New Freedom)	17349	Sylvan Dell	17701	Three Springs	17264
Stormstown	16870	Summit Hill	18250	Sylvan Grove	16858	Three Tuns	19002
Stormville	18360	Summit Lawn	18103	Sylvan Hills	16648	Throop	18512
Stouchsburg	19567	Summit Mills	15552	Sylvania (Bradford		Thumptown	16901
Stoufferstown	17201	Summit Station	17979	County)	16945	Thurston	18657
Stoughstown	17257	Sumneytown	18084	Sylvania (Potter County)		Tiadaghton	16901
Stover	16686	Sunbrook	16635	(Township)	16720	Tidal	16259
Stoverdale	17036	Sunbury	17801	Sylvis	16692	Tide	15748
Stoverstown	17362	Suncliff	15765	Syner	17003	Tidioute	16351
Stowe (Allegheny County)		Sundale	18920	Table Rock	17307	Tiffany	18801
(Township)	15136	Sunderlinville	16943	Tacony (Part of		Tilden (Township)	19526
Stowe (Montgomery		Sunnybrook	19075	Philadelphia)	19135	Tillotson	16438
County)	19464	Sunnyburn	17302	Tafton	18464	Timber Lakes	19067
Stowell	18623	Sunny Point	18428	Talmage	17580	Timberly Heights	16001
Stoystown	15563	Sunny Side (Allegheny		Talmar	17814	Timblin	15778
Straban (Township)	17325	County)	15063	Tamanend	18252	Timbuck	16738
Strabane	15363	Sunnyside (Armstrong		Tamaqua	18252	Time	15337
Strafford	19087	County)	16201	Tamarack	17764	Tinicum (Bucks County)	18947
Strangford	15717	Sunny Side (Bedford		Tamiment	18371	Tinicum (Bucks County)	
Strasburg	17579	County)	16650	Tanglewood Lakes	18426	(Township)	18947
Strasburg (Township)	17602	Sunnyside (Lawrence		Tanguy	19342	Tinicum (Deleware	
Strattanville	16258	County)	16101	Tank	18249	County) (Township)	19029
Strausstown	19559	Sunnyside (Lebanon		Tanners Falls	18431	Tioga	16946
Strawberry Ridge	17821	County)	17042	Tannersville	18372	Tioga (Township)	16946
Strawberry Square (Part		Sunnyside		Tannery (Carbon County)	18661	Tioga Junction	16946
of Harrisburg)	17101	(Northumberland		Tannery (Luzerne County)	18661	Tiona	16352
Strawbridge	17758	County)	17872	Tanoma	15728	Tionesta	16353
Strickersville	19350	Sunrise Lake	18337	Tarentum	15084	Tionesta (Township)	16353
Strickhousers	17360	Sunset Acres	15701	Tarrs	15688	Tippecanoe	15480
Stricklerstown	17073	Sunset Grove	19380	Tarrtown	16210	Tippery	16301
Strinestown	17345	Sunset Hills (Part of		Tatamy	18085	Tipton	16684
Stringtown (Armstrong		Economy)	15042	Tatesville	15537	Tire Hill	15959
County)	16226	Sunset Manor	17405	Taylor (Blair County)		Titusville	16354
Stringtown (Greene		Sunset Pines (Part of		(Township)	16673	Tivoli	17737
County)	15320	Lock Haven)	17745	Taylor (Centre County)		Toboyne (Township)	17071
Strobleton	16353	Sunset Valley	15642	(Township)	16686	Toby (Clarion County)	
Strodes Mills	17044	Sunset Village	18451	Taylor (Fulton County)		(Township)	16248
Stronach	16833	Sunshine	18655	(Township)	16689	Toby (Elk County)	15846
Strong	17851	Sun Valley	18330	Taylor (Lackawanna		Toby Farms (Part of	
Strongstown	15957	Sun Village (Part of		County)	18517	Chester)	19015
Stroud (Township)	18360	Chester)	19013	Taylor (Lawrence County)		Tobyhanna	18466
Stroudsburg	18360	Sunville	16317	(Township)	16160	Tobyhanna (Township)	18350
Stroudsburg West	18360	Superior (Fayette County)	15417	Taylor Highlands (Part of		Tobyhanna Army Depot	18466
Studa	15312	Superior (Westmoreland		Huntingdon)	16652	Todd (Fulton County)	
Stull	18636	County)	15627	Tayloria	19363	(Township)	17233
Stump Creek	15863	Suplee	19371	Taylorstown	15365	Todd (Huntingdon	
Stumptown	16666	Surveyor Mine	16830	Taylorsville	15729	County)	16685
Sturgeon	15082	Suscon	18641	Taylorville	17921	Todd (Huntingdon	
Sturgeon-Noblestown	15082	Susquehanna (Cambria		Teagarden Homes	15322	County) (Township)	16685
Sturgis (Part of Archbald)	18447	County) (Township)	15714	Tearing Run	15748	Toddesville	17325
Suburban Village	19380	Susquehanna (Dauphin		Teedyskung Lake	18428	Toftrees	16803
Suedburg	17963	County) (Township)	17109	Teepleville	16403	Toland	17324
Sugarcreek (Armstrong		Susquehanna (Juniata		Telescope	16922	Tolna	17349
County) (Township)	16025	County) (Township)	17045	Telford	18969	Tomb	17740
Sugarcreek (Venango		Susquehanna (Lycoming		Tell (Township)	17213	Tompkinsville	18433
County)	16323	County) (Township)	17701	Temple	19560	Tomstown	17268
Sugar Grove (Mercer		Susquehanna		Templeton	16259	Tooley Corners	18444
County) (Township)	16125	(Susquehanna County)	18847	Ten Mile	15311	Topton	19562
Sugar Grove (Warren		Susquehanna Bridge	16830	Tenth Avenue (Part of		Torpedo	16340
County)	16350	Susquehanna Trails	17314	Bethlehem)	18018	Torrance	15779
Sugar Grove (Warren		Susquehanna Valley Mall	17831	Terminal	19082	Torrance State Hospital	15779
County) (Township)	16350	Sutersville	15083	Terney Plan	15650	Torresdale (Part of	
Sugar Hill	15824	Swales	17049	Terrace Acres	18052	Philadelphia)	19114
Sugarloaf (Columbia		Swampoot	16127	Terre Hill	17581	Torresdale Manor	19020
County) (Township)	17814	Swanville	16415	Terry (Township)	18853	Torrey	18473
Sugarloaf (Luzerne		Swart	15364	Terrytown	18853	Toughkenamon	19374
County)	18249	Swarthmore	19081	Texas (Township)	18431	Towamencin (Township)	19443
Sugarloaf (Luzerne		Swartzville	17569	Tharptown	17872	Towamensing (Township)	18071
County) (Township)	18251	Swatara (Dauphin County)		The Hideout	18436	Towamensing Trails	18210
Sugar Notch	18706	(Township)	17111	The Meadows	16865	Towanda	18848
Sugar Run	18846	Swatara (Lebanon		The Pines	17350	Towanda (Township)	18848
Sugartown	19355	County) (Township)	17038	The Woodlands	16033	Tower City	17980
Sullivan (Township)	16932	Swatara Station	17033	Thieleman Crossroads	16046	Tower Hill	18914
Summerdale	17093	Swede Hill	15601	Thomas	15330	Tower Hill No. One	15475
Summerhill (Cambria		Swedeland	19401	Thomasdale	15935	Tower Hill No. Two	15417
County)	15958	Sweden (Township)	16915	Thomas Mills	15935	Towerville	19320
Summerhill (Cambria		Sweden Valley	16915	Thomasville	17364	Town Hill	18655
County) (Township)	15921	Swedesburg	19405	Thompson (Fulton		Town Line	18655
Summer Hill (Columbia		Swedetown	16646	County) (Township)	17236	Townville	16360
County)	18603	Sweeney Plan	15012	Thompson (Susquehanna		Traces of Lattimore	18328
Summerhill (Crawford		Sweeneys Crossroads	15012	County)	18465	Trachsville	18071
County) (Township)	16406	Sweet Valley	18656	Thompson (Susquehanna		Trade City	16256
				County) (Township)	18462		

	ZIP
Tradesville	18914
Trafford	15085
Trailwood	18702
Trainer	19013
Transfer	16154
Trappe	19426
Trauger	15650
Traymore	18974
Traymore Manor	18974
Treasure Lake	15801
Tredyffrin (Township)	19312
Treehaven (Part of Bethel Park)	15102
Trees Mills	15601
Treichlers	18086
Tremont	17981
Tremont (Township)	17963
Trent	15557
Trenton	17948
Tresckow	18254
Tresslarville	18436
Trevorton	17881
Trevose	19047
Trevose Heights	19047
Trexler	19529
Trexlertown	18087
Trimmer Manor	17405
Trindle Spring	17055
Trinity Park	15301
Tripoli	15927
Triumph (Township)	16340
Trooper	19401
Trotter	15425
Trout Run	17771
Trouts Corners (Part of Hermitage)	16148
Trouts Crossing	15666
Troutville	15866
Trowbridge	16936
Troxelville	17882
Troy (Bradford County)	16947
Troy (Bradford County) (Township)	16947
Troy (Clearfield County)	16866
Troy (Crawford County) (Township)	16404
Troy Center	16404
Troy Hill	16201
Truce	17566
Trucksville	18708
Trucksville Gardens	18708
Truemans	16347
Truesdale Terrace	18706
Truittsburg	16224
Truman	15834
Trumbauersville	18970
Trunkeyville	16351
Truxall	15613
Tryonville	16404
Tuckerton	19605
Tullytown	19007
Tulpehocken (Township)	19550
Tuna	16701
Tunkhannock (Monroe County) (Township)	18610
Tunkhannock (Wyoming County)	18657
Tunkhannock (Wyoming County) (Township)	18657
Tunnel	18661
Tunnel Hill	16641
Tunnelton	15681
Turbett (Township)	17082
Turbot (Township)	17847
Turbotville	17772
Turkey City	16058
Turkeyfoot (Franklin County)	17201
Turkeyfoot (Washington County)	15332
Turkey Run (Part of Shenandoah)	17976
Turkeytown	15089
Turnersville	16134
Turnip Hole	16373
Turnpike (Part of Shrewsbury)	17361
Turtle Creek	15145
Turtlepoint	16750
Tuscarora (Bradford County) (Township)	18623
Tuscarora (Juniata County)	17082
Tuscarora (Juniata County) (Township)	17035
Tuscarora (Perry County) (Township)	17062
Tuscarora (Schuylkill County)	17982
Tusculam	17257

	ZIP
Tusseyville	16828
Twenty Row	15927
Twilight	15022
Twin Bridge Farm	19380
Twin Bridges	15022
Twin Brooks	17405
Twin Lakes	18458
Twin Oaks (Adams County)	17325
Twin Oaks (Bucks County)	19056
Twin Oaks (Delaware County)	19014
Twin Oaks (Venango County)	16319
Twin Oaks Farms	19014
Twin Rocks	15960
Two Taverns	17325
Tyler	15849
Tylerdale (Part of Washington)	15301
Tyler Hill	18469
Tyler Run-Queens Gate	17403
Tylersburg	16361
Tylersport	18971
Tylersville	17773
Tyre	15126
Tyrone (Adams County) (Township)	17325
Tyrone (Blair County)	16686
Tyrone (Blair County) (Township)	16686
Tyrone (Perry County) (Township)	17040
Uhlerstown	18972
Uledi	15484
Ulhers	18040
Ulrichtown	17340
Ulster	18850
Ulster (Township)	18850
Ulysses	16948
Ulysses (Township)	16948
Unamis	15411
Unicorn	17566
Union (Adams County) (Township)	17331
Union (Berks County) (Township)	19508
Union (Centre County) (Township)	16844
Union (Clearfield County) (Township)	15856
Union (Crawford County) (Township)	16335
Union (Erie County) (Township)	16438
Union (Fulton County) (Township)	17267
Union (Huntingdon County) (Township)	17052
Union (Jefferson County) (Township)	15829
Union (rural) (Lancaster County)	17560
Union (Lancaster County)	17536
Union (Lawrence County) (Township)	16101
Union (Lebanon County) (Township)	17038
Union (Luzerne County) (Township)	18655
Union (Mifflin County) (Township)	17004
Union (Schuylkill County) (Township)	17967
Union (Snyder County) (Township)	17864
Union (Tioga County) (Township)	17724
Union (Union County) (Township)	17889
Union (Washington County) (Township)	15332
Union Center	17724
Union City	16438
Union Dale	18470
Union Deposit	17033
Union Furnace	16686
Union Grove	17519
Union Hill	18235
Union Mills	17004
Union Square	17545
Uniontown (Fayette County)	15401
Uniontown (Indiana County)	15724
Uniontown (Venango County)	16323
Uniontown (York County)	17019

	ZIP
Union Valley (Lawrence County)	16157
Union Valley (Washington County)	15332
Unionville (Beaver County)	15074
Unionville (Berks County)	19518
Unionville (Butler County)	16001
Unionville (Chester County)	19375
Union Water Works	17003
United	15689
Unity (Allegheny County)	15239
Unity (Westmoreland County) (Township)	15650
Unity House	18373
Unity Junction (Part of Plum)	15239
Unityville	17774
Universal	15235
University City (Part of Philadelphia)	19104
University Heights	18015
University Park (Part of State College)	16802
Upland	19015
Upland Terrace	19004
Upper Allen (Township)	17055
Upper Augusta (Township)	17801
Upper Bern (Township)	19506
Upper Black Eddy	18972
Upper Brownville	17976
Upper Burrell (Township)	15068
Upper Chichester (Township)	19061
Upper Darby	19082-83
For specific Upper Darby Zip Codes call (215) 352-0800, or your local postmaster.	
Upper Dublin (Township)	19034
Upper Exeter	18643
Upper Fairfield (Township)	17754
Upper Frankford (Township)	17241
Upper Frederick (Township)	18074
Upper Glasgow	19464
Upper Gwynedd (Township)	19454
Upper Hanover (Township)	18041
Upper Hillville	16248
Upper Lawn	17078
Upper Leacock (Township)	17540
Upper Lehigh	18224
Upper Macungie (Township)	18087
Upper Mahanoy (Township)	17836
Upper Mahantango (Township)	17941
Upper Makefield (Township)	18940
Upper Merion (Township)	19406
Upper Middletown	15480
Upper Mifflin (Township)	17241
Upper Milford (Township)	18092
Upper Mill (Part of Mount Holly Springs)	17065
Upper Moreland (Township)	19090
Upper Mount Bethel (Township)	18013
Upper Nazareth (Township)	18064
Upper Orchard	19056
Upper Oxford (Township)	19363
Upper Paxton (Township)	17061
Upper Peanut	15480
Upper Pottsgrove (Township)	19464
Upper Providence (Delaware County) (Township)	19063
Upper Providence (Montgomery County) (Township)	19456
Upper Reese	16648
Upper Sagon	17877
Upper Salford (Township)	18957
Upper Saucon (Township)	18034
Upper Southampton (Township)	18966
Upper St. Clair (Township)	15241
Upperstrasburg	17265
Upper Tulpehocken (Township)	19559
Upper Turkeyfoot (Township)	15557

	ZIP
Upper Two Lick	15701
Upper Tyrone (Township)	15631
Upper Uwchlan (Township)	19335
Upper Wheel	15698
Upper Yoder (Township)	15905
Upton	17225
Uptown (Part of Pittsburgh)	15219
Urban	17830
Urey	15742
Uriah	17324
Ursina	15485
Ursina Junction (Part of Confluence)	15424
Utahville	16627
Utica	16362
Utopia	15613
Uwchlan (Township)	19341
Uwchland	19480
Vail	16686
Valemont Heights	15147
Valencia	16059
Valier	15780
Vallamont Hills (Part of Williamsport)	17701
Valley (Armstrong County) (Township)	16201
Valley (Chester County) (Township)	19320
Valley (Montour County) (Township)	17821
Valley Camp (Part of New Kensington)	15068
Valley Falls	19006
Valley Forge	19481-85
For specific Valley Forge Zip Codes call (215) 783-0232, or your local postmaster.	
Valley Forge Christian College	19460
Valley Forge Estates	19087
Valley Forge Homes	19406
Valley Forge Manor	19460
Valley Furnace	17959
Valley Green	17319
Valley Green Estates	17319
Valley Green Heights	17319
Valley Green West	17319
Valley-Hi	15533
Valley Stream	18707
Valley View (Centre County)	16823
Valley View (Chester County)	19344
Valley View (Lancaster County)	17545
Valley View (Schuylkill County)	17983
Valley View (York County)	17403
Valley View Heights	16226
Van	16319
Van Buren	15329
Vance	15301
Vances Mill	15401
Vanceville	15330
Vanderbilt	15486
Vandergrift	15690
Vandling	18421
Vandyke	17082
Van Emman	15317
Vankirk	15301
Van Meter	15479
Van Ormer	16639
Vanport (Township)	15009
Van Voorhis	15366
Van Wert	17059
Varden	18436
Vawter	18810
Venango (Butler County) (Township)	16049
Venango (Crawford County)	16440
Venango (Crawford County) (Township)	16440
Venango (Erie County) (Township)	16442
Venetia	15367
Venice	15057
Venturetown	16365
Venus	16364
Vera Cruz	18049
Verdilla	17870
Vere Cruz	17569
Vermilion Hill	19054
Vernfield	19438
Vernon (Crawford County) (Township)	16335
Vernon (Wyoming County)	18657
Vernondale	16505

* Area Zip Code   † Post Office Boxes

	ZIP
Vernon Park (Part of Philadelphia)	19144
Verona	15147
Versailles	15132
Vestaburg	15368
Vesta Heights	15333
Veterans Administration Hospital (Butler County)	16001
Veterans Administration Medical Center (Lebanon County)	17042
Veterans Hospital (Allegheny County)	15240
Veterans Hospital (Chester County)	19320
Veterans Hospital (Luzerne County)	18702
Vicksburg (Blair County)	16648
Vicksburg (Union County)	17883
Victory (Township)	16342
Victory Heights	16323
Victory Hills	15063
Viewmont Mall (Part of Dickson City)	18519
Village	15241
Village Green	19013
Village Green-Green Ridge	19013
Village of Cross Creek	17402
Village of Olde Hickory	17601
Village of the Four Seasons	18470
Village of Westover	17055
Village Shires	18966
Villa Green	17403
Villa Maria	16155
Villanova	19085
Vinco	15909
Vinemont	17569
Vintage	17562
Vintondale	15961
Violet Hill	17403
Violet Wood	19057
Vira	17044
Virginia Farms	15717
Virginia Hills West	15126
Virginia Mills	17320
Virginville	19564
Voganville	17522
Vogleyville	16001
Volant	16156
Vosburg	18657
Vowinckel	16260
Vulcan	18214
Wadesville	17901
Wadsworth (Part of Philadelphia)	19150
Wagner	17841
Wagnersville	18040
Wagontown	19376
Wahlville	16033
Wahnetah (Part of Jim Thorpe)	18229
Wakena	15681
Walbert	18104
Walcksville	18235
Walden Woods	15126
Walkchalk	16201
Walker (Centre County) (Township)	16841
Walker (Huntingdon County) (Township)	16652
Walker (Juniata County) (Township)	17059
Walker (Schuylkill County) (Township)	18252
Walkers Mill	15106
Walkertown	15427
Wall	15148
Wallace (Township)	19343
Wallace Junction (Part of Girard)	16417
Wallaceton	16876
Wallaceville	16354
Wallenpaupack Lake Estates	18436
Waller	17814
Wallingford	19086
Wallis Run	17771
Walls Corners	18414
Wallsville	18414
Walltown	16838
Walmo	16101
Walnut	17082
Walnut Bend	16301
Walnut Bottom	17266
Walnut Gardens	18052
Walnut Grove	17074
Walnut Hill (Fayette County)	15401

	ZIP
Walnut Hill (Greene County)	15327
Walnut Hill (Montgomery County)	19001
Walnutport	18088
Walnuttown	19522
Walsall	15904
Walston	15781
Walston Junction (Part of Punxsutawney)	15767
Walters	18045
Waltersburg	15488
Waltonville	17036
Waltz	15679
Waltz Landing	18428
Wampum	16157
Wanamakers	19529
Wanamie	18634
Wandin	15729
Wanneta	16401
Wapwallopen	18660
Ward (Delaware County)	19331
Ward (Tioga County) (Township)	17724
Wardville	17062
Warfordsburg	17267
Warminster	18974
Warminster (Township)	18974
Warminster Heights	18974
Warner	15022
Warren (Bradford County) (Township)	18851
Warren (Franklin County) (Township)	17236
Warren (Warren County)	16365
Warren Center	18851
Warrendale	15086
Warren South	16365
Warren State Hospital	16365
Warrensville	17701
Warrington (Bucks County)	18976
Warrington (Bucks County) (Township)	18976
Warrington (York County) (Township)	17019
Warrior Ridge	16669
Warrior Run	18706
Warriors Mark	16877
Warriors Mark (Township)	16686
Warsaw (Jefferson County) (Township)	15825
Warsaw (Lackawanna County)	18512
Warsaw (Luzerne County)	18702
Warwick (Bucks County) (Township)	18929
Warwick (Chester County)	19520
Warwick (Chester County) (Township)	19520
Warwick (Lancaster County) (Township)	17543
Washington (Armstrong County) (Township)	16218
Washington (Berks County) (Township)	19512
Washington (Butler County) (Township)	16061
Washington (Cambria County) (Township)	15938
Washington (Clarion County) (Township)	16326
Washington (Cumberland County)	17241
Washington (Dauphin County) (Township)	17048
Washington (Erie County) (Township)	16412
Washington (Fayette County) (Township)	15012
Washington (Franklin County) (Township)	17268
Washington (Greene County) (Township)	15370
Washington (Indiana County) (Township)	15732
Washington (Jefferson County) (Township)	15840
Washington (Lawrence County) (Township)	16156
Washington (Lehigh County) (Township)	18080
Washington (Lycoming County) (Township)	17810
Washington (Northampton County) (Township)	18013
Washington (Northumberland County) (Township)	17867

	ZIP
Washington (Schuylkill County) (Township)	17963
Washington (Snyder County) (Township)	17842
Washington (Washington County)	15301
Washington (Westmoreland County)	15613
Washington (Wyoming County)	18657
Washington (York County) (Township)	17316
Washington Boro	17582
Washington Crossing	18977
Washington Heights (Part of Lemoyne)	17043
Washington Hill (Part of Pottstown)	19464
Washington Square Gardens	19401
Washingtonville	17884
Wassergass	18055
Waterfall	16689
Waterford (Erie County)	16441
Waterford (Erie County) (Township)	16441
Waterford (Westmoreland County)	15658
Waterford (York County)	17402
Waterloo	17021
Waterloo Mills	19333
Waterman	15748
Waterside	16695
Waterson	16258
Water Street	16611
Waterton	18655
Waterville	17776
Waterworks, The	15238
Watkins	15775
Watrous	16921
Watrous Corners	18801
Watson (Lycoming County) (Township)	17740
Watson (Warren County) (Township)	16351
Watson Farm	16239
Watson Run	16316
Watsontown	17777
Watters	16033
Wattersonville	16218
Watts (Township)	17020
Wattsburg	16442
Waverly	18471
Wawa (Part of Chester Heights)	19017
Wawaset	19380
Wayland	16335
Waymart	18472
Wayne (Armstrong County) (Township)	16222
Wayne (Clinton County) (Township)	17748
Wayne (Crawford County) (Township)	16314
Wayne (Dauphin County) (Township)	17032
Wayne (Delaware County)	19087
Wayne (Erie County) (Township)	16407
Wayne (Greene County) (Township)	15362
Wayne (Lawrence County) (Township)	16117
Wayne (Mifflin County) (Township)	17051
Wayne (Schuylkill County) (Township)	17933
Waynecastle	17225
Wayne Heights	17268
Waynesboro	17268
Waynesburg	15370
Waynesburg Lakes	15329
Waynesville	17032
Weatherly	18255
Weaverland	17519
Weaversville	18067
Weavertown (Berks County)	19518
Weavertown (Lancaster County)	17505
Weavertown (Lebanon County)	17046
Weavertown (Washington County)	15317
Webster	15087
Webster Mills	17233
Weedville	15868
Wegley	15642

	ZIP
Wehnwood (Part of Altoona)	16601
Weidasville	18078
Weidmanville	17522
Weigelstown	17315
Weikert	17885
Weilersville	18011
Weinel's Crossroads	15656
Weir Lake	18058
Weisel	18944
Weisenberg (Township)	18066
Weishample	17938
Weissport	18235
Weissport East	18235
Weldbank	16313
Weldon	19006
Wellersburg	15564
Wellington Estates	18901
Welliversville	17815
Wells (Bradford County) (Township)	16925
Wells (Fulton County) (Township)	16691
Wellsboro	16901
Wellsboro Junction	16901
Wells Creek	15541
Wells Tannery	16691
Wellsville	17365
Welsh Hill	18470
Welsh Run	17225
Welty	15666
Wendel	15691
Wendover	15601
Wenks	17304
Wentlings Corners	16232
Werleys Corner	18066
Wernersville	19565
Wernersville Heights	19565
Wernersville State Hospital	19565
Wertz	16693
Wertzville	17055
Wescosville	18106
Wesley	16038
Wesley Chapel	15909
Wesleyville	16510
Wessex Hills	15108
West (Township)	16669
West Abington (Township)	18419
West Acres	17837
West Alexander	15376
West Aliquippa (Part of Aliquippa)	15001
West Ambler	19002
West Annville	17003
West Auburn	18623
West Bangor (Northampton County)	18072
West Bangor (York County)	17314
West Beaver (Township)	17841
West Belt Junction (Part of Pittsburgh)	15230
West Bend	15433
West Berwick (Part of Berwick)	18603
West Bethlehem (Township)	15345
West Bingham	16923
West Bolivar	15923
West Bradford (Township)	19335
West Branch (Cambria County)	15714
West Branch (Potter County) (Township)	16922
West Brandywine (Township)	19320
West Bristol	19007
West Brownsville	15417
West Brunswick (Township)	17961
West Buffalo (Township)	17844
West Burlington	16947
West Burlington (Township)	16914
Westbury	15071
West Cain (Township)	19376
West Cameron	17872
West Cameron (Township)	17872
West Carroll (Township)	15737
West Catasauqua	18052
West Chester	19380-83
For specific West Chester Zip Codes call (610) 696-4808, or your local postmaster.	
West Chillisquaque (Township)	17850
West Clifford	18470
West Cocalico (Township)	17578
Westcolang	18428

	ZIP
West Conshohocken	19428
West Cornwall (Township)	17042
West Creek	15834
West Creek Hills	17011
West Cressona (Part of Cressona)	17929
West Damascus	18469
West Decatur	16878
West Deer (Township)	15044
West Derry	15627
West Donegal (Township)	17022
West Earl (Township)	17508
West Easton	18042
West Eldred	16731
West Elizabeth	15088
West Ellwood Junction (Part of Koppel)	16136
West End (Allegheny County)	15220
West End (Dauphin County)	17102
West End (Washington County)	15301
West Enola	17025
West Fairfield	15944
West Fairview	17025
Westfall (Township)	18336
West Fallowfield (Chester County) (Township)	19330
West Fallowfield (Crawford County) (Township)	16131
West Falls	18615
West Fayetteville	17222
Westfield	16950
Westfield (Township)	16950
Westfield Terrace	17070
West Finley	15377
West Finley (Township)	15377
Westford	16134
West Franklin (Armstrong County) (Township)	16262
West Franklin (Bradford County)	18832
West Freedom	16049
Westgate Hills	18017
West Goshen	19380
West Goshen (Township)	19380
West Goshen Hills	19380
West Goshen Park	19380
West Grove	19390
West Hamburg	19526
West Hanover (Township)	17112
West Hazleton	18201
West Hemlock (Township)	17821
West Hempfield (Township)	17601
West Hickory	16370
West Hill	17013
West Hills (Armstrong County)	16201
West Hills (Mifflin County)	17044
West Hills Estates	17701
West Homestead	15120
Westinghouse Village	19029
West Jeannette (Part of Jeannette)	15644
West Jonestown	17038
West Keating (Township)	16871
West Kittanning	16201
West Lampeter (Township)	17537
West Lancaster	17603
Westland	15378
West Lawn (Berks County)	19609
West Lawn (Union County)	17837
West Lebanon (Indiana County)	15783
West Lebanon (Lebanon County) (Township)	17046
West Lebanon (Lebanon County)	17046
West Leechburg	15656
West Leisenring	15489
West Lenox	18826
West Leroy	17724
West Liberty (Allegheny County)	15226
West Liberty (Butler County)	16057
West Liberty (Clearfield County)	15801
Westline	16751
West Mahanoy (Township)	17976
West Mahoning (Township)	16256
West Manayunk	19151

	ZIP
West Manchester (Township)	17404
West Manchester Mall (Part of York)	17404
West Manheim (Township)	17331
West Market (Part of Philadelphia)	19139
West Marlborough (Township)	19348
West Mayfield	15010
West Mead (Township)	16335
West Middlesex	16159
West Middletown	15379
West Mifflin	15122
West Milton	17886
Westminster (Erie County)	16506
Westminster (Luzerne County)	18702
West Monocacy	19518
Westmont (Cambria County)	15905
Westmont (Lebanon County)	17042
West Monterey	16049
Westmont Plan	16201
Westmoreland City	15692
West Moshannon	16651
West Myerstown	17067
West Nanticoke	18634
West Nantmeal (Township)	19520
West New Kensington	15030
West Newton	15089
West Nicholson	18446
West Norriton	19401
West Norriton (Township)	19401
West Nottingham (Township)	19362
Weston	18256
Weston Place	17976
Westover (Bucks County)	19067
Westover (Clearfield County)	16692
West Overton	15683
Westover Woods	19401
West Park (Allegheny County)	15136
West Park (Philadelphia County)	19131
West Pen Argyl	18072
West Penn (Township)	17960
West Pennsboro (Township)	17241
West Perry (Township)	17086
West Philadelphia (Part of Philadelphia)	19104
West Pike	16922
West Pikeland (Township)	19425
West Pike Run (Township)	15427
West Pittsburg	16160
West Pittston	18643
West Point (Cambria County)	15942
West Point (Montgomery County)	19486
West Point (Westmoreland County)	15601
Westport	17778
West Pottsgrove	19464
West Pottsgrove (Township)	19464
West Providence (Township)	15537
West Reading	19611
West Renovo	17764
West Ridge	17603
West Rockhill (Township)	18960
West Sadsbury (Township)	19365
West Salem (Township)	16125
West Salisbury	15565
West Scranton (Part of Scranton)	18504
West Shenango (Township)	16134
Westside (Part of Bethlehem)	18018
West Spring Creek	16407
West Springfield	16443
West St. Clair (Township)	15521
West Sunbury	16061
West Tarentum (Part of Tarentum)	15084
West Taylor (Township)	15906
West Telford (Part of Telford)	18969
Westtown	19395
Westtown (Township)	19395
Westtown Acres	19380

	ZIP
West Union	15364
West Valley	16201
West Vandergrift	15690
West View (Allegheny County)	15229
Westview (Beaver County)	15009
Westview Heights	16101
Westville	15824
West Vincent (Township)	19425
West Warren	13812
West Wayne	19087
West Waynesburg	15370
West Wheatfield (Township)	15944
West Whiteland (Township)	19341
West William Penn	17976
West Willow	17583
West Wilmerding	15137
West Winfield	16023
Westwood (Allegheny County)	15205
Westwood (Cambria County)	15905
Westwood (Chester County)	19320
Westwood Park	19083
West Wyoming	18644
West Wyomissing	19609
West York	17404
West Zollarsville	15345
Wetherills Corner	19460
Wetmore	16735
Wetmore (Township)	16735
Wetona	16914
Wexford	15090
Weyant	16655
Wharton (Fayette County) (Township)	15437
Wharton (Potter County)	16720
Wharton (Potter County) (Township)	16720
Wheatfield (Township)	17020
Wheatland	16161
Wheatland Hills	17604
Wheat Sheaf	19067
Wheeler	15425
Wheelerville	17724
Whig Hill	16353
Whiskerville	16040
Whitaker	15120
White (Beaver County) (Township)	15010
White (Cambria County) (Township)	16639
White (Fayette County)	15490
White (Indiana County)	15681
White (Indiana County) (Township)	15701
White Bear	19508
White Cottage	15341
White Deer	17887
White Deer (Township)	17887
Whitehall (Adams County)	17340
Whitehall (Allegheny County)	15227
White Hall (Dauphin County)	17110
Whitehall (Lehigh County)	18052
Whitehall (Lehigh County) (Township)	18052
White Hall (Montour County)	17821
Whitehall Mall	18052
Whitehall Park	19401
White Haven	18661
White Hill	17011
White Horse (Chester County)	19073
White Horse (Lancaster County)	17527
White House	15478
Whiteland Crest	19341
Whiteland Farms	19355
Whiteley (Township)	15370
Whitemarsh (Township)	19428
Whitemarsh Downs	19075
White Mills	18473
White Oak (Allegheny County)	15131
White Oak (Lancaster County)	17545
White Oak (Westmoreland County)	15068
White Oak Manor	18040
White Oaks	18701
White Pine	17771
Whitesburg	16201
Whites Corner	16927
Whites Crossing	18407

	ZIP
Whites Ferry	18657
Whiteside	16651
Whitesprings	17844
White Squaw Mission	17353
Whitestown	16052
Whites Valley	18453
White Valley (Part of Murrysville)	15632
Whitewood	19057
Whitfield	19609
Whitford Hills	19341
Whitney	15693
Whitney Lake	18428
Whitneyville	16901
Whitpain (Township)	19422
Whitsett	15473
Wick	16057
Wickerham Manor	15063
Wickerham Manor-Fisher	15063
Wickerton	19390
Wickham Village	15001
Wickhaven	15492
Wiconisco	17097
Wiconisco (Township)	17097
Widener College (Part of Chester)	19013
Widnoon	16261
Wiegletown	16101
Wiggans	17948
Wigwam	16731
Wila	17074
Wilawana	18840
Wilber	15563
Wilburton	17888
Wilco Hill	15087
Wilcox	15870
Wild Acres Country Club	18328
Wildcat	16248
Wilden Acres	18045
Wildwood	15091
Wildwood Terrace	18701
Wiley	17363
Wilgus	15742
Wilkes-Barre	18701-06
	18708
	18710-73
For specific Wilkes-Barre Zip Codes call (717) 829-5468, or your local postmaster.	
Wilkes-Barre (Township)	18702
Wilkes Manor	18977
Wilkins (Township)	15145
Wilkinsburg	15221
Wilkins Township	15145
Willet	15732
William Penn Annex	19107
William Penn Manor	18017
Williams (Dauphin County) (Township)	17098
Williams (Northampton County) (Township)	18042
Williamsburg (Blair County)	16693
Williamsburg (Clarion County)	16214
Williams Grove	17055
Williamson	17270
Williamsport	17701*
	17703†
Williamstown (Dauphin County)	17098
Williamstown (Washington County)	15322
Willistown (Township)	19355
Willopenn	18966
Willowbrook	19061
Willowburn	19085
Willowdale	19348
Willow Grove (Lawrence County)	16101
Willow Grove (Montgomery County)	19090
Willow Grove Naval Air Station	19090
Willow Grove Park	19090
Willow Hill	17271
Willow Lake	17901
Will-O-Wood	19007
Willow Springs (Columbia County)	17815
Willow Springs (Westmoreland County)	15642
Willow Street	17584
Willow View Heights	17584
Wills Creek	15545
Wilmer	19460
Wilmerding	15148
Wilmington (Lawrence County) (Township)	16105

*** Area Zip Code** **† Post Office Boxes**

	ZIP
Wilmington (Mercer County) (Township) ...	16142
Wilmore	15962
Wilmore Heights	15958
Wilmot (Township)	18846
Wilpen	15658
Wilshire Hills (Lancaster County)	17603
Wilshire Hills (York County)	17402
Wilson (Allegheny County)	15025
Wilson (Berks County) ...	19608
Wilson (Northampton County)	18042
Wilson Creek	15557
Wilson Heights	18426
Wilsons Corners	19460
Wimmers	18436
Winburne	16879
Windber	15963
Winder Village	19007
Windfall	17724
Windgap	18091
Windham (Bradford County) (Township) ...	18837
Windham (Wyoming County) (Township)	18623
Windham Center	18837
Winding Brook Manor	18062
Winding Hill	17055
Winding Hill Heights	17055
Windom	17603
Wind Ridge	15380
Windsor (Berks County) (Township)	19526
Windsor (York County)...	17366
Windsor (York County) (Township)	17356
Windsor Castle	19526
Windsor Farms	17110
Windsor Park (Cumberland County)	17055
Windsor Park (York County)	17403
Windward Heights	16001
Winfield (Butler County) (Township)	16023
Winfield (Union County)	17889
Wingate	16823
Wingerton	17268
Winslow	15767
Winslow (Township)	15851
Winstead	15474
Winterburne	15849
Winterdale	18461
Winterstown	17356
Wintersville	17087
Wireton	15001
Wiscasset	18344
Wishaw	15851
Wismer	18947
Wissahickon Village	19444
Wissingertown	15902
Wissinoming (Part of Philadelphia)	19135
Witinski Villa	18706
Witmer	17585
Wittenberg	15552
Wittmer	15116
Wolf (Township)	17737

	ZIP
Wolf Creek (Township)	16127
Wolfdale	15301
Wolfe Store	16872
Wolf Run	16749
Wolfsburg	15522
Wolfs Corners	16353
Wolfs Crossroads	17801
Womelsdorf	19567
Wood	16694
Wood (Township)	16674
Woodale	18301
Woodbine	17302
Woodbourne	19047
Woodbridgetown	15478
Woodbury (Bedford County)	16695
Woodbury (Bedford County) (Township)	16695
Woodbury (Blair County) (Township)	16693
Woodchoppertown	19512
Woodcock	16433
Woodcock (Township)	16433
Woodcock Grange	16433
Woodcrest	19380
Wooddale	15425
Woodglen	15442
Woodhaven Estates	15001
Woodhill	18940
Woodland (Clearfield County)	16881
Woodland (Mifflin County)	17084
Woodland Heights	16301
Woodland Park	17701
Woodland View	17402
Woodlawn (Lancaster County)	17603
Woodlawn (Lehigh County)	18104
Woodlawn Park	15001
Woodlyn	19094
Woodlyn Park	19094
Woodrow	15340
Woodruff	15341
Woodside (Bucks County)	19067
Woodside (Fayette County)	15478
Woodside (Luzerne County)	18224
Woodside-Drifton	18221
Woods of Sandy Ridge	18901
Woodvale (Part of Johnstown)	15901
Woodvale Heights	15909
Woodville (Allegheny County)	15106
Woodville (Chester County)	19318
Woodville State Hospital	15106
Woodward (Centre County)	16882
Woodward (Clearfield County) (Township) ...	16651
Woodward (Clinton County) (Township) ...	17745
Woodward (Lycoming County) (Township) ...	17744
Woodward Acres	15601
Woodycrest	16803

	ZIP
Woolrich	17779
Wopsononock	16636
Worcester	19490
Worcester (Township) ...	19490
Worden Place (Part of Harveys Lake)	18618
Worleytown	17225
Worman	19518
Wormleysburg	17043
Worth (Butler County) (Township)	16057
Worth (Centre County) (Township)	16870
Worth (Mercer County) (Township)	16133
Worthington	16262
Worthville	15784
Woxall	18979
Wright (Township)	18707
Wrights	16743
Wrights Corners	16749
Wrightsdale	17563
Wrightstown	18940
Wrightstown (Township)	18980
Wrightsville (Warren County)	16340
Wrightsville (York County)	17368
Wurtemburg	16117
Wurtemburg Heights	16117
Wyalusing	18853
Wyalusing (Township) ...	18853
Wyano	15695
Wyattville (Part of Sugarcreek)	16323
Wycombe	18980
Wydnor	18015
Wyebrooke	19344
Wylandville	15330
Wylie	15037
Wylie (Part of Pittsburgh)	15219
Wyncote	19095
Wyncote Hills	19095
Wyncroft	19063
Wyndham Hills	17403
Wyndmoor	19118
Wyndmoor Valley	19075
Wynnewood (Bucks County)	19067
Wynnewood (Montgomery County)	19096
Wynnewood Shopping Center	19096
Wyoming	18644
Wyoming Camp Ground	18643
Wyoming Valley Mall (Part of Wilkes-Barre)	18702
Wyomissing	19610
Wyomissing Hills	19609
Wyomissing Junction (Part of Wyomissing)	19610
Wysox	18854
Wysox (Township)	18854
Yardley	19067
Yardley Farms	19067
Yardley Hunt	19067
Yarnell	16823
Yatesboro	16263
Yatesville (Luzerne County)	18640

	ZIP
Yatesville (Schuylkill County)	17976
Yeadon	19050
Yeagertown	17099
Yellow Creek	16650
Yellow Hammer	16353
Yellow House	19518
Yellowwood	19007
Yerkes	19426
Yocumtown	17319
Yoe	17313
York	17401-07
For specific York Zip Codes call (717) 848-2381, or your local postmaster.	
York (Township)	17403
Yorkana	17402
York County	17402
York Haven	17370
Yorklyn	17402
York Mall	17402
York New Salem	17371
York Road (Bucks County)	18974
York Road (York County)	17331
York Run	15401
Yorkshire	17402
York Springs	17372
Yostville	18444
Young (Indiana County) (Township)	15725
Young (Jefferson County) (Township)	15767
Youngdale	17748
Youngsburg	19320
Youngstown (Fayette County)	15456
Youngstown (Luzerne County)	18221
Youngstown (Westmoreland County)	15696
Youngsville (Northampton County)	18038
Youngsville (Warren County)	16371
Youngwood	15697
Yount	15522
Yukon	15698
Zebleys Corner	19061
Zehners	17960
Zelienople	16063
Zerbe (Northumberland County) (Township) ...	17881
Zerbe (Schuylkill County)	17981
Zieglerville	19492
Zimmerman	15501
Zion	16823
Zion Grove	17985
Zionhill	18981
Zions View	17404
Zionsville	18092
Zollarsville	15345
Zooks Corner	17602
Zooks Dam	17059
Zora	17320
Zucksville	18040
Zullinger	17272

	ZIP		ZIP		ZIP		ZIP
Abbott Run Valley	02864	Coasters Harbor (Part of		Greystone	02911	Nausauket (Part of	
Adamsville	02801	Newport)	02840	Hamilton	02852	Warwick)	02886
Albion	02802	Coggeshall	02885	Hampden Meadows	02806	Naval Construction	
Allendale	02911	Coles (Part of Warwick)	02889	Harmony	02829	Battalion Center	02854
Allenton	02852	Columbia Heights	02875	Harris	02816	Nayatt	02806
Alton	02894	Common Fence Point	02871	Harrisville	02830	New Harbor	02807
Annawomscutt	02806	Commons	02837	Haversham	02891	Newport	02840
Annex (Part of		Comstock Gardens (Part		Highland Beach (Part of		Newport East	02840
Providence)	02903	of Cranston)	02910	Warwick)	02889	New Shoreham (Town)	02807
Anthony	02816	Conanicut Park	02835	Hill's Grove (Part of		Nichols Corner	02818
Apple Blossom (Part of		Conimicut (Part of		Warwick)	02886	Nooseneck	02816
Cranston)	02920	Warwick)	02889	Hog Island	02809	North (Part of Providence)	02908
Arcadia	02832	Corey's Lane	02871	Homestead	02872	North Foster	02825
Arctic	02893	Coventry	02816	Hope	02831	North Kingstown	02852*
Arkwright	02816	Coventry (Town)	02816	Hope Valley	02832		02854†
Arlington (Part of		Coventry Center	02816	Hopkins Hollow	02827	North Providence	02911
Cranston)	02920	Cowesett (Part of		Hopkinton	02833	North Providence (Town)	02911
Arnold Mills	02864	Warwick)	02886	Hopkinton (Town)	02833	North Quidnessett	02852
Arnold's Neck (Part of		Cranston	02920-21	Howard (Part of Cranston)	02920	North Scituate	02857
Warwick)	02886		02910	Hoxsie (Part of Warwick)	02889	North Smithfield (Town)	02896
Ashaway	02804	For specific Cranston Zip		Hughesdale	02919	Norwood (Part of	
Ashton	02864	Codes call (401) 781-0249, or		Indian Lake Shores	02879	Warwick)	02888
Auburn (Part of Cranston)	02910	your local postmaster.		India Point (Part of		Oakland	02830
Austin	02822	Crescent Park (Part of		Providence)	02903	Oakland Beach (Part of	
Avondale	02891	East Providence)	02914	Island Park	02871	Warwick)	02886
Barberville	02832	Crompton	02893	Jackson	02823	Oak Lawn (Part of	
Barrington	02806	Cross Mills	02813	Jamestown	02835	Cranston)	02920
Barrington (Town)	02806	Cumberland	02864	Jamestown (Town)	02835	Old Harbor	02807
Bayridge (Part of		Cumberland (Town)	02864	Jamestown Center	02835	Olney Arnold Estates (Part	
Warwick)	02818	Cumberland Hill	02864	Jamestown Shores	02835	of Cranston)	02920
Bayside (Part of Warwick)	02889	Curtis Corners	02883	Jerusalem	02879	Olneyville (Part of	
Bay Spring	02806	Darlington (Part of		Johnston (Town)	02919	Providence)	02909
Bay View (Part of East		Pawtucket)	02861	Johnston	02919	Palace Garden (Part of	
Providence)	02914	Davisville	02852	Kent Corner (Part of East		Warwick)	02888
Beach Terrace	02809	Davisville (Part of North		Providence)	02914	Parcel Post Annex	02891
Bellefonte (Part of		Kingston)	02854	Kent Heights (Part of East		Pascoag	02859
Cranston)	02920	Diamond Hill	02864	Providence)	02914	Pawtucket	02860-62
Belleville	02852	Dunns Corners	02891	Kenyon	02836	For specific Pawtucket Zip	
Berkeley	02864	Durfee Hill	02814	Kingston	02881	Codes call (401) 729-7800, or	
Beverage Hill (Part of		Eagleville	02878	Knightsville (Part of		your local postmaster.	
Pawtucket)	02860	East Greenwich	02818	Cranston)	02920	Peace Dale	02883
Bishops Heights	02857	East Greenwich (Town)	02818	La Fayette	02852	Perryville	02879
Black Plain	02822	East Matunuck	02879	Lake Bel Air	02896	Pettaquamscutt Lake	
Block Island	02807	East Natick (Part of		Lake Mishnock	02817	Shores	02874
Bonnet Shores	02882	Warwick)	02893	Lakewood (Part of		Phenix	02893
Boon Lake	02822	East Providence	02914	Warwick)	02888	Phillipsdale (Part of East	
Bowdish Lake	02814	East Providence Wharf		Langworthy Corner	02891	Providence)	02914
Bradford	02808	(Part of East		Laurel Hill	02859	Pilgrim (Part of Warwick)	02888
Branch Village	02896	Providence)	02914	Laurel Park	02885	Pine Hill	02822
Brenton Village (Part of		East Side (Part of		Leonard Corner (Part of		Pleasant View (Part of	
Newport)	02840	Providence)	02906	East Providence)	02914	Pawtucket)	02860
Bridgeport	02878	East Warren	02885	Liberty	02877	Plum Beach	02874
Bridgetown	02874	Echo Lake	02814	Limerock	02865	Plum Point	02874
Briggs Beach	02837	Eden Park (Part of		Lincoln	02865	Poccasett Heights	02871
Bristol	02809	Cranston)	02920	Lincoln (Town)	02860	Point Judith	02882
Bristol (Town)	02809	Edgewood (Part of		Lincoln Park (Part of		Pontiac (Part of Warwick)	02886
Bristol Colony	02872	Cranston)	02905	Warwick)	02888	Popasquash Point	02809
Bristol Ferry	02871	Elmwood (Part of		Lippit	02893	Portsmouth	02871
Bristol Highlands	02809	Providence)	02907	Lippitt Estate	02864	Portsmouth (Town)	02871
Bristol Narrows	02809	Enos (Part of Cranston)	02920	Little Compton	02837	Potowomut (Part of	
Broadway (Part of		Escoheag	02822	Little Compton (Town)	02837	Warwick)	02818
Newport)	02840	Esmond	02917	Lockwood Corner (Part of		Potter Hill	02891
Brookfield (Part of		Exeter	02822	Warwick)	02889	Primrose	02896
Cranston)	02920	Exeter (Town)	02822	Longmeadow (Part of		Print Works (Part of	
Brush Neck Cove (Part of		Fairbanks Corner	02827	Warwick)	02889	Cranston)	02920
Warwick)	02886	Finast (Part of East		Lonsdale	02865	Providence	02901-09
Bryant College	02917	Providence)	02914	Lonsdale (Part of Valley			02940
Bullocks Point (Part of		Fiskeville (Part of		Falls)	02864	For specific Providence Zip	
East Providence)	02914	Cranston)	02823	Lymansville	02911	Codes call (401) 276-6850, or	
Burdickville	02808	Fogland Point	02878	Manton (Part of		your local postmaster.	
Burrillville (Town)	02830	Forestdale	02824	Providence)	02909	Prudence Island	02872
Buttonwoods (Part of		Fort Adams (Part of		Manville	02838	Prudence Park	02872
Warwick)	02886	Newport)	02840	Maple Root Village	02816	Quidnessett	02852
Canonchet	02832	Foster	02825	Mapleville	02839	Quidnick	02816
Carnegie Heights	02865	Foster (Town)	02825	Marieville	02904	Quinnville	02865
Carolina	02812	Fox Point (Part of		Matunuck	02879	Quonochontaug	02813
Carpenters Beach	02879	Providence)	02906	Melville	02871	Rhode Island Mall (Part of	
Cedar Grove Estates	02822	Frenchtown	02818	Melville	02871	Warwick)	02886
Cedar Point	02835	Fruit Hill	02911	Meshanticut (Part of		Rice City	02827
Cedar Tree Point (Part of		Galilee	02882	Cranston)	02920	Rice Plat	02857
Warwick)	02886	Garden City (Part of		Middletown (Town)	02842	Richmond (Town)	02812
Centerville (Kent County)	02893	Cranston)	02920	Middletown	02842	River Point	02893
Centerville (Washington		Garden City Center (Part		Misquamicut	02891	Riverside (Part of East	
County)	02832	of Cranston)	02920	Mohegan	02830	Providence)	02915
Central Falls	02863	Gazzaville	02839	Mohegan Bluffs	02807	River Vue (Part of	
Centredale	02911	Geneva	02911	Mooresfield	02874	Warwick)	02889
Charlestown	02813	Georgiaville	02917	Moosup Valley	02827	Rockville	02873
Charlestown (Town)	02813	Glendale	02826	Moscow	02832	Rocky Point (Part of	
Charlestown Beach	02813	Glocester (Town)	02814	Mount Pleasant (Part of		Warwick)	02889
Chepachet	02814	Goat Island (Part of		Providence)	02908	Rumford (Part of East	
Chepiwanoxet (Part of		Newport)	02840	Mount Vernon	02825	Providence)	02916
Warwick)	02886	Goulds	02883	Mount View	02852	Rumstick Point	02806
Cherry Valley	02814	Graniteville	02911	Nannaquaket	02878	Sakonnet	02837
Cherry Valley Beach	02814	Grants Mills	02838	Narragansett	02882	Sandy Point (Kent	
Chopmist	02857	Greene	02827	Narragansett (Town)	02882	County)	02818
Clarke's Village	02835	Green Hill	02879	Narragansett Heights	02878	Sandy Point (Newport	
Clayville	02815	Greenville	02828	Nasonville	02830	County)	02872
Clyde	02893	Greenwood (Part of		Natick (Part of Warwick)	02893	Sandy Point (Washington	
		Warwick)	02886			County)	02807

	ZIP
Saunderstown	02874
Saundersville	02857
Saylesville	02865
Scituate (Town)	02857
Shady Harbor	02891
Shannock	02875
Shawomet (Part of Warwick)	02889
Shelter Harbor	02891
Shores Acres	02852
Silver Lake (Part of Providence)	02909
Simmonsville	02919
Slatersville	02876
Slocum	02877
Smithfield (Town)	02917
Smith Hill (Part of Providence)	02908
Sockannosset (Part of Cranston)	02920
South Foster	02825
South Hopkinton	02813
South Kingstown (Town)	02879
South Providence (Part of Providence)	02905
South Warren	02885
Spragueville	02828

	ZIP
Spring Green (Part of Warwick)	02888
Spring Grove	02814
Spring Lake Beach	02826
Squantum (Part of East Providence)	02914
Stillwater	02917
Summit	02827
Tarkiln	02830
The Anchorage	02842
The Hummocks	02871
Thornton	02919
Tiverton	02878
Tiverton (Town)	02878
Tiverton Four Corners	02878
Tockwotten (Part of Providence)	02903
Tonomy Hill (Part of Newport)	02840
Touisset Highlands	02885
Tuckertown	02879
Tunipus	02837
Union Village	02896
Usquepaug	02892
Valley Falls	02864
Vaughn Hollow	02827
Wakefield	02879*

	ZIP
	02880†
Wakefield-Peacedale	02883
Walnut Hill (Part of Woonsocket)	02895
Warren	02885
Warren (Town)	02885
Warren Point	02837
Warwick	02886-89
For specific Warwick Zip Codes call (401) 737-6200, or your local postmaster.	
Warwick Mall (Part of Warwick)	02886
Warwick Neck (Part of Warwick)	02889
Washington Park (Part of Cranston)	02905
Watch Hill	02891
Watchmocket Square (Part of East Providence)	02914
Waterford	01504
Waterman Four Corners	02857
Weekapaug	02891
West Barrington	02806
Westcott (Part of Warwick)	02893

	ZIP
Westcott Beach	02814
Westerly	02891
Westerly (Town)	02891
West Glocester	06260
West Greenville	02828
West Greenwich (Town)	02817
West Greenwich Center	02827
West Kingston	02892
West Warwick	02893
West Warwick (Town)	02893
Weybosset Hill (Part of Providence)	02903
Whipple	02830
White Rock	02891
Wickford Junction	02852
Wildes Corner (Part of Warwick)	02886
Wood Estates	02816
Wood River Junction	02894
Woodville (Providence County)	02911
Woodville (Washington County)	02832
Woonsocket	02895
Wyoming	02898
Yorktown Manor	02852

* Area Zip Code   **† Post Office Boxes**

	ZIP
Abbeville	29620
Abney	29067
Academy Acres	29488
Adamsburg	29379
Adams Run	29426
Adamsville	29570
Adger	29180
Adrian	29526
Aiken	29801-04
For specific Aiken Zip Codes	
call (803) 648-2351, or your	
local postmaster.	
Aiken Estates	29803
Aiken West	29801
Alcolu	29001
Alcot	29010
Allen	29511
Allendale	29810
Allendale Correctional	
Institute	29827
Allsbrook	29569
Alvin	29479
Anderson	29621-25
For specific Anderson Zip	
Codes call (803) 226-1595, or	
your local postmaster.	
Anderson Mall (Part of	
Anderson)	29621
Andrews	29510
Angelus	29718
Angle Siding	29902
Anne Village	29440
Ansel	29651
Antioch (Kershaw County)	29020
Antioch (Lancaster	
County)	29720
Antreville	29655
Appleton	29810
Appleton Mills	29625
Aragon Mills (Part of Rock	
Hill)	29730
Arcadia	29320
Arcadia Lakes	29206
Arial	29640
Ariel Crossroads	29574
Arkwright	29301
Arlington	29651
Armenia	29706
Arthurtown	29201
Asbury	29340
Ashepoo	29446
Ashland	29010
Ashleigh	29817
Ashley Forest	29407
Ashley Hall (Part of	
Charleston)	29401
Ashley Heights	29405
Ashley Junction (Part of	
North Charleston)	29406
Ashton	29082
Ashwood	29010
Aspen Heights	29646
Atkins	29080
Atlantic Beach	29582
Auburn	29550
Augusta Road (Part of	
Greenville)	29604
Avondale	29407
Awendaw	29429
Aynor	29511
Badham	29471
Baileys Landing	29936
Baker Crossroads	29569
Bald Rock	29379
Baldwin	29706
Ballentine	29002
Balltown	29801
Bamberg	29003
Barkersville	29916
Barksdale	29360
Barnes	29655
Barnwell	29812
Barrineau	29560
Bartell Crossroads	29554
Barton	29827
Bascomville	29729
Batesburg	29006
Bath	29816
Baton Rouge	29706
Baxter Forks	29569
Bayboro	29569
Bay Shores	29665
Bay Springs	29584
Bay View	29204
Beaufort	29901-05
For specific Beaufort Zip Codes	
call (803) 524-4746, or your	
local postmaster.	
Beaufort Marine Corps Air	
Station	29904

	ZIP
Beckhamville	29055
Beech Island	29842
Bel-Clear Heights	29841
Beldoc	29836
Belle Isle Gardens	29440
Belle Meade (Greenville	
County)	29603
Belle Meade (Lexington	
County)	29172
Bellinger	29927
Bells	29475
Belmont	29203
Belton	29627
Belvedere (Aiken County)	29841
Belvedere (Richland	
County)	29204
Ben Avon	29302
Bendale (Part of	
Columbia)	29203
Beneventum	29440
Bennett	29405
Bennettsville	29512
Bent Tree	29678
Berea	29611
Berlin	29137
Bethany	29710
Bethera	29430
Bethesda	29584
Bethune	29009
Beufordtown	29453
Beverly Hills	29445
Beverly Woods	29301
Bingham	29565
Birdtown Crossroads	29550
Bishopville	29010
Blackjack	29180
Blacks	29166
Blacksburg	29702
Blackstock	29014
Blackville	29817
Blair	29015
Blakedale	29649
Blenheim	29516
Bloomingvale	29510
Bloomville	29102
Blossom	29583
Blue Heaven	29638
Blue Ridge Community	
Pre-Release Center	29609
Blue Town	29512
Bluff	29142
Bluff Estates	29209
Bluffton	29910
Blythewood	29016
Bob Jones University	
(Part of Greenville)	29614
Bob Marina	29163
Boiling Springs	29316
Bolentown	29115
Bon Aire	29902
Bon Air Terrace	29150
Bonham	29379
Bonneau	29431
Bonneau Beach	29431
Bonniview Estates	29803
Boones Creek	29676
Bordeaux	29835
Borden	29017
Boulder Bluff	29445
Bounty Land	29672
Bowling Green	29703
Bowman	29018
Bowyer	29059
Boyden Arbor	29206
Boykin (Kershaw County)	29128
Boykin (Marlboro County)	28343
Bradley	29819
Bradleyville	29841
Branchville	29432
Brand	29360
Brandon	29611
Branwood (Part of	
Greenville)	29610
Brasstown	29658
Brattonsville	29726
Brazen Crossroads	29583
Breeze Hill (Part of	
Burnettown)	29834
Breezewood	29819
Brentwood	29405
Brewerton	29692
Briarcliffe Acres	29572
Briarcreek	29340
Brighton	29922
Brighton Beach	29910
Brightsville	28343
Bristow	29516
Britton	29153
Brittons Neck	29546

	ZIP
Broad Street (Part of	
Sumter)	29150
Broadway Lake	29621
Brock	29691
Brock Circle	29654
Brockington	29556
Brogdon	29150
Brookdale	29115
Brook Forest	29605
Brook Green Park	29501
Brookhaven Estates	29801
Brooklyn	29720
Brooksville	29582
Brownsville (Dorchester	
County)	29483
Brownsville (Marlboro	
County)	29516
Brownway	29526
Bruner	29061
Brunson	29911
Brunsons Crossroads	29554
Bryans Crossroads	29590
Buckeye Forest	29377
Buck Hall	29429
Buckingham Landing	29928
Bucksport	29526
Bucksville	29526
Buffalo (McCormick	
County)	29835
Buffalo (Union County)	29321
Buford	29720
Buford Crossroads	29720
Bufords Bridge	29843
Bullock Creek	29742
Bunker Hill	29536
Burgess	29576
Burnettown	29834
Burnt Church Crossroads	29474
Burton	29902
Bynum	29556
Byrd	29477
Byrds Crossroads	28114
Cades	29518
Caesars Head	28718
Caldwell Street (Part of	
Rock Hill)	29731
Calhoun (Part of	
Clemson)	29631
Calhoun Falls	29628
Callison	29819
Camden	29020
Cameron	29030
Campbell Work Release	
Center	29210
Camp Creek	29720
Camp Croft	29302
Campobello	29322
Campton	29349
Canaan (Orangeburg	
County)	29038
Canaan (Spartanburg	
County)	29302
Canadys	29433
Cane Savannah	29154
Canterbury	29673
Capitol (Part of Columbia)	29211
Capitol View	29209
Carlisle	29031
Carmel	29058
Carolina Circle	29488
Caromi Village	29456
Carters Crossroads	29554
Cartersville	29161
Carver Heights	29204
Carvers Bay	29554
Cash	29520
Cashville	29388
Cassatt	29032
Catarrah	29718
Catawba	29704
Cateechee	29667
Catholic Hill	29488
Cave	29810
Cayce	29033
Cedar Grove	29526
Cedar Hill	29835
Cedar Springs	29455
Cedar Terrace	29209
Celriver	29732
Cementon	29059
Centenary	29519
Center Crossroads	29554
Centerville (Anderson	
County)	29621
Centerville (Dillon County)	29565
Central	29630
Central Pacolet	29372
Challedon	29210
Chaparral Ranches	29461
Chapin	29036

	ZIP
Chappells	29037
Charleston	29401-25
For specific Charleston Zip	
Codes call (803) 760-5300, or	
your local postmaster.	
Charleston Heights (Part	
of North Charleston)	29405
Charleston Southern	
University	29411
Charles Towne Square	
(Part of North	
Charleston)	29406
Chartwell	29210
Cheddar	29627
Cheraw	29520
Cherokee	29302
Cherokee Falls	29702
Cherokee Forest	29687
Cherokee Gardens	29672
Cherry Grove Beach (Part	
of North Myrtle Beach)	29582
Cherry Hill Estates	29902
Cherry Road (Part of	
Rock Hill)	29732
Cherryvale	29154
Chesnee	29323
Chester	29706
Chesterfield	29709
Chestnut Hills	29605
Chickasaw Point	29693
Chicora Place (Part of	
North Charleston)	29405
Choppee	29440
Citadel (Part of	
Charleston)	29409
Citadel Mall (Part of	
Charleston)	29407
City View	29611
Claremont	29150
Clarks Hill	29821
Claussen	29505
Clayton	29015
Clearmont	29693
Clear Pond	29003
Clearspring	29681
Clearwater	29822
Cleburne	29440
Clemson	29631-34
For specific Clemson Zip Codes	
call (803) 654-2531, or your	
local postmaster.	
Clemson University	29631
Cleora	29824
Cleveland	29635
Clifton	29324
Clinton	29325
Clio	29525
Clover	29710
Clubhouse Crossroads	
(Dorchester County)	29472
Club House Crossroads	
(Lexington County)	29054
Clyde	29101
Coastal (Part of North	
Myrtle Beach)	29582
Coastal Work Release	
Center	29405
Cochrantown	29526
Cokesbury	29653
Cold Point	29360
Coldstream	29210
College Acres	29803
Colliers	29838
Colonial Heights	29902
Colonial Village	29715
Columbia	29201-92
For specific Columbia Zip	
Codes call (803) 926-6000, or	
your local postmaster.	
Columbia Bible College	
and Seminary	29203
Columbia Mall	29204
Coneross	29693
Conestee	29636
Congaree	29044
Connecticut Park	29341
Converse	29329
Conway	29526-27
For specific Conway Zip Codes	
call (803) 248-6313, or your	
local postmaster.	
Cooks Crossroads	29644
Cool Branch	29031
Cooley Springs	29323
Cool Spring	29511
Coosaw	29940
Coosawhatchie	29912
Cope	29038
Cordesville	29434
Cordova	29039

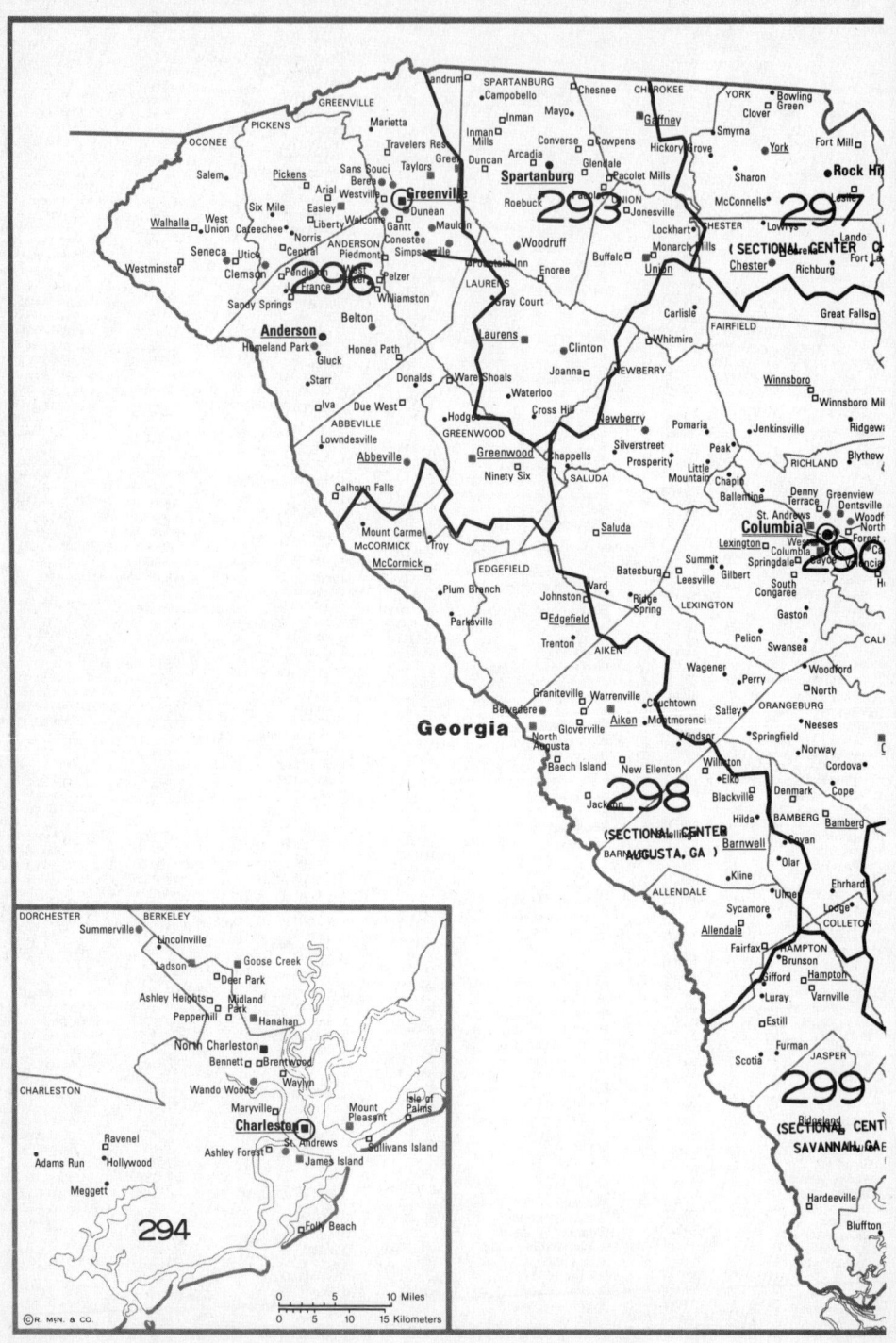

Landrum · SPARTANBURG · Chesnee · CHEROKEE · YORK · Bowling Green · Clover
GREENVILLE · Campobello · Mayo · Gaffney · Smyrna · York · Fort Mill
Marietta · Inman Mills · Inman · Cowpens · Hickory Grove · Sharon · Rock Hill
OCONEE · PICKENS · Travelers Rest · Greer · Duncan · Glenlake · Pacolet Mills · McConnells
Salem · Pickens · Sans Souci · Taylors · Spartanburg · 293 · York
West Union · Arial · Berea · Greenville · Roebuck · UNION · Jonesville · Lockhart · Monarch Mills · Chester · 297
Walhalla · Six Mile · Easley · Westville · Welcome · Dunean · Mauldin · Conestee · Woodruff · Enoree · Buffalo · Union · SECTIONAL CENTER
Seneca · Utica · Central · ANDERSON · Piedmont · Simpsonville · LAURENS · Carlisle · Chester · Richburg
Westminster · Clemson · Pelzer · Williamston · Gray Court · Laurens · Whitmire · FAIRFIELD · Great Falls
Sandy Springs · 96 · France · Belton · Clinton · NEWBERRY · Winnsboro · Winnsboro
Anderson · Homeland Park · Honea Path · Donalds · Ware Shoals · Joanna · Pomaria · Jenkinsville · Ridgeway
Gluck · Starr · Iva · Due West · ABBEVILLE · Hodges · Cross Hill · Newberry · Silverstreet · Prosperity · Peak · RICHLAND · Blythewood
Lowndesville · GREENWOOD · Ninety Six · SALUDA · Little Mountain · Chapin · Ballentine · Denny Terrace · Greenview · Dentsville
Abbeville · Greenwood · Chappells · Saluda · St. Andrews · Columbia · North Forest
Calhoun Falls · Mount Carmel · Troy · Batesburg · Summit · Lexington · West Columbia · Cayce · Gilbert · Springdale · South Congaree · Gaston
McCormick · Ward · Ridge Spring · LEXINGTON · Pelion · Swansea
Plum Branch · Johnston · AIKEN · Wagener · Perry · Woodford
Parksville · Trenton · EDGEFIELD · North · ORANGEBURG · Neeses
Graniteville · Warrenville · Couchtown · Salley · Springfield · Norway · Cordova
Belvedere · Gloverville · Aiken · Montmorenci · Windsor · Willston · Elko · Denmark · Cope
Georgia · North Augusta · Beech Island · New Ellenton · Jackson · 298 · Blackville · Hilda · BAMBERG · Govan · Bamberg
SECTIONAL CENTER AUGUSTA, GA · BARNWELL · Barnwell · Olar · Ehrhard
Kline · Ulme · Lodge · COLLETON
ALLENDALE · Sycamore · Allendale · HAMPTON · Fairfax · Brunson · Hampton
Luray · Varnville · Estill · JASPER · 299
Furman · Scotia · SECTIONAL CENTER SAVANNAH, GA
Ridgeland · Hardeeville · Bluffton

DORCHESTER · BERKELEY
Summerville · Lincolnville
Ladson · Goose Creek
Ashley Heights · Deer Park · Midland Park
Pepperhill · Hanahan
North Charleston · Bennett · Brentwood
CHARLESTON · Wando Woods · Waylyn
Maryville · Mount Pleasant · Isle of Palms
Ravenel · Charleston · St. Andrews · Sullivans Island
Adams Run · Hollywood · Ashley Forest · James Island
Meggett · 294 · Folly Beach

0 · 5 · 10 Miles
0 · 5 · 10 · 15 Kilometers

© R. MCN. & CO.

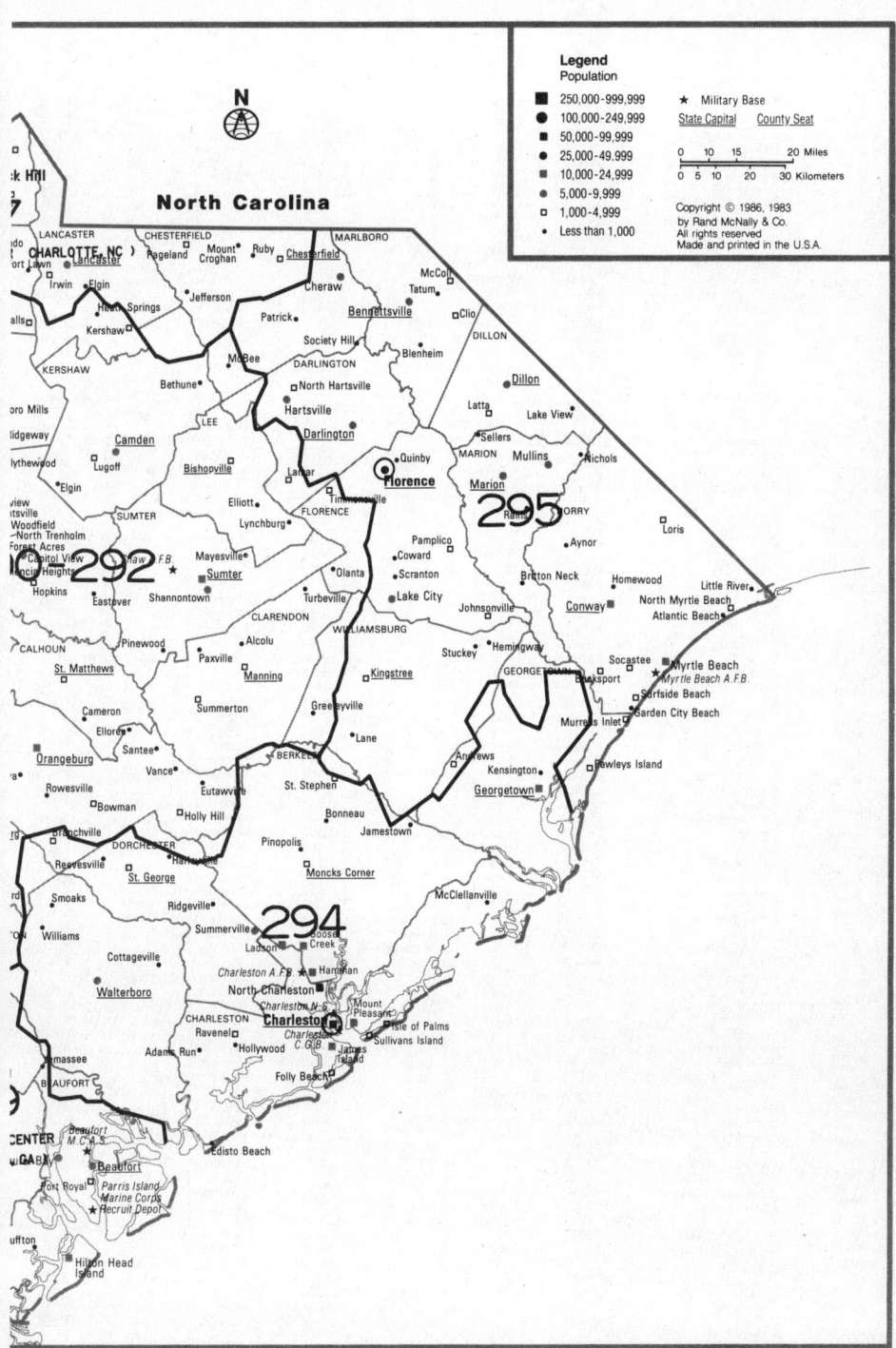

Legend

Population

■ 250,000-999,999
● 100,000-249,999
■ 50,000-99,999
● 25,000-49,999
■ 10,000-24,999
● 5,000-9,999
□ 1,000-4,999
• Less than 1,000

★ Military Base

State Capital   County Seat

0   10   15   20 Miles
0 5 10   20   30 Kilometers

North Carolina

LANCASTER   CHESTERFIELD   MARLBORO
CHARLOTTE, NC   Pageland   Mount   Ruby   Chesterfield
Irwin   Elgin   Croghan
Heath Springs   Jefferson   Cheraw   McColl   Tatum
Kershaw   Patrick   Society Hill   Bennettsville   Clio
                                    DILLON
KERSHAW   McBee   Blenheim   Dillon
Bethune   North Hartsville   Latta   Lake View
Camden   Hartsville   DARLINGTON   Sellers
LEE   Darlington   MARION   Mullins   Nichols
Bishopville   Lamar   Quinby   Florence   Marion   295   HORRY
Elliott   Timmonsville   FLORENCE   Rains   Loris
SUMTER   Lynchburg   Pamplico   Aynor
Mayesville   Olanta   Coward   Scranton   Britton Neck   Homewood   Little River
Sumter   Turbeville   Lake City   Johnsonville   Conway   North Myrtle Beach
Shannontown   CLARENDON   WILLIAMSBURG   Socastee   Atlantic Beach
Eastover   Stuckey   Hemingway   Myrtle Beach
CALHOUN   Pinewood   Alcolu   GEORGETOWN   Bucksport   Surfside Beach
St. Matthews   Paxville   Kingstree   Garden City Beach
Cameron   Manning   Murrells Inlet
Ellore   Summerton   Greeleyville   Lane
Orangeburg   Santee   Andrews   Kensington   Pawleys Island
Vance   Eutawville   BERKELEY   Georgetown
Bowman   St. Stephen   Bonneau   Jamestown
Holly Hill   DORCHESTER   Pinopolis   McClellanville
Reevesville   Harleyville   294
St. George   Ridgeville   Summerville   Goose   Ladson   Creek
Smoaks   Cottageville   Charleston A.F.B.   Hanahan
Williams   North Charleston   Mount
Walterboro   Charleston N.S.   Pleasant
CHARLESTON   Charleston   Isle of Palms
Ravenel   C.G.B.   Sullivans Island
Adams Run   Hollywood   James   Island
Folly Beach
BEAUFORT
CENTER   Beaufort M.C.A.S.
GABAY   Beaufort
Port Royal   Parris Island   Marine Corps   Edisto Beach
Recruit Depot
ufton   Hilton Head   Island

	ZIP
Cornwell	29014
Coronaca	29649
Cottageville	29435
Couchtown	29801
Country Club Estates	29730
Country Homes	29646
Courtenay	29672
Coward	29530
Cowpens	29330
Crafts-Farrow	29203
Crane Forest	29203
Crescent	29388
Crescent Beach (Part of North Myrtle Beach)	29582
Creston	29030
Crestview	29501
Crocketts Crossroads	29720
Crocketville	29913
Crooks Crossroads	29554
Crosland Park (Part of Aiken)	29801
Cross	29436
Cross Anchor	29331
Cross Anchor Correctional Institution	29335
Crosscreek Mall (Part of Greenwood)	29646
Cross Hill	29332
Cross Keys	29379
Crosswell	29640
Cummings	29944
Cusaac Crossroads	29541
Cypress Crossroads	29069
Cypress Fork	29001
Dacusville	29640
Daisy	29569
Dale	29914
Dalewood	29653
Dalzell	29040
Danwood	29541
Darlington	29532
	29540

For specific Darlington Zip Codes call (803) 303-3223, or your local postmaster.

	ZIP
Daufuskie Island	29915
Davis Crossroads	29148
Davis Station	29041
Deans	29684
De Bordieu Colony	29440
Deer Park	29405
DeKalb	29175
Delemar Crossroads	29470
Delmar	29070
Delphos	29745
Delta	29178
Denmark	29042
Denny Terrace	29203
Dentsville	29204
Denver	29625
Deweys Hill (Part of North Charleston)	29406
Dillon	29536
Dinkins	29150
Dinkins Mill	29128
Dixiana	29172
Dixie	29720
Dog Bluff	29511
Donalds	29638
Dongola	29526
Dorange	29471
Dorchester	29437
Dorchester Estates	29485
Dorchester Terrace	29405
Douglass	29014
Dovesville	29540
Drake	29516
Drawdy	29488
Drayton (Charleston County)	29407
Drayton (Spartanburg County)	29333
Draytonville	29340
Drexel Lake Hills	29206
Dry Branch	29803
Dubose	29150
Du Bose Crossroads	29153
Du Bose Park	29020
Dudley	29728
Due West	29639
Duford	29581
Dunbar (Georgetown County)	29440
Dunbar (Marlboro County)	29525
Duncan	29334
Dunean	29601
Dunes (Part of Myrtle Beach)	29577
Dupont	29407

	ZIP
Dusty Bend (Part of Camden)	29020
Dutch Fork	29210
Dutchman	29374
Dutchman Correctional Institution	29335
Dutch Square	29210
Dutch Village	29063
Dyson	29666
Eadytown	29468
Earle Homes	29624
Earles	29510
Earles Grove	29678
Earlwood Park	29532
Early Branch	29916
Easley	29640-42

For specific Easley Zip Codes call (803) 859-9411, or your local postmaster.

	ZIP
East Bay (Part of Charleston)	29403
East Gaffney	29340
East Gantt	29609
East Greer	29651
East Hartsville	29550
Eastmont	29209
Eastover	29044
East Side Acres	29488
East Sumter	29150
East View	29669
Eau Claire (Part of Columbia)	29203
Ebenezer (Florence County)	29501
Ebenezer (York County)	29732
Eden	29645
Edenwood	29033
Edgefield	29824
Edgemoor	29712
Edgewood (Part of Columbia)	29204
Edisto	29038
Edisto Beach	29438
Edisto Island	29438
Edmund	29073
Effingham	29541
Ehrhardt	29081
Elgin (Kershaw County)	29045
Elgin (Lancaster County)	29720
Elko	29826
Elliott	29046
Elloree	29047
Elmwood Park	29803
Emanuelville	29536
Emerald Place	29646
Emerald Valley	29210
Emory	29138
Enchanted Hills	29672
Enoree	29335
Epworth	29666
Equinox Mill	29625
Estill	29918
Eureka	29847
Eureka Mill	29706
Eutaw Springs	29048
Eutawville	29048
Evans Crossroad	29720
Evergreen	29541
Evergreen Hills	29625
Fairfax	29827
Fairfield (Part of Hilton Head Island)	29928
Fairfield Terrace	29203
Fair Forest (Greenwood County)	29646
Fairforest (Spartanburg County)	29336
Fairmont	29301
Fair Play	29643
Fairview (Greenville County)	29651
Fairview (Oconee County)	29672
Fairview Crossroads	29070
Farrel Crossroads	29432
Farrow Terrace	29203
Fechtig	29916
Federal (Florence County)	29503
Federal (Greenville County)	29603
Felderville	29047
Fenwick Hills	29455
Ferndale (Charleston County)	29406
Ferndale (Spartanburg County)	29301
Filbert	29710
Fingerville	29338
Finklea	29569
Finland	29042
Fisher Hill	29520

	ZIP
Five Forks (Anderson County)	29621
Five Forks (Greenville County)	29681
Five Forks (Pickens County)	29657
Five Points (Oconee County)	29693
Five Points (Richland County)	29205
Flamingo Acres	29512
Flat Rock	29624
Flat Shoals	29691
Fletcher	29570
Florence	29501-06

For specific Florence Zip Codes call (803) 679-2465, or your local postmaster.

	ZIP
Florence Mall (Part of Florence)	29501
Floyd Dale	29542
Floyds Crossroads	29581
Folly Beach	29439
Folly Field (Part of Hilton Head Island)	29928
Forest	29437
Forest Acres (Oconee County)	29691
Forest Acres (Richland County)	29206
Forest Beach (Part of Hilton Head Island)	29928
Forestbrook	29577
Forest Lake (Richland County)	29206
Forest Lake (York County)	29715
Foreston	29102
Forest Park	29642
Fork	29543
Fork Shoals	29645
Forrest Hills (Part of Latta)	29565
Fort Lawn	29714
Fort Mill	29715*
	29716†
Fort Motte	29135
Fountain Inn	29644
Fountain Lake	29048
Four Holes	29115
Four Mile	29464
Fowler	29556
Foxtown	29801
Foxwood Hills	29693
Francis Marion College	29506
Fraserville	29585
Friarsgate (Part of Irmo)	29063
Friendfield	29591
Friendship	29678
Fripp Island	29920
Fruit Hill	29138
Furman	29921
Furman University	29613
Gable	29051
Gadsden	29052
Gaffney	29340-42

For specific Gaffney Zip Codes call (803) 489-7144, or your local postmaster.

	ZIP
Gaillard Crossroads	29400
Galavon	29536
Galaxy	29209
Galivants Ferry	29544
Gantt	29605
Gapway	29574
Garden City	29576
Garden City Beach	29576
Gardens Corner	29945
Garnett	29922
Gaston	29053
Gem Lake Estates	29801
Georgetown	29440-42

For specific Georgetown Zip Codes call (803) 546-5515, or your local postmaster.

	ZIP
Georgetown	29640
Gifford	29923
Gilbert	29054
Gillisonville	29936
Givhans	29472
Glass Hill	29526
Glendale	29346
Glenn Springs	29374
Gloverville	29828
Gluck	29624
Glymphville	29126
Godsey	29666
Golden Grove	29673
Golightly	29302
Gooches	29720
Goodwins Crossroads	29325
Goose Creek	29445

	ZIP
Goretown	29569
Gourdin	29564
Govan	29843
Gowensville	29322
Grace	29720
Grahamville (Horry County)	29526
Grahamville (Jasper County)	29936
Gramling	29348
Graniteville	29829
Graves	29440
Gray Court	29645
Grays	29916
Grays Hill	29902
Great Falls	29055
Greeleyville	29056
Green Bay	29450
Greenbriar	29678
Greenbrier	29180
Green Pond (Colleton County)	29446
Green Pond (Spartanburg County)	29388
Green Sea	29545
Greenview	29203
Greenville	29601-16

For specific Greenville Zip Codes call (803) 282-8401, or your local postmaster.

	ZIP
Greenwood	29646-49

For specific Greenwood Zip Codes call (803) 223-2321, or your local postmaster.

	ZIP
Greenwood Correctional Center	29646
Greenwood Shores	29666
Greer	29650-52

For specific Greer Zip Codes call (803) 877-6423, or your local postmaster.

	ZIP
Grenadier	29210
Gresham	29546
Grice Ferry	29574
Grove Park	29501
Grover	29447
Guess	29727
Gurley	29569
Guthries	29726
Hagood	29128
Hamburg (Part of North Augusta)	29841
Hamer	29547
Hammond	29624
Hammond Crossroads	29135
Hampton	29924
Hampton Drive	29488
Hampton Heights	29687
Hampton Park Terrace (Part of Charleston)	29403
Hanahan	29406
Hannah	29583
Hanover Hills	29672
Harbison	29212
Harbour Town (Part of Hilton Head Island)	29928
Hardeeville	29927
Harleyville	29448
Harmony (Edgefield County)	29832
Harmony (York County)	29704
Harmony Hill	29341
Harris	29646
Hartsville	29550
Harveytown	29365
Haskell Heights	29203
Hayne	29301
Hayne Junction	29301
Hazelwood Acres	29209
H & B Village (Part of Hampton)	29924
Heatherwood	29640
Heathley Wood (Part of Sumter)	29150
Heath Springs	29058
Hebron	29518
Helena	29108
Hemingway	29554
Hendersonville	29488
Hendricks Corner	29526
Hibernia	29105
Hickory Grove (Florence County)	29501
Hickory Grove (Horry County)	29526
Hickory Grove (York County)	29717
Hickory Hill	29446
Hickory Tavern	29645
High Point	29627

Place	ZIP
Hilda	29813
Hillcrest (Part of Spartanburg)	29318
Hillcrest Acres (Part of Belton)	29627
Hillcrest Heights (Part of Williamston)	29697
Hillcrest Mall (Part of Spartanburg)	29302
Hilton	29036
Hilton Head Island	29925-26
	29928
	29938

For specific Hilton Head Island Zip Codes call (803) 785-2179, or your local postmaster.

Place	ZIP
Hobcaw Point	29464
Hodges	29653
Hollands Store	29684
Hollydale	29115
Holly Hill	29059
Holly Springs (Oconee County)	29693
Holly Springs (Spartanburg County)	29349
Hollywood (Charleston County)	29449
Hollywood (Saluda County)	29138
Hollywood Hills	29203
Holmsville	29563
Holtson Crossroads	29006
Homeland Park	29621
Homewood	29526
Homewood Park	29520
Honea Path	29654
Honey Hill	29479
Hoodtown	29742
Hopewell	29717
Hopkins	29061
Horatio	29062
Horeb	29180
Horrel Hill	29061
Horry	29511
Horsegall	29944
Howard	29569
Hudsontown	29477
Huger	29450
Hunley Park (Part of North Charleston)	29404
Huntington Estates	29841
Hyman	29583
Independents	29209
India Hook	29730
Indiantown	29554
Industrial (Part of Rock Hill)	29730
Ingleside	29356
Inman	29349
Inman Mills	29349
Irmo	29063
Irvines Landing	29649
Irwin	29720
Isgett Circle	29520
Islandton	29929
Isle of Palms	29451
Italy	29510
Iva	29655
Jackson	29831
Jacksonboro	29452
Jackson Mill (Part of Wellford)	29385
Jacksonville	29834
Jalapa	29108
James Island	29412
Jamestown (Berkeley County)	29453
Jamestown (Horry County)	29526
Jamison	29115
Jedburg	29483
Jefferson	29718
Jenkinsville	29065
Jennys	29827
Jericho	29426
Joanna	29351
Jocassee	29676
Johns Island	29455*
	29457†
Johnson City	29301
Johnson Crossroads	29809
Johnsonville	29555
Johnston	29832
Johnstown	29816
Johnsville	29481
Jones Crossroads (Aiken County)	29105
Jones Crossroads (Lancaster County)	29720
Jonesville	29353
Jordan	29102
Jordania	29678
Jordanville	29544
Judson	29611
Judson No. 2	29611
Juniper Bay	29526
Kathwood (Part of West Columbia)	29169
Kelly	29379
Kellytown	29550
Kelton	29353
Kemper	29563
Kensington	29440
Keowee (Abbeville County)	29654
Keowee (Oconee County)	29672
Kershaw	29067
Ketchuptown	29581
Kiawah Island	29455
Kilgore	29335
Killian	29203
Kinards	29355
King Circle	29720
Kingsburg	29555
Kings Creek	29719
Kingstree	29556
Kingswood	29210
Kirkland	29020
Kirkland Correctional Institute	29210
Kirksey	29848
Kitchings Mill	29137
Kittredge	29434
Kline	29814
Klondike Crossroads	29526
Kneece	29006
Knightsville	29483
Knollwood Acres	29512
Knox	29706
Ladson	29456
La France	29656
Lake City	29560
Lake Forest (Greenville County)	29606
Lake Forest (Pickens County)	29640
Lake Forest Estates	29841
Lake Lanier	29356
Lakemont	29635
Lake Murray Shores	29070
Lake Shores	29649
Lakeview (Chester County)	29714
Lake View (Dillon County)	29563
Lakewood	29732
Lakewood Manor	29301
Lake Wylie	29710
Lamar	29069
Lambertown	29510
Lambs (Part of North Charleston)	29405
Lancaster	29720*
	29721†
Lancaster Mill	29720
Lando	29724
Landrum	29356
Landsford	29704
Lane	29564
Lanford	29335
Langley	29834
Larkin	29377
Lathem (Part of Easley)	29640
Latimer	29628
Latta	29565
Laurel Bay	29902
Laurens	29360
Leawood	29601
Lebanon (Anderson County)	29621
Lebanon (Fairfield County)	29180
Leeds	29031
Leesburg (Part of Columbia)	29209
Leesville	29070
Legareville	29455
Lena	29918
Leo	29560
Lesslie	29730
Lester	29512
Level Land	29655
Lewis	29706
Lewis Crossroads	29532
Lexington	29071-73

For specific Lexington Zip Codes call (803) 359-9355, or your local postmaster.

Place	ZIP
Liberty	29657
Liberty Hill (Charleston County)	29406
Liberty Hill (Kershaw County)	29074
Liberty Hill (McCormick County)	29835
Lieber Correctional Institution	29472
Limehouse	29927
Limestone	29115
Lincoln Shire	29203
Lincolnville	29483
Lions Beach	29461
Litchfield Beach	29585
Little Africa	29323
Little Camden	29201
Little Chicago	29322
Little Eastatoe	29685
Little Mountain	29075
Little River	29566
Little Rock	29567
Little Texas	29690
Livingston	29076
Lobeco	29931
Lockhart	29364
Lockhart Junction	29353
Lodge	29082
Lone Star	29077
Long Bay Estates	29572
Long Branch	29853
Longcreek (Oconee County)	29658
Long Creek (Pickens County)	29640
Long Leaf	29488
Long Point	29569
Longs	29568
Longtown	29130
Loris	29569
Lowenstein Mills	29621
Lowndesville	29659
Lowrys	29706
Lucknow	29010
Lugoff	29078
Luray	29932
Lydia	29079
Lydia Mills	29325
Lykesland	29061
Lyman	29365
Lynchburg	29080
Lyndhurst	29812
Lynwood	29816
McAlister Square (Part of Greenville)	29607
Mac Arthurs Junction	29638
McBee	29101
McBeth	29431
McClellanville	29458
McColl	29570
McConnells	29726
McCormick	29835
McCormick Correctional Institution	29835
McCormick Crossroads	29536
McCutchen Crossroads	29010
McDonald	29440
MacDougall Youth Correction Center	29472
Macedonia	29330
McKellar Farms	29646
McKenzie Crossroads	29114
McPhersonville	29916
Maddens	29360
Madison (Aiken County)	29829
Madison (Oconee County)	29693
Magnolia Park	29853
Mallory	29565
Manning	29102
Manning Crossroads	29536
Manville	29010
Maple Crossroads	29526
Maplewood	29340
Marietta	29661
Marine Corps Air Station	29904
Marion	29571
Marlboro	29512
Mars Bluff	29506
Martin	29836
Maryville (Charleston County)	29407
Maryville (Georgetown County)	29440
Masons Crossroads	29621
Mathews (Part of Greenwood)	29646
Mathews Heights	29646
Mauldin	29662
Mayesville	29104
Mayfair	29687
Mayfair Mill (Part of Pickens)	29671
Mayo	29368
Mayo Mills	29368
Mayson	29138
Meadowlake	29203
Mechanicsville	29532
Meggett	29449
Melrose	29803
Merchant	29138
Middendorf	29550
Midland Park	29405
Midland Valley	29829
Midway (Bamberg County)	29003
Midway (Kershaw County)	29032
Midway (Lancaster County)	29720
Midway Crossroads	29554
Midway Village	29577
Miley	29933
Mill Creek	29163
Millers Crossroads	29838
Millett	29836
Mill Village (Part of Bennettsville)	29512
Millwood (Sumter County)	29150
Millwood (Williamsburg County)	29556
Millwood Gardens	29150
Milton	29325
Mink Point Plantation	29902
Minturn	29573
Mitchellville	29936
Mitford	29055
Modoc	29838
Monaghan	29611
Monarch Mill	29379
Moncks Corner	29461
Monetta	29105
Monroe Crossroads	29512
Montague	29601
Mont Clare	29532
Monticello	29106
Montmorenci	29839
Montrose	29520
Moore	29369
Moores Crossroads	29518
Moreland	29407
Morgan	29927
Morningside	29607
Morris Acres	29455
Moselle	29929
Mountain Brook	29209
Mountain Lakes	29706
Mountain Rest	29664
Mountain View	29323
Mount Carmel	29840
Mount Croghan	29727
Mount Gallagher	29692
Mount Holly	29445
Mount Olive	29581
Mount Pleasant	29464*
	29465†
Mount View	29687
Mountville	29370
Mt. Calvary	29536
Mulberry	29150
Mullins	29574
Murphy Estates	29841
Murrells Inlet	29576
Myrtle Beach	29572
	29575
	29577-78

For specific Myrtle Beach Zip Codes call (803) 626-9533, or your local postmaster.

Place	ZIP
Myrtle Beach Air Force Base	29579
Myrtle Island	29910
Myrtle Square (Part of Myrtle Beach)	29577
Naval Hospital	29902
Naval Weapons	29445
Naval Weapons Station	29408
Neeses	29107
Nesmith	29580
Nevitt Forest	29621
Newberry	29108
New Cut	29720
New Easley Highway (Part of Greenville)	29611
New Ellenton	29809
New Holland Crossroads	29006
New Hope	29530
Newport	29732
New Prospect	29349
New Road	29945
Newry	29665
Newtonville	29512
New Town	29536
New Zion	29111
Neyles	29488

	ZIP
Nichols	29581
Nicholson Village	29801
Nimmons	29685
Nine Times	29685
Ninety Six	29666
Nixons Crossroads	29566
Nixonville	29526
Nixville	29944
Norris	29667
North	29112
North Aiken (Part of Aiken)	29801
North Anderson (Part of Anderson)	29623
North Augusta	29841
Northbridge (Part of Charleston)	29407
North Bridge Terrace (Part of Charleston)	29405
North Charleston	29418-20

For specific North Charleston Zip Codes call (803) 569-2610, or your local postmaster.

	ZIP
North Conway (Part of Conway)	29526
North Forest Beach (Part of Hilton Head Island)	29928
Northgate (Cherokee County)	29341
Northgate (Florence County)	29501
North Greenwood	29649
North Hartsville	29550
Northlake	29621
North Litchfield Beach	29585
North Mullins (Part of Mullins)	29574
North Myrtle Beach	29582
	29597-98

For specific North Myrtle Beach Zip Codes call (803) 249-1023, or your local postmaster.

	ZIP
North Pacolet	29322
North Santee	29458
Northside Correctional Center	29303
North Summerville (Part of Summerville)	29483
North Trenholm	29206
North Winyah Heights (Part of Georgetown)	29440
Northwood Estates	29405
Northwoods Mall (Part of Charleston)	29405
Norway	29113
Oakbank (Cherokee County)	29330
Oak Dale (Clarendon County)	29111
Oakdale (Florence County)	29501
Oakdale (York County)	29730
Oak Grove (Dillon County)	29565
Oak Grove (Lexington County)	29073
Oak Hill	29801
Oakland (Beaufort County)	29902
Oakland (Sumter County)	29150
Oakland Crossroads	29547
Oakland Mill (Part of Newberry)	29108
Oakley	29461
Oak Ridge	29058
Oaks Crossroads	29142
Oakvale	29673
Oakway	29693
Oakwood	29801
Oatland	29440
Oats	29069
Ocean Drive Beach (Part of North Myrtle Beach)	29582
Ocean Forest (Part of Myrtle Beach)	29577
Oceanview	29412
Oconee Estates	29672
Oconee Station	29691
Ogden	29730
Olanta	29114
Olar	29843
Old House	29936
Old Madison	29693
Olympia	29201
Ora	29360
Orangeburg	29115-17

For specific Orangeburg Zip Codes call (803) 536-1720, or your local postmaster.

	ZIP
Orchard Park (Part of Greenville)	29615
Orr Mill	29621
Orrville	29621
Orum	29583
Osborn	29426
Osceola	29744
Oswego	29150
Otranto	29405
Outland	29554
Owings	29645
Oyster Point	29412
Pacolet	29372
Pacolet Mills	29373
Pacolet Park (Part of Pacolet Mills)	29373
Padgetts	29481
Pageland	29728
Palmer Work Release Center	29501
Palmetto	29532
Palmetto Estates	29902
Palmetto Fort	29464
Pamplico	29583
Panola (Clarendon County)	29125
Panola (Greenwood County)	29646
Paramount Park	29605
Paris	29609
Parker	29611
Parkers Ferry	29426
Parkersville	29585
Park Place	29609
Parksville	29844
Parler	29142
Parr	29065
Parris Island	29905
Parris Island Marine Corps Recruit Depot	29905
Parrot Point	29412
Patrick	29584
Pauline	29374
Pawleys Island	29585
Paxville	29102
Peach Valley	29303
Peak	29122
Pecan Terrace	29605
Pecan Way Terrace (Part of Orangeburg)	29115
Pee Dee	29571
Pelham	29651
Pelion	29123
Pelzer	29669
Pendleton	29670
Peniel Crossroads	29161
Pepperhill (Part of North Charleston)	29418
Percival Crossroads	29693
Perry	29124
Perry Correctional Institution	29669
Philip	29464
Phoenix	29646
Pickens	29671
Pickett Post	29691
Piedmont	29673
Piercetown	29697
Pierpont	29407
Pimlico	29461
Pine Grove (Darlington County)	29532
Pine Grove (Hampton County)	29924
Pinehaven (Part of Charleston)	29405
Pinehurst (Dorchester County)	29483
Pinehurst (Greenwood County)	29646
Pine Island	29577
Pineland (Charleston County)	29429
Pineland (Jasper County)	29934
Pineridge (Darlington County)	29101
Pineridge (Lexington County)	29172
Pine Valley	29210
Pineville	29468
Pinewood (Spartanburg County)	29303
Pinewood (Sumter County)	29125
Pinopolis	29469
Pisgah	29128
Plantation Pines	29180
Plantersville	29440
Playcards	29569
Plaza (Part of Sumter)	29150

	ZIP
Pleasantburg (Part of Greenville)	29606
Pleasant Grove	29671
Pleasant Hill (Georgetown County)	29554
Pleasant Hill (Lancaster County)	29058
Pleasant Lane	29824
Pleasant Valley	29605
Pleasant View	29569
Plum Branch	29845
Pocotaligo	29945
Poe	29609
Polaris Missile Facility Atlantic	29408
Polk Village	29902
Pomaria	29126
Pontiac	29045
Poovey Farm	29720
Poplar Springs	29369
Port Royal	29935
Port Royal Plantation (Part of Hilton Head Island)	29928
Poston	29555
Powdersville	29673
Pregnall	29437
Primus	29720
Princeton	29654
Pritchardville	29910
Promised Land	29819
Prospect Crossroads	29560
Prosperity	29127
Providence	29059
Pumpkintown	29671
Puncheon Creek	29510
Purysburg Landing	29927
Quail Hollow	29169
Quinby	29506
Quinby Estates (Part of Quinby)	29506
Quinby Forest (Part of Quinby)	29501
Rabon Crossroads	29511
Rains	29589
Rantowles	29449
Ravenel	29470
Ravenwood (Part of Forest Acres)	29206
Red Bank	29073
Red Bank Landing	29048
Red Bluff Crossroads	29569
Red Hill (Horry County)	29526
Red Hill (rural) (Horry County)	29544
Red Hill (Lee County)	29020
Red Top	29455
Reevesville	29471
Rehobeth	29544
Reid Park	29520
Reidville	29375
Rembert	29128
Remount (Part of North Charleston)	29406
Renfrew	29690
Renno	29325
Retreat	29693
Return	29678
Reynold	29817
Rhems	29440
Ribault Park (Part of Beaufort)	29902
Richburg	29729
Rich Hill Crossroads	29058
Richland	29675
Richland Mall (Part of Forest Acres)	29206
Richland Springs	29138
Richmond Hills	29609
Richtex	29180
Ridgecrest	29801
Ridgeland	29936
Ridge Spring	29129
Ridgeville	29472
Ridgeway	29130
Ridgewood (Charleston County)	29456
Ridgewood (Oconee County)	29678
Ridgewood (Richland County)	29203
Rimini	29125
Ringle Heights	29440
Rion	29132
Ritter	29488
Riverdale	29536
River Falls	29661
Riverland	29412
Riverland Terrace	29412
Rivermont	29210

	ZIP
Rivers General Mail Facility (Part of North Charleston)	29411
Riverside (Abbeville County)	29692
Riverside (Anderson County)	29624
Riverside (Greenville County)	29611
Riverside (Lancaster County)	29720
Riverside Park	29210
Riverview	29715
Robat	29379
Robbins	29831
Robbins Circle	29706
Robertville	29922
Robinson	29101
Rock Bluff	29556
Rockbridge	29206
Rock Hill (Fairfield County)	29065
Rock Hill (York County)	29730-34

For specific Rock Hill Zip Codes call (803) 327-4187, or your local postmaster.

	ZIP
Rockton	29180
Rockville	29487
Rocky Bottom	29685
Roddy	29704
Rodman	29706
Roebuck	29376
Rogers Fallout	29544
Rosehill Park	29340
Roseida	29902
Rosinville	29477
Round O	29474
Rowell	29704
Rowesville	29133
Ruby	29741
Ruffin	29475
Russellville	29476
St. Andrews (Charleston County)	29407
St. Andrews (Richland County)	29210
St. Charles	29104
St. George	29477
St. Helena Island	29920
St. Julian	29048
St. Matthews	29135
St. Paul	29148
St. Paul Forks	29526
St. Stephen	29479
Salak	29646
Salem (Florence County)	29583
Salem (Oconee County)	29676
Salem Crossroads	29015
Salley	29137
Salters	29590
Saluca	29646
Saluda	29138
Saluda Gardens (Part of West Columbia)	29169
Saluda Terrace (Part of West Columbia)	29169
Samaria	29006
Sampit	29440
Sanders Corner	29062
Sandridge (Berkeley County)	29059
Sand Ridge (Horry County)	29526
Sandwood	29206
Sandy Flat	29687
Sandy Ridge	29666
Sandy Springs	29677
Sans Souci	29609
Sans Souci Heights	29609
Santee	29142
Santee Circle	29461
Santuc	29379
Sardinia	29143
Sardis	29161
Satchel Ford Terrace	29206
Savannah Bluff	29526
Sawyerdale	29112
Saxon	29301
Saylors Crossroads	29627
Scanlonville	29464
Schofield	29843
Schultz Hill (Part of North Augusta)	29841
Scotia	29939
Scottsville	29104
Scranton	29591
Seabrook	29940
Seabrook Island	29455
Sea Pines (Part of Hilton Head Island)	29928
Seaside	29412

	ZIP		ZIP		ZIP		ZIP
Secessionville	29412	Springdale (Lancaster		Thor	29123	West Gantt	29605
Sedalia	29379	County)	29720	Three Trees	29412	Westgate (Part of	
Seiglers Crossroads	29801	Springdale (Lexington		Tibwin	29458	Spartanburg)	29301
Seigling	29810	County)	29170	Tifton	29532	Westgate Mall (Part of	
Seivern	29164	Springfield (Orangeburg		Tigerville	29688	Spartanburg)	29301
Sellers	29592	County)	29146	Tillman	29943	West Marion	29571
Selma	29536	Springfield (Spartanburg		Timberlake	29678	Westminster	29693
Seneca	29678*	County)	29349	Timmonsville	29161	Westover Acres (Part of	
	29679†	Spring Hill (Lee County)	29128	Tirzah	29745	West Columbia)	29169
Seneca Landing	29678	Spring Hill (Richland		Toddville	29526	West Pelzer	29669
Seven Mile (Part of North		County)	29177	Tokeena Crossroads	29678	West Springs	29353
Charleston)	29405	Springmaid Beach	29577	Toney Creek	29627	West Union	29696
Seven Oaks	29210	Spring Mills	29067	Townville	29689	Westview	29301
Shady Rest (Part of		Springtown	29481	Toxaway (Part of		Westville (Greenville	
Bennettsville)	29512	Spring Valley	29646	Anderson)	29621	County)	29611
Shalimar	29341	Springwood	29204	Tradesville	29720	Westville (Kershaw	
Shannon Hill	29010	Stallsville	29485	Tranquil Acres	29456	County)	29175
Shannontown	29150	Stark Terrace	29203	Travelers Rest	29690	Whetstone	29664
Sharon	29742	Starmount	29172	Trenton	29847	Whipper Barony (Part of	
Shaw Air Force Base	29152	Starr	29684	Triangle (Part of Belton)	29627	North Charleston)	29405
Shaw Heights	29152	Startex	29377	Trio	29595	White Bluff Crossroads	29067
Sheldon	29941	Stateburg	29150	Troy	29848	White Hall (Colleton	
Shell	29526	State College (Part of		Tuckertown	29031	County)	29446
Shell Point	29902	Orangeburg)	29115	Tugtown	29059	Whitehall (Greenwood	
Shepard	29032	State Farm	29128	Turbeville	29162	County)	29646
Sheppard Park	29483	Steedman	29070	Twin Lake Hill	29209	Whitehall (Lexington	
Sherwood Acres	29301	Stiefeltown	29851	Tyler	29536	County)	29210
Shiloh (Oconee County)	29678	Stokes	29488	Ulmer	29849	White Oak	29176
Shiloh (Sumter County)	29080	Stokes Bridge	29010	Una (Darlington County)	29069	White Plains (Anderson	
Shiloh Estates	29678	Stomp Springs	29325	Una (Spartanburg County)	29378	County)	29697
Shipyard Plantation (Part		Stoneboro	29058	Union	29379	White Plains (Chesterfield	
of Hilton Head Island)	29928	Stoney Hill	29127	Union Bleachery	29609	County)	29718
Shirley	29922	Stono	29412	Union Crossroads	29111	White Pond	29853
Shoals Junction	29638	Stover	29014	Unity	28173	White Rock	29177
Shulerville	29479	Stratford Hall	29803	University (Part of		White Stone	29386
Silver	29102	Stratton Capers	29405	Columbia)	29208	Whitesville	29461
Silver Bluff Estates	29803	Strawberry	29461	University of South		Whitetown	29845
Silverstreet	29145	Stuart Point	29940	Carolina at Coastal		Whitmire	29178
Simpson	29130	Stuckey	29554	Carolina	29526	Whitney	29303
Simpsonville	29680-81	Sullivans Island	29482	Utica	29678	Wilder	29431
For specific Simpsonville Zip		Summer Hill (Part of North		Valencia Heights	29205	Wilkinson Heights	29115
Codes call (803) 963-5909, or		Augusta)	29841	Valley Falls	29303	Wilkinsville	29340
your local postmaster.		Summerland (Part of		Vance	29163	Wilksburg	29706
Singing Pines	29678	Batesburg)	29006	Van Wyck	29744	Williams	29493
Singleton	29135	Summerton	29148	Varnville	29944	Williams Estate	29720
Six Mile	29682	Summerville	29483-85	Vaucluse	29850	Williamston	29697
Six Points	29801	For specific Summerville Zip		Verdery	29819	Willington	29835
Skyview Terrace	29210	Codes call (803) 873-3571, or		Victor Mills (Part of Greer)	29651	Williston	29853
Slansville	29483	your local postmaster.		Village Creek	29678	Willowbrook	29445
Slater	29683	Summit	29070	Virginia Acres	29803	Wilson	29102
Slater-Marietta	29661	Sumter	29150-51	Voorhees College	29042	Wilson Creek	29646
Slighs	29127		29153-54	Waddell Gardens (Part of		Wilsons Cross Roads	29532
Smallwood (Fairfield		For specific Sumter Zip Codes		Beaufort)	29902	Windsor	29856
County)	29130	call (803) 773-9312, or your		Wade Hampton	29607	Windsor Estates	29204
Smallwood (Laurens		local postmaster.		Wadmalaw Island	29487	Windsor Forest	29501
County)	29325	Sunnyside (Part of Greer)	29651	Wadsworth	29301	Windsor Lake Park	29206
Smith	29730	Sunset	29685	Wagener	29164	Windsor Park	29520
Smithboro	29574	Surfside Beach	29575	Walden Correctional		Windsor Plantation	29440
Smith Mills	29554	Suttons	29510	Institute	29210	Windwood	29461
Smoaks	29481	Swansea	29160	Walhalla	29691	Windy Hill	29506
Smyrna	29743	Sweden	29042	Wallace	29596	Windy Hill Beach (Part of	
Snelling	29812	Sweetwater (Aiken		Walnut Grove	29374	North Myrtle Beach)	29582
Sniders Crossroads	29475	County)	29841	Walterboro	29488	Winnsboro	29180
Snowden	29464	Sweetwater (Barnwell		Wampee	29568	Winnsboro Mills	29180
Socastee	29577	County)	29812	Wando	29492	Winona	29506
Society Hill	29593	Switzer	29369	Wando Woods	29405	Winthrop College (Part of	
South Anderson (Part of		Switzerland	29936	Ward	29166	York)	29730
Anderson)	29624	Sycamore	29846	Ware Place	29669	Wisacky	29010
South Congaree	29172	Syracuse	29532	Ware Shoals	29692	Wolfton	29112
Southern Meadows	29678	Talatha	29803	Warren Crossroads	29470	Women's Correctional	
Southern Shops	29303	Tall Pines	29536	Warrenville	29851	Center	29210
South Forest Estates	29605	Tamassee	29686	Warsaw	29510	Woodburn Hills	29301
South Greenwood (Part of		Tanglewood (Beaufort		Wateree	29044	Woodfield	29206
Greenwood)	29646	County)	29902	Waterford Estates	29440	Woodfields	29605
South Hartsville	29550	Tanglewood (Greenville		Waterloo	29384	Woodford	29112
South Hills	29379	County)	29611	Watkins Store	29803	Woodland Hills	29210
South Lynchburg	29080	Tanglewood (Oconee		Watson Village (Part of		Woodrow	29040
South Lynchburg (Part of		County)	29672	Anderson)	29624	Woodruff	29388
Mullins)	29574	Tanglewood (Orangeburg		Watts Mills	29360	Woodside	29610
South Park (Part of		County)	29115	Waverly Mills	29585	Woodville	29669
Florence)	29505	Tarboro	29943	Waylyn	29405	Woodward	29014
Southpark Shopping		Tatum	29594	Wedgefield	29168	Workman	29111
Center (Part of		Taxahaw	29067	Welcome (Anderson		Yarn Mill	29520
Florence)	29505	Taylors	29687	County)	29621	Yauhannah	29440
Southside	29505	Tega Cay	29715	Welcome (Greenville		Yeamans Hall (Part of	
South Sumter	29150	Temperance Hill	29571	County)	29611	Hanahan)	29410
South Windermere (Part		Ten Mile	29464	Wellford	29385	Yemassee	29945
of Charleston)	29407	Ten Mile (Part of		Wellington Mill	29624	Yenome	29812
Soviet Union	29693	Charleston)	29406	Wesleyan	29630	Yonges Island	29449
Spartanburg	29301-18	Terrells Crossroads	29518	West Andrews (Part of		York	29745
For specific Spartanburg Zip		Texas	29477	Andrews)	29510	Yorkshire	29209
Codes call (803) 585-0301, or		The Farms (Part of		West Columbia	29169-72	Yoruba Village	29941
your local postmaster.		Hanahan)	29410	For specific West Columbia Zip		Youngs	29388
Spaulding Heights	29501	The Groves (Part of		Codes call (803) 796-0455, or		Zion	29574
Spiderweb	29841	Mount Pleasant)	29464	your local postmaster.			
Spring Branch	29571	The Meadows	29678				

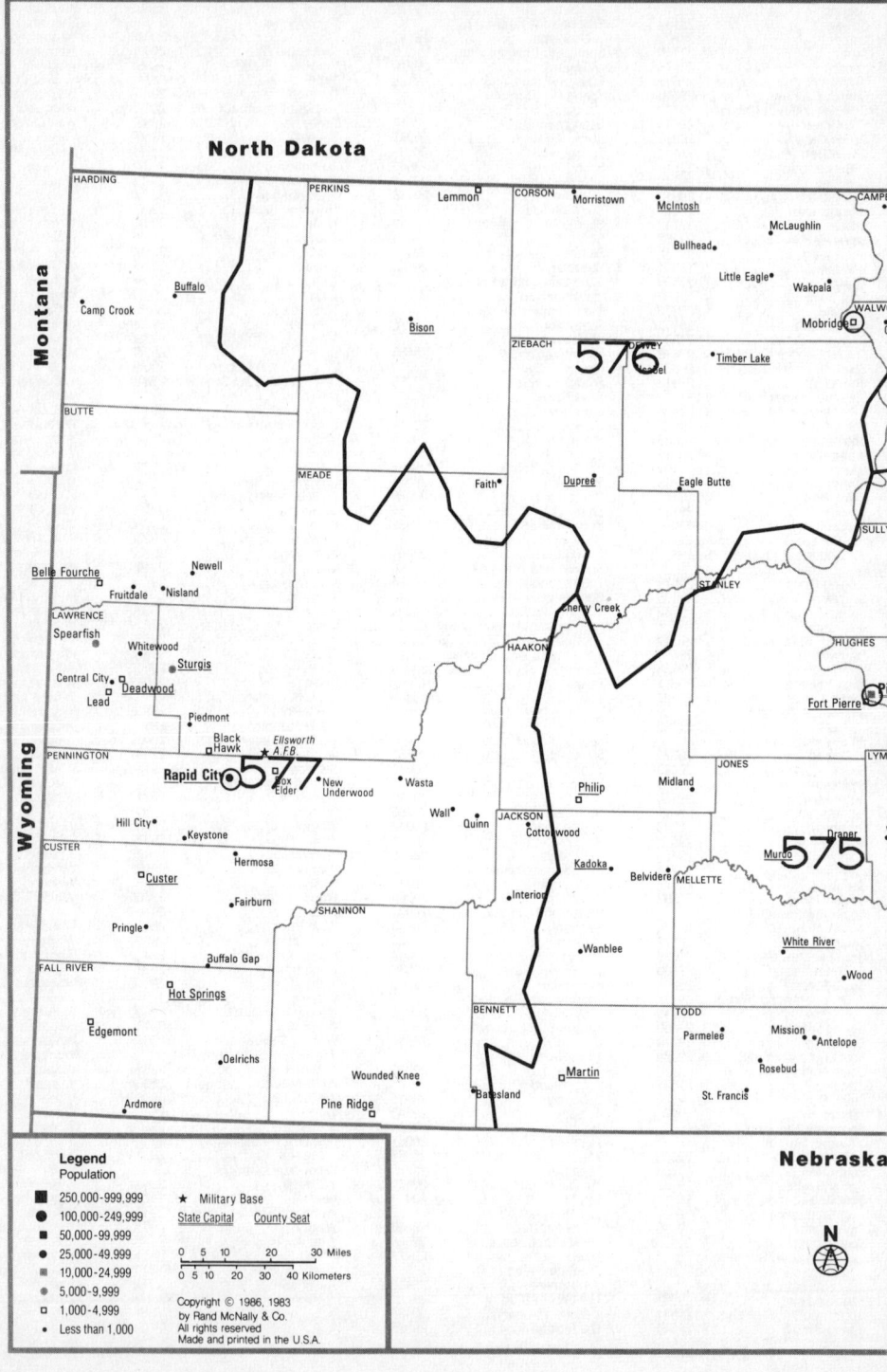

North Dakota

HARDING

PERKINS

Lemmon

CORSON   Morristown   McIntosh

CAMPB

McLaughlin

Bullhead

Little Eagle   Wakpala

Buffalo

Camp Crook

Bison

MALWC

Mobridge

G

ZIEBACH   **576**   DEWEY   Timber Lake

Isabel

BUTTE

MEADE   Faith   Dupree   Eagle Butte

ISULLY

Belle Fourche   Newell

Fruitdale   Nisland

LAWRENCE   Cherry Creek   STANLEY   HUGHES

Spearfish   HAAKON

Whitewood   Sturgis

Central City   Deadwood

Lead   Fort Pierre   Pi

Piedmont

Black   Ellsworth   JONES   LYM

Hawk   A.F.B.

PENNINGTON   Box   New   Wasta   Philip   Midland

Rapid City   **577**   Elder   Underwood

Wall   Quinn   JACKSON   **575**

Hill City   Keystone   Cottonwood   Murdo   Draper

CUSTER   Kadoka   Belvidere   MELLETTE

Hermosa

Custer   Interior

Fairburn   White River

SHANNON

Pringle   Wanblee   Wood

Buffalo Gap

FALL RIVER

Hot Springs   BENNETT   TODD

Edgemont   Parmelee   Mission   Antelope

Oelrichs   Rosebud

Wounded Knee   Martin   St. Francis

Ardmore   Pine Ridge   Batesland

Montana

Wyoming

Nebraska

N

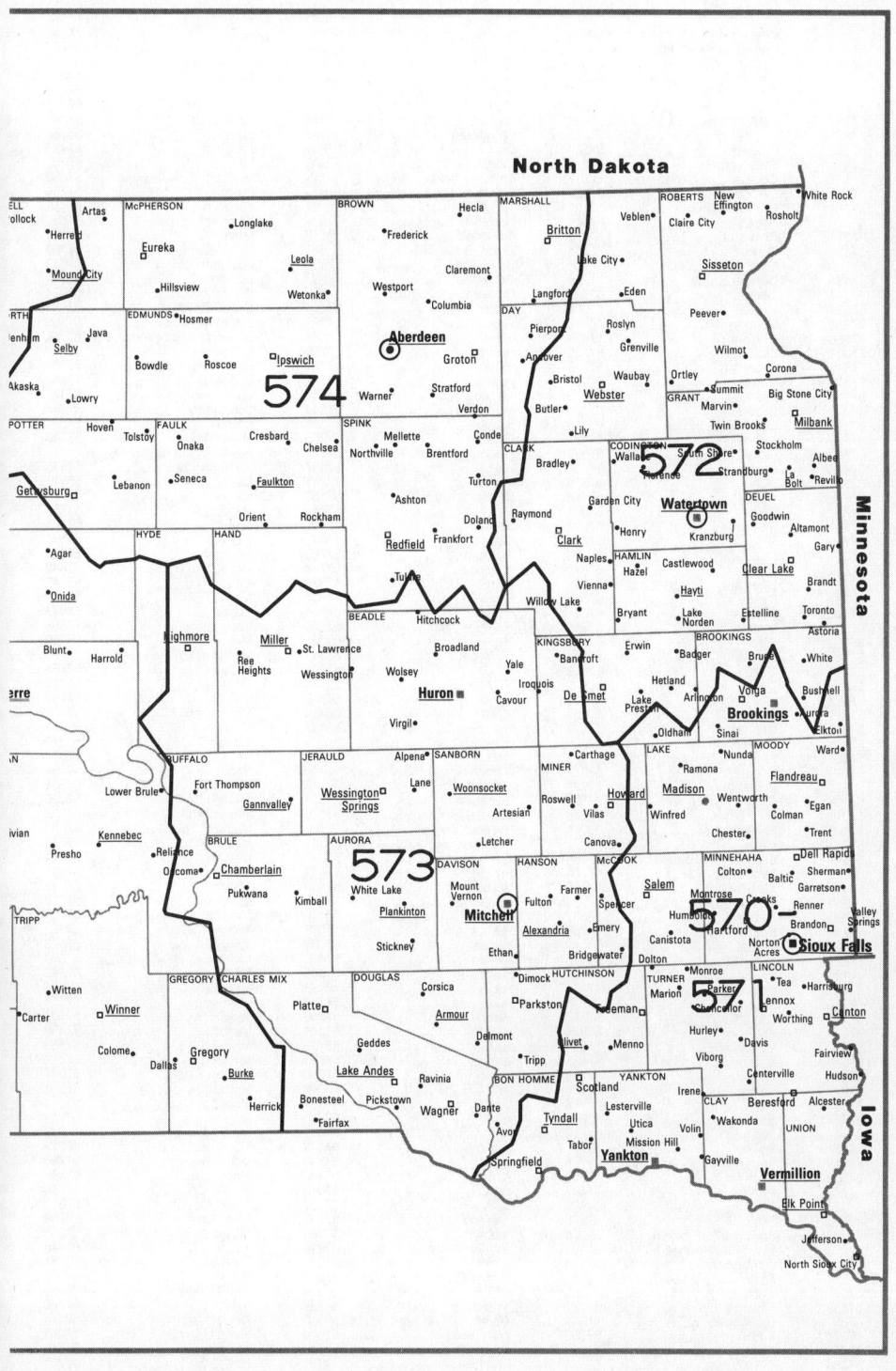

North Dakota

ROBERTS

MARSHALL

BROWN

McPHERSON

Minnesota

Iowa

	ZIP		ZIP		ZIP		ZIP
Aberdeen	57401*	Chautauqua	57042	Freeman	57029	Kingsburg	57062
	57402†	Chelsea	57465	Froehlich Addition	57104	Kones Corner	57223
Academy	57369	Cherry Creek	57622	Fruitdale	57742	Kranzburg	57245
Agar	57520	Chester	57016	Fulton	57340	Kyle	57752
Agency Village	57262	Cheyenne Crossing	57754	Galena	57732	La Bolt	57246
Akaska	57420	Cheyenne River Indian		Gannvalley	57341	Ladner	57720
Albee	57259	Reservation	57625	Garden City	57236	Lake Andes	57356
Alcester	57001	Claire City	57224	Garretson	57030	Lake Campbell	57006
Alexandria	57311	Claremont	57432	Gary	57237	Lake City	57247
Allen	57714	Clark	57225	Gayville	57031	Lake Norden	57248
Alpena	57312	Clark Colony	57258	Geddes	57342	Lake Preston	57249
Altamont	57226	Clayton	57332	Gettysburg	57442	Lane	57358
Ames	57362	Clearfield	57580	Glad Valley	57629	Langford	57454
Amherst	57421	Clear Lake	57226	Glencross	57630	Lantry	57636
Andover	57422	Colman	57017	Glendale Colony	57440	La Plant	57652
Antelope	57555	Colome	57528	Glenham	57631	Lead	57754
Ardmore	57715	Colonial Pine Hills	57701	Goodwin	57238	Lebanon	57455
Arlington	57212	Colton	57018	Graceville Colony	57076	Lemmon	57638
Arlington Beach	57212	Columbia	57433	Greenfield	57010	Lennox	57039
Armour	57313	Conde	57434	Green Grass	57625	Leola	57456
Arpan	57762	Corn Creek	57560	Greenwood	57380	Lesterville	57040
Artas	57437	Corona	57227	Gregory	57533	Letcher	57359
Artesian	57314	Corsica	57328	Grenville	57239	Lily	57274
Ashton	57424	Corson	57005	Groton	57445	Linden Beach	57227
Astoria	57213	Cottonwood	57775	Grover	57201	Littleburg	57555
Athol	57424	Crandall	57434	Hamill	57534	Little Eagle	57639
Aurora	57002	Crazy Horse	57730	Hammer	57255	Lodgepole	57640
Aurora Center	57375	Creighton	57729	Hanna	57754	Lone Tree	57024
Avon	57315	Cresbard	57435	Harrington	57551	Longlake	57457
Badger	57214	Crocker	57229	Harrisburg	57032	Long Lake Colony	57481
Baltic	57003	Crooks	57020	Harrison	57344	Long Valley	57547
Bancroft	57316	Crow Creek Indian		Harrold	57536	Loomis	57301
Barnard	57426	Reservation	57339	Hartford	57033	Lower Brule	57548
Batesland	57716	Crow Lake	57382	Hartford Beach	57227	Lower Brule Indian	
Bath	57427	Custer	57730	Hayes	57537	Reservation	57548
Bear Butte	57785	Dallas	57529	Hayti	57241	Lowry	57472
Bear Creek	57636	Dante	57329	Hayward Addition	57106	Lucas	57523
Belle Fourche	57717	Davis	57021	Hazel	57242	Ludlow	57755
Belvidere	57521	Deadwood	57732	Hecla	57446	Lyons	57041
Bemis	57238	De Grey	57501	Henry	57243	McCook Lake	57038
Beresford	57004	Dell Rapids	57022	Hereford	57785	McIntosh	57641
Bethlehem	57708	Delmont	57330	Hermosa	57744	McLaughlin	57642
Big Bend	57702	Dempster	57234	Herreid	57632	Madison	57042
Big Springs	57001	Denby	57716	Herrick	57538	Madsen Beach	57279
Big Stone City	57216	De Smet	57231	Hetland	57244	Mahto	57643
Bijou Hills	57370	Dimock	57331	Hiawatha Beach	57279	Manchester	57353
Bison	57620	Dixon	57533	Hidden Timber	69201	Manderson	57756
Black Hawk	57718	Doland	57436	Highmore	57345	Manderson-White Horse	
Blacktail	57754	Dolton	57319	Hill City	57745	Creek	57756
Blumengard Colony	57438	Downtown (Part of		Hillhead	57270	Mansfield	57460
Blunt	57522	Aberdeen)	57401	Hillside	57328	Marcus	57757
Bonesteel	57317	Draper	57531	Hillside Colony	57436	Marcy Colony	57366
Bon Homme Colony	57063	Dupree	57623	Hillsview	57437	Marion	57043
Bonilla	57348	Eagle Butte	57625	Hisega	57701	Marlow	57270
Bowdle	57428	East Sioux Falls	57101	Hisle	57577	Martin	57551
Box Elder	57719	Eden	57232	Hitchcock	57348	Marty	57361
Bradley	57217	Edgemont	57735	Holabird	57540	Marvin	57251
Brandon	57005	Egan	57024	Holmquist	57274	Maurine	57626
Brandt	57218	Elk Point	57025	Hooker	57070	Maxwell Colony	57059
Brentford	57429	Elkton	57026	Hoover	57760	Mayfield	57037
Bridger	57748	Ellis	57107	Hosmer	57448	Meadow	57644
Bridgewater	57319	Ellsworth Air Force Base	57706	Hot Springs	57747	Meckling	57044
Bristol	57219	Elmore	57754	Houghton	57449	Mellette	57461
Britton	57430	Elm Springs	57736	Hoven	57450	Menno	57045
Broadland	57350	Elm Springs Colony	57334	Howard	57349	Midland	57552
Brookings	57006	Emery	57332	Howes	57748	Midway	57037
Brownsville	57754	Empire	57788	Hub City	57069	Milbank	57252
Bruce	57220	Empire, The (Part of		Hudson	57034	Milesville	57553
Bryant	57221	Falls)	57116	Huffton	57432	Millboro	57580
Buffalo	57720	Enning	57737	Humboldt	57035	Miller	57362
Buffalo Gap	57722	Epiphany	57321	Hurley	57036	Miller Dale Colony	57362
Buffalo Ridge	57115	Erwin	57233	Huron	57350	Milltown	57366
Buffalo Trading Post	57018	Esmond	57353	Huron Colony	57350	Mina	57462
Bullhead	57621	Estelline	57234	Ideal	57541	Miranda	57438
Burbank	57010	Ethan	57334	Igloo	57735	Mission	57555
Burke	57523	Eureka	57437	Imlay	57780	Mission Hill	57046
Bushnell	57276	Fairburn	57738	Interior	57750	Mission Ridge	57532
Butler	57219	Fairfax	57335	Iona	57542	Mitchell	57301
Cactus Flat	57567	Fairpoint	57787	Ipswich	57451	Mobridge	57601
Camp Crook	57724	Fairview	57027	Irene	57037	Monroe	57047
Canistota	57012	Faith	57626	Iron Lightning	57623	Montrose	57048
Canova	57321	Farmer	57311	Iroquois	57353	Morningside	57350
Canton	57013	Farmingdale	57725	Isabel	57633	Morristown	57645
Capa	57552	Faulkton	57438	James	57445	Mosher	57580
Caputa	57725	Fedora	57337	Java	57452	Mound City	57646
Carpenter	57322	Ferney	57439	Jefferson	57038	Mount Vernon	57363
Carter	57526	Firesteel	57628	Johnson Siding	57701	Mud Butte	57758
Carthage	57323	Flandreau	57028	Joubert	57344	Murdo	57559
Castle Rock	57760	Flandreau Indian		Junction City	57010	Mystic	57745
Castlewood	57223	Reservation	57028	Junius	57042	Naples	57271
Cavour	57324	Fleetwood (Part of		Kadoka	57543	Nemo	57759
Cedar Butte	57579	Brandon)	57005	Kaylor	57354	New Effington	57255
Cedar Grove Colony	57369	Florence	57235	Keldron	57634	Newell	57760
Center	57058	Forestburg	57314	Kenel	57642	New Holland	57364
Center Point	57070	Fort Pierre	57532	Kennebec	57544	New Underwood	57761
Centerville	57014	Fort Thompson	57339	Keyapaha	57545	Nisland	57762
Central City	57754	Frankfort	57440	Keystone	57751	Nora	57001
Chamberlain	57325	Franklin	57042	Kidder	57430	Norbeck	57438
Chancellor	57015	Frederick	57441	Kimball	57355	Norris	57560

	ZIP		ZIP		ZIP		ZIP
North Eagle Butte	57625	Ralph	57650	Sisseton Indian		Vermillion	57069
North Sioux City	57049	Ramona	57054	Reservation	57262	Vetal	57551
North Spearfish	57783	Rapid City	57701-02	Smiths Park	57075	Viborg	57070
Northville	57465		57709	Smithwick	57782	Victor	57260
Norton Acres	57104	For specific Rapid City Zip		So Dak Park	57279	Vienna	57271
Nunda	57050	Codes call (605) 394-8600, or		Soldier Creek	57555	Vilas	57349
Oacoma	57365	your local postmaster.		Sorum	57620	Villa Trailer Court	57706
Oelrichs	57763	Rapid Valley	57701	South Shore	57263	Virgil	57379
Ogala Lakota College	57752	Ravinia	57357	Spearfish	57783	Vivian	57576
Oglala	57764	Raymond	57258	Spencer	57374	Volga	57071
Okaton	57562	Red Elm	57623	Spink	57025	Volin	57072
Okreek	57563	Redfield	57469	Spink Colony	57440	Wagner	57380
Ola	57325	Redig	57776	Spring Creek	57572	Wakonda	57073
Oldham	57051	Redowl	57777	Spring Creek Colony	58439	Wakpala	57658
Olivet	57052	Red Scaffold	57626	Springfield	57062	Wakpamani	57716
Olsonville	69201	Red Shirt	57744	Spring Valley	57036	Walker	57601
Onaka	57466	Ree Heights	57371	Spring Valley Colony	57382	Wall	57790
Onida	57564	Reliance	57569	Standing Rock Indian		Wallace	57272
Opal	57765	Renner	57055	Reservation	58538	Wanblee	57577
Oral	57766	Reva	57651	Stanley Corner	57319	Ward	57074
Ordway	57433	Revillo	57259	Stephan	57346	Warner	57479
Orient	57467	Richland	57025	Stickney	57375	Wasta	57791
Orland	57042	Ridgeview	57652	Stockholm	57264	Watauga	57660
Ortley	57256	Riverside	57301	Stone Bridge	57223	Watertown	57201
Osceola	57316	Riverside Colony	57350	Stoneville	57787	Waubay	57273
Owanka	57767	Rochford	57778	Storla	57359	Waverly	57202
Parade	57647	Rockerville	57701	Strandburg	57265	Webster	57274
Parker	57053	Rockham	57470	Stratford	57474	Webster Grove	57106
Parkston	57366	Rockport	57311	Sturgis	57785	Wecota	57438
Parmelee	57566	Roscoe	57471	Summit	57266	Wentworth	57075
Patricia	57551	Rosebud	57570	Sunnyview	57006	Wessington	57381
Pearl Creek Colony	57353	Rosebud Indian		Swett	57551	Wessington Springs	57382
Pearsons Corner	57070	Reservation	57570	Tabor	57063	Western Mall (Part of	
Pedro	57729	Rosedale Colony	57301	Tacoma Park	57433	Sioux Falls)	57105
Peever	57257	Rosholt	57260	Tea	57064	Westerville	57069
Peninsula Park	57075	Roslyn	57261	Thomas	57241	Westport	57481
Perkins	57062	Roswell	57349	Thunder Butte	57623	Wetonka	57481
Philip	57567	Roubaix	57754	Thunder Hawk	57638	Wewela	57578
Pickerel	57239	Rowena	57056	Tilford	57769	White	57276
Pickstown	57367	Rumford	57774	Timber Lake	57656	White Butte	57638
Piedmont	57769	Rumpus Ridge	57012	Tolstoy	57475	Whitehorse (Dewey	
Pierpont	57468	Running Water	57062	Toronto	57268	County)	57661
Pierre	57501	Rushmore Mall (Part of		Trail City	57657	White Horse (Todd	
Pine Ridge	57770	Rapid City)	57701	Trent	57065	County)	57555
Pine Ridge Indian		Rutland	57057	Tripp	57376	White Lake	57383
Reservation	57770	St. Charles	57571	Trojan	57754	White Owl	57792
Plainview	57748	St. Francis	57572	Troy	57265	White River	57579
Plainview Colony	57451	St. Lawrence	57373	Tschetter Colony	57052	White Rock	57260
Plankinton	57368	St. Onge	57779	Tulare	57476	Whitewood	57793
Plano	57340	Salem	57058	Turkey Ridge	57036	Wicksville	57767
Platte	57369	Sanator	57730	Turton	57477	Willow Lake	57278
Platte Colony	57369	Savoy	57754	Tuthill	57574	Wilmot	57279
Pluma	57732	Scenic	57780	Twin Brooks	57269	Winfred	57076
Pollock	57648	Scotland	57059	Two Strike	57570	Winner	57580
Polo	57467	Selby	57472	Tyndall	57066	Witten	57584
Porcupine	57772	Seneca	57473	Union Center	57787	Wolf Creek Colony	57052
Potato Creek	57750	Shadehill	57653	Unityville	57058	Wolsey	57384
Prairie City	57649	Shady Beach	57227	University (Part of		Wood	57585
Prairie Village	57042	Sharps Corner	57752	Brookings)	57007	Woonsocket	57385
Presho	57568	Sherman	57060	Usta	57626	Worthing	57077
Pringle	57773	Silver City	57701	Utica	57067	Wounded Knee	57794
Promise	57601	Sinai	57061	Vale	57788	Yale	57386
Provo	57774	Sioux Falls	57101-07	Valley Springs	57068	Yankton	57078
Pukwana	57370		57116-18	Valley View	57072	Yankton Indian	
Pumpkin Center	57035	For specific Sioux Falls Zip		Vayland	57381	Reservation	57380
Putney	57445	Codes call (605) 332-8360, or		Veblen	57270	Zell	57483
Quinn	57775	your local postmaster.		Vedin Corner	57037	Zeona	57795
Quinn Table	57790	Sisseton	57262	Verdon	57434		

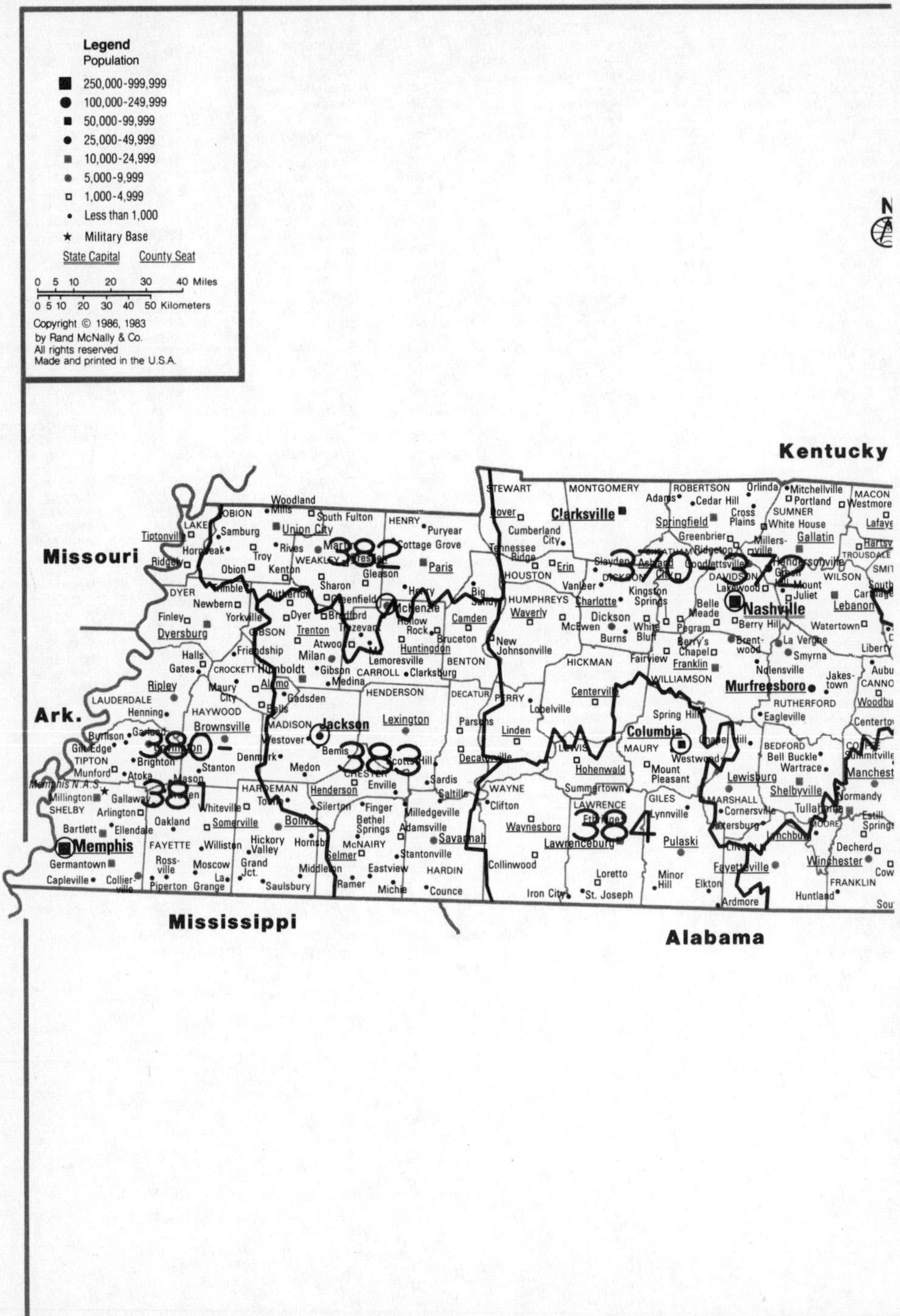

Legend
Population

- ■ 250,000 - 999,999
- ● 100,000 - 249,999
- ■ 50,000 - 99,999
- ● 25,000 - 49,999
- ■ 10,000 - 24,999
- ● 5,000 - 9,999
- □ 1,000 - 4,999
- · Less than 1,000
- ★ Military Base

State Capital   County Seat

0 5 10   20   30   40 Miles
0 5 10 20   30 40   50 Kilometers

Kentucky

Missouri

Ark.

Memphis

Mississippi

Alabama

Nashville

Clarksville

Murfreesboro

Columbia

Jackson

382

380-381

383

384

372

N

N

Virginia

385

I-75

Knoxville

Chattanooga

Georgia

North Carolina

370 Nashville

373 **374**

372

377-379 Knoxville

373 **374** Chattanooga

Georgia

380- Memphis

381 Ark.

Place	ZIP	Place	ZIP	Place	ZIP	Place	ZIP
Acklen (Part of Nashville)	37212	Asbury (Coffee County)	37355	Bear Creek (Part of Oneida)	37892	Bethel (DeKalb County)	37166
Acton	38357	Asbury (Haywood County)	38069	Beardstown (Part of Lobelville)	37097	Bethel (Giles County)	38477
Adair	38301	Asbury (Knox County)	37914	Bear Spring	37058	Bethel (Haywood County)	38012
Adams	37010	Asbury (Lauderdale County)	38063	Beartown	37660	Bethel (Maury County)	38482
Adams Crossroads	37055	Asbury (Pickett County)	38577	Bearwallow	37015	Bethel (Perry County)	37096
Adamsville	38310	Asbury (Stewart County)	37175	Beasley	37034	Bethel (Rutherford County)	37129
Adolphus	37774	Asbury Estates	37804	Beauty Hill	38315	Bethel Springs	38315
Aetna	37033	Ashburn	37172	Beaver	38011	Bethesda (Greene County)	37641
Afton	37616	Ash Hill	37046	Beaverdam Springs	37147	Bethesda (Williamson County)	37046
Airport	37110	Ashland	38485	Beaver Hill	38580	Bethlehem (Bedford County)	37160
Airport Estates (Part of Nashville)	37217	Ashland City	37015	Beaver Ridge	37921	Bethlehem (Campbell County)	37766
Airport Mail Facility (Davidson County)	37217	Ashport	38063	Beckwith	37122	Bethlehem (Hardin County)	38310
Airport Mail Facility (Shelby County)	38130	Ashwood	38401	Bedford	37160	Bethlehem (Henry County)	38222
Akard Addition	37620	Asia	37398	Beech	38261	Bethlehem (Monroe County)	37354
Alamo	38001	Aspen Hill	38478	Beech Bluff	38313	Bethlehem (Williamson County)	37064
Alanthus Hill	37879	Athendale	38401	Beech Bottom	37083	Bethpage	37022
Albany	37743	Athens	37303*	Beech Fork	37714	Betsy Willis	37342
Alcoa	37701		37371†	Beech Grove (Anderson County)	37769	Beulah (Greene County)	37810
Alder Branch	37876	Atkins	37079	Beechgrove (Coffee County)	37018	Beulah (Union County)	37807
Alder Springs (Campbell County)	37766	Atoka	38004	Beech Grove (Grainger County)	37881	Beverly	37918
Alder Springs (Union County)	37807	Atwood	38220	Beech Grove (Hawkins County)	37711	Bible Hill	38363
Alexander Springs	38456	Auburntown	37016	Beech Grove (Trousdale County)	37074	Bidwell	37144
Alexandria	37012	Aulon (Part of Memphis)	38101	Beech Grove (Weakley County)	38230	Big Boy Junction	38030
Algood	38506	Austin Peay State University (Part of Clarksville)	37040	Beech Hill (Franklin County)	37398	Bigbyville	38401
Allardt	38504	Austin Springs (Washington County)	37601	Beech Hill (Giles County)	38478	Big Creek (Hancock County)	37869
Allens	38012	Austin Springs (Weakley County)	38226	Beech Hill (Macon County)	37074	Big Creek (Hawkins County)	37857
Allens Chapel	37166	Avoca (Part of Bristol)	37620	Beechnut City	37617	Big Creek (Monroe County)	37354
Allensville	37876	Avondale (Grainger County)	37861	Beech Springs	37764	Big Ivy	38372
Allisona	37046	Avondale (Sumner County)	37075	Beechwood	37020	Big Lick	38555
Allons	38541	Avondale Springs	37861	Beersheba Springs	37305	Big Mountain	37840
Alloway	37337	Ayers	38030	Bel Air	38261	Big Piney	37774
Allred	38542	Bacchus	37879	Bel Aire (Coffee County)	37388	Big Ridge Park	37807
Almaville	37014	Bacon Gap	37763	Bel Aire (Rutherford County)	37130	Big Rock	37023
Almy	37755	Bagdad	37145	Bel-Aire Heights (Part of Winchester)	37398	Big Sandy	38221
Alpha	37814	Baggettsville	37172	Belfast	37019	Big Sinks	37866
Alpha Heights	37814	Bailey	38017	Belinda City	37122	Big Spring (Blount County)	37737
Alpine	38543	Baileyton	37745	Belk	37166	Big Spring (Carter County)	37643
Altamont	37301	Bailey Town	37821	Bella Mara Estates	37854	Big Spring (Meigs County)	37322
Alto	37324	Bain	38320	Bell Buckle	37020	Big Springs (Hancock County)	37731
Alton Park (Part of Chattanooga)	37409	Bairds Mills	37090	Bell Campground	37849	Big Springs (Overton County)	38570
Altonville	37857	Baker Crossroads	38555	Belle Aire (Knox County)	37922	Big Springs (Rutherford County)	37037
Alumwell	37857	Bakers (Part of Nashville)	37072	Belle Aire (White County)	38583	Big Spring Union	37752
Alynwick	37804	Bakers Crossroads	38583	Belle Brook Estate (Part of Bristol)	37620	Biltmore	37643
Amherst (Part of Knoxville)	37931	Bakersworks	37029	Belle Eagle	38012	Binfield	37804
Amity Heights	37620	Bakerton	37150	Belle Founte	37312	Bingham	37064
Amqui (Part of Nashville)	37115	Bakertown (Davidson County)	37013	Belle Meade (Blount County)	37801	Binghamton (Part of Memphis)	38112
Anark	38344	Bakertown (Moore County)	37352	Belle Meade (Davidson County)	37205	Birchwood	37308
Anderson (Franklin County)	37376	Bakerville	37185	Belleville	37334	Bird Crossroad	37876
Anderson (Overton County)	38574	Bakewell	37304	Bellevue (Part of Nashville)	37221	Bird Song	38320
Anderson Heights	37617	Bald Point	37881	Bellevue Center (Part of Nashville)	37221	Bishop	38024
Andersonville	37705	Ball Camp	37921	Bellevue Estates	37331	Bivens	38472
Anes	37091	Ballplay (Monroe County)	37385	Bell Mill	37363	Black Center (Part of Camden)	38320
Angeltown	37022	Ball Play (Polk County)	37362	Bells	38006	Black Creek	37852
Anglers Cove	37763	Balltown	37331	Bellsburg	37036	Black Fox (Bradley County)	37311
Annadale (Part of Cleveland)	37312	Baltimore	37843	Bell Town (Cheatham County)	37082	Black Fox (Grainger County)	37888
Annadel	37770	Baneberry	37890	Belltown (Monroe County)	37385	Black Jack	37355
Anthony Hill	38460	Bangham	38506	Belltown (Polk County)	37317	Blackman	37129
Antioch (Part of Nashville)	37011†	Banner	37738	Bellview (Bledsoe County)	37367	Black Oak	37841
	37013*	Banner Hill	37650	Bellview (Lincoln County)	37334	Blackwell	37861
Antioch (DeKalb County)	37166	Banner Springs	38556	Bellwood	37087	Blaine	37709
Antioch (Jackson County)	38562	Baptist (Part of Nashville)	37203	Belmont (Anderson County)	37705	Blair	37748
Antioch (Loudon County)	37771	Baptist Ridge	38568	Belmont (Coffee County)	37355	Blair Gap	37660
Antioch (Montgomery County)	37040	Barefoot	37186	Belmont (Jefferson County)	37725	Blair Lane	37087
Antioch (Polk County)	37307	Barfield	37129	Belmont West	37919	Blakeville	37144
Antioch (Tipton County)	38011	Bargerton	38351	Belvidere	37306	Blanche	38488
Apison	37302	Barkertown	37365	Bernis (Part of Jackson)	38314	Blanche Chapel	38449
Appleton	38457	Barnardsville	37763	Bending Chestnut	37064	Blaney Forest (Part of East Ridge)	37412
Arcade (Part of Nashville)	37219	Barnes	38573	Benton	37307	Blanton Chapel	37355
Arcadia	37660	Barnesville	38483	Benton Springs	37307	Bledsoe (Lincoln County)	37144
Archer	37091	Barr	38040	Berclair (Part of Memphis)	38117	Bledsoe (Sumner County)	37022
Archville	37369	Barren Plain	37172	Berea (Giles County)	38478	Block City (Part of Mount Carmel)	37642
Arcott	38551	Barretville	38053	Berea (Warren County)	38581	Blockhouse	37801
Ardmore	38449	Barthelia	37031	Berlin	37091	Blondy (Part of Hohenwald)	38462
Arkland	38487	Bartlebaugh	37416	Berry Hill	37204	Bloomingdale	37660
Arlington (Houston County)	37061	Bartlett	38133-35	Berrys Chapel	37064	Bloomington	38549
Arlington (Knox County)	37917	For specific Bartlett Zip Codes call (901) 388-1713, or your local postmaster.		Bessie	38079	Bloomington Heights	37660
Arlington (Shelby County)	38002	Barton Springs	37813	Bethany	37110	Bloomington Springs	38545
Armathwaite	38504	Bates Hill	37110	Bethel (Anderson County)	37716	Blount Hills	37804
Armona	37804	Bath Springs	38311	Bethel (Benton County)	38320	Blountville	37617
Armour	38401	Batley	37716	Bethel (Blount County)	37882	Blowing Cave Mill	37876
Arno	38461	Battlewood Estates	37064	Bethel (Carroll County)	38344		
Arnold Air Force Base	37389	Baugh	38449	Bethel (Cheatham County)	37015		
Arnold Engineering Development Center	37389	Baugh Spring	37353				
Arnolds Chapel	38544	Baxter	38544				
Arp	38063	Bazel Town (Part of Harriman)	37748				
Arrington	37014	Beacon	38363				
Arrowhead	37920	Beamswitch	38230				
Arrowhead Estates	37381	Beans Creek	37345				
Arthur	37707	Bean Station	37708				

	ZIP
Blowing Springs	37716
Bluebank	38079
Blue Creek	38472
Bluefields (Part of Nashville)	37214
Blue Goose	38351
Blue Grass	37922
Blue Hill	37110
Blue Ridge (Part of Bristol)	37620
Blue Spring	37643
Blue Springs (DeKalb County)	37166
Blue Springs (Hamilton County)	37341
Blue Springs (Jefferson County)	37871
Bluff City	37618
Bluff Creek	38547
Bluff Springs	37110
Bluhmtown	37166
Blunts Landing	37096
Blythe Ferry	37321
Board Valley	38583
Boatland	38556
Bodenham	38478
Boggs	37861
Bogota	38007
Bohannon Addition (Part of Athens)	37303
Boiling Springs	38544
Bold Spring	37101
Bolivar	38008
Bolton	38002
Boma	38544
Bon Air (Sumner County)	37022
Bon Air (White County)	38583
Bon Aqua	37025
Bon Aqua Junction	37098
Bon De Croft	38583
Bone Cave	38581
Bonicord	38024
Bonnertown	38457
Bonny Kate	37920
Bonsack	38554
Bonwood (Part of Jackson)	38301
Boom	38573
Boone	37601
Boones Creek	37615
Booneville	37334
Boonshill	38459
Boothspoint	38030
Bordeaux (Part of Nashville)	37218
Borden Mills (Part of Kingsport)	37660
Boston	37064
Bowen	37861
Bowling	38555
Bowman	38555
Bowmantown	37690
Boxwood Hills	37922
Boyd	37922
Boyd Mill Estates (Part of Franklin)	37064
Boyds Creek	37876
Brace	38483
Brackentown	37148
Bradburn Hill	37745
Bradbury	37763
Braden (Fayette County)	38010
Braden (Union County)	37870
Bradford	38316
Bradley Square (Part of Cleveland)	37312
Bradleytown	38030
Bradshaw (Giles County)	38478
Bradshaw (Hawkins County)	37857
Bradyville	37026
Braemar	37658
Braid Cove	37087
Brainerd (Part of Chattanooga)	37411
Brakebill	37354
Bransford	37022
Bratcher's Croosroads	37110
Brattontown (Part of Lafayette)	37083
Bray	37883
Brayton	37338
Braytown	37710
Brazil	38382
Breckinredge South	37064
Brentlawn (Part of Springfield)	37172
Brentwood (Hamblen County)	37814
Brentwood (Williamson County)	37024

	ZIP
	37027
For specific Brentwood Zip Codes call (615) 373-1661, or your local postmaster.	
Brewer Addition (Part of Athens)	37303
Brewstertown	37852
Briar Thicket	37713
Briarwood	37040
Briceville	37710
Brick Church	38478
Bride	38019
Bridgeport	37821
Bridwell Heights	37617
Bright Hope	37743
Brighton (Lincoln County)	37335
Brighton (Tipton County)	38011
Brims Corner	38001
Bristol	37620-25
For specific Bristol Zip Codes call (615) 968-2355, or your local postmaster.	
Britton Ford	38256
Brittontown	37616
Britts Landing	37097
Brittsville	37336
Broad Acres	37849
Broadmoor	38024
Broadview (Crockett County)	38034
Broadview (Franklin County)	37398
Broadway (Davidson County)	37203
Broadway (Henderson County)	38351
Brockdell	37367
Brockland Acres	37813
Brock's	38230
Brookhaven (Part of Crossville)	38555
Brooks (Part of Hohenwald)	38462
Brookwood	38464
Brotherton	38506
Browder (Part of Jasper)	37347
Brown Crossroads	38469
Brown Ellis	37748
Brownington	37398
Browns	37083
Browns Chapel	37377
Brownsville	38012
Browntown	38578
Brownwood Acres	37064
Broylesville	37681
Bruceton	38317
Bruner Grove	37713
Brunswick	38014
Brush Creek (Sequatchie County)	37327
Brush Creek (Smith County)	38547
Brush Creek (Williamson County)	37062
Brushy Mountain State Penitentiary	37845
Bruton Branch	38365
Bryan Hill (Part of Dayton)	37321
Bryant Station	37091
Bryson	38449
Bryson Mountain	40965
Buchanan	38222
Buck Lodge	37148
Buckner	37166
Bucksnort	37140
Bucktown (Hardin County)	38372
Bucktown (Loudon County)	37771
Buena Vista	38318
Buffalo (Humphreys County)	37078
Buffalo (Scott County)	37756
Buffalo Springs	37861
Buffalo Valley	38548
Bufords	38472
Bugscuffle	37183
Buladeen	37643
Bullards Creek	38562
Bull Creek	37756
Bullet Creek	37369
Bull Run (Anderson County)	37849
Bull Run (Davidson County)	37015
Bulls Gap	37711
Bumpus Cove	37650
Bumpus Mills	37028
Buncombe	37617
Bungalow Town	37804
Bunker Hill	38478
Buntontown	37640
Burbank	37687

	ZIP
Burchfield Heights	37830
Burem	37857
Burgen	37026
Burgess	38506
Burke	37367
Burlington (Part of Knoxville)	37914
Burlington Heights (Part of Cleveland)	37312
Burlison	38015
Burnett	38501
Burns	37029
Burnt Church	38372
Burristown	38562
Burrville	37872
Burt	37190
Burton (Part of Rogersville)	37857
Burwood	37179
Busby (Part of Loretto)	38469
Bush Grove	38002
Busseltown	37771
Busseltown	38363
Butler	37640
Butlers Landing	38551
Bybee (Cocke County)	37713
Bybee (Warren County)	37110
Byrdstown	38549
Cabin Row	37171
Cabo	38332
Cades	38358
Cades Cove	37882
Cadet (Part of Franklin)	37064
Cagle	37327
Cain Mill	37860
Cainsville	37085
Cairo (Crockett County)	38001
Cairo (Sumner County)	37066
Cairo Bend	37087
Calderwood	37801
Calfkiller	38574
Calhoun	37309
Calico	37322
Calista	37049
Callins	38230
Calls	37330
Calvin Estates	38301
Camargo	37334
Cambria	37325
Cambridge	38581
Camden	38320
Camelot (Cumberland County)	38555
Camelot (Hawkins County)	37857
Camilla Homes	38004
Campaign	38550
Camp Austin	37829
Campbell Army Airfield	42223
Campbell Junction	38555
Campbells	38451
Campbellsville	38478
Camp Creek	37743
Camp Ground (Fentress County)	38553
Camp Ground (Weakley County)	38237
Camp Marymount	37062
Camp Monterey Lake	38574
Camp Nakanawa	38555
Camp Relax	37166
Camps	37869
Camp Ta-Pa-Win-Go	37694
Camp Woodlee	37110
Canadaville	38028
Cane Ridge (Part of Nashville)	37013
Caney Branch	37743
Caney Creek (Hamblen County)	37891
Caney Creek (Hawkins County)	37857
Caney Ford	37748
Caney Spring	37091
Caney Valley	37879
Cantrell	38485
Capitol Hill (Franklin County)	37330
Capitol Hill (Scott County)	37756
Capleville	38118
Caravelle Estates	37122
Cardiff (Part of Rockwood)	37854
Carlisle	37058
Carlock (Jackson County)	38562
Carlock (McMinn County)	37331
Carnegie (Part of Johnson City)	37601
Carpenter Campground	37804
Carr Branch	37825
Carroll	37087

	ZIP
Carroll Reece (Part of Johnson City)	37601
Carson Spring	37821
Carter	37643
Carter Chapel	37818
Carters Creek	38401
Carthage	37030
Carthage Junction (Part of Gordonsville)	38567
Cartwright (Sequatchie County)	37397
Cartwright (Smith County)	37145
Caryville	37714
Cash Point	38449
Cassville	38583
Castalian Springs	37031
Castle Heights	37821
Cataska	37385
Cat Corner	38240
Cates	38079
Cates Trailor	37764
Catlettsburg (Part of Sevierville)	37876
Cato	37057
Catons Grove	37722
Catoosa	37770
Cave	38559
Cave Spring	37879
Cedar Bluff	37876
Cedar Bluff Two	37922
Cedar Chapel	38075
Cedar Creek	37743
Cedar Creek Landing	37096
Cedarcrest	37857
Cedarfork (Claiborne County)	37879
Cedar Fork (Loudon County)	37846
Cedar Grove (Bedford County)	37034
Cedar Grove (Carroll County)	38321
Cedar Grove (Carter County)	37601
Cedar Grove (Henderson County)	38371
Cedar Grove (Humphreys County)	37078
Cedar Grove (Pickett County)	38577
Cedar Grove (Roane County)	37763
Cedar Grove (Rutherford County)	37060
Cedar Grove (Sullivan County)	37660
Cedar Grove (rural) (Sullivan County)	37618
Cedar Grove (Wilson County)	37087
Cedar Hill (Putnam County)	38544
Cedar Hill (Robertson County)	37032
Cedar Springs	37303
Cedar Valley (Part of Bristol)	37620
Celina	38551
Center (Crockett County)	38337
Center (Lawrence County)	38464
Center (Monroe County)	37385
Center Grove (Franklin County)	37388
Center Grove (Jackson County)	38562
Center Hill (Cannon County)	37190
Center Hill (Henderson County)	38368
Center Hill Loop	38368
Center Point (Chester County)	38332
Center Point (Giles County)	38478
Center Point (Hardeman County)	38042
Center Point (Lawrence County)	38468
Center Point (Sequatchie County)	37327
Center Point (Stewart County)	37058
Center Point (White County)	38587
Center Star	38454
Centersville (Greene County)	37861
Centersville (Loudon County)	37742
Centertown	37110
Centerville (Hickman County)	37033

	ZIP		ZIP		ZIP		ZIP
Centerville (Wilson County)	37087	 37424		Cold Spring (Bledsoe County)	37367	County Line (Sevier County)	37865
Central (Carter County)	37601	For specific Chickamauga Zip Codes call (615) 892-8047, or your local postmaster.		Cold Spring (Johnson County)	37683	Courtland	37172
Central (Gibson County)	38382					Cove Creek (Campbell County)	37714
Central (Lauderdale County)	38063	Chickasaw Heights (Part of Paris)	38242	Cold Springs (Blount County)	37886	Cove Creek (Carter County)	37687
Central (Obion County)	38253	Childers Hill	38326	Cold Springs (Hawkins County)	37873	Cove Creek Cascades...	37862
Central Heights	37617	Chilhowee View	37803	Coldwater	37334	Cove Lake Estates (Part of Caryville)	37714
Central Point	37861	China Grove	38233	Colesburg	37055	Covington	38019
Central State Psychiatric Hospital (Part of Nashville)	37217	Chinquapin Grove	37618	Coles Ferry	37087	Cowan	37318
		Chinubee	38486	Coles Store	38544	Cowanstown	37640
Central View	37587	Chipman	37022	Coletown	37317	Coxville	38343
Cerro Gordo	38372	Chittum	37879	College	37367	Cozette	38380
Chalklevel (Benton County)	38320	Choptack	37857	Collegedale	37315	Crab Orchard	37723
Chalk Level (Hawkins County)	37857	Chota	37801	College Grove	37046	Crabtree	37687
		Choto Estates	37922	College Grove Estates	37854	Crackers Neck	37683
Chambers	38261	Choto Hills	37777	College Hill (Part of Dayton)	37321	Craggie Hope	37082
Champ	37359	Christiana	37037			Craigfield	37025
Chanceytown	37391	Christian Bend	37642	College Park	37601	Crandull	37688
Chandler	37777	Christianburg	37874	College Park Estates	37803	Cranmore Cove	37321
Chantay Acres (Part of Columbia)	38401	Christian Chapel	38343	College Square Mall (Part of Morristown)	37813	Cravenston	38589
Chanute	38577	Christie Hill	37801	Colliers Corner	37760	Crawfish Valley	38464
Chapel Hill (Marshall County)	37034	Christmasville (Carroll County)	38201	Collierville	38017*	Crawford	38554
					38027†	Creek Store	37810
Chapel Hill (Maury County)	38461	Christmasville (Haywood County)	38012	Collins (Grundy County)	37365	Creekwood (Bedford County)	37160
Chapman Grove	37763	Chuckey	37641	Collins (Hawkins County)	37857		
Chapmans	38478	Church Hill	37642	Collinwood	38450	Creekwood (Wilson County)	37122
Chapmansboro	37035	Churchton	38059	Colonial Acres	38225	Crenshaw	37920
Charity (Part of Lynchburg)	37334	Citico Beach	37885	Colonial Circle	37865	Crescent	37129
Charles Creek Estates...	37110	Clacks Gap	37748	Colonial Heights	37663	Creson (Part of Fayetteville)	37334
Charleston (Bradley County)	37310	Clairfield	37715	Colonial Village (Part of Knoxville)	37920	Creston	38555
		Clark Addition	37804	Columbia	38401*	Crestwood	37763
Charleston (Tipton County)	38069	Clarkrange	38553		38402†	Crestwood Hills	37918
Charleys Branch	37710	Clarksburg	38324	Columbia Hill	38574	Crewstown	38464
Charlotte	37036	Clarksville	37040-44	Columbus Hill	38562	Crieve Hall (Part of Nashville)	37211
Charlotte Park (Part of Nashville)	37209	For specific Clarksville Zip Codes call (615) 647-3392, or your local postmaster.		Comfort	37380	Crippen Gap	37918
				Commerce	37184	Crisp Spring	37357
Charlton Green (Part of Franklin)	37064	Clarksville Base	42223	Community Acres	37180	Crockett	38253
Chaska	37766	Clarktown	38583	Como	38223	Crockett Mills	38021
Chattanooga	37401-50	Claxton (Anderson County)	37849	Compton	37130	Cromwell Crossroads...	38450
For specific Chattanooga Zip Codes call (615) 499-8256, or your local postmaster.		Claxton (McMinn County)	37303	Conasauga	37316	Cronanville	38079
		Claybrook	38301	Concord (Carroll County)	38344	Crooked Creek	37097
Cherokee	38380	Clay Hill	37892	Concord (Gibson County)	38382	Cross	37617
Cherokee Harshaw	37743	Claylick	37187	Concord (Humphreys County)	37185	Cross Anchor	37743
Cherokee Heights	37801	Clayton	38260	Concord (Knox County)	37922	Cross Bridges	38474
Cherokee Hills (Roane County)	37763	Clearbranch	37650	Concord (Rhea County)	37332	Cross Keys	37046
		Clear Creek Mill	37332	Concord (Rutherford County)	37153	Crossland	42049
Cherokee Hills (Part of Sevierville)	37862	Clearmont	37110	Conklin	37659	Cross Lanes	37186
Cherokee Hills (Sevier County)	37865	Clear Springs (Knox County)	37806	Conner Heights (Part of Pigeon Forge)	37863	Cross Plains	37049
						Cross Road	37841
Cherry	38041	Clear Springs (McMinn County)	37309	Conyersville	38251	Crossroads (Benton County)	38320
Cherry Acres (Part of Gruetli-Laager)	37339	Clearview	37048	Cookeville	38501-03	Cross Roads (Cannon County)	37190
Cherrybrook	37912	Clearwater	37303		38505-06		
Cherry Chapel	38372	Clements Lake Estates (Part of Fairview)	37062	For specific Cookeville Zip Codes call (615) 526-7141, or your local postmaster.		Crossroads (Crockett County)	38006
Cherry Creek	38583	Clementsville	37150			Cross Roads (DeKalb County)	37059
Cherry Grove	38333	Cleveland	37311-12	Coolspring Galleria (Part of Franklin)	37064	Cross Roads (Dyer County)	38034
Cherry Hill	38582		37320	Cool Springs	38259		
Cherry Valley	37184		37323	Cooper	38556	Cross Roads (Fentress County)	38556
Chesney	37848		37364	Coopers	38317	Crossroads (Hardin County)	38372
Chester Estates (Part of Fairview)	37062	For specific Cleveland Zip Codes call (615) 472-6597, or your local postmaster.		Coopertown	37172	Cross Roads (Lawrence County)	38456
				Copperhill	37317		
Chesterfield	38351	Clevenger	37821	Corbin Hill	37840	Crossroads (Lawrence County)	38468
Chestnut Bluff	38040	Cliff Springs	38574	Cordell	37756		
Chestnut Glade	38237	Clifftops	37356	Corders Crossroads	37348	Cross Roads (Macon County)	37186
Chestnut Grove (Jefferson County)	37725	Cliffwood	38464	Cordova	38018*		
		Clifton	38425		38088†	Crossroads (Shelby County)	38017
Chestnut Grove (Perry County)	37096	Clifton Junction	38425	Corinth (Knox County)	37918		
		Clifty	38583	Corinth (Sumner County)	37148	Cross Roads (Stewart County)	37175
Chestnut Grove (Robertson County)	37073	Clinton	37716*	Cornersville	37047		
			37717†	Coro Lake (Part of Memphis)	38109	Crossroads (Wayne County)	38450
Chestnut Grove (Stewart County)	37058	Clopton	38011	Corona	72338		
Chestnut Grove (Sumner County)	37148	Cloud Creek	37857	Corryton	37721	Crosstown (Part of Memphis)	38104
		Clouds	37879	Cortner	37360	Crossville	38055
Chestnut Grove (Union County)	37807	Clouse Hill	37387	Cosby	37722		38057-58
		Clovercroft	37064	Coster (Part of Knoxville)	37917	For specific Crossville Zip Codes call (615) 484-6521, or your local postmaster.	
Chestnut Hill (Cumberland County)	38555	Cloverdale (Obion County)	38240	Cotham	38382		
		Cloverdale (Shelby County)	38053	Cottage Grove	38224	Crosswinds	37122
Chestnut Hill (Jefferson County)	37725	Cloverdale (White County)	38583	Cottage Home	37095	Crowley Store	38230
		Clover Hill (Blount County)	37804	Cottonport	37322	Crown Point Estates	37122
Chestnut Hill (Sumner County)	37148	Cloverhill (Davidson County)	37214	Cottontown	37048	Crucifer	38345
		Cloverport	38381	Cottonwood Estates	37064	Crump	38327
Chestnut Mound	38552	Club Springs	38560	Cottonwood Grove	38080	Crunk	37073
Chestnut Orchard	37172	Coal Chute	37643	Cotula	37766	Crystal	38261
Chestnut Ridge	37641	Coalfield	37719	Couchville (Part of Nashville)	37214	Crystal Springs	37348
Chestoa	37650	Coal Hill (Morgan County)	37872	Coulterville	37373	Cuba (Hawkins County)	37811
Chestua	37354	Coal Hill (Scott County)	37852	Counce	38326	Cuba (Shelby County)	38053
Chestuee	37312	Coaling	37036	Country Club	38008	Cuba Landing	37185
Chewalla	38393	Coalmont	37313	Country Haven Estates	37179	Cub Creek	38562
Chic	38030	Coble	37033	Country Roads	37064	Culleoka	38451
Chickamauga (Part of Chattanooga)	37421-22	Coffee Landing	38310	Countrywood Estates	37064	Culpepper	37149
		Coffee Ridge	37650	Countyline (Moore County)	37352		
		Cog Hill	37325				
		Cokercreek	37314				

Place	ZIP
Cumberland City	37050
Cumberland Estates (Part of Knoxville)	37921
Cumberland Furnace	37051
Cumberland Gap	37724
Cumberland Heights (Grundy County)	37313
Cumberland Heights (Montgomery County)	37040
Cumberland Springs	37321
Cumberland View	37757
Cumberland View Estates	37769
Cummings	38583
Cummingsville	38585
Cunningham	37052
Cupp Mill	37825
Curlee	37190
Curve	38063
Cusick	37865
Cuzick	37772
Cypress	38006
Cypress Creek	38222
Cypress Inn	38452
Daisy (Part of Soddy-Daisy)	37379
Dale Hollow	38551
Dalewood (Part of Nashville)	37207
Dallas Gardens	37379
Dallas Hills	37379
Dalton Heights (Part of Morristown)	37814
Dancyville	38069
Dandridge	37725
Dante	37921
Darden	38328
Darks Mill	38401
Daugherty Estates	37062
Daus	37327
Davenport	37110
Davidson	38589
Davidson Chapel	38382
Davis Chapel (Campbell County)	37766
Davis Chapel (Carroll County)	38344
Davis Springs	37692
Daylight	37110
Days Crossroads	37083
Daysville	37854
Dayton	37321
Dayton Spur	38555
Deanburg	38366
Deans	37033
DeArmond	37748
Deason	37020
De Busk	37743
Decatur	37322
Decaturville	38329
Decherd	37324
Deep Springs	37725
Deerfield (Lawrence County)	38464
Deerfield (Williamson County)	37064
Deerfield Acres	37620
Deer Lodge	37726
Deermont	37829
Defeated	37030
Defense Depot (Part of Memphis)	38114
Delano	37325
Delina	37047
Dellrose	38453
Dellwood	37804
Del Rio	37727
Demory	37766
Denmark	38391
Dennis Cove	37658
Denton	37722
Dentville	37325
Denver (Cannon County)	37149
Denver (Humphreys County)	37054
De Priest Bend (Part of Lobelville)	37097
De Rossett	38583
Detroit	38015
Devonia	37710
Diana	37047
Dibrell	37110
Dickel (Part of Tullahoma)	37388
Dickey Bluff Peninsula	37381
Dickson	37055*
	37056†
Dickson Town	38455
Difficult	37145
Dill	37367
Dilley	37730
Dillton	37130
Disco	37737
Dismal	37095
Disney	37769
Ditty	38506
Dixie	38261
Dixie Lee Junction (Part of Farragut)	37922
Dixon Springs	37057
Dixonville	38053
Doaks Crossroads	37090
Dobson Branch	38501
Dockery	37310
Dodson (Roane County)	37748
Dodson (White County)	38583
Dodson Estates (Part of Nashville)	37076
Dodsons	38472
Doeville	37640
Dog Hill	38034
Dogtown (Carter County)	37643
Dog Town (Grundy County)	37313
Dogtown (Polk County)	37391
Dogwood	37763
Dogwood Heights	37879
Dogwood Shores	37763
Dollar	38318
Donelson (Part of Nashville)	37214
Donnel Chapel	37149
Donoho	37030
Doran Addition	37660
Dorton	38555
Dossett	37716
Dotson	37888
Dotsontown	37681
Dotsonville	37191
Doty Chapel	37616
Double Bridges	38040
Double Springs (McMinn County)	37303
Double Springs (Putnam County)	38544
Double Top	38556
Douglas	37064
Douglas Estates	37725
Dover (Hamblen County)	37813
Dover (Stewart County)	37058
Dowelltown	37059
Dowler Heights	37377
Downtown (Part of Chattanooga)	37401-03
For specific Downtown Zip Codes call (615) 499-8231, or your local postmaster.	
Downtown (Part of Cleveland)	37311
Downtown (Part of Knox)	37901
Downtown (Part of Maryville)	37801
Doyle	38559
Drapers Crossroads	37083
Dresden	38225
Driftwood (Part of Bristol)	37620
Dripping Springs	37398
Drop	38583
Drummonds	38023
Dry Branch	37869
Dry Creek	37659
Dry Hill (Johnson County)	37640
Dry Hill (Lauderdale County)	38040
Dry Hollow (Part of Kingsport)	37660
Duck Creek	37869
Duck River	38454
Ducktown (Polk County)	37326
Ducktown (Washington County)	37681
Dudney Hill	38562
Due West (Part of Nashville)	37115
Duff	37729
Dukedom	38226
Dulaney	37743
Dull	37036
Dumplin	37820
Dunbar	38311
Duncantown	37330
Dunlap	37327
Duplex	37064
Du Pont	37865
Durhamville	38063
Dutch	37888
Dutch Valley	37716
Dyer	38330
Dyersburg	38024*
	38025†
Dykes Crossroads	38555
Dyllis	37748
Dyson Grove	37640
Eads	38028
Eagan	37730
Eagle Creek	38341
Eagle Furnace	37854
Eagleton Village	37804
Eagleville	37060
Earleyville	37110
East (Part of Nashville)	37206
East Acres	38053
East Brainerd	37421
Eastbrook (Part of Estill Springs)	37330
East Chattanooga (Part of Chattanooga)	37406
East Cleveland	37311
East Cyruston	37334
East Due West (Part of Nashville)	37115
Easter Seal	37122
East Etowah	37331
East Fork	37876
Eastgate Mall (Part of Chattanooga)	37411
Eastgate Shopping Center (Part of Memphis)	38117
East Jamestown	38556
East Junction (Part of Memphis)	38101
East Lake (Part of Chattanooga)	37407
Eastland	38583
East Memphis (Part of Memphis)	38111
East Miller's Cove	37886
Eastport	38573
East Ridge	37412
Eastside (Cannon County)	37190
East Side (Carter County)	37643
East Side (Dickson County)	37029
Eastside (Sullivan County)	37664
Eastside (Warren County)	38581
East Springbrook (Part of Alcoa)	37701
East Sweetwater	37874
East Union	38301
Eastview (Greene County)	37745
Eastview (McNairy County)	38367
East View (Meigs County)	37336
Eastwood (Part of La Vergne)	37086
Eaton	38331
Eaton Crossroad	37771
Eaton Forest	37771
Ebenezer (Marion County)	37347
Ebenezer (Monroe County)	37329
Echo Hills	37743
Eddie Hill	37090
Edenwold (Part of Nashville)	37115
Edgefield (Part of Bristol)	37620
Edgemont (Cocke County)	37821
Edgemont (Sullivan County)	37620
Edgemoor	37716
Edgewater (Rhea County)	37321
Edgewater (Wilson County)	37122
Edgewood (Dyer County)	38059
Edgewood (Sullivan County)	37660
Edgewood Acres	37804
Edgewood Heights	37849
Edison	38343
Edith	38063
Edward Grove	38063
Edwards Point	37377
Edwina	37821
Egam	37334
Egypt (Part of Memphis)	38128
Eidson	37731
Elba	38066
Elbethel	37160
Elbridge	38240
Elgin	37732
Elizabeth	38034
Elizabethton	37643*
	37644††
Elkhead	37366
Elkhorn	38242
Elk Mills	37640
Elk Mill Village (Part of Fayetteville)	37334
Elkmont	37738
Elkmont Springs	38449
Elkton	38455
Elk Valley	37847
Ellejoy	37865
Ellendale (Part of Bartlett)	38029
Ellington Park	37064
Ellis Mills	37050
Ellisville	38004
Elm Grove	38015
Elm Springs	37888
Elmwood	38560
Elora	37328
Elverton	37748
Elza	37830
Embreeville	37650
Emerald Acres	37814
Emerts Cove (Part of Pittman Center)	37862
Emery Mill	37367
Emmanuel School of Religion	37601
Emmett	37620
Emory Gap (Part of Harriman)	37748
Emory Heights (Part of Harriman)	37748
Englewood (McMinn County)	37329
Englewood (Obion County)	38260
English Mountain Resort	37876
Enigma	38548
Eno	37055
Enon	37150
Ensor (Part of Baxter)	38544
Enterprise (Hawkins County)	37857
Enterprise (Maury County)	38474
Enville	38332
Epperson	37385
Erasmus	38555
Erie	37846
Erin	37061
Erlanger (Part of Chattanooga)	37403
Ernestville	37650
Erwin	37650
Essary Springs	38061
Estes Kefauver (Part of Johnson City)	37601
Estes Woods	37381
Estill Springs	37330
Ethridge	38456
Etowah	37331
Etter	38549
Eucebia	37865
Eulia	37186
Eureka (Bradley County)	37323
Eureka (Hardin County)	38372
Eureka (Roane County)	37854
Eurekaton	38075
Eva	38333
Evansville	38024
Evensville	37332
Evergreen	37687
Evins Mill	37166
Ewingville (Part of Franklin)	37064
Excell	37040
Executive Estates	38464
Factory	38485
Fair Acres (Hickman County)	37025
Fair Acres (Sullivan County)	37660
Fairfield (Bedford County)	37183
Fairfield (Hickman County)	37033
Fairfield (Sumner County)	37186
Fairfield Acres	37814
Fairfield Glade	38558
Fair Garden	37876
Fairgrounds (Part of Shelbyville)	37160
Fairlane Estates (Part of Shelbyville)	37160
Fairmont (Part of Bristol)	37620
Fairmount	37377
Fairview (Blount County)	37803
Fairview (Bradley County)	37312
Fairview (Carroll County)	38201
Fairview (Carter County)	37658
Fairview (Clay County)	38541
Fairview (Coffee County)	37360
Fairview (Fentress County)	38556
Fairview (Greene County) (mail Mohawk)	37810
Fairview (Greene County) (mail Afton)	37616
Fairview (Lawrence County) (mail Afton)	38469
Fair View (Lincoln County)	37334
Fairview (Macon County)	37186
Fairview (Madison County)	38343
Fairview (McMinn County)	37303
Fairview (Meigs County)	37322
Fairview (Pickett County)	38549
Fairview (Roane County)	37763
Fairview (Scott County)	37756

* Area Zip Code   † Post Office Boxes

Name	ZIP
Fairview (Stewart County)	37058
Fairview (Warren County)	37110
Fairview (Washington County)	37659
Fairview (Wayne County)	38463
Fairview (White County)	38583
Fairview (Williamson County)	37062
Fairview Heights (Jefferson County)	37725
Fairview Heights (Williamson County)	37062
Fairyland	38555
Faix	38549
Falcon	38375
Fall Branch	37656
Fall Creek	37160
Falling Water	37343
Fall River	38468
Falls Mill	37306
Fanchers Mills	38583
Fancy Meadows	37871
Farmers Exchange	38462
Farmers Valley	37096
Farmington (Marshall County)	37091
Farmington (Williamson County)	37064
Farner	37333
Farragut	37922
Farris Chapel	37398
Farrport (Part of Alcoa)	37701
Faulkner Springs	37110
Faxon	38221
Fayette Corners	38075
Fayetteville	37334
Federal Correctional Institution	38116
Federal Reserve (Part of Nashville)	37203
Fellowship	37122
Fernvale	37064
Fernwood	37814
Few Chapel	37101
Fielden Store	37820
Fincastle	37766
Findlay (Part of Sparta)	38583
Finger	38334
Finley	38030
Fisherville	38017
Fishery	37650
Fish Springs	37640
Fisk University (Part of Nashville)	37203
Five Points (Giles County)	38478
Five Points (Lawrence County)	38457
Five Points (Madison County)	38366
Five Points (Rhea County)	37321
Flag Branch	37743
Flag Pond	37657
Flat Branch Junction	37387
Flat Creek (Bedford County)	37160
Flat Creek (Overton County)	38570
Flat Gap (Hancock County)	37883
Flatgap (Jefferson County)	37760
Flat Hollow	37870
Flat Rock (Morgan County)	37726
Flat Rock (Smith County)	37090
Flattop	37379
Flatwood (Tipton County)	38015
Flatwood (Warren County)	37110
Flatwoods (Lawrence County)	38456
Flatwoods (Perry County)	37096
Flewellyn	37172
Flintville	37335
Flippin	38063
Floraton	37149
Florence	37129
Flourville	37601
Flowertown	37360
Fly	38482
Flynns Lick	38562
Foothills Mall (Part of Maryville)	37804
Forbus	38577
Ford	37772
Ford Chapel	37825
Fordtown (Campbell County)	37766
Fordtown (Sullivan County)	37663
Forest Chapel	37186
Forest Grove (Davidson County)	37080

Name	ZIP
Forest Grove (Meigs County)	37322
Forest Hill (Blount County)	37803
Forest Hill (Shelby County)	38139
Forest Hills (Bedford County)	37160
Forest Hills (Davidson County)	37215
Forest Hills (Knox County)	37919
Forest Hills (Sullivan County)	37620
Forest Home	37064
Forest Home Farms	37064
Forest Mill	37355
Forge Ridge	37752
Forked Deer	38037
Fork Mountain	37710
Fork of Pike	37095
Fork Ridge	40965
Forrest Park (Part of Tullahoma)	37388
Forsythe (Part of Memphis)	38101
Fort Campbell	42223
Fort Campbell South	42223
Fort Donelson Shores	37058
Fort Henry Mall (Part of Kingsport)	37664
Fort Loudon Estates	37772
Fort Pillow Prison and State Farm	38041
Fort Robinson (Part of Kingsport)	37660
Forty Forks	38315
Fosterville	37063
Foundry Hill	38251
Fountain City (Part of Knoxville)	37918
Fountain Head	37148
Fountain Heights	38401
Fourmile Board Hill	38485
Four Points	37820
Fowler Grove	37713
Fowlkes	38033
Fox Bluff	37015
Fox Branch	37869
Foxfire	38555
Frankewing	38459
Frankfort	37770
Franklin	37064-65
	37068
For specific Franklin Zip Codes call (615) 794-2784, or your local postmaster.	
Franklin East	37064
Fraterville	37769
Frayser (Part of Memphis)	38127
Fredonia (Coffee County)	37355
Fredonia (Haywood County)	38069
Fredonia (Montgomery County)	37040
Free Communion	38573
Free Hill	38551
Freeland	38222
Free State	38562
Freewill	38562
Fremont	38261
French Broad	37727
Frettin	38052
Friendship (Bledsoe County)	37381
Friendship (Crockett County)	38034
Friendship (Hamilton County)	37341
Friendship (Hawkins County)	37881
Friendship (Sullivan County)	37620
Friends Station	37820
Friendsville	37737
Frisco	37642
Frog Jump (Crockett County)	38040
Frog Jump (Gibson County)	38382
Frog Level	37731
Frog Pond	37083
Front Street (Part of Memphis)	38103
Frost Bottom	37840
Fruitland	38343
Fruitvale	38336
Fulton	38041
Gabtown	37656
Gadsden	38337
Gainesboro	38562
Gainsville	38049
Gaitherville	38464

Name	ZIP
Galaxy Heights (Part of Chattanooga)	37343
Galbraith Springs	37811
Galen	37083
Gallatin	37066
Gallaway	38036
Gandy	38464
Gann	38358
Gapcreek	37643
Gap of the Ridge	37083
Gardner	38237
Garland	38019
Gassaway	37095
Gates	38037
Gath	37110
Gatlinburg	37738
Gattistown	37359
Gause	37035
Gay	37110
General Mail Facility (Part of Knoxville)	37950
Gentry	38544
Georgetown (Gibson County)	38382
Georgetown (Hamilton County)	37336
Georgetown (McMinn County)	37370
George W. Lee (Part of Memphis)	38126
Georgia Crossing	37398
Germantown	38138-39
	38183
For specific Germantown Zip Codes call (901) 754-7818, or your local postmaster.	
Germantown (Part of Nashville)	37189
Gerren Heights	37367
Gibbs (Part of Union City)	38261
Gibbs Crossroads	37145
Gibson	38338
Gibson Hall	37879
Gibsontown (Part of Kingsport)	37660
Gibson Wells	38343
Gift	38019
Gilbreath	37818
Gilchrist	38310
Gildfield	38002
Gilfield	37686
Gilliśes Mills	38372
Gilmore	38301
Gilt Edge	38015
Gin House Lake	38011
Gladdice	38562
Glade Creek	38583
Glades (Morgan County)	37726
Glades (Sevier County)	37738
Gladeville	37071
Glass	38240
Gleason	38229
Glen	37342
Glen Alice	37854
Glencliff (Part of Nashville)	37211
Glendale (Hamilton County)	37405
Glendale (Lawrence County)	38469
Glendale (Loudon County)	37742
Glendale (Maury County)	38401
Glendale (Washington County)	37681
Glendale Estates	38478
Glen Del Acres	37860
Glenhaven (Part of Fairview)	37062
Glen Mary	37852
Glenmore Estates	37853
Glen Oaks	37122
Glenobey	38556
Glenview (Part of Nashville)	37217
Glenwood	37185
Glenwylde	37051
Glimp	38041
Glover	37172
Glover Hill (Part of Jasper)	37347
Glynnwood Lake	38028
Gnat Hill	37355
Goat City	38355
Godwin	38401
Goffton	38501
Goin	37825
Golddust	38063
Goldpoint (Part of Chattanooga)	37343
Goodbars	38581
Goodfield	37322
Good Hope (Campbell County)	37762
Good Hope (Dyer County)	38059

Name	ZIP
Goodlettsville	37070†
	37072*
Good Luck	38369
Goodspring	38460
Good Springs	37331
Goose Horn	38588
Gooseneck	37705
Gordon (Part of Pulaski)	38478
Gordonsburg	38462
Gordonsville	38563
Gorman	37101
Goshen	37642
Gossburg	37018
Grabal	38358
Graball	37148
Graham	37137
Grammer Estates	37062
Grand Junction	38039
Grand Valley	38067
Grandview (Greene County)	37641
Grandview (Knox County)	37920
Grandview (Rhea County)	37337
Grandview Estates	37764
Grandview Terrace	37620
Granite	37716
Grannys Branch	38221
Grant	38563
Grantsboro	37766
Granville	38564
Grasshopper	37308
Grassland	37064
Grassy Cove	38555
Grassy Creek	37317
Grassy Fork	37753
Grassy Valley	37743
Gratio	38240
Gravel Hill (McNairy County)	38339
Gravel Hill (Washington County)	37681
Gravelly Hill (Part of Jefferson City)	37760
Graveltown	37145
Graveston	37721
Gray	37615
Gray Acres	37620
Graysville	37338
Graytown	37033
Graywinds	37122
Green Ack	37840
Green Acres (Giles County)	38478
Green Acres (Knox County)	37921
Green Acres (Roane County)	37763
Green Acres (Sullivan County)	37660
Greenback	37742
Greenbriar	37185
Greenbriar Village (Part of Crossville)	38555
Greenbrier (Cheatham County)	37015
Green Brier (Pickett County)	38549
Greenbrier (Robertson County)	37073
Greenbrier (Williamson County)	37064
Greenbrier Lake	37087
Greeneville	37743-45
For specific Greeneville Zip Codes call (615) 638-2221, or your local postmaster.	
Greenfield	38230
Greenfield Bend	38487
Greenfields (Part of Kingsport)	37660
Green Grove	37074
Green Harbor	37138
Greenhaw	37324
Green Hill (Jefferson County)	37725
Green Hill (Warren County)	37110
Green Hill (Wilson County)	37138
Green Hills (Part of Nashville)	37215
Greenland	37642
Green Meadow (Blount County)	37701
Green Meadow (Bradley County)	37311
Green Meadows	38556
Green Pond	38554
Greens Crossroads	37110
Greens Mill	37343
Greentown	37387
Greenvale	37184

* Area Zip Code   † Post Office Boxes

Place	ZIP
Huron	38345
Hurricane (Houston County)	37175
Hurricane (Jackson County)	38562
Hurricane (Wilson County)	37090
Hurricane Hill	38063
Hurricane Mills	37078
Hustburg	37134
Hutsell (Part of Athens)	37303
Hygeia Springs	37073
Hyndsver	38237
Iconium	37190
Idaho	38468
Idaville	38004
Ideal Valley	37381
Idlewild (Gibson County)	38346
Idlewild (McMinn County)	37303
Idlewood (Part of Franklin)	37064
Ilemar	37122
Imperial Estates	37921
Independence (Hancock County)	37731
Independence (Overton County)	38573
Independence Estates	37087
India	38242
Indian Bluff	37710
Indian Cave	37709
Indian Creek	37757
Indian Hills	37087
Indian Mound (DeKalb County)	38583
Indian Mound (Stewart County)	37079
Indian Ridge (Grainger County)	37709
Indian Ridge (Washington County)	37601
Indian Springs	37617
Ingleside Hill (Part of Athens)	37303
Inglewood (Part of Nashville)	37216
Inskip (Part of Knoxville)	37912
Interstate Park	37032
Irish Cut	37821
Iron City	38463
Ironsburg	37385
Irving College	37110
Irwinton Shores	37880
Isabella	37346
Isham (Part of Winfield)	37892
Island Home (Part of Knoxville)	37920
Island Park	37618
Isoline	38555
Isom	38461
Ivy	37369
Ivy Bluff	37110
Ivydell	37766
Ivy Point (Part of Nashville)	37072
Ivyton	38543
Jacksboro	37757
Jacks Creek	38347
Jackson	38301-08
	38314

For specific Jackson Zip Codes call (901) 422-5369, or your local postmaster.

Place	ZIP
Jackson Heights (Part of Murfreesboro)	37129
Jackson Ridge	37060
Jacksons Chapel	37036
Jackson Square (Part of Oak Ridge)	37830
Jacobs Hill	37090
Jakestown	37130
Jamestown (Fentress County)	38556
Jamestown (Tipton County)	38015
Jarrell	38201
Jasper	37347
Jaybird (Cocke County)	37821
Jaybird (Hamblen County)	37814
Jeannette	38363
Jearoldstown	37641
Jefferson	37166
Jefferson City	37760
Jefferson Estates	37877
Jefferson Springs	37167
Jellico	37762
Jena	37742
Jenkins Hill (Part of Sevierville)	37862
Jenkinsville	38024
Jere Baxter (Part of Nashville)	37216
Jernigan Town	37188

Place	ZIP
Jersey (Part of Chattanooga)	37416
Jessie	37110
Jewell	38225
Jewett	37337
Jimtown	37821
Jockey	37681
Joelton (Part of Nashville)	37080
John Sevier	37914
Johnson Bible College	37920
Johnson City	37601-15

For specific Johnson City Zip Codes call (615) 461-8251, or your local postmaster.

Place	ZIP
Johnsons	37048
Johnsons Chapel	38583
Johnsons Grove	38006
Johntown	37074
Jones	38006
Jonesborough	37659
Jones Chapel	38549
Jones Cove	37876
Jones Mill	38224
Jones Valley	38482
Jonesville (Fentress County)	38553
Jonesville (Roane County)	37840
Joppa (Grainger County)	37861
Joppa (White County)	38587
Jordonia (Part of Nashville)	37218
Jug Town	37130
Juno	38351
Kagley	37801
Kansas (Jefferson County)	37760
Kansas (Sumner County)	37066
Karns	37921
Kaywood (Part of Tullahoma)	37388
Kedron (Giles County)	38477
Kedron (Maury County)	37174
Keefe	38080
Keeling	38069
Keenburg	37643
Keese (Part of Decherd)	37324
Keith Springs	37398
Kellertown	37183
Kelley Town (Part of Oliver Springs)	37840
Kelso	37348
Keltonburg	37166
Kemmer Hill (Part of Spring City)	37381
Kempville	37030
Kendricks Creek	37663
Kennedy Creek	37016
Kenneytown	37745
Kenton	38233
Kepler	37857
Kerrville	38053
Kettle Mills	38461
Key	38583
Key Corner	38040
Keystone (Part of Johnson City)	37601
Killians Chapel (Part of Altamont)	37301
Kilsyth	37766
Kimball	37347
Kimberly Heights	37920
Kimberly Acres	37122
Kimbrough Crossroad	37890
Kimery	38230
Kimmins	38462
Kimsey	37391
Kin Cove	37122
Kinderhook	38476
Kingfield	37064
Kingsport	37660-65

For specific Kingsport Zip Codes call (615) 245-5111, or your local postmaster.

Place	ZIP
King Springs (Part of Johnson City)	37601
Kings Ridge (Part of Chattanooga)	37343
Kingston	37763
Kingston Heights	37763
Kingston Hills	37919
Kingston Mill	37160
Kingston Springs	37082
Kingston Woods	37919
Kinneys	37172
Kinzel Springs	37882
Kirk	38017
Kirkland (Lincoln County)	38488
Kirkland (Williamson County)	37046
Kirkwood	37040
Kite	37857
Kittrell	37149

Place	ZIP
Kleburne	37174
Klondike	37857
Knapp	37769
Knob Creek (Lauderdale County)	38063
Knob Creek (Sevier County)	37865
Knoxville	37901-50

For specific Knoxville Zip Codes call (615) 558-4528, or your local postmaster.

Place	ZIP
Knoxville College (Part of Knoxville)	37921
Kodak	37764
Kodak Estates	37764
KoKo	38069
Kontika	37087
Kyles Ford	37765
Laager (Part of Gruetli-Laager)	37339
Laconia	38045
Lacy	38052
Lafayette	37083
La Follette	37766
La Grange	38046
Laguardo	37087
Lake City	37769
Lake Colonial Estates	37014
Lake Crest	37663
Lake Drive	38079
Lake Farm Estates	37167
Lake Forest (Grainger County)	37861
Lake Forest (Hamilton County)	37343
Lake Forest (Knox County)	37920
Lakeharbor	37763
Lake Harbor Estates	37416
Lake Haven	37087
Lake Hills (Part of Tullahoma)	37388
Lakeland	38002
Lakemont	37777
Lakemont Cabin Area	37811
Lakemont Heights (Part of Rockwood)	37854
Lakemoor	37920
Lakemoore (Part of Morristown)	37814
Lake Placid	38340
Lake Road (Part of Fairview)	37062
Lakeshore Estates	37416
Lake Side (Jefferson County)	37890
Lakeside (Monroe County)	37885
Lakeside Estates (Part of Estill Springs)	37330
Lakeside Heights	37890
Lakeside Park	37343
Lakesite	37379
Lake Tansi Village	38555
Lake Tullahoma Estates (Part of Tullahoma)	37388
Lakeview (Blount County)	37777
Lakeview (Claiborne County)	37825
Lakeview (Roane County)	37763
Lakeview (Robertson County)	37172
Lakeview Commercial Park (Part of Franklin)	37064
Lakeview Estates	37777
Lake View Heights (Part of Harriman)	37748
Lakeview Manor	38256
Lakeview Park (Part of Dandridge)	37725
Lakewood	37138
Lakewood Village	37381
Lamar (Shelby County)	38114
Lamar (Washington County)	37659
Lambert	38068
Lamont	37172
Lamontville	37309
Lancaster	38569
Lancaster Hill	38567
Lancelot Acres	38478
Lancing	37770
Lane	38240
Laneview	38382
Langford Farms	37138
Lanier	37801
Lantana	38555
Lapata	38059
Lascassas	37085
Lassiter Corner	38232
Latham	38225
Laurel (Anderson County)	37716
Laurel (Sevier County)	37876

Place	ZIP
Laurel Bloomery	37680
Laurel Bluff	37763
Laurel Brook	37321
Laurelburg	38581
Laurel Cove	38581
Laurel Grove	37710
La Vergne	37086
Lavinia	38348
Law	38351
Law Chapel	37801
Lawnville	37763
Lawrenceburg	38464
Lawson Crossroad	37882
Lawton	38375
Leach	38344
Leadvale (Cocke County)	37890
Leadvale (Jefferson County)	37890
Leana	37129
Leapwood	38310
Lea Springs	37709
Leatherwood	38485
Lebanon	37087-90

For specific Lebanon Zip Codes call (615) 444-2672, or your local postmaster.

Place	ZIP
Ledgemere (Part of Shelbyville)	37160
Lee	37367
Lee College (Part of Cleveland)	37311
Leeland	37064
Leemans Corner	37090
Leesburg	37659
Lee Valley	37869
Leeville	37090
Leewood (Part of Memphis)	38101
Leftwich	38401
Legate	37079
Leighs	38019
Leighton	38391
Leinart	37716
Leipers Fork	37064
Lenoir City	37771-72

For specific Lenoir City Zip Codes call (615) 986-3225, or your local postmaster.

Place	ZIP
Lenow	38018
Lenox	38047
Leoma	38468
Leonardtown	37620
Leoni	37190
Lewisburg	37091
Lewis Chapel	37327
Lexie	37306
Lexie Crossroads	37306
Lexington	38351
Liberty (Benton County)	38320
Liberty (Decatur County)	38329
Liberty (DeKalb County)	37095
Liberty (Franklin County)	37398
Liberty (Giles County)	38477
Liberty (Jackson County)	38564
Liberty (Lincoln County)	37334
Liberty (Morgan County)	37887
Liberty (Sequatchie County)	37397
Liberty (Sumner County) (mail Bethpage)	37022
Liberty (Sumner County) (mail Gallatin)	37066
Liberty (Washington County)	37641
Liberty (Weakley County)	38229
Liberty Grove	38469
Liberty Hill (Giles County)	38456
Liberty Hill (Grainger County)	37888
Liberty Hill (Greene County)	37641
Liberty Hill (McMinn County)	37329
Liberty Hill (Williamson County)	37025
Liberty Hill (Wilson County)	37012
Lick Creek (Benton County)	38221
Lick Creek (Decatur County)	38363
Lickskillet	37807
Lickton (Part of Nashville)	37189
Lightfoot	38063
Lillamay	37015
Lillydale	37650
Lily Grove	37825
Limestone	37681
Limestone Cove	37692
Linary	38555
Lincoln	37334

* Area Zip Code   † Post Office Boxes

	ZIP
Lincoln Park (Part of Knoxville)	37917
Lincoya Hills (Part of Nashville)	37214
Linden	37096
Lindsay Mill	37769
Link	37037
Linsdale	37325
Linton (Part of Nashville)	37216
Linwood	37090
Lisbon	38052
Little Barren	37825
Littlebrook (Part of Rockford)	37853
Littlecrab	38556
Little Creek	37752
Little Doe	37640
Little Emory	37748
Little Hope (Rutherford County)	37129
Little Hope (Wayne County)	38485
Littlelot	38454
Little Milligan	37640
Little River	37804
Little White Oak	37766
Litton	37367
Litz Manor (Part of Kingsport)	37660
Liverwort	37040
Livesay Mill	37731
Livingston	38570
Lobelville	37097
Locke	38053
Lockertsville	37015
Lockmiller Addition (Part of Athens)	37303
Locust Grove	38059
Locust Mount	37659
Locust Springs	37616
Lodge	37380
Lodi	38486
Logans Lake	38334
Lois (Part of Lynchburg)	37359
Lomax Crossroads	38462
Lone Mountain (Claiborne County)	37825
Lone Mountain (Scott County)	37852
Lone Oak	37377
Lone Oaks (Part of Atoka)	38004
Lone Star	37660
Lonewood	38585
Long Branch (Hamilton County)	37343
Long Branch (Lawrence County)	38464
Long Creek	37843
Long Hollow (Part of La Follette)	37766
Long Island (Part of Kingsport)	37660
Long Rock	38344
Longs Mills (Part of Athens)	37303
Longtown	38049
Longview	37020
Longwood	37064
Lonsdale (Part of Knoxville)	37921
Lookout Mountain	37350
Lookout Valley (Part of Chattanooga)	37419
Loon Bay	37028
Loretto	38469
Lorraine	37381
Lost Creek (Decatur County)	38329
Lost Creek (White County)	38583
Lost Mountain	37745
Loudon	37774
Louise	37051
Louisville	37777
Lovejoy	38574
Lovelace	37641
Love Lady	38549
Loveland (Part of Knoxville)	37924
Lovell Heights	37922
Love Station	37650
Lovetown	38474
Lower Mill	37343
Lower Mockeson	38468
Lowland	37778
Lowryville	38372
Luckett	38063
Lucky	37110
Lucy	38053
Luna	37019
Lunns Store	37034

	ZIP
Lupton City (Part of Chattanooga)	37351
Luray	38352
Lusk	37327
Luskville	37309
Luther	37869
Luttrell (Loudon County)	37846
Luttrell (Union County)	37779
Lutts	38471
Lyles	37098
Lynchburg	37352
Lynn Garden	37665
Lynn Point	38316
Lynnville	38472
Lyons View (Part of Knoxville)	37919
McAllister Hill	37346
McAllisters Crossroads	37171
McAnna	38260
McBurg	38459
McCains	38401
McClamerys Stand (Part of Collinwood)	38450
McCloud	37857
McClures Bend	37030
McCoinsville	38562
McConnell	38237
McCullough	38024
Mc Donald	37353
McDonald Hill	37857
Macedonia (Carroll County)	38201
Macedonia (McMinn County)	37329
Macedonia (Obion County)	38233
Macedonia (White County)	38583
McElroy	38559
Mace's Hill	37057
McEwen	37101
McGeetown	37317
McIlwain	38341
McKenzie	38201
McKinley	37601
McKinnon	37175
McLemoresville	38235
McLin's Corner	38034
McMahan (Part of Sevierville)	37862
McMillan	37914
McMinnville	37110
McNairy	38315
Macon	38048
McPheeter Bend	37642
Maddox	38372
Madge	38002
Madie	38080
Madison	37115*
	37116†
Madison College (Part of Nashville)	37115
Madison Hall	38301
Madison Square (Part of Nashville)	37115
Madisonville	37354
Maggart	38560
Magnolia	37175
Magnolia Place (Part of Franklin)	37064
Major	37090
Malesus (Part of Jackson)	38301
Mall at Green Hills, The (Part of Nashville)	37215
Mall at Johnson City, The (Part of Johnson City)	37601
Mall of Memphis, The (Part of Memphis)	38118
Mallory (Part of Memphis)	38109
Mallorys (Part of Franklin)	37064
Maloney Heights	37920
Maloneyville	37918
Manchester	37355
Manila	37329
Mankinville	37130
Manlyville	38256
Mansfield	38236
Mansfield Gap	37877
Manson	38556
Maple Grove (Clay County)	38541
Maple Grove (Macon County)	37083
Maple Grove (Meigs County)	37880
Maple Hill	37620
Maplehurst	37618
Maplewood (Part of Nashville)	37216
Marble City (Part of Knoxville)	37919
Marbledale	37914

	ZIP
Marble Hall	37857
Marble Hill (Blount County)	37737
Marble Hill (Moore County)	37398
Marble Plains	37398
Marbleton	37692
Marguerite	37814
Marion (Claiborne County)	37715
Marion (Montgomery County)	37051
Markham	38079
Marlborough	38317
Marlow	37716
Marlyn Hills (Part of Bristol)	37620
Marrowbone	37015
Mars Hill (Lawrence County)	38464
Mars Hill (Rhea County)	37381
Martel Estates	37772
Martha	37090
Marthas Chapel	37040
Martha Washington	38553
Martin	38237
Martin Creek (Hancock County)	37879
Martin Creek (Putnam County)	38544
Martin Springs	37380
Marvin	37818
Marys Grove	38488
Maryville	37801-04
For specific Maryville Zip Codes call (615) 983-7801, or your local postmaster.	
Maryville College (Part of Maryville)	37801
Mascot	37806
Mason	38049
Mason Grove	38343
Mason Hall	38233
Masseyville	38315
Matheny Grove	38225
Maupin Row (Part of Johnson City)	37601
Maury City	38050
Maxey	38059
Maxwell	37306
Maxwell Chapel	38568
May Acres	37877
Mayhome	37184
Mayland	38555
Maymead	37683
Maynardville	37807
Mayview Heights	37849
McCutchen Heights	38261
Mc Donald	37810
Meacham	38024
Meades Quarry (Part of Knoxville)	37920
Meadorville	37083
Meadow	37742
Meadowbrook (Blount County)	37804
Meadowbrook (Greene County)	37616
Meadow Brook (Warren County)	37110
Meadow Green Acres	37064
Meadow Mead (Part of Paris)	38242
Meadow View (Hamilton County)	37336
Meadowview (Lawrence County)	38464
Meadowview Gardens (Part of Harriman)	37748
Meadowwood Acres (Part of Fairview)	37062
Medford	37769
Medina	38355
Medon	38356
Melrose (Blount County)	37886
Melrose (Davidson County)	37204
Melville Hill (Part of Soddy-Daisy)	37379
Melvine	37367
Memphis	38101-90
For specific Memphis Zip Codes call (901) 775-3872, or your local postmaster.	

COLLEGES & UNIVERSITIES

Christian Brothers College	38104
Memphis State University	38152
Rhodes College	38112
University of Tennessee-Memphis	38163

	ZIP
### FINANCIAL INSTITUTIONS	
Bank of Bartlett	38128
Boatmen's Bank of Tennessee	38119
Community Bank of Germantown	38119
First American National Bank	38103
First Tennessee Bank, National Association	38103
Leader Federal Bank for Savings	38103
National Bank of Commerce	38150
Nationsbank of Tennessee, N.A.	38112
Union Planters National Bank	38103
United American Bank of Memphis	38119
### HOSPITALS	
Baptist Memorial Hospital	38146
Methodist Hospital of Memphis	38104
Regional Medical Center at Memphis	38103
St. Francis Hospital	38119
St. Joseph Hospital and Health Centers	38105
Veterans Affairs Medical Center	38104
### HOTELS/MOTELS	
Hampton Inn-Medical Center	38104
Holiday Inn International Airport	38116
Holiday Inn Midtown/Medical Center	38104
Ramada Hotel Convention Center	38103
Ramada Southwest	38116
### MILITARY INSTALLATIONS	
Defense Distribution Depot, Memphis	38114
Tennessee Air National Guard, FB6422, Memphis International Airport	38118
United States Army Engineer District, Memphis	38103
Memphis State University (Part of Memphis)	38152
Mendenhall (Part of Memphis)	38117
Mengelwood	38047
Mentor	37777
Mercer	38392
Meredith Cave	37766
Merry Oaks (Part of Nashville)	37214
Michie	38357
Middlebrook Heights (Part of Knoxville)	37919
Middleburg (Hardeman County)	38008
Middleburg (Henderson County)	38374
Middle City	38024
Middle Creek	37862
Middle Fork	38345
Middle Settlement	37777
Middleton	38052
Middle Valley	37343
Middle Valley Estates	37343
Midfields	37665
Midland	37020
Midtown	37748
Midtown Heights	37748
Midway (Cannon County)	37026
Midway (Cocke County)	37727
Midway (Cumberland County)	38555
Midway (DeKalb County)	37166
Midway (Dyer County)	38030
Midway (Franklin County)	37375
Midway (Greene County)	37809
Midway (Johnson County)	37640
Midway (Knox County)	37871
Midway (Obion County)	38261
Midway (Roane County)	37763
Midway (Warren County)	37110
Midway (Washington County)	37601
Mifflin	38352
Milan	38358
Milan Army Ammunition Plant	38358

* Area Zip Code   † Post Office Boxes

	ZIP
Milburnton	37681
Miles Crossroads	37150
Mile Straight (Part of Soddy-Daisy)	37379
Milky Way	38478
Mill Brook	37681
Mill Creek (Anderson County)	37705
Mill Creek (Morgan County)	37872
Mill Creek (Putnam County)	38506
Mildale	37172
Milledgeville	38359
Miller's Store	38225
Millersville	37072
Millertown	37914
Millican Grove	37876
Milligan College	37682
Millington	38053-54
	38083
For specific Millington Zip Codes call (901) 872-3278, or your local postmaster.	
Millsfield	38024
Mill Spring	37820
Milltown (Humphreys County)	37101
Milltown (Jackson County)	38588
Milltown (Macon County)	37150
Milltown (Marshall County)	37091
Millview	37064
Milo	37381
Milton	37118
Mimms (Part of Nashville)	37211
Mimosa	37334
Mimosa Estates	37777
Mimosa Heights	37777
Mineral Park	37353
Mineral Springs	38574
Mink	38485
Minnick	38240
Minor Hill	38473
Mint	37803
Miser Station	37737
Miston	38056
Mitchell	37148
Mitchellville	37119
Mixie	38342
Moccasin	38485
Mohawk	37810
Mohawk Crossroad	37711
Molino	37334
Mon	37087
Mona	37129
Monoville	37030
Monroe	38573
Montague (Davidson County)	37216
Montague (Rhea County)	37321
Monteagle	37356
Monterey	38574
Montezuma	38340
Montgomery Junction	37756
Monticello (Williamson County)	37064
Monticello (Wilson County)	37122
Montpier Farms	37064
Montvale	37803
Moodyville	38549
Mooneyham	38585
Moons	38256
Moon Shadows	37341
Mooreland Heights (Part of Knoxville)	37920
Mooresburg	37811
Mooresburg Springs	37811
Moores Chapel	38358
Moores College	38581
Mooresville	37091
Mooretown	37190
Mooring	38079
Morgan Springs	37321
Morganton	37742
Morgantown	37321
Morganville	37397
Morley	37766
Morny (Part of Nashville)	37080
Morris Chapel (Benton County)	38320
Morris Chapel (Hardin County)	38361
Morrison	37357
Morrison City	37665
Morrison Creek	38562
Morristown	37813-16
For specific Morristown Zip Codes call (615) 586-1291, or your local postmaster.	
Moscow	38057
Mosheim	37818

	ZIP
Moss	38575
Mossy Grove	37748
Mountain City	37683
Mountain Dale	37650
Mountain Home (Part of Johnson City)	37684
Mountain View (Rhea County)	37321
Mountain View (Scott County)	37852
Mountain View Acres (Part of Winchester)	37398
Mount Airy	37327
Mount Ararat	37095
Mount Carmel (Decatur County)	38329
Mount Carmel (Greene County)	37711
Mount Carmel (Hawkins County)	37645
Mount Carmel (Tipton County)	38019
Mount Carmel (Washington County)	37641
Mount Crest	37367
Mount Cumberland	37329
Mount Denson	37172
Mount Gilead (Henderson County)	38321
Mount Gilead (White County)	38583
Mount Harmony (McMinn County)	37826
Mount Harmony (Monroe County)	37385
Mount Helen	38504
Mount Herman (Bedford County)	37160
Mount Herman (Weakley County)	38230
Mount Hope	38485
Mount Horeb	37760
Mount Joy	38474
Mount Juliet	37122
Mount Lebanon (Lawrence County)	38464
Mount Lebanon (Tipton County)	38019
Mount Leo (Part of McMinnville)	37110
Mount Moriah	38320
Mount Nebo	38463
Mount Olive (Grundy County)	37110
Mount Olive (Knox County)	37920
Mount Olive (Marion County)	37397
Mount Olive (Rutherford County)	37130
Mount Pelia	38237
Mount Pisgah	38587
Mount Pleasant (Greene County)	37743
Mount Pleasant (Henry County)	38222
Mount Pleasant (Maury County)	38474
Mount Pleasant (Putnam County)	38506
Mount Pleasant (Scott County)	37852
Mount Tabor	37804
Mount Tucker Addition	37617
Mount Union (Jackson County)	38564
Mount Union (Pickett County)	38549
Mount Vernon (Monroe County)	37358
Mount Vernon (Rutherford County)	37153
Mount Vernon (Sumner County)	37022
Mount View (Davidson County)	37211
Mount View (Grundy County)	37366
Mount Vinson	38379
Mount Zion (Cheatham County)	37015
Mount Zion (Monroe County)	37885
Mount Zion (Montgomery County)	37051
Mount Zion (Obion County)	38232
Mount Zion (Warren County)	37110
Mourberry	38583
Mowbray	37379
Mt. Carmel	37345

	ZIP
Mt. Lebanon	38329
Mt. Vernon	37388
Mud Creek (McNairy County)	38310
Mud Creek (Warren County)	38581
Muddy Pond	38574
Mudsink	37064
Mulberry	37359
Mulberry Gap	37869
Mulberry Hill	37058
Mulloy	37048
Munford	38058
Murfreesboro	37129-33
For specific Murfreesboro Zip Codes call (615) 893-2201, or your local postmaster.	
Murray-Lake Hills (Part of Chattanooga)	37416
Murray Store	37826
Myers (Part of Winchester)	37398
Nameless	38545
Nance	38001
Nance Ferry	37709
Nances Grove	37820
Nankipoo	38040
Napier	38462
Narrows of the Harpeth	37082
Narrow Valley	37861
Nash	38544
Nashville	37201-50
For specific Nashville Zip Codes call (615) 885-1005, or your local postmaster.	

COLLEGES & UNIVERSITIES

	ZIP
Belmont University	37212
David Lipscomb College	37204
Tennessee State University	37209
Vanderbilt University	37240

FINANCIAL INSTITUTIONS

	ZIP
First American National Bank	37237
First Union National Bank of Tennessee	37203
Nationsbank of Tennessee	37219
Third National Bank in Nashville	37219

HOSPITALS

	ZIP
Baptist Hospital	37236
Centennial Medical Center	37202
Nashville Metropolitan Bordeaux Hospital	37218
St. Thomas Hospital	37205
Vanderbilt University Hospital and Clinic	37232
Veterans Affairs Medical Center	37212

HOTELS/MOTELS

	ZIP
Doubletree Hotel	37219
Holiday Inn-Briley Parkway	37219
Holiday Inn-Crowne Plaza	37219
Loews Vanderbilt Plaza Hotel	37203
Nashville Airport Marriott	37214
Regal Maxwell House	37228
Sheraton Music City	37214

MILITARY INSTALLATIONS

	ZIP
Tennessee Air National Guard, FB6421, Nashville International Airport	37217
United States Army Engineer District, Nashville	37202
United States Property and Fiscal Office for Tennessee	37204
Natco (Part of Columbia)	38401
National Cemetery (Part of Memphis)	38122
Natural Bridge	37843
Nauvoo	38024
Neapolis	38401
Neboville	38059
Needmore (Hamblen County)	37891
Needmore (Marshall County)	37091
Needmore (Maury County)	38474
Needmore (Montgomery County)	37079

	ZIP
Needmore (Wilson County)	37138
Neely	38391
Neely Crossroads	38551
Nelsontown (Part of Kingsport)	37660
Nemo	37887
Nenny	37891
Neptune	37015
Neubert	37920
Neva	37683
Newbern	38059
New Bethel	37331
New Canton	37642
New Castle	38075
Newcomb	37819
New Corinth	37861
New Deal	37048
New Dellrose	38453
New Due West (Part of Nashville)	37115
Newell Station	37865
New Enterprise	38338
New Era	38555
New Harmony (Bledsoe County)	37367
New Harmony (Macon County)	37074
New Haven (Lawrence County)	38464
New Haven (Scott County)	37841
New Herman	37160
New Hope (Cheatham County)	37080
New Hope (Hancock County)	37869
New Hope (Hardin County)	38310
New Hope (Hawkins County)	37857
New Hope (Houston County)	37175
New Hope (Humphreys County)	37101
New Hope (Jackson County)	38568
New Hope (Lincoln County)	37334
New Hope (Marion County)	37380
New Hope (McNairy County)	38339
New Hope (Roane County)	37854
New Hope (Williamson County)	37062
New Hope (Wilson County)	37087
New Johnsonville	37134
New Line	37814
New Loyston	37807
Newmansville	37616
New Market	37820
New Markham	38079
New Middleton	38563
New Midway	37763
Newport	37821
New Prospect	38464
New Providence (Loudon County)	37774
New Providence (Montgomery County)	37042
New River	37755
New Safford	38328
New Salem (Hamilton County)	37379
New Salem (Jackson County)	38562
New Salem (Scott County)	37841
New Tazewell	37825
Newton	38555
New Town (Marshall County)	37047
New Town (Maury County)	37174
Newtown (Polk County)	37317
Newtown (Rutherford County)	37153
New Union	37355
New Victory	37659
New Zion (Carroll County)	38344
New Zion (Macon County)	37186
Nickletown	37347
Nicks Creek	37756
Nine Mile	37367
Ninth Model	37357
Niota	37826
Nixon	38372
Noah	37355
Nobles	38242

* Area Zip Code   † Post Office Boxes

	ZIP
Nolensville	37135
Nonaburg	37329
Nonaville	37122
Nonconnah (Part of Memphis)	38116
Norene	37136
Norma	37756
Normandy	37360
Norris	37828
North (Part of Memphis)	38107
North (Part of Nashville)	37208
North Chattanooga (Part of Chattanooga)	37405
Northcott	37660
Northcutts Cove (Grundy County)	37110
Northcutt's Cove (Warren County)	37110
Northeast (Part of Nashville)	37207
Northeast Correctional Center	37683
Northern Hills (Part of Chattanooga)	37343
Northgate Mall (Part of Chattanooga)	37415
Northgate Shopping Center (Part of Memphis)	38127
North Glen Estates (Part of Chattanooga)	37343
North Hills (Part of Knoxville)	37917
North Johnson City (Part of Johnson City)	37601
North Knoxville (Part of Knoxville)	37917
Northpoint	37874
North Riverside	38462
Northside (Part of Jackson)	38301
North Springs	38588
Northwest Correctional Center	38079
Norwood (Anderson County)	37840
Norwood (Knox County)	37912
Notchy Creek	37354
Nough	37727
Nubia	37186
Nucarbon	38468
Number One (Part of Gallatin)	37066
Nunnelly	37137
Nutbush	38012
Oak City	37865
Oak Court Mall (Part of Memphis)	38117
Oakdale (Hawkins County)	37873
Oakdale (Macon County)	37186
Oakdale (Morgan County)	37829
Oak Dale (Overton County)	38573
Oakdale (White County)	38583
Oakfield	38362
Oak Grove (Campbell County)	37769
Oak Grove (Carter County)	37643
Oak Grove (Claiborne County)	37752
Oak Grove (Clay County)	38575
Oak Grove (Dickson County)	37055
Oak Grove (Franklin County)	37324
Oak Grove (Giles County)	38460
Oak Grove (Hardin County)	38372
Oak Grove (Henry County)	38222
Oak Grove (Jefferson County)	37725
Oak Grove (Lewis County)	38462
Oak Grove (Madison County)	38301
Oak Grove (Marion County)	37397
Oak Grove (Monroe County)	37354
Oak Grove (Overton County) (mail Hilham)	38568
Oak Grove (Overton County) (mail Livingston)	38570
Oak Grove (Pickett County)	38573
Oak Grove (Polk County)	37307
Oak Grove (Sumner County)	37022

	ZIP
Oak Grove (Tipton County)	38019
Oak Grove (Union County)	37866
Oak Grove (Warren County)	37357
Oak Grove (Washington County)	37615
Oak Grove (Weakley County)	38237
Oak Grove Heights	37921
Oakhaven (Part of Memphis)	38116
Oak Hill (Carter County)	37658
Oak Hill (Cocke County)	37843
Oak Hill (Cumberland County)	38555
Oak Hill (Davidson County)	37220
Oak Hill (Overton County)	38580
Oak Hill (Pickett County)	38549
Oak Hill (Sullivan County)	37620
Oak Hill (Washington County)	37659
Oakhurst (Part of Maryville)	37803
Oakland (Fayette County)	38060
Oakland (Grainger County)	37861
Oakland (Henry County)	38242
Oakland (Jefferson County)	37760
Oakland (Knox County)	37918
Oakland (Robertson County)	37172
Oakland (Warren County)	37110
Oakland (Washington County)	37690
Oaklawn	37166
Oakleigh Estates	37620
Oakley	38541
Oaklyn	38555
Oak Park (Part of Tullahoma)	37388
Oak Plains	37040
Oak Ridge	37830*
	37831†
Oak Ridge Mall (Part of Oak Ridge)	37830
Oak Tree	37062
Oak View	37886
Oakville (Part of Memphis)	38118
Oakwood (Knox County)	37917
Oakwood (Montgomery County)	37191
Oakwood Estates	37064
Obion	38240
Ocana	37075
Ocoee	37361
O'Connors	38583
Odd Fellows Hall	38478
Officers Chapel	38506
Offutt	37716
Ogden	37321
Okalona	38570
Okolona (Carter County)	37601
Okolona (Hawkins County)	37642
Old Antioch	38562
Old Chihowee	37865
Olde Mill	37343
Oldfort	37362
Old Glory	37804
Old Hickory (Part of Nashville)	37138
Old Hickory Mall (Part of Jackson)	38301
Old Kingsport (Part of Kingsport)	37660
Old Laguardo	37122
Old Lawton	38375
Old Salem	37345
Old Springville	38256
Old Sweetwater	37874
Old Washington	37321
Old Winesap	38555
Old Zion	38583
Olivehill	38475
Oliver Springs	37840
Olivet	38372
One Hundred Oaks Mall (Part of Nashville)	37204
Oneida	37841
Only	37140
Ooltewah	37363
Opossum	38063
Opossum Creek Pines	37379
Oral	37771
Orchard View	37840
Orebank	37664
Ore Spring	38225
Orgains Crossroads	37040

	ZIP
Orlinda	37141
Orme	37380
Orysa	38063
Osage	38242
Osemont Chapel	37190
Ostella	37091
Oswego	37762
Otes	37857
Otter Creek Junction	38555
Ottway	37745
Overall	37130
Overlook	37804
Ovilla	38464
Ovoca	37388
Owens Chapel	37172
Owl City	38079
Owl Hoot	38080
Ozone (Cumberland County)	37842
Ozone (Overton County)	38573
Pactolus	37663
Pailo	37327
Paint Rock	37846
Palestine (Henderson County)	38351
Palestine (Robertson County)	37172
Pall Mall	38577
Palmer	37365
Palmersville	38241
Palmyra	37142
Pandora	37640
Paperville (Part of Bristol)	37620
Paradise Acres	37122
Paragon Mills (Part of Nashville)	37211
Paris	38242
Parkburg	38366
Park City (Knox County)	37914
Park City (Lincoln County)	37334
Parker	38577
Parker's Cross Roads	38388
Park Grove	38464
Park Settlement	37862
Parkshore Estates	37343
Parksville	37307
Parkview	37854
Parkway (Part of Maryville)	37801
Parkway Village (Part of Memphis)	38118
Parragon	38506
Parrottsville	37843
Parsons	38363
Pasquo (Part of Nashville)	37221
Pate Hill	37818
Patterson	37153
Patterson Crossroads	37752
Pattie Gap	37846
Patty	37325
Paulette	37807
Paw Paw Ridge	38030
Payne Cove	37366
Paynes Store	37022
Peabody	37766
Peak	37716
Peakland	37322
Peanut	37843
Pea Ridge (DeKalb County)	37095
Pea Ridge (Lawrence County)	38464
Pearl City	37334
Peavine	38555
Pebble Hill	38357
Peckerwood Point	38004
Peeled Chestnut	38583
Pegram	37143
Pelham	37366
Penile Hill	37324
Pennine	37381
Pennington Bend (Part of Nashville)	37214
Pennington Chapel	37888
Peppertown	38469
Perrin Hollow	37709
Perryville	38363
Persia	37857
Petersburg (Hawkins County)	37857
Petersburg (Lincoln County)	37144
Peters Landing	38425
Petros	37845
Petway	37015
Peytonville	37064
Philadelphia (Jackson County)	38545
Philadelphia (Loudon County)	37846
Philadelphia (Washington County)	37641

	ZIP
Philippi	37166
Phillippy	38079
Pickwatina Place (Part of Athens)	37303
Pickwick Dam	38365
Piedmont	37725
Pierce	38257
Pierce Town	37640
Pigeon Forge	37863*
	37868†
Pigeon River Estates (Part of Sevierville)	37862
Pigeon Roost	37185
Pikeville	37367
Pillowville	38201
Pilot Knob	37711
Pilot Mountain	37770
Pine Bluff	37398
Pinebrook Estates	37341
Pine Crest (Campbell County)	37757
Pine Crest (Carter County)	37601
Pine Grove (Greene County)	37743
Pine Grove (Loudon County)	37774
Pine Grove (Rhea County)	37381
Pine Grove (Sevier County)	37863
Pine Grove (Van Buren County)	38585
Pine Haven (Fentress County)	38556
Pinehaven (Shelby County)	38053
Pine Hill (Bradley County)	37353
Pine Hill (Clay County)	38575
Pine Hill (Marion County)	37397
Pine Hill (Scott County)	37841
Pine Lake	38002
Pineland	37322
Pine Orchard	37829
Pine Point	38256
Pine Ridge (Jefferson County)	37890
Pine Ridge (Polk County)	37333
Pine Top	37772
Pine Tree Estates	37343
Pineview	37096
Pineville (Part of Morristown)	37814
Pinewood (Cheatham County)	37015
Pinewood (Hickman County)	37137
Piney (Loudon County)	37774
Piney (Van Buren County)	38585
Piney Flats	37686
Piney Grove (McMinn County)	37303
Piney Grove (Scott County)	37892
Piney Grove (Washington County)	37601
Piney Shores Estates	37381
Pinhook (Putnam County)	38574
Pinhook (Union County)	37807
Pinnacle (Part of Pittman Center)	37876
Pinson	38366
Pioneer	37847
Pipers Chapel	37148
Piperton	38017
Pisgah (DeKalb County)	37166
Pisgah (Giles County)	38478
Pisgah (Shelby County)	38018
Pisgah (Weakley County)	38225
Pittman Center	37862
Plainfield (Part of Maryville)	37804
Plain Grove	38573
Plainview (Rutherford County)	37037
Plainview (Union County)	37779
Plant	37134
Plantation Hills (Part of Knoxville)	37917
Plateau	38555
Pleasant Green	37726
Pleasant Grove (Bedford County)	37160
Pleasant Grove (Cocke County)	37821
Pleasant Grove (Lincoln County)	37334
Pleasant Grove (Marion County)	37347
Pleasant Grove (Scott County)	37892
Pleasant Grove (Sumner County)	37186

* Area Zip Code   **† Post Office Boxes**

***Area Zip Code** †**Post Office Boxes**

	ZIP		ZIP		ZIP		ZIP
Royal Oaks (Williamson County)	37068	Sequoyah Hills	37343	Shirley	38504	South Fulton	38257
Royal Oaks (Wilson County)	37122	Sequoyah Village (Part of Madisonville)	37354	Shirleyton	37397	Southgate Shopping Center (Part of Memphis)	38109
Royer Estates (Part of Murfreesboro)	37130	Serles	38052	Shooks Gap	37920	South Green	37743
Rucker	37130	Settlers Point	37064	Shop Springs	37184	South Hall (Part of Alcoa)	37701
Rudderville	37064	Seven Islands	37920	Shore Acres	37379	South Harriman (Part of Harriman)	37748
Rudolph	38012	Seven Oaks	37922	Short Creek	37037	South Johnson City (Part of Johnson City)	37601
Rugby	37733	Sevier Home	37920	Short Mountain	37190	South Knoxville (Part of Knoxville)	37920
Rugby Hills (Part of Memphis)	38127	Sevierville	37862	Short Tail Springs	37341	Southland Mall (Part of Memphis)	38116
Rural Hill (Davidson County)	37217		37864	Shouns (Part of Mountain City)	37683	South Liberty	37303
Rural Hill (Wilson County)	37071		37876	Shubert	38462	South Pittsburg	37380
Rural Vale	37385	For specific Sevierville Zip Codes call (615) 453-2981, or your local postmaster.		Siam	37643	Southport	38451
Russel Fork	37766			Sidonia	38255	Southside (Hardin County)	38326
Russell Crossroad	37743			Signal Hills (Part of Chattanooga)	37405	Southside (Montgomery County)	37171
Russell Hill	37145	Sewanee	37375	Signal Mountain	37377	South Tunnel	37066
Russellville	37860	Sewee	37826	Silerton	38377	Spain's Hill	37085
Rusty (Part of Fairview)	37062	Seymour	37865	Silica	37714	Sparkmantown	38559
Rutherford	38369	Shackle Island	37075	Siloam	37186	Sparta	38583
Rutherford Estates	38401	Shacklett	37082	Silvacola	37617	Speedwell	37870
Ruthton	37620	Shades Bridge	38230	Silver City	37860	Spencer	38585
Ruthville	38237	Shady Grove (Coffee County)	37357	Silver Grove	37618	Spencer Creek (Part of Franklin)	37064
Rutledge	37861	Shady Grove (Hamilton County)	37379	Silverhill	37087	Spencer Hill	38474
Rutledge Falls	37355	Shady Grove (Jackson County)	38562	Silver Point	38582	Spencers Mill	37029
Rutledge Hill	37342	Shady Grove (Jefferson County)	37725	Silver Ridge (Part of Lenoir City)	37771	Sportman Acres	37122
Ryall Springs	37421	Shady Grove (Knox County)	37922	Silver Springs	37122	Spot	37140
Sadie	37643	Shady Grove (Lincoln County)	37335	Silvertop	37101	Spout Springs	38232
Sadlers	37010	Shady Grove (Montgomery County)	37040	Sims Spring	37160	Springbrook (Blount County)	37701
Safley	37110	Shady Grove (Morgan County)	37770	Singleton (Bedford County)	37160	Springbrook (Madison County)	38301
Sagewood Estates	38401	Shady Grove (Putnam County)	38574	Singleton (Blount County)	37777	Spring City	37381
Sailors Rest	37050	Shady Grove (Trousdale County)	37074	Sinking Cove	37376	Spring Creek (Hardeman County)	38067
St. Andrews	37372	Shady Grove (White County)	38587	Sitka	38358	Spring Creek (Madison County)	38378
St. Bethlehem (Part of Clarksville)	37155	Shady Grove Shores	37379	Sixmile	37803	Spring Creek (McMinn County)	37303
St. Clair (Hawkins County)	37711	Shady Hill	38351	Skaggston	37806	Spring Creek (Perry County)	37096
St. Clair (Rhea County)	37381	Shady Rest	37110	Skinem	37334	Spring Creek (Wilson County)	37087
St Elmo (Part of Chattanooga)	37409	Shady Valley	37688	Skinner Crossroad	38574	Springdale (Claiborne County)	37879
St. James	37743	Shafter	38230	Skullbone	38316	Springdale (Sullivan County)	37663
St. Joseph	38481	Shake Rag Hill	38485	Skyline	38063	Springfield	37172
St. Paul	38023	Shallowford	37650	Skyline Park (Part of Signal Mountain)	37377	Spring Hill (Anderson County)	37716
Saint Peters	38012	Shandy	38008	Slayden	37165	Spring Hill (Henderson County)	38345
Sainville	37355	Shannondale (Part of Knoxville)	37918	Slick Rock	37852	Spring Hill (Maury County)	37174
Sale Creek	37373	Shannon Hills	37343	Slide	37857	Spring Hill (White County)	38583
Salem (Cocke County)	37843	Sharon	38255	Smartt	37378	Spring Lake	38134
Salem (Lewis County)	37033	Sharondale (Part of Tullahoma)	37388	Smithfield	37385	Springmont	37138
Salem (Montgomery County)	37040	Sharp Place	38556	Smith Fork	38475	Spring Place	37914
Salem (Tipton County)	38004	Sharps Chapel	37866	Smithland	37348	Springs Chapel	38553
Salem (Weakley County)	38255	Sharpsville	37130	Smith Mill	37334	Springtown	37369
Saltillo	38370	Shaver Town	38563	Smiths Chapel	37150	Springvale	37813
Samburg	38254	Shawanee	37867	Smith Springs (Part of Nashville)	37217	Spring View (Blount County)	37801
Sampson	37367	Shawnette	38450	Smithtown (Bledsoe County)	38338	Springview (Williamson County)	37064
Sanders	37387	Shawtown	38232	Smithtown (Marion County)	37380	Springville	38256
Sandhill	38229	Shelby Center (Part of Bartlett)	38134	Smithville	37166	Spruce Pine	37811
Sandlick	37825	Shelby Farms (Part of Memphis)	38101	Smithwood (Part of Knoxville)	37918	Spurgeon	37615
Sand Ridge	38351	Shelbyville	37160	Smoky Junction	37756	Squirrel Flat	38556
Sand Springs	38574	Shelbyville Mills	37160	Smoky View Estates	37804	Staffords Store	38230
Sand Switch	37375	Shell Creek	37687	Smyrna (Carroll County)	38344	Staffordtown	37317
Sandy	38589	Shellmound	37347	Smyrna (Pickett County)	38549	Stainville	37710
Sandy Hook	38474	Shellsford	37110	Smyrna (Rutherford County)	37167	Stanfill	37847
Sandy Lane	37385	Shenandoah Heights	37601	Smyrna (Warren County)	37110	Stanley Junction	37841
Sandy Point	38320	Shenandoah	37865	Sneed Forest Estates	37064	Stanton	38069
Sandy Ridge	37725	Shepp	38069	Sneed Glen	37064	Stantonville	38379
Sandy Spring	37032	Sherrill Heights (Part of Madisonville)	37354	Sneedville	37869	Star Point	38549
Sanford	37370	Sherrilltown	37184	Snow Hill	37363	State Capitol (Part of Nashville)	37219
Sanford Hill (Part of Henderson)	38340	Sherwood	37376	Snows Hill	37059	State Line	37334
Sango	37040	Sherwood Estates	37716	Soddy-Daisy	37379	Statesville	37184
Santa Fe	38482	Sheybogan	37190	Solo	38019	State University (Part of Johnson City)	37601
Saratoga Springs	37367	Shiloh (Bedford County)	37183	Solway	37931	Static	38549
Sardis	38371	Shiloh (Carroll County)	38341	Somerville	38068	Stayton	37051
Saulsbury	38067	Shiloh (Cumberland County)	38555	South (Part of Chattanooga)	37409-10	Stella	38460
Saundersville (Part of Hendersonville)	37075	Shiloh (Grainger County)	37861		37419	Stephen Holston (Part of Bristol)	37620
Savannah	38372	Shiloh (Hardin County)	38376	For specific South Zip Codes call (615) 821-3781, or your local postmaster.		Stephens	37840
Sawdust	38401	Shiloh (Hawkins County)	37869			Stephenson	37342
Sawyers Mill	38320	Shiloh (Humphreys County)	37101	South (Part of Nashville)	37210	Steppsville	37110
Scandlyn	37840	Shiloh (Jackson County)	38506	Southall	37064	Sterling Park	37343
Scarboro (Part of Oak Ridge)	37830	Shiloh (Montgomery County)	37051	South Berlin	37091	Stewart (Houston County)	37175
Scattersville	37148	Shiloh (Overton County)	38554	South Carthage	37030	Stewart (Warren County)	37110
Scenic Point Estates	37777	Shiloh (Rutherford County)	37130	South Cleveland	37311	Stewart Chapel	37335
Scoot Mill	37810	Shiloh (Sumner County)	37066	South Clinton (Part of Clinton)	37716	Stinking Creek	37766
Scottsboro (Part of Nashville)	37218	Shiloh (Wilson County)	37138	South Columbia (Part of Columbia)	38401	Stiversville	38451
Scotts Hill	38374	Shingleton	37683	South Covington (Part of Covington)	38019	Stock Creek	37920
Screamer	38474	Shining Rock	37766	South Daisy (Part of Soddy-Daisy)	37379		
Seeber Flats	37710	Shipetown	37806	South Dyersburg	38024		
Selmer	38375	Shipley	38506	Southeastern Tennessee State Regional Correctional	37367		
Sengtown	37148	Shipps Bend	37033	Southern Hills (Part of Columbia)	38401		
Sentinel Heights (Part of Dayton)	37363			South Etowah	37331		
Sequatchie	37374						
Sequoia Grove (Part of Cleveland)	37312						
Sequoia Hills	37743						
Sequoyah Estates (Part of Madisonville)	37354						

	ZIP
Stockton	38556
Stockton Valley	37774
Stokes	38034
Stone	38562
Stonebrook	37135
Stone River (Part of Nashville)	37076
Stone River Estates (Part of Nashville)	37214
Stones River Homes (Part of Smyrna)	37167
Stonewall	38560
Stoney Fork	37714
Stoney Point	37181
Stony Gap	37869
Stony Point	37873
Strahl	37857
Straight Fork	37847
Strawberry Plains	37871
Striggersville	37857
Stringtown (Gibson County)	38233
Stringtown (Montgomery County)	37191
Stroudsville	37032
Stump Hollow	37381
Suburban Hills (Knox County)	37901
Suburban Hills (McMinn County)	37370
Suck Creek	37405
Sugar Creek (Jackson County)	38562
Sugar Creek (Johnson County)	37683
Sugar Forks (Part of Dandridge)	37725
Sugar Grove (Bradley County)	37323
Sugar Grove (Roane County)	37748
Sugar Grove (Sumner County)	37186
Sugarlimb	37771
Sugar Tree	38380
Suggs Creek	37122
Sullivan Gardens	37663
Sulphur	38570
Sulphura	37148
Sulphur Creek	37147
Sulphur Springs (Anderson County)	37716
Sulphur Springs (Hamblen County)	37814
Sulphur Springs (Lincoln County)	37334
Sulphur Springs (Marion County)	37397
Sulphur Springs (McNairy County)	38375
Sulphur Springs (Washington County)	37659
Sumac	38478
Summer City	37367
Summerfield	37387
Summer Shade	38541
Summertown (Hamilton County)	37377
Summertown (Lawrence County)	38483
Summit (Hamilton County)	37363
Summit (Hawkins County)	37711
Summitville	37382
Sunbright	37872
Sunkist Beach	38079
Sunny Brook (Part of Bristol)	37620
Sunny Hill	38012
Sunny Hills	37620
Sunnyside (Greene County)	37743
Sunnyside (Hancock County)	37869
Sunnyside (Sullivan County)	37617
Sunrise (Hickman County)	37033
Sunrise (Macon County)	37150
Sunset (Grainger County)	37861
Sunset (Pickett County)	38549
Sunset Gap	37722
Sunset Hills (Hamblen County)	37814
Sunset Hills (Sullivan County)	37660
Surgoinsville	37873
Sutherland	24236
Swan (Part of Hohenwald)	38462
Swan Bluff	37033
Swann Chapel	37725
Swannsylvania	37725
Sweet Lips	38340

	ZIP
Sweeton Hill (Part of Coalmont)	37313
Sweetwater (Lewis County)	38462
Sweetwater (Monroe County)	37874
Swift	38372
Sycamore (Cheatham County)	37015
Sycamore (Putnam County)	38501
Sycamore Landing	37185
Sycamore Valley (Cheatham County)	37015
Sycamore Valley (Macon County)	37083
Sykes	38547
Sylvia	37055
Tabernacle (Haywood County)	38012
Tabernacle (Tipton County)	38019
Tabor	38555
Tackett Creek	37766
Taft	38488
Talbott	37877
Tallassee	37801
Talley	37144
Tampico	37861
Tanglewood (Monroe County)	37874
Tanglewood (Smith County)	37030
Tara Estates (Part of Tullahoma)	37388
Tarbett	37853
Tarlton	37110
Tarpley	38478
Tarsus	37142
Tasso	37312
Tate	38344
Tate Springs	37708
Tatesville	37365
Tatumville	38059
Taylor Chapel	37058
Taylor Crossroads	37160
Taylor Hill (Part of Dayton)	37321
Taylor Place	38556
Taylors Crossroads	38573
Taylorsville (Maury County)	38461
Taylorsville (Wilson County)	37087
Taylortown	38459
Tazewell	37879
Teague	38381
Tekoa	37931
Telford	37690
Tellico Hills (Part of Athens)	37303
Tellico Plains	37385
Temperance Hall	37095
Temple Hill	37650
Temple Hills Country Club Estates	37064
Templeton	38059
Templow	37022
Tenchtown	38556
Ten Mile	37880
Ten Mile Center (Part of Knoxville)	37930
Tennemo	38056
Tennessee City	37055
Tennessee Hills (Part of Bristol)	37620
Tennessee Ridge	37178
Tennessee Tech (Part of Cookeville)	38505
Terrace Hills	37122
Terrace View	37381
Terrell	38237
Terry	38321
Terry Creek	37847
Theodore (Part of Hohenwald)	38462
Theta	38401
The Wye	37769
Thick	37034
Thomas	38544
Thomas Addition	37665
Thomas Bridge	37618
Thomasville	37015
Thompsons Station	37179
Thompsons Store	38551
Thorngrove	37871
Thorn Hill	37881
Thornton (Part of Farragut)	37722
Three Churches	38450
Three Oaks	38456
Three Point	38041
Three Points	37918

	ZIP
Three Springs	37860
Throckmorton	37079
Thula	37810
Thurman Addition (Part of Pigeon Forge)	37863
Tibbs	38012
Tidwell	37025
Tiftona (Part of Chattanooga)	37419
Tiger Valley	37658
Tigrett	38070
Tilghman	38233
Timberlake (Hawkins County)	37857
Timberlake (Henderson County)	38351
Timesville	37377
Timothy	38568
Tin Cup	38320
Tinsleys Bottom	38551
Tiprell	37724
Tipton	38071
Tiptonville	38079
Tishamingo	37122
Tobaccoport	37028
Tom Murray (Part of Jackson)	38301
Toone	38381
Top of the World Estates	37878
Topside	37920
Topsy	38485
Toqua	37885
Tottys	38454
Toulon	38063
Towee	37369
Towering Oaks	38464
Town Acres (Part of Greeneville)	37745
Town Creek	37870
Towne Hills (Part of Chattanooga)	37343
Townsend	37882
Trace End Estates	37064
Traceview	37064
Tracy City	37387
Trade	37691
Tradewinds	37122
Trails End	37122
Tranquility	37303
Travisville	38577
Treadway	37883
Trenton	38382
Trent Valley	37869
Trentville	37871
Trevecca College (Part of Nashville)	37210
Trezevant	38258
Tri-Angle	37160
Trigonia	37801
Trimble	38259
Trinity	37064
Triune	37014
Trousdale	37357
Troy	38260
Trundel Crossroad	37865
Tuckahoe	37871
Tuckers Crossroads	37087
Tucker Springs	37353
Tullahoma	37388
Tulu	38357
Tumbling	38201
Tuppertown (Part of Oliver Springs)	37840
Turley	37714
Turners Station	37186
Turnersville	37032
Turnpike	38012
Turtletown	37391
Tusculum (Part of Nashville)	37211
Tusculum College	37745
Twin Bridges	37726
Twin Cove	37714
Twin Oak	38544
Twin Oaks	37620
Twinton	38554
Twomey (Part of Centerville)	37033
Tylersville	38030
Tyner Hills (Part of Chattanooga)	37421
Tyson Store	38233
Una (Part of Nashville)	37217
Unaka Springs	37650
Underwood (Macon County)	37083
Underwood (Sevier County)	37764
Unicoi (Monroe County)	37385
Unicoi (Unicoi County)	37692
Union (Hardin County)	38310
Union (Haywood County)	38012

	ZIP
Union (Morgan County)	37840
Union (Roane County)	37763
Union (Union County)	37866
Union (Warren County)	38581
Union Central	38358
Union City	38261*
	38281†
Union Grove (Blount County)	37737
Union Grove (McMinn County)	37826
Union Grove (Meigs County)	37322
Union Heights	37813
Union Hill (Clay County)	38575
Union Hill (Davidson County)	37080
Union Hill (Lawrence County)	38468
Union Hill (Sumner County)	37066
Union Hill (Tipton County)	38004
Union Ridge	37183
Union Temple	37616
Union Valley	37865
Unionville (Bedford County)	37180
Unionville (Dyer County)	38040
Unitia	37772
University (Part of Knoxville)	37916
University of Tennessee (Part of Martin)	38238
University of the South	37375
Upchurch	37616
Upper Mockeson	38468
Upper Shell Creek	37687
Upper Sinking	37147
Uptonville	38392
Vale	38317
Valleybrook (Hamilton County)	37343
Valley Brook (Wilson County)	37122
Valley Creek	37715
Valley Forge	37643
Valley Hills (Part of Bristol)	37620
Valley View	37716
Van Buren	38042
Vandever	38555
Van Dyke	38242
Van Hill	37857
Vanleer	37181
Vannatta	37160
Vanntown	37335
Vardy	37869
Vasper	37714
Vaughn's Gap (Part of Nashville)	37205
Vaughns Grove	38382
Verdun	37841
Vernon	37137
Vernon Heights	37664
Verona	37091
Verona Hills	37122
Versailles	37153
Vesta	37090
Vestal (Part of Knoxville)	37920
Veterans Administration (Part of Murfreesboro)	37129
Veto	38477
Viar	38024
Victoria	37397
Victory	37766
Vildo	38075
Villa Gardens (Part of Knoxville)	37918
Village Green (Part of Farragut)	37922
Vine	37090
Vinegar Hill	37620
Vine Ridge	38554
Viola	37394
Virtue (Part of Farragut)	37922
Vise	38329
Vison Cross Roads	37110
Volunteer Heights (Part of Crossville)	38555
Vonore	37885
Vose (Part of Alcoa)	37701
Waco	38472
Walden	37377
Walden Creek	37862
Waldens Ridge (Bledsoe County)	37381
Waldens Ridge (Rhea County)	37321
Wales	38478
Walkertown (Greene County)	37616
Walkertown (Hardin County)	38372

* Area Zip Code   † Post Office Boxes

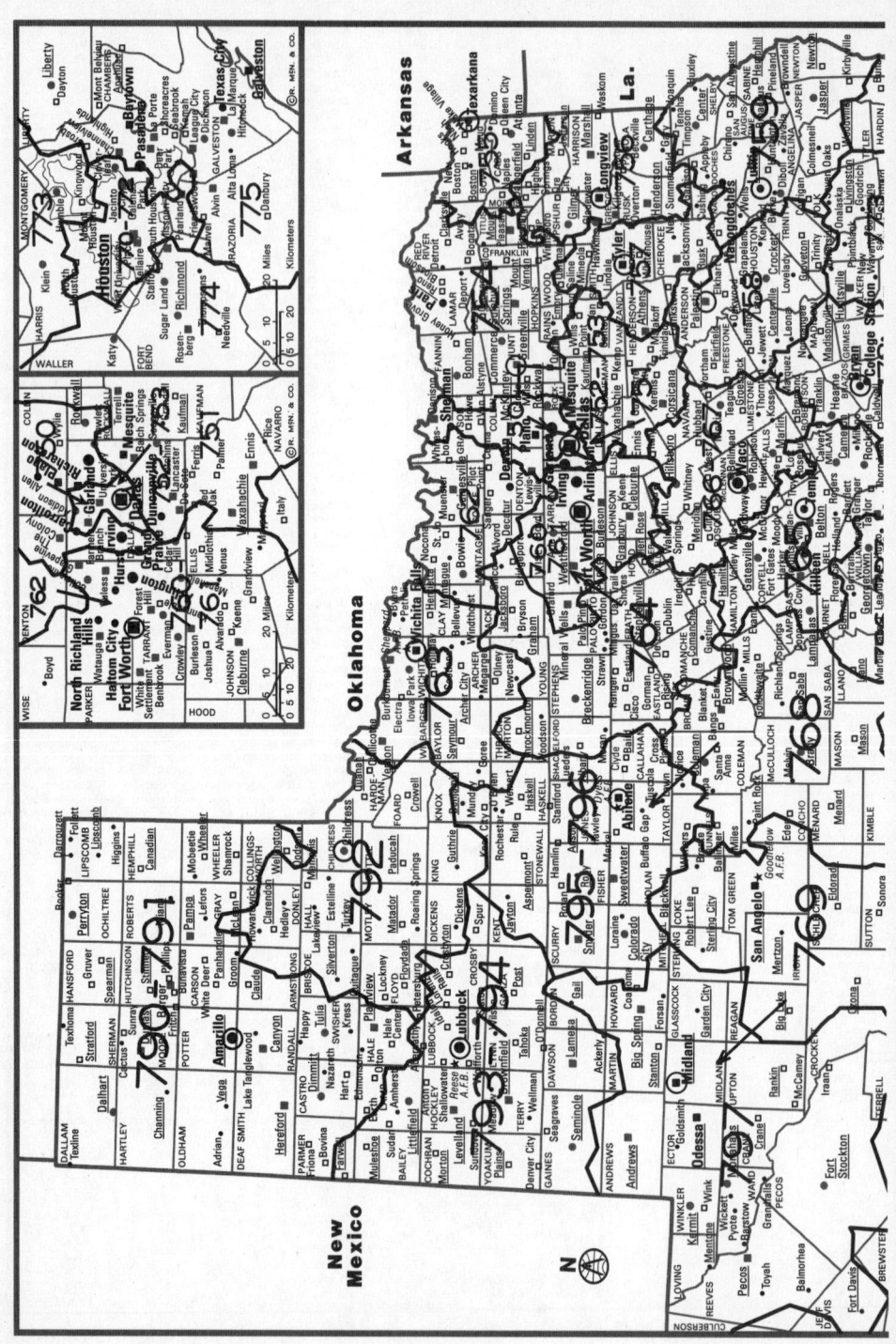

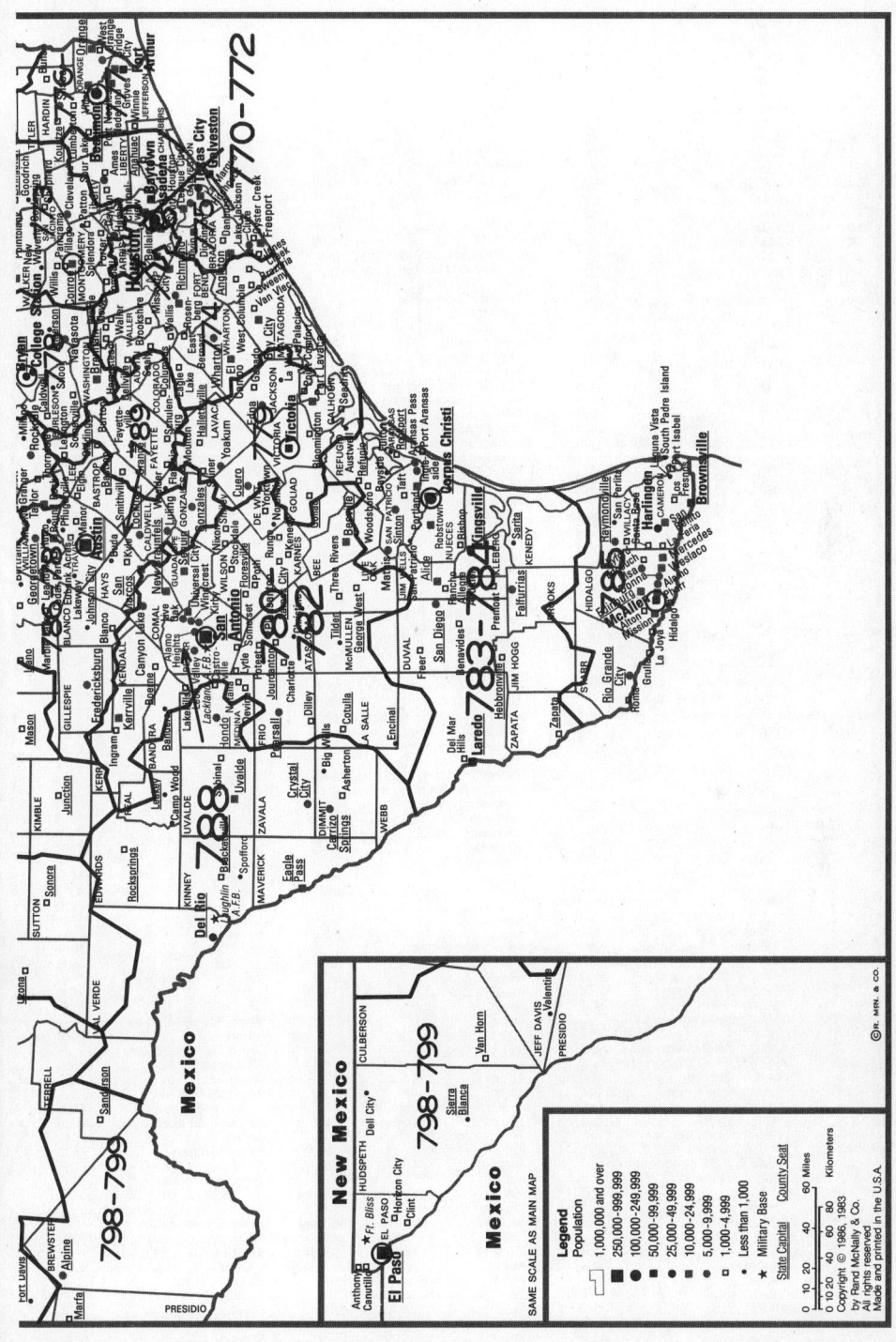

	ZIP
Abbott	76621
Aberfoyle	75496
Abernathy	79311
Abilene	79601-06
For specific Abilene Zip Codes call (915) 673-6485, or your local postmaster.	
Abilene Christian College (Part of Abilene)	79699
Ables Springs	75160
Abner	75142
Abram	78572
Abram-Perezville	78572
Acala	79839
Ace	77326
Ackerly	79713
Acton	76048
Acuff	79401
Acworth	75426
Adams Gardens	78550
Adams Hill	78245
Adams Oaks	77365
Adamsville	76550
Addicks	77079
Addicks Barker (Part of Houston)	77218
Addielou	75412
Addison	75001
Addran	75482
Adell	76088
Ad Hall	76520
Adina	78947
Adkins	78101
Admiral	79504
Adrian	79001
Adsul	75956
Afton	79220
Aggieland (Part of College Station)	77844
Agnes	76082
Agua Dulce	78330
Agua Nueva	78361
Aguilares	78369
Aiken (Floyd County)	79221
Aiken (Shelby County)	75935
Airlawn (Part of Dallas)	75235
Airport City	78108
Airport Mail Facility (Part of Houston)	77205
Airville	76501
Alabama and Coushatta Indian Reservation	77351
Alamo	78516
Alamo Alto	79853
Alamo Beach (Bandera County)	78063
Alamo Beach (Calhoun County)	77979
Alamo Heights	78208-09
For specific Alamo Heights Zip Codes call (210) 826-0461, or your local postmaster.	
Alamo Ranchettos	79735
Alanreed	79002
Alazan	75961
Alba	75410
Albany	76430
Albert	78671
Albert Thomas (Part of Nassau Bay)	77058
Albion	75426
Alco	75949
Alderbranch	75801
Aldine	77039
Aldine Estates	77039
Aldine Gardens	77039
Aldine Meadows	77039
Aledo	76008
Aleman	76531
Alexander	76446
Aley	75143
Alfred	78332
Algerita	76877
Algoa	77511
Alice	78332*
	78333†
Alief (Part of Houston)	77411
Allamore	79855
Allen	75002
Allenfarm	77868
Allenhurst	77414
Allens Chapel	75492
Allens Point	75446
Alleyton	78935
Allison	79003
Allmon	79250
Alma	75119
Almeda (Part of Houston)	77045

	ZIP
Almeda Mall (Part of Houston)	77075
Almont	75559
Aloe	77905
Alpine	79830*
	79831†
Alsa	75169
Alsdorf	75119
Altair	77412
Alta Loma (Part of Santa Fe)	77510
Alto	75925
Altoga	75069
Alton	78572
Alto Springs	76653
Alum	78160
Alum Creek	78957
Alvarado	76009
Alvin	77511*
	77512†
Alvord	76225
Amarillo	79101-89
For specific Amarillo Zip Codes call (806) 379-2140, or your local postmaster.	
Ambia	75460
Ambrose	75414
American Technological University	76540
Ames (Coryell County)	76528
Ames (Liberty County)	77575
Amherst (Lamar County)	75460
Amherst (Lamb County)	79312
Amigoland Mall (Part of Brownsville)	78520
Ammansville	78945
Amon Carter Boulevard (Part of Fort Worth)	76155
Amy	75432
Anadarko	75667
Anahuac	77514
Anchor	77515
Anchorage	78065
Ander	77963
Anderson	77830
Anderson Mill	78750
Andice	78628
Andrews	79714
Andrewsville	75683
Angelo State University (Part of San Angelo)	76909
Angleton	77515*
	77516†
Angus	75110
Angus Valley (Part of Austin)	78758
Anna	75409
Annarose	78022
Annetta	76008
Annetta North	76087
Annetta South	76008
Anneville	76023
Annona	75550
Anson	79501
Anson Jones (Part of Houston)	77009
Antelope	76389
Anthony	88021
Anthony Harbor	75929
Antioch (Cass County)	75551
Antioch (Delta County)	75432
Antioch (Henderson County)	75758
Antioch (Houston County)	75851
Antioch (Jasper County)	77612
Antioch (Madison County)	75852
Antioch (Rusk County)	75652
Antioch (Shelby County) (mail Center)	75935
Antioch (Shelby County) (mail Timpson)	75975
Anton	79313
Apache Addition (Part of Seguin)	78155
Apache Shores	78734
Apolonia	77830
Apparel Mart (Part of Dallas)	75207
Appelt Hill	77964
Appleby	75961
Apple Springs	75926
Aquilla	76622
Aransas Pass	78335†
	78336*
Arbala	75482
Arbor	75847
Arbor Oaks (Part of Houston)	77088

	ZIP
Arcadia (Galveston County)	77517
Arcadia (Shelby County)	75935
Archer City	76351
Arcola	77583
Arden	76901
Argenta	78368
Argo	75558
Argyle	76226
Argyle Plaza (Part of Houston)	77035
Ariola	77625
Arizona	77367
Arlam	75946
Arledge Ridge	75418
Arlington	76003-07
	76010-18
	76094
	76096
For specific Arlington Zip Codes call (817) 274-3385, or your local postmaster.	
Arlington Downs (Part of Arlington)	76010
Arlington Heights (Part of Fort Worth)	76147
Armstrong	78338
Arneckeville	77954
Arnett (Coryell County)	76528
Arnett (Hockley County)	79336
Arp	75750
Arrowhead Lake	77378
Arrowhead Shores	76048
Arrowhead Village	78130
Arroyo (Part of Harlingen)	78550
Arroyo City	78586
Arsenal (Part of San Antonio)	78283
Art	76820
Artesian Forest	77304
Artesia Wells	78001
Arthur City	75411
Arvana	79331
Asa	76707
Ash (Henderson County)	75751
Ash (Houston County)	75835
Ashby	77465
Asherton	78827
Ashford West (Part of Houston)	77077
Ashland	75640
Ashmore	79342
Ashtola	79226
Ashworth	75142
Asia	75939
Aspermont	79502
Astrodome (Part of Houston)	77025
Astro Hills	78130
Atascocita (Part of Humble)	77346
Atascosa	78002
Ater	76528
Athens	75751
Atlanta	75551
Atlas	75460
Atoy	75785
Atreco (Part of Port Arthur)	77640
Attoyac	75961
Atwell	76437
Aubrey	76227
Auburn	76050
Audobon Park (Part of Houston)	77338
Augusta	75844
Aurora	76078
Austin	78701-69
For specific Austin Zip Codes call (512) 929-1255, or your local postmaster.	
Austin Lake Estates	78759
Austonio	75835
Austwell	77950
Authon	76088
Autumn Woods	77362
Avalon	76623
Avery	75554
Avinger	75630
Avoca	79503
Avonbell (Part of Amarillo)	79106
Avondale	76179
Avon Park	76708
Axtell	76624
Azle	76020*
	76098†
Bacliff	77518
Bagby	75446
Bagwell	75412

	ZIP
Bailey	75413
Baileyboro	79371
Bailey's Prairie	77515
Baileyville	76570
Bainer	79339
Bainville	78119
Baird	79504
Baker	76087
Bakersfield	79752
Balch	79358
Balch Springs	75180
Balcones (Part of Austin)	78759
Balcones Heights	78201
Balcones Village	78750
Bald Hill	75901
Bald Prairie	77856
Baldwin	75661
Ballinger	76821
Balmorhea	79718
Balsora	76426
Bammel	77040
Bammel Timbers	77040
Banana Junction	76708
Bancroft (Part of Pinehurst)	77630
Bandera	78003
Bandera Falls	78063
Bangs	76823
Banquete	78339
Barbarosa	78130
Barclay	76656
Bardin Road (Part of Arlington)	76018
Bardwell	75101
Barker	77413
Barksdale	78828
Barnes	75960
Barnhart	76930
Barnum	75939
Barrett	77532
Barrington Oaks (Part of Austin)	78759
Barry	75102
Barstow	79719
Bartlett	76511
Bartley Woods	75492
Barton Creek Square (Part of Austin)	78746
Bartons Chapel	76458
Bartonville	76226
Barwise	79235
Bascom	75705
Basin	79834
Basin Springs	76264
Bassett	75574
Bassett Center (Part of El Paso)	79925
Bastrop	78602
Bastrop Bayou	77515
Bastrop Beach	77515
Bateman	78662
Batesville (Red River County)	75426
Batesville (Zavala County)	78829
Batson	77519
Battle	76664
Baxter	75751
Bay City	77414
Bay Harbor	77554
Baylor University (Part of Waco)	76706
Bay Oaks	77571
Bayou Bend (Part of Houston)	77088
Bayou Chantilly (Part of Dickinson)	77539
Bayou Vista	77563
Bay Plaza (Part of Baytown)	77521
Bayport (Part of Houston)	77058
Bayside	78340
Bayside Terrace	77571
Baytown	77520-22
For specific Baytown Zip Codes call (713) 420-2508, or your local postmaster.	
Bayview (Cameron County)	78566
Bay View (Galveston County)	77518
Bayview Estates	76945
Bayway (Part of Baytown)	77520
Baywood (Part of Seabrook)	77586
Bazette	75144
Beach	77301
Beach City	77520
Beacon Hill (Part of San Antonio)	78201

	ZIP
Beadle	77414
Bear Creek (Part of Houston)	77084
Bear Grass	75846
Beasley	77417
Beattie	76442
Beaukiss	78621
Beaumont	77701-08
	77710
	77713-26
For specific Beaumont Zip Codes call (409) 842-7200, or your local postmaster.	
Beaumont Place	77028
Beauxart Gardens	77705
Beaver Dam	75559
Bebe	78603
Becker	75142
Beckville	75631
Becton	79343
Bedford	76021-22
	76095
For specific Bedford Zip Codes call (214) 647-2996, or your local postmaster.	
Bedias	77831
Bee Cave	78733
Beech Grove	75951
Beechnut (Part of Houston)	77072
Beechwood	75948
Bee House	76525
Beeville	78102*
	78104†
Belcherville	76255
Belfalls	76579
Belgrade	75928
Belk	75411
Bellaire	77401*
	77402†
Bellaire Addition	75704
Bellaire West (Part of Houston)	77072
Bell Branch	76651
Bellevue	76228
Bellmead	76704-05
For specific Bellmead Zip Codes call (817) 799-1546, or your local postmaster.	
Bells	75414
Bellview	75410
Bellville	77418
Belmar (Part of Amarillo)	79106
Belmena	76520
Belmont	78604
Belott	75835
Belton	76513
Ben Arnold	76519
Benavides	78341
Ben Bolt	78342
Benbrook	76126
Benchley	77801
Bend	76824
Bending Bough	77373
Ben Franklin	75415
Ben Hur	76664
Benjamin	79505
Bennett	76066
Bennett Estates	77302
Benoit	76882
Bent Tree (Part of Dallas)	75287
Bentwood (Part of San Angelo)	76904
Bentwood Acres	75076
Ben Wheeler	75754
Berclair	78107
Berea (Houston County)	75835
Berea (Marion County)	75657
Bergheim	78004
Bergstrom Air Force Base	78743
Berlin	77833
Bernardo	78933
Berry Street	76110
Berryville	75763
Bertram	78605
Bessmay	77612
Best	76932
Bethany	71007
Bethel (Anderson County)	75861
Bethel (Ellis County)	75165
Bethel (Henderson County)	75751
Bethlehem (Bowie County)	75559
Bethlehem (Collin County)	75442
Bethlehem (Upshur County)	75644
Bethsaida	75551
Beto Unit	75861

	ZIP
Beto 2 Unit	75801
Bettie	75644
Beulah	75941
Beverly	76711
Beverly Hills (Part of Dallas)	75211
Bevil Oaks	77706
Bevilport	75951
Beyersville	78615
Biardstown	75462
Big Bend National Park	79834
Bigfoot	78005
Biggs Army Air Base	79908
Big Lake	76932
Big Oaks	75630
Big Sandy	75755
Big Spring	79720*
	79721†
Big Square	79027
Big Thiket	77369
Big Town Regional Mall (Part of Mesquite)	75149
Big Valley Ranchettes	76522
Big Wells	78830
Billington	76624
Billpark (Part of Houston)	77012
Biloxi	75928
Birch	77879
Birdville (Part of Haltom City)	76117
Birnam Woods	77379
Birome	76673
Birthright	75482
Biry	78016
Bisbee	76063
Bishop	78343
Bivins	75555
Black	79035
Blackfoot	75853
Black Hills	75110
Black Jack (Cherokee County)	75789
Black Jack (Robertson County)	77859
Blackland	75189
Blackoak	75431
Blackwell	79506
Blakeney	75412
Blanchard	77351
Blanco	78606
Blanconia	78102
Blandlake	75972
Blanket	76432
Bleakwood	75956
Bledsoe	79314
Bleiblerville	78931
Blessing	77419
Blevins	76524
Blewett	78801
Blodgett	75686
Bloomburg	75556
Bloomdale	75069
Bloomfield	76258
Blooming Grove	76626
Bloomington	77951
Blossom	75416
Blue	78947
Bluebonnet (Part of Austin)	78758
Bluegrove	76352
Blue Haven Estates	75169
Blue Lake Estates	78654
Blue Mound	76131
Blue Ridge (Collin County)	75424
Blue Ridge (Falls County)	76661
Blueroan	77434
Bluetown	78592
Blue Water Key	75758
Bluff Dale	76433
Bluff Springs (Parker County)	76020
Bluff Springs (Travis County)	78744
Bluffton	78607
Blum	76627
Blumenthal	78624
Bluntzer	78380
Board	76442
Bob Harris (Part of Pasadena)	77506
Bob Lyons (Part of Galveston)	77554
Bobo	75974
Bobville	77333
Boca Chica (Part of Brownsville)	78520
Boerne	78006
Bogata	75417
Bois D'Arc	75801

	ZIP
Boling	77420
Boling-Iago	77420
Bolivar	76266
Bolton	75686
Bomarton	76380
Bon Ami	75956
Bonanza (Hill County)	76692
Bonanza (Hopkins County)	75420
Bonanza Beach	78611
Bonham	75418
Bonita	76255
Bonnerville	75840
Bonney	77583
Bonnie View	78393
Bono	76031
Bon Wier	75928
Booker	79005
Boonsville	76426
Booth	77469
Boquillas	79834
Borden	78962
Borderland	79932
Bordersville (Part of Houston)	77338
Borger	79007*
	79008†
Bosqueville	76708
Boston (Part of New Boston)	75570
Boswell	77340
Bovina	79009
Bowie	76230
Bowser	76872
Box Church	76642
Boxelder	75550
Boxwood	75683
Boyce	75165
Boyd (Fannin County)	75418
Boyd (Wise County)	76023
Boys Ranch	79010
Boz	75165
Brachfield	75681
Bracken	78266
Brackettville	78832
Brad	76475
Bradfield	75656
Bradford	75853
Bradshaw	79567
Brady (McCulloch County)	76825
Brady (Shelby County)	75935
Branch	75407
Branchville	76520
Brandon	76628
Bransford (Part of Colleyville)	76034
Branton	76471
Brashear	75420
Brazoria	77422
Brazos	76472
Brazos Mall (Part of Lake Jackson)	77566
Brazos Point	76652
Breckenridge	76424
Bremond	76629
Brenham	77833*
	77834†
Brentwood Manor	77904
Breslau	77964
Briar	76020
Briarcliff	78669
Briaroaks	76028
Briary	76570
Brice	79226
Bridge Chapel	75455
Bridge City	77611
Bridgeport	76426
Brierwood Bay	75763
Briggs	78608
Bright Star (Rains County)	75410
Bright Star (Van Zandt County)	75169
Briscoe	79011
Briscoe Unit	78017
Bristol	75119
Britton	76063
Broaddus	75929
Broadway (Crosby County)	79243
Broadway (Harris County)	77207
Broadway (Lamar County)	75460
Broadway Junction	75460
Broadway Square (Part of Tyler)	75703
Brock	76087
Brock Junction	76087
Brogado	79718
Bronco	79355
Bronson	75930

	ZIP
Bronte	76933
Brookeland	75931
Brookesmith	76827
Brook Forest	77357
Brook Glen Addition (Part of La Porte)	77571
Brookhollow (Part of Dallas)	75247
Brookshier	76933
Brookshire	77423
Brookside Village	77581
Brookston	75421
Broom City	75839
Broome	76951
Brown College	77880
Browndell	75931
Brownfield	79316
Browning	75705
Brownsboro (Caldwell County)	78644
Brownsboro (Henderson County)	75756
Brownsville	78520-26
For specific Brownsville Zip Codes call (210) 546-2411, or your local postmaster.	
Brownwood	76801-04
For specific Brownwood Zip Codes call (915) 646-0656, or your local postmaster.	
Brownwood (Part of Orange)	77630
Broyles	75801
Bruceville (Part of Bruceville-Eddy)	76630
Bruceville-Eddy	76630
Brumley	75686
Brundage	78834
Bruni	78344
Brunswick	75925
Brushie Prairie	76641
Brushy Bend Park	78681
Brushy Creek (Anderson County)	75801
Brushy Creek (Williamson County)	78681
Brushy Creek North	78681
Bryan	77801-08
For specific Bryan Zip Codes call (409) 779-1988, or your local postmaster.	
Bryans Mill	75568
Bryson	76427
Buchanan Dam	78609
Buchanan Lake Village	78672
Buchel	77954
Buck Creek	75949
Buckeye	77414
Buckholts	76518
Buckhorn (Austin County)	77418
Buckhorn (Newton County)	75928
Buckingham	75080
Buckner	76462
Buda	78610
Buena Vista (Bexar County)	78221
Buena Vista (Burnet County)	78611
Buena Vista (Shelby County)	75975
Buffalo	75831
Buffalo Gap (Taylor County)	79508
Buffalo Gap (Travis County)	78734
Buffalo Springs	76228
Buford	79512
Bugbee Heights	79078
Bug Tussle	75449
Bula	79320
Bullard	75757
Bullock	76470
Bulverde	78163
Buna	77612
Bunavista (Part of Borger)	79007
Buncomb	75633
Bunger	76450
Bunker Hill	75486
Bunker Hill Village	77024
Bunyan	76446
Burkburnett	76354
Burke	75941
Burkett	76828
Burkeville	75932
Burleigh	77418
Burleson	76028*
	76097†
Burlington	76519

	ZIP
Burnell	78119
Burnet	78611
Burns (Bowie County)	75561
Burns (Cooke County)	76258
Burr	77488
Burris Crossing	79853
Burrow	75189
Burton	77835
Busby	79543
Bushland	79012
Bushwhacker Peninsula	75147
Bushy	77845
Bustamante	78361
Busterville	79358
Butler (Bastrop County)	78621
Butler (Freestone County)	75855
Byers	76357
Bynum	76631
Byrd	75119
Byrds	76801
Cabot Kingsmill	79065
Cactus	79013
Caddo	76429
Caddo Mills	75135
Cadiz	78102
Cain City	78624
Calaveras	78114
Caldwell	77836
Caledonia	75946
Calf Creek	76825
Call	75933
Calliham	78007
Callisburg	76240
Call Junction	75933
Calvary	75773
Calvert	77837
Camden	75934
Camelot	78239
Cameron	76520
Cameron Park	78521
Camey	75034
Camilla	77331
Camp Air	76856
Campbell	75422
Campbellton	78008
Camp Dallas	75034
Camp Maxey	75473
Campo Alto	78516
Camp Ruby	77351
Camp San Saba	76825
Camp Springs	79526
Camp Stanley	78206
Camp Strake	77301
Camp Swift	78602
Campti	75935
Camp Valley	78140
Camp Verde	78010
Camp Wood	78833
Cana	75169
Canada Verde	78114
Canadian	79014
Canal City	77617
Candelaria	79843
Candlelight Oaks (Part of Houston)	77088
Caney	77414
Caney City	75148
Caney Creek Estates	77357
Cannon	75495
Canton	75103
Canutillo	79835
Canyon (Lubbock County)	79408
Canyon (Randall County)	79015
Canyon City	78130
Canyon Creek (Part of Richardson)	75080
Canyon Creek Estates	78130
Canyon Lake	78130
Canyon Lake Acres	78130
Canyon Lake Estates	78130
Canyon Lake Forest	78130
Canyon Lake Hills	78130
Canyon Lake Island	78130
Canyon Lake Mobile Home Estates	78130
Canyon Lake Shores	78130
Canyon Lake Village	78130
Canyon Lake Village West	78130
Canyon Springs Resort	78130
Canyon Valley	79356
Canyon View Acres	78163
Capital Plaza (Part of Austin)	78723
Capitol (Part of Austin)	78701
Caplen	77617
Capps Corner	76265
Cap Rock	79357
Caprock Shopping Center (Part of Lubbock)	79404

	ZIP
Caps	79606
Caradan	76844
Carancahua	77465
Carbon	76435
Carbondale	75567
Cardinal (Part of Athens)	75751
Carey	79222
Carey Estates (Part of Seabrook)	77586
Carlisle	75862
Carlos	77830
Carl Range (Part of Irving)	75062
Carlsbad	76934
Carl's Corner	76645
Carlton	76436
Carmine	78932
Carmona	75939
Caro	75961
Carolina Cove	77367
Carpenter	78101
Carpenters Bluff	75020
Carricitos	78586
Carrizo Springs	78834
Carroll	75771
Carroll Springs	75853
Carrollton	75006-08
	75010-11
For specific Carrollton Zip Codes call (214) 418-7858, or your local postmaster.	
Carrollton Park Two (Part of Dallas)	75006
Carson	75488
Carta Valley	78840
Carterville	75563
Carthage	75633
Cartwright (Kaufman County)	75142
Cartwright (Wood County)	75494
Casa Piedra	79843
Casa View (Part of Dallas)	75228
Cash	75402
Cason	75636
Cass	75556
Cassie	78611
Castell	76831
Castle Hills	78213
Castlewood	77039
Castolon	79834
Castroville	78009
Catarina	78836
Cat Spring	78933
Causeway Beach	75143
Cave Creek	78624
Cave Springs	75670
Caviness	75460
Cawthon	77868
Cayote	76689
Cayuga	75832
Cedar Branch (Henderson County)	75147
Cedar Branch (Houston County)	75844
Cedar Creek (Anderson County)	75839
Cedar Creek (Bastrop County)	78612
Cedar Elm (Part of San Antonio)	78249
Cedar Grove (Cass County)	75560
Cedar Grove (Coryell County)	76522
Cedar Grove (El Paso County)	79915
Cedar Grove (Harris County)	77532
Cedar Hill (Dallas County)	75104*
	75106†
Cedar Hill (Floyd County)	79241
Cedar Hills	78621
Cedar Lake	77414
Cedar Lane	77415
Cedar Mills Resort	76245
Cedar Park	78613*
	78630†
Cedar Point	77520
Cedar Shores Estates	76671
Cedar Springs (Falls County)	76570
Cedar Springs (Upshur County)	75683
Cedar Valley	78736
Cedarview	75104
Cee Vee	79223
Cego	76524
Cele	78653
Celeste	75423
Celina	75009

	ZIP
Center (Limestone County)	76642
Center (Shelby County)	75935
Center City	76844
Center Grove	75455
Center Line	77879
Center Point (Camp County)	75686
Center Point (Ellis County)	76651
Center Point (Kerr County)	78010
Center Point (Panola County)	75691
Center Point (Parker County) (mail Azle)	76020
Center Point (Parker County) (mail Weatherford)	76087
Center Point (Titus County)	75455
Center Point (Upshur County)	75755
Centerview	75833
Centerville (Leon County)	75833
Centerville (Trinity County)	75845
Central (Angelina County)	75969
Central (Tarrant County)	76102
Central Gardens	77627
Central Heights (Jefferson County)	77627
Central Heights (Nacogdoches County)	75961
Central High	75925
Centralia	75834
Central Mall (Bowie County)	75501
Central Mall (Jefferson County)	77640
Central Park (Bexar County)	78216
Central Park (Harris County)	77011
Central Unit	77478
Cestohowa	78113
Chaffee Village	76544
Chalk	79248
Chalk Bluff	76705
Chalk Mountain	76401
Chalybeate	75494
Chambersville	75069
Chambliss	75409
Champion Forest	77303
Chances Store	77839
Chandler	75758
Channelview	77530
Channelwood	77530
Channing	79018
Chaparral Hills	78840
Chaparral Park	78652
Chapman	75652
Chapman Ranch	78347
Chappel	76877
Chappell Hill	77426
Charco	77963
Charleston	75432
Charlie	76306
Charlotte	78011
Chase Field Naval Air Station	78102
Chat	76645
Chateau Woods	77301
Chatfield	75105
Cheapside	77954
Cheek	77705
Cherokee	76832
Cherry Mound	75020
Cherry Spring	78624
Chester	75936
Chesterville	77435
Chico	76431
Chicota	75425
Chief	75142
Chihuahua	78572
Childress	79201
Chillicothe	79225
Chilton	76632
Chimney Corners (Part of Austin)	78731
China	77613
China Grove (Bexar County)	78223
China Grove (Scurry County)	79526
China Spring	76633
Chinati	79843
Chireno	75937
Chita	75862
Choate	78119
Chocolate Bayou	77511

	ZIP
Choice	75935
Chriesman	77838
Christine	78012
Christoval	76935
C H Rouse Estates	77365
Church Hill (Cherokee County)	75766
Church Hill (Rusk County)	75652
Churchill Bridge	77422
Cibolo	78108
Cielo Vista (Part of El Paso)	79925
Cielo Vista Mall (Part of El Paso)	79925
Cienegas Terrace	78840
Circle	79064
Circle Back	79371
Circle D-KC Estates	78602
Circleville (Titus County)	77736
Circleville (Williamson County)	76574
Cisco	76437
Cistern	78941
Citrus City	78572
Citrus Grove	77465
Civic Center (Part of Houston)	77208
Clairemont	79549
Clairette	76457
Clardy	75468
Clarendon	79226
Clareville	78102
Clark	77327
Clarks	77979
Clarksville	75426
Clarksville City	75647
Clarkwood (Part of Corpus Christi)	78406
Claude	79019
Clauene	79336
Clawson	75904
Clay	77839
Claydesta Station (Part of Midland)	79710
Clayton (Jefferson County)	77627
Clayton (Panola County)	75637
Claytonville (Fisher County)	79556
Claytonville (Swisher County)	79052
Clear Creek	76544
Clear Lake City (Part of Houston)	77058
Clear Lake Shores	77565
Clear Spring	78130
Clearview	78602
Cleburne	76031*
	76033†
Clegg	78022
Clemens Unit	77422
Clemons	77423
Clemville	77414
Cleveland	77327*
	77328†
Clever Creek	75935
Cliffside	79106
Clifton (Bosque County)	76634
Clifton (Van Zandt County)	75169
Climax	75407
Cline	78801
Clint	79836
Clinton (DeWitt County)	77954
Clinton (Hunt County)	75135
Clodine	77469
Close City	79356
Cloverleaf	77015
Club Lake Estates	75708
Clute	77531
Clyde	79510
Coady	77520
Coahoma	79511
Coal Mine (Part of Lytle)	78052
Cobb Creek	75852
Cobb Switch	75160
Cochran	77418
Cockrell Hill	75211
Coffee City	75763
Coffeeville	75683
Coffield Unit	75861
Coit	76653
Coke	75431
Coldhill	75708
Coldspring	77331
Coleman	76834
Coleman Cove	75929
Colfax	75103
College Country Estates	75020

* Area Zip Code † Post Office Boxes

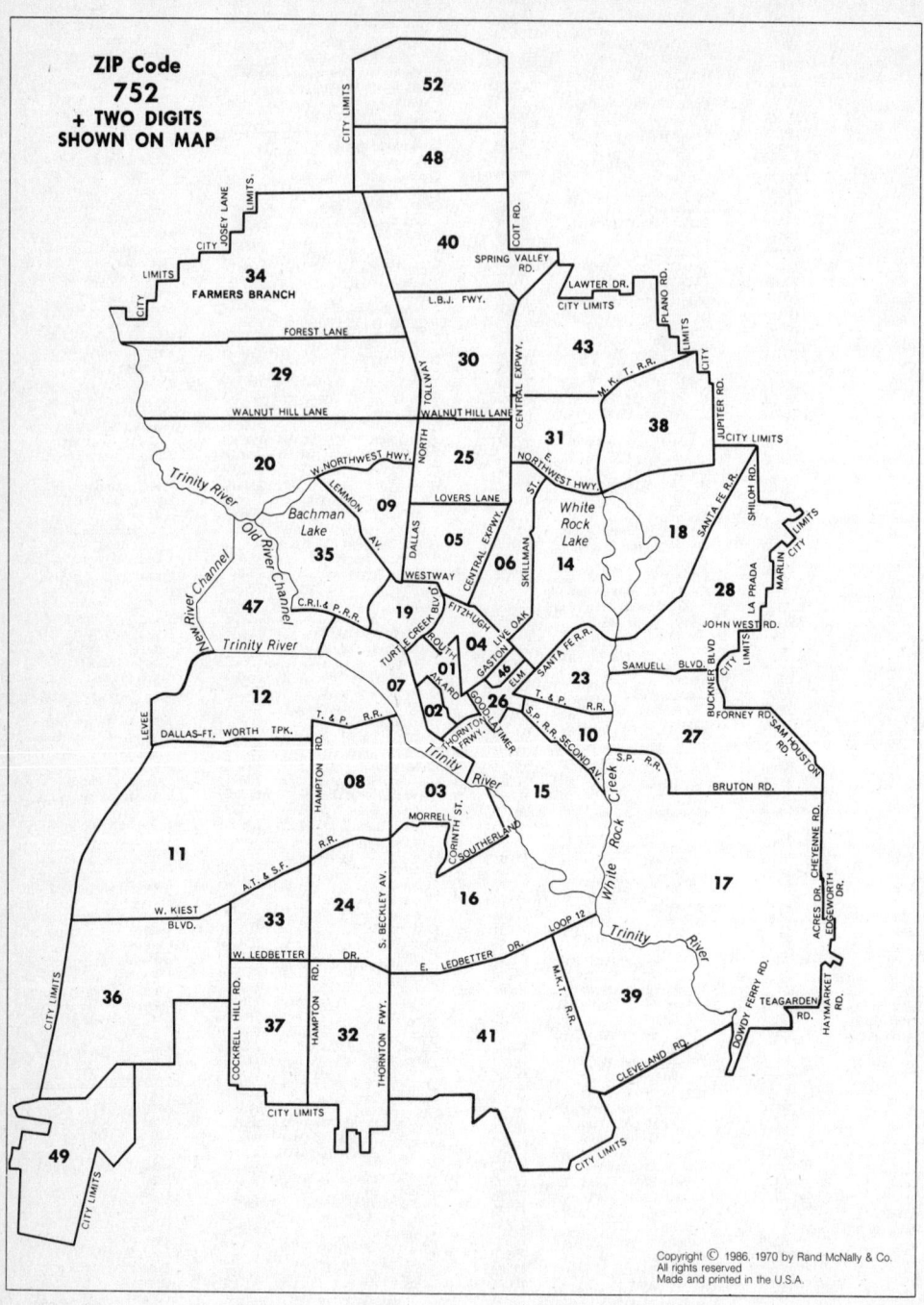

ZIP Code
752
**+ TWO DIGITS
SHOWN ON MAP**

52

48

40

34
FARMERS BRANCH

30

29

43

38

20

25

31

09

05

06

14

18

35

28

47

19

04

23

12

07

01

02

26

10

27

08

03

15

11

33

24

16

17

36

37

32

41

39

49

Column 1

	ZIP
Deer Haven	78654
Deer Park	77536
Deerwood East	77445
De Kalb	75559
Delba	75452
Delbert L. Atkinson (Part of Pasadena)	77505
De Leon	76444
Delhi	78953
Delia	76635
Dell City	79837
Del Mar Hills (Part of Laredo)	78041
Delmita	78536
Del Monte	77627
Delray	75633
Del Rio	78840-42

For specific Del Rio Zip Codes call (210) 775-3571, or your local postmaster.

	ZIP
Delrose	75644
Del Valle	78617
Demi-John Island	77541
Democrat (Comanche County)	76442
Democrat (Mills County)	76442
De Moss (Part of Houston)	77036
Denhawken	78160
Denison	75020*
	75021†
Denning	75972
Dennis	76439
Denny	76653
Denson Springs	75844
Denton	76201-07

For specific Denton Zip Codes call (817) 387-8555, or your local postmaster.

	ZIP
Denton	79510
Denver City	79323
Denver Harbor (Part of Houston)	77020
Deport	75435
Derby	78017
Dermott	79549
Desdemona	76445
Desert	75424
De Soto	75115
	75123

For specific De Soto Zip Codes call (214) 223-6500, or your local postmaster.

	ZIP
Dessau	78753
Detmold	76577
Detroit	75436
Devers	77538
Devils Pocket	77612
Devine	78016
Dew	75860
Dewalt	77478
Dewees	78114
Deweyville	77614
Dewville	78140
Dexter	76240
D'Hanis	78850
Dial (Fannin County)	75446
Dial (Hutchinson County)	79007
Dialville	75785
Diamondhead	77356
Diana	75640
Diboll	75941
Dicey	76086
Dickens	79229
Dickinson	77539
Dido	76179
Dies	75979
Dike	75437
Dilley	78017
Dilworth (Gonzales County)	78629
Dilworth (Red River County)	75426
Dime Box	77853
Dimmitt	79027
Dimple	75426
Dinero	78022
Ding Dong	76542
Dinsmore	77488
Direct	75486
Dirgin	75691
Divide	75420
Divot	78017
Dixie (Grayson County)	76273
Dixie (Jasper County)	75951
Dixon	75402
Doans	76384
Dobbin	77333
Dobrowolski	78026

Column 2

	ZIP
Dodd	79347
Dodd City	75438
Dodge	77334
Dodson	79230
Dogwood	75979
Dogwood Acres (Part of Houston)	77022
Dogwood City	75762
Dolen	77327
Dominion	78257
Domino	75572
Donall Estates	78611
Donie	75838
Donna	78537
Don Tol	77420
Doole	76836
Dorchester	75459
Doss	78618
Dot	76524
Dothan	76437
Dotson	75669
Double Bayou	77514
Double Diamond Estates	79036
Double Oak	75226
Doucette	75942
Dougherty	79231
Douglass	75943
Douglassville	75560
Downing	76442
Downsville	76706
Downtown (Part of Amarillo)	79105
Downtown (Part of Austin)	78767-68

For specific Downtown Zip Codes call (512) 477-7907, or your local postmaster.

	ZIP
Downtown (Part of Beaumont)	77704
Downtown (Part of Brownsville)	78522
Downtown (Part of Bryan)	77801
Downtown (Part of Corpus Christi)	78401-03
	78407-08

For specific Downtown Zip Codes call (512) 883-0651, or your local postmaster.

	ZIP
Downtown (Part of Dallas)	75201-02

For specific Downtown Zip Codes call (214) 953-3045, or your local postmaster.

	ZIP
Downtown (Part of El Paso)	79901
Downtown (Part of Ft. Worth)	76101-02
	76113

For specific Downtown Zip Codes call (817) 870-8102, or your local postmaster.

	ZIP
Downtown (Part of Freeport)	77541
Downtown (Part of Irving)	75017†
	75060*
Downtown (Part of Longview)	75606
Downtown (Part of Lubbock)	79401*
	79408†
Downtown (Part of McAllen)	78501*
	78505†
Downtown (Part of San Antonio)	78205
	78291-99

For specific Downtown Zip Codes call (210) 227-3399, or your local postmaster.

	ZIP
Downtown (Part of Tyler)	75710
Downtown (Part of Waco)	76701
	76703
	76706
	76711

For specific Downtown Zip Codes call (817) 757-6541, or your local postmaster.

	ZIP
Doyle	76642
Dozier	79079
Drasco	79567
Draw	79373
Dreka	75973
Dresden	75102
Dreyer	77984
Driftwood (Hays County)	78619
Driftwood (Henderson County)	75143
Driners	75937
Dripping Springs	78620
Driscoll	78351
Drop	76247

Column 3

	ZIP
Dryden	78851
Dubina	78956
Dublin	76446
Dudley	79601
Duffau	76457
Dugas Addition	77611
Dugger	78155
Dumas	79029
Dumont	79232
Dunbar	75440
Duncanville	75116
	75137-38

For specific Duncanville Zip Codes call (214) 298-3603, or your local postmaster.

	ZIP
Dundee	76366
Dunlap	79248
Dunlay	78861
Dunn	79516
Dunnan (Part of Houston)	77022
Duplex	75447
Durango	76656
Duster	76444
Dye Mound	76265
Dyersdale	77016
Eagle Lake	77434
Eagle Mountain	76135
Eagle Mountain Acres	76020
Eagle Pass	78852*
	78853†
Earles Camp	79521
Earles Chapel	75764
Early	76802
Earlywine	77833
Earth	79031
East Afton	79220
East Amarillo (Part of Amarillo)	79104
East Arlington (Part of Arlington)	76007
East Austin (Part of Austin)	78702
East Bernard	77435
East Caney	75482
East Center	75140
East Columbia	77486
East Delta	75450
East Donna (Part of Donna)	78537
Easterly	77856
Eastex Oaks Village (Part of Houston)	77338
Eastgate	77535
East Glen (Part of El Paso)	79936
East Grand (Part of Dallas)	75223
East Hamilton	75973
East Houston (Part of Houston)	77028
Eastland	76448
East Liberty	75935
East Mayfield (Part of Hemphill)	75948
East Mountain	75644
Easton	75641
East Point	75494
East Ridge (Part of Amarillo)	79107
East Side	75639
East Tawakoni	75453
East Tempe	77351
East Texas (Part of Commerce)	75428
Eastvale	75056
East View (Part of Kilgore)	75662
Eastview Terrace	78101
Eastwood (Part of Houston)	77023
Eastwood Heights (Part of El Paso)	79925
Eaton	77856
Ebenezer (Camp County)	75686
Ebenezer (Jasper County)	75951
Ebony	76864
Echo (Coleman County)	76834
Echo (Orange County)	77630
Echo Hills	75763
Eckert	78675
Ecleto	78111
Ector	75439
Edcouch	78538
Eddy (Part of Bruceville-Eddy)	76524
Eden	76837
Edgar	77954
Edge	77808
Edgecliff	76134
Edgewater Estates	78368

Column 4

	ZIP
Edgewood	75117
Edgeworth	76569
Edhube	75418
Edinburg	78539*
	78540†
Edith	76945
Edmonson	79032
Edna	77957
Edna Hill	76446
Edom	75756
Edroy	78352
Egan	76031
Egypt (Leon County)	75833
Egypt (Montgomery County)	77355
Egypt (Wharton County)	77436
Elam (Part of Dallas)	75217
Elam Springs	75755
Elbert	76372
El Calmino	75948
El Campo	77437
El Campo Club	77465
El Campo South	77437
El Cenizo	78043
El Centro (Part of Laredo)	78042
El Centro Mall (Part of Pharr)	78577
Eldorado	76936
Eldorado Center	76569
Eldridge (Part of Sugar Land)	77478
Electra	76360
Electric City	79007
Elevation	76556
El Gato	78516
Elgin	78621
Eliasville	76481
El Indio	78860
El Jardin (Part of Brownsville)	78520
El Jardin Del Mar (Part of Pasadena)	77586
Elk	76624
Elkhart	75839
El Lago	77586
Ellinger	78938
Ellington Air Force Base (Part of Houston)	77209
Elliott (Robertson County)	77859
Elliott (Wilbarger County)	76364
Ellis (Part of Levelland)	79338
Ellis Unit	77340
Elmaton	77440
Elmdale	79601
Elmendorf	78112
Elm Flat	75144
Elm Grove (Cherokee County)	75785
Elm Grove (Fayette County)	78959
Elm Grove (San Saba County)	76872
Elm Grove (Wharton County)	77434
Elm Mott	76640
Elmo	75118
Elmont	75495
Elm Ridge (Grayson County)	75020
Elm Ridge (Milam County)	76520
Elmtown	75801
Elmwood (Anderson County)	75801
Elmwood (Guadalupe County)	78155
Eloise	76680
El Oso	78119
El Paso (El Paso County)	79901-99

For specific El Paso Zip Codes call (915) 775-7542, or your local postmaster.

	ZIP
El Paso (Fisher County)	79543
El Pinon Estates	75929
El Ranchito	79766
El Rancho Estates	76008
El Refugio	78582
Elroy	78617
Elsa	78543
El Sauz	78582
El Toro	77957
Elwood (Fannin County)	75447
Elwood (Madison County)	75852
Ely	75439
Elysian Fields	75642
Emberson	75486
Emblem	75482
Emerald Valley	78250
Emhouse	75110
Emmett	76641

---

* Area Zip Code   **† Post Office Boxes**

	ZIP		ZIP		ZIP		ZIP
Emory	75440	Faker	75686		78480	MILITARY INSTALLATIONS	
Encantada	78586	Falcon	78564	For specific Flour Bluff Zip			
Encantada-Ranchito El		Falcon Heights	78545	Codes call (512) 937-3530, or		Carswell Air Force Base	76127
Calaboz	78520	Falcon Mesa	78076	your local postmaster.		United States Army	
Enchanted Oaks (Harris		Falcon Village	78545	Flower Hill	78934	Engineer District, Fort	
County)	77373	Falfurrias	78355	Flower Mound	75028	Worth	76102
Enchanted Oaks		Fallon	76667	Floy	78941	United States Property	
(Henderson County)	75147	Falls City	78113	Floyd	75401	and Fiscal Office for	
Enchanted River Estates	78003	Fambrough	76424	Floydada	79235	Fort Worth	76108
Encinal	78019	Famuliner	79346	Fluvanna	79517		
Encino	78353	Fannett	77705	Flynn	77855	Fort Worth Town Center	
Energy	76452	Fannin	77960	Fodice	75851	(Part of Fort Worth)	76115
Engle	78956	Fargo	76384	Follett	79034	Forum 303 Mall (Part of	
English	75426	Farmer	76460	Folley	79255	Arlington)	76010
Enloe	75441	Farmers Branch	75234	Fondren (Part of Webster)	77598	Foster (Fort Bend County)	77469
Ennis	75119*	Farmers Valley	76384	Fords Corner	75972	Foster (Terry County)	79316
	75120†	Farmersville	75442	Fordtran	77995	Foster Hills	75951
Enoch	75644	Farmington	75058	Forest	75925	Foster Place (Part of	
Enochs	79324	Farnsworth	79033	Forestburg	76239	Houston)	77021
Ensign	75119	Farr Addition	79756	Forest Chapel	75411	Fosters Store	77836
Enterprise (Cherokee		Farrar	75838	Forest Glade	76667	Fouke	75765
County)	75766	Farrsville	75977	Forest Grove (Collin		Fountain (Part of Grand	
Enterprise (Van Zandt		Farwell	79325	County)	75069	Prairie)	75050
County)	75169	Fashing	78008	Forest Grove (Henderson		Fountain View	77032
Eola	76937	Fate	75132	County)	75758	Four Corners (Brazoria	
Eolian	76424	Faught	75462	Forest Heights	77630	County)	77422
Era	76238	Faulkner	75416	Forest Hill (Lamar County)	75446	Four Corners (Fort Bend	
Erath	76708	Fawil	75928	Forest Hill (Potter County)	79107	County)	77469
Erin	75951	Fayburg	75424	Forest Hill (Tarrant		Four Corners	
Erwin	77830	Fayetteville	78940	County)	76119	(Montgomery County)	77301
Escobares	78582	Faysville	78539	Forest Hill (Wood County)	75783	Four Way	79018
Escobas	78361	Federal Correctional		Forest Hill Estates	76528	Fowlerton	78021
Eskota	79561	Institution (Bastrop		Forest Hills (Part of Tyler)	75702	Fox	76088
Esmond Estates (Part of		County)	78602	Forest North Estates	78729	Fox Landing	75938
Odessa)	79762	Federal Correctional		Forest Spring	77351	Fox Run	77373
Esperanza	79839	Institution (Bowie		Forney	75126	Foxwood	77362
Esquire Estates	75147	County)	75501	Forreston	76041	Frame Switch	76574
Esseville	78008	Federal Correctional		Forsan	79733	Francis (Part of West	
Estacado	79343	Institution (Dallas		Fort Bliss	79906	Orange)	77630
Estacado Estates (Part of		County)	75159		79908	Francitas	77961
Amarillo)	79109	Federal Correctional			79916	Frankell	76470
Estelline	79233	Institution (Live Oak			79918	Franklin	77856
Estes	78382	County)	78071	For specific Fort Bliss Zip		Frankston	75763
Estes Addition	76071	Federal Correctional		Codes call (915) 562-4036, or		Fred	77616
Ethel	76233	Institution (Tarrant		your local postmaster.		Fredericksburg	78624
Etoile	75944	County)	76119	Fort Bliss (El Paso		Fredonia (Gregg County)	75662
Etter	79029	Federal Prison Camp	79720	County)	79916	Fredonia (Mason County)	76842
Eubank Acres	78753	Fedor	78947	Fort Clark Springs	78832	Fredonia Hill (Part of	
Eula	79510	Fellowship	75961	Fort Davis	79734	Nacogdoches)	75961
Eulalie	75975	Fentress	78622	Fort Gates	76528	Freedom (Lubbock	
Euless	76039-40	Ferris	75125	Fort Hancock	79839	County)	79412
For specific Euless Zip Codes		Fetzer	77363	Fort Hood	76544	Freedom (Rains County)	75440
call (817) 283-6636, or your		Fiddlers Green	75034	Fort McKavett	76841	Freeneytown	75667
local postmaster.		Field Creek	76869	Fort Ringgold (Part of Rio		Freeport	77541
Eulogy	76652	Fieldton	79326	Grande City)	78582	Freer	78357
Eureka	75110	Fife	76825	Fort Spunky	76031	Freestone	75838
Eustace	75124	Files Valley	76055	Fort Stockton	79735	Freeway Oaks Estates	77365
Evadale	77615	Fincastle	75763			Freheit	78130
Evant	76525	Fink	75076	**Fort Worth**	76101-26	Frelsburg	78950
Evergreen (Grimes		Finney (Hale County)	79072		76131-85	French Creek Village (Part	
County)	77861	Finney (King County)	79248	For specific Fort Worth Zip		of San Antonio)	78240
Evergreen (San Jacinto		First Colony	77479	Codes call (817) 625-3628, or		Frenstat	77836
County)	77327	Fischer	78623	your local postmaster.		Fresenius	77656
Evergreen Park	77662	Fisk	76834			Fresno	77545
Everitt	77327	Fitze	75946	COLLEGES & UNIVERSITIES		Freyburg	78956
Everman	76140	Fitzhugh	78703			Friday	75845
Ewell	75644	Five Points (El Paso		Southwestern Baptist		Friendship (Jasper	
Exchange Park (Part of		County)	79903*	Theological Seminary	76122	County)	75966
Dallas)	75245		79923†	Texas Christian University	76129	Friendship (Lamb County)	79371
Eylau	75501	Five Points (Ellis County)	75165	Texas Wesleyan		Friendship (Leon County)	75846
Ezzell	77964	Flagg	79027	University	76105	Friendship (Smith County)	75647
Fabens	79838	Flamingo Bay (Part of				Friendship (Upshur	
Fairbanks (Part of		Seabrook)	77586	FINANCIAL INSTITUTIONS		County)	75644
Houston)	77040-41	Flanagan	75691	Bank of Commerce	76102	Friendship (Van Zandt	
For specific Fairbanks Zip		Flat	76526	Bank One, Texas, N.A.	76102	County)	75140
Codes call (713) 937-7691, or		Flat Fork	75974	Central Bank & Trust	76104	Friendswood	77546
your local postmaster.		Flatonia	78941	Comerica Bank-Texas	76107	Friona	79035
Fairchilds	77469	Flat Prairie	77835	First Interstate Bank of		Frisco	75034
Fairfield	75840	Flats	75472	Texas, N.A.	76102	Fritch	79036
Fairgreen	77039	Flatwood	75754	Overton Bank & Trust,		Frog	75160
Fairland	78654	Fleetwood Oaks	77079	N.A.	76109	Frognot	75424
Fairlie	75428	Fletcher	77657	Southwest Bank	76133	Frontier Lakes	77378
Fairmount	75948	Flint	75762	Summit National Bank	76102	Fronton	78582
Fairoaks	75838	Flint Creek	76450	Texas Commerce Bank,		Frosa	76678
Fair Oaks Ranch	78006	Flo	75831	National Association	76102	Frost	76641
Fair Park (Part of Dallas)	75210	Flomot	79234			Fruitland	76230
Fair Play	75631	Flora	75437	HOSPITALS		Fruitvale	75127
Fairview (Bailey County)	79371	Florence	76527	All Saints Episcopal		Frydek	77474
Fairview (Bosque County)	76689	Florence Hill (Part of		Hospital of Fort Worth	76104	Frys Gap	75766
Fairview (Brazos County)	77807	Grand Prairie)	75052	Harris Methodist-Fort		Fulbright	75436
Fairview (Cass County)	75563	Floresville	78114	Worth	76104	Fuller Springs	75901
Fairview (Collin County)	75002	Florey	79714	HCA Medical Plaza		Fulshear	77441
Fairview (Gaines County)	79360	Florine (Part of San		Hospital	76104	Fulton	78358
Fairview (Harris County)	77006	Antonio)	78209	Saint Joseph Hospital	76104	Fulton Beach (Part of	
Fairview (Howard County)	79720	Flour Bluff (Part of Corpus		Tarrant County Hospital		Fulton)	78358
Fairview (Rusk County)	75784	Christi)	78418-19	District	76104	Funston	79501
Fairview (Wilson County)	78114					Furney Richardson	75860
Fairview (Wise County)	76078			HOTELS/MOTELS		Gail	79738
Fairy	76457			Residence Inn	76107	Gainesville	76240*
				Worthington	76102		

	ZIP
Galena Park	77547
Galilee	77340
Gallatin	75764
Gallaway	71049
Galle (Part of Dallas)	78638
Galleria (Part of Dallas)	75240
Galleria, The (Part of Houston)	77056
Galveston	77550-54
For specific Galveston Zip Codes call (409) 763-1819, or your local postmaster.	
Galvez Mall (Part of Galveston)	77551
Ganado	77962
Garceno	78582
Garciasville	78547
Garden Acres (Part of Fort Worth)	76028
Garden City (Glasscock County)	79739
Garden City (Harris County)	77018
Gardendale (Ector County)	79758
Gardendale (La Salle County)	78014
Garden Oaks (Part of Houston)	77206
Garden Ridge	78266
Garden Valley	75771
Garden Villas	77904
Garfield (DeWitt County)	78164
Garfield (Travis County)	78617
Garland (Bowie County)	75559
Garland (Dallas County)	75040-49
For specific Garland Zip Codes call (214) 272-5541, or your local postmaster.	
Garland (Red River County)	75550
Garner	76088
Garrett	75119
Garretts Bluff	75411
Garrison	75946
Garth	77520
Garvin	76023
Garwood	77442
Gary	75643
Gasoline	79255
Gastonia	75114
Gatesville	76528
Gatesville Unit	76528
Gateway Shopping City (Part of Beaumont)	77701
Gatewood	77039
Gause	77857
Gay Hill (Fayette County)	78945
Gay Hill (Washington County)	77833
General Mail Facility (Part of Austin)	78710
Geneva	75947
Geneva Estates	78736
Genoa (Part of Houston)	77034
George	77871
Georges Creek	76031
Georgetown	78626-28
For specific Georgetown Zip Codes call (512) 863-2325, or your local postmaster.	
George West	78022
George W. Singer (Part of Lubbock)	79424
Georgia	75486
Gerald	76640
Geronimo	78115
Geronimo Forest	78254
Geronimo Village	78253
Gethsemane	75657
Gholson	76705
Gibtown	76486
Giddings	78942
Gilchrist	77617
Gill	75670
Gillett	78116
Gilliland	79260
Gilmer	75644
Gilpin	79370
Ginger	75410
Girard	79518
Girvin	79740
Givens	75462
Gladewater (Gregg County)	75647
Gladewater (Titus County)	75455
Glass	76690
Glaze City	77984

	ZIP
Glazier	79014
Glen Cove (Coleman County)	76834
Glen Cove (Galveston County)	77565
Glencrest (Part of Fort Worth)	76119
Glendale	75862
Glenfawn	75760
Glen Flora	77443
Glenn Heights	75115
Glen Rose	76043
Glenwood (Potter County)	79103
Glenwood (Upshur County)	75644
Glidden	78943
Globe	75486
Glory	75462
Gober	75443
Godley	76044
Gold	78624
Golden	75444
Golden Beach	78643
Golden Oaks	78628
Golden Triangle Mall (Part of Denton)	76206
Goldfinch	78005
Goldsboro	79519
Goldsmith	79741
Goldthwaite	76844
Goliad	77963
Golinda	76655
Gomez	79316
Gonzales	78629
Goober Hill	75973
Goodfellow Air Force Base	76908
Good Hope	77964
Goodland	79371
Goodlett	79252
Goodlow	75144
Goodlow Park	75144
Goodnight (Armstrong County)	79226
Goodnight (Navarro County)	75144
Goodrich	77335
Good Springs	75667
Goodville	76632
Gordon (Lynn County)	79356
Gordon (Palo Pinto County)	76453
Gordonville	76245
Goree	76363
Goree Unit	77340
Gorman	76454
Goshen	77340
Gough	75448
Gould	75766
Gouldbusk	76845
Graceton	75644
Graford	76449
Graham (Garza County)	79356
Graham (Jasper County)	75951
Graham (Young County)	76450
Granada Estates	78737
Granbury	76048-49
For specific Granbury Zip Codes call (817) 573-5515, or your local postmaster.	
Grand Bluff	75631
Grandfalls	79742
Grand Prairie	75050-54
For specific Grand Prairie Zip Codes call (214) 264-5751, or your local postmaster.	
Grand Saline	75140
Grandview (Dawson County)	79351
Grand View (El Paso County)	79930
Grandview (Gray County)	79039
Grandview (Johnson County)	76050
Grange Hall	75670
Granger	76530
Grangerland	77302
Granite Shoals	78654
Granjeno	78572
Granview Beach	78611
Granville W. Elder (Part of Houston)	77013
Grape Creek	76901
Grapeland	75844
Grapetown	78624
Grapevine	76051
	76092

	ZIP
	76099
For specific Grapevine Zip Codes call (817) 488-9012, or your local postmaster.	
Grassland	79356
Graves (Part of Midland)	79708
Gray	75657
Grayback	76360
Grayburg	77659
Grays Chapel	75801
Grays Prairie	75158
Graytown	78114
Great Northwest	78250
Great Oaks	78681
Great Southwest (Part of Arlington)	76005
Green	78119
Green Acres	77058
Greenbriar (Part of Houston)	77098
Green Hill	75455
Green Lake	77979
Green Pastures	78640
Greenridge (Part of Houston)	77022
Greens Bayou (Part of Houston)	77015
Greens Camp	79521
Greens Creek	76446
Greens North (Part of Houston)	77067
Greenspoint Mall (Part of Houston)	77060
Green Valley	77227
Greenview	75420
Greenview Hills (Part of Irving)	75062
Greenview Manor	77032
Greenville	75401-04
For specific Greenville Zip Codes call (903) 455-5363, or your local postmaster.	
Greenville Avenue (Part of Dallas)	75206
Greenvine	77835
Greenway	78223
Greenway Plaza (Part of Houston)	77046
Greenwood (Hopkins County)	75478
Greenwood (Midland County)	79701
Greenwood (Parker County)	76088
Greenwood (Wise County)	76246
Greenwood Acres (Llano County)	78609
Greenwood Acres (Orange County)	77626
Greenwood Forest	77028
Greenwood Village	77093
Greggton (Part of Longview)	75604
Gregory	78359
Gresham	75703
Grey Forest	78023
Gribble (Part of Farmers Branch)	75234
Grice	75644
Griffin	75789
Griffing (Part of Port Arthur)	77640
Griffing Park (Part of Port Arthur)	77640
Griffith (Cochran County)	79346
Griffith (Ellis County)	76084
Grigsby	75935
Grit (Mason County)	76856
Grit (Rains County)	75410
Groceville	77301
Groesbeck	76642
Groom	79039
Grosvenor	76801
Groves	77619
Groveton	75845
Grow	79248
Gruenau	78164
Gruene	78130
Grulla	78548
Gruver	79040
Guadalupe	77905
Guadalupe Heights	78028
Guajillo	78332
Guerra	78360
Gulf Camp	79756
Gulfgate Mall (Part of Houston)	77087
Gulfway (Part of Corpus Christi)	78412

	ZIP
Gum Springs (Cass County)	75560
Gum Springs (Harrison County)	75601
Gun Barrel City	75147
Gunsight	76437
Gunter (Grayson County)	75058
Gunter (Wood County)	75410
Gussettville	78022
Gustine	76455
Guthrie	79236
Guy	77444
Guys Store	75833
Hacienda Heights (Part of El Paso)	79915
Hackberry (Bexar County)	78210
Hackberry (Cottle County)	79248
Hackberry (Denton County)	75068
Hackberry (Garza County)	79356
Hackberry (Lavaca County)	78956
Hagansport	75487
Hagerman	75090
Hagerville	75847
Hail	75492
Hainesville	75773
Halbert	75973
Hale Center	79041
Halesboro	75417
Halfway	79072
Hall (Marion County)	75657
Hall (San Saba County)	76871
Hallettsville	77964
Halloway Heights	77047
Halls Bluff	75835
Hallsburg	76705
Halls Store	71007
Hallsville	75650
Halsell	76365
Haltom City	76117
Hamby	79601
Hamilton	76531
Hamlin	79520
Hamon	78629
Hampton	75936
Hamshire	77622
Hancock Oak Hills	78130
Hancock Shopping Center (Part of Austin)	78751
Handley (Part of Fort Worth)	76124
Hankamer	77560
Hannibal	76401
Hanover	76520
Hansford	79081
Happy	79042
Happy Hill	76009
Happy Union	79072
Happy Valley	79566
Harbin	76446
Harbor Grove (Part of Hickory Creek)	75065
Harborlight	75948
Hardin	77561
Hardin-Simmons (Part of Abilene)	79698
Hardy	76265
Hare	76574
Hargill	78549
Harker Heights	76543
Harkeyville	76877
Harlandale (Part of San Antonio)	78214
Harlem	77469
Harleton	75651
Harlingen	78550-53
For specific Harlingen Zip Codes call (210) 423-1464, or your local postmaster.	
Harmon	75446
Harmony (Anderson County)	75801
Harmony (Parker County)	76087
Harmony (Rusk County)	75684
Harmony Grove	77340
Harmony Hill	75691
Harper	78631
Harriet	78548
Harrisburg (Harris County)	77012
Harrisburg (Jasper County)	75951
Harrison	76682
Harrold	76364
Hart	79043
Hartburg	77630
Hart Camp	79339
Hartley	79044
Harts Bluff	75455

	ZIP
Hart Spur (Part of Hurst)	76053
Hartzo	75657
Harvard	75686
Harvest Acres (Montgomery County)	77372
Harvest Acres (Tom Green County)	76905
Harvest Heights	77088
Harvey	77845
Harwood	78632
Haskell	79521
Haslam	75954
Haslet	76052
Hasse	76456
Hatchel	79567
Hatchetville	75437
Havana	78572
Hawkins	75765
Hawkinsville	77414
Hawley	79525
Hawthorne	77358
Hayden	75169
Haynesville	76360
Hays	78666
Hazy Hollow	77355
Headlea Estates (Part of Odessa)	79762
Headsville	76653
Heald	79057
Hearne	77859
Heath	75087
Hebbronville	78361
Hebco (Part of San Antonio)	78218
Hebron	75056
Heckville	79329
Hedley	79237
Hedwig Village	77024
Heidelberg	78570
Heidenheimer	76533
Heights (Galveston County)	77590
Heights (Harris County)	77248
Helena	78118
Helmic	75845
Helotes	78023
Hemphill	75948
Hempstead	77445
Henderson	75652*
	75653†
Henderson Chapel	76866
Henderson Heights	79763
Henkhaus	77984
Henly	78620
Henning	75946
Henrietta	76365
Henrys Chapel	75789
Hereford	79045
Heritage Northwest	78245
Heritage Oaks	77365
Hermleigh	79526
Herring (Part of San Angelo)	76901
Herty (Part of Lufkin)	75901
Hewitt	76643
Hext	76848
Hickey	75667
Hickory Creek (Denton County)	75065
Hickory Creek (Hunt County)	75423
Hickory Hill	75686
Hickory Hills	77356
Hickory Hollow	75929
Hickston	78959
Hico	76457
Hidalgo	78557
Hidden Echo	77336
Hidden Forest (Part of San Antonio)	78232
Hidden Hill	75065
Hidden Hills Harbor	75147
Hidden Valley (Part of Houston)	77088
Hide-A-Way Lake	75771
Higginbotham	79360
Higgins	79046
Highbank	76680
High Hill	78956
High Island	77623
Highland (Erath County)	76446
Highland (Johnson County)	76031
Highland Acres (Grayson County)	75076
Highland Acres (Harris County)	77018
Highland Acres (Hunt County)	75453

	ZIP
Highland Addition (Harris County)	77018
Highland Addition (Parker County)	76082
Highland Creek Lakes	78736
Highland Estates (Part of Victoria)	77904
Highland Haven	78654
Highland Hills (Bexar County)	78223
Highland Hills (Dallas County)	75241
Highland Mall (Part of Austin)	78752
Highland Park	75205
Highland Range Estates	76901
Highlands	77562
Highland Village	75067
Highland Waters	78003
Highpoint	77093
Highsaw	75763
Hi Ho	77630
Hiland Shores	75076
Hill and Dale Acres	77372
Hill City	76476
Hill Country Village	78232
Hillcrest	75511
Hillebrandt	77705
Hillister	77624
Hillje	77455
Hills	78659
Hillsboro	76645
Hillside Estates	75763
Hillside Gardens	77039
Hilltop (Coryell County)	76528
Hilltop (Gillespie County)	78624
Hilltop (Grayson County)	75020
Hilltop Acres	78253
Hilltop Lakes	77871
Hilshire Village	77055
Hinckley	75460
Hindes	78026
Hines	76384
Hinkles Ferry	77422
Hiram	75160
Hitchcock	77563
Hitchland	73942
Hoard	75773
Hobbs	75926
Hobson	78117
Hochheim	77967
Hockley	77447
Hodges	79525
Hodgson	75559
Hoen	76691
Hogan Acres	76028
Hogansville	75410
Hogg	77836
Holiday Beach	78382
Holiday Estates	75169
Holiday Harbor	75630
Holiday Hills	75453
Holiday Hills Estates	76424
Holiday Lake Estates	77335
Holiday Lakes	77515
Holiday Oaks	77372
Holland (Bell County)	76534
Holland (Hardin County)	77625
Holland Quarters	75633
Holliday	76366
Hollis	77864
Holly	75851
Holly Grove	77351
Holly Springs (Camp County)	75686
Holly Springs (Jasper County)	75951
Holly Springs (Nacogdoches County)	75946
Holly Springs (Van Zandt County)	75754
Holly Terrace	77365
Hollywood Addition	77627
Hollywood Heights	77627
Hollywood Park	78232
Holman	78962
Holt	76872
Homer (Angelina County)	75901
Homer (Jasper County)	75951
Homestead Meadows	79927
Homewood	75951
Hondo	78861
Honea	77356
Honey Grove (Cass County)	75551
Honey Grove (Fannin County)	75446
Honey Island	77625
Hood	76240

	ZIP
Hooks	75561
Hoover	79065
Hoovers Valley	78611
Hope	77995
Hopewell (Franklin County)	75457
Hopewell (Houston County)	75835
Hopewell (Leon County)	75833
Horizon City	79927
Horn Hill	76642
Horseshoe Bay	78654
Horseshoe Bay South	78654
Horseshoe Bay West	78654
Horseshoe Falls	78130
Hortense	77351
Horton (Delta County)	75428
Horton (Jasper County)	75951
Horton (Panola County)	75639
Hostyn	78945
Hot Wells	79851
Houmont Park	77044
Houseman Addition	77662
Houston	77001-99
	77101-99
	77201-99

For specific Houston Zip Codes call (713) 227-1474, or your local postmaster.

COLLEGES & UNIVERSITIES

	ZIP
Houston Baptist University	77074
Rice University	77251
South Texas College of Law	77002
Texas Southern University	77004
University of Houston-Clear Lake	77058
University of Houston-Downtown	77002
University of St. Thomas	77006
University of Texas Health Science Center at Houston	77225

FINANCIAL INSTITUTIONS

	ZIP
American Bank	77002
Bank of Houston	77002
Bank One, Texas, N.A.	77002
BankTEXAS, National Association	77063
Bank United of Texas, F.S.B.	77027
Charter National Bank-Houston	77008
Compass Bank-Houston	77210
Cullen Center Bank & Trust	77002
Enterprise Bank-Houston	77023
First Interstate	77002
Guardian Savings & Loan Association	77057
Harrisburg Bank, Houston	77012
Lockwood National Bank of Houston	77020
Med Center Bank	77030
Merchants Bank	77008
NationsBank of Texas, National Association	77002
Northwest Bank	77092
Post Oak Bank	77056
Texas Commerce Bank, National Association	77002
University State Bank	77005

HOSPITALS

	ZIP
AMI Park Plaza Hospital	77004
AMI Twelve Oaks Hospital	77027
Harris County Hospital District	77030
HCA Spring Branch Medical Center	77055
Hermann Hospital	77030
Houston Northwest Medical Center	77090
Memorial City Medical Center	77024
Memorial Hospital System	77074
Methodist Hospital	77030
St. Joseph Hospital	77002
St. Luke's Episcopal Hospital	77030
Texas Children's Hospital	77030
University of Texas M.D. Anderson Cancer Center	77030
Veterans Affairs Medical Center	77030

HOTELS/MOTELS

	ZIP
Adam's Mark Houston	77042
Embassy Suites Hotel	77074
Four Seasons Hotel, Houston	77010
Holiday Inn Crowne Plaza-Galleria	77027
Holiday Inn-Houston Intercontinental	77032
Houston Marriott Airport	77032
Houston Marriott Medical Center	77030
Houston Marriott Westside	77079
Hyatt Regency Houston	77002
J.W. Marriott Hotel	77056
Quality Inn-Intercontinental Airport	77205
Residence Inn	77030
Ritz Carlton, Houston	77027
Westchase Hilton & Towers	77042
Westin Galleria	77056
Westin Oaks	77056

MILITARY INSTALLATIONS

	ZIP
Coast Guard Air Station, Houston	77034
Lyndon B. Johnson Space Center	77058
Texas Air National Guard, FB6433, Ellington Field	77034

	ZIP
Howard	75165
Howardwick	79226
Howe	75459
Howland	75460
Hoxie	76574
Hoyt (Part of Alba)	75410
Hoyte	76520
Hub	79035
Hubbard	76648
Huckabay	76401
Hudson	75904
Hudson Oaks	76087
Huffines	75555
Huffman	77336
Hufsmith	77337
Hughes Springs	75656
Hughey	75662
Hulen Mall (Part of Fort Worth)	76132
Hulen Park (Part of Texas City)	77590
Hull	77564
Humble	77325
	77338-39
	77345-47
	77396

For specific Humble Zip Codes call (713) 446-3152, or your local postmaster.

	ZIP
Humble Camp	78377
Humble Heights (Part of Houston)	77338
Hungerford	77448
Hunt	78024
Hunter	78130
Hunters Creek Village	77024
Hunters Retreat	77355
Huntington	75949
Huntsville	77340-42

For specific Huntsville Zip Codes call (409) 295-7741, or your local postmaster.

	ZIP
Hurlwood	79407
Hurnville	76365
Huron	76692
Hurst	76053-54

For specific Hurst Zip Codes call (817) 284-3464, or your local postmaster.

	ZIP
Hurstown	75973
Hurst Springs	76634
Hutchins	75141
Hutto	78634
Huxley	75973
Huxley Bay	75973
Hye	78635
Hylton	79506
Iago	77420
Ida	75491
Idalou	79329
Idle Hour Acres	78728
Ike	75165
Illinois Bend	76265
Impact	79603
Imperial	79743

Name	ZIP	Name	ZIP	Name	ZIP	Name	ZIP
Imperial Valley (Part of Houston)	77022	Jean	76374		76248*	Kountze	77625
Inadale	79545	Jeddo	78953	Kellerville	79057	Kovar	78941
Independence	77833	Jefferson	75657	Kelly	75409	Kress	79052
India	75125	Jefferson City Shopping Center (Part of Port Arthur)	77640	Kellyville	75657	Kreutzberg	78006
Indian Creek	76801			Kelsey	75644	Krugerville	76227
Indian Gap	76531	Jefferson Heights (Part of San Angelo)	76901	Kelton	79096	Krum	76249
Indian Harbor Estates	76048			Keltys (Part of Lufkin)	75903	Kubala Store	78164
Indian Hill	75977	Jenkins	75638	Kemah	77565	Kurten	77862
Indian Hills	78006	Jennings	75462	Kemp	75143	Kuykendahl Village (Part of Houston)	77068
Indian Lake (Cameron County)	78586	Jensen Drive (Part of Houston)	77026	Kempner	76539		
Indian Lake (Newton County)	77630	Jensens Point	77465	Kendalia	78027	Kyle	78640
Indian Lodge	76652	Jericho	79226	Kendleton	77451	Kyote	78005
Indian Oaks (Henderson County)	75163	Jermyn	76459	Kenedy	78119	Labatt	78114
Indian Oaks (Waller County)	77466	Jerrys Quarters	77833	Kenefick	77535	La Blanca	78558
Indianola	77979	Jersey Village	77040	Kennard	75847	La Casita	78582
Indian Rock	75644	Jerusalem	77422	Kennedale	76060	La Casita-Garciasville	78547
Indian Shores	75532	Jester Unit	77469	Kenney	77452	Laceola	77864
Indian Springs	77351	Jewett	75846	Kensing	75450	Lackland Air Force Base	78236
Indian Trails (Part of Victoria)	77904	J. Frank Dobie (Part of San Antonio)	78220	Kent	79855	Lackland Heights	78227
Indian Village	77351	Jiba	75142	Kentuckytown	75491	Lackland Terrace (Part of San Antonio)	78227
Indian Waters	78003	Joaquin	75954	Kenwood Place	77339	La Coste	78039
Indian Woods	77355	Joe Pool (Part of Dallas)	75244	Kerens	75144	La Cuchilla (Part of Mission)	78572
Industrial (Part of Dallas)	75207	John Dunlop (Part of Houston)	77063	Kermit	79745	Lacy	75845
Industry	78944	John Foster (Part of Pasadena)	77502	Kerrick	79051	Lacy-Lakeview	76705
Inez	77968	Johnson	79316	Kerrville	78028* 78029†	Ladonia	75449
Ingleside	78362	Johnson City	78636			LaFayette	75686
Ingleside on the Bay	78362	Johnsons Station (Part of Arlington)	76015	Kessler Park (Part of Dallas)	75208	La Feria	78559
Ingram	78025	Johnstown	75169	Kevin	77327	Lagarto	78022
Ingram Park Mall (Part of San Antonio)	78238	Johnsville	76401	Key	79331	La Gloria	78591
Inks Lake Village	78609	Johntown	75417	Key Ranch Estates	75163	Lago	78586
Inwood (Part of Dallas)	75209	Joiner	78945	Keystone Park (Part of Dallas)	75240	Lago Vista	78645
Inwood Forest (Part of Houston)	77088	Jolnerville	75658	Kickapoo	75763	La Grange	78945
Inwood Place	77016	Joliet	76848	Kildare	75562	Laguna Heights	78578
Inwood Village (Part of Dallas)	75206	Jolly	76303	Kildare Junction	75555	Laguna Park	76634
Iola	77861	Jollyville	78729	Kilgore	75662* 75663†	Laguna Tres Estates	76049
Iowa Colony	77583	Jonah	78626			Laguna Vista	78578
Iowa Park	76367	Jones	75140	Killeen	76540-47	Laguna Vista Estates	75751
Ira	79527	Jonesboro	76538	For specific Killeen Zip Codes call (817) 634-0281, or your local postmaster.		La Hacienda Estates	78759
Iraan	79744	Jones Creek (Brazoria County)	77541			La Homa	78572
Irby	79521			Killeen Mall (Part of Killeen)	76543	Laird Hill	75666
Iredell	76649	Jones Creek (Wharton County)	77437	Kilowatt (Part of Orange)	77630	Lajitas	79852
Ireland	76538	Jones Prairie	76520	Kimball	76652	La Joya	78560
Irene	76650	Jonestown	78645	Kimbro	78653	La Junta	76020
Ironton	75766	Jonesville	75659	Kinard Estates	77630	Lake Air Center (Part of Waco)	76710
Irving	75014-17 75038-39 75060-63	Joplin	76458	King (Coryell County)	76528		
		Joppa	76605	King (Red River County)	75550	Lake Barbara (Part of Clute)	77531
For specific Irving Zip Codes call (214) 986-6557, or your local postmaster.		Jordan (Part of Amarillo)	79159	King City (Part of Cleveland)	77327	Lake Bonanza	77356
		Josephine	75164			Lake Bridgeport	76426
Irving Mall (Part of Irving)	75062	Joshua	76058	King Ranch	78363	Lake Brownwood	76801
Irvington (Part of Houston)	77022	Josserand	75845	Kingsbury	78638	Lake Chateau Woods	77302
Island (Galveston County)	77550	Jot 'Em Down	75469	Kings Cove	78611	Lake Cherokee	75652
Island (Madison County)	75852	Jourdanton	78026	Kingsland	78639	Lake City	78387
Italy	76651	Joy (Clay County)	76365	Kingsland Estates	78639	Lake Conroe Forrest	77301
Itasca	76055	Joy (Smith County)	75647	Kingsley (Part of Garland)	75041	Lake Conroe West	77301
Ivan	76424	Jozye	77864	Kings Mill	79065	Lake Corsicana (Part of Corsicana)	75110
Ivanhoe	75447	Juanita Craft (Part of Dallas)	75315	Kings Point	78073		
Iveys Crossing	79853			Kingston	75401	Lake Creek	75450
Ivy	76854	Jubilee Springs	76502	Kings Village	78727	Lake Creek Estates	77355
Izoro	76522	Jud	79544	Kingsville	78363* 78364†	Lake Dallas	75065
Jacinto City	77029	Judson	75660			Lake Gardens	76901
Jack D Watson (Part of Fort Worth)	76161	Juliff	77583	Kingsville Naval Station	78363	Lake Halbert (Part of Corsicana)	75110
Jacksboro	76458	Julius Melcher (Part of Houston)	77027	Kingswood	75104		
Jackson (Marion County)	75657			Kingtown	75961	Lake Highlands (Part of Dallas)	75238
Jackson (Shelby County)	75954	Jumbo	75669	Kingwood	77339	Lakehills	78063
Jackson (Van Zandt County)	75103	Junction	76849	Kinkler	77964	Lake Jackson	77566
Jacksonville	75766	Juno	76943	Kiomatia	75436	Lake Jackson Farms	77566
Jacobia	75401	Jupiter Pharmacy (Part of Richardson)	75080	Kirby	78219	Lake Kiowa	76240
Jamaica Beach	77554			Kirbyville	75956	Lakeland	77302
James	75935	Justiceburg	79330	Kirkland	79201	Lakeland Heights (Part of Grand Prairie)	75050
James Griffith (Part of Houston)	77080	Justin	76247	Kirkpatrick Addition	75704		
		Kadane Corner	76360	Kirtley	78957	Lakeland Park	78759
James Moody (Part of Victoria)	77904	Kalgary	79370	Kirvin	75848	Lake Livingston	77376
		Kamay	76369	Kittrell	75862	Lake Meredith Estates	79036
Jamestown (Newton County)	75966	Karney	77979	Kleberg (Part of Dallas)	75253	Lake Pauline	79252
		Kanawha	75436	Klein	77379	Lake Placid	78155
Jamestown (Smith County)	75140	Karen	77355	Klondike (Dawson County)	79331	Lakeport	75603
Jaques Spur (Part of Denison)	75020	Karnack	75661	Klondike (Delta County)	75448	Lake Ransom Canyon Village	79366
Jardin	75428	Karnes City	78118	Klump	77833		
Jarrell	76537	Katemcy	76825	Knapp	79527	Lake Rolling Wood	77301
Jarvis Christian College	75765	Katy	77449-50 77491-94	Knickerbocker	76939	Lake Shadows	77532
Jasper	75951			Knippa	78870	Lake Shore	76801
Jasper Heights (Part of Marshall)	75670	For specific Katy Zip Codes call (713) 578-0942, or your local postmaster.		Knob Hill	75034	Lakeshore Estates	75630
				Knollwood	75090	Lakeshore Estates West	75630
Jayton	79528	Kaufman	75142	Knott	79748	Lake Shore Gardens	78368
		Kayare (Part of Harlingen)	78550	Knox City	79529	Lakeside (Galveston County)	77565
		Keechi	75831	Koerth	77964		
		Keenan	77356	Kohrville	77040	Lakeside (San Patricio County)	78368
		Keene	76059	Kokomo	76454	Lakeside (Tarrant County)	76108
		Keeter	76023	Komensky	77975	Lakeside Acres	78006
		Keith	77861	Kona Kai	77650	Lakeside Beach	78669
		Keller	76244†	Kopernik Shores	78520	Lakeside City	76308
				Kopperl	76652	Lakeside Heights	78639
				Kosciusko	78160	Lakeside Park	77530
				Kosse	76653	Lakeside Village	76671

* Area Zip Code   † Post Office Boxes

* Area Zip Code   † Post Office Boxes

	ZIP
McCoy (Atascosa County)	78053
McCoy (Floyd County)...	79235
McCoy (Panola County)	75643
McCreless Mall (Part of San Antonio)	78223
McDade	78650
McDade Estates	77304
Macdona	78054
Macedonia (Austin County)	77474
Macedonia (Bowie County)	75501
Macedonia (Brazoria County)	77422
Macedonia (Liberty County)	77327
McElroy	75968
McFaddin	77973
McGalin	77612
McGee Landing	75948
McGregor	76657
McKenzie	75630
McKibben	79081
McKinney	75069-70
For specific McKinney Zip Codes call (214) 542-5031, or your local postmaster.	
McKnight	75652
McLean	79057
McLendon (Part of McLendon-Chisholm)	75087
McLendon-Chisholm	75087
McLeod	75565
McMahan	78616
McMillin	76877
McMurray (Part of Abilene)	79697
McNair	77520
McNair Village	76544
McNary	79839
McNeil (Caldwell County)	78648
McNeil (Travis County)...	78651
Macon	75457
McQueeney	78123
Mc Rea Lake	77302
Macune	75972
Macy	77882
Madero	78572
Madisonville	77864
Madras	75426
Magasco	75968
Magic (Part of San Antonio)	78229*
	78280†
Magnet	77488
Magnolia	77355
Magnolia Beach	77979
Magnolia Bend	77302
Magnolia Gardens	77044
Magnolia Hills	77355
Magnolia Springs	75957
Magpetco (Part of Port Neches)	77651
Mahl	75961
Mahomet	78605
Mahoney	75482
Main Place (Part of Dallas)	75202
Majors	75457
Malakoff	75148
Mallard	76251
Mall Del Norte (Part of Laredo)	78040
Mall of Abilene (Part of Abilene)	79606
Malone	76660
Malta	75570
Mambrino	76048
Manchaca	78652
Manchester	75412
Manda	78653
Manheim	78659
Mankin	75163
Mankins	76366
Manor	78653
Manor East Shopping Center (Part of Bryan)	77801
Mansfield	76063
Manvel	77578
Maple (Bailey County)...	79344
Maple (Red River County)	75417
Maple Crest Acres (Part of Vidor)	77662
Maple Springs	75455
Mapleton	75835
Marathon	79842
Marble Falls	78654
March Trailer Court	75169
Marfa	79843
Margaret	79227

	ZIP
Marie	76933
Marietta	75566
Marilee	75058
Marion	78124
Markham	77456
Markley	76460
Marlin	76661
Marquez	77865
Marshall	75670*
	75671†
Marshall Creek	76262
Marshall Ford	78732
Marshall Meadows (Part of San Antonio)	78240
Marshall Springs	75455
Mart	76664
Martindale	78655
Martinez	78219
Martin Luther King (Part of Houston)	77033
Martins Mills	75754
Martin Springs	75482
Martinsville	75958
Marvin	75462
Mary Hardin-Baylor (Part of Belton)	76513
Maryneal	79535
Marysville	76252
Mason	76856
Mason Lake Estates	77327
Massey Lake	75861
Masterson	79058
Matador	79244
Matagorda	77457
Mathews	77434
Mathis	78368
Matinburg	75686
Maud	75567
Mauriceville	77626
Maverick	76865
Maxdale	76542
Maxey	75421
Maxwell	78656
May	76857
Maydelle	75772
Mayfair (Part of Houston)	77022
Mayfield (Hale County)...	79041
Mayfield (Hill County)	76055
Mayflower (Newton County)	75977
Mayflower (Rusk County)	75691
Mayhill	76205
Maynard	77358
Maypearl	76064
Maysfield	76555
Meador Grove	76557
Meadow	79345
Meadowcreek (Part of San Angelo)	76904
Meadowlakes	78611
Meadowood Acres	78252
Meadows	77477
Mecca	77871
Medical Center (Part of Houston)	77054
Medicine Mound	79252
Medill	75460
Medina	78055
Medio (Part of Houston)	77022
Meeker	77706
Meek Estates	75163
Meeks	76519
Megargel	76370
Megaron (Part of Lubbock)	79423
Melear (Part of Arlington)	76013
	76015-17
For specific Melear Zip Codes call (817) 465-3868, or your local postmaster.	
Melissa	75454
Melody Hills (Part of Fort Worth)	76111
Melrose (Gregg County)	75662
Melrose (Nacogdoches County)	75961
Melrose Heights	77018
Melvin	76858
Melwood Place	77016
Memorial City Shopping Center (Part of Houston)	77024
Memorial Park (Part of Houston)	77024
Memphis	79245
Menard	76859
Mendoza	78644
Menlow	76621
Mentone	79754

	ZIP
Mentz	78935
Mercedes	78570
Mercer's Gap	76442
Merchandise Mart (Part of Dallas)	75201
Mercury	76872
Mereta	76940
Meridian	76665
Merit	75458
Merkel	79536
Merle	77879
Mertens	76666
Mertzon	76941
Mesa Verde (Part of Amarillo)	79107
Meskill (Part of Texas City)	77590
Mesquite	75149-50
	75180-87
For specific Mesquite Zip Codes call (214) 288-4476, or your local postmaster.	
Metcalf Gap	76475
Meusebach Creek	78624
Mexia	76667
Mexico	75474
Meyerland Plaza Shopping Center (Part of Houston)	77096
Meyersville	77974
Miami	79059
Michael Unit	75861
Mickey	79241
Mico	78056
Midcity	75473
Middleton	75833
Middletowne (Part of Seguin)	78155
Middle Water	79022
Midfield	77458
Midkiff	79755
Mid Lake Village	75948
Midland	79701-12
For specific Midland Zip Codes call (915) 560-5105, or your local postmaster.	
Midland Park Mall (Part of Midland)	79705
Midline	77327
Midlothian	76065
Midway (Dawson County)	79331
Midway (Fannin County)	75418
Midway (Hill County)	76645
Midway (Jim Wells County)	78372
Midway (Lavaca County)	77984
Midway (Lubbock County)	79364
Midway (Madison County)	75852
Midway (Montgomery County)	77327
Midway (Scurry County)	79526
Midway (Smith County)	75792
Midway (Titus County)	75455
Midway (Upshur County)	75644
Midway (Van Zandt County)	75754
Midway Mall (Part of Sherman)	75090
Midyett	75639
Miguel	78005
Mila Doce	78543
Milam	75959
Milano	76556
Milburn	76872
Mildred	75110
Mile High	79851
Miles	76861
Milford	76670
Mill Creek	77833
Mill Creek Forest	77355
Miller Grove (Camp County)	75686
Miller Grove (Hopkins County)	75433
Miller's Cove	75455
Millersview	76862
Millett	78014
Millheim	77474
Millican	77866
Millsap	76066
Millsville	78362
Milton	75435
Minden	75680
Mineola	75773
Mineral	78125
Mineral Wells	76067*
	76068†
Minerva	76567
Mings Chapel	75644

	ZIP
Mingus	76463
Minimaz (Part of Alvin)...	77511
Minter	75468
Mirando City	78369
Mission	78572*
	78573†
Mission Bend	77083
Mission Valley	77905
Missouri City	77459
	77489
For specific Missouri City Zip Codes call (713) 499-6502, or your local postmaster.	
Mitchell Avenue (Part of Waco)	76708
Mixon	75789
Mobeetie	79061
Mobile City	75087
Mobile Meadows Park	77630
Mockingbird (Part of Austin)	78745
Moffat	76502
Moffett	75901
Monahans	79756
Monaville	77445
Monkstown	75488
Monroe	75662
Monroe City	77514
Monroe Street (Part of Wichita Falls)	76309
Mont	77964
Montague	76251
Montague Ranch Estates	78003
Montalba	75853
Mont Belvieu	77580
Monte Alto	78538
Montell	78801
Monte Oaks	77357
Monteola	78119
Montgomery	77356
Montgomery Gardens	75708
Monthalia	78614
Monticello	75455
Montopolis (Part of Austin)	78741
Moody	76557
Moonshine Hill	77338
Moore (Frio County)	78057
Moore (Jasper County)	75951
Moore's Chapel	75418
Moores Crossing	78617
Moore Station	75770
Mooreville	76632
Mooring	77801
Morales	77957
Moran	76464
Moravia	78956
Morgan	76671
Morgan Creek	78611
Morgan Mill	76465
Morgan's Point	77571
Morgan's Point Resort	76513
Morningside Heights (Part of El Paso)	79930
Morrill	77925
Morris Ranch	78624
Morse	79062
Morton (Cochran County)	79346
Morton (Harrison County)	75640
Moscow	75960
Mosheim	76689
Moss Bluff	77575
Moss Hill	77575
Mostyn	77355
Moulton	77975
Mound	76558
Mound City	75844
Mountain	76528
Mountain City	78610
Mountain Home	78058
Mountain Peak	76065
Mountain Springs (Cooke County)	76258
Mountain Springs (Hill County)	76645
Mountain Valley Estates	76058
Mountain View (Part of El Paso)	79904
Mountain View Unit	76528
Mount Blanco	79322
Mount Calm	76673
Mount Carmel	76360
Mount Enterprise (Rusk County)	75681
Mount Enterprise (Wood County)	75773
Mount Haven	75766
Mount Houston	77016
Mount Joy	75441

* Area Zip Code   **† Post Office Boxes**

Place	ZIP	Place	ZIP
Mount Lookout	78130	New Boston	75570
Mount Lucas	78022	New Braunfels	78130-33
Mount Mitchell	75571	For specific New Braunfels Zip	
Mount Moriah	75571	Codes call (210) 625-7736, or	
Mount Olive	77995	your local postmaster.	
Mount Pleasant	75455*	New Bremen	78950
	75456†	Newburg	76442
Mount Selman	75757	Newby	75846
Mount Sylvan	75771	New Caney	77357
Mount Union	75956	New Caney Heights	77357
Mount Vernon	75457	Newcastle	76372
Mozelle	76834	New Chapel Hill	75701
Muddig	75449	New Clarkson	76570
Mudville	77801	New Colony	75563
Muellersville	77833	New Corn Hill	76537
Muenster	76252	New Deal	79350
Mulberry	75476	New Fountain	78861
Muldoon	78949	Newgulf	77462
Muleshoe	79347	New Harmony (Shelby	
Mulkey	79027	County)	75973
Mullin	76864	New Harmony (Smith	
Mullins Prairie	78945	County)	75704
Mumford	77867	Newharp	76239
Muncy	79241	New Hebron	75685
Munday	76371	New Home	79383
Munson	75189	New Hope (Cherokee	
Murchison	75778	County)	75766
Murphy	75094	New Hope (Collin County)	75069
Murray	76450	New Hope (Dallas	
Murryhill (Part of Lubbock)	79413	County)	75149
Musgrove	75494	New Hope (Henderson	
Mustang (Denton County)	76258	County)	75756
Mustang (Navarro County)	75110	New Hope (Jones	
Mustang Mott Store	77954	County)	79553
Mustang Ridge	78610	New Hope (Rusk County)	75662
Mykawa Road (Part of		New Hope (San Jacinto	
Houston)	77033	County)	77327
Myra	76253	New Hope (Smith County)	75703
Myrtle Springs	75169	New Hope (Wood	
Naaman (Part of Garland)	75040	County)	75773
Nacalina		New Katy	78653
Nacogdoches	75961-64	Newlin	79245
For specific Nacogdoches Zip		New London	75682
Codes call (409) 564-3737, or		New Lynn	79381
your local postmaster.		New Mine	75686
Nada	77460	New Moore	79351
Nadeau (Part of Texas		Newport (Clay County)	76230
City)	77590	Newport (Harris County)	77532
Nancy	75980	New Prospect (Rusk	
Naples	75568	County)	75652
Naruna	76550	New Prospect (Shelby	
Nash (Bowie County)	75569	County)	75975
Nash (Ellis County)	75165	New River Lake Estates	77327
Nassau Bay (Harris		New Salem (Falls County)	76570
County)	77058	New Salem (Palo Pinto	
Nassau Bay (Hood		County)	76472
County)	76049	New Salem (Rusk County)	75652
Nasworthy Hills (Part of		Newsome	75451
San Angelo)	76904	New Summerfield	75780
Nat	75760	New Sweden (McCulloch	
Natalia	78059	County)	76825
Naval Air (Part of Corpus		New Sweden (Travis	
Christi)	78419	County)	78653
Navarro	75151	New Taiton	77437
Navarro Mills	76679	Newton	75966
Navasota	77868-69	New Ulm	78950
For specific Navasota Zip		New Waverly	77358
Codes call (409) 825-6812, or		New Wehdem	77833
your local postmaster.		New Willard	77351
Navo	76227	New York	75770
Nazareth	79063	Neylandville	75401
Nebgen	78624	Nickel	76629
Necessity	76424	Nickelberry	75566
Nechanitz	78946	Nickel Creek	88220
Neches	75779	Niederwald	78640
Neches Indian Village	75925	Nigton	75926
Neches Junction (Part of		Nimitz (Part of San	
Port Arthur)	77640	Antonio)	78216*
Nederland	77627		78279†
Needmore (Bailey County)	79371	Nimrod	76437
Needmore (Delta County)	75448	Nineveh	75833
Needville	77461	Nix	76550
Negley	75426	Nixon	78140
Neinda	79520	Noack	76574
Nell	78119	Nobility	75424
Nelson City	78006	Noble	75470
Nelsonville	77418	Nockenut	78160
Nelta	75437	Nocona	76255
Nemo	76070	Nogalus	75845
Nesbitt (Harrison County)	75670	Nolan	79537
Nesbitt (Robertson		Nolanville	76559
County)	76629	Nolte	78155
Neuville	75935	Nome	77629
Nevada	75173	Nona	77625
Newark	76071	Noodle	79536
New Baden	77870	Noonday	75762
New Berlin	78121	Nopal	78164
New Bielau	78962	Nordheim	78141
New Birthright	75482	Norias	78338

Place	ZIP	Place	ZIP
Norman Crossing	76574	North Zulch	77872
Normandy	78877	Norton	76865
Normangee	77871	Norwood	75972
Normanna	78142	Notrees	79759
Norse	76634	Nottingham Forest	77630
North (Part of Garland)	77044*	Nottingham Woods	75835
	77045†	Novice (Coleman County)	79538
North Amarillo (Part of		Novice (Lamar County)	75462
Amarillo)	79117	Novohrad	77975
Northampton	77379	Noxville	78631
North Austin (Part of		Nugent	79601
Austin)	78751	Nursery	77976
Northaven (Part of Dallas)	75229	Oakalla	76542
North Beach (Part of		Oak Canyon	77302
Corpus Christi)	78402	Oak Creek Addition (Part	
North Bonami	75956	of Grapevine)	76051
North Branch (Part of		Oak Crest Estates	78628
Dallas)	75244	Oak Dale (Erath County)	76401
North Broadway (Part of		Oakdale (Hopkins County)	75482
San Antonio)	78217	Oak Flat (Angelina	
North Caney	75482	County)	75949
North Cedar	75926	Oak Flat (Nacogdoches	
North Cleveland	77327	County)	75760
Northcliff	78108	Oak Flat (Rusk County)	75681
North Concho Lake		Oak Forest (Harris	
Estates	76901	County)	77018
Northcrest	76705	Oak Forest (Travis	
Northcrest Estates (Part of		County)	78759
Victoria)	77904	Oak Grove (Bowie	
Northcross Mall (Part of		County)	75554
Austin)	78757	Oak Grove (Camp	
Northeast (Part of Austin)	78752	County)	75686
North East Mall (Part of		Oak Grove (Ellis County)	75119
Hurst)	76053	Oak Grove (Kaufman	
Northeast Station (Part of		County)	75142
Odessa)	79764	Oak Grove (Tarrant	
Northern Hills	75020	County)	76028
Northfield	79201	Oak Grove (Wood	
Northgate (El Paso		County)	75783
County)	79914†	Oak Hill (Jasper County)	75951
	79924*	Oak Hill (Johnson County)	76031
Northgate (Victoria		Oak Hill (Rusk County)	75652
County)	77904	Oak Hill (Travis County)	78735
North Groesbeck	79252	Oak Hills Acres	77362
North Heights (Part of		Oakhill Station (Part of	
Amarillo)	79107	Austin)	78749
North Hills Mall (Part of		Oakhurst	77359
North Richland Hills)	76180	Oak Island	77514
North Houston	77086	Oak Lake	76705
North Houston General		Oakland (Cherokee	
Mail Facility (Part of		County)	75785
Houston)	77315	Oakland (Colorado	
North Houston Heights	77039	County)	78951
North Lake (Dallas		Oakland (Rusk County)	75652
County)	75238	Oakland (Van Zandt	
Northlake (Denton		County)	75103
County)	76247	Oak Lawn (Part of Dallas)	75219
Northlake Estates	78628	Oaklawn Village (Part of	
North Line Oaks	77301	Texarkana)	75501
Northline Shopping Center		Oak Leaf	75154
(Part of Houston)	77022	Oak Point	75034
Northline Terrace	77093	Oak Ridge (Cooke	
North Oaks	78753	County)	76240
North Orange Heights	77630	Oak Ridge (Kaufman	
Northpark Center (Part of		County)	75160
Dallas)	75225	Oak Ridge (Llano County)	78654
Northpark Mall (Part of El		Oak Ridge (Nacogdoches	
Paso)	79924	County)	75961
North Port Arthur (Part of		Oak Ridge (Parker	
Port Arthur)	77642	County)	76087
North Richland Hills	76118	Oak Ridge North	77302
Northrup	78942	Oaks (Bee County)	78119
North Rusk (Part of Rusk)	75785	Oaks (Tarrant County)	76114
North San Antonio Hills	78253	Oaks North	78260
North San Pedro	78880	Oak Terrace	77365
North Shepherd (Part of		Oak Trail Shores	76048
Houston)	77088	Oak Valley	75110
Northside Village (Part of		Oakview	77611
Houston)	77015	Oak Village North	78266
North Springs	77373	Oakville	78060
North Star Mall (Part of		Oakwilde	77093
San Antonio)	78216	Oakwood (Leon County)	75855
Northtown Mall (Part of		Oakwood (Tarrant	
Dallas)	75234	County)	76012
Northwest (Part of Austin)	78756-57	Oakwood Village and	
	78766	Westwood Plaza (Part	
For specific Northwest Zip		of Abilene)	79603
Codes call (512) 454-4581, or		Oatmeal	78605
your local postmaster.		O'Brien	79539
Northwest (Part of Dallas)	75220	Oceanshore	77650
Northwest Hills	78024	Ocee	76638
Northwest Mall (Part of		Odell	79247
Houston)	77292	Odell Addition (Part of	
Northwest Park	77086	Grapevine)	76051
Northwest Plaza (Part of		Odem	78370
Dallas)	75238	Odessa	79760-69
Northwood	78758	For specific Odessa Zip Codes	
Northwood Hills Village		call (915) 332-6436, or your	
(Part of Dallas)	75240	local postmaster.	

* **Area Zip Code**   † **Post Office Boxes**

Place	ZIP
Odom	75147
Odonnell	79351
Oenaville	76501
O'Farrell	75551
Oglesby	76561
Oilla	77630
Oilton	78371
Oklahoma	77355
Oklahoma Flat	79339
Oklahoma Lane	79325
Oklaunion	76373
Okra	76435
Ola	75142
Old Boston	75570
Old Bowling	77865
Old Brazoria (Part of Brazoria)	77422
Old Dime Box	77853
Olden	76466
Oldenburg	78945
Old Ferry	78669
Old Glory	79540
Old Ivy	75847
Old Kinkler	77964
Old Larissa	75757
Old London	75682
Old Mill (Part of Leon Valley)	78238
Old Mobeetie (Part of Mobeetie)	79061
Old Moulton	77975
Old Ocean	77463
Old River Lake	77327
Old River Terrace	77530
Old River-Winfree	77520
Olds	75951
Old Sabinetown	75948
Old Salem	75933
Old Union (Bowie County)	75574
Old Union (Limestone County)	76687
Old Union (Titus County)	75455
Old Waverly	77358
Oletha	76687
Olfen	76875
Olin	76457
Olive	77625
Olivia	77979
Olmito	78575
Olmos (Bee County)	78389
Olmos (Starr County)	78582
Olmos Park	78212
Olney	76374
Olton	79064
Omaha	75571
Omen	75789
Onalaska	77360
One Seventy Seven Lake Estates	77356
Onion Creek	78747
Opdyke	79336
Opdyke West	79336
Opelika	75778
Oplin	79510
O'Quinn	78945
Ora	75949
Oran	76449
Orange	77630-32
For specific Orange Zip Codes call (409) 883-9351, or your local postmaster.	
Orangedale	78102
Orangefield	77639
Orange Grove (Harris County)	77039
Orange Grove (Jim Wells County)	78372
Orangeville	75491
Orchard	77464
Ore City	75683
Orient	76901
Orla	79770
Orme (Part of Arlington)	76010
Osage	76528
Oscar	76501
Osceola	76055
Ottine	78658
Otto	76675
Ovalo	79541
Overland Plaza (Part of Arlington)	76003
Overton	75684
Ovilla	75154
Owens (Brown County)	76801
Owens (Crosby County)	79357
Owensville	77856
Owentown	75708
Oyster Creek	77541
Ozona	76943
Pacio	75450
Pack Unit	77868
Padgett	76374
Padre-Staples Mall (Part of Corpus Christi)	78411
Paducah	79248
Pagoda	75862
Paige	78659
Paint Rock	76866
Pakan	79079
Palacios	77465
Palava	79556
Palestine (Anderson County)	75801*
	75802†
Palestine (Polk County)	75936
Palito Blanco	78332
Palmer	75152
Palmetto (Part of Oakhurst)	77359
Palm Harbor	78382
Palmhurst	78572
Palm Park	78223
Palm Valley	78550
Palmview	78572
Palo Alto	78343
Paloduro	79226
Palo Pinto	76484
Paluxy	76467
Pampa	79065*
	79066†
Pancake	76528
Pandale	76943
Pandora	78143
Panhandle	79068
Panna Maria	78144
Panola	75685
Panorama Estates	75169
Panorama Village	77301
Pantego	76094
Papalote	78387
Paradise	76073
Paradise Bay	75143
Paradise Hills	75929
Paris	75460-62
For specific Paris Zip Codes call (903) 784-3381, or your local postmaster.	
Park	78945
Park Cities (Part of University Park)	75205
Parkdale (Part of Dallas)	75227
Parkdale Mall (Part of Beaumont)	77706
Parkdale Plaza (Part of Corpus Christi)	78411
Parker (Collin County)	75002
Parker (Johnson County)	76050
Parker Point	75980
Parker Square (Part of Wichita Falls)	76308
Park Forest (Part of Dallas)	75240
Park Glen (Part of Houston)	77072
Park Place (Part of Houston)	77017
Park Row (Part of Katy)	77449
Parks at Arlington, The (Part of Arlington)	76015
Park Springs	76270
Parkview (Part of Fort Stockton)	79735
Parkview Estates	78155
Parkwood	77612
Parkwood Estates	77032
Parnell	79201
Parvin	75009
Pasadena	77501-08
For specific Pasadena Zip Codes call (713) 475-5140, or your local postmaster.	
Pasadena Town Square (Part of Pasadena)	77506
Patilo	76462
Patman	75656
Patrich	75652
Patricia	79331
Patrick (Dallas County)	75125
Patrick (McLennan County)	76708
Patroon	75973
Pattison	77466
Patton	76689
Pattonfield	75644
Patton Park	76544
Patton Village	77372
Pattonville	75468
Pauline	75124
Pauls Store	75973
Pawelekville	78113
Pawnee	78145
Paxton	75954
Paynes Corner	79360
Payne Springs	75124
Payton Colony	78606
Peach Creek	77488
Peach Creek Estates	77372
Peach Tree (Brazos County)	77801
Peachtree (Jasper County)	75951
Peacock	79502
Peadenville	76067
Pearl	76528
Pearland	77581
	77584
	77588
For specific Pearland Zip Codes call (713) 485-2814, or your local postmaster.	
Pearl City	77995
Pear Ridge (Part of Port Arthur)	77640
Pearsall	78061
Pearsons Chapel	75851
Pear Valley	76867
Peaster	76485
Pebble Beach	75121
Pebble Hills (Part of El Paso)	79925
Pecan (Part of Del Rio)	78840
Pecan Acres (Orange County)	77662
Pecan Acres (Wise County)	76071
Pecan Gap	75469
Pecangrove (Coryell County)	76528
Pecan Grove (Fort Bend County)	77469
Pecan Hill	75154
Pecan Lake Area	77835
Pecan Plantation	76048
Pecos	79772
Peeltown	75158
Peerless	75482
Peggy	78062
Pelham	76648
Pelican Bay	76020
Pendleton	76564
Pendleton Harbor	75948
Penelope	76676
Peniel (Part of Greenville)	75401
Penitas	78576
Pennington	75856
Penwell	79776
Peoria	76645
Pep	79353
Percilla	75844
Perezville	78572
Perico	79087
Permian Mall (Part of Odessa)	79762
Pernitas Point	78022
Perrin	76486
Perrin Field	75020
Perrin Heights	75020
Perry	76677
Perry Landing (Part of Jones Creek)	77541
Perryton	79070
Perryville	75494
Pershing (Part of Austin)	78702
Pershing Park	76544
Personville	76642
Pert	75801
Peters	77474
Petersburg	79250
Peterson	77627
Peters Prairie	75426
Petersville	77995
Petrolia	76377
Petronila	78380
Petteway	76629
Pettibone	76520
Pettit	77336
Pettus	78146
Petty (Lamar County)	75470
Petty (Lynn County)	79373
Petty's Chapel	75110
Pflugerville	78660*
	78691†
Phalba	75147
Pharr	78577
Phelan	78602
Phelps	77340
Phillips	79007
Phillipsburg	77426
Pickens	75751
Pickett	75110
Pickton	75471
Pidcoke	76528
Piedmont (Grimes County)	77830
Piedmont (Upshur County)	75644
Pierce	77467
Pierces Chapel	75766
Piggly Wiggly (Part of Bryan)	77801
Pike	75424
Pilgrim Ridge	77367
Pilgrims Rest	75410
Pilot Grove	75491
Pilot Knob	78744
Pilot Point	76258
Pine	75686
Pine Acres	77357
Pine Branch	75417
Pine Crest	77301
Pine Forest (Hopkins County)	75471
Pine Forest (Orange County)	77662
Pine Grove (Cherokee County)	75766
Pine Grove (Newton County)	75966
Pine Grove (Orange County)	77630
Pine Hill (Cherokee County)	75766
Pinehill (Rusk County)	75652
Pinehurst (Montgomery County)	77362
Pinehurst (Orange County)	77630
Pine Island	77445
Pine Lake	77356
Pineland	75968
Pine Mills	75773
Pine Park	75948
Pine Prairie	77340
Pine Ridge	77625
Pine Springs (Culberson County)	88220
Pine Springs (Smith County)	75702
Pine Trail Shores	75762
Pine Valley	75941
Pineview	75494
Pinewood (Part of Longview)	75601
Pinewood Estates (Hardin County)	77706
Pinewood Estates (Montgomery County)	77372
Pinewood Village	77093
Piney	77418
Piney Grove (Cass County)	75551
Piney Grove (Upshur County)	75451
Piney Point (Harris County)	77024
Piney Point (Montgomery County)	77301
Piney Point (Sabine County)	75959
Piney Woods	75951
Pinnacle	75644
Pioneer	76471
Pioneer Trails	77302
Pipe Creek	78063
Pirtle	75684
Pisgah	75929
Pitner Junction	75684
Pitts	77338
Pittsburg	75686
Placation Estates	75959
Placedo	77977
Placid	76872
Plains (Borden County)	79351
Plains (Yoakum County)	79355
Plainview (Denton County)	76249
Plainview (Hale County)	79072*
	79073†
Plainview (Sabine County)	75968
Plainview (Wharton County)	77455
Plano	75022-23
	75074-75
	75086
	75093-94
For specific Plano Zip Codes call (214) 423-4260, or your local postmaster.	
Plantersville	77363

* Area Zip Code   **† Post Office Boxes**

	ZIP
Plaska	79245
Plateau	79855
Pleak	77469
Pleasant Farms	79763
Pleasant Grove (Bowie County)	75501
Pleasant Grove (Dallas County)	75217
Pleasant Grove (Falls County)	76570
Pleasant Grove (Upshur County)	75755
Pleasant Grove (Wood County)	75494
Pleasant Hill (Blanco County)	78636
Pleasant Hill (Eastland County)	76437
Pleasant Hill (Nacogdoches County)	75946
Pleasant Hill (Polk County)	75939
Pleasant Hill (Washington County)	77833
Pleasanton	78064
Pleasant Point	76009
Pleasant Ridge (Henderson County)	75763
Pleasant Ridge (Leon County)	75833
Pleasant Ridge (Montague County)	76230
Pleasant Ridge (Panola County)	75633
Pleasant Springs	75833
Pleasant Valley (Dallas County)	75040
Pleasant Valley (Garza County)	79356
Pleasant Valley (Lamb County)	79347
Pleasant Valley (Palo Pinto County)	76067
Pleasant Valley (Potter County)	79108
Pleasant Valley (Wichita County)	76305
Pleasant Valley Acres	77355
Pledger (Fisher County)	79543
Pledger (Matagorda County)	77468
Pluck	75939
Plum	78952
Plum Creek	75831
Plum Grove	77327
Plum Ridge	75980
Plymouth Park Shopping Center (Part of Irving)	75061
Poe Prairie	76066
Poesville	76671
Poetry	75160
Point	75472
Pointblank	77364
Point Comfort	77978
Point Enterprise	76667
Point Loma	78368
Point Royal	75758
Point Venture	78641
Polar	79549
Pollok	75969
Polytechnic (Part of Fort Worth)	76105
Ponder	76259
Pond Springs	78729
Pone	75667
Ponta	75766
Pontotoc	76869
Poole	75440
Poolville	76487
Porfirio	78580
Port Acres (Part of Port Arthur)	77640
Portairs (Part of Corpus Christi)	78405
Port Alto	77979
Port Aransas	78373
Port Arthur	77640-43
For specific Port Arthur Zip Codes call (409) 983-3266, or your local postmaster.	
Port Bolivar	77650
Porter	77365
Porter Heights	77365
Porter Springs	75835
Porterville Timbers	77365
Port Isabel	78578
Portland	78374
Port Lavaca	77979
Port Mansfield	78598
Port Neches	77651

	ZIP
Port O'Connor	77982
Porvenir	77854
Posey (Hopkins County)	75482
Posey (Lubbock County)	79364
Possum Kingdom	76449
Post	79356
Post Oak (Blanco County)	78636
Post Oak (Delta County)	75432
Postoak (Freestone County)	75840
Postoak (Jack County)	76230
Postoak (Lamar County)	75416
Post Oak (Robertson County)	76629
Post Oak Bend City	75142
Post Oak Mall (Part of College Station)	77840
Post Oak Point	78950
Poteet	78065
Poth	78147
Potosi	79601
Potters Point	75657
Pottsboro	75076
Pottsville	76565
Powderly	75473
Powell	75153
Powell Point	77451
Poynor	75782
Prade Ranch	78058
Praesel	76567
Praha	78941
Prairie Dell	76571
Prairie Grove (Angelina County)	75941
Prairie Grove (Limestone County)	76667
Prairie Hill (Limestone County)	76678
Prairie Hill (Washington County)	77833
Prairie Lea	78661
Prairie Mountain	78643
Prairie Point	76239
Prairie Valley (Fayette County)	78952
Prairie Valley (Montague County)	76255
Prairie View	77446
Prairieville	75147
Prattville	75432
Premont	78375
Presidio	79845*
	79846†
Preston (Part of Dallas)	75225
Preston Shores	75076
Prestonwood (Dallas County)	75248
Prestonwood (Tarrant County)	76012
Prestonwood Town Center (Part of Dallas)	75240
Price (Jefferson County)	77627
Price (Rusk County)	75687
Priddy	76870
Primera	78550
Primrose	75754
Princeton	75407
Pringle	79083
Pritchett	75644
Proctor	76468
Proffitt	76372
Progreso	78579
Progreso Lakes	78579
Progress (Bailey County)	79347
Progress (Palo Pinto County)	76067
Promenade (Part of Richardson)	75080
Prospect	75657
Prosper	75078
Providence (Angelina County)	75904
Providence (Hardin County)	77625
Providence (Polk County)	77351
Providence (Van Zandt County)	75140
Provident City	77455
Pruitt (Cass County)	75657
Pruitt (Van Zandt County)	75140
Puckett Place (Part of Amarillo)	79109
Puckett West (Part of Amarillo)	79109
Puerto Rico	78563
Pumphrey	79567
Pumpkin	77358
Pumpkin Center	79331
Pumpville	78851

	ZIP
Punkin Center	76087
Purdon	76679
Purley	75457
Purmela	76566
Pursley	76679
Purves	76446
Putnam	76469
Pyote	79777
Pyron	79545
Quail	79251
Quail Run (Part of Fort Stockton)	79735
Quail Valley	78626
Quanah	79252
Quarry	77833
Queen City	75572
Quemado	78877
Quicksand	75966
Quihi	78861
Quinlan	75474
Quintana	77541
Quitaque	79255
Quite Village	77662
Quitman	75783
Rabb	78380
Rabbit Center	76401
Rabbs	77964
Rabbs Prairie	78945
Rachal	78353
Radium	79501
Ragtown	75411
Rainbow	76077
Rainbow Hills	78227
Raisin	77905
Raleigh	76641
Ralls	79357
Ramah	75974
Rambo	75555
Ramireno	78067
Ramirez	78376
Ranch Harbor Estates	76692
Ranchito	78586
Ranchland (Part of El Paso)	79915*
	79926†
Ranchland Acres	79703
Rancho Alegre	78332
Rancho de la Parita	78372
Rancho Viejo (Cameron County)	78520
Rancho Viejo (Jim Hogg County)	78361
Randolph	75475
Randolph Air Force Base	78148
	78150
For specific Randolph Air Force Base Zip Codes call (210) 652-5409, or your local postmaster.	
Ranger	76470
Rangerville	78586
Rankin (Ellis County)	75119
Rankin (Upton County)	79778
Ratama	78017
Ratcliff (Houston County)	75858
Ratcliff (San Augustine County)	75972
Ratcliffe	78164
Ratibor	76501
Rattan	75432
Ravenna	75476
Rayburn	77327
Rayburn Hideaway	75937
Rayford	77373
Rayland	76384
Raymondville	78580
Ray Point	78071
Raywood	77582
Reagan	76680
Reagan Wells	78801
Reagor Springs	75165
Realitos	78376
Reata Trails	78628
Redbank	75561
Red Bird Mall (Part of Dallas)	75237
Red Bluff	79770
Red Branch	75855
Redford	79846
Red Gate	78539
Red Hill (Cass County)	75560
Red Hill (Lamar County)	75473
Red Lake	75855
Redland (Angelina County)	75901
	75904
For specific Redland Zip Codes call (409) 634-7749, or your local postmaster.	
Redland (Leon County)	75833

	ZIP
Redland (Van Zandt County)	75754
Redlawn	75925
Redlick	75501
Redmond Terrace (Part of College Station)	77840
Red Oak (Ellis County)	75154
Red Oak (Kaufman County)	75142
Red Ranger	76569
Red River Army Depot	75501
Red Rock	78662
Red Springs (Baylor County)	76380
Red Springs (Bowie County)	75501
Red Springs (Smith County)	75701
Red Top	76450
Redtown (Anderson County)	75839
Red Town (Angelina County)	75904
Redwater	75573
Redwood	78666
Reedville	78656
Reese	75766
Reese Air Force Base	79489
Refugio	78377
Regency	76864
Rehburg	77835
Rehobeth	75633
Reilly Springs	75482
Rek Hill	78940
Reklaw	75784
Relampago	78570
Reliance	77801
Remolino	78582
Rendon	76028
Reno (Lamar County)	75462
Reno (Parker County)	76020
Retreat (Grimes County)	77868
Retreat (Hill County)	76627
Retreat (Navarro County)	75110
Retrieve Unit	77515
Retta	76028
Rhea	79035
Rhea Mills	75069
Rhineland	76371
Rhome	76078
Rhonesboro	75494
Ricardo	78363
Rice (Navarro County)	75155
Rice (Smith County)	75701
Rices Crossing	76574
Richards	77873
Richardson	75080-85
For specific Richardson Zip Codes call (214) 235-8353, or your local postmaster.	
Richardson Square (Part of Richardson)	75081
Rich Hill (Part of Houston)	77057
Richland (Dallas County)	75243
Richland (Navarro County)	76681
Richland (Rains County)	75472
Richland Hills	76118
Richland Mall (Part of Waco)	76710
Richland Park (Part of Fort Worth)	76118
Richland Plaza (Part of North Richland Hills)	76118
Richland Springs	76871
Richmond	77406†
	77469*
Richwood	77531
Riderville	75633
Ridge (Mills County)	76864
Ridge (Robertson County)	77856
Ridgecrest (Part of Amarillo)	79109
Ridgecrest Addition	77630
Ridgeheights	79701
Ridgemere (Part of Amarillo)	79109
Ridgeway	75482
Ridglea (Part of Fort Worth)	76116
Ridgmar Mall (Part of Fort Worth)	76116
Ridings	75476
Riesel	76682
Rimwick Forrest	77355
Rincon	78582
Ringgold	76261
Rio del Sol	78522
Rio Farms	78538
Rio Frio	78879

	ZIP		ZIP		ZIP		ZIP
Rio Grande City	78582	Roman Forest	77357	St. Jo	76265	Fort Sam Houston	78234
Rio Hondo	78583	Roman Hills	77356	Saint John	78956	Kelly Air Force Base	78241
Rio Llano Ranch	78643	Romayor	77368	Saint John Colony	78616	Lackland Air Force Base	78236
Rio Medina	78066	Romero	79022	St. Lawrence	79739	Texas Air National Guard,	
Rio Pecos	79740	Romney	76471	St. Louis (Part of Tyler)	75702	FB6432, Kelly Air Force	
Rios	78349	Roosevelt (Kimble		St. Paul (Brazoria County)	77422	Base	78241
Rio Vista	76093	County)	76874	St. Paul (Collin County)	75098		
Rising Star	76471	Roosevelt (Lubbock		St. Paul (Falls County)	76661	San Augustine	75972
Rita	77857	County)	79401	St. Paul (San Patricio		San Benito	78586
River Bend (Newton		Ropesville	79358	County)	78387	San Carlos	78539
County)	75932	Rosalie	75417	Salado	76571	Sanco	76945
River Bend (Sabine		Rosanky	78953	Salem (Bastrop County)	78953	Sanctuary	76020
County)	75948	Roscoe	79545	Salem (Milam County)	76520	Sanderson	79848
River Bend Estates	78003	Rosebud	76570	Salem (Smith County)	75789	Sand Flat (Rains County)	75440
River Brook	77302	Rose City	77662	Salesville	76067	Sandflat (Smith County)	75706
Riverby	75488	Rosedale	76661	Salineno	78585	Sand Flat (Van Zandt	
Rivercenter (Part of San		Rose Hill (Harris County)	77375	Salmon	75839	County)	75140
Antonio)	78205	Rose Hill (San Jacinto		Salona	76230	Sand Hill (Floyd County)	79235
Riverdrive Mall (Part of		County)	77331	Salt Flat	79847	Sand Hill (Upshur County)	75644
Laredo)	78040	Rose Hill (Wood County)	75773	Salt Gap	76836	Sandia	78383
River Hill	75633	Rose Hill Acres	77657	Saltillo	75478	San Diego	78384
Riverland	76365	Rosenberg	77471	Sam Houston (Part of		Sandjack	75928
River Oak Lake Estates	78758	Rosenthal	76655	Houston)	77002	Sand Lake	75119
River Oaks (Harris		Rosevine	75930	Sam Houston College		Sandoval	76574
County)	77019	Rosewood	75644	(Part of Huntsville)	77341	Sand Ridge (Houston	
River Oaks (Tarrant		Rosharon	77583	Samnorwood	79077	County)	75835
County)	76114	Rosita (Duval County)	78384	Sam Rayburn	75951	Sand Ridge (Wharton	
River Oaks Ranch	78063	Rosita (Starr County)	78582	Sanaloma Estates	78628	County)	77434
River Plantation	77302	Ross	76684	San Angelo	76901-08	Sand Springs (Howard	
River Ridge	75951	Rosser	75157	For specific San Angelo Zip		County)	79720
Riverside (Tarrant County)	76111	Rosston	76263	Codes call (915) 659-7700, or		Sand Springs (Wood	
Riverside (Walker County)	77367	Rossville	78065	your local postmaster.		County)	75773
Riverside Crest (Part of		Rotan	79546			Sandusky	76273
Houston)	77338	Round Mountain	78663	**San Antonio**	78201-99	Sandy	78665
River Woods Estates	77050	Round Prairie	75144	For specific San Antonio Zip		Sandy Acres	79703
Riviera	78379	Round Rock	78664	Codes call (512) 657-8302, or		Sandy Corner	77437
Riviera Beach	78379		78680-81	your local postmaster.		Sandy Creek	78556
Roach	75551	For specific Round Rock Zip				Sandy Fork	78632
Roach Town	75758	Codes call (512) 255-3516, or		COLLEGES & UNIVERSITIES		Sandy Harbor	78654
Roane	75110	your local postmaster.		Incarnate Word College	78209	Sandy Hill	77833
Roanoke	76262	Round Timber	76380	Our Lady of the Lake		Sandy Point	77583
Roans Prairie	77875	Round Top	78954	University of San		Sandy Ridge	77351
Roaring Springs	79256	Roundup	79313	Antonio	78207	San Elizario	79849
Robbins	75846	Rowden	79504	St. Mary's University	78228	San Felipe	77473
Robert Lee	76945	Rowena	76875	Trinity University	78212	Sanford	79078
Robertson	79343	Rowlett	75030*	University of Texas Health		Sanford Estates	79036
Robinson	76706		75088†	Science Center at San		San Gabriel	76577
Robinson Plaza (Part of		Roxton	75477	Antonio	78284	San Gabriel Heights	78628
Robinson)	76706	Royal Forest	77303	University of Texas at San		Sanger	76266
Robstown	78380	Royal Lane (Part of		Antonio	78249	San Geronimo	78023
Roby	79543	Dallas)	75230			San Isidro	78588
Rochelle	76872	Royal Oaks (Henderson		FINANCIAL INSTITUTIONS		San Jacinto (Part of	
Rochester	79544	County)	75143	Bank One, Texas, N.A.	78205	Amarillo)	79106
Rock Creek	76708	Royal Oaks (Llano		Bank of San Antonio	78205	San Jose	78332
Rockdale	76567	County)	78639	Bank of the West	78207	San Juan (Hidalgo	
Rockett	75165	Royal Oaks (Orange		Broadway National Bank	78209	County)	78589
Rockford	75462	County)	77626	First Federal Savings		San Juan (Nueces	
Rock Harbor	76048	Royalty	79779	Bank	78209	County)	78406
Rockhill (Collin County)	75069	Royalwood	77028	Frost National Bank of		San Leanna	78748
Rock Hill (Jasper County)	75951	Roy Miller (Part of Corpus		San Antonio	78205	San Leon	77539
Rock Hill (Wood County)	75783	Christi)	78465	Groos Bank, National		San Marcos	78666*
Rockhouse	78950	Roy Royall (Part of		Association	78216		78667†
Rock Island (Colorado		Houston)	77016	International Bank of		San Patricio	78368
County)	77470	Royse City	75189	Commerce	78209	San Pedro	78520
Rock Island (Polk County)	75939	Royston	79543	Jefferson State Bank	78201	San Perlita	78590
Rockland	75938	Rucker	76444	Kelly Field National Bank	78238	San Saba	76877
Rockne	78602	Rufe Jordan	79065	Nationsbank of Texas,		Sansom Park	76114
Rockport	78381*	Rugby	75435	N.A.	78205	Santa Anna	76878
	78382†	Ruidosa	79843	Texas Commerce Bank-		Santa Catarina	78582
Rock Prairie	77801	Rule	79547	San Antonio, N.A.	78209	Santa Cruz	78582
Rocksprings	78880	Rumley	76539	U.S.A.A. Federal Savings		Santa Elena	78591
Rockwall	75087	Run	78537	Bank	78288	Santa Fe	77510
Rockwood	76873	Runaway Bay	76426				77517
Rocky Branch	75638	Runge	78151	HOSPITALS		For specific Santa Fe Zip	
Rocky Creek Park	77835	Rural Shade	75144	Audie L. Murphy Memorial		Codes call (409) 925-2934, or	
Rocky Hill	76661	Rushwood	77067	Veterans Hospital	78284	your local postmaster.	
Rocky Mound	75686	Rusk	75785	Baptist Medical Center	78205	Santa Maria	78592
Rocky Point	75440	Rutersville	78945	Bexar County Hospital		Santa Monica	78580
Rocky Springs (Angelina		Ruth Springs	75163	District	78229	Santa Rita (Part of San	
County)	75949	Ryanville	78377	San Antonio Regional		Angelo)	76901
Rocky Springs (Tyler		Rye	77369	Hospital	78229	Santa Rosa	78593
County)	75938	Sabanna	76437	Santa Rosa Health Care		Santo	76472
Roddy	75147	Sabathany	76086	Corporation	78207	San Ygnacio	78067
Rodney	76639	Sabinal	78881	Southwest Texas		Saragosa	79780
Roganville	75956	Sabine	77640	Methodist Hospital	78229	Saratoga	77585
Rogers	76569	Sabine Pass	77655			Sarco	77963
Rogers Hill	76691	Sabine Sands	75928	HOTELS/MOTELS		Sardis (Cass County)	75656
Rolling Hills (Hunt County)	75453	Sabinetown	75948	Hilton Palacio del Rio	78205	Sardis (Ellis County)	76065
Rolling Hills (Potter		Sachse	75048	Holiday Inn Riverwalk		Sargent	77414
County)	79108	Sacul	75788	North	78205	Sarita	78385
Rolling Hills (Waller		Saddle and Surrey	77356	Hotel St. Anthony	78205	Sash	75446
County)	77445	Sadler	76264	Marriott Riverwalk	78205	Saspamco	78112
Rolling Hills Shores	76087	Sagerton	79548	Ramada Inn Airport	78209	Satin	76685
Rolling Meadows	75603	Saginaw	76179			Satsuma	77040
Rolling Oaks	75169	St. Claire Cove	77650	MILITARY INSTALLATIONS		Sattler	78130
Rolling Oaks Mall (Part of		St. Elmo	75859	Brooks Air Force Base	78235	Sauney Stand	77426
San Antonio)	78247	St. Francis	79107	Camp Bullis	78234	Savage	79357
Rollingwood	78746	St. Francis Village	76036	Camp Stanley Storage		Savoy	75479
Roma	78584	St. Hedwig	78152	Activity	78269	Sayers	78602

	ZIP
Scallorn	76853
Scenic Heights	78130
Scenic Hills	78108
Scenic Oaks	78023
Scenic Terrace	78130
Schattel	78005
Schertz	78154
Schicke Point	77465
Schoolerville	76531
School Land	78140
Schroeder	77963
Schulenburg	78956
Schumansville	78130
Schwab City	77351
Schwertner	76573
Scissors	78537
Scotland	76379
Scotsdale (Ector County)	79762
Scotsdale (El Paso County)	79925
Scott	75169
Scottsville	75688
Scranton	76437
Scrappin Valley	75977
Scroggins	75480
Scurry	75158
Seabrook	77586
Sea Crest Park	77520
Seadrift	77983
Seagoville	75159
Seagraves	79359
Sea Isle	77554
Seale	76687
Sealy	77474
Seaton	76501
Seawillow	78644
Sebastian	78594
Sebastopol	75862
Seco Mines	78852
Security	77327
Sedalia	75495
Segno	77351
Segovia	76849
Seguin	78155*
	78156†
Sejita	78376
Selden	76401
Selfs	75446
Selma	78209
Selman City	75689
Seminary Hill (Part of Fort Worth)	76115
Seminole	79360
Senate	76458
Senior	78073
Sequoia Estates	77032
Serbin	78942
Serenada	78628
Serna (Part of San Antonio)	78218
	78266

For specific Serna Zip Codes call (210) 655-0151, or your local postmaster.

	ZIP
Seth Ward	79072
Seven Oaks	77350
Seven Pines	75601
Seven Points	75143
Seven Sisters	78357
Sexton	75972
Sexton City	75684
Seymore	75482
Seymour	76380
Shadow Glen	77530
Shadow Lake Estates	77365
Shadowland	75435
Shadowland Retreat	77365
Shady Acres (Brazoria County)	77422
Shady Acres (Burnet County)	78654
Shady Brook Acres	77355
Shady Grove (Angelina County)	75941
Shady Grove (Cherokee County)	75785
Shady Grove (Dallas County)	75050
Shady Grove (Kerr County)	78028
Shady Grove (Marion County)	75657
Shady Grove (Nacogdoches County)	75961
Shady Grove (Navarro County)	76679
Shady Grove (Panola County)	75669

	ZIP
Shady Grove (Rains County)	75440
Shady Grove (Smith County)	75706
Shady Grove (Upshur County)	75755
Shady Hollow	78739
Shady Oaks (Henderson County)	75751
Shady Oaks (Tarrant County)	76053
Shady Shores (Denton County)	76205
Shady Shores (Henderson County)	75147
Shady Trees (Part of Houston)	77338
Shafter	79850
Shallowater	79363
Shamrock	79079
Shamrock Shores	76801
Shankleville	75932
Shannon	76365
Sharon	75701
Sharp	76518
Sharpstown (Part of Houston)	77036
Sharpstown Center (Part of Houston)	77036
Sharyland (Part of Mission)	78572
Shavano Park	78231
Shaw Bend	76877
Shawnee	75949
Shawnee Shores	75948
Shawnee Shores Estates	75474
Shaws Bend	78934
Sheffield	79781
Shelby	78940
Shelbyville	75973
Sheldon	77028
Shenandoah (Montgomery County)	77301
Shenandoah (Williamson County)	78613
Shep	79566
Shepherd	77371
Shepphard	77612
Shepton	75173
Sher-Den Mall (Part of Sherman)	75090
Sheridan	77475
Sherman	75090-92

For specific Sherman Zip Codes call (903) 892-3462, or your local postmaster.

	ZIP
Sherman-Hansford Plant	79040
Sherman Junction (Part of Denison)	75020
Sherry	75426
Sherwood	76941
Sherwood Forest	78258
Sherwood Place	77016
Sherwood Shores	78654
Shields	76845
Shiloh (Delta County)	75448
Shiloh (Leon County)	75855
Shiloh (Liberty County)	77575
Shiloh (Limestone County)	76667
Shiloh (Williamson County)	76578
Shiner	77984
Shipman Camp	75521
Shirley	75482
Shirley Creek	75937
Shiro	77876
Shive	76531
Shoreacres	77571
Short	75935
Sidney	76474
Sierra Blanca	79851
Siesta Shores (Travis County)	78669
Siesta Shores (Zapata County)	78076
Sikes Senter (Part of Wichita Falls)	76308
Silas	75975
Siloam	75559
Silsbee	77656-57

For specific Silsbee Zip Codes call (409) 385-3776, or your local postmaster.

	ZIP
Silver	76949
Silver City (Milam County)	76520
Silver City (Navarro County)	76679
Silver City (Red River County)	75426
Silver Creek Village	78611

	ZIP
Silver Creek Village No. 2	78611
Silver Hills	78006
Silver Lake	75140
Silverton	79257
Silver Valley	76834
Simmons	78071
Simms	75574
Simonton	77476
Simpsonville	77465
Simsboro	75860
Sinclair City	75789
Singing Sands	77617
Singletary Sites	75956
Singleton	77831
Sinton	78387
Sipe Springs	76442
Sisterdale	78006
Six Flags Mall (Part of Arlington)	76011
Six Mile	77979
Six Points (Part of Corpus Christi)	78404
Skellytown	79080
Skidmore	78389
Sky Harbor	76048
Skyview Unit	75785
Slabtown	75462
Slate Shoals	75462
Slaton	79364
Slide	79413
Slidell	76267
Sloan	76877
Slocum	75839
Small	75117
Smeltertown (Part of El Paso)	79927
Smetana	77801
Smiley	78159
Smithfield (Part of North Richland Hills)	76180
Smith Grove	75851
Smith Hill	75561
Smithland	75657
Smith Point	77514
Smiths Bend	76634
Smith Springs	76401
Smithville	78957
Smithwick	78654
Smitty (Part of Athens)	75751
Smyer	79367
Smyrna	75551
Snook	77878
Snow Hill (Collin County)	75442
Snow Hill (Polk County)	75939
Snow Hill (Upshur County)	75683
Snyder	79549*
	79550†
Socorro	79927
Soda	77351
Soda Springs	76066
Sodville	78387
Solms	78130
Somerset	78069
Somerville	77879
Sonoma (Part of Ennis)	75119
Sonora	76950
Soules Chapel	75644
Sour Gale	77659
South (Part of Garland)	75043
South Amarillo (Part of Amarillo)	79114
South Austin (Part of Austin)	78704
South Bend	76481
South Bosque	76710
South Brice	79226
South Dallas (Part of Dallas)	75215
Southeast (Part of Austin)	78741
	78744

For specific Southeast Zip Codes call (512) 444-3119, or your local postmaster.

	ZIP
Southeast Crossing (Part of Tyler)	75713
South Elm	76518
South End (Part of Beaumont)	77705
Southern Hills (Part of Abilene)	79605-08

For specific Southern Hills Zip Codes call (915) 698-7179, or your local postmaster.

	ZIP
Southern Methodist University (Part of University Park)	75275
South Gale	75020
South Groveton (Part of Groveton)	75845

	ZIP
South Haven	79720
South Houston	77587
Southlake	76092
Southland (Garza County)	79364
Southland (Wharton County)	77437
Southland Hills (Part of San Angelo)	76904
Southmayd	76268
Southmore (Part of Houston)	77004
South Mountain	76528
South Oak Cliff (Part of Dallas)	75216
South Padre Island	78597
South Park Mall (Part of San Antonio)	78224
South Plains	79258
South Plains Mall (Part of Lubbock)	79414
South Post Oak (Part of Houston)	77035
South Purmela	76566
Southridge Plaza (Part of Austin)	78745
South San Antonio (Part of San Antonio)	78211
South San Gabriel Ranches	78641
Southside (Part of Corpus Christi)	78413
Southside Estates (Part of Amarillo)	79110
Southside Place	77005
South Sulphur	75496
South Temple (Part of Temple)	76501
South Texas Medical Center (Part of San Antonio)	78229
Southton	78223
South View Estates	78737
Southwestern Baptist Theological Seminary (Part of Fort Worth)	76115
Southwest Freeway (Part of Houston)	77057
Sowells Bluff	75476
Sowers (Part of Irving)	75060
Spade	79369
Spanish Camp	77488
Spanish Fort	76255
Spanish Trail	76048
Sparenberg	79331
Sparks (Bell County)	76534
Sparks (El Paso County)	79927
Speaks	77985
Spearman	79081
Speegleville	76710
Spicewood	78669
Spicewood At Balcones Village	78750
Spicewood Beach	78669
Spillers Store	75850
Spillview Estates	75147
Spinwick Addition (Part of La Porte)	77571
Splawn	76520
Splendora	77372
Splendora Farms	77372
Spofford	78877
Spraberry	79702
Spring	77373
	77379-83
	77386-91

For specific Spring Zip Codes call (713) 288-6652, or your local postmaster.

	ZIP
Spring Branch	78070
Spring Creek (Gillespie County)	78624
Spring Creek (San Saba County)	76871
Spring Creek (Throckmorton County)	76370
Spring Creek Acres (Part of Victoria)	77904
Spring Creek Estates	77355
Springdale	75572
Spring Dell	77373
Springfield (Anderson County)	75801
Springfield (Limestone County)	76667
Spring Forest	77373
Spring Hill (Bowie County)	75559
Spring Hill (Camp County)	75686
Spring Hill (Gregg County)	75603

* Area Zip Code   † Post Office Boxes

	ZIP
Spring Hill (Guadalupe County)	78155
Spring Hill (Jasper County)	75951
Springhill (Navarro County)	76639
Spring Hills	77373
Springlake	79082
Spring Seat	75846
Springtown	76082
Spring Valley (Dallas County)	75240
Spring Valley (Harris County)	77024
Spring Valley (McLennan County)	76655
Sprinkle	78754
Spur	79370
Spurger	77660
Stacy	76836
Stafford	77477
Stagecoach	77355
Stage Coach Farms	77355
Stage Coach Hills	78255
Stairtown	78648
Staley	77359
Stamford	79553
Stamps	75644
Stanfield	76365
Stanger Springs	75754
Stanton	79782
Staples	78670
Star	76880
Star Harbor	75148
Star Route	79346
Starrville	75792
Startzville	78130
Steeltown (Part of Groves)	77619
Steep Hollow	77801
Stellar	78949
Stephen F. Austin University (Part of Nacogdoches)	75962
Stephenville	76401
Sterley	79241
Sterling City	76951
Sterlings Island	77367
Sterrett	75165
Stewards Mill	75840
Stewart	75691
Stewart Heights (Part of Baytown)	77520
Stieren	78632
Stilson	77535
Stinnett	79083
Stith	79536
Stockard	75751
Stockdale	78160
Stockman	75975
Stock Yards (Part of Fort Worth)	76106
Stoneburg	76230
Stoneham	77868
Stonewall	78671
Stonewall Mall	78409-10
	78426
For specific Stonewall Mall Zip Codes call (512) 886-2200, or your local postmaster.	
Stony	76259
Stout	75494
Stowell	77661
Stranger	76653
Stratford	79084
Stratton	77954
Stratton Ridge	77531
Strawn	76475
Streetman	75859
Strickland	75968
String Prairie	78953
Structure	78621
Stuart Place	78550
Study Butte	79852
Stumptown	75931
Sturdivant	76067
Sturgeon	76273
Styx	75143
Sublett (Part of Arlington)	76063
Sublime	77986
Sudan	79371
Suffolk	75644
Sugar Land	77478-79
	77487
For specific Sugar Land Zip Codes call (713) 494-2042, or your local postmaster.	
Sugar Valley	77480
Sullivan City	78595
Sulphur Bluff	75481

	ZIP
Sulphur Springs (Angelina County)	75980
Sulphur Springs (Hopkins County)	75482*
	75483†
Sulphur Springs (Rusk County)	75760
Summerall	75147
Summerfield (Castro County)	79085
Summerfield (Upshur County)	75644
Summer Hill	75751
Summit Heights (Part of El Paso)	79930*
	79931†
Sumner	75486
Sun (Part of Denison)	75020
Sundown	79372
Sunnyside (Castro County)	79027
Sunny Side (Waller County)	77445
Sunnyslope (Part of Texarkana)	75501
Sunnyvale	75149
Sunray	79086
Sunrise (El Paso County)	79904
Sunrise (Falls County)	76661
Sunrise Acres (Part of El Paso)	79904
Sunrise Beach	78643
Sunrise Mall (Cameron County)	78521
Sunrise Mall (Nueces County)	78412
Sunset (Lubbock County)	79416
Sunset (Montague County)	76270
Sunset Mall (Part of San Angelo)	76904
Sunset Marketown (Part of Amarillo)	79102
Sunset Ridge	77301
Sunset Valley	78745
Sunshine Hill	76360
Sun Valley (El Paso County)	79924
Sun Valley (Lamar County)	75462
Surf Oaks (Part of Seabrook)	77586
Surfside Beach	77541
Sutherland Springs	78161
Swamp City	75647
Swan	75706
Swan Lagoon (Part of Nassau Bay)	77058
Swanson Hill	75801
Sweeny	77480
Sweeny Switch	78368
Sweet Home (Guadalupe County)	78155
Sweet Home (Lavaca County)	77987
Sweetwater (Comanche County)	76442
Sweetwater (Nolan County)	79556
Swenson	79502
Swift	75961
Swiss Alp	78956
Swiss Village	78611
Sycamore	75932
Sylvan	75462
Sylvan Beach (Part of La Porte)	77571
Sylvester	79560
Tabor	77801
Tacoma	75633
Tadmor	75847
Taft	78390
Taft Southwest	78390
Tahoka	79373
Talco	75487
Tall Pines	75630
Talpa	76882
Talty	75160
Tamega	78605
Tamina	77302
Tandy Center (Part of Fort Worth)	76102
Tanglewood	78947
Tanglewood Forest	78748
Tanglewood Island	78424
Tanglewood Manor	77357
Tankersly	76901
Tarkington Acres	77327
Tarkington Prairie	77327

	ZIP
Tarleton (Part of Stephenville)	76402
Tarpley	78883
Tarrant (Part of Fort Worth)	76039
Tarzan	79783
Tate Springs (Part of Arlington)	76003
Tatum	75691
Tavener	77435
Taylor	76574
Taylor Lake Village	77586
Taylorsville	78662
Taylor Town	75462
Taylorville	75452
Teague	75860
Teaselville	75757
Tecula	75766
Tehuacana	76686
Telegraph	76883
Telephone	75488
Telferner	77988
Telico	75119
Tell	79259
Temple	76501-05
For specific Temple Zip Codes call (817) 773-0792, or your local postmaster.	
Temple Mall (Part of Temple)	76502
Temple Springs	75951
Tenaha	75974
Tennessee	75975
Tennessee Colony	75861
Tennyson	76953
Terlingua	79852
Terrell	75160
Terrell Hills	78209
Terrell Station	79781
Terrell Wells (Part of San Antonio)	78221
Terrys Chapel	76570
Terryville	77995
Texarkana	75501-05
For specific Texarkana Zip Codes call (903) 838-9537, or your local postmaster.	
Texas Christian University (Part of Fort Worth)	76119
Texas City	77590-92
For specific Texas City Zip Codes call (409) 948-2591, or your local postmaster.	
Texas City Junction (Part of Hitchcock)	77563
Texas City Junction (Part of Texas City)	77590
Texas Lutheran (Part of Seguin)	78155
Texas Womans University (Part of Denton)	76204
Texhoma	73949
Texline	79087
Texon	76932
Thalia	79227
Thayer	78570
The Bluffs (Part of San Angelo)	76901
The Colony	75056
Thedford	75771
The Grove	76576
The Heights (Part of Alvin)	77511
The Homestead	78736
The Knobbs	78650
Thelma (Bexar County)	78221
Thelma (Limestone County)	76642
The Meadows (Part of Meadows)	77477
The Oaks	78130
Theon	76537
Thermo	75482
The Shores (Part of Amarillo)	79110
The Woodlands	77380
Thicket	77374
Thomas	75644
Thomas Manor (Part of El Paso)	79915
Thomaston	77989
Thompson	77040
Thompson Heights	75020
Thompsons	77481
Thompsonville	78959
Thornberry	76306
Thorndale	76577
Thornton	76687
Thorntonville	79756
Thorp Spring	76048

	ZIP
Thousand Oaks (Part of San Antonio)	78270
Thrall	76578
Three Leagues	79331
Three Points	78660
Three Rivers	78071
Three Way	76401
Thrifty	76801
Throckmorton	76483
Thurber	76463
Tidwell	75401
Tidwell Prairie	76629
Tierra Linda Ranch	78028
Tigertown	75446
Tiki Island	77554
Tilden	78072
Tilmon	78616
Timber Cove (Part of Taylor Lake Village)	77586
Timberlake	77429
Timberlake Acres	77365
Timber Lakes Estates	77380
Timber Ridge (Bexar County)	78251
Timber Ridge (Montgomery County)	77380
Timberwood Park	78258
	78260
For specific Timberwood Park Zip Codes call (210) 657-8302, or your local postmaster.	
Timothy	75105
Timpson	75975
Tin Top	76087
Tioga	76271
Tira	75482
Tivoli	77990
Tivydale	78624
Tobe Hahn (Part of Beaumont)	77706
Toco	75421
Tod (Part of Seabrook)	77586
Todd City	75801
Todd Mission	77363
Togo	78957
Tokio	79376
Tolar	76476
Tolbert	76384
Toledo Village (Newton County)	75932
Toledo Village (Sabine County)	75948
Tolosa	75143
Tomball	77375*
	77377†
Tom Bean	75489
Tonkowon Country	78628
Tool	75143
Topsey	76522
Tornillo	79853
Tours	76691
Tow	78672
Town and Country Center (Part of Houston)	77024
Town Bluff	75979
Town East Mall (Part of Mesquite)	75150
Town Oaks (Part of Marshall)	75670
Town Plaza (Part of Victoria)	77901
Town West	77478
Toyah	79785
Toyahvale	79786
Tracy	75667
Tradewinds	75143
Trail Lake (Part of Fort Worth)	76162
Trammells	77045
Travis	76656
Travis Peak	78654
Trawick	75961
Trent	79561
Trenton	75490
Trevat	75845
Tri Cities	75751
Trickham	76878
Tri-Lake Estates	77356
Trimmier Friendship	76542
Trinidad	75163
Trinity	75862
Trinity Park	75098
Trinity River (Part of Fort Worth)	76109
Trophy Club	76262
Tropical Acres	77904
Troup	75789
Trout Creek	75933
Troy	76579

* Area Zip Code   **† Post Office Boxes**

	ZIP		ZIP		ZIP		ZIP
Truby	79525	Valleycreek	75452	Vistula	75851	Webster (Harris County)	77598
Truce	76230	Valley Hi (Part of San		Voca	76887	Webster (Wood County)	75494
Trumbull	75125	Antonio)	78227	Volente	78641	Weches	75844
Truscott	79260	Valley Lodge (Part of		Von Ormy	78073	Wedgewood (Part of Fort	
Tucker	75801	Simonton)	77476	Voss	76888	Worth)	76163
Tuleta	78162	Valley Mills	76689	Votaw	77376	Weedhaven	77979
Tulia	79088	Valley Spring	76885	Voth (Part of Beaumont)	77709	Weeping Mary	75925
Tulip	75447	Valley View (Comal		Vsetin	77964	Weesatche	77993
Tulsita	78119	County)	78130	Waco	76701-98	Weimar	78962
Tundra	75103	Valley View (Cooke		For specific Waco Zip Codes		Weinert	76388
Tunis	77836	County)	76272	call (817) 757-6585, or your		Weir	78674
Tupelo	75155	Valley View (McLennan		local postmaster.		Weirville	75482
Turkey	79261	County)	76701	Wade	78372	Welch	79377
Turkey Creek (Part of		Valley View (Mitchell		Wadsworth	77483	Welch Store	75973
Copperas Cove)	76522	County)	79512	Waelder	78959	Welcome	78944
Turlington	75840	Valley View (Runnels		Wainwright (Part of San		Weldon	75851
Turnersville	76528	County)	76821	Antonio)	78208	Welfare	78006
Turnertown	75689	Valley View (Upshur		Wainwright Heights	76544	Wellborn	77881
Turney	75766	County)	75644	Waka	79093	Wellington	79095
Turtle Bayou	77514	Valley View (Wichita		Wake	79243	Wellman	79378
Tuscola	79562	County)	76367	Wakefield	75939	Wells (Cherokee County)	75976
Tuttle Addition	77488	Valley View Center (Part		Wake Village	75501	Wells (Lynn County)	79351
Tuxedo	79553	of Dallas)	75240	Walburg	78673	Wells Branch	78728
Twine Cedar Retreat	75948	Valley Wells	78830	Waldeck	78946		78753
Twin Shores	77378	Val Verde	76518	Walden	77356	For specific Wells Branch Zip	
Twin Valley Terrace	78073	Val Verde Park Estates	78840	Walden Place	77093	Codes call (915) 622-4566, or	
Twitty	79079	Van	75790	Walden Woods (Part of		your local postmaster.	
Tye	79563	Van Alstyne	75495	Houston)	77012	Wellswood	75929
Tyler	75701-13	Vance	78828	Waldrip	76852	Wentworth	75103
For specific Tyler Zip Codes		Vancourt	76955	Walhalla	78954	Weser	77963
call (903) 595-8621, or your		Vandalia	75426	Walkers Mill	75650	Weslaco	78596
local postmaster.		Vanderbilt	77991	Walker Village	76544	Weslayan (Part of	
Tynan	78391	Vanderpool	78885	Wall	76957	Houston)	77277
Type	78621	Vandyke	76442	Wallace	75103	Wesley	77833
Uhland	78640	Vanetia	77865	Wallace Chapel	75686	Wesley Grove	77831
Umbarger	79091	Van Horn	79855	Waller	77484	West	76691
Uncertain	75661	Van Vleck	77482	Wallis	77485	West Austin (Part of	
Union (Brazos County)	77801	Varisco	77801	Wallisville	77597	Austin)	78763
Union (Franklin County)	75478	Vasco	75450	Walnut Bend	76273	West Baytown (Part of	
Union (Lubbock County)	79364	Vashti	76228	Walnut Creek	77355	Baytown)	77520
Union (Scurry County)	79549	Vattmannville	78379	Walnut Forest	78753	West Bluff	77630
Union (Terry County)	79316	Vaughan	76645	Walnut Grove (Collin		Westbrae (Part of	
Union (Wilson County)	78140	Vealmoor	79720	County)	75069	Houston)	77031
Union Academy	75801	Veal Station	76082	Walnut Grove (Smith		Westbrook	79565
Union Bluff	76645	Vedas Camp	75521	County)	75703	West Camp	79325
Union Bower (Part of		Vega	79092	Walnut Hill (Part of Dallas)	75220	Westchase (Part of	
Irving)	75060	Venable Village	76544	Walnut Hills	77303	Houston)	77215
Union Center	76471	Ventura	77355	Walnut Springs (Bosque		Westchester (Part of	
Union Grove (Bell County)	76513	Venus	76084	County)	76690	Grand Prairie)	75054
Union Grove (Cherokee		Vera	76383	Walnut Springs		Westcliff	76513
County)	75766	Verbena	79356	(Montgomery County)	77355	West Cliff Park (Part of	
Union Grove (Upshur		Verdi	78064	Walston Springs	75801	Amarillo)	79124
County)	75647	Verhalen	79772	Walton (Cass County)	71082	West Columbia	77486
Union High	76639	Verhelle	77954	Walton (Van Zandt		West Delta	75448
Union Hill (Bosque		Veribest	76886	County)	75751	Western Hills (Part of	
County)	76652	Vernon	76384*	Wamba	75503	Copperas Cove)	76522
Union Hill (Henderson			76385†	Waneta	75844	Western Plaza Mall (Part	
County)	75756	Verona	75424	Waples	76048	of Amarillo)	79101
Union Hill (Upshur		Veterans Administration		Warda	78960	Westfield (Harris County)	77090
County)	75644	(Part of Waco)	76711	Ward Prairie	75840	Westfield (Wharton	
Union Springs	75961	Viboras	78361	Wards Creek	75574	County)	77437
Union Valley	75189	Vick	76937	Waring	78074	Westfield Estates	77093
Unity	75486	Vickery (Part of Dallas)	75231	Warren	77664	West Galveston (Part of	
Universal City	78148	Victoria (Limestone		Warren City	75647	Jamaica Beach)	77551
University (Part of Austin)	78712*	County)	76664	Warrenton	78961	Westgate (Harris County)	77429
	78713†	Victoria (Victoria County)	77901-05	Warsaw	75142	Westgate (Tom Green	
University (Part of Dallas)	75205-06	For specific Victoria Zip Codes		Washburn	79019	County)	76901
	75372	call (512) 575-2363, or your		Washington	77880	Westgate Mall (Potter	
For specific University Zip		local postmaster.		Waskom	75692	County)	79160
Codes call (214) 647-2996, or		Victoria Mall (Part of		Wastella	79545	Westgate Mall (Travis	
your local postmaster.		Victoria)	77904	Watauga	76148	County)	78704
University of Dallas (Part		Victory City	75561	Water Front Park	78130	Westgate Towne Centre	
of Irving)	75061	Victory Gardens	77630	Waterloo (Grayson		(Part of Abilene)	79605
University of Texas at El		Vidauri	78377	County)	75020	Westhaven	78130
Paso (Part of El Paso)	79902	Vidor	77662*	Waterloo (Williamson		Westheimer (Part of	
University Park (Bexar			77670†	County)	76574	Houston)	77042
County)	78228	Vienna	77964	Waterman	75935	Westhill Addition	77437
University Park (Dallas		View	79606	Waters Bluff	75792	Westhoff	77994
County)	75205	Viewpoint	75460	Water Valley	76958	West Lake (Jasper	
University Park (Wichita		Vigo Park	79088	Waterwood (San Jacinto		County)	75951
County)	76308	Vilas	76534	County)	77359	Westlake (Tarrant County)	76248
University Place (Part of		Villa Cavazos	78520	Waterwood (Walker		Westlake (Travis County)	78746
Nacogdoches)	75961	Village (Part of Highland		County)	77340	West Lake Hills	78746
Upper Meyersville	78164	Park)	75205	Watkins	75103	Westlakes (Part of San	
Upshaw	75943	Village Mills	77663	Watson	76550	Antonio)	78245
Upton	78957	Village Shores	78130	Watson Community (Part		Westlakes Mercado (Part	
Urbana	77371	Village Station (Part of		of Arlington)	76006	of San Antonio)	78227
Utility (Part of San		Midland)	79704	Watsonville	76063	Westlawn	77630
Antonio)	78219	Villa Nueva	78520	Watt	76664	Westminster	75485
Utley	78602	Villareales	78582	Waxahachie	75165	West Mountain	75647
Utopia	78884	Vincent	79511	Wayside	79094	West Odessa	79764
Uvalde	78801*	Vineyard	76458	Wealthy	77871		79769
	78802†	Vinton	79821	Weatherford	76086-88	For specific West Odessa Zip	
Valdasta	75424	Violet	78380	For specific Weatherford Zip		Codes call (915) 381-6707, or	
Valentine	79854	Virginia Point	77554	Codes call (817) 594-3072, or		your local postmaster.	
Valera	76884	Vista del Sol (Part of El		your local postmaster.		Weston	75097
Valle de Oro	79010	Paso)	79935	Weaver	75478	West Orange	77630
Valle Vista Mall (Part of		Vista Ridge Mall (Part of		Webberville	78653	Westover	76380
Harlingen)	78552	Lewisville)	75067	Webbville	76828	Westover Hills	76107

* Area Zip Code **† Post Office Boxes**

	ZIP
West Payne	77437
Westphalia	76656
West Point (Fayette County)	78963
West Point (Lynn County)	79373
West Sinton	78370
West Tawakoni	75474
West Texas State University (Part of Canyon)	79016
West University Place	77005
West Vernon (Part of Vernon)	76384
Westview (Part of Waco)	76710
Westville	75862
West Waco (Part of Waco)	76710
Westway	79835
Westwood	75951
Westwood Mall (Part of Houston)	77036
Westworth Village	76114
Wetmore (Part of San Antonio)	78247
Wetsel	75069
Wexford Park	77662
Whaley	75570
Wharton	77488
Whatley	75657
Wheatland	76116
Wheeler	79096
Wheeler Springs	75835
Wheelock	77882
Whispering Oaks (Bexar County)	78230
Whispering Oaks (Rains County)	75453
Whispering Pines (Montgomery County)	77302
Whispering Pines (Walker County)	77358
Whispering Winds	78264
Whisperwood (Part of Lubbock)	79416
White City (San Augustine County)	75929
White City (Wilbarger County)	76384
White Deer	79097
Whiteface	79379
Whiteflat	79234
White Hall (Bell County)	76557
White Hall (Coryell County)	76528
White Hall (Grimes County)	77868
Whitehall (Kaufman County)	75147
Whitehouse	75791
Whiteland	76858
White Mound	75090
White Oak (Gregg County)	75693
White Oak (Montgomery County)	77365
White Oak (Morris County)	75571
White Oak (Titus County)	75455
White Oak Valley Estates	77301
White Rock (Dallas County)	75218
White Rock (Grayson County)	75491

	ZIP
White Rock (Hunt County)	75423
White Rock (Red River County)	75426
White Rock (Robertson County)	76629
White Rock (San Augustine County)	75972
Whitesboro	76273
White Settlement	76108
Whitestar	79234
White Stone (Part of Cedar Park)	78641
Whitetail	78628
Whiteway	76538
Whitewright	75491
Whitharral	79380
Whitman	77833
Whitney	76692
Whitsett	78075
Whitt	76490
Whitton	75103
Whon	76878
Wichita Falls	76301-11
For specific Wichita Falls Zip Codes call (817) 766-4188, or your local postmaster.	
Wichita Valley Farms	76301
Wickett	79788
Wiedeville	77833
Wieland	75402
Wiergate	75977
Wiggins	76691
Wigginsville	77301
Wilcox	77879
Wildcat (Part of Plano)	75023
Wilderville	76570
Wild Horse	79855
Wild Hurst	75925
Wildorado	79098
Wild Peach Village	77422
Wildwood (Hardin County)	77663
Wildwood (Walker County)	77367
Wilford Hall U.S. Air Force Hospital (Part of San Antonio)	78236
Wilkins	75755
Wilkinson	75455
Willacy County Housing Authority	78580
Willamar	78580
William Beaumont Army Medical Center	79920
William Penn	77833
William Rice (Part of Houston)	77005
Williams	76471
Williamsburg (Lamar County)	75460
Williamsburg (Lavaca County)	77964
William Spear Addition	75704
Willis	77378
Willow City	78675
Willow Grove (McLennan County)	76712
Willow Grove (Shelby County)	75954
Willow Park	76087
Willow Place (Part of Houston)	77070
Willow Point	76426

	ZIP
Willow Springs (Fayette County)	78940
Willow Springs (Rains County)	75440
Willow Springs (San Jacinto County)	77331
Wills Point	75169
Wilmer	75172
Wilmeth	79567
Wilson (Falls County)	76519
Wilson (Lynn County)	79381
Wilson Lake	77351
Wimberley	78676
Winchell	76827
Winchester	78964
Windcrest	78239
Windcrest Mall (Part of San Antonio)	78221
Windemere (Burnet County)	78669
Windemere (Travis County)	78660
Windmill (Part of Houston)	77075
Windom	75492
Windsor Park Mall (Part of San Antonio)	78218
Windthorst	76389
Winedale	77835
Winfield	75493
Winfree (Chambers County)	77535
Winfree (Orange County)	77630
Wingate	79566
Wink	79789
Winkler	75859
Winnie	77665
Winningkoff (Part of Lucas)	75069
Winnsboro	75494
Winona	75792
Winter Haven	78839
Winter Hill	75943
Winters	79567
Winwood Mall (Part of Odessa)	79762
Witting	77975
Wixon Valley	77808
Wizard Wells	76458
Woden	75978
Wolfe City	75496
Wolfforth	79382
Womack	76634
Woodbine	76240
Woodbranch	77357
Woodbury	76645
Wood-Canyon Waters	75147
Woodcreek	78676
Woodcreek North	78676
Woodcrest	77301
Woodhaven Estates	77304
Wood Hollow	77365
Woodlake (Bexar County)	78244
Woodlake (Grayson County)	75020
Woodlake (Trinity County)	75865
Woodland (Bell County)	76513
Woodland (Red River County)	75436
Woodland Estates	75948
Woodland Hills (Henderson County)	75143

	ZIP
Woodland Hills (Hill County)	76692
Woodland Lakes	77355
Woodland Shores	75630
Woodlawn (Angelina County)	75904
Woodlawn (Harrison County)	75694
Woodlawn Lakes	77355
Woodley	75670
Woodloch	77301
Woodridge Park	78264
Woodrow (Fort Bend County)	77430
Woodrow (Lubbock County)	79401
Woods	75974
Woodsboro	78393
Woods of Shavano (Part of San Antonio)	78249
Woodson	76491
Wood Springs	75701
Woodville	75979
Woodway (McLennan County)	76712
Woodway (Victoria County)	77904
Woody Acres	77365
Woosley	75472
World Trade Center (Part of Dallas)	75207
Wortham	76693
Worthing	77964
Wright City	75684
Wrightsboro	78677
Wyldwood	78612
Wylie (Collin County)	75098
Wylie (Franklin County)	75494
Wylie (Taylor County)	79606
Wynne Unit	77340
Wynnewood Village Shopping Center (Part of Dallas)	75224
Wynnrock Estates	78737
Yancey	78886
Yantis	75497
Yarboro	77868
Yarbrough Plaza (Part of El Paso)	79912
Yard	75861
Yarrelton	76518
Yaupon Cove	77351
Yellowpine	75948
Yoakum	77995
Yorktown	78164
Young	75840
Youngsport	76542
Yowell	75428
Ysleta (Part of El Paso)	79907*
	79917†
Zabcikville	76501
Zapata	78076
Zavalla	75980
Zephyr	76890
Zionsville	77833
Zippville	78155
Zorn	78666
Zuehl	78124
Zunkerville	78119
Zybach	79011

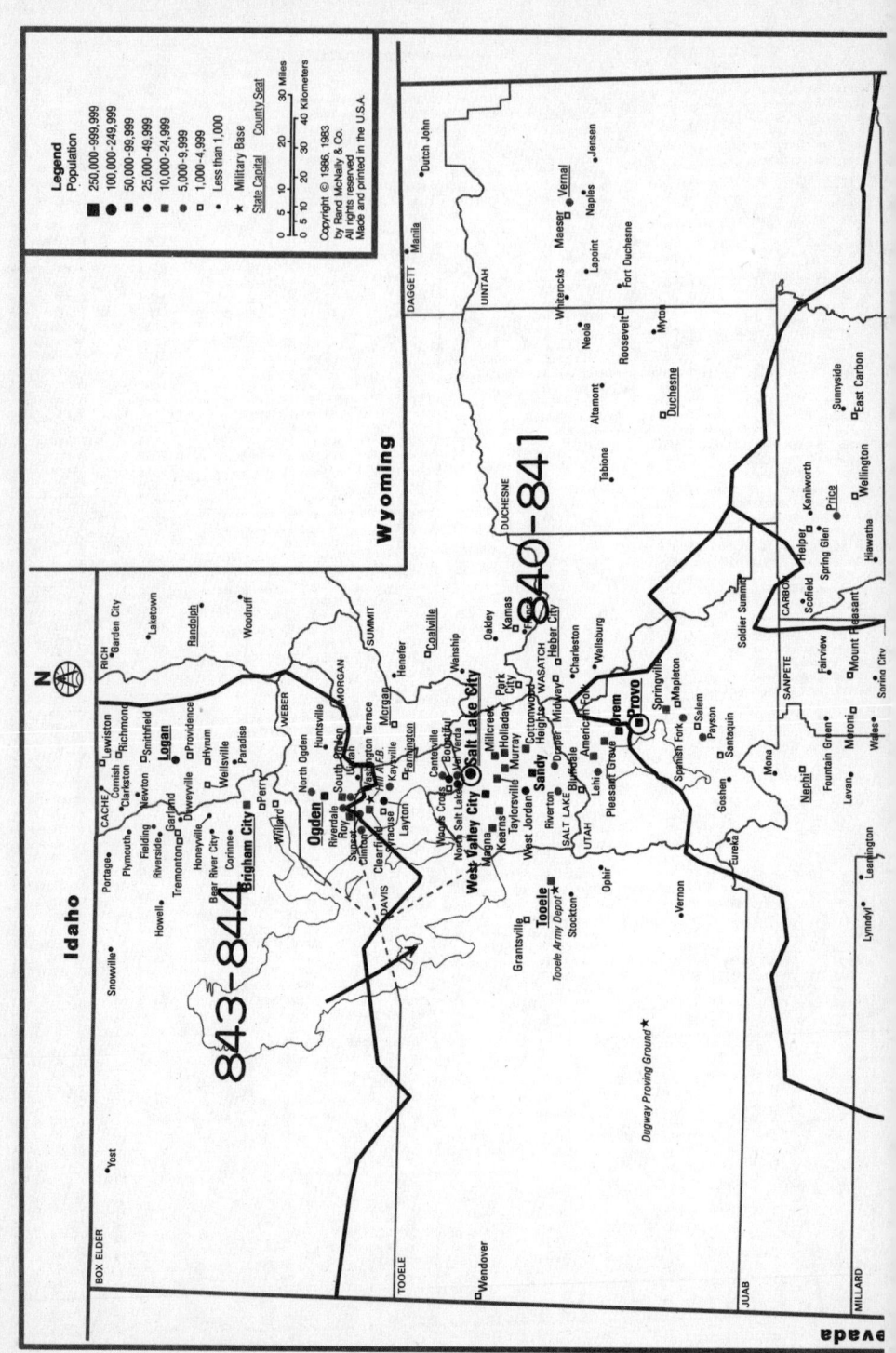

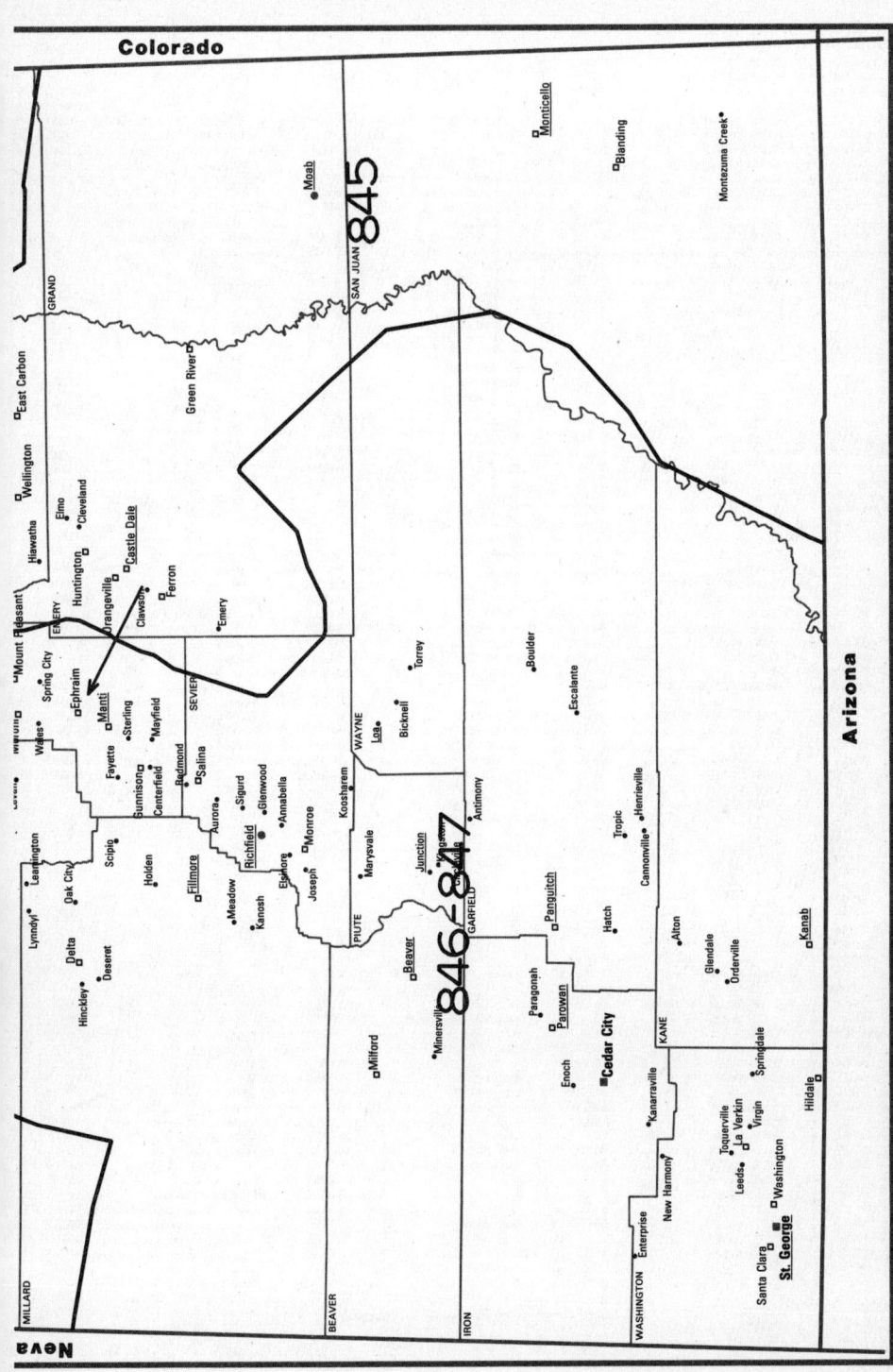

Place	ZIP
Abraham	84635
Adamsville	84731
Alpine	84004
Alta	84092
Altamont	84001
Alton	84710
Altonah	84002
Amalga	84335
American Fork	84003
Aneth	84510
Angle	84712
Annabella	84711
Antimony	84712
Arcadia	84012
Arsenal (Part of Sunset)	84015
Aspen Acres	84055
Atwood (Part of Murray)	84107
Aurora	84620
Austin	84754
Avon	84328
Axtell	84621
Ballard	84066
Bauer	84071
Bear River City	84301
Beaver	84713
Beaverdam	84306
Belmont Heights (Part of Sandy)	84070
Benjamin	84660
Ben Lomond (Part of Ogden)	84404
Bennion	84118
	84123

For specific Bennion Zip Codes call (801) 974-2200, or your local postmaster.

Place	ZIP
Benson	84335
Beryl	84714
Beryl Junction	84714
Bicknell	84715
Big Water	84741
Bingham Canyon	84006
Birdseye	84629
Blanding	84511
Bloomington	84770
Bluebell	84007
Bluff	84512
Bluffdale	84065
Bonanza	84008
Boneta	84051
Bonnie (Part of Orem)	84057
Bothwell	84337
Boulder	84716
Bountiful	84010*
	84011†
Bowery Haven	84701
Brendel	84540
Brian Head	84719
Bridgeland	84012
Brigham City	84302
Brighton	84121
Brooklyn	84754
Bryce	84764
Bryce Canyon	84717
Bullfrog	84533
Burbank	84751
Burmester	84029
Burrville	84701
Bushnell (Part of Brigham City)	84302
Cache Junction	84304
Cache Valley Mall (Part of Logan)	84321
Caineville	84775
Callao	84034
Call Fort	84302
Cannonville	84718
Canyon Rim	84106
Carbonville	84501
Castle Dale	84513
Castleton	84532
Castle Valley	84532
Cedar City	84720*
	84721†
Cedar Hills	84062
Cedar Valley	84013
Cedarview	84066
Center Creek	84032
Centerfield	84622
Centerville	84014
Central (Sevier County)	84754
Central (Washington County)	84722
Charleston	84032
Chester	84623
Circleville	84723
Cisco	84515
Clarkston	84305
Clawson	84516
Clear Creek (Box Elder County)	83342
Clear Creek (Carbon County)	84526
Clearfield	84015*
	84016†
Cleveland	84518
Clinton	84015
Clover	84069
Clyde (Part of Orem)	84057
Coalville	84017
College Ward	84321
Collinston	84306
Columbia	84520
Columbia Junction (Part of East Carbon)	84520
Copperton	84006
Corinne	84307
Cornish	84308
Cottonwood	84121
Cottonwood Heights	84121
Cottonwood Mall	84117
Cottonwood West	84117
	84121

For specific Cottonwood West Zip Codes call (801) 974-2200, or your local postmaster.

Place	ZIP
Cove	84320
Crescent (Part of Sandy)	84070
Crossroads Plaza Mall & Tower (Part of Salt Lake City)	84144
Croydon	84018
Cushing (Part of Midvale)	84047
Dammeron Valley	84783
Daniel	84032
Defas Park	84031
Delta	84624
Deseret	84624
Devils Slide	84050
Deweyville	84309
Downtown (Part of Salt Lake City)	84101
Draper	84020
Dry Fork	84078
Duchesne	84021
Duck Creek Village	84762
Dugway	84022
Dugway Proving Ground	84022
Dutch John	84023
East Bay (Part of Provo)	84605
East Carbon	84520
Eastland	84535
East Midvale	84047
East Millcreek	84117
East Portal	84032
Eastwood Hills	84106
Echo	84024
Eden	84310
Elberta	84626
Elgin	84525
Elk Ridge	84660
Elmo	84521
Elsinore	84724
Elwood	84337
Emery	84522
Emory	84024
Enoch	84720
Enterprise (Morgan County)	84050
Enterprise (Washington County)	84725
Ephraim	84627
Erda	84074
Escalante	84726
Esk Dale	84728
Etna	84313
Eureka	84628
Fairfield	84013
Fairgrounds (Part of Salt Lake City)	84116
Fairview	84629
Family Center at Midvalley, The	84123
Farmington	84025
Farr West	84404
Fashion Place (Part of Murray)	84107
Faust	84080
Fayette	84630
Ferron	84523
Fielding	84311
Fillmore	84631
Fish Lake	84701
Flowell	84631
Foothill (Part of Salt Lake City)	84108
Fort Duchesne	84026
Fountain Green	84632
Francis	84036
Freedom	84646
Freeport Center (Part of Clearfield)	84016
Fremont	84747
Fruita	84775
Fruit Heights	84037
Fruitland	84027
Gandy	84728
Garden City	84028
Garland	84312
Garrison	84728
Genola	84655
Glendale	84729
Glenwood	84730
Goshen	84633
Goshute Indian Reservation	84034
Gouldings Trading Post	86033
Grand Vu	84532
Granger (Part of West Valley City)	84119
Granite	84092
Grantsville	84029
Greendale	84023
Green Lake	84023
Green River	84525
Greenville	84731
Greenwich	84732
Grouse Creek	84313
Grover	84773
Gunlock	84733
Gunnison	84634
Gusher	84030
Hailstone	84032
Halchita	84531
Halls Crossing	84533
Hamilton Fort	84720
Hanksville	84734
Hanna	84031
Hardy (Part of Lindon)	84062
Harrisburg Junction	84770
Harrisville	84404
Hatch	84735
Hatton	84637
Hayden	84053
Heber City	84032
Helper	84526
Henefer	84033
Henrieville	84736
Herriman	84065
Hiawatha	84527
Hidden Lake	84055
Highland	84003
Highlands	84050
Hildale	84784
Hill Air Force Base	84056
Hinckley	84635
Hite	84533
Holden	84636
Holiday Park	84055
Holladay	84117
Holladay-Cottonwood	84117
	84121

For specific Holladay-Cottonwood Zip Codes call (801) 974-2200, or your local postmaster.

Place	ZIP
Honeyville	84314
Hooper	84315
Hoovers	84750
Howell	84316
Hoytsville	84017
Hunter (Part of West Valley City)	84120
Huntington	84528
Huntsville	84317
Hurricane	84737
Hyde Park	84318
Hyrum	84319
Ibapah	84034
Indianola	84629
Ioka	84066
Ivins	84738
Jensen	84035
Jerusalem	84646
Joseph	84739
Junction	84740
Kamas	84036
Kanab	84741
Kanarraville	84742
Kanosh	84637
Kaysville	84037
Kearns	84118
Keetley	84032
Kelton	84336
Kenilworth	84529
Kimball Junction	84060
Kingston	84743
Koosharem	84744
Lake Point	84074
Lake Powell	84533
Lake Shore	84601
Lakeside Resort	84701
Laketown	84038
Lakeview	84601
Lapoint	84039
Lark	84065
La Sal	84530
La Sal Junction	84530
La Verkin	84745
Lawrence	84528
Layton	84040-41

For specific Layton Zip Codes call (801) 544-1203, or your local postmaster.

Place	ZIP
Layton Hills Mall (Part of Layton)	84041
Leamington	84638
Leeds	84746
Leeton	84066
Lehi	84043
Leland	84660
Levan	84639
Lewiston	84320
Liberty	84310
Lincoln	84074
Lindon	84042
Little Bonanza	84078
Little Cottonwood Creek Valley	84121
Littleton	84050
Loa	84747
Logan	84321-23

For specific Logan Zip Codes call (801) 752-7246, or your local postmaster.

Place	ZIP
Long Valley Junction	84758
Lund	84720
Lyman	84749
Lynn	83346
Lynndyl	84640
Madsen (Part of Honeyville)	84314
Maeser	84078
Magna	84044
Mammoth	84601
Manderfield	84713
Manila	84046
Manti	84642
Mantua	84324
Mapleton	84664
Marion	84036
Marriott	84404
Martin	84526
Marysvale	84750
Mayfield	84643
Meadow	84644
Meadowville	84038
Mendon	84325
Mexican Hat	84531
Middleton	84770
Midvale	84047
Midway	84049
Milburn	84629
Milford	84751
Millcreek (Grand County)	84532
Millcreek (Salt Lake County)	84109
Mills	84639
Millville	84326
Milton	84050
Minersville	84752
Moab	84532
Modena	84753
Molen	84523
Mona	84645
Monarch	84066
Monroe	84754
Montezuma Creek	84534
Monticello	84535
Monti Verdi	84050
Monument Valley	84536
Moore	84523
Morgan	84050
Moroni	84646
Mountain Green	84050
Mountain Home	84051
Mount Carmel	84755
Mount Carmel Junction	84755
Mount Emmons	84001
Mount Olympus	84117
Mount Pleasant	84647
Murray	84107
Myton	84052
Naples	84078
Navajo Indian Reservation	86515
Neola	84053

* Area Zip Code † Post Office Boxes

	ZIP		ZIP		ZIP		ZIP
Nephi	84648	Polls	84050	Snowbird	84092	Tropic	84776
Newcastle	84756	Portage	84331	Snowville	84336	Trout Creek	84083
New Harmony	84757	Portersville	84050	Snyderville	84060	Ucolo	84535
Newton	84327	Price	84501	Soldier Summit	84601	Uintah	84405
Nibley	84321	Promontory	84307	South Jordan	84095	Uintah and Ouray Indian	
North Creek	84713	Providence	84332	South Ogden	84403	Reservation	84026
North Logan	84341	Provo	84601-06	South Salt Lake	84115	Union	84047
North Ogden	84404	For specific Provo Zip Codes		South Weber	84405	University (Part of Provo)	84602
North Salt Lake	84054	call (801) 374-2000, or your		Spanish Fork	84660	University Mall (Part of	
Oak City	84649	local postmaster.		Spring City	84662	Orem)	84057
Oak Creek	84629	Randlett	84063	Springdale	84767	Upalco	84007
Oakley	84055	Randolph	84064	Springdell	84604	Upton	84017
Oasis	84650	Redmond	84652	Spring Glen	84526	Utah State Prison	84020
Ogden	84401-14	Red Wash	84078	Spring Lake	84651	Utah State University (Part	
For specific Ogden Zip Codes		Redwood (Part of West		Springville	84663	of Logan)	84322
call (801) 627-4437, or your		Valley City)	84119	Standrod	83342	Utida (Part of Cornish)	84308
local postmaster.		Richfield	84701	Stansbury Park	84074	Uvada	84753
Ogden ALC Hardness		Richmond	84333	Starr	84645	Val Verda	84010
Test Center	84401	Richville	84050	Sterling	84665	Venice	84701
Ogden City Mall (Part of		Riverdale	84405	Stockton	84071	Vermillion	84657
Ogden)	84401	River Heights	84321	Stoddard	84050	Vernal	84078*
Oljato	86033	Riverside	84334	Sugar House (Part of Salt			84079†
Olmstead	84604	Riverton	84065	Lake City)	84106	Vernon	84080
Ophir	84071	Rockville	84763	Sugarville	84624	Veyo	84782
Oquirrh	84084	Roosevelt	84066	Summit	84772	Vineyard	84057
Orangeville	84537	Roper (Part of South Salt		Summit Point	84535	Virgin	84779
Orderville	84758	Lake)	84115	Sunnyside	84539	Vivian Park	84604
Orem	84057-59	Rosette	84329	Sunset	84015	Wales	84667
For specific Orem Zip Codes		Round Valley	84038	Sutherland	84624	Wallsburg	84082
call (801) 225-2071, or your		Roy	84067	Swan Creek	84028	Wanship	84017
local postmaster.		Rush Valley	84069	Syracuse	84075	Warren	84404
Ouray	84063	St. George	84770*	Tabiona	84072	Washington	84780
Pallas (Part of Murray)	84107		84771†	Talmage	84073	Washington Terrace	84403
Palmyra	84660	Salem	84653	Taylor	84401	Wellington	84542
Panguitch	84759	Salina	84654	Taylorsville	84118-19	Wellsville	84339
Paradise	84328	Salt Lake City	84101-80		84123	Wendover	84083
Paragonah	84760	For specific Salt Lake City Zip		For specific Taylorsville Zip		West Bountiful	84087
Park City	84060*	Codes call (801) 974-2200, or		Codes call (801) 974-2200, or		West Haven	84067
	84068†	your local postmaster.		your local postmaster.		West Jordan	84084
Park Terrace	84106	Samak	84036	Taylorsville-Bennion	84118-19		84088
Park Valley	84329	Sandy	84070		84123	West Point	84015
Parowan	84761		84090-94	For specific Taylorsville-Bennion		West Valley City	84120
Partoun	84083	For specific Sandy Zip Codes		Zip Codes call (801) 974-2200,		West Warren	84404
Payson	84651	call (801) 255-4022, or your		or your local postmaster.		West Weber	84401
Penrose	84337	local postmaster.		Teasdale	84773	Wheelon	84306
Peoa	84061	Santa Clara	84765	Terra	84022	White City	84070
Perry	84302	Santaquin	84655	Thatcher	84337	Whiterocks	84085
Peruvian Park (Part of		Scipio	84656	Thompson	84540	Wildwood	84604
Sandy)	84093	Scofield	84526	Thompsonville	84750	Willard	84340
Peterson	84050	Sevier	84766	Ticaboo	84533	Wilson (Part of West	
Pickelville (Part of Garden		Sherwood Park (Part of		Tooele	84074	Haven)	84401
City)	84028	Sandy)	84093	Tooele Army Depot	84074	Woodland	84036
Pine Mountain	84055	Shivwits	84765	Toquerville	84774	Woodland Hills	84653
Pine Valley	84781	Sigurd	84657	Torrey	84775	Woodruff	84086
Pintura	84720	Silver Fork	84121	Town (Part of Ogden)	84402	Woods Cross	84087
Pioneer (Part of Salt Lake		Silver Reef	84746	Tremonton	84337	Yost	83342
City)	84147	Skull Valley Indian		Trenton	84338	ZCMI Center (Part of Salt	
Plain City	84404	Reservation	84029	Tridell	84076	Lake City)	84111
Pleasant Grove	84062	Slaterville	84404	Trolley Square (Part of		Zion National Park	84767
Pleasant View	84404	Smithfield	84335	Salt Lake City)	84102		
Plymouth	84330						

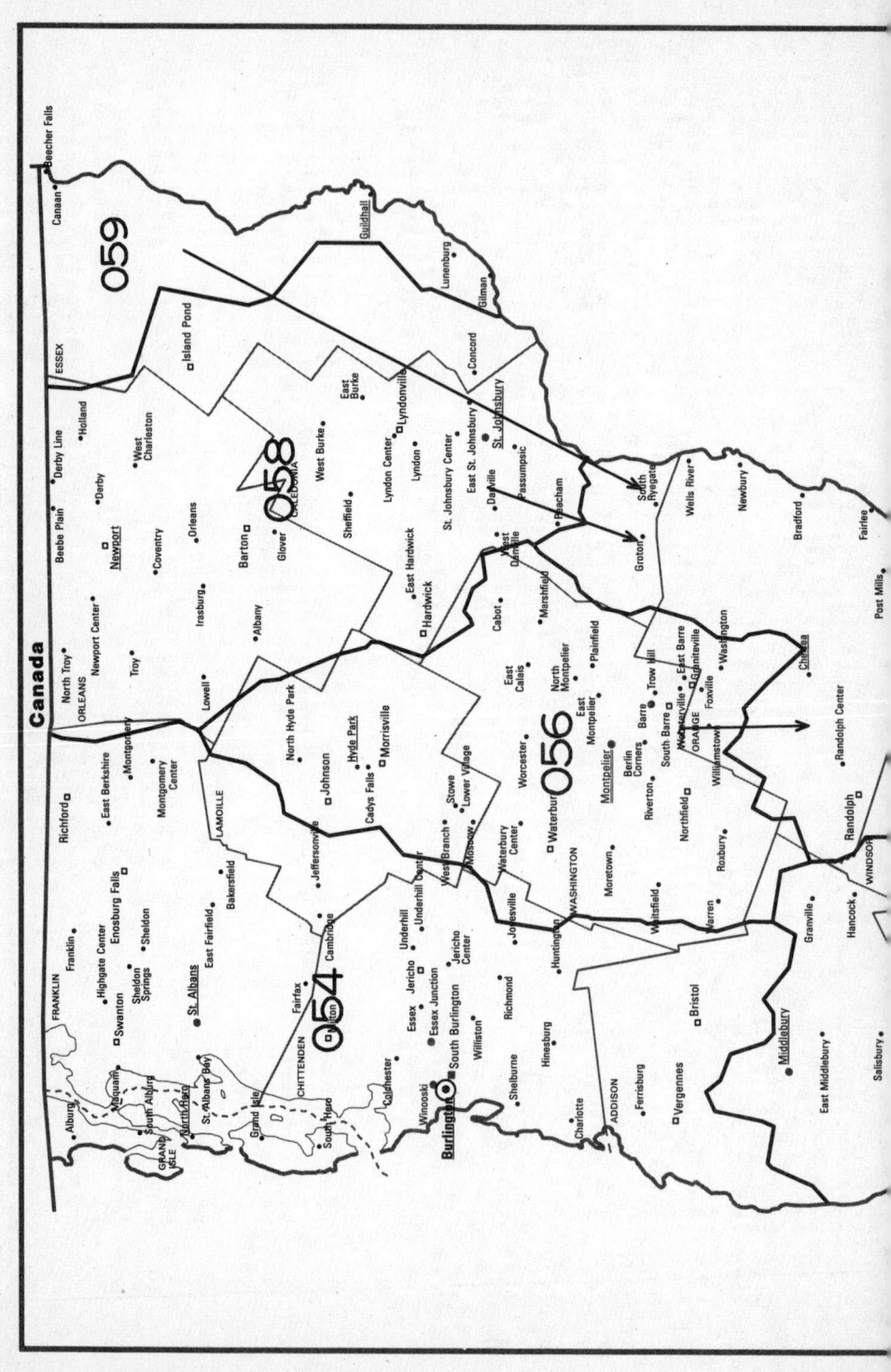

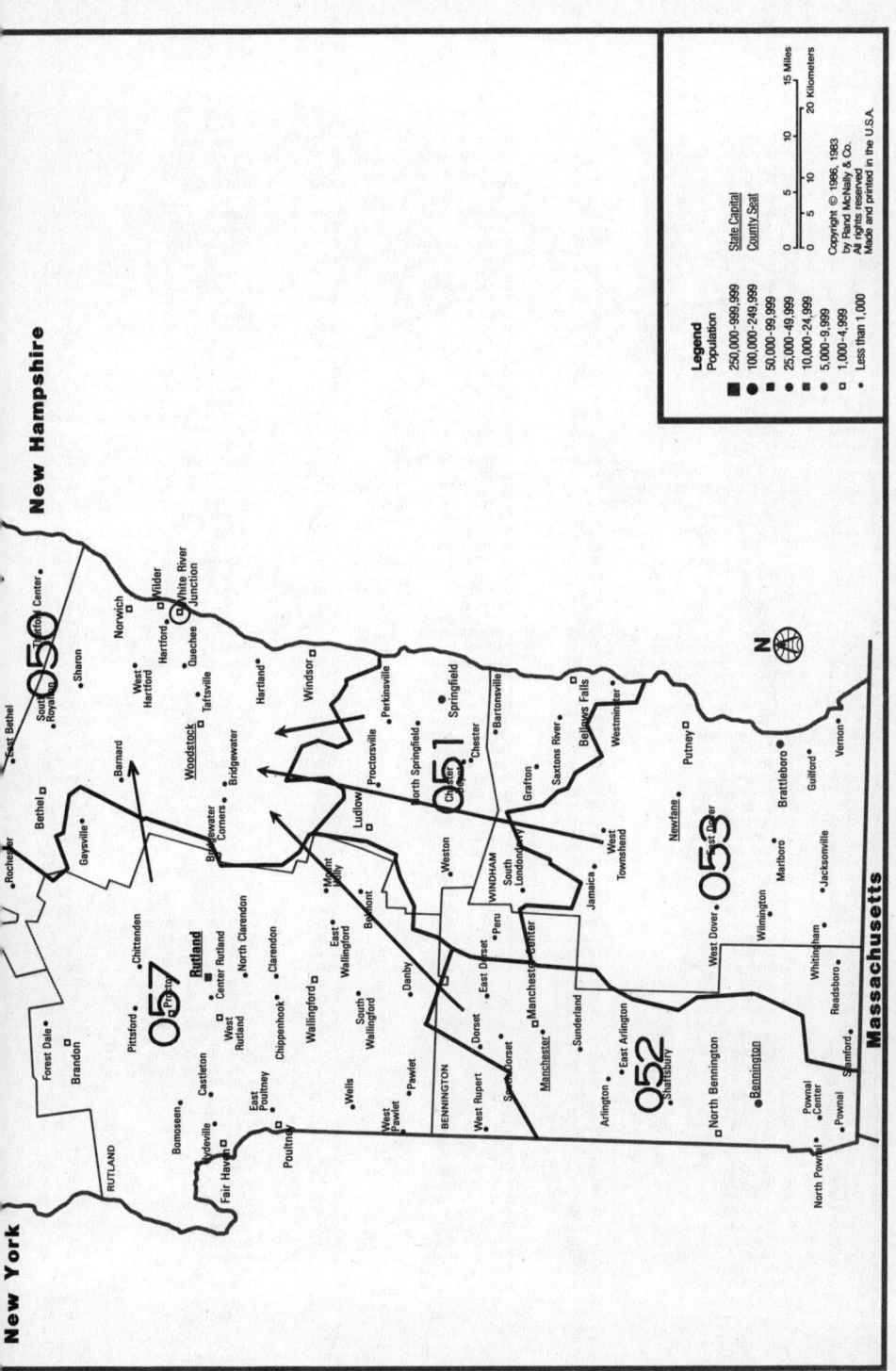

New Hampshire

New York

Massachusetts

Legend
Population
250,000-999,999
100,000-249,999
50,000-99,999
25,000-49,999
10,000-24,999
5,000-9,999
1,000-4,999
Less than 1,000

State Capital
County Seat

	ZIP		ZIP		ZIP		ZIP
Abnaki	05474	Bridgewater	05034	Corinth (Town)	05039	Enosburg (Town)	05450
Adamant	05640	Bridgewater (Town)	05034	Corinth Center	05039	Enosburg Center	05450
Addison	05491	Bridgewater Center	05035	Corinth Corners	05039	Enosburg Falls	05450
Addison (Town)	05491	Bridgewater Corners	05035	Cornwall	05753	Essex (Town)	05451
Albany	05820	Bridport	05734	Cornwall (Town)	05753	Essex Center	05451
Albany (Town)	05820	Bridport (Town)	05734	Coventry	05825	Essex Junction	05452*
Albany Center	05845	Brighton (Town)	05846	Coventry (Town)	05825		05453†
Alburg	05440	Brimstone Corner	05083	Craftsbury	05826	Ethan Allen Shopping	
Alburg (Town)	05440	Brimstone Corners	05761	Craftsbury (Town)	05826	Center (Part of	
Alburg Center	05440	Bristol	05443	Craftsbury Common	05827	Burlington)	05404
Alburg Springs	05440	Bristol (Town)	05443	Cream Hill	05734	Evansville	05860
Alfrecha	05759	Brockways Mills	05143	Crystal Beach	05732	Fairfax	05454
Alpine Village	05674	Brookfield	05036	Cuttingsville	05738	Fairfax (Town)	05454
Ames Hill	05344	Brookfield (Town)	05036	Danby	05739	Fairfax Falls	05454
Amsden	05151	Brookfield Center	05036	Danby (Town)	05739	Fairfield	05455
Andover (Town)	05143	Brookline (Town)	05345	Danby Corners	05739	Fairfield (Town)	05455
Arlington	05250	Brookside (Chittenden		Danville	05828	Fairfield Station	05455
Arlington (Town)	05250	County)	05494	Danville (Town)	05828	Fair Haven (Town)	05743
Arlington	05250	Brookside (Windham		Danville Center	05828	Fair Haven	05743
Arnold Bay	05491	County)	05341	Derby	05829	Fairlee	05045
Ascutney	05030	Brooksville	05753	Derby (Town)	05829	Fairlee (Town)	05045
Athens	05143	Brownington	05860	Derby Line	05830	Fays Corner	05477
Athens (Town)	05143	Brownington (Town)	05860	Deweys Mills	05059	Fayston (Town)	05660
Avalon Beach	05750	Brownington Center	05860	Dorset	05251	Ferdinand (Town)	05905
Averill	05901	Brownsville	05037	Dorset (Town)	05251	Fernville	05733
Averill (Town)	05901	Brunswick (Town)	03590	Dover	05341	Ferrisburg	05456
Avery's Gore (Town)	05903	Buck Hollow	05454	Dover (Town)	05341	Ferrisburg (Town)	05456
Bailey's Mills	05062	Buels (Town)	05487	Downers	05151	Fieldsville	05089
Bakersfield	05441	Burke	05871	Downingville	05443	Fletcher	05444
Bakersfield (Town)	05441	Burke (Town)	05871	Dows Crossing	05836	Fletcher (Town)	05444
Baltimore (Town)	05143	Burke Mountain	05832	Dowsville	05660	Florence	05744
Barnard	05031	Burlington	05401-02	Dummerston	05346	Fonda	05488
Barnard (Town)	05031		05405-06	Dummerston (Town)	05346	Forest Dale	05745
Barnet	05821	For specific Burlington Zip		Duxbury	05676	Foxville	05654
Barnet (Town)	05821	Codes call (802) 863-6033, or		Duxbury (Town)	05676	Franklin	05457
Barnet Center	05821	your local postmaster.		Eagle Point	05855	Franklin (Town)	05457
Barnumtown	05472	Burnham Hill	05843	East Albany	05845	Freedleyville	05253
Barre	05641	Burnham Hollow	05757	East Alburg	05440	Gallup Mills	05858
Barre (Town)	05678	Butlers Corners	05452	East Arlington	05252	Garfield	05661
Barre Transfer (Part of		Butternut Bend	05761	East Barnard	05068	Gassetts	05143
Montpelier)	05602	Button Bay	05491	East Barre	05649	Gaysville	05746
Barton	05822	Cabot	05647	East Berkshire	05447	Georgia	05454
Barton (Town)	05822	Cabot (Town)	05647	East Bethel	05032	Georgia (Town)	05478
Bartonsville	05143	Cadys Falls	05661	East Braintree	05060	Georgia Center	05478
Basin Harbor	05491	Calais	05648	East Brookfield	05036	Georgia Plains	05468
Bayside	05404	Calais (Town)	05648	East Burke	05832	Gilman	05904
Beanville	05060	Cambridge	05444	East Cabot	05647	Glastenbury (Town)	05262
Beaulieu's Corner	05459	Cambridge (Town)	05444	East Calais	05650	Glover	05839
Beebe Plain	05823	Cambridge Junction	05464	East Cambridge	05464	Glover (Town)	05839
Beecher Falls	05902	Cambridgeport	05141	East Charleston	05833	Goodrich Four Corners	05055
Bellows Falls	05101	Canaan	05903	East Charlotte	05445	Goose City	05341
Belmont	05730	Canaan (Town)	05903	East Clarendon	05759	Goose Green	05039
Belvidere (Town)	05492	Castleton	05735	East Concord	05906	Gordon Landing	05458
Belvidere Center	05492	Castleton (Town)	05735	East Corinth	05040	Goshen	05733
Belvidere Corners	05492	Cavendish	05142	East Craftsbury	05826	Goshen (Town)	05733
Belvidere Junction	05492	Cavendish (Town)	05142	East Dorset	05253	Goulds Mills	05156
Bennington	05201	Cavendish Center	05142	East Dover	05341	Grafton	05146
Bennington (Town)	05201	Cedar Beach	05445	East Dummerston	05346	Grafton (Town)	05146
Bennington College (Part		Center Rutland	05736	East Enosburg	05450	Grahamville	05149
of North Bennington)	05201	Centerville (Lamoille		East Fairfield	05448	Granby	05840
Benson	05731	County)	05655	East Fletcher	05464	Granby (Town)	05840
Benson (Town)	05731	Centerville (Windsor		East Franklin	05457	Grand Isle	05458
Benson Landing	05743	County)	05001	East Granville	05669	Grand Isle (Town)	05458
Berkshire	05447	Champlain (Part of South		East Hardwick	05836	Graniteville	05654
Berkshire (Town)	05450	Burlington)	05401	East Haven	05837	Graniteville-East Barre	05654
Berlin (Town)	05602	Charleston (Town)	05872	East Haven (Town)	05837	Granville-East Barre	05747
Berlin Corners	05602	Charlotte	05445	East Highgate	05459	Granville	05747
Bethel	05032	Charlotte (Town)	05445	East Hubbardton	05735	Green Acres	05477
Bethel (Town)	05032	Checkerberry	05468	East Jamaica	05343	Green Bay	05046
Bethel Gilead	05060	Chelsea	05038	East Johnson	05656	Greenbush	05151
Binghamville	05444	Chelsea (Town)	05038	East Lyndon	05851	Green River	05301
Birdland	05474	Chelsea West Hill	05041	East Middlebury	05740	Greensboro	05841
Bliss Pond	05640	Chester	05143	East Monkton	05443	Greensboro (Town)	05841
Blissville	05764	Chester (Town)	05143	East Montpelier	05651	Greensboro Bend	05842
Bloomfield	03590	Chester-Chester Depot	05143	East Montpelier (Town)	05651	Greens Corners	05478
Bloomfield (Town)	03590	Chester Depot	05144	East Montpelier Center	05602	Groton	05046
Blossoms Corners	05775	Chimney Corner	05446	East Orange	05086	Groton (Town)	05046
Bolton	05676	Chimney Point	05491	East Peacham	05862	Guildhall	05905
Bolton (Town)	05676	Chipman Lake	05739	East Pittsford	05701	Guildhall (Town)	05905
Bolton Valley	05477	Chipmans Point	05760	East Poultney	05741	Guilford	05301
Boltonville	05081	Chippenhook	05777	East Putney	05346	Guilford (Town)	05301
Bomoseen	05732	Chiselville	05250	East Randolph	05041	Guilford Center	05301
Bondville	05340	Chittenden	05737	East Richford	05476	Halifax	05358
Bordoville	05450	Chittenden (Town)	05737	East Roxbury	05663	Halifax (Town)	05358
Bowlsville	05742	Clarendon	05759	East Rupert	05761	Halls Lake	05062
Bradford	05033	Clarendon (Town)	05759	East Ryegate	05042	Hammondsville	05062
Bradford (Town)	05033	Clarendon Springs	05777	East Sheldon	05450	Hancock	05748
Bragg	05055	Cleveland Corner	05661	East Shoreham	05770	Hancock (Town)	05748
Braintree	05060	Cloverdale	05489	East St. Johnsbury	05838	Hanksville	05487
Braintree (Town)	05060	Colbyville	05676	East Sutton Ridge	05867	Hardscrabble	05156
Braintree Hill	05060	Colchester	05446*	East Thetford	05043	Hardwick	05843
Brandon	05733		05449†	East Wallingford	05742	Hardwick (Town)	05843
Brandon (Town)	05733	Colchester (Town)	05446	East Warren	05674	Hardwick Center	05843
Brattleboro	05301-04	Cold River	05738	Eden	05652	Hardwick Steet	05836
For specific Brattleboro Zip		Concord	05824	Eden (Town)	05652	Harmonyville	05353
Codes call (802) 254-4110, or		Concord (Town)	05824	Eden Mills	05653	Harrisville	05301
your local postmaster.		Concord Corner	05824	Egypt	05448	Hartford	05047
Brattleboro Center	05301	Copperfield	05079	Elmore (Town)	05657	Hartford (Town)	05047
Bread Loaf	05753	Corinth	05039	Ely	05044	Hartland	05048

	ZIP		ZIP		ZIP		ZIP
Hartland (Town)	05048	Lower Plain	05033	New Haven Mills	05443	Poultney (Town)	05764
Hartland Four Corners	05049	Lower Village	05672	Newport	05855	Pownal	05261
Harvey	05828	Lower Waterford	05848	Newport (Town)	05857	Pownal (Town)	05261
Healdville	05758	Lower Websterville	05641	Newport Center	05857	Pownal Center	05261
Heartwellville	05350	Ludlow	05149	North Bennington	05257	Prindle Corner	05445
Hectorville	05471	Ludlow (Town)	05149	North Brattleboro	05304	Proctor (Town)	05765
Hewitts Corners	05053	Lunenburg	05906	North Burlington (Part of		Proctor	05765
Highgate (Town)	05459	Lunenburg (Town)	05906	Burlington)	05401	Proctorsville	05153
Highgate Center	05459	Lyman	05001	North Calais	05650	Prosper	05091
Highgate Falls	05459	Lympus	05032	North Cambridge	05464	Putnamville	05602
Highgate Springs	05460	Lyndon	05849	North Chester	05143	Putney	05346
Hinesburg	05461	Lyndon (Town)	05849	North Clarendon	05759	Putney (Town)	05346
Hinesburg (Town)	05461	Lyndon Center	05850	North Concord	05858	Quechee	05059
Hinesburg	05301	Lyndon State College	05851	North Danville	05819	Queen City Park (Part of	
Holden	05763	Lyndonville	05851	North Derby	05855	South Burlington)	05401
Holland	05830	McIndoe Falls	05050	North Dorset	05253	Ralston Corner	05824
Holland (Town)	05830	Mackville	05843	North Duxbury	05676	Randolph	05060
Hortonia	05760	Mad River Glen	05673	North Fairfax	05454	Randolph (Town)	05060
Hortonville	05758	Maidstone (Town)	05905	North Fayston	05660	Randolph Center	05061
Houghtonville	05146	Maidstone Lake	03590	North Ferrisburg	05473	Rawsonville	05155
Hubbard Corner	05478	Mallets Bay	05404	Northfield	05663	Reading	05062
Hubbardton	05732	Manchester (Town)	05254	Northfield (Town)	05663	Reading (Town)	05062
Hubbardton (Town)	05732	Manchester	05254	Northfield Center	05663	Reading Center	05062
Huntington	05462	Manchester (Manchester		Northfield Falls	05664	Readsboro	05350
Huntington (Town)	05462	Depot) (railroad station)	05255	North Hartland	05052	Readsboro (Town)	05350
Huntington Center	05462	Manchester Center	05255	North Hero	05474	Readsboro Falls	05350
Huntville	05454	Maple Dell	05156	North Hero (Town)	05474	Red Village	05851
Hutchins	05471	Maquam	05488	North Hyde Park	05665	Reedville	05143
Hyde Park	05655	Marlboro	05344	North Montpelier	05666	Rhode Island Corner	05477
Hyde Park (Town)	05655	Marlboro (Town)	05344	North Orwell	05760	Rices Mills	05075
Hydeville	05750	Marshfield	05658	North Pomfret	05053	Richford	05476
Indian Point (Part of		Marshfield (Town)	05658	North Pownal	05260	Richford (Town)	05476
Newport)	05855	Mary Meyer	05353	North Randolph	05041	Richmond	05477
Inwood	05821	Mechanicsville	05461	North Royalton	05068	Richmond (Town)	05477
Ira	05777	Medburyville	05363	North Rupert	05761	Ricker Mills	05046
Ira (Town)	05777	Melville	05478	North Sheldon	05485	Ripton	05766
Irasburg	05845	Mendon	05701	North Sherburne	05751	Ripton (Town)	05766
Irasburg (Town)	05845	Mendon (Town)	05701	North Shrewsbury	05738	Riverton	05663
Irasville	05673	Merrill Corner	05845	North Springfield	05150	Robinson	05767
Island Pond	05846	Middlebury	05753	North Thetford	05054	Rochester	05767
Isle La Motte	05463	Middlebury (Town)	05753	North Troy	05859	Rochester (Town)	05767
Isle La Motte (Town)	05463	Middlesex	05602	North Tunbridge	05077	Rockingham	05101
Jacksonville	05342	Middlesex (Town)	05602	North Vernon	05354	Rockingham (Town)	05101
Jamaica	05343	Middlesex Center	05602	North Westminster	05101	Rockville	05443
Jamaica (Town)	05343	Middletown	05143	North Windham	05148	Rocky Dale	05443
Jay	05859	Middletown Springs	05757	North Wolcott	05680	Round Pond	05069
Jay (Town)	05859	Middletown Springs		Norton	05907	Roxbury	05669
Jay Peak	05859	(Town)	05757	Norton (Town)	05907	Roxbury (Town)	05669
Jeffersonville	05464	Mile Point	05491	Norwich	05055	Roxbury Flat	05669
Jenneville	05089	Miles Pond	05858	Norwich (Town)	05055	Royalton	05068
Jericho	05465	Millbrook	05053	Norwich University (Part		Royalton (Town)	05068
Jericho (Town)	05465	Mill Village (Orange		of Northfield)	05663	Rupert	05768
Jericho Center	05465	County)	05079	Oakland	05478	Rupert (Town)	05768
Jerusalem	05443	Mill Village (Orleans		Oil City	05072	Russellville	05738
Joes Pond	05873	County)	05827	Old Bennington	05201	Russtown	05001
Johnson	05656	Milton	05468	Old Church	05060	Rutland	05701*
Johnson (Town)	05656	Milton (Town)	05468	Orange	05641		05702†
Jonesville	05466	Miltonboro	05468	Orange (Town)	05641	Ryegate	05042
Kansas	05252	Monkton	05469	Orchard Lane	05156	Ryegate (Town)	05042
Keeler Bay	05486	Monkton (Town)	05469	Orleans	05860	St. Albans	05478
Kendall	05043	Monkton Ridge	05473	Orwell	05760	St. Albans (Town)	05481
Kendricks Corner	05150	Montgomery	05470	Orwell (Town)	05760	St. Albans Bay	05481
Killington	05751	Montgomery (Town)	05470	Panton	05491	St. Albans Hill	05478
Kimball	05822	Montgomery Center	05471	Panton (Town)	05491	St. Albans Shopping	
Kirby (Town)	05824	Montpelier	05601*	Paper Mill Village	05257	Center (Part of St.	
Kirby Corner	05495		05602†	Passumpsic	05861	Albans)	05478
Lake Dunmore	05769	Moretown	05660	Pawlet	05761	St. George (Town)	05495
Lake Elmore	05657	Moretown (Town)	05660	Pawlet (Town)	05761	St. Johnsbury	05819
Lake Fairlee	05044	Moretown Common	05660	Peacham	05862	St. Johnsbury (Town)	05819
Lake Hortonia	05743	Morgan	05853	Peacham (Town)	05862	St. Johnsbury Center	05863
Lake Morey	05045	Morgan (Town)	05853	Pearl	05458	Saint Michael's College	05404
Lake Park	05855	Morgan Center	05853	Peaseville	05143	St. Rocks	05478
Lake Raponda	05363	Morristown	05661	Pedden Acres	05156	Salisbury (Town)	05769
Lake Rescue	05149	Morristown (Town)	05661	Pekin	05667	Salisbury	05769
Lake St. Catherine	05764	Morrisville	05661	Perkinsville	05151	Samsonville	05450
Lakewood	05488	Moscow	05662	Peru	05152	Sanderson Corner	05454
Landgrove	05148	Mosquitoville	05042	Peru (Town)	05152	Sandgate	05250
Landgrove (Town)	05148	Mount Holly	05758	Peth	05060	Sandgate (Town)	05250
Lapham Bay	05734	Mount Holly (Town)	05758	Pierces Corner	05759	Saxtons River	05154
Larrabees Point	05770	Mount Snow	05356	Pikes Falls	05343	Scottsville	05739
Leicester	05733	Mount Tabor	05739	Pittsfield	05762	Searsburg	05363
Leicester (Town)	05733	Mount Tabor (Town)	05739	Pittsfield (Town)	05762	Searsburg (Town)	05363
Leicester Junction	05778	Nashville	05465	Pittsford	05763	Seymour Lake	05853
Lemington	03576	Neshobe Beach	05732	Pittsford (Town)	05763	Shadow Lake	05839
Lemington (Town)	03576	Newark	05871	Plainfield	05667	Shady Rill	05602
Lewis (Town)	05905	Newark (Town)	05871	Plainfield (Town)	05667	Shaftsbury	05262
Lewiston	05055	Newark Hollow	05871	Pleasant Valley	05444	Shaftsbury (Town)	05262
Lilliesville	05032	New Boston (Norwich		Plymouth	05056	Shaftsbury Center	05262
Lincoln	05443	Town)	05772	Plymouth (Town)	05056	Sharon	05065
Lincoln (Town)	05443	New Boston (Stockbridge		Plymouth Kingdom	05149	Sharon (Town)	05065
Lindsay Beach	05855	Town)	05055	Plymouth Union	05056	Shawville	05457
Londonderry	05148	Newbury	05051	Pomfret	05053	Sheddsville	05089
Londonderry (Town)	05148	Newbury (Town)	05051	Pomfret (Town)	05053	Sheffield	05866
Long Point	05473	Newbury Center	05081	Post Mills	05058	Sheffield (Town)	05866
Lowell	05847	Newfane	05345	Potash Bay	05491	Sheffield Square	05866
Lowell (Town)	05847	Newfane (Town)	05345	Potash Point	05491	Shelburne	05482
Lower Branch	05060	New Haven (Town)	05472	Pottersville	05680	Shelburne (Town)	05482
Lower Cabot	05658	New Haven	05472	Poultney	05764	Shelburne Falls	05482
Lower Granville	05747						

	ZIP		ZIP		ZIP		ZIP
Shelburne Road Section		Stevens Mills	05476	Waits River	05086	Westminster	05158
(Part of South		Stevensville	05489	Walden	05873	Westminster (Town)	05158
Burlington)	05401	Stockbridge	05772	Walden (Town)	05873	Westminster Station (Part	
Sheldon	05483	Stockbridge (Town)	05772	Walden Heights	05873	of Westminster)	05159
Sheldon (Town)	05483	Stowe	05672	Wallace Pond	05903	Westminster West	05346
Sheldon Junction	05483	Stowe (Town)	05672	Wallingford	05773	Westmore	05860
Sheldon Springs	05485	Strafford	05072	Wallingford (Town)	05773	Westmore (Town)	05860
Sherburne (Town)	05751	Strafford (Town)	05072	Waltham (Town)	05491	West Newbury	05085
Shoreham	05770	Stratton (Town)	05360	Wardsboro	05355	West Norwich	05055
Shoreham (Town)	05770	Stratton Mountain	05155	Wardsboro (Town)	05355	Weston	05161
Shoreham Center	05770	Sudbury	05733	Wardsboro Center	05355	Weston (Town)	05161
Shrewsbury	05738	Sudbury (Town)	05733	Warners (Town)	05903	Weston Priory	05161
Shrewsbury (Town)	05738	Sugarbush Valley	05674	Warren	05674	West Pawlet	05775
Simonsville	05143	Summer Point	05491	Warren (Town)	05674	West Rupert	05776
Simpsonville	05353	Summit	05758	Warren's (Town)	05903	West Rutland (Town)	05777
Smithville	05149	Sunderland	05250	Washington	05675	West Rutland	05777
Smugglers Notch	05464	Sunderland (Town)	05250	Washington (Town)	05675	West Salisbury	05769
Sodom	05257	Sutton	05867	Washington Heights	05657	West Springfield	05156
Somerset (Town)	05345	Sutton (Town)	05867	Waterbury	05676	West Swanton	05488
South Albany	05875	Swanton	05488	Waterbury (Town)	05676	West Topsham	05086
South Alburg	05440	Swanton (Town)	05488	Waterbury Center	05677	West Townshend	05359
South Barre	05670	Tafts Corner	05495	Waterford (Town)	05848	West Wardsboro	05360
South Burlington	05403	Taftsville	05073	Waterville	05492	West Waterford	05819
South Cabot	05658	Talcville	05767	Waterville (Town)	05492	West Windsor (Town)	05037
South Cambridge	05464	Tarbellville	05742	Weathersfield (Town)	05151	West Woodstock	05091
South Corinth	05039	The Bluffs (Part of		Weathersfield Bow	05156	Weybridge	05753
South Danville	05828	Newport)	05855	Weathersfield Center	05151	Weybridge (Town)	05753
South Dorset	05251	The Island	05161	Websterville	05678	Weybridge Hill	05753
South Duxbury	05660	Thetford	05074	Wells	05774	Wheelock	05851
South End	05739	Thetford (Town)	05074	Wells (Town)	05774	Wheelock (Town)	05851
Southern Vermont College	05201	Thetford Center	05075	Wells River	05081	White River Junction	05001
South Hero	05486	Thompsonburg	05148	West Addison	05491	Whitesville	05142
South Hero (Town)	05486	Thompson's Point	05445	West Arlington	05250	Whiting	05778
South Lincoln	05443	Tinmouth	05773	West Barnet	05821	Whiting (Town)	05778
South Londonderry	05155	Tinmouth (Town)	05773	West Berkshire	05450	Whitingham	05361
South Lunenburg	05906	Topsham	05076	West Bolton	05465	Whitingham (Town)	05361
South Newbury	05051	Topsham (Town)	05076	West Branch	05672	Wilder	05088
South Newfane	05351	Topsham Four Corners	05040	West Brattleboro	05301	Williamstown	05679
South Northfield	05663	Townshend	05353	West Bridgewater	05035	Williamstown (Town)	05679
South Peacham	05821	Townshend (Town)	05353	West Bridport	05734	Williamsville	05362
South Pomfret	05067	Trow Hill	05641	West Brookfield	05060	Williston (Town)	05495
South Poultney	05764	Troy	05868	West Burke	05871	Williston	05495
South Randolph	05041	Troy (Town)	05868	West Castleton	05743	Williston Road Section	
South Reading	05153	Tunbridge	05077	West Charleston	05872	(Part of South	
South Richford	05476	Tunbridge (Town)	05077	West Corinth	05039	Burlington)	05401
South Royalton	05068	Tyson	05149	West Cornwall	05753	Wilmington	05363
South Ryegate	05069	Una Bella	05201	West Danville	05873	Wilmington (Town)	05363
South Starksboro	05487	Underhill	05489	West Dover	05356	Windham	05359
South Strafford	05070	Underhill (Town)	05489	West Dummerston	05357	Windham (Town)	05359
South Tunbridge	05068	Underhill Center	05490	West Enosburg	05450	Windsor (Town)	05089
South Vershire	05079	Union Village	05043	West Fairlee	05083	Windsor	05089
South Walden	05843	University Mall (Part of		West Fairlee (Town)	05083	Winhall (Town)	05340
South Wallingford	05773	South Burlington)	05403	West Fairlee Center	05044	Winooski	05404
South Wardsboro	05355	University of Vermont		Westfield	05874	Winooski Park	05404
South Washington	05675	(Part of Burlington)	05405	Westfield (Town)	05874	Wolcott	05680
South Wheelock	05851	Upper Graniteville	05654	Westford	05494	Wolcott (Town)	05680
South Windham	05359	Vergennes	05491	Westford (Town)	05494	Woodbury	05681
South Woodbury	05681	Vernon	05354	West Georgia	05478	Woodbury (Town)	05681
South Woodstock	05071	Vernon (Town)	05354	West Glover	05875	Woodford	05201
Spoonerville	05143	Vershire	05079	West Groton	05046	Woodford (Town)	05201
Springfield	05156	Vershire (Town)	05079	West Halifax	05358	Woodford Hollow	05201
Springfield (Town)	05156	Vershire Center	05079	West Hartford	05084	Woodstock	05091
Stamford	05352	Vershire Heights	05079	West Haven	05743	Woodstock (Town)	05091
Stamford (Town)	05352	Victory (Town)	05858	West Haven (Town)	05743	Worcester	05682
Stannard	05842	Waitsfield	05673	West Hill	05450	Worcester (Town)	05682
Stannard (Town)	05842	Waitsfield (Town)	05673	West Lincoln	05443	Wrightsville (Part of	
Starksboro	05487	Waitsfield Common	05673	West Milton	05468	Montpelier)	05602
Starksboro (Town)	05487						

Place	ZIP
Aarons Creek	24598
Abbey Oaks	22180
Abbott	24127
Abilene	23923
Abingdon	24210-12
For specific Abingdon Zip Codes call (703) 628-1121, or your local postmaster.	
Accomac	23301
Accotink	22060
Accotink Heights	22003
Achilles	23001
Achsah	22727
Acorn	22469
Acredale (Part of Virginia Beach)	23464*
	23467†
Acree Acres	23692
Ada	22115
Addison Heights	22202
Aden	22123
Adial	22938
Adkins Store	23140
Adner	23149
Adria	24630
Adsit	23856
Advance Mills	22968
Adwolf	24354
Afton	22920
Agricola	24574
Aiken Summit	24054
Aily	24237
Air Mail Facility (Part of Norfolk)	23519
Airmont	22141
Ajax	24161
Alanthus	22714
Alanton (Part of Virginia Beach)	23450
Albemarle (Part of Norfolk)	23503
Alberene	22959
Alberta	23821
Albin	22603
Alcoma	23921
Aldie	22001
Alexander Corner (Part of Portsmouth)	23707
Alexandria	22301-32
For specific Alexandria Zip Codes call (703) 549-4201, or your local postmaster.	
Alfonso	22421
Algonquin Park (Part of Norfolk)	23505
Alhambra	22951
Alice Heights	23234
Alleghany	24426
Alleghany Spring	24162
Allen	24226
Allencrest	22207
Allens Creek	24553
Allenslevel	23936
Allentown	23301
Allison Gap	24370
Allisonia	24347
Allmondsville	23061
Allwood	24521
Alma	22851
Almagro (Part of Danville)	24541
Almira (Part of Pound)	24279
Alonzaville	22644
Alpha	23936
Alpine	22003
Alps	22514
Alsop	22553
Altavista	24517
Alto	24483
Alton	24520
Alum Ridge	24091
Alvarado	24211
Amburg	23043
Amelia Court House	23002
Amherst (Amherst County)	24521
Amherst (Fairfax County)	22015
Amissville	22002
Ammon	23822
Amonate	24601
Ampthill	23234
Ampthill Heights (Part of Richmond)	23234
Amsterdam	24175
Andersonville	23911
Andover	24215
Andrew Lewis Place	24153
Angola	23901
Ankum	23868
Annalee Heights	22042
Annandale	22003
Annandale Acres	22003
Annandale Gardens	22003
Annandale Terrace	22003
Annex	24401
Ante	23847
Antioch	24590
Appalachia	24216
Apple Blossom Mall (Part of Winchester)	22601
Apple Grove	23117
Appomattox	24522
Aqua	24435
Aquia Harbor	22554
Aragona Village (Part of Virginia Beach)	23455
Ararat	24053
Arbor Estates (Part of Suffolk)	23434
Arborhill	24401
Arcadia	24066
Arch Mills	24066
Arcola	22010
Arcturus	22308
Ardmore (Part of Fairfax)	22030
Argyle Heights	22405
Ark	23003
Arlington	22201-19
For specific Arlington Zip Codes call (703) 525-4838, or your local postmaster.	
Arlington (Part of Hopewell)	23860
Arlington Forest	22203
Arlington Hall	22212
Arlington Heights	22204
Arlington Village	22204
Arlingwood	22207
Armel	22602
Armistead Forest (Part of Portsmouth)	23703
Armstrong	24460
Armstrong Gardens (Part of Hampton)	23669
Aroda	22709
Arrington	22922
Arrowhead (Part of Virginia Beach)	23462
Arthur	24162
Artillery Ridge	22408
Artrip	22225
Arvonia	23004
Asberrys	24377
Ashburn	22011
Ashby	23040
Ashland	23005
Ashton Heights	22201
Ashville	22115
Ashwood	24445
Aspen	23959
Aspenwall	24528
Assawoman	23302
Atkins	24311
Atlantic (Accomack County)	23303
Atlantic (Part of Virginia Beach)	23458
Atlantic Park (Part of Virginia Beach)	23451
Atlee	23111
Atoka	22115
Attoway	24354
Auburn	22019
Augusta Correctional Center	24430
Augusta Springs	24411
Aurora Hills	22202
Austinville	24312
Avalon	22473
Avalon Terrace (Part of Virginia Beach)	23462
Averett	24580
Avon	22920
Avondale	23111
Avon Forest	22039
Axtel	24562
Axton	24054
Aylett	23009
Aylor	22727
Azalea Acres (Part of Norfolk)	23518
Azalea Court	23227
Azalea Gardens (Part of Hampton)	23669
Bachelors Hall	24541
Backbay (Part of Virginia Beach)	23457
Bacons Castle	23883
Bacons Fork	23950
Bacova	24412
Bacova Junction	24445
Baden	24228
Bagby	22514
Bagleys Mills	23970
Bailey	24605
Baileys Crossroads	22041
Balcony Falls (Part of Glasgow)	24555
Ballards Crossroads	23315
Ballentine Place (Part of Norfolk)	23509
Balls Hills	22101
Ballston	22203
Ballston Common	22203
Ballsville	23139
Baltimore Corner	23850
Balty	22546
Banco	22711
Bandy	24602
Bane	24134
Banner	24230
Banners Corner	24224
Barbours Creek	24127
Barboursville	22923
Barcroft	22204
Barfoot	24151
Barham	23881
Barhamsville	23011
Barley	23847
Barnesville	23964
Barnett	24266
Barnetts	23030
Barracks	22901
Barracks Road (Part of Charlottesville)	22903
Barren Ridge	24401
Barren Springs	24313
Barrett Acres (Part of Suffolk)	23434
Bartlett	23314
Bartlick	24256
Bartons Crossroad	24378
Bartonsville	22602
Barytes (Part of Bristol)	24201
Basham	24138
Basic (Part of Waynesboro)	22980
Baskerville	23915
Baskerville Correctional Unit	23915
Bassett	24055
Bassett Forks	24055
Bastian	24314
Basye	22810
Batesville	22924
Bath Alum	24460
Battersea (Part of Petersburg)	23803
Battery	22560
Battery Park (Henrico County)	23228
Battery Park (Isle of Wight County)	23304
Battle Beach	23851
Battle Creek	22851
Battlefield Green	22407
Battlefield Park (Part of Petersburg)	23805
Bavon	23138
Bayberry Estates	22485
Bay Colony (Part of Virginia Beach)	23451
Bayford	23354
Bay Island (Part of Virginia Beach)	23451
Bay Lake Beach (Part of Virginia Beach)	23455
Baylake Pines (Part of Virginia Beach)	23455
Baynesville	22520
Bayport	23079
Bayside (Accomack County)	23417
Bayside (Part of Virginia Beach)	23455
Bay View	23310
Bayville Park (Part of Virginia Beach)	23455
Baywood	24333
Beach	23838
Beach Grove	22967
Beaconsdale (Part of Newport News)	23607
Bealeton	22712
Beamamantown (Part of Big Stone Gap)	24219
Beamon (Part of Suffolk)	23434
Bear Wallow	24622
Beaufont Hills (Part of Richmond)	23225
Beaumont	23014
Beaverdam	23015
Beaverlett	23109
Beazley	22560
Beckham	24538
Bedford	24523
Bee	24217
Beech Fork	23974
Beech Springs	24263
Beechwood	23919
Beechwood Hills (Arlington County)	22207
Beechwood Hills (Campbell County)	24502
Beechwood Manor	23860
Bel Air	22042
Belaire (Part of Norfolk)	23518
Beldor	22827
Belfast Mills	24609
Bellair (Albemarle County)	22903
Bell Air (Stafford County)	22405
Bellamy (Gloucester County)	23017
Bellamy (Scott County)	24251
Bellamy Manor (Part of Virginia Beach)	23464
Bellbluff (railroad station)	23219
Bellbluff	23234
Belle Haven (Accomack County)	23306
Belle Haven (Fairfax County)	22307
Belle Haven (Part of Virginia Beach)	23452
Belle Meade (Fauquier County)	22642
Bellemeade (Part of Richmond)	23224
Belle Meadows (Part of Bristol)	24201
Belle View	22307
Belleville (Part of Suffolk)	23435
Bellevue (Part of Richmond)	23227
Bellevue Forest	22207
Bells Cross Road (Spotsylvania County)	22553
Bells Cross Roads (Louisa County)	23093
Bell Spur (Carroll County)	24120
Bell Spur (Patrick County)	24120
Bells Valley	24439
Bellwood	23234
Bellwood Manor	23234
Belmont (Loudoun County)	22011
Belmont (Prince William County)	22191
Belmont (Spotsylvania County)	22553
Belmont Acres	23234
Belmont Circle	23901
Belmont Farms (Part of Christiansburg)	24073
Belmont Park	22079
Belmont Place (Part of Norfolk)	23505
Belona	23139
Belspring	24058
Belvedere (Fairfax County)	22041
Belvedere (Part of Norfolk)	23504
Belvidere Beach	22405
Belvoir	22115
Bena	23018
Benhams	24202
Ben Hur	24218
Benmoreel (Part of Norfolk)	23505
Bennetts Creek (Part of Suffolk)	23435
Bennetts Harbor (Part of Suffolk)	23434
Bennett Springs	24153
Benns Church	23430
Bensley	23234
Bent Creek	24553
Bent Mountain	24059
Bentonville	22610
Bergton	22811
Berkeley	22901
Berkley (Part of Norfolk)	23523
Berkshire	22207
Berlin	23866
Berryville	22611
Berton	24134
Bestland	22454
Betana Park	22090
Bethany	24412
Bethel (Fauquier County)	22186
Bethel (Halifax County)	24589

* Area Zip Code   † Post Office Boxes

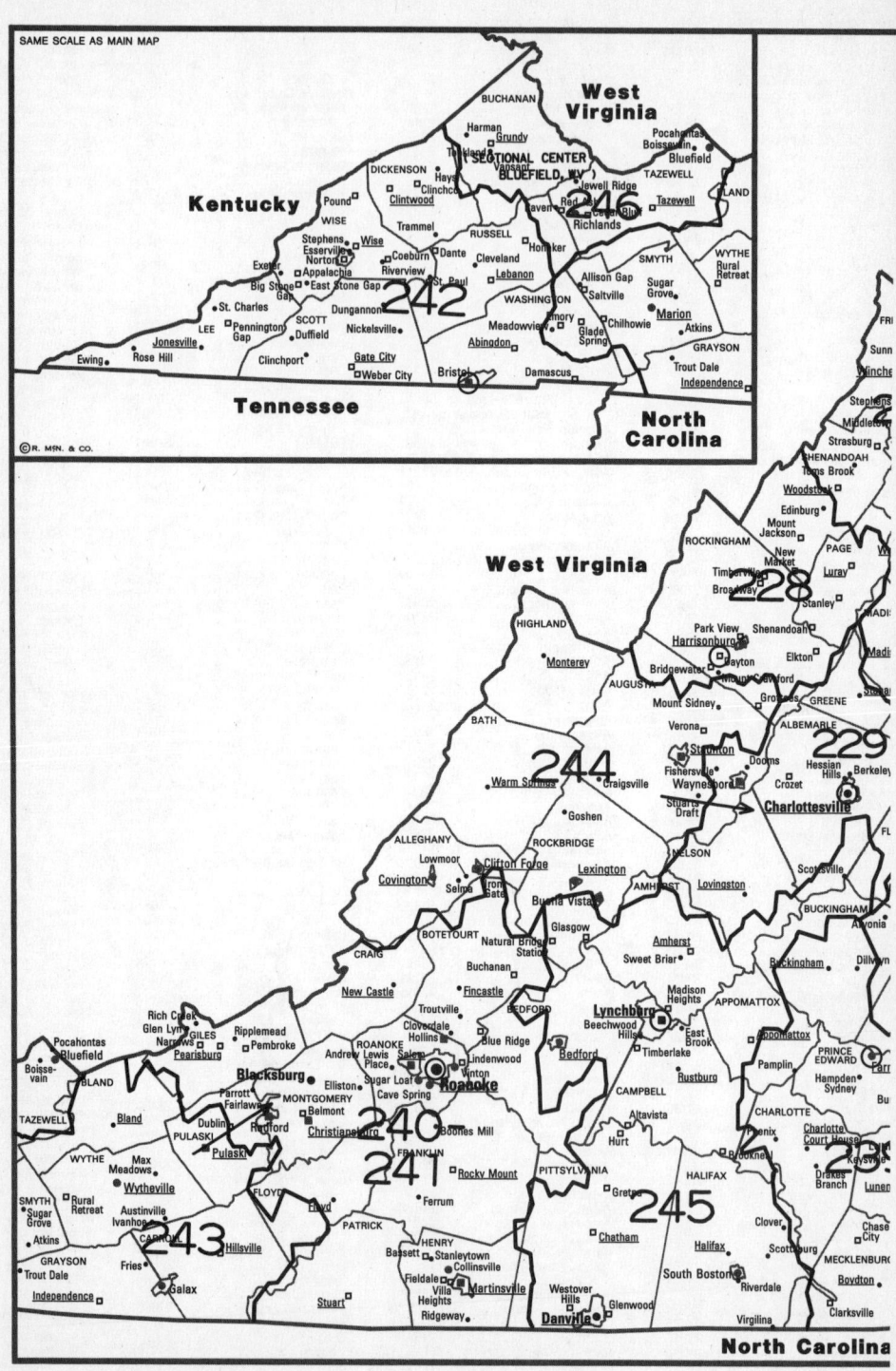

SAME SCALE AS MAIN MAP

BUCHANAN

West Virginia

Harman
Grundy

DICKENSON
Thlass
SECTIONAL CENTER
BLUEFIELD, WV
Vansant
Hays
Clinchco

Pocahontas
Boissevain
Bluefield

TAZEWELL

Kentucky

Pound
Clintwood

Jewell Ridge
Raven
Cedar Bluff
Richlands

246

Tazewell

LAND

WISE
Trammel

RUSSELL

WYTHE
Rural
Retreat

Stephens
Esserville
Norton
Appalachia
East Stone Gap

Wise
Coeburn
Riverview

Dante
Cleveland

Homaker

SMYTH

Exeter

St. Paul

Allison Gap
Saltville

Sugar
Grove

Big Stone
Gap

Dungannon

WASHINGTON

Marion
Atkins

St. Charles

LEE
Pennington
Gap

SCOTT
Duffield
Nickelsville

242

Lebanon

Meadowview
Emory
Glade
Spring

Chilhowie

GRAYSON

Jonesville

Clinchport

Gate City
Weber City

Abingdon

Damascus

Trout Dale
Independence

Ewing
Rose Hill

Bristol

Sunn

Winche

©R. M⁹N. & CO.

Tennessee

**North
Carolina**

Stephens
Middleto
Strasburg
SHENANDOAH
Toms Brook

FRI

Woodstock

Edinburg
Mount
Jackson

West Virginia

ROCKINGHAM

New
Market

Luray

PAGE

W

HIGHLAND

Timberville
Broadway

228

Stanley

MADI

Monterey

Park View
Harrisonburg

Shenandoah

Bridgewater
Dayton
Mt. Craw Crawford

Elkton

Madi

AUGUSTA

Mount Sidney

GREENE

BATH

Verona

Groatoba

244

Staunton

ALBEMARLE

Berkeley

Dooms

Hessian
Hills

229

Warm Springs

Fishersville
Waynesboro

Crozet

Stuarts
Draft

Charlottesville

Goshen

FL

ALLEGHANY

ROCKBRIDGE

NELSON

Scottsville

Lowmoor
Clifton Forge

Lexington

Lovingston

BUCKINGHAM

Covington
Selma
Iron
Gate

AMHERST

Alvonia

Buena Vista

Dillwyn

Glasgow

Amherst
Sweet Briar

Buckingham

BOTETOURT

Natural Bridge
Station

CRAIG

Buchanan

Madison
Heights

APPOMATTOX

New Castle

Fincastle

Troutville

BEDFORD

Lynchburg

Appomattox

Rich Creek
Glen Lyn
GILES
Narrows
Pembroke

Ripplemead

Cloverdale
Hollins

Blue Ridge

Beechwood
Hills

East
Brook

PRINCE
EDWARD

Parr

Pocahontas
Boissevain

Pearisburg

ROANOKE
Andrew Lewis
Place
Salem

Lindenwood

Bedford

Timberlake

Pamplin

Hampden
Sydney

BLAND

Blacksburg

Sugar Loaf
Cave Spring

Roanoke

Rustburg

CHARLOTTE

TAZEWELL

Bland

Parrott
Fairlawn
Elliston
MONTGOMERY
Belmont

CAMPBELL

Phenix

Charlotte
Court House

Dublin
Radford
Christiansburg

240

Boones Mill

Altavista

Brookneal

Max
Meadows

PULASKI

Hurt

Drakes
Branch

WYTHE

Pulaski

241

FRANKLIN

Rocky Mount

PITTSYLVANIA

HALIFAX

Lunen

Rural
Retreat

Wytheville

FLOYD

Ferrum

Greta

245

SMYTH
Sugar
Grove

Austinville
Ivanhoe

Floyd

PATRICK

HENRY

Chatham

Clover

Chase
City

Atkins

CARROLL

243

Hillsville

Bassett
Stanleytown
Collinsville

Halifax

Scottsburg

MECKLENBURG

GRAYSON
Trout Dale

Fries

Galax

Fieldale
Villa
Heights

Martinsville

Westover
Hills

South Boston

Riverdale

Boydton

Independence

Stuart

Ridgeway

Glenwood

Virgilina

Clarksville

Danville

North Carolina

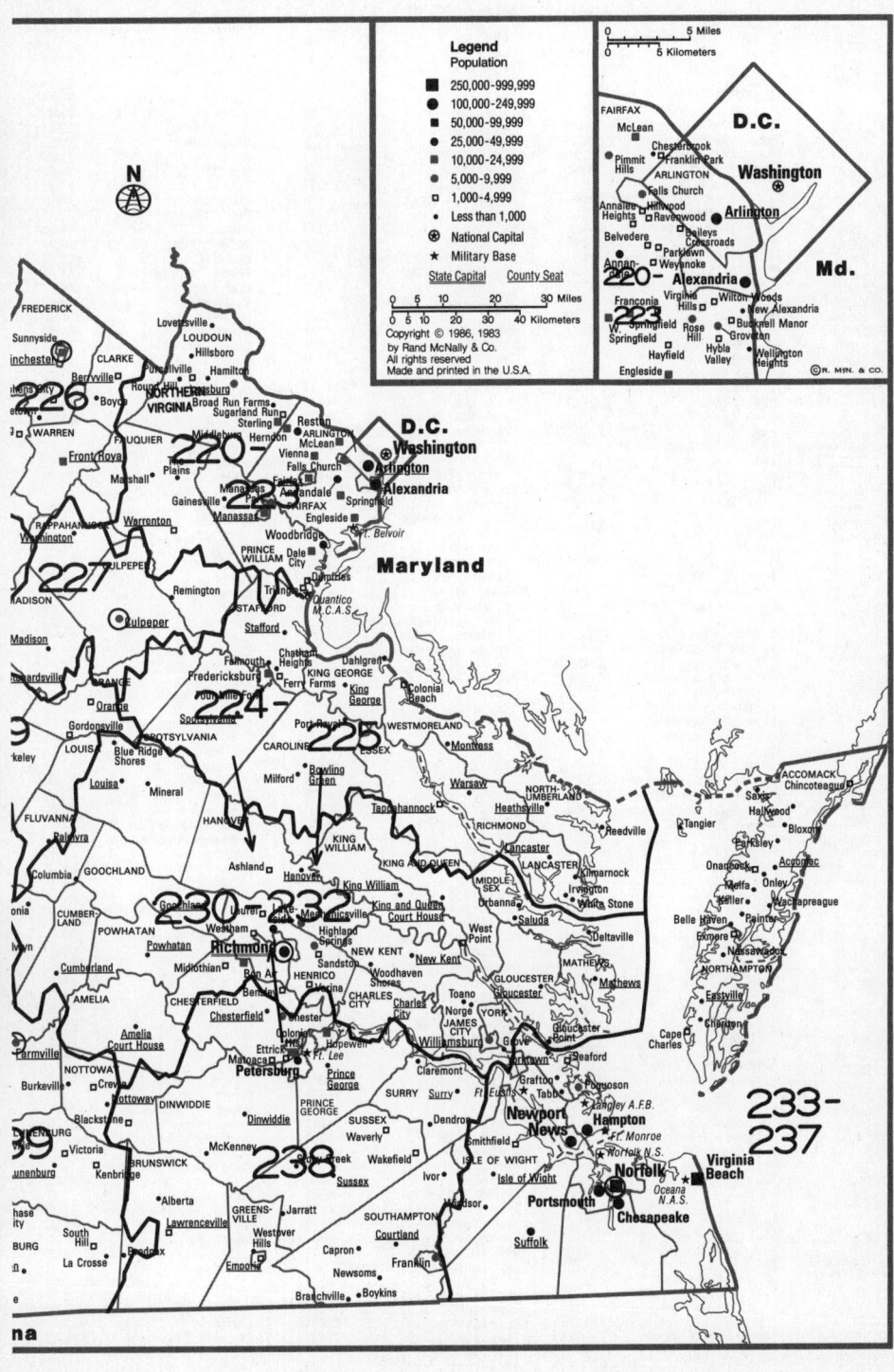

Legend
Population
- 250,000-999,999
- 100,000-249,999
- 50,000-99,999
- 25,000-49,999
- 10,000-24,999
- 5,000-9,999
- 1,000-4,999
- Less than 1,000
- ✪ National Capital
- ★ Military Base
- State Capital   County Seat

0 5 10   20   30 Miles
0 5 10 20   30   40 Kilometers

Copyright © 1986, 1983
by Rand McNally & Co.
All rights reserved
Made and printed in the U.S.A.

0   5 Miles
0   5 Kilometers

	ZIP		ZIP		ZIP		ZIP
Bethel (Prince William County)	22191	Bon Air (Chesterfield County)	23235-36	Broad Bay Colony (Part of Virginia Beach)	23451	Burkes Garden	24608
Bethel (Warren County)	22630	For specific Bon Air Zip Codes		Broad Creek (Part of Norfolk)	23502	Burkes Shop	22580
Bethel Manor (Part of Hampton)	23665	call (804) 272-2987, or your local postmaster.		Broadford	24316	Burketown	24486
Beulah Church	22560	Bonbrook	24065	Broad Meadows	23060	Burkeville	23922
Beulah Village	23234	Bondtown (Part of Coeburn)	24230	Broad Rock (Part of Richmond)	23224	Burks Garden (Part of Tazewell)	24651
Beulahville	23009	Bonny Blue	24282	Broad Run	22014	Burnam Woods	23168
Beverley Hills (Part of Alexandria)	22305	Bonsack	24012	Broad Run Farms	20165	Burnleys	22923
Beverly Forest	22150	Boones Mill	24065	Broadway	22815	Burnside Farms	23111
Beverly Heights (Part of Salem)	24153	Boonesville	22932	Brockroad	22553	Burnsville	24487
Beverly Hills	23229	Boonsboro	24503	Brodnax	23920	Burnt Chimney	24184
Beverly Manor	22101	Bordeaux	22090	Brokenburg	22553	Burnt Store	23950
Beverlyville	22539	Boston (Accomack County)	23420	Broken Hill	22065	Burnt Tree	22960
Big Bethel (Part of Hampton)	23666	Boston (Culpeper County)	22713	Brookbury (Part of Richmond)	23234	Burr Hill	22433
Big Fork	23970	Boston (Part of Suffolk)	23434	Brooke	22430	Burrowsville	23842
Big Island	24526	Boswells Tavern	22942	Brookeshire	23181	Burson Place	24202
Big Laurel	24293	Botetourt Correctional Unit	24175	Brookfield (Fairfax County)	22021	Burton (Part of Virginia Beach)	23455
Big River	24439	Botha	22186	Brookfield (Stafford County)	22405	Burtons Shop	24651
Big Rock	24603	Bottoms Bridge	23150	Brookfield Park (Part of Norfolk)	23503	Bush Hill	22310
Big Spring	22650	Boudar Gardens	23228	Brookhaven	22101	Bush Hill Woods	22310
Big Stone Gap	24219	Boulevard Estates	22031	Brook Hill	23227	Bush Mill	24271
Big Vein	24635	Bowers Corner	23893	Brookland Estates	22310	Busthead	24609
Biltmore	23060	Bowers Hill (Part of Chesapeake)	23321	Brookland Gardens	23228	Bustleburg	24450
Binns Hall	23030	Bowlers Wharf	22560	Brooklyn	22594	Butterworth	23840
Birch	24592	Bowling	24263	Brookneal	24528	Butts Corner	22039
Birchett Estate	23875	Bowling Green	22427	Brook Vale	22503	Butylo	22504
Birchland Park	24592	Bowling Park (Part of Norfolk)	23504	Brookville (Part of Alexandria)	22304	Bybee	22963
Birchleaf	24220	Bowmans Crossing	22824	Brookwood (Part of Virginia Beach)	23452	Byllesby	24350
Birch Town	23336	Boxley Hills	24012	Brookwood Manor	23141	Bynum Store	23924
Birchwood Park	23185	Boxwood	24054	Brosville	24541	Byrdton	22482
Birdneck Acres (Part of Virginia Beach)	23451	Boyce	22620	Brown Field (Part of Quantico)	22134	Cabin Point	23881
Birdsnest	23307	Boyd Tavern	22947	Brown Grove	23005	Cadet (Part of Big Stone Gap)	24219
Birmingham	24609	Boydton	23917	Brownsburg	24415	Cady	23069
Biscoe	23148	Boykins	23827	Browns Corner	23141	Caira	23040
Bishop	24604	Boys Home	24426	Browns Cove	22932	Caledonia	23038
Bishops Corner	23938	Bracey	23919	Browns Store	22473	Callaghan	24426
Blackberry	24055	Braddock (Part of Alexandria)	22302	Brown Town (Amherst County)	24521	Callands	24530
Black Branch	23924	Braddock Heights (Part of Alexandria)	22302	Browntown (Warren County)	22610	Callao	22435
Black Creek	23851	Braddock Hills	22003	Broyhill Crest	22003	Callaville	23856
Blackford	24260	Bradford Acres (Part of Virginia Beach)	23455	Broyhill Forest	22207	Callaway	24067
Blacklick	24368	Bradley Acres	23150	Broyhill Park	22042	Callison	24445
Blackridge	23950	Bradley Forest	22110	Brucetown	22622	Calno	23069
Blacksburg (Montgomery County)	24060-63	Bradshaw	24087	Bruington	23023	Calvary	22664
For specific Blacksburg Zip Codes call (703) 552-2751, or your local postmaster.		Brambleton (Part of Norfolk)	23504	Brumley Gap	24210	Calverton	22016
Blacksburg (Rockbridge County)	24416	Branchville	23828	Bruno	24258	Cambria (Part of Christiansburg)	24073
Blacksburg (Washington County)	24340	Brand	24401	Brunswick	23868	Cambridge	23235
Blackstone	23824	Brandon	23881	Brush Tavern	24502	Camden Heights (Part of Norfolk)	23502
Blackwater (Lee County)	24221	Brandon Heights (Part of Newport News)	23601	Bryan Park	23228	Camellia Shores (Part of Norfolk)	23518
Blackwater (Part of Virginia Beach)	23457	Brandon Place (Part of Norfolk)	23513	Bryan Parkway	23228	Camelot	22003
Blackwater Bridge (Part of Virginia Beach)	23457	Brandons Store	23824	Bryant	22967	Cameron (Part of Alexandria)	22304
Blackwells Chapel	24361	Brandon Village	22203	Bryants Corner	23847	Cameron Station (Part of Alexandria)	22304
Blackwood	24273	Brandy Creek Estates	23111	Bryn Mawr	22101	Cameron Valley (Part of Alexandria)	22314
Blainville	22835	Brandy Station	22714	Buchanan	24066	Camp	24375
Blairs	24527	Brattons Bridge	24460	Buckhall	22110	Camp Barrett	22134
Blakes	23035	Brays	22560	Buckingham (Arlington County)	22203	Campbell	22947
Bland	24315	Brayshore Park	23072	Buckingham (Buckingham County)	23921	Camp Creek	24091
Bland Correctional Center	24315	Breaks	24607	Buckingham (Chesterfield County)	23112	Campostella Heights (Part of Norfolk)	23523
Blandford (Part of Petersburg)	23803	Brecon Ridge	22030	Buckingham Circle	22903	Camps Mill (Part of Suffolk)	23434
Blanks Store	23030	Bremo Bluff	23022	Buckland	22065	Camptown	24528
Blanks Tavern	23030	Bren Mar Park	22312	Bucknell Heights	22307	Cana	24317
Bleak	22728	Brentsville	22013	Bucknell Manor	22307	Candlewax	24260
Blevinstown	22030	Brentwood	23234	Buckner	23024	Cannady	24656
Bloomfield	22012	Brentwood Forest (Part of Norfolk)	23518	Buckroe Beach (Part of Hampton)	23664	Canova	22110
Bloomingdale	23228	Briarcliff (Part of Vinton)	24179	Buckton	22657	Canterburg	22655
Blowing Rock	24228	Briarwood (Part of Bristol)	24201	Buena	22733	Canterbury	23229
Bloxom	23308	Briarwood (Part of Portsmouth)	23703	Buena Vista	24416	Canterbury Hills	22901
Bluefield	24605	Bridgetown	23405	Buffalo Forge	24555	Canterbury Woods	22003
Blue Grass	24413	Bridgewater	22812	Buffalo Gap	24479	Canton	24221
Bluemont	22012	Bridle Creek	24348	Buffalo Hill	24521	Capahosic	23061
Blue Mountain	22630	Briery	23947	Buffalo Hills	22044	Cape Charles	23310
Blue Ridge	24064	Briery Branch	22821	Buffalo Junction	24529	Cape Henry (Part of Virginia Beach)	23454
Blue Ridge Mountain Estates	22630	Briggs	22611	Buffalo Ridge	24171	Cape Henry Shores (Part of Virginia Beach)	23451
Blue Ridge Shores	23093	Brights	24557	Buffalo Springs	24529	Cape Story by the Sea (Part of Virginia Beach)	23451
Bluestone	23927	Brightwood	22715	Bufford Cross Roads	23847	Capeville	23313
Blundon Corner	22456	Brilyn Park	22046	Bull Run	22110	Capitol (Part of Richmond)	23201-19
Bocock	24501	Brink	23847	Bull Run Mountain Estates	22069	For specific Capitol Zip Codes call (804) 783-0825, or your local postmaster.	
Body Camp	24523	Bristol	24201-03	Bumpass	23024		
Bohannon	23021	For specific Bristol Zip Codes call (615) 968-2355, or your local postmaster.		Bundy	24265	Capon Road	22657
Boiling Spring	24426	Bristol Mall (Part of Bristol)	24201	Bunker Hill	24523	Capron	23829
Boissevain	24606	Bristow (Fairfax County)	22003	Burdette	23851	Captain's Cove	23356
Bolar	24484	Bristow (Prince William County)	22013	Burgess	22432	Carbo	24225
Bolsters Store	23882	Britain	22080	Burgundy Village	22303	Cardinal	23025
Bolton	24266	Britton Hills Farms	23230	Burke	22009†	Cardinal Forest	22152
Bon Air (Arlington County)	22205	Brittonwood	23234	Burke Heights	22015*	Cardova	22701
				Burke Hills	22015	Cardwell	23039

* Area Zip Code † Post Office Boxes

	ZIP
Cardwell Town	24370
Caret	22436
Carfax	24230
Carloover	24445
Carolanne Farms (Part of Virginia Beach)	23462
Caroline Correctional Unit	23069
Caroline Pines	22546
Carriage Hill (Fairfax County)	22181
Carriage Hill (Part of Virginia Beach)	23452
Carrie	24225
Carrollton	23314
Carrsbrook	22901
Carrsville	23315
Carsley	23890
Carson	23830
Carsonville	24348
Carters Mills	24053
Cartersville	23027
Carterton	24266
Carver Court (Part of Hampton)	23669
Carver Gardens	23185
Carysbrook	23055
Casanova	22017
Cascade	24069
Cash	23061
Cash Corner	22942
Cashville	23417
Caskie	24553
Castle Craig	24550
Castle Heights	23917
Castleton	22716
Castlewood	24224
Catalpa	22701
Catawba (Halifax County)	24577
Catawba (Roanoke County)	24070
Catharpin	22018
Catherton (Part of Manassas)	22110
Catlett	22019
Cats Bridge	23420
Cauthornville	23029
Cavalcade	22003
Cavalier Park (Part of Virginia Beach)	23451
Cave Mountain	24579
Cave Spring	24018
Cavetown	22835
Caylor	24248
Cedar Bluff (Tazewell County)	24609
Cedar Bluff (Washington County)	24236
Cedar Branch (Part of Saltville)	24370
Cedar Forest	24569
Cedar Fork	22546
Cedar Green	24401
Cedar Grove (Halifax County)	24520
Cedar Grove (Mecklenburg County)	23970
Cedar Grove (Northampton County)	23310
Cedar Grove Acres (Part of Chesapeake)	23320
Cedarhill	24565
Cedar Lawn	23231
Cedar Level (Part of Hopewell)	23860
Cedar Point	23063
Cedar Springs	24368
Cedarville (Warren County)	22630
Cedarville (Washington County)	24361
Cedon	22580
Celt	22973
Centenary	24590
Center Cross	22437
Center Star	23841
Centerville (Accomack County)	23412
Centerville (Augusta County)	22812
Centerville (Bedford County)	24523
Centerville (Goochland County)	23103
Centerville (Halifax County)	24592
Centerville (James City County)	23188
Centerville (Louisa County)	23117

	ZIP
Central (Part of Richmond)	23241
Central Facility	22079
Central Garage	23086
Central Gardens	23223
Central Hill	23487
Centralia	23831
Centralia Gardens	23234
Central Martinsville (Part of Martinsville)	24112
Central Plains	22963
Central Point	22514
Central State Hospital	23803
Centre Heights	22020
Centreville	22020
Centreville Farms	22020
Ceres	24318
Chadswyck (Part of Chesapeake)	23321
Chalet Woods	22020
Chalk Level	24557
Chamberlain Village	22134
Chamberlayne	23227
Chamberlayne Farms	23227
Chamberlayne Heights	23227
Chamberlayne North	23227
Chamblissburg	24179
Champlain	22438
Chance	22439
Chancellor	22407
Chancellors Green	22407
Chancellorsville	22553
Chaneys	24565
Chantilly	22021*
	22022†
Chantilly Estates	22021
Chapel	24124
Chapel Acres	22153
Chapel Hill (Part of Alexandria)	22302
Chapel Park (Part of Newport News)	23606
Chapel Square	22003
Charity	24185
Charlemont	24526
Charles City	23030
Charlie Hope	23920
Charlotte Court House	23923
Charlottesville	22901-06
For specific Charlottesville Zip Codes call (804) 286-2282, or your local postmaster.	
Chase City	23924
Chatham	24531
Chatham Correctional Unit	24531
Chatham Heights	24405
Chatham Hill	24370
Chatmoss	24112
Chatmoss-Laurel Park	24112
Cheapside	23310
Check	24072
Cheriton	23316
Cherokee Heights (Part of Norfolk)	23518
Cherry Acres (Part of Hampton)	23669
Cherrydale	22207
Cherry Hill (Charles City County)	23030
Cherry Hill (Dinwiddie County)	23872
Cherry Hill (Prince William County)	22026
Chesapeake (Independent City)	23320-28
For specific Chesapeake Zip Codes call (804) 547-2144, or your local postmaster.	
Chesapeake (Northampton County)	23310
Chesapeake Beach (Northumberland County)	22539
Chesapeake Beach (Part of Virginia Beach)	23455
Chesapeake Heights (Part of Hampton)	23664
Chesapeake Manor (Part of Norfolk)	23513
Chesapeake Square (Part of Chesapeake)	23321
Chesconessex	23417
Chesdin Manor	23885
Chesopeian Colony (Part of Virginia Beach)	23452
Chesswood	23234
Chester	23831
Chesterbrook	22101
Chesterbrook Gardens	22101
Chesterbrook Woods	22101

	ZIP
Chester Estates (Part of Bristol)	24201
Chesterfield	23832
	23838
For specific Chesterfield Zip Codes call (804) 748-6031, or your local postmaster.	
Chesterfield Heights (Part of Norfolk)	23504
Chesterfield Work Release	23832
Chester Gap	22623
Chestnut Hill (Fairfax County)	22003
Chestnut Hill (King George County)	22485
Chestnut Knob	24112
Chestnut Level	24527
Chestnut Yard	24381
Chevalle	22110
Chewings Corner	22534
Chickahominy Haven	23089
Chickahominy Shores	23089
Childress	24073
Childry	24577
Chilesburg	22546
Chilhowie	24319
Chiltons	22520
Chimney Run	24484
Chincoteague	23336-37
For specific Chincoteague Zip Codes call (804) 336-6400, or your local postmaster.	
Chinquapin Village (Part of Alexandria)	22302
Chisford	22520
Christchurch	23031
Christensons Corner	23188
Christians	24479
Christiansburg	24068†
	24073*
Christie	24598
Chuckatuck (Part of Suffolk)	23432
Chula	23002
Church Hill (Part of Richmond)	23223
Churchill	22043
Churchland (Part of Portsmouth)	23703
Church Road	23833
Church View	23032
Churchville	24421
Cifax	24556
Circlewoods	22031
Cismont	22947
Civic Center (Part of Richmond)	23240
Clam	23308
Clancie	23156
Claraville	22473
Claremont (Arlington County)	22206
Claremont (Surry County)	23899
Clarendon	22201
Claresville	23847
Clarkes Gap	22075
Clarksville (Mecklenburg County)	23927
Clarksville (Washington County)	24340
Clarkton	24577
Clary	22657
Claudville	24076
Clay Bank	23061
Claypool Hill	24609
Clays Mill	24589
Clayville	23139
Clear Brook (Frederick County)	22624
Clearbrook (Roanoke County)	24014
Clearfield	22151
Clearfork	24314
Clearview Manor	22101
Clearwater Park	24426
Clell	24631
Clermont Woods	22310
Cleveland	24225
Cliffield	24637
Clifford	24533
Cliffview	24333
Clifton (Fairfax County)	22024
Clifton (Orange County)	22733
Cliftondale	24422
Clifton Forge	24422
Climax	24531
Clinchburg	24361
Clinchco	24226
Clinchport	24244
Clintwood	24228

	ZIP
Clito	24330
Clover (Part of Alexandria)	22314
Clover (Halifax County)	24534
Cloverdale (Botetourt County)	24077
Cloverdale (Fluvanna County)	23022
Clover Hill	22821
Club Court	23227
Cluster Springs	24535
Coalcreek	24333
Coaldan	24641
Coal Kiln	23420
Coal Mine	22657
Coan Stage	22473
Cobbdale (Part of Fairfax)	22030
Cobbs Creek	23035
Cobham	22929
Cobham Park	22572
Cobham Wharf	23883
Cochran	23821
Cody	24577
Coeburn	24230
Coffee	24551
Cohasset	23055
Cohoke	23181
Coke	23072
Colchester	22079
Cold Harbor Farms	23111
Cold Springs Correctional Unit	24440
Coldwater	23108
Coleman Falls	24536
Coleman Place (Part of Norfolk)	23504
Coles Creek	24151
Coles Point	22442
Coliseum Mall (Part of Hampton)	23666
Colleen	22922
College (Part of Fredericksburg)	22401*
	22404†
College Park (Part of Alexandria)	22314
College Park (Part of Staunton)	24401
College Park (Part of Suffolk)	23703
Colley	24220
Collierstown	24450
Collingwood	22308
Collins Crossing	22580
Collinsville	24078
Collinwood	24266
Cologne	23037
Colonial Beach	22443
Colonial Forest	23111
Colonial Heights (Independent City)	23834
Colonial Heights (Part of Hampton)	23664
Colonial Heights (Part of Norfolk)	23518
Colonial Heights (Washington County)	24202
Colonial Place (Part of Norfolk)	23508
Colonial Village	22201
Colonial Williamsburg (Part of Williamsburg)	23185
Colosse	23315
Colthurst	22901
Coltons Mill	24523
Columbia	23038
Columbia Forest	22204
Columbia Furnace	22824
Columbia Heights	22204
Columbia Park (Part of Hopewell)	23860
Columbia Pines	22003
Colvin Run	22066
Comans Well	23897
Comers Rock	24326
Comet	23430
Commodore Park (Part of Norfolk)	23503
Commonwealth	22901
Commonwealth Acres	23875
Community	22306
Comorn	22405
Compton	22650
Conaway	24603
Concord (Brunswick County)	23876
Concord (Campbell County)	24538
Concord Heights	22401
Conde	22115
Confederate Heights	23222

	ZIP		ZIP		ZIP		ZIP
Conicville	22842	Crouch	22437	Del Ray (Part of		Dugspur	24325
Conners Grove	24380	Crows	24426	Alexandria)	22301	Dugwell	24151
Conners Valley	24324	Crozet	22932	Delta (Part of Alexandria)	22304	Duke Gardens (Part of	
Contra	22437	Crozier	23039	Deltaville	23043	Alexandria)	22304
Cookstown	22553	Crymes Store	23974	Delton	24324	Dumbarton	23228
Coolwell	24521	Crystal City	22202	Denaro	23002	Dumfries	22026
Cooper	23092	Crystal Hill	24539	Denbigh (Part of Newport		Dunavant	22401
Cootes Store	22815	Crystal Spring Knolls	22207	News)	23602	Dunbar	24216
Copper Hill	24079	Cuckoo	23117	Denby Park (Part of		Dunbar Gardens (Part of	
Copper Valley	24141	Cullen	23934	Norfolk)	23505	Hampton)	23666
Corbin	22446	Culmore	22041	Dendron	23839	Dunbrooke	22560
Corinth	23866	Culpeper	22701	Denmark	24450	Duncan Gap	24293
Corn Valley	24260	Cumberland	23040	Denniston	24520	Duncans Mills	22435
Cornwall	24416	Cummings Heights	24210	Dentons Corner	23921	Duncanville	24210
Coronado (Part of Norfolk)	23513	Cumnor	23085	Derby	24216	Dundalow (Part of Suffolk)	23434
Cottage Heights (Part of		Cunningham	22963	Desha	22560	Dundas	23938
Norfolk)	23504	Curdsville	23936	Detrick	22652	Dunford Town	24602
Cottage Park (Part of		Currioman Landing	22520	Devon Manor (Part of		Dungadin Heights	22630
Norfolk)	23503	Currituck Farms	23150	Norfolk)	23503	Dungannon	24245
Cottage Road Park (Part		Cuscowilla	23917	Devonshire Gardens	22042	Dunlop (Part of Colonial	
of Norfolk)	23505	Customhouse (Part of		Dewey	24279	Heights)	23834
Coulson	24381	Norfolk)	23514	DeWitt	23840	Dunn Loring	22027
Coulwood	24260	Cypress Chapel (Part of		Dewitt Hospital	22060	Dunn Loring Woods	22180
Council	24260	Suffolk)	23434	Diamond Springs (Part of		Dunnsville	22454
Countis Corner	24202	Cypress Manor	23851	Virginia Beach)	23455	Durrett Town	22920
Country Club Hills		Cypress Point (James		Diascund	23089	Dutton	23050
(Arlington County)	22207	City County)	23089	Dickensdale	23230	Duty	24217
Country Club Hills (Part of		Cypress Point (Surry		Dickensonville	24224	Dwale	24228
Fairfax)	22030	County)	23899	Diggs	23045	Dwina	24230
Country Club Manor	22207	Dabney Estates	23885	Diggs Park (Part of		Dye	24649
Country Club View	22032	Dabneys	23102	Norfolk)	23523	Dyers Store	24112
Country Creek	22181	Dahlgren	22448	Dillard's Landing	23140	Dyke	22935
Countryside	20165	Dahlia	27866	Dillwyn	23936	Eads	22202
Counts	24237	Dalbys	23310	Dinwiddie	23841	Eagle Rock	24085
County Line Cross Roads	23923	Dale City	22193	Dinwiddie Correctional		Earlhurst	24426
Court House	22216	Dalecrest (Part of		Unit	23833	Earls	23002
Courtland	23837	Alexandria)	22304	Dinwiddie Gardens	23803	Earlysville	22936
Courtland Park	22041	Dale Enterprise	22801	Disputanta	23842	East Aberdeen Gardens	
Courtney	23060	Daleville	24083	Ditchley	22482	(Part of Hampton)	23666
Cove Colony	22503	Damascus	24236	Dixie (Fluvanna County)	23055	East Brook	24501
Cove Creek (Bland		Dam Neck (Part of		Dixie (Mathews County)	23050	East End (Part of	
County)	24314	Virginia Beach)	23461	Dixie Hill	22030	Richmond)	23223
Cove Creek (Tazewell		Dam Neck Corner (Part of		Dockery	23970	Eastern Park (Part of	
County)	24651	Virginia Beach)	23454	Doe Hill	24433	Virginia Beach)	23452
Covesville	22931	Danbury Forest	22151	Dogtown	23063	Eastern State Hospital	23185
Covingston Corner	23047	Dandy	23694	Dogue	22451	East Falls Church	22205
Covington	24426	Daniel	22960	Dogue Creek Village	22060	Eastham	22901
Cox's Chapel	24363	Daniel Boone	24251	Dogwood Hill (Part of		East Hampton (Part of	
Crab Orchard	24230	Danieltown	23821	Staunton)	24401	Hampton)	23669
Crackers Neck (Scott		Danripple	24592	Dogwood Knoll	23111	East Highland Park	23222
County)	24271	Dante	24237	Dolphin	23843	East Hilton (Part of	
Crackers Neck (Wise		Danville	24540-43	Donna Lee Gardens	22046	Newport News)	23607
County)	24219	For specific Danville Zip Codes		Dooms	22980	East Lexington	24450
Craddockville	23341	call (804) 792-2246, or your		Doran	24612	Eastmoreland	23231
Cradock (Part of		local postmaster.		Dorchester (Part of		East Norton (Part of	
Portsmouth)	23702	Dare	23692	Richmond)	23234	Norton)	24273
Craigs Mills	24202	Darlington Heights	23935	Dorchester (Wise County)	24273	East Norview (Part of	
Craig Springs	24127	Darnell Town	24265	Dorchester Junction	24273	Norfolk)	23513
Craigsville	24430	Darvills	23824	Dorset Woods	23075	East Ocean View (Part of	
Crandon	24315	Darwin	24228	Doswell	23047	Norfolk)	23503
Cranes Nest	24230	Daugherty	23301	Dot	24277	Easton Place (Part of	
Craney Island Estates	23111	Davenport	24239	Double Tollgate	22663	Norfolk)	23502
Creeds (Part of Virginia		Davis	24472	Douglas Park (Part of		Eastover (Part of Suffolk)	23434
Beach)	23457	Davis Corner (Part of		Portsmouth)	23701	Eastover Gardens	23231
Crescent Hill (Part of		Virginia Beach)	23462	Douglass Park	22204	East Point (Accomack	
Hopewell)	23860	Davis Wharf	23345	Doveville	22032	County)	23417
Crescent Hills	22207	Dawley Corner (Part of		Dowden Terrace	22311	East Point (Rockingham	
Cresthill	22639	Virginia Beach)	23457	Downings	22460	County)	22827
Crestview (Henrico		Dawn	23047	Downtown (Part of		East Radford (Part of	
County)	23226	Dayton	22821	Blacksburg)	24063	Radford)	24141
Crestview (Prince Edward		Deans (Part of Suffolk)	23435	Downtown (Part of		East Stone Gap	24246
County)	23901	Deatonville	23083	Charlottesville)	22902	East Suffolk Gardens	
Crestwood Manor	22003	De Bree (Part of Norfolk)	23517	Downtown (Part of		(Part of Suffolk)	23434
Crewe	23930	De Busk Mill	24340	Leesburg)	22075	Eastville	23347
Criders	22820	Deel	24656	Downtown (Part of		Eastville Station (Part of	
Criglersville	22727	Deep Bottom	23075	Lynchburg)	24505	Eastville)	23347
Crimora	24431	Deep Creek (Accomack		Downtown (Part of		Ebenezer	24565
Cripple Creek	24322	County)	23417	Manassas)	22110	Ebony	23845
Crittenden (Part of		Deep Creek (Part of		Downtown (Part of		Eclipse (Part of Suffolk)	23433
Suffolk)	23433	Chesapeake)	23323	Roanoke)	24001	Edge	24554
Critz	24082	Deep Creek (Part of		Doylesville	22932	Edgehill (King George	
Croaker	23188	Newport News)	23606	Drakes Branch	23937	County)	22485
Croatan Beach (Part of		Deep Hole	23336	Dranesville	22070	Edgehill (Southampton	
Virginia Beach)	23451	Deerborne (Part of		Draper	24324	County)	23851
Crockett	24323	Richmond)	23234	Drewryville	23844	Edgehill Park	23803
Crockett Springs	24162	Deerfield	24432	Drill	24260	Edgemont (Part of	
Crofton	24179	Deerfield Correctional		Driver (Part of Suffolk)	23435	Covington)	24426
Cromwell (Part of Norfolk)	23509	Center	23829	Drouin Hill	23075	Edgemont Park	24210
Crooked Oak	24343	Deerfield Estates	23832	Drum Bay	22469	Edgerton	23868
Crossbrook	24215	Deer Park (Part of		Dry Branch	24132	Edgewater (Part of	
Crosses Corner	23069	Manassas)	22110	Dryburg	24589	Norfolk)	23508
Cross Junction	22625	Deer Park Groove (Part of		Dryden	24243	Edgewood (Part of	
Crosskeys	22841	Newport News)	23607	Dry Fork (Pittsylvania		Petersburg)	23805
Crossroads (Albemarle		Deerrock	22938	County)	24549	Edinburg	22824
County)	22959	Defense General Supply		Dry Fork (Wise County)	24230	Ednam Forest	22901
Crossroads (Halifax		Center	23297	Drytown	24630	Edom	22834
County)	24577	De Jarnett	22514	Duane	23009	Edsall Park	22151
Crossroads Mall (Part of		Delaplane	22025	Dublin	24084	Edwards Shop	22718
Roanoke)	24012	Delaware	23851	Dudley	24558	Edwardsville	22456
Crosswinds	22153	Delmar	24236	Duffield	24244	Effinger	24450

	ZIP
Eggleston	24086
Eheart	22923
Elam	23960
Elberon	23846
Elephant Fork (Part of Suffolk)	23434
Elevon	22438
Elizabeth Park (Part of Norfolk)	23502
Elizabeth River Shores (Part of Virginia Beach)	23464
Elizabeth River Terrace (Part of Virginia Beach)	23464
Elk Creek	24326
Elk Garden	24266
Elk Hill	23063
Elko	23150
Elkrun	22728
Elkton	22827
Elkwood	22718
Ellett	24073
Elliston	24087
Elliston-Lafayette	24087
Ellisville	23093
Ellsworth (Part of Norfolk)	23505
Elma	22971
Elmhurst (Part of Norfolk)	23513
Elmo	24592
Elmont	23005
Elmwood Estates	22101
El-Nido	22101
Elon	24572
Elsom	23181
Eltham	23181
Elysian Woods	22192
Emmerton	22572
Emory	24327
Emory-Meadow View	24327
Emporia	23847
Endicott	24088
Enfield	23106
Engleside	22309
English Hills	23228
Enonville	23936
Eppes Fork	27584
Erica	22520
Esmont	22937
Esnon	23924
Esserville	24273
Estabrook (Part of Norfolk)	23509
Estabrook Park (Part of Norfolk)	23513
Estaline	24430
Estes	22716
Ethel	22572
Ethridge Estates	23805
Etlan	22719
Ettrick	23803
Euclid (Part of Virginia Beach)	23462
Euclid Place (Part of Virginia Beach)	23462
Euclid Terrace (Part of Virginia Beach)	23462
Eureka	23947
Eureka Park (Part of Virginia Beach)	23452
Eustaces Corner	22728
Euwanee Park (Part of Norfolk)	23503
Everets (Part of Suffolk)	23434
Evergreen	23939
Evergreen Hills	24202
Evergreen Shores	23696
Evington	24550
Ewell	23185
Ewing	24248
Exeter	24216
Exmore	23350
Faber	22938
Fagg	24073
Fairchester (Part of Fairfax)	22030
Fair City Mall (Part of Fairfax)	22031
Fairfax	22030-39
For specific Fairfax Zip Codes call (703) 273-5571, or your local postmaster.	
Fairfax Acres	22030
Fairfax Circle (Part of Fairfax)	22031
Fairfax Forest	22031
Fairfax Station	22039
Fairfax Villa	22030
Fairfax Woods (Part of Fairfax)	22030
Fairfield (Essex County)	22454

	ZIP
Fairfield (Rockbridge County)	24435
Fairhaven	22303
Fair Hill	22031
Fairland	22312
Fairlawn (Part of Covington)	24426
Fairlawn (Pulaski County)	24141
Fairlawn Estates (Part of Norfolk)	23502
Fairlawn Heights	23075
Fairlee	22031
Fair Meadows (Part of Virginia Beach)	23462
Fair Meadows Estates (Part of Virginia Beach)	23462
Fairmont Manor (Part of Norfolk)	23509
Fairmount Park (Part of Norfolk)	23509
Fair Oaks (Part of Fairfax)	22032
Fair Oaks (Henrico County)	23075
Fair Port	22539
Fairview (Fairfax County)	22306
Fairview (Part of Fairfax)	22031
Fairview (Mecklenburg County)	23924
Fairview (Montgomery County)	24149
Fairview (Northampton County)	23310
Fairview (Page County)	22835
Fairview (Scott County)	24244
Fairview Beach	22405
Fairview Heights (Part of Clifton Forge)	24422
Fairview Heights (Part of Lexington)	24450
Fairwood	24378
Fairwood Acres	22039
Falconbridge	23234
Falconerville	24521
Falling Creek	23234
Falling Spring	24445
Falls Church	22040-46
For specific Falls Church Zip Codes call (703) 532-8822, or your local postmaster.	
Falls Hill	22043
Falls Mills	24613
Fallville	24326
Falmouth	22405
Fancy Gap	24328
Fancy Hill	24521
Farmers	22580
Farmers Fork (Essex County)	22509
Farmers Fork (Richmond County)	22572
Farmers Store	24360
Farmingdale (Part of Hopewell)	23860
Farmington (Albemarle County)	22903
Farmington (Henrico County)	23229
Farmville	23901
Farnham	22460
Fauquier Springs	22186
Favonia	24382
Fawcett Gap	22602
Fayette Park	23222
Featherstone	22191
Featherstone Shores	22191
Federal Correctional Institution	23803
Federal Reserve (Part of Richmond)	23219
Fentress (Part of Chesapeake)	23322
Fentress (Part of Virginia Beach)	23451
Fenwick Park	22042
Fergusonville	23930
Ferncliff	23084
Ferndale Gardens	23803
Ferndale Park	23803
Ferrum	24088
Ferry Farms	22405
Fieldale	24089
Fife	23054
Figsboro	24112
File	22427
Fincastle	24090
Finchley	23927
Fine Creek Mills	23139
Finneywood	23924
First Colony	23185

	ZIP
First Street (Part of Radford)	24141
Fishers Hill	22626
Fishersville	22939
Five Forks (Amherst County)	24521
Five Forks (Bedford County)	24523
Five Forks (Carroll County)	24343
Five Forks (Dinwiddie County)	23833
Five Forks (Halifax County)	24592
Five Forks (Part of Hopewell)	23860
Five Forks (James City County)	23185
Five Forks (Madison County)	22960
Five Forks (Nelson County)	24553
Five Forks (Prince Edward County)	23958
Five Lakes	23141
Five Mile Fork	22407
Five Oaks	24630
Flactem Manor	23805
Flagpond	24221
Flat Gap	24279
Flat Iron	22520
Flatridge	24378
Flat Rock (Powhatan County)	23139
Flatrock (Russell County)	24260
Flat Run	22508
Flat Spur	24237
Flat Top	24230
Flatwood	24312
Flatwoods	24090
Fleeburg	22849
Fleenors	24202
Fleenortown	24263
Fleet (Part of Norfolk)	23511
Fleeton	22539
Flemington	24228
Fletcher	22973
Fletcherville	22186
Flint Hill (Bedford County)	24121
Flint Hill (Rappahannock County)	22627
Flood	24458
Floris	22071
Floyd	24091
Foneswood	22461
Fontaine	24148
Ford	23850
Fordham (Part of Hampton)	23663
Forest	24551
Forest Acres	23805
Forest Hill (Part of Richmond)	23225
Forest Hills (Part of Virginia Beach)	23450
Forest Lake Hills	23111
Forest Park (Part of Hampton)	23666
Forest Park (Part of Norfolk)	23518
Forestville (Fairfax County)	22066
Forestville (Shenandoah County)	22847
Fork Ridge	24639
Forks of Buffalo	24521
Forks Of Water	24413
Forksville	23950
Fork Union	23055
Formosa	23962
Fort Belvoir	22060
Fort Blackmore	24250
Fort Chiswell	24360
Fort Defiance	24437
Fortener Addition	24354
Fort Hill (Henrico County)	23226
Fort Hill (Part of Lynchburg)	24502
Fort Hunt	22306
Fort Lee (Henrico County)	23075
Fort Lee (Prince George County)	23801
Fort Lewis Terrace (Part of Salem)	24153
Fort Mitchell	23941
Fort Myer	22211
Fort Myer Heights	22209
Fort Pickett	23824
Fort Valley	22652
Foster	23056
Fosters Falls	24360

	ZIP
Four Corners	22182
Four Mile Fork	22408
Fourway (Part of Tazewell)	24630
Fox	24348
Foxhall (Part of Norfolk)	23502
Fox Hill (Part of Hampton)	23664
Fox Mill Estates	22070
Foxwells	22578
Fractionville	24210
Fraleytown	24244
Franconia	22310
Franconia Commons	22310
Franklin	23851
Franklin Farms	23805
Franklin Forest	22101
Franklin Heights	24151
Franklin Junction (Part of Suffolk)	23438
Franklin Park	22101
Franks Mill	24401
Franktown	23354
Frederick Hall	23117
Frederick Heights	22602
Fredericksburg	22401-08
For specific Fredericksburg Zip Codes call (703) 373-6543, or your local postmaster.	
Fredericksburg (rural Rockbridge County)	24473
Freeman	23856
Freemont	24343
Freeport	23061
Freeshade Corner	23071
Free Union	22940
Fremac (Part of Virginia Beach)	23451
Friendship	24340
Fries	24330
Fringer	24066
Frogtown	22012
Front Royal	22630
	22651
For specific Front Royal Zip Codes call (703) 635-4540, or your local postmaster.	
Frytown	22186
Fuqua Farms	23234
Fulks Run	22830
Fulton (Part of Richmond)	23231
Furnace	22827
Furnace Hill	24354
Furnace Mountain	22075
Gainesboro	22603
Gaines Mill Estates	23111
Gainesville	22065
Gala	24085
Galax	24333
Gallops Corner (Part of Virginia Beach)	23464
Galts Mill	24572
Gammons Store	23102
Garden City (Arlington County)	22207
Garden City (Part of Hampton)	23661
Garden Wood Park (Part of Virginia Beach)	23455
Gardner	24260
Gardners Crossroads	23117
Garfield Estates	22191
Gargatha	23421
Garland Heights	23234
Garrisonville	22463
Garrisonville Estates	22554
Garysville	23860
Gasburg	23857
Gate City	24251
Gatewood	22534
Gatewood Park (Part of Virginia Beach)	23454
Gaylord	22611
Gaynor Heights	24112
Gayton	23075
Geer	22973
Genito	23139
Genoa	22830
George Mason University	22030
Georges Fork	24228
Georges Mill	22080
Georges Tavern	23063
Georgetown	22842
Georgetown South (Part of Manassas)	22110
Georgetown Village	22191
George Washington (Part of Alexandria)	22305
George Washington Village	22060
Georgian Hamlet	22110

	ZIP		ZIP		ZIP		ZIP
Gether	22514	Grassy Creek (Russell		Grundy	24614	Hayes	23072
Getz	22842	County)	24224	Guilford (Accomack		Hayfield (Fairfax County)	22310
Ghent (Part of Norfolk)	23517	Gratton	24651	County)	23308	Hayfield (Frederick	
Gholsonville	23893	Gravel Hill (Part of		Guilford (Fairfax County)	22310	County)	22638
Gibson Station	24248	Richmond)	23225	Guilford Heights	23899	Haymarket	22069
Gidsville	24521	Graves Mill	22721	Guinea	22580	Haynesville	22472
Gilbert Gardens	23231	Graves Store	24104	Guinea Mills	23040	Haynesville Correctional	
Gilmore Mills	24579	Gray	23897	Gum Spring	23065	Unit	24472
Ginter Park (Part of		Graysontown	24141	Gum Tree	23005	Haysi	24256
Richmond)	23227	Gray's Pointe	22033	Gunn Hall Manor (Part of		Hayters Gap	24210
Gladehill	24092	Graysville	23301	Virginia Beach)	23454	Haywood	22722
Gladesboro	24343	Great Bridge (Part of		Gunston Heights	22079	Hazel	24237
Glade Spring	24340	Chesapeake)	23320*	Gunston Manor	22079	Hazel Heights (Part of	
Gladstone	24553		23328†	Gunton Park	24360	Bristol)	24201
Gladys	24554	Great Falls	22066	Gwathmey	23005	Head Waters	24442
Glamorgan	24293	Great Neck Manor (Part		Gwynn	23066	Healing Springs	24445
Glasgow	24555	of Virginia Beach)	23450	Hacksneck	23358	Health Science (Part of	
Glass	23072	Green Acres (Part of		Haddonfield	24279	Richmond)	23219
Glebe Point	22432	Fairfax)	22030	Hadensville	23067	Healys	23071
Gleedsville	22075	Greenbackville	23356	Hagans	24263	Heards	22920
Glen Alden	22030	Green Bay	23942	Hague	22469	Heathsville	22473
Glen Allen	23058-60	Greenbriar (Chesterfield		Hale Creek	24634	Hebron (Augusta County)	24401
For specific Glen Allen Zip		County)	23831	Halemhurst (Part of		Hebron (Carroll County)	24333
Codes call (804) 270-2846, or		Greenbriar (Fairfax		Fairfax)	22032	Hebron (Dinwiddie	
your local postmaster.		County)	22033	Hales Bottom	24605	County)	23894
Glenbrook Hills	23075	Greenbrier Mall (Part of		Halfway	22171	Hechler Village	23223
Glencarlyn	22204	Chesapeake)	23320	Halifax	24558	Heights (Part of	
Glendale (Part of Newport		Greenbush	23357	Halifax Correctional Unit	24558	Petersburg)	23803
News)	23607	Green Cove	24236	Hall Addition	24354	Helmet	23148
Glendale Acres	23030	Greendale (Henrico		Hallieford	23068	Hematite	24426
Glen Echo	23223	County)	23228	Hallowing Point Estates	22079	Hendricks Store	24121
Glenford	24210	Greendale (Washington		Hallsboro	23113	Henry	24102
Glen Forest	22041	County)	24210	Halls Hill	22207	Henry Clay Heights	23111
Glenita	24244	Greendale Manor	24330	Hallwood (Accomack		Henry Fork	24151
Glen Lyn	24093	Greenes Corner	23024	County)	23359	Henrytown (Part of	
Glenmore	24562	Greenfield (Nelson		Hallwood (Part of		Saltville)	24370
Glenns	23149	County)	22920	Hampton)	23664	Hepners	22842
Glen Oaks	22015	Greenfield (Pittsylvania		Hamburg (Page County)	22835	Herald	24230
Glenrochie	24211	County)	24557	Hamburg (Shenandoah		Heritage Court	23228
Glen Rock (Part of		Greenfield (Washington		County)	22824	Heritage Square	22003
Norfolk)	23502	County)	24361	Hamilton	22068	Heritage Village	22003
Glen Roy Estates	23061	Greenfield Farms (Part of		Hamiltontown	24273	Herman	23967
Glenshellah (Part of		Portsmouth)	23703	Hamlin	24224	Hermitage	22980
Portsmouth)	23707	Greenlee	24579	Hampden Sydney	23943	Hermitage Farms	23228
Glenvar	24153	Greenmount	22801	Hampton	23651-70	Hermitage Park	23228
Glen Wilton	24438	Green Oaks (Part of		For specific Hampton Zip		Hermosa	24577
Glenwood (Part of		Newport News)	23601	Codes call (804) 826-7586, or		Herndon	22070-71
Danville)	24541	Green Pond	24531	your local postmaster.		For specific Herndon Zip Codes	
Glenwood Farms	23223	Greens Folly Apartments	24592	Hampton Institute (Part of		call (703) 437-3740, or your	
Glenwood Park (Part of		Green Spring	22603	Hampton)	23668	local postmaster.	
Norfolk)	23505	Green Springs (Louisa		Hampton Terrace (Part of		Hessian Hills	22901
Gloucester	23061	County)	22942	Hampton)	23669	Hewlett	22546
Gloucester Banks	23062	Green Springs		Hanckel	24361	Hickory Flat	24333
Gloucester Courthouse	23061	(Washington County)	24211	Handsom	23859	Hickory Ground (Part of	
Gloucester Point	23062	Green Valley (Part of		Hanging Rock	24153	Chesapeake)	23322
Goblintown	24171	Bristol)	24202	Hanover	23069	Hickory Grove Acres	22069
Goddin Hill	23005	Greenville (Augusta		Hanover Heights	23111	Hickory Haven	23103
Gogginsville	24151	County)	24440	Hansonville	24266	Hickory Hill	22901
Goldbond	24094	Greenville (Fauquier		Happy Creek	22630	Hickory Junction	24260
Golddale	22568	County)	22123	Harbors of Newport	22191	Hicks Island	23089
Gold Hill	23123	Greenville Correctional		Harborton	23389	Hicksville	24314
Goldvein	22720	Unit	24440	Harbor View	22079	Hiddenbrook	22070
Gonyon	22473	Greenway Downs	22042	Hardings	22482	Hideaway Park	22031
Goochland	23063	Greenway Hills (Part of		Hardware	24590	Hidenwood (Part of	
Goodall	23192	Fairfax)	22030	Hardwood	24245	Newport News)	23606
Goode	24556	Greenwich (Prince William		Hardy	24101	High Knob	22630
Goods Mills	24471	County)	22123	Hardyville	23070	Highland	24084
Goodview	24095	Greenwich (Part of		Hare Valley	23350	Highland Gardens	23222
Goodwins Ferry	24128	Virginia Beach)	23462	Harless	24073	Highland Homes	22405
Goose Pimple Junction	24202	Greenwood (Albemarle		Harman (Buchanan		Highland Park (Arlington	
Gordonsville	22942	County)	22943	County)	24618	County)	22205
Gore	22637	Greenwood (Henrico		Harman (Tazewell County)	24602	Highland Park (Part of	
Goshen	24439	County)	23060	Harman Junction	24614	Hopewell)	23860
Goshen Cross Road	23015	Greenwood (Part of		Harmony (Halifax County)	24520	Highland Park (Part of	
Gossan Mines	24333	Norfolk)	23513	Harmony (Shenandoah		Portsmouth)	23707
Gouldin	23192	Greenwood (Rockingham		County)	22824	Highland Park (Prince	
Gowrie Park (Part of		County)	22827	Harpersville (Part of		William County)	22110
Norfolk)	23509	Greenwood Farms (Part		Newport News)	23607	Highland Park (Part of	
Grady	24530	of Hampton)	23666	Harrell Siding (Part of		Richmond)	23222
Grafton	23692	Gregory Corner	23968	Suffolk)	23434	Highlands	22201
Grafton Village	22405	Gressitt	23156	Harris Grove	23692	Highland Springs	23075
Grahams Forge	24360	Gretna	24557	Harrisonburg	22801	High Meadows	24202
Granby Shores (Part of		Griffinsburg	22701	Harriston	24441	High Point (Part of	
Norfolk)	23503	Griffith	24422	Harrisville	22660	Hopewell)	23860
Grandin Road (Part of		Grimes	22624	Harrowgate	23831	Hightown (Highland	
Roanoke)	24015	Grimsleyville	24639	Harryhogan	22435	County)	24444
Grand View (Part of		Grimstead	23064	Hartfield	23071	Hightown (Rockingham	
Hampton)	23664	Grindall Creek	23234	Harts Shop	23117	County)	22834
Grangeville	23410	Grit	24563	Hartwood	22471	Highview Park	22207
Granite Hills (Part of		Grizzard	23879	Harvey	24219	Hilander Park	24202
Richmond)	23225	Groseclose	24368	Hassen Heights (Part of		Hill	24251
Granite Springs	22553	Grotons	23399	Bristol)	24201	Hillbrook	22003
Grant	24378	Groton Town	23359	Hatchers	23139	Hillcrest	23040
Grant's Field	23803	Grottoes	24441	Hat Creek	24528	Hillcrest Estates	22110
Granville	23030	Grove	23185	Hatton	24590	Hillsboro	22132
Grapefield	24314	Grove Hill	22849	Haven Heights (Part of		Hillsdale (Part of Suffolk)	23434
Grassland	22733	Grove Park (Part of		Virginia Beach)	23462	Hillsman Corner	24502
Grass Ridge	22101	Portsmouth)	23707	Hawkinstown	22842	Hillsville	24343
Grassy Creek (Henry		Groveton (Fairfax County)	22306	Hawthorne (Part of		Hill Top (Part of	
County)	24112	Groveton Heights	22306	Norton)	24273	Martinsville)	24112

* Area Zip Code   † Post Office Boxes

	ZIP
Hilltop (Part of Suffolk)	23451
Hilltop Manor (Part of Virginia Beach)	23454
Hilltop-Oceana (Part of Virginia Beach)	23454
Hilltown	24330
Hillwood	22042
Hiltons	24258
Hilton Village (Part of Newport News)	23601
Hinesville	24549
Hinnom	22520
Hinton	22831
Hitesburg	24598
Hiwassee	24347
Hixburg	23958
Hoadly	22191
Hobson (Part of Suffolk)	23436
Hockley	23156
Hockman (Part of Bluefield)	24605
Hodges	24554
Hodges Manor (Part of Portsmouth)	23701
Hodgesville	24151
Hoges Chapel	24136
Holcomb Rock	24503
Holdcroft	23030
Holiday Hills (Part of Richmond)	23235
Holiday Point Estates (Part of Suffolk)	23434
Holland (Part of Suffolk)	23437
Hollindale	22306
Hollin Hall	22308
Hollin Hills	22307
Hollins	24019
Hollins College	24020
Holly Brook	24315
Holly Forest	22039
Holly Grove	23024
Holly Hills	23139
Hollymead	22901
Holly Park	22032
Holly Point	23430
Hollywood (Part of Suffolk)	23434
Holman	22853
Holmes Run Acres	22042
Holmes Run Heights	22003
Holmes Run Park	22042
Holston	24210
Holston Mill	24354
Holts Crossing	24554
Home Creek	24614
Homeville	23890
Homewood	22015
Honaker	24260
Honey Branch	24283
Honeyville	22851
Hood	22723
Hopeton	23421
Hopewell (Independent City)	23860
Hopewell (Pittsylvania County)	24549
Hopkins	23421
Horizon Hills (Part of Bristol)	24201
Horners	22520
Hornsbyville	23692
Horntown	23395
Horse Gap (Part of Pound)	24279
Horse Head	22473
Horse Pasture	24112
Horsepen	24619
Horsey	23396
Hotchkiss	24460
Hot Springs	24445
Howardsville (Albemarle County)	24562
Howardsville (Loudoun County)	22012
Howellsville	22630
Howertons	22454
Howland	22473
Hubbard Springs	24263
Huckleberry Hills	23805
Huddle	24382
Huddleston	24104
Hudgins	23076
Hudson Crossroads	22842
Hudson Terrace (Part of Newport News)	23607
Huffman	24128
Huffville	24138
Hughes Store	23030
Hull Street (Part of Richmond)	23224
Hume	22639
Hunterdale	23851
Hunter Estates	22079
Hunters Valley	22181
Huntersville (Part of Norfolk)	23504
Huntersville (Part of Suffolk)	23435
Huntingcreek Hills	23234
Huntington (Fairfax County)	22303
Huntington (Henrico County)	23229
Huntington Heights (Part of Newport News)	23607
Huntly	22640
Hunton	23060
Hunts Village	22032
Hupp	22853
Hurley	24620
Hurricane	24293
Hurt	24563
Huske	23882
Hustle	22476
Hyacinth	22435
Hybla Valley	22306
Hybla Valley Farms	22306
Hyco	24592
Hylas	23146
Hylton Park	23235
Iberis	22503
Ida	22835
Idlewilde (Part of Covington)	24426
Idylwood	22043
Igo	22405
Imboden	24216
Independence	24348
Independent Hill	22110
Index	22485
Indian Field	22572
Indian Gap	24656
Indian Neck	23148
Indian River (Part of Chesapeake)	23325
Indian River Estates (Part of Virginia Beach)	23462
Indian Rock	24066
Indian Run Park	22312
Indian Springs (Chesterfield County)	23234
Indian Springs (Fairfax County)	22312
Indian Valley	24105
Indika	23487
Ingham	22849
Ingleside (Part of Norfolk)	23502
Ingram	24597
Inlet	22701
Inman	24216
Ino	22437
Interior	24094
Intervale	24426
Ira	24620
Irisburg	24054
Irondale	24219
Iron Gate (Alleghany County)	24448
Irongate (Prince William County)	22110
Ironto	24087
Irving	24174
Irvington	22480
Irwin	23063
Isaac	23851
Island Creek	24343
Island Farm	22560
Island Ford	22827
Isle of Wight	23397
Isom	24228
Ivakota	22024
Ivanhoe	24350
Ivondale	22572
Ivor	23866
Ivy	22945
Jacksons Ferry	24312
Jamaica	23079
James River Estates	23238
James Store	23080
Jamesville	23398
Janaf Shopping Center (Part of Norfolk)	23502
Janey	24631
Jarratt	23867
Jasper	24244
Java	24565
Jefferson (Fairfax County)	22042
Jefferson (Powhatan County)	23139
Jefferson Manor	22303
Jefferson Mews (Part of Herndon)	22070
Jefferson Park	23860
Jeffersonton	22724
Jefferson Village	22042
Jeffress	23927
Jenkins Bridge	23399
Jenkins Neck	23072
Jennings	23930
Jennings Gap	24421
Jennings Mission	24251
Jennings Store	24244
Jericho (Carroll County)	24381
Jericho (Part of Suffolk)	23434
Jerome	22824
Jersey	22481
Jessup Farms	23234
Jester Gardens (Part of Chesapeake)	23320
Jetersville	23083
Jewell Hollow	22835
Jewell Ridge	24622
Jewell Valley	24622
Johnsontown	23405
Joliff (Part of Chesapeake)	23321
Jolivue	24401
Jollett	22827
Jones	22553
Jonesboro	23824
Jones Corner	22427
Jones Creek (Part of Martinsville)	24112
Jonesville	24263
Jordan Mines	24449
Josephine	24273
Joyce Heights (Part of Fairfax)	22030
Joyner	23829
Justisville	23421
Ka	24245
Karo	22630
Kathmoor	22310
Keats	27553
Kecoughtan (Part of Hampton)	23667
Keeling	24566
Keene	22946
Keene Mill Manor	22152
Keen Mountain	24624
Keen Mountain Correctional Center	24631
Keezletown	22832
Keith	23009
Keller	23401
Kells Corner	23924
Kelsa	24620
Kemmerer Gem No. 2	24282
Kemp's Place	23231
Kempsville (Part of Virginia Beach)	23462
Kempsville Colony (Part of Virginia Beach)	23464
Kempsville Gardens (Part of Virginia Beach)	23462
Kempsville Heights (Part of Virginia Beach)	23462
Kenbridge	23944
Kendall Acres	23234
Kendall Grove	23347
Kenilworth (Part of Norfolk)	23503
Kennard	22572
Kennelworth (Part of Petersburg)	23803
Kent	24382
Kent Gardens	22101
Kent Park (Part of Norfolk)	23509
Kents Store	23084
Kentuck	24586
Kenwood (Hanover County)	23005
Kenwood (Part of Hopewell)	23860
Keokee	24265
Kerfoot	22025
Kermit	24251
Kerns	24250
Kernstown (Part of Winchester)	22602
Kerrs Creek	24450
Keswick	22947
Keysville	23947
Key West	22901
Kibler	24053
Kidds Fork	22514
Kidd's Store	24590
Kidville	22939
Kiels Gardens	22030
Kiger Hill	24450
Kilby (Part of Suffolk)	23434
Kilby Shores (Part of Suffolk)	23434
Kildare Annex	23230
Kilmarnock	22482
Kilmarnock Wharf	22482
Kimages	23030
Kimballton	24150
Kimberley Hills	23901
Kimberling	24315
Kimberly Acres	23234
Kinderhook	22973
Kindrick	24382
King and Queen Court House	23085
King George	22485
Kingsbury Manor	22980
Kings Corner	23089
Kings Crossroads	23964
Kingsdale	23851
Kings Fork (Part of Suffolk)	23434
Kings Grant (Part of Virginia Beach)	23452
Kings Hill	23231
Kingsland	23234
Kings Park	22151
Kings Park West	22032
Kings Point	23185
Kings Store	24091
Kingston	24550
Kingston Chase	22070
Kingstown	24019
Kingsville	23901
Kingswood	23185
Kingswood Court	23111
Kingtown (Part of Bristol)	24201
King William	23086
Kino	22560
Kinsale	22488
Kiptopeke	23310
Kire	24094
Kirkside	22306
Klotz	24150
Knightly	24437
Knob Hill (Part of Virginia Beach)	23464
Koehler	24112
Koger Executive Center (Part of Norfolk)	23506
Konnarock	24236
Laburnum Manor	23222
Lacey Forest	22205
Lacey Spring	22833
Lackey	23694
La Crosse	23950
Ladd	22980
Ladysmith	22501
Lafayette	24087
Lafayette Boulevard (Part of Norfolk)	23509
Lafayette Park (Part of Norfolk)	23509
Lahore	22502
Lake	22511
Lake Barcroft	22044
Lake Caroline	22546
Lake Crystal Farms	23235
Lake Jackson	22110
Lake Monticello	22963
Lake Of The Woods	22508
Lake Ridge	22192
Lakeside (Henrico County)	23228
Lakeside (Part of Newport News)	23606
Lakeside (Part of Salem)	24153
Lakeside Heights	23692
Lakeside Hills	23228
Lakeside Village	23038
Lakeview Acres	23901
Lakeville Estates (Part of Virginia Beach)	23464
Lakewood (Fairfax County)	22041
Lakewood (James City County)	23185
Lakewood (Part of Norfolk)	23509
Lakewood (Pittsylvania County)	24541
Lamberts Point (Part of Norfolk)	23508
Lambsburg	24351
Lanahan	24088
Lancaster	22503
Landmark Center (Part of Alexandria)	22304
Landmark Plaza (Part of Alexandria)	22312

*** Area Zip Code** **† Post Office Boxes**

	ZIP
Landmark Square (Part of Manassas)	22110
Land of Promise (Part of Virginia Beach)	23457
Land O'Pines	23832
Landtown (Part of Virginia Beach)	23456
Lanes Corner (Hanover County)	23005
Lanes Corner (Spotsylvania County)	22553
Lanesville	23086
Laneview	22504
Lanexa	23089
Langhorne Acres	22031
Langley	22101
Langley Forest	22101
Langley Research Center (Part of Hampton)	23665
Langley View (Part of Hampton)	23669
Lankford Corner	22473
Lantz Mills	22824
Lara	22503
Larchmont (Arlington County)	22201
Larchmont (Part of Norfolk)	23508
Larkspur (Part of Virginia Beach)	23462
Larrys Store	24598
Larwood Acres	24202
Lassiter Courts (Part of Newport News)	23607
Laswell	24360
Latanes	22443
Laurel (Henrico County)	23060
Laurel (Russell County)	24260
Laurel Branch	24091
Laureldale	24236
Laurel Dell	23228
Laurel Fork	24352
Laurel Grove	24594
Laurel Grove Estates	23111
Laurel Hill (Augusta County)	24482
Laurel Hill (Shenandoah County)	22641
Laurel Manor (Part of Virginia Beach)	23451
Laurel Mills	22716
Laurel Oak	23234
Laurel Park (Henrico County)	23228
Laurel Park (Henry County)	24112
Lawndale Farms	23231
Lawrenceville	23868
Lawrenceville Hills	23868
Lawson	23430
Lawson Forest (Part of Virginia Beach)	23455
Lawson's Store (Mecklenburg County)	23924
Lawsons Store (Russell County)	24224
Lawyers	24501
Laymantown	24064
L C Page (Part of Norfolk)	23518
Leaksville	22835
Leatherwood	24112
Lebanon	24266
Lebanon Church	22641
Leck	24230
Leda	24577
Lee	23039
Lee Acres	23875
Lee Boulevard Heights	22044
Leedstown	22443
Lee Forest	22030
Lee Hall (Part of Newport News)	23603
Lee Heights	22207
Lee-Hi Village	22030
Leemaster	24656
Lee Meadows	22032
Lee Mont	23403
Lee Park	23150
Leesburg	22075
Leesville	24571
Lee Town	24614
Leewood	22151
Lenah	22001
Lennig	24577
Lenox (Part of Norfolk)	23503
Lenox (Part of Virginia Beach)	23451
Leon	22725
Lerty	22520
Lester Manor	23086

	ZIP
Level Run	24563
Lewinsville	22101
Lewinsville Heights	22101
Lewisetta	22505
Lewis Park	22030
Lewiston	23005
Lewisville	22611
Lexington	24450
Liberia Woods (Part of Manassas)	22110
Liberty (Halifax County)	24577
Liberty (Tazewell County)	24651
Lick Fork	24230
Lick Run	24085
Lick Skillet	24370
Lightfoot	23090
Lignum	22726
Lilian	22539
Lilly	22821
Lime Hill	24202
Limeton	22610
Lincoln	22078
Lincolnia (Part of Alexandria)	22312
Lincolnia (Fairfax County)	22311-12
For specific Lincolnia Zip Codes call (703) 354-1622, or your local postmaster.	
Lincolnia Heights	22312
Lincolnia Park	22312
Lincoln Park (Fairfax County)	22030
Lincoln Park (Part of Norfolk)	23513
Lindell	24210
Linden	22642
Lindenwood	24179
Lindsay	22942
Linkhorn (Part of Virginia Beach)	23454
Linkhorn Estates (Part of Virginia Beach)	23454
Linkhorn Shores (Part of Virginia Beach)	23451
Linlier (Part of Virginia Beach)	23451
Linville	22834
Lipps	24273
Lithia	24066
Little Haven (Part of Virginia Beach)	23452
Little Plymouth	23091
Little River Hills (Part of Fairfax)	22031
Little River Pines	22031
Little River Shopping Center	22003
Little Rocky Run	22024
Littleton	23890
Little Vienna Estates	22181
Litwalton	22503
Litz	24340
Lively	22507
Lloyd Place (Part of Suffolk)	23434
Loch Laird (Part of Buena Vista)	24416
Loch Lomond	22110-11
For specific Loch Lomond Zip Codes call (703) 368-2145, or your local postmaster.	
Lockhart Flats	24228
Locust Creek	23024
Locust Dale	22948
Locust Grove	22508
Locust Hill (Middlesex County)	23092
Locust Hill (Wythe County)	24360
Locust Mound	23410
Locustville	23404
Lodge	22435
Lodi	24340
Lodore	23002
Lofton	24472
Logan	22553
Loisdale Estates	22150
Lombardy Grove	23970
London Bridge (Part of Virginia Beach)	23454
London Towne	22020
Lone Fountain	24421
Lone Gum	24104
Longbottom (Part of Grundy)	24614
Long Branch	24237
Long Dale (Alleghany County)	24422
Longdale (Henrico County)	23060

	ZIP
Longdale Furnace	24422
Long Island	24569
Long Point (Part of Portsmouth)	23703
Longshop	24060
Long Spur	24084
Longview	23430
Looney's Creek	24614
Loretto	22509
Lorfax Heights	22079
Lorne	22546
Lorraine	23075
Lorton	22079
	22199
For specific Lorton Zip Codes call (703) 339-6128, or your local postmaster.	
Lost Corner	22663
Lost Forest	23234
Lottsburg	22511
Loudoun Heights	25425
Louisa	23093
Love	22952
Loves Mill	24319
Loves Shop	24558
Lovettsville	22080
Lovingston	22949
Lower Brandon	23881
Lower Elk Creek	24326
Lower Exeter	24216
Lowery Hills	24202
Lowesville	22951
Lowmoor	24457
Lowry	24570
Loxley Place (Part of Portsmouth)	23702
Luck	24565
Lucketts	22075
Lumberton	23890
Lummis (Part of Suffolk)	23434
Lunenburg	23952
Luray	22835
Lurich	24124
Lusters Gate	24060
Luttrellville	22435
Lydia	22973
Lyells	22572
Lyman Park	22134
Lynchburg	24501-06
For specific Lynchburg Zip Codes call (804) 528-8900, or your local postmaster.	
Lynch Station	24571
Lyndhurst	22952
Lynhaven (Part of Alexandria)	22305
Lynn Grove	23222
Lynnhaven (Part of Hampton)	23666
Lynnhaven (Part of Virginia Beach)	23450
Lynnhaven Acres (Part of Virginia Beach)	23452
Lynnhaven Colony (Part of Virginia Beach)	23451
Lynnhaven Mall (Part of Virginia Beach)	23452
Lynn Shores (Part of Virginia Beach)	23452
Lynn Spring	24649
Lynnwood (Rockingham County)	24471
Lynnwood (Part of Virginia Beach)	23452
Lynwood	22191
Lyon Park	22201
Lyon Village	22201
Mabe	24244
McAdam	24301
Macanie	22842
McCall Gap	24340
McChesney Heights (Part of Bristol)	24201
McClung	24460
McClure	24269
McConnell	24251
McCoy	24111
McCrady	24370
McDonalds Mill	24060
McDonald's Small Farms	23060
McDowell	24458
Macedonia	23308
Maces Springs	24258
McGaheysville	22840
McHenry	22553
Machipongo	23405
McKendree	24558
McKenney	23872
McKinley	24459
McLean	22101-02

	ZIP
	22106
For specific McLean Zip Codes call (703) 790-9100, or your local postmaster.	
McLean Estates	22101
McLean Hamlet	22102
McLean Manor	22101
McMullen	22973
McNeals Corner	22503
Macon	23101
Madison	22727
Madison College (Part of Harrisonburg)	22801
Madison Heights	24572
Madison Manor	22205
Madison Mills	22953
Madison Run	22942
Madisonville	23958
Madrid	22980
Madrillon Farms	22182
Maggie	24127
Magnolia (Part of Suffolk)	23434
Magnolia Gardens (Part of Suffolk)	23434
Maidens	23102
Major	24526
Makemie Park	23442
Malbrook	22044
Malcolm	24202
Malibu (Part of Virginia Beach)	23452
Mallow	24426
Malmaison	24527
Manakin	23103
Manakin Farms	23103
Manakin Sabot	23103
Manassas	22110-11
For specific Manassas Zip Codes call (703) 368-2145, or your local postmaster.	
Manassas Park	22111
Manbur	23150
Manchester Mills	23875
Maness	24282
Mangohick	23104
Mannboro	23105
Manquin	23106
Manry	23888
Mantua	22031
Mantua Hills	22031
Manville	24251
Maple Grove (Rockbridge County)	24450
Maple Grove (Spotsylvania County)	22407
Maple Grove (Westmoreland County)	22443
Maplewood	23002
Mappsburg	23420
Mappsville	23407
Marble Valley	24432
Marcem (Part of Gate City)	24251
Marengo	23950
Margo	22553
Marion	24354
Marion Hill	23231
Marionville	23408
Markham (Fauquier County)	22643
Markham (Pittsylvania County)	24557
Mark Haven Beach	22454
Marksville	22851
Marlan Forest	22307
Marlbank	23692
Marlboro	23224
Marlbrook	24483
Marrowbone Heights	24148
Marshall	22115
Marshall Heights	23072
Marsh Run	22712
Marstella Estates	22186
Martha Gap	24256
Martin Siding	23405
Martins Store	22920
Martinsville	24112-15
For specific Martinsville Zip Codes call (703) 632-4745, or your local postmaster.	
Marumsco Acres	22191
Marumsco Hills	22191
Marumsco Plaza	22191
Marumsco Village	22191
Marumsco Woods	22191
Marvin	24639
Marye	22553
Marysville	24554
Maryus	23107
Mascot	23108

* Area Zip Code   **† Post Office Boxes**

	ZIP
Mason Cove	24153
Mason Creek (Part of Salem)	24153
Masonville	22003
Massanetta Springs	22801
Massanutten	22840
Massaponax	22407
Massies Mill	22954
Mathews	23109
Matoaca	23803
Mattaponi	23110
Maurertown	22644
Maury Place (Part of Newport News)	23601
Mavisdale	24627
Max Creek	24347
Maxie	24628
Maximum Security Facility	22079
Max Meadows	24360
Maxwell	24651
Mayberry	24120
Maybrook	24136
Mayfair Place	23223
Mayfield	23230
Mayfield Farms	23111
Mayflower	24521
Mayo (Halifax County)	24598
Mayo (Henry County)	24165
Maytown (Part of Coeburn)	24230
Meade	22560
Meadowbrook (Chesterfield County)	23234
Meadowbrook (Part of Norfolk)	23505
Meadowbrook Forest (Part of Norfolk)	23518
Meadowcrest (Part of Bristol)	24201
Meadowood	23227
Meadows of Dan	24120
Meadows of Newgate	22020
Meadow View (Chesterfield County)	23234
Meadowview (Washington County)	24361
Meadville	24558
Mears	23409
Mears Station	23409
Mearsville	23409
Mechanicsburg	24315
Mechanicsville (Hanover County)	23111
Mechanicsville (Rockingham County)	22853
Mechums River	22901
Mecklenburg Correctional Center	23917
Media Park	23231
Meetze	22186
Meherrin	23954
Melfa	23410
Melrose (Campbell County)	24554
Melrose (Part of Roanoke)	24017
Melrose Gardens	22172
Melton	22942
Memorial Heights	22306
Mendota	24270
Mentow	24104
Meredithville	23873
Meridian Park	22046
Merrifield	22081*
	22116†
Merrimac	24060
Merrimack Park (Part of Norfolk)	23503
Merrimac Shores (Part of Hampton)	23669
Merry Point	22513
Messongo	23399
Metomkin	23421
Mew	24224
Michaux	23139
Midcity Shopping Center (Part of Portsmouth)	23707
Middlebrook	24459
Middleburg	22117
Middleridge	22032
Middleton	23228
Middleton Gardens (Part of Salem)	24153
Middletown (Frederick County)	22645
Middletown (Northampton County)	23413
Middletowne Farms	23185
Midland	22728

	ZIP
Midlothian	23112-13
For specific Midlothian Zip Codes call (804) 794-5177, or your local postmaster.	
Midway (Halifax County)	24598
Midway (Mecklenburg County)	23915
Midway (Tazewell County)	24609
Mike	24538
Mila	24473
Milan (Part of Norfolk)	23508
Miles	23025
Milford	22514
Military Circle Center (Part of Norfolk)	23502
Millboro	24460
Millboro Spring	24460
Mill Creek Park	22003
Millenbeck	22503
Miller Park (Part of Lynchburg)	24501
Millers Tavern	23115
Mill Gap	24465
Mill Garden	22553
Milltown	22080
Millwood	22646
Milteer Acres (Part of Suffolk)	23434
Mineral	23117
Mine Run	22568
Minimum Security Facility	22079
Minnieville	22193
Minor	22560
Mint Spring	24463
Miona	23415
Miskimon	22473
Mission Home	22940
Mitchells	22729
Mitchelltown	22445
Mobjack	23118
Modern (Part of Hampton)	23666
Modest Town	23412
Moffats Creek	24459
Mogarts Beach	23430
Mollusk	22517
Monaskon	22503
Moneta	24121
Moneys Corner	22070
Monroe	24574
Monroe Gardens (Part of Hampton)	23669
Monroe Hall	22443
Montague	22504
Montclair	22026
Montebello	24464
Monterey	24465
Montevideo	22840
Montezuma	22821
Montezuma Gardens	23223
Montford	22960
Montgomery	24023
Monticello Park (Part of Alexandria)	22305
Monticello Village (Part of Norfolk)	23509
Monticello Woods	22150
Montpelier (Charles City County)	23030
Montpelier (Hanover County)	23192
Montpelier Station	22957
Montrose	23231
Montrose Heights (Part of Richmond)	23231
Montrose Terrace	23231
Montross	22520
Montvale	24122
Montvue	22901
Monument Heights	23226
Moon	23119
Mooreland	23075
Mooreland Farms	23229
Moores Corner	22554
Moorings	23839
Moran	23966
Morattico	22523
Morefield	24283
Morningside Hills	24210
Morning Star	22835
Morrisdale	23831
Morrison (Part of Newport News)	23601
Morrisonville	22080
Morrisville	22712
Morven	23002
Mosby	22042
Mosby Woods (Part of Fairfax)	22030
Moscow	22843
Moseley	23120

	ZIP
Moss Run	24426
Mossy Creek	22812
Motley	24563
Motleys Mill	24531
Motorun	23163
Mountain Falls	22602
Mountain Gap	22075
Mountain Grove	24484
Mountain Hill	24586
Mountain Lake	24136
Mountain Valley	24112
Mountain View (Giles County)	24134
Mountain View (King George County)	22406
Mountain View (Pulaski County)	24084
Mountain View (Rockbridge County)	24416
Mountain View (Washington County)	24211
Mount Airy	24557
Mount Alto	22937
Mount Carmel (Halifax County)	24520
Mount Carmel (Smyth County)	24354
Mountcastle	23140
Mount Clifton	22842
Mount Clinton	22801
Mount Crawford	22841
Mountfair	22932
Mount Garland	23117
Mount Hermon	24541
Mount Heron	24631
Mount Holly	22524
Mount Jackson	22842
Mount Landing	22560
Mount Laurel	24534
Mount Meridian	24441
Mount Nebo	22235
Mount Olive	22660
Mount Pisgah	24467
Mount Pleasant	24521
Mount Pleasant Estates	22405
Mount Sidney	24467
Mount Solon	22843
Mount Vernon	22121
Mount Vernon Forest	22309
Mount Vernon Park	22309
Mount Vernon Square	22306
Mount Vernon Terrace	22309
Mount Vernon Valley	22309
Mount Vernon Woods	22309
Mountville	22117
Mount Vinco	23921
Mount Williams	22602
Mount Zephyr	22309
Mount Zion	24554
Mouth of Laurel	24609
Mouth of Wilson	24363
Mt. Ararat	23927
Mt. Cross	24540
Mt. View	24354
Mud Fork	24630
Mulch	22460
Munden (Part of Virginia Beach)	23457
Mundy Point	22435
Munson Hill	22041
Murat	24450
Murpheyville	24368
Murphy	24656
Murrayfield	24319
Museville	24531
Mustoe	24468
Mutton Hunk	23421
Myndus	22949
Myrtle (Part of Suffolk)	23434
Nace	24175
Naffs	24065
Nahor	22963
Nain	22603
Namozine Store	23833
Nancy Wrights Corner	22580
Nandua	23420
Nansemond (Part of Suffolk)	23434
Nansemond Shores (Part of Suffolk)	23434
Naola	24574
Narrows	24124
Naruna	24576
Nash Ford	24225
Nasons	22733
Nassawadox	23413
Nathalie	24577
National Airport	20001
National Heights	23231
Natural Bridge	24578

	ZIP
Natural Bridge Station	24579
Natural Well	24445
Naval Base (Part of Norfolk)	23511
Naval Weapons Laboratory	22448
Naval Weapons Station	23691
Navy Annex	20370
Naxera	23122
Naylors Beach	22572
Nealy Ridge	24226
Nebo	24318
Needmore (Smyth County)	24319
Needmore (Wise County)	24273
Neenah	22520
Neersville	22132
Negro Foot	23192
Nellysford	22958
Nelson	24580
Nelson Estates	23231
Nelsonia	23414
Nelson Park	23185
Nesting	23079
Nethers	22740
Nettleridge	24171
New Alexandria	22307
New Baltimore	22186
Newbern	24126
Newberry	20165
New Birchett Estates	23875
New Bohemia	23842
New Canton	23123
New Castle	24127
New Church	23415
Newcomb Hall (Part of Charlottesville)	22904
New Design (Part of Danville)	24541
New Ellett	24060
New Glasgow	24521
New Gosport (Part of Portsmouth)	23702
New Hampden	24413
New Hope (Augusta County)	24469
New Hope (Charles City County)	23030
Newington	22122
Newington Station	22153
Newington Woods	22153
New Kent	23124
Newland	22572
New London	24551
New Market	22844
Newmarket Fair (Part of Newport News)	23605
New Point	23125
Newport (Giles County)	24128
Newport (Page County)	22849
Newport News	23601-12
For specific Newport News Zip Codes call (804) 247-5241, or your local postmaster.	
New Post	22408
New River	24129
News Ferry	24592
Newsoms	23874
Newstead Farm	23875
New Store	23901
Newton Park (Part of Norfolk)	23523
Newtown (King and Queen County)	23126
Newtown (Lancaster County)	22503
Newtown (Rockbridge County)	24450
Newtown (Rockingham County)	22827
Newville (Prince George County)	23842
Newville (Sussex County)	23890
Nicelytown	24422
Nickelsville	24271
Niday	24124
Nimrod Hall	24460
Ninde	22526
Nineveh	22630
Nokesville	22123
Nomini Grove	22572
Nora	24272
Norfolk	23501-41
For specific Norfolk Zip Codes call (804) 629-2198, or your local postmaster.	
COLLEGES & UNIVERSITIES	
Norfolk State University	23504

* Area Zip Code   **† Post Office Boxes**

	ZIP
FINANCIAL INSTITUTIONS	
First Union National Bank of Virginia	23510
First Virginia Bank of Tidewater	23510
Life Savings Bank, F.S.B.	23510
HOSPITALS	
DePaul Medical Center	23505
Lake Taylor Hospital	23502
Sentara Leigh Hospital	23502
Sentara Norfolk General Hospital	23507
HOTELS/MOTELS	
Best Western Center Inn	23502
Holiday Inn	23503
Norfolk Airport Hilton	23502
Omni Waterside	23510
Quality Inn-Lake Wright	23502
Ramada Inn-Airport	23502
MILITARY INSTALLATIONS	
Armed Forces Staff College	23511
Naval Air Station, Norfolk	23511
Naval Amphibious Base, Little Creek	23521
Naval Supply Center, Norfolk, Material Operations Department, Ocean Terminal	23512
Navy Material Transportation Office, Norfolk	23511
United States Army Engineer District, Norfolk	23510
Norge	23127
Norland	24228
Norman	22701
North (Arlington County)	22207
	22213
For specific North Zip Codes call (703) 536-1828, or your local postmaster.	
North (Mathews County)	23128
North Bristol (Part of Bristol)	24201
North Fairlington	22206
Northfields	22901
North Fork	22132
North Gap	24366
North Garden	22959
North Halifax	24577
North Holston	24370
North Jericho (Part of Suffolk)	23434
North Linkhorn Park (Part of Virginia Beach)	23451
North Post	22060
North Rolleston (Part of Norfolk)	23502
North Run Hills	23228
Northside (Part of Richmond)	23222
North Springfield	22151
North Stanton	24577
North Tazewell (Part of Tazewell)	24630
North View	23970
North Virginia Beach (Part of Virginia Beach)	23451
North Weems	22576
North Wellville	23824
Northwest (Part of Chesapeake)	23322
North Woodley	22042
Norton	24273
Nortonsville	22935
Norvello	23917
Norview (Part of Norfolk)	23513
Norwood (Bedford County)	24551
Norwood (Nelson County)	24581
Nottingham (Part of Richmond)	23235
Nottingham (Scott County)	24251
Nottoway	23955
Nottoway Correctional Center	23922
Novelty	24137
Novum	22735
Nurney (Part of Suffolk)	23434
Nurneysville (Part of Suffolk)	23434
Nutbush	23942
Nuttall	23061

	ZIP
Nuttsville	22528
Oakcrest (Part of Alexandria)	22302
Oakcrest (Arlington County)	22202
Oakdale	24450
Oakdale Farms (Part of Norfolk)	23505
Oak Forest	23040
Oak Grove (Carroll County)	24381
Oak Grove (Loudoun County)	20166
Oak Grove (Spotsylvania County)	22407
Oak Grove (Washington County)	24202
Oak Grove (Westmoreland County)	22443
Oak Hall	23416
Oak Hill (Augusta County)	22980
Oak Hill (Grayson County)	24363
Oak Hill (Henrico County)	23223
Oak Hill (Page County)	22650
Oak Hill Estates	23005
Oakhurst (Part of Petersburg)	23805
Oakland (Part of Suffolk)	23432
Oakland Park	23350
Oakleaf Terrace (Part of Norfolk)	23523
Oak Level (Halifax County)	24558
Oaklevel (Henry County)	24055
Oakley	22437
Oakpark	22730
Oak Ridge (Fairfax County)	22180
Oakridge (Part of Suffolk)	23434
Oakridge Estates (Prince William County)	22110
Oakridge Estates (Part of Suffolk)	23434
Oakton	22124
Oak Valley Estates	22181
Oakville	24522
Oakwood (Arlington County)	22213
Oakwood (Buchanan County)	24631
Oakwood (Fairfax County)	22310
Oakwood (Part of Norfolk)	23513
Oakwood Forest	24426
Oatlands	22075
Occoquan	22125
Occoquan Facility	22079
Occupacia	22476
Oceana (Part of Virginia Beach)	23454
Ocean Park (Part of Virginia Beach)	23455
Ocean View (Part of Norfolk)	23503
Ocoonita	24263
Ocran	22578
Oilville	23129
Old Courthouse	22182
Old Creek Estates	22032
Old Dominion	22969
Old Dominion Gardens	22101
Olde Forge	22032
Oldewood	22043
Oldfield (Part of Virginia Beach)	23451
Old Glade Spring	24340
Old Hampton (Part of Hampton)	23669
Oldhams	22529
Old Somerset	22972
Old Tavern	22171
Oldtown	24333
Old Well	23959
Olinger	24219
Olive (Part of Portsmouth)	23701
Omaha	24228
Omega	24592
Onancock	23417
Onemo	23130
Onley	23418
Ontario	23937
Opal	22186
Opequon	22602
Ophelia	22530
Oranda	22657
Orange	22960
Orange Hunt	22152-53
For specific Orange Hunt Zip Codes call (703) 451-1533, or your local postmaster.	
Orapax Farms	23141

	ZIP
Orbit	23487
Orchard Hill	23234
Orchid	23117
Orchid Lake	23065
Ordinary	23131
Oregon Acres (Part of Portsmouth)	23707
Oreton	24219
Oriskany	24130
Orkney Springs	22845
Orlando (Part of Suffolk)	23434
Orlean	22128
Orleans Village	22312
Oronoco	24483
Osaka	24216
Osbornes Chapel	24221
Osborns Gap	24228
Osceola	24211
Osso	22405
Othma	23153
Otter Hill	24523
Otter River	24571
Otterville	24523
Ottobine	22821
Ottoman	22503
Overall	22610
Overbrook (Part of Norfolk)	23513
Overlee Knolls	22205
Owens	22485
Owens Brooke (Part of Manassas)	22110
Owenton	23148
Oxford (Part of Richmond)	23235
Oyster	23419
Oyster Point (Part of Newport News)	23606
Ozeana	22454
Paces	24592
Paeonian Springs	22129
Page	24631
Page Hollow	24370
Paige	22580
Paineville	23083
Paint Bank	24131
Painter	23420
Paint Lick	24637
Palls	23086
Palmer	22578
Palmer Crossroads	27563
Palmer Springs	23917
Palmyra (Fluvanna County)	22963
Palmyra (Part of Suffolk)	23434
Pamlico (Part of Norfolk)	23503
Pamplin	23958
Panoramic Hills	22003
Pardee	24216
Paris	22130
Park (Part of Waynesboro)	22980
Parker	22508
Parkers Shores	22577
Parkfairfax (Part of Alexandria)	22302
Parkglen	22204
Parklawn	22312
Park Lee Place	23234
Park Place (Part of Norfolk)	23508
Parksley	23421
Parkview (Part of Newport News)	23605
Park View (Part of Portsmouth)	23707
Parkview (Rockingham County)	22801
Parkview Hills	22101
Parkwood	22408
Parnassus	24421
Parrott	24132
Parsonage	24224
Partlow	22534
Passapatanzy	22405
Passing	22427
Pastoria	23421
Patna	24487
Patrician Manor (Part of Hampton)	23666
Patrick Henry Correctional Unit	24148
Patrick Henry Heights	23111
Patrick Henry Mall (Part of Newport News)	23607
Patrick Springs	24133
Patterson (Buchanan County)	24631
Patterson (Wythe County)	24343
Pattonsville	24244
Pauls Cross Roads	22560
Paynes Store	22553

	ZIP
Paytes	22553
Peach Bottom	24333
Peaks	23069
Peapatch	24622
Pearisburg	24134
Pearly	24614
Peary	23138
Pedlar Mills	24574
Pedro	22559
Pemberton	23063
Pembroke	24136
Pembroke Mall (Part of Virginia Beach)	23462
Pembroke Manor (Part of Virginia Beach)	23455
Pender	22033
Penderbrook	22033
Pendleton	23117
Penhook	24137
Penn Acres	23235
Penn Daw	22306
Penn Daw Terrace	22307
Pennington Gap	24277
Penn Laird	22846
Penn Lee	24282
Penns Store	24165
Pennsytown (Part of Norfolk)	23513
Penola	22546
Pentagon	20301
Penvir	24124
Peola Mills	22740
Pepper	24141
Perrin	23072
Perrowville	24551
Perryville (Part of Saltville)	24370
Perth	24577
Petersburg	23803-05
For specific Petersburg Zip Codes call (804) 732-4631, or your local postmaster.	
Peterson Chapel	24244
Petunia	24382
Peytonsburg	24565
Phenix	23959
Philadelphia (Part of Suffolk)	23434
Philbeck Crossroads	23968
Phillip	24202
Phillis	23917
Philomont	22131
Philpott	24055
Phoebus (Part of Hampton)	23663
Piankatank Shores	23071
Pickaway	24597
Pico	24066
Piedmont	24441
Piedmont Mall (Part of Danville)	24540
Pierces Corner	22503
Pierces Shop	22960
Pigeon Hill	22611
Pilgrams Knob	24634
Pilot	24138
Pimmit	22043
Pimmit Hills	22043
Pine	24324
Pineaire (Part of Suffolk)	23434
Pine Chapel Village (Part of Hampton)	23666
Pinecrest	22312
Pinecrest Heights	22003
Pinedale	23229
Pine Grove (Clarke County)	22012
Pine Grove (Page County)	22851
Pine Grove (Washington County)	24270
Pine Grove Court (Part of Hampton)	23669
Pine Grove Terrace (Part of Hampton)	23669
Pine Hill	23111
Pinehurst (Part of Portsmouth)	23703
Pine Ridge (mail Annandale)	22003
Pine Ridge (mail Fairfax)	22031
Pinero	23061
Pine Springs	22042
Pine Tree	23027
Pinetta	23061
Pineville	22840
Pinewood Lake	22309
Pinewood Lawns	22309
Pinewood Park (Part of Manassas Park)	22110
Pinewood South	22309
Piney Grove	24589

* Area Zip Code   † Post Office Boxes

	ZIP
Piney River	22964
Pinners Point (Part of Portsmouth)	23707
Pipers Gap	24333
Pisgah	24651
Pitmans Corner	22576
Pittmantown (Part of Suffolk)	23438
Pittsville	24139
Pizarro	24091
Plain View	23156
Plantersville	23937
Plasterco	24370
Plaza, The (Part of Lynchburg)	24501
Pleasant Gap	24549
Pleasant Grove (Henry County)	24112
Pleasant Grove (Lunenburg County)	23947
Pleasant Grove (Mecklenburg County)	23970
Pleasant Grove Estates	23920
Pleasant Heights	24370
Pleasant Hill (Part of Harrisonburg)	22801
Pleasant Hill (Part of Suffolk)	23434
Pleasant Ridge (Fairfax County)	22003
Pleasant Ridge (Part of Virginia Beach)	23451
Pleasant Shade	23847
Pleasant Valley (Buckingham County)	23936
Pleasant Valley (Fairfax County)	22021
Pleasant Valley (Rockingham County)	22848
Pleasantview	24574
Plum Creek	24340
Plum Point	23181
Plum Tree	23024
Plymouth	23974
Poages Mill	24018
Pocahontas (Part of Petersburg)	23803
Pocahontas (Tazewell County)	24635
Pocahontas Correctional Unit	23832
Pocket	24282
Poetown (Part of Grundy)	24614
Poff	24091
Pohick Estates	22079
Point Breeze	22454
Point Eastern	22546
Point Pleasant	24315
Pons	23866
Poole Siding	23833
Pope	23829
Poplar Camp	24360
Poplar Cove	23417
Poplar Heights	22046
Poplar Hill (Fairfax County)	22003
Poplar Hill (Giles County)	24134
Poplar Inn	22546
Poplar Springs	23075
Poquoson	23662
Porter	22937
Porters Cross Roads	24382
Port Haywood	23138
Portlock (Part of Chesapeake)	23324
Port Norfolk (Part of Portsmouth)	23707
Port-O-Dumfries	22172
Port Republic	24471
Port Royal	22535
Portside (Part of Portsmouth)	23705
Portsmouth	23701-09
For specific Portsmouth Zip Codes call (804) 397-4607, or your local postmaster.	
Portsmouth Heights (Part of Portsmouth)	23707
Post Oak	22553
Potato Creek	24363
Potomac (Part of Alexandria)	22301
Potomac Beach (Part of Colonial Beach)	22443
Potomac Farms	22011
Potomac Hills	22101
Potomac Mills (Prince William County)	22192
Potomac Mills (Westmoreland County)	22520

	ZIP
Potters Flats	41522
Pound	24279
Pounding Mill	24637
Powcan	23023
Powells Store (Albemarle County)	22937
Powells Store (Bedford County)	24526
Powhatan	23139
Prater	24656
Pratts	22731
Premier	24640
Prentiss Place (Part of Portsmouth)	23707
Preston	24112
Preston Hills	24202
Preston King	22205
Prices Fork	24073
Prices Store	24572
Prilliman	24088
Prince George	23875
Prince George Woods Estates	23875
Princess Anne (Part of Virginia Beach)	23456
Proffit	22901
Prospect	23960
Prospectdale	24134
Providence (Grayson County)	24330
Providence (Halifax County)	24577
Providence Church (Part of Suffolk)	23434
Providence Forge	23140
Providence Park	23222
Provost	23139
Public Fork	23967
Pughsville (Part of Suffolk)	23435
Pulaski	24301
Pulaski Correctional Unit	24084
Pumpkin Center	24315
Pungo (Part of Virginia Beach)	23456
Pungoteague	23422
Purcell	24225
Purcellville	22132
Purchase	24244
Purdy	23847
Purvis (Part of Suffolk)	23437
Puryear Corner	23927
Putnam	24260
Quail Oaks	23234
Quantico	22134
Quantico Marine Corps Air Station	22134
Quantico Station	22134
Quarry	24370
Quebec	24354
Queens Lake	23185
Quicksburg	22847
Quicks Mill	24401
Quinby	23423
Quinque	22965
Quinton	23141
Rabat	24577
Raccoon Ford	22701
Racefield	23168
Radford	24141-43
For specific Radford Zip Codes call (703) 639-3531, or your local postmaster.	
Radford Army Ammunition Plant	24141
Radford University (Part of Radford)	24142
Radiant	22732
Radnor Heights	22209
Ragged Point Beach	22442
Raines Tavern	23901
Rainswood	22473
Raketown	24350
Raleigh Place (Part of Chesapeake)	23320
Raleigh Terrace (Part of Hampton)	23661
Ramoth	22554
Ramsey (Part of Norton)	24273
Randolph	23962
Random Hills	22030
Rangeley	24089
Ransons	23936
Raphine	24472
Rapidan	22733
Rappahannock Academy	22538
Rappahannock Estates	22454
Rappahannock Shores	22454
Rapps Mill	24450
Raven	24639
Ravensworth	22151

	ZIP
Ravensworth Grove	22003
Ravensworth Park	22003
Ravenwood (Fairfax County)	22044
Ravenwood (Prince William County)	22110
Ravenwood Park	22044
Rawhide	24265
Rawley Springs	22831
Rawlings	23876
Raymondale	22042
Raynor	23866
Rayon Terrace (Part of Covington)	24426
Readus	22824
Reams	23803
Reba	24523
Rectortown	22140
Red Apple Orchard	22971
Redart	23076
Red Ash	24640
Red Bank (Halifax County)	24598
Red Bank (Northampton County)	23408
Redd Shop	23901
Red Eye	24531
Red Fox Forest	22003
Red Hill (Albemarle County)	22959
Red Hill (Charlotte County)	24528
Red House	23963
Red Lane	23139
Redlawn	23919
Red Mills	24431
Red Oak	23964
Red Top (Part of Suffolk)	23434
Red Valley	24065
Redwood	24146
Reed Creek	24265
Reedville	22539
Reesedale	24087
Reese Shop	23967
Refuge	22655
Regina	22540
Rehoboth	23974
Rehoboth Church	22482
Reids Ferry (Part of Suffolk)	23434
Reids Grove	22101
Reliance	22649
Remington	22734
Remlik	23175
Remo	22579
Renan	24557
Republican Grove	24585
Rescue	23424
Reservoir Hill (Part of Covington)	24426
Rest	22624
Reston	22090-91
For specific Reston Zip Codes call (703) 437-6677, or your local postmaster.	
Retreat	24151
Reva	22735
Revis	23175
Rexburg	22560
Reynolds Store	22625
Rhoadesville	22542
Rice	23966
Riceville	24565
Richardson	24343
Richardsville	22736
Rich Creek	24147
Richlands	24641
Richmond	23201-98
For specific Richmond Zip Codes call (804) 775-6140, or your local postmaster.	
Richmond Beach	22560
Richmond Heights	23231
Rich Neck	22472
Richpatch	24426
Rich Valley	24370
Ridge	23233*
	23242†
Ridgecrest	22124
Ridgelea Estates	22031
Ridge View	22310
Ridgeway (Halifax County)	24597
Ridgeway (Henry County)	24148
Ridgeway (Pittsylvania County)	24139
Riggs	22435
Riggs	22650
Rileyville	24149
Riner	24149
Ringgold	24586
Rio	22901

	ZIP
Ripplemead	24150
Rip Rap	24598
Rivanna	22936
River Bend Estates	22190
Riverdale (Halifax County)	24592
Riverdale (Part of Hampton)	23666
Riverdale (Southampton County)	23851
Riverhill	24333
River Hills	23075
Rivermont (Augusta County)	24477
Rivermont (Chesterfield County)	23831
Rivermont (Part of Covington)	24426
Rivermont (Part of Lynchburg)	24503
Rivermont (Part of Newport News)	23601
River Oaks	22101
River Park (Part of Portsmouth)	23707
River Ridge Mall (Part of Lynchburg)	24502
Rivers Edge	23860
Riverside	24416
Riverside Estates	22309
Riverside Gardens	22308
Riverton (Part of Front Royal)	22651
Riverview (Part of Norfolk)	23504
Riverview (Wise County)	24230
Riverville	24553
Riverwood	22207
Rixeyville	22737
Roanes	23061
Roanoke	24001-38
For specific Roanoke Zip Codes call (703) 985-8765, or your local postmaster.	
Roaringfork	24216
Roaring Run	24066
Robbins Chapel	24265
Roberts Mill	24375
Robertsons	24523
Robin Ridge	23111
Robinwood	23231
Robley	22460
Robnel (Part of Manassas)	22110
Rochelle	22738
Rockbridge Baths	24473
Rock Castle	23063
Rockfish	22971
Rockland	22630
Rockland Village	22021
Rock Mills	22716
Rock Springs (Chesterfield County)	23234
Rock Springs (Fauquier County)	22186
Rocktown	24202
Rockville	23146
Rocky Bar	22827
Rocky Gap	24366
Rocky Mount	24151
Roda	24216
Rodden	24577
Rodophil	23083
Roebuck	24210
Roetown	24236
Rogers	24073
Roland Park (Part of Norfolk)	23509
Rolling Brook	22192
Rolling Hills	22309
Rolling Meadows	23875
Rolling Valley	22015
Rollins Fork	22544
Rondo	24531
Roosevelt Gardens (Part of Norfolk)	23513
Roseann	24614
Rose Bower	24522
Rosedale	24280
Rose Hill (Fairfax County)	22310
Rose Hill (Lee County)	24281
Rose Hill Farms	22310
Roseland	22967
Rosemont (Part of Alexandria)	22301
Rosemont (Fairfax County)	22101
Rosemont (Part of Suffolk)	23434
Rosemont (Part of Virginia Beach)	23452
Roseville	22554
Roslyn Hills	23229

	ZIP
Rosslyn (Part of Arlington)	22209*
	22219†
Roth	24631
Rough Creek	23959
Round Bottom	24124
Round Hill	22141
Round Top	24293
Roundtree	22042
Rowe	24646
Roxbury (Charles City County)	23140
Roxbury (Henrico County)	23229
Royal City (Part of Grundy)	24614
Royal Court	22003
Ruark	23043
Rubermont	23974
Ruby	22545
Ruckersville	22968
Rudee Inlet (Part of Virginia Beach)	23451
Rue	23421
Ruff	23109
Rugby	24363
Rural Retreat	24368
Rushmere	23430
Rushmere Shores	23430
Russell	24260
Russell Creek	24283
Rustburg	24588
Rustburg Correctional Unit	24588
Rustic	23030
Rutherford	22032
Ruther Glen	22546
Ruthland	23228
Ruthville	23147
Ryan	22011
Rye Cove	24244
Sabot	23103
Sadler Heights (Part of Suffolk)	23434
Sago	24137
St. Brides (Part of Chesapeake)	23322
St. Charles	24282
St. Clair	24605
St. Clair Bottom	24319
St. Davids Church	22652
St. Elmo (Part of Alexandria)	22305
St. Joy	23921
St. Just	22567
St. Louis	22117
St. Luke	22664
St. Paul	24283
St. Stephens	22019
St. Stephens Church	23148
Salem (Culpeper County)	22701
Salem (Independent City)	24153
Salem Woods	23234
Salisbury	23113
Salona Village	22101
Saltpetre	24085
Saltville	24370
Saluda	23149
Salvia	23148
Samos	23180
Sanburne Park	23150
Sand Bridge (Part of Virginia Beach)	23456
Sandidges	24521
Sands	23874
Sandston	23150
Sandy Bottom (Part of Suffolk)	23432
Sandy Fork	23927
Sandy Hook	23153
Sandy Level	24161
Sandy Point	22579
Sandy River	24054
Sanford	23426
Sangerville	22812
Sanville	24055
Sarah	23130
Saratoga	22153
Saratoga Place (Part of Suffolk)	23434
Saumsville	22644
Saunders (Part of Richmond)	23220
Savage Crossing (Part of Suffolk)	23434
Savageville	23417
Savedge	23881
Saxe	23967
Saxis	23427
Sayersville	24602
Scarborough Neck	23306
Scenic Park (Part of Bristol)	24201

	ZIP
Schley	23154
Schoolfield (Part of Danville)	24541
Schuyler	22969
Scotland	23883
Scott Addition	24210
Scottie Farms	23075
Scottsburg	24589
Scotts Crossroads	23924
Scotts Fork	23002
Scottsville	24590
Scottswood	23851
Scrabble	22749
Scruggs	24121
Seaboard	24641
Seaford	23696
Seaford Shores	23696
Sealston	22547
Seapines (Part of Virginia Beach)	23451
Searcy	23831
Seatack (Part of Virginia Beach)	23451
Seaview	23429
Seawright Spring	24467
Sebrell	23837
Sedalia	24526
Sedgefield (Part of Newport News)	23607
Sedgefield Manor	23228
Sedley	23878
Selden	23061
Selma	24474
Seminary	24219
Seminary Valley (Part of Alexandria)	22304
Senora	22503
Seven Corners	22044
Seven Corners Shopping Center	22044
Seven Fountains	22652
Seven Mile Ford	24373
Seven Pines	23150
Seven Pines Villa	23150
Severn	23155
Severn Manor	23072
Shacklefords	23156
Shacklefords Fork	23156
Shadow	23163
Shadow Valley (Part of Bristol)	24201
Shadwell	22947
Shady Grove (Greene County)	22940
Shady Grove (Halifax County)	24598
Shady Grove (Washington County)	24210
Shady Oak	22066
Shadyside	23405
Shanghai	23110
Shannondale	24630
Shannon Hills	24148
Shannon Park	22577
Sharps	22548
Shawnee Land	22602
Shawsville	24162
Shawver Mill	24651
Shea Terrace (Part of Portsmouth)	23707
Sheep Town	24312
Sheffield Court	23235
Sheffield Terrace	24148
Shelby	22727
Shelfar	23117
Shelors Mill	24091
Shelton (Part of Virginia Beach)	23455
Shenandoah (Part of Hopewell)	23860
Shenandoah (Page County)	22849
Shenandoah Farms	22630
Shenandoah Place	23226
Shenandoah Retreat	22012
Shenandoah Shores	22630
Shepherds Hill	24265
Shepherds Store	23038
Sheppards	23901
Sherando	22952
Sherwill	24538
Sherwood Forest	24401
Sheva	24531
Shields	23306
Shiloh (King George County)	22549
Shiloh (Southampton County)	23827
Shiny Rock	23927
Shipman	22971

	ZIP
Shirley	23030
Shirley Duke (Part of Alexandria)	22304
Shirley Gate Park	22030
Shirlington	22206
Shockoe	24531
Shores	22963
Short Lane	23061
Short Pump	23060
Shorts Creek	24312
Short Gap	24647
Shoulders Hill (Part of Suffolk)	23435
Shrevewood	22043
Shumansville	22514
Shumate	24124
Siddon	24580
Sigma (Part of Virginia Beach)	23456
Signpine	23061
Sign Post	23395
Siler	22603
Silva	23415
Silver Beach	23398
Silver Springs	22310
Silverwood (Part of Chesapeake)	23320
Simeon	22901
Simmonsville	24127
Simons Corner	22572
Simonsdale (Part of Portsmouth)	23701
Simonson	22460
Simpkins	23310
Simpsons	24072
Sinai	24592
Sinclair Farms (Part of Hampton)	23669
Singers Glen	22850
Sinking Creek	24127
Sinnickson	23395
Sissons Corner	22473
Sixmile Post	24151
Skeetrock	24228
Skeggs	24646
Skinquarter	23120
Skippers	23879
Skipwith	23968
Skipwith Farms (Henrico County)	23229
Skipwith Farms (Part of Williamsburg)	23185
Skyland	22835
Skyland Estates	22642
Skymont (Part of Staunton)	24401
Slabtown	24251
Slate	24614
Slate Mills	22740
Sleepy Hole (Part of Suffolk)	23435
Sleepy Hollow	22042
Sleepy Hollow Estates (Fairfax County)	22044
Sleepy Hollow Estates (Henrico County)	23229
Sleepy Hollow Manor	22044
Sleepy Hollow Run	22003
Sleepy Hollow Woods	22003
Sliders	23936
Sloantown	24244
Smithfield	23430
Smiths Cross Roads	23970
Smoky Ordinary	23868
Snake Creek	24343
Snapp	24340
Snell	22553
Snowden (Amherst County)	24526
Snowden (Fairfax County)	22308
Snowflake	24251
Snow Hill	23156
Snowville	24347
Soles	23050
Solomons Store	23060
Solsburg	22827
Somers	22503
Somerset	22972
Somerton (Part of Suffolk)	23438
Somerville	22739
Sonans	24531
Sorocco (Part of Suffolk)	23434
Soudan	23927
South	22204
Southampton (Part of Hampton)	23669
Southampton Correctional Center	23829
South Anna	23117
South Boston	24592

	ZIP
South Chesconessex	23417
South Clinchfield	24225
Southern Estates	23805
Southern Pine	23803
South Fairlington	22206
South Garden	22959
South Hill	23970
South Jackson	22842
South Martinsville (Part of Martinsville)	24112
South Norfolk (Part of Chesapeake)	23324
South Plains (Part of Petersburg)	23805
Southport	22191
Southridge	22101
South Roanoke (Part of Roanoke)	24014
Southside (Part of Richmond)	23224
South Suffolk (Part of Suffolk)	23434
South Woodley	22042
Spainville	23824
Sparkling Springs	22834
Sparta	22552
Speedwell	24374
Speegleville (Part of Hampton)	23666
Spencer	24165
Sperryville	22740
Spitler	22835
Spivey Store	24251
Splash Dam	24256
Spotsylvania	22553
Spotsylvania Courthouse	22553
Spottswood	24475
Spout Spring	24593
Springbrook Forest	22003
Spring City	24225
Springcreek	22812
Springdale (Part of Bristol)	24201
Springdale (Henrico County)	23222
Springfield (Fairfax County)	22150-53
For specific Springfield Zip Codes call (703) 451-1533, or your local postmaster.	
Springfield (Page County)	22835
Springfield (Rockbridge County)	24066
Springfield Estates	22150
Springfield Forest	22150
Springfield Mall Regional Shopping Center	22150
Springfield Plaza	22150
Spring Garden (Part of Bristol)	24201
Spring Garden (Pittsylvania County)	24527
Spring Grove	23881
Springhaven Estates	22102
Spring Hill	24401
Spring Meadows	23111
Spring Mills	24538
Springvale	22066
Spring Valley (Grayson County)	24330
Spring Valley (Stafford County)	22405
Springville	24630
Springwood	24066
Sprouses Corner	23936
Stacy	24614
Stafford	22554*
	22555†
Stafford Correctional Unit	22554
Staffordshire	23235
Staffordsville	24167
Stage Junction	23038
Staleys Cross Roads	24368
Stanardsville	22973
Stanley	22851
Stanleytown (Henry County)	24168
Stanleytown (Scott County)	22435
Stapleton	24572
Starkey	24018
Starnes	24250
Star Tannery	22654
Statesville	23874
Station Hills	22039
Staunton	24401*
	24402†
Staunton Park (Part of Staunton)	24401
Steeleburg	24609
Steeles Tavern	24476

*Area Zip Code † Post Office Boxes

	ZIP		ZIP		ZIP		ZIP
Steinman	24226	Sunnyside (Frederick		Three Forks	24588	University (Part of	
Stella	24133	County)	22603	Threemile Corner	23117	Charlottesville)	22903
Stemphleytown	22821	Sunny View	22309	Three Springs	24202	University Heights	
Stephens	24293	Sunset Heights	23231	Three Square (Goochland		(Albemarle County)	22901
Stephens City	22655	Sunset Hills	22090	County)	23063	University Heights	
Stephenson	22656	Sunset Manor	22312	Three Square (Louisa		(Henrico County)	23229
Sterling	20164-67	Sunset Village (Part of		County)	23024	University of Richmond	
For specific Sterling Zip Codes		Salem)	24153	Threeway	22469	(Part of Richmond)	23173
call (703) 430-6363, or your		Supply	22559	Tibbstown	22942	Uno	22738
local postmaster.		Surrey Square	22032	Tibitha	22539	Upper Brandon	23881
Sterling Point (Part of		Surry	23883	Ticktown	23301	Upperville	22176
Portsmouth)	23703	Susan	23163	Tidemill	23072	Upright	22454
Stevensburg	22741	Sussex	23884	Tidewater	22572	Upshaw	23009
Stevens Creek	24330	Sussex Hilton (Part of		Tidwells	22520	Urbanna	23175
Stevensville	23161	Newport News)	23605	Tight Squeeze	24531	Vails Mill	24236
Stewart (Part of		Sutherland (Dinwiddie		Tignor	22514	Vale	22124
Richmond)	23221	County)	23885	Timberlake	24502	Valentine Hills	23228
Stewartsburg	24416	Sutherland (Wise County)	24273	Timberly Heights (Part of		Valentines	23887
Stewartsville	24179	Sutherland Manor	23885	Petersburg)	23803	Valley Brook	22042
Stickleyville	24244	Sutherlin	24594	Timber Ridge	24450	Valley Creek	24271
Stingray Point	23043	Sutton Place	22031	Timberville	22853	Valley Mall (Part of	
Stith	24534	Sutton Woods	22181	Timothy Park	22309	Harrisonburg)	22801
Stockton	24054	Swansea Manor (Part of		Tiny	24220	Valley Mills	24479
Stoddert	23901	Newport News)	23601	Tiptop	24630	Valley Ridge	24426
Stokesland (Part of		Swansonville	24549	Tito	24244	Valley View	22306
Danville)	24541	Sweet Briar	24595	Tivis	24256	Valley View Mall (Part of	
Stokesville	22843	Sweet Briar Park	23075	Toano	23168	Roanoke)	24012
Stone Bridge	22663	Sweet Chalybeate	24426	Tobaccoville	23139	Valleywood	22191
Stone Creek	24277	Sweet Hall	23181	Todds Tavern	22553	Van Buren Furnace	22644
Stonega	24285	Swift Creek (Part of		Toga	23936	Vanderpool	24465
Stone Mountain	24523	Colonial Heights)	23834	Tola	23959	Vandola	24541
Stones Mill	24382	Swift Run	22827	Toms Bottom	24256	Vandyke (Buchanan	
Stone Springs (Part of		Switch Back	22445	Toms Brook	22660	County)	24639
Harrisonburg)	22801	Swoope	24479	Toms Creek	24230	Van Dyke (Tazewell	
Stonewall	24538	Swords Creek	24649	Tookland	24614	County)	24609
Stonewall Acres	22110	Sycamore	24557	Topnot	22657	Vannoy Acres	22030
Stonewall Manor	22180	Sydnorsville	24151	Topping	23169	Vannoy Park	22024
Stoneybrook	22553	Sylvania Heights	22408	Toshes	24139	Vansant	24656
Stony	24245	Sylvatus	24343	Totaro	23856	Varina	23231
Stony Battery	24354	Syria	22743	Tower Mall (Part of		Varina Grove	23075
Stony Creek	23882	Syringa	23169	Portsmouth)	23701	Vaucluse	22655
Stony Man	22835	Tabb	23693	Town and Country		Vaughn	22835
Stony Point	22901	Tabscott	23038	Estates	22180	Vawter Corner	23093
Stony Point Mills	23040	Tacoma	24230	Townsend	23443	Velma	23108
Stony Ridge	24630	Taft	22578	Trade Center (Part of		Venia	24260
Stormont	23149	Talbot Park (Part of		Alexandria)	22304	Vera	24522
Story	23837	Norfolk)	23505	Trammel	24289	Verbena	22827
Stott	23898	Tall Oaks	22003	Trapp	22176	Verdi	22435
Stovall	24577	Tallysville	23124	Treemont	23234	Vernon Hill	24597
Stover	24421	Tamworth	23027	Treherneville	23307	Verona	24482
Straightstone	24569	Tangier	23440	Tremont Gardens	22042	Vertain Park	22032
Strasburg	22657	Tannersville	24377	Trenholm	23139	Vesta	24177
Strasburg Junction	22657	Tappahannock	22560	Trents Mill	23040	Vests Store	23139
Stratford	22558	Tara	22205	Trevilians	23170	Vesuvius	24483
Stratford Hills (Arlington		Taro	23934	Triangle	22172	Vicey	24256
County)	22207	Tarpon	24228	Trigg	24134	Vicker	24073
Stratford Hills (Part of		Tasley	23441	Trinity	24175	Vicker Heights	24073
Richmond)	23225	Tatum	22567	Triplet	23868	Vicksville	23878
Stratford Landing	22308	Tauxemont	22308	Trout Dale	24378	Victoria	23974
Stratford-on-the-Potomac	22308	Taylors Store	24184	Troutville	24175	Vienna	22180-83
Stratford Village	23222	Taylorstown	22075	Trower	23480	For specific Vienna Zip Codes	
Strathmeade Springs	22003	Taylors Valley	24236	Troy	22974	call (703) 938-2125, or your	
Strathmore	23022	Taylorsville	23047	Trueblue	22701	local postmaster.	
Stringtown	22611	Tazewell	24651	Truxillo	23002		
Stroupes Store	24382	Tazewell Correctional Unit	24651	Tuckahoe	23229	Viers	24256
Stuart	24171	Teas	24375	Tuckahoe Park	23229	Viewtown	22746
Stuarts Draft	24477	Temperanceville	23442	Tuckahoe Village	23229	Village	22570
Stubbs	22553	Temple Hall Estates	23168	Tucker Hill	22488	Villa Heights	24112
Studley	23162	Temple Hill (Part of		Tuggle	23901	Villamay	22307
Stukeley Hall Farms	23227	Castlewood)	24224	Tunstall	23124	Villamont	24178
Stumptown (Loudoun		Templeman	22520	Turbeville	24596	Villboro	22580
County)	22075	Tenso	24226	Turnbull	22186	Vint Hill Farms	22186
Stumptown (Northampton		Tenth Legion	22815	Turners Crossroads	23879	Vint Hill Farms Station	22186
County)	23347	Terrys Fork	24138	Turner Store	23873	Vinton	24179
Suburban Apartments	23230	Tetotum	22485	Turnpike (Part of Fairfax)	22031	Virgilina	24598
Sudley	22110	Thaxton	24174	Tuscarora	22454	Virginia Beach	23450-67
Sudley Manor	22110	The English Hills	22039	Twin Pines (Part of		For specific Virginia Beach Zip	
Suffolk	23432-39	The Hollow	24053	Portsmouth)	23703	Codes call (804) 340-6227, or	
For specific Suffolk Zip Codes		The Knolls	22191	Twin Poplars	22938	your local postmaster.	
call (804) 539-5191, or your		Thelma	22942	Twin Springs	24271	Virginia City	24283
local postmaster.		The Manors	22192	Twymans Mill	22727	Virginia Forest (Part of	
Sugar Grove	24375	Theological Seminary		Tye River	22922	Falls Church)	22046
Sugar Hill	24528	(Part of Alexandria)	22304	Tyler Gardens (Part of		Virginia Gardens (Part of	
Sugarland Run	20164	The Plains	22171	Falls Church)	22046	Norfolk)	23505
Sugar Loaf	24018	The Ridge	23917	Tyler Park	22042	Virginia Heights (Arlington	
Suiter	24314	Thessalia	24134	Tylerton	22405	County)	22204
Sulgrave Manor	22309	The Timbers	22152	Tyro	22976	Virginia Heights (Henrico	
Sumerduck	22742	The Villas	22191	Tysons Corner	22103	County)	23231
Summerdeon	24479	Thomas Bridge	24354	Tysons Corner Center	22102	Virginia Highlands	22202
Summit (Smyth County)	24375	Thomas Corner (Part of		Tysons Green	22182	Virginia Hills (Part of	
Summit (Spotsylvania		Norfolk)	23502	Union (Bedford County)	24174	Bristol)	24201
County)	22408	Thomasson Park	22134	Union (Floyd County)	24380	Virginia Hills (Fairfax	
Sun	24224	Thomas Terrace	24504	Union Hall	24176	County)	22310
Sunbeam	23851	Thomastown	24445	Union Level	23970	Virginia State University	
Sunnybank	22539	Thompson Valley	24651	Unionville	22567	(Part of Petersburg)	23803
Sunnybrook	22182	Thornburg	22565	Unison	22141	Virginia Union University	
Sunnybrook Estates	22110	Thornhill	22960	United States Marine		(Part of Richmond)	23220
Sunnyside (Cumberland		Thoroughfare	22014	Reservation	22134	Vir-Mar Beach	22473
County)	23040	Thoroughgood (Part of		Unity	23898	Volens	24577
		Virginia Beach)	23455			Volney	24379
						Vulcan	22567

Place	ZIP	Place	ZIP	Place	ZIP	Place	ZIP
Wabun	24153	West Augusta	24485	White Oak (Stafford County)	22405	Wolfglade	24333
Wachapreague	23480	West Bottom	23022	White Oaks	22307	Wolford	24658
Wadesville	22611	Westbourne	23230	White Oak Swamp	23150	Wolftown	22748
Wake	23176	Westbriar	23075	White Plains	23893	Wolf Trap (Fairfax County)	22182
Wakefield (Part of Alexandria)	*	Westchester (Chesterfield County)	23235	White Post	22663	Wolf Trap (Halifax County)	24592
Wakefield (Sussex County)	22304	Westchester (Fairfax County)	22031	White Shop	23086	Womacks	23923
Wakefield (Sussex County)	23888	Westdale	23229	White Stone	22578	Wood	24250
Wakefield Chapel	22003	West Dante	24272	Whitesville	23421	Woodberry Forest	22989
Wakefield Forest	22003	West End Manor	23229	Whitethorne	24060	Woodberry Hills (Part of Danville)	24541
Wake Forest	24060	Western (Part of Petersburg)	23803	Whitetop	24292	Woodbridge	22191-94
Wakenva	24237	West Falls Church (Part of Falls Church)	22046	Whiteville	23040	For specific Woodbridge Zip Codes call (703) 494-6427, or your local postmaster.	
Waldrop	22942	Westfield (Part of Bristol)	24201	Whitewood	24657	Woodbrook	22901
Walhaven	22310	West Fork	24069	Whitley	23487	Woodford	22580
Walkers	23089	West Fredericksburg (Part of Fredericksburg)	22401	Whitlock	22942	Woodhaven Shores	23141
Walker Store	23924	West Galax (Part of Galax)	24333	Whitmell	24549	Woodland Hills	24210
Walkers Well	24531	West Gate	22110	Whittle	24531	Woodlawn (Carroll County)	24381
Walkerton	23177	West Gate of Lomond	22110	Wickford	22310	Woodlawn (Part of Hopewell)	23860
Wallace	24202	West Ghent (Part of Norfolk)	23507	Wicomico	23184	Woodlawn Manor	22309
Wallaces Store	23937	Westgrove	22307	Wicomico Church	22579	Woodlawn Mansion	22060
Wallops Flight Center	23337	Westham	23229	Wide Water	22554	Woodlawn Park	22309
Wallops Island	23337	Westhampton (Fairfax County)	22043	Widewater Beach	22554	Woodlawn Terrace (Fairfax County)	22309
Walnut Grove	24270	Westhampton (Part of Richmond)	23226	Wightman	23924	Woodlawn Terrace (Henrico County)	23150
Walnut Hill (Part of Petersburg)	23805	Westhaven (Part of Portsmouth)	23707	Wilburdale	22003	Woodlawn Village	22060
Walters	23315	West Hope	23882	Wilda	24477	Woodlee (Part of Staunton)	24401
Walters Woods	22044	Westland	22578	Wilde Acres	22602	Woodley Hills	22306
Walton	24141	West Langley	22101	Wilderness	22553	Woodley Hills (Part of Engleside)	22309
Walton Furnace	24360	Westlawn	22042	Wilderness Corner	22553	Woodman Terrace	23228
Walton Park	23112	West Leigh	22901	Wildwood (Fluvanna County)	22963	Woodmont (Arlington County)	22207
Waltons Store	24104	West Lexington (Part of Covington)	24450	Wildwood (Henrico County)	23227	Woodmont (Chesterfield County)	23235
Wan	23061	Westmoreland (Albemarle County)	22901	Wildwood Farms	23842	Woodridge	24590
Ward	24620	Westmoreland (Westmoreland County)	22577	Wilkinsons Store	23833	Woodrow Wilson	22939
Wardell	24609	Westmoreland Heights	22043	Wilkinson Terrace	23234	Woodrum (Part of Staunton)	24401
Wards Corner (Part of Norfolk)	23505	Westmoreland Park	22046	Willard Park (Part of Norfolk)	23509	Woods Cross Roads	23190
Wards Mill	24333	West Norfolk (Part of Portsmouth)	23703	Williamsburg	23185-88	Woodside Estates	22102
Wardtown	23482	Westover (Arlington County)	22205	For specific Williamsburg Zip Codes call (804) 229-4668, or your local postmaster.		Woods Mill	22938
Ware Neck	23178	Westover (Charles City County)	23030	Williamsburg Manor	22308	Woodson	22951
Wares Crossroads	23117	Westover Hills (Augusta County)	22980	Williams Mill	24251	Woods Store	24091
Wares Wharf	22454	Westover Hills (Part of Danville)	24541	Williamson Road (Part of Roanoke)	24012	Woodstock	22664
Warfield	23889	Westover Hills (Greensville County)	23847	Williamsville	24487	Woodville	22749
Warminster	24599	Westover Hills (Part of Richmond)	23225	Willis	24380	Woodway	24277
Warm Springs	24484	West Petersburg	23803	Willisville	22176	Woolwine	24185
Warner	23179	West Piney	24382	Willis Wharf	23486	Worlds	24530
Warren	24590	West Point	23181	Willoughby Terrace (Part of Norfolk)	23503	Worsham	23901
Warrenton	22186	West Raven	24639	Willow	24521	Worshams	23139
Warren Woods (Part of Fairfax)	22030	West Springfield	22152	Willowbrook	23024	Wren	23959
Warsaw	22572	Wests Store	24577	Willow Hill	23881	Wright (Part of Norfolk)	23505
Warwick (Part of Newport News)	23601	Westview (Augusta County)	24479	Willow Lakes (Part of Chesapeake)	23320	Wrights Shop	24572
Warwick on the James (Part of Newport News)	23601	West View (Goochland County)	23063	Willow Lawn	23230	Wrightsville	22427
Warwick Village (Part of Alexandria)	22305	Westview Hills	22152	Willow Run	22003	Wurno	24301
Washington	22747	West Warm Springs	24484	Willow Spring	24266	Wylliesburg	23976
Washington Corner	22580	Westwood	23226	Willow Woods	22003	Wyndale	24210
Washington Gardens (Part of Hampton)	23669	Westwood Estates	24211	Wills Corner	23430	Wythe (Part of Hampton)	23661
Washington National Airport	22201	Westwood Forest	22182	Willston	22044	Wytheville	24382
Washington Park	23847	Westwood Park	22046	Wilmington	22963	Yacht Haven Estates	22309
Watauga	24211	Westwood Place	24426	Wilroy (Part of Suffolk)	23434	Yale	23897
Waterford	22190	Weyanoke	22312	Wilsons	23894	Yancey Mills	22932
Waterlick	22657	Weyers Cave	24486	Wilson Springs	24473	Yanceyville	23093
Waterloo	22663	Whaley (Part of Suffolk)	23438	Wilton Woods	22310	Yards	24659
Water View (Middlesex County)	23180	Whaleyville (Part of Suffolk)	23438	Winchester	22601-04	Yellow Branch	24550
Waterview (Part of Portsmouth)	23707	Wheatfield	22641	For specific Winchester Zip Codes call (703) 662-2553, or your local postmaster.		Yellow Springs	24361
Watson	22075	Wheatland	22132	Windmill Point	22578	Yellow Sulphur Springs	24073
Wattsville	23483	Wheeler	24248	Windsor	23487	Yellow Tavern	23060
Waugh	24526	Whitacre	22625	Windsordale	23229	York Manor	23075
Waverly	23890	White City	23847	Windsor Estates	22310	Yorkshire	22110
Waverly Hills	22207	White Gate	24134	Windsor Farms (Part of Richmond)	23221	Yorkshire Acres	22110
Waverly Village	22407	White Hall (Albemarle County)	22987	Windsor Park	22310	Yorkshire Park	22110
Waxpool	22010	Whitehall (Frederick County)	22603	Windsor Place	23075	York Terrace	23185
Wayland	23235	White Head Hall	23828	Windsor Shades	23140	Yorktown	23690-93
Waynesboro	22980	White Hill	24477	Windy Hill Estates	23111	For specific Yorktown Zip Codes call (804) 898-3098, or your local postmaster.	
Waynewood	22308	White House	24580	Winesap	24572	Yorktown Naval Weapons Station	23691
Wayside	23030	White Marsh	23183	Winfall	24554	Yost	24460
Weal	24531	White Mill	24210	Wingina	24599	Youngers Store	24558
Webbtown	22611	White Oak (Halifax County)	24558	Winona (Part of Norfolk)	23509	Yuma	24251
Weber City (Fluvanna County)	23022			Winslow Hills	22310	Zacata	22581
Weber City (Scott County)	24290			Winston	22701	Zack	24459
Wedgewood	23229			Wintergreen	22958	Zanoni	23191
Weedonville	22485			Winterham	23002	Zenda	22801
Weems	22576			Winterpock	23832	Zepp	22644
Weirwood	23413			Wirtz	24184	Zion	22942
Welchs	22580			Wise	24293	Zion Crossroads	22942
Welcome	22485			Wisharts Point	23303	Ziontown	23075
Wellford	22572			Wistar Farms	23228	Zuni	23898
Wellington (Fairfax County)	22308			Witch Duck (Part of Suffolk)	23462*		
Wellington (Prince William County)	22110				23466†		
Wellington Heights	22308			Withams	23488		
West Arlington	22213			Wittens Mills	24630		

* Area Zip Code   † Post Office Boxes

Place	ZIP
Aberdeen	98520
Aberdeen Gardens	98520
Academy	99031
Acme	98220
Adamsview Park	98951
Addy	99101
Adelaide (Part of Federal Way)	98003
Adelma Beach	98368
Admiral's Cove	98239
Adna	98522
Adrian	98851
Aeneas	98855
Agate Point	98110
Agnew	98362
Ahtanum	98903
Airway Heights	99001
Ajlune	98564
Albion	99102
Alder	98328
Alder Terrace	98926
Alderton	98371
Alderwood	98225
Alderwood Manor	98036
Alderwood Manor-Bothell North	98021
Alexander Beach	98221
Alger	98233
Algona	98001
Allen	98232
Allentown	98178
Allyn	98524
Allyn-Grapeview	98524
Almira	99103
Aloha	98571
Alpental	98068
Alpha	98570
Altoona	98643
Amanda Park	98526
Amber	99004
Amboy	98601
American Lake	98498
Anacortes	98221
Anatone	99401
Anderson Island	98303
Angle Lake (Part of SeaTac)	98188
Annapolis (Part of Port Orchard)	98366
Appleton	98602
Arbor Heights (Part of Seattle)	98146
Arcadia	98584
Arden	99114
Ardenvoir	98811
Argyle	98250
Ariel	98603
Arletta	98335
Arlington	98223
Arlington Heights	98223
Armar	98270
Arrowhead (King County)	98011
Arrowhead (Pierce County)	98498
Arrowhead Beach	98292
Artic	98537
Artondale	98335
Ashford	98304
Asotin	99402
Auburn	98001-02
	98071
	98092
For specific Auburn Zip Codes call (206) 833-0540, or your local postmaster.	
Auburn Twin Lakes (Part of Federal Way)	98023
Ault Field	98277
Avery	98617
Avon	98273
Ayer	99348
Azwell	98846
Baby Island Heights	98260
Baileysburg	98328
Bainbridge Island	98110
Baker Heights	98273
Ballard (Part of Seattle)	98107
B and G	98201
Bangor	98315
Bangor Submarine Base	98315
Bangor Trident Base	98315
Barberton	98665
Baring	98224
Barstow	99141
Basin City	99343
Battle Ground	98604
Battle Point	98110
Bay Center	98527
Bay City	98520
Bayne	98022
Bay Shore	98584
Bay View (Island County)	98260
Bayview (Skagit County)	98273
Bazinet Eddition	98532
Beachcombers Hidden Beach	98253
Beachcrest	98501
Beacon Hill	98632
Beaux Arts Village	98004
Beaver	98305
Beaver Valley	98365
Beckett Point	98368
Belfair	98528
Bellevue	98004-09
	98015
For specific Bellevue Zip Codes call (206) 454-2489, or your local postmaster.	
Bellevue Square (Part of Bellevue)	98004
Bellingham	98225-28
For specific Bellingham Zip Codes call (206) 676-8303, or your local postmaster.	
Bellis Fair (Part of Bellingham)	98226
Belmont	99104
Belvidere	99116
Bench Drive (Part of Aberdeen)	98520
Benge	99105
Benson Hill	98055
Benton City	99320
Bethel	98366
Beverly	99321
Beverly Beach	98249
Beverly Park (Part of Everett)	98203
Bickleton	99322
Big Bend	98251
Big Lake	98273
Bingen	98605
Birch Bay	98230
Birchfield	98901
Birdsview	98237
Bissell	99137
Bitter Lake (Part of Seattle)	98133
Biz Point	98221
Black Diamond	98010
Black Lake	99114
Black River (Part of Skyway)	98178
Black River (Part of Renton)	98055
Black River Junction (Part of Renton)	98055
Blaine	98230*
	98231†
Blakely Island	98222
Blanchard	98232
Blewett	98826
Blockhouse	98620
Blue Creek	99109
Blue Lake	99115
Blueslide	99180
Blyn	98382
Boise	98022
Bonneville Spur (Part of Bellingham)	98225
Bonney Lake	98390
Bordeaux	98556
Bossburg	99126
Boston Harbor	98506
Bothell	98011-12
	98021
	98041
For specific Bothell Zip Codes call (206) 486-3243, or your local postmaster.	
Boulevard Park	98188
Bow	98232
Bowman Beach	98381
Boyds	99107
Brady	98563
Breidablick	98370
Bremerton	98310-12
For specific Bremerton Zip Codes call (206) 373-1456, or your local postmaster.	
Brewster	98812
Briarwood	98031
Bridgeport	98813
Brief	98822
Brier	98036
Brinnon	98320
Broadmoor (Part of Seattle)	98112
Broadway (Part of Seattle)	98102
Brookdale	98444
Brooklane Village	98926
Brooklyn	98537
Browns Point	98422
Brownstown	98920
Brownsville	98310
Bruceport	98586
Brush Prairie	98606
Bryant	98223
Bryn Mawr	98178
Bryn Mawr-Skyway	98178
Buckeye	99005
Buckhorn	98245
Buckley	98321
Bucoda	98530
Buena	98921
Buena Vista	98292
Bunker	98532
Burbank	99323
Burbank Heights	99301
Burien	98146-48
	98166-68
For specific Burien Zip Codes call (206) 242-8920, or your local postmaster.	
Burley	98322
Burlington	98233
Burnett	98321
Burton	98013
Bush Point	98249
Butler Acres	98626
Butler Cove	98501
BZ Corner	98672
Cabin Creek	98925
Camaloch	98292
Camano City	98292
Camano Country Club	98292
Camas	98607
Camelot	98001
Campbell's Glen	98236
Camp Murray	98498
Camp Union	98312
Campus (Part of Bellingham)	98225
Canal Tract	98320
Cape George	98368
Capital Mall (Part of Olympia)	98502
Capitol City Country Club	98501
Capitol Hill (Part of Seattle)	98102
Cap Sante (Part of Anacortes)	98221
Carbonado	98323
Care Free Loop	98331
Carlisle	98536
Carlsborg	98324
Carlton	98814
Carnation	98014
Carrier Annex (Part of Everett)	98204
Carrolls	98609
Carson	98610
Carson River Valley	98610
Carylon Beach	98501
Cascade-Fairwood	98055
Cascade Mall	98055
Cascade Park East	98684
Cascade Park West	98684
Cascade Terrace	98371
Cascade Valley	98837
Cascade Vista	98058
Cashmere	98815
Castle Rock	98611
Cathan	98270
Cathcart	98290
Cathlamet	98612
Cavelero Beach	98292
Cedar Creek Corrections Center	98556
Cedardale	98273
Cedar Falls	98045
Cedar Grove	98038
Cedarhome	98292
Cedar Mountain	98055
Cedarview	98390
Cedarville	98568
Cedonia	99137
Center	98376
Centerville	98613
Central (Part of Yakima)	98901
Centralia	98531
Central Park	98520
Central Valley	98370
Ceres	98532
Charleston (Part of Bremerton)	98312
Charleston Beach	98312
Charter Oak	98604
Chattaroy	99003
Chehalis	98532
Chehalis Indian Reservation	98568
Chehalis Village	98568
Chelan	98816
Chelan Falls	98817
Chelatchie	98601
Cheney	99004
Cherokee Bay Park	98038
Cherry Crest (Part of Bellevue)	98004
Cherry Gardens	98019
Cherry Grove	98604
Cherry Point	98230
Chesaw	98844
Chewelah	99109
Chico	98312
Chimacum	98325
Chinook	98614
Christopher (Part of Auburn)	98002
Chuckanut Village (Part of Bellingham)	98225
Chumstick	98826
Churchlake	98390
Cicero	98223
Cinebar	98533
Cispus	98377
City Center (Part of Bellingham)	98225
Clallam Bay	98326
Claquato	98532
Claremont (Part of Everett)	98201
Clarkston	99403
Clarkston Heights	99403
Clarkston Heights-Vineland	99403
Clay City	98328
Clayton	99110
Clearbrook	98247
Clear Lake (Pierce County)	98328
Clearlake (Skagit County)	98235
Clear Lake (Spokane County)	99022
Clearview	98290
Clearwater	98331
Cle Elum	98922
Cleveland	99356
Cliffdell	98937
Cline (Part of Springdale)	99173
Clinton	98236
Clipper	98244
Cloverland	98402
Clover Park	98499
Clyde Hill	98004
Coal Creek	98632
Coalfield	98059
Cohasset Beach	98595
Colbert	99005
Colby	98366
Colchester	98366
Coles Corner	98826
Colfax	99111
College (Part of Pullman)	99163
College Place	99324
Colton	99113
Columbia (Part of Seattle)	98118
Columbia Beach	98236
Columbia Center (Part of Kennewick)	99336
Columbia Heights	98632
Columbia Valley Gardens	98632
Colville	99114
Colville Indian Agency	99155
Colville Indian Reservation	99155
Conconully	98819
Concora (Part of Tukwila)	98188
Concrete	98237
Conifer View (Part of Bothell)	98011
Connell	99326
Conway	98238
Cook	98605
Cooper Point	98501
Copalis Beach	98535
Copalis Crossing	98536
Cornwall (Part of Bellingham)	98225
Cosmopolis	98537
Cottage Lake	98072
Cottage Lake Bridle Trail	98033
Cottonwood Beach	98230
Cougar	98616
Coulee City	99115
Coulee Dam	99116

* Area Zip Code   † Post Office Boxes

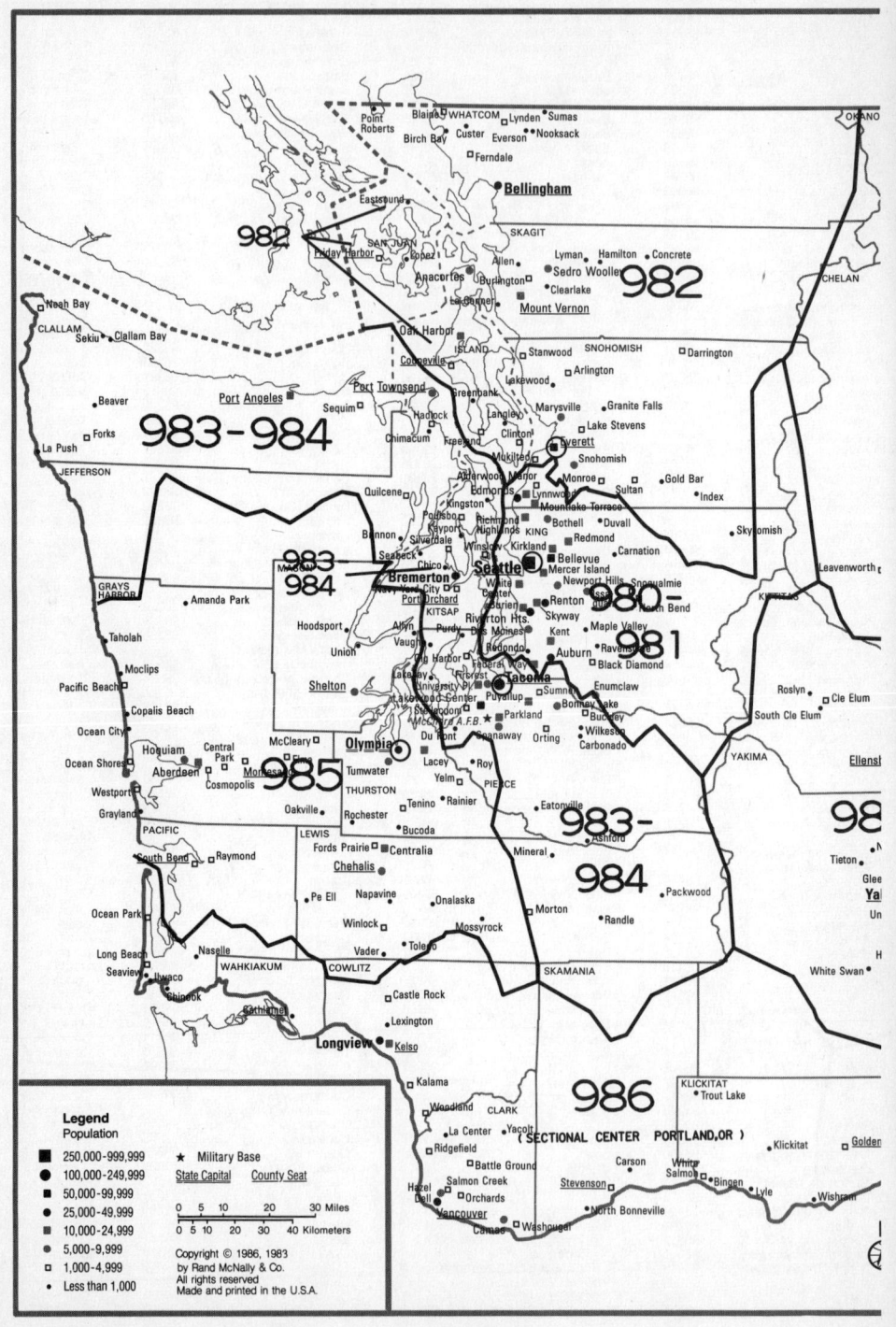

982

982

Point Roberts · Blaine · WHATCOM · Lynden · Sumas
· Custer · Everson · Nooksack
Birch Bay
· Ferndale
Bellingham
Eastsound
SAN JUAN · Lyman · Hamilton · Concrete
Friday Harbor · Lopez · Allen · Sedro Woolley
· Anacortes · Burlington · Clearlake
La Conner · **Mount Vernon**

Neah Bay · CLALLAM · Clallam Bay
Sekiu · Stanwood · SNOHOMISH · Darrington
Coupeville
ISLAND · Lakewood · Arlington
· Beaver · Port Angeles · Sequim
Port Townsend · Greenbank · Marysville · Granite Falls
· Langley · Lake Stevens

983–984
· Forks · Hadlock · Clinton · **Everett**
La Push · Chimacum · Freeland · Mukilteo · Snohomish
JEFFERSON · Quilcene · Alderwood Manor · Monroe · Gold Bar
· Edmonds · Lynnwood · Sultan
· Kingston · Mountlake Terrace · · Index
· Poulsbo · Richmond · Bothell · Duvall
· Silverdale · Highlands · KING · Redmond
Bangor · Keyport · Winslow · Kirkland · Carnation · Skykomish
· Seabeck · **Seattle** · Bellevue · Leavenworth
· Chico · White · Mercer Island
983–984 · **Bremerton** · Center · Newport Hills · Snoqualmie
GRAYS · Amanda Park · Port Orchard · Burien · Renton · North Bend
HARBOR · KITSAP · Skyway
· Hoodsport · Allyn · Purdy · Des Moines · Kent · Maple Valley
· Taholah · Union · Vaughn · Redondo · Ravensdale
· Moclips · Fife · Federal Way · Auburn · Black Diamond
Pacific Beach · Gig Harbor · Fircrest · **Tacoma** · Sumner · Enumclaw · Roslyn · Cle Elum
Copalis Beach · Lakewood Center · Puyallup · Bonney Lake · South Cle Elum
Ocean City · McCleary · University Pl · Steilacoom · Buckley
Ocean Shores · Central · Steilacoom · Parkland · Wilkeson · YAKIMA
· Hoquiam · Park · Fircrest · McChord A.F.B. · Orting · Carbonado
Aberdeen · Montesano · **985** · Du Pont · Spanaway
Westport · Cosmopolis · **Olympia** · Lacey · Roy
Grayland · Tumwater · Yelm · Rainier
PACIFIC · THURSTON · PIERCE · **983–**
· Oakville · Tenino · · Eatonville
· Raymond · Rochester · Bucoda · Ashford · **984**
South Bend · LEWIS · Fords Prairie · Centralia · Mineral · Packwood
· Pe Ell · **Chehalis** · Morton · Randle
Ocean Park · Napavine · Onalaska
· Winlock · Mossyrock
Long Beach · Naselle · Vader · Toledo · White Swan
Seaview · Ilwaco · WAHKIAKUM · COWLITZ · SKAMANIA
Chinook · · Castle Rock
· Lexington
Longview · Kelso
· Kalama · KLICKITAT
· Woodland · CLARK · **986** · Trout Lake
· La Center · Yacolt (SECTIONAL CENTER PORTLAND, OR)
· Ridgefield · Battle Ground · Carson · White · Klickitat
Hazel · Salmon Creek · Salmon · Bingen · Lyle
Dell · Orchards **Stevenson** · North Bonneville
Vancouver · Washougal
Camas

Legend
Population
■ 250,000-999,999   ★ Military Base
● 100,000-249,999   State Capital   County Seat
■ 50,000-99,999
■ 25,000-49,999   0 5 10   20   30 Miles
■ 10,000-24,999   0 5 10   20   30   40 Kilometers
• 5,000-9,999
□ 1,000-4,999   Copyright © 1986, 1983
· Less than 1,000   by Rand McNally & Co.
                        All rights reserved
                        Made and printed in the U.S.A.

OKANO
CHELAN
KITTITAS
Ellensb
98
Tieton · Glee
Ya
Un

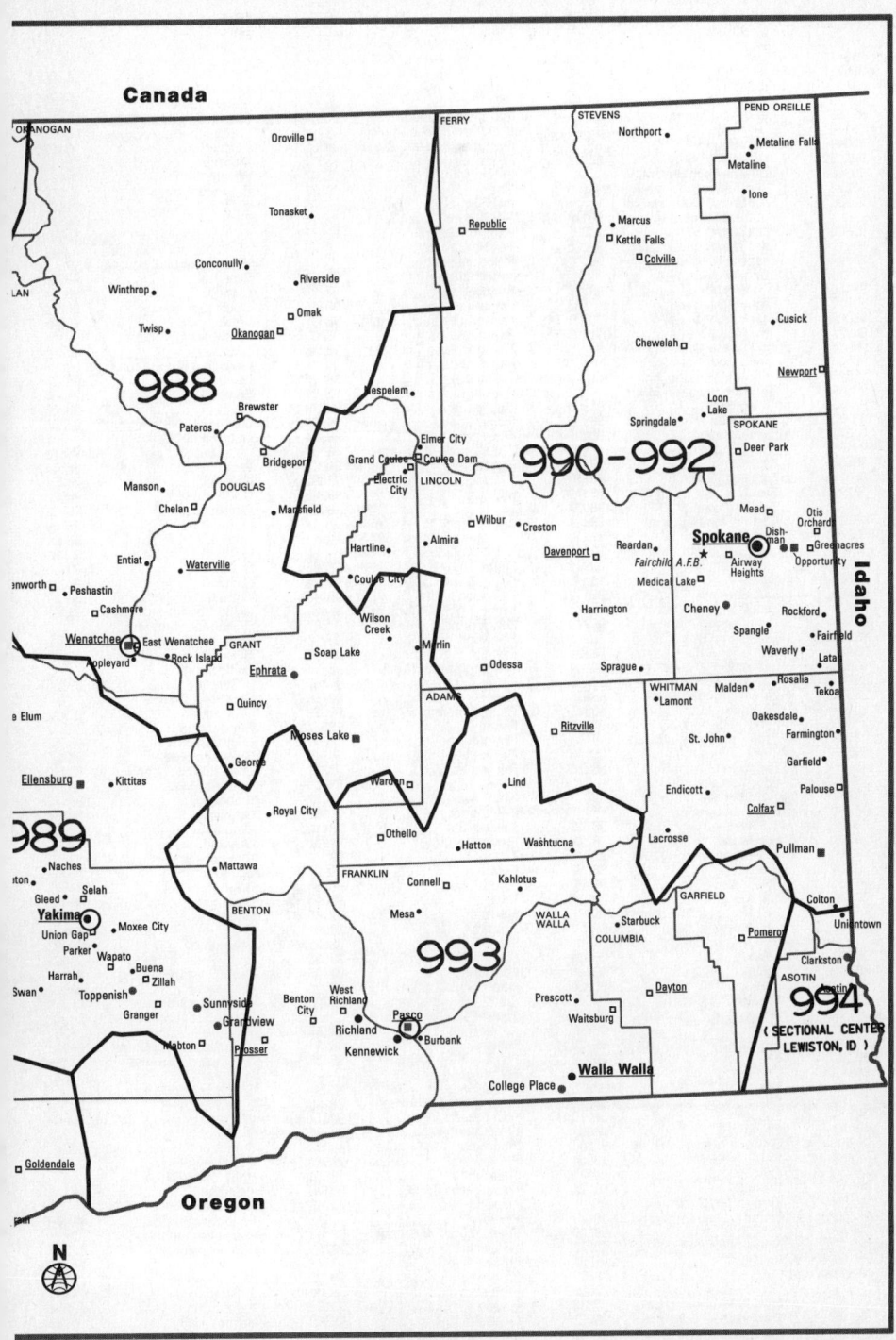

Canada

OKANOGAN

FERRY

STEVENS

PEND OREILLE

Oroville □

Northport □

Metaline Falls □

Metaline □

Ione □

Tonasket □

Republic □

Marcus □

Cusick □

Conconully □

Riverside □

Kettle Falls □

Colville □

Winthrop □

Omak □

Chewelah □

Newport □

Twisp □

Okanogan □

988

Jespelem □

Loon Lake □

SPOKANE

Brewster □

Elmer City □

Springdale □

Deer Park □

Pateros □

Grand Coulee □ Coulee Dam □

990-992

Bridgeport □

Electric City □

LINCOLN

Manson □

DOUGLAS

Mansfield □

Wilbur □ Creston □

Mead □

Otis Orchards □

Greenacres □

Chelan □

Hartline □

Almira □

Davenport □

Reardan □

Dishman □

Spokane ⊙

Opportunity □

Entiat □

Waterville □

Fairchild A.F.B.

Airway Heights

Peshastin □

Coulee City □

Medical Lake □

Cheney □

Rockford □

enworth □

Cashmere □

Wilson Creek □

Harrington □

Spangle □

Fairfield □

Wenatchee ⊡ East Wenatchee

GRANT

Marlin □

Waverly □

Latah

Appleyard □ Rock Island

Soap Lake □

Odessa □

Sprague □

WHITMAN

Malden □

Rosalia □

Tekoa

Ephrata □

ADAMS

Lamont □

e Elum

Quincy □

Oakesdale □

Moses Lake ■

Ritzville □

St. John □

Farmington □

Ellensburg ■

Kittitas □

Royal City □

Ward□n □

Lind □

Endicott □

Garfield □

Palouse □

Colfax □

989

Mattawa □

FRANKLIN

Othello □

Hatton □

Washtucna □

Lacrosse □

Pullman □

Naches □

Connell □

Kahlotus □

GARFIELD

Colton □

Gleed □ Selah □

Mesa □

Starbuck □

Uniontown □

Yakima ⊙

Moxee City □

WALLA WALLA

COLUMBIA

Pomeroy □

Clarkston □

Union Gap □

Parker □

Wapato □

Buena

Zillah □

993

Prescott □

Dayton □

ASOTIN

994

Harrah □

Toppenish □

Swan

West Richland □

Waitsburg □

(SECTIONAL CENTER LEWISTON, ID)

Granger □

Sunnyside □

Benton City □

Pasco ⊡

Grandview □

Richland □ Burbank □

Mabton □

Prosser □

Kennewick □

Goldendale □

College Place □

Walla Walla

Oregon

N

BENTON

LINCOLN

Place	ZIP	Place	ZIP	Place	ZIP	Place	ZIP
Country Homes	99218	Dumas Bay-Twin Lakes (Part of Federal Way)	98023	Eureka (Whatcom County)	98225	Garfield	99130
Countryside Beach	98501	Dungeness	98382	Evaline	98596	Garland (Part of Spokane)	99205
Coupeville	98239	Du Pont	98327	Evans	99126	Garrett	99362
Covington	98042	Dusty	99143	Everett	98201-08	Gate	98579
Covington-Sawyer-Wilderness	98042	Duvall	98019	For specific Everett Zip Codes call (206) 355-9505, or your local postmaster.		Geiger Heights	99204
Cowiche	98923	Duwamish	98188	Everett Mall (Part of Everett)	98208	Geneva	98226
Coyote Ridge Corrections Center	99326	Eagledale	98110	Evergreen (Clark County)	98684	George	98824
Cozy Nook	99109	Eaglemount	98368	Evergreen (Pierce County)	98411	Georgetown (mail Ravensdale)	98051
Creosote	98110	Earlington (Part of Renton)	98055	Evergreen Estates	98501	Georgetown (Part of Seattle)	98108
Crescent Bar	98848	Earlmount (Part of Redmond)	98052	Evergreen Shores	98501	Getchell	98223
Creston	99117	East Aberdeen (Part of Aberdeen)	98520	Everson	98247	Gibraltar	98221
Crocker	98360	East Coulee Dam (Part of Coulee Dam)	99116	Ewan	99127	Gifford	99131
Crockett Lake Estates	98239	East Everett	98205	Factoria	98006	Gig Harbor	98329
Cromwell	98335	East Farms	99025	Fairchild Air Force Base	99011		98332
Crossroads (Part of Bellevue)	98008	Eastgate (King County)	98007	Fairfield	99012		98335
Crown Hill (Part of Seattle)	98117	Eastgate (Walla Walla County)	99362	Fair Harbor	98546	For specific Gig Harbor Zip Codes call (206) 858-2700, or your local postmaster.	
Crystal Mountain	98022	East Heights	99133	Fairhaven (Part of Bellingham)	98225	Gilberton	98310
Crystal Spring	98110	East Hill-Meridian	98031	Fairmont	98204	Glacier	98244
Crystal Springs	98466		98042	Fairview (Kitsap County)	98310	Glacier Springs	98244
Crystal Village	98022	For specific East Hill-Meridian Zip Codes call (206) 852-3950, or your local postmaster.		Fairview (Yakima County)	98901	Gleed	98904
Cumberland	98022	East Hoquiam (Part of Hoquiam)	98550	Fairview-Sumach	98903	Glen Cove (Jefferson County)	98368
Cunningham	99327	East Kittitas	98926	Fairwood (King County)	98058	Glencove (Pierce County)	98329
Curlew	99118	Eastmont	98205	Fairwood (Spokane County)	99218	Glendale	98236
Curtis	98538	East Olympia	98540	Fall City	98024	Glenoma	98336
Cushman Dam	98548	Easton	98925	Fargher Lake	98675	Glenrose	99203
Cusick	99119	East Port Orchard	98366	Farmington	99128	Glenwood (Kitsap County)	98366
Custer (Pierce County)	98413	East Quilcene	98376	Fawn Lake	98584	Glenwood (Klickitat County)	98619
Custer (Whatcom County)	98240	East Raymond	98577	Federal (Part of Seattle)	98104	Globe	98554
Dabob	98376	East Renton Highlands	98024	Federal Way	98003	Gold Bar	98251
Daisy	99167	East Seattle (Part of Mercer Island)	98040		98023	Goldendale	98620
Dalkena	99156	East Selah	98901		98063	Gooseberry Point	98262
Dallesport	98617	Eastsound	98245		98093	Goose Prairie	98929
Danville	99121	East Spokane	99212	For specific Federal Way Zip Codes call (206) 927-8100, or your local postmaster.		Gorst	98337
Darlington (Part of Everett)	98203	East Stanwood (Part of Stanwood)	98292	Felida	98685	Goss Lake	98260
Darrington	98241	East Union (Part of Seattle)	98122	Felton Stone Lodge	99026	Govan	99185
Dash Point	98402	Eastview Hills	98204	Ferndale	98248	Graham	98338
Davenport	99122	East Wenatchee	98802	Fern Hill (Part of Tacoma)	98412	Graham Point	98584
Day Creek	98284	East Wenatchee Bench	98801	Fern Prairie	98607	Grand Coulee	99133
Day Island	98466	Eatonville	98328	Fernwood	98366	Grand Mound (census designated place)	98579
Dayton (Columbia County)	99328	Echo	99114	Fife	98424	Grand Mound	98501
Dayton (Mason County)	98584	Echo Lake	98133	Fife Heights	98424	Grandview (Clallam County)	98363
Decatur	98221	Eden	98643	Finley	99337	Grandview (Yakima County)	98930
Deep Creek	99022	Edgecomb	98223	Fircrest	98466	Granger	98932
Deep River	98638	Edgemoor (Part of Bellingham)	98225	Fircrest Eddition	98532	Granite Falls	98252
Deer Harbor	98243	Edgewater (Part of Everett)	98203	Firdale	98577	Grant Orchards	98851
Deer Island	98390	Edgewood	98372	Firgrove	98204	Grant Road Addition	98802
Deer Lake	99148	Edgewood-North Hill	98371	Fir Tree	98540	Granville Grange	98252
Deer Park	99006	Edison	98232	Firwood	98371	Grapeview	98546
Delano	99133	Edmonds	98020	Fisher	98607	Grassmere	98237
Delano Beach	98349		98026	Fish Town	98257	Gravelly Lake	98499
Delphi	98501	For specific Edmonds Zip Codes call (206) 774-6667, or your local postmaster.		Five Corners	98662	Grayland	98547
Delphi Country Club	98501	Edwall	99008	Fletcher Bay	98110	Grays Harbor City	98550
Del Ridge	98501	Eglon	98346	Florence	98292	Grays Landing	99009
Deming	98244	Elbe	98330	Fobes Hill	98205	Grays River	98621
Denison	99006	Elberton	99130	Foothill	99207	Greenacres	99016
Denny Creek	98045	Eldon	98555	Forbes	98584	Greenbank	98253
Denny Park	98011	Eldorado Hills	98312	Ford	99013	Greenbank Estates	98253
Desert Aire	99349	Electric City	99123	Fordair	99115	Green Bluff	99003
Des Moines	98188	Elk	99009	Ford Park	98331	Green River Gorge	98022
	98198	Elk Plain	98387	Fords Prairie	98531	Greens Landing	98816
For specific Des Moines Zip Codes call (206) 285-1650, or your local postmaster.		Ellensburg	98926	Forest	98532	Greenwater	98022
Devereaux Lake	98528	Ellisford	98855	Forest Beach	98335	Greenwater Meadows	98251
Dewey	98221	Ellisport	98070	Forest Glen	98501	Greenwood (Grays Harbor County)	98520
Dexter by the Sea	98590	Ellsworth	98664	Forest Hills Addition	99208	Greenwood (King County)	98103
Diablo	98283	Ellsworth North	98664	Forest Park (Part of Lake Forest Park)	98155	Greenwood (Stevens County)	99141
Diamond	99111	Ellsworth South	98664	Forks	98331	Greenwood (Whatcom County)	98264
Diamond Lake	99156	Elma	98541	Fort Lewis	98433	Grisdale	98563
Dieringer	98390	Elmer City	99124	Fort Wright (Part of Spokane)	99204	Gromore	98903
Dines Point	98253	Eltopia	99330	Foster (Part of Tukwila)	98188	Grotto	98288
Disautel	98841	Endicott	99125	Four Lakes	99014	Guemes	98221
Discovery Bay	98368	Enterprise	99129	Fox Island	98333	Haller Lake (Part of Seattle)	98133
Dishman	99213	Entiat	98822	Fragaria	98359	Hamilton	98255
Dixie	99329	Enumclaw	98022	Frances	98577	Hansville	98340
Dockton	98070	Ephrata	98823	Frankfort	98638	Happy Valley (Part of Bellingham)	98225
Dodge	99347	Erlands Point	98312	Frederickson	98446	Harbor Center	98249
Doe Bay	98279	Erlands Point-Kitsap Lake	98312	Freeland	98249	Harbor Heights (Part of Gig Harbor)	98338
Dollar's Corner	98604	Espanola	99022	Freeman	99015	Harbour Pointe	98204
Donald	98951	Esperance	98043	Fremont (Part of Seattle)	98103	Harmon Heights	98045
Doty	98539	Ethel	98542	Friday Harbor	98250	Harper	98366
Douglas	98858	Etna	98674	Frisken Wye	98541	Harrah	98933
Downing	98812	Eufaula Heights	98632	Fruitland	99129	Harrington	99134
Downtown (Part of Kent)	98032	Eureka (Walla Walla County)	99348	Fruitvale	98902	Hartford (Part of Lake Stevens)	98258
Downtown (Part of Tacoma)	98402			Furport	99156	Hartland	98635
Downtown (Part of Vancouver)	98660			Gales Addition	98362		
Draper Spring	98619			Galvin	98544		
Driftwood Acres	98940			Gamblewood	98346		
Driftwood Point	98390			Gardena	99360		
Driftwood Shores	98292			Garden City (Part of McCleary)	98557		
Dryad	98532			Gardiner	98382		
Dryden	98821						
Duluth	98642						

* Area Zip Code † Post Office Boxes

	ZIP
Hartline	99135
Hartstene	98584
Harwood	98908
Hatton	99332
Havillah	98855
Hawk Acres	98501
Hay	99136
Hayford	99204
Haynes Acres	98501
Hays Park (Part of Spokane)	99207
Hazel	98223
Hazel Dell	98665
Hazel Dell North	98665
Hazel Dell South	98665
Hazelwood	98055
Heather Downs (Part of Renton)	98055
Heisson	98622
Herron Island	98349
Hidden Valley	98304
Highland (Asotin County)	99403
Highland (Benton County)	99337
Highland (Clark County)	98629
Highland (Snohomish County)	98258
Highland Estates	98584
Highland Heights	98571
Highland Park (Part of Seattle)	98106
Highlands (Part of Renton)	98056
High Point (mail Issaquah)	98126
High Point (Part of Seattle)	98027
High Valley	98027
Hilltop	98004
Hillyard (Part of Spokane)	99207
Hintzville	98312
Hobart	98025
Hockinson	98606
Hogans Corner	98550
Hoh Indian Reservation	98331
Hoko	98326
Holcomb	98577
Holden Village	98816
Holiday Valley Estates	98501
Holly	98312
Hollywood	98072
Hollywood Beach	98816
Holman	98644
Holmes Harbor Estates	98253
Home	98349
Home Acres	98205
Home Valley	98648
Honeymoon Vista Bay	98253
Hood	98651
Hoodsport	98548
Hoogdal	98284
Hooper	99333
Hope	98333
Hoquiam	98550
Horseshoe Lake	98366
Houghton (Part of Kirkland)	98033
Humptulips	98552
Hunters	99137
Hunts Point	98004
Huntsville	99328
Husum	98623
Hyak	98068
Illahee (Grays Harbor County)	98569
Illahee (Kitsap County)	98310
Ilwaco	98624
Image	98662
Impach	99138
Inchelium	99138
Index	98256
Indian Beach	98292
Indianola	98342
Indian Village	98221
Inglewood	98011
Inglewood-Finn Hill	98011
Inlet Island	98390
Innis Arden	98160
Interbay (Part of Seattle)	98119
Intercity	98203
Interlaken	98438
International (Part of Seattle)	98104
Ione	99139
Irby	99159
Ireland	98607
Irondale	98339
Iron Springs	98535
Isabella Lake	98584
Island Center	98110
Island Lake	98370
Island View	98381

	ZIP
Issaquah	98027
Jared	99180
John Sam Lake	98270
Johnson	99113
Johnson Point	98501
Jordan	98223
Jovita	98371
Joyce	98343
Juanita (Part of Kirkland)	98033
Junction City	98520
Juniper Beach	98292
Kachees Ridge	98925
Kahlotus	99335
Kalama	98625
Kala Point	98368
Kalispel Indian Reservation	99180
Kamilche	98584
Kanaskat	98051
Kangley	98051
Kapowsin	98344
Keller	99140
Kellogg Marsh	98223
Kellys Korner	98501
Kelso	98626
Kendall	98295
Kenmore	98028
Kennard Corner	98012
Kennedys Lagoon	98239
Kennewick	99336-37
For specific Kennewick Zip Codes call (509) 582-5000, or your local postmaster.	
Kennydale (Part of Renton)	98056
Kenroy	98802
Kent	98031-32
	98035
	98042
	98064
For specific Kent Zip Codes call (206) 852-3950, or your local postmaster.	
Kettle Falls	99141
Kewa	99138
Key Center	98329
Keyport	98345
Keyport Naval Torpedo Station	98345
Keystone	98849
Kid Valley	98649
Kingsgate	98011
Kings Lakeside	98603
Kingston	98346
Kiona	99320
Kirkland	98033-34
	98083
For specific Kirkland Zip Codes call (206) 822-2292, or your local postmaster.	
Kitsap Lake	98312
Kittitas	98934
Klaber	98538
Klaus	98532
Klickitat	98628
Klipsan Beach	98640
Knab	98591
Knappton	98638
Koontzville	99116
Kooskooskie	99362
Kozy Kamp	98642
Krain	98022
Kruse	98271
Kruse Junction	98271
K Street (Part of Tacoma)	98405*
	98415†
Kummer	98010
Lacamas	98570
La Center	98629
Lacey	98503
	98513
	98516
For specific Lacey Zip Codes call (206) 459-2371, or your local postmaster.	
La Conner	98257
Lacrosse	99136
	99143
For specific Lacrosse Zip Codes call (509) 549-3848, or your local postmaster.	
Lagoon Point	98253
La Grande	98348
Lake Alice	98024
Lakebay	98349
Lake City (Part of Seattle)	98125
Lake Crescent	98363
Lakedale	98940
Lake Dolloff	98001

	ZIP
Lake Forest North	98155
Lake Forest Park	98155
Lake Goodwin	98292
Lake Heights	98002
Lake Hills (Part of Bellevue)	98007
Lake Howard	98292
Lake Joy	98014
Lake Kachees	98925
Lake Kathleen	98055
Lake Ki	98223
Lakeland North	98001
Lakeland South	98002
Lakeland Village (Part of Medical Lake)	99022
Lake Leota	98072
Lake Loma	98271
Lake Louise	98498
Lake Lucerne	98038
Lake Martha	98037
Lake McDonald	98055
Lake Meridian	98042
Lake Pattison	98501
Lake Retreat	98051
Lakeridge	98178
Lake Sawyer	98042
Lakes District	98439
	98498-99
For specific Lakes District Zip Codes call (206) 471-6198, or your local postmaster.	
Lake Serene-North Lynnwood	98037
Lake Shore	98665
	98685
For specific Lake Shore Zip Codes call (206) 695-4462, or your local postmaster.	
Lake Stevens	98258
Lakeview	98499
Lakeview Park	98851
Lakeview Terrace	99133
Lake Wilderness	98038
Lakewood	98259
Lakewood Mall (Part of Tacoma)	98402
Lakota (Part of Federal Way)	98003
Lamoine	98858
Lamona	99144
Lamont	99017
Langley	98260
La Push	98350
Larch Corrections Center	98675
Larchmont (Part of Tacoma)	98409
Larimers Corner	98290
Latah	99018
Laurel (Klickitat County)	98619
Laurel (Whatcom County)	98225
Laurel Heights (Part of Everett)	98203
Laurelhurst (Part of Seattle)	98105
Laurier	99146
Lawrence (Pierce County)	98409
Lawrence (Whatcom County)	98247
Laws Corner	98672
Lazy C	98320
Leadpoint	99114
Lea Hill	98092
Leavenworth	98826
Lebam	98554
Ledgewood Beach	98239
Leland	98376
Lemolo	98370
Lexington	98626
Liberty	98922
Liberty Lake	99019
Liberty Park (Part of Spokane)	99202
Lilliwaup	98555
Lincoln (Kitsap County)	98370
Lincoln (Lincoln County)	99147
Lind	99341
Littell	98532
Little Boston	98346
Little Falls	99013
Littlerock	98556
Lochsloy	98258
Lockamas Heights	98607
Locke	99119
Lofall	98370
Lone Lake Shores	98260
Lone Pine	99116
Long Beach	98631
Longbranch	98349

	ZIP
Long Lake (Kitsap County)	98366
Long Lake (Lincoln County)	99013
Longmire	98397
Long Point Manor	98239
Longview	98632
Longview Heights	98632
Longview Junction (Part of Kelso)	98626
Loomis	98827
Loon Lake	99148
Lopez	98261
Lost Creek	99180
Lost Lake	98292
Loveland	98387
Lowden	99360
Lowell (Part of Everett)	98203
Lower Elwha Indian Reservation	98363
Loyal Heights (Part of Seattle)	98117
Lucerne	98816
Lummi Indian Reservation	98226
Lummi Island	98262
Lummi Point	98262
Lyle	98635
Lyman	98263
Lynden	98264
Lynnwood	98036-37
	98046
For specific Lynnwood Zip Codes call (206) 778-2154, or your local postmaster.	
Lynwood Center	98110
Mabana	98292
Mabton	98935
McChord Air Force Base	98438
McCleary	98557
McDonald	98837
McGinnis Lake	99116
McGowan	98614
Machias	98290
McKees Beach	98292
Mckenna	98558
McMicken Heights (Part of SeaTac)	98188
McMillin	98360
McNeil Island	98388
Madigan Hospital	98431
Madison Park (Part of Seattle)	98112
Madrona Beach	98292
Madrona Point (Part of Bremerton)	98312
Mae	98837
Magnolia (Part of Seattle)	98199
Main Office (Part of Seattle)	98111
Makah Air Force Station 758th Radar Squadron	98357
Makah Indian Reservation	98357
Malaga	98828
Malden	99149
Malo	99150
Malone	98559
Malott	98829
Maltby	98290
Manchester	98353
Manito (Part of Spokane)	99203
Manito Club Estates	99203
Manitou Beach	98061
Manor	98604
Mansfield	98830
Manson	98831
Manzanita	98110
Maple Beach	98281
Maple Falls	98266
Maple Grove	98363
Maple Hills	98031
Maple Valley	98038
Maple Valley Heights	98055
Maplewood (Part of Renton)	98055
Maplewood Heights	98055
Marblemount	98267
Marcus	99151
Marengo	99169
Marietta	98226
Marietta-Alderwood	98225
Marine Drive (Part of Bremerton)	98312
Marine Hills (Part of Federal Way)	98003
Marine View Estates (Part of Federal Way)	98003
Marketown	98277
Markham	98520
Marlin	98832

	ZIP		ZIP		ZIP		ZIP
Marshall	99020	Mount Brook	98672	Ocean Grove	98571	Ping	99347
Martha Lake	98012	Mount Hope	99012	Ocean Park	98640	Pioneer	98642
Martin Luther King Jr Way		Mountlake Terrace	98043	Ocean Shores	98569	Pioneer Square (Part of	
(Part of Tacoma)	98405	Mount Pleasant	98362	Ocosta	98520	Seattle)	98104
Maryhill	98620	Mount Tahoma Estate	98501	Odessa	99159	Pipe Lake	98038
Marys Corner	98532	Mount Vernon	98273	Offutt Lake	98589	Plain	98826
Marysville	98270-71	Moxee	98936	Okanogan	98840	Plaza	99170
For specific Marysville Zip		Muckleshoot Indian		Olalla	98359	Pleasant Harbor	98320
Codes call (206) 659-1260, or		Reservation	98092	Olalla Valley	98359	Pleasant Hill	98626
your local postmaster.		Mukilteo	98275	Oldport	98501	Pleasant Prairie	99207
Matlock	98560	Munson Point	98584	Old Tacoma (Part of		Pleasant Valley	98665
Matneys Spur	99141	Murdock	98617	Tacoma)	98466	Plymouth	99346
Mattawa	99344	Murphy's Corner	98012	Old Willapa	98577	Pocahontas Bay	99009
Maxwelton	98236	Mushroom Corner	98501	Olga	98279	Point Roberts	98281
May Creek	98251	Naches	98937	Olympia	98501-16	Point White	98110
Mays Pond	98012	Nahcotta	98637	For specific Olympia Zip Codes		Pomeroy	99347
Maytown	98502	Nahwatzel Lake	98584	call (206) 357-2286, or your		Pomona	98901
Mazama	98833	Napavine	98565	local postmaster.		Pomona Heights	98903
Mead	99021	Naselle	98638	Olympic Corrections		Ponder	98499
Meadow Brook (King		National	98304	Center	98331	Ponderosa Estates	98390
County)	98065	Naval Supply Center		Olympic View	98383	Pontius Park	99021
Meadowbrook (Yakima		Puget Sound	98314	Olympus Ocean Estates	98571	Portage	98070
County)	98903	Naval Torpedo Station	98345	Omak	98841	Portage Point	98262
Meadowdale (Kitsap		Navy Yard City	98312	Onalaska	98570	Port Angeles	98362-63
County)	98310	Neah Bay	98357	Oneida	98643	For specific Port Angeles Zip	
Meadowdale (Snohomish		Neilton	98566	Onion Creek	99114	Codes call (206) 452-9275, or	
County)	98020	Nemah	98586	Opportunity	99206	your local postmaster.	
Meadow Glade	98604	Nespelem	99155	Orcas	98280	Port Angeles East	98362
Meadow Grange	98273	Nespelem Community	99155	Orchard Avenue	99211	Port Blakely	98110
Medical Lake	99022	Newaukum	98092	Orchard Prairie	99207	Port Discovery	98368
Medina	98039	Newcastle	98055	Orchards	98662	Porter	98541
Meeker (Part of Puyallup)	98371	Newhalem	98283	Orchards North	98662	Port Gamble	98364
Melbourne	98563	New London	98550	Orchards South	98662	Port Gamble Indian	
Menlo	98561	Newman Lake	99025	Orient	99160	Reservation	98346
Mercer Island	98040	Newport (King County)	98004	Orillia (Part of Kent)	98032	Port Hadlock	98339
Meredith (Part of Auburn)	98001	Newport (Pend Oreille		Orin	99114	Port Ludlow	98365
Meridian Heights	98042	County)	99156	Orondo	98843	Port Madison	98110
Merritt	98826	Newport Hills	98006	Oroville	98844	Port Madison Indian	
Mesa	99343	Newport Shores (Part of		Orting	98360	Reservation	98310
Metaline	99152	Bellevue)	98004	Osceola	98022	Port Orchard	98366
Metaline Falls	99153	Newton	98550	Oso	98223	Port Stanley	98261
Methow	98834	Nighthawk	98827	Ostrander	98626	Port Townsend	98368
Metreco	98438	Nile	98937	Othello	98327	Possession	98236
Miami Beach	98380	Nine Mile Falls	99026	Otis Orchards	99027	Possession Shores	98236
Mica	99023	Nisqually Indian		Otis Orchards-East Farms	99025	Potlatch	98584
Midlakes (Part of		Community	98513	Outlook	98938	Poulsbo	98370
Bellevue)	98015	Nisqually Indian		Oyhut	98550	Poverty Bay (Part of	
Midland	98404	Reservation	98597	Oysterville	98641	Federal Way)	98003
	98444-45	Nisson	98550	Ozette	98326	Prairie	98284
For specific Midland Zip Codes		Nooksack	98276	Pacific	98047	Prairie Center (Part of	
call (206) 471-6175, or your		Nordland	98358	Pacific Beach	98571	Coupeville)	98239
local postmaster.		Norma Beach	98020	Packwood	98361	Prairie Ridge	98390
Midland Acres (Part of		Norman	98292	Paine Field-Lake Stickney	98204	Prescott	99348
Camas)	98607	Normandy Park	98166	Painted Hills	99206	Preston	98050
Midvale Corner	98236	North Beach	98245	Palisades	98845	Priest Point	98271
Midway (King County)	98035	North Bend	98045	Palmer	98051	Proctor (Part of Tacoma)	98407
Midway (Pierce County)	98335	North Bonneville	98639	Palouse	99161	Proebstel	98662
Milan	99003	North City	98155	Panhandle Lake	98584	Prosser	99350
Milco (Part of Kelso)	98626	North City-Ridgecrest	98155	Paradise Estates	98304	Prune Hill	98607
Miles	99122	North Cove	98547	Paradise Inn	98398	Puget Island	98612
Mill A	98605	North Creek-Canyon Park		Park	98284	Puget Sound Naval Base	98314
Mill Creek	98012		98021	Parker	98939	Puget Sound Naval	
Miller River	98288	For specific North Creek-		Parkland	98444-46	Shipyard	98314
Millwood	99212	Canyon Park Zip Codes call		For specific Parkland Zip Codes		Pullman	99163-65
Milton	98354	(206) 486-3243, or your local		call (206) 471-6144, or your		For specific Pullman Zip Codes	
Mima	98501	postmaster.		local postmaster.		call (509) 334-3212, or your	
Mineral	98355	North Fort Lewis	98434	Park Orchard	98031	local postmaster.	
Minnehaha	98661	Northgate (Part of Seattle)	98125	Park Rapids	99114	Purdy	98332
Mirror Lake (Part of		Northgate Shopping		Parkwater (Spokane		Purdy Treatment Center	
Federal Way)	98003	Center (Part of Seattle)	98125	County)	99211	for Women	98332
Mirrormont	98027	North Hill	98166	Parkway Plaza (Part of		Puyallup	98371-74
Mission Beach	98271	North Lake	98001	Tukwila)	98188	For specific Puyallup Zip Codes	
Misty Meadows	98012	North Lynnwood	98036	Parkwood	98366	call (206) 845-2334, or your	
Mobase	98433	North Marysville	98271	Pasadena Park	99206	local postmaster.	
Moclips	98562	North Omak	98841	Pasco	99301*	Queen Anne (Part of	
Mohler	99154	Northport	99157		99302†	Seattle)	98109
Mold	99115	North Prosser	99350	Pataha City	99347	Queensborough	98021
Molson	98844	North Puyallup	98372	Pateros	98846	Queets	98331
Mondovi	99122	Northrup (Part of Bellevue)	98008	Paterson	99345	Quendall (Part of Renton)	98055
Monitor	98836	North Town (Part of		Peach Acres	98465	Quilcene	98376
Monohon	98027	Spokane)	99207	Pearcot	98801	Quileute Indian	
Monroe	98272	Northtown Mall (Part of		Pearson	98370	Reservation	98350
Monse	98812	Spokane)	99207	Pe Ell	98572	Quinault	98575
Monta Vista	98499	Northwood	98264	Pend Orielle Village	99153	Quinault Indian	
Montborne	98273	Northwoods	98616	Penn Cove Park	98277	Reservation	98587
Montesano	98563	North Yelm	98597	Peone	99021	Quincy	98848
Moore	98816	Norwood Village (Part of		Perrinville (Part of		Rainer Valley (Part of	
Moorlands	98011	Bellevue)	98004	Edmonds)	98020	Seattle)	98118
Moran Prairie	99203	Novelty	98019	Peshastin	98847	Rainier	98576
Morgan Acres	99207	Nugents Corner	98247	Picnic Point	98335	Rainier Beach (Part of	
Morganville (Part of Black		Oakbrook	98497	Pillar Rock	98643	Seattle)	98102
Diamond)	98010	Oakesdale	99158	Pinebrook (Part of		Rainier Terrace	98371
Morton	98356	Oak Harbor	98277	Vancouver)	98660	Ralston	99169
Moses Lake	98837	Oakland (Part of Tacoma)	98409	Pine City	99170	Rambler Park	98908
Moses Lake North	98837	Oak Park (Part of Camas)	98607	Pinecliff	98937	Randle	98377
Mossyrock	98564	Oakville	98568	Pinecroft	99214	Raugust	98837
Mountain Home Park	99328	O'Brien (Part of Kent)	98032	Pine Glen	98925	Ravensdale	98051
Mountain View	98273	Obstruction Pass	98279	Pinehurst (Part of Everett)	98203	Raymond	98577
Mountain View Beach	98292	Ocean City	98569	Pine Lake	98027	Reardan	99029

	ZIP
Redmond	98052-53
	98073
For specific Redmond Zip Codes call (206) 885-1296, or your local postmaster.	
Redondo	98054
Rees Corner	98290
Regal (Part of Spokane)	99208
Reintree	98072
Renton	98055-59
For specific Renton Zip Codes call (206) 255-8920, or your local postmaster.	
Renton Village (Part of Renton)	98055
Republic	99166
Retsil	98378
Rhodesia Beach	98527
Rhododendron Park	98390
Rice	99167
Richland	99352
Richmond Beach	98160
Richmond Beach-Innis Arden	98160
Richmond Highlands	98133
Ridgecrest	98155
Ridgefield	98642
Ridgetop	98383
Riiho Park	98640
Rimrock	98937
Ritzville	99169
Riverbend	98821
Rivercrest	98204
Riverside (Okanogan County)	98849
Riverside (Spokane County)	99201
Riverton Heights	98188
Riverview Hills	99005
Robe	98252
Robinswood (Part of Bellevue)	98008
Roche Harbor	98250
Rochester	98579
Rockford	99030
Rock Island	98850
Rockport	98283
Rocky Butte	98812
Rocky Point (Cowlitz County)	98626
Rocky Point (Island County)	98292
Rocky Point (Kitsap County)	98312
Rocky Woods	98387
Rodena Beach	98239
Rollingbay	98061
Rolling Hills	98277
Ronald	98940
Roosevelt (Klickitat County)	99356
Roosevelt (Snohomish County)	98290
Roosevelt Beach	98571
Rosalia	99170
Rosario	98245
Rosario Beach	98221
Rosburg	98643
Rosedale	98335
Rose Hill (Part of Kirkland)	98033
Rose Valley	98626
Rosewood	99208
Roslyn	98941
Roy	98580
Royal Camp	99344
Royal City	99357
Ruby	99119
Ruff	98832
Ruston	98407
Ryderwood	98581
Sahalee	98052-53
For specific Sahalee Zip Codes call (206) 285-1650, or your local postmaster.	
St. Andrews	99115
St. John	99171
St. Urbans	98596
Salkum	98582
Salmon Beach (Part of Tacoma)	98424
Salmon Creek (census designated place)	98685-86
For specific Salmon Creek Zip Codes call (206) 695-4462, or your local postmaster.	
Salmon Creek	98665
Saltwater	98188
Samish Island	98232
Samish Lake	98226

	ZIP
San de Fuca	98239
Sandy Hook	98236
Sandy Hook Park	98370
Sandy Point	98260
Santiago Beach	98587
Sappho	98305
Sara	98642
Saratoga Beach	98260
Saratoga Heights	98260
Saratoga Shores	98292
Satsop	98583
Satus	98948
Sauk River Estates	98283
Sawyer	98951
Scandia	98370
Scatchet Head	98236
Schawana	99321
Schneiders Prairie	98502
Schwarder	98908
Scopa (Part of Renton)	98055
Scott Lake	98501
Sea Acres	98279
Seabeck	98380
Seabold	98110
Sea First (Part of Seattle)	98104
Seahurst (Part of Burien)	98062
Seal Rock	98320
Seamount Estates	98320
SeaTac	98158
Seatac Mall (Part of Federal Way)	98003
Seatons Grove	99116
Seattle	98101-09
	98111-99
For specific Seattle Zip Codes call (206) 285-1650, or your local postmaster.	
COLLEGES & UNIVERSITIES	
Griffin College	98121
Seattle University	98122
University of Washington	98195
FINANCIAL INSTITUTIONS	
American Marine Bank	98104
First Interstate Bank of Washington, N.A.	98104
Key Bank of Washington	98104
Metropolitan Federal Savings & Loan Association of Seattle	98101
Seattle-First National Bank	98104
U.S. Bank of Washington, National Association	98101
Washington Federal Savings & Loan Association	98101
Washington Mutual Savings Bank	98101
HOSPITALS	
Group Health Cooperative Central Hospital	98112
Harborview Medical Center	98104
Providence Medical Center	98122
Swedish Medical Center-Seattle	98104
University of Washington Medical Center	98195
Veterans Affairs Medical Center	98108
Virginia Mason Medical Center	98101
HOTELS/MOTELS	
Edgewater Inn	98121
Holiday Inn Crowne Plaza	98101
Ramada Inn-Downtown Seattle	98121
Red Lion Hotel-SeaTac	98188
Sea-Tac Marriott	98188
Seattle Airport Hilton	98188
Seattle Hilton	98101
Seattle Sheraton Hotel & Towers	98101
Sorrento Hotel	98104
Westin Hotel-Seattle	98101
MILITARY INSTALLATIONS	
Air Force Water Port Logistics Office	98134
Coast Guard Support Center, Seattle	98134
Fort Lawton	98433
(MTMC) Pacific Northwest Outpost	98134

	ZIP
Naval Station, Puget Sound	98115
Supervisor of Shipbuilding, Conversion and Repair, Seattle	98115
United States Engineer District, Seattle	98124
13th Coast Guard District, Seattle	98134
Seattle Heights (Part of Edmonds)	98036
Seaview	98644
Sedro Woolley	98284
Sekiu	98381
Selah	98942
Selleck	98051
Sequim	98382
Sequioa	98031
Seven Bays	99122
Seven Mile	99026
Shadle Center (Part of Spokane)	99205
Shaker Church	98271
Shana Park	98501
Shangri-La Shores	98239
Shaw Island	98286
Shawnee	99111
Shelter Bay	98257
Shelton	98584
Sheridan Beach	98155
Sheridan Park (Part of Bremerton)	98310
Sherwood Forest (Part of Bellevue)	98008
Shine	98365
Shoalwater Indian Reservation	98590
Shore Acres	98335
Shorewood	98106
Shorewood Beach	98333
Shrine Beach	98816
Shuwah	98331
Sierra Division	98239
Sifton	98662
Sightly	98649
Silcott	99403
Silvana	98287
Silvana Terraces	98292
Silver Beach (Part of Bellingham)	98225
Silver Brook	98377
Silver Creek	98585
Silverdale	98383
Silverlake (Cowlitz County)	98645
Silver Lake (Snohomish County)	98208
Silver Lake (Spokane County)	99022
Silver Lake-Firecrest	98201
Similk Beach	98221
Sisco Heights	98223
Skagit City	98273
Skagit Country Club	98233
Skamania	98648
Skamokawa	98647
Skokomish	98584
Skokomish Indian Reservation	98584
Skykomish	98288
Skyway	98178
Sleepy Hollow	98647
Smithville	98635
Smokey Point	98223
Smyrna	99357
Snee Oosh	98257
Snohomish	98290*
	98291†
Snoqualmie	98065
Snoqualmie Pass	98068
Soap Lake	98851
South Aberdeen (Part of Aberdeen)	98520
South Bay	98501
South Beach (Kitsap County)	98110
South Beach (Whatcom County)	98281
South Bellingham (Part of Bellingham)	98225
South Bend	98586
South Broadway	98902
Southcenter (Part of Tukwila)	98188
South Cle Elum	98943
South Colby	98384
South Elma	98541
Southgate (Pierce County)	98499

	ZIP
Southgate (Thurston County)	98501
South Hill	98373
South Hill Mall (Part of Puyallup)	98371
South Montesano	98563
South Park (Part of Seattle)	98108
South Park Village	98366
South Point	98365
South Prairie	98385
South Seattle (Part of Seattle)	98102
Southshore Mall (Part of Aberdeen)	98520
Southside (Part of Everett)	98208
South Snohomish	98290
South Sound Center (Part of Lacey)	98503
South Tacoma (Part of Tacoma)	98409
South Union	98501
South Wenatchee	98801
Southworth	98386
Spanaway	98387
Spangle	99031
Special Offender Center	98272
Spokane	99201-28
For specific Spokane Zip Codes call (509) 459-0222, or your local postmaster.	
Spokane Indian Reservation	99129
Sprague	99032
Spring Creek	98940
Springdale	99173
Spring Glen	98024
Squaxin Island Indian Reservation	98584
Stabler	98610
Stanwood	98292
Starbuck	99359
Star Lake	98001
Startup	98293
Station A (Part of Tacoma)	98408*
	98418†
Stehekin	98852
Steilacoom	98388
Steptoe	99174
Sterling	98284
Stevenson	98648
Stiebels Corner	98346
Stillwater	98014
Stimson Crossing	98223
Strandell (Part of Everson)	98247
Stratford	98853
Streeters	98611
Stringtown	98624
Sudden Valley	98226
Sultan	98294
Sumach	98901
Sumas	98295
Summerwood	99005
Summit	98373
Summit Lake	98501
Summit Park	98221
Sumner	98390
Suncrest	99026
Sundale	99356
Sundins Beach	98292
Sun Island	98925
Sunland Estates	98824
Sunlight Beach	98236
Sunlight Shores	98236
Sunny Bay	98335
Sunnydale (Part of Burien)	98155
Sunnyside (Snohomish County)	98205
Sunnyside (Yakima County)	98944
Sunnyside Beach (Part of Steilacoom)	98388
Sunnyslope (Chelan County)	98801
Sunnyslope (Kitsap County)	98366
Sunrise Beach	98335
Sunrise Point	98292
Sunset	99171
Sunset Bay	99034
Sunset Beach (Grays Harbor County)	98571
Sunset Beach (Island County)	98292
Sunset Beach (Mason County)	98528
Sunset Beach (Pierce County)	98466

* Area Zip Code   † Post Office Boxes

	ZIP
Sunset West (Lewis County)	98532
Sunset West (Yakima County)	98903
Sun Village (Part of Kirkland)	98012
Sunwood Lakes	98501
Suquamish	98392
Swan Trail	98205
Swede Hill	98332
Swinomish Indian Reservation	98257
Swinomish Village	98257
Swofford	98564
Sylvan	98333
Synarep	98849
Tacoma	98401-99
For specific Tacoma Zip Codes call (206) 471-6175, or your local postmaster.	
Tacoma Junction (Part of Fife)	98424
Tacoma Mall (Part of Tacoma)	98409
Tacoma Point	98390
Tahlequah	98070
Taholah	98587
Tahuya	98588
Tampico	98903
Tanglewilde	98503
Tanglewilde East	98516
Tanglewilde-Thompson Place	98506
Tanner	98045
Teanaway	98922
Tekoa	99033
Telma	98826
Tenino	98589
Terminal Annex (Part of Spokane)	99202
Terminal Finance (Part of Seattle)	98134
Teronda West	98239
Terrace Heights	98901
Terrill Beach	98245
Terry Avenue (Part of Seattle)	98109
Terrys Corner	98292
Thomas	98032
Thompson Place	98516
Thornton	99176
Thorp	98946
Thrashers Corner	98021
Three Lakes	98290
Three Rivers Mall (Part of Kelso)	98626
Thrift	98338
Tieton	98947
Tiger	99180
Tillicum	98492
Tillicum Beach	98292
Tillicum Siding	98492
Timber Lakes	98584
Timberlane	98042
Tokeland	98590
Toledo	98591
Tonasket	98855
Toppenish	98948
Totem Lake (Part of Kirkland)	98033
Touchet	99360
Toutle	98649
Town and Country	99210
Tracyton	98393
Trafton	98223
Treasure Island	98546
Trend (Part of Kirkland)	98033
Trentwood	99215

	ZIP
Triangle Shopping Mall (Part of Longview)	98632
Tri-Cities (Part of Pasco)	99302
Trinidad	98848
Triton	98555
Trout Lake	98650
Tukwila	98108
Tulalip	98271
Tulalip Bay	98270-71
For specific Tulalip Bay Zip Codes call (206) 355-9505, or your local postmaster.	
Tulalip Indian Reservation	98271
Tumtum	99034
Tumwater	98502
Turner	98238
Turner Corner	98072
Twin Rivers Corrections Center	98272
Twisp	98856
Tyler	99004
Umtanum	98926
Underwood	98651
Union	98592
Union Gap	98903
Union Mill	98501
Uniontown	99179
University (Part of Seattle)	98105
University Place	98464†
	98465*
University Village (Part of Seattle)	98105
Upper Preston	98027
Uranium City	99013
Urban	98221
Useless Bay Country Club	98260
Usk	99180
Utsalady	98292
Vader	98593
Valley	99181
Valleyford	99036
Valley Mall (Part of Union Gap)	98903
Valley Ridge (Part of SeaTac)	98188
Valley View	98331
Van Asselt (Part of Seattle)	98108
Van Buren	98247
Vancouver	98660-68
	98682-86
For specific Vancouver Zip Codes call (206) 695-4462, or your local postmaster.	
Vancouver Mall	98662
Van Horn	98237
Vantage	98950
Van Zandt	98244
Vashon	98070
Vashon Center	98070
Vashon Heights	98070
Vaughn	98394
Veazie	98002
Venersborg	98604
Venice	98110
Veradale	99037
Verlot	98252
Vesta	98537
Veterans Administration Hospital (Part of Vancouver)	98661
View	98629
View Park	98366
View Ridge (Part of Seattle)	98115
Villa Beach	98303
Villa Plaza	98499
Vinland	98370

	ZIP
Virginia	98370
Vision Acres	98626
Wabash	98022
Wahkiacus	98670
Waitsburg	99361
Waitts Lake	99181
Waldron	98297
Walla Walla	99362
Walla Walla East	99362
Waller	98443
Wallingford (Part of Seattle)	98103
Wallula	99363
Wallula Junction	99363
Walnut Grove	98662
Wanapum Village	99321
Wapato	98951
Warden	98857
Warm Beach	98292
Warnick	98244
Warren	98335
Washington Corrections Center	98584
Washington State Reformatory	98272
Washougal	98671
Washtucna	99371
Waterman	98366
Waterville	98858
Wauconda	98859
Waukon	99008
Wauna	98395
Waunch Prairie (Part of Centralia)	98531
Wautauga Beach	98366
Waverly	99039
Wawawai	99113
Weallup Lake	98270
Wedgwood (Part of Seattle)	98115
Wegoe	98433
Weikel	98902
Welcome	98244
Wellpinit	99040
Wenatchee	98801-07
For specific Wenatchee Zip Codes call (509) 662-7663, or your local postmaster.	
Wenatchee Heights	98802
West Beach	98245
West Blakely	98110
West Clarkston	99403
West Clarkston-Highland	99403
West Coulee (Part of Coulee Dam)	99116
Westfair Shopping Center (Part of Federal Way)	98023
Westhaven (Part of Westport)	98595
Westlake Center (Part of Seattle)	98101
West Lake Sammamish	98008
West Lake Stevens	98258
West Longview	98632
Westmont Acres	98851
West Park (Part of Bremerton)	98312
West Pasco	99301
Westport	98595
West Port Madison	98110
West Richland	99352
West Seattle (Part of Seattle)	98116
West Side Highway	98632
West Sound	98245
West Tapps	98390
West Valley	98903

	ZIP
	98908
For specific West Valley Zip Codes call (509) 454-2450, or your local postmaster.	
Westward Siding (Part of Tacoma)	98406
West Wenatchee	98802
Westwood (King County)	98126
Westwood (Kitsap County)	98110
Wheeler	98837
Whidbey Island Naval Air Station	98278
White Center	98106
White Center-Shorewood	98106
White Pass	98937
Whites	98541
White Salmon	98672
White Swan	98952
Whitney Esttes	98532
Whitstran	99350
Wickersham	98220
Wilbur	99185
Wilburton (Part of Bellevue)	98004
Wildcat Lake	98312
Wilderness	98501
Wiley	98908
Wilkeson	98396
Willada	99171
Willapa	98577
Willard	98605
Willow Grove	98632
Wilson Creek	98860
Winchester	98848
Winlock	98596
Winona	99125
Winthrop	98862
Winton	98826
Wishkah	98520
Wishram	98673
Wishram Heights	98673
Withrow	98858
Wollochet	98335
Woodinville	98072
Woodland	98674
Woodland Beach	98292
Woodland Creek	98501
Woodland Park	98603
Woodlawn (Part of Hoquiam)	98550
Woodmont Beach	98032
Woodsmuir	98501
Woodway	98020
Wycoff (Part of Bremerton)	98312
Wye Lake	98366
Yacht Haven	98250
Yacolt	98675
Yakima	98901-09
For specific Yakima Zip Codes call (509) 454-2450, or your local postmaster.	
Yakima Indian Reservation	98948
Yakima Mall (Part of Yakima)	98901
Yale	98603
Yardley	99202
Yarrow Point	98004
Yelm	98597
Yeomalt	98110
Yesler Terrace (Part of Seattle)	98104
Yokeko Point	98221
Yoman Ferry	98303
Zenith	98188
Zillah	98953

Place	ZIP
Aarrons Fork	25071
Abbott	26201
Abney	25847
Abraham	25918
Accoville	25606
Acme	25122
Ada	24701
Adaline	26033
Adamston (Part of Clarksburg)	26301
Adamsville	26431
Adlai	26170
Adolph	26280
Adrian	26210
Advent	25231
Afton	26764
Aggregate	26241
Airport Road	25813
Ajax	25676
Albright	26519
Alderson	24910
Alexander	26218
Algoma	24868
Alice	26342
Alkol	25501
Allendale	26003
Allen Junction	25810
Allensville	25427
Alister	26167
Alloy	25002
Alma	26320
Alpena	26254
Alpha	26408
Alpheus (Part of Gary)	24836
Alpoca	24710
Alta	26656
Altizer	25234
Alton	26210
Alum Bridge	26321
Alum Creek (Kanawha County)	25003
Alum Creek (Lincoln County)	25003
Alvon	24986
Alvy	26322
Amandaville	25177
Amboy	26705
Ambrosia	25550
Ameagle	25004
Amelia	25160
Amherstdale	25607
Amherstdale-Robinette	25607
Amigo	25811
Amma	25005
Anawalt	24808
Andersonville	26033
Andrew	25154
Angel Terrace (Part of Charleston)	25303
Angerona	25241
Anjean	25984
Anmoore	26323
Annamoriah	26141
Annamoriah Flats	26141
Ansted	25812
Anthony	24938
Antioch (Doddridge County)	26456
Antioch (Mineral County)	26743
Aplin	25244
Apple Farm	25274
Apple Grove (Mason County)	25502
Apple Grove (McDowell County)	24844
Aracoma	25601
Arborland Acres	25177
Arbovale	24915
Arbuckle	25123
Arbutus Park (Part of Clarksburg)	26301
Archer	26377
Archer Heights	26035
Arcola	26206
Ardel	25570
Arden (Barbour County)	26405
Arden (Berkeley County)	25401
Argonne	25649
Argyle	25654
Arkansas	26801
Arlee	25106
Arlington (Harrison County)	26301
Arlington (McDowell County)	24810
Arlington (Upshur County)	26234
Arnett	25007
Arnette	26619
Arnettsville	26505
Arnold Hill	26241
Arnoldsburg	25234
Arroyo	26047
Arthur	26816
Arthurdale	26520
Artie	25008
Arvilla	26135
Asbury	24916
Asbury Church	26801
Asco	24828
Ashford	25009
Ashland	24810
Ashley	26456
Ashton	25503
Aspinall	26412
Astor	26347
Astor Junction (Part of Flemington)	26347
Atenville	25524
Athens	24712
Atwell	24813
Atwood	26167
Auburn	26325
Augusta (Hampshire County)	26704
Augusta (Mercer County)	24740
Aurora	26705
Austen	26410
Austin	24917
Auto	24844
Auville (Part of Iaeger)	24844
Auviltown	26290
Avis (Part of Hinton)	25951
Avon	26411
Avondale (Doddridge County)	26456
Avondale (McDowell County)	24811
Bablin	26376
Backus	25976
Baden	25123
Baisden (Logan County)	25652
Baisden (Mingo County)	25608
Baker	26801
Baker Heights	25401
Baker Park	25177
Baker Ridge	26505
Bakerton	25410
Bald Knob	25010
Baldwin	26351
Ballard	24918
Ballengee	24919
Balls Gap	25541
Bancroft	25011
Bandytown	25204
Barboursville	25504
Bardane	25430
Bargers Springs	24935
Barker	26419
Barksdale	25951
Barn	25841
Barnabus	25638
Barnet Run	26610
Barrackville	26559
Barrett	25013
Barrs	25276
Barry Mine	26347
Bartley	24813
Bartow	24920
Basin	24726
Basnettsville	26570
Basore	26812
Bass	26836
Baxter	26560
Bayard	26707
Bear Creek	26624
Beard Heights	24954
Beards Fork	25014
Bear Mountain Mine	26334
Bearsville	26149
Beason	26415
Beatrice	26178
Beatysville	26133
Beaver	25813
Bebee	26155
Becco	25607
Beckley	25801*
	25802†
Beckley Junction (Part of Mabscott)	25871
Beckwith	25814
Bedington	25401
Beebe	25625
Beech Bottom	26030
Beech Creek	25682
Beech Glen	26656
Beechgrove	26415
Beech Hill	25187
Beechwood	25810
Beelick Knob	25976
Beeson	24714
Belgrove	25248
Belington	26250
Bellburn	25958
Belle	25015
Bellepoint (Part of Hinton)	25951
Belleville	26133
Bellmeade	25550
Bellview (Part of Fairmont)	26554
Bellwood	25962
Belmont	26134
Belva	26656
Belvedere Heights	25414
Bemis	26268
Benbush	26292
Bendale	26452
Ben Lomond	25515
Bennett	26423
Benson	26378
Benson Park	25302
Bens Run	26135
Benton Ferry	26554
Bentree	25018
Benwood	26031
Benwood Junction (Part of Benwood)	26031
Berea	26327
Bergoo	26298
Berkeley	25401
Berkeley Springs	25411
Berlin	26452
Bernie	25521
Berryburg	26347
Berry Siding	26621
Berryville	25411
Bertha Hill	26541
Berwind	24815
Beryl	26726
Besoco	25857
Bessemer	25401
Bethany	26032
Bethel Place	26181
Bethesda	25570
Bethlehem (Harrison County)	26431
Bethlehem (Ohio County)	26003
Betty Zane	26003
Beverly	26253
Beverly Hills (Cabell County)	25705
Beverly Hills (Marion County)	26554
Bias	25670
Bickmore	25019
Big Battle	26426
Bigbend	26136
Big Chimney	25302
Big Creek	25505
Big Four	24853
Big Isaac	26426
Big Moses	26320
Big Mountain (Part of Cedar Grove)	25039
Big Otter	25113
Big Run (Marion County)	26582
Big Run (Marshall County)	26033
Big Run (Webster County)	26217
Big Run (Wetzel County)	26561
Big Sandy	24816
Bigson	25206
Big Springs	26137
Big Sycamore	25111
Billings	25270
Bim	25021
Bingamon	26591
Bingamon Junction	26591
Bingham	25958
Birch River	26610
Birchton	25209
Birds Creek	26410
Bishop	24604
Bismarck	26739
Blackberry City	25678
Black Betsy	25159
Black Bottom	25601
Black Eagle	25882
Blackhawk	25306
Blacksville	26521
Black Wolf	24871
Blaine	26717
Blair (Jefferson County)	25432
Blair (Logan County)	25022
Blairton	25401
Blakeley	25160
Blandville	26328
Blaser	26444
Blennerhassett	26101
Blocton	25685
Bloomery (Hampshire County)	26817
Bloomery (Jefferson County)	25414
Bloomingrose	25024
Blount	25025
Blue	26149
Blue Creek	25026
Bluefield	24701
Blue Jay	25816
Blue Ridge Acres	25425
Blue Rock	26280
Bluestone	24701
Blue Sulphur Springs	24910
Blueville (Part of Grafton)	26354
Bluewell	24701
Blundon	25071
Board	25253
Boaz	26187
Bob White	25028
Boggs	26299
Bolair	26288
Bolivar	25425
Bolt	25817
Bomont	25030
Bona Vista (Part of Charleston)	25311
Bonnie	26619
Bonnivale	26150
Booher	26320
Boomer	25031
Boonesborough (Part of Gauley Bridge)	25057
Booth	26522
Boothsville	26554
Borderland	25665
Boreman	26101
Borgman	26444
Bottom Creek	24853
Boulder	26201
Bowan Ridge	25701
Bowden	26254
Bowlby	26541
Bowles	25523
Boyd	26234
Boyer	24915
Bozoo	24923
Bradley (Boone County)	25051
Bradley (Raleigh County)	25818
Bradshaw	24817
Braeholm	25607
Bragg	25918
Bramwell	24715
Branchland	25506
Brandonville	26523
Brandywine	26802
Braxton	26619
Bream	25071
Breeden	25666
Brenton	24818
Bretz (Preston County)	26524
Bretz (Tucker County)	26287
Brewsterdale	24619
Briarwood Estates	26101
Brick Church	25514
Bridgeport	26330
Bridgeport Hill (Part of Bridgeport)	26330
Bridgeway	26149
Brink	26582
Bristol	26332
Broaddus (Part of Philippi)	26416
Broadmoor	26181
Broad Oaks (Part of Clarksburg)	26301
Brohard	26138
Brookhaven (Kanawha County)	25143
Brookhaven (Monongalia County)	26505
Brooklyn	25840
Brooklyn Junction (Part of New Martinsville)	26155
Brooks	25957
Brookside	26705
Brounland	25314
Brown	26448
Brownlow	26354
Brownsburg	24954
Browns Mills	26505
Brownsville (Fayette County)	25085
Brownsville (Lewis County)	26452
Brownton	26334
Brownwood	25864
Bruceton Mills	26525
Bruno	25611
Brush Fork	24701
Brushyrun	26866
Brydon	26435
Bryson	25865
Bubbling Spring	26865
Buck	25951

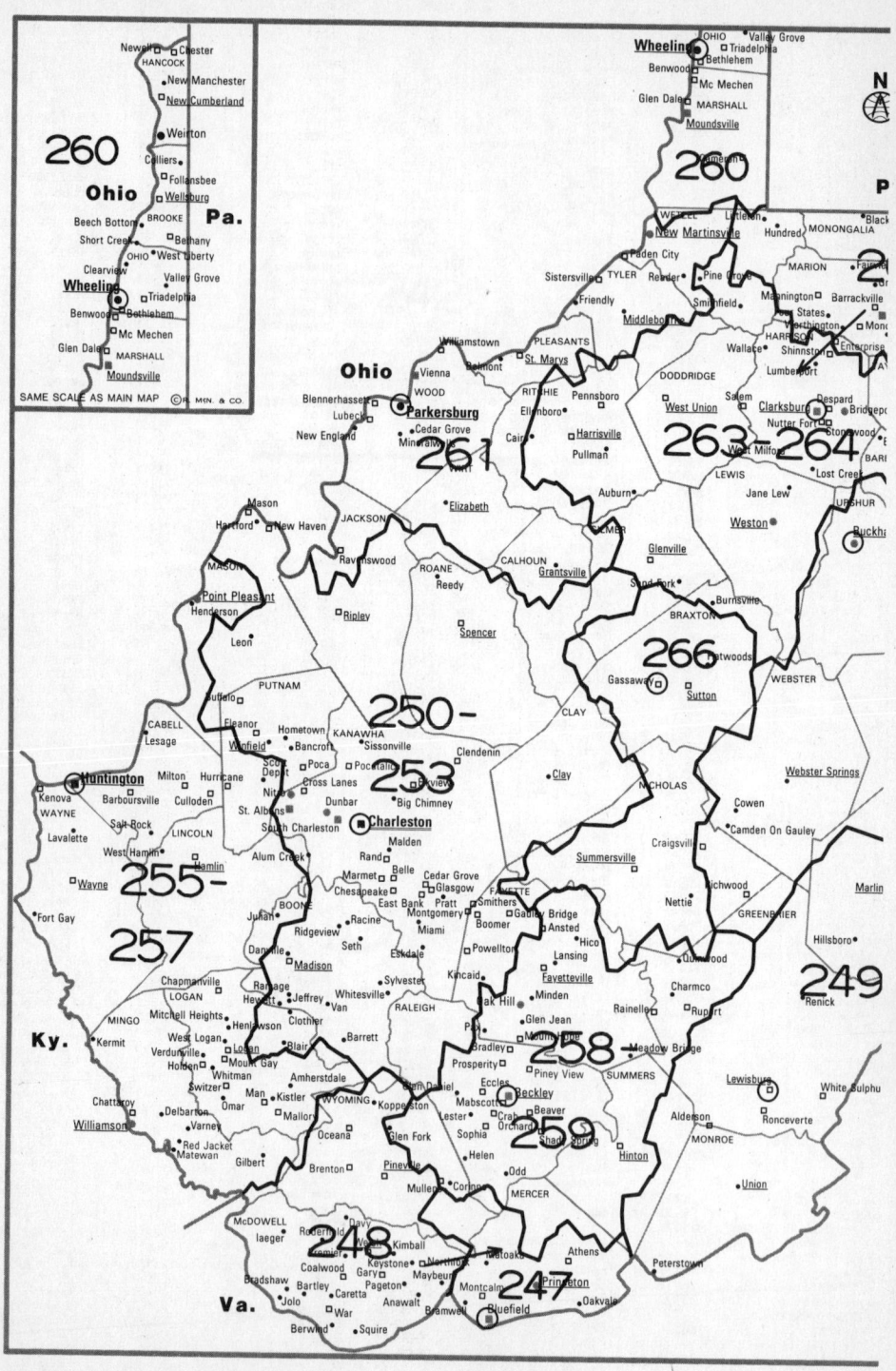

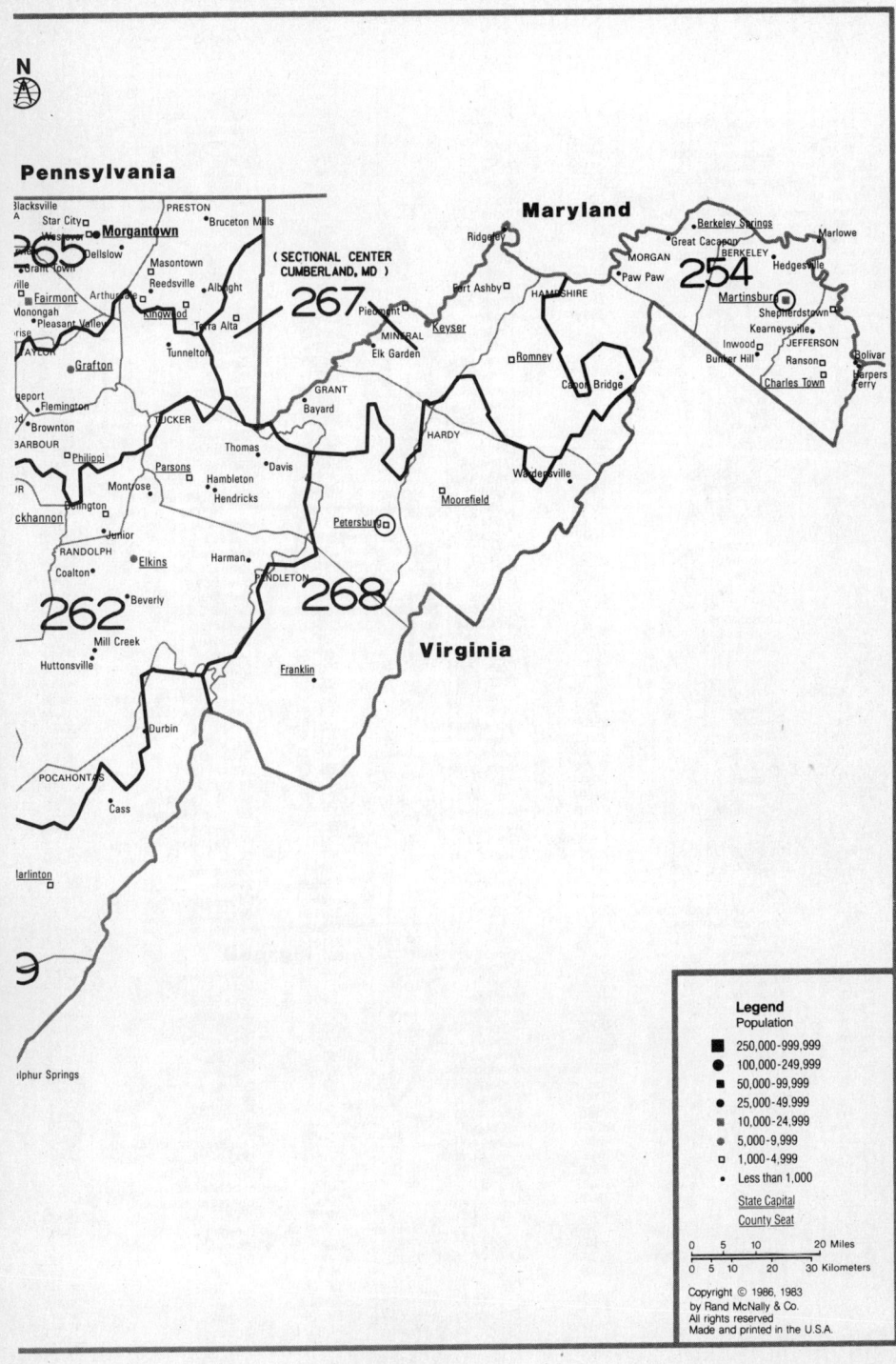

N

Pennsylvania

Blacksville
Star City
Morgantown
Wesover
Dellslow
265
rant own
ville
Fairmont
Monongah
Pleasant Valley
rise
TAYLOR
Grafton
eport
Flemington
Brownton
BARBOUR
Philippi
UR
Montrose
ington
ckhannon
Junior
RANDOLPH
Elkins
Coalton
262
Mill Creek
Huttonsville
Durbin
POCAHONTAS
Cass
larlinton
9
lphur Springs

PRESTON
Bruceton Mills
Masontown
Reedsville
Albright
Kingwood
Terra Alta
Tunnelton

(SECTIONAL CENTER
CUMBERLAND, MD)
267

Arthurdale

TUCKER
Thomas
Davis
Parsons
Hambleton
Hendricks

Harman
FINDLETON
268

Beverly

Franklin

Virginia

Piedmont
MINERAL
Keyser
Elk Garden

GRANT
Bayard

HARDY

Moorefield

Petersburg

Ridgeley

Fort Ashby

HAMPSHIRE

Romney

Capon Bridge

Wardensville

Maryland

Berkeley Springs
Great Cacapon
MORGAN
Paw Paw

254
Martinsburg

Marlowe
Hedgesville
BERKELEY
Shepherdstown
Kearneysville
Inwood
JEFFERSON
Bunker Hill
Ranson
Charles Town
Bolivar
Harpers
Ferry

Place	ZIP
Buckeye	24924
Buckhannon	26201
Bud	24716
Buena Vista	25320
Buffalo	25033
Buffalo Creek	25530
Buff Lick	25039
Bula	26521
Bulger	25501
Bull	25669
Bull Run	26547
Bulltown	26631
Bunker Hill (Berkeley County)	25413
Bunker Hill (Kanawha County)	25309
Bunners Ridge	26554
Burchfield	26562
Burlington	26710
Burning Springs (Kanawha County)	25015
Burning Springs (Wirt County)	26141
Burnsville	26335
Burnsville Junction (Part of Burnsville)	26335
Burnt Factory	25411
Burnt House	26178
Burnwell	25034
Burton	26562
Butchersville	26452
Cabell	25871
Cabin Creek	25035
Cabins	26855
Cabot	25163
Cabot Station	26147
Cairo	26337
Caldwell	24925
Calis	26033
Callaway	25880
Calvert (Part of St. Albans)	25177
Calvin	26660
Cambria	26386
Camden	26338
Camden On Gauley	26208
Cameron	26033
Camp	26320
Campbelltown	24954
Camp Creek	25820
Campus	24827
Canaan	26234
Canaan Heights	26260
Canaan Valley	26260
Canebrake	24819
Cane Fork	25075
Canfield (Braxton County)	26601
Canfield (Randolph County)	26241
Cannelton	25036
Canton	26456
Cantwell	26362
Canvas	26662
Canyon	26505
Capehart	25123
Capels	24820
Capitol (Part of Charleston)	25311
Capon Bridge	26711
Capon Springs	26823
Carbon	25122
Carbondale	25036
Caretta	24821
Carl	26676
Carlisle	25917
Carl Lee Ray	26181
Carlos	24844
Carolina	26563
Carolina Heights	25177
Carpendale	26753
Carrollton	26238
Carswell	24853
Carter	26218
Cascade	26547
Cashmere	24918
Cass	24927
Cassity	26278
Cassville	26527
Catawba	26554
Cave	26807
Cazy	25028
Cedar Grove (Kanawha County)	25039
Cedar Grove (Wood County)	26101
Cedarville	26611
Center Hill	26143
Center Point	26339
Centerville	25555
Central	26101
Centralia	26612
Central Station	26456
Century	26214
Century No. 2	26238
Ceredo	25507
Ceres	24701
Cham	25654
Chapel	26624
Chapman (Braxton County)	26412
Chapman (Webster County)	26288
Chapman Addition	26070
Chapmanville	25508
Charleston	25301-75
For specific Charleston Zip Codes call (800) 677-8777, or your local postmaster.	
Charleston Ordnance Center (Part of South Charleston)	25303
Charleston Town Center (Part of Charleston)	25375
Charles Town	25414
Charlton Heights (Part of Gauley Bridge)	25040
Charmco	25958
Chatham Hill	26571
Chattaroy	25667
Chauncey	25612
Cheat Lake	26505
Cheat Neck	26505
Chelyan	25035
Cherokee	25122
Cherry Falls	26288
Cherry Grove	26804
Cherry Run	25427
Chesapeake (Kanawha County)	25315
Chesapeake (Marion County)	26554
Chester	26034
Chesterville	26150
Chestnut Heights	26070
Chestnut Hill (Part of Weirton)	26062
Chestnut Ridge	26505
Chiefton	26301
Childs	26162
Chimney Corner	25085
Chloe	25235
Christian	25611
Churchville	26338
Cicerone	25243
Cinco	25306
Cinderella	25661
Circleville	26804
Cirtsville	25801
Cisco	26161
Claremont	25936
Clarence	25244
Clarksburg	26301*
	26302†
Clay	25043
Claypool (Logan County)	25617
Claypool (Summers County)	25976
Claysville	26743
Clayton	24910
Clear Creek	25044
Clear Fork	24822
Clearview	26003
Clem	26623
Clemtown	26405
Clendenin	25045
Cleveland	26215
Clifftop	25831
Clifton	25237
Clifton Mills	26525
Clinton (Boone County)	25013
Clinton (Ohio County)	26059
Clintonville	24928
Clio	25046
Clothier	25047
Clouston	26033
Clover	25276
Cloverdale	24963
Clover Lick	24927
Clyde (Kanawha County)	25302
Clyde (Wetzel County)	26186
Coal Branch Heights (Part of Charleston)	25301
Coalburg	25035
Coal City	25823
Coaldale	24724
Coal Fork	25306
Coal Mountain	24823
Coalton	26257
Coal Valley	25047
Coalwood	24824
Coburn	26562
Coco	25071
Cofoco	25147
Coketon	26292
Colcord	25048
Cold Stream	26711
Coldwater	26411
Colebank	26405
Coleman	25517
Colfax	26566
Colliers	26035
Collinsdale	25034
Columbia	25118
Combs Addition	25617
Comfort	25049
Conaway	26149
Concord	26410
Confidence	25168
Congo	26050
Conings	26443
Cool Ridge	25825
Cooper (Part of Bramwell)	24715
Coopertown	25148
Copen	26615
Copley	26452
Cora	25614
Cordova	24966
Core	26529
Corinne	25826
Corinth	26713
Corley (Barbour County)	26250
Corley (Braxton County)	26621
Corliss	25962
Cornstalk	24901
Cornwallis	26337
Cortland	26260
Corton	25045
Costa	25051
Cottageville	25239
Cottle	26207
Cotton	25046
Cottontown	26562
Country Club Acres (Part of South Charleston)	25309
Countsville	25243
Courtright	26330
Cove (Part of Weirton)	26062
Cove Creek	25534
Cove Gap	25534
Covel	24719
Cowen	26206
Cox Landing	25537
Coxs Mills	26342
Coxtown (Part of Weston)	26452
Crab Orchard	25827
Crag	25962
Craigmoor	26408
Craigsville	26205
Cranberry	25828
Craneco	25630
Cranesville	26764
Crany	24870
Crawford	26343
Crawley	24931
Creamery	24910
Crede	25302
Cremo	26141
Crescent	25136
Cressmont	25043
Creston	26141
Crichton	25961
Crickmer	25831
Crooked Creek	25639
Crosby	25125
Cross Lanes	25313
Crossroads	26589
Crow	25813
Crown (Logan County)	25606
Crown (Monongalia County)	26505
Crown Hill	25052
Crow Summit	26164
Crum	25669
Crumpler	24825
Crystal	24747
Crystal Lake	26456
Crystal Springs (Randolph County)	26241
Crystal Springs (Wood County)	26181
Cubana	26237
Cucumber	24826
Culloden	25510
Cumberland Heights	24701
Cunard	25840
Curtin	26288
Curtisville	26582
Cusicks Crossing	26562
Custer Addition	26301
Cutlips	26619
Cuzzart	26530
Cyclone	24827
Cyrus	25530
Czar	26224
Dabney	25654
Dahmer	26807
Dailey	26259
Daisy	25505
Dakota	26554
Dale	26377
Dallas	26036
Dallison	26180
Dameron	25849
Danese	25831
Daniels	25832
Dans Run	26763
Danville	25053
Darkesville	25428
Dartmont	25009
Dartmoor	26250
Davenport	26175
Davin	25617
Davis (Logan County)	25625
Davis (Tucker County)	26260
Davis Creek	25003
Davisville	26142
Davy	24828
Dawes	25054
Dawmont	26344
Dawson	24910
Daybrook	26570
Daysville	26201
Deansville	26201
Deanville	26452
Decota	25122
Deep Valley (Marion County)	26582
Deep Valley (Tyler County)	26360
Deep Water	25057
Deer Creek	24927
Deer Run	26807
Deer Walk	26180
Dehue	25654
Delbarton	25670
Dellslow	26531
Delong	26170
Delray	26714
Dempsey	25840
Denver (Marshall County)	26033
Denver (Preston County)	26444
Denver Heights	26033
Derryhale	25846
Despard	26301
Dessie	26623
Devon	25682
Dewitt	25901
Diamond (Kanawha County)	25015
Diamond (Logan County)	25625
Diana	26217
Dickinson	25015
Dickson	25535
Dille	26617
Dingess	25671
Dingy	26623
Dink	25113
Dixie	25059
Doane	25511
Dobra	25183
Dock	25177
Dog Patch	25636
Dog Run	25043
Dola	26386
Donaldson	26206
Doortown	26288
Dorcas	26847
Dorothy	25060
Dothan	25833
Dott	24736
Douglas (Calhoun County)	25235
Douglas (Tucker County)	26292
Downtown (Part of Huntington)	25701
Downtown (Part of Wheeling)	26003
Drennen	26667
Drews Creek	25140
Droop	24966
Drybranch	25061
Dry Creek	25062
Dryfork	26263
Dry Hill	25801
Duck	25063
Dudeon	25248
Dudley Gap	25541
Duffields	25442
Duffy	26376
Duhring	24747
Dukes	25252

---

* Area Zip Code † Post Office Boxes

* Area Zip Code   † Post Office Boxes

Place	ZIP
Green Valley (Nicholas County)	25981
Greenview	25053
Greenville	24945
Greenwood (Boone County)	25010
Greenwood (Doddridge County)	26360
Greer (Mason County)	25550
Greer (Monongalia County)	26505
Greggsville (Part of Wheeling)	26003
Grey Eagle	25674
Griffithsville	25521
Grimms Landing	25095
Grippe	25314
Grove	26411
Groves	25063
Grubbs Corner	25401
Guardian	26217
Gum Spring	26505
Gunville	25123
Guthrie	25312
Guyandotte (Part of Huntington)	25702
Guyan Estates	25504
Guyan Terrace	25601
Gypsy	26361
Hacker Valley	26222
Hagans	26529
Hager	25563
Hales Gap	24701
Hall	26201
Hallburg	25063
Halleck	26505
Halltown	25423
Halo	26206
Hambleton	26269
Hamlin	25523
Hammond	26566
Hampden	25623
Hampton	26201
Hampton Heights (Part of Charleston)	25314
Hancock	25411
Handley	25102
Hanna	26180
Hannahsville	26290
Hanover	24839
Hansford	25103
Hany	25511
Harding	26250
Hardy	24740
Harewood Mine	25031
Harlin	26456
Harman	26270
Harmco (Part of Mullens)	25882
Harmony	25246
Harmony Grove	26505
Harper (Pendleton County)	26807
Harper (Raleigh County)	25851
Harper Heights	25801
Harpers Ferry	25425
Harpertown	26241
Harris Ferry	26181
Harrison	25105
Harrisville	26362
Harters Hill	26591
Hartford	25247
Hartland	25043
Hartmansville	26717
Harts	25524
Harvey	25901
Harveytown (Part of Huntington)	25704
Hastings	26377
Hatcher (Mercer County)	24740
Hatcher (Wyoming County)	24870
Hatfield Bottom (Part of Matewan)	25678
Havaco	24841
Haywood	26366
Haywood Junction	26431
Hazelgreen	26367
Hazelton	26535
Hazelwood	26241
Hazy	25189
Headsville	26710
Heaters	26627
Heatherfield	25443
Heavener Grove	26201
Hebron	26346
Hedgesville	25427
Hedgeview	25637
Heizer	25159
Helen	25853
Helens Run	26591

Place	ZIP
Helvetia	26224
Hemlock	26224
Hemphill (Part of Welch)	24842
Henderson	25106
Hendricks	26271
Henlawson	25624
Henning	24938
Henrietta	26147
Hensley	24843
Hensley Heights	25635
Hepzibah (Harrison County)	26369
Hepzibah (Taylor County)	26330
Hereford	25252
Herndon	24726
Herndon Heights	24726
Hernshaw	25107
Herold	26601
Herring	26547
Hettie	26376
Hetzel	25076
Hewett	25108
Hiawatha	24729
Hickman Run	26554
Hickory Chapel	25550
Hico	25854
Highland	26346
Highland Lake Terrace	26181
Highland Park	26241
Highlawns (Part of Rivesville)	26588
High View	26808
Hildebrand	26505
Hillcrest (Part of Fairmont)	26554
Hilldale	25951
Hillsboro	24946
Hillsdale	24976
Hilltop	25855
Hillview (Cabell County)	25702
Hillview (Marion County)	26554
Hillview Terrace	26041
Hilton Village	25962
Hinch	25682
Hines	25967
Hinkleville	26201
Hinton	25951
Hiorra	26410
Hite	26588
Hitop	25160
Hix	25951
Hodgesville	26201
Hogsett	25515
Hokes Mill	24970
Holbrook	26456
Holcomb	26261
Holden	25625
Holly	25122
Holly Grove	25103
Hollywood	24983
Homeland	26378
Hometown	25109
Homewood	26452
Hominy Falls	26679
Hoodsville	26588
Hoo Hoo	25865
Hookersville	26651
Hooverson Heights	26037
Hoover Town	26218
Hopemont	26764
Hopeville	26855
Hopewell (Barbour County)	26416
Hopewell (Fayette County)	25938
Hopewell (Marion County)	26554
Hopewell (Preston County)	26525
Hopkins Fork	25181
Horner	26372
Horsepen	24619
Horse Shoe Run	26769
Horton	26296
Hosterman	26264
Hotchkiss	25920
Hoult	26554
Howells Mill	25545
Howesville	26444
Hoy	26704
Hubball	25506
Hubbardstown	25555
Hudson	26519
Huff Junction	25634
Hughart	24928
Hughes	26404
Hugheston	25110
Hugo	25168
Hull	24844
Humphrey	26133
Hundred	26575
Hunt	25635

Place	ZIP
Hunter's Ridge (Part of Charleston)	25314
Huntersville	24954
Hunting Ground	26804
Huntington	25701-79
For specific Huntington Zip Codes call (304) 526-9600, or your local postmaster.	
Huntington Mall (Part of Barboursville)	25504
Hur	26151
Hurricane	25526
Hurst	26321
Hutchinson	26591
Huttonsville	26273
Huttonsville Correctional Center	26273
Iaeger	24844
Idamay	26576
Ikes Fork	24845
Independence (Clay County)	25125
Independence (Jackson County)	25275
Independence (Preston County)	26374
Indian (Part of St. Albans)	25177
Indian Meadows	25545
Indian Mills	24935
Indore	25111
Industrial	26375
Industrial (Part of Clarksburg)	26301
Industry	26152
Ingleside	24740
Ingram Branch	25119
Inkerman	26801
Institute	25112
Intermont	26851
Inwood	25428
Ireland	26376
Irona	26537
Iroquis	25928
Isaban	24846
Isom	25121
Israel	26444
Itmann	24847
Iuka	26149
Ivy	26201
Ivydale	25113
Jacksonburg	26377
Jackson Flats	24873
Jacksons Mills	26452
Jacobs Fork	24884
Jacox	24946
Jamestown	25446
Jamison Mine No. Nine	26571
Jane Lew	26378
Janie	25209
Jarrolds Valley (Part of Whitesville)	25209
Jarvisville	26332
Jawood	25811
Jayenn	26554
Jeffrey	25114
Jenkinjones	24848
Jenks	25563
Jennington	26254
Jenny Gap	25865
Jere	26546
Jerrys Run	26133
Jesse	24849
Jimtown (Harrison County)	26386
Jimtown (Morgan County)	25411
Job	26270
Jockeycamp Run	26456
Jodie	26674
Joetown	26582
Johnnycake	24844
Johnsontown (Berkeley County)	25427
Johnsontown (Jefferson County)	25430
Johnstown	26385
Joker	26141
Jolo	24850
Jonben	25856
Jones Springs	25427
Jordan	26554
Jordan Run	26833
Josephine	25857
Josephs Mills	26320
Joy	26456
Judson	24910
Judy Gap	26814
Julia	24966
Julian	25529
Jumping Branch	25969
Junction	26824
Junior	26275

Place	ZIP
Justice	24851
Justice Addition	25601
Kabletown	25414
Kalamazoo	26416
Kanawha	26142
Kanawha City (Part of Charleston)	25304
Kanawha Drive	26351
Kanawha Estates (Part of Charleston)	25304
Kanawha Falls	25115
Kanawha Head	26228
Kanawha Station	26142
Kansooth	26033
Kasson	26405
Katy	26554
Katy Lick	26301
Kayford	25122
Kearneysville	25430
Kedron	26201
Keeler Glade	26525
Keenan	24983
Kegley	24731
Keister	24901
Keith	25148
Kelly	25022
Kelly Hill	25045
Kellysville	24732
Kenna	25248
Kenova	25530
Kent	26055
Kentuck	25249
Kera Landing	25262
Kerens	26276
Kermit	25674
Keslers Cross Lanes	26675
Kessler	25984
Kettle	25243
Key	26814
Keyrock	24874
Keyser	26726
Keystone	24852
Kiahsville	25534
Kidwell	26149
Kieffer	24950
Kilarm Junction	26554
Killarney	25915
Kilsyth	25859
Kimball	24853
Kimberly	25118
Kincaid	25119
Kincheloe	26378
Kinder	25540
Kingmont	26578
Kingston	25120
Kingstown	25561
Kingsville	26257
Kingwood	26537
Kirby	26729
Kirby Addition	24740
Kirbyton	25181
Kirk	25671
Kirt	26283
Kistler	25628
Kitchen	25508
Kitsonville (Part of Weston)	26452
Kline	26866
Klines Gap	26833
Knawl	26447
Knob Fork	26581
Knobs	26451
Knollwood	25302
Knottsville	26354
Kodol	26186
Kopperston	24854
Kyle	24855
Lacoma	24827
La Frank (Part of Richwood)	26261
Lahmansville	26731
Lake	25121
Lake Floyd	26332
Lake Ridge	26630
Lake Ron	26181
Lake Washington	25526
Lakin	25250
Lamberton	26346
Lanark	25860
Landes	26847
Landgraff	24829
Landisburg	25831
Lando Mines	25670
Landville	25635
Laneville	26263
Lanham	25159
Lansing	25862
Largent	25422
Larkmead	26101
Lashmeet	24733

	ZIP
Lauckport (Part of Parkersburg)	26101
Laura Lee Mine	26386
Laurel Branch	24131
Laurel Dale	26743
Laurel Fork	26601
Laurel Iron Works	26505
Laurel Park	26301
Laurel Point	26505
Laurel Valley	26301
Lavalette	25535
Lawn	25976
Lawrenceville (Part of Chester)	26034
Layland	25864
Leachtown	26143
Lead Mine	26290
Leadsville	26241
Leander	25912
Leckie	24856
Lee	25880
Lee Creek	26181
Leet	25524
Leetown	25430
Leevale	25209
Leewood	25122
Leewood Park	26003
Left Hand	25251
Lego	25857
Lehew	26865
Leivasy	26676
Lenore	25676
Lenox	26519
Leon	25123
Leonard	24966
Leopold	26443
Lerona	25971
Le Roy	25252
Lesage	25537
Leslie	25972
Lester	25865
Letart	25253
Letherbark	25234
Letter Gap	25255
Levels	25431
Lewisburg	24901
Lex	24817
Liberty (Harrison County)	26301
Liberty (Putnam County)	25124
Lick Creek	25979
Lick Fork	25840
Lico	25314
Lightburn	26378
Lila	24808
Lilac Hills	24740
Lillybrook	25857
Lillydale (Monroe County)	24945
Lillydale (Wyoming County)	24822
Lilly Grove	24740
Lillyhaven	24854
Lilly Park	25962
Lima	26383
Limestone (Marshall County)	26041
Limestone (Mineral County)	26726
Limestone Hill	26143
Linden	25256
Lindside	24951
Lindytown	25204
Link	26167
Linn	26384
Linwood	26291
Little	26146
Little Birch	26629
Little Falls	26505
Little Italy (Clay County)	25113
Little Italy (Randolph County)	26296
Little Laurel Creek (Part of Richwood)	26261
Little Pittsburg	26434
Littlesburg	24701
Littleton	26581
Lively	25917
Liverpool	25252
Livingston	25083
Lizemores	25125
Lloydsville	26619
Lobata	25678
Lobelia	24946
Lochgelly	25866
Lockbridge	25973
Lockhart	25275
Lockney	25258
Lockwood	26651
Lodgeville	26330
Logan	25601
Logansport	26582

	ZIP
Lomax	24899
London	25126
Lonetree	26149
Longacre	25186
Long Branch (Fayette County)	25867
Long Branch (Wyoming County)	24882
Longdale	25253
Longpole	24844
Long Run	26426
Longview	26238
Lookout	25868
Loom	26704
Looneyville	25259
Lorado	25630
Lorentz	26229
Lorton Lick	24701
Lost City	26810
Lost Creek	26385
Lost River	26810
Loudenville	26033
Loudon Heights (Part of Charleston)	25314
Louise	26070
Loveridge	24966
Lovern	24740
Lowdell	26169
Lowell	24962
Lower Belle	25015
Lower Falls	25177
Lower Nicut	26633
Low Gap	25130
Lowney	25666
Lowsville	26533
Lubeck	26101
Lucas	25938
Lucretia	26354
Lumberport	26386
Lundale	25631
Lyburn	25632
Lynco	24857
Lynn	25678
Lynn Camp	26039
Lynwinn	25823
Lyonsville	26651
Maben	25870
Mabie	26278
Mabscott	25871
MacAlpin	25921
MacArthur	25873
McCauley	26801
McClellan	26582
McCloud	25671
Mc Comas	24735
McConnell	25646
McCorkle	25564
McCreery	25934
Macdale	26521
Macdonald	25880
Mc Dowell	24810
MacDunn	25161
Mace	26294
Macfarlan	26148
McGee	26354
Mc Graws	25875
McGuire Park	26452
McIntire	26369
McKeefrey	26041
McKinleyville	26070
Macksville	26884
McMechen	26040
Macomber	26425
McRoss	25962
Mc Whorter	26401
Madam Creek	25951
Madeline	25811
Madison	25130
Madison Run	26705
Magnolia (Morgan County)	25422
Magnolia (Upshur County)	26218
Mahan	25131
Maher	25661
Mahone	26362
Maidsville	26541
Maitland	24886
Majorsville	26036
Malcom Spring Heights	25541
Malden	25306
Mallory	25634
Mammoth	25132
Man	25635
M and K Junction (Part of Rowlesburg)	26425
Manheim	26425
Manila	25508
Manleys Church	26554
Mannings	25425
Mannington	26582
Manown	26537

	ZIP
Mansfield (Part of Philippi)	26416
Manus	25649
Maple Acres	24701
Maple Fork	25880
Maple Lake	26330
Maple Meadow	25865
Maple Point (Part of Barrackville)	26559
Maple View	24701
Maplewood	25874
Marfrance	25981
Margaret	26448
Marianna	24859
Marie	24918
Marie Heights	26101
Marine	24828
Market	26411
Markwood	26710
Marlaing Addition	25177
Marlinton	24954
Marlowe	25419
Marmet	25315
Marquess	26444
Marrtown	26101
Marshall	25252
Marshall Terrace	26070
Marshall University (Part of Huntington)	25703
Marshville	26332
Martha	25504
Martin	26743
Martinsburg	25401
Marvel	25812
Marytown	24889
Mason	25260
Masontown	26542
Masonville	26847
Masseyville	25174
Matewan	25678
Matheny (Wood County)	26181
Matheny (Wyoming County)	24860
Mathias	26812
Matoaka	24736
Maud	26155
Maxine	25049
Maxwell	26170
Maxwell Acres	26041
Maxwelton	24957
Maybeury	24861
Maynor	25801
Maysel	25133
Maysville	26833
Mead	25915
Meadland	26330
Meador	25682
Meadow Bluff	24958
Meadow Bridge	25976
Meadowbrook (Harrison County)	26404
Meadowbrook (Kanawha County)	25311
Meadowbrook (Mason County)	25550
Meadow Creek	25977
Meadowdale	26554
Meadowville	26250
Meadville	26135
Mechanicstown	25414
Mechlenberg Heights	25443
Medina	26164
Medley	26734
Melissa	25504
Mellin	26362
Melrose (Mercer County)	24712
Melrose (Wood County)	26181
Melville	25646
Mercers Bottom	25123
Meredith Springs	26554
Meriden	26416
Merrimac	25661
Metz	26585
Meyerstown	25414
Miami	25134
Micco	25647
Middlebourne	26149
Middle Grave Creek	26041
Middle Run	26623
Middletown (Part of Richwood)	26261
Midkiff	25540
Midland	26241
Midway (Barbour County)	26250
Midway (Mercer County)	24701
Midway (Putnam County)	25168
Midway (Raleigh County)	25878
Mifflin	25047
Milam (Hardy County)	26838
Milam (Wyoming County)	25875
Mile Branch	24811

	ZIP
Millard	25276
Millbrook	26711
Mill Creek	26280
Millersville	26554
Millertown	26354
Milliken	25071
Mill Point	24946
Mill Run	26271
Millstone (Calhoun County)	25261
Millstone (Mingo County)	25670
Milltown	25163
Millville	25432
Millwood	25262
Milo	25256
Milton	25541
Minden	25879
Mineral City	25617
Mineralwells (census designated place)	26150
Mineral Wells	26150
Mingo	26294
Mink Shoals	25302
Minnehaha Springs	24954
Minnie	26155
Minnora	25268
Miracle Run	26570
Missouri Branch	25511
Mitchell	26807
Mitchell Branch	25692
Mitchell Heights	25601
Moatstown	26813
Moatsville	26405
Mobley	26437
Mohawk	24862
Mohegan	24820
Moler Crossroads	25443
Monarch	25039
Monaville	25636
Monclo	25183
Monitor	24976
Monkeytown	26814
Monongah	26554
Monson	24836
Montana Mines	26586
Montcalm	24737
Montcoal	25135
Monterville	26282
Montgomery	25136
Montgomery Heights	25057
Montpelier (Part of Clarksburg)	26301
Montrose (Kanawha County)	25303
Montrose (Randolph County)	26283
Moore	26283
Moorefield	26836
Mooresville	26529
Morgan	26164
Morgan Heights (Part of Westover)	26505
Morgansville	26456
Morgantown	26502-07
For specific Morgantown Zip Codes call (304) 291-1035, or your local postmaster.	
Morning Star	25276
Morrall Mine	26416
Morristown	26143
Morrisvale	25565
Mossy	25917
Moundsville	26041
Mountain	26407
Mountain Cove	25938
Mountaindale	26525
Mountaineer Mall (Part of Morgantown)	26505
Mountain Mission	25425
Mountain View	26444
Mount Alto	25264
Mount Carbon	25139
Mount Clare	26408
Mount De Chantel (Part of Wheeling)	26003
Mount Echo	26060
Mount Gay	25637
Mount Gay-Shamrock	25601
Mount Harmony	26554
Mount Home	25113
Mount Hope (Fayette County)	25880
Mount Hope (Roane County)	25286
Mount Hope (Wood County)	26160
Mount Liberty	26416
Mount Lookout	26678
Mount Nebo	26679

* Area Zip Code   † Post Office Boxes

Name	ZIP	Name	ZIP	Name	ZIP	Name	ZIP
Mount Olive (Mason County)	25503	Nollville	25401		26102†	Poe	26683
Mount Olive (Roane County)	25276	Normantown	25267	Parkview (Ohio County)	26003	Point Lick Junction	25306
Mount Olivet (Marshall County)	26003	North Berkeley	25411	Parkview (Taylor County)	26354	Point Mills (Part of Valley Grove)	26059
Mount Olivet (Mercer County)	24747	North Charleston (Part of Charleston)	25312	Par Metta Crest	26184	Point Pleasant	25550
Mount Pleasant	25446	North Fairmont (Part of Fairmont)	26554	Parsley Bottom	25676	Points	25437
Mount Storm	26739	Northfork	24868	Parsons	26287	Polard	26149
Mount Tabor	25801	North Hills	26101	Patterson Creek	26753	Polemic	26601
Mount Vernon (Preston County)	26547	North Matewan	25688	Paw Paw	25434	Polk Gap	25870
Mount Vernon (Putnam County)	25526	North Mitchell Heights	25601	Pax	25904	Pondco	25208
Mountview	25825	North Mountain	25427	Paynesville	24873	Pond Creek	26133
Mount Welcome	25286	North Parkersburg (Part of Parkersburg)	26104	Peach Creek	25639	Pond Gap	25160
Mount Zion (Calhoun County)	26151	North River Mills	26711	Peanut	26582	Pond Junction (Part of Madison)	25130
Mount Zion (Tucker County)	26290	North Spring	24869	Pear	25918	Pool	26684
Moyers	26813	North View (Part of Clarksburg)	26301	Pea Ridge	25705	Port Amherst	25306
Mozart	26003	Norton	26285	Pecks Mill	25547	Porters Falls	26162
Mozer	26866	Norway	26554	Pecks Run	26201	Porterwood	26283
Mud	25565	Norwood (Part of Fairmont)	26554	Peeltree	26238	Porto Rico	26411
Muddlety	26651	Numan	26426	Peewee	25252	Posey	25180
Mudfork (Calhoun County)	25235	Nuriva (Part of Mullens)	25882	Pemberton	25878	Potomac	15376
Mudfork (Logan County)	25649	Nursery Gap	25514	Pence Springs	24962	Potomac Manor	26717
Mullens	25882	Nutter Farm	26161	Peniel	25270	Potomac Park	26419
Mullensville	24874	Nutter Fort	26301	Pennsboro	26415	Powell	26554
Munday	26152	Nutter Fort Stonewood (Part of Nutter Fort)	26301	Pentress	26544	Powell Creek	25130
Munson	24883	Nutterville	25981	Peora	26431	Powellton	25161
Murphy	26201	Oak Acres	26181	Pepper	26330	Powhatan	24877
Murphytown	26142	Oakdale	26582	Perkins	26634	Pratt	25162
Murraysville	26164	Oak Flat	26802	Perry	26851	Premier	24878
Muses Bottom	26164	Oak Hill	25901	Persinger	26651	Prenter	25163
Mustang Acres (Part of Parkersburg)	26101	Oakmont (Mineral County)	26717	Petersburg	26847	Price	25540
Myra	25544	Oakmont (Ohio County)	26003	Peterson	26423	Price Hill (Boone County)	25130
Myrtle (Boone County)	25165	Oakvale	24739	Peterstown	24963	Price Hill (Raleigh County)	25818
Myrtle (Mingo County)	25670	Oakview Heights	25530	Petroleum	26161	Price Hill Junction (Part of Mount Hope)	25880
Nabob	25122	Oakwood Estates	26101	Pettit Heights	26070	Pricetown (Lewis County)	26452
Nallen	26680	O'Brion	25063	Pettry	24712	Pricetown (Wetzel County)	26437
Nancys Run	25276	Oceana	24870	Pettry Bottom	25189	Prichard	25555
Naoma	25140	Odaville	25275	Pettus	25209	Priestly	25003
Napier	26631	Odd	25902	Pettyville	26101	Prince	25907
National	26505	Ohley	25147	Peytona	25154	Princeton	24740
Natrium	26055	Olcott	25314	Pharoah	25555	Princewick	25908
Naugatuck	25685	Old Arthur	26816	Pheasant Run	26276	Procious	25164
Neal	25530	Old Fields	26845	Phico	25508	Proctor	26055
Neals Run	25444	Omar	25638	Philippi	26416	Propstburg	26802
Nebo (Clay County)	25141	Omps	25411	Piatt	25015	Prosperity	25909
Nebo (Upshur County)	26201	Ona	25545	Pickaway	24976	Prudence	25901
Needmore	26801	Onego	26886	Pickens	26230	Pruntytown	26354
Neibert	25632	O'Neil	26461	Pickle Street	26321	Pullman	26421
Nellis	25142	Oney Gap	24740	Pickshin	25857	Pumpkintown	26257
Nelson	25163	Onoto	24954	Pie	25670	Purgitsville	26852
Nemours	24738	Opekiska	26554	Piedmont	26750	Puritan	25670
Neola	24961	Oral Lake	26330	Pierce	26292	Pursglove	26546
Neptune	26164	Orchard	24918	Pierpont (Monongalia County)	26505	Pursley	26175
Nestlow	25512	Orchard Hill	25438	Pierpont (Wyoming County)	25870	Quaker	25511
Nestorville	26405	Organ Cave	24970	Pigeon	25164	Quarrier	25122
Nethkin	26726	Orgas	25148	Pike	26346	Queens	26237
Nettie	26681	Orient Hill	25958	Pikeside	25401	Queen Shoals	25045
Neville (Part of Beckley)	25801	Orlando	26412	Pinch	25156	Quick	25045
New	25918	Orleans Road	25422	Pine Bluff	26431	Quiet Dell	26408
Newark	26143	Orma	25268	Pine Creek	25625	Quinland	25205
Newberne	26409	Orr	26764	Pine Grove (Kanawha County)	25143	Quinnimont	25910
Newburg	26410	Ortin Heights	25143	Pine Grove (Marion County)	26554	Quinwood	25981
New Creek	26743	Orville	25654	Pine Grove (Wetzel County)	26419	Rachel	26587
New Cumberland	26047	Osage	26543	Pineknob	25140	Racine	25165
Newdale	26155	Osborne	25045	Pineville	24874	Racy	26161
Newell	26050	Osbornes Mills	25045	Piney	26167	Rada	26852
New England	26181	Oscar	24966	Piney View	25906	Radnor	25517
New England Heights	26181	O'Toole	24808	Pinoak	24733	Ragland	25690
New Era	25275	Otsego	25882	Pipestem	25979	Rainelle	25962
Newhall	24866	Ottawa	25149	Pisgah	25525	Raines Corner	24951
New Hamlin	25523	Otto	25276	Pleasant Creek	26416	Raintown	24946
New Haven	25265	Ovapa	25150	Pleasant Dale	26704	Raleigh	25911
New Hill (Marion County)	26591	Overfield	26416	Pleasant Hill	26147	Ramage	25114
New Hill (Monongalia County)	26527	Owings	26431	Pleasant Home	26133	Ramp	25985
New Hope	24740	Oxford	26456	Pleasant Valley (Hancock County)	26062	Ramsey	25912
Newlon	26236	Packs Branch	25880	Pleasant Valley (Marion County)	26554	Rand	25306
New Manchester	26056	Packsville	25209	Pleasant Valley (Marshall County)	26033	Randall	26543
New Martinsville	26155	Pad	25286	Pleasant Valley (Monongalia County)	26505	Ranger	25557
New Milton	26411	Paden City	26159	Pleasant Valley (Ohio County)	26003	Ranson	25438
New Richmond	24867	Page	25152	Pleasant View (Jackson County)	26164	Raven	26651
New Thacker	25694	Pageton	24871	Pleasant View (Lincoln County)	25506	Ravencliff	25913
Newton	25266	Paint Creek Junction (Part of Pratt)	25162	Pleasant View (Marion County)	26588	Raven Rock	26170
Newtown	25686	Palace Valley	26224	Pleasure Valley	26283	Raven Rocks	26763
Newville	26601	Palermo	25546	Pliny	25158	Ravenswood	26164
Next	26175	Palestine (Greenbrier County)	24910	Plum Orchard	25271	Rawl	25691
Nicolette	26101	Palestine (Wirt County)	26160	Pluto	25951	Rayburn	25550
Nicut	26633	Pansy	26847	Plymouth	25011	Raymond City	25159
Nimitz	25978	Panther	24872	Poca	25159	Raysal	24879
Nitro	25143	Paradise	25124	Pocatalico	25320	Reader	26167
Nitro Park Addition	25143	Parchment Valley	25271			Ream (Part of Gary)	24836
Nobe	26137	Parcoal	26288			Reamer	25045
Nolan	25687	Pardee	25630			Red Creek	26289
		Park Addition	26070			Redhill	26101
		Parkersburg	26101*			Red House	25168
						Red Jacket	25692
						Red Run	26271
						Red Spring	25976
						Redstar	25914

* Area Zip Code   † Post Office Boxes

Place	ZIP
Red Sulphur Springs	24918
Red Warrior Junction	25122
Reedson	25442
Reedsville	26547
Reedy	25270
Reedyville	25276
Reeses Mill	26726
Reger	26201
Renick	24966
Renicks Valley	24966
Rensford	25306
Replete	26222
Reston	25130
Reynoldsville	26422
Rhodell	25915
Richard	26505
Richardson	25234
Richland	24901
Richwood	26261
Rider	26385
Ridersville	25411
Ridgedale	26505
Ridge Farms	25588
Ridgeley	26753
Ridgeview (Boone County)	25169
Ridgeview (Logan County)	25637
Ridgeville	26710
Ridgeway	25440
Riffle	26601
Rift	24892
Rig	26836
Riley	25927
Rinehart	26448
Ringold	26505
Rio	26755
Ripley	25271
Ripley Landing	25262
Ripling Waters	25248
Rippon	25441
Rita	25632
Riverbend	25177
Riverlake Estates	25177
Riverlawn (Part of St. Albans)	25177
Riverside (Kanawha County)	25086
Riverside (Monongalia County)	26505
Riverton	26814
Rivesville	26588
Rivesville Junction (Part of Rivesville)	26588
Roach	25504
Roanoke	26423
Roberts	26456
Robertsburg	25172
Robey	26386
Robinette	25607
Robson	25173
Rock	24747
Rock Camp	24951
Rock Castle	25272
Rock Cave	26234
Rock Creek	25174
Rockford	26385
Rock Forge	26505
Rock Gap	25411
Rock Lake	26554
Rock Lake Village (Part of South Charleston)	25309
Rock Lick (Fayette County)	25879
Rocklick (Marshall County)	26033
Rock Oak	26801
Rockport	26169
Rockridge	24873
Rock Run	26456
Rocksdale	25234
Rockton	26623
Rock View	24880
Rockville	25540
Rocky Fork	25312
Rodemer	26764
Roderfield	24881
Rohr	26547
Rolfe	24897
Rollins Branch	24870
Romance	25248
Romines Mills	26385
Romney	26757
Romont	25812
Ronceverte	24970
Ronda	25182
Roneys Point	26059
Rosebud	26386
Roseby Rock	26041
Rosedale (Fayette County)	25901
Rosedale (Gilmer County)	26636

Place	ZIP
Rosedale (Monongalia County)	26541
Rosemont	26424
Roseville Addition	25177
Rossmore	25643
Rough Run	26866
Round Bottom	26575
Round Knob	25033
Rowlesburg	26425
Roxalana (Kanawha County)	25064
Roxalana (Roane County)	25259
Ruddle	26807
Rumble	25009
Runa	26679
Rupert	25984
Rush Creek	25276
Rush Run	25274
Rusk	26161
Russelldale	26710
Russellville	26680
Russellville Road	25981
Russett	26147
Ruth	25314
Ruthbelle	26519
Rutherford	26362
Rutledge	25311
Ryanville	26330
Rymer	26582
Sabine	25916
Sabraton (Part of Morgantown)	26505
Sago	26201
St. Albans	25177
St. Clara	26321
St. Cloud	26575
St. George	26290
St. Joe (Part of Albright)	26519
St. Joseph	26055
St. Marys	26170
Salem	26426
Salt Hill	25271
Saltlick Bridge	26627
Saltpetre	25514
Salt Rock	25559
Salt Sulphur Springs	24983
Saltwell	26330
Sam Black Church	24928
Sanderson	25045
Sand Fork	26430
Sand Hill	26003
Sandlick	24701
Sand Lick Junction	26435
Sand Ridge	25274
Sand Run	26201
Sandstone	25985
Sandy Huff	24844
Sandy Summit	25252
Sandyville	25275
Sanford	26554
Sanger	25901
Sanoma	26160
Sarah Ann	25644
Sardis	26301
Sarton	24973
Sassafras	25287
Sattes (Part of Nitro)	25143
Saulsbury	26150
Saulsville	25876
Saunders	25630
Saxman	26202
Saxon	25180
Scarbro	25917
Scarlet	25670
Scary	25177
Scherr	26726
Schrader	25071
Schultz	26170
Scott Depot	25560
Scrabble	25443
Seaman	25252
Secondcreek	24974
Security Hills	25414
Sedalia	26426
Seebert	24946
Selbyville	26236
Seminole	26361
Seneca Rocks	26884
Seng Creek	25209
Servia	25063
Seth	25181
Seven Pines	26582
Shadow Lawn (Part of Charleston)	25311
Shady Brook (Part of Weston)	26452
Shady Spring	25918
Shafer	26290
Shamrock	25614
Shanghai	25427

Place	ZIP
Shanks	26761
Shannondale	25425
Sharon	25182
Sharon Heights	25621
Sharples	25183
Shawvers Crossing	24931
Shegon	25649
Shenandoah Junction	25442
Shepherdstown	25443
Sheridan	25506
Sherman	26173
Sherrard	26003
Sherwood	26456
Shiloh (Raleigh County)	25844
Shiloh (Tyler County)	26146
Shinnston	26431
Shirley	26434
Shively	25508
Shoals	25562
Shock	26638
Short Creek	26058
Short Creek Valley	26003
Short Gap	26726
Short Line Junction (Part of Clarksburg)	26301
Shrewsbury	25015
Shriver	26546
Sias	25563
Sidneyville	25271
Sigman	25168
Silver Grove	25425
Silver Hill	26155
Silver Lake	26769
Silverton	26164
Simoda	26814
Simon	24882
Simpson	26435
Sinclair	26405
Sinks Grove	24976
Sir Johns Run	25411
Sissonville	25320
Sistersville	26175
Six	24824
Six Mile	25053
Skeetersville	25442
Skelton	25919
Skygusty	24883
Slab Fork	25920
Slabtown	25621
Slagle	25654
Slanesville	25444
Slate	26143
Slatyfork	26291
Sleepy Creek	25411
Smithburg	26436
Smith Crossroads	25411
Smithers	25186
Smithfield (Jefferson County)	25430
Smithfield (Wetzel County)	26437
Smithtown	26505
Smithville (Marion County)	26588
Smithville (Ritchie County)	26178
Smoke Hole	26866
Smoot	24977
Snider	26537
Snowden	25573
Snow Flake	24936
Snow Hill	25311
Snowshoe	26209
Sod	25564
Sodom	25183
Somerville	26181
Sophia	25921
South Charleston	25303
South Fork Junction	24883
South Hills (Kanawha County)	25314
South Hills (Monongalia County)	26505
South Madison (Part of Madison)	25130
South Malden	25306
South Park (Kanawha County)	25304
South Park (Lewis County)	26378
South Parkersburg (Part of Parkersburg)	26101
South Ruffner (Part of Charleston)	25304
Southside	25187
South Side Junction (Part of Thurmond)	25936
South Worthington	26591
Spangler	25160
Spanishburg	25922
Spaulding	25666
Spears	25540
Speed	25276

Place	ZIP
Speedway	24712
Spelter	26438
Spencer	25276
Spencer Hospital	25276
Spice	24946
Sprague	25926
Sprattsville	25621
Spread	25043
Sprigg	25693
Spring Creek	24966
Spring Dale (Fayette County)	25986
Springdale (Ohio County)	26003
Springfield	26763
Spring Gap	25444
Spring Hill (Harrison County)	26301
Spring Hill (Kanawha County)	25309
Springton	24736
Spring Valley	25701
Spurlockville	25565
Squire	24884
Stanaford	25927
Standard	25083
Star City	26505
Staten	25274
Statler Run	26570
Statts Mills	25279
Stealey (Part of Clarksburg)	26301
Steeles	24844
Steelton (Part of New Martinsville)	26155
Steep Gut Hollow	25687
Stephenson	25928
Steptown	25674
Stevenboro	26444
Stewart	26101
Stewart Chapel	26301
Stewartstown	26505
Stickney	25189
Stillman	26234
Stinson	25235
Stirrat	25645
Stohrs Cross Roads	25411
Stollings	25646
Stone Branch	25508
Stonecoal	25674
Stoneville	24834
Stonewall (Part of Charleston)	25302
Stonewood	26301
Stony Bottom	24927
Stony River	26739
Stotesbury	25921
Stotlers Crossroads	25411
Stouts Mills	26439
Stover	25844
Stowe	25607
Strange Creek	26639
Streby	26833
Streeter	25969
Stringtown (Barbour County)	26250
Stringtown (Marion County)	26582
Stringtown (Randolph County)	26263
Stringtown (Roane County)	25276
Strouds	26208
Stumptown	25280
Sturgisson	26505
Sugar Camp	26411
Sugar Grove	26815
Sugar Tree	25521
Sugar Valley (Pleasants County)	26135
Sugar Valley (Preston County)	26525
Sullivan (Raleigh County)	25847
Sullivan (Randolph County)	26241
Sully	26254
Sulphur	26717
Sulphur Spring	25625
Sumerco	25567
Summerlee	25931
Summers	26456
Summersville	26651
Summit (Lincoln County)	25567
Summit (Wood County)	26101
Summit Park	26301
Summit Point	25446
Sun	25846
Sunbeam	25076
Suncrest (Part of Morgantown)	26505
Sundial	25189

Place	ZIP	Place	ZIP	Place	ZIP	Place	ZIP
Sun Flower	25252	Trace	25671	Viropa	26431	Whiteoak (Ritchie County)	26421
Sun Hill	24822	Trace Fork	25320	Vivian	24853	White Oak Springs	26764
Sunlight	24991	Trace Junction	25625	Volcano	26180	White Pine	26147
Sunset Acres	26452	Tralee	24710	Volga	26238	White Rock	26554
Sunset Beach	26505	Traphill	25932	Vulcan	25697	Whites Addition	25637
Sunset Court	25508	Triadelphia	26059	Wadestown	26589	Whites Creek	25555
Sunshine	26582	Tribble	25123	Wadeville	26133	White Sulphur Springs	24986
Sun Valley (Hancock County)	26062	Triplett	25043	Wahoo	26554	Whitesville	25209
Sun Valley (Harrison County)	26301	Tripp	25669	Wainville	26206	Whitman	25652
Sun Valley (Kanawha County)	25177	Triune	26505	Waiteville	24984	Whitman Junction	25652
Superior	24886	Trout	24991	Waldeck	26452	Whitmer	26296
Superior Bottom	25638	Troy	26443	Walker	26180	Whittaker	25083
Surosa	25678	Troy Town	25649	Walker Lanes	26181	Wick	26149
Surveyor	25932	Trubada	26351	Walkersville	26447	Wickham	25871
Sutton	26601	True	25988	Wallace	26448	Widemouth	24736
Swamp Run	26201	Tuckahoe	24986	Wallace Heights	25312	Widen	25211
Swandale	25043	Tunnelton	26444	Wallback	25285	Wikel	24945
Sweeneysburg	25801	Turkey Gap	24736	Walnut	25235	Wilbur (Logan County)	25632
Sweetland	25568	Turkey Knob (Fayette County)	25880	Walnut Bottom	26818	Wilbur (Tyler County)	26320
Sweet Run	25530	Turkey Knob (Marion County)	26591	Walnut Grove	25414	Wilcoe (Part of Gary)	24895
Sweet Springs	24980	Turner Douglass	21550	Walnut Hill	25652	Wildcat	26376
Swiss	26690	Turnertown	26452	Walnut Valley Acres	25312	Wilding	26164
Switchback	24887	Turtle Creek	25203	Walton	25286	Wiley Ford	26767
Switzer	25647	Twilight	25204	Wana	26590	Wileyville	26186
Sycamore (Calhoun County)	25261	Twin Branch	24889	Wanda	25076	Wilkinson	25653
Sycamore (Harrison County)	26301	Two Lick	26378	War	24892	Willard	26431
Sycamore (Logan County)	25625	Two Mile (Part of Charleston)	25301	Ward	25039	William	26292
Sydnor Addition	25694	Two Run	26160	Warden	25927	Williamsburg	24991
Sylvester	25193	Tygart (Part of Parkersburg)	26101	Wardensville	26851	Williams Mountain	25163
Tablerock	25813	Tyler	26320	War Eagle	24844	Williamson	25661
Tablers	25428	Tyler Heights	25312	Warriormine (Part of War)	24894	Williamsport	26710
Tacy	26416	Tyler Mountain	25312	Warwood (Part of Wheeling)	26003	Williamstown	26187
Tad	25201	Tyrone	26505	Washburn	26362	Willis Branch	25880
Tague	26623	Uffington	26505	Washington	26181	Willow Bend	24983
Talbott	26250	Uler	25266	Washington Gardens	26181	Willow Island	26134
Talcott	24981	Uneeda	25205	Washington Heights	25130	Willowton	24740
Tallmansville	26237	Unger	25411	Washington Lake	26181	Wilmore	24844
Tamcliff	25621	Union	24983	Waterloo	25123	Wilsie	26641
Tams	25921	Union Addition	25136	Watson (Part of Fairmont)	26554	Wilson	26707
Tango	25523	Union City	24844	Waverly	26184	Wilsonburg	26461
Tanner	26179	Union Ridge	25520	Wayne	25570	Wilsondale	25699
Tannery	26836	United	25122	Wayside	24985	Wilsontown	26234
Taplin	25648	Unus	24938	Weaver	26250	Winding Gulf	25823
Tappan	26354	Upland (Mason County)	25082	Webb	25669	Windom	24859
Tarico Heights	25413	Upland (McDowell County)	24877	Weberwood (Part of South Charleston)	25303	Windsor Heights	26075
Tariff	25281	Upper Addis Run	26362	Webster	26354	Windy	26143
Tate	26623	Upperglade	26266	Webster Springs	26288	Winebrenners Crossroad	25401
Taylorville	25670	Upper Leatherwood	25019	Weircrest (Part of Weirton)	26062	Winfield (Marion County)	26554
Teaberry	24901	Upper Mingo	26294	Weirton	26062	Winfield (Putnam County)	25213
Teays	25569	Upper Tract	26866	Weirton Heights (Part of Weirton)	26062	Wingrove	25917
Teays Valley	25569	Upton Creek	25177	Welch	24801	Winifrede	25214
Tekram	25670	Ury	25853	Wellford	25045	Winifrede Junction (Part of Chesapeake)	25315
Tempa	24910	Utica	26133	Wellington Heights	26416	Winona	25942
Ten Mile	26237	Uvilla	25442	Wellsburg	26070	Wiseburg	25275
Tennerton	26201	Vadis	26321	Wendel	26347	Witcher	25015
Tera Rosa	26181	Vago	24938	Werner	26250	Wolfcreek	24993
Terra Alta	26764	Vale	25976	Werth	26651	Wolfe	24751
Terry	25934	Valley Bend (Barbour County)	26250	West Charleston (Part of Charleston)	25302	Wolf Pen	24896
Tesla	26629	Valley Bend (Randolph County)	26293	West Columbia	25287	Wolf Run	26033
Teter	26238	Valley Chapel	26446	West Dunbar	25064	Wolf Summit	26462
Teterton	26886	Valley Falls	26566	West End	26444	Wood	25123
Thacker	25694	Valley Fork	25283	West Gilbert (Part of Gilbert)	25621	Woodcliff Acres	26181
Thacker Mines	25694	Valley Furnace	26405	West Grafton (Part of Grafton)	26354	Woodland	26055
Thayer	25936	Valley Grove	26060	West Hamlin	25571	Woodland Heights (Part of Charleston)	25314
The Mileground	26505	Valley Head	26294	West Huntington (Part of Huntington)	25704	Woodland Park (Part of Parkersburg)	26101
The Y	25275	Valley Point	26519	West Junction	25206	Woodrow	24954
Thoburn	26554	Vallscreek	24819	West Liberty	26074	Woodruff	26033
Thomas	26292	Van	25206	West Logan	25601	Woodville	25572
Thompson Town	25637	Vanclevesville	25401	West Milford	26451	Woodward Woods (Part of Charleston)	25312
Thornhill	24735	Vandalia (Kanawha County)	25303	Weston	26452	Worth	24897
Thornton	26440	Vandalia (Lewis County)	26423	Westover	26505	Worthington	26591
Thornwood	24920	Van Junction	25206	West Pea Ridge	25705	Wriston	25840
Thorpe (Part of Gary)	24888	Vanville	25401	West Raleigh	25911	Wyatt	26463
Thousand Oaks (Part of Charleston)	25303	Van Vorhis	26505	West Romney	26757	Wyco	25943
Three Churches	26765	Varney	25696	West Union	26456	Wylo	25611
Threefork Bridge	26374	Vaucluse	26170	West Van Voorhis	26541	Wymer	26254
Three Mile	25071	Vaughan	26656	West Williamson (Part of Williamson)	25661	Wyoma	25515
Thurmond	25936	Vedra	24862	Weyanoke	24736	Wyoming	24898
Thursday	26178	Vegan	26267	Wharncliffe	25651	Yards	24659
Tichenal	26385	Venus (Part of Gary)	24836	Wharton	25208	Yates Crossing	25545
Tidewater	24853	Verdunville	25649	Wheeler	26222	Yawkey	25573
Tilden	25847	Verner	25650	Wheeling	26003	Yellow Creek	26136
Tioga	26691	Victor	25938	Wheeling Island (Part of Wheeling)	26003	Yellow Spring	26865
Tolleys (Part of Beckley)	25801	Victoria	26374	Whipple	25917	Yolyn	25654
Toll Gate	26415	Vienna	26105	Whirlwind	25524	Youngs Bottom	25071
Tomahawk	25427	Villa	25311	Whitby	25823	Yukon	24899
Toney	25524	Viola (Marion County)	26554	Whitehall	26554	Zela	26651
Toneyfork	24870	Viola (Marshall County)	26003	White Oak (Raleigh County)	25989	Zenith	24951
Tophet	25979	Virginia Heights	25177			Zevely	26537
Topins Grove	26164	Virginville	26035			Zigler	26807
Tornado	25202					Zinnia	26426
Tourison	25840					Zion	26218
Town Hill (Part of Petersburg)	26847						

	ZIP
Abbotsford	54405
Abells Corners	53121
Abrams	54101
Abrams (Town)	54101
Ackerville	53086
Ackley (Town)	54409
Ada	53020
Adams (Adams County)	53910
Adams (Adams County) (Town)	53934
Adams (Green County) (Town)	53504
Adams (Jackson County) (Town)	54615
Adams (Walworth County)	53120
Adams Beach	54929
Addison	53002
Addison (Town)	53002
Adell	53001
Adrian (Town)	54648
Advance	54111
Afton	53501
Agenda (Town)	54514
Ahnapee (Town)	54201
Ainsworth (Town)	54462
Airport Mail Center (Part of Milwaukee)	53237
Akan (Town)	54655
Alaska	54216
Alban (Town)	54473
Albany (Green County)	53502
Albany (Green County) (Town)	53502
Albany (Pepin County) (Town)	54755
Albertville	54730
Albion (Dane County)	53534
Albion (Dane County) (Town)	53534
Albion (Jackson County) (Town)	54615
Albion (Trempealeau County) (Town)	54738
Alden (Town)	54017
Alderley	53066
Algoma (Kewaunee County)	54201
Algoma (Winnebago County) (Town)	54901
Allen	54770
Allens Grove	53114
Allenton	53002
Allenville	54904
Allouez	54301
Alma (Buffalo County)	54610
Alma (Buffalo County) (Town)	54610
Alma (Jackson County) (Town)	54611
Alma Center	54611
Almena	54805
Almena (Town)	54826
Almon (Town)	54416
Almond	54909
Almond (Town)	54909
Alpha	54840
Alto	53919
Alto (Town)	53919
Altoona	54720
Alvin	54542
Alvin (Town)	54542
Amberg	54102
Amberg (Town)	54102
Amery	54001
Amherst	54406
Amherst (Town)	54977
Amherst Junction	54407
Amnicon (Town)	54874
Amnicon Falls	54874
Anacker	53901
Anderson (Burnett County) (Town)	54840
Anderson (Iron County) (Town)	54565
Angelica	54162
Angelica (Town)	54162
Angelo	54656
Angelo (Town)	54656
Angus	54817
Aniwa	54408
Aniwa (Town)	54414
Annaton	53825
Anson	54729
Anson (Town)	54748
Anston	54301
Anthony	54755
Antigo	54409
Antigo (Town)	54409
Applecreek	54911

	ZIP
Apple River (Town)	54810
Appleton	54911-15
For specific Appleton Zip Codes call (414) 734-7141, or your local postmaster.	
Applewood	53711
Arbor Vitae	54568
Arbor Vitae (Town)	54568
Arcade Acres	54971
Arcadia	54612
Arcadia (Town)	54612
Arena	53503
Arena (Town)	53503
Argonne	54511
Argonne (Town)	54511
Argyle	53504
Argyle (Town)	53504
Arkansaw	54721
Arkdale	54613
Arland	54004
Arland (Town)	54004
Arlington	53911
Arlington (Town)	53555
Armenia (Town)	54646
Armstrong (Fond du Lac County)	53079
Armstrong (Oconto County) (Town)	54149
Armstrong Creek	54103
Armstrong Creek (Town)	54103
Arnott	54481
Arpin	54410
Arpin (Town)	54410
Artesia Beach	53049
Arthur (Chippewa County) (Town)	54727
Arthur (Grant County)	53818
Ashford	53010
Ashford (Town)	53010
Ashippun	53003
Ashippun (Town)	53003
Ashland	54806
Ashland (Town)	54846
Ash Ridge	54664
Ashton	53562
Ashton Corners	53562
Ashwaubenon	54304
Askeaton	54126
Astico	53925
Athelstane	54104
Athelstane (Town)	54104
Athens	54411
Atlanta (Town)	54819
Atlas	54853
Attica	53502
Atwater	53922
Atwood	54460
Auburn (Chippewa County) (Town)	54757
Auburn (Fond du Lac County) (Town)	53040
Auburndale	54412
Auburndale (Town)	54412
Auburn Lake	53010
Augusta	54722
Aurora (Florence County)	49801
Aurora (Florence County) (Town)	49801
Aurora (Taylor County) (Town)	54433
Aurora (Waushara County) (Town)	54923
Auroraville	54923
Avalanche	54665
Avalon	53505
Avoca	53506
Avon (Town)	53520
Avon (Lafayette County)	53530
Avon (Rock County)	53520
Aztalan (Town)	53038
Babcock	54413
Badger Army Ammunition Plant	53913
Bad River Indian Reservation	54806
Bagley (Grant County)	53801
Bagley (Oconto County) (Town)	54161
Baileys Harbor	54202
Baileys Harbor (Town)	54202
Bakerville	54449
Baldwin	54002
Baldwin (Town)	54028
Balsam Lake	54810
Balsam Lake (Town)	54024
Bancroft	54921
Bangor	54614
Bangor (Town)	54653
Baraboo	53913

	ZIP
Baraboo (Town)	53951
Barksdale	54806
Barksdale (Town)	54806
Barnes (Town)	54873
Barneveld	53507
Barnum	54631
Barre (Town)	54601
Barre Mills	54601
Barron	54812
Barron (Town)	54812
Barronett (Barron County)	54813
Barronett (Washburn County) (Town)	54871
Barron Junction (Part of Barron)	54812
Bartelme (Town)	54416
Barton (Town)	53095
Barton	53095
Basco	53508
Bashaw (Burnett County)	54871
Bashaw (Washburn County) (Town)	54871
Bass Bay (Part of Muskego)	53150
Bassett	53101
Bass Lake (Sawyer County) (Town)	54843
Bass Lake (Washburn County) (Town)	54875
Basswood	53573
Batavia	53001
Bateman	54729
Bay City	54723
Bayfield	54814
Bayfield (Town)	54814
Bay Park Square (Part of Ashwaubenon)	54304
Bay Settlement (Part of Green Bay)	54301
Bay Shore Mall (Part of Glendale)	53217
Bayside	53217
Bayview (Town)	54891
Bay View Saint Francis (Part of Milwaukee)	53207
Beachs Corners	54627
Bear Bluff (Town)	54666
Bear Creek (Outagamie County)	54922
Bear Creek (Sauk County) (Town)	53577
Bear Creek (Waupaca County) (Town)	54922
Bear Lake (Barron County) (Town)	54868
Bear Lake (Rusk County)	54728
Bear Valley	53937
Beaver (Clark County) (Town)	54446
Beaver (Marinette County)	54114
Beaver (Marinette County) (Town)	54114
Beaver (Polk County) (Town)	54889
Beaver Brook (Town)	54871
Beaver Dam	53916
Beaver Dam (Town)	53916
Beaver Edge	53916
Beecher (Town)	54156
Beecher	54156
Beecher Lake	54156
Beechwood	53001
Beetown	53802
Beetown (Town)	53802
Beldenville	54003
Belgium	53004
Belgium (Town)	53004
Bell (Town)	54827
Bell Center	54631
Belle Plaine	54166
Belle Plaine (Town)	54166
Belleville	53508
Bellevue	54311
Bellevue (Town)	54311
Bellevue Town (census designated place)	54311
Bell Heights (Part of Appleton)	54911
Bellinger	54771
Bellwood	54820
Belmont (Lafayette County)	53510
Belmont (Lafayette County) (Town)	53818
Belmont (Portage County) (Town)	54909
Beloit	53511*
	53512†
Beloit Mall (Part of Beloit)	53511

	ZIP
Belvidere (Town)	54610
Benderville	54301
Benet Lake	53102
Bennett	54873
Bennett (Town)	54873
Benoit	54816
Benton	53803
Benton (Town)	53803
Bergen (Marathon County) (Town)	54455
Bergen (Vernon County) (Town)	54658
Berlin (Green Lake County)	54923
Berlin (Green Lake County) (Town)	54923
Berlin (Marathon County) (Town)	54401
Bern (Town)	54411
Berry (Town)	53528
Bethel	54410
Bethesda	53186
Bevent	54440
Bevent (Town)	54440
Big Bend (Rusk County) (Town)	54819
Big Bend (Waukesha County)	53103
Big Falls (Rusk County) (Town)	54848
Big Falls (Waupaca County)	54926
Big Flats	53934
Big Flats (Town)	54613
Big Patch	53818
Big Spring	53965
Billings Park (Part of Superior)	54880
Binghamton	54106
Birch (Ashland County)	54559
Birch (Lincoln County) (Town)	54442
Birch Creek (Town)	54745
Birchwood	54817
Birchwood (Town)	54817
Birchwood Lake	53010
Birnamwood	54414
Birnamwood (Town)	54414
Biron	54494
Black Brook (Town)	54005
Black Creek	54106
Black Creek (Town)	54106
Black Earth	53515
Black Earth (Town)	53560
Black Hawk	53588
Black River	53081
Black River Falls	54615
Blackwell	54541
Blackwell (Town)	54541
Black Wolf (Town)	54901
Blaine (Burnett County) (Town)	54830
Blaine (Portage County)	54909
Blair	54616
Blanchard (Town)	53516
Blanchardville	53516
Blenker	54415
Bloom (Town)	54639
Bloom City	54634
Bloomer	54724
Bloomer (Town)	54724
Bloomfield (Walworth County) (Town)	53128
Bloomfield (Waushara County) (Town)	54965
Bloomingdale	54667
Blooming Grove (Town)	53701
Bloomington	53804
Bloomington (Town)	53810
Bloomville	54435
Blueberry	54854
Blue Mounds	53517
Blue Mounds (Town)	53572
Blue River	53518
Bluff Siding	54629
Bluffview	53913
Boardman	54017
Boaz	53581
Bohners Lake	53105
Bolt	54208
Boltonville	53040
Bonduel	54107
Bone Lake (Town)	54837
Borth	54923
Boscobel	53805
Boscobel (Town)	53805
Bosstown	53581
Boulder Junction	54512
Boulder Junction (Town)	54512

* Area Zip Code   † Post Office Boxes

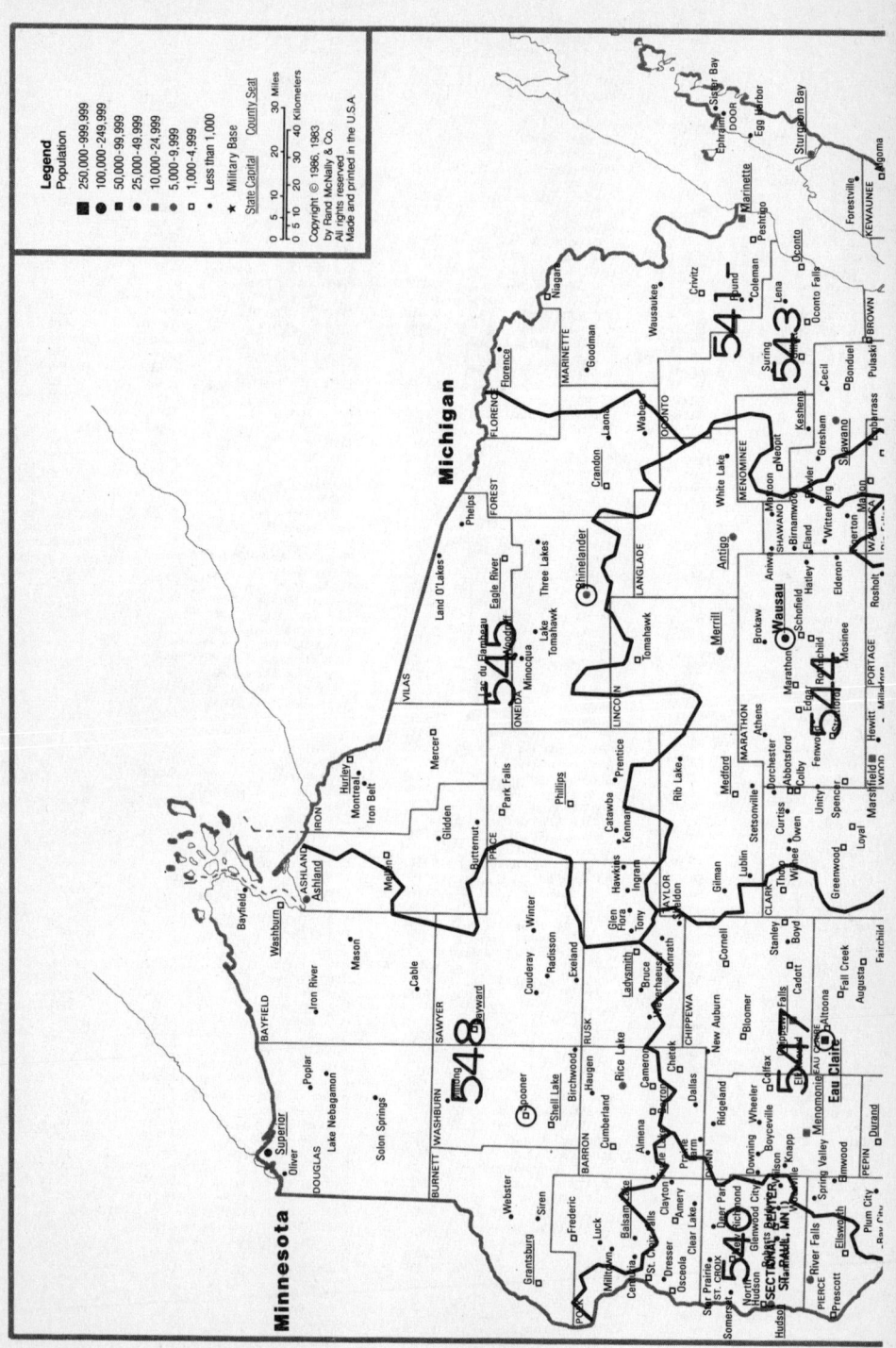

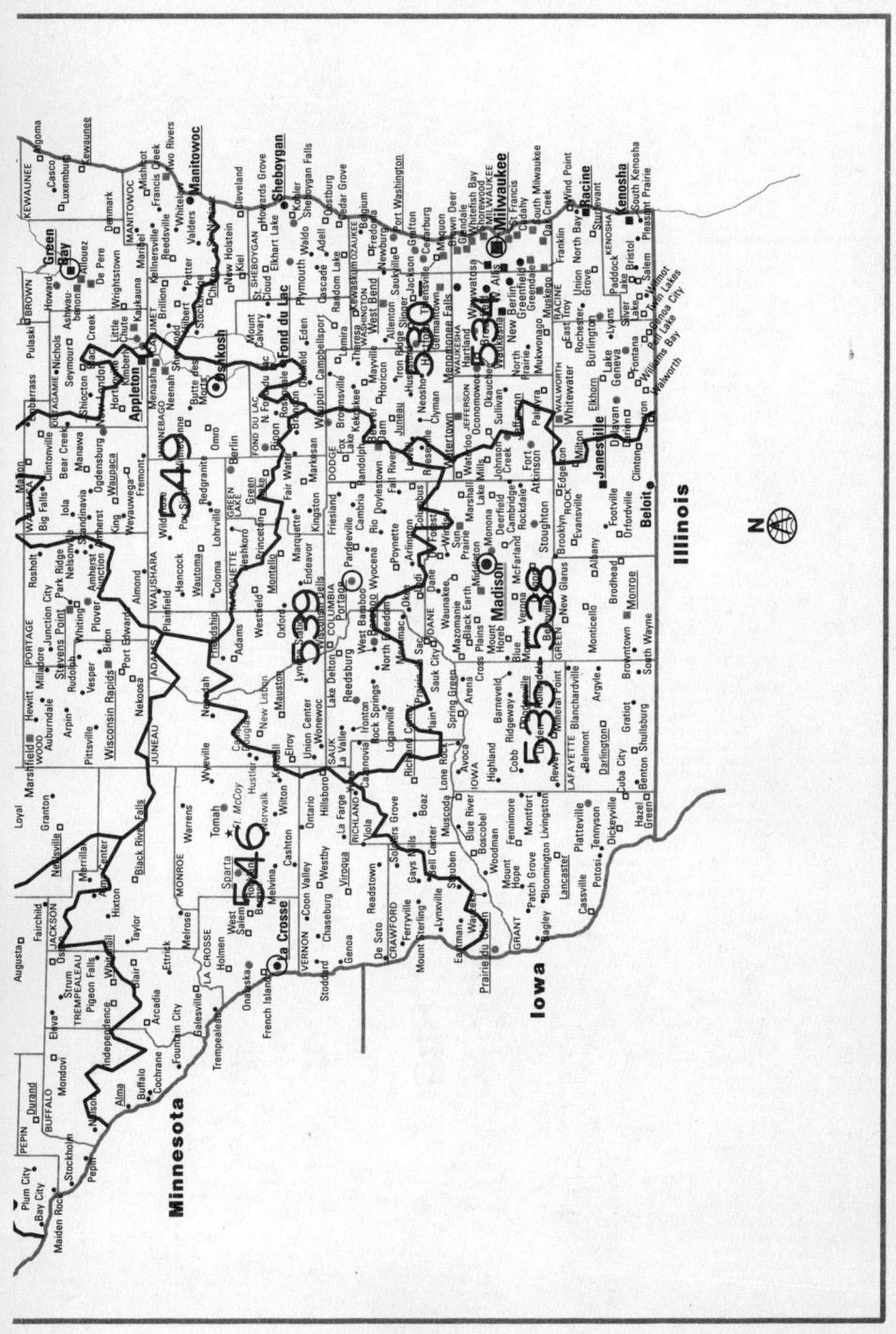

	ZIP
Bovina (Town)	54170
Bowers	53121
Bowler	54416
Boyceville	54725
Boyd	54726
Boydtown	53826
Brackett	54742
Bradford (Town)	53505
Bradley	53223-24

For specific Bradley Zip Codes call (414) 354-1470, or your local postmaster.

	ZIP
Bradley	54487
Bradley (Town)	54487
Branch	54203
Brandon	53919
Branstad	54840
Brant	53014
Brantwood	54513
Braund Addition	54660
Brazeau (Town)	54161
Breed	54174
Breed (Town)	54174
Briarcrest Estates	53545
Briarton	54162
Briarwood	53575
Brice Prairie	54650
Brickson Park	55558
Bridge Creek (Town)	54722
Bridgeport	53821
Bridgeport (Town)	53821
Briggsville	53920
Brigham (Town)	53507
Brighton	53139
Brighton (Town)	53139
Brighton (Town)	54488
Brill	54818
Brillion	54110
Brillion (Town)	54110
Bristol (Town)	53104
Bristol (Dane County) (Town)	53590
Bristol (Kenosha County)	53104
Bristow	54665
Brockway (Town)	54615
Brodhead	53520
Brodtville	53801
Brokaw	54417
Brookfield	53005
	53008
	53045

For specific Brookfield Zip Codes call (414) 782-5070, or your local postmaster.

	ZIP
Brookfield (Town)	53186
Brookfield Square (Part of Brookfield)	53005
Brookhaven	54494
Brooklyn (Green County)	53521
Brooklyn (Green County) (Town)	53521
Brooklyn (Green Lake County) (Town)	54941
Brooklyn (Washburn County) (Town)	54888
Brooks	53921
Brookside (Adams County)	53910
Brookside (Oconto County)	54101
Brookwood (Part of Madison)	53711
Brothertown	53014
Brothertown (Town)	53014
Brown Deer	53209
Browning (Town)	54451
Browns Lake	53105
Brownsville	53006
Browntown	53522
Bruce	54819
Bruemmerville	54201
Brule	54820
Brule (Town)	54820
Brunswick (Town)	54701
Brushville	54965
Brussels	54204
Brussels (Town)	54204
Bryant	54418
Buchanan (Town)	54911
Buck Creek	53581
Buckhorn Corner	53916
Buckman	54208
Budd	54665
Budsin	54960
Buena Park	53185
Buena Vista (Portage County) (Town)	54467
Buena Vista (Richland County) (Town)	53556

	ZIP
Buena Vista (Waukesha County)	53072
Buffalo (Buffalo County)	54622
Buffalo (Buffalo County) (Town)	54629
Buffalo (Marquette County) (Town)	53949
Buffalo Estates	53949
Bundy	54435
Bunker Hill	53924
Burke	53590
Burke (Town)	53590
Burkhardt	54016
Burlington	53105
Burlington (Town)	53105
Burnett	53922
Burnett (Town)	53922
Burnett Corners	53922
Burns (Town)	54614
Burns	54614
Burnside (Town)	54747
Burr Oak	54644
Burton	53820
Busseyville	53534
Butler (Clark County) (Town)	54771
Butler (Milwaukee County)	53213
Butler (Waukesha County)	53007
Butte des Morts	54927
Butternut	54514
Butternut Island	53039
Byrds Creek	53518
Byron	53009
Byron (Town)	53009
Byron (Town)	54618
Cable	54821
Cable (Town)	54821
Caddy Vista	53108
Cadiz (Town)	53522
Cadott	54727
Cady (Town)	54027
Cainville	53536
Calamine	53565
Calamus (Town)	53916
Caldwell	53149
Caledonia (Columbia County) (Town)	53901
Caledonia (Racine County)	53108
Caledonia (Racine County) (Town)	53108
Caledonia (Trempealeau County) (Town)	54630
Caledonia (Waupaca County) (Town)	54940
Calhoun (Part of New Berlin)	53151
Calumet (Town)	53049
Calumetville	53049
Calvary	53057
Cambria	53923
Cambridge	53523
Cameron (Barron County)	54822
Cameron (Wood County) (Town)	54449
Campbell (Town)	54601
Campbellsport	53010
Camp Douglas	54618
Campia	54868
Camp Lake	53109
Camp Leonard	53558
Canton (Barron County)	54868
Canton (Buffalo County) (Town)	54736
Capitol (Part of Madison)	53703
Capitol Court (Part of Milwaukee)	53216
Carey (Town)	54534
Carlisle	54235
Carlton (Town)	54216
Carnot	54213
Carol Beach Estates	53143
Caroline	54928
Carrollville (Part of Oak Creek)	53154
Carson (Town)	54443
Carter	54566
Carthage College	53140
Cary (Town)	54466
Caryville	54701
Cascade	53011
Casco	54205
Casco (Town)	54216
Casey (Town)	54801
Cashton	54619
Cassel (Town)	54426
Cassian (Town)	54529
Cassville	53806
Cassville (Town)	53806

	ZIP
Castle Rock (Town)	53809
Castle Rock	53569
Caswell (Town)	54511
Cataract	54620
Catawba	54515
Catawba (Town)	54459
Cato (Town)	54206
Cato	54206
Cavour	54511
Cayuga	54546
Cazenovia	53924
Cecil	54111
Cedar	54559
Cedarburg	53012
Cedarburg (Town)	53012
Cedar Creek	53095
Cedar Falls	54751
Cedar Grove	53013
Cedar Lake (Town)	54868
Cedar Rapids (Town)	54526
Center (Outagamie County) (Town)	54911
Center (Rock County) (Town)	53545
Center House	53946
Center Lake Woods	53179
Center Ninety (Part of Onalaska)	54650
Center Valley	54106
Centerville (Manitowoc County) (Town)	53015
Centerville (Trempealeau County)	54630
Central Avenue (Part of Superior)	54880
Central Park (Part of Superior)	54880
Centuria	54824
Chaffey	54836
Chain o' Lakes	54981
Chain o' Lakes-King	54981
Chambers Island	54212
Champion	54229
Chapel Ridge Heights	54301
Charlesburg	53014
Charlestown (Town)	53014
Charlie Bluff	53563
Chase	54171
Chase (Town)	54171
Chaseburg	54621
Chelsea	54419
Chelsea (Town)	54419
Chenequa	53029
Cherokee	54421
Cherrywood	53593
Chester (Town)	53963
Chetek	54728
Chetek (Town)	54728
Chicago Corners	54115
Chicog (Town)	54888
Chief Lake	54843
Chili	54420
Chilton	53014
Chilton (Town)	53014
Chimney Rock (Town)	54770
Chippewa (Town)	54514
Chippewa Falls	54729
Chiwaukee	53143
Christiana (Dane County) (Town)	53523
Christiana (Vernon County) (Town)	54667
Christie	54456
Cicero (Town)	54165
Cicero	54165
City Point	54466
City Point (Town)	54466
Clam Falls (Town)	54837
Clam Falls	54837
Clam Lake	54517
Clark	54498
Clark Mills	54206
Clarks Point	54986
Clarno	53566
Clarno (Town)	53566
Clay Banks (Town)	54201
Clayton (Crawford County) (Town)	54655
Clayton (Polk County)	54004
Clayton (Polk County) (Town)	54004
Clayton (Winnebago County) (Town)	54956
Clear Creek (Town)	54770
Clearfield (Town)	53950
Clear Lake (Polk County)	54005
Clear Lake (Polk County) (Town)	54005
Clear Lake (Rock County)	53563

	ZIP
Clearwater Lake	54521
Cleghorn	54738
Cleveland (Chippewa County) (Town)	54732
Cleveland (Jackson County) (Town)	54741
Cleveland (Manitowoc County)	53015
Cleveland (Marathon County) (Town)	54484
Cleveland (Taylor County) (Town)	54433
Clifford	54564
Clifton (Grant County) (Town)	53554
Clifton (Monroe County)	54618
Clifton (Monroe County) (Town)	54618
Clifton (Pierce County) (Town)	54022
Clinton (Barron County) (Town)	54805
Clinton (Rock County)	53525
Clinton (Rock County) (Town)	53525
Clinton (Vernon County) (Town)	54619
Clintonville	54929
Clover (Bayfield County) (Town)	54844
Clover (Manitowoc County)	54220
Cloverdale	54646
Cloverland (Douglas County) (Town)	54854
Cloverland (Vilas County) (Town)	54521
Clyde (Town)	53506
Clyde	53506
Clyman	53016
Clyman (Town)	53039
Cobb	53526
Cobban	54732
Cochrane	54622
Coddington	54467
Colburn (Adams County) (Town)	54943
Colburn (Chippewa County) (Town)	54726
Colburn (Chippewa County)	54726
Colby	54421
Colby (Town)	54421
Cold Spring	53538
Cold Spring (Town)	53538
Coleman	54112
Colfax	54730
Colfax (Town)	54730
Colgate	53017
Collins	54207
Coloma	54930
Coloma (Town)	54930
Coloma Corners	54930
Columbia	54456
Columbus	53925
Columbus (Town)	53925
Combined Locks	54113
Commonwealth	54121
Commonwealth (Town)	54121
Como	53147
Comstock	54826
Concord	53066
Concord (Town)	53066
Connorsville	54725
Conover	54519
Conover (Town)	54519
Conrath	54731
Cooks Valley (Town)	54724
Cooksville	53536
Coomer	54837
Coon (Town)	54621
Coon Rock	53503
Coon Valley	54623
Cooperstown	54208
Cooperstown (Town)	54227
Coral City	54773
Corinth	54411
Cormier (Part of Howard)	54301
Cornelia	53818
Cornell	54732
Corning (Town)	54452
Cornucopia	54827
Cottage Grove	53527
Cottage Grove (Town)	53527
Cottonville	53934
Couderay	54828
Couderay (Town)	54835
Country Estates	53105
County Line	54153

* Area Zip Code　　　† Post Office Boxes

	ZIP
Courtland (Town)	53932
Crandon	54520
Crandon (Town)	54520
Cranmoor	54495
Cranmoor (Town)	54495
Cream	54610
Crescent (Chippewa County)	54727
Crescent (Oneida County) (Town)	54501
Crescent Park	53558
Crestview	53402
Crivitz	54114
Cross (Town)	54629
Cross Lake	60002
Cross Plains	53528
Cross Plains (Town)	53528
Crystal (Town)	54801
Crystal Lake (Barron County) (Town)	54826
Crystal Lake (Marquette County) (Town)	54960
Crystal Lake Corners	54981
Cuba City	53807
Cudahy	53110
Cumberland	54829
Cumberland (Town)	54829
Curran (Jackson County) (Town)	54635
Curran (Kewaunee County)	54208
Curtiss	54422
Cushing	54006
Custer	54423
Cutler	54646
Cutler (Town)	54618
Cylon	54017
Cylon (Town)	54017
Czechville	54629
Dacada	53075
Dairyland	54830
Dairyland (Town)	54830
Dakota	54982
Dakota (Town)	54982
Dale	54931
Dale (Town)	54931
Daleyville	53572
Dallas	54733
Dallas (Town)	54733
Dalton	53926
Danbury	54830
Dancy	54455
Dane	53529
Dane (Town)	53555
Daniels (Town)	54872
Danville	53925
Darboy	54911
Darien	53114
Darien (Town)	53115
Darlington	53530
Darlington (Town)	53530
Davis Corners	53965
Day (Town)	54484
Dayton (Green County)	53508
Dayton (Richland County) (Town)	53581
Dayton (Waupaca County) (Town)	54981
Deansville	53559
Decatur (Town)	53520
Deckers Corner	53012
Decorah Prairie	54630
Dedham	54836
Deerbrook	54424
Deer Creek (Outagamie County) (Town)	54170
Deer Creek (Taylor County) (Town)	54480
Deerfield (Dane County)	53531
Deerfield (Dane County) (Town)	53531
Deerfield (Waushara County) (Town)	54943
Deer Park (Eau Claire County)	54742
Deer Park (St. Croix County)	54007
De Forest	53532
Dekorra (Town)	53955
Delafield	53018
Delafield (Town)	53072
Delavan	53115
Delavan (Town)	53115
Delavan Lake	53115
Dell	54667
Dellona (Town)	53965
Dell Prairie (Town)	53965
Dellwood	53927
Delmar (Town)	54726

	ZIP
Delta (Town)	54856
Delton (Town)	53959
Denmark	54208
Denoon (Part of Muskego)	53150
Denzer	53951
De Pere	54115
De Pere (Town)	54301
Deronda	54001
De Soto	54624
Dewey (Burnett County) (Town)	54845
Dewey (Douglas County)	54880
Dewey (Portage County) (Town)	54481
Dewey (Rusk County) (Town)	54563
Dewhurst (Town)	54456
Dexter (Town)	54466
Dexterville	54466
Diamond Bluff	54014
Diamond Bluff (Town)	54014
Dickeyville	53808
Diefenbach Corners	53086
Dilly	54634
Disco	54615
Dobie	54868
Dodge	54625
Dodge (Town)	54625
Dodge Correctional Institution	53963
Dodges Corners	53149
Dodgeville	53533
Dodgeville (Town)	53533
Doering	54435
Donald	54433
Dorchester	54425
Doty (Town)	54149
Dotyville	53057
Douglas (Town)	53930
Dousman	53118
Dover (Buffalo County) (Town)	54755
Dover (Racine County) (Town)	53182
Dovre (Town)	54757
Downing	54734
Downing Junction (Part of Downing)	54734
Downsville	54735
Downtown (Part of Green Bay)	54305
Downtown (Part of Oshkosh)	54901
Doyle (Town)	54868
Doylestown	53928
Drammen (Town)	54739
Draper (Town)	54896
Draper	54896
Dresser	54009
Dr. Martin Luther King, Jr. (Part of Milwaukee)	53212
Drummond (Town)	54832
Drummond	54832
Drywood	54727
Duck Creek (Part of Howard)	54301
Dudley	54435
Dunbar	54119
Dunbar (Town)	54156
Dunbarton	53586
Dundas	54130
Dundee	53010
Dunkirk (Town)	53589
Dunkirk	53589
Dunn (Dane County) (Town)	53558
Dunn (Dunn County) (Town)	54751
Duplainville	53186
Dupont (Town)	54950
Durand	54736
Durand (Town)	54736
Durham (Part of Muskego)	53130
Durham Hill (Part of Franklin)	53132
Duvall	54217
Dyckesville	54217
Eagle (Richland County) (Town)	53573
Eagle (Waukesha County)	53119
Eagle (Waukesha County) (Town)	53119
Eagle Corners	53573
Eagle Lake	53139
Eagle Lake Manor	53139
Eagle Point (Town)	54729
Eagle River	54521
Eagleton	54724
Eagleville	53149

	ZIP
Earl	54875
East Bristol	53925
East Delavan	53115
East Ellsworth (Part of Ellsworth)	54010
East End (Part of Superior)	54880
East Farmington	54020
East Friesland	53956
East Krok	54216
Eastman	54626
Eastman (Town)	53826
Easton	53910
Easton (Town)	53910
Easton (Town)	54471
East Side (Part of Madison)	53704
East Towne Mall (Part of Madison)	53704
East Troy	53120
East Troy (Town)	53120
East Waupun	53963
Eastwood	54494
Eaton (Brown County) (Town)	54217
Eaton (Clark County) (Town)	54437
Eaton (Manitowoc County) (Town)	53042
Eau Claire	54701-03
For specific Eau Claire Zip Codes call (715) 836-6470, or your local postmaster.	
Eau Galle (Dunn County)	54737
Eau Galle (Dunn County) (Town)	54737
Eau Galle (St. Croix County) (Town)	54028
Eau Pleine (Marathon County) (Town)	54484
Eau Pleine (Portage County) (Town)	54443
Eden (Fond du Lac County)	53019
Eden (Fond du Lac County) (Town)	53010
Eden (Iowa County) (Town)	53526
Edgar	54426
Edgerton	53534
Edgewater	54834
Edgewater (Town)	54834
Edgewood	53072
Edithton Beach	53143
Edmund	53535
Edson	54726
Edson (Town)	54726
Edwards	53015
Edwards Park (Part of McFarland)	53558
Egg Harbor	54209
Egg Harbor (Town)	54209
Eidsvold	54768
Eileen (Town)	54806
Eisenstein (Town)	54552
Eland	54427
Elba (Town)	53925
Elcho	54428
Elcho (Town)	54428
Elderon	54429
Elderon (Town)	54440
Eldorado	54932
Eldorado (Town)	54932
Eleva	54738
Elk (Town)	54555
Elk Creek	54747
Elk Grove (Town)	53807
Elk Grove	53807
Elkhart Lake	53020
Elkhorn	53121
Elk Mound	54739
Elk Mound (Town)	54739
Ella	54721
Ellenboro (Town)	53813
Ellington (Town)	54944
Ellis	54481
Ellison Bay	54210
Ellisville	54217
Ellsworth	54011
Ellsworth (Town)	54003
Elm Grove	53122
Elmhurst	54409
Elm Island	53185
Elmore	53010
Elm Tree Corners (Part of Howard)	54301
Elmwood	54740
Elmwood Park	53405

	ZIP
Elmwood Plaza (Part of Racine)	53403
El Paso	54003
El Paso (Town)	54003
Elroy	53929
Elton	54430
Embarrass	54933
Emerald	54012
Emerald (Town)	54012
Emerald Grove	53545
Emery (Town)	54513
Emmet (Dodge County) (Town)	53098
Emmet (Marathon County) (Town)	54426
Empire (Town)	54935
Enchanted Valley Estates	53562
Endeavor	53930
Enterprise	54463
Enterprise (Town)	54463
Ephraim	54211
Erdman	53083
Erin (St. Croix County)	54017
Erin (Washington County) (Town)	53027
Erin Prairie (Town)	54002
Esadore Lake	54451
Esdaile	54723
Esofea	54667
Estella (Town)	54732
Ettrick	54627
Ettrick (Town)	54627
Eureka (Polk County) (Town)	54024
Eureka (Winnebago County)	54934
Eureka Center	54024
Euren	54205
Evansville	53536
Evergreen (Langlade County) (Town)	54491
Evergreen (Marathon County)	54455
Evergreen (Washburn County) (Town)	54801
Excelsior (Richland County)	53518
Excelsior (Sauk County) (Town)	53961
Exeland	54835
Exeter (Town)	53508
Exile	54761
Fahey Heights	53575
Fairbanks (Town)	54486
Fairburn	54923
Fairchild	54741
Fairchild (Town)	54741
Fairfield (Rock County)	53114
Fairfield (Sauk County) (Town)	53913
Fairplay	53811
Fairview	54628
Fairview Beach	54901
Fair Water	53931
Fall City	54739
Fall Creek	54742
Fall River	53932
Falun	54840
Fargo	54665
Farmersville	53050
Farmhill	54740
Farmington (Jefferson County)	53094
Farmington (Jefferson County) (Town)	53094
Farmington (La Crosse County) (Town)	54644
Farmington (Polk County) (Town)	54017
Farmington (Washington County) (Town)	53040
Farmington (Waupaca County) (Town)	54981
Fayette	53530
Fayette (Town)	53530
Federal Correctional Institution	53952
Fence	54120
Fence (Town)	54120
Fennimore	53809
Fennimore (Town)	53809
Fenwood	54426
Fern (Town)	54121
Ferron Park	54801
Ferryville	54628
Fifield	54524
Fifield (Town)	54524
Fillmore	53021
Finley	54646

	ZIP
Finley (Town)	54646
Fish Creek	54212
Fisk	54904
Fitchburg	53711
Five Corners (Outagamie County)	54911
Five Corners (Ozaukee County)	53012
Five Points	53518
Flambeau (Price County) (Town)	54555
Flambeau (Rusk County)	54745
Flambeau (Rusk County) (Town)	54848
Flintville	54301
Florence	54121
Florence (Town)	54121
Folsom	54655
Fond du Lac	54935-37
For specific Fond du Lac Zip Codes call (414) 921-9300, or your local postmaster.	
Fontana	53125
Fontenoy	54208
Footville	53537
Ford (Town)	54433
Forest (Fond du Lac County) (Town)	54935
Forest (Richland County) (Town)	54664
Forest (St. Croix County)	54012
Forest (St. Croix County) (Town)	54012
Forest (Vernon County) (Town)	54639
Forest Junction	54123
Forest Mall (Part of Fond du Lac)	54935
Forestville	54213
Forestville (Town)	54213
Fort Atkinson	53538
Fort McCoy	54656
Fort Winnebago (Town)	53901
Forward	53572
Foster (Clark County) (Town)	54493
Foster (Eau Claire County)	54758
Fountain (Town)	53929
Fountain City	54629
Fountain Prairie (Town)	53932
Four Corners (Burnett County)	54837
Four Corners (Douglas County)	54880
Foxboro	54836
Fox Creek	54810
Fox Lake	53933
Fox Lake (Town)	53933
Fox Lake Correctional Institution	53933
Fox Point	53217
Fox River	53105
Fox River Mall (Part of Appleton)	54915
Francis Creek	54214
Frankfort (Marathon County) (Town)	54426
Frankfort (Pepin County) (Town)	54721
Franklin	54659
Franklin (Town)	54659
Franklin (Kewaunee County) (Town)	54216
Franklin (Manitowoc County) (Town)	54230
Franklin (Milwaukee County)	53132
Franklin (Sauk County) (Town)	53943
Franklin (Sheboygan County)	53073
Franklin (Vernon County) (Town)	54665
Franksville	53126
Franzen (Town)	54499
Frazer	54162
Frederic	54837
Fred John (Part of Milwaukee)	53225
Fredonia	53021
Fredonia (Town)	53075
Freedom (Forest County) (Town)	54566
Freedom (Outagamie County)	54131
Freedom (Outagamie County) (Town)	54131
Freedom (Sauk County) (Town)	53951

	ZIP
Freeman (Town)	54628
Freistadt (Part of Mequon)	53092
Fremont (Clark County) (Town)	54420
Fremont (Waupaca County)	54940
Fremont (Waupaca County) (Town)	54940
French Island	54601
Frenchville	54627
Friendship (Adams County)	53934
Friendship (Fond du Lac County) (Town)	54937
Friesland	53935
Frog Creek (Town)	54859
Fulton	53534
Fulton (Town)	53534
Fussville (Part of Menomonee Falls)	53051
Gale (Town)	54630
Galesville	54630
Galloway	54432
Garden Valley (Town)	54611
Garden Village	53511
Gardner (Town)	54204
Garfield (Jackson County) (Town)	54758
Garfield (Polk County) (Town)	54001
Garfield (Portage County)	54407
Garnet	53049
Gays Mills	54631
Genesee	53149
Genesee (Town)	53149
Genesee Depot	53127
Geneva (Town)	53121
Genevista	53147
Genoa	54632
Genoa (Town)	54624
Genoa City	53128
Georgetown (Grant County)	53807
Georgetown (Polk County) (Town)	54853
Georgetown (Price County) (Town)	54537
Germania (Iron County)	54550
Germania (Marquette County)	54960
Germania (Shawano County) (Town)	54486
Germantown (Juneau County) (Town)	53948
Germantown (Washington County)	53022
Germantown (Washington County) (Town)	53076
Gibbsville	53070
Gibraltar (Town)	54212
Gibson (Town)	54228
Gilbert	54487
Gile (Part of Montreal)	54525
Gillett	54124
Gillett (Town)	54124
Gillingham	53581
Gills Rock	54210
Gilman (Pierce County) (Town)	54767
Gilman (Taylor County)	54433
Gilmanton	54743
Gilmanton (Town)	54743
Gingles (Town)	54806
Glasgow	54627
Gleason	54435
Glenbeulah	53023
Glencoe (Town)	54629
Glendale (Milwaukee County)	53212
Glendale (Monroe County)	54638
Glendale (Monroe County) (Town)	54638
Glen Flora	54526
Glen Haven	53810
Glen Haven (Town)	53810
Glenmore (Town)	54208
Glenwood (Town)	54012
Glenwood City	54013
Glidden	54527
Globe	54456
Goetz (Town)	54727
Goodman	54125
Goodman (Town)	54125
Goodnow	54529
Goodrich	54451
Goodrich (Town)	54411
Gooseville	53075
Gordon (Ashland County) (Town)	54527

	ZIP
Gordon (Douglas County)	54838
Gordon (Douglas County) (Town)	54838
Gotham	53540
Grafton	53024
Grafton (Town)	53024
Grand Avenue, The (Part of Milwaukee)	53203
Grand Chute (Town)	54911
Grand Marsh	53936
Grand Rapids (Town)	54494
Grand View	54839
Grand View (Town)	54839
Granite Heights	54401
Grant (Clark County) (Town)	54436
Grant (Dunn County) (Town)	54730
Grant (Monroe County) (Town)	54666
Grant (Portage County) (Town)	54494
Grant (Rusk County) (Town)	54848
Grant (Shawano County) (Town)	54950
Granton	54436
Grantsburg	54840
Grantsburg (Town)	54840
Gratiot	53541
Gratiot (Town)	53541
Gravesville	53014
Green Acres	53121
Green Bay	54301-24
For specific Green Bay Zip Codes call (414) 496-8507, or your local postmaster.	
Green Bay (Town)	54229
Green Bay Plaza (Part of Green Bay)	54303
Greenbush	53026
Greenbush (Town)	53026
Greendale	53129
Greenfield (La Crosse County) (Town)	54623
Greenfield (Milwaukee County)	53219-21
For specific Greenfield Zip Codes call (414) 545-7240, or your local postmaster.	
Greenfield (Monroe County) (Town)	54660
Greenfield (Sauk County) (Town)	53913
Greenfield Park (Part of Fitchburg)	53711
Green Grove (Town)	54460
Green Lake	54941
Green Lake (Town)	54941
Green Lake Terrace	54941
Greenleaf	54126
Greenridge Park	53558
Greenstreet	54227
Green Valley (Marathon County) (Town)	54455
Green Valley (Shawano County)	54127
Green Valley (Shawano County) (Town)	54127
Greenville	54942
Greenville (Town)	54942
Greenwood (Clark County)	54437
Greenwood (Taylor County) (Town)	54451
Greenwood (Vernon County) (Town)	54634
Gregorville	54201
Grellton	53094
Gresham	54128
Grimms	54230
Grover (Marinette County) (Town)	54157
Grover (Taylor County) (Town)	54451
Grow (Town)	54563
Guenther (Town)	54455
Gull Lake (Town)	54875
Gurney	54528
Gurney (Town)	54528
Hackett (Town)	54555
Hager City	54014
Halder	54455
Hale	54758
Hale (Town)	54758
Hales Corners	53130
Hallie	54729
Hallie (Town)	54729
Halsey (Town)	54411

	ZIP
Hamburg	54411
Hamburg (Town)	54411
Hamburg (Town)	54621
Hamilton (Town)	54669
Hammel	54451
Hammond	54015
Hammond (Town)	54002
Hampden (Town)	53960
Hamples Corners	54911
Hampton (Part of Milwaukee)	53218
Hancock	54943
Hancock (Town)	54943
Haney (Town)	54631
Hannibal	54439
Hanover	53542
Hansen (Town)	54489
Hansonville	54822
Happy Corners	53807
Harbor (Part of Milwaukee)	53204
Harding (Town)	54452
Harmony (Marinette County)	54143
Harmony (Price County) (Town)	54515
Harmony (Rock County) (Town)	53545
Harmony (Vernon County) (Town)	54665
Harmony Grove	53555
Harris (Town)	53949
Harrison (Calumet County) (Town)	54911
Harrison (Grant County) (Town)	53818
Harrison (Lincoln County)	54435
Harrison (Lincoln County) (Town)	54435
Harrison (Marathon County) (Town)	54409
Harrison (Waupaca County) (Town)	54945
Harrisville	53949
Harshaw	54529
Hartford	53027
Hartford (Town)	53027
Hartland (Pierce County) (Town)	54011
Hartland (Shawano County) (Town)	54107
Hartland (Waukesha County)	53029
Harvey Estates	53589
Hatchville	54751
Hatfield	54754
Hatley	54440
Hauer	54876
Haugen	54841
Haven	53083
Hawkins	54530
Hawkins (Town)	54530
Hawthorne	54842
Hawthorne (Town)	54842
Hayes	54174
Hay River (Town)	54725
Hayton	53014
Hayward	54843
Hayward (Town)	54843
Hazel Green	53811
Hazel Green (Town)	53811
Hazelhurst	54531
Hazelhurst (Town)	54531
Heafford Junction	54532
Heart Prairie	53190
Hebel	54208
Hebron	53538
Hebron (Town)	53538
Hegg	54627
Helena	53503
Helenville	53137
Helvetia (Town)	54962
Hendren (Town)	54493
Henrietta (Town)	53924
Henrysville	54217
Herbster	54844
Herman (Dodge County) (Town)	53078
Herman (Shawano County) (Town)	54166
Herman (Sheboygan County) (Town)	53085
Herman Center	53050
Herold	54610
Hersey	54027
Hertel	54845
Hewitt (Town)	54456
Hewitt (Marathon County) (Town)	54401

	ZIP		ZIP		ZIP		ZIP
Hewitt (Wood County) ...	54441	Hull (Portage County)		Johnstown (Rock County)		Kroghville	53594
Hiawatha Trail Estates ...	53934	(Town)	54481	(Town)	53505	Krok	54216
Hickory Corners	54174	Humbird	54746	Johnstown Center	53545	Kronenwetter (Town)	54455
Hickory Grove (Town) ...	53805	Humboldt (Town)	54217	Jonesdale	53565	Kunesh	54162
Hickory Hill	53593	Humboldt	54229	Jordan (Green County)		Lac Courte Oreilles Indian	
Hickory Hill Estates	53719	Hunter (Town)	54843	(Town)	53504	Reservation	54876
Hickory Meadows	53597	Hunting	54486	Jordan (Portage County)	54481	Lac du Flambeau	54538
High Bridge	54846	Huntington	54017	Jordan Center	53504	Lac du Flambeau (Town)	54538
High Cliff	54952	Hurley	54534	Jordan Lake	53965	Lac du Flambeau Indian	
Highland (Douglas		Huron	54768	Juda	53550	Reservation	54538
County) (Town)	54849	Hurricane	53813	Jump River (Town)	54434	Lac La Belle	53066
Highland (Iowa County)	53543	Husher	53108	Jump River	54434	La Crosse	54601-03
Highland (Iowa County)		Hustisford	53034	Junction City	54443	For specific La Crosse Zip	
(Town)	53543	Hustisford (Town)	53039	Juneau (Part of		Codes call (608) 782-6034, or	
Highland Park	53049	Hustler	54637	Milwaukee)	53202-03	your local postmaster.	
Highland Shore	54904	Hutchins (Town)	54414	For specific Juneau Zip Codes		La Crosse Mall (Part of La	
Hika (Part of Cleveland)	53015	Hyde	53582	call (414) 289-8336, or your		Crosse)	54601
Hilbert	54129	Idlewild	54235	local postmaster.		Ladoga	53963
Hilbert Junction (Part of		Iduna	54627	Juneau (Dodge County)	53039	Ladysmith	54848
Hilbert)	54129	Imalone	54819	Kaiser	54552	La Farge	54639
Hiles (Forest County) ...	54511	Independence	54747	Kansasville	53139	Lafayette (Chippewa	
Hiles (Forest County)		Indian Creek	54837	Kaukauna	54130	County) (Town)	54729
(Town)	54511	Indianford	53534	Kaukauna (Town)	54130	Lafayette (Monroe	
Hiles (Wood County)		Indian Shores	54986	Keene	54921	County) (Town)	54656
(Town)	54466	Ingram	54526	Keenville	54901	Lafayette (Walworth	
Hill (Town)	54459	Inlet	53115	Kekoskee	53050	County) (Town)	53121
Hilldale (Part of Madison)	53705	Ino	54856	Kellner	54494	La Follette (Town)	54872
Hilldale Shopping Center		Institute	54235	Kellnersville	54215	La Grange (Monroe	
(Part of Madison)	53705	Iola	54945	Kelly (Bayfield County)		County) (Town)	54660
Hill Point	53937	Iola (Town)	54945	(Town)	54856	La Grange (Walworth	
Hillsboro	54634	Irma	54442	Kelly (Marathon County)	54476	County)	53190
Hillsboro (Town)	54638	Iron Belt	54536	Kempster	54444	La Grange (Walworth	
Hillsdale	54744	Iron Ridge	53035	Kendall (Lafayette County)		County) (Town)	53190
Hillside	53523	Iron River	54847	(Town)	53530	Lake (Marinette County)	
Hilltop (Part of Milwaukee)	53205	Iron River (Town)	54847	Kendall (Monroe County)	54638	(Town)	54159
	53233	Ironton	53941	Kennan	54537	Lake (Price County)	
For specific Hilltop Zip Codes		Ironton (Town)	53959	Kennan (Town)	54537	(Town)	54552
call (414) 342-3340, or your		Irving (Town)	54615	Kenosha	53140-44	Lake Beulah	53120
local postmaster.		Irvington	54751	For specific Kenosha Zip Codes		Lake Camelot	54475
Hines	54874	Isaar	54165	call (414) 657-3188, or your		Lake Church	53004
Hingham	53031	Isabelle (Town)	54723	local postmaster.		Lake Como Beach	53147
Hintz	54124	Island Beach	54901	Keshena	54135	Lake Delton	53940
Hixon (Town)	54498	Island Lake	54757	Keshena Falls	54135	Lake Eau Claire	54722
Hixton	54635	Island Park	54963	Kettle Moraine		Lake Emily	54407
Hixton (Town)	54635	Itasca (Part of Superior)	54880	Correctional Institution	53073	Lakefield	53024
Hoard (Town)	54422	Ithaca	53581	Kettle Moraine Lake	53010	Lake Five	53017
Hobart (Town)	54303	Ithaca (Town)	53581	Kewaskum	53040	Lake Geneva	53147
Hofa Park	54165	Ives (Part of Racine)	53404	Kewaskum (Town)	53040	Lake George (Kenosha	
Hoffman Corners	54638	Ives Grove	53177	Kewaunee	54216	County)	53104
Hogarty	54408	Ixonia	53036	Keyeser	53532	Lake George (Oneida	
Holcombe	54745	Ixonia (Town)	53036	Keyesville	53937	County)	54501
Holiday Heights	53934	Jackson (Adams County)		Keystone (Bayfield		Lake Hallie	54729
Holiday Hills	53511	(Town)	53952	County) (Town)	54806	Lake Holcombe (Town)	54745
Holland (Brown County)	54130	Jackson (Burnett County)		Keystone (Chippewa		Lake Ivanhoe	53147
Holland (Brown County)		(Town)	54893	County)	54732	Lake Keesus	53029
(Town)	54130	Jackson (Washington		Kickapoo (Town)	54652	Lakeland (Town)	54813
Holland (La Crosse		County)	53037	Kickapoo Center	54664	Lakeland College	53081
County) (Town)	54636	Jackson (Washington		Kiel	53042	Lake Lorraine	53115
Holland (Sheboygan		County) (Town)	53037	Kieler	53812	Lake Mills	53551
County) (Town)	53070	Jacksonport	54235	Kildare (Town)	53944	Lake Mills (Town)	53551
Hollandale	53544	Jacksonport (Town)	54235	Kimball (Town)	54534	Lake Nebagamon	54849
Hollister	54491	Jacobs (Town)	54527	Kimberly	54136	Lake Ripley	53523
Holmen	54636	Jamestown (Town)	53807	King (Lincoln County)		Lake Shangrila	60002
Holton (Town)	54405	Janesville	53545-47	(Town)	54487	Lake Sherwood	54457
Holway (Town)	54451	For specific Janesville Zip		King (Waupaca County)	54946	Lakeside (Town)	54874
Holy Cross	53004	Codes call (608) 754-5555, or		Kingsbridge	54241	Lake Tomahawk (Town)	54539
Homestead (Town)	54121	your local postmaster.		Kingston (Green Lake		Lake Tomahawk	54539
Honey Creek (Sauk		Janesville Mall (Part of		County)	53939	Laketown (Town)	54006
County) (Town)	53577	Janesville)	53545	Kingston (Green Lake		Lake Wazeecha	54494
Honey Creek (Walworth		Jefferson (Green County)		County) (Town)	53926	Lake Windsor	53598
County)	53138	(Town)	53550	Kingston (Juneau County)		Lake Wisconsin	53555
Honey Lake	53105	Jefferson (Jefferson		(Town)	54641	Lake Wissota	54729
Hoopers Mill	53551	County)	53549	Kinnickinnic (Town)	54022	Lakewood	54138
Hope	53527	Jefferson (Jefferson		Kirby	54666	Lakewood (Town)	54138
Horicon	53032	County) (Town)	53137	Kirchhayn	53012	Lamartine	53065
Horns Corners	53012	Jefferson (Monroe		Klevenville	53572	Lamartine (Town)	53065
Horse Creek	54026	County) (Town)	54619	Klondike	54112	Lamont	53530
Hortonia (Town)	54961	Jefferson (Vernon County)		Kloten	53014	Lamont (Town)	53530
Hortonville	54944	(Town)	54667	Knapp (Dunn County) ...	54749	Lampson	54888
Houlton	54082	Jefferson Junction	53549	Knapp (Jackson County)		Lanark (Town)	54981
How (Town)	54174	Jenkynsville	53807	(Town)	54666	Lancaster	53813
Howard (Brown County)	54303	Jennings	54463	Kneeland	53108	Land O'Lakes	54540
Howard (Chippewa		Jericho (Calumet County)	53014	Knellsville	53074	Land O'Lakes (Town)	54540
County) (Town)	54730	Jericho (Waukesha		Knight (Town)	54536	Landstad	54107
Howards Grove-Millersville	53083	County)	53119	Knowles	53048	Langes Corners	54208
Hubbard (Dodge County)		Jewett	54017	Knowlton	54455	Langlade	54491
(Town)	53032	Jim Falls	54748	Knowlton (Town)	54455	Langlade (Town)	54465
Hubbard (Rusk County)		Joel	54001	Knox (Town)	54513	Lannon	53046
(Town)	54848	Johannesburg	54017	Kodan	54201	Laona	54541
Hubbellton	53094	John P. Cofrin (Part of		Kohler	53044	Laona (Town)	54541
Hub City	53581	Green Bay)	54302	Kohlsville	53095	La Pointe	54850
Hubertus	53033	Johnsburg	53049	Kolberg	54213	La Pointe (Town)	54850
Hudson	54016	Johnson (Town)	54411	Komensky (Town)	54754	La Prairie (Town)	53545
Hudson (Town)	54016	Johnson Creek	53038	Koshkonong (Jefferson		Lark	54126
Hughes (Town)	54820	Johnsonville	53085	County) (Town)	53538	Larrabee (Manitowoc	
Huilsburg	53078	Johnstown (Polk County)		Koshkonong (Rock		County)	54241
Hull (Marathon County)		(Town)	54889	County)	53538	Larrabee (Waupaca	
(Town)	54421	Johnstown (Rock County)	53505	Kossuth (Town)	54220	County) (Town)	54929
				Krakow	54137	Larsen	54947

	ZIP		ZIP		ZIP		ZIP
LaRue	53951	Lind Center	54981	McFarland	53558	Marytown	53061
Lasleys Point	54986	Linden	53553	Mackford (Town)	53946	Mason	54856
Lauderdale	53121	Linden (Town)	53565	McKinley (Polk County)		Mason (Town)	54856
La Valle	53941	Lindina (Town)	53948	(Town)	54829	Mather	54641
La Valle (Town)	53941	Lindsey	54449	McKinley (Polk County)	54829	Matteson (Town)	54929
LaVerne Dilweg (Part of		Linn (Town)	60034	McKinley (Taylor County)		Mattoon	54450
Green Bay)	54303	Linton	53147	(Town)	54766	Mauston	53948
Lawrence (Brown County)		Linwood (Town)	54481	Mackville	54911	Maxville	54736
(Town)	54115	Lisbon (Juneau County)		McMillan (Town)	54449	Maxville (Town)	54736
Lawrence (Marquette		(Town)	53950	McNaughton	54543	May Corner	54157
County)	53964	Lisbon (Waukesha		Madge (Town)	54870	Mayfair Mall (Part of	
Lawrence (Rusk County)		County) (Town)	53089	Madison	53701-44	Wauwatosa)	53226
(Town)	54526	Little Black	54451	For specific Madison Zip Codes		Mayfield	53037
Lawton	54003	Little Black (Town)	54451	call (608) 246-1249, or your		Mayville (Clark County)	
Layton Park (Part of		Little Chicago	54448	local postmaster.		(Town)	54425
Milwaukee)	53215	Little Chute	54140	Madsen	54220	Mayville (Dodge County)	53050
Lead Mine	53807	Little Falls (Monroe		Magenta (Part of Eau		Mazomanie	53560
Lebanon (Dodge County)	53047	County) (Town)	54656	Claire)	54701	Mazomanie (Town)	53560
Lebanon (Dodge County)		Little Falls (Polk County)	54001	Magnolia	53536	Mead (Town)	54437
(Town)	53047	Little Grant (Town)	53813	Magnolia (Town)	53536	Meadowbrook (Town)	54835
Lebanon (Waupaca		Little Hope	54981	Maiden Rock	54750	Mecan (Town)	53949
County) (Town)	54961	Little Kohler	53021	Maiden Rock (Town)	54750	Medary (Town)	54650
Ledges	53532	Little Prairie	53119	Maine (Marathon County)		Medford	54451
Leeds	53571	Little Rapids	54115	(Town)	54401	Medford (Town)	54451
Leeds (Town)	53571	Little Rice (Town)	54564	Maine (Outagamie		Medina (Dane County)	
Leeds Center	53911	Little River (Town)	54153	County) (Town)	54170	(Town)	53559
Leeman	54170	Little Rose	54484	Mallwood	53534	Medina (Outagamie	
Leipsig	53916	Little Round Lake	54843	Malone	53049	County)	54951
Leland	53951	Little Sturgeon	54235	Manawa	54949	Meeker (Part of	
Lemington	54835	Little Suamico	54141	Manchester (Green Lake		Germantown)	53022
Lemonweir (Town)	53948	Little Suamico (Town)	54141	County)	53945	Meeme (Town)	53063
Lena	54139	Little Wolf (Town)	54949	Manchester (Green Lake		Meeme	53063
Lena (Town)	54139	Livingston	53554	County) (Town)	53945	Meenon (Town)	54893
Lenroot (Town)	54843	Loddes Mill	53583	Manchester (Jackson		Meggers	53061
Leola (Town)	54921	Lodi	53555	County) (Town)	54615	Mellen	54546
Leon	54656	Lodi (Town)	53555	Manitowish	54547	Melnik	54247
Leon (Town)	54646	Loganville	53943	Manitowish Waters (Town)	54545	Melrose	54642
Leon (Town)	54965	Lohrville	54970	Manitowish Waters	54545	Melrose (Town)	54642
Leonards Point	54904	Lombard	54771	Manitowoc	54220*	Melrose Park	54901
Leopolis	54948	Lomira	53048		54221†	Melvina	54619
LeRoy	53048	Lomira (Town)	53006	Manitowoc Rapids (Town)	54220	Memorial Mall (Part of	
LeRoy (Town)	53048	London	53523	Manitowoc Rapids (Part		Sheboygan)	53081
Leslie	53510	London Square Mall (Part		of Manitowoc)	54220	Menasha	54952
Lessor (Town)	54107	of Eau Claire)	54701	Maple	54854	Menasha (Town)	54952
Levis (Town)	54456	Lone Rock (Juneau		Maple (Town)	54854	Menchalville	54206
Lewis	54851	County)	54618	Maple Bluff	53704	Menekaunee (Part of	
Lewiston	53965	Lone Rock (Richland		Maple Creek (Town)	54961	Marinette)	54143
Lewiston (Town)	53965	County)	53556	Maple Grove (Barron		Menominee (Town)	54150
Leyden	53545	Long Lake (Florence		County) (Town)	54744	Menominee Indian	
Liberty (Grant County)		County)	54542	Maple Grove (Manitowoc		Reservation	54135
(Town)	53825	Long Lake (Florence		County)	54230	Menomonee Falls	53051*
Liberty (Manitowoc		County) (Town)	54542	Maple Grove (Manitowoc			53052†
County) (Town)	54245	Long Lake (Fond du Lac		County) (Town)	54110	Menomonie	54751
Liberty (Outagamie -		County)	53011	Maple Grove (Shawano		Menomonie (Town)	54751
County) (Town)	54170	Long Lake (Washburn		County) (Town)	54162	Menomonie Junction (Part	
Liberty (Vernon County)		County) (Town)	54817	Maple Heights	53014	of Menomonie)	54751
(Town)	54664	Longwood	54498	Maple Hills	53125	Mentor (Town)	54746
Liberty Grove (Town)	54202	Longwood (Town)	54498	Maplehurst (Town)	54498	Mequon	53092
Liberty Pole	54665	Lookout	54755	Maple Plain (Town)	54829	Mercer	54547
Liddell	54729	Loomis	54159	Mapleton	53066	Mercer (Town)	54547
Lilly Lake	53105	Lorain (Town)	54837	Maple Valley (Town)	54174	Meridean	54755
Lily	54445	Loretta	54896	Maplewood	54226	Merrill	54452
Lima (Grant County)		Lost Lake	53956	Marathon	54448	Merrill (Town)	54452
(Town)	53818	Louisburg	53807	Marathon (Town)	54448	Merrillan	54754
Lima (Pepin County)		Louis Corners	53042	Marblehead	53019	Merrimac	53561
(Town)	54736	Lowell	53557	Marcellon (Town)	53901	Merrimac (Town)	53561
Lima (Rock County)		Lowell (Town)	53579	March Rapids	54484	Merton	53056
(Town)	53190	Lower Nemahbin Lake	53066	Marengo	54855	Merton (Town)	53029
Lima (Sheboygan County)		Lowville (Town)	53955	Marengo (Town)	54855	Meteor (Town)	54835
(Town)	53085	Loyal	54446	Maribel	54227	Metomen (Town)	54971
Lima Center	53190	Loyal (Town)	54446	Mariotta (Town)	53805	Metz	54940
Limeridge	53942	Loyd	53924	Marinette	54143	Mid-City (Part of	
Lincoln (Adams County)		Lublin	54447	Marion (Grant County)		Milwaukee)	53208
(Town)	53964	Lucas (Town)	54751	(Town)	53805	Middle Inlet	54114
Lincoln (Bayfield County)		Luck	54853	Marion (Juneau County)		Middle Inlet (Town)	54114
(Town)	54856	Luck (Town)	54837	(Town)	53948	Middle Ridge	54614
Lincoln (Buffalo County)		Ludington	54742	Marion (Waushara County)	54950	Middleton	53562
(Town)	54610	Ludington (Town)	54742	Marion (Waushara		Middleton (Town)	53562
Lincoln (Burnett County)		Lugerville	54555	County) (Town)	54960	Middleton Junction	53719
(Town)	54893	Lund	54769	Markesan	53946	Midway (Brown County)	54301
Lincoln (Eau Claire		Lunds	54166	Marquette	53947	Midway (La Crosse	
County) (Town)	54722	Luxemburg	54217	Marquette (Town)	53946	County)	54650
Lincoln (Forest County)		Luxemburg (Town)	54217	Marshall (Dane County)	53559	Mifflin	53580
(Town)	54520	Lykens	54810	Marshall (Richland		Mifflin (Town)	53580
Lincoln (Kewaunee		Lymantown	54552	County) (Town)	53581	Mikana	54857
County)	54205	Lyndhurst	54128	Marshall (Rusk County)		Mikesville	54901
Lincoln (Kewaunee		Lyndon (Juneau County)		(Town)	54731	Milan	54453
County) (Town)	54205	(Town)	53944	Marshfield (Fond du Lac		Milford	53551
Lincoln (Monroe County)		Lyndon (Sheboygan		County) (Town)	53057	Milford (Town)	53551
(Town)	54666	County) (Town)	53073	Marshfield (Wood County)	54449	Milladore	54454
Lincoln (Polk County)		Lyndon Station	53944	Marshfield (Wood County)		Milladore (Town)	54412
(Town)	54001	Lynn	54436	(Town)	54449	Millard	53121
Lincoln (Trempealeau		Lynn (Town)	54436	Marshland	54629	Mill Center	54301
County) (Town)	54773	Lynne (Town)	54564	Martell	54767	Millersville (Part of	
Lincoln (Vilas County)		Lynxville	54640	Martell (Town)	54767	Howards Grove-	
(Town)	54521	Lyons	53148	Martinsville	53528	Millersville)	53083
Lincoln (Wood County)		Lyons (Town)	53148	Martintown	61089	Millhome	53042
(Town)	54449	McAllister	54177	Marxville	53560	Millston	54643
Lind (Town)	54983	McCartney	53806	Mary Lake	53597	Millston (Town)	54643

*Area Zip Code   † Post Office Boxes

	ZIP		ZIP		ZIP		ZIP
Millstone Heights	53532	Minong (Town)	54859	Nekoosa	54457	Northport (Waupaca	
Milltown	54858	Mishicot	54228	Nelma	49935	County)	54961
Milltown (Town)	54858	Mishicot (Town)	54228	Nelson	54756	North Prairie	53153
Millville	53827	Mitchell (Town)	53093	Nelson (Town)	54756	Northridge Mall (Part of	
Millville (Town)	53827	Modena	54755	Nelsonville	54458	Milwaukee)	53223
Milton (Buffalo County)		Modena (Town)	54755	Nenno	53002	North Shore (Part of	
(Town)	54629	Moeville	54011	Neopit	54150	Glendale)	53217
Milton (Rock County)	53563	Mole Lake	54520	Neosho	53059	North Tomah	54660
Milton (Rock County)		Mole Lake Indian		Nepeuskun (Town)	54971	Northway Mall (Part of	
(Town)	53563	Reservation	54520	Neshkoro	54960	Marshfield)	54449
Milton Junction (Part of		Molitor (Town)	54451	Neshkoro (Town)	54960	Northwoods Beach	54843
Milton)	53563	Monches	53029	Neuern	54217	North York	54846
		Mondovi	54755	Neva (Town)	54424	Norton	54730
Milwaukee	53201-34	Mondovi (Town)	54755	Neva Corners	54424	Norwalk	54648
	53237-95	Monico (Town)	54501	Newald	54511	Norway (Town)	53182
For specific Milwaukee Zip		Monico	54501	New Amsterdam	54636	Norway Grove	53532
Codes call (414) 291-2444, or		Monona	53716	Newark	53511	Norwegian Bay	54940
your local postmaster.		Monroe (Adams County)		Newark (Town)	53511	Norwood (Town)	54409
		(Town)	54613	New Auburn	54757	Nutterville	54401
COLLEGES & UNIVERSITIES		Monroe (Green County)	53566	New Berlin	53151	Nye	54020
Alverno College	53234	Monroe (Green County)		Newbold (Town)	54501	Oak Center	53065
Cardinal Stritch College	53217	(Town)	53566	Newburg	53060	Oak Creek	53154
Marquette University	53233	Monroe Center	54613	Newburg Corners	54614	Oakdale	54649
Milwaukee School of		Montana	54747	New Centerville	54002	Oakdale (Town)	54649
Engineering	53201	Montana (Town)	54747	New Chester (Town)	53936	Oakfield	53065
Mount Mary College	53222	Montello	53949	New Denmark (Town)	54208	Oakfield (Town)	53065
University of Wisconsin-		Montello (Town)	53949	New Diggings	61075	Oak Grove (Barron	
Milwaukee	53201	Monterey	53066	New Diggings (Town)	61075	County) (Town)	54868
		Montfort	53569	New Fane	53040	Oak Grove (Dodge	
FINANCIAL INSTITUTIONS		Monticello (Green County)	53570	New Franken	54229	County)	53039
Associated Bank	53201	Monticello (Lafayette		New Glarus	53574	Oak Grove (Dodge	
Badger Bank, S.S.B.	53211	County) (Town)	54810	New Glarus (Town)	53574	County) (Town)	53039
Bank One, Milwaukee,		Montpelier (Town)	54217	New Haven (Adams		Oak Grove (Pierce	
N.A.	53202	Montreal	54550	County) (Town)	53920	County) (Town)	54021
Continental Savings Bank,		Montrose (Town)	53508	New Haven (Dunn		Oak Hill	53156
S.A.	53202	Moon	54455	County) (Town)	54005	Oakhill Correctional	
Firstar Bank Milwaukee,		Moose Junction	54830	New Holstein	53061	Institution	53575
N.A.	53202	Moquah	54806	New Holstein (Town)	53061	Oakland (Burnett County)	
Firstar Trust Company	53202	Morgan (Town)	54154	New Hope (Town)	54407	(Town)	54893
First Bank, N.A.	53259	Morgan (Oconto County)	54154	New Lisbon	53950	Oakland (Douglas County)	
First Bank Southeast, N.A.	53202	Morgan (Shawano		New London	54961	(Town)	54874
Guaranty Bank, S.S.B.	53223	County)	54128	New Lyme (Town)	54656	Oakland (Jefferson	
Lincoln Savings Bank,		Morris (Town)	54486	New Miner	54646	County) (Town)	53538
S.A.	53215	Morrison	54126	New Munster	53152	Oakland (Jefferson	
M&I Marshall & Ilsley Bank	53202	Morrison (Town)	54126	New Odanah	54861	County)	53538
Maritime Savings Bank	53207	Morrisonville	53571	Newport (Town)	53965	Oakley	53550
Mutual Savings Bank	53223	Morris Park	53558	New Post	54828	Oakridge	53179
St. Francis Bank, F.S.B.	53235	Morse	54527	New Prospect	53010	Oak Shores	53125
Security Bank S.S.B.	53203	Morse (Town)	54546	New Richmond	54017	Oakwood (Part of Oak	
Valley Bank	53226	Moscow (Town)	53507	New Rome	54457	Creek)	53154
West Allis Savings Bank,		Mosel (Town)	53015	Newry	54619	Oakwood Mall (Part of	
S.A.	53221	Mosinee	54455	Newton (Manitowoc		Eau Claire)	54703
		Mosinee (Town)	54455	County)	53063	Oasis (Town)	54966
HOSPITALS		Mosling	54124	Newton (Manitowoc		Oconomowoc	53066
Columbia Hospital	53211	Moundville (Town)	53930	County) (Town)	53063	Oconomowoc (Town)	53069
Milwaukee County		Mountain	54149	Newton (Marquette		Oconomowoc Lake	53066
Medical Complex	53226	Mount Calvary	53057	County) (Town)	53964	Oconto	54153
St. Francis Hospital	53215	Mount Hope	53816	Newton (Vernon County)	54665	Oconto (Town)	54139
St. Joseph's Hospital	53210	Mount Hope (Town)	53816	Newtonburg	54220	Oconto Falls	54154
St. Luke's Medical Center	53215	Mount Horeb	53572	Newville	53534	Oconto Falls (Town)	54154
St. Mary's Hospital	53211	Mount Ida	53809	Niagara	54151	Odanah	54861
St. Michael Hospital	53209	Mount Ida (Town)	53809	Niagara (Town)	49870	Ogdensburg	54962
Sinai Samaritan Medical		Mount Morris	54982	Nichols	54152	Ogema	54459
Center	55233	Mount Morris (Town)	54982	Nippersink Manor	53128	Ogema (Town)	54459
Veterans Affairs Medical		Mount Pleasant (Green		Nokomis (Town)	54487	Oil City	54648
Center	53295	County) (Town)	53502	Nora	53531	Ojibwa	54862
		Mount Pleasant (Racine		Norman	54216	Ojibwa (Town)	54862
HOTELS/MOTELS		County) (Town)	53401	Norrie	54414	Okauchee	53069
Astor Hotel	53202	Mount Sterling	54645	Norrie (Town)	54414	Okauchee Lake	53058
Best Western Midway		Mount Tabor	54638	Norske	54945	Okee	53555
Hotel Highway 100	53226	Mount Vernon	53572	North Andover	53810	Old Albertville	54730
Grand Milwaukee Hotel	53207	Mount Zion	53805	North Bay (Door County)	54202	Old Ashippun	53003
Holiday Inn-South Airport	53221	Mukwa (Town)	54961	North Bay (Racine		Old Lebanon	53098
Howard Johnson Lodge		Mukwonago	53149	County)	53402	Oliver	54880
West	53226	Mukwonago (Town)	53149	North Bend	54642	Olivet	54767
Hyatt Regency Milwaukee	53203	Murphy Corner	54130	North Bend (Town)	54642	Oma (Town)	54534
Marc Plaza Hotel	53203	Murry (Town)	54819	North Branch	54611	Omro	54963
Pfister Hotel	53202	Muscoda	53573	North Bristol	53590	Omro (Town)	54901
		Muscoda (Town)	53573	North Cape	53126	Onalaska	54650
MILITARY INSTALLATIONS		Muskego	53150	Northeim	53063	Onalaska (Town)	54650
Coast Guard Group,		Myra	53095	Northfield	54635	Oneida (Town)	54155
Milwaukee	53207	Nabob	53095	Northfield (Town)	54635	Oneida	54155
Wisconsin Air National		Namakagon (Town)	54821	North Fond du Lac	54937	Oneida Indian Reservation	54155
Guard, FB6491,		Namur	54204	North Freedom	53951	Ono	54750
General Mitchell		Naples (Town)	54755	North Hudson	54016	Ontario	54651
International Airport	53207	Nasbro	53006	North Lake (Walworth		Oostburg	53070
84th Division (Training)	53218	Nasewaupee (Town)	54235	County)	53121	Orange (Town)	54618
440th Support Group,		Nashotah	53058	North Lake (Waukesha		Orange Mill	54618
General Mitchell		Nashville (Town)	54520	County)	53064	Oregon	53575
International Airport		Nasonville	54449	North Lancaster (Town)	53813	Oregon (Town)	53575
(AFRES)	53207	Navarino	54107	Northland	54945	Orfordville	53576
		Navarino (Town)	54107	Northland Mall (Part of		Orienta (Town)	54865
Mindoro	54644	Necedah	54646	Milwaukee)	53209	Orihula	54940
Mineral Point	53565	Necedah (Town)	54646	North Leeds	53911	Orion	53573
Mineral Point (Town)	53565	Neda	53035	North Lowell	53039	Orion (Town)	53573
Minnesota Junction	53032	Neenah	54956*	North Menomonie (Part of		Osborn (Town)	54165
Minocqua	54548		54957†	Menomonie)	54751	Osceola (Fond du Lac	
Minocqua (Town)	54548	Neillsville	54456	North Park	53402	County) (Town)	53010
Minong	54859	Nekimi (Town)	54901	Northport (Door County)	54210	Osceola (Polk County)	54020

* Area Zip Code † Post Office Boxes

	ZIP
Osceola (Polk County)	
(Town)	54020
Oshkosh	54901-04
For specific Oshkosh Zip Codes call (414) 236-0200, or your local postmaster.	
Osman	53063
Osseo	54758
Ostrander	54961
Otsego	53925
Otsego (Town)	53925
Ottawa (Town)	53118
Otter Creek (Dunn County) (Town)	54772
Otter Creek (Eau Claire County) (Town)	54722
Oulu (Town)	54847
Ourtown	53085
Owen	54460
Oxbo	54552
Oxford	53952
Oxford (Town)	53952
Pacific (Town)	53954
Packwaukee (Town)	53953
Packwaukee	53953
Paddock Lake	53168
Padus	54566
Palmyra	53156
Palmyra (Town)	53156
Paoli	53508
Pardeeville	53954
Parfreyville	54981
Paris (Grant County) (Town)	53807
Paris (Kenosa County)	53182
Paris (Kenosa County) (Town)	53182
Park Falls	54552
Parkland (Town)	54874
Parklawn (Part of Milwaukee)	53216
Park Plaza (Part of Oshkosh)	54902
Park Ridge	54481
Parrish	54435
Parrish (Town)	54435
Patch Grove	53817
Patch Grove (Town)	53821
Patzau	54836
Pearson	54462
Peck (Town)	54424
Pecks Station	53121
Peebles	54935
Peeksville (Town)	54527
Pelican (Town)	54501
Pelican Lake	54463
Pella	54950
Pella (Town)	54950
Pell Lake	53157
Pembine	54156
Pembine (Town)	54156
Pence	54550
Pence (Town)	54550
Peninsula Center	54202
Pensaukee	54153
Pensaukee (Town)	54153
Pepin	54759
Pepin (Town)	54759
Peplin	54455
Perkinstown	54451
Perry (Town)	53572
Pershing (Town)	54433
Peru (Dunn County) (Town)	54755
Peru (Portage County)	54407
Peshtigo	54157
Peshtigo (Town)	54143
Petersburg	54631
Petty Acres	53589
Pewaukee	53072
Pewaukee (Town)	53072
Phantom Lake	53149
Pheasant Branch (Part of Middleton)	53562
Phelps	54554
Phelps (Town)	54554
Phillips	54555
Phipps	54843
Phlox	54464
Piacenza	54986
Pickerel	54465
Pickett	54964
Piehl (Town)	54501
Pierce (Town)	54216
Pigeon (Town)	54773
Pigeon Falls	54760
Pike Lake	54440
Pilsen (Bayfield County) (Town)	54806

	ZIP
Pilsen (Kewaunee County)	54217
Pine Bluff	53528
Pine Creek	54625
Pine Grove (Brown County)	54301
Pine Grove (Portage County) (Town)	54921
Pine Lake (Iron County)	54534
Pine Lake (Oneida County) (Town)	54501
Pine River (Lincoln County) (Town)	54452
Pine River (Waushara County)	54965
Pine Tree Mall (Part of Marinette)	54143
Pine Valley (Town)	54456
Pipe	53049
Pipersville	53094
Pittsfield (Town)	54301
Pittsville	54466
Plain	53577
Plainfield	54966
Plainfield (Town)	54966
Plainville	53965
Plat	53017
Platteville	53818
Platteville (Town)	53818
Plaza 8 (Part of Sheboygan)	53081
Pleasant Prairie	53158
Pleasant Ridge	53533
Pleasant Springs (Town)	53589
Pleasant Valley (Eau Claire County) (Town)	54701
Pleasant Valley (St. Croix County) (Town)	54015
Pleasant Valley (Vernon County)	54658
Pleasant View	54615
Pleasantville	54758
Plover (Marathon County) (Town)	54414
Plover (Portage County)	54467
Plover (Portage County) (Town)	54467
Plugtown	53805
Plum City	54761
Plum Lake (Town)	54560
Plymouth (Juneau County) (Town)	53929
Plymouth (Rock County) (Town)	53545
Plymouth (Sheboygan County)	53073
Plymouth (Sheboygan County) (Town)	53073
Point Loomis Shopping Center (Part of Milwaukee)	53221
Poland	54301
Polar	54418
Polar (Town)	54418
Polifka Corners	54247
Polk (Town)	53076
Polley	54433
Polonia	54423
Poniatowski	54426
Poplar	54864
Popple Lake	54729
Popple River	54542
Popple River (Town)	54542
Porcupine	54721
Portage	53901
Port Andrew	53518
Port Edwards	54469
Port Edwards (Town)	54457
Porter (Town)	53545
Porterfield	54159
Porterfield (Town)	54159
Portland	53594
Portland (Town)	53594
Portland	54619
Portland (Town)	54619
Port Plaza Mall (Part of Green Bay)	54301
Port Washington	53074
Port Washington (Town)	53074
Port Wing	54865
Port Wing (Town)	54865
Poskin	54812
Post Lake	54428
Postville	53516
Potawatomi Indian Reservation	54520
Potosi	53820
Potosi (Town)	53820
Potter	54160
Potter Lake	53120

	ZIP
Potts Corners	54639
Pound	54161
Pound (Town)	54139
Powell	54547
Powers Lake	53159
Poygan (Town)	54963
Poynette	53955
Poy Sippi	54967
Poysippi (Town)	54967
Praag	54610
Prairie Corners	53807
Prairie du Chien	53821
Prairie du Chien (Town)	53821
Prairie du Sac	53578
Prairie du Sac (Town)	53583
Prairie Farm	54762
Prairie Farm (Town)	54762
Prairie Lake (Town)	54728
Pray	54466
Preble (Part of Green Bay)	54302
Prentice	54556
Prentice (Town)	54556
Prescott	54021
Presque Isle	54557
Presque Isle (Town)	54557
Preston (Adams County) (Town)	53934
Preston (Grant County)	53809
Preston (Trempealeau County) (Town)	54616
Price (Jackson County)	54741
Price (Langlade County) (Town)	54418
Primrose (Town)	53593
Princeton	54968
Princeton (Town)	54968
Prospect (Part of New Berlin)	53151
Pukana Beach	53049
Pulaski (Brown County)	54162
Pulaski (Iowa County) (Town)	53506
Pulcifer	54164
Purdy	54665
Quarry	54230
Quincy (Town)	53910
Quincy Details	53934
Quinney	53014
Racine	53401-08
For specific Racine Zip Codes call (414) 632-1661, or your local postmaster.	
Radisson	54867
Radisson (Town)	54867
Randall (Burnett County)	54840
Randall (Kenosha County) (Town)	60071
Randolph (Columbia County) (Town)	53923
Randolph (Dodge County)	53956
Random Lake	53075
Range	54001
Rankin	54201
Rantoul (Town)	53014
Rattman Heights	53701
Ravenoaks	53575
Rawson (Part of Oak Creek)	53172
Raymond	53126
Raymond (Town)	53126
Readfield	54969
Readstown	54652
Red Banks	54940
Red Cedar (Town)	54751
Red Cliff	54814
Red Cliff Indian Reservation	54806
Redgranite	54970
Red Mound	54624
Red River (Kewaunee County) (Town)	54205
Red River (Shawano County)	54166
Red Springs (Town)	54128
Redville	54498
Reedsburg	53959
Reedsburg (Town)	53959
Reedsville	54230
Reeseville	53579
Reeve	54004
Regency Mall (Part of Racine)	53406
Reid (Town)	54440
Reighmoor	54963
Remington (Town)	54413
Reseburg (Town)	54437
Reserve	54876
Retreat	54624

	ZIP
Rewey	53580
Rhine	53020
Rhine (Town)	53020
Rhinelander	54501
Rib Falls	54426
Rib Falls (Town)	54426
Rib Lake	54470
Rib Lake (Town)	54470
Rib Mountain (Town)	54401
Rib Mountain	54401
Rice Lake	54868
Rice Lake (Town)	54868
Richardson	54004
Richfield (Adams County) (Town)	53934
Richfield (Washington County)	53076
Richfield (Washington County) (Town)	53076
Richfield (Wood County) (Town)	54449
Richford	54930
Richford (Town)	54930
Richland (Richland County) (Town)	53581
Richland (Rusk County) (Town)	54526
Richland Center	53581
Richmond (Shawano County) (Town)	54166
Richmond (St. Croix County) (Town)	54017
Richmond (Walworth County)	53115
Richmond (Walworth County) (Town)	53115
Richwood (Dodge County)	53098
Richwood (Richland County) (Town)	53518
Ridgeland	54763
Ridgeville (Town)	54648
Ridgeway	53582
Ridgeway (Town)	53582
Rief's Mills	54247
Rietbrock (Town)	54411
Rileys	53593
Rileys Point	54235
Ringle	54471
Ringle (Town)	54471
Rio	53960
Rio Creek	54231
Riplinger	54479
Ripon	54971
Ripon (Town)	54971
Rising Sun	54628
River Falls	54022
River Falls (Town)	54022
River Hills	53209
	53217
For specific River Hills Zip Codes call (414) 962-8644, or your local postmaster.	
Rivermoor	54963
Riverside	53541
Riverview (Town)	54149
Riverwood	54613
River Wood Estates	53589
Roberts	54023
Robinson	53147
Rochester	53167
Rochester (Town)	53105
Rock (Rock County) (Town)	53545
Rock (Wood County) (Town)	54466
Rockbridge	53581
Rockbridge (Town)	53581
Rock Creek (Town)	54755
Rockdale	53523
Rock Elm	54740
Rock Elm (Town)	54740
Rock Falls (Dunn County)	54764
Rock Falls (Lincoln County) (Town)	54442
Rockfield	53077
Rock Lake	53179
Rockland (Brown County) (Town)	54115
Rockland (La Crosse County)	54653
Rockland (Manitowoc County) (Town)	54207
Rock Springs	53961
Rockton	54639
Rockville (Grant County)	53820
Rockville (Manitowoc County)	53042
Rockwood	54220

	ZIP		ZIP		ZIP		ZIP
Rocky Run	54481	St. Wendel (Part of Cleveland)	53015	Shanagolden	54527	South Chippewa (Part of Chippewa Falls)	54729
Rodell	54722	Salem (Kenosha County)	53168	Shanagolden (Town)	54527	South Fork (Town)	54530
Rogersville	54974	Salem (Kenosha County) (Town)	53168	Shantytown	54473	Southgate Mall (Part of Milwaukee)	53215
Rolling (Town)	54409	Salem (Pierce County) (Town)	54750	Sharon (Portage County) (Town)	54473	South Itasca (Part of Superior)	54880
Rolling Acres	53589	Salem Oaks	53168	Sharon (Walworth County)	53585	South Janesville (Part of Janesville)	53545
Rolling Ground	54655	Salvatorian Center (Part of New Holstein)	53062	Sharon (Walworth County) (Town)	53585	South Kenosha	53143
Rolling Prairie	53039	Sampson (Chippewa County) (Town)	54757	Shawano	54166	South Lancaster (Town)	53813
Rolling View	53589	Sampson (Oconto County)	54171	Shawano North Beach	54166	South Luxemburg (Part of Luxemburg)	54217
Romance	54632	Sanborn	54806	Sheboygan	53081-83	South Milwaukee	53172
Rome (Adams County) (Town)	54457	Sanborn (Town)	54861	For specific Sheboygan Zip Codes call (414) 458-3741, or your local postmaster.		South Necedah (Part of Necedah)	54646
Rome (Jefferson County)	53178	Sand Bay (Bayfield County)	54814	Sheboygan Falls	53085	South Randolph	53956
Roosevelt (Burnett County) (Town)	54813	Sand Bay (Door County)	54235	Sheboygan Falls (Town)	53085	South Range	54874
Roosevelt (Oneida County)	54501	Sand Creek	54765	Sheil	53575	Southridge Mall (Part of Greendale)	53129
Roosevelt (Taylor County) (Town)	54447	Sand Creek (Town)	54765	Shelby (Town)	54601	South Side (Part of Madison)	53715
Root River (Part of Milwaukee)	53227	Sand Lake (Burnett County) (Town)	54893	Sheldon (Monroe County) (Town)	54651	South Wayne	53587
Rose (Town)	54984	Sandlake (Polk County)	54009	Sheldon (Rusk County)	54766	Sparta	54656
Rosecrans	54227	Sand Lake (Sawyer County) (Town)	54876	Shell Lake	54871	Sparta (Town)	54656
Rose Lawn	54165	Sand Prairie	53518	Shennington	54618	Spaulding	54466
Rosemere (Part of Manitowoc)	54220	Sandusky	53937	Shepley	54499	Spencer	54479
Rosendale	54974	Saratoga (Town)	54494	Sheridan (Dunn County) (Town)	54725	Spencer (Town)	54479
Rosendale (Town)	54964	Sarona	54870	Sheridan (Waupaca County)	54981	Spider Lake (Town)	54843
Rosholt	54473	Sarona (Town)	54870	Sherman (Clark County) (Town)	54479	Spirit	54513
Rosiere	54205	Sauk City	53583	Sherman (Dunn County) (Town)	54751	Spirit (Town)	54513
Ross (Forest County) (Town)	54511	Saukville	53080	Sherman (Iron County) (Town)	54552	Spirit Falls	54564
Ross (Vernon County)	54665	Saukville (Town)	53074	Sherman (Sheboygan County) (Town)	53075	Split Rock	54486
Ross D. Sills	53125	Saxeville	54976	Sherman Center	53075	Spokeville	54479
Rostok	54216	Saxeville (Town)	54976	Sherry	54454	Spooner	54801
Rothschild	54474	Saxon	54559	Sherry (Town)	54454	Spooner (Town)	54801
Round Lake (Town)	54843	Saxon (Town)	54559	Sherwood (Calumet County)	54169	Sprague	54646
Rowleys Bay	54210	Saylesville (Dodge County)	53078	Sherwood (Clark County) (Town)	54466	Spread Eagle	54121
Roxbury	53583	Saylesville (Waukesha County)	53186	Shields (Dodge County) (Town)	53098	Spring Bluff	54930
Roxbury (Town)	53583	Sayner	54560	Shields (Marquette County) (Town)	53949	Springbrook (Town)	54875
Royalton	54975	Scandinavia	54977	Shiocton	54170	Spring Brook (Dunn County) (Town)	54751
Royalton (Town)	54975	Scandinavia (Town)	54977	Shirley	54115	Springbrook (Washburn County)	54875
Rozellville	54484	Scarboro	54217	Shopiere	53511	Springdale (Town)	53593
Rubicon (Town)	53078	Schleswig (Town)	53042	Shoreview	53179	Springfield (Dane County) (Town)	53528
Rubicon	53078	Schley (Town)	54452	Shorewood	53211	Springfield (Jackson County) (Town)	54659
Ruby (Town)	54745	Schnappsville	54411	Shorewood Hills	53705	Springfield (Marquette County) (Town)	53964
Rudolph	54475	Schoepke (Town)	54463	Shortville	54456	Springfield (St. Croix County) (Town)	54013
Rudolph (Town)	54475	Schofield	54476	Shoto	54241	Springfield (Walworth County)	53176
Rural	54981	School Hill	53042	Shullsburg	53586	Springfield Corners	53529
Rushford (Town)	54963	Schraven Circle	54937	Shullsburg (Town)	53586	Spring Green	53588
Rush Lake	54971	Scott (Brown County) (Town)	54229	Sidney	54456	Spring Green (Town)	53588
Rush River (Town)	54002	Scott (Burnett County) (Town)	54893	Sigel (Chippewa County) (Town)	54727	Spring Grove (Town)	53550
Rusk (Burnett County) (Town)	54801	Scott (Columbia County) (Town)	53923	Sigel (Wood County) (Town)	54494	Spring Hill Edition	53589
Rusk (Dunn County)	54751	Scott (Crawford County) (Town)	53518	Silica	53049	Spring Lake (Pierce County) (Town)	54767
Rusk (Rusk County) (Town)	54728	Scott (Lincoln County) (Town)	54452	Silver Cliff (Town)	54104	Spring Lake (Waushara County)	54960
Russell (Bayfield County) (Town)	54814	Scott (Monroe County) (Town)	54666	Silver Creek	53075	Spring Prairie	53121
Russell (Lincoln County) (Town)	54435	Scott (Sheboygan County) (Town)	53001	Silver Lake (Kenosha County)	53170	Spring Prairie (Town)	53121
Russell (Sheboygan County) (Town)	53079	Sechlerville	54635	Silver Lake (Walworth County)	53121	Springstead	54552
Russell (Trempealeau County)	54747	Seeleys	54843	Silver Lake (Waushara County)	54982	Springvale (Columbia County) (Town)	53960
Rutland (Town)	53589	Seif (Town)	54456	Sinsinawa	53824	Springvale (Fond du Lac County) (Town)	54974
Sabin	53581	Seneca (Crawford County)	54654	Sioux	54891	Spring Valley (Manitowoc County)	53063
Sacred Heart School of Theology	53130	Seneca (Crawford County) (Town)	54654	Sioux Creek (Town)	54728	Spring Valley (Pierce County)	54767
St. Anna	53061	Seneca (Green Lake County) (Town)	54923	Siren	54872	Spring Valley (Rock County) (Town)	53576
St. Anthony	53002	Seneca (Shawano County) (Town)	54978	Siren (Town)	54872	Springville (Adams County) (Town)	53965
St. Cloud	53079	Seneca (Wood County) (Town)	54494	Sister Bay	54234	Springville (Vernon County)	54665
St. Croix Falls	54024	Sequoia (Part of Milwaukee)	53223-24	Skanawan (Town)	54442	Springwater (Town)	54984
St. Croix Falls (Town)	54824	For specific Sequoia Zip Codes call (414) 354-6830, or your local postmaster.		Slab City	54107	Spruce	54139
St. Croix Indian Reservation	54830	Sevastopol (Town)	54235	Slabtown	53549	Spruce (Town)	54139
St. Francis	53235	Seven Mile Creek (Town)	53944	Slades Corner	53105	Stanberry	54875
Saint George	53085	Sextonville	53584	Slinger	53086	Standart	53533
St. Germain	54558	Seymour (Eau Claire County) (Town)	54701	Slovan	54205	Stanfold (Town)	54812
St. Germain (Town)	54558	Seymour (Eau Claire County)	54703	Smelser (Town)	53807	Stangelville	54208
St. John	54129	Seymour (Lafayette County) (Town)	53586	Sobieski	54171	Stanley (Barron County) (Town)	54822
St. Joseph (Fond du Lac County)	53079	Seymour (Outagamie County)	54165	Sobieski Corners	54141	Stanley (Chippewa County)	54768
St. Joseph (La Crosse County)	54601	Seymour (Outagamie County) (Town)	54165	Soldiers Grove	54655	Stanton (Dunn County) (Town)	54725
St. Joseph (St. Croix County) (Town)	54016	Shamrock	54615	Solon Springs	54873	Stanton (St. Croix County) (Town)	54017
St. Kilian	53010			Solon Springs (Town)	54873	Stark (Town)	54639
St. Lawrence (Washington County)	53027			Somers	53171	Starks	54501
St. Lawrence (Waupaca County) (Town)	54962			Somers (Town)	53171		
St. Marie (Town)	54968			Somerset	54025		
St. Martins (Part of Franklin)	53132			Somerset (Town)	55082		
St. Marys	54619			Somo (Town)	54564		
St. Michaels	53040			Soperton	54566		
St. Nazianz	54232			South Beaver Dam	53916		
St. Peter	53049			South Byron	53006		
				South Chase	54162		

	ZIP		ZIP		ZIP		ZIP
Starlake	54561	Tainter (Town)	54730	Turtle Lake (Walworth		Walhain	54217
Star Prairie	54026	Tainter Lake	54730	County)	53115	Walsh	54159
Star Prairie (Town)	54025	Tamarack	54612	Tustin	54940	Walworth	53184
Star Valley	54655	Tarrant	54736	Twelfth Street Junction		Walworth (Town)	53184
Starview Heights	53545	Taus	54206	(Part of Superior)	54880	Wandawega	53121
State Line	53140	Taycheedah	54935	Twelve Corners	54106	Wanderoos	54001
State Street (Part of		Taycheedah (Town)	54935	Twenty-Eighth Street		Warner (Town)	54437
Racine)	53404	Taycheedah Correctional		Junction (Part of		Warren (St. Croix County)	
Steffenrud Addition	54656	Institution	54935	Superior)	54880	(Town)	54023
Stella (Town)	54501	Taylor	54659	Twin Bluffs	53581	Warren (Waushara	
Stephenson (Town)	54114	Teegarden	54751	Twin Grove	53550	County) (Town)	54923
Stephenson Island (Part of		Tell	54610	Twin Lakes	53181	Warrens	54666
Marinette)	54143	Tennyson	53820	Two Creeks	54241	Warrentown	54750
Stephensville	54944	Terrace Park	53532	Two Creeks (Town)	54241	Wascott (Town)	54890
Sterling (Polk County)		Tess Corners (Part of		Two Rivers	54241	Wascott	54890
(Town)	54006	Muskego)	53130	Two Rivers (Town)	54241	Washburn (Bayfield	
Sterling (Vernon County)		Teutonia (Part of		Ubet	54009	County)	54891
(Town)	54624	Milwaukee)	53206	Underhill	54176	Washburn (Bayfield	
Stetsonville	54480	Texas (Town)	54401	Underhill (Town)	54176	County) (Town)	54891
Stettin (Town)	54401	Theresa	53091	Union (Burnett County)		Washburn (Clark County)	
Steuben	54657	Theresa (Town)	53050	(Town)	54830	(Town)	54456
Stevens Point	54481	Thiensville	53092	Union (Door County)		Washington (Door	
Stevenstown	54636		53097	(Town)	54204	County) (Town)	54246
Stiles	54139	For specific Thiensville Zip		Union (Eau Claire County)		Washington (Eau Claire	
Stiles (Town)	54139	Codes call (414) 242-1720, or		(Town)	54701	County) (Town)	54742
Stiles Junction	54139	your local postmaster.		Union (Grant County)	53818	Washington (Green	
Stinnett (Town)	54875			Union (Pierce County)		County) (Town)	53570
Stitzer	53825	Thiry Daems	54217	(Town)	54750	Washington (La Crosse	
Stockbridge	53088	Thompson	53027	Union (Rock County)	53536	County) (Town)	54619
Stockbridge (Town)	53014	Thompsonville	53126	Union (Rock County)		Washington (Rusk	
Stockbridge Indian		Thornapple (Town)	54819	(Town)	53536	County) (Town)	54819
Reservation	54416	Thornton	54166	Union (Vernon County)		Washington (Sauk	
Stockholm	54769	Thorp	54771	(Town)	54634	County) (Town)	53937
Stockholm (Town)	54769	Thorp (Town)	54768	Union (Waupaca County)		Washington (Shawano	
Stockton (Town)	54481	Three Lakes	54562	(Town)	54949	County) (Town)	54107
Stockton	54481	Three Lakes (Town)	54562	Union Center	53962	Washington (Vilas County)	
Stoddard	54658	Tibbets	53121	Union Church	53126	(Town)	54521
Stonebank	53066	Tichigan Lake	53185	Union Grove	53182	Washington Island	54246
Stone Lake	54876	Tiffany (Dunn County)		Unity (Clark County)		Waterford	53185
Stone Lake (Town)	54876	(Town)	54725	(Town)	54488	Waterford (Town)	53185
Stoughton	53589	Tiffany (Rock County)	53511	Unity (Marathon County)	54488	Waterford North	53185
Strader	54722	Tigerton	54486	Unity (Trempealeau		Waterford Woods	53185
Stratford	54484	Tilden	54729	County) (Town)	54770	Waterloo (Grant County)	
Strickland (Town)	54895	Tilden (Town)	54729	University (Part of		(Town)	53820
Strongs Prairie (Town)	54613	Tilleda	54978	Madison)	53715	Waterloo (Jefferson	
Strum	54770	Tipler	49935	Upham (Town)	54485	County)	53594
Stubbs (Town)	54819	Tipler (Town)	49935	Upper Third Street (Part		Waterloo (Jefferson	
Sturgeon Bay	54235	Tisch Mills	54240	of Milwaukee)	53212	County) (Town)	53551
Sturgeon Bay (Town)	54235	Token Creek	53532	Upson	54565	Watertown	53094
Sturtevant	53177	Tomah	54660	Uptown (Part of Racine)	53403		53098
Suamico	54173	Tomah (Town)	54660	Urne	54736	For specific Watertown Zip	
Suamico (Town)	54173	Tomahawk	54487	Utica (Crawford County)		Codes call (414) 261-5929, or	
Sugar Bush (Brown		Tomahawk (Town)	54487	(Town)	54655	your local postmaster.	
County)	54217	Tonet	54217	Utica (Dane County)	53523	Watertown (Town)	53094
Sugar Bush (Outagamie		Tony	54563	Utica (Waukesha County)	53066	Waterville (Pepin County)	
County)	54961	Towerville	54655	Utica (Winnebago County)		(Town)	54721
Sugar Camp	54501	Townsend	54175	(Town)	54964	Waterville (Waukesha	
Sugar Camp (Town)	54501	Townsend (Town)	54175	Valders	54245	County)	53066
Sugar Creek (Town)	53121	Trade Lake	54837	Valley	54639	Watterstown (Town)	53805
Sugar Grove	54655	Trade Lake (Town)	54837	Valley Junction	54660	Waubeek (Town)	54736
Sugar Island	53098	Trade River	54840	Valley View Mall (Part of		Waubeesee	53185
Sullivan	53178	Trego	54888	La Crosse)	54601	Waubeka	53021
Sullivan (Town)	53549	Trego (Town)	54888	Valmy	54235	Waubesa Heights	53558
Summit (Douglas County)		Trempealeau	54661	Valton	53968	Waucousta	53010
(Town)	54836	Trempealeau (Town)	54661	Van Buskirk	54534	Waukau	54980
Summit (Juneau County)		Trenton (Dodge County)		Vance Creek (Town)	54868	Waukechon (Town)	54166
(Town)	53948	(Town)	53916	Vandenbroek (Town)	54130	Waukesha	53186-88
Summit (Langlade		Trenton (Pierce County)		Vandyne	54979	For specific Waukesha Zip	
County) (Town)	54435	(Town)	54014	Vaudreuil	54615	Codes call (414) 542-5377, or	
Summit (Waukesha		Trenton (Washington		Veedum	54466	your local postmaster.	
County) (Town)	53058	County) (Town)	53095	Vermont (Town)	53515	Waumandee	54622
Summit Corners	53066	Trevor	53179	Vernon (Town)	53103	Waumandee (Town)	54622
Summit Lake	54485	Tri City (Part of Oak		Verona	53593	Waunakee	53597
Sumner (Town)	54868	Creek)	53154	Verona (Town)	53593	Waupaca	54981
Sumner (Barron County)	54822	Trimbelle	54011	Vesper	54489	Waupaca (Town)	54981
Sumner (Jefferson		Trimbelle (Town)	54011	Veterans Administration		Waupun (Dodge County)	53963
County) (Town)	53538	Tripoli	54564	Hospital (Part of		Waupun (Fond du Lac	
Sumner (Trempealeau		Tripp (Town)	54847	Shorewood Hills)	53705	County) (Town)	53963
County) (Town)	54758	Troy (Sauk County)		Victory	54624	Wausau	54401-03
Sumpter (Town)	53951	(Town)	53583	Vienna (Town)	53532	For specific Wausau Zip Codes	
Sunburst	53701	Troy (St. Croix County)		Vignes	54235	call (715) 842-0731, or your	
Sun Prairie	53590	(Town)	54022	Vilas (Dane County)	53527	local postmaster.	
Sun Prairie (Town)	53559	Troy (Walworth County)	53121	Vilas (Langlade County)		Wausau Center (Part of	
Sunset	54401	Troy (Walworth County)		(Town)	54424	Wausau)	54401
Sunset Beach	53916	(Town)	53120	Villard (Part of Milwaukee)	53209	Wausaukee	54177
Superior	54880	Troy Center	53120	Vineyard	53575	Wausaukee (Town)	54177
Superior (Town)	54880	True (Town)	54526	Vinland (Town)	54901	Wautoma	54982
Superior (Village)	54880	Truesdell	53143	Viola	54664	Wautoma (Town)	54982
Suring	54174	Truman	53530	Viroqua	54665	Wauwatosa	53210
Sussex	53089	Trusler Circle	53575	Viroqua (Town)	54665		53213
Swiss (Town)	54830	Tuckaway (Part of		Voltz Lake	53179		53222
Sylvan	54664	Milwaukee)	53221	Wabeno	54566		53226
Sylvan (Town)	54664	Tuleta Hills	53946	Wabeno (Town)	54566	For specific Wauwatosa Zip	
Sylvania	53177	Tunnel City	54662	Wagner (Town)	54177	Codes call (414) 258-9486, or	
Sylvester (Town)	53550	Turtle (Town)	53511	Waino	54820	your local postmaster.	
Symco	54949	Turtle Lake (Barron		Waldo	53093	Wauzeka	53826
Tabor	53404	County)	54889	Waldwick	53565	Wauzeka (Town)	53826
Taegesville	54401	Turtle Lake (Barron		Waldwick (Town)	53565	Waverly	54740
Taft (Town)	54771	County) (Town)	54004	Wales	53183		

* Area Zip Code   **† Post Office Boxes**

	ZIP		ZIP		ZIP		ZIP
Wayne (Lafayette County) (Town)	53587	Weston (Marathon County) (Town)	54476	Wilmot	53192	Wonewoc	53968
Wayne (Washington County)	53010	West Plainfield	54966	Wilson (Dunn County) (Town)	54733	Wonewoc (Town)	53929
Wayne (Washington County) (Town)	53010	West Point (Town)	53555	Wilson (Eau Claire County)	54726	Wood (Milwaukee County)	53295
Wayside	54126	Westport (Dane County) (Town)	53597	Wilson (Eau Claire County) (Town)	54726	Wood (Wood County) (Town)	54466
Webb Lake	54830	Westport (Richland County)	53518	Wilson (Lincoln County) (Town)	54487	Woodboro	54501
Webb Lake (Town)	54830	West Prairie	54665	Wilson (Rusk County) (Town)	54817	Woodboro (Town)	54501
Webster (Burnett County)	54893	West Racine (Part of Racine)	53405	Wilson (Sheboygan County) (Town)	53081	Wooddale	54817
Webster (Vernon County) (Town)	54639	West Rosendale	54974	Wilson (St. Croix County)	54027	Woodford	53599
Weirgor	54835	West Salem	54669	Wilton	54670	Woodhull	54932
Weirgor (Town)	54835	Westside (Part of Madison)	53711	Wilton (Town)	54670	Woodland (Dodge County)	53099
Wellington (Town)	54651	West Sweden (Town)	54837	Winchester	54545	Woodland (Sauk County) (Town)	53968
Wells (Town)	54656	West Towne Mall (Part of Madison)	53719	Winchester (Town)	54545	Woodman	53827
Wentworth	54874	Weyauwega	54983	Winchester	54947	Woodman (Town)	53827
Werley	53809	Weyauwega (Town)	54983	Winchester (Town)	54947	Woodmohr (Town)	54724
Wescott (Town)	54166	Weyerhaeuser	54895	Wind Lake	53185	Wood River (Town)	54840
West Allis	53214	Wheatland (Kenosha County)	53105	Wind Point	53402	Woodruff	54568
	53227	Wheatland (Kenosha County) (Town)	53105	Windsor	53598	Woodruff (Town)	54568
For specific West Allis Zip Codes call (414) 258-9454, or your local postmaster.		Wheatland (Vernon County) (Town)	54624	Windsor (Town)	53598	Woodstock	53581
West Baraboo	53913	Wheaton (Town)	54739	Windsor Hills	53532	Woodville (Calumet County) (Town)	54129
West Bend	53095	Wheeler	54772	Windsor Prairie	53532	Woodville (St. Croix County)	54028
West Bend (Town)	53095	Whitcomb	54486	Winfield (Town)	53959	Woodworth	53194
West Bloomfield	54983	White Creek	53965	Wingville (Town)	53569	Worcester (Town)	54555
Westboro	54490	Whitefish Bay (Door County)	54235	Winnebago	54985	Worden (Town)	54771
Westboro (Town)	54490	Whitefish Bay (Milwaukee County)	53217	Winnebago Heights	53049	Wrightstown	54180
Westby	54667	Whitehall	54773	Winnebago Indian Reservation	53965	Wrightstown (Town)	54115
West De Pere (Part of De Pere)	54115	White Lake	54491	Winnebago Mission	54615	Wuertsburg	54411
Western (Part of Milwaukee)	53210	Whitelaw	54247	Winneboujou	54820	Wyalusing	53801
Westfield (Marquette County)	53964	White Oak Springs (Town)	53586	Winneconne	54986	Wyalusing (Town)	53801
Westfield (Marquette County) (Town)	53964	White River (Town)	54855	Winneconne (Town)	54927	Wyeville	54660
Westfield (Sauk County) (Town)	53943	Whitestown (Town)	54639	Winter	54896	Wyocena	53969
Westford (Dodge County) (Town)	53916	Whitewater	53190	Winter (Town)	54896	Wyocena (Town)	53960
Westford (Richland County) (Town)	53924	Whitewater (Town)	53190	Wiota	53587	Wyoming (Iowa County) (Town)	53588
West Jacksonport	54209	Whiting	54481	Wiota (Town)	53587	Wyoming (Waupaca County) (Town)	54945
West Kewaunee (Town)	54216	Whittlesey	54451	Wiscona (Part of Glendale)	53209	Yahara Heights	53597
West Lima	54639	Wien (Town)	54426	Wisconsin Correctional Center System	53575	Yellow Lake	54830
Westlyn	54494	Wild Rose	54984	Wisconsin Dells	53965	York (Clark County) (Town)	54436
West Marshland (Town)	54840	Wildwood	54028	Wisconsin Rapids	54494-95	York (Dane County) (Town)	53925
West Milwaukee	53215	Wilkinson (Town)	54895	For specific Wisconsin Rapids Zip Codes call (715) 423-2130, or your local postmaster.		York (Green County) (Town)	53516
	53234	Willard (Clark County)	54493	Withee	54498	York (Jackson County)	54758
For specific West Milwaukee Zip Codes call (414) 643-0414, or your local postmaster.		Willard (Rusk County) (Town)	54731	Withee (Town)	54771	York Center	53559
Weston (Clark County) (Town)	54456	Williams Bay	53191	Wittenberg	54499	Yorkville	53182
Weston (Dunn County)	54751	Williamstown (Town)	53032	Wittenberg (Town)	54499	Yorkville (Town)	53182
Weston (Dunn County) (Town)	54751	Willow (Town)	53924	Witwen	53583	Young America	53095
Weston (Marathon County)	54476	Willow Springs (Lafayette County) (Town)	53565	Wolfcreek	54024	Yuba	54639
		Willow Springs (Waukesha County)	53051	Wolf Lake	53079	Zachow	54182
		Wilmore Heights	54971	Wolf River (Langlade County) (Town)	54491	Zander	54208
				Wolf River (Winnebago County) (Town)	54940	Zenda	53195
						Zittau	54940

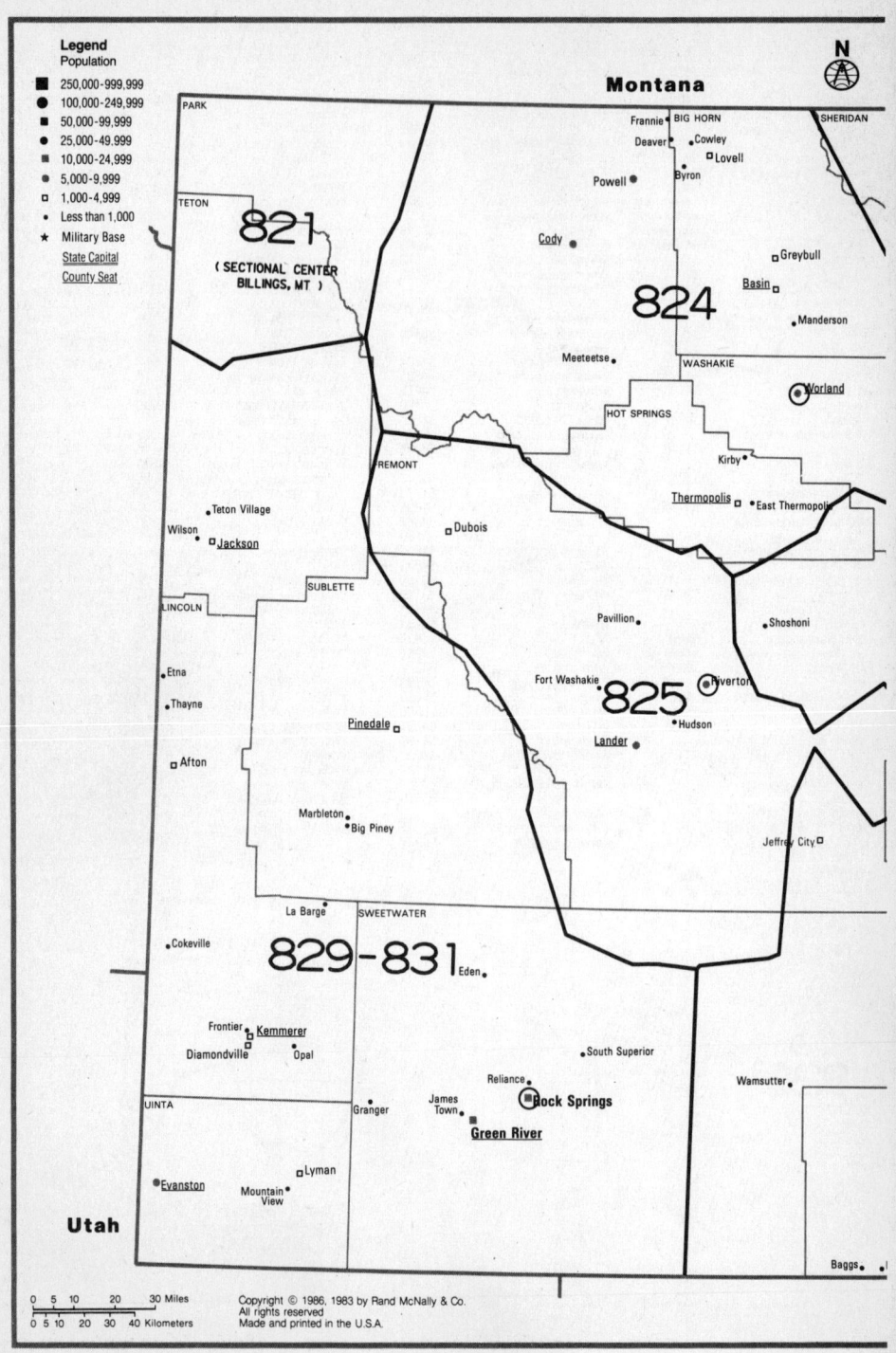

Legend
Population
- ■ 250,000-999,999
- ● 100,000-249,999
- ■ 50,000-99,999
- ● 25,000-49,999
- ■ 10,000-24,999
- ● 5,000-9,999
- □ 1,000-4,999
- • Less than 1,000
- ★ Military Base
- <u>State Capital</u>
- <u>County Seat</u>

N

Montana

PARK

TETON

821
(SECTIONAL CENTER
BILLINGS, MT)

BIG HORN

SHERIDAN

Frannie •
Deaver • • Cowley
• □ Lovell
Powell • ■ Byron

Cody • •

• <u>Greybull</u>
<u>Basin</u> □

824

• Manderson

Meeteetse • •

WASHAKIE

HOT SPRINGS

◎ <u>Worland</u>

FREMONT

• Kirby

<u>Thermopolis</u> □ • East Thermopolis

□ Dubois

• Teton Village
Wilson • □ <u>Jackson</u>

SUBLETTE

LINCOLN

Pavillion •

• Shoshoni

• Etna

• Thayne

Fort Washakie •
825 ◎ <u>Riverton</u>

<u>Pinedale</u> □

<u>Lander</u> • • Hudson

□ Afton

Marbleton •
• Big Piney

Jeffrey City □

La Barge •

SWEETWATER

• Cokeville

829-831 • Eden

Frontier • □ <u>Kemmerer</u>
Diamondville • • Opal

• South Superior

Wamsutter •

Reliance •
James • ■ **Rock Springs**
Town
Granger • <u>Green River</u>

UINTA

□ Lyman
• <u>Evanston</u> Mountain
View •

Baggs •

Utah

0 5 10   20   30 Miles
0 5 10   20   30   40 Kilometers

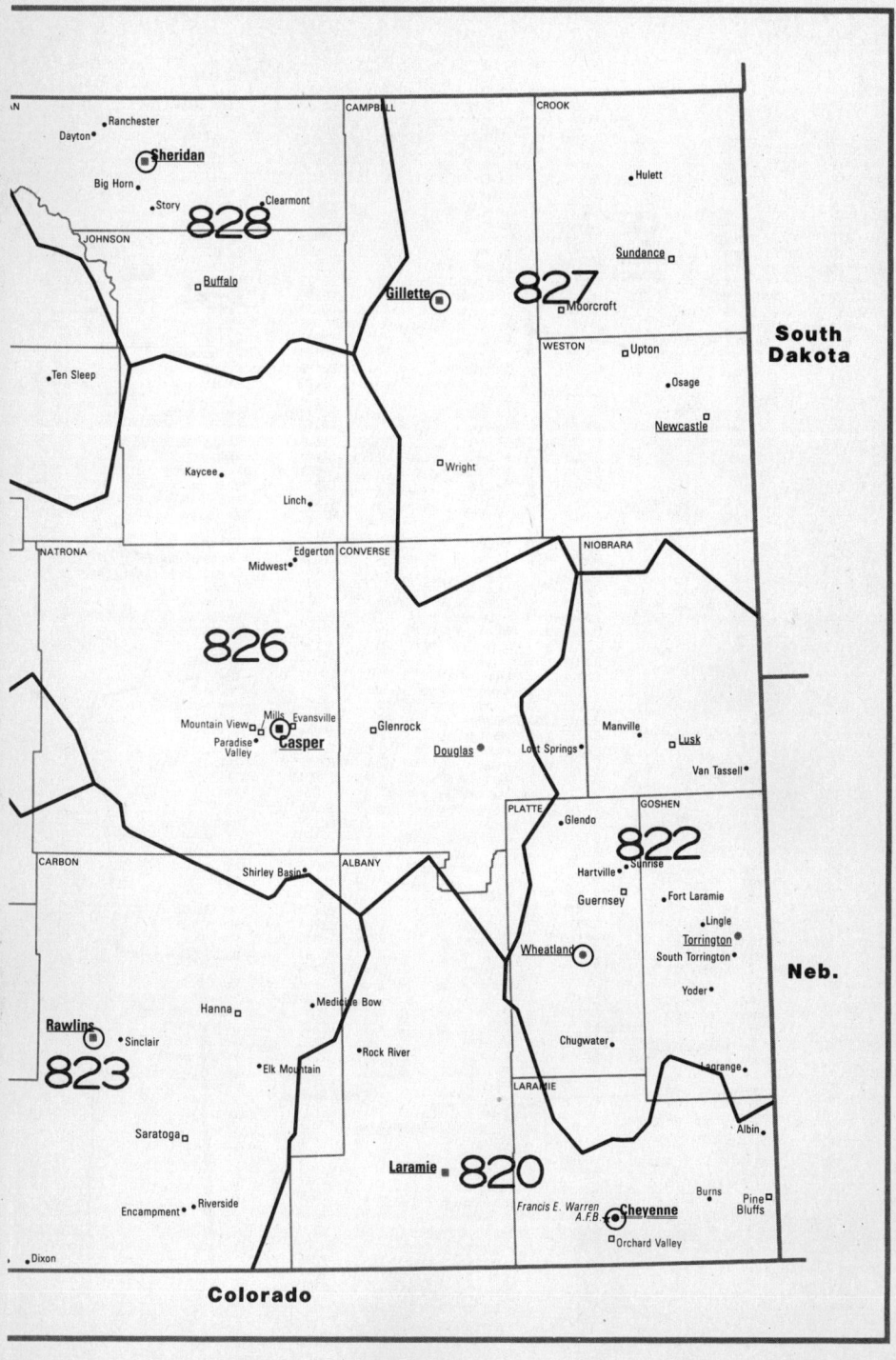

CAMPBELL

CROOK

Dayton •   • Ranchester

■ **Sheridan**

Big Horn •

Story •   • Clearmont

828

JOHNSON

□ Buffalo

Gillette ◉

• Ten Sleep

• Hulett

• Sundance □

827

• Moorcroft

WESTON

□ Upton

**South
Dakota**

• Osage

Newcastle □

Kaycee •

Wright □

Linch •

NATRONA   Edgerton CONVERSE

Midwest •   • Edgerton

NIOBRARA

826

Mountain View □ Mills • Evansville
Paradise • ◉ **Casper**
Valley

• Glenrock

Douglas •

Lost Springs •

• Manville

□ **Lusk**

Van Tassell •

PLATTE   GOSHEN

• Glendo

822

CARBON

Shirley Basin • ALBANY

Hartville □   • Sunrise

Guernsey •

Fort Laramie □

• Lingle

Torrington •
South Torrington •

Neb.

Wheatland ◉

Hanna □

• Medicine Bow

• Yoder

Rawlins ■ • Sinclair

823

• Elk Mountain

• Rock River

Chugwater •

Lagrange •

LARAMIE

Saratoga □

Albin •

Laramie ■ **820**

Encampment • • Riverside

Francis E. Warren
A.F.B. • ◉ **Cheyenne**

Burns •

Pine
Bluffs □

• Dixon

□ Orchard Valley

Colorado

	ZIP		ZIP		ZIP		ZIP
Adkins Valley	82801	East Thermopolis	82443	Lance Creek	82222	Red Buttes Village	82604
Afton	83110	Eden	82926	Lander	82520	Red Desert	82336
Airport (Part of Cheyenne)	82001	Edgerton	82635	Laramie	82070-71	Red Lane	82443
Aladdin	82710	Egbert	82053	For specific Laramie Zip Codes		Reliance	82943
Albany	82070	Elk Mountain	82324	call (307) 742-2109, or your		Reno (Part of Wright)	82732
Albin	82050	Elmo (Part of Hanna)	82327	local postmaster.		Reno Junction (Part of	
Alcova	82620	Emblem	82422	Leiter	82837	Wright)	82732
Allendale	82601	Encampment	82325	Leo	82327	Riovista	82935
Almy	82930	Esterbrook	82633	Linch	82640	Riverside	82325
Alpine	83128	Ethete	82520	Lingle	82223	Riverton	82501
Alpine Junction (Part of		Etna	83118	Little America	82929	Riverview	57735
Alpine)	83128	Evanston	82930*	Lonetree	82936	Robertson	82944
Alta	83422		82931†	Lost Cabin	82642	Rock River	82083
Alva	82711	Evansville	82636	Lost Springs	82224	Rockypoint	82724
Antelope Valley-Crestview	82718	Fairview	83119	Lovell	82431	Rolling Hills	82637
Arapahoe	82510	Farson	82932	Lucerne	82443	Rozet	82727
Arminto	82630	Fishing Bridge	82190	Lucky MacCamp	82501	Ryan Park	82331
Arrow Head Lodge	82836	Fontenelle	83101	Lusk	82225	Saddlestring	82840
Arvada	82831	Fort Bridger	82933	Lyman	82937	Sand Draw	82501
Atlantic City	82520	Fort Laramie	82212	Lysite	82642	Saratoga	82331
Auburn	83111	Fort Steele	82301	McFadden	82080	Savery	82332
Baggs	82321	Fort Washakie	82514	McKinley	82633	Seminoe Dam	82334
Bairoil	82322	Four Corners	82715	McKinnon	82938	Shawnee	82229
Banner	82832	Fox Farm-College	82007	Manderson	82432	Shell	82441
Barnum	82639	Foxpark	82070	Mantua	82435	Sheridan	82801
Bar Nunn	82601	Francis E. Warren Air		Manville	82227	Sheridan Gardens	82801
Basin	82410	Force Base	82001	Marbleton	83113	Shirley Basin	82615
Bear Lodge	82836	Frannie	82423	Mayoworth	82639	Shoshoni	82649
Beckton	82801	Freedom	83120	Medicine Bow	82329	Sinclair	82334
Bedford	83112	Frontier	83121	Meeteetse	82433	Slater	82201
Beulah	82712	Frontier Mall (Part of		Meriden	82081	Sleepy Hollow	82718
Big Horn	82833	Cheyenne)	82001	Merna	83115	Smoot	83126
Big Piney	83113	Garland	82435	Midvale	82501	South Greeley	82007
Bill	82631	Garrett	82058	Midwest	82643	South Jackson	83001
Bondurant	82922	Gas Camp 1	82643	Midwest Heights	82601	South Laramie	82070
Bonneville	82649	Gillette	82716-18	Milford	82520	South Pass City	82520
Bosler	82051	For specific Gillette Zip Codes		Mills	82644	South Torrington	82240
Bosler Junction	82051	call (307) 682-3727, or your		Moneta	82601	Spotted Horse	82831
Boulder	82923	local postmaster.		Moorcroft	82721	Story	82842
Boxelder	82637	Glendo	82213	Moose	83012	Sundance	82729
Bronx	83115	Glenrock	82637	Moran	83013	Sunrise (Natrona County)	82604
Brundage Place	82801	Granger	82934	Morton	82501	Sunrise (Platte County)	82215
Buffalo	82834	Granite Canon	82059	Mountain Home	82070	Sunshine	82433
Buford	82052	Grant Village	82190	Mountain View (Natrona		Superior	82945
Burlington	82411	Grass Creek	82443	County)	82604	Sussex	82639
Burns	82053	Green River	82935	Mountain View (Uinta		Sweetwater Station	82520
Burntfork	82938	Greybull	82426	County)	82936*	Taylor	82643
Burris	82512	Grover	83122		82939†	Ten Sleep	82442
Byron	82412	Guernsey	82214	Muddy Gap	82301	Teton Village	83025
Calpet	83123	Halfway	83113	Museum (Part of		Thayne	83127
Canyon	82190	Hamilton Dome	82427	Cheyenne)	82001	Thermopolis	82443
Carlile	82713	Hanna	82327	Natrona	82646	Three Forks	82301
Carpenter	82054	Happy Jack Ranchettes	82007	Newcastle	82701	Tie Siding	82084
Carter	82937	Harriman	82059	New Haven	82720	Torrington	82240
Casper	82601-09	Hartville	82215	Node	82228	Tower Junction	82190
For specific Casper Zip Codes		Hawk Springs	82217	North Rock Springs	82901	Turnerville	83112
call (307) 266-4000, or your		Hiland	82638	Number One (Part of		Ucross	82835
local postmaster.		Hillsdale	82060	Cheyenne)	82001	Ulm	82835
Centennial	82055	Hilltop (Part of Casper)	82609	O'Donnell Spur	82435	University (Part of	
Chatham	82401	Hoback Junction	83001	Old Faithful	82190	Laramie)	82071
Cheyenne	82001-09	Horse Creek	82061	Opal	83124	Upton	82730
For specific Cheyenne Zip		Hudson	82515	Orchard Valley	82007	Urie	82937
Codes call (307) 772-6583, or		Hulett	82720	Orin	82633	Uva	82201
your local postmaster.		Huntley	82218	Orpha	82633	Valley	82414
Chugwater	82210	Hyattville	82428	Osage	82723	Van Tassell	82242
Clareton	82701	Iron Mountain	82001	Oshoto	82724	Veteran	82243
Clark	59008	Jackson	83001-02	Osmond	83110	Walcott	82335
Clay	82723	For specific Jackson Zip Codes		Otto	82434	Wamsutter	82336
Clearmont	82835	call (307) 733-3650, or your		Pahaska	82414	Wapiti	82450
Cody	82414	local postmaster.		Paradise Valley (Part of		Wapiti Valley	82450
Cokeville	83114	Jackson Lake Lodge	83013	Casper)	82601	Warren Air Force Base	82005
Colony	57717	James Town	82935	Parkerton	82637	Western Hills (Part of	
Colter Bay	83001	Jay Em	82219	Parkman	82838	Cheyenne)	82001
Cora	82925	Jeffrey City	82310	Pavillion	82523	West Lance Creek	82222
Cowley	82420	Jelm	82063	Piedmont	82933	West Laramie	82070
Creston	82301	Jenny Lake	83012	Pine Bluffs	82082	Weston	82731
Creston Junction	82301	Kaycee	82639	Pinedale	82941	West Thumb	82190
Crowheart	82512	Kearny	82832	Pine Haven	82721	Wheatland	82201
Daniel	83115	Keeline	82220	Point of Rocks	82942	Willwood	82435
Dayton	82836	Kelly	83011	Powder River	82648	Wilson	83014
Deaver	82421	Kemmerer	83101	Powell	82435	Wind River Indian	
Devils Tower	82714	Keystone	82070	Prospector Village	82717	Reservation	82514
Diamondville	83116	Kinnear	82516	Rafter J Ranch	83001	Wolf	82844
Dixon	82323	Kirby	82430	Ralston	82440	Woods Landing	82063
Douglas	82633	La Barge	83123	Ranchester	82839	Worland	82401
Downer	82801	Lagrange	82221	Ranchettes	82009	Wright	82732
Dubois	82513	Lake	82190	Rawhide Village	82717	Wyarno	82845
Dwyer	82201	Lake Creek Resort	82070	Rawlins	82301	Wyodak	82718
Eastridge Mall (Part of		Lamont	82301	Recluse	82725		
Casper)	82601						